TABLE OF CONTENTS

TABLE OF CONTENTS

General Service Information Section

MOTOR
AUTO REPAIR MANUAL
49th Edition
First Printing

Michael J. Kromida, SAE
Editor

Warren Schildknecht, SAE
Special Projects Editor

Robert R. Savasta, SAE
Senior Associate Editor

Dan Irizarry, SAE
Production Editor

Michael E. Pallien, SAE
Associate Editor

Daniel E. Doku
Assistant Editor

Debra A. Luczak
Production Assistant

Mark E. Flynn, SAE
Associate Editor

Denver Steele
Assistant Editor

Jane Sennett
Production Assistant

Patrick Peyton, SAE
Associate Editor

James M. Garripoli
Assistant Editor

John R. Lypen, SAE
Associate Editor

John E. DeGroat
Assistant Editor

Thomas G. Gaeta
Assistant Editor

Published by
MOTOR

Frank A. Bennack, Jr.
President

Gordon L. Jones
*Vice President,
Hearst Books/Business
Publishing Group*

Philip D. Shalala
*Vice President,
Automotive Group*

Louis C. Forier, SAE
*Editorial Director
Motor Publications*

**Hearst Books/Business Publishing Group,
A Division of The Hearst Corp.**

555 West 57th St., New York, N.Y. 10019

Printed in the U.S.A. © Copyright 1985 by The Hearst Corporation

ISBN 0-87851-613-1

GASOLINE ENGINE TUNE UP SPECIFICATIONS

TABLE OF CONTENTS

GASOLINE ENGINE TUNE UP SPECIFICATIONS

TABLE OF CONTENTS

TABLE OF CONTENTS

GENERAL MOTORS CORPORATION—Continued

PONTIAC

PONTIAC—Continued

General Service Information Section

MOTOR AUTO REPAIR MANUAL

49th Edition

First Printing

Michael J. Kromida, SAE
Editor

Warren Schildknecht, SAE
Special Projects Editor

Robert R. Savasta, SAE
Senior Associate Editor

Dan Irizarry, SAE
Production Editor

Michael E. Pallien, SAE
Associate Editor

Daniel E. Doku
Assistant Editor

Debra A. Luczak
Production Assistant

Mark E. Flynn, SAE
Associate Editor

Denver Steele
Assistant Editor

Jane Sennett
Production Assistant

Patrick Peyton, SAE
Associate Editor

James M. Garripoli
Assistant Editor

John R. Lypen, SAE
Associate Editor

John E. DeGroat
Assistant Editor

Thomas G. Gaeta
Assistant Editor

Published by

MOTOR

Frank A. Bennac
President

Gordon L. Jor
*Vice President
Hearst Books/
Publishing G*

Philip D.
*Vice Pres
Automo*

Hearst Books/Business Publishing Group,
A Division of The Hearst Corp.

555 West 57th St., New York, N.Y. 10019

Printed in the U.S.A. © Copyright 1985 by The Hearst Corporation

ISBN 0-87851-613-1

TABLE OF CONTENTS—Continued

AMERICAN MOTORS

The following specifications are published from the latest information available. This data should be used only in the absence of a decal affixed in the engine compartment.

★ When checking ignition timing, disconnect vacuum hose at distributor and plug opening in hose so idle speed will not be affected. Also, on some computer controlled ignition systems, it may be necessary to disconnect certain vacuum hoses and/or electrical connectors. Refer to vehicle emission decal.

▲ Before removing wires from distributor cap, determine location of the No. 1 wire in cap, as distributor position may have been altered from that shown at the end of this chart.

Year & Engine/V.I.N.	Spark Plug Gap	Firing Order Fig. ▲	Ignition Timing BTDC ① ★ Man. Trans.	Ignition Timing BTDC ① ★ Auto. Trans.	Mark Fig.	Curb Idle Speed ② Man. Trans.	Curb Idle Speed ② Auto. Trans.	Fast Idle Speed Man. Trans.	Fast Idle Speed Auto. Trans.	Fuel Pump Pressure
1980										
4-151/B Exc. Calif.	.060	G	10°	12°	D	900	700D	2400㉔	2600㉔	6½–8
4-151/B Calif.	.060	G	12°	10°	D	㉓	⑳	2400㉔	2600㉔	6½–8
6-258/C Exc. Eagle	.035	F	6°	⑦	E	700	600D	1700④	1850④	4–5
6-258/C Eagle Exc. Calif.	.035	F	—	10°	E	—	600D	—	1850④	4–5
6-258/C Eagle Calif.	.035	F	—	8°	E	—	600D	—	1850④	4–5
1981										
4-151/B Concord & Spirit Exc. Calif.	.060	G	10°	12°	D	500/900	500/700D	2400㉔	2600㉔	6½–8
4-151/B Concord & Spirit Calif.	.060	G	10°	10°	D	500/900	500/700D	2400㉔	2600㉔	6½–8
4-151/B Eagle Exc. Calif.	.060	G	11°	12°	D	500/900	500/700D	2400㉔	2600㉔	6½–8
4-151/B Eagle Calif.	.060	G	10°	8°	D	500/900	500/700D	2400㉔	2600㉔	6½–8
6-258/C Concord & Spirit Exc. High Alt.	.035	F	6°	6°	E	650③	550D⑧	1700④	1850④	4–5
6-258/C Eagle Exc. Calif. & High Alt.	.035	F	8°	8°	E	650③	550D⑧	1700④	1850④	4–5
6-258/C Eagle Calif.	.035	F	4°	6°	E	650③	550D⑧	1700④	1850④	4–5
6-258/C High Alt.	.035	F	—	15°	E	—	550D⑧	—	1850④	4–5
1982										
4-151/B Concord & Spirit Exc. Calif. & High Alt.	.060	G	10°	10°	D	900⑪	700D⑨	2400	2400⑤	6½–8
4-151/B Eagle Exc. Calif. & High Alt.	.060	G	12°	12°	D	900⑪	700D⑨	2400	2500	6½–8
4-151/B Concord & Spirit Calif.	.060	G	8°	8°	D	900⑪	700D⑨	2400	2400⑤	6½–8
4-151/B Eagle Calif.	.060	G	8°	8°	D	900⑪	700D⑨	2500	2500	6½–8
4-151/B Concord & Spirit High Alt.	.060	G	15°	15°	D	900⑪	700D⑨	2400	2400⑤	6½–8
4-151/B Eagle High Alt.	.060	G	15°	15°	D	900⑪	700D⑨	2500	2500	6½–8
6-258/C Exc. High Alt.	.035	F	15°⑫㉑	15°⑫㉑	A	600③	500D⑧	1850	1850	4–5
6-258/C Concord & Spirit High Alt.	.035	F	19°⑫㉑	19°⑫㉑	A	600③	500D⑧	1850	1850	4–5
6-258/C Eagle High Alt.	.035	F	21°⑫㉑	21°⑫㉑	A	600③	500D⑧	1850	1850	4–5
1983										
4-150/U Exc. High Alt.	.035	B	12°⑩	12°⑩	C	500⑥	500D⑬	2000⑲	2300⑲	4–5
4-150/U High Alt.	.035	B	19°⑩	19°⑩	C	500⑥	500D⑬	2000⑲	2300⑲	4–5
4-151/B Exc. Calif.	.060	G	10°	10°	D	650/900	550/700D	2500㉔	2700㉔	6½–8
4-151/B Calif.	.060	G	12°	12°	D	650/900	550/700D	2500㉔	2700㉔	6½–8
6-258/C Concord & Spirit Exc. High Alt.	.035	F	6°	6°	A	650⑥	550D⑯	1700⑲	1850⑲	5–6½
6-258/C Eagle Exc. Calif. & High Alt.	.035	F	6°	6°	A	600⑥	500D⑯	1700⑲	1850⑲	5–6½
6-258/C Eagle Calif.	.035	F	6°	6°	A	650⑥	550D⑯	1700⑲	1850⑲	5–6½
6-258/C High Alt.	.035	F	13°	13°	A	700⑰	650D⑱	1700⑲	1850⑲	5–6½
1984										
4-150/U Exc. High Alt.	.035	B	12°⑩	12°⑩	C	⑥	⑬	2000⑲	2300⑲	4–5
4-150/U High Alt.	.035	F	19°⑩	19°⑩	A	⑥	⑬	2000⑲	2300⑲	4–5

continued

AMERICAN MOTORS—Continued

The following specifications are published from the latest information available. This data should be used only in the absence of a decal affixed in the engine compartment.

★ When checking ignition timing, disconnect vacuum hose at distributor and plug opening in hose so idle speed will not be affected. Also, on some computer controlled ignition systems, it may be necessary to disconnect certain vacuum hoses and/or electrical connectors. Refer to vehicle emission decal.

▲ Before removing wires from distributor cap, determine location of the No. 1 wire in cap, as distributor position may have been altered from that shown at the end of this chart.

| Year & Engine/V.I.N. | Spark Plug Gap | Firing Order Fig. ▲ | Ignition Timing BTDC①★ | | | Curb Idle Speed② | | Fast Idle Speed | | Fuel Pump Pressure |
			Man. Trans.	Auto. Trans.	Mark Fig.	Man. Trans.	Auto. Trans.	Man. Trans.	Auto. Trans.	
1984–85										
6-258/C Exc. High Alt.	.035	F	9°⑩	9°⑩	A	680⑭	600D⑮	1700⑲	1850⑲	5–6½
6-258/C High Alt.	.035	F	16°⑩	16°⑩	A	700⑭	650D⑮	1700⑲	1850⑲	5–6½

①—BTDC—Before top dead center.

②—Idle speed on man. trans. vehicles is adjusted in Neutral & on auto. trans. equipped vehicles is adjusted in Drive unless otherwise specified. When two idle speeds are listed, the higher speed is with the A/C or idle solenoid energized.

③—With holding solenoid energized, 750 RPM; with vacuum actuator energized, 900 RPM.

④—With stop screw on 2nd step of fast idle cam, TCS & EGR disconnected.

⑤—Models with A/C, 2600 RPM.

⑥—With holding solenoid energized, 750 RPM; with vacuum actuator energized, 750 RPM.

⑦—Concord & Spirit, 10° BTDC; Pacer, 8° BTDC.

⑧—With holding solenoid energized, 650D RPM; with vacuum actuator energized, 800D RPM.

⑨—On models equipped with A/C, with A/C off & solenoid disconnected, 500D RPM; with A/C on & solenoid connected, 1250D RPM.

⑩—At 1600 RPM with 3 wire electrical connector to vacuum input switches disconnected.

⑪—On models equipped with A/C, with A/C off & solenoid disconnected, 500 RPM; with A/C on & solenoid connected, 950 RPM.

⑫—At 1600 RPM.

⑬—With holding solenoid energized, 700D RPM; with vacuum actuator energized, 850D RPM.

⑭—With holding solenoid energized, 900 RPM; with vacuum actuator energized, 1100 RPM.

⑮—With holding solenoid energized, 800 RPM; with vacuum actuator energized, 900 RPM.

⑯—With holding solenoid energized, 650D RPM; with vacuum actuator energized, 850D RPM.

⑰—With holding solenoid energized, 750 RPM; with vacuum actuator energized, 1000 RPM.

⑱—With holding solenoid energized, 750D RPM; with vacuum actuator energized, 850D RPM.

⑲—With stop screw on 2nd step of fast idle cam and EGR disconnected.

⑳—With A/C, 700/950 RPM; less A/C, 500/700 RPM.

㉑—With ignition module electronic retard (two wire) connector disconnected and a jumper wire connected between the two module wire connector terminals.

㉒—On models with 2.37 rear axle ratio, set at 12° BTDC.

㉓—With A/C, 900/1250 RPM; less A/C, 500/900 RPM.

㉔—With fast idle screw on highest step of fast idle cam.

Fig. A

FIRING ORDER 1-3-4-2

Fig. B

Fig. C

Fig. D

Fig. E

FIRING ORDER 1-5-3-6-2-4

Fig. F

FIRING ORDER 1-3-4-2

Fig. G

continued

CHRYSLER CORP.
Front Wheel Drive

The following specifications are published from the latest information available. This data should be used only in the absence of a decal affixed in the engine compartment.

★ When checking ignition timing, disconnect vacuum hose at distributor and plug opening in hose so idle speed will not be affected. Also, on some computer controlled ignition systems, it may be necessary to disconnect certain vacuum hoses and/or electrical connectors. Refer to vehicle emission decal.

▲ Before removing wires from distributor cap, determine location of the No. 1 wire in cap, as distributor position may have been altered from that shown at the end of this chart.

Year & Engine/VIN Code	Spark Plug Gap	Firing Order Fig. ▲	Ignition Timing BTDC① Man. Trans.	Ignition Timing BTDC① Auto. Trans.	Mark Fig.	Curb Idle Speed Man. Trans.	Curb Idle Speed Auto. Trans. ②	Fast Idle Speed Man. Trans.	Fast Idle Speed Auto. Trans.	Fuel Pump Pressure
1980										
4-105/A Man. Trans.③	.035	A	12°	—	B	900	—	1400⑦	—	4–6
4-105/A Man. Trans.④	.035	A	10°	—	B	900	—	1400⑦	—	4–6
4-105/A Auto. Trans.③	.035	A	—	12°	C	—	900N	—	1700⑦	4–6
4-105/A Auto. Trans.④	.035	A	—	10°	C	—	900N	—	1700⑦	4–6
1981										
4-105/A Man. Trans.	.048	A	12°	—	B	900	—	1400⑨	—	4½–6
4-105/A Auto. Trans.	.048	A	—	10°	C	—	900N	—	1400⑨	4½–6
4-135/B Man. Trans.③	.035	D	10°	—	C	900	—	1100⑨	—	4½–6
4-135/B Auto. Trans.③	.035	D	—	10°	C	—	900N	—	1500⑩	4½–6
4-135/B Man. Trans.④	.035	D	10°	—	C	900	—	1100⑨	—	4½–6
4-135/B Auto. Trans.④	.035	D	—	10°	C	—	900N	—	1600⑩	4½–6
4-156/D	.041	F	—	7°	G	—	800N⑪	—	—	4½–6
1982										
4-105/A Man. Trans.	.035	A	20°⑫	—	B	850	—	1400	—	4½–6
4-105/A Auto. Trans.	.035	A	—	12°	C	—	900N	—	1400	4½–6
4-135/B Man. Trans.	.035	D	12°	—	C	850	—	1300	—	4½–6
4-135/B Auto. Trans.	.035	D	—	12°	C	—	900N	—	1600	4½–6
4-156/D	.041	F	—	7°	G	—	800N⑪	—	—	4½–6
1983										
4-97/A	.035	E	12°	—	H	⑭	—	1400	—	4½–6
4-105/B	.035	A	20°⑫	12°	⑬	850	900N	1400	1350	4½–6
4-135/C⑧	.035	D	10°	10°	C	775	900N	1400	1500	4½–6
4-135/C⑤	.035	D	6°	6°	C	900	850N	1350	1375	4½–6
4-135/F	.035	D	15°	—	C	850	—	1500	—	4½–6
4-135/D	.035	D	—	—	⑬	—	⑥	—	—	—
4-156/G	.040	F	—	7°	G	—	800N	—	—	4½–6
1984										
4-97/A	.035	E	12°	12°	H	850	1000N	—	—	4½–6
4-135/C	.035	D	10°	10°	⑬	800	900N	1500	1600	4½–6
4-135/F	.035	D	15°	—	C	850	—	1500	—	4½–6
4-135/D	.035	D	6°	6°	⑬	850⑥	750N⑥	—	—	34–38
4-135/E	.035	D	12°	12°	C	950⑥	800N⑥	—	—	51–55
4-156/G	.035–.040	F	—	7°	G	—	800N	—	950	4½–6
1985										
4-97/A	.035	E	12°	12°	H	850	1000N	1400	1400	4½–6
4-135/C	.035	D	10°	10°	—	800	900N	1700	1850	4½–6
4-135 H.P./C	.035	D	15°	—	C	850	—	1700	1850	4½–6
4-135 EFI/D	.035	D	12°	12°	—	850⑥	750N⑥	—	—	—
4-135 Turbo/E	.035	D	12°	12°	C	950⑥	950N⑥	—	—	—
4-156/G	.035–.040	F	—	7°	G	—	800N	—	950	4½–6

continued

CHRYSLER CORP.—Continued

The following specifications are published from the latest information available. This data should be used only in the absence of a decal affixed in the engine compartment.

★ When checking ignition timing, disconnect vacuum hose at distributor and plug opening in hose so idle speed will not be affected. Also, on some computer controlled ignition systems, it may be necessary to disconnect certain vacuum hoses and/or electrical connectors. Refer to vehicle emission decal.

▲ Before removing wires from distributor cap, determine location of the No. 1 wire in cap, as distributor position may have been altered from that shown at the end of this chart.

Year & Engine/VIN Code	Spark Plug Gap	Ignition Timing BTDC①				Curb Idle Speed		Fast Idle Speed		Fuel Pump Pressure
		Firing Order Fig.	Man. Trans.	Auto. Trans.	Mark Fig.	Man. Trans.	Auto. Trans. ②	Man. Trans.	Auto. Trans.	
FRONT WHEEL DRIVE—Continued										
1986										
4-97/A	.035	E	12°	—	H	800	—	—	—	4½–6
4-135 2 Bbl./C	.035	D	10°	10°	C	800	900N	—	—	4½–6
4-135 2 Bbl. H.O./C	.035	D	15°	—	C	850	—	—	—	4½–6
4-135 EFI/D	.035	D	12°	12°	C	900	700N	—	—	—
4-135 Turbo/E	.035	D	12°	12°	C	900	800N	—	—	—
4-153 EFI/K	.035	—	—	—	—	900	700N	—	—	—

①—BTDC—Before top dead center.
②—N: Neutral.
③—Exc. California
④—California
⑤—High altitude.
⑥—Idle speed controlled by Automatic Idle Speed (AIS) motor.
⑦—On lowest step of fast idle cam, w/ radiator fan operating, EGR & dist. vacuum advance disconnected & plugged & A/C off.
⑧—Exc. high altitude.
⑨—On 3rd step of fast idle cam (next to lowest), w/radiator fan operating, carb. switch grounded & EGR disconnected & plugged.
⑩—On 3rd step of fast idle cam (next to lowest), w/radiator fan operating,

carb. switch grounded, EGR disconnected & plugged & green duty cycle solenoid wire disconnected.
⑪—If mileage on vehicle is less than 300 mi., set at 750 RPM.
⑫—If an adjustable timing light is unavailable, use following procedure to mark flywheel for standard timing light:
  a. On models with A-412 manual transaxle, align 12° BTDC mark on flywheel with pointer on housing, cover flywheel timing marks with tape, then mark tape at 12° and 16° BTDC positions. Remove tape and reposition so that 12° BTDC mark on tape is aligned with 16° BTDC mark on flywheel. Permanently

mark flywheel at 16° BTDC mark on tape; a position which should correspond to 20° BTDC.
  b. On models with A-460 manual transaxle, align flywheel timing mark with 16° BTDC mark on housing, then scribe a line on flywheel aligned with 12° BTDC mark on housing. When checking or adjusting ignition timing, 20° BTDC will be indicated when scribed line is aligned with 16° BTDC mark on housing.
⑬—Exc. A-412 manual transaxle, Fig. C; A-412 manual transaxle, Fig. B.
⑭—Exc. high altitude, 900 RPM; high altitude, 850 RPM.

Fig. A

Fig. B

Fig. C

Fig. D

Fig. E

Fig. F

continued

CHRYSLER CORP.
Front Wheel Drive—Continued

MAGNETIC TIMING
PROBE
RECEPTACLE
Fig. G

Fig. H

Rear Wheel Drive

The following specifications are published from the latest information available. This data should be used only in the absence of a decal affixed in the engine compartment.

★ When checking ignition timing, disconnect vacuum hose at distributor and plug opening in hose so idle speed will not be affected. Also, on some computer controlled ignition systems, it may be necessary to disconnect certain vacuum hoses and/or electrical connectors. Refer to vehicle emission decal.

▲ Before removing wires from distributor cap, determine location of the No. 1 wire in cap, as distributor position may have been altered from that shown at the end of this chart.

Year & Engine/VIN Code	Spark Plug Gap	Ignition Timing BTDC①★				Curb Idle Speed		Fast Idle Speed		Fuel Pump Pressure
		Firing Order Fig. ▲	Man. Trans.	Auto. Trans.	Mark Fig.	Man. Trans.	Auto. Trans. ②	Man. Trans.	Auto. Trans.	
1980										
6-225/C Exc. Calif.	.035	B	—	12°	D	—	725N	—	1600④	3½–5
6-225/C Calif.	.035	B	—	12°	D	—	750N	—	—	3½–5
V8-318/G 2 Barrel	.035	C	—	12°	A	—	700N	—	1500④	5–7
V8-318/H 4 Barrel	.035	C	—	16°	A	—	700N	—	—	5–7
V8-360/K 2 Barrel	.035	C	—	12°	A	—	700N	—	1500④	5–7
V8-360/L 4 Barrel	.035	C	—	16°	A	—	750N	—	—	5–7
1981										
6-225/E Exc. Calif.	.035	B	—	12°	D	—	650N	—	1600④	4–5½
6-225/E Calif.	.035	B	—	16°	D	—	750N	—	2000④	4–5½
V8-318/K, M Less E.F.I.	.048③	C	—	16°	A	—	700N	—	1400④	5¾–7¼
V8-318/J E.F.I.	.035	C	—	12°	A	—	580N	—	—	7½–11½ ⑤
1982										
6-225/E Exc. Calif.	.035	B	—	12°	D	—	625N	—	1600④	4–5½
6-225/E Calif.	.035	B	—	12°	D	—	725N	—	1950④	4–5½
V8-318/K 2 Barrel	.035	C	—	16°	A	—	600N	—	1400④	5¾–7¼
V8-318/M 4 Barrel	.035	C	—	16°	A	—	650N	—	1400④	5¾–7¼
V8-318/J E.F.I.	.035	C	—	12°	A	—	580N	—	—	7½–11½ ⑤
1983										
6-225/H	.035	B	—	16°	D	—	750N	—	2000④	4–5½
V8-318/P 2 Barrel	.035	C	—	16°	A	—	700N	—	1400④	5¾–7½
V8-318/N E.F.I.	.035	C	—	12°	A	—	580D	—	—	7½–11½ ⑤

continued

The following specifications are published from the latest information available. This data should be used only in the absence of a decal affixed in the engine compartment.

★ When checking ignition timing, disconnect vacuum hose at distributor and plug opening in hose so idle speed will not be affected. Also, on some computer controlled ignition systems, it may be necessary to disconnect certain vacuum hoses and/or electrical connectors. Refer to vehicle emission decal.

▲ Before removing wires from distributor cap, determine location of the No. 1 wire in cap, as distributor position may have been altered from that shown at the end of this chart.

Year & Engine/VIN Code	Spark Plug Gap	Ignition Timing BTDC①★				Curb Idle Speed		Fast Idle Speed		Fuel Pump Pressure
		Firing Order Fig. ▲	Man. Trans.	Auto. Trans.	Mark Fig.	Man. Trans.	Auto. Trans. ②	Man. Trans.	Auto. Trans.	
REAR WHEEL DRIVE—Continued										
1984										
V8-318/P2 Barrel Exc. Calif.	.035	C	—	16°	A	—	700N	—	1400④	5¾—7¼
V8-318/P2 Barrel Calif.	.035	C	—	16°	A	—	730N	—	1400④	5¾—7¼
1985										
V8-318/P2 Barrel	.035	C	—	7°	A	—	680N	—	1700④	5¾—7¼
1986										
V8-318/2 Barrel	.035	C	—	—	A	—	680N	—	—	5¾—7¼

①—BTDC—Before top dead center.
②—N: Neutral. D: Drive.
③—If poor driveability condition is encountered during engine warmup on 1981 V8-318 2 Barrel engines built prior to Feb. 1, 1981, the spark plugs should be removed & regapped to .035 inch. These engines are equipped with spark plug type 65PR4 gapped at .048 inch. When replacing spark plugs, type 65PR gapped at .035 inch should be used.
④—With stop screw on second highest step of fast idle cam.
⑤—In tank electric fuel pump.

Fig. A

FIRING ORDER 1-5-3-6-2-4

Fig. B

FIRING ORDER 1-8-4-3-6-5-7-2

Fig. C

Fig. D

continued

FORD MOTOR COMPANY
Ford & Mercury Full Size Models

The following specifications are published from the latest information available. This data should be used only in the absence of a decal affixed in the engine compartment.

★ When checking ignition timing, disconnect vacuum hose at distributor and plug opening in hose so idle speed will not be affected. Also, on some computer controlled ignition systems, it may be necessary to disconnect certain vacuum hoses and/or electrical connectors. Refer to vehicle emission decal.

▲ Before removing wires from distributor cap, determine location of the No. 1 wire in cap, as distributor position may have been altered from that shown at the end of this chart.

Year & Engine/VIN Code	Spark Plug Gap	Firing Order Fig. ▲	Ignition Timing BTDC①★ Man. Trans.	Auto. Trans.	Mark Fig.	Curb Idle Speed② Man. Trans.	Auto. Trans.	Fast Idle Speed Man. Trans.	Auto. Trans.	Fuel Pump Pressure
1980										
V8-302/F Sedan Exc. Calif.⑥⑪⑫⑭	.050	A	—	6°	C	—	500D	—	1850③	6–8
V8-302/F Sedan Exc. Calif.⑥⑪⑬⑭	.050	A	—	8°	C	—	500D	—	1850③	6–8
V8-302/F Sta. Wag. Exc. Calif.⑪⑭	.050	A	—	6°	C	—	500D	—	③⑥⑮	6–8
V8-302/F Calif. & High Alt.⑯	.050	⑨	—	8°	C	—	500/650D	—	2000⑩	6–8
V8-351W/G Exc. High Output⑤⑯	.050	⑦	—	8°	C	—	550/640D	—	1650⑩	6–8
V8-351W/G High Output⑤⑯	.044	⑦	—	8°	C	—	550/700D	—	1500⑩	6–8
1981										
V8-255/D Exc. Calif.	.050	A	—	7°	C	—	500/650D	—	1800③	6–8
V8-255/D Calif.	.050	A	—	5°	C	—	500/650D	—	1800③	6–8
V8-302/F	.050	A	—	8°	C	—	500D	—	1800③	6–8
V8-351W/G⑤⑯	.050	⑦	—	—	C	—	550/640D	—	1650⑩	6–8
1982										
V8-255/D	.050	A	—	7°	C	—	500/650D	—	1800③	6–8
V8-302/F Exc. High Alt.	.050	A	—	8°	C	—	500D	—	1800③	6–8
V8-302/F High Alt.	.050	A	—	14°	C	—	500D	—	1800③	6–8
1983										
V8-302/F Exc. Calif.	.050	A	—	⑯	C	—	500D	—	2200③	—
V8-302/F Calif.	.050	A	—	⑯	C	—	550D	—	2400③	—
1984										
V8-302/F	.050	A	—	10°④	C	—	550D	—	2300③	—
1985										
V8-302/F Exc. Calif.	.050	A	—	10°	C	—	550D	—	2100	—
V8-302/F Calif.	.050	A	—	10°	B	—	550D	—	2300③	6–8
1986										
V8-302/	.050	A	—	—	B	—	600D	—	—	6½–8

①—BTDC—Before top dead center.
②—Idle speed on manual trans. vehicles is adjusted in Neutral & on auto. trans. equipped vehicles is adjusted in Drive unless otherwise specified. Where two idle speeds are listed, the higher speed is with the A/C or throttle solenoid energized. On models equipped with vacuum release brake, whenever adjusting ignition timing or idle speed, vacuum line to brake release mechanism must be disconnected & plugged to prevent parking brake from releasing when selector lever is moved to Drive.
③—On kickdown step of cam.
④—Disconnect single black wire connector near distributor, then start engine & check & adjust ignition timing as necessary. After completing adjustment, reconnect single black wire connector.
⑤—Windsor engine.
⑥—Refer to engine calibration code on engine identification label located at rear of left valve cover. The calibration code is located on the label after the engine code number and preceded by the letter C and the revision code is located below the calibration code and is preceded by the letter R.
⑦—Firing order, 1-3-7-2-6-5-4-8. Cylinder numbering (front to rear): Right bank 1-2-3-4, left bank 5-6-7-8. Refer to Fig. D for spark plug wire connections at distributor.
⑧—Engine cranking reference timing 10° BTDC. Ignition timing is not adjusta-

ble.
⑨—Firing order, 1-5-4-2-6-3-7-8. Cylinder numbering (front to rear): Right bank 1-2-3-4, left bank 5-6-7-8. Refer to Fig. D for spark plug wire connections at distributor.
⑩—On 2nd highest step of fast idle cam.
⑪—Except high altitude.
⑫—Calibration codes, 0-13A-R0, R11, R14 & 0-13F-R11.
⑬—Calibration codes, 0-13D-R0, R10, & R11.
⑭—Models less Electronic Engine Control (EEC) system.
⑮—Except calibration code 0-13A-R11, 1850 RPM; calibration code 0-13A-R11, 1700 RPM.
⑯—Models with Electronic Engine Control (EEC) System.

continued

FORD MOTOR COMPANY
Ford & Mercury Full Size Models—Continued

Fig. A

Fig. B

Fig. C

Fig. D

Ford & Mercury Compact & Intermediate Models

The following specifications are published from the latest information available. This data should be used only in the absence of a decal affixed in the engine compartment.

★ When checking ignition timing, disconnect vacuum hose at distributor and plug opening in hose so idle speed will not be affected. Also, on some computer controlled ignition systems, it may be necessary to disconnect certain vacuum hoses and/or electrical connectors. Refer to vehicle emission decal.

▲ Before removing wires from distributor cap, determine location of the No. 1 wire in cap, as distributor position may have been altered from that shown at the end of this chart.

Year & Engine/VIN Code	Spark Plug Gap	Ignition Timing BTDC①★				Curb Idle Speed②		Fast Idle Speed		Fuel Pump Pressure
		Firing Order Fig. ▲	Man. Trans.	Auto. Trans.	Mark Fig.	Man. Trans.	Auto. Trans.	Man. Trans.	Auto. Trans.	
1980										
4-140/A Exc. Calif.⑫⑬⑰⑱	.034	D	—	20°	E	—	800D	—	2000③	5–7�33
4-140/A Exc. Calif.⑫⑬⑰⑲	.034	D	—	17°	E	—	800D	—	2000③	5–7�33
4-140/A Exc. Calif.⑬⑳	.034	D	6°	6°	E	850	750D	1800③	2000③	5–7�33
4-140/A Calif.⑬	.034	D	6°	12°	E	850	750D	2000③	2000③	5–7�33
4-140/A⑭	.034	D	—	10°	E	—	800D	—	③⑫㉑	5–7�33
6-200/B Exc. Calif.⑫⑰㉒㊲	.050	F	—	7°	C	—	550/700D	—	2000③	5–7
6-200/B Exc. Calif.⑫⑰㉓㊲	.050	F	—	10°	C	—	550/700D	—	2000③	5–7

continued

FORD MOTOR COMPANY—Continued

The following specifications are published from the latest information available. This data should be used only in the absence of a decal affixed in the engine compartment.

★ When checking ignition timing, disconnect vacuum hose at distributor and plug opening in hose so idle speed will not be affected. Also, on some computer controlled ignition systems, it may be necessary to disconnect certain vacuum hoses and/or electrical connectors. Refer to vehicle emission decal.

▲ Before removing wires from distributor cap, determine location of the No. 1 wire in cap, as distributor position may have been altered from that shown at the end of this chart.

Year & Engine/VIN Code	Spark Plug Gap	Ignition Timing BTDC[1]★				Curb Idle Speed[2]		Fast Idle Speed		Fuel Pump Pressure
		Firing Order Fig. ▲	Man. Trans.	Auto. Trans.	Mark Fig.	Man. Trans.	Auto. Trans.	Man. Trans.	Auto. Trans.	
FORD & MERCURY COMPACT & INTERMEDIATE MODELS, 1980—Continued										
6-200/B Exc. Calif.[20][37]	.050	F	[12][24]	10°	C	700	550/700D	1600[3]	2000[3]	5-7
6-200/B Exc. Calif.[20][25]	.050	F	—	10°	C	—	625/700D	—	2000[3]	5-7
6-250/C[17]	.050	F	8°	—	A	600	—	1700[3]	—	5-7
6-250/C[20]	.050	F	4°	10°	A	700/800	550/650D	1700[3]	1700[3]	5-7
V8-255/D Exc. Calif. & High Alt.[26]	.050	G	—	6°	B	—	[12][27]	—	[4][12][28]	6-8
V8-255/D Calif.[8]	.050	G	—	6°	B	—	500/650D	—	1800[4]	6-8
V8-255/D Calif.[26]	.050	G	—	6°	B	—	[12][29]	—	2000[4]	6-8
V8-255/D High Alt.[37]	.050	G	—	6°	B	—	500/650D	—	2000[4]	6-8
V8-302/F Exc. Calif. & High Alt.[8]	.050	G	—	8°	B	—	[12][30]	—	2100[4]	6-8
V8-302/F Exc. Calif. & High Alt.[12][25][31]	.050	G	—	8°	B	—	[12][32]	—	2000[4]	6-8
V8-302/F Exc. Calif. & High Alt.[12][25][34]	.050	G	—	10°	B	—	500/650D	—	2000[4]	6-8
V8-302/F Calif.[8]	.050	G	—	6°	B	—	500/650D	—	2100[4]	6-8
V8-302/F Calif.[12][25][35]	.050	G	—	10°	B	—	500/650D	—	2000[4]	6-8
V8-302/F Calif.[12][26][38]	.050	G	—	6°	B	—	[12][39]	—	2100[4]	6-8
V8-302/F High Alt.[8]	.050	G	—	8°	B	—	500/650D	—	2000[4]	6-8
V8-302/F High Alt.[25]	.050	G	—	8°	B	—	[12][40]	—	2000[4]	6-8
1981										
4-140/A	.034	D	6°	12°	E	850[9]	750D[41]	2000[3]	2300[3]	5-7[33]
6-200/B[10][12]	.050	F	—	10°	C	—	600D	—	2000[3]	5-7[33]
6-200/B[11][12]	.050	F	—	12°	C	—	600D	—	2000[3]	5-7[33]
V8-255/D Exc. Calif.[16]	.050	G	—	10°	B	—	500D	—	1600[3]	6-8
V8-255/D Exc. Calif.[42]	.050	G	—	10°	B	—	500D	—	1700[3]	6-8
V8-255/D Calif.[16]	.050	G	—	8°	B	—	500/650D	—	1500[3]	6-8
V8-255/D Calif.[42]	.050	G	—	12°	B	—	500/650D	—	1500[3]	6-8
V8-302/F Exc. Calif.	.050	G	—	10°	B	—	500D	—	1600[3]	6-8
V8-302/F Calif.	.050	G	—	8°	B	—	500/675D	—	1600[3]	6-8
1982										
4-140/A Exc. Calif.	.034	D	6°	12°	E	850	800D	1800[3]	2000[3]	5-7[33]
4-140/A Calif.	.034	D	4°	12°	E	850	800D	1600[3]	1800[3]	5-7[33]
6-200/B Exc. High Alt.	.050	F	—	10°	C	—	450/600D	—	2000[3]	5-7[33]
6-200/B High Alt.	.050	F	—	12°	C	—	450/600D	—	2000[3]	5-7[33]
V6-232/3 Exc. Calif. & High Alt.	.044	I	—	[43]	J	—	550/650D	—	2200[4]	6-8
V6-232/3 Calif.	.044	I	—	12°	J	—	550/650D	—	1200[4]	6-8
V6-232/3 High Alt.	.044	I	—	12°	J	—	550/650D	—	2100[4]	6-8
V8-255/D Exc. High Alt.	.050	G	—	8°	B	—	500/650D	—	1500[3]	6-8
V8-255/D High Alt.	.050	G	—	14°	B	—	500/650D	—	1700[3]	6-8
1983										
4-140/A[13]	.044	D	9°	9°	E	850	800	1800[3]	2000[3]	5-7[33]
4-140/W[14]	.034	D	—	—	E	—	—	—	—	—

continued

FORD MOTOR COMPANY—Continued

The following specifications are published from the latest information available. This data should be used only in the absence of a decal affixed in the engine compartment.

★ When checking ignition timing, disconnect vacuum hose at distributor and plug opening in hose so idle speed will not be affected. Also, on some computer controlled ignition systems, it may be necessary to disconnect certain vacuum hoses and/or electrical connectors. Refer to vehicle emission decal.

▲ Before removing wires from distributor cap, determine location of the No. 1 wire in cap, as distributor position may have been altered from that shown at the end of this chart.

Year & Engine/VIN Code	Spark Plug Gap	Ignition Timing BTDC①★				Curb Idle Speed②		Fast Idle Speed		Fuel Pump Pressure
		Firing Order Fig. ▲	Man. Trans.	Auto. Trans.	Mark Fig.	Man. Trans.	Auto. Trans.	Man. Trans.	Auto. Trans.	
FORD & MERCURY COMPACT & INTERMEDIATE MODELS, 1983—Continued										
6-200/X Exc. High Alt.㊲	.050	F	—	10°	C	—	450/600	—	2000③	6–8
6-200/X High Alt.㊲	.050	F	—	12°	C	—	450/600	—	2000③	6–8
6-200/X Exc. Calif.㊹	.050	F	—	10°	C	—	450/550	—	2200③	6–8
6-200/X Calif.㊹	.050	F	—	10°	C	—	450/550	—	2100③	6–8
V6-232/3 Exc. Calif. & High Alt.	.044	I	—	12°	J	—	550/650	—	2200④	6–8㉝
V6-232/3 Calif.	.044	I	—	10°	J	—	550/700	—	2200④	6–8㉝
V6-232/3 High Alt.	.044	I	—	12°	J	—	550/700	—	2100④	6–8㉝
V8-302/F	.050	G	—	—	B	—	550	—	—	⑮
1984										
4-140/A⑬	.044	D	10°	10°	E	850	750D	2000	2200	5–7
4-140/W⑭	.034	D	10°	10°	E	825–975⑤	825–975⑤	⑤	⑤	—
V6-232/3	.044	I	—	10°	J	—	—	—	—	㊱
V8-302/F	.050	G	—	—	B	—	550D	—	⑥	⑮
V8-302 H.O./M	.044	H	—	—	B	—	550D	—		⑮
1985										
4-140/A⑬	.044	D	10°	10°	E	800	750D	2200	2200	5–7
4-140/W⑭	.034	D	10°	10°	E	⑤	⑤	⑤	⑤	—
V6-232/C	.044	I	—	10°	J	—	500–600D⑦	—	⑤	㊱
V8-302/F	.050	G	—	7°	B	—	550D	—	2200	⑮
V8-302 H.O./M	.044	H	—	10°	B	—	550D	—	2400	⑮
1986										
4-140/⑬	.044	D	—	—	E	800	750D	—	—	5½–6½
4-140/⑭	.034	D	—	—	E	—	—	—	—	—
V6-232/	.044	I	—	—	J	—	—	—	—	—
V8-302/	.050	—	—	—	B	—	—	—	—	—

①—BTDC—Before top dead center.
②—Idle speed on manual trans. vehicles is adjusted in Neutral & on auto. trans. equipped vehicles is adjusted in Drive unless otherwise specified. Where two idle speeds are listed, the higher speed is with the A/C or throttle solenoid energized. On models equipped with vacuum release brake, whenever adjusting ignition timing or idle speed, vacuum line to brake release mechanism must be disconnected & plugged to prevent parking brake from releasing when selector lever is moved to Drive.
③—On kickdown step of cam.
④—On high step of fast idle cam.
⑤—Controlled by idle speed control motor.
⑥—Calibration code 4-22F-R00, 2100 RPM; calibration codes 3-22D-R00, & 4-22F-R00, 2200 RPM; calibration codes 4-22C-R00, 4-22D-R00, 4-22D-R10, 4-22H-R00 & 4-22Q-R00, 2300 RPM.
⑦—With A/C on and clutch de-energized.
⑧—Granada.
⑨—If mileage on vehicle is less than 100 mi., set idle at 100 RPM less than specified.
⑩—Calibration code 1-12B-R0.
⑪—Calibration code 1-12B-R10.
⑫—Refer to engine calibration code on engine identification label, located at rear of left valve cover on V6 & V8 engines, on front of valve cover on in line 4 & 6 cyl. engines. The calibration code is located on the label after the engine code number is preceded by the letter C and the revision code is located below the calibration code and is preceded by the letter R.
⑬—Except turbocharged engine.
⑭—Turbocharged engine.
⑮—Fuel tank mounted pump, 6; frame mounted pump, 39.
⑯—Models less Automatic Overdrive Transmission.
⑰—Models less Thermactor pump.
⑱—Calibration code 9-21B-R10.
⑲—Calibration codes 0-21A-R0 & 0-21B-R0.
⑳—Models w/Thermactor pump.
㉑—Calibration codes 0-1H-R10, R11, R15 & 0-1S-R0, R10, R11, 2000 RPM; calibration codes 0-1H-R19, R20 & 0-1S-R15, 2150 RPM.
㉒—Calibration code 0-27A-R3.
㉓—Calibration code 0-27A-R10.
㉔—Calibration code 0-6A-R0, 10° BTDC; calibration code, 0-6B-R1, 12° BTDC.
㉕—Cougar XR-7 & Thunderbird.
㉖—Cougar, Fairmont, Thunderbird & Zephyr.
㉗—Calibration codes 0-16C-R0 & R15, 500/650D; calibration code 0-16C-R13, 550/700D; calibration code 0-16C-R18, 550/625D; calibration code 0-16C-R19, 500/625D.
㉘—Except calibration code 0-16C-R0, 1800 RPM; calibration code 0-16C-R0, 2000 RPM.
㉙—Calibration code 0-16S-R14, 500/650D RPM; calibration code 0-16S-R17, 500/625D RPM.
㉚—Calibration code 9-11C-R1, 600/675D RPM; calibration code 0-11D-R0, 500/650D RPM.
㉛—Calibration codes 0-11A-R0 & R10.
㉜—Calibration code 0-11A-R0, 500/650D RPM; calibration code 0-11A-R10, 500/625D RPM.
㉝—With pump to fuel tank return line pinched off & a new fuel filter in-

continued

FORD MOTOR COMPANY

Ford & Mercury Compact & Intermediate Models, Notes—Continued

㉞—stalled.
Calibration code 0-11B-R0.
㉟—Calibration codes 0-11P-R12 & R13.
㊱—Frame rail mounted pump, 40–45; intake manifold mounted pump, 30.5.
㊲—Fairmont & Zephyr.
㊳—Calibration codes 0-11N-R0, R10, R11

& R13.
㊴—Calibration codes 0-11N-R0 & R10, 500/650D RPM; calibration codes 0-11N-R11 & R13, 500/625D RPM.
㊵—Calibration code 0-11W-R0, 500/700D RPM; calibration code 0-11W-R10, 550/625D RPM.
㊶—If mileage on vehicle is less than 100

mi., set idle at 50 RPM less than specified.
㊷—Models with Automatic Overdrive Transmission.
㊸—Cougar & Granada, 10°BTDC; Cougar XR-7 & Thunderbird, 12°BTDC.
㊹—LTD & Marquis.

Fig. A

Fig. B

Fig. C

Fig. D

Fig. E

Fig. F

Fig. G

Fig. H

Fig. I

Fig. J

FORD MOTOR COMPANY—Continued

Ford Mustang & Pinto • Mercury Bobcat & Capri

The following specifications are published from the latest information available. This data should be used only in the absence of a decal affixed in the engine compartment.

★ When checking ignition timing, disconnect vacuum hose at distributor and plug opening in hose so idle speed will not be affected. Also, on some computer controlled ignition systems, it may be necessary to disconnect certain vacuum hoses and/or electrical connectors. Refer to vehicle emission decal.

▲ Before removing wires from distributor cap, determine location of the No. 1 wire in cap, as distributor position may have been altered from that shown at the end of this chart.

Year & Engine/VIN	Spark Plug Gap	Firing Order Fig. ▲	Ignition Timing BTDC①★ Man. Trans.	Ignition Timing BTDC①★ Auto. Trans.	Mark Fig.	Curb Idle Speed② Man. Trans.	Curb Idle Speed② Auto. Trans.	Fast Idle Speed Man. Trans.	Fast Idle Speed Auto. Trans.	Fuel Pump Pressure
1980										
4-140, 2300 cc/A Exc. Calif. ⑥⑧⑱⑳	.034	G	—	20°	E	—	600/800D	—	2000③	5–7④
4-140, 2300 cc/A Exc. Calif. ⑥⑧⑱㉑	.034	G	—	17°	E	—	650/800D	—	2000③	5–7④
4-140, 2300 cc/A Exc. Calif. ⑧⑲	.034	G	6°	6°	E	850	750D	2000③	1800③	5–7④
4-140, 2300 cc/A Calif. ⑧	.034	G	6°	12°	E	850	750D	2000③	2000③	5–7④
4-140, 2300 cc/T Exc. Calif. ⑨	.034	G	6°	10°	E	850	650/800D	1800③	③⑦㉒	④㉓
4-140, 2300 cc/T Calif. ⑨	.034	G	2°	10°	E	900	650/800D	1800③	③⑥㉔	④㉓
6-200/B Exc. Calif. ⑱	.050	A	—	⑥㉕	B	—	550/700D	—	2000③	5–7
6-200/B Exc. Calif. ⑲	.050	A	⑥㉖	10°	B	700/900	550/700D	1600③	2000③	5–7
6-200/B Calif.	.050	A	—	⑥㉗	B	—	600/700D	—	2300③	5–7
V8-255/D Exc. Calif. ⑥㉘㉙	.050	D	—	6°	C	—	500D	—	2000⑤	6–8
V8-255/D Exc. Calif. ⑥⑮㉘	.050	D	—	6°	C	—	550D	—	1800⑤	6–8
V8-255/D Calif.	.050	D	—	6°	C	—	550D	—	1800⑤	6–8
V8-255/D High Alt.	.050	D	—	6°	C	—	500D	—	2000⑤	6–8
1981										
4-140/A	.034	G	6°	12°	E	850⑯	750D	2000③	2300③	5–7④
6-200/B	.050	A	8°	⑥㉚	B	700	600D	1800③	2000③	5–7
V8-255/D Exc. Calif.	.050	D	—	10°	C	—	500/650D	—	1600③	6–8
V8-255/D Calif.	.050	D	—	8°	C	—	500/650D	—	1500③	6–8
1982										
4-140/A Exc. Calif. & High Alt.	.034	G	⑥㊱	12°	E	850	800D	③⑥㊳	2000③	5–7④
4-140/A Calif. ⑥㉝	.034	G	4°	—	E	850	—	1600③	—	5–7④
4-140/A Calif. ⑥㉞	.034	G	4°	12°	E	850	800D	1600③	1800③	5–7④
4-140/A High Alt.	.034	G	6°	12°	E	850	800D	1800③	2000③	5–7④
6-200/B	.050	A	—	㊲	B	—	450/600D	—	2000③	5–7
V8-255/D Exc. High Alt.	.050	D	—	8°	C	—	500/700D	—	1500③	6–8
V8-255/D High Alt.	.050	D	—	14°	C	—	500/700D	—	1600③	6–8
V8-302/F	.044	I	12°	—	C	700/900	—	1500③	—	6–8
1983										
4-140/A⑧	.044	G	9°	9°	E	850	800D	1800③	2000③	5–7
4-140/W⑨	.034	G	10°	—	E	825–975⑬	—	⑬	—	—
V6-232/3 Exc. Calif. & High Alt.	.044	F	—	10°	H	—	㊴	—	2200⑤	6–8⑩
V6-232/3 Calif.	.044	F	—	8°	H	—	㊴	—	2200⑤	6–8⑩
V6-232/3 High Alt.	.044	F	—	18°	H	—	㊴	—	2100⑤	6–8⑩
V8-302/F	.044	I	10°	—	C	700	—	2400⑤	—	6–8
1984										
4-140/A⑧	.044	G	10°	10°	E	850	750D	2000	2000	5–7⑩
4-140/W⑨	.034	G	10°	—	E	825–975⑬	—	⑬	⑬	—
V6-232/3	.044	F	—	10°	H	—	525	—	—	⑪

continued

GASOLINE ENGINE TUNE UP SPECIFICATIONS

FORD MOTOR COMPANY—Continued

The following specifications are published from the latest information available. This data should be used only in the absence of a decal affixed in the engine compartment.

★ When checking ignition timing, disconnect vacuum hose at distributor and plug opening in hose so idle speed will not be affected. Also, on some computer controlled ignition systems, it may be necessary to disconnect certain vacuum hoses and/or electrical connectors. Refer to vehicle emission decal.

▲ Before removing wires from distributor cap, determine location of the No. 1 wire in cap, as distributor position may have been altered from that shown at the end of this chart.

Year & Engine/VIN	Spark Plug Gap	Ignition Timing BTDC①★				Curb Idle Speed②		Fast Idle Speed		Fuel Pump Pressure
		Firing Order Fig. ▲	Man. Trans.	Auto. Trans.	Mark Fig.	Man. Trans.	Auto. Trans.	Man. Trans.	Auto. Trans.	
FORD MUSTANG & PINTO • MERCURY BOBCAT & CAPRI, 1984—Continued										
V8-302/M③①	.044	I	—	—	C	700	—	—	—	6–8
V8-302/M③②	.044	I	—	8°	C	—	550	—	2500	⑫
1985										
4-140/A⑧	.044	G	10°	10°	E	775	750D	2000③	2200③	5–7⑩
4-140/T⑨⑭	.034	G	10°	—	—	900	—	⑬	—	—
V6-232/3	.044	F	—	10°	H	—	525D⑬	—	⑬	⑪
V8-302/M Exc. Calif.	.044	I	12°	—	C	700	—	2400③	—	6–8
V8-302/M Calif.	.044	I	10°	—	C	700	—	2400③	—	6–8
V8-302/M Exc. Calif.⑥㉟	.044	I	—	8°	C	—	550D	—	2500	—
V8-302/M Exc. Calif.⑥⑰	.044	I	—	10°	C	—	550D	—	2400	—
V8-302/M Calif.	.044	I	—	6°	C	—	550D	—	2400	—
1986										
4-140/1 Barrel	.044	G	—	—	E	800	750D	—	—	5.5–6.5
4-140/Turbo	.034	G	—	—	—	—	—	—	—	—
V6-232/CFI	.054	F	—	—	H	—	550–625D③	—	—	—
V8-302/H.O.	.050	I	—	—	C	—	—	—	—	—

①—B.T.D.C.—Before top dead center.
②—Idle speed on manual trans. vehicles is adjusted in Neutral & on auto. trans. equipped vehicles is adjusted in Drive unless otherwise specified. Where two idle speeds are listed, the higher speed is with the A/C or throttle solenoid energized.
③—On kickdown step of cam.
④—With pump to fuel tank line pinched off & a new fuel filter installed.
⑤—On high step of fast idle cam.
⑥—Refer to engine calibration code on engine identification label located at rear of left valve cover on V6 & V8 engines, on front of valve cover on inline 4 & 6 cyl. engines. The calibration code is located on the label after the engine codes number & is preceded by the letter C & the revision code is located below the calibration code is preceded by the letter R.
⑦—With throttle solenoid energized. Higher idle speed is with A/C on & compressor clutch deenergized, if equipped.
⑧—Except turbocharged engine.
⑨—Turbocharged engine
⑩—If vehicle is equipped with Tripmind-er, return line should be pinched off when checking pressure.
⑪—Frame rail mounted pump, 40–45; intake manifold mounted pump, 30.5.
⑫—Fuel tank mounted pump, 6; frame mounted pump, 39.
⑬—Equipped w/ idle speed control.
⑭—Mustang SVO.
⑮—Calibration code 0-16A-R12.
⑯—If mileage on vehicle is less than 100 mi., set idle speed 100 RPM less than specified.
⑰—Calibration codes 5-22A-R0 & 5-22I-R0.
⑱—Models less Thermactor air pump.
⑲—Models with Thermactor air pump.
⑳—Calibration code, 9-21B-R10.
㉑—Calibration codes, 0-21A-R0 & 0-21B-R0 & R10.
㉒—Except calibration code 0-1H-R20, 2000 RPM; calibration code 0-1H-R20, 2150 RPM.
㉓—Manual trans., 5–7 psi.; auto. trans. models use an electric fuel pump.
㉔—Except calibration code 0-1S-R15, 2000 RPM; calibration code 0-1S-R15, 2150 RPM.
㉕—Calibration code 0-27A-R3, 7° BTDC; calibration code 0-27A-R10, 10° BTDC.
㉖—Calibration code 0-6A-R0, 10° BTDC; calibration code 0-6A-R1, 12° BTDC.
㉗—Except calibration code 0-7P-R11, 10° BTDC; calibration code 0-7P-R11, 7° BTDC.
㉘—Except high altitude.
㉙—Calibration code 0-16A-R0.
㉚—Except calibration code 1-12B-R10, 10° BTDC; calibration code 1-12B-R10, 12° BTDC.
㉛—Vehicles equipped with 5 speed manual trans.
㉜—Vehicles equipped with automatic overdrive trans.
㉝—Calibration code 2-5N-R0.
㉞—Exc. calibration code 2-5N-R0.
㉟—Calibration code 4-22A-R13.
㊱—Calibration codes 2-5A-R0 & 2-2B-R0, 6°; calibration codes 2-5C-R0 & 2-5C-R11, 4°.
㊲—Exc. high altitude, 10°; high altitude, 12°.
㊳—Calibration codes 2-5A-R0 & 2-5B-R0, 1800 RPM; calibration codes 2-5C-R0 & 2-5C-R11, 1600 RPM.
㊴—With A/C, 550/650D; less A/C, 450/550D.

continued

16

Fig. A

Fig. B

Fig. C

Fig. D

Fig. E

Fig. F

Fig. G

Fig. H

Fig. I

continued

FORD MOTOR COMPANY—Continued

Ford Escort, EXP & Tempo • Mercury LN7, Lynx & Topaz

The following specifications are published from the latest information available. This data should be used only in the absence of a decal affixed in the engine compartment.

★ When checking ignition timing, disconnect vacuum hose at distributor and plug opening in hose so idle speed will not be affected. Also, on some computer controlled ignition systems, it may be necessary to disconnect certain vacuum hoses and/or electrical connectors. Refer to vehicle emission decal.

▲ Before removing wires from distributor cap, determine location of the No. 1 wire in cap, as distributor position may have been altered from that shown at the end of this chart.

Year & Engine/VIN	Spark Plug Gap	Ignition Timing BTDC①★				Curb Idle Speed		Fast Idle Speed		Fuel Pump Pressure
		Firing Order Fig.▲	Man. Trans.	Auto. Trans.	Mark Fig.	Man. Trans.	Auto. Trans.②	Man. Trans.	Auto. Trans.	
1981										
4-97.6, 1.6L/2 Exc. Calif.	.044	A	10°⑦	10°⑦	B	900③⑧	750D④	2400⑤⑨	2400⑤	4–6⑥
4-97.6, 1.6L/2 Calif.	.044	A	10°⑦	6°⑦	B	900③⑧	750D④	2400⑤⑨	2400⑤	4–6⑥
1982										
4-97.6/2 Exc. Calif.⑩⑪⑫	.044	A	—	12°⑦	B	—	800D③	—	2400⑤	4½–6½⑥
4-96.6/2 Exc. Calif. & High Alt.⑪⑬⑭	.044	A	—	10°⑦	B	—	750D⑮	—	2400⑤	4½–6½⑥
4-97.6/2 Exc. High Alt.⑩⑪⑯	.044	A	6°⑦	—	B	800⑮	—	2400⑤	—	4½–6½⑥
4-97.6/2 Exc. High Alt.⑪⑬⑱	.044	A	14°⑦	—	B	800⑮	—	2400⑤	—	4½–6½⑥
4-97.6/2 Exc. High Alt.⑪⑬⑲⑳	.044	A	14°⑦	—	B	650/1300	—	2200⑤	—	4½–6½⑥
4-97.6/2 Exc. High Alt.⑪⑬㉑	.044	A	12°⑦	—	B	800⑮	—	2400⑤	—	4½–6½⑥
4-97.6/2 Exc. High Alt.⑪⑬㉒	.044	A	10°⑦	—	B	800⑮	—	2400⑤	—	4½–6½⑥
4-97.6/2 Calif.⑩⑪㉓	.044	A	—	12°⑦	B	—	800D③	—	2400⑤	4½–6½⑥
4-97.6/2 Calif.⑩⑪㉔	.044	A	—	8°⑦	B	—	800D③	—	2400⑤	4½–6½⑥
4-97.6/2 Calif.⑪⑬㉕	.044	A	—	8°⑦	B	—	750D⑮	—	2400⑤	4½–6½⑥
4-97.6/2 Calif.⑪⑬㉖	.044	A	—	10°⑦	B	—	750D⑮	—	2400⑤	4½–6½⑥
4-97.6/2 High Alt.⑩⑪㉗	.044	A	8°⑦	—	B	800⑯	—	2400⑤	—	4½–6½⑥
4-97.6/2 High Alt.⑪⑬㉘	.044	A	10°⑦	10°⑦	B	800⑯	750D⑮	2400⑤	2400⑤	4½–6½⑥
4-97.6 H.O./2㉙	.044	A	10°⑦	10°⑦	B	—	750D⑮	—	2200⑤	4½–6½⑥
1983										
4-97.6/2 Exc. High Alt.⑪㉚	.044	A	8°⑦	—	B	650	—	2100⑤	—	4½–6½⑥
4-97.6/2 Exc. High Alt.⑪㉙㉛	.044	A	10°⑦	—	B	800㉜/1200㉝	—	2400⑤⑨	—	4½–6½⑥
4-97.6/2 Exc. High Alt.⑪㉞	.044	A	—	10°⑦	B	—	750D	—	2400⑤	4½–6½⑥
4-97.6/2 Calif.⑪㊱	.044	A	8°⑦	10°⑦	B	800㉜/1200㉝	750D	2200㉟	2400⑤	4½–6½⑥
4-97.6/2 Calif.⑪㉙㊲	.044	A	—	14°⑦	B	—	750D	—	2400⑤	4½–6½⑥
4-97.6/2 High Alt.⑪㉙㊳	.044	A	10°⑦	—	B	900㉜/1500㉝	—	2400⑤⑨	—	4½–6½⑥
4-97.6/2 High Alt.⑪㉙㊹	.044	A	—	16°⑦	B	—	850D	—	2400⑤	4½–6½⑥
4-97.6 EFI/2⑪㊷	.044	A	13°	—	B	㊺	—	—	—	39
4-97.6 EFI/2⑪㊸	.044	A	15°	—	B	㊺	—	—	—	39
4-97.6 EFI/2 Exc. High Alt.⑪㊹	.044	A	—	15°	B	㊺	—	—	—	39
1984										
4-97.6 H.O./4 495⑪㊵㊿	.044	A	12°	—	B	800/1200㉝	—	2200㊴	—	4–6
4-97.6/2 49S⑪㊵㊼	.044	A	8°	—	B	720	—	2200㊴	—	4–6
4-97.6/2 49S⑪㊵㊽	.044	A	8°	—	B	700/1200㉝	—	2200㊴	—	4–6
4-97.6/2 Calif.⑪㊾	.044	A	8°	—	B	700/1200㉝	—	2200㊴	—	4–6
4-97.6 H.O./4 Calif.⑪㊿	.044	A	12°	—	B	800/1200㉝	—	2200㊴	—	4–6

continued

FORD MOTOR COMPANY—Continued

The following specifications are published from the latest information available. This data should be used only in the absence of a decal affixed in the engine compartment.

★ When checking ignition timing, disconnect vacuum hose at distributor and plug opening in hose so idle speed will not be affected. Also, on some computer controlled ignition systems, it may be necessary to disconnect certain vacuum hoses and/or electrical connectors. Refer to vehicle emission decal.

▲ Before removing wires from distributor cap, determine location of the No. 1 wire in cap, as distributor position may have been altered from that shown at the end of this chart.

Year & Engine/VIN	Spark Plug Gap	Ignition Timing BTDC [1] ★				Curb Idle Speed		Fast Idle Speed		Fuel Pump Pressure
		Firing Order Fig. ▲	Man. Trans.	Auto. Trans.	Mark Fig.	Man. Trans.	Auto. Trans. [2]	Man. Trans.	Auto. Trans.	
FORD ESCORT, EXP & TEMPO • MERCURY LN7, LYNX & TOPAZ, 1984—Continued										
4-97.6 H.O./4 49S & High Alt. [11][40][56]	.044	A	—	14°	B	—	700	—	2400[39]	4–6
4-97.6 H.O./4 Calif. [11][57]	.044	A	—	14°	B	—	700	—	2400[39]	4–6
4-97.6 EFI/5 Calif. [11][46][58]	.044	A	10°	—	B	800[45]	—	—	—	39
4-97.6 EFI/5 49S & High Alt. [11][47][48][59]	.044	A	10°	—	B	800[45]	—	—	—	39
4-97.6 EFI/5 49S & High Alt. [11][46][48][60]	.044	A	—	10°	B	—	750[45]	—	—	39
4-140/R	.044	C	15°	—	D	800	—	1900	—	4½–6½
4-140/R	.044	C	—	15°	E	—	700	—	2200	4½–6½
1985										
4-97.6/2	.044	A	8°[7]	—	B	[17]	—	2200[39]	—	5–7
4-97.6 H.O./4	.044	A	12°[7]	14°[7]	B	800/1200	700D	2200[39]	2400[39]	5–7
4-97.6 EFI/5	.044	A	10°	10°	B	800	750D	—	—	—
4-97.6 Turbo/8	.044	A	8°	—	B	800	—	—	—	—
4-116/9	.044	—	—	—	—	750	800D	—	—	4–6
4-140/X Exc. Calif.	.044	C	10°	10°	[49]	750	600D	—	—	—
4-140/X Calif.	.044	C	10°	10°	[49]	800	600D	—	—	—
4-140 H.O./S	.044	C	10°	—	[49]	800	—	—	—	—
1986										
4-116/9 2 Barrel	.044	—	—	—	—	750	800D	—	—	4–6
4-116/EFI	.044	—	—	—	—	1000	850D	—	—	—
4-140/	.044	C	—	—	[49]	800	—	—	—	—
4-140 H.O./	.044	C	—	—	[49]	800	—	—	—	—

① —BTDC—Before top dead center.
② —D: Drive.
③ —With A/C on, 1700 RPM, if equipped.
④ —With A/C on, 1850 RPM, if equipped.
⑤ —On kick down step of cam.
⑥ —With pump to tank return pinched off.
⑦ —At 800 RPM.
⑧ —If mileage on vehicle is less than 100 mi., set at 750 RPM.
⑨ —If mileage on vehicle is less than 100 mi., set at 2200 RPM.
⑩ —Early production EXP & LN7.
⑪ —Refer to engine calibration code on engine identification label, located at front of engine timing belt cover. The calibration code is located on the label below the engine sequence number (ESN) & is preceded by the letter C. The revision code is located next to the calibration code & is preceded by the letter R.
⑫ —Calibration code 1-4E-R0.
⑬ —Escort, Lynx & late production EXP & LN7.
⑭ —Calibration code 2-4C-R0.
⑮ —With A/C on, 1500N RPM, if equipped.
⑯ —Calibration codes 1-3S-R0 & 1-3S-R11.

⑰ —Less A/C, 720 RPM; with A/C, 700/1200 RPM.
⑱ —Calibration codes 2-3A-R10 & 2-3C-R0.
⑲ —Calibration codes 2-3D-R0, R1, R14 & R15.
⑳ —Models less A/C & power steering.
㉑ —Calibration code 2-3E-R0.
㉒ —Calibration code 2-3G-R0.
㉓ —Calibration code 1-4S-R0.
㉔ —Calibration code 1-4S-R10.
㉕ —Calibration code 2-4Q-R0.
㉖ —Calibration code 2-4Q-R10.
㉗ —Calibration code 1-3Y-R10.
㉘ —Calibration code, man. trans. 2-3X-R0; auto. trans., 2-4X-R0.
㉙ —High output engine.
㉚ —Calibration code 3-3D-R01.
㉛ —Calibration code 2-3B-R11.
㉜ —With VOTM "off".
㉝ —With VOTM "on".
㉞ —Calibration code 3-4C-R00.
㉟ —If mileage on vehicle is less than 100 miles, set at 2000 RPM.
㊱ —Calibration code, man. trans., 3-3C-R00; auto. trans., 3-4Q-R01.
㊲ —Calibration code 3-4T-R00.
㊳ —Calibration code 2-3Y-R11.
㊴ —On second step of fast idle cam.

㊵ —With electric cooling fan ON.
㊶ —Calibration code 3-4Y-R00.
㊷ —Calibration code 3-03A-R12.
㊸ —Calibration code 3-03A-R13.
㊹ —Calibration code 3-04A-R10.
㊺ —Idle speed not adjustable. Idle speed maintained by computer.
㊻ —Except turbocharged engine.
㊼ —Turbocharged engine.
㊽ —49S—All states exc. California.
㊾ —Refer to Fig. D for manual transaxle models or Fig. E for automatic transaxle models. On manual transaxle models, a cover plate retained by two screws must be removed to view timing marks. On automatic transaxle models, symbols are indented on outer face of flywheel.
㊿ —Calibration code 4-03A-R00.
51 —Calibration code 4-03F-R00.
52 —Calibration code 4-03K-R00.
53 —Calibration code 4-03P-R00.
54 —Calibration code 4-03S-R00.
55 —Calibration code 4-03A-R04.
56 —Calibration code 4-04S-R06.
57 —Calibration code 4-27A-R00.
58 —Calibration code 4-27T-R00.
59 —Calibration code 4-28A-R00.

continued

Fig. A

Fig. B

Fig. C

Fig. D

Fig. E

Ford Taurus & Mercury Sable

The following specifications are published from the latest information available. This data should be used only in the absence of a decal affixed in the engine compartment.

★ When checking ignition timing, disconnect vacuum hose at distributor and plug opening in hose so idle speed will not be affected. Also, on some computer controlled ignition systems, it may be necessary to disconnect certain vacuum hoses and/or electrical connectors. Refer to vehicle emission decal.

▲ Before removing wires from distributor cap, determine location of the No. 1 wire in cap, as distributor position may have been altered from that shown at the end of this chart.

| Year & Engine | Spark Plug Gap | Ignition Timing BTDC①★ | | | | Curb Idle Speed② | | Fast Idle Speed | | Fuel Pump Pressure |
		Firing Order Fig. ▲	Man. Trans.	Auto. Trans.	Mark Location	Man. Trans.	Auto. Trans.	Man. Trans.	Auto. Trans.	
1986										
4-153	.044	—	—	—	—	—	—	—	—	—
V6-182	.044	—	—	—	—	—	—	—	—	—

①—BTDC—Before top dead center.
②—Idle speed on manual trans. vehicles is adjusted in Neutral & on auto. trans. equipped vehicles is adjusted in Drive unless otherwise specified.

Where two idle speeds are listed, the higher speed is with the A/C or throttle solenoid energized. On models equipped with vacuum release brake, whenever adjusting ignition timing or

idle speed, vacuum line to brake release mechanism must be disconnected & plugged to prevent parking brake from releasing when selector is moved to Drive.

continued

FORD MOTOR COMPANY—Continued

Lincoln

The following specifications are published from the latest information available. This data should be used only in the absence of a decal affixed in the engine compartment.

★ When checking ignition timing, disconnect vacuum hose at distributor and plug opening in hose so idle speed will not be affected. Also, on some computer controlled ignition systems, it may be necessary to disconnect certain vacuum hoses and/or electrical connectors. Refer to vehicle emission decal.

▲ Before removing wires from distributor cap, determine location of the No. 1 wire in cap, as distributor position may have been altered from that shown at the end of this chart.

Year & Engine/VIN	Spark Plug Gap	Ignition Timing BTDC①★ Firing Order Fig.▲	Man. Trans.	Auto. Trans.	Mark Fig.	Curb Idle Speed② Man. Trans.	Auto. Trans.	Fast Idle Speed Man. Trans.	Auto. Trans.	Fuel Pump Pressure
1980										
V8-302/F Versailles Exc. High Alt.	.050	⑪	—	6°	B	—	550D	—	④⑥⑭	6–8
V8-302/F Versailles High Alt.	.050	⑪	—	8°	B	—	550D	—	2100④	6–8
V8-302/F E.F.I. Exc. Versailles	.050	⑪	—	⑦	B	—	550D	—	2100④	—
V8-351W/G⑤⑩	.050	⑪	—	—	B	—	550/640D	—	1650⑬	6–8
1981										
V8-302/F E.F.I. Exc. Calif.	.050	⑪	—	⑦	B	—	550D	—	2200⑬	—
V8-302/F E.F.I. Calif.	.050	⑪	—	⑦	B	—	550D	—	2150⑬	—
1982										
V6-232/3 Exc. Calif.	.044	A	—	12°	D	—	550/650D	—	2200④	6–8
V6-232/3 Calif.	.044	A	—	12°	D	—	550/650D	—	2200③	6–8
V8-302/F Exc. Calif.	.050	D	—	12°	B	—	550D	—	1700③	6–8
V8-302/F High Alt.	.050	D	—	12°	B	—	550D	—	1700③	6–8
V8-302/F Calif.	.050	⑪	—	—	B	—	550D	—	—	6–8
V8-302/F E.F.I. Exc. Calif.	.050	⑪	—	⑦	B	—	550D	—	2200⑫	—
V8-302/F E.F.I. Calif.	.050	⑪	—	⑦	B	—	550D	—	2150⑫	—
1983										
V8-302/F E.F.I. Exc. Calif.	.050	⑪	—	⑦	B	—	550D	—	2200④	39
V8-302/F E.F.I. Calif.	.050	⑪	—	⑦	B	—	550D	—	2200④	39
1984										
V8-302/F E.F.I. Exc. Calif.	.050	⑪	—	10°	B	—	550D	—	④⑥⑧	39
V8-302/F E.F.I. Calif.	.050	⑪	—	10°	B	—	550D	—	④⑥⑨	39
1985										
V8-302/F E.F.I.	.050	⑪	—	10°	B	—	550D	—	2300	39
V8-302 H.O./M E.F.I.	.050	⑪	—	10°	B	—	550D	—	2400	39
1986										
V8-302/E.F.I.	.050	⑪	—	—	B	—	—	—	—	—
V8-302 H.O./E.F.I.	.050	⑪	—	—	B	—	—	—	—	—

①—BTDC—Before top dead center.

②—Idle speed on manual trans. vehicles is adjusted in Neutral & on auto. trans. equipped vehicles is adjusted in Drive unless otherwise specified. Where two idle speeds are listed, the higher speed is with the A/C or throttle solenoid energized. On models equipped with vacuum release brake, whenever adjusting ignition timing or idle speed, vacuum line to brake release mechanism must be disconnected & plugged to prevent parking brake from releasing when selector is moved to Drive.

③—On kickdown step of cam.

④—On high step of fast idle cam.

⑤—Windsor engine.

⑥—Refer to engine calibration code on engine identification label, located at rear of left valve cover. The calibration code is located on the label after the engine code number and is preceded by the letter C and the revision code is located below the calibration code and is preceded by the letter R.

⑦—Ignition timing is not adjustable.

⑧—Calibration code 4-22B-R0, 2100 RPM; Exc. calibration code 4-22B-R0, 2300 RPM.

⑨—Calibration code 3-22D-R0, 2200 RPM; Calibration code 4-22Q-R0, 2300 RPM.

⑩—Models equipped with Electronic Engine Control (EEC) System.

⑪—Firing order for V8-302, 1-5-4-2-6-3-7-8. Firing order for V8-302 H.O., 351W, 1-3-7-2-6-5-4-8. Cylinder numbering (front to rear): Right bank 1-2-3-4, left bank 5-6-7-8. Refer to Fig. C for spark plug wire connections at distributor.

⑫—On 1st step of idle cam.

⑬—On 2nd highest step of fast idle cam.

⑭—Calibration code 0-11E-R0, 2100 RPM; calibration code 0-11E-R13, 2200 RPM.

continued

FORD MOTOR COMPANY
Lincoln—Continued

FIRING ORDER · 1 · 4 · 2 · 5 · 3 · 6

Fig. A

Fig. B

SPARK PLUG CONNECTIONS
5.8/6.6L (351/400 CID) V-8

SPARK PLUG CONNECTIONS
5.0L (302 CID) V-8

Fig. C

Fig. D

GENERAL MOTORS CORP.
Buick—Rear Wheel Drive Models & 1980–85 Riviera

The following specifications are published from the latest information available. This data should be used only in the absence of a decal affixed in the engine compartment.

★ When checking ignition timing, disconnect vacuum hose at distributor and plug opening in hose so idle speed will not be affected. Also, on some computer controlled ignition systems, it may be necessary to disconnect certain vacuum hoses and/or electrical connectors. Refer to vehicle emission decal.

▲ Before removing wires from distributor cap, determine location of the No. 1 wire in cap, as distributor position may have been altered from that shown at the end of this chart.

Year & Engine/V.I.N.	Spark Plug Gap	Ignition Timing BTDC①★				Curb Idle Speed②		Fast Idle Speed		Fuel Pump Pressure
		Firing Order Fig. ▲	Man. Trans.	Auto. Trans.	Mark Fig.	Man. Trans.	Auto. Trans.	Man. Trans.	Auto. Trans.	
1980										
V6-231/A, Exc. Calif.⑮⑳	.060	A	15°	15°	B⑬	600/800	③	2200	2000	3 Min.
V6-231/3, Exc. Calif.⑯⑳	.040	A	—	15°	B⑬	—	④	—	2200	5
V6-231/A, Calif.⑮	.060	A	—	15°	B⑬	—	⑥	—	2200	3 Min.
V6-231/3, Calif.⑯	.040	A	—	15°	B⑬	—	④	—	⑩	5
V6-252/4, Exc. Calif.	.060	A	—	15°	B⑬	—	⑭	—	2000	3 Min.
V8-265/S, Exc. Calif.	.060	K	—	10°	E	—	⑱	—	2200	7–8½
V8-301/W, Exc. Calif.	.060	K	—	12°	E	—	⑲	—	2500	7–8½
V8-305/H	.045	D	—	4°	⑤	—	⑱	—	2200	7½–9

continued

GENERAL MOTORS CORP.—Continued

The following specifications are published from the latest information available. This data should be used only in the absence of a decal affixed in the engine compartment.

★ When checking ignition timing, disconnect vacuum hose at distributor and plug opening in hose so idle speed will not be affected. Also, on some computer controlled ignition systems, it may be necessary to disconnect certain vacuum hoses and/or electrical connectors. Refer to vehicle emission decal.

▲ Before removing wires from distributor cap, determine location of the No. 1 wire in cap, as distributor position may have been altered from that shown at the end of this chart.

Year & Engine/V.I.N.	Spark Plug Gap	Firing Order Fig. ▲	Ignition Timing BTDC① ★		Mark Fig.	Curb Idle Speed②		Fast Idle Speed		Fuel Pump Pressure
			Man. Trans.	Auto. Trans.		Man. Trans.	Auto. Trans.	Man. Trans.	Auto. Trans.	
BUICK—REAR WHEEL DRIVE MODELS & 1980–85 RIVIERA, 1980—Continued										
V8-350/X, Exc. Calif.⑰	.060	F	—	15°	B⑬	—	③	—	1850	3 Min.
V8-350/R, Exc. Calif.㉑	.080	H	—	18°⑦	I	—	500/600D	—	700D	5½–6½
V8-350/, Exc. Calif.㉑	.080	H	—	⑫	I	—	550/650D	—	700D	5½–6½
1981										
V6-231/A⑮	.080	A	15°	15°	B⑬	800	⑪	2200	1800	3 Min.
V6-231/3⑯	.040	A	—	15°	B⑬	—	650D	—	2200	5
V6-252/4	.080	A	—	15°	B⑬	—	550/690D	—	2200	3 Min.
V8-265/S	.060	J	—	12°	E	—	450D	—	2300	7–8½
V8-307/Y	.080	H	—	15°⑦	I	—	⑪	—	650D	5½–6½
1982										
V6-231/A⑮	.080	A	—	15°	B⑬	—	500D⑪	—	2000	5½–6½
V6-231/C⑯	.060	A	—	15°	B⑬	—	500D	—	2000	5½–6½
V6-252/4	.080	A	—	15°	B⑬	—	500D⑪	—	2000	5½–6½
V8-307/Y	.080	H	—	20°⑦	I	—	⑪	—	650D	5½–6½
1983										
V6-231/A⑮	.080	A	—	15°	B⑬	—	⑪	—	2200	5½–6½
V6-231/8⑯	.060	A	—	15°	B⑬	—	⑪	—	2200	5½–6½
V6-252/4	.080	A	—	15°	B⑬	—	⑪	—	⑧	5½–6½
V8-307/Y	.080	H	—	20°⑦	I	—	⑪	—	900D	5½–6½
1984										
V6-231/A⑮	.080	A	—	15°	B⑬	—	⑪	—	2200	4¼–5¾
V6-231/9⑯	.060	J	—	—	—	—	⑨	—	—	—
V6-252/4	.080	A	—	15°	B⑬	—	⑪	—	⑧	5½–7
V8-307/Y	.080	H	—	20°⑦	I	—	⑪	—	900D	6–7½
1985										
V6-231/A⑮	.060	A	—	15°	B⑬	—	⑪	—	2200	4¼–5¾
V6-231/9⑯	.060	J	—	—	—	—	⑨	—	—	—
V8-307/Y	.080	H	—	20°⑦	I	—	⑪	—	550D	5½–6½
1986										
V6-231/A⑮	.060	A	—	—	B⑬	—	⑪	—	—	5½–7
V6-231/9⑯	.060	J	—	—	—	—	⑨	—	—	—
V8-307	—	H	—	—	I	—	⑪	—	—	6–7½

①—BTDC—Before top dead center.
②—Idle speed on man. trans. vehicles is adjusted in Neutral & on auto. trans. equipped vehicles is adjusted in Drive unless otherwise specified. Where two idle speeds are listed, the higher speed is with the A/C or idle solenoid energized.
③—Models less idle solenoid, 550D RPM; models w/idle solenoid, 550/670D RPM.
④—Except Riviera, 650D RPM; Riviera, 600/650D RPM.
⑤—Early models, Fig. C; late models, Fig. G.
⑥—Models less idle solenoid, 550D RPM; models w/idle solenoid, 550/620D RPM.
⑦—At 1100 RPM. ALDL test lead grounded.
⑧—Exc. Riviera, 2200 RPM; Riviera, 2100 RPM.
⑨—Idle speed controlled by Idle Air Control (IAC) valve.
⑩—Except Riviera, 2200 RPM; Riviera, 2500 RPM.
⑪—Idle speed is controlled by the idle speed control (ISC) motor or idle load compensator (ILC).
⑫—Electra & LeSabre, 18° BTDC; Riviera, 16° BTDC @ 1100 RPM.
⑬—The harmonic balancer on these engines has two timing marks. The timing mark measuring 1/16 in. is used when setting timing with a hand held timing light. The mark measuring ⅛ in. is used when setting timing with magnetic timing equipment.
⑭—Models less idle solenoid, 550D RPM; models w/idle solenoid, 550/680D RPM.
⑮—Except turbo charged engine.
⑯—Turbo charged engine.
⑰—Buick built engine. Distributor located at front of engine.
⑱—Models less idle solenoid, 550D RPM; models w/idle solenoid, 550/650D RPM.
⑲—Models less idle solenoid, 500D RPM; models w/idle solenoid, 500/650D RPM.

continued

Buick—Rear Wheel Drive & 1980–85 Riviera Notes—Continued

㉒—Except high altitude.   ㉑—Oldsmobile built engine. Distributor   located at rear of engine, counter-clockwise rotation.

Fig. A   Fig. B   Fig. C

Fig. D   Fig. E   Fig. F

Fig. G   Fig. H   Fig. I

Fig. K   Fig. J

continued

GENERAL MOTORS CORP.—Continued

1986 Buick Riviera, Cad. Eldorado & Seville & Olds. Toronado

The following specifications are published from the latest information available. This data should be used only in the absence of a decal affixed in the engine compartment.

★ When checking ignition timing, disconnect vacuum hose at distributor and plug opening in hose so idle speed will not be affected. Also, on some computer controlled ignition systems, it may be necessary to disconnect certain vacuum hoses and/or electrical connectors. Refer to vehicle emission decal.

▲ Before removing wires from distributor cap, determine location of the No. 1 wire in cap, as distributor position may have been altered from that shown at the end of this chart.

| Year & Engine | Spark Plug Gap | Ignition Timing BTDC①★ | | | | Curb Idle Speed | | Fast Idle Speed | | Fuel Pump Pressure |
		Firing Order Fig. ▲	Man. Trans.	Auto. Trans.	Location	Man. Trans.	Auto. Trans.	Man. Trans.	Auto. Trans.	
1986										
V6-231 SFI	.060	—	—	—	—	—	—	—	—	—
V8-250	—	—	—	—	—	—	—	—	—	—

①—BTDC—Before top dead center.

1985–86 Buick Electra & Park Avenue, Cad. DeVille & Fleetwood & Olds. 98 • 1986 Buick LeSabre & Olds. 88

The following specifications are published from the latest information available. This data should be used only in the absence of a decal affixed in the engine compartment.

★ When checking ignition timing, disconnect vacuum hose at distributor and plug opening in hose so idle speed will not be affected. Also, on some computer controlled ignition systems, it may be necessary to disconnect certain vacuum hoses and/or electrical connectors. Refer to vehicle emission decal.

▲ Before removing wires from distributor cap, determine location of the No. 1 wire in cap, as distributor position may have been altered from that shown at the end of this chart.

| Year & Engine/ V.I.N. Code | Spark Plug Gap | Ignition Timing BTDC①★ | | | | Curb Idle Speed② | | Fast Idle Speed | | Fuel Pump Pressure |
		Firing Order Fig. ▲	Man. Trans.	Auto. Trans.	Mark Fig.	Man. Trans.	Auto. Trans.	Man. Trans.	Auto. Trans.	
1985										
V6-181/E	.060	A	—	15°	B	—	③	—	2400	3.9–6.5
V6-231 MFI/3	.080	—	—	10°	—	—	③	—	③	—
V8-250 DFI/8	.060	—	—	10°	—	450④	—	—	—	—
1986										
V6-181 MFI	—	A	—	—	B	—	—	—	—	—
V6-231 SFI	.080	—	—	—	—	—	—	—	—	—
V8-250 DFI	.060	—	—	—	—	—	—	—	—	—

①—BTDC—Before top dead center.
②—D: Drive.
③—Idle speed is controlled by an idle speed control motor or idle air control motor.
④—Minimum RPM.

continued

GENERAL MOTORS CORP.

1985–86 Buick Electra & Park Avenue, Cad. DeVille & Fleetwood & Olds. 98 • 1986 Buick LeSabre & Olds. 88—Continued

Fig. A

Fig. B

1985–86 Buick Somerset Regal, Olds. Calais & Pont. Grand Am • 1986 Buick Skylark

The following specifications are published from the latest information available. This data should be used only in the absence of a decal affixed in the engine compartment.

★ When checking ignition timing, disconnect vacuum hose at distributor and plug opening in hose so idle speed will not be affected. Also, on some computer controlled ignition systems, it may be necessary to disconnect certain vacuum hoses and/or electrical connectors. Refer to vehicle emission decal.

▲ Before removing wires from distributor cap, determine location of the No. 1 wire in cap, as distributor position may have been altered from that shown at the end of this chart.

Year & Engine/ V.I.N.	Spark Plug Gap	Ignition Timing BTDC①★				Curb Idle Speed②		Fast Idle Speed		Fuel Pump Pressure
		Firing Order Fig. ▲	Man. Trans.	Auto. Trans.	Mark Fig.	Man. Trans.	Auto. Trans.	Man. Trans.	Auto. Trans.	
1985										
4-151/U	.060	A	8°③⑦	8°④⑦	B	⑤	⑤	—	⑤	—
V6-181/L	.040	C	—	⑥	D	—	⑤	⑤	⑤	—
1986										
4-151	.060	A	—	—	B	—	—	—	—	—
V6-181	.040	C	—	—	D	—	—	—	—	—

①—BTDC—Before top dead center.
②—D: Drive.
③—At 800 RPM.
④—At 750 RPM.
⑤—Controlled by idle air control motor.

⑥—Not adjustable.
⑦—Connect jumper wire between ALCL terminal A & B. The ALCL connector is located under the instrument panel.

Check average timing of cylinder numbers 1 & 4 & reset as necessary. After completing adjustment, remove jumper wire from ALCL connector.

Fig. A

Fig. B

continued

GENERAL MOTORS CORP.

1985—86 Buick Somerset Regal, Olds. Calais & Pont. Grand Am • 1986 Buick Skylark—Continued

Fig. C

FRONT OF ENGINE

SCREWS

SCREWS

FIRING ORDER
1 – 6 – 5 – 4 – 3 – 2

FRONT OF VEHICLE

Fig. D

Cadillac—Rear Wheel Drive Models & 1980—85 Eldorado & Seville

The following specifications are published from the latest information available. This data should be used only in the absence of a decal affixed in the engine compartment.

★ When checking ignition timing, disconnect vacuum hose at distributor and plug opening in hose so idle speed will not be affected. Also, on some computer controlled ignition systems, it may be necessary to disconnect certain vacuum hoses and/or electrical connectors. Refer to vehicle emission decal.

▲ Before removing wires from distributor cap, determine location of the No. 1 wire in cap, as distributor position may have been altered from that shown at the end of this chart.

Year & Engine/V.I.N.	Spark Plug Gap	Ignition Timing BTDC①★				Curb Idle Speed		Fast Idle Speed		Fuel Pump Pressure
		Firing Order Fig. ▲	Man. Trans.	Auto. Trans.	Mark Fig.	Man. Trans.	Auto. Trans.②	Man. Trans.	Auto. Trans.③	
1980										
V6-252/4, 4 Barrel	.060	E	—	15°	F	—	550/680D	—	2000	3 Min.
V8-350 E.F.I./8	.060	B	—	10°	A	—	600D	—	—	—
V8-368/6, 4 Barrel Exc. Calif.	.060	C	—	18°⑤	D	—	500/650D	—	1450	5¼—6½
V8-368/6, 4 Barrel Calif.	.060	C	—	18°⑤	D	—	575/650D	—	1350	5¼—6½
V8-368 D.E.F.I./9	.060	C	—	10°④	D	—	550D			
1981										
V6-252/4	.080	E	—	15°	F	—	550/690D	—	2200	3 Min.
V8-368 D.E.F.I./9	.060	C	—	10°	D	—	550D			
1982										
V6-252/4	.080	E	—	15°	F	—	⑥	—	⑥	4¼—5¾
V8-250 D.E.F.I./8	.060	G	—	10°	—	—	⑥	—	⑥	—
1983—84										
V8-250 D.E.F.I./8	.060	G	—	10°	—	—	⑥	—	⑥	—
1985—86										
V8-250 D.E.F.I./8	—	G	—	—	—	—	—	—	—	—

①—BTDC—Before top dead center.
②—Where two idle speeds are listed, the higher speed is with idle solenoid energized. Curb idle speed is adjusted with A/C off, while solenoid idle speed is adjusted with A/C on. Idle speed is adjusted in Drive unless otherwise specified.
③—With transmission in Park position & parking brake fully applied.
④—Engine wiring harness test lead, green connector, must be grounded.
⑤—At 1400 RPM.
⑥—Idle speed is controlled by an idle speed control motor or idle load compensator.

continued

GENERAL MOTORS CORP.

Cadillac—Rear Wheel Drive Models & 1980–85 Eldorado & Seville—Continued

Fig. A

Fig. B

Fig. C

Fig. D

Fig. E

Fig. F

Fig. G

Chevrolet—Camaro, Chevrolet, Corvette, Malibu & Monte Carlo

The following specifications are published from the latest information available. This data should be used only in the absence of a decal affixed in the engine compartment.

★ When checking ignition timing, disconnect vacuum hose at distributor and plug opening in hose so idle speed will not be affected. Also, on some computer controlled ignition systems, it may be necessary to disconnect certain vacuum hoses and/or electrical connectors. Refer to vehicle emission decal.

▲ Before removing wires from distributor cap, determine location of the No. 1 wire in cap, as distributor position may have been altered from that shown at the end of this chart.

Year & Engine/V.I.N.	Spark Plug Gap	Ignition Timing BTDC①★				Curb Idle Speed②		Fast Idle Speed		Fuel Pump Pressure
		Firing Order Fig. ▲	Man. Trans.	Auto. Trans.	Mark Fig.	Man. Trans.	Auto. Trans.	Man. Trans.	Auto. Trans.	
1980										
V6-229/K	.045	F	8°	12°	G	700/800	600/675D	1300	1750	4½—6
V6-231/A Exc. Calif.⑬	.060	D	—	15°	E⑪	—	560/670D	—	2200	4¼—5¾
V6-231/A Calif.⑬	.060	D	—	15°	E⑪	—	600D	—	2200	4¼—5¾
V6-231/3 Exc. Calif.⑭	.040	D	—	15°	E⑪	—	550D	—	2200	4¼—5¾
V6-231/3 Calif.⑭	.040	D	—	15°	E⑪	—	600D	—	2200	4¼—5¾
V8-267/J	.045	C	—	4°	④	—	500/600D	—	1850	7½—9
V8-305/H Exc. Calif.⑤	.045	C	4°	4°	④	700	500/600D	1500	1850	7½—9
V8-305/H Calif.⑤	.045	C	—	4°	④	—	550/650D	—	2200	7½—9
V8-305/H⑥	.045	C	—	4°	④	—	650D	—	—	7½—9
V8-350/L	.045	C	6°	6°	④	700	500/600D	1500	1850	7½—9
V8-350/8 Exc. High Alt.	.045	C	6°	6°	B	700	500/600D	1300	1600	7½—9
V8-350/8 High Alt.	.045	C	—	8°	B	—	600/650D	—	1750	7½—9
V8-350/6 High Perf.	.045	C	12°	12°	B	900	500/600D	1300	1600	7½—9

continued

GENERAL MOTORS CORP.—Continued

The following specifications are published from the latest information available. This data should be used only in the absence of a decal affixed in the engine compartment.

★ When checking ignition timing, disconnect vacuum hose at distributor and plug opening in hose so idle speed will not be affected. Also, on some computer controlled ignition systems, it may be necessary to disconnect certain vacuum hoses and/or electrical connectors. Refer to vehicle emission decal.

▲ Before removing wires from distributor cap, determine location of the No. 1 wire in cap, as distributor position may have been altered from that shown at the end of this chart.

Year & Engine/V.I.N.	Spark Plug Gap	Firing Order Fig. ▲	Ignition Timing BTDC ①★			Curb Idle Speed ②		Fast Idle Speed		Fuel Pump Pressure
			Man. Trans.	Auto. Trans.	Mark Fig.	Man. Trans.	Auto. Trans.	Man. Trans.	Auto. Trans.	
CHEVROLET—CAMARO, CHEVROLET, CORVETTE, MALIBU & MONTE CARLO—Continued										
1981										
V6-229/K	.045	F	6°	6°	G	③	③	2200	2200	4½-6
V6-231/A⑬	.080	D	—	15°	E⑪	—	③	—	1800	3 Min.
V6-231/3⑭	.040	D	—	15°	E⑪	—	650D	—	2200	5
V8-267/J	.045	C	—	6°	A	—	500/600D	—	2200	7½-9
V8-305/H	.045	C	6°	6°	A	700/800	500/600D	2200	2200	7½-9
V8-350/L	.045	C	—	6°	A	—	500/600D	—	2200	7½-9
V8-350/6	.045	C	6°	6°	B	700/800	500/600D	2200	2200	7½-9
1982										
4-151 E.F.I./2	.060	I	8°⑧	8°⑧	J	⑩	⑩	⑩	⑩	—
V6-173/1	.045	K	10°⑨	10°⑨	L	850⑫	600D⑮	2600	2500	6-7½
V6-229/K	.045	F	—	TDC	G		③	—	2200	4½-6
V6-231/A	.080	D	—	15°⑨	E⑪	—	③	—	1800	3 Min.
V8-267/J	.045	C	—	2°	A	—	500/600D	—	2200	7½-9
V8-305/H	.045	C	6°	6°⑨	A	700/800	500/600D	1800	2200	7½-9
V8-305 E.F.I./7	.045	C	—	6°⑦	A	—	⑩	—	⑩	—
V8-350/6	.045	C	—	6°⑦	A	—	⑩	—	⑩	—
1983										
4-151 E.F.I./2	.060	I	—	8°⑧	J	775N⑩	550D⑩	⑩	⑩	—
V6-173/1	.045	K	10°⑨	10°⑨	L	775/1100	600/750D	2500	2500	5½-6½
V6-229/9	.045	F	—	TDC	G	—	—	—	—	4½-6
V6-231/A	.080	D	—	15°⑨	E⑪	—	③	—	2200	4¼-4¾
V8-305/H	.045	C	6°⑨	6°⑨	A	700/800	500/650D	1800	2200	7½-9
V8-305 H.O./G	.045	C	6°⑨	6°⑨	A	700	500D	—	—	7½-9
V8-305 E.F.I./S	.045	C	6°	6°	A	⑩	⑩	⑩	⑩	—
1984										
4-151 E.F.I./2	.060	I	8°⑧	8°⑧	J	775⑩	500D⑩	⑩	⑩	—
V6-173/1	.045	K	10°⑨	10°⑨	L	775/1100	600/750D	2500	2500	5½-6½
V6-229/9	.045	F	—	TDC	G	—	—	—	—	4½-6
V6-231/A	.080	D	—	15°⑨	E⑪	—	③	—	2200	4¼-4¾
V8-305/H	.045	C	6°⑨	6°⑨	A	700/800	500/650D	1800	2200	7½-9
V8-305 H.O./G	.045	C	6°⑨	6°⑨	A	70/800	600/650D	1800	2200	7½-9
V8-350/8	.045	C	—	6°⑦	H	—	⑩	—	⑩	—
1985										
4-151/ E.F.I./2	.060	I	—	—	J	⑩	⑩	⑩	⑩	—
V6-173 M.F.I./S	.045	K	—	—	L	⑩	⑩	⑩	⑩	—
V6-262 E.F.I./Z	.035	—	—	—	—		⑩		⑩	—
V8-305/H	.045	C	—	—	A	700	500D	—	—	7½-9
V8-305 H.O./G	.045	C	—	—	A	700	600D	—	—	7½-9
V8-305 T.P.I./F	.045	C	—	—	A	⑩	⑩	⑩	⑩	—
V8-350/8	.045	C	—	—	H	⑩	⑩	⑩	⑩	—

continued

GENERAL MOTORS CORP.—Continued

The following specifications are published from the latest information available. This data should be used only in the absence of a decal affixed in the engine compartment.

★ When checking ignition timing, disconnect vacuum hose at distributor and plug opening in hose so idle speed will not be affected. Also, on some computer controlled ignition systems, it may be necessary to disconnect certain vacuum hoses and/or electrical connectors. Refer to vehicle emission decal.

▲ Before removing wires from distributor cap, determine location of the No. 1 wire in cap, as distributor position may have been altered from that shown at the end of this chart.

Year & Engine/V.I.N.	Spark Plug Gap	Firing Order Fig. ▲	Ignition Timing BTDC①★			Curb Idle Speed②		Fast Idle Speed		Fuel Pump Pressure
			Man. Trans.	Auto. Trans.	Mark Fig.	Man. Trans.	Auto. Trans.	Man. Trans.	Auto. Trans.	

CHEVROLET—CAMARO, CHEVROLET, CORVETTE, MALIBU & MONTE CARLO—Continued
1986

Year & Engine/V.I.N.	Spark Plug Gap	Firing Order Fig.	Man. Trans.	Auto. Trans.	Mark Fig.	Man. Trans.	Auto. Trans.	Man. Trans.	Auto. Trans.	Fuel Pump Pressure
4-151 E.F.I./2	.060	I	—	—	J	⑩	—	⑩	—	—
V6-173 M.F.I./S	.045	K	—	—	L	⑩	⑩	⑩	⑩	—
V6-262 E.F.I./Z	.035	—	—	—	—	—	⑩	—	⑩	—
V8-305 4 Barrel/H	.035	C	—	—	A	700	500D	—	—	7½—9
V8-305 H.O. 4 Barrel/G	.035	C	—	—	A	700	600D	—	—	7½—9
V8-305 T.P.I./F	.035	—	—	—	—	⑩	⑩	⑩	⑩	—
V8-350 T.P.I./8	—	C	—	—	H	⑩	⑩	⑩	⑩	—

①—BTDC—Before top dead center.
②—Idle speed on man. trans. vehicles is adjusted in Neutral and on auto. trans. equipped vehicles is adjusted in Drive unless otherwise specified. Where two idle speeds are listed, the higher speed is with A/C or idle solenoid energized.
③—Equipped with idle speed control motor.
④—Early models, Fig. G; late models, Fig. A.
⑤—Except Corvette.
⑥—Corvette.

⑦—When checking ignition timing, disconnect Electronic Spark Timing bypass connector (tan wire w/black stripe) to place EST in bypass mode.
⑧—Ground diagnostic connector located under dash. The check engine light should flash on & off when in diagnostic mode. Check average ignition timing of cylinder Nos. 1 & 4, & reset as necessary. After completing timing check, remove ground from diagnostic connector & ensure check engine light is off.
⑨—With distributor 4 wire connector disconnected.

connected.
⑩—Automatically controlled by Electronic Fuel Injection.
⑪—The harmonic balancer on these engines has two timing marks. The timing mark measuring 1/16 in. is used when setting timing with a hand held timing light. The mark measuring 1/8 in. is used when setting timing with magnetic timing equipment.
⑫—1100N with A/C.
⑬—Except turbocharged engine.
⑭—Turbocharged engine.
⑮—700D with A/C.

Fig. A   Fig. B   Fig. C   Fig. D

continued

Fig. E

Fig. F

Fig. G

Fig. H

Fig. I

Fig. J

Fig. K

Fig. L

continued

GENERAL MOTORS CORP.—Continued

Chevrolet Chevette & Pontiac 1000

The following specifications are published from the latest information available. This data should be used only in the absence of a decal affixed in the engine compartment.

★ When checking ignition timing, disconnect vacuum hose at distributor and plug opening in hose so idle speed will not be affected. Also, on some computer controlled ignition systems, it may be necessary to disconnect certain vacuum hoses and/or electrical connectors. Refer to vehicle emission decal.

▲ Before removing wires from distributor cap, determine location of the No. 1 wire in cap, as distributor position may have been altered from that shown at the end of this chart.

Year & Engine/V.I.N.	Spark Plug Gap	Firing Order Fig. ▲	Ignition Timing BTDC①★		Mark Fig.	Curb Idle Speed②		Fast Idle Speed		Fuel Pump Pressure
			Man. Trans.	Auto. Trans.		Man. Trans.	Auto. Trans.	Man. Trans.	Auto. Trans.	
1980										
4-97.6 Exc. Calif.⑤	.035	A	12°	18°	B	800/1150	750/1150	2500	2500	2½–6½
4-97.6 Calif.⑤	.035	A	12°	18°	B	800/1150	800/1150	2600	2500	2½–6½
1981										
4-97.6/9	.035	A	18°	18°	B	800/1150⑥	700D③	2500	2500	2½–6½
1982										
4-97.6/C	.035	A	4°	4°	B	700	700D	2500	2500	2½–6½
1983										
4-97.6/C	.035	A	6°	6°	B	800/1150	700/875D	2500	2500	2½–6½
1984										
4-97.6/C	.035	A	8°	8°	B	800④	700D	—	—	5–6½
1985										
4-97.6/C	.035	A	—	—	B	800	700D	—	—	5–6½
1986										
4-97.6/	.035	A	—	—	B	800	700D	—	—	—

①—BTDC—Before top dead center.
②—Idle speed on man. trans. vehicles is adjusted in Neutral & on auto. trans. equipped vehicles is adjusted in Drive unless otherwise specified. Where two idle speeds are listed, the higher speed is with the A/C or idle solenoid energized.
③—With solenoid energized, 1400 RPM with transmission in Park.
④—700 RPM with 3.36:1 axle.
⑤—On 4-97.6 C.I.D. engine, V.I.N. code is 9; 4-97.6 H.O. engine, V.I.N. code is O.
⑥—Models with carburetor No. 14023777, set at 700 RPM.

Fig. A

Fig. B

continued

GENERAL MOTORS CORP.—Continued

1982–86 Chev. Cavalier, Buick Skyhawk, Cad. Cimarron, Olds. Firenza & Pont. 2000 & Sunbird

The following specifications are published from the latest information available. This data should be used only in the absence of a decal affixed in the engine compartment.

★ When checking ignition timing, disconnect vacuum hose at distributor and plug opening in hose so idle speed will not be affected. Also, on some computer controlled ignition systems, it may be necessary to disconnect certain vacuum hoses and/or electrical connectors. Refer to vehicle emission decal.

▲ Before removing wires from distributor cap, determine location of the No. 1 wire in cap, as distributor position may have been altered from that shown at the end of this chart.

Year & Engine/V.I.N.	Spark Plug Gap	Ignition Timing BTDC①★				Curb Idle Speed		Fast Idle Speed		Fuel Pump Pressure
		Firing Order Fig.▲	Man. Trans.	Auto. Trans.	Mark Fig.	Man. Trans.	Auto. Trans.	Man. Trans.	Auto. Trans.	
1982										
4-112/G 2 Barrel③	.035	A	12°⑤	12°⑤	B⑥	⑦	⑦	2400	2300	4½⑧
4-112 E.F.I./O⑨	.060	C	8°⑩	8°⑩	D	④	④	④	④	—
4-121/B③	.035	A	—	12°⑤	B⑥	—	⑦	—	2300	4½⑧
1983										
4-112 E.F.I./O⑨	.035	C	8°⑩	8°⑩	D	④	④	④	④	—
4-121 E.F.I./P③	.035	A	TDC②	TDC②	B⑥	④	④	④	④	—
1984										
4-112 E.F.I./O⑨	.035	C	8°⑩	8°⑩	D	④	④	④	④	—
4-112 Turbo/J⑨	.035	C	8°⑩	8°⑩	D	④	④	④	④	—
4-121 E.F.I./P③	.035	A	6°②	6°②	B⑥	④	④	④	④	—
1985										
4-112 E.F.I./O⑨	.035	C	8°⑩	8°⑩	D	④	④	④	④	—
4-112 Turbo/J⑨	.035	C	8°⑩	8°⑩	D	④	④	④	④	—
4-121 E.F.I./P③	.035	A	6°⑤	6°⑤	B⑥	④	④	④	④	—
V6-173 M.F.I./W	.045	E	10°④	10°④	—	④	④	④	④	—
1986										
4-112 E.F.I./O⑨	.035	C	—	—	D	④	④	④	④	—
4-112 Turbo/J⑨	.035	C	—	—	D	④	④	④	④	—
4-121 E.F.I./P③	.035	A	—	—	B⑥	④	④	④	④	—
V6-173 M.F.I./W	.045	E	—	—	—	④	④	④	④	—

①—BTDC—Before top dead center.

②—Disconnect single wire from Electronic Spark Timing (EST) bypass connector to place system in ignition timing bypass mode. Do not disconnect three wire connector to distributor. Connect a suitable inductive pickup timing light to ignition coil high tension lead. When checking ignition timing, the pulley notch will appear to move slightly as each cylinder is fired during timing check. This slight pulley notch movement should be centered at the proper timing degree mark on the timing tab, see note 6. After timing check is complete, reconnect wire to EST bypass connector.

③—Overhead valve engine.

④—Idle speed is controlled by the idle air control assembly.

⑤—Disconnect 4 terminal Electronic Spark Timing (EST) wire connector to place system in ignition timing bypass mode. Connect a suitable inductive pickup timing light to ignition coil high tension lead near distributor. The pulley notch will appear to move slightly as each cylinder is fired during the timing check. This slight pulley notch movement should be centered at the proper timing degree mark on the timing tab, see note 6. After completing adjustment, reconnect EST wire connector.

⑥—The crankshaft pulley has two ignition timing notches located 180° apart. The notch for No. 1 cylinder is scribed across the three pulley sheave surfaces, while the second notch is scribed across the center sheave only.

⑦—Idle speeds are controlled by the idle speed control motor.

⑧—Minimum.

⑨—Overhead cam engine.

⑩—Ground diagnostic connector located under dash panel. The check engine light should begin flashing. Check average timing of cylinder Nos. 1 & 4. After completing adjustment, remove ground from diagnostic connector.

continued

GENERAL MOTORS CORP.

1982–86 Chev. Cavalier, Buick Skyhawk, Cad. Cimarron, Olds. Firenza & Pont. 2000 & Sunbird—Continued

Fig. A   Fig. B   Fig. C   Fig. D   Fig. E

1980–85 Chev. Citation, Buick Skylark, Olds. Omega & Pont. Phoenix

The following specifications are published from the latest information available. This data should be used only in the absence of a decal affixed in the engine compartment.

★ When checking ignition timing, disconnect vacuum hose at distributor and plug opening in hose so idle speed will not be affected. Also, on some computer controlled ignition systems, it may be necessary to disconnect certain vacuum hoses and/or electrical connectors. Refer to vehicle emission decal.

▲ Before removing wires from distributor cap, determine location of the No. 1 wire in cap, as distributor position may have been altered from that shown at the end of this chart.

Year & Engine/V.I.N.	Spark Plug Gap	Ignition Timing BTDC①★				Curb Idle Speed②		Fast Idle Speed		Fuel Pump Pressure
		Firing Order Fig. ▲	Man. Trans.	Auto. Trans.	Mark Fig.	Man. Trans.	Auto. Trans.	Man. Trans.	Auto. Trans.	
1980										
4-151/5 Exc. Calif.	.060	A	10°	10°	B	1000/1300	650/900D	2200	2600	6½–8
4-151/5 Calif.	.060	A	10°	10°	B	1000/1200	650/900D	2200	2600	6½–8
V6-173/7 Exc. Calif.	.045	C	2°	6°	D	750/1200	③	1900	2000	6–7½
V6-173/7 Calif.	.045	C	6°	10°	D	750	④	2000	2000	6–7½
1981										
4-151/5	.060	E	4°	4°	B	800/1000	550/675D	2600	2600	6½–8
V6-173/X⑤	.045	C	6°	10°	D	850/1100	600/850D	⑦	2600	6–7½
V6-173/Z H.O.⑧	.045	C	—	10°	D	—	650/850D	—	2400	6–7½

continued

GENERAL MOTORS CORP.—Continued

The following specifications are published from the latest information available. This data should be used only in the absence of a decal affixed in the engine compartment.

★ When checking ignition timing, disconnect vacuum hose at distributor and plug opening in hose so idle speed will not be affected. Also, on some computer controlled ignition systems, it may be necessary to disconnect certain vacuum hoses and/or electrical connectors. Refer to vehicle emission decal.

▲ Before removing wires from distributor cap, determine location of the No. 1 wire in cap, as distributor position may have been altered from that shown at the end of this chart.

Year & Engine/V.I.N.	Spark Plug Gap	Ignition Timing BTDC①★				Curb Idle Speed②		Fast Idle Speed		Fuel Pump Pressure
		Firing Order Fig. ▲	Man. Trans.	Auto. Trans.	Mark Fig.	Man. Trans.	Auto. Trans.	Man. Trans.	Auto. Trans.	

1980–85 CHEV. CITATION, BUICK SKYLARK, OLDS. OMEGA & PONT. PHOENIX—Continued

1982

Year & Engine/V.I.N.	Spark Plug Gap	Firing Order Fig.	Man. Trans.	Auto. Trans.	Mark Fig.	Man. Trans.	Auto. Trans.	Man. Trans.	Auto. Trans.	Fuel Pump Pressure
4-151/R	.060	E	8°⑨⑩	8°⑨⑩	B	⑪	⑪	⑪	⑪	—
V6-173/X Exc. H.O.	.045	C	10°⑫	10°⑫	D	800/1050	600/800D	⑦	2600	6—7½
V6-173/Z H.O.⑧	.045	C	6°⑫	10°⑫	D	850/1100	750/900D	2600	2800	6—7½

1983

Year & Engine/V.I.N.	Spark Plug Gap	Firing Order Fig.	Man. Trans.	Auto. Trans.	Mark Fig.	Man. Trans.	Auto. Trans.	Man. Trans.	Auto. Trans.	Fuel Pump Pressure
4-151/R	.060	E	8°⑨⑩	8°⑨⑩	B	⑪	⑪	⑪	⑪	—
V6-173/X Exc. H.O.	.045	C	10°⑫	10°⑫	D	775	600D	2500N	2500N	6—7½
V6-173/Z H.O.⑧	.045	C	10°⑫	10°⑫	D	800	725D	2600N	2700N	6—7½

1984

Year & Engine/V.I.N.	Spark Plug Gap	Firing Order Fig.	Man. Trans.	Auto. Trans.	Mark Fig.	Man. Trans.	Auto. Trans.	Man. Trans.	Auto. Trans.	Fuel Pump Pressure
4-151/R	.060	E	8⑩	8⑩	B	⑪	⑪	⑪	⑪	—
V6-173/X Exc. H.O.	.045	C	10°⑫	10°⑫	D	800/1100	600/750D	2500N	2500N	6—7½
V6-173/Z H.O.⑧	.045	C	10°⑫	10°⑫	D	800/1100	600/750D	2600N	2700N	6—7½

1985

Year & Engine/V.I.N.	Spark Plug Gap	Firing Order Fig.	Man. Trans.	Auto. Trans.	Mark Fig.	Man. Trans.	Auto. Trans.	Man. Trans.	Auto. Trans.	Fuel Pump Pressure
4-151/R	.060	E	8°⑥⑩	8°⑩⑬	B	⑪	⑪	⑪	⑪	—
V6-173/W	.045	C	10°⑫	10°⑫	D	⑪	⑪	⑪	⑪	—
V6-173/X	.045	C	10°⑭	10°⑭	D	800	600	—	—	6—7½

①—BTDC—Before top dead center.
②—Idle speed on man. trans. vehicles is adjusted in Neutral & on auto. trans. equipped vehicles is adjusted in Drive unless otherwise specified. Where two idle speeds are listed, the higher speed is with the A/C or idle solenoid energized.
③—Less A/C, 700D RPM; with A/C, 700/850D RPM.
④—Less A/C, 700D RPM; with A/C, 700/800D RPM.
⑤—Except Citation X-11 models.
⑥—At 900 RPM.
⑦—Models less A/C, 2400 RPM; models

with A/C 2600 RPM.
⑧—High output engine.
⑨—At 1050 RPM.
⑩—Ground diagnostic connector located under dash. The check engine light should flash on and off when in diagnostic mode. Check average ignition timing of cylinder Nos. 1 and 4, and reset as necessary. After completing ignition timing check, remove ground from diagnostic connector and ensure that check engine light is off.
⑪—Idle speed controlled by Idle Air Control (IAC) valve.

⑫—Disconnect 4 wire EST connector at distributor, then check & adjust basic ignition timing as needed. After checking timing, reconnect EST connector.
⑬—At 750 RPM.
⑭—Disconnect set timing connector, which is located in engine compartment near the blower housing along the cowl. This connector branches out if engine wiring harness near the bulkhead connector. After completing adjustment, reconnect set timing connector.

Fig. A

Fig. B

Fig. C

continued

GENERAL MOTORS CORP.

1980—85 Chev. Citation, Buick Skylark, Olds. Omega & Pont. Phoenix—Continued

Fig. D

Fig. E

1982—86 Chev. Celebrity, Buick Century, Olds. Cutlass Ciera, Pont. 6000 & 1984—86 Cutlass Cruiser

The following specifications are published from the latest information available. This data should be used only in the absence of a decal affixed in the engine compartment.

★ When checking ignition timing, disconnect vacuum hose at distributor and plug opening in hose so idle speed will not be affected. Also, on some computer controlled ignition systems, it may be necessary to disconnect certain vacuum hoses and/or electrical connectors. Refer to vehicle emission decal.

▲ Before removing wires from distributor cap, determine location of the No. 1 wire in cap, as distributor position may have been altered from that shown at the end of this chart.

Year & Engine/V.I.N.	Spark Plug Gap	Ignition Timing BTDC①★				Curb Idle Speed②		Fast Idle Speed		Fuel Pump Pressure
		Firing Order Fig. ▲	Man. Trans.	Auto. Trans.	Mark Fig.	Man. Trans.	Auto. Trans.	Man. Trans.	Auto. Trans.	
1982										
4-151/R	.060	A	—	8°③⑦	B	—	⑩	—	⑩	9–13
V6-173/X	.045	C	—	10°⑤	D	—	600D	—	2600N	6–7½
V6-181/E	.080	E	—	15°	F	—	⑩	—	2300P	6–7½
1983										
4-151/R	.060	A	—	8°⑦⑪	B	—	⑩	—	⑩	—
V6-173/X	.045	C	—	10°	D	—	600/750D	—	2500	5½–6½
V6-173 H.O./Z④	.045	C	—	10°	D	—	725/850D	—	2700	5½–6½
V6-181/E Exc. Calif.	.060	E	—	15°	F	—	⑩	—	2400	4–6½
V6-181/E Calif.	.060	E	—	15°	F	—	⑩	—	2300	4–6½
1984										
4-151/R	.060	A	—	8°⑦⑪	B	—	⑩	—	⑩	—
V6-173/X	.045	C	—	—	D	—	—	—	—	6–7½
V6-173 H.O./Z④	.045	C	—	—	D	—	—	—	—	6–7½
V6-181/E	.080	E	—	15°	F	—	⑩	—	2400	3.9–6.5
V6-231 MFI/3	.080	—	—	—	—	—	—	—	—	—
1985										
4-151/R	.060	A	—	8°⑦⑪	B	—	⑩	—	⑩	—
V6-173/X	.045	C	—	10°	D	—	600D	—	—	6½–7
V6-173 H.O. MFI/W④	.045	C	—	10°⑥	D	—	⑩	—	⑩	—
V6-181/E	.060	E	—	15°⑧	F	—	⑩	—	2400	3.9–6.5
V6-231 MFI/3	.080	—	—	15°⑨	—	—	⑩	—	⑩	—

continued

GENERAL MOTORS CORP.—Continued

The following specifications are published from the latest information available. This data should be used only in the absence of a decal affixed in the engine compartment.

★ When checking ignition timing, disconnect vacuum hose at distributor and plug opening in hose so idle speed will not be affected. Also, on some computer controlled ignition systems, it may be necessary to disconnect certain vacuum hoses and/or electrical connectors. Refer to vehicle emission decal.

▲ Before removing wires from distributor cap, determine location of the No. 1 wire in cap, as distributor position may have been altered from that shown at the end of this chart.

Year & Engine/V.I.N.	Spark Plug Gap	Ignition Timing BTDC① ★				Curb Idle Speed②		Fast Idle Speed		Fuel Pump Pressure
		Firing Order Fig. ▲	Man. Trans.	Auto. Trans.	Mark Fig.	Man. Trans.	Auto. Trans.	Man. Trans.	Auto. Trans.	

1982–86 CHEV. CELEBRITY, BUICK CENTURY, OLDS. CUTLASS CIERA, PONT. 6000 & 1984–86 CUTLASS CRUISER—Continued

1986

Year & Engine/V.I.N.	Spark Plug Gap	Firing Order Fig.	Man. Trans.	Auto. Trans.	Mark Fig.	Man. Trans.	Auto. Trans.	Man. Trans.	Auto. Trans.	Fuel Pump Pressure
4-151 EFI/R	.060	A	—	—	B	—	⑩	—	⑩	—
V6-173 2 Barrel/X	.045	C	—	—	D	—	600D	—	—	6–7½
V6-173 MFI/W	.045	C	—	—	D	—	⑩	—	⑩	—
V6-231 SFI/B, 3	—	—	—	—	—	—	⑩	—	⑩	—

①—BTDC—Before top dead center.
②—Idle speed on auto. trans. equipped vehicles is adjusted in Drive unless otherwise specified. Where two idle speeds are listed, the higher speed is with the A/C or idle solenoid energized.
③—At 1050N RPM.
④—High output engine.
⑤—At 600D RPM.
⑥—Disconnect set timing connector, which is located in engine compartment near blower housing along the cowl. This connector branches out of engine wiring harness near bulkhead connector. After completing adjustment, reconnect set timing connector.
⑦—Ground diagnostic connector located under dash. The check engine light should flash on & off when in diagnostic mode. Check average ignition timing of cylinder Nos. 1 & 4, reset as necessary. After completing ignition timing check, remove ground from diagnostic connector & ensure that check engine light is off.
⑧—With distributor 4 wire electrical connector disconnected. After completing adjustment, reconnect distributor wire connector.
⑨—With jumper wire connected between ALCL terminals A & B. The ALCL connector is located on the lower edge of the instrument panel to right of steering column. Remove jumper wire after completing adjustment.
⑩—Idle speeds are controlled by an idle speed control motor.
⑪—At 750 RPM.

Fig. A

Fig. B

Fig. C

Fig. D

Fig. E

Fig. F

continued

GENERAL MOTORS CORP.—Continued
1985–86 Chevrolet Nova

The following specifications are published from the latest information available. This data should be used only in the absence of a decal affixed in the engine compartment.

★ When checking ignition timing, disconnect vacuum hose at distributor and plug opening in hose so idle speed will not be affected. Also, on some computer controlled ignition systems, it may be necessary to disconnect certain vacuum hoses and/or electrical connectors. Refer to vehicle emission decal.

▲ Before removing wires from distributor cap, determine location of the No. 1 wire in cap, as distributor position may have been altered from that shown at the end of this chart.

Year & Engine/V.I.N.	Spark Plug Gap	Ignition Timing BTDC①★				Curb Idle Speed		Fast Idle Speed		Fuel Pump Pressure
		Firing Order Fig. ▲	Man. Trans.	Auto. Trans.	Mark Fig.	Man. Trans.	Auto. Trans.	Man. Trans.	Auto. Trans.	
1985										
4-97/4	.043	—	—	—	—	650	800	3000	3000	—
1986										
4-97/4	.043	—	—	—	—	650	750	—	—	—

①—BTDC—Before top dead center.

Oldsmobile—Rear Wheel Drive Models & 1980–85 Toronado

The following specifications are published from the latest information available. This data should be used only in the absence of a decal affixed in the engine compartment.

★ When checking ignition timing, disconnect vacuum hose at distributor and plug opening in hose so idle speed will not be affected. Also, on some computer controlled ignition systems, it may be necessary to disconnect certain vacuum hoses and/or electrical connectors. Refer to vehicle emission decal.

▲ Before removing wires from distributor cap, determine location of the No. 1 wire in cap, as distributor position may have been altered from that shown at the end of this chart.

Year & Engine/V.I.N.	Spark Plug Gap	Ignition Timing BTDC①★				Curb Idle Speed②		Fast Idle Speed		Fuel Pump Pressure
		Firing Order Fig. ▲	Man. Trans.	Auto. Trans.	Mark Fig.	Man. Trans.	Auto. Trans.	Man. Trans.	Auto. Trans.	
1980										
V6-231/A⑥⑧	.040	A	15°	15°	F⑮	600/800⑤	550/670D	2200	2000	3 Min.
V8-231/A⑧⑩	.060	A	—	15°	F⑮	—	550/620D	—	2200	3 Min.
V8-260/F	.080	B	—	⑰	G	—	500/625D	—	700D	5½–6½
V8-305/H, Exc. Calif.⑪	.045	C	—	4°	⑱	—	500/600D	—	1850	7½–9
V8-305/H, Calif.⑪	.045	C	—	4°	⑱	—	550/650D	—	2200	7½–9
V8-307/Y	.080	B	—	20°④	G	—	500/600D	—	700D	5½–6½
V8-350/R, Exc. Calif.	.080	B	—	18°④	G	—	500/600D	—	700D	5½–6½
V8-350/R, Calif.	.080	B	—	⑦	G	—	550/650D	—	700D	5½–6½
1981										
V6-231/A⑧	.080	A	15°	15°	F⑮	800	⑲	2200	1800	3 Min.
V6-252/4⑧	.080	A	—	15°	F⑮	—	550/690D	—	2200	3 Min.
V8-260/F	.080	B	—	⑳	G	—	⑲	—	700D	5½–6½
V8-307/Y, Exc. Calif.	.080	B	—	④⑬	G	—	⑲	—	650D	5½–6½
V8-307/Y, Calif.	.080	B	—	15°④	G	—	⑲	—	650D	5½–6½
1982										
V6-231/A	.080	A	—	15°	F⑮	—	⑲	—	2200	3 Min.
V6-252/4	.080	A	—	15°	F⑮	—	⑲	—	⑭	3 Min.
V8-260/8	.080	B	—	20°④	G	—	⑲	—	700D	5½–6½
V8-307/Y	.080	B	—	20°④	G	—	⑲	—	650D	5½–6½

continued

GENERAL MOTORS CORP.—Continued

The following specifications are published from the latest information available. This data should be used only in the absence of a decal affixed in the engine compartment.

★ When checking ignition timing, disconnect vacuum hose at distributor and plug opening in hose so idle speed will not be affected. Also, on some computer controlled ignition systems, it may be necessary to disconnect certain vacuum hoses and/or electrical connectors. Refer to vehicle emission decal.

▲ Before removing wires from distributor cap, determine location of the No. 1 wire in cap, as distributor position may have been altered from that shown at the end of this chart.

Year & Engine/V.I.N.	Spark Plug Gap	Ignition Timing BTDC①★				Curb Idle Speed②		Fast Idle Speed		Fuel Pump Pressure
		Firing Order Fig. ▲	Man. Trans.	Auto. Trans.	Mark Fig.	Man. Trans.	Auto. Trans.	Man. Trans.	Auto. Trans.	

OLDSMOBILE—REAR WHEEL DRIVE MODELS & 1980–85 TORONADO—Continued

Year & Engine/V.I.N.	Spark Plug Gap	Firing Order Fig. ▲	Man. Trans.	Auto. Trans.	Mark Fig.	Man. Trans.	Auto. Trans.	Man. Trans.	Auto. Trans.	Fuel Pump Pressure
1983										
V6-231/A	.080	A	—	15°	F⑮	—	⑲	—	2200	4¼–5¾
V6-252/4	.080	A	—	15°	F⑮	—	⑲	—	⑯	4¼–5¾
V8-307/Y③	.080	B	—	20°④	G	—	⑲	—	900D	6–7½
V8-307/9⑫	.080	B	—	20°④	G	—	500D	—	900D	6–7½
1984										
V6-231/A	.080	A	—	15°	F⑮	—	⑲	—	2200	4¼–5¾
V6-252/4	.080	A	—	15°	F⑮	—	⑲	—	⑯	4¼–5¾
V8-307/Y③	.080	B	—	20°④	G	—	⑲	—	700D	6–7½
V8-307/9⑫	.080	B	—	20°④	G	—	500D	—	900D	6–7½
1985										
V6-231/A	.060	A	—	15°	F⑮	—	⑲	—	2200	4¼–5¾
V8-307/Y③	.060	B	—	20°④	G	—	⑲	—	550D	5½–6½
V8-307/9⑫	.080	B	—	20°④	G	—	550/650D	—	750D	6–7½
1986										
V6-231/A	.060	A	—	—	F⑮	—	⑲	—	—	5½–7
V8-307/Y, 9	—	B	—	—	G	—	⑲	—	—	6–7½

①—BTDC—Before top dead center.
②—Idle speed on man. trans. vehicles is adjusted in Neutral & on auto. trans. equipped vehicles is adjusted in Drive unless otherwise specified. Where two idle speeds are listed, the higher speed is with the A/C or idle solenoid energized.
③—Exc. Hurst option.
④—At 1100 RPM ALDL test lead grounded.
⑤—Idle speed with solenoid energized is adjusted with A/C on & compressor clutch wires disconnected.
⑥—Except Calif. & models w/Computer Controlled Catalytic Converter (C4) System.
⑦—Except Toronado, 18° at 1100 RPM;

Toronado, 16° at 1100 RPM.
⑧—Buick built engine.
⑨—Injection timing, 7°ATDC at 1300 RPM.
⑩—California & models w/Computer Controlled Catalytic Converter (C4) system.
⑪—Chevrolet built engine.
⑫—Hurst option.
⑬—Toronado, 15°BTDC. 88, Custom Cruiser & Cutlass Cruiser, except engine codes TMK, TML, TMN & TMS, 15°BTDC; engine codes TMK, TML, TMN & TMS, 18°BTDC.
⑭—Except Toronado Calif. models, 2200 RPM; Toronado California models, 2100 RPM.
⑮—The harmonic balancer on these en-

gines has two timing marks. The timing mark measuring 1/16 in. is used when setting timing with a hand held timing light. The mark measuring 1/8 in. is used when setting timing with magnetic timing equipment.
⑯—Except Toronado, 2200 RPM; Toronado, 2100 RPM.
⑰—88 & Cutlass except sta. wag., 20° BTDC @ 1100 RPM; Cutlass sta. wag., 18° BTDC at 1100 RPM.
⑱—Early models, Fig. E; late models, Fig. D.
⑲—Idle speed is controlled by the idle speed control (ICS) motor or the idle load compensator (ILC).
⑳—Cutlass except sta. wag., 20°BTDC at 1100 RPM; Cutlass Cruiser & 88, 18°BTDC at 1100 RPM.

Fig. A

Fig. B

Fig. C

continued

GENERAL MOTORS CORP.

Oldsmobile—Rear Wheel Drive Models & 1980–85 Toronado— Continued

Fig. D

Fig. E

Fig. F

Fig. G

Pontiac—Rear Wheel Drive Models Exc. Fiero & 1000

The following specifications are published from the latest information available. This data should be used only in the absence of a decal affixed in the engine compartment.

★ When checking ignition timing, disconnect vacuum hose at distributor and plug opening in hose so idle speed will not be affected. Also, on some computer controlled ignition systems, it may be necessary to disconnect certain vacuum hoses and/or electrical connectors. Refer to vehicle emission decal.

▲ Before removing wires from distributor cap, determine location of the No. 1 wire in cap, as distributor position may have been altered from that shown at the end of this chart.

Year & Engine/V.I.N.	Spark Plug Gap	Ignition Timing BTDC①★				Curb Idle Speed②		Fast Idle Speed		Fuel Pump Pressure
		Firing Order Fig. ▲	Man. Trans.	Auto. Trans.	Mark Fig.	Man. Trans.	Auto. Trans.	Man. Trans.	Auto. Trans.	
1980										
V6-229/K	.045	L	10°	10°	M	700/750	600/675D	1750	1750	4½-6
V6-231/A Exc. Calif.	.040	B	15°	15°	C⑭	600/800	500/670D	2200	2000	3 Min.
V6-231/A Calif.	.060	B	—	15°	C⑭	—	550/620D	—	2200	3 Min.
V8-265/S	.060	J	—	10°	A	—	550/650D	—	2200	7-8½
V8-301/W⑩	.060	J	—	12°	A	—	550/650D	—	2500	7-8½
V8-301/W⑤	.060	J	—	12°	A	—	550D	—	2500	7-8½
V8-301/T⑧	.060	J	—	8°	A	—	600/650D	—	2400	7-8½
V8-305/H	.045	K	—	4°	④	—	550/650D	—	2200	7½-9
V8-350/X Exc. Calif.⑪	.060	I	—	15°	C⑭	—	550/670D	—	1850	3 Min.
V8-350/R Calif.⑯	.080	H	—	18°⑥	E	—	550/650D	—	700	5½-6½
1981										
V6-231/A	.080	B	15°	15°③	C⑭	800N	⑬	2200	1800	3 Min.
V8-265/S	.060	J	—	12°⑰	A	—	450D	—	2000	7-8½

continued

GENERAL MOTORS CORP.—Continued

The following specifications are published from the latest information available. This data should be used only in the absence of a decal affixed in the engine compartment.

★ When checking ignition timing, disconnect vacuum hose at distributor and plug opening in hose so idle speed will not be affected. Also, on some computer controlled ignition systems, it may be necessary to disconnect certain vacuum hoses and/or electrical connectors. Refer to vehicle emission decal.

▲ Before removing wires from distributor cap, determine location of the No. 1 wire in cap, as distributor position may have been altered from that shown at the end of this chart.

Year & Engine/V.I.N.	Spark Plug Gap	Ignition Timing BTDC①★ Firing Order Fig. ▲	Man. Trans.	Auto. Trans.	Mark Fig.	Curb Idle Speed② Man. Trans.	Auto. Trans.	Fast Idle Speed Man. Trans.	Auto. Trans.	Fuel Pump Pressure
PONTIAC—REAR WHEEL DRIVE MODELS EXC. FIERO & 1000, 1981—Continued										
V8-301/W Exc. Turbo	.060	J	—	12°⑰	A	—	450D	—	2000	7–8½
V8-301 Turbo/T	.060	J	—	6°⑰	A	—	450D	—	2400	7–8½
V8-305/H	.045	K	6°③	—	G	800N	—	2200	—	7½–9
V8-307/Y	.080	H	—	15°③⑥	E	—	⑬	—	650D	5½–6½
1982										
4-151 T.B.I./2	.060	F	8°⑨	8°⑨	N	⑦⑬	650D⑬	⑬	⑬	—
V6-173/1	.045	O	10°③	10°③	D	850/1100N	600/700D	2600	2500	6–7½
V6-231/A	.080	B	—	15°③	E⑭	—	500D	—	2000	4¼–5¾
V6-252/4	.080	B	—	15°③	E⑭	—	500D	—	—	4¼–5¾
V8-305/H	.045	K	6°③	6°③	G	700/800N	500/600D	1800⑫	2200⑫	7½–9
V8-305 T.B.I./7	.045	K	—	6°⑮	G	—	500D⑱	—	1000⑱	—
1983										
4-151 T.B.I./2	.060	F	—	8°⑨	N	—	⑬	—	⑬	—
V6-173/1	.045	O	10°③	10°③	D	775/1100N	600/750D	2500	2500	6–7½
V6-173 H.O./L	.045	O	10°③	10°③	D	800/1100N	725/850D	2600	2700	6–7½
V6-229/9	.045	L	—	TDC	M	—	⑬	—	⑬	4½–6
V6-231/A	.080	B	—	15°	C⑭	—	⑬	—	2200	4¼–5¾
V8-305/H	.045	K	6°③	6°③	G	700/800N	500/600D	1800⑫	2200⑫	7½–9
V8-305 T.B.I./S	.045	K	—	6°⑮	G	—	⑱	—	⑱	—
V8-305 H.O./G	.045	K	—	—	G	700	500D	—	—	7½–9
1984										
4-151/2	.060	F	8°⑨	8°⑨	N	⑬	⑬	⑬	⑬	—
V-173/1	.045	O	10°③	10°③	D	800/1100	600/750D	2600	2500	6–7½
V6-173/L	.045	O	10°③	10°③	D	800/1100	725/850D	2600	2700	6–7½
V6-231/A	.060	B	—	15°	C⑭	—	⑬	—	2200	4¼–5¾
V8-305/H	.045	K	6°③	6°③	G	700/800	500/650D	1800	2200	7½–9
V8-305 H.O./G	.045	K	6°③	6°③	G	700/800	600/650D	1800	2200	7½–9
1985										
4-151	.060	F	—	—	N	⑬	⑬	⑬	⑬	—
V6-173 MFI	.045	O	—	—	D	⑬	⑬	⑬	⑬	—
V6-231/A	.080	B	—	15°	C⑭	—	⑬	—	2200	4¼–5¾
V6-262/Z	.035		—	—	—	⑬	⑬	⑬	⑬	—
V8-305 4 BBL./H	.045	K	—	—	G	700	500D	—	—	7½–9
V8-305 4 BBL. H.O./G	.045	K	—	—	G	700	600D	—	—	7½–9
V8-305 TPI/6	.045		—	—		⑬	⑬	⑬	⑬	—
1986										
4-151 EFI/2	.060	F	—	—	N	⑬	—	⑬	—	—
V6-173 MFI/S	.045	O	—	—	D	⑬	⑬	⑬	⑬	—
V6-231/A	.060	B	—	—	C⑭	—	⑬	—	⑬	5½–7
V6-262 EFI/Z	.035		—	—		—	⑬	—	⑬	—
V8-305 4 Barrel/H	.035	K	—	—	G	700	500D	—	—	7½–9
V8-305 H.O. 4 Barrel/G	.035	K	—	—	G	700	600D	—	—	7½–9
V8-305 TPI/F	.035		—	—		⑬	⑬	⑬	⑬	—

①—BTDC—Before top dead center.
②—Idle speed on man. trans. vehicles is adjusted in Neutral & on auto. trans. equipped vehicles is adjusted in Drive unless otherwise specified. Where two idle speeds are listed, the higher speed is with the A/C or idle solenoid energized.

continued

GENERAL MOTORS CORP.
Pontiac—Rear Wheel Drive Models Exc. Fiero & 1000, Notes— Continued

③—With distributor 4-wire connector disconnected.
④—Early models, Fig. M; late models, Fig. G.
⑤—E/C (electronic control) engine.
⑥—At 1100 RPM.
⑦—Less A/C, 850 RPM; with A/C, 900 RPM.
⑧—Turbocharged engine.
⑨—Ground diagnostic connector located under dash. The check engine light should flash on & off when in diagnostic mode. Check average ignition timing of cylinder Nos. 1 & 4, and reset as necessary. After completing timing check, remove ground from

diagnostic connector & ensure check engine light is off.
⑩—Except E/C (electronic control) & turbocharged engines.
⑪—Distributor located at front of engine.
⑫—With EGR vacuum hose disconnected and plugged. Check adjustments within 15 seconds after placing throttle on high step of fast idle cam.
⑬—Idle speed is controlled by the idle speed control (ICS) motor or the idle load compensator (ILC).
⑭—The harmonic balancer on these engines has two timing marks. The mark measuring 1/16 in. is used when setting

timing with a hand held timing light. The mark measuring 1/8 in. is used when setting timing with magnetic timing equipment.
⑮—When checking ignition timing, disconnect Electric Spark Timing bypass connector (tan wire w/black stripe) to place EST in bypass mode.
⑯—Distributor located rear of engine, rotor rotation counter clockwise. Fuel located right side of engine.
⑰—With distributor by-pass pigtail (blue connector) grounded.
⑱—Idle speed controlled by Idle Air Control (IAC) assembly.

Fig. A

Fig. B

Fig. C

Fig. D

Fig. E

Fig. F

Fig. G

Fig. H

Fig. I

continued

Fig. J

Fig. K

Fig. L

Fig. M

Fig. N

Fig. O

continued

GENERAL MOTORS CORP.—Continued

Pontiac Fiero

The following specifications are published from the latest information available. This data should be used only in the absence of a decal affixed in the engine compartment.

★ When checking ignition timing, disconnect vacuum hose at distributor and plug opening in hose so idle speed will not be affected. Also, on some computer controlled ignition systems, it may be necessary to disconnect certain vacuum hoses and/or electrical connectors. Refer to vehicle emission decal.

▲ Before removing wires from distributor cap, determine location of the No. 1 wire in cap, as distributor position may have been altered from that shown at the end of this chart.

Year & Engine/V.I.N.	Spark Plug Gap	Ignition Timing BTDC①★				Curb Idle Speed②		Fast Idle Speed		Fuel Pump Pressure
		Firing Order Fig. ▲	Man. Trans.	Auto. Trans.	Mark Fig.	Man. Trans.	Auto. Trans.	Man. Trans.	Auto. Trans.	
1984										
4-151/R	.060	A	—	—	B	—	—	—	—	—
1985–86										
4-151/R	.060	A	—	—	B	—	—	—	—	—
V6-173 MFI	.045	A	—	—	—	—	—	—	—	—

①—BTDC—Before top dead center.
②—Idle speed on man. trans. vehicles is adjusted in Neutral, & on auto. trans. equipped vehicles is adjusted in Drive unless otherwise specified. Where two idle speeds are listed, the highest speed is with the A/C or idle solenoid energized.

FIRING ORDER 1-3-4-2

FRONT OF ENGINE

SCREW   SCREW

REAR OF VEHICLE

Fig. A

BEFORE

16 12 8 4

Fig. B

DIESEL ENGINE PERFORMANCE SPECIFICATIONS

TABLE OF CONTENTS

DIESEL ENGINE PERFORMANCE SPECIFICATIONS

FORD MOTOR COMPANY
Ford Escort & Tempo • Mercury Lynx & Topaz

Year & Engine/V.I.N.	Firing Order	Injection Timing	Injection Nozzle Pressure		Curb Idle Speed RPM	Fast Idle Speed RPM
			New	Used		
1984						
4-120/H	1-3-4-2	TDC①	1990–2105	1849–1990	750②	1500②
1985						
4-120/H	1-3-4-2	TDC①	1990–2105	1849–1990	—	–
1986						
4-120/	1-3-4-2	—	1914	—	—	–

①—With engine at operating temperature.   ②—With manual transmission.

Lincoln Continental & Mark VII

Year & Engine/V.I.N.	Firing Order	Injection Timing B.T.D.C.①	Injection Nozzle Opening Pressure②	Curb Idle Speed RPM	Fast Idle Speed RPM
1984–85					
6-149/L	1-5-3-6-2-4	5°③	2133	750–800	900–1050

①—B.T.D.C—Before top dead center.   ②—PSI.   ③—At 1500 RPM.

GENERAL MOTORS CORP.
Buick, Cadillac & Oldsmobile—Rear Wheel Drive Models & 1980–85 Eldorado, Riviera, Seville & Toronado

Year & Engine/V.I.N.	Firing Order	Injection Timing A.T.D.C.①	Curb Idle Speed RPM②	Fast Idle Speed RPM②
1980				
V8-350/N Exc. High Alt.	1-8-4-3-6-5-7-2	4½°③④	600D	750D
V8-350/N High Alt.	1-8-4-3-6-5-7-2	5½°③④	600D	750D
1981				
V8-350/N Exc. High Alt.	1-8-4-3-6-5-7-2	4°③④	600D	750D
V8-350/N High Alt.	1-8-4-3-6-5-7-2	5°③④	600D	750D
1982–83				
V6-262/V Exc. High Alt.	1-6-5-4-3-2	7°③⑤	650D	725D
V6-262/V High Alt.	1-6-5-4-3-2	7°③⑥	650D	725D
V8-350/N Exc. High Alt.	1-8-4-3-6-5-7-2	4°③⑦	600D	725D
V8-350/N High Alt.	1-8-4-3-6-5-7-2	4°③⑧	600D	725D
1984				
V6-262/V	1-6-5-4-3-2	7°③⑨	675D	775D
V8-350/N	1-8-4-3-6-5-7-2	4°③⑩	600D	750D
1985				
V8-350/N	1-8-4-3-6-5-7-2	5°③⑩	600D	750D

continued

GENERAL MOTORS CORP.
Buick, Cadillac & Oldsmobile—Rear Wheel Drive Models & 1980–85 Eldorado, Riviera, Seville & Toronado Notes—Continued

①—A.T.D.C.—After top dead center.
②—D: Drive.
③—Using diesel timing meter J-33075.
④—At 1200 RPM.
⑤—At 1300 RPM. At altitudes above 4000 ft., set at 8° ATDC.
⑥—At 1300 RPM. At altitudes below 4000 ft., set at 6° ATDC.
⑦—At 1250 RPM. At altitudes above 4000 ft., set at 5° ATDC.
⑧—At 1250 RPM. At altitudes below 4000 ft., set at 3° ATDC.
⑨—At 1300 RPM.
⑩—At 1250 RPM.

1985 Buick Electra & Park Avenue, Cad. DeVille & Fleetwood & Olds. 98

Year & Engine/V.I.N.	Firing Order	Injection Timing A.T.D.C.①	Curb Idle Speed RPM②	Fast Idle Speed RPM②
1985				
V6-262/T Exc. Calif.③	1-6-5-4-3-2	5½°④⑤	675D	750D
V6-262/T Calif.③	1-6-5-4-3-2	6½°④⑤	675D	750D
V6-262/T Exc. Calif.⑥	1-6-5-4-3-2	6°④⑤	675D	750D
V6-262/T Calif.⑥	1-6-5-4-3-2	7°④⑤	675D	750D

①—A.T.D.C.—After top dead center.
②—D: Drive.
③—Engines with external EGR.
④—Using diesel timing meter J-33075.
⑤—At 1300 RPM.
⑥—Engines with internal EGR.

Chevrolet & Pontiac—Rear Wheel Drive Models Exc. Chevette, Fiero & 1000

Year & Engine/V.I.N.	Firing Order	Injection Timing A.T.D.C.①	Curb Idle Speed RPM②	Fast Idle Speed RPM②
1980				
V8-350/N Exc. High Alt.	1-8-4-3-6-5-7-2	4½°③④	600D	750D
V8-350/N High Alt.	1-8-4-3-6-5-7-2	5½°③④	600D	750D
1981				
V8-350/N Exc. High Alt.	1-8-4-3-6-5-7-2	4°③④	600D	750D
V8-350/N High Alt.	1-8-4-3-6-5-7-2	5°③④	600D	750D
1982–83				
V6-262/V Exc. High Alt.	1-6-5-4-3-2	7°③⑤	650D	725D
V6-262/V High Alt.	1-6-5-4-3-2	7°③⑥	650D	725D
V8-350/N Exc. High Alt.	1-8-4-3-6-5-7-2	4°③⑦	600D	725D
V8-350/N High Alt.	1-8-4-3-6-5-7-2	4°③⑧	600D	725D
1984				
V8-350/N	1-8-4-3-6-5-7-2	4°③⑨	600D	750D
1985				
V8-350/N	1-8-4-3-6-5-7-2	5°③⑨	600D	750D

①—A.T.D.C.—After top dead center.
②—D: Drive.
③—Using diesel timing meter J-33075.
④—At 1200 RPM.
⑤—At 1300 RPM. At altitudes above 4000 ft., set at 8° ATDC.
⑥—At 1300 RPM. At altitudes below 4000 ft., set at 6° ATDC.
⑦—At 1250 RPM. At altitudes above 4000 ft., set at 5° ATDC.
⑧—At 1250 RPM. At altitudes below 4000 ft., set at 3° ATDC.
⑨—At 1250 RPM.

continued

GENERAL MOTORS CORP.—Continued

Chevrolet Chevette & Pontiac 1000

Year & Engine/V.I.N.	Injection Timing B.T.D.C.①	Curb Idle Speed RPM		Fast Idle Speed RPM	
		Man. Trans.	Auto. Trans.②	Man. Trans.	Auto. Trans.
1981					
4-110/D	18°③	625	725D	950	950
1982–83					
4-110/D	18°③	625	725N	950	950
1984					
4-110/D	18°③	625	725N	—	—
1985					
4-110/D	18°③	625	—	—	—
1986					
4-110/Exc. Calif.	—	700	725N	—	—
4-110/Calif.	—	625	725N	—	—

①—B.T.D.C—Before top dead center.   ②—D: Drive. N: Neutral.   ③—Static timing.

1982–85 Chev. Celebrity, Buick Century, Olds. Cutlass Ciera, Pont. 6000 & 1984–85 Cutlass Cruiser

Year & Engine/V.I.N.	Firing Order	Injection Timing A.T.D.C.①	Curb Idle Speed RPM②	Fast Idle Speed RPM②
1982				
V6-262/T	1-6-5-4-3-2	5°③④	650D	725D
1983–84				
V6-262/T	1-6-5-4-3-2	6°③④	675D	775D
1985				
V6-262/T Exc. Calif.	1-6-5-4-3-2	5½°③④	650D	750D
V6-262/T Calif.	1-6-5-4-3-2	6½°③④	650D	750D

①—A.T.D.C.—After top dead center.   ③—Using diesel timing meter J-33075.   ④—At 1300 RPM.
②—D: Drive.

TROUBLESHOOTING

TABLE OF CONTENTS

Introduction

STARTING A STALLED ENGINE

When an engine fails to start the chances are that 90 per cent of the cases will involve the ignition system and seldom the fuel system or other miscellaneous reasons. If a systematic procedure is followed the trouble can almost always be found without the use of special equipment.

To begin with, turn on the ignition switch and if the ammeter shows a slight discharge (or if the telltale lamp lights) it indicates that current is flowing. A glance at the gas gauge will indicate whether or not there is fuel in the tank.

Operate the starter and if the engine turns over freely, both the battery and starter are functioning properly. On the other hand, if the starter action is sluggish it may be due to a discharged or defective battery, loose, corroded or dirty battery terminals, mechanical failure in the starter, starter switch or starter drive. If the starter circuit is okay, skip this phase of the discussion and proceed to ignition.

STARTER CIRCUIT CHECKOUT

To determine which part of the starter circuit is at fault, turn on the light switch and again operate the starter. Should the lights go out or become dim, the trouble is either in the battery, its connections or cables. A hydrometer test of the battery should indicate better than 1.250 specific gravity, while a voltmeter, placed across the positive and negative posts, should indicate about 12 volts. If either of these tests prove okay, clean and tighten the battery connections and cable terminals or replace any cable which seems doubtful.

If the lights remain bright when the starter is operated, the trouble is between the battery and the starter, or the starter switch is at fault, since it is evident that there is no electrical connection between these points. If these connections are clean and tight, it is safe to assume that the starter or starter switch is defective.

NEUTRAL SAFETY SWITCH

If the ammeter shows a slight discharge (or if the telltale lamp lights) when the ignition is turned on, but the system goes dead when the starting circuit is closed, the neutral safety switch may be at fault. To check,

bypass the switch with a suitable jumper. If the engine now starts, adjust or replace the switch.

CAUTION: With the safety switch bypassed, the car can be started in any gear. Be sure the transmission is in neutral or park and the parking brake is applied.

PRIMARY IGNITION CHECKOUT

NOTE: For troubleshooting of electronic ignition systems, refer to Electronic Ignition section.

Let's assume that the battery and starter are doing their job, and that fuel is reaching the carburetor, but the car does not start, then the trouble must be somewhere in the ignition circuit. But first, before starting your diagnosis, it is advisable to give the whole system a visual inspection which might uncover obvious things such as broken or disconnected wires etc.

The best way to start tracing down ignition troubles is to begin with the primary circuit since this is where troubles show up most frequently. First remove the distributor cap and block the points open with a piece of cardboard, then turn on the ignition and with a test bulb or voltmeter check to see if there is current at the terminal on the distributor. If you do not get a reading at this point, the current is cut off somewhere in the connections leading back to the ignition switch or it may be that the condenser has an internal short to the ground. The latter possibility can be eliminated if you can restore current at the distributor terminal by disconnecting the condenser from the distributor plate so that its outside shell is not grounded. With the possibility of a bad condenser out of the way, work toward the ignition switch and test for current at each connection until you get to one where you get a reading. Between this connection and the distributor lies the trouble.

The foregoing steps in checking the primary circuit should include checking the ignition coil resistor for defects or loose connections. As this is done, bear in mind that while the starter cranks the engine, the resistor is by-passed by the starter switch on the American Motors 4-121 engine. This means that while the circuit through the resistor may be satisfactory, a broken connection or high resistance between the

starter switch by-pass terminal and the coil would prevent starting. On the other hand, a satisfactory by-pass circuit might start the engine while the engine would stall immediately upon releasing the starter switch if there was a defect in the coil resistance circuit.

If, to begin with, the test equipment shows a current reading at the distributor terminal, it is safe to assume that the trouble is in the unit itself, most likely burned or dirty breaker points. A final positive test for defective breaker points can be made very simply by removing the cardboard from between the points, and positioning the distributor cam by turning the engine to where the points are closed. With the points closed there should be no current at the distributor terminal. If there is current, replace the points.

In an emergency, the points can be cleaned by using the sanded side of a match box, a knife blade, or the sharp edge of a screwdriver to scrape the scale from the contact faces. After cleaning the points, if a gauge is not available to set the gap, a quick adjustment can be made by using four layers of a piece of newspaper. The thickness of the paper is equivalent to about .020", which is the approximate gap setting for most distributors. Of course, at the earliest opportunity, a precise point adjustment should be made.

If the procedure outlined under "Primary Ignition Checkout" does not uncover the trouble then it will be necessary to continue the tests into the secondary ignition circuit.

SECONDARY IGNITION CHECKOUT

First of all, remove the wire from one of the spark plugs, turn on the ignition and operate the starter. While the engine is cranking, hold the terminal of the spark plug wire about ¼ inch away from the engine or spark plug base. If the spark is strong and jumps the gap, the trouble is confined to either the spark plugs or lack of fuel. Before going any further, wipe the outside of the plugs to remove any dirt or dampness which would create an easy path for the current to flow, then try to start the engine again. If it still fails to start, remove one of the spark plugs and if it is wet around the base, it indicates that the fuel system is okay, so it naturally follows that the spark plugs are at fault. Remove all the plugs, clean them and set the gaps.

An emergency adjustment of spark plug gaps can be made by folding a piece of newspaper into 6 or 7 layers. When changing the gap, always bend the side (ground) electrode and never the center one as there is danger of breaking the insulation.

FUEL SYSTEM CHECKOUT

If the spark plug that was removed showed no indication of dampness on its base, check the fuel system. A quick check can be made by simply removing the carburetor air cleaner and looking down into the carburetor. Open and close the throttle manually and if fuel is present in the carburetor, the throttle will operate the accelerating pump, causing it to push gasoline through the pump jet. If it does, check the choke valve. If the engine is cold, the choke valve should be closed. If the choke won't close, the engine can be started by covering the carburetor throat while the engine is cranking, provided, of course, that fuel is reaching the carburetor.

Check the operation of the fuel pump by disconnecting the fuel lines from the pump to the carburetor. Crank the engine and if the pump is working, fuel will pulsate out of the line. If not, either the pump isn't working or the line from the tank to the pump is clogged. Before blaming the pump, however, disconnect the line at the inlet side of the pump which leads to the tank and, while a companion listens at the tank blow through the line. If a gurgling sound is heard back in the tank, the line is open and the trouble is in the pump. Remove the sediment bowl, if so equipped and clean the screen, then replace the bowl and screen, being sure that you have an airtight fit. If the pump still refuses to function, it should be removed and repaired.

The foregoing discussion will, in most cases, uncover the cause of why an engine won't start. However, if further diagnosis is necessary, the following list will undoubtedly provide the answer.

ENGINE NOISE TESTS
LOOSE MAIN BEARING

A loose main bearing is indicated by a powerful but dull thud or knock when the engine is pulling. If all main bearings are loose a noticeable clatter will be audible.

The thud occurs regularly every other revolution. The knock can be confirmed by shorting spark plugs on cylinders adjacent to the bearing. Knock will disappear or be less when plugs are shorted. This test should be made at a fast idle equivalent to 15 mph in high gear. If bearing is not quite loose enough to produce a knock by itself, the bearing may knock if oil is too thin or if there is no oil at the bearing.

LOOSE FLYWHEEL

A loose flywheel is indicated by a thud or click which is usually irregular. To test, idle the engine at about 20 mph and shut off the ignition. If thud is heard, the flywheel may be loose.

LOOSE ROD BEARING

A loose rod bearing is indicated by a metallic knock which is usually loudest at about 30 mph with throttle closed. Knock can be reduced or even eliminated by shorting spark plug. If bearing is not loose enough to produce a knock by itself, the bearing may knock if oil is too thin or if there is no oil at the bearing.

PISTON PIN

Piston pin, piston and connecting rod noises are difficult to tell apart.

A loose piston pin causes a sharp double knock which is usually heard when engine is idling. Severity of knock should increase when spark plug to this cylinder is short-circuited. However, on some engines the knock becomes more noticeable at 25 to 35 mph on the road.

Piston pin rubs against cylinder wall, caused by lock screw being loose or snap ring broken.

HYDRAULIC LIFTERS

The malfunctioning of a hydraulic valve lifter is almost always accompanied by a clicking or tapping noise. More or less hydraulic lifter noise may be expected when the engine is cold but if lifters are functioning properly the noise should disappear when the engine warms up.

If all or nearly all lifters are noisy, they may be stuck because of dirty or gummy oil.

If all lifters are noisy, oil pressure to them may be inadequate. Foaming oil may also cause this trouble. If oil foams there will be bubbles on the oil level dipstick. Foaming may be caused by water in the oil or by too high an oil level or by a very low oil level.

If the hydraulic plungers require an initial adjustment, they will be noisy if this adjustment is incorrect.

If one lifter is noisy the cause may be:
1. Plunger too tight in lifter body.
2. Weak or broken plunger spring.
3. Ball valve leaks.
4. Plunger worn.
5. Lock ring (if any) improperly installed or missing.
6. Lack of oil pressure to this plunger.

If ball valve leaks, clean plunger in special solvent such as acetone and reinstall. Too often, plungers are condemned as faulty when all they need is a thorough cleaning.

Gum and dirty oil are the most common causes of hydraulic valve lifter trouble. Engine oil must be free of dirt. Select a standard brand of engine oil and use no other. Mixing up one standard brand with another may cause gummy oil and sticking plungers. Do not use any special oils unless recommended by the car manufacturer and change oil filter or element at recommended intervals.

LOOSE ENGINE MOUNTINGS

Occasional thud with car in operation. Most likely to be noticed at the moment the throttle is opened or closed.

EXCESSIVE CRANKSHAFT END PLAY

A rather sharp rap which occurs at idling speed but may be heard at higher speeds also. The noise should disappear when clutch is disengaged.

FUEL PUMP NOISE

Diagnosis of fuel pumps suspected as noisy requires that some form of sounding device be used. Judgment by ear alone is not sufficient, otherwise a fuel pump may be needlessly replaced in attempting to correct noise contributed by some other component. Use of a stethoscope, a long screwdriver, or a sounding rod is recommended to locate the area or component causing the noise. The sounding rod can easily be made from a length of copper tubing $\frac{1}{4}$ to $\frac{3}{8}$ inch in diameter.

If the noise has been isolated to the fuel pump, remove the pump and run the engine with the fuel remaining in the carburetor bowl. If the noise level does not change, the source of the noise is elsewhere and the original fuel pump should be reinstalled. On models using a fuel pump push rod, check for excessive wear and/or galling of the push rod.

VAPOR LOCK

The term vapor lock means the flow of fuel to the mixing chamber in the carburetor has been stopped (locked) by the formation of vaporized fuel pockets or bubbles caused by overheating the fuel by hot fuel pump, hot fuel lines or hot carburetor.

The more volatile the fuel the greater the tendency for it to vapor lock. Vapor lock is encouraged by high atmospheric temperature, hard driving, defective engine cooling and high altitude.

A mild case of vapor lock will cause missing and hard starting when engine is warm. Somewhat more severe vapor lock will stop the engine which cannot be started again until it has cooled off enough so that any vaporized fuel has condensed to a liquid.

SERVICE NOTE: Some cars have a vapor bypass system. These cars have a special fuel filter which has a metering outlet in the top. Any vapor which forms is bled off and returned to the fuel tank through a separate line alongside the fuel supply line. This system greatly reduces the possibility of vapor lock. However, if vapor lock is suspected examine the bypass valve to see if it is functioning.

PERCOLATION

Percolation means simply that gasoline in the carburetor bowl is boiling over into the intake manifold. This condition is most apt to occur immediately after a hot engine is shut off. Most carburetors have a provision for relieving the vapor pressure of overheated fuel in the carburetor bowl by

TROUBLESHOOTING

means of ports. If, however, percolation should take place, the engine may be started by allowing it to cool slightly and then holding the throttle wide open while cranking to clear the intake manifold of excess fuel.

SPARK KNOCK, PING, DETONATION

All three expressions mean the same thing. It is a sharp metallic knock caused by vibration of the cylinder head and block. The vibration is due to split-second high-pressure waves resulting from almost instantaneous abnormal combustion instead of the slower normal combustion.

The ping may be mild or loud. A mild ping does no harm but a severe ping will reduce power. A very severe ping may shatter spark plugs, break valves or crack pistons.

Pinging is most likely to occur on open throttle at low or moderate engine speed. Pinging is encouraged by:
1. Overheated engine.
2. Low octane fuel.
3. Too high compression.
4. Spark advanced too far.
5. Hot mixture due to hot engine or hot weather.
6. Heavy carbon deposit which increases the compression pressure.
7. Clogged or restricted EGR passages.

Tendency to ping increases with mixture temperature including high atmospheric temperature; intake manifold heater valve "on" when engine is warm; hot cooling water; hot interior engine surfaces due to sluggish water circulation or water jackets clogged with rust or dirt especially around exhaust valves. Some of these troubles may be confined to one or two cylinders.

If an engine pings objectionably even when using the highest octane fuel available, retard the spark setting, but first be sure the EGR system is functioning, the cooling system is in good condition, the mixture is not too lean, and the combustion chambers are free of carbon deposits.

PRE-IGNITION

Pre-ignition means that the mixture is set on fire before the spark occurs, being ignited by a red hot spot in the combustion chamber such as an incandescent particle of carbon; a thin piece of protruding metal; an overheated spark plug, or a bright red hot exhaust valve. The result is reduction of power and overheating accompanied by pinging. The bright red hot exhaust valve may be due to a leak, to lack of tappet clearance, to valve sticking, or to a weak or broken spring.

Pre-ignition may not be noticed if not severe. Severe pre-ignition results in severe pinging. The most common cause of pre-ignition is a badly overheated engine.

When the engine won't stop when the ignition is shut off, the cause is often due to red hot carbon particles resting on heavy carbon deposit in a very hot engine.

AFTER-BURNING

A subdued put-putting at the exhaust tail pipe may be due to leaky exhaust valves which permit the mixture to finish combustion in the muffler. If exhaust pipe or muffler is red hot, better let it cool, as there is some danger of setting the car on fire. Most likely to occur when mixture is lean.

ENGINE CONTINUES TO RUN AFTER IGNITION IS TURNED OFF

This condition, known as "dieseling," "run on," or "after running," is caused by improper idle speed and/or high temperature. Idle speed and engine temperature are affected by:

Carburetor Adjustment:
High idle speed will increase the tendency to diesel because of the inertia of the engine crankshaft and flywheel. Too low an idle speed, particularly with a lean mixture, will result in an increase in engine temperature, especially if the engine is allowed to idle for long periods of time.

Ignition Timing:
Because advanced ignition timing causes a corresponding increase in idle speed and retarded timing reduces idle speed, ignition timing influences the tendency to diesel in the same manner as Carburetor Adjustment.

Fuel Mixture:
Enriching the idle fuel mixture decreases the tendency to diesel by causing the engine to run cooler.

Fuel Content:
High octane fuels tend to reduce dieseling. Increased fuel content of lead alkyl increases the tendency to diesel. Phosphates and nickel fuel additives help prevent dieseling.

Spark Plugs:
Plugs of too high a heat range for the engine in question can cause dieseling.

Throttle Plates:
If the throttle plates are not properly aligned in the carburetor bore, a resulting leanness in fuel mixture occurs, contributing to dieseling.

Electrical System:
Normally, during dieseling, ignition is self-supplied by a "hot spot," self-igniting fuel, etc. However, there is a possibility of the vehicle's electrical system supplying the necessary ignition. When the ignition switch is turned off, a small amount of current can flow from the generator into the primary of the ignition coil through the generator tell-tale light. This is particularly true when the warning light bulb has been changed for one of increased wattage.

NOTE: "Run on" is more prevalent in an engine when the ignition is turned off before the engine is allowed to return to idle. Therefore, it can be reduced by letting the engine return to idle before shutting off the ignition. "Run on" incidence can be reduced on automatic transmission units by turning off the engine when in gear.

A certain amount of "run on" can be expected from any gasoline engine regardless of make, size or configuration. (Diesel engines operate on this principle.) However, if the above suggestions are correctly employed, "Run on" will be reduced to an unnoticeable level.

ENGINE

Condition	Possible Cause	Correction
ENGINE WILL NOT START	1. Weak battery.	1. Test battery specific gravity. Recharge or replace as necessary.
	2. Corroded or loose battery connections.	2. Clean and tighten battery connections. Apply a coat of petroleum to terminals.
	3. Faulty starter.	3. Repair starter motor.
	4. Moisture on ignition wires and distributor cap.	4. Wipe wires and cap clean and dry.
	5. Faulty ignition cables.	5. Replace any cracked or shorted cables.
	6. Open or shorted primary ignition circuit.	6. Trace primary ignition circuit and repair as necessary.
	7. Malfunctioning ignition points or condensor.	7. Replace ignition points & condensor as necessary.

ENGINE—Continued

Condition	Possible Cause	Correction
ENGINE WILL NOT START, continued	8. Faulty coil.	8. Test and replace if necessary.
	9. Incorrect spark plug gap.	9. Set gap correctly.
	10. Incorrect ignition timing.	10. Reset timing.
	11. Dirt or water in fuel line or carburetor.	11. Clean lines and carburetor. Replace filter.
	12. Carburetor flooded.	12. Adjust float level—check seats.
	13. Incorrect carburetor float setting.	13. Adjust float level—check seats.
	14. Faulty fuel pump.	14. Install new fuel pump.
	15. Carburetor percolating. No fuel in the carburetor.	15. Measure float level. Adjust bowl vent. Inspect operation of manifold heat control valve.
ENGINE STALLS	1. Idle speed set too low.	1. Adjust carburetor.
	2. Incorrect choke adjustment.	2. Adjust choke.
	3. Idle mixture too lean or too rich.	3. Adjust carburetor.
	4. Incorrect carburetor float setting.	4. Adjust float setting.
	5. Leak in intake manifold.	5. Inspect intake manifold gasket and replace if necessary.
	6. Worn or burned distributor rotor.	6. Install new rotor.
	7. Incorrect ignition wiring.	7. Install correct wiring.
	8. Faulty coil.	8. Test and replace if necessary.
	9. Incorrect tappet lash.	9. Adjust to specifications.
ENGINE LOSS OF POWER	1. Incorrect ignition timing.	1. Reset timing.
	2. Worn or burned distributor rotor.	2. Install new rotor.
	3. Worn distributor shaft.	3. Remove and repair distributor.
	4. Dirty or incorrectly gapped spark plugs.	4. Clean plugs and set gap.
	5. Dirt or water in fuel line, carburetor or filter.	5. Clean lines, carburetor and replace filter.
	6. Incorrect carburetor float setting.	6. Adjust float level.
	7. Faulty fuel pump.	7. Install new pump.
	8. Incorrect valve timing.	8. Check and correct valve timing.
	9. Blown cylinder head gasket.	9. Install new head gasket.
	10. Low compression.	10. Test compression of each cylinder.
	11. Burned, warped or pitted valves.	11. Install new valves.
	12. Plugged or restricted exhaust system.	12. Install new parts as necessary.
	13. Faulty ignition cables.	13. Replace any cracked or shorted cables.
	14. Faulty coil.	14. Test and replace as necessary.
ENGINE MISSES ON ACCELERATION	1. Dirty, or gap too wide in spark plugs.	1. Clean spark plugs and set gap.
	2. Incorrect ignition timing.	2. Reset timing.
	3. Dirt in carburetor.	3. Clean carburetor and replace filter.
	4. Acceleration pump in carburetor.	4. Install new pump.
	5. Burned, warped or pitted valves.	5. Install new valves.
	6. Faulty coil.	6. Test and replace if necessary.
ENGINE MISSES AT HIGH SPEED	1. Dirty or gap set too wide in spark plug.	1. Clean spark plugs and set gap.
	2. Worn distributor shaft.	2. Remove and repair distributor.
	3. Worn or burned distributor rotor.	3. Install new rotor.
	4. Faulty coil.	4. Test and replace if necessary.
	5. Incorrect ignition timing.	5. Reset timing.
	6. Dirty jets in carburetor.	6. Clean carburetor, replace filter.
	7. Dirt or water in fuel line, carburetor or filter.	7. Clean lines, carburetor and replace filter.
NOISY VALVES	1. High or low oil level in crankcase.	1. Check for correct oil level.
	2. Thin or diluted oil.	2. Change oil.
	3. Low oil pressure.	3. Check engine oil level.
	4. Dirt in valve lifters.	4. Clean lifters.
	5. Bent push rod.	5. Install new push rods.
	6. Worn rocker arms.	6. Inspect oil supply to rockers.
	7. Worn tappets.	7. Install new tappets.
	8. Worn valve guides.	8. Ream and install new valves with O/S Stems.
	9. Excessive run-out of valve seats or valve faces.	9. Grind valve seats and valves.
	10. Incorrect tappet lash.	10. Adjust to specifications.

TROUBLESHOOTING

ENGINE—Continued

Condition	Possible Cause	Correction
CONNECTING ROD NOISE	1. Insufficient oil supply. 2. Low oil pressure. 3. Thin or diluted oil. 4. Excessive bearing clearance. 5. Connecting rod journals out-of-round. 6. Misaligned (bent) connecting rods.	1. Check engine oil level. 2. Check engine oil level. Inspect oil pump relief valve and spring. 3. Change oil to correct viscosity. 4. Measure bearings for correct clearance. 5. Replace crankshaft or regrind journals. 6. Replace bent connecting rods.
MAIN BEARING NOISE	1. Insufficient oil supply. 2. Low oil pressure. 3. Thin or diluted oil. 4. Excessive bearing clearance. 5. Excessive end play. 6. Crankshaft journal worn out-of-round. 7. Loose flywheel or torque converter.	1. Check engine oil level. 2. Check engine oil level. Inspect oil pump relief valve and spring. 3. Change oil to correct viscosity. 4. Measure bearings for correct clearances. 5. Check thrust bearing for wear on flanges. 6. Replace crankshaft or regrind journals. 7. Tighten to correct torque.
OIL PUMPING AT RINGS	1. Worn, scuffed, or broken rings. 2. Carbon in oil ring slot. 3. Rings fitted too tight in grooves.	1. Hone cylinder bores and install new rings. 2. Install new rings. 3. Remove the rings. Check grooves. If groove is not proper width, replace piston.
OIL PRESSURE DROP	1. Low oil level. 2. Faulty oil pressure sending unit. 3. Clogged oil filter. 4. Worn parts in oil pump. 5. Thin or diluted oil. 6. Excessive bearing clearance. 7. Oil pump relief valve stuck. 8. Oil pump suction tube loose, bent or cracked.	1. Check engine oil level. 2. Install new sending unit. 3. Install new oil filter. 4. Replace worn parts or pump. 5. Change oil to correct viscosity. 6. Measure bearings for correct clearance. 7. Remove valve and inspect, clean, and reinstall. 8. Remove oil pan and install new tube if necessary.
NO OIL PRESSURE	1. Low oil level. 2. Oil pressure gauge or sending unit inaccurate. 3. Oil pump malfunction. 4. Oil pressure relief valve sticking. 5. Oil passages on pressure side of pump obstructed. 6. Oil pickup screen or tube obstructed.	1. Add oil to correct level. 2. Replace defective unit. 3. Repair oil pump. 4. Remove and inspect oil pressure relief valve assembly. 5. Inspect oil passages for obstructions. 6. Inspect oil pickup for obstructions.
LOW OIL PRESSURE	1. Low oil level. 2. Oil excessively thin due to dilution, poor quality, or improper grade. 3. Oil pressure relief spring weak or sticking. 4. Oil pickup tube and screen assembly has restriction or air leak. 5. Excessive oil pump clearance. 6. Excessive main, rod, or camshaft bearing clearance.	1. Add oil to correct level. 2. Drain and refill crankcase with recommended oil. 3. Remove and inspect oil pressure relief valve assembly. 4. Remove and inspect oil inlet tube and screen assembly. (Fill pickup with lacquer thinner to find leaks.) 5. Check clearances. 6. Measure bearing clearances, repair as necessary.
HIGH OIL PRESSURE	1. Improper grade oil. 2. Oil pressure gauge or sending unit inaccurate. 3. Oil pressure relief valve sticking closed.	1. Drain and refill crankcase with correct grade oil. 2. Replace defective unit. 3. Remove and inspect oil pressure relief valve assembly.
EXTERNAL OIL LEAK	1. Fuel pump gasket broken or improperly seated.	1. Replace gasket.

54

ENGINE—Continued

Condition	Possible Cause	Correction
EXTERNAL OIL LEAK, continued	2. Cylinder head cover gasket broken or improperly seated.	2. Replace gasket; check cylinder head cover gasket flange and cylinder head gasket surface for distortion.
	3. Oil filter gasket broken or improperly seated.	3. Replace oil filter.
	4. Oil pan side gasket broken or improperly seated.	4. Replace gasket; check oil pan gasket flange for distortion.
	5. Oil pan front oil seal broken or improperly seated.	5. Replace seal; check timing chain cover and oil pan seal flange for distortion.
	6. Oil pan rear oil seal broken or improperly seated.	6. Replace seal; check oil pan rear oil seal flange; check rear main bearing cap for cracks, plugged oil return channels, or distortion in seal groove.
	7. Timing chain cover oil seal broken or improperly seated.	7. Replace seal.
	8. Oil pan drain plug loose or has stripped threads.	8. Repair as necessary and tighten.
	9. Rear oil gallery plug loose.	9. Use appropriate sealant on gallery plug and tighten.
	10. Rear camshaft plug loose or improperly seated.	10. Seat camshaft plug or replace and seal, as necessary.
EXCESSIVE OIL CONSUMPTION	1. Oil level too high.	1. Lower oil level to specifications.
	2. Oil too thin.	2. Replace with specified oil.
	3. Valve stem oil seals are damaged, missing, or incorrect type.	3. Replace valve stem oil seals.
	4. Valve stems or valve guides worn.	4. Check stem-to-guide clearance and repair as necessary.
	5. Piston rings broken, missing.	5. Replace missing or broken rings.
	6. Piston rings incorrect size.	6. Check ring gap, repair as necessary.
	7. Piston rings sticking or excessively loose in grooves.	7. Check ring side clearance, repair as necessary.
	8. Compression rings installed upside down.	8. Repair as necessary.
	9. Cylinder walls worn, scored, or glazed.	9. Repair as necessary.
	10. Piston ring gaps not properly staggered.	10. Repair as necessary.
	11. Excessive main or connecting rod bearing clearance.	11. Check bearing clearance, repair as necessary.

OIL PRESSURE INDICATOR

LIGHT NOT LIT, IGNITION ON AND ENGINE NOT RUNNING.	1. Bulb burned out.	1. Replace bulb.
	2. Open in light circuit.	2. Locate and correct open.
	3. Defective oil pressure switch.	3. Replace oil pressure switch.
LIGHT ON, ENGINE RUNNING ABOVE IDLE SPEED.	1. Grounded wiring between light and switch.	1. Locate and repair ground.
	2. Defective oil pressure switch.	2. Replace oil pressure switch.
	3. Low oil pressure.	3. Locate cause of low oil pressure and correct.

IGNITION, STARTER & FUEL

Condition	Possible Cause	Correction
NOTHING HAPPENS WHEN START ATTEMPT IS MADE	1. Undercharged or defective battery.	1. Check condition of battery and recharge or replace as required.
	2. Loose battery cables.	2. Clean and tighten cable connections.
	3. Burned fusible link in starting circuit.	3. Check for burned fusible link. Correct wiring problem.
	4. Incorrectly positioned or defective neutral start switch.	4. Check neutral start switch adjustment. If O.K., replace switch.

IGNITION, STARTER & FUEL—Continued

Condition	Possible Cause	Correction
NOTHING HAPPENS WHEN START ATTEMPT IS MADE, continued	5. Loose or defective wiring between neutral start switch and ignition switch.	5. Check for loose connections and opens between battery, horn relay, ignition switch, and solenoid "S" terminal. Check battery ground cable. Replace or repair defective item.
	6. Defective starter motor.	6. Repair or replace starter motor.
	7. Defective starter interlock system.	7. Use emergency button under hood. If car starts, repair circuit in interlock system. If car does not start, check and repair starter circuit.
SOLENOID SWITCH CLICKS BUT STARTER DOES NOT CRANK	1. Undercharged or defective battery.	1. Test battery. Recharge or replace battery.
	2. Loose battery cables.	2. Check and tighten battery connections.
	3. Loose or defective wiring at starter.	3. Tighten connections or repair wiring as required.
	4. Defective solenoid.	4. Replace solenoid.
	5. "Hot stall" condition.	5. Check engine cooling system.
	6. Excessive engine rotational torque caused by mechanical problem within engine.	6. Check engine torque for excessive friction.
	7. Defective starter motor.	7. Repair or replace starter motor.
SLOW CRANKING	1. Vehicle is overheating.	1. Check engine cooling system and repair as required.
	2. Undercharged or defective battery.	2. Recharge or replace battery.
	3. Loose or defective wiring between battery and engine block.	3. Repair or replace wiring.
	4. Loose or defective wiring between battery and solenoid "Bat" terminal.	4. Repair or replace wiring.
	5. Defective starter motor.	5. Repair or replace starter.
STARTER SPINS AND/OR MAKES LOUD GRINDING NOISE BUT DOES NOT TURN ENGINE	1. Defective starter motor.	1. Repair or replace starter motor.
	2. Defective ring gear.	2. Replace ring gear.
STARTER KEEPS RUNNING AFTER IGNITION SWITCH IS RELEASED— FROM "START" TO "RUN" POSITION	1. Defective ignition switch.	1. Replace ignition switch.
	2. Defective solenoid.	2. Replace solenoid.
STARTER ENGAGES ("Clunks") BUT ENGINE DOES NOT CRANK	1. Open circuit in solenoid armature or field coils.	1. Repair or replace solenoid or starter motor.
	2. Short or ground in field coil or armature.	2. Repair or replace starter motor.
HARD STARTING (Engine Cranks Normally)	1. Binding linkage, choke valve or choke piston.	1. Repair as necessary.
	2. Restricted choke vacuum and hot air passages.	2. Clean passages.
	3. Improper fuel level.	3. Adjust float level.
	4. Dirty, worn or faulty needle valve and seat.	4. Repair as necessary.
	5. Float sticking.	5. Repair as necessary.
	6. Exhaust manifold heat valve stuck.	6. Repair as necessary.
	7. Faulty fuel pump.	7. Replace fuel pump.
	8. Incorrect choke cover adjustment.	8. Adjust choke cover.
	9. Inadequate unloader adjustment.	9. Adjust unloader.
	10. Faulty ignition coil.	10. Test and replace as necessary.
	11. Improper spark plug gap.	11. Adjust gap.
	12. Incorrect initial timing.	12. Adjust timing.
	13. Incorrect valve timing.	13. Check valve timing; repair as necessary.
ROUGH IDLE OR STALLING	1. Incorrect curb or fast idle speed.	1. Adjust curb or fast idle speed.
	2. Incorrect initial timing.	2. Adjust timing to specifications.
	3. Improper idle mixture adjustment.	3. Adjust idle mixture.
	4. Damaged tip on idle mixture screw(s).	4. Replace mixture screw(s).
	5. Improper fast idle cam adjustment.	5. Adjust fast idle.
	6. Faulty PCV valve air flow.	6. Test PCV valve and replace as necessary.

IGNITION, STARTER & FUEL—Continued

Condition	Possible Cause	Correction
ROUGH IDLE OR STALLING, continued	7. Exhaust manifold heat valve inoperative.	7. Lubricate or replace heat valve as necessary.
	8. Choke binding.	8. Locate and eliminate binding condition.
	9. Improper choke setting.	9. Adjust choke.
	10. Vacuum leak.	10. Check manifold vacuum and repair as necessary.
	11. Improper fuel level.	11. Adjust fuel level.
	12. Faulty distributor rotor or cap.	12. Replace rotor or cap.
	13. Leaking engine valves.	13. Check cylinder leakdown rate or compression and repair as necessary.
	14. Incorrect ignition wiring.	14. Check wiring and correct as necessary.
	15. Faulty coil.	15. Test coil and replace as necessary.
	16. Clogged air bleed or idle passages.	16. Clean passages.
	17. Restricted air cleaner.	17. Clean or replace air cleaner.
	18. Faulty EGR valve operation if equipped.	18. Test EGR system and replace as necessary if equipped.
FAULTY LOW-SPEED OPERATION	1. Clogged idle transfer slots.	1. Clean transfer slots.
	2. Restricted idle air bleeds and passages.	2. Clean air bleeds and passages.
	3. Restricted air cleaner.	3. Clean or replace air cleaner.
	4. Improper fuel level.	4. Adjust fuel level.
	5. Faulty spark plugs.	5. Clean or replace spark plugs.
	6. Dirty, corroded, or loose secondary circuit connections.	6. Clean or tighten secondary circuit connections.
	7. Faulty ignition cable.	7. Replace ignition cable.
	8. Faulty distributor cap.	8. Replace cap.
FAULTY ACCELERATION	1. Improper pump stroke.	1. Adjust pump stroke.
	2. Incorrect ignition timing.	2. Adjust timing.
	3. Inoperative pump discharge check ball or needle.	3. Clean or replace as necessary.
	4. Worn or damaged pump diaphragm or piston.	4. Replace diaphragm or piston.
	5. Leaking main body cover gasket.	5. Replace gasket.
	6. Engine cold and choke too lean.	6. Adjust choke.
	7. Faulty spark plug(s).	7. Clean or replace spark plug(s).
	8. Leaking engine valves.	8. Check cylinder leakdown rate or compression, repair as necessary.
	9. Faulty coil.	9. Test coil and replace as necessary.
FAULTY HIGH-SPEED OPERATION	1. Incorrect ignition timing.	1. Adjust timing.
	2. Faulty distributor centrifugal advance.	2. Check centrifugal advance and repair as necessary.
	3. Faulty distributor vacuum advance.	3. Check vacuum advance and repair as necessary.
	4. Low fuel pump volume.	4. Replace fuel pump.
	5. Improper spark plug gap.	5. Adjust gap.
	6. Faulty choke operation.	6. Adjust choke.
	7. Partially restricted exhaust manifold, exhaust pipe, muffler, or tailpipe.	7. Eliminate restriction.
	8. Clogged vacuum passages.	8. Clean passages.
	9. Improper size or obstructed main jets.	9. Clean or replace as necessary.
	10. Restricted air cleaner.	10. Clean or replace as necessary.
	11. Faulty distributor rotor or cap.	11. Replace rotor or cap.
	12. Worn distributor shaft.	12. Replace shaft.
	13. Faulty coil.	13. Test coil and replace as necessary.
	14. Leaking engine valve(s).	14. Check cylinder leakdown or compression and repair as necessary.
	15. Faulty valve spring(s).	15. Inspect and test valve spring tension and replace as necessary.
	16. Incorrect valve timing.	16. Check valve timing and repair as necessary.
	17. Intake manifold restricted.	17. Pass chain through passages.
MISFIRE AT ALL SPEEDS	1. Faulty spark plug(s).	1. Clean or replace spark plug(s).
	2. Faulty spark plug cable(s).	2. Replace as necessary.
	3. Faulty distributor cap or rotor.	3. Replace cap or rotor.
	4. Faulty coil.	4. Test coil and replace as necessary.

IGNITION, STARTER & FUEL—Continued

Condition	Possible Cause	Correction
MISFIRE AT ALL SPEEDS, continued	5. Primary circuit shorted or open intermittently.	5. Trace primary circuit and repair as necessary.
	6. Leaking engine valve(s).	6. Check cylinder leakdown rate or compression and repair as necessary.
	7. Faulty hydraulic tappet(s).	7. Clean or replace tappet(s).
	8. Faulty valve spring(s).	8. Inspect and test valve spring tension, repair as necessary.
	9. Worn lobes on camshaft.	9. Replace camshaft.
	10. Vacuum leak.	10. Check manifold vacuum and repair as necessary.
	11. Improper carburetor settings.	11. Adjust carburetor.
	12. Fuel pump volume or pressure low.	12. Replace fuel pump.
	13. Blown cylinder head gasket.	13. Replace gasket.
	14. Intake or exhaust manifold passage(s) restricted.	14. Pass chain through passages.
POWER NOT UP TO NORMAL	1. Incorrect ignition timing.	1. Adjust timing.
	2. Faulty distributor rotor.	2. Replace rotor.
	3. Worn distributor shaft.	3. Replace shaft.
	4. Incorrect spark plug gap.	4. Adjust gap.
	5. Faulty fuel pump.	5. Replace fuel pump.
	6. Incorrect valve timing.	6. Check valve timing and repair as necessary.
	7. Faulty coil.	7. Test coil and replace as necessary.
	8. Faulty ignition cables.	8. Test cables and replace as necessary.
	9. Leaking engine valves.	9. Check cylinder leakdown rate or compression and repair as necessary.
	10. Blown cylinder head gasket.	10. Replace gasket.
	11. Leaking piston rings.	11. Check compression and repair as necessary.
INTAKE BACKFIRE	1. Improper ignition timing.	1. Adjust timing.
	2. Faulty accelerator pump discharge.	2. Repair as necessary.
	3. Improper choke operation.	3. Repair as necessary.
	4. Lean fuel mixture.	4. Check float level or manifold vacuum for vacuum leak.
EXHAUST BACKFIRE	1. Vacuum leak.	1. Check manifold vacuum and repair as necessary.
	2. Faulty A.I.R. diverter valve.	2. Test diverter valve and replace as necessary.
	3. Faulty choke operation.	3. Repair as necessary.
	4. Exhaust leak.	4. Locate and eliminate leak.
PING OR SPARK KNOCK	1. Incorrect ignition timing.	1. Adjust timing.
	2. Distributor centrifugal or vacuum advance malfunction.	2. Check advance and repair as necessary.
	3. Excessive combustion chamber deposits.	3. Use combustion chamber cleaner.
	4. Carburetor set too lean.	4. Adjust carburetor.
	5. Vacuum leak.	5. Check manifold vacuum and repair as necessary.
	6. Excessively high compression.	6. Check compression and repair as necessary.
	7. Fuel octane rating excessively low.	7. Try alternate fuel source.
	8. Heat riser stuck in heat on position.	8. Free-up or replace heat riser.
	9. Insufficient EGR flow.	9. Check EGR system operation.
SURGING (Cruising Speeds To Top Speeds)	1. Low fuel level.	1. Adjust fuel level.
	2. Low fuel pump pressure or volume.	2. Replace fuel pump.
	3. Improper PCV valve air flow.	3. Test PCV valve and replace as necessary.
	4. Vacuum leak.	4. Check manifold vacuum and repair as necessary.
	5. Dirt in carburetor.	5. Clean carburetor, replace filter.
	6. Undersize main jets.	6. Replace main jet(s).
	7. Clogged fuel filter screen.	7. Replace fuel filter.
	8. Restricted air cleaner.	8. Clean or replace air cleaner.
	9. Excessive EGR valve flow.	9. Check EGR system operation.

CHARGING SYSTEM

Condition	Possible Cause	Correction
ALTERNATOR FAILS TO CHARGE (No Output or Low Output)	1. Alternator drive belt loose. 2. Regulator base improperly grounded. 3. Worn brushes and/or slip rings. 4. Sticking brushes. 5. Open field circuit. 6. Open charging circuit. 7. Open circuit in stator windings. 8. Open rectifiers.	1. Adjust drive belt to specifications. 2. Connect regulator to a good ground. 3. Install new brushes and/or slip rings. 4. Clean slip rings and brush holders. Install new brushes if necessary. 5. Test all the field circuit connections, and correct as required. 6. Inspect all connections in charging circuit, and correct as required. 7. Remove alternator and disassemble. Test stator windings. Install new stator if necessary. 8. Remove alternator and disassemble. Test the rectifiers. Install new rectifier assemblies if necessary.
LOW, UNSTEADY CHARGING RATE	1. High resistance in body to engine ground lead. 2. Alternator drive belt loose. 3. High resistance at battery terminals. 4. High resistance in charging circuit. 5. Open stator winding.	1. Tighten ground lead connections. Install new ground lead if necessary. 2. Adjust alternator drive belt. 3. Clean and tighten battery terminals. 4. Test charging circuit resistance. Correct as required. 5. Remove and disassemble alternator. Test stator windings. Install new stator if necessary.
LOW OUTPUT AND A LOW BATTERY	1. High resistance in charging circuit. 2. Shorted rectifier. Open rectifier. 3. Grounded stator windings. 4. Faulty voltage regulator.	1. Test charging circuit resistance and correct as required. 2. Perform current output test. Test the rectifiers and install new rectifier heat sink assembly as required. Remove and disassemble the alternator. 3. Remove and disassemble alternator. Test stator windings. Install new stator if necessary. 4. Test voltage regulator. Replace as necessary.
EXCESSIVE CHARGING RATE TO A FULLY CHARGED BATTERY	1. Faulty ignition switch. 2. Faulty voltage regulator.	1. Install new ignition switch. 2. Test voltage regulator. Replace as necessary.
NOISY ALTERNATOR	1. Alternator mounting loose. 2. Worn of frayed drive belt. 3. Worn bearings. 4. Interference between rotor fan and stator leads. 5. Rotor or rotor fan damaged. 6. Open or shorted rectifer. 7. Open or shorted winding in stator.	1. Properly install and tighten alternator mounting. 2. Install a new drive belt and adjust to specifications. 3. Remove and disassemble alternator. Install new bearings as required. 4. Remove and disassemble alternator. Correct interference as required. 5. Remove and disassemble alternator. Install new rotor. 6. Remove and disassemble alternator. Test rectifers. Install new rectifier heat sink assemble as required. 7. Remove and disassemble alternator. Test stator windings. Install new stator if necessary.
EXCESSIVE AMMETER FLUCTUATION	1. High resistance in the alternator and voltage regulator circuit.	1. Clean and tighten all connections as necessary.

CHARGING SYSTEM INDICATOR

Condition	Possible Cause	Correction
LIGHT ON, IGNITION OFF	1. Shorted positive diode.	1. Locate and replace shorted diode.
LIGHT NOT ON, IGNITION ON AND ENGINE NOT RUNNING	1. Bulb burned out. 2. Open in light circuit. 3. Open in field.	1. Replace bulb. 2. Locate and correct open. 3. Replace rotor.
LIGHT ON, ENGINE RUNNING ABOVE IDLE SPEED	1. No generator output. 2. Shorted negative diode. 3. Loose or broken generator belt.	1. Check and correct cause of no output. 2. Locate and replace shorted diode. 3. Tighten or replace and tighten generator belt.

COOLING SYSTEM

Condition	Possible Cause	Correction
HIGH TEMPERATURE INDICATION—OVERHEATING	1. Coolant level low. 2. Fan belt loose. 3. Radiator hose(s) collapsed. 4. Radiator blocked to airflow. 5. Faulty radiator cap. 6. Car overloaded. 7. Ignition timing incorrect. 8. Idle speed low. 9. Air trapped in cooling system. 10. Car in heavy traffic. 11. Incorrect cooling system component(s) installed. 12. Faulty thermostat. 13. Water pump shaft broken or impeller loose. 14. Radiator tubes clogged. 15. Cooling system clogged. 16. Casting flash in cooling passages. 17. Brakes dragging. 18. Excessive engine friction. 19. Car working beyond cooling system capacity. 20. Antifreeze concentration over 68%. 21. Low anti-freeze concentration.	1. Replenish coolant level. 2. Adjust fan belt. 3. Replace hose(s). 4. Remove restriction. 5. Replace cap. 6. Reduce load. 7. Adjust ignition timing. 8. Adjust idle speed. 9. Purge air. 10. Operate at fast idle intermittently to cool engine. 11. Install proper component(s). 12. Replace thermostat. 13. Replace water pump. 14. Flush radiator. 15. Flush system. 16. Repair or replace as necessary. Flash may be visible by removing cooling system components or removing core plugs. 17. Repair brakes. 18. Repair engine. 19. Install heavy-duty cooling fan and/or radiator. 20. Lower antifreeze content. 21. Add anti-freeze to provide a minimum 50% concentration.
LOW TEMPERATURE INDICATION—OVERCOOLING	1. Improper fan being used. 2. Improper radiator. 3. Thermostat stuck open. 4. Improper fan pulley (too small).	1. Install proper fan. 2. Install proper radiator. 3. Replace thermostat. 4. Install proper pulley.
COOLANT LOSS—BOILOVER<hr>**NOTE:** Immediately after shutdown, the engine enters a period known as heat soak. This is caused because the cooling system is inoperative but engine temperature is still high. If coolant temperature rises above boiling point, it may push some coolant out of the radiator overflow tube. If this does not occur frequently, it is considered normal.	Refer to Overheating Causes in addition to the following: 1. Overfilled cooling system. 2. Quick shutdown after hard (hot) run. 3. Air in system resulting in occasional "burping" of coolant. 4. Insufficient antifreeze allowing coolant boiling point to be too low. 5. Antifreeze deteriorated because of age or contamination. 6. Leaks due to loose hose clamps, loose nuts, bolts, drain plugs, faulty hoses, or defective radiator. 7. Faulty head gasket. 8. Cracked head, manifold, or block.	 1. Reduce coolant level to proper specification. 2. Allow engine to run at fast idle prior to shutdown. 3. Purge system. 4. Add antifreeze to raise boiling point. 5. Replace coolant. 6. Pressure test system to locate leak then repair as necessary. 7. Replace head gasket. 8. Replace as necessary.
COOLANT ENTRY INTO CRANKCASE OR CYLINDER	1. Faulty head gasket. 2. Crack in head, manifold or block.	1. Replace head gasket. 2. Replace as necessary.
COOLANT RECOVERY SYSTEM INOPERATIVE	1. Coolant level low. 2. Leak in system. 3. Pressure cap not tight or gasket missing or leaking. 4. Pressure cap defective. 5. Overflow tube clogged or leaking. 6. Recovery bottle vent plugged.	1. Replenish coolant. 2. Pressure test to isolate leak and repair as necessary. 3. Repair as necessary. 4. Replace cap. 5. Repair as necessary. 6. Remove restriction.

COOLING SYSTEM—Continued

Condition	Possible Cause	Correction
NOISE	1. Fan contacting shroud. 2. Loose water pump impeller. 3. Dry fan belt. 4. Loose fan belt. 5. Rough surface on drive pulley. 6. Water pump bearing worn.	1. Reposition shroud and check engine mounts. 2. Replace pump. 3. Apply belt dressing or replace belt. 4. Adjust fan belt. 5. Replace pulley. 6. Remove belt to isolate. Replace pump.
NO COOLANT FLOW THROUGH HEATER CORE	1. Plugged return pipe in water pump. 2. Heater hose collapsed or plugged. 3. Plugged heater core. 4. Plugged outlet in thermostat housing. 5. Heater bypass hole in cylinder head plugged.	1. Remove obstruction. 2. Remove obstruction or replace hose. 3. Remove obstruction or replace core. 4. Remove flash or obstruction. 5. Remove obstruction.

COOLANT TEMPERATURE INDICATOR

Condition	Possible Cause	Correction
"HOT" INDICATOR; LIGHT NOT LIT WHEN CRANKING ENGINE	1. Bulb burned out. 2. Open in light circuit. 3. Defective ignition switch.	1. Replace bulb. 2. Locate and correct open. 3. Replace ignition switch.
LIGHT ON, ENGINE RUNNING	1. Wiring grounded between light and switch. 2. Defective temperature switch. 3. Defective ignition switch. 4. High coolant temperature.	1. Locate and correct grounded wiring. 2. Replace temperature switch. 3. Replace ignition switch. 4. Locate and correct cause of high coolant temperature.

EXHAUST SYSTEM

Condition	Possible Cause	Correction
LEAKING EXHAUST GASES	1. Leaks at pipe joints. 2. Damaged or improperly installed seals or packing. 3. Loose exhaust pipe heat tube extension connections. 4. Burned or rusted out exhaust pipe heat tube extensions.	1. Tighten U-bolt nuts at leaking joints. 2. Replace seals or packing as necessary. 3. Replace seals or packing as required. Tighten stud nuts or bolts. 4. Replace heat tube extensions as required.
EXHAUST NOISES	1. Leaks at manifold or pipe connections. 2. Burned or blown out muffler. 3. Burned or rusted out exhaust pipe. 4. Exhaust pipe leaking at manifold flange. 5. Exhaust manifold cracked or broken. 6. Leak between manifold and cylinder head.	1. Tighten clamps at leaking connections to specified torque. Replace gasket or packing as required. 2. Replace muffler assembly. 3. Replace exhaust pipe. 4. Tighten attaching bolt nuts. 5. Replace manifold. 6. Tighten manifold to cylinder head stud nuts or bolts.
LOSS OF ENGINE POWER AND/OR INTERNAL RATTLES IN MUFFLER	1. Dislodged turning tubes and or baffles in muffler.	1. Replace muffler.
LOSS OF ENGINE POWER	1. Imploding (inner wall collapse) of exhaust pipe.	1. Replace exhaust pipe.
ENGINE HARD TO WARM UP OR WILL NOT RETURN TO NORMAL IDLE	1. Heat control valve frozen in the open position.	1. Free up manifold heat control using a suitable manifold heat control solvent.
MANIFOLD HEAT CONTROL VALVE NOISE	1. Thermostat broken. 2. Broken, weak or missing anti-rattle spring.	1. Replace thermostat. 2. Replace spring.

CLUTCH & SYNCHRO-MESH TRANSMISSION

Condition	Possible Cause	Correction
CLUTCH CHATTER	1. Worn or damaged disc assembly. 2. Grease or oil on disc facings. 3. Improperly adjusted cover assembly. 4. Broken or loose engine mounts. 5. Misaligned clutch housing.	1. Replace disc assembly. 2. Replace disc assembly and correct cause of contamination. 3. Replace cover assembly. 4. Replace or tighten mounts. 5. Align clutch housing.
CLUTCH SLIPPING	1. Insufficient pedal free play. 2. Burned, worn, or oil soaked facings. 3. Weak or broken pressure springs.	1. Adjust release fork rod. 2. Replace disc assembly and correct cause of contamination. 3. Replace cover assembly.
DIFFICULT GEAR SHIFTING	1. Excessive pedal free play. 2. Excessive deflection in linkage or firewall. 3. Worn or damaged disc assembly. 4. Improperly adjusted cover assembly. 5. Clutch disc splines sticking. 6. Worn or dry pilot bushing. 7. Clutch housing misaligned.	1. Adjust release fork rod. 2. Repair or replace linkage. 3. Replace disc assembly. 4. Replace cover assembly. 5. Remove disc assembly and free up splines or replace disc. 6. Lubricate or replace bushing. 7. Align clutch housing.
CLUTCH NOISY	1. Dry clutch linkage. 2. Worn release bearing. 3. Worn disc assembly. 4. Worn release levers. 5. Worn or dry pilot bushing. 6. Dry contact-pressure plate lugs in cover.	1. Lubricate where necessary. 2. Replace release bearing. 3. Replace disc assembly. 4. Replace cover assembly. 5. Lubricate or replace bushing. 6. Lubricate very lightly.
TRANSMISSION SHIFTS HARD	1. Incorrect clutch adjustment. 2. Clutch linkage binding. 3. Gearshift linkage incorrectly adjusted, bent, or binding. 4. Bind in steering column, or column is misaligned. 5. Incorrect lubricant. 6. Internal bind in transmissions—e.g. shift rails, interlocks, shift forks, synchronizer teeth. 7. Clutch housing misalignment.	1. Adjust clutch pedal free-play. 2. Lubricate or repair linkage as required. 3. Adjust linkage—correct any bind. Replace bent parts. 4. Disconnect shift rods at column. Check for bind/misalignment between tube and jacket by shifting lever into all positions. Correct as required. 5. Drain and refill transmission. 6. Remove transmission and inspect shift mechanism. Repair as required. 7. Check runout at rear face of clutch housing.
GEAR CLASH WHEN SHIFTING FROM ONE FORWARD GEAR TO ANOTHER	1. Incorrect clutch adjustment. 2. Clutch linkage binding. 3. Gear shift linkage incorrectly adjusted, bent, or binding. 4. Clutch housing misalignment. 5. Damaged or worn transmission components: shift forks, synchronizers, shift rails and interlocks. Excessive end play due to worn thrust washers.	1. Adjust clutch. 2. Lubricate or repair linkage as required. 3. Adjust linkage, correct binds, replace bent parts. 4. Check runout at rear face of clutch housing. 5. Inspect components. Repair or replace as required.
TRANSMISSION NOISY	1. Insufficient lubricant. 2. Incorrect lubricant. 3. Clutch housing to engine or transmission to clutch housing bolts loose. 4. Dirt, chips in lubricant. 5. Gearshift linkage incorrectly adjusted, or bent or binding. 6. Clutch housing misalignment. 7. Worn transmission components: front-rear bearings, worn gear teeth, damaged gear teeth or synchronizer components.	1. Check lubricant level and replenish as required. 2. Replace with proper lubricant. 3. Check and correct bolt torque as required. 4. Drain and flush transmission. 5. Adjust linkage, correct binds, replace bent parts. 6. Check runout at rear face of clutch housing. 7. Inspect components and repair as required.

CLUTCH & SYNCHRO-MESH TRANSMISSION—Continued

Condition	Possible Cause	Correction
JUMPS OUT OF GEAR	1. Gearshift linkage incorrectly adjusted. 2. Gearshift linkage bent or binding. 3. Clutch housing misaligned. 4. Worn pilot bushing. 5. Worn or damaged clutch shaft roller bearings. 6. Worn, tapered gear teeth; synchronizer parts worn. 7. Shifter forks, shift rails, or detent-interlock parts worn, missing, etc. 8. Excessive end play of output shaft gear train, countershaft gear or reverse idler gear.	1. Adjust linkage. 2. Correct bind, replace bent parts. 3. Check runout at rear face of clutch housing. 4. Replace bushing. 5. Replace bearings. 6. Inspect and replace as required. 7. Inspect and replace as required. 8. Replace thrust washers, and snap rings (output shaft gear train).
WILL NOT SHIFT INTO ONE GEAR—ALL OTHERS OK	1. Gearshift linkage not adjusted correctly. 2. Bent shift rod at transmission. 3. Transmission shifter levers reversed. 4. Worn or damaged shift rails, shift forks, detent-interlock plugs, loose setscrew in shifter fork, worn synchronizer parts.	1. Adjust linkage. 2. Replace rod. 3. Correctly position levers. 4. Inspect and repair or replace parts as required.
LOCKED IN ONE GEAR—CANNOT BE SHIFTED OUT OF THAT GEAR	1. Gearshift linkage binding or bent. 2. Transmission shifter lever attaching nuts loose or levers are worn at shifter fork shaft hole. 3. Shift rails worn or broken, shifter fork bent, setscrew loose, detent-interlock plug missing or worn. 4. Broken gear teeth on countershaft gear, clutch shaft, or reverse idler gear.	1. Correct bind, replace bent components. 2. Tighten nuts, replace worn levers. 3. Inspect and replace worn or damaged parts. 4. Inspect and replace damaged part.

BRAKES

Condition	Possible Cause	Correction
LOW BRAKE PEDAL **(Excessive pedal travel required to apply brake)**	1. Excessive clearance between linings and drums caused by inoperative automatic adjusters. 2. Worn brake lining. 3. Bent, distorted brakeshoes. 4. Caliper pistons corroded. 5. Power unit push rod height incorrect.	1. Make 10 to 15 firm forward and reverse brake stops to adjust brakes. If brake pedal does not come up, repair or replace adjuster parts as necessary. 2. Inspect and replace lining if worn beyond minimum thickness specification. 3. Replace brakeshoes in axle sets. 4. Repair or replace calipers. 5. Check height with gauge (only). Replace power unit if push rod height is not within specifications.
LOW BRAKE PEDAL **(Pedal may go to floor under steady pressure)**	1. Leak in hydraulic system. 2. Air in hydraulic system. 3. Incorrect or non-recommended brake fluid (fluid boils away at below normal temp.).	1. Fill master cylinder to within 1/4-inch of rim; have helper apply brakes and check calipers, wheel cylinders combination valve, tubes, hoses and fittings for leaks. Repair or replace parts as necessary. 2. Bleed air from system. Refer to Brake Bleeding. 3. Flush hydraulic system with clean brake fluid. Refill with correct-type fluid.

TROUBLESHOOTING

BRAKES—Continued

Condition	Possible Cause	Correction
LOW BRAKE PEDAL **(Pedal goes to floor on first application—OK on subsequent applications)**	1. Disc brakeshoe (pad) knock back; shoes push caliper piston back into bore. Caused by loose wheel bearings or excessive lateral runout of rotor (rotor wobble). 2. Calipers sticking on mounting surfaces of caliper and anchor. Caused by buildup of dirt, rust, or corrosion on abutment.	1. Adjust wheel bearings and check lateral runout of rotor(s). Refinish rotors if runout is over limits. Replace rotor if refinishing would cause rotor to fall below minimum thickness limit. 2. Clean mounting surfaces and lubricate surfaces with molydisulphide grease or equivalent.
FADING BRAKE PEDAL **(Pedal falls away under steady pressure)**	1. Leak in hydraulic system. 2. Master cylinder piston cups worn, or master cylinder bore is scored, worn or corroded.	1. Fill master cylinder reservoirs to within ¼-inch of rim; have helper apply brakes, check master cylinder, calipers, wheel cylinders combination valve, tubes, hoses, and fittings for leaks. Repair or replace parts as necessary. 2. Repair or replace master cylinder.

DECREASING BRAKE PEDAL TRAVEL
(Pedal travel required to apply brakes decreases, may be accompanied by hard pedal)
	1. Caliper or wheel cylinder pistons sticking or seized.
	2. Master cylinder compensator ports blocked (preventing fluid return to reservoirs) or pistons sticking or seized in master cylinder bore.
	3. Power brake unit binding internally.
	
	4. Incorrect power unit push rod height.
		1. Repair or replace calipers, or wheel cylinders.
		2. Repair or replace master cylinder.
		
		3. Test unit as follows:
		  a. Raise hood, shift transmission into neutral and start engine.
		  b. Increase engine speed to 1500 RPM, close throttle and fully depress brake pedal.
		  c. Slowly release brake pedal and stop engine.
		  d. Remove vacuum check valve and hose from power unit. Observe for backward movement of brake pedal or power unit-to-brake pedal push rod.
		  e. If pedal or push rod moves backward, power unit has internal bind—replace power brake unit.
		4. Adjust push rod height.

SPONGY BRAKE PEDAL **(Pedal has abnormally soft, springy, spongy feel when depressed)**	1. Air in hydraulic system. 2. Brakeshoes bent or distorted. 3. Brake lining not yet seated to drums and rotors.	1. Bleed brakes. 2. Replace brakeshoes. 3. Burnish brakes.
HARD BRAKE PEDAL **(Excessive pedal pressure required to stop car. May be accompanied by brake fade)**	1. Loose or leaking power brake unit vacuum hose. 2. Brake lining contaminated by grease or brake fluid. 3. Incorrect or poor quality brake lining. 4. Bent, broken, distorted brakeshoes. 5. Calipers binding or dragging on anchor. Rear brakeshoes dragging on support plate. 6. Rear brake drum(s) bell mouthed, flared or barrel shaped (distorted). 7. Caliper, wheel cylinder, or master cylinder pistons sticking or seized.	1. Tighten connections or replace leaking hose. 2. Determine cause of contaminations and correct. Replace contaminated brake lining in axle sets. 3. Replace lining in axle sets. 4. Replace brakeshoes and lining. 5. Sand or wire brush anchors and caliper mounting surfaces and lubricate surfaces lightly. Clean rust or burrs from rear brake support plate ledges and lubricate ledges. **NOTE:** If ledges are deeply grooved or scored, do not attempt to sand or grind them smooth—replace support plate. 6. Replace rear drum(s). 7. Repair or replace parts as necessary.

64

BRAKES—Continued

Condition	Possible Cause	Correction

HARD BRAKE PEDAL, continued	8. Power brake unit vacuum check valve malfunction.	8. Test valve as follows:
		  a. Start engine, increase engine speed to 1500 RPM, close throttle and immediately stop engine.
		  b. Wait at least 90 seconds then try brake action.
		  c. If brakes are not vacuum assisted for 2 or more applications, check valve is faulty.

	9. Power brake unit has internal bind or incorrect push rod height (too long).	9. Test unit as follows:
		  a. With engine stopped, apply brakes several times to exhaust all vacuum in system.
		  b. Shift transmission into neutral, depress brake pedal and start engine.
		  c. If pedal falls away under foot pressure and less pressure is required to hold pedal in applied position, power unit vacuum system is working. Test power unit as outlined in item (3) under Decreasing Brake Pedal Travel. If power unit exhibits bind condition, replace power unit.
		  d. If power unit does not exhibit bind condition, disconnect master cylinder and check push rod height with appropriate gauge. If height is not within specifications, replace power unit.

	10. Master cylinder compensator ports (at bottom of reservoirs) blocked by dirt, scale, rust, or have small burrs (blocked ports prevent fluid return to reservoirs).	10. Repair or replace master cylinder. **CAUTION:** Do not attempt to clean blocked ports with wire, pencils, or similar implements.
	11. Brake hoses, tubes, fittings clogged or restricted.	11. Use compressed air to check or unclog parts. Replace any damaged parts.
	12. Brake fluid contaminated with improper fluids (motor oil, transmission fluid, or poor quality brake fluid) causing rubber components to swell and stick in bores.	12. Replace all rubber components and hoses. Flush entire brake system. Refill with recommended brake fluid.
GRABBING BRAKES **(Severe reaction to brake pedal pressure)**	1. Brake lining(s) contaminated by grease or brake fluid.	1. Determine and correct cause of contamination and replace brakeshoes and linings in axle sets.
	2. Parking brake cables incorrectly adjusted or seized.	2. Adjust cables. Free up or replace seized cables.
	3. Power brake unit binding internally or push rod height incorrect.	3. Test unit as outlined in item (3) under Decreasing Brake Pedal Travel. If o.k., check push rod height. If unit has internal bind or incorrect push rod height, replace unit.
	4. Incorrect brake lining or lining loose on brakeshoes.	4. Replace brakeshoes in axle sets.
	5. Brakeshoes bent, cracked, distorted.	5. Replace brakeshoes in axle sets.
	6. Caliper anchor plate bolts loose.	6. Tighten bolts.
	7. Rear brakeshoes binding on support plate ledges.	7. Clean and lubricate ledges. Replace support plate(s) if ledges are deeply grooved. Do not attempt to smooth ledges by grinding.
	8. Rear brake support plates loose.	8. Tighten mounting bolts.
	9. Caliper or wheel cylinder piston sticking or seized.	9. Repair or replace parts as necessary.
	10. Master cylinder pistons sticking or seized in bore.	10. Repair or replace master cylinder.

BRAKES—Continued

Condition	Possible Cause	Correction
BRAKES GRAB, PULL, OR WON'T HOLD IN WET WEATHER	1. Brake lining water soaked.	1. Drive car with brakes lightly applied to dry out lining. If problem persists after lining has dried, replace brakeshoe lining in axle sets.
	2. Rear brake support plate bent allowing excessive amount of water to enter drum.	2. Replace support plate.
DRAGGING BRAKES (Slow or incomplete release of brakes)	1. Brake pedal binding at pivot.	1. Free up and lubricate.
	2. Power brake unit push rod height incorrect (too high) or unit has internal bind.	2. Replace unit if push rod height is incorrect. If height is o.k., check for internal bind as outlined in item (3) under Decreasing Brake Pedal Travel.
	3. Parking brake cables incorrectly adjusted or seized.	3. Adjust cables. Free up or replace seized cables.
	4. Brakeshoe return springs weak or broken.	4. Replace return springs. Replace brakeshoe if necessary in axle sets.
	5. Automatic adjusters malfunctioning.	5. Repair or replace adjuster parts as required.
	6. Caliper, wheel cylinder or master cylinder pistons sticking or seized.	6. Repair or replace parts as necessary.
	7. Master cylinder compensating ports blocked (fluid does not return to reservoirs).	7. Use compressed air to clear ports. Do not use wire, pencils, or similar objects to open blocked ports.
CAR PULLS TO ONE SIDE WHEN BRAKES ARE APPLIED	1. Incorrect front tire pressure.	1. Inflate to recommended cold (reduced load) inflation pressures.
	2. Incorrect front wheel bearing adjustment or worn—damaged wheel bearings.	2. Adjust wheel bearings. Replace worn, damaged bearings.
	3. Brakeshoe lining on one side contaminated.	3. Determine and correct cause of contamination and replace brakeshoe lining in axle sets.
	4. Brakeshoes on one side bent, distorted, or lining loose on shoe.	4. Replace brakeshoes in axle sets.
	5. Support plate bent or loose on one side.	5. Tighten or replace support plate.
	6. Brake lining not yet seated to drums and rotors.	6. Burnish brakes.
	7. Caliper anchor plate loose on one side.	7. Tighten anchor plate bolts.
	8. Caliper or wheel cylinder piston sticking or seized.	8. Repair or replace caliper or wheel cylinder.
	9. Brakeshoe linings watersoaked.	9. Drive car with brakes lightly applied to dry linings. Replace brakeshoes in axle sets if problem persists.
	10. Loose suspension component attaching or mounting bolts, incorrect front end alignment. Worn suspension parts.	10. Tighten suspension bolts. Replace worn suspension components. Check and correct alignment as necessary.
CHATTER OR SHUDDER WHEN BRAKES ARE APPLIED (Pedal pulsation and roughness may also occur)	1. Front wheel bearings loose.	1. Adjust wheel bearings.
	2. Brakeshoes distorted, bent, contaminated, or worn.	2. Replace brakeshoes in axle sets.
	3. Caliper anchor plate or support plate loose.	3. Tighten mounting bolts.
	4. Excessive thickness variation or lateral rim out of rotor.	4. Refinish or replace rotor.
	5. Rear drum(s) out of round, sharp spots.	5. Refinish or replace drum.
	6. Loose suspension component attaching or mounting bolts, incorrect front end alignment. Worn suspension parts.	6. Tighten suspension bolts. Replace worn suspension components. Check and correct alignment as necessary.
NOISY BRAKES (Squealing, clicking, scraping sound when brakes are applied)	1. Bent, broken, distorted brakeshoes.	1. Replace brakeshoes in axle sets.
	2. Brake lining worn out—shoes contacting drum or rotor.	2. Replace brakeshoes and lining in axle sets. Refinish or replace drums or rotors.
	3. Foreign material imbedded in brake lining.	3. Replace brake lining.

BRAKES—Continued

Condition	Possible Cause	Correction
NOISY BRAKES, continued	4. Broken or loose hold-down or return springs. 5. Rough or dry drum brake support plate ledges. 6. Cracked, grooved, or scored rotor(s) or drum(s).	4. Replace parts as necessary. 5. Lubricate support plate ledges. 6. Replace rotor(s) or drum(s). Replace brakeshoes and lining in axle sets if necessary.
PULSATING BRAKE PEDAL	1. Out of round drums or excessive thickness variation or lateral runout in disc brake rotor(s). 2. Bent rear axle shaft.	1. Refinish or replace drums or rotors. 2. Replace axle shaft.

SUSPENSION & STEERING

Condition	Possible Cause	Correction
HARD OR ERRATIC STEERING	1. Incorrect tire pressure. 2. Insufficient or incorrect lubrication. 3. Suspension, steering or linkage parts damaged or misaligned. 4. Improper front wheel alignment. 5. Incorrect steering gear adjustment. 6. Sagging springs.	1. Inflate tires to recommended pressures. 2. Lubricate as required. 3. Repair or replace parts as necessary. 4. Adjust wheel alignment angles. 5. Adjust steering gear. 6. Replace springs.
PLAY OR LOOSENESS IN STEERING	1. Steering wheel loose. 2. Steering linkage or attaching parts loose or worn. 3. Pitman arm loose. 4. Steering gear attaching bolts loose. 5. Loose or worn wheel bearings. 6. Steering gear adjustment incorrect or parts badly worn.	1. Inspect splines and repair as necessary. Tighten steering wheel nut. 2. Tighten, adjust, or replace faulty components. 3. Inspect shaft splines and repair as necessary. Torque attaching nut and stake in place. 4. Tighten bolts. 5. Adjust or replace bearings. 6. Adjust gear or replace defective parts.
WHEEL SHIMMY OR TRAMP	1. Improper tire pressure. 2. Wheels, tires, or brake drums out-of-balance or out-of-round. 3. Inoperative, worn, or loose shock absorbers or mounting parts. 4. Loose or worn steering or suspension parts. 5. Loose or worn wheel bearings. 6. Incorrect steering gear adjustments. 7. Incorrect front wheel alignment.	1. Inflate tires to recommended pressures. 2. Inspect parts and replace unacceptable out-of-round parts. Rebalance parts. 3. Repair or replace shocks or mountings. 4. Tighten or replace as necessary. 5. Adjust or replace bearings. 6. Adjust steering gear. 7. Correct front wheel alignment.
TIRE WEAR	1. Improper tire pressure. 2. Failure to rotate tires. 3. Brakes grabbing. 4. Incorrect front wheel alignment. 5. Broken or damaged steering and suspension parts. 6. Wheel runout. 7. Excessive speed on turns.	1. Inflate tires to recommended pressures. 2. Rotate tires. 3. Adjust or repair brakes. 4. Align incorrect angles. 5. Repair or replace defective parts. 6. Replace faulty wheel. 7. Make driver aware of condition.
CAR LEADS TO ONE SIDE	1. Improper tire pressures. 2. Front tires with uneven tread depth, wear pattern, or different cord design (i.e., one bias ply and one belted tire on front wheels). 3. Incorrect front wheel alignment. 4. Brakes dragging. 5. Faulty power steering gear valve assembly.	1. Inflate tires to recommended pressures. 2. Install tires of same cord construction and reasonably even tread depth and wear pattern. 3. Align incorrect angles. 4. Adjust or repair brakes. 5. Replace valve assembly.

TROUBLESHOOTING

SUSPENSION & STEERING—Continued

Condition	Possible Cause	Correction
CAR LEADS TO ONE SIDE, continued	6. Pulling due to uneven tire construction.	6. Replace faulty tire.

HEADLAMPS

Condition	Possible Cause	Correction
ONE HEADLAMP INOPERATIVE OR INTERMITTENT	1. Loose connection.	1. Secure connections to sealed beam including ground.
	2. Defective sealed beam.	2. Replace sealed beam.
ONE OR MORE HEADLIGHTS ARE DIM	1. Open ground connection at headlight.	1. Repair ground wire connection between sealed beam and body ground.
	2. Ground wire mislocated in headlight connector (type 2 sealed beam).	2. Relocate ground wire in connector.
ONE OR MORE HEADLIGHTS SHORT LIFE	1. Voltage regulator maladjusted.	1. Readjust regulator to specifications.
ALL HEADLIGHTS INOPERATIVE OR INTERMITTENT	1. Loose connection.	1. Check and secure connections at dimmer switch and light switch.
	2. Defective dimmer switch.	2. Check voltage at dimmer switch with test lamp. If test lamp bulb lights only at switch "Hot" wire terminal, replace dimmer switch.
	3. Open wiring—light switch to dimmer switch.	3. Check wiring with test lamp. If bulb lights at light switch wire terminal, but not at dimmer switch, repair open wire.
	4. Open wiring—light switch to battery.	4. Check "Hot" wire terminal at light switch with test lamp. If lamp does not light, repair open wire circuit to battery (possible open fusible link).
	5. Shorted ground circuit.	5. If, after a few minutes operation, headlights flicker "ON" and "OFF" and/or a thumping noise can be heard from the light switch (circuit breaker opening and closing), repair short to ground in circuit between light switch and headlights. After repairing short, check for headlight flickering after one minute operation. If flickering occurs, the circuit breaker has been damaged and light switch must be replaced.
	6. Defective light switch.	6. Check light switch. Replace light switch, if defective.
UPPER OR LOWER BEAM WILL NOT LIGHT OR INTERMITTENT	1. Open connection or defective dimmer switch.	1. Check dimmer switch terminals with test lamp. If bulb lights at all wire terminals, repair open wiring between dimmer switch and headlights. If bulb will not light at one of these terminals, replace dimmer switch.
	2. Short circuit to ground.	2. Follow diagnosis above (all headlights inoperative or intermittent).

SIDE MARKER LAMPS

Condition	Possible Cause	Correction
ONE LAMP INOPERATIVE	1. Turn signal bulb burnt out (front lamp).	1. Switch turn signals on. If signal bulb does not light, replace bulb.
	2. Side marker bulb burnt out.	2. Replace bulb.
	3. Loose connection or open in wiring.	3. Using test lamp, check "Hot" wire terminal at bulb socket. If test lamp lights, repair open ground circuit. If lamp does not light, repair open "Hot" wire circuit.

SIDE MARKER LAMPS—Continued

Condition	Possible Cause	Correction
FRONT OR REAR LAMPS INOPERATIVE	1. Loose connection or open ground connection.	1. If associated tail or park lamps do not operate, secure all connectors in "Hot" wire circuit. If park and turn lamps operate, repair open ground connections.
	2. Multiple bulbs burnt out.	2. Replace burnt out bulbs.
ALL LAMPS INOPERATIVE	1. Blown fuse.	1. If park and tail lamps do not operate, replace blown fuse. If new fuse blows, check for short to ground between fuse panel and lamps.
	2. Loose connection.	2. Secure connector to light switch.
	3. Open in wiring.	3. Check tail light fuse with test lamp. If test lamp lights, repair open wiring between fuse and light switch. If not, repair open wiring between fuse and battery (possible open fusible link).
	4. Defective light switch.	4. Check light switch. Replace light switch, if defective.

TAIL, PARK AND LICENSE LAMPS

Condition	Possible Cause	Correction
ONE SIDE INOPERATIVE	1. Bulb burnt out.	1. Replace bulb.
	2. Open ground connection at bulb socket or ground wire terminal.	2. Jump bulb base socket connection to ground. If lamp lights, repair open ground circuit.
BOTH SIDES INOPERATIVE	1. Tail lamp fuse blown.	1. Replace fuse. If new fuse blows, repair short to ground in "Hot" wire circuit between fuse panel through light switch to lamps.
	2. Loose connection.	2. Secure connector at light switch.
	3. Open wiring.	3. Using test light, check circuit on both sides of fuse. If lamp does not light on either side, repair open circuit between fuse panel and battery (possible open fusible link). If test lamp lights at light switch terminal, repair open wiring between light switch and lamps.
	4. Multiple bulb burnout.	4. If test lamp lights at lamp socket "Hot" wire terminal, replace bulbs.
	5. Defective light switch.	5. Check light switch. Replace light switch, if defective.

TURN SIGNAL AND HAZARD WARNING LAMP

Condition	Possible Cause	Correction
TURN SIGNALS INOPERATIVE ONE SIDE	1. Bulb(s) burnt out (flasher cannot be heard).	1. Turn hazard warning system on. If one or more bulbs are inoperative replace necessary bulbs.
	2. Open wiring or ground connection.	2. Turn hazard warning system on. If one or more bulbs are inoperative, use test lamp and check circuit at lamp socket. If test lamp lights, repair open ground connection. If not, repair open wiring between bulb socket and turn signal switch.
	3. Improper bulb or defective turn signal switch.	3. Turn hazard warning system on. If all front and rear lamps operate, check for improper bulb. If bulbs are OK, replace defective turn signal switch.
	4. Short to ground (flasher can be heard, no bulbs operate).	4. Locate and repair short to ground by disconnecting front and rear circuits separately.

TROUBLESHOOTING

TURN SIGNAL AND HAZARD WARNING LAMP—Continued

Condition	Possible Cause	Correction
TURN SIGNALS INOPERATIVE	1. Blown turn signal fuse.	1. Turn hazard warning system on. If all lamps operate, replace blown fuse. If new fuse blows, repair short to ground between fuse and lamps.
	2. Defective flasher.	2. If turn signal fuse is OK and hazard warning system will operate lamps, replace defective turn signal flasher.
	3. Loose connection.	3. Secure steering column connector.
HAZARD WARNING LAMPS INOPERATIVE	1. Blown fuse.	1. Switch turn signals on. If lamps operate, replace fuse if blown. If new fuse blows, repair short to ground. (could be in stop light circuit).
	2. Defective hazard warning flasher.	2. If fuse is OK, switch turn signals on. If lamps operate, replace defective hazard flasher.
	3. Open in wiring or defective turn signal switch.	3. Using test lamp, check hazard switch feed wire in turn signal steering column connector. If lamp does not light on either side of connector, repair open circuit between flasher and connector. If lamp lights only on feed side of connector, clean connector contacts. If lamp lights on both sides of connector, replace defective turn signal switch assembly.

BACK-UP LAMP

Condition	Possible Cause	Correction
ONE LAMP INOPERATIVE OR INTERMITTENT	1. Loose or burnt out bulb. 2. Loose connection. 3. Open ground connections.	1. Secure or replace bulb. 2. Tighten connectors. 3. Repair bulb ground circuit.
BOTH LAMPS INOPERATIVE OR INTERMITTENT	1. Neutral start or back-up lamp switch maladjusted. 2. Loose connection or open circuit.	1. Readjust or replace bulb. 2. Secure all connectors. If OK, check continuity of circuit from fuse to lamps with test lamp. If lamp does not light on either side of fuse, correct open circuit from battery to fuse.
	3. Blown fuse.	3. Replace fuse. If new fuse blows, repair short to ground in circuit from fuse through neutral start switch to back-up lamps.
	4. Defective neutral start or back-up lamp switch. 5. Defective ignition switch.	4. Check switch. Replace neutral start or back-up lamp switch, if defective. 5. If test lamp lights at ignition switch battery terminal but not at output terminal, replace ignition switch.
LAMP WILL NOT TURN OFF	1. Neutral start or back-up switch maladjusted. 2. Defective neutral start or back-up lamp switch.	1. Readjust neutral start or back-up lamp switch. 2. Check switch. Replace neutral start or back-up lamp switch, if defective.

STOP LIGHTS

Condition	Possible Cause	Correction
ONE BULB INOPERATIVE	1. Bulb burnt out.	1. Replace bulb.
ONE SIDE INOPERATIVE	1. Loose connection, open wiring or defective bulbs.	1. Turn on directional signal. If lamp does not operate, check bulbs. If bulbs are OK, secure all connections. If lamp still does not operate, use test lamp and check for open wiring.

STOP LIGHTS—Continued

Condition	Possible Cause	Correction
ONE SIDE INOPERATIVE, continued	2. Defective directional signal switch or canceling cam.	2. If lamp will operate by turning directional signal on, the switch is not centering properly during canceling operation. Replace defective cancelling cam or directional signal switch.
ALL INOPERATIVE	1. Blown fuse.	1. Replace fuse. If new fuse blows, repair short to ground in circuit between fuse and lamps.
	2. Stop-switch maladjusted or defective.	2. Check stop switch. Adjust or replace stop switch, if required.
WILL NOT TURN OFF	1. Stop switch maladjusted or defective.	1. Readjust switch. If switch still malfunctions, replace.

HORNS

Condition	Possible Cause	Correction
HORNS WILL NOT OPERATE	1. Loose connections in circuit.	1. Check and tighten connections. Be sure to check ground straps.
	2. Defective horn switch.	2. Replace defective parts.
	3. Defective horn relay.	3. Replace relay.
	4. Defects within horn.	4. Replace horn.
HORNS HAVE POOR TONE	1. Low available voltage at horn, or defects within horn.	1. Check battery and charging circuit. Although horn should blow at any voltage above 7.0 volts, a weak or poor tone may occur at operating voltage below 11.0 volts. If horn has weak or poor tone at operating voltage of 11.0 volts or higher, remove horn and replace.
HORNS OPERATE INTERMITTENTLY	1. Loose or intermittent connections in horn relay or horn switch.	1. Check and tighten connections.
	2. Defective horn switch.	2. Replace switch.
	3. Defective relay.	3. Replace relay.
	4. Defects within horn.	4. Replace horn.
HORNS BLOW CONSTANTLY	1. Sticking horn relay.	1. Replace relay.
	2. Horn relay energized by grounded or shorted wiring.	2. Check and adjust wiring.
	3. Horn button can be grounded by sticking closed.	3. Adjust or replace damaged parts.

SPEEDOMETER

Condition	Possible Cause	Correction
SPEEDOMETER NOT OPERATING PROPERLY	1. Noisy speedometer cable.	1. Loosen over-tightened casing nuts and snap-on at speedometer head. Replace housing and core. Replace broken cable.
	2. Pointer and odometer inoperative. Inaccurate reading.	2. Check tire size. Check for correct speedometer driven gear.
	3. Kinked cable.	3. Replace cable. Reroute casing so that bends have no less than 6" radius.
	4. Defective speedometer head.	4. Replace speedometer.
	5. Casing connector loose on speedometer case.	5. Tighten connector.

Fig. 1   Checking axle flange run-out

Fig. 2   Checking drum/rotor pilot radial run-out

NOISE, VIBRATION & HARSHNESS

ROAD TEST

A road test and customer interview can provide much of the information needed to identify the specific condition which must be dealt with.

1. Make notes during diagnosis routine. This will ensure diagnosis is complete and systematic. Take care not to overlook details.
2. Road test vehicle and study condition by reproducing it several times during test.
3. When condition is reproduced, perform road test checks immediately. Refer to "Road Test Quick Checks" to identify proper section of diagnostic procedure. Perform checks several times to ensure valid conclusions. While the quick checks may not locate the problem, they will indicate the areas where there are no problems.
4. Do not make changes or adjustments before a road test and inspection of vehicle are performed. Any changes made can hide problems or add additional problems. Check and note tire pressures, any leaks, loose nuts or bolts, shiny spots where components may be rubbing, and if any unusually heavy items are in trunk.

ROAD TEST QUICK CHECKS

1. **25–50 mph**—Under light acceleration, a moaning noise can be heard possibly accompanied by a vibration in floor. Refer to "Tip-In Moan" diagnostic procedure.
2. **25–45 mph**—Under steady to heavy acceleration, a rumbling noise can be heard. Refer to "Incorrect Driveline Angle" diagnostic procedure.
3. **High Speed**—Under slow acceleration and deceleration, shaking is noticeable in steering column or wheel, seats, floor pan, trim panels, or front end sheet metal. Refer to "High Speed Shake" procedure.

4. **High Speed**—Vibration can be felt in floor pan or seats, with no visible shaking but with rumble, buzz, hum, or booming noise. Refer to "Driveline Vibration" procedure.
5. **High Speed**—Coast with clutch disengaged or with automatic transmission in neutral and engine idling. If vibration is present, refer to "Driveline Vibration" procedure. If vibration is no longer present, refer to "Engine and Accessory Vibration" or "High Speed Shake" procedures.
6. **0–High Speed**—Vibration can be felt when engine reaches particular RPM. Vibration can also be felt when vehicle is stationary. Refer to "Engine and Accessory Vibration."

TYPES OF CONDITIONS

High Speed Shake (35 mph)

This condition involves a visible shake and pumping feeling in steering column, seats, or floor pan. The vibration is of low frequency (about 9–15 cycles per second) and may be seen as front end sheet metal shake. The condition may or may not be intensified by lightly applying brakes.

Tip-In Moan (15–50 mph)

Acceleration between 15–50 mph is accompanied by vibration which causes moan or high frequency resonance in floor pan. This condition is usually worse at a particular engine speed and at a particular throttle opening during acceleration at that speed. A moaning sound may also be caused depending on which component is producing the noise.

Driveline Vibration (50 mph)

This condition does not involve a visible vibration, but is felt in floor pan as rumble, buzz, hum, drone, or boom. This condition is independent of engine speed and will occur at same speed in any gear, and is not sensitive to acceleration or deceleration and cannot be reduced by coasting in neutral. The condition can be duplicated by supporting vehicle on axle-type hoist and operating driveline in gear at appropriate speed.

Engine or Accessory Vibration (All Speeds)

This condition can occur at any vehicle speed but always at same engine RPM. Vibration will disappear during neutral coast and can be duplicated by operating engine at problem RPM with vehicle stationary. The condition can be caused by any component turning at engine speed when vehicle is stationary.

HIGH SPEED SHAKE

1. Apply brakes gently. If shake increases, proceed to step 2; if shake does not increase, proceed to step 10.
2. Lightly apply parking brake. If shake increases, proceed to step 3; if shake does not increase, proceed to step 6.
3. Check clearance between rear drum and brake shoe. Loosen cable tension if necessary. If clearance is correct, proceed to step 4; if clearance is not correct, proceed to step 7.
4. Using dial indicator, check axle flange run-out, **Fig. 1.** If run-out is acceptable, proceed to step 5. If run-out is unacceptable, proceed to step 8.
5. Check run-out of rear brake drum or disc. If run-out is acceptable, proceed to step 10. If run-out is unacceptable, proceed to step 9.
6. Check run-out of front brake disc. If run-out is acceptable, proceed to step 10. If run-out is unacceptable, proceed to step 9.
7. Adjust parking brake cable tension and road test vehicle. If shake is not eliminated, proceed to step 4.
8. Replace axle shaft and road test vehicle. If shake is not eliminated, proceed to step 5.
9. Replace or machine brake drums or discs and road test vehicle. If shake is not eliminated, proceed to step 10.
10. Raise and support vehicle. Turn wheels by hand and check for abnormal wear, damage, wheel bearing play or roughness. If abnormal wear or damage is found, proceed to step 12. If wheel bearing displays excessive play or roughness, proceed to step 13. If brakes drag proceed to steps 5 and 6.

11. Road test vehicle, noting carefully which area of vehicle is shaking. If front end sheet metal is shaking heavily, proceed to step 14. If shaking is felt more in floor pan, seat and steering column, proceed to step 15.
12. Replace worn or damaged tires and check for any other damaged components such as shock absorbers. Road test vehicle. If vehicle still shakes, proceed to step 15.
13. Check and adjust wheel bearings. Replace damaged wheel bearings and road test vehicle. If shake is not eliminated, proceed to step 15.
14. Check and tighten all major front end sheet metal attaching bolts and adjust hood rests. Road test vehicle. If shake is not eliminated, proceed to step 15.
15. Balance wheels on vehicle and check tires and rims for run-out. If wheel balancing is not necessary, proceed to step 16. If wheel and tire run-out are found, proceed to step 19.
16. Road test vehicle at speed at which condition was most apparent. If shake is not eliminated, proceed to step 17.
17. Install a known good set of wheels and tires on vehicle and road test. If shake is eliminated, proceed to step 18. If shake is not eliminated, proceed to step 23.
18. If one or more of the tires has a construction irregularity which causes tire to contact the road in an irregular manner, substitute known good tires until irregular tires are located.
19. Attempt to reduce run-out by mounting wheel in different position in relation to axle. If run-out is now acceptable, proceed to step 16. If run-out is still excessive, proceed to step 17. If repositioning indicates axle shaft run-out, proceed to step 22. If repositioning indicates tire and wheel run-out, proceed to step 20.
20. Attempt to correct run-out by repositioning tire on rim. If run-out is acceptable, proceed to step 15. If run-out is still excessive, proceed to step 21.
21. Replace component shown to be unserviceable and recheck run-out. If run-out is acceptable, proceed to step 15. if run-out is excessive, proceed to step 22.
22. Measure axle shaft run-out, **Fig. 2.** Replace shaft if run-out is excessive and check run-out of new shaft. Install wheel and check run-out again. If run-out is acceptable, proceed to step 15. If run-out is excessive, proceed to step 20.
23. Raise and support vehicle. Remove rear wheels and tires. Check all axle and brake rotor run-out measurements if not already checked. If axle and brake run-out are acceptable, proceed to step 24. If axle run-out is excessive, proceed to step 8. If brake disc run-out is excessive, proceed to step 9.
24. Check driveshaft run-out. If run-out is acceptable, proceed to step 25. if run-out is excessive, proceed to step 27.
25. Remove driveshaft and inspect universal joints. If joints are OK, proceed to step 26. If joints are defective, replace joints.
26. Install driveshaft and check for vibration. If vibration is unacceptable, proceed to step 27.
27. Measure ring gear run-out. If run-out is excessive, proceed to step 28.
28. Install new ring and pinion. Check run-out to ensure parts are within specifications. Recheck for vibration.

MOANING NOISE DURING LIGHT ACCELERATION

1. Inspect air cleaner for correct positioning of gasket, lid and gasket, element and duct. Correct if necessary and check condition. If noise is unacceptable, proceed to step 2.
2. On vehicles where a transmission extension housing damper is specified, ensure damper is installed. Recheck condition, if noise is unacceptable, proceed to step 3.
3. Loosen engine mounts, start engine, and shift from Neutral to Drive and back to normalize engine mounts. Tighten engine mounts and check condition; if noise is unacceptable, proceed to step 4.
4. With exhaust system hot, loosen hangers, and operate engine while shifting from Neutral to Drive and back to normalize exhaust system. Tighten hangers and recheck condition; if noise is unacceptable, proceed to step 5.
5. Inspect accessory drive belts for proper tension and accessory brackets for proper bolt torques. Adjust or tighten if necessary and check condition, if noise is unacceptable, proceed to step 6.
6. Loosen all bell housing bolts ¾ turn to test if noise is reduced. If noise is reduced, recheck step 2.

DRIVELINE VIBRATION

1. Raise and support vehicle with drive wheels free. Operate driveline at problem speed. If vibration is present, proceed to step 3; if vibration is not present, proceed to step 2.
2. Retest vehicle to observe reported condition.
3. Evaluate noise and vibration by operating driveline at problem speed. If audible boom or rumble occurs above 30 mph, proceed to step 4. If buzzy feel occurs in floor pan above 30 mph, proceed to step 5. If a gravelly feel or grinding sound occurs at low speeds, proceed to step 4.
4. Install rear spring dampers if available for vehicle. If condition is still unacceptable or dampers are not available, proceed to step 5.
5. Scribe a line to index rear axle companion flange to driveshaft flange. Inspect drive shaft for dents, undercoating, proper seating of U-joint bearing caps, and tight U-joints. If driveshaft is in acceptable condition, proceed to step 6. Replace driveshaft if damaged. Replace U-joints if worn or improperly positioned.
6. Inspect wheel bearings. If bearings are OK, proceed to step 10; if wheel bearings are not in acceptable condition, proceed to step 7.
7. Replace wheel bearings and retest for vibration. If vibration is unacceptable proceed to step 10.
8. Repair or replace driveshaft. If vibration is unacceptable proceed to step 10.
9. Reposition U-joint bearing caps or replace U-joints. If vibration is unacceptable, proceed to step 10.
10. Disconnect driveshaft from rear axle companion flange and reconnect 180° from original position. Operate driveline at problem speed. If vibration is unacceptable, install rear axle pinion nose damper if available for vehicle. If pinion damper is not available or vibration is still unacceptable, proceed to step 11.
11. Disconnect driveshaft and return to original position. Refer to "Driveshaft Run-out, Check" procedure and check run-out at front, center, and rear of driveshaft. If run-out is less than .035 inch at all positions, proceed to step 15 of "High Speed Shake" diagnosis. If run-out at front and/or center of driveshaft exceeds .035 inch while rear of shaft is acceptable, proceed to step 8. If run-out at rear of driveshaft exceeds .035 inch, proceed to "Driveshaft Run-out Check" procedure.
12. Balance driveshaft on vehicle and test vehicle at problem speed. If vibration is still unacceptable, proceed to step 17 of "High Speed Shake" diagnosis.

INCORRECT PINION ANGLE

1. Ensure U-joints are tight and all bearing caps are in plate. If U-joints are in good condition, proceed to step 3; if not, proceed to step 2.
2. Make an index mark on driveshaft and rear axle companion flange. Remove driveshaft and replace U-joints. Retest vehicle; if vibration is unacceptable, proceed to step 3.
3. Refer to "Driveline Pinion Angle Check" procedure to check pinion angle.
4. If pinion angle is correct, proceed to step 1 of "Driveline Vibration."

ENGINE OR ACCESSORY VIBRATION

1. With vehicle stationary, run engine at problem speed to check for condition. If vibration is present, proceed to step 2; if not, proceed to step 1 of "Driveline Vibration" diagnosis.
2. Inspect drive belts to check for wear or fraying. Ensure pulleys are not damaged or bent. Replace any damaged components and operate engine at problem speed. If vibration is present, proceed to step 3.
3. Check drive belt tension and adjust if necessary. Operate engine at problem speed. If vibration is still present, proceed to step 4.
4. Check torque of all accessory bracket bolts and retorque as necessary. Operate engine at problem speed; if vibration is still present, proceed to step 5.

Fig. 3   Checking tire/wheel radial run-out

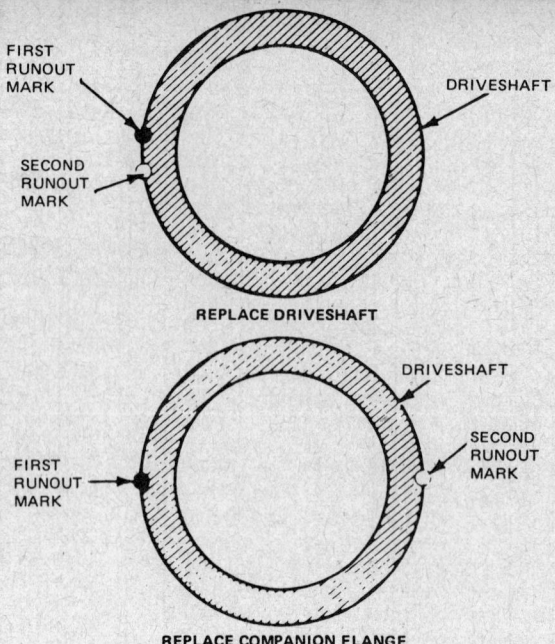

Fig. 4   Checking driveshaft run-out

5. Check pulley alignment and run-out visually at idle. Realign or replace pulleys if necessary. Operate engine at problem speed; if condition is still present, proceed to step 6.
6. Inspect belts for severe whipping at problem speed. If whip cannot be corrected by adjusting tension, replace belts. Operate engine at problem speed; if condition is still present, proceed to step 7.
7. Check engine accessories for noise while operating engine at problem speed. If vibration is still present, proceed to step 9. If vibration is not present, proceed to step 8.
8. Repair or replace noisy accessory. Connect and tension drive belt. Operate engine at problem speed; if vibration is still present, proceed to step 9.
9. Remove accessory from bracket. Inspect all hardware and bracket. Repair or replace as necessary.

CHECKS & ADJUSTMENTS

TIRE/WHEEL RUN-OUT

1. After road test, promptly raise car on hoist to prevent flat spots in tires. Spin front wheels by hand to check for rough wheel bearings. Ensure bearings are not loose and adjust if necessary. If bearings are OK, proceed to step 2. If bearings have rough feel, proceed to step 2.
2. Check total radial and lateral run-out of tire and wheel assembly, **Fig. 3.** If both run-out measurements are less than .070 inch, balance tires. If lateral run-out exceeds .070 inch, proceed to step 3. If radial run-out exceeds .070 inch, proceed to step 4.
3. Check wheel rim lateral run-out. If run-out is less than .045 inch, replace tire and proceed to step 2. If run-out exceeds .045 inch, replace wheel and proceed to step 2.

4. Mark point of maximum run-out on tire thread. Check radial run-out of wheel. If radial run-out of wheel exceeds .045 inch, replace wheel and proceed to step 2. If radial run-out of wheel is less than .045 inch, proceed to step 5.
5. Mark point of least run-out on wheel. Remove tire from wheel and match point of maximum tire run-out with point of least run-out on wheel. Mount tire in this position and check total radial run-out of wheel and tire assembly. If total radial run-out is less than .070 inch, balance tires. If run-out exceeds .070 inch, replace tire and proceed to step 2.

DRIVESHAFT RUN-OUT

1. Raise and support vehicle. Mark position of rear wheels in relation to mounting studs to ensure reinstallation in same position.
2. Turn driveshaft by turning rear drum or disc. Measure run-out at front, center, and rear of driveshaft. Mark point of highest run-out at each location. If run-out measurement at front or center of driveshaft is greater than .035 inch, install new driveshaft and retest vehicle. If run-out measurement at all three positions is less than .035 inch, balance driveshaft. If run-out measurement is less than .035 inch at front and center of driveshaft, but greater than .045 at rear of driveshaft, proceed to step 3.
3. Make mark indexing rear axle companion flange to driveshaft. Disconnect driveshaft at flange, turn 180°, and reconnect. Check run-out at rear of driveshaft and mark high point. If run-out measures less than .035 inch and vibration is unacceptable, balance driveshaft. If run-out measures more than .035 inch, proceed to step 4.
4. Check position of run-out marks from steps 2 and 3, **Fig. 4.** If marks are

about 1 inch apart, replace driveshaft. If marks are about 180° apart, replace rear axle companion flange and proceed to step 2.

DRIVESHAFT BALANCE

Two methods are possible depending on the method of connecting the driveshaft to the differential. Some vehicles are equipped with a drilled companion flange at the differential which allows re-indexing of the driveshaft in 45° increments. Driveshafts not equipped with this style flange can be balanced using worm-drive hose clamps, **Fig. 5.**

Re-indexing Method

1. Mark one hole of rear U-joint yoke flange with letter A. Number rear axle pinion flange holes 1 through 8 starting with hole opposite yoke flange hole A, **Fig. 6.** Position A-1 will be considered original index position.

NOTE: Check U-joints for binding while re-indexing.

2. Index driveshaft 180° to position A-5. Road test vehicle. If condition is still unsatisfactory, check condition in position A-3 and position A-7.
3. If further improvement is necessary, evaluate remaining positions that are located between best of previous positions A-3 and A-7.
4. Coat flange bolts with suitable thread locking compound and torque to 70–95 ft. lbs.

Hose Clamp Method

1. Make a mark to index rear axle companion flange to driveshaft. Disconnect driveshaft at flange, turn 180° and reconnect. If vibration increases, return driveshaft to original position. If vibration is reduced, proceed to step 2.
2. Mark rear of driveshaft with 4 equal

Fig. 5 Balancing driveshaft using hose clamps

DRIVESHAFT
PILOTING YOKE

CIRCULAR
FLANGE

HOLE POSITION
"A"

Fig. 6 Driveshaft indexing

sections numbered 1 through 4. Install a worm-drive hose clamp with screw at position 1 on driveshaft, **Fig. 7.** Operate driveline at problem speed. Check with clamp in each position. If vibration is worse in each position, proceed to step 5. If vibration is reduced in any one position, proceed to step 3. If vibration is reduced in any 2 positions, turn clamp between those positions and proceed to step 3.

3. Install additional clamp with screw in same position as first clamp in its best position. Operate driveline at problem speed. If vibration is same or increased, proceed to step 4.

4. Rotate each clamp screw ½ inch away in opposite directions, **Fig. 8.** If vibration is reduced, continue to move

clamp screws apart until vibration is minimal. If vibration is still excessive, proceed to step 5.

5. Install wheels and road test vehicle to check if vibration might be acceptable on road. If vibration is unacceptable, proceed to step 17 of "High Speed Shake" diagnosis procedure.

DRIVELINE PINION ANGLE CHECKING

1. Raise vehicle on drive-on hoist, ensuring vehicle is at proper controlled height, **Fig. 9.**

2. Turn driveshaft so pinion U-joint bearing cap is facing down.

3. Place Vee magnet from pinion angle measuring tool T68P-4602-A or equivalent on driveshaft. Working from left side of vehicle, position pinion angle

gauge on Vee magnet with adjusting screw towards front of vehicle. Adjust screw so bubble just contacts zero line, **Fig. 10.**

4. Move gauge to U-joint bearing cap with tool in same relative position as it was on Vee magnet, **Fig. 11.**

5. Read position on left edge of bubble on scale to determine driveshaft pinion angle. If pinion angle is not correct, adjust. Recheck and proceed to step 6.

6. Position Vee magnet on front of driveshaft and position gauge on magnet. Zero bubble and move gauge to downward facing U-joint bearing cap at rear of transmission. Read driveline angle and compare with specification.

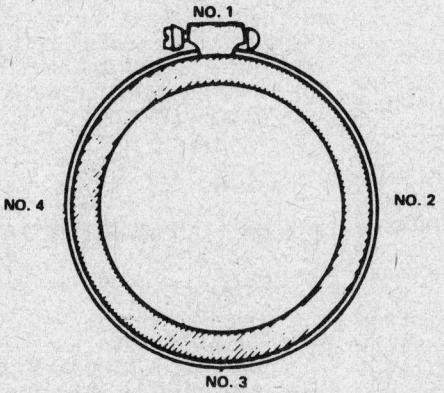

NO. 1

NO. 4

NO. 2

NO. 3

Fig. 7 Installing hose clamp

ROTATE EACH CLAMP
1/2 INCH FROM
THE BEST POSITION

BEST POSITION

Fig. 8 Optimizing clamp location

FRONT

AXLE BUMPER

CONTROLLED HEIGHT

AXLE

Fig. 9 Controlled height

Fig. 10 Positioning driveline angle gauge on driveshaft

Fig. 11 Positioning driveline angle gauge on pinion U-joint cap

Electrical

CIRCUIT MALFUNCTIONS

There are three types of electrical malfunctions that cause an inoperative circuit. They are the open circuit, short circuit and grounded circuit.

OPEN CIRCUIT

When there is a complete break in the normal current patch such as a broken wire, **Fig. 1,** it prevents the flow of electricity from the source of power to the electrical unit or from the electrical unit to the ground. In the automotive electrical circuit, the current usually flows through wires or cables, through switches and an electrical component. The component may be grounded through its mounting attachments or another wire to ground and back to the source. A break anywhere along this route results in an open circuit and a complete loss of power. A break in the circuit is an infinite high resistance. However, symptoms will appear different than the typical high resistance circuit. For example, there will be no heat created by this type of malfunction since there is no current flow. An ammeter will not produce a reading since there is no current flow. A voltmeter, depending on where it is placed in the circuit in relation to the "Open", may

or may not register a reading.

A high resistance in a circuit reduces current flow and causes the unit to operate intermittently or not at all. An open or high resistance circuit may be caused by a broken wire in the wiring harness, loose connections at terminals, broken leads or wiring within the units or poor ground connections between the unit and the ground.

SHORT CIRCUIT

A short circuit, **Fig. 2,** is basically one that is completed the wrong way, such as two bare wires contacting each other so the current bypasses part of the circuit. When the current bypasses part of the circuit, it has found the path of least resistance and a higher current flow results. This causes blown fuses, wiring and component overheating, burned components and insulation, and inoperative components.

A short circuit causes more current flow through the conductor than the conductor can handle. This causes the conductor to overheat and, if the overload is severe or lasts long enough, will melt the wire and burn the insulation. If the wire melts through, there is no path for the current to flow and the circuit becomes an open circuit.

GROUNDED CIRCUIT

A grounded circuit, **Fig. 3,** is similar to the short circuit since a grounded circuit also bypasses part of the normal circuit. However, the current flows directly to ground. A grounded circuit may be caused by a bare wire contacting the ground, or part of the circuit within a component contacting the frame or housing of the component. A grounded circuit may also be caused by deposits of dirt, oil or moisture around the connections or terminals since these deposits provide a path for the current to flow to ground. The current follows the path of least resistance to complete the circuit back to ground.

CIRCUIT PROTECTION
FUSES

The most common circuit protector in the automotive electrical system is the fuse. The fuse consists of a thin wire or strip of metal enclosed in a glass tube. Some vehicles use a new type fuse where the wire is enclosed in plastic. The wire or metal strip melts when there is an overload caused by a short or grounded circuit. The fuse is designed to melt before the wiring or elec-

Fig. 1   Open circuit

Fig. 2   Short circuit

Fig. 3   Grounded circuit

trical components are damaged. The cause of the overload must be located and repaired before the new fuse is installed since the new fuse will also blow.

Fuses are rated in amperes. Since different circuits carry various amounts of current, depending upon load components and wire gauge, the properly rated fuse must be installed in the circuit. Never install a fuse with a higher amperage rating than the original.

CIRCUIT BREAKERS

Circuit breakers incorporate a bimetallic strip which, when heated by an overloaded circuit, moves and opens the contacts to break the circuit. When the bimetallic strip cools, it returns to the original position, closing the contacts and completing the circuit. The circuit breaker will open and close the circuit until the overload is located and repaired or the circuit is opened with a switch.

FUSIBLE LINK

A fusible link is a short length of wire connected into a heavy feed circuit of the wiring system. The wire is generally four gauge sizes smaller than the circuit being protected and is used when the circuit is not protected by a fuse or circuit breaker. The fusible link is designed to melt in event of an overload before damage can occur to the circuit. Fusible links are marked on the insulation with the wire gauge size since the heavy insulation causes the link to appear heavier in wire size. Engine compartment wiring harnesses incorporate fusible links. When replacing a fusible link, the overload must be located and repaired and the same size fusible link installed in the circuit.

Fig. 4   12 volt test light

Fig. 5   Checking for power w/12 volt test light

TROUBLESHOOTING

Fig. 6 Self powered test light

TEST LAMP
UNPOWERED TYPE

A test light consists of a 12 volt lamp bulb fitted with a pair of convenient test leads or one lead and a probe, **Fig. 4.** This test light is used with the power "On."

Check for Power
1. Connect one of the leads to a good ground or the battery negative terminal, **Fig. 5.**
2. Use the other test lead to check for power at the suspected wires, connectors or components.
3. If the light illuminates, power exists at the location being tested.

Blown Fuse Condition Check
1. Turn off all equipment powered through the fuse.

Fig. 7 Checking for continuity w/self powered test light

2. Disconnect all load items powered through the fuse. If a motor is present in the circuit, disconnect the motor connector. If a light is present in the circuit, remove the lamp bulb.
3. Turn ignition switch to "Run" position if necessary to supply power to the fuse, then turn "On" the equipment switches.
4. Connect one test lead to the "Hot" end

of the blown fuse and the other lead to a good ground. The light should illuminate, indicating power to the fuse.
5. Disconnect the test lead connected to ground and connect lead to the other end of the blown fuse. If the light does not illuminate, it indicates that the short circuit has been removed by disconnecting the equipment. If the light illuminates, it indicates that a ground

Fig. 8 Typical jumper wires

Fig. 9 Bypassing part of circuit w/jumper wire

VOLTMETER

Fig. 10 Voltmeter & connection into circuit

OHMMETER

Fig. 11 Ohmmeter & connection into circuit

AMMETER

Fig. 12 Ammeter & connection into circuit

is present in the wiring. Isolate the ground by disconnecting the connectors in the circuit one at a time. Refer to the "Power Check".

SELF-POWERED TYPE

The self-powered test light is a light and battery holder assembly fitted with test leads, or a test lead and a probe, **Fig. 6.**

The light battery and test leads are connected in series so when the test leads are connected to two points of a continuous circuit, the light will illuminate, **Fig. 7.** This test light is used with the power "Off".

Continuity Check

Connect test leads to the ends of the

suspected circuit. If the light illuminates, it indicates that the circuit is continuous and not broken. This test light may also be used to test a switch or other component. Connect the test leads to the switch terminals. If the light illuminates, the switch contacts are closed. At least one of the switch

Fig. 13 Digital multimeter

Fig. 14 Short circuit tester construction

Fig. 15 Connecting a short circuit tester into circuit

Fig. 16 Connecting circuit breaker into circuit in place of fuse

terminals should be disconnected from the normal switch circuit, so that only the switch is checked.

Ground Check

Connect one test lead to the suspected point and the other lead to the ground. If the light illuminates, it indicates that the point is grounded.

JUMPER WIRE

A jumper wire is simply a length of wire with terminals at both ends, usually alligator clips, and is used to connect two points of a circuit or component, **Fig. 8.** The jumper wire is used for bypassing a portion of the circuit to temporarily prevent it from causing an open circuit. The jumper wire is used with the power "On".

In an open circuit consisting of a switch in series with a light or other load component, connect the jumper wire to the switch terminals and apply power to the circuit, **Fig. 9.** If the connection of the jumper wire causes the circuit to operate, this indicates that the switch is open.

CAUTION: Do not use the jumper wire as a substitute for high resistance loads such as motors that are connected between the hot circuit and the ground.

TEST EQUIPMENT

VOLTMETER

A DC voltmeter is used to measure DC voltage to ground. Connect the negative lead of the voltmeter to the ground and the positive lead to the point where voltage is to be measured, **Fig. 10.** This is called a parallel connection. The voltmeter is used with the power "On".

OHMMETER

The ohmmeter is used to measure resistance between two points in a circuit. Connect one lead of the ohmmeter to one point in the circuit and the other lead to the second point in the circuit being checked, **Fig. 11.** The ohmmeter is also used to check continuity of a circuit. For example, if you connect the ohmmeter leads to both ends of a length of wire, the reading will indicate some resistance or simply, a reading will be obtained. Now if the same length of wire is cut in half, the circuit is broken or open and no reading will be obtained, indicating an open circuit. The ohmmeter is used with the power "Off".

AMMETER

A DC ammeter indicates current flow in amperes. The ammeter is connected into the circuit in series. Connect the positive lead of the ammeter to the power source and the negative lead into the remaining circuit so that all current must flow through the ammeter, **Fig. 12.** The ammeter is used with the power "On".

Some ammeters are equipped with a clamp-on probe. These ammeters are used to measure starter current.

DIGITAL MULTIMETER

This test instrument, **Fig. 13,** combines the functions of all the above analog style instruments. The digital reading ensures more accurate voltage read out, which is especially important when testing low voltage circuits often used in microprocessor systems. When using such a device to test voltage or current of an unknown magnitude, be sure to set the range selector to the highest range first. Reduce setting as necessary to obtain satisfactory reading.

SHORT CIRCUIT TESTER

A home-made short circuit tester can be made with a sealed beam, flasher or 7 amp. circuit breaker, wire and/or a buzzer as follows:
1. Connect test lead to two lengths of wire.

Fig. 17 Three speed blower motor circuit, typical

Fig. 18 Measuring voltage drop through one resistor

Fig. 19 Measuring voltage drop through two resistors

2. Connect one wire to the ground terminal of the sealed beam, **Fig. 14.**

NOTE: It is desirable that a sealed beam connector be obtained since it will be easier to replace the sealed beam when it fails.

---

3. Wire the high and low beam terminals and attach a length of wire to them.
4. Connect the flasher or circuit breaker in series with the sealed beam.
5. It is desirable but not necessary to connect a buzzer in parallel with the flasher. Also, an "On-Off" switch

installed in one of the buzzer leads will make the signal optional during testing.

6. Various adapters can be made from old wiring harnesses so the tester leads can be connected at various points of the circuit such as fuse panel, connectors, etc.

To Use the Tester

Connect the tester in series with the circuit being tested, using battery power as feed current, **Fig. 15.** When the circuit is closed and full power is supplied, the sealed beam will flash brightly and also, the buzzer will sound intermittently if connected in the circuit.

COMPASS

An ordinary magnetic compass may be used for locating grounded circuits. The use of the compass utilizes the principle that a current carrying conductor creates a magnetic field.

In circuits protected by a circuit breaker, a short or ground can be located quickly. Activate the circuit and follow the conductor with the compass. The compass will oscillate each time the circuit breaker closes. When the compass passes the point of the short or ground, the compass will stop oscillating, indicating the location of the malfunction.

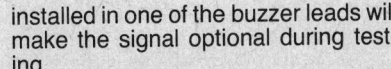

Fig. 20 Measuring voltage drop directly

Fig. 21 Measuring no-load voltage

Fig. 22   Measuring current draw from battery

Fig. 23   Measuring blower motor current draw

The compass can be used without removing trim, cover plates or tape. If the circuit is protected by a fuse, the defect can be found with the compass by substituting a circuit breaker for the fuse.

FUSE SUBSTITUTION

By using a circuit breaker in place of the fuse in the circuit being tested, **Fig. 16**, other tools can be effectively used. A turn signal flasher may be used as a circuit breaker. Solder a lead to each terminal of the flasher, solder the leads to each end cap of blown fuse. This unit may be installed in the fuse block in place of the fuse normally used. However, when attempting to locate a short or ground when using a magnetic compass, the flasher may operate too quickly to produce satisfactory needle deflection. To slow the flasher operation, insert a generator field control rheostat in series in one flasher lead. By adding additional resistance, the rate of flasher operation may be reduced to produce satisfactory compass needle deflection.

CURRENT DRAW & VOLTAGE DROP

AVAILABLE VOLTAGE & VOLTAGE DROP

Voltage drop is the amount of voltage lost as electricity passes through a resistance (lamp bulb, blower motor, resistor) and is measured using a voltmeter. The principle of voltage drop can best be demonstrated using a heater blower circuit where resistors are used to deliberately create voltage drops. In a typical three speed blower circuit the blower motor is powered through a speed control switch. The switch has three wires leading to the resistor pack, **Fig. 17**. The amount of voltage available to the motor depends on

which wire is fed from the switch. Resistors in the blower circuit allow for a change in blower speed by causing a voltage drop ahead of the motor. It must be remembered that available voltage and voltage drop must be measured under load; that is, with the circuit operating a load component such as a motor, or light bulb. In **Fig. 17** power to the blower is through wire A, by-passing the resistors. The blower is now operating at maximum speed. Available voltage may be measured by connecting a voltmeter negative lead to a ground and moving the positive lead various points along the blower circuit, **Fig. 17**. Battery voltage is available at the motor because there is little resistance in the circuit up to this point. Available voltage from the motor is zero volts because the circuit has used up the full 12 volts to operate the motor.

VOLTAGE DROP IN A SERIES CIRCUIT

If the blower switch is positioned for medium speed, power to the motor must travel through wire B and through one of the resistors in the resistor pack, **Fig. 18**. A resistor has now been placed in series with the motor. The voltage drop is four volts through the resistor and eight volts through the motor for a total voltage drop of 12 volts. The motor now operates slower because there are only eight volts available to operate it.

NOTE: When resistances are connected in series, the voltage drops add up to the total available voltage at the source. Each voltage drop is proportional to the resistance of component the electricity flows through.

When the blower switch is positioned for low speed, the switch feeds wire C and there are now two resistors in series with

the motor, **Fig. 19**. The available voltages are 12 volts into the resistor block, eight volts into resistor B and 4 volts into the motor. The voltage drops are four volts at resistor A, four volts at resistor B and four volts at the motor for a total voltage drop of 12 volts. In each case zero volts are available out of the motor because the ground circuit has no resistance. If the ground circuit had resistance caused by a faulty ground connection, there would be a positive reading out of the motor. Also, each of the resistors would have proportionately lower voltage drops.

Measuring Voltage Drop Directly

Voltage drop may be read directly from the meter by connecting the meter across the component or segment of the circuit, **Fig. 20**. Check that the voltmeter positive lead is connected to the battery side of the circuit and the negative lead is connected to the ground side. **Fig. 20** shows voltmeter connections for reading voltage drop across the resistor pack on the low blower circuit. The combined voltage drop through both resistors is eight volts.

No Load Voltage

With the blower circuit operating on low blower and the motor disconnected from the circuit, connect two voltmeters as shown in **Fig. 21**. Meter A is connected as if to read resistor pack voltage drop. It will read zero because there is no voltage drop in a non-operating circuit. Meter B is connected as if to read available voltage. It is actually reading battery no load voltage. The circuit must be operating, that is, under load, to read voltage drop directly and to read available voltage in order to compute voltage drop. If the circuit is not under load, there will be no voltage drop.

CURRENT DRAW

Current draw, or current, is the amount

of electrical flow or volume and is measured using an ammeter. The ammeter is connected into the circuit, in series with the load, switch or resistor. It will measure current draw only when the circuit is closed and electricity is flowing. In **Fig. 22**, the ammeter is connected as if to read current draw from the battery. The positive battery cable is disconnected so that any current flowing must go through the meter. If the vehicle's electrical systems were turned on one at a time, the meter would measure how much current each draws. The ammeter may be connected anywhere in a circuit, even between load and ground, as long as it is connected in series and correct polarity is observed.

High Resistance Short To Ground

When a short circuit occurs and the current draw is not sufficient to cause the fuse to blow, but does cause a drain on the battery, an ammeter may be used to locate the short. If a current draw exists with everything off, then there is a short to ground.

NOTE: On some vehicles equipped with

an electric clock, there will be a slight current draw at all times with all accessories off. This current draw should be taken into consideration when diagnosing a short circuit with an ammeter.

To locate the short, remove fuses one at a time until the meter reads zero. If this occurs, trouble shoot that circuit for a short to ground.

Electric Motor Current Draw

Using the previous example of a blower circuit, an ammeter connected in series between the resistor pack and blower motor with the blower switch on high, **Fig. 23**, will show a reading of eight amps. This is a typical current draw for this type of motor. When the blower switch is moved to the medium position, the blower is being fed through a resistor and this reduces available voltage to the motor. The motor now draws about six amps and the motor operates slower. On low blower speed, the draw would decrease to 3 or 4 amps. If the

switch were turned off, the ammeter would read zero.

NOTE: Current draw is highest with no resistance and reduces as resistances are added in series.

If a second blower motor were connected in parallel and both were operated from the same switch, the electrical load would be doubled. The current draw, in the high speed position, would be 16 amps. Whenever electrical loads are added in parallel, the current draw increases. The effective resistance of the circuit decreases as parallel loads are added. If the two motors were connected in series, both would operate at reduced speed because one would act as a resistor for the other.

When an electric motor or solenoid has to work harder due to mechanical resistance, it draws more current. If the resistance is great, the motor will draw more current than that which can be safely handled by the circuit's fuse or circuit breaker. In this case the fuse blows or circuit breaker opens and interrupts the flow of current.

FUEL, IGNITION & GENERAL MAINTENANCE

INDEX
Page No.

Fuel System Service

DESCRIPTION

All vehicles covered in this manual that are equipped with gasoline engines use either carburetors or some type of fuel injection system.

On carbureted models, the carburetor receives gasoline from the fuel pump and combines it with air to form an explosive substance. This air/fuel mixture is then drawn through the intake manifold into the combustion chamber by the downward movement of the piston on the intake stroke.

On fuel injected models, the fuel injectors receive fuel under pressure from fuel rails or fuel lines, which are supplied by the fuel pump. The amount of fuel injected is controlled by a computer or electronic module, as is the amount of air introduced, to maintain a near perfect air/fuel ratio.

The ideal air/fuel ratio is approximately

15 parts air to each part gasoline. The carburetor or fuel injection system constantly adjusts the air fuel ratio which varies as the engine operates over a range of loads, speeds and temperatures.

On carbureted models, most of the work performed by the carburetor is performed internally, but there are several simple external adjustments that will provide easier starts, smoother running and better gas mileage. All carbureted vehicles use both an air filter and a gas filter. If these filters are not changed at regular intervals, the vehicle will lose power and waste gasoline. The choke changes the air/fuel mixture when the engine is cold. It should be periodically cleaned and checked for proper adjustment. The fast idle speed works in conjunction with the choke, and must be set so that the engine does not stall when cold.

On fuel injected models, the operation of

the fuel injection system is generally controlled by some type of electronic unit and should be serviced by a qualified technician. All fuel injection systems also use gas filters that should be changed at regular intervals.

There are several emission control devices that may affect operation of the carburetor or fuel injection system. The PCV (positive crankcase ventilation) valve meters gases from the engine crankcase back through the intake manifold to be burned. If the PCV valve is not working properly, it can alter the air/fuel ratio and cause the vehicle to idle rough. Gasoline vapors from the fuel tank and carburetor, or fuel injection system, are directed to a charcoal canister. Some of these canisters contain a filter that should be changed at manufacturer's recommended intervals. Exhaust gases are recycled through an EGR (exhaust gas recirculation) valve

Fig. 1   Pressure testing fuel pump

Fig. 2   Disconnecting fuel line

back into the intake manifold. The EGR valve should be serviced at manufacturer's recommended intervals.

AIR FILTER

All carbureted and some gasoline powered fuel injected models use dry type air filters that should be changed periodically to maintain optimum engine performance. Consult owner's manual for proper replacement intervals. The air filter is contained inside the air filter housing. To gain access to the air filter, remove air filter housing cover. Depending on make and model of vehicle, the housing cover is retained by bolt(s), nut(s), wing nut(s) or spring clips. Many air filter housings also contain other filters, such as vent filters, which can be replaced when replacing air filter.

CARBURETOR & FUEL INJECTION SYSTEM ADJUSTMENTS

While the carburetor or fuel injection system is generally assumed to be the cause of poor engine performance or rough idle, there are other factors to be considered before attempting any adjustments:
1. Faulty distributor
2. Misadjusted timing
3. Faulty spark plugs and/or wires
4. Faulty air cleaner
5. Defective evaporative emission system
6. Defective early fuel evaporative emission system
7. Defective positive crankcase ventilation system

8. Defective exhaust gas recirculation system
9. Insufficient engine compression
10. Leaking vacuum at intake manifold, vacuum hoses and connections
11. Loose carburetor mounting bolts or nuts
   It is advisable to seek professional advice before assuming the carburetor or fuel injection system is at fault.

While various carburetor or fuel injection system adjusting specifications and some adjusting procedures are given on the vehicle emission control information label, it is advisable not to attempt adjustment. Most carburetors or fuel injection components in use today have various limiting devices installed on them as required by Federal law. As a general rule, these limiting devices should only be removed during overhaul procedures, and then only by a qualified technician. While various settings can be checked against specifications, it is advisable to seek professional advice whenever adjustments are required.

CHARCOAL CANISTER

Most gasoline powered vehicles have an evaporative emission system to control the escape of gasoline vapors into the atmosphere. All evaporative emission systems use charcoal canisters. Most charcoal canisters are nonserviceable. A few canisters of the open bottom type are used on vehicles such as Chevrolet. These open bottom type canisters require periodic filter replacement. Consult owners manual for filter replacement intervals and applicability and change filter as described below.
1. Mark all canister hoses for proper assembly, then remove all hoses from top of canister.

CAUTION: Charcoal canisters are made of plastic and are easily subject to breakage. When removing hoses from canister, use extreme care to avoid damaging canister.

2. Carefully remove canister from vehicle.
3. Remove filter element by squeezing it out from under lip surface at bottom of canister, and from under retainer bar, if applicable.
4. Squeeze new element under retainer bar, if applicable, and position it evenly around entire bottom of canister, tucking edges under lip of canister.
5. Install canister in original position in vehicle.
6. Connect canister hoses to proper locations on top of canister.

FUEL FILLER CAP

The fuel filler cap used on vehicles without an evaporative emission system incorporates an anti-surge mechanism that prevents fuel spillage through the cap due to surge when cornering. Atmospheric air and fuel vapor are normally allowed to pass into and out of the fuel system, preventing tank collapse and/or excess pressure build up. In some cases the anti-surge mechanism can prevent fuel vapor from passing through the cap but pressure cannot build to excess levels.

The fuel filler cap used on vehicles with an evaporative emission system has a pressure-vacuum valve that vents air into the tank as fuel is consumed to prevent fuel tank collapse. Fuel vapor will not vent into the atmosphere until a predetermined pressure above atmospheric has been reached.

Fig. 3 Thermostatically operated heated air intake system (typical)

Fig. 4 Vacuum operated heated air intake system (typical)

Use of an improper filler cap can result in damage to the fuel system or poor vehicle performance.

FUEL PUMP PRESSURE TEST

NOTE: This procedure is used on carbureted vehicles with mechanical fuel pump. It is advised to seek professional assistance concerning electric fuel pumps or fuel pumps used on vehicles equipped with fuel injection.

To perform pressure test, disconnect fuel pipe at carburetor inlet and attach pressure gauge and hose between carburetor inlet and disconnected fuel pipe, **Fig. 1.** Take pressure reading with engine running. The pressure should be within the limits listed in the individual car chapters. The pressure should remain constant or return very slowly to zero when the engine is stopped.

GAS FILTER

All gasoline powered vehicles use a gas filter to prevent entry of dirt or other foreign matter into carburetor or fuel injection components. All filters on carbureted models and some filters on fuel injected models are serviceable and these filters should be changed periodically, as a clogged gas filter may cause stalling or hesitation. On fuel injected vehicles, serviceable fuel filters are generally of either the self contained in-line type, or an in-line paper element in a canister, located downstream from fuel pump. On carbureted vehicles, some filters are the self-contained in-line type located between the carburetor and the fuel pump, while others are installed at the carburetor inlet.

It should be noted that some fuel injection systems maintain fuel under high pressure at all times. When replacing fuel filters on fuel injected models, it is adviseable to bleed system as necessary before removing filter.

To change in-line paper type elements, unscrew bottom portion of canister and remove old element. When installing bottom portion of canister, ensure that gasket is properly seated, if used.

To change self contained in-line filters, proceed as follows:
1. Loosen spring clips or clamps at outer ends of hoses and slide toward gas filter until they clear flanges on fuel line.
2. Remove filter with hoses and clamps attached.

NOTE: If replacement hoses and clamps are provided with replacement filter, removal of old filter assembly can be facilitated by slicing original hoses lengthwise to prevent unnecessary distortion of fuel line.

3. If replacement hoses and clamps are not provided with replacement filter, loosen spring clips or clamps on hoses and slide them past flanges of gas filter, remove hoses from old filter and install them on replacement filter, and secure with spring clips or clamps, ensuring that spring clips or clamps are inboard of filter flanges.
4. Install replacement filter assembly in gas line, ensuring that arrow on filter points toward carburetor. Secure with spring clips or clamps, ensuring that they are outboard of gas line flanges.

To change gas filters installed externally at carburetor inlet, proceed as follows:
1. Loosen spring clip or clamp at fuel line end of hose and slide upward over flange of fuel line.
2. Unscrew filter from carburetor and remove filter with hose from vehicle.
3. Screw new filter into carburetor.

CAUTION: Screw new filter in only until snug. Filter usually will not fit flush against carburetor. Overtightening of filter will cause breakage with neck of filter becoming lodged in carburetor.

4. Install new hose, if provided, or original hose on filter and insert fuel line into other end of hose, securing with spring clips or clamps.

To change gas filters installed internally at carburetor inlet, proceed as follows, **Fig. 2:**
1. Hold large nut with suitable wrench and loosen small nut.

CAUTION: Use a flare nut wrench on small nut. Use of a conventional wrench will distort nut. Break nut loose by manually rapping wrench rather than pushing or pulling it.

2. Remove large nut together with gas filter, spring, and gaskets, noting installed direction of filter.
3. Install paper gasket in large nut, then the replacement filter, ensuring that filter is installed in correct direction.
4. Insert spring into carburetor inlet, then the nut with filter. Ensure that gasket is properly positioned on nut.
5. Tighten nut until snug.
6. Hand start fuel line flare nut into large nut.
7. Hold large nut with suitable wrench, and tighten flare nut until snug.

After changing any gas filter, start the engine and check for leaks.

HEATED AIR INTAKE SYSTEM

All gasoline powered carbureted vehicles use a heated air intake system to improve driveability and maximize gas mileage. This system is either thermostatically or vacuum controlled, **Figs. 3 and 4.** There are several visual checks that can be made to check for proper system operation.
1. Disconnect air cleaner duct system as necessary to allow viewing of air door, usually located in air cleaner snorkel.
2. With engine cold, check position of air door, using a flashlight and/or mirror to facilitate viewing as necessary. Air door should be in up position, blocking entry of outside air and allowing entry of heated air from exhaust manifold.
3. Start engine and run at idle. As engine warms up, air door should lower gradually until it is in a fully down position when engine reaches operating temperature.
4. If air door does not work as described in steps 2 and 3, check air door for sticking or binding and check spring for weakness or distortion.
5. If air door is free and spring is satisfactory, check duct work for leaks or loose connections and, on vacuum operated systems, check vacuum hoses for cracks, leaks, or loose connections.
6. If system still does not work, seek professional advice.

PCV VALVE

The PCV valve is part of the positive crankcase ventilation system. This system regulates the venting of engine crankcase gasses back into the intake manifold where they are burned. A malfunctioning valve will cause the engine to idle rough or stall. The PCV valve should be changed at recommended intervals. The PCV system can be checked as follows:

1. Remove PCV from intake manifold and rocker arm cover.
2. Run engine at idle.
3. Place thumb over end of valve and check for vacuum.
4. If there is no vacuum, check for clogged hoses or valve.
5. Shut off engine.
6. Shake valve. If valve does not rattle, replace it.
7. When installing new PCV valve, check engine idle and adjust as necessary.

VACUUM HOSES

Many problems encountered in the fuel system can be caused by the vacuum hoses. All vacuum hoses should be checked for cracks, leaks, breakage, or faulty connections. Replace any suspect vacuum hoses. Check the vacuum hose routings referring to the emission control sticker, if available. This sticker is usually located on a valve cover, adjacent to the radiator, on the underside of the hood, or on a shock tower. The vacuum hose routing is color coded and, for the most part, the actual hose colors correspond to the color coding. However, an individual hose color may differ from the color coding.

General Maintenance

LUBRICATION & OIL CHANGE

ENGINE OIL & FILTER CHANGE

NOTE: Engine oil and filter should be changed at intervals recommended by the vehicle manufacturer.

1. Operate engine and allow to reach operating temperature, then turn ignition off.
2. Place drain pan under engine oil pan, then using a suitable wrench remove drain plug.
3. Allow engine oil to thoroughly drain into pan, then replace drain plug.

NOTE: Do not overtighten drain plug, as this can strip the threads in oil pan.

4. If oil filter is to be replaced, position drain pan under filter, then install oil filter wrench and remove filter by turning counterclockwise, **Fig. 1.**

NOTE: Ensure old oil filter gasket is not on the filter adapter on the engine. Clean adapter before installing new filter.

5. Coat new oil filter gasket with engine oil, then position filter on adapter, **Fig. 2.** Hand tighten filter until gasket contacts adapter face, then tighten filter one additional turn. Wipe filter and adapter with a clean cloth.

NOTE: Ensure gasket is in position on filter before tightening. Do not use oil filter wrench to tighten filter. Hand tighten only.

6. Remove oil filter cap and add quantity of oil specified by manufacturer, then install filler cap.

NOTE: Only add oil which meets the vehicle manufacturer's specifications.

7. Start engine and check to ensure oil

Fig. 1   Oil filter removal (typical)

Coat Gasket With Engine Oil

Fig. 2   Oil filter installation (typical)

Fig. 3 Typical fitting locations

Fig. 4   Identifying grease fittings (typical). If vehicle is equipped with plugs, the plugs must be removed and a grease fitting installed prior to lubricating

filter and drain plug are not leaking, then turn ignition off.

8. Check oil level to ensure crankcase is full but not overfilled. Add oil as necessary.

NOTE: Do not bring oil level above "Full" mark on dipstick. Overfilling could result in damage to engine gaskets or seals causing leaks.

EGR VALVE, CHECK

1. Start engine and allow to warm up.
2. With engine at curb idle speed, disconnect vacuum hose from EGR valve and plug hose to prevent vacuum leak.
3. Attach hand vacuum pump to EGR valve fitting.
4. Operate pump to apply at least 4 inches of vacuum to valve.
5. Observe that engine begins to misfire and run roughly. If there is no change in engine performance, EGR valve is defective or gas passages are clogged with exhaust deposits.
6. Disconnect vacuum hose from valve.
7. Remove the two bolts holding valve to manifold or spacer, and remove valve.
8. Clean old gasket off mating surface with scraper and wire brush.
9. Inspect and clean out gas passages in manifold or spacer with wire gun-bore brush or small round wire brush.
10. Exhaust deposits can be removed from EGR valve with wire brush or by tapping side of valve with soft mallet.
11. Ensure valve stem and diaphragm can move freely by pushing on diaphragm.
12. Check diaphragm for leakage by applying vacuum with hand vacuum pump.
13. Install new valve or reinstall old valve with new gasket and tighten bolts.
14. Reconnect vacuum hose and check operation. With engine warmed up, valve should be seen or felt to operate when throttle opening is increased beyond idle.

CHASSIS LUBRICATING

The first time you perform a grease job, you will spend much of the time looking for the fittings, **Figs. 3 and 4.**

As you find a fitting, wipe it off with a clean rag. This will help you spot it later and also prevent you from injecting dirt with the grease.

The injection tip of the grease gun should be a catch fit on the fitting nipple. That is, once in place it will not slip off. Slight, straight-on pressure is all that is necessary for the gun tip to engage the fitting. Once that is done, pump the handle. To ensure proper lubrication and to prevent damage to the seals, pump slowly until rubber boot or seal can be felt or seen to swell slightly.

NOTE: If the fitting fails to take grease, the lubricant will ooze out between fitting and top of the gun. Do not just keep pumping, hoping some grease is getting in, or you will have a mess. It is normal for a bit of grease to seep out. However, if the fitting is obviously not taking grease, it should be replaced.

REPACKING FRONT WHEEL BEARINGS

1. Remove inner and outer bearings as outlined in car chapters.
2. Clean old lubricant from hub and spindle.
3. Clean inner and outer bearings and bearing races with kerosene.

NOTE: Ensure all old lubricant is removed before repacking. Allow bearings and races to dry thoroughly. Do not use compressed air to clean bearings.

4. Inspect cones, rollers and races for cracks, nicks and wear, and replace as necessary

NOTE: Bearings and race must be replaced as a unit.

5. Place a small amount of wheel bearing grease in palm of hand, then force grease into large end of roller cage until grease protrudes from small end.

NOTE: Use only wheel bearing grease which meets the vehicle manufacturer's specifications.

6. Lubricate remaining bearings in the same manner, then install and adjust bearings as outlined in truck chapter.

NOTE: Apply a light film of grease to lips of grease retainer before installing.

CHECKING & MAINTAINING FLUID LEVELS

NOTE: When checking fluid levels, ensure vehicle is on a level surface. If vehicle is not level, an accurate fluid level reading cannot be obtained.

ENGINE OIL LEVEL

1. Warm up engine, then turn ignition off and allow a few minutes for oil to return to crankcase.
2. Remove dipstick and wipe off.
3. Replace dipstick and ensure it is seated in tube.
4. Remove dipstick and inspect to see if oil level is between "Add" and "Full" marks.

Fig. 5   Replacing thermostat (typical)

Vacuum Valve

Pressure Valve Gasket

Pressure Valve

Cap Inside Perimeter Gasket

Fig. 6   Radiator cap (typical)

NOTE: Add oil only if level is at or below "Add" mark.

5. If oil level is at "Add" mark, one quart of oil will bring level to "Full" mark. If oil level is below "Add" mark, add sufficent amount of oil to bring level between "Add" & "Full" marks.

NOTE: Do not bring oil level above "Full" mark, as overfilling of crankcase could result in damage to engine gaskets and seals and cause leaks. Only add oil meeting the vehicle manufacturer's specifications.

6. Replace dipstick.

BATTERY

1. Remove filler cap and check fluid level in each cell.

NOTE: Keep flame and sparks away from top of battery as combustible gases present may explode. Do not allow battery electrolyte to contact skin, eyes, fabric or painted surfaces. Flush contacted area with water immediately and thoroughly and seek medical attention if necessary. Wear eye protection when working on or near battery. Do not wear rings or other metal jewelry when working on or near battery.

2. Add water as required to bring fluid level of each cell up to split ring located at bottom of filler well.

NOTE: In areas where water is known to

be hard or have a high mineral or alkali content, distilled water must be used. If water is added during freezing temperatures, the vehicle should be driven several miles afterwards to mix the water and battery electrolyte.

3. Install filler caps.

COOLING SYSTEM

NOTE: Add only permanent type antifreeze which meets the vehicle manufacturer's specifications.

CAUTION: Never add large quantities of water into radiator if vehicle has overheated before engine has cooled off. If necessary to service at this time, start engine and add water to coolant slowly. this will avoid damage to the engine.

Less Coolant Recovery System

NOTE: Avoid checking coolant level if engine is hot. If coolant level must be checked when engine is hot, muffle radiator cap with a thick cloth, then turn cap counterclockwise until pressure starts to escape. After pressure has been completely relieved, finish removing cap.

1. With engine cold, remove radiator cap and inspect coolant level.
2. Coolant level should be approximately 1 inch below bottom of filler neck.
3. Add solution of 50% water–50% antifreeze as required.
4. Install radiator cap.

With Coolant Recovery System

NOTE: On these type systems, do not remove radiator cap to check coolant level.

1. Start engine and allow to reach operating temperature.
2. Visually inspect coolant level in plastic reservoir.
3. On all models except Chrysler Corp. vehicles, coolant level should be between "Full" and "Add" marks or at "Full Hot" mark, depending on reservoir. On Chrysler Corp. vehicles, coolant level should be between the one and two quart marks with engine operating at idle speed.
4. Remove reservoir filler cap and add solution of 50% water–50% antifreeze as required.
5. Install reservoir filler cap.

BRAKE MASTER CYLINDER RESERVOIR

1. Clean master cylinder reservoir cover, then using a screwdriver, unsnap retainer(s) and remove cover.

NOTE: Do not hold cover over vehicle, as brake fluid may damage finish.

2. Brake fluid level should be ¼ inch from top of master cylinder reservoir.

NOTE: If brake fluid level is excessively low, the brake linings should be inspected for wear and brake system checked for leaks. Fluid level in reservoirs servicing

Fig. 7   Radiator cap with pressure release mechanism (typical)

Fig. 8   Factory installed coolant recovery system (typical)

disc brakes will decrease as disc brake pads wear.

3. Add brake fluid as required.

NOTE: Only add brake fluid which meets the vehicle manufacturer's specifications. Use only brake fluid which has been in a tightly closed container to prevent contamination from dirt and moisture. Do not allow petroleum base fluids to contaminate brake fluid, as seal damage may result.

4. Install cover and snap retainer into place.

NOTE: Ensure retainer is locked into cover grooves.

POWER STEERING PUMP RESERVOIR

1. Start engine and allow to reach operating temperature, then turn ignition off.
2. Clean area around filler cap or dipstick, then remove filler cap or dipstick and inspect fluid level.
3. Fluid level should be between "Full" mark and end of dipstick.

NOTE: On models without dipstick, fluid level should be half way up filler neck.

4. Add fluid as necessary, then install filler cap or dipstick.

NOTE: Only add fluid recommended by the vehicle manufacturer.

AUTOMATIC TRANSMISSION

1. Firmly apply parking brake, then start

and run engine for approximately 10 minutes to bring transmission fluid to operating temperature.

NOTE: Do not run engine in unventilated area. Exhaust gases contain carbon monoxide which could be deadly in unventilated areas.

2. With engine running at idle speed, shift selector through all positions, then place lever in Neutral or Park as recommended by owner's manual.
3. Clean dipstick cap, then remove dipstick and wipe off.
4. Replace dipstick and ensure it is seated in tube.
5. Remove dipstick and inspect to see if fluid level is between "Add" and "Full" marks.

NOTE: Add fluid only if level is at or below "Add" mark.

6. If fluid level is at "Add" mark, one pint of transmission fluid will bring level to "Full" mark. If fluid level is below "Add" mark, add sufficient amount of fluid to bring level between "Add" and "Full" marks. Transmission fluid is added through the dipstick tube.

NOTE: Do not bring level above "Full" mark, as overfilling could result in damage to transmission. Only add automatic transmission fluid of type and specification recommended by the vehicle manufacturer.

7. Replace dipstick and ensure it is seated in tube.

MANUAL TRANSMISSION

1. Set parking brake and block wheels.
2. Clean area around filler plug, then

using a suitable wrench or ratchet, remove filler plug.
3. Fluid should be level with bottom of filler plug hole.
4. Add fluid as required, then install filler plug.

NOTE: Only add lubricant recommended by the vehicle manufacturer.

REAR AXLE

1. Set parking brake and block wheels.
2. Clean area around filler plug, then using a suitable ratchet, remove filler plug.
3. Fluid level should be approximately ½ inch below bottom of filler plug hole.
4. Add fluid as required, then install filler plug.

NOTE: Only add lubricant recommended by vehicle manufacturer.

COOLING SYSTEM SERVICE

CAUTION: Do not attempt to perform any system servicing when the engine is hot or the cooling system is pressurized. Even a simple operation such as removing the radiator cap should be avoided since personal injury and loss of coolant may result.

DRAINING THE SYSTEM

Most cooling systems incorporate a radiator petcock usually located on the engine side of the radiator at either of the lower corners. Some radiator petcocks are locat-

Fig. 9 Aftermarket coolant recovery system installation (typical)

Belt Tension Gauge

Drive Belt

Fig. 10 Checking belt tension with a tension gauge

ed on the side of the radiator. Not all cooling systems are equipped with a radiator petcock.

1. Place a suitable container under radiator to catch coolant.
2. On systems equipped with a radiator petcock, turn the tangs (ears) to open the petcock. However, do not apply excessive pressure in either direction as damage to the petcock may result because some petcocks turn clockwise and others counterclockwise to open.
3. On systems not equipped with a radiator petcock, it will be necessary to remove the lower hose from the radiator.
4. Dispose of coolant.

FLUSHING THE SYSTEM

There are two flushing methods which can be performed without the use of special equipment. One method outlined below requires the use of a garden hose only. The second method requires the use of the garden hose and a "Tee" fitting spliced into one of the heater hoses. The "Tee" fitting and other items and instructions needed to perform this type of flushing are available through aftermarket manufacturers.

1. With coolant system drained, remove thermostat as outlined below:
   a. To located the thermostat housing on most engines follow the upper radiator hose from the radiator to the engine block. On some engines, follow the lower radiator hose from the radiator to the engine block. The point at which these hoses connect is the thermostat housing.
   b. The thermostat housing is usually retained by two bolts or nuts. Remove these bolts or nuts and remove the housing.

c. Lift the thermostat from the mounting flange, **Fig. 5**, noting the position in which it was installed. This is important to avoid reinstalling the thermostat upside down.
   d. Reinstall thermostat housing, however do not reinstall thermostat. Tighten retaining bolt.
2. Insert garden hose into radiator filler opening, open radiator petcock and turn on water.
3. Start engine and run engine for a few minutes. This should flush out any loose particles in the system.
4. Turn off engine and remove the garden hose.
5. Remove thermostat housing. Thoroughly clean the thermostat housing and engine-surfaces of old gasket and sealer. This is necessary to prevent leakage between the housing and engine surfaces.
6. Install new thermostat housing gasket and the thermostat. Make certain the thermostat is installed exactly in the same position as it was removed.
7. Install thermostat housing and tighten retaining bolts and nuts.
8. Allow radiator to drain.
9. Close radiator petcock, if equipped.
10. Remove coolant overflow tank, if equipped. Thoroughly clean the inside of the tank and reinstall.

REFILLING THE SYSTEM

1. Determine the amount of anti-freeze required to achive a 50/50 solution in

the cooling system. Refer to the "Cooling System & Capacity Data" tables in the individual car chapters. Take the total number of quarts listed in the tables and divide by two. This number is the amount of anti-freeze, in quarts, required to achieve the 50/50 solution. This solution will generally provide protection to −35 degrees F.
2. Add the amount of anti-freeze to the radiator determined in the preceding step. If radiator fills before required amount of anti-freeze is installed, start engine and turn on heater. Add the anti-freeze as the coolant level sinks in the radiator.
3. Continue to run engine with the radiator cap removed until the upper radiator hose becomes hot to the touch.
4. Top up the coolant level in the radiator to the bottom of the filler neck with a 50/50 mixture of anti-freeze and water.
5. If equipped with an overflow tank, add a 50/50 mixture of anti-freeze and water to the cold level as marked on the side of the tank.

RADIATOR CAP

The radiator filler cap contains a pressure relief valve and a vacuum relief valve, **Fig. 6**. The pressure relief valve is held against its seat by a spring, which when compressed relieves excessive pressure out the radiator outflow. The vacumm valve is held against its seat by a spring which when compressed opens the valve to

Fig. 11 Pivot bolt and adjusting bolt arrangement

Fig. 12 Loosening adjusting bolt and pivot bolt

Fig. 13 Adjustment bolt and adjustment slot arrangement

relieve the vacuum created when the system cools.

NOTE: Some aftermarket radiator caps incorporate a pressure release mechanism to relieve cooling system pressure before rotating cap, **Fig. 7.**

The radiator cap should be washed with clean water and pressure checked at regular tune-up intervals. Inspect rubber seal on cap for tears or cracks. If the pressure cap will not hold pressure or does not release at the proper pressure, replace the cap.

COOLANT RECOVERY SYSTEM

The coolant recovery system supplements the standard cooling system in that additional coolant is available from a plastic reservoir, **Fig. 8.**

As the coolant is heated it expands within the cooling system and overflows into the plastic reservoir. As the engine cools, the coolant contacts and is drawn back into the radiator by vacuum. In this way, the radiator is filled to capacity at all times, resulting in increased cooling efficiency.

Air or vapor entering the system will be forced to the reservoir under the coolant and will exit through the reservoir cap.

A special radiator cap is designed to discourage inadvertent removal. The finger grips have been eliminated, replaced by a round configuration.

Overflow Kit

If your vehicle does not have an overflow reservoir, it is easy to fit it with one, **Fig. 9.** A kit should include the following:
1. A clear plastic reservoir with quart markings to indicate fluid level.
2. A replacement radiator cap, with an air sealing gasket in the cap's inside

perimeter.
3. Necessary hoses and fittings.

HOSE REPLACEMENT

The radiator, heater and the coolant bypass hoses are held at each end by a clamp. All clamps but the spring design can be loosened with a screwdriver. To save yourself time after you have removed the hose from your radiator or heater, buy the replacement hose and any necessary clamps before starting the job.

Removal
1. Drain the radiator as outlined previously. Use a clean container, large enough to hold the coolant from your cooling system after replacing the hose. If you are removing the radiator upper hose or heater hoses, you need only drain the radiator. If you are removing the lower hose, also drain the block as follows: disconnect the lower hose at the radiator, bend it down and use it as a drain spout.
2. Loosen the clamps with a screwdriver at each end of the hose to be removed. If the clamps are old and corroded, they may be stuck to the hose. Loosening the screw may not be enough on some designs, in which case you'll have to pry the clamp.

CAUTION: Be very careful when prying under the clamp. The fittings are extremely fragile and might bend or break if too much force is exerted.

If the hose is held by spring clamps, you may be in for a struggle unless you have spring clamp pliers. There are many types of pliers designed for these clamps, including ordinary slip-joint pliers with recesses cut into the jaws to grip each end of the clamp. To release the clamp you must squeeze the ends together, and if you try to use ordinary pliers, the ends may split off. The best procedure is to discard the spring type and install a wormdrive band clamp, but if you insist in reusing the one you have, at least invest in a pair of special pliers.

Fig. 14 Serpentine drive belt with spring loaded tensioner

Fig. 15 Checking belt tension without belt tension gauge

3. Twist the hose back and forth to loosen it from the connector. Slide the hose off the connections. If the hose is stuck, shove in a screwdriver and try to pry loose. If the working angle is poor for the screwdriver, or if the hose is really stuck, cut the hose off the neck with a single-edge razor blade. If the hose being removed is dried and cracked and remnants of it remain on either connection, clean the connection thoroughly with a scraper or putty knife.

Installation
1. With the old hose removed, wire brush the hose connections to remove foreign material.
2. To ease installation, coat hose neck with a soap solution.
3. Slide the hose in position so it is completely on the neck at each end, to avoid possibility of kinking and to provide room for proper positiong of the clamp. Except for the wormdrive clamp, which can be opened completely, the clamp must be loosely placed over the hose prior to fitting its end on the neck.
4. Make sure the clamps are beyond the head and placed in the center of the clamping surface of the connections.
5. Tighten the clamps.
6. Refill the cooling system as outlined previously.

COOLING SYSTEM LEAKS

If the coolant level must be adjusted frequently, the cooling system may be leaking either internally or externally. To determine if the system is leaking internally, special equipment must be used such as a pressure tester. To determine if the system is leaking externally, check for leakage in the following locations: radiator and its seams, hoses and their connections, heater core, water pump, coolant temperature sending unit, thermostat housing, hot water choke housing, heater water valve, coolant recovery tank and core plugs.

DRIVE BELTS

Proper belt tension is important not only to minimize noise and prolong belt life, but also to protect the accessories being driven.

Belts which are adjusted too tight may cause failure to the bearing of the accessory which it drives. Premature wear and breakage of the belt may also result. Belts which are too loose will slip on their pulleys and cause a screeching sound. Loose belts can also cause the battery to go dead, the engine to overheat, steering to become hard (if equipped with power steering) and air conditioner to malfunction.

DRIVE BELT TENSION GAUGE

The use of a belt tension gauge will quickly indicate whether a belt is properly adjusted or not. Low cost tension gauges give spot readings while the more expensive ones give continuous readings as the belt tension is adjusted, **Fig. 10.**

DRIVE BELT INSPECTION

All belts should be inspected at regular intervals for uneven wear, fraying and glazing.

CAUTION: Do not inspect belts while engine is running.

Small cracks on the underside of the belt can be enlarged for inspection by flexing the belt. Cracks expose the interior to damage, leading to breakage without warning.

Grease rots ordinary rubber belts. It also causes the belts to slip.

Glazed belts, indicated with a shiny friction surface cause the belts to slip. This can cause overheating, a low charging rate, and hard steering in the case of vehicles with power steering.

Always make sure to inspect the underside of belts. Belts that appear sound from the top, may be severely split on the sides and bottom, ready to fail.

DRIVE BELT TENSION ADJUSTMENT

1. Run engine until it reaches normal operating temperature, then turn engine off.

CAUTION: Do not attempt to check or adjust any drive belt while engine is running. Turn engine off.

2. Using belt tension gauge following manufacturer's instructions, check tension of each belt, individually. Refer to individual vehicle chapter for belt tension specifications.
3. If adjustment is necessary, proceed as follows:
   a. Pivot Bolt and Adjusting Bolt, **Figs. 11 and 12:** using a suitable wrench, loosen adjusting bolt and pivot bolt, then using a pry bar, move accessory toward or away from engine until tension gauge reaches specified reading. Make sure to tighten bolts before relieving force applied to pry bar.

CAUTION: Do not pry against power steering housing or air pump housing.

   b. Adjusting Bolt and Adjusting Bolt Slots, **Fig. 13,** loosen adjusting slot bolts, then loosen or tighten adjusting bolt until tension gauge reaches specified reading. Make sure to tighten adjusting slot bolts.
   c. Idler Pulley Pivot Bolt and Adjusting Bolt: loosen idler pulley pivot bolt and adjusting bolt, then insert a ½ inch flex handle into pulley arm slot and apply force on handle until

Fig. 16 Disconnecting lower shock absorber mount (typical)

Fig. 17 Possible source of shock absorber leakage

tension gauge reaches specified reading. Make sure to tighten pivot and adjusting bolt before relieving force on handle.

NOTE: Some later models use a serpentine drive belt which incorporates a spring loaded tensioner, eliminating the need for adjustment, **Fig. 14.**

4. To check tension on a belt without a belt tension gauge, proceed as follows:
   a. Place a straight edge along the belt from pulley to pulley, **Fig. 15.**
   b. Using a ruler, depress belt at midpoint between pulleys. Measure amount of deflection. For belt with a free span of less than 12 inches between pulleys, amount of deflection should be ¼ inch. For belts with a free span of more than 12 inches between pulleys, amount of deflection should be ½ inch.
   c. Adjust belt tension, if necessary, as described previously.
5. Recheck belt tension, and readjust if necessary.

DRIVE BELT REPLACEMENT

To replace a belt on models not equipped with a serpentine belt with spring loaded tensioner, loosen the adjusting bolt and pivot bolt. Move accessory as required to obtain maximum slack on belt. Remove belt by lifting off the pulleys and working it around the fan or other accessories, as

necessary. Occasionally on multiple belt arrangements, it will be necessary to remove one or more additional belts in order to remove the defective belt. To install belt, reverse removal procedure and adjust belt tension as described previously.

NOTE: On accessories which are driven by dual belts, it is adviseable to replace both belts even if only one needs replacement.

To replace a belt on models equipped with a serpentine belt with spring loaded tensioner, lift the tensioner, using a half inch breaker bar.

SHOCK ABSORBERS
ON VEHICLE CHECKS

Bounce Test

Check each shock absorber by bouncing each corner of vehicle. This is best accomplished by alternately lifting up and pushing down at corner of vehicle until maximum up and down movement is reached. Let go of vehicle and ensure movement stops very quickly. Relative damping of shocks should be compared side to side but not front to rear.

Shock Mounts

If noise appears to come from shock mounts, raise vehicle on hoist that supports wheels and check mountings for the following:
1. Worn or defective grommets.

2. Loose mounting nuts or bolts.
3. Possible interference condition.
4. Missing bump stops.

If no apparent faults can be found but noise condition exists when vehicle is bounced, proceed to next check.

Leak Inspection & Manual Operation Check

1. Disconnect each shock lower mount, **Fig. 16,** and pull down on shock absorber until fully extended.
2. Check for leaks in seal cover area, **Fig. 17.** Shock absorber oil is a very thin hydraulic fluid that has a characteristic odor and dark brown color.

NOTE: Shock absorber seals are intended to allow slight seepage to lubricate rod. A trace of oil around seal cover area is not cause for shock absorber replacement since the unit has sufficient reserve fluid to compensate for this seepage.

Ensure oil spray is not from some other source. To check, wipe wet area clean and manually operate shock absorber as described in following step. Fluid will reappear if shock absorber is leaking.

NOTE: Air line must be disconnected from air adjustable shocks before they are manually operated.

3. If necessary, fabricate bracket or handle to enable a secure grip on shock absorber end, **Fig. 18.**
4. Check for internal binding, leakage, and improper or defective valving by pulling down and pushing up shock absorber. Compare rebound resistance (downward) of both shock absorbers, then compression resistance. If any noticeable difference is detected during either stroke, the weaker unit is usually at fault.
5. If shock absorber operates noisily, it

Fig. 18   Methods of gripping shock absorbers

Fig. 19   Purging air from shock absorbers

should be replaced. Noise conditions that require shock asorber replacement are as follows:

a. Grunt or squeal after full stroke in both directions.
b. Clicking noise during fast direction reversal.
c. Skip or lag when reversing direction in mid-stroke.

BENCH CHECKS

If a suitable hoist is not available to perform on-vehicle shock absorber checks, or there is still doubt as to whether the units are defective, the following bench test can be performed.

Spiral Groove Reservoir Shock Absorbers

NOTE: If this style shock absorber is stored or left to lie in a horizontal position for any length of time, an air pocket will form in pressure chamber. If air pocket is not purged, shock absorber may be misdiagnosed as faulty. Purge air from pressure chamber as follows:

a. Extend shock absorber while holding it vertically and right side up, **Fig. 19.**
b. Invert shock absorber and fully compress unit.
c. Repeat steps a and b at least 5 times to ensure air is completely purged.

1. Obtain known good shock absorber with same part number.
2. Hold both shock absorbers in vertical position and clamp bottom mounts in vise. Do not clamp on mounting threads or on reservoir tube.
3. Operate shock absorbers by hand at different speeds and compare resistance of known good shock to the other. Rebound resistance (extension) is usually greater than compression resistance (about 2:1). Resistance should be smooth and consistent for each stroke rate.
4. Check for the following conditions which indicate a defective shock absorber:

Fig. 20   Supporting control arm on vehicles with spring on lower control arm

a. Skip or lag when reversing direction in mid-stroke.
b. Seizing or binding except at extreme end of stroke.
c. Noises such as grunt or squeal after completing full stroke in either direction.
d. Clicking noise at fast reversal.
e. Fluid leakage.
5. Check for loose piston by extending shock absorber to full rebound position, then give an extra hard pull. If any give is present, piston is loose and unit must be replaced.

Gas Cell Shock Absorbers

These shock absorbers are equipped with a gas-filled cell which takes the place of air in the reservoir. Foaming of the fluid is eliminated since air and fluid cannot mix. Because of this feature, these style shock absorbers must be tested in an upside down position. If a lag is noticed when unit is stroked, gas cell has ruptured and unit must be replaced.

Air Adjustable Shock Absorbers

These shock absorbers have an air chamber similar to the spiral groove reservoir type which must be purged. Refer to note under "Spiral Groove Reservoir Shock Absorbers" to purge air from shock absorbers.

1. Place shock absorber in vise in vertical position with larger diameter tube at top, and clamp at lower mounting ring.
2. Operate unit manually at different speeds. A consistent degree of resistance should be felt through length of stroke A gurgling noise is normal since unit is normally pressurized.
3. Refer to "Spiral Groove Reservoir Shock Absorbers" test procedure for remainder of bench checks.

FRONT SUSPENSION & STEERING CHECKS

To perform the following wear checks, tension must be removed from the suspension parts. Raise the vehicle and support with jack stands. Relieve load from suspension as follows: on vehicles with the spring or torsion bar on the lower control arm, place a floor jack or single piston hydraulic jack under lower arm control as close to ball joint as possible, **Fig. 20,** and raise control arm until vehicle chassis is about to lift off jack stand, then stop; on vehicles with spring on upper control arm, jack up lower control arm as described previously, place block of wood between upper control arm and frame, **Fig. 21,** and

Fig. 21 Blocking control arm of vehicles with spring on upper control arm

slowly lower jack from lower control arm, making sure that neither upper control nor wooden block move. Wooden block must be removed after inspection is completed.

UPPER & LOWER CONTROL ARM BUSHINGS CHECK

1. Have assistant sit in vehicle and apply brake to lock front wheels.
2. Grasp front wheel with both hands and vigorously attempt to rotate it forward

Fig. 22 Tire rotation chart

Fig. 23 Tire tread wear patterns

Fig. 24   Battery construction

Fig. 25   Typical maintenance free battery

and backward. Observe control arms for excessive front-to-rear movement.

3. Repeat procedure on other front wheel.

UPPER BALL JOINT CHECK

1. Grasp front wheel at top with one hand and at bottom with other.
2. Pull wheel out at bottom while simultaneously pushing in at top. Have assistant watch for play in upper ball joint.
3. Repeat on other front wheel.

LOWER BALL JOINT CHECK

1. Place suitable bar or pipe directly under center of tire.
2. Wedge pipe against ground and lift. Several tries may be necessary to get a good check.
3. Repeat procedure on other wheel.

STEERING LINKAGE CHECK

1. Grasp wheel with both hands and vigorously shake tire from right to left. Have assistant check for wear in tie-rod ends, center link, and idler arm. Idler arm should not move up and down.
2. Repeat procedure on other wheel.

TIRE CARE

TIRE ROTATION

The purpose of tire rotation is to equalize normal wear. By equalizing this wear evenly over the entire tread surface, you extend tire life. Recommended rotation patterns are shown in **Fig. 22.**

It is wise to provide snow tires with rims of their own. They can be kept on rims of their own during both storage and use. In this way, you will protect tires from the bead damage which becomes a possibility when you break a tire away from a rim.

A studded snow tire should always be mounted on the same wheel of the car year

after year. When storing studded snow tires, mark tire in chalk for either Right or Left, depending upon which side of the car the tire was mounted.

When storing tires, lay them flat, off the tread to prevent flat spots from developing. Keep tires away from electricity-producing machinery which creates ozone and can damage rubber.

TIRE MAINTENANCE

Tires should be inspected regularly for excessive or abnormal tread wear, fabric breaks, cuts or other damage, **Fig. 23.** A bulge or bump in the sidewall or tread is reason for discarding a tire. A bulge indicates that the tread or sidewall has separated from the tire body. The tire is a candidate for a blowout. Look also for small stones or other foreign bodies wedged in the tread. These can be removed by prying them out carefully with a screwdriver.

BATTERY SERVICE

NOTE: All vehicles are available with a standard two terminal battery. Some later model General Motors vehicles have an optional Power Reserve Battery System. If the battery in your vehicle appears to have three battery terminals, refer to "Power Reserve Battery System" for further information.

CONSTRUCTION & OPERATION

To understand why batteries malfunction, some knowledge of batteries is important. Simply stated, the battery is constructed of two unlike materials, a positive plate and a negative plate with a porous separator between the two plates, **Fig. 24.** This assembly placed in a suitable battery

case and filled slightly above the top of the plates with electrolyte (sulphuric acid and distilled water) forms a cell. The 12 volt battery is composed of 6 cells interconnected by plate straps. Note that batteries have varying number of plates per cell, but each cell in any given battery has the same number of plates.

The battery performs the following four basic functions in a vehicle:

1. Supplies electrical energy to the starter motor to crank and start the engine and also to the ignition system while the engine is being started.
2. Supplies electrical energy for accessories such as radio, tape deck, heater, and lights when engine is not running and the ignition switch is in the "OFF" or the "Accessory" position.
3. Supplies additional electrical energy for accessories while the engine is running when the output alternator is exceeded by the various accessories.
4. Stabilizes voltage in the electrical system. Satisfactory operation of the ignition system and any other electrical device is impossible with a damaged, weak or even underpowered (low rating) battery.

Sealed Batteries

Sealed batteries, called "Maintenance Free" or "Freedom" batteries, **Fig. 25,** are available on some vehicles, and can also be purchased from other sources.

The sealed batteries have unique chemistry and construction methods which provide advantages.

Water never needs to be added to the battery.

The battery is completely sealed except for two small vent holes on the side. The vent holes allow what small amount of gases are produced in the battery to escape. The special chemical composition inside the battery reduces the production of gas to an extremely small amount at normal charging voltages.

Fig. 26 Battery energy versus falling temperature comparison chart

Watt Rating	5 Amperes	10 Amperes	20 Amperes	30 Amperes	40 Amperes	50 Amperes
Below 2450	10 Hours	5 Hours	2½ Hours	2 Hours		
2450–2950	12 Hours	6 Hours	3 Hours	2 Hours	1½ Hours	
Above 2950	15 Hours	7½ Hours	3¾ Hours	2 Hours	1¾ Hours	1½ Hours

Fig. 27 Battery charging guide

Fig. 28 Cleaning battery terminals

The battery has a very strong ability to withstand damaging effects of overcharge, and the terminals are tightly sealed to minimize leakage. A charge indicator in the cover indicates state of charge.

Compared to a conventional battery in which performance decreases steadily with age, the sealed battery delivers more available power at any time during its life. The battery has a reduced tendency to self-discharge as compared to a conventional battery.

SAFETY PRECAUTIONS

CAUTION: Electrolyte solution in the battery is a strong and dangerous acid. it is extremely harmful to eyes, skin and clothing. If acid contacts any part of the body, flush immediately with water for a period not less than 15 minutes. If acid is accidentally swallowed, drink large quantities of milk or water, followed by milk of magnesia, a beaten raw egg or vegetable oil. Call physician immediately.

When batteries are being charged, highly explosive hydrogen and oxygen gases form in each battery cell. Some of this gas escapes through the vent holes in the plugs on top of battery case and forms an explosive atmosphere surrounding the battery. This explosive gas will remain in and/or around the battery for several hours after the battery has been charged. Sparks or flames can ignite this gas and cause a dangerous battery explosion.

The following precautions must be observed to avoid battery explosion, personal harm and damage to the vehicle's electrical system.
1. Do not smoke near batteries being charged or those which have been recently charged. It is a good practice never to smoke near a battery even though the battery is in the vehicle.
2. Always shield your eyes when working with batteries.
3. Do not disconnect live (working) circuits (lights or accessories operating) at the terminals of batteries since sparking usually occurs at a point where such a circuit is disconnected.
4. Use extreme caution when connecting or disconnecting booster leads or cable clamps from battery chargers. Make sure live (working) circuits are disconnected before connecting or disconnecting the booster leads or cable clamps. Poor booster lead connections are a common cause of electrical arcing causing battery explosions.

CAUSES OF DISCHARGED BATTERIES

There are numerous reasons that could cause a battery to discharge and appear to be defective, therefore the battery should not be targeted as the primary source of electrical and/or starting problems before it has been tested.

The following are some common conditions that could discharge a good battery:
1. Lights left "ON" or doors not closed properly, leaving dome light "ON."
2. Excessive use of accessories with the engine not running.
3. Improper installation of after market accessories.
4. Alternator belt loose or damaged.
5. Dirty battery case causing a self-discharge condition.
6. Loose battery cable terminals.
7. Low alternator output.
8. High resistance in charging circuits caused by other loose electrical connections.

BATTERY RATING & CAPACITY

The two most commonly used ratings are the 20 hour rating of 80° F and the cold cranking load capacity of the battery at 0° F, specified in amps. Batteries are also rated by watts in the Peak Watt Rating (PWR) which is actually the cold cranking ability of the battery at 0° F.

Another battery rating method is the reserve capacity rating in minutes. The purpose of this rating is to determine the length of time a vehicle can be operated with a faulty charging system (malfunctioning alternator or regulator). Batteries are normally marketed by the Ampere-Hour rating which is based on the 20 hour rating. The Ampere-Hour rating is also normally stamped on the battery case or on a label attached to the battery. A battery capable of furnishing 4 amps for a period of 20 hours is classified as an 80 ampere hour battery (4 amps × 20 hour = 80).

The Ampere-Hour rating should not be confused with the cranking performance of a battery at 0° F. Batteries with the same Ampere-Hour ratings can have various 0° F cranking capacities. The higher quality battery will have a higher Ampere-Hour rating and a higher cranking capacity will increase with larger number of plates per cell, larger size of plates, and larger battery case size allowing for more electrolyte solution.

SELECTING A REPLACEMENT BATTERY

Long and troublefree service can be better assured when the capacity or wattage rating of the replacement battery is at least equal to the wattage rating of the battery originally engineered for the application by the manufacturer.

FUEL, IGNITION & GENERAL MAINTENANCE

Fig. 29   Removing side type battery terminal

Fig. 30   Removing bolt type terminal

The use of an undersized battery may result in poor performance and early failure. **Fig. 26** shows how battery power shrinks while the need for engine cranking power increases with falling temperatures. Sub-zero temperatures reduce capacity of a fully charged battery to 45% of its normal power and at the same time increase cranking load to 3½ times the normal warm weather load.

Hot weather can also place excessive electrical loads on the battery. Difficulty in starting may occur when cranking is attempted shortly after a hot engine has been turned off or stalls. High compression engines can be as difficult to start under such conditions as on the coldest day. Consequently, good performance can be obtained only if the battery has ample capacity to cope with these conditions.

A battery of greater capacity should be considered if the electrical load has been increased through the addition of accessories, or if driving conditions are such that the generator cannot keep the battery charged.

On applications where heavy electrical loads are encountered, a higher output generator that will supply a charge during low speed operation may be required to increase battery life and improve battery performance.

TESTING BATTERY (SPECIFIC GRAVITY)

NOTE: The specific gravity of a sealed battery cannot be checked.

A hydrometer can be used to measure the specific gravity of the electrolyte in each cell. There are several types of hydrometers available, the least expensive consisting of a glass tube, a rubber bulb at the end of the tube and several balls within the tube. To use this type, the specific gravity of the battery must be interpreted by the number of balls which float to the

Fig. 31   Removing spread type terminal

surface of the electrolyte, according to the manufacturer's instructions.

The hydrometer indicates the concentration of the electrolyte.

BOOST STARTING A VEHICLE WITH A DISCHARGED BATTERY

1. Be sure the ignition key is in the off position and all accessories and lights are off.
2. Shield eyes. Use goggles or similar eye protection.
3. Connect the booster cables from the positive (+) battery terminal of the dis-

charged battery (vehicle to be started) to the positive (+) battery terminal of the vehicle used as the booster.
4. Connect one end of the other cable to negative (−) terminal of the good battery.
5. Connect one end of the other cable to engine bolthead or similar good contact spot on the vehicle being started.

CAUTION: Never connect to negative terminal of dead battery.

NOTE: To prevent damage to other electrical components on the vehicle being

Fig. 32   Removing battery cable terminal using cable terminal puller

1	CONTROLLER
2	ACCESSORY BATTERY POSITIVE TERMINAL (A+)
3	NEGATIVE TERMINAL (−) FOR BOTH BATTERIES
4	RESERVE CRANKING BATTERY POSITIVE TERMINAL (C+)

Fig. 33   Posipower battery and controller

VOLTAGE AND ELECTROLYTE TEMPERATURE	
ESTIMATED ELECTROLYTE TEMPERATURE	MINIMUM REQUIRED VOLTAGE UNDER 15 SECOND LOAD
70°F (21°C) & ABOVE	9.6
50°F (10°C)	9.4
30°F (1-1°C)	9.1
15°F (−10°C)	8.8
0°F (−18°C)	8.5
BELOW 0°F	8.0

Fig. 34   Power reserve voltage chart

started, make certain engine is at idle speed before connecting jumper cables.

CHARGING THE BATTERY

There are two separate methods of recharging batteries which differ basically in the rate of charge.

Slow Charging Method

Slow charging is the best and only method of completely recharging a battery. This method, when properly applied, may be used safely under all possible conditions providing the electrolyte is at proper level and the battery is capable of being fully charged. The normal charging rate is 5 amperes.

A fully charged battery is indicated when all cell specific gravities do not increase when checked at three one-hour intervals and all cells are gassing freely.

Charge periods of 24 hours or more may be required because of the low charging rate. See charging guide, **Fig. 27.**

Quick Charging Method

In order to get a car back on the road in the least amount of time, it is sometimes necessary to quick charge a battery. The battery cannot be brought up to full charged condition by the quick charge method. It can, however, be substantially recharged or boosted but, in order to bring it to a fully charged condition, the charging cycle must be finished by charging at a low or normal rate. Some quick chargers have a provision for finishing the charging cycle at a low rate to bring the battery up to a fully charged condition.

CAUTION: Too high a current during quick charging will damage battery plates.

BATTERY CABLE SERVICE

NOTE: At regular intervals, perform a visual inspection of the battery.

This inspection should be performed when any of the underhood maintenance items such as engine oil, transmission fluid or radiator coolant level are checked.

1. Clean any heavy accumulation of dirt or corrosion on the battery terminals and battery tray with a wire brush, **Fig. 28.** Finish cleaning with a solution of baking soda and water. Diluted ammonia can also be used as a washing agent. Thoroughly flush battery with clean water.

NOTE: Baking soda and ammonia neutralize battery acid. Therefore make sure

Fig. 35 Headlamp adjusting screws (typical)

LOW BEAM ADJUSTMENT PATTERN
(VISUAL AIM AT 25 FEET)
5-3/4" TYPE 2 LAMPS (OUTBOARD ONLY) AND 7" TYPE 2 LAMPS

LINE 1	HIGH INTENSITY ZONES.
LINE 2	HORIZONTAL AND VERTICAL AT CENTER OF HEADLAMPS.
LINES 3 & 5	VERTICAL AT CENTER OF HEADLAMPS.
LINE 4	VERTICAL AT CENTER OF CAR.

HIGH BEAM ADJUSTMENT PATTERN
(VISUAL AIM AT 25 FEET)
5-3/4" TYPE 1 LAMPS (INBOARD ONLY)

Fig. 36 Headlamp aiming

these agents are kept out of the battery by keeping the battery caps tightly in place.

2. Check for damaged cable insulation. Damaged insulation can cause the cable to short out against the body of the vehicle or other accessories. Cables in this condition should be replaced immediately.
3. Check level of electrolyte. If required, add water as described further on.
4. Make sure battery is securely held in place. A loose or broken bracket can result in battery damage (both internally and externally) from excessive vibration.

Battery Cable, Replace

NOTE: When disconnecting battery cables, first make sure all accessories are off, disconnect the negative battery cable and then the positive cable. Make sure to reconnect cables in the reverse order of removal.

1. On side terminal batteries, loosen the retaining bolts using a 5/8-inch wrench, and disconnect the cable from the battery, **Fig. 29.**
2. On all other type batteries, loosen the cable retaining bolt using a 1/2 inch or 9/16 inch box wrench, **Fig. 30,** and lift the cable off the battery posts. Some cables can be removed by squeezing the tabs on the cable terminal using a pair of pliers, **Fig. 31,** and lifting the cable off the battery posts.
3. If the battery terminals are difficult to remove, use a terminal puller, **Fig. 32.** Place the legs of the puller underneath the terminal and tighten the puller screw until the terminal is removed.
4. Clean the cable terminals and battery posts using a terminal and post wire brush, **Fig. 28.**
5. Clean the battery top using a solution of soda and water. Ensure the battery

is thoroughly cleaned and dried. Make sure you cover the battery caps to avoid entry of the soda and water solution into the battery.

6. To install the cables on a side terminal battery, place the cables onto the battery and tighten the retaining screws using a 5/16 inch wrench.
7. To install the cables on all other types of batteries, place the cables on the battery post and force them all the way down. if the cable is not completely bottomed, spread the cable terminal slightly with a screwdriver, until the terminal is properly positioned.
8. Tighten the terminal bolts using a 1/2 inch or 9/16 inch box wrench.
9. Coat the outside of the terminals with petroleum jelly to prevent corrosion.

REPLACING BATTERY

Careless installation of a new battery can ruin the battery. In removing the old battery, note the location of the positive battery post so the new battery can be installed in the same position. Always remove the negative (ground) cable first.

Use an open-end wrench to loosen the clamp. If the nut is very tight, use one wrench on the head of the bolt and the other on the nut to avoid straining and possibly cracking the battery cover. A pair of tire pliers can be used to loosen the nut, but a wrench should always be used on the head of the bolt.

If a cable terminal is corroded to the post, do not try to loosen it by hammering, or by resting a tool on the battery and prying—either method can break the battery container. Use a screw type terminal puller, **Fig. 32,** or spread the cable terminals slightly with a screwdriver.

Clean any corrosion from the cables, battery case, or hold-downs, and inspect them. Paint any corroded steel parts with acid-proof paint. Make sure the cable is of the correct size and that its insulation and clamp terminal are in good condition.

Put the new battery in position, making sure it sits level, and tighten the hold-down a little at a time, alternately, to avoid distorting and breaking the battery case. The hold-downs should be snug enough to prevent bouncing, but should not be too tight.

NOTE: Before connecting the cables, check the battery terminals to be sure the battery is not reversed.

Clean the battery post bright with sandpaper or a wire brush.

Don't hammer the terminals down on the posts, as the battery case may crack. Spread the terminals slightly if necessary. Connect the starter cable first and the negative (ground) cable last, tightening the terminal bolts after making sure the cables don't interfere with the vent plugs or rub against the hold-downs.

POWER RESERVE BATTERY SYSTEM

This system, available as an option on some later model General Motors vehicles, is made up of a control box, three battery cables and a Posipower battery case that contains two separate batteries, **Fig. 33.** The terminal marked "A+" is the positive terminal of the "Accessory Battery." It operates as the normal battery in a car, handling all voltage requirements of the vehicle. The terminal marked "C+" is the positive terminal of the "Reserve Cranking Battery". This portion of the battery is used to assist the Accessory Battery for normal starting and to start the engine if the Accessory Battery is run down, due to lights or other accessories being left on, or a malfunction in the electrical section.

The center terminal is the common ground for both batteries. The controller couples the two batteries together when the ignition switch is turned to "START". When the ignition switch is returned to "RUN", the controller removes the Reserve Cranking Battery from the circuit and the Accessory Battery handles all voltage requirements for the vehicle.

If the Accessory Battery is low due to one or more accessories being left on or an electrical malfunction, the Accessory Battery will not be able to start the vehicle. If this is the case, turn the ignition switch to "RUN" or "ON", then "PRESS" and "RELEASE" the Battery Reserve push button switch on the lower instrument panel. The controller will now engage the Reserve Cranking Battery into the system to start the engine. Now turn ignition switch to "START" position and start the engine in the usual manner. After starting, the two batteries will stay coupled together and be charged by the alternator. The two batteries will remain coupled together until the ignition is turned "OFF".

Testing & Charging Posipower Battery

NOTE: The following procedures apply to both batteries contained in the Posipower battery case. Test and charge each battery separately.

1. Check for visible damage, such as cracked or broken case, replacing battery as necessary.
2. Disconnect all load from battery, then, using accurate digital voltmeter, read Open Circuit Voltage (OCV).
3. If OCV is at least 12.4 volts, proceed to "Load Test". If OCV is less than 12.4 volts, proceed to "Charging", then to "Load Test".

Load Test

1. With all other load disconnected from battery, connect a carbon pile load and voltmeter across battery.
2. Adjust carbon pile to obtain load current of 110 amps for Accessory Battery (A+ terminal) or 200 amps for Reserve Cranking Battery (C+ terminal).
3. Observe voltage after 15 seconds with load applied.
4. If voltage is below listed value, **Fig. 34,** replace battery.

Charging

NOTE: Each battery may be charged at any rate in amperes as long as battery temperature does not exceed 125°F. and gassing or spewing of electrolyte does not occur. If either of these conditions occur, reduce charging rate.

1. Using suitable charger, set initial rate at highest rate and charge for one hour.
2. Disconnect charger.
3. Connect carbon pile load and adjust to obtained ampere values of 110 amps (A+ terminal) or 200 amps (C+ terminal) for 15 seconds to remove surface charge.

4. After 15 seconds, disconnect carbon pile load, then wait 45 seconds.
5. Using digital voltmeter, read OCV. If OCV is below 12.4 volts, repeat charging procedure. If OCV is at least 12.4 volts, proceed to "Load Test".

NOTE: The recharge time required to bring OCV to 12.4 volts or above varies according to state of charge at beginning of charge period, battery temperature (the lower the temperature of the battery, the longer the charging time required) or the capacity of the charger.

HEADLAMP AIMING

It is recommended that headlamps be checked for proper aim every 12 months or whenever front body work is repaired. On most vehicles, aiming can be performed without removing headlamp bezels. Vertical adjustment is usually accomplished with a screw at the top of the sealed beam retaining ring (12 o'clock position). Horizontal adjustment is provided by a screw at the right or left (3 or 9 o'clock position) of the sealed beam unit, **Fig. 35.** Headlamp aiming can be performed visually with a screen as follows:

1. Vehicle should be on level floor so headlamps are 25 ft. from screen or light colored wall. Fuel tank should be ½ full. Any heavy loads that are normally in vehicle should remain there. Driver and passengers should not be in vehicle during aiming. Tires should be inflated to specified pressures and headlamps lenses should be cleaned.
2. Mark screen or wall with four lines as shown in **Fig. 36.**
3. Adjust low beam pattern only as shown in top diagram in **Fig. 36.**
4. On vehicles with four headlamp systems, cover low beam (outboard or upper lamps) and adjust high beam lamp pattern as shown in bottom diagram of **Fig. 36.**

Ignition System Service

BASIC OPERATION

Combustion of air/fuel mixtures in gasoline engines is initiated by spark ignition. Complete burning (combustion) of the air/fuel mixtures is essential for proper engine performance, acceptable driveability and fuel economy, and exhaust emission control. In order to ensure that the air/fuel mixtures burn completely, the spark that begins combustion must be of sufficient heat (voltage) and duration, and it must be applied at exactly the right moment during each cylinder's operating cycle.

The part of the vehicle electrical system that produces spark to ignite the air/fuel mixtures is the ignition system. Spark is created by producing an electric arc between electrodes of the spark plug, **Fig. 1,** which is installed in the combustion chamber of each cylinder. Depending upon engine design and operating conditions, 5000 to 30,000 volts of electricity are required to produce a spark of sufficient energy to ensure proper combustion of air/fuel mixtures.

The ignition system receives energy to produce spark from the vehicle battery and charging system. Since the nominal voltage of most automotive electrical systems is 12 volts, one of the main functions of the ignition system is to increase battery voltage to the voltage required to produce an arc across the spark plug of sufficient heat and duration. The other main function of ignition systems is to deliver these "stepped-up" voltages to the spark plug of each cylinder at exactly the right time to ensure that air/fuel mixtures burn completely and transfer the maximum amount of energy to produce power.

Ignition systems are broken down into two main sub-systems which relate to the two main system functions. The primary (low voltage) side of the system performs the function of increasing battery voltage to the levels necessary to produce spark. The secondary side of the system delivers the high voltage to the spark plugs.

The ignition coil is the transformer that steps-up battery voltage to produce spark, and also the division point between primary and secondary ignition circuits. The coil consists of two coils of wire, insulated from each other, which are wound around an iron core, **Fig. 2.** The primary windings consist of a few turns of large diameter wire, while the secondary windings consist of many turns of fine wire. The coil creates high voltages necessary to produce spark through magnetic induction.

As battery voltage (current) flows through the coil primary windings, a magnetic field is produced. When current flow through the primary windings is momentarily interrupted, the magnetic field instantly collapses and high voltage is induced in the coil secondary windings. This induced voltage is discharged through the spark plug, creating spark to initiate combustion.

Fig. 1   Typical spark plug, cross-sectional view

Secondary voltage strength is determined by the strength of the magnetic field created by current flow in the primary windings, the speed with which the magnetic field collapses and the difference between the number of turns of wire in the primary and secondary sides of the coil. The longer current flows in the primary windings (dwell period), the stronger the magnetic field created will be. The stronger the magnetic field is and the quicker it collapses, the higher the voltages in the secondary circuit will be. In addition, secondary voltages increase as the difference between the number of turns of wire in the primary and secondary windings increases.

The ignition distributor, **Fig. 3,** acts as both the switch that turns current flow on and off in the primary circuit, and as the mechanism that delivers secondary (high) voltages to each spark plug at the right time. The distributor is driven by the engine and synchronized to the engine's mechanical operation. When the distributor is properly installed and adjusted, it will momentarily stop current flow in the primary circuit and connect the coil secondary windings to the spark plug of each cylinder just as the piston in that cylinder is reaching top dead

center on the compression stroke. This synchronization between ignition system electrical operation and engine mechanical operation is referred to as ignition timing.

Common practice is to relate the ignition firing point to the rotation of the crankshaft, and to express this relationship in degrees. The point of crankshaft rotation where the piston is at Top Dead Center (TDC) is expressed as zero degrees. Generally, the ignition system is adjusted so that the firing point will occur before TDC, which is referred to as ignition advance. If the firing point is set to occur after TDC, it is referred to as spark retard.

In order for air/fuel mixtures to transfer maximum energy to the engine, the mixture must reach the point of complete combustion just after each piston has reached TDC on its compression stroke. Because there is a slight lag between the time that the mixture begins to burn (ignition) and the time that complete combustion is achieved, ignition must occur before the piston has reached TDC and begun its downward travel. If the spark occurs too late, energy is lost because the piston is already moving downward when the mixture reaches its maximum explosive force. If spark occurs too early, the piston must fight against the explosive force in order to rise, which absorbs energy and ultimately causes damage to engine components. Therefore, correct timing of the ignition system is essential for efficient engine operation.

Basic ignition timing is determined by the installation position of the distributor. However, ideal ignition timing to ensure proper combustion varies constantly with changing engine operating conditions. Ignition systems have built in electronic, mechanical and/or vacuum operated devices which advance or retard ignition timing from the basic setting to compensate for changing loads, air/fuel mixtures and engine speeds.

ELECTRONIC IGNITION SYSTEMS

In order to properly ignite air/fuel mixtures required for exhaust emission control under all operating conditions, most vehicles covered in this manual use electronic ignition systems. On electronic systems, the breaker points, operating cam and condenser used on older systems to control primary circuit voltage have been replaced by a non-mechanical triggering mechanism and an electronic control unit (module). This allows the electronic systems to control current flow through the ignition primary circuit with more flexibility and precision, resulting in higher secondary voltages and more precise ignition timing. In addition, because there is no mechanical triggering mechanism to wear out, electronic systems require less maintenance.

Fig. 2   Typical ignition coil construction & operation

IRON CORE
SECONDARY WINDING
PRIMARY WINDING
MAGNETIC FIELD BUILD-UP
MAGNETIC FIELD COLLAPSE

Fig. 3 Conventional coil ignition system schematic

Although electronic ignition components differ in design from manufacturer to manufacturer, or even within a single manufacturer's vehicle line, all current systems operate in a similar manner. Each system consists of a control module which controls current flow in the primary circuit, and on some systems ignition timing; a distributor which contains a magnetic trigger and sensor mechanism, and on some models the module, coil and mechanical and/or vacuum operated advance mechanisms; a coil which steps-up battery voltages to produce spark; a distributor cap with terminals for each cylinder and a rotor which directs secondary voltages to the proper cap terminal; specially insulated wires to carry secondary voltages from the distributor

cap to each spark plug; primary (low voltage) wiring that links the control module, trigger sensor, ignition coil and the vehicle electrical system. Installation and mouting of these components varies from vehicle to vehicle.

The electronic ignition coil consists of primary and secondary windings like coils used with breaker point systems. Current flow through the coil primary windings is switched on and off by the electronic control module, which on most systems, has the ability to vary the "on" time (dwell period) to match secondary voltages to engine operating conditions. Module operation is controlled by a magnetic "impulse" type mechanism which consists of a trigger wheel mounted on the distributor shaft and

a sensor coil which detects trigger wheel position.

AMERICAN MOTORS SOLID STATE IGNITION SYSTEM

This ignition system, **Fig. 4,** is used on 1980–86 vehicles except those equipped with the four cylinder engine. The solid state ignition system consists of the ignition switch, electronic ignition control unit, ignition coil, primary resistance wire and bypass, distributor, spark plugs and on some 1983–86 models, a knock sensor and a MCU unit.

The electronic ignition control unit is a solid state, moisture resistant module. The component parts are sealed in a potting

Fig. 4 Solid State Ignition (SSI) system schematic. American Motor models less fuel control computer (models w/fuel control computer similar)

IGNITION SWITCH

DISTRIBUTOR

DUAL BALLAST
RESISTOR

ELECTRONIC
CONTROL
UNIT

BATTERY

IGNITION COIL

Fig. 5   Electronic ignition system schematic. 1980 Chrysler Corporation

START PICK-UP

CAP CLIP

RUN
PICK-UP
CONNECTOR

NON MAGNETIC
FEELER GAUGE

RELUCTOR

START
PICK-UP
CONNECTOR

RUN
PICK-UP

CAP CLIP

Fig. 6   Dual pick-up distributor. Chrysler Corporation V8 engines (6 cyl. engines similar)

PRINTED CIRCUIT BOARD

CONNECTOR

VACUUM TRANSDUCER

Fig. 7 Spark Control Computer (SCC). Chrysler Corporation

material to resist vibration and environmental conditions. The control unit is incorporated with reverse polarity protection and transient voltage protection.

The distributor incorporates a sensor and trigger wheel. Current flowing through the ignition coil creates a magnetic field in the primary windings. When the circuit is opened, the magnetic field collapses and induces a high voltage in the coil secondary windings. This circuit is electronically controlled by the electronic ignition control unit. The distributor sensor and trigger wheel provide the signal to operate the control unit. The trigger wheel is mounted on the distributor shaft and has one tooth for each cylinder. The sensor, a coil of fine wire mounted to a permanent magnet, develops an electromagnetic force that is sensitive to the presence of ferrous metal. The sensor detects the trigger wheel teeth as the teeth pass the sensor. When a trigger wheel tooth approaches the pole piece of the sensor, it reduces the reluctance of the magnetic field, increasing field

strength. Field strength decreases as the tooth moves away from the pole piece. This increase and decrease of field strength generates an alternating current which is interpreted by the electronic ignition control unit. The control unit then opens and closes the ignition coil primary circuit.

Since there are no contacting surfaces and no wear occurs, dwell angle requires no adjustment. The dwell angle is electronically controlled by the electronic ignition control unit. When the coil circuit is switched open, an electronic timer in the control unit keeps the circuit open only long enough for the spark to discharge. Then, it automatically closes the ignition coil primary circuit.

On some 1983–86 models, the knock sensor detects audible spark knock about to occur, then sends a signal to the MCU unit to retard ignition timing.

NOTE: Due to design characteristics of the knock sensor system, occasional audible spark knock of low intensity and short duration is considered normal. Do not attempt to correct audible spark knock unless duration is lengthy or constant and occurs primarily above 3000 RPM.

CHRYSLER CORPORATION

1980 MODELS

These models use a conventional electronic ignition system, **Fig. 5,** which consists of a remote mounted electronic control unit (module) and conventional ignition coil, external ballast resistor and a distributor in which breaker points, cam and condenser have been replaced by a magnetic pick-up and reluctor (trigger wheel). During normal operation, battery voltage is supplied to the ignition coil through the ballast resistor, which acts as a voltage stabilizer. However, during cranking the ballast resistor is by-passed and the coil receives full

battery voltage. On 1980 models, the module has a built-in current regulator, and receives full battery voltage.

The ignition coil primary circuit is completed to ground through a switching transistor in the control module. The single pole magnetic pick-up controls operation of the module switching transistor. As the reluctor rotates with the distributor shaft, the reluctor poles pass the pick-up pole each time a spark plug should be fired. As the reluctor poles pass the pick-up, a voltage signal is produced in the pick-up coil which is transmitted to the control module. Each time the module receives this signal, the transistor momentarily interrupts current flow through the coil primary circuit, causing high voltage to be induced in the secondary circuit. Secondary voltages are distributed to the spark plugs through a conventional distributor cap and rotor, and specially insulated spark plug wires.

Spark advance is controlled by both a centrifugal advance mechanism and a vacuum diaphragm. The centrifugal advance,

ROTOR

SHUTTER BLADE

HALL EFFECT SWITCH UNIT

GROUND STRAP

Fig. 8 Hall effect distributor. Chrysler Corporation 4-135 (2.2L) engines

STATOR

CONTROL MODULE

MAGNETIC PICK-UP

Fig. 9 Electronic ignition distributor with integral control module. Chrysler Corporation 4-156 (2.6L) engines

Fig. 10   Dura Spark II system schematic, typical. Dura Spark I similar

located under the breaker plate, advances the position of the reluctor (trigger wheel) in relation to the magnetic pick-up as engine speed increases. The vacuum diaphragm operates the magnetic pick-up mounting plate (breaker plate), changing the position of the pick-up in relation to the reluctor, depending upon the strength of the vacuum signal.

1981–86 6-225 & V8 ENGINES

All 1981–85 models except V8 models with manual transmissions use a dual pick-up distributor, **Fig. 6**, in which one magnetic pick-up provides signal voltage to the electronic control module only during starting, and signals from the other pick-up are used only during normal running. In addition, all models with the 6-225 engine and some 1983–86 models with the V8-318 engine are equipped with the Electronic Spark Control (ESC) system. The ignition system used on V8 models with manual transmissions operates the same way as the 1980 system.

Dual Pick-Up Distributor

The dual pick-up distributor allows basic ignition timing during normal running to be advanced for improved performance, while allowing the spark advance to be reduced during cranking for easier starting. On models with ESC, the dual pick-up distributor operation is controlled by a spark control computer. On models without ESC, the signal pulses from the two magnetic pick-up assemblies are controlled by a relay.

When the ignition switch is in the start position, the dual pick-up relay is energized through the starter solenoid, and the control module is operated by pulse signals from the start pick-up. When the igni-

tion switch is in the on (run) position, the relay is de-energized and module operation is controlled by the run pick-up. The remainder of the ignition system on models without ESC operates the same way as the 1980 system.

Electronic Spark Control (ESC)

The ESC system uses a micro-processor control module (computer) to control ignition timing, and air/fuel mixtures and Exhaust Gas Recirculation (EGR) in order to ensure optimum engine performance under all operating conditions. ESC system components include the spark control computer with an integral vacuum transducer (sensor), a dual pick-up distributor, coolant and charge (air/fuel mixture) temperature sensors, and a throttle position sensor. The distributor used with ESC systems does not have centrifugal or vacuum advance mechanisms, as all ignition timing functions are controlled by the computer.

The spark control computer assembly, **Fig. 7**, consists of a printed circuit board, vacuum sensor and an electronic control module (computer) which are contained in a housing attached to the air cleaner. The module computes optimum ignition timing for all operating conditions, based on input from the various sensors. Ignition timing is controlled by the module by controlling current switching in the ignition coil primary circuit.

The computer operates in two basic modes, start and run. The start mode only functions when the ignition switch is in the start position or when the run mode is disabled. The run mode only functions when the ignition switch is in the on (run) position. The two operating modes cannot function at the same time.

During cranking, computer operation is controlled by pulse signals from the distributor start pick-up and the run mode is bypassed. Ignition timing remains fixed at the value determined by start pick-up installation position. The amount of spark advance available in this mode is determined by distributor installation position.

During normal running, the start mode is by-passed, and the computer uses pulse signals from the distributor run pick-up as a reference signal and to compute engine RPM and crankshaft position. Whenever the throttle is moved away from idle position (throttle position switch open), the computer constantly alters ignition timing based on input from vehicle sensors. When the throttle is returned to idle position (throttle position switch closed), ignition timing is maintained at a fixed value.

If there is a malfunction in the computer run circuit, the system will switch to the start mode but performance and fuel economy will be reduced. However, if the start pick-up is defective, or if there is a failure in the computer start circuit, the engine will not start or run.

4-135 (2.2L) ENGINE

Ignition system operation and spark timing on vehicles equipped with the 4-135 (2.2L) engine is controlled by the Electronic Fuel Control (EFC) system. Ignition system components include the spark control computer, Hall effect distributor, conventional type ignition coil, specially insulated distributor cap, rotor and spark plug wires, and various sensors that provide vehicle operating information to the computer. The spark control computer controls both ignition timing and air/fuel mixtures to ensure

Fig. 11 Dura Spark II distributor

proper combustion under all operating conditions.

The spark control computer assembly, **Fig. 7,** consists of a printed circuit board, vacuum sensor and electronic control module (computer). It controls ignition timing under all operating conditions, based on information from vehicle sensors. The computer controls ignition timing by controlling current switching in the ignition coil primary circuit.

System operation on these models is similar to the operation of the ESC system used on six and eight cylinder engines, but the control signals are generated by a Hall effect sensor in the distributor, rather than by separate pick-up coils. During cranking, the computer maintains ignition timing at a fixed value, based on distributor installation position. During normal running, the computer uses distributor signals as a reference to compute engine RPM and crankshaft position. As long as the throttle position switch is open (off-idle position), the computer adjusts ignition timing based on sensor signals. When the throttle switch is closed (idle position), the computer maintains ignition timing at a fixed value.

Hall Effect Distributor

The Hall effect sensor consists of a small integrated circuit and semi-conductor sensor assembly, and a permanent magnet which is mounted facing the sensor and separated by an air gap, **Fig. 8.** Four metal "shutter" plates attached to the distributor rotor pass through this air gap as the distributor rotates. When the semi-conductor sensor is exposed to the magnetic field (no plate in the air gap), a voltage signal is generated on the sensor. When the magnetic field is blocked by the presence of a plate in the air gap, no voltage signal is generated. The voltage signal cycle is converted to a sharp "on/off" signal by the integrated circuit attached to the sensor. This on/off signal is used by the spark control computer to control ignition system operation and compute RPM and crankshaft position.

4-156 (2.6L) ENGINE

This system consists of a conventional ignition coil, specially insulated distributor cap, rotor and spark plug wires, and a distributor, **Fig. 9,** which contains an electronic control module (IC igniter), magnetic pick-up assembly, and centrifugal and vacuum advance mechanisms. Ignition coil primary current is controlled by the module in response to timing signals generated by the magnetic pick-up. System and component operation is typical of conventional electronic ignition systems.

1980—86 HIGH ENERGY IGNITION SYSTEM (H.E.I.)

The H.E.I. system utilizes an all-electronic module, pickup coil and timer core in place of the conventional ignition points and condenser (the condenser is used for noise suppression only). Point pitting and rubbing block wear resulting in retarded ignition timing, are eliminated.

The magnetic pickup consists of a rotating timer core attached to the distributor shaft, a stationary pole piece, permanent magnet and pickup coil.

When the distributor shaft rotates, the teeth of the timer core line up and pass the teeth of the pole piece inducing voltage in the pickup coil which signals the all-electronic module to open the ignition coil primary circuit. Maximum inductance occurs at the moment the timer core teeth are lined up with the teeth on the pole piece. At the instant the timer core teeth start to pass the pole teeth, the primary current decreases and a high voltage is induced in the ignition coil secondary winding and is directed through the rotor and high voltage leads to fire the spark plugs.

NOTE: Since this is a full 12 volt system it does not require a resistance wire.

The vacuum diaphragm is connected by linkage to the pole piece. When the diaphragm moves against spring pressure it rotates the pole piece allowing the poles to

advance relative to the timer core. The timer core is rotated about the shaft by conventional advance weights, thus providing centrifugal advance.

CAUTION: Never connect a wire directly between the "Tach" terminal of the distributor connector and the ground since this will damage the electronic circuitry of the module.

A convenient tachometer connection is incorporated in the wiring connector on the side of the distributor. However due to its transistorized design, the high energy ignition system will not trigger some models of engine tachometers.

NOTE: A diagnostic connector is used on some 1980 vehicles. This connector is located in the engine compartment on the left front fender or skirt and can be identified by its bright orange color. On vehicles equipped with this connector, a tachometer may be connected between terminals 6 and G.

CAUTION: When using a timing light to adjust ignition timing, the connection should be made at the No. 1 spark plug. Forcing foreign objects through the boot at the No. 1 terminal of the distributor cap will damage the boot and could cause engine misfiring.

The spark plug boot has been designed to form a tight seal around the spark plug and should be twisted ½ turn before removal.

Electronic Spark Timing (EST) System

This system is used on some 1980 GM models and can be identified by the addition of a four-wire distributor connector. The H.E.I. distributor used in this system is a modified unit and does not have a vacuum advance unit or centrifugal weights. The electronic module has seven pins. A spark shield is used under the rotor to protect the electronic circuits from false impulses.

Fig. 12   Thick Film Ignition (TFI-IV) system schematic

The EST system consists of a digital computer (ECM) and engine sensors. EST controls the ignition timing in relation to crankshaft position and spark dwell. Crankshaft position is determined by distributor reference pulses received from the pick-up coil. Engine timing advance is determined by the engine speed and its load. This advance is then modified by the engine coolant temperature during starting, the actual engine coolant temperature, the barometric pressure, manifold pressure and throttle switch.

The following input signals determine the spark advance signal to the distributor:

a. System power.
b. Ignition on signal.
c. Engine crank signal.
d. Throttle switch.
e. Distributor references pulses.
f. Manifold absolute pressure (MAP).
g. Ambient pressure.
h. Engine coolant temperature.

1981–86 HIGH ENERGY IGNITION W/ELECTRONIC SPARK TIMING (HEI-EST) SYSTEM

The High Energy Ignition System with Electronic Spark Timing (HEI-EST) is used on all 1981–86 GM models except 1981 Chevrolet V6-229 (V.I.N. code K), which uses Electronic Module Retard (EMR).

The HEI-EST system consists of an electronic distributor with the ignition coil mounted on the distributor cap on 6 and 8 cylinder models, or with an externally mounted coil on 4 cylinder models. All spark timing changes in the HEI-EST system are performed electronically by the

Electronic Control Module (ECM). The ECM monitors information from various engine sensors, determines the correct spark timing and signals the distributor to change timing as necessary. A secondary spark advance system is incorporated into the system to signal the ignition module in case of ECM failure. The HEI-EST system does not use vacuum or mechanical advance.

On some HEI-EST systems, Electronic Spark Control (ESC) is used to retard spark advance when detonation occurs. The spark is retarded for 20 seconds, then the spark control returns to EST.

The ESC system consists of three basic components: sensor, distributor and controller. The ESC sensor is an accelerometer or magneto-strictive device, mounted on the engine block. It detects presence, or absence, and intensity of detonation by vibration characteristics of the engine. The sensor's output is an electrical signal which is sent to the controller. A failure of the sensor would allow no retard.

The distributor is an HEI-EST unit with an electronic module modified so that it can respond to ESC controller signal. The command is delayed when detonation is detected, providing the level of retard required. The amount of retard is determined by the severity of detonation.

The ESC controller processes the sensor signal into a command signal to the distributor to adjust spark timing. This is a continuous process monitoring and controlling detonation. The controller is a hard-wired signal processor and amplifier which operates from 6 to 16 volts. Controller failure would be indicated by no ignition, no retard of full retard.

NOTE: Since this is a full 12 volt system,

no resistance wire is used. Also, a diagnostic connector is used on some models. This connector is located in the engine compartment on the left side front fender skirt. On vehicles equipped with this connector, a tachometer may be connected between terminals 6 and G.

A tachometer connection is incorporated in the wiring connector on the side of the distributor on 6 and 8 cylinder models, next to the coil battery terminal on Chevette and 1000 models, at the coil brown wire connector on Century, Citation, Cutlass Ciera, Omega, Phoenix, Skylark and 6000 models or at the tach connector taped to the engine wiring harness at the engine compartment side of the firewall on Cavalier, Cimarron, Firenza, 2000 and Skyhawk models. On AMC vehicles with HEI, the tach terminal is located opposite the positive terminal on the ignition coil. If vehicle is not equipped with a tachometer, there is a remote tach terminal located above the heater fan motor housing also.

CAUTION: Never connect a wire directly between the Tach terminal of the distributor connector and ground as this will damage the electronic circuitry of the module. When using a timing light to adjust ignition timing, the connection should be made at the No. 1 spark plug. Forcing foreign objects through the boot at the No. 1 spark plug terminal will damage the boot and cause engine misfire.

1980–81 ELECTRONIC MODULE RETARD SYSTEM (EMR)

This system is used on early 1980 Olds-

1	THROTTLE BODY ASM
2	IDLE AIR CONTROL (IAC)
3	THROTTLE POSITION SENSOR (TPS)
4	DETONATION SENSOR
5	MASS AIR FLOW CONNECTOR

Fig. 13 Computer Controlled Coil Ignition system components

Fig. 17 Distributor cap removal. W/bale clip type retainers

CLIP

mobile models with V8-260 (V.I.N. code F) and V8-307 (V.I.N. code Y), also on Oldsmobile and Pontiac models with V8-350 (V.I.N. code R) and on 1981 Chevrolet V6-229 (V.I.N. code K).

The Electronic Module Retard System (EMR) is comprised of a five terminal ignition module located in the distributor, an EMR vacuum switch and six port Thermal Vacuum Switch (TVS) on Oldsmobile except V8-350 California models and a vacuum operated electrical switch on Chevrolet models. On Oldsmobile and Pontiac V8-350 California models, the EMR function is controlled by the C-4 system Electronic Control Module (ECM).

On Oldsmobile except V8-350 California models, during engine operation below 120°F. the six port TVS directs engine vacuum to the EMR switch, closing the switch contacts. With the EMR vacuum switch contacts closed, the EMR module is grounded and timing is retarded 10° ± 2°. During periods of cold engine operation when engine vacuum drops below 4 in. Hg., the EMR vacuum switch contacts will open, allowing normal timing advance.

When engine is operating at normal temperature the TVS is closed, therefore no vacuum reaches the EMR vacuum valve and the engine operates with normal timing advance.

On Chevrolet models, a vacuum operated vacuum switch controls EMR module grounding. When the EMR module is grounded, the timing is retarded a calibrated number of crankshaft degrees. When the retard circuit is opened, the distributor operates in a conventional manner, using vacuum and centrifugal advance mechanisms to control ignition timing.

NOTE: If the EMR module is removed or replaced for any reason, the ignition timing must be checked and reset to specifications as necessary.

FORD 1980–1983 DURA SPARK I & II SOLID STATE IGNITION SYSTEMS

The Dura Spark ignition systems are controlled by an electronic module, **Fig.**

10. The Dura Spark systems produce higher spark plug voltages, permitting the use of wider spark plug gaps required to ignite the leaner air/fuel mixtures.

The distributor shaft and armature rotation, **Fig. 11,** causes the armature poles to pass by the core of the magnetic pick-up assembly. As an armature tooth approaches the pole piece, it reduces the reluctance of the magnetic circuit, thus increasing the field strength. The resulting alternating voltage is applied to the ignition module at a rate proportional to engine speed. The ignition module shuts off the primary circuit each time it receives a pulse from the magnetic pick-up. The timing circuitry in the module leaves the circuit "Off" just long enough for the coil to discharge into the secondary circuit then turns the

Fig. 14 Magnetic pick-up air gap

Fig. 15 Spark plug wire retainer. GM-HEI type systems

Fig. 16 Distributor cap removal. GM-HEI type systems

FUEL, IGNITION & GENERAL MAINTENANCE

Fig. 18 Distributor cap & rotor inspection

primary circuit "On" again. Maximum time is allowed for the coil to discharge.

Special low resistance ignition coils are used, therefore conventional ignition coils are not to be used on these systems. The ignition coil can be identified by its blue color and the terminals are marked differently.

The electronic module is the brain of this system and is well protected from outside elements such as heat and shock. The heat sink containing all the electronic devices is sealed in a mixture of epoxy and sand. This module cannot be disassembled and must be replaced if malfunctioning.

The ignition system is protected against electrical current produced during normal vehicle operation and against reverse polarity or high voltage accidentally applied if vehicle is jump started.

CAUTION: The ignition system will be damaged if other than volt-ohm test procedures are used to check alternator output. This alternator test procedure is outlined in the "Ford Motorcraft Alternator" section, under "Voltmeter Test."

Do not use the volt-amp test procedure or any other test that utilizes a knife switch on the battery terminal.

FORD 1980–1986 DURA SPARK III SOLID STATE IGNITION SYSTEM

The Dura Spark III system is used on

engines equipped with Electronic Engine Control (EEC). The system primary side consists of the battery, ignition switch, primary wiring, EEC system input and an ignition module. The secondary side consists of a distributor, distributor cap, adapter and rotor, spark plug cables and spark plugs. When the ignition switch is in the On position, the primary circuit and the ignition coil are energized. The EEC system provides a signal which tells the ignition module to turn off the coil primary circuit. The off and on times of the primary circuit are controlled by the EEC computer. When the circuit is turned Off, the magnetic field built up in the ignition coil collapses, inducing a high voltage into the coil secondary windings. This high voltage is then delivered to the spark plugs by the rotor and secondary ignition wires.

FORD 1982–86 THICK FILM INTEGRATED (TFI) IV IGNITION SYSTEM ESCORT, EXP, LN7, LYNX, TEMPO & TOPAZ

On this system, the ignition module is attached to a mounting pad located on the distributor bowl, **Fig. 12.** The ignition coil is potted in plastic and has external laminations similar to a transformer.

NOTE: On these units, do not reapply or remove any of the silicone coating from the distributor cap electrodes.

COMPUTER CONTROLLED COIL IGNITION (C³I) SYSTEM

This system, used on 1985–86 Buicks with V6-181 and V6-231 turbocharged engines and some 1986 General Motors vehicles, consists of an electronic control module (ECM), camshaft and crankshaft sensors and connecting wires, **Fig. 13.** On the V6-181 engine, the camshaft and crankshaft sensors are combined into one sensor. A sealed 14-pin connector is used at the ignition module which goes directly to the ECM. There are no connections between the ECM and the module.

This distributorless ignition system uses a waste spark method of spark distribution. Each cylinder is paired with the one opposite it and the spark occurs simultaneously in both cylinders. The cylinder on exhaust requires very little of the available voltage to arc. The remaining high voltage is used as required by the compressing cylinder. The process is repeated when the cylinders reverse roles. There are three coils for a six cylinder engine.

The spark distribution is synchronized by a signal from a hall switch activated crankshaft sensor. This signal is used by the ignition module to trigger each coil at the proper time.

The V6-231 turbo also uses a separate camshaft sensor that provides the ECM with a voltage signal when the No. 1 cylinder is on the compression stroke. This information is used by the ECM to properly time the fuel injection and spark.

An ECM fuse is used to provide a low current source that provides voltage for the sensors and internal circuitry. A separate C³I fuse is used to provide voltage for the ignition coils.

ELECTRONIC IGNITION SERVICE

IGNITION SYSTEM TUNE-UP

The following is an outline of the visual inspections and repair procedures necessary to ensure proper operation of the ignition systems described previously. Refer to appropriate headings for actual repair, replacement and inspection procedures for each component or sub-assembly. Follow all listed precautions to ensure successful repairs.

1. Inspect battery, cables and connections.
2. Ensure that battery is fully charged, connections are tight and free from corrosion, and that cables are not frayed or damaged.

NOTE: Refer to "General Maintenance Section" for battery service procedures.

3. Inspect wiring and connections between the distributor and remotely mounted ignition coil, control module and fuel control computer, if equipped.
4. Ensure that all connections are tight and free from corrosion, and that wiring is properly routed and not pinched or damaged.

NOTE: An electrically conductive silicone grease is used in the wiring connectors of most electronic ignition systems. Do not remove this grease from the connectors.

5. Inspect spark plug wires. Ensure that wires are properly retained in the clamps provided to keep them away from other engine components.
6. Spark plug wires that are cracked, broken, burned or saturated with oil should be replaced.
7. Inspect distributor cap and rotor for cracks, burned terminals and insulation, and carbon tracking.
8. Check air gap between the magnetic pick-up and trigger wheel, if equipped, using a non-magnetic feeler gauge as shown in **Fig. 14.**

NOTE: Although the distributor air gap is not adjustable on many models, the correct air gap is essential for proper ignition system operation.

CAUTION: Using a ferrous metal (steel, iron, etc.) gauge to check the distributor air gap will damage ignition system components.

9. Inspect ignition coil, noting the following:
   a. Coil should be replaced if terminals are burned or damaged.
   b. Oil filled coils should be replaced if there are signs of leakage or cracks around the high tension tower or primary terminals.
   c. On open type coils, used on GM-HEI and Ford TFI-IV, replace coil if windings are burned or terminals are loose.

NOTE: Slight play in the windings of open type coils is normal, and does not indicate a defective coil.

10. Remove and inspect spark plugs, and replace as needed.
11. Check basic ignition timing.
12. Check operation of centrifugal, vacuum and/or electronic ignition timing control mechanisms.

DISTRIBUTOR CAP & ROTOR, REPLACE

Observe the following precautions when replacing the cap and rotor:

1. Note installation position of the No. 1 spark plug wire on the distributor cap.
2. Mark each spark plug wire with the corresponding cylinder number, using tape, paint etc. If wiring positions become confused, refer to the "Tune Up Specifications" section in the individual truck chapters.
3. Note the installation position of the cap on the distributor housing, and ensure that the cap is properly seated during installation.
4. Note the rotor installation position on the distributor shaft, and ensure that the rotor is properly indexed and seated during installation.

CAUTION: If the cap and/or rotor are improperly installed, cranking the engine will damage distributor components. If the ignition wires are incorrectly installed, the engine may back-fire, resulting in component damage and a possible engine compartment fire.

Removal

1. Disconnect battery ground cable.
2. On models equipped with GM-Delco HEI type systems, proceed as follows:
   a. If spark plug wires are secured by a retainer, **Fig. 15,** release retainer latches and remove retainer and plug wires from cap as an assembly.
   b. On models with an integral coil, release latches securing battery lead and distributor connector, then disconnect electrical connectors from cap.

CAUTION: Release plug wire retainer and electrical connector latches carefully to avoid breakage.

3. Release distributor cap from housing as follows:
   a. On models with GM-HEI type systems, press each latch down with a flat blade screw driver, then turn latch counterclockwise ¼–½ turn, **Fig. 16.**
   b. On Dodge and Plymouth V8 and 6 cylinder models, and all International models, insert a flat blade screw driver between each bale clip and the cap, **Fig. 17,** and pry clips away from cap.
   c. On Dodge and Plymouth 4 cylinder models and Jeep models with BID or SSI, turn retaining screws counterclockwise until they are released from the distributor housing.
   d. On Ford Models with a two piece cap, release bale clips holding cap to adapter. On models with a one piece cap, turn screws counterclockwise until they are released from the distributor housing.
4. Lift cap from distributor housing, taking care not to damage rotor or carbon button in center of cap.
5. If spark plug wires are still connected to cap, invert cap for inspection, taking care not to stretch or dislodge wires.
6. Remove screws securing rotor, if equipped, then remove rotor from distributor shaft.

Inspection

1. Inspect cap as shown in **Fig. 18.** Cap should be replaced if it is cracked, carbon tracked, burnt, or if terminals are excessively worn or corroded.
2. Inspect rotor contacts and replace rotor if contacts are damaged or severely pitted.
3. Inspect rotor body and replace rotor if plastic is cracked or if there are signs of burning (indicated by gray-white spots).

Installation

1. Install rotor on distributor shaft, ensuring that all locating tabs and notches are aligned, and that rotor is fully seated. Tighten retaining screws evenly, if equipped.
2. If cap is to be replaced, transfer spark plug wires, one at a time, to proper terminals on replacement cap.
3. Position cap on distributor housing, ensuring that all locating tabs are engaged in their respective slots and that cap is fully seated.
4. Secure cap to distributor as follows:
   a. On GM-HEI type systems, depress each retainer with a flat blade screw driver, then turn retainer clockwise until it contacts distributor housing. Ensure that retainers are engaged in slots on housing.
   b. On caps retained with bale clips, press each clip into its slot by hand, while holding cap in position.
   c. On caps retained with screws, tighten screws securely and evenly, but do not over tighten screws as cap may be damaged.
5. Check installation position of cap and wires against firing order diagram shown in "Tune-Up Specifications" section before starting engine.

SPARK PLUGS, REPLACE

1. Mark each spark plug wire with the corresponding cylinder number, using tape, paint, etc. Refer to "Tune-Up

Specifications" for cylinder numbering.

2. Disconnect wires from each spark plug as follows:
   a. Grasp wire boot firmly and twist boot back and forth approximately ½ turn to free boot from plug.
   b. Still holding boot, pull wire away from plug with a slight twisting motion.
   c. Pull wires off by the boot only. Pulling on the wires may cause internal breakage.
3. Blow out loose dirt adjacent to spark plugs before loosening each plug.

NOTE: If compressed air is not available, remove dirt by blowing through a straw or short length of hose.

4. Install a suitable spark plug socket (13/16 inch or 5/8 inch) over spark plug.
5. Connect ratchet to spark plug socket using extensions, if necessary, to allow ratchet handle to swing, then turn plug counterclockwise until loose (approximately 1 full turn).
6. Loosen each plug as outlined in steps 4 and 5, then briefly crank engine to "blow out" loosened carbon.
7. Remove spark plugs by hand, using plug socket and a suitable extension to reach plugs.
8. If a spark plug cannot be turned by hand after performing steps 4–6, proceed as follows:
   a. Apply penetrating oil to plug threads and retighten plug with ratchet.
   b. Wait 1–2 minutes, then attempt to remove plug as outlined previously.
   c. If plug is still too tight to be unscrewed by hand, alternately tighten and loosen plug (steps "a" and "b") until it becomes free.

CAUTION: If spark plug does not loosen after performing steps "a" and "b" a few times, plug may be incorrectly installed, siezed, or damaged. Retighten plug and have plug removed by a professional technician.

9. Inspect plugs, referring to **Fig. 19,** and replace as needed. Correct any problem causing abnormal spark plug condition.
10. Adjust gaps for each spark plug to be installed using a round, wire type feeler gauge, **Fig. 20,** and a suitable bending tool.

CAUTION: Always use a suitable tool to adjust spark plug gap. Tapping ground electrode against a hard surface or prying against the center electrode may damage spark plug. Never install a spark plug without first checking the electrode gap.

11. Install spark plugs, using the plug socket and extension to turn each plug clockwise, by hand, until plug is seated against cylinder head.

NOTE: If plugs cannot be installed by

GAP BRIDGED	OIL FOULED	CARBON FOULED
IDENTIFIED BY DEPOSIT BUILD-UP CLOSING GAP BETWEEN ELECTRODES. CAUSED BY OIL OR CARBON FOULING. IF DEPOSITS ARE NOT EXCESSIVE, THE PLUG CAN BE CLEANED.	IDENTIFIED BY WET BLACK DEPOSITS ON THE INSULATOR SHELL BORE ELECTRODES CAUSED BY EXCESSIVE OIL ENTERING COMBUSTION CHAMBER THROUGH WORN RINGS AND PISTONS, EXCESSIVE CLEARANCE BETWEEN VALVE GUIDES AND STEMS, OR WORN OR LOOSE BEARINGS. CAN BE CLEANED IF ENGINE IS NOT REPAIRED, USE A HOTTER PLUG.	IDENTIFIED BY BLACK, DRY FLUFFY CARBON DEPOSITS ON INSULATOR TIPS, EXPOSED SHELL SURFACES AND ELECTRODES. CAUSED BY TOO COLD A PLUG, WEAK IGNITION, DIRTY AIR CLEANER, DEFECTIVE FUEL PUMP, TOO RICH A FUEL MIXTURE, IMPROPERLY OPERATING HEAT RISER OR EXCESSIVE IDLING. CAN BE CLEANED.
WORN	NORMAL	LEAD FOULED
IDENTIFIED BY SEVERELY ERODED OR WORN ELECTRODES. CAUSED BY NORMAL WEAR, SHOULD BE REPLACED	IDENTIFIED BY LIGHT TAN OR GRAY DEPOSITS ON THE FIRING TIP. CAN BE CLEANED.	IDENTIFIED BY DARK GRAY, BLACK, YELLOW OR TAN DEPOSITS OR A FUSED GLAZED COATING ON THE INSULATOR TIP. CAUSED BY HIGHLY LEADED GASOLINE. CAN BE CLEANED.
PRE-IGNITION	OVERHEATING	FUSED SPOT DEPOSIT
IDENTIFIED BY MELTED ELECTRODES AND POSSIBLY BLISTERED INSULATOR. METALLIC DEPOSITS ON INSULATOR INDICATE ENGINE DAMAGE. CAUSED BY WRONG TYPE OF FUEL, INCORRECT IGNITION TIMING OR ADVANCE, TOO HOT A PLUG, BURNT VALVES OR ENGINE OVERHEATING. REPLACE THE PLUG.	IDENTIFIED BY A WHITE OR LIGHT GRAY INSULATOR WITH SMALL BLACK OR GRAY BROWN SPOTS AND WITH BLUISH-BURNT APPEARANCE OF ELECTRODES, CAUSED BY ENGINE OVERHEATING. WRONG TYPE OF FUEL, LOOSE SPARK PLUGS, TOO HOT A PLUG, LOW FUEL PUMP PRESSURE OR INCORRECT IGNITION TIMING. REPLACE THE PLUG.	IDENTIFIED BY MELTED OR SPOTTY DEPOSITS RESEMBLING BUBBLES OR BLISTERS. CAUSED BY SUDDEN ACCELERATION. CAN BE CLEANED.

Fig. 19   Spark plug inspection

hand, ensure that threads in cylinder head are free from dirt and damage. If threads are damaged, have engine repaired by a competent technician.

12. Torque spark plugs to specifications found in individual truck chapters. If torque wrench is not available, turn each taper-seat type plug 1/16 turn clockwise from hand tight position; turn each gasket seat plug 1/4 turn.
13. Lightly coat inside of each plug wire boot with a suitable silicone grease to prevent boots from seizing on plugs, then reconnect wires.
14. Check installation position of plug wires against engine firing order. Ensure that wires are properly connected before starting engine.

Fig. 20   Spark plug gap measurement

SPARK PLUG WIRES, REPLACE

1. Remove spark plug wires individually, even if the entire set is being replaced, to ensure that each wire is routed properly.
2. On GM-HEI type systems where wires are held in a retainer, release clips securing retainer to cap, free wires from cap terminals by turning boot back and forth, and allow assembly to rest in position on distributor.
3. On all models, disconnect spark plug wire at distributor, noting installation position.
4. Release wire from all looms and clamps between distributor and spark plug, then disconnect wire from plug.
5. Select a replacement wire of the same length and type, and having the same type terminals (straight, angled, etc.) as the wire that was removed.
6. Lightly coat inside of spark plug terminal boot with a suitable silicone grease to prevent wire from seizing on plug, then connect new wire to plug.

NOTE: Ensure that wire is fully seated on spark plug terminal end.

7. Route replacement wire through all looms and clamps installed to prevent wire from contacting hot or moving engine components, **Figs. 21 through 23.**
8. Lightly lubricate inside of distributor terminal boot with suitable silicone grease, then connect wire to distributor cap terminal.

NOTE: On GM-HEI type systems so equipped, engage wire in proper retainer hole.

9. Repeat procedure with remaining wires that must be replaced.
10. Check installation position of all wires against engine firing order.
11. Ensure that wires are properly installed and fully seated before starting engine.
12. On GM-HEI type system with a wire retainer, press retainer and wire assembly onto cap evenly until latches "click" into place.

DISTRIBUTOR, REPLACE

The following is a general procedure which includes many of the precautions that must be observed whenever an ignition distributor is removed and installed on a gasoline engine. Steps 1 through 7 of the removal procedure can be used to check whether distributor installation position is correct, or to properly index the engine for distributor installation if the engine has been rotated with the distributor removed. However, because distributor installation position is critical to proper engine performance, and because there are many possible mistakes that can result in severe engine damage and even personal injury, removal and installation of the distributor should not be attempted by the beginner.

Read the procedure and included precautions carefully, noting each step that may (or may not) apply to your vehicle. If there is any doubt as to whether you possess the required mechanical skills or the proper tools to perform the steps as outlined, seek the assistance of a professional technician.

Removal
1. Disconnect spark plug wire and remove No. 1 spark plug on all except International models with V8 engines. On International V8 engines, remove No. 8 spark plug.

NOTE: Refer to "Tune-Up Specifications" for firing order and cylinder numbering.

2. Disable ignition system to prevent engine from starting as follows:
   a. Disconnect ignition coil secondary lead from distributor cap, if equipped, then ground lead to engine using a suitable jumper wire.
   b. On GM-HEI type systems with an integral coil, release latch and disconnect battery lead (heavy gauge red wire) from distributor cap.
3. Crank engine in short bursts, holding thumb over spark plug opening, until compression pressure can be felt at opening.
4. When compression pressure can be felt at opening, disengage starter and observe timing marks.

NOTE: Refer to "Tune-Up Specifications" for timing mark locations.

FRONT

SPARK PLUG WIRES MUST BE ROUTED TO AVOID CONTACT OR RUBBING AGAINST EACH OTHER OR OTHER OBJECT.

Fig. 21   Typical spark plug wire installation. 4 cyl. engines

FRONT

SPARK PLUG WIRES MUST BE ROUTED TO AVOID CONTACT OR RUBBING AGAINST EACH OTHER OR OTHER OBJECT.

Fig. 22 Typical spark plug wire installation. Inline 6 cyl. engines

Fig. 23 Typical spark plug wire installation. V8 engines

5. Stationary and movable marks should be quite close to each other. Rotate engine by hand, as needed, to align timing marks at 0° (TDC) position.
6. Mark position of No. 1 spark plug wire terminal (No. 8 on International V8) on distributor housing, then remove distributor cap.
7. If rotor contact is pointing at mark made in step 6, proceed to next step; if not, proceed as follows:
   a. If contact is pointing directly away from mark (180° out), rotate engine exactly 1 full revolution, until timing marks are aligned at TDC, then proceed to step 8.
   b. If rotor contact is not pointing at or directly away from housing reference mark with timing marks aligned at TDC, distributor is incorrectly installed or defective, or engine timing chain may be defective. Engine should be checked by a professional technician.
8. Disconnect battery ground cable, then mark position of rotor contact and housing reference mark on engine using chalk, paint, etc.
9. Disconnect electrical connectors to distributor, then remove hold-down bolt and clamp.

NOTE: Special hold down bolts are used on some models to prevent distributor position adjustment. Do not attempt to remove these bolts unless you have the proper tool.

10. Lift distributor straight out of engine while observing rotor. Rotor may move away from reference position due to design of distributor drive gear. Note position of rotor when distributor is fully withdrawn.

CAUTION: Do not rotate engine with distributor removed. If engine is rotated, it will be necessary to return engine to TDC on the compression stroke of the reference cylinder before the distributor can be reinstalled.

Installation
1. Ensure that engine position has not changed while distributor was removed.
2. If distributor is being replaced, temporarily install cap on replacement distributor and mark position of cap reference terminal on housing.
3. Rotate distributor shaft so that rotor contact is pointing at reference mark on distributor housing.

NOTE: If rotor position changed as distributor was removed from engine, position rotor as noted in step 10 of removal procedure.

4. Align mark on distributor housing with mark on engine, then insert distributor into engine.
5. Distributor should seat fully in engine, and rotor contact mark on engine and mark on distributor housing should be aligned.

NOTE: If so equipped, ensure that oil pump driveshaft is properly engaged with distributor shaft. It may be necessary to crank engine with starter after distributor drive gear is partially engaged in order to engage oil pump shaft and allow distributor to seat.

6. Install distributor hold down clamp and retaining bolts.

NOTE: If it was necessary to rotate engine to allow full engagement of distributor shaft, recheck that distributor housing reference mark and rotor contact are aligned with reference cylinder at TDC on the compression stroke.

7. Reconnect electrical connectors and reinstall distributor cap.
8. Check basic ignition timing and adjust as needed.

NOTE: On Ford Models with Dura Spark III or TFI-IV, ensure that rotor is properly indexed to distributor.

METRIC–ENGLISH CONVERSION TABLE

Multiply	by	to get equivalent number of:
LENGTH		
Inch	25.4	millimetres (mm)
Foot	0.304 8	metres (m)
Yard	0.914 4	metres
Mile	1.609	kilometres (km)
AREA		
Inch²	645.2	millimetres² (mm²)
	6.45	centimetres² (cm²)
Foot²	0.092 9	metres² (m²)
Yard²	0.836 1	metres²
VOLUME		
Inch³	16 387.	mm³
	16.387	cm³
	0.016 4	litres (l)
Quart	0.946 4	litres
Gallon	3.785 4	litres
Yard³	0.764 6	metres³ (m³)
MASS		
Pound	0.453 6	kilograms (kg)
Ton	907.18	kilograms (kg)
Ton	0.907	tonne (t)
FORCE		
Kilogram	9.807	newtons (N)
Ounce	0.278 0	newtons
Pound	4.448	newtons
TEMPERATURE		
Degree Fahrenheit	(†°F-32) ÷ 1.8	degree Celsius (C)

°F -40 0 32 40 80 98.6 120 160 200 212
°C -40 -20 0 20 37 40 60 80 100

Multiply	by	to get equivalent number of:
ACCELERATION		
Foot/sec²	0.304 8	metre/sec² (m/s²)
Inch/sec²	0.025 4	metre/sec²
TORQUE		
Pound-inch	0.112 98	newton-metres (N·m)
Pound-foot	1.355 8	newton-metres
POWER		
Horsepower	0.746	kilowatts (kW)
PRESSURE OR STRESS		
Inches of water	0.249 1	kilopascals (kPa)
Pounds/sq. in.	6.895	kilopascals
ENERGY OR WORK		
BTU	1 055.	joules (J)
Foot-pound	1.355 8	joules
Kilowatt-hour	3 600 000. or 3.6×10^6	joules (J = one W's)
LIGHT		
Foot candle	1.076 4	lumens/metre² (lm/m²)
FUEL PERFORMANCE		
Miles/gal	0.425 1	kilometres/litre (km/l)
Gal/mile	2.352 7	litres/kilometre (l/km)
VELOCITY		
Miles/hour	1.609 3	kilometres/hr. (km/h)

METRIC CONVERSION

HOW TO USE CONVERSION CHARTS

Left Column is units of 10, (0, 10, 20, 30 etc.);
Top Row is in units of one (0, 1, 2, 3, etc).

EXAMPLE: Feet to Inches Conversion Chart

feet	0	1	2	3	4	5	6	7	8	9	feet
	inches	inches	inches	inches	inches	inches	inches	inches	inches	inches	
--		12	24	36	48	60	72	84	96	108	--
10	120	132	144	156	168	180	192	204	216	228	10
20	240	252	264	276	288	300	312	324	336	348	20
30	360	372	384	396	408	420	432	444	456	468	30
40	480	492	504	516	528	540	552	564	576	588	40
50	600	612	624	636	648	660	672	684	696	708	50

12 feet equals 144 inches. Read across from 10 and down from 2.
6 feet equals 72 inches. Read down from 6.

FEET TO METRES

ft	0	1	2	3	4	5	6	7	8	9	ft
	m	m	m	m	m	m	m	m	m	m	
--		0.305	0.610	0.914	1.219	1.524	1.829	2.134	2.438	2.743	--
10	3.048	3.353	3.658	3.962	4.267	4.572	4.877	5.182	5.486	5.791	10
20	6.096	6.401	6.706	7.010	7.315	7.620	7.925	8.230	8.534	8.839	20
30	9.144	9.449	9.754	10.058	10.363	10.668	10.973	11.278	11.582	11.887	30
40	12.192	12.497	12.802	13.106	13.411	13.716	14.021	14.326	14.630	14.935	40
50	15.240	15.545	15.850	16.154	16.459	16.764	17.069	17.374	17.678	17.983	50
60	18.288	18.593	18.898	19.202	19.507	19.812	20.117	20.422	20.726	21.031	60
70	21.336	21.641	21.946	22.250	22.555	22.860	23.165	23.470	23.774	24.079	70
80	24.384	24.689	24.994	25.298	25.603	25.908	26.213	26.518	26.822	27.127	80
90	27.432	27.737	28.042	28.346	28.651	28.956	29.261	29.566	29.870	30.175	90
100	30.480	30.785	31.090	31.394	31.699	32.004	32.309	32.614	32.918	33.223	100

METRES TO FEET

m	0	1	2	3	4	5	6	7	8	9	m
	ft	ft	ft	ft	ft	ft	ft	ft	ft	ft	
--		3.2808	6.5617	9.8425	13.1234	16.4042	19.6850	22.9659	26.2467	29.5276	--
10	32.8084	36.0892	39.3701	42.6509	45.9318	49.2126	52.4934	55.7743	59.0551	62.3360	10
20	65.6168	68.8976	72.1785	75.4593	78.7402	82.0210	85.3018	88.5827	91.8635	95.1444	20
30	98.4252	101.7060	104.9869	108.2677	111.5486	114.8294	118.1102	121.3911	124.6719	127.9528	30
40	131.2336	134.5144	137.7953	141.0761	144.3570	147.6378	150.9186	154.1995	157.4803	160.7612	40
50	164.0420	167.3228	170.6037	173.8845	177.1654	180.4462	183.7270	187.0079	190.2887	193.5696	50
60	196.8504	200.1312	203.4121	206.6929	209.9738	213.2546	216.5354	219.8163	223.0971	226.3780	60
70	229.6588	232.9396	236.2205	239.5013	242.7822	246.0630	249.3438	252.6247	255.9055	259.1864	70
80	262.4672	265.7480	269.0289	272.3097	275.5906	278.8714	282.1522	285.4331	288.7139	291.9948	80
90	295.2756	298.5564	301.8373	305.1181	308.3990	311.6798	314.9606	318.2415	321.5223	324.8032	90
100	328.0840	331.3648	334.6457	337.9265	341.2074	344.4882	347.7690	351.0499	354.3307	357.6116	100

MILES TO KILOMETRES

mile	0	1	2	3	4	5	6	7	8	9	mile
	km	km	km	km	km	km	km	km	km	km	
--		1.609	3.219	4.828	6.437	8.047	9.656	11.265	12.875	14.484	--
10	16.093	17.703	19.312	20.921	22.531	24.140	25.750	27.359	28.968	30.578	10
20	32.187	33.796	35.406	37.015	38.624	40.234	41.843	43.452	45.062	46.671	20
30	48.280	49.890	51.499	53.108	54.718	56.327	57.936	59.546	61.155	62.764	30
40	64.374	65.983	67.593	69.202	70.811	72.421	74.030	75.639	77.249	78.858	40
50	80.467	82.077	83.686	85.295	86.905	88.514	90.123	91.733	93.342	94.951	50
60	96.561	98.170	99.779	101.39	103.00	104.61	106.22	107.83	109.44	111.04	60
70	112.65	114.26	115.87	117.48	119.09	120.70	122.31	123.92	125.53	127.14	70
80	128.75	130.36	131.97	133.58	135.19	136.79	138.40	140.01	141.62	143.23	80
90	144.84	146.45	148.06	149.67	151.28	152.89	154.50	156.11	157.72	159.33	90
100	160.93	162.54	164.15	165.76	167.37	168.98	170.59	172.20	173.81	175.42	100

KILOMETRES TO MILES

km	0	1	2	3	4	5	6	7	8	9	km
	mil	mil	mil	mil	mil	mil	mil	mil	mil	mil	
--		0.621	1.243	1.864	2.486	3.107	3.728	4.350	4.971	5.592	--
10	6.214	6.835	7.457	8.078	8.699	9.321	9.942	10.562	11.185	11.805	10
20	12.427	13.049	13.670	14.292	14.913	15.534	16.156	16.776	17.399	18.019	20
30	18.641	19.263	19.884	20.506	21.127	21.748	22.370	22.990	23.613	24.233	30
40	24.855	25.477	26.098	26.720	27.341	27.962	28.584	29.204	29.827	30.447	40
50	31.069	31.690	32.311	32.933	33.554	34.175	34.797	35.417	36.040	36.660	50
60	37.282	37.904	38.525	39.147	39.768	40.389	41.011	41.631	42.254	42.874	60
70	43.497	44.118	44.739	45.361	45.982	46.603	47.225	47.845	48.468	49.088	70
80	49.711	50.332	50.953	51.575	52.196	52.817	53.439	54.059	54.682	55.302	80
90	55.924	56.545	57.166	57.788	58.409	59.030	59.652	60.272	60.895	61.515	90
100	62.138	62.759	63.380	64.002	64.623	65.244	65.866	66.486	67.109	67.729	100

GALLONS (U.S.) TO LITRES

U.S. gal	0	1	2	3	4	5	6	7	8	9	U.S. gal
	L	L	L	L	L	L	L	L	L	L	
--		3.7854	7.5709	11.3563	15.1417	18.9271	22.7126	26.4980	30.2834	34.0638	--
10	37.8543	41.6397	45.4251	49.2105	52.9960	56.7814	60.5668	64.3523	68.1377	71.9231	10
20	75.7085	79.4940	83.2794	87.0648	90.8502	94.6357	98.4211	102.2065	105.9920	109.7774	20
30	113.5528	117.3482	121.1337	124.9191	128.7045	132.4899	136.2754	140.0608	143.8462	147.6316	30
40	151.4171	155.2025	158.9879	162.7734	166.5588	170.3442	174.1296	177.9151	181.7005	185.4859	40
50	189.2713	193.0568	196.8422	200.6276	204.4131	208.1985	211.9839	215.7693	219.5548	223.3402	50
60	227.1256	230.9110	234.6965	238.4819	242.2673	246.0527	249.8382	253.6236	257.4090	261.1945	60
70	264.9799	268.7653	272.5507	276.3362	280.1216	283.9070	287.6924	291.4779	295.2633	299.0487	70
80	302.8342	306.6196	310.4050	314.1904	317.9759	321.7613	325.5467	329.3321	333.1176	336.9030	80
90	340.6884	344.4738	348.2593	352.0447	355.8301	359.6156	363.4010	367.1864	370.9718	374.7573	90
100	378.5427	382.3281	386.1135	389.8990	393.6844	397.4698	401.2553	405.0407	408.8261	412.6115	100

METRIC CONVERSION

LITRES TO GALLONS (U.S.)

L	0	1	2	3	4	5	6	7	8	9	L
	gal	gal	gal	gal	gal	gal	gal	gal	gal	gal	
--		0.2642	0.5283	0.7925	1.0567	1.3209	1.5850	1.8492	2.1134	2.3775	--
10	2.6417	2.9059	3.1701	3.4342	3.6984	3.9626	4.2267	4.4909	4.7551	5.0192	10
20	5.2834	5.5476	5.8118	6.0759	6.3401	6.6043	6.8684	7.1326	7.3968	7.6610	20
30	7.9251	8.1893	8.4535	8.7176	8.9818	9.2460	9.5102	9.7743	10.0385	10.3027	30
40	10.5668	10.8310	11.0952	11.3594	11.6235	11.8877	12.1519	12.4160	12.6802	12.9444	40
50	13.2086	13.4727	13.7369	14.0011	14.2652	14.5294	14.7936	15.0577	15.3219	15.5861	50
60	15.8503	16.1144	16.3786	16.6428	16.9069	17.1711	17.4353	17.6995	17.9636	18.2278	60
70	18.4920	18.7561	19.0203	19.2845	19.5487	19.8128	20.0770	20.3412	20.6053	20.8695	70
80	21.1337	21.3979	21.6620	21.9262	22.1904	22.4545	22.7187	22.9829	23.2470	23.5112	80
90	23.7754	24.0396	24.3037	24.5679	24.8321	25.0962	25.3604	25.6246	25.8888	26.1529	90
100	26.4171	26.6813	26.9454	27.2096	27.4738	27.7380	28.0021	28.2663	28.5305	28.7946	100

GALLONS (IMP.) TO LITRES

IMP gal	0	1	2	3	4	5	6	7	8	9	IMP gal
	L	L	L	L	L	L	L	L	L	L	
--		4.5460	9.0919	13.6379	18.1838	22.7298	27.2758	31.8217	36.3677	40.9136	--
10	45.4596	50.0056	54.5515	59.0975	63.6434	68.1894	72.2354	77.2813	81.8275	86.3732	10
20	90.9192	95.4652	100.0111	104.5571	109.1030	113.6490	118.1950	122.7409	127.2869	131.8328	20
30	136.3788	140.9248	145.4707	150.0167	154.5626	159.1086	163.6546	168.0005	172.7465	177.2924	30
40	181.8384	186.3844	190.9303	195.4763	200.0222	204.5682	209.1142	213.6601	218.2061	222.7520	40
50	227.2980	231.8440	236.3899	240.9359	245.4818	250.0278	254.5738	259.1197	263.6657	268.2116	50
60	272.7576	277.3036	281.8495	286.3955	290.9414	295.4874	300.0334	304.5793	309.1253	313.6712	60
70	318.2172	322.7632	327.3091	331.8551	336.4010	340.9470	345.4930	350.0389	354.5849	359.1308	70
80	363.6768	368.2223	372.7687	377.3147	381.8606	386.4066	390.9526	395.4985	400.0445	404.5904	80
90	409.1364	413.6824	418.2283	422.7743	427.3202	431.8662	436.4122	440.9581	445.9041	450.0500	90
100	454.5960	459.1420	463.6879	468.2339	472.7798	477.3258	481.8718	486.4177	490.9637	495.5096	100

LITRES TO GALLONS (IMP.)

L	0	1	2	3	4	5	6	7	8	9	L
	gal	gal	gal	gal	gal	gal	gal	gal	gal	gal	
--		0.2200	0.4400	0.6599	0.8799	1.0999	1.3199	1.5398	1.7598	1.9798	--
10	2.1998	2.4197	2.6397	2.8597	3.0797	3.2996	3.5196	3.7396	3.9596	4.1795	10
20	4.3995	4.6195	4.8395	5.0594	5.2794	5.4994	5.7194	5.9394	6.1593	6.3793	20
30	6.5593	6.8193	7.0392	7.2592	7.4792	7.6992	7.9191	8.1391	8.3591	8.5791	30
40	8.7990	9.0190	9.2390	9.4590	9.6789	9.8989	10.9189	10.3389	10.5588	10.7788	40
50	10.9988	11.2188	11.4388	11.6587	11.8787	12.0987	12.3187	12.5386	12.7586	12.9786	50
60	13.1986	13.4185	13.6385	13.8585	14.0785	14.2984	14.5184	14.7384	14.9584	15.1783	60
70	15.3983	15.6183	15.8383	16.0582	16.2782	16.4982	16.7182	16.9382	17.1581	17.3781	70
80	17.5981	17.8181	18.0380	18.2580	18.4780	18.6980	18.9179	19.1379	19.3579	19.5779	80
90	19.7978	20.0178	20.2378	20.4578	20.6777	20.8977	21.1177	21.3377	21.5576	21.7776	90
100	21.9976	22.2176	22.4376	22.6575	22.8775	23.0975	23.3175	23.5374	23.7574	23.9774	100

POUNDS TO KILOGRAMS

lb	0	1	2	3	4	5	6	7	8	9	lb
	kg	kg	kg	kg	kg	kg	kg	kg	kg	kg	
..		0.454	0.907	1.361	1.814	2.268	2.722	3.175	3.629	4.082	..
10	4.536	4.990	5.443	5.897	6.350	6.804	7.257	7.711	8.165	8.618	10
20	9.072	9.525	9.979	10.433	10.886	11.340	11.793	12.247	12.701	13.154	20
30	13.608	14.061	14.515	14.969	15.422	15.876	16.329	16.783	17.237	17.690	30
40	18.144	18.597	19.051	19.504	19.958	20.412	20.865	21.319	21.772	22.226	40
50	22.680	23.133	23.587	24.040	24.494	24.948	25.401	25.855	26.308	26.762	50
60	27.216	27.669	28.123	28.576	29.030	29.484	29.937	30.391	30.844	31.298	60
70	31.751	32.205	32.659	33.112	33.566	34.019	34.473	34.927	35.380	35.834	70
80	36.287	36.741	37.195	37.648	38.102	38.555	39.009	39.463	39.916	40.370	80
90	40.823	41.277	41.730	42.184	42.638	43.092	43.545	43.998	44.453	44.906	90
100	45.359	45.813	46.266	46.720	47.174	47.627	48.081	48.534	48.988	49.442	100

KILOGRAMS TO POUNDS

kg	0	1	2	3	4	5	6	7	8	9	kg
	lb	lb	lb	lb	lb	lb	lb	lb	lb	lb	
..		2.205	4.409	6.614	8.818	11.023	13.228	15.432	17.637	19.842	..
10	22.046	24.251	26.455	28.660	30.865	33.069	35.274	37.479	39.683	41.888	10
20	44.092	46.297	48.502	50.706	52.911	55.116	57.320	59.525	61.729	63.934	20
30	66.139	68.343	70.548	72.752	74.957	77.162	79.366	81.571	83.776	85.980	30
40	88.185	90.389	92.594	94.799	97.003	99.208	101.41	103.62	105.82	108.03	40
50	110.23	112.44	114.64	116.84	119.05	121.25	123.46	125.66	127.87	130.07	50
60	132.28	134.48	136.69	138.89	141.10	143.30	145.51	147.71	149.91	152.12	60
70	154.32	156.53	158.73	160.94	163.14	165.35	167.55	169.76	171.96	174.17	70
80	176.37	178.57	180.78	182.98	185.19	187.39	189.60	191.80	194.01	196.21	80
90	198.42	200.62	202.83	205.03	207.23	209.44	211.64	213.85	216.05	218.26	90
100	220.46	222.67	224.87	227.08	229.28	231.49	233.69	235.89	238.10	240.30	100

POUNDS PER SQUARE INCHES TO KILOPASCALS

lb/in^2	0	1	2	3	4	5	6	7	8	9	lb/in^2
	kPa	kPa	kPa	kPa	kPa	kPa	kPa	kPa	kPa	kPa	
..	0.0000	6.8948	13.7895	20.6843	27.5790	34.4738	41.3685	48.2663	55.1581	62.0528	..
10	68.9476	75.8423	82.7371	89.6318	96.5266	103.4214	110.3161	117.2109	124.1056	131.0004	10
20	137.8951	144.7899	151.6847	158.5794	165.4742	172.3689	179.2637	186.1584	193.0532	199.9480	20
30	206.8427	213.7375	220.6322	227.5270	234.4217	241.3165	248.2113	255.1060	262.0008	268.8955	30
40	275.7903	282.6850	289.5798	296.4746	303.3693	310.2641	317.1588	324.0536	330.9483	337.8431	40
50	344.7379	351.6326	358.5274	365.4221	372.3169	379.2116	386.1064	393.0012	399.8959	406.7907	50
60	412.6854	420.5802	427.4749	434.3697	441.2645	448.1592	455.0540	461.9487	468.8435	475.7382	60
70	482.6330	489.5278	496.4225	503.3173	510.2120	517.1068	524.0015	530.8963	537.7911	544.6858	70
80	551.5806	558.4753	565.3701	572.2648	579.1596	586.0544	592.9491	599.8439	606.7386	613.6334	80
90	620.5281	627.4229	634.3177	641.2124	648.1072	655.0019	661.8967	668.7914	675.6862	682.5810	90
100	689.4757	696.3705	703.2653	710.1601	717.0549	723.9497	730.8445	737.7393	744.6341	751.5289	100

119

KILOPASCALS TO POUNDS PER SQUARE INCHES

kPa	0	1	2	3	4	5	6	7	8	9	kPa
	lb/in^2	lb/in^2	lb/in^2	lb/in^2	lb/in^2	lb/in^2	lb/in^2	lb/in^2	lb/in^2	lb/in^2	
--		.1450	.2901	.4351	.5801	.7252	.8702	1.0153	1.1603	1.3053	--
10	1.4504	1.5954	1.7404	1.8855	2.0305	2.1556	2.3206	2.4656	2.6107	2.7557	10
20	2.9007	3.0458	3.1908	3.3359	3.4809	3.6259	3.7710	3.9160	4.0610	4.2061	20
30	4.3511	4.4961	4.6412	4.7862	4.9313	5.0763	5.2213	5.3664	5.5114	5.6564	30
40	5.8015	5.9465	6.0916	6.2366	6.3816	6.5267	6.6717	6.8167	6.9618	7.1068	40
50	7.2518	7.3969	7.5419	7.6870	7.8320	7.9770	8.1221	8.2671	8.4121	8.5572	50
60	8.7022	8.8473	8.9923	9.1373	9.1824	9.4274	9.5724	9.7175	9.8625	10.0076	60
70	10.1526	10.2976	10.4427	10.5877	10.7327	10.8778	11.0228	11.1678	11.3129	11.4579	70
80	11.6030	11.7480	11.8930	12.0381	12.1831	12.3281	12.4732	12.6182	12.7633	12.9083	80
90	13.0533	13.1984	13.3434	13.4884	13.6335	13.7785	13.9236	14.0686	14.2136	14.3587	90
100	14.5037	14.6487	14.7938	14.9388	15.0838	15.2289	15.3739	15.5190	15.6640	15.8090	100

POUND FEET TO NEWTON-METRES

ft-lb	0	1	2	3	4	5	6	7	8	9	ft-lb
	N·m	N·m	N·m	N·m	N·m	N·m	N·m	N·m	N·m	N·m	
--		1.3558	2.7116	4.0675	5.4233	6.7791	8.1349	9.4907	10.8465	12.2024	--
10	13.5582	14.9140	16.2698	17.6256	18.9815	20.3373	21.6931	23.0489	24.4047	25.7605	10
20	27.1164	28.4722	29.8280	31.1838	32.5396	33.8954	35.2513	36.6071	37.9629	39.3187	20
30	40.6745	42.0304	43.3862	44.7420	46.0978	47.4536	48.8094	50.1653	51.5211	52.8769	30
40	54.2327	55.5885	56.9444	58.3002	59.6560	61.0118	62.3676	63.7234	65.0793	66.4351	40
50	67.7909	69.1467	70.5025	71.8584	73.2142	74.5700	75.9258	77.2816	78.6374	79.9933	50
60	81.3491	82.7049	84.0607	85.4165	86.7724	88.1282	89.4840	90.3898	92.1956	93.5514	60
70	94.9073	96.2631	97.6189	98.9747	100.3305	101.6863	103.0422	104.3980	105.7538	107.1096	70
80	108.4654	109.8213	111.1771	112.5329	113.8887	115.2445	116.6003	117.9562	119.3120	120.6678	80
90	122.0236	123.3794	124.7353	126.0911	127.4469	128.8027	130.1585	131.5143	132.8702	134.2260	90
100	135.5818	136.9376	138.2934	139.6493	141.0051	142.3609	143.7167	145.0725	146.4283	147.7842	100

NEWTON-METRES TO POUND FEET

N·m	0	1	2	3	4	5	6	7	8	9	N·m
	ft-lb	ft-lb	ft-lb	ft-lb	ft-lb	ft-lb	ft-lb	ft-lb	ft-lb	ft-lb	
--		.7376	1.4751	2.2127	2.9502	3.6878	4.4254	5.1692	5.9005	6.6381	--
10	7.3756	8.1132	8.8507	9.5883	10.3258	11.0634	11.8010	12.5385	13.2761	14.0136	10
20	14.7512	15.4888	16.2264	16.9639	17.7015	18.4390	19.1766	19.9142	20.6517	21.3893	20
30	22.1269	22.8644	23.6020	24.3395	25.0771	25.8147	26.5522	27.2898	28.0274	28.7649	30
40	29.5025	30.2400	30.9776	31.7152	32.4527	33.1903	33.9279	34.6654	35.4030	36.1405	40
50	36.8781	37.6157	38.3532	39.0908	39.8283	40.5659	41.3035	42.0410	42.7786	43.5162	50
60	44.2537	44.9913	45.7288	46.4664	47.2040	47.9415	48.6791	49.4167	50.1542	50.8918	60
70	51.6293	52.3669	53.1045	53.8420	54.5796	55.3171	56.0547	56.7923	57.5298	58.2674	70
80	59.0050	59.7425	60.4801	61.2176	61.9552	62.6928	63.4303	64.1679	64.9055	65.6430	80
90	66.3806	67.1181	67.8557	68.5933	69.3308	70.0684	70.8060	71.5435	72.2811	73.0186	90
100	73.7562	74.4938	75.2313	75.9689	76.7064	77.4440	78.1816	78.9191	79.6567	80.3943	100

AMERICAN MOTORS

INDEX OF SERVICE OPERATIONS

NOTE: Refer to the rear of this manual for vehicle manufacturer's special service tool suppliers.

Vehicle Identification Number Location

Plate is attached to top of instrument panel, on driver's side.

Engine Identification

4-150 (1983–84): The engine code is located on a machined surface on the right side of the cylinder block between number three and four cylinders. The letter "U" denotes the 4-150 engine.

4-151 (1980–83): The engine code is located on a pad at the right front of the cylinder block below the cylinder head. The letter B denotes the 4-151 engine.

6-258 (1980–86): The engine code is located on a pad between number two and three cylinders. The letter "A" denotes the 258 engine with one barrel carburetor. The letter "C" denotes the 258 engine with two barrel carburetor. The letter "E" denotes the 232 engine.

Grille Identification

1980 Pacer

1980 AMX

1980 Eagle

1980 Spirit

1980 Concord

1980 Eagle Sport

1981–83 Concord

1981–83 Spirit

1981–83 Eagle SX/4 Sport

1981–86 Eagle

continued

General Engine Specifications

Year	Engine CID①/Liter	V.I.N. Code②	Carburetor	Bore and Stroke	Compression Ratio	Net H. P. @ R.P.M.③	Maximum Torque Ft. Lbs. @ R.P.M.	Normal Oil Pressure Pounds
1980	4-151, 2.5L	B	2SE, 2 Bbl.⑤	4.0 × 3.0	8.24	—	—	36–41
	6-258, 4.23L	C	BBD, 2 Bbl.④	3.75 × 3.90	8.3	—	—	37–75
1981	4-151, 2.5L	B	2SE, 2 Bbl.⑤⑥	4.0 × 3.0	8.24	—	—	36–41
	6-258, 4.23L	C	BBD, 2 Bbl.④	3.75 × 3.90	8.0	—	—	37–75
1982	4-151, 2.5L	B	2SE, 2 Bbl.⑤	4.0 × 3.0	8.24	—	—	36–41
	4-151, 2.5L	B	E2SE, 2 Bbl.⑤⑦	4.0 × 3.0	8.24	—	—	36–41
	6-258, 4.23L	C	BBD, 2 Bbl.④	3.75 × 3.90	8.6	—	—	37–75
1983	4-151, 2.5L	B	2SE, 2 Bbl.⑤⑥	4.0 × 3.0	8.2	—	—	36–41
1983–84	4-150, 2.46L	U	YFA, 1 Bbl.④⑧	3.88 × 3.19	9.2	—	132 @ 3200	37–75
1983–86	6-258, 4.23L	C	BBD, 2 Bbl.④	3.75 × 3.90	9.2	—	—	37–75

①—CID—cubic inch displacement.
②—On 1980 models, the seventh digit denotes engine code. On 1981–86 models, the fourth digit denotes engine code.
③—Ratings are net-as installed on vehicle.
④—Carter.
⑤—Rochester.
⑥—Calif. vehicles equipped with E2SE.
⑦—Calif. & auto trans. only.
⑧—Electronic Feedback Carburetor.

Valve Specifications

Year	Model/V.I.N.	Valve Lash Int.	Valve Lash Exh.	Valve Angles Seat	Valve Angles Face	Valve Spring Installed Height	Valve Spring Pressure Lbs. @ In.	Stem Clearance Intake	Stem Clearance Exhaust	Stem Diameter Intake	Stem Diameter Exhaust
1980–83	4-151/B	Hydraulic②	Hydraulic②	46	45	1.66	176 @ 1.254	.0010–.0027	.0010–.0027	.3418–.3425	.3418–.3425
1980–86	6-258/C	Hydraulic②	Hydraulic②	③	①	1.786	195 @ 1.411	.001–.003	.001–.003	.3715–.3725	.3715–.3725
1983–84	4-150/U	Hydraulic②	Hydraulic②	44½	44	1.625	213 @ 1.20	.001–.003	.001–.003	.3110–.3120	.3110–.3120

①—Intake 29°, exhaust 44°.
②—No adjustment.
③—Intake 30°, exhaust 44½°.

Pistons, Pins, Rings, Crankshaft & Bearings

Year	Model/ V.I.N.	Piston Clearance Top of Skirt	Ring End Gap① Comp.	Ring End Gap① Oil	Wrist-pin Diameter	Rod Bearings Shaft Diameter	Rod Bearings Bearing Clearance	Main Bearings Shaft Diameter	Main Bearings Bearing Clearance	Thrust on Bear. No.	Shaft End Play
1980–83	4-151/B	.0025–.0033	.010	.015	.92725	2.000	.0005–.0026	2.2998	.0005–.0022	5	.0035–.0085
1980–86	6-258/C	.0009–.0017	.010	.010	.9307	2.0934–2.0955	.001–.003	2.4986–2.5001	.001–.003	3	.0015–.0065
1983–84	4-150/U	.0009–.0017	.010	.010	.9307	2.0934–2.0955	.001–.003	2.4986–2.5001	.001–.002	2	.0015–.0065

①—Fit rings in tapered bores for clearance listed in tightest portion of ring travel.

continued

Engine Tightening Specifications★

★ Torque specifications are for clean and lightly lubricated threads only. Dry or dirty threads produce increased friction which prevents accurate measurement of tightness.

Year	Engine Model/V.I.N.	Spark Plugs Ft. Lbs.	Cylinder Head Bolts Ft. Lbs.	Intake Manifold Ft. Lbs.	Exhaust Manifold Ft. Lbs.	Rocker Arm Shaft Bracket Ft. Lbs.	Rocker Arm Cover Ft. Lbs.	Connecting Rod Cap Bolts Ft. Lbs.	Main Bearing Cap Bolts Ft. Lbs.	Flywheel to Crankshaft Ft. Lbs.	Vibration Damper or Pulley Ft. Lbs.
1983–84	4-150/U	27	85②	23	23	19③	28①	33	80	⑦	80⑤
1980	4-151/B	11	92	37	39	20④	7	30	65	68	160
1981–82	4-151/B	11	92	37	37	20③	7	30	65	68	160
1983	4-151/B	11	92	26	37	20③	7	30	65	68	162
1980	6-258/⑥	28	105	23	23	19③	50①	33	80	105	80⑤
1981	6-258/C	11	85	23	23	19③	28①	33	65	105	80⑤
1982–86	6-258/C	11	85②	23	23	19③	28①	33	80	105	80⑤

①—Inch pounds.
②—Coat underside of cylinder head bolt heads & threads with a suitable sealing compound.
③—Rocker arm cap screw.
④—Rocker arm stud nut.
⑤—Lubricate bolt threads lightly before assembly.
⑥—For V.I.N. code, refer to the "General Engine Specifications" at the front of chapter.
⑦—Torque bolts to 50 ft. lbs., then tighten bolts an additional 60 degrees.

Cooling System & Capacity Data

Year	Model or Engine/V.I.N.	Cooling Capacity, Qts.		Radiator Cap Relief Pressure, Lbs.	Thermo. Opening Temp.	Fuel Tank Gals.	Engine Oil Refill Qts. ①	Transmission Oil			Rear Axle Oils Pint
		Less A/C	With A/C					3 Speed Pints	4 & 5 Speed Pints	Auto. Trans. Qts. ②	
1980	4-151/B Spirit & Concord	6.5	6.5	14	195	13⑦	3⑨	—	3.3	7.1	3
	6-258/C Spirit, AMX & Concord	11	14	14	195	21⑦	4	—	3.3	8.5	3
	6-258/C Pacer	14	14	14	195	21	4	—	3.3	8.5	3
	6-258/C Eagle	11	14	14	195	22⑫	4	—	—	8.5⑥	3③
1981	4-151/B Spirit & Concord	6.5	6.5	15	195	21⑦	3⑨	—	3.3	7.1	3
	4-151/B Eagle	6.5	6.5	15	195	22⑫	3⑨	—	3.3⑥	7.1⑥	3③
	6-258/C Spirit & Concord	11⑪	14	15	195	21⑦	4	—	3.3	8.5	3
	6-258/C Eagle	14	14	15	195	22⑫	4	—	3.3⑥	8.5⑥	3③
1982	4-151/B Spirit & Concord	6.5	6.5	15	195	21⑦	3⑨	—	④	7.1	3
	4-151/B Eagle	6.5	6.5	15	195	22⑫	3⑨	—	④⑥	7.1⑥	3③
	6-258/C Spirit & Concord	11⑪	14	15	195	21⑦	4	—	④	8.5	3
	6-258/C Eagle	11⑪	14	15	195	22⑫	4	—	④⑥	8.5⑥	3③
1983	4-150/U Eagle	6.5	6.5	15	195	21	3½⑤	—	④⑥	7.1⑥	3③
	4-151/B Eagle	6.5	6.5	15	195	⑩	3⑨	—	④⑥	7.1⑥	3③
	6-258/C Spirit & Concord	11⑪	14	15	195	21⑦	4	—	⑧	8.5	3
	6-258/C Eagle	14	14	15	195	⑩	4	—	④⑥	8.5⑥	3③
1984	4-150/U Eagle	9	9	15	195	22	3½⑤	—	④⑥	7⑥	3③
	6-258/C Eagle	14	14	15	195	22	4	—	④⑥	7⑥	3③
1985–86	6-258/C Eagle	14	14	15	195	22	4	—	4	8.5⑥	3③

①—Add one quart with filter change.
②—Approximate. Make final check with dipstick.
③—Front Axle, 2.5 pts.
④—Four speed man. trans., 3.5 pts.; five speed man. trans., 4.0 pts.
⑤—Add ½ qt. with filter change.
⑥—Transfer Case, 3.0 qts.
⑦—Concord, 22 gal.
⑧—Four speed man. trans., 4 pts.; five speed man. trans., 4.5 pts.
⑨—With or without filter change.
⑩—Except SX-4, 22 gals.; SX-4, 21 gals.
⑪—With heavy duty cooling system, 14 qts.
⑫—Kammback & SX-4, 21 gals.

continued

Wheel Alignment Specifications

Year	Model	Caster Angle, Degrees		Camber Angle, Degrees				Toe In. Inch	Toe Out on Turns, Deg.①	
		Limits	Desired	Limits		Desired			Outer Wheel	Inner Wheel
				Left	Right	Left	Right			
1980	Eagle	+3 to +5	+4	−⅜ to +⅜	−⅜ to +⅜	Zero	Zero	¹⁄₁₆ to ³⁄₁₆	③	38
	Pacer	+1 to +3½	+2	0 to +¾	0 to +¾	+⅜	+⅜	¹⁄₁₆ to ³⁄₁₆	③	35
	AMX, Concord & Spirit	0 to +2½	+1	+⅛ to +¾	−⅛ to +½	+⅜	+⅛	¹⁄₁₆ to ³⁄₁₆	③	38
1981	Concord & Spirit	0 to +2½	+1	+⅛ to +¾	−⅛ to +½	+⅜	+⅛	¹⁄₁₆ to ³⁄₁₆	③	38
	Eagle	+2 to +3	+2½	−⅛ to +⅝	−⅛ to +⅝	+⅜	+⅜	②	③	38
1982–83	Concord & Spirit	+3½ to +5	+4½	+⅛ to +¾	−⅛ to +½	+⅜	+⅛	¹⁄₁₆ to ³⁄₁₆	—	—
1983–86	Eagle	+3 to +5	+4	+⅛ to +⅝	−⅛ to +⅝	+⅜	+⅜	¹⁄₁₆ to ³⁄₁₆	③	38

①—Incorrect toe-out when other adjustments are correct, indicates bent steering arms. ②—With Select Drive System, ⅛" toe-in; less Select Drive System ⅛" toe-out. ③—Wheels at full turn.

Alternator Specifications

Year	Alternator							Regulator			
	Make	Model	Ground Polarity	Rated Output		Field Current ①		Model	Regulator Test @ 120°F.		
				Amperes	Volts	Amperes	Volts		Ampere Load	Altern. R.P.M.	Volts
1980	Delco	—	Negative	42	—	4.0–5.0	—	1116387③	—	—	13.4–14.4
	Delco	—	Negative	55	—	4.0–5.0	—	1116387③	—	—	13.4–14.4
	Bosch	—	Negative	65	14	3.5–5.0	—	②	—	—	13.4–14.4
1981–82	Delco	—	Negative	42	—	4.0–5.0	—	1116387③	—	—	13.4–14.4
	Delco	—	Negative	55	—	4.0–5.0	—	1116387③	—	—	13.4–14.4
	Delco	—	Negative	63	—	4.0–5.0	—	1116387③	—	—	13.4–14.4
	Delco	—	Negative	70	—	4.0–5.0	—	1116387③	—	—	13.4–14.4
1983–86	Delco	—	Negative	42	—	4.0–5.0	—	1116387③	—	—	13.4–14.4
	Delco	—	Negative	56	—	4.0–5.0	—	1116387③	—	—	13.4–14.4
	Delco	—	Negative	66	—	4.0–5.0	—	1116387③	—	—	13.4–14.4
	Delco	—	Negative	78	—	4.0–5.0	—	1116387③	—	—	13.4–14.4

①—Excessive current drawn indicates shorted field winding. No current draw indicates an open winding. ②—B192052193B B14V3. ③—Integral regulator.

Starting Motor Applications

Year	Engine/V.I.N.	Starter Ident. No.
1980	6-258/A,C	3231372①
1980–83	4-151/B	1109526②
	4-151/B	3236659②
1981	6-258/C	3238665①
1982–86	6-258/C	E1FF-BA①
1983–84	4-150/U	E1FF-BA①

①—Motorcraft.
②—Delco-Remy.

Drive Axle Specifications

Year	Model	Carrier Type ②	Ring Gear & Pinion Backlash		Pinion Bearing Preload			Differential Bearing Preload		
			Method	Adjustment	Method	New Bearings Inch-Lbs.	Used Bearings Inch-Lbs.	Method	New Bearings Inch-Lbs.	Used Bearings Inch-Lbs.
1980–86	7⁹⁄₁₆" Dr. Gr.③	Integral	Shims	.005–.009	Sleeve	15–25①	15–25①	Shims	.008	.008
	MODEL 30④	Integral	Shims	.005–.010	Shims	20–40①	15–25①	Shims	.015	.015

①—Adjust at drive pinion flange nut with inch-pound torque wrench. Eagle front axle shaft end play, .003 inch. ③—Rear Axle.
②—Rear axle shaft end play, .006 inch. ④—Eagle front axle.

Electrical Section

STARTER
REPLACE

NOTE: If shims are used to position starter motor, note location of shims, as shims must be reinstalled in the same locations during starter installation.

EXCEPT EAGLE 6-258 & 1980—83 4-151

1. Disconnect battery ground cable.
2. Disconnect cable from starter motor terminal.
3. Remove attaching bolts and remove starter.
4. Reverse procedure to install.

EAGLE 6-258

Man. Trans.
1. Disconnect battery ground cable.
2. Disconnect cable from starter motor terminal.
3. Detach vibration bracket at front axle tube.
4. Remove bolts attaching bracket to flywheel housing, then loosen bolt at starter motor.
5. Swing bracket downward, away from starter motor, then remove remaining attaching bolt and starter motor.
6. Reverse procedure to install.

Auto. Trans.
1. Disconnect battery ground cable.
2. Disconnect cable from starter motor terminal.
3. Detach front section of bracket from front axle tube, then detach rear section of bracket from converter housing.
4. Remove attaching bolts and starter motor.
5. Reverse procedure to install.

Fig. 1   Lock cylinder removal

1980—83 4-151

1. Disconnect battery ground cable, then remove starter motor to engine brace. On Eagle models it may be necessary to remove an additional brace to remove starter motor.
2. Remove two starter motor to engine attaching bolts, then lower starter motor and disconnect wiring from solenoid.
3. Remove starter motor from vehicle.
4. Reverse procedure to install. Reinstall any shims that were removed.

IGNITION LOCK
REPLACE

1. Remove turn signal switch as described further on.
2. Place key lock in "Lock" position and using a small flat blade screwdriver to depress the lock cylinder retaining tab,

remove the lock cylinder, **Fig. 1.**
3. Reverse procedure to install.

IGNITION SWITCH
REPLACE

NOTE: On Pacer models, it may be necessary to remove steering tube cover and A/C duct to gain access to ignition switch. On Concord, Eagle and Spirit models, remove package tray, if equipped.

The ignition switch, **Fig. 2,** is mounted on the lower section of the steering column of all models and is connected to the steering lock by a remote control rod.

REMOVAL

1. Disconnect battery ground cable.
2. Place ignition lock in "Off-Lock" position and remove switch attaching screws.
3. Disconnect switch from control rod and wiring connectors from switch, then remove switch from steering column.

INSTALLATION

1. On standard steering columns, move slider to extreme left and on tilt steering columns, move slider to extreme right. This places the switch in the "Accessory" position.
2. Place actuator rod in slider hole and install switch on steering column without moving slider out of detent. Hold key in "Accessory" position and push switch downward to remove slack in linkage and tighten screws.
3. Connect battery ground cable and check for proper operation.

Fig. 2   Ignition switch installation (typical)

Fig. 3   Stoplight switch (typical)

Fig. 4   Compressing lock plate & removing retaining ring

Fig. 5   Turn signal switch

Fig. 6   Taping turn signal connector & wires

LIGHT SWITCH
REPLACE

CONCORD, EAGLE & SPIRIT

1. Disconnect battery ground cable.
2. Remove package tray, if equipped, and disconnect speedometer cable.
3. Remove instrument cluster bezel attaching screws and tilt bezel away from instrument panel.
4. With switch in full "On" position, press release button on switch and remove shaft and knob assembly.
5. Remove switch mounting sleeve nut.
6. Disconnect electrical connectors from switch and remove switch from vehicle.
7. Reverse procedure to install.

PACER

1. Disconnect battery ground cable.
2. Remove switch overlay attaching screws and pull overlay assembly rearward.
3. With switch in full "On" position, press release button on switch and remove shaft and knob assembly.
4. Remove switch mounting sleeve nut.
5. Disconnect electrical connectors from switch and remove switch from vehicle.
6. Reverse procedure to install.

STOP LIGHT SWITCH
REPLACE

1. Disconnect battery ground cable.
2. On Concord, Eagle and Spirit models, remove package tray, if equipped.
3. On Pacer models, remove steering column tube cover and intermediate duct under instrument panel, if equipped with A/C.
4. On all models, disconnect wire connector from switch.
5. Remove brake pedal pivot bolt, nylon retaining rings, sleeve, and remove switch.

6. When installing switch, be sure dimple on switch is opposite the bushing collar, **Fig. 3**.

NOTE: There are two bolt holes on the brake pedal. On models equipped with power brakes, install bolt in lower hole. On models less power brakes, install bolt in upper hole.

7. Reverse procedure to install.

Fig. 7   Instrument cluster (typical). Concord, Eagle & Spirit

AMERICAN MOTORS

NEUTRAL SAFETY SWITCH
REPLACE

EXCEPT 1980–83 4-151

1. Raise and support vehicle.
2. Disconnect wiring from switch and unscrew from transmission. Allow fluid to drain into a container.
3. Move shift linkage to park and neutral positions and check switch operating fingers for proper positioning.
4. Reverse procedure to install. Correct transmission fluid level as required.

TURN SIGNAL SWITCH
REPLACE

1. Disconnect battery ground cable, then remove steering wheel.
2. Using lock plate compressor tool No. J-23653, depress lock plate and remove and pry round wire snap ring from steering shaft groove, **Fig. 4.**

NOTE: On some models, the steering shaft has metric threads and is identified by a blue colored steering wheel nut and/or a groove cut into the steering shaft splines. If shaft has metric threads, replace compressor forcing screw with metric forcing screw J-23653-4 to depress lock plate.

3. Remove lock plate compressor tool, snap ring, lock plate and directional signal canceling cam from steering shaft.
4. Place directional signal lever in the right turn position, then remove lever and directional signal switch mounting screws, **Fig. 5.**
5. Depress hazard warning switch and remove button by turning in counter clockwise direction.
6. Remove directional signal switch wiring harness connector from mounting bracket on right side of lower column.
7. On Concord, Eagle, Pacer & Spirit models, remove steering tube cover.
8. Remove steering column lower bracket bolts, then loosen steering column bracket nuts.
9. Fold connector over harness and wrap with tape to avoid snagging, **Fig. 6.** Raise column and pull harness out of column.

NOTE: On models with tilt column, raise column and remove plastic wiring harness protector.

10. On Concord models, with column shift, automatic transmission, use stiff wire, such as a paper clip, to depress lock tab which retains shift quadrant light wire to wiring harness connector. The shift quadrant light wire is the grey wire connected to terminal D on wiring harness connector.
11. Reverse procedure to install.

HORN SOUNDER & STEERING WHEEL
REPLACE

1. Disconnect battery ground cable.
2. On steering wheels with horn buttons, remove button by first lifting button upward, and then pulling button out. On steering wheels equipped with horn ring or bar, remove screws from back of steering wheel, then pull wire plastic retainer out of directional signal canceling cam and remove horn ring or bar.
3. Remove steering wheel nut and washer. Note alignment marks on steering wheel and shaft for use during installation. If marks are not present, paint alignment marks on shaft and steering wheel.

NOTE: Some steering shafts have metric steering wheel nut threads. Metric steering wheel nuts are color coded blue for identification and steering shafts will have an identifying groove on shaft steering wheel splines.

4. Using a suitable puller, remove steering wheel.
5. Reverse procedure to install.

INSTRUMENT CLUSTER
REPLACE

AMX, CONCORD, EAGLE & SPIRIT

1. Disconnect battery ground cable.
2. On 1980–85 Concord, Eagle and Spirit models, remove lower steering column cover. On models equipped with column shift automatic transmission, remove gear selector dial actuator cable from steering column shift shroud.
3. On all models, remove instrument cluster bezel attaching screws across top of bezel, above radio and behind glove box door.
4. Tip top of bezel outward and disengage tabs along bottom edge of bezel.
5. If equipped, disconnect glove box lamp wire connector.
6. Depress speedometer cable locking tab and disconnect speedometer cable.
7. Push downward on three illumination lamp housings above bezel, until lamp housings are clear of instrument panel.
8. Disconnect headlamp switch and wiper control connectors and switch lamp.

NOTE: To disconnect headlamp switch connector, lift two locking tabs.

9. Twist and remove cluster illumination lamp sockets, then disconnect instru-

ment cluster wire connectors.
10. Remove clock or tachometer attaching screws, if equipped. It is not necessary to remove clock adjusting knob.
11. Disconnect clock or tachometer feed wires from circuit board, if equipped.
12. Remove cluster housing and circuit board to bezel attaching screws.
13. Remove cluster housing and circuit board assembly from bezel, **Fig. 7.** If equipped with clock or tachometer, position aside as necessary.

PACER

1. Disconnect battery ground cable.
2. Remove cluster bezel.
3. Remove radio knobs and nuts, then remove radio overlay.
4. Remove headlamp switch overlay retaining screws, then pull overlay back so that speedometer cable can be removed.
5. Remove cluster retaining screws, disconnect wiring harness and gear selector cable if equipped, then remove cluster assembly, **Fig. 8.**

NOTE: On models equipped with automatic transmission, remove steering tube cover.

6. Reverse procedure to install.

W/S WIPER MOTOR
REPLACE

PACER

1. Disconnect battery ground cable and disconnect linkage drive arm from motor crankpin.
2. Remove vacuum canister and mounting bracket assembly, if necessary.
3. On models equipped with air conditioning, remove two nuts from left side of heater housing and one nut from the right side of the housing.
4. On models not equipped with air conditioning, remove two nuts and one screw from left side of heater housing and one nut from the right side of the housing.
5. On all models, remove screw from heater housing support.
6. Pull heater housing forward.
7. Remove screws from wiper motor mounting plate and disconnect wiring harness.
8. Remove attaching screws and wiper motor.
9. Reverse procedure to install.

NOTE: Ensure output arm is in parked position before installing wiper motor.

EXC. PACER

1. Disconnect battery ground cable. Remove wiper arms and blades.
2. Remove four screws holding motor to dash.

3. Separate harness connector at the motor.
4. Pull motor and linkage out of opening to expose the drive link to crank stud retaining clip. Raise up the lock tab of the clip with a flat bladed screwdriver and slide clip off stud.
5. Reverse procedure to install.

LIFTGATE WIPER MOTOR
REPLACE

1. Disconnect battery ground cable. Remove wiper arm and blade.
2. Remove liftgate trim pad.
3. Disconnect wiring harness and ground wire.
4. Remove nut and pad securing wiper motor shaft to liftgate.
5. Remove screws securing wiper motor bracket, then separate bracket from motor.
6. Reverse procedure to install.

W/S WIPER TRANSMISSION
REPLACE

PACER

1. Disconnect battery ground cable and remove wiper arms and blades.
2. Remove pivot shaft bodies to cowl screws using tool No. J-25359-02.
3. Disconnect linkage from motor output arm, then remove pivot shaft body assembly.
4. Reverse procedure to install.

AMX, CONCORD, EAGLE, & SPIRIT

1. Disconnect battery ground cable. Remove wiper arms and blades.
2. Remove pivot shaft-to-cowl top nuts.
3. Remove wiper motor.
4. Slide pivot shaft body and link assembly to the left to clear right pivot shaft opening and move assembly to the right side of car to remove as a unit.
5. Reverse procedure to install.

NOTE: When installing pivot shafts to cowl top, flat side of pivot shaft indexes flat side of hole in cowl top when pivot shaft is in up position.

W/S WIPER SWITCH
REPLACE

PACER

1. Disconnect battery ground cable. Using a small screwdriver, remove knob from switch by releasing tension on clip.
2. Remove bezel from instrument cluster by pulling toward rear of vehicle.
3. Remove four screws attaching head-

Fig. 8   Instrument cluster (typical). Pacer

lamp switch overlay, then pull toward rear of vehicle to gain access to rear of w/s wiper switch.
4. Remove connector from rear of switch.
5. Remove two screws attaching switch to instrument panel, then remove switch.
6. Reverse procedure to install.

ALL EXC. PACER

1. Disconnect battery ground cable.
2. Locate small notch at base of knob and insert a small screwdriver and apply pressure to release spring and pull knob from shaft.
3. Remove slotted trim nut from front of switch.
4. Push switch through instrument panel, then disconnect wiring harness and remove switch.
5. Reverse procedure to install.

RADIO
REPLACE

NOTE: When installing radio, be sure to adjust antenna trimmer for peak performance.

CONCORD, EAGLE & SPIRIT

1. Disconnect battery ground cable.
2. Remove radio knobs and retaining nuts. On models equipped with C.B. radio, remove radio bezel.
3. Remove instrument cluster center

housing retaining screws, then remove center housing.
4. Disconnect power and speaker wiring and antenna lead, then remove radio.
5. Reverse procedure to install.

PACER

1. Disconnect battery ground cable.
2. Remove radio knobs, nuts and bezels, then the radio overlay.
3. Loosen radio attaching screws and lift radio from mounting bracket.
4. Disconnect antenna lead and wire connectors and remove radio.
5. Reverse procedure to install.

HEATER CORE
REPLACE

PACER

1. Disconnect battery ground cable.
2. Drain approximately 2 qts. from cooling system.
3. Remove heater hoses and install plugs in hoses and core openings, **Fig. 2**.
4. Position vacuum hoses away from core housing.
5. On models with A/C, disconnect outside air door vacuum hose from vacuum motor.
6. Remove core housing cover screws, disconnect overcenter spring and remove cover.
7. Remove screws attaching core to

housing and remove core.

8. Reverse procedure to install.

AMX, CONCORD, EAGLE & SPIRIT

1. Disconnect battery ground cable, then drain about 2 qts. from cooling system.
2. Disconnect heater hoses and plug heater core tubes.
3. Remove blower motor and fan.
4. Remove housing attaching nut(s) from inside engine compartment.
5. Remove package tray if so equipped.
6. Disconnect wire connector at resistor.
7. On models with A/C, remove instrument panel bezel, outlet and duct.
8. Disconnect control cables from damper levers.
9. Remove right side windshield pillar moulding and the instrument panel upper attaching screws and right side cap screw at the door hinge post.
10. Remove right side kick panel and heater housing attaching screws.
11. Pull the right side of the instrument panel slightly rearward and remove the housing.
12. Remove cover and screws attaching heater core to housing, then remove heater core from housing.
13. Reverse procedure to install.

Fig. 9   Heater & blower housing assembly. Pacer (Typical)

BLOWER MOTOR
REPLACE

PACER

Less Air Conditioning
1. Disconnect battery ground cable.
2. Remove right side windshield moulding, then the instrument panel crash pad.
3. Remove right scuff plate and cowl panel.
4. Remove lower instrument panel to pillar attaching screws, then pull instrument panel rearward and reinstall attaching screws, allowing panel to rest on screws.
5. Remove heater core housing attaching nuts and screw, position vacuum lines aside, disconnect air door, then pull housing forward and position on upper control arm.
6. Remove blower motor attaching screws, disconnect relay ground wire and resistor wiring.
7. Remove blower motor brace.
8. Loosen heater housing to instrument panel attaching nuts.
9. Pull blower motor housing rearward and downward, disconnect vacuum hoses from motors and remove blower housing.
10. Remove housing cover, disconnect wire and remove blower to housing attaching screws.
11. Remove blower from housing, then separate fan and mounting bracket from motor.
12. Reverse procedure to install.

With Air Conditioning
1. Disconnect battery ground cable.
2. Remove right scuff plate and cowl panel.
3. Remove radio overlay, then the instrument panel crash pad.
4. Remove instrument panel to right pillar attaching screws, then the upper to lower instrument panel attaching screws, located above glove box.
5. Disconnect air door cable from heater core housing and remove housing to floor pan brace screw.
6. Disconnect wires from blower motor resistor and vacuum lines from vacuum motors.
7. Remove heater core housing attaching nuts and screw, position vacuum lines aside, then pull housing forward and position on upper control arm.
8. Remove floor duct.

Fig. 10   Centering adjusting screw location.

9. Disconnect wires from blower motor relay and remove blower motor housing attaching screw from firewall.
10. Loosen evaporator housing to dash panel attaching nuts, remove blower motor housing attaching screw from dash panel, then pull blower housing rearward and downward.
11. Pull right side of instrument panel rearward and remove blower motor.
12. Remove blower housing cover.
13. Remove blower motor from housing, the separate fan and mounting bracket from motor.
14. Reverse procedure to install.

AMX, CONCORD, EAGLE & SPIRIT

1. Disconnect battery ground cable.
2. Working in engine compartment, disconnect blower motor wire.
3. Remove three retaining nuts for blower scroll cover to which blower assembly is attached and remove blower motor and fan.
4. Reverse procedure to install.

SPEED CONTROL
ADJUST

CENTERING ADJUSTMENT

This adjustment is made by turning the centering adjusting screw on the regulator, **Fig. 10.** If speed control engages at two or more mph higher than selected speed, turn centering adjusting screw counter clockwise a small amount. If engagement speed is two or more mph below selected speed, turn centering adjusting screw clockwise a

small amount. Check for proper centering adjustment on a level road after making each adjustment.

VACUUM DUMP VALVE

While holding brake pedal in the depressed position, move vacuum dump valve toward pedal bracket as far as possible, then release brake pedal.

4-150 Engine Section

ENGINE MOUNTS
REPLACE

Removal or replacement of any cushion can be accomplished by supporting the weight of the engine or transmission at the area of the cushion to be replaced.

ENGINE
REPLACE

The engine is removed without the transmission as follows:
1. Drain cooling system.
2. Mark hood hinge locations, disconnect underhood lamp, if equipped, and remove hood.
3. Disconnect battery cables, and remove battery.
4. Disconnect alternator wiring and the ignition coil, distributor and oil pressure sender leads.
5. Remove TCS switch bracket from cylinder block, if equipped.
6. Disconnect flexible fuel line from fuel pump and plug line and pump port.
7. Disconnect engine ground strap.
8. Remove the right front engine support cushion to bracket screw.
9. If equipped with air conditioning:
   a. Remove service valve covers and front seat valves.
   b. Loosen service valve to compressor attaching nuts.
   c. Bleed compressor refrigerant charge.
   d. Remove service valves and cap compressor ports and service valves.
   e. Disconnect clutch feed wire.
10. Remove starter.
11. Remove air cleaner and disconnect purge hose from canister and TAC vacuum hose from manifold, if equipped.
12. Disconnect throttle stop solenoid lead, if equipped.
13. Disconnect fuel return hose from fuel filter and the carburetor bowl vent hose from canister.
14. Disconnect throttle cable and remove from bracket. Disconnect throttle valve rod at carburetor and the bellcrank.
15. Disconnect heater and air conditioning system vacuum hose from intake manifold.
16. Disconnect temperature sender wire and TCS vacuum solenoid wiring harness.
17. Disconnect radiator hoses from radiator and the heater hoses from engine.

18. Disconnect transmission oil cooler lines from radiator, if equipped.
19. Remove fan shroud attaching screws, then the radiator and shroud.
20. Remove fan and spacer. Install a 5/16 × 1/2 inch capscrew through fan pulley, into water pump flange.
21. Remove power brake vacuum check valve from power brake unit, if equipped.
22. If equipped with power steering, disconnect hoses from gear and drain reservoir. Cap gear ports and hoses.
23. Remove transmission filler tube bracket screw, if equipped.
24. Raise and support vehicle on jackstands.
25. If equipped with automatic transmission:
   a. Remove converter housing spacer cover.
   b. Remove converter attaching screws.
   c. Remove exhaust pipe support from converter housing. This also supports the inner end of the transmission linkage.
26. If equipped with manual transmission:
   a. Remove clutch housing cover and clutch bellcrank inner support screws.
   b. Disconnect springs and remove bellcrank.
   c. Remove outer bellcrank to strut rod bracket retainer.
   d. Disconnect back-up lamp switch wiring harness under hood at dash panel to gain access to clutch housing screw.
27. On all models, remove engine mount cushion to bracket screws.
28. To remove front axle assembly, proceed as follows:
   a. Support axle assembly, then remove half shaft to axle flange attaching bolts.
   b. Compress half shafts inward, toward wheels, and secure to

frame side sills with wire.
   c. Remove axle bracket attaching bolts at axle tube and right hand engine mount, then remove axle bracket.
   d. Remove axle bracket attaching bolts at pinion end of axle.
   e. Remove left engine mount support to front axle bracket attaching bolts.
   f. Disconnect axle vent hose, then lower axle assembly and remove from vehicle.
29. Disconnect exhaust pipe from manifold.
30. Remove upper converter or clutch housing screws and loosen the bottom screws.
31. Raise vehicle and support on jackstands.
32. Remove air conditioning compressor drive belt idler pulley and the compressor mounting bracket, if equipped.
33. Install suitable engine lifting equipment and slightly raise engine. Support transmission with a suitable jack.
34. Remove remaining converter or clutch housing screws.
35. Remove engine from vehicle.
36. Reverse procedure to install.

CYLINDER HEAD
REPLACE

1. Disconnect battery ground cable, then drain cooling system.
2. Remove intake and exhaust manifold bolts. Remove manifolds and intake manifold gasket.
3. Remove valve cover bolts and valve cover.
4. Alternately loosen rocker arm capscrews, then remove bridges, pivots and rocker arms.
5. Remove push rods and spark plugs.
6. Remove cylinder head bolts and cylinder head.
7. Reverse procedure to install. Coat cylinder head gasket with a suitable sealer and install gasket with the word "TOP" facing upward. Install cylinder head bolts and torque to specifications in sequence, **Fig. 1.** Coat threads of stud No. 8 with a suitable sealer and torque nut to 75 ft. lbs. Torque intake and exhaust manifold bolts to 23 ft. lbs. in sequence, **Fig. 2.**

Fig. 1 Cylinder head tightening sequence. 4-150

VALVE ARRANGEMENT

FRONT TO REAR

4-150 .... E-I-I-E-E-I-I-E

VALVE LIFT SPECS.

Engine	Year	Intake	Exhaust
4-150	1983–84	.424	.424

VALVE TIMING SPECS.

Intake Opens Before TDC

Engine	Year	Degrees
4-150	1983–84	12

ROCKER ARMS
REPLACE

1. Remove rocker arm cover attaching screws, then remove rocker arm cover.

NOTE: RTV sealant is used between rocker arm cover and cylinder head mating surfaces. To avoid damaging rocker arm cover, do not pry cover upward until seal has been completely broken. When prying cover upward, pry only in areas marked "Pry Here," which are located near rocker arm cover bolt holes.

2. Alternately loosen the rocker arm cap screws one turn at a time to prevent damage to bridge, **Fig. 3**.
3. After removing rocker arm cap screws, remove bridge, pivots, rocker arms and push rods.

Fig. 3 Rocker arm, bridge & pivot assembly. 4-150

Fig. 2 Intake & exhaust manifold tightening sequence. 4-150

NOTE: Tag all components so they can be reinstalled in the same position as removed.

4. Reverse procedure to install. When installing rocker arm cap screws, tighten each screw alternately and evenly approximately one turn at a time to prevent damage to bridge.

VALVE GUIDES

The valve guides are an integral part of the cylinder head. If valve stem to guide clearance is excessive, the guide should be reamed to the next oversize and the appropriate oversize valve installed. Valves are available in standard size and oversizes of .003 inch and .015 inch.

VALVE LIFTERS
REPLACE

1. Remove cylinder head cover.
2. Alternately loosen each capscrew one turn at a time, then remove bridge and pivot assemblies, rocker arms and push rods.

NOTE: Tag all components so they can be reinstalled in the same positions.

3. Using tool No. J-21884 or equivalent, remove valve lifters through push rod openings in cylinder head, **Fig. 4**.

NOTE: If lifters are to be reused, retain in same order as removed.

4. Reverse procedure to install. Before installing, dip each lifter in American Motors Engine Oil Supplement or equivalent. Tighten bridge and pivot assembly capscrews one turn at a time to prevent damage to bridge.

TIMING CASE COVER & TIMING CHAIN
REPLACE

REMOVAL

1. Disconnect battery ground cable, then

drain cooling system.
2. Remove bolts securing water and fuel pumps to engine, then remove water and fuel pumps.
3. Remove crankshaft pulley bolts and pulley.
4. Using tool No. J-9256 or equivalent, remove timing chain cover seal.
5. Remove timing chain cover bolts and cover.
6. Remove timing chain tensioner, **Fig. 5**.
7. Remove crankshaft oil slinger.
8. Remove camshaft sprocket retaining bolt and washer, then lift off camshaft sprocket, crankshaft sprocket and timing chain as an assembly, **Fig. 6**.

INSTALLATION

1. Install crankshaft sprocket, camshaft sprocket and timing chain as an assembly. Ensure crankshaft and camshaft sprocket timing marks are aligned, **Fig. 7**.
2. Install camshaft sprocket retaining bolt and washer. Torque camshaft sprocket retaining bolt to 50 ft. lbs.

NOTE: To verify correct installation of timing chain, rotate crankshaft to position camshaft sprocket timing mark at one o'clock, **Fig. 8**. The crankshaft sprocket timing mark should now be at the three o'clock position. There should be 20 timing chain pins between the timing marks of both sprockets.

3. Install timing chain tensioner as follows:
   a. Turn tensioner lever to unlock (down) position, **Fig. 9**.

Fig. 4 Hydraulic valve lifter assembly. 4-150

Exploded view of cylinder head, intake & exhaust manifolds. 4-150

OIL FILLER CAP

VENTILATION VALVE

GROMMET

CYLINDER HEAD (ROCKER) COVER

BRIDGE

PIVOT

VALVE LOCKS

ROCKER ARM

VALVE SPRING

RETAINER

OIL DEFLECTOR

PUSH ROD

CYLINDER HEAD STUD

CYLINDER HEAD BOLT

CYLINDER HEAD CORE PLUG

CYLINDER HEAD

PLUG

DOWEL PIN

SNAP RING

TAPPET

INTAKE MANIFOLD GASKET

HOSE FITTING

VALVE

INTAKE MANIFOLD

PLUG

EXHAUST MANIFOLD

O-RING

GASKET

INTAKE MANIFOLD HEATER

HEAT STOVE

Fig. 5   Removing timing chain cover. 4-150

Fig. 7   Valve timing marks. 4-150

Fig. 9   Position timing chain tensioner in the unlock position. 4-150

Fig. 6   Removing timing chain & gear sprockets. 4-150

Fig. 8   Timing chain installation check. 4-150

Fig. 10   Using tool No. J-22248 to align timing case cover. 4-150

b. Pull tensioner block toward tensioner lever. Hold tensioner block and turn tensioner lever to lock (up) position.

c. Install timing chain tensioner on cylinder block and torque bolts to 14 ft. lbs.

d. Turn timing chain lever to unlock (down) position. Ensure tensioner is released before installing timing chain cover.

4. Install oil slinger.

5. Using tool No. J-22248 or equivalent for timing chain cover alignment, install timing chain cover, **Fig. 10.** Torque cover bolts to 5 ft. lbs.

6. Coat outside diameter of the timing chain cover seal with suitable sealer and install cover seal. With cover seal in position, coat inside diameter of seal lip with clean engine oil.

7. Insert draw screw of tool No. J-91632 or equivalent into tool No. J-22248, **Fig. 11.** Tighten draw screw nut until tool comes in contact with timing chain cover.

8. Reverse steps 1 through 3 to complete installation procedure.

CAMSHAFT
REPLACE

1. Drain cooling system, then remove radiator.

2. Remove A/C condenser and receiver assembly with refrigerant hoses attached and position aside. Do not discharge system.

3. Remove valve lifters as described under "Valve Lifters, Replace."

4. Remove timing case cover and timing chain as described under "Timing Case Cover and Timing Chain, Replace."

5. Remove camshaft.

6. Reverse procedure to install.

PISTON & ROD ASSEMBLE

Pistons are marked with an arrow on the

Fig. 11   Installing timing case cover front seal. 4-150

top perimeter, **Fig. 12.** When installing piston in engine, the arrow must face toward front of engine. Always assemble rods and caps with oil squirt holes facing camshaft. Check side clearance between connecting rod and crankshaft journal. Clearance should be .010 to .019 inch.

MAIN BEARINGS

The main bearing journal size (diameter) is identified by a color coded paint mark on adjacent cheek toward flanged (rear) end of crankshaft, except for rear main journal which is on crankshaft rear flange. Color codes used to indicate journal and corresponding bearing sizes are listed in **Figs. 13 and 14.**

CONNECTING ROD BEARINGS

The connecting rod journal is identified by a color coded paint mark on adjacent cheek or counterweight toward flanged (rear) end of crankshaft. Color codes used to indicate journal sizes and corresponding bearing sizes are listed in **Fig. 15.**

NOTE: Do not intermix the bearing caps. Each connecting rod and its bearing cap are stamped with the corresponding cylinder number.

RING SET

PISTON

PIN SET

CONNECTING ROD

OIL LEVEL GAUGE
(DIPSTICK) AND TUBE

PLUGS

OIL CHANNEL
PLUG

CYLINDER BLOCK

CAMSHAFT

FLYWHEEL AND RING GEAR
(W/MANUAL TRANSMISSION)

PIN

PILOT BUSHING
(WITH MANUAL
TRANSMISSION)

CRANKSHAFT

CAMSHAFT
SPROCKET

TIMING
CHAIN
TENSIONER

KEYS

TIMING CHAIN

WASHER

BUSHING OIL WICK (WITH
MANUAL TRANSMISSION)

MAIN BEARING CAP SEAL
KIT (REAR)

MAIN BEARING CAP
(REAR)

MAIN
BEARINGS

CRANKSHAFT
SPROCKET

CONNECTING
ROD
BEARING
CAP

CONNECTING ROD
BEARING

OIL SHEDDER
(SLINGER)

MAIN
BEARINGS
CAPS

VIBRATION DAMPER
PULLEY

GASKET

WASHER

TIMING CASE COVER

SEAL

VIBRATION DAMPER

Exploded view of cylinder block & components. 4-150

OIL PAN
REPLACE

1. Disconnect battery ground cable.
2. Drain engine oil.
3. Lock steering wheel and remove air cleaner.
4. Support engine using a suitable holding fixture.
5. Raise vehicle and support on side sills.
6. Mark for assembly reference and disconnect front driveshaft.
7. Remove engine cushion bolts.
8. Remove bolts from sill-to-crossmember and position bar aside.
9. Loosen pitman arm at gear, then loosen idler arm at steering linkage.
10. Remove bolt from steering damper at crossmember.
11. Loosen sway bar bolts and lower sway bar bolts and lower sway bar.
12. Disconnect half shafts from axle.

NOTE: Compress half shafts in toward wheels, secure in compressed position with wire attached to frame sills.

13. Remove bolts from right bracket at axle tube bolt bars, then remove bolts from left upper axle bracket at upper end, and bolts from pinion end bracket at pinion.
14. Remove vent hose and remove axle assembly.
15. Support crossmembers with jack and remove crossmember nuts and bolts, then lower crossmember assembly for clearance.
16. Remove starter motor, then the torque converter housing access cover.
17. Remove oil pan screws and remove oil pan, **Fig. 16.**
18. Reverse procedure to install.

ARROW TOWARD FRONT OF ENGINE

OIL HOLE TOWARD CAMSHAFT

Fig. 12   Piston & rod assemble. 4-150

OIL PUMP
REPLACE

1. Drain crankcase, then remove oil pan, **Fig. 16.**
2. Remove bolts attaching oil pump to cylinder block, then remove oil pump and gasket.

NOTE: Do not disturb positioning of oil pump strainer and tube. If tube is moved a replacement tube and screen assembly must be installed.

3. Reverse procedure to install. Torque short attaching bolts to 10 ft. lbs. and long attaching bolts to 17 ft. lbs.

OIL PUMP SERVICE

1. Remove oil pump cover retaining screws, then remove cover from pump body.
2. Check gear end clearance as follows:
   a. Place straight edge across ends of gears and pump body, **Fig. 17.**
   b. Check clearance using a suitable feeler gauge.
   c. Clearance should be .002 to .006 inch. If clearance is not within limits, replace oil pump assembly.
3. Check gear to pump body clearance as follows:
   a. Insert a suitable feeler gauge between gear tooth and pump body, **Fig. 18.**
   b. Clearance should be .002 to .004 inch. If clearance is not within limits, replace idler gear, idler shaft and drive gear assembly.
4. If pressure relief valve is to be checked, move pickup tube and screen assembly out of way. Remove spring retainer, spring and oil pressure relief valve plunger. Check pressure relief valve components for binding and clean or replace as necessary. After reinstalling relief valve components, install a replacement pickup tube and screen assembly.

NOTE: When replacing relief valve plung-

Crankshaft No. 1 Main Bearing Journal Color Codes and Diameter in Inches (mm)	Cylinder Block No. 1 Main Bearing Bore Color Code and Size in Inches (mm)		Bearing Insert Color Code	
			Upper Insert Size	Lower Insert Size
Yellow — 2.5001 to 2.4996 (Standard) (63.5025 to 63.4898 mm)	Yellow —	2.6910 to 2.6915 (68.3514 to 68.3641 mm)	Yellow — Standard	Yellow — Standard
	Black —	2.6915 to 2.6920 (68.3641 to 68.3768 mm)	Yellow — Standard	Black — 0.001-inch Undersize (0.025 mm)
Orange — 2.4996 to 2.4991 (0.0005 Undersize) (63.4898 to 63.4771 mm)	Yellow —	2.6910 to 2.6915 (68.3514 to 68.3641 mm)	Yellow — Standard	Black — 0.001-inch Undersize — (0.001 mm)
	Black —	2.6915 to 2.6920 (68.3461 to 68.3768 mm)	Black — 0.001-inch Undersize (0.025 mm)	Black — 0.001-inch Undersize (0.025 mm)
Black — 2.4991 to 2.4986 (0.001 Undersize) (63.4771 to 63.4644 mm)	Yellow —	2.6910 to 2.6915 (68.3514 to 68.3641 mm)	Black — 0.001-inch Undersize — (0.025 mm)	Black — 0.001-inch Undersize — (0.025 mm)
	Black —	2.6915 to 2.6920 (68.3461 to 68.3768 mm)	Black — 0.001-inch Undersize (0.025 mm)	Green — 0.002-inch Undersize (0.051 mm)
Green — 2.4986 to 2.4981 (0.0015 Undersize) (63.4644 to 63.4517 mm)	Yellow —	2.6910 to 2.6915 (68.3514 to 68.3641 mm)	Black — 0.001-inch Undersize — (0.025 mm)	Green — 0.002-inch Undersize (0.051 mm)
Red — 2.4901 to 2.4896 (0.010 Undersize) (63.2485 to 63.2358 mm)	Yellow —	2.6910 to 2.6915 (68.3514 to 68.3641 mm)	Red — 0.010-inch Undersize (0.254 mm)	Red — 0.010-inch Undersize — (0.254 mm)

Fig. 13   Main bearing selection chart. 4-150 No. 1 main bearing

Crankshaft Main Bearing Journal 2-3-4-5 Color Code and Diameter in Inches (Journal Size)	Bearing Insert Color Code	
	Upper Insert Size	Lower Insert Size
Yellow — 2.5001 to 2.4996 (Standard) (63.5025 to 63.4898 mm)	Yellow — Standard	Yellow — Standard
Orange — 2.4996 to 2.4991 (0.0005 Undersize) (63.4898 to 63.4771 mm)	Yellow — Standard	Black — 0.001-inch Undersize (0.025mm)
Black — 2.4991 to 2.4986 (0.001 Undersize) (63.4771 to 63.4644 mm)	Black — 0.001-inch Undersize (0.025 mm)	Black — 0.001-inch Undersize (0.025 mm)
Green — 2.4986 to 2.4981 (0.0015 Undersize) (63.4644 to 63.4517 mm)	Black — 0.001-inch Undersize (0.025 mm)	Green — 0.002-inch Undersize (0.051 mm)
Red — 2.4901 to 2.4896 (0.010 Undersize) (63.2485 to 63.2358 mm)	Red — 0.010-inch Undersize (0.054 mm)	Red — 0.010-inch Undersize (0.254 mm)

Fig. 14   Main bearing selection chart. 4-150 Nos. 2,3,4,5 main bearings

Connecting Rod Bearing Journal 2-3-4-5 Color Code and Diameter in Inches (Journal Size)	Bearing Insert Color Code	
	Upper Insert Size	Lower Insert Size
Yellow — 2.0955 to 2.0948 (53.2257 - 53.2079 mm) (Standard) Orange — 2.0948 to 2.0941 (53.2079 - 53.1901 mm) (0.0007 Undersize) Black — 2.0941 to 2.0943 (53.1901 to 53.1723 mm) (0.0014 Undersize) Red — 2.0855 to 2.0848 (53.9717 to 53.9539 mm) (0.010 Undersize)	Yellow — Standard Yellow — Standard Black — 0.001-inch (0.025 mm) Undersize Red — 0.010-inch (0.254 mm) Undersize	Yellow — Standard Black — 0.001-inch (0.025 mm) Undersize Black — 0.001-inch (0.025 mm) Undersize Red — 0.010-inch (0.245 mm) Undersize

Fig. 15   Connecting rod bearing selection chart. 4-150

er, ensure correct size is installed. Plungers are available in standard size and .010 inch oversize.

5. If a replacement pickup tube is to be installed, apply a light coating of Permatex No. 2 sealant or equivalent to end of tube. Install pickup tube and screen using tool No. J-21882, **Fig. 19.**
6. Before installing pump cover, fill pump with petroleum jelly.
7. When installing pump cover, torque attaching screws to 70 inch lbs.

BELT TENSION DATA

	New Lbs.	Used Lbs.
V Type Belts		
A/C Comp.	125–155	90–115
Air Pump		
Less Power Steer.	125–155	90–115
W/Power Steer.	65–75	60–70
Alternator	125–155	90–115
Power Steer.	125–155	90–115
Serpentine Type Belt	180–200	140–160

WATER PUMP
REPLACE

1. Drain cooling system.
2. Disconnect radiator and heater hoses from water pump.
3. Remove drive belts.

Fig. 16   Oil pan & oil pump. 4-150

Fig. 17 Checking oil pump gear end clearance. 4-150

Fig. 18 Checking oil pump gear to body clearance. 4-150

Fig. 19 Installing oil pump pickup screen & tube assembly. 4-150

4. If equipped, remove fan shroud attaching screws, then remove fan and fan shroud.
5. Remove water pump attaching bolts, then remove water pump and gasket.
6. Reverse procedure to install. Torque water pump attaching bolts to 13 ft. lbs.

FUEL PUMP
REPLACE

1. Disconnect fuel lines from pump.
2. Remove retaining screws and fuel

pump.
3. Remove all gasket material from the pump and block gasket surfaces. Apply sealer to both sides of new gasket.
4. Position gasket on pump flange and hold pump in position against its mounting surface. Make sure rocker arm is riding on camshaft eccentric.
5. Press pump tight against its mounting.

Install retaining screws and tighten them alternately.
6. Connect fuel lines. Then operate engine and check for leaks.

NOTE: When installing pump, crank engine to place camshaft eccentric in a position as to place the least amount of tension on fuel pump rocker arm. This will ease pump installation.

4-151 Engine Section

NOTE: Refer to Section 10 for service procedures not covered in this section.

ENGINE MOUNTS
REPLACE

NOTE: Remove fan shroud to radiator attaching screws to prevent damage to shroud.

1980–82 CONCORD & SPIRIT

Removal or replacement of any cushion can be accomplished by supporting the weight of the engine at the area of the cushion to be replaced.

1980–83 EAGLE
Left Side

1. Disconnect heated air tube from air cleaner and exhaust manifold.
2. Remove bolts attaching engine cushion bracket to axle housing.
3. Remove engine mount through bolt,

then support engine using a suitable jack.
4. Remove engine cushion support bracket, then remove engine mount attaching bolts and engine mount.
5. Reverse procedure to install. Torque engine mount to engine bolts to 33 ft lbs., cushion support bracket to engine bolts to 40 ft. lbs. and engine mount through bolt to 45 ft. lbs.

Right Side

1. Disconnect battery ground cable, then loosen left hand side engine mount through bolt.
2. Loosen bolts attaching engine cushion bracket to axle housing.
3. Remove right side engine mount through bolt, then remove engine cushion to bracket attaching bolts.
4. Disconnect axle tube at right hand side, then disconnect axle at pinion support.
5. Position a suitable jack under engine and raise engine slightly, then remove

engine mount.
6. Reverse procedure to install. Torque engine mount to engine bolts to 33 ft. lbs., cushion bracket bolts to 40 ft. lbs. and engine mount through bolts to 45 ft. lbs.

ENGINE
REPLACE

1980–82 CONCORD & SPIRIT

NOTE: On these models, the engine and transmission are removed as an assembly.

1. Disconnect battery ground cable, then drain cooling system.

CAUTION: Do not loosen cylinder block drain plug with system hot and under pressure because serious burns from coolant can occur.

2. Disconnect upper and lower radiator hoses at radiator.
3. Mark location of hinges on hood, then remove hood.
4. Remove air cleaner, fan and fan shroud.
5. On models equipped with automatic transmission, disconnect fluid cooler lines from radiator.
6. Remove radiator to support attaching bolts, then remove radiator.
7. Remove power steering pump drive belt, if equipped.
8. On models less A/C, disconnect wire connector from alternator.
9. On models with A/C, remove compressor and condenser attaching bolts, then position compressor and condenser out of way with refrigerant lines connected. Remove evaporator to dryer line from sill clips.
10. Disconnect heater hose from intake manifold, then remove throttle cable clip and remove cable from bracket.
11. On models with A/C, disconnect wire connector from alternator and pull wiring through tube.
12. Disconnect pressure and return hoses from power steering gear, if equipped.
13. Disconnect module control solenoid, choke heater, idle speed solenoid and temperature sending unit wire connectors.
14. Detach dipstick tube from exhaust manifold, then remove tube and dipstick from block.
15. Remove engine mount nuts at crossmember and ground cable from left hand engine cushion bracket at engine.
16. Disconnect fuel hose from steel tube on right hand frame side rail.
17. Disconnect wiring from starter solenoid, distributor and oil pressure sending unit.
18. Loosen crossmember attaching bolts and lower crossmember slightly, then remove transmission oil cooler lines, if equipped, speedometer cable from transmission, transmission linkage, backup light switch wire connector, transmission rear mount and crossmember.
19. Disconnect exhaust pipe from exhaust manifold, then suspend exhaust pipe from strut rod bushing with wire.
20. On models equipped with manual transmission, disconnect clutch linkage.
21. Mark propeller shaft and pinion flange so they can be installed in the same position, then remove propeller shaft.
22. Using a suitable engine lifting device, remove engine and transmission from vehicle.
23. Reverse procedure to install.

1980–83 EAGLE

NOTE: On these models, the engine is removed separately from the transmission.

1. Refer to the 1980–82 Concord and Spirit Engine, Replace procedure and perform steps 1 through 14.
2. Remove left front engine mount bracket to axle housing attaching bolts.
3. Raise and support vehicle, then remove splash shield and disconnect both half shafts from front axle. Compress half shafts inward, toward wheels and secure to frame side sills with wire.
4. Mark front drive shaft so it can be installed in the same position, then remove front driveshaft.
5. Using a suitable jack, support front axle, then disconnect axle at right hand tube support and at pinion end of axle.
6. Disconnect axle vent tube, then remove front axle.
7. Remove axle support bracket from cylinder block, then remove starter motor and shims.
8. Disconnect wiring from distributor, oil pressure sending unit and backup light switch.
9. Disconnect fuel hose from steel line.
10. On models with manual transmission, disconnect clutch release cylinder from clutch housing. Position a wooden block between transfer case and skid plate, then remove clutch housing to engine attaching bolts.
11. On models with automatic transmission, disconnect manual linkage, then remove converter housing inspection cover and remove converter to flywheel attaching nuts. Remove converter housing to engine attaching bolts.
12. Disconnect exhaust pipe from exhaust manifold, then lower vehicle.
13. Remove engine mount attaching bolts, then attach a suitable engine lifting device and raise engine slightly.
14. Remove left engine mount bracket, then remove engine from vehicle.
15. Reverse procedure to install.

OIL PAN
REPLACE

1. Disconnect battery ground cable, then remove fan shroud attaching screws and slide shroud toward engine.
2. Raise vehicle and support at frame side sills, then drain crankcase.
3. On Eagle models proceed as follows:
   a. Using a suitable jack, support front axle.
   b. Mark front drive shaft so it can be installed in the same position, then remove drive shaft.
   c. Disconnect both half shafts from axle. Compress shafts inward, toward wheels, and secure to frame side sills with wire.
   d. Disconnect axle assembly at right hand axle tube, at left hand engine mount and at pinion mount.
   e. Lower axle assembly slightly and

disconnect vent tube, then remove axle assembly.
4. Remove starter motor, then remove flywheel housing inspection cover.
5. Remove engine mount to crossmember attaching nuts.
6. Position a suitable jack under vibration damper and raise engine approximately 1 to 2 inches.
7. Remove crossmember right hand nut and screws and loosen left hand nut, then lower right side of front crossmember.
8. Remove oil pan attaching bolts, then pry crossmember downward on right side and remove oil pan.
9. Reverse procedure to install.

FUEL PUMP
REPLACE

1981–83 EAGLE

1. Disconnect battery ground cable.
2. Remove alternator and harness as an assembly and position aside, then disconnect mounting bracket from cylinder block and intake manifold.
3. Loosen bottom bolt of intake manifold-to-right side engine cushion bracket and move bracket toward fender panel.
4. Disconnect carburetor vent hose and position aside.
5. Temporarily move coolant hoses to heater core to gain clearance, then disconnect vacuum hoses after tagging them.
6. Disconnect fuel inlet pipe at fuel pump, then disconnect fuel pump-to-carburetor pipe at pump.
7. Install engine holding fixture and remove right engine cushion through bolt and raise engine slightly.
8. Raise and support vehicle.
9. Disconnect right side engine cushion bracket from block and axle bracket, then lower vehicle.
10. Raise engine and position bracket to gain access clearance to fuel pump bolts, then remove fuel pump bolts and fuel pump.
11. Clean all gasket material from fuel pump-to-block mating surface, then install new gasket and fuel pump and torque to 15 ft. lbs.
12. Connect fuel pipes to fuel pump.
13. Connect engine cushion bracket to cylinder block and axle bracket, then lower engine onto cushion and remove holding fixture.
14. Install engine cushion through bolt and nut, then connect vacuum hoses and route heater hoses to original locations.
15. Install intake manifold-to-cushion bracket.
16. Install alternator mounting bracket and alternator, then install and adjust belts and reconnect battery ground cable.

6-258 Engine Section

ENGINE MARKINGS

A letter code is used to denote size of the bore, main bearings and rod bearings. This code is located on a boss above the oil filter. This letter code is as follows:

Letter "B"
Cyl. bore .010 inch oversize

Letter "M"
Main bearings .010 inch undersize

Letter "P"
Rod bearings .010 inch undersize

Letter "C"
Camshaft block bore .010 inch over-size

Letters "PM"
Main and rod bearings .010 inch under-size

ENGINE MOUNTS
REPLACE

Removal or replacement of any cushion can be accomplished by supporting the weight of the engine or transmission at the area of the cushion to be replaced, **Figs. 1, 2 and 3.**

Fig. 1   Engine mounts. Exc. Pacer & 1981—86 Eagle (typical)

ENGINE
REPLACE

AMX, CONCORD, EAGLE & SPIRIT

The engine is removed without the transmission as follows:
1. Drain cooling system.

Fig. 2   Engine mounts. Pacer

Fig. 3   Engine mounts. 1981—86 6 cyl. Eagle

2. Mark hood hinge locations, disconnect underhood lamp, if equipped, and remove hood.
3. Disconnect battery cables and remove battery.
4. Disconnect alternator wiring and the ignition coil, distributor and oil pressure sender leads.
5. Remove TCS switch bracket from cylinder block, if equipped.
6. Disconnect flexible fuel line from fuel pump and plug line and pump port.
7. Disconnect engine ground strap.
8. Remove the right front engine support cushion to bracket screw.
9. If equipped with air conditioning:
   a. Remove service valve covers and front-seat valves.
   b. Loosen service valve to compressor attaching nuts.
   c. Bleed compressor refrigerant charge.
   d. Remove service valves and cap compressor ports and service valves.
   e. Disconnect clutch feed wire.
10. Remove starter.
11. Remove air cleaner and disconnect purge hose from canister and TAC vacuum hose from manifold, if equipped.
12. Disconnect throttle stop solenoid lead, if equipped.
13. Disconnect fuel return hose from fuel filter and the carburetor bowl vent hose from canister.
14. Disconnect throttle cable and remove from bracket. Disconnect throttle valve rod at carburetor and the bellcrank.
15. Disconnect carburetor stepper motor and oxygen sensor electrical connectors, if equipped.
16. Disconnect heater and air conditioning system vacuum hose from intake manifold.
17. Disconnect temperature sender wire and TCS vacuum solenoid wiring harness.
18. Disconnect radiator hoses from radiator and the heater hoses from engine.
19. Disconnect transmission oil cooler lines from radiator, if equipped.
20. Remove fan shroud attaching screws, then the radiator and shroud.
21. Remove fan and spacer. Install a 5/16 × 1/2 inch capscrew through fan pulley, into water pump flange.
22. Remove power brake vacuum check valve from power brake unit, if equipped.
23. If equipped with power steering, disconnect hoses from gear and drain reservoir. Cap gear ports and hoses.
24. Remove transmission filler tube bracket screw, if equipped.
25. Raise and support vehicle on jackstands.
26. If equipped with automatic transmission:
   a. Remove converter housing spacer cover.
   b. Remove converter attaching screws.
   c. Remove exhaust pipe support from converter housing. This also sup-

ports the inner end of the transmission linkage.
27. If equipped with manual transmission:
   a. Remove clutch housing cover and clutch bellcrank inner support screws.
   b. Disconnect springs and remove bellcrank.
   c. Remove outer bellcrank to strut rod bracket retainer.
   d. Disconnect back-up lamp switch wiring harness under hood at dash panel to gain access to clutch housing screw.
28. On all models, remove engine mount cushion to bracket screws.
29. On Eagle models proceed as follows:
   a. Support axle assembly, then remove half shaft to axle flange attaching bolts.
   b. Compress half shafts inward, toward wheels, and secure to frame side sills with wire.
   c. Remove axle bracket attaching bolts at axle tube and right hand engine mount, then remove axle bracket.
   d. Remove axle bracket attaching bolts at pinion end of axle.
   e. Remove left engine mount support to front axle bracket attaching bolts.
   f. Disconnect axle vent hose, then lower axle assembly and remove from vehicle.
30. Disconnect exhaust pipe from manifold.
31. Remove upper converter or clutch housing screws and loosen the bottom screws.
32. Raise vehicle and support on jackstands.
33. Remove air conditioning compressor drive belt idler pulley and the compressor mounting bracket, if equipped.
34. Install suitable engine lifting equipment and slightly raise engine. Support transmission with a suitable jack.
35. Remove remaining converter or clutch housing screws.
36. Remove engine from vehicle.
37. Reverse procedure to install.

PACER

The engine and transmission are removed as an assembly.
1. Mark hood hinge locations, disconnect underhood lamp, if equipped, and remove hood.
2. Drain cooling system and oil pan.
3. Disconnect heater and radiator hoses from engine.
4. Park W/S wiper at center of windshield to provide clearance for valve cover removal.
5. Remove battery.
6. Disconnect and cap transmission oil cooler lines, if equipped.
7. Remove fan shroud and radiator.
8. If equipped with air conditioning:
   a. Remove service valve covers and front-seat the valves.

   b. Bleed refrigerant charge from compressor by loosening service valve fittings.
   c. Disconnect and cap condenser and evaporator lines from compressor. Cap the service valves.
   d. Disconnect receiver outlet at coupling.
   e. Remove condenser and receiver assembly.
9. Remove air cleaner assembly.
10. Disconnect wiring at the following components, if equipped: starter, ignition coil, distributor, alternator, A/C compressor, temperature sensing unit, oil pressure sending unit, solenoid vacuum valve, TCS solenoid control switch, throttle stop solenoid and brake warning lamp switch.
11. Disconnect the following lines, if equipped: fuel pump suction, power brake vacuum supply from manifold, fuel filter return, heater and A/C system vacuum supply from manifold, carburetor pressure vent and power steering.
12. Remove carburetor and cover intake manifold opening.
13. Remove valve cover and vibration damper.
14. Disconnect accelerator cable at control cable bracket.
15. Raise and support vehicle with jackstands.
16. Disconnect exhaust pipe at manifold.
17. Disconnect transmission linkage and, if equipped, clutch linkage.
18. Disconnect speedometer cable from transmission.
19. Remove propeller shaft and cap transmission output shaft.
20. Support transmission with a suitable jack and remove rear crossmember.
21. Install suitable engine lifting equipment and support engine weight.
22. Remove engine mount bracket to front support cushion attaching bolts, then the front support cushions.
23. Lower jack from transmission.
24. Raise vehicle with a suitable positioned under front crossmember until bottom of front bumper is approximately three feet from floor, then support vehicle at that height with jackstands.
25. Remove oil filter and starter.
26. Raise front of engine and partially remove assembly by pulling upward until rear of cylinder head clears cowl.
27. Lower the vehicle and remove engine-transmission assembly.
28. Reverse procedure to install.

CYLINDER HEAD
REPLACE

Tighten cylinder head bolts a little at a time in three steps in the sequence shown in the illustrations. Final tightening should be to the torque specifications listed in the Engine Tightening table.

NOTE: On Pacer models, park windshield wiper blades at center of windshield to aid

Fig. 4 Cylinder head tightening sequence. The No. 11 bolt must be sealed to prevent coolant leakage.

Fig. 5 Manifold tightening sequence. 1980

Fig. 6 Manifold tightening sequence. 1981—86

ROCKER ARMS

All engines have the intake and exhaust rocker arms pivoting on a bridged pivot assembly which is secured to the cylinder head by two cap screws, **Fig. 7.** When installing cap screws, turn each screw one turn at a time to avoid breaking the bridge. Torque cap screws to 19 ft. lbs.

The push rods are hollow, serving as oil galleries for lubricating each individual rocker arm assembly. Prior to installing, the push rods should be cleaned thoroughly, inspected for wear and deposits which may restrict the flow of oil to the rocker arm.

The push rods also serve as guides to maintain correct rocker arm to valve stem relationship; therefore, a contact pattern on the push rods where they contact the cylinder head is normal.

Lubrication to each rocker arm is supplied by the corresponding hydraulic valve lifter. A metering system located in each valve lifter consists of a stepped lower sur-

in removal cylinder head.

1. Drain cooling system and disconnect hoses at thermostat housing.
2. Remove air cleaner and disconnect fuel line and vacuum advance line.
3. Remove valve cover and gasket.

NOTE: During removal of valve cover, use a suitable putty knife or razor blade and break silicone seal between valve cover and cylinder head. Do not pry valve cover upward until seal has been completely broken.

4. Remove rocker arms and bridged pivot assemblies. Alternately loosen each cap screw one turn at a time to prevent damage to bridge.

NOTE: Label push rods, rocker arms and bridge pivots so they can be installed in the same position.

5. Disconnect power steering pump and air pump and position pumps and brackets aside. Do not disconnect hoses from pumps.
6. Remove intake and exhaust manifold assembly from cylinder head.
7. On models equipped with A/C, remove A/C drive belt idler bracket from cylinder head. Loosen alternator drive belt, then remove alternator bracket to cylinder head mounting bolt. Remove bolts from compressor mounting bracket and position compressor aside.
8. Disconnect ignition wires and remove spark plugs.
9. Disconnect temperature sending unit wire and battery ground cable.
10. Remove ignition coil and bracket assembly.

11. Remove cylinder head bolts, cylinder head and gasket.
12. Reverse procedure to install. Torque cylinder head bolts in sequence shown in **Fig. 4** and torque manifold bolts in sequence shown in **Figs. 5 and 6.**

VALVE ARRANGEMENT
FRONT TO REAR

6-258 . . . . E-I-I-E-I-E-E-I-E-I-I-E

VALVE LIFT SPECS.

Year	Engine	Intake	Exhaust
1980 –86	6-258	.405	.405

VALVE TIMING
Intake Opens Before TDC

Year	Engine	Degrees
1980	6-258①	12.12
1980	6-258②	14.58
1981–86	6-258②	9

①—1 barrel carb.
②—2 barrel carb.

Fig. 7 Rocker arms, push rod and pivot assembly

LUBRICATION SUPPLY TO PUSH ROD

Fig. 8 Hydraulic lifter identification

Lock Ring
Plunger Cap
Push Rod Socket
Metering Disc
Plunger
Valve Seat
Valve
Valve Spring
Valve Retainer
Plunger Return Spring
Tappet Body

Fig. 9 Hydraulic valve lifter

face on the push rod cap that contacts a flat plate, causing a restriction, **Fig. 8.** The restriction meters the amount of oil flow through the push rod cap, hollow push rod, and upper valve train components. A loss of lubrication to the rocker arm could be caused by a restricted or plugged push rod or a defective hydraulic valve lifter.

CAUTION: Correct installation of push rods in these engines is critical and more than normal care must be taken upon installation. When placing the push rods through the guide hole in the cylinder head, it is important that the push rod end is inserted in the plunger cap socket. It is possible that the push rod may seat itself on the edge of the plunger cap which will restrict valve lifter rotation and lubrication to rocker arms.

It is recommended that, just prior to installation of the cylinder head covers, the engine be operated and the supply of lubrication to each rocker arm be visually inspected. if inspection reveals that an individual rocker arm is not being supplied with lubrication, the push rod and/or valve lifter must be inspected to determine the cause.

VALVE GUIDES

Excessive valve stem-to-guide clearance will cause lack of power, rough idling and noisy valves, and may cause valve breakage. Insufficient clearance will result in noisy and sticky functioning of valves and disturb engine smoothness of operation.

Valve stem-to-guide clearances are listed in the Engine Valve Specifications table. By using a micrometer and a suitable telescope hole gauge, check the diameter of the valve stem in three places (top, center and bottom). Insert telescope hole gauge in valve guide bore, measuring at the center. Subtract the highest reading of valve stem diameter from valve guide bore center diameter to obtain valve-to-guide clearance. If clearance is not within specified limits, use the next oversize valve and ream bore to fit. Valves with oversize stems are available in .003 inch, .015 inch and .030 inch.

HYDRAULIC LIFTERS

Valve lifters may be removed from their bores after removing the cylinder head cover. Using Valve Tappet Removal and Installation Tool J-21884 remove the tappets through the push rod openings in the cylinder head. The type of lifter used on these engines is illustrated in **Fig. 9.**

TIMING CASE COVER
REPLACE

1. Remove drive belts, fan and pulley.
2. Remove vibration damper.
3. Remove oil pan-to-timing chain cover screws and cover-to-block screws.

Fig. 10 Valve timing

4. Raise the cover and pull the oil pan front seal up enough to pull the retaining nibs from the holes in the cover.
5. Remove timing chain cover gasket from block. Cut off seal tab flush with front face of cylinder block. Clean gasket surfaces.
6. Remove oil seal.
7. Place gasket in position on cylinder block. Install new oil pan front seal, cut off protruding tab of seal to match portion of the original seal.
8. Insert suitable aligning tool in cover seal bore and on crankshaft. Install cover-to-oil pan screws and tighten lightly. Install cover screws and tighten.
9. Retighten all screws and install new cover seal.

ARROW TOWARD FRONT OF ENGINE

OIL HOLE TOWARD CAMSHAFT

Fig. 11 Piston & rod assembly

TIMING CHAIN

When installing a timing chain, see that the timing marks on the sprockets are in line as shown in **Fig. 10.**

CAMSHAFT
REPLACE

1. Remove distributor and ignition wires and the fuel pump.
2. Remove radiator from vehicle. If equipped with A/C, remove condenser and receiver with refrigerant lines attached and position out of way.
3. Remove cylinder head and valve lifters.
4. Remove timing chain cover.
5. Rotate crankshaft until timing marks on sprockets are aligned, **Fig. 10.**
6. Remove sprockets and chain.
7. On all models except Pacer, remove front bumper or grille as required to remove camshaft.
8. On Pacer models, remove hood and raise engine sufficiently to permit camshaft removal.

NOTE: Mark hinge locations on hood panel for alignment during installation.

9. Remove camshaft.
10. Reverse procedure to install.

PISTONS & RODS
ASSEMBLE

Pistons are marked with a depression notch or arrow on the top perimeter, **Fig. 11.** When installed in the engine, this notch or arrow must be toward the front of the engine. Always assemble rods and caps with the cylinder numbers facing the camshaft side of engine. Check side clearance between connecting rod and crankshaft journals. Clearance should be .005–.014 inch on 1980 models and .010–.019 inch on 1981–86 models.

PISTONS, PINS & RINGS

Pistons are furnished in standard sizes and oversizes of .002, .005, .010 and .020 inch.

Piston pins are furnished in oversizes of .003 and .005 inch.

Piston rings are available in .020 inch oversizes.

MAIN & ROD BEARINGS

Both main and rod bearings are supplied in undersizes of .001, .002, .010 and .012 inch.

Fig. 12 Rear main bearing sealing

Fig. 13 Engine lifting fixture

CRANKSHAFT REAR OIL SEAL
REPLACE

1. To replace the seal, **Fig. 12**, remove oil pan and scrape oil pan surfaces clean.
2. Remove rear main bearing cap.
3. Remove and discard old seals.
4. Clean cap thoroughly.
5. Loosen all remaining main bearing cap screws.
6. With a brass drift and hammer, tap upper seal until sufficient seal is protruding to permit pulling seal out completely with pliers.
7. Wipe seal surface of crankshaft clean, then oil lightly.
8. Coat back surface of upper seal with soap, and lip of seal with engine oil.
9. Install upper seal into cylinder block. Lip of seal must face to front of engine.
10. Coat cap and cylinder block mating surface portion of seal with RTV Silicone or equivalent, being careful not to apply sealer on lip of seal.
11. Coat back surface of lower seal with soap, and lip of seal with No. 40 engine oil. Place into cap, seating seal firmly into seal recess in cap.
12. Place RTV Silicone or equivalent on both chamfered edges of rear main bearing cap.
13. Install main bearings and install cap. Tighten all caps to correct torque as listed in the Engine Tightening Specifications table.
14. Cement oil pan gasket to cylinder block with tongue of gasket at each end coated with RTV Silicone or equivalent before installing into rear main bearing cap at joint of tongue and oil pan front neoprene seal.
15. Coat oil pan rear seal with soap. Place into recess of rear main bearing cap, making certain seal is firmly and evenly seated.
16. Install oil pan and tighten drain plug securely.

OIL PAN
REPLACE

PACER

1. Drain oil, then install engine holding fixture.
2. Disconnect steering shaft flexible coupling and position out of way.
3. Raise vehicle and support on side sills.
4. Remove front engine mount through bolts.
5. Disconnect brake lines from front wheel cylinders, then disconnect upper ball joints from spindles.

NOTE: Ensure shock absorber is securely attached.

6. Remove upper control arm and position aside.

7. Support front crossmember with jack, then remove nuts from rear mounts and swing crossmember forward.
8. Remove starter.
9. Remove oil pan and front and rear oil pan seals.
10. Reverse procedure to install.

1980–83 ALL EXC. PACER & EAGLE

1. Disconnect battery ground cable.
2. Turn steering wheel to full left lock.
3. Support engine using a suitable holding fixture, **Fig. 13**.
4. Raise vehicle and support on side sills.
5. Disconnect steering idler arm at side sill.
6. Disconnect engine front support cushions at engine brackets.
7. Loosen sway bar link nuts to end of

Engine oiling system

threads, if equipped.

8. Remove front crossmember to side sill attaching bolts, then pull crossmember down.
9. Remove engine right support bracket from engine.
10. Loosen strut rods at lower control arms; do not remove screws.
11. Remove starter motor.
12. Drain crankcase, then remove oil pan attaching bolts and oil pan.
13. Clean gasket surfaces of oil pan and engine block. Remove all sludge and dirt from oil pan sump.
14. Reverse procedure to install.

1980–83 EAGLE

1. Disconnect battery ground cable.
2. Drain engine oil.
3. Lock steering wheel and remove air cleaner.
4. Support engine using a suitable holding fixture.
5. Raise vehicle and support on side sills.
6. Mark for assembly reference and disconnect front driveshaft.
7. Remove engine cushion bolts.
8. Remove bolts from sill-to-crossmember and position bar aside.
9. Loosen pitman arm at gear, then loosen idler arm at steering linkage.
10. Remove bolt from steering damper at crossmember.
11. Loosen sway bar bolts and lower sway bar bolts and lower sway bar.
12. Disconnect half shafts from axle.

NOTE: Compress half shafts in toward wheels, secure in compressed position with wire attached to frame sills.

13. Remove bolts from right bracket at axle tube bolt bars, then remove bolts from left upper axle bracket at upper end, and bolts from pinion end bracket at pinion.
14. Remove vent hose and remove axle assembly.
15. Support crossmembers with jack and remove crossmember nuts and bolts, then lower crossmember assembly for clearance.
16. Remove starter motor, then the torque converter housing access cover.
17. Remove oil pan screws and remove oil pan.
18. Reverse procedure to install.

1984–86 EAGLE

1. Disconnect battery ground cable.
2. Lock steering wheel, then raise and support vehicle at side sills.

3. Drain engine oil, then mark front driveshaft to ensure correct alignment during assembly.
4. Disconnect driveshaft, then support axle assembly with a suitable jack.
5. Disconnect half shafts from axle.

NOTE: Compress half shafts in toward wheels, secure in compressed position with wire attached to frame sills.

6. Remove bolt from right bracket at axle tube bolt bars, then the bolts from left upper axle bracket at the upper end.
7. Remove pinion end bracket to pinion attaching bolts.
8. Remove vent hose and axle assembly.
9. Remove starter motor, then the torque converter housing access cover.
10. Remove oil pan attaching screws, then the oil pan.
11. Reverse procedure to install.

OIL PUMP

NOTE: When servicing oil pump, if inlet tube is moved out of position a new inlet tube and screen assembly must be installed.

The oil pump is located in the oil pan thus necessitating removal of the pan to gain access to the pump.

Oil pump removal or replacement will not affect distributor timing as the distributor drive gear remains in mesh with the camshaft gear.

Upon disassembly of the oil pump, place a straightedge across gears and pump body and check clearance between straightedge and pump body which should be .004–.008 inch for 1980 engines and .006–.004 inch for 1981–86 engines. Clearance between gears and pump housing should be .0005–.0025 inch.

NOTE: The pump cover should be installed with the pump out of the engine and pump checked for freedom of operation before installation.

The oil pressure relief valve, which is built into the pump, is not adjustable, the correct pressure being built into the relief valve spring.

BELT TENSION DATA

	New Lbs.	Used Lbs.
Air Conditioning	125–155	90–115
Air Pump	65–75	60–70
Fan and Power Steering	125–155	90–115
Serpentine Type Belt	180–200	140–160

WATER PUMP
REPLACE

NOTE: On engines equipped with a serpentine drive belt, the water pump and fan drive assembly will operate in the reverse rotation of an engine not equipped with a serpentine drive belt. Water pumps for use on these engines can be identified by the letters "REV" cast into the pump body, while fan components can be identified by the word "REVERSE" stamped on the fan drive and on the inner side of the fan.

1. Disconnect battery ground cable.
2. Drain cooling system and disconnect radiator and heater hoses from pump.
3. Remove drive belts.

NOTE: On some models it will be necessary to remove alternator front bracket and place alternator aside, without disconnecting wires.

4. Remove fan shroud attaching bolts, then remove fan, hub and shroud.
5. Remove water pump and gasket.
6. Reverse procedure to install.

FUEL PUMP
REPLACE

1. Disconnect fuel lines from pump.
2. Remove retaining screws and fuel pump.
3. Remove all gasket material from the pump and block gasket surfaces. Apply sealer to both sides of new gasket.
4. Position gasket on pump flange and hold pump in position against its mounting surface. Make sure rocker arm is riding on camshaft eccentric.
5. Press pump tight against its mounting. Install retaining screws and tighten them alternately.
6. Connect fuel lines. Then operate engine and check for leaks.

NOTE: When installing pump, crank engine to place camshaft eccentric in a position as to place the least amount of tension on fuel pump rocker arm. This will ease pump installation.

Clutch, Manual Transmission & Transfer Case Section

CLUTCH PEDAL
ADJUST

PEDAL FREE PLAY

1980—83 4-151, 1981—86 Eagle w/6-258 & 1983—84 4-150

These models are equipped with a hydraulic actuated clutch and no adjustment is required.

Exc. 4-150, 151 & 1981—86 w/6-258

In order to provide sufficient free movement of the clutch release bearing when the clutch is engaged and pedal fully released, free pedal play should be 7/8 inch to 1 1/8 inch with desired free play of 1 1/8 inch.

Adjustment for free pedal play is made by varying the length of the beam or link to the release lever rod. Lengthening this rod reduces pedal travel; shortening it increases pedal play, **Fig. 1**.

CLUTCH
REPLACE

Fig. 1   Typical clutch linkage

4-151, 1981—86 6-258 & 1983—84 4-150

Exc. Eagle
1. Remove transmission as described under Transmission, Replace.
2. Remove clutch housing to engine attaching bolts, then the clutch housing.
3. Remove throwout bearing, then mark pressure plate and flywheel for reassembly.
4. Remove pressure plate to flywheel attaching bolts, then remove pressure plate and clutch disc.

NOTE: Loosen pressure plate to flywheel bolts alternately and evenly to prevent distorting pressure plate.

5. Reverse procedure to install. Position clutch and pressure plate on flywheel and install attaching bolts finger tight. Align clutch disc using a suitable alignment tool, then tighten pressure plate attaching bolts alternately and evenly to 23 ft. lbs. Torque clutch housing to engine and transmission to clutch housing attaching bolts to 54 ft. lbs.

Eagle
1. Remove transmission as described under Transmission, Replace.
2. Remove right hand brace rod and starter motor, then disconnect clutch release cylinder spring from clutch fork.
3. Remove clutch release cylinder, with hydraulic line attached, and clutch housing inspection cover.

4. Disconnect exhaust pipe at exhaust manifold, then remove clutch housing to engine attaching bolts and remove clutch housing.
5. Mark pressure plate and flywheel for reassembly, then remove pressure plate attaching bolts and remove pressure plate and clutch disc.

NOTE: Loosen pressure plate attaching bolts alternately and evenly to prevent distorting pressure plate.

6. Reverse procedure to install. Position clutch disc and pressure plate on flywheel and install attaching bolts finger tight. Align clutch disc using a suitable alignment tool, then tighten pressure plate attaching bolts alternately and evenly to 28 ft. lbs. Torque clutch housing to engine upper attaching bolts to 27 ft. lbs. Torque clutch housing lower attaching bolts and dowel bolts to 43 ft. lbs. Torque transmission to engine attaching bolts to 55 ft. lbs.

1980 6 CYL.
Removal
1. Remove transmission as described further on.
2. Remove starter, clutch housing, throwout lever, bearing and sleeve assembly.

NOTE: Mark clutch cover, pressure plate and flywheel to insure correct alignment during installation.

3. Remove clutch cover and pressure

plate assembly.

NOTE: When removing clutch cover and pressure plate assembly from flywheel, loosen screws evenly until spring tension is released, as cover could be warped by improper removal, resulting in clutch chatter when reassembled.

4. Remove pilot bushing lubricating wick and soak in engine oil.

NOTE: Unless special clutch rebuilding equipment is available, it is recommended that the clutch assembly be exchanged for a rebuilt unit should the clutch require rebuilding. The driven disc, however, may be replaced without special equipment. If clutch rebuilding equipment is available, follow the equipment manufacturer's instructions.

Installation
1. Inspect clutch release lever height and correct as necessary. If used, lubricate pilot bushing wick with engine oil.
2. Install clutch disc and cover on flywheel and loosely install bolts. Using clutch aligning tool or transmission clutch shaft, align clutch disc.
3. Tighten cover retaining bolts several turns at a time to prevent cover distortion, then torque bolts to 28 ft. lbs.
4. Install throwout lever, bearing and sleeve assembly, clutch housing and starter.

MANUAL TRANS.
REPLACE

EXC. EAGLE

4-151 & 1981–84 6-258
1. Remove console, if equipped, then remove gearshift lever, bezel and boot.
2. Mark propeller shaft and rear axle pinion flange so they can be installed in the same position, then remove propeller shaft.
3. Disconnect speedometer cable and backup lamp switch wire connector.
4. Disconnect exhaust pipe, if necessary.
5. Remove starter motor, then disconnect clutch release cylinder spring at clutch fork.
6. Remove inspection cover from clutch housing, then remove bolts attaching catalytic converter support bracket to transmission rear support bracket, if equipped.
7. Place support under front of engine, then remove bolts attaching transmission mount to rear crossmember.
8. Remove nuts attaching rear crossmember to frame side sills, then remove crossmember.
9. Remove transmission to clutch housing attaching bolts, then remove transmission.
10. Reverse procedure to install. Torque transmission to clutch housing attaching bolts to 54 ft. lbs.

1980 6-258
1. Remove knob, bezel, boot and gear shift lever.
2. Open hood and raise vehicle.
3. Mark rear universal joint and propeller shaft to ensure proper alignment at time of installation, then remove propeller shaft.
4. Disconnect speedometer cable and backup lamp switch and TCS switch wires, if equipped.
5. If equipped with four speed transmission, release back-up lamp switch wires from clip on transmission top cover.
6. Install support stand under clutch housing to support engine when crossmember and transmission are removed.
7. On Pacer models, disconnect ground strap at support cushion bolt.
8. On all models, remove rear crossmember to frame side sill attaching nuts.
9. Remove catalytic converter support bracket, if equipped.
10. On AMX, Concord and Spirit models, remove rear support cushion to crossmember attaching bolts and remove crossmember.

NOTE: On Pacer models, crossmember is removed with transmission.

11. On all models remove two lower transmission to clutch housing attaching bolts.
12. Remove two upper transmission to

clutch housing attaching bolts and remove transmission.

NOTE: Care must be taken not to damage clutch shaft, pilot bushing or clutch disc.

EAGLE

4-151 & 6-258
1. Place transmission shift lever in the neutral position, then remove console, if equipped.
2. Remove gearshift lever bezel and boot, then remove gearshift lever from mounting cover on transmission.
3. Remove skid plate, then mark position of speedometer adapter for reassembly, then disconnect speedometer cable. Plug adapter opening in transfer case to prevent lubricant spillage.
4. Mark propeller shafts and axle yokes for reassembly, then disconnect propeller shafts at transfer case.
5. Disconnect backup lamp switch wire connector, then support engine using a suitable jack.
6. Support transmission and transfer case using a suitable transmission jack, then remove rear crossmember.
7. Remove catalytic converter support bracket from transfer case.
8. Remove transmission to clutch housing attaching bolts, then remove transmission and transfer case as an assembly.
9. Remove nuts from transfer case mounting studs, then separate transfer case from transmission.
10. Reverse procedure to install. Torque transfer case to transmission adapter housing stud nuts to 33 ft. lbs. Torque transmission to clutch housing bolts to 55 ft. lbs.

TRANSFER CASE
REPLACE

WITH AUTO. TRANS.
1. Raise and support vehicle.
2. Support engine and transmission with a suitable jack or jack stand.
3. Disconnect catalytic converter support bracket from adapter housing.
4. Remove skid plate.
5. Disconnect speedometer cable and adapter from transfer case. Discard adapter O-ring.
6. Mark propeller shafts and transfer case yoke for assembly reference. Then, disconnect propeller shafts from yokes. Secure shafts aside.
7. Disconnect gearshift and throttle linkage from transmission.
8. Remove rear crossmember.
9. Remove transfer case to adapter housing nuts.
10. Remove transfer case from vehicle.
11. Install transfer case on adapter housing.
12. Install and torque transfer case to adapter housing nuts to 33 ft. lbs.
13. Install rear crossmember.

14. On 1981–86 models, install rear brace rod.
15. Remove jack or jack stand, supporting engine and transmission.
16. Connect gearshift and throttle linkage to transmission.
17. Connect propeller shafts to transfer case yokes.
18. Install new O-ring on speedometer adapter, then the adapter and speedometer cable to transfer case.
19. Install skid plate.
20. Connect catalytic converter support bracket to adapter housing.
21. Check transfer case lubricant level and adjust, if necessary. Also, check transmission linkage adjustments.

WITH MANUAL TRANS.
1. Shift transmission into neutral.
2. Remove screws attaching gear shift lever bezel to floorpan or console, (if equipped).
3. Slide bezel and boot up on gear shift lever to gain access to lever attaching bolts, then remove bolts and remove lever.
4. Remove bolts attaching gear shift lever mounting cover to transmission adapter housing and remove cover.
5. Remove nut from transfer case mounting stud from inside transmission adapter housing.
6. Raise and support vehicle.
7. Remove skid plate and stiffening brace, or rear brace rod on 1982–86 models.
8. Remove speedometer adapter retainer attaching bolt and remove retainer, adapter and cable, then plug adapter opening in transfer case to avoid excessive oil leakage.

NOTE: Before removing speedometer adapter, mark position for reference during assembly.

9. Mark propeller shafts and axle yokes for assembly reference and disconnect propeller shafts at transfer case.
10. On 1981–86 models only, remove transfer case shift motor vacuum harness.
11. Support transfer case with transmission jack, then remove nuts from transfer case mounting studs and remove transfer case.
12. Align transmission output and transfer case input shafts and install transfer case on transmission adapter housing, then install and torque transfer case mounting stud nuts to 33 ft. lbs.
13. Remove jack supporting transfer case.
14. Connect propeller shafts to axle yokes and torque clamp strap bolts to 15 ft. lbs.
15. Install new O-ring on speedometer adapter, then install adapter and cable and retainer, torque retainer bolt to 100 inch lbs.
16. Install skid plate amd stiffening brace, or rear brace rod on 1982–86 models, and torque retaining bolts to 30 ft. lbs.

17. On 1981–86 models only, install transfer case shift motor vacuum harness.
18. Check and correct fluid levels in transmission and transfer case, then lower vehicle.
19. Install nut on transfer case mounting stud inside transmission adapter housing, torque nut to 33 ft. lbs.
20. Install gear shift lever mounting cover on transmission adapter housing, then install gear shift lever on mounting cover.
21. Position gear shift lever boot and bezel on floorpan of console (if equipped), and install bezel attaching screws.

NOTE: On 1982–86 models, steps 1 through 5 and 19 through 21 apply to SR-4 transmission only.

Rear Axle, Propeller Shaft & Brakes

REAR AXLES

Figs. 1 and 2 illustrate the rear axle assembly used on these cars. When necessary to overhaul the unit, refer to the Rear Axle Specifications table in this chapter.

DESCRIPTION

In these rear axles, **Figs. 1 and 2,** the drive pinion is mounted in two tapered roller bearings. These bearings are preloaded by a washer behind the front bearing. The pinion is positioned by shims located in front of the rear bearing. The differential is supported in the carrier by two tapered roller side bearings. These bearings are preloaded by shims located between the bearings and carrier housing. The differential assembly is positioned for proper ring gear and pinion backlash by varying the position of these shims. The differential case houses two side gears in mesh with two pinions mounted on a pinion shaft which is held in place by a lock pin. The side gears and pinions are backed by thrust washers.

It is not necessary to remove the rear axle assembly. However, the underbody should be washed to prevent particles of road dirt from contaminating the parts.

REAR AXLE & PROP. SHAFT
REPLACE

1. Remove cotter pins and remove axle shaft nuts.
2. Raise vehicle and position support stands under rear frame side sills.
3. Remove wheels and brake drum retaining screws.
4. Remove brake drums, then disconnect brake lines at wheel cylinders.
5. Using a suitable puller, remove support plates, oil seal, retainer and end play shims.

NOTE: Axle shaft end play shims are installed at left side of axle only.

6. Using a suitable puller, remove axle shafts.
7. Remove axle housing cover and drain lubricant, then reinstall cover.
8. Disconnect parking brake cables at

1. BOLT	16. PINION NUT	30. DIFFERENTIAL CASE
2. WASHER	17. BREATHER	31. RING GEAR BOLT
3. AXLE SHAFT OIL SEAL AND RETAINER ASSEMBLY	18. BREATHER HOSE	32. DIFFERENTIAL PINION WASHER
4. AXLE SHAFT BEARING SHIM	19. BREATHER	33. DIFFERENTIAL PINION
5. AXLE SHAFT BEARING CUP	20. PINION DEPTH ADJUSTING SHIM	34. DIFFERENTIAL SIDE GEAR
6. AXLE SHAFT BEARING	21. PINION REAR BEARING CUP	35. DIFFERENTIAL SIDE GEAR THRUST WASHER
7. AXLE SHAFT	22. PINION BEARING-REAR	36. DIFFERENTIAL PINION SHAFT THRUST BLOCK
8. AXLE SHAFT INNER OIL SEAL	23. PINION GEAR	37. DIFFERENTIAL PINION SHAFT PIN
9. NUT	24. DIFFERENTIAL BEARING	38. DIFFERENTIAL PINION SHAFT
10. AXLE HOUSING	25. DIFFERENTIAL BEARING CUP	39. AXLE HOUSING COVER GASKET
11. COLLAPSIBLE SPACER	26. DIFFERENTIAL BEARING SHIM	40. AXLE HOUSING COVER
12. PINION BEARING CUP-FRONT	27. DIFFERENTIAL BEARING CAP	41. AXLE IDENTIFICATION TAG
13. PINION BEARING-FRONT	28. DIFFERENTIAL BEARING CAP BOLT	42. BOLT
14. PINION OIL SEAL	29. RING GEAR	43. AXLE HOUSING COVER FILL PLUG
15. UNIVERSAL JOINT YOKE		44. WASHER

Fig. 1   Rear axle assembly (typical). 7⁹⁄₁₆ in. axle

equalizer.
9. Mark universal joint and rear axle yokes for reassembly, then disconnect propeller at rear yoke.
10. Remove stabilizer bar, if equipped.
11. Disconnect brake hose at body floor pan bracket.
12. Disconnect vent tube from axle tube.
13. Support axle assembly using a suitable jack.
14. Disconnect shock absorbers at spring plates.
15. Remove spring U-bolts, spring plates and spring clip plate, if equipped with a stabilizer bar.

16. Rotate axle until it clears springs, then lower axle assembly and remove from vehicle.
17. Reverse procedure to install.

AXLE SHAFTS
REPLACE

DISASSEMBLY

The hub and drum are separate units, and the hub and axle shaft are serrated to mate and fit together on the taper. Both are punched marked to insure correct assembly, **Fig. 3.** The axle shaft and bearing may be removed as follows:

1. Remove rear wheel, drum and hub, then disconnect parking brake cable at equalizer.
2. Disconnect brake tube from wheel cylinder and remove brake support plate assembly, oil seal and axle shims from axle shaft.

NOTE: Axle shaft end play shims are located on the left side only.

3. Using suitable puller, pull axle shaft and bearing from axle tube, then remove and discard inner oil seal.

NOTE: The bearing cone must be pressed off the shaft, using an arbor press.

CAUTION: On models equipped with Twin Grip differential, do not rotate differential unless both axle shafts are in place.

ASSEMBLY

When installing hub onto axle, install two well lubricated thrust washers and axle shaft nut. Tighten axle shaft nut until hub is installed to the dimensions shown in **Fig. 3.** Remove axle shaft nut and one thrust washer. Reinstall axle shaft nut and tighten to 250 ft. lbs. If cotter pin hole is not aligned, tighten the nut to the next castellation and install cotter pin.

NOTE: Do not use an original hub on a replacement axle shaft; use a new hub. A new hub may be installed on an original axle shaft providing the serrations on the shaft are not worn or damaged. Be certain that the hub and axle shaft are punch marked to insure proper alignment on installation. A replacement hub, which is not serrated, can be installed and serrations will be cut in the hub when installed on the shaft due to the difference in hardness of the shaft and the hub.

Replace the parts in the reverse order of their removal. If the old parts are replaced and the shims have not been disturbed, the axle shaft end play should be correct when the parts are assembled. However, if a new shaft, bearing, differential carrier or housing has been installed, it will be necessary to check the end play.

The end play can be checked when all parts have been replaced except the wheel and hub. To make this check, rap each axle shaft after the nuts are tight to be sure the bearing cups are seated. Then place a dial indicator so that its stem contacts the end of the shaft and work the shaft in and out to determine the amount of existing end play. Axle shaft end play should be .004–.008 inch. If an adjustment is necessary, remove the outer oil seal and brake support and add or remove shims as required. When making this adjustment, add or subtract shims on left side of axle only.

NOTE: The application of a bead of seal-

1. BOLT
2. WASHER
3. AXLE SHAFT OIL SEAL RETAINER
4. AXLE SHAFT OIL SEAL
5. AXLE SHAFT BEARING SHIM
6. AXLE SHAFT BEARING CUP
7. AXLE BEARING
8. AXLE BOLT
9. AXLE SHAFT INNER OIL SEAL
10. PINION COLLAPSIBLE SPACER
11. FILLER PLUG
12. FRONT PINION BEARING CUP
13. PINION OIL SEAL
14. UNIVERSAL JOINT YOKE
15. PINION NUT
16. FRONT PINION BEARING
17. BREATHER
18. BREATHER HOSE
19. NUT
20. REAR AXLE HOUSING
21. DRIVE PINION DEPTH ADJUSTING SHIM
22. REAR PINION BEARING CUP
23. REAR PINION BEARING
24. PINION GEAR
25. DIFFERENTIAL BEARING
26. DIFFERENTIAL BEARING CUP
27. DIFFERENTIAL BEARING SHIM
28. DIFFERENTIAL BEARING CUP
29. BOLT
30. BOLT
31. HOUSING COVER
32. HOUSING COVER GASKET
33. DIFFERENTIAL PINION SHAFT
34. DIFFERENTIAL PINION GEAR THRUST WASHER
35. DIFFERENTIAL SIDE GEAR THRUST WASHER
36. DIFFERENTIAL PINION GEAR
37. DIFFERENTIAL SIDE GEAR
38. DIFFERENTIAL PINION SHAFT THRUST BLOCK
39. BOLT
40. DIFFERENTIAL CASE
41. DIFFERENTIAL PINION SHAFT PIN
42. RING GEAR

Fig. 2   Rear axle assembly (typical). 8⅞ in. axle

ALIGNING MARKS

SERRATIONS

1-3/16 (30.14 mm) (7 9/16 AXLE)
1-5/16 (33.32 mm) (8 7/8 AXLE)

Fig. 3   Installing hub on axle

ing material such as "Pliobond" or "Permatex" to the outer diameter of axle tube flange and the brake support contact area is recommended. The sealing material will be used in addition to the gasket for improved sealing.

BRAKE ADJUSTMENTS

These brakes, have self-adjusting mechanisms that assure correct lining-to-drum clearances at all times. The automatic adjusters operate only when the brakes are applied as the car is moving rearward.

Although the brakes are self-adjusting, an initial adjustment is necessary after the brake shoes have been relined or replaced, or when the length of the star wheel adjusting screw has been changed during some other service operation.

Frequent usage of an automatic transmission forward range to halt reverse vehicle motion may prevent the automatic adjusters from functioning, thereby inducing low pedal heights. Should low pedal heights be encountered on these models, it is recommended that numerous forward and reverse stops be made until satisfactory pedal height is obtained.

NOTE: If a low pedal condition cannot be

AMERICAN MOTORS

corrected by making numerous stops (provided the hydraulic system is free of air) it indicates that the self-adjusting mechanism is not functioning. Therefore, it will be necessary to remove the brake drum, clean, free up and lubricate the adjusting mechanisms. Then adjust the brakes as follows, being sure the parking brake is fully released.

ADJUSTMENT

1. Remove access slot cover from brake support plate.
2. Using brake adjusting tool or screwdriver, rotate adjuster screw until wheel is locked.
3. Back off adjuster screw one complete turn.

NOTE: To back off adjuster screw, insert a piece of ⅛ inch rod past adjuster screw and force adjusting lever off adjuster screw.

4. Install rubber access slot cover.
5. Following the initial adjustment and final assembly, check the brake pedal height to insure brake operation. Then drive the car forward and reverse, making 10 to 15 brake applications prior to road testing. This action balances the adjustment of the four brake units and raises the brake pedal.

PARKING BRAKE
ADJUST

PACER

1. Make sure service brakes are properly adjusted.
2. Apply and release parking brake several times.
3. Place parking lever in first notch from fully released position and place transmission in neutral.

4. Raise and support vehicle at rear axle using jack stands.
5. Loosen locknut and tighten cable adjuster until there is a heavy brake drag at rear wheels.
6. Loosen adjuster until heavy drag is just eliminated and tighten locknut.

EXC. PACER

With Adjustment Gauge J-23462
1. Make sure service brakes are properly adjusted.
2. Apply and release parking brake several times.
3. Raise and support vehicle at rear axle using jack stands.
4. Place parking brake in first notch from fully released position.
5. Place an inch lb. torque wrench on Parking Brake Cable Adjustment Gauge J-23462 and place gauge on from parking brake cable, centered between cable housing ferrule and cable equalizer.
6. Apply 50 inch lbs. of torque and note indicator reading. If reading is not within the green band, adjust parking brake at equalizer until satisfactory reading is obtained.
7. Release parking brake and check for brake drag. If brake drag is evident, inspect actuating cables and equalizer for freedom of movement and proper operation. Inspect cable condition, especially at areas where cable passes near exhaust components. Correct as necessary and readjust parking brake cable.

Less Adjustment Gauge J-23462
1. With service brakes properly adjusted, set parking brake pedal on the first notch from fully released position.
2. Adjust front cable at equalizer to obtain .0001–.005 inch (.003–.127mm) clearance between parking brake lever strut and primary brake shoe at both rear brakes.

3. Release pedal and check for rear wheel drag—wheels should rotate freely.

BRAKE MASTER CYLINDER
REPLACE

1. Disconnect brake lines from master cylinder. Cap lines and master cylinder ports.
2. On models with manual brakes, disconnect master cylinder push rod at brake pedal.
3. On all models, remove nuts or bolts attaching master cylinder to dash panel or brake booster and remove master cylinder. On Pacer models, remove mounting bracket and boot retainer plate.
4. Install in the reverse order of removal and bleed the brake system.

POWER BRAKE UNIT
REPLACE

1. Disconnect booster push rod from brake pedal.
2. Remove vacuum hose from check valve.
3. Remove nuts and washers securing master cylinder to booster unit, then separate master cylinder from booster unit.

NOTE: Do not disconnect brake lines from master cylinder.

4. Remove booster unit to firewall attaching nuts and remove booster unit.
5. Reverse procedure to install.

Rear Suspension

SHOCK ABSORBER
REPLACE

1. With the rear axle supported properly, disconnect lower end of shock absorber from stud on mounting bracket.
2. Remove upper mounting bracket from underbody.
3. Reverse procedure to install.

LEAF SPRINGS
REPLACE

1. Support rear axle, removing tension from springs.
2. Disconnect lower end of shock absorber from stud on mounting bracket, **Figs. 1 and 2.**

3. Remove "U" bolts securing spring plate and spring to axle tube.
4. Disassemble rear shackle and remove eye bolt from spring forward mounting bracket.

NOTE: On Pacer, remove nuts attaching rear hanger bracket to mounting studs on side sill and remove spring.

5. Reverse procedure to install. Replace bushings as necessary.

CONTROL ARMS & BUSHINGS
REPLACE

NOTE: Replace control arms one at a time

to prevent axle assembly misalignment, making installation difficult.

UPPER CONTROL ARMS

1. Support vehicle at frame.
2. Remove control arm bolts from frame crossmember and axle tube bracket.
3. To replace axle tube bracket bushings, refer to **Figs. 3 and 4.**
4. Reverse procedure to install.

LOWER CONTROL ARMS

1. Support vehicle at rear axle.
2. Remove stabilizer bar, if equipped.
3. Remove control arm mount bolts from frame and axle tube brackets.
4. Reverse procedure to install.

NOTE: Lower control arm bushings are

Fig. 1 Rear suspension assembly. AMX, Concord, Pacer & Spirit

Fig. 3 Upper control arm rear bushing removal

Fig. 4 Upper control arm rear bushing installation

not serviceable.

STABILIZER BAR
REPLACE

CONCORD, EAGLE & SPIRIT

1. Raise and support rear of vehicle, then remove nuts and grommets attaching stabilizer to connecting links, **Figs. 5 and 6.**
2. Remove bolts attaching stabilizer bar mounting clamps to spring clip plates and remove stabilizer bar.
3. Reverse procedure to install. Torque link lock nuts to 7 ft. lbs. and mounting clamp bolts to 25 ft. lbs.

Fig. 5 Rear stabilizer bar. Concord & Spirit

Fig. 2 Rear suspension assembly. Eagle

Fig. 6 Rear stabilizer bar. Eagle

Front End & Steering Section

DESCRIPTION

EAGLE

These models use an independent front coil spring suspension system, **Fig. 1.** The wheels are suspended on upper and lower control arms with a coil spring located between the upper control arm and a spring seat beneath the wheel housing panels.

Direct acting telescoping shock absorbers are located inside the coil springs. A stabilizer bar attached to each control arm with stabilizer links provides stability, and a dampener dampens steering oscillations.

PACER

These models have an independent front coil spring front suspension system using unequal length upper and lower control arms, **Fig. 2.** The coil springs are mounted between the lower control arms and the front crossmember with the lower arm functioning as the loaded member.

EXC. EAGLE & PACER

The front suspension, **Figs. 3 and 4** is an independent linked type, with the coil springs located between seats in the wheel house panels and seats attached to the upper control arms.

Directing acting telescoping shock absorbers are located inside the coil springs.

Each upper control arm assembly has two rubber bushings attached to the wheel house panel and a ball joint attached to the steering knuckle.

Each lower control arm has a rubber bushing attached to the front crossmember and a Ball joint attached to the steering knuckle.

The lower control arm strut rods are attached to the lower control arms and body side sill brackets.

WHEEL ALIGNMENT

PACER

Caster is adjusted by rotating the rear pivot bolt eccentric, **Fig. 5.** After adjustment, torque locknut to 110 ft. lbs.

Camber is adjusted by rotating both front and rear lower control arm pivot bolt eccentrics, **Fig. 5.** After adjustment, torque locknut to 110 ft. lbs.

EXC. PACER

Caster is obtained by moving the two adjusting nuts on the threaded strut rod, **Fig. 6.** One nut is on each side of the mounting bracket. Therefore, moving the nuts on the rod will move the lower control arm to front or rear for desired caster angle. After adjustment, torque adjusting nuts to 65 ft. lbs. Torque locknuts to 75 ft. lbs.

Camber is obtained by turning on the

Fig. 1   Front suspension view. Eagle

Fig. 2   Front suspension. Pacer (Typical)

Fig. 3   Front suspension upper control arm components. Exc. Eagle & Pacer

Fig. 4   Front suspension lower control arm components. Exc. Eagle & Pacer

would otherwise result in noise problems or damage.

eccentric lower control arm bolt, **Fig. 7.** After adjustment, torque lock nut to 110 ft. lbs.

TOE-IN
ADJUST

To adjust toe-in, loosen the clamps at both ends of the adjustable tubes on each tie rod. Turn the tubes an equal amount until the toe-in is correct. Turning the right tube in the direction the wheels revolve when the car is going forward increases the toe-in and turning the left tube in the opposite direction increases toe-in. To decrease toe-in turn the right tube backward and the left tube forward. It is important that both tubes be turned an equal amount in order to maintain the correct position of the steering wheel. When adjustment is complete, tighten all clamp bolts.

NOTE: In performing service operations on the steering linkage or when adjusting toe-in, be sure to square the tie rod ball sockets on the studs and align the tie rod stud in the center, or slightly above center, of the cross tube opening, before tightening the steering linkage adjusting tube. This will prevent the stud from contacting the side of the cross tube opening, which

WHEEL BEARINGS
ADJUST

1980–83 EXC. EAGLE

1. To adjust bearings tighten spindle nut to 25 ft. lbs. while rotating the wheel to seat bearings.
2. Then loosen spindle nut 1/3 turn and with wheel rotating, retorque spindle nut to 6 inch pounds.
3. Place the nut retainer on spindle nut with the slots of the retainer aligned with the cotter pin hole on the spindle.
4. Install cotter pin and dust cap.

WHEEL BEARINGS
REPLACE

DISC BRAKES

Exc. Eagle
1. Remove two thirds of the total fluid capacity of the master cylinder reservoir to prevent fluid overflow when the cal-

Fig. 5   Caster and camber adjustment. Pacer

Fig. 6   Caster adjustment, Exc. Pacer

Fig. 7   Camber adjustment. Exc. Pacer

iper pistons are pushed back on their bores.

2. Raise car and remove front wheels.
3. Disconnect hydraulic tube from mounting bracket. Do not disconnect any hydraulic fitting.
4. Holding the lower edge of the caliper, remove the lower bolt. Any shims that fall out at this point should be labeled to insure that they be replaced in their original position.
5. Holding the upper edge of the caliper, remove the upper bolt, tag these shims.
6. Hang caliper from upper suspension to prevent strain being placed on brake hose.
7. Remove spindle nut and hub and disc assembly. Grease retainer and inner bearing can now be removed.
8. Reverse procedure to install.

CHECKING BALL JOINTS FOR WEAR
PACER

Lower Ball Joint
1. Position vehicle on level surface and remove lower ball joint lubrication plug.
2. Insert a 2 to 3 in. piece of stiff wire or thin rod into plug hole until it contacts ball stud, then accurately scribe mark on wire or rod at outer edge of plug hole.
3. If distance from ball stud to outer edge of plug hole is 7/16 in. or more, replace ball joint.

Upper Ball Joint
1. Position suitable jack under lower control arm and raise vehicle until wheel is off floor.
2. Move top of wire toward and away from center of vehicle, if any looseness or play is present, replace ball joint.
3. Using a suitable tool, move upper control arm up and down. If looseness or play is present, replace ball joint.

EXCEPT PACER

Before checking ball joints for wear, make sure the front wheel bearings are properly adjusted and that the control arms are tight.

Referring to **Fig. 8,** raise wheel with a jack placed under the frame as shown. Then test by moving the wheel up and down to check axial play, and rocking it at the top and bottom to measure radial play.

The upper ball joint should be replaced if total travel when rocking and tire exceeds 160 inch.

The lower ball joint is spring loaded and should be replaced if there is any noticeable lateral shake.

NOTE: On Eagle models, if lower ball joint is worn excessively, the lower control arm and ball joint must be replaced as an assembly.

Fig. 8   Check ball joints for wear. Exc. Pacer

BALL JOINTS
REPLACE

PACER

Upper Ball Joint
1. Raise vehicle and remove wheel and tire assembly.
2. Using suitable jack, raise lower control arm approximately 1 in.
3. Remove cotter pin and retaining nut from upper ball joint stud.
4. Install tool J-9656 onto ball joint stud.
5. Lower jack supporting control arm slightly, then strike tool with hammer to loosen ball stud in steering knuckle.
6. Chisel heads from rivets attaching ball joint to upper control arm, then drive rivets out using a punch.
7. Remove tool from ball stud, then remove ball joint assembly.
8. Position ball joint on upper control arm and install nuts and bolts.

NOTE: Install bolts from bottom with nuts on top. Torque nuts to 25 ft. lbs.

9. Reverse procedure to assemble. Torque ball joint stud to 75 ft. lbs.

Lower Ball Joint
1. Raise vehicle and remove wheel and tire assembly.

2. Remove brake drum or caliper and rotor assembly.

NOTE: When removing caliper do not damage brake tubing or hose. Secure caliper to frame with wire.

3. Remove steering arm to steering knuckle attaching bolts and position steering arm aside.
4. Disconnect stabilizer bar link bolt at lower control arm, if equipped.
5. Support lower control arm with a suitable jack and remove cotter pin and nut from lower ball joint stud.
6. Install tool No. J-9656 on ball stud and remove jack.
7. Strike tool with hammer to loosen ball stud in steering knuckle.
8. Support lower control arm with jack and remove tool.
9. Disengage ball stud from steering knuckle and position components aside.

NOTE: Use wire to suspend components from upper control arm.

10. Chisel heads from rivets attaching ball joint to lower control arm, then drive rivets out using a punch and remove ball joint.
11. Position ball joint on lower control arm and install nuts and bolts.

NOTE: Install bolts from top with nuts on bottom. Torque bolts to 25 ft. lbs.

12. Reverse procedure to assemble. Torque lower ball joint stud nut to 75 ft. lbs., steering arm to knuckle bolts to 55 ft. lbs., and the stabilizer bar link bolt to 7 ft. lbs.

EXC. PACER

UPPER BALL JOINT
1. Position a 2x4x5 in. block of wood on side sill under upper control arm.
2. Raise vehicle and support at frame side sills.
3. Remove wheel, brake drum, caliper and rotor assembly.

NOTE: When removing caliper do not damage brake tubing or hose. Secure caliper to frame with wire.

4. Remove cotter pin and retaining nut from upper ball joint stud.
5. Install tool No. J-9656 on ball stud, then using a hammer strike tool to loosen ball stud in steering knuckle.
6. Support lower control arm with a suitable jack.
7. Chisel heads from rivets attaching ball joint to upper control arm, then drive rivets out using a punch.
8. Remove tool from ball stud and ball joint from steering knuckle.
9. Position ball joint on control arm and install nuts and bolts. Torque bolts to 25 ft. lbs.
10. Reverse procedure to assemble. Torque ball joint stud nut to 75 ft. lbs.

LOWER BALL JOINT

Exc. Eagle

1. Position a 2x4x5 in. block of wood on side sill under upper control arm.
2. Raise vehicle and support at frame side sills.
3. Remove wheel and brake drum or caliper and rotor assembly.

NOTE: When removing caliper do not damage brake tubing or hose. Secure caliper to frame with wire.

4. Disconnect strut rod from lower control arm and steering arm from steering knuckle.
5. Remove lower ball joint stud cotter pin and retaining nut.
6. Install tool No. 9656 on ball stud, then strike tool with hammer to loosen ball stud in steering knuckle.
7. Support lower control arm with a suitable jack.
8. Chisel heads from rivets attaching ball joint to upper control arm, then drive rivets out using a punch.
9. Remove tool from ball stud and ball joint from steering knuckle and lower control arm.
10. Position ball joint on lower control arm and install attaching bolts loosely.
11. Connect strut to lower control arm and torque bolts to 75 ft. lbs.
12. Torque ball joint to lower control arm attaching bolts to 25 ft. lbs.
13. Lubricate steering stop, then install ball stud on steering knuckle. Torque stud nut to 75 ft. lbs. Install cotter pin.
14. Install wheel and brake drum or caliper and rotor and lower vehicle.

Eagle

NOTE: On these models, the lower control arm and lower ball joint must be replaced as an assembly.

1. Remove cotter pin, nut lock and hub nut, then raise and support front of vehicle.
2. Remove wheel, caliper and rotor.
3. Remove lower ball joint cotter pin and retaining nut.
4. Using tool No. J-9656, disconnect lower ball joint from steering knuckle.
5. Remove half shaft flange bolts, then remove half shaft.
6. Remove bolts attaching strut rod to lower control arm, then disconnect stabilizer bar from lower control arm.
7. Remove inner pivot bolt, then remove lower control arm from crossmember.
8. Position control arm on cross member, then install inner pivot bolt. Do not tighten inner pivot bolt at this time.
9. Position lower ball joint on steering knuckle, then install ball joint stud nut. Torque ball joint stud nut to 75 ft. lbs., then install cotter pin.
10. Connect stabilizer bar to lower control arm and torque lock nut to 7 ft. lbs.
11. Connect strut rod to lower control arm and torque attaching bolts to 75 ft. lbs.
12. Install half shaft to axle flange and

Fig. 9   Installing Spring compressor. Pacer

torque bolts to 45 ft. lbs.
13. Position a suitable jack under control arm and raise control arm slightly to compress coil spring, then tighten inner pivot bolt to 110 ft. lbs.
14. Install rotor, caliper and hub nut. Torque hub nut to 180 ft. lbs., then install nut lock and cotter pin.
15. Install wheel and tire assembly, then lower vehicle and check wheel alignment.

Fig. 10   Compressing spring. Pacer

SHOCK ABSORBER
REPLACE

PACER

1. Disconnect shock absorber at upper mounting.
2. Raise and support vehicle.
3. Disconnect shock absorber at lower mounting.
4. Remove shock absorber.
5. Reverse procedure to install.

EXC. PACER

After disconnecting shock absorber from wheelhouse panel at top and lower spring seat at the bottom, withdraw shock absorber out of top of wheelhouse.

SPRING
REPLACE

PACER

1. Remove shock absorber, then the stabilizer bar link bolt at lower control arm, if equipped.
2. On models with drum brakes, remove wheel, tire and drum. On disc brake models, remove wheel, tire, caliper and rotor.
3. Remove steering arm to knuckle attaching bolts and position arm aside.
4. Compress spring, **Figs. 9 and 10.**
5. Remove cotter pin and nut from lower ball joint, then using tool J-9656 and a hammer, disengage stud from steering knuckle and position knuckle aside.

NOTE: Use wire to support steering knuckle otherwise brake hoses may be damaged.

6. Position lower control arm aside and relieve spring tension. When all tension is relieved, remove tool and spring.
7. Reverse procedure to install.

EXC. PACER

1. Remove shock absorber.
2. Install spring compressor tool J-23474 through upper spring seat opening, **Fig. 11.** Place tool lower attaching screws through shock absorber mounting holes in the lower spring seat. Install tool lower retainer.
3. Remove lower spring seat pivot retaining nuts.
4. Tighten compressor until spring is compressed approximately 1 inch.
5. Raise and support front of car under frame allowing control arms to fall free of lower spring seat. Remove wheel.
6. Pull lower spring seat away from car. Loosen compressor and allow lower spring seat to come out.
7. When all spring tension is released, remove tool lower retainer spring seat and spring.
8. Reverse procedure to install.

American Motors

STABILIZER BAR
REPLACE

1. Raise and support front of vehicle, then remove right side wheel.
2. Disconnect idler arm at frame side sill.
3. Remove stabilizer bar mounting clamps at the frame side sills.
4. Disconnect stabilizer bar link at lower control arms, then remove link bolts, rubber grommets, spacer and retainers.
5. Remove stabilizer bar from right side of vehicle. Move steering linkage and left side wheel, as necessary, to obtain clearance.
6. Reverse procedure to install.

Fig. 11 Installation of spring compressor Exc. Pacer

STEERING GEAR
REPLACE

PACER

1. Unlock steering column, then raise and support vehicle.
2. Remove reinforcement brace to cross-member and left engine support bracket attaching bolts, then remove brace.
3. On models with power steering, position a drain pan under steering gear housing and disconnect power steering hoses at gear.

NOTE: Cap hoses and connections to prevent entry of dirt.

4. Remove flexible coupling pinch bolt,

1. HALF-SHAFT ASSEMBLY
2. AXLE MOUNTING BRACKETS
3. VENT HOSE
4. PINION AND FRONT BEARING CUP
5. WASHER
6. YOKE AND SEAL
7. OUTER BOOT AND RETAINER
8. RZEPPA JOINT ASSEMBLY
9. SPINDLE
10. HALF-SHAFT
11. INNER BOOT AND RETAINER
12. TRI-POT JOINT ASSEMBLY
13. TRI-POT HOUSING
14. AXLE SHAFT (SHORT)
15. BALL BEARING AND SEAL
16. AXLE HOUSING
17. AXLE SHAFT (LONG)
18. NEEDLE BEARING AND SEAL
19. PRELOAD SHIM
20. WASHER
21. DEPTH SHIM
22. PINION REAR BEARING AND CUP
23. SLINGER
24. PINION GEAR
25. COVER
26. DIFFERENTIAL BEARING AND CUP
27. DIFFERENTIAL PINION AND THRUST WASHER
28. PINION MATE SHAFT
29. SIDE GEAR, THRUST WASHER AND LOCKRING
30. BEARING CAP
31. RING GEAR
32. DIFFERENTIAL CASE

Fig. 12 Front axle assembly. 1980–84 Eagle less Select Drive System

then disconnect coupling from steering pinion shaft.

5. Turn wheels in direction of tie rod to be disconnected, then using a floor jack, raise lower control arm at least 2 in. Remove cotter pin and retaining nut from tie rod end and using tool J-3295, disconnect tie rod from steering arm.
6. Remove bolts attaching steering gear mounting clamp to right side of crossmember.
7. Remove steering gear housing to crossmember attaching nuts, then using a blunt punch, remove bolts, washers, sleeves and grommets from gear housing.
8. Rotate bottom of gear housing toward front of front of vehicle until pinion shaft is parallel with skid plate, then slide gear toward right side of vehicle until housing and tube clear mounting plate.
9. Reverse procedure to install.

EXCEPT PACER

Manual Steering
1. Remove flexible coupling bolts.
2. Remove pitman arm, using a suitable puller.
3. Remove mounting screws and lower steering gear from vehicle.
4. Reverse procedure to install.

Power Steering
1. Disconnect pressure and return hoses from gear. Raise hoses above pump level to keep oil from draining out of pump.
2. Remove flexible coupling bolt nuts, noting the different nut sizes to insure correct assembly.
3. On Eagle models, remove skid plate, if equipped, then remove left hand crossmember to sill support brace and stabilizer bar bracket from frame.
4. Remove pitman arm with a suitable puller.
5. Remove gear attaching bolts.
6. Slide lower shaft free of coupling flange, then remove gear.
7. Reverse procedure to install.

POWER STEERING PUMP
REPLACE

MODELS w/4 CYL. ENGINE
1. Remove air induction hose, then remove power steering pump adjusting bracket mounting bolts.
2. Move power steering pump toward engine and remove drive belt.
3. Loosen return hose clamp and slide back along hose, then pull power steering pump forward and disconnect both pressure and return lines.
4. Remove bolts attaching power steering pump front mounting bracket to rear mounting bracket and engine.
5. Remove power steering pump, pivot bracket and front mounting bracket as an assembly.
6. Reverse procedure to install.

Fig. 13   Front axle assembly. 1980—84 Eagle w/Select Drive System

MODELS w/6 CYL. ENGINE

Less A/C
1. On 1980–83 models, remove air pump drive belt, then remove air pump pivot stud nut.
2. On all models, remove power steering pump adjusting stud nuts and pivot bolt, then remove pump drive belt.
3. Disconnect pressure and return lines, then remove bolts attaching power steering pump bracket to engine and remove pump.
4. Reverse procedure to install.

With A/C
1. Remove air induction hoses
2. On 1980–83 models, remove air pump adjusting bolt and pivot stud, then remove air pump drive belt.
3. Remove A/C compressor drive belt, then remove compressor pulley and pulley bracket as an assembly.
4. Remove power steering pump pivot bolt attaching lower edge of pump to engine.
5. Remove power steering pump adjusting bracket stud nuts and bolt attaching pump to rear bracket, then slide drive belt from pulley.
6. Pull power steering pump and front

mounting bracket forward until bracket clears air pump pivot stud.
7. On 1980–83 models, remove air pump pivot stud and position air pump aside.
8. On all models, disconnect power steering pump pressure and return lines, then remove pump.
9. Reverse procedure to install.

EAGLE FRONT AXLE SERVICE

NOTE: Refer to **Figs. 12, 13** and **14** during front axle service procedures.

AXLE, REPLACE

Removal
1. Raise and support vehicle.
2. Install half shaft boot protectors J-28712 onto boots.
3. Remove half shaft to axle flange bolts and secure half shaft to vehicle underbody.
4. Insert wire through half shaft flange bolt holes, then compress half shaft

1. HALF-SHAFT ASSEMBLY
2. AXLE MOUNTING BRACKETS
3. VENT HOSE
4. PINION AND FRONT BEARING CUP
5. WASHER
6. YOKE AND SEAL
7. OUTER BOOT AND RETAINER
8. RZEPPA JOINT ASSEMBLY
9. SPINDLE
10. HALF-SHAFT
11. INNER BOOT AND RETAINER

12. TRI-POT JOINT ASSEMBLY
13. TRI-POT HOUSING
14. AXLE SHAFT (SHORT)
15. BALL BEARING AND SEAL
16. AXLE HOUSING
17. AXLE SHAFT (LONG)
18. NEEDLE BEARING AND SEAL
19. PRELOAD SHIM
20. WASHER
21. DEPTH SHIM
22. PINION REAR BEARING
     AND CUP

23. SLINGER
24. PINION GEAR
25. COVER
26. DIFFERENTIAL BEARING AND CUP
27. DIFFERENTIAL PINION AND THRUST
     WASHER
28. PINION MATE SHAFT
29. SIDE GEAR, THRUST WASHER AND
     LOCKRING
30. BEARING CAP
31. RING GEAR
32. DIFFERENTIAL CASE

Fig. 14   Front axle assembly.
1985–86 Eagle

and wrap wire between boots to prevent half shaft from separating.
5. Mark propeller shaft and axle yoke for reference during reassembly and remove propeller shaft.
6. Support axle assembly using suitable jack.
7. On models equipped with Select Drive System, remove brace rod and shift motor shield.
8. On all models, remove axle mounting bolts. On models less Select Drive System, the axle is secured to the engine block with five bolts. On models with Select Drive System, the axle is secured to the engine block by five bolts on the left hand side and one bolt on the right hand side.
9. On models equipped with Select Drive System, disconnect vacuum hose from axle shift motor, then partially lower axle assembly and disconnect vent hose.

10. On all models, lower axle assembly to allow access to vent hose and remove hose.
11. Remove axle assembly from vehicle.

NOTE: Do not apply any load or weight on the hub assembly whenever the half shafts are not securely attached to the axle shaft flanges.

Installation

1. Support axle assembly on suitable jack and position assembly under vehicle.
2. Raise axle assembly slightly and install vent hose.
3. Continue raising axle assembly until properly positioned and install axle mounting bolts. Torque bolts to 50 ft. lbs.
4. Connect propeller shaft to axle yoke. Ensure shaft and yoke are aligned.

CARRIER
O-RING

HUB

CARRIER TO
HUB SEAL

SHOULDERED
BEARING

HUB AND
BEARING CARRIER

SHOULDERED
BEARING

HUB
SPACER

STEERING
KNUCKLE PIN

HUB ASSEMBLY
WITH SHOULDERED
BEARING

**Fig. 15   Disassembled view of
axle hub. Eagle**

5. Remove wire used to prevent half shafts from separating, then install half shaft to axle flange bolts and torque to 45 ft. lbs.
6. On models equipped with Select Drive System, connect vacuum harness on axle shift motor shield.
7. On all models, remove half shaft boot protectors.
8. On models equipped with Select Drive, connect brace rod to axle.

AXLE SHAFT SEAL, REPLACE

NOTE: On 1985–86 models, removal of the right hand shaft seal is the same as that of the left hand shaft seal.

1. Remove axle assembly.
2. Remove axle housing cover and drain lubricant.
3. Remove axle shaft retaining clip, then the axle shaft.
4. Remove axle shaft seal using suitable screwdriver.
5. Install replacement axle shaft seal using Installer J-29152 for right hand side axle shaft and Installer J-29154 for left hand side axle shaft.
6. Install axle shaft, then the axle shaft retaining clip.
7. Apply suitable sealant to axle housing cover and install cover. Torque cover bolts to 20 ft. lbs.
8. Fill axle with 2½ pints of SAE 85W-90 lubricant, then install assembly onto vehicle. Refer to Axle, Installation for procedures.

AXLE HUB & BEARING

Removal
1. Raise and support vehicle, then remove wheel, caliper and rotor.
2. Remove bolts attaching axle shaft flange to half shaft.

NOTE: Insert wire through half shaft flange bolt holes, then compress half shaft and wrap wire between boots to prevent half shaft from separating.

3. Remove cotter pin, lock nut and axle shaft nut, then the half shaft.
4. Remove steering arm from steering knuckle.
5. Remove caliper anchor plate from steering knuckle, then the three torx head bolts retaining hub assembly using tool J-26359.
6. Remove hub assembly from steering knuckle and clean grease from steering knuckle cavity.

Disassemble
1. Press hub from bearing carrier, then remove bearings, hub spacer, steering knuckle pin seal, carrier to hub seal, carrier O-ring and bearing spacer, if equipped, **Fig. 15.**
2. Clean all components and inspect for wear and damage and replace as necessary.

NOTE: If hub incorporates ball bearings,

the entire hub assembly must be replaced if damage to internal components is indicated. If hub incorporates tapered bearings, internal hub components may be replaced as necessary. Bearings and races must be replaced in matched sets.

3. Press bearing races from hub carrier, if necessary. Install replacement bearing races using a brass drift or suitable press.

Assemble
1. Fill steering knuckle pin, hub, bearing carrier and lip type seal cavities with lithium base wheel bearing lubricant.
2. Pack bearings with lithium base wheel bearing lubricant, then install bearings into hub carrier, **Fig. 15.**
3. Install seal onto hub side of bearing carrier, then press hub into carrier and install hub spacer on end of hub shaft.

NOTE: Do not install bearing carrier O-ring at this time.

4. Install inner seal into steering knuckle pin.
5. Install splash shield onto hub and bearing carrier, then install bearing carrier O-ring.
6. Install splash shield and bearing carrier into steering knuckle pin, then install carrier attaching bolts and torque to 75 ft. lbs.

Installation
1. Partially fill hub cavity of steering knuckle with chassis lubricant and install hub assembly onto steering knuckle. Torque hub torx head bolts to 75 ft. lbs.
2. Install caliper anchor plate and torque plate retaining bolts to 100 ft. lbs.
3. Install steering arm onto steering knuckle and torque retaining bolts to 100 ft. lbs.
4. Install half shaft, then the axle flange to shaft bolts and hub nut. Torque half shaft to flange bolts to 45 ft. lbs and hub nut 175 ft. lbs.
5. Install lock nut, replacement cotter pin, rotor, caliper and wheel.

AXLE SHAFT, REPLACE

NOTE: On 1985–86 models, removal of

the right hand shaft is the same as that of the left hand shaft.

1. Refer to Axle Shaft Seal, Replace. Perform steps 1 through 3 for axle shaft removal and steps 6 through 8 for axle shaft installation.

AXLE SHAFT BEARING, REPLACE

NOTE: Two different style axle shaft bearings are used on the Eagle front axle. The left side axle shaft uses a ball bearing. The right side axle shaft uses a needle bearing. On 1985–86 models, removal of the right hand side bearing is the same as that of the left hand bearing.

1. Remove axle assembly. Refer to Axle, Removal for procedure.
2. Remove axle housing cover and drain lubricant.
3. Remove axle shaft retaining clip, then the axle shaft.
4. Remove axle shaft seal using suitable screwdriver.
5. Remove needle bearing using Tools J-29173 and J-2619-1. Remove ball bearing using suitable brass punch and hammer.

NOTE: If needle bearing tools are not available, remove the differential, then the bearing using a 15/16 in. socket and three foot extension bar.

6. Install axle shaft bearings. Use tool J-29153 to install needle bearing and tool J-29154 to install ball bearing.
7. Install axle shaft seals using Installer J-29152 for the right hand side axle shaft and Installer J-29154 for left hand side axle shaft.
8. Install axle shafts, then the retaining clips.
9. Apply suitable sealant to axle housing cover and install cover. Torque cover bolts to 20 ft. lbs.
10. Fill axle with 2½ pints of SAE 85W-90 lubricant, then install asembly onto vehicle. Refer to Axle, Installation for procedure.

1984–86 HALF SHAFT SERVICE

Disassemble
1. Using a suitable tool cut and remove both outer boot clamps, then roll outer boot from constant velocity joint.
2. Position a wooden block against constant velocity joint inner race and drive joint from shaft. If half shaft is to be positioned in a vise, use protective vise jaws.
3. Using a brass drift, tap constant velocity joint cage until cage is tilted outward far enough to remove first ball, then remove remaining balls in the same manner.
4. Align two outer constant velocity joint oblong holes with slots located on interior wall of spindle housing and remove cage and inner race.
5. Align shoulder between race grooves with inside of oblong cage holes, then rotate inner race out of cage using the larger of the two openings.
6. Remove two snap rings from shaft, then remove outer boot.
7. Remove rubber retaining ring from small end of inner boot.
8. Cut inner boot retaining strap, then remove strap from tripod housing. Slide boot away from housing.
9. Remove tripod joint and shaft from housing.
10. Remove snap ring that retains tripod joint on shaft using suitable pliers, then remove tripod joint.
11. Remove inner boot from shaft if replacement is required.
12. Remove any remaining snap rings from shaft, if not removed previously.

Inspection

Clean all components in a suitable solvent and dry with compressed air. Check all components for wear and damage and joints for rough operation, replace components as necessary.

NOTE: Outer constant velocity joint and inner tripod joint are replaced as an assembly.

Assemble

1. Pack spindle hub with chassis grease.
2. Install outer constant velocity joint inner into cage, then install cage and race assembly into spindle hub. The smaller diameter of the cage and stopping groove of race must face outward.
3. Using a brass drift, tilt cage outward until first ball can be installed into cage, then install remaining balls in the same manner.
4. Pack constant velocity joint with chassis grease, then install outer boot on half shaft.
5. Install inner and outer snap rings, then constant velocity joint onto shaft until inner race contacts inner snap ring.
6. Position boot over constant velocity joint, then install both boot clamps using tool No. J-22716 or equivalent.

NOTE: Check and adjust installed length of boot. Total installed length should be 4.134 inch (105 mm). Move small end of boot in or out on shaft to obtain specified length.

7. Pack tripod joint housing with chassis grease, then install inner small retainer ring, boot and large retainer ring onto half shaft.
8. Install tripod joint and snap ring onto shaft, then install tripod joint and shaft into housing.
9. Position boot and install rubber retainer ring over small end of boot.
10. Install large end boot clamp using a suitable tool.

INTERMEDIATE SHAFT, OUTER AXLE SHAFT & SHIFT HOUSING, REPLACE

Models w/Select Drive System

1. Raise and support front of vehicle.
2. Remove front axle assembly, then drain lubricant.
3. Remove bolts securing shift housing and remove shift fork, shifting housing and shift motor as an assembly, **Figs. 13 and 14.**
4. Working through access hole in the outer axle shaft flange, remove screws securing axle tube cover.
5. Remove outer axle shaft assembly by tapping shaft flange with a rubber or plastic mallet.
6. Remove intermediate shaft snap ring, then remove intermediate shaft and shift collar.
7. Using a suitable puller and slide hammer, remove outer axle shaft bearing race.
8. Using adapter tool No. J-26225 and slide hammer J-6471-2, remove intermediate shaft needle bearing from axle tube end.
9. Using spreader tool No. J-29369-1 and slide hammer No. J-2619-01, remove intermediate shaft gear bearing.

NOTE: The intermediate shaft gear is retained on the axle shaft by an internal type expandable snap ring. When removing the bearing from the gear be sure to support the gear face on vise jaws to avoid pulling the gear off the shaft. The gear and shaft are serviced only as an assembly.

10. Remove outer axle shaft retaining "E" ring.
11. Make a reference mark on outer axle shaft gear (for assembly purposes) and remove gear from shaft.
12. Remove outer axle shaft bearing using an arbor press.
13. Remove axle oil seal and tube cover.
14. Clean and carefully inspect all components for wear or damage. Replace all necessary components.
15. Install axle oil seal and tube cover on axle shaft.
16. Using an arbor press, install axle shaft bearing and race on shaft.
17. Install axle shaft gear on shaft using an arbor press. Be sure to align reference mark. Also ensure gear splines are facing outward.
18. Install axle shaft "E" ring.
19. Using tool No. J-29153, install intermediate shaft needle bearing.
20. Install intermediate shaft gear needle bearing in gear bore using an arbor press.
21. Install intermediate shaft, then install shift collar, and seat shaft in differential.
22. Install intermediate shaft lock ring.
23. Install outer axle shaft assembly, torque axle tube cover bolts evenly and in a cross sequence. Torque bolts 144 inch-pounds.
24. Install gasket on shift housing cover and install.

NOTE: Check to ensure the shift fork tabs are aligned in the shift collar.

25. Torque shift housing cover bolts to 108 inch-pounds.
26. Install axle cover using a new gasket. Torque bolts to 20 ft. lbs.
27. Fill shift housing with five ozs. of specified lubricant, then fill axle housing.

SELECT DRIVE SYSTEM

The Select Drive is a system which permits the full time four wheel drive power train to be operated in a two wheel drive mode. When the vehicle is stopped, the system can be changed from two wheel drive to four wheel or four wheel drive to two wheel drive, by pulling the instrument panel control switch pull release pin downward and moving the control switch lever to the desired position. The two major components of this system are a shifting device in the transfer case and a disconnecting mechanism in the front axle, which are controlled by the instrument panel switch through a series of vacuum actuators.

The vacuum actuated shifter mechanism located on the transfer case slides a splined clutch, located on the transfer case main shaft, rearward to engage or forward to disengage power to the front drive chain sprocket. In the two wheel drive position, the shifter mechanism also locks the transfer case differential. Also the main shaft and differential assembly will turn as a unit, transferring power to the rear driveshaft, while front output shaft, chain and sprocket remain stationary.

A vacuum actuated disconnect device is used to engage or disengage a splined clutch that connects the right hand driveshaft to the right hand half shaft. When four wheel drive is selected, the spline clutch is engaged and the front drive axle operates in a normal manner. When two wheel is selected, the vacuum actuator releases the spline clutch, which releases drive to the right hand half shaft and allows the right hand driveshaft to rotate freely. Due to the design of the differential, to equalize torque between left and right axle shafts, disconnecting the right axle shaft will allow the left axle shaft to rotate freely. The axle disconnect will not release all front drive components in the two wheel drive mode. Half shafts and different side gears will continue to rotate with the front wheels as the vehicle is driven.

AXLE SHIFT MOTOR, REPLACE

Models w/Select Drive System

1. Make a reference mark on fork and housing for assembly purposes.
2. Rotate shift motor and remove retaining snap rings using a suitable screwdriver.
3. Remove shift motor from housing and remove O-ring from motor.
4. Reverse procedure to install.

NOTE: The following models are covered in this chapter: CHRYSLER—Cordoba (1980–83), Fifth Avenue (1984–86), Imperial (1981–83), LeBaron (1980–81), Newport (1980–81), New Yorker (1980–82), New Yorker Fifth Avenue (1983), Town & Country (1980–81); DODGE—Aspen (1980), Diplomat (1980–85), Mirada (1980–83), St. Regis (1980–81); PLYMOUTH—Gran Fury (1980–86), Volaré (1980).

INDEX OF SERVICE OPERATIONS

NOTE: Refer to the rear of this manual for vehicle manufacturer's special service tool suppliers.

Vehicle Number Location

1980–86: On plate attached to dash pad and visible through windshield.

Engine Number Location

1980–83 Six: Right front of block below cylinder head.

1980–86 318, 360: Left front of block below cylinder head.

1980 V8-400: Upper right front of cylinder block.

Engine Identification Code

1980–86 engines are identified by the cubic inch displacement found within the engine number stamped on the pad.

Chrysler & Imperial Grille Identification

1980 Newport	1980 New Yorker	1980 Cordoba
1980 LeBaron	1981 LeBaron	1981–83 Cordoba
1981 Newport	1981 New Yorker	1981–83 Imperial
1981 "300" & 1982 Cordoba LS	1982 New Yorker & 1983 New Yorker Fifth Avenue	1984–1986 Fifth Avenue

continued

Dodge Grille Identification

| 1980–81 St. Regis | 1980 Aspen | 1980–82 Diplomat |
| 1980–83 Mirada | 1983–84 Diplomat | 1985–86 Diplomat SE |

Plymouth Grille Identification

| 1980 Volaré | 1980–81 Gran Fury | 1982–86 Gran Fury |

General Engine Specifications

Year	Engine CID①/Liter	Engine V.I.N. Code②	Carburetor	Bore and Stroke	Compression Ratio	Net H.P. @ R.P.M.③	Maximum Torque Ft. Lbs. @ R.P.M.	Normal Oil Pressure Pounds
CHRYSLER & IMPERIAL								
1980	6-225, 3.7L	C	1945, 1 Bbl.⑦	3.40 × 4.12	8.4	90 @ 3600	160 @ 1600	30–70
	V8-318, 5.2L	G	BBD, 2 Bbl.⑤	3.91 × 3.31	8.5	120 @ 3600	245 @ 1600	30–80
	V8-318, 5.2L	H	TQ, 4 Bbl.⑤	3.91 × 3.31	8.5	155 @ 4000	240 @ 2000	30–80
	V8-360, 5.9L	K	BBD, 2 Bbl.⑤	4.00 × 3.58	8.4	130 @ 3200	—	30–80
	V8-360, 5.9L⑧	L	TQ, 4 Bbl.⑤	4.00 × 3.58	8.0	185 @ 4000	275 @ 2000	30–80
1981	6-225, 3.7L⑥	E	1945, 1 Bbl.⑦	3.40 × 4.12	8.4	85 @ 3600	165 @ 1600	30–70
	6-225, 3.7L④	E	6145, 1 Bbl.⑦	3.40 × 4.12	8.4	85 @ 3600	165 @ 1600	30–70
	V8-318, 5.2L⑥	K	BBD, 2 Bbl.⑤	3.91 × 3.31	8.6	130 @ 4000	230 @ 2000	30–80
	V8-318, 5.2L④	M	TQ, 4 Bbl.⑤	3.91 × 3.31	8.6	165 @ 4000	240 @ 2000	30–80
	V8-318, 5.2L	J	E.F.I⑨	3.91 × 3.31	8.4	140 @ 4000	240 @ 2000	30–80
1982	6-225, 3.7L⑥	E	1945, 1 Bbl.⑦	3.40 × 4.12	8.4	90 @ 3600	160 @ 1600	30–70
	6-225, 3.7L④	E	6145, 1 Bbl.⑦	3.40 × 4.12	8.4	90 @ 3600	160 @ 1600	30–70
	V8-318, 5.2L⑥	K	BBD, 2 Bbl.⑤	3.91 × 3.31	8.5	130 @ 4000	230 @ 2000	30–80
	V8-318, 5.2L④	M	TQ, 4 Bbl.⑤	3.91 × 3.31	8.5	165 @ 4000	240 @ 2000	30–80
	V8-318, 5.2L	J	E.F.I.⑨	3.91 × 3.31	8.5	140 @ 4000	245 @ 2000	30–80
1983	6-225, 3.7L	H	6145, 1 Bbl.⑦	3.40 × 4.12	8.4	90 @ 3600	165 @ 1600	30–70
	V8-318, 5.2L	P	BBD, 2 Bbl.⑤	3.91 × 3.31	8.5	130 @ 4000	230 @ 1600	30–80
	V8-318, 5.2L	N	E.F.I.⑨	3.91 × 3.31	8.5	140 @ 4000	245 @ 2000	30–80
1984	V8-318, 5.2L	P	BBD, 2 Bbl.⑤	3.91 × 3.31	8.6	130 @ 4000	235 @ 1600	30–80
1985–86	V8-318, 5.2L	P	6280, 2 Bbl.⑦	3.91 × 3.31	9.0	140 @ 3600	265 @ 1600	30–80
DODGE								
1980	6-225, 3.7L	C	1945, 1 Bbl.⑦	3.40 × 4.12	8.4	90 @ 3600	160 @ 1600	30–70
	V8-318, 5.2L	G	BBD, 2 Bbl.⑤	3.91 × 3.31	8.5	120 @ 3600	245 @ 1600	30–80
	V8-318, 5.2L	H	TQ, 4 Bbl.⑤	3.91 × 3.31	8.5	155 @ 4000	240 @ 2000	30–80
	V8-360, 5.9L	K	BBD, 2 Bbl.⑤	4.00 × 3.58	8.4	130 @ 3200	—	30–80
	V8-360, 5.9L	L	TQ, 4 Bbl.⑤	4.00 × 3.58	8.4	185 @ 4000	275 @ 2000	30–80
	V8-360, 5.9L⑧	L	TQ, 4 Bbl.⑤	4.00 × 3.58	8.0	185 @ 4000	275 @ 2000	30–80
1981	6-225, 3.7L⑥	E	1945, 1 Bbl.⑦	3.40 × 4.12	8.4	85 @ 3600	83 @ 2400	35–65
	6-225, 3.7L④	E	6145, 1 Bbl.⑦	3.40 × 4.12	8.4	85 @ 3600	165 @ 1600	30–70
	V8-318, 5.2L⑥	K	BBD, 2 Bbl.⑤	3.91 × 3.31	8.6	130 @ 4000	230 @ 2000	35–65
	V8-318, 5.2L	M	TQ, 4 Bbl.⑤	3.91 × 3.31	8.6	165 @ 4000	240 @ 2000	35–65
1982	6-225, 3.7L⑥	E	1945, 1 Bbl.⑦	3.40 × 4.12	8.4	90 @ 3600	160 @ 1600	30–70
	6-225, 3.7L④	E	6145, 1 Bbl.⑦	3.40 × 4.12	8.4	90 @ 3600	160 @ 1600	30–70
	V8-318, 5.2L⑥	K	BBD, 2 Bbl.⑤	3.91 × 3.31	8.5	130 @ 4000	230 @ 2000	30–80
	V8-318, 5.2L④	M	TQ, 4 Bbl.⑤	3.91 × 3.31	8.5	165 @ 4000	240 @ 2000	30–80
1983	6-225, 3.7L	H	6145, 1 Bbl.⑦	3.40 × 4.12	8.4	90 @ 3600	165 @ 1600	30–70
	V8-318, 5.2L	P	BBD, 2 Bbl.⑤	3.91 × 3.31	8.5	130 @ 4000	230 @ 1600	30–70
1984	V8-318, 5.2L	P	BBD, 2 Bbl.⑤	3.91 × 3.31	8.6	135 @ 4000	230 @ 1600	30–80
1985–86	V8-318, 5.2L	P	6280, 2 Bbl.⑦	3.91 × 3.31	9.0	140 @ 3600	265 @ 1600	30–80

continued

GENERAL ENGINE SPECIFICATIONS—Continued

Year	Engine CID①/Liter	Engine V.I.N. Code②	Carburetor	Bore and Stroke	Compression Ratio	Net H.P. @ R.P.M.③	Maximum Torque Ft. Lbs. @ R.P.M.	Normal Oil Pressure Pounds
PLYMOUTH								
1980	6-225, 3.7L	C	1945, 1 Bbl.⑦	3.40 × 4.12	8.4	90 @ 3600	160 @ 1600	30–70
	V8-318, 5.2L	G	BBD, 2 Bbl.⑤	3.91 × 3.31	8.5	120 @ 3600	245 @ 1600	30–80
	V8-318, 5.2L	H	TQ, 4 Bbl.⑤	3.91 × 3.31	8.5	155 @ 4000	240 @ 2000	30–80
	V8-360, 5.9L	K	BBD, 2 Bbl.⑤	4.00 × 3.58	8.4	130 @ 3200	—	30–80
	V8-360, 5.9L	L	TQ, 4 Bbl.⑤	4.00 × 3.58	8.4	185 @ 4000	275 @ 2000	30–80
1981	6-225, 3.7L⑥	E	1945, 1 Bbl.⑦	3.40 × 4.12	8.4	85 @ 3600	165 @ 1600	30–70
	6-225, 3.7L④	E	6145, 1 Bbl.⑦	3.40 × 4.12	8.4	85 @ 3600	165 @ 1600	30–70
	V8-318, 5.2L⑥	K	BBD, 2 Bbl.⑤	3.91 × 3.31	8.6	130 @ 4000	230 @ 2000	35–65
	V8-318, 5.2L	M	TQ, 4 Bbl.⑤	3.91 × 3.31	8.6	165 @ 4000	240 @ 2000	35–65
1982	6-225, 3.7L⑥	E	1945, 1 Bbl.⑦	3.40 × 4.12	8.4	90 @ 3600	160 @ 1600	30–70
	6-225, 3.7L④	E	6145, 1 Bbl.⑦	3.40 × 4.12	8.4	90 @ 3600	160 @ 1600	30–70
	V8-318, 5.2L⑥	K	BBD, 2 Bbl.⑤	3.91 × 3.31	8.5	130 @ 4000	230 @ 2000	30–80
	V8-318, 5.2L④	M	TQ, 4 Bbl.⑤	3.91 × 3.31	8.5	165 @ 4000	240 @ 2000	30–80
1983	6-225, 3.7L	H	6145, 1 Bbl.⑦	3.40 × 4.12	8.4	90 @ 3600	165 @ 1600	30–70
	V8-318, 5.2L	P	BBD, 2 Bbl.⑤	3.91 × 3.31	8.5	130 @ 4000	230 @ 1600	30–80
1984	V8-318, 5.2L	P	BBD, 2 Bbl.⑤	3.91 × 3.31	8.6	130 @ 4000	235 @ 1600	30–80
1985–86	V8-318, 5.2L	P	6280, 2 Bbl.⑤	3.91 × 3.31	9.0	140 @ 3600	265 @ 1600	30–80

①—CID—Cubic Inch Displacement.
②—On 1980 vehicles, the fifth digit in the VIN denotes engine code. On 1981–86 vehicles, the eighth digit in the VIN denotes engine code.
③—Ratings are net—as installed in vehicle.
④—California.
⑤—Carter.
⑥—Exc. California.
⑦—Holley.
⑧—With dual exhaust.
⑨—Electronic Fuel Injection.

Valve Specifications

Year	Engine/ V.I.N.	Valve Lash Int.	Valve Lash Exh.	Valve Angles Seat	Valve Angles Face	Valve Spring Installed Height	Valve Spring Pressure Lbs. @ In.	Stem Clearance Intake	Stem Clearance Exhaust	Stem Diameter Intake	Stem Diameter Exhaust
CHRYSLER & IMPERIAL											
1980	6-225/C,D	.010H	.020H	45	②	1¹¹⁄₁₆	144 @ 1⁵⁄₁₆	.001–.003	.002–.004	.372–.373	.371–.372
	V8-318/G,H	Hydraulic①		45	45	1¹¹⁄₁₆	177 @ 1⁵⁄₁₆	.001–.003	.002–.004	.372–.373	.371–.372
	V8-360/K,J	Hydraulic①		45	45	1¹¹⁄₁₆	177 @ 1⁵⁄₁₆	.001–.003	.002–.004	.372–.373	.371–.372
	V8-360/L③	Hydraulic①		45	45	1²¹⁄₃₂	193 @ 1¼	.0015–.0035	.0025–.0045	.3715–.3725	.3705–.3715
1981–83	6-225/E,H,P	Hydraulic①		45	②	1¹¹⁄₁₆	144 @ 1⁵⁄₁₆	.001–.003	.002–.004	.372–.373	.371–.372
	V8-318⑤⑥	Hydraulic①		45–45½	44½–45	1¹¹⁄₁₆	177 @ 1⁵⁄₁₆	.001–.003	.002–.004	.372–.373	.371–.372
	V8-318④⑥	Hydraulic①		45–45½	44½–45	1²¹⁄₃₂	193 @ 1¼	.0015–.0035	.0025–.0045	.3715–.3725	.3705–.3715
1984–86	V8-318/P	Hydraulic①		45–45½	44½–45	1¹¹⁄₁₆	177 @ 1⁵⁄₁₆	.001–.003	.002–.004	.372–.373	.371–.372
DODGE & PLYMOUTH											
1980	6-225/C,D	.010H	.020H	45	②	1¹¹⁄₁₆	144 @ 1⁵⁄₁₆	.001–.003	.002–.004	.372–.373	.371–.372
	V8-318/G,H	Hydraulic①		45	45	1¹¹⁄₁₆	177 @ 1⁵⁄₁₆	.001–.003	.002–.004	.372–.373	.371–.372
	V8-360/K,J	Hydraulic①		45	45	1¹¹⁄₁₆	177 @ 1⁵⁄₁₆	.001–.003	.002–.004	.372–.373	.371–.372
	V8-360/L③	Hydraulic①		45	45	1²¹⁄₃₂	193 @ 1¼	.0015–.0035	.0025–.0045	.3715–.3725	.3705–.3715
1981–83	6-225/E,H	Hydraulic①		45	②	1¹¹⁄₁₆	144 @ 1⁵⁄₁₆	.001–.003	.002–.004	.372–.373	.371–.372
	V8-318/ K,M,P	Hydraulic①		45–45½	44½–45	1¹¹⁄₁₆	177 @ 1⁵⁄₁₆	.001–.003	.002–.004	.372–.373	.371–.372
1984–86	V8-318/P	Hydraulic①		45–45½	44½–45	1¹¹⁄₁₆	177 @ 1⁵⁄₁₆	.001–.003	.002–.004	.372–.373	.371–.372

①—No adjustment.
②—Intake 45°, exhaust 43°.
③—High Performance.
④—With Electronic Fuel Injection.
⑤—Less Electronic Fuel Injection.
⑥—Refer to General Engine Specifications for V.I.N. code.

continued

Pistons, Pins, Rings, Crankshaft & Bearings

Year	Engine/ V.I.N.	Piston Clearance Top of Skirt	Ring End Gap①		Wrist- pin Diam- eter	Rod Bearings		Main Bearings		Thrust on Bear. No.	Shaft End Play
			Comp.	Oil		Shaft Diameter	Bearing Clearance	Shaft Diameter	Bearing Clearance		
CHRYSLER & IMPERIAL											
1980	6-225/C	.0005–.0015	.010	.015	.9008	2.1865–2.1875	.0005–.0025	2.7495–2.7505	.0005–.0020	3	.002–.009
	V8-318/G,H	.0005–.0015	.010	.015	.9842	2.1240–2.1250	.0005–.0025	2.4995–2.5005	②	3	.002–.009
	V8-360/J,K,L	③	.010	.015	.9842	2.1240–2.1250	.0005–.0025	2.8095–2.8105	②	3	.002–.009
1981–83	6-225/E,H	.0005–.0015	.010	.015	.9008	2.1865–2.1875	.0010–.0025	2.7495–2.7505	.0010–.0025	3	.0035– .0095
	V8-318④	.0005–.0015	.010	.015	.9842	2.124–2.125	.0005–.0025	2.4995–2.5005	②	3	.002–.009
1984–86	V8-318/P	.0005–.0015	.010	.015	.9482	2.124–2.125	.0005–.0025	2.4995–2.5005	②	3	—
DODGE & PLYMOUTH											
1980	6-225/C	.0005–.0015	.010	.015	.9008	2.1865–2.1875	.0005–.0025	2.7495–2.7505	.0005–.0020	3	.002–.009
	V8-318/G,H	.0005–.0015	.010	.015	.9842	2.1240–2.1250	.0005–.0025	2.4995–2.5005	②	3	.002–.009
	V8-360/J,K,L	③	.010	.015	.9842	2.1240–2.1250	.0005–.0025	2.8095–2.8105	②	3	.002–.009
1981–83	6-225/E,H	.0005–.0015	.010	.015	.9008	2.1865–2.1875	.0010–.0025	2.7495–2.7505	.0010–.0025	3	.0035– .0095
	V8-318④	.0005–.0015	.010	.015	.9842	2.124–2.125	.0005–.0025	2.4995–2.5005	②	3	.002–.009
1984–86	V8-318/P	.0005–.0015	.010	.015	.9842	2.124–2.125	.0005–.0025	2.4995–2.5005	②	3	—

①—Fit rings in tapered bores for clearance listed in tightest portion of ring travel.
②—No. 1, .0005–.0015"; No. 2, 3, 4 & 5, .0005–.0020".
③—With 2 bbl. carb., .0005–.0015"; with 4 bbl. carb., .001"–.002".
④—Refer to General Engine Specifications for V.I.N. code.

Alternator & Regulator Specifications

Year	Unit Number	Ground Polarity	Field Coil Draw Amperes	Current Output			Operating Voltage			Voltage Regulator Point Gap	Regulator Armature Air Gap
				Engine R.P.M.	Amperes	Volts	Engine R.P.M.	Volts	Voltage @ 80°F ①		
1980	Bronze Tag	Negative	4.5–6.5②	1250	40⑤	15	1250	15	13.9–14.6	—	—
	Natural Tag	Negative	4.5–6.5②	1250	47⑤	15	1250	15	13.9–14.6	—	—
	Violet Tag	Negative	4.5–6.5②	1250	40⑤	15	1250	15	13.9–14.6	—	—
1980–81	Yellow Tag③	Negative	4.5–6.5②	1250	57⑤	15	1250	15	13.9–14.6	—	—
	Brown Tag	Negative	4.5–6.5②	1250	62⑤	15	1250	15	13.9–14.6	—	—
	Yellow Tag④	Negative	4.75–6.0②	900	72⑤	13	900	13	13.9–14.6	—	—
1982–83	Yellow Tag③	Negative	4.5–6.5②	1250	47⑤	15	1250	15	13.9–14.6	—	—
	Brown Tag	Negative	4.5–6.5②	1250	58⑤	15	1250	15	13.9–14.6	—	—
	Yellow Tag⑥	Negative	4.75–6.0②	900	97⑤	13	900	13	13.9–14.6	—	—
1984–86	Yellow Tag③	Negative	2.5–5.0②	1250	47⑤	15	1250	15	13.9–14.6	—	—
	Brown Tag	Negative	2.5–5.0②	1250	58⑤	15	1250	15	13.9–14.6	—	—
	Yellow Tag⑥	Negative	2.5–5.0②	900	97⑤	13	900	13	13.9–14.6	—	—

①—For each 10 degree rise in temperature subtract .04 volt. Temperature is checked with thermometer two inches from installed voltage regulator cover.
②—Current draw at 12 volts while turning rotor shaft by hand.
③—60 amp rating.
④—100 amp rating.
⑤—Minimum output.
⑥—114 amp rating.

continued

Starting Motor Applications

Year	Engine	Starter Ident. No.
1980	6-225①, V8-318	4118855
	6-225②, V8-360	4111860
1981–83	6-225, V8-318	4111860
1984–86	V8-318	4111860

①—Except Diplomat & LeBaron.
②—Diplomat & LeBaron.

Engine Tightening Specifications★

★ Torque specifications are for clean and lightly lubricated threads only. Dry or dirty threads produce increased friction which prevents accurate measurement of tightness.

Year	Engine/V.I.N	Spark Plugs Ft. Lbs.	Cylinder Head Bolts Ft. Lbs.	Intake Manifold Ft. Lbs.	Exhaust Manifold Ft. Lbs.	Rocker Arm Shaft Bracket Ft. Lbs.	Rocker Arm Cover In. Lbs.	Connecting Rod Cap Bolts Ft. Lbs.	Main Bearing Cap Bolts Ft. Lbs.	Flywheel to Crankshaft Ft. Lbs.	Vibration Damper to Crankshaft Ft. Lbs.
1980	6-225/C,D	10	70	④	120①	24	40	45	85	55	②
1980	V8-318/G,H, 360/J,K,L	30	95	40	③	200①	40	45	85	55	100
1981–83	6-225/E,H	10	70	④	120①	24	80	45	85	55	②
	V8-318⑤	30	95	45	③	200①	80	45	85	55	100
1984–86	V8-318/P	30	95	45	③	200①	95	45	85	55	100

①—Inch pounds.
②—Press fit.
③—Screw, 20 ft. lbs.; Nut, 15 ft. lbs.
④—Intake to exhaust manifold stud nut 240 in. lbs., Intake to exhaust manifold bolts 200 in. lbs.
⑤—Refer to General Engine Specifications for V.I.N. code.

Rear Axle Specifications

Year	Model	Carrier Type	Ring Gear & Pinion Backlash		Pinion Bearing Preload			Differential Bearing Preload		
			Method	Adjustment	Method	New Bearings Inch-Lbs.	Used Bearings Inch-Lbs.	Method	New Bearings Inch-Lbs.	Used Bearings Inch-Lbs.
1980–83	8¼"⑤	Integral	②	.006–.008	①	20–35④	10–25④	②	③	③
	9¼"⑤	Integral	②	.006–.008	①	20–35④	10–25④	②	③	③
	7¼"⑤	Integral	②	.004–.006	①	15–25	—	②	③	③
1984–86	7¼"	Integral	②	.006–.008	①	20–35④	10–25④	②	③	③
	8¼"	Integral	②	.006–.008	①	20–35④	10–25④	②	③	③

①—Collapsible spacer.
②—Threaded adjusters.
③—Preload is correct when ring gear & pinion backlash is properly adjusted.
④—Adjust by turning pinion shaft nut with an inch-pound torque wrench with seal removed.
⑤—"C" lock type.

continued

Wheel Alignment Specifications

NOTE: See that riding height is correct before checking wheel alignment

Year	Model	Caster Angle, Degrees		Camber Angle, Degrees				Toe-In. Inch	Toe-Out on Turns, Deg.	
		Limits	Desired	Limits		Desired			Outer Wheel	Inner Wheel
				Left	Right	Left	Right			
CHRYSLER & IMPERIAL										
1980–81	Cordoba, LeBaron	+1¼ to +3¾	+2½	−¼ to +1¼	−¼ to +1¼	+½	+½	¹⁄₁₆ to ³⁄₁₆	18	20
	Newport, New Yorker	−¼ to +2¼	+1	−¼ to +1¼	−¼ to +1¼	+½	+½	¹⁄₁₆ to ³⁄₁₆	18	20
1981	Imperial	+1¼ to +3¾	+2½	−¼ to 1¼	−¼ to +1¼	+½	+½	¹⁄₁₆ to ³⁄₁₆	18	20
1982–86	All	+1¼ to +3¾	+2½	−¼ to +1¼	−¼ to +1¼	+½	+½	¹⁄₁₆ to ³⁄₁₆	18	20
DODGE										
1980–81	Aspen, Diplomat & Mirada	+1¼ to +3¾	+2½	−¼ to +1¼	−¼ to +1¼	+½	+½	¹⁄₁₆ to ³⁄₁₆	18	20
	St. Regis	−¼ to +2¼	+1	−¼ to +1¼	−¼ to +1¼	+½	+½	¹⁄₁₆ to ³⁄₁₆	18	20
1982–86	All	+1¼ to +3¾	+2½	−¼ to +1¼	−¼ to +1¼	+½	+½	¹⁄₁₆ to ³⁄₁₆	18	20

①—Except Aspen & Diplomat.

Year	Model	Caster Angle, Degrees		Camber Angle, Degrees				Toe-In. Inch	Toe-Out on Turns, Deg.	
PLYMOUTH										
1980	Gran Fury	−¼ to +2¼	+1	−¼ to +1¼	−¼ to +1¼	+½	+½	¹⁄₁₆ to ³⁄₁₆	18	20
	Volaré	+1¼ to +3¾	+2½	−¼ to +1¼	−¼ to +1¼	+½	+½	¹⁄₁₆ to ³⁄₁₆	18	20
1981	Gran Fury	−¼ to +2¼	+1	−¼ to +1¼	−¼ to +1¼	+½	+½	¹⁄₁₆ to ³⁄₁₆	18	20
1982–86	All	+1¼ to +3¾	+2½	−¼ to +1¼	−¼ to +1¼	+½	+½	¹⁄₁₆ to ³⁄₁₆	18	20

Cooling System & Capacity Data

Year	Model or Engine/V.I.N.	Cooling Capacity, Qts.		Radiator Cap Relief Pressure, Lbs.	Thermo. Opening Temp.	Fuel Tank Gals.	Engine Oil Refill Qts. ①	Transmission Oil			Rear Axle Oil Pints
		Less A/C	With A/C					3 Speed Pints	4 Speed Pints	Auto. Trans. Qts. ②	
CHRYSLER											
1980	LeBaron 6-225/C	11½	12½	16	195	18	4	—	—	8.15	③
	LeBaron V0-010/G,H	15	15½	16	195	18	4	—	—	8.15	③
	Cordoba 6-225/C	11½	12½	16	195	21	4	—	—	8.15	4½
	Cordoba V8-318/G,H	15	15½	16	195	21	4	—	—	8.15	4½
	Cordoba V8-360/K,L	14	14	16	195	21	4	—	—	8.15	4½
	Newport, New Yorker 6-225/C	11½	14½	16	195	21	4	—	—	8.15	4½
	Newport, New Yorker V8-318/G,H	15	17½	16	195	21	4	—	—	8.15	4½
	Newport, New Yorker V8-360/K,L	16	16	16	195	21	4	—	—	8.15	4½

continued

COOLING SYSTEM & CAPACITY DATA—Continued

Year	Model or Engine/V.I.N.	Cooling Capacity, Qts.		Radiator Cap Relief Pressure, Lbs.	Thermo. Opening Temp.	Fuel Tank Gals.	Engine Oil Refill Qts. ①	Transmission Oil			Rear Axle Oil Pints
		Less A/C	With A/C					3 Speed Pints	4 Speed Pints	Auto. Trans. Qts. ②	
CHRYSLER—Continued											
1981	LeBaron 6-225/E	11½	12½	16	195	18	4	—	—	8.15	④
	LeBaron V8-318/K,M	15	15½	16	195	18	4	—	—	8.15	④
	Cordoba 6-225/E	11½	14½	16	195	18	4	—	—	8.15	④
	Cordoba V8-318/K,M	15	17½	16	195	18	4	—	—	8.15	④
	Newport, New Yorker 6-225/E	11½	14½	16	195	21	4	—	—	8.15	④
	Newport, New Yorker V8-318/K,M	15	17½	16	195	21	4	—	—	8.15	④
1982–83	Cordoba 6-225/E,H	11½	15	16	195	18	4	—	—	8½	④
	Cordoba V8-318⑪	15	15½	16	195	18	4	—	—	8½	④
	New Yorker 6-225/E,H	11½	12½	16	195	18	4	—	—	8½	④
	New Yorker V8-318⑪	15	15½	16	195	18	4	—	—	8½	④
1984–86	Fifth Avenue V8-318/P	15½⑦	15½⑦	16	195	18	4	—	—	⑧⑨	⑩
IMPERIAL											
1981	All	15	17.5	16	195	18	4	—	—	8.15	4.4
1982–83	All	15½	16½	16	195	18	4	—	—	8½	4.4
DODGE											
1980	Aspen, Diplomat 6-225/C	11½	12½	16	195	18	4	4¾	—	8.15	③
	Aspen, Diplomat V8-318/G,H	15	15½	16	195	18	4	—	—	8.15	③
	Aspen V8-360/K,L	14	14	16	195	18	4	—	—	8.15	③
	Mirada 6-225/C	11½	12½	16	195	21	4	—	—	8.15	4½
	Mirada V8-318/G,H	15	15½	16	195	21	4	—	—	8.15	4½
	Mirada V8-360/K,L	14	14	16	195	21	4	—	—	8.15	4½
	St. Regis 6-225/C	11½	14½	16	195	21	4	—	—	8.15	4½
	St. Regis V8-318/G,H	15	17½	16	195	21	4	—	—	8.15	4½
	St. Regis V8-360/K,L	16	16	16	195	21	4	—	—	8.15	4½
1981	All 6-225/E	11.5	⑫	16	195	⑬	4	—	—	8.15	④
	All V8-318/KM	15	⑤	16	195	⑬	4	—	—	8.15	④
1982–83	Diplomat 6-225/E,H	11½	⑥	16	195	18	4	—	—	8½	④
	Diplomat V8-318⑪	15	15½	16	195	18	4	—	—	8½	④
	Mirada 6-225/E,H	11½	12½	16	195	18	4	—	—	8½	④
	Mirada V8-318⑪	15	15½	16	195	18	4	—	—	8½	④
1984–86	Diplomat V8-318/P	15½⑦	15½⑦	16	195	18	4	—	—	⑧⑨	⑩

continued

COOLING SYSTEM & CAPACITY DATA—Continued

Year	Model or Engine/V.I.N.	Cooling Capacity, Qts.		Radiator Cap Relief Pressure, Lbs.	Thermo. Opening Temp.	Fuel Tank Gals.	Engine Oil Refill Qts. ①	Transmission Oil			Rear Axle Oil Pints
		Less A/C	With A/C					3 Speed Pints	4 Speed Pints	Auto. Trans. Qts. ②	
PLYMOUTH											
1980	Gran Fury 6-225/C	11½	14½	16	195	21	4	—	—	8.15	4½
	Gran Fury V8-318/G,H	15	17½	16	195	21	4	—	—	8.15	4½
	Gran Fury V8-360/K,L	16	16	16	195	21	4	—	—	8.15	4½
1981	Gran Fury 6-225/E	11½	14½	16	195	21	4	—	—	8.15	④
	Gran Fury V8-318/K,M	15	17½	16	195	21	4	—	—	8.15	④
1982–83	Gran Fury 6-225/E,H	11½	12½	16	195	18	4	—	—	8½	④
	Gran Fury V8-318⑪	15	15½	16	195	18	4	—	—	8½	④
1984–86	Gran Fury V8-318/P	15½⑦	15½⑦	16	195	18	4	—	—	⑧⑨	⑩
VOLARÉ											
1980	Volaré 6-225/C	11½	12½	16	195	18	4	4¾	—	8.15	③
	Volaré V8-318/G,H	15	15½	16	195	18	4	—	—	8.15	③
	Volaré V8-360/K,L	14	14	16	195	18	4	—	—	8.15	③

①—Add 1 qt. with filter change.
②—Approximate. Make final check with dipstick.
③—With 7¼ inch ring gear, 2 pts.; 8¼ inch ring gear, 4½ pts.
④—With 7¼" ring gear, 2½ pts.; with 8¼" ring gear, 4.4 pts.; with 9¼" ring gear, 4½ pts.
⑤—Except Diplomat, 17½ qts.; Diplomat, 15½ qts.
⑥—1982, 15 qts.; 1983, 12½ qts.
⑦—Heavy duty cooling system, 16½ qts.
⑧—A904 trans., 8.15 qts., A727 trans., 8 qts.
⑨—Add an additional ¼ qt. with auxiliary cooler.
⑩—7¼ inch axle, 2.5 pts.; 8¼ inch axle, 4.4 pts.
⑪—Refer to General Engine Specifications for V.I.N. code.
⑫—Except Diplomat, 14½ qts.; Diplomat, 12½ qts.
⑬—Diplomat & Mirada, 18 gals.; St. Regis, 21 gals.

Electrical Section

Fig. 1 Ignition lock removal. Model less tilt column

Fig. 2 Ignition lock removal. Models w/tilt column

STARTER
REPLACE

1. Disconnect ground cable at battery.
2. Remove cable at starter.
3. Disconnect wires at solenoid.
4. Remove one stud nut and one bolt attaching starter motor to flywheel housing.
5. Slide transmission oil cooler bracket off stud (if so equipped).
6. Remove starter motor and removeble seal.
7. Reverse above procedure to install.

NOTE: When tightening attaching bolt and nut be sure to hold starter away from engine to insure proper alignment.

CLUTCH SWITCH

1980

A clutch switch is used which necessitates depressing the clutch pedal before the engine can be started.

IGNITION SWITCH & LOCK
REPLACE

1980–86

1. Disconnect battery ground cable and remove turn signal switch as outlined elsewhere in this chapter.
2. Remove ignition key lamp assembly retaining screw and the assembly.
3. Remove snap ring from upper end of steering shaft.
4. Remove bearing housing to lock housing retaining screws, then the bearing housing from shaft.
5. Remove bearing lower snap ring from

shaft.
6. Pry sleeve from steering shaft lock plate hub, then, using a suitable punch, drive lock plate groove pin from lock plate.

NOTE: Drive pin from end without grooves.

7. Remove lock plate from shaft, then the shaft through lower end of column.
8. Remove shift indicator pointer screw, if equipped.
9. Remove buzzer switch retaining screw and the switch.
10. Remove lock lever guide plate retaining screws and the guide plate.
11. Place lock cylinder in the "Lock" position and remove key. With a suitable tool, depress spring loaded lock retainer and pull lock cylinder from housing bore, **Figs. 1 and 2.**
12. Remove ignition switch retaining screws and the ignition switch.
13. Reverse procedure to install.

IGNITION SWITCH
ADJUST

1980–86 EXCEPT CORDOBA & MIRADA

1. Disconnect battery ground cable.
2. Place transmission in Park and ignition lock in the lock position.
3. If switch was not removed from column, loosen two mounting bolts and insert a lock pin into hole on switch marked lock. If switch was removed from column, pin switch in the lock position, then place switch into rod and rotate 90 degrees over mounting holes. Loosely install mounting bolts. Replacement switches are supplied with locking pins.
4. Apply light upward pressure to align rod and switch and hold switch in this

position while tightening retaining bolts. Remove locking pin.
5. Remove lock pin from switch.
6. Reverse procedure to install.

COLUMN MOUNTED DIMMER SWITCH
ADJUST

1980–81 GRAN FURY, NEWPORT, NEW YORKER & ST. REGIS; 1980–83 CORDOBA & MIRADA; 1981–83 IMPERIAL

1. Loosen two switch mounting screws, then depress switch plunger slightly and insert locking pin.
2. Apply light upward pressure to remove free play between switch and rod.
3. While holding switch with slight upward pressure tighten the two mounting screws.
4. Remove locking pin and check switch for proper operation.

LIGHT SWITCH
REPLACE

1980–81 GRAN FURY, NEWPORT, NEW YORKER & ST. REGIS; 1980–83 CORDOBA & MIRADA; 1981–83 IMPERIAL

1. If equipped, remove intermittent wipe and power antenna module assembly.
2. Disconnect battery ground cable.
3. Depress switch stem release button and pull knob and stem from switch.
4. Using a small screwdriver, snap out switch trim bezel, then remove mounting nut.

5. Pull switch from cluster and disconnect wire connector.
6. Reverse procedure to install.

1980 ASPEN & VOLARE, 1980–81 LEBARON, 1980–86 DIPLOMAT, 1982 NEW YORKER, 1982–86 GRAN FURY, 1983 NEW YORKER FIFTH AVENUE & 1984–86 FIFTH AVENUE

1. Disconnect battery ground cable.
2. Remove cluster bezel.
3. Remove switch mounting plate attaching screws and pull switch and plate assembly outward.
4. Depress headlight switch stem, then depress release button and pull knob and stem from switch.
5. Remove switch mounting nut, then disconnect electrical connector and remove switch.
6. Reverse procedure to install.

STOP LIGHT SWITCH
REPLACE

1980–86

1. Disconnect battery ground cable.
2. Disconnect wiring from switch and remove switch from brake pedal bracket.
3. Reverse procedure to install.

NEUTRAL SAFETY & BACK-UP SWITCH
REPLACE

1980–86

1. Unscrew switch from transmission case, allowing fluid to drain into a container, **Fig. 3.**
2. Move shift lever to "Park" and then to "Neutral" positions and inspect to see that switch operating lever is centered in switch opening in case.
3. Screw switch into transmission case and torque to 24 ft. lbs.
4. Add fluid to proper level.
5. Check to see that switch operates only in "Park" and "Neutral".

HORN SOUNDER & STEERING WHEEL
REPLACE

1980–86

1. Disconnect ground cable at battery.
2. On steering wheels with center horn button, remove button by pulling outwards. On steering wheels with pressure sensitive switch pad, remove mounting screws from underside of wheel, then disconnect horn wire when removing pad.
3. On models with center horn button,

Fig. 3   Neutral safety switch.

disconnect horn switch wire and remove switch and ring.
4. On all models, remove steering wheel nut and use a suitable puller to remove steering wheel.

CAUTION: Do not bump or hammer on steering shaft to remove wheel as damage to shaft may result.

5. Reverse procedure to install.

TURN SIGNAL SWITCH
REPLACE

1981–86

1. Disconnect battery ground cable.
2. Remove steering wheel as described under "Steering Wheel, Replace".
3. On models equipped with tilt column, remove lock plate cover and lock plate.
4. On all models, remove lower instrument panel bezel.
5. On 1981 LeBaron, 1981–86 Diplomat, 1982 New Yorker, 1982–86 Gran Fury, and 1983 New Yorker Fifth Avenue and 1984–86 Fifth Avenue models equipped with tilt column, remove gear shift indicator, then the two steering column to lower instrument panel reinforcement retaining screws. Remove mounting bracket from steering column.
6. On all models, unsnap four plastic retainers and remove wiring through steering column.
7. Disconnect light blue wire connector, then remove turn signal lever attaching screw and allow lever assembly to hang loosely from column.
8. Remove turn signal/hazard warning switch attaching screws, then pull switch from steering column, while carefully guiding wires up through column opening.
9. Reverse procedure to install.

1980

1. Disconnect battery ground cable and remove steering wheel.
2. Remove steering column cover. On Charger and Cordoba, it is necessary to remove the lower instrument panel bezel.
3. On models with tilt column proceed as follows:
   a. On all models except Charger and Cordoba, remove gearshift indicator.
   b. On all models, remove steering

column to lower panel reinforcement nuts.
   c. Remove mounting bracket attaching bolts and the mounting bracket from steering column.
   d. Remove wiring trough screws and the wiring trough.
4. On all except models with Tilt columns, unsnap retainer clips attaching wiring trough to steering column and remove wiring trough.
5. Position shift lever at the full clockwise position except on Tilt columns. On Tilt columns, position shift lever at the midpoint.
6. Disconnect turn signal switch wiring harness connector.
7. Remove turn signal lever attaching screw and the lever.

NOTE: On models equipped with speed control, it is not necessary to remove lever but allow lever to hang.

8. Remove hazard warning switch and upper bearing retainer mounting screws.
9. Carefully pull switch from column, guiding wires through column opening.
10. Reverse procedure to install.

INSTRUMENT CLUSTER
REPLACE

1981–83 IMPERIAL

1. Disconnect battery ground cable.
2. Remove cigar lighter and ash tray from instrument panel, **Fig. 4.**
3. Remove instrument panel cluster overlay attaching screws, then remove overlay.
4. Remove lower instrument panel cluster bezel attaching screws, then remove bezel.
5. Remove instrument cluster bezel attaching screws and bezel then remove plastic pins retaining cluster mask to cluster and remove mask.
6. Remove instrument cluster to panel attaching screws, then pull cluster forward and disconnect wire connectors from cluster.
7. Remove cluster assembly.
8. Reverse procedure to install.

1980–81 GRAN FURY, NEWPORT, NEW YORKER & ST. REGIS; 1980–83 CORDOBA & MIRADA

1. Disconnect battery ground cable.
2. Remove five hood and brake release beel screws, then the bezel.
3. Remove four accessory switch bezel screws, then the bezel.
4. Pull gearshift pointer cable from steering column.
5. Remove the lower left and right hand bezels and the gearshift pointer cable.
6. Remove three steering column toe plate bolts at firewall, then the nuts

Fig. 4 Electronic instrument cluster. 1981–83 Imperial

and washers attaching steering column bracket to instrument panel steering column support bracket. Lower the steering column, allowing steering wheel to rest on seat.
7. Disconnect speedometer cable and the right hand mirror control cable.
8. Remove five screws securing instrument cluster to panel, **Fig. 5.**
9. Roll cluster downward and disconnect headlamp switch electrical connector and instrument cluster wiring.
10. Remove instrument cluster from vehicle.
11. Reverse procedure to install.

1980–81 LEBARON, 1980–86 DIPLOMAT, 1982 NEW YORKER, 1982–86 GRAN FURY, 1983 NEW YORKER FIFTH AVENUE & 1984–86 FIFTH AVENUE

1. Disconnect battery ground cable.
2. Remove lower panel assembly.
3. Remove left lower reinforcement by removing two screws located at left end.
4. Remove gear shift indicator.
5. Remove steering column toe plate mounting bolts and upper steering column mounting nuts, then lower steering column.
6. Disconnect speedometer cable.
7. Remove two mounting screws and detach fuse block from mid reinforcement.
8. Remove one screw attaching radio to mid reinforcement.
9. Remove four upper and four lower cluster mounting screws, **Fig. 6.**
10. Pull cluster out from instrument panel and disconnect wire connectors, control cables and vacuum harness, then remove cluster assembly.
11. Reverse procedure to install.

1980 ASPEN & VOLARÉ

1. Disconnect battery ground cable.
2. Remove steering column cover and instrument panel end cap.
3. Remove lower left reinforcement and remove gearshift indicator.
4. Remove steering column toe plate bolts, then remove the two upper mounting nuts and lower steering column.
5. Remove left side cowl mouldings, then disconnect speedometer cable.
6. Remove two mounting screws, then detach fuse block from mid reinforcement.
7. Remove 1 screw attaching radio to mid-reinforcement, 4 screws at bottom of cluster and 3 screws at top of cluster, **Fig. 7.**
8. Pull cluster from panel, then disconnect all electrical connectors, control cables and vacuum hoses and remove cluster.
9. Reverse procedure to install.

W/S WIPER MOTOR
REPLACE

1. Disconnect battery ground cable.
2. Remove wiper arm and blades.
3. Remove cowl screen.
4. Remove drive crank arm retaining nut and drive crank. Disconnect wiring to motor.
5. Unfasten and remove wiper motor.
6. Reverse procedure to install.

W/S WIPER TRANSMISSION
REPLACE

1. Disconnect battery ground cable.
2. On all models except Aspen & Volaré, remove top plastic screen. On Aspen and Volaré, disconnect washer hose to gain access to drive crank.
3. On all models, remove the arm and

blade assemblies.

4. Remove the drive crank from the moldingser motor by removing the attaching nut.
5. On all models except Aspen, Diplomat, LeBaron, Volare, 1982 New Yorker, 1982–86 Gran Fury, 1983 New Yorker Fifth Avenue and 1984–86 Fifth Avenue, remove six pivot mounting screws.
6. On Aspen, Diplomat, LeBaron, Volare, 1982 New Yorker, 1982–86 Gran Fury, 1983 New Yorker Fifth Avenue and 1984–86 Fifth Avenue, remove pivot mounting nut and washer.
7. Reverse procedure to install.

W/S WIPER SWITCH
REPLACE

1980 ASPEN, VOLARÉ, 1980–81 LEBARON & DIPLOMAT

1. Disconnect battery ground cable.
2. Remove instrument cluster bezel.

Fig. 5 Instrument cluster removal. 1980–81 Gran Fury, Newport, New Yorker & St. Regis; 1980–83 Cordoba & Mirada

CARRIER AND CLUSTER ASSEMBLY

MOUNTING NUT   STUD

RADIO

GROUND STRAP

VIEW IN DIRECTION OF ARROW Z

KNOBS

GROUND STRAP

KNOBS

WINDSHIELD WIPER SWITCH

CONNECTOR

HEATED REAR WINDOW INDICATOR LAMP

U-CLIP

MOUNTING SCREWS

HEADLAMP SWITCH

PLATE

MOUNTING SCREW

PLATE

BEZEL

MOUNTING SCREW

DOOR AJAR BULB

CARRIER AND CLUSTER ASSEMBLY

KNOBS

MOUNTING NUT

BEZEL

KNOB AND SHAFT

VIEW IN DIRECTION OF ARROW Y

TAILGATE AJAR BULB

SOCKETS

LOW WASHER FLUID BULB

Fig. 6 Instrument cluster. (Typical) 1980–81 LeBaron, 1980–86 Diplomat, 1982 New Yorker, 1982–86 Gran Fury, 1983 New Yorker Fifth Avenue & 1984–86 Fifth Avenue

LOWER PANEL ASSEMBLY

CLUSTER CARRIER ASSEMBLY

END CAP

Fig. 7 Instrument cluster. 1980 Aspen & Volaré

3. Remove switch module assembly attaching screws, then pull assembly out and let hang in order to gain access to switch.
4. Remove switch knob from stem, then remove switch mounting screws.
5. Disconnect switch wire connector and remove switch.
6. Reverse procedure to install.

1980–81 NEWPORT; 1980–82 NEW YORKER & ST. REGIS; 1980–86 GRAN FURY; 1980–83 CORDOBA & MIRADA; 1981–83 IMPERIAL; 1983 NEW YORKER FIFTH AVENUE; 1982–86 DIPLOMAT & 1984–86 FIFTH AVENUE

Refer to 'Turn Signal Switch, Replace' procedure.

RADIO
REPLACE

NOTE: When installing radio, be sure to adjust antenna trimmer for peak performance.

1980–81 GRAN FURY, NEWPORT, NEW YORKER & ST. REGIS; 1980–83 CORDOBA & MIRADA; 1981–83 IMPERIAL

1. Disconnect battery ground cable.
2. Remove center bezel, then remove radio to panel attaching screws.
3. Pull radio from instrument panel, then disconnect antenna and electrical leads.
4. Reverse procedure to install.

1980 ASPEN & VOLARE; 1980–81 LEBARON; 1980–86 DIPLOMAT; 1982 NEW YORKER; 1982–84 GRAN FURY; 1983 NEW YORKER FIFTH AVENUE & 1984–86 FIFTH AVENUE

1. Disconnect battery ground cable.
2. Remove instrument cluster bezel, then the radio mounting screws.
3. Pull radio from panel and disconnect all wiring, then remove radio from vehicle.
4. Reverse procedure to install.

VACUUM LINES TO WATER VALVE AND MANIFOLD VACUUM TEE

HEATER ASSEMBLY TO PLENUM MOUNTING BRACE

BLOWER MOTOR ASSEMBLY

CENTER DISTRIBUTION DUCT

HEATER DISTRIBUTION HOUSING

VIEW IN DIRECTION OF ARROW X

Fig. 8 Heater core & blower motor assembly (less A/C). 1980–81 Gran Fury, Mirada, Newport, New Yorker, St. Regis & Cordoba

Fig. 9 Heater core & blower motor assembly (less A/C). 1982–83 Cordoba & Mirada

HEATER CORE
REPLACE

Before attempting to remove a heater core, disconnect the battery ground cable, drain the radiator and remove inlet and outlet hoses from heater assembly in engine compartment.

1980–81 GRAN FURY, NEWPORT, NEW YORKER & ST. REGIS; 1980–83 CORDOBA & MIRADA; 1981–83 IMPERIAL

Less Air Conditioning
1. Disconnect battery ground cable and drain cooling system.
2. Disconnect heater hoses from heater core.
3. Disconnect vacuum hoses from water valve and manifold tee, then push hoses and grommet through dash panel.
4. Remove four nuts securing heater assembly to dash panel.
5. Move front seat rearward and remove console, if equipped.
6. On models except Cordoba, Imperial and Mirada, remove heater control and disconnect vacuum harness from extension harness.
7. On all models, remove glove box, ash tray and housing, right hand lap cooler duct, lower right hand trim panel or bezel, and the right hand cowl trim pad.
8. Disconnect blower motor electrical connections.
9. Disconnect temperature control cable from heater housing, then remove heater distribution housing, **Figs. 8 and 9**.
10. Support heater housing and remove the heater housing to plenum mounting brace. Pull housing rearward and move toward right side to remove.
11. Remove heater housing top cover, then the heater core retaining screw.
12. Lift heater core from housing.
13. Reverse procedure to install.

With Air Conditioning
1. Disconnect battery ground cable and drain cooling system.
2. Discharge air conditioning refrigerant system.
3. Disconnect heater hoses from heater core.

Fig. 10 Heater core & blower motor assembly (with A/C). 1980–81 Gran Fury, Mirada, Newport, New Yorker, St. Regis & Cordoba & 1981 Imperial

4. Remove "H" valve and cap refrigerant lines. Remove condensate drain tube.
5. Disconnect vacuum lines from engine compartment and push grommet and vacuum lines through dash panel.

NOTE: On manual air conditioning systems, the vacuum lines are connected to the manifold vacuum tee and water valve. On semi-automatic air conditioning systems, the vacuum lines are connected to the vacuum reservoir and water valve.

6. Remove four nuts attaching evaporator heater assembly to dash panel.
7. Move front seat rearward and remove console, if equipped.
8. On models except Cordoba, Imperial and Mirada, remove air conditioning switch control from dash panel and disconnect vacuum harness from harness extension.
9. On all models, remove ash tray and housing and the glove box assembly.
10. Disconnect right hand lap cooler tube from lap cooler and remove the right hand trim panel or bezel.
11. Remove right hand cowl trim pad and disconnect blower motor electrical connections.
12. On Cordoba, Imperial and Mirada, disconnect vacuum harness from harness extension, then remove heater distribution housing.
13. On all models, disconnect temperature control cable from evaporator heater housing.
14. On models except Cordoba, Imperial Mirada, remove heater distribution housing and the center distribution duct.
15. On all models, remove the hi/lo door

Fig. 11 Heater core & blower motor assembly (with A/C). 1982–83 Cordoba, Imperial & Mirada

Fig. 12 Speed Control lock-in screw adjustment

actuator, **Figs. 10 and 11.**

16. On models with semi-automatic air conditioning system, remove vacuum servo actuator from housing and the in-car air hose from compensator.
17. On all models, support housing and remove brace between housing and plenum. Then, pull housing rearward and move toward right aide to remove.
18. Remove housing top cover and the heater core retaining screw.
19. Lift heater core from housing.
20. Reverse procedure to install.

1980 ASPEN & VOLARE; 1980–81 LEBARON; 1980–86 DIPLOMAT; 1982 NEW YORKER; 1982–86 GRAN FURY; 1983 NEW YORKER FIFTH AVENUE; 1984–86 FIFTH AVENUE

Less Air Conditioning

1. Disconnect battery ground cable and drain cooling system.
2. Disconnect and plug heater hoses from dash panel.
3. Remove heater core tube dash panel seals and retainer.
4. Remove instrument cluster bezel as-

sembly, upper cover, steering column cover, right intermediate side cowl trim panel and the lower instrument panel.
5. Remove instrument panel center to lower reinforcement.
6. Remove right vent control cable from unit.
7. Disconnect temperature and mode door control cables from unit, then the blower motor resistor block wiring.
8. Remove heater assembly mounting nuts in engine compartment.
9. Remove heater support to plenum bracket and pull heater unit from dash panel.
10. Separate heater housing by removing retainer clips.
11. Remove heater core tube support clamp and slide heater core from housing.
12. Reverse procedure to install.

With Air Conditioning

1. Disconnect battery ground cable and drain cooling system.
2. Discharge refrigerant system.
3. Remove air cleaner, then disconnect heater hoses from heater core. Install plugs in heater core tubes to prevent coolant from spilling when removing unit.
4. Remove "H" valve, then cap refrigerant lines to prevent dirt and moisture from entering.
5. Remove instrument cluster bezel as-

sembly.
6. Remove instrument panel upper cover, steering column cover and right intermediate side cowl trim panel.
7. Remove lower instrument panel.
8. Remove instrument center to lower reinforcement.
9. Remove floor console, if equipped.
10. Remove right center air distribution duct.
11. Disconnect locking tab on defroster distribution duct.
12. Disconnect temperature control cable from evaporator housing.
13. Disconnect blower motor resistor block wire connector.
14. Disconnect vacuum lines from water valve and vacuum source tee.
15. Remove wiring from evaporator housing and vacuum lines from inlet air housing, then disconnect vacuum harness coupling.
16. Remove drain tube from engine compartment.
17. Remove nuts from evaporator housing mounting studs on engine side of dash panel.
18. Remove hanger strap from plenum stud above evaporator housing, then tilt evaporator housing back to clear dash panel and remove housing from vehicle.
19. Remove blend air door lever from shaft.
20. Remove top cover screws and the cover.
21. Remove heater core from housing.
22. Reverse procedure to install.

BLOWER MOTOR
REPLACE

1982 NEW YORKER; 1982–86 DIPLOMAT, GRAN FURY; 1983 NEW YORKER FIFTH AVENUE & 1984–86 FIFTH AVENUE

NOTE: The blower motor is accessible from under right side of instrument panel.

Less A/C

1. Disconnect battery ground cable.
2. Disconnect blower motor ground and feed wires.
3. Remove blower motor to heater housing attaching screws, then remove blower motor.

Fig. 13 Speed Control servo cable throttle adjustment

4. Reverse procedure to install.

With A/C

1. Disconnect battery ground cable.
2. Disconnect blower motor feed wire, then remove blower motor housing to recirculation housing attaching nuts and separate blower motor housing from upper housing.
3. Remove blower motor plate attaching screws, then remove wire grommet, mounting plate and blower motor and wheel as an assembly.
4. Reverse procedure to install.

1980–81 GRAN FURY, NEWPORT, NEW YORKER & ST. REGIS; 1980–83 CORDOBA & MIRADA; 1981–83 IMPERIAL

NOTE: The blower motor is accessible from under right side of instrument panel.

1. Disconnect battery ground cable.
2. Remove glove box assembly.
3. Disconnect blower motor electrical connections.
4. Remove heater housing or evaporator-heater housing to plenum brace.
5. Remove blower motor mounting screws and the blower motor, **Figs. 8 through 11.**
6. Reverse procedure to install.

1980 ASPEN & VOLARÉ; 1980–81 LEBARON & DIPLOMAT

Less Air Conditioning

1. Remove heater assembly and heater

core as outlined under "Heater Core, Replace".
2. Remove blower motor vent tube.
3. Remove blower motor mounting nuts and the blower motor.
4. Reverse procedure to install.

With Air Conditioning

NOTE: All service to the blower motor is performed under the right side of the instrument panel.

1. Disconnect battery ground cable and the blower motor feed wire.
2. Remove blower motor mounting nuts from bottom of recirculation housing.
3. Separate upper and lower blower motor housing, then remove blower motor mounting plate screws.
4. Remove wire grommet, mounting plate and blower motor.
5. Reverse procedure to install.

SPEED CONTROLS
ADJUST

Lock-in Screw Adjustment, Fig. 12

Lock-in accuracy will be affected by poor engine performance (need for tune-up), loaded gross weight of car (trailering), improper slack in control cable. After the foregoing items have been considered and the speed sags or drops more than 2 to 3 mph when the speed control is activated, the lock-in adjusting screw should be turned counter-clockwise approximately ¼ turn per one mph correction required.

If a speed increase of more than 2 to 3

mph occurs, the lock-in adjusting screw should be turned clockwise ¼ turn per one mph correction required.

CAUTION: This adjustment must not exceed two turns in either direction or damage to the unit may occur.

Throttle Cable Adjustment, Fig. 13

Optimum servo performance is obtained with a given amount of free play in the throttle control cable. To obtain proper free play, insert a ¹⁄₁₆ inch diameter pin between forward end of slot in cable end of carburetor linkage pin (hair pin clip removed from linkage pin). With choke in full open position and carburetor at curb idle, pull cable back toward dash panel without moving carburetor linkage until all free play is removed. Tighten cable clamp bolt to 45 inch-pounds, remove ¹⁄₁₆ inch pin and install hair pin clip.

Brake Switch Adjustment

1. Loosen switch bracket.
2. Insert proper spacer gauge between brake push rod and switch with pedal in free position. On 1980–81 Gran Fury, Newport, New Yorker and St. Regis models, a .150 inch spacer is used. On 1980–81 models except Gran Fury, Newport, New Yorker and St. Regis and all 1982–86 models, a .130 inch spacer is used.
3. Push switch bracket assembly toward brake push rod until plunger is fully depressed and switch contacts spacer.
4. Tighten bracket bolt to 75 in-lbs. and remove spacer.

Engine Section

ENGINE MOUNTS
REPLACE

1. Disconnect throttle linkage at transmission and at carburetor.
2. Raise hood and position fan to clear radiator hose and radiator top tank.
3. Remove torque nuts from insulator studs.
4. Raise engine just enough to remove front engine mount.
5. Reverse above to install.

ENGINE
REPLACE

ALL V8 ENGINES

1. Scribe a line on hinge brackets on hood to assure proper adjustments when installing. Then remove hood.
2. Remove battery, drain cooling system, remove all hoses, fan shroud, disconnect oil cooler lines and remove radiator.
3. On models with A/C, remove com-

pressor from mounting bracket and position on right fender.

NOTE: Do not tilt compressor when removed from mounting bracket. Before installing compressor turn pulley several revolutions by hand to ensure all oil is back in compressor oil sump.

4. On all models, remove distributor cap, vacuum lines and wiring.
5. Remove carburetor, linkage, starter wires and oil pressure wire.
6. Disconnect power steering hoses, if equipped.
7. Remove starter, alternator, charcoal canister and horns.
8. Disconnect exhaust pipe at manifold.
9. On vehicles with automatic transmission:
   a. Mark converter and drive plate to aid in installation.
   b. Remove torque converter drive plate bolts.
   c. Install a C-clamp on bottom front of torque converter, to assure that converter remains properly positioned in transmission housing.

d. Remove converter housing to engine bolts.
   e. Support transmission in its normal position to assure ease of installation.
10. On vehicles with manual transmission, remove transmission.
11. Attach engine lifting fixture.
12. Remove engine front mounting bolts, then raise and work engine out of chassis.
13. Reverse procedure to install.

6-225

1. Scribe hood hinge outlines on hood and remove hood.
2. Drain cooling system and remove battery and carburetor air cleaner.
3. Disconnect transmission cooler lines at radiator (if equipped).
4. Remove radiator and hoses.
5. On models with A/C, remove compressor from mounting bracket and position on right fender.

NOTE: Do not tilt compressor when removed from mounting bracket. Before

Fig. 1 Cylinder head tightening sequence. 6-225

Fig. 2 Intake manifold tightening sequence. V8-318, 360

Fig. 3 Cylinder head tightening sequence. V8-318, 360

installing compressor turn pulley several revolutions by hand to ensure all oil is back in compressor sump.

6. On all models, remove closed ventilation system and evaporative control system from cylinder head cover.
7. Disconnect fuel lines, vacuum lines, carburetor linkage and wiring to engine.
8. Disconnect power steering hoses, if equipped.
9. Remove starter, alternator and horns.
10. Disconnect exhaust pipe at manifold.
11. Remove converter cover plate.
12. On manual transmission equipped vehicles disconnect propeller shaft, tie out of the way and disconnect wires and linkage at transmission.
13. On manual transmission equipped vehicles attach engine support fixture, remove engine rear crossmember and remove transmission.
14. On automatic transmission equipped vehicles disconnect torque converter drive plate from engine. Mark converter and drive plate to aid in installation.

Support transmission in its normal position in relation to the vehicle, to insure ease of installation.
15. Attach lifting fixture to cylinder head and attach chain hoist.
16. Remove engine support and front engine mounting bolts and lift engine from chassis.
17. Reverse procedure to install.

CYLINDER HEAD
REPLACE

6-225

1. Drain cooling system.
2. Remove carburetor air cleaner and fuel line.
3. Disconnect accelerator linkage.
4. Remove vacuum control tube at carburetor and distributor.
5. Disconnect spark plug wires, heater hose and clamp holding by-pass hose.
6. Disconnect heat indicator sending unit wire.

NOTE: On models equipped with air pump, disconnect diverter valve vacuum line from intake manifold and remove air tubes from cylinder head.

7. Disconnect exhaust pipe at manifold.
8. On all models, remove closed vent system and rocker arm cover.
9. Remove rocker shaft assembly and push rods.

NOTE: During disassembly note location of push rods so they can be installed in the same position.

10. Remove cylinder head bolts, then remove cylinder head and intake and exhaust manifold as an assembly.
11. Install the head in the reverse order of removal, and tighten the bolts in the sequence shown in **Fig. 1**.
12. When installing the manifolds, loosen the three bolts holding the intake and exhaust manifolds together. This is required to maintain proper alignment. Install intake and exhaust manifolds with cup side of the conical washers against the manifolds.

V8-318, 360

NOTE: The intake manifold attaching bolts on some engines are tilted upward about 30 degrees at an angle to the manifold-to-cylinder head gasket face. The purpose of this design is to provide more effective sealing at the cylinder block end gaskets. If the intake manifold is removed the installation should be such that the bolt tightening is done evenly and in the sequence shown in **Fig. 2**.

With gaskets in place start all bolts, leaving them loose. Run bolts 1 through 4 down so the heads just touch manifold. Then tighten these four bolts to 25 foot-pounds torque. After checking to see that gaskets are properly seated at all surfaces, tighten remaining bolts to 25 foot-pounds. Finally tighten all bolts in the sequence shown to specifications.

1. Drain cooling system and disconnect battery ground cable.
2. Remove alternator, carburetor air cleaner and fuel line. Disconnect accelerator linkage.
3. Remove vacuum advance hose and distributor cap and wires.
4. Disconnect coil wires, heat indicator wire, heater and by-pass hoses.
5. Remove closed ventilation system and rocker arm covers.
6. Remove intake manifold, coil and carburetor as an assembly.

Fig. 4 Cylinder head bolt hole identification. V8-318 engines.

Fig. 5   Rocker arm and shaft assembly. 6-225

7. Remove exhaust manifolds.
8. Remove rocker arm and shaft assemblies. Remove push rods.

NOTE: During disassembly note location of push rods so they can be installed in the same position.

9. Remove head bolts and cylinder heads.
10. Reverse procedure to install heads and tighten bolts in sequence, **Fig. 3.**

SERVICE NOTE: V8-318 engines have cylinder head bolt holes drilled through the block into the water jacket in certain locations, **Fig. 4.** Cylinder head bolts in these locations must have sealer 4057989 or equivalent applied to the threads to prevent engine coolant leakage. Ensure old sealer is cleaned from the threads before applying new sealer.

VALVES
ADJUST

1980 6-225

Before the final valve lash adjustment is made, operate the engine for 5 minutes at a fast idle to stabilize engine temperatures.

Before starting the adjustment procedure, make two chalk marks on the vibration damper. Space the marks approximately 120° apart (⅓ of circumference) so that with the timing mark the damper is divided into three equal parts. Adjust the valves for No. 1 cylinder. Repeat the procedure for the remaining valves, turning the crankshaft ⅓ turn in the direction of normal rotation while adjusting the valves in the firing order sequence of 153624.

VALVE ARRANGEMENT
FRONT TO REAR

V8-318, 360 . . . . E-I-I-E-E-I-I-E
6-225 . . . . E-I-E-I-E-I-I-E-I-E-I-E

VALVE LIFT SPECS.

Engine	Year	Intake	Exhaust
6-225	1980	.406	.414
	1981–83	.378	.378
V8-318	1980–86	.373	.400
V8-360	1980	.410	.410

Fig. 6   Rocker arm and shaft assembly installed. V8-318 & 360

VALVE TIMING SPECS.
INTAKE OPENS BEFORE TDC

Engine	Year	Degrees
6-225	1980	16
	1981–83	6
8-318	1980–86	10
8-360	1980	18

ROCKER ARMS
REPLACE

6-225

Removal
1. Remove closed ventilation and evaporation control systems.
2. Remove rocker arm cover.
3. Remove rocker shaft bolts and retainers.
4. Lift off rocker arms and shaft.

Inspection

Clean all parts with a suitable solvent. Be sure the inside of the shaft is clean and the oil holes are open. The drilled oil hole in the bore of the rocker arm must be open to the trough and valve end of the arms. The trough also feeds oil to the adjusting screw and push rod.

The shaft should be free from excessive wear in arm contact areas. The shaft should be smooth in retainer contact areas. The adjusting screws in the rocker arms should have a uniform round end. The drag torque should be smooth and uniform. The retainers should be smooth and undamaged in the shaft contact area.

Fig. 7   Hydraulic roller lifter installation. 1985—86 V8-318

Fig. 8   Hydraulic roller lifter exploded view. 1985—86 V8-318

Fig. 9   Hydraulic valve lifter. 1979—84

Assembly & Installation

1. Referring to **Fig. 5,** note position of oil hole on forward end of shaft which denotes the upper side of shaft. Rocker arms must be put on the shaft with the adjusting screw to the right side of the engine. Place one of the small retainers on the one long bolt and install the bolt in the rear hole in the shaft from the top side.
2. Install one rocker arm and one spacer; then two rocker arms and a spacer. Continue in same sequence until all rocker arms and spacers are on the shaft.
3. Place a bolt and small retainer in front hole in shaft.
4. Place a bolt and the one wide retainer through the center hole in the shaft with six rocker arms on each side of center.
5. Install remaining bolts and retainers.
6. Locate the assembly on the cylinder head and position rocker arm adjusting screws in push rods.
7. Tighten bolts finger tight, bringing retainers in contact with the shaft between rocker arms.
8. Tighten bolts to specified torque.
9. On 1980 models, adjust valve lash to specifications after running engine to normal operating temperature.
10. Reverse remaining procedure to complete installation.

Fig. 10   Removing valve lifter

V8-318, 360

To provide correct lubrication for the rocker arms on these engines, the rocker shafts have a small notch machined at one end and these notches must always face inward toward the center of the engine when installed. In other words, the notched end must be toward the rear of the engine on the right bank, and to the front of the engine on the left bank.

Rocker arms must be correctly positioned on the shaft prior to installation on cylinder head, **Fig. 6.**

It is also important when installing the rocker shaft assembly on the cylinder head to position the short retainers at each end and in the center, and to place long retainers in the two remaining positions.

VALVE GUIDES

Valves operate in guide holes bored directly in the cylinder head. When valve stem-to-guide clearance becomes excessive, valves with oversize stems of .005, .015 and .030 inch are available for service replacement. When necessary to install valves with oversize stems the valve bores should be reamed to provide the proper operating clearance.

VALVE LIFTERS
REPLACE

1985—86 V8-318

NOTE: 1985—86 V8-318 engines are equipped with roller type hydraulic lifters.

Removal

1. Remove valve covers, rocker shaft

Fig. 11   Valve timing marks aligned for correct valve timing. All Sixes

assembly and push rods, noting installation position so that components can be installed in original position.
2. Remove intake manifold as outlined in 'Cylinder Head, Replace'.
3. Remove yoke retainer and aligning yokes, **Fig. 7.**
4. Insert puller C-4129 or equivalent through opening in cylinder head, seat tool securely in head of lifter, then pull lifter from bore.

NOTE: If more than one lifter is to be removed, identify lifters to ensure reinstallation in original position.

Inspection

1. Inspect bore in cylinder block, and if bore is scored or shows signs of wear or sticking, ream bore and install oversized lifter assembly.
2. Pry out plunger retaining, then disassemble lifter as shown in **Fig. 8.**

NOTE: Plunger and body assemblies are not interchangeable, and plunger valve must always be installed in original body. Disassemble only one lifter at a time to

Fig. 12   Valve timing marks aligned for correct valve timing. All V8s

Fig. 13   Camshaft and related parts. 6-225

Fig. 14   Piston and rod assembly. 6-225

Fig. 15 Piston and rod assembly. V8 engines

Fig. 16 Lower oil seal & retainer. 6-225

---

avoid mixing components.

3. Clean components with solvent suitable for removing all varnish and blow dry with compressed air.
4. Inspect plunger for scoring, wear and pitting, and inspect valve seat for any condition that may prevent seating. If any defect is found, replace lifter assembly.
5. Coat components with clean engine oil or suitable assembly lubricant, then reassemble lifter as shown in **Fig. 8.**

Installation
1. Lubricate lifters, then install in original bores.
2. Install aligning yokes ensuring that arrow points toward camshaft, **Fig. 7.**
3. Install yoke retainers and torque screws to 200 inch lbs.
4. Reverse remaining procedure to complete installation, start engine and run at approximately 15000RPM until it reaches normal operating temperature.

CAUTION: To prevent engine damage, do not run engine above fast idle until all lifters have filled with oil and become quiet.

Exc. 1985—86 V8-318

After taking off rocker arm and shaft assembly, lift out push rods. The valve lifters, **Fig. 9,** may then be removed with a suitably long magnet rod. If the lifters cannot be removed with the magnet rod, a special tool (C-4129) may be used, **Fig. 10.** Insert the tool through the push rod opening in the cylinder head and into lifter. Turn the handle to expand the tool in the lifter, then with a twisting motion remove the lifter from its bore.

TIMING CHAIN COVER
REPLACE

6-225
1. To remove cover, drain cooling system and remove radiator and fan.
2. Remove vibration damper with a puller.
3. Loosen oil pan bolts to allow clearance and remove chain case cover.
4. Reverse above procedure to install cover.

V8-318, 360
1. Remove radiator, fan and belt.
2. Remove water pump and housing as a unit.
3. Remove power steering pump, if necessary.
4. Remove crankshaft pulley.
5. Remove key from crankshaft.
6. Remove fuel pump.
7. Loosen oil pan bolts and remove front bolt at each side.
8. Remove chain case cover and gasket, using extreme caution to avoid damaging oil pan gasket otherwise oil pan will have to be removed. It is normal to find particles of neoprene collected between crankshaft seal retainer and oil slinger.
9. Reverse procedure to install.

TIMING CHAIN
REPLACE

6-225
Removal
1. After removing chain case cover as outlined above, take off camshaft sprocket attaching bolt.
2. Remove chain with camshaft sprocket.
3. Clean all parts and dry with compressed air.
4. Inspect timing chain for broken or

damaged links. Inspect sprockets for cracks and chipped, worn or damaged teeth.

Installation
1. Turn crankshaft so sprocket timing mark is toward and directly in line with centerline of camshaft.
2. Temporarily install camshaft sprocket. Rotate camshaft to position sprocket timing mark toward and directly in line with centerline of crankshaft; then remove camshaft sprocket.
3. Place chain on crankshaft sprocket and position camshaft sprocket in chain so sprocket can be installed with timing marks aligned without moving camshaft, **Fig. 11.**
4. Install parts removed in reverse order of removal.

V8 ENGINES

To install chain and sprockets, lay both the camshaft and crankshaft sprockets on the bench. Position the sprockets so that the timing marks are next to each other. Place the chain on both sprockets, then push the gears apart as far as the chain will permit. Use a straightedge to form a line through the exact centers of both gears. The timing marks must be on this line, **Fig. 12.**

Slide the chain with both sprockets on the camshaft and crankshaft at the same time; then recheck the alignment.

NOTE: On V8 engines, use tool No. C-3509 to prevent camshaft from contacting welch plug in rear of engine block. Remove distributor and oil pump-distributor drive gear. Position tool against rear side of cam gear and attach tool with distributor retainer plate bolt.

CAMSHAFT & BEARINGS
REPLACE

6-225

The camshaft is supported by four precision type, steel backed, babbitt-lined bearings. Rearward thrust is taken by the rear face of the sprocket hub contacting the front of the engine block.

The camshaft, **Fig. 13,** can be removed after removing the grille, radiator and timing chain. To remove the camshaft bearings, the engine must be removed from the vehicle.

1. Remove valve lifters, oil pump, fuel pump and distributor.
2. Install a long bolt into front of camshaft to aid removal. Remove camshaft using care not to damage bearings.
3. Remove welch plug back of rear camshaft bearing.
4. Remove bearings with suitable puller equipment.
5. Install new bearings, being sure the oil holes in bearings line up with the corresponding oil holes in the crankcase.

NOTE: Install No. 1 camshaft bearing $\frac{3}{32}$ in. inward from front face of cylinder block.

6. Apply sealer to welch plug and plug bore, then install plug at rear of camshaft.

V8 ENGINES

To remove the camshaft, remove all valve lifters, timing chain and sprockets. Remove distributor and oil pump-distributor drive gear. Remove fuel pump and see that push rod has moved away from eccentric drive cam. Remove thrust plate, noting installation position of timing chain oil tab so it can be installed in the same manner. Withdraw camshaft from engine, using care to see that camshaft lobes do not damage the camshaft bearings.

If camshaft bearings are to be replaced, it is recommended that the engine be removed from the chassis and the crankshaft taken out in order that any chips or foreign material may be removed from the oil passages.

PISTON & ROD
ASSEMBLE

6-225

Piston and rod assemblies must be installed as shown in **Fig. 14.**

V8 ENGINES

When installing piston and rod assemblies in the cylinders, the compression ring gaps should be diametrically opposite one another and not in line with the oil ring gap. The oil ring expander gap should be toward the outside of the "V" of the engine. The oil ring gap should be turned toward the inside of the engine "V".

Immerse the piston head and rings in clean engine oil and, with a suitable piston ring compressor, insert the piston and rod assembly into the bore. Tap the piston down into the bore, using the handle of a hammer.

Assemble the pistons to the rods as shown in **Fig. 15.**

PISTONS, PINS & RINGS

Pistons are available in standard sizes and the following oversize: .020.

Pins are available in the following oversizes: V8-318 & 360, .003, .008 inch. Not furnished on all other engines.

Rings are available in the following oversizes: std. to .009, .020–.029, .040–.049 inch.

MAIN & ROD BEARINGS

Main bearings are furnished in standard sizes and the following undersizes: .001, .002, .003, .010, .012 inch.

Rod bearings are furnished in standard sizes and the following undersizes: .001, .002, .003, .010, .012 inch.

6-225 engines may be equipped with either a cast or forged crankshaft. The following parts are not interchangeable between cast and forged crankshaft engines: crankshaft, crankshaft bearings, connecting rods and bearings and cylinder block. On models equipped with manual transmission, cast crankshaft engine vibration damper is not interchangeable with forged crankshaft engine and requires that a crankshaft screw and washer be used and torqued to 135 ft. lbs. On models equipped with automatic transmission, vibration damper and torque converter are interchangeable between cast and forged crankshaft engines.

CRANKSHAFT REAR OIL SEAL
REPLACE

6-225

SERVICE BULLETIN: Crankshaft oil seal leaks on 1981–83 6-225 engines can sometimes be difficult to locate and repair without proper diagnosis. When a seal leak is suspected, always perform an air test to verify the condition and location before you begin disassembly. Test for oil leaks as follows:

NOTE: Only regulated air adjusted to 4 psi should be used to air test engine.

1. Remove crankcase vent valve and cap and plug valve cover holes.
2. Remove dipstick, then install rubber hose connected to air source into dipstick tube.
3. Raise and support vehicle, then remove torque convertor or clutch housing cover.
4. Visually inspect rear of engine block for leakage. Leakage between rear seal and crankshaft will cause oil spray in a circular pattern. Leakage

from retainer side seals, retainer joint face or back side of rear seal will tend to run straight down. Other possible leak paths are a porous block and rear cam and gallery plugs.
5. Apply air pressure to crankcase and check seal area for leaks. If leakage is evident, check seal or seal retainer. If no leakage is detected, rotate crankshaft and watch for leakage. If a leak is detected while crankshaft is being rotated, check crankcase seal surface for damage or scratches. If no leakage is detected, pressurize lubrication system and check for leaking oil passage.
6. Remove rear seal retainer. Inspect retainer and seal sides for proper sealing and half round seal for correct positioning. If leak is evident only when crankshaft is rotated, inspect crankshaft for nicks, scratches or cuts in seal area. Polish nicks or scratches with emery cloth.
7. Clean old sealer from seal retainer and block, and remove upper seal half. Ensure seal was not installed backwards, since this can cause leakage. Check outside diameter of seal for cuts or peeled rubber.

Replacement seals are of two piece rubber type composition which make possible the replacement of upper rear seal without removing crankshaft. Both halves must be used. After removing oil pan, rear main bearing cap and seal retainer, pry lower rope seal from retainer with small screwdriver. Screw a special tool into upper rope seal and carefully pull to remove seal while rotating crankshaft. Install upper half of new seal into block, making sure stripe on seal faces rear of engine. Shim stock or equivalent may be used to protect back side of seal against sharp side of block. Rotate crankshaft to ease installation. Apply a $\frac{1}{8}$ inch bead of RTV sealant into groove in retainer, starting and ending $\frac{1}{2}$ inch from ends of groove. Install other half of seal into retainer, ensuring stripe on seal faces rearward, then install rear main bearing cap and torque to specifications. Install side seals onto retainer using bonder part #4057988 or equivalent. Apply a small amount of RTV sealer to retainer in areas shown in **Fig. 16.** Install retainer and torque to 30 ft. lbs.

NOTE: Do not apply sealer to seal lip surface, as leakage may result.

V8-318 & 360

Replacement of rear main bearing oil seals is similar to procedure given above for 6 cylinder engines. A seal retainer is not found on these engines; lower half of seal is installed into groove in rear main bearing cap.

The 318 engine has cap seals in addition to lower seal secured by rear main bearing cap. Cap seal with yellow paint is installed, narrow sealing edge up, into right side with bearing cap in engine position. Cap seals must be flush with shoulder of bearing cap to prevent oil leakage.

The 360 engine requires sealer to be applied adjacent to rear main bearing oil

Fig. 17   Rear main bearing caps. V8-318 & 360

Fig. 18   Oil pump. 6-225

seal as cap seals are not used, **Fig. 17.** After applying sealer, quickly assemble rear main bearing cap to block and torque to specifications.

OIL PAN
REPLACE

6-225

1. Drain radiator, disconnect battery ground cable and radiator hoses and remove oil dipstick.
2. Remove shroud attaching screws, separate shroud from radiator and position rearward on engine.
3. Raise vehicle and drain oil pan.
4. Remove engine to transmission support bracket.
5. Disconnect exhaust pipe, then torque converter inspection shield.
6. Remove center link from steering arm and idler arm ball joints.
7. Support front of engine with a jack stand placed under the right front corner of oil pan.
8. Remove engine front mount bolts. Raise engine approx. 1½ to 2 inch.
9. Remove oil pan attaching screws, rotate engine crankshaft to clear counterweights and remove oil pan.
10. Reverse procedure to install.

V8-318, 360
1980–81 Newport, New Yorker & St. Regis

1. Disconnect battery ground cable and remove oil level dipstick.
2. Raise vehicle and drain crankcase, then remove engine to torque convert-
3. Remove steering idler arm ball joints from center link.
4. Disconnect exhaust pipes from exhaust manifolds.
5. Remove oil pan attaching bolts.
6. Position a suitable jack under transmission remove rear engine mount to transmission extension attaching bolts.
7. Raise transmission until rear of oil pan can be lowered to clear transmission.

8. Reverse procedure to install.

1980 Aspen & Volare; 1980–81 LeBaron; 1980–86 Diplomat; 1980–83 Cordoba & Mirada; 1981–83 Imperial; 1982 New Yorker; 1982–86 Gran Fury; 1983 New Yorker Fifth Avenue & 1984–86 Fifth Avenue

1. Disconnect battery ground cable and remove engine oil level dipstick.
2. Raise vehicle and drain crankcase.
3. Remove exhaust crossover pipe, then disconnect and lower center link.
4. Remove starter and starter mounting stud.
5. Remove torque converter inspection cover.
6. Remove oil pan attaching bolts and oil pan.
7. Reverse procedure to install.

1980 V8-360 4 Bar. Carb.

1. Disconnect battery ground cable and remove oil dipstick.
2. Remove fan shroud attaching bolts and place shroud over fan.
3. Raise vehicle and disconnect steering linkage center link.
4. Remove oil pan bolts.
5. Raise transmission slightly with a suitable jack and remove rear engine mount to transmission bolts.
6. Lower rear of oil pan until clear of transmission.
7. Lower transmission and loosely install the rear engine mount bolts.
8. Loosen front engine mounts from frame.
9. Raise engine with a suitable jack approximately one inch and remove oil pan.
10. Reverse procedure to install.

OIL PUMP
REPLACE

SIX CYLINDER

1. Drain radiator and disconnect upper and lower hoses.
2. Remove fan shroud (if equipped).
3. Raise vehicle on a hoist, support front of engine with a jack stand place

under right front corner of engine oil pan. Do not support engine at crankshaft pulley or vibration damper.
4. Remove front engine mounts.
5. Raise engine 1½ to 2 inches.
6. Remove oil filter, pump attaching bolts and remove pump assembly.
7. Reverse procedure to install.

V8 ENGINES

SERVICE BULLETIN: 1980 V8-318, 360 Low Oil Pressure: An incorrectly installed oil line plug, part number 3462871, may cause low or dropping oil pressure. To check plug for proper position:

1. Remove oil pressure sending unit from rear of cylinder block.
2. Insert a ⅛ inch wire into sensing unit hole to measure distance between plug and top of machined surface of oil pressure sending unit hole.
3. The distance should be 7½ to 7¹¹⁄₁₆ inches.
4. If measurement is less than 7½ inches, use a suitable dowel drift to drive plug into proper position.
5. If measurement is greater than 7¹¹⁄₁₆ inches, remove oil pan and the No. 5 main bearing cap. Drive plug upward to properly position.

On V8-318, 360 engines, remove oil pan as outlined, then remove pump from rear main bearing cap. Reverse procedure to install, torquing retaining bolts to 30 ft. lbs.

OIL PUMP SERVICE
6-225

To disassemble, remove the pump cover seal ring, **Fig. 18.** Press off the drive gear, supporting the gear to keep load off aluminum body. Remove rotor and shaft and lift out outer pump rotor. Remove oil pressure relief valve plug and lift out spring and plunger. Remove oil pressure sending unit.

Inspection

1. The rotor contact area and the bores

Fig. 19   Oil pump. V8-318 & 360

Engine oiling system. 6-225

for the shaft and valve in the pump body should be smooth, free from scratches, scoring or excessive wear.

2. The pump cover should be smooth, flat and free from scoring or ridges. Lay a straightedge across the cover. If a .0015 inch feeler gauge can be inserted under the straightedge, the cover should be replaced.

3. All surfaces of the outer rotor should be smooth and uniform, free from ridges, scratches or uneven wear. Discard a rotor less than .649 inch thick for 1980 or .825 inch thick for 1981–83 and/or less than 2.469 inch in diameter.

4. The inner rotor and shaft assembly should be smooth, free from scoring and uneven wear. Discard rotors less than .649 inch thick for 1980 or .825 inch thick for 1981–83.

5. Place outer rotor in pump body and measure clearance between rotor and body. Discard pump body if clearance is more than .014 inch.

6. Install inner rotor and shaft in pump body. Shaft should turn freely but without side play. If clearance between rotor teeth is more than .010 inch, replace both rotors.

7. Measure rotor end clearance. If feeler gauge of more than .004 inch can be inserted between straightedge and rotors, install a new pump body.

8. The oil pressure relief valve should be smooth, free from scratches or scoring, and should be a free fit in its bore.

9. The relief valve spring has a free length of 2¼ inches and should test between 22.3 and 23.3 pounds when compressed to 1¹⁹⁄₃₂ inch. If not, replace the spring.

Assembly and Installation

1. With pump rotors in body, press drive gear on shaft, flush with end of shaft.

2. Install seal ring in groove in body and install cover. Tighten bolts to 95 inch lbs. Test pump for free turning.

3. Install oil pressure relief valve spring. Use new washer (gasket) and tighten plug securely.

4. If pump shaft turns freely, remove pump cover and outer rotor before

installation of pump on engine.

5. Install oil pressure sending unit and tighten to 60 inch lbs. (5 ft. lbs.)

6. Using a new gasket, install pump on engine and tighten bolts to 200 inch lbs. (16 ft. lbs.)

7. Install oil filter reservoir on pump. Install filter element and tighten cover nuts to 25 ft. lbs.

8. Connect oil pressure sending unit wire.

9. Complete the installation by reversing steps as given under Oil Pump, Replace.

V8-318, 360

After removing the pump from the engine, it should be disassembled, cleaned and inspected for wear, **Fig. 19**.

1. To remove the relief valve, remove the cotter pin and drill a ⅛ inch hole into the relief valve retainer cap and install a self-threading sheet metal screw.

2. Clamp screw into vise and tap on housing lightly with a soft hammer to remove the retaining cap, then remove the relief valve spring and valve.

3. Remove the oil pump cover and discard the oil seal ring.

4. Remove pump rotor, shaft and lift out outer rotor.

5. Mating surface of the pump cover should be smooth. If scratched or grooved, replace the pump.

6. Lay a straight edge across the cover. If a .0015 inch feeler gauge can be inserted between the cover and the straight edge, replace the pump.

7. Measure thickness and diameter of outer rotor. If rotor thickness is .825 inch or less on V8-318 engines, or .943 inch or less on V8-360 engines or if the diameter of the rotor is 2.429 inches or less, replace the outer

rotor.

8. If the inner rotor is .825 inch or less on V8-318 engines, or .943 inch or less on V8-360 engines, replace the inner rotor and shaft assembly.

9. Install the outer rotor into the housing. Press rotor to one side with the fingers and measure the clearance between the rotor and body with a feeler gauge. If the measurement is .014 inch or greater, replace the pump.

10. Place the inner rotor and shaft into the pump. If clearance between the rotors is .010 inch or greater, replace the shaft and both rotors.

11. Place a straightedge across the face of the pump between bolt holes. If a feeler gauge of .004 inch or greater can be inserted, replace the pump.

12. Check the oil pump relief valve plunger for scoring and free operation in the bore. Small marks may be removed with 400-grit sand paper.

13. The relief valve spring should have a free length of 2¹⁄₃₂ to 2³⁄₆₄ inch and should test between 16.2 and 17.2 pounds when compressed to 1¹¹⁄₃₂ inch. If not, replace the spring.

BELT TENSION DATA

	New①	Used①
1980–86 All	120	70

①—Belt tension in lbs.

WATER PUMP
REPLACE

CAUTION: When it becomes necessary to remove a fan clutch of the silicone type, the assembly must be supported in the vertical position to prevent leaks of silicone

ROCKER SHAFT

OIL SUPPLY TO PUSH ROD

OIL FEED HOLE

OIL FLOWS TO ONLY ONE BRACKET ON EACH HEAD. BRACKET IS SECOND FROM REAR ON RIGHT HEAD. BRACKET IS SECOND FROM FRONT ON LEFT HEAD

ROCKER SHAFT OIL PASSAGE

TO MAIN BEARINGS

TO CAMSHAFT BEARINGS

OIL GALLERY

ROCKER SHAFT BRACKET

OIL PASSAGE FOR OIL PRESSURE INDICATOR LIGHT

RIGHT OIL GALLERY

PASSAGE TO CAMSHAFT REAR BEARING

PLUG

OIL FROM FILTER TO SYSTEM

OIL TO FILTER

CRANKSHAFT

FROM OIL PUMP

OIL FILTER

OIL PUMP

OIL INTAKE

TO CONNECTING ROD BEARINGS

OIL GALLERY

PASSAGE TO CYLINDER HEAD

TAPPET

FEED FROM OIL GALLERY TO #2 MAIN BEARING AND PASSAGE TO HEAD MAIN

Engine Oiling System. V8-318 & 360

fluid from the clutch mechanism. This loss of fluid will render the fan clutch inoperative.

6-225

1. Drain cooling system, then remove battery, upper and lower radiator hoses and fan shroud.
2. Remove all drive belts, then remove fan attaching bolts, fan, spacer and pulley.
3. Remove A/C compressor and air pump bracket to water pump attaching bolts, then position compressor and air pump aside. Keep compressor in upright position.
4. Disconnect by-pass and heater hoses from water pump.
5. Remove water pump attaching bolts and remove pump assembly.
6. Reverse procedure to install.

V8-318, 360

1. Drain cooling system and disconnect battery ground cable.
2. Remove all drive belts, then remove radiator shroud and position over fan.
3. Remove fan assembly, pulley and fan shroud.
4. Remove alternator adjusting strap and

mounting bolts and position alternator aside.
5. Remove A/C compressor with mounting brackets and position aside, if equipped. Keep compressor in upright position.
6. Remove power steering pump mounting bolts and position pump aside, if equipped.
7. Remove air pump and mounting brackets, if equipped. Disconnect air hose at pump fittings.
8. Disconnect by-pass and heater hoses at water pump.
9. Disconnect lower radiator hose from pump.
10. Remove remaining water pump attaching bolts and remove pump assembly.
11. Reverse procedure to install.

SERVICE BULLETIN: CORE HOLE PLUG SIZES: When replacing a cup-type core hole plug in an engine, the size of the hole in the cylinder head, water jacket or rear bearing bore for the camshaft should be checked. At these locations a 1/16 inch oversize hole is sometimes bored in production and an oversize core plug installed.

Core plugs 1/16 inch oversize are available for replacement should they be

required at these locations.

FUEL PUMP
REPLACE

SERVICE NOTE: Before installing the pump, it is good practice to crank the engine so that the nose of the camshaft eccentric is out of the way of the fuel pump rocker arm when the pump is installed. In this way there will be the least amount of tension on the rocker arm, thereby easing the installation of the pump.

1. Disconnect fuel lines from fuel pump.
2. Remove fuel pump attaching bolts and fuel pump.
3. Remove all gasket material from the pump and block gasket surfaces. Apply sealer to both sides of new gasket.
4. Position gasket on pump flange and hold pump in position against its mounting surface. Make sure rocker arm is riding on camshaft eccentric.
5. Press pump tight against its mounting. Install retaining screws and tighten them alternately.
6. Connect fuel lines. Then operate engine and check for leaks.

Clutch & Transmission Section

CLUTCH PEDAL
ADJUST

1. Inspect condition of clutch pedal rubber stop, if stop is damaged install a new one.
2. Where necessary, disconnect interlock clutch rod at transmission end.
3. Adjust linkage by turning self-locking adjusting nut to provide $5/32$ inch free movement at outer end of fork. This movement will provide the prescribed one-inch free play at pedal.
4. Assemble interlock clutch rod (if used) to transmission pawl.

CLUTCH
REPLACE

REMOVAL

1. Remove transmission and clutch housing pan.
2. Remove return spring from clutch release fork and clutch housing or torque shaft lever.
3. Remove spring washer securing fork rod to torque shaft lever and remove rod from torque shaft and release fork.
4. Remove clutch release bearing assembly, release fork and boot from

CROSS-OVER BLADE IN NEUTRAL

Fig. 1 Gearshift lever adjustment. Three speed transmission w/column mounted shifter

clutch housing.
5. Mark clutch cover and flywheel so that they may be assembled in their original position to maintain balance.
6. Loosen clutch cover retaining screws one or two turns at a time in succession until cover is loose and remove screws.

7. Remove clutch assembly and disc from clutch housing using care to avoid contaminating the friction surfaces.

INSTALLATION

1. Lubricate pilot bushing in crankshaft with Multi-Purpose Grease number 2932524 or equivalent.
2. Clean surfaces of flywheel and pressure plate, making certain no oil or grease remains on these parts.
3. Hold cover plate and disc in place and insert a special clutch aligning tool or a spare clutch shaft through the hub of the disc and into the crankshaft pilot bearing.
4. Bolt clutch cover loosely to flywheel, being sure marks previously made are lined up.
5. To avoid distortion of clutch cover, tighten cover bolts a few turns each in progression until all are tight. The final tightening should be 200 inch lbs.

THREE SPEED TRANSMISSION
REPLACE

1. Disconnect shift rods from transmission levers.

NOTE: If shift rods are retained by plastic grommets, disconnect the shift levers from the transmission to avoid replacing the grommets.

2. Drain lubricant from transmission and disconnect propeller shaft.
3. Disconnect speedometer cable and backup light switch connector.
4. If necessary, disconnect exhaust pipes from exhaust manifolds.
5. Raise engine slightly using a suitable support fixture or jack and disconnect extension housing from center crossmember.
6. Support transmission with a suitable jack and remove center crossmember.
7. Remove transmission to clutch housing retaining bolts, then slide transmission rearward until input shaft clears clutch disc and remove transmission.
8. Reverse procedure to install.

FOUR SPEED & OVERDRIVE TRANSMISSION
REPLACE

1. Remove console and shift components.
2. Drain fluid from transmission.
3. Disconnect propeller shaft at rear universal joint and carefully pull yoke out of extension housing. Be careful not to

SCREW AND WASHER ASSEMBLY (3)
SPACER (3)
GROMMET (3)
SCREW (4)
KNOB
NUT
SCREW (4)
COVER
CLIP
BOOT ASSEMBLY
GEARSHIFT SELECTOR LEVER
SPACER (3)
MECHANISM
PLATE
2ND AND 3RD ROD
BOLT (3)
1ST AND REVERSE ROD
CLIP
BOLT
LOCK WASHER
SWIVEL (2)
LEVER ALIGNMENT SLOT

5/8
2-3/8 1/16
LEVER ALIGNMENT TOOL (SHEET METAL)

Fig. 2 Gearshift linkage adjustment. Three speed transmission w/floor mounted shifter

scratch or nick ground surface on sliding spline yoke during removal and installation of shaft.

4. Disconnect speedometer cable and stop light switch leads.
5. Disconnect left-hand exhaust pipe (dual exhaust) from manifold.
6. Disconnect parking cable where necessary.
7. Support rear of engine with a jack.
8. Raise engine slightly and disconnect extension housing from removable center crossmember.
9. Support transmission with a suitable jack and remove center crossmember.
10. Remove transmission-to-clutch housing bolts.
11. Slide transmission rearward and out of vehicle.
12. Reverse procedure to install.

SHIFT LINKAGE
ADJUST

THREE SPEED TRANS.

Column Shift
1. Loosen both shift rod swivels.
2. With transmission shift levers in neutral (middle detent), move shift lever to align locating slots in bottom of steering column shift housing and bearing

Fig. 3 Gearshift linkage adjustment. Four speed transmission

housing. Install suitable tool in slot to maintain alignment.
3. Place screwdriver or other suitable tool between crossover blade and 2nd-3rd lever at steering column so that both lever pins are engaged by crossover blade, **Fig. 1.**
4. Torque both shift rod swivel bolts to 125 inch lbs.
5. Remove gearshift housing locating tool and remove tool from crossover blade at steering column.
6. Shift through all gears to check adjustment and crossover smoothness. Check for operation of steering column lock in reverse and other gear positions. If properly adjusted, ignition should lock in reverse position only without having to force shift lever.

Floor Shift
1. Place shift lever in neutral position and disconnect shift rods from levers.
2. Fabricate alignment tool from 1/16 in. thick sheet metal as shown in **Fig. 2.**
3. Insert alignment tool into slots in levers and frame to hold levers in neutral position, **Fig. 2.**
4. Place transmission levers in neutral position and adjust shift rod swivels so that rods will install freely into levers.
5. Secure rods with washers and clips, then remove alignment tool and check shifter operation.

FOUR SPEED TRANS.

1. Install floor shift lever aligning tool, **Fig. 3,** to hold levers in neutral position. Crossover alignment tool shown in **Fig. 3,** will have to be fabricated.
2. With all rods disconnected from transmission shift levers, place levers in neutral position.
3. Starting with 1-2 shift rod, rotate shift rods until ends of rods enter shift levers. It may be necessary to remove clip at shifter end to rotate rods.
4. Replace washers and clips, then remove aligning tool and check shifting action.

Rear Axle, Propeller Shaft & Brakes

NOTE: Figs. 1 and 2 illustrate the various rear axle assemblies used on these models. When necessary to overhaul any of these units, refer to the Rear Axle Specifications table in this chapter.

tubes to lubricate the axle shaft roller bearings, **Fig. 3.**

Servicing the late design 7¼ inch rear axle is the same as the early design 7¼ differential, except for the axle shaft and axle shaft bearing. When replacing axle shaft or axle shaft bearing refer to "Axle

Shaft, Replace (Fig. 2 Type)" for service procedures.

Two types of integral carrier axles are used. In both types, the drive pinion is mounted in two opposing tapered roller bearings which are preloaded by a spacer

INTEGRAL TYPE REAR AXLE

NOTE: The following changes have been made in the design of the 7¼ inch rear axle during the 1982 model year for all models except Imperial.

1. The inboard ends of the 8¼ inch axle shaft tubes are swedged down in size and pressed into the 7¼ inch carrier, **Fig. 2.**
2. The 7¼ inch axle shafts ball bearings are replaced with the 8¼ inch axle shaft roller bearings.
3. The axle shafts are retained with the standard 8¼ inch axle "C" lock washer, **Fig. 3.**
4. The 7¼ inch differential side gears now have a counterbore to incorporate the "C" lock washers. These side gears can be used on the early design 7¼ inch axles, but the early design side gears cannot be used on the later design 7¼ inch axle.
5. The late design carrier has two cast holes to allow lube to flow into the

Fig. 1 Integral carrier rear axle exploded view. 1980—81 & early production 1982 w/7¼ inch ring gear

Fig. 2 Integral carrier rear axle exploded view. Models w/8¼ inch ring gear, late production 1982–86 models w/7¼ inch ring gear similar

positioned between them.

In the unit shown in **Fig. 1,** the differential is supported by two tapered roller side bearings. These bearings are preloaded by spacers located between the bearings and carrier housing. The differential assembly is positioned for ring and pinion backlash by varying these spacers.

Axle shafts in this unit are held in place by retainers at the outer ends of the shafts. These retainers are bolted through the brake backing plates to the rear axle tubes.

In the unit shown in **Fig. 2,** the differential is also supported by two tapered roller bearings. A threaded differential bearing adjuster is located in each bearing pedestal cap to eliminate differential side play, adjust and maintain ring and pinion backlash and provide a means of obtaining differential bearing preload.

Axles are retained by means of a "C" washer which is installed into a groove in the inner end of the axle shaft inside the differential unit.

On both these units, a removable stamped steel cover, bolted to the rear of the carrier, permits inspection and service of the differential without removal of the complete axle assembly from the vehicle.

NOTE: 7¼ and 8¼ in. axle differentials have balanced side and pinion gears. Any attempt to mix these side or pinion gears with previously manufactured ones will result in lock up or excessive differential backlash. Side and pinion gears must be replaced as a set.

REAR AXLE
REPLACE

1. Raise rear of vehicle and position safety stands at front of rear springs.

Fig. 3 Typical axle shaft 'C' lock installation & 7¼ inch axle housing identification

2. Remove rear wheels, then disconnect brake lines at wheel cylinders. Cap brake line fittings to prevent loss of fluid.
3. Disconnect parking brake cables.
4. Mark drive shaft and pinion flanges for reassembly, then remove drive shaft.
5. Disconnect shock absorbers from spring plate studs, then loosen rear spring U-bolt nuts and remove U-bolts.
6. Remove axle assembly from vehicle.

AXLE SHAFT
REPLACE

FIG. 1 TYPE

1. With wheel removed, remove clips holding brake drum on wheel studs and remove drum.
2. Disconnect brake lines at wheel cylinders.
3. Using access hole in axle flange, remove retainer nuts from end of housing.
4. Remove axle shaft and brake assembly, using a slide hammer-type puller.
5. Remove brake assembly from axle shaft with care to avoid damaging shaft in seal contact area.
6. Remove oil seal from axle housing.
7. Remove axle shaft bearings only when necessary. Removal of bearings makes them unfit for further use.
8. Axle shaft end play is pre-set and not adjustable. End play is accomplished by the amount of end play built into the bearings. The two axle housing brake support plate gaskets on each side are used for sealing purposes only. Always replace the gaskets once they have been removed.
9. Press bearing and collar on shaft firmly against shoulders on shaft.
10. Install new oil seal in housing.
11. Install brake assembly on axle housing and carefully slide axle shaft through oil seal and into side gear splines.
12. Tap end of axle shaft lightly to position axle shaft bearing into bearing bore and attach retainer plate to housing.
13. Install brake drums and wheels.

FIG. 2 TYPE

1. With wheel and brake drum removed, or caliper and rotor assembly removed, loosen differential housing cover and drain lubricant. Remove cover.
2. Turn differential case to make pinion shaft lock screw accessible and remove lock screw and shaft.
3. Push axle shaft inward toward center of car and remove "C" washer from groove in axle shaft, **Fig. 3.**
4. Remove axle shaft from housing, being careful not to damage the axle bearing, which will remain in the housing.
5. The axle bearing and/or seal can now

be removed if necessary.

6. Reverse procedure to install.

PROPELLER SHAFT
REPLACE

1. Remove both rear universal joint roller and bushing assembly clamps from pinion yoke. Do not disturb retaining strap holding roller assemblies on cross.
2. Lower front of vehicle slightly to prevent loss of transmission oil and pull drive shaft out as an assembly.
3. To install, carefully slide yoke into splines on transmission output shaft.
4. Align rear of propeller shaft with pinion yoke and position roller and bushing assemblies into seats of pinion yoke.
5. Install bushing clamps and tighten clamp bolts to 170 inch lbs.

BRAKE ADJUSTMENTS

1980—86 SELF ADJUSTING BRAKES

These brakes, **Fig. 4,** have self-adjusting shoe mechanisms that assure correct lining-to-drum clearances at all times. The automatic adjusters operate only when the brakes are applied as the car is moving rearward.

Although the brakes are self-adjusting, an initial adjustment is necessary when the brake shoes have been relined or replaced, or when the length of the star wheel adjuster has been changed during some other service operation.

Frequent usage of an automatic transmission forward range to halt reverse vehicle motion may prevent the automatic adjusters from functioning, thereby inducing low pedal heights. Should low pedal heights be encountered, it is recommended that numerous forward and reverse stops be made until satisfactory pedal height is obtained.

SERVICE NOTE: If a low pedal height condition cannot be corrected by making numerous reverse stops (provided the hydraulic system is free of air) it indicates that the self-adjusting mechanism is not functioning. Therefore, it will be necessary to remove the drum, clean, free up and lubricate the adjusting mechanism. Then adjust the brakes, being sure the parking brake is fully released.

ADJUSTMENT

1. Each backing plate has two adjusting hole covers; remove the rear cover and turn the adjusting screw upward with a screwdriver or other suitable tool to expand the shoes until a slight drag is felt when the drum is rotated.
2. While holding the adjusting lever out of engagement with the adjusting screw, **Fig. 5,** back off the adjusting screw until wheel rotates freely with no drag.

Fig. 4   Left rear brake

3. Install wheel and adjusting hole cover. Adjust brakes on remaining wheels in the same manner.
4. If pedal height is not satisfactory, drive the vehicle and make sufficient reverse stops until proper pedal height is obtained.

PARKING BRAKE
ADJUST

1. Release parking brake lever and loosen cable adjusting nut to be sure cable is slack.
2. With rear wheel brakes properly adjusted tighten cable adjusting nut until a slight drag is felt when the rear wheels are rotated. Then loosen the cable adjusting nut until both rear wheels can be rotated freely.
3. To complete the operation, back off an additional two turns of the cable adjusting nut.

Fig. 5   Releasing brake lever with screwdriver while adjusting star wheel

4. Apply and release parking brake several times to be sure rear wheels are not dragging when cable is in released position.

BRAKE MASTER CYLINDER
REPLACE

MANUAL BRAKES

1. Disconnect brake lines from master cylinder. Install plugs in outlets to prevent fluid leakage.
2. From under instrument panel, disconnect stop lamp switch mounting bracket and position aside.
3. Grasp brake pedal and pull backward to disengage push rod from master cylinder piston.

NOTE: This will require a pull of about 50 pounds. Also, the retention grommet will be destroyed.

4. Remove master cylinder to cowl retaining nuts and remove master cylinder by pulling straight out.

CAUTION: Make sure to remove all traces of old grommet from push rod groove and master cylinder piston.

5. Reverse procedure to install. Install new grommet on push rod, then lubricate grommet with water and align push rod with master cylinder piston. Using brake pedal, apply pressure to fully seat push rod into piston.

POWER BRAKES

1. Disconnect primary and secondary

brake tubes from master cylinder, then cap lines and master cylinder fitting.
2. Remove nuts attaching master cylinder to power brake unit, then slide master cylinder from power brake unit.
3. Reverse procedure to install.

POWER BRAKE UNIT
REPLACE

1. Remove master cylinder retaining nuts, then carefully slide out master cylinder from power brake and allow it to rest on fender shield.
2. Disconnect vacuum hose from power

brake.
3. From under instrument panel, disconnect push rod from brake pedal. On linkage type power brake unit, also remove lower pivot retaining bolt.
4. Remove power brake retaining nuts and remove power brake unit.
5. Reverse procedure to install.

Rear Suspension

Fig. 1   Rear spring isolator

Fig. 2   Rear spring (typical)

Fig. 3   Spring pivot bushing replacement

SHOCK ABSORBER
REPLACE

To replace shock absorber, support rear axle properly and disconnect shock absorber at upper and lower mountings.

Fig. 4   Sway bar installation. 1980 Aspen & Volare, 1980—81 LeBaron, 1980—86 Diplomat, 1980—83 Cordoba & Mirada, 1981—83 Imperial, 1982 New Yorker, 1982—86 Gran Fury, 1983 New Yorker Fifth Avenue & 1984—86 Fifth Avenue

LEAF SPRINGS & BUSHINGS
REPLACE

1. Support rear axle, relieving tension from spring.
2. Disconnect shock absorber from lower mounting.
3. Remove "U" bolts and spring plate, or lower spring seat isolator retainer and isolator, **Fig. 1.**
4. Remove spring front hanger to body mount bracket nuts, **Fig. 2.**
5. Remove rear shackle bolts, lower spring, thus pulling spring front hanger bolts out of holes.
6. Remove front hanger and rear shackle from spring. To replace pivot bushings, refer to **Fig. 3.** Bushing replacement is accomplished in one operation.
7. Reverse procedure to install.

LEAF SPRING SERVICE

To replace interliners, remove spring alignment clips and on all models except Imperial, discard alignment clips. Separate spring leaves with a screwdriver or other suitable tool and remove interliners. Thoroughly clean spring surfaces before installation of new interliners.

To replace zinc interleaves, clamp spring in a vise and remove center bolt. Open vise carefully, allowing spring to expand. Interleaves can now be serviced. Install a drift through spring center bolt holes and clamp spring in a vise. Remove drift and install center bolt.

SWAY BAR
REPLACE

1. Remove nuts, retainers and rubber insulators from sway bar upper links, **Figs. 4 and 5.**
2. Disconnect sway bar brackets from frame.
3. Remove link from support assembly and replace insulators. Reverse procedure to install.

Fig. 5   Sway bar installation. Except 1980 Aspen & Volare, 1980—81 LeBaron, 1980—86 Diplomat, 1980—83 Cordoba & Mirada, 1981—83 Imperial, 1982 New Yorker, 1982—86 Gran Fury, 1983 New Yorker Fifth Avenue & 1984—86 Fifth Avenue

Front Suspension & Steering Section

FRONT SUSPENSION

MODELS WITH TRANSVERSE TORSION BAR FRONT SUSPENSION

This front suspension, **Fig. 1**, incorporates two transverse torsion bars which react on the outboard end of the lower control arms. The torsion bars are anchored in the front crossmember opposite the affected wheel. The torsion bars are mounted parallel to the front crossmember through a "Pivot Cushion Bushing", attached to the crossmember, and turns and extends rearward to the lower control arm. The torsion bar ends are provided with an isolated bushing, bolted to the lower control arm and sway bar, which acts as the lower control arm strut.

Riding height is controlled by the torsion bar adjusting bolts on the anchor end of the torsion bar. The right torsion bar is adjusted from the left side and the left torsion bar is adjusted from the right side.

The torsion bar assembly incorporates the "Pivot Cushion Bushing" and "Bushing to Lower Control Arm". The lower control arm inner ends are bolted to the crossmember and pivots through bushings.

Caster and camber settings are made by loosening the upper control arm pivot bar bolt nuts and adjusting as necessary.

MODELS WITH LONGITUDINAL TORSION BAR FRONT SUSPENSION

This suspension, **Figs. 2 and 3**, consists of two torsion bar springs (right and left), two sets of upper and lower control arms, four ball joints and two struts.

The front ends of the torsion bar springs engage the lower control arms at the inner pivot points. The rear end of the torsion bars engage adjustable anchor and cam assemblies that are supported by brackets welded to the frame side rails and a removable crossmember.

The upper control arms are mounted on removable brackets that are bolted to the frame side rails. The lower control arms are attached to the frame front crossmember by a pivot shaft and bushing assembly. The pivot shafts are mounted in replaceable rubber bushings.

The steering knuckles are connected to the upper and lower control arms by means of ball joints. To prevent the possibility of fore and aft movement of the lower control arms, a strut is attached to the front crossmember and to the lower control arm.

This suspension has a rubber mounted crossmember, a torsion bar crossmember, more serviceable struts and a lower control arm with pressed in ball joints. Caster and camber settings are made by loosening the upper control arm pivot bar bolt nuts and adjusting as necessary.

Fig. 1 Transverse torsion bar front suspension.

WHEEL ALIGNMENT

NOTE: Front suspension height must be checked and corrected as necessary before performing wheel alignment.

1. Remove all foreign material from exposed threads of cam adjusting bolt nuts or pivot bar adjusting bolt nuts.
2. Record initial camber and caster readings before loosening cam bolt nuts or pivot bar bolt nuts.
3. On vehicles using cam bolts, the camber and caster is adjusted by loosening the cam bolt nuts and turning the cam bolts as necessary until the desired setting is obtained. On vehicles using pivot bars, tool C-4576 is required to adjust caster and camber. When performing adjustments, the camber settings should be held as close as possible to the "desired" setting, and the caster setting should be held as nearly equal as possible on both wheels.

Fig. 2 Upper control arm & steering knuckle (Typical).

SERVICE NOTE: There may be cases when the vehicle may not have sufficient positive camber adjustment. Upper control arm plate spacers are available that will allow more positive camber adjustment, if required. If this condition is encountered, use spacer 1-4014352 for front suspension upper control arm front pivot support and spacer 1-4014353 for the rear pivot support. To install spacers, proceed as follows:

1. Loosen but do not remove caster/camber adjustment nut.
2. Raise vehicle and remove wheel and tire assembly.
3. Loosen but do not remove shock absorber upper mounting nut.
4. Remove two support plate bolts at front end of plate, then loosen two rear bolts enough to slide front spacer between support plate and frame.
5. Align holes in spacer with holes in support plate and frame.
6. Insert two front bolts and start threads. Do not tighten.
7. Repeat steps 4 through 6 for rear spacer.
8. Torque the four support plate bolts to 65 ft. lbs. and the shock absorber upper nut to 25 ft. lbs.
9. Lower vehicle and adjust alignment on side that spacers were installed.

TOE-IN
ADJUST

With the front wheels in straight ahead position, loosen the clamps at each end of both adjusting tubes. Adjust toe-in by turning the tie rod sleeve which will "center" the steering wheel spokes. If the steering wheel was centered, make the toe-in adjustment by turning both sleeves an

Fig. 3 Longitudinal torsion bar & lower control arm (Typical).

Fig. 4 Checking lower ball joint for wear

equal amount. Position the clamps so they are on the bottom and tighten bolts to 15 ft. lbs.

WHEEL BEARINGS
ADJUST

1. Tighten adjusting nut to 20–25 ft. lbs. while rotating wheel.
2. On 1980 models, back off adjusting nut to completely release bearing. On 1981–86 models, back off adjusting nut ¼ turn.
3. Finger tighten adjusting nut while rotating wheel, then align nut lock with cotter pin slot and install cotter pin.
4. The resulting adjustment should be .0001–.003 end play.

WHEEL BEARINGS
REPLACE

1. Raise car and remove front wheels.
2. Remove grease cap, cotter pin, lock nut and bearing adjusting nut.
3. Remove bolts that attach caliper to steering knuckle.
4. Slowly slide caliper up and away from disc and support caliper on steering knuckle arm.

NOTE: Do not allow caliper to hang by brake hose.

5. Remove thrust washer and outer bearing cone. Remove hub and disc assembly. Grease retainer and inner bearing can now be removed.
6. Reverse procedure to install.

CHECKING BALL JOINTS FOR WEAR
UPPER BALL JOINT

1. Position a suitable jack under lower control arm and raise wheel and tire assembly clear of floor, then remove wheel cover and wheel bearing dust cover and cotter pin.

2. Tighten wheel bearing adjusting nut just enough to remove all play between hub, bearings and spindle.
3. Lower jack positioned under lower control arm to allow tire to lightly contact floor.
4. Grasp top of tire and move wheel and tire assembly inward and outward. While moving tire inward and outward, check for movement at ball joints between steering knuckle and upper control arm.
5. If any lateral movement is present, the upper ball joint should be replaced.
6. After completing upper ball joint check, readjust wheel bearing as described under "Wheel Bearings, Adjust".

LOWER BALL JOINT

NOTE: If loose ball joints are suspected, first make sure the front wheel bearings are properly adjusted and that the control arms are tight.

1. Raise front of vehicle and place jack stands underneath each lower control arm as far out as possible.

NOTE: The upper control arms must not contact the rubber rebound bumpers.

2. With weight of vehicle on lower control arms, attach dial indicator onto lower control arm, **Fig. 4.**
3. Place dial indicator plunger tip against ball joint housing and zero dial indicator.
4. Using a pry bar under the center of the tire, raise and lower the tire and measure the axial travel of the ball joint housing with respect to the ball joint. If the axial travel is .030 inch or more than specified, the ball joint should be replaced.

BALL JOINTS
REPLACE

UPPER BALL JOINT

1. Place ignition switch in the "Off" posi-

tion.
2. Using a suitable jack raise front of vehicle and position a jack stand under lower control arm as close to wheel and tire assembly as possible. Check to ensure that jack stand is not in contact with brake splash shield. Also check to ensure that rubber rebound bumper is not in contact with frame.

NOTE: The torsion bar will remain in the loaded position.

3. Remove wheel and tire assembly.
4. Remove cotter pin and nut from lower ball joint stud. Position tool No. C3564-A over lower ball joint stud, allowing tool to rest on knuckle arm, then set tool securely against upper ball joint stud.
5. Tighten tool to apply pressure against upper ball joint stud, then strike knuckle with hammer to loosen stud.
6. Remove tool, then detach upper ball joint from knuckle.

NOTE: Support knuckle and brake assembly to prevent damage to lower ball joint and brake hoses.

7. Remove upper ball joint from upper control arm, using tool No. C3560.
8. Reverse procedure to install. Thread upper ball joint into control arm as far as possible by hand. Torque upper ball joint into control arm to 100 ft. lbs. After tightening lower ball joint stud nut, install cotter pin.

NOTE: Ball joint seals should be replaced whenever they have been removed.

LOWER BALL JOINT

1. Place ignition switch in the "Off" position.
2. Raise vehicle and support so front suspension is in the full rebound position. Position jack stands under front frame for additional support.
3. Remove wheel and tire assembly, then remove disc brake caliper and support with wire hook to prevent brake hose from becoming damaged.
4. Remove disc brake hub and rotor assembly and splash shield, then disconnect shock absorber at lower mounting.

5. Release load on torsion bar by rotating adjusting bolt counter-clockwise.
6. Remove upper and lower ball joint stud nuts and cotter pin, then position tool No. C3564-A over upper ball joint stud so that tool is resting on steering knuckle.
7. Rotate threaded portion of tool to lock it against lower ball joint stud. Tighten tool to place pressure on lower ball joint stud, then strike steering knuckle with a hammer to loosen stud. Remove tool and disconnect lower ball joint.
8. Use tool No. C4212 to press ball joint from lower control arm.
9. Position replacement ball joint on lower control arm, then press into control arm using tool No. C4212.
10. Install seal over lower ball joint. Use tool No. C4039 to press retainer portion of seal until it is locked in position.
11. Position lower ball joint to steering knuckle, then install upper and lower stud nuts and torque to 100 ft. lbs. After tightening stud nuts, install cotter pin.
12. Place tension on torsion bar by rotating adjusting bolt clockwise.
13. Install disc brake assembly and wheel and tire assembly, then adjust front wheel bearing as described under "Wheel Bearings, Adjust".
14. Lubricate ball joint, then lower vehicle and adjust vehicle riding height.

TORSION BAR
REPLACE

MODELS W/TRANSVERSE TORSION BARS
Removal
1. Raise vehicle and support so front suspension is in full rebound position.

Fig. 5 Measuring front suspension height. 1981 Newport, New Yorker & St. Regis

2. Rotate anchor adjusting bolts located in frame crossmember, counter-clockwise to release load on both torsion bars. Then, remove anchor adjusting bolt from torsion bar to be removed.
3. Raise lower control arms until 2⅞ inch clearance is obtained between crossmember ledge at jounce bumper and the torsion bar end bushing and support lower arms at this height.

NOTE: This procedure will align the sway bar and the lower control arm attaching points for disassembly and component re-alignment and attachment during assembly.

4. Remove sway bar to control arm attaching bolt and retainers, then the two bolts securing torsion bar end bushing to lower control arm.
5. Remove two bolts securing torsion bar pivot cushion bushing to crossmember, then the torsion bar and anchor assembly from crossmember.
6. Separate anchor from torsion bar.

Inspection
1. Inspect seal for damage and replace, if necessary.
2. Inspect bushing to lower control arm and pivot cushion bushing. Inspect seals on cushion bushing for cuts, tears or severe deterioration that may allow moisture to enter under cushion. If corrosion is evident, replace torsion bar assembly.
3. Inspect torsion bars for paint damage and touch up, if necessary.
4. Clean anchor hex openings and torsion bar hex ends.
5. Inspect torsion bar adjusting bolt and swivel for damage or corrosion and replace, if necessary.

Installation
1. Slide balloon seal over torsion bar end with cupped end facing toward hex.
2. Lubricate torsion bar hex end with lubricant, P/N 2525035, and install hex end into anchor bracket. With the torsion bar in horizontal position, the anchor bracket ears should be positioned nearly straight upward. Position

Fig. 6 Measuring front suspension height. 1981 LeBaron, 1981–83 Cordoba, Imperial, Mirada, 1981–86 Diplomat, 1982 New Yorker, 1982–86 Gran Fury, 1983 New Yorker Fifth Avenue & 1984–86 Fifth Avenue

Fig. 7 Measuring front suspension height. 1980 models

swivel into anchor bracket ears.

3. Install torsion bar anchor bracket assembly into crossmember anchor retainer, then the anchor adjusting bolt and bearing.

4. Install two bolt and washer assemblies securing pivot cushion bushing to crossmember. Leave assemblies loose enough to install friction plates.

5. With lower control arms supported as outlined in step 3 under "Removal", install the two bolt and nut assemblies securing torsion bar bushing to lower control arm and torque nuts to 70 ft. lbs.

6. Ensure that torsion bar anchor bracket is fully seated in crossmember. Then install friction plates between cross-member and pivot cushion bushing with open end of slot to rear and bottomed out on mounting bolt. Tighten cushion bushing bolts to 85 ft. lbs. Place balloon seal over anchor bracket.

7. Install new bolt through sway bar, retainer cushions and sleeve and attach to lower control arm end bushing, then torque bolt to 50 ft. lbs.

8. Rotate anchor adjusting bolt clockwise to load torsion bar.

9. Lower vehicle and adjust riding height.

MODELS W/LONGITUDINAL TORSION BARS

The torsion bars are not interchangeable side for side. The bars are marked either right or left by an "R" or an "L" stamped on one end of the bar. The general procedure for replacing a torsion bar is as follows:

Removal

1. Remove upper control arm rebound bumper.

2. If vehicle is to be raised on a hoist, make sure it is lifted on the body only so suspension is in full rebound position (no load).

3. Release all load from torsion bar by turning anchor adjusting bolt counter-clockwise.

4. Slide rear anchor balloon seal off of rear anchor and remove lock ring from anchor.

5. Remove torsion bar, by sliding bar out through rear of rear anchor. Use care not to damage balloon seal when it is removed from torsion bar.

NOTE: On some models, it may be necessary to remove transmission torque shaft to provide clearance.

Inspection

1. Inspect balloon seal for damage and replace if necessary.

2. Inspect torsion bar for scores or nicks. Dress down all scratches and nicks to remove sharp edges, then paint repaired areas with a rust preventive.

3. Remove all foreign material from hex openings in anchors and from hex ends of torsion bars.

4. Inspect adjusting bolt and swivel and replace if there is any sign of corrosion or other damage. Lubricate for easy operation.

Installation

1. Insert torsion bar through rear anchor.

2. Slide balloon seal over torsion bar with cupped end toward rear of bar.

3. Coat both ends of torsion bar with a long mileage lubricant.

4. Slide torsion bar in hex opening of lower control arm.

5. Install lock ring, making sure it is seated in groove.

6. Pack annular opening in rear anchor completely full of a long mileage lubricant.

7. Position lip of balloon seal in groove of anchor.

8. Turn adjusting bolt clockwise to place a load on torsion bar.

9. Lower vehicle to floor and adjust front suspension height.

10. Install upper control arm rebound bumper.

SWAY BAR
REPLACE

1980 ASPEN & VOLARE; 1980—81 CORDOBA, DIPLOMAT & LEBARON & MIRADA; 1981 IMPERIAL; 1982—86 ALL MODELS

1. Raise and support front of vehicle.

NOTE: Sway bar to lower control arm attaching points are aligned only when lower control arms are at design height. If frame contact or twin post hoist is used, release load on torsion bar by turning adjuster bolts counter-clockwise, then raise lower control arms until clearance between crossmember ledge and torsion bar to lower control arm bushing is 2⅞ inches. Support lower control arms with jack stand during sway bar removal and installation.

2. With lower control arms properly supported, remove sway bar to torsion bar bushing attaching bolts, retainers, cushions and sleeves.

3. Remove retainer assembly strap bolts and retainer straps, then remove sway bar.

4. Reverse procedure to install. Inspect cushions and bushings for excessive wear or deterioration and replace as necessary.

1980—81 EXC. ASPEN, CORDOBA, DIPLOMAT, LEBARON, MIRADA, VOLARE & 1981 IMPERIAL

1. Place ignition switch in off or unlocked position.

2. Raise vehicle on hoist to place front suspension in rebound position.

3. Remove wheel cover and wheel and tire assembly.

4. Remove nut and bolt on each end of

bar attaching sway bar to strut clamp. Remove nut and bolt from both sway bar link straps to free sway bar from links.

5. Remove sway bar by pulling unit out through frame crossmember openings in direction of area where wheel has been removed.

6. Reverse procedure to install. Inspect cushions and bushing for excessive wear or deterioration and replace as necessary.

RIDING HEIGHT
ADJUST

Before taking measurements, grasp the bumpers at the center (rear bumper first) and jounce the car up and down several times. Jounce the car at the front bumper the same number of times and release the bumper at the same point in the cycle each time.

1981—86 MODELS

1. On 1981 Newport, New Yorker and St. Regis models, the height is measured from the bottom of the frame side rail, between radiator yoke and forward edge of crossmember, to ground, **Fig. 5.**

2. On 1981 LeBaron, 1981—83 Cordoba, Imperial & Mirada, 1981—86 Diplomat, 1982 New Yorker, 1982—86 Gran Fury, 1983 New Yorker Fifth Avenue & 1984—86 Fifth Avenue, the height is measured from the head of the front suspension front crossmember insulator bolt to ground, **Fig. 6.**

3. If necessary, turn torsion bar adjusting bolt clockwise to increase height and counterclockwise to decrease height.

4. After completing adjustment, jounce vehicle and recheck riding height. Both sides must be measured even though only one side may have been adjusted. Front vehicle height should not vary more than ¼ inch from the specified riding height. Riding height should also be within ¼ inch side to side.

1980 MODELS

1. On all models except Aspen, Volaré, Diplomat and LeBaron, measure distance from a point 1 inch forward of rear face of torsion bar anchor to the floor (Measurement A), **Fig. 7.** The distance should be as listed below.

2. On 1980 Aspen, Volaré, Diplomat and LeBaron, measure distance from lowest point of lower control arm inner pivot bushing to the floor, **Fig. 7.** The distance should be as listed below.

3. Measure the other side in the same manner.

4. Adjust by turning the torsion bar anchor adjusting nut clockwise to increase the height and counterclockwise to decrease the height. The difference from side-to-side should not exceed ⅛ inch.

5. After adjusting, jounce the car and recheck the measurements on both

CHRYSLER CORP.—Rear Wheel Drive

sides, even if only one side may have been adjusted.

Chrysler & Imperial

Year	Model	
1980	LeBaron	10¼ inch
1980	Newport, New Yorker	10¾ inch
1980	Cordoba	10¼ inch
1981	Newport, New Yorker	16¾ inch
1981–83	Cordoba, LeBaron	12½ inch
1981–83	Imperial	12½ inch
1982	New Yorker	12½ inch
1983	New Yorker Fifth Ave.	12½ inch
1984–86	Fifth Avenue	12½ inch

Dodge

Year	Model	
1980	Aspen	10¼ inch
1980	Diplomat	10¼ inch
1980	St. Regis	10¾ inch
1980	Mirada	10¼ inch
1981	St. Regis	16¾ inch
1981–83	Diplomat, Mirada	12½ inch
1984–86	Diplomat	12½ inch

Plymouth

Year	Model	
1980	Volare	10¼ inch
1980	Gran Fury	10¾ inch
1981	Gran Fury	16¾ inch
1982–86	Gran Fury	12½ inch

MANUAL STEERING GEAR
REPLACE

CAUTION: To avoid damage to the energy absorbing steering column, it is recommended that the steering column be completely detached from floor and instrument panel before steering gear is removed.

1. Use a suitable puller to remove steering arm from under vehicle.
2. Remove gear to frame retaining bolts and remove gear.
3. Reverse procedure to install.

POWER STEERING GEAR
REPLACE

1. Disconnect battery ground cable.
2. Remove steering column.
3. Disconnect fluid hoses from steering gear and support free ends above pump to avoid loss of fluid. Plug fittings on gear.
4. Disconnect steering arm from gear with suitable puller.
5. Remove gear to frame retaining bolts or nuts and remove gear.
6. Reverse procedure to install.

POWER STEERING PUMP
REPLACE

1. Loosen power steering pump mounting and locking bolts, then remove drive belt.
2. Disconnect pressure and return lines at power steering pump.
3. Remove pump mounting bolts, then remove pump and mounting bracket.
4. Reverse procedure to install.

CHRYSLER CORP. FRONT WHEEL DRIVE

NOTE: The following models are covered in this chapter: CHRYSLER—E-Class (1983–84), Executive (1983–85), Laser (1984–86), LeBaron (1982–86), LeBaron GTS (1986), New Yorker (1983–86), Town & Country (1982–86); DODGE—Aries (1981–86), Charger (1983–86), Daytona (1984–86), 400 (1982–83), Lancer (1985–86), Omni (1980–86), 024 (1980–82), Shelby Charger (1983–86), 600 (1983–86); PLYMOUTH—Caravelle (1985–86), Horizon (1980–86), Reliant (1981–86), TC-3 (1980–82), Turismo (1983–86).

INDEX OF SERVICE OPERATIONS

NOTE: Refer to the rear of this manual for vehicle manufacturer's special service tool suppliers.

3-1

Grille Identification

1980 Omni (4 Door)

1980 Horizon (4 Door)

1980 Omni 024 (2 Door)

1980—81 Horizon TC3 (2 Door)

1981 Omni (4 Door)

1981 Horizon (4 Door)

1981—82 Omni 024 (2 Door)

1981—82 Reliant

1981—83 Aries

1982 Horizon TC3 (2 Door)

1982—83 400

1982—83 Horizon (4 Door)

1982—83 Omni (4 Door)

1982—85 LeBaron, Town & Country & Convertible

1983 Charger 2.2

1983 Reliant

1983 Turismo

1983—84 E Class, 1983—85 Executive & 1983—86 New Yorker

1984 Aries

1984—86 Daytona & Laser Turbo

1984—86 Horizon

continued

1984—86 Daytona & Laser Less Turbo

1984—86 Omni

1984 Reliant

1983—85 600

1984—86 Charger & Turismo

1985—86 Aries

1985—86 Caravelle

1985—86 Lancer

1985—86 LeBaron GTS

1985—86 Omni GLH

1985—86 Reliant

1985—86 Shelby Charger

1986 Dodge 600

1986 Chrysler LeBaron

continued

General Engine Specifications

Year	Engine CID①/Liter	VIN Code②	Carburetor	Bore and Stroke Inch (Millimeters)	Compression Ratio	Net H.P. @ R.P.M.③	Maximum Torque Ft. Lbs. @ R.P.M.	Normal Oil Pressure Pounds @ 2000 RPM
1980	4-105, 1.7L④⑥	A	5220, 2 Bbl.⑦	3.13 × 3.40 (79.5 × 86.4)	8.2	65 @ 5200	85 @ 2400	60–90
	4-105, 1.7L⑤⑥	A	5220, 2 Bbl.⑦	3.13 × 3.40 (79.5 × 86.4)	8.2	65 @ 5200	85 @ 2400	60–90
1981	4-105, 1.7L⑥	A	6520, 2 Bbl.⑦	3.13 × 3.40 (79.5 × 86.4)	8.2	63 @ 5200	83 @ 2400	60–90
	4-135, 2.2L⑧	B	6520, 2 Bbl.⑦	3.44 × 3.62 (87.5 × 92)	8.5	84 @ 4800	111 @ 2500	50
	4-156, 2.6L⑨	D	Mikuni, 2 Bbl.	3.59 × 3.86 (91.1 × 98)	8.2	92 @ 4800	131 @ 2500	57
1982	4-105, 1.7L⑥	A	6520, 2 Bbl.⑦	3.13 × 3.40 (79.5 × 86.4)	8.2	63 @ 4800	83 @ 2400	60–90
	4-135, 2.2L⑧	B	6520, 2 Bbl.⑦	3.44 × 3.62 (87.5 × 92)	8.5	84 @ 4800	111 @ 2400	50
	4-156, 2.6L⑨	D	Mikuni, 2 Bbl.	3.59 × 3.86 (91.1 × 98)	8.2	92 @ 4500	131 @ 2500	57
1983	4-97, 1.6L⑩	A	6520, 2 Bbl.⑦	3.17 × 3.07 (80.6 × 78)	8.8	62 @ 4800	86 @ 3200	58–87⑪
	4-105, 1.7L⑥	B	6520, 2 Bbl.⑦	3.13 × 3.40 (79.5 × 86.4)	8.2	63 @ 4800	83 @ 2400	60–90
	4-135, 2.2L⑧	C	6520, 2 Bbl.⑦	3.44 × 3.62 (87.5 × 92.0)	9.0	94 @ 5200	117 @ 3200	50
	4-135, 2.2L⑧⑫	F	6520, 2 Bbl.⑦	3.44 × 3.62 (87.5 × 92)	9.6	107 @ 5600	126 @ 3600	50
	4-135, 2.2L⑧	D	E.F.I.⑬	3.44 × 3.62 (87.5 × 92)	9.0	94 @ 5200	120 @ 3200	50
	4-156, 2.6L⑨	G	Mikuni, 2 Bbl.	3.59 × 3.86 (91.1 × 98.0)	8.2	93 @ 4500	131 @ 2500	57
1984	4-97, 1.6L⑩	A	6520, 2 Bbl.⑦	3.17 × 3.07 (80.6 × 78)	8.8	64 @ 4800	87 @ 2800	58–87⑪
	4-135, 2.2L⑧	C	6520, 2 Bbl.⑦	3.44 × 3.62 (87.5 × 92)	9.0	96 @ 5200	119 @ 3200	50
	4-135, 2.2L⑧⑫	F	6520, 2 Bbl.⑦	3.44 × 3.62 (87.5 × 92)	10.0	110 @ 5600	129 @ 3600	50
	4-135, 2.2L⑧	D	E.F.I.⑬	3.44 × 3.62 (87.5 × 92)	9.0	99 @ 5600	121 @ 3200	50
	4-135, 2.2L⑧⑭	E	E.F.I.⑬	3.44 × 3.62 (87.5 × 92)	8.5	142 @ 5600	160 @ 3600	50
	4-156, 2.6L⑨	G	Mikuni, 2 Bbl.	3.59 × 3.86 (91.1 × 98)	8.7	101 @ 4800	140 @ 2800	85⑮
1985	4-97, 1.6L⑩	A	6520, 2 Bbl.⑦	3.17 × 3.07 (80.6 × 78)	8.8	64 @ 4800	87 @ 2800	40–90⑪
	4-135, 2.2L⑧	C	6520, 2 Bbl.⑦	3.44 × 3.62 (87.5 × 92)	9.5	96 @ 5200	119 @ 3200	25–90⑪
	4-135, 2.2L⑧⑫	F	6520, 2 Bbl.⑦	3.44 × 3.62 (87.5 × 92)	10	110 @ 5600	129 @ 3600	25–90⑪
	4-135, 2.2L⑧	D	E.F.I.⑬		9.0	99 @ 5600	121 @ 3200	25–90⑪
	4-135, 2.2L⑧⑭	E	E.F.I.⑬	3.44 × 3.62 (87.5 × 92)	8.5	146 @ 5200	168 @ 3600	25–90⑪
	4-156, 2.6L⑨	G	Mikuni, 2 Bbl.	3.59 × 3.86 (91.1 × 98)	8.7	101 @ 4800	140 @ 2800	45–90⑪
1986	4-97, 1.6L⑩	A	6520, 2 Bbl.⑦	3.17 × 3.07 (80.6 × 78)	8.8	64 @ 4800	87 @ 2800	72.5
	4-135, 2.2L⑧	C	6520, 2 Bbl.⑦	3.44 × 3.62 (87.5 × 92)	9.5	96 @ 5200	119 @ 3200	50
	4-135, 2.2L⑧⑫	F	6520, 2 Bbl.⑦	3.44 × 3.62 (87.5 × 92)	9.6	110 @ 5600	129 @ 3600	50
	4-135, 2.2L⑧	D	E.F.I.⑬		9.0	97 @ 5200	122 @ 3200	50
	4-135, 2.2L⑧⑭	E	E.F.I.⑬	3.44 × 3.62 (87.5 × 92)	8.1	146 @ 5200	170 @ 3600	50
	4-153, 2.5L	K	E.F.I.⑬	3.44 × 4.09 (87.5 × 104)	9.0	100 @ 4800	136 @ 2800	50

continued

GENERAL ENGINE SPECIFICATIONS NOTES—Continued

①—CID—cubic inch displacement.
②—On 1980 models, the 5th digit of the V.I.N. denotes engine code. On 1981-84 models, the 8th digit of the V.I.N. denotes engine code.
③—Ratings are net—as installed in vehicle.

④—Calif. & high altitude.
⑤—Exc. Calif. & high altitude.
⑥—1700 cc.
⑦—Holley.
⑧—2200 cc.
⑨—2600 cc.

⑩—1600 cc.
⑪—At 3000 RPM.
⑫—High output engine.
⑬—Electronic fuel injection.
⑭—Turbocharged engine.
⑮—At 2500 RPM.

Valve Specifications

| Year | Engine/ VIN | Valve Lash | | Valve Angles | | Valve Spring Installed Height Inch (Millimeters) | Valve Spring Pressure Lbs. @ In. | Stem Clearance | | Stem Diameter | |
		Int. in. (MM)	Exh. in. (MM)	Seat	Face			Intake Inch (Millimeters) ①	Exhaust Inch (Millimeters) ①	Intake Inch (Millimeters)	Exhaust Inch (Millimeters)
1980	4-105/A (1700 cc)	.008C (.20C)	.016C (.30C)	45°	45°	③	④	.020 (.5)	.027 (.7)	.314 (7.97)	.313 (7.95)
1981-83	4-105/A (1700 cc)	.010H (.25H)	.018H (.45H)	45°	45°	③	④	.020 (.5)	.027 (.7)	.314 (7.97)	.313 (7.95)
1981-84	4-135/⑤ (2200 cc)	Hydraulic		45°	45°	1.65 (41.9)	⑦	.0009-.0026 (.022-.065)	⑥	.312-.313 (7.935-7.953)	.311-.312 (7.906-7.924)
	4-156/⑤ (2600 cc)	.006H② (.15H)	.010H (.25H)	45°	45°	1.59 (40.4)	61 @ 1.59	.0012-.0024 (.03-.06)	.0020-.0035 (.05-.09)	.300 (8)	.300 (8)
1983-84	4-97/A (1600 cc)	.010C (.25C)	.012C (.35C)	46°	45°	—	—	.0015-.00275 (.037-.070)	.00225-.0035 (.057-.090)	.3137 (7.970)	.3129 (7.950)
1985	4-97/A (1600 cc)	.010C (.25C)	.010C (.25C)	46°	45°	—	—	.0005-.0018 (.012-.045)	.0013-.0014 (.032-.035)	.3147-.3153 (7.995-8.010)	.3139-.3145 (7.975-7.990)
	4-135/⑤ (2200 cc)	Hydraulic		45°	45°	1.65 (41.9)	⑧	.0009-.0026 (.022-.065)	.0030-.0047 (.076-.119)	.3124 (7.935)	.3103 (7.881)
	4-156/G (2600 cc)	.006H⑨ (.15H)	.010H (.25H)	45°	45°	1.59 (40.4)	61 @ 1.591	.0012-.0024 (.03-.06)	.0020-.0035 (.05-.09)	.300⑩ (8)	.300 (8)
1986	4-97/A (1600 cc)	.010C (.25C)	.010C (.25C)	46°	45°	—	—	.0005-.0018 (.012-.045)	.0013-.0014 (.032-.035)	.3147-.3153 (7.995-8.010)	.3139-.3145 (7.975-7.990)
	4-135/⑤ (2200 cc)	Hydraulic		45°	45°	1.65 (41.9)	⑧	.0009-.0026 (.022-.065)	.0030-.0047 (.076-.119)	.3124 (7.935)	.3103 (7.881)
	4-153/K (2500 cc)	Hydraulic		45°	45°	1.65 (41.9)	175 @ 1.22	.0009-.0026 (.022-.065)	.0030-.0047 (.076-.119)	.3124 (7.935)	.3103 (7.881)

①—Refer to text.
②—Jet valve clearance, .006H.
③—Inner valve spring, 1.13 inch (28.6 mm); outer valve spring, 1.28 inch (32.6 mm).
④—Inner valve spring, 48 @ .720; outer valve spring, 100 @ .878.

⑤—For V.I.N. code, refer to the "General Engine Specifications" at the front of the chapter.
⑥—On 1981-82 stem clearance is .0028-.0044 (.070-.113) & on 1983-84 stem clearance is .0030-.0047 (.076-.119).
⑦—Exc. 1984 VIN codes C & D, 175 lbs. @

1.22 in.; 1984 VIN codes C & D, 135 lbs. @ 1.22 in.
⑧—Exc. 1985-86 VIN codes C & D, 175 lbs. @ 1.22 in.; 1985-86 VIN codes C & D, 150 lbs. @ 1.22 in.
⑨—Jet valve clearance, .010H.
⑩—Jet valve stem diameter, .169 (4.3).

continued

Engine Tightening Specifications★

★ Torque specifications are for clean and lightly lubricated threads only. Dry or dirty threads produce increased friction which prevents accurate measurement of tightness.

Year	Engine Model/VIN	Spark Plugs Ft. Lbs.	Cylinder Head Bolts Ft. Lbs.	Intake Manifold Inch Lbs.	Exhaust Manifold Inch Lbs.	Camshaft Cover Inch Lbs.	Connecting Rod Cap Bolts Ft. Lbs.	Main Bearing Cap Bolts Ft. Lbs.	Flywheel to Crankshaft Ft. Lbs.	Crankshaft Pulley Ft. Lbs.
1980	4-105/A 1700 cc	20	60①	200②	150	48	35	47	52	58
1981–83	4-105/④ 1700 cc	20	60①	200②	200	48	35	47	⑤	58
1981–85	4-135/④ 2200 cc	26	45①	200	200	105	40①	30①	65	20.8
	4-156/④ 2600 cc	18.3	③	150	150	53	34	58	100	87
1983–86	4-97/A 1600 cc	⑦	52	133	180	44⑥	28	48	—	110
1986	4-135/④	26	45①	200	200	105	40①	30①	—	—
	4-153/K	26	45①	200	200	105	40①	30①	—	—

①—Turn torque wrench an additional 90 degrees after the specified torque has been achieved.
②—Intake to exhaust manifold inboard nut, 150 inch lbs. Intake to exhaust manifold outboard nut, 200 inch lbs.

③—Cold engine, 69 ft. lbs.; warm engine, 76 ft. lbs.
④—For V.I.N code, refer to the "General Engine Specifications" at the front of the chapter.

⑤—Man. trans., 60 ft. lbs.; auto. trans., 40 ft. lbs.
⑥—Rocker arm covers.
⑦—1983 models, 20 ft. lbs.; 1984–86 models, 22 ft. lbs.

Pistons, Pins, Rings, Crankshaft & Bearings

Year	Engine Model/ VIN	Piston Clearance Top of Skirt Inch (Millimeter)	Ring End Gap① Comp. Inch (Millimeter)	Ring End Gap① Oil Inch (Millimeter)	Wristpin Diameter Inch (Millimeter)	Rod Bearings Shaft Diameter Inch (Millimeter)	Rod Bearings Bearing Clearance Inch (Millimeter)	Main Bearings Shaft Diameter Inch (Millimeter)	Main Bearings Bearing Clearance Inch (Millimeter)	Thrust on Bear. No.	Shaft End Play Inch (Millimeter)
1980	4-105/A 1700 cc	.0004–.0015 (.011–.039)	.012 (.3)	.012 (.3)	.866 (21.997–22.001)	1.81 (46)	.0004–.0025 (.010–.064)	2.12 (54)	.0008–.0030 (.020–.080)	3	.003–.007 (.07–.18)
1981–83	4-105/A 1700 cc	.0004–.0015 (.011–.039)	.012 (.3)	.016 (.41)	.866 (21.997–22.001)	1.8087–1.8094 (45.94–45.96)	.0011–.0034 (.028–.088)	2.1236–2.1244 (53.94–53.96)	.0008–.0030 (.020–.080)	3	.003–.007 (.07–.18)
1981	4-135/B 2200 cc	.0005–.0015 (.013–.038)	.011 (.28)	.015 (.38)	.9008 (22.88)	1.968–1.969 (49.987–50.013)	.0004–.0026 (.011–.067)	2.362–2.363 (59.987–60.013)	.0004–.0026 (.011–.067)	3	.002–.007 (.05–.18)
1982–85	4-135/② 2200 cc	.0005–.0015 (.013–.038)	.011 (.28)	.015 (.38)	—	1.968–1.969 (49.987–50.013)	③	④	⑤	3	.002–007 (.05–.18)
1981–85	4-156/② 2600 cc	.0008–.0016 (.02–.04)	.010 (.25)	.0078 (.2)	.866 (22)	2.0866 (53)	.0008–.0028 (.02–.07)	2.3622 (60)	.0008–.0028 (.02–.07)	3	.002–.007 (.05–.18)
1983–86	4-97/A 1600 cc	.0016–.0020 (.041–.051)	.012 (.3)	.010 (.25)	.866 (21.991–21.995)	1.6124–1.6127 (40.957–40.965)	.001–.0025 (.025–.064)	2.046–2.047 (51.975–51.985)	.0009–.0031 (.04–.078)	3	.0035–.011 (.09–.27)
1986	4-135/② 2200 cc	⑥	⑦	.015 (.38)	—	1.968–1.969 (49.987–50.013)	③	④	⑤	3	.002–.007 (.05–.18)
	4-153/K 2500 cc	.0005–.0015 (.013–.038)	.011 (.28)	.015 (.38)	—	1.968–1.969 (49.987–50.013)	.0008–.0034 (.019–.087)	2.362–2.363 (59.987–60.013)	.0003–.0031 (.007–.080)	3	.002–.007 (.05–.18)

①—Minimum.
②—For V.I.N. code, refer to the "General Engine Specifications" at the front of the chapter.
③—1982–84 models & 1985–86 exc. turbocharged engine, .0008–.0034 (.019–.087; 1985–86 turbocharged engine, .0008–.0031 (.019–.079).

④—1982–84 models & 1985–86 exc. turbocharged engine, 2.362–2.363 (59.987–60.013); 1985–86 turbocharged engine, 2.3622–2.3627 (60.00–60.013).
⑤—1982–84 models & 1985 exc. turbocharged engine, .0003–.0031 (.007–.080); 1985 turbocharged engine,

.0004–.0023 (.11–.54).
⑥—Exc. turbocharged, .0005–.0015 (.013–.038); turbocharged, .0015–.0025 (.0381–.0635).
⑦—Exc. turbocharged, .011 (.28); turbocharged, upper comp. ring .010 (.28), lower comp. ring .009 (.23).

continued

3–6

Alternator & Regulator Specifications

Year	Alternator				Regulator						
	Part Number	Rated Hot Output Amps.	Field Current 12 Volts @ 80° F.	Output @ 15 Volts 1250 R.P.M.	Part Number	Field Relay			Voltage Regulator		
						Air Gap In.	Point Gap In.	Closing Voltage	Air Gap In.	Point Gap In.	Voltage @ 80° F.
1980–81	Yellow①	60	5	57	4091050	—	—	—	—	—	13.9–14.6
	Brown①	65	5	62	—	—	—	—	—	—	13.9–14.6
1981–85	A4T25191②	75	—	63–70③	Integral	—	—	—	—	—	14.1–14.7④
1982–83	Yellow①	60	4.5–6.5	45	4111990	—	—	—	—	—	13.9–14.6
	Brown①	78	4.5–6.5	56	4111990	—	—	—	—	—	13.9–14.6
1983–86	K1⑤	65	2.5–5.0	50	—	—	—	—	—	—	—
1984–85	Yellow	60	2.5–5.0	45	—	—	—	—	—	—	13.9–14.6
	Brown	78	2.5–5.0	56	—	—	—	—	—	—	13.9–14.6
	B120 427 850MP⑤	90	—	78–85③	Integral	—	—	—	—	—	13.8–14.2⑥
1985	①⑦	40/90	2.5–5.0	96	—	—	—	—	—	—	—
	⑤⑦	40/90	2.5–5.0	87	—	—	—	—	—	—	—
1986	Yellow	60	2.5–5.0	45	—	—	—	—	—	—	13.9–14.6
	Brown	78	2.5–5.0	56	—	—	—	—	—	—	13.9–14.6
	①⑦	40/90	2.5–5.0	87	—	—	—	—	—	—	—
	⑤⑦	40/90	2.5–5.0	80	—	—	—	—	—	—	—
	⑤⑧	40/100	2.5–5.0	87	—	—	—	—	—	—	—

①—Chrysler alternator.
②—Mitsubishi alternator.
③—At 13.5 volts & 1000 RPM.
④—At 68° F.
⑤—Bosch alternator.
⑥—At 77° F.
⑦—40/90 AMP alternator w/ voltage regulator in engine electronics.
⑧—40/90 AMP alternator w/voltage regulator in engine electronics.

Starting Motor Applications

Year	Engine/VIN	Model	Ident. Number	Year	Engine/VIN	Model	Ident. Number
1980	4-105/A (1700 cc)①	Bosch	5206260		4-135 (2200 cc)①③	Bosch	5213045
	4-105/A (1700 cc)①	Nippondenso	5206270		4-135 (2200 cc)②③	Bosch	5213395
1979–83	4-105 (1700 cc)②③	Bosch	5206255		4-135 (2200 cc)③	Nippondenso	5213645
	4-105 (1700 cc)②③	Nippondenso	5206265	1983–86	4-97/A (1600 cc)	Mitsubishi	5213301
1981	4-105/A (1700 cc)①	Bosch	5213080	1984–85	4-135 (2200 cc)④	Bosch	5213045
	4-105/A (1700 cc)①	Nippondenso	5213085		4-135 (2200 cc)④	Nippondenso	5213645
	4-135/B (2200 cc)	Bosch	5213045		4-135/E (2200 cc)	Bosch	5213450
	4-135/B (2200 cc)	Nippondenso	5213190	1986	4-135④	Bosch	5226442
1981–85	4-156/③ (2600 cc)	Nippondenso	5213235		4-135④	Nippondenso	5226742
1982–83	4-105 (1700 cc)①③	Bosch	5213395		4-135④	Bosch	5226441
	4-105 (1700 cc)①③	Nippondenso	5213295		4-153/K	Bosch	5226444

①—Automatic Transmission.
②—Manual Transmission.
③—For V.I.N. code, refer to the "General Engine Specifications" at the front of the chapter.
④—VIN codes C, D & F.

continued

Wheel Alignment Specifications

Year	Model	Caster Angle, Degrees		Camber Angle, Degrees				Toe In Inch	Toe Out on Turns, Deg.	
		Limits	Desired	Limits		Desired			Outer Wheel	Inner Wheel
				Left	Right	Left	Right			
1980–83	Horizon & Omni①	—	—	−¼ to +¾	−¼ to +¾	+5/16	+5/16	②	—	—
	Horizon & Omni③	—	—	⑦	⑦	⑦	⑦	④	—	—
1981	Aries & Reliant①	—	—	−¼ to +¾	−¼ to +¾	+5/16	+5/16	⑤	—	—
	Aries & Reliant③	—	—	−1 to 0	−1 to 0	−½	−½	⑥	—	—
1982–83	Aries & Reliant①	—	—	−¼ to +¾	−¼ to +¾	+5/16	+5/16	⑤	—	—
	Aries & Reliant③	—	—	−1 to 0	−1 to 0	−½	−½	⑥	—	—
	LeBaron & 400①	—	—	−¼ to +¾	−¼ to +¾	+5/16	+5/16	⑤	—	—
	LeBaron & 400③	—	—	−1 to 0	−1 to 0	−½	−½	⑥	—	—
1983	Charger & Turismo①	—	—	−¼ to +¾	−¼ to +¾	+5/16	+5/16	⑤	—	—
	Charger & Turismo③	—	—	−¼ to −1¼	−¼ to −1¼	−¾	−¾	④	—	—
	New Yorker, E Class & 600①	—	—	−¼ to +¾	−¼ to +¾	+5/16	+5/16	⑤	—	—
	New Yorker, E Class & 600③	—	—	−1 to 0	−1 to 0	−½	−½	⑥	—	—
1984–85	All①	—	—	−¼ to +¾	−¼ to +¾	+5/16	+5/16	⑤	—	—
	Charger, Horizon, Omni & Turismo③	—	—	−1¼ to −¼	−1¼ to −¼	−¾	−¾	④	—	—
	Exc. Charger, Horizon, Omni & Turismo③	—	—	−1 to 0	−1 to 0	−½	−½	⑥	—	—
1986	All①	—	—	−¼ to +¾	−¼ to +¾	+5/16	+5/16	⑤	—	—
	Charger, Horizon, Omni & Turismo③	—	—	−1¼ to −¼	−1¼ to −¼	−½	−½	⑧	—	—
	Exc. Charger, Horizon, Omni & Turismo③	—	—	−1¼ to +¼	−1¼ to +¼	+½	+½	⑨	—	—

①—Front wheel alignment.
②—1980, 5/32″ out to ⅛″ in (.3° out to .2° in); 1981–83, 7/32″ out to ⅛″ in (.4° out to .2° in).
③—Rear wheel alignment.
④—5/32″ out to 11/32″ in (.3° out to .7° in).
⑤—7/32″ out to ⅛″ in (.4° out to .2° in).
⑥—3/16″ out to 3/16″ in (.38° out to .38° in).
⑦—1980–81 Limits, −1¼° to −½°; Desired, −1°. 1982–83 Limits, −1¼° to −¼°; Desired, −¾°.
⑧—3/16″ out to 13/32″ in (.40 out to .8° in).
⑨—5/16″ out to 5/16″ in (.60 out to .60° in).

Cooling System & Capacity Data

Year	Model or Engine/VIN	Cooling Capacity		Radiator Cap Relief Pressure, Lbs.	Thermo. Opening Temp. Degrees F. (Centigrade)	Fuel Tank Gals. (Litres)	Engine Oil Refill Qts. (Litres)	Transmission Oil		Final Drive Pints (Litres)②
		Less A/C Qts. (Litres)	With A/C Qts. (Litres)					4 & 5 Speed Pints (Litres)	Auto. Trans. Qts. (Litres)①	
1980	All/⑧	6 (5.7)	⑨	16	195 (90.6)	13 (49)	4④ (3.8)	2.8 (1.25)	7.3③ (6.9)	2.4 (1.1)
1981–82	4-105/A (1.7L)	6 (5.7)	6 (5.7)	16	195 (90.6)	13 (49)	4④ (3.8)	3 (1.4)	7.3⑤ (6.9)	2.4 (1.1)
	4-135/B (2.2L)	7 (6.6)	7 (6.6)	16	195 (90.6)	13 (49)	4④ (3.8)	4 (1.8)	7.5⑤ (7.1)	2.4 (1.1)
	4-156/D (2.6L)	8.5 (8.1)	8.5 (8.1)	16	190 (88)	13 (49)	5⑥ (5)	4 (1.8)	8.5⑤ (8.1)	2.4 (1.1)
1983	4-97 (1.6L)/A	7 (6.6)	7 (6.6)	16	195 (90.6)	13 (49)	3.5⑥ (3.3)	⑪	—	—
	4-105 (1.7L)/B	6 (5.7)	6 (5.7)	16	195 (90.6)	13 (49)	4④ (3.8)	⑪	8.4⑦ (7.9)	2.4 (1.1)
	4-135 (2.2L)/⑧	9 (8.5)	9 (8.5)	16	195 (90.6)	13⑩ (49)	4④ (3.8)	⑪	8.9⑦⑫ (8.4)	2.4 (1.1)
	4-156 (2.6L)/G	9 (8.5)	9 (8.5)	16	190 (88)	13 (49)	4④ (3.8)	⑪	8.9⑦⑫ (8.4)	2.4 (1.1)
1984–85	4-97 (1.6L)/A	6.8 (6.4)	6.8 (6.4)	16	195 (90.6)	13 (49)	3.5⑥ (3.3)	3.8⑬ (1.7)	8.9⑦ (8.4)	2.4 (1.1)
	4-135 (2.2L)/⑧	9 (8.5)	9 (8.5)	16	195 (90.6)	⑨	4.0④ (3.8)	4.0⑬ (1.8)	8.9⑦⑫ (8.4)	2.4 (1.1)
	4-156 (2.6L)/G	9 (8.5)	9 (8.5)	16	190 (88)	14 (53)	5.0⑥ (4.8)	—	8.9⑦⑫ (8.4)	2.4 (1.1)

continued

COOLING SYSTEM & CAPACITY DATA—Continued

Year	Model or Engine/VIN	Cooling Capacity		Radiator Cap Relief Pressure, Lbs.	Thermo. Opening Temp. Degrees F. (Centigrade)	Fuel Tank Gals. (Litres)	Engine Oil Refill Qts. (Litres)	Transmission Oil		Final Drive Pints (Litres)②
		Less A/C Qts. (Litres)	With A/C Qts. (Litres)					4 & 5 Speed Pints (Litres)	Auto. Trans. Qts. (Litres)①	
1986	4-97 (1.6L)/A	6.8 (6.4)	6.8 (6.4)	16	195 (90.6)	13 (49)	3.5⑥ (3.3)	3.8⑬ (1.7)	8.9⑦ (8.4)	2.4 (1.1)
	4-135 (2.2L)/⑧	9 (8.5)	9 (8.5)	16	195 (90.6)	⑨	4.0④ (3.8)	4.0⑬ (1.8)	8.9⑦⑫ (8.4)	2.4 (1.1)
	4-153 (2.5L)/K	9 (8.5)	9 (8.5)	16	195 (90.6)	14 (53)	4.0 (3.8)	4.0⑬ (1.8)	8.9⑫ (8.4)	2.4 (1.1)

①—Approximate. Make final check with dipstick.
②—Automatic trans. only.
③—Drain & refill, 2.5 qts.
④—With or without filter change.
⑤—Drain & refill, 3 qts.
⑥—Includes ½ qt. for filter change.
⑦—Drain & refill, 4 qts.
⑧—For V.I.N. code, refer to "General Engine Specifications" at the front of the chapter.
⑨—Exc. Charger, Horizon, Omni & Turismo—14.0 gals.; Charger, Horizon, Omni & Turismo—13.0 gals.
⑩—EFI models, 14.0 gals.
⑪—A-412, 3.0 pts.; A-460, 4.0 pts.; A-465 (5 spd.), 4.6 pts.
⑫—Vehicles with fleet option package, 9.2 qts.
⑬—5 spd. transaxle, 4.6 pts.

Electrical Section

Fig. 1 Ignition lock cylinder removal. Models with standard column exc. 1980–86 Horizon & Omni; 1983–86 Charger & Turismo

Fig. 2 Ignition lock cylinder removal. Models with tilt column exc. 1980–86 Horizon & Omni; 1983–86 Charger & Turismo

Fig. 3 Ignition lock cylinder retaining pin removal. 1980–86 Horizon & Omni; 1983–86 Charger & Turismo

Fig. 4 Ignition switch replacement. Exc. 1980–86 Horizon & Omni; 1983–86 Charger & Turismo

STARTER
REPLACE

4-153, 4-97, 4-135 & 1981–83 4-105

1. Disconnect battery ground cable.
2. Remove starter to flywheel housing and rear bracket to engine or transaxle attaching bolts.
3. On models equipped with 4-135 engine, loosen air pump tube at exhaust manifold, then position tube bracket away from starter motor.
4. If equipped, remove heat shield clamp and heat shield.
5. Disconnect starter cable at starter motor and solenoid leads at solenoid, then remove starter motor.
6. Reverse procedure to install.

4-156 & 1980 4-105

1. Disconnect battery ground cable.
2. Disconnect starter cable at starter.
3. Disconnect solenoid lead wire from solenoid.
4. Remove starter attaching bolts and the starter.
5. Reverse procedure to install.

IGNITION LOCK
REPLACE

EXC. 1980–86 HORIZON & OMNI; 1983–86 CHARGER & TURISMO

Models Less Tilt Column

1. Disconnect battery ground cable.
2. Remove turn signal switch as described under "Turn Signal Switch, Replace."
3. Disconnect horn and ignition key lamp ground wires, then remove ignition key lamp attaching screw and lamp.
4. Remove four screws attaching upper bearing housing to lock housing, then remove snap ring from upper end of steering shaft and remove upper bearing housing.
5. Remove lock plate spring and lock plate from steering shaft.
6. Position lock cylinder in Lock position and remove ignition key.
7. Remove key waring buzzer attaching screws, then remove buzzer.
8. Remove two screws attaching ignition switch to steering column, then remove switch by rotating switch 90° and sliding from rod.
9. Remove two screws attaching dimmer switch, then disengage dimmer switch from actuator rod.
10. Remove two bellcrank attaching screws, then slide bellcrank up into lock housing until it can be disconnected from ignition switch actuator rod.
11. With lock cylinder in Lock position, insert a small diameter screwdriver into lock cylinder release holes and push inward until spring loaded lock cylinder retainers release, **Fig. 1.**
12. Grasp lock cylinder and pull from lock housing bore.
13. Reverse procedure to install. The lock cylinder and ignition switch must be in the Lock position.

Models W/Tilt Column

1. Disconnect battery ground cable.
2. Remove turn signal switch as described under "Turn Signal Switch, Replace."
3. Remove ignition key lamp.
4. Position ignition lock cylinder in the Lock position, then remove ignition key.
5. Insert a thin screwdriver into lock cylinder release slot and depress spring latch which releases lock cylinder, then grasp lock cylinder and remove from column, **Fig. 2.**
6. Reverse procedure to install.

1980–86 HORIZON & OMNI; 1983–86 CHARGER & TURISMO

1. Remove steering wheel, column covers and turn signal switch.
2. With a hack saw blade, cut the upper ¼ inch from the retainer pin boss, **Fig. 3.**
3. Using a suitable drift, drive roll pin from housing and remove lock cylinder.
4. Insert new cylinder into housing, ensuring that it engages the lug or ignition switch driver.
5. Install roll pin.
6. Check for proper operation.

IGNITION SWITCH
REPLACE

EXC. 1980–86 HORIZON & OMNI; 1983–86 CHARGER & TURISMO

1. Disconnect battery ground cable.
2. Remove under panel sound deadener.
3. Disconnect speed control switch.
4. Remove two screws attaching switch to column.
5. Rotate switch 90° and pull-up to disengage from ignition switch rod, **Fig. 4.**
6. Reverse procedure to install. When installing new switch push up gently on switch to take up slack in rod system.

Fig. 5 Ignition switch replacement. 1980–86 Omni & Horizon; 1983–86 Charger & Turismo

Fig. 6 Light switch replacement (Typical)

Fig. 7 Dimmer switch replacement. Exc. 1980–86 Horizon & Omni; 1983–86 Charger & Turismo; models less tilt column

7. Reverse procedure to install.

1980–86 HORIZON & OMNI; 1983–86 CHARGER & TURISMO

1. Disconnect battery ground cable.
2. Remove connector from ignition switch.
3. Place ignition lock in "Lock" position and remove key.
4. Remove the two ignition switch mounting screws and permit the switch and push rod to drop below the column jacket, **Fig. 5.**
5. Rotate the switch 90° for removal of switch from push rod.
6. Position ignition switch in "Lock" position, the second detent from the top of the switch.
7. Place switch at right angle to column and insert push rod.
8. Align switch on bracket and loosely install screws.
9. With a light rearward load on the switch, tighten attaching screws.
10. Connect ignition switch wiring connector and battery ground cable.
11. Check for proper operation.

LIGHT SWITCH
REPLACE

EXC. 1980–86 HORIZON & OMNI; 1983–86 CHARGER & TURISMO, 1985–86 LANCER & LEBARON

1. Disconnect battery ground cable, then place gearshift lever in "1" position.
2. Remove left upper and lower instrument cluster bezel attaching screws, then detach bezel from five retaining clips and remove bezel.
3. Remove three screws attaching headlamp switch retainer plate to instrument panel.
4. Pull headlamp switch and retainer plate rearward and disconnect wire connector, then depress button on switch and remove switch knob and stem.
5. Remove switch retainer plate escutcheon, then remove nut attaching switch to plate.
6. Reverse procedure to install.

Fig. 8 Dimmer switch installation. 1980–86 Horizon & Omni; 1983–86 Charger & Turismo; Models w/Tilt Column

1980–86 HORIZON & OMNI; 1983–86 CHARGER & TURISMO

1. Disconnect battery ground cable.
2. Reach under instrument panel and depress light switch knob release button, then pull light switch knob and shaft from switch.
3. Remove four bezel attaching screws and the bezel.
4. Remove switch attaching screws and disconnect electrical connector from switch, **Fig. 6.**
5. Remove switch from panel.
6. Reverse procedure to install.

1985–86 LANCER & LEBARON

1. Disconnect battery ground cable.
2. Remove cluster bezel attaching screws, then the cluster bezel.
3. Remove headlight and accessory switch module attaching screws, then pull module assembly away from dash panel and remove all electrical connectors.
4. Depress button on bottom of headlight switch, then remove switch knob and stem.
5. Remove switch assembly to switch module attaching screws.
6. Remove switch assembly from module, then the switch assembly retaining plate from switch.

DIMMER SWITCH
REPLACE

EXC. 1980–86 HORIZON & OMNI; 1983–86 CHARGER & TURISMO

Models Less Tilt Column

1. Disconnect battery ground cable, then disconnect electrical connector from switch.
2. Remove two screws attaching switch to column, **Fig. 7.**
3. Reverse procedure to install. During installation, gently push up on switch to take up slack on rod.

Models w/Tilt Column

Refer to "1980–86 Horizon & Omni; 1983–86 Charger & Turismo" for Dimmer Switch, Replace procedure.

1980–86 HORIZON & OMNI; 1983–86 CHARGER & TURISMO

1. Disconnect battery ground cable, then disconnect connector from switch.
2. Remove the two switch mounting screws and disengage switch from push rod, **Fig. 8.**
3. To install switch, firmly seat push rod into switch, then compress switch until two .093 inch drill shanks can be inserted into alignment holes. Position upper end of push rod in pocket of wash/wipe switch.

NOTE: This can be done by feel, or if necessary, by removing lower column cover.

4. Apply a light rearward pressure on switch, then install screws and remove drills.

NOTE: The switch should click when lever is lifted, and again as lever returns, just before it reaches its stop in the down position.

5. Reconnect wiring connector to switch and connect battery ground cable.

Fig. 9 Lock plate removal. Models with tilt column exc. 1980–86 Horizon & Omni; 1983–86 Charger & Turismo

Fig. 10 Turn signal switch replacement. Exc. 1980–86 Horizon & Omni; 1983–86 Charger & Turismo

Fig. 11 Turn signal switch replacement. 1980–86 Horizon & Omni; 1983–86 Charger & Turismo

TURN SIGNAL SWITCH
REPLACE

EXC. 1980–86 HORIZON & OMNI; 1983–86 CHARGER & TURISMO

1. Disconnect battery ground cable.
2. Remove horn button and switch and steering wheel nut, then remove steering wheel using a suitable puller.
3. Remove instrument panel lower bezel and steering column cover.
4. On models with tilt steering column, remove transmission gearshift indicator, then remove two nuts attaching steering column to lower panel. Remove four attaching bolts, then remove bracket from column.
5. On models less tilt column, position gearshift lever into its full clockwise position. On models with tilt column, place gearshift lever to its midway position.
6. On models with tilt column, carefully remove plastic cover from lock plate, then depress lock plate with tool No. C-4156 and remove snap ring, **Fig. 9.** Remove lock plate, canceling cam and upper bearing spring from steering shaft.

Fig. 12 Instrument panel, exploded view (Typical). 1981–84 Aries & Reliant; 1982–83 LeBaron & 400; 1983 E Class, Executive, New Yorker & 600

Fig. 13 Instrument cluster removal. 1984 E Class & LeBaron; 1984–85 Executive; 1984–86 New Yorker & 600; 1985–86 Aries, Caravelle, LeBaron Exc. GTS, Town & Country & Reliant

Fig. 14 Instrument panel pad removal. 1984 E Class & LeBaron; 1984–85 Executive; 1984—86 New Yorker & 600; 1985–86 Aries, Caravelle, LeBaron Exc. GTS, Town & Country & Reliant

7. Remove turn signal lever attaching screws, then remove lever. On models with speed control allow lever to hang from column.
8. Remove turn signal switch and upper bearing attaching screws, then carefully remove turn signal switch, while guiding wire up through column opening, **Fig. 10.**
9. Reverse procedure to install.

1980–86 HORIZON & OMNI; 1983–86 CHARGER & TURISMO

Removal

1. Disconnect battery ground cable.
2. Remove horn button or horn pad, then the horn switch.
3. Remove steering wheel nut and the steering wheel with a suitable puller.
4. Remove four screws from the lower steering column cover and the cover.
5. Remove screw securing washer-wiper switch and position switch aside.
6. Disconnect turn signal and hazard warning wiring connector, disengage wiring harness from support bracket and remove vinyl tape securing key in buzzer wires to turn signal harness.
7. Remove three turn signal switch retainer screws, **Fig. 11.**
8. Remove turn signal and hazard warning switch while guiding wiring harness out from column.

Installation

1. Guide wiring harness downward through column until the switch is properly seated.
2. Install switch retainer and the three screws.
3. Snap plastic harness retainer into support bracket, connect harness connector and tape key in buzzer wires to harness.

4. Install washer-wiper switch and retaining screw.
5. Install lower steering column cover.
6. Install steering wheel, horn switch and horn button.
7. Connect battery ground cable.

INSTRUMENT CLUSTER
REPLACE

1981–84 ARIES, RELIANT; 1982–83 LEBARON, 400; 1983 E CLASS, EXECUTIVE, NEW YORKER & 600

1. Disconnect battery ground cable.
2. Remove screws securing instrument cluster bezel and pull bezel from retaining clips, **Fig. 12.**
3. Remove screws securing upper right bezel and the bezel.
4. Remove screws securing instrument panel pad, as needed, and raise pad slightly to allow cluster removal.
5. Remove 4 screws securing instrument cluster and pull cluster away from dash.
6. Disconnect electrical connectors and speedometer cable, then remove cluster.
7. Reverse procedure to install.

1984 E CLASS & LEBARON, 1984–85 EXECUTIVE, 1984–86 NEW YORKER & 600 & 1985–86 ARIES, CARAVELLE, LEBARON EXC. GTS, TOWN & COUNTRY & RELIANT

1. Disconnect battery ground cable.
2. Remove screws securing instrument cluster bezel, **Fig. 13,** and the bezel.
3. Remove screws securing instrument panel pad, **Fig. 14,** and raise pad slightly to allow cluster removal.
4. Remove 4 screws securing cluster and pull cluster from dash.
5. Disconnect electrical connectors and speedometer cable, if equipped, then remove cluster.
6. Reverse procedure to install.

Fig. 15 Instrument panel, exploded view (Typical). 1980–83 Horizon & Omni; 1983 Charger & Turismo

1984–86 DAYTONA & LASER

1. Disconnect battery ground cable.
2. Remove screws securing cluster bezel and the bezel.
3. Remove 4 screws securing cluster and pull cluster away from dash.
4. Disconnect electrical connectors and speedometer cable, if equipped, then remove cluster.
5. Reverse procedure to install.

1980–83 HORIZON, OMNI; 1983 CHARGER & TURISMO

1. Disconnect battery ground cable.
2. Remove two mask-lens assembly lower attaching spring pins by pulling rearward with suitable pliers.
3. Pull mask-lens rearward, lower slightly and remove from cluster.
4. Disconnect speedometer cable.
5. Remove two speedometer attaching screws and the speedometer.
6. Disengage two wiring harness connectors. On Rallye cluster disconnect three harness connectors.
7. Remove two cluster attaching screws, **Fig. 15.** On Rallye cluster remove four screws.
8. Remove cluster upper attaching spring pins and pull cluster from panel.
9. Disconnect clock wiring, if equipped.
10. Remove cluster from vehicle.
11. Reverse procedure to install.

1984–86 CHARGER, HORIZON, OMNI & TURISMO

1. Disconnect battery ground cable.
2. Remove 2 lower cluster bezel retaining screws, **Fig. 16.**
3. Allow bezel to drop slightly, then remove bezel.
4. Remove 4 screws securing instrument cluster and pull cluster away from dash.
5. Disconnect electrical connectors and speedometer cable, then remove cluster.
6. Reverse procedure to install.

1985–86 LANCER & LEBARON GTS

1. Disconnect battery ground cable.
2. Place gear selector lever in lowest position, then remove instrument cluster bezel attaching screws and bezel.
3. Remove lower steering column cover, then disconnect gear selector cable at steering column shift housing.
4. Remove mask and lens assembly.
5. Remove speedometer assembly, then disconnect speedometer cable.
6. Remove cluster assembly attaching screws, then pull cluster assembly away from dash panel.
7. Disconnect all electrical connectors from cluster assembly, then remove cluster, **Fig. 17.**

Fig. 16   Instrument cluster & bezel. 1984–86 Charger, Horizon, Omni & Turismo

Fig. 17   Instrument cluster assembly. 1985–86 Lancer & LeBaron GTS

8. Reverse procedure to install.

WIPER SWITCH
REPLACE

FRONT

Exc. 1980–86 Horizon & Omni; 1983–86 Charger and Turismo

1. Disconnect battery ground cable and remove steering wheel, using a suitable puller.
2. On models equipped with intermittent wiper system, remove two screws attaching turn signal lever cover to lock housing and remove turn signal lever cover.
3. Remove screw attaching W/S wiper switch and the switch, **Fig. 18.**
4. Reverse procedure to install.

1980–86 Horizon & Omni; 1983–86 Charger & Turismo

1. Disconnect battery ground cable.
2. Disconnect wiper switch and turn signal switch wiring harness connectors.
3. Remove lower column cover.
4. Remove horn button.
5. Place ignition lock in "Off" position and turn steering wheel so the access hole in the hub area is at the 9 o'clock position on 1983–85 models, and in the 3 o'clock position on 1980–82 models.
6. With a suitable screwdriver, loosen turn signal lever screw through access hole.
7. Disengage dimmer push rod from wiper switch.
8. Unsnap wiring clip and remove wiper switch.
9. Reverse procedure to install.

REAR

Exc. Charger, Horizon, Omni, Turismo & 1985—86 Lancer & LeBaron GTS

1. Disconnect battery ground cable.
2. Remove cluster bezel, then seven lower trim bezel attaching screws.
3. Remove trim bezel by unsnapping two retaining clips.
4. Disconnect switch assembly electrical connector.
5. Remove two switch attaching screws, then the switch.
6. Reverse procedure to install.

Charger, Horizon, Omni & Turismo

1. Disconnect battery ground cable.
2. Depress two spring clips on top of bezel, using a thin blade screwdriver.
3. Tip bezel rearward and pull out switch assembly.
4. Remove switch and lamp electrical connector, then remove switch assembly.
5. Reverse procedure to install.

1985—86 Lancer & LeBaron GTS

1. Disconnect battery ground cable.
2. Remove headlight and accessory switch module from instrument panel.
3. Remove two rear wiper and washer switch attaching screws from module, then the switch.
4. Reverse procedure to install.

WINDSHIELD WIPER MOTOR
REPLACE

FRONT

Exc. 1980—86 Horizon & Omni; 1983—86 Charger & Turismo

1. Disconnect battery ground cable, then remove wiper arms and pivot attaching nuts.
2. Remove plastic screen covering cowl, if equipped, and disconnect reservoir hose from "T" connector on Daytona and Laser.
3. Remove wiper motor cover and disconnect electrical connectors to motor.
4. Push pivots downward into plenum chamber, then pull motor outward to clear mounting stud. Move wiper motor toward driver's side of vehicle as far as possible and pull right hand pivot and link assembly through opening, then move motor toward passenger side of vehicle and remove wiper motor, and left hand pivot and link assembly.
5. Remove nut from end of motor shaft and remove motor crank.
6. Reverse procedure to install.

1980—86 Horizon & Omni; 1983—86 Charger & Turismo

1. Remove wiper arm assemblies.
2. Remove the nuts from the left and right pivots.
3. Remove wiper motor plastic cover.

Fig. 18   W/S wiper switch removal. Exc. 1980—86 Horizon & Omni; 1983—86 Charger & Turismo

4. Disconnect wiper motor wiring harness.
5. Remove three bolts from wiper motor mounting bracket.
6. Disengage the pivots from cowl top mounting positions.
7. Remove wiper motor, cranks, pivots and drive link assembly from cowl plenum chamber.
8. Remove wiper motor from drive crank linkage.
9. Reverse procedure to install.

REAR

1981—86 Aries, Reliant, 1982—86 LeBaron, 1985 Executive & 1985—86 Lancer & Town & Country

1. Disconnect battery ground cable.
2. Remove wiper arm and blade assembly.
3. Remove wiper motor cover, then disconnect wire connector from motor.
4. Remove four screws attaching wiper motor bracket to liftgate, then remove wiper motor.
5. Reverse procedure to install.

1984—86 Daytona and Laser

1. Disconnect battery ground cable.
2. Raise wiper arm, release latch and remove arm assembly.
3. Remove inner trim panel and disconnect electrical connector to motor.
4. Remove grommet from liftgate glass.
5. Remove 2 screws securing motor and the motor.
6. Reverse procedure to install.

1980—86 Horizon & Omni; 1983—85 Charger & Turismo

1. Disconnect battery ground cable and remove wiper arm assembly.
2. Remove pivot shaft nut, bezel and seal.
3. Remove wiper motor cover and disconnect electrical connector to motor.
4. Remove screws securing wiper motor and the motor.
5. Reverse procedure to install.

RADIO
REPLACE

1981—84 ARIES, RELIANT; 1982—83 LEBARON, 400; 1983 E CLASS, EXECUTIVE, NEW YORKER & 600

1. Disconnect battery ground cable, then remove center bezel.
2. On vehicles equipped with monospeaker, remove speaker, then disconnect from radio.
3. Remove two screws attaching radio to base panel, then pull radio through front face of base panel.
4. Disconnect wiring harness, antenna lead and ground strap.
5. Reverse procedure to install.

1984 E CLASS, EXECUTIVE SEDAN, LEBARON, NEW YORKER & 600

1. Disconnect battery ground cable.
2. Remove screws securing instrument cluster bezel, **Fig. 13**, and the bezel.
3. Remove screws securing radio and pull radio away from dash panel.
4. Disconnect electrical connectors and antenna lead, then remove radio.
5. Reverse procedure to install.

1984—86 DAYTONA & LASER

1. Disconnect battery ground cable.
2. Remove 2 screws securing bottom of console bezel, then lift bezel from console.
3. Remove 2 screws securing radio and pull radio away from console.
4. Disconnect electrical connectors and antenna lead, then remove radio.
5. Reverse procedure to install.

1980—86 HORIZON & OMNI; 1983—86 CHARGER & TURISMO

1. Disconnect battery ground cable.
2. Remove right bezel attaching screws and open the glove box.
3. Remove bezel, guiding the right end around glove box as needed.
4. Remove radio mounting screws.
5. Pull radio from panel and disconnect wiring, ground strap and antenna lead from radio.
6. Remove radio from vehicle.
7. Reverse procedure to install.

1985—86 ARIES, CARAVELLE, EXECUTIVE, LEBARON EXC. GTS, NEW YORKER, RELIANT, TOWN & COUNTRY & 600

1. Disconnect battery ground cable.
2. Remove left instrument bezel attaching screws, then the bezel.
3. Remove two radio and radio bezel to base panel attaching screws.
4. Pull radio through front face of base panel, then disconnect electrical con-

nectors, antenna lead and ground strap.
5. Remove radio from vehicle.
6. Reverse procedure to install.

1985—86 LANCER & LEBARON GTS

1. Disconnect battery ground cable.
2. Remove cluster bezel attaching screws, then the cluster bezel.
3. Remove radio attaching screws, then pull radio away from dash panel.
4. Disconnect electrical connectors, antenna lead and ground strap.
5. Remove radio from vehicle.
6. Reverse procedure to install.

HEATER CORE
REPLACE

LESS A/C

Exc. 1980—86 Horizon & Omni; 1983—86 Charger & Turismo

1. Disconnect battery ground cable, then drain cooling system.
2. Disconnect wire connector from blower motor, then disconnect control cable from mode door.
3. Disconnect heater hoses from heater core, then cap heater core tube openings to prevent coolant spillage.
4. Remove glove box, then remove nut attaching hanger bracket to heater assembly through glove box opening.

NOTE: On Daytona, Lancer, Laser & LeBaron GTS, remove 2 screws and disconnect demister adapter from top of heater case.

5. From engine compartment of dash panel, remove two nuts attaching heater assembly.
6. Carefully slide heater assembly out from under instrument panel, **Figs. 19 and 20.**
7. Remove insulation from around heater core tubes, then remove upper core mounting screw.
8. Using a screwdriver, pry retainer tabs from outer edges of heater housing cover, then remove cover.
9. Remove lower heater core to housing attaching screws, then slide heater core from housing.
10. Reverse procedure to install.

1980—86 Horizon & Omni; 1983—86 Charger & Turismo

1. Disconnect battery ground cable, then drain cooling system.
2. Disconnect blower motor electrical connector, then remove ash tray.
3. Depress red color coded tab on end of temperature control cable, and pull control cable out of receiver on heater assembly.
4. Remove glove box and door assembly.
5. Disconnect heater hoses and plug heater core tube openings.
6. Remove two heater assembly to dash panel attaching nuts, **Fig. 21.**
7. Disconnect blower resistor electrical

Fig. 19 Heater assembly. Models less A/C exc. 1980—86 Horizon & Omni; 1983—86 Charger & Turismo; 1985—86 Daytona, Lancer, Laser & LeBaron GTS

Fig. 20 Heater assembly. Models less A/C 1985—86 Daytona, Lancer, Laser & LeBaron GTS

connector, then remove heater support brace to instrument panel attaching screws.
8. Remove heater support bracket nut, then disconnect strap from plenum stud and lower heater assembly from under instrument panel.
9. Depress yellow color coded tab on end of mode door control cable out of receiver on heater assembly.
10. Move heater unit toward right side of vehicle, then out from under instrument panel.
11. Remove left heater outlet duct attaching screws, then the heater outlet duct.
12. Remove four blower motor mounting plate attaching screws, then the blow-

er motor assembly.
13. Remove four outside air and defroster door cover attaching screws, then the door cover.
14. Remove defroster door assembly, then lift defroster door control rod out of heater assembly.
15. Remove 8 heater core cover attaching screws, then the core cover.
16. Slide heater core up and out of heater assembly.
17. Reverse procedure to install.

WITH A/C

Exc. 1980—86 Horizon & Omni; 1983—86 Charger & Turismo

1. Disconnect battery ground cable,

Fig. 21 Heater assembly. 1980—86 Horizon & Omni; 1983—86 Charger & Turismo less A/C

Fig. 22 Heater assembly. Models with A/C exc. 1980—86 Horizon & Omni; 1983—86 Charger & Turismo

12. Pull unit rearward so that mounting studs clear dash panel, then carefully remove unit from under instrument panel.
13. Place evaporator heater assembly on workbench, then on 1980—82 models, remove ¼-20 nut from mode door actuator arm on top cover. On 1983—86 models, remove actuator arm by squeezing it off its mounting clips.
14. Remove two retaining clips from front edge of cover.
15. Remove two mode door actuator to cover attaching screws, then the actuator.
16. Remove 15 screws securing cover to evaporator heater assembly, then lift off cover, **Fig. 22.**
17. Lift mode door out of unit.
18. Remove screw from heater core tube retaining bracket, then the heater core from evaporator heater assembly.
19. Reverse procedure to install.

1980—83 Horizon & Omni; 1983 Charger & Turismo
1. Disconnect battery ground cable, then drain cooling system and discharge A/C system.
2. Disconnect heater hose at heater core. Plug heater core tube opening.
3. Disconnect vacuum lines at engine intake manifold and water valve, **Fig. 23.**
4. Remove expansion valve ("H" valve), **Fig. 23,** as follows:
   a. Disconnect low pressure cut-off switch electrical connector, located on side of "H" valve.
   b. Remove hex head bolt from center of plumbing sealing plate.
   c. Pull refrigerant line assembly toward front of vehicle.
   d. Remove two allen head cap screws, then carefully remove the disassembled valve.
5. Remove hose clamp, then the condensate drain tube from evaporator heater assembly.
6. Remove evaporator heater assembly to dash panel attaching nuts, then depress red color coded tab on end of temperature control cable and pull control cable out of receiver on heater assembly.
7. Remove glove box and door assembly, then disconnect vacuum harness from heater A/C control, located under instrument panel.

Fig. 23 Air conditioning & heater hose routing. 1980—86 Horizon; 1983—86 Charger & Turismo

drain cooling system and discharge A/C system.
2. Disconnect heater hoses from heater core, then cap heater core tube openings to prevent coolant spillage.
3. Disconnect vacuum lines at engine intake manifold and water valve.
4. Remove right scuff plate and cowl side trim panel.
5. Remove A/C control panel, then the center console, if equipped.
6. Remove forward console mounting bracket, if equipped.
7. Remove center distribution duct, then the demister adapter on Daytona,

Lancer, Laser & LeBaron Hatchback.
8. Remove defroster duct from under panel, then disconnect condensation drain tube from engine side of dash panel.
9. Disconnect electrical connectors and control cables from A/C and heater housing.
10. Remove right side cowl to plenum brace, then pull carpet rearward from under unit.
11. Remove A/C and heater housing hanger bracket attaching screw, then the four nuts attaching unit to dash panel from engine compartment.

Fig. 24   Heater assembly. 1980–86 Horizon & Omni; 1983–86 Charger & Turismo with A/C

Fig. 25   Blower motor replacement. 1980–86 Horizon & Omni; 1983–86 Charger & Turismo less A/C

Fig. 26   Blower motor replacement. Models with A/C

8. Disconnect blower motor electrical connector.
9. Remove right trim bezel to instrument panel attaching screws, then the right trim bezel.
10. Remove center distribution duct to instrument panel attaching screws, then the distribution duct.
11. Remove defroster duct adapter, then the panel support bracket.
12. Remove right side cowl lower panel, then the right side instrument panel pivot bracket screw.
13. Remove screws attaching lower instrument panel to steering column, then pull carpet from under evaporator heater assembly as far rearward as possible.
14. Remove nut attaching evaporator heater assembly to plenum mounting brace and blower motor ground cable, then support heater assembly with hands and remove mounting brace from its stud, **Fig. 24.**
15. Lift and pull evaporator heater assembly rearward to clear dash panel and liner. The panel will also have to be pulled rearward to allow assembly clearance.
16. Remove evaporator heater assembly from dash panel, taking care to prevent dash panel attaching studs from hanging up in dash liner.
17. Place evaporator assembly on work bench, then remove nut from mode door actuator arm on top cover.
18. Remove two retaining clips from front edge of cover, then the mode door actuator to cover attaching screws and mode door actuator.

19. Remove 15 heater assembly cover attaching screws, then lift cover door out of heater assembly.
20. Remove heater core tube retaining bracket attaching screw, then lift core from heater assembly.
21. Reverse procedure to install.

1984–86 Charger, Horizon, Omni & Turismo

1. Disconnect battery ground cable, then drain cooling system and discharge A/C system.
2. Disconnect blend air door cable and disengage from clip on heater air duct.
3. Remove glove box and door assembly.
4. Remove center bezel attaching screws, then the center bezel.
5. Remove center distribution duct and defroster duct adapter.
6. Disconnect heater hoses and A/C lines. Plug heater core tube openings.
7. Disconnect vacuum lines at engine and water valve, **Fig. 23.**
8. Remove four dash retaining nuts, then the right side cowl trim panel.
9. Remove right instrument panel pivot bracket attaching screw, then the two screws attaching lower instrument panel at steering column.
10. Remove panel top cover.
11. Remove all but left panel to fenceline attaching screw, then pull carpet from under A/C unit as far rearward as possible.
12. Remove support strap attaching nut and blower motor ground cable, then

support heater unit with hands and remove strap from its plenum stud, **Fig. 24.**
13. Lift and pull evaporator heater assembly rearward to clear dash panel and liner. The panel will also have to be pulled rearward to allow assembly clearance.
14. Remove evaporator heater assembly from dash panel, taking care to prevent dash panel attaching studs from hanging up in dash liner.
15. Place evaporator heater assembly on work bench, then remove nut from mode door actuator arm on top cover.
16. Remove two retaining clips from front edge of cover, then the mode door actuator to cover attaching screws and mode door actuator.
17. Remove 15 heater unit cover attaching screws, then the cover. Lift mode door out of heater assembly.
18. Remove heater core tube retaining bracket attaching screw, then lift core from heater assembly.
19. Reverse procedure to install.

BLOWER MOTOR
REPLACE

LESS A/C

Exc. 1980–86 Horizon & Omni; 1983–86 Charger & Turismo

1. Perform steps 1 through 14 as described under "Heater Core, Replace."
2. Remove blower motor to heater housing attaching screws, then remove blower motor.

Fig. 27   Speed control lock-in screw adjustment

3. Remove clamp retaining blower motor wheel to shaft, then remove two nuts attaching retainer plate to blower motor and remove plate.
4. Reverse procedure to install.

1980—86 Horizon & Omni; 1983—86 Charger & Turismo

1. Disconnect battery ground cable.
2. Disconnect blower motor wiring connector.
3. Remove left heater outlet duct.
4. Remove screws retaining blower motor mounting plate to heater unit.
5. Remove blower motor assembly, **Fig. 25.**
6. Reverse procedure to install.

WITH A/C

1. Disconnect battery ground cable.
2. Remove three screws securing glove box to instrument panel and the glove box.
3. Disconnect blower motor feed and ground wires. Remove wires from retaining clip on recirculating housing.
4. Disconnect blower motor vent tube from A/C unit.
5. Loosen recirculation door actuator from bracket and remove actuator from housing. Do not disconnect vacuum lines.
6. Remove seven screws securing recirculating housing to A/C unit, then the housing.

7. Remove three blower motor mounting flange nuts and the blower motor, **Fig. 26.**
8. Reverse procedure to install.

SPEED CONTROL
LOCK-IN SCREW ADJUSTMENT

Lock-in accuracy will be affected by poor engine performance (need for tune-up), loaded gross weight of car (trailering), improper slack in control cable. After the foregoing items have been considered and the speed sags or drops more than 2 to 3 mph when the speed control is activated, the lock-in adjusting screw should be turned counter-clockwise approximately 1/4 turn per one mph correction required, **Fig. 27.**

If a speed increase of more than 2 to 3 mph occurs, the lock-in adjusting screw should be turned clockwise 1/4 turn per one mph correction required.

CAUTION: This adjustment must not exceed two turns in either direction or damage to the unit may occur.

THROTTLE CABLE ADJUSTMENT

Optimum servo performance is obtained with a given amount of free play in the throttle control cable. To obtain proper free play, insert a 1/16 inch diameter pin, **Fig. 28,** between forward end of slot in cable end of carburetor linkage pin (hair pin clip removed from linkage pin). With choke in full open position and carburetor at curb idle, pull cable back toward dash panel without moving carburetor linkage until all free play is removed. Tighten cable clamp bolt to 45 inch-pounds, remove 1/16 inch pin and install hair pin clip.

Fig. 28   Speed control servo throttle cable adjustment (Typical)

BRAKE SWITCH ADJUSTMENT

Exc. 1980—86 Horizon & Omni; 1983—85 Charger & Turismo

Position stop light switch to retaining bracket, then with brake pedal depressed, push switch forward into retaining bracket until it is fully seated. Slowly release brake pedal and allow pedal striker to rachet switch rearward in bracket to the correct position. No further adjustment is necessary.

1980—86 Horizon & Omni; 1983—86 Charger & Turismo

1. Loosen switch bracket.
2. Insert .130 spacer gauge between brake push rod and switch with pedal in free position.
3. Push switch bracket assembly toward brake push rod until plunger is fully depressed and switch contacts spacer.
4. Tighten bracket bolt to 75 in-lbs. and remove spacer.

4-97 Engine Section

ENGINE MOUNTS
REPLACE

NOTE: When positioning the engine on 1983–86 models, check driveshaft's length as outlined in the "Front Suspension & Steering Section" under "Driveshaft Length, Adjust." The engine mounts incorporate slotted bolt holes to permit side-to-side positioning of the engine thereby affecting the length of the driveshaft. Failure to properly position engine may result in extensive damage to the engine.

Refer to **Figs. 1 and 2** when replacing engine mounts.

ENGINE
REPLACE

MANUAL TRANS.

NOTE: The engine and transmission are removed as an assembly.

1. Disconnect battery cables and drain cooling system.
2. Scribe hood hinge locations and remove hood.
3. Remove radiator hoses, then the radiator and shroud assembly.
4. Remove air cleaner.
5. Remove A/C compressor mounting bolts and position compressor aside, if equipped.
6. Disconnect all wiring, hoses, lines and cables from engine.
7. Remove air diverter valve and lines from air pump.
8. Remove alternator belt and alternator.
9. Disconnect clutch and speedometer cables.
10. Raise and support vehicle.
11. Disconnect drive shafts from transmission and secure aside with wire.
12. Disconnect exhaust pipe from manifold.
13. Remove air pump hoses and lines, then the air pump belt and the air pump.
14. Disconnect transmission linkage.
15. Lower vehicle.
16. Attach suitable engine lifting equipment to engine.
17. Raise engine slightly and remove front engine mount bolt.
18. Remove right and left engine mount bolts.
19. Remove engine and transmission assembly from vehicle.
20. Reverse procedure to install.

AUTO. TRANS.

NOTE: The engine is removed without the transmission.

	TIGHTENING TORQUE	
A	54 N·m	40 FT. LB.
B	28 N·m	250 IN. LB.
C	37 N·m	325 IN. LB.
D	14 N·m	130 IN. LB.
E	75 N·m	55 FT. LB.
F	95 N·m	70 FT. LB.
G	54 N·m	40 FT. LB.
H	28 N·m	250 IN. LB.

Fig. 1   Engine mount replacement. 1983

	TIGHTENING TORQUE			
A	28 N·m	250 IN. LB.	C	68 N·m	50 FT. LB.
B	95 N·m	70 FT. LB.	D	54 N·m	40 FT. LB.

Fig. 2   Engine mount replacement. 1984–86

Fig. 3 Cylinder head bolt removal sequence

Fig. 4 Rocker arm assembly removal

Fig. 5 Cylinder head bolt tightening sequence

Fig. 6 Checking valve clearance

1. Disconnect battery cables and drain cooling system.
2. Scribe hood hinge locations and remove hood.
3. Remove radiator hoses and the air cleaner.
4. Remove A/C compressor mounting bolts and position compressor aside, if equipped.
5. Disconnect all wiring, hoses, lines and cables from engine.
6. Remove air diverter valve and lines from air pump, if equipped.
7. Remove alternator belt and the alternator.
8. Remove upper bellhousing bolts.
9. Raise and support vehicle and remove front wheels.
10. Remove left and right splash shields.
11. Remove power steering pump belt and pump mounting bolts. Position pump aside.
12. Remove water pump and crankshaft pulleys.
13. Remove front engine mounting bolt.
14. Remove transmission inspection cover, then the flex plate bolts.
15. Remove starter motor.
16. Remove lower bellhousing bolts.
17. Lower vehicle and support transmission with a suitable jack.
18. Attach suitable engine lifting equipment to engine.
19. Remove engine oil filter and the right engine mount.
20. Lift and remove engine from vehicle.
21. Reverse procedure to install.

CYLINDER HEAD
REPLACE

NOTE: Cylinder head must be cool prior to removal to avoid cylinder head distortion.

1. Drain cooling system.
2. Remove intake and exhaust manifolds from cylinder head.
3. Remove rocker arm cover.
4. Remove cylinder head bolts evenly in sequence, **Fig. 3.**

NOTE: Rocker arm supporting brackets are located on dowels and are retained by head bolts. Only brackets 2 and 4 are pinned to rocker arm shaft.

5. Tie rocker arm assembly together with suitable wire, then remove, **Fig. 4.**
6. Remove push rods, noting location of each to facilitate installation, then remove cylinder head.
7. Reverse procedure to install.

NOTE: Refer to **Fig. 5** for cylinder head bolt tightening sequence. Bolts are to be torqued progressively to 52 ft. lbs.

VALVE ARRANGEMENT
FRONT TO REAR

4-97 . . . . I-E-I-E-I-E-I

VALVE TIMING
INTAKE OPENS BEFORE TDC

Engine	Year	Degrees
4-97	1983	13
4-97	1984–86	16½

VALVES
ADJUST

NOTE: For proper clearance, valve adjustment must be set with piston at TDC on the compression stroke with engine cold.

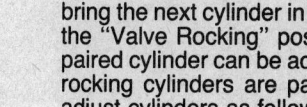

Fig. 7 Checking valve guide wear

1. Rotate crankshaft noting exhaust valve movement. When one valve begins to close continue turning slowly until intake valve on same cylinder just starts to open. This is the "Valve Rocking" position. In this position, the clearance in the opposite cylinder can be adjusted.
2. After checking both clearances, **Fig. 6,** rotate crankshaft one half turn to bring the next cylinder in firing order to the "Valve Rocking" position and the paired cylinder can be adjusted. Valve rocking cylinders are paired to valve adjust cylinders as follows: 4–1, 2–3, 1–4, 3–2.
3. Adjust valve clearance by loosening locknut and turning screw until a sliding fit is obtained between valve stem and rocker, **Fig. 6.**

VALVE GUIDE
SERVICE

NOTE: Remove varnish and carbon deposits from valve guide interior with a suitable guide cleaner.

VALVE GUIDE WEAR

1. Insert valve into guide leaving .400 inch above cylinder gasket surface.
2. Firmly attach a dial indicator to cylinder head so indicator needle is in contact with valve margin.
3. Move valve to and from indicator and note total indicator reading, **Fig. 7.**
4. Total indicator reading shows valve guide wear. Wear must not exceed .020 inch for intake valves, or .027 inch for exhaust valves.

Fig. 8 Distributor drive slot marking

Fig. 9 Oil pump driveshaft assembly

CAMSHAFT
REPLACE

1. Remove oil filter, then the 7 oil pump attaching screws and pull assembly from block.
2. Remove distributor and drive housing and mark crankcase in relation to drive slot, **Fig. 8.**
3. Remove distributor drive from drive shaft spindle using a suitable magnet, **Fig. 9.**
4. Remove shaft drive gear circlip.

NOTE: Insert a shop towel into cavity around gear to prevent circlip from falling into crankcase during removal or installation.

5. Remove driveshaft toward pump side of crankcase with a tapping motion until gear is free of spline, and remove gear.
6. Remove fuel pump and tappets, noting location of tappets to facilitate proper installation.
7. Remove camshaft thrust plate and camshaft.
8. Reverse procedure to install.

PISTON & ROD ASSEMBLY

When installing piston and connecting rod assembly, the notches on pistons 1 and 3 must face toward flywheel end of engine and the notches on pistons 2 and 4 must be facing timing chain, **Fig. 10.**

TIMING CHAIN COVER
REPLACE

1. Disconnect battery ground cable.
2. Loosen AIR pump adjusting screw and bracket and remove belt.
3. Raise vehicle and remove right inner splash shield.
4. Loosen alternator adjusting screw, then move alternator inward and remove alternator/water pump drive belt.
5. Remove crankshaft pulley belt, washer and pulley.
6. Drain cooling system and remove water pump to timing cover hose.

7. Slightly raise and support engine at the timing cover end and remove engine mount bracket to timing cover and block attaching bolts.
8. Remove crankcase extension to cover screws, then the cover to block attaching screws.

NOTE: Two cover to block screws extend through tubular locating dowels, **Fig. 11.** During removal, ensure dowels do not fall into crankcase extension.

9. Remove timing cover.
10. Reverse procedures to install.

TIMING COVER SEAL
REPLACE

1. Perform steps 1 through 5 under "Timing Chain Cover, Replace".
2. Using tool No. C-4762-1 on 1983 models, or C-748 on 1984–86 models, and a suitable wrench, insert tool over crankshaft nose and turn tool

Fig. 10 Piston installation

Fig. 11 Tubular dowel location

Fig. 12   Measuring timing chain stretch

Fig. 13   Crankshaft sprocket removal

Fig. 14   Timing mark alignment

Fig. 15   Crankshaft rear oil seal removal

Fig. 16   Crankshaft rear oil seal installation

firmly into seal.

3. Tighten thrust screw to remove seal, then tap side of thrust screw to remove seal.
4. Using tool No. C-4761 and a new seal drive seal into timing cover with the lips of seal toward engine until tool stops aginst cover.
5. Examine pulley hub for dirt and defects and polish with 400 grit sandpaper as necessary.
6. Lubricate pully hub and seal lip using a suitable lubricant, then align keyway and install crankshaft pulley, washer and bolt.
7. Torque retaining bolt to 110 ft. lbs.
8. Reverse steps 1 through 4 to assemble.

TIMING CHAIN
REPLACE

1. Remove timing chain cover as described under "Timing Chain Cover, Replace."
2. Before removing timing chain, check timing chain stretch as follows:

a. Rotate crankshaft until one of the three camshaft sprocket bolts is located at top of crankshaft and camshaft centerlines.
b. Using a suitable size socket and torque wrench, apply torque in direction of crankshaft rotation to the camshaft sprocket bolt, **Fig. 12.** Apply 30 ft. lbs. of torque if cylinder head is installed on engine and 15 ft. lbs. of torque if cylinder head is removed from engine.

NOTE: Do not allow engine to turn while applying torque.

c. Hold a ruler alongside a link in the chain and apply same torque as described previously in opposite direction and note amount of chain movement, **Fig. 12.** If movement exceeds ⅛ inch, timing chain must be replaced.
3. Remove camshaft sprocket attaching bolts, sprocket and chain.
4. Remove crankshaft sprocket using tools C-4760 (adapter) and C-3894-A (puller) or equivalent, **Fig. 13.**
5. Align crankshaft sprocket with key and drive firmly onto crankshaft.
6. Loosely install camshaft sprocket onto camshaft.
7. Rotate crankshaft and camshaft until timing marks on both sprockets are on a line passing through crankshaft and camshaft centerlines, **Fig. 14.**
8. Remove camshaft sprocket without disturbing timing marks, then reinstall sprocket and timing chain making sure marks are aligned as described previously.
9. Install camshaft sprocket bolts and torque to 113 inch lbs.
10. Reverse remainder of procedure to assemble.

REAR CRANKSHAFT OIL SEAL SERVICE

1. Place inner surface of seal housing on spacers to allow clearance for seal removal.
2. Install tool No. C-4759 or equivalent and drive seal from housing, **Fig. 15.**

NOTE: Tool No. C-4759 with universal driver C-4171 is used as both a seal remover and, when reversed, a seal installer, **Figs. 15 and 16.**

3. Place outer seal housing on a flat surface, **Fig. 16.**
4. Using tool No. C-4759 with tool No. C-4171 (driver) tap seal into housing to full depth.

OIL PAN
REPLACE

1. Drain engine oil.
2. Remove 16 oil pan attaching screws.
3. Remove pan and gasket.
4. Clean pan and gasket surfaces.
5. Install new gasket and reinstall pan.
6. Torque oil pan attaching screws to 9.4 ft. lbs. (111 inch lbs.) for 1983–84 models or 7.4 ft. lbs. (89 inch lbs.) for 1985–86 models.
7. Refill engine oil.

Fig. 17 Oil pump replacement

Fig. 18 Exploded view of oil pump

Fig. 19 Exploded view of oil pressure relief valve

OIL PUMP
REPLACE

REMOVAL

1. Remove oil filter.
2. Remove the seven oil pump mounting bolts while holding pump together as an assembly, **Fig. 17.**
3. Pull assembly from block.

REPLACE

NOTE: Seal all oil pump attaching bolt threads with suitable sealer before installation.

1. Install new housing to block and housing to cover gaskets.
2. Place cover on housing and insert two bolts to maintain alignment.
3. Install housing into block, then rotate assembly as necessary to engage drive gear shaft with slot in driveshaft.
4. Align bolt pattern, install remaining bolts and torque bolts to 9.4 ft. lbs. (111 inch lbs.)

OIL PUMP SERVICE
DISASSEMBLY

1. For oil pump disassembly, refer to **Fig. 18.**
2. Disassemble oil pressure relief valve by unscrewing dome nut and removing sealing washer, **Fig. 19.**

3. Remove relief valve sleeve using a suitable allen wrench.
4. Remove spring and ball.

NOTE: Examine the ball for defects such as grooves or scuffing. Check ball for roundness using a micrometer and replace if defective.

ASSEMBLY

1. Place ball on its seat in relief valve cover, then using a soft rod, tap ball into place with a small hammer.
2. Insert spring into sleeve and screw sleeve into cover and torque to 62 inch lbs, **Fig. 19.**
3. Install sealing washer and dome nut and torque to 30 ft. lbs, **Fig. 19.**
4. Refer to **Fig. 18** to reassemble oil pump.

FUEL PUMP
REPLACE

1. Disconnect battery ground cable.
2. Disconnect fuel lines from fuel pump.
3. Remove fuel pump mounting bolts.
4. Remove fuel pump from vehicle.
5. Reverse procedure to install.

WATER PUMP
REMOVAL

1. Disconnect battery ground cable.
2. Remove radiator cap and drain cooling system from water pump drain plug.
3. Remove pump to block coolant hose at water pump.

4. Loosen alternator/water pump drive belt, then remove pump pulley.
5. Remove 4 pump to crankcase extension screws and pull assembly from crankcase.

INSTALLATION

1. Position water pump on crankcase extension with new gasket.
2. Install 4 pump to crankcase extension screws and torque to 9 ft. lbs.
3. Install pump to block hose and torque clamp to 35 inch lbs.
4. Install drain plug and torque to 13 ft. lbs.
5. Install pump pulley and adjust belt tension to specifications, then refill cooling system.

BELT TENSION DATA

	New	Used
1983		
Air Pump	95	70
Alternator/Water Pump	115	95
Power Steering	95	70
1984–86		
Air Pump	95	70
Alternator/Water Pump	115	80
Power Steering	95	70

4-105 Engine Section

Fig. 1   Front engine mount

Fig. 2   Right side engine mount. 1980

Fig. 3   Left engine mount. 1980

Fig. 4   Right engine mount. 1981–83

Fig. 5   Left engine mount. 1981–82

Fig. 6   Left engine mount. 1983

ENGINE MOUNTS

NOTE: When positioning the engine on 1981–83 models, check driveshaft length as outlined in the "Front Suspension & Steering Section" under "Driveshaft Length, Adjust." The engine mounts incorporate slotted bolt holes to permit side-to-side positioning of the engine thereby affecting the length of the driveshaft. Failure to properly position engine may result in extensive damage to the engine.

Refer to Figs. 1 through 7 when replacing the engine mounts.

NOTE: The left engine mount is attached with two types of mounting screws. Two of the three are of the pilot type with extended tips. Extended tip screws must be installed

Fig. 7   Correct positioning of extended tip mount bolts

in the proper position, **Fig. 7.** Damage to the shift cover or difficult shifting may occur if the screws are incorrectly installed.

ENGINE
REPLACE

MANUAL TRANS.

NOTE: The engine and transmission are removed as an assembly.

1. Disconnect battery cables and drain cooling system.
2. Scribe hood hinge locations and remove hood.
3. Remove radiator hoses, then the radiator and shroud assembly.
4. Remove air cleaner.
5. Remove A/C compressor mounting bolts and position compressor aside, if equipped.
6. Disconnect all wiring, hoses, lines and cables from engine.
7. Remove air diverter valve and lines from air pump.

Fig. 8 Cylinder head tightening sequence

8. Remove alternator belt and alternator.
9. Disconnect clutch and speedometer cables.
10. Raise and support vehicle.
11. On models with A-412 transaxle, disconnect drive shaft from transaxle and secure aside. On models with A-460 transaxle, remove driveshafts as outlined in "Front Suspension and Steering."
12. Disconnect exhaust pipe from manifold.
13. Remove air pump hoses and lines, then the air pump belt and the air pump.
14. Disconnect transmission linkage.
15. Lower vehicle.
16. Attach suitable engine lifting equipment to engine.
17. Raise engine slightly and remove front engine mount bolt.
18. Remove right and left engine mount bolts.
19. Remove engine and transmission assembly from vehicle.
20. Reverse procedure to install. Align engine as outlined in "Front Suspension And Steering," to ensure proper driveshaft length.

AUTO. TRANS.

NOTE: The engine is removed without the transmission.

1. Disconnect battery cables and drain cooling system.
2. Scribe hood hinge locations and remove hood.
3. Disconnect transmission cooler lines and radiator hoses, then remove radiator, hoses and cooling fan.
4. Remove air cleaner assembly, then remove A/C compressor, if equipped, and position aside.
5. Disconnect all wiring, hoses, lines and cables from engine.
6. Remove air diverter valve and lines from air pump, if equipped.
7. Remove alternator belt and the alternator.
8. Remove upper bellhousing bolts.
9. Raise and support vehicle and remove front wheels.
10. Remove left and right splash shields.
11. Remove power steering pump belt and pump mounting bolts. Position pump aside.
12. Remove water pump and crankshaft pulleys.
13. Remove front engine mounting bolt.

Fig. 9 Cylinder head assembly, exploded view

14. Remove transmission inspection cover, then the flex plate bolts.
15. Remove starter motor.
16. Remove lower bellhousing bolts.
17. Lower vehicle and support transmission with a suitable jack.
18. Attach suitable engine lifting equipment to engine.
19. Remove engine oil filter and the right engine mount.
20. Lift and remove engine from vehicle.
21. Reverse procedure to install. Align engine as outlined in "Front Suspension And Steering," to ensure proper driveshaft length.

CYLINDER HEAD
REPLACE

1. Drain cooling system and perform Steps 1 through 15 as outlined under "Timing Belt, Replace" procedure.
2. Remove intake and exhaust manifolds from cylinder head.
3. Disconnect all wiring, hoses and cables attached to cylinder head.
4. Remove cam cover bolts and the cam cover.
5. Loosen cylinder head attaching bolts in reverse sequence found in **Fig. 8.**
6. Remove cylinder head from engine, **Fig. 9.**
7. Reverse procedure to install. Insert bolts No. 8 and 10 first, to center the cylinder head on engine block. Torque bolts to specifications in sequence, **Fig. 8.** To properly tension the timing belt, perform Steps 16 through 22 as outlined under "Timing Belt, Replace" procedure.

VALVE ARRANGEMENT
FRONT TO REAR

4-105 . . . . E-I-E-I-I-E-I-E

Fig. 10 Checking valve clearance

Fig. 13 Piston indentification markings

VALVE LIFT SPECS.

Engine	Year	Intake	Exhaust
4-105	1980–83	.406	.406

VALVE TIMING
Intake Opens Before TDC

Engine	Year	Degrees
4-105	1980–83	14

VALVES
ADJUST

1. Using feeler gauges, check valve clearance with cam lobe in position shown in **Fig. 10**.

NOTE: Engine should be at normal operating temperature, with thermostat open and coolant temperature approximately 195°F. If necessary to check valve clearance with cylinder head cold, use following specifications: Intake, .006–.010 inch; Exhaust, .014–.018 inch, then recheck after engine has reached normal operating temperature.

2. If valve clearance is greater than specified, remove valve adjusting disc and insert a thicker disc to obtain proper clearance.

Fig. 11 Valve adjusting disc replacement

3. If valve clearance is less than specified, remove valve adjusting disc and insert a thinner disc to obtain proper clearance.
4. To replace valve adjusting disc, depress cam follower with tool L-4417 or equivalent and remove with a narrow screwdriver, **Fig. 11,** and a magnet. Install new disc and recheck clearance.
5. Valve adjusting discs are available in thicknesses of 3.00 mm to 4.25 mm in increments of .05 mm.

VALVE GUIDES

The valve guides may be removed by pressing out from the combustion chamber side. Coat the new valve guide with oil and press into cold cylinder head until the shoulder is seated. The replacement valve guides have a shoulder. Do not exert a pressure greater than one ton after the valve guide shoulder is seated since the shoulder may break. Ream valve guide to .315–.316 inch.

CAMSHAFT
REPLACE

1. Remove timing belt as outlined under "Timing Belt, Replace".
2. Remove camshaft sprocket.
3. Remove bearing caps 5, 1 and 3, **Fig. 12**.
4. Diagonally loosen and remove bearing caps 2 and 4, **Fig. 12**.
5. Remove camshaft from cylinder head.
6. Lubricate bearing shells, journals and contact faces of bearing caps.
7. Install caps in proper order, observing off center bearing position.
8. Reverse Steps 1 through 5 to complete installation.

PISTON & ROD ASSEMBLY

When installing the piston and connecting rod assembly the arrow on top of the piston must face toward the front of engine, **Fig. 13,** and the forged mark on the connecting rod must face toward the intermediate shaft, **Fig. 14**.

Connecting rod side clearance should be .015 inch maximum.

Fig. 12 Camshaft bearing cap indentification

Fig. 14 Connecting rod assemblies

NOTE: There are two types of connecting rod assemblies. One uses a stud and nut to retain the bearing cap and the other uses a bolt to retain the bearing cap, **Fig. 14**.

PISTONS, RINGS & PINS

Pistons are available in standard sizes and oversizes of 0.25, 0.50 and 1.0 mm.

Rings are available in standard sizes and oversizes of 0.25, 0.50 and 1.0 mm.

MAIN & ROD BEARINGS

Main bearings are available in standard sizes and undersizes of 0.25, 0.50 and 0.75 mm. Refer to **Fig. 15** for bearing installation.

Rod bearings are available in standard sizes and undersizes of 0.25, 0.50 and 0.75 mm.

TIMING BELT
REPLACE

1. Disconnect battery ground cable.
2. Remove A/C compressor adjusting strap screws and the drive belt, if equipped. Remove screws from compressor mount and stabilizer brackets, then position compressor aside. Remove compressor bracket from

alternator and the compressor mount bracket.

3. Loosen alternator adjusting strap and remove drive belt.
4. Remove alternator mount bolts and position alternator aside.
5. Remove alternator and compressor mounting bracket from retainer bracket.
6. Loosen power steering pump drive belt, if equipped.
7. Raise and support vehicle.
8. Remove inner fender shield.
9. Remove air compressor, water pump and air pump drive belts, if equipped.
10. Remove idler pulley assembly.
11. Remove crankshaft pulley, **Fig. 16**, and power steering belt, if equipped.
12. Remove lower plastic timing belt cover.
13. Lower vehicle and support engine with a suitable jack.
14. Remove right engine mounting bolt and raise engine slightly.
15. Loosen timing belt tensioner and remove timing belt.
16. Rotate crankshaft and intermediate sprockets until markings are aligned on sprockets, **Fig. 17**.
17. Rotate camshaft sprocket until marking on sprocket is aligned with cylinder head cover, **Fig. 18**.
18. Install timing belt.
19. Install belt tensioning tool L-4502 on large belt tensioner nut in horizontal position, **Fig. 19**.
20. Reset tool index, as needed, to maintain axis within 15° of horizontal with tensioner bearing against belt.
21. Rotate engine clockwise, 2 full revolutions, then tighten tensioner lock nut.

NOTE: Ensure that timing marks are properly aligned with No. 1 cylinder at TDC of compression stroke.

22. Remove tensioning tool, then reverse remaining procedure to complete installation.

FRONT ENGINE OIL SEAL SERVICE

Refer to **Figs. 20 and 21** to replace the crankshaft, intermediate shaft or camshaft seal.

REAR CRANKSHAFT OIL SEAL SERVICE

1. Using a suitable screwdriver, pry oil seal out. Use caution not to nick or damage crankshaft flange seal surface.
2. Place tool L-4455-1 over crankshaft, **Fig. 22**.
3. Place replacement oil seal over tool and tap seal into position with a mallet.

Fig. 15 Crankshaft & bearing assembly, exploded view

Fig. 17 Aligning timing marks on crankshaft & intermediate shaft sprockets

Fig. 18 Aligning timing mark on camshaft sprocket

OIL PUMP
REPLACE

REMOVAL

1. Remove oil pan and gasket.
2. Remove oil pump mounting screws, then the oil pump from engine block, **Fig. 23**.

INSTALLATION

1. Install oil pump with shaft in bore until pump mounting face contacts engine block. It may be necessary to rotate pump body to engage pump shaft tongue in distributor shaft groove.
2. Install oil pump mounting screws.
3. Install oil pan gasket and oil pan.

Front Wheel Drive—CHRYSLER CORP.

CAUTION
IF TIMING BELT WAS REMOVED OR REPLACED, RECHECK VALVE TIMING.

NOTE
ALL PARTS SHOWN IN THIS ILLUSTRATION CAN BE REMOVED AND INSTALLED WITH ENGINE IN CAR.

TIMING BELT SPROCKET ON CAMSHAFT DO NOT REMOVE WHEN REPLACING TIMING BELT, DRIVE OR ADJUSTING VALVE TIMING

79 N·m (58 ft lb)

TENSIONER FOR TIMING BELT CHECK FOR FREE MOVEMENT

TIMING BELT CHECK FOR WEAR/ADJUSTING INSTALLING: REMOVE WATER PUMP PULLEY

43 N·m (32 ft lb)
24 N·m (18 ft lb)

V-BELT CHECK FOR WEAR ADJUSTING TENSION

OIL SEAL FOR INTERMEDIATE SHAFT

CRANKSHAFT PULLEY NOTE POSITION WHEN INSTALLING DRIVE BELT

OIL SEAL FOR CRANKSHAFT

79 N·m (58 ft lb)

79 N·m (58 ft lb)

TIMING BELT SPROCKET ON INTERMEDIATE SHAFT

TIMING BELT SPROCKET ON CRANKSHAFT

27 N·m (20 ft lb)
REMOVE ONLY WHEN SEPARATING V-BELT PULLEY FROM DRIVE BELT SPROCKET

14 N·m (10 ft lb)

Fig. 16 Timing belt & sprocket assembly, exploded view

Fig. 19 Timing belt tensioner tool installation

Fig. 20 Front engine oil seal removal

OIL PUMP SERVICE
DISASSEMBLY

1. Lightly clamp oil pump in a vise with shaft facing downward.
2. Remove two screws from cover.
3. Push shaft upward and remove shaft and drive gear assembly.
4. Pry deflector plate from assembly and remove strainer.

NOTE: The relief valve is staked in place and is not serviceable.

INSPECTION

1. Check end play, **Fig. 24.** End play should be .001–.006 inch.
2. Check gear backlash, **Fig. 25.** Backlash should be .002–.008 inch. If not, replace pump gears.
3. Check cover for flatness with a .002 inch feeler gauge, **Fig. 26.**
4. Use compressed air to check relief valve for proper movement, **Fig. 27.**

ASSEMBLY

1. Lightly lubricate all parts.
2. Install driven gear and the drive gear/shaft assembly.
3. Place cover on pump body and install cover screws.
4. Rotate shaft in each direction. If any binding is detected, disassemble pump and inspect for nicks on gears and/or foreign material.

FUEL PUMP
REPLACE

1. Disconnect fuel lines from fuel pump.
2. Remove fuel pump mounting bolts.
3. Remove fuel pump from vehicle.
4. Reverse procedure to install.

WATER PUMP
REPLACE

1. Disconnect battery ground cable.
2. Drain cooling system.
3. Disconnect radiator hoses and bypass hose from water pump.
4. Remove A/C compressor from mounting brackets and position aside with refrigerant lines attached, if equipped.
5. Remove alternator.
6. Disconnect diverter valve hose at valve, then remove the rear air pump bracket and front air pump bracket, if equipped.
7. Remove alternator bracket from water pump.
8. Remove timing belt cover bolt and two top water pump attaching bolts.
9. Remove water pump from vehicle.
10. Reverse procedure to install.

Fig. 21 Front engine oil seal installation

Fig. 22 Rear crankshaft seal installation

OIL DIPSTICK

OIL PRESSURE AND CHOKE HEAT SWITCH 10 N•m (84 IN. LB.)

19 N•m (168 IN. LB.)

20 N•m (180 IN. LB.)

OIL FILTER
NOTE
TIGHTEN ¾ TO 1 TURN AFTER GASKET CONTACTS BASE.

ENGINE OIL FILLING CAPACITIES:
WITH OIL FILTER CHANGE OR WITHOUT OIL FILTER CHANGE

4.0 LITRES (4.0 QUARTS)
(3 IMP. QTS.)

OIL PUMP DRIVE GEAR AND SHAFT ASSEMBLY

OIL PUMP DRIVEN GEAR

10 N•m (84 IN. LB.)

19 N•m (168 IN. LB.)

STRAINER

OIL DEFLECTOR PLATE
PRY OFF WITH SCREWDRIVER

OIL PAN GASKET ALWAYS REPLACE

OIL PAN BOLT

30 N•m (22 IN. LB.)

Fig. 23 Engine lubrication system, exploded view

BELT TENSION DATA

		New	Used
1980	Air Cond.	55	40
	Air Pump	65	45
	Alternator	75	55
	Power Steer.	40	25
1981–83	Air Cond.	90	45
	Air Pump	70	40
	Alternator	65	40
	Power Steer.	80	50

Fig. 24 Checking oil pump gear end play

Fig. 25 Checking oil pump gear backlash

Fig. 26 Checking oil pump gear cover flatness

Fig. 27 Checking oil pump relief valve with compressed air

4-135 & 4-153 Engine Section

A	54 N•m (40 FT. LBS.)
B	28 N•m (250 IN. LBS.)
C	95 N•m (70 FT. LBS.)
D	15 N•m (130 IN. LBS.)

Fig. 1 Engine mount. 1981—83 right side

| A | 54 N•m (40 FT. LBS.) |
| B | 95 N•m (70 FT. LBS.) |

Fig. 2 Front engine mount. 1981—83

A	54 N•m (40 FT. LBS.)
B	68 N•m (50 FT. LBS.)
C	75 N•m (55 FT. LBS.)

Fig. 3 Engine mount. 1981—83 left side Automatic Transaxle

A	54 N•m (40 FT. LBS.)
B	68 N•m (50 FT. LBS.)
C	75 N•m (55 FT. LBS.)

Fig. 4 Engine mount. 1981—83 left side Manual Transaxle

A—28 N•m (250 IN. LBS.)
B—95 N•m (70 FT. LBS.)

STRUT AND 2 SPACERS TURBOCHARGED ENGINE ONLY

Fig. 5 Engine mount. 1984—85 right side shown, 1986 similar

A—95 N•m (70 FT. LBS.)
B—54 N•m (40 FT. LBS.)

Fig. 6 Front engine mount. 1984—85 shown, 1986 similar

ENGINE MOUNTS

NOTE: When positioning the engine on 1981—86 models, check driveshaft length as outlined in the "Front Suspension & Steering Section" under "Driveshaft Length, Adjust." The engine mounts incorporate slotted bolt holes to permit side-to-side positioning of the engine thereby affecting the length of the driveshaft. Failure to properly position engine may result in extensive damage to the engine.

Refer to **Figs. 1 through 8** when replacing the engine mounts.

NOTE: On 1981—83 vehicles, the left engine mount is attached with two types of mounting screws. Two of the three are of the pilot type with extended tips. Extended tip screws must be installed in the proper position, **Fig. 8**. Damage to the shift cover or difficult shifting may occur if the screws are incorrectly installed.

Fig. 7 Engine mount. 1984—85 left side shown, 1986 similar

Fig. 8 Correct positioning of extended tip screws

Fig. 9 Anti roll strut & damper

Fig. 10 Alternator & compressor mounting bracket, replacement. 1981—84

Fig. 11 Accessory & solid mount compressor bracket, replacement. 1985—86

ENGINE
REPLACE

1981—83

1. Disconnect battery ground cable.
2. Scribe alignment marks on hood and hood hinge, then remove hood.
3. Drain cooling system, then disconnect radiator hoses at radiator and engine.
4. Remove radiator and fan shroud, then remove air cleaner.
5. Remove A/C compressor from mounting bracket and position aside with hoses attached, if equipped.
6. Remove power steering pump from mounting bracket and position aside with hoses attached, if equipped.
7. Drain crankcase and remove oil filter.
8. Disconnect wire connectors at alternator, carburetor and engine.
9. Disconnect fuel line, heater hose and accelerator cable.
10. Remove alternator from mounting bracket and position aside.

11. On models equipped with manual transmission, disconnect clutch cable, then remove transmission lower cover.
12. On all models, disconnect exhaust pipe from exhaust manifold, then remove starter motor.
13. On models equipped with automatic transmission, remove transmission case lower cover and place alignment marks on flex plate and torque converter, then remove converter to flex plate attaching screws. Attach a C-clamp to front lower portion of converter housing to retain torque converter in housing when engine is being removed.
14. On all models, install a suitable transmission holding fixture and attach a suitable engine lifting device.
15. Remove right hand inner splash shield, then disconnect ground strap.
16. Remove right hand engine mount to insulator through bolt.
17. Remove transmission case to engine block attaching bolts.

18. Remove front engine mount to bracket bolt, then carefully lift engine from vehicle.
19. Reverse procedure to install.

1984—86

1. Perform steps 1 through 15 for 1981—83 models.
2. Remove long bolt through yoke bracket and insulator.

CAUTION: If insulator screws are to be removed, mark position on side rail for exact reinstallation.

3. Remove transmission case to cylinder block mounting screws.
4. Remove front engine mount screw and nut.
5. On vehicles with manual transmission, remove anti roll strut or damper, **Fig. 9.**
6. On vehicles with manual transmission, remove insulator through bolt from inside wheel house, or the insulator

	TORQUES	
A	54 N•m	40 FT. LBS.
B	41 N•m	30 FT. LBS.

**Fig. 12   Power steering pump &
mounting bracket, replacement**

**Fig. 13   Timing belt cover
removal. 1981—85**

**Fig.14   Timing belt cover
removal. 1986**

**Fig. 15   Crankshaft,
intermediate shaft & camshaft
oil seal removal**

1985—86
1. Disconnect battery ground cable and drain cooling system.
2. On models equipped with turbocharger, remove right engine mount bolt attaching isolator support bracket to engine mount bracket.
3. On all models, remove five side mounting bolts No. 1, 4, 5, 6 and 7, **Fig. 11.**
4. Remove front mounting nut No. 2 and loosen front bolt No. 3, **Fig. 11.**

NOTE: Coolant may leak from No. 3 bolt hole.

5. Rotate solid mount bracket away from engine and slide on stud until free. Front mounting bolt, spacer and strut, if equipped with turbocharger, will be removed with bracket.
6. Reverse procedure to install. Attaching bolts should be tightened in sequence and to specified torque as follows:
   a. Bolt No. 1 to 30 inch lbs.
   b. Nut No. 2 and Bolt No. 3 to 40 ft. lbs.
   c. Bolts No. 1 (second tightening), 4 and 5 to 40 ft. lbs.
   d. Bolts No. 6 and 7 to 40 ft. lbs.

POWER STEERING PUMP MOUNTING BRACKET

1. Remove pump locking screw, **Fig. 12.**
2. Remove pivot bolt and pivot nut, then the drive belt.
3. Remove power steering pump and lay aside.
4. Remove mounting bracket bolts, then the bracket.
5. Reverse procedure to install.

CRANKSHAFT PULLEY & WATER PUMP PULLEY

1. Remove screws retaining water pump pulley to pump shaft.

**Fig. 16   Cranskhaft,
intermediate shaft & camshaft
oil seal installation**

2. Remove bolts retaining crankshaft pulley.
3. Raise and support front of vehicle, then remove right inner splash shield and remove crankshaft pulley.
4. Reverse procedure to install

TIMING BELT COVER

SERVICE BULLETIN: Timing belt tooth skipping on 1981—83 models less A/C may be caused by snow and/or ice being injested into the timing belt area. This condition may happen when operating in very deep snow or during blizzard conditions. A timing cover sealing package, part No. 4293186, should be used to correct this problem.

1. Remove nuts securing cover to cylinder head, **Figs. 13 and 14.**
2. Remove screws securing cover to cylinder head, then remove both halves of timing belt cover.

bracket to transmission screws.
7. On all vehicles, carefully lift engine from vehicle.
8. Reverse procedure to install.

TIMING SPROCKETS & OIL SEALS

ALTERNATOR BELT REMOVAL

1. Disconnect battery ground cable.
2. Loosen alternator locking screw, then loosen adjusting screw and remove belt.
3. Reverse procedure to install.

ALTERNATOR & COMPRESSOR MOUNTING BRACKET

1981—84
For replacement of alternator and compressor mounting bracket refer to **Fig. 10.**

Fig. 17 Aligning crankshaft & intermediate shaft timing marks. 1981—84

Fig. 18 Aligning crankshaft & intermediate shaft timing marks. 1985—86

Fig. 19 Aligning camshaft timing marks

Fig. 20 Camshaft & intermediate shaft sprocket replacement

3. Position a suitable jack under engine, then remove right hand engine mount bolt and raise engine slightly.
4. Loosen timing belt tensioner, then remove timing belt.
5. Reverse procedure to install.

CRANKSHAFT SPROCKET

1. With timing belt removed from engine, remove the crankshaft sprocket bolt.
2. Remove crankshaft sprocket using a suitable puller.

CRANKSHAFT, INTERMEDIATE SHAFT & CAMSHAFT OIL SEAL SERVICE

Refer to **Figs. 15 and 16** for removal and installation of crankshaft, intermediate shaft or camshaft seals.

NOTE: On late model 1981 2.2L engines, the camshaft oil seals were changed from

steel backed to uni-directional rubber backed type seals. This change made necessary an increase in the cylinder rear seal bore to prevent accidental mixing of the uni-directional front and rear seals.

The replacement seal for early built 2.2L engines will also be rubber backed with arrows indicating the direction of rotation and location in the head marked on the seal. The seals must be installed as indicated.

CRANKSHAFT & INTERMEDIATE SHAFT TIMING

1. Rotate crankshaft and intermediate shaft until markings on sprockets are aligned, **Figs. 17 and 18.**

CAMSHAFT TIMING

1. Rotate camshaft until arrows on hub are aligned with No. 1 camshaft cap to cylinder head line, **Fig. 19.** Small hole must be located along vertical center line.
2. Install timing belt. Refer to "Adjusting Drive Belt Tension" described elsewhere for proper drive belt adjustment.
3. Rotate crankshaft two full revolutions and recheck timing.

NOTE: Do not allow oil or solvents to contact the timing belt since they will deteriorate the rubber and cause tooth skippage.

CAMSHAFT & INTERMEDIATE SHAFT REMOVAI & INSTALLATION

Refer to **Fig. 20** for removal and installation of camshaft and intermediate shaft sprocket.

Fig. 21 Adjusting drive belt tension

ADJUSTING DRIVE BELT TENSION

1. Remove spark plugs then rotate crankshaft to TDC position.
2. Using a suitable tool, loosen tensioner lock nut, **Fig. 21.**
3. Reset belt tension so that belt tensioning tool axis is within 15° of horizontal.
4. Rotate crankshaft two revolutions in clockwise direction and position at TDC, then tighten tensioner lock nut.

BALANCE SHAFTS

The 4-153 engine is equipped with two balance shafts installed in a carrier attached to the lower crankcase.

The shafts are interconnected through gears to rotate in opposite directions. These gears are driven by a short chain from the crankshaft, to rotate at two times crankshaft speed. This counterbalances certain engine reciprocating masses.

Fig. 22   Removing chain cover, guide & tensioner

Fig. 23   Removing drive chain & sprockets

Fig. 24   Setting gear timing

Fig. 25   Setting balance shaft timing

Fig. 26   Adjusting chain tension

SHAFT, REPLACE

1. Remove oil pan, oil pickup, timing belt cover, belt, crankshaft belt sprocket and front crankshaft oil seal retainer.
2. Remove chain cover, guide and tensioner, **Fig. 22.**
3. Remove balance shaft gear and chain sprocket retaining screws and the crankshaft chain sprocket torx screws, then the chain and sprocket assembly, **Fig. 23.**
4. Remove double ended gear cover retaining stud, then the cover and balance shaft gears.
5. Remove carrier rear cover and the balance shafts.
6. Remove six carrier to crankshaft attaching bolts to separate carrier.
7. Reverse procedure to install, then adjust crankshaft to balance shaft timing.

CARRIER ASSEMBLY, REPLACE

NOTE: The gear cover, gears, balance shafts and rear cover will remain intact during carrier removal.

1. Remove chain cover and driven balance shaft chain sprocket screw.
2. Loosen tensioner pivot and adjusting screws, then move driven balance shaft inboard (through) driven chain sprocket. Sprocket will hang in lower chain loop.
3. Remove carrier to crankshaft attaching bolts and the carrier.
4. Reverse procedure to install, then adjust crankshaft to balance shaft timing.

TIMING, ADJUST

1. With balance shafts installed in carrier, position carrier on crankshaft and install six attaching bolts, torquing to 40 ft. lbs.
2. Rotate balance shafts until both shaft keyways are parallel to vertical centerline of engine, then install short hub drive gear on sprocket driven shaft. After installation, gear and balance shaft keyways must face up with gear timing marks meshed as shown, **Fig. 24.**
3. Install gear cover and torque double ended stud/washer fastener to 105 inch lbs.
4. Install crankshaft sprocket and torque socket head torx screws to 130 inch lbs.
5. Rotate crankshaft until number one cylinder is at top dead center (TDC). The timing marks on the chain sprocket should line up with the parting line on the left side of number one main bearing cap, **Fig. 25.**
6. Place chain over crankshaft sprocket so that nickel plated link of chain is over the timing mark on the crankshaft sprocket, **Fig. 25.**

7. Place balance shaft sprocket into timing chain so that timing mark on the sprocket (yellow dot) mates with yellow painted link on chain.
8. With balance shaft keyways at 12 o'clock, slide balance shaft sprocket onto nose of balance shaft. Balance shaft may have to be pushed in slightly to allow for clearance.

NOTE: Balance shaft timing is correct if the timing mark on sprocket, the painted link and the arrow on the side of the gear cover are aligned.

9. If sprockets are timed correctly, install balance shaft bolts, torquing to 250 inch lbs. A wood block placed between crankcase and crankshaft counterbalance will prevent gear rotation.

TENSIONING CHAIN

1. Install chain tensioner loosely assembled.
2. Place a .039 inch thick by 2.75 inch long shim between tensioner and chain, push tensioner and shim up against chain and apply firm pressure directly behind the adjustment slot to take up all slack. Chain must have shoe radius contact as shown, **Fig. 26.**

Fig. 27 Air cleaner box & support, hoses, & throttle body adaptor

Fig. 28 Accelerator linkage & throttle body

Fig. 29 Valve spring, replace

Fig. 30 Cylinder head bolt removal sequence

3. With load applied, tighten top tensioner bolt first, then bottom pivot bolt, torquing both to 105 inch lbs., then remove shim.
4. Position guide on double ended stud, ensuring tab on guide fits into slot on gear cover, then install nut/washer assembly, torquing to 105 inch lbs.
5. Install carrier covers, torquing screws to 105 inch lbs.

INTAKE & EXHAUST MANIFOLD
EXCEPT TURBO

1. Disconnect battery ground cable and drain coolant system.
2. Remove air cleaner and disconnect all vacuum and fuel lines and electrical connectors from carburetor.
3. Disconnect throttle linkage, then remove power steering pump drive belt.
4. Disconnect power brake vacuum hose from manifold, if equipped.
5. Disconnect hoses from water crossover, then raise and support vehicle and disconnect exhaust pipe from exhaust manifold.
6. Remove power steering pump and position aside, then remove intake manifold support bracket.
7. Remove EGR tube, then the intake manifold retaining screws.
8. Lower vehicle and remove intake manifold.
9. Remove exhaust manifold retaining nuts, then the exhaust manifold.
10. Reverse procedure to install.

TURBO

1. Disconnect battery ground cable and drain cooling system.
2. Raise and support vehicle.
3. Disconnect exhaust pipe at articulated joint and disconnect oxygen sensor at electrical connectors.
4. Remove turbocharger to block support bracket.
5. Loosen oil drain back tube connector hose clamps and move tube down on block fitting.
6. Disconnect turbocharger coolant inlet tube at cylinder block and disconnect tube support bracket.
7. Lower vehicle.
8. Remove air cleaner assembly including throttle body adaptor, hose, and air cleaner box with support bracket, **Fig. 27.**
9. Disconnect accelerator linkage, throttle body electrical connector, and vacuum hoses, **Fig. 28.**
10. Remove four bracket to intake manifold screws and two bracket to heat shield retaining clips, then lift and secure fuel rail, with injectors, wiring harness, and fuel lines intact, up out of way.
11. Disconnect turbocharger oil feed line at oil sending unit tee.
12. Disconnect upper radiator hose at thermostat housing.
13. Remove cylinder head with manifolds and turbocharger as an assembly as described under "Cylinder Head & Valve Assembly".
14. Reverse procedure to install.

CYLINDER HEAD & VALVE ASSEMBLY
REMOVING & INSTALLING VALVE SPRINGS
Cylinder Head Off Engine

1. Using suitable tool to hold valves in head, compress valve spring enough to remove and install valve bead locks, **Fig. 29.**

Fig. 31 Cylinder head bolt tightening sequence

Cylinder Head On Engine

1. Rotate crankshaft until piston is at TDC on compression stroke.
2. Apply 90–100 psi. of compressed air into spark plug hole of valve being removed.
3. Using suitable tool, compress valve spring enough to remove valve stem locks.
4. Remove valve spring and spring seat.
5. Remove valve seal.

CYLINDER HEAD BOLT REMOVE SEQUENCE

When removing cylinder head, remove cylinder head bolts in proper sequence, **Fig. 30.**

CYLINDER HEAD BOLT TIGHTENING SEQUENCE

1. Referring to bolt tightening sequence, **Fig. 31,** tighten cylinder head bolts in three steps as follows:
   a. Torque bolts to 30 ft. lbs.
   b. Torque bolts to 45 ft. lbs.
   c. Advance each bolt an additional ¼ turn (90 degrees).

CAMSHAFT BEARING CAPS

1. With caps removed from engine, check oil holes for obstructions.

Fig. 32 Camshaft bearing cap installation

INDENT-ASSEMBLE TOWARD FRONT OF ENGINE

OIL HOLE-ASSEMBLE TOWARD FRONT OF ENGINE

MARK

Fig. 33 Piston & connecting rod assembly. 1981—85

OIL HOLE-ASSEMBLE TOWARD FRONT OF ENGINE

VALVE CUT(S) TOWARDS MANIFOLD SIDE OF ENGINE

MARK

2.2L

2.2L TURBOCHARGED PISTON - DISHED WITH ARROW OR DIMPLE TOWARDS FRONT OF ENGINE

2.5L

DISHED WITH VALVE CUTOUTS

Fig. 34 Piston & connecting rod assembly. 1986

SCREW 23 N•m (200 IN. LBS.)

Fig. 35 Oil pump replacement. 1981—84

TO FILTER CAVITY

MOUNTING SCREWS 23 N•m (200 IN. LBS.)

MACHINED SURFACES (BLOCK AND PUMP INTERFACE.)

PUMP INSTALLATION
INSTALL PUMP FULL DEPTH AND ROTATE BACK AND FORTH SLIGHTLY TO ENSURE POSITIVE FULL SURFACE CONTACT BETWEEN PUMP MOUNTING FACE AND BLOCK MACHINED SURFACES - WHILE CONTINUING TO SUPPORT THE PUMP, INSTALL AND TIGHTEN MOUNTING SCREWS

Fig. 36 Oil pump replacement. 1985—86

STRAIGHT EDGE

FEELER GAUGE

Fig. 37 Measuring oil pump end play

MICROMETER

OUTER ROTOR

Fig. 38 Measuring oil pump outer rotor thickness

FEELER GAUGE

INNER ROTOR

OUTER ROTOR

Fig. 39 Measuring clearance between oil pump rotors

2. With caps aligned in proper sequence, ensure arrow on caps 1, 2, 3 and 4 point toward timing belt, **Fig. 32.**
3. Apply suitable sealant to No. 1 and No. 5 bearing cap.
4. Install caps before installing camshaft seals, then torque cap bolts to 160 inch lbs.

NOTE: Some 1983–84 engines may be equipped with oversize camshaft bearings. Engines with oversize camshaft bearings can be identified by green markings on cylinder head and camshaft at AIR pump side of engine.

VALVE LIFT SPECS.

Engine	Year	Intake	Exhaust
4-135	1981–85	.430	.430

VALVE TIMING
Intake Opens Before TDC

Engine	Year	Degrees
4-135	1981–82	12
	1983	16
	1984–85 exc. Shelby Opt. & Turbocharged	16
	Shelby	10.5
	Turbocharged	10
	1986 exc. Turbocharged	16
	Turbocharged	10
4-153	1986	12

Fig. 40   Measuring oil pump outer rotor clearance

Fig. 41   Measuring oil pump cover clearance

Fig. 42   Section view of Garret-AiResearch T3 type turbocharger

Fig. 43   Turbocharger water cooling system

PISTON & ROD ASSEMBLY

1981-85

When installing the piston and rod assembly, indentation on top of piston must face towards timing belt side of engine, **Fig. 33.** The oil hole on the connecting rod must face timing belt side of engine and be on the same side as the indented mark on the piston.

Connecting rod clearance should be .005—.013 inch.

1986

When installing piston and rod assembly, valve cut must face toward manifold side of engine, **Fig. 34.** Turbocharged engine pistons will have an arrow or dimple toward front of engine. Oil hole on connecting rod must face timing belt side of engine.

Connecting rod clearance should be .005—.013 inch.

ENGINE LUBRICATION SYSTEM

OIL PUMP ASSEMBLY

1981-84

1. With oil pan removed, remove screw securing oil pump to cylinder block, **Fig. 35.**

2. Reverse procedure to install. Torque oil pump attaching screws to 200 inch lbs.

NOTE: The oil pump must fully seat on the cylinder block before the mounting bolts are tightened. Check for proper seating by rotating the pump body on the block. The pump body should move a few degrees in both directions with no further movement into the block. If not, the mating surfaces should be cleaned of any foreign material preventing proper seating, otherwise damage to the oil pump, pump driveshaft and gear, or distributor drive may result.

1985-86

1. With oil pan removed, remove two screws securing oil pump to cylinder block assembly, **Fig. 36.**
2. Apply suitable sealant to pump to block interface.
3. Lubricate oil pump rotor and shaft and the drive gear.
4. Install pump full depth and rotate back and forth slightly to ensure proper positioning and alignment through full surface contact of pump and block machined interface surfaces.

CAUTION: Pump must be held in fully seated position while installing screws.

5. Torque attaching screws to 200 inch lbs.

OIL PUMP SERVICE

1. Measure the following oil pump clearances:
   a. End play, **Fig. 37.** End play should be .001–.006 in on 1981–82 models, .001–.004 in. on 1983–85 models or .001–.004 in. on 1986 models.
   b. Outer rotor thickness, **Fig. 38.** Thickness should be .825 in. minimum on 1981–85 models or .944 in. minimum on 1986 models. Install outer rotor with chamfered edge in pump body.
   c. Clearance between rotors, **Fig. 39,** should be .010 in. maximum on 1981–85 models or .008 in. maximum on 1986 models.
   d. Outer rotor clearance, **Fig. 40.** Clearance should be .014 in. maximum.
   e. Oil pump cover, **Fig. 41.** Clearance should be .015 in. maximum on 1981–82 models or .003 in. maximum on 1983–86 models.
   f. Oil pressure relief valve spring length should be 1.95 in.

WATER PUMP
REPLACE

1. Disconnect battery ground cable.
2. Drain cooling system, and remove upper radiator hose.
3. Remove A/C compressor from mounting brackets and position aside with refrigerant lines attached, if equipped.
4. Remove alternator.
5. Disconnect lower radiator hose, bypass hose and four water pump to engine attaching screws, then remove water pump.
6. Reverse procedure to install.

BELT TENSION DATA

	New	Used
1981–84		
Air Cond.	95	80
Air Pump	GC—	GC—
Alternator	GC115	GC80
Power Steer.	GC95	GC80
1985–86		
Air Cond.	GC105	80
Air Pump	GC—	GC—
Alternator	GC115	GC80
Power Steer.	GC105	GC80

TURBOCHARGER

The turbocharged engine is similar to the standard 4-135 engine. However, many components have been upgraded in order to withstand the more than fifty percent higher power output generated by the turbocharger. This upgrading includes more durable intake and exhaust valve materials, better sealing piston rings, a larger capacity oil pump, select-fit bearings, and a revised camshaft. Dished piston tops are incorporated to lower the compression ratio.

The turbocharged engine integrates a Garrett-AiResearch T-3 center housing and wastegate assembly with a Chrysler built compressor and turbine housing, and exhaust outlet elbow, **Fig. 42.** The wastegate is calibrated to regulate maximum boost pressure at 7.5 psi. Turbo boost begins at 1200 RPM, rises to 7.2 psi at 2050 RPM, and peaks at 7.5 psi at 6000 RPM.

This turbocharger also incorporates a water cooled turbine end shaft bearing which lowers bearing temperatures, especially after a hot shut-off, to increase the durability of the turbocharger, **Fig. 43.**

4-156 Engine Section

ENGINE MOUNTS

NOTE: When positioning the engine on 1981–85 models, check driveshaft length as outlined in the "Front Suspension & Steering Section" under "Driveshaft Length, Adjust." The engine mounts incorporate slotted bolt holes to permit side-to-side positioning of the engine thereby affecting the length of the driveshaft. Failure to properly position engine may result in extensive damage to the engine.

Refer to **Figs. 1 through 5** when replacing the engine mounts.

NOTE: The left engine mount is attached with two types of mounting screws. Two of the three are of the pilot type with extended tips. Extended tip screws must be installed in the proper position, **Fig. 6.** Damage to the shift cover or difficult shifting may occur if the screws are incorrectly installed.

ENGINE
REPLACE

1. Disconnect battery ground cable.
2. Scribe alignment marks on hood and hood hinge, then remove hood.
3. Drain cooling system, then disconnect radiator hoses at radiator and engine.
4. Remove radiator and fan shroud, then remove air cleaner.
5. Remove A/C compressor from mounting bracket and position aside with hoses attached, if equipped.
6. Remove power steering pump from mounting bracket and position aside with hoses attached, if equipped.
7. Drain crankcase and remove oil filter.
8. Disconnect wire connectors at alternator, carburetor and engine.
9. Disconnect fuel line, heater hose and accelerator cable.
10. Remove alternator from mounting bracket and position aside.
11. Disconnect exhaust pipe from exhaust manifold, then remove starter motor.
12. Remove transmission case lower cover and place alignment marks on flex plate and torque converter, then remove converter to flex plate attaching screws. Attach a C-clamp to front lower portion of converter housing to retain torque converter in housing when engine is being removed.
13. Install a suitable transmission holding fixture and attach a suitable engine lifting device.
14. Remove right hand inner splash shield, then disconnect ground strap.
15. Remove right hand engine mount to insulator through bolt.
16. Remove transmission case to engine block attaching bolts.
17. Remove front engine mount to bracket bolt, then carefully lift engine from vehicle.
18. Reverse procedure to install.

A	54 N·m (40 FT. LBS.)
B	28 N·m (250 IN. LBS.)
C	95 N·m (70 FT. LBS.)
D	15 N·m (130 IN. LBS.)

Fig. 1 Engine mount. Right side. 1981–83

Fig. 4 Engine mount. Left side. 1984–85

A-28 N·m (250 IN. LBS.)
B-C★ 102 N·m (75 IN. LBS.)
★CAUTION: NUT "C" MUST BE TIGHTENED BEFORE BOLT "B"

Fig. 2 Engine mount. Right side. 1984–85

| A | 54 N·m (40 FT. LBS.) |
| B | 61 N·m (45 FT. LBS.) |

Fig. 5 Front engine mount

A	54 N·m (40 FT. LBS.)
B	68 N·m (50 FT. LBS.)
C	75 N·m (55 FT. LBS.)

Fig. 3 Engine mount. Left side. 1981–83

Fig. 6 Correct positioning of extended tip screws

TIMING GEARS & OIL SEALS

TIMING CHAIN CASE COVER, REMOVAL

1. Disconnect battery ground cable.
2. Remove alternator locking screw, then loosen jam nut and adjusting screw. Remove drive belt.
3. Remove distributor retaining nut, then remove distributor from cylinder head and position aside.
4. Remove front and rear A/C compressor to bracket attaching screws, then remove A/C compressor and position aside.
5. Remove power steering pump pivot and lock screws, then remove drive belt.
6. Remove power steering pump mounting screw and nut, then position power steering pump aside.
7. Remove power steering pump bracket to engine attaching screws, then remove bracket.
8. Raise vehicle and remove right inner splash shield.
9. Drain crankcase, then remove crankshaft drive pulley.

10. Lower vehicle and position a suitable jack under engine.
11. Remove engine mount to frame side rail through bolt, then remove engine oil dipstick.
12. Remove air cleaner assembly.
13. Disconnect battery ground cable, then the spark plug wires.
14. Disconnect vacuum hoses from cylinder head cover.
15. Remove cylinder head cover screws, then the cylinder head cover.
16. Remove oil pan attaching screws, then remove oil pan.
17. Remove timing indicator plate from timing chain case cover.
18. Remove engine mounting plate from timing chain case cover.
19. Remove cylinder head cover as previously described.
20. Remove two front cylinder head screws. Do not disturb any other cylinder head bolts.
21. Refer to **Fig. 7** and remove remaining screws securing chain case cover to engine.

SILENT SHAFT DRIVE CHAIN, REMOVAL

1. Remove chain case cover as previously described.
2. Remove sprocket screws, then the drive chain, crankshaft sprocket and silent shaft sprocket, **Fig. 8.**

CAMSHAFT DRIVE CHAIN, REMOVAL

1. Remove chain case cover as previously described.
2. Remove camshaft sprocket holder, then the left and right timing chain guides, **Fig. 9.**
3. Depress tensioner to remove drive chain.
4. Remove crankshaft and camshaft sprockets.

CAMSHAFT INSTALLATION

1. With camshaft bearing caps installed, rotate camshaft until timing marks are aligned as shown in **Fig. 10.**

TIMING CHAIN INSTALLATION

1. Install sprocket holder, then left and right chain guides, **Fig. 8.**
2. Rotate crankshaft until No. 1 piston is at TDC on compression stroke.
3. Install tensioner spring assembly onto oil pump body, **Fig. 9.**
4. Install timing chain on camshaft sprocket and crankshaft sprocket. Ensure timing marks are aligned, **Fig. 11.** Timing marks on sprockets are punch marks on the teeth while timing marks on chain are plated links.
5. Align crankshaft sprocket to the crankshaft keyway and slide into place. Align camshaft sprocket dowel hole to camshaft dowel hole.

Timing gears & chain assembly. 1981–84

- 18 N·m (156 IN. LBS.)
- 34 N·m (25 FT. LBS.)
- *SAME—MATCH HUB DIRECTION
- SILENT SHAFT SPROCKET (LOWER*)
- CAMSHAFT SPROCKET
- CRANKSHAFT (SILENT SHAFTS) SPROCKET
- 18 N·m (156 IN. LBS.)
- 18 N·m (156 IN. LBS.)
- 54 N·m (40 FT. LBS.)
- CRANKSHAFT SPROCKET
- 34 N·m (25 FT. LBS.)
- SILENT SHAFT SPROCKET (UPPER*)

Timing gears & chain assembly. 1985

- BOLT "B" 20 N·m (14 FT. LBS.)
- CHAIN GUIDE "B"
- BOLT "A" 9 N·m (1 FT. LBS.)
- WASHER SPRING
- FLANGE BOLTS 18 N·m (156 IN. LBS.)
- FLANGE BOLT (2) 34 N·m (25 FT. LBS.)
- SILENT SHAFT "B" SPROCKETS (SAME, MATCH HUB DIRECTION)
- SPACER
- CHAIN "B"
- CHAIN GUIDE "C"
- CRANKSHAFT (SILENT SHAFT) SPROCKET
- FLANGE BOLTS 18 N·m (156 IN. LBS.)
- CHAIN GUIDE
- DISTRIBUTOR GEAR
- CAMSHAFT SPROCKET
- SPRING PIN
- LOOSE SIDE GUIDE
- 54 N·m (40 FT. LBS.)
- SPROCKET HOLDER
- SPRING
- RUBBER WASHER
- FLANGE BOLT (2)
- TENSIONER
- TIMING CHAIN
- CRANKSHAFT SPROCKET
- TENSION GUIDE
- FLANGE BOLT

Fig. 7 Chain case cover removal

- BOLT 18 N·m (160 IN. LBS.)
- CHAIN CASE COVER GASKET
- GASKET
- COVER
- SCREW
- BOLT 18 N·m (160 IN. LBS.)
- SEAL
- BOLT 18 N·m (160 IN. LBS.)
- CHAIN CASE COVER

Fig. 8 Silent shaft drive chain, replace

- CHAIN GUIDE C
- CHAIN GUIDE B
- SPROCKET B
- SPROCKET B
- CHAIN B
- CHAIN GUIDE A

Fig. 9 Camshaft drive chain, replace

- DISTRIBUTOR DRIVE GEAR
- LOCATING DOWEL
- CAMSHAFT SPROCKET
- CAMSHAFT SPROCKET HOLDER
- WASHER
- SCREW
- TENSIONER
- SCREW 54 N·m (40 FT. LBS.)
- CRANKSHAFT SPROCKET
- SCREW
- DRIVE CHAIN
- CHAIN GUIDE

6. Install dowel pin, then the distributor drive gear. Install sprocket screw onto camshaft and torque to 40 ft. lbs.

SILENT SHAFT CHAIN INSTALLATION & ADJUSTMENT

1. Install silent shaft chain drive pulley onto crankshaft.

2. Install silent shaft chain onto oil pump sprocket and silent shaft sprocket, **Fig. 12**.
3. Ensure timing marks are aligned. Timing marks on the sprockets are punch marks on the teeth, while timing marks on the chain are plated links.
4. Align crankshaft sprocket plated link with punch mark on sprocket.
5. Position chain on crankshaft sprocket,

then install oil pump sprocket and silent shaft sprockets on their respective shafts.
6. Install oil pump and silent shaft sprocket screws and torque to 25 ft. lbs.
7. Install three chain guides. Snug tighten retaining bolts.
8. Refer to **Fig. 12** and adjust silent shaft chain tension as follows:

Fig. 10   Camshaft timing mark alignment

Fig. 11   Timing chain installation

Fig. 12   Silent Shaft chain adjustment & installation with engine removed

a. Tighten chain guide "A" mounting screws.

b. Tighten chain guide "C" mounting screws.

c. Shake oil pump and silent shaft sprockets to collect slack at point "P".

d. Adjust position of chain guide "B" so that when the chain is pulled in direction of arrow "F", clearance between chain guide "B" and chain links will be .4–.14 in. Tighten chain guide "B" mounting screws.

9. Install new gasket on chain case, coat gasket with suitable sealant, then install chain case to block and torque attaching screws to 156 in. lbs.

TENSION ADJUSTMENT WITH ENGINE INSTALLED

1. Remove cover over access hole in chain case cover, **Fig. 13.**
2. Loosen bolt "B", **Fig. 13.**
3. Apply pressure by hand on boss indicated in **Fig. 13**, then torque bolt "B" to 160 in. lbs.

CRANKSHAFT, BEARINGS & SILENT SHAFT

REAR OIL SEAL, REPLACE

1. Remove screws attaching crankshaft rear oil seal retainer, then the retainer, **Fig. 14.**
2. Remove separator from retainer, then the oil seal.
3. Install new seal into retainer, then the separator. Ensure oil hole is positioned at separator bottom.

MAIN BEARING CAPS

1. Install main bearing caps in sequence and ensure arrows on caps are pointed in direction of timing chain, **Fig. 15.**

Crankshaft, bearings & silent shaft assembly

Fig. 13 Silent Shaft chain adjustment with engine installed

Fig. 14 Rear oil seal, replace

Fig. 15 Main bearing cap installation

Fig. 16 Oil pump & Silent Shaft, removal

Fig. 17 Piston & Rod assembly

Fig. 18 Piston ring installation

Fig. 19 Installing oil ring side rail

Fig. 20 Piston ring end gap location

OIL PUMP & SILENT SHAFT

1. Refer to **Fig. 16** and remove silent shaft screw, then the silent shaft.
2. Remove oil pump to cylinder block screw, then the oil pump.

SILENT SHAFT CLEARANCES

Before installing silent shaft, measure outer diameter to outer bearing clearance. Clearance should be .0008–.0024 in. (.02–.06mm). Measure inner diameter to inner bearing clearance. Clearance should be .0020–.0035 in. (.05–.09mm).

PISTON & ROD ASSEMBLY

During installation of piston and rod assembly, arrow at top of piston must face toward front of engine (timing chain), **Fig. 17.** Refer to **Fig. 18** for correct piston ring installation and note the following groove clearances:

1. No. 1 upper: .0024–.0039 in. (.06–.10 mm). wear limit: .004 in. (.1 mm).
2. No. 2 intermediate: .0008–.0024 in. (.02–.06 mm). Wear limit: .004 in. (.1 mm).

3. Oil ring upper: .010–.018 in. (.25–.45 mm). Wear limit: .039 in. (.1 mm).
4. Oil ring intermediate: .010–.018 in. (.25–.45 mm). Wear limit: .039 in. (.1 mm).
5. Oil ring side rail: .008–.035 in. (.2–.4 mm) Wear limit: .059 in. (.15 mm). Connecting rod side clearance should be .004–.010 inch.

INSTALLING PISTON RING SIDE RAIL

1. Place one end of side rail between piston ring groove and spacer expander, **Fig. 19.**

3–43

Fig. 21 Cylinder head bolt removal sequence

94 N•m (69 FT. LBS.) COLD ENGINE
103 N•m (75 FT. LBS.) HOT ENGINE

18 N•m (156 IN. LBS.)

Fig. 22 Cylinder head bolt tightening sequence

IDENTIFICATION MARK (CENTER CAP ONLY)
(2: NO. 2, 3: NO. 3, 4: NO. 4)

ROCKER SHAFT, RIGHT — ROCKER SHAFT, LEFT

MATING MARK ON THE SHAFT — MATING MARK ON THE SHAFT

MATING MARK ON THE CAP — ARROW INDICATING THE FRONT — MATING MARK ON THE CAP

Fig. 23 Camshaft bearing cap installation

2. Hold end of ring firmly and press downward on portion to be installed until side rail is in position. Do not use a piston ring expander.
3. Install upper side rail first, then the lower side rail.

PISTON RING END GAP LOCATION

1. Position piston ring end gaps as shown in **Fig. 20**.
2. Position oil ring expander gap at least 45° from side rail gaps but not on piston pin center line or in thrust direction.

CYLINDER HEAD & VALVE ASSEMBLY

CYLINDER HEAD, REPLACE

1. Disconnect battery ground cable, then drain cooling system. Disconnect upper radiator hose and heater hoses.
2. Disconnect spark plug wires from

6 N•m (53 IN. LBS.)

12 N•m (105 IN. LBS.)

54 N•m (40 FT. LBS.)

103 N•m (HOT) (76 FT. LBS.)

54 N•m (40 FT. LBS.)

18 N•m (156 IN. LBS.)

Cylinder head & valve assembly

spark plugs, then remove distributor.
3. Remove carburetor to valve cover bracket.
4. Disconnect fuel lines from fuel pump, then remove fuel pump.
5. Remove cylinder head cover bolts, then the cylinder head cover.
6. Disconnect all electrical connectors and vacuum lines from cylinder head.
7. Disconnect throttle linkage from carburetor.
8. Remove water pump belt and pulley.
9. Rotate crankshaft until No. 1 piston is at TDC.
10. Paint a white reference mark on the timing chain in line with the timing mark on camshaft sprocket.
11. Remove camshaft sprocket bolt, sprocket and distributor drive gear.

12. Raise and support vehicle.
13. Disconnect air feed lines.
14. Remove power steering pump and position aside.
15. Disconnect ground strap and remove dipstick tube.
16. Remove exhaust manifold heat shield, then disconnect exhaust pipe from catalytic converter. Lower vehicle.
17. Remove cylinder head bolts in sequence shown in **Fig. 21**.
18. Reverse procedure to install. Refer to cylinder head bolt tightening sequence, **Fig. 22**, tighten cylinder head bolts in three steps as follows:
   a. Torque all bolts except No. 11 to 35 ft. lbs.
   b. Torque all bolts except No. 11 to 69 ft. lbs. on a cold engine or 75 ft. lbs. on a hot engine.

Fig. 24   Rocker arm shaft assembly

Fig. 25   Measuring installed valve spring height

Fig. 26   Adjusting valve clearance

Fig. 27   Adjusting jet valve clearance

Fig. 28   Oil pump gear alignment

c. Torque cylinder head to chain case cover bolts (No. 11) to 156 in. lbs.

CAMSHAFT BEARING CAP

1. Align camshaft bearing caps with arrows pointing toward timing chain, **Fig. 23.** Install caps in numerical order.

ROCKER ARM SHAFT ASSEMBLY

1. Refer to **Fig. 24** and install bolts into front bearing caps.
2. Install wave washers, rocker arms, bearing caps and springs in order shown, **Fig. 24.**
3. Place rocker shaft assembly into position, then rotate camshaft until dowel pin hole is at vertical centerline, **Fig. 10.**
4. Tighten camshaft bearing cap bolts in the following order:
   a. No. 3 cap bolts to 85 inch. lbs.
   b. No. 2 cap bolts to 85 inch. lbs.
   c. No. 4 cap bolts to 85 inch. lbs.
   d. Front cap bolts to 85 inch. lbs.
   e. Rear cap bolts to 85 inch. lbs.
5. Repeat step 4, increasing torque to 175 inch lbs.

INSTALLED VALVE SPRING HEIGHT

1. Measure installed height of valve spring between spring seat and spring retainer, **Fig. 25.** Installed height should be 1.590 in. If height is greater than 1.629 in., replace spring.

VALVE CLEARANCE ADJUSTMENT

NOTE: Check hot torque on cylinder head bolts before performing valve adjustments.

1. With engine at operating temperature, position piston at TDC on compression stroke.
2. Loosen valve adjuster lock nut, then adjust valve clearance by rotating adjusting screw while measuring with a feeler gauge, **Fig. 26.**
3. Valve clearance should be as follows: Intake—.006 in; Exhaust—.010 in.
4. Tighten lock nut securely while holding adjusting screw with screwdriver.

JET VALVE SERVICE

1. Install jet valve assembly into cylinder head.

2. Using suitable socket, torque jet valve to 168 inch lbs., (14 ft. lbs.).

NOTE: Ensure that socket wrench is not tilted with respect to centerline of jet valve as damage to the valve stem may result. Check hot torque on cylinder head bolts before performing jet valve adjustments.

3. With engine at operating temperature, position piston at TDC of compression stroke.
4. Loosen jet valve adjuster lock nut, **Fig. 27.**
5. Proper valve clearance is obtained by rotating adjusting screw while measuring clearance with feeler gauge.
6. Valve clearance should be .006 in.
7. Tighten lock nut securely while holding adjusting screw with screwdriver.

INTAKE MANIFOLD, REPLACE

1. Disconnect battery ground cable and drain coolant system.
2. Disconnect hose between water pump and intake manifold.
3. Disconnect carburetor air horn and position aside.
4. Disconnect carburetor and intake manifold vacuum hoses, throttle linkage, and fuel line.

5. Remove fuel filter and fuel pump and position aside.
Remove mounting nuts and washers securing intake manifold, then the intake manifold.

VALVE LIFT SPECS.

Engine	Year	Intake	Exhaust
4-156	1981–85	.410	.410

VALVE TIMING

INTAKE OPENS BEFORE TDC

Engine	Year	Degrees
4-156	1981–85	25

ENGINE LUBRICATION SYSTEM

OIL PUMP CLEARANCES

Refer to **Fig. 16** and measure the following clearances:

1. Drive gear to body—.0043–.0059 in. (.11–.15 mm).
2. Driven gear end play—.0024–.0047 in. (.06–.10 mm) for 1984–85 models.
3. Driven gear end play—.0024–.0047 in. (.06–.12 mm) for 1981–83 models; .0016–.0039 in. (.04–.10 mm) for 1984–85 models.
4. Drive gear end play—.0016–.0028 in. (.04–.07 mm) for 1981–83 models; .0020–.0043 in. (.05–.11 mm) for 1984–85 models.
5. Drive gear to body clearance—.0043–.0059 in. (.11–.15 mm).
6. Drive gear to bearing—.0008–.0020 in (.02–.05 mm).
7. Relief valve spring length—1.850 in. (47 mm).
8. Relief valve spring load—9.5 lbs. at 1.575 in. (40 mm).

Refer to **Fig. 28** and align mating marks of drive and driven gears, then prime pump with clean oil and install onto engine.

WATER PUMP
REPLACE

1. Disconnect battery ground cable.
2. Drain cooling system.
3. Disconnect radiator hose, bypass hose, and heater hose from water pump.
4. Remove drive pulley shield.
5. Remove locking screw and pivot screws.
6. Remove drive belt and remove water pump from engine.
7. Reverse procedure to install.

Cylinder block, piston & connecting rod assembly

BELT TENSION DATA

	New	Used
1981–85		
Power Steer.	95	80
Alternator	115	80
Air Cond.	115	80

Clutch & Manual Transaxle Section

CLUTCH
ADJUST

1981—86 MODELS W/4-135 ENGINE & 1983—86 MODELS W/4-97 ENGINE

The clutch release cable, **Fig. 1**, on these models cannot be adjusted. When the cable is properly routed, the spring between the clutch pedal and positioner adjuster will hold the clutch cable in the proper position. An adjuster pivot is used to hold release cable in place to ensure complete clutch release when the clutch pedal is depressed.

1980—83 MODELS W/4-105 ENGINE

1. Pull upward on clutch cable at housing attachment, **Fig. 2**.
2. Rotate sleeve downward until sleeve snugly contacts grommet.
3. Rotate sleeve so end of sleeve seats into rectangular groove in grommet.
4. Check for proper operation.

CLUTCH
REPLACE

1981—86 MODELS W/4-135 ENGINE & 1983—86 MODELS W/4-97 ENGINE

1. Remove transaxle as outlined under "Manual Transaxle, Replace" procedure.
2. Mark relationship between clutch cover and flywheel for reference during reassembly, then insert suitable clutch disc aligning tool through clutch disc hub.
3. Gradually loosen clutch cover attaching bolts, then remove pressure plate and cover assembly and disc from flywheel.
4. Remove clutch release shaft and slide release bearing assembly off input shaft seal retainer. Remove fork from release bearing thrust plate.
5. Reverse procedure to install. Align reference marks made during disassembly, then using a clutch disc alignment tool, install disc, plate and cover to flywheel. Refer to **Figs. 3 and 4** for torque specifications.

1980—83 MODELS W/4-105 ENGINE

Removal

1. Remove transaxle as outlined under "Manual Transaxle, Replace" procedure.
2. Gradually loosen and remove bolts attaching flywheel to pressure plate.
3. Remove flywheel and clutch disc, **Fig. 5.**

Fig. 1 Clutch cable routing. 1981—86 models w/4-135 engine & 1983—86 models w/4-97 engine

Fig. 2 Clutch pedal free play adjustment. 1980—83 models w/4-105 engine

4. Remove retaining ring and release plate.
5. Mark position of pressure plate on crankshaft.
6. Gradually loosen and remove bolts attaching pressure plate to flywheel.
7. Remove spacer and pressure plate.

Installation

1. Thoroughly clean surfaces of flywheel and pressure plate with fine sandpaper or crocus cloth. Also, ensure that all oil or grease has been removed.
2. Align marks on pressure plate and crankshaft and install pressure plate and spacer on crankshaft. Install and torque attaching bolts to 55 ft. lbs. (75 Nm).
3. Install release plate and retaining ring.
4. Using tool L-4533 to center clutch disc, **Fig. 6,** install disc and flywheel onto pressure plate. Ensure the drilled mark on flywheel is at the top so the two dowels in the flywheel align the proper holes in the pressure plate.
5. Install and torque flywheel to pressure plate attaching bolts to 15 ft. lbs. (20 Nm).
6. Remove centering tool.
7. Install transaxle and adjust clutch.
8. Check for proper operation.

Fig. 3 Clutch assembly. 1981—86 models w/4-135 engine

Fig. 6 Centering clutch disc. 1980—83 models w/4-105 engine

Fig. 4 Clutch assembly. 1983—86 models w/4-97 engine

Fig. 7 Lock pin removal & installation. 1981—86 models w/4-135 engine & 1983—86 models w/4-97 engine

Fig. 5 Clutch assembly. 1980—83 models w/4-105 engine

Fig. 8 Adjusting rod-type gear shift linkage. 1981—86 models w/4-135 engine & 1983—86 models w/4-97 engine

LET.	TORQUE	
	N•M	IN. LBS.
Ⓐ	28	250
Ⓑ	8	70
Ⓒ	7	60
Ⓓ	3	30

Fig. 9   Cable operated gearshift linkage. 1981—83 models w/4-135 engine

LET.	TORQUE	
	N•m	LBS.
Ⓐ	28	250 IN.
Ⓑ	6	55 IN.
Ⓒ	8	75 IN.
Ⓓ	4	35 IN.
Ⓔ	95	70 FT.

Fig. 10   Cable operated gearshift linkage. 1984—86 models w/4-135 engine

Fig. 11   Cable adjusting pins

Fig. 12   Adjusting selector cable

Fig. 13   Adjusting crossover cable

GEARSHIFT LINKAGE
ADJUST

1981—86 MODELS W/4-135 ENGINE & 1983—86 MODELS W/4-97 ENGINE

Rod Linkage

1. Remove lock pin from transaxle selector shaft housing, **Fig. 7**.
2. Reverse lock pin so long end is facing downward, and insert pin into same threaded hole while pushing selector shaft into selector housing.

3. Raise and support vehicle then loosen clamp bolt that secures gearshift tube to gearshift rod.
4. Check that gearshift connector slides and rotates freely in gearshift tube.
5. Position shifter mechanism connector assembly so that isolator is spaced .050 inch away from upstanding flange, while rib on isolator is aligned fore and aft with hole in blocker bracket. Hold connector isolator in this position and torque clamp bolt on gearshift tube to 170 inch lbs. No significant force should be placed on linkage during this procedure, **Fig. 8**.

6. Lower vehicle, remove lock pin from selector shaft housing and reinstall lock pin in reversed position. Torque pin to 105 in. lbs.
7. Check for proper operation.

1981—86 MODELS W/4-135 ENGINE

Cable Linkage, Figs. 9 & 10

1. Remove lock pin from transaxle selector shaft housing, **Fig. 7**.
2. Reverse lock pin so long end is down, and insert lock pin into same threaded

Fig. 14 Aligning slider & block bracket marks. 1980–83 models w/4-105 engine

Fig. 15 Installing spacer. 1980–83 models w/4-105 engine

Fig. 16 Revised gearshift blocker bracket. 1980–83 models w/4-105 engine

hole while pushing selector shaft in 1–2 neutral position.

3. Remove gearshift knob, retaining nut and pull-up ring.
4. On all models except 1984–86 Daytona and Laser, remove console attaching screws and the console.
5. On 1984–86 Daytona and Laser models, remove console as follows:
   a. Remove front seat assemblies.
   b. Remove 2 forward console bezel attaching screws and the bezel.
   c. Remove carpet retaining clips from console.
   d. Remove console attaching bolts and screws.
   e. Disconnect electrical connectors from console, then remove console from vehicle.
6. On all models, fabricate 2 cable adjusting pins as shown in **Fig. 11.**
7. Adjust selector cable and torque adjusting screw to 60 inch lbs. (7 Nm) on 1981–83 models, or 55 inch lbs. (6 Nm) on 1984–86 models, **Fig. 12.**

NOTE: The selector cable adjusting screw must be properly torqued.

8. Adjust crossover cable and torque adjusting screw to 60 inch lbs. (7 Nm) on 1981–83 models, or 55 inch lbs. (6 Nm) on 1984–86 models, **Fig. 13.**

NOTE: The crossover cable adjusting screw must be properly torqued.

9. Remove lock pin from selector shaft housing and reinstall lock pin so long end is up in selector shaft housing, **Fig. 7.**
10. Check for proper operation and reinstall console, pull-up ring, retaining nut and gearshift knob.

1980–83 MODELS W/4-105 ENGINE

1. Place shift lever in neutral at 3-4 position.
2. Loosen shift tube clamp.

Fig. 17 Removing anti-rotational link

3. Align tab on slider with hole in blocker bracket, **Fig. 14.**
4. Install a ½ inch spacer, **Fig. 15,** to set gearshift unit lock-out.

NOTE: If the blocker bracket has a ⅝ stamp imprint at the forward vertical face of the reinforcement strap, **Fig. 16,** it indicates that a ⅝ inch spacer must be used in place of the ½ inch spacer.

5. Tighten shift tube clamp and remove spacer.
6. Check for proper operation.

MANUAL TRANSAXLE
REPLACE

1981–86 MODELS W/4-135 ENGINE & 1983–86 MODELS

W/4-97 ENGINE

1. Disconnect battery ground cable.
2. Raise and support vehicle and install suitable engine support fixture.
3. Disconnect gearshift linkage and clutch cable from transaxle.
4. Remove front wheel and tire assemblies.

5. Remove left front splash shield, then the impact bracket from transaxle if so equipped.
6. Refer to "Driveshafts, Replace" to disconnect driveshafts.
7. Support transaxle and remove upper clutch housing bolts.
8. Remove left engine mount from transaxle noting location of bolts.
9. Remove anti-rotational link, **Fig. 17.**
10. Remove engine to transaxle toward left side of vehicle until mainshaft clears clutch and lower and remove transaxle.
12. Reverse procedure to install. When installing left engine mount, refer to "Engine mounts" section.

1980–83 MODELS W/4-105 ENGINE

1. Disconnect battery ground cable.
2. Disconnect shift linkage rods, starter wiring and backup lamp switch wiring.
3. Remove starter and disconnect clutch cable.
4. Remove bolt attaching speedometer adapter to transaxle.
5. With speedometer cable housing connected, pull adapter and pinion from transaxle.
6. Raise and support vehicle. Also, support engine with suitable equipment.
7. Disconnect right hand drive shaft and position aside.
8. Remove left hand drive shaft.
9. Remove left splash shield.
10. Drain transaxle fluid.
11. Remove bolts from left engine mount.
12. Remove transaxle to engine attaching nuts and bolts.
13. Slide transaxle toward left side of vehicle until mainshaft clears clutch.
14. Lower and remove transaxle from vehicle.
15. Reverse procedure to install.

Rear Axle, Rear Suspension & Brakes Section

Fig. 1   Parking brake cable & brake tube assemblies. 1981—86 Aries & Reliant; 1982—83 400; 1982—86 LeBaron; 1983—86 New Yorker & 600; 1983-85 E Class & Executive; 1984—86 Daytona & Laser; 1985—86 Caravelle & Lancer; 1985 Town & Country

TORQUE		
Ⓐ	54 N·m	40 FT. LBS.
Ⓑ	108 N·m	80 FT. LBS.
Ⓒ	61 N·m	45 FT. LBS.
Ⓓ	8 N·m	70 IN. LBS.

Fig. 2   Rear axle & suspension assembly. 1981—83 Aries & Reliant; 1982—83 LeBaron & 400; 1983 New Yorker, E Class, Executive & 600

REAR AXLE
REPLACE
EXC. 1980—86 HORIZON, OMNI, 1983—86 CHARGER, TURISMO, & 1986 TOWN & COUNTRY

1. Raise and support vehicle, support rear axle, and remove rear wheels.
2. Disconnect parking brake cable at connector and cable housing at floor pan bracket, **Fig. 1**.
3. Disconnect brake tube assembly from brake line on trailing arm support bracket, and remove lock.
4. On 1986 models equipped with automatic load leveling, disconnect link from sensor to track bar.
5. Disconnect shock absorbers and track bar at rear axle. Support track bar end.
6. Lower axle until spring and isolator assemblies, **Figs. 2, 3 and 4**, come free and can be removed.
7. Support pivot ends of trailing arms and remove pivot bracket bolts. Lower and remove axle from vehicle.
8. Reverse procedure to install. Torque brake tube assembly to hose fitting to 140 inch lbs. Torque other components as shown in **Figs. 2, 3 and 4**.

1980—86 HORIZON & OMNI & 1983—86 CHARGER & TURISMO

1. Raise and support vehicle.
2. Remove wheels.
3. Removing brake fitting and retaining clips securing flexible brake line.
4. Remove parking brake cable adjusting connection nut.

5. Release parking brake cables from bracket by slipping ball-end of cables through brake connectors.
6. Pull parking brake cable through bracket.
7. Remove brake drums.
8. Remove brake assembly and spindle retaining bolts, **Fig. 5**.
9. Position spindle aside using a piece of wire.
10. Support axle and suspension with a suitable jack.
11. Remove shock absorber mounting bolts.
12. Remove trailing arm to hanger bracket mounting bolt.
13. Lower rear axle from vehicle.
14. Reverse procedure to install.

SHOCK ABSORBER & COIL SPRING
REPLACE
EXC. 1980—86 HORIZON, OMNI, 1983—86 CHARGER, TURISMO, & 1986 TOWN & COUNTRY

Removal
1. Raise and support vehicle.
2. Support axle assembly and remove both upper and lower shock absorber

attaching bolts and the shock absorbers. On 1986 models equipped with automatic load leveling, remove link from track bar to sensor.
3. Lower axle assembly until spring and spring upper isolater can be removed, **Figs. 2, 3 and 4**.

Installation
1. Position jounce bumper to rail, install and torque attaching screws to 70 in. lbs. (7Nm).
2. Install isolator over jounce bumper and install spring.
3. Raise axle and install shock absorber. Loosely assemble lower shock absorber attaching bolts and torque upper attaching bolts to 40 ft. lbs. On 1986 models with load leveling, attach link to track bar
4. With suspension supporting vehicle, torque shock absorber attaching screws to 40 ft. lbs. (54 Nm.).

1980—86 HORIZON & OMNI; 1983—86 CHARGER & TURISMO

Replacement
1. Remove upper shock absorber mounting protective cap, located inside vehicle at upper rear wheel well area.

CHRYSLER CORP.—Front Wheel Drive

NOTE: On two door models, it is necessary to remove the lower rear quarter trim panel for access.

2. Remove upper shock absorber mounting nut, isolator retainer and upper isolator, **Fig. 5.**
3. Raise and support vehicle.
4. Remove shock absorber lower mounting bolt.
5. Remove shock absorber and coil spring assembly from vehicle.
6. Reverse procedure to install.

Service
1. Install coil spring retractors, tool L-4514, or equivalent, on coil spring and support in a vise, **Fig. 6.** Grip 4 or 5 coils of the spring in the retractors. Also, do not extend retractors more than 9¼ inches.
2. Tighten retractors evenly until spring pressure is released from upper spring seat.
3. Hold flat end of push rod and loosen retaining nut.

CAUTION: Ensure that spring is properly compressed before loosening retaining nut since personal injury may result.

4. Remove lower isolator, push rod sleeve and upper spring seat.
5. Remove shock absorber from coil spring.
6. Remove jounce bumper and dust shield from push rod, **Fig. 7.**
7. Remove lower spring seat. **Fig. 7.**
8. Reverse procedure to assemble.

REAR WHEEL ALIGNMENT

Due to the design of the rear suspension and the incorporation of stub axles or wheel spindles, it is possible to adjust the camber and toe of the rear wheels on these vehicles. Adjustment is controlled by adding shims approximately .010 inch thick between the spindle mounting surface and spindle mounting plate. The amount of adjustment is approximately 0° 18' per shim. Refer to **Figs. 8 through 11** for proper placement of the shims.

REAR WHEEL BEARING
ADJUST
1. Torque adjusting nut to 270 inch lbs. (30 Nm) while rotating wheel.
2. Stop wheel and loosen adjusting nut, **Fig. 12.**
3. Tighten adjusting nut finger tight. End play should be .001–.003 inch.
4. Install castle lock with slots aligned with cotter pin hole.
5. Install cotter pin and grease cap.

TORQUE		
A	40 FT. LBS.	54 N·m
B	50 FT. LBS.	68 N·m
C	55 FT. LBS.	75 N·m
D	70 IN. LBS.	8 N·m

Fig. 3 Rear axle & suspension assembly. 1984–85 Aries, Reliant, Daytona, Laser, New Yorker, Caravelle, Lancer, LeBaron & 600; 1985 Executive & Town & Country

TORQUE		
A	40 FT. LBS.	54 N·m
B	45 FT. LBS.	61 N·m
C	55 FT. LBS.	75 N·m
D	70 IN. LBS.	8 N·m
E	70 FT. LBS.	95 N·m

Fig. 4 Rear axle & suspension assembly. 1986 Aries, Reliant, Daytona, Laser, New Yorker, Carvelle, Lancer, Lebaron, 600 & Town & Country

3–52

LET	TORQUE	
Ⓐ	20 FT LBS	27 N·m
Ⓑ	40 FT LBS	54 N·m
Ⓒ	45 FT LBS	61 N·m
Ⓓ	80 FT LBS	108 N·m

Fig. 5 Rear axle & suspension assembly. 1980—86 Horizon & Omni; 1983—86 Charger & Turismo

Fig. 6 Retracting coil spring

Fig. 7 Jounce bumper, dust shield & lower spring seat replacement

Fig. 8 Shim installation for toe-out

Fig. 9 Shim installation for toe-in

Fig. 10 Shim installation for positive camber

SERVICE BRAKES
ADJUST

The rear brakes on 1983—86 models are self-adjusting and no adjustment is necessary. On 1980—82 models, the rear brakes are not self-adjusting and periodic adjustment is required as follows:

1. Raise and support vehicle.
2. Remove adjusting hole covers from brake supports.
3. Release parking brake and back off cable adjustment to slacken cable.
4. Insert a narrow screwdriver into adjusting nut hole. Move screwdriver handle downward on left side or upward on right side until wheels are locked, **Fig. 13.**
5. Back off nut 10 clicks.
6. Adjust parking brake.

PARKING BRAKE
ADJUST

1. Raise and support vehicle.
2. Release parking brake and back off adjustment to slacken cable.
3. Tighten cable adjusting nut until a slight drag is obtained while rotating wheels.

Fig. 11 Shim installation for negative camber

Fig. 12   Wheel bearing assembly

4. Loosen cable adjusting nut until the wheels rotate freely, then an additional two turns.
5. Apply and release parking brake to check for proper operation. The rear wheels should rotate without dragging.

MASTER CYLINDER
REPLACE
MANUAL BRAKES

1. Disconnect and plug brake tubes from master cylinder. Cap master cylinder ports.
2. Disconnect stop lamp switch mounting bracket from beneath instrument panel.

3. Pull brake pedal rearward to disengage push rod from master cylinder.

NOTE: Pulling the brake pedal rearward will destroy the grommet. Install a new grommet when installing the push rod.

4. Remove master cylinder attaching nuts.
5. Remove master cylinder from vehicle.
6. Reverse procedure to install.

POWER BRAKES

1. Disconnect and plug brake tubes from master cylinder. Cap master cylinder ports.
2. Remove master cylinder attaching nuts.
3. Remove master cylinder from power brake unit.
4. Reverse procedure to install.

POWER BRAKE UNIT
REPLACE

1. Remove master cylinder attaching nuts, slide master cylinder from mounting studs and support on fender shield. Do not disconnect brake tubes from master cylinder.

Fig. 13   Adjusting service brakes

2. Remove clutch cable mounting bracket, if equipped.
3. Disconnect vacuum hose from power brake unit.
4. From beneath instrument panel, install a suitable screwdriver between the center tang on retainer clip and the brake pedal pin. Rotate the screwdriver so the retainer center tang will pass over brake pedal pin. Pull retainer clip from pin.
5. Remove stop light switch and striker plate, if equipped.
6. Remove power brake unit attaching nuts and the power brake unit from vehicle.
7. Reverse procedure to install.

Front Suspension & Steering Section

DESCRIPTION

These vehicles use a MacPherson type front suspension with the vertical shock absorber struts attached to the upper fender reinforcement and the steering knuckle, **Fig. 1.** The lower control arms are attached inboard to a crossmember and outboard to the steering knuckle through a ball joint to provide lower steering knuckle position. During steering maneuvers, the strut and steering knuckle rotate as an assembly.

The drive shafts are attached inboard to the transaxle output drive flanges and outboard to the driven wheel hub.

WHEEL ALIGNMENT

NOTE: Prior to wheel alignment ensure tires are at recommended pressure, are of equal size and have approximately the same wear pattern. Check front wheel and tire assembly for radial runout and inspect lower ball joints and steering linkage for looseness. Check front and rear springs for sagging or damage. Front suspension inspections should be performed on a level floor or alignment rack with fuel tank at capacity and vehicle free of luggage and passenger compartment load.

Fig. 1   Front suspension

Fig. 2 Camber adjustment. 1980—83 All & 1984—86 Charger, Horizon, Omni & Turismo

Fig. 4 Toe-in adjustment

Fig. 3 Camber adjustment. 1984—86 exc. Charger, Horizon, Omni & Turismo

Prior to each alignment reading the vehicle should be bounced an equal number of times from the center of the bumper alternately, first from the rear, then the front, releasing at bottom of down cycle.

CASTER

The caster angle on these vehicles cannot be adjusted.

CAMBER

To adjust camber, loosen the cam and through bolts, **Figs. 2 and 3.** On 1985—86 Lancer and LeBaron GTS, remove rear washer plate and one of the knuckle bolts and replace with a new cam bolt. On all models, rotate cam bolt to move top of wheel in or out to obtain specified camber angle. On all 1980—83 models and 1984—86 Charger, Horizon, Omni and Turismo, torque cam bolt nuts to 45 ft. lbs., then advance nuts an additional ¼ turn. On 1984—86 models except Charger, Horizon, Omni and Turismo, torque nuts to 75 ft. lbs., then advance an additional ¼ turn.

TOE-IN

To adjust toe-in, center the steering wheel and hold in position with a suitable tool. Loosen the tie rod lock nuts and rotate the rod, **Fig. 4,** to adjust toe-in to specifications. Use care not to twist the steering gear rubber boots. Torque the tie rod lock nuts to 55 ft. lbs. (75 Nm). Adjust position of steering gear rubber boots. Remove steering wheel holding tool.

Fig. 5 Strut damper replacement. 1980—83

STRUT DAMPER ASSEMBLY
REPLACE

REMOVAL

1. Raise and support vehicle, then remove front wheels.
2. On all models exc. 1985—86 Lancer

TORQUE 27 N•m (20 FT. LBS.)

TORQUE NUTS TO 61 N•m (45 FT. LBS.) PLUS ¼ TURN

CAM BOLT

WASHER PLATE

KNUCKLE BOLT

Fig. 6   Strut damper replacement. 1984–86 Charger, Horizon, Omni & Turismo

TORQUE 27 N•m (20 FT. LBS.)

TORQUE 13 N•m (10 FT. LBS.)

KNUCKLE BOLT

CAM BOLT

WASHER PLATE

TORQUE NUTS TO 100 N•m (75 FT. LBS.) PLUS ¼ TURN

Fig. 7   Strut damper replacement. 1984 E-Class; 1984–85 Executive; 1984–86 Aries, Daytona, Laser, LeBaron Exc. GTS, New Yorker, Reliant, Town & Country & 600; 1985–86 Caravelle

and LeBaron GTS, mark position of camber adjusting cam for proper alignment during installation.

3. On 1985–86 Lancer and LaBaron GTS, mark outline of strut on knuckle for proper alignment during installation.

4. On all models, remove cam bolt, knuckle bolt or bolts, washer plate and brake hose to damper bracket attaching screw, **Figs. 5 through 8.**

NOTE: On 1985 Lancer and LeBaron GTS, discard one knuckle bolt and washer plate.

5. Remove strut damper to fender shield attaching nut and washer assemblies.
6. Remove strut damper from vehicle.

INSTALLATION

1. Position strut assembly into fender reinforcement, then install retaining nuts and washers and torque to 20 ft. lbs.
2. Position steering knuckle and washer plate to strut, then install upper cam and lower through bolts.

NOTE: On 1985 Lancer and LeBaron GTS, replace one knuckle bolt with a new cam bolt.

3. Install brake hose retainer on damper, then index alignment marks made during removal.
4. Position a 4 inch or larger C-clamp on steering knuckle and strut, **Fig. 9,** then tighten clamp just enough to eliminate any looseness between strut and

TORQUE 27 N•m (20 FT. LBS.)

KNUCKLE BOLT

WASHER PLATE

TORQUE 13 N•m (10 FT. LBS.)

WASHER PLATE

TORQUE NUTS TO 100 N•m (75 FT. LBS.) PLUS ¼ TURN

Fig. 8   Strut damper replacement. 1985–86 Lancer & LeBaron GTS

knuckle. Check alignment of marks made during removal. On all 1980–83 models and 1984–86 Charger, Horizon, Omni and Turismo, torque cam bolt nuts to 45 ft. lbs., then advance nuts an additional ¼ turn. On 1984–86 models except Charger, Horizon, Omni and Turismo, torque nuts to 75 ft. lbs., then advance an additional ¼ turn.

5. Remove C-clamp, then install wheel and tire assembly.

Fig. 9 Strut damper installation

Fig. 10 Strut damper assembly. 1980–83

COIL SPRING
REPLACE

1. Remove strut damper assembly as outlined previously.
2. Using a suitable tool, compress coil spring.
3. Remove strut rod nut while holding strut rod to prevent rotation.
4. Remove the mount assembly, **Figs. 10 through 12.**
5. Remove coil spring from strut damper.
6. Inspect mount assembly for deterioration of rubber isolator, retainers for cracks and distortion and bearings for binding.
7. Install the bumper dust shield assembly.
8. Install spring and seat, upper spring retainer, bearing and spacer, mount assembly and the rebound bumper, retainer and rod nut upper.

NOTE: On all 1980–83 models and 1984–86 exc. Charger, Horizon, Omni and Turismo, position the spring upper retainer tab or notch parallel to the damper lower attaching bracket, **Fig. 13.** On 1984–86 Charger, Horizon, Omni and Turismo, position the spring upper retainer tab 180° to the damper lower attaching bracket, **Fig. 14.**

9. Torque strut rod nut to 60 ft. lbs. (81 Nm). Do not release spring compressor before torquing nut.
10. Remove spring compressor.

BALL JOINTS

The lower control arm ball joints operate with no free play. On 1980 models, the ball joints are bolted to the lower control arm. On these models, the ball joint can be replaced without replacing the entire lower control arm. When installing ball joint to lower control arm, tighten attaching bolt to 60 ft. lbs. On 1981–86 models, the ball joint is pressed into the lower control arm. On these models, the ball joint can be pressed from the lower control arm using a 1¹⁄₁₆ inch deep socket and tool No. C-4699-2. When pressing ball joint into lower control arm, use tool Nos. C-4699-1 and C-4699-2. Install ball joint seal using a 1½ socket and tool No. C-4699-2.

NOTE: On some models the ball joint is welded to the lower control arm. On these models the ball joint and lower control arm must be replaced as an assembly.

Fig. 11 Strut damper assembly. 1984–86 Charger, Horizon, Omni & Turismo

Fig. 12 Dual path strut damper assembly. Exc. 1984–86 Charger, Horizon, Omni & Turismo

Fig. 13 Spring seat & retainer position. 1980—83 models & 1984—86 Exc. Charger, Horizon, Omni & Turismo

Fig. 14 Spring seat & retainer position. 1984—86 Charger, Horizon, Omni & Turismo

CHECKING BALL JOINTS

1981—86

With weight of vehicle resting on wheel and tire assembly, attempt to move grease fitting with fingers, **Fig. 15.** Do not use a tool or added force to attempt to move grease fitting. If grease fitting moves freely, then ball joint is worn and should be replaced.

1980

1. Raise and support vehicle.
2. With suspension in full rebound position, attach a dial indicator to lower control arm with the plunger resting against steering knuckle leg, **Fig. 16.**
3. Place a pry bar on top of the ball joint housing to lower control arm bolt with tip of bar under the steering knuckle leg.
4. With the pry bar, raise and lower the steering knuckle to measure the axial travel.
5. If measurement is .050 inch or greater, the ball joint should be replaced.

LOWER CONTROL ARM

REPLACE

REMOVAL

1. Raise and support vehicle.
2. Remove the front inner pivot through bolt, the rear stub strut nut, retainer and bushing and the ball joint to steering knuckle clamp bolt, **Figs. 17 and 18.**
3. Separate the ball joint from the steering knuckle by prying between the ball stud retainer and the lower control arm.

NOTE: Pulling the steering knuckle "Out" from vehicle after releasing from ball joint can separate inner C/V joint.

4. Remove sway bar to control arm nut and reinforcement and rotate control arm over sway bar. Remove rear stub strut bushing, sleeve and retainer.

Fig. 15 Checking ball joint for wear. 1981—86

Fig. 16 Checking lower ball joint. 1980

Fig. 17 Lower control arm assembly. 1980

Fig. 18   Lower control assembly. 1981–86

Fig. 20   Hub removal

strut nut to 70 ft. lbs. (94 Nm).

STEERING KNUCKLE
REPLACE

REMOVAL

1. Remove cotter pin and nut lock.
2. Loosen hub nut with brakes applied, **Fig. 19.**

NOTE: The nub and driveshaft are splined together through the knuckle (Bearing) and retained by the hub nut.

3. Raise and support vehicle, then remove front wheel.
4. Remove hub nut. Ensure that the splined driveshaft is free to separate from spline in hub during knuckle removal. A pulling force on the shaft can separate the inner C/V joint. Tap lightly with a brass drift, if required.
5. Disconnect the tie rod end from steering arm with a suitable puller.
6. Disconnect brake hose retainer from strut damper.
7. Remove clamp bolt securing ball joint stud into steering knuckle and brake caliper adapter screw and washer assemblies.
8. Support caliper with a piece of wire. Do not hang by brake hose.
9. Remove rotor.
10. Mark position of camber cam upper adjusting bolt and loosen both bolts.
11. Support steering knuckle and remove cam adjusting and through bolts. Move upper knuckle "Leg" from strut damper bracket and lift knuckle from ball joint stud.

NOTE: Support driveshaft during knuckle removal. Do not permit driveshaft to hang after separating steering knuckle from vehicle.

INSTALLATION

1. Place steering knuckle on lower ball joint stud and the driveshaft through hub.
2. Position upper "Leg" of knuckle into strut damper bracket and install cam and through bolts. Place cam in original position. Place a 4 inch or larger C-clamp on strut and steering knuckle,

Fig. 19   Steering knuckle assembly. 1980–86

INSTALLATION

1. Install retainer, bushing and sleeve on stub strut.
2. Position control arm over sway bar and install rear stub strut and front pivot into crossmember.
3. Install front pivot bolt and loosely assemble nut, **Figs. 17 and 18.**
4. Install stub strut bushing and retainer and loosely assemble nut.
5. Place sway bar bracket stud through control arm and install retainer and nut. Torque nut to 70 ft. lbs. (94 Nm)

on 1980 vehicles, 22 ft. lbs. (30 Nm) on 1981–83 vehicles, or 25 ft. lbs. (34 Nm) on 1984–86 vehicles.
6. Install ball joint stud into steering knuckle, then the clamp bolt. Torque bolt to 50 ft. lbs. (68 Nm) on all 1980–83 vehicles and 1984 Charger, Horizon, Omni and Turismo, or 70 ft. lbs. (94 Nm) on all 1984 models except Charger, Horizon, Omni and Turismo and all 1985–86 models.
7. Lower vehicle and with suspension support vehicle torque front pivot bolt to 105 ft. lbs. (142 Nm) and the stub

then tighten clamp just enough to eliminate looseness between knuckle and strut. Ensure cam alignment marks are aligned. On all 1980–83 models and 1984–86 Charger, Horizon, Omni and Turismo, torque cam bolt nuts to 45 ft. lbs. (61 Nm), then advance nuts an additional ¼ turn. On 1984–86 models except Charger, Horizon, Omni and Turismo, torque nuts to 75 ft. lbs. (100 Nm), then advance an additional ¼ turn.

3. Install and torque ball joint to steering knuckle clamp bolt to 50 ft. lbs. (68 Nm) on all 1983 models and 1984 Charger, Horizon, Omni and Turismo, or 70 ft. lbs. (95 Nm) on 1984 models except Charger, Horizon, Omni and Turismo and all 1985–86 models.
4. Install tie rod end into steering arm and torque nut to 35 ft. lbs. (47 Nm). Install cotter pin.
5. Install rotor.
6. Install caliper over rotor and position adapter to steering knuckle. Install adapter to knuckle bolts and torque to 85 ft. lbs. (115 Nm) on 1980–82 models, or 160 ft. lbs (216 Nm) on 1983–85 models.
7. Attach brake hose retainer to strut damper and torque screw to 10 ft. lbs. (13 Nm).
8. Install washer and hub nut.
9. Torque hub nut to 180 ft. lbs. (245 Nm) with brakes applied.
10. Install nut lock and new cotter pin.

HUB & BEARING
REPLACE

NOTE: If 1980 Horizon and Omni models show premature wheel bearing failures, an improperly grounded engine may be the cause. When this problem is encountered, a high pitch whining noise will be emitted from the bearing and the bearing outer race and bearing balls will appear black due to arcing across the race. Also a wear pattern will be indicated on the outer surface of the bearing race. Check for the following proper ground conditions: battery ground cable to transmission mounting bolt, battery ground cable to body ground, braided strap from right hand motor mount to frame side rail and braided strap from right rear of engine to firewall. If all ground cables and straps are properly installed, check for a broken or separated battery ground cable or body ground cable and replace as necessary. After correcting the improper engine ground condition, replace wheel bearing and race.

SERVICE BULLETIN: On 1984 Models except Charger, Horizon, Omni and Turismo there are two designs or types of front knuckle/hub bearings used, tapered roller or ball bearing design. It is possible to have either or both types of bearings on the same vehicle. No functional problems result from a mixed bearing condition, however, a service problem may arise as a result of the different characteristics of these bearings.

If there is movement noted on one or both wheels but no bearing noise, measure movement at wheel outer rim diameter with a dial gauge. The maximum allowable movement on a 13 inch wheel at the rim lip is .020 inch, on a 14 inch wheel .023 inch and .025 inch on a 15 inch wheel. Do not replace bearings for looseness if the movement is as specified. Also do not over torque the axle retaining nut beyond 180 ft. lbs. to minimize bearing free play.

Fig. 21   Sway bar assembly. 1980–81

Fig. 22   Sway bar assembly. 1982–83. (1984–86 similar)

REMOVAL

1. Remove steering knuckle as described under "Steering Knuckle, Replace."
2. Remove hub from bearing using tool No. C-4811 or equivalent, **Fig. 20.**

NOTE: Back out three bearing attaching screws from knuckle until hub is unseated.

Fig. 23 Driveshaft identification

Labels in figure: EXPOSED BOOT RETENTION COLLAR; ONE PIECE "TRIPLE RAIL" EXTRUSION; A.C.I.; INNER BOOT; ANGLE; OUTER BOOT; RADIUS; THREE PIECE CONSTRUCTION; G.K.N.; WELDED CONSTRUCTION; CITROEN; INNER BOOT; ANGLE; OUTER BOOT; ANGLE; ONE PIECE EXTRUSION; S.S.G.

Also install adapter screw into rear attaching screw threads and place thrust button inside hub bore.

3. Remove three screws and bearing retainer from knuckle.
4. Pry bearing seal from machined recess in knuckle.
5. Press bearing out of knuckle using tool No. C-4811 or equivalent.

INSTALLATION

1. Press new bearing into knuckle using tool No. C-4811 or equivalent.
2. On 1980–83 models, install brake dust shield.
3. On all models, install new seal and bearing retainer. Torque retainer screws to 20 ft. lbs. (27 Nm).
4. Press hub into bearing using tool No. C-4811 or equivalent.
5. Install new bearing seal using tool No. C-4698 or equivalent.

SERVICE BULLETIN: A new front wheel bearing seal is available for 1980 Omni and Horizon that replaces the original slinger assembly. The new seal assembly should be installed in place of the original slinger any time a bearing or outer CV joint is serviced. The sealing surface must be thoroughly cleaned. The seal and knuckle contact surfaces must be packed with Mopar Multi Mileage Grease or equivalent.

SWAY BAR
REPLACE

REMOVAL

1. Raise and support front of vehicle.
2. On 1980–81 models, remove end bushing to control arm nut and reinforcement plate, **Fig. 21.** On 1982–86 models, remove nuts, bolts and retainer at control arm, **Fig. 22.**
3. On 1980–81 models, remove sway bar to crossmember linkage (nut, retainer and insulators at top of crossmember). Bushing are permanently installed on sway bars. On 1982–86 models, remove bolts at crossmember clamps, then remove clamps.
4. Remove sway bar.

NOTE: On 1980–81 models it may be necessary to disassemble the intermediate linkage.

INSTALLATION

NOTE: 1982–86 vehicles have a linkless sway bar in the front suspension. The new sway bar is nearly symmetric looking and it is possible to install the sway bar improperly in the vehicle when it is removed for service. Always mark the sway bar prior to removal to assure proper installation. Sway bars used for production and service replacement are marked on the left (driver side) by a daub or stripe of paint.

Fig. 24 Driveshaft assemblies. 1980

Labels in figure: SHAFT RETAINER; SIDE GEAR; TRIPOD JOINT; DIFFERENTIAL UNIT; STRUT DAMPER; KNUCKLE; AUTOMATIC; MANUAL; HUB; RZEPPA JOINT; BEARING; HUB NUT; TRIPOD JOINT; CONNECTING SHAFT (LEFT); WASHER

Fig. 26 Drive shaft assembly. Late 1982 & 1983—86 except models w/A412 manual transaxle

Fig. 25 Driveshaft assemblies. 1981 & early 1982

1. On 1980–1981 models, loosely assemble intermediate links and straps to sway bar, and sleeve, retainer and isolators to links. On 1982–86 models, position crossmember bushings on bar with curved surface up and split to front of vehicle. Set upper clamps onto crossmember bushings, lift bar assembly into crossmember and install lower clamps and bolts.
2. On 1980–81 models, position link ends through crossmember and install upper isolators, retainers and nut. On 1982–86 models, position retainers at control arms, then insert bolts and install nuts.
3. With lower control arms raised to design height, tighten bolts, **Figs. 21 and 22.** Refer to **Fig. 21** for bolt torques on 1980–81 models. Torque bolts to 22 ft. lbs. (30 Nm) on 1982–83 models, or 25 ft. lbs. (34 Nm) on 1984–86 models.

NOTE: A bushing retainer is not used on 1984–86 models.

DRIVESHAFT IDENTIFICATION

Driveshafts are identified as "A.C.I.", "CITROEN", "G.K.N." or "S.S.G." assemblies, **Fig. 23.** Vehicles can be equipped with any of these assemblies, however they should not be intermixed.

Two different driveshaft systems are used. All 1984–86 turbocharged models use an "equal length" system while all others use an "unequal length" system. The "equal length" system has short solid interconnecting shafts of equal length on the left and right sides. The "unequal length" system has a short solid interconnecting shaft on the left side with a longer tubular interconnecting shaft on the right.

Procedures for installation and removal of driveshafts are essentially the same for all types of assemblies used.

DRIVESHAFTS
REPLACE

1980—83 MODELS W/A412 MANUAL TRANSAXLE
Removal
1. Remove hub nut as outlined under "Steering Knuckle, Replace" procedure.
2. Remove clamp bolt securing ball joint stud into steering knuckle.
3. Separate ball joint stud from steering knuckle.
4. Separate outer C/V joint splined shaft from hub while moving knuckle/hub assembly away from C/V joint, **Figs. 24 and 25.**

NOTE: The separated outer joint and shaft must be supported during inner joint separation from transaxle drive flange. Secure assembly to control arm during next step. Also, the grease slonger must not be bent or damaged during service procedures. Do not attempt to remove, repair or replace.

5. Using a suitable tool or tool L-4550, remove six 8mm allen head screws attaching inner C/V joint to transaxle drive flange. Clean foreign material from C/V joint and drive flange.

NOTE: Remove plastic caps installed over allen head screws.

6. Release outer assembly from control arm.
7. To remove driveshaft assembly, hold both inner and outer housings parallel and rotate outer assembly downward and the inner assembly upward at drive flange.
8. Remove driveshaft from vehicle.

Installation
1. If lubricant was lost during handling, fill C/V joint housing with lubricant, P/N 4131389 or equivalent.
2. Clean grease from joint housing, face, screw holes and transaxle drive flange

prior to installation.
3. Support assembly vertically with inner housing upward.

NOTE: Do not move inner joint in or out during reassembly to drive flange since this movement can force the lubricant from the joint.

4. Position inner housing to drive flange and rotate assembly upward. Locate inner housing in drive flange. Support the outer end of driveshaft, **Fig. 24.** Do not permit assembly to hang.
5. Secure inner C/V joint to drive flange with new allen head screws. Then, using tool L-4550 or equivalent, torque the six screws to 440 inch lbs. (50 Nm). Install plastic caps over allen head screws.

NOTE: Failure to properly torque screws may result in failure during vehicle operation.

6. Push knuckle/hub assembly out and install splined outer C/V joint shaft into hub.
7. Install knuckle assembly on ball joint stud. Install and torque clamp bolt to 50 ft. lbs. (68 Nm).
8. Install washer and hub nut. Torque nut to 180 ft. lbs. (245 Nm). Install nut lock and cotter pin.
9. If, after attaching driveshaft assembly in the vehicle the inboard boot appears collapsed or deformed, vent the inner boot by inserting a round tipped, small diameter rod between the boot and shaft. As venting occurs, the boot will return to the normal shape.

NOTE: After installation of driveshaft, check the driveshaft length as outlined in "Driveshaft Length, Adjust."

EXCEPT 1980—83 MODELS W/A412 MANUAL TRANSAXLE
Removal

NOTE: On 1980–81 and early 1982 mod-

Fig. 27 Speed pinion replacement. Except 1980–83 models w/A412 manual transaxle

Fig. 28 Circlips exposed. 1980–81 & early 1982 models less A412 manual transaxle

Fig. 29 Compressing circlip. 1980–81 & early 1982 models less A412 manual transaxle

Fig. 30 Circlip installation. 1980–81 & early 1982 models less A412 manual transaxle

els, the inboard C/V joints have stub shafts splined into the differential side gears and are retained with circlips, **Figs. 24 and 25.** The circlip "Tangs" are located on a machined surface on the inner end of the stub shafts and are removed and installed with the shaft. On late 1982 & 1983–86 models, the driveshafts are spring loaded and are retained to the side gears by constant spring pressure provided by the spring contained in the C/V joints, **Fig. 26.**

1. On 1980–81 and early 1982 models, drain transaxle differential unit and remove cover.
2. On all models, if removing the right hand driveshaft, the speedometer pinion must be removed prior to driveshaft removal, **Fig. 27.**
3. On 1980–81 and early 1982 models, rotate driveshaft to expose circlip tangs, **Fig. 28.** Using needle nose pliers, compress circlip tangs while prying shaft into side gear splined cavity, **Fig. 29.** The circlip will be compressed in the cavity with the shaft.
4. On all models, remove clamp bolt securing ball joint clamp bolt to steering knuckle, then separate ball joint stud from steering knuckle. Do not damage ball joint or C/V joint boots.
5. Separate outer C/V joint splined shaft from hub by holding C/V housing while moving knuckle/hub assembly away from C/V joint.

NOTE: Do not damage slinger on outer C/V joint. Do not attempt to remove, repair or replace.

6. Support assembly at C/V joint housings and remove by pulling outward on the inner C/V joint housing. Do not pull on the shaft.

NOTE: If removing left hand driveshaft assembly, the removal may be aided by inserting a screwdriver blade between the differential pinion shaft and carefully prying against the end face of stub.

7. Remove driveshaft assembly from vehicle.

Installation

NOTE: On 1980–81 and early 1982 units, install new circlips on inner joint shaft before installation, **Fig. 30.**

1. On 1980–81 and early 1982 units, ensure tang on circlips are aligned with flattened end of shaft before inserting shaft into transaxle. If not, this can cause jamming or component damage.
2. On all models, hold inner joint assembly at housing while aligning and guiding the inner joint spline into transaxle.
3. On 1980–81 and early 1982 units, while holding the inner joint housing, quickly thrust the shaft into the differential. This will complete the lock-up of the driveshaft to the axle side gear.

NOTE: On 1980–81 and early 1982 models, inspect circlip positioning in side gears to verify lock-up.

4. On all models, push knuckle/hub assembly out and install splined outer C/V joint shaft into hub.

5. Install knuckle assembly on ball joint stud.
6. Install clamp bolt. Torque to 50 ft. lbs. (68 Nm) on all 1980–83 models and 1984 Charger, Horizon, Omni and Turismo, or 70 ft. lbs. (95 Nm) on all 1984 models except Charger, Horizon, Omni and Turismo and 1985–86 models.
7. Install speedometer pinion, **Fig. 27.**
8. On 1980–81 and early 1982 models, apply a 1/16 inch bead of silicone sealant, part number 4026070, to differential cover sealing surface and mating surface of transaxle case after both have been properly cleaned and inspected.
9. On 1980–81 and early 1982 models, install differential cover and torque retaining screws to 250 inch lbs. (28 Nm).
10. On all models, fill differential to bottom of filler plug hole with Dexron automatic transmission fluid.
11. On 1980–86 models, install washer and hub nut. Torque hub nut to 180 ft. lbs. (245 Nm). Install nut lock and cotter pin.
12. If, after attaching driveshaft assembly in vehicle the inboard boot appears collapsed or deformed, vent the inner boot by inserting a round tipped, small diameter rod between the boot and shaft. As venting occurs, the boot will return to the normal shape.

NOTE: After installation of driveshaft, check the driveshaft length as outlined in "Driveshaft Length, Adjust."

DRIVESHAFT LENGTH ADJUST

If the vertical bolts on both engine mounts have been loosened, or the vehicle has experienced front structural damage, driveshaft length must be checked.

The engine mounts incorporate slotted bolt holes to permit side-to-side positioning of the engine, thereby affecting the length of the driveshaft. To check driveshaft length proceed as follows.

Fig. 31 Right side driveshaft length. 1981

Fig. 32 Measuring clearance between bushing and support bracket. 1981

1981–82

NOTE: Measuring of the right driveshaft (passenger side) will indicate proper positioning of both sides.

1. Position the vehicle so that the weight of the body is on all four wheels.
2. Using a tape measure or other suitable measuring device, measure direct distance from inner edge of outboard boot to inner edge of inboard boot, **Fig. 31.**
3. If measurement matches length shown in **Fig. 31,** no further action is required. If measurement is not within given range, engine position must be corrected as follows:
   a. Remove load on engine motor mounts by carefully supporting engine and transmission assembly with a floor jack.
   b. Loosen right and left engine mount vertical fasteners and front engine mount bracket to front crossmember bolts.

Fig. 33 Measuring driveshaft. 1983–85

NOTE: The right and left engine mount rubber bushings should be positioned to provide approximately .06–.14 inch clearance between the bushing and the supporting bracket, **Fig. 32.** When bracket movement is required, it will be necessary to obtain proper bushing to bracket clearance as well as proper driveshaft length.

   c. Pry engine right or left as required

to achieve proper driveshaft assembly length. A total of .47 inch is available for driveshaft length adjustment. Insert 3mm thick spacers adjacent to isolator snubber on each side. These spacers must be in place when engine mount fasteners are tightened, **Fig. 32.**
   d. Torque right and left engine mount vertical bolts to 250 inch lbs. and torque front engine mount bolts to 40 ft. lbs.

Body	Engine	Driveshaft Identification			"A" Dimension	
		Type	Side	Tape Color	mm	Inch
CHARGER, HORIZON, OMNI & TURISMO	1.6L/2.2L	G.K.N.	Right	Yellow	498-509	19.6-20.0
			Left	Yellow	240-253	9.5-10.0
		A.C.I.	Right	Red	469-478	18.5-19.0
			Left	Red	208-218	8.2- 8.6
EXC. CHARGER, DAY-TONA, HORIZON, LASER, OMNI & TURISMO	2.2L	G.K.N.	Right	Blue	505-515	19.9-20.3
			Left	Blue	259-277	10.2-10.9
		A.C.I.	Right	Green	477-485	18.8-19.1
			Left	Green	229-244	9.0- 9.6
		G.K.N./A.C.I.	Right	Orange	492-500	19.4-19.7
			Left	Orange	243-258	9.6-10.2
		Citroen	Right	White	480-492	18.9-19.4
			Left	White	238-255	9.4-10.0
	2.6L	G.K.N.	Right	Silver	501-510	19.7-20.1
			Left	Silver	254-269	10.0-10.6
		Citroen	Right	Yellow	480-492	18.9-19.4
			Left	Yellow	238-255	9.4-10.0
EXC. CHARGER, HORIZON, OMNI & TURISMO	2.2L Turbo	G.K.N.	Right	Tan	257-265	10.1-10.4
			Left	Silver	254-269	10.0-10.6
		Citroen	Right	Red	241-251	9.5- 9.9
			Left	Yellow	238-255	9.4-10.0

Fig. 34   Driveshaft length specifications. 1984

Body	Engine	Driveshaft Identification			"A" Dimension	
		Type	Side	Tape Color	mm	Inch
CHARGER, HORIZON, OMNI & TURISMO	1.6L/2.2L	G.K.N.	Right	Yellow	498-509	19.6-20.0
			Left	Yellow	240-253	9.5-10.0
		A.C.I.	Right	Red	469-478	18.5-19.0
			Left	Red	208-218	8.2- 8.6
	2.2L Turbo	Citroen	Right	Orange	211-220	8.3-8.7
			Left	Orange	211-220	8.3-8.7
CHARGER, DAYTONA, HORIZON, LANCER, LASER, LEBARON GTS, OMNI & TURISMO	2.2L	Citroen	Right	Green	465-477	18.3-18.8
			Left	Green	211-220	8.3-8.7
		A.C.I.	Right	Blue	463-472	18.2-18.6
			Left	Blue	204-213	8.0-8.4
EXC. CHARGER, HORIZON, OMNI & TURISMO	2.2L	G.K.N.	Right	Blue	505-515	19.9-20.3
			Left	Blue	259-277	10.2-10.9
		A.C.I.	Right	Green	477-485	18.8-19.1
			Left	Green	229-244	9.0- 9.6
		G.K.N./A.C.I.	Right	Orange	492-500	19.4-19.7
			Left	Orange	243-258	9.6-10.2
		Citroen	Right	White	480-492	18.9-19.4
			Left	White	238-255	9.4-10.0
	2.6L	G.K.N.	Right	Silver	501-510	19.7-20.1
			Left	Silver	254-269	10.0-10.6
		Citroen	Right	Yellow	480-492	18.9-19.4
			Left	Yellow	238-255	9.4-10.0
EXC. CHARGER, HORIZON, OMNI & TURISMO	2.2L Turbo	G.K.N.	Right	Tan	257-265	10.1-10.4
			Left	Silver	254-269	10.0-10.6
		Citroen	Right	Red	241-251	9.5- 9.9
			Left	Yellow	238-255	9.4-10.0

Fig. 35   Driveshaft length specifications. 1985

		Driveshaft Identification			"A" Dimension	
Body	Engine	Type	Side	Tape Color	mm	Inch
CHARGER, HORIZON OMNI & TURISMO	1.6L/2.2L	G.K.N.	Right	Yellow	498-509	19.6-20.0
			Left	Yellow	240-253	9.5-10.0
		A.C.I.	Right	Red	469-478	18.5-19.0
			Left	Red	208-218	8.2- 8.6
	2.2L Turbo	Citroen	Right	Orange	211-220	8.3-8.7
			Left	Orange	211-220	8.3-8.7
CHARGER, DAYTONA, HORIZON, LANCER, LASER, LEBARON GTS, OMNI & TURISMO	2.2L	Citroen	Right	Green	465-477	18.3-18.8
			Left	Green	211-220	8.3-8.7
		A.C.I.	Right	Blue	463-472	18.2-18.6
			Left	Blue	204-213	8.0-8.4
EXC. CHARGER, HORIZON, OMNI & TURISMO	2.2L/2.5L	G.K.N.	Right	Blue	505-515	19.9-20.3
			Left	Blue	259-277	10.2-10.9
		A.C.I.	Right	Green	477-485	18.8-19.1
			Left	Green	229-244	9.0- 9.6
		G.K.N./A.C.I.	Right	Orange	492-500	19.4-19.7
			Left	Orange	243-258	9.6-10.2
		Citroen	Right	White	480-492	18.9-19.4
			Left	White	238-255	9.4-10.0
		S.S.G	Right	Gold	457-469	17.9-18.5
			Left	Gold	216-232	8.5- 9.1
	2.6L	G.K.N.	Right	Silver	501-510	19.7-20.1
			Left	Silver	254-269	10.0-10.6
		Citroen	Right	Yellow	480-492	18.9-19.4
			Left	Yellow	238-255	9.4-10.0
EXC. CHARGER, HORIZON, OMNI, & TURISMO	2.2L Turbo	G.K.N.	Right	Tan	257-265	10.1-10.4
			Left	Silver	254-269	10.0-10.6
		Citroen	Right	Red	241-251	9.5- 9.9
			Left	Yellow	238-255	9.4-10.0

Fig. 36   Driveshaft length specifications. 1986

1983-85

1. Position vehicle with wheels straight ahead and body weight distributed on all 4 tires.
2. Measure direct distance between inner edge of outboard boot to inner edge of inboard boot on both driveshafts, **Fig. 33.**

NOTE: On 1983 models equipped with 4-105 engine and manual transaxle, measure from outer edge of inboard flange.

3. Driveshaft length must be within specifications in chart, **Figs. 34 through 36.** If measurement is not within specifications, engine position must be corrected as follows:
   a. Remove load from engine mounts by carefully supporting engine and transmission assembly with a suitable jack.
   b. Loosen right and left engine mount vertical bolts (1984-85 models, right only) and the front engine mount bracket-to-crossmember attaching bolts.
   c. Pry engine to the right or left as

Fig. 37   Left engine mount adjustment. 1984-86

necessary to bring driveshaft length within specifications.

NOTE: On 1984-85 models, the left engine mount is sleeved over long support bolt and shaft, **Fig. 37,** to provide lateral adjustment whether or not engine weight is removed.

   d. Torque engine mount vertical bolts to 250 inch lbs. and front engine mount bolts to 40 ft. lbs.
   e. On 1984-85 models, center left engine mount.

INNER CONSTANT VELOCITY JOINT SERVICE

1981-86

Disassemble

1. Remove clamp and boot from joint and discard, **Fig. 38.**
2. On Citroen units, separate tripod from housing by slightly deforming retaining ring at three locations, **Fig. 39.** If necessary, cut retaining ring from housing and install replacement retaining ring with inner flange rolled, then stake into machined groove with a suitable punch.

NOTE: When removing tripod from housing, secure rollers. After tripod has been removed, secure assembly with tape.

3. On 1981 and early 1982 G.K.N. non-spring loaded units, slide tripod from housing, **Fig. 40.** On late 1982-86 G.K.N. spring loaded units, bend tabs on joint cover using needle nose pliers, then remove tripod from housing, **Fig. 41.**
4. On 1984 A.C.I. units, position housing so all 3 rollers are flush with retaining

Fig. 38   Driveshaft components. 1981–83 (1984–86 similar)

Fig. 39   Removing 3 ball tripod housing. 1981–86 Citroen inner C/V joint

Fig. 40   Removing 3 ball tripod housing. 1981 & early 1982 G.K.N. inner C/V joint

Fig. 41   Removing 3 ball tripod housing. Late 1982–86 G.K.N. inner C/V joint

Fig. 42   Removing 3 ball tripod housing. 1984 A.C.I. inner C/V joint

Fig. 43   Removing 3 ball tripod housing. 1985–86 A.C.I. inner C/V joint

Fig. 44   Separating tripod from housing. 1986 S.S.G. inner C/V joint

tabs. Pull housing out by hand at a slight angle to pop one roller at a time out of the retaining tabs, **Fig. 42.** Do not hold joint at too severe an angle, as the rollers may be damaged.

NOTE: The retaining tabs must not be bent during removal or installation of the housing.

5. On 1985–86 A.C.I. units, hold housing and lightly compress C/V joint retention spring while bending tabs back

with a pair of pliers, **Fig. 43.** Support housing, then separate tripod from housing.

6. On 1986 S.S.G. units, use flathead screwdriver to pry wire ring out of groove and slide tripod from housing, **Fig. 44.**

CAUTION: When removing the housing

from the tripod, hold the rollers in place on the trunion studs to prevent the rollers and needle bearings from falling out. After tripod is out of housing, secure rollers in place with tape.

7. Remove snap ring from end of shaft, then remove tripod using brass punch.

Fig. 45 Slinger installation. 1984 w/ turbocharged engine

Fig. 46 Driveshaft components. 1980

Fig. 48 Remove snap ring & tripod. Inner C/V joints

Fig. 47 Removing 3-ball tripod, housing & shaft assembly. 1980 inner C/V joints

Inspection

Remove grease from assembly and inspect bearing race and tripod components for wear and damage and replace as necessary. On late 1982–86 spring loaded joints inspect spring, spring cup and sperical end of connecting shaft for wear and damage and replace as necessary.

NOTE: Components of spring loaded and nonspring loaded inner C/V joints cannot be interchanged.

Assemble

1. On 1984 models equipped with turbocharged engine, install a new slinger, **Fig. 45.** Tap slinger down until collar is flush with journal, then on 1984–86 models, slide rubber seal over stub shaft and into groove.
2. On all models, slide small end of boot over shaft. On Tubular type shafts, align boot lip with mark on shaft outer diameter. On solid type shafts, position small end of boot in groove on

shaft.
3. Place rubber clamp over groove on boot.
4. Install tripod on shaft with non-chamfered face of tripod body facing shaft retainer groove.
5. Lock tripod assembly on shaft by installing retaining ring in shaft groove.
6. Distribute two packets of grease provided with boot and clamp kit into boot assembly on G.K.N. units, one packet on A.C.I. units, ⅔ packet on Citroen units or ½ packet on S.S.G. units.
7. On 1981–83 models with 4-105 engine and manual transaxle, install joint housing over tripod, then position large end of boot in groove in housing. Add two additional packets of grease after boot has been secured to housing.
8. On 1981 and early 1982 models less 4-105 engine with manual transaxle, distribute one packet of grease in housing before positioning housing over tripod. On Citroen units, reform retainer ring. On all units, secure boot

to housing with boot clamp.
9. On late 1982 & 1983–86 models less 4-105 engine and manual transaxle, distribute remaining grease supplied into housing. Position spring, with spring cup attached to exposed end, into spring pocket. Place a small amount of grease on spring cup, then position housing over tripod. On Citroen units, reform or replace retainer ring. On G.K.N. units, bend retaining tabs. On 1984 A.C.I. units, align rollers with retaining tabs and housing tracks and pop one roller at a time through the retaining tabs. On 1985–86 A.C.I. units, slide tripod onto housing. On 1986 S.S.G. units, slip tripod into housing and install tripod wire retaining ring into position, ensuring retaining ring retains tripod in housing. Care must be taken to ensure proper spring positioning. The spring must remain centered in the housing spring pocket when the tripod is installed and seated in spring cup.

Do not bend retaining tabs back to original position at this time, the tripod

Fig. 49 Outer C/V joint disassembled. 1981–86

Fig. 50 Outer C/V joint disassembled. 1980

Fig. 51 Removing joint from shaft. Outer C/V joints

Fig. 52 Circlip removal. Outer C/V joints

must be engaged in the housing when driveshaft is installed. On all units, position boot over boot groove in housing, then install clamp.

NOTE: When installing housing, check to insure that spring remains in pocket and centered in housing. Also ensure that spring cup contacts spherical end of connecting shaft.

1980

Disassembly
1. Cut the metal clamps from the boot and discard boot, **Fig. 46.**
2. Remove grease from inside of joint housing and 3-ball and trunion assembly, **Fig. 47.**
3. Remove retaining rings from shaft-end groove, then the tripod with a brass drift, **Fig. 48.**

Inspection
Inspect the joint housing ball raceway and tripod components for excessive wear. Replace if necessary.

Assembly
1. To install new boot, slide small rubber clamp onto shaft, then the small end of boot over the shaft, **Fig. 46.**

NOTE: On tubular shafts, position the boot lip face in line with the mark on the shaft outside diameter. On solid shafts, position the small boot end in the machined groove.

2. Clamp the small boot end by placing the rubber clamp over the boot groove.
3. Install the tripod on the shaft with the non-chamfered face of the tripod body facing the shaft retainer groove.
4. Install the retaining ring in the groove to lock the tripod assembly on the shaft.
5. Distribute two packets of grease in the boot. The packets of proper lubricant are provided in the boot joint kits.
6. On manual driveshafts, install the joint housing over the tripod and position the large end of boot in the groove on the housing. Two additional packets of grease are to be added after the boot is secured to the housing.
7. On automatic driveshafts, position housing over tripod and position boot over housing groove. One additional packet of grease is to be added after securing boot to housing.
8. On all driveshafts, install large metal clamp on boot, ensuring that the boot is properly located on the shaft and is not twisted.
9. Install the clamp tags in the slots and tighten clamp by hand.
10. Clamp bridge with tool C-4124 and squeeze to complete tightening the clamp. Do not cut through the clamp bridge and/or damage the boot.
11. On manual driveshafts, distribute two additional packets of grease in the joint housing. First push forward gently on the housing to provide space to accommodate volume of grease required.

OUTER CONSTANT VELOCITY JOINT SERVICE

DISASSEMBLY
1. Cut boot clamps from boot and discard boot and clamps, **Figs. 49 and 50.**
2. Clean grease from joint.
3. Exc. on S.S.G. units support shaft in a soft jawed vise, support the outer joint

Fig. 53 Ball removal. Outer C/V joints

and tap with a mallet to dislodge joint from internal circlip installed in a groove at the outer end of the shaft, **Fig. 51.** Do not remove slinger from housing.
4. On S.S.G. units, loosen damper weight bolts and slide weight and the boot toward inner joint, then expand circlip with suitable pliers, slide joint from shaft and reinstall damper weight.
5. Remove circlip from shaft groove and discard, **Fig. 52.**
6. Unless the shaft requires replacement, do not remove the heavy lock ring from the shaft, **Fig. 52.**
7. If the constant velocity joint was operating satisfactorily and the grease does not appear contaminated, proceed to "Assembly" procedure, Step 8.
8. If the constant velocity joint is noisy or badly worn, replace entire unit. The repair kit will include boot, clamps, circlip and lubricant. Clean and inspect the joint outlined in the following steps.
9. Clean surplus grease and mark relative position of inner cross, cage and housing with a dab of paint.
10. Hold joint vertically in a soft jawed vise.
11. Press downward on one side of the inner race to tilt cage and remove ball from opposite side, **Fig. 53.** If joint is

Fig. 54 Cage & cross assembly removal. Outer C/V joints

Fig. 55 Removing cross from cage. Outer C/V joints

Fig. 56 Cage & cross assembly. Outer C/V joints

Fig. 57 Compressing circlip. Outer C/V joints

tight, use a hammer and a brass drift to tap inner race. Do not strike the cage. Repeat this step until all six balls are removed. A screwdriver may be used to pry the balls loose.

12. Tilt the cage assembly vertically and position the two opposing, elongated cage windows in area between ball grooves. Remove cage and inner race assembly by pulling upward from the housing, **Fig. 54.**

13. Rotate inner cross 90 degrees to cage and align one of the race spherical lands with an elongated cage window. Raise land into cage window and remove inner race by swinging outward, **Fig. 55.**

INSPECTION

1. Check housing ball races for excessive wear.
2. Check splined shaft and nut threads for damage.
3. Inspect the balls for pitting, cracks, scouring and wear. Dulling of the surface is normal.
4. Inspect cage for excessive wear on inner and outer spherical surfaces, heavy brinelling of cage, window cracks and chipping.

5. Inspect inner race (Cross) for excessive wear or scouring of ball races.
6. If any of the defects listed in Steps 1 through 5, are found, replace the C/V assembly as a unit.

NOTE: Polished areas in races (Cross and housing) and on cage spheres are normal and does not indicate a need for joint replacement unless they are suspected of causing noise and vibration.

ASSEMBLY

1981–84
1. If removed, position wear sleeve on joint housing, then tap sleeve onto housing using tool No. C-4698.
2. Lightly oil components, then align marks made during disassembly.
3. Align one of the inner race lands with elongated window of cage, then insert race into cage and pivot 90°.
4. Align elongated cage windows with housing land, then pivot cage 90°.
5. Lubricate ball races with one packet of grease from kit.
6. Tilt cage and inner race assembly and insert balls.
7. With shaft supported in a soft jawed vise, install boot. On G.K.N. and A.C.I. units, slip small clamp over spacer ring and shaft.
8. Slide small end of boot over spacer ring and shaft, then position boot end in machined groove.

NOTE: On Citroen units, position vent sleeve under boot at clamp area.

9. Install snap ring on shaft. When installing use care not to overexpand snap ring.
10. Position joint housing on shaft, then engage by tapping sharply with a soft faced mallet.
11. Check to ensure that snap ring is properly seated, by attempting to pull joint from shaft.
12. Locate large end of boot over housing.

Fig. 58 Positioning joint into shaft splined. Outer C/V joints

13. On G.K.N. and A.C.I. units, secure boot clamps using tool No. C-4124. On Citroen units, secure boot clamps using tool C-4653.

NOTE: G.K.N. and A.C.I. units use steel clamps, while Citroen units use a strap type clamp.

1980
1. Lightly lubricate all components before assembling joint.
2. Align parts according to paint markings.
3. Insert one inner race (Cross) lands into an elongated cage window and feed race into cage. Pivot cross 90 degrees to complete cage assembly.
4. Align opposite elongated cage windows with housing land and insert cage assembly into housing. Pivot cage 90 degrees to complete installation.

NOTE: When properly assembled, the curved side of the elongated cage windows and the inner cross counterbore should face outward from the joint, **Fig. 56.**

5. Apply lubricant to ball races between all sides of ball grooves.

Fig. 59 Intermediate shaft assembly. 1984–86 turbocharged models

Fig. 60 Removing speedometer pinion from extension housing

6. Insert balls into raceway by tilting cage and inner race assembly. Ensure that locking ring is seated in the groove.
7. To install new boot, slide small metal clamp over lock ring and shaft.
8. Slide end of boot over lock ring and shaft, then position in machined groove.
9. Place small metal clamp over boot groove. Locate clamp tags in slots and hand tighten. Clamp bridge with tool C-4124 and squeeze to complete tightening.
10. Insert new circlip in shaft groove. Do not expand or twist circlip during assembly.
11. Position tool L-4538 on shaft splines with the tapered end outboard and compress circlip, **Fig. 57.** Ensure that sufficient spline area is left ahead of the tool to provide entry of outer joint onto shaft, **Fig. 58.**
12. Place outer joint on splined end, engage splines and rap with a mallet, allowing tool to slide along with the joint.
13. Remove tool and check that circlip is properly seated by attempting to pull joint from shaft.
14. Place large end of boot over joint housing, ensuring that boot is not twisted.
15. Place large metal clamp over boot and locate clamp tags in slots, hand tightening the clamp.
16. Clamp bridge with tool L-4124 and squeeze to complete tightening. Do not cut through clamp bridge and/or damage boot.

INTERMEDIATE SHAFT ASSEMBLY

NOTE: The intermediate shaft assembly, **Fig. 59,** is used on all 1984–86 turbocharged models.

REMOVAL

1. Remove right driveshaft, refer to "Driveshaft, Replace" procedure.
2. Remove speedometer pinion from extension housing, **Fig. 60.**
3. Remove two screws from bearing assembly bracket to engine block, **Fig. 59.**
4. Remove intermediate shaft assembly from transaxle extension by pulling yoke outward.

SUB-ASSEMBLY SERVICE

UNIVERSAL JOINT & ROLLER

Disassemble
1. Mark relationship of shafts to insure proper alignment during assembly. Apply penetrating oil to bushing, then remove snap rings.
2. Support yoke in vise, then position 1⅛ inch socket over bushing on top of yoke.
3. Strike socket with a suitable hammer until bushing moves up out of yoke into socket.
4. Turn assembly in vise and remove remaining bushings in same manner.

Assemble
1. Hold cross in position between yoke ears with one hand and start one bushing assembly into yoke with other hand.
2. Hammer bushing assembly into yoke, then install snap ring.
3. Install remaining bushing assemblies in same manner.

BRACKET, BEARING & SLINGER ASSEMBLY

Disassemble
1. Remove two bearing assembly to support bracket attaching screws, then separate bearing from bracket.
2. Press intermediate shaft out of bearing assembly and outer slinger.

NOTE: Do not dent or damage inner slinger or end of stub shaft.

3. If either slinger is damaged, it should be replaced by carefully pressing shaft through slinger.

NOTE: The bearing assembly is not serviceable and must be replaced as an assembly.

Assemble
1. Place new slinger on stub shaft, then using a suitable tool, drive slinger down until it bottoms out on shoulder of shaft. Ensure slinger is properly seated.
2. Press bearing assembly onto shaft, leaving a minimum of ⅟₃₂ inch (1mm) clearance between slinger and bearing assembly.

NOTE: Apply pressure only to the inner race of the bearing assembly during installation.

3. Press outer slinger into position using a suitable tool. The slinger must bottom out on the shoulder of the shaft.

INSTALLATION

1. Attach bracket loosely to bearing assembly.
2. Hold stub yoke and install spline into transaxle.
3. Attach bracket to engine. Torque attaching screws to 40 ft. lbs. (54 Nm).
4. Push intermediate shaft assembly into transaxle as far as it can travel, then torque bracket to bearing attaching screws to 21 ft. lbs. (28 Nm).
5. Apply suitable grease inside spline and pilot bore on bearing end of intermediate shaft.
6. Install speedometer pinion, then the right drive shaft, refer to "Driveshaft, Replace" procedure.

RACK & PINION STEERING GEAR
REPLACE

NOTE: 1980 vehicles are equipped with manual steering gears supplied by two manufacturers, Burman and Cam Gears. The replacement rubber boots for these gears are not interchangeable.

The Burman gear can be identified by the name "Burman" cast on the housing, and is visible from under the hood.

The Cam Gear steering gear has no identification markings.

1. Raise and support vehicle, then remove front wheels.
2. Remove tie rod ends with a suitable puller.
3. On all models except Omni, Horizon, Charger and Turismo, remove steering column as follows:
   a. Disconnect battery ground cable.
   b. On column shift vehicles, disconnect cable rod by prying rod out of grommet in shift lever.
   c. Disconnect all wiring connectors at steering column jacket and remove steering wheel center pad.
   d. Disconnect horn wires and horn switch, then pull steering wheel from column.
   e. Expose steering column bracket, remove instrument panel steering column cover and lower reinforcement. Remove bezel.
   f. Remove indicator set screw and shaft indicator pointer from shift housing.
   g. Remove nuts attaching steering column bracket to instrument panel support, then lower the bracket support to the floor.

CAUTION: Do not remove roll pin to remove steering column assembly.

   h. Pull steering column rearward, and disconnect lower shaft from coupling.
   i. Reinstall anti-rattle clips into lower coupling tube slot.

   j. Remove column assembly out through passenger compartment, being careful not to damage paint or trim.
   k. Cut plastic grommets from shift levers and install new grommets from rod side of lever using pliers and a backup washer. Apply grease to grommets.
4. On Omni, Horizon, Charger and Turismo, drive out lower roll pin attaching pinion shaft to lower universal joint.
5. On all models except Omni, Horizon, Charger and Turismo, support the front suspension crossmember with a suitable jack, then remove bolts attaching steering gear to front crossmember. Lower crossmember from vehicle frame.
6. On Omni, Horizon, Charger and Turismo, remove 2 rear crossmember nuts and loosen 2 front bolts, then lower crossmember slightly to gain access to boot seal shields.
7. Remove splash shields and boot seal shields.
8. On power steering units, disconnect hoses from steering gear.
9. Disconnect tie rod ends from steering knuckles.
10. Remove gear to front suspension crossmember attaching bolts, then remove gear from left side of engine.
11. Reverse procedure to install. On all models except Omni, Horizon, Charger and Turismo, reinstall steering column as follows:
    a. Align and insert lower stub shaft into coupling, raise column into position and loosely install bracket nuts. Pull column assembly rearward and torque nuts to 105 inch lbs.
    b. With needle nose pliers, pull coupling spring upward until it touches the universal flange.
    c. Snap gearshift rods into grommets.
    d. Readjust gearshift linkage as necessary.
    e. Install steering wheel and torque nut to 60 ft. lbs. except on 1982–86 models. On 1982–86 models, torque nut to 45 ft. lbs.
    f. Install horn switch and horn switch wire.
    g. Connect all wiring connectors at steering column jacket and install steering wheel pad.
    h. Connect battery ground cable and test operation of lights and horn.
    i. On column shift vehicles, connect gearshift indicator pointer to its approximate original location. Slowly move gear shift lever from 1 (low) to park, pausing briefly at each position. The indicator pointer must align with each selector position. If necessary, loosen and readjust pointer correctly.
    j. Install instrument panel steering column cover.

POWER STEERING PUMP
REPLACE

4-97 ENGINE

1. Loosen pressure hose connector at pump.
2. Remove drive belt adjustment nut from top rubber isolator stud, then loosen 3 lock nuts on rear studs.
3. Place a suitable container on top of radiator yoke to catch any spilled fluid.
4. Remove drive belt and 3 lock nuts, then lift pump and bracket assembly from vehicle.
5. Remove pump reservoir cap and drain fluid, then disconnect hoses from pump. Plug pump ports and hose ends to prevent contamination.
6. Reverse procedure to install.

4-105, 135 & 153 ENGINES

1. Remove power steering pump drive belt adjusting bolt and nut, then remove nut attaching pump end hose bracket, if equipped.
2. Raise and support vehicle, then remove nut attaching pump pressure hose locating bracket to crossmember.
3. Disconnect pressure hose from steering gear and allow fluid to drain into a suitable container.
4. Remove drive belt splash shield, then disconnect both pressure and return hoses at power steering pump. Cap hoses and fitting to prevent entry of dirt.
5. Remove lower stud nut and pivot bolt from power steering pump, then lower vehicle.
6. Remove drive belt pulley from pump, then move pump rearward to clear mounting bracket and remove adjusting bracket.
7. Rotate pump so that pulley faces rear of vehicle, then lift pump assembly from vehicle.
8. Reverse procedure to install.

4-156 ENGINE

1. Disconnect pressure and return lines from pump. Cap all lines and fittings.
2. Remove belt adjustment and pivot bolts, then remove drive belt from pulley.
3. Remove power steering pump and mounting bracket as an assembly from vehicle.
4. Reverse procedure to install.

FORD & MERCURY
Full Size Models

NOTE: This chapter includes service procedures for the 1980–82 LTD, Marquis & 1983–86 LTD Crown Victoria & Grand Marquis.

For service procedures on the 1983–86 LTD & Marquis models, refer to the "Ford & Mercury—Compact Intermediate Models Chapter."

Refer to the rear of this manual for vehicle manufacturer's special service tool suppliers.

INDEX OF SERVICE OPERATIONS

Engine & Serial Number Location

Engine code is fifth digit of serial number on 1980 models, or eighth digit of serial number on 1981–86 models. The serial number is stamped on a metal tag located on top left side dash and visible through windshield.

Grille Identification

1980–82 Ford LTD

1980–82 Ford LTD Landau & Country Squire

1980–82 Mercury Marquis

1983–84 Ford LTD Crown Victoria & Country Squire

1983–86 Mercury Grand Marquis

1985–86 Ford LTD Crown Victoria & Country Squire

General Engine Specifications

Year	Engine C.I.D.①/Liter	V.I.N. Code②	Carburetor	Bore and Stroke	Compression Ratio	Net H.P. @ R.P.M.③	Maximum Torque Ft. Lbs. @ R.P.M.	Normal Oil Pressure Pounds
FORD								
1980	V8-302, 5.0L	F	2700VV, 2 Bbl.④	4.00 × 3.00	8.4	130 @ 3600	230 @ 1600	40–60
	V8-351W, 5.8L⑥	G	7200VV, 2 Bbl.④	4.00 × 3.50	8.3	140 @ 3400	265 @ 2000	40–60
	V8-351W, 5.8L H.O. ⑥⑧	G	7200VV, 2 Bbl.④	4.00 × 3.50	8.3	—	—	40–60
1981	V8-255, 4.2L	D	7200VV, 2 Bbl.④	3.68 × 3.00	8.2	120 @ 3400	205 @ 2600	40–60
	V8-302, 5.0L⑦	F	7200VV, 2 Bbl.④	4.00 × 3.00	8.4	130 @ 3400	230 @ 2200	40–60
	V8-302, 5.0L⑤	F	7200VV, 2 Bbl.④	4.00 × 3.00	8.4	130 @ 3400	235 @ 1800	40–60
	V8-351W, 5.8L⑥	G	7200VV, 2 Bbl.④	4.00 × 3.50	8.3	145 @ 3200	270 @ 1800	40–60
	V8-351W, 5.8L H.O. ⑥⑧	G	7200VV, 2 Bbl.④	4.00 × 3.50	8.3	165 @ 3600	285 @ 2200	40–60
1982	V8-255, 4.2L	D	7200VV, 2 Bbl.④	3.68 × 3.00	8.2	122 @ 3400	209 @ 2400	40–60
	V8-302, 5.0L	F	7200VV, 2 Bbl.④	4.00 × 3.00	8.4	132 @ 3400	236 @ 1800	40–60
1983–85	V8-302, 5.0L	F	E.F.I.⑨	4.00 × 3.00	8.4	140 @ 3200	250 @ 1600	40–60
1986	V8-302, 5.0L	—	S.E.F.I.⑩	4.00 × 3.00	8.9	—	—	40–60

continued

GENERAL ENGINE SPECIFICATIONS

Year	Engine C.I.D.①/Liter	Engine V.I.N. Code②	Carburetor	Bore and Stroke	Compression Ratio	Net H.P. @ R.P.M.③	Maximum Torque Ft. Lbs. @ R.P.M.	Normal Oil Pressure Pounds
MERCURY								
1980	V8-302, 5.0L	F	2700VV, 2 Bbl.④	4.00 × 3.00	8.4	130 @ 3600	230 @ 1600	40–60
	V8-351W, 5.8L⑥	G	7200VV, 2 Bbl.④	4.00 × 3.50	8.3	140 @ 3400	265 @ 2000	40–60
	V8-351W, 5.8L H.O. ⑥⑧	G	7200VV, 2 Bbl.④	4.00 × 3.50	8.3			40–60
1981	V8-255, 4.2L	D	7200VV, 2 Bbl.④	3.68 × 3.00	8.2	120 @ 3400	205 @ 2600	40–60
	V8-302, 5.0L⑦	F	7200VV, 2 Bbl.④	4.00 × 3.00	8.4	130 @ 3400	230 @ 2200	40–60
	V8-302, 5.0L⑤	F	7200VV, 2 Bbl.④	4.00 × 3.00	8.4	130 @ 3400	235 @ 1800	40–60
	V8-351W, 5.8L⑥	G	7200VV, 2 Bbl.④	4.00 × 3.50	8.3	145 @ 3200	270 @ 1800	40–60
	V8-351W, 5.8L H.O. ⑥⑧	G	7200VV, 2 Bbl.④	4.00 × 3.50	8.3	165 @ 3600	285 @ 2200	40–60
1982	V8-255, 4.2L	D	7200VV, 2 Bbl.④	3.68 × 3.00	8.2	122 @ 3400	209 @ 2400	40–60
	V8-302, 5.0L	F	7200VV, 2 Bbl.④	4.00 × 3.00	8.4	132 @ 3400	236 @ 1800	40–60
1983–85	V8-302, 5.0L	F	E.F.I.⑨	4.00 × 3.00	8.4	140 @ 3200	250 @ 1600	40–60
1986	V8-302, 5.0L	—	S.E.F.I.⑩	4.00 × 3.00	8.9	—	—	40–60

①—C.I.D.—cubic inch displacement.
②—On 1980 models the fifth digit of V.I.N. denotes engine code. On 1981–86 models, the eighth digit of V.I.N. denotes engine code.
③—Ratings are net—as installed in vehicle.
④—Motorcraft.
⑤—Exc. Calif.
⑥—Windsor engine.
⑦—Calif. only.
⑧—High Output engine.
⑨—E.F.I.—electronic fuel injection.
⑩—S.E.F.I.—sequential electronic fuel injection.

Starting Motor Applications

Year	Engine/V.I.N.	Ident. No.	Year	Engine/V.I.N.	Ident. No.
1980	V8-255/D, 302/F②	D8OF-AA	1981–82	V8-255/D, 302/F	E1AF-BA
	V8-351W/G①②	D8OF-AA	1983	V8-302/F	E3AF-AA
	V8-255/D, 302F③	E1AF-BA	1984	V8-302/F	④
	V8-351/W/G①③	E1AF-BA	1985–86	V8-302/F	E4AF-AA

①—Windsor engine.
②—Models built prior to March 2, 1981.
③—Models built from March 2, 1981.
④—E3AF-AA, models built prior to December, 1983; E4AF-AA, models built from December, 1983.

Alternator & Regulator Specifications

Year	Stamp Color Code	Current Rating Amperes	Current Rating Volts	Field Current @ 75°F. Amperes	Field Current @ 75°F. Volts	Voltage Regulator Part No. (10316)	Voltage Regulator Voltage @ 75°F.
1980–81	Orange②④	40	15	4.0	12	D9BF-AB①	13.8–14.6
	Black②④	65	15	4.0	12	D9BF-AB①	13.8–14.6
	Green②④	60	15	4.0	12	D9BF-AB①	13.8–14.6
	Black③④	70	15	4.0	12	D9BF-AB①	13.8–14.6
	Red③④	100	15	4.0	12	D9BF-AB①	13.8–14.6
1982	Orange②④	40	15	4.0	12	E1AF-BA①	13.8–14.6
	Black②④	65	15	4.0	12	E1AF-BA①	13.8–14.6
	Green②④	60	15	4.0	12	E1AF-BA①	13.8–14.6
	Black③④	70	15	4.0	12	E1AF-BA①	13.8–14.6
	Red③④	100	15	4.0	12	E1AF-BA①	13.8–14.6
1983	Orange②④	40	15	4.25	12	E2AF-AA①	—
	Black②④	65	15	4.25	12	E2AF-AA①	—
	Green②④	60	15	4.25	12	E2AF-AA①	—
	Black③④	70	15	4.25	12	E2AF-AA①	—
	Red③④	100	15	4.25	12	E2AF-AA①	—

continued

ALTERNATOR & REGULATOR SPECIFICATIONS—Continued

Year	Stamp Color Code	Current Rating		Field Current @ 75°F.		Voltage Regulator	
		Amperes	Volts	Amperes	Volts	Part No. (10316)	Voltage @ 75°F.
1984–85	Orange②④	40	15	4.25	12	E4AF-AA①	—
	Green②④	60	15	4.25	12	E4AF-AA①	—
	Black③④	70	15	4.25	12	E4AF-AA①	—
	Red③④	100	15	4.25	12	E4AF-AA①	—
1986	—	—	—	—	—	E6AF-AA	—

①—Electronic voltage regulator. These units are color coded black for systems w/warning indicator lamp & blue for systems w/ammeter.

①—Stamp color code.
②—Rear terminal alternator.
③—Side terminal alternator.
④—Solid state alternator.

Rear Axle Specifications

Year	Carrier Type	Ring Gear & Pinion Backlash Inch	Nominal Pinion Locating Shim, Inch	Pinion Bearing Preload				Differential Bearing Preload	Pinion Nut Torque Ft.-Lbs.①
				New Bearings With Seal Inch-Lbs.	Used Bearings With Seal Inch-Lbs.	New Bearings Less Seal Inch-Lbs.	Used Bearings Less Seal Inch-Lbs.		
1980	Integral	.008–.015	.030	17–27	8–14	—	—	.008–.012	140
1981–83	Integral	.008–.015	.030	16–29	8–14	—	—	.016②	③
1984–86	Integral	.008–.015	.030	11–19	8–14	—	—	16②	③

①—If torque cannot be obtained, install new spacer.

②—Differential case spread.
③—With 7.5 inch ring gear, 170 ft.-lbs.;

with 8.5 & 8.8 inch ring gear, 140 ft.-lbs.

Valve Specifications

Year	Engine Model/V.I.N.	Valve Lash		Valve Angles		Valve Spring Installed Height	Valve Spring Pressure Lbs. @ In.	Stem Clearance		Stem Diameter	
		Int.	Exh.	Seat	Face			Intake	Exhaust	Intake	Exhaust
1980	V8-302/F	.096–.163		45	44	⑦	⑨	.0010–.0027	.0015–.0032	.3416–.3423	.3411–.3418
	V8-351W/G②	.096–.163③		45	44	⑦	⑨	.0010–.0027	.0015–.0032	.3416–.3423	.3411–.3418
1980–81	V8-351W H.O./G②⑪	.096–.146③		45	44	⑦	⑫	.0010–.0027	.0015–.0032	.3416–.3423	.3411–.3418
1981	V8-351W/G②	.096–.146③		45	44	⑦	⑨	.0010–.0027	.0015–.0032	.3416–.3423	.3411–.3418
	V8-255, 302⑱	.096–.146③		45	44	⑩	⑨	.0010–.0027	.0015–.0032	.3416–.3423	.3411–.3418
1982	V8-255/D, 302/F	.096–.146③		45	44	⑩	⑬	.0010–.0027	.0015–.0032	.3416–.3423	.3411–.3418
1983–85	V8-302/F	.096–.146③		45	44	⑩	①	.0010–.0027	.0015–.0032	.3416–.3423	.3411–.3418
1986	V8-302	.096–.146③		45	44	⑩	①	.0010–.0027	.0015–.0032	.3416–.3423	.3411–.3418

①—Intake, 205 @ 1.36; exhaust, 205 @ 1.05.
②—Windsor engine.
③—Clearance specified is obtainable at valve stem tip with lifter collapsed. See "Valves, Adjust" text.
④—Intake, 200 @ 1.34; exhaust, 200 @ 1.20.
⑤—Intake, 1²⁵⁄₃₂; exhaust 1¹¹⁄₁₆.
⑥—Intake, 1¹¹⁄₁₆; exhaust, 1³⁹⁄₆₄.
⑦—Intake, 1²⁵⁄₃₂; exhaust, 1³⁹⁄₆₄.
⑧—Intake, 226 @ 1.39; exhaust, 200 @ 1.20.
⑨—Intake, 205 @ 1.36; exhaust, 200 @ 1.20.
⑩—Intake, 1¹¹⁄₁₆; exhaust, 1¹⁹⁄₃₂.
⑪—High output engine.
⑫—Intake, 204 @ 1.33; exhaust, 205 @ 1.15.
⑬—Intake, 205 @ 1.36; exhaust, 205 @ 1.15.

continued

Pistons, Pins, Rings, Crankshaft & Bearings

Year	Engine Model/V.I.N.	Piston Clearance	Ring End Gap①		Wrist-pin Diameter	Rod Bearings		Main Bearings		Thrust on Bear. No.	Shaft End Play
			Comp.	Oil		Shaft Diameter	Bearing Clearance	Shaft Diameter	Bearing Clearance		
1980	V8-302/F	.0018–.0026	.010	.015	.9122	2.1228–2.1236	.0008–.0026	2.2486	②	3	.004–.008
	V8-351W/G ③	.0018–.0026	.010	.015	.9122	2.1228–2.1236	.0008–.0026	2.9998	.0008–.0015	3	.004–.008
1981	V8-255/D	.0014–.0024	.010	.015	.9122	2.1228–2.1236	.0008–.0024	2.2482–2.2490	②	3	.004–.008
	V8-302/F	.0018–.0026	.010	.015	.9122	2.1228–2.1236	.0008–.0024	2.2482–2.2490	②	3	.004–.008
	V8-351W/G ③	.0018–.0026	.010	.015	.9122	2.3103–2.3111	.0007–.0025	2.9994–3.0002	.0008–.0015	3	.004–.008
1982	V8-255/D	.0014–.0024	.010	.015	.9122	2.1228–2.1236	.0008–.0015	2.2482–2.2490	.0005–.0015	3	.004–.008
1982–83	V8-302/F	.0018–.0026	.010	.015	.9122	2.1228–2.1236	.0008–.0015	2.2482–2.2490	.0005–.0015	3	.004–.008
1984–85	V8-302/F	.0018–.0026	.010	.015	.9122	2.1228–2.1236	.0008–.0015	2.2482–2.2490	④	3	.004–.008
1986	V8-302	.0018–.0026	.010	.015	.9122	2.1228–2.1236	.0008–.0015	2.2482–2.2490	④	3	.004–.008

①—Fit rings in tapered bores for clearance listed in tightest portion of ring travel.
②—No. 1, .0001–.0015; all others, .0004–.0015.
③—Windsor engine.
④—No. 1, .0004–.0025; all others, .0004–.0015.

Engine Tightening Specifications★

★ Torque specifications are for clean and lightly lubricated threads only. Dry or dirty threads produce increased friction which prevents accurate measurement of tightness.

Year	Engine Model/V.I.N.	Spark Plugs Ft. Lbs.	Cylinder Head Bolts Ft. Lbs.	Intake Manifold Ft. Lbs.	Exhaust Manifold Ft. Lbs.	Rocker Arm Stud Nut or Bolt Ft. Lbs.	Rocker Arm Cover Ft. Lbs.	Connecting Rod Cap Bolts Ft. Lbs.	Main Bearing Cap Bolts Ft. Lbs.	Flywheel to Crankshaft Ft. Lbs.	Vibration Damper or Pulley Ft. Lbs.
1980	V8-302/F	10–15	65–72	23–25	18–24	18–25	3–5	19–24	60–70	75–85	70–90
	V8-351W/H,G①	10–15	105–112	23–25	18–24	18–25	3–5	40–45	95–105	75–85	70–90
1981	V8-351W/G①	10–15	105–112	23–25	18–24	18–25	3–5	40–45	95–105	75–85	70–90
1981–82	V8-255/D	10–15	65–72	18–20	18–24	18–25	3–5	19–24	60–70	75–85	70–90
1981–85	V8-302/F	10–15	65–72	23–25	18–24	18–25	3–5	19–24	60–70	75–85	70–90
1986	V8-302	10–15	65–72	23–25	18–24	18–25	3–5	19–24	60–70	75–85	70–90

①—Windsor engine.

Wheel Alignment Specifications

Year	Model	Caster Angle, Degrees		Camber Angle, Degrees				Toe-In. Inch	Toe-Out on Turns, Deg.	
		Limits	Desired	Limits		Desired			Outer Wheel	Inner Wheel
				Left	Right	Left	Right			
1980–82	All	+2¼ to +3¾	+3	−¼ to +1¼	−¼ to +1¼	+½	+½	3/16①	18.51	20
1983–86	All	+2¼ to +4	+3	−¼ to +1¼	−¼ to +1¼	+½	+½	1/16	18.51	20

①—1980–82, 1/16 inch.

continued

Cooling System & Capacity Data

Year	Model or Engine/V.I.N.	Cooling Capacity, Qts.		Radiator Cap Relief Pressure, Lbs.	Thermo. Opening Temp.	Fuel Tank Gals.	Engine Oil Refill Qts. ①	Transmission Oil			Rear Axle Oil Pints
		Less A/C	With A/C					3 Speed Pints	4 Speed Pints	Auto. Trans. Qts. ②	
FORD											
1980	V8-302/F	13	13.3	16	196	19⑥	4⑦	—	—	⑨	⑩
	V8-351W/G	13.9	14	16	196	19⑥	4⑦	—	—	⑧	⑩
1981	V8-255/D	13.8	13.8	16	191	20	4⑦	—	—	12	⑩
	V8-302/F	13	13.4	16	196	20	4⑦	—	—	12	⑩
	V8-351W/G	13.8	13.8⑤	16	196	20	4⑦	—	—	12	⑩
1982	V8-255/D	14.7	15	16	191	20	4⑦	—	—	12	3¾
1982–83	V8-302/F	13	13.4	16	196	20	4⑦	—	—	12	3¾
1984–85	V8-302/F	13	13.4③	16	196	18④	4⑦	—	—	12.3	4
1986	V8-302	13	13.4③	16	196	18	4⑦	—	—	12.3	3.75
MERCURY											
1980	V8-302/F	13	13.3	16	196	19⑥	4⑦	—	—	⑨	⑩
	V8-351W/G	13.9	14	16	196	19⑥	4⑦	—	—	⑧	⑩
1981	V8-255/D	13.8	13.8	16	191	20	4⑦	—	.—	12	⑩
	V8-302/F	13	13.4	16	196	20	4⑦	—	—	12	⑩
	V8-351W/G	13.8	13.8⑤	16	196	20	4⑦	—	—	12	⑩
1982	V8-255/D	14.7	15	16	191	20	4⑦	—	—	12	3¾
1982–83	V8-302/F	13	13.4	16	196	20	4⑦	—	—	12	3¾
1984–85	V8-302/F	13	13.4③	16	196	18④	4⑦	—	—	12.3	4
1986	V8-302	13	13.4③	16	196	18	4⑦	—	—	12.3	3.75

①—Add one quart with filter change.
②—Approximate. Make final check with dipstick.
③—Trailer tow, 14.6 qts.
④—Sta. Wag., 18.5 gals.
⑤—Trailer tow, 15 qts.
⑥—Station wagon, 20 gal.

⑦—When changing engine oil on these models, both drain plugs must be removed to fully drain crankcase. One drain plug is located at the front of the oil pan, while the other drain plug is located at rear left side of the oil pan.

⑧—C4, 10 qts.; FMX, 11 qts.; F10D Overdrive auto. trans., 12 qts.
⑨—C4, 10 qts.; FMX, 11 qts.; C6, 11.8 qts.; Overdrive auto. trans., 12 qts.
⑩—7½″ ring gear, 3½ pts.; 8½″ ring gear, 4 pts.

Electrical Section

Fig. 1 Ignition switch. 1980—86

This will permit the retaining pin to extend into the lock cylinder housing hole.

7. Rotate key to check for proper mechanical operation.
8. Connect key warning switch electrical connector.
9. Connect battery ground cable.
10. Check for proper operation.

IGNITION SWITCH
REPLACE

1980—86

1. Disconnect battery ground cable.
2. Remove upper column shroud.
3. Disconnect ignition switch electrical connector.
4. With a ⅛ inch twist drill, drill out the switch retaining bolt heads. Then, remove the bolts with a "Easy Out" or equivalent.
5. Disengage ignition switch from actuator and remove from vehicle, Fig. 1.
6. On 1980—81 models, adjust ignition switch to "Lock" position. On 1982—86 models, adjust ignition switch to "Run" position. Insert a .050 inch drill or equivalent through the switch housing and into the carrier to prevent movement.

NOTE: A replacement ignition switch includes an installed adjusting pin.

7. On 1980—81 models, rotate ignition key to "Lock" position. On 1982—86 models, place lock cylinder in the "Run" position, which is approximately 90° from the "Lock" position.
8. Install ignition switch on actuator pin.
9. Install switch break-off head mounting bolts and tighten until the bolt heads shear.
10. Remove adjusting pin or drill.
11. Connect ignition switch electrical connector.
12. Connect battery ground cable and check for proper operation.
13. Install column shroud.

LIGHT SWITCH
REPLACE

1980—86

1. Disconnect battery ground cable.
2. Under instrument panel, depress light switch knob and shaft retainer button on side of switch and, while holding button in, pull knob and shaft assembly from switch, **Fig. 2.**
3. Unscrew trim bezel and remove lock nut.
4. From under instrument panel, pull switch from panel while tilting downward, disconnect electrical connector and remove switch.
5. Reverse procedure to install.

Fig. 2 Light switch. (Typical)

STOP LIGHT SWITCH
REPLACE

1. Referring to **Fig. 3**, disconnect wires at connector.
2. Remove hairpin retainer and slide switch, push rod and nylon washers and bushing away from pedal, and remove switch.
3. Position the new switch, push rod, bushing and washers on brake pedal pin and secure with hairpin retainer.
4. Connect wires at connector and install wires in retaining clip.

TURN SIGNAL SWITCH
REPLACE

1980—86

1. Disconnect battery ground cable.
2. On models with tilt column, unsnap extension shroud, located below steering wheel, from retaining clip. On all models, remove five attaching screws, then remove steering column trim shroud.
3. Remove turn signal switch lever by grasping lever and using a pulling twisting motion of the hand, while pulling lever straight out of switch.
4. Peel foam sight shield from switch, then disconnect two turn signal switch wire connectors.
5. Remove two screws attaching turn signal switch to lock cylinder housing, then disengage switch from housing.
6. Reverse procedure to install.

NEUTRAL SAFETY SWITCH

EXC. MODELS W/AUTOMATIC OVERDRIVE TRANSMISSION

The neutral safety switch has been eliminated and is replaced by a series of steps incorporated into the steering column selector lever hub casting.

MODELS W/AUTOMATIC OVERDRIVE TRANSMISSION

1. Disconnect battery ground cable.

STARTER
REPLACE

SERVICE BULLETIN: STARTER PROBLEMS: If the starter is noisy or if it locks up, before condemning the starter, loosen the three mounting bolts enough to hand fit the starter properly into the pilot plate. Then tighten the mounting bolts, starting with the top bolt.

1. Disconnect battery ground cable.
2. Raise and support vehicle.
3. Disconnect starter cable from motor.
4. Remove mounting bolts and starter.

NOTE: On some models it may be necessary to turn the wheels right or left to remove starter.

5. Reverse procedure to install. Torque bolts to 15—20 ft. lbs.

IGNITION LOCK
REPLACE

1980—86

1. Disconnect battery ground cable.
2. Remove steering column trim shroud.
3. Disconnect key warning switch electrical connector.
4. Turn ignition lock to "On" position.
5. Using a ⅛ inch pin or punch located in the 4 o'clock hole and 1¼ inch from outer edge of lock cylinder housing, depress retaining pin while pulling the lock cylinder from housing.
6. Turn lock cylinder to "On" position and insert cylinder into housing. Ensure that the lock cylinder is fully seated and aligned into the interlocking washer before turning key to "Off" position.

2. Remove air cleaner assembly.
3. Place transmission selector lever in manual low position, then disconnect neutral safety switch electrical connector from switch. Lift connector straight off without any side-to-side motion.
4. Remove switch and O-ring using a 24 inch extension, universal adapter and socket No. T74P-77247-A.

NOTE: Use of any tools other than those specified may result in damage to the vehicle.

5. Reverse procedure to install. Torque switch to 7–10 ft. lbs.

HORN SOUNDER
REPLACE

1980—86

Refer to "TURN SIGNAL SWITCH, REPLACE" for horn switch replacement.

INSTRUMENT CLUSTER
REPLACE

1980—86

1. Disconnect battery ground cable.
2. Disconnect speedometer cable.
3. Remove instrument cluster trim cover attaching screws and the trim cover.
4. Remove the two lower steering column cover attaching screws and the cover.
5. Remove steering column shroud lower half.
6. Remove screws securing transmission indicator column bracket to steering column. Detach cable loop from pin on shift lever and remove bracket from column.
7. Remove four instrument cluster attaching screws.
8. Disconnect cluster feed plug and remove cluster assembly from vehicle.
9. Reverse procedure to install.

W/S WIPER MOTOR
REPLACE

1980—86

1. Disconnect battery ground cable.
2. On 1982–86 models, disconnect right side washer nozzle hose and remove right side wiper arm and blade assembly from pivot shaft.
3. On all models, remove wiper motor and linkage cover.
4. Disconnect linkage drive arm from the motor output arm crankpin by removing retaining clip.
5. Disconnect the wiring connectors from the motor.
6. Remove three bolts retaining the

Fig. 3 Mechanical stop light switch.

motor to the dash panel extension and the motor.
7. Reverse procedure to install.

W/S WIPER SWITCH
REPLACE

1980—86

1. Disconnect battery ground cable.
2. Remove the steering column cover screws and separate the two halves.
3. Remove wiper switch retaining screws, disconnect wiring connector and remove switch.
4. Reverse procedure to install.

W/S WIPER TRANSMISSION
REPLACE

1980—86

1. Disconnect battery ground cable.
2. Remove wiper arm and blade assemblies from the pivot shafts. Remove rear hood seal.
3. Remove wiper motor and linkage cover for access to linkage.
4. Disconnect the linkage drive arm from the motor crank pin by removing the retaining clip.
5. Remove the six bolts retaining the left and right pivot shafts to the cowl, and remove the complete linkage assembly.
6. Reverse procedure to install.

RADIO
REPLACE

NOTE: When installing radio, be sure to

adjust antenna trimmer for peak performance.

1980—86

NOTE: For an all-electronic radio, perform step 6 first.

1. Disconnect battery ground cable.
2. Remove radio knobs and screws attaching the bezel to instrument panel.
3. Remove the radio mounting plate attaching screws.
4. Pull radio to disengage it from the lower rear support bracket.
5. Disconnect radio wiring and remove radio.
6. Remove the radio to mounting plate retaining nuts and washers and remove the mounting plate.
7. Remove the rear upper support retaining nut and remove the support.
8. Reverse procedure to install. Perform step 6 first if equipped with all-electronic radio.

HEATER CORE
REPLACE

1980—86

1. Disconnect battery ground cable, then drain cooling system.
2. Disconnect heater hoses from heater core. Plug heater hoses and core fittings to prevent coolant spillage.
3. Remove bolt located below w/s wiper motor, attaching left end of plenum to dash panel.
4. Remove nut attaching upper left hand corner of evaporator or heater case to dash panel.
5. Disconnect vacuum control system supply hose from vacuum source,

Fig. 4   Plenum assembly removal (Typical). 1980–86

Fig. 5   Heater core removal (Typical). 1980–86

then push grommet and hose into passenger compartment.

6. Remove glove box, then loosen right hand door sill plate and remove side cowl trim panel.

7. Remove bolt attaching right hand side of instrument panel to side cowl.

8. Remove instrument panel pad as follows:
   a. Remove two screws from each defroster nozzle opening in pad.
   b. From front lower edge of panel pad, remove five attaching screws.
   c. From each end of pad, remove one attaching screw.
   d. On 1980–81 models, remove screw from lower end of pad through glove box door opening.
   e. Lift pad assembly from instrument panel.

9. On models less ATC, disconnect temperature control cable from plenum bracket and blend air door crank.

10. On models equipped with ATC, disconnect temperature control cable and vacuum harness connector from ATC sensor. Disconnect ATC sensor tube from sensor and evaporator case connector, then disconnect wire connector from EV relay.

11. On all models, remove push clip attaching center duct bracket to plenum, then rotate bracket upward and to the right.

12. Disconnect vacuum harness at vacuum connector near floor air distribution duct.

13. Disconnect the white vacuum hose from the outside recirculating air door vacuum motor.

14. Remove two screws from rear side of floor air distribution duct to plenum, **Fig. 4.** To remove the right hand screw, it may be necessary to remove the two screws attaching the lower panel door vacuum motor to the mounting bracket.

15. Remove push fastener attaching floor air distribution duct to left end of plenum, then remove floor air distribution duct.

16. Remove two nuts located along lower flange of plenum.

17. Carefully move plenum rearward, so that heater core tubes and plenum case upper stud clear openings in dash panel, then remove plenum from vehicle by rotating upper portion of the plenum forward, down and out from under instrument panel. It may be necessary to carefully pull the lower edge of the instrument panel rearward while the plenum is being removed from behind the instrument panel.

18. Remove retaining screws from heater core cover, then the cover from the plenum assembly, **Fig. 5.**

19. Remove retaining screw from heater core inlet and outlet tube bracket.

20. Pull heater core and seal assembly from plenum assembly.

21. Reverse procedure to install.

BLOWER MOTOR
REPLACE

1980–86

1. Disconnect battery ground cable.

2. Disconnect blower motor ground wire and the engine ground wire and position wiring aside.

3. Disconnect blower motor lead connector from wiring harness hard shell connector.

4. Remove blower motor cooling tube from blower motor.

5. Remove blower motor retaining screws.

6. Rotate blower motor slightly to the right so the bottom edge of the mounting plate follows the contour of the wheelwell splash panel. Then, lift blower motor up and out of housing assembly.

7. Reverse procedure to install.

SPEED CONTROLS
1980–86

Actuator Cable Adjustment

1. Remove cable retaining clip.
2. Deactivate the throttle positioner.
3. Set carburetor at hot idle.
4. Pull the actuator cable to remove slack.
5. While maintaining light tension on the actuator cable, insert the cable retaining clip.

Vacuum Dump Valve

The vacuum dump valve is mounted on a moveable mounting bracket. The valve should be adjusted so that it is closed when the brake pedal is not depressed and opens when the brake pedal is depressed.

Engine Section

Fig. 1 Engine mount. 1980—86 V8-255, 302 & 351W

ENGINE MOUNTS
REPLACE

CAUTION: Whenever self-locking mounting bolts and nuts are removed, they must be replaced with new self-locking bolts and nuts.

1980—86 V8-255, 302 & 351W

1. On 1982—86 models, remove fan shroud attaching screw.
2. On all models, remove nut and through bolt attaching insulator to support bracket, **Fig. 1.**
3. Raise the engine slightly with a jack and a wood block placed under the oil pan.
4. Remove the engine insulator assembly to cylinder block attaching bolts. Remove the engine insulator assembly and the heat shield, if so equipped.
5. Reverse procedure to install.

ENGINE
REPLACE

NOTE: Because of engine compartment tolerances, the engine should not be removed and installed with the transmission attached.

1980—86

1. Disconnect battery and alternator ground cables.
2. Drain cooling system and oil pan.
3. Remove hood.
4. Remove air cleaner and intake duct assembly.
5. Disconnect radiator hoses from engine.
6. Disconnect transmission oil cooler lines from radiator.
7. Remove fan shroud attaching bolts, then the radiator, fan, spacer, pulley and shroud.
8. Remove alternator mounting bolts and position alternator aside.

9. Disconnect oil pressure sending unit electrical connector.
10. Disconnect fuel tank line at fuel pump and plug line.
11. Disconnect accelerator cable and speed control cable, if equipped, from carburetor.
12. Disconnect throttle valve vacuum line from intake manifold.
13. Disconnect manual shift rod and retracting spring at shift rod stud.
14. Disconnect transmission filler tube bracket from engine block.
15. Isolate and remove A/C compressor from vehicle, if equipped.
16. Disconnect power steering pump bracket from cylinder head and water pump and position aside, if equipped.
17. Disconnect power brake vacuum line from intake manifold, if equipped.
18. Disconnect heater hoses from engine.
19. Disconnect coolant temperature sending unit electrical connector.
20. Remove upper converter housing to engine attaching bolts.
21. Disconnect ignition coil and distributor wiring. Remove harness from left hand rocker arm cover and position aside. Disconnect ground strap from engine block.
22. Raise and support front of vehicle.
23. Disconnect starter motor wiring and remove starter motor.
24. Disconnect exhaust pipes from manifold.
25. Disconnect engine mounts from frame brackets.
26. Disconnect secondary air line to catalytic converter, if equipped.
27. Disconnect transmission oil cooler lines from retainer.
28. Remove converter housing inspection cover.
29. Disconnect converter from flywheel. Secure converter in housing.
30. Remove remaining converter housing to engine bolts.
31. Lower vehicle and support transmission. Attach suitable engine lifting equipment to engine.
32. Raise engine slightly and pull forward to disengage from transmission.
33. Remove engine from vehicle.
34. Reverse procedure to install.

CYLINDER HEAD
REPLACE

Tighten cylinder head bolts a little at a time in three steps in the sequence shown in **Fig. 2.** Final tightening should be to the torque specifications listed in the "Engine Tightening" table. After bolts have been tightened to specifications, they should not be disturbed.

1980—86 V8-255, 302 & 351W

1. Disconnect battery ground cable.

Fig. 2 Cylinder head tightening sequence.

2. Remove intake manifold and carburetor as an assembly.
3. Remove rocker arm cover.
4. If left cylinder head is being removed, isolate and remove A/C compressor, if equipped.
5. Remove EGR cooler, if equipped with V8-351W and EEC system.
6. If left cylinder head is being removed, disconnect power steering pump bracket from cylinder head and engine block and position assembly aside.
7. Remove Thermactor crossover tube from rear of cylinder heads.
8. If right cylinder head is being removed, remove alternator bracket bolt and spacer and, if equipped, the A/C compressor mounting bracket.
9. Loosen rocker arm stud nuts or bolts so that rocker arms can be rotated to the side.
10. Remove push rods, keeping them in sequence so they may be returned to their original locations. Remove exhaust valve stem caps.
11. Disconnect exhaust pipes from exhaust manifold.
12. Unfasten and remove cylinder head.
13. Reverse removal procedure to install the head. Tighten cylinder head down in the sequence shown in **Fig. 2.** When installing intake manifold refer to **Fig. 3** for bolt tightening sequence.

NOTE: On V8-255 engines, when installing intake manifold, a 1/8 in. bead of RTV sealer should be applied at mating surfaces of intake manifold, cylinder head and cylinder block, **Fig. 4.** After intake manifold seals and gaskets have been positioned, apply a 1/16 in. bead of RTV sealer to the outer end of each intake manifold seal for the entire width of the seal, **Fig. 4.**

SERVICE NOTE: On V8-302 engines equipped with cork intake manifold seals, both the front and rear seals should be replaced with RTV sealer. Apply a 1/4 inch bead of sealer to front and rear sealing surfaces of engine block.

VALVE ARRANGEMENT
FRONT TO REAR

Right . . . . I-E-I-E-I-E-I-E
Left . . . . E-I-E-I-E-I-E-I

Fig. 3 Intake manifold tightening sequence. V8-255, 302 & 351W

VALVE LIFT SPECS.

Engine	Year	Intake	Exhaust
V8-255	1982	.375	.375
V8-302	1980–86	.375	.391
V8-351	1980–81①	.411	.411
V8-351 H.O.	1980–81①②	.442	.450

VALVE TIMING

Intake Opens Before TDC

Engine	Year	Degrees
V8-255	1981–82	16
V8-302	1980–86	16
V8-351	1980①	23

①—Windsor engine

VALVES
ADJUST

To eliminate the need of adjusting valve lash, a positive stop fulcrum bolt and seat is used on 1980–86 V8-255, 302 and 351W engines, **Fig. 5**.

It is very important that the correct push rod be used and all components be installed and torqued as follows:
1. Position the piston of the cylinder being worked on at TDC of its compression stroke.
2. On 1980–86 V8-255, 302 and 351W engines, install rocker arm, fulcrum seat and oil deflector. Install fulcrum bolt and torque to 18–25 ft. lbs.

A .060 inch shorter push rod or a .060 inch longer rod are available for service to provide a means of compensating for dimensional changes in the valve mechanism. Valve stem-to-rocker arm clearance

Fig. 4 Applying RTV sealer for intake manifold installation. V8-255

should be as listed in the " Valve Specifications" table, with the hydraulic lifter completely collapsed, **Fig. 6**. Repeated valve grind jobs will decrease this clearance to the point that if not compensated for the lifters will cease to function.

When checking valve clearance, if the clearance is less than the minimum, the .060 inch shorter push rod should be used. If clearance is more than the maximum, the .060 inch longer push rod should be used. (See Valve Specifications table.) To check valve clearance, proceed as follows:
1. Mark crankshaft pulley at three locations, with number 1 location at TDC timing mark (end of compression stroke), number 2 location one half turn (180°) clockwise from TDC and number 3 location three quarter turn clockwise (270°) from number 2 location.
2. Turn the crankshaft to the number 1 location and check the clearance on the following valves:

   V8-255 & 302
No. 1 Intake	No. 1 Exhaust
No. 7 Intake	No. 5 Exhaust
No. 8 Intake	No. 4 Exhaust

   V8-351W & 351M
No. 1 Intake	No. 1 Exhaust
No. 4 Intake	No. 3 Exhaust
No. 8 Intake	No. 7 Exhaust

3. Turn the crankshaft to the number 2 location and check the clearance on the following valves:

   V8-255 & 302
No. 5 Intake	No. 2 Exhaust
No. 4 Intake	No. 6 Exhaust

   V8-351W & 351M
No. 3 Intake	No. 2 Exhaust
No. 7 Intake	No. 6 Exhaust

4. Turn the crankshaft to the number 3 location and check the clearance on the following valves:

   V8-255 & 302
No. 2 Intake	No. 7 Exhaust
No. 3 Intake	No. 3 Exhaust
No. 6 Intake	No. 8 Exhaust

   V8-351W & 351M
No. 2 Intake	No. 4 Exhaust
No. 5 Intake	No. 5 Exhaust
No. 6 Intake	No. 8 Exhaust

Fig. 5 Rocker arm. 1980–86 V8-255, 302 & 351W

VALVE GUIDES

Valve guides in these engines are an integral part of the head and, therefore, cannot be removed. For service, guides can be reamed oversize to accommodate one of three service valves with oversize stems (.003 inch, .015 inch and .030 inch).

Check the valve stem clearance of each valve (after cleaning) in its respective valve guide. If the clearance exceeds the service limits of .0055 inch, ream the valve guides to accommodate the next oversize diameter valve.

ROCKER ARMS
1980–86 V8-255, 302 & 351W

These engines use a bolt and fulcrum attachment, **Fig. 5**. To remove, remove attaching bolt, then the fulcrum, rocker arm and fulcrum guide, if the other rocker arm is being removed.

SERVICE NOTE: Some 1981–82 models equipped with low profile rocker arm fulcrums (part No. E1TZ-6A528-A) may experience excessive oil displacement when engine is operated for extended periods during high ambient temperatures. This problem may be corrected by replacing original rocker arm fulcrums with part No. D7AZ-6A528-A.

VALVE LIFTERS
REPLACE

NOTE: The internal parts of each hydraulic valve lifter assembly are a matched set. If these are mixed, improper valve operation may result. Therefore, disassemble, inspect and test each assembly separately to prevent mixing the parts.

Fig. 7 illustrates the type of hydraulic lifter used. See the "Trouble Shooting Chapter" under the heading Engine Noises for causes of hydraulic valve lifter noise.

Fig. 6   Checking valve clearance on models with hydraulic lifters

Fig. 7   Hydraulic valve lifter disassembled (typical)

1. Remove intake manifold and related parts.
2. Remove rocker arm covers.
3. Loosen rocker arm stud nuts or bolts and rotate rocker arms to the side.
4. Lift out push rods, keeping them in sequence in a rack so they may be installed in their original location.
5. Using a magnet rod, remove valve lifters and place them in sequence in a rack so they may be installed in their original location.
6. Reverse procedure to install.

TIMING CASE COVER
REPLACE

NOTE: To replace the seal in the timing gear cover, it is necessary to remove the cover as outlined below.

V8-255, 302 & 351

1. Drain cooling system and oil pan.
2. Disconnect lower radiator hose from water pump.
3. Disconnect heater hose from water pump and slide water pump bypass hose clamp toward pump.
4. Unfasten and position alternator and bracket out of way.
5. If equipped with power steering or air conditioning, remove the drive belts.
6. Remove the fan, spacer, pulley and drive belt.
7. Remove crankshaft pulley and vibration damper.

NOTE: If equipped with EEC II system, disconnect crankshaft position sensor electrical connector.

8. Disconnect fuel pump outlet line from pump and remove pump retaining bolts and lay pump to one side with flex line attached.
9. Remove oil dipstick and the oil pan to front cover attaching bolts.
10. Unfasten and remove the front cover and water pump as an assembly.
11. Reverse procedure to install.

Fig. 8   Timing marks aligned for correct valve timing

TIMING CHAIN
REPLACE

V8-255, 302 & 351

After removing the cover as outlined above, crank the engine until the timing marks are aligned as shown in **Fig. 8.** Remove camshaft sprocket retaining bolt, washer and fuel pump eccentric and, on 1981–86 models with electronic fuel injection, remove spacer. Slide both sprockets and chain forward and remove them as an assembly.

Reverse procedure to install the chain and sprockets, being sure the timing marks are aligned.

CAMSHAFT
REPLACE

NOTE: It may be necessary to remove or reposition radiator, A/C compressor and grille components to provide adequate clearance.

1. To remove camshaft, remove cylinder front cover and timing chain.
2. Remove distributor cap and spark plug wires, then remove distributor.
3. Disconnect automatic transmission oil cooler lines from radiator and remove radiator.
4. Remove intake manifold and carburetor as an assembly.
5. Remove rocker arm covers.
6. Loosen rocker arm stud nuts or bolts and rotate rocker arms to one side.
7. Remove push rods, keeping them in sequence in a rack so they may be installed in their original location.
8. Using a magnet, remove valve lifters and place them in a rack in sequence so they may be installed in their original location.
9. Remove camshaft thrust plate, **Fig. 9** and carefully pull camshaft from engine, using care to avoid damaging camshaft bearings.
10. Reverse procedure to install.

CAMSHAFT BEARINGS

When necessary to replace camshaft bearings, the engine will have to be removed from the vehicle and the plug at the rear of the cylinder block will have to be removed in order to utilize the special camshaft bearing removing and installing tools required to do this job. If properly installed, camshaft bearings require no reaming—nor should this type bearing be reamed or altered in any manner in an attempt to fit bearings.

PISTON & ROD
ASSEMBLE

Assemble the pistons to the rods so the notch or arrow faces toward the front of engine and the numbered side of rod faces away from center of engine, **Fig. 10.** After installation, check side clearance between connecting rods at each crankshaft journal. Clearance should be .010–.020 in.

Fig. 9   Camshaft & related parts

Fig. 10   Piston & rod assembly

Fig. 11   Split-lip rear crankshaft seal installation

PISTONS, PINS & RINGS

Pistons and rings are available in standard sizes and oversizes of .003, .020, .030 and .040 inch.

Oversize piston pins of .001 and .002 inch are available.

MAIN & ROD BEARINGS

Main and rod bearings are available in standard sizes and the following undersizes: .001, .002, .010, .020, .030, .040 inch.

CRANKSHAFT OIL SEAL
REPLACE

A rubber split-lip rear crankshaft oil seal is available for service. This seal can be installed without removal of the crankshaft and also eliminates the necessity of seal installation tools.

1. Remove oil pan and, if necessary, the oil pump.
2. Remove rear main bearing cap.
3. Loosen remaining bearing caps, allowing crankshaft to drop down about 1/32 inch.
4. Remove old seals from both cylinder block and rear main bearing cap. Use a brass rod to drift upper half of seal from cylinder block groove. Rotate crankshaft while drifting to facilitate removal.
5. Carefully clean seal groove in block with a brush and solvent. Also clean seal groove in bearing cap. Remove the oil seal retaining pin from the bearing cap if so equipped. The pin is not used with the split-lip seal.
6. Dip seal halves in clean engine oil.
7. Carefully install upper seal half in its groove with undercut side of seal toward front of engine, **Fig. 11**, by rotating it on shaft journal of crankshaft until approximately 3/8 inch protrudes below the parting surface. Be sure no rubber has been shaved from outside diameter of seal by bottom edge of groove.
8. Retighten main bearing caps and torque to specifications.
9. Install lower seal in main bearing cap with undercut side of seal toward front of engine, and allow seal to protrude about 3/8 inch above parting surface to mate with upper seal upon cap installation.
10. Apply suitable sealer to parting faces of cap and block. Install cap and torque to specifications.

NOTE: If difficulty is encountered in installing the upper half of the seal in position, lightly lap (sandpaper) the side of the seal opposite the lip side using a medium grit paper. After sanding, the seal must be washed in solvent, then dipped in clean engine oil prior to installation.

Fig. 12   Crankshaft rear oil seals

SERVICE BULLETIN: A revised crankshaft rear oil seal has been released for service. This new seal may be received when ordering an oil pan gasket kit and is installed in the same manner as described previously, **Fig. 12**.

OIL PAN
REPLACE

1980—86 V8-255, 302 & 351W

1. Disconnect battery ground cable and remove air cleaner assembly.
2. Disconnect accelerator cable and kickdown rod from carburetor.
3. Remove accelerator mounting bracket bolts and bracket.
4. Remove fan shroud attaching screws and position shroud over fan.

Fig. 13   Oil pump. V8-255, 302 & 351W

Engine oiling system (typical)

5. Disconnect wiper motor electrical connector and remove wiper motor.
6. Disconnect windshield washer hose.
7. Remove wiper motor mounting cover.
8. Remove oil level dipstick, then the dipstick tube retaining bolt from exhaust manifold.
9. If equipped with EGR cooler or EEC, remove Thermactor air dump tube retaining clamp, then the Thermactor crossover tube at rear of engine.
10. On all models, raise and support vehicle.
11. Drain oil pan.
12. On vehicles equipped with EGR cooler or EEC, remove filler tube from transmission oil pan and drain transmission, then remove starter motor.
13. Disconnect fuel line at fuel pump and plug line.

NOTE: Vehicles equipped with electronic fuel injection use a high pressure electric fuel pump. Prior to disconnecting fuel lines from the pump, pressure must be released at the Schrader valve on the fuel charging assembly.

14. Disconnect exhaust pipes from manifolds.
15. If equipped with EGR cooler or EEC, remove exhaust gas sensor from exhaust manifold, then the Thermactor secondary air tube to converter housing clamps.
16. On all models, remove dipstick tube from oil pan.
17. Loosen rear engine mount attaching nuts.
18. Remove engine mount through bolts.
19. Remove shift crossover bolts at transmission.
20. If equipped with EGR cooler or EEC, disconnect exhaust pipes from catalytic converter outlet, then the catalytic converter secondary air tube and inlet pipes to exhaust manifold.
21. On all models, disconnect transmission kickdown rod.

22. Remove torque converter housing cover.
23. Remove brake line retainer from front crossmember.
24. With a suitable jack, raise engine as far as possible.
25. Place a block of wood between each engine mount and chassis bracket. When engine is secured in this position, remove jack.
26. Remove oil pan attaching bolts and lower the oil pan.
27. Remove oil pick-up tube bolts and lower tube in oil pan.
28. Remove oil pan from vehicle.
29. Reverse procedure to install.

OIL PUMP
REPLACE

1. Remove oil pan as described under "Oil Pan, Replace" procedure.
2. On V8-255, 302 and 351W engine, remove oil inlet pickup tube and screen assembly.
3. On all engines, remove oil pump attaching bolts and remove oil pump and intermediate drive shaft.
4. Reverse procedure to install. Prime oil pump with engine oil before installing. Position intermediate drive shaft into distributor sprocket. With intermediate drive shaft firmly seated, the stop on the shaft should contact crankcase surface. Remove shaft and adjust as necessary. Position pump with intermediate drive shaft insert to cylinder block, then install and torque attaching bolts to 22 to 32 ft. lbs.

NOTE: Do not force oil pump into position on cylinder block. If pump drive shaft is misaligned with distributor shaft, rotate drive shaft to a new position.

OIL PUMP
SERVICE

1. With all parts clean and dry, check the inside of the pump housing and the outer race and rotor for damage or excessive wear, **Fig. 13.**
2. Check the mating surface of the pump cover for wear. If this surface is worn, scored or grooved, replace the pump.
3. Measure the clearance between the outer race and housing. This clearance should be .001–.013 inch.
4. With the rotor assembly installed in the housing, place a straight edge over the rotor assembly and housing. Measure the clearance between the straight edge and the rotor and outer race. Maximum recommended limits is .004 inch. The outer race, shaft and rotor are furnished only as an assembly.
5. Check the drive shaft-to-housing bearing clearance by measuring the O.D. of the shaft and the I.D. of the housing bearing. The recommended clearance limits are .0015–.0030 inch.
6. Inspect the relief valve spring for a collapsed or worn condition.
7. Check the relief valve piston for scores and free operation in the bore. The specified piston clearance is .0015–.0030 inch.

BELT TENSION DATA

	New Lbs.	Used Lbs.
1980		
Exc. ¼ inch	140	110
¼ inch inch	65	50
1980		
Ribbed belt w/o tensioner	155	150
Ribbed belt with tensioner	130	130
¼ inch V Belt	65	50
1981		
All other V Belts	140	105
V Ribbed Belts		
4K①	110	100
5K②	125	120
5K③	108	108
6K④	165	150
6K⑤	113	113
1982–86		
¼ inch V Belt	65	50
All other V Belts	140	105
V Ribbed Belt		
4K Exc. Air Pump①	130	115
4K Air Pump①	110	105
5K②	150	135
6K⑤	113	110
6K⑥	160	145

①—4 grooves.
②—5 grooves fixed.
③—5 grooves with absorber.
④—6 grooves with absorber.
⑤—6 grooves with tensioner.
⑥—6 grooves fixed.

WATER PUMP
REPLACE

1. Drain cooling system, then remove carburetor air inlet tube.
2. On models equipped with a fan shroud, remove shroud attaching bolts and place shroud over fan and spacer. Remove fan and spacer from water pump shaft, then remove fan shroud.
3. Remove alternator drive belt, A/C drive belt and idler pulley bracket, if so equipped. Remove power steering drive belt and power steering pump, if so equipped. Remove all brackets from water pump, then remove water pump.
4. Disconnect radiator lower hose and heater hose at water pump.
5. Remove drive belt, fan, spacer or fan drive clutch and pulley.
6. Reverse procedure to install.

FUEL PUMP
REPLACE

MECHANICAL TYPE

1. Loosen, then retighten fuel line connection(s) using a suitable wrench. Do not disconnect lines at this time.
2. Loosen fuel pump attaching bolts one or two turns. Apply hand force to pump to loosen gasket.
3. Rotate engine until fuel pump cam lobe is near low position to reduce pressure on pump.
4. Disconnect fuel lines and, if equipped, the vapor return line from pump.
5. Remove fuel pump attaching bolts and pump. Remove and discard gasket.
6. Clean all gasket material from engine and fuel pump.
7. Install attaching bolts into fuel pump. Then install new gasket over bolts.
8. Install pump and tighten attaching bolts alternately and evenly.
9. Connect fuel lines and vapor return line, if equipped, then operate engine and check for leaks.

Rear Axle, Propeller Shaft & Brakes

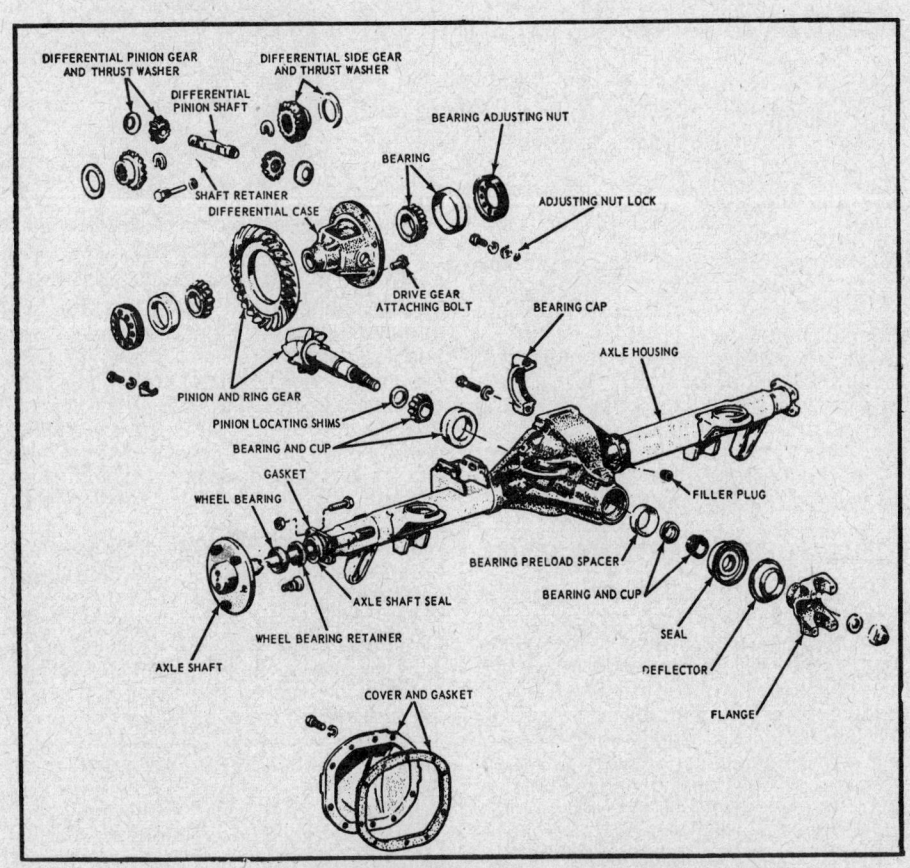

Fig. 1 Integral type rear axle assembly (typical)

REAR AXLES

Figs. 1 and 2 illustrate the rear axle assemblies used on these cars. When necessary to overhaul either of these units, refer to the "Rear Axle Specifications" table in this chapter.

INTEGRAL CARRIER TYPE

The gear set consists of a ring gear and an overhung drive pinion which is supported by two opposed tapered roller bearings, **Fig. 1.** The differential case is a one-piece design with openings allowing assembly of the internal parts and lubricant flow. The differential pinion shaft is retained with a threaded bolt (lock) assembled to the case.

The roller type wheel bearings have no inner race, and the rollers directly contact the bearing journals of the axle shafts. The axle shafts do not use an inner and outer bearing retainer. Rather, they are held in the axle by means of C-locks, **Fig. 3.** These C-locks also fit into a machined recess in the differential side gears within the differential case. There is no retainer bolt access hole in the axle shaft flange.

Rear Axle, Replace
1. Raise vehicle and support using jack stands under both frame side rails.
2. Mark drive shaft and pinion flange for reassembly, then disconnect drive shaft at pinion flange and remove drive shaft from transmission exten-

Fig. 2 Removable carrier type of rear axle assembly (typical)

Fig. 3 Axle shaft C locks. Integral type axle

Fig. 4 Using hook-type tool to remove oil seal

Fig. 5 Using special driver to install oil seal

sion housing. Install seal replacer tool in extension housing to prevent leakage.

3. Disconnect parking brake cable and brake lines. Cover brake lines to prevent contamination.

4. Support axle with jack, then lower axle far enough to relieve spring tension.

5. Disconnect shock absorbers at lower mounting brackets.

6. If equipped, disconnect track bar from axle housing stud.

7. Remove nuts, washers and pivot bolts connecting lower suspension arms to axle housing, then disconnect both arms from housing.

8. Remove nuts, bolts, washers and two eccentric washers, then disconnect upper suspension arm from axle housing.

9. Lower rear axle and remove from vehicle.

Axle Shaft, Bearing & Seal, Replace

1. Raise car on hoist and remove wheels.

2. Drain differential lubricant.

3. Remove brake drums.

4. Remove differential housing cover.

5. Position safety stands under rear frame member and lower hoist to allow axle to lower as far as possible.

6. Working through differential case opening, remove pinion shaft lock bolt and pinion shaft.

7. Push axle shaft(s) inward toward center of axle housing and remove C-lock(s) from housing, Fig. 3.

8. Remove axle shaft, using extreme care to avoid contact of shaft seal lip with any portion of axle shaft except seal journal.

9. Use a hook-type puller to remove seal and bearing, Fig. 4.

10. Reverse procedure to install, using suitable driving tools, Fig. 5, to install seal and bearing. New seals are prepacked with lubricant and do not require oil soaking before installation.

REMOVABLE CARRIER TYPE

In these axles, Fig. 2, the drive pinion is straddle-mounted by two opposed tapered roller bearings which support the pinion shaft at the rear of the pinion gear. The drive pinion is assembled in a pinion retainer that is bolted to the differential carrier. The tapered roller bearings are preloaded by a collapsible spacer between the bearings. The pinion is positioned by a shim or shims located between the drive pinion retainer and the differential carrier.

The differential is supported in the carrier by two tapered roller side bearings.

These bearings are preloaded by two threaded ring nuts or sleeves between the bearings and pedestals. The differential assembly is positioned for proper ring gear and pinion backlash by varying the adjustment of these ring nuts. The differential case houses two side gears in mesh with two pinions mounted on a pinion shaft which is held in place by a pin. The side gears and pinions are backed by thrust washers. With high performance engines, an optional rear axle having a four-pinion differential is also used.

The axle shafts are of unequal length, the left shaft being shorter than the right. The axle shafts are mounted on sealed ball bearings or tapered roller bearings which are pressed on the shafts.

SERVICE BULLETIN: All Ford Built Rear Axles: Recent manufacturing changes have eliminated the need for marking rear axle drive pinions for individual variations from nominal shim thicknesses. In the past, these pinion markings,

Fig. 6 Removing axle shaft with slide hammer-type puller

Fig. 7 Splitting bearing inner retainer for bearing removal

JUST SET TO DRUM DIAMETER HERE FIND CORRECT BRAKE SHOE DIAMETER HERE

Fig. 8 Brake adjustment gauge

with the aid of a shim selection table, were used as a guide to select correct shim thicknesses when a gear set or carrier assembly replacement was performed.

With the elimination of pinion markings, use of the shim selection table is no longer possible and the methods outlined below must be used.

1. Measure the thickness of the original pinion depth shim removed from the axle. Use the same thickness upon installation of the replacement carrier or drive pinion. If any further shim change is necessary, it will be indicated in the tooth pattern check.
2. If the original shim is lost, substitute a nominal shim for the original and use the tooth pattern check to determine if further shim changes are required.

Rear Axle, Replace

1. Raise rear of vehicle and remove wheel and tire assembly.
2. On models equipped with rear drum brakes, remove brake drums.
3. On models equipped with rear disc brakes, remove calipers from anchor plates, then remove two retaining nuts and slide rotors off axle shafts.

NOTE: Secure calipers to frame with wire.

4. Make marks on drive shaft yoke and pinion flange for reassembly, then disconnect drive shaft at rear axle U-joint and remove drive shaft from transmission extension housing. Install seal replacer tool in extension housing to prevent leakage.
5. Disconnect anti-skid sensor, if equipped.
6. Position safety stands under frame rear members, then support axle housing using a suitable jack.
7. Disconnect brake hydraulic lines from axle housing retaining clips.
8. Disconnect vent tube from rear housing.
9. Disconnect shock absorbers from lower mounting brackets.
10. Disconnect track bar from mounting stud on rear axle housing bracket.

NOTE: The axle housing mounting bracket has two holes, the track bar should be attached to the lower hole.

11. Lower rear axle housing until coil springs are released, then remove springs and insulators.
12. Disconnect suspension lower arms from axle housing, then disconnect suspension upper arms from housing.
13. Lower axle housing and remove from vehicle.

Axle Shaft, Bearing & Seal, Replace

1. Remove rear wheel assembly, then the brake drum or caliper and rotor assembly.
2. Remove axle shaft retainer nuts and bolts.
3. Pull axle shaft assembly from housing. It may be necessary to use a suitable slide hammer type puller, **Fig. 6**.
4. To replace wheel bearing on models equipped with tapered roller bearings:
   a. Drill a ¼ inch hole in inner bearing retainer approximately ¾ of the thickness of the bearing retainer deep.

NOTE: Do not drill completely through the bearing retainer since damage to the axle shaft may result.

   b. Place a cold chisel across the drilled hole and strike with a hammer to break retainer, then discard retainer, **Fig. 7**.
   c. Using suitable press and plates, press bearing from axle shaft. Do not apply heat since the heat will weaken the axle shaft bearing journal area.
   d. Install lubricated seal and bearing on axle shaft, ensuring the cup rib ring faces toward the axle flange.

NOTE: The lubricated seal of the bearing assembly used with drum brake installations is of a different length than the seal used on disc brake installations and are not interchangeable. For identification, the seal used on drum brake installations has a grey color outer rim and on disc brake installations, the seal has a black oxide appearance.

   e. Press new bearing into place, then the bearing retainer firmly against the bearing.

   f. Remove old bearing cup from axle housing with a suitable puller. Place new bearing cup on bearing and apply lubricant to outside diameter of seal and bearing cup and install in axle housing.
5. To replace wheel bearing on models equipped with ball bearings:
   a. Remove oil seal from axle housing, **Fig. 4**.
   b. Loosen bearing inner retainer by striking retainer ring in several places with a cold chisel and slide off shaft, **Fig. 7**.

NOTE: On some models, it may be necessary to drill a ¼ inch hole in inner bearing retainer approximately ¾ of the thickness of the bearing retainer deep before using the cold chisel.

   c. Using suitable press and plates, press bearing from shaft. Do not heat axle shaft since the heat will damage the shaft.
   d. Install outer retainer on shaft and press bearing into place. Press inner retainer onto shaft until firmly seated against bearing.
   e. Install oil seal into axle housing, **Fig. 5**.
6. On all units, slide axle shaft assembly into housing, engaging axle shaft splines in the side gear.

SERVICE NOTE: If replacing an axle shaft and bearing assembly of the sealed ball bearing design, the replacement assembly will have a tapered roller bearing. This tapered roller bearing is interchangeable with the ball bearing as an assembly only, however the inner oil seal must be removed before the tapered bearing shaft can be installed into the housing bore. The housing wheel bearing bore should be sanded with emery cloth before installing the bearing to provide a good sealing surface for the seal.

When removing a tapered roller bearing axle shaft, the outer bearing race may separate from the retainer ring and remain in the housing bore. If this occurs, the bearing must be removed and reinstalled on the shaft to prevent damage to the seal.

Fig. 9   Rear drum type brakes

Fig. 10   Backing off brake adjustment by disengaging adjusting lever with screwdriver

PROPELLER SHAFT
REPLACE

1. Mark the relationship of the driveshaft to pinion flange, then disconnect rear U-joint or companion flange from drive pinion flange.
2. Pull drive shaft toward rear of car until front U-joint yoke clears transmission extension housing and output shaft.
3. Install a suitable tool, such as a seal driver, in seal to prevent lube from leaking from transmission.
4. Before installing, check U-joints for freedom of movement. If a bind has resulted from misalignment after overhauling the U-joints, tap the ears of the drive shaft sharply to relieve the bind.
5. If rubber seal installed on end of transmission extension housing is damaged, install a new seal.
6. Lubricate yoke spline with special spline lubricant. This spline is sealed so that transmission fluid does not "wash" away spline lubricant.
7. Install yoke on transmission output shaft.
8. Align marks on driveshaft and pinion flange, then install U-bolts and nuts which attach U-joint to pinion flange. Tighten U-bolts evenly to prevent binding U-joint bearings.

BRAKE ADJUSTMENTS

1. Use the brake shoe adjustment gauge shown in **Fig. 8** to obtain the drum inside diameter as shown. Tighten the adjusting knob on the gauge to hold this setting.
2. Place the opposite side of the gauge over the brake shoes and adjust the shoes by turning the adjuster screw until the gauge just slides over the linings. Rotate the gauge around the lining surface to assure proper lining diameter adjustment and clearance.
3. Install brake drum and wheel. Final adjustment is accomplished by mak-

ing several firm reverse stops, using the brake pedal.

SELF-ADJUSTING BRAKES

These brakes, **Fig. 9,** have self-adjusting shoe mechanisms that assure correct lining-to-drum clearances at all times. The automatic adjusters operate only when the brakes are applied as the car is moving rearward.

Although the brakes are self-adjusting, an initial adjustment is necessary after the brake shoes have been relined or replaced, or when the length of the star wheel adjuster has been changed during some other service operation.

Frequent usage of an automatic transmission forward range to halt reverse vehicle motion may prevent the automatic adjusters from functioning, thereby inducing low pedal heights. Should low pedal heights be encountered, it is recommended that numerous forward and reverse stops be performed with a firm pedal effort until satisfactory pedal height is obtained.

NOTE: If a low pedal height condition cannot be corrected by making numerous reverse stops (provided the hydraulic system is free of air), it indicates that the self-adjusting mechanism is not functioning. Therefore, it will be necessary to remove the brake drums, clean, free up and lubricate the adjusting mechanism. Then adjust the brakes, being sure the parking brake is fully released.

INITIAL ADJUSTMENT

1. Remove adjusting hole cover from brake backing plate and, from the backing plate side, turn the adjusting screw upward with a screwdriver or other suitable tool to expand the shoes until a slight drag is felt when the drums are rotated.
2. Remove the drum.
3. While holding the adjusting lever out of engagement with the adjusting screw, **Fig. 10,** back off the adjusting

screw about one full turn with the fingers.

NOTE: If finger movement will not turn the screw, free it up. If this is not done, the adjusting lever will not turn the screw during vehicle operation. Lubricate the screw with oil and coat with wheel bearing grease. Any other adjustment procedure may cause damage to the adjusting screw with consequent self-adjuster problems.

4. Install wheel and drum, and adjusting hole cover. Adjust brakes on remaining wheels in the same manner.
5. If pedal height is not satisfactory, drive the vehicle and make sufficient reverse stops with a firm pedal effort until proper pedal height is obtained.

PARKING BRAKE
ADJUST

Check parking brake cables when brakes are fully released. If cables are loose, adjust as follows:

1980—86 REAR DRUM BRAKES

1. Make sure parking brake is released.
2. Place transmission in neutral and raise the vehicle.
3. Tighten the adjusting nut against the cable equalizer to cause rear brakes to drag.
4. Then loosen the adjusting nut until the rear wheels are fully released. There should be no drag.
5. Lower vehicle and check operation.

VACUUM RELEASE PARKING BRAKE

The vacuum power unit will release the parking brakes automatically when the shift lever is moved into any drive position with the engine running. The brakes will not release automatically, however, when the shift lever is in neutral or park position with the engine running, or in any position with the engine off.

The power unit piston rod is attached to the release lever. Since the release lever pivots against the pawl, a slight movement of the release lever will disengage the pawl from the ratchet, allowing the brakes to release. The release lever pivots on a rivet pin in the pedal mount.

As shown in **Fig. 11**, hoses connect the power unit and the engine manifold to a vacuum release valve in the transmission neutral safety switch. Moving the transmission selector lever into any drive position with the engine running will open the release valve to connect engine manifold vacuum to one side of the actuating piston in the power unit. The pressure differential thus created will cause the piston and link to pull the release lever.

MASTER CYLINDER
REPLACE

1. Disconnect brake lines from master cylinder.
2. Remove nuts retaining master cylinder to brake booster.
3. Remove master cylinder.
4. Reverse procedure to install.

HYDRO-BOOST BRAKE BOOSTER
REPLACE

1. Working from inside of car under instrument panel, disconnect booster push rod link from brake pedal. To do this, proceed as follows:

Fig. 11 Connections for automatic parking brake release. Typical

2. Disconnect stop light switch wires at connector. Remove hairpin retainer. Slide switch off brake pedal pin just far enough for switch outer hole to clear pin. Then lift switch straight upward from pin. Slide master cylinder push rod and nylon washers and bushing off brake pedal pin.
3. Open hood and disconnect brake line at master cylinder outlet fitting.
4. Disconnect the pressure, steering gear and return lines, then plug lines and ports.
5. Remove Hydro-Boost to dash panel nuts and remove assembly from panel, sliding push rod link from engine side of dash panel.
6. Reverse procedure to install. To purge system, disconnect coil wire so that

engine will not start. Fill power steering pump reservoir, then while engaging starter, pump brake pedal. Do not cycle steering wheel until all residual air has been purged from the hydro boost unit. Check fluid level, then connect coil wire and start engine. Apply brakes with a pumping action and cycle steering wheel, then check system for leaks.

VACUUM BRAKE BOOSTER
REPLACE

1. Disconnect battery ground cable.
2. Disconnect master cylinder from booster and position aside.

NOTE: It is not necessary to disconnect brake lines, but care should be taken to avoid twisting or kinking lines.

3. Disconnect manifold vacuum hose from booster check valve.
4. Working inside vehicle, disconnect stop lamp switch electrical connector under instrument panel.
5. Remove stop lamp switch retaining pin. Slide switch off brake pedal pin enough so outer plate of switch clears the pin, then remove switch from pin.
6. Remove booster-to-dash panel attaching screws.
7. Slide booster pushrod, nylon washers and bushing off brake pedal pin.
8. Slide pushrod out from engine side of dash panel and remove booster from vehicle.
9. Reverse procedure to install.

Rear Suspension

SHOCK ABSORBER
REPLACE

1. With the rear axle supported properly disconnect shock absorber at upper mounting and compress it to clear hole in spring seat.
2. Disconnect shock absorber from stud on axle bracket.
3. Reverse procedure to install.

COIL SPRING
REPLACE

1. Raise rear of vehicle and support at frame. Support rear axle with a suitable jack.
2. Disconnect shock absorbers at lower mountings.
3. Disconnect brake line from rear brake hose and remove hose to bracket clip.

4. Lower axle to remove springs.

NOTE: On some models, it may be necessary to disconnect the right hand parking brake cable from right hand upper arm retainer before lowering axle.

5. Reverse procedure to install. Install an insulator between upper seat and spring on 1980–86 models.

CONTROL ARMS
REPLACE

NOTE: Control arms must be replaced in pairs.

1. Raise rear of vehicle and support at frame. Support axle with a suitable jack.
2. Remove stabilizer bar.
3. Lower axle and install a second jack under differential pinion nose.

4. Disconnect parking brake cable from upper arm retainer.
5. Disconnect control arm from axle bracket. On upper arms, disconnect arm from crossmember and on lower arms, disconnect arm from frame attachment bracket.
6. Reverse procedure to install.

STABILIZER BAR
REPLACE

1980–86

1. Raise and support vehicle at frame side rails.
2. Support rear axle with a suitable jack and position axle so the shock absorbers are fully extended.
3. Remove bolts, nuts and spacers attaching stabilizer bar to lower arms, **Fig. 1.**
4. Remove stabilizer bar from vehicle.
5. Reverse procedure to install.

Fig. 1   Rear suspension. 1980—86

Front Suspension & Steering Section

FRONT SPRING POSITIONING

HOLE "A"   HOLE "B"
END OF SPRING MUST CLEAR
HOLE "A" AND COVER HOLE "B"

Fig. 1   Front suspension. 1980—86

Fig. 2   Adjusting caster & camber. 1980—86

Caster and camber can be adjusted by loosening the bolts that attach the upper suspension arm to the shaft at the frame side rail, and moving the arm assembly in or out in the elongated bolt holes, **Fig. 2.** Since any movement of the arm affects both caster and camber, both factors should be balanced against one another when making the adjustment.

NOTE: On 1980—86 models, use alignment tool T79P-3000A, **Fig. 2.** Install the tool with the pins in the frame holes and the hooks over the upper arm inner shaft. Tighten the hook nuts snug before loosening the upper arm inner shaft attaching bolts.

CASTER, ADJUST

1. Tighten the tool front hook nut or loosen the rear hook nut as required to increase caster to the desired angle.
2. To decrease caster, tighten the rear hook nut or loosen the front hook nut as required.

NOTE: The caster angle can be checked without tightening the inner shaft retaining bolts.

3. Check the camber angle to be sure it did not change during the caster adjustment and adjust if necessary.
4. Torque the upper arm inner shaft retaining bolts to 120—140 ft. lbs. and remove tool.

CAMBER, ADJUST

1. Loosen both inner shaft retaining bolts.
2. Tighten or loosen the hook nuts as necessary to increase or decrease camber.
3. Recheck caster and readjust if necessary.
4. Torque upper arm inner shaft retaining bolts to 120—140 ft. lbs.

TOE-IN
ADJUST

Position the front wheels in their straight-ahead position. Then turn both tie rod adjusting sleeves an equal amount until

FRONT SUSPENSION

1980—86

Referring to **Fig. 1,** note that the lower control arms pivot on two bolts and bushings attached to the crossmember. Previous models used only one bolt and bushing to attach the lower control arm to the suspension crossmember.

WHEEL ALIGNMENT

SERVICE BULLETIN: WHEEL BALANCING DIFFERS: On cars with disc brakes, dynamic balancing of the wheel-and-tire assembly on the car should not be attempted without first pulling back the shoe and lining assemblies from the rotor. If this is not done, brake drag may burn out the motor on the wheel spinner.

The drag can be eliminated by removing the wheel, taking out the two bolts holding the caliper splash shield, and detaching the shield. Then push the pistons into their cylinder bores by applying steady pressure on the shoes on each side of the rotor for at least a minute. If necessary, use water-pump pliers to apply the pressure.

After the pistons have been retracted, reinstall the splash shield and wheel. The wheel-and-tire assembly can then be dynamically balanced in the usual way. After the balancing job has been completed, be sure to pump the brake pedal several times until the shoes are seated and a firm brake pedal is obtained.

the desired toe-in setting is obtained. Torque tie rod sleeve clamp bolt to 20–22 ft. lbs.

WHEEL BEARINGS
ADJUST

1. Raise and support vehicle so front wheels are free to turn.
2. Remove wheel cover, then the grease cap from hub.
3. Clean excess grease from end of spindle, then remove cotter pin and nut lock.
4. Back off adjusting nut three turns, then rock wheel assembly in and out several times to push shoe and linings away from rotor.
5. Torque adjusting nut to 17–25 ft. lbs. while rotating the wheel assembly.
6. Back off adjusting nut ½ turn, then retighten nut to 10–15 inch lbs.
7. Install nut lock on nut so castellations on lock are aligned with cotter pin hole in spindle, then install cotter pin.
8. Check wheel rotation. If wheel rotates roughly or makes noise, lubricate or replace bearings as necessary.

WHEEL BEARINGS
REPLACE

1. Raise and support front of vehicle, then remove tire and wheel assemblies.
2. Remove caliper mounting bolts.

NOTE: It is not necessary to disconnect the brake lines for this operation.

3. Slide caliper off of disc, inserting a spacer between the shoes to hold them in their bores after the caliper is removed. Position caliper assembly out of the way.

NOTE: Do not allow caliper to hang by brake hose.

4. Remove hub and disc assembly. Grease retainer and inner bearing can now be removed.
5. Reverse procedure to install.

CHECKING BALL JOINTS FOR WEAR
UPPER BALL JOINT

1. Raise car on floor jacks placed beneath lower control arms.
2. Grasp lower edge of tire and move wheel in and out.
3. As wheel is being moved in and out, observe upper end of spindle and upper arm.
4. Any movement between upper end of spindle and upper arm indicates ball joint wear and loss of preload. If any such movement is observed, replace upper ball joint.

NOTE: During the foregoing check, the lower ball joint will be unloaded and may

Fig. 3 Lower ball joint wear indicators. 1980–86

move. Disregard all such movement of the lower ball joint. Also, do not mistake loose wheel bearings for a worn ball joint.

LOWER BALL JOINT
1980–86

These models are equipped with lower ball joint wear indicators, **Fig. 3.** To check ball joint for wear, support vehicle in normal driving position with both ball joints loaded. Observe the checking surface of the ball joint. If the checking surface is inside the cover, **Fig. 3,** replace the ball joint.

SHOCK ABSORBER
REPLACE

1. Remove nut, washer and bushing from shock absorber upper end.
2. Raise vehicle and install safety stands.
3. Remove two thread-cutting screws from lower end of shock absorber, then remove shock absorber.
4. Reverse procedure to install.

NOTE: If threads in lower arm become damaged, re-use original thread-cutting screws along with ⁵⁄₁₆-18 locknuts.

COIL SPRING
REPLACE
1980–86

1. Raise and support vehicle.
2. Remove wheel.
3. Disconnect stabilizer bar link from lower control arm.
4. Remove shock absorber.
5. Remove steering center link from pitman arm.
6. Compress coil spring with a suitable spring compressor, tool D-78P-5310-A or equivalent.
7. Remove two lower control arm pivot bolts and disengage arm from crossmember.
8. Remove spring from vehicle.
9. Reverse procedure to install. Torque stabilizer bar to lower control arm nuts to 9–12 ft. lbs. Torque lower control

arm to crossmember bolts to 120–140 ft. lbs.

BALL JOINTS
REPLACE

NOTE: Ford Motor Company recommends that new ball joints should not be installed on used control arms and that the control arm be replaced if ball joint replacement is required. However, aftermarket ball joint repair kits which do not require control arm replacement, are available and can be installed using the following procedure.

The ball joints are riveted to the upper and lower control arms. The ball joints can be replaced on the car by removing the rivets and retaining the new ball joint to the control arm with the attaching bolts, nuts and washers furnished with the ball joint kit.

When removing a ball joint, use a suitable pressing tool to force the ball joint out of the spindle.

POWER STEERING GEAR
REPLACE

1. Remove stone shield, if equipped.
2. Disconnect pressure and return lines from steering gear. Plug lines and ports in gear to prevent entry of dirt.
3. Remove two bolts that secure flex coupling to steering gear and to column.
4. Raise car and remove sector shaft nut.
5. Use a puller to remove pitman arm.
6. Support steering gear, then remove attaching bolts.
7. Work steering gear free of flex coupling and remove it from car.
8. Reverse procedure to install.

POWER STEERING PUMP
REPLACE
1980–86 MODELS

1. Disconnect power steering pump return line and allow power steering pump fluid to drain into a suitable container.
2. Disconnect power steering pump pressure hose from pump fitting.
3. Disconnect drive belt from power steering pump pulley, remove pulley, then remove pump.
4. Reverse procedure to install. Torque pump to mounting bracket bolts to 30–45 ft. lbs.

NOTE: On Ford model CII power steering pump, torque pressure hose to pump fitting to 10–15 ft. lbs. End play on this fitting is normal and does not indicate a loose fitting.

FORD & MERCURY
Compact & Intermediate Models

NOTE: The Ford Mustang, Pinto, Mercury Bobcat and Capri are located elsewhere in this manual. Refer to the rear of this manual for vehicle manufacturer's special service tool suppliers.

INDEX OF SERVICE OPERATIONS

Engine & Serial Number Location

Engine code is fifth digit of serial number on 1980 models, or eighth digit of serial number on 1981–86 models. The serial number is stamped on a metal tag located on top left side dash and visible through windshield.

Grille Identification

1980 Cougar

1980 Granada

1980 Monarch

1980 Thunderbird

1980–81 Fairmont

1980–81 Fairmont Futura

1980–83 Zephyr

1981 Cougar & 1982 Cougar Sta. Wag.

1981 Granada

1981–82 Thunderbird

1982 Cougar Exc. Sta. Wag

1982 Granada

1982–83 Fairmont

1983–84 Cougar

1983–84 Thunderbird

1983–84 Mercury Marquis

1983–85 Ford LTD

1985–86 Cougar
continued

GRILLE IDENTIFICATION—Continued

1985—86 Cougar XR-7

1985—86 Ford LTD

1985—86 Mercury Marquis

1985—86 Thunderbird

1985—86 Thunderbird Turbo Coupe

General Engine Specifications

Year	Engine CID①/Liter	Engine V.I.N. Code②	Carburetor	Bore and Stroke	Compression Ratio	Net H.P. @ R.P.M.③	Maximum Torque Lbs. Ft. @ R.P.M.	Normal Oil Pressure Pounds
1980	4-140, 2.3L④⑤	A	5200, 2 Bbl.⑪	3.781 × 3.126	9.0	88 @ 4600	119 @ 2600	40–60
	4-140, 2.3L⑤⑧	A	6500, 2 Bbl.⑫	3.781 × 3.126	9.0	89 @ 4800	122 @ 2600	40–60
	4-140, 2.3L④⑦	A	5200, 2 Bbl.⑫	3.781 × 3.126	9.0	—	—	40–60
	4-140, 2.3L⑦⑧	A	6500, 2 Bbl.⑫	3.781 × 3.126	9.0	—	—	40–60
	6-200, 3.3L④	B	1946, 1 Bbl.⑫	3.68 × 3.13	8.6	91 @ 3800	160 @ 1600	30–50
	6-200, 3.3L⑧	B	1946C, 1 Bbl.⑫	3.68 × 3.13	8.6	—	—	30–50
	6-250, 4.1L④⑨	C	YFA, 1 Bbl.⑥	3.68 × 3.91	8.6	90 @ 3200	194 @ 1660	40–60
	V8-255, 4.2L⑮	D	2150, 2 Bbl.⑪	3.68 × 3.00	8.8	119 @ 3800	194 @ 2200	40–60
	V8-255, 4.2L⑬⑭	D	2150, 2 Bbl.⑪	3.68 × 3.00	8.8	115 @ 3800	191 @ 2000	40–60
	V8-255, 4.2L⑧⑨	D	2150, 2 Bbl.⑪	3.68 × 3.00	8.8	117 @ 3800	193 @ 2000	40–60
	V8-302, 5.0L⑨	F	2150, 2 Bbl.⑪	4.00 × 3.00	8.4	134 @ 3600	232 @ 1600	40–60
	V8-302, 5.0L④⑬⑭	F	2150, 2 Bbl.⑪	4.00 × 3.00	8.4	131 @ 3600	231 @ 1600	40–60
	V8-302, 5.0L⑧⑬⑭	F	2150, 2 Bbl.⑪	4.00 × 3.00	8.4	132 @ 3600	232 @ 1400	40–60
1981	4-140, 2.3L	A	6500, 2 Bbl.⑫	3.781 × 3.126	9.0	88 @ 4600	118 @ 2600	40–60
	6-200, 3.3L	B	1946, 1 Bbl.⑫	3.68 × 3.13	8.6	88 @ 3800	154 @ 1400	30–50
	V8-255, 4.2L④	D	2150, 2 Bbl.⑪	3.68 × 3.00	8.2	115 @ 3400	195 @ 2200	40–60
	V8-255, 4.2L⑧	D	7200VV, 2 Bbl.⑪	3.68 × 3.00	8.2	120 @ 3400	205 @ 2600	40–60
	V8-302, 5.0L④	F	2150, 2 Bbl.⑪	4.00 × 3.00	8.4	130 @ 3400	235 @ 1600	40–60
	V8-302, 5.0L⑧	F	7200VV, 2 Bbl.⑪	4.00 × 3.00	8.4	130 @ 3400	235 @ 1800	40–60
1982	4-140, 2.3L	A	6500, 2 Bbl.⑫	3.781 × 3.126	9.0	86 @ 4600	117 @ 2600	40–60
	6-200, 3.3L	B	1946, 1 Bbl.⑫	3.68 × 3.13	8.6	87 @ 3800	154 @ 1400	30–50
	V6-232, 3.8L④	3	2150, 2 Bbl.⑪	3.81 × 3.39	8.8	112 @ 4000	175 @ 2600	54–59
	V6-232, 3.8L⑧	3	7200VV, 2 Bbl.⑪	3.81 × 3.39	8.8	118 @ 4000	186 @ 2600	54–59
	V8-255, 4.2L④	D	2150, 2 Bbl.⑪	3.68 × 3.00	8.2	122 @ 3400	209 @ 2400	40–60
	V8-255, 4.2L⑧	D	7200VV, 2 Bbl.⑪	3.68 × 3.00	—	—	—	40–60
1983	4-140, 2.3L⑤	A	YFA, 1 Bbl.⑥	3.78 × 3.12	9.0	86 @ 4600	117 @ 2600	50
	4-140, 2.3L⑦	W	E.F.I.⑩	3.78 × 3.12	8.0	—	—	55
	6-200, 3.3L	X	1946, 1 Bbl.⑫	3.68 × 3.12	8.6	87 @ 3800	154 @ 1400	50
	V6-232, 3.8L	3	2150, 2 Bbl.⑪	3.8 × 3.4	8.7	112 @ 4000	175 @ 2600	40–60
	V8-302, 5.0L	F	E.F.I.⑩	4.00 × 3.00	—	—	—	40–60
1984–85	4-140, 2.3L⑤	A	YFA, 1Bbl.⑥	3.78 × 3.12	9.0	88 @ 4000	1220 @ 2400	50
	4-140, 2.3L⑦	W	E.F.I.⑩	3.78 × 3.12	8.0	145 @ 4600	180 @ 3600	55
	V6-232, 3.8L	3	E.F.I.⑩	3.80 × 3.40	8.7	120 @ 3600	205 @ 1600	40–60
	V8-302, 5.0L	F	E.F.I.⑩	4.00 × 3.00	8.4	140 @ 3200	250 @ 1600	40–60
	V8-302, H.O., 5.0L	M	E.F.I.⑩	4.00 × 3.00	8.3	165 @ 3800	245 @ 2000	40–60

continued

FORD & MERCURY—Compact & Intermediate Models

GENERAL ENGINE SPECIFICATIONS—Continued

Year	Engine CID①/Liter	Engine V.I.N. Code②	Carburetor	Bore and Stroke	Compression Ratio	Net H.P. @ R.P.M.③	Maximum Torque Lbs. Ft. @ R.P.M.	Normal Oil Pressure Pounds
1986	4-140, 2.3L⑤	—	YFA, 1Bbl.⑥	3.78 × 3.12	9.5	88 @ 4200	122 @ 2600	50
	4-140, 2.3L⑦⑰	—	E.F.I.⑩	3.78 × 3.12	8.0	145 @ 4400	180 @ 3000	55
	4-140, 2.3L⑦⑱	—	E.F.I.⑩	3.78 × 3.12	8.0	155 @ 4600	190 @ 2800	55
	V6-232, 3.8L	—	E.F.I.⑩	3.80 × 3.40	8.7	120 @ 3600	205 @ 1600	40–60
	V8-302, 5.0L	—	S.E.F.I.⑯	4.00 × 3.00	8.9	150 @ 3400	270 @ 2000	40–60

①—CID—cubic inch displacement.
②—On 1980 models, the fifth digit of the V.I.N. denotes engine code. On 1981–85 models, the eighth digit of the V.I.N. denotes engine code.
③—Ratings are NET—as installed on vehicle.
④—Except California.
⑤—Non-Turbocharged.
⑥—Carter.
⑦—Turbocharged.
⑧—California.
⑨—Granada & Monarch.
⑩—Electronic fuel injection.
⑪—Motorcraft.
⑫—Holley.
⑬—Thunderbird.
⑭—Cougar XR-7.
⑮—Fairmont & Zephyr.
⑯—Sequential electronic fuel injection.
⑰—Auto. trans.
⑱—Man. trans.

Starting Motor Applications

Year	Engine/V.I.N.	Ident. No.	Year	Engine/V.I.N.	Ident. No.
1980	4-140/A	D8EF-AA		6-200/X③	E3AF-AA
	6-200/B①	D8BF-CA		6-200/X④	E1BF-BA
	6-200/B②	D8BF-AA		V6-232/3	E25F-AA
	6-250/C	D8OF-AA		V8-302/F	E3AF-AA
	V8-255/D, V8-302/F⑨	D8OF-AA	1984	4-140/A⑤	E2BF-AA
	V8-255/D, V8-302/F⑩	E1AF-BA		4-140/A⑧	E4DF-AA
1981	4-140/A⑪	E1ZF-AA		4-140/W	E4SF-AA
	4-140/A⑫	E1ZF-BA		V6-232/3	E25F-AA
	4-140/A⑬	E2BF-AA		V8-302/F⑤	E3AF-AA
	6-200/B⑭	E1BF-BA		V8-302/F⑧	E4AF-AA
	6-200/B⑪⑮	E1BF-BA		V8-302 H.O./M	—
	6-200/B⑮⑯	E1AF-BA	1985	4-140/A	E4DF-AA
	V8-255/D, V8-302/F	E1AF-BA		4-140/W	—
1982	4-140/A	E2BF-AA		V6-232/3	E4DF-BA
	6-200/B⑰	E1AF-BA		V8-302/F	E4AF-AA
	6-200/B⑱	E1BF-BA		V8-302 H.O./M	—
	V6-232/3⑲	E2SF-AA	1986	4-140㉑	—
	V6-232/3⑳	E25F-AA		4-140㉒	E4SF-AA
	V8-255/D⑥	E1AF-BA		V6-232	E4DF-BA
	V8-255/D⑦	E3AF-AA		V8-302	E4AF-AA
1983	4-140/A,W	E2BF-AA			

①—Automatic trans.
②—Manual trans.
③—Except Fairmont & Zephyr high alt.
④—Fairmont & Zephyr high alt.
⑤—Vehicles manufactured before 12/83.
⑥—Vehicles manufactured before 5-17-82.
⑦—Vehicles manufactured after 5-16-82.
⑧—Vehicles manufactured from 12/83.
⑨—Vehicles manufactured before 3-24-80.
⑩—Vehicles manufactured after 3-23-80.
⑪—Vehicles manufactured before 3-21-81.
⑫—Vehicles manufactured between 3-21-81 and 5-1-81.
⑬—Vehicles manufactured after 5-1-81.
⑭—Thunderbird & XR-7.
⑮—Except Thunderbird & XR-7.
⑯—Vehicles manufactured after 3-20-81.
⑰—Except Thunderbird & XR-7 with C5 automatic trans., serial no. PEB-Z2.
⑱—Thunderbird & XR-7 with C5 automatic trans., serial no. PEB-Z2.
⑲—Vehicles manufactured before 1-18-82.
⑳—Vehicles manufactured after 1-17-82.
㉑—Non-Turbocharged.
㉒—Turbocharged.

continued

Alternator & Regulator Specifications

Year	Color Code Stamp	Current Rating① Amperes	Volts	Field Current @ 75°F. Amperes	Volts	Voltage Regulator Model No. (10316)	Voltage @ 75°F.	Contact Gap	Armature Air Gap	Field Relay Armature Air Gap	Closing Voltage @ 75°F.
1980–81	Orange③⑤⑦	40	15	4.0	12	D9BF-AB⑥	13.8–14.6	④	④	④	—
	Green③⑤⑦	60	15	4.0	12	D9BF-AB⑥	13.8–14.6	④	④	④	—
	Black③⑤⑦	65	15	4.0	12	D9BF-AB⑥	13.8–14.6	④	④	④	—
	Black③⑤⑧	70	15	4.0	12	D9BF-AB⑥	13.8–14.6	④	④	④	—
	Red③⑤⑧	100	15	4.0	12	D9BF-AB⑥	13.8–14.6	④	④	④	—
1982	Orange③⑤⑦	40	15	4.0	12	E1AF-AA⑥	13.8–14.6	④	④	④	—
	Green③⑤⑦	60	15	4.0	12	E1AF-AA⑥	13.8–14.6	④	④	④	—
	Black③⑤⑦	65	15	4.0	12	E1AF-AA⑥	13.8–14.6	④	④	④	—
	Black③⑤⑧	70	15	4.0	12	E1AF-AA⑥	13.8–14.6	④	④	④	—
	Red③⑤⑧	100	15	4.0	12	E1AF-AA⑥	13.8–14.6	④	④	④	—
1983	Orange③⑤⑦	40	15	4.25	12	—	—	—	—	—	—
	Black③⑤⑦	65	15	4.25	12	—	—	—	—	—	—
	Green③⑤⑦	60	15	4.25	12	—	—	—	—	—	—
	Black③⑤⑧	70	15	4.25	12	—	—	—	—	—	—
	Red③⑤⑧	100	15	4.25	12	—	—	—	—	—	—
1984	Orange③⑤⑦	40	15	4.25	12	—	—	—	—	—	—
	Green③⑤⑦	60	15	4.25	12	—	—	—	—	—	—
	Black③⑤⑧	70	15	4.25	12	—	—	—	—	—	—
	Red③⑤⑧	100	15	4.25	12	—	—	—	—	—	—
1985–86	Orange③⑤⑦	40	15	4.25	12	E4AF-AA⑥	—	④	④	④	—
	Green③⑤⑦	60	15	4.25	12	E4TF-AA⑥	—	④	④	④	—
	Black③⑤⑧	70	15	4.25	12	E4AF-AA⑥	—	④	④	④	—
	Red③⑤⑧	100	15	4.25	12	E4AF-AA⑥	—	④	④	④	—

①—Current rating stamped on housing.
②—Voltage regulation stamped on cover.
③—Stamp color.
④—Not adjustable.
⑤—Solid state alternator.
⑥—Electronic voltage regulator. These units are color coded black for systems w/warning indicator lamp & blue for systems w/ammeter.
⑦—Rear terminal alternator.
⑧—Side terminal alternator.

Valve Specifications

Year	Engine/V.I.N.	Valve Lash Int.	Exh.	Valve Angles Seat	Face	Valve Spring Installed Height	Valve Spring Pressure Lbs. @ In.	Stem Clearance Intake	Exhaust	Stem Diameter, Standard Intake	Exhaust
1980	4-140/A	.040–.050②	45	44	1 9/16	167 @ 1.16	.0010–.0027	.0015–.0032	.3416–.3423	.3411–.3418
	6-200/B	.110–.184①	45	44	1 37/64	150 @ 1.22	.0008–.0025	.0010–.0027	.3100–.3107	.3098–.3105
	6-250/C	.096–.160①	45	44	1 37/64	150 @ 1.22	.0008–.0025	.0010–.0027	.3100–.3107	.3098–.3105
	V8-255/D	.071–.193①	45	44	⑤	⑥	.0010–.0027	.0015–.0032	.3416–.3423	.3411–.3418
	V8-302/F	.071–.193①	45	44	⑤	③	.0010–.0027	.0015–.0032	.3416–.3423	.3411–.3418
1981	4-140/A	.040–.050②	45	44	1 9/16	167 @ 1.16	.0010–.0027	.0015–.0032	.3416–.3423	.3411–.3418
	6-200/B	.110–.160①	45	44	1 37/64	150 @ 1.22	.0008–.0025	.0010–.0027	.3100–.3107	.3098–.3105
	V8-255/D	.096–.146①	45	44	⑤	④	.0010–.0027	.0015–.0032	.3416–.3423	.3411–.3418
	V8-302/F	.096–.146①	45	44	⑤	④	.0010–.0027	.0015–.0032	.3416–.3423	.3411–.3418
1982	4-140/A	.040–.050②	45	44	1 9/16	167 @ 1.16	.0010–.0027	.0015–.0032	.3416–.3423	.3411–.3418
	6-200/B	.110–.184①	45	44	1 19/32	150 @ 1.22	.0008–.0025	.0010–.0027	.3100–.3107	.3098–.3105
	V6-232/3	.088–.189①	45	44	1 47/64	215 @ 1.40	.0010–.0027	.0015–.0032	.3416–.3423	.3411–.3418
	V8-255/D	.096–.146①	45	44	⑤	⑨	.0010–.0027	.0015–.0032	.3416–.3423	.3411–.3418
1983	4-140/A,W	.040–.050②	45	44	1 9/16	149 @ 1.12	.0010–.0027	.0015–.0032	.3416–.3423	.3411–.3418
	6-200/X	.110–.184①	45	44	1 19/32	150 @ 1.22	.0008–.0025	.0010–.0027	.3100–.3107	.3098–.3105
	V6-232/3	.088–.189①	45	44	1 47/64	215 @ 1.40	.0010–.0027	.0015–.0032	.3416–.3423	.3411–.3418
	V8-302/F	.096–.146①	45	44	⑤	⑦	.0010–.0027	.0015–.0032	.3416–.3423	.3411–.3418
1984–85	4-140/A,W	.040–.050②	45	44	1 9/16	154 @ 1.52	.0010–.0027	.0015–.0032	.3416–.3423	.3411–.3418
	V6-232/3	.088–.189①	45	44	1 37/50	215 @ 1.79	.0010–.0027	.0015–.0032	.3416–.3423	.3411–.3418
	V8-302/F	.096–.146①	45	44	⑤	⑦	.0010–.0027	.0015–.0032	.3416–.3423	.3411–.3418
	V8-302 H.O./M	.123–.146①	45	44	—	⑧	.0010–.0027	.0015–.0032	.3416–.3423	.3411–.3418

VALVE SPECIFICATIONS—Continued

Year	Engine/V.I.N.	Valve Lash Int.	Valve Lash Exh.	Valve Angles Seat	Valve Angles Face	Valve Spring Installed Height	Valve Spring Pressure Lbs. @ In.	Stem Clearance Intake	Stem Clearance Exhaust	Stem Diameter, Standard Intake	Stem Diameter, Standard Exhaust
1986	4-140	.040–.050②	—	45	44	1⁹⁄₁₆	154 @ 1.52	.0010–.0027	.0015–.0032	.3416–.3423	.3411–.3418
	V6-232	.088–.189①	—	45	44	1³⁷⁄₅₀	215 @ 1.79	.0010–.0027	.0015–.0032	.3416–.3423	.3411–.3418
	V8-302	.096–.146①	—	45	44	⑤	⑦	.0010–.0027	.0015–.0032	.3416–.3423	.3411–.3418

①—Clearance is obtained at valve stem tip with hydraulic lifter collapsed. If clearance is less than the minimum install an undersize push rod; if clearance is greater than the maximum install on oversize push rod.
②—Measured at cam with hydraulic lifter completely collapsed.
③—Intake, 204 @ 1.36; exhaust, 200 @ 1.20.
④—Intake, 205 @ 1.36; exhaust, 200 @ 1.20.
⑤—Intake, 1¹¹⁄₁₆ in.; exhaust, 1¹⁹⁄₃₂ in.
⑥—Intake, 201 @ 1.36; exhaust, 200 @ 1.20.
⑦—Intake, 205 @ 1.36; exhaust, 205 @ 1.05.
⑧—Intake, 225 @ 1.33; exhaust, 220 @ 1.15.
⑨—Intake, 205 @ 1.36; exhaust, 205 @ 1.15.

Pistons, Pins, Rings, Crankshaft & Bearings

Year	Engine/ V.I.N.	Piston Clearance	Ring End Gap① Comp.	Ring End Gap① Oil	Wrist-pin Diameter	Rod Bearings Shaft Diameter	Rod Bearings Bearing Clearance	Main Bearings Shaft Diameter	Main Bearings Bearing Clearance	Main Bearings Thrust on Bear. No.	Shaft End Play
1980	4-140/A③	.0014–.0022	.010	.015	.9121	2.0462–2.0472	.0008–.0015	2.3982–2.3990	.0008–.0015	3	.004–.008
	4-140/A⑤	.0034–.0042	.010	.015	.9121	2.0462–2.0472	.0008–.0015	2.3982–2.3990	.0008–.0015	3	.004–.008
	6-200/B	.0013–.0021	.008	.015	.9121	2.1232–2.1240	.0008–.0015	2.2482–2.2490	.0008–.0015	5	.004–.008
	6-250/C	.0013–.0021	.008	.015	.9121	2.1232–2.1240	.0008–.0015	2.3982–2.3990	.0008–.0015	5	.004–.008
	V8-255/D	.0018–.0026	.010	.015	.9121	2.1228–2.1236	.0008–.0015	2.2482–2.2490	⑥	3	.004–.008
	V8-302/F	.0018–.0026	.010	.015	.9121	2.1228–2.1236	.0008–.0015	2.2482–2.2490	⑥	3	.004–.008
1981	4-140/A	.0014–.0022	.010	.015	.9121	2.0462–2.0472	.0008–.0015	2.3982–2.3990	.0008–.0015	3	.004–.008
	6-200/B	.0013–.0021	.008	.015	.9121	2.1232–2.1240	.0008–.0015	2.2482–2.2490	.0008–.0015	5	.004–.008
	V8-255/D	.0004–.0024	.010	.015	.9121	2.1228–2.1236	.0008–.0015	2.2482–2.2490	⑥	3	.004–.008
	V8-302/F	.0018–.0026	.010	.015	.9121	2.1228–2.1236	.0008–.0015	2.2482–2.2490	⑥	3	.004–.008
1982	4-140/A	.0014–.0022	.010	.015	.9121	2.0465–2.0472	.0008–.0015	2.3982–2.3990	.0008–.0015	3	.004–.008
	6-200/B	.0013–.0021	.008	.015	.9121	2.1232–2.1240	.0008–.0015	2.2482–2.2490	.0008–.0015	5	.004–.008
	V6-232/3	.0014–.0022	.010	.015	.9121	2.3103–2.3111	.0010–.0014	2.5190–2.5198	.0010–.0014	3	.004–.008
	V8-255/D	.0014–.0024	.010	.015	.9121	2.1228–2.1236	.0008–.0015	2.2482–2.2490	②	3	.004–.008
1983	4-140/A,W	.0014–.0022	.010	.015	.9121	2.0462–2.0472	.0008–.0015	2.3982–2.3990	.0008–.0015	5	.004–.008
	6-200/X	.0013–.0021	.008	.015	.9121	2.1232–2.1240	.0008–.0015	2.3982–2.2490	.0008–.0015	3	.004–.008
	V6-232/3	.0014–.0022	.010	.015	.9121	2.3103–2.3111	.0010–.0014	2.5190–2.5198	.0010–.0014	3	.004–.008
	V8-302/F	.0018–.0026	.010	.015	.9121	2.1228–2.1236	.0008–.0015	2.2482–2.2490	④	3	.004–.008

continued

PISTONS, PINS, RINGS, CRANKSHAFT & BEARINGS—Continued

Year	Engine/V.I.N.	Piston Clearance	Ring End Gap① Comp.	Ring End Gap① Oil	Wrist-pin Diameter	Rod Bearings Shaft Diameter	Rod Bearings Bearing Clearance	Main Bearings Shaft Diameter	Main Bearings Bearing Clearance	Main Bearings Thrust on Bear. No.	Shaft End Play
1984–85	4-140/A,W	.0030–.0038	.010	.015	.9121	2.0465–2.0472	.0008–.0015	2.3982–2.3990	.0008–.0015	5	.004–.008
	V6-232/3	.0014–.0032	.010	.015	.9121	2.3103–2.3111	.0010–.0014	2.5190–2.5198	.0010–.0014	3	.004–.008
	V8-302/F	.0018–.0026	.010	.015	.9121	2.1228–2.1236	.0008–.0015	2.2482–2.2490	④⑦	3	.004–.008
	V8-302 H.O./M	.0018–.0026	.010	.015	.9121	2.1228–2.1236	.0008–.0015	2.2482–2.2490	④⑦	3	.004–.008
1986	4-140	.0030–.0038	.010	.015	.9121	2.0465–2.0472	.0008–.0015	2.3982–2.3990	.0008–.0015	5	.004–.008
	V6-232	.0014–.0032	.010	.015	.9121	2.3103–2.3111	.0010–.0014	2.5190–2.5198	.0010–.0014	3	.004–.008
	V8-302	.0018–.0026	.010	.015	.9121	2.1228–2.1236	.0008–.0015	2.2482–2.2490	.0004–.0015	3	.004–.008

①—Fit rings in tapered bores for clearance listed in tightest portion of ring travel.
②—No. 1, .0004–.0025; No. 2, 3, 4, 5, .0004–.0015.
③—Non-Turbocharged.
④—No. 1, .0004–.0025; No. 2, 3, 4, 5, .0004–.0015.
⑤—Turbocharged.
⑥—No. 1: .0001–.0015; No. 2, 3, 4, 5: .0004–.0015.
⑦—1985, .0004–.0015.

Engine Tightening Specifications★

★ Torque specifications are for clean and lightly lubricated threads only. Dry or dirty threads produce increased friction which prevents accurate measurement of tightness.

Year	Engine/V.I.N.	Spark Plugs Ft. Lbs.	Cylinder Head Bolts Ft. Lbs.	Intake Manifold Ft. Lbs.	Exhaust Manifold Ft. Lbs.	Rocker Arm Shaft Bracket Ft. Lbs.	Rocker Arm Cover Ft. Lbs.	Connecting Rod Cap Bolts Ft. Lbs.	Main Bearing Cap Bolts Ft. Lbs.	Flywheel to Crankshaft Ft. Lbs.	Vibration Damper or Pulley Ft. Lbs.
1980	4-140/A	5–10	80–90	⑦	16–23	—	6–8	30–36	80–90	56–64	100–120
	6-200/B	10–15	70–75	—	18–24	30–35	3–5	21–26	60–70	75–85	85–100
	6-250/C	10–15	70–75	—	18–24	30–35	3–5	21–26	60–70	75–85	85–100
	V8-255/D	10–15	65–72	23–25	18–24	18–25⑥	3–5	19–24	60–70	75–85	70–90
	V8-302/F	10–15	65–72	23–25	18–24	18–25⑥	3–5	19–24	60–70	75–85	70–90
1981	4-140/A	5–10	80–90	14–21	16–23	—	6–8	30–36	80–90	56–64	100–120
	6-200/B	10–15	70–75	—	18–24	30–35	3–5	21–26	60–70	75–85	85–100
	V8-255/D	10–15	65–72	18–20	18–24	18–25⑥	3–5	19–24	60–70	75–85	70–90
	V8-302/F	10–15	65–72	23–25	18–24	18–25⑥	3–5	19–24	60–70	75–85	70–90
1982	4-140/A	5–10	80–90	14–21	16–23	—	5–8	30–36	80–90	56–64	100–120
	6-200/B	10–15	70–75	—	18–24	30–35	3–5	21–26	60–70	75–85	85–100
	V6-232/3	15–22	②	18.4	15–22	18.4–25.8	3–5	31–36	65–81	54–64	93–121
	V8-255/D	10–15	65–72	18–20	18–24	18–25⑥	3–5	19–24	60–70	75–85	70–90
1983	4-140/A,W	5–10	80–90	14–21	16–23	—	5–8	30–36	80–90	56–64	100–120
	6-200/X	10–15	70–75	—	18–24	30–35	3–5	21–26	60–70	75–85	85–100
	V6-232/3	5–11	②	18.4	15–22	18.4–25.8	3–5	31–36	65–81	54–64	93–121
	V8-302/F	10–15	65–72	23–25	18–24	18–25⑥	3–5	19–24	60–70	75–85	70–90
1984	4-140/A,W	5–10	80–90	14–21	16–23	—	5–8	30–36	80–90	56–64	100–120
	V6-232/3	5–11	⑤	⑧	15–22	18.4–25.8⑥	6.6–8.8	31–36	65–81	56–64	93–121
	V8-302/F	10–15	65–72	23–25	18–24	18–25⑥	3–5	19–24	60–70	75–85	70–90
	V8-302H.O./M	10–15	④	23–25	18–24	18–25⑥	3–5	19–24	60–70	75–85	70–90
1985	4-140/A,W	5–10	⑨	14–21	⑩	—	5–8	⑪	⑫	56–64	100–120
	V6-232/3	5–11	⑤	⑧	15–22	①⑥	80–106③	31–36	65–81	54–64	93–121
	V8-302/F	10–15	⑮	23–25	18–24	18–25⑥	3–5	19–24	60–70	75–85	70–90
	V8-302/M	10–15	⑮	23–25	18–24	18–25⑥	3–5	19–24	60–70	75–85	70–90

continued

5–7

ENGINE TIGHTENING SPECIFICATIONS—Continued

★ Torque specifications are for clean and lightly lubricated threads only. Dry or dirty threads produce increased friction which prevents accurate measurement of tightness.

Year	Engine/V.I.N.	Spark Plugs Ft. Lbs.	Cylinder Head Bolts Ft. Lbs.	Intake Manifold Ft. Lbs.	Exhaust Manifold Ft. Lbs.	Rocker Arm Shaft Bracket Ft. Lbs.	Rocker Arm Cover Ft. Lbs.	Connecting Rod Cap Bolts Ft. Lbs.	Main Bearing Cap Bolts Ft. Lbs.	Flywheel to Crankshaft Ft. Lbs.	Vibration Damper or Pulley Ft. Lbs.
1986	4-140	5–10	⑨	14–21	⑩	—	5–8	⑪	⑫	56–64	100–120
	V6-232	5–11	⑤	⑧	15–22	①⑥	80–106③	31–36	65–81	54–64	93–121
	V8-302	10–15	⑮	23–25	18–24	18–25⑥	3–5	19–24	60–70	75–85	70–90

①—Torque in 2 steps: 1, 5–11 ft. lbs.; 2, 18.4–25.8 ft. lbs.
②—Tighten in 4 steps: 1, 47 ft. lbs.; 2, 55 ft. lbs.; 3, 63 ft. lbs.; 4, 74 ft. lbs. Back off all bolts 2–3 turns, retorque in 4 steps.
③—Inch lbs.
④—Torque in 2 steps: 1, 55–65 ft. lbs.; 2, 65–72 ft. lbs.

⑤—Tighten in 4 steps: 1, 37 ft. lbs.; 2, 45 ft. lbs.; 3, 52 ft. lbs.; 4, 59 ft. lbs. Back off all bolts 2–3 turns, retorque in 4 steps.
⑥—Fulcrum bolt to cylinder head.
⑦—Except turbocharged engine, 14–21 ft. lbs; turbocharged engine, 13–18 ft. lbs.
⑧—Torque in 3 steps: 1, 7 ft. lbs.; 2, 15 ft.

lbs.; 3, 24 ft. lbs.
⑨—Torque in 2 steps: 1, 50–60 ft. lbs.; 2, 80–90 ft. lbs.
⑩—Torque in 2 steps: 1, 5–7 ft. lbs.; 2, 16–23 ft. lbs.
⑪—Torque in 2 steps: 1, 25–30 ft. lbs.; 2, 30–36 ft. lbs.
⑫—Torque in 2 steps: 1, 50–60 ft. lbs.; 2, 80–90 ft. lbs.

Wheel Alignment Specifications

Year	Model	Caster Angle, Degrees		Camber Angle, Degrees				Toe-In. Inch	Toe-Out on Turns, Deg.	
		Limits	Desired	Limits		Desired			Outer Wheel	Inner Wheel
				Left	Right	Left	Right			
1980	Cougar XR-7	+⅛ to +1⅞	+1	−½ to +1¼	−½ to +1¼	+⅜	+⅜	3/16	19.84	20
	Fairmont, Sedan	+⅛ to +1⅞	+1	−5/16 to +13/16	−5/16 to +13/16	+7/16	+7/16	3/16	19.74	20
	Fairmont, Sta. Wag.	−⅛ to +1⅝	+¾	−¼ to +1¼	−¼ to +1¼	+½	+½	3/16	19.74	20
	Granada	−1¼ to +¼	−½	−½ to +1	−½ to +1	+¼	+¼	⅛	18.43①	20
	Monarch	−1¼ to +¼	−½	−½ to +1	−½ to +1	+¼	+¼	⅛	18.43①	20
	Thunderbird	+⅛ to +1⅞	+1	−½ to +1¼	−½ to +1¼	+⅜	+⅜	3/16	19.84	20
	Zephyr, Sedan	+⅛ to +1⅞	+1	−5/16 to +13/16	−5/16 to +13/16	+7/16	+7/16	3/16	19.74	20
	Zephyr, Sta. Wag.	−⅛ to +1⅝	+¾	−¼ to +1¼	−¼ to +1¼	+½	+½	3/16	19.74	20
1981	Cougar	+⅛ to +1⅞	+1	−5/16 to +13/16	−5/16 to +13/16	+7/16	+7/16	3/16	19.84	20
	Cougar XR-7	+⅛ to +1⅞	+1	−½ to +1¼	−½ to +1¼	+⅜	+⅜	3/16	19.77	20
	Fairmont, Sedan	+⅛ to +1⅞	+1	−5/16 to +13/16	−5/16 to +13/16	+7/16	+7/16	3/16	19.84	20
	Fairmont, Sta. Wag.	−⅛ to +1⅝	+¾	−¼ to +1¼	−¼ to +1¼	+½	+½	3/16	19.84	20
	Granada	+⅛ to +1⅞	+1	−5/16 to +13/16	−5/16 to +13/16	+7/16	+7/16	3/16	19.84	20
	Thunderbird	+⅛ to +1⅞	+1	−½ to +1¼	−½ to +1¼	+⅜	+⅜	3/16	19.77	20
	Zephyr, Sedan	+⅛ to +1⅞	+1	−5/16 to +13/16	−5/16 to +13/16	+7/16	+7/16	3/16	19.84	20
	Zephyr, Sta. Wag.	−⅛ to +1⅝	+¾	−¼ to +1¼	−¼ to +1¼	+½	+½	3/16	19.84	20
1982	Cougar Sedan	+⅛ to +1⅞	+1	−5/16 to +13/16	−5/16 to +13/16	+7/16	+7/16	3/16	19.84	20
	Cougar Sta. Wag.	+⅛ to +1⅝	+¾	−¼ to +1¼	−¼ to +1¼	+½	+½	3/16	19.84	20
	Cougar XR-7	+⅛ to +1⅞	+1	−½ to +1¼	−½ to +1¼	+⅜	+⅜	3/16	19.73	20
	Fairmont	+⅛ to +1⅞	+1	−5/16 to +13/16	−5/16 to +13/16	+7/16	+7/16	3/16	19.84	20
	Granada Sedan	+⅛ to +1⅞	+1	−5/16 to +13/16	−5/16 to +13/16	+7/16	+7/16	3/16	19.84	20
	Granada Sta. Wag.	+⅛ to +1⅝	+¾	−¼ to +1¼	−¼ to +1¼	+½	+½	3/16	19.84	20
	Thunderbird	+⅛ to +1⅞	+1	−½ to +1¼	−½ to +1¼	+⅜	+⅜	3/16	19.73	20
	Zephyr	+⅛ to +1⅞	+1	−5/16 to +13/16	−5/16 to +13/16	+7/16	+7/16	3/16	19.84	20
1983	Cougar	+½ to +2	+1¼	−½ to +1	−½ to +1	+¼	+¼	3/16	19.73	20
	Fairmont	+⅜ to +2⅛	+1⅛	−5/16 to +13/16	−5/16 to +13/16	+7/16	+7/16	3/16	19.84	20
	LTD Sedan	+⅜ to +2⅛	+1⅛	−5/16 to +13/16	−5/16 to +13/16	+7/16	+7/16	3/16	19.84	20
	LTD Sta. Wagon	−⅛ to +1⅞	+⅞	−¼ to +1¼	−¼ to +1¼	+½	+½	3/16	19.84	20

continued

WHEEL ALIGNMENT SPECIFICATIONS—Continued

Year	Model	Caster Angle, Degrees		Camber Angle, Degrees				Toe-In. Inch	Toe-Out on Turns, Deg.	
		Limits	Desired	Limits		Desired			Outer Wheel	Inner Wheel
				Left	Right	Left	Right			
1983 cont'd	Marquis Sedan	+⅛ to +2⅛	+1⅛	−5⁄16 to +13⁄16	−5⁄16 to +13⁄16	+7⁄16	+7⁄16	³⁄16	19.84	20
	Marquis Sta. Wagon	−⅛ to +1⅞	+⅞	−¼ to +1¼	−¼ to +1¼	+½	+½	³⁄16	19.84	20
	Thunderbird	+½ to +2	+1¼	−½ to +1	−½ to +1	+¼	+¼	³⁄16	19.73	20
	Zephyr	+⅛ to +2⅛	+1⅛	−5⁄16 to +13⁄16	−5⁄16 to +13⁄16	+7⁄16	+7⁄16	³⁄16	19.84	20
1984	Cougar	+¼ to +1¾	+1	−½ to +1	−½ to +1	+¼	+¼	³⁄16	19.73	20
	LTD Sedan	+¼ to +2¼	+1	−¼ to +1¼	−¼ to +1¼	+½	+½	³⁄16	19.84	20
	LTD Sta. Wagon	+¼ to +2¼	+1	−¼ to +1¼	−¼ to +1¼	+½	+½	³⁄16	19.84	20
	Marquis Sedan	+¼ to +2¼	+1	−¼ to +1¼	−¼ to +1¼	+½	+½	³⁄16	19.84	20
	Marquis Sta. Wagon	+¼ to +2¼	+1	−¼ to +1¼	−¼ to +1¼	+½	+½	³⁄16	19.84	20
	Thunderbird	+¼ to +1¾	+1	−½ to +1	−½ to +1	+¼	+¼	³⁄16	19.73	20
1985–86	Cougar	0 to +1½	+¾	−½ to +1	−½ to +1	+¼	+¼	³⁄16	19.73	20
	LTD Sedan	+⅛ to +2⅛	+⅞	−⅜ to +1⅛	−⅜ to +1⅛	+⅜	+⅜	³⁄16	19.84	20
	LTD Sta. Wagon	0 to +2	+¾	−5⁄16 to +13⁄16	−5⁄16 to +13⁄16	+7⁄16	+7⁄16	³⁄16	19.84	20
	Marquis Sedan	+⅛ to +2⅛	+⅞	−⅜ to +1⅛	−⅜ to +1⅛	+⅜	+⅜	³⁄16	19.84	20
	Marquis Sta. Wagon	0 to +2	+¾	−5⁄16 to +13⁄16	−5⁄16 to +13⁄16	+7⁄16	+7⁄16	³⁄16	19.84	20
	Thunderbird	0 to +1½	+¾	−½ to +1	−½ to +1	+¼	+¼	³⁄16	19.73	20

①—Power steering 18.20°.

Cooling System & Capacity Data

Year	Model or Engine/V.I.N.	Cooling Capacity Qts.		Radiator Cap Relief Pressure, Lbs.	Thermo. Opening Temp.	Fuel Tank Gals.	Engine Oil Refill Qts. ①	Transmission Oil			Rear Axle Oil Pints
		Less A/C	With A/C					3 Speed Pints	4 & 5 Speed Pints	Auto. Trans. Qts. ②	
1980	4-140/A	8.6	9	⑧	191	14	4	—	2.8	6.7	⑤
	4-140/A⑫	9.2	9.2	⑧	191	12.7	4½	—	3.5	—	⑤
	6-200/B	8.1	8.1	16	196	14	4	—	4½	㉑	⑤
	6-250/C	10.6	10.8	16	196	18	4	—	4½	㉒	㉖
	V8-255/D⑦	13.4	13.5	16	196	14	4⑱	—	—	10	⑤
	V8-255/D④	14.6	14.7	16	196	18	4	—	—	9.6	㉖
	V8-255/D③	13.2	13.3	16	196	17½	4⑱	—	—	10.1	5
	V8-302/F④	14.2	14.3	16	196	18	4	—	—	9.6	㉖
	V8-302/F③	12.7	12.8	16	196	17½	4⑱	—	—	㉓	5
1981	4-140/A⑦	8.6	9.2	⑧	191	14	4	—	2.8	㉔	⑤
	4-140/A③	8.6	9.2	⑧	191	14	4	—	4.5	6.8	3½
	6-200/B⑦	8.4	8.5	16	196	16	4	—	—	㉕	⑤
	6-200/B③	8.4	8.5	16	196	16	4	—	—	㉕	3½
	6-200/B③	8.4	8.5	16	196	17½	4	—	—	7.7	3½
	V8-255/D⑦	14.8	15.2	16	191	16	4⑱	—	—	9.6	⑤
	V8-255/D③	14.8	15.2	16	196	16	4⑱	—	—	9.6	3½
	V8-255/D③	14.9	15	16	191	18	4⑱	—	—	㉓	3½
	V8-302/F③	13.2	13.4	16	196	18	4⑱	—	—	12	3½
1982	4-140/A⑦	8.6	9.4	⑧	191	④	4	—	2.8	8	⑤
	4-140/A⑲	8.4	8.5	⑧	191	④	4	—	2.8	8	3.2
	6-200/B⑦⑲	8.4	8.5	16	196	④	4	—	2.8	⑥	⑤
	6-200/B⑮	8.4	8.5	16	196	21	4	—	—	⑨	3.2
	V6-232/3	10.7	10.8	16	196	⑩	4	—	—	⑨	3.2

continued

COOLING SYSTEM & CAPACITY DATA—Continued

Year	Model or Engine/V.I.N.	Cooling Capacity Qts. Less A/C	Cooling Capacity Qts. With A/C	Radiator Cap Relief Pressure, Lbs.	Thermo. Opening Temp.	Fuel Tank Gals.	Engine Oil Refill Qts. [1]	Transmission Oil 3 Speed Pints	Transmission Oil 4 & 5 Speed Pints	Transmission Oil Auto. Trans. Qts. [2]	Rear Axle Oil Pints
1982 cont'd	V8-255/D [7]	15.2	15.2	16	191	[4]	4 [18]	—	—	11	[5]
	V8-255/D [15]	14.9	14.0	16	191	21	4 [18]	—	—	[9]	3.2
1983	4-140/A [7][14]	8.6	9.4	[8]	191	[4]	4 [13]	—	2.8	8	3.25
	4-140 [3][12]	8.4	8.7	[8]	191	18	4.5 [13][17]	—	4.75	—	3.25
	6-200/X [7]	8.4	8.5	16	191	[4]	4	—	—	[11][25]	3.25
	6-200/X [14]	8.4	8.5	16	191	[4]	4	—	—	[16]	3.25
	V6-232/3 [14]	10.7	10.8	16	196	[4]	4	—	—	[20]	3.25
	V6-232/3 [3]	10.7	10.8	16	196	21	4	—	—	[20]	3.25
1984	4-140/A [14]	8.6	9.4	16	191	[4]	4 [13]	—	2.8	8	3.5
	4-140/W [3][12]	10.5	10.5	16	191	21	4.5 [13][17]	—	5.6	8	3.5
	V6-232/3 [14]	10.7	10.8	16	196	[4]	4	—	—	11	3.5
	V6-232/3 [3]	10.7	10.8	16	196	21	4	—	—	[20]	3.5
	V8-302/F [3]	14	14.2	16	196	21	4 [18]	—	—	12.3	3.5
1985	4-140/A [14]	9.5	10.2	16	191	[4]	4 [13]	—	—	8	3.5
	4-140/W [3][12]	10.8	10.8	16	191	21	4.5 [13][17]	—	5.6	8	3.5
	V6-232/3 [14]	11.5	11.5	16	196	[4]	4	—	—	11	3.5
	V6-232/3 [3]	11.7	11.7	16	196	21	4	—	—	[20]	3.5
	V8-302/F [3]	14.2	14.2	16	196	21	4 [18]	—	—	12.3	3.5
1986	4-140 [25]	8.6	9.2	14	191	16	4	—	—	8	3.25
	4-140 [26]	8.9	8.9	[13]	191	19	4.5 [13]	—	—	8	3.5
	V6-232	10.7	10.8	16	197	22	4	—	—	12	3.25
	V8-302	13.3	13.4	16	197	22	4	—	—	12	3.25

①—Add 1 qt. with filter change.
②—Approximate. Make final check with dipstick.
③—Cougar & Thunderbird.
④—Standard, 16.0 gals.; optional 20.0 gals.
⑤—With 7.5 inch ring gear, 3.2 pts.; with 6.75 inch ring gear, 2.5 pts.
⑥—With C-3 trans., 8.0 qts.; with C-5 trans., 11.0 qts.
⑦—Fairmont & Zephyr.
⑧—Less A/C, 13 psi.; with A/C 16 psi.
⑨—With C-5 trans., 11.0 qts.; with F10-D automatic overdrive trans., 12.0 qts.
⑩—Cougar & Granada standard, 16 gals.; optional 20 gals. Cougar XR-7 & Thunderbird, 21 gals.
⑪—C3, 8 qts. C5, except high altitude models, 11 qts.; high altitude models, 7.5 qts.
⑫—Turbocharged engine.
⑬—Add ½ qt. with filter change.
⑭—LTD & Marquis.
⑮—Cougar, XR-7 & Thunderbird.
⑯—C3, 8 qts. C5, except Calif., 10.3 qts.; California, 7.5 qts.
⑰—Before starting engine after changing oil, disconnect ignition switch connector from distributor & crank engine several times (not longer than 30 seconds for each cranking interval) until oil lamp goes out or a steady oil pressure reading is observed, then reconnect switch connector & start engine.
⑱—Dual sump oil pan. Remove both drain plugs to fully drain oil. One drain plug located at front of oil pan. Second drain plug located at left side of oil pan.
⑲—Cougar & Granada.
⑳—C5, 11 qts. Automatic overdrive transmission, 12 qts.
㉑—C3, 8 qts.; C4, 7.1 qts.
㉒—Jatco, 8.6 qts.; C4, 9.6 qts.
㉓—C4, 10.1 qts.; F10-D auto. overdrive trans., 12 qts.
㉔—7.5 inch ring gear, 3.5 pts.; 8.5 inch ring gear, 3.8 pts.
㉕—LTD & Marquis, 16 gal.; Thunderbird & Cougar, 21 gal.
㉖—8 inch ring gear, 4.5 pts.; 9 inch ring gear, 5 pts.

Rear Axle Specifications

Year	Ring Gear Diameter	Carrier Type	Ring Gear & Pinion Backlash Inch	Nominal Pinion Locating Shim, Inch	Pinion Bearing Preload New Bearings With Seal Inch-Lbs.	Pinion Bearing Preload Used Bearings With Seal Inch-Lbs.	Pinion Bearing Preload New Bearings Less Seal Inch-Lbs.	Pinion Bearing Preload Used Bearings Less Seal Inch-Lbs.	Differential Bearing Preload	Pinion Nut Torque Ft.-Lbs. [1]
1980	6¾″	Integral	.008–.012	.030	17–27	6–12	—	—	.016 [2]	140
	7½″ WGX [3]	Integral	.008–.012	.030	16–29	8–14	—	—	.016 [2]	170
	9″	Removal	.008–.015	.030	17–27	8–14	—	—	.008–.012 [2]	170
1981	6¾″ WGG [3]	Integral	.008–.015	.030	16–29	8–14	—	—	.016 [2]	140
1981–86	7½″ WGX, WGZ [3]	Integral	.008–.015	.030	16–29	8–14	—	—	.016 [2]	170

①—If torque cannot be obtained, install new spacer. ②—Case spread across differential. ③—Indentification tag prefix.

Electrical Section

STARTER
REPLACE

1980–81 FAIRMONT, ZEPHYR, GRANADA & 1981 COUGAR w/4-140 ENGINE & ALL 1982–86 VEHICLES

1. Disconnect battery ground cable.
2. Raise vehicle on hoist.
3. Remove starter shield, if equipped.
4. Disconnect starter cable from motor.
5. Remove starter attaching bolts and remove starter.

1980–81 COUGAR XR-7 & THUNDERBIRD w/V8-255, 302 ENGINES

1. Disconnect battery ground cable.
2. Raise and support vehicle.
3. Remove starter motor attaching bolts, then lower starter motor and disconnect starter cable.
4. Reverse procedure to install.

1980–81 FAIRMONT, ZEPHYR, GRANADA & 1981 COUGAR w/6-200 ENGINE

1. Disconnect battery ground cable, then raise and support vehicle and remove upper starter attaching bolt.
2. Remove exhaust heat shield, then disconnect starter cable from starter motor.
3. Remove lower starter mounting bolts, then remove starter motor.
4. Reverse procedure to install.

1980 GRANADA & MONARCH V8-302

1. Disconnect battery ground cable.
2. Disconnect starter cable from starter.
3. Remove engine mount through bolt and nut.
4. Remove two bolts retaining insulator to block and remove insulator.
5. Position a suitable jack under engine and raise engine.
6. Remove starter attaching bolts and starter.

NOTE: On engines equipped with a solenoid actuated starter, turn wheel to full right and remove the idler arm to frame bolts. On some models, it may be necessary to turn wheels aside to aid starter removal.

SERVICE BULLETIN: NOISY STARTER OR STARTER LOCKUP: If either of these situations occur, loosen the three mounting bolts enough to hand fit the starter properly into pilot plate. Then tighten starter mounting bolts, starting with top bolt. Starter should not be replaced until it has been proven noisy after proper alignment has been established by the above method.

Fig. 1   Ignition switch. 1980–83 Fairmont, Zephyr, 1980–82 Cougar XR-7, 1980–86 Thunderbird, 1981–82 Granada, 1981–86 Cougar, 1983–86 LTD & Marquis

IGNITION LOCK
REPLACE

1. Disconnect battery ground cable.
2. On 1980 models, remove trim shroud.
3. On 1981–86 models equipped with tilt column, remove upper extension shroud by detaching from retaining clip at 9 o'clock position.
4. On 1981–86 models, remove both trim shroud halves.
5. On all models, disconnect key warning switch electrical connector.
6. Turn ignition key to "Run." Place gear shift lever in "Park" if equipped with column shift.
7. Insert a ⅛ inch diameter wire pin into hole in casting around lock cylinder. Remove lock cylinder while depressing retaining pin with wire.
8. Reverse procedure to install. Lock cylinder must be in "Run" and retaining pin depressed during installation. Following installation, turn the key to check for correct operation in all positions.

IGNITION SWITCH
REPLACE

1980–83 FAIRMONT & ZEPHYR; 1980–82 COUGAR XR-7, 1980–86 THUNDERBIRD; 1981–82 GRANADA; 1981–86 COUGAR; 1983–86 LTD & MARQUIS

1. Disconnect battery ground cable.

2. On 1981–86 models equipped with tilt column, remove upper extension shroud by detaching from retaining clip at 9 o'clock position.
3. On 1981–86 models, remove both trim shroud halves.
4. Disconnect ignition switch wire connector.
5. Drill out bolts that attach switch to lock cylinder housing using a ⅛ in. drill. Remove the two bolts using an easy-out or equivalent.
6. Disengage ignition switch from actuator pin, **Fig. 1.**
7. Adjust switch by sliding carrier to "Lock" position and inserting a drill bit through switch housing and into carrier. On 1980–81 models, insert a .050 inch drill bit.
8. On 1982–86 models, adjust switch by sliding carrier to "Run" position and inserting a ⅛ inch drill bit through housing and into carrier.
9. On 1980–81 models, rotate ignition key to "Lock" position, then install switch on actuator pin.
10. On 1982–86 models, rotate ignition key to the run position, which is approximately 90° from Lock position, then install ignition switch on actuator pin.
11. Install new switch to lock cylinder housing break away bolts and torque bolt until heads break away.
12. Remove drill bit from switch housing, then connect switch wire connector.
13. Connect battery ground cable and check switch for proper operation, then install steering column trim shroud.

EXCEPT 1980–83 FAIRMONT & ZEPHYR; 1980–82 COUGAR XR-7, 1980–86 THUNDERBIRD; 1981–82 GRANADA; 1981–86 COUGAR; 1983–86 LTD & MARQUIS

1. Remove steering column shroud and lower steering column from brake support bracket.
2. Disconnect battery cable.
3. Disconnect switch wiring and remove two switch retaining nuts. Disconnect switch from actuator and remove switch, **Fig. 2.**
4. Move shift lever to "Park" position on automatic transmissions and Reverse on standard transmission units. Place ignition key in "Lock" position and remove the key.

NOTE: New replacement switches are pinned in the "Lock" position by a plastic shipping pin inserted in a locking hole in the switch. For an existing switch, pull plunger out as far as it will go then back one detent to "Lock" position and insert a 3/32 inch drill in locking hole to retain switch in Lock position.

ACTUATING ROD

LOCKING TABS

Fig. 2   Ignition switch installation. 1980 Granada & Monarch

HEADLIGHT KNOB
AND SHAFT ASSEMBLY

INSERT HOOKED
TOOL INTO KNOB SLOT
TO DEPRESS SPRING;
THEN PULL OFF SHAFT.

Fig. 3   Light switch knob removal. 1980 Granada & Monarch

KNOB RELEASE BUTTON

Fig. 4   Light switches. Exc. 1985-86 Thunderbird & Cougar

5. With locking pin in place, install switch on steering column, determine mid position of actuator lash and tighten retaining bolts.
6. Remove locking pin.

LIGHT SWITCH
REPLACE

EXC. 1985–86 THUNDERBIRD & COUGAR

1. Disconnect battery ground cable.
2. On 1980 Granada and Monarch models, to remove light switch knob, bend a discarded bowden cable into shape shown in **Fig. 3.** Insert hooked end of cable into knob slot to depress spring, then pull knob from shaft.
3. On all other models, remove control knob and shaft assembly, by placing knob in full "On" position, then pressing knob release button on switch and pulling out knob and shaft, **Fig. 4.** To gain access to the release button on Fairmont and Zephyr models with air conditioning it may be necessary to first disconnect the left A/C duct.
4. On all models, remove bezel nut. Disconnect multiple plug connector, vacuum hoses if vehicle is equipped with headlight doors and remove switch.
5. Reverse procedure to install. On 1980 Granada and Monarch models, align triangular holes in knob and shaft, then press knob onto shaft until knob bottoms. On all other models, install knob and shaft by inserting shaft into the switch until a distinct click is heard. In some instances it may be neces-

sary to rotate the shaft slightly until it engages the switch carrier.

1985–86 THUNDERBIRD & COUGAR

1. Disconnect battery ground cable.
2. Remove lens assembly attaching screws and the lens assembly, **Fig. 5.**
3. Remove switch assembly attaching screws from instrument panel, pull switch from panel, then disconnect electrical connector.

NOTE: On vehicles equipped with auto lamp/dimmer switch, remove this switch before removing light switch.

4. Reverse procedure to install.

STOP LIGHT SWITCH
REPLACE

1. Disconnect battery ground cable and disconnect wires at switch connector.

NOTE: On 1980 Granada and Monarch models with vacuum power brake units, loosen brake booster nut ¼ turn, thereby eliminating binding during removal.

2. Remove hairpin retainer and slide stop light switch, push rod, nylon washers and bushings away from brake pedal, and remove switch, **Fig. 6.**
3. Reverse procedure to install and on 1980 Granada and Monarch models, torque brake booster retaining nuts to 13–25 ft. lbs.

NEUTRAL SAFETY SWITCH
REPLACE

TRANSMISSION MOUNTED SWITCH

Except Automatic Overdrive Transmission

1. Remove downshift linkage rod from transmission downshift lever.
2. Apply penetrating oil to downshift lever shaft and nut; then remove downshift outer lever.
3. Remove switch attaching bolts.
4. Disconnect multiple wire connector and remove switch from transmission.
5. Install new switch.
6. With transmission manual lever in neutral, rotate switch and install gauge pin (#43 drill) into gauge pin holes, **Fig. 7.**

NOTE: The shank end of the drill must be inserted 31/64 in. (15/32 in., 1983–86 models) into each of the gauge pin holes.

7. Tighten switch attaching bolts and remove gauge pin.
8. Complete the installation in reverse order of removal.

Automatic Overdrive Transmission

1. Disconnect battery ground cable.
2. Place transmission gear selector in manual low position.
3. Raise and support vehicle.

Fig. 5 Removing headlamp switch. 1985-86 Thunderbird & Cougar

Fig. 6 Mechanical stop light switch

Fig. 7 Neutral safety switch. Transmission mounted

4. Disconnect electrical connector from neutral start switch. Lift connector straight up off switch using a long screwdriver under the rubber plug of connector.
5. Remove switch and "O" ring using socket No. T74P-77247-A or equivalent.

NOTE: Use of any tools other than those specified may result in damage to the vehicle.

6. Reverse procedure to install. Torque switch to 7–10 ft. lbs.

TURN SIGNAL SWITCH
REPLACE

1980–83 FAIRMONT & ZEPHYR; 1980–82 COUGAR XR-7; 1980–86 THUNDERBIRD; 1981–82 GRANADA; 1981–86 COUGAR; 1983–86 LTD & MARQUIS

1. Disconnect battery ground cable.
2. On 1981–84 models with tilt column, remove upper extension shroud. Unsnap shroud from retaining clip located at the 9 o'clock position.
3. On all models, remove trim shroud or shroud halves.
4. Remove turn signal switch lever from switch. Grasp lever and use a pulling and twisting motion while pulling lever straight out from switch.

5. Peel back foam shield from turn signal switch, then disconnect two electrical connectors from switch.
6. Remove turn signal switch attaching screws and the switch from vehicle.
7. Reverse procedure to install.

EXCEPT 1980–83 FAIRMONT & ZEPHYR; 1980–82 COUGAR XR-7; 1980–86 THUNDERBIRD; 1981–82 GRANADA; 1980–86 COUGAR; 1983–86 LTD & MARQUIS

1. Remove retaining screw from underside of steering wheel spokes and lift off pad horn switch/trim cover and medallion as an assembly.
2. Disconnect horn switch wires from terminals.
3. Remove steering wheel retaining nut and remove steering wheel with suitable puller.
4. Remove turn signal switch lever by unscrewing it from steering column.
5. Remove shroud from under steering column.
6. Disconnect steering column wiring connector plugs and remove screws that secure switch to column.
7. On tilt column, remove wires and terminals from column plug. Record color code and position of wires before removing. A hole provided in the flange casting on fixed columns makes it unnecessary to separate wires from plug as the plug with wires can be guided through hole.

8. Remove plastic cover sleeve from wiring harness and remove switch from top of column.

HORN SOUNDER
REPLACE

NOTE: On some models, the horn sounder is located on the turn signal, headlight dimmer and horn lever. Refer to Turn Signal Switch Replace, when replacing switch.

The horn button used on some models may be removed by twisting the button counter-clockwise. The horn switch on some models is part of the trim cover assembly and if defective, the trim cover must be replaced. The horn sounder on rim-blow steering wheels equipped with speed control cannot be replaced and if defective, the steering wheel assembly must be replaced. On rim-blow steering wheels without speed control, the horn sounder (plastic strip and copper insert) may be replaced using the following procedure:
1. Remove trim pad and disconnect lead wires.
2. Remove plastic cover and lift out horn insert on inner diameter of steering wheel.
3. Reverse procedure to install.

STEERING WHEEL
REPLACE

1. Disconnect battery ground cable.
2. Remove steering wheel trim pad, horn button or ring.

NOTE: On 1981–83 models with 4-spoke steering wheel, alternately push out on the cover retaining posts using a ⁹⁄₃₂ inch rod through two access holes in back of steering wheel.

3. Disconnect horn and speed control wiring, if equipped.
4. Remove steering wheel nut.
5. Mark relationship between steering shaft and steering wheel hub for proper reinstallation.
6. Remove steering wheel with a suitable puller.
7. Reverse procedure to install.

INSTRUMENT CLUSTER
REPLACE

1985–86 THUNDERBIRD, COUGAR, LTD & MARQUIS

STANDARD CLUSTER

Thunderbird & Cougar Exc. Turbo Coupe

1. Disconnect battery ground cable.
2. Remove two lower trim covers.
3. Remove steering column cover, then disconnect shift indicator bracket and cable assembly from steering column.
4. Move shift lever, then remove cluster trim cover.
5. Remove 4 cluster attaching screws, then pull bottom of cluster toward steering wheel.
6. Working from behind and underneath cluster, disconnect the two electrical connectors.
7. Swing bottom of cluster outward to gain adequate clearance, then remove cluster from vehicle.
8. Reverse procedure to install ensuring that shift indicator is properly adjusted.

Turbo Coupe

1. Disconnect battery ground.
2. Remove steering column shroud, if applicable.
3. Remove the ten retaining screws, then the cluster trim cover.
4. Remove the four instrument cluster to instrument panel attaching screws, then pull cluster outward.
5. Disconnect cluster feed plug from receptacle and boost gauge rubber tube from gauge nipple.
6. Remove cluster from vehicle.
7. Reverse procedure to install.

LTD & Marquis

1. Disconnect battery ground cable.
2. Disconnect speedometer cable from cluster.
3. Remove instrument trim cover, then the steering column shroud.

Fig. 8   Instrument cluster 1980 Granada & Monarch (Typical)

4. Remove shift control cable clamp retaining screw, then disconnect cable loop from shift cane lever pin. Remove plastic clamp from steering column.
5. Remove the four cluster attaching screws, then disconnect feed plug from receptacle.
6. Disconnect engine warning lamp, then remove cluster from vehicle.
7. Reverse procedure to install, noting the following:
   a. When reconnecting shift control cable, place loop of cable over pin on shift cane lever.
   b. Position shift lever in Drive, then rotate cable clamp until indicator pointer is centrally located on D. Torque cable clamp retaining screw to 20–30 inch lbs.
   c. Move shift lever through all shift positions and check indicator pointer for proper position.

ELECTRONIC CLUSTER

Thunderbird & Cougar Exc. Turbo Coupe

Refer to "Standard Cluster" for removal procedures on the above mentioned vehicles.

1980–82 COUGAR XR-7, 1980–84 THUNDERBIRD & 1983–84 COUGAR, LTD & MARQUIS

STANDARD CLUSTER

1983–84 Cougar & Thunderbird

1. Disconnect battery ground cable.
2. Remove steering column shroud and instrument cluster trim cover.
3. Remove 6 instrument cluster-to-instrument panel attaching screws.
4. Pull cluster away from instrument panel and disconnect speedometer cable and cluster feed plugs.
5. Remove instrument cluster from vehicle.
6. Reverse procedure to install.

1981–84 Exc. 1983–84 Cougar & Thunderbird

1. Disconnect battery ground cable.
2. Disconnect speedometer cable, then remove instrument panel trim cover and steering column shroud.
3. Remove screw attaching transmission shift lever indicator cable bracket to steering column, then detach cable loop from pin on shift cane lever and remove plastic clamp from around steering column.
4. Remove four instrument cluster retaining screws, then disconnect cluster feed plug and remove instrument cluster.
5. Reverse procedure to install.

1980 Models

1. Disconnect battery ground cable.
2. Disconnect speedometer cable.
3. Remove steering column shroud and instrument cluster trim cover.
4. Remove six instrument cluster lens and mask attaching screws, then remove lens and mask.
5. Remove four instrument cluster attaching screws.
6. Disconnect cluster feed plug from printed circuit connector, then remove cluster assembly.
7. Reverse procedure to install.

ELECTRONIC CLUSTER

1. Disconnect battery ground cable.
2. Remove four instrument panel lower trim cover attaching screws, then remove trim cover.
3. Remove steering column shroud.
4. Remove six instrument cluster trim panel attaching screws, then remove trim panel.
5. Remove four instrument cluster to instrument panel attaching screws.
6. Remove screw attaching transmission selector lever indicator cable bracket to steering column, then detach cable loop from pin on steering column.
7. Carefully pull cluster assembly away from instrument panel.

Fig. 9   Instrument panel. 1983—86 Cougar & Thunderbird

8. Disconnect speedometer cable and cluster feed plug and ground wire from cluster back plate, then remove cluster assembly.
9. Reverse procedure to install.

1980—83 FAIRMONT, ZEPHYR & 1981—82 COUGAR & GRANADA

1. Disconnect battery ground cable.
2. Remove steering column shroud.
3. Remove instrument cluster trim cover.
4. Remove screw retaining PRND21 control cable clamp to steering column. Then, disconnect the cable from pin on steering column. Remove plastic clamp from steering column.

5. Remove two upper and two lower screws retaining instrument cluster to instrument panel.
6. Pull cluster from instrument panel and disconnect speedometer cable.
7. Disconnect electrical connectors from instrument cluster.
8. Remove instrument cluster from vehicle.
9. Reverse procedure to install.

1980 GRANADA & MONARCH

1. Disconnect battery ground cable.
2. Remove lower cluster cover from below steering column.
3. Remove steering column shroud.
4. On all models, remove headlamp

switch knob and shaft assembly and bezel.
5. Remove four cluster finish panel attaching screws.
6. Using a right angle screwdriver, pry along edges of finish panel, thereby removing studs from retainers and remove finish panel.
7. Disconnect automatic transmission indicator cable and speedometer cable.
8. Remove four screws retaining cluster to instrument panel, then pull cluster out and disconnect feed plug from printed circuit, **Fig. 8.**
9. Disconnect wires from fuel gauge if equipped with low fuel warning light and remove cluster.
10. Reverse procedure to install

W/S WIPER MOTOR
REPLACE

1980–82 COUGAR XR-7; 1980–86 THUNDERBIRD; 1981–82 GRANADA; 1981–86 COUGAR; 1981–83 FAIRMONT & ZEPHYR; 1983–86 LTD & MARQUIS

1. On 1983–86 Cougar and Thunderbird models, operate wipers and turn ignition key off when blades are straight up on the windshield.
2. On all models, disconnect battery ground cable.
3. On 1980–82 Cougar XR-7 and Thunderbird, and 1983–86 LTD and Marquis models, remove right hand wiper and blade assembly. On Fairmont, Granada, Zephyr, 1981–86 Cougar and 1983–86 Thunderbird models, remove both wiper arm and blade assemblies.
4. Remove cowl grille or trash screen attaching screws, then remove cowl grille or trash screen.
5. Remove clip, then disconnect linkage drive arm from motor crankpin.
6. Disconnect wire connector from wiper motor, then remove wiper motor attaching bolts and lift motor from cowl opening.

1980 FAIRMONT & ZEPHYR

1. Disconnect battery ground cable.
2. Remove left hand wiper arm from pivot shaft and place on cowl grille.
3. Remove cowl grille attaching screws, then raise left hand corner of cowl grille to gain access to linkage drive arm.
4. Disconnect linkage arm from motor output arm pin by removing retaining clip.
5. Disconnect wiper motor wire connector.
6. Remove wiper motor to cowl attaching bolts, then remove wiper motor.

1980–81 FAIRMONT, ZEPHYR, 1982 COUGAR, GRANADA & 1983–86 LTD & MARQUIS STA. WAG. LIFTGATE WIPER MOTOR

1. Disconnect battery ground cable.
2. Remove wiper arm and blade assembly.
3. Remove pivot shaft attaching nut and spacers.
4. On 1982–86 models, remove liftgate inner trim panel.
5. On all models, remove license plate housing attaching screws, then disconnect lamp electrical connector and remove housing.
6. Disconnect wiper motor wire connector.
7. Remove linkage arm lock clip, then pry off arm and remove linkage.
8. Remove wiper motor and bracket attaching bolts, then remove motor and bracket.

1980 GRANADA & MONARCH

1. Disconnect battery ground cable.
2. Remove instrument panel pad.
3. Remove speaker mounting bracket, then disconnect wire connector and remove speaker.
4. Remove defroster nozzle and air distribution duct.
5. Remove wiper motor to cowl attaching bolts, then remove wiper motor.

W/S WIPER, TRANSMISSION REPLACE

1980–83 FAIRMONT & ZEPHYR; 1980–82 COUGAR XR-7; 1980–86 THUNDERBIRD; 1981–82 GRANADA; 1981–86 COUGAR; 1983–86 LTD & MARQUIS

1. On 1983–86 Cougar and Thunderbird models, operate wipers and turn ignition key off when blades are straight up on windshield.
2. On all models, disconnect battery ground cable.
3. On all models except 1983–86 Cougar and Thunderbird, remove both wiper arm and blade assemblies.
4. On 1983–86 Cougar and Thunderbird models, remove right wiper arm and blade assembly.
5. On all models, remove cowl grille or left trash screen attaching screws then the cowl grille or screen.
6. Remove retaining clip, then disconnect linkage drive arm from wiper motor crankpin.
7. On Fairmont, Granada, Zephyr and 1981–82 Cougar models, remove 4 bolts attaching left and right pivot shafts to cowl, then remove linkage assembly.
8. On Cougar XR-7, Thunderbird and 1983–86 LTD and Marquis models, remove 2 bolts attaching right pivot shaft to cowl, then remove nut, washer and spacer from left pivot shaft and remove linkage assembly.
9. On 1983–86 Cougar and Thunderbird models, remove pivot shaft attaching screws, then remove linkage assembly out through cowl chamber.
10. Reverse procedure to install.

1980 GRANADA & MONARCH

Left Side
1. Remove instrument cluster.
2. Remove wiper arm and blade.
3. Working through cluster opening, disconnect both pivot shaft links from motor drive arm by removing retaining clip.
4. Remove three pivot shaft assembly retaining bolts and remove assembly through cluster opening.
5. Reverse procedure to install.

Right Side
1. Disconnect battery ground cable and remove wiper blade and arm.
2. On air conditioned units, remove right duct assembly.
3. From under the instrument panel, disconnect first left then right pivot shaft link from motor drive arm.
4. Reaching between utility shelf and instrument panel, remove pivot shaft retaining bolts and lower assembly out from under panel.
5. Reverse procedure to install.

W/S WIPER SWITCH
REPLACE

1980–83 FAIRMONT & ZEPHYR; 1980–82 COUGAR XR-7; 1980–86 THUNDERBIRD; 1981–82 GRANADA; 1981–86 COUGAR; 1983–86 LTD & MARQUIS

1. Disconnect battery ground cable.
2. Remove four steering column shroud attaching screws, then grasp top and bottom of shroud and separate.
3. Using a screwdriver, disconnect wire connector from wiper switch.
4. Remove two wiper switch attaching screws, then remove switch.
5. Reverse procedure to install.

1980–81 FAIRMONT, ZEPHYR, 1982 COUGAR, GRANADA & 1983–86 LTD & MARQUIS STA. WAG. LIFTGATE WIPER MOTOR

1. Disconnect battery ground cable.
2. Remove wiper switch knob, then remove two bezel retaining screws.
3. Pull switch retainer away from instrument panel.
4. Remove wiper switch retaining nut, then separate switch from retainer.
5. Disconnect wire connector from wiper switch, then remove switch.
6. Reverse procedure to install.

1980 GRANADA, MONARCH COLUMN MOUNTED SWITCH

1. Disconnect battery ground cable.
2. Disconnect turn signal and wiper/washer switch wire connector.
3. Remove lower instrument panel shield.
4. Remove two screws and separate steering column cover halves.
5. Pull wire cover from bottom on column and remove cover.
6. With a screwdriver, disengage wiring shield tang and pry shield to remove.
7. Remove screw securing turn signal and windshield wiper/washer switch assembly to column, then remove the assembly.
8. Reverse procedure to install.

RADIO
REPLACE

NOTE: When installing radio, be sure to adjust antenna trimmer for peak performance.

1980—82 COUGAR XR-7, 1980—86 THUNDERBIRD & 1983—86 COUGAR, LTD & MARQUIS

1. Disconnect battery ground cable.
2. Remove radio knobs, then remove instrument panel center trim panel.
3. Remove radio mounting plate attaching screws.
4. Pull radio to disengage from lower rear support bracket, then disconnect power antenna, speaker leads and floor switch lead, if equipped and remove radio.
5. Reverse procedure to install.

1980—83 FAIRMONT, ZEPHYR & 1981—82 COUGAR & GRANADA

1. Disconnect battery ground cable.
2. Disconnect power lead, speaker leads and antenna lead from radio.
3. Remove control knobs, discs, control knob shaft nuts and washers.
4. Remove ash tray and bracket.
5. Remove radio rear support attaching nut.
6. Remove instrument panel lower reinforcement.
7. Remove heater or A/C floor ducts.
8. Remove radio from bezel and rear support, then lower radio from instrument panel.
9. Reverse procedure to install.

1980 GRANADA & MONARCH

1. Disconnect battery ground cable.
2. Remove headlamp switch.
3. Remove knobs from heater and A/C control, windshield wiper switch and radio.
4. Remove instrument panel applique.
5. Disconnect antenna lead.
6. Remove radio bezel to instrument panel screws, then pull radio and bezel out to disconnect remaining electrical leads and remove radio from panel.
7. Remove rear support bracket and bezel from radio.
8. Reverse procedure to install.

HEATER CORE
REPLACE

1983—86 COUGAR & THUNDERBIRD

Less Air Conditioning
1. Disconnect battery ground cable.
2. Remove steering column cover, then the instrument panel reinforcement under steering column opening.

3. Remove 2 nuts securing hood latch release handle mounting bracket to brake pedal support under steering column.
4. Remove sound insulator from lower left side of instrument panel, **Fig. 9.**
5. Remove 2 steering column clamp attaching nuts and lower steering column to rest on front seat.
6. Remove instrument panel pad attaching screws and the pad.
7. Disconnect speedometer cable from speedometer.
8. Remove console cover or tray.
9. Remove 4 console switch panel cover attaching screws, then disconnect electrical connectors and remove switch panel.
10. Remove console attaching screws, then disengage console from instrument panel and position aside.
11. Remove 2 pins attaching glove compartment door straps to glove compartment and allow door to hang down on hinge.
12. Remove instrument panel brace attaching bolt from glove compartment opening.
13. Remove brake pedal support attaching nut from lower edge of instrument panel.
14. Remove instrument panel brace attaching bolt from lower edge of instrument panel on left side of console extension.
15. Remove instrument panel-to-cowl side panel attaching bolt from both sides of instrument panel.
16. Support instrument panel and remove 3 instrument panel-to-cowl top panel attaching screws.
17. Move instrument panel rearward, disconnect necessary electrical connectors and vacuum hoses, and rest panel on front seat.
18. Drain cooling system, then disconnect hoses from heater core. Cover hoses and heater core tubes to prevent leakage.
19. Remove 2 nuts securing heater case to dash panel from engine compartment.
20. Working in passenger compartment, remove screws attaching heater case support bracket and air inlet duct support bracket to cowl top panel.
21. Remove nut retaining bracket at left end of heater case to dash panel and nut securing bracket below case to dash panel.
22. Pull heater case away from dash panel to gain access to heater core access cover attaching screws.
23. Remove heater core access cover attaching screws and the cover.
24. Remove heater core and seals from heater case, **Fig. 10.**
25. Remove the 2 seals from heater core tubes.
26. Reverse procedure to install.

With Air Conditioning
1. Perform steps 1 through 17 as described under "Heater Core, Replace," "1983—86 Cougar & Thunderbird, Less Air Conditioning."
2. Discharge refrigerant from A/C system at the service valve on suction line.

When system is fully discharged, disconnect and cap high and low pressure lines.
3. Drain cooling system, then disconnect hoses from heater core. Cover hoses and heater core tubes to prevent leakage.
4. Remove screw securing air inlet duct and blower housing assembly support brace to cowl top panel.
5. Disconnect black vacuum supply hose from in-line check valve in engine compartment.
6. Disconnect blower motor electrical connectors from harness.
7. Remove 2 evaporator case-to-dash panel attaching nuts from engine compartment.
8. Working in passenger compartment, remove evaporator case support bracket-to-cowl top panel attaching screw.
9. Remove nut securing bracket below evaporator case to dash panel.
10. Carefully remove evaporator case assembly from vehicle.
11. Remove 5 heater core access cover attaching screws and the cover.
12. Remove heater core and seals from evaporator case, **Fig. 11.**
13. Remove the 2 seals from heater core tubes.
14. Reverse procedure to install.

1980—82 COUGAR XR-7, THUNDERBIRD, 1983—86 LTD & MARQUIS

1. Disconnect battery ground cable.
2. Remove steering column cover assembly, then remove left and right finish panels, **Fig. 12.**
3. Remove two screws from sides of instrument panel pad and retainer assembly.
4. Remove pad and retainer assembly and upper finish panel.
5. Remove steering column attaching bolts, then carefully lower steering column just enough to allow access to transmission gear selector lever cable assembly. Reach between steering column and instrument panel, then carefully lift selector lever cable from lever and remove cable clamp from steering column tube.
6. Lower steering column and allow to rest on front seat.
7. Remove screw attaching instrument panel to brake pedal support through steering column opening.
8. Disconnect temperature door cable from door and heater/evaporator cable bracket.
9. Disconnect vacuum hose connectors at evaporator housing.
10. Disconnect blower motor resistor wire from resistor on heater/evaporator case and blower motor feed wire at inline connector.
11. Support instrument panel, then remove three screws attaching top of instrument panel to cowl.
12. Remove one screw attaching each end of instrument panel to cowl side panels, then remove two screws attaching instrument panel to floor.

DOOR SHAFT
-19B752-

VACUUM MOTOR
-18A318-

ACCESS COVER
-18N277-

SEAL -18C676-

SEAL
-18A597-

DOOR SHAFT
-18A293-

HEATER CORE
-18476-

RESTRICTOR
DOOR
-19A555-

UPPER CASE
-19A626-

SEAL
-19B588-

HEAT-DEFROST
DOOR
-19B749-

DOOR SHAFT
-19D846-

TEMPERATURE BLEND
DOOR
-19D843-

VACUUM
MOTOR
18A318-

SEAL
-19A672-

CLIP
-19A779-

BAFFLE
-19A999-

SEAL
-19B739-

BLOWER RESISTOR
-19A706-

DRAIN
-19874-

LOWER CASE
-19C831-

Fig. 10   Heater core less air conditioning. 1980—82 Cougar XR-7, 1980—86 Thunderbird, 1983—86 Cougar, LTD & Marquis

Fig. 11 Heater core with air conditioning. 1980—83 Fairmont, Zephyr, 1980—82 Cougar XR-7, 1980—86 Thunderbird, 1981—82 Granada, 1981—86 Cougar & 1983—86 LTD & Marquis

Fig. 12   Instrument panel trim panel (Typical). 1980—82 Cougar XR-7, Thunderbird & 1983—86 LTD & Marquis

BLOWER
MOTOR

BLOWER
WHEEL

RESISTOR
ASSEMBLY

HEATER CORE
SUPPORT BRACKET

SCREW

SCREW

CLAMP

HEATER CORE
AND SEAL

TEMPERATURE
BLEND DOOR

HEATER CORE COVER

Fig. 13   Heater core assembly built after 11-1-81. 1982—83 Fairmont & Zephyr & 1982 Cougar & Granada

13. Move instrument panel rearward and disconnect speedometer cable and any wires that will prevent instrument panel from being placed on front seat.

NOTE: Use care when removing instrument panel to prevent damage to panel or steering column surfaces.

14. On all 1980—81 models and 1982—86 models less A/C, perform steps 18 through 26 under "Heater Core, Replace," 1983—86 Cougar & Thunderbird, Less Air Conditioning."
15. On 1983—86 models with A/C, perform steps 2 through 14 under "Heater Core, Replace," "1983—86 Cougar & Thunderbird, With Air Conditioning."

1980—83 FAIRMONT, ZEPHYR & 1981—82 COUGAR & GRANADA

SERVICE BULLETIN: Models with heat-er cases built after 11-1-81 use a one piece case, **Fig. 13.** This type case cannot be separated and all interior case components must be removed and installed through openings in case.

Less Air Conditioning
1. Disconnect battery ground cable and drain cooling system.
2. Disconnect heater hoses from heater core and seal the core tubes.
3. Remove glove box liner.
4. Remove instrument panel to cowl brace retaining screws and brace.
5. Place temperature control lever in the warm position.
6. Remove heater core cover retaining screws and the cover, **Figs. 13 and 14.**
7. From engine compartment, remove heater case assembly mounting stud nuts.
8. Push heater core tubes and seal toward passenger compartment to loosen heater core from case assem-bly.
9. Remove heater core through glove box opening.
10. Reverse procedure to install.

With Air Conditioning
1. Disconnect battery ground cable.
2. Remove screws attaching instrument cluster trim panel to instrument panel pad.
3. Remove instrument panel pad to instrument panel screws at each defroster opening.
4. Remove instrument panel pad edge to instrument panel screws, and pad.
5. Remove steering column lower cover to instrument panel screws then the cover.
6. On 1980—83 models, proceed as follows:
   a. Remove steering column trim shroud attaching screws and the trim shrouds.
   b. Remove steering column attaching nuts, then carefully lower steering column just enough to allow ac-

Fig. 14 Heater case assembly built prior to 11-1-81. 1980—82 Fairmont, Zephyr, 1981—82 Cougar & Granada

cess to transmission gear selector lever cable assembly. Reach between steering column and instrument panel and carefully lift selector lever cable from lever and remove cable clamp from steering column tube.

c. Lower steering column and allow to rest on front seat.

7. On all models, remove instrument panel to brake pedal support screw at steering column opening.

8. Remove screw attaching lower brace to lower edge of instrument panel below radio.

9. Remove screw attaching the brace to lower edge of instrument panel.

10. Disconnect temperature control cable from blend door and evaporator case bracket.

11. Disconnect vacuum hose connectors from evaporator case.

12. Disconnect blower resistor wire connector from resistor on evaporator

housing, then the blower motor feed wire at in-line connector.

13. Support instrument panel and, with an angle Phillips screwdriver, remove three screws attaching top of instrument panel to the cowl.

14. Remove screws attaching instrument panel to cowl side panels.

15. Move instrument panel rearward and disconnect speedometer cable and any wiring that will not permit the instrument panel to be positioned on the front seat.

16. On 1980—81 models, proceed as follows:

a. Drain cooling system, then disconnect hoses from heater core and seal core tubes.

b. From engine compartment, remove nuts retaining evaporator case to dash panel.

c. From passenger compartment, remove screws attaching evaporator case support bracket and air inlet duct support bracket to cowl top

panel.

d. Remove one nut retaining bracket at left end of evaporator case to dash panel and one nut retaining bracket beneath the case to dash panel.

e. Pull evaporator case assembly from dash panel.

17. On 1982—83 models, proceed as follows:

a. Discharge refrigerant from A/C system at the service valve on suction line. When system is fully discharged, disconnect and cap high and lower pressure lines.

b. Drain cooling system, then disconnect hoses from heater core. Cover hoses and heater core tubes to prevent leakage.

c. Remove screw securing air inlet duct and blower housing assembly support brace to cowl top panel.

d. Disconnect black vacuum supply hose from in-line check valve in engine compartment.

SELF-TAPPING SCREW—42127-S8
#10-12 x 1/2 HEX. WASHER HD.
4 REQUIRED

GROMMET

CORE ASSEMBLY

CORE COVER PLATE

SELF-TAPPING SCREW—42127-S8
#10-12 x 1/2 HEX. WASHER HD.
4 REQUIRED

BLOWER MOTOR AND WHEEL ASSEMBLY

ALIGNMENT DIMPLES

HEATER CASE ASSEMBLY

ALIGNMENT HOLES

POLYURETHANE MOUNTING PADS

Fig. 15 Heater core & blower motor less air conditioning. 1980 Granada & Monarch

e. Disconnect blower motor electrical connectors from harness.
f. Disconnect electrical connector from blower motor resistor.
g. Remove two evaporator case-to-dash panel attaching nuts from engine compartment.
h. Working in passenger compartment, remove evaporator case support bracket-to-cowl top panel attaching screws.
i. Remove screw retaining bracket below evaporator case to dash panel.
j. Carefully remove evaporator case assembly from vehicle.
18. On all models, remove five heater core access cover attaching screws and the access cover, **Fig. 11.**
19. Remove heater core and seals from evaporator case.
20. Remove the two seals from heater core tubes.
21. Reverse procedure to install.

1980 GRANADA & MONARCH

Less Air Conditioning
1. Drain cooling system and disconnect heater hoses from heater core.
2. Remove glove box and the right and floor air distribution ducts.
3. Disconnect heater control cables and wiring harness from resistor assembly. Remove right vent cable bracket from instrument panel.
4. Remove vent duct to upper cowl mounting bolt.
5. Remove heater case to dash panel

nuts, then the heater case and vent duct assembly.
6. Remove core cover and seal, then slide core from case, **Fig. 15.**

With Air Conditioning
1. Disconnect battery ground cable and drain coolant system, then disconnect heater hoses from core at engine side of dash panel.

NOTE: Easier access may be obtained by first disconnecting suction hose and moving it out of the way.

2. Remove heat distribution duct from instrument panel, seat belt interlock module and glove box liner, then loosen right door sill scuff plate and remove right cowl side from trim panel.
3. Loosen instrument panel to right cowl side bolt and remove instrument panel brace bolt at lower rail under glove box.
4. Remove tunnel to cowl brace, located to left of evaporator plenum assembly, if equipped.
5. Remove defroster nozzle by removing instrument panel crash pad, removing radio speaker or panel cowl brace, removing four nozzle to cowl bracket screws and lifting defroster nozzle upward through crash panel, **Fig. 16.**
6. Disconnect vacuum hoses from A/C-Defrost and A/C-Heat door motors and remove vacuum harness to plenum clip screw, then remove the two A/C-Heat mounting nuts and swing door rearward on crankarm.
7. Remove two plenum to left mounting

bracket screws and remove the two screws and three clips securing plenum to evaporator case.
8. Swing bottom of plenum away from evaporator case and disengage S-clip on forward flange of plenum, then raise plenum to clear tabs on top of evaporator case.
9. Move plenum to left as far as possible (about 4 inches), pulling rearward on instrument panel to gain clearance.

NOTE: Use extreme care when pulling back on instrument panel to avoid cracking plastic panel. Also, there is very little clearance between plenum and wiper motor assembly.

10. Using tab molded into rear heater core seal, pull heater core to left, then as rear surface of heater core clears evaporator case, pull core rearward and downward to clear instrument panel.
11. Reverse procedure to install, making certain that heater core tube to dash panel seal is in place between evaporator case and dash panel.

BLOWER MOTOR
REPLACE

1980–83 FAIRMONT & ZEPHYR & 1981–82 COUGAR & GRANADA LESS AIR CONDITIONING
1. Disconnect battery ground cable.
2. Remove screw securing right register duct mounting bracket to lower edge of instrument panel.
3. Remove screws securing ventilator control cable lever assembly to lower edge of instrument panel.
4. Remove glove box liner.
5. Remove plastic rivets securing grille to ventilator floor outlet, then the grille from the bottom of the ventilator assembly.
6. Remove right register duct and register assembly.
7. Remove screws securing ventilator assembly to blower housing portion of the heater case assembly.
8. Slide ventilator assembly toward the right, then downward to remove from under instrument panel.
9. Remove push nut from door crank arm.
10. Remove control cable housing retaining screw, then control cable assembly from ventilator assembly.
11. On 1980–81 models, disconnect blower lead wire from case and push through hole in case. Remove right side cowl trim panel and the ground terminal lug retaining screw.
12. On 1982–83 models, remove hub clamp spring from blower wheel hub, then slide wheel off shaft.
13. On all models, remove blower motor attaching screws and the blower motor. On 1982–83 models, disconnect motor electrical connector before removing from vehicle.
14. Reverse procedure to install.

Fig. 16   Heater core. 1980 Granada & Monarch with air conditioning

Fig. 17   Blower motor. 1980—83 Fairmont, Zephyr w/air conditioning. 1980—82 Cougar XR-7, 1980—86 Thunderbird, 1983—86 Cougar, LTD & Marquis

SUPPLY VACUUM
CHECK VALVE

VACUUM HOSE TO
VACUUM RESERVOIR

BALL CHAIN
RETAINING PIN

ACTUATOR VACUUM LINE

SERVO ASSEMBLY
(THROTTLE ACTUATOR)

UPPER
SPEEDOMETER
CABLE

ACTUATOR
BRACKET

BEAD CHAIN
ADJUSTER ASSEMBLY

BLUE CONNECTOR

RED CONNECTOR

BEAD CHAIN ADJUST TO
MAINTAIN .06 TO .250
SERVO ARM FREE TRAVEL
WITH ENGINE ON HOT IDLE

SPEED SENSOR

LOWER
SPEEDOMETER
CABLE

Fig. 18 Servo assembly & throttle linkage (typical)

1980—83 FAIRMONT, ZEPHYR WITH AIR CONDITIONING, 1980—82 COUGAR XR-7, 1980—86 THUNDERBIRD, 1983—86 COUGAR & 1983—86 LTD & MARQUIS

1. Disconnect battery ground cable.
2. Remove glove box and disconnect vacuum hose from outside—recirc air door motor.
3. Remove instrument panel lower right to side attaching bolt.
4. Remove screw attaching support brace to top of air inlet duct.
5. Disconnect blower motor lead wire.
6. Remove nut securing blower motor housing lower bracket to evaporator case.
7. Remove side cowl trim panel and the blower ground wire screw.
8. Remove screw securing top of air inlet duct to evaporator case.
9. Move air inlet duct and blower housing assembly downward from evaporator case, **Fig. 17.**
10. Remove blower motor mounting plate screws and the blower motor.

NOTE: Do not remove mounting plate from motor.

11. Reverse procedure to install.

1980 GRANADA & MONARCH

Less Air Conditioning
Remove heater case as outlined in the "1980 Granada & Monarch" procedure under "Heater Core, Removal," then remove screws securing blower motor to case, **Fig. 15**

With Air Conditioning
1. Disconnect battery ground cable.
2. Loosen right door sill scuff plate and remove right cowl side trim panel, then remove right lower instrument panel to cowl side bolt.
3. Remove cowl to loosen instrument panel brace bolt, then disconnect wiring harness connectors from blower motor and remove cooling tube from motor.
4. Remove the four blower motor attaching screws and remove blower motor from scroll by pulling on lower edge of instrument panel to gain clearance.

NOTE: Use extreme care when pulling back on instrument panel to avoid cracking plastic panel.

5. Reverse procedure to install.

SPEED CONTROLS

EXCEPT 1980—83 FAIRMONT, ZEPHYR, 1980—82 COUGAR XR-7, 1980—86 THUNDERBIRD, 1981—82 GRANADA, 1981—86 COUGAR & 1983—86 LTD & MARQUIS

Adjust bead chain to obtain .06—.25 inch actuator arm free travel when engine is at hot idle. The adjustment should be made to take as much slack as possible out of the chain without restricting the carburetor lever from returning to idle, **Fig. 18.**

On vehicles with a solenoid anti-diesel valve, perform adjustment with ignition switch in the "ON" position.

1980—83 FAIRMONT, ZEPHYR, 1980—82 COUGAR XR-7, 1980—86 THUNDERBIRD, 1981—82 GRANADA, 1981—86 COUGAR & 1983—86 LTD & MARQUIS

Bead Chain Adjustment
This adjustment should be made to remove as much slack as possible from the chain without restricting the carburetor lever from returning to the idle speed position. On vehicles equipped with a solenoid throttle positioner, the adjustment should be performed with the throttle positioner disengaged.

Vacuum Dump Valve
The vacuum dump valve is mounted on a moveable mounting bracket. The valve should be adjusted so that it is closed when the brake pedal is not depressed and opens when the brake pedal is depressed.

Actuator Cable Adjustment
1. Remove cable retaining clip.
2. On all carbureted models, deactivate the throttle positioner and set carburetor at hot idle.
3. On all models, pull the actuator cable to remove slack.
4. Insert cable retaining clip while maintaining light tension on the actuator cable.

Engine Section

NOTE: Refer to "FORD MUSTANG & PINTO ● MERCURY BOBCAT & CAPRI" Section for service procedures on the 2300 cc (4-140) engine not covered in this section.

ENGINE MOUNTS

CAUTION: Whenever self-locking mounting bolts and nuts are removed, they must be replaced with new self-locking bolts and nuts.

SERVICE BULLETIN: On some 1982 Granada, 1982–83 Cougar and Thunderbird and 1983 LTD and Marquis models, a Silver colored flange nut which retains the engine mounts to No. 2 crossmember has replaced the black nut previously used. Reduce torque on this type nut to 50–65 ft. lbs.

1985–86 COUGAR, LTD, MARQUIS & THUNDERBIRD 4-140

1. Support engine using a suitable jack and wooden block placed under oil pan.
2. On LTD and Marquis models, remove bolt securing lower end of engine damper to No. 2 crossmember bracket, **Fig. 3.**
3. On turbocharged engine, remove through bolts attaching both insulators to No. 2 crossmember bracket
4. On all models, remove nuts and washers attaching both insulators to No. 2 crossmember.
5. Disconnect shift linkage, then raise engine just enough to disengage insulator from crossmember bracket.
6. Remove insulator and bracket attaching bolts, then the insulator and bracket assembly, **Figs. 3 and 4.**
7. Reverse procedure to install.

1983–84 COUGAR, LTD, MARQUIS & THUNDERBIRD 4-140

1. Support engine using a suitable jack and wooden block placed under oil pan.
2. Remove fuel pump shield attaching screw, if equipped, from left hand engine support bracket.
3. On LTD and Marquis models, remove bolt securing lower end of engine damper to No. 2 crossmember bracket, **Fig. 1.**
4. On Cougar and Thunderbird models, remove through bolts from bottom of mounts, **Fig. 2.**
5. Remove nuts and washers attaching both insulators to No. 2 crossmember.
6. Raise engine just enough to clear insulator studs from crossmember.
7. Remove insulator and bracket attaching bolts, then the insulator and bracket assembly from vehicle.
8. Reverse procedure to install.

Fig. 1   Engine mounts. 1983–84 LTD & Marquis 4-140

Fig. 2   Engine mounts. 1983–84 Cougar & Thunderbird 4-140

Fig. 3 Engine mounts. 1985—86 LTD & Marquis 4-140

Fig. 4 Engine mounts. 1985—86 Cougar & Thunderbird 4-140

1980—83 FAIRMONT, ZEPHYR, 1980—82 THUNDERBIRD, COUGAR XR-7, 1981—82 COUGAR, GRANADA & 1983 LTD & MARQUIS 6-200

1. Remove fan shroud screws.
2. Support engine with suitable jack and wooden block.
3. On LTD and Marquis models, remove engine damper lower bolt and No. 2 crossmember bracket, **Fig. 5.**
4. On all models, remove nut and washer assemblies from insulators at No. 2 crossmember.
5. Raise engine with jack until insulator studs clear crossmember.
6. Disconnect bracket from engine and remove engine mount.
7. Reverse procedure to install. Torque fasteners according to **Figs. 5 and 6.**

1980 GRANADA & MONARCH w/6-250

1. Remove the insulator to support bracket retaining nuts, **Fig. 7.**
2. Using a wood block placed under the oil pan, raise the engine enough to clear the insulator.
3. Remove the retaining screws and nuts from the insulator(s). Remove the insulator(s).
4. Reverse procedure to install.

1983—86 V6-232

1. Remove fan shroud attaching screws.
2. Support engine using a suitable jack and wooden block placed under oil pan.
3. Remove nuts and washers attaching insulators to No. 2 crossmember, **Fig. 8.**
4. On LTD and Marquis models, remove bolt securing lower end of engine damper to No. 2 crossmember bracket, if necessary.
5. Disconnect shift linkage, if necessary.
6. On all models, raise engine sufficiently to clear insulator studs from crossmember.
7. Remove fuel pump shield, if equipped, from right hand side of engine.
8. Disconnect oil cooler line attaching clips and starter ground cable from right hand engine support bracket.
9. Remove insulator and bracket attaching bolts, then the insulator and bracket assembly from vehicle.
10. Reverse procedure to install.

1982 V6-232

1. Support engine using a suitable jack and wooden block placed under oil pan.
2. Remove nut and washer attaching mount to chassis, then raise engine slightly, **Fig. 9.**
3. Remove bolts attaching engine mount and bracket to engine, then remove mount.
4. Reverse procedure to install.

Fig. 5 Engine mounts. 1983 LTD & Marquis 6-200

1981 COUGAR & GRANADA V8-255

1. Remove fan shroud attaching screws, then position shroud over fan.
2. Using a suitable jack with a wooden block placed under oil pan, support engine.
3. Remove nut and through bolt attaching insulator to support bracket, **Fig. 10.**
4. Raise engine slightly, then remove insulator and bracket assembly to cylinder block attaching bolts.
5. Remove insulator assembly and heat shield, if equipped.
6. Reverse procedure to install.

1984–86 LTD & MARQUIS V8-302

1. Remove fan shroud attaching screws.
2. Position block of wood under oil pan, then support engine with suitable jack.
3. Remove insulator to crossmember attaching nuts.
4. Disconnect shift linkage, then raise engine and remove insulator.
5. Reverse procedure to install.

Fig. 6 Engine mounts. 1980–83 Fairmont, Zephyr, 1980–82 Cougar, XR-7, Thunderbird & 1981–82 Granada 6-200

Fig. 7 Engine mounts. 1980 Granada & Monarch w/6-250

Fig. 8 Engine mounts 1983—86 LTD & Marquis V6-232 (Typical of 1983—86 Cougar & Thunderbird)

1980—82 COUGAR XR-7, 1983—86 COUGAR & 1980—86 THUNDERBIRD V8-255 & 302

1. Remove fan shroud attaching screws.
2. Using a suitable jack with a wooden block placed under oil pan, support engine.
3. Remove nut and through bolt attaching insulator to frame crossmember.
4. On 1983—86 models, disconnect shift linkage.
5. Raise engine slightly, then remove insulator and heat shield, if equipped, **Fig. 10.**
6. Reverse procedure to install.

1980—81 FAIRMONT & ZEPHYR V8-255 & 302

1. Remove fan shroud attaching screws.
2. Remove nuts attaching insulators to lower bracket, **Fig. 10.**
3. Raise engine slightly using a block of wood placed under the oil pan and a suitable jack.
4. Remove bolts attaching insulator to engine block.
5. Remove insulator assembly.
6. Reverse procedure to install.

1980 GRANADA & MONARCH V8-255, 302

1. Using a block of wood and jack placed under oil pan, support engine.
2. Remove through bolt attaching motor mount to crossmember, **Fig. 11.**

3. Remove engine mount to engine attaching bolts.
4. Raise engine slightly and remove engine mount and heat shield (if used).
5. Reverse procedure to install.

ENGINE
REPLACE

6-200 & 250

1. Remove battery ground cable.
2. Remove hood assembly.

Fig. 10 Engine mounts (typical). 1980—81 Fairmont, Zephyr, 1980—82 Cougar XR-7, 1983—86 Cougar, 1980—86 Thunderbird & 1981 Cougar & Granada V8-255, 302

Fig. 9 Engine mount. 1982 V6-232

Fig. 11 Engine mounts. 1980 Granada & Monarch V8-255, 302

5-29

3. Drain cooling system and oil pan.
4. Disconnect crankcase ventilation hose and remove air cleaner.
5. Disconnect canister purge hose from P.C.V. valve.
6. Disconnect radiator and heater hoses and remove all drive belts.
7. If equipped with automatic transmission, disconnect transmission oil cooler lines from radiator.
8. On all models, remove radiator, then the fan, spacer and pulley.
9. Disconnect alternator and starter wiring, then the accelerator cable from carburetor.
10. If equipped with Thermactor system, remove or disconnect components that may interfere with engine replacement.
11. If equipped with A/C, remove compressor from mounting bracket and position aside with refrigerant line attached.
12. On all models, disconnect and plug fuel pump inlet line.
13. Disconnect ignition coil wires, then the oil pressure and water temperature wiring from sending units.
14. Remove starter motor.
15. If equipped with manual transmission, disconnect clutch retracting spring, then the clutch equalizer shaft and arm bracket from underbody rail. Remove arm bracket and equalizer shaft.
16. On all models, raise vehicle and remove flywheel or converter housing upper attaching bolts.
17. Disconnect exhaust pipe from manifold. Loosen exhaust pipe clamp and slide off support bracket on engine.
18. Disconnect front engine mounts from underbody bracket.
19. Remove flywheel or converter housing cover.
20. If equipped with manual transmission, remove flywheel housing lower attaching bolts.
21. If equipped with automatic transmission, remove converter to flywheel bolts, then the converter housing lower attaching bolts.
22. On all models, lower vehicle and support transmission and flywheel or converter housing with a suitable jack.
23. Attach suitable lifting equipment to engine and remove engine from vehicle.
24. Reverse procedure to install.

V6-232

1. Disconnect battery ground cable, then drain cooling system and crankcase.
2. On models equipped with underhood light, disconnect electrical connector from the light.
3. Mark position of hood hinges, then remove hood.
4. Remove air cleaner, air inlet duct and heat tube.
5. Remove fan shroud and fan assembly, then loosen accessory drive belt idler and remove drive belt and water pump pulley.
6. Disconnect upper and lower radiator hoses at radiator.
7. Disconnect Thermactor hose at air

tube check valve, then remove air tube valve bracket attaching bolt at rear of right hand cylinder head.
8. Remove secondary wire from ignition coil.
9. Remove bolts attaching power steering pump mounting bracket, then remove pump and bracket assembly and position aside with hoses attached, if equipped.
10. On models with A/C, remove compressor mounting bracket attaching bolts, then remove compressor and mounting bracket assembly and secure to right hand shock absorber tower with refrigerant lines attached.
11. Remove alternator and position aside.
12. Disconnect heater hoses from water pump and heater tube.
13. On models equipped with speed control, disconnect servo chain at carburetor, then remove servo bracket attaching bolts and servo.
14. Disconnect all necessary vacuum hoses and wiring connectors.
15. Remove engine ground strap to dash panel attaching screw.
16. Disconnect transmission downshift linkage, throttle cable from carburetor, or fuel charging assembly, then remove throttle cable bracket attaching bolts.
17. Disconnect fuel line and PCV valve hose from carburetor, or flexible fuel lines from steel lines over the rocker arm cover, on models equipped with fuel injection.
18. Remove carburetor assembly from intake manifold. On models equipped with 7200 VV two barrel carburetor, remove spark knock intensity sensor and adapter assembly which is located between carburetor and thermostat housing.
19. With EGR spacer and phenolic gasket in position, install engine lifting plate T75T-6000-A or equivalent over carburetor mounting studs, then install nuts.
20. Raise vehicle and disconnect fuel inlet hose from fuel pump. Cap fuel hose to prevent entry of dirt.
21. Remove inspection cover from torque converter housing, then remove nuts attaching flex plate to torque converter.
22. Remove starter motor.
23. Remove transmission cooler line retaining clips, then disconnect exhaust pipe from exhaust manifold.
24. Remove four lower engine to transmission attaching bolts, then lower vehicle.
25. Remove engine mount to crossmember attaching nuts.
26. Lower vehicle and position a suitable transmission jack under transmission. Raise jack just enough to support weight of transmission.
27. Remove two upper engine to transmission attaching bolts, then place a ¼ inch piece of plywood or other suitable material between engine and radiator to prevent damage to radiator.
28. Carefully raise engine slightly, then pull away transmission and lift from

vehicle.

V8-255, 302

1. Disconnect battery ground cable.
2. Remove hood.
3. Drain cooling system and oil pan.
4. Remove air cleaner and intake duct assembly.
5. Disconnect radiator and heater hoses, then remove all drive belts.
6. If equipped with automatic transmission, disconnect transmission oil cooler lines from radiator.
7. On all models, remove fan shroud attaching bolts, then the radiator, fan, spacer, pulley and shroud.
8. Remove alternator mounting bolts and position alternator aside with wiring attached.
9. Disconnect oil pressure and water temperature wiring from sending units, then the accelerator cable from carburetor.
10. Disconnect and plug fuel pump inlet line.
11. If equipped with automatic transmission, disconnect throttle valve vacuum line from intake manifold. Disconnect manual shift rod and the retracting spring at shift rod stud. Disconnect transmission filler tube bracket from engine block.
12. If equipped with Thermactor system, remove or disconnect components that may interfere with engine replacement.
13. If equipped with A/C, isolate and remove compressor.
14. If equipped with power steering, disconnect pump bracket from cylinder head and position assembly aside.
15. If equipped with power brakes, disconnect brake vacuum line from intake manifold.
16. On all models, remove flywheel or converter housing upper attaching bolts.
17. Disconnect ignition coil wiring.
18. On models equipped with EEC IV system, disconnect air charge temperature sensor, engine coolant temperature sensor and exhaust gas oxygen sensor electrical connectors.
19. On all models, disconnect wiring harness from left side rocker arm cover and position aside. Disconnect ground strap from engine block.
20. Raise front of vehicle. Disconnect starter wiring, then remove starter motor.
21. Disconnect exhaust pipes from manifolds.
22. Disconnect engine mounts from brackets on frame.
23. If equipped with manual transmission, remove bolts attaching clutch equalizer bar to frame rail, then the equalizer from engine block. Remove remaining flywheel housing to engine bolts.
24. If equipped with automatic transmission, disconnect transmission oil cooler lines from retainer and remove converter housing inspection cover. Remove converter to flywheel bolts and secure converter in housing. Remove remaining converter housing to engine bolts.

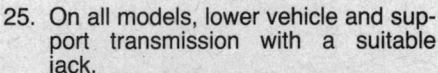

Fig. 12 Cylinder head tightening sequence. 1980–83 6-200 & 250

Fig. 13 Cylinder head tightening sequence. 1982–86 V6-232

Fig. 14 Intake manifold tightening sequence. 1982–86 V6-232

25. On all models, lower vehicle and support transmission with a suitable jack.
26. Attach suitable engine lifting equipment to engine.
27. Lift engine slightly and pull forward to disengage from transmission, then remove engine from vehicle.
28. Reverse procedure to install.

CYLINDER HEAD
REPLACE

Tighten cylinder head bolts a little at a time in three steps in the sequence shown in the illustrations. Final tightening should be to the torque specifications listed in the Engine Tightening table. After tightening the bolts to specifications, they should not be disturbed.

6-200 & 250

1. Drain cooling system and remove air cleaner.
2. Disconnect exhaust pipe from manifold and pull it down.
3. Disconnect accelerator cable and transmission downshift rod from carburetor.
4. Disconnect fuel inlet line at fuel filter hose, and distributor vacuum line at carburetor.
5. Disconnect coolant lines at carburetor spacer, if equipped. Remove radiator upper hose at outlet housing.
6. Disconnect distributor vacuum line at distributor. Disconnect carburetor fuel inlet line at fuel pump. Remove lines as an assembly.
7. Disconnect spark plug wires at plugs and temperature sending unit wire at sending unit.
8. Remove crankcase ventilation system. Remove hoses from Thermactor system as necessary for accessability.
9. Remove valve rocker arm cover.
10. Remove rocker arm shaft assembly.
11. Remove valve push rods.
12. Remove remaining cylinder head bolts and lift off head.
13. Reverse procedure to install. Torque cylinder head according to sequence shown in Fig. 12 in three steps: step 1, 50–55 ft. lbs.; step 2, 60–65 ft. lbs.; step 3, 70–75 ft. lbs.

V6-232

1. Disconnect battery ground cable, then drain cooling system.

2. Remove air cleaner, air intake duct and heat tube.
3. Loosen accessory drive belt idler and remove drive belt.
4. If left cylinder head is to be removed, proceed as follows:
   a. Remove oil filler cap.
   b. If equipped with power steering, remove pump bracket attaching bolts, then remove pump and bracket assembly and position pump aside with hoses attached.
   c. If equipped with A/C, remove compressor bracket attaching bolts, then position compressor and bracket assembly aside with refrigerant lines attached.
5. If right cylinder head is to be removed, proceed as follows:
   a. Remove Thermactor diverter valve and hose assembly.
   b. Remove accessory drive belt idler, then remove alternator.
   c. Remove Thermactor pump pulley, then remove Thermactor pump.
   d. Remove alternator mounting bracket.

NOTE: On models equipped with Tripminder, the fuel supply line from the fuel pump to the fuel sensor will have to be disconnected to gain access to the upper alternator bracket bolt.

   e. Remove PCV valve.
6. Remove intake manifold and exhaust manifolds.
7. Remove rocker arm cover attaching screws, then loosen cover by using a putty knife under cover flange and remove cover. Do not use excess force when loosening rocker arm cover as cover may become damaged.
8. Loosen rocker arm fulcrum bolt enough to allow rocker arms to be rotated to one side, then remove push rods.

NOTE: Tag push rods so they can be installed in the same position.

9. Remove cylinder head attaching bolts, then remove cylinder head and gasket.
10. Reverse procedure to install. Apply a thin coating of pipe sealant D8AZ-19558-A or equivalent to the shorter cylinder head bolts which are installed on the exhaust manifold side of the cylinder head. Do not apply pipe sealant to long bolts which are installed on the intake manifold side of the cylinder head. Tighten cylinder head bolts in

four steps to torque listed under Engine Tightening Specifications using sequence shown in **Fig. 13.** On 1982–83 models: step 1, 47 ft. lbs.; step 2, 55 ft. lbs.; step 3, 63 ft. lbs.; step 4, 74 ft. lbs. On 1984–86 models: step 1, 37 ft. lbs.; step 2, 45 ft. lbs.; step 3, 52 ft. lbs.; step 4, 59 ft. lbs. Loosen cylinder bolts approximately 2 to 3 turns, then retighten bolts in four steps to specified torque in sequence, **Fig. 13.** When installing intake manifold, tighten mounting bolts to torque specified under Engine Tightening Specifications in sequence shown in **Fig. 14.**

NOTE: Before installing intake manifold, apply a ⅛ inch bead of silicone rubber sealer D6AZ-19562-B or equivalent at mating surfaces of intake manifold, cylinder heads and cylinder block, **Fig. 15.** Also apply a ⅛ inch bead of sealer to the outer end of each intake manifold seal for the full width of the seal.

V8-255, 302

1. Remove intake manifold and carburetor as an assembly.
2. Disconnect battery ground cable at cylinder head.
3. If left head is being removed, remove A/C compressor (if equipped). Also remove and wire power steering pump out of the way. If equipped with Thermactor System, disconnect hose from air manifold on left cylinder head.
4. If right head is to be removed, remove alternator mounting bracket bolt and spacer, ground wire and air cleaner inlet duct.
5. If right head is to be removed on an engine with Thermactor System, remove air pump from bracket. Disconnect hose from air manifold.
6. Disconnect exhaust manifolds at exhaust pipes.
7. Remove rocker arm covers. If equipped with Thermactor System, remove check valve from air manifold.
8. Remove fulcrum bolts, oil deflector (if used), fulcrum and rocker arms. On all engines, remove push rods. Keep push rods and rocker arm components in order so they may be installed in original position.
9. Remove head bolts and lift head off block.

1/8" DIA. BEAD C3AZ-19528-A (OR -B) SEALER (4-JOINTS)

INTAKE MANIFOLD GASKET

CYLINDER HEAD

INTAKE MANIFOLD SEAL

1/16" DIA. BEAD C3AZ-19526-A (OR -B) SEALER (4-SEAL ENDS)

SEAL MOUNTING SURFACE OF CYLINDER BLOCK

Fig. 15   Applying RTV sealer for intake manifold installation. 1980—86 V8-255, 302 & 1982—86 V6-232

Fig. 18   Compressing lifter to check valve clearance. V8 engines (typical of 6 cylinder engines)

10. Reverse procedure to install. Torque cylinder head bolts in sequence shown in **Fig. 16,** and torque intake manifold bolts in sequence shown in **Fig. 17.**

NOTE: On 1980—86 V8-255, 302 engines, before installing intake manifold, apply a ⅛ in. bead of silicone rubber sealer D6AZ-19563-A or B or equivalent at mating surfaces of intake manifold, cylinder heads and cylinder block, **Fig. 15.** Also apply a 1/16 in. bead of sealer to the outer end of each intake manifold seal for the full width of the seal.

SERVICE BULLETIN: On V8-302 engines equipped with cork intake manifold seals, both the front and rear seals should be replaced with RTV sealer. Apply a ¼ inch bead of sealer to the front and rear sealing surfaces of engine block.

Fig. 16   Cylinder head tightening. V8 engines

VALVE ARRANGEMENT
FRONT TO REAR

4-140 . . . . E-I-E-I-E-I-E-I
6-200, 250 . . . . E-I-I-E-I-E-I-E-I-E-I-I-E
V6-232 Right . . . . I-E-I-E-I-E
V6-232 Left . . . . E-I-E-I-E-I
V8-255, 302 Right . . . . I-E-I-E-I-E-I-E
V8-255, 302 Left . . . . E-I-E-I-E-I-E-I

VALVE LIFT SPECS

Engine	Year	Intake	Exhaust
4-140	1980—86	.3997	.3997
6-200	1980—83	.372	.372
6-250	1980	.372	.372
V6-232	1982—86	.415	.417
V8-255	1980—82	.3753	.3753
V8-302	1980—81	.3753	.3909
	1983—86	.3753	.3909
V8-302H.O.	1984—86	.4130	.4420

VALVE TIMING
INTAKE OPENS BEFORE TDC

Engine	Year	Degrees
4-140	1980—86	22
6-200	1980—82	20
6-250	1980	18
V6-232	1982—86	13
V8-255	1980—82	16
V8-302	1980—81	16
(Exc. H.O.)	& 1983—86	

VALVES
ADJUST

6-200 & 250

A .060 inch longer or a .060 inch shorter push rod is available to compensate for dimensional changes in the valve train. If clearance is less than the minimum, the .060 inch shorter push rod should be used. If clearance is more than the maximum, the .060 inch longer push rod should be used.

The procedure used to check the valve clearance is to rotate the crankshaft with an auxiliary starter switch until the No. 1 piston is near TDC at the end of the compression stroke, and then compress the valve lifter using tool 6513-K or equivalent, **Fig. 18.** At this point the following valves can be checked:

FRONT

Fig. 17   Intake manifold tightening sequence V8-255, 302

No. 1 Intake No. 3 Exhaust
No. 1 Exhaust No. 4 Intake
No. 2 Intake No. 5 Exhaust

After the clearance of these valves have been checked, rotate the crankshaft until the No. 6 piston is on TDC at the end of its compression stroke (1 revolution of the crankshaft), and then compress the valve lifter using tool 6513-K or equivalent, **Fig. 18,** and check the following valves:

No. 2 Exhaust No. 5 Intake
No. 3 Intake No. 6 Intake
No. 4 Exhaust No. 6 Exhaust

V6-232

A .060 inch longer or a .060 inch shorter push rod is available to compensate for dimensional changes in the valve train. If clearance is less than specified, the .060 inch shorter push rod should be used. If clearance is more than the maximum specified, the .060 inch longer push rod should be used.

Using an auxiliary starter switch crankshaft until No. 1 cylinder is at TDC compression stroke, then compress valve lifter using tool T82C-6500-A or equivalent, **Fig. 18.** At this point, the following valves can be checked:

No. 1 Intake No. 3 Intake
No. 1 Exhaust No. 4 Exhaust
No. 2 Exhaust No. 6 Intake

After clearance on these valves has been checked, rotate crankshaft until No. 5 cylinder is at TDC compression stroke (1 revolution of crankshaft), and then compress valve lifter using tool No. T82C-6500-A or equivalent, **Fig. 18,** and check the following valves:

No. 2 Intake No. 5 Intake
No. 3 Exhaust No. 5 Exhaust
No. 4 Intake No. 6 Exhaust

Fig. 19   Rocker arm assembly. V6-232, V8-255, 302

Fig. 20   Rocker arm shaft assembly. 6-200 & 250

Magnet

Fig. 21   Removing valve lifter with magnetic rod

V8 ENGINES

For these engines, a .060 inch longer or a .060 inch shorter push rod is available to provide a means of compensating for dimensional changes in the valve train and rocker arm. If the clearance is less than the minimum, the .060 inch shorter push rod should be used. If clearance is more than the maximum the .060 inch longer push rod should be used.

All engines use a bolt and fulcrum attachment, **Fig. 19.**

To check valve clearance, proceed as follows:
1. Mark crankshaft pulley at three locations with number 1 location at TDC timing mark (end of compression stroke), number 2 location one half turn (180°) clockwise from TDC and number 3 location three quarter turn clockwise (270°) from TDC.
2. Turn the crankshaft to the number 1 location, then compress valve lifter using tool T71P-6513-A or equivalent, **Fig. 18,** and check the clearance on the following valves:
   V8-255, 302 (Exc. H.O.)
   No. 1 Intake   SNo. 1 Exhaust
   No. 7 Intake   SNo. 5 Exhaust
   No. 8 Intake   SNo. 4 Exhaust
   V8-302 (H.O.)
   No. 1 Intake   SNo. 1 Exhaust
   No. 4 Intake   SNo. 3 Exhaust
   No. 8 Intake   SNo. 7 Exhaust

3. Turn the crankshaft to the number 2 location, then compress valve lifter using tool T71P-6513-A or equivalent, **Fig. 18,** and check the clearance on the following valves:
   V8-255, 302 (Exc. H.O.)
   No. 4 Intake   SNo. 2 Exhaust
   No. 5 Intake   SNo. 6 Exhaust
   V8-302 (H.O.)
   No. 3 Intake   SNo. 2 Exhaust
   No. 7 Intake   SNo. 6 Exhaust
4. Turn the crankshaft to the number 3 location, then compress valve lifter using tool T71P-6513-A or equivalent, **Fig. 18,** and check the clearance on the following valves:
   V8-255, 302 (Exc. H.O.)
   No. 2 Intake   SNo. 3 Exhaust
   No. 3 Intake   SNo. 7 Exhaust
   No. 6 Intake   SNo. 8 Exhaust
   V8-302 (H.O.)
   No. 2 Intake   SNo. 4 Exhaust
   No. 5 Intake   SNo. 5 Exhaust
   No. 6 Intake   SNo. 8 Exhaust
   adjust valve lash.

VALVE GUIDES

Valve guides consist of holes bored in the cylinder head. For service the guide holes can be reamed oversize to accommodate valves with oversize stems of .015 and .030 inch.

ROCKER ARM SERVICE

6-200 & 250

Disassemble
1. To disassemble, remove pin and spring washer from each end of rocker shaft, **Fig. 20.**
2. Slide rocker arms, springs and supports off the shaft, being sure to identify location of parts for reassembly.
3. If it is necessary to remove the plugs from the shaft ends, drill or pierce the plug on one end. Then use a steel rod to knock out the plug on the opposite end. Working from the open end, knock out the remaining plug.

Assemble
1. Lubricate all parts with engine oil. Apply Lubriplate to the rocker arm

Fig. 22   Hydraulic valve lifter

pads.
2. If plugs were removed from shaft ends, use a blunt tool or large diameter pin punch and install a plug (cup side out) in each end of shaft.
3. Install spring washer and pin on one end of shaft.
4. Install rocker arms, supports and springs in order shown in **Fig. 20.** Be sure oil holes in shaft are facing downward.
5. Complete the assembly by installing remaining spring washer and pin.

V6-232

These engines use stamped steel rocker arms retained by a fulcrum seat which bolts directly to the cylinder head and guides the rocker arm. Torque fulcrum bolts in two steps as follows: For each valve rotate crankshaft until tappet rests on heel (base circle) of camshaft lobe and torque fulcrum bolt to 5–11 ft. lbs. After initial torquing all fulcrum bolts, final torque to 19–25 ft. lbs. Final torque may be done with camshaft in any position.

V8-255, 1980—81 V8-302 & 1983—86 V8-302

These engines use stamped steel rocker arms retained by a fulcrum seat, **Fig. 19.** The fulcrum seat bolts directly to the cylinder head and guides the rocker arm.

SERVICE BULLETIN: Some 1981 V8-255 and V8-302 engines equipped with low profile rocker arm fulcrums (part No. E1TZ-

Fig. 23 Front cover attaching bolt locations. 1982—86 V6-232

6A528-A) may experience excessive oil displacement when engine is operated for extended periods during high ambient temperatures. This problem may be corrected by replacing original rocker fulcrums with part No. D7AZ-6A528-A.

VALVE LIFTERS
REPLACE

6-200 & 250

When necessary to replace valve lifters, remove cylinder head and related parts as outlined previously. Then, using a magnet rod, **Fig. 21,** remove and install one lifter at a time to be sure they are placed in their original bores.

When installing, apply Lubriplate to each lifter foot and coat the remainder of lifter with oil before installation.

V6-232, V8-255, 302

1. On V6-232 engine, disconnect secondary ignition wires from spark plugs using wire remover T74P-6666-A or equivalent. Remove ignition wire routing clips from rocker arm cover attaching bolt studs and position wires aside.
2. On all models, remove intake manifold.
3. Remove rocker arm covers. On engines with stud mounted rocker arms, loosen stud nuts and rotate rocker arms to one side. On other engines, remove fulcrum bolt, fulcrum, rocker arm and fulcrum guide (if used).
4. Remove push rods in sequence so they can be installed in their original bores.

NOTE: On 1985–86 V8 engines equipped with roller lifters, the push rods have a collar at the upper end and can only be installed one way. When installing lifters, ensure that lifter is correctly oriented so that roller rotates in same direction.

5. Using a magnet rod, **Fig. 21,** remove the lifters and place them in a numbered rack so they can be installed in their original bores. If the lifters are stuck in their bores by excessive varnish, etc., it may be necessary to use a

plier-type tool to remove them. Rotate the lifter back and forth to loosen it from the gum or varnish.
6. The internal parts of each lifter are matched sets. Do not intermix parts. Keep the assemblies intact until they are to be cleaned, **Fig. 22.**

TIMING CASE COVER
REPLACE

NOTE: To replace the seal in the timing gear cover, it is necessary to remove the cover as outlined below.

6-200 & 250
Removal

1. Disconnect battery ground cable.
2. Drain cooling system and oil pan.
3. Disconnect radiator hoses from engine, then the transmission oil cooler lines from radiator, if equipped.
4. Remove radiator, then the drive belt, fan and pulley.
5. If equipped with A/C, remove condenser attaching bolts and position condenser forward with refrigerant lines attached. Remove compressor drive belt.
6. On all models, remove accessory drive pulley and the crankshaft damper with a suitable puller.
7. On 6-200 engines, remove front cover attaching screws from cover and oil pan. Pry cover from cylinder block slightly and cut oil pan gasket flush with front face of cylinder block.
8. On 6-250 engines, remove oil pan, then the front cover.
9. On all models, clean mating surfaces of cylinder block and front cover.

Installation

1. Apply oil resistant sealer to new front cover gasket and position gasket on front cover. Apply sealer to exposed area of gasket.
2. On 6-200 engines, apply sealer to gasket surface of oil pan. Cut and position the required portions of a new gasket on oil pan. Apply sealer to exposed areas of gasket, including the corners where contact is made with the front cover gasket.
3. On all models, install front cover.
4. Lubricate hub of crankshaft damper with Lubriplate or equivalent, then install damper. Torque attaching bolt to specifications.
5. On 6-250 engines, install oil pan.
6. On all models, install accessory drive pulley.
7. Reverse "Removal" steps 1 through 5 to complete installation.

V6-232

1. Disconnect battery ground cable, then drain cooling system.
2. Remove air cleaner and air intake duct.
3. Remove fan shroud attaching screws and fan and fan clutch attaching bolts, then remove fan and clutch assembly and shroud.

Fig. 24 Timing marks aligned for correct valve timing. 6-200 & 250

4. Loosen accessory drive belt idler, then remove drive belt and water pump pulley.
5. On models equipped with power steering, remove pump bracket attaching bolts, then position pump aside with hoses attached.
6. On models equipped with A/C, remove compressor front support bracket.
7. Disconnect coolant bypass hose and heater hose at water pump and upper radiator hose at thermostat housing.
8. Disconnect ignition coil secondary wire from distributor cap, then remove distributor cap with ignition wires attached.
9. With No. 1 cylinder at TDC compression stroke, mark position of rotor to distributor housing and position of distributor housing to front cover.
10. Remove distributor hold down clamp, then lift distributor from front cover.
11. On models equipped with Tripminder, remove fuel flow meter support bracket. Do not remove flow meter or disconnect fuel lines.
12. On 1982–86 models, raise and support front of vehicle, then remove crankshaft pulley using a suitable puller.
13. On 1982–83 models, remove fuel pump shield, if equipped, then disconnect fuel pump to carburetor fuel line at fuel pump.
14. On all models, remove fuel pump attaching bolts and position aside with fuel hose attached.
15. Remove oil filter, then disconnect lower radiator hose from water pump.
16. Remove oil pan as described under "Oil Pan, Replace."
17. Lower vehicle and remove front cover attaching bolts, **Fig. 23.**

NOTE: One of the front cover attaching bolts is located behind the oil filter adapter. Also tag bolts as they are removed so that they can be installed at the same location.

18. Remove ignition timing indicator, then remove front cover and water pump as an assembly.
19. Remove camshaft thrust button and spring from camshaft.
20. Reverse procedure to install. Before installing front cover attaching bolts at location 10, **Fig. 23,** coat threads of bolt with pipe sealant D8AZ-19558-A

Fig. 25 Timing marks aligned for correct valve timing. 1982–86 V6-232

or equivalent. Also lubricate camshaft thrust button with polyethylene grease before installing. Torque front cover attaching bolts to 15 to 22 ft. lbs.

NOTE: If a replacement front cover is to be installed, the water pump, oil pump, oil filter adapter and intermediate shaft must be removed from the front cover to be replaced and reinstalled on the replacement front cover. Also it may be necessary to rotate crankshaft 180° from the No. 1 cylinder TDC location to position fuel pump eccentric for fuel pump installation. When installing distributor, No. 1 cylinder must be at TDC position and marks made during removal must be aligned.

V8 ENGINES

1. To remove cover, drain cooling system and crankcase. Remove air cleaner and disconnect battery ground cable.
2. Remove water hose as necessary.
3. Remove generator support bolt at water pump, and loosen generator mounting bolts.
4. Remove fan, spacer and pulley.
5. Remove power steering drive belt (if equipped). If air conditioned, remove compressor drive belt.
6. Remove crankshaft pulley and adapter.
7. Remove fuel pump and lay it to one

side with flexible fuel line attached.
8. Remove oil level dipstick tube bracket and oil filler tube bracket.
9. Remove oil pan-to-front cover bolts.
10. Remove cover and water pump as an assembly.
11. Drive out cover seal with a pin punch. Clean out recess in cover.
12. Coat a new seal with grease and drive seal in until it is fully seated in recess. Check seal after installation to be sure spring is properly positioned in seal.
13. Reverse removal procedure to install cover.

TIMING CHAIN

After removing the cover as outlined above, remove the crankshaft front oil slinger. Crank the engine until the timing marks are aligned as shown in **Figs. 24, 25 and 26.** Remove camshaft sprocket retaining bolt(s) and washer. Slide both sprockets and chain forward and remove them as an assembly.

Reverse the order of the foregoing procedure to install the chain and sprockets, being sure the timing marks are aligned.

CAMSHAFT
REPLACE

6-200 & 250

1. Remove air cleaner, then drain cooling system and crankcase.
2. Remove radiator and grille.
3. On models equipped with A/C, remove condensor attaching bolts and position condensor aside.

NOTE: Do not disconnect refrigerant lines from condensor.

4. On 1980–84 models, disconnect accelerator control cable from carburetor and bracket, then the bracket from carburetor.
5. On all models, disconnect fuel inlet line from fuel filter.
6. Disconnect connectors and vacuum hoses connected to cylinder head from carburetor.

Fig. 26 Timing marks aligned for correct valve timing. V8 engines

7. Disconnect exhaust pipe from manifold. Pull pipe down and remove gasket.
8. On all models, disconnect carburetor fuel inlet line from fuel pump.
9. Disconnect ignition wires from spark plugs and the high tension lead from ignition coil.
10. On all models, disconnect engine temperature sending unit electrical connector from sending unit.
11. On 1980 models, disconnect and plug flexible fuel line from fuel pump.
12. On all models, remove distributor, fuel pump and oil filter.
13. Remove crankcase vent hose, regulator valve, rocker arm cover, cylinder head and lifters.
14. Remove drive belt, fan and pulley, then the damper using a suitable puller.
15. On 1980 models, remove oil level dipstick.
16. On models with 6-250 engine, remove oil pan.
17. On 1980 models, remove oil pump and inlet tube assembly.
18. On all models, remove front cover, gasket, timing chain and sprockets.
19. Remove camshaft thrust plate, then the camshaft by pulling toward front of engine, **Fig. 27.**

CAUTION: Use care to avoid damaging crankshaft bearings.

Fig. 27 Camshaft and related parts. 6-200 & 250

Fig. 28 Camshaft and related parts. V8 engines

Fig. 30   Piston & rod assembly. 1982—86 V6-232

Fig. 29   Piston & rod assembly. 6-200 & 250 engines

Fig. 31   Piston & rod assembly. V8s

20. Reverse procedure to install.

V6 & V8 ENGINES

1. Drain cooling system and remove radiator and grille.
2. If equipped with air conditioning:
   a. On 255 and 302 engines, remove condensor retaining bolts and position condensor aside without disconnecting refrigerant lines.
   b. On V6-232 engine, purge refrigerant from system and remove condensor.
3. Remove front cover, timing chain and sprockets.
4. Remove intake manifold.
5. Remove push rods and lifters.
6. On V6-232 engine, remove oil pan.
7. Remove thrust plate, then carefully remove camshaft by pulling toward front of engine, **Fig. 28.**

CAUTION: Use care to avoid damaging camshaft bearings.

8. Reverse procedure to install.

PISTON & ROD ASSEMBLY

When installed, piston and rod assembly should have the notch or arrow in piston head toward front of engine with connecting rod numbers positioned as shown in **Figs. 29, 30 and 31.** Check side clearance between connecting rods at each crankshaft journal. Clearance should be .0035–.0105 for 4-140, 6-200 and 6-250 engines, .0047–.0114 for V6-232 engine, and .010–.020 for V8-302 engine.

PISTONS, PINS & RINGS

Pistons are available in standard sizes

and oversizes of .003, .020, .030 and .040 in. Piston rings are available in standard sizes and oversizes of .020, .030 and .040 in. Piston pins are available in standard size and oversizes of .001 and .002 in.

MAIN & ROD BEARINGS

Main and rod bearings are available in standard sizes and undersizes of .001, .002, .010, .020 and .030 in.

CRANKSHAFT REAR OIL SEAL
REPLACE

1980–83

1. On all except V6-232 engines, remove oil pan and oil pump as described under "Oil Pan, Replace" and "Oil Pump, Replace."
2. Loosen all main bearing cap bolts, allowing crankshaft to drop slightly. Do not let crankshaft drop more than 1/32 inch.
3. Remove rear main bearing cap.
4. Remove old seals from both cylinder block and rear main bearing cap. To remove block half of seal, use a seal removal tool or install a small screw in one end of seal and pull on screw to remove seal.

NOTE: Use care to prevent damaging the crankshaft seal surfaces.

5. Carefully clean seal groove in block with a brush and solvent. Also clean seal groove in bearing cap. Remove the oil seal retaining pin from the bearing cap if so equipped. The pin is not used with the split-lip seal.

6. Dip seal halves in clean engine oil.
7. Carefully install upper seal half in its groove with undercut side of seal toward front of engine, **Fig. 32,** by rotating it on shaft journal of crankshaft until approximately 3/8 inch protrudes below the parting surface. Be sure no rubber has been shaved from outside diameter of seal by bottom edge of groove.

NOTE: On V6-232 engines, seal ends should be flush with the block and cap.

8. Retighten main bearing caps and torque to specifications.
9. Install lower seal in main bearing cap with undercut side of seal toward front of engine, and allow seal to protrude about 3/8 inch above parting surface to mate with upper seal upon cap installation.

NOTE: On V6-232 engines, install seals with locating tab facing rear of engine, then remove the tab, **Fig. 33.**

10. Apply suitable sealer to parting faces of cap and block. Install cap and torque to specifications.

NOTE: If difficulty is encountered in installing the upper half of the seal in position, lightly lap (sandpaper) the side of the seal opposite the lip side using a medium grit paper. After sanding, the seal must be washed in solvent, then dipped in clean engine oil prior to installation.

SERVICE BULLETIN: A new crankshaft rear oil seal has been released for service. This new seal may be received when ordering an oil pan gasket kit and is installed in the same manner as described above, **Fig. 34.**

1984–86

1. Using a sharp tool, punch one hole

3/8"

SEAL HALVES TO PROTRUDE BEYOND PARTING FACES
THIS DISTANCE TO ALLOW FOR CAP TO BLOCK
ALIGNMENT

3/8"

REAR FACE OF REAR MAIN
BEARING CAP AND CYLINDER BLOCK

INSTALL SEAL WITH THIS
UNDERCUT TOWARDS FRONT
OF ENGINE

REAR OF ENGINE   FRONT OF ENGINE

VIEW LOOKING AT PARTING FACE
OF SPLIT-LIP REAR C/S SEAL

Fig. 32 Crankshaft rear seal installation. 1980—83 exc. 1982—83 V6-232

REAR BEARING CAP

REAR OIL SEAL

LOCATING TAB

APPLY SEALER AS SHOWN SEE NOTE BELOW

FRONT OF ENGINE

PRELUBE SEAL AND JOURNAL WITH LUBRIPLATE

TAB

UPPER AND LOWER SEAL ENDS TO BE FLUSH IN BLOCK AND CAP

SEALER NOTE: CLEAN THE AREA WHERE SEALER IS TO BE APPLIED BEFORE INSTALLING THE SEALS. USE FORD SPOT REMOVER B7A-19521-A OR EQUIVALENT. AFTER THE SEALS ARE IN PLACE, APPLY A 1/16 INCH BEAD OF D6AZ-19562-A OR -B SEALER AS SHOWN. SEALER MUST NOT CONTACT SEALS.

Fig. 33 Crankshaft rear seal installation. 1982—83 V6-232

APPLY SILICONE RUBBER SEALER IN THIS AREA (C3AZ-19562-A OR B)

NEW STYLE SEAL

APPLY SILICON RUBBER SEALER IN THIS AREA (C3AZ-19562-A OR B)

OLD STYLE SEAL

Fig. 34 Crankshaft oil seals

into seal metal surface between seal lip and engine block.
2. Remove seal using slide hammer No. T82L-9533-B or equivalent. Use care to prevent damaging the sealing surface.
3. Lubricate new seal with clean engine oil and install using tool No. T82L-6701-A or equivalent. Tighten bolts alternately to seat seal properly, **Fig. 35.**

OIL PAN
REPLACE

1980—83 FAIRMONT & ZEPHYR, 1981—82 GRANADA & COUGAR & 1983—86 COUGAR, LTD, MARQUIS & THUNDERBIRD 4-140

1. Disconnect battery ground cable.
2. Raise and support vehicle.
3. Drain cooling system and crankcase.
4. Remove right and left engine support nuts and washers or bolts.
5. Raise engine as far as possible using a suitable jack. Place wooden blocks between the mounts and chassis bracket or No. 2 crossmember pedestals, then remove jack.
6. Remove steering gear attaching nuts and bolts and the steering gear-to-flex coupling attaching bolt. Position steering gear forward and down.
7. Remove shake brace, then the starter motor.

8. Remove engine rear support-to-cross-member attaching nuts.
9. Raise and support transmission with a suitable jack.
10. Remove oil pan attaching bolts and the oil pan.
11. Reverse procedure to install.

1980—83 FAIRMONT, ZEPHYR, 1980—82 COUGAR XR-7, THUNDERBIRD & 1981—82 COUGAR & GRANADA 6-200 & 250

1. If equipped with automatic transmission, disconnect transmission oil cooler lines at radiator.
2. On all models, remove radiator top support, then the oil level dipstick.
3. Raise and support vehicle, and drain oil pan.
4. Remove nuts and bolts attaching sway bar to chassis and allow sway bar to hang downward.
5. Remove "K" brace.
6. Lower rack and pinion steering gear.
7. Remove starter motor.
8. Remove nuts attaching engine mounts to support brackets.
9. Loosen rear insulator to crossmember attaching bolts.
10. Slightly raise engine and place a ¼ inch spacer between engine support insulator and chassis bracket.

NOTE: Loosen fan shroud attaching screws to prevent damage to fan when raising engine.

11. Support and raise transmission slightly with a suitable jack.
12. Remove oil pan attaching bolts and lower oil pan to crossmember.
13. Remove oil pump intermediate driveshaft, pick-up tube and screen assembly and allow components to drop into oil pan.
14. Position transmission oil cooler lines aside, if equipped, and remove oil pan from vehicle. It may be necessary to

rotate crankshaft.
15. Reverse procedure to install.

1980 GRANADA & MONARCH 6-250

1. On automatic transmission vehicles, disconnect transmission oil cooler lines at radiator.
2. Remove both radiator top support bolts, then raise vehicle and drain crankcase.
3. Remove the four bolts and nuts retaining sway bar to chassis and allow bar to hang down.
4. Remove starter motor, then remove both engine mount retaining nuts to support brackets.
5. Loosen but do not remove both rear mount insulator to crossmember bolts.
6. Raise front of engine and place 1¼ inch wooden blocks between engine mount and chassis bracket.
7. Lower engine and raise transmission slightly, then remove oil pan bolts and lower oil pan to crossmember.
8. Position crankshaft rear throw in the up position, then position transmission oil cooler lines aside and remove oil pan.
9. Reverse procedure to install.

1982 COUGAR XR-7 & GRANADA, 1982—86 COUGAR & THUNDERBIRD & 1983—86 LTD & MARQUIS V6-232

1. Disconnect battery ground cable, then remove air cleaner and air intake duct.
2. Remove fan shroud attaching screws and position shroud over fan, then remove engine oil dipstick.
3. Remove vacuum solenoid(s) from dash panel and position on engine

Fig. 35   Crankshaft rear seal installation. 1984–86

Fig. 36   Oil pump assembly. V6-232

with vacuum hoses attached.
4. Raise and support front of vehicle, then remove exhaust pipe to exhaust manifold attaching nuts.
5. Drain crankcase, then remove oil filter.
6. Remove shift linkage bracket to converter housing attaching bolts.
7. Disconnect transmission oil cooler lines at radiator. Remove four converter cover attaching bolts, then remove converter cover.
8. Remove bolts attaching engine damper to No. 2 crossmember.
9. Disconnect steering gear at flex coupling, then remove steering gear to main crossmember attaching bolts and allow steering gear to rest on frame.
10. Remove nuts and bolts attaching from engine mounts to chassis, then raise engine approximately 2 to 3 inches and insert wooden block between engine mounts and frame.

NOTE: On some models, it may be necessary to raise engine as much as 5 inches to provide clearance for oil pan removal. On these models, transmission fluid dipstick tube may contact Thermactor air tube. If contact occurs, lower engine and remove dipstick and air tube.

11. Remove oil pan attaching bolts, then lower oil pan to crossmember.
12. Remove oil pump pickup tube attaching bolts and pickup tube bracket attaching nut, then lower pickup tube into oil pan.
13. Remove oil pan through front of vehicle, then remove oil pan gaskets and seals.
14. Reverse procedure to install. Using a small screwdriver, work tabs of oil pan seal into gap between rear main bearing cap and cylinder block, then with tabs positioned, work seal into groove on rear main bearing cap. Apply a ⅛ inch bead of silicone sealer D6AZ-19562-B or equivalent where front cover and cylinder block join and where rear main bearing cap and cyl-

inder block join. Apply a ⅛ inch bead along oil pan rail surface of cylinder block and a ¼ inch bead along front cover to oil pan surface.

1983–86 COUGAR & THUNDERBIRD, 1984–86 LTD, MARQUIS V8-302

1. Disconnect battery ground cable.
2. Remove oil level indicator from left side of rear oil sump.
3. Remove air cleaner assembly.
4. Remove fan shroud attaching bolts and position shroud over fan.
5. Raise and support vehicle.
6. Drain engine oil and transmission fluid.
7. Disconnect driveshaft, then remove speedometer cable from transmission.
8. Remove transmission shift linkage lever from transmission.
9. Remove flywheel housing cover attaching bolts and the cover.
10. Remove flywheel-to-converter attaching bolts, then the transmission kickdown control shaft.
11. Remove gear selector valve rod, then the starter motor.
12. Remove catalytic converter and muffler inlet pipes.
13. Support transmission with a suitable jack and remove converter housing-to-cylinder block attaching bolts.
14. Remove No. 3 crossmember and rear insulator support assemblies.
15. Disconnect neutral start switch electrical connector from transmission.
16. Disconnect transmission oil cooler lines, then lower transmission and converter assembly from vehicle.
17. Remove flywheel attaching bolts, then the engine rear cover plate.
18. Remove steering gear attaching bolts and position gear aside.
19. Raise engine sufficiently to provide clearance for oil pan removal.
20. Remove oil pan attaching bolts and the oil pan.
21. Reverse procedure to install.

1980–82 COUGAR XR-7 & THUNDERBIRD V8-255 & 302

1. Disconnect battery ground cable.
2. Remove fan shroud attaching screws and position shroud over fan, then remove dipstick and tube assembly.
3. Raise vehicle and drain crankcase.
4. Disconnect steering flex coupling, then remove two bolts attaching steering gear to main crossmember and let steering gear rest on frame away from oil pan.
5. Unclip and position splash pan away from ends of stabilizer.
6. Remove brackets attaching stabilizer bar to frame, then pull bar downward.
7. Remove transmission shift linkage bracket from frame rail.
8. Remove engine mount attaching bolts, then disconnect and plug transmission oil cooler lines.
9. Disconnect exhaust pipe at exhaust manifolds.
10. Loosen transmission mount nuts, then position a suitable jack under engine and raise engine until engine mount bolts clear frame mounts and pry engine as far forward as it will slide on the transmission mounts.
11. Position two wooden blocks between engine mounts and frame.
12. Remove oil pan attaching bolts, then lower oil pan to frame.
13. Remove oil pump attaching bolts and inlet tube attaching nut, then lower oil pump assembly into oil pan.
14. Remove oil pan. When removing, pull pan forward of stabilizer bar and steering gear flex coupling.

NOTE: It may be necessary to rotate the crankshaft so that oil pan will clear crankshaft counterweights.

15. Reverse procedure to install.

Fig. 37 Oil pump assembly. 6-200 & 250

1980–81 FAIRMONT, ZEPHYR & 1981 COUGAR & GRANADA V8-255 & 302

1. Remove fan shroud attaching bolts and position shroud over fan.
2. Raise and support vehicle, then drain oil pan.
3. Remove two bolts attaching steering gear to main crossmember and let steering gear rest on frame away from oil pan.
4. Remove engine mount attaching bolts.
5. Raise engine with a suitable jack and place wood blocks between engine mounts and frame.
6. Remove rear "K" braces.
7. Remove oil pan attaching bolts and lower oil pan to frame.
8. Remove oil pump attaching bolts and the inlet tube attaching nut, then lower pump into oil pan.
9. Remove oil pan, rotating crankshaft as necessary to provide clearance for oil pan.
10. Reverse procedure to install.

1980 GRANADA & MONARCH V8-302

1. Raise and support vehicle, then drain oil pan.
2. Remove stabilizer bar from chassis.
3. Remove engine front support through bolts, then the supports. If equipped, remove bolt and nut securing power steering lines to rear side of lower arm.
4. Remove idler arm bracket retaining bolts and pull linkage downward and aside.
5. Remove oil pan attaching bolts and the oil pan.
6. Reverse procedure to install.

OIL PUMP
REPLACE

6-200 & 250

1. Remove oil pan and related parts as directed above.
2. Unfasten and remove pump, gasket and intermediate drive shaft.
3. Prime pump by filling either the inlet or outlet port with engine oil. Rotate pump shaft to distribute oil within pump body.
4. Position intermediate drive shaft into distributor socket.
5. Position new gasket on pump housing. Insert intermediate drive shaft into oil pump.
6. Install pump and shaft as an assembly.
7. Install oil pan.

V6-232

On these engines, the oil pump is contained within the front cover, **Fig. 36.**

V8-255, 302

1. Remove oil pan as outlined above.
2. Remove pump inlet tube and screen.
3. Remove pump retaining bolts and remove pump, gasket and intermediate shaft.
4. To install, position intermediate drive shaft into distributor socket. With shaft seated in socket, stop on shaft should touch roof of crankcase. Remove shaft and position stop as necessary.
5. With new gasket on pump housing and stop properly positioned, insert intermediate shaft into oil pump. Install pump and shaft as a unit. Do not force pump into position if it will not seat readily. The drive shaft hex may be misaligned with distributor shaft. To align, rotate shaft into new position.
6. Prime pump by filling either inlet or outlet port with engine oil. Rotate pump shaft to distribute oil within pump body.
7. Position new gasket on pump housing.
8. Insert intermediate drive shaft into oil pump.
9. Install pump and shaft as a unit.
10. Complete installation in reverse order of removal.

OIL PUMP, REPAIRS
V8-255, 302 & ALL SIXES

Referring to **Figs. 36 through 38**, disassemble pump. To remove the oil pressure relief valve, insert a self-threading sheet metal screw of the proper diameter into the oil pressure relief valve chamber cap and pull cap out of chamber. Remove spring and plunger.

The inner rotor and shaft and the outer race are serviced as an assembly. One part should not be replaced without replacing the other.

Fig. 38 Oil pump assembly. V8-255, 302

BELT TENSION DATA

	New	Used
1980–81		
Exc. ¼ inch Belts.	140	105
¼ inch Belts.	65	50
1981		
V Ribbed Belts		
4K①	105	100
5K②	125	120
5K③	108	108
6K②	155	150
6K④	113	113
1982–86		
Except ¼ inch Belts	140	105
¼ inch Belts		
Except Air Pump	65	50
Air Pump	110	105
Ribbed Belt		
4 Rib		
Except Air Pump	130	115
Air Pump	110	105
5 Rib	150	135
6 Rib		
V6	175	145
V8	113	110

①—4 groves.
②—5 grooves fixed.
③—W/ absorber.
④—W/ tensioner.

WATER PUMP
REPLACE

6-200 & 250

1. Drain cooling system, then remove Thermactor pump, power steering and A/C drive belts, if equipped.
2. Disconnect lower radiator hose, then remove fan belt, fan and drive clutch and water pump pulley.
3. Disconnect heater hose at water pump.
4. Remove water pump attaching bolts,

Engine oiling system. 6-200 & 250

Engine oiling system. V8-255, 302

then remove water pump.
5. Reverse procedure to install.

V6-232

1. Drain cooling system, then remove air cleaner and air intake duct.
2. Remove fan shroud attaching screws then the fan and fan clutch attaching bolts. Remove fan and fan clutch and shroud.
3. Loosen accessory drive belt idler, then remove drive belt and water pump pulley.
4. On models equipped with power steering, remove pump mounting bracket attaching bolts, position pump aside with hoses attached.
5. On models equipped with A/C, remove compressor front support bracket.
6. Disconnect lower radiator hose, coolant bypass hose and heat hose from water pump.
7. On models equipped with Tripminder,

remove fuel flow sensor support bracket. Do not disconnect fuel lines.
8. Remove water pump attaching bolts, then remove water pump.
9. Reverse procedure to install.

V8-255, 302

1. Drain cooling system.
2. Remove air inlet tube.
3. On models equipped with a fan shroud, remove shroud attaching bolts and position shroud over fan.
4. On all models remove fan, spacer and fan shroud.
5. Remove A/C compressor drive belt and idler pulley bracket, if equipped.
6. Remove alternator drive belt, then remove power steering drive belt and pump, if equipped.
7. Remove all accessory brackets attached to water pump, then remove water pump pulley.
8. Disconnect lower radiator hose, heater hose and bypass hose from water

pump.
9. Remove water pump to front cover attaching bolts, then remove water pump.
10. Reverse procedure to install.

FUEL PUMP
REPLACE

1. Loosen fuel line connections, then retighten hand tight. Do not disconnect lines at this time.
2. Loosen fuel pump attaching bolts one or two turns. Apply hand force to break pump free from gasket.
3. Rotate engine slightly until pump cam lobe is near lowest position.
4. Disconnect inlet and outlet lines and the vapor return line from pump, if equipped.
5. Remove fuel pump attaching bolts and pump. Remove and discard gasket.
6. Reverse procedure to install.

Clutch & Transmission Section

COWL SIDE TRIM PANEL – REMOVE FOR CARPET RELOCATION

WHEN INSTALLING BOOT, BE SURE CARPET IS NEXT TO METAL RETAINER AS SHOWN

CARPET–ROLL BACK AS SHOWN TO GAIN ACCESS TO BOOT SCREWS

TRANSMISSION GEAR SHIFT LEVER BOOT.

SCUFF PLATE REMOVE TWO FRONT SCREWS

SECTIONAL VIEW

SHOWING POSITION OF CARPETING IN RELATIONSHIP TO BOOT

Fig. 1 Shift lever boot removal. 1980–83 Fairmont, Zephyr, 1981–82 Cougar, Granada & 1983 LTD & Marquis

CLUTCH PEDAL, ADJUST

1981–83 FAIRMONT, ZEPHYR, 1981–82 COUGAR, GRANADA, 1983 LTD, MARQUIS, 1983–86 THUNDERBIRD & 1984–86 COUGAR

These models incorporate a self adjusting clutch mechanism. The adjust mechanism consists of a spring loaded rachet quadrant attached to the clutch cable. To accomplish this adjustment, grasp clutch pedal and pull upward, then slowly depress clutch pedal. If a click is heard during the procedure, an adjustment was necessary and has been accomplished. This procedure should be performed at least every 5000 miles.

1980 FAIRMONT & ZEPHYR

1980 4-140 & V8-302

1. Remove dust shield, then loosen clutch cable locknut.
2. Turn adjusting nut as necessary to obtain a total clutch pedal stroke of 5.3 inches on models with 4-140 engines, and 6.5 inches on models with V8-302 engines.

NOTE: Turning adjusting nut clockwise will raise pedal and counterclockwise will lower pedal.

3. Tighten locknut against adjusting nut using care not to disturb the adjustment. Apply and release the clutch pedal several times and recheck pedal height.
4. Install dust shield.

1980 6-200

1. Pull cable toward front of vehicle until adjusting nut can be rotated. Do not rotate nylon adjusting nut until it is free of rubber insulator. To release nut from rubber insulator, it may be necessary to block the clutch release forward so the clutch is partially disengaged.
2. Rotate nut clockwise until 5.3 inches of clutch pedal stroke can be obtained when the nut has been reinstalled in the rubber insulator. Cycle the clutch pedal several times and recheck the adjustment.

NOTE: This negative free play is normal and is required to provide for clutch facing wear.

EXC. 1980–83 FAIRMONT, ZEPHYR, 1981–82 COUGAR, GRANADA, 1983 LTD, MARQUIS, 1983–86 THUNDERBIRD & 1984–86 COUGAR

1. Disconnect clutch return spring from release lever.
2. On 1980 models remove locking pin, then on all models loosen adjusting nut.
3. Move release lever rearward until release bearing lightly contacts clutch pressure plate release fingers.
4. Slide rod until it seats in release lever pocket.
5. Insert .136 inch feeler gauge (see below) between adjusting nut and swivel sleeve, then tighten adjusting nut finger tight against feeler gauge.
6. On 1980 models, rotate rod slightly to align flat with pin hole in adjusting nut, then install locking pin and remove feeler gauge.
7. On all models, connect return spring to release lever.
8. Depress clutch pedal a minimum of five times, then recheck free play setting with the feeler gauge. Check free travel of pedal which should be ⅞ to 1⅛ inch.

CLUTCH
REPLACE

1980–83 FAIRMONT, ZEPHYR, 1981–82 COUGAR, GRANADA, 1983 LTD, MARQUIS, 1983–86 THUNDERBIRD & 1984–86 COUGAR

NOTE: On 1981–86 models lift clutch pedal upward to disengage clutch cable self adjuster pawl and quadrant. Push quadrant forward, then detach cable from quadrant and allow quadrant to swing rearward slowly.

4-140

1. Raise vehicle and remove release lever spring and dust shield.
2. Loosen clutch cable lock nut and adjusting nut, then disconnect clutch cable from release lever.
3. Remove retaining clip, then remove clutch cable from clutch housing.
4. Remove starter motor.
5. Remove bolts attaching engine rear plate to lower front portion of fly-wheel housing.
6. Remove transmission and flywheel housing as described under "Transmission, Replace."
7. Remove clutch release lever from housing by pulling lever through opening in housing until retainer spring is disengaged from pivot.
8. On 1982–86 models, remove release bearing from release lever.
9. Remove pressure plate cover attaching bolts.

NOTE: Loosen bolts evenly to relieve spring tension without distorting cover. Mark cover and flywheel so that pressure plate can be installed in the same position.

10. Remove pressure plate and clutch disc from flywheel.
11. Reverse procedure to install. Adjust clutch pedal as described under "Clutch Pedal, Adjust."

NOTE: Prior to installing throw-out bearing, apply a light film of lithium base lubricant No. C1AZ-19590-B or equivalent to transmission front bearing retainer outside diameter, the clutch release fork and anti-rattle spring where they contact the release bearing hub and to the throw-out bearing where the bearing contacts the pressure plate release fingers. In addition, fill the throw-out bearing grease groove with the same lubricant. Clean up all excess lubricant.

6-200 & V8-302

1. Raise vehicle, then remove transmission as described under "Transmission, Replace."
2. Remove dust shield and loosen clutch cable adjusting nut, then disengage clutch cable from release lever.
3. Disengage clutch cable from flywheel housing.
4. Remove starter.
5. Remove bolts attaching engine rear plate to front lower portion of flywheel housing.
6. Remove bolts attaching housing to cylinder block.
7. Move housing back just far enough to clear pressure plate and remove housing.
8. Remove clutch release lever from housing by pulling lever through housing opening until retainer spring is disengaged from pivot.
9. Remove pressure plate cover attaching bolts.

NOTE: Loosen bolts evenly to relieve spring tension without distorting cover. Mark cover and flywheel so that pressure plate can be installed in the same position.

10. Remove pressure plate and clutch disc from flywheel.
11. Reverse procedure to install. Adjust clutch pedal as described under "Clutch Pedal, Adjust."

NOTE: Prior to installing throw-out bearing, apply a light film of lithium base lubricant No. C1AZ-19590-B or equivalent to transmission front bearing retainer outside diameter, the clutch release fork and anti-rattle spring where they contact the release bearing hub and to the throw-out bearing where the bearing contacts the pressure plate release fingers. In addition, fill the throw-out bearing grease groove with the same lubricant. Clean up all excess lubricant.

EXC. 1980–83 FAIRMONT, ZEPHYR, 1981–82 COUGAR, GRANADA, 1983 LTD, MARQUIS, 1983–86 THUNDERBIRD & 1984–86 COUGAR

1. Remove transmission as described under Transmission, Replace.
2. Disconnect clutch release lever retaining spring.
3. Loosen clutch adjusting rod nuts and remove adjusting rod.
4. Remove starter motor.
5. Remove engine rear plate to lower flywheel housing attaching bolts.

Fig. 2   Shift lever installation. 1980–83 Fairmont, Zephyr, 1981–82 Cougar, Granada & 1983 LTD & Marquis

6. Remove flywheel housing to engine attaching bolts and clutch equalizer bar pivot bracket, if equipped.
7. Move flywheel housing back just far enough to clear pressure plate and remove housing.

NOTE: Use care not to disturb clutch linkage.

8. Pull clutch release lever through opening in housing until retainer spring is disengaged from pivot.
9. Remove pressure plate cover attaching bolts.

NOTE: Loosen bolts evenly to relieve spring tension without distorting cover. Mark cover and flywheel so that pressure plate can be installed in the same position.

10. Remove pressure plate and clutch disc from flywheel.
11. Reverse removal procedure to install the clutch and adjust the pedal as outlined under "Clutch Pedal, Adjust".

FOUR SPEED OVERDRIVE TRANSMISSION
REPLACE

1980 FAIRMONT, GRANADA, MONARCH & ZEPHYR

1. Raise vehicle and mark drive shaft so it can be installed in the same position, then disconnect driveshaft at rear U-joint flange. Slide driveshaft from transmission output shaft, then install an extension housing seal installation tool into extension housing opening to prevent lubricant spillage.
2. Disconnect speedometer cable from extension housing.
3. Remove shifter tower to turret assembly attaching screws, then remove shift tower.
4. Support engine using a suitable jack, then remove extension housing to engine rear support attaching bolts.
5. Raise rear of engine slightly to relieve weight from crossmember, then remove crossmember to frame side support attaching bolts and remove crossmember.
6. Support transmission using a suitable jack, then remove bolts attaching transmission to flywheel housing.
7. Move transmission rearward until input shaft clears flywheel, then lower transmission from vehicle. It may be necessary to lower engine slightly to obtain clearance for transmission removal.
8. Reverse procedure to install.

FOUR SPEED TRANS.
REPLACE

1980–83 FAIRMONT, ZEPHYR, 1981–82 COUGAR, GRANADA & 1983 LTD & MARQUIS

1. Remove coin tray, then remove four

screws attaching boot to floor pan and pull boot up on shift lever. Remove three lever attaching screws, then remove shift lever and boot assembly, **Figs. 1 and 2.**
2. From under hood, remove flywheel housing to engine block upper attaching bolts or nuts.
3. Raise and support vehicle.
4. Mark driveshaft so that it can be installed in the same position, then remove driveshaft and install a plug in transmission extension housing to prevent lubricant leakage.
5. Remove clutch release lever dust cover, then disconnect clutch cable from release lever.
6. Remove starter motor.
7. Remove speedometer cable attaching screw, then lift cable from extension housing.
8. Support rear of engine using a suitable jack, then remove bolts attaching crossmember to body.
9. Remove bolts attaching crossmember to extension housing and remove crossmember.
10. Lower engine as required to permit removal of bolts attaching flywheel housing to engine. Slide transmission rearward from engine and lower from vehicle.

NOTE: It may be necessary to slide mounting bracket forward from catalytic converter heat shield to provide clearance to move transmission rearward for removal.

11. Remove cover attaching bolts and drain lubricant.
12. Remove flywheel housing to transmission attaching bolts, then remove flywheel housing.
13. Reverse procedure to install.

FIVE SPEED TRANS.
REPLACE

1983—86 THUNDERBIRD & 1984—86 COUGAR

1. Raise and support vehicle.
2. Mark driveshaft for assembly reference, then disconnect driveshaft from rear U-joint flange. Slide driveshaft from transmission output shaft, then install an extension housing seal installation tool into extension housing

opening to prevent lubricant spillage.
3. Remove 4 catalytic converter attaching bolts and the converter with inlet pipe.
4. Remove rear transmission support attaching bolts.
5. Support engine and transmission using a suitable jack, then remove crossmember attaching bolts. Raise engine slightly and remove crossmember.
6. Lower transmission to gain access to 2 shift handle attaching bolts, then remove the bolts and shift handle.
7. Disconnect backup light electrical connector.
8. Remove speedometer cable retainer bolt, then the speedometer driven gear from transmission.
9. Remove transmission-to-flywheel attaching bolts.
10. Move transmission rearward until input shaft clears flywheel housing, then lower transmission from vehicle. It may be necessary to lower engine slightly to provide clearance for transmission removal.

NOTE: Do not depress clutch pedal while transmission is removed from vehicle.

11. Reverse procedure to install.

Rear Axle, Propeller Shaft & Brakes

REAR AXLES

FORD WGF & WGG (6¾ inch RING GEAR) INTEGRAL CARRIER

This rear axle, **Fig. 1,** is an integral design hypoid with the centerline of the pinion set below the centerline of the ring gear. The semi-floating axle shafts are retained in the housing by ball bearings and bearing retainers at axle ends.

The differential is mounted on two opposed tapered roller bearings which are retained in the housing by removable caps. Differential bearing preload and drive gear backlash is adjusted by nuts located behind each differential bearing cup.

The drive pinion assembly is mounted on two opposed tapered roller bearings. Pinion bearing preload is adjusted by a collapsible spacer on the pinion shaft. Pinion and ring gear tooth contact is adjusted by shims between the rear bearing cone and pinion gear.

FORD WGX & WGZ INTEGRAL CARRIER

The gear set, **Fig. 2,** consist of a ring gear and an overhung drive pinion which is supported by two opposed tapered roller bearings. Pinion bearing preload is maintained by a collapsible spacer on the pinion shaft and adjusted by the pinion nut. The

Fig. 1 Disassembled view of Ford WGF & WGG (6¾ inch Ring Gear) integral carrier type rear axle assembly

differential case is a one piece design with two openings to allow assembly of internal components and lubricant flow. The pinion shaft is retained with a threaded bolt assembled to the case. The differential case is mounted in the carrier between two opposed tapered roller bearings. The bearings are retained in the carrier by removable bearing caps. Differential bearing preload and ring gear backlash are adjusted by the use of shims located between the differential bearing cups and the carrier housing. Axle shafts are held in the housing by C-locks positioned in a slot on the axle shaft splined end, **Fig. 3.**

REMOVABLE CARRIER TYPE

In these axles, **Fig. 4,** the drive pinion is straddle-mounted by two opposed tapered roller bearings which support the pinion shaft in front of the drive pinion gear, and a straight roller bearing that supports the pinion shaft at the rear of the pinion gear. The drive pinion is assembled in a pinion retainer that is bolted to the differential carrier. The tapered roller bearings are preloaded by a collapsible spacer between the bearings. The pinion is positioned by a shim or shims located between the drive pinion retainer and the differential carrier.

The differential is supported in the carrier by two tapered roller side bearings. These bearings are preloaded by two threaded ring nuts or sleeves between the bearings and the pedestals. The differential assembly is positioned for proper ring gear and pinion backlash by varying the adjustment of these ring nuts. The differential case houses two side gears in mesh with two pinions mounted on a pinion shaft which are held in place by a pin. The side gears and pinions are backed by thrust washers.

The axle shafts are of unequal length, the left shaft being shorter than the right. The axle shafts are mounted in sealed ball bearings which are pressed on the shafts.

REAR AXLE
REPLACE

LEAF SPRING SUSPENSION

1. Raise vehicle and support at rear frame members.
2. Drain lubricant from axle.
3. Mark drive shaft and pinion flanges for reassembly, then disconnect drive shaft at rear axle U-joint and remove drive shaft from transmission extension housing. Install seal replacer tool in extension housing to prevent leakage.
4. Disconnect shock absorbers at lower mountings.
5. Remove rear wheels and brake drums, then disconnect brake lines at wheel cylinders.
6. Disconnect vent hose from vent tube, then remove vent tube from brake junction and axle housing.
7. Remove clips retaining brake lines to axle housing.
8. Support rear axle housing using a suit-

Fig. 2 Disassembled view of Ford WGX & WGZ integral carrier type rear axle assembly

able jack, remove U-bolts and plates.
9. Lower rear axle and remove vehicle.
10. Reverse procedure to install.

COIL SPRING SUSPENSION

1. Raise rear of vehicle support at frame members and rear axle, then remove wheel and tire assembly.
2. Remove brake drums and disconnect brake lines at wheel cylinders.
3. Make marks on drive shaft yoke and pinion flange for reassembly, then disconnect drive shaft at rear U-joint and remove drive shaft from transmission extension housing. Install seal replacer tool in extension housing to prevent leakage.
4. Position a drain pan under differential carrier, then remove carrier attaching bolts and allow differential to drain.
5. Disconnect stabilizer bar, if equipped.
6. Disconnect shock absorbers from lower mountings.
7. Remove brake lines from retaining clips on rear axle housing, then remove brake line junction block retaining screw.

8. Position a suitable jack under axle housing to prevent housing from tilting when removing control arms.
9. Disconnect lower control arms from axle housing and position control arms downward.
10. Disconnect upper control arms from axle housing and position control arms upward.
11. Disconnect air vent line.
12. Lower axle slightly and remove coil springs and insulators.
13. Lower axle housing and remove from vehicle.

AXLE SHAFT
REPLACE

REMOVABLE CARRIER TYPE
Removal
1. Remove wheel assembly.
2. Remove brake drum or rotor and caliper assembly.
3. Working through hole provided in axle shaft flange, **Fig. 5,** remove nuts that secure wheel bearing retainer.
4. Pull axle shaft out of housing. If bear-

Fig. 3   Axle shaft C-lock. WGX & WGZ integral type rear axle

Fig. 5   Removing nuts from wheel bearing retainer

Fig. 4   Rear axle assembly with removable carrier

ing is a tight fit in axle housing use a slide hammer-type puller, **Fig. 6.** Remove brake backing plate and secure to frame rail with wire.

5. If the axle shaft bearing is to be replaced, loosen the inner retainer by nicking it deeply with a chisel in several places, **Fig. 7.** The bearing will then slide off easily.
6. Press bearing from axle shaft.
7. Inspect machined surface of axle shaft and housing for rough spots that would affect sealing action of the oil seal. Carefully remove any burrs or rough spots.
8. Press new bearing on shaft until it seats firmly against shoulder on shaft.
9. Press inner bearing retainer on shaft until it seats firmly against bearing.
10. If oil seal is to be replaced, use a hook-

type tool to pull it out of housing, **Fig. 8.** Wipe a small amount of oil resistant sealer on outer edge of seal before it is installed, **Fig. 9.**

Installation
1. Place a new gasket on each side of brake carrier plate and slide axle shaft into housing.
2. Start the splines into the differential side gear and push the shaft in until bearing bottoms in housing.
3. Install retainer. On all 1980 models,

torque retaining nuts to 20 to 40 ft. lbs.
4. Install brake drum or caliper and rotor and wheel assembly.

FORD WGF & WGG INTEGRAL CARRIER TYPE

1. Remove wheel and tire assembly, then remove nuts attaching brake drum to axle shaft flange and remove brake drum.

Fig. 6   Removing axle shaft with slide hammer-type puller

Fig. 7   Splitting bearing inner retainer for bearing removal

Fig. 8   Using hook-type tool to remove oil seal

Fig. 9   Using special driver to install oil seal

Fig. 10   Axle shaft bearing identification. WGX & WGZ integral type rear axle

Fig. 11   Revised brake adjustment

2. Working through opening in axle shaft flange, remove nuts securing axle shaft bearing retainer, **Fig. 5.**
3. Using a suitable puller, pull axle shaft from housing, **Fig. 6.**
4. Remove brake backing plate and attach to frame side rail with a piece of wire.
5. If rear wheel bearing is to be replaced, loosen inner retainer ring by nicking it deeply in several places with a chisel, **Fig. 7,** then slide retainer from axle shaft.
6. Press bearing from axle shaft using tool No. T71P-4621-B.
7. Using a hook type puller, remove oil seal from axle housing, **Fig. 8.**
8. Position bearing retainer and bearing on axle shaft, then using tool No. T62F-4621-A, press bearing onto shaft until firmly seated against shoulder.
9. Using bearing installation tool, press inner retainer onto shaft until retainer is firmly seated against bearing.
10. Wipe all lubricant from oil seal area of axle housing, then install oil seal using tool No. T79P-1177-A, **Fig. 9.**
11. Install gasket on housing flange, then install brake backing plate.
12. Carefully slide axle shaft into housing using care not to damage oil seal, then install bearing retainer attaching nuts and torque to 20 to 40 ft. lbs.
13. Install brake drum and retaining nuts, then install wheel and tire assembly.

FORD WGX & WGZ INTEGRAL CARRIER TYPE

1. Raise and support rear of vehicle.
2. Remove wheel and tire assembly and brake drum.
3. Remove rear axle housing cover and drain lubricant.
4. Remove differential pinion lock screw and differential pinion shaft.
5. Push axle shafts inward and remove C-locks, **Fig. 3.**
6. Remove axle shaft from housing using care not to damage oil seal.
7. Remove bearing and seal as an assembly using a suitable slide hammer, **Fig. 8,** if necessary.

NOTE: Two types of bearing are used,

Fig. 10. One requires a light press fit in the housing flange, while on the other a loose fit is acceptable. Therefore, if a loose fitting bearing is encountered, it does not indicate excessive wear or damage.

8. Lubricate bearing with rear axle lubricant and install bearing into housing bore using tool No. T78P-1225-A.
9. Install axle shaft seal into housing using tool No. T78P-1177-A, **Fig. 9.**
10. Reverse procedure to install axle shaft.

PROPELLER SHAFT
REPLACE

1. Mark relationship of driveshaft to pinion flange, then disconnect rear U-joint or companion flange from drive pinion flange.
2. Pull drive shaft toward rear of car until front U-joint yoke clears transmission extension housing and output shaft.
3. Install a suitable tool, such as a seal driver, in seal to prevent lube from leaking from transmission.
4. Before installing, check U-joints for freedom of movement. If a bind has resulted from misalignment after overhauling the U-joints, tap the ears of the drive shaft sharply to relieve the bind.
5. If rubber seal installed on end of transmission extension housing is damaged, install a new seal.
6. On a manual shift transmission, lubricate yoke spline with conventional transmission grease. On an automatic transmission, lubricate yoke spline with special spline grease. This spline is sealed so that transmission fluid does not "wash" away spline lubricant.
7. Install yoke on transmission output shaft.

8. Install U-bolts and nuts which attach U-joint to pinion flange. Tighten U-bolts evenly to prevent binding U-joint bearings.

BRAKE ADJUSTMENTS

SERVICE BULLETIN: REVISED BRAKE ADJUSTMENT PROCEDURE: Some models use a new front and rear brake backing plate which omits the adjusting slot for manual brake adjustment. The backing plates have a partially stamped knock-out slot for use ONLY when the brake drums cannot be removed in a normal manner. The open slot is then covered with a rubber plug as used in the past to prevent contamination of the brakes.

When servicing a vehicle requiring a brake adjustment, the metal knock-out plugs should NOT be removed. Rather the drums should be removed and brakes inspected for a malfunction.

Although the brakes are self-adjusting, an initial adjustment will be necessary after a brake repair, such as relining or replacement. The initial adjustment can be obtained by the new procedure which follows:

1. Use the brake shoe adjustment gauge shown in **Fig. 11** to obtain the drum inside diameter as shown. Tighten the adjusting knob on the gauge to hold this setting.
2. Place the opposite side of the gauge over the brake shoes and adjust the shoes by turning the adjuster screw until the gauge just slides over the linings. Rotate the gauge around the lining surface to assure proper lining diameter adjustment and clearance.
3. Install brake drum and wheel. Final adjustment is accomplished by making several firm reverse stops, using the brake pedal.

SELF-ADJUSTING BRAKES

These brakes, **Fig. 12** have self-adjusting shoe mechanisms that assure correct lining-to-drum clearances at all times. The

Shoe Guide (Anchor Pin) Plate — Anchor Pin — FORWARD
Parking Brake Link
Washer
Parking Brake Lever Retaining Clip
Secondary Shoe
Shoe Hold-Down Spring
Brake Parking Lever
Cable Hook
Parking Brake Cable And Housing
Link Spring
Primary Shoe
Parking Brake Cable Housing Retainer
Automatic Adjuster Spring
REAR BRAKE

Fig. 12 Rear drum brake mechanism

automatic adjusters operate only when the brakes are applied as the car is moving rearward.

Although the brakes are self-adjusting, an initial adjustment is necessary after the brake shoes have been relined or replaced, or when the length of the star wheel adjuster has been changed during some other service operation.

Frequent usage of an automatic transmission forward range to halt reverse vehicle motion may prevent the automatic adjusters from functioning, thereby inducing low pedal heights. Should low pedal heights be encountered, it is recommended that numerous forward and reverse stops be made until satisfactory pedal height is obtained.

NOTE: If a low pedal condition cannot be corrected by making numerous reverse stops (provided the hydraulic system is free of air) it indicates that the self-adjusting mechanism is not functioning. Therefore, it will be necessary to remove the brake drum, clean, free up and lubricate the adjusting mechanism. Then adjust the brake, being sure the parking brake is fully released.

PARKING BRAKE
ADJUST

REAR DRUM BRAKES

1. Make sure parking brake is released.
2. Place transmission in neutral and raise the vehicle.
3. Tighten the adjusting nut against the cable equalizer to cause rear brakes to drag.
4. Then loosen the adjusting nut until the rear wheels are fully released. There should be no drag.
5. Lower vehicle and check operation.

REAR DISC BRAKES

1. Fully release parking brake, then place transmission in neutral and support vehicle at rear axle.
2. Tighten adjuster nut until levers on calipers just start to move, then loosen

the nut just enough to obtain full travel to the off position.

NOTE: If brake cables are replaced in any system having a foot-actuated control assembly, stroke parking brake control with about 100 pounds pedal effort, then repeat adjustment.

3. The lever is in the off position when a ¼ inch diameter pin can be freely inserted past the side of the lever into the ¼ inch diameter holes in the cast iron housing.
4. Apply and release the parking brake, then apply and release the service brake pedal with moderate force. Check parking brake levers on calipers to determine if they are fully returned to the off position.

NOTE: If the ¼ inch pin cannot be freely inserted, the adjustment is too tight. Repeat adjustment procedure. Also, if levers do not return to off position, parking and service brake function will be affected as the vehicle is driven.

VACUUM RELEASE UNIT

The vacuum power unit will release the parking brake automatically when the transmission selector lever is moved into any driving position with the engine running. The brakes will not release automatically, however, when the selector lever is in neutral or park position with the engine running, or in any other position with the engine off.

The lower end of the release handle extends out for alternate manual release in the event of vacuum power failure or for optional manual release at any time.

MASTER CYLINDER
REPLACE

1980–82 LESS POWER BRAKES

1. Disconnect battery ground cable.
2. Disconnect stop light switch wires, re-

move hairpin retainer and slide stop light switch off brake pedal pin just far enough to clear end of pin. Then lift switch straight upward from pin.
3. Slide master cylinder push rod with nylon washers and bushings from brake pedal pin.
4. Remove brake tubes from outlet ports of master cylinder.
5. Remove lock nuts that secure master cylinder to dash panel and lift cylinder forward and upward from vehicle.
6. Reverse procedure to install.

1980–86 WITH POWER BRAKES

1. Disconnect brake lines from master cylinder.
2. Disconnect brake warning lamp electrical connector, if equipped.
3. On all models, remove master cylinder to power brake unit attaching nuts, then lift master cylinder from mounting studs.
4. Reverse procedure to install.

POWER BRAKE UNIT
REPLACE

EXC. HYDRO-BOOST

Exc. 1985–86 4-140

1. Disconnect battery ground cable and remove air cleaner.
2. On 1980–84 models equipped with 4-140 engine, disconnect accelerator cable from carburetor, then remove screw that secures accelerator cable to to shaft bracket and remove cable bracket. Remove two screws that secure accelerator shaft bracket to manifold and rotate bracket toward engine. Remove RPO horn, if equipped.
3. On all models, disconnect manifold vacuum hose from booster check valve.
4. Disconnect brake lines from primary and secondary outlet ports of master cylinder.
5. Remove master cylinder-to-booster attaching nuts and the master cylinder.
6. Working under instrument panel, disconnect electrical connector from stop lamp switch.
7. Remove hairpin type retainer. Slide stop lamp switch off brake pedal pin just far enough for the switch outer hole to clear the pin, then lower switch away from pin.
8. Remove booster-to-dash panel attaching nuts.
9. On models equipped with speed control, unfasten control amplifier from lower outboard booster stud and position aside.
10. On all models, slide booster pushrod, bushing and inner nylon washer off brake pedal pin.
11. Move booster forward in engine compartment until booster studs clear dash panel, then rotate front of booster toward engine and remove booster.

5–47

12. Reverse procedure to install.

1985–86 4-140

1. Disconnect battery ground cable and remove air cleaner.
2. Disconnect accelerator cable from throttle plate.
3. Remove screw that secures accelerator cable to shaft bracket and remove cable from bracket.
4. REmove two screws that secure accelerator shaft bracket to manifold and rotate bracket toward engine.
5. On LTD and Marquis models, remove RPO horn.
6. On Cougar and Thunderbird models, release fuel system pressure, then disconnect the two manifold injector connectors located near oil dipstick retaining bracket. Disconnect two fuel lines to fuel supply manifold assembly.
7. On all models, remove engine oil dipstick tube and bracket.
8. Remove windshield wiper motor.
9. Disconnect vacuum lines located over brake booster at dash panel vacuum tee.
10. REmove bolt securing clutch cable stand, then move bracket to side rail at fender inner panel.
11. On models equipped with speed control, move speed control cable to one side to clear booster.
12. On all models, disconnect manifold booster line from booster check valve.
13. Disconnect brake lines from master cylinder, then remove master cylinder attaching nuts and the master cylinder.
14. Working under instrument panel, disconnect electrical connector from stop lamp switch.
15. Remove hairpin type retainer and outer nylon washer from brake pedal pin, then slide stop lamp switch off brake pedal pin just enough for outer arm to clear pin.
16. On models equipped with speed control, unfasten control amplifier from lower outboard booster stud and position aside.
17. On all models, slide booster push rod link and nylon washers off brake pedal pin.
18. Move booster forward in engine compartment until booster studs clear dash panel, then rotate front of booster toward engine and remove booster.
11. Reverse procedure to install.

HYDRO-BOOST

1. Disconnect stoplight switch wires at connector and remove hairpin retainer, then slide stoplight switch off brake pedal pin far enough for switch outer hole to clear pin and remove pin from switch.
2. Slide hydro-boost push rod and nylon washers and bushing off brake pedal pin.
3. Remove master cylinder and position to one side without disturbing hydraulic lines.

NOTE: It is not necessary to disconnect brake lines, but care should be taken not to deform lines.

4. Disconnect pressure, steering gear and return lines from booster, then plug lines and ports in hydro-boost to prevent entry of dirt.
5. Remove hydro-boost retaining nuts, and remove assembly sliding push rod link from engine side of dash panel.
6. Reverse procedure to install. To purge system, disconnect coil wire so that engine will not start. Fill power steering pump reservoir, then while engaging starter, pump brake pedal. Do not cycle steering wheel until all residual air has been purged from the hydro boost unit. Check fluid level, then connect coil wire and start engine. Apply brakes with a pumping action and cycle steering wheel, then check system for leaks.

Rear Suspension

SHOCK ABSORBER, REPLACE

1980–83 FAIRMONT & ZEPHYR; 1980–82 COUGAR XR-7; 1980–86 THUNDERBIRD; 1981–82 GRANADA; 1981–86 COUGAR; 1983–86 LTD & MARQUIS

1. On sedans, open trunk to gain access to upper shock absorber attachment. On station wagons, remove side panel trim covers.
2. Remove rubber cap from shock absorber stud.
3. On all models, remove shock absorber attaching nut, washer and insulator.
4. Raise vehicle and support rear axle.
5. Compress shock absorber to clear hole in upper shock absorber tower.
6. On 1980–83 Fairmont and Zephyr, 1981–82 Cougar and Granada and 1983–86 LTD and Marquis models, remove nut or bolt and washer from shock absorber lower mounting stud, then the shock absorber. On 1980–82 Cougar XR-7, 1980–86 Thunderbird and 1983–86 Cougar models, remove shock absorber protective cover, then the shock absorber attaching bolt and shock absorber.
7. Reverse procedure to install. Torque upper shock mount to 14–26 ft. lbs. on 1980–81 models, or 26 ft. lbs. on 1982–86 models. Torque lower attaching bolt to 40–55 ft. lbs. on 1980 models, 65–70 ft. lbs. on 1981 models, 60–65 ft. lbs. on 1982 models, or 55–70 ft. lbs. on 1983–86 models.

NOTE: On 1984–86 Thunderbird and Cougar models equipped with optional handling package, torque lower attaching bolt to 45–60 ft. lbs.

EXC. 1980–83 FAIRMONT & ZEPHYR; 1980–82 Cougar XR-7; 1980–86 THUNDERBIRD; 1981–82 GRANADA; 1981–86 COUGAR; 1983–86 LTD & MARQUIS

1. Raise and properly support vehicle.
2. Disconnect shock absorber from its lower and upper mounting, then remove shock absorber.
3. Reverse procedure to install.

AXLE DAMPER
REPLACE

1984–86 THUNDERBIRD & COUGAR w/4-140 TURBOCHARGED ENGINE

1. Raise and support vehicle at rear axle.
2. Remove wheel.
3. Remove axle damper front attaching nut and pivot bolt.
4. Remove rear attaching nut, then the axle damper and spacer.
5. Reverse procedure to install. Torque all attaching nuts and bolts to 55–70 ft. lbs.

LEAF SPRINGS & BUSHINGS
REPLACE

1980 GRANADA & MONARCH

1. Raise rear of vehicle and support at frame. Support axle with a suitable jack.
2. Disconnect shock absorbers from lower mountings.

Fig. 1   Leaf spring suspension (typical)

Fig. 2   Spring front bushing removal

Fig. 3   Spring front bushing installation

3. Lower jack and remove spring plate "U" bolts and spring plate, **Fig. 1.**
4. Raise axle to remove weight from spring and disassemble rear shackle.
5. Remove spring front mount bolt.
6. Replace spring front eye bushings as necessary, **Figs. 2 and 3.**
7. Reverse procedure to install.

STABILIZER BAR
REPLACE

1980—83 FAIRMONT & ZEPHYR; 1980—82 COUGAR XR-7; 1980—86 THUNDERBIRD; 1981—82 GRANADA; 1981—86 COUGAR; 1983—86 LTD & MARQUIS

1. Raise and support rear of vehicle.
2. Remove four bolts attaching stabilizer bar to lower control arms.
3. Remove stabilizer bar from vehicle.

COIL SPRING
REPLACE

1980—83 FAIRMONT & ZEPHYR; 1980—82 COUGAR XR-7; 1980—86 THUNDERBIRD; 1981—82 GRANADA; 1981—86 COUGAR; 1983—86 LTD & MARQUIS

1. Remove stabilizer bar as described under "Stabilizer Bar, Replace," if equipped.
2. Position a suitable jack under rear axle, then raise vehicle and support body at rear body crossmember.
3. Lower axle until shock absorbers are fully extended.

NOTE: Support axle with jack stands or a suitable jack.

4. Position a suitable jack under lower control arm pivot bolt and remove nut and bolt. Carefully and slowly lower the control arm until all spring tension is relieved.
5. Remove coil spring and insulators from vehicle, **Fig. 4.**

CONTROL ARMS
REPLACE

NOTE: Upper and lower control arms must be replaced in pairs.

1980–83 FAIRMONT & ZEPHYR; 1980–82 COUGAR XR-7; 1980–86 THUNDERBIRD; 1981–82 GRANADA; 1981–86 COUGAR; 1983–86 LTD & MARQUIS

Upper Arm

1. Raise vehicle and support body at rear body crossmember.
2. Remove upper arm pivot bolt and nut, **Fig. 4.**
3. Remove front pivot bolt and nut, then remove upper arm from vehicle.

Lower Arm

1. Remove stabilizer bar as described under "Stabilizer Bar, Replace," if equipped.
2. Position a suitable jack under rear axle, then raise vehicle and support body at rear body crossmember.
3. Lower axle until shock absorbers are fully extended.

NOTE: Support axle with jack stands or a suitable jack.

4. Position a suitable jack under lower control arm rear pivot bolt and remove nut and bolt, **Fig. 5.** Carefully and slowly lower the control arm until all spring tension is relieved, then remove coil spring and insulators.
5. Remove lower control arm front pivot bolt and nut, then remove lower control arm assembly.

Fig. 4   Rear suspension (typical)

Front Suspension & Steering Section

FRONT SUSPENSION

1980–83 FAIRMONT & ZEPHYR; 1980–82 COUGAR XR-7; 1980–86 THUNDERBIRD; 1981–82 GRANADA; 1981–86 COUGAR; 1983–86 LTD & MARQUIS

This suspension, **Fig. 1,** is a modified McPherson strut design, which uses shock struts and coil springs. The springs are mounted between the lower control arm and a spring pocket in the crossmember.

1980 GRANADA & MONARCH

Referring to **Fig. 2,** each front wheel rotates on a spindle. The upper and lower ends of the spindle are attached to ball joints that are mounted to an upper and lower control arm. The upper arm pivots on a bushing and shaft assembly that is bolted to the underbody. The lower arm pivots on a bolt that is located in an underbody bracket.

A coil spring seats between the upper arm and the top of the spring housing. A double-acting shock absorber is bolted to the arm and the top of the spring housing.

Struts, which are connected between the lower control arms and the underbody, prevent the arms from moving fore and aft.

WHEEL ALIGNMENT

1983 FAIRMONT & ZEPHYR & 1983–86 COUGAR, LTD, MARQUIS & THUNDERBIRD

Caster

The caster angle of this suspension is factory pre-set and cannot be adjusted.

Camber

1. Remove pop rivet from camber plate.
2. Loosen 3 camber plate-to-body apron nuts.
3. Move top of shock strut as needed to

bring camber angle within specifications, then tighten nuts.

NOTE: It is not necessary to replace the pop rivet.

1980–82 FAIRMONT & ZEPHYR; 1980–82 COUGAR XR-7; 1980–82 THUNDERBIRD; 1981–82 GRANADA; 1981–82 COUGAR

Caster & Camber

The caster and camber angles of this suspension are factory pre-set and cannot be adjusted in the field.

1980 GRANADA & MONARCH

As shown in **Fig. 3,** caster is controlled by the front suspension strut. To obtain positive caster, loosen the strut rear nut and tighten the strut front nut against the bushing. To obtain negative caster, loosen the strut front nut and tighten the strut rear nut against the bushing. Torque strut to

VIEW Z

VIEW Z

Fig. 1   Front suspension (typical). 1980—83 Fairmont & Zephyr, 1980—82 Cougar XR-7, 1980—86 Thunderbird, 1981—82 Granada, 1981—86 Cougar & 1983—86 LTD & Marquis

SHOCK ABSORBER
UPPER MOUNTING
BRACKET

SHOCK ABSORBER

SPRING

BUMPER

UPPER BALL JOINT

UPPER ARM

SPINDLE

ECCENTRIC
AND BOLT

STABILIZER
BAR

STABILIZER
LINK

INSULATOR
WASHERS

NUT

STRUT

LOWER
ARM

FRONT
RETAINING BOLT

LOWER
BALL JOINT

Fig. 2   Front suspension (typical). 1980 Granada & Monarch

Turn Nuts Forward/Negative Caster

Turn Nuts Rearward/Positive Caster

Front Adjustment Nut
Inner Sleeve
Washers

Outer Sleeve

Front Insulator

Rear Insulator

Rear Adjustment Nut

Strut

Caster Adjustment Nuts

Camber Adjustment

Guide

Spread This Member At Lower Arm Pivot Bushing

Fig. 3   Caster and camber adjustments. 1980 Granada & Monarch

FORD & MERCURY—Compact & Intermediate Models

underbody nut to 70–80 ft. lbs.

Camber is controlled by the eccentric cam located at the lower arm attachment to the side rail. To adjust camber, loosen the camber adjustment bolt nut at the rear of the body bracket. Spread the body bracket at the camber adjustment bolt area just enough to permit lateral travel of the arm when the adjustment bolt is turned. Rotate the bolt and eccentric clockwise from the high position to increase camber or counterclockwise to decrease it. Torque lower arm to underbody bolt to 85–100 ft. lbs.

TOE-IN
ADJUST

1980–83 FAIRMONT & ZEPHYR; 1980–82 COUGAR XR-7; 1980–86 THUNDERBIRD; 1981–82 GRANADA; 1981–86 COUGAR; 1983–86 LTD & MARQUIS

1. Check to see that steering shaft and steering wheel marks are in alignment and in the top position.
2. Loosen clamp screw on the tie rod bellows and free the seal on the rod to prevent twisting of the bellows, **Fig. 4.**
3. Place opened end wrench on flats of tie rod socket to prevent socket from turning, then loosen tie rod jam nuts.
4. Use suitable pliers to turn the tie rod inner end to correct the adjustment to specifications. Do not use pliers on tie rod threads. Turning to reduce number of threads showing will increase toe-in. Turning in the opposite direction will reduce toe-in.
5. Torque tie rod jam nuts to 33–50 ft. lbs. on 1980–81 models, or 43–50 ft. lbs. on 1982–86 models.

EXC. 1980–83 FAIRMONT & ZEPHYR; 1980–82 COUGAR XR-7; 1980–86 THUNDERBIRD; 1981–82 GRANADA; 1981–86 COUGAR; 1983–86 LTD & MARQUIS

Check the steering wheel spoke position when the front wheels are in the straight-ahead position. If the spokes are not in the normal position, they can be adjusted while toe-in is being adjusted.
1. Loosen clamp bolts on each tie rod end sleeve.
2. Adjust toe-in. If steering wheel spokes are in their normal position, lengthen or shorten both rods equally to obtain correct toe-in. If spokes are not in normal position, make necessary rod adjustments to obtain correct toe-in and steering wheel spoke alignment.

WHEEL BEARINGS
ADJUST

1. With wheel rotating, tighten adjusting nut to 17–25 ft. lbs.

Fig. 4   Toe-in adjustment. 1980–83 Fairmont, Zephyr, 1980–82 Cougar XR-7, 1980–86 Thunderbird, 1981–82 Granada, 1981–86 Cougar & 1983–86 LTD & Marquis

Fig. 5   Front wheel bearing adjustment

2. Back off adjusting nut ½ turn, then retighten nut to 10–15 inch lbs. on 1980–83 models, or 10–12 inch lbs. on 1984–86 models.
3. Place nut lock on nut so that castellations on lock are aligned with cotter pin hole in spindle and install cotter pin, **Fig. 5.**
4. Check front wheel rotation, if it rotates noisily or rough, clean, inspect or replace wheel bearings as necessary.

WHEEL BEARINGS
REPLACE

DISC BRAKES
1. Raise car and remove front wheels.
2. Remove caliper mounting bolts.

NOTE: It is not necessary to disconnect the brake lines for this operation.

3. Slide caliper off of disc, inserting a clean spacer between the shoes to hold them in their bores after the caliper is removed. Position caliper out of the way.

NOTE: Do not allow caliper to hang by brake hose.

4. Remove hub and disc assembly. Grease retainer and inner bearing can now be removed.

CHECKING BALL JOINTS FOR WEAR
UPPER BALL JOINT

1980 Granada & Monarch
1. Raise car on frame contact hoist or by floor jacks placed beneath underbody until wheel falls to full down position.
2. Grasp the lower edge of tire and move the wheel in and out.
3. While the wheel is being moved observe any movement between the upper end of the spindle and upper arm. If any movement is observed replace the ball joint.

LOWER BALL JOINT

1980–83 Fairmont & Zephyr; 1980–82 Cougar XR-7; 1980–86 Thunderbird; 1981–82 Granada; 1981–86 Cougar; 1983–86 LTD & Marquis
1. Support vehicle in normal driving position with both ball joints loaded.
2. Clean area around grease fitting and checking surface.

NOTE: The checking surface is the round boss into which the grease fitting is installed.

3. The checking surface should project outside the cover, **Fig. 6.** If surface is inside cover replace lower arm assembly.

1980 Granada & Monarch

1. With car jacked up as directed above, grasp the lower edge of the tire and move it in and out.
2. As wheel is being moved in and out, observe lower end of spindle and lower arm.
3. Any movement between lower end of spindle and lower arm indicates ball joint wear and loss of preload. If such movement is observed, replace lower arm and/or ball joint.

NOTE: During the foregoing check, the ball joints will be unloaded and may move. Therefore disregard any movement of the upper ball joint when checking the lower ball joint and any movement of the lower ball joint when checking the upper ball joint. Also, do not mistake loose wheel bearings for a worn ball joint.

BALL JOINT COVER

NEW   WORN

CHECKING SURFACE

Fig. 6 Checking lower ball joint. 1980–83 Fairmont, Zephyr, 1980–82 Cougar XR-7, 1980–86 Thunderbird, 1981–82 Granada, 1981–86 Cougar & 1983–86 LTD & Marquis

BALL JOINTS
REPLACE

NOTE: Ford Motor Company recommends that new ball joints should not be installed on used control arms and that the control arm be replaced if ball joint replacement is required. However, aftermarket ball joint repair kits which do not require control arm replacement, are available and can be installed using the following procedure.

1980–83 FAIRMONT & ZEPHYR; 1980–82 COUGAR XR-7; 1980–86 THUNDERBIRD; 1981–82 GRANADA; 1981–86 COUGAR; 1983–86 LTD & MARQUIS

These ball joints are not serviceable. If they require replacement, the control arm and ball joint must be replaced as an assembly.

EXC. 1980–83 FAIRMONT & ZEPHYR; 1980–82 COUGAR XR-7; 1980–86 THUNDERBIRD; 1981–82 GRANADA; 1981–86 COUGAR; 1983–86 LTD & MARQUIS

The ball joints are riveted to the upper and lower control arms. The upper ball joint can be replaced by removing the rivets and retaining the new ball joint to the upper control arm with bolts, nuts and washers furnished with the ball joint repair kit. When removing an upper ball joint, use a suitable pressing tool to loosen the ball joint from the spindle.

SHOCK STRUT
REPLACE

1980–83 FAIRMONT & ZEPHYR; 1980–82 COUGAR XR-7; 1980–86 THUNDERBIRD; 1981–82 GRANADA; 1981–86 COUGAR; 1983–86 LTD & MARQUIS

1. Place ignition switch in the Unlocked position so that front wheels are free to move.
2. From engine compartment, remove one strut to upper mounting nut. Use a screwdriver in rod slot to hold rod stationary when removing nut.
3. Raise front of vehicle by lower control arms, then place safety stands under frame jack pads located rearward of wheels.
4. Remove wheel and tire assembly, then remove brake caliper, rotor assembly and dust shield.
5. Remove two nuts and bolts attaching lower strut to spindle.

NOTE: Gas pressurized struts (1983–86 Cougar, LTD, Marquis, and Thunderbird) must be held firmly during removal of the last spindle-to-strut bolt since gas pressure will cause strut to extend fully when bolt is removed.

6. Lift strut upward from spindle to compress rod, then pull downward and remove strut.
7. On 1983–86 models, remove jounce bumper.
8. Reverse procedure to install. Torque upper mount attaching nut to 60–75 ft. lbs. on 1980–82 models, or 55–92 ft. lbs. on 1983–86 models. Remove suspension load from lower control arm by lowering front of vehicle, then torque lower mounting nuts to 150–180 ft. lbs. on 1980–82 models, or 120–179 ft. lbs. on 1983–86 models.

SHOCK ABSORBER
REPLACE

1980 GRANADA & MONARCH

1. Raise hood and remove upper mounting bracket-to-spring tower retaining nuts.
2. Raise front of car and place safety stands under lower control arms.
3. Remove shock absorber lower retaining nuts and washers.
4. Lift shock absorber from spring tower.
5. Reverse procedure to install. Torque shock absorber upper attachment bolts to 10–16 ft. lbs., shock absorber upper bracket to body nuts to 32–48 ft. lbs. and shock absorber to spring seat to 8–12 ft. lbs.

COIL SPRING
REPLACE

1980–83 FAIRMONT & ZEPHYR; 1980–82 COUGAR XR-7; 1980–86 THUNDERBIRD; 1981–82 GRANADA; 1981–86 COUGAR; 1983–86 LTD & MARQUIS

1. Raise front of vehicle and position safety stands under jack pads located rearward of wheels, then remove wheel and tire assembly.
2. On 1982–86 models, disconnect caliper and wire it out of the way without disconnecting brake lines.
3. On all models, disconnect stabilizer bar link from lower control arm.
4. Remove steering gear attaching bolts, and position gear aside.
5. Disconnect tie rod from spindle using tool 3290-C, or equivalent.
6. Using spring compressor D78P-5310-A on 1980–81 models, or T82P-5310-A on 1982–86 models, compress spring until it is free from lower seat.
7. Remove two lower control arm pivot bolts and disengage control arm from frame, then remove spring from seat. If a replacement spring is to be installed, measure compressed length of spring being removed to assist in compressing and installing the replacement spring.
8. Reverse procedure to install. When installing spring, locate lower end of coil between two holes in lower control arm spring pocket. On 1980–81 models, torque control arm pivot bolt nuts to 200–220 ft. lbs., stabilizer bar link nut to 9 to 12 ft. lbs. and steering gear

to crossmember attaching bolts to 90 to 100 ft. lbs. On 1982 models, torque lower control arm pivot nuts to 215 to 260 ft. lbs., stabilizer bar to lower control arm nut 6 to 12 ft. lbs. and steering gear to crossmember bolts to 90 to 100 ft. lbs. On 1983–86 models, torque control arm pivot nuts to 150–180 ft. lbs., stabilizer bar link nut to 6–12 ft. lbs., steering gear to crossmember nuts to 90–100 ft. lbs., and tie rod end to 35 ft. lbs.

1980 GRANADA & MONARCH

1. Remove shock absorber and upper mounting bracket as an assembly.
2. Raise car on hoist and install safety stands.
3. Remove wheel, hub and drum or caliper and rotor.
4. Install a suitable spring compressor and compress spring.
5. Remove two upper-arm-to-spring tower retaining nuts and swing upper arm outward from spring.
6. Release spring compressor. Then remove spring.
7. Reverse procedure to install. Torque upper arm and inner shaft to body nuts to 85–100 ft. lbs.

STABILIZER BAR AND/OR INSULATOR

1980–83 FAIRMONT & ZEPHYR; 1980–82 COUGAR XR-7; 1980–86 THUNDERBIRD; 1981–82 GRANADA; 1981–86 COUGAR; 1983–86 LTD & MARQUIS

1. Raise vehicle and place jack stands under lower control arms.
2. Disconnect stabilizer bar from links, then remove stabilizer insulator retaining clamps and remove stabilizer.
3. To remove insulator, cut insulators and plastic sleeves from stabilizer bar. Before installing new insulators, coat the necessary parts of the stabilizer with grease, then install the insulators and sleeves.
4. Reverse procedure to install stabilizer bar. Install new stabilizer link bolts with heads facing down and torque to 9–12 ft. lbs. on 1980–81 models, 6 to 12 ft. lbs. on 1982–86 models. Using new bolts, install stabilizer insulator retaining clamps and torque to 14 to 16 ft. lbs. on 1980 models, 25 to 30 ft. lbs. on 1981 models, 20 to 25 ft. lbs. on 1982–86 models.

POWER STEERING GEAR
REPLACE

INTEGRAL POWER RACK & PINION

1. Disconnect battery ground cable.

---

2. Remove bolt retaining flexible coupling to input shaft.
3. Turn ignition key "ON" and raise vehicle.
4. Remove the two tie rod end retaining nuts, then separate studs from spindle arms, using a suitable tool.
5. Support gear and remove attaching bolts, then lower gear enough to gain access to pressure and return lines, and remove bolt attaching the hose bracket to the gear.
6. Disconnect pressure and return lines and remove steering gear. Plug lines and ports to prevent entry of dirt.
7. Reverse procedure to install. Torque pressure and return line fittings to 10–15 ft. lbs., gear housing to crossmember mounting bolt to 80–100 ft. lbs., steering flex coupling bolt to 20–30 ft. lbs. and tie rod end to spindle arm nut to 35–47 ft. lbs.

NOTE: On some models, hoses can swivel when torqued properly. Do not over tighten.

INTEGRAL POWER STEERING GEAR

1. Disconnect pressure and return lines from gear and plug openings to prevent entry of dirt.
2. Remove two bolts that secure flex coupling to gear and column.
3. Raise vehicle and remove pitman arm with suitable puller.
4. If vehicle is equipped with synchromesh transmission, remove clutch release retracting spring to provide clearance to remove gear.
5. Support gear and remove three gear attaching bolts.

MANUAL STEERING GEAR
REPLACE

RACK & PINION

1. Disconnect battery ground cable, turn ignition "On" and raise vehicle.
2. Remove tie rod end retaining nuts and using ball joint separator, separate tie rod ends from spindle arms.
3. Remove pinion shaft to flexible coupling bolt and the bolts securing steering gear to crossmember.
4. Turn front wheels, then remove steering gear from left side of vehicle.
5. Reverse procedure to install. Torque connecting rod end to spindle arm nut to 35–47 ft. lbs. on 1980 models and 41–47 ft. lbs. on 1981–84 models. Torque flex coupling to 20–37 ft. lbs. and torque steering gear to crossmember bolts to 80–100 ft. lbs. on 1980 models and 90–100 ft. lbs. on 1981–86 models.

EXC. RACK & PINION

1. Remove flex coupling bolts.
2. Remove pitman arm nut and remove arm from shaft using a puller.
3. With manual transmission it may be necessary to disconnect the clutch linkage and on V8 models it may be necessary to lower the exhaust system.
4. Unfasten and remove steering gear.
5. Reverse procedure to install. Torque steering gear to side rail bolts to 50–60 ft. lbs. and pitman arm to sector shaft nut to 200–225 ft. lbs.

POWER STEERING PUMP
REPLACE

1. Disconnect return hose from power steering pump and allow fluid to drain into a suitable container.
2. Remove pressure hose from power steering pump fitting.
3. On models less fixed pump, remove mounting bracket attaching bolts, then disconnect drive belt from pulley and remove pump.
4. On models with fixed pump, remove drive belt from pulley, then remove pulley and lift pump from engine compartment.
5. Reverse procedure to install.

CONTROL VALVE
REPLACE

NON-INTEGRAL POWER STEERING

1. Disconnect fluid fittings at control valve and drain fluid from lines by turning wheels to left and right.
2. Loosen clamp at right-hand end of sleeve. Remove roll pin from steering arm-to-idler arm rod through slot in sleeve.
3. Using tool 3290-C, remove ball stud from sector shaft arm.

NOTE: The use of any other tool may result in damage to the control valve assembly.

4. Turn wheels fully to left and unthread control valve from idler arm rod.
5. Reverse procedure to install. Measure distance between center of left spindle connect-rod hole in idler arm to edge of control valve. Distance must be 2.55–2.65 inches. Torque valve sleeve clamp nut to 13–17 ft. lbs., ball stud nut to 35–47 ft. lbs., worm screw hose clamp to 30–60 in. lbs., return line to control valve to 16–25 ft. lbs., pressure line to control valve to 15–19 ft. lbs. and pressure and return lines to power cylinder to 15–19 ft. lbs. Connect short control valve to power cylinder hose to valve port "C" and other hose to valve port "A".

INDEX OF SERVICE OPERATIONS

NOTE: Refer to the rear of this manual for vehicle manufacturer's special service tool suppliers.

Engine Identification

Engine code is eighth digit in serial
number (VIN) located on left side dash.

Grille Identification

1981 Escort

1981 Lynx

**1982 Escort; 1983 Escort GL, GLX,
L & Sta. Wag; 1984 Escort GL & L**

1982–84 EXP

1982–83 LN7

1982 Lynx

**1983 Escort GT
1984 Escort GT & LX**

**1983 Lynx RS
1984 Lynx RS & LTS**

**1983 Lynx GS, L, LS & Sta. Wag.
1984 Lynx GS, L & Sta. Wag.**

1984–85 Ford Tempo

1984–85 Mercury Topaz

continued

General Engine Specifications

Year	Engine CID①/Liter	Engine VIN Code②	Carburetor	Bore and Stroke	Compression Ratio	Net H.P. @ R.P.M.③	Maximum Torque Ft. Lbs. @ R.P.M.	Normal Oil Pressure Pounds
1981	97.6, 1.6 L	2	740, 2 Bbl.④	3.15 × 3.13	8.8	65 @ 5200	85 @ 3000	40
1982	97.6, 1.6 L	2	740, 2 Bbl.④	3.15 × 3.13	8.8	70 @ 4600	89 @ 3000	30—50
1983	97.6, 1.6 L	2	740, 2 Bbl.④	3.15 × 3.13	8.8	70 @ 4600	89 @ 3000	30—50
	97.6, 1.6 L	2	EFI	3.15 × 3.13	9.5	88 @ 5400	—	30—50
	97.6, 1.6 L H.O.	2	740, 2 Bbl.④	3.15 × 3.13	—	—	—	—
1984	97.6, 1.6 L	2	740, 2 Bbl.④	3.15 × 3.13	8.8	70 @ 4600	88 @ 2600	30—50
	97.6, 1.6 L	5	EFI	3.15 × 3.13	9.5	80 @ 5400	88 @ 3000	30—50
	97.6, 1.6 L H.O.	4	740, 2 Bbl.④	3.15 × 3.13	9.0	80 @ 5400	88 @ 3000	30—50
	120, 2.0 L⑥	H	Fuel Injection	3.39 × 3.39	22.5	52 @ 3600	82 @ 2400	—
	140, 2.3 L⑦	R	6149, 1 Bbl.⑤	3.68 × 3.30	9.0	84 @ 4600	118 @ 2600	55—70
1985	97.6, 1.6L	2	740, 2 Bbl.④	3.15 × 3.13	9.0	70 @ 4600	88 @ 2600	30—50
	97.6, 1.6L H.O.	4	740, 2 Bbl.④	3.15 × 3.13	9.0	80 @ 5400	88 @ 3000	30—50
	97.6, 1.6L⑧	5	EFI	3.15 × 3.13	9.0	84 @ 5200	90 @ 2800	30—50
	97.6, 1.6L⑨	5	EFI	3.15 × 3.13	8.0	120 @ 5200	120 @ 3400	30—50
	120, 2.0L⑥	H	Fuel Injection	3.39 × 3.39	22.5	52 @ 3600	82 @ 2400	—
	140, 2.3L⑦	S,X	EFI	3.68 × 3.30	9.0	100 @ 4600	125 @ 3200	55—70
1986	113.5, 1.9L		2 Bbl.⑤	3.23 × 3.46	—	—	—	35—65
	113.5, 1.9L		EFI	3.23 × 3.46	9.0	115 @ 5400	115 @ 4600	35—65
	120, 2.0L⑥	H	Fuel Injection	3.39 × 3.39	22.5	—	—	—
	140, 2.3L⑦	S,X	EFI	3.68 × 3.30	—	—	—	55—70

①—CID—Cubic inch displacement.
②—The eighth digit in the VIN denotes engine code.
③—Ratings are net—as installed in vehicle.
④—Motorcraft.
⑤—Holley.
⑥—Diesel.
⑦—Tempo & Topaz.
⑧—Exc. turbocharged engine.
⑨—Turbocharged engine.

Starting Motor Applications

Year	Engine Model/V.I.N.	Ident. No.①	Year	Engine Model/V.I.N.	Ident. No.①
1981	4-97.6, 1.6L/2	EIEF-AB	1985	4-97.6, 1.6L/②	E4EF-BA
1982	4-97.6, 1.6L/2	EIEF-AD		4-120, 2.0L/H	E4EF-AA
1983	4-97.6, 1.6L/2	E3EF-AA		4-140, 2.3L/S,X	E43F-AA
		E4EF-BA	1986	4-97.6, 1.6L/②	EFEF-BA
1984	4-97.6, 1.6L/②	E3EF-AA		4-113.5, 1.9L	E6EF-AA
		E4EF-BA		4-120, 2.0L/H	EFEF-AA
	4-120, 2.0L/H	E4EF-AA		4-140, 2.3L/S,X	E43F-AA
	4-140, 2.3L/R	E43F-AA			

①—Basic Ident. No., 11001. ②—V.I.N. Codes, 2, 5 and 4.

Alternator & Regulator Specifications

Year	Ident. Stamp Color	Current Rating Amperes	Current Rating Volts	Field Current @ 75°F. Amperes	Field Current @ 75°F. Volts	Voltage Regulator Ident. No.①	Voltage Regulator Voltage @ 75°F	Voltage Regulator Contact Gap	Voltage Regulator Armature Air Gap	Field Relay Armature Air Gap	Field Relay Closing Voltage @ 75°F.
1981	Orange	40	15	4	12	D9BF-AB	13.8—14.6	—	—	—	—
	Green	60	15	4	12	D9BF-AB	13.8—14.6	—	—	—	—
	Black	65	15	4	12	D9BF-AB	13.8—14.6	—	—	—	—
1982—83	Orange	40	15	4	12	②	13.8—14.6	—	—	—	—
	Green	60	15	4	12	②	13.8—14.6	—	—	—	—
	Black	65	15	4	12	②	13.8—14.6	—	—	—	—
1984—86	Orange	40	15	4.25	12	—	—	—	—	—	—
	Green	60	15	4.25	12	—	—	—	—	—	—
	Black	65	15	4.25	12	—	—	—	—	—	—

①—Basic Ident. No., 10316.
②—1982 Escort & Lynx, EIAF-AA; 1982 EXP & LN7, EITF-AA; 1983 Escort & Lynx, E2AF-AA; 1983 EXP & LN7, E2TF-AA.

continued

Valve Specifications

Year	Engine	Valve Lash Int.	Valve Lash Exh.	Valve Angles Seat	Valve Angles Face	Valve Spring Installed Height	Valve Spring Pressure Lbs. @ In.	Stem Clearance Intake	Stem Clearance Exhaust	Stem Diameter Intake	Stem Diameter Exhaust
1981	4-97.6, 1.6L/2	.059–.194①		45	44	1.46	180 @ 1.09	.0008–.0027	.0015–.0032	.316	.315
1982	4-97.6, 1.6L/2	.059–.194①		45	44	1.46	180 @ 1.09	.0008–.0027	.0018–.0037	.316	.315
1983	4-97.6, 1.6L/2	.059–.194①		45	45.6	1.46	200 @ 1.09	.0008–.0027	.0018–.0037	.316	.315
	4-97.6, 1.6L/2 E.F.I. & H.O.	.059–.194①		45	45.6	1.46	206 @ 1.09	.0008–.0027	.0018–.0037	.316	.315
1984	4-97.6, 1.6L/2	.059–.194①		45	45.6	1.46	200 @ 1.09	.0008–.0027	.0018–.0037	.316	.315
	4-97.6, 1.6L/4 H.O.	.059–.194①		45	45.6	1.46	200 @ 1.09	.0008–.0027	.0018–.0037	.316	.315
	4-97.6, 1.6L/5 E.F.I.	.059–.194①		45	45.6	1.46	200 @ 1.09	.0008–.0027	.0018–.0037	.316	.315
	4-120, 2.0L/H Diesel	③		45	45	—	—	.0016–.0029	.0018–.0031	.3141	.3140
	4-140, 2.3L/R②	.070–.170①		45	45.75	1.49	182 @ 1.10	.0018	.0023	.3415–.3422	.3411–.3418
1985	4-97.6, 1.6L/2,4,5	.059–.194①		45	45.6	1.46	200 @ 1.09	.0008–.0027	.0018–.0037	.3167	.3156
	4-120, 2.0L/H Diesel	③		45	45	—	—	.0016–.0029	.0018–.0031	.3141	.3140
	4-140, 2.3L/S,X	.070–.170①		45	45.75	1.49	182 @ 1.10	.0018	.0023	.3415–.3422	.3411–.3418
1986	4-97.6, 1.6L/2,4,5	.059–.194①		45	45.6	1.46	200 @ 1.09	.0008–.0027	.0018–.0037	.3167	.3156
	4-113.5, 1.9L	—	—	—	—	—	—	—	—	—	—
	4-120, 2.0L/H Diesel	③		45	45	—	—	.0016–.0029	.0018–.0031	.3141	.3140
	4-140, 2.3L/S,X	.070–.170①		45	45.75	1.49	182 @ 1.10	.0018	.0023	.3415–.3422	.3411–.3418

①—With hydraulic valve lash adjuster completely collapsed.   ②—Tempo & Topaz.   ③—Intake, .008–.011; Exhaust, .011–.015. Refer to text for procedure.

Pistons, Pins, Rings, Crankshaft & Bearings

Year	Engine/VIN	Piston Clearance	Ring End Gap① Comp.	Ring End Gap① Oil	Wristpin Diameter	Rod Bearings Shaft Diameter	Rod Bearings Bearing Clearance	Main Bearings Shaft Diameter	Main Bearings Bearing Clearance	Thrust on Bear. No.	Shaft End Play
1981–83	4-97.6, 1.6L/2	.0008–.0016	.012	.016	.8119–.8124	1.885–1.886	.0008–.0015	2.2826–2.2834	.0008–.0015	3	.004–.008
1984–85	4-97.6, 1.6L/2	.0018–.0026	.012	.016	.8119–.8124	1.885–1.886	.0008–.0015	2.2826–2.2834	.0008–.0015	3	.004–.008
	4-97.6, 1.6L/4 H.O.	.0018–.0026	.012	.016	.8119–.8124	1.885–1.886	.0008–.0015	2.2826–2.2834	.0008–.0015	3	.004–.008
	4-97.6, 1.6L/5 E.F.I.	.0018–.0026	.012	.016	.8119–.8124	1.885–1.886	.0008–.0015	2.2826–2.2834	.0008–.0015	3	.004–.008
	4-120, 2.0L/H Diesel	.0013–.0020	.0079	.0079	.9843–1.0234	2.005–2.006	.0012–.0020	2.359–2.360	.0012–.0020	3	.0016–.0111
	4-140, 2.3L/R,S,X②	.0012–.0022	.008	.015	.9119–.9124	2.123–2.124	.0008–.0015	2.248–2.249	.0008–.0015	3	.004–.008
1986	4-97.6, 1.6L/2,4,5	.0018–.0026	.012	.016	.8119–.8124	1.885–1.886	.0008–.0015	2.2826–2.2834	.0008–.0015	3	.004–.008
	4-113.5, 1.9L	—	—	—	—	—	—	—	—	—	—
	4-120, 2.0L/H Diesel	.0013–.0020	.0079	.0079	.9843–1.0234	2.805–2.006	.0012–.0020	2.359–2.360	.0012–.0020	3	.0016–.0111
	4-140, 2.3L/R,S,X②	.0012–.0022	.008	.015	.9119–.9124	2.123–2.124	.0008–.0015	2.248–2.249	.0008–.0015	3	.004–.008

continued

PISTONS, PINS, RINGS, CRANKSHAFT & BEARINGS, NOTES—Continued

①—Fit rings in tapered bores for clearance listed in tightest portion of ring travel.

②—Tempo & Topaz.

Engine Tightening Specifications

Year	Engine/VIN	Spark Plugs Ft. Lbs.	Cylinder Head Bolts Ft. Lbs.	Intake Manifold Ft. Lbs.	Exhaust Manifold Ft. Lbs.	Rocker Arm Shaft Bracket Ft. Lbs.	Rocker Arm Cover Ft. Lbs.	Connecting Rod Cap Bolts Ft. Lbs.	Main Bearing Cap Bolts Ft. Lbs.	Flywheel to Crankshaft Ft. Lbs.	Vibration Damper or Pulley Ft. Lbs.
1981–82	4-97.6, 1.6L/2	17–23	44①	12–15	15–20	7–11②	6–8	19–25	67–80	59–69	74–90
1983	4-97.6, 1.6L/2	8–15	44①	12–15	15–20	7–11②	6–8	19–25	67–80	54–64	74–90
1984	4-97.6, 1.6L/2, 4 & 5	8–15	③	12–15	15–20	7–11②	6–8	19–25	67–80	54–64	74–90
	4-120, 2.0L/H Diesel	④	—	11–16	15–19	—	⑤	50–54	60–65	130–137	115–123
	4-140, 2.3L/R, S,X⑥	5–10	⑦⑫	15–23	⑧	⑨⑩	3–5	21–26⑪	60–74	54–64	82–103
1985	4-97.6, 1.6L/2,4,5,	8–15	⑮	12–15	15–20	7–11②	6–8	19–25	67–80	54–64	74–90
	4-120, 2.0L/H Diesel	④	—	12–17	16–20	—	⑤	48–51	61–65	130–137	116–123
	4-140, 2.3L/RSX ⑥	5–10	⑫	15–23	⑧	⑨⑩	21–26⑪	51–66	51–66	54–64	140–170
1986	4-97.6, 1.6L/2,4,5	8–15	⑮	12–15	15–20	7–11②	6–8	19–25	67–80	54–64	74–90
	4-113.5, 1.9L	—	—	—	—	—	—	—	—	—	—
	4-120, 2.0L/H Diesel	④	—	12–17	16–20	—	⑤	48–51	61–65	130–137	116–123
	4-140, 2.3L/R,S,X ⑥	5–10	⑫	15–23	⑧	⑨⑩	21–26⑪	51–66	51–66	54–64	140–170

①—Then tighten bolts an additional ½ turn in ¼ turn increments after specified torque has been obtained.

②—Rocker arm stud to cylinder head.

③—Torque bolts to 30–45 ft. lbs., then turn bolts an additional 180 degrees in 90 degree increments.

④—Glow plug torque, 10–14 ft. lbs.

⑤—Cylinder head cover torque, 5–7 ft. lbs.

⑥—Tempo & Topaz.

⑦—Tighten bolts in 2 steps. Final torque of bolts must be 81 ft. lbs.

⑧—Tighten bolts in 2 steps. First to 5–7 ft. lbs., then 20–30 ft. lbs.

⑨—Tighten bolts in 2 steps. First to 4–7 ft. lbs., then 19–26 ft. lbs.

⑩—Rocker arm fulcrum bolt to cylinder head.

⑪—Connecting rod cap nut.

⑫—Torque bolts in 2 steps. First to 51–59 ft. lbs., then 70–76 ft. lbs.

⑬—Torque to 44 ft. lbs., then loosen 2 turns and retorque to 44 ft. lbs.

Wheel Alignment Specifications

Year	Model	Caster Angle, Degrees Limits	Caster Angle, Degrees Desired	Camber Angle, Degrees Limits Left	Camber Angle, Degrees Limits Right	Camber Angle, Degrees Desired Left	Camber Angle, Degrees Desired Right	Toe-In Inch	Toe-Out on Turns, Deg. Outer Wheel	Toe-Out on Turns, Deg. Inner Wheel
1981	Front	+.55 to +2.05	+1.3	+1.4 to +2.9	+.95 to +2.45	+2.15	+1.7	①	②	20
	Rear	—	—	−1.45 to +.25	−1.45 to +.25	−.6	−.6	0–.36	—	—
1982–83	Front	+.55 to +2.05	+1.3	+1.4 to +2.9	+.95 to +2.45	+2.15	+1.7	①	③	20
	Rear	—	—	−1.45 to +.25	−1.45 to +.25	−.6	−.6	.09	—	—
1984	Front④	+.65 to +2.15	+1.4	+1.4 to +2.9	+.95 to +2.45	+2.15	+1.7	①	—	—
	Rear④	—	—	−2.1 to +.4	−1.45 to +.25	−1.25	−.6	1/16	—	—
	Front⑤	+.55 to +2.05	+1.3	+1.12 to +2.63	+.7 to +2.2	+1.9	+1.5	①	—	—
	Rear⑤	—	—	−.1 to +.5	−1 to +.5	−.25	−.25	1/16	—	—
1985–86	Front④⑥	—	—	—	—	—	—	—	—	—
	Rear④⑥	—	—	−11/32 to +21/32	−11/32 to +21/32	−13/16	−13/16	+3/32	—	—
	Front④⑦	—	—	—	—	—	—	—	—	—
	Rear④⑦	—	—	−25/32 to +15/32	−25/32 to +15/32	−15/16	−15/16	+3/32	—	—
	Front⑤	+½ to +2	+1¼	+1¼ to +2¾	+¾ to +2¼	+2	+1½	−1/10	—	—
	Rear⑤	—	—	—	—	—	—	+3/16	—	—

continued

WHEEL ALIGNMENT SPECIFICATIONS, NOTES—Continued

①—Toe out, .10 inch.
②—Left wheel, 19.97°; right wheel, 17.04°.
③—Left wheel, 20°; right wheel, 17°.
④—All models, Except Tempo & Topaz.
⑤—Tempo & Topaz.
⑥—Except turbocharged engine.
⑦—Turbocharged engine.

Cooling System & Capacity Data

Year	Model or Engine/VIN	Cooling Capacity, Qts.		Radiator Cap Relief Pressure, Lbs.	Thermo. Opening Temp.	Fuel Tank Gals.	Engine Refill Qts. ①	Transaxle Oil	
		Less A/C	With A/C					4 & 5 Speed Pints	Auto Trans. Qts. ①
1981	4-97.6, 1.6L/2	6.3	6.4	16	191	②	4③	5	9.8
1982	4-97.6, 1.6L/2	8	8	16	191	11.3	4③	5	9.8
1983	4-97.6, 1.6L/2	6.7	8	16	191	11.3	4③	④	8.3
1984	4-97.6, 1.6L/2	6.7	8.1	16	192	13	3.5	④	7.8
	4-120, 2.0/H	8.1	8.1	16	190	13	5	6.1	7.8
	4-140, 2.3/R	8.1	8.1	16	192	14	4	④	8.3
1985	4-97.6, 1.6L/2,4,5	6.7	8.1	16	192	13	3.5	④	7.8
	4-120, 2.0L/H⑤	9.2	9.2	16	190	13	5.28	6.1	—
	4-120, 2.0L/H⑥	9.2	9.2	16	190	15.2	5.28	6.1	—
	4-140, 2.3L/S,X⑥	8.1	8.1	16	192	15.2	4	6.1	7.8
1986	4-97.6, 1.6L/2,4,5	6.7	8.1	16	192	13	3.5	④	7.4
	4-113.5, 1.9L	6.5	7.1	16	—	13	3.5	6.1	7.4
	4-120, 2.0L/H⑤	9.2	9.2	16	190	13	5.28	6.1	—
	4-120, 2.0L/H⑥	9.2	9.2	16	190	15.2	5.28	6.1	—
	4-140, 2.3L/S,X⑥	8.1	8.1	16	192	15.2	4	6.1	7.8

①—Approximate. Make final check with dipstick.
②—Models w/man. trans., 9 gals.; models w/ auto. trans., 10 gals.; models w/ extended range option, 11.3 gals.
③—Includes filter.
④—4 speed trans., 5 pints; 5 speed trans., 6.1 pints.
⑤—Escort & Lynx.
⑥—Tempo & Topaz.

continued

Electrical Section

Fig. 1 Ignition switch removal. 1981

STARTER
REPLACE

EXCEPT DIESEL ENGINE

1. Disconnect battery ground cable and raise and support vehicle. Disconnect starter cable from starter motor terminal.
2. On vehicles equipped with manual transmission, remove three nuts attaching roll restrictor brace to transmission-side starter studs and remove brace.
3. Remove two bolts attaching starter rear support bracket. Remove retaining nut from rear of starter stud bolt, then remove bracket.
4. Remove three starter mounting nuts or bolts and the starter.
5. Reverse procedure to install.

DIESEL ENGINE

1. Remove battery cover, then disconnect battery ground cable located in luggage compartment.
2. Disconnect cable assembly from fender apron relay and starter solenoid.
3. Remove upper starter mounting stud bolt.
4. Raise and support vehicle.
5. Disconnect vacuum hose from vacuum pump.
6. Remove starter support bracket attaching screws, then the bracket.
7. Remove power steering hose bracket.
8. Remove ground wire assembly and cable support from starter bolt studs.
9. Remove 2 starter mounting studs.
10. Remove vacuum pump bracket.
11. Remove starter.
12. Reverse procedure to install.

IGNITION SWITCH
REPLACE

1981

1. Disconnect battery ground cable.

2. Remove steering column upper and lower trim shroud. It may be necessary to loosen four steering column attaching nuts to facilitate shroud removal.
3. Disconnect ignition switch electrical connector, **Fig. 1.**
4. Using a ⅛ in. drill, drill out the break-off head bolts attaching the switch to the lock cylinder.
5. Remove two switch retaining bolts using an easy out, then disengage the ignition switch from the actuator pin.
6. Adjust ignition switch by sliding carrier to the switch lock position, then insert a ¹⁄₁₆ in. drill bit through switch housing and into carrier.

NOTE: A replacement switch assembly includes an adjusting pin already installed.

7. Rotate lock cylinder to lock position and install switch onto actuator pin. Then install new break-off head bolts. Hand tighten the bolts.
8. Locate ignition switch upward on steering column until all travel in screw slots is used.
9. Hold switch in this position and tighten break off head bolts until heads break off. Remove adjustment drill bit, connect electrical connector, then install upper and lower trim shroud.

1982–86

1. Disconnect battery ground cable, then remove five steering column shroud attaching screws.
2. Remove two bolts and two nuts attaching steering column to column bracket, then lower steering column assembly to seat and remove column shrouds.
3. Disconnect ignition switch wire connector, then rotate ignition switch lock cylinder to the Run position.
4. Using a ⅛ inch drill bit, drill out shear bolts retaining ignition switch to lock cylinder housing.
5. Remove the two shear bolts using an easy out.
6. Detach ignition switch from actuator pin, then remove switch.
7. Check to ensure that ignition switch actuator pin slot and ignition switch lock cylinder are in the Run position.

NOTE: Replacement ignition switches are set in the Run position. The Run position on the ignition switch lock cylinder is located approximately 90° from the lock position.

8. Position ignition switch on actuator pin. It may be necessary to move switch slightly to align switch to column mounting bolt holes, **Fig. 2.**
9. Install and tighten shear bolts until heads break-off.
10. Connect wire connector to ignition switch, then connect battery ground cable and check ignition switch for proper operation.

Fig. 2 Ignition switch. 1982–86

11. Position upper shroud on column, then raise steering column and install column mounting bracket to instrument panel attaching bolts. Torque bolts to 15 to 25 ft. lbs.
12. Position lower shroud on column and install attaching bolts.

STOPLIGHT SWITCH
REPLACE

1981–86

1. Disconnect battery ground cable.
2. Disconnect electrical connector from switch.

NOTE: On vehicles equipped with standard brakes, the locking tab must be lifted before electrical connector can be removed.

3. On vehicles equipped with standard brakes, remove retainer, then slide the switch, push rod, white nylon washer and bushing away from pedal. Remove switch from vehicle, **Fig. 3.**
4. On vehicles equipped with power brakes, remove retainer and outer white nylon washer from pedal pin. Slide switch off brake pedal pin far enough so that outer side of plate of switch clears pin. Remove switch, **Fig. 3.**

TURN SIGNAL, HAZARD, HORN, FLASH-TO-PASS & DIMMER SWITCH
REPLACE

1. Disconnect battery ground cable.
2. Remove 5 shroud screws, then the lower shroud.

Fig. 3   Stop light switch

Fig. 4   Turn signal, hazard, horn, flash-to-pass & dimmer switch

Fig. 5   Instrument cluster removal. Exc. 1984—86 Tempo & Topaz

3. Remove upper shroud assembly.
4. Grasp switch lever and pull lever straight out from switch assembly, **Fig. 4.**
5. Peel back foam switch cover from turn signal switch.
6. Disconnect 2 electrical connectors.
7. Remove 2 self tapping screws attaching switch assembly to lock cylinder housing, then disconnect switch from housing.
8. Reverse procedure to install.

INSTRUMENT CLUSTER
REPLACE

1981—86

1. Disconnect battery ground cable, then remove steering column lower cover.
2. On Tempo and Topaz models, remove eight instrument cluster finish panel retaining screws and radio knobs, then the finish panel.
3. On Escort EXP, LN7 & Lynx models, remove four cluster opening finish panel retainer screws, then the finish panel.
4. From under instrument panel, disconnect speedometer cable, then pull cluster away from instrument panel, **Figs. 5 and 6.**
5. Disconnect cluster electrical connector from printed circuit.
5. Reverse procedure to install.

Fig. 6   Instrument cluster removal. 1984—86 Tempo & Topaz

AUXILIARY CLUSTER, REPLACE

EXP, LN7 & Tempo

1. Disconnect battery ground cable.
2. Pull trim cover at bottom edge and slide out of tabs at top edge.
3. Remove three cluster to console attaching screws. On Tempo models, remove four cluster to console attaching screws, then pull cluster outward and disconnect electrical connector.
4. Remove cluster from console.
5. Reverse procedure to install.

TEMPERATURE GAUGE, REPLACE

Topaz

1. Disconnect battery ground cable.
2. Remove instrument cluster as described under "Instrument Cluster, Replace".
3. Remove retaining screws, mask and lens from cluster backplate.
4. Remove two gauge retaining nuts and gauge.
5. Reverse procedure to install.

GRAPHIC WARNING DISPLAY, REPLACE

Escort, Lynx, Tempo & Topaz

1. Disconnect battery ground cable, then remove console finish panel by prying at bottom edge to disengage retainers.
2. Remove module to console attaching screws, then pull module outward and disconnect electrical connector.
3. Remove module from console.
4. Reverse procedure to install.

STEERING WHEEL
REPLACE

1. Disconnect battery ground cable.
2. Remove steering hub cover assembly, then the steering wheel attaching nut. Discard nut.
3. Remove steering wheel from steering shaft using tool T67L3600A. Do not use a knock-off type steering wheel puller or strike end of steering column with a hammer since damage to steering column bearings will result.
4. Reverse procedure to install. Install new wheel retaining nut, then torque to 30–40 ft. lbs. On non-tilt models, install steering wheel cover, then insert attaching bolts and torque to 13–20 inch lbs.

HORN SOUNDER
REPLACE

NOTE: On these models, the horn sounder is located on the turn signal, headlight dimmer and horn lever. Refer to Turn Signal, Hazard, Horn, Flash-To-Pass & Dimmer Switch, Replace when replacing lever.

SCREW (3)
WIPER MOTOR
WIRING

Fig. 7 Windshield wiper motor

HEADLAMP SWITCH
REPLACE

1981–83

1. Disconnect battery ground cable, then on vehicles without A/C, the left hand air vent control cable from the instrument panel.
2. Remove screws securing fuse panel bracket and position fuse panel to the side.
3. Place headlamp switch in the "On" position and depress the headlamp knob and shaft retainer button on headlamp switch. Remove knob and shaft assembly.
4. Remove headlamp switch bezel and disconnect electrical connector, then remove switch.
5. Reverse procedure to install.

1984–86

1. Disconnect battery ground cable.
2. Insert a thin flat blade under flange at side of headlamp switch to depress spring retaining clip. Twist blade to remove switch from one side.
3. Repeat step 2 for other side of headlamp switch.
4. Pull headlamp switch and electrical connector outward from instrument panel.
5. Disconnect headlamp switch electrical connector.
6. Reverse procedure to install.

RADIO
REPLACE

1981–83

1. Disconnect battery ground cable.
2. Remove A/C floor duct, if equipped.
3. Disconnect power, speaker and antenna leads from radio.
4. Remove knobs, discs, control shaft, nuts and washers from radio.
5. Remove ash tray and bracket, then the radio.
6. Remove radio rear support attaching nut.
7. Reverse procedure to install.

1984–86

1. Disconnect battery ground cable.
2. Remove radio knobs and instrument panel center trim panel.
3. Remove radio mounting plate screws, then pull radio outward to disengage lower rear support bracket.
4. Disconnect antenna and speaker leads from radio, then remove radio.
5. Remove nuts and washers from radio control shafts. Remove mounting plate.
6. Remove rear support retaining nut and support.
7. Reverse procedure to install.

W/S WIPER SWITCH
1981–86

NOTE: The switch handle is an integral part of the switch and cannot be removed separately.

1. Disconnect battery ground cable.
2. Remove upper steering column trim shroud, then disconnect electrical connector.
3. Pull back shield, then remove two screws securing switch. Remove switch.
4. Reverse procedure to install.

W/S WIPER MOTOR
REPLACE

1981–86

1. Disconnect battery ground cable.
2. Lift passenger side water shield cover from cowl, then disconnect motor electrical connector.
3. Remove linkage retaining clip from motor arm, then the three bolts attaching motor to mounting bracket, **Fig. 7.**
4. Disconnect operating arm from motor, then separate motor from mounting bracket and remove from vehicle.
5. Reverse procedure to install.

REAR WIPER MOTOR
REPLACE

ESCORT, LYNX, EXP & LN7

1. Disconnect battery ground cable.
2. Remove liftgate inner trim panel.
3. On station wagon models, remove license plate housing attaching screws, disconnect lamp electrical connector, then the housing.
4. Pull wiper motor electrical connector clip out from retaining hole.
5. Disconnect electrical connector halves.
6. Remove motor.
7. Reverse procedure to install.

W/S WIPER TRANSMISSION
REPLACE

1981–86

1. Remove wiper arm and blade assemblies from pivot shaft.
2. Disconnect battery ground cable, then remove clip and disconnect linkage drive arm from motor crank pin.
3. On Tempo and Topaz models, remove top grille from left and right cowl, then the pivot to cowl attaching screws.
4. On Escort, EXP, LN7 and Lynx models, remove pivot shaft retaining nuts.
5. On all models, remove linkage and pivots from cowl chamber, **Figs. 8 and 9.**
6. Reverse procedure to install.

Fig. 8 Windshield wiper linkage replace, Exc. 1984–86 Tempo & Topaz

HEATER CORE
REPLACE

LESS AIR CONDITIONING

1. Disconnect battery ground cable and drain cooling system.
2. Disconnect heater hoses from heater core and plug all open lines and fittings to prevent spillage.
3. Remove glove box and liner and move temperature lever to warm position.
4. Remove heater core cover, then working from engine compartment, loosen two nuts attaching heater case assembly to dash panel.
5. Push heater core toward passenger compartment, then pull heater core through glove box opening and remove from vehicle, **Fig. 10.**
6. Reverse procedure to install.

WITH AIR CONDITIONING

1. Disconnect battery ground cable and drain cooling system.
2. Disconnect heater hoses from heater core and plug all lines and fittings.
3. Remove floor duct from plenum.
4. Remove screws attaching heater core cover to plenum, then the cover and heater core, **Fig. 11.**
5. Reverse procedure to install.

BLOWER MOTOR
REPLACE

LESS AIR CONDITIONING

1. Disconnect battery ground cable.
2. Remove screws securing right ventilator control cable to instrument panel.
3. Remove screw securing right register duct to lower right edge of instrument

Fig. 9 Windshield wiper linkage replace, 1984–86 Tempo & Topaz

Fig. 10   Heater core removal, less air conditioning

Fig. 11   Heater core removal, with air conditioning

panel.
4. Remove glove box and hinge bar from instrument panel.
5. Pull right register duct from installed position between air inlet duct and right register opening, **Figs. 12 and 13.**
6. Remove ventilator grille from bottom of ventilator assembly, then screws securing right ventilator assembly to blower housing.
7. Remove hub clamp spring from blower wheel hub, **Fig. 14.**
8. Pull blower wheel from blower shaft, then remove three blower motor flange attaching screws.
9. Pull blower motor from housing, disconnect electrical connector, then remove motor from vehicle.
10. Reverse procedure to install.

WITH AIR CONDITIONING

1. Disconnect battery ground cable.
2. Remove glove box door and instrument panel lower reinforcement from instrument panel.
3. Disconnect blower motor electrical connector, then remove blower motor and mounting plate from evaporator housing.
4. Rotate motor until mounting plate flats clear edge of glove box opening, then remove motor.
5. Remove hub clamp wheel spring from blower wheel hub and remove blower wheel from motor shaft.
6. Reverse procedure to install.

SPEED CONTROLS

ACTUATOR CABLE ADJUSTMENT

Escort, EXP, LN7 & Lynx
1. Remove cable retaining clip, then disengage throttle positioner.
2. Place carburetor throttle lever at the curb idle speed position.
3. Pull on actuator cable end tube to remove slack from cable, **Fig. 15.**

4. While maintaining light tension on actuator cable, insert cable retaining clip.

Tempo & Topaz
1. With ignition "Off," adjust carburetor so throttle plate is closed and choke linkage is completely off cam.
2. Remove beaded chain locking pin, then pull bead chain through adjuster.
3. Insert locking pin into hole which allows greatest tension on bead chain, without opening throttle plate.

Vacuum Dump Valve Adjustment
1. Firmly depress brake pedal and hold in position.
2. Pull inward on dump valve until collar contacts retaining clip.
3. Position a .050 to .100 inch shim between pedal and dump valve button.
4. Pull brake pedal rearward to its normal position and allow dump valve to rachet into retaining clip.

Clutch Switch Adjustment

NOTE: This adjustment should be performed on models with manual transmission, when speed control will not engage.

1. Position and support clutch pedal in the full upward position against pedal stop.
2. Loosen switch attaching screw and slide switch forward toward clutch pedal, until clearance between switch plunger cap and switch housing is .030 inch, then tighten attaching screw.
3. Remove support holding clutch pedal in the full upward position and check speed control for proper operation. Ensure that speed control disengages when clutch pedal is depressed.

Fig. 12   Vent assembly removal. 1981–83

Fig. 13 Vent assembly removal. 1984—86

Fig. 14 Blower motor removal. Less air conditioning

Fig. 15 Speed control actuator cable assembly

Fig. 1 Left hand front No. 1 insulator. 5 speed manual transaxle

Fig. 1A Left hand front No. 1 insulator. 4 speed manual transaxle

Fig. 1B Left hand front No. 1 insulator. Automatic transaxle

Fig. 1C Left hand rear No. 4 insulator. Automatic transaxle

Fig. 1D Left hand rear No. 4 insulator. Manual transaxle

Fig. 1E Right hand No. 3A insulator. All

ENGINE MOUNTS

Refer to **Figs. 1 through 1E** when replacing the engine mounts.

ENGINE
REPLACE

EXCEPT TURBOCHARGED ENGINE

1. Disconnect battery ground cable, then mark location of hinges and remove hood.
2. Remove air cleaner, fresh air intake tube and hot air tube.
3. Drain cooling system, then disconnect secondary coil wire from distributor.
4. Remove alternator and thermactor pump.
5. Disconnect A/C compressor clutch wire from compressor.
6. On models with automatic transaxle, disconnect upper and lower oil cooler lines at radiator, then remove transmission oil cooler line clips.
7. Disconnect upper and lower radiator hoses.
8. Disconnect heater hoses from engine.
9. Disconnect wire connector from electric cooling fan and remove fan motor and shroud assembly, then remove radiator.
10. Remove power steering pump filler tube and cap pump opening to prevent fluid spillage, if equipped.
11. Disconnect all necessary vacuum hose and electrical connections.
12. Disconnect fuel supply and return hoses at metal connector to engine.
13. On models with automatic transaxle, disconnect throttle kickdown linkage.
14. Disconnect vacuum hose at power brake booster, if equipped.
15. Disconnect hose to thermactor valve, then disconnect accelerator cable at carburetor and bracket.
16. Disconnect fuel evaporation hose at metal tube located on left hand fender.
17. Loosen upper power steering pump pivot bolt, then remove upper pump to adjusting bracket attaching bolts, if equipped.
18. Remove upper rear thermactor pump bracket bolt, then install lifting eye.
19. Remove upper A/C compressor to mounting bracket attaching bolts, then remove clip retaining A/C compressor inlet line to exhaust manifold.
20. Raise and support vehicle, then loos-
en power steering pump lower adjusting bolt and remove drive belt. Remove power steering pump to lower bracket attaching bolts, then remove pump from bracket by passing pulley through adjusting bracket opening. Secure power steering pump against dash panel.
21. Remove heater supply and return tube clamps.
22. Remove starter motor ground cable and engine ground strap, then remove knee brace located at front of starter motor.
23. On models with manual transaxle, remove roll restrictor.
24. Remove starter motor and knee brace rear section, then disconnect exhaust pipe at inlet connector.
25. On models with automatic transaxle, remove converter cover and bracket. On models with manual transaxle, remove lower flywheel cover and brackets.
26. Using tool No. T81P-6312-A, remove crankshaft pulley.
27. On models with automatic transaxle, remove converter to flywheel attaching nuts, then remove lower converter housing to engine attaching bolts.

28. On models with manual transaxle, remove lower clutch housing to engine attaching bolts.
29. Remove coolant by pass hose from intake manifold, then remove lower No. 3-A engine mount bolt and nut from under insulator, **Fig. 1.**
30. Remove A/C compressor lower bracket bolt, if equipped.
31. Lower vehicle and attach a suitable lifting device to engine. Attach lifting device to engine using a 10mm bolt to exhaust side of cylinder head at the transaxle end and at lifting eye of thermacter pump bracket. A stabilizer chain may also be attached to alternator bracket bolt.
32. Remove engine mount No. 3-A through bolt, then remove engine mount, **Fig. 1.**
33. Remove A/C compressor bracket, if equipped.
34. On models with manual transaxle, remove timing belt cover.
35. Position a suitable transmission jack under transaxle.
36. On models with automatic transaxle, remove upper converter housing to engine attaching bolts. On models with manual transaxle, remove upper clutch housing to engine attaching bolts.
37. Remove engine from vehicle.

NOTE: On models with automatic transaxle, check to ensure that torque converter studs are free from flywheel before removing engine.

W/TURBOCHARGED ENGINE

1. Mark position of hood hinges and remove hood.
2. Disconnect battery ground cable.
3. Remove air cleaner and air intake tube assembly.
4. Drain cooling system.
5. Disconnect secondary wire from ignition coil.
6. Remove alternator drive belt, alternator mounting bolts, then position alternator aside.
7. Disconnect upper and lower radiator hoses from engine.
8. Disconnect heater hoses from engine.
9. Remove radiator guard, then the radiator assembly from vehicle.
10. Disconnect heater assembly from metal tube.
11. Mark then disconnect all electrical connectors and vacuum hoses from engine.
12. Disconnect fuel supply and return lines from intake manifold brackets.
13. On models with power brakes, disconnect power booster vacuum hose from engine.
14. Disconnect accelerator cable from air throttle body assembly, then remove cable routing bracket attaching screws.
15. Disconnect vapor hose from carbon canister tube.
16. Disconnect purge hose from canister purge solenoid.
17. Raise and support vehicle.

18. Remove oil cooler assembly.
19. Remove clamp from heater supply and return lines.
20. Disconnect battery cable from starter motor.
21. Remove brace from front of starter motor.
22. Remove starter motor assembly from engine.
23. Disconnect exhaust pipe from turbocharger assembly.
24. Remove inspection cover, exhaust pipe support bracket and crankshaft pulley.
25. Remove timing belt cover lower attaching bolts.
26. Remove flywheel housing lower attaching bolts.
27. Remove bolt securing battery ground cable to cylinder block.
28. Remove nut and bolt attaching No. 3A insulator bracket to the engine bracket located at front of engine, **Fig. 1E.**
29. Disconnect EGR tube from intake manifold.
30. Disconnect pulse air hose at check valve and air cleaner assembly.
31. Lower vehicle.
32. Install suitable engine lifting equipment onto engine lifting eyes.
33. Remove nuts attaching casting to No. 3A insulator, then the casting.
34. Remove remaining timing belt cover attaching bolts, then the cover.
35. Position a suitable jack under transaxle assembly. Raise jack enough to support the weight of the transaxle.
36. Remove flywheel housing upper attaching bolts.
37. Remove engine from vehicle.
38. Reverse procedure to install.

CYLINDER HEAD
REPLACE

NOTE: Some engines may have an oversize camshaft. Engines having an oversize camshaft will be identified by a stamping marked ".38/OC" on the outside of the cylinder head above the No. 4 exhaust port. The camshaft will also be stamped ".38/OC" at the distributor drive end. If a cylinder head necessitating replacement incorporates an oversize camshaft, a standard size camshaft must be used with the replacement cylinder head.

1. Disconnect battery ground cable.
2. On except turbocharged engine models, drain cooling system and disconnect heater hose from intake manifold.
3. On turbocharged engine models, disconnect radiator upper hose from intake manifold.
4. Disconnect electrical connector from cooling fan switch.
5. On except turbocharged engine models, remove air cleaner assembly.
6. On turbocharged engine models, remove air supply hose from air throttle body assembly.
7. Remove PCV oil separator, if equipped.
8. Disconnect PCV hose from air cleaner

assembly.
9. Remove rocker arm cover.
10. Remove drive belts, crankshaft pulley and timing belt cover.
11. Set engine No. 1 cylinder to TDC of compression stroke, then remove distributor cap and spark plug wire assembly.
12. Using a suitable tool, loosen both timing belt tensioner attaching bolts.
13. Position timing belt tensioner as far left as possible.
14. Remove timing belt.
15. Disconnect EGR tube from EGR valve.
16. Mark then disconnect PVS hose connectors.
17. Disconnect choke cap to electrical connector, if equipped.
18. Disconnect fuel supply and return lines from engine.
19. Disconnect accelerator cable and speed control cable, if equipped.
20. On turbocharged engine models, disconnect EGO electrical connector and EGR valve vacuum hose.
21. On power steering models, remove thermactor pump drive belt, pump and pump mounting bracket.
22. Disconnect altitude compensator from dash panel, if equipped.
23. Disconnect alternator air intake tube, if equipped and electrical connector.
24. Remove alternator and mounting bracket.
25. On turbocharged engine models, disconnect turbocharger air intake tube. Disconnect turbocharger oil supply tube from coolant outlet.
26. Raise and support vehicle.
27. Disconnect exhaust pipe from exhaust manifold or turbocharger mounting flange.
28. On turbocharged engine models, disconnect turbocharger oil drain from turbocharger.
29. Lower vehicle.
30. Remove cylinder head bolts and washers. Discard bolts and washers.
31. Remove cylinder head, exhaust manifold, intake manifold and turbocharger, if equipped as an assembly.
32. Reverse procedure to install. Torque cylinder head bolts in sequence shown in **Fig. 2.** After tightening bolts to specifications, refer to "Timing Belt, Replace" for belt tensioning data.

NOTE: Before installing cylinder head, the crankshaft must be rotated to position No. 1 piston at 90 degrees before top dead center. To position the piston, rotate crankshaft until pulley keyway is at the nine o'clock position. To time the valve train to this piston position, rotate camshaft until keyway is at the six o'clock position. The camshaft and crankshaft must not be rotated from this position until after the timing belt and gears have been installed.

VALVE ARRANGEMENT
FRONT TO REAR

1.6 L . . . . I-E-I-E-I-E-I-E

FRONT OF
VEHICLE ↓

**Fig. 2 Cylinder head bolt
tightening sequence**

CAM LOBE LIFT SPECS

Engine	Year	Intake	Exhaust
1.6L	1981–86	.229	.229
1.6L, E.F.I. & H.O.	1983–86	.240	.240

VALVE LIFT SPECS

Engine	Year	Intake	Exhaust
1.6 L	1981–86	.377	.377
1.6 L, E.F.I., H.O. & Turbo-charged.	1983–86	.396	.396

VALVE TIMING

INTAKE OPENS BEFORE TDC

Engine	Year	Degrees
1.6 L	1981	16
1.6 L	1982	20

VALVES
ADJUST

The 1.6L engines are equipped with overhead camshafts and hydraulic lash adjusters. Valve stem to rocker arm clearance is measured with the tappet completely collapsed. Perform the following procedure when measuring valve tappet clearance:

1. Rotate engine until No. 1 piston is on TDC of compression stroke.
2. Position suitable hydraulic lifter compressor tool onto rocker arm and slowly apply pressure to bleed tappet. Continue applying pressure until lifter plunger bottoms. Hold tappet in this position and check clearance between rocker arm and valve stem tip with feeler gauge. Collapsed tappet gap should be .059–.194 in. If clearance is less than specified, check for worn or damaged fulcrums, tappets or camshaft lobes.
3. With No. 1 piston on TDC of compression stroke, check the following valves for 1981 models:
No. 1 intake & No. 1 exhaust.
No. 2 intake & No. 3 exhaust.
Rotate crankshaft 180° clockwise from above position and check the following valves:

No. 2 exhaust & No. 3 intake.
No. 4 intake & No. 4 exhaust.
4. With No. 1 piston on TDC of compression stroke, check the following valves for 1982–86 models:
No. 1 intake & No. 1 exhaust.
No. 2 intake.
Rotate crankshaft 180° from above position and check the following valves:
No. 3 intake & No. 3 exhaust
Rotate crankshaft another 180° from above position and check the following valves:
No. 4 intake & No. 4 exhaust.
No. 2 exhaust.

VALVE GUIDES

Valve guide reamers are available in oversizes of .003, .015 and .030 in. When reaming a valve guide to an oversize, use the reamer in sequence from the smallest oversize first, to the next largest, etc. Always reface the valve seat after the valve guide has been reamed and use a suitable tool to remove the corner that forms on the inner diameter of the top of the valve guide.

CAMSHAFT
REPLACE

1. Disconnect battery ground cable and remove air cleaner assembly.

Fig. 3 Timing belt cover removal

2. Disconnect PCV hose and remove accessory drive belts.
3. Remove crankshaft pulley, then the timing belt cover, **Fig. 3.**
4. Remove valve cover, then rotate engine until No. 1 piston is on TDC of compression stroke.
5. Remove rocker arm hex flange nuts, fulcrums and rocker arms.
6. Remove fulcrum washers, then the tappets.
7. Remove crankshaft sprocket, then the timing belt. Refer to "Timing Belt, Replace" for procedure.
8. Remove camshaft sprocket, key and distributor assembly.
9. Loosen both timing belt tensioner attaching bolts using tool T81P-6254A or equivalent.
10. Remove camshaft thrust plate, then the fuel pump.
11. Remove ignition coil and bracket.
12. Remove camshaft from back of head towards transaxle.
13. Reverse procedure to install. Lubricate camshaft with suitable oil before installing. Check camshaft seal for damage and wear.

PISTON & ROD ASSEMBLE

Assemble the piston to the rod with arrow or lug facing front of engine and numbered side of rod facing exhaust man-

ARROW OR LUG TOWARD FRONT OF ENGINE

OIL SQUIRT HOLE

Fig. 4   Piston & rod assembly

CAMSHAFT POINTER MUST BE ALIGNED WITH THE TIMING MARK.

TURN THE CRANKSHAFT UNTIL KEYWAY IS AT 12 O'CLOCK.

Fig. 5   Aligning camshaft to cylinder head timing marks

PRESSURE IS RELIEVED FROM THE BELT

PRY THE TENSIONER AWAY FROM THE BELT AND TIGHTEN ONE OF THE ATTACHING BOLTS

Fig. 6   Relieving timing belt tension

ifold side of engine, **Fig. 4.** Check side clearance between connecting rods at each connecting rod crankshaft journal. Clearance should be .004–.011 in.

PISTONS, RINGS & PINS

Standard size pistons and rings are color coded red or blue and oversize pistons and rings have .004 OS stamped on their dome. Piston to bore clearance should be .0008–.0016 in. on 1981 models, .0012–.0020 in. on 1982 models and .0018–.0026 in. on 1983–86 models. Measure cylinder bore and select a piston to ensure proper clearance. When the piston to bore clearance is in the lower 1/3 of the specified range, a red piston should be used; in the middle 1/3 range a blue piston should be used and in the upper 1/3 range a .004 OS piston should be used. Piston pins are not available in oversize.

MAIN & ROD BEARINGS

Main and rod bearings are available in standard size and undersizes of .001 and .002 in.

TIMING BELT
REPLACE

NOTE: Replacement of the timing belt when the belt tension is released is not necessary. Replace a damaged timing belt as required.

1. Disconnect battery ground cable and remove accessory drive belts.

2. Remove timing belt cover, **Fig. 3.**

NOTE: Align timing mark on camshaft sprocket with timing mark on cylinder head, **Fig. 5.**

3. Install timing belt cover and insure that timing mark on crankshaft pulley aligns with TDC mark on front cover. Remove timing belt cover.
4. Loosen both timing belt tensioner attaching bolts using tool T81P-6254A or equivalent.
5. Position belt tensioner away from belt as far as possible, then tighten one of the tensioner attaching bolts, **Fig. 6.**
6. Remove crankshaft pulley, then the timing belt. Discard timing belt, if damaged.
7. Install timing belt over gears in counterclockwise direction starting at crankshaft. Ensure belt span between crankshaft and camshaft is kept tight as belt is installed over remaining gears, **Fig. 7.**
8. Loosen belt tensioner attaching bolts and allow tensioner to locate against belt.
9. Tighten one tensioner attaching bolt using tool T81P-6254A or equivalent.
10. Install crankshaft pulley, drive plate and pulley attaching bolt.
11. Hold crankshaft pulley stationary using tool YA-826 or equivalent and torque pulley attaching bolt to 74–90 ft. lbs. (100–121 Nm).
12. To seat timing belt on sprocket teeth, proceed as follows:
    a. Connect battery ground cable.
    b. Crank engine for approximately 30 seconds.
    c. Disconnect battery ground cable.
    d. Turn crankshaft to align timing pointer on camshaft sprocket with timing mark on cylinder head.
    e. Position timing belt cover on engine and confirm timing mark on crankshaft aligns with TDC pointer on the cover.

NOTE: If timing marks do not align, remove timing belt, align timing marks and repeat steps 7 thru 12.

13. Loosen belt tensioner attaching bolt tightened in step 9.
14. Secure crankshaft so it cannot rotate, then using tool No. D81P-6256 or equivalent and a torque wrench, turn camshaft sprocket counterclockwise. Tighten timing belt tensioner attaching bolt when torque wrench reads 27–32 ft. lbs., for a new timing belt and 10 ft. lbs., for a used timing belt.

NOTE: The engine must be cold when torque is applied to the camshaft sprocket. Do not set torque on a hot engine.

15. Remove crankshaft pulley and install timing belt cover.
16. Install accessory drive belts, crankshaft pulley and connect battery ground cable.

FRONT ENGINE OIL SEAL SERVICE

1. Remove timing belt as described under "Timing Belt, Replace".
2. Remove camshaft sprocket or crankshaft pulley as necessary.
3. Remove appropriate seal, **Figs. 8 and 9.**
4. Reverse procedure to install.

REAR CRANKSHAFT OIL SEAL SERVICE

1. Remove engine as described under "Engine, Replace".
2. Remove rear cover plate, **Fig. 10,** then the flywheel.
3. Using suitable tool, pierce seal metal casing.

Fig. 8 Camshaft front oil seal installation

Fig. 9 Crankshaft front oil seal installation

NOTE: WHEN THE CRANKSHAFT KEYWAY IS AT THE 12 O'CLOCK POSITION, NUMBER ONE PISTON IS AT TDC. WHEN THE KEY-WAY IS AT THE 9 O'CLOCK POSITION, NUMBER ONE PISTON IS 90° BEFORE TDC.

Fig. 7 Timing belt installed

4. Insert sheet metal screw into hole until screw forces seal out of retainer.
5. Reverse procedure to install using suitable seal installation tool to install seal.

INTAKE MANIFOLD
REPLACE

EXCEPT TURBOCHARGED ENGINE

1. Disconnect battery ground cable and drain coolant system.
2. Disconnect heater hose from intake manifold and remove air cleaner assembly.
3. Disconnect vacuum hoses as necessary, then the electrical connectors from idle fuel solenoid, bowl vent and choke.
4. Remove EGR supply tube.
5. Raise and support vehicle, then disconnect PVS hose using tool T81P-8564A or equivalent.

6. Remove intake manifold nuts Nos. 2, 3, and 6, **Fig. 11,** then lower vehicle.
7. Disconnect fuel line at fuel filter and return line at carburetor.
8. Disconnect accelerator cable and, if equipped, speed control cable.
9. On vehicles equipped with automatic transmission, disconnect throttle valve linkage at carburetor, then remove cable bracket attaching bolts.
10. On vehicles equipped with power steering, remove thermactor pump drive belt, thermactor pump, mounting bracket and by-pass hose.
11. Remove fuel pump, then three remaining manifold attaching nuts. Remove intake manifold.

NOTE: Do not place manifold on flat surface as damage to gasket surfaces may result.

12. Reverse procedure to install. Tighten intake manifold stud nuts in sequence shown in **Fig. 11** to torque listed in Engine Tightening Specifications.

W/TURBOCHARGED ENGINE

1. Disconnect battery ground cable.
2. Remove air supply hose from throttle body assembly.
3. Mark then disconnect all electrical connectors and vacuum hoses from intake manifold.
4. Remove EGR supply tube.
5. Disconnect electrical connector from throttle air bypass solenoid.
6. Raise and support vehicle.
7. Remove the bottom 3 intake manifold attaching nuts, **Fig. 12.**
8. Lower vehicle.
9. Disconnect fuel supply and return

Fig. 10 Rear cover plate, removal

Fig. 11 Intake manifold bolt tightening sequence

PLUG
TIGHTEN TO
6.5-11.0 N·m
(4.8-8.1 LB-FT)

STUD
TIGHTEN TO
2.0-10.0 N·m
(1.5-7.3 LB-FT)

FITTING ASSEMBLY
9A474
TIGHTEN TO
16.0-24.0 N·m
(12-17 LB-FT)

GASKET
9439

STUD
TIGHTEN TO 2.0-10.0 N·m
(1.5-7.3 LB-FT)

NUT
TIGHTEN TO
16.0-20.0 N·m
(12-14 LB-FT)

NUT
TIGHTEN TO
16.0-20.0 N·m
(12-14 LB-FT)

INTAKE MANIFOLD
CHARGING ASSEMBLY
9H487

FRONT OF VEHICLE

Fig. 12   Intake manifold assembly. Turbocharged engine

lines from intake manifold.
10. Disconnect accelerator cable from throttle body assembly.
11. Disconnect engine wiring harness from shock tower bracket.
12. Disconnect PCV hose from rocker cover and intake manifold.
13. Remove PCV valve.
14. Remove remaining 3 intake manifold attaching nuts, intake manifold and gasket.
15. Reverse procedure to install. Tighten intake manifold stud nuts in sequence shown in **Fig. 11** to torque listed in Engine Tightening Specifications.

EXHAUST MANIFOLD
REPLACE

EXCEPT TURBOCHARGED ENGINE

1. Disconnect battery ground cable.
2. Remove air cleaner.
3. Disconnect electrical connector from fan switch.
4. Remove radiator shroud bolts, then the shroud.
5. Disconnect EGR tube from exhaust

manifold.
6. Disconnect thermactor tube from exhaust manifold.
7. Remove A/C hose bracket, if equipped.
8. Remove exhaust manifold heat stove.
9. Remove exhaust manifold attaching nuts, **Fig. 13.**
10. Raise and support vehicle.
11. Remove anti-roll brace.
12. Disconnect water tube mounting brackets.
13. Disconnect exhaust pipe from exhaust manifold.

NOTE:
NUTS DRIVEN AFTER HEAT
SHROUD INSTALLATION

TIGHTEN
TO
21.0-26.5
N·m
(15.5-19.5
LB-FT)

GASKET

EXHAUST
MANIFOLD

GASKET

EXHAUST
MANIFOLD

20-30 N·m
(15-22 LB-FT)

MUFFLER INLET
PIPE BRACKET
TIGHTEN TO
9-13 N·m
(7-10 LB-FT)

HIGH-OUTPUT AND EFI
ENGINES

TIGHTEN THE ATTACHING
NUTS TO 21-26.4 N·m
(15-20 LB-FT)

GASKET

MONOLITHIC TIMING
PROBE PLUG
TIGHTEN TO 20-34 N·m
(15-25 LB-FT)

Fig. 13   Exhaust manifold assembly. Except turbocharged engine

BOLT TIGHTEN TO 8.0-11.0 N·m (5.9-8.1 LB-FT)

1/8-27 PIPE PLUG TIGHTEN TO 7.0-11.0 N·m (5.2-8.1 LB-FT) APPLY ESG-M4G194-A SEALER PRIOR TO ASSEMBLY

SHIELD 12A087

FRONT OF VEHICLE

EXHAUST MANIFOLD 9428

GASKET 9448

NUT TIGHTEN TO 21.0-26.0 N·m (15.5-19.1 LB-FT) (12 REQ'D)

VERIFY THAT TAB PROTRUDES UPPER RIGHT HAND CORNER AFTER INSTALLATION

GASKET 68898

EGO SENSOR ASSEMBLY 9F472 TIGHTEN TO 36.6-44.7 N·m (27-33 LB-FT)

OIL RETURN LINE – 9G441

TURBOCHARGER ASSEMBLY 9G438

STUD TIGHTEN TO 2.0-1.0 N·m (1.5-7.3 LB-FT) SHORT END INTO EXHAUST MANIFOLD

APPLY ESE-M4G4167-A3 PRIOR TO ASSEMBLY

SCREW AND WASHER ASSEMBLY TIGHTEN TO 8.0-11.0 N·m (5.9-8.1 LB-FT)

Fig. 14   Exhaust manifold assembly. Turbocharged engine

14. Remove exhaust manifold.
15. Reverse procedure to install.

W/TURBOCHARGED ENGINE

1. Disconnect battery ground cable.
2. Remove cooling fan shield from radiator support.
3. Loosen compressor outlet hose clamp from throttle housing.

4. Disconnect hose from turbocharger compressor inlet.
5. Remove alternator and bracket assembly.
6. Disconnect EGO sensor electrical connector, **Fig. 14.**
7. Raise and support vehicle.
8. Disconnect oil supply line from turbocharger coolant outlet.
9. Disconnect oil return line from cylinder block.
10. Remove exhaust pipe to turbocharger assembly attaching nuts, then position exhaust pipe away from mounting studs.
11. Remove exhaust shield from water outlet connector.
12. Remove nuts attaching exhaust manifold to cylinder head. Slide exhaust manifold and turbocharger assembly away from cylinder head.
13. Remove turbocharger and exhaust manifold as an assembly.

NOTE: If exhaust manifold is being replaced, replace EGO sensor.

14. Reverse procedure to install. Torque exhaust manifold nuts to 16–19 ft. lbs.

OIL PAN
REPLACE

1. Disconnect battery ground cable, then raise and support vehicle.
2. Drain engine oil, then disconnect starter electrical connectors.
3. Remove knee brace, then the starter.

DRAIN PLUG

⑦ ⑥ ⑤ ④ ③ ② ①
⑰ ③ ⑯ ⑰ ⑯ ⑮ ⑯ ⑬ ⑫ ① ⑱
⑱ ④ ⑤ ⑦ ⑨ ⑩ ② ⑮
⑨ ⑧ ⑩ ⑪ ⑫ ⑬ ⑭

TIGHTEN THE ATTACHING BOLTS USING THE SEQUENCE INSIDE THE DIAGRAM RETIGHTEN THE ATTACHING BOLTS USING THE SEQUENCE OUTSIDE THE DIAGRAM

Fig. 15   Oil pan bolt tightening sequence

4. Remove transaxle knee braces, then the oil pan retaining bolts. Remove the oil pan and discard gaskets.
5. On turbocharged engines, remove EGR tubes from exhaust inlet pipe. Disconnect exhaust inlet pipe from exhaust manifold. Remove exhaust inlet pipe support bracket and pipe.
6. Reverse procedure to install using suitable sealant on all pan gaskets. Refer to **Fig. 15** for oil pan bolt tightening sequence.

OIL PUMP
REPLACE

1. Perform steps 1 thru 4 as described under "Timing Belt, Replace".
2. Remove timing belt from camshaft and crankshaft pulleys and water pump gear.
3. Raise and support vehicle, then drain engine oil.
4. Remove crankshaft pulley, then the timing belt. Discard timing belt.
5. Remove crankshaft drive plate assembly, then the crankshaft pulley and gear.
6. Disconnect starter electrical connectors, then remove knee brace from engine.
7. Remove starter, then the rear section of knee brace. Remove transmission inspection plate.
8. Remove oil pan retaining bolts, then the oil pan.
9. Remove oil pick up tube brace to cylinder block bolt.
10. Remove oil pump attaching bolts, oil pump and gaskets, **Fig. 16.**
11. Reverse procedure to install using

ATTACHING BOLT (6) TIGHTEN TO 8-11 N·m (6-8 LB-FT)

SUPPORT BRACE

GASKET

OIL PUMP

PICK-UP TUBE

BRACE ATTACHING BOLT TIGHTEN TO 14-17 N·m (10-13 LB-FT)

Fig. 16   Oil pump removal

GASKET

PUMP HOUSING

PRESSURE RELIEF VALVE

GASKET

PICK-UP TUBE AND SCREEN ASSEMBLY

OUTER RACE

ROTOR

RETURN TUBE

PUMP COVER

Fig. 17   Oil pump

CRESCENT PUMP   GEROTOR

Fig. 18   Crescent & gerotor type oil pumps

suitable sealant on all pan gaskets.

OIL PUMP SERVICE

Refer to **Fig. 17** and measure the following clearances:
a. Outer race to housing: .0027–.0055 in. (.069–.140 mm).
b. Outer race and rotor to cover: .001–.0025 in. (.040–.66 mm.).
c. Relief valve to bore: .007–.0031 in. (.02–.08 mm).

NOTE: An engine oil leak at the oil pump hex socket plug on some 1981–82 vehicles may be serviced by applying sealer to the oil pump hex plug threads above the pressure relief valve plug. Remove hex plug and clean plug threads with a suitable solvent. Apply sealer No. E0AZ-19554A or equivalent to the plug threads. Engines built prior to September of 1981 will have a ⅜ hex plug. Torque plug to 6–9 ft. lbs. Engines built after September of 1981 will have a shouldered hex plug with a white plastic sealing ring. Torque plug to 21–24

ft. lbs. These plugs are not interchangeable and must not be overtorqued.

NOTE: On some engines built after March 31, 1983, a new gerotor gear design oil pump is being used, **Fig. 18.** The oil pump, oil pan and crankshaft used on models equipped with gerotor gear type oil pumps are not interchangeable with those used with the crescent type oil pump.

OIL COOLER
REPLACE

W/TURBOCHARGED ENGINES ONLY

1. Disconnect battery ground cable.
2. Drain engine oil and remove oil filter.
3. Drain cooling system.
4. Remove clamps retaining coolant hoses onto oil cooler, then the hoses.
5. Remove oil filter adapter insert, then the oil cooler from engine.
6. Reverse procedure to install

FUEL PUMP
REPLACE

MECHANICAL

1. Loosen fuel supply attaching nut at fuel pump outlet and the fuel pump mounting bolts.
2. Manually rotate engine until pump push rod is positioned on low side of cam.
3. Disconnect fuel lines from fuel pump.
4. Remove pump mounting bolts, then the pump and gasket.
5. Reverse procedure to install.

ELECTRIC

NOTE: Fuel supply lines will remain pressurized for long periods of time after engine shut-down. This pressure must be relieved before any service is attempted. A valve is provided on the fuel rail assembly for this purpose. To relieve system pressure, remove air cleaner assembly and connect pressure gauge tool No. T80L-9974-A or equivalent, onto fuel diagnostic valve on the fuel rail assembly. Gradually release fuel system pressure.

1. Disconnect battery ground cable.
2. Depressurize fuel system as described previously.
3. Raise and support vehicle.
4. Loosen fuel pump mounting bolt until fuel pump can be removed from vehicle.
5. Remove parking brake cable from pump clip.
6. Disconnect electrical connector and fuel pump outlet fitting.
7. Disconnect fuel pump inlet line from pump.

NOTE: Either drain fuel tank or raise end of fuel line above fuel level in tank to prevent fuel siphon action.

8. Remove pump from vehicle.
9. Reverse procedure to install. To pressurize fuel system, proceed as follows:
   a. Install pressure tool gauge No. T80L-9974-A or equivalent onto fuel rail pressure fitting.
   b. Turn ignition switch to ON position for 2 seconds and repeat turning ignition switch ON and OFF at 2 second intervals until gauge tool indicates approximately 35 psi.

WATER PUMP
REPLACE

1. Disconnect battery ground cable and drain coolant system.
2. Remove accessory drive belts, then the engine front timing cover.

3. Position No. 1 cylinder at TDC, then loosen both belt tensioner attaching bolts.
4. Secure tensioner as far left as possible, then remove timing belt. Discard timing belt.
5. Remove camshaft sprocket, then the rearward front timing cover stud.
6. Disconnect heater return tube hose connection at water pump inlet tube.
7. Remove water pump inlet tube fasteners, then the tube and gasket.
8. Remove water pump to cylinder block bolts, then the water pump.
9. Reverse procedure to install. Refer to "Timing Belt, Replace" for proper belt tensioning procedures.

BELT TENSION DATA

	New	Used
1981		
¼ inch	50–80	40–60
4 ribbed	90–120	90–110
5 ribbed	110–140	110–130
1982–83		
¼ inch	50–80	40–60
Air Pump		
4 ribbed	90–130	90–120
All Others		
4 ribbed	110–150	100–130
5 ribbed	130–170	120–150
1984–86		
Air Pump (Low Mount)	90–130	80–100
Less Power Steering Air Pump (High Mount) & Power Steering Pump	50–90	40–60
Alternator	150–190	140–160

TURBOCHARGER

The turbocharger is used to increase engine power on a demand basis. As engine load increases and the throttle opens, more air-fuel mixture flows into the combustion chambers. As the increased flow is burned a larger volume of high energy exhaust gases enters the engine exhaust system and is directed through the turbocharged turbine housing. Some of the exhaust gas energy is used to increase the speed of the turbine wheel which is connected to the compressor wheel. The increased speed of the compressor wheel compresses the air-fuel mixture and delivers the compressed air-fuel mixture to the intake manifold. The high pressure in the intake manifold allows a denser charge to enter the combustion chambers, in turn developing more engine power during the combustion cycle. Turbocharger output is governed by an integral wastegate which controls the passage of exhaust gas past the turbine. The electronic fuel injection system provides precise air-fuel mixture control. The fuel injectors at each cylinder intake port deliver more fuel when needed for high turbocharger boost power output.

The EEC-1V electronic engine control system provides precise control of fuel injection response to throttle position, air temperature, engine temperature, altitude and engine emission levels. The EEC-1V system also controls spark timing, exhaust gas recirculation and automatically shuts-off the air conditioner compressor at wide-open throttle to eliminate engine power drag when full engine output is needed.

4-113.5 Gasoline Engine Section

Fig. 1 Right hand No. 3A insulator

Fig. 2 Left hand rear No. 4 insulator

ENGINE MOUNTS

Refer to **Figs. 1 through 3** when replacing engine mounts.

ENGINE
REPLACE

1. Mark position of hood hinges, then remove hood.
2. Disconnect battery ground cable, then remove air cleaner, intake duct and heat tube.
3. Remove alternator air intake tube, then drain engine coolant.
4. Remove secondary coil wire, then the alternator drive belt.
5. Remove alternator mount bolts, then position alternator aside.
6. Disconnect thermactor air supply hose at pump, then remove pump.
7. On models with automatic transaxle, disconnect cooler lines at radiator.
8. On all models, disconnect the engine coolant hoses at radiator, then the heater hoses at engine block.
9. Disconnect electric cooling fan, then remove fan and shroud as an assembly.
10. On models with automatic transaxle, remove transaxle coolant line routing clip at radiator.
11. On all models, remove radiator.
12. Disconnect heater at metal tube, then the necessary engine electrical connectors.
13. Esconnect vacuum hoses, then the fuel pump supply and return lines.
14. On models with power assist brakes,

disconnect brake booster vacuum hose at engine.
15. On models with automatic transaxle, disconnect kickdown rod at carburetor.
16. On all models, disconnect vacuum hose at thermactor valve.
17. Disconnect accelerator cable at carburetor, then remove cable routing bracket attaching screws.
18 Disconnect vapor hose at carbon canister, then raise and support vehicle.
19. Remove clamp from heater supply and return tubes, then disconnect starter battery cable.
20. Remove knee brace from front of starter motor, then pull starter from vehicle.
21. Disconnect exhaust pipe, then remove support bracket.
22. Remove converter cover on automatic transaxle models or inspection cover on manual transaxle models, then the crankshaft pulley.
23. On models with automatic transaxle, remove torque converter to flywheel attaching bolts, then the converter housing lower attaching bolts.
24. On models with manual transaxle, remove timing belt cover lower attaching bolts, then the flywheel attaching bolts.
25. On all models, loosen coolant bypass hose clamp, then disconnect hose from intake manifold.
26. Remove battery ground cable to engine block attaching bolt, then the No. 3A casting bracket to engine bracket attaching nut and bolt, **Fig. 1.**
27. Lower vehicle, then attach suitable lifting brackets to engine, then attach lifting device to engine brackets.
28. Remove No. 3A casting to insulator retaining nut, then the casting.
29. On models with manual transaxle, remove remaining timing belt cover attaching bolts, then the cover.
30. On all models, remove insulator attaching bracket from engine, then support transaxle with a suitable jack.

31. Remove upper attaching bolts from converter housing on models with automatic transaxle or flywheel housing on models with manual transaxle.
32. On all models, remove engine from vehicle.
33. Reverse procedure to install.

CYLINDER HEAD
REPLACE

1. Raise and support hood in open position, then disconnect battery ground cable.
2. Drain cooling system, then disconnect coolant and heater hoses from intake manifold.
3. Disconnect cooling fan switch electrical connectors, then remove air cleaner assembly.
4. Remove PCV hose at air cleaner assembly, then disconnect vacuum hoses.
5. Remove rocker arm cover, then disconnect accessory drive belts.
6. Remove crankshaft pulley, then the timing belt cover.
7. Place No. 1 cylinder at T.D.C. of compression stroke by turning crankshaft until pulley keyway is at 12 o'clock and camshaft sprocket keyway is at 6 o'clock, then remove distributor cap and spark plug wires as an assembly.
8. Remove both belt tensioner attaching bolts using suitable torque wrench adapter, then position tensioner as far left toward front of vehicle as possible.
9. Remove timing belt, then disconnect EGR tube at valve
10. Disconnect PVS hose connectors, if equipped, using valve replace tool No. T81P-8564-A or equivalent, then label connectors and position aside.
11. Disconnect choke cap wire, if equipped, then the fuel supply and return lines from right side of engine

Fig. 3   Left hand front No. 1 insulator

Fig. 4   Cylinder head bolt tightening sequence

12. Disconnect accelerator cable, then the speed control cable, if equipped.
13. On models with power steering, remove thermactor pump drive belt, pump then the mounting bracket.
14. Disconnect altitude compensator, if equipped, and position aside.
15. Disconnect alternator air intake tube, if equipped, then the electrical connector.
16. Remove alternator and attaching bracket, then raise and support vehicle.
17. Disconnect exhaust pipe at manifold, then lower vehicle.
18. Remove cylinder head attaching bolts and washers, then discard.
19. Remove cylinder head, exhaust and intake manifolds as an assembly.
20. Remove and discard gasket.

NOTE: Before installing cylinder head, rotate crankshaft so pulley keyway is positioned at 9 o'clock (viewed from front of engine). Turn camshaft to position its keyway at 6 o'clock, then install cylinder head. Turn crankshaft so pulley keyway is positioned at 12 o'clock. The camshaft and crankshaft are now properly timed and should not be rotated from this position until after timing belt and sprockets have been installed.

21. Reverse procedure to install, noting the following:
    a. Install new cylinder head gasket on cylinder block.
    b. Apply light coating of engine oil to new cylinder head bolts prior to installation.
    c. Torque bolts to 44 ft. lbs. following sequence shown, **Fig. 4,** then loosen bolts approximately two turns and retorque to 44 ft. lbs.

VALVE ARRANGEMENT
FRONT TO REAR

1.9L	I-E-I-E-I-E-I-E

CAM LOBE LIFT SPECS

Engine	Year	Intake	Exhaust
1.9L	1986	.240	.240

VALVE LIFT SPECS

Engine	Year	Intake	Exhaust
1.9L	1986	.396	.396

VALVES
ADJUST

The 1.9L engine is equipped with an overhead camshaft and hydraulic lash adjuster. Valve stem to rocker arm clearance is measured with tappet completely collapsed. Perform the following procedure when measuring valve tappet clearance:

1. Rotate engine until piston of No. 1 cylinder is at TDC of compression stroke.
2. Position suitable hydraulic lifter compressor tool onto rocker arm, then slowly apply pressure to bleed tappet. Continue to apply pressure until lifter plunger bottoms. Hold tappet in this position and check clearance between rocker arm and valve stem tip using a suitable feeler gauge with less than a ⅜ inch width. Collapsed tappet gap clearance should be .059–.194 inch. If clearance is less than specified, check for worn ar damaged fulcrums, tappets or camshaft lobes.
3. With No. 1 piston on TDC of compression stroke, check the following valves as outlined:
    No. 1 intake & No. 1 exhaust.
    No. 2 intake.
    Rotate crankshaft 180° from present position, then check the following valves:
    No. 3 intake & No.3 exhaust.
    Rotate crankshaft 180° from present position, then check the following valves:
    No. 4 intake & No. 4 exhaust.
    No. 2 exhaust.

CAMSHAFT
REPLACE

1. Disconnect battery ground cable, then remove air cleaner assembly.
2. Remove PCV hose, then the accessory drive belts.
3. Remove crankshaft pulley, then the timing belt cover.
4. Remove valve cover attaching bolts and studs, then the valve cover.
5. Set piston of No. 1 cylinder at TDC of compression stroke, then remove rocker arm hex flange nuts, fulcrums and rocker arms.
6. Remove fulcrum washers, then the tappets.
7. Remove distributor assembly, then loosen timing belt tensioner attaching bolts using torque wrench adapter tool No. T81P-6254-A or equivalent.
8. Remove timing belt, then the camshaft sprocket and key.
9. Remove thrust plate, then the fuel pump.
10. Remove ignition coil and coil bracket.
11. Remove camshaft through rear of head, toward transaxle.
12. Reverse procedure to install.
13. Apply a suitable lubricant to camshaft prior to installation, then check seal for wear and damage and replace as necessary.

PISTON & ROD
ASSEMBLE

Position locator tool D85P-6135-A or equivalent into center hole of sleeve T71P-6135-P1, **Fig. 5,** then place piston onto locator. Locator will align pin bores in piston and rods and will also serve as a pilot for piston pin. Press piston into place using tool No. T81P-6135-A2 or equivalent. Assemble piston to rod with arrow facing front of engine and numbered side of rod facing exhaust manifold side of engine, **Fig. 6.** Check side clearance between connecting rods at eachcrankshaft journal. Clearance should be .004–.011 inch.

TIMING BELT
REPLACE

1. Disconnect battery ground cable, then remove accessory drive belts.
2. Remove timing cover.

NOTE: Align timing mark on camshaft sprocket with timing mark on cylinder head.

Legend:

1. SPARK PLUG CABLE SET
2. BOLT/STUD, COVER ATTACHING (2)
3. ROCKER ARM COVER
4. SCREW, COVER ATTACHING (7)
5. NUT, FULCRUM ATTACHING (8)
6. FULCRUM, ROCKER ARM
7. ROCKER ARM
8. WASHER, FULCRUM (8)
9. BOLT, CYLINDER HEAD ATTACHING (10)
10. SCREW, ROTOR ATTACHING (2)
11. STUD, FULCRUM ATTACHING (8)
12. KEYS, VALVE SPRING RETAINER
13. RETAINER, VALVE SPRING
14. VALVE SPRING
15. SEAL, VALVE STEM
16. SEAT, VALVE SPRING
17. HYDRAULIC TAPPET
18. SPARK PLUG
19. PLATE, CAMSHAFT THRUST
20. STUD, MANIFOLD ATTACHING (8)
21. GASKET, EXHAUST MANIFOLD
22. NUT, MANIFOLD ATTACHING (8)
23. EGR TUBE
24. CHECK VALVE, AIR INJECTION
25. EXHAUST MANIFOLD
26. SHAFT KEY, CAM SPROCKET
27. BOLT/WASHER SPROCKET ATTACHING (1)
28. SPROCKET, CAMSHAFT
29. SEAL, CAMSHAFT
30. CAMSHAFT
31. BOLT, THRUST PLATE ATTACHING (2)
32. INTAKE VALVE
33. EXHAUST VALVE
34. GASKET, CYLINDER HEAD

35. CYLINDER BLOCK
36. BOLTS (2) & NUTS (2), COVER ATTACHING
37. TIMING BELT COVER
38. ENGINE MOUNT
39. CRANKCASE VENTILATION BAFFLE
40. GASKET, INTAKE MANIFOLD
41. DOWEL, CYLINDER HEAD ALIGNMENT (2)
42. STUD, MANIFOLD ATTACHING (6)
43. FUEL PUMP
44. GASKET, FUEL PUMP
45. PUSH ROD, FUEL PUMP
46. INTAKE MANIFOLD
47. NUT, MANIFOLD ATTACHING (6)
48. STUD, VALVE ATTACHING (2)
49. GASKET, EGR VALVE
50. EGR VALVE
51. NUT, VALVE ATTACHING (2)
52. STUD, CARBURETOR ATTACHING (4)
53. GASKET, CARBURETOR MOUNTING
54. CARBURETOR
55. FUEL LINE
56. SCREW, CAP ATTACHING (2)
57. DISTRIBUTOR CAP
58. ROTOR
59. BOLT, DISTRIBUTOR ATTACHING (3)
60. NUT, CARBURETOR ATTACHING (4)
61. BOLT, PUMP ATTACHING (2)
62. THERMOSTAT HOUSING
63. THERMOSTAT
64. GASKET, HOUSING
65. BOLT, HOUSING ATTACHING (2)
66. DISTRIBUTOR

Cylinder head assembly & related components exploded view

1. DOWEL, PRESSURE PLATE ALIGNMENT
2. FLYWHEEL
3. SEAL, CRANKSHAFT REAR
4. BOLT, RETAINER ATTACHING (6)
5. SEAL RETAINER
6. GASKET, RETAINER
7. CYLINDER BLOCK
8. ENGINE LIFTING EYE
9. PLUG AND GASKET, MONOLITHIC TIMING
10. PLUG, COOLANT DRAIN
11. GASKET, PUMP (OIL)
12. OIL PUMP
13. GASKET, PUMP (WATER)
14. WATER PUMP
15. BOLT, PUMP (WATER) ATTACHING (4)
16. TIMING BELT — INSTALLED VIEW
17. SPRING, TENSIONER
18. BRACKET AND IDLER, TENSIONER
19. BOLT, TENSIONER ATTACHING (2)
20. TIMING BELT COVER
21. CRANKSHAFT PULLEY
22. WASHER, PULLEY BOLT (1)
23. BOLT, PULLEY ATTACHING (1)
24. BOLT, COVER ATTACHING (4)
25. OIL PUMP ASSEMBLY
26. GASKET, PICKUP TUBE
27. SCREEN AND COVER ASSEMBLY
28. BOLT, PICK UP ATTACHING (2)
29. SPROCKET, CRANKSHAFT

30. GUIDE, TIMING BELT
31. SEAL, CRANKSHAFT FRONT
32. BOLT, PUMP (OIL) ATTACHING (6)
33. BOLT, BRACE ATTACHING (1)
34. SEAL, PAN FRONT
35. GASKET, PAN SIDE
36. OIL PAN
37. SEAL, DRAIN PLUG
38. PLUG, OIL PAN DRAIN
39. BOLT, PAN ATTACHING (18)
40. GASKET, PAN SIDE
41. SEAL, PAN REAR
42. BOLT, CAP ATTACHING (10)
43. MAIN BEARING CAPS
44. MAIN BEARING INSERTS, LOWER (NON-GROOVED)
45. CRANKSHAFT
46. MAIN BEARING INSERTS, UPPER
47. OIL PRESSURE SENDING UNIT
48. DOWEL, TRANSMISSION ALIGNMENT
49. ADAPTER, OIL FILTER
50. OIL FILTER
51. PISTON
52. PISTON PIN
53. CONNECTING ROD
54. CONNECTING ROD BEARINGS
55. CONNECTING ROD CAP
56. NUT, CAP ATTACHING
57. BOLT, CAP ATTACHING

Cylinder block, crankshaft & related components exploded view

Fig. 5 Assembling piston to rod

Fig. 6 Piston & rod assembly

3. Install timing belt cover, then ensure timing mark on crankshaft pulley aligns with TDC mark on front cover.
4. Remove timing belt cover.
5. Loosen both timing tensioner attaching bolts using torque wrench adapter T81P-6254-A or equivalent.
6. Pry tensioner away from belt as far as possible, then tighten one attaching bolt.
7. Remove crankshaft pulley, then the timing belt. Discard timing belt if damaged.
8. Install timing belt over sprockets in a counterclockwise direction starting at crankshaft. Ensure belt span between crankshaft and camshaft is kept tight as belt is installed over remaining sprocket.
9. Loosen belt tensioner attaching bolt and allow to locate against belt.
10. Tighten one tensioner attaching bolt using previously mentioned tool, then install crankshaft pulley, drive plate and pulley attaching bolt.
11. Retain crankshaft pulley using tool No. YA-826, then torque pulley nut to 74–90 ft. lbs.
12. To seat timing belt on sprocket teeth, proceed as follows:
    a. Connect battery ground cable, then crank engine for approximately 30 seconds.
    b. Disconnect battery ground cable, then rotate crankshaft as necessary to align timing pointer on cam sprocket with timing mark on cylinder head.
    c. Position timing belt cover on engine, then ensure timing mark on crankshaft aligns with TDC pointer on cover.
    d. If timing marks do not align, remove belt, align timing marks and repeat steps 8–12.
13. Loosen tensioner attaching bolt, then secure crankshaft and ensure it will not rotate.

14. Using tool No. D81P-6256-A or equivalent and a suitable torque wrench, turn camshaft sprocket counterclockwise. Torque belt tensioner attaching bolt to 27–32 ft. lbs for new belt or 10 ft. lbs. on new belt.

NOTE: Ensure engine is cold when applying torque to camshaft sprocket. Do not set torque on hot engine.

15. Install timing belt cover, accessory drive belts, then connect battery ground cable.

FRONT CRANKSHAFT OIL SEAL SERVICE

1. Remove timing belt as described under "Timing Belt, Replace."
2. Remove crankshaft pulley, then the front seal.
3. Install new front seal using tool No. T81P-6700-A or equivalent.
4. Install crankshaft pulley, then the timing belt.

Fig. 7 Intake manifold bolt tightening sequence

EXHAUST MANIFOLD

GASKET

GASKET

TIGHTEN ATTACHING NUTS TO 24-32 N·m (18-23 LB-FT)

MONOLITHIC TIMING PROBE PLUG TIGHTEN TO 20-34 N·m (15-25 LB-FT)

A6954 f

Fig. 8   Exhaust manifold assembly

REAR CRANKSHAFT OIL SEAL SERVICE

1. Remove transaxle assembly.
2. Remove rear cover plate, then the fly-wheel.
3. Using a suitable tool, punch a hole into seal metal surface between lip and block. Screw in threaded end of suitable slide hammer, then remove seal. Use care not to damage oil seal surface.
4. Inspect crankshaft seal area for damage that may cause new seal to leak. If damage is present, repair or replace crankshaft as necessary.
5. Apply a suitable lubricant to new seal, then install seal using tool No. T81P-6701-A or equivalent.
6. Tighten bolts evenly as to allow seal to seat straight, then install flywheel and torque attaching bolts to 54–64 ft. lbs.
7. Install rear cover plate, then the trans-axle.

INTAKE MANIFOLD
REPLACE

1. Raise and secure hood in open position, then disconnect battery ground cable.
2. Partially drain cooling system, then disconnect heater hose from intake manifold.
3. Remove air cleaner assembly, then disconnect vacuum hoses.
4. Disconnect electrical connectors from choke cap wire, bowl vent and idle fuel solenoid, then remove EGR supply tube.
5. Raise and support vehicle, then remove PVS hose connectors using tool No. T81P-8564-A or equivalent. Lable connectors, then position aside.
6. Remove bottom three intake manifold attaching nuts, then lower vehicle.
7. Disconnect fuel line at fuel filter, then the return line at carburetor.

8. Disconnect accelerator, then the speed control cable, if equipped.
9. On models with automatic transaxle, Disconnect throttle valve linkage at carburetor, then remove cable bracket attaching bolts.
10. On models with power steering, remove thermactoer pump drive belt, pump, pump mounting bracket, then the thermactor bypass hose.
11. Remove fuel pump, then the remaining intake valve attaching bolts.
12. Reverse procedures to install. Tighten retaining nuts in sequence shown, **Fig. 7**, to torque value listed in Engine Tightening Specifications.

EXHAUST MANIFOLD
REPLACE

1. Disconnect battery ground cable, then remove air cleaner tray.
2. Disconnect electric cooling fan electrical connector, then remove radiator shroud attaching bolts and shroud.
3. Disconnect thermactor tube at exhaust manifold, then remove air conditioning hose bracket.
4. Remove exhaust manifold retaining nuts, then raise and support vehicle.
5. Remove anti-roll brace, then disconnect water tube brackets.
6. Disconnect exhaust pipe at catalytic converter, then remove exhaust manifold.
7. Reverse procedure to install. Refer to **Fig. 8**, during installation procedure.

OIL PUMP
REPLACE

1. Secure hood in open position, then disconnect battery ground cable.
2. Loosen alternator bolt at adjusting arm, then remove accessory drive belt.
3. Remove timing belt cover. Place No. 1 cylinder at T.D.C. of compression stroke by turning crankshaft until pulley keyway is at 12 o'clock and camshaft sprocket keyway is at 6 o'clock. Loosen belt tensioner, then pry tensioner away from belt and tighten one attaching bolt.
4. Disengage timing belt from camshaft sprocket, water pump sprocket and crankshaft sprocket. Raise vehicle on a suitable hoist, then drain crankcase.
5. Remove timing belt, then the crankshaft drive plate assembly.
6. Remove crankshaft pulley, then the crankshaft sprocket.
7. Disconnect starter cable at starter, then remove knee brace from engine.
8. Remove starter, then the rear section of knee brace and inspection plate at transaxle.
9. Remove oil pan retaining bolts, then the oil pan.

10. Remove front and rear oil pan seals and side gaskets, then the oil pump attaching bolts, oil pump and gasket.
11. Remove oil pump seal.
12. Reverse procedure to install. Apply a suitable sealant to oil pan gasket surfaces. Torque oil pump screen and pickup tube attaching bolts to 6–9 ft. lbs. Torque oil pump attaching bolts to 5–7 ft. lbs. Torque oil pan attaching bolts to 15–20 ft. lbs.

FUEL PUMP
REPLACE

1. Loosen fuel supply attaching nuts at fuel pump outlet using suitable tool.
2. Loosen fuel pump attaching bolts approximately two turns, then manually rotate engine to position pump push rod on low side of cam.
3. Remove rubber hose and clamp from fuel pump inlet, then disconnect fuel line from fuel pump inlet.
4. Disconnect fuel line from fuel pump outlet, then remove pump attaching bolts, fuel pump gasket and push rod.
5. Reverse procedure to install.

WATER PUMP
REPLACE

1. Disconnect battery ground cable, then drain cooling system.
2. Remove accessory drive belts, then the engine front timing cover.
3. Place No. 1 cylinder at T.D.C. of compression stroke by turning crankshaft until pulley keyway is at 12 o'clock and camshaft sprocket keyway is at 6 o'clock. Loosen belt tensioner, then pry tensioner away from belt and tighten one attaching bolt.
4. Secure tensioner as far left as possible, then remove timing belt.
5. Remove camshaft sprocket, then the rearward front timing cover stud.
6. Disconnect heater return tube hose connection at water pump inlet tube.
7. Remove water pump inlet tube fasteners, then the tube and gasket.
8. Remove water pump to cylinder block bolts, then the water pump.
9. Reverse procedure to install. Refer to "Timing Belt, Replace" for proper belt tensioning procedures.

BELT TENSION DATA

	New lbs.	Used lbs.
1986		
Air Pump (Low Mount) Less Power Steering	90–130	80–100
Air Pump (High Mount) & Power Steering Pump	50–90	40–60
Alternator	150–190	140–160

4-140 Gasoline Engine Section

LEFT HAND FRONT NO. 1 INSULATOR
MTX 4 AND 5-SPEED APPLICATIONS

Fig. 1   Left hand front No. 1 insulator. 4 & 5 speed manual transaxle

LEFT HAND FRONT NO. 1 INSULATOR
ATX APPLICATIONS

Fig. 2   Left hand front No. 1 insulator. Automatic transaxle

Fig. 3   Left hand rear No. 4 insulator. 4 speed manual transaxle

ENGINE MOUNTS
REPLACE

Refer to **Figs. 1 through 5** when replacing engine mounts.

ENGINE
REPLACE

NOTE: Engine and transaxle are removed as an assembly.

LEFT HAND REAR NO. 4 INSULATOR
MTX 5-SPEED AND ATX APPLIATIONS
(SAME AS MTX 4-SPEED EXCEPT AS SHOWN)

Fig. 4   Left hand rear No. 4 insulator. 5 speed manual & automatic transaxle

1. Mark position of hood hinges, then remove hood.
2. Disconnect battery ground cable, then remove air cleaner assembly.
3. Remove lower radiator hose and drain coolant from engine. Remove upper radiator hose from engine.
4. On models equipped with automatic transaxle, disconnect transaxle cooler lines from rubber hoses below radiator.
5. Remove coil assembly from cylinder head. Disconnect coolant fan electrical connector.
6. Remove radiator shroud, cooling fan and radiator.
7. Carefully discharge refrigerant from air conditioning system, if equipped. Remove inlet and outlet lines from compressor.
8. Mark and disconnect all electrical and vacuum lines from engine.
9. On models equipped with automatic transaxle, disconnect TV linkage from transaxle. On models equipped with manual transaxle, disconnect clutch cable from transaxle shift lever.
10. Disconnect accelerator linkage, fuel supply and return lines from engine.
11. Disconnect thermactor pump discharge hose from pump.
12. Disconnect power steering pressure and return lines from pump, if equipped. Remove power steering line bracket from cylinder head.
13. Install engine support tool No. D79P-6000-A or equivalent, to engine lifting eye.
14. Raise and support vehicle.
15. Remove starter cable from starter.
16. Remove air hose from catalytic converter.
17. Remove bolt securing exhaust pipe bracket to oil pan. Remove two exhaust pipes to exhaust manifold

nuts, then pull exhaust pipe out of rubber insulating grommets and position aside.
18. Disconnect speedometer cable from transaxle.
19. Remove water pump inlet hose from engine.
20. Remove bolts securing control arms to body. Remove stabilizer bar bracket bolts and brackets.
21. Remove halfshaft assembly from transaxle.

ALL APPLICATIONS

Fig. 5   Right hand No. 3A insulator. All

Fig. 6   Cylinder head bolt tightening sequence

Fig. 7   Front cover removal

22. On models equipped with manual transaxle, remove roll restrictor nuts from transaxle. Remove shift stabilizer bar to transaxle bolts. Remove shift mechanism to shift shaft nut and bolt from transaxle.
23. On models equipped with automatic transaxle, disconnect manual shift cable clip from transaxle shift lever. Remove manual shift linkage bracket bolts and bracket from transaxle.
24. Remove nuts and left hand rear No. 4 insulator mount bracket from body bracket.
25. Lower vehicle and install suitable lifting hoist to engine.

NOTE: Do not allow front wheels to touch floor.

26. Remove engine support tool No. D79L-6000-A or equivalent from engine.
27. Remove right hand No. 3 insulator intermediate bracket to engine bracket bolts and intermediate bracket to insulator nuts. Remove nut on the bottom of double ended stud which secures intermediate bracket to engine bracket. Remove bracket.
28. Carefully lower engine and transaxle assembly from vehicle.

CYLINDER HEAD
REPLACE

1. Disconnect battery ground cable.
2. Remove lower radiator hose and drain coolant from engine.
3. Disconnect heater hose from fitting located under intake manifold.
4. Disconnect upper radiator hose from cylinder head.
5. Disconnect electric cooling fan switch from electrical connector.
6. Remove air cleaner assembly from engine.
7. Mark and disconnect all vacuum hoses from cylinder head.
8. Remove rocker arm cover.
9. Remove all accessory drive belts from engine.
10. Remove distributor cap and spark plug wires as an assembly.

11. Disconnect EGR tube from EGR valve. Disconnect choke cap wire.
12. Disconnect fuel supply and return lines from rubber connector.
13. Disconnect accelerator cable and speed control cable, if equipped.
14. Loosen thermactor pump belt pulley.
15. Raise and support vehicle.
16. Disconnect exhaust system from exhaust pipe. Lower vehicle.
17. Remove cylinder head bolts, cylinder head and gasket with thermactor pump, exhaust and intake manifolds attached.

NOTE: Do not lay cylinder head flat. Damage to spark plugs or gasket surfaces may result.

18. Reverse procedure to install. Torque cylinder head bolts in sequence shown in **Fig. 6,** to 53–59 ft. lbs. on early 1984 production models, 81 ft. lbs on later production 1984 models or 70–76 ft. lbs on 1985–86 models.

VALVE ARRANGEMENT
FRONT TO REAR

4-140 . . . . I-E-I-E-I-E-I

HYDRAULIC VALVE LIFTERS
REPLACE

NOTE: Before replacing a hydraulic valve lifter for noisy operation, ensure the noise is not caused by improper collapsed tappet gap, worn rocker arms, pushrods or valve tips.

1. Remove cylinder head as described previously.
2. Using a suitable magnet, remove lifters from lifter bores.
3. Place valve lifters in a rack so they can be installed in their original positions.

NOTE: If the lifters are stuck in their bores by excessive varnish or gum buildup, use tool No. T70L-6500-A or equivalent to remove valve lifters.

4. Reverse procedure to install.

ROCKER ARM COVER
REPLACE

1. Disconnect battery ground cable.
2. Remove oil filler cap.
3. Disconnect PCV hose from PCV valve.
4. Disconnect throttle linkage cable from rocker arm cover.
5. Disconnect speed control cable from rocker arm cover, if equipped.
6. Remove rocker arm cover bolts and cover.
7. Reverse procedure to install.

FRONT COVER OIL SEAL
REMOVAL

NOTE: The following removal and installation procedure can only be performed with the engine removed from the vehicle. Remove engine as described under "Engine, Replace".

1. Remove bolt and washer from crankshaft pulley.
2. Using tool No. T77F-4220-B1 or equivalent, remove crankshaft pulley.
3. Using tool No. T74P-6700-A or equivalent, remove front cover oil seal.

INSTALLATION

1. Coat new front cover oil seal with a suitable lubricant.
2. Using tool No. T83T-4676-A or equivalent, install oil seal into front cover. Drive oil seal in until it is fully seated into front cover recess. Check oil seal after installation to ensure spring is properly positioned in oil seal.

Cylinder head assembly & components

1 VACUUM TUBE
2 VENT VALVE ASSEMBLY
3 TUBE ASSEMBLY
4 GROMMET
5 ROCKER ARM COVER
6 ROCKER ARM COVER GASKET
7 SPARK PLUG WIRES
8 DISTRIBUTOR CAP
9 FUEL LINES
10 FUEL LINES
11 FUEL FILTER
12 FUEL FILTER LINES
13 FUEL FILTER LINES
14 FUEL PUMP GASKET
15 FUEL PUMP ASSEMBLY

16 DIPSTICK
17 DIPSTICK TUBE ASSEMBLY
18 DISTRIBUTOR
19 CYLINDER HEAD BOLTS
20 ENGINE LIFTING EYE
21 SPARK PLUG
22 ROCKER ARM FULCRUM
23 ROCKER ARM
24 PUSHROD
25 EXHAUST VALVE STEM SEAL
26 KEY
27 SPRING RETAINER
28 SPRING
29 INTAKE VALVE STEM SEAL

30 TEMPERATURE SENSOR
31 FAN SWITCH
32 WATER OUTLET CONNECTION
33 WATER OUTLET CONNECTION GASKET
34 THERMOSTAT ASSEMBLY
35 INTAKE VALVE
36 EXHAUST VALVE
37 CYLINDER HEAD
38 CARBURETOR FUEL LINE
39 CARBURETOR ASSEMBLY
40 CARBURETOR GASKET
41 BRACKET
42 BRACKET
43 ACCELERATOR SHAFT BRACKET

44 EGR VALVE ASSEMBLY
45 EGR VALVE GASKET
46 VACUUM FITTING
47 SENSOR
48 VACUUM FITTING
49 BRACE
50 INTAKE MANIFOLD ASSEMBLY
51 VACUUM FITTING
52 TUBE ASSEMBLY
53 TUBE ASSEMBLY
54 EXHAUST MANIFOLD
55 HEAT SHIELD
56 CYLINDER BLOCK
57 CYLINDER HEAD GASKET

Cylinder block assembly & components

1 REINFORCEMENT PLATE
2 FLYWHEEL
3 REAR COVER PLATE
4 CAMSHAFT BEARING
5 CAMSHAFT BEARING
6 CAMSHAFT BEARING
7 COIL
8 TAPPET ASSEMBLY
9 CLAMP
10 ROTOR
11 DISTRIBUTOR ASSEMBLY
12 TUBE
13 OIL DIPSTICK
14 OIL FILTER
15 INSERT
16 OIL PRESSURE SWITCH

17 FUEL PUMP PUSHROD
18 FUEL PUMP GASKET
19 FUEL PUMP
20 RETAINER ASSEMBLY
21 COVER
22 GASKET
23 DOWEL
24 WATER PUMP ASSEMBLY
25 WATER PUMP GASKET
26 TENSIONER ASSEMBLY
27 CAMSHAFT
28 THRUST PLATE
29 CAMSHAFT SPROCKET
30 CRANKSHAFT SPROCKET
31 TIMING CHAIN ASSEMBLY
32 WASHER

33 TIMING CHAIN DAMPER
34 FRONT COVER GASKET
35 FRONT COVER
36 SEAL
37 CRANKSHAFT PULLEY ASSEMBLY
38 INTERMEDIATE DRIVESHAFT
39 OIL PUMP ASSEMBLY
40 PICK-UP TUBE GASKET
41 PICK-UP TUBE ASSEMBLY
42 UPPER MAIN BEARING
43 UPPER THRUST BEARING
44 UPPER MAIN BEARING FRONT
45 CRANKSHAFT
46 LOWER MAIN BEARING
47 REAR MAIN BEARING CAP
48 MAIN BEARING CAP

49 MAIN BEARING CAP
50 MAIN BEARING CAP
51 MAIN BEARING CAP FRONT
52 BOLT
53 OIL PAN ASSEMBLY
54 DRAIN PLUG
55 WASHER
56 PISTON RINGS
57 PISTON
58 PISTON PIN
59 CONNECTING ROD
60 STUD
61 ROD BEARINGS
62 ROD CAP
63 NUT

Fig. 8   Valve timing marks

3. Install crankshaft pulley, washer and bolt. Torque crankshaft pulley bolt to specification.

FRONT COVER, TIMING CHAIN & SPROCKETS
REPLACE

NOTE: The following procedure can only be performed with the engine removed from the vehicle. Remove engine as described under "Engine, Replace".

1. Remove dipstick, crankshaft pulley bolt, washer and pulley.
2. Remove front cover bolts and front cover, **Fig. 7**.
3. Align camshaft and crankshaft sprocket timing marks as shown in **Fig. 8.**
4. Remove camshaft sprocket bolt and washer.
5. Remove sprockets and timing chain from engine as an assembly, **Fig. 9**. Check timing chain vibration damper for wear. Replace if necessary.
6. Remove oil pan.
7. Reverse procedure to install. Ensure to align timing marks as shown in **Fig. 7.**

CAMSHAFT
REPLACE

NOTE: The following procedure can only be performed with the engine removed from the vehicle. Remove engine as described under "Engine, Replace".

1. Remove dipstick. Drain coolant and oil from engine.
2. Remove accessory drive belts and pulleys.
3. Position No. 1 piston at TDC with distributor rotor at No. 1 firing position, then remove distributor.
4. Remove cylinder head as described under "Cylinder Head, Replace".
5. Using a suitable magnet, remove hydraulic tappets and position in order so that they can be installed in their original locations. If tappets are stuck in their bores, use tool No. T70L-6500A or equivalent to remove tappets.

Fig. 9   Timing chain & sprockets removal

6. Loosen then remove fan drive belt, fan and crankshaft pulley.
7. Remove front cover as described under "Front Cover, Timing Chain & Sprockets, Replace".
8. Remove fuel pump, gasket and fuel pump push rod.
9. Remove timing chain, sprockets and timing chain tensioner as described under "Front Cover, Timing Chain & Sprockets, Replace".
10. Remove camshaft thrust plate. Carefully remove camshaft from engine to avoid damaging camshaft bearings, journals and lobes.
11. Reverse procedure to install. Lubricate camshaft with suitable oil before installing. Ensure No. 1 piston is at TDC with distributor rotor at No. 1 firing position.

MAIN BEARINGS

Main bearings are available in standard sizes and undersizes of .010, .020, .030 and .040 inch.

CRANKSHAFT REAR OIL SEAL
REPLACE

1. Remove engine and transaxle from vehicle as described under "Engine, Replace".
2. Remove transaxle from engine.
3. Remove rear cover plate.
4. Using a suitable tool, punch a hole into the seal metal surface between the lip and block. Using Tool No. T77L-9533-B or equivalent, remove seal.
5. Reverse procedure to install.

INTAKE & EXHAUST MANIFOLD
REPLACE

1. Disconnect battery ground cable and drain coolant from engine.

2. Disconnect accelerator cable.
3. Remove air cleaner assembly and heat stove duct from heat shield.
4. Disconnect all vacuum lines from intake manifold.
5. Remove thermactor belt from pulley, thermactor hose and thermactor pump from engine.
6. Remove exhaust pipe to exhaust manifold nuts and disconnect exhaust pipe from exhaust manifold.
7. Remove exhaust manifold heat shield.
8. Disconnect EGO sensor electrical connector.
9. Disconnect thermactor check valve hose from tube assembly. Remove EGR valve bracket nuts and EGR valve bracket.
10. Disconnect water inlet hose from intake manifold.
11. Disconnect EGR hose from EGR valve.
12. Remove bolts, intake manifold and gasket from engine.
13. Remove bolts and exhaust manifold from engine.
14. Reverse procedure to install. Torque exhaust manifold bolts in two steps. Torque bolts in sequence shown in **Fig. 10** to 7–10 ft. lbs., then 20–30 ft. lbs. Torque intake manifold bolts in sequence shown in **Fig. 11** to 15–23 ft. lbs.

OIL PAN
REPLACE

1. Disconnect battery ground cable.
2. Raise and support vehicle.
3. Drain coolant and oil from engine.
4. On models equipped with manual transaxle, remove roll restrictor.
5. Remove starter from engine.
6. Disconnect exhaust pipe from oil pan.
7. Remove engine coolant tube located at the lower radiator hose, at the water pump and from tabs on oil pan.
8. Remove oil pan bolts and oil pan, **Fig. 12,** from engine.
9. Reverse procedure to install.

Fig. 10   Exhaust manifold bolt tightening sequence

Fig. 11   Intake manifold bolt tightening sequence

Fig. 13   Oil pump removal

Fig. 12   Oil pan removal

OIL PUMP
REPLACE

1. Disconnect battery ground cable.
2. Remove oil pan as described under "Oil Pan, Replace".
3. Remove oil pump bolts and oil pump, **Fig. 13**, from engine. Remove intermediate driveshaft from oil pump.
4. Reverse procedure to install.

WATER PUMP
REPLACE

1. Disconnect battery ground cable and drain coolant from engine.
2. Loosen thermactor pump adjusting bolt and remove belt.
3. Remove thermactor air pump hose clamp, thermactor pump bracket bolts, pump and bracket assembly from engine.
4. Loosen water pump idler pulley bolt and remove belt from water pump pulley.
5. Remove water pump inlet tube.
6. Remove water pump bolts and water pump, **Fig. 14**.
7. Reverse procedure to install.

FUEL PUMP
REPLACE

NOTE: Fuel supply lines will remain pressurized for long periods of time after engine shut-down. This pressure must be relieved before any service is attempted. A valve is provided on the fuel rail assembly for this purpose. To relieve system pressure, remove air cleaner assembly and connect pressure gauge tool No. T80L-9974-A or equivalent onto fuel valve on fuel rail assembly.

1. Disconnect battery ground cable.
2. Depressurize fuel system as described previously.
3. Remove fuel from fuel tank by pumping fuel out of fuel filler neck.
4. Raise and support vehicle.
5. Disconnect then remove fuel filler neck.
6. Support fuel tank, then remove tank support straps. Lower fuel tank partially and remove fuel lines, electrical connectors and vent lines from tank.
7. Turn fuel pump locking ring counterclockwise and remove locking ring.
8. Remove fuel pump, bracket and gasket assembly.
9. Reverse procedure to install. To pressurize fuel system, proceed as follows:
   a. Install pressure gauge tool No. T80L-9974-A or equivalent onto fuel rail pressure fitting.
   b. Turn ignition switch to ON position for 3 seconds, repeatedly 5 to 10 times until pressure gauge indicates 13 psi.

-8507-
GASKET

FRONT OF
ENGINE

-8501-
WATER PUMP
ASSEMBLY

M8 X 1.25 X 25.0 BOLT

M8 X 1.25 X 90.0 BOLT

Fig. 14 Water pump removal

BELT TENSION DATA

	New Lbs.	Used Lbs.
Alternator, Power Steering & Air Conditioning	150–190	140–160
Water Pump & Air Pump	50–90	40–60

ENGINE MOUNTS

Refer to **Fig. 1** when replacing the engine mounts.

ENGINE
REPLACE

NOTE: Engine and transaxle are removed from vehicle as an assembly.

1. Disconnect battery ground cable located in luggage compartment.
2. Remove air cleaner assembly.
3. Remove lower radiator hose, then drain coolant from engine.
4. Disconnect cooling fan electrical connector.
5. Remove radiator shroud, cooling fan and radiator from vehicle.
6. Remove starter cable from starter.
7. Carefully discharge refrigerant from air conditioning system, if equipped.

Disconnect pressure and return lines from compressor.
8. Mark then disconnect all electrical and vacuum lines from engine.
9. Disconnect clutch cable from transaxle shift lever.
10. Disconnect injection pump throttle linkage. Disconnect fuel supply and return lines from engine.
11. Disconnect power steering pressure and return lines from power steering pump, if equipped. Remove power

PART NO.	DESCRIPTION			
1	6B712	NUT	14	6051	GASKET
2	99239-0516	WOODRUFF KEY	15	6049	HEAD ASSEMBLY (CYLINDER)
3	6700	SEAL	16	6K258	STUD (CAMSHAFT BEARING CAP
4	6250	CAMSHAFT	17	6515	SHIM, VALVE ADJUSTING
5	6065	BOLT	18	6500	TAPPET ASSEMBLY
6	9A451	GLOW PLUG HARNESS	19	6518	KEY (VALVE SPRING RETAINING)
7	9A564	FUEL RETURN PIPE	20	6514	RETAINER
8	9K540	WASHER	21	6513	SPRING
9	9E527	INJECTOR NOZZLE	22	6A536	VALVE SPRING SEAT
10	9E529	WASHER	23	6571	VALVE STEM SEAL
11	9C991	GASKET	24	6510	VALVE GUIDE ASSEMBLY
12	12A342	GLOW PLUG	25	6505	EXHAUST VALVE
13	6057	INSERT ASSEMBLY (COMBUSTION CHAMBER)	26	6507	INTAKE VALVE

Cylinder head & components

Fig. 1 Engine mount assembly

PART NO.	DESCRIPTION			
1	6A008	DOWEL PIN (CYLINDER HEAD TO CYLINDER BLOCK)	10	6211	BEARING, ROD
2	6010	BLOCK ASSEMBLY (CYLINDER)	11	6C327	OIL JET ASSEMBLY (PISTON COOLING)
3	6754 (LOWER)	TUBE ASSEMBLY (OIL LEVEL INDICATOR)	12	6K757	BOLT
4	6148	PISTON RINGS	13	6333	BEARING, MAIN
5	6135	PISTON PIN	14	6334	BEARING, THRUST
6	6108	PISTON	15	6337	BEARING, MAIN
7	6214	BOLT	16	6303	CRANKSHAFT
8	6200	ROD ASSEMBLY	17	6701	SEAL (CRANKSHAFT REAR OIL)
9	6212	NUT	18	6345	BOLT

Cylinder block & components

steering line bracket from cylinder head.
12. Install engine support tool D79P-6000A or equivalent to engine lifting eye.
13. Raise and support vehicle.
14. Remove bolt securing exhaust pipe bracket to oil pan. Remove exhaust pipe to exhaust manifold nuts, then disconnect exhaust pipe from exhaust manifold.
15. Disconnect speedometer cable from transaxle.
16. Disconnect heater hoses from heater

and oil cooler.
17. Remove bolts securing control arms to body. Remove stabilizer bar bracket bolts and bracket.
18. Remove halfshaft assembly from transaxle.
19. On models equipped with manual transaxle, remove shift stabilizer bar to transaxle bolts. Remove shift shaft nut and bolt from transaxle.
20. Remove lefthand rear No. 4 insulator mount bracket nuts and bracket from body bracket.
21. Remove lefthand front No. 1 insulator

to transaxle mounting bolts.
22. Lower vehicle. Do not allow front wheels to touch floor.
23. Remove engine support tool D79P-6000A from engine lifting eye.
24. Remove righthand No. 3A insulator intermediate bracket to engine bracket bolts, intermediate bracket to insulator nuts and bottom nut of double ended stud securing intermediate bracket to engine bracket. Remove bracket.
25. Lower engine and transaxle from vehicle.
26. Reverse procedure to install.

PART NO.	DESCRIPTION			
1	6E006	COVER ASSEMBLY (TIMING BELT REAR OUTER)	12 6766	CAP ASSEMBLY (OIL FILLER)
2	6268	BELT (TIMING)	13 6584	GASKET
3	6K252	BOLT	14 8501	WATER PUMP
4	6278	WASHER	15 6019	COVER ASSEMBLY (TIMING BELT)
5	6256	SPROCKET, CAMSHAFT	16 6020	SEAL (TIMING BELT COVER)
6	6K254	TENSIONER (TIMING BELT)	17 6K282	BOLT
7	6L273	SPRING (TENSIONER)	18 6306	SPROCKET, CRANKSHAFT
8	9M564	SPROCKET, INJECTION PUMP	19 6378	WASHER
9	6K291	SPACER	20 6A340	BOLT
10	6E004	COVER ASSEMBLY (TIMING BELT REAR INNER)	21 6A312	PULLEY ASSEMBLY (CRANKSHAFT)
11	6582	COVER ASSEMBLY (VALVE ROCKER ARM)		

Timing belt, sprockets & related components

CYLINDER HEAD & PRE-CHAMBER
REPLACE

1. Disconnect battery ground cable and drain cooling system.
2. Remove camshaft cover, front and rear timing belt covers and belts.
3. Raise and support vehicle.
4. Disconnect exhaust pipe from exhaust manifold.
5. Lower vehicle.
6. Remove air inlet duct from air cleaner and intake manifold. Install cap, **Fig. 2,** onto intake manifold.
7. Disconnect all electrical connectors and vacuum hoses from temperature sensors.

8. Remove upper and lower coolant hoses and upper radiator hose from thermostat housing.
9. Remove injection lines from injection pump and nozzles. Cap all lines and fittings with cap set No. T84P-9395 or equivalent, **Fig. 3.**
10. Disconnect glow plug harness from engine harness.
11. Loosen cylinder head bolts in sequence shown in **Fig. 4,** then remove cylinder head.
12. Remove glow plugs.
13. Using a brass drift and hammer, remove pre-chambers from cylinder head, **Fig. 5.**
14. Clean pre-chamber cups, pre-chambers, cylinder head and crankcase gasket surfaces.

15. Install pre-chambers into cylinder head. Ensure pins are aligned with slots, **Fig. 5.**
16. Install glow plugs and torque to specification. Note the following:
   a. Using compressed air, blow out cylinder head bolt threads in crankcase.
   b. Install new cylinder head gasket. Ensure cylinder head oil feed hole is not restricted, **Fig. 6.**
   c. Measure dimension A, **Fig. 7,** of each cylinder head bolt. If dimension A is more than 4.5 in., replace cylinder head bolt.
   d. Rotate camshaft until both intake and exhaust valves for No. 1 cylinder are closed. Rotate crankshaft clockwise until No. 1 piston is half-

PART NO.		DESCRIPTION
1	9C674	INLET, AIR
2	12A344	
3	8575	THERMOSTAT
4	8B607	TEMPERATURE SENSOR
5	8A564	TEMPERATURE SWITCH, VACUUM
6	6A664	HOSE
7	9439	GASKET, INTAKE
8	18472	HOSE
9	9B552	BRACKET, INJECTION PUMP
10	9A543	INJECTION PUMP
11	9B552	BRACKET, INJECTION PUMP
12	9A555	FUEL LINES
13	6B850	HOSE ASSEMBLY (OIL BY-PASS INLET)
14	6B856	OIL COOLER ASSEMBLY
15	6K834	ENGINE OIL COOLER ASSEMBLY
16	6731	OIL FILTER ASSEMBLY
17	18B402	TUBE, COOLANT
18	9448	GASKET, EXHAUST
19	9430	MANIFOLD, EXHAUST
20	9A462	SHIELD, MANIFOLD
21	9424	MANIFOLD, INTAKE
22	8255	GASKET
23	8592	HOUSING, THERMOSTAT

Intake manifold, exhaust manifold & injection pump components

way up in the cylinder bore toward TDC.

e. Install cylinder head.

f. Before installing cylinder head bolts, paint a white reference mark on each bolt, **Fig. 8,** then apply a light coat of clean engine oil to bolt threads.

g. Torque cylinder head bolts in sequence shown in **Fig. 9** to 22 ft. lbs. Using the painted reference marks, tighten each cylinder head bolt in sequence an additional 90°,

Fig. 8. Tighten cylinder head bolts another 90° to complete cylinder head bolt installation.

17. Reverse procedure to install.

INTAKE MANIFOLD
REPLACE

1. Disconnect battery ground cable and drain cooling system.
2. Remove air inlet duct from air cleaner and intake manifold. Install cap, **Fig.**

2, onto intake manifold.
3. Disconnect resistor electrical connectors from glow plugs.
4. Remove breather hose from engine and upper radiator hose from thermostat housing.
5. Disconnect upper and lower coolant hoses from thermostat housing.
6. Disconnect electrical connectors from temperature sensors.
7. Remove intake manifold to cylinder head bolts, then the intake manifold.
8. Reverse procedure to install.

Fig. 2   Intake manifold removal

Fig. 5   Pre-chamber removal

Fig. 6   Cylinder head gasket installation

Fig. 3   Injection nozzle protective cap set

Fig. 4   Cylinder head bolt loosening sequence

DIMENSION A
NEW: 113 ± 0.03 mm
(4.45 ± 0.01 INCH)
USED MAX.: 114.5 mm (4.51 INCHES)

Fig. 7   Cylinder head bolt dimension A

EXHAUST MANIFOLD
REPLACE

1. Disconnect battery ground cable.
2. Disconnect exhaust pipe from exhaust manifold.
3. Remove bolts securing heat shield to exhaust manifold.
4. Remove exhaust manifold to cylinder head nuts, then the exhaust manifold.
5. Reverse procedure to install.

VALVES
ADJUST

1. Disconnect breather hose from intake manifold and remove camshaft cover.
2. Rotate crankshaft until No. 1 piston is at TDC.
3. Using a suitable feeler gauge, check valve shim to cam lobe clearance for Nos. 1 and 2 intake valves and Nos. 1 and 3 exhaust valves, **Fig. 10**. Intake valve clearance should be .008–.011 in., exhaust valves clearance should be .011–.015 in.
4. Rotate crankshaft one complete revolution. Measure valve clearance for Nos. 3 and 4 intake valves and Nos. 2 and 4 exhaust valves. If measured clearance is not to specification, proceed as follows:

a. Rotate crankshaft until lobe of valve to be adjusted is facing downward.
b. Install cam follower retainer tool No. T84P-6513B or equivalent as shown in **Fig. 11**.
c. Rotate crankshaft until cam lobe is on base circle as shown in **Fig. 12**. Using tool No. T71P-19703C or equivalent, pry valve adjusting shim out of the cam follower, **Fig. 12**.

NOTE: Valve shims are available in thicknesses ranging from .134–.181 in. (3.40–4.60mm)

If the valve was tight, select a shim with a smaller thickness. If the valve was loose, select a shim with a larger thickness.

Fig. 8   Cylinder head bolt tightening steps

Fig. 9   Cylinder head bolt tightening sequence

Fig. 10   Checking valve clearance

Fig. 11 Installing cam follower retainer

Fig. 12 Positioning cam lobe on base circle for valve shim removal

Fig. 13 Valve shim sizes

NOTE: Shim thickness is stamped on valve shim, **Fig. 13.** Install shim with numbers facing downward.

5. Rotate crankshaft until cam lobe is facing downward and remove cam follower retainer.
6. Recheck valve clearance. Repeat steps 2 thru 4 for each valve to be adjusted.

CAMSHAFT
REPLACE

1. Disconnect battery ground cable.
2. Disconnect breather hose from camshaft cover.
3. Remove camshaft cover bolts, then the camshaft cover.
4. Remove flywheel timing mark cover from clutch housing.
5. Rotate crankshaft until No. 1 cylinder is at TDC.
6. Remove front and rear timing belt covers.
7. Loosen front timing belt tensioner, then remove timing belt from camshaft sprocket.
8. Install an adjustable wrench onto camshaft boss, then loosen front camshaft sprocket bolt.
9. Hold camshaft with wrench then remove rear camshaft sprocket bolt.
10. Using tool Nos. T77F-4220B1 and D80L-625-4 or equivalents, remove camshaft sprockets. Retain camshaft sprocket woodruff keys.
11. Remove No. 1, 3 and 5 camshaft bearing caps.
12. Remove No. 2 and 4 camshaft bearing caps as follows:
    a. Loosen one of the camshaft bearing nuts two or three turns.
    b. Loosen the remaining camshaft bearing nuts one at a time, two or three turns.
    c. Repeat steps 12a and 12b, turning each nut two or three turns at a time, until all camshaft bearing cap nuts are loose.
13. Remove camshaft and discard camshaft seals.
14. Remove cam followers and note their

location for installation in their original positions.
15. Reverse procedure to install. For installation of camshaft bearings, proceed as follows:

NOTE: Install camshaft bearings with arrows pointing toward front of engine. No. 2, 3 and 4 camshaft bearing caps have their numbers stamped on the top surface of the bearing cap. No. 1 and 5 bearing caps are not marked. No. 1 bearing cap has a slot to fit over camshaft thrust flange.

    a. Install No. 2 and 4 bearing caps, tightening one of the nuts two or three turns.
    b. Tighten the remaining nuts one at a time, two or three turns.
    c. Repeat steps 15a and 15b, turning each nut two or three turns at a time until No. 2 and 4 bearing caps are seated.
    d. Install No. 1, 3 and 5 bearing caps, and torque nuts to 15–19 ft. lbs.

FRONT TIMING BELT
REMOVAL

1. With engine removed from vehicle, remove front timing belt upper cover bolts, then the upper cover.
2. Install flywheel holding tool T84P-6375 or equivalent onto flywheel.
3. Remove crankshaft pulley to crankshaft sprocket bolts.
4. Using tool Nos. T58P-6316 and T74P-6700B or equivalents, remove crankshaft pulley.
5. Remove front timing belt lower cover bolts, then the lower cover. Loosen tensioner pulley, then remove timing belt.

INSTALLATION

1. Align camshaft sprocket with timing marks as shown in **Fig. 14.**

NOTE: Ensure crankshaft sprocket timing marks are aligned, **Fig. 15.**

2. Remove tensioner spring from front timing belt upper cover, then install spring into tensioner lever slot and over crankcase stud, **Fig. 16.**
3. Push tensioner lever toward water pump and tighten lock bolt.
4. Install timing belt as shown in **Fig. 14.** Adjust timing belt as described in "FRONT TIMING BELT, ADJUST".
5. Install front timing belt lower cover. Torque lower cover bolts to 5–7 ft. lbs.
6. Install crankshaft pulley. Torque pulley bolts to 17–24 ft. lbs.
7. Install front timing belt upper cover. Torque upper cover bolts to 5–7 ft. lbs.

REAR TIMING BELT
REPLACE

1. With engine removed from vehicle, remove rear timing belt cover bolts, then the rear cover.
2. Remove flywheel timing mark cover from clutch housing.
3. Rotate crankshaft until flywheel timing mark is at TDC on No. 1 cylinder, **Fig. 17.**

NOTE: Ensure injection pump and camshaft sprocket timing marks are aligned with their marks, **Fig. 18.**

4. Loosen tensioner locknut. Using a suitable tool, insert tool into tensioner slot, **Fig. 19.** Rotate tensioner clockwise, then tighten lock nut.
5. Remove rear timing belt.
6. Install rear timing belt as shown in **Fig. 20.**
7. Loosen tensioner lock nut and adjust timing belt as described under "REAR TIMING BELT, ADJUST".
8. Install rear timing belt cover. Torque the 6mm rear cover bolts to 5–9 ft. lbs., torque the 8mm rear cover bolts to 12–16 ft. lbs.

FRONT TIMING BELT
ADJUST

1. Remove flywheel timing mark cover.
2. Remove front timing belt upper cover.
3. Remove timing belt tension spring from front cover.
4. Install tensioner spring into belt tensioner lever and over crankcase stud, **Fig. 16.**
5. Loosen tensioner pulley lock bolt.
6. Rotate crankshaft pulley two revolutions clockwise until flywheel TDC timing mark aligns with pointer on rear cover plate, **Fig. 17.**

Fig. 14 Front timing belt installation

NOTE: TIMING BELT LOWER COVER REMOVED FOR CLARITY.

Fig. 15 Crankshaft pulley timing marks

Fig. 16 Front timing belt tensioner spring installation

Fig. 17 Flywheel timing marks

NOTE: Ensure front camshaft sprocket is aligned with its timing mark, **Fig. 21.**

7. Torque tensioner lock bolt to 23–34 ft. lbs. Using a suitable belt tension gauge, check belt tension, **Fig. 14.** Belt tension should be 33–44 lbs.
8. Remove tensioner spring and install spring into front cover.
9. Install front cover. Torque front cover bolts to 5–7 ft. lbs.
10. Install flywheel timing mark cover.

REAR TIMING BELT
ADJUST

1. Remove flywheel timing mark cover.
2. Remove rear timing belt cover.
3. Rotate crankshaft pulley two revolutions clockwise until flywheel TDC timing mark aligns with pointer on rear cover plate, **Fig. 17.**

NOTE: Ensure injection pump and camshaft sprocket timing marks are aligned with their marks, **Fig. 18.**

Fig. 18 Camshaft and injection pump timing marks

4. Torque tensioner lock nut to 15–20 ft. lbs.
5. Using a suitable belt tension gauge, check belt tension, **Fig. 20.** Belt tension should be 22–33 lbs.
6. Install rear timing belt cover. Torque the 6mm rear cover bolts to 5–9 ft. lbs., torque the 8mm rear cover bolts to 12–16 ft. lbs.
7. Install flywheel timing mark cover.

INJECTION PUMP
REPLACE

1. Disconnect battery ground cable located in luggage compartment.
2. Disconnect air inlet duct from air cleaner and intake manifold. Install cap, **Fig. 2,** onto intake manifold.

Fig. 19 Loosening tensioner pulley

3. Remove rear timing belt cover and flywheel timing mark cover.
4. Remove rear timing belt as described under "REAR TIMING BELT, REPLACE".
5. Disconnect throttle and speed control cable, if equipped.
6. Disconnect vacuum lines from altitude compensator and cold start diaphragm.
7. Disconnect fuel supply and return lines from injection pump.
8. Disconnect electrical connector from fuel cut-off solenoid.
9. Remove injection lines from injection pump and nozzles. Cap all lines and fittings with cap set No. T84P-9395 or equivalent, **Fig. 3.**

Fig. 20   Rear timing belt tensioner

Fig. 21   Camshaft timing mark

Fig. 22   Injection pump sprocket removal

Fig. 23   Piston alignment

Fig. 24   Connecting rod cap alignment marks

an "F" mark, **Fig. 23,** on piston toward front of engine. Connecting rods have alignment marks stamped on one side of main bearing bore boss, **Fig. 24.** After piston and connecting rod assemblies have been installed, check side clearance between connecting rods on each crankshaft journal. Clearance should be .0043–.0103 inch.

MAIN & ROD BEARINGS

Main bearings are available in standard size and undersizes of .010, .020 and .030 inch. Connecting rod bearings are available in standard sizes and undersizes of .003, .010, .020, and .030 inch.

CRANKSHAFT REAR OIL SEAL
REPLACE

1. Disconnect battery ground cable.
2. Remove transaxle and clutch assemblies from engine.
3. Install flywheel holding tool No. T84P-6375A or equivalent, and remove flywheel bolts and flywheel.
4. Remove oil seal from crankshaft.
5. Reverse procedure to install.

OIL PAN
REPLACE

1. Disconnect battery ground cable.
2. Raise and support vehicle.
3. Remove oil pan bolts, then the oil pan.
4. Reverse procedure to install.

10. Rotate injection pump sprocket until injection pump and camshaft sprocket timing marks align with their marks, **Fig. 18.**
11. Install two M8 × 1.25 bolts into injection pump sprocket holes, **Fig. 22,** to secure injection pump sprocket. Remove injection pump sprocket bolt.
12. Using tool Nos. T77F-4220B1 and D80L-625-4 or equivalents, remove injection pump sprocket.
13. Remove bolt securing injection pump to pump front bracket.
14. Remove injection pump nuts, then the injection pump.
15. Reverse procedure to install.

PISTON & ROD ASSEMBLE

Pistons are available in standard size and oversize of .020 in. Install piston with

OIL PUMP
REPLACE

1. Disconnect battery ground cable.
2. With engine removed from vehicle, remove accessory drive belts.
3. Drain engine oil and remove oil pan.
4. Remove crankshaft pulley, front timing belt, front timing belt tensioner and crankshaft sprocket.
5. Remove bolts securing oil pump to crankcase, then the oil pump.
6. Reverse procedure to install.

BELT TENSION DATA

	New Lbs.	Used Lbs.
Alternator Exc. V ribbed	120–160	110–130
Power Steering & Air Conditioning	150–190	140–160

Clutch & Manual Transaxle Section

CLUTCH
ADJUST

The cable operated clutch control system, **Fig. 1**, is self adjusting and periodic adjustments are not required. If the clutch cable is replaced for any reason, an initial adjustment is performed by pulling the clutch pedal to its full upward position.

CLUTCH
REPLACE

1. Remove transmission as described under "Manual Transaxle, Replace" procedure.
2. Loosen pressure plate cover attaching bolts evenly to avoid distorting cover. If same pressure plate and cover are to be installed, mark cover and flywheel so pressure plate can be installed in original position.
3. Remove pressure plate and clutch disc from flywheel, **Fig. 2**.
4. Position clutch disc and pressure plate onto flywheel with flatter side of clutch disc facing toward flywheel.
5. Ensure three dowel pins on flywheel are aligned with dowel pins on pressure plate.
6. Snug tighten cover attaching bolts, then align clutch disc using tool T81P-7550A or equivalent. Torque bolts to 12–24 ft. lbs. (17–32 N.m.).
7. Remove alignment tool, then install transaxle and perform initial clutch adjustment.

GEARSHIFT LINKAGE
ADJUST

Adjustment of the external gearshift linkage is not necessary and no provision is made for adjustment, **Fig. 3**.

MANUAL TRANSAXLE
REPLACE

4 SPEED

Except Tempo & Topaz
1. Disconnect battery ground cable.
2. Remove 2 top transaxle to engine mounting bolts.
3. Grasp and pull clutch cable forward, disconnecting cable from clutch release lever.
4. Remove clutch cable casing from rib on the top surface of transaxle case.
5. Raise and support vehicle.
6. Remove brake hose routing clip to suspension strut bracket mounting bolt.
7. Remove bolt securing lower control arm ball joint onto steering knuckle assembly. Pry lower control arm away from knuckle.

8. Using tool No. D83P-4026-A or equivalent, pry right inboard CV joint assembly from transaxle.
9. Remove inner CV joint from transaxle by grasping right hand steering knuckle and swing knuckle and shaft outward from transaxle.
10. Wire halfshaft assembly in level position to prevent over-extending CV joint.
11. Repeat steps 8 through 10 on left inboard CV joint assembly.

NOTE: If the CV joint cannot be pried from the transaxle, insert tool T81P-4026-A or equivalent through right side of case and tap CV joint out.

12. Remove both front stabilizer bar to

control arm attaching nut and washer.
13. Remove 2 front stabilizer bar mounting brackets, then the stabilizer bar.
14. Disconnect speedometer cable from transaxle.
15. Disconnect back-up light switch electrical connector from transaxle switch.
16. Remove clutch housing stiffener brace attaching bolts.
17. Remove shift mechanism stabilizer bar to transaxle attaching bolt.
18. Disconnect then remove transaxle control selector indicator switch and bracket.
19. Remove shift mechanism to shift shaft attaching bolt, then the shift mechanism.
20. Position a suitable jack under transaxle assembly.
21. Loosen rear mount stud nut, then

Fig. 1   Clutch linkage

Fig. 2   Clutch assembly

DISASSEMBLED VIEW

FRONT OF VEHICLE

1. KNOB – GEAR SHIFT LEVER
2. NUT – SHIFT KNOB LOCKING
3. UPPER BOOT ASSEMBLY – GEAR SHIFT LEVER
4. SCREW – TAPPING (4 REQUIRED)
5. LOWER BOOT ASSEMBLY – GEAR SHIFT LEVER
6. BOOT RETAINER ASSEMBLY – GEAR SHIFT LEVER
7. BOLT – BOOT RETAINER (4 REQUIRED)
8. NUT – SPRING (4 REQUIRED)
9. LEVER ASSEMBLY – GEARSHIFT
10. BOLT – TAPPING (4 REQUIRED)
11. SCREW – TAPPING (4 REQUIRED)
12. SUPPORT ASSEMBLY (SHIFT STABILIZER BAR)
13. BUSHING – GEAR SHIFT STABILIZER BAR

14. SLEEVE – GEAR SHIFT ROD
15. SCREW – TAPPING (2 REQUIRED)
16. COVER – CONTROL SELECTOR
17. BUSHING – ANTI TIZZ
18. HOUSING – CONTROL SELECTOR
19. ASSEMBLY – SHIFT ROD AND CLEVIS
20. ASSEMBLY – CLAMP
21. CLAMP – GEAR SHIFT LEVER (2 REQUIRED)
22. NUT – CLAMP ASSEMBLY
23. RETAINING SPRING – GEAR SHIFT TUBE
24. BOLT -- STABILIZER BAR ATTACHING
25. WASHER – FLAT (2 REQUIRED)
26. ASSEMBLY – NUT/WASHER (4 REQUIRED)

Fig. 3 Gearshift linkage

remove bottom rear mount attaching bolt.
22. Remove 3 bolts securing front mount to transaxle case.
23. Lower transaxle slightly until transaxle clears rear mount.
24. Position a suitable jack under engine oil pan.
25. Remove remaining 4 transaxle to engine attaching bolts.
26. Lower transaxle from vehicle.
27. Reverse procedure to install.

NOTE: During installation of transaxle assembly, ensure transaxle is flush with rear face of engine before installing and tightening attaching bolts.

Tempo & Topaz
1. Disconnect battery ground cable.
2. Position a suitable block of wood approximately 7 inches of length under clutch pedal to hold clutch pedal up.
3. Grasp and pull clutch cable forward, disconnecting cable from clutch release shaft lever assembly.
4. Remove clutch casing from top rib of transaxle case.
5. Remove 2 top transaxle to engine attaching bolts.
6. Remove air cleaner assembly.
7. Raise and support vehicle, then remove front stabilizer bar to control arm

attaching nut and washer.
8. Remove stabilizer bar mounting brackets.
9. Remove nut and bolt attaching lower control ball joint to steering knuckle assembly.
10. Using a suitable tool, pry lower control arm away from steering knuckle.
11. Using tool D83P-4026-A or equivalent, pry left inboard CV joint assembly from transaxle. Remove inboard CV joint from transaxle by grasping the lefthand steering knuckle and swinging the knuckle and halfshaft outward from transaxle.

NOTE: If the CV joint cannot be pried from transaxle, insert tool T81P-4026-A or equivalent through right side of case and tap CV joint out.

12. Wire halfshaft assembly in level position to prevent over-extending CV joint.
13. Repeat steps 10 through 12 for other CV joint.
14. Remove back-up light switch electrical connector from transaxle.
15. Remove starter motor and position aside.
16. Remove engine roll restrictor.
17. Remove shift mechanism, shift indicator and bracket assembly.

18. Disconnect speedometer cable from transaxle.
19. Remove oil pan to clutch housing stiffener brace attaching bolts.
20. Position a suitable jack under transaxle assembly.
21. Remove 2 nuts securing lefthand rear No. 4 insulator to body bracket.
22. Remove bolts securing lefthand front No. 1 insulator to body bracket.
23. Lower transaxle slightly until transaxle clears rear mount.
24. Position a suitable jack under engine.
25. Remove 4 transaxle to engine attaching bolts.
26. Lower transaxle from vehicle.
27. Reverse procedure to install.

5 SPEED

1. Disconnect battery ground cable and drain transaxle fluid.
2. Wedge a seven inch wood block under clutch pedal.
3. Disconnect clutch cable from clutch release shaft assembly, then remove the clutch cable casing from rib on top surface of transaxle case.
4. Remove two top transaxle to engine mounting bolts.
5. Remove top bolt that secures air management valve bracket to transaxle.
6. Raise vehicle, then remove lower control arm ball joint to steering knuckle attaching nut and bolt. Discard nut and bolt and repeat procedure on opposite side.
7. Pry lower control arm from knuckle on both sides of vehicle using suitable pry bar. Use care not to damage or cut ball joint.
8. Pry left inboard CV joint assembly from transaxle using suitable pry bar.

NOTE: Lubricant will drain from the seal at this time. Install two plugs.

9. Remove inboard CV joint from transaxle. Repeat procedure on other side.

NOTE: If the CV joint assembly cannot be pried from the transaxle, insert tool T81P-4026-A or other suitable tool through the left side and tap the joint out. Tool can be used from either side of the transaxle.

10. Wire left and right half shaft assemblies in level position.
11. Remove backup lamp switch connector from transaxle backup lamp switch.
12. Remove engine roll restrictor bracket.
13. Remove three heater pipe bracket attaching screws, then remove engine roll restrictor.
14. Remove starter.
15. Disconnect shift mechanism from shaft.
16. Disconnect and remove control selector indicator switch arm from shift shaft.
17. Remove shift mechanism stabilizer bar to transaxle attaching bolt, then remove control selector indicator switch and bracket.

18. Remove speedometer cable from transaxle.
19. Remove two stiffener brace attaching bolts from lower position of clutch housing.
20. Position a jack under transaxle.
21. Remove two rear mount and air management valve to transaxle securing bolts, then remove three bolts attaching front mount to transaxle.
22. Lower transaxle support jack until

transaxle clears rear mount and support engine with suitable jack. Use a suitable piece of wood between the jack and engine.
23. Remove remaining four engine-to-transaxle attaching bolts.
24. Remove transaxle from rear face of the engine and lower it from vehicle.

NOTE: The transaxle case casting may

have sharp edges. Wear protective gloves when handling the transaxle assembly.

25. Reverse procedure to install. Torque the following as specified, engine-to-transaxle bolts 26–31 ft. lbs., front transaxle mount bolts 25–35 ft. lbs., rear transaxle mount bolts 40–51 ft. lbs., starter stud bolts 30–40 ft. lbs., starter nuts 25–30 ft. lbs.

Rear Suspension & Brakes Section

DESCRIPTION
EXCEPT TEMPO & TOPAZ

These vehicles use a modified MacPherson strut independent rear suspension, **Fig. 1.** Each side consists of a shock strut, lower control arm, tie rod, spindle and a coil spring mounted between the lower control arm and body crossmember side rail.

TEMPO & TOPAZ

These vehicles use a new MacPherson strut independent rear suspension, **Fig. 2.** Each side consists of a shock absorber strut assembly, two parallel control arms per side, tie rod, spindle and a jounce bumper and bracket.

The shock absorber strut assembly includes a rubber isolated top mount, upper spring seat, coil spring insulator, coil spring and a lower spring seat. the strut assembly is attached at the top by two studs, which retain the top mount of the strut to the inner body side panel. The lower end of the assembly is bolted to the spindle. The two control arms are attached to the underbody and spindle with nuts and bolts. The tie rod is attached to the underbody and the spindle. The jounce bumper bracket is bolted to the strut.

SHOCK STRUT
REPLACE

EXCEPT TEMPO & TOPAZ

1. Raise and support vehicle.
2. Remove rear compartment access panels. On four-door models, remove quarter trim panel.
3. Loosen top shock strut attaching nut, then remove wheel assembly.
4. Remove clip retaining brake hose to rear shock and position hose aside.
5. Loosen but do not remove two nuts and bolts securing shock strut to spindle.
6. Remove top mounting nut, washer and rubber insulator, **Fig. 3.**
7. Remove two bottom mounting bolts, then the shock strut from the vehicle.
8. Reverse procedure to install.

FRONT OF VEHICLE

NOTE: ALL BOLTS MUST BE INSTALLED IN DIRECTION SHOWN

Fig. 1   Rear suspension, exploded view. Except Tempo & Topaz

SPRING

STRUT

TOP MOUNT

INSULATOR, SPRING

JOUNCE BUMPER AND BRACKET ASSEMBLY

SPINDLE

ARM AND BUSHING ASSEMBLY 4 REQ'D.

TIE ROD

Fig. 2   Rear suspension components. Tempo & Topaz

Fig. 3   Shock absorber strut upper mounting components. Except Tempo & Topaz

Fig. 4   Strut, spring & upper mount components. Tempo & Topaz

Fig. 5   Installing control arm. Tempo & Topaz

SHOCK STRUT, UPPER MOUNT & SPRING
REPLACE

TEMPO & TOPAZ

1. Raise and support vehicle. Loosen upper strut mount to body nuts located in luggage compartment.
2. Remove wheel assembly.
3. Place a suitable jack under control arms.
4. Remove brake hose bracket to strut bolt and position brake hose bracket aside.
5. Remove jounce bumper bracket.
6. Remove two upper mount to body nuts, then the strut.
7. Place strut, spring and upper mount assembly into a suitable spring compressor tool.

NOTE: Do not remove the spring from the strut without first compressing the spring.

8. With spring compressed, remove strut shaft to mount nuts. Remove spring, strut and mount, **Fig. 4**, from spring compressor tool.
9. Reverse procedure to install. Torque shaft nut to 35–50 ft. lbs., torque jounce bumper bracket to strut mount bolts to 70–96 ft. lbs., torque top mount to body nuts to 25–30 ft. lbs.

LOWER CONTROL ARM
REPLACE

EXCEPT TEMPO & TOPAZ

1. Raise and support vehicle, then remove wheel assembly.

2. Place a suitable jack under lower control arm between spring and spindle mounting.

NOTE: Rear suspension should be at full rebound and the shock strut fully extended.

3. Remove control arm to body mounting nuts, then the control arm to spindle mounting nuts. Do not remove bolts.
4. Remove spindle end mounting bolt, then slowly lower jack until spring and spring insulator can be removed.
5. Remove bolts from body mountings, then the control arm from vehicle.
6. Reverse procedure to install.

TEMPO & TOPAZ

1. Raise and support vehicle.
2. Remove wheel assembly.
3. Remove control arm to spindle nut and bolt.
4. Remove center mounting nut and bolt.
5. Remove control arm from vehicle.
6. Reverse procedure to install. Torque control arm to body bolt to 40–55 ft. lbs., torque control arm to spindle nut to 60–86 ft. lbs.

NOTE: When installing new control arms the bushing with the 10mm hole is installed toward the center of the vehicle and the bushing with the 12mm hole toward the spindle. The offset on the control arm must

face up on the right side of the vehicle and down on the left side of the vehicle, **Fig. 5**. The flanged edge of the control arm stamping must face the rear of the vehicle.

TIE ROD
REPLACE

EXCEPT TEMPO & TOPAZ

1. Raise and support vehicle.
2. Scribe a reference mark on tie rod front bracket at bolt head centerline for use during reassembly.
3. Remove nut, washer and insulators attaching tie rod to spindle.
4. Remove nut and bolt attaching tie rod to body bracket, then the tie rod.

NOTE: It may be necessary to pry front bracket sheet metal apart slightly to remove tie rod from body.

5. Place a new dished washer over tie rod end with flange toward middle of rod, **Fig. 6**.
6. Install tie rod through spindle bushings and place eye of rod into body bracket. Secure rod to bracket using a new nut and bolt. Do not tighten.
7. Place another dished washer over end of rod with flange toward end of rod, then install a new nut and torque to 65–75 ft. lbs.
8. Using suitable jack, raise lower control arm to curb height.
9. Align center of bolt head with reference mark on body bracket, then torque tie rod front bolt to 90–100 ft. lbs. This bolt must be installed with head inboard on vehicle.
10. Lower vehicle to ground.

TEMPO & TOPAZ

1. Raise and support vehicle.
2. From inside of luggage compartment, loosen two strut top mount to body nuts.
3. Raise vehicle. Position a suitable jack under lower control arm with a piece of wood between jack and control arm.
4. Remove wheel assembly.
5. Remove two top mount studs, then tie rod to spindle retaining nut.

Fig. 6   Tie rod installation

Fig. 7   Rear brake assembly. Models w/7 inch brake drum dia.

6. Remove tie rod to body retaining nut.
7. Lower jack until upper strut mount studs clear body mount holes.
8. Move spindle rearward until tie rod can be removed.
9. Place new washers and bushings on both ends of tie rod, **Fig. 6.**

NOTE: Front and rear bushings are not interchangeable. The rear bushings have indentations incorporated in them.

10. Insert tie rod into body bracket, then install new bushing, washer and nut. Do not tighten nut.
11. Pull back on spindle until tie rod can be installed into the spindle. Install new bushing, washer and nut. Do not tighten nut.
12. Raise jack enough to secure the two strut mounting studs in place.
13. Install two strut to body mount nuts. Torque nuts to 20—30 ft. lbs.
14. Using a suitable jack, raise lower control arm to curb height. Install tie rod nuts and torque to 52—74 ft. lbs.
15. Remove jack and install wheel assembly. Lower vehicle.

SPINDLE
REPLACE

EXCEPT TEMPO & TOPAZ

1. Raise and support vehicle.
2. Remove wheel assembly, then the brake drum and wheel bearings.
3. Remove brake backing plate assembly, then the tie rod retaining nut and dished washer.
4. Remove two nuts and bolts securing strut to spindle.
5. Remove nut and bolt securing lower control arm to spindle, then the spindle.
6. Reverse procedure to install.

TEMPO & TOPAZ

1. Raise and support vehicle.
2. Remove wheel assembly.
3. Remove brake drum. Remove brake flex hose bracket to strut bolt.
4. Remove brake backing plate to spin-

Fig. 8   Rear brake assembly. Models w/8 inch brake drum dia.

dle bolts, then the brake backing plate.
5. Remove lower control arm to spindle bolt, washer and nut.
6. Remove tie rod nut, bushing and washer.
7. Remove spindle to strut bolts, then the spindle.
8. Reverse procedure to install. Torque spindle to strut bolts to 70—96 ft. lbs. Torque tie rod nut to 52—74 ft. lbs. Torque lower control arm to spindle nut to 60—86 ft. lbs.

COIL SPRING
REPLACE

EXCEPT TEMPO & TOPAZ

1. Raise and support vehicle. Support lower control arm with suitable jack.
2. Remove tire and wheel assembly.
3. Remove nut, bolt and washer securing lower control arm to spindle.
4. Lower control arm until spring can be removed.
5. Reverse procedure to install. A new spring insulator must be used when replacing the spring.

BRAKE ADJUSTMENTS

Although the brakes are self-adjusting, **Figs. 7 and 8,** an initial adjustment will be necessary after a brake repair. The initial adjustment can be obtained as follows:

1. On 7 in. brakes, pivot adjuster quadrant until it meshes with knurled pin and is in third or fourth notch of the outboard end of the quadrant, **Fig. 9.**
2. On 8 in. brakes, determine inside diameter of drum brake surface using brake shoe gauge tool D81L-1103-A or equivalent. Adjust brake shoe diameter to fit gauge. Hold automatic adjusting lever out of engagement while rotating adjusting screw and ensure that screw rotates freely.
3. Install drum and wheel assembly, then adjust wheel bearings as described in **Fig. 10.**
4. Complete adjustment by applying brakes several times, then check brake operation by making several stops from varying speeds.

NOTE: If brake drum cannot be removed for brake servicing, remove rubber plug from backing plate inspection hole. On 7 in.

SET QUADRANT ON THIRD OR FOURTH NOTCH PRIOR TO ASSEMBLY

THIRD OR FOURTH NOTCH

180 mm (7-INCH) REAR BRAKE

Fig. 9   Initial brake adjustment

Fig. 10   Rear wheel bearing, assembly

brakes, insert a suitable tool into the hole until it contacts adjuster assembly pivot. Apply pressure sideways on the pivot point allowing adjuster quadrant to ratchet and release the brake adjustment. On 8 in. brakes remove the brake line to axle retention bracket. This will allow sufficient room for insertion of a suitable tool to disengage adjusting lever and back off the adjusting screw.

PARKING BRAKE
ADJUST

1. Pump brake pedal three times before making adjustment.
2. Place transmission in neutral, then raise and support vehicle.
3. Position parking brake control assembly in 12th notch position (two notches from full application). Tighten adjusting nut until rear wheel brakes drag slightly with control assembly fully released. Repeat procedure as necessary to ensure proper adjustment.
4. Reposition control assembly in 12th notch, then loosen adjusting nut enough to eliminate rear brake drag with the control assembly fully released.
5. Lower vehicle and check operation of parking brake.

MASTER CYLINDER
REPLACE

LESS POWER BRAKES

1. Disconnect battery ground cable.
2. Disconnect stoplamp switch electrical connector and remove switch retainer.
3. Slide stoplamp switch off pedal pin far enough to clear end of pin, then remove switch from pin.
4. From inside engine compartment loosen two master cylinder attaching nuts, then slide master cylinder push rod, nylon washers and bushings from brake pedal pin.
5. Disconnect brake lines from master cylinder, then remove nuts securing master cylinder to dash panel. List cylinder forward and upward and remove from vehicle.
6. Reverse procedure to install.

WITH POWER BRAKES

1. Disconnect brake lines from master cylinder. Cap all lines and fittings.
2. On late 1983 models and all 1984–86 models, disconnect brake warning lamp switch wire connector.
3. Remove master cylinder to power brake unit attaching nuts, then remove master cylinder.
4. Reverse procedure to install.

POWER BRAKE UNIT
REPLACE

1. Remove master cylinder as described

under Master Cylinder, Replace, Power Brakes.
2. From inside passenger compartment, disconnect stoplamp switch electrical connector.
3. Remove pushrod retainer and outer nylon washer from pedal pin, then slide switch along brake pedal far enough for outer hole to clear pin. Slide switch upward and remove.
4. Remove booster to dash panel attaching nuts, then slide booster pushrod and pushrod bushing from brake pedal pin.
5. From inside engine compartment, disconnect manifold vacuum hose from booster check valve.
6. Move booster forward until booster studs clear dash panel, then remove booster.
7. Reverse procedure to install.

REAR WHEEL BEARING
ADJUST

1. Raise and support vehicle. Remove dust cover from hub. Remove wheel assembly, if necessary.
2. Remove cotter pin and nut retainer.
3. Back off adjusting nut 1 full turn.
4. Torque adjusting nut, **Fig. 10**, to 17–25 ft. lbs., while rotating drum assembly.
5. Back off adjusting nut ½ turn, then retighten adjusting nut to 10–15 inch lbs. Position adjusting nut retainer over nut so slots are aligned with cotter pin hole, then install cotter pin.
6. Install dust cover, wheel assembly, if necessary and lower vehicle to ground.

6-49

Front Suspension & Steering Section

Fig. 1 Front suspension

Fig. 2 Installing coil spring compressor. Except Tempo & Topaz

DESCRIPTION

These vehicles use a MacPherson type front suspension with the vertical shock absorber struts attached to the upper fender reinforcements and the steering knuckle, **Fig. 1.** The lower control arms are attached inboard to a crossmember and outboard to the steering knuckle through a ball joint to provide lower steering knuckle position.

WHEEL ALIGNMENT
CASTER & CAMBER

Caster and camber angles are preset at the factory and cannot be adjusted.

TOE-IN

To adjust toe-in, lock steering wheel in the straight ahead position using suitable steering wheel holder. Remove small outer clamp from steering boot to prevent boot from twisting during adjustment procedure. Loosen tie rod adjusting nuts, then adjust left and right tie rods until each wheel has ½ the desired total toe specification. Tighten tie rod adjusting nuts, replace steering gear rubber boots and tighten clamp. Remove steering wheel holding tool.

STRUT ASSEMBLY
REPLACE

1. Raise and support vehicle, then remove tire and wheel assembly.

2. Remove brake hose retaining bracket from strut.
3. On Tempo and Topaz models, remove brake caliper, brake rotor, and tie-rod end.
4. Place suitable jack under lower control arm and raise strut as far as possible without raising vehicle.
5. On models except Tempo and Topaz, install spring compressor tool No. T81P-5310A or equivalent by placing top jaw on second coil from top and bottom jaw so as to grip a total of 5 coils, then compress spring until there is about ⅛ inch between any 2 coils, **Fig. 2.**
6. On Tempo and Topaz models, install spring compressor tool No. 14-0259 or 86-0016 by placing top jaw on 5th or 6th coil from bottom, then compress spring a minimum of 3½ inches, **Fig. 3.**

NOTE: Spring must be compressed before strut is removed to insure that no excessive force is applied to constant velocity universal joints.

7. Remove steering knuckle-to-strut pinch bolt, then loosen two top mount to apron nuts and top strut shaft nut.

NOTE: When loosening or tightening strut-to-mount nut, hold 6mm Allen wrench, **Fig. 4,** or hold 8mm hex with a deep socket ¼-inch drive wrench, **Figs. 5 and 6,** and turn only the nut.

8. Lower jack from control arm, then using a large screwdriver, spread

knuckle-to-strut pinch joint.
9. Place block of wood 2 × 4 × 7½ inches against knuckle shoulder. Using suitable pry bar between wood block and lower spring seat, separate strut from knuckle, **Fig. 7.**
10. Remove two top mounting nuts, then the strut, spring, and top mount assembly from vehicle.
11. On 1981–82 vehicles, install 18mm deep socket onto strut shaft nut. Insert 6mm Allen wrench into shaft end, then clamp mount into vise, **Fig. 4.**
12. On 1983–86 except Tempo and Topaz, place 18mm deep socket tool No. D81P-18045-A1 or equivalent on strut shaft nut. Place an 8mm deep socket, ¼ inch drive onto shaft end and clamp mount into vise, **Fig. 5.**
13. On Tempo and Topaz, place 18mm deep socket tool No. D81P-18045-A1 or equivalent on strut shaft nut. Insert an 8mm hex deep socket with ¼-inch drive wrench and clamp strut into vise, **Fig. 6.**
14. On all vehicles, remove top shaft mounting nut from shaft while holding Allen wrench or ¼-inch drive socket.

NOTE: Do not clamp directly on strut with vise as damage to strut may result.

15. Remove strut top mount components and, except on Tempo and Topaz, spring.

NOTE: On Tempo and Topaz models, check spring insulator for damage to splash shield.

16. On Tempo and Topaz models, remove spring compressor from strut and remove spring.
17. Reverse procedure to install. Refer to **Figs. 8 and 9** for proper installation

Fig. 3 Installing coil spring compressor. Tempo & Topaz

Fig. 4 Removing shock absorber strut top mounting nut. 1981–82

Fig. 5 Removing shock absorber strut top mounting nut. 1983–86 exc. Tempo & Topaz

Fig. 6 Removing shock absorber strut top mounting nut. Tempo & Topaz

Fig. 7 Separating shock absorber strut from knuckle

1 DUST CAP 18A179
2 NUT AND WASHER N801442
3 UPPER MOUNT 18183
4 THRUST PLATE 3K048
5 BEARING AND SEAL 3B155
6 SPRING SEAT 5A324
7 NUT N801310-S100 (2)
8 SPRING INSULATOR 5415
9 SPRING 5310
10 JOUNCE BUMPER, FRONT 18A085
11 SHOCK ABSORBER STRUT 18045

Fig. 8 Installation of shock absorber strut top mounting components. Except Tempo & Topaz

sequence of top mount components. On except Tempo and Topaz models, torque strut shaft nut to 48–62 ft. lbs., on Tempo and Topaz models, torque strut shaft nut to 35–50 ft. lbs. Install new steering knuckle pinch nut and torque to 66–81 ft. lbs. On except Tempo and Topaz models, torque two top mount attaching nuts to 22–29 ft. lbs. On Tempo and Topaz models, torque two top mount attaching nuts to 25–30 ft. lbs.

CHECKING BALL JOINTS

1. Raise and support vehicle.
2. With suspension in full rebound position, grasp lower edge of tire and move wheel in and out, **Fig. 10.**
3. Observe lower end of knuckle and lower control arm as wheel is being moved in and out. Any movement between lower end of knuckle and lower arm indicates excessive ball joint wear.

4. If any movement is observed, install a new lower control arm assembly. The lower ball joint and control arm are serviced as an assembly only. Refer to Lower Control Arm, Replace in this section.

LOWER CONTROL ARM
REPLACE

1. Raise and support vehicle.
2. Remove nut from stabilizer bar, then the large dished washer.
3. Remove lower control arm inner pivot bolt and nut.
4. Remove lower control arm ball joint pinch bolt, then using a screwdriver, separate the control arm from the steering knuckle and remove from vehicle.

NOTE: Ensure steering column is in unlocked position. Do not use a hammer to separate ball joint from knuckle.

5. Reverse procedure to install. Torque pinch bolt and nut to 37–44 ft. lbs. On 1981–83 vehicles, torque lower control arm inner pivot nut to 44–55 ft. lbs. On 1984–86 vehicles, torque lower control arm inner pivot nut to 50–60 ft. lbs. Torque stabilizer bar nut to 98–115 ft. lbs.

STEERING KNUCKLE
REPLACE

1. Raise and support vehicle, then remove wheel assembly.
2. Remove cotter pin from tie rod end stud, then the slotted nut.
3. Using tool 3290C and adapter T81P3504W, remove tie rod end from knuckle.
4. Remove brake caliper, then the hub from the driveshaft.
5. On 1984-86 vehicles, loosen two top mount nuts. Do not remove nuts.
6. On all vehicles, remove pinch bolt and nut securing lower arm to steering

Fig. 9   Installation of shock absorber strut top mounting components. Tempo & Topaz

knuckle, then using a screwdriver, separate lower arm from knuckle.

NOTE: Ensure steering column is in unlocked position. Do not use a hammer to separate ball joint from knuckle.

7. Remove shock absorber strut to steering knuckle pinch bolt, then using a screwdriver, slightly open knuckle to strut pinch joint.
8. Remove steering knuckle from shock absorber strut, **Fig. 7,** then from the vehicle.
9. Reverse procedure to install. Torque steering knuckle to shock strut assembly pinch bolt to 66–81 ft. lbs., torque lower control arm to steering knuckle pinch bolt to 37–44 ft. lbs. On 1984–86 vehicles, torque two top mount nuts to 25–30 ft. lbs. Install new slotted nut then torque to 23–35 ft. lbs.

STABILIZER BAR
REPLACE

1. Raise and support vehicle.
2. Remove stabilizer insulator mounting bracket bolts.
3. Remove stabilizer bar to control arm attaching bolts, then the stabilizer bar assembly.
4. Remove worn insulators from stabilizer bar.
5. Reverse procedure to install. Torque stabilizer bar to control arm attaching bolt to 98–115 ft. lbs. Torque stabilizer insulator mounting bracket bolts to 60–70 ft. lbs.

STEERING GEAR
REPLACE

MANUAL STEERING

1. Disconnect battery ground cable, then turn ignition switch to "On" position.
2. Remove access panel from dash below steering column.
3. Remove intermediate shaft bolts at gear input shaft and at steering column shaft.
4. Using a wide blade screwdriver, spread slots enough to loosen intermediate shaft at both ends.
5. Turn steering wheel fully left to allow clearance for tie rod removal.
6. Remove tie rod ends from steering knuckles using tool 3290C and adapter T81P3504W. Turn right wheel to full left position.
7. Remove left tie rod end from tie rod, then on vehicles equipped with automatic transmission disconnect speedometer cable at transmission.
8. Disconnect secondary air tube at check valve, then exhaust pipes from exhaust manifold.
9. Remove exhaust hanger bracket from below steering gear. Wire exhaust system aside.
10. Remove gear mounting brackets and insulators, then separate gear from intermediate shaft while simultaneously pulling upward on shaft from inside vehicle.

NOTE: Right and left hand brackets and insulators are not interchangeable.

11. Rotate gear forward and downward to clear input shaft.
12. Ensure input shaft is in full left turn position, then remove gear through right side apron opening until left tie rod clears shift linkage.
13. Lower left side of gear and remove gear from vehicle.
14. Reverse procedure to install. Ensure input shaft is at full left turn stop and right wheel assembly is in full left turn position. Use caution not to damage steering gear bellows.

POWER STEERING

1. Disconnect battery ground cable, then turn ignition switch to On position.
2. Remove access panel from dash below steering column.
3. Remove four screws from dash panel steering column boot, then slide boot along intermediate shaft.
4. Remove intermediate shaft bolts at gear input shaft and from steering column shaft.
5. Using wide blade screwdriver, spread slot wide enough to loosen intermediate shaft at both ends.
6. Turn steering wheel to full left stop to facilitate gear removal.
7. On all 1981–82 vehicles except 1.6 L. engine and manual transmission without air conditioning, remove pressure switch electrical connector, then the switch.

NOTE: AS WHEEL IS BEING MOVED IN AND OUT, OBSERVE THE LOWER END OF THE KNUCKLE AND THE LOWER CONTROL ARM. ANY MOVEMENT BETWEEN LOWER END OF THE KNUCKLE AND THE LOWER ARM INDICATES ABNORMAL BALL JOINT WEAR

Fig. 10   Checking lower ball joint

8. On 1984–86 vehicles, remove air cleaner.
9. On vehicles equipped with air conditioning, except Tempo and Topaz models, secure liquid line above dash opening.
10. Disconnect secondary air tube at check valve, then the exhaust pipes from exhaust manifold. Secure exhaust system to the side.
11. Remove exhaust hanger brackets from below steering gear and from side apron.
12. Disconnect pressure and return lines from intermediate connector and drain fluid.
13. Remove tie rod ends from steering knuckles using tool 3290C and adapter T81P3504W. Turn right wheel to full left turn position.
14. On vehicles equipped with manual transmission, remove left tie rod end from tie rod.
15. On vehicles equipped with automatic transmission, disconnect speedometer cable from transmission.
16. On vehicles equipped with automatic transmission, disconnect shift cable assembly from transmission.
17. Except on Tempo and Topaz models, remove screws securing heater water tube to brace below oil pan.
18. Except on Tempo and Topaz models, remove nut from lower bolt securing engine mounting bracket to transmission housing. Tap bolt out as far as possible.
19. Remove gear mounting brackets and insulators.
20. Remove gear from intermediate shaft by pushing upward on shaft with bar while pulling gear downward.
21. Rotate gear downward and forward to clear input shaft.
22. Ensure input shaft is in full left turn position, then move gear through right side apron opening until left tie rod clears opening. Use caution to avoid damaging bellows.
23. Lower left side of gear and remove gear from vehicle.
24. Reverse procedure to install.

NOTE: EXERCISE CARE NOT TO DAMAGE OR CUT BALL JOINT BOOT. PRY BAR MUST NOT CONTACT LOWER ARM.

Fig. 11   Separating ball joint from steering knuckle

Fig. 12   Removing halfshaft from differential housing

Fig. 13   Separating outer constant velocity joint from hub

POWER STEERING PUMP
REPLACE

WITH DIESEL ENGINE

1. Remove drive belts.
2. On vehicles with air conditioning, remove alternator.
3. On vehicles with air conditioning, remove both braces from support bracket.
4. Disconnect power steering lines and drain fluid from pump.
5. Remove four bracket mounting bolts.
6. Install pulley removal tool No. T69L-10300-B or equivalent on pulley hub. Hold small hex head of tool and turn tool nut counterclockwise to remove pulley.
7. Remove pump from bracket.
8. Reverse procedure to install.

WITH GASOLINE ENGINE

Escort, EXP, LN7 & Lynx
1. Remove air cleaner, thermactor pump drive belt and thermactor pump.
2. Remove power steering reservoir filler extension. Cover opening to prevent entry of dirt.
3. From underneath vehicle, loosen one power steering pump adjusting bolt and remove one pump to mounting bracket bolt, then disconnect return hose.
4. Form engine compartment, loosen one power steering pump adjusting bolt, then loosen pivot and remove drive belts.
5. Remove the remaining two power steering pump to bracket retaining bolts, then remove pump from bracket by passing pulley through adjusting bracket opening.
6. Disconnect pressure hose from power steering pump, then remove pump.
7. Reverse procedure to install.

Tempo & Topaz
1. Remove alternator drive belt.
2. Place alternator in upper most position.
3. Remove radiator overflow bottle.
4. Remove power steering pump drive belt.
5. Disconnect return line from pump.
6. Completely back off power steering pump pressure line nut. The pressure line will separate when the pump bracket is removed.

7. Remove power steering pump mounting bolts and pump.
8. Reverse procedure to install.

DRIVESHAFTS
REPLACE

NOTE: If removing both right and left side halfshafts, plugs T81P-1177B or equivalent must be installed. Failure to do so may result in dislocation of differential side gears, necessitating transaxle disassembly to re-align the gears. Also, halfshaft removal and installation procedures are the same for manual and automatic transaxles except for the following: due to automatic transaxle case configuration the right side halfshaft assembly must be removed first. Tool T81P-4026A or equivalent is then inserted into transaxle to remove left side inner constant velocity joint assembly from transaxle. If only the left side halfshaft is to be removed from the vehicle, remove right side halfshaft assembly from the transaxle case only and secure to underside of vehicle, then remove left halfshaft assembly. The hub nut and lower control arm to steering knuckle attaching bolt and nut must be discarded after removal and new nuts and bolts installed.

1. Loosen hub nut without unstaking. Use of a chisel or similar tool to unstake nut may damage spindle threads.
2. Raise and support vehicle and remove wheel assemblies.
3. Remove bolt attaching brake hose routing clip to suspension strut.
4. Remove nut from ball joint to steering knuckle attaching bolt, then drive bolt from knuckle using suitable punch and hammer.
5. Separate ball joint from steering knuckle using pry bar, **Fig. 11.**

NOTE: Lower ball joints fit into a pocket formed in the plastic disc brake shield. The shield must be positioned away from the ball joint while removing ball joint from steering knuckle.

6. Remove halfshaft from differential housing using suitable pry bar. Use caution not to damage dust deflector located between shaft and case, **Fig. 12.** If an automatic transaxle halfshaft

assembly cannot be removed from differential by using a pry bar, insert a large bladed screwdriver between differential pinion shaft and inboard constant velocity joint stub shaft. Sharply tap on screwdriver handle, to free halfshaft from differential.

NOTE: Use caution not to damage differential oil seal, constant velocity joint boot or constant velocity joint dust deflector.

7. Separate outer constant velocity joint from hub using puller T81P-1104C or equivalent, **Fig. 13,** and adapters T81P-1104B and T81P-1104A or equivalent.

NOTE: Do not use a hammer to separate outboard constant velocity joint stub shaft from hub as damage to internal components may result.

8. Reverse procedure to install. Install new circlip on inboard constant velocity joint stub shaft. Align splines of inboard constant velocity joint stub shaft with splines in differential. Push joint into differential until circlip seats in side gear, **Fig. 14.** Torque new control arm to steering knuckle nut to 37-44 ft. lbs. Torque new hub nut to 180-200 ft. lbs., and stake nut, **Fig. 15.**

NOTE: If the hub nut cracks or splits during staking, remove and replace hub nut.

CONSTANT VELOCITY JOINT SERVICE

Replacement
1981–82 & EARLY 1983 MODELS
REMOVAL

NOTE: Service is the same for both inner and outer constant velocity joints.

1. Place halfshaft in suitable vice. Use caution not to damage boot or clamp.

Fig. 14   Installing inner constant velocity joint into differential side gear

Fig. 15   Hub nut staking tool fabrication

2. Cut large boot clamp and remove from boot, **Fig. 16,** then position boot upward on shaft. If boot only is being replaced due to damage, check joint grease for contamination. If joints were operating satisfactorily and grease is not contaminated, add grease and install new boot. If grease is contaminated, joint must be completely disassembled.

3. Separate constant velocity joint from shaft using tool T81P-3514A or equivalent, **Fig. 17.** If necessary, boot may be removed from shaft by cutting remaining clamp and removing boot.

4. Remove circlip from end of shaft and discard. Inspect stop ring for damage and replace as necessary, **Fig. 18.**

LEGEND:

1. OUTER BEARING RACE AND STUB SHAFT ASSEMBLY
2. BEARING CAGE
3. BALL BEARINGS (6)
4. INNER BEARING RACE
5. BOOT CLAMP (LARGE)
6. BOOT
7. BOOT CLAMP (SMALL)
8. CIRCLIP
9. STOP RING
10. INTERCONNECTING SHAFT
11. STOP RING
12. CIRCLIP
13. BOOT CLAMP (SMALL)
14. BOOT
15. BOOT CLAMP (LARGE)
16. BEARING RETAINER
17. BEARING CAGE
18. BALL BEARINGS (6)
19. INNER BEARING RACE
20. OUTER BEARING RACE AND STUB SHAFT ASSEMBLY
21. CIRCLIP
22. DUST DEFLECTOR

Fig. 16   Halfshaft assemblies. 1981—82 & 1983 Early Models

Fig. 17   Separating constant velocity joint from shaft. 1981—82 & 1983 Early Models

Fig. 18   Stub shaft stop ring

Fig. 19   Assembling constant velocity joints onto halfshafts

Fig. 21 Halfshaft assembled length. 1981—82 & 1983 Early Models

Fig. 20 Installing constant velocity joint clamp

Fig. 23 Separating constant velocity joint from shaft. Late 1983 & 1984—86 models

Fig. 22 Halfshaft assemblies. Late 1983 & 1984—86 models

NOTE: WHEN REPLACING A BOOT, CV JOINT, INTERCONNECTING SHAFT, OR COMPLETE HALFSHAFT ASSEMBLY, BE WELL ACQUAINTED WITH THE TRANSAXLE TYPE, TRANSAXLE RATIO, ENGINE SIZE AND SPECIFY RIGHT OR LEFT SIDE INBOARD OR OUTBOARD END.

LEGEND:

1. OUTER BEARING RACE AND STUB SHAFT ASSEMBLY
2. BEARING CAGE
3. BALL BEARINGS (6)
4. INNER BEARING RACE
5. BOOT CLAMP (LARGE)
6. BOOT
7. BOOT CLAMP (SMALL)
8. CIRCLIP
9. STOP RING
10. INTERCONNECTING SHAFT
11. STOP RING
12. CIRCLIP
13. BOOT CLAMP (SMALL)
14. BOOT
15. BOOT CLAMP (LARGE)
16. BEARING RETAINER (MTX 5-SPEED ONLY)
17. BEARING RETAINER (MTX 4-SPEED AND ATX)
18. BEARING CAGE
19. BALL BEARINGS (6)
20. INNER BEARING RACE
21. OUTER BEARING RACE AND STUB SHAFT ASSEMBLY
22. CIRCLIP
23. DUST SEAL

INSTALLATION

1. Inspect splines at each end of shaft for damage and wear. Inner constant velocity joint must be installed onto longer splines, **Fig. 19.**
2. Ensure stop ring is in proper position, then install new circlip into groove nearest end of shaft.
3. Install joint boot until it seats in its groove, then install clamp. Tighten clamp securely but do not damage boot or cut clamp bridge, **Fig. 20.**
4. Position boot upward towards end of shaft, then position constant velocity joint onto shaft and tap into position using plastic mallet. Joint is fully seated when circlip locks in groove cut into joint bearing inner race. Check for proper seating by trying to pull joint from shaft.
5. Lubricate joints with lubricant packs supplied with service kit. On outer joint, fill boot with ⅔ packet and pack joint with 1⅓ packet of lubricant. On inner joint, fill boot with one packet and pack joint with one packet of lubricant. Use lubricant D8RZ-19590A or equivalent only.
6. Position boot over joint, then pry end of boot upward to release any trapped air.
7. Position joint inward or outward as necessary to adjust halfshaft to length shown in **Fig. 21.**
8. Ensure boot is seated in groove, then refer to step 3 for clamp installation.

LATE 1983 & 1984—86 MODELS

REMOVAL

Except Inboard Constant Velocity Joint & Boot, 5-Speed Manual Transaxle

1. Place halfshaft in suitable vise. Use caution not to damage boot or clamp.
2. Cut large boot clamp and remove from boot, **Fig. 22,** then position boot upward on shaft. If boot only is being replaced due to damage, check joint grease for contamination. If joints were operating satisfactorily and grease is not contaminated, add grease and install new boot. If grease is contaminated, joint must be completely disassembled.
3. Place interconnecting shaft in a suitable vise and angle constant velocity joint so that inner bearing race is exposed, **Fig. 23.**
4. Using suitable drift and hammer, tap inner bearing race to dislodge internal circlip and separate constant velocity joint from interconnecting shaft, being careful not to drop joint.
5. Remove boot from shaft, cutting remaining clamp as necessary.
6. Remove circlip from end of shaft and discard. Inspect stop ring for damage and replace as necessary, **Fig. 18.**

Inboard Constant Velocity Joint & Boot, 5-Speed Manual Transaxle

1. Remove large boot clamp, roll boot back, and wipe away excess grease.
2. Remove wire ring bearing retainer from outer race, then remove outer race.
3. Pull inner race and bearing assembly out until it rests on circlip, then, using suitable pliers, spread stop ring and move it back on shaft.
4. Slide inner race and bearing assembly down shaft to expose circlip, then remove circlip.
5. Remove inner race and bearing assembly and, if necessary, remove boot.

INSTALLATION

Except Inboard Constant Velocity Joint & Boot, 5-Speed Manual Transmission

1. Install new stop ring, if removed. Ensure that stop ring is properly seated in groove.

LEFT HAND HALF SHAFT ASSEMBLY

432mm
(17.0 INCHES)

TEMPO/TOPAZ, ESCORT/LYNX, EXP
MTX 4-SPEED, MTX 5-SPEED (ALL ENGINES)

LONG STUB

LEFT HAND HALF SHAFT ASSEMBLY

408mm
(16.1 INCHES)

TEMPO/TOPAZ, ESCORT/LYNX, EXP, ATX (ALL ENGINES)

RIGHT HAND HALF SHAFT ASSEMBLY

763mm
(30.0 INCHES)

TEMPO/TOPAZ (DIESEL ENGINE)
ESCORT/LYNX, EXP (ALL ENGINES)

RIGHT HAND HALF SHAFT ASSEMBLY

763mm
(30.0 INCHES)

TEMPO/TOPAZ (2.3L ENGINE ONLY)

Fig. 24   Halfshaft assembled lengths. Late 1983 & 1984—86 models

2. Install new circlip in groove nearest end of shaft. To avoid over-expansion or twisting of circlip, start one end in groove and work circlip over stub shaft end and into groove.

NOTE: Interconnecting shafts are different depending on application. These shafts are non-symmetrical. Outboard end is approximately ¼ inch longer, from end of shaft to end of boot groove, than inboard end. Be careful to install inboard and outboard constant velocity joints to proper ends of shaft.

3. Install constant velocity joint boot, if removed, ensuring that boot is seated in groove. Tighten clamp securely, but not too tight.
4. Before positioning boot over constant velocity joint, pack joint and boot as follows:
   a. On inboard constant velocity joint, fill boot with 45 grams of grease and pack joint with 90 grams of grease.
   b. On outboard constant velocity joint, fill boot with 45 grams of grease and pack joint with 45 grams of grease.

CAUTION: Use only lubricant E2FZ-19590-A or equivalent.

Fig. 25   Right hand interconnecting shaft. Late 1983 & 1984—86 models

Fig. 26   Outer constant velocity joint bearing cage configuration

Fig. 27 Removing outer constant velocity joint bearings

Fig. 28 Removing bearing cage and inner race assembly from outer constant velocity joint

Fig. 29 Aligning inner cage and bearing race

Fig. 30 Removing inner race from bearing cage

Fig. 31 Counterbore positioning and ball groove & window alignment

8. Ensure that boot is seated in groove, then install clamp securely but not too tight.

Inboard Constant Velocity Joint & Boot, 5-Speed Manual Transmission
1. Move circlip and stop ring back into their respective grooves on shaft.

NOTE: Left hand interconnecting shaft is symmetrical and inboard and outboard constant velocity joints may be installed on either end. Right hand interconnecting shaft is non-symmetrical and care must be taken so that inboard and outboard constant velocity joints are correctly installed, **Fig. 25.**

2. Install constant velocity joint boot, if removed. Ensure that boot is seated in groove, then install clamp securely but not too tight.
3. Install new circlip in groove nearest end of shaft. To avoid over-expansion or twisting of circlip, start one end in groove and work circlip over stub shaft end and into groove.
4. Fill boot with 45 grams of grease and fill outer race with 90 grams of grease. Use only lubricant E2FZ-19590-A or equivalent.

5. Position boot upward toward end of shaft, then position constant velocity joint onto shaft and tap into position using plastic mallet. Joint is fully seated when circlip locks in groove cut into joint bearing inner race. Check for proper seating by trying to pull joint from shaft.
6. Remove all excess grease from external surfaces of constant velocity joint, then position boot over constant velocity joint and move joint in or out to adjust to proper length, **Fig. 24.**
7. Before installing boot clamp, insert dulled screwdriver blade between boot and outer bearing race to allow trapped air to escape.

5. Push inner race and bearing assembly into outer race by hand.
6. Install ball retainer into groove inside outer race.
7. With boot positioned upward toward end of shaft, install constant velocity joint using suitable hammer. Ensure that splines are aligned before hammering constant velocity joint onto shaft.
8. Remove all excess grease from external surfaces of constant velocity joint, then position boot over constant velocity joint and move joint in or out to adjust to proper length, **Fig. 24.**
9. Before installing boot clamp, insert dulled screwdriver blade between boot and outer bearing race to allow trapped air to escape.
10. Ensure that boot is seated in groove, then install clamp securely but not too tight.

DISASSEMBLY & ASSEMBLY
Outer Joint

NOTE: Two different bearing cages are used on the outer joints. One type contains four equal sized windows and two elongated windows while the other type contains six windows of equal size, **Fig. 26.**

1. Position stub shaft in suitable vise with bearing facing upward.
2. Press downward on inner race until bearing can be removed, **Fig. 27.** Remove all six bearings in this manner.
3. Pivot bearing cage and inner race assembly into position shown in **Fig. 28.** Align cage windows with outer

Fig. 32 Inner constant velocity joint assembly. Roll crimp ball retainer type

Fig. 33 Inner constant velocity joint assembly. Wire ring ball retainer type

Fig. 34 Removing inner constant velocity joint outer ball retainer

Fig. 35 Removing inner constant velocity joint inner race and bearing assembly

Fig. 36 Removing bearings from cage

Fig. 37 Removing inner race from bearing cage

race lands while pivoting cage, **Fig. 29,** then remove from outer race.

4. To separate inner race from cage, determine cage design and proceed as follows: on cages with six equal windows rotate inner race upward and remove from cage. On cages with two elongated windows, pivot inner race until it is in position shown in **Fig. 28,** then align one inner race band with one elongated window and position race through the window. Rotate inner race upward and remove from cage, **Fig. 30.**

5. Reverse procedure to assemble. Refer to **Fig. 31** for ball groove and window alignment and proper counter-bore positioning.

INNER JOINT

Roll Crimp Ball Retainer Type, Fig. 32

NOTE: On late 1983 and 1984–86 models with 5-speed manual transmission, disassembly of inboard constant velocity joint, **Fig. 33,** is performed during removal. Assembly of inboard constant velocity joint is performed during installation as previously described.

1. Remove circlip from end of joint stub shaft, then using suitable cutters, cut and remove ball retainer, **Fig. 34.** Discard retainer since a new retainer is not required for assembly.

2. Gently tap joint on work surface until assembly can be removed by hand, **Fig. 35.**

3. Remove bearings from cage by prying with a dulled screwdriver. Use caution not to damage or scratch any components, **Fig. 36.**

4. Rotate inner race to align lands with cage windows, then remove race from bearing cage through wider end of cage, **Fig. 37.**

5. Reverse procedure to assemble.

Wire Ring Ball Retainer Type

1. Remove large clamp, then slide boot back and wipe excess grease.

2. Using a suitable tool, remove wire ring ball retainer from race.

3. Remove outer race.

4. Pull inner race and bearing assembly out until race contacts snap ring.

5. Using suitable pliers, spread then slide snap ring back onto shaft.

6. Slide inner race and bearing assembly down the shaft to allow access to the snap ring.

7. Using a suitable screwdriver, remove snap ring.

8. Remove inner race and bearing assembly.

9. Reverse procedure to assemble.

FORD MUSTANG & PINTO
MERCURY BOBCAT & CAPRI

INDEX OF SERVICE OPERATIONS

NOTE: Refer to the rear of this manual for vehicle manufacturer's special service tool suppliers.

Engine & Serial Number Location

Engine code is fifth digit of serial number on 1980 models, or eighth digit of serial number on 1981–86 models. The serial number is stamped on a metal tag located on top left side dash and visible through windshield.

Grille Identification

1980 Bobcat

1980–81 Capri

1980–82 Mustang

1980 Pinto

1981 Mustang Cobra

1982 Capri

1982 Mustang GT

1983–84 Capri

**1983 Mustang
1984 Mustang Exc. S.V.O.**

1984 Mustang S.V.O.

1985–86 Mustang GT

continued

General Engine Specifications

Year	Engine CID[1]/Liter	V.I.N. Code[2]	Carburetor	Bore and Stroke	Compression Ratio	Net H.P. @ R.P.M.[3]	Maximum Torque Ft. Lbs. @ R.P.M.	Normal Oil Pressure Pounds
1980	4-140, 2.3L[8]	A	5200, 2 Bbl.[5]	3.781 × 3.126	9.0	[13]	[14]	50
	4-140, 2.3L[9]	T	6500, 2 Bbl.[4]	3.781 × 3.126	9.0	—	—	55
	6-200, 3.3L[7]	B	1946, 1 Bbl.[4]	3.68 × 3.126	8.5	—	—	30–50
	V8-255, 4.2L[7]	D	2150, 2 Bbl.[5]	3.68 × 3.00	8.8	131 @ 2600	—	40–60
1981	4-140, 2.3L	A	5200, 2 Bbl.[5][10]	3.781 × 3.126	9.0	88 @ 4600	118 @ 2600	40–60
	6-200, 3.3L[7]	B	1946, 1 Bbl.[4]	3.68 × 3.13	8.6	94 @ 4000	158 @ 1400	30–50
	V8-255, 4.2L[7][12]	D	2150, 2 Bbl.[5]	3.68 × 3.00	8.2	120 @ 3400	205 @ 2600	40–60
	V8-255, 4.2L[7][11]	D	7200VV, 2 Bbl.[5]	3.68 × 3.00	8.2	115 @ 3400	195 @ 2200	40–60
1982	4-140, 2.3L	A	5200, 2 Bbl.[5][10]	3.781 × 3.126	9.0	[15]	[16]	40–60
	6-200, 3.3L	B	1946, 1 Bbl.[4]	3.68 × 3.13	8.6	87 @ 3800	154 @ 1400	40–60
	V8-255, 4.2L[11]	D	2150, 2 Bbl.[5]	3.68 × 3.00	8.2	83 @ 111	194 @ 1600	30–50
	V8-255, 4.2L[12]	D	7200VV, 2 Bbl.[5]	3.68 × 3.00	8.2	83 @ 111	194 @ 1600	40–60
	V8-302, 5.0L H.O.	F	2150A, 2 Bbl.[5]	4.00 × 3.00	8.4	160 @ 4200	247 @ 2400	40–60
1983	4-140, 2.3L[8]	A	YFA, 1 Bbl.[20]	3.781 × 3.126	9.0	90 @ 4600	122 @ 2600	40–60
	4-140, 2.3L[9]	W	E.F.I[19]	3.781 × 3.126	8.0	—	—	40–60
	V6-232, 3.8L	3	2150, 2 Bbl.[5]	3.8 × 3.4	8.7	112 @ 4000	175 @ 2600	54–59
	V8-302 H.O., 5.0L	F	4180, 4 Bbl.[4]	4.0 × 3.0	8.3	174 @ 4200	244 @ 2400	40–60
1984	4-140, 2.3L[8]	A	YFA, 1 Bbl.[20]	3.781 × 3.126	9.0	88 @ 4000	122 @ 2400	40–60
	4-140, 2.3L[9]	W	E.F.I[19]	3.781 × 3.126	8.0	175 @ 4400	210 @ 3000	40–60
	V6-232, 3.8L	3	E.F.I.[19]	3.8 × 3.4	8.7	120 @ 3600	205 @ 1600	54–59
	V8-302 H.O., 5.0L[17]	M	4180-C[4]	4.0 × 3.0	8.3	[21]	[22]	40–60
	V8-302 H.O., 5.0L[18]	M	E.F.I.[19]	4.0 × 3.0	8.3	165 @ 3800	245 @ 2000	40–60
1985	4-140, 2.3L[8]	A	YFA, 1 Bbl.[20]	3.781 × 3.126	9.0	88 @ 4000	122 @ 2400	50
	4-140, 2.3L[9]	T	E.F.I[19]	3.781 × 3.126	8.0	200 @ 5000	240 @ 3000	50
	V6-232, 3.8L	3	C.F.I.[23]	3.8 × 3.4	8.7	120 @ 3600	205 @ 1600	40–60
	V8-302, 5.0L[18]	M	C.F.I.[23]	4.0 × 3.0	8.3	180 @ 4200	260 @ 2600	40–60
	V8-302, 5.0L[6]	M	4180-C[4]	4.0 × 3.0	8.3	210 @ 4400	270 @ 3200	40–60
1986	4-140, 2.3L[8]	A	YFA, 1 Bbl.[20]	3.781 × 3.126	9.5	88 @ 4200	122 @ 2600	50
	4-140, 2.3L[9]	T	E.F.I[19]	3.781 × 3.126	8.0	200 @ 5000	240 @ 3200	50
	V6-232, 3.8L	3	C.F.I.[23]	3.8 × 3.4	8.7	120 @ 3600	205 @ 1600	40–60
	V8-302, 5.0L	—	S.E.F.I.[24]	4.0 × 3.0	9.2	200 @ 4000	285 @ 3000	40–60

[1]—CID—cubic inch displacement.
[2]—On 1980 vehicles the fifth digit in the VIN denotes engine code. On 1981–86 vehicles the eighth digit denotes engine code.
[3]—Net rating—as installed on vehicle.
[4]—Holley.
[5]—Motorcraft.
[6]—Vehicles equipped with 5 speed manual overdrive trans.
[7]—Refer to the Ford & Mercury—Compact & Intermediate Chapter for Service procedures on this engine.
[8]—Non-Turbocharged.

[9]—Turbocharged.
[10]—Some vehicles equipped with model 6500 Feedback Carburetor.
[11]—Exc. Calif.
[12]—Calif. only.
[13]—Exc. Calif., 88 @ 4600; Calif., 89 @ 4800.
[14]—Exc. Calif., 119 @ 2600; Calif. 122 @ 2600.
[15]—Vehicles less A/C, 86 @ 4600; vehicles with A/C, 92 @ 4600.
[16]—Vehicles less A/C, 117 @ 2600; vehicles with A/C, 119 @ 2600.

[17]—Vehicles equipped with 5 speed manual trans.
[18]—Vehicles equipped with automatic overdrive trans.
[19]—Electronic fuel injection.
[20]—Carter.
[21]—Prior to 12/1/83, 175 @ 4000; from 12/1/83, 205 @ 4400.
[22]—Prior to 12/1/83, 245 @ 2200; from 12/1/83, 265 @ 3200.
[23]—C.F.I.—Central fuel injection.
[24]—S.E.F.I.—Sequential electronic fuel injection.

continued

Starting Motor Applications

Year	Engine Model/V.I.N.	Ident. No.	Year	Engine Model/V.I.N.	Ident. No.	Year	Engine Model/V.I.N.	Ident. No.
1980	4-140/A	D8EF-AA		6-200/B	E1AF-BA		V8-302/M①	E3AF-AA
	6-200/B⑤	D8BF-CA		V8-255/D⑫	E1AF-BA		V8-302/M②	E4AF-AA
	6-200/B⑥	D8BF-AA		V8-255/D⑬	E3AF-AA	1985	4-140/A③	E4DF-AA
	V8-255/D	D8OF-AA		V8-302/F⑫	E1AF-BA		4-140/T④	E4SF-AA
1981	4-140/A⑦	E1ZF-AA		V8-302/F⑬	E3AF-AA		V6-232/3	E4DF-BA
	4-140/A⑧	E1ZF-AB	1983	4-140/A	E2BF-AA		V8-302/M	E4AF-AA
	4-140/A⑨	E2BF-AA		V6-232/A	E25F-AA	1986	4-140/A③	—
	6-200/B⑤⑩	E1BF-BA		V8-302/F	E3AF-AA		4-140/T④	—
	6-200/B⑤⑪	E1AF-BA	1984	4-140/A①	E2BF-AA		V6-232/3	—
	6-200/B⑥	E1BF-AA		4-140/A②	E4DF-AA		V8-302/	—
	V8-255/D	E1AF-BA		4-140/W②	E4SF-AA			
1982	4-140/A	E2BF-AA		V6-232/3	E25F-AA			

①—Vehicles manufactured before December 1983.
②—Vehicles manufactured after December 1983.
③—Except turbocharged engine.
④—Turbocharged engine.
⑤—Automatic trans.
⑥—Manual trans.
⑦—Vehicles manufactured before 3-2-81.
⑧—Vehicles manufactured between 3-2-81 and 5-1-81.
⑨—Vehicles manufactured after 5-1-81.
⑩—Vehicles manufactured before 3-2-81.
⑪—Vehicles manufactured after 3-1-81.
⑫—Vehicles manufactured before 5-17-82.
⑬—Vehicles manufactured after 5-16-82.

Alternator & Regulator Specifications

Year	Make or Model	Current Rating		Field Current @ 75°F.		Voltage Regulator		Field Relay
		Amperes	Volts	Amperes	Volts	Make or Model	Voltage @ 75°F.	Closing Voltage @ 75°F.
1980	Orange①④⑥	40	15	4.0	12	D9VF-AB③⑦	13.8–14.6	—
	Green①④⑥	60	15	4.0	12	D9VF-AB③⑦	13.8–14.6	—
	Black①④⑥	65	15	4.0	12	D9VF-AB③⑦	13.8–14.6	—
	Black①⑤⑥	70	15	4.0	12	D9VF-AB③⑦	13.8–14.6	—
1981	Orange①④⑥	40	15	4.0	12	—	13.8–14.6	—
	Green①④⑥	60	15	4.0	12	—	13.8–14.6	—
	Black①④⑥	65	15	4.0	12	—	13.8–14.6	—
	Black①⑤⑥	70	15	4.0	12	—	13.8–14.6	—
	Red①⑤⑥	100	15	4.0	12	—	13.8–14.6	—
1982	Orange①④⑥	40	15	4.0	12	E1TF-AA	13.8–14.6	—
	Green①④⑥	60	15	4.0	12	E1TF-AA	13.8–14.6	—
	Black①④⑥	65	15	4.0	12	E1TF-AA	13.8–14.6	—
	Black①⑤⑥	70	15	4.0	12	E1TF-AA	13.8–14.6	—
	Red①⑤⑥	90	15	4.0	12	E1TF-AA	13.8–14.6	—
1983	Orange①④⑥	40	15	4.25	12	E2TF-AA	—	—
	Green①④⑥	60	15	4.25	12	E2TF-AA	—	—
	Black①④⑥	65	15	4.25	12	E2TF-AA	—	—
	Black①⑤⑥	70	15	4.25	12	E2TF-AA	—	—
	Red①⑤⑥	100	15	4.25	12	E2TF-AA	—	—
1984–86	Orange①④⑥	40	15	4.25	12	E4TF-AA	—	—
	Green①④⑥	60	15	4.25	12	E4TF-AA	—	—
	Black①⑤⑥	70	15	4.25	12	E4TF-AA	—	—
	Red①⑤⑥	100	15	4.25	12	E4TF-AA	—	—

①—Color of identification tag.
②—Pinto & Bobcat use D8BF-AA.
③—Pinto & Bobcat use D9BF-AB.
④—Rear terminal alternator.
⑤—Side terminal alternator.
⑥—Solid state alternator.
⑦—Electronic voltage regulator. These units are color coded black for systems w/warning indicator lamp & blue for system w/ammeter.

continued

Pistons, Pins, Rings, Crankshaft & Bearings

Year	Engine/ V.I.N.	Piston Clearance	Ring End Gap①		Wrist-pin Diameter	Rod Bearings		Main Bearings		Thrust on Bear. No.	Shaft End Play
			Comp.	Oil		Shaft Diameter	Bearing Clearance	Shaft Diameter	Bearing Clearance		
1980	4-140/A⑤	.0014–.0022	.010	.015	.9121	2.0462–2.0472	.0008–.0015	2.3982–2.3990	.0008–.0015	3	.004–.008
	4-140/T④	.0034–.0042	.010	.015	.9121	2.0462–2.0472	.0008–.0015	2.3982–2.3990	.0008–.0015	3	.004–.008
	6-200/B③	.0013–.0021	.008	.015	.9121	2.1232–2.1240	.0008–.0015	2.2482–2.2490	.0008–.0015	3	.004–.008
	V8-255/D③	.0018–.0026	.010	.015	.9121	2.1328–2.1236	.0008–.0015	2.2482–2.2490	②	3	.004–.008
1981	4-140/A	.0014–.0022	.010	.015	.9121	2.0462–2.0472	.0008–.0015	2.3982–2.3990	.0008–.0015	3	.004–.008
	6-200/B③	.0013–.0021	.008	.015	.9121	2.1232–2.1240	.0008–.0015	2.2482–2.2490	.0008–.0015	3	.004–.008
	V8-255/D③	.0014–.0024	.010	.015	.9121	2.1328–2.1236	.0008–.0015	2.2482–2.2490	②	3	.004–.008
1982	4-140/A	.0014–.0022	.010	.015	.9121	2.0465–2.0472	.0008–.0015	2.3982–2.3990	.0008–.0015	3	.004–.008
	6-200/B③	.0013–.0021	.008	.015	.9121	2.1232–2.1240	.0008–.0015	2.2482–2.2490	.0008–.0015	3	.004–.008
	V8-255/D③	.0014–.0024	.010	.015	.9121	2.1228–2.1236	.0008–.0015	2.2482–2.2490	⑥	3	.004–.008
	V8-302 H.O./F③	.0018–.0026	.010	.015	.9121	2.1228–2.1236	.0008–.0015	2.2482–2.2490	⑥	3	.004–.008
1983	4-140/A⑤	.0014–.0022	.010	.015	.9121	2.0465–2.0472	.0008–.0015	2.3982–2.3990	.0008–.0015	3	.004–.008
	4-140/W④	.0030–.0038	.010	.015	.9121	2.0465–2.0472	.0008–.0015	2.3982–2.3990	.0008–.0015	3	.004–.008
	V6-232/3	.0014–.0022	.010	.015	.9121	2.3103–2.3111	.0010–.0014	2.5190–2.5198	.0010–.0014	3	.004–.008
	V8-302 H.O./F	.0018–.0026	.010	.015	.9121	2.1228–2.1236	.0008–.0015	2.2482–2.2490	⑥	3	.004–.008
1984	4-140/A⑤	.0030–.0038	.010	.015	.9121	2.0465–2.0472	.0008–.0015	2.3982–2.3990	.0008–.0015	3	.004–.008
	4-140/W④	.0030–.0038	.010	.015	.9121	2.0465–2.0472	.0008–.0015	2.3982–2.3990	.0008–.0015	3	.004–.008
	V6-232/3	.0014–.0032	.010	.015	.9122	2.3103–2.3111	.0010–.0014	2.5190–2.5198	.0010–.0014	3	.004–.008
	V8-302 H.O./M	.0018–.0026	.010	.015	.9122	2.1228–2.1236	.0008–.0015	2.2482–2.2490	⑥	3	.004–.008
1985	4-140/A,T	.0030–.0038	.010	.015	.9121	2.0465–2.0472	.0008–.0015	2.3982–2.3990	.0008–.0015	3	.004–.008
	V6-232/3	.0014–.0032	.010	.015	.9122	2.3103–2.3111	.0010–.0014	2.5190–2.5198	.0010–.0014	3	.004–.008
	V8-302/M	.0018–.0026	.010	.015	.9122	2.1228–2.1236	.0008–.0015	2.2482–2.2490	.0004–.0015	3	.004–.008

①—Fit rings in tapered bores for clearance listed in tightest portion of ring travel.
②—No. 1, .0001–.0015; others, .0004–.0015.
③—Refer to the Ford & Mercury—Compact & Intermediate chapter for service procedures on this engine.
④—Turbocharged engine.
⑤—Except turbocharged engine.
⑥—No. 1, .0004–.0025; others, .0004–.0015.

Valve Specifications

Year	Engine/V.I.N.	Valve Lash		Valve Angles		Valve Spring Installed Height	Valve Spring Pressure Lbs. @ In.	Stem Clearance		Stem Diameter, Standard	
		Int.	Exh.	Seat	Face			Intake	Exhaust	Intake	Exhaust
1980	4-140/A,T	.040–.050②		45	44	1.56	167 @ 1.16	.0010–.0027	.0015–.0032	.3416–.3423	.3411–.3418
	6-200/B④	.110–.184⑤		45	44	1.578	150 @ 1.22	.0008–.0025	.0010–.0027	.3100–.3107	.3098–.3105
	V8-255/D④	.123–.173⑤		45	44	③	①	.0010–.0027	.0015–.0032	.3416–.3423	.3411–.3418
1981	4-140/A	.040–.050②		45	44	1.56	167 @ 1.16	.0010–.0027	.0015–.0032	.3416–.3423	.3411–.3418
	6-200/B④	.110–.184⑤		45	44	1.58	150 @ 1.22	.0008–.0025	.0010–.0027	.3100–.3107	.3098–.3105
	V8-255/D④	.096–.146⑤		45	44	③	⑥	.0010–.0027	.0015–.0032	.3416–.3423	.3411–.3418
1982	4-140/A	.040–.050②		45	44	1.56	167 @ 1.16	.0010–.0027	.0015–.0032	.3416–.3423	.3411–.3418
	6-200/B④	.110–.184⑤		45	44	1.58	150 @ 1.22	.0008–.0025	.0010–.0027	.3100–.3107	.3098–.3105
	V8-255/D④	.096–.146⑤		45	44	③	⑦	.0010–.0027	.0015–.0032	.3416–.3423	.3411–.3418
	V8-302 H.O./F④	.096–.146⑤		45	44	③	⑦	.0010–.0027	.0015–.0032	.3416–.3423	.3411–.3418
1983	4-140/A,W	.040–.050②		45	44	1.56	167 @ 1.16	.0010–.0027	.0015–.0032	.3416–.3423	.3411–.3418
	V6-232/3④	.088–.189⑤		45	44	1.74	215 @ 1.40	.0010–.0027	.0015–.0032	.3416–.3423	.3411–.3418
	V8-302 H.O./F④	.123–.146⑤		45	44	⑧	⑨	.0010–.0027	.0015–.0032	.3416–.3423	.3411–.3418
1984–85	4-140/A,W,T	.040–.050②		45	44	1⁹⁄₁₆	154 @ 1.16	.0010–.0027	.0015–.0032	.3416–.3423	.3411–.3418
	V6-232/3④	.088–.189		45	44	³⁷⁄₅₀	215 @ 1.79	.0010–.0027	.0015–.0032	.3416–.3423	.3411–.3418
	V8-302 H.O./M	.123–.146⑤		45	44	⑧	⑨	.0010–.0027	.0015–.0032	.3416–.3423	.3411–.3418

continued

VALVE SPECIFICATIONS, NOTES—Continued

①—Intake, 201 @ 1.36; exhaust, 200 @ 1.20.
②—Measured at cam with hydraulic valve lash adjuster completely collapsed.
③—Intake, 1¹¹⁄₁₆; exhaust, 1¹⁹⁄₃₂.
④—Refer to the Ford & Mercury—Compact & Intermediate Chapter for service procedures on this engine.
⑤—Clearance is obtained at valve stem tip with hydraulic lifter collapsed. If clearance is less than the minimum install an undersize push rod; if clearance is greater than the maximum install an oversize push rod.
⑥—Intake, 205 @ 1.36; exhaust, 200 @ 1.20.
⑦—Intake, 205 @ 1.36; exhaust, 205 @ 1.15.
⑧—Intake, 1²⁵⁄₃₂; exhaust, 1³⁹⁄₆₄.
⑨—Intake, 204 @ 1.33; exhaust, 205 @ 1.05.

Engine Tightening Specifications★

★ Torque specifications are for clean and lightly lubricated threads only. Dry or dirty threads produce increased friction which prevents accurate measurement of tightness.

Year	Engine Model/V.I.N.	Spark Plugs Ft. Lbs.	Cylinder Head Bolts Ft. Lbs.	Intake Manifold Ft. Lbs.	Exhaust Manifold Ft. Lbs.	Rocker Arm Shaft Bracket Ft. Lbs.	Rocker Arm Cover Ft. Lbs.	Connecting Rod Cap Bolts Ft. Lbs.	Main Bearing Cap Bolts Ft. Lbs.	Flywheel to Crankshaft Ft. Lbs.	Vibration Damper or Pulley Ft. Lbs.
1980–81	4-140/A⑥	5–10	80–90	14–21	16–23	—	6–8	30–36	80–90	56–64	100–120
	4-140/T⑦	5–10	80–90	13–18	16–23	—	6–8	30–36	80–90	56–64	100–120
	6-200/B①	10–15	70–75	—	18–24	30–35	3–5	21–26	60–70	75–85	85–100
	V8-255/D①	10–15	65–72	④	18–24	18–25③	3–5	19–24	60–70	75–85	70–90
1982	4-140/A	5–10	80–90	14–21	16–23	—	5–8	30–36	80–90	56–64	100–120
	6-200/B	10–15	70–75	—	18–24	30–35	3–5	21–26	60–70	75–85	85–100
	V8-255/D①	10–15	65–72	18–20	18–24	18–25③	3–5	19–24	60–70	75–85	70–90
	V8-302 H.O./F①	10–15	65–72	23–25	18–24	18–25③	3–5	19–24	60–70	75–85	70–90
1983	4-140/A⑥	5–10	80–90	14–21	16–23	—	5–8	30–36	80–90	56–64	100–120
	4-140/W⑦	5–10	80–90	14–21	16–23	—	5–8	30–36	80–90	54–64	100–120
	V6-232/3	5–11	⑤	18.4	15–22	18.4–25.8 ③	3–5	31–36	65–81	56–64	93–121
	V8-302 H.O./F	10–15	65–72	23–25	18–24	18–25③	3–5	19–24	60–70	75–85	70–90
1984	4-140/A⑥	5–10	80–90	14–21	16–23	—	5–8	30–36	80–90	56–64	100–120
	4-140/W⑦	5–10	80–90	14–21	16–23	—	5–8	30–36	80–90	56–64	100–120
	V6-232/3	5–11	⑧	24	15–22	18.4–25.8 ③	80–106 ⑨	31–36	65–81	54–64	93–121
	V8-302 H.O./M	10–15	65–72	23–25	18–24	18–25③	3–5	19–24	60–70	75–85	70–90
1985–86	4-140/A,T	5–10	⑩	14–21	⑬	—	5–8	⑯	②	56–64	100–120
	V6-232/3	5–11	⑧	⑫	15–22	③⑭	80–106 ⑮	31–36	65–81	54–64	93–121
	V8-302/M	10–15	⑪	23–25	18–24	18–25③	3–5	19–24	60–70	75–85	70–90

①—Refer to the Ford & Mercury—Compact & Intermediate Chapter for service procedures.
②—Torque in 2 steps: 1, 50–60 ft. lbs.; 2, 80–90 ft. lbs.
③—Rocker fulcrum bolt to cylinder head.
④—1980, 23–25 ft. lbs.; 1981, 18–20 ft. lbs.
⑤—Tighten in (4) steps: (1) 47 ft. lbs., (2) 55 ft. lbs., (3) 63 ft. lbs., (4) 74 ft. lbs., then back off all bolts 2–3 revolutions

and repeat steps 1 through 4.
⑥—Except turbocharged engine.
⑦—Turbocharged engine.
⑧—Tighten in (4) steps: (1) 37 ft. lbs., (2) 45 ft. lbs., (3) 52 ft. lbs., (4) 59 ft. lbs., then back off all bolts 2–3 revolutions & repeat steps 1 through 4.
⑨—Inch lbs.
⑩—Torque in 2 steps: 1, 50–60 ft. lbs.; 2, 80–90 ft. lbs.
⑪—Torque in 2 steps: 1, 55–65 ft. lbs.; 2,

65–72 ft. lbs.
⑫—Torque in 3 steps: 1, 7 ft. lbs.; 2, 15 ft. lbs.; 3, 24 ft. lbs.
⑬—Torque in 2 steps: 1, 5–7 ft. lbs.; 2, 16–23 ft. lbs.
⑭—Torque in 2 steps: 1, 5–11 ft. lbs.; 2, 18.4–25.8 ft. lbs.
⑮—Inch lbs.
⑯—Torque in 2 steps: 1, 25–30 ft. lbs.; 2, 30–36 ft. lbs.

continued

Rear Axle Specifications

Year	Ring Gear Diameter	Carrier Type	Ring Gear & Pinion Backlash Inch	Nominal Pinion Locating Shim, Inch	Pinion Bearing Preload				Differential Bearing Preload	Pinion Nut Torque Ft. Lbs.
					New Bearings With Seal Inch-Lbs.	Used Bearings With Seal Inch-Lbs.	New Bearings Less Seal Inch-Lbs.	Used Bearings Less Seal Inch-Lbs.		
1980	7½" WGX, WGZ②	Integral	.008–.012	.030	17–27	8–14	—	—	.016③	140
	8, 9"	Removable	.008–.012	④	17–27	8–14	—	—	.005–.008①	170
	6¾" WGF, WGG②	Integral	.008–.015	.030	17–27	6–12	—	—	.016③	140
1981–82	7½" WGX②	Integral	.008–.015	.030	16–29	8–14	—	—	.016③	170
	6¾" WGG②	Integral	.008–.015	.030	16–29	8–14	—	—	.016③	140
1983–86	7½" WGX②	Integral	.008–.015	.030	16–29	8–14	—	—	.016③	170
	8.8	Integral	.008–.015	.030	16–29	8–14	—	—	—	—

①—Case spread with new bearings; with used bearings, .003–.005".
②—Identification tag code.
③—Case spread.
④—8 inch ring gear, .022"; 9 inch ring gear, .015".

Wheel Alignment Specifications

Year	Model	Caster Angle, Degrees		Camber Angle Degrees				Toe-In Inch	Toe-Out on Turns, Deg.	
		Limits	Desired	Limits		Desired			Outer Wheel	Inner Wheel
				Left	Right	Left	Right			
1980	Bobcat & Pinto ①	+¼ to +1¾	+1	−¼ to +1¼	−¼ to +1¼	+½	+½	⅛	18.84	20
	Bobcat & Pinto ②	−¾ to +1¼	+¼	−¼ to +1¼	−¼ to +1¼	+½	+½	⅛	18.84	20
1980–81	Capri & Mustang	+¼ to +1¾	+1	−½ to +1	−½ to +1	+¼	+¼	3/16	19.84	20
1982	Capri & Mustang	+⅜ to +1⅞	+1⅛	−½ to +1	−½ to +1	+¼	+¼	3/16	19.84	20
1983	Capri & Mustang	+½ to +2	+1¼	−¾ to +¾	−¾ to +¾	Zero	Zero	3/16	19.84	20
1984	Capri & Mustang	+½ to +2	+1¼	−¾ to +¾	−¾ to +¾	Zero	Zero	3/16	19.84	20
	Mustang SVO	+⅛ to +1⅞	+1	−¾ to +¾	−¾ to +¾	Zero	Zero	⅛	19.84	20
1985–86	All	+¼ to +1¾	+1	−¾ to +¾	−¾ to +¾	Zero	Zero	3/16	19.84	20

①—Exc. sta. wag.
②—Sta. wag.

continued

Cooling System & Capacity Data

Year	Model or Engine/V.I.N.	Cooling Capacity, Qts.		Radiator Cap Relief Pressure, Lbs.	Thermo. Opening Temp.	Fuel Tank Gals.	Engine Oil Refill Qts. [1]	Transmission Oil			Rear Axle Oil Pints
		Less A/C	With A/C					4 Speed Pints	5 Speed Pints	Auto. Trans. Qts. [2]	
1980	4-140/A[3]	8.6	8.9	13	191	[8]	4	2.8	—	[10]	[9]
	4-140/A[5][6]	8.6	9	[13]	191	11.5	4	2.8	3.7	6.7	[9]
	4-140/T[5][7]	9.2	9.2	16	191	12.5[11]	4½	3.5	3.7	6.7	[9]
	6-200/B[5]	8.1	8.1	16	191	12.5	4	4.5	—	[4]	[9]
	V8-255/D[5]	13.4	13.5	16	196	12.5	4[12]	—	—	10	[9]
1981	4-140/A[5]	8.6	9	[13]	191	12.5	4	2.8	3.7	[10]	—
	6-200/B[5]	8.4	8.4	16	196	12.5	4	4.5	—	[15]	[14]
	V8-255/D[5]	14.7	15	16	191	12.5	4[12]	—	—	9.6	[14]
1982	4-140/A[5]	8.6	9.4	[13]	191	15.4	4	2.8	3.7	8	[14]
	6-200/B[5]	8.4	8.4	16	196	15.4	4	—	—	[20]	[14]
	V8-255/D[5]	14.7	15	16	191	15.4	4[12]	—	—	11	[14]
	V8-302 H.O./F[5]	13.1	13.4	16	196	15.4	4[12]	4.5	—	—	[14]
1983	4-140/A[6]	8.6	9.4	[13]	191	15.4	4	2.8	—	8	[16]
	4-140/W[7]	10.5	10.5	[13]	191	15.4	4	—	5.6	—	[16]
	V6-232/3	—	—	16	196	15.4	4	—	—	11	[16]
	V8-302/F	13.1	13.4	16	196	15.4	4[12]	4.5	—	—	3.5
1984	4-140/A[6]	8.6	9.4	[13]	191	15.4	4	2.8	—	8	[16]
	4-140/W[7]	10.5	10.5	[13]	191	15.4	4	—	5.6	8	[16]
	V6-232/3	10.7	10.8	16	196	15.4	4	—	—	11	[16]
	V8-302/M	13.1	13.4	16	196	15.4	4[12]	—	—	11	3.5
1985	4-140/A[6]	8.6	9.2	[13]	191	15.4	4	2.8	—	8	3.25
	4-140/T[7]	10.8	10.8	16	192	15.4	4	—	5.6	—	3.25
	V6-232/3	10.7	10.8	16	198	15.4	4	—	—	11	3.25
	V8-302/M[17]	14.1	14.1	16	198	15.4	4[12]	—	5.6	—	3.25
	V8-302/M[18]	14.1	14.1	16	198	15.4	4[12]	—	—	12.3	3.25
1986	4-140/A[6]	8.6	9.2	[19]	191	15.4	4	2.8	—	8	3.25
	4-140/T[7]	9	9	[19]	191	15.4	4	—	5.6	—	3.25
	V6-232/3	10.7	10.8	16	196	15.4	4	—	—	12.3	3.25
	V8-302/	14.1	14.1	16	198	15.4	4	—	5.6	12.3	3.75

[1]—Add 1 qt. with filter change unless otherwise noted.
[2]—Approximate. Make final check with dipstick.
[3]—Bobcat & Pinto.
[4]—C3 trans., 8 qts.; C4 trans., 7 qts.
[5]—Capri & Mustang.
[6]—Non-turbocharged.
[7]—Turbocharged.
[8]—Exc. Sta. Wag. & Calif. auto. trans. sedan, 13 gals.; Calif. auto. trans. sedan, 11.7 gals.; Sta. Wag., 14 gals.
[9]—6¾ inch axle, 2.5; 7½ inch axle, 3.5; 8 inch axle, 4.5.
[10]—C3, 8 qts.; C4, 6.7 qts.
[11]—Automatic transmission, 11.9 gal.
[12]—Dual sump oil. When draining oil, it is necessary to remove both drain plugs. One drain plug is located at front of oil pan. The second plug is located on left side of oil pan.
[13]—Less A/C, 13 psi.; with A/C, 16 psi.
[14]—6¾" ring gear axle, 2.5 pts.; 7½" ring gear axle, 3.5 pts.
[15]—C3, 8 qts.; C4 w/10¼ in. torque converter, 7.2 qts.; C4 w/12 in. torque converter, 9.6 qts.
[16]—Standard rear axle, 3.25 pts.; traction-lok rear axle, 3.55 pts.
[17]—Except fuel injected engine.
[18]—Fuel injected engine.
[19]—Less A/C, 14 psi.; with A/C, 16 psi.
[20]—C3, 8 qts.; C4 trans., 10 qts.

Electrical Section

STARTER
REPLACE

EXCEPT 1980 BOBCAT & PINTO

1. Disconnect battery ground cable.
2. Raise and support front of vehicle.
3. On 1980–81 models with V8-255 engine, remove wishbone brace.
4. On 1981 models with 4-140 or 6-200 engine, remove starter heat shield.

NOTE: On models with 6-200 engine, remove heat shield by loosening lower starter attaching bolt and removing nut from stud.

5. On all models, disconnect starter cable from starter.
6. Remove starter motor attaching bolts and the starter.
7. Reverse procedure to install.

1980 BOBCAT & PINTO

1. Disconnect battery ground cable.
2. Raise vehicle and remove four bolts from crossmember under bell housing.
3. Remove flex coupling clamping screw from steering gear, then the three bolts attaching steering gear to crossmember.
4. Disconnect steering gear from flex coupling and pull gear down to gain access to starter.
5. Disconnect starter cable and remove three attaching bolts and starter.
6. Reverse procedure to install.

Fig. 1   Ignition switch. 1980–86 Capri, Mustang & Mustang SVO

IGNITION LOCK
REPLACE

1980–86

1. Disconnect battery ground cable.
2. On 1981–86 models with tilt steering column, remove upper extension shroud. Unsnap shroud from retaining clip located at the 9 o'clock position.
3. On all models, remove trim shroud or shroud halves, then disconnect key warning switch electrical connector.
4. Place gear shift lever in PARK on models with automatic trans. or in any gear on models with manual trans.
5. Insert a ⅛ inch diameter pin in the hole in casting surrounding lock cylinder. Pull lock cylinder out of housing while depressing retaining pin.
6. To install, turn lock cylinder to RUN position and depress retaining pin.

7. Install lock cylinder into housing. Turn key to OFF position after checking that cylinder is fully seated and aligned in the interlocking washer.
8. Turn the key to check for proper operation in all positions.
9. Install trim shroud and extension shroud if applicable.
10. Reconnect battery ground cable.

IGNITION SWITCH
REPLACE

1982–86 CAPRI, MUSTANG & MUSTANG SVO

Removal

1. Disconnect battery ground cable.
2. Remove steering column trim shroud.

NOTE: For tilt column only, remove upper extension shroud.

3. Disconnect electrical connector from switch, **Fig. 1.**
4. Rotate ignition key to On (Run) position.
5. Drill out bolt heads securing switch to lock cylinder using a ⅛ inch twist drill. Remove bolts using an "Easy Out" or equivalent.
6. Disengage switch from the actuator pin.

Installation

1. Adjust switch by sliding the carrier to the switch On (Run) position.
2. Check to ensure that the ignition key lock cylinder is in the On (Run) position by rotating the key lock cylinder approximately 90 degrees from the Lock position.
3. Install switch onto the actuator pin.
4. Secure the switch with new break-off head bolts. Tighten bolts until heads shear.
5. Connect electrical connector to switch.
6. Install steering column trim shroud.

NOTE: For tilt column only, install upper extension shroud.

7. Connect battery ground cable.
8. Check for proper operation.

1980–81 CAPRI & MUSTANG

Removal

1. Disconnect battery ground cable.
2. Rotate ignition key to "Lock" position.
3. Remove steering column trim shroud.
4. Using a ⅛ inch twist drill, drill out the bolt heads securing the switch to the lock cylinder. Then, remove the bolts using an "Easy Out" or equivalent, **Fig. 1.**
5. Disengage the actuator rod from switch.

Fig. 2   Ignition switch installation. 1980 Bobcat & Pinto

Fig. 3 Stoplight switch installation.

Fig. 4 Neutral safety switch adjustment. C4 units

2. Remove hairpin retainer, slide switch, push rod and nylon washers and bushing away from the pedal and remove the switch, **Fig. 3.**
3. Reverse procedure to install.

NEUTRAL SAFETY, SWITCH
REPLACE

Removal
1. Remove downshift linkage rod from transmission downshift lever.
2. Remove downshift outer lever retaining nut and lever.
3. Remove two switch attaching bolts.
4. Disconnect wire connector and remove switch.

Installation
1. Install switch on transmission and replace attaching bolts.
2. With transmission manual lever in neutral, rotate switch and install gauge pin (No. 43 drill) into gauge pin hole, **Fig. 4.**
3. Tighten switch attaching bolts and remove gauge pin.
4. Install outer downshift lever and attaching nut.
5. Install downshift linkage rod to downshift lever.
6. Install switch wire connector and check operation of switch. The engine should start only with lever in NEUTRAL or PARK.

LIGHT SWITCH
REPLACE

1. Disconnect battery ground cable.
2. Depress shaft release button by inserting a screwdriver through hole in underside of instrument panel, then remove knob and shaft.
3. Remove bezel nut, lower switch, disconnect electrical connector and remove switch.

---

6. Disconnect electrical connector from switch.
7. Remove switch from vehicle.

Installation
1. With ignition key in "Lock" position, place switch on actuator rod.
2. Secure the switch with two new "Break-Off Head" bolts. Tighten the bolts until the heads shear.
3. Remove the locking pin from new switch, if installed.
4. Connect switch electrical connector.
5. Connect battery ground cable.
6. Check for proper operation.

EXC. 1980–86 CAPRI, MUSTANG & MUSTANG SVO

1. Remove shrouding from steering column and detach and lower steering column from brake support bracket.
2. Disconnect battery ground cable.
3. Disconnect switch wiring at plug, **Fig. 2.**
4. Remove two nuts that retain switch to column.
5. Lift switch vertically upward to disengage actuator rod from switch.
6. To install switch, both the locking mechanism at top of column and the switch must be in LOCK position for correct adjustment.
7. Move shift lever into PARK (with automatic transmission) or REVERSE (with manual transmission), turn the key to LOCK position and remove the key.

NOTE: New switches, when received, are already pinned in LOCK position by a plastic shipping pin inserted in a locking hole on top of switch.

8. Position the hole in the end of switch plunger to the hole in the actuator and install the connecting pin.
9. Position switch on column and install retaining nuts, but do not tighten them.
10. Move switch up and down along column to locate the mid-position of rod lash and then tighten nuts.
11. Remove the plastic or substitute locking pin, connect battery and check switch for proper start in PARK or NEUTRAL.

STOP LIGHT SWITCH
REPLACE

1. Disconnect wires at connector.

Fig. 5 Instrument cluster (Typical) 1980—86 Capri, Mustang & Mustang SVO

TURN SIGNAL SWITCH
REPLACE

1980—86 CAPRI, MUSTANG & MUSTANG SVO

1. Disconnect battery ground cable.
2. On models with tilt column, remove upper extension shroud by unsnapping shroud retaining clips at the 9 o'clock position.
3. Remove five attaching screws, then separate and remove two trim shroud halves.
4. Grasp turn signal switch lever by grasping and using a twisting pulling motion while pulling lever outward.
5. Peel back foam shield from turn signal switch, then disconnect two turn signal switch electrical connectors.
6. Remove two screws attaching turn signal switch to lock housing, then disengage switch from housing and remove.
7. Reverse procedure to install.

1980 BOBCAT & PINTO

1. Disconnect battery ground cable.
2. Remove steering wheel.
3. Unscrew turn signal switch lever from column.
4. Remove shroud from under steering column.

5. Disconnect steering column wiring connector plugs from bracket.
6. Remove turn signal switch attaching screws.
7. Remove plastic cover sleeve from wiring harness.
8. Pull switch and wiring up from steering columns.
9. Reverse procedure to install.

HORN SOUNDER
REPLACE

1980—86 CAPRI, MUSTANG & MUSTANG SVO

1. Disconnect battery ground cable, then remove steering column cover attaching screws and steering column cover.
2. With wire connectors exposed, carefully lift connector retaining tabs and disconnect connectors.
3. Remove switch attaching screws and the switch.
4. Reverse procedure to install.

1980 BOBCAT & PINTO

The horn sounder can be removed by depressing it and turning counter-clockwise or by removing retaining screws from under steering wheel spokes.

INSTRUMENT CLUSTER
REPLACE

1980—86 CAPRI, MUSTANG & MUSTANG SVO

1. Disconnect battery ground cable.
2. Remove three upper retaining screws from instrument cluster trim cover, then the trim cover.
3. On Mustang SVO models, remove four screws retaining instrument cluster to instrument panel. Disconnect turbo-boost pressure hose from retaining brace.
4. Remove upper and lower screws retaining instrument cluster to instrument panel.
5. Pull cluster from panel slightly and disconnect speedometer cable and the printed circuit electrical connectors.
6. Remove instrument clusters from instrument panel, **Fig. 5.**
7. Reverse procedure to install.

1980 BOBCAT & PINTO
Main Cluster
1. Remove two screws attaching upper half to lower half of steering column shroud, then remove lower half shroud.
2. Loosen forward steering column

attaching nuts one or two turns.
3. Loosen rearward steering column attaching nuts ⅜ to ½ inch.
4. Disconnect wire connectors at printed circuit board and tachometer.
5. Disconnect speedometer cable.
6. Remove four cluster attaching screws and pull cluster out along angle of steering column, **Fig. 6.**

Auxiliary Cluster
1. Remove main cluster as described above.
2. Remove two screws attaching auxiliary cluster to instrument panel.
3. Remove auxiliary cluster mask from front of instrument panel.
4. Disconnect wire connector from printed circuit board, then remove auxiliary cluster through access provided by removal of main instrument cluster.

WINDSHIELD WIPER MOTOR
REPLACE

1981-86

1. Disconnect battery ground cable, then remove right hand wiper arm and blade assembly.
2. Remove cowl grille, then remove clip and disconnect linkage drive arm from motor crank pin.
3. Disconnect wiper motor wire connector, then remove three motor attaching screws and pull motor through opening.
4. Reverse procedure to install.

1980

1. Loosen two nuts and disconnect wiper pivot shaft and link from the motor drive arm ball, on Bobcat and Pinto models. A link retaining clip is used on Capri & Mustang models.
2. Remove three motor attaching screws and lower motor away from under the left side of the instrument panel.
3. Disconnect wiper motor wires and remove motor.

WINDSHIELD WIPER TRANSMISSION
REPLACE

1981-86 CAPRI, MUSTANG & MUSTANG SVO

1. Disconnect battery ground cable, then remove right wiper arm and blade assembly from pivot shaft.
2. Remove cowl grille, then remove clip and disconnect linkage drive arm from wiper motor crank pin.
3. Remove two screws retaining right hand pivot shaft to cowl and large nut and spacer from left pivot shaft, then remove linkage assembly.
4. Reverse procedure to install.

MULTIPLE CONNECTOR   NUT—45257-S

CLUSTER—10849

SCREW—52818-S   K2724-A

Fig. 6 Instrument-cluster removal (Typical). 1980 Bobcat & Pinto

1980 CAPRI & MUSTANG

1. Remove wiper motor and linkage cover for access to linkage.
2. Disconnect linkage drive arm from motor crank pin by removing the clip.
3. Remove bolts retaining right pivot shaft and the nut retaining left pivot shaft.
4. Remove assembly from vehicle.
5. Reverse procedure to install.

1980 BOBCAT & PINTO

1. Disconnect battery ground cable, then remove wiper arms and blades from pivot shafts.
2. Remove heater control cover from instrument panel to floor brace, then remove brace.
3. Remove glove box and door, trim panel located below glove box, floor heat distribution duct and center register.
4. Remove two wiring loom retainer attaching screws and pull wiring loom down and out of way.
5. Remove A/C defroster air distribution duct.
6. Loosen two nuts retaining wiper pivot shaft and link assembly to motor drive arm ball, then remove screws attaching both pivots.
7. Remove pivot shaft and link assembly from under left side of instrument panel.
8. Reverse procedure to install. Apply a ³⁄₁₆ in. bead of sealer around each

screw and main pivot stem before installing gasket.

WINDSHIELD WIPER SWITCH
REPLACE

1980-86 CAPRI, MUSTANG & MUSTANG SVO

1. Disconnect battery ground cable.
2. Remove steering column shroud attaching screws and the shroud.
3. Disconnect electrical connector from wiper switch.
4. Remove wiper switch attaching screws and the switch.
5. Reverse procedure to install.

1980 BOBCAT & PINTO

1. Remove instrument cluster as outlined previously.
2. Insert a thin bladed screwdriver into the slot in the switch knob and depress the spring. Then pull the knob from the switch shaft.
3. Remove wiper switch bezel nut. Then unplug wires and remove switch.

REAR WIPER MOTOR & LINKAGE
REPLACE

1980-82 MUSTANG & CAPRI

1. Disconnect battery ground cable.
2. Remove wiper arm and blade assembly.
3. Remove pivot shaft attaching nut and spacers.
4. Remove liftgate inner trim panel.
5. Disconnect electrical connector from wiper motor.
6. Remove 3 motor bracket attaching screws.
7. Remove motor, bracket and linkage assembly from vehicle.
8. Reverse procedure to install.

REAR WIPER SWITCH
REPLACE

1980-82 MUSTANG & CAPRI

1. Disconnect battery ground cable.
2. Remove wiper switch knob.
3. Remove 2 bezel attaching screws, then pull switch retainer away from instrument panel.
4. Remove switch retaining nut and separate switch from retainer.
5. Disconnect electrical connector from switch and remove switch from vehicle.
6. Reverse procedure to install.

BOLT AND WASHER ASSEMBLY – 57030-S

INSTRUMENT PANEL TO-COWL BRACE – 54043A50

RETAINING SCREW

HEATER CORE AND SEAL – 18B539

COVER RETAINING SCREW (4) – 42134-S2

COVER – 18B300

Fig. 7   Heater core replacement. 1980–86 Capri, Mustang & Mustang SVO less A/C

HEATER CORE
REPLACE

LESS AIR CONDITIONING

1980–86 Capri, Mustang & Mustang SVO

1. Drain cooling system and disconnect battery ground cable.
2. Disconnect heater hoses from heater core and plug core openings.
3. Remove glove box liner.
4. Remove instrument panel to cowl brace retaining screws and the brace.
5. Move temperature control lever to warm position.
6. Remove the four heater core cover retaining screws, then the cover through the glove box opening.
7. Remove heater core assembly mounting stud nuts from engine compartment.
8. Push core tubes and seal toward passenger compartment to loosen core from case assembly.
9. Remove heater core from case through the glove box opening, **Fig. 7.**
10. Reverse procedure to install.

Exc. 1980–86 Capri, Mustang & Mustang SVO

1. Drain coolant and disconnect battery.
2. Disconnect blower motor ground wire at engine side of dash.
3. Disconnect heater hoses at engine block.
4. Remove four heater assembly-to-dash mounting nuts from the engine side of the dash.
5. Remove the glove box.
6. Disconnect control cables from heater. Remove mounting bracket clips and disconnect cables from door crank arms.
7. Remove radio as outlined previously.
8. Working inside car, remove snap rivet that attaches the forward side of the defroster air duct to the plenum chamber. Move the air duct back into the defroster nozzle to disengage it from the tabs on the plenum chamber. Now, tilt the forward edge of the duct up and forward to disengage it from the nozzle and remove it from the left side of the heater assembly.
9. Remove heater case-to-instrument panel support bracket mounting screw and remove the heater case. At the same time, pull the two heater hoses in through the dash panel. Then disconnect the hoses from the heater core in the case.
10. Remove compression gasket from cowl air inlet.
11. Remove eleven clips from around the front and rear case flanges and separate the front and rear halves of the case, **Fig. 8.**
12. Lift heater core from front half of case.

RADIO
REPLACE

NOTE: When installing radio, be sure to adjust antenna trimmer for peak performance.

1980–86 CAPRI, MUSTANG & MUSTANG SVO

1. Disconnect battery ground cable.
2. On 1982–86 models with console, remove console as follows:
   a. Remove gear shift lever opening plate. Lift plate up at front end and disengage from clip.
   b. Remove console panel moulding from center of console.
   c. Remove front ash tray.
   d. Remove 2 console-to-floor pan attaching screws located under the ash tray.
   e. Open console storage compartment door and remove 4 console-to-floor pan attaching screws.
   f. Disconnect all electrical connectors from console, then remove console from vehicle.
3. On all models, disconnect all electrical connectors from radio.
4. Remove control knobs, discs, control shaft nuts and washers.
5. Remove ash tray and bracket.
6. Remove radio rear support attaching nut.
7. Remove instrument panel lower reinforcement.
8. Remove A/C or heater floor ducts.
9. Remove radio from bezel and rear support, then lower from instrument panel.
10. Reverse procedure to install.

1980 BOBCAT & PINTO

1. Disconnect battery ground cable.
2. Remove instrument panel trim brace cover.
3. Remove rear support to radio attaching bolt.
4. Remove four screws attaching the bezel to the instrument panel opening.
5. Pull radio out from instrument panel and disconnect speaker, power and antenna wires and remove radio.

WITH AIR CONDITIONING

1980–86 Capri, Mustang & Mustang SVO

1. Disconnect battery ground cable.
2. Remove screws securing the left side of instrument panel pad retaining tabs to the instrument panel, in the upper right and left corners of the instrument panel cluster area.
3. Remove screws securing the right side of instrument panel pad retaining tabs to instrument panel, located in the two openings at the top edge of the right instrument panel trim applique, above the glove box.
4. Remove screws securing leading edge of instrument panel pad to defroster openings. Use a magnetic or locking tang type phillips screwdriver. Do not let screws drop into defroster openings since plenum door damage may result.
5. Raise the overhanging edge of the instrument panel pad to clear retaining tabs and pull pad rearward to remove from top of instrument panel.
6. Remove screws attaching steering column opening lower cover to instrument panel, then the cover.
7. Remove steering column trim shrouds.
8. Remove nuts securing steering column to brake pedal support and lower steering column for access to gearshift selector lever and cable assembly.
9. Reach between steering column and instrument panel and lift selector lever cable off selector lever. Then, remove cable clamp from steering column tube.
10. Rest steering column on front seat.
11. Remove screw attaching instrument panel to brake pedal support at steering column opening.
12. Remove screw attaching lower brace to lower edge of instrument panel, below the radio.
13. Remove screw attaching brace to lower edge of instrument panel.
14. Disconnect temperature control cable from temperature blend door and evaporator case bracket.
15. Disconnect seven-port vacuum hose connectors at evaporator case.
16. Disconnect blower resistor wire connector from resistor and the blower motor feed wire at in-line connector near the blower resistor wire connector.
17. Support instrument panel and remove three screws securing top of instrument panel to the cowl.
18. Remove screw at each side of instrument panel securing instrument panel to cowl side panels.
19. Move instrument panel rearward and disconnect speedometer cable and any wiring that will not permit the panel to lay on the front seat.
21. Drain cooling system.
22. On 1980–81 models, proceed as follows:
    a. Disconnect hoses from heater core. Cover hoses and heater core tubes to prevent leakage.

b. Remove 2 nuts securing evaporator case to dash panel from engine compartment.
c. Working in passenger compartment, remove screws attaching evaporator case support bracket and air inlet duct support bracket to cowl top panel.
d. Remove nut retaining bracket at left end of evaporator case to dash panel and nut securing bracket below case to dash panel.
e. Pull evaporator case assembly from dash panel to gain access to heater core access cover-to-evaporator case attaching screws.

23. On 1982–86 models, proceed as follows:
    a. Discharge refrigerant from A/C system at the service valve on suction line. When system is fully discharged, disconnect and cap high and low pressure lines.
    b. Disconnect hoses from heater core. Cover hoses and heater core tubes to prevent leakage.

Fig. 8   Heater core removal. 1980 Bobcat & Pinto less A/C

Fig. 9   A/C defrost air distribution duct fold down door. 1980 Bobcat & Pinto

HEATER ASSEMBLY

BLOWER HOUSING

SPRING CAP NUT

RIGHT VENTILATOR

RIGHT VENTILATOR CONTROL ASSEMBLY

RIGHT REGISTER DUCT

VENTILATOR GRILLE

RETAINING SCREW

Fig. 10   Right ventilator assembly removal. 1980—86 Capri, Mustang & Mustang SVO less A/C

hose in engine compartment.
4. Remove glove box.
5. Disconnect vacuum hoses from evaporator case and temperature control cable from blend door crank arm.
6. Remove heat distribution duct.
7. Remove staples retaining fold down door on plenum, **Fig. 9.** Bend fold down door from locating tabs on plenum and remove adapter duct.

NOTE: During installation, position fold down door between locating tabs and tape in place with two pieces of black tape, **Fig. 9.**

8. Remove blower motor and wheel from blower scroll.
9. Install a ¼-20 hex washer head screw in mounting tab of inlet duct to upper cowl bracket, holding inlet duct in place.

NOTE: Leave screw in position during installation of case assembly.

10. Remove inlet duct to evaporator case screws.

NOTE: One upper case to inlet duct screw is located under outside-recirc. motor mounting bracket.

11. Remove evaporator to cowl bracket screws and the evaporator to dash panel nuts in engine compartment. Rotate evaporator down and away from instrument panel and remove from under panel.
12. Remove upper to lower case screws and rubber seal from heater core tubes.
13. Remove upper half of evaporator case and move rubber seal on evaporator core forward and pull evaporator core from lower case.
14. Remove heater core upper straps, air deflector mounting screw, then remove air deflector and heater core.

BLOWER MOTOR
REPLACE

LESS AIR CONDITIONING
1980—86 Capri, Mustang & Mustang SVO
1. Disconnect battery ground cable.
2. Remove right ventilator assembly as follows:
   a. Remove screw securing right register duct to lower edge of instrument panel, **Fig. 10.**
   b. Remove 2 screws securing ventilator control cable lever assembly to lower edge of instrument panel.
   c. Remove glove compartment liner to gain access to upper left ventilator attaching screw.
   d. Remove 2 plastic rivets securing grille to ventilator floor outlet opening. Remove grille from bottom of ventilator assembly to gain access to lower right ventilator assembly attaching screw.

c. Remove screw securing air inlet duct and blower housing assembly support brace to cowl top panel.
d. Disconnect black vacuum supply hose from in-line check valve in engine compartment.
e. Disconnect blower motor electrical connectors from harness.
f. Disconnect electrical connector from blower motor resistor.
g. Remove 2 evaporator case-to-dash panel attaching nuts from engine compartment.
h. Working in passenger compartment, remove 2 evaporator case support bracket-to-cowl top panel attaching screws.
i. Remove screw securing bracket below evaporator case to dash panel.
j. Carefully remove evaporator case assembly from vehicle.

24. On all models, remove 5 heater core access cover attaching screws and the access cover.
25. Remove heater core and seals from evaporator case.
26. Remove the 2 seals from heater core tubes.
27. Reverse procedure to install.

1980 Bobcat & Pinto
1. Disconnect battery ground cable, drain radiator and discharge refrigerant from A/C system.
2. Remove refrigerant lines and the front half of refrigerant manifold.

NOTE: Remove manifold mounting stud to ensure clearance for removal of evaporator case.

3. Disconnect heater hoses from core tubes and remove condensation drain

e. Remove right register duct and register assembly to gain access to upper right ventilator attaching screw.

f. Remove 4 screws securing ventilator assembly to blower housing section of heater case.

g. Move ventilator assembly to the right and down and remove from under instrument panel.

h. Remove push nut from door crank arm.

i. Remove control cable snap lock tab and the control cable assembly from ventilator assembly.

3. On 1980–81 models, remove blower motor as follows:

a. Disconnect blower motor electrical connector from spade terminal of resistor assembly and push back through hole in case.

b. Remove right side trim panel to gain access to blower ground lug, then remove ground terminal lug attaching screw.

c. Remove blower motor flange attaching screws from inside blower housing.

d. Remove blower motor from housing.

4. On 1982–86 models, remove blower motor as follows:

a. Remove hub clamp spring from blower wheel hub.

b. Remove blower wheel from shaft.

c. Remove blower motor flange attaching screws from inside blower housing.

d. Slide blower motor out of housing and disconnect electrical connectors from motor.

e. Remove blower motor from vehicle.

5. Reverse procedure to install.

Exc. 1980–86 Capri, Mustang & Mustang SVO

1. Follow procedure to remove the heater core as described previously.

2. Disconnect the blower motor lead wire (orange) from the resistor.

3. Remove the four blower mounting plate nuts and remove the motor and wheel assembly, **Fig. 11.**

4. Reverse procedure to install.

WITH AIR CONDITIONING

1980–86 Capri, Mustang & Mustang SVO

1. Disconnect battery ground cable.

2. Remove glove box and disconnect hose from outside-recirculation door vacuum motor.

3. Remove instrument panel lower right to side cowl attaching bolt.

4. Remove screw attaching support brace to top of air inlet duct.

Fig. 11   Blower motor. (Typical)

5. Disconnect blower motor feed wire at connector.

6. Remove nut retaining blower housing lower support bracket to evaporator case.

7. Remove side cowl trim panel.

8. Remove blower motor ground wire screw.

9. Remove screw attaching top of air inlet duct to evaporator case.

10. Pull air inlet duct and blower housing assembly downward and away from evaporator case.

11. Remove four blower motor mounting plate screws, then the blower motor assembly from blower housing.

NOTE: Do not remove mounting plate from motor.

12. Reverse procedure to install.

Exc. 1980–86 Capri, Mustang & Mustang SVO

1. Remove glove box.

2. Remove four screws retaining blower motor and wheel to blower scroll.

3. Remove blower motor and wheel assembly.

NOTE: On 1980 models, it may be necessary to remove bolt securing instrument panel to right side cowl and pull instrument panel rearward to provide clearance for blower motor removal.

SPEED CONTROL
BEAD CHAIN ADJUSTMENT

Adjust bead chain to obtain a taut chain with the engine at hot idle. The adjustment should be made as to remove as much slack as possible from the bead chain without restricting the carburetor lever from returning to idle. On vehicles equipped with a solenoid throttle positioner, perform adjustment with throttle positioner deactivated.

ACTUATOR CABLE ADJUSTMENT

1. Deactivate the throttle positioner.

2. Set carburetor at hot idle.

3. Pull the actuator cable to remove slack.

4. While maintaining light tension on the actuator cable, insert the cable retaining clip.

VACUUM DUMP VALVE

The vacuum dump valve is mounted on a moveable mounting bracket. The valve should be adjusted so that it is closed when the brake pedal is not depressed and opens when the brake pedal is depressed.

2300 cc Engine Section

Fig. 1   Engine mounts. 1980—86 Capri, Mustang & Mustang SVO

NOTE: This U.S. built engine is designed to metric specifications and therefore metric tooling will be required.

ENGINE MOUNTS
REPLACE

1980—86 CAPRI, MUSTANG & MUSTANG SVO

1. Support engine using a wood block and jack placed under the engine.
2. Remove fan shroud, if necessary.
3. Remove screw attaching fuel pump shield to left hand support bracket, if so equipped.
4. Remove nut and washer assemblies attaching both insulators to the crossmember, **Figs. 1 and 2.**
5. Disconnect transmission shift linkage.
6. Raise engine sufficiently to clear the insulator studs from the crossmember.
7. Remove bolts attaching insulator and bracket assembly from engine and remove insulator and bracket assembly.
8. Reverse procedure to install. Torque insulator and bracket assembly to 33—45 ft. lbs. Torque crossmember nut

assemblies onto insulator studs to 70—100 ft. lbs.

1980 BOBCAT & PINTO

1. Remove fan shroud screws and support engine with a suitable jack and place a piece of wood under oil pan.
2. Remove insulator to support bracket through bolt, **Fig. 3.**
3. Remove support bracket mounting bolts, raise engine slightly, then remove support bracket.
4. Remove insulator to engine block bolts and insulator.
5. Reverse procedure to install.

ENGINE
REPLACE

1. Raise hood and secure in vertical position.
2. Drain coolant from radiator and oil from crankcase.
3. Remove air cleaner and exhaust manifold shroud.
4. Disconnect battery ground cable.
5. Remove radiator hoses and remove radiator and fan.
6. Disconnect heater hoses from water pump and carburetor choke fitting.
7. Disconnect wires from alternator and

starter and disconnect accelerator cable from carburetor. On A/C vehicles, remove compressor from bracket and position it out of way with lines attached.
8. Disconnect flex fuel line from tank line and plug tank line.
9. Disconnect primary wire at coil and disconnect oil pressure and temperature sending unit wires at sending units.
10. Remove starter and raise vehicle to remove the flywheel or converter housing upper attaching bolts.
11. Disconnect inlet pipe at exhaust manifold. Disconnect engine mounts at underbody bracket and remove flywheel or converter housing cover.
12. On vehicle with manual shift, remove flywheel housing lower attaching bolts.
13. On vehicle with automatic transmission, disconnect converter from flywheel and remove converter housing lower attaching bolts. Disconnect transmission oil cooler lines if attached to engine at pan rail.
14. Lower vehicle and support transmission and flywheel or converter housing with a jack.
15. Attach engine lifting hooks to brackets and carefully lift engine out of engine compartment.

Fig. 2   Engine mount installation. 1983–86 4-140 turbocharged engine

CYLINDER HEAD
REPLACE

NOTE: On Mustang SVO models, loosen and disconnect intercooler clamps from intercooler air ducts.

1. Drain cooling system, then remove air cleaner assembly.
2. Remove heater hose-to-rocker arm cover retaining screw.
3. Remove distributor cap and ignition wires.
4. Remove spark plugs.
5. Disconnect all vacuum hoses necessary for cylinder head removal
6. Remove engine oil dipstick.

7. Remove rocker arm cover attaching bolts and the cover.
8. Remove intake manifold attaching bolts, then the intake manifold and carburetor as an assembly.
9. Remove alternator drive belt, then the alternator mounting bracket attaching bolts.
10. Removing timing belt cover attaching bolts and the cover.
11. Loosen cam idler attaching bolts. Move idler to the unloaded position and retighten attaching bolts.
12. Remove timing belt from camshaft and auxiliary sprockets.
13. Remove heat stove from exhaust manifold.
14. Remove exhaust manifold, then the timing belt idler and two bracket

bolts.
15. Remove timing belt idler spring stop from cylinder head, then disconnect oil sending unit electrical connector.
16. Remove cylinder head attaching bolts

TORQUE THE CYLINDER HEAD BOLTS TO SPECIFICATIONS IN TWO PROGRESSIVE STEPS IN THE SEQUENCE SHOWN.

WHEN INSTALLING CYLINDER HEAD, POSITION THE CAMSHAFT AS SHOWN TO AVOID DAMAGE TO PROTRUDING VALVES.

Fig. 4   Cylinder head installation. 2300 cc engine

Fig. 3   Engine mount installation (typical). 1980 Bobcat & Pinto

GASKET

FITTINGS

FRONT OF ENGINE

LIFTING EYE

TORQUE THE MANIFOLD BOLTS TO SPECIFICATIONS IN TWO PROGRESSIVE STEPS IN THE SEQUENCE SHOWN

Fig. 5   Intake manifold tightening sequence. 2300 cc engine

and the cylinder head.

17. Reverse procedure to install. Torque cylinder head bolts to specifications in sequence shown in **Fig. 4** and intake manifold attaching bolts in sequence shown in **Fig. 5**.

NOTE: When installing cylinder head, position camshaft in the 5 o'clock position, **Fig. 4**, allowing minimum protrusion of valves from cylinder head.

VALVE ARRANGEMENT
FRONT TO REAR

2300 cc Engine . . . . E-I-E-I-E-I-E-I

Fig. 6   Valve train installation. 2300 cc engine

VALVE LIFT SPECS.

Engine	Year	Intake	Exhaust
2300 cc	1980–83	.3997	.3997
2300 cc	1984–85	.3900	.3900

VALVE TIMING
INTAKE OPENS BEFORE TDC

Engine	Year	Degrees
2300 cc	1980–85	22

VALVES
ADJUST

The valve lash on this engine cannot be adjusted due to the use of hydraulic valve lash adjusters, **Fig. 6.** However, the valve train can be checked for wear as follows:

1. Crank engine to position camshaft with flat section of lobe facing rocker arm of valve being checked.
2. Remove rocker arm retaining spring.

NOTE: Late models do not incorporate the retaining spring.

3. Collapse lash adjuster with tool T74P-6565B and insert correct size feeler gauge between rocker arm and camshaft lobe, **Fig. 7.** If clearance is not as listed in the "Valve Specifications" chart in front of this chapter, remove rocker arm and check for wear and replace as necessary. If rocker arm is found satisfactory, check valve spring assembled height and adjust as needed. If valve spring assembled height is within specifications listed in the front of this chapter, remove lash adjuster and clean or replace as necessary.

VALVE GUIDES

Valve guides consist of holes bored in the cylinder head. For service the guides can be reamed oversize to accommodate valves with oversize stems of .003, .015 and .030 inch.

ROCKER ARM SERVICE

1. Remove rocker arm cover.
2. Rotate camshaft until flat section of lobe faces rocker arm being removed.
3. With tool T74P-6565B, collapse lash adjuster and, if necessary, valve spring and slide rocker arm over lash adjuster.
4. Reverse procedure to install.

NOTE: Before rotating camshaft, ensure that lash adjuster is collapsed to prevent valve train damage.

LASH ADJUSTER
REPLACE

The hydraulic valve lash adjusters can be removed after rocker arm removal. There are two types of lash adjusters available, Type 1, being the standard lash adjuster, **Fig. 8,** and Type II, having a .020 inch oversize outside diameter, **Fig. 9.**

FRONT ENGINE SEALS
REPLACE

To gain access to the front engine seals,

Fig. 7 Checking valve clearance. 2300 cc engine

Fig. 8 Valve lash adjuster, Type I. 2300 cc engine

remove the timing belt cover and proceed as follows:

Crankshaft Oil Seal
1. Without removing cylinder front cover, remove crankshaft sprocket with tool T74P-6306A, **Fig. 10.**
2. Remove crankshaft oil seal with tool T74P-6700B, **Fig. 11.**
3. Install a new crankshaft oil seal with tool T74P-6150A, **Fig. 12.**
4. Install crankshaft sprocket with recess facing engine block, **Fig. 13.**

Camshaft & Auxiliary Shaft Oil Seals
1. Remove camshaft or auxiliary shaft sprocket with tool T74P-6256A, **Fig. 14.**
2. Remove oil seal with tool T74P-6700B, **Fig. 15.**
3. Install a new oil seal with tool T74P-6150A, **Fig. 12.**
4. Install camshaft or auxiliary shaft sprocket with tool T74P-6256A with center arbor removed.

TIMING BELT
1. Position crankshaft at TDC, No. 1 cylinder compression stroke.
2. Remove timing belt cover, loosen belt tensioner, and remove belt from sprockets, **Fig. 16.** Tighten tensioner bolt, holding tensioner in position.

NOTE: Do not rotate crankshaft or camshaft after belt is removed. Rotating either component will result in improper valve timing.

3. To install belt, ensure timing marks are aligned, **Fig. 17,** and place belt over sprockets.
4. Loosen tensioner bolt, allowing tensioner to move against belt.
5. Rotate crankshaft two complete turns, removing slack from belt. Torque tensioner adjustment and pivot bolts and check alignment of timing marks, **Fig. 17.**
6. Install timing belt cover.

CAMSHAFT
REPLACE
1. Drain cooling system, then remove air cleaner assembly.
2. Disconnect ignition wires from spark plugs and rocker arm cover and position aside.
3. Disconnect all vacuum hoses necessary for camshaft removal.
4. Remove rocker arm cover attaching bolts and the cover.
5. Remove alternator drive belt.
6. Remove alternator mounting bracket attaching bolts and position bracket aside.
7. Remove upper radiator hose and disconnect lower hose.
8. Remove fan shroud. On models

equipped with electric fan, remove fan and shroud as an assembly.
9. Remove timing belt cover attaching bolts and the cover.
10. Loosen cam idler attaching bolts. Move idler to the unloaded position and retighten attaching bolts.
11. Remove timing belt from camshaft and auxiliary sprockets.
12. Raise and support vehicle.
13. Remove right and left engine mount nuts and washers.
14. Raise engine as far as possible using a suitable transmission jack with a block of wood positioned between jack and engine. Install wood blocks between No. 2 crossmember pedestals and engine mounts, then remove jack and lower vehicle.
15. Depress valve springs using tool No. T74P-6565-A or equivalent and remove camshaft followers.
16. Remove camshaft sprocket attaching

Fig. 10 Crankshaft sprocket removal. 2300 cc engine

Fig. 9 Valve lash adjuster, Type II. 2300 cc engine

Fig. 11 Crankshaft front oil seal removal. 2300 cc engine

Fig. 12 Engine front seals installation. 2300 cc engine

bolt, then the sprocket using tool No. T-74P-6565-A, or equivalent.
17. Remove seal using tool No. T74P-6700-A, or equivalent.
18. Remove camshaft retainer attaching screws and the retainer.
19. Remove camshaft from cylinder head, **Fig. 18.**
20. Reverse procedure to install.

NOTE: The camshaft sprocket attaching bolt should be replaced. If a new bolt is not available, coat threads of original bolt with D8AZ-19554-A sealer or equivalent, or wrap teflon tape around threads prior to installation.

PISTON & ROD
ASSEMBLE

Assemble the rod to the piston with the arrow or notch on top of piston facing front of engine, **Fig. 19.**

Check side clearance between connecting rods at each connecting rod crankshaft journal. Clearance should be .0035–.0105 in.

PISTONS, PINS & RINGS

Oversize pistons are available in oversizes of .003 inch, .020 inch, .030 inch and .040 inch. Oversize rings are available in .020 inch, .030 inch and .040 inch oversizes. Oversize pins are not available.

MAIN & ROD BEARINGS

Undersize main bearings are available in .002 inch, .020 inch, .030 inch and .040 inch undersizes. Undersize rod bearings

are available in undersizes of .002 inch, .010 inch, .020 inch, .030 inch and .040 inch.

The crankshaft and main bearings are installed with arrows on main bearing caps facing front of engine, **Fig. 20.** Install PCV baffle between bearing journals No. 3 and 4.

CRANKSHAFT OIL SEAL
1983—86

1. Remove oil pump, if necessary, as described under "Oil Pump, Replace".
2. Punch one hole into metal surface between seal and block using a sharp awl.
3. Screw the threaded end of slide hammer, tool No. T77L-9533-B or equivalent, into seal and remove seal. Use care to avoid damaging oil seal mating surface.
4. Apply suitable sealer to seal and block mating surfaces.
5. Position seal on tool No. T82L-6701-A or equivalent, **Fig. 21,** and install seal.

Fig. 13 Crankshaft sprocket installation. 2300 cc engine

Fig. 14 Camshaft & auxiliary shaft sprockets removal. 2300 cc engine

Fig. 15 Camshaft & auxiliary shaft seals removal. 2300 cc engine

Fig. 16 Drive belt & sprockets installation. 2300 cc engine

Tighten bolts alternately to ensure proper seating of the seal.
6. Install oil pump if previously removed.

1980–81

1. Remove oil pan.
2. Remove rear main bearing cap.
3. Loosen remaining bearing caps, allowing crankshaft to drop down about 1/32 inch.
4. Install a sheet metal screw into seal and pull screw to remove seal.
5. Carefully clean seal groove in block with a brush and solvent. Also clean seal groove in bearing cap.
6. Dip seal halves in clean engine oil.
7. Carefully install upper seal half in its groove with locating tab toward rear of engine, **Fig. 22**, by rotating it on shaft journal of crankshaft until approximately 3/8 inch protrudes below the

parting surface. Be sure no rubber has been shaved from outside diameter of seal by bottom edge of groove.
8. Retighten main bearing caps and torque to specifications.
9. Install lower seal in main bearing cap with undercut side of seal toward front of engine, and allow seal to protrude about 3/8 inch above parting surface to mate with upper seal upon cap installation.
10. Apply suitable sealer to parting faces of cap and block. Install cap and torque to specifications.

NOTE: If difficulty is encountered in installing the upper half of the seal in position, lightly lap (sandpaper) the side of the seal opposite the lip side using a medium grit paper. After sanding, the seal must be washed in solvent, then dipped in clean engine oil prior to installation.

OIL PAN
REPLACE

1980–86

1. Disconnect battery ground cable.
2. Remove fan shroud. If equipped with electric fan, remove fan and shroud as an assembly.
3. On 1983–86 models, drain cooling system, then disconnect upper and lower hoses from radiator.
4. On all models, raise and support vehicle.
5. Drain engine oil, then remove right and left engine mount nuts and bolts or washers.
6. Raise engine as far as possible using a suitable jack with a block of wood positioned between jack and engine. Install wood blocks between mounts and chassis brackets or No. 2 cross-

Fig. 17 Valve timing marks.
2300 cc engine

Fig. 18 Camshaft replacement. 2300 cc engine

member pedestals, then remove jack.
7. Remove shake brace, then the sway bar attaching bolts and lower the sway bar.
8. Remove starter motor.
9. Remove steering gear attaching bolts and lower the gear.
10. Remove oil pan attaching bolts and the oil pan.

NOTE: The number four piston must be in the up position to allow clearance between crankshaft and rear of oil pan for oil pan removal.

11. Reverse procedure to install.

1979

1. Drain crankcase and remove oil dipstick and flywheel inspection cover.
2. Disconnect steering cable from rack and pinion, then rack and pinion from crossmember and move forward to provide clearance.
3. Unfasten and remove oil pan. To install oil pan, refer to **Fig. 23.**

OIL PUMP
REPLACE

The oil pump, **Fig. 24,** can be removed after oil pan removal, **Fig. 25.**

OIL PUMP REPAIRS

1. Remove end plate and withdraw O ring from groove in body.
2. Check clearance between inner rotor tip and outer rotor lobe, **Fig. 26.** This

should not exceed .012 inch. Rotors are supplied only in a matched pair.
3. Check clearance between outer rotor and the housing, **Fig. 27.** This should not exceed .013 inch.
4. Place a straightedge across face of pump body, **Fig. 28.** Clearance between face of rotors and straightedge should not exceed .004 inch.
5. If necessary to replace rotor or drive shaft, remove outer rotor and then drive out retaining pin securing the skew gear to drive shaft and pull off the gear.
6. Withdraw inner rotor and drive shaft.

WATER PUMP
REPLACE

1. Drain cooling system and disconnect hoses from pump.
2. Loosen alternator and remove drive belt.
3. Remove fan, spacer and pulley.

NOTCH POINTING TOWARDS
FRONT OF ENGINE

SQUIRT HOLE

Fig. 19 Piston & rod. 2300 cc engine

4. Remove water pump attaching bolts and water pump after removing drive belt cover.

FUEL PUMP
REPLACE

1. Loosen fuel line connectors, then retighten hand tight. Do not disconnect lines at this time.
2. Loosen fuel pump attaching bolts one or two turns. Apply hand force to break pump free from gasket.
3. Rotate engine slightly until pump cam lobe is near it's lowest position.
4. Disconnect inlet and outlet lines and the vapor return line, if equipped, from pump.
5. Remove fuel pump attaching bolts and the pump. Remove and discard gasket.
6. Reverse procedure to install.

BELT TENSION DATA

	New Lbs.	Used Lbs.
1980		
Exc. ¼ inch	140	110
¼ inch	65	50
1980		
Ribbed Belt w/o Tensioner	155	150
Ribbed Belt w/ Tensioner	130	130
1981		
Except ¼ inch	140	110
¼ inch	65	40
V Ribbed Belt		
4K	105	100
5K①	125	120
5K②	108	108
6K①	155	150
6K②	113	113

Fig. 20   Crankshaft & main bearing installation. 2300 cc engine

Fig. 21   Crankshaft rear oil seal installation. 1983–86 2300 cc engine

Fig. 22   Crankshaft rear oil seal installation. 1980–82 2300 cc engine

1982–86

Except ¼ inch	140	105
¼ inch	65	50
V Ribbed Belt		
4 Rib		
Except Air Pump	130	115
Air Pump	110	105
5 Rib	150	135
6 Rib ①	113	110
6 Rib ③	160	145

①—W/ tensioner.
②—W/ absorber.
③—Fixed.

TURBOCHARGER

The turbocharger, **Figs. 29 through 33,** is an exhaust driven device which compresses the air-fuel mixture that is used to increase engine power on a demand basis, allowing a smaller, more economical engine to be used. An optional turbocharger is available on 1980 and 1984 Capri, Mustang and 1984–86 Mustang SVO models equipped with the 4-140 (2300cc) engine.

A turbine in the exhaust gas flow is connected through a shaft to the impeller (compressor). During normal, steady operation, the turbine does not rotate with sufficient speed to boost pressure to compress the air-fuel mixture. As the speed increases, the mixture is compressed, allowing the denser mixture to enter the combustion chambers and develop more engine power during the combustion cycle.

The intake manifold pressure (boost) is controlled by a wastegate valve which is used to bypass a portion of the exhaust gasses around the turbine at a predetermined point in the cycle, limiting the boost

DRAIN PLUG

OIL PAN-6675

M6X 16.0 LONG SCREW
AND WASHER-18 PLACES

M8X 20.0 LONG
SCREW AND WASHER
- 4 PLACES

PAN GASKET,R.
6710

SEAL-6723
SEE NOTE BELOW

PAN GASKET L.
6711

SEE BONDING NOTE BELOW

GUIDE PINS

SEAL-6722

OIL-RESISTANT SEALER APPROX. 0.125" WIDE BEAD
TO JOINT OF BLOCK AND FRONT COVER

OIL PAN GASKET

BLOCK

FRONT COVER
OR REAR CAP

SEAL TAB

1. APPLY GASKET ADHESIVE EVENLY TO OIL PAN FLANGE AND TO PAN SIDE
   GASKETS. ALLOW ADHESIVE TO DRY PAST WET STAGE, THEN INSTALL
   GASKETS TO OIL PAN.
2. APPLY SEALER TO JOINT OF BLOCK AND FRONT COVER. INSTALL SEALS TO
   FRONT COVER AND REAR BEARING CAP AND PRESS SEAL TABS FIRMLY INTO
   BLOCK. BE SURE TO INSTALL THE REAR SEAL BEFORE THE REAR MAIN
   BEARING CAP SEALER HAS CURED.
3. POSITION 2 GUIDE PINS AND INSTALL THE OIL PAN. SECURE THE PAN WITH
   THE FOUR M8 BOLTS SHOWN ABOVE.
4. REMOVE THE GUIDE PINS AND INSTALL AND TORQUE THE EIGHTEEN M6 BOLTS,
   BEGINNING AT HOLE A AND WORKING CLOCKWISE AROUND THE PAN.

Fig. 23   Oil pan installation. 2300 cc engine

SCREW AND WASHER

6600-OIL PUMP

6A618-SHAFT ASSY
OIL PUMP INTERMEDIATE

Fig. 25   Oil pump installation. 2300 cc engine

IDENTIFICATION
MARKS

Fig. 24   Oil pump. 2300 cc engine

pressure.

A green light on the instrument panel
indicates that the turbocharger is in a safe
boost condition. A red light and buzzer are
used to indicate a malfunction or if boost
pressure exceeds a predetermined level.

The turbocharger used on 1984–86
Mustang SVO models, is similar to the one
used on the Mustang and Capri. However,
the Mustang SVO is equipped with a
charge air cooler (intercooler) mounted
between the turbocharger and throttle
body assemblies. The intercooler, cools
the air flowing out of the turbocharger. The
Mustang SVO also uses a turbo boost con-

**Fig. 26   Checking inner rotor tip
clearance**

Engine oiling system. 2300 cc engine

Fig. 27 Checking outer rotor to housing clearance. 2300 cc engine

trol system which along with the intercooler, allows higher turbo boost pressures, increased combustion efficiency, engine horsepower and torque.

The turbocharger boost control system used on Mustang SVO, is designed to provide electronic variable boost control. The boost control system provides regulation of the wastegate actuator signal allowing up to 14 psi of turbo boost pressure. The system includes a control module, solenoid/hose assembly, calibrated tee fitting and a relay/switch assembly.

Turbochargers are lubricated from the engine oil system. These turbochargers

CENTER HOUSING

COMPRESSOR

OUTLET ELBOW

ACTUATOR

TURBINE

Fig. 29 Turbocharger

Straight Edge

Feeler Gauge

Fig. 28 Checking rotor end play. 2300 cc engine

EXH. TO TURBO
EXH. FROM TURBO
ATMOSPHERIC AIR
PRESSURIZED AIR

Fig. 30 Turbocharger air flow. 1980

Fig. 31 Turbocharger air flow. 1984

operate at speeds up to 120,000 RPM which makes the lubrication of the bearings which support the shaft important for cooling as well as friction.

The oil enters the turbocharger through an inlet fitting in the center housing. This inlet fitting directs oil to the center housing bearings, the oil then drains from the turbocharger through a return hole in the center housing. When changing oil and filter on a turbocharged engine disconnect the ignition switch connector from the distributor then crank engine several times until the oil light goes out. Reconnect the ignition wire to the distributor. This procedure will aid in the filling of the oil system before starting engine.

NOTE: Engine oil on 1980 turbocharged engines must be changed every 3000 miles since turbocharger bearing damage may occur from oil contamination.

INTAKE MANIFOLD is redesigned.

OIL SUPPLY and RETURN lines are new.

TURBOCHARGER is an exhaust driven device which compresses the air/fuel mixture.

EGR TUBE and VALVE are new.

CROSSOVER PIPE moves exhaust gas from one side of the engine to the other, and DOWN PIPE connects the exhaust system to the turbocharger.

NEW INTAKE and EXHAUST VALVES and CYLINDER HEAD GASKET handle increased loads, stresses, and temperatures.

UPGRADED RADIATOR enhances engine cooling.

OIL CAPACITY is increased by 1/2 quart.

TURBO BOOST/OVERBOOST AND ENGINE OIL OVERTEMPERATURE WARNING SYSTEM is new.

ELECTRONIC PRESSURE RETARD SYSTEM retards spark to eliminate possibility of detonation.

FORGED PISTONS increase durability. The pin offset is decreased, and the second land width and bore clearance increased. The TOP RING is ductile iron, and the LOWER COMPRESSION RING is chromed.

MAIN BEARINGS AND ROD BEARINGS have increased load capacity.

The OIL PUMP has a stiffer relief valve spring to maintain normal oil pressure.

Fig. 32 Turbocharger system. 1980

INTERCOOLER

THROTTLE BODY

CLAMP

BOLTS

UPPER FRONT BRACKET

CLAMP

INTERCOOLER BRACKET

TURBOCHARGER

Fig. 33 Intercooler assembly. Mustang SVO

6-200 Engine Section

Refer to the Ford & Mercury—Compact & Intermediate chapter for service procedures on this engine not included in this section.

OIL PAN, REPLACE

1. If equipped with automatic transmission, disconnect transmission oil cooler lines from radiator, then remove the radiator top support.
2. Remove dipstick, then raise and support vehicle and drain crankcase.
3. Remove the four bolts and nuts retaining sway bar to chassis and allow sway bar to hang down.
4. Remove K-brace, then lower the rack and pinion steering gear.
5. Remove starter motor, then remove the two engine mounts to support bracket nuts and loosen the two rear insulator to crossmember retaining bolts.
6. Raise engine and place a 1¼ inch wooden block between each engine support insulator and chassis bracket, then lower engine onto wood blocks.
7. Using floor jack, raise transmission slightly, then remove the oil pan retaining bolts and lower oil pan onto crossmember.
8. Position transmission oil cooler lines aside and remove oil pan. If necessary, rotate engine so crankshaft throws clear oil pan rail.
9. Reverse procedure to install.

V6-232 Engine Section

Refer to Ford & Mercury—Compact & Intermediate chapter for service procedures on this engine.

Fig. 1   Engine mount. 1980—85 Capri & Mustang

Fig. 2   Serpentine drive belt

Fig. 3   Serpentine drive belt tensioner alignment marks

V8 Engine Section

NOTE: Refer to the Ford & Mercury—Compact & Intermediate chapter for service procedures on this engine not included in this section.

ENGINE MOUNTS
REPLACE

1980–85 CAPRI & MUSTANG

NOTE: Late 1985 and 1986 models, use viscous type engine mounts.

1. Remove fan shroud attaching screws, if necessary.
2. Remove nuts attaching insulators to lower bracket, **Fig. 1.**
3. Raise engine with a suitable jack and a block of wood placed under oil pan.
4. Remove insulator to engine block attaching bolts.
5. Remove insulator from vehicle.
6. Reverse procedure to install.

VALVES
ADJUST

The firing order of the 1982–86 V8-302 H.O. engine is 1-3-7-2-6-5-4-8, while the firing order for the 1980–81 V8-302 and 1980–82 V8-255 engines is 1-5-4-2-6-3-7-8. Therefore when adjusting valves on the 1982–86 V8-302 H.O. engine, refer to the procedure for the V8-351 engine in the "Ford & Mercury—Compact & Intermediate" chapter.

OIL PAN
REPLACE

1. Disconnect battery cables.

2. Remove fan shroud retaining bolts and position fan shroud over fan.
3. On 1981–86 models, remove dipstick and tube assembly.
4. On all models, raise and support vehicle, then drain crankcase.

NOTE: Some oil pans have dual oil sumps. Make sure to remove both drain plugs to thoroughly drain oil.

5. Remove the two bolts retaining steering gear to main crossmember and allow steering gear to rest on frame away from oil pan.
6. Remove engine mount retaining bolts, then raise engine and place a 2 x 4 inch wooden block between each engine mount and vehicle frame.
7. Remove rear K-braces
8. Remove oil pan retaining bolts and lower oil pan onto frame.
9. Remove oil pump retaining bolts and the inlet tube retaining nut from No. 3 main bearing cap stud. Lower the oil pump assembly into the oil pan.
10. Remove oil pan. If necessary, rotate engine so that crankshaft throws clear oil pan rail.
11. Reverse procedure to install.

SERPENTINE DRIVE BELT

Some engines are equipped with a serpentine drive belt, **Fig. 2,** to drive the accessories in place of the usual arrangement. This "V" ribbed belt drives the fan/water pump, alternator, secondary air pump, optional A/C compressor and optional power steering pump.

The tensioner arm should be checked to ensure that the top edge of the arm is located between the two index marks scribed on the circumference next to the slot of the tensioner housing, **Fig. 3.** If the tensioner arm is not properly aligned, the drive belt and pulleys should be inspected for wear and binding. If the drive belt and pulleys are satisfactory, the tensioner must be replaced as outlined in the following procedure.

Drive Belt & Tensioner, Replace

1. Insert a 16 inch pry bar or equivalent in the slot of the tensioner bracket, and using the tensioner housing as a fulcrum, push the pry bar downward to force the tensioner pulley upward, relieving tension on belt, **Fig. 2.**
2. Remove drive belt.
3. Remove bolt securing tensioner assembly to alternator bracket.
4. Remove tensioner assembly.
5. Position tensioner assembly so the tang, located on the rear of the assembly, is placed to fit in the hole or slot in alternator bracket.
6. Install the tensioner assembly bolt through the hole in the alternator bracket and torque bolt to 55-80 ft. lbs.
7. Install drive belt by inserting the pry bar as outlined in Step 1. Refer to decal located on top of the windshield washer/coolant expansion reservoir for proper belt routing.
8. Remove pry bar.
9. The drive belt is automatically tensioned when the tensioner arm is located between the two index marks, **Fig. 3.**

Clutch & Transmission Section

CLUTCH PEDAL
ADJUST

1981–85 CAPRI, MUSTANG SVO & MUSTANG

These models incorporate a self adjusting clutch mechanism. The adjust mechanism consists of a spring loaded rachet quadrant attached to the clutch cable. To accomplish this adjustment, grasp clutch pedal and pull upward, then slowly depress clutch pedal. If a click is heard during the procedure, an adjustment was necessary and has been accomplished. This procedure should be performed at least every 5000 miles.

1980 CAPRI & MUSTANG

NOTE: These models do not require a free play adjustment. A clutch pedal height adjustment will be required instead.

1. From under vehicle remove dust shield.
2. Loosen clutch cable lock nut. Turn adjusting nut clockwise to raise clutch pedal and counter clockwise to lower clutch pedal. The total clutch pedal stroke should be 5.3 in. for 4-140 en-

gine and 6.5 in. for V8-302 engine.
3. Torque lock nut to 5 to 8 ft. lbs., using care not to disturb adjustment.
4. Cycle clutch pedal several times, then recheck pedal height.
5. When clutch system is properly adjusted the clutch pedal can be raised approximately 2.7 in. on 4-140 engines and 1.5 in. for V8-302 engines, before contacting the clutch pedal stop.

1980 BOBCAT & PINTO

1. Loosen clutch cable lock nut at flywheel housing.

2. Pull cable toward front of vehicle so the nylon adjuster nut tabs are clear of the housing boss, then rotate nut toward vehicle front approximately ¼ inch.
3. Release the cable, neutralizing the system, and pull cable forward again so release lever free movement is eliminated.
4. Rotate the adjusting nut until contact is made between index tab face and the housing, then index the tabs to engage the nearest housing groove.
5. Torque lock nut to 15 ft. lbs.

CLUTCH
REPLACE

NOTE: Prior to installing throw-out bearing, apply a light film of lithium base lubricant part No. C1AZ-19590-B or equivalent to transmission front bearing retainer outside diameter, the clutch release fork and antirattle spring where they contact the release bearing hub and to the throw-out bearing where the bearing contacts the pressure plate release fingers. In addition, fill the throw-out bearing grease groove with the same lubricant. Wipe off all excess lubricant.

1980 BOBCAT & PINTO

1. Remove shift lever by removing knob and boot, then compress rubber spring and remove retaining snap ring. Bend shift lever lock tabs up and remove plastic dome nut from extension housing.
2. Raise vehicle on a hoist.
3. Disconnect drive shaft from U joint flange and slide drive shaft off transmission output shaft. Insert tool over output shaft to prevent loss of lubricant.
4. Disconnect speedometer cable and backup light switch wire connector from extension housing.
5. Disconnect lower end of clutch cable at release lever.
6. Remove starter motor.
7. Remove bolts securing engine rear plate to front lower part of flywheel housing.
8. Support rear of engine using a suitable jack, then remove bolt attaching engine rear support. Also remove crossmember attaching bolts and remove the crossmember.
9. Remove bolts attaching flywheel housing to engine block.
10. Move transmission and flywheel housing assembly rearward until housing clears the clutch pressure plate. Lower transmission and remove.
11. Unfasten and remove the pressure plate, marking same to assure correct

assembly.

1980–86 CAPRI & MUSTANG

NOTE: On 1981–86 Capri and Mustang, lift clutch pedal upward to disengage clutch cable self adjuster pawl and quadrant. Push quadrant forward, then detach cable from quadrant and allow quadrant to slowly swing rearward.

1. Loosen clutch cable adjusting nut to allow slack in cable. On all models, disconnect cable from release lever.
2. Position gear shift lever in neutral, then remove lever attaching screws and the lever.
3. Raise and support vehicle.
4. On all models, remove dust shield.
5. On all models, remove driveshaft. Cover extension housing to prevent leakage.
6. Disconnect electrical leads and speedometer cable from transmission.
7. Support rear of engine and remove crossmember, then lower engine as necessary and remove transmission attaching bolts and transmission.
8. Disconnect clutch release cable from lever and flywheel housing.
9. Disconnect starter cable and remove starter motor.
10. On models with V6 engine, remove number 2A crossmember. This crossmember is located behind the number 2 crossmember which supports the engine.
11. On all models, remove flywheel housing.
12. Evenly loosen and remove pressure plate attaching screws to prevent distortion of pressure plate. If pressure plate is to be reused, mark pressure plate and flywheel to assure correct assembly.

1984–86 MUSTANG SVO

1. Lift clutch pedal to its uppermost position, then disconnect pawl and quadrant. Push quadrant forward, disconnect cable from quadrant and allow quadrant to slowly swing rearward.
2. Raise and support vehicle, then disconnect shift linkage assembly from transmission.
3. Remove retainer and clevis pins from lower end of bellcrank.
4. Separate clevis from cable end.
5. Remove retaining clip and cable from flywheel housing.
6. Remove starter cable and starter motor from flywheel housing.
7. Remove engine rear plate attaching bolts from front lower portion of flywheel housing.

8. Disconnect drive shaft from U-joint flange and slide drive shaft from transmission output shaft. Insert output shaft cap tool onto transmission output shaft.
9. Position a suitable jack under transmission, then remove transmission to bellhousing attaching bolts. Disconnect speedometer cable and electrical connectors from transmission.
10. Lower transmission assembly from vehicle.
11. Remove housing to cylinder block attaching bolts. Pull housing rearward to clear pressure plate, then remove housing.
12. Disconnect the short cable from release lever by pushing cable and release lever boot approximately ½ inch toward release bearing. Pull cable rearward through release lever boot hole.
13. Remove release lever boot from flywheel housing.
14. Remove clutch release lever from housing by pulling lever through housing window until retainer spring is disengaged from pivot.
15. Remove release bearing from release lever.
16. Loosen the six pressure plate cover attaching bolts evenly to gradually release spring tension and avoid damaging the pressure plate cover.
17. If the same pressure plate and cover are to be reused, mark pressure plate cover and flywheel so pressure plate can be installed in its original position.
18. Remove pressure plate and clutch disc assembly from flywheel.
19. Reverse procedure to install.
20. During installation of pressure plate assembly, proceed as follows:
    a. Using a suitable clutch alignment tool, align clutch disc.
    b. Alternately tighten the bolts a few turns at a time, until bolts are tight.
    c. Torque the six pressure plate cover bolts to 12–24 ft. lbs, then remove clutch alignment tool.
    d. Apply a light film of grease part No. C1AZ-19590-B or equivalent, onto the outside diameter of transmission front bearing retainer, release lever fork and anti-rattle spring where they contact the release bearing hub, release bearing surface, release lever ball pivot and lever pocket.

4 & 5 SPEED TRANS.
REPLACE

Remove transmission assembly as described under "Clutch, Replace".

Rear Axle, Propeller Shaft & Brakes

Fig. 1 Disassembled integral rear axle. 6¾ inch ring gear. 1980—83

REAR AXLE
INTEGRAL TYPE

This rear axle, **Figs. 1 and 2** is an integral design hypoid with the centerline of the pinion set below the centerline of the ring gear. The semi-floating axle shafts are retained in the housing by ball bearings and bearing retainers at axle ends.

The differential is mounted on two opposed tapered roller bearings which are retained in the housing by removable caps. Differential bearing preload and drive gear backlash is adjusted by nuts located behind each differential bearing cup.

The drive pinion assembly is mounted on two opposed tapered roller bearings. Pinion bearing preload is adjusted by a collapsible spacer on the pinion shaft. Pinion and ring gear tooth contact is adjusted by shims bebetween the rear bearing cone and pinion gear.

REMOVABLE CARRIER TYPE

In these axles, **Fig. 3**, the drive pinion is straddle-mounted by two opposed tapered roller bearings which support the pinion shaft in front of the drive pinion gear, and a straight roller bearing that supports the pinion shaft at the rear of the pinion gear. The drive pinion is assembled in a pinion retainer that is bolted to the differential carrier. The tapered roller bearings are preloaded by a collapsible spacer between the bearings. The pinion is positioned by a shim or shims located between the drive pinion retainer and the differential carrier.

The differential is supported in the carrier by two tapered roller side bearings. These bearings are preloaded by two threaded ring nuts or sleeves between the bearings and the pedestals. The differential assembly is positioned for proper ring gear and pinion backlash by varying the adjustment of these ring nuts. The differential case houses two side gears in mesh with two pinions mounted on a pinion shaft which is held in place by a pin. The side gears and pinions are backed by thrust washers.

The axle shafts are of unequal length, the left shaft being shorter than the right. The axle shafts are mounted in sealed ball bearings which are pressed on the shafts.

REAR AXLE
REPLACE

1. Raise vehicle and support at rear frame members.
2. Drain lubricant from axle.
3. Mark drive shaft and pinion flanges for reassembly, then disconnect drive shaft at rear axle U-joint and remove drive shaft from transmission extension housing. Install seal replacer tool in extension housing to prevent leakage.
4. Disconnect shock absorbers at lower mountings.
5. Remove rear wheels and brake drums, then disconnect brake lines at wheel cylinders.
6. Disconnect vent hose from vent tube, then remove vent tube from brake junction and axle housing.
7. Remove clips retaining brake lines to axle housing.
8. Support rear axle housing using a suitable jack.
9. On models with coil springs, disconnect upper control arms from mount-

Fig. 2   Disassembled integral rear axle. 7½ inch ring gear

Fig. 3 Disassembled rear axle with removable carrier (typical)

ings on axle housing, then carefully lower axle assembly until spring tension is relieved and remove coil springs. Disconnect lower control arms from axle housing.
10. On models with leaf springs, remove U-bolts and plates.
11. Lower rear axle and remove from vehicle.
12. Reverse procedure to install.

AXLE SHAFT, BEARING & OIL SEAL REPLACE

INTEGRAL TYPE

6¾ Inch Ring Gear
1. Remove wheel and tire from brake drum.
2. Remove Tinnerman nuts that secure brake drum to axle flange and remove brake drum.
3. Working through hole in each axle flange, remove nuts that secure wheel bearing retainer plate. Then pull the axle shaft assembly out of the housing being careful not to cut or rough up the seal.

NOTE: The brake backing plate must not be dislodged. Replace one nut to hold the

plate in place after shaft is removed.

4. If wheel bearing is to be replaced, loosen inner retainer ring by nicking it deeply with a chisel in several places. It will then slide off.
5. Remove bearing from shaft.

7½ Inch Ring Gear
1. Raise and support vehicle.
2. Remove wheel and tire assembly, then the brake drum.
3. Clean all dirt from carrier cover area.
4. Remove housing cover to drain lubricant from rear axle.
5. Remove differential pinion shaft lock bolt and the shaft.
6. Move flanged end of axle shafts toward center of vehicle and remove "C" clip from button end of shaft.
7. Remove axle shaft from housing. Use care to avoid damaging the oil seal.
8. Remove bearing and seal as an assembly using a suitable slide hammer.
9. Reverse procedure to install. Lubricate new bearing with rear axle lubricant prior to installation. Apply suitable grease between lips of oil seal.

NOTE: The bearing should be installed using tool No. T78P-1225-A or equivalent, and the seal using tool No. T78P-1177-A or equivalent. If proper tools are not used, early bearing or seal failure may result. If seal becomes cocked in the bore during in-

stallation, it must be removed and replaced with a new one.

8.8 Inch Ring Gear
1. Raise and support vehicle, then remove rear wheel and tire assembly.
2. Clean all dirt from carrier cover area with a wire brush and/or cloth.
3. Remove axle housing cover and drain lubricant from axle, **Fig. 4.**
4. Remove differential pinion shaft lock bolt and differential pinion shaft.
5. Push flanged end of axle shaft toward center of the vehicle, then remove C-lock from button end of axle shaft assembly.
6. Remove axle shaft from housing. Ensure not to damage oil seal.
7. Insert tool 1175-AC or equivalent, into housing bore and position it behind bearing so tangs on tool engage bearing outer race. Using slide hammer tool T50T-100-A or equivalent, remove bearing and seal as a unit.
8. Reverse procedure to install, noting the following:
   a. Lubricate new bearing with lubricant E0AZ-19580-A or equivalent, and install bearing into housing bore using tool T78P-1225-A or equivalent.
   b. Install axle shaft seal using tool T78P-1177-A or equivalent. Apply

Fig. 4   Disassembled integral rear axle. 8.8 inch ring gear

lubricant C1AZ-19590-B or equivalent, between the lips of the seal.

NOTE: Installation of bearing or seal assembly without proper tool may result in an early bearing or seal failure. If seal becomes cocked in bore during installation, remove it and install a new one.

c. Check for presence of axle shaft O-ring on the spline end of the shaft and install if not present.

Removable Carrier Type

1. Remove wheel assembly.
2. Remove brake drum from flange.
3. Working through hole provided in axle shaft flange, remove nuts that secure wheel bearing retainer.
4. Pull axle shaft out of housing. If bearing is a tight fit in axle housing use a slide hammer-type puller.
5. Remove brake backing plate.
6. If the axle shaft bearing is to be replaced, loosen the inner retainer by nicking it deeply with a chisel in several places. The bearing will then slide off easily.
7. Press bearing from axle shaft.
8. Inspect machined surface of axle shaft and housing for rough spots that would affect sealing action of the oil seal. Carefully remove any burrs or rough spots.

9. Press new inner bearing retainer on shaft until it seats firmly against shoulder on shaft.
10. Press inner bearing retainer on shaft until it seats firmly against bearing.
11. If oil seal is to be replaced, use a hook-type tool to pull it out of housing. Wipe a small amount of oil resistant sealer on outer edge of seal before it is installed.

Installation
1. Place a new gasket on each side of brake carrier plate and slide axle shaft into housing. Start the splines into the differential side gear and push the shaft in until bearing bottoms in housing.
2. Install retainer and tighten nuts to 20–40 ft. lbs.
3. Install brake drum and wheel.

PROPELLER SHAFT
REPLACE

1. To maintain balance, mark relationship of rear drive shaft yoke and the drive pinion flange of the axle if alignment marks are not visible.
2. Disconnect rear U-joint from companion flange, **Fig. 5.** Wrap tape around loose bearing caps to prevent them from falling off spider. Pull drive shaft toward rear of car until slip yoke clears

transmission extension housing and the seal. Install tool in extension housing to prevent lubricant leakage.

BRAKE ADJUSTMENTS

The hydraulic drum brakes, **Fig. 6,** are self-adjusting and require a manual adjustment only after brake shoes have been replaced. The adjustment is made as follows:

1. Using tool No. 11-0001 on 1980–82 models, or tool No. D81L-1103-A on 1983–86 models, determine inside diameter of brake drum, **Fig. 6.**
2. Reverse tool and adjust brake shoes to fit the gauge. Hold automatic adjusting lever out of engagement while rotating adjusting screw, to prevent burring slots in screw.

PARKING BRAKE
ADJUST

1. Release parking brake.
2. Place transmission in Neutral and raise vehicle until rear wheels clear floor.
3. Tighten adjusting nut on equalizer rod at the control, **Fig. 7,** to cause the rear wheel brakes to drag.

Fig. 5 Drive shaft and universal joints disassembled. Single Cardan type U-joint

Fig. 6 Brake adjustment

4. Loosen adjusting nut until rear brakes are just free.

MASTER CYLINDER
REPLACE

EXC. POWER BRAKES

1. Disconnect battery ground cable.
2. Disconnect stoplight switch wires at connector. Remove spring retainer and slide stop light switch off brake pedal pin just far enough to clear end of pin, then lift switch straight upward from the pin.
3. Slide master cylinder push rod and nylon washers and bushings off brake pedal pin.
4. Remove brake tubes from master cylinder ports.
5. Unfasten and remove master cylinder

by lifting forward and upward from vehicle.

POWER BRAKES

Disconnect brake tubes from master cylinder, then remove attaching nuts and slide master cylinder forward and upward from vehicle.

POWER BRAKE UNIT
REPLACE

1. Remove stoplight switch and slide booster push rod, bushing and inner nylon washer from brake pedal pin.
2. Remove air cleaner.
3. On all except Capri and Mustang with V8 engine, disconnect accelerator cable from carburetor. Remove screws securing accelerator cable bracket to engine and rotate bracket toward engine. On models with 4-140

engine, disconnect inlet hose of choke water cover and position aside.
4. On Bobcat and Pinto, disconnect vacuum hoses from solenoid on fender apron, then remove the solenoid.
5. On all models, disconnect vacuum hose from power brake unit.
6. Disconnect hydraulic lines from master cylinder and cap open lines and ports.
7. Remove master cylinder.
8. From inside vehicle, remove power brake unit to dash panel attaching nuts.
9. On models with speed control, remove control amplifier which is mounted on the lower outboard booster stud and set aside.
10. On all models, work from engine compartment and move booster forward until booster studs clear the dash panel, then raise front of unit and remove from vehicle.

Fig. 7 Parking brake adjustment

Rear Suspension

SHOCK ABSORBER
REPLACE

1980–86 CAPRI, MUSTANG & MUSTANG SVO

NOTE: On hatchback models, the upper shock absorber upper mounting is accessible from the luggage compartment. On hatchback and fastback models, remove side panel trim covers to gain access to the upper shock absorber mounting.

1. Disconnect shock absorber from upper mounting.
2. Raise vehicle and support rear axle.
3. Compress shock absorber to clear hole in upper shock absorber tower.
4. Disconnect shock absorber from lower mounting and remove shock absorber from vehicle.
5. Reverse procedure to install.

1980 BOBCAT & PINTO

1. With rear axle supported properly disconnect shock absorber from lower mounting.
2. Remove bolts securing upper mounting bracket to underbody.
3. Remove bracket from shock absorber.
4. Reverse procedure to install.

LEAF SPRINGS & BUSHINGS
REPLACE

1980 BOBCAT & PINTO

1. Raise rear of vehicle and support at frame. Support axle with a suitable jack.
2. Disconnect shock absorbers from lower mountings.
3. Lower jack and remove spring plate "U" bolts and spring plate, **Fig. 1**.
4. Raise axle to remove weight from spring and disassemble rear shackle.
5. Remove spring front mount bolt.
6. Replace spring front eye bushing as necessary, **Figs. 2 and 3**.
7. Reverse procedure to install.

COIL SPRING
REPLACE

1980–86 CAPRI, MUSTANG & MUSTANG SVO

1. Raise rear of vehicle and support at rear body crossmember.
2. Remove stabilizer bar, if equipped, **Fig. 4**.
3. Lower axle housing until shock absorbers are fully extended.

Fig. 1   Leaf spring rear suspension. 1980 Bobcat & Pinto

NOTE: The axle housing must be supported with a suitable jack.

4. Position a suitable jack under lower control arm rear pivot bolt to support control arm, then remove pivot bolt.
5. Carefully lower the lower control arm until spring tension is relieved, then remove coil spring and insulator.
6. Reverse procedure to install. Torque lower control arm pivot bolt to 70 to 100 ft. 1980 and 1983–86 models, or 90–100 ft. lbs. on 1981–82 models,

with suspension at curb height.

CONTROL ARMS & BUSHINGS
REPLACE

1980–86 CAPRI, MUSTANG & MUSTANG SVO

Upper Control Arm
1. Raise rear of vehicle and support at

Fig. 2   Spring, front bushing removal. 1980 Bobcat & Pinto

Fig. 3   Spring, front bushing installation. 1980 Bobcat & Pinto

rear body crossmember.
2. Remove upper control arm rear and front pivot bolts, then remove control arm.
3. If control arm axle bracket bushings are to be replaced, refer to **Figs. 5 and 6.**
4. Position upper control arm into side rail bracket, then install front pivot bolt. Do not tighten bolt at this time.
5. Raise rear axle until upper control arm rear pivot bolt hole is aligned with hole in axle housing, then install rear pivot bolt. Do not tighten bolt at this time.
6. Position suspension at curb height. Torque front pivot bolt to 70–100 ft. lbs. on 1983–86 models, 85–120 ft. lbs. on 1980 models, or 100 ft. lbs. on 1981–82 models. Torque rear pivot bolt to 70–100 ft. lbs. on 1980 models, 100 ft. lbs. on 1981–82 models, or 80–104 ft. lbs. on 1983–86 models.

Lower Control Arms
1. Remove coil spring as described under "Coil Spring, Replace."

2. Remove lower control arm front pivot bolt and nut, then remove control arm.
3. Reverse procedure to install. Torque front pivot bolt to 85–120 ft. lbs. on 1980 models, 100 ft. lbs. on 1981–82 models, or 80–104 ft. lbs. on 1983–86 models. Torque rear pivot bolt to 70–100 ft. lbs. on 1980 and 1983–86 models, or 100 ft. lbs. on 1981–82 models.

STABILIZER BAR
REPLACE

1980–86 CAPRI, MUSTANG & MUSTANG SVO

1. Raise and support rear of vehicle.
2. Remove four bolts attaching stabilizer bar to brackets on lower control arms.
3. Remove stabilizer bar from vehicle.

4. Reverse procedure to install. Torque all bolts to 15–20 ft. lbs. on 1980 models, 20 ft. lbs. on 1981 models, or 45–50 ft. lbs. on 1982–86 models.

AXLE DAMPERS
REPLACE

1984–86 MUSTANG GT, CAPRI RS, GS & MUSTANG SVO

1. Raise vehicle and support rear axle.
2. Remove rear wheel, then the axle damper rear attaching nut and pivot bolt, **Fig. 7.**
3. Remove axle damper forward attaching nut, the axle damper and spacer.
4. Reverse procedure to install. Torque attaching bolts to 50–60 ft. lbs.

TRACTION BAR
REPLACE

1984 MUSTANG & CAPRI WITH 2300CC TURBOCHARGED OR V8-302 H.O. ENGINES

1. Raise vehicle and support rear axle.
2. Remove traction bar to rear axle attaching bolts, then the traction bar, adjusting shims and "U" bolt, **Fig. 8.**
3. Remove cotter pin and washer, then the rubber bumper if necessary.
4. Reverse procedure to install, noting the following:
   a. If rubber bumper is replaced, use tire mounting solution ESAM-1B6B or equivalent to ease installation.
   b. Torque traction bar attaching nuts to 85–105 ft. lbs.
   c. Adjust traction bar, as needed, by adding or subtracting shims, **Fig. 8.**

Fig. 4   Coil spring rear suspension (typical). 1980–86 Capri, Mustang & Mustang SVO

Fig. 5 Upper control arm axle bracket bushing installation. 1980—86 Capri, Mustang & Mustang SVO

Fig. 6 Upper control arm axle bracket bushing removal. 1980—86 Capri, Mustang & Mustang SVO

Fig. 7 Axle damper assembly. 1984—86 Mustang GT, Capri RS, GS & Mustang SVO

Fig. 8 Traction bar assembly. 1984 Mustang & Capri with 2300cc turbocharged or V8-302 H.O. engines

Front Suspension & Steering Section

FRONT SUSPENSION

1980—86 CAPRI, MUSTANG & MUSTANG SVO

The front suspension, **Fig. 1**, is of the modified McPherson strut design, which uses shock struts and coil springs. The springs are mounted between the lower control and a spring pocket in the cross-member.

1980 BOBCAT & PINTO

The upper and lower ends of the spindle are attached to upper and lower ball joints which are mounted in upper and lower arms. The upper arm pivots on a bushing and shaft assembly which is bolted to the frame. The lower arm pivots on a bolt in the front crossmember, **Fig. 2**.

WHEEL ALIGNMENT

1980—86 CAPRI, MUSTANG & MUSTANG SVO

Caster
The caster angle of this suspension is factory pre-set and cannot be adjusted.

Camber
1. Remove pop rivet from camber plate.
2. Loosen 3 camber plate-to-body apron nuts.
3. Move top of shock strut as needed to bring camber angle within specifications, then tighten nuts.

NOTE: It is not necessary to replace the pop rivet.

1980 BOBCAT & PINTO

Caster and Camber
1. Working inside front wheel housing, install special tool, one at each end of the upper arm inner shaft. Turn the special tool bolts inward until the bolt ends contact the body metal, **Fig. 3**.
2. Loosen the two upper arm inner shaft-to-body bolts. The upper shaft will move inboard until stopped by the tool bolt ends solidly contacting the body metal.
3. Turn the special tool bolts inward or outward until caster and camber are within specifications. Tightening these

Fig. 1 Front suspension assembly. 1980—86 Capri, Mustang & Mustang SVO

bolts on the special tool forces the arm outward; while loosening the bolts on the tools permits the arm and inner shaft to move inboard due to weight force.

4. When properly adjusted, torque shaft-to-body bolts to 95–120 ft. lbs., then remove the special tools.

TOE-IN
ADJUST

1. Check to see that steering shaft and steering wheel marks are in alignment and in the top position.
2. Loosen clamp screw on the tie rod bellows and free the seal on the rod to prevent twisting of the bellows, **Fig. 4.**
3. Loosen tie rod jam nut.
4. Use suitable pliers to turn the tie rod inner end to correct the adjustment to specifications. Do not use pliers on tie rod threads. Turning to reduce number of threads showing will increase toe-in. Turning in the opposite direction will reduce toe-in. On 1980–81 models, torque tie rod jam nuts to 35–50 ft. lbs. On 1982–86 models, torque

to 43–50 ft. lbs.

WHEEL BEARINGS
ADJUST

1. Raise vehicle until wheel and tire clear floor.
2. Remove wheel cover and dust cap from hub.
3. Remove cotter pin and lock nut.
4. Loosen adjusting nut 3 turns, then rock wheel, hub and rotor assembly in and out several times to move shoe and linings away from rotor.
5. While rotating wheel assembly, torque the adjusting nut to 17–25 ft. lbs. to seat the bearings.
6. Back off the adjusting nut one half turn. Retighten the nut to 10–15 in. lbs. with a torque wrench or finger tight.
7. Locate the nut lock on the adjusting nut so the castellations on the lock are aligned with the cotter pin hole in the spindle.
8. Install new cotter pin and replace dust cap and wheel cover.

WHEEL BEARINGS
REPLACE

(DISC BRAKES) 1980—86 CAPRI, MUSTANG & MUSTANG SVO

1. Raise vehicle and remove front wheels.
2. Remove caliper mounting bolts.

NOTE: It is not necessary to disconnect the brake lines for this operation.

3. Slide caliper off of disc, inserting a clean spacer between the shoes to hold them in their bores after the caliper is removed. Position caliper out of the way.

NOTE: Do not allow caliper to hang by brake hose.

4. Remove hub and disc assembly. Grease retainer and inner bearing can now be removed.
5. Reverse procedure to install.

1980 BOBCAT & PINTO

1. Raise car and remove front wheels.
2. Use a ¾ inch wrench to loosen the large bolt at top of caliper assembly and washer at the front of the caliper. Loosen it until it can be turned with the fingers.
3. Remove the smaller bolt at bottom of caliper with a ⅝ inch wrench.
4. Insert a strong piece of wire carefully through the upper opening in the caliper and fasten it. Position the free end of the wire over the suspension upper arm.
5. When removing caliper from disc the brake pads must be held apart. Do this by inserting a piece of wood or cardboard. While holding the caliper, remove the large bolt in front. Now carefully slide the caliper back and slightly upward to remove it. While doing this, insert the wood or cardboard between the brake pads.
6. Carefully move caliper back to suspension upper arm and fasten loose end of wire so caliper will not drop.
7. Dust cap can now be removed from hub. Remove nut lock, etc. and rock disc to ease out washer and outer bearing. Disc can now be removed to service grease seal or inner bearing.

CHECKING BALL JOINTS FOR WEAR

UPPER BALL JOINT

1980 Bobcat & Pinto

1. Raise car and place floor jacks beneath lower arms.
2. Grasp lower edge of tire and move wheel in and out.
3. As the wheel is being moved, notice any movement between the upper end of the spindle and the upper arm. If movement is present, replace the ball joint.

LOWER BALL JOINT

1980—86 Capri, Mustang & Mustang SVO

Support vehicle in normal driving position with both ball joints loaded. Clean area around grease fitting and checking surface. The checking surface is the round boss into which the grease fitting is installed. The checking surface should project outside the ball joint cover, **Fig. 5**. If checking surface is inside the cover replace the lower control arm assembly.

1980 Bobcat & Pinto

1. Raise vehicle and place jacks under lower arms as shown in **Fig. 6**.
2. Be sure wheel bearings are properly adjusted.
3. Attach a dial indicator to lower arm and position indicator so that plunger rests against inner side of wheel rim near lower ball joint.
4. Grasp tire at top and bottom and slowly move tire in and out. If the reading exceeds .250 inch, replace the joint.

Fig. 2   Front suspension assembly (typical). 1980 Bobcat & Pinto

Fig. 3   Caster & camber adjustment. 1980 Bobcat & Pinto

Fig. 4 Toe-in adjustment (typical)

CHECKING SURFACE

Fig. 5 Checking lower ball joint for wear. 1980–86 Capri, Mustang & Mustang SVO

SHOCK STRUT
REPLACE

1980–84 CAPRI, MUSTANG & MUSTANG SVO

1. Place ignition switch in the unlocked position.
2. From engine compartment, remove upper shock absorber mounting nut.
3. Raise front of vehicle and support lower control arms. Position safety stands under frame jacking pads located rearward of wheels.
4. Remove wheel and tire assembly.
5. Remove caliper, rotor and dust shield.
6. Remove two bolts attaching shock absorber to spindle.
7. Lift strut upward from spindle to compress rod, then pull downward and remove shock absorber.
8. On 1983–86 models, remove jounce bumper.
9. Reverse procedure to install. Torque upper mounting nut to 60–75 ft. lbs. on 1979–82 models, or 55–92 ft. lbs. on 1983–86 models. Torque lower mounting nuts to 150–180 ft. lbs. on 1980–82 models, or 120–179 ft. lbs. on 1983–86 models.

SHOCK ABSORBER
REPLACE

1980 BOBCAT & PINTO

1. Disconnect upper end of the shock.

2. Raise vehicle and install safety stands.
3. Disconnect lower end of shock. It may be necessary to use a pry bar to free "T" shaped end of the shock from the lower end.
4. Reverse procedure to install. Torque shock absorber to lower arm nut to 70 ft. lbs. and shock absorber upper attachment to 26 ft. lbs.

COIL SPRING
REPLACE

1980–86 CAPRI, MUSTANG & MUSTANG SVO

1. Raise front of vehicle and place safety stands under jack pads located rearward of wheels, then remove wheel and tire assembly.
2. Disconnect stabilizer bar link from lower control arm.
3. Remove steering gear attaching bolts and position gear out of way.
4. Using tool 3290-C, disconnect tie rod from spindle.
5. Install spring compressor D78P-5310-A on 1980–81 models, or T82P-5310A on 1982–86 models and compress coil spring until it is free of the spring seat.

NOTE: Ensure spring compressor is properly installed before compressing spring. Also ensure spring is sufficiently compressed to permit removal of lower control arm pivot bolts.

6. Remove two lower control arm pivot

bolts, then disengage lower control arm and remove spring assembly, **Fig. 1.**

NOTE: Measure compressed length of spring and amount of curvature to aid in compressing and installing spring.

7. Reverse procedure to install. Ensure lower spring end is positioned between two holes in lower control arm spring pocket. Torque stabilizer bar to lower arm to 9 ft. lbs., steering gear to No. 2 crossmember to 95 ft. lbs. and tie rod to spindle to 40 ft. lbs. on 1980–81 models, or 35 ft. lbs. on 1982–86 models.

1980 BOBCAT & PINTO

1. Raise vehicle and support front end with safety stands.
2. Place a jack under lower arm to support it.
3. Disconnect lower end of shock.
4. Remove bolts that attach strut to lower arm.
5. Remove nut that retains shock to crossmember and remove the shock.
6. Remove nut and bolt that secures inner end of lower arm to crossmember.
7. Carefully lower jack to relieve pressure from spring and remove spring.
8. Reverse procedure to install. Torque shock to lower arm nut to 70 ft. lbs.,

MAXIMUM TOLERANCE

Fig. 6 Measuring lower ball joint play

POWER

385506-5100
3 REQ'D

72035-S
2 REQ'D

385508-52
3 REQ'D

385505-S100
2 REQ'D
80-100 LB. FT.

385002-52
2 REQ'D
35-47 LB. FT.

MANUAL

385032-52
35-50 LB. FT.

Fig. 7 Steering gear installation (typical)

strut to lower arm bolts to 40–60 ft. lbs., shock to crossmember nut to 22–30 ft. lbs. and lower arm to crossmember to 40–60 ft. lbs.

BALL JOINTS
REPLACE

1980–86 CAPRI, MUSTANG & MUSTANG SVO

On these models, the lower ball joint and lower control arm must be replaced as an assembly.

1980 BOBCAT & PINTO

NOTE: Ford Motor Company recommends that new ball joints should not be installed on used control arms and that the control arm be replaced if ball joint replacement is required. However, aftermarket ball joint repair kits which do not require control arm replacement, are available and can be installed using the following procedure.

The ball joints are riveted to the control arms. The ball joints can be replaced on the car by removing the rivets and replacing them with new attaching bolts, nuts and washers furnished with the kit.

When removing a ball joint, use a suitable pressing tool to force the ball joint out of the spindle.

STEERING GEAR
REPLACE

1980–86 CAPRI, MUSTANG & MUSTANG SVO

1. Disconnect battery ground cable.

2. Remove bolt attaching flexible coupling to input shaft.
3. Place ignition switch in the On position, then raise and support front of vehicle.
4. Remove cotter pins and nuts from tie rod ends, then using a suitable tool separate tie rods from spindle arms, **Fig. 7.**
5. Support steering gear, then remove two nuts, bolts and washers attaching steering gear to crossmember. On power steering gears, lower gear slightly and disconnect pressure and return lines. Cap lines and fittings to prevent entry of dirt.
6. Remove steering gear from vehicle.
7. Reverse procedure to install. Torque flexible coupling to input shaft bolt to 20–30 ft. lbs., tie rod to spindle arm nuts to 35–47 ft. lbs. and steering gear to crossmember bolts to 80–100 ft. lbs. Torque pressure line fitting at gear housing to 10–15 ft. lbs.

1980 BOBCAT & PINTO
Manual Steering Gear
1. Disconnect battery ground cable, turn ignition "On" and raise vehicle.
2. Remove tie rod end retaining nuts and using ball joint separator (tool 329OC), separate tie rod ends from spindle arms, **Fig. 7.**
3. Remove pinion shaft to flexible coupling bolt and the bolts securing steering gear to crossmember.
4. Turn front wheels, then remove steering gear from left side of vehicle.

Power Steering Gear
1. Disconnect battery ground cable.
2. Remove bolt retaining flexible coupling to input shaft.
3. Turn ignition key "On" and raise vehicle.

4. Remove the two tie rod end retaining nuts, then separate studs from spindle arms, using a suitable tool.
5. On Mustang models, remove the number 2A crossmember located behind the front crossmember to allow removal of steering gear retaining bolts.
6. Support gear and remove attaching bolts, then lower gear enough to gain access to pressure and return lines, and remove bolt attaching the hose bracket to the gear.
7. Disconnect pressure and return lines and remove steering gear. Plug lines and ports to prevent entry of dirt.

POWER STEERING PUMP
REPLACE

1980–86

1. Disconnect return hose from power steering pump reservoir and allow fluid to drain into a suitable container.
2. Disconnect pressure hose from power steering pump fitting, then remove pump mounting bracket and disconnect drive belt from pulley.
3. On 2.3L, 3.8L and 5.0L engines which incorporate a fixed pump system, remove the belt from the pulley, and remove the pulley.
4. On all models, remove power steering pump.
5. Reverse procedure to install. Torque pump to mounting bracket bolts to 30–45 ft. lbs. and pressure hose to pump tube nut to 10–15 ft. lbs.

NOTE: End play of pressure hose to pump fitting is normal and does not indicate a loose fitting. Do not overtorque.

INDEX OF SERVICE OPERATIONS

NOTE: Refer to rear of this manual for vehicle manufacturer's special service tool suppliers.

General Engine Specifications

Year	Engine CID①/Liter	Engine V.I.N. Code②	Carburetor	Bore & Stroke	Compression Ratio	Net H.P. @ R.P.M.③	Maximum Torque Ft. Lbs. @ R.P.M.	Normal Oil Pressure Pounds
1986	4-153 (2.5L)	—	C.F.I.④	3.7 × 3.6	9.0	92 @ 4000	132 @ 3000	55–70
	V6-182 (3.0L)	—	E.F.I.⑤	3.5 × 3.1	9.25	140 @ 4600	160 @ 3000	55–70

①—CID—Cubic inch displacement.
②—The eighth digit of the V.I.N. denotes engine code.
③—Ratings are net—as installed in vehicle.
④—Central Fuel Injection.
⑤—Electric Fuel Injection.

Alternator & Regulator Specifications

Year	Ident. No.	Current Rating① Amperes	Current Rating① Volts	Voltage Regulator
1986	E6DF-AA	64	15	Integral
	E6DF-BA	75	15	Integral
	E6DF-CA	70	15	Integral
	E6DF-DA	64	15	Integral

①—Stamped on alternator housing.

Starting Motor Applications

Year	Engine/V.I.N.	Ident. No.
1986	4-153/	—
	V6-182/	—

Valve Specifications

Year	Engine/V.I.N.	Valve Lash Int.	Valve Lash Exh.	Valve Angles Seat	Valve Angles Face	Valve Spring Installed Height	Valve Spring Pressure Lbs. @ In.	Stem Clearance Intake	Stem Clearance Exhaust	Stem Diameter, Std. Intake	Stem Diameter, Std. Exhaust
1986	4-153/	—	—	—	—	—	—	—	—	—	—
	V6-182/	.086–.188	—	—	—	1.46	—	.0010–.0027	.0015–.0032	—	—

Pistons, Pins, Rings, Crankshaft & Bearings

Year	Engine/ V.I.N.	Piston Clearance	Ring End Gap Comp.	Ring End Gap Oil	Wristpin Diameter	Rod Bearings Shaft Diameter	Rod Bearings Bearing Clearance	Main Bearings Shaft Diameter	Main Bearings Bearing Clearance	Thrust on Bearing No.	Shaft End Play
1986	4-153/	—	—	—	—	—	—	—	—	3	—
	V6-182/	.0014–.0022	—	—	—	—	.0008–.0026	—	.0008–.0026	3	—

Engine Tightening Specifications★

★ Torque specifications are for clean and lightly lubricated threads only. Dry or dirty threads produce increased friction which prevents accurate measurement of tightness.

Year	Engine/ V.I.N.	Spark Plugs Ft. Lbs.	Cylinder Head Bolts Ft. Lbs.	Intake Manifold Ft. Lbs.	Exhaust Manifold Ft. Lbs.	Rocker Arm Ft. Lbs.	Rocker Arm Cover Ft. Lbs.	Connecting Rod Cap Bolts Ft. Lbs.	Main Bearings Cap Bolts Ft. Lbs.	Flywheel to Crankshaft Ft. Lbs.	Vibration Damper or Pulley Ft. Lbs.
1986	4-153/	—	—	—	—	—	—	—	—	—	—
	V6-182/	5–10	63–81	19–28	15–22	5–11	6–9	19–25	65–81	54–64	92–122

Front Wheel Alignment Specifications

Year	Model	Caster Angle, Degrees		Camber Angle, Degrees				Toe-Out Inch	Toe-Out on Turns, Deg.	
		Limits	Desired	Limits		Desired			Outer Wheel	Inner Wheel
				Left	Right	Left	Right			
1986	Sable Sedan	+2⅞° to +5⅞°	+3⅞°	−1³⁄₃₂° to +³⁄₃₂°	−1³⁄₃₂° to +³⁄₃₂°	−½°	−½°	¹⁄₁₀	—	—
	Taurus Sedan	+3° to +6°	+4°	−1³⁄₃₂° to +³⁄₃₂°	−1³⁄₃₂° to +³⁄₃₂°	−½°	−½°	¹⁄₁₀	—	—
	Sta. Wag.	+2¹³⁄₁₆° to +5¹³⁄₁₆°	+3¹³⁄₁₆°	−1¹⁄₃₂° to +⁵⁄₃₂°	−1¹⁄₃₂° to +⁵⁄₃₂°	−⁷⁄₁₆	−⁷⁄₁₆	¹⁄₁₀	—	—

Rear Wheel Alignment Specifications

Year	Model	Camber Angle, Degrees		Toe-In Inch
		Limits	Desired	
1986	Sable Sedan	−1⁹⁄₁₆° to −³⁄₁₆°	−⁷⁄₈°	⅛
	Taurus Sedan	−1⅝° to −¼°	−¹⁵⁄₁₆°	⅛
	Sta. Wag.	−1⅝° to −¼°	−¹⁵⁄₁₆°	⅛

Cooling System & Capacity Data

Year	Model or Engine/V.I.N.	Cooling Capacity, Qts.		Radiator Cap Relief Pressure, Lbs.	Thermo. Opening Temp.	Fuel Tank Gals.	Engine Oil Refill, Qts.	Transaxle Capacity	
		Less A/C	With A/C					Manual Pts.	Automatic Qts.①
1986	4-153/	8.5	8.5	16	192	16	4②	6.1	7.8
	V6-182/	10	10	16	197	16	4②	—	10.4

①—Approximate, make final check with dipstick. ②—Add ½ qt. with filter change.

Service Information

3.0L Engine Service

Refer to **Figs. 1 through 23** for service procedures on this engine.

Suspension

FRONT

These vehicles utilize a MacPherson strut front suspension with a stabilizer bar, **Fig. 24**. The struts are nitrogen gas-filled which minimizes fluid aeration. The top of the coil springs are seated in a ball bearing mount, reducing friction during steering movement and as the spring compresses and expands. The spring is offset relative to the strut.

Caster and camber are factory preset and do not require adjustment during normal vehicle operation. The spring towers incorporate adjustable plate and tower markings to assist in suspension realignment to facilatate collision repairs. The entire front suspension can be removed with the front sub-frame, engine and transaxle.

The stabilizer bar is mounted in teflon-lined insulators to reduce friction. The tension-type drag struts, linking the front suspension to the front sub-frame, are mounted in rubber bushings, thereby minimizing road noise and vibration transmission to the vehicle body.

REAR

These vehicles utilize different rear suspension systems for sedan, **Fig. 25**, and station wagon models, **Fig. 26**.

The sedan model, **Fig. 25**, uses MacPherson struts with longitudinal tie rods and parallel transverse suspension arms to control the position of the wheel spindles at the lower end of the struts. Double isolated drag struts and a stabilizer bar are also used on these models.

The station wagon, **Fig. 26**, uses a short-and-long-arm-type rear suspension. Variable rate coil springs and nitrogen gas-filled shock absorbers are also used.

M5 X 0.8 X 27.0 HEX HD.PLT.
SCREW AND WASHER ASSY.
TORQUE TO 2.03-2.60 Nm.

PARALLEL TO
C OF ENGINE

VIEW A

3.0-V6

-12106-
HOUSING ASSY.
DISTRIBUTOR
TERMINAL

-12281-
WIRE & BRACKET
ASSY. L.H.

DISTRIBUTOR ASSY.
(REF.)

-12A310-
COIL & BRACKET
ASSY.

FRONT OF ENGINE

M10 X 20.0 BOLT
TORQUE TO 40.0 - 55.0 Nm.

-12A012-
SUPPRESSOR WIRE ASSY. VIEW A
(ROUTED UNDER WIRES
2 & 5)

-12A310-
COIL & BRACKET
ASSY.

FRONT OF ENGINE

-12280-
WIRE & BRACKET ASSY. R.H.

FIRING ORDER: 1-4-2-5-3-6

Fig. 1   Ignition coil & spark plug wires installation

M6 X 1.0 X 18.0 BOLT
TORQUE TO 8.0 - 12.0 Nm.
(4) PLACES

-9F792-
FUEL RAIL ASSY.

INLET END

-9F593-(GREY)
FUEL INJECTOR ASSY.
(6) PLACES
APPLY ESE-M2C39-F OIL
TO "O" RINGS PRIOR TO
INSTALLATION.

OUTLET END

-9J447-
INTAKE MANIFOLD ASSY.
LOWER

FRONT OF ENGINE

ASSEMBLY PROCEDURE

1. APPLY ESE-M2C39-F OIL TO INJECTOR HOLES IN FUEL RAIL ASSY. (-9F792-)

2. INJECTORS WILL BE SUPPLIED PRE-SORTED (RICH, MEAN, LEAN) BY A DOT ON FLAT
    SURFACE AND MUST BE INSTALLED WITHOUT MIXING.

3. REMOVE PROTECTIVE CAPS FROM INLET SIDE OF FUEL INJECTORS (-9F593-) AND PRESS
    INTO FUEL RAIL ASSY.

4. APPLY ESE-M2C39-F OIL TO INJECTOR HOLES IN INTAKE MANIFOLD ASSY. (-9J447-),
    REMOVE PROTECTIVE CAPS FROM OUTLET END OF INJECTORS AND PRESS INJECTORS WITH
    FUEL RAIL ASSY. INTO INJECTOR HOLES IN INTAKE MANIFOLD.

5. INSTALL BOLTS (2) PER SIDE AND TORQUE TO SPECIFICATIONS SHOWN.

Fig. 2   Fuel injectors & rail installation

M8 X 1.25 X 1.35
BOLT-HEX FLANGE HD.
TORQUE TO 20.0-30.0 Nm.
(2) PLACES

M8 X 1.25 X 105.0
BOLT-HEX FLANGE HD.
TORQUE TO 20.0-30.0 Nm.
(2) PLACES

M8 X 1.25 X 99.3
STUD BOLT-HEX FLANGE HD.
TORQUE TO 20.0-30.0 Nm.

M8 X 1.25 X 70.0
BOLT-HEX FLANGE HD.
TORQUE TO 20.0-30.0 Nm.

-9E926-
AIR INTAKE THROTTLE
BODY ASSY.

-9H486-
GASKET-AIR INTAKE
THROTTLE BODY ASSY.

GUIDE PINS
(2) PLACES

3.0-V6

FRONT OF ENGINE

ASSEMBLY PROCEDURE

1. INSTALL GUIDE PINS IN FRONT AND REAR HOLES OF ENGINE
   MOUNTING PAD FOR THROTTLE BODY.

2. INSTALL GASKET (-9H486-) OVER GUIDE PINS.

3. POSITION THROTTLE BODY (-9E926-) ON ENGINE OVER GUIDE PINS.

4. INSTALL CENTRAL BOLTS (4) PLACES AND HAND TIGHTEN M8 X 1.25 X 1.35
   BOLTS (2) PLACES AND M8 X 1.25 X 105.0 BOLTS (2) PLACES.

5. REMOVE GUIDE PINS.

6. INSTALL (1) M8 X 1.25 X 70.0 BOLT AND (1) M8 X 1.25 X 99.3 STUD
   BOLT AND HAND TIGHT.

7. TORQUE ALL (6) BOLTS SIMULTANEOUSLY TO SPECIFICATION NOTED ABOVE.

Fig. 3 Throttle body installation

-6051-
RIGHT HAND GASKET

-6083-
LEFT HAND GASKET

"V" CUT HERE
INDICATES GASKET
IS FOR TRUCK

-6051-
RH. & LH.

"V" CUT HERE
INDICATES GASKET IS
FOR PASSENGER CAR

HOLLOW
DOWEL
(2) PLACES

FRONT OF ENGINE

HOLLOW
DOWEL
(MUST BE BOTTOMED OUT)

9.8-8.8 REF.

SECTION A

Fig. 4 Cylinder head gasket installation

FORD TAURUS • MERCURY SABLE

M11 X 1.50 X 100.0 BOLT
12 POINT FLANGE
(8) PLACES PER HEAD
SEE NOTE FOR TORQUE

-6049-
CYLINDER HEAD ASSY.

-6010-
CYLINDER
BLOCK ASSY

LOCATING PIN
(2) PLACES
(FOR SINGLE WRENCH
METHOD ONLY)

LEFT SIDE ——————— SHOWN
RIGHT SIDE ——————— TYPICAL

FRONT OF ENGINE

ASSEMBLY PROCEDURE

1. INSTALL CYLINDER HEAD ASSEMBLY (-6049-) OVER LOCATING PINS & DOWELS

2. HAND START MINIMUM OF TWO BOLTS IN EACH HEAD

3. REMOVE LOCATING PINS AND INSTALL REMAINING BOLTS

4. TORQUE BOLTS IN SEQUENCE SHOWN ABOVE IN TWO STEPS.
   STEP #1 : 65.0-75.0 Nm.
   STEP #2 : 85.0-110.0 Nm.

Fig. 5 Cylinder head installation

-9439-
INTAKE MANIFOLD GASKET
(2) PLACES

-9A424-
SEAL-INTAKE
MANIFOLD REAR

FRONT OF ENGINE

-9A425-
SEAL-INTAKE MANIFOLD FRONT

ESE-M4G195-A SEALER
(4) PLACES
BEFORE END SEAL
INSTALLATION

-9439-
INTAKE MANIFOLD GASKET

VIEW A

-6049-
CYLINDER HEAD ASSY.

ESE-M4G195-A SEALER

-6010-
CYLINDER BLOCK ASSY.

ESE-M4G195-A
SEALER
(4) PLACES
AFTER END SEAL
INSTALLATION

-6051-
CYLINDER HEAD
GASKET

SECTION B

-6051-
CYLINDER HEAD GASKET

VIEW A

FRONT OF
ENGINE

ASSEMBLY PROCEDURE

1. APPLY ESE-M4G195-A SEALER TO INTERSECTION OF
   CYLINDER BLOCK ASSY. AND HEAD ASSY.(4) PLACES
   AS SHOWN IN SECTION B.

2. POSITION INTAKE MANIFOLD GASKETS (-9439-) AND INSERT
   LOCKING TABS OVER TABS ON CYLINDER HEAD GASKETS
   AS SHOWN IN VIEW A

3. INSTALL FRONT INTAKE MANIFOLD SEAL (-9A425-) AND
   REAR INTAKE MANIFOLD SEAL (-9A424-) SECURE WITH
   RETAINING FEATURES.

4. APPLY ESE-M4G195-A SEALER AS SHOWN IN VIEW A AFTER
   GASKET INSTALLATION.

Fig. 6   Intake manifold gasket installation

MB X 1.25 X 55.0
BOLT-TORX HEAD
TORQUE TO
26.0-38.0 Nm.
(8) PLACES

INTAKE
LOWER 2.13+
HEAD 1.0 -
BLOCK

SECTION-A

END RAIL GAP
AS INSTALLED

-9J447-
LOWER INTAKE
MANIFOLD ASSY.

FRONT OF ENGINE

ASSEMBLY PROCEDURE

1. LOCATE INTAKE MANIFOLD ASSY. ON ENGINE.

2. INSTALL BOLTS IN ALL HOLES AND TORQUE IN ABOVE SEQUENCE TO
   26.0-38.0 Nm.
   THREE STEPS AS FOLLOWS:
   STEP #1. TORQUE TO 15 Nm.
   STEP #2. TORQUE TO 25 Nm.
   STEP #3. TORQUE TO 33 Nm.

Fig. 7   Intake manifold installation

-9430-
EXHAUST MANIFOLD R.H.

M8 X 1.25 X 69.25
STUD BOLT HEX
FLANGE H.D.
TORQUE TO
20.0-30.0 Nm.

M8 X 1.25 X 45.0
SCREW & WASHER ASSY.
TORQUE TO 20.0-30.0 Nm..
(5)PLACES

FRONT OF ENGINE

-9431-
EXHAUST MANIFOLD L.H.

M8 X 45.0
SCREW & WASHER
ASSY. TORQUE TO
20.0-30.0 Nm.
(3) PLACES

M8 X 45.0 X 25.0
STUD BOLT HEX FLANGE
TORQUE TO 20.0-30.0 Nm.
(2) PLACES

M8 X 1.25 X 90.0
SCREW & WASHER ASSY.
TORQUE TO 20.0-30.0 Nm.

FRONT OF ENGINE

Fig. 8 Exhaust manifold installation

M6 X 1.00 X 2.0
SCREW & WASHER ASSY.
TORQUE TO 8.0 - 12.0 Nm.
(5) PLACES AS SHOWN LEFT SIDE
(5) PLACES AS SHOWN RIGHT SIDE

M6 X 1.00 X 49.3 STUD
TORQUE TO 8.0 - 12.0 Nm.
(3) PLACES AS SHOWN LEFT SIDE
(3) PLACES AS SHOWN RIGHT SIDE

-6A505- (L.H.)
ROCKER ARM
COVER ASSY.

-6582- (R.H.)
ROCKER ARM
COVER ASSY.

LOCATING PINS
(OPTIONAL)
(2) PLACES

-6584-
GASKET - VALVE
ROCKER ARM COVER
(2) PLACES

ESE-M4G195-A
SEALER
(2) PLACES
EACH SIDE

INTAKE MANIFOLD ASSY.

INTERSECTION OF HEAD AND
INTAKE MANIFOLD MUST BE
FLUSH TO WITHIN ± 1.0 mm
GASKET MUST NOT PROTRUDE
ABOVE HIGHEST SURFACE.

CYLINDER HEAD ASSY.

FRONT OF ENGINE

SECTION A

QUALITY AUDIT CHECK

ASSEMBLY PROCEDURE

1. APPLY ESE-M4G195-A SEALER TO INTERSECTION OF HEAD ASSY.
   AND INTAKE MANIFOLD ASSY.-(2) PLACES EACH SIDE.

2. INSTALL LOCATING PINS AS SHOWN (OPTIONAL).

3. POSITION ROCKER ARM COVER GASKET (-6584-) AND SECURE WITH
   RETAINING FEATURES.

4. INSTALL ROCKER ARM COVER (-6A505- L.H. & -6582-R.H.).

5. INSTALL (2) BOLTS/STUDS IN EACH ROCKER ARM COVER AND
   REMOVE LOCATING PINS. INSTALL REMAINING FASTENERS
   AND TORQUE ALL FASTENERS TO SPECIFICATION.

Fig. 9   Rocker arm cover installation

ASSEMBLY PROCEDURE

1. ROTATE CAMSHAFT TO POSITION "A" AS SHOWN.

2. INSTALL PUSHRODS (-6565-) (12) PLACES-PUSHRODS MUST BE SEATED PROPERLY ON TAPPET ASSY.

3. INSTALL ROCKER ARMS (-6564-), FULCRUMS (-6A528-), AND BOLTS IN LOCATIONS AS SPECIFIED IN CAMSHAFT POSITION "A," TORQUE BOLTS TO 7.0-15.0 Nm, AS REQ'D TO SEAT FULCRUMS IN CYLINDER HEAD.

4. ROTATE CRANKSHAFT 120° TO POSITION "B"

5. INSTALL ROCKER ARMS (-6564-), FULCRUMS (-6A528-), AND BOLTS IN LOCATIONS AS SPECIFIED IN CAMSHAFT POSITION "B", TORQUE BOLTS TO 7.0-15.0 Nm. AS REQ'D TO SEAT FULCRUMS IN CYLINDER HEAD
   NOTE:
   FULCRUMS MUST BE FULLY SEATED IN CYLINDER HEADS AND PUSHRODS MUST BE FULLY SEATED IN ROCKER ARM SOCKETS PRIOR TO FINAL TORQUE.

6. APPLY ESE-M2C39-F OIL TO ROCKER ARM ASSEMBLIES.

7. FINAL TORQUE BOLTS TO 26.0-38.0 Nm., (CAMSHAFT MAY BE IN ANY POSITION.)
   NOTE:
   CAMSHAFT POSITIONS "A" AND "B" ARE REQUIRED TO PLACE TAPPET ASSY. ON BASE CIRCLE OF CAMSHAFT LOBE TO CHECK COLLAPSED TAPPET GAP.

FULCRUM AND BOLT MUST BE FULLY SEATED AFTER FINAL TORQUE

4.69-2.15 WITH TAPPET FULLY COLLAPSED ON BASE CIRCLE OF CAM LOBE AFTER ASSEMBLY REF. QUALITY AUDIT ONLY.

CYL. NO.	CAMSHAFT POSITION	
	A	B
	SET GAP OF VALVES NOTED	
1	INT.	EXH.
2	EXH.	INT.
3	NONE	INT.-EXH.
4	INT.	EXH.
5	EXH.	INT.
6	NONE	INT.-EXH.

Fig. 10 Rocker arm & push rod installation

-6518-
KEY-VALVE SPRING RETAINER
(12) PLACES
KEY MUST BE
PROPERLY SEATED

-6514-
VALVE SPRING RETAINER
(6) PLACES

-6A511-
VALVE SPRING & DAMPER ASSY.
(6) PLACES

-6A517- (INTAKE)
VALVE STEM SEAL
(3) PLACES
(VIOLET BAND)

-6A517- (EXHAUST)
VALVE STEM SEAL
(3) PLACES
(BROWN BAND)

-6049-
CYLINDER HEAD

FRONT OF ENGINE

NOTE:
APPLY ESE-M2C74-B OIL TO VALVE GUIDES
PRIOR TO ASSEMBLY
DIP THE VALVE FOOT AND STEM IN ESE-M2C123-A
OIL FROM A MAXIMUM OF THREE QUARTERS TO A
MINIMUM OF ONE HALF OF THE VALVE STEM LENGTH
PRIOR TO ASSEMBLY

-6507-
INTAKE VALVE
(3) PLACES

-6505-
EXHAUST VALVE
(3) PLACES

VALVE STEM TO GUIDE CLEARANCES
INTAKE VALVE = 0.026-0.068
EXHAUST VALVE = 0.038-0.081

CHECKING VALVE SPRING INSTALLED HEIGHT

BOTTOM OF
RETAINER

INSTALLED
SPRING HEIGHT
(SEE CHART)

SPRING SEAT

MAINTAIN SPECIFIED VALVE SPRING
INSTALLED HEIGHT BY VARYING
THIS DEMENSION PER AFFECTED
CYLINDER HEAD DETAIL

GAGE LINE

	VALVES	INTAKE AND EXHAUST ALL
INSTALLED SPRING HEIGHT	FOR 95% PRODUCTION	40.92-39.23
	FOR 100% PRODUCTION	

Fig. 11 Valve installation

-6500-
TAPPET
COAT TAPPET BORES
WITH ESE-M2C39-F OIL
PRIOR TO INSTALLING TAPPETS
(12) PLACES

FRONT OF ENGINE

NOTE:
APPLY ESE-M2C39-F OIL TO CAMSHAFT LOBES
PRIOR TO INSTALLING TAPPETS
TAPPET TO BORE CLEARANCE 0.018 - 0.069

Fig. 12   Hydraulic valve lifter installation

-6378-
FLAT WASHER

M14 X 1.5 X 40.0 BOLT
TORQUE TO 125 - 165 Nm.
ADD ESE-M4G195-A
SEALER TO DAMPER
KEYWAY PRIOR TO
INSTALLATION

-6316-
CRANKSHAFT VIBRATION
DAMPER LUBRICATE
OUTSIDE OF DAMPER HUB
WITH ESE-M2C39-F OIL
OR ESE-M1C104-A GREASE
PRIOR TO INSTALLATION.
SEAL SURFACE MUST BE
FREE OF DIRT OR GRIT.

APPLY ESE-M4G195-A SEALER
TO SLOT

FRONT OF ENGINE

Fig. 13 Crankshaft damper installation

-6019-
FRONT COVER ASSY.

-8501-
WATER PUMP ASSY.

-6020-
GASKET-FRONT COVER

LOCATING PIN
(2) PLACES
AS REQ'D.

DOWEL (REF.)
(2) PLACES

CRANKSHAFT
SEAL PROTECTOR

-6010-
BLOCK ASSY.-CYLINDER

FRONT OF ENGINE

ASSEMBLY PROCEDURE

1. INSTALL FRONT COVER GASKET (-6020-) OVER DOWELS.

2. INSTALL LOCATING PINS AS REQ'D ON FRONT FACE OF CYLINDER
   BLOCK HOLES # 4 & 12 TYPICAL AND POSITION SEAL PROTECTOR
   OVER END OF CRANKSHAFT.

3. INSTALL FRONT COVER (-6059-) & WATER PUMP (-8501-) ASSY.

4. INSTALL BOLTS IN HOLES # 1,6,10, & 15
   AND REMOVE CRANKSHAFT SEAL PROTECTOR.

5. INSTALL REMAINING BOLTS AND TORQUE ALL WATER PUMP AND FRONT
   COVER BOLTS

Fig. 14 Engine front cover installation

BEARING CLEARANCES 0.025-0.075
END PLAY MUST BE 0.05-0.18

-6306-
CRANKSHAFT
SPROCKET

-6268-
TIMING CHAIN

VIEW A

-6278-
WASHER-CAM
SPROCKET

FRONT OF ENGINE

-6256-
CAMSHAFT
SPROCKET

NOTE:
CAM SPROCKET KEY IS INTEGAL
WITH CAM SPROCKET

-6279-
M11 X 30.0
BOLT-HEX
TORQUE TO 55.0-70.0Nm

-6268-
TIMING CHAIN

-6306-
CRANKSHAFT SPROCKET

-6256-
CAMSHAFT
SPROCKET

TIMING MARKES MUST BE IN
POSITION SHOWN WITH
#1 PISTON AT TOP DEAD CENTER
FIRING

VIEW - A
POSITION OF TIMING MARKS

Fig. 15   Timing chain installation

M11 X 1.50 X 80.0
BOLT TORQUE
TO 88.0-110.0 Nm.
(4) PLACES

M11 X 1.50 X 117.5 X 30.0
STUD
TORQUE TO
88.0-110.0Nm
(4) PLACES

-6325-
REAR CAP
THE REAR MAIN BEARING
CAP MUST BE INSTALLED
SO THAT THE CAP IS FLUSH
TO 0.5 FORWARD OF THE
REAR FACE OF BLOCK

-6327-
REAR INTERMEDIATE CAP

-6W332-
MAIN BEARING
REAR-LOWER

-6A339-
MAIN THRUST BEARING-LOWER

-6334-
FRONT
INTERMEDIATE CAP

-6329-
FRONT CAP
ASSEMBLE CAPS
WITH ARROWS ON
CAPS POINTING
FORWARD.
CAPS ARE
IDENTIFIED
1 THRU 4
FRONT TO
REAR

-6303-
CRANKSHAFT
END PLAY AFTER
INSTALLATION 0.1-0.2

-6A338-
MAIN
BEARING-LOWER
(2) PLACES

-6W331-
MAIN BEARING
REAR-UPPER

-6337-
MAIN THRUST
BEARING -UPPER

KEY
[3/16 X 1.75]
PART OF
CRANKSHAFT

ADD DAB OF ESE-M4G195-A
SEALER BETWEEN REAR CAP
AND CYLINDER BLOCK.
(2) PLACES AS SHOWN

-6010-
BLOCK
ASSY-CYLINDER

-6333-
MAIN
BEARING-UPPER
(2) PLACES

FRONT OF ENGINE

NOTE:
MAIN BEARING VERTICAL ASSEMBLED CLEARANCES FOR #1-2-3-4 JOURNALS 0.020-0.066 [.0008-.0026].
ALL SADDLES IN CYLINDER BLOCK AND MAIN BEARING CAPS MUST BE CLEAN AND FREE OF CHIPS, DIRT, PAINT AND
OTHER FOREIGN MATERIAL.
OIL ALL UPPER BEARING SURFACES (INCLUDING THRUST FACE) WITH ESE-M2C39-F OIL PRIOR TO INSTALLING
BEARING CAPS.
BEARING CAPS MUST BE FULLY SEATED IN SADDLE AND THRUST BEARING FACES MUST BE ALIGNED AND SEATED
PRIOR TO BEARING CAP BOLT RUNDOWN. SEAT BEARING THRUST FACES FORWARD AGAINST BLOCK BY
APPLYING A LOAD REARWARD ON THE CRANKSHAFT TO ALIGN BEARING FACES AND THEN FORWARD TO FULLY
SEAT BEARING ON BLOCK THRUST SURFACE. (LOAD ON CRANKSHAFT MUST NOT EXCEED 2767 N AND SHOULD BE
APPLIED AXIALLY).

CRANKSHAFT MUST NOT BE ROTATED UNTIL ALL MAIN BEARING CAP BOLTS ARE TORQUED TO SPECIFICATION UNLESS
SUFFICIENT FORCE IS APPLIED TO EACH MAIN BEARING CAP TO PREVENT MAIN BEARINGS FROM MOVING.

Fig. 16 Crankshaft & main bearing installation

M8 X 1.0 NUT-HEX
TORQUING PROCESS

1. START NUTS WITH NON-TORQUING HAND TOOL.

2. TORQUE NUTS TO 26.0-38.0 Nm.

3. BACK OFF NUTS MINIMUM OF (2) REVOLUTIONS

4. FINAL TORQUE TO 26.0-34.0 Nm.

-6210-
ROD CAP
(6)PLACES

-6211-
ROD BEARING
(6)PLACES

GUIDE TOOL

FRONT OF ENGINE

PISTON RING COMPRESSION TOOL

-6211-
ROD BEARING
(6)PLACES

-6100-
PISTON AND ROD ASSY.
(6)PLACES

NOTE:
COAT ALL CRANKSHAFT PIN JOURNALS, CYLINDER BORE SURFACES AND/OR PISTON & ROD ASSEMBLIES WITH ESE-M2C39-F OIL PRIOR TO INSTALLING PISTON & ROD ASSEMBLIES.
INSTALL PISTON AND CONNECTING ROD ASSEMBLIES IN THE FOLLOWING ORDER:
1. PISTON & ROD ASSY. # 3 & #4
2. PISTON & ROD ASSY. # 1 & # 5
3. PISTON & ROD ASSY. # 2 & # 6

Fig. 17 Piston & connecting rod installation

0.25-0.75 PISTON TO DECK
CLEARANCE WITH PISTON AT T.D.C.
MEASURED PARALLEL TO CRANKSHAFT
ON TRUE CENTERLINE OF PISTON
(AVERAGE OF TWO READINGS)

-6010- CYLINDER BLOCK

32.0 GAGE

64.0 GAGE

STAMP CORRELATION
NUMBERS ON CAP AND ROD
IN AREAS SHOWN
FOR NUMBER SIZE REFER TO
-6100- PISTON AND ROD ASSY.

PISTON TO BORE CLEARANCE AS
MEASURED AT "W" DIMENSION
ON PISTON AND LOCATION SPECIFIED
ON CYLINDER BLOCK 0.036-0.056
[.0014-.0022]

1.5 MINIMUM
NO DISTORTION OF
PARTING SURFACE
PERMITTED

FRONT OF ENGINE

CONNECTING ROD TO CRANKSHAFT
SIDE CLEARANCE 0.15-0.35
[.006-.014]

VIEW A & B

-6100- PISTON AND ROD ASSY.

NOTCH ON PISTON DOME AND BUTTON ON
CONNECTING ROD IDENTIFICATION MARKS
MUST BE ON SAME SIDE AND TOWARDS
FRONT OF ENGINE.

MACHINE LOCATING BOSS

VIEW A

VIEW B

VIEW - FRONT OF ENGINE

NOTE:
-6211- CONNECTING ROD BEARING VERTICAL ASSEMBLED
CLEARANCE (ACTUAL MEASUREMENT) 0.020-0.066
[.0008-.0026]

NOTE:
MAXIMUM TURNING TORQUE 21.0 Nm.

Fig. 18 Piston & connecting rod clearances

-6266-
CUP PLUG
APPLY ESE-M4G217-A SEALER
TO CUP PLUG OR BLOCK (OPT.)
CUP PLUG MUST BE PRESSED
FLUSH TO BLOCK

REAR VIEW

FRONT OF ENGINE

-6250-
CAMSHAFT
COAT ALL CAMSHAFT JOURNALS
OR CYLINDER BLOCK BEARINGS (OPT.)
WITH ESE-M2C39-F OIL
OPTIONAL-DIP ENTIRE CAMSHAFT IN
ESE-M2C39-F OIL PRIOR TO INSTALLATION

FRONT OF ENGINE

-6269-
THRUST PLATE

M6- X 1.0 X 14.0
BOLT-HEX HD.
TORQUE T0
8.0-12.0Nm
(2) PLACES

Fig. 19 Camshaft installation

REAR FACE OF BLOCK
0.0 (DO NOT BOTTOM)
0.5
-6701-
SEAL ASSY.

SECTION-A
SEAL
INSTALLED HEIGHT

-6303-
CRANKSHAFT

-6325-
REAR MAIN
BEARING CAP.

-6701-
SEAL ASSY.

INSTALLATION TOOL

ASSEMBLY PROCEDURE

1. LUBRICATE SEAL AND SEAL SURFACE ON CRANKSHAFT WITH ESE-M2C39-F OIL.

2. INSTALL SEAL ON INSTALLATION TOOL WITH FLAT SIDE TO REAR (SPRING SIDE TOWARDS ENGINE).

3. PLACE SEAL INSTALLATION TOOL WITH SEAL OVER PILOT DIAMETER OF CRANKSHAFT AND SLIDE SEAL ONTO CRANKSHAFT.

4. PRESS SEAL INTO SEAL BORE WITH AUTOMATIC HYDRULIC PRESS UNTIL TOOL CONTACTS REAR FACE OF BLOCK OR CAP. REAR FACE OF SEAL MUST BE WITHIN 0.508/0.000 [.020/.000] IN RELATION TO REAR FACE OF BLOCK.

5. CHECK REAR SEAL SQUARENESS. SEAL FACE SURFACE MUST NOT EXCEED 0.532 [.021] TIR IN RELATION TO REAR FACE OF BLOCK AFTER INSTALLATION.

6. CRANKSHAFT TORQUE TO TURN AFTER SEAL INSTALLATION IS NOT TO EXCEED (6 Nm.)

Fig. 20   Crankshaft rear oil seal installation

-6C624-
OIL LEVEL SENSOR
TORQUE TO 34.0 - 47.5 Nm

-6C626-
GASKET

M6 - 1.0 X 14.0
SCREW & WASHER ASSY.
TORQUE TO 8.0 - 12.0 Nm
(16) PLACES

-6675-
OIL PAN ASSY.

-6710-
OIL PAN GASKET

GUIDE PINS
(2) PLACES

ESE-M4G195-A
SEALER
(2) PLACES

FRONT OF ENGINE

ESE-M4G195-A
SEALER
(2) PLACES

ASSEMBLY PROCEDURE

1. APPLY ESE-M4G195-A SEALER AT JUNCTION OF REAR MAIN BEARING CAP AND CYLINDER BLOCK AND JUNCTION OF FRONT COVER ASSY. AND CYLINDER BLOCK

2. INSTALL GUIDE PINS (OPTIONAL)

3. LOCATE OIL PAN GASKET (-6710-) TO CYLINDER BLOCK PAN RAIL AND SECURE RETAINING FEATURES.

4. LOCATE OIL PAN (-6675-) OVER GUIDE PINS, START AND SEAT (14) FASTENERS, REMOVE GUIDE PINS, START AND SEAT REMAINING (2) FASTENERS.

5. TORQUING PROCESS:

   TORQUE (4) CORNER FASTENERS ("A") TO SPECIFICATION THEN REMAINING (12) FASTENERS TO SPECIFICATIONS. BACK OFF AND RETORQUE (16) FASTENERS TO SPECIFICATIONS.

6. INSTALL OIL LEVEL SENSOR (-6C624-) AND GASKET (-60626-) AND TORQUE TO SPECIFICATION.

Fig. 21   Oil pan installation

M10- 1.5 X 55.0 BOLT
TORQUE TO 40.0 - 55.0 Nm.

-6600-
OIL PUMP ASSY.

VIEW A

-6A751-
RETAINER

-6A605-
OIL PUMP
INTERMEDIATE SHAFT

VIEW A

-6A618-
OIL PUMP
INTERMEDIATE SHAFT ASSY.

M10 X 1.5 NUT - HEX
TORQUE TO
40.0 - 55.0 Nm.
(4) PLACES

-6687-
OIL PAN BAFFLE

FRONT OF ENGINE

ASSEMBLY PROCEDURE

1. INSERT OIL PUMP INTERMEDIATE SHAFT ASSY. INTO HEX DRIVE HOLE IN OIL PUMP UNTIL RETAINER "CLICKS" INTO PLACE.

2. PILOT OIL PUMP WITH INTERMEDIATE SHAFT THROUGH INTERMEDIATE SHAFT HOLE IN REAR MAIN BEARING CAP, POSITION PUMP OVER PINS.

3. INSTALL BOLT AND TORQUE TO SPECIFICATION NOTED ABOVE.

4. POSITION OIL PAN BAFFLE (-6687-) ON STUDS AND SECURE WITH NUTS - TORQUE TO SPECIFICATION

Fig. 22   Oil pump installation

-6019-
FRONT COVER ASSY.

OPTIONAL:
USE OF (2)
LOCATING PINS
AND THEIR
LOCATION

M6 X 1.0 X 25.0
BOLT

-8507-
GASKET-WATER PUMP

-8501-
WATER PUMP ASSY.

ASSEMBLY PROCEDURE

1. INSTALL LOCATING PINS INTO FRONT COVER (-6059-) BOLT HOLES
   (LOCATION OPTIONAL).

2. INSTALL WATER PUMP GASKET (-8507-) AND WATER PUMP ASSY.
   (-8501-) OVER LOCATING PINS.

3. INSTALL BOLTS # 3,5,8,9 & 11,REMOVE LOCATING PINS

Fig. 23 Water pump installation

Fig. 24   Front suspension

Fig. 25   Rear suspension. Sedan

7A-28

Fig. 26   Rear suspension, Station Wagon

LINCOLN

INDEX OF SERVICE OPERATIONS

NOTE: Refer to the rear of this manual for vehicle manufacturer's special service tool suppliers.

Serial & Engine Number Location

Engine code is fifth digit of serial number on 1980 models, or eighth digit of serial number on 1981–86 models. The serial number is stamped on a metal tag located on top left side dash and visible through windshield.

Grille Identification

1980 Versailles

1980 Continental

1980–82 Mark VI

1980–82 Mark VI w/Auxiliary Lamps

1981 Continental & 1982–84 Lincoln Town Car

1982–83 Lincoln Continental

1983 Mark VI

1984–86 Continental Mark VII

1984–86 Lincoln Continental

1985–86 Lincoln Town Car

continued

General Engine Specifications

Year	Engine C.I.D./Liter①	V.I.N. Code②	Fuel System	Bore and Stroke	Compression Ratio	Net H.P. @ R.P.M.③	Maximum Torque Ft. Lbs. @ R.P.M.	Normal Oil Pressure Pounds
1980	V8-302/5.0L	F	2150, 2 Bbl.④	4.00 × 3.00	8.4	132 @ 3600	232 @ 1400	40–60
	V8-302/5.0L	F	⑦	4.00 × 3.00	8.4	129 @ 3600	231 @ 2000	40–60
	V8-351W/5.8L	G	7200VV, 2 Bbl.④	4.00 × 3.50	8.3	140 @ 3400	265 @ 2000	40–60
1981	V8-302/5.0L	F	⑦	4.00 × 3.00	8.4	130 @ 3400	230 @ 2000	40–60
1982	V6-232/3.8L⑤	3	2150, 2 Bbl.④	3.81 × 3.39	8.8	112 @ 4000	175 @ 2600	54–59
	V6-232/3.8L⑥	3	7200VV, 2 Bbl.④	3.81 × 3.39	8.8	118 @ 4000	186 @ 2600	54–59
	V8-302/5.0L⑤	F	2150, 2 Bbl.④	4.00 × 3.00	8.4	—	—	40–60
	V8-302/5.0L⑥	F	7200VV, 2 Bbl.④	4.00 × 3.00	8.4	131 @ 3400	229 @ 1200	40–60
	V8-302/5.0L	F	⑦	4.00 × 3.00	8.4	134 @ 3400	232 @ 3200	40–60
1983	V8-302/5.0L⑤	F	⑦	4.00 × 3.00	8.4	⑧	⑨	40–60
	V8-302/5.0L⑥	F	⑦	4.00 × 3.00	8.4	130 @ 3200	240 @ 2000	40–60
	6-149/2.4L⑩	L	—	3.15 × 3.19	22	144 @ 4800	150 @ 2400	58
1984	V8-302/5.0L	F	⑦	4.00 × 3.00	8.4	⑪	⑫	40–60
1985	6-149/2.4L⑩	L	⑬	3.15 × 3.19	22	114 @ 4800	150 @ 2400	58
	V8-302/5.0L	F	⑦	4.00 × 3.00	8.4	⑪	⑫	40–60
	V8-302 H.O./5.0L	M	⑦	4.00 × 3.00	8.3	180 @ 4200	260 @ 2600	40–60
1986	V8-302/5.0L	—	⑦	4.00 × 3.00	8.9	150 @ 3400	270 @ 2000	40–60
	V8-302 H.O./5.0L	—	⑦	4.00 × 3.00	9.2	200 @ 4000	285 @ 3000	40–60

①—C.I.D.—cubic inch displacement.
②—On 1980 vehicles the fifth digit in the VIN denotes engine code. On 1981–86 vehicles the eighth digit denotes engine code.
③—Ratings are net—as installed in vehicle.
④—Motorcraft.
⑤—Exc. Calif.
⑥—Calif.
⑦—Electronic Fuel Injection.
⑧—Single exhaust, 103 @ 3200; Dual exhaust 145 @ 3600.
⑨—Single exhaust, 240 @ 2000; Dual exhaust 245 @ 2200.
⑩—Turbocharged diesel engine.
⑪—Single exhaust, 140 @ 3200; Dual exhaust, 155 @ 3600.
⑫—Single exhaust, 250 @ 1600; Dual exhaust, 265 @ 2000.
⑬—Fuel injection.

Valve Specifications

Year	Engine Model/V.I.N.	Valve Lash① Int.	Valve Lash① Exh.	Valve Angles Seat	Valve Angles Face	Valve Spring Installed Height	Valve Spring Pressure Lbs. @ In.	Stem Clearance Intake	Stem Clearance Exhaust	Stem Diameter Intake	Stem Diameter Exhaust
1980	V8-302/F	.096–.163①		45	44	③	⑥	.001–.0027	.0015–.0032	.3416–.3423	.3411–.3418
	V8-351W/G	.096–.163①		45	44	④	⑥	.001–.0027	.0015–.0032	.3416–.3423	.3411–.3418
1981	V8-302/F	.096–.146①		45	44	③	⑥	.001–.0027	.0015–.0032	.3416–.3423	.3411–.3418
1982	V6-232/3	.088–.189①		45	44	1¾	215 @ 1.40	.001–.0027	.0015–.0032	.3416–.3423	.3411–.3418
	V8-302/F	.096–.146①		45	44	③	⑦	.001–.0027	.0015–.0032	.3416–.3423	.3411–.3418
1983	V8-302/F	.096–.146①		45	44	⑧	⑨	.001–.0027	.0015–.0032	.3416–.3423	.3411–.3418
1984	V8-302/F	.096–.146①		45	44	⑧	⑨	.001–.0027	.0015–.0032	.3416–.3423	.3411–.3418
1984–85	6-149/L②	.012C	.012C	45	45	—	—	.010⑩	.010⑩	—	—
1985	V8-305/F	.096–.146①		45	44	⑧	⑨	.001–.0027	.0015–.0032	.3416–.3423	.3411–.3418
	V8-305 H.O./M	.123–.146①		45	44	⑪	⑤	.001–.0027	.0015–.0032	.3416–.3423	.3411–.3418

①—Clearance is obtained at valve stem tip with hydraulic lifter collapsed. If clearance is less than minimum, install an undersize push rod; if clearance is greater than maximum, install an oversize push rod.
②—Diesel engine.
③—Intake, 1¹¹⁄₁₆; exhaust, 1¹⁹⁄₃₂.
④—Intake, 1⁵¹⁄₆₄; exhaust, 1³⁹⁄₆₄.
⑤—Intake, 194–214 @ 1.33; exhaust 195–215 @ 1.05.
⑥—Intake, 204 @ 1.36; exhaust, 200 @ 1.20.
⑦—Intake, 186–214 @ 1.36; exhaust, 195–215 @ 1.15.
⑧—Intake, 1⁴³⁄₆₄–1⁴⁵⁄₆₄; exhaust, 1³⁷⁄₆₄–1³⁹⁄₆₄.
⑨—Intake, 196–214 @ 1.36; exhaust, 195–215 @ 1.05.
⑩—Maximum.
⑪—Intake, 1.79; exhaust 1.60.

continued

Pistons, Pins, Rings, Crankshaft & Bearings

Year	Engine/VIN	Piston Clearance	Ring End Gap①		Wrist-pin Diam-eter	Rod Bearings		Main Bearings		Thrust on Bear. No.	Shaft End Play
			Comp.	Oil		Shaft Diameter	Bearing Clearance	Shaft Diameter	Bearing Clearance		
1980	V8-351W④	.0018–.0026	.010	.015	.9121	2.3103–2.3111	.0008–.0015	2.9994–3.0002	.0008–.0015	3	.004–.008
1980–81	V8-302/F	.0018–.0026	.010	.015	.9121	2.1228–2.1236	.0008–.0015	2.2482–2.2490	③	3	.004–.008
1982	V6-232/3	.0014–.0022	.010	.015	.9121	2.3103–2.3111	.001–.0014	2.5198–2.5190	.001–.0014	3	.004–.008
1982–83	V8-302/F	.0018–.0026	.010	.015	.9121	2.1228–2.1236	.0008–.0015	2.2482–2.2490	②	3	.004–.008
1984	V8-302/F	.0018–.0026	.010	.015	.9121	2.1228–2.1236	.0008–.0015	2.2482–2.2490	②	3	.004–.008⑤
1984–85	6-149/L⑥	⑦	.008	.010	—	—	—	⑧	.0008–.0018	6	.003–.006
1985	V8-302/F,M	.0018–.0026	.010	.015	.9121	2.1228–2.1236	.0008–.0015	2.2482–2.2490	.0004–.0015	3	.004–.008⑤

①—Fit rings in tapered bores for clearance listed in tightest portion of ring travel.
②—#1, .0004–.0025; others, .0004–.0015.
③—#1, .0001–.0015; others, .0005–.0015.
④—1979, H; 1980, G.
⑤—.012 Maximum.
⑥—Diesel engine.
⑦—Alcan-Nural pistons, .0010–.0021; KS pistons, .0016–.0027; Mahle pistons, .0018–.0029.
⑧—Refer to Diesel Engine Section.

Engine Tightening Specifications★

★ Torque specifications are for clean and lightly lubricated threads only. Dry or dirty threads produce increased friction which prevents accurate measurement of tightness.

Year	Engine/V.I.N.	Spark Plugs Ft. Lbs.	Cylinder Head Bolts Ft. Lbs.	Intake Manifold Ft. Lbs.	Exhaust Manifold Ft. Lbs.	Rocker Arm Stud Nut or Bolt Ft. Lbs.	Rocker Arm Cover Ft. Lbs.	Connecting Rod Cap Bolts Ft. Lbs.	Main Bearing Cap Bolts Ft. Lbs.	Flywheel to Crankshaft Ft. Lbs.	Vibration Damper or Pulley Ft. Lbs.
1980	V8-351W/G	10–15	105–112	23–25	18–24	③	3–5	40–45	95–105	75–85	70–90
1980–86	V8-302/F,M	10–15	⑨	23–25	18–24	③	3–5	19–24	60–70	75–85	70–90
1982	V6-232/3	17–23	④	⑤	15–22	⑥	⑦	31–36	65–81	54–64	93–121
1984–85	6-149/L⑧	—	②	14–17	14–17		6–7	①	43–48	77–85	282–311

①—Torque in two steps: #1, 14 ft. lbs.; #2, torque bolts an additional 70° from step 1.
②—Torque in four steps: #1, 22–29 ft. lbs.; #2, 36–43 ft. lbs.; #3, torque bolts an additional 70° from step 2; #4, start engine and allow to run 25 minutes, then torque bolts an additional 90° from step 3.
③—Rocker arm fulcrum bolt to cylinder head, 18–25 ft. lbs.
④—Tighten bolts in 4 steps; #1, 47 ft. lbs.; #2, 55 ft. lbs.; #3, 63 ft. lbs.; #4, 74 ft. lbs.; then back off all bolts 2–3 turns and repeat sequence.
⑤—Tighten bolts in three steps; #1, 5.1 ft. lbs.; #2, 10.3 ft. lbs.; #3, 18.4 ft. lbs.
⑥—Rocker arm fulcrum bolt to cylinder head, tighten bolts in two steps; #1, 5.1–11.0 ft. lbs.; #2, 18.4–25.8 ft. lbs.
⑦—36–61 in. lbs.
⑧—Diesel engine.
⑨—Tighten bolts in two steps; #1, 55–65 ft. lbs.; #2, 65–72 ft. lbs.

Rear Axle Specifications

Year	Model	Carrier Type	Ring Gear & Pinion Backlash Inch	Nominal Pinion Locating Shim, Inch	Pinion Bearing Preload				Differential Bearing Preload	Pinion Nut Torque Ft.-Lbs.
					New Bearings With Seal Inch-Lbs.	Used Bearings With Seal Inch-Lbs.	New Bearings Less Seal Inch-Lbs.	Used Bearings Less Seal Inch-Lbs.		
1980	All	Removable	.008–.012	④	17–27①	8–14①	—	—	②⑥	③
1980–86	All	Integral	.008–.015	.030	16–29	8–14	—	—	.016⑥	⑤

①—Bearing set with collapsible spacer; with solid spacer 13–33 inch-lbs.
②—With new bearings, .008–.012 inch; with used bearings, .005–.008 inch.
③—With collapsible spacer 170 ft. lbs., with solid spacer 200 ft. lbs.
④—With 8 inch ring gear, .022 inch; with 9 inch ring gear, .015 inch.
⑤—With 7.5 inch ring gear, 170 ft. lbs., with 8.5 and 8.8 inch ring gear, 140 ft. lbs.
⑥—Case spread.

continued

Wheel Alignment Specifications

Year	Model	Caster Angle, Degrees		Camber Angle, Degrees				Toe-In Inch	Toe-Out on Turns, Deg.①	
		Limits	Desired	Limits		Desired			Outer Wheel	Inner Wheel
				Left	Right	Left	Right			
1980	Versailles	−1¼ to +¼	−½	−½ to +1	−½ to +1	+¼	+¼	⅛	②	20
1980–81	Lincoln	+2¼ to +3¾	+3	−¼ to +1¼	−¼ to +1¼	+½	+½	1/16	18.51	20
	Mark VI	+2¼ to +3¾	+3	−¼ to +1¼	−¼ to +1¼	+½	+½	1/16	18.51	20
1982	Town Car	+2¼ to +3¾	+3	−¼ to +1¼	−¼ to +1¼	+½	+½	1/16	18.51	20
	Mark VI	+2¼ to +3¾	+3	−¼ to +1¼	−¼ to +1¼	+½	+½	1/16	18.51	20
	Continental	+⅛ to +1⅞	+1	−½ to +1¼	−½ to +1¼	+⅜	+⅜	3/16	19.13	20
1983	Town Car	+2¼ to +4	+3	−¼ to +1¼	−¼ to +1¼	+½	+½	1/16	18.51	20
	Mark VI	+2¼ to +4	+3	−¼ to +1¼	−¼ to +1¼	+½	+½	1/16	18.51	20
	Continental	+⅜ to +2⅛	+1¼	−½ to +1¼	−½ to +1¼	+⅜	+⅜	⅛	19.13	20
1984	Town Car	+2½ to +4	+3	−¼ to +1¼	−¼ to +1¼	+½	+½	1/16	18.51	20
	Mark VII③	+7/10 to +2½	+1¾	−¾ to +¾	−¾ to +¾	0	0	⅛	17.14	20
	Continental③	+7/10 to +2½	+1¾	−¾ to +¾	−¾ to +¾	0	0	⅛	17.14	20
1985–86	Town Car	+2¼ to +4	+3	−¼ to +1¼	−¼ to +1¼	+½	+½	1/16	18.51	20
	Mark VII③	+⅝ to +2¾	+1½	−¾ to +¾	−¾ to +1¾	0	0	⅛	17.41	20
	Continental③	+⅝ to +2¾	+1½	−¾ to +¾	−¾ to +1¾	0	0	⅛	17.41	20

①—Incorrect toe-out, when other adjustments are correct, indicates bent steering arms.
②—With power steering; 18.20 & Without 18.43.
③—Set ride height before performing alignment check.

Cooling System & Capacity Data

Year	Model or Engine	Cooling Capacity, Qts.		Radiator Cap Relief Pressure, Lbs.	Thermo. Opening Temp.	Fuel Tank Gals.	Engine Oil Refill Qts.①	Transmission Oil		Auto. Trans. Qts.②	Rear Axle Oil Pints
		Less A/C	With A/C					3 Speed Pints	4 Speed Pints		
1980	Lincoln	—	13.4	16	196	18⑥	4	—	—	12	⑦
	Mark VI	—	13.4	16	196	18⑥	4	—	—	12	⑦
	Versailles	—	13.4	16	196	19.2	4	—	—	9.6	5
1981	Lincoln & Mark VI	—	13.4	16	195	18	4	—	—	12	4
1982–83	Town Car	—	13.4	16	195	18	4	—	—	12.0	3.75
	Mark VI	—	13.4	16	195	18	4	—	—	12.0	3.75
	Continental	—	④	16	195	⑧	4	—	—	12.0	3.25
1984–85	Town Car	—	13.4	16	195	18	4	—	—	12	3.75
	Mark VII	—	③	⑨	195	22.3	⑤	—	—	12	3.5
	Continental	—	③	⑨	195	22.3	⑤	—	—	12	3.5
1986	Town Car	—	13.4	16	195	18	4	—	—	12	3.75
	Mark VII	—	14.1	16	195	22.3	4	—	—	12	3.5
	Continental	—	14.1	16	195	22.3	4	—	—	12	3.5

①—Add one quart with filter change.
②—Approximate. Make final check with dipstick.
③—Exc. diesel engine, 13.4; diesel engine, 11.8.
④—V8-302, 13.4 qts; V6-232, 11.1 qts.
⑤—Gasoline engines, 4.0 qts.; diesel engine 6.5 qts. less oil filter.
⑥—V8-351W, 20 gal.
⑦—7.5 inch axle, 3.5 pts; 8.5 inch axle, 4 pts.
⑧—V8-302, 22.6 gals; V6-232, 20 gals.
⑨—Gasoline engines, 16 lbs.; diesel engines, 15 lbs.

continued

Starting Motor Applications

Year	Application	Ident. No.	Year	Application	Ident. No.
1980–81	All	E1AF-AA		Gas Models④⑤	E4DF-BA
1982	Exc. Continental①	E1AF-BA		Gas Models④⑥	E4AF-AA
	Exc. Continental②	E3AF-AA	1985	Diesel Models⑦	E4LB-AB
	Continental	E25F-AA		Diesel Models⑧	E5LF-AA
1983	All	E3AF-AA		Gas Models	E4AF-AA
1984	Diesel Models	E4LF-AB	1986	All	E4AF-AA
	Gas Models③	E3AF-AA			

①—To 5/82.
②—From 5/82.
③—To 12/83.
④—From 12/83.
⑤—Exc. Town Car.
⑥—Town Car.
⑦—To 1/85.
⑧—From 1/85.

Alternator & Regulator Specifications

Year	Ident. No.①	Current Rating②		Field Current @ 75°F.		Voltage Regulator	
		Amperes	Volts	Amperes	Volts	Ident. No. ③⑥	Voltage @ 75°F.
1980–81	Orange④⑦	40	15	4.0	12	E2PZ-A⑧	13.8–14.6
	Black④⑦	65	15	4.0	12	E2PZ-A⑧	13.8–14.6
	Green④⑦	60	15	4.0	12	E2PZ-A⑧	13.8–14.6
	Black⑤⑦	70	15	4.0	12	E2PZ-A⑧	13.8–14.6
	Red⑤⑦	100	15	4.0	12	E2PZ-A⑧	13.8–14.6
1982	Orange④⑦	40	15	4.0	12	E2PZ-A⑧	13.8–14.6
	Black④⑦	65	15	4.0	12	E2PZ-A⑧	13.8–14.6
	Green④⑦	60	15	4.0	12	E2PZ-A⑧	13.8–14.6
	Black⑤⑦	70	15	4.0	12	E2PZ-A⑧	13.8–14.6
	Red⑤⑦	100	15	4.0	12	E2PZ-A⑧	13.8–14.6
1983	Orange④⑦	40	15	4.25	12	E2PZ-A⑧	—
	Black④⑦	65	15	4.25	12	E2PZ-A⑧	—
	Green④⑦	60	15	4.25	12	E2PZ-A⑧	—
	Black⑤⑦	70	15	4.25	12	E2PZ-A⑧	—
	Red⑤⑦	100	15	4.25	12	E2PZ-A⑧	—
1984–86	Orange④⑦	40	15	4.25	12	E2PZ-A	—
	Green④⑦	60	15	4.25	12	E2PZ-A	—
	Black⑤⑦	70	15	4.25	12	E2PZ-A	—
	Red⑤⑦	100	15	4.25	12	E2PZ-A	—

①—Basic No. 10300.
②—Stamped on housing.
③—Stamped on cover.
④—Rear terminal alternator.
⑤—Side terminal alternator.
⑥—Basic No. 10316.
⑦—Solid state alternator.
⑧—Electronic voltage regulator. These units are color coded black for system w/warning indicator lamp & blue for systems w/ammeter.

Electrical Section

Fig. 1 Ignition lock cylinder. Versailles

Fig. 2 Ignition switch installation. Exc. Versailles

STARTER
REPLACE
VERSAILLES

1. Disconnect battery ground cable, then raise vehicle on a hoist.
2. Disconnect starter cable at starter terminal.
3. Remove through bolt and nut attaching motor mount insulator to mounting bracket.
4. Using a suitable jack, raise engine.
5. Remove starter mounting bolts, then the starter.
6. Reverse procedure to install.

EXC. VERSAILLES & DIESEL ENGINE MODELS

1. Disconnect battery ground cable, then raise and support vehicle.
2. Disconnect starter cable at starter terminal, then remove starter mounting bolts.
3. Remove starter. On some models, it may be necessary to turn wheels to the left or right to gain clearance for removal.
4. Reverse procedure to install. Torque starter cable to starter motor bolt to 70–110 inch lbs.

DIESEL ENGINE MODELS

1. Disconnect battery ground cables.
2. Raise and support vehicle, then remove starter retaining bolts.
3. Lower vehicle, then disconnect starter motor relay to solenoid wire assembly.
4. Remove oil level indicator tube assembly retaining bolts.
5. Disconnect accelerator pedal from throttle cable assembly.
6. Remove starter from vehicle.
7. Reverse procedure to install.

IGNITION LOCK
REPLACE
EXC. VERSAILLES

1. Disconnect battery ground cable.

2. On models with tilt wheel, remove upper column extension shroud by unsnapping from retaining clip at 9 o'clock position.
3. Remove steering column trim shroud.
4. Disconnect key warning switch electrical connector.
5. Turn ignition lock to "On" position.
6. Using a ⅛ inch pin or punch located in the 4 o'clock hole and 1¼ inch from outer edge of lock cylinder housing, depress retaining pin while pulling the lock cylinder from housing.
7. Turn lock cylinder to "On" position and insert cylinder into housing. Ensure that the lock cylinder is fully seated and aligned into the interlocking washer before turning key to "Off" position. This will permit the retaining pin to extend into the lock cylinder housing hole.
8. Rotate key to check for proper mechanical operation.
9. Connect key warning switch electrical connector.
10. Connect battery ground cable.
11. Check for proper operation.

VERSAILLES

1. Disconnect the battery ground cable.
2. **Units With Fixed Steering Columns:** Remove the steering wheel trim pad and steering wheel. Insert a wire pin in the hole located inside the column halfway down the lock cylinder housing, **Fig. 1.**
   Units With Tilt Steering Columns: Insert wire pin in the hole located on the outside of the flange casting next to the emergency flasher button, **Fig. 1.**
3. Place the gear shift lever in Park position, and turn the lock cylinder with the ignition key to the Run position.
4. Depress the wire pin while pulling up on the lock cylinder to remove. Remove the wire pin.
5. To install, insert the lock cylinder into the housing in the flange casting, and turn the key to the Off position. Be certain that the cylinder is fully

inserted before turning to the Off position. This action will extend the cylinder retaining pin into the cylinder housing.
6. Turn the key to check for correct operation in all positions.
7. Install the steering wheel and trim pad on fixed column units.
8. Connect the battery ground cable.

IGNITION SWITCH
REPLACE
1982–86

1. Disconnect battery ground cable.
2. For tilt wheel only, remove upper column extension shroud by unsnapping from retaining clip at 9 o'clock position.
3. Remove steering column trim shrouds.
4. Disconnect ignition switch electrical connector. Turn the lock cylinder to the "On" position.
5. With a ⅛ inch drill, drill out the switch retaining bolt heads. Then, remove the bolts with an "Easy Out" or equivalent.
6. Disengage ignition switch from actuator and remove from vehicle, **Fig. 2.**
7. Adjust ignition switch by sliding the carrier to the switch "On" position.

NOTE: A replacement ignition switch will be pre-set in the "On" position.

8. Ensure the lock cylinder is in approximately the "On" position and install the ignition switch onto the actuator pin.
9. Install switch break-off head mounting bolts and tighten until heads shear.
10. Reconnect switch electrical connector and battery ground cable. Check the ignition switch for proper operation in all switch positions. Be sure the column is locked in the lock position.
11. Reinstall shrouds.

Fig. 3   Ignition switch installation. Versailles

Fig. 4   Light switch replacement. 1984–86 Continental & Mark VII

1980–81 CONTINENTAL & MARK VI

1. Disconnect battery ground cable.
2. Remove upper column shroud.
3. Disconnect ignition switch electrical connector.
4. With a ⅛ inch diameter twist drill, drill out the switch retaining bolt heads. Then, remove the bolts with a "Easy Out" or equivalent.
5. Disengage ignition switch from actuator and remove from vehicle, **Fig. 2.**
6. Adjust ignition switch by sliding the carrier to the switch "Lock" position. Insert a .050 inch drill or equivalent through the switch housing and into the carrier to prevent movement.

NOTE: A replacement ignition switch includes an installed adjusting pin.

7. Rotate ignition key to "Lock" position.
8. Install ignition switch on actuator pin.
9. Install switch break-off head mounting bolts and tighten until the bolt heads shear.
10. Remove adjusting pin or drill.
11. Connect ignition switch electrical connector.
12. Connect battery ground cable and check for proper operation.
13. Install column shroud.

VERSAILLES

1. Disconnect battery ground cable.
2. Remove steering column shroud, then detach and lower steering column from brake support bracket.
3. Disconnect switch wiring, then remove two nuts retaining switch to steering column, **Fig. 3.**
4. Lift switch vertically upward to disengage actuator rod, then remove switch.
5. When installing ignition switch, both locking mechanism at top of column and ignition switch must be in Lock position for correct adjustment. To hold mechanical parts in column in Lock position, move shift lever to Park, then turn key to Lock position and remove key.

NOTE: New replacement switches are pinned in Lock position by a metal pin inserted in locking hole located on side of switch. For existing switch, move switch carrier using a .010 in. diameter rod to lock detent. Insert a ⁵⁄₆₄ in. drill bit into lock hole on side of switch to hold switch in Lock position.

6. Connect switch plunger to actuator rod.
7. Position switch on column and install retaining nuts, but do not tighten.
8. Move switch up and down along column to locate mid-position of rod lash, then tighten switch retaining nuts.
9. Remove locking pin, then connect battery ground cable and check switch for proper operation.
10. Attaching steering column to brake support and install steering column shroud.

LIGHT SWITCH
REPLACE
1984–86 CONTINENTAL & MARK VII

1. Remove lens assembly attaching screws and the lens assembly.
2. Remove switch assembly attaching screws, then pull switch out from instrument panel, **Fig. 4.**
3. Disconnect switch electrical connector and remove switch.
4. Reverse procedure to install.

1982–83 CONTINENTAL

1. Disconnect battery ground cable.
2. Remove steering column trim shrouds.
3. Unsnap the instrument panel cluster lower moulding to expose five screws along bottom of cluster lens and remove.
4. Remove the left hand lower pad retaining screws and carefully tilt the pad out from under the cluster lens.
5. Disconnect the headlamp switch wiring connectors.
6. Insert a hooked tool into headlight switch knob slot and remove spring tension on knob, then pull off.
7. Remove switch retaining nut and lens.
8. Remove second nut and screw retaining the switch to lower pad and remove.
9. Reverse procedure to install.

1982–83 MARK VI & 1982–86 TOWN CAR

1. Disconnect battery ground cable.
2. Insert a hooked tool into headlight switch knob slot and remove spring tension on knob, then pull off.
3. Remove steering column lower shroud and lower left hand instrument panel trim bezel.
4. Remove five headlight switch mounting bracket retaining screws.
5. Carefully pull switch and bracket from instrument panel and disconnect switch wiring.

Fig. 5 Light switch. Versailles & 1980–81 Continental & Mark VII

Fig. 7 Neutral safety switch. Versailles

Fig. 6 Stop light switch 1980–86 (typical)

6. On Mark VI models, mark and remove vacuum hoses from switch distributor valve.
7. Remove locknut and screw retaining switch to switch bracket.
8. Reverse procedure to install.

1980–81 CONTINENTAL & MARK VI

1. Disconnect battery ground cable.
2. From instrument panel, depress light switch knob and shaft retainer button on side of switch and, while holding button in, pull knob and shaft assembly from switch, **Fig. 5**.
3. Unscrew trim bezel and remove lock nut.
4. From under instrument panel, pull switch from panel while tilting downward, disconnect electrical connector and remove switch.
5. Reverse procedure to install.

VERSAILLES

1. Disconnect battery ground cable.
2. Remove control knob and shaft by pressing knob release button and pulling it out of switch housing, **Fig. 5**.
3. Remove bezel nut and lower switch assembly.
4. Disconnect multiple plug and vacuum hoses at switch body and remove switch.
5. Reverse procedure to install.

STOP LIGHT SWITCH
REPLACE

1980–86

1. Disconnect wires at switch connector.
2. Remove hairpin retainer, slide switch, push rod and nylon washers and bushing away from brake pedal, and remove switch, **Fig. 6**.

NOTE: On Versailles models, loosen brake booster nuts at pedal support approximately ¼ inch so booster is free to move to eliminate binding during switch removal.

3. Reverse above procedure to install.

NEUTRAL SAFETY SWITCH
REPLACE

1980–86 CONTINENTAL & 1984–86 MARK VII WITH AOD TRANSMISSION

1. Disconnect battery ground cable.
2. Position transmission selector lever in "Lo" position.
3. Raise and support vehicle, then working from underneath vehicle, disconnect electrical harness from switch by lifting harness straight up off switch.
4. Using tool T74P-77247-A or equivalent, remove neutral start switch and O-ring seal by positioning tool over the extension housing area to gain access to switch.
5. Reverse procedure to install. Torque switch to 7–10 ft. lbs. using tool mentioned above.

1980–86 TOWN CAR & 1980–83 MARK VI WITH AOD TRANSMISSION

1. Disconnect battery ground cable, then remove air cleaner assembly.
2. Position transmission selector lever in "Lo."
3. Disconnect electrical harness from switch by lifting harness straight up off switch.
4. Using tool T74P-77247-A or equivalent, remove neutral start switch and O-ring seal through access path at left side of dash panel.
5. Reverse procedure to install. Torque switch to 7–10 ft. lbs. using tool mentioned above.

VERSAILLES W/FLOOR SHIFT

Transmission Mounted Switch
1. Remove downshift linkage rod from transmission downshift lever.
2. Apply penetrating oil to downshift lever shaft and nut; then remove downshift outer lever.
3. Remove switch attaching bolts.
4. Disconnect multiple wire connector and remove switch from transmission.
5. Install new switch.
6. With transmission manual lever in neutral, rotate switch and install gauge pin (#43 drill) into gauge pin holes, **Fig. 7**.
7. Tighten switch attaching bolts and remove gauge pin.
8. Complete the installation in reverse order of removal.

TURN SIGNAL SWITCH
REPLACE

1. Disconnect battery ground cable.
2. On models with tilt wheels, remove upper column extension shroud by unsnapping from retaining clip at 9

LINCOLN

o'clock position.
3. Remove steering column cover attaching screws and the cover, then the signal lever.
4. Carefully lift wiring connector plug retainer tabs and disconnect the plugs from switch.
5. Remove switch retaining screws and lift up switch assembly.
6. Reverse procedure to install.

HORN SOUNDER & STEERING WHEEL
REPLACE

EXC. VERSAILLES

Refer to "Turn Signal Switch, Replace" for horn switch replacement.
1. Working from behind steering wheel, remove steering wheel hub cover by pushing retaining posts outward with a suitable drift.
2. Remove steering wheel to shaft retaining nut. Discard nut.
3. If no marks are present, scribe alignment marks on steering wheel and shaft to aid in installation.
4. Using a suitable puller, remove steering wheel from shaft.
5. Reverse procedure to install. Torque new retaining nut to 30–40 ft. lbs.

NOTE: On vehicles equipped with speed control, check slip ring for damage and slip ring grease for contamination before installing steering wheel.

VERSAILLES

1. Disconnect battery ground cable.
2. Remove screws from behind wheel spoke holding crash pad to wheel. Lift pad and disconnect horn wires. Disconnect speed control wires if used and remove pad.
3. Remove steering wheel nut. Install a suitable puller and remove steering wheel.
4. Reverse procedure to install.

INSTRUMENT CLUSTER
REPLACE

1984–86 MARK VII

1. Remove the four finish panel retaining screws, then rotate top of panel towards steering wheel and remove from vehicle, **Fig. 8.**
2. Remove the six instrument panel pad retaining screws, then rotate pad toward steering wheel and remove from vehicle.
3. Remove the four instrument cluster to instrument panel retaining screws, then pull cluster away from instrument panel.
4. Disconnect cluster electrical connec-

Fig. 8   Electronic instrument cluster. 1984–86 Mark VII

Fig. 9   Electronic instrument panel. 1982–86 Continental

tor and remove cluster.
5. Reverse procedure to install.

1982–86 CONTINENTAL

1. Disconnect battery ground cable.
2. Remove steering column shroud.
3. Snap off instrument panel mouldings.
4. Remove seventeen instrument panel assembly to instrument panel and instrument panel pad retaining screws, then remove trim assembly, **Fig. 9.**
5. Disconnect transmission indicator cable from steering column.
6. Remove four cluster retaining screws from instrument panel and move cluster away from instrument panel.
7. Disconnect wiring harness connector and remove cluster.
8. Reverse procedure to install.

Fig. 10 Electronic instrument cluster. 1980—81 Continental & Mark VI, 1982—83 Mark VI & 1982—86 Town Car

1980—81 CONTINENTAL & MARK VI; 1982—83 MARK VI & 1982—86 TOWN CAR

Less Electronic Cluster

1. Disconnect battery ground cable.
2. Disconnect speedometer cable, then remove trim cover screws and remove trim cover.
3. Remove lower steering column cover screws and remove cover.
4. Remove transmission indicator bracket retaining screw, then disconnect cable loop and bracket pin from steering column. Also remove the column bracket from column.
5. Remove cluster retaining screws, then disconnect electrical feed plug from connector and remove cluster.

With Electronic Cluster

1. Disconnect battery ground cable.
2. Remove steering column cover, lower instrument panel trim cover, keyboard trim panel and panel on left of column.
3. Remove the ten instrument cluster trim cover retaining screws, then remove trim cover.
4. Remove the four screws retaining instrument cluster to instrument panel and pull cluster forward. Disconnect both electrical plugs and ground wire from their receptacles, then disconnect speedometer cable by pressing on flat surface of plastic connector.
5. Remove transmission indicator cable bracket retaining screw, then disconnect cable loop and bracket pin from steering column.
6. Remove plastic clamp from around steering column, then remove cluster, **Fig. 10.**
7. Reverse procedure to install.

VERSAILLES

1. Disconnect battery ground cable.

2. Remove screws securing lower cluster applique beneath steering column.
3. Remove steering column shroud.
4. Remove headlamp switch knob and shaft assembly, then the switch bezel.
5. Remove four screws from cluster front cover.
6. Using a right angle screwdriver, pry along edges of finish panel, thereby removing studs from retainers and remove finish panel.
7. Pull front cover slightly outward at top, then rearward at bottom to disengage cover to panel retainers.
8. Remove cluster front cover.
9. Remove screw attaching transmission indicator cable bracket to steering column and detach cable loop from pin on column.
10. Disconnect speedometer cable connector.
11. Remove four screws securing cluster to instrument panel.
12. Pull cluster from instrument panel and disconnect electrical connectors, **Fig. 12.**
13. Remove cluster from vehicle.
14. Reverse procedure to install.

W/S WIPER MOTOR
REPLACE

1984—86 MARK VII

1. Turn wipers on, then with wiper blades straight up on windshield, turn ignition key to "off" position.
2. Disconnect battery ground cable and remove arm and blade assemblies.
3. Remove left side cowl top grille.

Fig. 11 Instrument cluster. Versailles

LINCOLN

4. Remove drive arm to motor crankpin retaining clip, then disconnect drive arm from crankpin.
5. Disconnect wiper motor electrical connector, then remove wiper motor retaining screws and the wiper motor from opening.
6. Reverse procedure to install.

1982–86 CONTINENTAL

1. Disconnect battery ground cable.
2. Remove right hand side wiper and blade assembly.
3. Remove cowl top grille retaining screws and grille.
4. Disconnect linkage drive arm from the motor output arm crankpin by removing retainer clip.
5. Disconnect electrical connector and remove three motor attaching screws.
6. Pull the motor from the opening.
7. Reverse procedure to install.

1980–81 CONTINENTAL & MARK VI; 1982–83 MARK VI & 1982–86 TOWN CAR

1. Disconnect battery ground cable.
2. Disconnect right side washer nozzle hose clip and remove right side wiper arm and blade assembly from pivot shaft.
3. Remove wiper motor linkage cover.
4. Disconnect linkage drive arm from the motor output arm crankpin by removing retainer clip.
5. Disconnect the wiring connectors from the motor.
6. Remove three bolts retaining the motor to the dash panel extension and the motor.
7. Reverse procedure to install.

VERSAILLES

1. Disconnect battery ground cable.
2. Remove eight instrument panel pad attaching screws, then remove pad.
3. Remove speaker mounting bracket, then disconnect wire connector and remove speaker.
4. Remove defroster nozzle and air distribution duct. Remove interlock module from bracket and disconnect multiple connector.
5. Remove wiper bracket to cowl attaching bolts and drive arm clip, then remove wiper motor.
6. Reverse procedure to install.

W/S WIPER TRANSMISSION
REPLACE

1984–86 MARK VII

NOTE: The wiper transmission is mounted below the cowl top panel and can be reached by raising the hood. Because the pivot shaft and transmission assemblies are connected with unremovable plastic ball joints, the right and left pivot shafts and transmission are serviced as a unit.

1. Perform steps 1 and 2 as outlined under "W/S Wiper Motor, Replace" procedure.
2. Raise hood, then remove left and right cowl top grilles.
3. Remove drive arm to wiper motor crankpin retaining clip, then disconnect drive arm from crankpin.
4. Remove pivot shaft attaching screws, then guide transmission and pivots from cowl chamber.
5. Reverse procedure to install, ensuring wiper motor is in "Park" position.

1982–86 CONTINENTAL

1. Disconnect battery ground cable.
2. Remove right hand side wiper arm and blade assembly.
3. Remove cowl top grille retaining screws and remove grille.
4. Disconnect linkage drive arm from the motor output arm crankpin by removing retainer clip.
5. Remove the right side pivot shaft retaining screws then, remove the large nut and spacer from the left side pivot shaft.
6. Remove linkage.
7. Reverse procedure to install.

1980–81 CONTINENTAL & MARK VI; 1982–83 MARK VI & 1982–86 TOWN CAR

1. Disconnect battery ground cable.
2. Remove wiper arm and blade assemblies from the pivot shafts.
3. Remove wiper motor and linkage cover for access to linkage.
4. Disconnect the linkage drive arm from the motor crank pin by removing the retaining clip.
5. Remove the six bolts retaining the left and right pivot shafts to the cowl, and remove the complete linkage assembly.
6. Reverse procedure to install.

VERSAILLES

Left Side
1. Remove instrument cluster.
2. Remove wiper arm and blade.
3. Working through cluster opening, disconnect both pivot shaft links from motor drive arm by removing retaining clip.
4. Remove three pivot shaft assembly retaining bolts and remove assembly through cluster opening.
5. Reverse procedure to install.

Right Side
1. Disconnect battery ground cable and remove wiper blade and wiper arm.
2. If air conditioned, remove right duct assembly by unclipping duct from right connector and sliding left end out of plenum chamber. Lower duct assembly out from under instrument panel.
3. From under the instrument panel, disconnect first left then right pivot shaft link from motor drive arm.
4. Reaching between utility shelf and instrument panel, remove pivot shaft retaining bolts and lower assembly out from under panel.
5. Reverse procedure to install.

W/S WIPER SWITCH
REPLACE

Exc. Versailles

1. Disconnect battery ground cable.
2. Remove the steering column cover screws and separate the two halves.
3. Remove wiper switch retaining screws, disconnect wiring connector and remove switch.
4. Reverse procedure to install.

VERSAILLES

NOTE: The wiper/washer switch is an integral part of the turn signal arm and cannot be replaced separately.

1. Disconnect battery ground cable.
2. Disconnect wiper/washer and turn signal electrical connector from under instrument panel.
3. Remove lower instrument panel shield retaining screws and shield.
4. Remove steering column cover screws and separate cover halves.
5. Remove wiring cover by pulling it, then remove wiring shield by prying out.
6. Using an internal bit screwdriver, remove wiper/washer and turn signal arm assembly.
7. Reverse procedure to install.

RADIO
REPLACE

NOTE: When installing radio, be sure to adjust antenna trimmer for peak performance.

1982–86 CONTINENTAL & 1984–86 MARK VII

1. Disconnect battery ground cable.
2. Remove center instrument panel trim panel.
3. Remove four radio and mounting bracket to instrument panel retaining screws.
4. Push radio towards the front of vehicle and raise back end slightly so rear support bracket clears clip in instrument panel and carefully pull out radio.
5. Disconnect radio wiring and remove radio.
6. Remove rear support bracket.
7. Reverse procedure to install.

1980–81 CONTINENTAL & MARK VI, 1982–83 MARK VI & 1982–86 TOWN CAR

1. Disconnect battery ground able.
2. Remove radio plate to instrument panel retaining screws.
3. Pull radio rearward until the rear support bracket is clear of instrument panel.
4. Disconnect radio wiring and antenna lead. Remove radio.
5. Remove screws securing front bracket

Fig. 12 Servo assembly & throttle linkage installation. 1980—86 (typical)

Fig. 13 Vacuum dump valve adjustment (typical)

to radio and remove, remove rear support bracket.
6. Reverse procedure to install.

VERSAILLES

1. Disconnect battery ground cable.
2. Remove headlamp switch.
3. Remove knobs from heater and A/C control, windshield wiper switch and radio.
4. Remove instrument panel applique.
5. Remove radio bezel to instrument panel screws, then pull radio and bezel out to disconnect antenna lead and electrical leads, then remove radio from panel.
6. Remove rear support bracket and bezel from radio.
7. Reverse procedure to install.

SPEED CONTROLS
ADJUST

1980—86

Bead Chain

Adjust bead chain cable to obtain desired free travel with engine warm and carburetor at idle position. Desired free travel is 1/8—1/4 inch, **Fig. 12.** The adjustment should be made to take as much slack as possible out of the bead chain without restricting the carburetor lever from returning to idle. On vehicles with solenoid anti-diesel valve, perform the adjustment with the ignition switch in the ON position.

Actuator Cable

1. Remove actuator cable retaining clip from speed control connection adjuster.
2. Disengage throttle positioner.

3. With carburetor in hot idle position, pull the actuator cable end tube until all slack is removed from cable.
4. While maintaining light tension on cable, install cable retaining clip.

Vacuum Dump Valve

The vacuum dump valve is fully adjustable in its mounting bracket. When correctly adjusted, the valve should be closed when the brake pedal is in the released position, enabling the black housing of the valve to clear the adapter or pad on the brake pedal. If adjustment is necessary, hold the brake pedal down and push the dump valve forward through its adjustment collar. Position a .050 inch shim on the adapter or pad, **Fig. 13,** then pull brake pedal fully rearward. Release brake pedal and remove shim. The white plunger on the valve should be in contact with the adapter or pad, while the threaded black housing should have sufficient clearance away from it.

HEATER CORE
REPLACE

1984—86 MARK VII

1. Remove instrument panel.
2. Discharge refrigerant from A/C system, then disconnect high and low pressure hoses. Cap hose ends to prevent entry of dirt and moisture.
3. Drain coolant and disconnect hoses from heater core. Plug hoses and core to prevent spillage.
4. Remove air inlet duct/blower housing assembly support brace to cowl top panel retaining screw.
5. Disconnect A/C wiring, if necessary, then working from engine compart-

ment, remove the two evaporator case to dash panel retaining nuts.
6. Working from passenger compartment, remove evaporator case support bracket to cowl panel attaching screw.
7. Carefully pull evaporator case away from dash panel and remove from vehicle.
8. Remove heater core access cover to evaporator case attaching screws.
9. Remove heater core and seals from case, then remove seals from heater core tubes.
10. Reverse procedure to install.

1982—86 CONTINENTAL

1. Disconnect battery ground cable.
2. Remove steering column cover assembly, then remove left and right finish panels, **Fig. 9.**
3. Remove two screws from sides of instrument panel pad and retainer assembly.
4. Remove pad and retainer assembly and upper finish panel.
5. Remove steering column attaching bolts, then carefully lower steering column just enough to allow access to transmission gear selector lever cable assembly. Reach between steering column and instrument panel, then carefully lift selector lever cable from lever and remove cable clamp from steering column tube.
6. Lower steering column and allow to rest on front seat.
7. Remove screw attaching instrument panel to brake pedal support through steering column opening.
8. Disconnect temperature door cable from door and heater/evaporator cable bracket.
9. Disconnect vacuum hose connectors at evaporator housing.
10. Disconnect blower motor resistor wire from resistor on heater/evaporator case and blower motor feed wire at inline connector.
11. Support instrument panel, then remove three screws attaching top of instrument panel to cowl.
12. Remove one screw attaching each end of instrument panel to cowl side panels, then remove two screws attaching instrument panel to floor.
13. Move instrument panel rearward and disconnect speedometer cable and any wires that will prevent instrument

Fig. 14 Plenum & air inlet duct assembly. 1980–81 Continental & Mark VI, 1982–83 Mark VI & 1982–86 Town Car

panel from being placed on front seat.

NOTE: Use care when removing instrument panel to prevent damage to panel or steering column surfaces.

14. Drain cooling system, then disconnect heater hoses from heater core. Plug heater core tubes to prevent coolant spillage.
15. Discharge A/C system, then remove high and low side pressure hoses. Cap the hose openings to prevent entry of dirt or moisture.
16. From engine compartment, remove two nuts attaching heater/evaporator case to dash panel.
17. From passenger compartment, remove bolts attaching heater/evaporator case and air inlet duct support brackets to cowl top panel.
18. Remove one nut attaching bracket at left side of heater/evaporator case to dash panel, then remove one nut retaining bracket below case to dash panel.
19. Carefully pull case away from dash panel to gain access to heater core cover attaching bolts.
20. Remove five heater core cover attaching bolts, then remove cover.
21. Remove heater core and seals from case, then remove seals from heater core tubes.
22. Reverse procedure to install.

1980–81 CONTINENTAL & MARK VI; 1982–83 MARK VI & 1982–86 TOWN CAR

1. Disconnect battery ground cable.
2. Disconnect heater hoses from core. Plug hoses and heater core tubes to prevent coolant loss during core removal.
3. Remove one bolt located below the windshield wiper motor retaining left end of plenum to dash panel.
4. Remove one nut retaining the upper left corner of evaporator case to dash panel.
5. Disconnect vacuum supply hose from vacuum source, then push grommet and hose into passenger compartment.
6. Remove glove compartment, then loosen door sill plates and remove side cowl trim panels.

NOTE: On some models, it may be necessary to lower the steering column to remove the instrument panel. On these models, disconnect harnesses from multiple connectors and transmission shift indicator from column, then remove steering column to instrument panel brace attaching nuts and lower steering column to seat.

7. Disconnect speedometer cable from speedometer and antenna lead from radio.
8. Remove bolt retaining lower right end of instrument panel to side cowl, then remove instrument panel pad as follows:

a. Remove screws retaining instrument panel pad to instrument panel at each defroster opening.
b. Remove the one screw retaining each outboard end of pad to instrument panel.
c. Remove the five screws retaining lower edge of instrument panel pad, then pull instrument panel pad rearward and remove it.
9. Disconnect temperature control cable housing from bracket at top of plenum, then disconnect cable from temperature blend door crank arm.
10. Remove push clip retaining the center register duct bracket to the plenum and rotate bracket to the right.
11. Disconnect vacuum jumper harness at multiple vacuum connector near the floor air distribution duct, then disconnect white vacuum hose from the outside-recirculating door vacuum motor.
12. Remove screws retaining the passenger side of floor air distribution duct to the plenum. It may be necessary to remove the two screws retaining the partial (lower) panel door vacuum motor to mounting bracket to gain access to right screw.
13. Remove the plastic push fastener retaining floor air distribution duct to left end of plenum and remove floor air distribution duct.
14. Remove nuts from the two studs along lower edge of plenum.
15. Carefully move plenum rearward to allow heater core tubes and stud at top of plenum to clear holes in dash panel. Remove plenum by rotating top of ple-

num forward, down and out from under instrument panel. Carefully pull lower edge of instrument panel rearward as necessary while rolling the plenum from behind the instrument panel, Fig 14.
16. Remove the four retaining screws from heater core cover and remove cover from plenum, Fig. 15.
17. Remove heater core retaining screw then pull core and seal assembly from plenum assembly.
18. Reverse procedure to install.

VERSAILLES

1. Disconnect battery ground cable and drain cooling system.
2. Disconnect hoses from heater core. Plug heater core tubes to prevent coolant leakage.
3. Remove washer nut from plenum assembly mounting stud on engine side of dash panel.
4. Remove floor duct, seat belt interlock module and bracket, glove box liner and shields.
5. Loosen right door sill scuff plate, right A-pillar trim cover and right cowl side trim panel.
6. Loosen instrument panel to right cowl side bolt and remove instrument panel brace at lower rail below glove box opening.
7. If used, remove tunnel to cowl brace located on left side of plenum assembly.
8. Disconnect vacuum hoses from A/C-Defrost and Heat/Defrost door motors. Remove screw from clip retaining vacuum harness to plenum.
9. Remove the two Heat/Defrost door motor mounting nuts and swing motor rearward on door crankarm.
10. Remove the two screws retaining plenum to left mounting bracket, then remove the two screws and three clips retaining plenum to evaporator case.
11. Swing bottom of plenum away from evaporator case to disengage S-clip on forward flange of plenum, then raise plenum to clear tabs on top of evaporator case.
12. Move plenum to left while pulling instrument rearward to gain clearance. Use care to avoid cracking plastic.

NOTE: There is very little clearance between plenum and wiper motor assembly.

13. Pull heater core to the left, then as rear

Fig. 15   Heater core removal. 1980–81 Continental & Mark VI, 1982–83 Mark VI & 1982–86 Town Car

surface of heater core clears evaporator case, pull core rearward and downward to clear instrument panel.
14. Reverse procedure to install. Before installing core, make sure that heater core tube to dash panel seal is in place.

BLOWER MOTOR
REPLACE

1982–86 CONTINENTAL & 1984–86 MARK VII

1. Disconnect battery ground cable.
2. Remove glove box and shield, then disconnect vacuum hose from outside-recirculating air door vacuum motor.
3. Remove instrument panel lower right to side cowl attaching bolt then, remove screw attaching support brace to top of air inlet duct.
4. Disconnect blower motor power lead at wire connector.
5. Remove blower motor housing lower support bracket to heater/evaporator

attaching nut.
6. Remove side cowl trim panel.
7. Remove ashtray receptacle, then remove two screws securing instrument panel to transmission tunnel inside ashtray opening.
8. Remove screw attaching top of air inlet duct to heater/evaporator case.
9. Remove air inlet duct and blower housing assembly down and away from the evaporator case.
10. Remove assembly from vehicle, then remove four blower motor mounting plate screws and remove blower motor from housing.
11. Reverse procedure to install.

1980–81 CONTINENTAL & MARK VI; 1982–83 MARK VI & 1982–86 TOWN CAR

1. Disconnect battery ground cable.
2. Disconnect blower motor lead from wiring harness, then remove blower motor cooling tube from blower motor.
3. Remove the four blower motor retaining screws.
4. Rotate motor and wheel assembly slightly to the right so that bottom edge of mounting plate follows contour of wheel well splash panel, then lift the motor and wheel assembly up and out of housing.
5. Reverse procedure to install.

VERSAILLES

1. Disconnect battery ground cable.
2. Remove glove box.
3. Loosen right door sill scuff plate, right A-pillar trim cover and remove right cowl side trim panel.
4. Remove right lower instrument panel to cowl side bolt.
5. Remove cowl to lower instrument panel brace bolt.
6. Disconnect electrical connector from motor.
7. Remove blower motor assembly retaining screws and then blower motor. Pull rearward on lower edge of instrument panel to gain clearance.

NOTE: Do not remove mounting plate from blower motor, as the plate location is critical and should not be changed.

8. Reverse procedure to install.

Gasoline Engine Section

ENGINE MOUNTS
REPLACE

CAUTION: Whenever self-locking mounting bolts and nuts are removed, they must be replaced with new self-locking bolts and nuts.

1980–83 MARK VI, 1980–86 CONTINENTAL, 1982–86 TOWN CAR & 1984–86 MARK VII

1. Remove fan shroud attaching screws, if necessary.
2. Remove the nut and through bolt attaching the insulator to the support bracket, **Figs. 1, 2 and 3.**
3. Raise the engine slightly with a jack and a wood block placed under the oil pan.
4. Remove the engine insulator assembly to cylinder block attaching bolts. Remove the engine insulator assembly and the heat shield, if so equipped.
5. Reverse procedure to install.

VERSAILLES

1. Disconnect fan shroud from radiator and set shroud back on the fan. On all models, support engine using a jack and block of wood placed under oil pan.
2. Remove through bolt attaching insulator to insulator support bracket, **Fig. 4.**
3. Raise engine slightly and remove insulator and support bracket to engine attaching bolts.
4. Remove insulator and support bracket assembly.
5. Reverse procedure to install.

Fig. 2   Engine mounts. 1982–86 Continental & 1984–86 Mark VII V8-302

ENGINE
REPLACE

1982 CONTINENTAL V6-232

1. Disconnect battery ground cable, then drain cooling system and crankcase.
2. Mark position of hood hinges, then remove hood.
3. Remove air cleaner, air inlet duct and heat tube.
4. Remove fan shroud and fan assembly, then loosen accessory drive belt idler and remove drive belt and water pump pulley.
5. Disconnect upper and lower radiator hoses at radiator.
6. Disconnect Thermactor hose at air tube check valve, then remove air tube valve bracket attaching bolt at rear of right hand cylinder head.
7. Remove secondary wire from ignition coil.
8. Remove bolts attaching power steering pump mounting bracket, then remove pump and bracket assembly and position aside with hoses attached if equipped.

9. On models with A/C, remove compressor mounting bracket attaching bolts, then remove compressor and mounting bracket assembly and secure to right hand shock absorber tower with refrigerant lines attached.
10. Remove alternator and position aside.
11. Disconnect heater hoses from water pump and heater tube.
12. On models equipped with speed control, disconnect servo chain at carburetor, then remove servo bracket attaching bolts and servo.
13. Disconnect all necessary vacuum hoses and wiring connectors.
14. Remove engine ground strap to dash panel attaching screw.
15. Disconnect transmission downshift linkage, throttle cable from carburetor, then remove throttle cable bracket attaching bolts.
16. Disconnect fuel line and PCV valve hose from carburetor.
17. Remove carburetor assembly from intake manifold. On models equipped with 7200 VV two barrel carburetor, remove spark knock intensity sensor and adapter assembly which is located between carburetor and thermostat housing.
18. With EGR spacer and phenolic gasket in position, install engine lifting plate T75T-6000-A or equivalent over carburetor mounting studs, then install nuts.
19. Raise vehicle and disconnect fuel inlet hose from fuel pump. Cap fuel hose to prevent entry of dirt.
20. Remove inspection cover from torque converter housing, then remove nuts attaching flex plate to torque converter.
21. Remove starter motor.
22. Remove transmission cooler line retaining clips, then disconnect ex-

Fig. 3   Engine mounts. 1980–81 Continental, 1980–83 Mark VI & 1982–86 Town Car V8-302, 351W

Fig. 4   Engine mounts. Versailles

REAR SUPPORT

NO. 3 CROSSMEMBER

NO. 2 CROSSMEMBER

FRONT SUPPORT (RIGHT)

FRONT SUPPORT (LEFT)

Fig. 1 Engine mounts. 1982 Continental V6-232

Fig. 5 Cylinder head tightening sequence. V6-232

Fig. 6 Intake manifold tightening sequence. V6-232

Fig. 7 Cylinder head tightening. V8 Engines

haust pipe from exhaust manifold.
23. Remove four lower engine to transmission attaching bolts, then lower vehicle.
24. Remove engine mount to crossmember attaching nuts.
25. Lower vehicle and position a suitable transmission jack under transmission. Raise jack just enough to support weight of transmission,
26. Remove two upper engine to transmission attaching bolts, then place a ¼ inch piece of plywood or other suitable material between engine and radiator to prevent damage to radiator.
27. Carefully raise engine slightly, then pull away from transmission and lift from vehicle.
28. Reverse procedure to install. Torque fasteners according to numbers in **Fig. 1:** 1, 35–50 ft. lbs.; 2, 50–70 ft. lbs.; 3, 35–60 ft. lbs.; 4, 35–60 ft. lbs.; 5, 70–90 ft. lbs.; 6, 35–50 ft. lbs.; 7, 70–90 ft. lbs.

VERSAILLES, 1980–83 MARK VI, 1980–86 CONTINENTAL, 1982–86 TOWN CAR & 1984–86 MARK VII

NOTE: On models equipped with Thermactor system, remove or disconnect components that will interfere with engine removal or installation.

1. Drain cooling system and crankcase.
2. Remove hood, then disconnect battery and alternator ground cables from cylinder block.
3. Remove air cleaner and duct assembly.
4. Disconnect upper and lower radiator hoses from engine block and transmission oil cooler lines from radiator.
5. Remove bolts attaching fan shroud to radiator.
6. Remove radiator, fan, spacer, pulley and fan shroud.
7. Remove alternator mounting bolts and position alternator aside.
8. Disconnect oil pressure sending unit wire connector and fuel line at fuel pump. Plug fuel tank line.

NOTE: On models equipped with electronic fuel injection, relieve pressure at the schrader type valve on the fuel charging valve before disconnecting fuel lines.

9. Disconnect accelerator cable from throttle and throttle valve vacuum line

at intake manifold.
10. Disconnect transmission manual shift rod, then disconnect retracting spring at shift rod stud.
11. Disconnect transmission oil filler tube bracket from engine block.
12. On models equipped with A/C, isolate and remove compressor.
13. Remove power steering pump bracket from cylinder head and position pump aside. Position pump so that fluid will not drain from reservoir.
14. Disconnect heater hoses from water pump and intake manifold and temperature sending unit wire connector.
15. Remove converter housing to engine upper attaching bolts.
16. Disconnect primary wire connector from ignition coil, then remove wiring harness from left rocker arm cover and position out of way. Disconnect ground strap from block. On EEC-IV equipped vehicles, disconnect wiring at sensors.
17. Raise front of vehicle and remove starter.
18. Disconnect exhaust pipes from exhaust manifold, then remove engine support insulators from brackets on frame.
19. Disconnect transmission oil cooler lines from retainer and remove converter housing inspection cover.
20. Disconnect flywheel from converter, secure converter to converter housing.
21. Remove remaining converter housing to engine attaching bolts, then lower vehicle and support transmission using a suitable jack.
22. Attach engine lifting device to lifting brackets on intake manifold, then raise engine slightly and disconnect from transmission.
23. Carefully lift engine from engine compartment.
24. Reverse procedure to install.

CYLINDER HEAD
REPLACE

NOTE: Before installing cylinder head, wipe off engine block gasket surface and be certain no foreign material has fallen into cylinder bores, bolt holes or in the valve lifter area. It is good practice to clean out bolt holes with compressed air.

Some cylinder head gaskets are coated with a special lacquer to provide a good

seal once the parts have warmed up. Do not use any additional sealer on such gaskets. If the gasket does not have this lacquer coating, apply suitable sealer to both sides.

Tighten cylinder head bolts a little at a time in three steps in the sequence shown in the illustrations. Final tightening should be to the torque specifications listed in the Engine Tightening table. After the bolts have been torqued to specifications, they should not be disturbed.

V6-232

1. Disconnect battery ground cable, then drain cooling system.
2. Remove air cleaner, air intake duct and heat tube.
3. Loosen accessory drive belt idler and remove drive belt.
4. If left cylinder head is to be removed, proceed as follows:
   a. Remove oil filler cap.
   b. If equipped with power steering, remove pump bracket attaching bolts, then remove pump and bracket assembly and position pump aside with hoses attached.
   c. If equipped with A/C, remove compressor bracket attaching bolts, then position compressor and bracket assembly aside with refrigerant lines attached.
5. If right cylinder head is to be removed, proceed as follows:
   a. Remove Thermactor diverter valve and hose assembly.
   b. Remove accessory drive belt idler, then remove alternator.
   c. Remove Thermactor pump pulley, then remove Thermactor pump.
   d. Remove alternator mounting bracket.

NOTE: On models equipped with Tripminder, then fuel supply line from the fuel pump to the fuel sensor will have to be disconnected to gain access to the upper alternator bracket bolt.

   e. Remove PCV valve.
6. Remove intake manifold, and exhaust manifolds.
7. Remove rocker arm cover and attaching screws, then loosen cover by using a putty knife under cover flange and remove cover. Do not use excess force when loosening rocker arm cover as cover may become damaged.
8. Loosen rocker fulcrum bolt enough to allow rocker arms to be rotated to one side, then remove push rods.

Fig. 8 Intake manifold tightening sequence. V8-302 & 351W

NOTE: Tag push rods so they can be installed in the same position.

9. Remove cylinder head attaching bolts, then remove cylinder head and gasket.
10. Reverse procedure to install. Apply a thin coating of pipe sealant D8AZ-19558-A or equivalent to the shorter cylinder head bolts which are installed on the exhaust manifold side of the cylinder head. Do not apply pipe sealant to long bolts which are installed on the intake manifold side of the cylinder head. Tighten cylinder head bolts in four steps to torque listed under Engine Tightening Specifications using sequence shown in **Fig. 5.** Loosen cylinder bolts approximately 2 to 3 turns, then retighten bolts in four steps to specified torque in sequence, **Fig. 5.** When installing intake manifold, tighten mounting bolts to torque specified under Engine Tightening Specifications in sequence shown in **Fig. 6.**

NOTE: Before installing intake manifold, apply a ⅛ inch bead of silicone rubber sealer D6AZ-19562-B or equivalent at mating surfaces of intake manifold, cylinder heads and cylinder block. Also apply a ⅛ inch bead of sealer to the outer end of each intake manifold seal for the full width of the seal.

V8-302 & 351W

1. Remove intake manifold and carburetor (if equipped) as an assembly.
2. Disconnect battery ground cable at cylinder head.

Fig. 9 Compressing lifter to check valve clearance

3. If left head is being removed, remove A/C compressor (if equipped). Also remove and wire power steering pump out of the way. If equipped with Thermactor System, disconnect hose from air manifold on left cylinder head.
4. If right head is to be removed, remove alternator mounting bracket bolt and spacer, ground wire and air cleaner inlet duct, and A/C compressor bracket.
5. If right head is to be removed on an engine with Thermactor System, remove air pump from bracket. Disconnect hose from air manifold.
6. Disconnect exhaust manifolds at exhaust pipes.
7. Remove rocker arm covers. If equipped with Thermactor System, remove check valve from air manifold.
8. Remove fulcrum bolts, oil deflectors (if used), fulcrums and rocker arms. On all engines, remove push rods. Keep rocker arms and push rods in order so they can be installed in the same position.
9. Remove head bolts and lift head off block.
10. Reverse procedure to install. Torque cylinder head bolts in sequence shown in **Fig. 7,** and torque intake manifold bolts in sequence shown in **Fig. 8.**

SERVICE BULLETIN: Some V8-302 engines may exhibit engine oil leakage at the front or rear intake manifold end seals. To correct this condition, RTV sealer should be used instead of the conventional cork seals provided in the gasket set.

Remove intake manifold and gaskets, then clean cylinder block and intake manifold sealing surfaces with suitable solvent. Install side runner gaskets onto cylinder block, then apply a ¼ inch bead of RTV sealer across the front and rear sealing surfaces of the cylinder block. When applying the sealer, ensure sealer does not get inside engine, as damage may result. Install manifold and torque bolts to specifications.

SERVICE BULLETIN: Some 1981–82

Fig. 10 Rocker arm & related parts. V6-232, V8-302 & 351W

V8-302 engines may exhibit excessive oil consumption caused by low profile rocker arm fulcrums, Part No. E1TZ-6A528-A, allowing excessive oil displacement when the engine is operated for an extended period during high ambient temperatures. To service the above problem, replace the fulcrums indicated above with new fulcrums, Part No. D7AZ-6A528-A.

VALVES
ADJUST

V6-232

A .060 inch longer or a .060 inch shorter push rod is available to compensate for dimensional changes in the valve train. If clearance is less than specified, the .060 inch shorter push rod should be used. If clearance is more than the maximum specified, the .060 inch longer push rod should be used.

Using an auxiliary starter switch crankshaft until No. 1 cylinder is at TDC compression stroke, then compress valve lifter using tool T82C-6500-A or equivalent, **Fig. 9.** At this point, the following valves can be checked:

No. 1 Intake	No. 3 Intake
No. 1 Exhaust	No. 4 Exhaust
No. 2 Exhaust	No. 6 Intake

After clearance on these valves has been checked, rotate crankshaft until No. 5 cylinder is at TDC compression stroke (1 revolution of crankshaft), and then compress valve lifter using tool No. T82C-6500-A or equivalent, **Fig. 9,** and check the following valves:

No. 2 Intake	No. 5 Intake
No. 3 Exhaust	No. 5 Exhaust
No. 4 Intake	No. 6 Exhaust

V8-302 & 351

To eliminate the need of adjusting valve lash, a positive stop nut fulcrum bolt and seat is used on these engines, **Fig. 10.**

It is very important that the correct push rod be used and all components be

Fig. 11 Hydraulic valve lifter disassembled (typical)

Fig. 12 Hydraulic roller valve lifter disassembled

installed and torqued as follows:
1. Position the piston of the cylinder being worked on at TDC of its compression stroke.
2. Install rocker arm, fulcrum seat and oil deflector. Install fulcrum bolt and torque to 18–25 ft. lbs.

A .060 inch shorter push rod or a .060 inch longer rod is available for service to provide a means of compensating for dimensional changes in the valve mechanism. Valve stem-to-rocker arm clearance should be as listed in the Valve Specifications table, with the hydraulic lifter completely collapsed, **Fig. 9.** Repeated valve grind jobs will decrease this clearance to the point that if not compensated for the lifters will cease to function.

When checking valve clearance, if the clearance is less than the minimum, the .060 inch shorter push rod should be used. If clearance is more than the maximum, the .060 inch longer push rod should be used. (See Valve Specifications table.) To check valve clearance, proceed as follows:
1. Mark crankshaft pulley at three locations, with number 1 location at TDC timing mark (end of compression stroke), number 2 location one half turn (180°) clockwise from TDC and number 3 location three quarter turn clockwise (270°) from number 2 location.
2. Turn the crankshaft to the number 1 location and check the clearance on the following valves:
V8-302
No. 1 Intake	No. 1 Exhaust
No. 7 Intake	No. 5 Exhaust
No. 8 Intake	No. 4 Exhaust
V8-302 H.O. & 351
No. 1 Intake	No. 1 Exhaust
No. 4 Intake	No. 3 Exhaust
No. 8 Intake	No. 7 Exhaust
3. Turn the crankshaft to the number 2 location and check the clearance on the following valves:
V8-302
No. 5 Intake	No. 2 Exhaust
No. 4 Intake	No. 6 Exhaust

V8-302 H.O. & 351
No. 3 Intake	No. 2 Exhaust
No. 7 Intake	No. 6 Exhaust
4. Turn the crankshaft to the number 3 location and check the clearance on the following valves:
V8-302
No. 2 Intake	No. 7 Exhaust
No. 3 Intake	No. 3 Exhaust
No. 6 Intake	No. 8 Exhaust
V8-302 H.O. & 351
No. 2 Intake	No. 4 Exhaust
No. 5 Intake	No. 5 Exhaust
No. 6 Intake	No. 8 Exhaust

VALVE ARRANGEMENT
FRONT TO REAR

V6 Engine Right Bank	I-E-I-E-I-E
V6 Engine Left Bank	E-I-E-I-E-I
V8 Engine Right Bank	I-E-I-E-I-E-I-E
V8 Engine Left Bank	E-I-E-I-E-I-E-I

VALVE LIFT SPECS.

Engine	Year	Intake	Exhaust
V6-232	1982	.415	.417
V8-302	1980–86	.375	.390
V8-302H.O.	1985–86	.413	.442
V8-351W	1980	.411	.411

VALVE TIMING
INTAKE OPENS BEFORE TDC

Engine	Year	Degrees
V6-232	1982	13
V8-302①	1980–82	16
V8-302②	1980–81	17
V8-302②	1982	16
V8-351W	1980	23

①—Less EFI.
②—With EFI.

ROCKER ARM
REPLACE
V6-232, V8-302 & 351W

The rocker arm is supported by a fulcrum bolt which fits through the fulcrum seat and threads into the cylinder head. To disassemble, remove the bolt, fulcrum seat, fulcrum guide and rocker arm, **Fig. 9.**

VALVE GUIDES

Valve guides in these engines are an integral part of the head and, therefore, cannot be removed. For service, guides can be reamed oversize to accommodate one of three service valves with oversize stems (.003 inch, .015 inch and .030 inch).

Check the valve stem clearance of each valve (after cleaning) in its respective valve guide. If the clearance exceeds the service limits of .0055 inch, ream the valve guides to accommodate the next oversize diameter valve.

HYDRAULIC VALVE LIFTERS
REPLACE

NOTE: The internal parts of each hydraulic valve lifter assembly are a matched set. If these are mixed, improper valve operation may result. Therefore, disassemble, inspect and test each assembly separately to prevent mixing the parts.

Fig. 11, illustrates a conventional type hydraulic lifter used on 1980-85 engines exc. 1985 V8-302 H.O. Fig. 12, illustrates a roller type hydraulic lifter used on 1985 V8-302 H.O. and all 1986 V8-302 engines. See the Trouble Shooting Chapter under the heading Engine Noises for causes of hydraulic valve lifter noise. To replace valve lifters, proceed as follows:

Fig. 13   Front cover attaching bolt location. V6-232

Fig. 14   Valve timing marks. V6-232

Fig. 15   Valve timing marks. V8 Engines

1. Remove intake manifold and related parts.
2. Remove rocker arm covers.
3. Loosen rocker arm stud nuts or bolts and rotate rocker arms to the side.
4. Lift out push rods, keeping them in sequence in a rack so they may be installed in their original location.

NOTE: 1985 V8-302 H.O. and all 1986 engines are equipped with roller hydraulic lifters, **Fig. 12.** Push rods used on these engines have a collar at the upper end and must be installed in this position.

5. Using a magnet rod, remove valve lifters and place them in sequence in a rack so they may be installed in their original location.
6. Reverse procedure to install.

TIMING CASE COVER
REPLACE

NOTE: If necessary to replace the cover oil seal the cover must first be removed.

V6-232

1. Disconnect battery ground cable and drain cooling.
2. Remove air cleaner and air duct assembly.
3. Remove fan shroud attaching, then remove fan and clutch assembly and fan shroud.
4. Loosen accessory drive belt idler, then remove drive belt and water pump pulley.
5. On models equipped with power steering, remove pump bracket attaching bolts, then position pump and bracket assembly aside with hoses attached.
6. If equipped with A/C, remove compressor front support bracket.
7. Disconnect by-pass hose, heater hoses and upper radiator hose from engine.
8. Position No. 1 cylinder at TDC compression stroke, then disconnect coil wire from distributor cap. Remove distributor cap and mark position of rotor to distributor body and distributor body to front cover. Remove distributor hold down clamp, then remove distributor.

9. On models equipped with Tripminder, remove fuel flow meter support bracket.
10. Raise vehicle and support, then remove crankshaft damper using a suitable puller.
11. Remove fuel pump shield, then remove fuel pump attaching bolts and position pump aside with fuel hose attached.
12. Remove oil filter, then disconnect lower radiator hose at water pump.
13. Remove oil pan as described under Oil Pan, Replace.
14. Lower vehicle, then remove front cover attaching bolts, **Fig. 13.**

NOTE: One of the front cover attaching bolts is located behind the oil filter adapter.

15. Remove ignition timing indicator, then remove front cover and water pump as an assembly.
16. Reverse procedure to install. Coat threads of bolt located at position 10, **Fig. 13,** with a suitable sealer before installing. Torque front cover attaching bolts to 15 to 22 ft. lbs.

NOTE: Lubricate camshaft thrust button with Polyethylene grease before installing front cover. Also ensure that thrust button and spring are properly seated.

V8-302, 351W

1. Drain cooling system and crankcase.
2. Remove fan shroud attaching bolts and position shroud over engine fan.
3. Remove engine fan, spacer and shroud.
4. Remove drive belts and A/C idler pulley bracket.
5. Remove power steering pump and position aside.
6. Remove all accessory brackets attached to water pump, then remove water pump pulley.
7. Disconnect lower radiator hose, heater hose and by-pass hose from water pump.
8. Remove crankshaft pulley from vibra-

tion damper.
9. Remove damper attaching screw and washer, then using a suitable puller, remove damper.
10. Disconnect fuel pump outlet line, then remove fuel pump attaching bolts and position pump aside.
11. Remove oil level dip stick.
12. Remove oil pan to front cover attaching bolts.
13. Remove front cover to engine block attaching bolts, then remove front cover and water pump as an assembly.

NOTE: Use a thin blade knife to cut oil pan gasket flush with cylinder block face prior to separating front cover from cylinder block.

14. Reverse procedure to install.

TIMING CHAIN
REPLACE

1. To remove the chain, first take off the timing chain cover as outlined previously.
2. Crank the engine until the timing mark on the camshaft sprocket is adjacent to the timing mark on the crankshaft sprocket, **Figs. 14 & 15.**
3. Remove cap screws, lock plate and fuel pump eccentric from front of camshaft.
4. Place a screwdriver behind the camshaft sprocket and carefully pry the sprocket and chain off the camshaft.
5. Reverse the foregoing procedure to install the chain, being sure to align the timing marks as shown in **Figs. 14 and 15.**

CAMSHAFT
REPLACE

If it is necessary to replace the camshaft only it may be accomplished without removing the engine from the chassis. But if the camshaft bearings are to be replaced the engine will have to be removed. To remove the camshaft, proceed as follows:

Fig. 16 Camshaft & related parts (typical). V8 engines

Fig. 17 Piston & rod assembly. V6-232

Exc. Versailles

NOTE: It may be necessary to remove or reposition radiator, A/C compressor and grille components to provide adequate clearance.

1. To remove camshaft, remove front cover and timing chain.
2. Remove distributor cap and spark plug wires, then remove distributor.
3. Disconnect automatic transmission oil cooler lines from radiator and remove radiator.
4. Remove intake manifold and carburetor (if equipped) as an assembly.
5. Remove rocker arm covers.
6. Loosen rocker arm fulcrum or bolts and rotate rocker arms to one side.
7. Remove push rods, keeping them in sequence in a rack so they may be installed in their original location.
8. Using a magnet, remove valve lifters and place them in a rack in sequence so they may be installed in their original location.
9. Remove camshaft thrust plate, and carefully pull camshaft from engine, using care to avoid damaging camshaft bearings, **Fig. 16**.
10. Reverse procedure to install.

NOTE: Prior to installation of the camshaft, lubricate push rods and camshaft lobes with lubricant part No. D9AZ-19579-C or equivalent on V6-232 engines and D0AZ-19584-A or equivalent for V8-302 & 351W engines. Using engine oil SF, lubricate valve tappets & bores.

VERSAILLES

1. Remove hood latch assembly, then disconnect A/C ambient temperature sensor wire connector and remove hood latch support brackets.
2. Remove condenser to radiator support attaching bolts, then remove fender to radiator support braces at each side of engine compartment.
3. Remove air dam and gasket located between radiator support and grille opening panel.

Fig. 18 Piston & rod assembly. V8 Engines

4. Carefully lift condenser upward until clearance is obtained to remove camshaft.
5. Remove cylinder front cover and timing chain as outlined previously.
6. Remove intake manifold and carburetor as an assembly.
7. Remove rocker covers. Loosen rocker arm stud nuts or fulcrum bolts and rotate rocker arms to the side.
8. Remove push rods and valve lifters in sequence so they can be installed in the same position.
9. Remove camshaft thrust plate, then carefully remove camshaft from engine, **Fig. 16**.

NOTE: When removing camshaft, use care not to damage camshaft bearings.

10. Reverse procedure to install.

PISTON & ROD
ASSEMBLE

If the old pistons are serviceable, make certain that they are installed on the rods from which they were removed. The assembly must be assembled as shown in

Figs. 17 and 18.
Check side clearance between connecting rods and crankshaft journal. Clearance should be .010–.020 inch for all engines except V6-232. V6-232 clearance should be .0047–.0114 inch.

PISTONS, RINGS & PINS

Pistons are available in oversizes of .003, .020, .030 and .040 inch.
Piston pins are available in oversizes of .001 and .002 inch.
Rings are available in oversizes of .020, .030 and .040 inch.

MAIN & ROD BEARINGS

Main and rod bearings are available in standard size and undersizes of .001, .002, .010, 020, .030 and .040 inch.

CRANKSHAFT REAR OIL SEAL
REPLACE

1980—83

1. Remove oil pan and oil pump, if necessary.
2. Remove rear bearing cap, **Fig. 19**.
3. Loosen remaining bearing caps, allowing crankshaft to drop down about 1/32 inch.
4. Remove old seals from both cylinder block and rear main bearing cap. Use a brass rod to drift upper half of seal from cylinder block groove. Rotate crankshaft while drifting to facilitate removal.
5. Carefully clean seal groove in block with a brush and solvent. Also clean seal groove in bearing cap. Remove the oil seal retaining pin from the bearing cap if so equipped. The pin is not used with the split-lip seal.

Fig. 19 Crankshaft & related parts. V8 Engines

Fig. 20 Rear crankshaft seal installation. 1980—83

Fig. 21 Rear oil seal installation. 1984—86

3. Lubricate new seal with engine oil, then position seal on installer tool T82L-6701-A, or equivalent, **Fig. 21.**
4. With spring end of seal facing towards engine, install tool, then alternately tighten bolts until rear face of seal is within .005 inch of the engine block.

OIL PAN
REPLACE

1982 CONTINENTAL V6-232

1. Disconnect battery ground cable, then remove air cleaner and air intake duct.
2. Remove fan shroud attaching screws and position shroud over fan, then remove engine oil dipstick.
3. Remove vacuum solenoid from dash panel and position on engine with vacuum hoses attached.
4. Raise and support front of vehicle, then remove exhaust pipe to exhaust manifold attaching nuts.
5. Drain crankcase, then remove oil filter.
6. Remove shift linkage bracket to converter housing attaching bolts.
7. Disconnect transmission oil cooler lines at radiator. Remove four converter cover attaching bolts, then remove converter cover.
8. Remove bolts attaching engine damper to No. 2 crossmember.
9. Disconnect steering gear at flex coupling, then remove steering gear to main crossmember attaching bolts and allow steering gear to rest on frame.
10. Remove nuts and bolts attaching from engine mounts to chassis, then raise engine approximately 2 to 3 inches and insert wooden block between engine mounts and frame.

NOTE: On some models, it may be necessary to raise engine as much as 5 inches to provide clearance for oil pan removal. On these models, transmission fluid dipstick tube may contact Thermactor air tube. If contact occurs, lower engine and remove dipstick and air tube.

6. Dip seal halves in clean engine oil.
7. Carefully install upper seal half in its groove with undercut side of seal toward front of engine, **Fig. 20,** by rotating it on shaft journal of crankshaft until approximately ⅜ inch protrudes below the parting surface. Be sure no rubber has been shaved from outside diameter or seal by bottom edge of groove.
8. Retighten main bearing caps and torque to specifications.
9. Install lower seal in main bearing cap with undercut side of seal toward front of engine, and allow seal to protrude about ⅜ inch above parting surface to mate with upper seal upon cap installation.
10. Apply suitable sealer to parting faces of cap and block. Install cap and torque to specifications.

NOTE: If difficulty is encountered in installing the upper half of the seal in position, lightly lap (sandpaper) the side of the seal opposite the lip side using a medium grit paper. After sanding, the seal must be washed in solvent, then dipped in clean engine oil prior to installation.

1984—86
A new one-piece rear oil seal is used on 1984—86 engines. To replace the new type seal, proceed as follows:
1. Using a sharp awl, punch one hole into seal metal surface between seal lip and engine block.
2. Using slide hammer tool T82L-9533-B or equivalent, screw tool into hole in seal and remove seal by gently pulling rearward. Use caution to avoid damaging sealing surface.

8-23

Fig. 22   Oil pump assembly. V6-232

Fig. 23   Oil pump assembly.
V8-302 & 351W

11. Remove oil pan attaching bolts, then lower oil pan to crossmember.
12. Remove oil pump pickup tube attaching bolts and pickup tube bracket attaching nut, then lower pickup tube into oil pan.
13. Remove oil pan through front of vehicle, then remove oil pan gaskets and seals.
14. Reverse procedure to install. Using a small screwdriver, work tabs of oil pan seal into gap between rear main bearing cap and cylinder block, then with tabs positioned, work seal into groove on rear main bearing cap. Apply a ⅛ inch bead of silicone sealer D6AZ-19562-B or equivalent where front cover and cylinder block join and where rear main bearing cap and cylinder block join. Apply a ⅛ inch bead along oil pan rail surface of cylinder block and a ¼ inch bead along front cover to oil pan surface.

NOTE: When using silicone sealant, assembly must occur within 15 minutes after sealant application. After this time, the sealer may start to set, and its sealing effectiveness may be reduced.

1980–83 MARK VI, 1980–86 CONTINENTAL, 1982–86 TOWN CAR & 1984–86 MARK VII

1. Disconnect battery ground cable and remove air cleaner assembly.
2. Disconnect accelerator cable and kickdown rod from throttle.
3. Remove accelerator mounting bracket bolts and bracket, then the EGR valve and cooler, if applicable.
4. Remove fan shroud attaching screws and position shroud over fan.
5. Disconnect wiper motor electrical connector and remove wiper motor.
6. Disconnect windshield washer hose.
7. Remove wiper motor mounting cover.
8. Remove oil level dipstick, then the dip-

stick tube retaining bolt from exhaust manifold.
9. If equipped with EGR cooler, remove Thermactor air dump tube retaining clamp, then the Thermactor crossover tube at rear of engine.
10. Raise and support vehicle, then drain engine oil.
11. On models equipped with EEC, remove transmission filler tube from oil pan and drain transmission fluid, then remove starter.
12. Disconnect fuel tank fuel line at fuel pump and plug line.

NOTE: Vehicles equipped with electronic fuel injection have high pressure at the electric fuel pump. Pressure must be relieved at the schrader type valve on the fuel charging assembly before disconnecting fuel supply and return lines.

13. Disconnect exhaust pipes from manifolds. Remove oxygen sensor, if applicable.
14. If equipped with EGR cooler, remove exhaust gas sensor from exhaust manifold, then the Thermactor secondary air tube to converter housing clamps.
15. On all models, remove dipstick tube from oil pan.
16. Loosen rear engine mount attaching nuts.
17. Remove engine mount through bolts.
18. Remove shift crossover bolts at transmission.
19. If equipped with EGR cooler, disconnect exhaust pipes from catalytic converter outlet, then the catalytic converter secondary air tube and inlet pipes to exhaust manifold.
20. On all models, disconnect transmission kickdown rod.
21. Remove torque converter housing cover.
22. Remove brake line retainer from front crossmember.
23. With a suitable jack, raise engine as

far as possible.
24. Place a block of wood between each engine mount and chassis bracket. When engine is secured in this position, remove jack, then the low oil level sensor, if equipped.
25. Remove oil pan attaching bolts and lower the oil pan.
26. Remove oil pick-up tube bolts and lower tube in oil pan.
27. Remove oil pan from vehicle.
28. Reverse procedure to install.

VERSAILLES

1. Disconnect battery ground cable.
2. Remove two fan shroud attaching screws and loosen shroud to prevent damage when raising engine.
3. Raise vehicle and drain crankcase.
4. Remove stabilizer bar from chassis.
5. Remove right and left engine mount through bolts.
6. Loosen transmission oil cooler lines and move aside.
7. Raise engine and position 2 × 4 in. wooden blocks under engine mounts.
8. Remove oil pan attaching bolts and oil pan.

NOTE: It will be necessary to rotate the crankshaft during removal so that rear crankshaft throw is in horizontal position to clear rear oil pan flange.

9. Reverse procedure to install.

OIL PUMP
REPLACE

V6-232

On these engines, the oil pump is contained within the front cover, **Fig. 22.**

V8 ENGINES

1. Remove oil pan as previously

Engine lubrication (typical). V8 engine

5. Check the drive shaft-to-housing bearing clearance by measuring the O.D. of the shaft and the I.D. of the housing bearing. The recommended clearance limits are .0015–.0030 inch.
6. Inspect the relief valve spring for a collapsed or worn condition.
7. Check the relief valve piston for scores and free operation in the bore. The specified clearance is .0015–.0030 inch.

BELT TENSION DATA

	New	Used
1980 ¼ inch	65	50
Exc. ¼ inch	140	110
1981		
Except ¼ inch	140	110
¼ inch	65	40
V Ribbed Belt		
4 Rib	105	100
5 Rib①	125	120
5 Rib②	108	108
6 Rib①	155	150
6 Rib②	113	113
1982–86		
Except ¼ inch	140	105
¼ inch	65	50
V Ribbed Belt		
4 Rib		
Except Air Pump	130	115
Air Pump	110	105
5 Rib	150	135
6 Rib①	160	145
6 Rib②	113	110

①—W/ tensioner
②—W/ absorber

described under "Oil Pan, Replace".
2. Remove the two attaching bolts and remove the oil pump assembly with gasket and drive shaft.
3. Reverse procedure to install.

OIL PUMP
SERVICE

V6-232 ENGINE

To disassemble, remove oil filter (if necessary), oil pump, cover bolts and cover. Lift oil pump gears from front cover pocket and remove cover gasket. Remove cotter pin from relief valve plug in pump housing. Drill a small hole and insert a self-tapping screw into the plug, then using pliers, remove plug from pump housing. Remove retainer spring and relief valve from pump housing. Using a suitable solvent, thoroughly clean oil pump components. Inspect oil pump as follows:
1. Check oil pump cover gasket surface. Remove any remaining gasket material, burrs and nicks.
2. Position a straightedge across oil pump gears and gasket surface.
3. Using a feeler gauge, measure clearance between straightedge and gasket surface. Clearance should be .002–.005 inch. If clearance is less than .002 inch, proceed to step 4.
4. Using a micrometer, measure oil pump gear thickness. Gear thickness should be .872–.873 inch. If gear is less than .872 inch, replace gear and check reading.
5. Measure front cover gear pocket depth. Depth should be .868–.870 inch. If depth exceeds .870 inch, replace oil pump front cover.

6. Using a feeler gauge, measure side clearance between gear tooth and gear pocket side wall. Clearance should be .002–.005 inch. If clearance exceeds .005 inch, proceed to step 7.
7. Using a micrometer, measure gear diameter. Gear diameter should be 1.664–1.666 inch. If gear diameter is less than 1.664 inch, replace gear and check reading.
8. Measure front cover gear pocket width. Width should be 1.671–1.674 inch. If width is less than 1.671, replace front cover.

V8 ENGINES

To disassemble, remove the pump cover plate, **Fig. 23,** and lift out the rotor and shaft. Remove cotter pin that secures relief valve plug in pump housing. Drill a small hole and insert a self-tapping screw into plug, then using pliers remove plug from pump housing. Then remove the retainer spring and relief valve from the pump housing. Inspect the pump as follows:
1. With all parts clean and dry, check the inside of the pump housing and the outer race and rotor for damage or excessive wear.
2. Check the mating surface of the pump cover for wear. If this surface is worn, scored or grooved, replace the cover.
3. Measure the clearance between the outer race and housing. This clearance should be .001–.013.
4. With the rotor assembly installed in the housing, place a straight edge over the rotor assembly and housing. Measure the clearance between the straight edge and the rotor and outer race. Recommended limits are .0016–

WATER PUMP
REPLACE

V6-232

1. Drain cooling system, then remove air cleaner and air intake duct.
2. Remove fan shroud attaching screws and fan and fan clutch attaching bolts, then remove fan and fan clutch and shroud.
3. Loosen accessory drive belt idler, then remove drive belt and water pump pulley.
4. On models equipped with power steering, remove pump mounting bracket attaching bolts, position pump aside with hoses attached.
5. On models equipped with A/C, remove compressor front support bracket.
6. Disconnect lower radiator hose, coolant bypass hose and heat hose from water pump.
7. On models equipped with Tripminder, remove fuel flow sensor support bracket. Do not disconnect fuel lines.
8. Remove water pump attaching bolts, then remove water pump.
9. Reverse procedure to install.

V8-302 & 351W

1. Drain cooling system, then remove fan

shroud attaching bolts and position shroud over fan.
2. Remove fan, spacer and shroud.
3. Remove drive belts, then remove A/C idler pulley bracket.
4. Remove power steering pump and position aside.
5. Remove all accessory brackets which attach to water pump, then remove water pump pulley.
6. Remove lower radiator hose, heater hose and by-pass hose from water pump.
7. Remove water pump to front cover attaching bolts, then remove water pump.
8. Reverse procedure to install.

FUEL PUMP
REPLACE

MECHANICAL TYPE

1. Disconnect fuel lines from fuel pump.
2. Remove fuel pump attaching bolts and the fuel pump and gasket.
3. Remove all gasket material from the pump and block gasket surfaces. Apply sealer to both sides of new gasket.
4. Position gasket on pump flange and hold pump in position against its mounting surface. Make sure rocker arm is riding on camshaft eccentric.
5. Press pump tight against its mounting. Install retaining screws and tighten them alternately.
6. Connect fuel lines. Then operate engine and check for leaks.

NOTE: Before installing the pump, it is good practice to crank the engine so that the nose of the camshaft eccentric is out of the way of the fuel pump rocker arm when the pump is installed. In this way there will be the least amount of tension on the rocker arm, thereby easing the installation of the pump.

ELECTRIC TYPE

NOTE: When the electric fuel pump is removed from the fuel tank, all the rubber hoses, clamps and mounting gaskets should be replaced, as exposure to the air causes the hoses to become brittle and will lead to premature failure.

Removal

1. Remove air cleaner.
2. Attach tool T80L-9974-A or equivalent, to fuel diagnostic valve on the fuel charging assembly, then slowly depressurize fuel system.
3. Siphon fuel from fuel tank, then raise and support vehicle.
4. Disconnect fuel supply, return and vent lines at the left and right side rear axle frame kickdowns.
5. Disconnect electrical connector in front of fuel tank.
6. Disconnect and remove fuel filler tube.
7. Remove fuel tank support straps, then the fuel tank.
8. Clean all dirt accumulated around fuel pump attaching flange, then disconnect supply and return line fittings and the electrical connector.
9. Turn fuel pump lockring counterclockwise and remove lockring.
10. Remove fuel pump and bracket assembly from fuel tank. Discard seal ring.

Installation

1. Clean fuel tank mounting surface and seal ring groove.
2. Lightly coat new seal ring with heavy grease to hold it in place, then install into fuel ring groove.
3. Carefully install fuel pump and bracket assembly into tank, ensuring filter is not damaged during installation. Ensure locating keys are positioned in keyways and seal ring remains in groove.
4. Holding pump assembly in place, install lockring finger tight, ensuring all locking tabs are positioned under fuel tank ring tabs. Continue to turn lock ringing clockwise until ring contacts stop.
5. Connect fuel pump electrical connector, then lubricate fittings and reconnect fuel lines.
6. Install fuel tank and tighten support straps.
7. Reconnect fuel sender and fuel pump wiring harness, then lower vehicle.
8. Install fuel filler tube and reconnect vent line.
9. Lubricate fittings at right and left hand side of rear axle frame, reconnect finger tight, then tighten an additional ¼ turn.
10. Fill fuel tank with at least 10 gallons of fuel and check for leaks.
11. Connect tool Y80L-9974-A or equivalent, onto fuel charging assembly diagnostic valve. Turn ignition key "ON" for approximately 3 seconds. Turn key "OFF," then back "ON" for another 3 seconds. Continue to perform this operation until gauge reads at least 35 psi. Check for leaks at all fittings. Correct as necessary.
12. Remove tool, start engine and recheck for leaks.

Diesel Engine Section

ENGINE MOUNTS
REPLACE

1. Raise and support vehicle.
2. Remove insulator to crossmember attaching nuts, then raise engine with suitable jack, **Fig 1.**
3. Remove insulator to bracket attaching bolts and the insulator.
4. Reverse procedure to install. Refer to **Fig. 1,** for proper torque specifications.

ENGINE
REPLACE

1. Disconnect battery ground cable.
2. Disconnect under hood lamp wiring connector.
3. Scribe hinge mark locations, then remove hood.
4. Drain cooling system and oil pan, then remove air cleaner assembly.
5. Remove fan shroud attaching bolts, then the fan shroud.
6. Remove cooling fan, then disconnect upper and lower radiator hoses.
7. Disconnect transmission oil cooler lines, then remove radiator.
8. Discharge A/C system, then disconnect hoses from compressor. Plug hoses to prevent dirt entry.
9. Disconnect muffler inlet pipe.
10. Disconnect vacuum hoses and wiring harnesses that will interfere with engine removal.
11. Disconnect engine oil cooler lines.
12. Disconnect accelerator cable and fuel line from injection pump.
13. Disconnect transmission shift linkage.
14. Disconnect ground cable at engine.
15. Remove coolant expansion bottle and position aside.
16. Disconnect heater hoses at dash panel.
17. Disconnect electrical lead at A/C compressor.
18. Disconnect power steering pump and position aside.
19. Disconnect fuel lines from injectors.
20. Disconnect instrument panel wiring harness.
21. Install engine support tool D79F-6000-A or equivalent, then raise and support vehicle.
22. Remove muffler inlet pipe, then the engine oil cooler bracket and brace.
23. Remove stabilizer bar bracket attaching bolts and position stabilizer bar forward.
24. Remove left fender splash shield, then disconnect steering column shaft coupling from steering gear.
25. Remove engine mount insulator retaining nuts, then raise engine with suitable jack.

Fig. 1   Engine mount removal & installation

Fig. 2   Diagnostic connector

Fig. 3   TDC aligning pin installed

CYLINDER HEAD
REPLACE

1. Disconnect battery ground cable and drain cooling system.
2. Disconnect heater hose, then remove accessory drive belts.
3. Remove valve cover, then disconnect diagnostic connectors, **Fig. 2.**
4. Disconnect coolant temperature switch and glow plug electrical connectors.
5. Disconnect breather hose and bracket.
6. Remove oil dipstick tube to intake manifold attaching clamp and position tube aside.
7. Disconnect boost pressure switch electrical connector.

26. Position steering gear, as necessary, then lower engine.
27. Remove converter housing cover, then the converter to drive plate retaining nuts. Position locking pliers in housing to support converter.
28. Remove crossmember retaining nuts, then the transmission shift lever bellcrank.
29. Raise transmission with suitable jack, then remove crossmember retaining bolts.
30. Lower transmission, then remove engine to converter housing retaining bolts.
31. Reinstall crossmember retaining bolts, then lower vehicle.
32. Install suitable engine lifting equipment, then remove engine support tool.
33. Lift engine and remove from vehicle.
34. Reverse procedure to install.

Fig. 4 Cylinder head bolt removal & installation

☐REMOVAL ○INSTALLATION

GASKET CODE—
NUMBER OF HOLES

HIGHEST PISTON PROTRUSION OF ALL 6 PISTONS mm	CYL. HEAD GASKET CODE NO. OF HOLES	THICKNESS OF CYL. HEAD GASKET mm
0.60 – 0.70	1	1.4
0.70 – 0.85	2	1.5
0.85 – 1.00	3	1.6

Fig. 5 Cylinder head gasket selection chart

8. Disconnect radiator hose from cylinder head, then the idle boost coolant hose.
9. Remove vacuum pump from cylinder head.
10. Disconnect No. 1 injector nozzle to injection pump leak hose.
11. Using tool T84P-9395-B or equivalent, disconnect injection lines from nozzles and injection pump. Cap nozzles and lines to prevent dirt entry.
12. Disconnect turbocharger oil lines.
13. Rotate crankshaft pulley until No. 1 cylinder is at TDC, compression stroke, then install TDC aligning pin, tool No. T84P-6400-A or equivalent between cylinder block flange and flywheel, **Fig. 3.**
14. Loosen camshaft drive sprocket retaining bolt, then camshaft drive belt tensioning roller nut and bolt. Remove drive belt.
15. Loosen cylinder head attaching bolts following sequence shown in **Fig. 4,** then remove cylinder head.
16. Clean cylinder head and crankcase sealing surfaces using suitable spray solvent.

NOTE: Do not score or scratch sealing surfaces, since leakage may occur due to high compression pressures.

17. Check cylinder head for warpage. If warpage exceeds .006 inch, replace cylinder head.
18. Select cylinder head gasket thickness as follows:
    a. Mount dial indicator D82L-4201-A and height gauge D84P-6100-A so that indicator pointer is on top of No. 1 position.
    b. Rotate crankshaft until piston is at TDC.
    c. Zero indicator on crankcase, then move indicator pointer to front of piston. Record measurement. Move pointer to rear of piston and again record measurement. Average the two measurements.
    d. Repeat steps a through c for remaining pistons.
    e. Using measurement of highest piston, select the correct cylinder head gasket using chart shown, **Fig. 5.**

19. Clean carbon and oil deposits from head bolts.

NOTE: Keep oil and/or antifreeze from entering cylinder head bolt holes, since damage to crankcase may result. If either enters bolt holes, blow out using compressed air.

20. Position head gasket onto crankcase, then install cylinder head.
21. Install and torque cylinder head bolts in sequence shown, **Fig. 4.**
22. Reverse steps 1 through 13 to complete installation, noting the following:
    a. Torque turbocharger oil lines to 14-17 ft. lbs.
    b. Torque injection line fittings to nozzles and pump to 14-18 ft. lbs.
    c. Torque vacuum pump-to-cylinder head attaching bolts to 6-7 ft. lbs.
    d. After installation is complete, start and run engine for 15 minutes, checking for any fuel, coolant or oil leaks. Repair as necessary.
    e. After running engine for 25 minutes, stop engine and remove valve cover. Using a suitable breaker bar, tighten cylinder head bolts an additional quarter turn (90 degrees). Adjust valves to specifications, then install valve cover.

INTAKE MANIFOLD
REPLACE

1. Disconnect battery ground cable.
2. Remove diagnostic plug bracket and position aside, **Fig. 2.**
3. Disconnect turbocharger boost pressure indicator connector.
4. Remove oil dipstick tube to intake manifold attaching clamp and position tube aside.
5. Loosen turbocharger crossover pipe boot clamp.
6. Remove intake manifold to cylinder head attaching bolts, then the intake manifold.
7. Reverse procedure to install.

EXHAUST MANIFOLD
REPLACE

1. Disconnect battery ground cable, then remove air cleaner assembly.
2. Disconnect muffler inlet pipe from turbocharger outlet. Plug outlet to prevent dirt entry.
3. Disconnect EGR valve vacuum line.
4. Disconnect inlet duct from turbocharger. Plug inlet to prevent dirt entry.
5. Loosen turbocharger crossover pipe boot clamp, then remove oil feed tube to exhaust manifold retaining clamp.
6. Remove oil feed line to turbocharger attaching bolts. Plug oil feed line and oil inlet port on turbocharger to prevent contamination of turbocharger oiling system.
7. Disconnect oil return line from turbocharger oil drain port. Plug line and port to prevent contamination of turbocharger oiling system.
8. Remove exhaust manifold to cylinder head attaching bolts, then the exhaust manifold and turbocharger assembly. Plug crossover pipe to prevent dirt entry.
9. Reverse procedure to install. Torque manifold attaching bolts and oil feed line to 14–17 ft. lbs., oil return line to 29–36 ft. lbs. and muffler inlet pipe to turbocharger outlet bolts to 31–35 ft. lbs.

VALVE TIMING
INTAKE OPENS BEFORE TOP DEAD CENTER

Engine	Year	Degrees
6-149	1984–85	6

VALVE LIFT SPECS

Engine	Year	Intake	Exhaust
6-149	1984–85	.374	.376

Fig. 7   Camshaft positioning tool installation

Fig. 6   Loosening adjustment eccentric

ROCKER ARM
REPLACE

1. Remove valve cover and vacuum pump.
2. Rotate engine until cam lobe for rocker arm being replaced faces upward.
3. Remove rocker arm retaining clip.
4. Using tool T84P-6513-C or equivalent, compress valve spring.
5. Remove rocker arm assembly.

NOTE: Ensure valve spring retainer remain locked in valve stem.

6. Reverse procedure to install. Coat barrel of pivot ball pin with Loctite 270 or equivalent, before installing rocker arm.
7. Adjust valve clearances as outlined in "Valves, Adjust" procedure.

VALVES
ADJUST

1. Remove valve cover.

Fig. 8   Injection pump timing aligning pin installation

2. Rotate engine until camshaft lobe of valve being adjusted faces upward.
3. Using tool T84P-6575-A or equivalent and a 12 mm open end wrench, loosen adjusting eccentric locknut, **Fig. 6.**
4. Position feeler gauge, then rotate eccentric with a suitable punch until clearance is within specifications.
5. Tighten adjusting eccentric locknut.

TIMING BELT
REPLACE

1. Disconnect battery ground cable, then drain cooling system.
2. Disconnect upper radiator hose, then remove fan shroud.
3. Remove accessory drive belts, then the fan and clutch assembly.
4. Remove crankshaft pulley and vibration damper retaining bolts, then the pulley and damper.
5. Disconnect heater hose from thermostat housing.
6. Remove timing belt cover-to-crankcase attaching bolts, then the cover.
7. Remove valve cover.
8. Rotate engine until No. 1 cylinder is at TDC compression stroke, then install TDC aligning pin, T84P-6400-A or equivalent, **Fig. 3.**
9. Install camshaft positioning tool T84P-6256-A or equivalent onto cylinder head, **Fig. 7.**

NOTE: Flat side of nut or cam position tool should be facing down.

10. Loosen camshaft sprocket bolt.
11. If old belt will be re-installed, mark direction of engine rotation on belt.
12. Loosen belt tensioner attaching bolts, then remove timing belt.
13. If using new belt or belt with less than 10,000 miles, insert .098 inch feeler gauge between camshaft positioning tool, **Fig. 7,** and right corner of cylinder head.
14. Install injection pump aligning pin T84P-9000-A or equivalent, through injection pump sprocket, **Fig. 8.**
15. Rotate camshaft sprocket clockwise against aligning pin, then install timing belt. Starting at crankshaft sprocket, route belt around intermediate shaft sprocket, injection pump sprocket, camshaft sprocket and tension roller, **Fig. 9.**

NOTE: Ensure V side of belt is correctly positioned in pulley V.

16. Hand tighten belt tensioner until all slack is removed from timing belt.
17. Remove injection pump aligning pin.
18. Torque belt tensioner to 35 ft. lbs. for belts with less than 10,000 miles, or 24 ft. lbs. for belts greater than 10,000 miles.
19. Torque belt tensioner attaching bolts to 17 ft. lbs.
20. Torque camshaft sprocket bolt to 44 ft. lbs.
21. Reverse steps 1 through 9 to complete installation. Torque crankshaft pulley and vibration damper retaining bolts to 15–22 ft. lbs.
22. Adjust injection pump timing.

Fig. 9   Timing belt installation

Fig. 10   Aligning Allen head screws

CAMSHAFT
REPLACE

1. Disconnect battery ground cable, then remove valve cover.
2. Remove vacuum pump, cooling fan and fan clutch.
3. Remove accessory drive belts and tensioner, then the camshaft drive belt cover.
4. Remove rocker arms as outlined previously.
5. Rotate engine until cylinder No. 1 is at TDC compression stroke, then install TDC aligning pin, tool No. T84P-6400-A or equivalent, between cylinder block flange and flywheel, **Fig. 3.**
6. Loosen camshaft sprocket bolt, then the timing belt tensioner roller nut and bolt.
4. Remove camshaft sprocket retaining bolt and the sprocket.
5. Scribe alignment marks on camshaft bearing caps and cylinder head so that they can be installed in original position.
6. Remove bearing cap retaining nuts, then the bearing caps.
7. Remove camshaft.
8. Position camshaft onto cylinder head.
9. Install bearing caps and retaining nuts. Torque 6 mm nuts to 7 ft. lbs. and 8 mm nuts to 16 ft. lbs.
10. Loosely install camshaft sprocket, then install timing belt.
11. Torque camshaft sprocket retaining bolt to 44 ft. lbs.
12. Remove TDC alignment pin, then install rocker arms.
13. Install camshaft drive belt cover. Torque bolts to 6-7 ft. lbs.
14. Install accessory drive belt tensioner, drive belts, fan and fan clutch.
15. Install vacuum pump and rocker arm cover.
16. Connect battery ground, then run engine while checking for oil, intake air and coolant leaks.

Fig. 11   Vibration damper sprocket removal

ENGINE FRONT COVER
REPLACE

1. Perform steps 1 through 6 of "Timing Belt, Replace" procedure.
2. Remove intermediate shaft sprocket retaining bolt using tool T84P-6316-A or equivalent, **Fig. 10.**

NOTE: Ensure allen head screws are aligned with holes in intermediate shaft sprocket, **Fig. 10.**

3. Remove vibration damper flange and sprocket retaining bolt. Using tool T67L-3600-A or equivalent, remove flange and sprocket, **Fig. 11.**

4. Remove the three oil pan to front cover attaching bolts, then loosen the remaining oil pan bolts.
5. Remove the six front cover to crankcase attaching bolts, then the front cover.
6. Clean front cover and crankcase mating surfaces.
7. Inspect and, if necessary, replace crankshaft and intermediate shaft oil seals.
8. Install new front cover gasket. Coat areas where front cover gasket meets oil pan gasket with a ¼ inch bead of RTV sealant.
9. Position front cover onto crankcase and install attaching bolts. Torque 6mm bolts to 7 ft. lbs. and 8mm bolts to 16 ft. lbs.
10. Install the three front cover to oil pan attaching bolts. Torque all bolts to 7 ft. lbs.
11. Install vibration damper flange and sprocket onto crankshaft with shoulder facing toward front of vehicle.
12. Position intermediate shaft sprocket onto intermediate shaft, guiding locating pin into bore.
13. Install holding tool T84P-6316-A or equivalent, ensuring that Allen head screws in tool align with holes in intermediate shaft.
14. Install vibration damper flange and sprocket retaining bolt. Torque bolt to 282–311 ft. lbs.
15. Install intermediate shaft sprocket retaining bolt and torque to 44 ft. lbs.
16. Install and adjust timing belt as outlined previously.
17. Perform steps 1 through 6 of "Timing Belt, Replace" procedure in reverse sequence to complete installation.

INJECTION PUMP
REPLACE

1. Remove timing belt as outlined previously.
2. Install injection pump sprocket aligning pin T84P-9000-A or equivalent,

Fig. 12 Rear cover removal

REAR COVER BOLTS (6)

OIL PAN BOLTS (4)

then remove sprocket retaining nut and washer.
3. Using suitable puller, remove sprocket from injection pump.
4. Remove woodruff key from pump shaft.
5. Remove oil dipstick tube to intake manifold attaching clamp, then position dipstick tube aside.
6. Disconnect turbo pressure switch indicator electrical connector.
7. Remove diagnostic plug bracket and position aside, **Fig. 2.**
8. Loosen turbo crossover pipe boot to intake manifold attaching clamp.
9. Remove intake manifold to cylinder head attaching bolts, then the intake manifold.
10. Disconnect and plug fuel lines from injection nozzles.
11. Remove fuel lines from injection pump. Note location of each line to aid reassembly.
12. Disconnect coolant hoses from idle speed boost housing.
13. Disconnect electrical connectors from fuel shut-off solenoid, micro-switch and injection timing solenoid.
14. Disconnect nozzle return line from injection pump and fuel return hose from fuel return line on left fender apron.
15. Disconnect fuel inlet hose from fuel return line on left fender apron.
16. Disconnect vacuum hoses from altitude compensation valve. Note location of hoses to aid reassembly.
17. Disconnect throttle cable and speed control cable, if equipped, from injection pump.
18. Remove injection pump attaching nuts and bolts, then the injection pump.
19. Reverse procedure to install. When installing injection pump, ensure that mark on front cover aligns with mark on injection pump mounting boss Bleed fuel system as outlined under "Fuel System Bleeding".

FUEL SYSTEM BLEEDING

1. Ensure that vent screw is closed and that power is available to fuel shut-off solenoid.

2. Turn ignition "On" and allow pump to operate for approximately two minutes, then start engine. If engine runs correctly, system does require bleeding. If engine does not run correctly, proceed to next step.
3. Loosen coupling nuts on injector nozzles, then crank engine until all air is bled from lines.

NOTE: Use extreme caution not to allow high pressure fuel to contact skin.

4. Start engine. If engine runs correctly, no further bleeding is required. If engine does not run correctly, proceed to next step.
5. Crank engine and bleed system in the following locations:
   a. Fuel return line banjo bolt (labeled OUT).
   b. Injection pump distributor head plug bolt.
   c. Fuel shut-off solenoid.
   d. Fuel lines at injection pump.

PISTON & ROD ASSEMBLE

Pistons are supplied by three different manufacturers, Alcan-Nural, KS and Mahle. Both standard size and oversize pistons are available, however pistons can be replaced only in sets of six.

Numbers on connecting rod and bearing cap must be on same side when installing piston. Install piston with arrow facing toward front of engine.

MAIN BEARINGS

Main bearings are available in standard size and undersizes of .010 and .020 inch. The different main bearing thicknesses are identified by a color code on the edge of the bearing shell. The correct bearings to use for each journal are determined during production and are shown by paint marks in the crankcase for bearings in the block; and by paint marks on the crankshaft counterweights, for bearings in the main caps.

CRANKSHAFT REAR OIL SEAL
REPLACE

1. Raise and support vehicle.
2. Remove transmission.
3. Remove drive plate assembly.
4. Remove the four oil pan to rear engine cover attaching bolts.
5. Loosen, but do not remove, the remaining oil pan bolts.
6. Remove rear cover attaching bolts, then the rear cover, **Fig. 12.**
7. Clean crankcase and rear engine cover mating surfaces.
8. Press oil seal from rear cover using an arbor press.
9. Using seal replacer T84P-6701-A or equivalent, press new seal into rear cover.
10. Lubricate sealing lips with engine oil, then install new cover gasket onto crankcase.
11. Apply gasket sealer at points where rear cover gasket meets oil pan gasket.
12. Install rear cover onto crankcase. Torque 6mm bolts to 7 ft. lbs. and 8mm bolts to 16 ft. lbs.
13. Install the four oil pan to rear cover attaching bolts, then torque all oil pan bolts to 7 ft. lbs.
14. Install drive plate assembly.
15. Install transmission, then lower vehicle.
16. Start engine and check for oil leaks.

OIL PAN & PUMP
REPLACE

1. Remove engine as outlined in "Engine, Replace" procedure.
2. Remove oil pan attaching bolts, then the oil pan.
3. Remove oil pump to crankcase attaching bolts, then the oil pump and shaft.
4. Install oil pump shaft, ensuring that it is fully engaged with intermediate shaft.
5. Install oil pump and attaching bolts, then torque bolts to 16 ft. lbs.
6. Clean oil pan and crankcase mating surfaces, then apply a ¼ inch bead of RTV sealant on split lines of engine front and rear covers and crankcase.
7. Position new oil pan gasket onto oil pan, then install oil pan and attaching bolts. Torque bolts to 7 ft. lbs.

WATER PUMP
REPLACE

1. Drain cooling system into suitable container.
2. Remove drive belts, then the cooling fan and clutch assembly.
3. Remove water pump pulley, then disconnect heater hose from thermostat housing.
4. Remove timing belt cover.
5. Remove water pump attaching bolts, then the water pump.
6. Reverse procedure to install.

Rear Axle, Propeller Shaft & Brakes

REAR AXLES

Figs. 1 & 2 illustrate the rear axle assemblies used on these vehicles. When necessary to overhaul either one of these units, refer to the rear axle specifications table at the beginning of this chapter.

1980–86 INTEGRAL CARRIER TYPE

The gear set consists of a ring gear and an overhung drive pinion which is supported by two opposed tapered roller bearings, **Fig. 1**. The differential case is a one-piece design with openings allowing assembly of the internal parts and lubricant flow. The differential pinion shaft is retained with a threaded bolt (lock) assembled to the case.

The roller type wheel bearings have no inner race, and the rollers directly contact the bearing journals of the axle shafts. The axle shafts do not use an inner and outer bearing retainer. Rather, they are held in the axle by means of C-locks. These C-locks also fit into a machined recess in the differential side gears within the differential case. There is no retainer bolt access hole in the axle shaft flange.

1980 REMOVABLE CARRIER TYPE

In these axles, **Fig. 2,** the drive pinion is straddle-mounted by two opposed tapered roller bearings which support the pinion shaft in front of the drive pinion gear, and straight roller bearing that supports the pinion shaft at the rear of the pinion gear. The drive pinion is assembled in a pinion retainer that is bolted to the differential carrier. The tapered roller bearings are preloaded by a collapsible spacer between the bearings. The pinion is positioned by a shim or shims located between the drive pinion retainer and the differential carrier.

The differential is supported in the carrier by two tapered roller side bearings. These bearings are preloaded by two threaded ring nuts or sleeves between the bearings and pedestals. The differential assembly is positioned for proper ring gear and pinion backlash by varying the adjustment of these ring nuts. The differential case houses two side gears in mesh with two pinions mounted on a pinion shaft which is held in place by a pin. The side gears and pinions are backed by thrust washers.

The axle shafts are of unequal length, the left shaft being shorter than the right. The axle shafts are mounted in tapered roller or ball bearings that are pressed on the shafts.

SERVICE BULLETIN: All Ford Built Rear Axles: Recent manufacturing changes have eliminated the need for marking rear axle drive pinions for individual variations from nominal shim thicknesses. In the past, these pinion markings,

with the aid of a shim selection table, were used as a guide to select correct shim thicknesses when a gear set or carrier assembly replacement was performed.

With the elimination of pinion markings, use of the shim selection table is no longer possible and the methods outlined below must be used.

1. Measure the thickness of the original pinion depth shim removed from the axle. Use the same thickness upon installation of the replacement carrier or drive pinion. If any further shim change is necessary, it will be indicated in the tooth pattern check.
2. If the original shim is lost, substitute a nominal shim for the original and use the tooth pattern check to determine if further shim changes are required.

Fig. 1   Integral carrier type rear axle assembly (typical). 1980–86

Fig. 2   Removable carrier type rear axle assembly (typical). 1980

REAR AXLE
REPLACE

1980–83 MARK VI, 1980–86 CONTINENTAL, 1982–86 TOWN CAR & 1984–86 MARK VII

1. Raise vehicle and position safety stands under the rear frame crossmember.
2. Disconnect drive shaft at companion flange and secure it to vehicle using wire.
3. Remove wheels and brake drums. If equipped with rear disc brakes,

Fig. 3   Removing axle shaft with slide hammer-type puller

T66L-4234-A OR T7IP-4234-A
TOOL T50T-100-A

Fig. 4   Splitting bearing inner retainer for bearing removal

TOOL 1175-AC

Fig. 5   Using hook-type tool to remove oil seal

remove calipers from anchor plates and rotors from shafts.

4. Support axle housing with floor jack.
5. Disconnect brake line from clips that retain line to axle housing, then disconnect vent from rear axle housing.

NOTE: Some axle vents may be secured to the housing assembly through the brake junction block. When reinstalling, apply thread locking compound E0AZ-19554-B or equivalent to ensure proper retention.

6. Disconnect shock absorbers from axle housing.
7. Disconnect upper control arms from mountings on axle housing.
8. Lower axle housing assembly until coils springs are released, then remove springs.
9. Disconnect lower control arms from mountings on axle housing, then lower the axle housing and remove it from vehicle.
10. Reverse procedure to install.

VERSAILLES

1. Raise vehicle and position safety stands under rear frame members.
2. Mark drive shaft yoke and pinion flange for reassembly, then disconnect drive shaft at rear axle U-joint and remove drive shaft from transmission extension housing. Install seal replacer tool in extension housing to prevent leakage.
3. Disconnect shock absorbers from lower mountings.
4. Remove wheel and tire assembly.
5. Remove calipers from anchor plates, then remove two retaining nuts and slide rotors off axle shafts.

NOTE: Secure calipers to frame with wire.

6. Remove vent tube from axle housing.
7. Remove brake lines from axle housing clips.
8. Support axle housing using a suitable jack, then remove spring clip nuts and plates.
9. Lower rear axle assembly and remove from vehicle.
10. Reverse procedure to install.

AXLE SHAFTS & BEARINGS
REPLACE

REMOVABLE CARRIER

1. Remove rear wheel assembly, then the brake drum or caliper and rotor assembly.
2. Remove axle shaft retainer nuts and bolts.
3. Pull axle shaft assembly from housing. It may be necessary to use a suitable slide hammer type puller, **Fig. 3.**
4. To replace wheel bearing on models equipped with tapered roller bearings:
   a. Drill a ¼ inch hole in inner bearing retainer approximately ¾ of the thickness of the bearing retainer deep.

NOTE: Do not drill completely through the bearing retainer since damage to the axle shaft may result.

   b. Place a cold chisel across the drilled hole and strike with a hammer to break retainer, then discard retainer, **Fig. 4.**
   c. Using suitable press and plates, press bearing from axle shaft. Do not apply heat since the heat will weaken the axle shaft bearing journal area.
   d. Install lubricated seal and bearing on axle shaft, ensuring the cup rib ring faces toward the axle flange.

NOTE: The lubricated seal of the bearing assembly used with drum brake installations is of a different length than the seal used on disc brake installations and are not interchangeable. For identification, the seal used on drum brake installations has a grey color outer rim and on disc brake installations, the seal has a black oxide appearance.

   e. Press new bearing into place, then the bearing retainer firmly against the bearing.

   f. Remove old bearing cup from axle housing with a suitable puller. Place new bearing cup on bearing and apply lubricant to outside diameter of seal and bearing cup and install in axle housing.
5. To replace wheel bearing on models equipped with ball bearings:
   a. Remove oil seal from axle housing, **Fig. 5.**
   b. Loosen bearing inner retainer by striking retainer ring in several places with a cold chisel and slide off shaft, **Fig. 4.**

NOTE: On some models, it may be necessary to drill a ¼ inch hole in inner bearing retainer approximately ¾ of the thickness of the bearing retainer deep before using the cold chisel.

   c. Using suitable press and plates, press bearing from shaft. Do not heat axle shaft since the heat will damage the shaft.
   d. Install outer retainer on shaft and press bearing into place. Press inner retainer onto shaft until firmly seated against bearing.
   e. Install oil seal into axle housing, **Fig. 6.**
6. On all units, slide axle shaft assembly into housing, engaging axle shaft splines in the side gear.
7. Install and torque axle shaft retainer nuts and bolts to 20—40 ft. lbs.

INTEGRAL CARRIER

1. Raise car on hoist and remove wheels.
2. Drain differential lubricant.
3. Remove brake drums.
4. Remove differential housing cover.
5. Position safety stands under rear frame member and lower hoist to allow axle to lower as far as possible.
6. Working through differential case opening, remove pinion shaft lock bolt and pinion shaft.
7. Push axle shaft(s) inward toward cen-

Fig. 6 Using special driver to install oil seal

TOOL T50T-100-A   T58L-101-A
                         TOOL-1175-AC

Fig. 8 Removing axle shaft seal and bearing

AXLE SHAFTS

C-LOCKS

Fig. 7 Axle shaft "C" locks

ter of axle housing and remove C-lock(s) from housing, **Fig. 7.**

8. Remove axle shaft, using extreme care to avoid contact of shaft seal lip with any portion of axle shaft except seal journal.
9. Use a hook-type puller to remove seal and bearing, **Fig. 8.**
10. Reverse procedure to install, using suitable driving tools to install seal and bearing. Lubricate new bearing with rear axle lubricant and apply grease between the lips of the seal. Apply silicone sealant to carrier casting face as shown, **Fig. 9,** then install housing cover. Torque cover bolts to 30 ft. lbs.

PROPELLER SHAFT
REPLACE

To maintain proper drive line balance, mark the drive shaft, universal joints, slip yoke and companion flange before removing the shaft assembly so it can be reinstalled in its original position.

1. On Continental, Town Car, Versailles and Mark VI and VII vehicles, remove companion flange to drive pinion flange attaching bolts.
2. Pull drive shaft rearward until slip yoke clears transmission extension housing.
3. Reverse procedure to install.

DRUM BRAKE ADJUSTMENTS

These brakes have self-adjusting shoe mechanisms that assure correct lining-to-drum clearances at all times. The automatic adjusters operate only when the brakes are applied when the car is moving rearward.

Although the brakes are self-adjusting, an initial adjustment is necessary when the brake shoes have been relined or replaced, or when the length of the star wheel adjuster has been changed during some other service operation.

Frequent usage of an automatic transmission forward range to halt reverse vehicle motion may prevent the automatic adjusters from functioning, thereby inducing low pedal heights. Should low pedal heights be encountered, it is recommended that numerous forward and reverse stops be made until satisfactory pedal height is obtained.

NOTE: If a low pedal height condition cannot be corrected by making numerous reverse stops (provided the hydraulic system is free of air) it indicates that the automatic adjusting mechanism is not functioning. Therefore, it will be necessary to remove the brake drum, clean, free up and lubricate the adjusting mechanism. Then adjust the brakes, being sure the parking brake is fully released.

ADJUSTMENT

SERVICE BULLETIN: When servicing a vehicle requiring a brake adjustment, the metal knock-out plugs should NOT be removed. Rather the drums should be removed and brakes inspected for a malfunction.

Although the brakes are self-adjusting, an initial adjustment will be necessary after

CARRIER CASTING FACE

1/8" TO 3/16" WIDE CONTINUOUS BEAD OF SILICONE RUBBER SEALANT (D6AZ-19562-A OR -B OR EQUIVALENT) TYPICAL BEAD INSTALLATION. PARTS MUST BE ASSEMBLED WITHIN 1/4 HOUR AFTER APPLICATION OF SEALANT. GASKET SURFACE OF HOUSING AND CARRIER MUST BE FREE OF OIL.

Fig. 9 Applying sealant to carrier casting face

Fig. 10   Backing off brake adjustment by disengaging adjuster lever with screwdriver

Fig. 11   Brake adjustment with gauge

a brake repair, such as relining or replacement. The initial adjustment can be obtained by the new procedure which follows:

NOTE: If after removing brake drum retainers, the brake drum cannot be removed, remove steel knock-out plugs (if equipped) with suitable hammer and chisel. If equipped with rubber plugs, pry plug from backing plate. Insert a narrow screwdriver through hole in backing plate and disengage lever from adjusting screw. While holding lever away from adjusting screw, back off adjusting screw using a suitable tool to retract brake shoes, **Fig. 10.**

1. Use the brake shoe adjustment gauge shown in **Fig. 11** to obtain the drum inside diameter as shown. Tighten the adjusting knob on the gauge to hold this setting.
2. Place the opposite side of the gauge over the brake shoes and adjust the shoes by turning the adjuster screw until the gauge just slides over the linings. Rotate the gauge around the lining surface to assure proper lining diameter adjustment and clearance.
3. Install brake drum and wheel. Final adjustment is accomplished by making several firm reverse stops, using the brake pedal.

PARKING BRAKES
ADJUST

REAR DISC BRAKES

1. Fully release parking brake, then place transmission in neutral and support vehicle at rear axle.
2. Tighten adjuster nut until levers on calipers just begin to move, then loosen adjuster nut until levers just return to stop position.

3. Apply and release parking brake. Check levers on caliper to determine if they are fully returned by attempting to pull lever rearward. If lever moves, the adjustment is too tight and must be readjusted.

REAR DRUM BRAKES

1. Make sure the parking brake is fully released.
2. Place transmission in neutral and raise the vehicle.
3. Tighten the adjusting nut against the cable equalizer to cause rear wheel brake drag. Then loosen the adjusting nut until the rear brakes are fully released. There should be no brake drag.
4. Lower the vehicle and check operation.

VACUUM RELEASE UNIT

The vacuum power unit will release the parking brake automatically when the transmission selector lever is moved into any driving position with the engine running. The brakes will not release automatically, however, when the selector lever is in neutral or park position with the engine running, or in any other position with the engine off.

The lower end of the release handle extends out for alternate manual release in the event of vacuum power failure or for optional manual release at any time.

To detect leaks in the vacuum release parking brake lines or to find disconnected or an improperly connected line, listen for a hissing sound along the line routings.

NOTE: Do not apply compressed air to the vacuum system when conducting a leak test. The actuator diaphragm in the parking brake vacuum motor may be damaged.

Perform the following to detect leaks in the vacuum release system:

1. Start and operate engine at idle. Position transmission gear shift lever into Neutral and apply parking brake.
2. Position transmission gear shift lever into Drive and check parking brake sector to insure sector returns to its stop (zero travel position), when the parking brake releases.

NOTE: The parking brake vacuum release does not operate with the transmission in Reverse.

3. If parking brake does not release, disconnect vacuum line from parking brake release vacuum motor and connect a suitable vacuum gauge to the line. A minimum of 10 inches Hg is required to actuate the parking brake vacuum motor. If a minimum reading is obtained, replace parking brake release vacuum line. If a minimum reading is not obtained, replace parking brake vacuum release motor.

MASTER CYLINDER
REPLACE

1. Disconnect brake lines from master cylinder.
2. Remove two nuts attaching master cylinder to power brake unit.
3. Slide master cylinder off mounting studs and remove from vehicle.
4. Reverse procedure to install.

POWER BRAKE UNIT
REPLACE

1. Disconnect battery ground cable, then remove air cleaner.
2. Disconnect vacuum hose from power brake unit check valve.
3. Disconnect brake lines from master cylinder, then remove two nuts attach-

ing master cylinder to power brake unit and remove master cylinder.

4. Working from under instrument panel, disconnect stop lamp switch wire connector, then remove clip and washer from brake pedal pin. Slide brake lamp switch off brake pedal pin just far enough for outer arm to clear pin, then remove switch. Slide power brake push rod and washer from brake pedal pin.

5. On models equipped with speed control, remove amplifier unit from lower power brake unit mounting stud.

6. Move power brake unit forward until studs clear dash panel, then remove unit.

7. Reverse procedure to install.

Rear Suspension

Fig. 1   Rear suspension (typical). Versailles

Fig. 2   Spring front bushing removal. Versailles

SHOCK ABSORBER
REPLACE

1982—86 CONTINENTAL & 1984—86 MARK VII

NOTE: On 1984—86 vehicles, turn air suspension switch off before replacing shock absorber.

1. Open trunk to gain access to upper shock absorber attachment.
2. Remove rubber cap if equipped, from shock absorber stud, then remove nut, washer and insulator.
3. Raise vehicle and support rear axle.
4. Remove lower shock absorber protective cover, then remove cross bolt and nut from lower shock absorber mounting bracket.
5. From underneath vehicle, compress shock absorber to clear hole in upper shock tower, then remove shock absorber.

NOTE: These models are equipped with gas pressurized shock absorbers which extend unassisted during removal. Do not apply heat or flame to the shock absorber tube during removal.

6. Reverse procedure to install. While holding shock absorber in position, torque lower cross bolt to 59 ft. lbs. Lower vehicle and install upper mounting nut, washer and insulator and torque nut to 24 to 26 ft. lbs.

EXC. 1982—86 CONTINENTAL & 1984—86 MARK VII

1. With the rear axle supported properly disconnect shock absorber at upper mounting and compress it to clear hole.
2. Disconnect shock absorber from lower attachment.
3. Reverse procedure to install.

NOTE: The 1984—86 Town Car is equipped with gas pressurized shock absorbers which extend unassisted during removal. Do not apply heat or flame to the shock absorber tube during removal.

LEAF SPRINGS & BUSHINGS
REPLACE

VERSAILLES

1. Raise rear of vehicle and support at frame. Support axle with a suitable jack.

Fig. 3   Spring front bushing installation. Versailles

2. Disconnect shock absorbers from lower mountings.
3. Lower jack and remove spring plate "U" bolts and spring plate, **Fig. 1.**
4. Raise axle to remove weight from spring and disassemble rear shackle.
5. Remove spring front mount bolt.
6. Replace spring front eye bushings as necessary, **Figs. 2 and 3.**
7. Reverse procedure to install.

COIL SPRINGS
REPLACE

1982—83 CONTINENTAL

1. Remove stabilizer bar as described under Stabilizer Bar, Replace, if equipped.
2. Position a suitable jack under rear axle, then raise vehicle and support body at rear body crossmember.
3. Lower axle until shock absorbers are fully extended.

NOTE: Support axle with jack stands or a suitable jack.

4. Position a suitable jack under lower control arm pivot bolt and remove nut and bolt. Carefully and slowly lower the control arm until all spring tension is relieved.
5. Remove coil spring and insulators from vehicle, **Fig. 4.**

Fig. 4   Rear suspension. 1982–83 Continental

1980–81 CONTINENTAL, 1980–83 MARK VI & 1982–86 TOWN CAR

1. Raise rear of vehicle and support at frame side sills. Support rear axle with a suitable jack.
2. Disconnect shock absorbers and stabilizer bar from axle housing, **Fig. 5.**
3. Disconnect right hand parking brake cable from right hand upper arm retainer.
4. Lower the axle housing until coil springs are released.
5. Remove springs and insulators, **Fig. 5.**
6. Reverse procedure to install.

CONTROL ARMS
REPLACE

1984–86 CONTINENTAL & MARK VII
Upper Arm

NOTE: Always replace control arm in pairs. If one arm requires replacement, replace the same arm on the opposite side of the vehicle.

1. Turn air suspension switch off.

2. Raise and support vehicle, then disconnect rear height sensor from side arm. Note position of sensor adjustment bracket to aid in reassembly.
3. Remove upper arm to axle and upper arm to frame bracket pivot bolts and nuts.
4. Remove upper control arm.
5. Reverse procedure to install. Torque pivot bolts to 100 ft. lbs.

Lower Arm

1. Turn air suspension switch to off position, then raise and support vehicle and remove wheel assembly.
2. Vent air springs to atmosphere by removing air spring solenoid.
3. Remove the two air spring to lower control arm retaining bolts, and remove air spring from lower arm.
4. Remove control arm to frame and control arm to axle bracket pivot bolts and nuts.
5. Remove lower control arm.
6. Reverse procedure to install. Torque pivot bolts to 100 ft. lbs.

1982–83 CONTINENTAL
Upper Arm

NOTE: Always replace control arms in pairs. Therefore, if one arm requires replacement, replace the same arm on the opposite side of the vehicle.

1. Raise vehicle and support body at rear body crossmember.
2. Remove upper arm pivot bolt and nut, **Fig. 4.**
3. Remove front pivot bolt and nut, then remove upper arm from vehicle.
4. Reverse procedure to install. Torque upper arm pivot and front pivot bolts to 100 ft. lbs.

Lower Arm

NOTE: Always replace control arms in pairs. Therefore, if one arm requires replacement, replace the same arm on the opposite side of the vehicle.

1. Remove stabilizer bar as described under Stabilizer Bar, Replace, if equipped.
2. Position a suitable jack under rear axle, then raise vehicle and support body at rear body crossmember.
3. Lower axle until shock absorbers are fully extended.

NOTE: Support axle with jack stands or a suitable jack.

4. Position a suitable jack under lower control arm rear pivot bolt and remove nut bolt, **Fig. 4.** Carefully and slowly lower the control arm until all spring tension is relieved, then remove coil spring and insulators.

384485-S2
2 REQ'D.

18041
2 REQ'D.

18198
2 REQ'D.

5536
2 REQ'D.

18198
2 REQ'D.

5560
2 REQ'D.

18171
2 REQ'D.

18080
2 REQ'D.

4730
2 REQ'D.

N800414-S100
4 REQ'D.

VIEW A

N800523-S100
4 REQ'D.

N800185-S2
4 REQ'D.

N800937-S100
4 REQ'D.

N801670-S100

5538 ASSY.
2 REQ'D.

5500
2 REQ'D.

N800523-S100
4 REQ'D.

N800523-S100
2 REQ'D.

N800169
2 REQ'D.

N801670-S100
2 REQ'D.

N801670-S100
4 REQ'D.

N800523-S100
2 REQ'D.

5A638
2 REQ'D.

N801670-S100
2 REQ'D.

VIEW A

Fig. 5   Rear suspension. 1980—81 Continental, 1980—83 Mark VI & 1982—86 Town Car

5. Remove lower control arm front pivot bolt and nut, then remove lower control arm assembly.

1980—81 CONTINENTAL, 1980—83 MARK VI & 1982—86 TOWN CAR

NOTE: Always replace control arms in pairs. Therefore, if one arm requires replacement, replace the same arm on the opposite side of vehicle. Also, if both upper and lower control arms are to be removed at the same time, first remove both coil springs.

1. Raise vehicle and support at frame side rails with jack stands.
2. If removing lower control arm, disconnect stabilizer bar from arm (if equipped).
3. With shock absorbers fully extended, support axle under differential pinion nose and under axle. If removing upper arm, disconnect parking brake

cable from retainer.
4. Remove pivot bolts and nuts from axle and frame brackets, **Fig. 5.**
5. Remove control arm from vehicle.
6. Reverse procedure to install. Torque lower arm to axle bracket pivot bolt to 118 ft. lbs. and lower arm to frame pivot bolt to 135 ft. lbs.

STABILIZER BAR
REPLACE

1984—86 CONTINENTAL & MARK VII

1. Turn air suspension switch off, then raise and support vehicle.
2. Remove stabilizer bar to link attaching nuts.
3. Remove stabilizer bar to bushing "U" clamp attaching nuts, then the stabilizer bar.
4. Reverse procedure to install.

1980—81 CONTINENTAL, 1980—83 MARK VI & 1982—86 TOWN CAR

Referring to **Fig. 3,** each wheel rotates on a spindle. The upper and lower ends of the spindle are attached to upper and lower ball joints that are mounted to an upper and lower control arm. The upper control arm pivots on a shaft assembly that is bolted to the frame. The lower control arm pivots on a bolt in the front crossmember.

1982—83 CONTINENTAL

1. Raise and support rear of vehicle.
2. Remove four stabilizer bar to lower control arm attaching bolts.
3. Remove stabilizer bar from vehicle.
4. Reverse procedure to install. Torque stabilizer bar to lower control arm attaching bolts to 45 to 50 ft. lbs.

1980—81 CONTINENTAL, 1980—83 MARK VI & 1982—86 TOWN CAR

1. Raise rear of vehicle and support at frame side sills.
2. Lower axle housing until shock absorbers are fully extended.
3. Remove the four bolts, nuts and spacers retaining stabilizer bar lower control arms, then remove stabilizer bar, **Fig. 5.**
4. Reverse procedure to install. Torque bolts to 70—92 ft. lbs.

Front Suspension & Steering Section

FRONT SUSPENSION

1984-86 CONTINENTAL & MARK VII

This suspension is a modified MacPherson strut design which is very similar to the suspension used in the 1982-83 Continental. The difference is a stamped lower control arm and the use of air bags in place of the coil springs.

1982—83 CONTINENTAL

This suspension, **Fig. 1,** is a modified MacPherson strut design, which uses shock struts and coil springs. The springs are mounted between the lower control arm and a spring pocket in the crossmember.

VERSAILLES

Referring to **Fig. 2,** each front wheel rotates on a spindle. The upper and lower ends of the spindle are attached to ball joints that are mounted to an upper and lower control arm. The upper arm pivots on a bushing and shaft assembly that is bolted to the under body. The lower arm pivots on a bolt that is located in an under body bracket.

A coil spring seats between the upper arm and the top of the spring housing. A double-acting shock absorber is bolted to the arm and the top of the spring housing.

Struts, which are connected between the lower control arms and the under body, prevent the arms from moving fore and aft.

Fig. 2   Front suspension (typical). Versailles

WHEEL ALIGNMENT

1984—86 CONTINENTAL & MARK VII

NOTE: Before performing wheel alignment check on these vehicles, ensure vehicle ride height is correct.

Caster & Camber

Caster is pre-set at the factory and is not adjustable.

To adjust camber, drill out pop rivet

380335-S

N620483-S2
6 REQD
81-102 N·m
(60-75 LB-FT)

3B391
2 REQD

N800280-S7
8-15 N·m
(6-12 LB-FT)

FENDER APRON

81-102 N·m
(60-75 LB-FT)

N800265-S2

18A084

5B482

5482

N800236-S100
203-244 N·m
(150-180 LB-FT)

N800234-S100

5486

381612-S100
136-163 N·m
(100-120 LB-FT)

3108 LH
3107 RH

N801923-S2
27-34 N·m
(20-25 LB-FT)

72045-S2

N800264-S2

VIEW Y

3051 LH ASSY.
3042 RH ASSY.

5493

VIEW Z

NOTE:
LINK BOLT, SPACER, AND
WASHER PART NUMBERS
VARY FOR EACH
VEHICLE LINE.

5415

N800277-S2

N800799-S100

5310

VIEW X

5414
ASSEMBLE FLUSH TO
1.4" OUT FROM END
OF SPRING

N800237-S100
292-353 N·m
(215-260 LB-FT)

5414
INSULATOR

3051 & 3042

5310

HOLE "A"

HOLE "B"

END OF SPRING MUST CLEAR
HOLE "A" AND COVER HOLE "B"

VIEW Z

VIEW X

Fig. 1 Front suspension. 1982—83 Continental

Fig. 4   Caster & camber adjustment. Versailles

Fig. 3   Front suspension. 1980—81 Continental, 1980—83 Mark VI & 1982—86 Town Car

Fig. 5   Caster & camber adjusting tools. 1980—81 Continental, 1980—83 Mark VI & 1982—86 Town Car

1980—81 CONTINENTAL 1980—83 MARK VI & 1982—85 TOWN CAR

Caster and camber can be adjusted by loosening the bolts that attach the upper suspension arm to the shaft at the frame side rail, and moving the arm assembly in or out in the elongated bolt holes, **Fig. 3.** Since any movement of the arm affects both caster and camber, both factors should be balanced against one another when making the adjustment.

Caster, Adjust
1. To adjust caster, install the adjusting tool as shown in **Fig. 5.**
2. Loosen both upper arm inner shaft retaining bolts and move either front or rear of the shaft in or out as necessary to increase or decrease caster angle. Then tighten bolt to retain adjustment.

Camber, Adjust
1. Loosen both upper arm inner retaining bolts and move both front and rear ends of shaft inward or outward as necessary to increase or decrease camber angle.
2. Tighten bolts and recheck caster and readjust if necessary.

located on top of camber plate. Loosen the camber plate to body apron retaining nuts, then move the top of the shock strut to the desired location. Retighten the retaining nuts. It is not necessary to replace the pop rivet after the camber adjustment is completed.

1982—83 CONTINENTAL

Caster & Camber
The caster and camber angles of this suspension are factory pre-set and cannot be adjusted in the field.

VERSAILLES

Caster & Camber
As shown in **Fig. 4,** caster is controlled by the front suspension strut. To obtain positive caster, loosen the strut rear nut and tighten the strut front nut against the bushing. To obtain negative caster, loosen the strut front nut and tighten the strut rear nut against the bushing.

Camber is controlled by the eccentric cam located at the lower arm attachment to the side rail. To adjust camber, loosen the camber adjustment bolt nut at the rear of the body bracket. Spread the body bracket at the camber adjustment bolt area just enough to permit lateral travel of the arm when the adjustment bolt is turned. Rotate the bolt and eccentric clockwise from the high position to increase camber or counterclockwise to decrease it.

Fig. 7 Lower ball joint wear indicator. 1982–86 Continental & 1984–86 Mark VII

Fig. 6 Toe-in adjustment. 1982–86 Continental & 1984–86 Mark VII

Fig. 8 Lower ball joint wear indicator. 1980–81 Continental, 1980–83 Mark VI & 1982–86 Town Car

TOE-IN
ADJUST

1982–86 CONTINENTAL & 1984–86 MARK VII

1. Check to see that steering shaft and steering wheel marks are in alignment and in the top position.
2. Loosen clamp screw on the tie rod bellows and free the seal on the rod to prevent twisting of the bellows, **Fig. 6.**
3. Place opened end wrench on flats of tie rod socket to prevent socket from turning, then loosen tie rod jam nuts.
4. Use suitable pliers to turn the tie rod inner end to correct the adjustment to specifications. Do not use pliers on tie rod threads. Turning to reduce number of threads showing will increase toe-in. Turning in the opposite direction will reduce toe-in.

Exc. 1982–86 CONTINENTAL & 1984–86 MARK VII

Position the front wheels in their straight-ahead position. Then turn both tie rod adjusting sleeves an equal amount until the desired toe-in setting is obtained.

WHEEL BEARINGS
ADJUST

1. With wheel rotating, tighten adjusting nut to 17–25 ft. lbs.
2. Back off adjusting nut ½ turn and re-tighten nut to 10–15 inch lbs.
3. Place nut lock on nut so that castellations on lock are aligned with cotter pin hole in spindle and install cotter pin.
4. Check front wheel rotation, if it rotates noisily or rough, clean, inspect or replace wheel bearings as necessary.

WHEEL BEARINGS
REPLACE

1. Raise car and remove front wheels.
2. Remove caliper mounting bolts.

NOTE: It is not necessary to disconnect the brake line for this operation.

3. Slide caliper off of the disc, inserting a spacer between the shoes to hold them in their bores after the caliper is removed. Position caliper assembly out of the way.

NOTE: Do not allow caliper to hang by brake hose.

4. Remove hub and disc. Grease retainer and inner bearing can now be removed.
5. Reverse procedure to install.

CHECKING BALL JOINTS FOR WEAR
UPPER BALL JOINT

Versailles

1. Raise car on frame contact hoist or by floor jacks placed beneath under body until wheel falls to full down position.
2. Grasp the lower edge of tire and move the wheel in and out.
3. While the wheel is being moved observe any movement between the upper end of the spindle and upper arm. If any movement is observed replace the ball joint.

1980–81 Continental, 1980–83 Mark VI & 1982–86 Town Car

1. Raise car on floor jacks placed beneath lower control arms.
2. Grasp lower edge of tire and move wheel in and out.
3. As wheel is being moved in and out, observe upper end of spindle and upper arm.
4. Any movement between upper end of spindle and upper arm indicates ball joint wear and loss of preload. If such movement is observed, replace upper ball joint.

NOTE: During the foregoing check, the lower ball joint will be unloaded and may move. Disregard all such movement of the lower joint. Also, do not mistake loose wheel bearings for a worn ball joint.

LOWER BALL JOINT

1982–86 Continental & 1984–86 Mark VII

1. Support vehicle in normal driving position with both ball joints loaded.
2. Clean area around grease fitting and checking surface.

NOTE: The checking surface is the round boss into which the grease fitting is installed.

3. The checking surface should project outside the cover, **Fig. 7.** If surface is inside cover replace lower arm assembly.

Fig. 9 Ford CII Power steering pump installation. 1980—86

1980—81 Continental, 1980—83 Mark VI & 1982—86 Town Car

These models are equipped with lower ball joint wear indicators, **Fig. 8.** To check ball joint for wear, support vehicle in normal driving position with both ball joints loaded. Observe the checking surface of the ball joint. If the checking surface is inside the cover, replace the ball joint.

Versailles

1. With car jacked up as directed above, grasp the lower edge of the tire and move it in and out.
2. As wheel is being moved in and out, observe lower end of spindle and lower arm.
3. Any movement between lower end of spindle and lower arm indicates ball joint wear and loss of preload. If such movement is observed, replace lower arm and/or ball joint.

NOTE: During the foregoing check, the ball joints will be unloaded and may move. Therefore disregard any movement of the upper ball joint when checking the lower ball joint and any movement of the lower ball joint when checking the upper ball joint. Also, do not mistake loose wheel bearings for a worn ball joint.

BALL JOINTS
REPLACE

1982—86 CONTINENTAL & 1984—86 MARK VII

These ball joints are not serviceable. If they require replacement, the control arm and ball joint must be replaced as an assembly. Torque ball joint stud nut to 100—120 ft. lbs.

EXCEPT 1982—86 CONTINENTAL & 1984—86 MARK VII

NOTE: Ford Motor Company recommends that new ball joints should not be installed on used control arms and that the control arm be replaced if ball joint replacement is required. However, aftermarket ball joint repair kits which do not require control arm replacement, are available and can be installed using the following procedure.

When replacing a riveted joint, remove the rivets and retain the new joint in its control arm with the bolts, nuts and washers furnished with the ball joint kit.

Use a suitable pressing tool to force the ball joint from the spindle.

SHOCK STRUT
REPLACE

1982—86 CONTINENTAL & 1984—86 MARK VII

NOTE: On 1984—86 vehicles, turn air suspension switch off before removing shock strut.

1. Place ignition switch in the Unlocked position so that front wheels are free to move.
2. From engine compartment, remove one strut to upper mounting nut. Use a screwdriver in rod slot to hold rod stationary when removing nut.
3. Raise front of vehicle by lower control arms, then place safety stands under frame jack pads located rearward of wheels.
4. Remove wheel and tire assembly, then remove brake caliper, rotor assembly and dust shield.
5. Remove two nuts and bolts attaching lower strut to spindle.

NOTE: When removing the second lower strut to spindle nut, hold strut firmly as gas pressure will cause strut to fully extend.

6. Lift strut upward from spindle to com-

press rod, then pull downward and remove strut.

7. Reverse procedure to install. Torque upper mount attaching nut to 60 to 75 ft. lbs. Remove suspension load from lower control arm by lowering front of vehicle, then torque lower mounting nuts to 150 to 180 ft. lbs.

SHOCK ABSORBER
REPLACE

VERSAILLES

1. Raise hood and remove upper mounting bracket-to-spring tower retaining nuts.
2. Raise front of car and place safety stands under lower control arms.
3. Remove shock absorber lower retaining nuts and washers.
4. Lift shock absorber from spring tower.
5. Reverse procedure to install.

1980–81 CONTINENTAL, 1980–83 MARK VI & 1982–86 TOWN CAR

1. Remove nut, washer and bushing from upper end of shock absorber.
2. Raise vehicle and support on stands.
3. Remove screws retaining shock absorber to lower control arm and remove shock absorber.
4. Reverse procedure to install.

COIL SPRING
REPLACE

1982–83 CONTINENTAL

1. Raise front of vehicle and position safety stands under jack pads located rearward of wheels, then remove wheel and tire assembly.
2. Disconnect stabilizer bar link from lower control arm.
3. Remove steering gear attaching bolts, then position gear out of way.
4. Using tool 3290-C or equivalent, disconnect tie rod from spindle.
5. Using spring compressor D78P-5310-A or equivalent, compress spring until it is free from lower seat.
6. Remove two lower control arm pivot bolts and disengage control arm from frame, then remove spring from seat. If a replacement spring is to be installed, measure compressed length of spring being removed to assist in compressing and installing the replacement spring.
7. Reverse procedure to install. When installing spring, locate lower end of coil between two holes in lower control arm spring pocket. Torque control arm pivot bolt nuts to 215 to 260 ft.lbs., stabilizer bar link nut to 6 to 12 ft. lbs. and steering gear to crossmember attaching bolts to 90 to 100 ft. lbs.

1980–81 CONTINENTAL, 1980–83 MARK VI & 1982–85 TOWN CAR

1. Raise and support vehicle.
2. Remove wheel.
3. Disconnect stabilizer bar link from lower control arm.
4. Remove shock absorber.
5. Remove steering center link from pitman arm.
6. Compress coil spring with a suitable spring compressor, tool D-78P-5310-A or equivalent.
7. Remove two lower control arm pivot bolts and disengage arm from crossmember.
8. Remove spring from vehicle.
9. Reverse procedure to install. Torque pivot bolts to 120–140 ft. lbs.

NOTE: Tail end of spring must be positioned as shown in **Fig. 3.**

VERSAILLES

1. Remove shock absorber and upper mounting bracket as an assembly.
2. Raise car on hoist and install safety stands.
3. Remove wheel, tire, rotor and caliper assembly from spindle.
4. Install a suitable spring compressor and compress spring.
5. Remove two upper-arm-to-spring tower retaining nuts and swing upper arm outward from spring.
6. Release spring compressor, then remove spring.
7. Reverse procedure to install.

POWER STEERING GEAR
REPLACE

INTEGRAL POWER RACK & PINION

1982–86 Continental & 1984–86 Mark VII

1. Disconnect battery ground cable.
2. Remove bolt retaining flexible coupling to input shaft.
3. Turn ignition key "On" and raise vehicle.
4. Remove the tie rod end retaining nuts, then separate studs from spindle arms.
5. Support gear and remove attaching bolts, then lower gear enough to gain access to pressure and return lines, and remove bolt attaching the hose bracket to the gear, and bolts from the crossmember.
6. Disconnect and cap pressure and return lines, then remove steering gear.
7. Reverse procedure to install. Torque pressure and return line fittings to 15–20 ft. lbs. Torque steering gear to crossmember bolts to 80–100 ft. lbs. Torque tie rod ends to spindle arm nuts to 35–47 ft. lbs.

1980–86 INTEGRAL POWER STEERING GEAR

Exc. Versailles, 1982–86 Continental & 1984–86 Mark VII

1. Disconnect lines from steering gear and plug lines and ports.
2. Remove the two bolts securing flex coupling to steering gear and to column.
3. Raise vehicle and remove sector shaft nut and pitman arm.

NOTE: Do not damage the seals.

4. Support steering gear and remove three attaching bolts. Remove flex coupling clamp bolt and work steering gear free of coupling, then remove steering gear.
5. Reverse procedure to install.

CONTROL VALVE, REPLACE

Versailles

1. Disconnect fluid fittings at control valve and drain fluid from lines.
2. Loosen clamp at right-hand end of sleeve. Remove roll pin from steering arm-to-idler arm rod through slot in sleeve.
3. Using tool 3290-C, remove ball stud from sector shaft arm.

NOTE: The use of any other tool may result in damage to the control valve assembly.

4. Turn wheels fully to left and unthread control valve from idler arm rod.
5. Reverse procedure to install.

POWER STEERING PUMP
REPLACE

1980–86 FORD C11

1. Disconnect fluid return hose at reservoir and drain power steering fluid into a container.
2. Remove pressure hose from pump fitting. Do not remove fitting from pump.
3. Disconnect belt from pulley. If necessary, remove pulley from pump installing pulley remover tool T75L-3733-A or equivalent so small diameter threads engage in pump shaft. While holding small hex head, rotate tool nut to remove pulley. Do not apply in and out pressure on pump shaft as this will damage the internal thrust areas, **Fig. 9.**
4. Remove pump.
5. If pulley was removed, install tool and while holding small hex head, turn tool nut clockwise to install pulley. Pulley must be flush within .010 inch of the end of the pump shaft. Do not apply in and out pressure on shaft. Remove tool.

BUICK—REAR WHEEL DRIVE MODELS & 1980-85 RIVIERA

INDEX OF SERVICE OPERATIONS

NOTE: Refer to the rear of this manual for vehicle manufacturer's special service tool suppliers.

Engine Identification

Buick engines are stamped with two different sets of numbers. One is the engine production code which identifies the engine and its approximate production date. The other is the engine serial number which is the same number that is found on the vehicle identification plate. To identify an engine, look for the production code prefix letters, then refer to the following table for its identification.

Buick built engines have the distributor located at the front of the engine. On all 1980 V8 models, the engine production code is located on the right front of block. On 1980-86 V6 models, the production

code is located on the left rear of block. On 1980 vehicles, the fifth digit in the VIN denotes engine code. On 1981-86 vehicles the eighth digit in the VIN denotes engine code.

Chevrolet built V8 engines have the distributor located at rear of engine with clockwise rotor rotation; the code is stamped on the engine case pad located below the cylinder head on the right hand side of the engine.

Oldsmobile built gasoline engines have the distributor located at the rear of the engine with counter-clockwise rotor rotation and right side mounted fuel pump. All

Oldsmobile built gasoline engines and all diesel engines except 1983-85 V6-262 have the identification codes stamped on the front left side of the engine block. On 1983-85 V6-262 engines, the primary identification code is stamped on the right front of the engine and a secondary number may be stamped on the left front of the engine.

Pontiac built V8 engines, have the distributor located at the rear of the engine with counter-clockwise rotor rotation and left side mounted fuel pump. The engine production code is located on the right front of the cylinder block.

Engine Codes

Engine	VIN	Code Prefix
1980		
V6-231③⑥	A	EA, EB, EC, ED, EK, EM, EP, OV, OW, OX, OY
V6-231④⑦	3	EE, EH, EJ, ER, EU, EV, EW, OS
V6-252④	4	MF
V8-301①④	W	X3, XT, XW
V8-305②④	H	CEC, CMM
V8-350②④	X	MB, MT, MU
V8-350④⑤	R	UAD, UAF, UAS, UAT
V8-350⑤⑧	N	VBM, VBN, VBS, VBT, VBU, VCD, VCH
1981		
V6-231③⑥	A	NA, NB, NC, ND, NF, NJ, NK, NL, NZ, LZ, RA, RB, RK, RL, RC, RD
V6-231④⑦	3	NE, NR, NG, RO, RR
V6-252④	4	SA, SB, SC, SD, SF, SG, SJ, SK, SL, SM, SN, SP, SQ
V8-265①③	S	AW, DB, DC, AZ, BA, DH, DJ
V8-307④⑤	Y	TKA, TKB, TKC, TKL, TKM, TKP, TKT, TKU, TKX, TKY, TKZ, TLA, TLB, TLD, TLF, TLH, TLJ, TLK, TLL, TLM, TLN, TLP, TLR, TLT, TMF, TMH, TMJ
V8-350⑤⑧	N	VKB, VKC, VKH, VKJ, VKN, VKR, VKU, VKY, VLA, VLC, VLD, VLK, VLL, VLN, VLP, VL8, VLY, VMJ, VMT, VMX, VMY, VNA, VNB, VNC, VND, VNE, VNF, VNJ, VNK, VNL, VNR, VNT, VNV, VNZ, VPA, VPK, VPL, VPR, VPS, VPT, VPV, VPX, VPY, VPZ, VRP, VRH
1982		
V6-231③⑥	A	MA, MC, MG, MK, ML, MM
V6-231④⑦	3	MB, MF, MH
V6-252④	4	FA, FB, FC, FD, FE, FF, FG, FH, FJ, FK
V6-262⑤⑧	V	UAA, UAD, UAJ
V8-307④⑤	Y	TAA, TAB, TAC, TAD, TAF, TAK, TAM, TAW, TAX, TAY, TAZ, TBA, TBB

Engine	VIN	Code Prefix
V8-350⑤⑧	N	VAB, VAC, VAD, VAK, VAL, VAM, VAN, VAP, VAS, VAU, VAW, VAX, VAY, VAZ, VBA, VBB, VBC, VBP, VBU, VBW
1983		
V6-231③⑥	A	ND, NG, NH, NJ, NL
V6-231④⑦	8	NB, NC, NK
V6-252④	4	SA, SB, SC, SD, SF, SG, SH
V6-262⑤⑧	V	UKA, UKB, UKC, UKJ, UKK
V8-307④⑤	Y	TKA, TKB, TKD, TKH, TKK, TKL, TKM, TKN, TKP, TKS, TKT, TKY
V8-350⑤⑧	N	VKB, VKC, VKD, VKK, VKL, VKR, VKS, VKT, VKZ, VLA, VLB, VLP, VLS, VLT, VLW
1984		
V6-231③⑥	A	FRA, FSA, FUA, FWA, FXA, FYA, FZA
V6-231⑦	9	FAA, FJA
V6-252④	4	HAC, HBC, HCC, HDC, HHC, H3B
V6-262⑤⑧	V	UAW, UAX, UAY, UA2, UBZ, UCZ, ULR, ULS, ULT, ULW
V8-307④⑤	Y	PAA, PAB, PAC, PAH, PAK, PAL, PAT, PAW, PAY
V8-350④⑧	N	RAA, RAB, RAF, RAH, RAJ, RAM, RAN, RAP, RAT, RAU, RAX, RAY, RAZ, RBL, RBM, RBR, RBS, RBT, RBU, RBW, RBX, RBY, RBZ, RCA, RCB, RCC, RCD, RCF, RCH, RCJ

①—Pontiac built engine.
②—Chevrolet built engine.
③—Two barrel carb.
④—Four barrel carb.
⑤—Oldsmobile built engine.
⑥—Except turbocharged engine.
⑦—Turbocharged engine.
⑧—Diesel.

1980 Riviera

1980 Century

1980 Century Ltd.

1980 Regal

1980 LeSabre

1980 Electra

1981 Century

1981 Regal Limited

1981–83 Regal Sport Coupe

1981 LeSabre

1981 Electra & Estate Wagon

1981–82 Riviera 1983 Riviera Exc. "T" Type

1982 Regal Limited Sedan & Estate Wagon 1983 Regal "T" Type

1982–84 Electra

1982–83 LeSabre

1983 Regal Limited

1983 Riviera "T" Type

1984–85 Regal "T" Type

1984—85 LeSabre

1984—85 Riviera

1984—86 Regal

1984—86 Regal Grand National

General Engine Specifications

Year	Engine CID①/Liter	V.I.N. Code②	Carburetor	Bore and Stroke	Compression Ratio	Net H.P. @ R.P.M.③	Maximum Torque Lbs. Ft. @ R.P.M.	Normal Oil Pressure Pounds
1980	V6-231, 3.8L	A	M2ME, 2 Bbl.④	3.80 × 3.40	8.0	110 @ 3800	190 @ 1600	37
	V6-231, 3.8L⑩	3	E4ME, 4 Bbl.④	3.80 × 3.40	8.0	170 @ 4000	265 @ 2400	37
	V6-252, 4.1L	4	M4ME, 4 Bbl.④	3.97 × 3.40	8.1	125 @ 4000	205 @ 2000	37
	V8-265, 4.3L⑧	S	M2ME, 2 Bbl.④	3.75 × 3.00	8.2	120 @ 3600	210 @ 1600	40
	V8-301, 4.9L⑧	W	M4ME, 4 Bbl.④	4.00 × 3.00	8.2	150 @ 4000	240 @ 2000	38—42
	V8-305, 5.0L⑨	H	E4ME, 4 Bbl.④	3.736 × 3.48	8.5	155 @ 4000	230 @ 2400	32—40
	V8-350, 5.7L	X	M4MC, 4 Bbl.④⑬	3.80 × 3.85	8.0	155 @ 3400	280 @ 1600	34
	V8-350, 5.7L⑤⑫	R	M4MC, 4 Bbl.④⑬	4.057 × 3.385	8.3	160 @ 3600	270 @ 2000	30—45
	V8-350, 5.7L⑤⑭	N	Fuel Injection	4.057 × 3.385	22.5	105 @ 3200	205 @ 1600	30—45
1981	V6-231, 3.8L	A	M2ME, 2 Bbl.④	3.80 × 3.40	8.0	110 @ 3800	190 @ 1600	37
	V6-231, 3.8L⑩	3	E4ME, 4 Bbl.④	3.80 × 3.40	8.0	⑮	⑯	37
	V6-252, 4.1L	4	E4ME, 4 Bbl.④	3.97 × 3.40	8.0	125 @ 4000	205 @ 2000	37
	V8-265, 4.3L⑧	S	M2ME, 2 Bbl.④	3.75 × 3.00	8.0	119 @ 4000	204 @ 2000	37
	V8-307, 5.0L⑤	Y	M4MC, 4 Bbl.④	3.80 × 3.385	8.0	150 @ 3600	245 @ 1600	37
	V8-350, 5.7L⑤⑭	N	Fuel Injection	4.057 × 3.385	22.5	105 @ 3200	205 @ 1600	30—45
1982	V6-231, 3.8L	A	E2ME, 2 Bbl.④	3.80 × 3.40	8.0	110 @ 3800	190 @ 1600	37
	V6-231, 3.8L⑩	3	E4ME, 4 Bbl.④	3.80 × 3.40	8.0	⑮	⑯	37
	V6-252, 4.1L	4	E4ME, 4 Bbl.④	3.97 × 3.40	8.0	125 @ 4000	205 @ 2000	37
	V6-262, 4.3L⑤⑭	V	Fuel Injection	4.057 × 3.385	21.6	85 @ 3600	165 @ 1600	35
	V8-307, 5.0L⑤	Y	E4ME, 4 Bbl.④	3.80 × 3.385	8.5	140 @ 3600	240 @ 1600	35
	V8-350, 5.7L⑤⑭	N	Fuel Injection	4.057 × 3.385	22.5	105 @ 3200	200 @ 1600	35
1983	V6-231, 3.8L	A	2 Bbl.④	3.80 × 3.40	8.0	110 @ 3800	190 @ 1600	37
	V6-231, 3.8L⑩	8	4 Bbl.④	3.80 × 3.40	8.0	180 @ 4000	⑰	37
	V6-252, 4.1L	4	4 Bbl.④	3.965 × 3.40	8.0	125 @ 4000	205 @ 2000	37
	V6-262, 4.3L⑤⑭	V	Fuel Injection	4.057 × 3.385	22.5	85 @ 3600	165 @ 1600	30—45
	V8-307, 5.0L⑤	Y	4 Bbl.④	3.80 × 3.385	8.0	140 @ 3600	240 @ 1600	30—45
	V8-350, 5.7L⑤⑭	N	Fuel Injection	4.057 × 3.385	22.5	105 @ 3200	200 @ 1600	30—45

continued

GENERAL ENGINE SPECIFICATIONS—Continued

Year	Engine CID①/Liter	V.I.N. Code②	Carburetor	Bore and Stroke	Compression Ratio	Net H.P. @ R.P.M.③	Maximum Torque Lbs. Ft. @ R.P.M.	Normal Oil Pressure Pounds
1984	V6-231, 3.8L	A	2 Bbl.④	3.80 × 3.40	8.0	110 @ 3800	190 @ 1600	37
	V6-231, 3.8L⑩	9	Fuel Injection	3.80 × 3.40	8.0	190 @ 4000	300 @ 2400	37
	V6-252, 4.1L	4	4 Bbl.④	3.965 × 3.40	8.0	125 @ 4000	205 @ 2000	37
	V6-262, 4.3L⑤⑭	V	Fuel Injection	4.057 × 3.385	21.6	85 @ 3600	165 @ 1600	30–45
	V8-307, 5.0L⑤	Y	4 Bbl.④	3.800 × 3.385	8.0	140 @ 3600	240 @ 1600	30–45
	V8-350, 5.7L⑤⑭	N	Fuel Injection	4.057 × 3.385	21.6	105 @ 3200	200 @ 1600	30–45
1985	V6-231, 3.8L	A	2 Bbl.④	3.800 × 3.400	8.0	110 @ 3800	190 @ 1600	37⑥
	V6-231, 3.8L⑩	9	Fuel Injection	3.800 × 3.400	8.0	⑪	300 @ 2400	37⑥
	V6-262, 4.3L⑤⑭	V	Fuel Injection	4.057 × 3.385	21.6	85 @ 3600	165 @ 1600	30⑦
	V8-307, 5.0L⑤	Y	4 Bbl.④	3.800 × 3.385	8.0	140 @ 3600	240 @ 1600	30⑦
	V8-350, 5.7L⑤⑭	N	Fuel Injection	4.057 × 3.385	22.5	105 @ 3200	200 @ 1600	30⑦
1986	V6-231, 3.0L	A	2 Bbl.④	3.800 × 3.400	8.0	110 @ 3800	190 @ 1600	37
	V6-231, 3.0L⑩	9	Fuel Injection	3.800 × 3.400	8.0	235 @ 4400	330 @ 2800	37
	V8-307, 5.0L	Y	4 Bbl.④	3.800 × 3.385	8.0	140 @ 3200	255 @ 2000	30

①—CID—cubic inch displacement.
②—The fifth digit in the V.I.N. denotes engine code on 1980 vehicles. The eighth digit in the V.I.N. denotes engine code on 1981–85 vehicles.
③—Ratings are net—as installed in the vehicle.
④—Rochester.
⑤—See Oldsmobile chapter for service procedures on this engine.
⑥—At 2400 RPM.
⑦—Minimum at 1500 RPM.
⑧—See Pontiac chapter for service procedures on this engine.
⑨—See Chevrolet chapter for service procedures on this engine.
⑩—Turbocharged engine.
⑪—Regal, 200 @ 4000; Riviera, 190 @ 4000.
⑫—Riviera.
⑬—Vehicles equipped with C-4 system-E4ME.
⑭—Diesel.
⑮—Regal, 170 @ 4000; Riviera, 180 @ 4000.
⑯—Regal, 275 @ 2400; Riviera, 270 @ 2400.
⑰—Regal, 280 @ 2400; Riviera, 290 @ 2400.

Drive Axle Specifications

Year	Model	Carrier Type	Ring Gear & Pinion Backlash		Pinion Bearing Preload			Differential Bearing Preload		
			Method	Adjustment	Method	Adjustment New Bearings Inch-Lbs.	Adjustment Used Bearings Inch-Lbs.	Method	Adjustment New Bearings Inch-Lbs.	Adjustment Used Bearings Inch-Lbs.
1980–84	Exc. Riviera	Integral	Shims	.006–.008	Spacer	20–25①	10–15①	Shims	35–40②	20–25②
1980–85	Riviera	Integral	Shims	.005–.009	Spacer	18–24	③	Shims	④	④
1985–86	Exc. Riviera	Integral	Shims	.005–.009	Spacer	20–25①	10–15①	Shims	35–40②	20–25②

①—Measured with torque wrench at pinion flange nut.
②—Total preload measured with torque wrench at pinion flange nut with new seal installed.
③—Pre-check reading plus 5 inch lbs.
④—Slip fit plus .003 inch preload on each side.

Alternator Specifications

Year	Model	Rated Hot Output Amps.	Field Current 12 Volts @ 80 F.	Year	Model	Rated Hot Output Amps.	Field Current 12 Volts @ 80 F.	Year	Model	Rated Hot Output Amps.	Field Current 12 Volts @ 80 F.
1980	1100110	42	—		1100284	85	—		1105566	66	—
	1100111	63	—		1101037	70	—		1105567	78	—
	1101038	70	—		1101045	85	—	1985	1100200	78	—
	1101044	70	—		1101056	—	—		1100206	56	—
	1101080	80	—		1101082	70	—		1100208	66	—
	1101071	70	—		1101084	85	—		1100217	78	—
	1103088	55	—		1101088	70	—		1100239	56	—
	1103100	55	—		1101098	70	—		1100247	66	—
	1103101	37	—		1103119	63	—		1100257	78	—
	1103102	63	—	1983	1100200	78	—		1100260	78	—
	1103103	63	—		1100230	42	—		1104446	94	—
	1103104	42	—		1100239	55	—		1105028	78	—
	1103105	42	—		1100240	63	—		1105085	108	—
	1103106	63	—		1100260	78	—		1105197	70	—
	1103112	63	—		1100297	42	—		1105200	85	—
	1103186	63	—		1100300	63	—		1105329	85	—
1981	1100110	42	—		1105022	78	—		1105428	94	—
	1100121	63	—		1105025	63	—		1105441	94	—
	1100156	55	—		1105034	63	—		1105443	94	—
	1100164	55	—		1105040	85	—		1105444	94	—
	1101037	70	—		1105198	85	—		1105447	94	—
	1101045	85	—		1105250	70	—		1105493	94	—
	1101082	70	—	1984	1100200	78	—		1105494	78	—
	1101084	85	—		1100239	56	—		1105496	94	—
	1101085	85	—		1100260	78	—		1105497	108	—
	1101437	70	—		1105028	78	—		1105509	108	—
	1103088	55	—		1105041	78	—		1105541	94	—
	1103119	63	—		1105197	70	—		1105548	85	—
1982	1100110	42	—		1105250	70	—		1105552	85	—
	1100111	63	—		1105443	94	—		1105553	97	—
	1100121	63	—		1105444	94	—		1105562	66	—
	1100156	55	—		1105493	94	—		1105592	94	—
	1100164	55	—		1105547	94	—		1105617	94	—
	1100165	60	—		1105548	85	—	1986	1100200	78	—
	1100190	76	—		1105549	108	—		1100239	55	—
	1100194	70	—		1105561	94	—		1105197	70	—
	1100198	38	—		1105562	94	—		1105565	78	—
	1100281	63	—		1105564	66	—				
					1105565	78	—				

Engine Tightening Specifications★

★ Torque specifications are for clean and lightly lubricated threads only. Dry or dirty threads produce increased friction which prevents accurate measurement of tightness.

Year	Engine/V.I.N.	Spark Plugs Ft. Lbs.	Cylinder Head Bolts Ft. Lbs.	Intake Manifold Ft. Lbs.	Exhaust Manifold Ft. Lbs.	Rocker Arm Shaft Bracket Ft. Lbs.	Rocker Arm Cover Ft. Lbs.	Connecting Rod Cap Bolts Ft. Lbs.	Main Bearing Cap Bolts Ft. Lbs.	Flywheel to Crankshaft Ft. Lbs.	Vibration Damper or Pulley Ft. Lbs.
1980–83	V6-231⑭	15	80	45	25	30	4	40	100	60	225
	V8-265, 301⑭	15	95	40	35	20⑪	6	35	②	95	160
	V8-305⑭	22	65	30	20	—	4	45	70	60	60
	V8-350/L⑥	22	65	30	20	—	4	45	70	60	60
	V8-350/X⑤	15	80	45	25	30	4	40	100	60	225
	V8-350/R⑦	25	130⑩	40⑩	25	28④	⑫	42	③	⑧	255
1980–83	V6-252/4	15	80	45	25	30	4	40	100	60	225
	V8-307/Y⑦	25	130⑩	40⑩	25	28④	⑫	42	③	60	200–310
	V8-350/N⑨	—	130⑩	40⑩	25	28④	⑫	42	120	60	200–310
1982–83	V6-262/V⑨	—	⑬	41	29	29④	⑫	42	①	65	160–350
1984	V6-231/A,9	15	80	45	25	30	4	40	100	60	225
	V6-252/4	15	80	45	25	30	4	40	100	60	225
	V6-262/V⑨	—	⑬	41	31	28④	—	42	105	57	203–350
1984–85	V8-307/Y⑦	25	125⑩	40⑩	25	28④	—	42	③	60	200–310
	V8-350/N⑨	—	130⑩	40⑩	25	28④	—	42	120	60	200–310
1985	V6-231/A,9	15	80	47	25	25	6	40	100	60	200
	V6-262/V	—	⑬	41	28	28④	6	42	⑮	57	203–350
1986	V6-231/A,9	20	80	32	37	43	7	40	100	60	200
	V8-307	25	125⑩	40⑩	25	28④	90⑯	42	③	60	200–310

①—1982, 107 ft. lbs.; 1983, 89 ft. lbs.
②—Rear main 100 ft. lbs; all others, 70 ft. lbs.
③—Nos. 1, 2, 3, 4—80 ft. lbs., No. 5—120 ft. lbs.
④—Rocker arm pivot bolt to head.
⑤—Buick built engine. Distributor located at front of engine.
⑥—Chevrolet built engine. Distributor located at rear of engine, clockwise rotation.
⑦—Oldsmobile built engine. Distributor located at rear of engine, counterclockwise rotation.
⑧—Auto. trans. 60 ft. lbs.; man. trans., 90 ft. lbs.
⑨—Oldsmobile built diesel engine.
⑩—Clean and dip entire engine bolt in engine oil before installing and tightening.
⑪—Rocker arm to stud nut.
⑫—Fully driven, seated and not stripped.
⑬—Torque inner 8 bolts to 142 ft. lbs. Torque outer 6 bolts (bolts nearest intake & exhaust manifolds) to cylinder head mating surfaces) to 59 ft. lbs.
⑭—For V.I.N. code identification refer to the "General Engine Specifications" at the beginning of the chapter.
⑮—Engines w/2 bolt caps, 89 ft. lbs. Engines w/4 bolt main caps: Exc. caps 2 & 3 outer, 89 ft. lbs.; caps 2 & 3 outer, 52 ft. lbs.
⑯—Inch pounds.

Pistons, Pins, Rings, Crankshaft & Bearings

Year	Engine/ V.I.N.	Piston Clearance	Ring End Gap① Comp.	Ring End Gap① Oil	Wrist-pin Diameter	Rod Bearings Shaft Diameter	Rod Bearings Bearing Clearance	Main Bearings Shaft Diameter	Main Bearings Bearing Clearance	Thrust on Bear. No.	Shaft End Play
1980	V6-231⑯	.0008–.0020	.013	.015	.9393	2.2487–2.2495	.0005–.0026	2.4995	.0003–.0018	2	.003–.009
	V8-265/S⑦	.0017–.0025	.010	.035	.940	2.00	.0005–.0025	3.00	.0002–.0018	4	.003–.009
	V8-301⑦⑯	.0025–.0033	.010	.035	.927	2.25	.0005–.0025	3.00	.0004–.0020	4	.006–.020
	V8-305②⑯	.0007–.0017	.010	.015	.9272	2.099–2.100	.0013–.0035	⑪	⑫	5	.002–.006
	V8-350/X③	.0008–.0020	.013	.015	.9393	1.991–2.000	.0005–.0026	3.0000	.0004–.0015	3	.003–.009
	V8-350/L②	.0007–.0017	.010	.015	.9272	2.099–2.100	.0013–.0035	⑪	⑫	5	.002–.006
	V8-350/R④	.00075–.00175	.010	.015	.9805	2.1238–2.1248	.0004–.0033	⑤	.005–.021⑥	3	.0035–.0135
1980–81	V6-252/4	.0008–.0020	.013	.015	.9393	2.2487–2.2495	.0005–.0026	2.4995	.0003–.0018	2	.003–.009
	V8-350/N⑧	.005–.006	.015	.015	1.0951	2.1238–2.1248	.0005–.0026	2.9998	.005–.0021⑥	3	.0035–.0135

continued

PISTONS, PINS, RINGS, CRANKSHAFT & BEARINGS—Continued

Year	Engine/ V.I.N.	Piston Clearance	Ring End Gap①		Wrist-pin Diam-eter	Rod Bearings		Main Bearings			
			Comp.	Oil		Shaft Diameter	Bearing Clearance	Shaft Diameter	Bearing Clearance	Thrust on Bear. No.	Shaft End Play
1981	V6-231⑯	.0008–.0020	.013	.015	.9393	2.2487–2.2495	.0005–.0026	2.4995	.0003–.0018	2	.003–.009
	V8-265/S⑦	.0017–.0025	.010	.035	.940	2.00	.0005–.0025	3.00	.0002–.0018	4	.003–.009
	V8-307/Y④	.00075–.00175	.010	.015	.9805	2.1238–2.1248	.0004–.0033	⑨	⑩	3	.0035–.0135
	V8-350/N⑧	.005–.006	.015	.015	1.0951	2.1238–2.1248	.0005–.0026	2.9998	.005–.0021⑥	3	.0035–.0135
1982	V6-231/A⑬	.0008–.0020	.013	.015	.9393	2.2487–2.2495	.0005–.0026	2.4995	.0003–.0018	2	.003–.009
	V6-231/3⑭	.0022–.0034	.013	.015	.9393	2.2487–2.2495	.0005–.0026	2.4995	.0003–.0018	2	.003–.009
	V6-252/4	.0008–.0020	.013	.015	.9393	2.2487–2.2495	.0005–.0026	2.4995	.0003–.0018	2	.003–.009
	V6-262/V⑧	.003–.004	.015	.015	1.0950	2.2490–2.2510	.0003–.0035	2.9993–3.0003	⑮	3	.0035–.0135
	V8-307/Y④	.00075–.00175	.010	.015	.9805	2.1238–2.1248	.0004–.0033	⑨	⑩	3	.0035–.0135
	V8-350/N⑧	.003–.004	.015	.015	1.0951	2.1238–2.1248	.0005–.0026	2.9993–3.0003	⑲	3	.0035–.0135
1983	V6-231/A⑬	.0008–.0020	.010	.015	.9393	2.2487–2.2495	.0005–.0026	2.4995	.0003–.0018	2	.003–.009
	V6-231/8⑭	.0022–.0034	.010	.015	.9393	2.2487–2.2495	.0005–.0026	2.4995	.0003–.0018	2	.003–.009
	V6-252/4	.0008–.0020	.010	.015	.9393	2.2487–2.2495	.0005–.0026	2.4995	.0003–.0018	2	.003–.009
	V6-262/V⑧	.0035–.0045	⑰	.015	1.0950	2.2490–2.2510	.0003–.0025	2.9993–3.0003	⑮	3	.0035–.0135
	V8-307/Y④	.00075–.00175	.010	.015	.9805	2.1238–2.1248	.0004–.0033	⑨	⑩	3	.0035–.0135
	V8-350/N⑧	.003–.004	⑰	.015	1.0951	2.1238–2.1248	.0005–.0026	2.9993–3.0003	⑲	3	.0035–.0135
1984	V6-231/A⑬	.0008–.0020	.010	.015	.9392	2.2487–2.2495	.0005–.0026	2.4995	.0003–.0018	2	.003–.011
	V6-231/9⑭	.0022–.0034⑱	.010	.015	.9392	2.2487–2.2495	.0005–.0026	2.4995	.0003–.0018	2	.003–.011
	V6-252/4	.0008–.0020	.010	.015	.9392	2.2487–2.2495	.0005–.0026	2.4995	.0003–.0018	2	.003–.011
	V6-262/V⑧	.0035–.0045	⑰	.010	1.0951	2.2490–2.2500	.0005–.0025	2.9993–3.0003	⑮	3	.0035–.0135
	V8-307/Y④	.00075–.00175	.010	.015	.9805	2.1238–2.1248	.0004–.0033	⑨	⑩	3	.0035–.0135
	V8-350/N⑧	.0035–.0045	⑰	.010	1.0951	2.1238–2.1248	.0005–.0026	2.9993–3.0003	⑲	3	.0035–.0135
1985	V6-231/A⑬	.0008–.0020	.010	.015	.9392	2.2487–2.2495	.0005–.0026	2.4995	.0003–.0018	2	.003–.011
	V6-231/9⑭	.0022–.0034⑱	.010	.015	.9392	2.2487–2.2495	.0005–.0026	2.4995	.0003–.0018	2	.003–.011
	V6-262/V⑧	.0035–.0045	⑰	.015	1.0951	2.2488–2.2498	.0004–.0026	2.9993–3.0003	⑮	3	.0035–.0135
	V8-307/Y④	.00075–.00175	.009	.015	.9805	2.1238–2.1248	.0004–.0033	⑳	㉑	3	.0035–.0135
	V8-350/N⑧	.0035–.0045	.015	.015	1.0951	2.1238–2.1248	.0005–.00256	2.9993–3.0003	⑮	3	.0035–.0135
1986	V6-231/A⑬	.0008–.0020	.010	.015	.9392	2.2487–2.2495	.0005–.0026	2.4995	.0003–.0018	2	.003–.011
	V6-231/9⑭	.0022–.0034⑱	.010	.015	.9392	2.2487–2.2495	.0005–.0026	2.4995	.0003–.0018	2	.003–.011
	V8-307/Y	.00075–.00175	.009	.015	.9805	2.1238–2.1248	.0004–.0033	⑳	㉑	3	.0035–.0135

①—Fit rings in tapered bores for clearance given in tightest portion of ring travel. Clearances specified are minimum gaps.
②—Chevrolet built engine. Distributor located at rear of engine, clockwise rotation.
③—Buick built engine.
④—Oldsmobile built engine. Distributor located at rear of engine, counterclockwise rotation.
⑤—No. 1: 2.4988–2.4998 inch; Nos. 2, 3, 4, 5: 2.4985–2.4995 inch.
⑥—Rear, .0015–.0031 inch.
⑦—Pontiac built engine. Distributor located at rear of engine, counterclockwise rotation.
⑧—Olds. built diesel engine.
⑨—No. 1, 2.4993–2.4998 inch; Nos. 2, 3, 4, 5, 2.4990–2.4995 inch.
⑩—No. 5, .0015–.0031 inch; Nos. 1, 2, 3, 4, .0005–.0021 inch.
⑪—No. 1: 2.4484–2.4493 inch; Nos. 2, 3, 4: 2.4481–2.4490 inch; No. 5: 2.4479–2.4488 inch.
⑫—No. 1: .0008–.0020 inch; Nos. 2, 3, 4: .0011–.0023 inch; No. 5: .0017–.0032 inch.
⑬—Except turbocharged engine.
⑭—Turbocharged engine.
⑮—Nos. 1, 2 & 3, .0005–.0020 inch; No. 4, .0020–.0034 inch.
⑯—For V.I.N. code, refer to the "General Engine Specifications" at the beginning of the chapter.
⑰—Top ring, .019 inch; 2nd ring, .015 inch.
⑱—At piston pin centerline.
⑲—Nos. 1, 2, 3 & 4, .0005–.0021; No. 5, .0020–.0034.
⑳—No. 1, 2.4988–2.4998 inch; Nos. 2, 3, 4 & 5, 2.4985–2.4995 inch.
㉑—No. 5, .0016–.0032 inch; Nos. 1, 2, 3 & 4, .0005–.0021 inch.

Valve Specifications

Year	Model/V.I.N.	Valve Lash		Valve Angles		Valve Spring Installed Height ①	Valve Spring Pressure Lbs. @ In.	Stem Clearance		Stem Diameter	
		Int.	Exh.	Seat	Face			Intake	Exhaust	Intake	Exhaust
1980	V6-231, 252②	Hydraulic⑥		45	45	1.727	⑭	.0015–.0035	.0015–.0032	.3401–.3412	.3405–.3412
	V8-265, 301②	Hydraulic⑥		46	45	1.69	170 @ 1.26	.0017–.0020	.0017–.0020	.3400	.3400
	V8-305④②	1 Turn⑤		46	45	1.70	200 @ 1.25	.0010–.0027	.0010–.0027	.3410–.3417	.3410–.3417
	V8-350/X⑪	Hydraulic⑥		45	45	1.727	⑬	.0015–.0035	.0015–.0032	.3720–.3730	.3723–.3730
	V8-350/L④	1 Turn⑤		46	45	1.70	200 @ 1.25	.0010–.0027	.0010–.0027	.3410–.3417	.3410–.3417
	V8-350/R⑦	Hydraulic⑥		⑧	⑨	1.67	187 @ 1.27	.0010–.0027	.0015–.0032	.3425–.3432	.3420–.3427
	V8-350/N⑦⑫	Hydraulic⑥		⑧	⑨	1.67	152 @ 1.30	.0010–.0027	.0015–.0032	.3425–.3432	.3420–.3427
1981	V6-231②	Hydraulic⑥		45	45	1.727	⑭	.0015–.0035	.0015–.0032	.3402–.3412	.3405–.3412
	V6-252/4	Hydraulic⑥		45	45	1.727	⑭	.0015–.0035	.0015–.0032	.3402–.3412	.3405–.3412
	V8-265/S⑩	Hydraulic⑥		46	45	1.66	187 @ 1.296	.0010–.0027	.0010–.0027	.3418–.3425	.3418–.3425
	V8-307/Y⑦	Hydraulic⑥		⑧	⑨	1.67	189 @ 1.27	.0010–.0027	.0015–.0032	.3425–.3432	.3420–.3427
	V8-350/N⑦⑫	Hydraulic⑥		⑧	⑨	1.67	⑭	.0010–.0027	.0015–.0032	.3425–.3432	.3420–.3427
1982–83	V6-231②	Hydraulic⑥		45	45	1.727	182 @ 1.34	.0015–.0035	.0015–.0032	.3401–.3412	.3405–.3412
	V6-252/4	Hydraulic⑥		45	45	1.727	182 @ 1.34	.0015–.0035	.0015–.0032	.3401–.3412	.3405–.3412
	V6-262/V	Hydraulic⑥		⑧	⑨	1.670	210 @ 1.220	.0010–.0027	.0015–.0032	.3425–.3432	.3420–.3427
	V8-307/Y	Hydraulic⑥		⑧	⑨	1.670	187 @ 1.27	.0010–.0027	.0015–.0032	.3425–.3432	.3420–.3427
	V8-350/N	Hydraulic⑥		⑧	⑨	1.670	210 @ 1.220	.0010–.0027	.0015–.0032	.3425–.3432	.3420–.3427
1984	V6-231/A	Hydraulic⑥		45	45	1.727	182 @ 1.34	.0015–.0032	.0015–.0032	.3401–.3412	.3405–.3412
	V6-231/9③	Hydraulic⑥		45	45	1.727	220 @ 1.34	.0015–.0032	.0015–.0032	.3401–.3412	.3405–.3412
	V6-252/4	Hydraulic⑥		45	45	1.727	182 @ 1.34	.0015–.0032	.0015–.0032	.3401–.3412	.3405–.3412
	V6-262/V	Hydraulic⑥		⑧	⑨	1.670	210 @ 1.22	.0010–.0027	.0015–.0032	.3425–.3432	.3420–.3427
	V8-307/Y	Hydraulic⑥		⑧	⑨	1.670	187 @ 1.27	.0010–.0027	.0015–.0032	.3425–.3432	.3420–.3427
	V8-350/N	Hydraulic⑥		⑧	⑨	1.670	210 @ 1.22	.0010–.0027	.0015–.0032	.3425–.3432	.3420–.3427
1985	V6-231/A	Hydraulic⑥		45	45	1.727	182 @ 1.34	.0015–.0035	.0015–.0032	.3401–.3412	.3405–.3412
	V6-231/9③	Hydraulic⑥		45	45	1.727	⑮	.0015–.0035	.0015–.0032	.3401–.3412	.3405–.3412
	V6-262/V⑫	Hydraulic⑥		⑧	⑨	1.670	210 @ 1.220	.0010–.0027	.0015–.0032	.3425–.3432	.3420–.3428
	V8-307/Y⑦	Hydraulic⑥		⑯	⑰	1.670	187 @ 1.270	.0010–.0027	.0015–.0032	.3425–.3432	.3420–.3427
	V8-350/N⑫	Hydraulic⑥		⑧	⑨	1.670	210 @ 1.220	.0010–.0027	.0015–.0032	.3424–.3432	.3420–.3428
1986	V6-231/A	Hydraulic⑥		45	45	1.727	182 @ 1.34	.0015–.0035	.0015–.0032	.3401–.3412	.3405–.3412
	V6-231/9③	Hydraulic⑥		45	45	1.727	185 @ 1.34	.0015–.0035	.0015–.0032	.3401–.3412	.3405–.3412
	V8-307/Y⑦	Hydraulic⑥		⑯	⑰	1.670	187 @ 1.270	.0010–.0027	.0015–.0032	.3425–.3432	.3420–.3427

①—Outer spring.
②—For VIN code, refer to "General Engine Specifications" at the beginning of the chapter.
③—Turbocharged engine.
④—Chevrolet built engine. Distributor located at rear of engine, clockwise rotation.
⑤—Turn rocker arm stud nut until all lash is eliminated, then tighten nut the additional turn listed.

⑥—No adjustment.
⑦—Oldsmobile built engine. Distributor located at rear of engine, counterclockwise rotation.
⑧—Intake, 45°; exhaust 31°.
⑨—Intake 44°; exhaust, 30°.
⑩—Pontiac built engine. Distributor located at rear of engine, clockwise rotation.
⑪—Buick built engine. Distributor located at front of engine.

⑫—Diesel engine.
⑬—Intake, 180 @ 1.34; exhaust, 177 @ 1.45.
⑭—Intake, 164 @ 1.34; exhaust, 182 @ 1.34.
⑮—Regal, 185 lbs. @ 1.340 inches; Riviera, 220 lbs. @ 1.340 inches.
⑯—Intake, 45°; exhaust, 59°.
⑰—Intake, 46°; exhaust, 60°.

Starting Motor Applications

Year	Engine/V.I.N.	Starter Number	Year	Engine/V.I.N.	Starter Number
1980	V6-231⑦⑨	1109061		V8-350⑦⑨	1109072
	V6-231⑧⑨	1998204		V8-350⑧⑨	1998205
	V6-252/4	1109062		V8-350/N④⑦	1100215
	V8-265, 301⑨	1109523		V8-350/N④⑧	1100214
	V8-305 2 Bbl. Carb.⑨	1109064	1981	V6-231⑦⑨	1109061
	V8-305/H, 4 Bbl. Carb.	1109524		V6-231⑧⑨	1998204
	V8-350/X①	1109062		V6-252/4⑦	1998227
	V8-350/L②⑤	1109524		V6-252/4⑧	1998205
	V8-350/L②⑥	1109065		V8-265, 301⑨	1109523

continued

STARTING MOTOR APPLICATIONS—Continued

Year	Engine/V.I.N.	Starter Number	Year	Engine/V.I.N.	Starter Number
1981 cont'd	V8-307/Y	1998205		V6-262/V④	1998556
	V8-350/N④⑦	1109216			22511854
	V8-350/N④⑧	1109218		V8-307/Y⑦	1109544
1982	V6-231/3⑦	1998234		V8-307/Y⑧	1998237
	V6-231/3⑧	1998237		V8-350/N④⑦	1998553
1982–83	V6-231/A	1998234			22523207
	V6-252/4⑦	1998234		V8-350/N④⑧	1109495
	V6-252/4⑧	1998237	1985	V6-231/A	1998236
	V8-262/V	1998552		V6-231/9⑦	1998236
	V8-307/Y⑦	1109544		V6-231/9⑧	1998237
	V8-307/Y⑧	1998237		V6-262/V	22511854
	V8-350/N④⑦	1998552		V8-307/Y⑦	1109544
	V8-350/N④⑧	1109495		V8-307/Y⑧	1998237
1983	V6-231/8⑦	1998234		V8-350/N⑦	1998553
	V6-231/8⑧	1998237		V8-350/N⑧	1109495
1984	V6-231/A,9⑦	1998236	1986	V6-231/A	1998516
	V6-231/9③⑧	1998237		V6-231/9	—
	V6-252/4⑦	1998234		V8-307/Y	1998536
	V6-252/4⑧	1998237			

①—Distributor at front of engine.
②—Distributor at rear of engine, clockwise rotation.
③—Distributor at rear of engine, counterclockwise rotation.
④—Diesel engine.
⑤—Exc. Skylark.
⑥—Skylark.
⑦—Exc. Riviera.
⑧—Riviera.
⑨—For V.I.N. code, refer to the "General Engine Specifications" at the beginning of the chapter.

Cooling System & Capacity Data

Year	Model or Engine/V.I.N.	Cooling Capacity, Qts.		Radiator Cap Relief Pressure, Lbs.	Thermo. Opening Temp.	Fuel Tank Gals.	Engine Oil Refill Qts. ①	Transmission Oil			Rear Axle Oil Pints
		Less A/C	With A/C					3 Speed Pints	4 Speed Pints	Auto. Trans. Qts. ②	
1980	V6-231⑪⑥	13.3	13.3	15	195	18.1	4	3.5	3.5	㉛	㊳
	V6-231⑩⑥	13	13	15	195	25	4	3.5	—	㉛	㊳
	V6-231 Turbo/3⑪	13.7㉟	13.8㉟	15	195	18.1	4	3.5	—	㉛	㊳
	V6-231 Turbo/3⑩	13.4㉞	13.4㉞	15	195	25	4	—	—	㉛	㊳
	V6-231 Turbo/3⑬	—	13.66㉖	15	195	21	4	—	—	⑨	3.2⑧
	V6-252/4⑩⑭	13	13	15	195	25	4	—	—	㉛	㊳
	V8-301/W⑪	20.3㉗	21	15	195	18.1	4㉙	3.5	—	㉛	㊳
	V8-301/W⑩⑭	18.9	18.9	15	195	25③	4㉙	3.5	—	㉛	㊳
	V8-305/H⑪	—	17.6㊱	15	195	18.1	4	—	—	㉛	㊳
	V8-350/X⑩⑭㉓㊴	14.3㉔	14.2㉔	15	195	25③	4	—	—	㉛	㊳
	V8-350/R⑩⑭㉘㊵	—	14.5㉒	15	195	25③	4	—	—	㉛	㊳
	V8-350⑬⑥	—	15.5	15	195	21	4	—	—	⑨	3.2⑧
	V8-350 Diesel/N⑩⑭	18.3	18	15	195	27③	7㉑	—	—	㉛	㊳
1981	V6-231/A⑪	13	13	15	195	18.1	4	3.5	—	⑫	3½
	V6-231/A⑩	13	13	15	195	25	4	3.5	—	⑫	3½
	V6-231 Turbo/3⑪	13.4㉞	13.4㉞	15	195	18.1	4	—	—	⑫	3½
	V6-231 Turbo/3⑬	13.6㉟	13.6㉟	15	195	21	4	—	—	⑫	3.3⑧
	V6-252/4⑩⑭	13	13	15	195	25	4	—	—	⑫	3½
	V6-252/4⑬	13	13	15	195	21	4	—	—	⑫	3.3⑧
	V8-265/S⑪	20.2㉗	20.2㉗	15	195	18.1	4㉙	3.5	—	⑫	3½
	V8-307/Y⑩⑭	18.9	18.9	15	195	25③	4	—	—	⑫	3½
	V8-307/Y⑬	16.4	16.4	15	195	22	4	—	—	⑫	3.3⑧
	V8-350 Diesel/N⑩⑭	17.3	17	15	195	27③	7㉑	—	—	⑫	3½
	V8-350 Diesel/N⑬	18.2	18.2	15	195	27	7㉑	—	—	⑫	3½

continued

Year	Model or Engine/V.I.N.	Cooling Capacity, Qts. Less A/C	Cooling Capacity, Qts. With A/C	Radiator Cap Relief Pressure, Lbs.	Thermo. Opening Temp.	Fuel Tank Gals.	Engine Oil Refill Qts. [1]	3 Speed Pints	4 Speed Pints	Auto. Trans. Qts. [2]	Rear Axle Oil Pints
1982	V6-231/A[50]	12.98	13.02	15	195	18	4	—	—	[19]	[38]
	V6-231/A[10]	13	13	15	195	25[3]	4	—	—	[19]	[38]
	V6-231 Turbo/3[50]	13.44[34]	13.44[34]	15	195	25[3]	4	—	—	[19]	[38]
	V6-231 Turbo/3[13]	13.6[35]	13.6[35]	15	195	21	4	—	—	[19]	3.2[8]
	V6-252/4[50]	12.98	13.02	15	195	18	4	—	—	[19]	[38]
	V6-252/4[10][14]	13	13	15	195	25[3]	4	—	—	[19]	[38]
	V6-252/4[13]	13	13	15	195	21	4	—	—	[19]	3.2[8]
	V6-262 Diesel/V[20]	14.8	14.8	15	195	20	6.5[21]	—	—	[19]	[38]
	V8-307/Y[10][14]	18.9	18.9	15	195	25[3]	4	—	—	[19]	[38]
	V8-307/Y[13]	18.8	18.95	15	195	21	4	—	—	[19]	3.2[8]
	V8-350 Diesel/N[20]	17.33	17.33	15	195	20	7[21]	—	—	[19]	[38]
	V8-350 Diesel/N[10][14]	17	17	15	195	27[3]	7[21]	—	—	[19]	[38]
	V8-350 Diesel/N[13]	18.2	18.2	15	195	23	7[21]	—	—	[19]	3.2[8]
1983	V6-231/A[20]	12.9	13	15	195	[53]	4	—	—	[19]	[38]
	V6-231/A[10]	12.9	13	15	195	25[3]	4	—	—	[19]	[38]
	V6-231 Turbo/8[50]	13.4	13.4[34]	15	195	19.8	4	—	—	[19]	[38]
	V6-231 Turbo/8[13]	—	13.6[35]	15	195	21.1	4	—	—	[19]	3.2[8]
	V6-252/4[20]	12.9	13	15	195	[53]	4	—	—	[19]	[38]
	V6-252/4[10][14]	12.9	13	15	195	25[3]	4	—	—	[19]	[38]
	V6-252/4[13]	—	13	15	195	21.1	4	—	—	[19]	3.2[8]
	V6-262 Diesel/V[20]	—	14.7	18.5	195	[53]	6.5[21]	—	—	[19]	[38]
	V8-307/Y[10][14]	15.4[18]	16[18]	15	195	25[3]	4	—	—	[19]	[38]
	V8-307/Y[13]	—	16[18]	15	195	21.1	4	—	—	[19]	3.2[8]
	V8-350 Diesel/N[20]	—	17.3	15	195	[53]	6.5[21]	—	—	[19]	[38]
	V8-350 Diesel/N[10][14]	—	17.9	15	195	26[3]	6.5[21]	—	—	[19]	[38]
	V8-350 Diesel/N[13]	—	18	15	195	22.8	6.5[21]	—	—	[19]	3.2[8]
1984	V6-231/A[20]	12.9	13	15	195	19.8	4	—	—	[19]	3.5
	V6-231/A[10]	13	13	15	195	25[3]	4	—	—	[19]	[38]
	V6-231 Turbo/9[20]	13	13	15	180	19.8	5	—	—	[19]	3.5
	V6-231 Turbo/9[13]	—	12.9[34]	15	180	21.1	5	—	—	[19]	3.3[8]
	V6-252/4[20]	13	13	15	195	19.8	4	—	—	[19]	3.5
	V6-252/4[10][14]	13	13	15	195	25[3]	4	—	—	[19]	[38]
	V6-252/4[13]	—	12.6	15	195	21.1	4	—	—	[19]	3.3[8]
	V6-262 Diesel/V[20]	13.6	14.4	15	195	[53]	6[21]	—	—	[19]	3.5
	V8-307/Y[10][14]	15.4	16	15	195	25[3]	4	—	—	[19]	[38]
	V8-307/Y[13]	—	16	15	195	21.1	4	—	—	[19]	3.3[8]
	V8-350 Diesel/N[10][14]	18.3	17.9	15	195	26[3]	7[21]	—	—	[19]	[38]
	V8-350 Diesel/N[13]	18.2	18.2	15	195	22.8	7[21]	—	—	[19]	3.3[8]
1985	V6-231/A[10]	13.0	13.0	15	195	25[3]	4	—	—	[19]	[38]
	V6-231/A[20]	12.9	13.0	15	195	18.1	4	—	—	[19]	[38]
	V6-231/9[20]	13.0	13.0	15	180	18.1	5	—	—	[19]	[38]
	V6-231/9[13]	—	12.9[34]	15	180	21.1	5	—	—	[19]	3.3[8]
	V6-262 Diesel/V	13.6[43]	14.4	16–18.5	195	19.8	6[21]	—	—	[19]	[38]
	V8-307/Y[16]	15.4[18]	16.0	15	195	25[3]	4	—	—	[19]	[38]
	V8-307/Y[13]	—	16.0	15	195	21.1	4	—	—	[19]	3.3[8]
	V8-350 Diesel/N[16]	18.0	18.3	15	195	26[3]	7[21]	—	—	[19]	[38]
	V8-350 Diesel/N[13]	18.2	18.2	15	195	22.8	7[21]	—	—	[19]	3.3[8]
1986	V6-231/A	12.9	13.0	15	195	18.1	4	—	—	[19]	[38]
	V6-231/9	13.0	13.0	15	180	18.1	5	—	—	[19]	[38]
	V8-307/Y	15.4[18]	16.0	15	195	22	4	—	—	[19]	[38]

continued

COOLING SYSTEM & CAPACITY DATA NOTES

①—Add one quart with filter change.
②—Approximate. Make final check with dipstick.
③—Estate Wagon 22 gallons.
④—With heavy duty cooling system, 14.5 qts.
⑤—With heavy duty cooling system, 21.6 qts.
⑥—For VIN code, refer to "General Engine Specifications" at the front of the chapter.
⑦—Skylark.
⑧—Final drive.
⑨—Total 12 qts. Oil pan only 5 qts.
⑩—LeSabre.
⑪—Century & Regal.
⑫—THM 200C—total 9½ qts., pan only 3½ qts.; THM 325—total 12 qts., pan only 5 qts.; THM 250C—total 10¾ qts., pan only 4 qts.; THM 350C—total 10 qts., pan only 3⅛ qts.; THM 2004R—total 11 qts., pan only 3½ qts.
⑬—Riviera.
⑭—Electra.
⑮—Total 10 qts.; pan only 3 qts.
⑯—Exc. Riviera.
⑰—Exc. wagon, 19.8 gals.; wagon, 18.2 gals.
⑱—With heavy duty cooling, 16.0 qts.
⑲—THM 200C—total 9.4 qts., pan only 3.48 qts. THM 200-4R—total 11.05 qts., pan only, 3.48 qts. THM 250C—total 10.04 qts., pan only 4.0 qts. THM 325-4L—total 11.75 qts., pan only 4.86 qts. THM 350C—total 10.04 qts., pan only 3.17 qts.
⑳—Regal.
㉑—Includes oil filter. For 1980 models, use recommended diesel oil, designated SE/CC. For 1981 models use recommended diesel oil designated SF/CC, SF/CD or SE/CC. For 1982–85 models use recommended diesel oil designated SF/CC or SF/CD.
㉒—With heavy duty cooling, 15.2 qts.
㉓—Distributor at front of engine.
㉔—With heavy duty cooling, 15.0 qts.
㉕—With heavy duty cooling system, 15 qts.
㉖—With heavy duty cooling, 14.17 qts.
㉗—With heavy duty cooling system, 20.8 qts.
㉘—Distributor at rear of engine.
㉙—With or without filter change.
㉚—With heavy duty cooling system, 15.4 qts.
㉛—THM 200—total 9.5 qts., pan only 3.5 qts. THM 250C—total 10 qts., pan only 4 qts. THM 350—total 12.25 qts., pan only 3.25 qts. THM 400—total 10 qts., pan only 3 qts.
㉜—With heavy duty cooling system, 16.6 qts.
㉝—With heavy duty cooling system, 16.9 qts.
㉞—With heavy duty cooling, 13.7 qts.
㉟—With heavy duty cooling, 14.1 qts.
㊱—With heavy duty cooling system, 18.0 qts.
㊲—4 Barrel Carb.
㊳—7½ inch axle, 3.5 pts.; 8½ inch axle, 4.25 pts.; 8¾ inch axle, 5.4 pts.
㊴—Buick built engine.
㊵—Oldsmobile built engine.
㊶—THM 200—total 9.5 qts.; oil pan only 3.5 qts. THM 350—total capacity 10 qts; oil pan only 3 qts.
㊷—Electra, 25.3 gal.
㊸—With heavy duty cooling, 14.4 qts.

Wheel Alignment Specifications

| Year | Model | Caster Angle, Degrees | | Camber Angle, Degrees | | | | Toe-In Inch | Toe Out on Turns, Deg. | |
| | | Limits | Desired | Limits | | Desired | | | Outer Wheel | Inner Wheel |
				Left	Right	Left	Right			
1980	Century, Regal①	+.5 to +1.5	+1	0 to +1	0 to +1	+.5	+.5	1/16 to 3/16	—	—
	Century, Regal②	+2.5 to +3.5	+3	0 to +1	0 to +1	+.5	+.5	1/16 to 3/16	—	—
	Riviera	+2 to +3	+2.5	−.5 to +.5	−.5 to +.5	Zero	Zero	③	—	—
	Others	+2.5 to +3.5	+3	+.3 to +1.3	+.3 to +1.3	+.8	+.8	1/16 to 3/16	—	—
1981	Century, Regal②	+2.5 to +3.5	+3	0 to +1	0 to +1	+.5	+.5	1/16 to 3/16	—	—
	Riviera	+2 to +3	+2.5	−.5 to +.5	−.5 to +.5	Zero	Zero	③	—	—
	Others	+2.5 to +3.5	+3	+.3 to +1.3	+.3 to +1.3	+.8	+.8	1/16 to 3/16	—	—
1982	Regal	+2.5 to +3.5	+3	0 to +1	0 to +1	+.5	+.5	1/16 to 3/16	—	—
	Riviera	+2 to +3	+2.5	−.5 to +.5	−.5 to +.5	Zero	Zero	③	—	—
	Others	+2.5 to +3.5	+3	+.3 to +1.3	+.3 to +1.3	+.8	+.8	1/16 to 3/16	—	—
1983–84	Regal	+2.5 to +3.5	+3	0 to +1	0 to +1	+.5	+.5	1/16 to 3/16	—	—
	Riviera	+2 to +3	+2.5	−.5 to +.5	−.5 to +.5	Zero	Zero	③	—	—
	Others	+2.5 to +3.5	+3	+.3 to +1.3	+.3 to +1.3	+.8	+.8	1/16 to 3/16	—	—
1985	Regal	+2 to +4	+3	−.3 to +1.3	−.3 to +1.3	+½	+½	1/16 to 1/4	—	—
	Riviera	+1.5 to +3.5	+2.5	−.8 to +.8	−.8 to +.8	0	0	−⅛ to +⅛	—	—
	Others	+2 to +4	+3	0 to +1.6	0 to +1.6	+.8	+.8	1/16 to 1/4	—	—
1986	Regal	+2 to +4	+3	−.3 to +1.3	−.3 to +1.3	+½	+½	1/16 to 1/4	—	—
	Estate Wagon	+2 to +4	+3	0 to +1.6	0 to +1.6	+.8	+.8	1/16 to 1/4	—	—

①—Manual steering.   ②—Power steering.   ③—1/16" toe-in to 1/16" toe-out.

Electrical Section

STARTER
REPLACE

To remove the starter, disconnect ground cable from battery. Disconnect cable and solenoid lead wire from solenoid switch. Remove flywheel inspection cover. Remove starter attaching bolts and remove starter.

LIGHT SWITCH
REPLACE

1980–84 ELECTRA & LESABRE; 1985–86 ELECTRA ESTATE, 1985 LESABRE & 1986 LESABRE ESTATE

1. Disconnect battery ground cable.
2. Remove left lower instrument panel trim and A/C ducts as required.
3. Pull headlamp switch to full on position.
4. On 1980–81 models, remove knob and stem by depressing retainer on switch frame. On 1982–86 models, depress retainer through slot in rear of knob and pull knob from stem.
5. Remove switch stem escutcheon and instrument cluster bezel.
6. Remove nut securing switch, lower switch from rear of instrument panel, then disconnect electrical connector from switch.
7. Reverse procedure to install.

1980–85 RIVIERA, 1980–81 CENTURY & 1980–83 REGAL

1. Disconnect battery ground cable.
2. Depress retainer through slot in rear of switch knob, then pull knob from stem.
3. Remove switch escutcheon, then the instrument cluster bezel.
4. Remove screws securing switch to instrument panel, then pull switch away from panel.

NOTE: Disconnect twilight sentinal harness, if equipped, prior to pulling switch from instrument panel.

5. On Century and Regal models, disconnect electrical connector from switch.
6. On all models, reverse procedure to install.

1984–86 REGAL

1. Disconnect battery ground cable.
2. Remove instrument cluster bezel by carefully pulling it away from instrument panel.

NOTE: Place column mounted gear selector lever in low position and lower tilt wheel, if equipped, to aid removal of bezel.

3. Remove 3 retaining screws, then pull switch assembly from instrument panel.
4. Reverse procedure to install, ensuring that switch is properly seated in instrument panel socket.

COLUMN-MOUNTED DIMMER SWITCH
REPLACE

1. Disconnect battery ground cable.
2. Remove instrument panel lower trim and on models with A/C, remove A/C duct extension at column.
3. Disconnect shift indicator from column and remove toe-plate cover screws.
4. Remove two nuts from instrument panel support bracket studs and lower steering column, resting steering wheel on front seat.
5. Remove dimmer switch retaining screw(s) and the switch. Tape actuator rod to column and separate switch from rod.
6. Reverse procedure to install. To adjust switch, depress dimmer switch slightly and install a 3/32 inch twist drill to lock the switch to the body. Force switch upward to remove lash between switch and pivot. Torque switch retaining screw(s) to 35 inch lbs. and remove tape from actuator rod. Remove twist drill and check for proper operation.

IGNITION LOCK
REPLACE

1. Remove steering wheel as described under Horn Sounder and Steering Wheel, Replace.
2. Remove turn signal switch as described under Turn Signal Switch, Replace, then remove buzzer switch.
3. Place ignition switch in Run position, then remove lock cylinder retaining screw and lock cylinder.
4. To install, rotate lock cylinder to stop while holding housing, **Fig. 1.** Align cylinder key with keyway in housing, then push lock cylinder assembly into housing until fully seated.
5. Install lock cylinder retaining screw. Torque screw to 40 in. lbs. for standard columns. On adjustable columns, torque retaining screw to 22 in. lbs.
6. Install buzzer switch, turn signal switch and steering wheel.

IGNITION SWITCH
REPLACE

The ignition switch is located on the top of the steering column under the instrument panel. To replace it the steering column must be lowered as follows:

1. Lower steering column as outlined in "Column Mounted Dimmer Switch,

Fig. 1   Ignition lock removal

Fig. 2   Clutch start switch installation. 1980–81

Fig. 3 Turn signal & hazard warning switch assembly

Replace."
2. Remove column mounted dimmer switch, if equipped.
3. Disconnect electrical connector from switch. On models equipped with standard column and key release feature or tilt column except key release, ensure switch is in "Accessory" position. On models equipped with standard column except key release or tilt column with key release, ensure switch is in "Off-Unlock" position.
4. Remove two screws securing switch, then remove switch.
5. On models equipped with standard column and key release feature or tilt column except key release, position switch slider and lock in the "Accessory" position. On models equipped with standard column except key release or tilt column with key release, position switch slider and lock at "Accessory" position, then move slider and lock two detents to the "Off-Unlock" position.
6. Fit actuator rod into switch and assemble to column.
7. Complete assembly in reverse of removal procedure.

Fig. 4 Lock plate retainer removal

STOP LIGHT SWITCH
REPLACE

The stop lights are controlled by a mechanical switch mounted on the brake pedal bracket. This spring loaded switch makes contact whenever the brake pedal is applied. When the brake pedal is released it depresses the switch to open the contacts and turn brake lights off.

CLUTCH START SWITCH
1980-81

A clutch start switch is installed on all manual transmission cars. The switch is mounted on the clutch pedal bracket and it prevents the car from being started until the clutch pedal is depressed, **Fig. 3.**

TURN SIGNAL SWITCH
REPLACE

As shown in **Fig. 3,** the assembly is a turn signal switch and hazard warning switch. It is mounted in a housing at the upper end of the steering column mast jacket, just below the steering wheel. Therefore to get at the switch the steering

Fig. 5 Turn signal switch harness removal

wheel will have to be removed.
Also, on models equipped with tilt steering columns, it is necessary to lower the column assembly from instrument panel.
1. Disconnect battery ground cable.
2. Remove steering wheel and lock plate cover. On tilt columns, remove tilt lever.
3. With a suitable compressor, compress lock plate and spring, then remove snap ring from shaft, **Fig. 5.**
4. Remove lock plate cover with a suitable screwdriver.
5. Remove lock plate, cancelling cam, preload spring and thrust washer.
6. Remove turn signal lever and hazard warning switch knob.
7. Disconnect switch wiring connector and wrap a piece of tape around connector upper end and wiring harness, preventing snagging when removing switch, **Fig. 5.**
8. Remove three switch retaining screws and switch.
9. Reverse procedure to install.

NEUTRAL START SWITCH
EXC. MODELS W/KEY RELEASE LEVER

Actuation of the ignition switch is prevented by a mechanical lockout system, **Figs. 6 and 7,** which prevents the lock cylinder from rotating when the selector lever is out of Park or Neutral. When the selector lever is in Park or Neutral, the

Fig. 6 Mechanical neutral start mechanism. Standard column

Fig. 7 Mechanical neutral start mechanism. Tilt column

Fig. 8 Mechanical neutral start mechanism. Shown in park position

Fig. 9 Neutral start & back-up lamp switch installation. 1980-81

Fig. 10 Neutral start & back-up lamp switch installation. 1982-86

Fig. 11 Tilt & telescoping steering wheel assembly exploded view

slots in the bowl plate and the finger on the actuator rod align allowing the finger to pass through the bowl plate in turn actuating the ignition switch, **Fig. 8.** If the selector lever is in any position other than Park or Neutral, the finger contacts the bowl plate when the lock cylinder is rotated, thereby preventing full travel of the lock cylinder.

NEUTRAL START & BACK-UP LIGHT SWITCH
REPLACE

NOTE: Some models use a combination neutral start & back-up light switch, while other models use a back-up light switch. Both type switches are serviced by the following procedures.

1980-81 MODELS

1. On automatic transmission equipped models, place gear selector in "Neutral" for column shift, or "Park" for console shift. On manual transmission models, place gearshift in "Reverse".
2. Remove screws attaching switch to steering column, then remove switch.
3. Disconnect wiring connectors. Connect wiring connectors to new switch.
4. Position new switch on steering column, aligning the switch carrier tang in the switch tube slot.
5. Install attaching screws and tighten.

NOTE: No adjustment is required. The switch is pinned in the proper position with a plastic shear pin.

6. If adjustment is required:
   a. On models with automatic transmission, place gear selector in "Neutral" for column shift, or "Park" for console shift. On models with manual transmission, place gearshift in "Reverse".
   b. Loosen switch adjusting screws.
   c. On models with column shift, while rotating switch on column, insert a

.096 inch gage pin in neutral gage hole a depth of ⅜ inch, **Fig. 9.** On models with console shift, while rotating switch on column, insert .096 inch gage pin in park gage hole a depth of ⅜ inch, **Fig. 9.**
   d. Tighten attaching screws and remove gage pin.

1982-86 MODELS

1. Place gear selector in "Neutral".
2. Gently rock switch out of steering column.
3. Disconnect wiring connectors. Connect wiring connectors to new switch.
4. Align switch actuator with hole in shift tube, **Fig. 10.**
5. Position connector side of switch into lower jacket cut out.
6. Push down front of switch, ensuring switch tangs snap into holes in steering column jacket.
7. Adjust switch by placing gear selector in "Park" position. The switch main housing and housing back should ratchet, providing proper adjustment.

STANDARD HORN SOUNDER & STEERING WHEEL
REPLACE

1. Remove horn cap or actuator bar.
2. Remove steering wheel nut retainer, if used.
3. On all models, back off nut until flush with top of steering shaft.
4. Use a suitable puller to remove wheel.

TILT & TELESCOPE STEERING WHEEL
REPLACE

REMOVAL

1. Disconnect battery ground cable.
2. Remove screws, **Fig. 11,** and lift pad assembly up, then disconnect horn wiring electrical connector by pushing in and turning counterclockwise.
3. Push locking lever counterclockwise until full release position is obtained.
4. Scribe plate assembly where the two screws secure plate assembly to locking lever.
5. Remove screws and plate assembly.
6. Remove steering wheel nut retainer and nut.
7. Using tool No. J185903, remove steering wheel assembly.

NOTE: Use of a steering wheel puller other than the one recommended in Step 7, or a sharp blow on the end of the steering shaft or shift lever could shear or loosen the plastic fasteners which maintain steering column rigidity.

INSTALLATION

1. Install a suitable set screw into upper shaft at the full extended position and lock.
2. Align scribe mark on steering wheel hub with mark on end of shaft and install steering wheel. Ensure unsecured end of horn upper contact assembly is completely seated against top of horn contact carrier assembly.
3. Install nut onto upper steering shaft and torque to 30 ft. lbs. Install nut retainer.
4. Remove set screw and install plate assembly and screws. Tighten screws finger tight.
5. Position locking lever in vertical position and move lever counterclockwise until plate holes align with holes in lever. Install plate securing screws.
6. Align pad assembly with holes in steering wheel and install screws.
7. Connect battery ground cable. Ensure locking lever securely locks steering wheel travel and that steering wheel travel is free in the unlocked position.

Fig. 12 Instrument cluster trim cover. 1980-85 Riviera

Fig. 13 Windshield wiper switch removal. 1982-86 models w/tilt column

INSTRUMENT CLUSTER
REPLACE

1980-82 RIVIERA

1. Disconnect ground cable from battery and speedometer cable from transaxle or cruise control transducer.
2. Disconnect parking brake release cable and lap cooler hose, as equipped, then remove left lower instrument panel trim.
3. Remove headlamp switch knob, escutcheon and instrument cluster bezel, Fig. 12.
4. Disconnect shift indicator cable from steering column, remove 2 nuts securing column bracket, then lower steering column.
5. Remove cluster retaining screws, then pull cluster from instrument panel.
6. Disconnect speedometer cable and electrical connectors from cluster, then remove cluster.
7. Reverse procedure to install.

1983-85 RIVIERA
Standard Cluster
1. Disconnect ground cable from battery and speedometer cable at transaxle, cruise control transducer or union in engine compartment.

2. Remove center trim bezel, headlamp switch knob and escutcheon, and left (cluster) trim bezel, Fig. 12, pulling bezels straight away from instrument panel.
3. Remove 2 screws securing leading edge of lower instrument panel cover, then disconnect shift indicator cable from steering column.
4. Remove 4 screws securing cluster, then tilt top of cluster away from instrument panel.
5. Remove "Check Engine" bulb and socket from cluster and disconnect speedometer cable.
6. Place gear selector lever in low, then pull cluster away from instrument panel just far enough to gain access to Vehicle Speed Sensor (VSS).
7. Remove screw securing VSS optic head and the optic head, then lift cluster from instrument panel.
8. Reverse procedure to install.

Digital Cluster
1. Perform steps 1-5 as outlined for "Standard Cluster."
2. Disconnect wiring harness from cluster by depressing lock tab on connector and pulling connector away from cluster.
3. Remove screw securing cluster ground strap to instrument panel brace.
4. Place gear selector lever in low, pull cluster out just enough to gain access to Vehicle Speed Sensor (VSS), then remove screw securing VSS optic head and the optic head from cluster.
5. Reverse procedure to install.

Fig. 14 Windshield wiper switch removal. 1982-86 models w/standard column

Fig. 15 Heater housing installation. 1980-85 Riviera

GROUND WIRE
BLOWER MOTOR
BLOWER FAN
CORE COVER
TEMPERATURE VALVE
HEATER CORE
R.H. VENT VALVE
POWER VENT VALVE
BLOWER AIR INLET CASE
DEFROSTER VALVE
PLENUM AND MOUNTING CASE
DRAIN COVER (FLAPPER)
WATER BAFFLE
MOUNTING BAFFLE
L.H. VENT VALVE
DISTRIBUTOR CASE
MODULE TO COWL MOUNTING GASKET
ASSEMBLED

Fig. 16 Heater module assembly exploded view. 1980–81 Century & 1980–86 Regal less A/C

1. Disconnect battery ground cable.
2. If speedometer is to be removed, disconnect speedometer cable from transmission, cruise control transducer or union in engine compartment.
3. Pull steering column filler forward and remove headlamp switch knob as outlined previously.
4. Remove left (cluster) trim bezel, grasping bezel on both sides and pulling straight away from instrument panel.
5. Remove fuel gauge as follows:
   a. Remove 4 screws securing gauge.
   b. Withdraw gauge assembly from carrier, then remove bulb sockets and disconnect electrical connector from gauge.
6. Remove speedometer as follows:
   a. Remove 4 screws securing speedometer.
   b. Withdraw speedometer just far enough to gain access to cable and electrical connections.
   c. Remove bulb sockets and disconnect cable from speedometer.
   d. On 1982–86 models, remove screws securing speed sensor optic head and disconnect sensor from speedometer.
   e. Remove speedometer.
7. Reverse procedure to install components.

1980–81 CENTURY; 1980–82 REGAL

1. Disconnect battery ground cable.
2. Remove headlamp switch knob and escutcheon.
3. Carefully pry out and remove cluster trim plate.
4. Remove five cluster lens attaching screws, then remove cluster lens.
5. To remove speedometer, remove two speedometer retaining screws. Disconnect speedometer cable and wire connector, then lift speedometer from instrument cluster.
6. To replace fuel gauge or clock, remove attaching screws, then slide gauge or clock from cluster and disconnect wire connector.

1983 REGAL

1. Disconnect ground cable from battery and speedometer cable from transmission or cruise control transducer.
2. Remove headlamp switch knob and pull knob from rear defogger switch, if equipped.
3. Remove left (cluster) bezel, grasping bezel with both hands and pulling it straight away from instrument panel.
4. Remove 5 screws securing cluster lense, trip odometer knob and the lense assembly.
5. Remove clock and fuel gauge.
6. Remove speedometer retaining screws and withdraw speedometer just enough to gain access to Vehicle Speed Sensor (VSS).
7. Disconnect speedometer cable, remove screw securing VSS optic head, then withdraw speedometer head from cluster.
8. Remove steering column cover, then disconnect shift indicator cable from steering column.
9. Remove 4 cluster retaining screws and the cluster.
10. Reverse procedure to install.

1984–86 REGAL

1. Disconnect ground cable from battery and speedometer cable from transmission or cruise control transducer.

2. Place gear selector lever in low and lower tilt wheel if equipped, then grasp left (cluster) trim bezel with both hands and pull bezel straight away from instrument panel.
3. Remove steering column lower cover, then disconnect shift indicator cable from steering column.
4. Remove 2 nuts securing column bracket, then lower steering column.
5. Remove 4 cluster retaining screws, then disconnect speedometer cable and any "hard wired" bulb sockets from cluster.
6. Pull cluster away from instrument panel just enough to gain access to Vehicle Speed Sensor (VSS), then remove screw securing VSS optic head to speedometer.
7. On models with digital cluster, release harness connector, then disconnect connector from cluster and remove screw securing cluster ground strap.
8. On all models, remove cluster.
9. Reverse procedure to install.

1980–86 FULL SIZE EXC. RIVIERA

NOTE: On these models, the speedometer and fuel gauge are removed from the instrument panel carrier as separate assemblies

W/S WIPER MOTOR REPLACE

1. Disconnect battery and remove cowl screen.
2. Loosen nuts on wiper drive link to motor cranking arm and slip drive link off cranking arm.
3. Disconnect washer hoses and electrical connections.
4. Unfasten motor and remove.

NOTE: On models with round motor, the motor must be in "Park" position when assembling crank arm to transmission drive link.

W/S WIPER TRANSMISSION
REPLACE

1. Disconnect battery ground cable and remove cowl vent screen or grille.
2. Disconnect wiper motor electrical connector.
3. Remove wiper arm and blade assemblies.
4. Loosen transmission drive link to motor crank arm attaching nuts, then disconnect drive link from crank arm.
5. Remove right and left transmission to body retaining screws and guide transmission and linkage through cowl opening.

NOTE: On full size models equipped with round motor, remove transmission retaining screws from transmission being removed.

6. Reverse procedure to install.

W/S WIPER SWITCH
REPLACE

MODELS W/COLUMN MOUNTED SWITCH

1. Remove steering wheel as described under "Horn Sounder and Steering Wheel, Replace."
2. Remove turn signal switch as described under "Turn Signal Switch, Replace."
3. Remove ignition lock and buzzer as described under "Ignition Lock, Replace."
4. Remove and install cover and wiper switch as shown in **Figs. 13 & 14.**
5. Reverse remaining procedure to install.

1980-81 RIVIERA

1. Disconnect battery ground cable.
2. Remove left hand trim cover, **Fig. 12.**
3. Remove two switch to cluster attaching screws.
4. Pull switch rearward and remove.

1980-81 CENTURY & 1980-82 REGAL

1. Remove headlamp switch knob and escutcheon.
2. Remove trim plate.
3. Remove two switch attaching screws, then disconnect wire connector and remove switch.
4. Reverse procedure to install.

1980-81 FULL SIZE EXC. RIVIERA

1. Remove left trim plate.
2. Remove switch attaching screws.
3. Disconnect electrical connector from switch and remove switch from vehi-

Fig. 17 Heater module assembly exploded view. 1980-81 Century & 1980-86 Regal with A/C

cle.
4. Reverse procedure to install.

RADIO
REPLACE

NOTE: When installing radio, be sure to adjust antenna trimmer for peak performance.

1981-85 RIVIERA

1. Disconnect battery ground cable.
2. Remove center trim plate by grasping firmly and pulling rearward.
3. Remove six screws from radio mounting bracket.
4. Remove six screws from instrument panel lower cover assembly, then pull cover assembly out from instrument panel enough to gain access to two screws attaching radio bracket to instrument panel lower tie bar. Remove screws.
5. Carefully pull radio assembly rearward

to remove.
6. Disconnect radio harness connectors and antenna lead.
7. Reverse procedure to install.

1980 RIVIERA

1. Disconnect battery ground cable.
2. Remove center trim cover.
3. Remove four screws attaching radio mounting plate to instrument panel.
4. Disconnect radio wire connector and antenna lead.
5. Pull radio and mounting plate rearward and remove radio.

1980-81 CENTURY & 1980-86 REGAL

1. Disconnect battery ground cable.
2. Remove cigar lighter, then the radio control knobs and escutcheons, as needed.
3. Remove center trim plate by grasping firmly and pulling rearward.

NOTE: A flat blade screwdriver or putty

Fig. 18 Heater module assembly exploded view. 1980-86 Full Size exc. Riviera & models with A/C

knife can be used to pry up a corner of the center trim plate to aid in removal.

4. Remove four screws attaching radio bracket to instrument panel.
5. Open glove box door and release spring retainers, then allow door to open fully.
6. Working through glove box door, loosen holding bracket nut on right rear side of radio, then remove antenna lead.
7. Carefully pull radio assembly rearward to remove.
8. Disconnect radio harness connectors, then remove bracket.
9. Reverse procedure to install.

1981-86 FULL SIZE EXC. RIVIERA

1. Disconnect battery ground cable.
2. Remove radio knobs, escutcheons and if equipped with rear defogger, rear defogger knob.
3. Remove left hand instrument panel trim plate by removing headlight knob, then place gear selector in low. Using a suitable flat bladed screwdriver or putty knife, remove trim plate by gently prying edge, then lifting straight out.
4. Remove center trim plate attaching screws, then trim plate.
5. Remove screws attaching radio to radio bracket, then carefully pull radio rearward out of instrument panel.

Fig. 19 Heater module assembly exploded view. 1980–86 Full Size with A/C exc. Riviera

6. Disconnect radio harness connectors and antenna lead.
7. Reverse procedure to install.

1980 FULL SIZE EXC. RIVIERA

1. Disconnect battery ground cable.
2. Remove ash tray and bracket.

3. Remove radio knobs and escutcheons from shafts.
4. Remove lower left-hand air duct.
5. Remove retaining nuts from radio control shafts.
6. Disconnect electrical connections from radio.
7. Remove rear radio attaching nut, then the radio from vehicle.
8. Reverse procedure to install.

HEATER CORE
REPLACE

1980–85 RIVIERA

1. Disconnect battery ground cable and drain cooling system.
2. Disconnect heater hoses from heater core and install plugs in heater core

outlets.

3. Remove instrument panel sound absorbers, then lower steering column.
4. Remove instrument cluster as described under Instrument Cluster, Replace.
5. Remove radio front speakers.
6. Remove screws attaching manifold to heater case.
7. Remove upper and lower instrument panel attaching screws.
8. Disconnect parking brake release cable.
9. Disconnect instrument panel wiring harness from dash wiring harness.
10. Disconnect right hand remote control mirror cable from instrument panel pad.
11. Disconnect speedometer cable and temperate control cable at heater case.
12. Disconnect radio, A/C wiring and vacuum lines, and all wiring necessary to remove instrument panel assembly. If equipped with pulse wiper, remove wiper switch, unlock wire connector from cluster carrier and separate pulse wiper jumper harness from wiper switch wire connector.
13. Remove instrument panel and harness assembly.
14. Remove defroster ducts, then remove blower motor resistor.
15. Remove A/C-heater housing to dash panel nuts, **Fig. 15.**
16. Remove housing to dash screw and clip from inside vehicle, then remove housing assembly from dash.
17. Remove heater core from housing assembly.

1980–81 CENTURY & 1980–86 REGAL

Without Air Conditioning
1. Disconnect battery ground cable and partially drain cooling system.
2. Disconnect hoses from heater core, then the electrical connectors.
3. Remove front module retaining screws and module cover.
4. Remove heater core, **Fig. 16.**
5. Reverse procedure to install.

With Air Conditioning
1. Disconnect battery ground cable and partially drain cooling system.
2. Disconnect hoses from heater core, then the electrical connectors from module.
3. Remove retaining bracket, ground strap, module rubber seal and screen.
4. Remove right hand windshield wiper arm.
5. Remove retaining screws from diagnostic connector, hi-blower relay and thermostatic switch.

6. Remove module top cover, then heater core, **Fig. 17.**
7. Reverse procedure to install.

1980–86 FULL SIZE EXC. RIVIERA

Without Air Conditioning
1. Disconnect battery ground cable and drain radiator.
2. Disconnect heater hoses from module, then the electrical connections from module front case.
3. Remove module front case attaching screws, then the heater core, **Fig. 18.**
4. Reverse procedure to install.

With Air Conditioning
1. Disconnect battery ground cable and drain radiator.
2. Disconnect heater hoses from module.
3. Remove diagnostic connector and thermostatic switch from module.
4. Remove weather seal from top of module cover, then the cowl screen and windshield washer nozzle.
5. Remove module cover attaching screws.
6. Remove heater core retaining clip and the heater core from vehicle, **Fig. 19.**
7. Reverse procedure to install.

BLOWER MOTOR
REPLACE

RIVIERA
1. Disconnect battery ground cable.
2. Remove right fender skirt to provide clearance for blower motor removal.
3. Disconnect wire connector and cooling hose.
4. Remove blower motor attaching screws and blower motor.

EXC. RIVIERA
1. Disconnect blower motor wiring.
2. Remove blower motor attaching screws and the blower motor, **Figs. 16, 17, 18 and 19.**

SPEED CONTROL
POWER UNIT, ADJUST

Units With Bead Chain
1. Make sure that engine hot idle speed is properly adjusted, then shut off engine and set carburetor choke to hot idle position.
2. Check slack in chain by disconnecting swivel from ball stud and holding chain

taut at ball stud. Center of swivel should extend ⅛ inch beyond center of ball stud.
3. To adjust bead chain slack, remove retainer from swivel and chain assembly, then place chain into swivel cavities which permits chain to have slight slack.
4. Install retainer over swivel and chain assembly.

Units With Servo Rod
1. Make sure that engine hot idle speed is properly adjusted, then shut off engine and set carburetor choke to hot idle position.
2. Remove servo rod retainer, then adjust rod and install retainer in hole which provides some clearance between retainer and servo bushing. Clearance must not exceed width of one hole.

Units With Cable
1. Make sure that engine hot idle speed is properly adjusted, then shut off engine and set carburetor choke to hot idle position.
2. Remove cable pin retainer, then pull power unit end of cable toward power unit as far as it will go. If one of four holes in power unit tab aligns with cable pin, connect pin to tab with retainer.
3. If tab does not align with pin, move cable away from power unit until next closest tab hole aligns and connect pin to tab with retainer.

CAUTION: Do not force cable to make adjustment, as this will prevent engine from returning to idle.

CRUISE SPEED ADJUSTMENT

1980–82
The cruise speed adjustment can be set as follows:
1. If car cruises below engagement speed, screw orifice tube on transducer outward.
2. If car cruises above engagement speed, screw orifice tube inward.

NOTE: Each ¼ turn of the orifice tube will change cruise speed about one mile per hour. Snug up lock nut after each adjustment.

BRAKE RELEASE SWITCH ADJUSTMENT

Fully depress brake pedal, then push switch and valve forward to contact bracket or arm. Pull pedal rearward with approximately 15 to 20 pounds of force to adjust switch and valve properly.

Gasoline Engine Section

NOTE: For service procedures see Chevrolet Chapter for V8-305 and V8-350 with the distributor located at the rear of engine, clockwise distributor rotor rotation; Oldsmobile Chapter for V8-307 and V8-350 with distributor located at the rear of engine, counter clockwise distributor rotor rotation; Pontiac Chapter for V8-265 and V8-301.

Fig. 1 V6 engine mounts. Exc. Riviera

ENGINE MOUNTS
REPLACE

1. Raise car and provide frame support at front of car.
2. Support weight of engine at forward edge of pan.
3. Remove mount to engine block or frame bolts. Raise engine slightly and remove mount to mount bracket bolt and nut, **Figs. 1 through 3.** Remove mount.
4. Reverse above procedure to install.

ENGINE
REPLACE

1980–85 RIVIERA

1. Remove hood. Scribe alignment marks on hood around hinge areas for alignment during installation.
2. Disconnect battery ground cable and remove air cleaner.
3. Drain cooling system and disconnect heater hoses.
4. Remove fan, pulleys and belts.
5. Remove upper and lower radiator hoses and fan shroud.
6. Disconnect transmission cooler lines from radiator, then remove radiator.
7. Remove air conditioning compressor.
8. Disconnect all electrical wires and vacuum hoses.
9. On turbocharged engines:
   a. Disconnect accelerator cable at carburetor.
   b. Disconnect fuel pump lines and plug lines to prevent spilling fuel.
   c. Remove power steering pump mounting bolts and position pump assembly aside.
   d. Remove alternator, then disconnect engine to body ground straps.
   e. Disconnect turbocharger outlet

exhaust pipe from turbocharger.
10. On all except turbocharged engines:
    a. Disconnect accelerator rod and throttle valve cable.
    b. Disconnect fuel lines and plug lines to prevent spilling fuel.
    c. Remove power steering pump.
    d. Remove transmission cooler line bracket.
    e. Disconnect left exhaust pipe.
11. Raise and properly support vehicle.
12. Drain engine oil, then remove starter.
13. Remove converter shield, then the flywheel to converter bolts.
14. On all except turbocharged engines, disconnect right exhaust pipe and remove splash shield.
15. Remove the right transmission to engine bolts.
16. Remove right output shaft support bolts, then lower vehicle.
17. Support the final drive using a chain, then remove the remaining transmission to engine bolts.
18. Remove front motor mount support bolts.
19. Remove final drive to engine bracket.
20. Remove engine using a suitable hoist.
21. Reverse procedure to install.

EXC. 1980–85 RIVIERA

1. Remove hood and drain radiator.
2. Disconnect battery ground cable.
3. Remove fan shroud, radiator and air cleaner.
4. If equipped with A/C, disconnect compressor brackets and position out of way.
5. Remove power steering from bracket and position out of way.
6. Disconnect all hoses, linkages and electrical connections from engine.
7. Disconnect exhaust pipes and remove

1	ENGINE MOUNT	5	NUT 35 N·m (26 FT. LB.)
2	BRACKET	6	WASHER
3	WASHER	7	RETAINER
4	BOLT 90 N·m (66 FT. LB.)	8	NUT 90 N·m (66 FT. LB.)

Fig. 2 Engine mounts exploded view. Riviera

converter cover.
8. Remove flywheel to converter or pressure plate bolts, engine to transmission bolts and motor mount bolts.
9. Support transmission and remove engine.

CYLINDER HEAD
REPLACE

Prior to reinstalling the cylinder head bolts on V6 engines, coat the head bolts with a suitable heavy body thread sealer. This is to prevent coolant leakage, as the head bolt holes extend into the water jacket.

Fig. 3 Engine mounts. V8-350/X

Fig. 4 Cylinder head tightening sequence. V8-350/X

An accurate torque wrench should be used when installing head bolts. Uneven tightening of the head bolts can distort the cylinder bores, causing compression loss and excessive oil consumption.
1. Drain coolant and disconnect battery.
2. Remove intake manifold.

NOTE: On models equipped with V6 engine, remove distributor cap and rotor to gain access to left hand intake manifold torx head bolt. Use tool J-24394 to remove torx head bolt.

3. When removing right cylinder head, remove Delcotron and/or A/C compressor with mounting bracket and move out of the way. Do not disconnect hoses from A/C compressor.
4. When removing left cylinder head, remove oil dipstick and power steering pump, and secure pump aside leaving hoses connected.
5. Disconnect exhaust manifold from head to be removed.
6. Remove rocker arm shaft and lift out push rods.
7. Remove cylinder head.
8. Reverse procedure to install and tighten bolts gradually and evenly in the sequence shown in **Figs. 4 through 6.**

NOTE: When installing intake manifold, refer to **Figs. 7 and 8** for bolt tightening sequence.

ROCKER ARMS
V6-231 & 252; V8-350/X

A nylon retainer is used to retain the

rocker arm. Break them below their heads with a chisel, or pry out with channel locks, **Fig. 9.** Production rocker arms can be installed in any sequence since the arms are identical.

Replacement rocker arms for all engines are identified with a stamping, right (R) and left (L), **Fig. 10** and must be installed as shown in **Fig. 11.**

To install rocker arms, position arm on rocker shaft, centering it over the ¼ inch hole in the rocker shaft. Install new rocker arm retainers in the provided holes using a ½ inch or larger drift to seat them.

VALVE ARRANGEMENT
FRONT TO REAR

Engine	Arrangement
V6-231 & 252	E-I-I-E-I-E
V8-350/X	E-I-I-E-E-I-I-E

VALVE LIFT SPECS.

Engine	Year	Intake	Exhaust
V6-231①	1980-84	.3570	.3660
V6-231②	1980-81	.3410	.3660
V6-252	1980-84	.3570	.3660
V8-265	1980-81	.3570	.3660
V8-301	1980	.3570	.3660
	1981	.3500	.3500
V8-305	1980	.3727	.4100
V8-307	1981-86	.4000	.4000
V8-350③	1980	.3570	.3390
			.3660

① —Exc. turbo charged engine.
② —Turbo charged engine.
③ —Distributor located at front of engine.

VALVE TIMING
INTAKE OPENS BEFORE TDC

Engine	Year	Degrees
V6-231	1980-84	16
V6-252	1980-84	16
V8-265	1980	27
	1981	16
V8-301	1980	16
V8-305	1980	28
V8-307	1981	20
V8-350①	1980	16

① —Distributor located at front of engine.

VALVE GUIDES

SERVICE NOTE: Abnormal oil consumption or detonation on 1980-82 V6-252 engines may be caused by intake valve seals that have lifted off the valve guide. To correct this condition, a smaller replacement seal, Part No. 25516279, should be installed onto valve guide. Since valve guide outside diameter must be reduced from .605 to .552 to accept the new seal, it will be necessary to rework the valve guides prior to seal installation. Using

Fig. 5 Cylinder head tightening sequence. 1980-83 V6-231 & 252

Fig. 6 Cylinder bolt tightening sequence. 1984 V6-252 & 1984-86 V6-231

Fig. 7 Intake manifold tightening sequence. V8-350/X

Fig. 8   Intake manifold tightening sequence. V6-231 & 252

1 ROCKER ARM RETAINERS

Fig. 9   Rocker arm retainer removal. V6-231 & 252; V8-350/X

valve guide cutting tool KL1440, or equivalent, perform the following operation.

1. Remove cylinder head as outlined in "Cylinder Head, Replace" procedure.
2. Remove all intake and exhaust valves from cylinder head to prevent metal chips from lodging in exhaust guide mechanism.
3. Insert cutting tool into chuck of low speed drill, oil tool pilot, then insert pilot into intake valve guide.
4. Applying steady pressure to cutting tool, machine valve guide until small cutter block in tool has cut chamfer on top of valve guide.
5. Thoroughly clean cylinder head and guides, then remove any burrs from valve stem and guides with a fine stone.
6. Oil valves and install them into guides.
7. Install new seals onto valve guides, then reassemble cylinder head assembly.
8. Install cylinder head.

The valve guides are an integral part of the cylinder head and cannot be replaced.

If valve stem clearance is excessive, the valve guide must be reamed and an oversize valve installed. Valves are available in the oversize of .010 inch.

HYDRAULIC VALVE LIFTERS

Failure of hydraulic valve lifters, **Fig. 12**, is generally caused by an inadequate oil supply or dirt. An air leak at the intake side of the oil pump or too much oil in the engine will cause air bubbles in the oil supply to the lifters, causing them to collapse. This is a probable cause of trouble if several lifters fail to function, but air in the oil is an unlikely cause of failure of a single unit.

The valve lifters may be lifted out of their bores after removing the rocker arms, push rods and intake manifold. Adjustable pliers with taped jaws may be used to remove lifters that are stuck due to varnish, carbon, etc. **Fig. 12** illustrates the type of lifter used.

TIMING CASE COVER REPLACE

V6-231, 252 & V8-350/X

1. Drain cooling system and remove

radiator and heater return hose.
2. Remove fan, pulleys and belts.
3. Remove crankshaft pulley and balancer.
4. If equipped with power steering, remove any pump bracket bolts attached to timing chain cover and loosen and remove any other bolts necessary that will allow pump and brackets to be moved out of the way.
5. Remove fuel pump.
6. Remove Delcotron and brackets.
7. Remove distributor cap and pull spark plug wire retainers off brackets on rocker arm cover. Swing distributor cap with wires attached out of the way. Disconnect distributor primary lead.
8. Remove distributor. If chain and sprockets are not to be disturbed, note position of distributor rotor for installation in the same position.
9. Loosen and slide clamp on thermostat by-pass hose rearward.
10. Remove bolts attaching chain cover to block.
11. Remove two oil pan-to-chain cover bolts and remove cover.
12. Reverse procedure to install, noting data shown in **Figs. 13 and 14.**

RIGHT AND LEFT MARKING

Fig. 10   Service rocker arm identification. V6-231 & 252; V8-350/X

Fig. 11   Service rocker arms installation. V6-231 & 252; V8-350/X

Fig. 12 Hydraulic valve lifter parts exploded view

IMPORTANT: Remove the oil pump cover and pack the space around the oil pump gears completely full of vaseline. There must be no air space left inside the pump. Reinstall the cover using a new gasket. This step is very important as the oil pump may lose its prime whenever the pump, pump cover or timing chain cover is disturbed. If the pump is not packed it may not begin to pump oil as soon as the engine is started.

TIMING CHAIN
REPLACE

V6-231, 252 & V8-350/X

1. With the timing case cover removed as outlined above, temporarily install the vibration damper bolt and washer in end of crankshaft.
2. Turn crankshaft so sprockets are positioned as shown in **Fig. 15.** Use a sharp rap on a wrench handle to start the vibration damper bolt out without disturbing the position of the sprockets.
3. Remove oil slinger.
4. Remove distributor drive gear and fuel pump eccentric.
6. Use two large screwdrivers to alternately pry the camshaft sprocket then the crankshaft sprocket forward until the camshaft sprocket is free. Then

Fig. 13 Timing chain cover installation. V6-231 & 252

remove camshaft sprocket and chain, and crankshaft sprocket off crankshaft.
7. To install, assemble chain on sprockets and slide sprockets on their respective shafts with the "O" marks on the sprockets lined up as shown.
8. Complete the installation in the reverse order of removal.

CAMSHAFT
REPLACE

NOTE: If engine is in the car, the radiator, grille and A/C components will have to be removed. If engine is out of car, proceed as follows:

1. To remove camshaft, remove intake manifold, rocker arm/shaft assemblies, push rods and valve lifters.
2. Remove timing chain and sprockets.
3. Slide camshaft out of engine, using care not to mar the bearing surfaces.

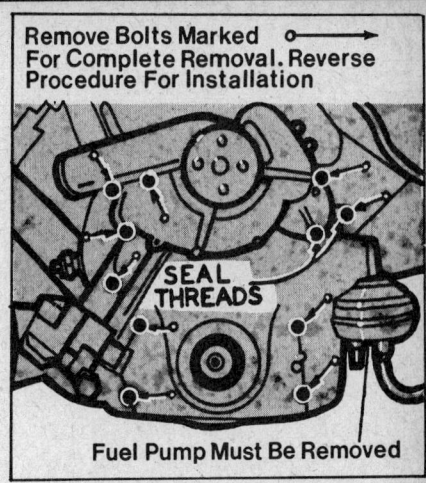

Fig. 14 Timing chain cover installation. V8-350/X

PISTONS & RODS
ASSEMBLE

SERVICE NOTE: Some 1980–82 V6-231 (Vin A) and V6-252 engines may exhibit engine noise just above idle with transmission in gear. The noise can best be described as a light ticking sound, similar to overhead valve noise, but appears to come from the bottom portion of the engine and is most pronounced at the rear of the front wheel opening. This noise may be caused by excessive side clearance between the connecting rod and the crankshaft journal thrust surfaces on the number one, three or five cylinder. The clearance should be checked using a dial indicator or feeler gauge. If a feeler gauge is used, the gauge should be placed next to the thrust surface on the counterweight and not next to the thin wall section between two adjacent rods. Make sure the feeler gauge is fully seated on the journal and not on top of the narrow raised thrust surface. Clearance measurements should be made at several places around the journal. If rod clearance exceeds .015 inch on the above mentioned cylinders, the rod should be replaced. A new rod, Part No. 25516444, is available which is .010 inch thicker than

Fig. 15 Valve timing mark alignment. V6-231 & 252; V8-350/X

Fig. 16 Piston and connecting rod installation. V6-231 & 252

Fig. 17 Piston and connecting rod installation. V8-350/X

Fig. 18 Connecting rod and main bearing insert identification

Fig. 19 Oil pump cover and relief valve exploded view

CHECK CLEARANCE BETWEEN STRAIGHT EDGE & GASKET SURFACE SHOULD BE BETWEEN .002" & .006"

Fig. 20 Checking oil pump gear and cover clearance

the original. The new rod will reduce the clearance to the low side of the specified limits.

Rods and pistons should be assembled and installed as shown in **Figs. 16 and 17.**

Measure connecting rod side clearance using a suitable feeler gauge. Clearance obtained should be .006–.023 for 1980–84, or .003–.015 inch for 1985–86.

PISTONS, PINS & RINGS

Pistons are available in standard sizes and oversizes of .005, .010 and .030 inch.

Rings are furnished in standard sizes and oversizes of .010 and .030 inch.

Piston pins are supplied in standard sizes only.

OIL PAN
REPLACE

V6-231 & 252

Exc. 1981–85 Riviera
1. Raise and support front of vehicle.
2. Remove flywheel cover and exhaust crossover pipe. On 1982–86 models, raise engine with a suitable lifting device to gain clearance.
3. Drain engine oil into a suitable container.
4. Remove oil pan bolts, then pan.
5. Reverse procedure to install.

NOTE: Some engines use R.T.V. silicone

sealer instead of a cork gasket for oil pan to crankcase sealing. When replacing the oil pan or sealing material on these engines, either R.T.V. sealer or a cork gasket can be used during reassembly. If R.T.V. sealer is used, the pan rail and block sealing surfaces should be cleaned thoroughly and a ¼ inch bead of sealant applied evenly to the pan rail, avoiding any breaks or gaps in the sealer during application.

1981–85 Riviera
1. Disconnect battery ground cable.
2. Remove one final drive to transmission bolts.
3. Install suitable engine support fixture.
4. Raise and support vehicle.
5. Remove idler arm bracket from frame, then position steering wheel at left lock.
6. Disconnect drive axles from output shafts, then battery cable support from output shaft support.
7. Disconnect output shaft support from engine block.
8. Remove remaining final drive to transmission bolts.
9. Position suitable transmission jack under final drive, then remove final drive cover and final drive unit.
10. Remove starter, then flywheel cover.
11. Remove oil pan bolts, then oil pan.
12. Reverse procedure to install.

NOTE: Some engines use R.T.V. silicone sealer instead of a cork gasket for oil pan to crankcase sealing. When replacing the oil pan or sealing material on these engines, either R.T.V. sealer or a cork gasket can be used during reassembly. If R.T.V. sealer is used, the pan rail and block sealing surfaces should be cleaned thoroughly and a ¼ inch bead of sealant applied evenly to the pan rail, avoiding any breaks or gaps in the sealer during application.

1980 V8-350
1. Disconnect battery and drain oil.
2. Remove fan shroud to radiator tie bar screws.
3. Remove air cleaner and disconnect linkage to throttle.
4. Raise and support car on stands.
5. With manual transmission, loosen clutch equalizer bracket to frame bolts. Disconnect crossover pipe at engine.

Fig. 21 Typical turbocharger assembly exploded view

Fig. 22   Turbocharger system schematic. V6-231

Engine lubrication system. V8-350

6. With automatic transmission, remove lower flywheel housing. Remove shift linkage attaching bolt and swing out of way. Disconnect crossover pipe at engine. Disconnect idler arm at frame and push steering linkage forward to crossmember. Remove front engine mount bolts and raise engine by placing jack under crankshaft pulley mounting.

NOTE: If car is air conditioned, at this point it will be necessary to place a support under right side of transmission prior to raising engine to prevent transmission from cocking to the right when raised.

7. Remove oil pan. It may be necessary to position crankshaft so 1 and 2 crankpin and counterweight will not interfere with front of pan.

MAIN & ROD BEARINGS

Main bearings are available in standard sizes and undersizes of .001, .002, and .010 inch.

Rod bearings are furnished in standard sizes and undersizes of .001, .002 and .010 inch, **Fig. 18.**

CRANKSHAFT OIL SEAL REPAIR

Since the braided fabric seal used on these engines can be replaced only when the crankshaft is removed, the following repair procedure is recommended.
1. Remove oil pan and bearing cap.
2. Drive end of old seal gently into groove, using a suitable tool, until packed tight. This may vary between ¼ and ¾ inch depending on amount of pack required.
3. Repeat previous step for other end of seal.

4. Measure and note amount that seal was driven up on one side. Using the old seal removed from bearing cap, cut a length of seal the amount previously noted plus ¹⁄₁₆ inch.
5. Repeat previous step for other side of seal.
6. Pack cut lengths of seal into appropriate side of seal groove. A guide tool, J-21526-1, and packing tool, J-21526-2, may be used since these tools have been machined to provide a built-in stop.
7. Install new seal in bearing cap.
8. Apply thin coat of suitable sealer to block contact surfaces of bearing cap, then install cap and torque bolts to specifications.

OIL PUMP
REMOVAL

1. To remove pump, take off oil filter.
2. Disconnect wire from oil pressure indicator switch in filter by-pass valve cap (if so equipped).
3. Remove screws attaching oil pump cover to timing chain cover. Remove cover and slide out pump gears. Replace any parts not serviceable.
4. Check relief valve in its bore in cover. Valve should have no more clearance than an easy slip fit. If any perceptible side shake can be felt, the valve and/or cover should be replaced.
5. The filter by-pass valve should be flat and free of nicks and scratches.

ASSEMBLY & INSTALLATION

1. Lubricate and install pressure relief valve and spring in bore of pump cover. Install cap and gasket. Torque cap to 30-35 ft. lbs.
2. Install pump gears and shaft in pump body section of timing chain cover to check gear end clearance. Check

clearance as shown in **Fig. 20.** If clearance is less than .002 inch, check timing chain cover for evidence of wear.
3. If gear end clearance is satisfactory, remove gears and pack gear pocket full of petroleum jelly, not chassis lube.
4. Reinstall gears so petroleum jelly is forced into every cavity of gear pocket and between teeth of gears. Unless pump is properly packed, it may not prime when engine is started.
5. Install cover and tighten screws alternately and evenly. Final tightening is 10-15 ft-lbs. torque. Install filter on nipple.

BELT TENSION DATA

1980-86—	New lbs.	Used lbs.
⁵⁄₁₆ in.	80	50
³⁄₈ in. exc. cogged belt	140	70
³⁄₈ in. cogged belt		60
¹⁵⁄₃₂ in.	165	90

WATER PUMP
REPLACE

Drain cooling system, being sure to drain into a clean container if antifreeze solution is to be saved. Remove the fan belt and disconnect all hoses from water pump. Remove water pump.

FUEL PUMP
REPLACE

ELECTRIC PUMP

CAUTION: The fuel system on models with fuel injected engines is under high pressure, which must be relieved prior to opening the system. To relieve system pressure: remove "Fuel Pump" fuse from fuse block, start and run engine until fuel remaining in lines is consumed, crank engine for approximately 3 seconds to ensure complete pressure relief, then turn off ignition and reinstall fuse.

1. Disconnect battery ground cable.
2. Raise and support vehicle.

NOTE: If vehicle is raised on center post type hoist, place suitable supports under front of vehicle to aid stability when fuel tank is removed.

3. Support fuel tank, then remove retaining straps and screw securing ground strap to chassis.
4. Lower tank, disconnect fuel and vapor lines and electrical connectors from sending unit, then remove tank from under vehicle.
5. Release cam lock retainer securing sending unit using a J-24187 or equivalent, then withdraw sending unit/pump assembly from tank.
6. Slide pump up into connector hose and separate pump from bottom retainer.
7. When pump clears bottom retainer, pull pump from connecting hose to remove.
8. Reverse procedure to install.

MECHANICAL PUMP

NOTE: Before installing the pump, it is good practice to crank the engine so that the nose of the camshaft eccentric is out of the way of the fuel pump rocker arm when the pump is installed. In this way there will be the least amount of tension on the rocker arm, thereby easing the installation of the pump.

1. Disconnect fuel lines from fuel pump.

2. Remove fuel pump mounting bolts and the fuel pump.
3. Remove all gasket material from the pump and block gasket surfaces. Apply sealer to both sides of new gasket.
4. Position gasket on pump flange and hold pump in position against its mounting surface. Make sure rocker arm is riding on camshaft eccentric.
5. Press pump tight against its mounting. Install retaining screws and tighten them alternately.
6. Connect fuel lines. Then operate engine and check for leaks.

TURBOCHARGER

The turbocharger, **Fig. 21,** is used to increase engine power on a demand basis, therefore allowing a smaller, more economical engine to be used. The turbocharged V6-231 is available with either two or four barrel carburetion on 1980-83 models and with sequential port fuel injection on 1984-86 models.

As engine load increases and the throttle opens, more air-fuel mixture is drawn into the combustion chambers. As the increased volume is burned, a larger volume of high energy exhaust gasses enters the engine exhaust system and is directed through the turbocharger turbine housing, **Fig. 22.** Some of the exhaust gas energy is used to increase the speed of the turbine wheel which is connected to the compressor wheel. The increased speed of the compressor wheel compresses the air-fuel mixture and delivers the compressed air-fuel mixture to the intake manifold, **Fig. 22.** The high pressure in the intake manifold allows a denser charge to enter the combustion chambers, in turn developing more engine power during the combustion cycle.

The intake manifold pressure (Boost) is controlled to a maximum value by an exhaust gas bypass valve (Wastegate). The wastegate allows a portion of the exhaust gas to bypass the turbine wheel, thereby not increasing turbine speed. On 1980-83 models, the wastegate is operated by a spring loaded diaphragm device sensing the pressure differential across the compressor. When intake manifold pressure reaches a set value above ambient pressure, the wastegate begins to bypass the exhaust gas. On 1984-86 models, an electronic wastegate is used. In this system, a pulse width modulated solenoid has been positioned between the manifold and wastegate diaphragm. Information regarding air flow, engine RPM, transmission gear and detonation is collected and analyzed by the Electronic Control Module. If the engine will tolerate additional boost, the solenoid signals the wastegate accordingly. Inside the wastegate, the exhaust divert valve is normally closed, allowing boost pressure to rise until the mass air flow called for by the ECM is satisfied. When air flow reaches this level, the exhaust divert valve opens, allowing the exhaust gas to divert around the turbine and flow directly into the exhaust system.

NOTE: Engine oil on 1980-81 turbocharged engines must be changed every 3000 miles, otherwise, turbocharger bearing damage may occur from oil contamination. On 1982-86 turbocharged engines the recommended oil and oil filter change interval is every 7500 miles or 12 months, whichever comes first. This change is due to increased oil capacity, a higher output oil pump and a revised turbocharger oil passage.

Diesel Engine Section

REFER TO THE OLDSMOBILE CHAPTER FOR SERVICE PROCEDURES ON THE V6-262 & V8-350 DIESEL ENGINES, NOT FOUND IN THIS SECTION.

ENGINE
REPLACE

V8-350 ENGINE
Exc. Riviera
1. Disconnect ground cable from batteries and drain cooling system.
2. Remove air cleaner.
3. Scribe hood hinge locations and remove hood.
4. Disconnect ground wires at inner fender and the engine ground strap at right cylinder head.
5. Disconnect radiator hoses, oil cooler

lines, heater hoses, vacuum hoses, power steering hoses from gear, A/C compressor with brackets and hoses attached, fuel pump hose from fuel pump and the wiring.
6. Remove hairpin clip from bellcrank.
7. Remove throttle and throttle valve cables from intake manifold brackets and position cables aside.
8. Remove upper radiator support and the radiator.
9. Raise and support vehicle.
10. Disconnect exhaust pipes from exhaust manifold.
11. Remove torque converter cover and

the three bolts securing torque converter to flywheel.
12. Remove engine mount bolts or nuts.
13. Remove three engine to transmission bolts on the right side.
14. Disconnect starter wiring and remove starter.
15. Lower vehicle.
16. Attach suitable engine lifting equipment to engine. Support transmission with a suitable jack.
17. Remove the three engine to transmission bolts on the left side.
18. Remove engine from vehicle.
19. Reverse procedure to install.

Riviera

1. Disconnect battery ground cable and drain cooling system.
2. Remove radiator upper support.
3. Remove air cleaner assembly.
4. Scribe hood hinge locations and remove hood.
5. Disconnect engine ground strap.
6. Disconnect upper and lower radiator hoses from engine.
7. Disconnect transmission oil cooler lines from radiator.
8. Disconnect heater hoses from water pump and water control valve.
9. Remove radiator, fan and the shroud.
10. Disconnect power steering pump bracket from engine and position aside without disconnecting lines.
11. Disconnect A/C compressor bracket from engine and position aside without disconnecting lines.
12. Disconnect fuel lines.
13. Disconnect throttle cable, vacuum hoses and electrical connections.
14. Disconnect left hand exhaust pipe from manifold.
15. On left side of engine, remove through bolt and bracket securing final drive to engine.
16. Raise and support engine.
17. Remove flywheel shield.
18. Disconnect right hand exhaust pipe from manifold.
19. Disconnect starter motor wiring and remove starter motor.
20. Remove converter to flywheel bolts. Mark location of converter on flywheel for alignment during installation.
21. Remove splash shield.
22. Remove engine front mounting attaching nuts.
23. Remove two bolts securing right hand output shaft support brackets. Using a sharp tool, scribe a mark around the washers as far as possible. Use these scribe marks to position bracket upon installation.
24. Remove lower right hand transmission to engine attaching bolts. One bolt retains the modulator line clip.
25. Use a suitable length of chain to retain final drive in vehicle.
26. Lower vehicle and attach suitable engine lifting equipment to engine.
27. Remove the remaining transmission to engine bolts. It may be necessary to raise or lower transmission with a suitable jack to facilitate bolt removal.
28. Raise engine and remove from vehicle.
29. Reverse procedure to install.

V6-262 ENGINE

1. Disconnect battery ground cable and drain cooling system.
2. Scribe reference marks, then remove hood from vehicle.
3. Disconnect all hoses, lines and electrical connectors from engine.

NOTE: Do not disconnect wires from the starter.

4. Disconnect throttle cable, transmission T.V. or detent cable at injection pump and engine brackets.
5. Remove upper radiator support and radiator from vehicle.
6. Raise and support vehicle.
7. Disconnect exhaust pipes at exhaust manifold.
8. Remove torque converter flywheel cover and three torque converter to flywheel bolts.
9. Remove starter and two engine mount bolts.
10. From the right side of the vehicle, remove three engine to transmission bolts.
11. Lower vehicle and position suitable lifting equipment onto engine.
12. Using a suitable jack, raise transmission enough to gain access to the other three transmission to engine bolts. Remove bolts and lift engine from vehicle.
13. Reverse procedure to install. Torque flywheel to torque converter bolts to 35 ft. lbs. Torque two engine mount bolts to 55 ft. lbs.

Clutch & Manual Transmission Section

CLUTCH PEDAL
ADJUST

1. Disconnect return spring from clutch fork.
2. Rotate clutch lever and shaft assembly until pedal is against rubber bumper on dash brace.
3. Push outer end of clutch fork rearward until throwout bearing lightly contacts pressure plate fingers.
4. Install lower push rod in gauge hole and increase length until all lash is removed.
5. Install swivel or rod in hole furthest from centerline of lever and shaft assembly, then install retainer.
6. Tighten lock nut and spacer against swivel and connect clutch fork return spring.
7. Check clutch pedal free travel. Free play should be 45/64 to 1 5/16 inch.

CLUTCH
REPLACE

1. Remove transmission.
2. Remove pedal return spring from clutch fork and disconnect rod assembly from clutch fork.
3. Remove flywheel housing.
4. Remove clutch throw-out bearing from clutch fork.
5. Disconnect clutch fork from ball stud by moving it toward center of flywheel housing.
6. Mark clutch cover and flywheel so it can be installed in the same position.
7. Loosen clutch cover to flywheel bolts one turn at a time to avoid bending of clutch cover flange until spring pressure is released.
8. Support pressure place and cover assembly while removing last bolts, then remove pressure plate and driven plate.
9. Reverse procedure to install being sure to line up marks made in removal.

3 SPEED TRANS.
REPLACE

1. Disconnect speedometer cable from driven gear fitting.
2. Disconnect shift control rods from shifter levers at transmission.
3. Remove propeller shaft.
4. Support rear of engine and remove transmission crossmember.
5. Remove two top transmission attaching bolts and insert guide pins in these holes.
6. Remove two lower bolts and slide transmission straight back and out of vehicle.
7. Reverse procedure to install.

3 SPEED TRANS.
SHIFT LINKAGE

Column Shift

1. Place column selector lever in Reverse detent, making sure the steering column selector plate engages lower most column lever (1st-reverse).
2. Loosen 1st-reverse adjusting clamp.
3. Shift transmission lever into reverse and tighten the 1st-reverse clamp.
4. Shift transmission levers into neutral and loosen 2nd-3rd clamp.
5. Install 3/16 inch diameter rod through 2nd-3rd lever selector plate and the 1st-reverse lever and alignment plate.
6. Tighten 2nd-3rd shift rod clamp.

Floor Shift

1. Place transmission levers in Neutral.
2. Loosen shift rod adjusting clamp bolts on shifter assembly.

3. Insert ¼ inch drill rod through shift assembly and shift levers.
4. Tighten clamp bolts.

4 SPEED TRANS.
REPLACE

1. Disconnect speedometer cable and remove driven gear.
2. Disconnect shift control rods from transmission.
3. Remove propeller shaft.
4. Support rear of engine and remove transmission support.
5. Remove two top transmission-to-flywheel housing bolts and insert guide pins.
6. Remove two lower bolts.
7. Slide transmission back and out.
8. Reverse procedure to install.

4 SPEED TRANS.
SHIFT LINKAGE

Floor Shift
1. Place transmission in neutral.
2. Adjust all three shift rods so a ¼ inch drill rod can be installed through shifter assembly and shift levers.
3. Tighten swivel nuts.

Rear Axle, Propeller Shaft & Brakes

REAR AXLES

Fig. 1 illustrates the type rear drive axle assembly used on Buicks. When necessary to overhaul any of these units, refer to the Rear Axle Specifications table in this chapter.

In this rear axle, Fig. 1, the drive pinion is mounted in two tapered roller bearings which are preloaded by a collapsible spacer. The pinion is positioned by shims located between a shoulder on the drive pinion and the rear bearing. The front bearing is held in place by a large nut.

The differential is supported in the carrier by two tapered roller side bearings. These are preloaded by inserting shims between the bearings and the pedestals. The differential assembly is positioned for proper ring gear and pinion backlash by varying these shims. The ring gear is bolted to the case. The case houses two side gears in mesh with two pinions mounted on a pinion axle which is anchored in the case by a spring pin. The pinions and side gears are backed by thrust washers.

REAR AXLE
ASSEMBLY
REPLACE

It is not necessary to remove the rear axle assembly for any normal repairs but if the housing must be replaced the assembly may be removed as follows:
1. Raise vehicle and support using jack stands under both frame side rails.
2. Mark rear universal joint and flange for

Fig. 1   Differential assembly cross-sectional view

Fig. 2 Rear wheel bearing. Riviera w/rear disc brakes

Fig. 3 Rear wheel bearing. Riviera w/rear drum brakes

proper reassembly and disconnect rear joint.
3. Push propeller shaft as far forward as possible and wire up out of way.
4. Disconnect parking brake cables and rear brake hose. Cover brake hose opening to prevent entrance of dirt.
5. Support axle with jack and disconnect shock absorbers at lower ends.
6. Disconnect upper control arms at axle housing, then lower axle and remove coil springs.
7. Disconnect lower control arms and remove axle assembly.

AXLE SHAFT
REPLACE

NOTE: Design allows for axle shaft end play of .025 inch on "C", "G", "K", "O" and "P" (7½ inch) axles, and .032 inch on "P" (except 7½ inch). These axles may be identified by the third letter located on the right rear tube on the forward side. This end play can be checked with the wheel and brake drum removed by measuring the difference between the end of the housing and the axle shaft flange while moving the axle shaft in and out by hand.

End play over this is excessive. Compensating for all the end play by inserting a shim inboard of the bearing in the housing is not recommended since it ignores the end play of the bearing itself, and may result in improper seating of the gasket or backing plate against the housing. If end play is excessive, the axle shaft and bearing assembly should be removed and the cause of the excessive end play determined and corrected.

REMOVING AXLE SHAFT

1. Remove wheels and brake drums.
2. Remove bolts and differential cover and allow lubricant to drain.
3. Remove pinion shaft lock bolt and pinion shaft then push axle shafts inward, remove C-lock and axle shaft.

REPLACING AXLE SHAFT BEARINGS & SEALS

1. Using a suitable pry bar, remove seal from housing.

NOTE: Do not damage axle housing.

2. Position tool No. J-23689 behind bearing bore so tangs on tool engage bearing outer race, then using a suitable slide hammer attached to tool No. J-23689, remove bearing.
3. Using suitable gear lubricant, lubricate bearing. Then, using axle bearing installer J-23690, install bearing. Bearing is properly seated when tool bottoms against housing shoulder.
4. Lubricate seal with suitable gear lubricant, then using seal installer J-21128, tap seal into position until seal is flush with axle tube.
5. Install axle.

AXLE SHAFT, INSTALL

1. Apply a coat of wheel bearing grease in wheel bearing and seal recess.
2. Install axle shaft through seal and bearing and through side gear as far in as possible.

NOTE: Do not let shaft drag across seal lip and apply grease between seal lips.

3. Install C-lock and move axle shaft outward to bottom C-lock in recess of side gear.
4. Install pinion shaft and torque lock bolt to 20 ft. lbs.
5. Install gasket and cover and torque bolts to 30 ft. lbs. After 20 minutes, retorque bolts to 30 ft. lbs.
6. Install correct type and amount of lubricant.
7. Install brake drum and wheel.

REAR WHEEL BEARING & SPINDLE
REPLACE (1980-85 RIVIERA)

NOTE: The rear wheel bearing is a sealed

unit. This bearing is not serviceable for repacking or adjustment. The bearing must not be subjected to heat or early bearing failure may result.

REAR DISC BRAKES
Removal

1. Raise and support rear of vehicle.
2. Remove tire and wheel assembly.
3. Mark a wheel stud and a corresponding place on the rotor to assist in installation if bearing is not replaced.
4. Disconnect brake line at bracket on control arm.
5. Remove caliper and rotor assembly.
6. Remove four nuts and bolts securing the spindle to the control arm and remove bearing assembly, **Fig. 2.**

Installation

NOTE: Before installing bearing, remove all rust and corrosion from bearing mounting surfaces. Lack of a flat surface may result in early bearing failure. A slip fit must exist between the bearing and the control arm assembly.

1. Install rear spindle, shield and plate to lower control arm. Torque nuts to 35 ft. lbs., **Fig. 2.**
2. If bearing was not replaced, install rotor using reference marks made at time of removal.
3. Install brake caliper assembly.
4. Connect brake line at bracket on control arm, tighten and bleed brake system.
5. Install wheel and tire assembly.
6. Remove support and lower car.

REAR DRUM BRAKES
Removal

1. Raise and support rear of vehicle.
2. Remove tire and wheel assembly.
3. Remove brake drum.
4. Remove four nuts attaching rear wheel bearing assembly to control arm.
5. Remove wheel bearing and four attaching bolts **Fig. 3.**

Installation

NOTE: Before installing bearing, remove

all rust and corrosion from bearing mounting surfaces. Lack of a flat surface for any reason may result in early bearing failure. A slip fit must exist between the bearing and the control arm assembly.

1. Install four nuts and bolts attaching wheel bearing to rear control arm assembly **Fig. 3.** Torque nuts to 35 ft. lbs.
2. Install brake drum.
3. Install wheel and tire assembly.
4. Remove supports and lower car.

PROPELLER SHAFT
REPLACE

NOTE: When service is required, the propeller shaft must be removed from the car as a complete assembly. While handling it out of the car, the assembly must be supported on a straight line as nearly as possible to avoid jamming or bending any of the parts.

Two attachment methods are used to secure the propeller shaft to the pinion flange or end yoke, a pair of bolted straps or a set of bolted flanges.

1. Scribe alignment marks between propeller shaft and pinion flange or end yoke to aid reassembly.
2. Remove strap or flange bolts at rear of propeller shaft. Tape bearing cups to prevent loss of needle bearings.
3. Slide shaft assembly rearward, disengaging front yoke from transmission output shaft splines and lower from vehicle.
4. Reverse procedure to install.

NOTE: Prior to installing propeller shaft, lubricate all shaft splines with engine oil. When installing propeller shaft, do not attempt to drive in place with hammer. If shaft will not slip into place, inspect for burrs on transmission output shaft splines, twisted slip yoke splines or the wrong U-joint yoke. Repair as necessary.

PROPELLER SHAFT BALANCE

A wheel balancer of the type equipped with a strobe light can be used to facilitate balancing of the driveshaft. The pick-up unit should be placed directly under the nose of the rear axle carrier and as far forward as possible.

1. Place car on twin post lift so rear of car is supported on the rear axle housing and rear wheels are free to rotate.
2. Remove both rear wheels and tire assemblies and reinstall wheel lug nuts with flat side next to drum.
3. Mark and number driveshaft at four points 90° apart at rear of shaft just forward of balance weights.
4. Place strobe light pick-up under nose of differential.
5. With car running in gear at car speed where unbalance is at its peak, allow

driveline to stabilize by holding at constant speed. Point strobe light at spinning shaft and note position of one of the reference marks.
6. Shut off engine and position shaft so reference mark will be in position noted when car was running.

CAUTION: Do not run car on hoist for extended periods due to danger of overheating transmission or engine.

7. When strobe light flashed, the heaviest point of the shaft was down. To balance shaft it will be necessary to apply weight 180° away. Screw type hose clamps can be used as weights as shown in **Fig. 4.**

BRAKE ADJUSTMENTS
SELF-ADJUSTING DRUM BRAKES

These brakes have self-adjusting shoe mechanisms that assure correct lining-to-drum clearances at all times. The automatic adjusters operate only when the brakes are applied as the car is moving rearward.

Although the brakes are self-adjusting, an initial adjustment is necessary after the brake shoes have been relined or replaced, or when the length of the adjusting screw has been changed during some other service operation.

Frequent usage of an automatic transmission forward range to halt reverse vehicle motion may prevent the automatic adjusters from functioning, thereby inducing low pedal heights. Should low pedal heights be encountered, it is recommended that numerous forward and reverse stops be made until satisfactory pedal height is obtained.

NOTE: If a low pedal condition cannot be corrected by making numerous reverse stops (provided the hydraulic system is free of air) it indicates that the self-adjusting mechanism is not functioning. Therefore, it will be necessary to remove the brake drum, clean, free up and lubricate the adjusting mechanism. Then adjust the brakes as follows, being sure the parking brake is fully released.

Adjustment

1. Remove adjusting hole cover from backing plate. Turn brake adjusting screw to expand shoes until wheel can just be turned by hand.
2. Using suitable tool to hold actuator away from adjuster, **Fig. 5,** and back off adjuster 30 notches. If shoes still drag, back off one or two additional notches.

NOTE: Brakes should be free of drag when adjuster has been backed off approximately 12 notches. Heavy drag at this point indicates tight parking brake cables.

3. Install adjusting hole cover and check parking adjustment.

CAUTION: If finger movement will not turn the screw, free it up. If this is not done, the actuator will not turn the screw during subsequent vehicle operation. Lubricate the screw with oil and coat with wheel bearing grease. Any other adjustment procedure may cause damage to the adjusting screw with consequent self-adjuster problems.

4. Install wheel and drum, and adjusting hole cover. Adjust brakes on remaining wheels in the same manner.
5. If pedal height is not satisfactory, drive the vehicle and make sufficient reverse stops until proper pedal height is obtained.

PARKING BRAKE
ADJUST

1980–85 W/REAR DISC BRAKES

1. Lubricate parking brake cables at equalizer and underbody rub points. Check all cables for freedom of operation.
2. Fully release parking brake and raise vehicle.
3. Hold cable stud from turning and tighten equalizer nut until cable slack is removed and levers are against stops on caliper housing. If levers are off stops, loosen cable until levers return to stop.
4. Operate parking brake several times to check adjustment. When properly adjusted, the parking brake pedal should move 5¼ inch to 6¾ inch when a force of approximately 125 pounds is applied on all except Riviera. On Riviera, the parking brake pedal should move ¼ inch to 5½ inch when a force of approximately 125 pounds is applied.

1980–86 W/REAR DRUM BRAKES

Need for parking brake adjustment is indicated if the service brake operates with good pedal reserve but the parking brake pedal can be depressed a minimum of 9 ratchet clicks but not more than 16 under heavy foot pressure. After making sure that the service brakes are properly adjusted, adjust the parking brake as follows:

1. Depress parking brake exactly three ratchet clicks on 1985–86 models or two ratchet clicks on 1980–84 models.
2. Loosen jam nut, and tighten adjusting nut until rear wheels can just be turned rearward using both hands but are locked when forward motion is attempted.
3. Tighten jam nut and release parking brake. Rear wheels should turn freely in either direction with no brake drag.

STEP 1
DETERMINE POINT
OF UNBALANCE

STEP 2
ADD HOSE CLAMPS 180°
FROM POINT OF UNBALANCE
UNITL THEY BECOME
HEAVY SPOT

STEP 3
ROTATE TWO CLAMPS EQUALLY
AWAY FROM EACH OTHER
UNTIL BEST BALANCE
IS ACHIEVED

Fig. 4   Positioning clamps to balance propeller shaft

BACKING PLATE
J-21281
J-6166 WRENCH
TO EXPAND SHOES
MOVE END OF TOOL UPWARD

Fig. 5   Typical drum brake adjustment

MASTER CYLINDER
REPLACE

1. Disconnect brake pipes from master cylinder and tape end of pipes to prevent entrance of dirt.
2. On manual brakes, disconnect brake pedal from master cylinder push rod.
3. Remove two nuts holding master cylinder to dash or power cylinder and remove master cylinder from car.

POWER BRAKE UNIT
REPLACE

EXC. HYDRO-BOOST

1. Remove two nuts attaching master cylinder to brake unit, then position master cylinder away from brake unit with brake lines attached.

NOTE: Use care not to bend or kink brake lines.

2. Disconnect vacuum hose from check valve. Plug vacuum hose to prevent dirt from entering.
3. Remove four nuts holding power unit to dash.
4. Remove retainer and washer from brake pedal pin and disengage push rod eye or clevis.
5. Remove power unit from car.

HYDRO-BOOST

NOTE: Pump brake pedal several times with engine off to deplete accumulator of fluid.

1. Remove two nuts attaching master cylinder to booster, then move master cylinder away from booster with brake lines attached.
2. Remove three hydraulic lines from booster. Plug and cap all lines and outlets.
3. Remove retainer and washer securing booster push rod to brake pedal arm.

4. Remove four nuts attaching booster unit to dash panel.
5. From engine compartment, loosen booster from dash panel and move booster push rod inboard until it disconnects from brake pedal arm. Remove spring washer from brake pedal arm.
6. Remove booster unit from vehicle.
7. Reverse procedure to install. To purge system, disconnect feed wire from injection pump or ignition system. Fill power steering pump reservoir, then crank engine for several seconds and recheck power steering pump fluid level. Connect feed wire and start engine, then cycle steering wheel from stop to stop twice and stop engine. Discharge accumulator by depressing brake pedal several times, then check fluid level. Start engine, then turn steering wheel from stop to stop and turn engine off. Check fluid level and add fluid as necessary. If foaming occurs, stop engine and wait for approximately one hour for foam to dissipate, then recheck fluid level.

Rear Suspension

SHOCK ABSORBER
REPLACE

1. With the rear axle supported properly, disconnect shock absorber from lower mounting bracket. On models equipped with automatic level control, disconnect air hose from shock absorber.
2. Disconnect shock absorber upper end from underbody attachment.
3. Reverse procedure to install.

COIL SPRINGS
REPLACE

1980–85 RIVIERA

1. Raise and support rear of vehicle.

[A] LOCATE BOTTOM END OF SPRING BETWEEN DIMPLES ON CONTROL ARM ASSEMBLY.

[B] USE EITHER ALL HIGH LIMIT, OR ALL LOW LIMIT SPRINGS. DO NOT INTERMIX BETWEEN LEFT AND RIGHT REAR POSITIONS. (LOW LIMIT SPRINGS HAVE A CIRCLE AROUND THE CODE LETTERS. HIGH LIMIT SPRINGS DO NOT).

FRONT OF CAR
INSULATOR
[B] [A] SPRINGS
INSULATOR
CONTROL ARM ASSEMBLY
FRAME
[A]
VIEW A

Fig. 1   Coil spring installation. Riviera

Fig. 2   Typical coil spring suspension. Exc. Riviera

2. Using a suitable jack support lower control arm.
3. Disconnect automatic level control air hose from shock absorber. If removing spring from left hand side of vehicle, disconnect level control link from control arm.
4. Disconnect shock absorber from upper mounting.
5. Lower the control arm until all spring tension is relieved, then remove spring.
6. Reverse procedure to install. Locate spring as shown in **Fig. 1.**

EXC. 1980—85 RIVIERA

1. Support vehicle at frame and support rear axle with a suitable jack.
2. Disconnect shock absorbers from lower mounting brackets, **Fig. 2,** then the brake hose from the axle housing.
3. Disconnect upper control arms at differential.
4. Lower jack fully, extending springs, then remove springs.

NOTE: Do not allow the brake hose to become kinked or stretched.

5. Reverse procedure to install. Refer to **Fig. 3,** for correct coil spring staggering. After installation, bleed brakes.

Fig. 3   Coil spring installation. Exc. Riviera

Fig. 4   Control arm assembly. Riviera

Fig. 5   Rear stabilizer installation. Riviera   **Fig. 6   Rear stabilizer installation. Exc. Riviera**

CONTROL ARMS
REPLACE

NOTE: Remove and replace one control arm at a time as axle assembly may slip sideways, making installation difficult.

1980—85 RIVIERA

1. Raise and support rear of vehicle, then remove wheel and tire assembly.
2. Disconnect brake line at bracket on control arm.
3. Remove stabilizer bar. Refer to "Stabilizer Bar, Replace".
4. Remove rear wheel bearing and spindle. Refer to "Rear Wheel Bearing And Spindle, Replace" in Rear Axle, Propeller Shaft and Brakes Section.
5. If removing left hand control arm, disconnect automatic level control link from control arm.
6. Using a suitable jack, support control arm.
7. Disconnect air hose from shock absorber, then detach shock absorber from upper and lower mountings.
8. Lower control arm until all spring tension is relieved, then remove spring and insulators.
9. Remove two bolts attaching control arm to frame and remove control arm, **Fig. 4.**

EXCEPT 1980—85 RIVIERA
Upper Control Arms
1. Support vehicle at frame and rear axle.
2. Remove control arm mount bolts from frame and axle housing attachments, **Fig. 2.**
3. Reverse procedure to install.

NOTE: Control arm bolts must be tightened with vehicle at curb height.

Lower Control Arm
Lower control arms may be removed and replaced using the "Upper Control Arms" procedure. However, it may be necessary to reposition the jack farther forward under carrier to aid in removing rear mount bolt. Also, a brass drift may be needed to remove mount bolts.

STABILIZER BAR
REPLACE

1980—85 RIVIERA

1. Raise and support rear of vehicle.
2. Remove bolts attaching front of stabilizer bar to control arms, **Fig. 5.**
3. Remove inside nut and bolt from each side of stabilizer bar link, then loosen nut and bolt on outside of link.
4. Rotate bottom parts of link to one side and slide stabilizer bar out of bushings.

EXC. 1980—85 RIVIERA

1. Support vehicle at rear axle.
2. Remove stabilizer bar attaching bolts from brackets on lower control arms, **Fig. 6.**
3. Reverse procedure to install.

Front Suspension & Steering Section

For front suspension & steering service procedures on Riviera models refer to Cadillac, "Front End & Steering Section, 1980—85 Eldorado & Seville."

FRONT SUSPENSION

On this type front suspension, **Fig. 1,** each wheel is connected independently to the vehicle frame by upper and lower control arms, ball joints and a steering knuckle. The upper and lower control arms are designed and positioned to allow the steering knuckles to move in a prescribed three dimensional arc. Tie rods, connected to the steering knuckles, ensure the front wheels are held in the proper relationship to each other.

A ball joint is riveted to the outer end of the upper arm and is spring loaded to insure proper alignment of the ball in the socket.

The inner end of the lower control arm has pressed-in bushings. Two bolts, passing through the bushings, attach the arm to the frame. The lower ball joint is a press fit in the arm and attaches to the steering knuckle with a castellated nut that is retained with a cotter pin.

Rubber seals are provided on upper and lower shafts and at ball socket assemblies to exclude dirt and moisture from bearing surfaces. Grease fittings are provided at all bearing locations.

WHEEL ALIGNMENT

NOTE: Prior to checking or resetting caster and camber angles, bounce the front end at least twice to allow vehicle to return to normal trim height.

Caster and camber are adjusted by shimming at the upper control arm shaft attaching points.

Adding shims at the front locations will change caster toward negative with practically no change in camber. Adding shims at the rear locations will change caster toward positive and camber toward negative. Adding equal shims at both front and rear locations will not change caster but will change camber toward negative.

To adjust, loosen both front and rear nuts to free shims for removal or addition. After installing or removing shims, torque shaft nuts to 75 ft. lbs. on all except Century and Regal, and 46 ft. lbs. for Century and Regal.

NOTE: A normal service shim pack should leave at least two threads exposed beyond the shaft nuts after final tightening. The difference between front and rear shim packs should not exceed .40 inch.

TOE-IN
ADJUST

NOTE: Prior to checking or resetting toe-in, bounce the front end at least twice to allow vehicle to return to normal trim height.

1. Ensure wheel bearings are adjusted properly. Refer to "Wheel Bearings, Adjust".
2. Using suitable alignment equipment, with steering wheel in the straight ahead position, check toe-in.
3. If toe-in is not within specifications, loosen tie rod adjustment sleeve clamp bolts.
4. Turn tie rod adjustable sleeves an equal amount of turns but in opposite directions to bring toe-in within specifications.
5. Ensure tie rod end housings are at right angles to the steering arm, then position and torque tie rod adjustable sleeve clamps as shown in **Fig. 2.**

WHEEL BEARINGS
ADJUST

1. Raise and support front of vehicle.
2. Remove wheel hub dust cap.
3. Remove spindle nut cotter pin, then while rotating wheel assembly forward, torque spindle nut to 12 ft. lbs. to seat bearings.
4. Loosen spindle nut slightly to "the just loose" position.
5. Hand tighten spindle nut, then install

Fig. 1 Typical Front suspension exploded view

BOLTS MUST BE INSTALLED IN DIRECTION SHOWN. ROTATE BOTH INNER AND OUTER TIE ROD HOUSINGS REARWARD TO THE LIMIT OF BALL JOINT TRAVEL BEFORE TIGHTENING CLAMPS. WITH THIS SAME REARWARD ROTATION ALL BOLT CENTERLINES MUST BE BETWEEN ANGLES SHOWN AFTER TIGHTENING CLAMPS.

CLAMP ENDS MAY TOUCH WHEN NUT IS TORQUED TO SPECIFICATIONS, BUT GAP MUST BE VISIBLE ADJACENT TO ADJUSTER SLEEVE.

DO NOT LOCATE ADJUSTER TUBE SLOT IN THIS AREA

20 N·m (15 FT. LBS.)

CLAMP MUST BE BETWEEN AND CLEAR OF DIMPLES. TORQUE NUTS TO SPECIFICATION.

Fig. 2 Tie rod adjustment sleeve & clamp installation

CHECKING BALL JOINTS FOR WEAR

If loose ball joints are suspected, first be sure front wheel bearings are properly adjusted and that control arms are tight.

cotter pin. If cotter pin cannot be installed, loosen spindle nut until hole in the spindle lines up with a slot in the nut. Do not loosen more then ½ flat of the nut.
6. With wheel bearings properly adjusted, end play should be .001 to .005 inch.

WHEEL BEARINGS
REPLACE

1. Raise and support vehicle and remove front wheels.
2. Remove brake tube support bracket bolt. Do not disconnect hydraulic tube or hose.
3. Remove caliper to mounting bracket bolts. Hang caliper from upper suspension.

NOTE: Do not place strain on brake line.

4. Remove spindle nut and hub and disc assembly. Inner wheel bearing and grease retainer can now be removed.

Then check ball joints as follows:

UPPER BALL JOINT

1. Raise front of vehicle with jacks placed between coil spring pockets and ball joint of lower control arm.
2. Position suitable dial indicator at top of wheel rim, then grasp wheel top and bottom, while pulling out top, push in bottom and read dial indicator. Reverse the push-pull procedure and read dial indicator.

3. If dial indicator reading exceeds .125 inch, the upper ball joint should be replaced.

LOWER BALL JOINT

A wear indicator is built into the ball joint. Remove dirt deposits around service plug and observe position of nipple. Refer to **Fig. 3** for wear tolerance.

BALL JOINTS
REPLACE

NOTE: On all models the upper ball joint is spring-loaded in its socket. If the ball stud has any perceptible shake or if it can be twisted with the fingers, the ball joint should be replaced.

On all models, the lower ball joint is not spring-loaded and depends upon car weight to load the ball. The lower ball joint should never be replaced merely because it "feels" loose when in an unloaded condition.

FRONT SUSPENSION BALL JOINT WEAR INDICATOR

WORN

NEW

SINTERED IRON BEARING

WEAR SURFACES

HOUSING SOCKET

RUBBER PRESSURE RING

WEAR INDICATOR

.050 INCH

WHEN BALL JOINT WEAR CAUSES WEAR INDICATOR SHOULDER TO RECEDE WITHIN THE SOCKET HOUSING REPLACEMENT IS REQUIRED

Fig. 3 Lower ball joint check

Fig. 4 Removing ball joint stud from steering knuckle

Upper ball joints on all models are riveted to the control arm and can be replaced.

Lower ball joints on all models are pressed into the control arm and can be replaced with a suitable ball joint tool.

CAUTION: When servicing lower ball joints, be sure to support lower control arm with a suitable jack. If lower control arm is not supported and steering knuckle is disconnected from control arm, the heavily compressed front spring will be completely released.

UPPER BALL JOINT

1. Support vehicle at frame and remove wheel assembly.
2. Remove cotter pin from upper ball joint stud, loosen nut approximately 2 turns, do not remove nut.
3. Position tool as shown in **Fig. 4,** turn threaded end of tool until stud disengages knuckle.
4. Position jack under lower control arm at spring seat, raise jack until compression is relieved from upper control arm bumper.
5. Remove stud nut, lift control arm from steering knuckle and place a block of wood between control arm and frame.
6. On all models,
   a. Center punch rivet head as close to center as possible.
   b. Using a ⅛ inch twist drill, drill through center of rivet approximately ½ rivet length deep.
   c. Enlarge hole using a 7/32 inch drill.
   d. Using a chisel, remove rivet heads, then drive rivets out using a suitable punch.
7. Position ball joint on upper control arm. Install bolts through bottom of control arm with nuts on top, torque to 8 ft. lbs.
8. On all models, position ball joint stud so cotter pin hole is facing forward and remove wooden block from between control arm and frame.
9. Place wheels in straight ahead position, raise jack under lower control until ball joint stud can be installed in steering knuckle.
10. Install castellated nut on ball joint stud. Torque nut to 65 ft. lbs.

NOTE: If cotter pin holes do not align, do not loosen nut, however, tighten until cotter pin can be installed.

11. Install wheel assembly and lower vehicle.

LOWER BALL JOINT

1. Support vehicle under frame side rails.

NOTE: Position jack under lower control at outboard end, raise jack until it is ½ inch below control arm.

2. Remove cotter pin, loosen ball joint stud nut approximately 2 turns, do not remove nut.
3. Position tool as shown in **Fig. 4,** turn threaded end of tool until ball joint stud is disengaged from steering knuckle.
4. Position jack under lower control arm at spring seat and raise jack until compression is removed from upper control arm bumper.
5. Remove lower ball joint stud nut and position steering knuckle aside.
6. Using tool No. J-9519-10, remove ball joint from lower control arm.
7. Position ball joint on control arm with bleed vent on rubber boot facing inward.
8. Install tool J-9519-10 and turn threaded end of tool until ball joint is fully seated in lower control arm.
9. Position new ball joint stud so cotter pin hole is facing forward.

Fig. 5 Removing front coil spring

10. Place wheels in the straight ahead position and install ball joint stud on steering knuckle.
11. Install stud nut torque nut to 81 ft. lbs., then install cotter pin.

NOTE: If cotter pin holes do not align do not loosen stud nut, tighten nut until cotter pin can be installed.

12. Install wheel assembly.

SHOCK ABSORBER
REPLACE

Unfasten shock absorber at top and bottom and remove it through the spring seat. Check shock absorber for obvious physical damage or oil leakage. Push and pull

SPRING

FORWARD

NOTE SPRING TO BE INSTALLED WITH TAPE AT LOWEST POSITION. BOTTOM OF SPRING IS COILED HELICAL, AND THE TOP IS COILED FLAT WITH A GRIPPER NOTCH NEAR END OF WIRE (TAPE LOCATION OPTIONAL)

NOTE: AFTER ASSEMBLY, END OF SPRING COIL MUST COVER ALL OR PART OF ONE INSPECTION DRAIN HOLE. THE OTHER HOLE MUST BE PARTLY EXPOSED OR COMPLETELY UNCOVERED.

FORWARD

FORWARD

VIEW A

SPRING

FORWARD

WHEN A PORTION OF COILS ARE COMPRESSED THE COIL TO COIL GAP MUST NEVER BE LESS THAN 23.3mm. (29/32")

WHEN ENTIRE SPRING IS COMPRESSED THE OVERALL DIMENSION MUST NEVER BE LESS THAN 205.5 mm. (3.2/32")

VIEW B

Fig. 6 Coil spring installation. All exc. Full size models

shock absorber in an upright position. If smooth hydraulic resistance is not present in both directions, replace shock absorber.

COIL SPRING
REPLACE

1. Raise and support vehicle at frame.
2. Remove shock absorber lower mount, then push shock up through control arm and into spring.
3. Remove stabilizer bar from lower control arm. Refer to "Stabilizer Bar, Replace".
4. Position a tool No. J-23028 at lower control arm pivot bolts, **Fig. 5.**
5. Position a suitable jack under tool installed in step 4 and chain together, then raise jack slightly to remove tension from lower control arm pivot bolts.
6. Using a suitable chain, secure lower control arm and coil spring together.
7. Remove rear lower control arm pivot bolt, then front bolt.
8. Slowly lower jack with lower control arm and spring attached.
9. When spring compression is relieved, remove spring.
10. Reverse procedure to install. Refer to **Figs. 6 and 7,** for proper installation.

STABILIZER BAR
REPLACE

1. Raise and support front of vehicle.
2. Remove nut, link bolt, retainers, grommets, spacer and stabilizer linkage from lower control arms.
3. Remove bracket to frame bolts, then remove stabilizer shaft, rubber bushings and brackets. On 1980–81 Century and 1980–86 Regal models, use tool No. J-25359-20 to remove stabilizer shaft bolt.
4. Reverse procedure to install. Note the following:
   a. When installing rubber bushings, bushings should be positioned squarely in the brackets with the bushing slit facing front of vehicle.

Fig. 7 Coil spring installation. Full size models

b. Torque stabilizer link nut to 13 ft. lbs. and bracket bolts to 25 ft. lbs.

MANUAL STEERING GEAR
REPLACE

1. Remove two nuts or pinch bolt securing lower coupling to steering shaft flange.
2. Use a suitable puller to remove pitman arm.
3. Unfasten gear (3 bolts) from frame and remove from car.
4. Reverse procedure to install.

POWER STEERING, GEAR REPLACE

1. Disconnect pressure and return line hoses at steering gear and elevate ends of hoses higher than pump to prevent oil from draining out of pump.
2. Remove pinch bolt securing coupling to steering gear.

3. Jack up car and remove pitman shaft nut, then use a suitable puller to remove pitman arm.
4. On full size models, remove sheet metal baffle that covers frame-to-gear attaching bolts, if equipped.
5. Loosen the three frame-to-steering gear bolts and remove steering gear.
6. Reverse procedure to install.

POWER STEERING PUMP
REPLACE

1. Disconnect battery ground cable.
2. Remove steering pump belt, alternator belt and air conditioning compressor belt, if equipped.
3. On 1980–81 models, remove steering pump pulley using tool J-25304 or equivalent.
4. On all models disconnect steering pump hoses from pump and plug all open lines and fittings to prevent entry of dirt.
5. Remove pump or pump with brackets from engine.
6. Reverse procedure to install.

1982-86 CHEV. CELEBRITY • BUICK CENTURY • OLDS. CUTLASS CIERA • PONT. 6000 • 1984-86 OLDS. CUTLASS CRUISER

Refer to chapter 13 for service procedures not covered in this chapter.

INDEX OF SERVICE OPERATIONS

NOTE: Refer to the rear of this manual for vehicle manufacturer's special service tool suppliers.

Vehicle Identification Number Location

On top of instrument panel, left front.

Engine Number Location

On 4-151, V6-173, V6-181, V6-231 engines, the engine code stamping is located on vertical pad on engine to transmission mounting flange located on forward side of block. On V6-262 diesel engines, the engine code stamping is located on vertical pad located on right side of engine front cover.

Engine V.I.N. Code

The eighth digit of the seventeen digit V.I.N. code denotes engine code.

Engine Identification Codes

Year	Engine	V.I.N. Code	Code
1982	4-151①	R	3M, 3S, 3J
	4-151①	R	3K, 3L, 3P
	V6-173②	X	CAY, CAZ, CBA
	V6-173②	X	CBC, CBD, CBF
	V6-173②	X	CBH, CBJ, CBK
	V6-173②	X	CMC, CMF, CMH
	V6-173②	X	CMJ, CMM, CMS
	V6-173②	X	C7N, C7R, C7S
	V6-173②	X	C7T, C7U, C7W
	V6-173②	X	D2A, D2B, D2C
	V6-173②	X	D2D, D2F, D2H
	V6-181③	E	EA, EB
	V6-262④	T	UAC, UAH, UAL
1983	4-151①	R	YAA, YAL, YAP
	V6-173②	X	D2J, D2K, D2M
	V6-173②	X	D2N, D2R, D2S
	V6-173②	X	DCA, DCB, DCC
	V6-173②	X	DCD, DCF, DCH
	V6-173②	X	DCJ, DCK, DCM
	V6-173②	X	DCN, DCR, DCS
	V6-173②	X	DCT, DCV
	V6-173②	X	DCW, DC
	V6-173 HO②⑤	Z	DFA, DFB, DFC
	V6-173 HO②⑤	Z	DFD, DFF, DFH
	V6-173 HO②⑤	Z	DTA, DTB, DTC
	V6-173 HO②⑤	Z	DTJ, DTK
	V6-181③	E	RA, RB, RC
	V6-262④	T	ULJ, ULK, ULL
	V6-262④	T	ULM, ULN, ULP
1984	4-151①	R	Z3J, Z3K, Z3L
	4-151①	R	Z5C, Z5L, Z5M
	V6-173②	X	C4F, C4H, C4J
	V6-173②	X	C4K, C4M, C4X
	V6-173②	X	C4Y, C4Z, C44
	V6-173②	X	C5C, C5D, C5F
	V6-173②	X	C5H, C5J, C5K
	V6-173②	X	C5M, C5N, C5O
	V6-173②	X	SCC, SCH, SCK
	V6-173②	X	SCM, SCS, SCT
	V6-173②	X	SCU, SC
	V6-173 HO②⑤	Z	SFA, SFB, SFC
	V6-173 HO②⑤	Z	SFF, SFM, SFN
	V6-173 HO②⑤	Z	SFR, SFS
	V6-181③	E	MAB, MBB, MCA
	V6-181③	E	MDA, MFA
	V6-231 MFI③	3	FCB, FFC
	V6-262④	T	UAA, UAB, UAC
	V6-262④	T	UAM, UAP, UAS
	V6-262④	T	UBA, UBB, UBD
	V6-262④	T	UBF, UBH, UBJ
	V6-262④	T	UBK, UBL, UBM
	V6-262④	T	UBN, UBP, UBR
	V6-262④	T	UBS, UBT, UCB
	V6-262④	T	UCC, UCD, UCF
	V6-262④	T	UKS, UKT, UKU
	V6-262④	T	UKX, ULX, ULY
	V6-262④	T	ULZ, UMB
1985	4-151①	R	AAF, AAR, ABY
	4-151①	R	ACC, ACM
	4-151①	R	ADJ, ADK
	V6-173②	X	C5R, C5S, C5T
	V6-173②	X	C8R, C8S, C8T
	V6-173②	X	C8U, CAS, CAX
	V6-173②	X	CDA, CDB, CDC
	V6-173 HO MFI②⑤	W	CAA, CAB, CAC
	V6-173 HO MFI②⑤	W	CAH, CAK, CAL
	V6-181③	E	MAC, MLA
	V6-181③	E	WBA, WDA
	V6-231 MFI③	3	NAA, NBB, NRA
	V6-262④	T	UDB, UDC, UDH
	V6-262④	T	UMM, UMN, UMT
	V6-262④	T	UNC, UND

①—Pontiac built engine.
②—Chevrolet built engine.
③—Buick built engine.
④—Oldsmobile built diesel engine.
⑤—High output engine.

Grille Identification

1982–83 Buick Century Exc. "T" Type

1982–83 Chevrolet Celebrity

1982–83 Olds. Cutlass Ciera Exc. Brougham, ES & LS

1982–83 Olds. Cutlass Ciera Brougham & LS

1982–83 Pontiac 6000 Exc. "STE"

1983 Buick Century "T" Type

1983 Pontiac 6000 "STE"

1984 Buick Century Exc. "T" Type

1984 Buick Century "T" Type

1984 Chevrolet Celebrity

1984 Pontiac 6000 LF 4 Door & Station Wagon

1984 Olds. Cutlass Ciera & Cruiser, 1985 Olds. Ciera Holiday

1985 Buick Century Custom & Wagon

1985 Buick Century T-Type

1985 Olds. Cutlass Ciera

1985 Olds. Cutlass Cruiser

1985–86 Pontiac 6000 LE & Wagon

1986 Buick Century

1986 Chevrolet Celebrity

1986 Olds. Cutlass Ciera Exc. ES

1986 Olds. Cutlass Ciera ES

1986 Pontiac 6000 STE

General Engine Specifications

Year	Engine CID①/Liter	V.I.N. Code②	Carburetor	Bore and Stroke	Com-pression Ratio	Net H.P. @ R.P.M.③	Maximum Torque Ft. Lbs. @ R.P.M.	Normal Oil Pressure Pounds
1982	4-151, 2.5L	R	T.B.I	4.00 × 3.00	8.2	90 @ 4000	132 @ 2800	36–41
	V6-173, 2.8L	X	E2SE, 2 Bbl④	3.50 × 2.99	8.5	112 @ 5100	145 @ 2400	50–65
	V6-181, 3.0L	E	E2ME, 2 Bbl④	3.80 × 2.66	8.45	110 @ 4800	145 @ 2600	37
	V6-262, 4.3L⑤	T	Fuel Injection	4.05 × 3.385	21.6	85 @ 3600	165 @ 1600	30–45
1983	4-151, 2.5L	R	T.B.I	4.00 × 3.00	8.2	90 @ 4000	135 @ 2800	36–41
	V6-173, 2.8L	X	E2SE, 2 Bbl④	3.50 × 2.99	8.5	112 @ 4800	145 @ 2400	50–65
	V6-173 H.O., 2.8L⑥	Z	E2SE, 2 Bbl④	3.50 × 2.99	8.9	130 @ 5400	145 @ 2400	50–65
	V6-181, 3.0L	E	E2ME, 2 Bbl④	3.80 × 2.66	8.45	110 @ 4800	145 @ 2600	37
	V6-262, 4.3L⑤	T	Fuel Injection	4.05 × 3.385	21.6	85 @ 3600	165 @ 1600	30–45
1984	4-151, 2.5L	R	T.B.I	4.00 × 3.00	8.2	90 @ 4000	134 @ 2400	36–41
	V6-173, 2.8L	X	E2SE, 2 Bbl④	3.50 × 2.99	8.5	112 @ 5100	148 @ 2400	50–65
	V6-173 H.O., 2.8L⑥	Z	E2SE, 2 Bbl④	3.50 × 2.99	8.9	130 @ 5400	145 @ 2400	50–65
	V6-181, 3.0L	E	E2ME, 2 Bbl④	3.80 × 2.666	8.45	110 @ 4800	145 @ 2600	37
	V6-231 MFI, 3.8L	3	Fuel Injection	3.80 × 3.40	8.0	125 @ 4400	195 @ 2000	37
	V6-262, 4.3L⑤	T	Fuel Injection	4.05 × 3.385	21.6	85 @ 3600	165 @ 1600	30–45
1985	4-151, 2.5L	R	T.B.I	4.00 × 3.00	9.0	92 @ 4400	134 @ 2800	37.5
	V6-173, 2.8L	X	E2SE, 2 Bbl④	3.50 × 2.99	8.5	112 @ 4800	148 @ 2400	50–65
	V6-173 H.O. MFI, 2.8L⑥	W	Fuel Injection	3.50 × 2.99	8.9	125 @ 4500	145 @ 2400	50–65
	V6-181, 3.0L	E	E2ME, 2 Bbl④	3.80 × 2.666	8.45	110 @ 4800	145 @ 2600	37
	V6-231 MFI, 3.8L	3	Fuel Injection	3.80 × 3.40	8.0	125 @ 4400	195 @ 2000	37
	V6-262, 4.3L⑤	T	Fuel Injection	4.057 × 3.385	22.8	85 @ 3600	165 @ 1600	30–45
1986	4-151, 2.5L	R	T.B.I	4.00 × 3.00	9.0	92 @ 4400	134 @ 2800	—
	V6-173, 2.8L	X	E2SE, 2 Bbl	3.50 × 2.99	—	—	—	—
	V6-173 MFI, 2.8L	W	Fuel Injection	3.50 × 2.99	8.5	130 @ 4800	—	—
	V6-231 SFI, 3.8L	3, B	Fuel Injection	3.80 × 3.40	8.5	150 @ 4400	200 @ 2000	—

①—CID—cubic inch displacement.
②—The eighth digit denotes engine code.
③—Ratings are net—as installed in vehi-cle.
④—Rochester.
⑤—Diesel engine.
⑥—High output engine.

Starting Motor Applications

Year	Engine/V.I.N.	Starter Ident. No.	Year	Engine/V.I.N.	Starter Ident. No.
1982	4-151, V6-173, V6-181①	1109530②		V6-231 MFI/3	1998445①
	V6-262 Diesel/T	1998553②		V6-262 Diesel/T	1998553②
	V6-262 Diesel/T	22515863③		V6-262 Diesel/T	22515863③
1983	4-151/R	1109556①	1985	4-151/R	1998450②
	V6-173/X,Z	1109533①		V6-173/X,W	1109564②
	V6-173/X,Z	1109564①		V6-181/E	1998448②
	V6-181	1109560①		V6-231/3	1998445②
	V6-262 Diesel/T	1998553②		V6-262 Diesel/T	2252209②
	V6-262 Diesel/T	22515863③		V6-262 Diesel/T	22523207③
1984	4-151/R	1109556①	1986	4-151/R	1109564②
	V6-173/X,Z	1109564①		V6-173/X, W	1109564②
	V6-181/E	1998448①		V6-231/3, B	1998521②

①—For V.I.N. code, refer to the "General Engine Specifications" at the begin-ning of chapter.
②—Delco-Remy.
③—Mitsubishi.

continued

Alternator Specifications

Year	Model	Rated Hot Output Amps.	Year	Model	Rated Hot Output Amps.	Year	Model	Rated Hot Output Amps.
1982	1100113	63		1105190	85		01105428	94
	1100164	55		1105196	85		01105441	94
	1100166	63		1105199	85		01105444	94
	1100174	55		1105200	85		01105509	108
	1100192	85		1105244	42		01105552	85
	1100193	85		1105245	78		01105553	97
	1100196	63	1984	1100200	78		01105587	97
	1101037	70		1100206	56		01105588	78
	1101039	70		1100208	66		01105590	56
	1101044	70		1100217	78		01105592	94
	1101067	70		1100233	42		01105600	66
	1101084	85		1100235	42		01105603	66
	1101086	85		1100239	56	1985	01100200	78
	1101448	80		1100243	66		01100206	56
	1103197	63		1100247	66		01100208	66
1983	1100200	78		1100252	66		01100217	78
	1100208	63		1100254	66		01100239	56
	1100217	78		1100268	78	1986	1100206	56
	1100231	42		1100272	78		1100208	63
	1100232	42		1105425	94		1100217	78
	1100233	42		1105428	94		1100666	85
	1100235	42		1105441	94		1101113	97
	1100239	55		1105443	94		1105588	78
	1100240	63		1105444	94		1105590	56
	1100243	63		1105509	108		1105592	94
	1100252	63		1105542	94		1105603	66
	1100254	63		1105552	85		1105610	66
	1100260	78		1105553	97		1105615	108
	1100272	78		01100243	66		1105667	100
	1105023	63		01100247	66			
	1105189	85		01105425	94			

Valve Specifications

Year	Engine/V.I.N.	Valve Lash Int.	Valve Lash Exh.	Valve Angles Seat	Valve Angles Face	Valve Spring Installed Height	Valve Spring Pressure Lbs. @ In.	Stem Clearance Intake	Stem Clearance Exhaust	Stem Diameter Intake	Stem Diameter Exhaust
1982–84	4-151/R	Hydraulic①		46	45	1.66	151 @ 1.254	.0010–.0027	.0010–.0032	.3418–.3425	.3418–.3425
	V6-173/X	1½ Turns②		46	45	1.57	195 @ 1.180	.0010–.0027	.0010–.0027	.3410–.3417	.3410–.3417
	V6-181/E	Hydraulic①		45	45	1.727	220 @ 1.340	.0015–.0035	.0015–.0032	.3401–.3412	.3405–.3412
	V6-262 Diesel/T	Hydraulic①		③	④	1.67	210 @ 1.220	.0010–.0027	.0015–.0032	.3425–.3432	.3420–.3427
1984	V6-231/3	Hydraulic①		45	45	1.727	210 @ 1.340	.0015–.0035	.0015–.0032	.3401–.3412	.3405–.3412
1985	4-151/R	Hydraulic①		46	45	1.69	151 @ 1.254	.0010–.0027	⑤	.3418–.3425	.3418–.3425
	V6-173/W,X	1½ Turns②		46	45	1.57	195 @ 1.180	.0010–.0027	.0010–.0027	.3410–.3417	.3410–.3417
	V6-181/E	Hydraulic①		45	45	1.727	220 @ 1.340	.0015–.0035	.0015–.0032	.3401–.3412	.3405–.3412
	V6-231/3	Hydraulic①		45	45	1.727	182 @ 1.340	.0015–.0035	.0015–.0032	.3401–.3412	.3405–.3412
	V6-262 Diesel/T	Hydraulic①		③	④	1.670	210 @ 1.22	.0010–.0027	.0015–.0032	.3425–.3432	.3420–.3428
1986	4-151/R	Hydraulic①		46	45	1.69	151 @ 1.254	.0010–.0027	⑤	.3418–.3425	.3418–.3425
	V6-173/W, X	1½ Turns②		46	45	1.57	195 @ 1.181	.0010–.0027	.0010–.0027	.3410–.3417	.3410–.3417
	V6-231/3, B	Hydraulic①		45	45	1.727	—	.0015–.0035	.0015–.0032	.3401–.3412	.3405–.3412

①—No adjustment.
②—Turn rocker arm stud nut until all lash is eliminated, then tieghten nut the additional turns listed.
③—Intake, 45°; Exhaust, 31°.
④—Intake, 44°; Exhaust, 30°.
⑤—Top, .0010–.0027 inch; Bottom, .0020–.0037 inch.

continued

Pistons, Pins, Rings, Crankshaft & Bearings

| Year | Engine Model/V.I.N. | Piston Clearance | Ring Gap[1] | | Wristpin Diameter | Rod Bearings | | Main Bearings | | | |
			Comp.	Oil		Shaft Diameter	Bearing Clearance	Shaft Diameter	Bearing Clearance	Thrust on Bear. No.	Shaft End Play
1982	4-151/R	.0025–.0033	.010	.015	.9400	2.000	.0005–.0026	2.300	.0005–.0022	5	.0035–.0085
	V6-173/X	.0017–.0027	.010	.020	.9199	2.0303–2.0314	.0014–.0036	2.5336–2.5346	.0018–.0030	3	.0020–.0068
	V6-181/E	.0008–.0020	.013	.015	.9392	2.2487–2.2495	.0005–.0026	2.4995	.0003–.0018	3	.0030–.0090
	V6-262/T[2]	.0030–.0040	.015	.015	1.095	2.2490–2.2510	.0003–.0025	2.9993–3.0003	[3]	3	.0035–.0135
1983	4-151/R	.0025–.0033	.010	.015	.9400	2.000	.0005–.0026	2.300	.0005–.0022	5	.0035–.0085
	V6-173/X,Z	.0007–.0017	.010	.020	.9199	2.0303–2.0314	.0014–.0038	[4]	.0016–.0032	3	.0020–.0068
	V6-181/E	.0008–.0020	.010	.015	.9392	2.2487–2.2495	.0005–.0026	2.4995	.0003–.0018	3	.0030–.0110
	V6-262/T[2]	.0035–.0045	[5]	.015	1.095	2.2490–2.2510	.0003–.0025	2.9993–3.0003	[3]	3	.0035–.0135
1984	4-151/R	.0025–.0030	.010	.020	.9400	2.000	.0005–.0026	2.300	.0005–.0022	5	.0035–.0085
	V6-173/X,Z	.0007–.0017	.010	.020	.9199	2.0303–2.0314	.0014–.0038	[4]	.0016–.0032	3	.0024–.0084
	V6-181/E	.0008–.0020	.010	.015	.9392	2.2487–2.2495	.0005–.0026	2.4995	.0003–.0018	3	.0030–.0110
	V6-231/3	.0008–.0020	.010	.015	.9392	2.2487–2.2495	.0005–.0026	2.4995	.0003–.0018	3	.0030–.0110
	V6-262/T[2]	.0035–.0045	[5]	.015	1.095	2.2490–2.2510	.0003–.0025	2.9993–3.0003	[3]	3	.0035–.0135
1985	4-151/R	.0025–.0033	.010	.010	.9400	2.000	.0005–.0026	2.300	.0005–.0022	3	.0035–.0085
	V6-173/W	.0007–.0017	.010	.010	.9199	1.9983–1.9993	.0014–.0038	2.6477	.0016–.0032	3	.0024–.0084
	V6-173/X	.0007–.0017	.010	.010	.9199	1.9983–1.9993	.0014–.0038	[6]	.0016–.0032	3	.0024–.0084
	V6-181/E	.0008–.0020	.010	.015	.9392	2.2487–2.2495	.0005–.0026	2.4995	.0003–.0018	3	.003–.011
	V6-231/3	.0008–.0020	.010	.015	.9392	2.2487–2.2495	.0005–.0026	2.4995	.0003–.0018	3	.003–.011
	V6-262/T[2]	.0035–.0045	[5]	.010	1.095	2.2490–2.2500	.0005–.0025	2.9993–3.0003	[3]	3	.001–.007
1986	4-151/R	.0025–.0033	.010	.010	.9400	2.000	.0005–.0026	2.300	.0005–.0022	3	.0035–.0085
	V6-173/X	.0007–.0017	.010	.020	.9054	1.9983–1.9993	.0014–.0037	[7]	.0016–.0033	3	.0020–.0033
	V6-173/W	.0010–.0020	.010	.020	.9054	1.9983–1.9993	.0014–.0037	[7]	.0016–.0033	3	.0020–.0033

[1]—Fit rings in tapered bores for clearances given in tightest portion of ring travel. Clearances specified are minimum gaps.
[2]—Diesel engine.
[3]—Nos. 1, 2 & 3, .005–.0021 inch; No. 4, .0020–.0034 inch.
[4]—Nos. 1, 2 & 4, 2.5336–2.5346 inch; No. 3, 2.5331–2.5340 inch.
[5]—Top ring, .019 inch; 2nd ring, .013 inch.
[6]—Nos. 1, 2 & 4, 2.4936–2.4946 inch; No. 3, 2.4931–2.4941 inch.
[7]—Engines stamped A or T, 2.6473–2.6483 inch; engines stamped K, 2.4937–2.4947 inch. Engine identification stamp (A, K or T) on cylinder block at top front flange or below exhaust manifold on front of engine. The letter stamp will appear beside engine code & unit number.

Engine Tightening Specifications★

★ Torque specifications are for clean and lightly lubricated threads only. Dry or dirty threads produce increased friction which prevents accurate measurement of tightness.

Year	Engine Model/ V.I.N.	Spark Plugs Ft. Lbs.	Cylinder Head Bolts Ft. Lbs.	Intake Manifold Ft. Lbs.	Exhaust Manifold Ft. Lbs.	Rocker Arm Stud Ft. Lbs.	Rocker Arm Cover Ft. Lbs.	Connecting Rod Cap Bolts Ft. Lbs.	Main Bearing Cap Bolts Ft. Lbs.	Flywheel to Crankshaft Ft. Lbs.	Vibration Damper or Pulley Ft. Lbs.
1982	4-151/R	15	85[8]	29	44	20[6]	6	32	70	44	200
	V6-173/X	7–15	65–75	20–25	22–28	43–49	6–9	34–40	63–74	45–55	66–84
	V6-181/E	15	80	45	25	30[7]	4	40	100	60	225
	V6-262/T[1]	—	[2][3]	41	29	[4]	[5]	42	107	76	160–350
1983	4-151/R	15	85[8]	29	44	20[6]	6	32	70	63	200
	V6-173/X,Z	7–15	65–75	20–25	22–28	43–49	6–9	34–40	63–74	45–55	66–84
	V6-181/E	15	80	45	25	30[7]	4	40	100	60	225
	V6-262/T[1]	—	[2][3]	41	29	[4]	[5]	42	89	76	160–350
1984	4-151/R	15	92[8]	29	44	20[6]	6	32	70	44	200
	V6-173/X,Z	7–15	65–75	20–25	22–28	43–49	6–9	34–40	63–74	45–55	66–84
	V6-181/E	15	80	45	25	30[7]	4	40	100	60	225
	V6-231/3	15	80	45	25	30[7]	4	40	100	60	225
	V6-262/T[1]	—	[2][3]	41	31	[4]	[5]	42	89	76	203–350

continued

ENGINE TIGHTENING SPECIFICATIONS—Continued

★ Torque specifications are for clean and lightly lubricated threads only. Dry or dirty threads produce increased friction which prevents accurate measurement of tightness.

Year	Engine Model/ V.I.N.	Spark Plugs Ft. Lbs.	Cylinder Head Bolts Ft. Lbs.	Intake Manifold Ft. Lbs.	Exhaust Manifold Ft. Lbs.	Rocker Arm Stud Ft. Lbs.	Rocker Arm Cover Ft. Lbs.	Connecting Rod Cap Bolts Ft. Lbs.	Main Bearing Cap Bolts Ft. Lbs.	Flywheel to Crankshaft Ft. Lbs.	Vibration Damper or Pulley Ft. Lbs.
1985	4-151/R	15	85⑧	29	44	20⑥	6	32	70	44	200
	V6-173/W,X	7–15	65–75	20–25	22–28	43–49	6–9	34–40	63–74	45–55	66–84
	V6-181/E	15	80	47	25	25⑦	6	40	100	60	200
	V6-231/3	15	80	47	25	25⑦	6	40	100	60	200
	V6-262/T①	—	②⑨	41	31	④	⑤	42	89	76	203–350
1986	4-151/R	15	85⑧	29	44	20⑥	6	32	70	44	200
	V6-173/W, X	11	65–90	20–25	22–28	43–49	6–9	34–40	63–74	40–52	67–85
	V6-231/3, B	20	—	32	37	43⑥	7	40	100	60	200

①—Diesel engine.
②—Clean & dip entire bolt in engine oil before tightening to obtain a correct torque reading.
③—Torque inner 8 bolts to 142 ft. lbs. Torque outer 6 bolts (bolts nearest intake & exhaust manifold to cylinder block mating surfaces) to 59 ft. lbs.
④—Rocker arm pivot studs, 11 ft. lbs.; rocker arm nuts, 28 ft. lbs.
⑤—Fully driven, seated & not stripped.
⑥—Rocker arm bolt.
⑦—Rocker arm shaft.
⑧—Requires thread sealer on bolt threads and underside of bolt heads.
⑨—Refer to text for proper torque and sequence procedure.

Cooling System & Capacity Data

Year	Model & Engine/V.I.N.	Cooling Capacity, Qts.		Radiator Cap Relief Pressure, Lbs.	Thermo. Opening Temp.	Fuel Tank Gals.	Engine Oil Refill Qts.	Transaxle Oil	
		Less A/C	With A/C					Manual Transaxle Pts.	Auto. Transaxle Qts.①
1982	4-151/R	9.4	9.7	15	195	16	3②	—	5
	V6-173/X	11.4	11.7	15	195	16	4②	—	5
	V6-181/E	13.5	14.25	15	195	16	4③	—	5
	V6-262/T⑤	13.2	13.7	15	195	16	6④	—	5
1983	4-151/R	9.4⑥	9.7⑥	15	195	16	3②	—	⑦
	V6-173/X,Z	11.9⑧	12.4⑧	15	195	16	4②	—	⑦
	V6-181/E	13.5⑨	14.4	15	195	16	4③	—	⑦
	V6-262/T⑤	13⑩	13.9	16–18.5	195	16	6④	—	⑦
1984	4-151/R	9.4⑥	9.7⑥	15	195	15.7	3②	6	⑦
	V6-173/X,Z	12.5⑬	12.6⑬	15	195	15.7	4②	6	⑦
	V6-181/E	12.8⑪	13.1⑪	15	195	15.7	4③	6	⑦
	V6-231 MFI/3	12.1	12.6	15	195	15.7	4③	6	⑦
	V6-262/T⑤	12.4⑫	12.6	16–18.5	185	16.4	6④	6	⑦
1985	4-151/R	9.4⑥	9.7⑥	15	195	15.7	3②	—	⑦
	V6-173/W,X	—	—	15	195	15.7	4②	—	—
	V6-181/E	12.8⑪	13.1⑪	15	195	15.7	4③	—	⑦
	V6-231/3	12.1	12.6	15	195	15.7	4③	—	⑦
	V6-262/T⑤	12.4⑫	12.6⑫	16–18.5	185	16.4	6④	—	⑦
1986	4-151/R	9.4	9.7	15	195	15.7	3.0②	—	⑦
	V6-173/W, X	11.8	12	15	195	16.4	4.0②	—	⑦
	V6-231/3, B	12	12.7	15	195	15.7	4.0③	—	⑦

①—Approximate, make final check with dipstick.
②—With or without filter change.
③—Add 1 qt. with filter change.
④—Includes filter. Use recommended diesel engine oil, designated SF/CC or SF/CD.
⑤—Diesel Engine.
⑥—W/heavy duty cooling system, 12 qts.
⑦—Oil pan only, 4 qts.; total capacity, 6 qts.
⑧—W/heavy duty cooling system, 12.7 qts.
⑨—W/heavy duty cooling system, 14 qts.
⑩—W/heavy duty cooling system, 13.9 qts.
⑪—Heavy duty, 13.3 qts.
⑫—Heavy duty, 12.6 qts.
⑬—Heavy duty, 12.8 qts.

Wheel Alignment Specifications

Year	Model	Caster Angle, Degrees		Camber Angle, Degrees				Toe-In Inch	Toe-Out on Turns, Deg.	
		Limits	Desired	Limits		Desired			Outer Wheel	Inner Wheel
				Left	Right	Left	Right			
1982–83	All	0°–+4°	+2°	−½° to +½°	−½° to +½°	0°	0°	0	—	—
1984–86	All	.9° to 2.9°	1.9°	−½° to +½°	−½° to +½°	0°	0°	0	—	—

Electrical Section

STARTER
REPLACE

NOTE: Upon removal of starter, note if any shims are used. If shims are used, they should be reinstalled in their original location during installation.

If starter is noisy during cranking, remove one .015 inch double shim or add one .015 inch single shim to the outer bolt. If starter makes a high pitched whine after firing, add .015 inch double shims until noise ceases.

EXCEPT V6-262 DIESEL

1. Disconnect battery ground cable.
2. Raise and support vehicle.
3. From beneath vehicle, remove two starter motor to engine bolts and lower starter. On 4-151 engine remove nut securing starter bracket to rear of starter.
4. Disconnect solenoid wires and battery cable then, remove starter.
5. Reverse procedure to install.

V6-262 DIESEL

1. Disconnect battery ground cable. On engines with heavy duty option there will be two batteries. Install a suitable engine holding device.
2. Raise and support vehicle. Remove left and center engine mount stud nuts, then 2 front cradle mount bolts and lower cradle. Remove flywheel cover.
3. Remove starter lower shield nut and starter flex shield for removal accessibility.
4. Disconnect wires from starter noting position of wires for installation.
5. Remove starter attaching bolts, then remove starter.

STEERING WHEEL
REPLACE

1. Disconnect battery ground cable.
2. Remove horn button or pad.
3. Remove retainer and steering wheel retaining nut.
4. Remove steering wheel with a suitable puller (tool No. J-1859-03 or BT-61-9).
5. Reverse procedure to install.

IGNITION LOCK
REPLACE

1. Remove steering wheel as outlined under "Steering Wheel, Replace" procedure.
2. Remove turn signal switch as outlined under "Turn Signal Switch, Replace" procedure.
3. Remove buzzer switch and spring clip.

Tighten nut until tool slightly depresses lock plate

Fig. 1   Compressing lock plate

4. Turn lock cylinder to "Run" position, then remove lock cylinder retaining screw and the lock cylinder.
5. To install, rotate lock cylinder to the stop while holding housing. Align cylinder key with keyway in housing, then push lock cylinder into housing until fully seated.
6. Install lock cylinder retaining screw, then the buzzer switch, turn signal switch and steering wheel.

TURN SIGNAL SWITCH
REPLACE

1. Disconnect battery ground cable.
2. Remove steering wheel as outlined under "Steering Wheel, Replace" procedure.
3. Using a screwdriver, pry cover from housing.
4. Using lock plate compressing tool J-23653, compress lock plate, and pry snap ring from groove on shaft, **Fig. 1**. Slowly release lock plate compressing tool, then remove tool and lock plate from shaft end.
5. Slide canceling cam and upper bearing preload spring from end of shaft.
6. Remove turn signal (multi-function) lever.
7. Remove hazard warning knob retaining screw, button, spring and knob.
8. Remove pivot arm.
9. Wrap upper part of electrical connector with tape to prevent snagging of wires during switch removal.
10. Remove switch retaining screws and pull switch up from column, guiding wire harness through column.
11. Reverse procedure to install.

IGNITION & DIMMER SWITCHES
REPLACE

1. Remove turn signal switch as outlined under "Turn Signal Switch, Replace" procedure.
2. Refer to **Figs. 2 and 3** to remove ignition and dimmer switches.

NOTE: On 1985–86 models with tilt column, position ignition switch slider to extreme right for key release feature, one detent to left for park lock feature or two detents to left for all other columns.

3. When installing dimmer switch, depress switch slightly to install a $3/32$ inch twist drill. Force switch upward to remove lash and tighten retaining screw.

WIPER SWITCH
REPLACE

WINDSHIELD

1. Remove turn signal switch as outlined under "Turn Signal Switch, Replace" procedure.
2. Refer to **Figs. 4 and 5** for wiper switch replacement.

REAR WINDOW

1. Disconnect battery ground cable.
2. Remove left hand trim panel, then right side switch trim cover.
3. Remove switch attaching screws, then switch.
4. Reverse procedure to install.

STOPLAMP SWITCH
ADJUST

Insert switch into tubular clip until the switch body seats on the tube clip. Pull the brake pedal rearward against internal pedal stop. This will properly position switch in tubular clip.

NEUTRAL SAFETY SWITCH
REPLACE

1982–86 MODELS WITH AUTO. TRANS & KEY RELEASE

1. Disconnect battery ground cable.
2. Place gear selector in Neutral.
3. Gently rock switch out of steering column.
4. Disconnect electrical connectors, then remove switch from vehicle.
5. Connect electrical connectors to new switch.
6. Align switch actuator with hole in shift tube.
7. Position connector side of switch into lower jacket cutout.
8. Push down front of switch, ensuring switch tangs snap into holes in steering column jacket.
9. Adjust switch by placing gear selector in Park position. The switch main housing and housing back should ratchet, providing proper adjustment.
10. If readjustment is needed, move hous-

REMOVE
1. Remove parts as shown.

INSTALL
1. Install parts as shown.
2. Position rod in slider hole and install ignition switch. Install lower stud and tighten to 3.9 N•m (35 in. lbs.)
3. Install dimmer switch and depress switch slightly to insert 3/32" drill. Force switch up to remove lash, then tighten screw, and nut to 3.9 N•m (35 in. lbs.).
4. Place shifter in neutral and install shift lever.

EXC. KEY RELEASE

MOVE SWITCH SLIDER TO EXTREME LEFT (ACC.) POSITION. THEN MOVE SLIDER TWO DETENTS TO THE RIGHT TO "OFF UNLOCK" POSITION.

KEY RELEASE

MOVE SWITCH SLIDER TO EXTREME LEFT (ACC.) POSITION THEN

INSTALL IGNITION SWITCH

Fig. 2   Ignition & dimmer switch removal & installation (Typical). Except tilt column.

ing as far as possible toward Low gear position, then repeat step 9.

1982-86 MODELS WITH AUTO. TRANS. LESS KEY RELEASE

These vehicles do not use a neutral safety switch. A mechanical block on the transmission gear selector prevents starting the engine when the transmission is in any gear other than Park or Neutral.

HEADLAMP SWITCH
REPLACE

CELEBRITY

1. Disconnect battery ground cable.
2. Remove headlamp switch knob.
3. Remove instrument cluster trim cover.
4. Remove screws attaching headlamp switch mounting plate to instrument cluster carrier.

5. Disconnect headlamp switch connector.
6. Remove headlamp switch from mounting plate.
7. Reverse procedure to install.

CENTURY

1982-84
1. Disconnect battery ground cable.
2. Pry trim panel and center trim cover outward using a suitable tool.
3. Remove three screws in steering column trim collar, then the collar.
4. Remove ash tray, then the six screws attaching trim pad to instrument panel.
5. Remove trim pad, then the three switch to instrument panel attaching screws.
6. Pull switch rearward and remove.
7. Reverse procedure to install.

1985-86
1. Disconnect battery ground cable.
2. Pry steering column collar rearward,

using a suitable tool, and remove.
3. Remove two outer ducts, then the two screws behind the ducts.
4. Remove screw from behind steering column collar.
5. On models less console, open ash tray and remove two screws.
6. On models with console, remove two screws from ash tray cover and trim plate.
7. On all models, pull trim plate rearward to release clips, then remove trim plate.
8. Remove switch to instrument panel attaching screws, then pull switch rearward and remove.
9. Reverse procedure to install.

6000

1. Disconnect battery ground cable.
2. Remove steering column trim cover, headlight rod and knob assembly.
3. Remove left trim plate.
4. Remove three screws attaching switch and bracket assembly to instru-

10-9

REMOVE

1. Remove parts as shown.

INSTALL

1. Install parts as shown.
2. Position rod in slider hole and install ignition switch. Install lower stud and tighten to 3.9 N•m (35 in. lbs.)
3. Install dimmer switch and depress switch slightly to insert 3/32'' drill. Force switch up to remove lash, then tighten screw, and nut to 3.9 N•m (35 in. lbs.).
4. Place shifter in neutral and install shift lever.

Fig. 3   Ignition & dimmer switch removal & installation (Typical). Tilt column.

ment panel, disconnect electrical connector and remove switch/bracket assembly.
5. Loosen bezel and remove switch from bracket.
6. Reverse procedure to install.

INSTRUMENT CLUSTER
REPLACE

CELEBRITY

1. Disconnect battery ground cable.
2. Remove headlamp switch knob, then remove ten screws attaching trim

plate to carrier and remove trim plate, **Fig. 6.**
3. Remove three screws at underside of trim pad, then remove upper screw at right of trim pad opening and two screws at right end of trim pad. Remove trim pad, **Fig. 7.**
4. Remove six cluster lens to carrier attaching screws, **Fig. 8.**
5. Tilt cluster rearward slightly and disconnect all electrical connectors and speedometer cable. Remove cluster.
6. Reverse procedure to install.

CENTURY
1982
1. Disconnect battery ground cable.

2. Disconnect speedometer cable at cruise control transducer (if equipped). If not equipped with cruise control, disconnect cable at upper and lower cable connections.
3. Remove nine screws retaining trim plate to cluster, then put gear shift lever in low and gently pull on trim plate to remove.
4. Remove shift indicator cable clip from shift bowl.
5. Remove lap vent trim cover by removing two attaching screws.
6. Lower steering column by removing front two retaining bolts.
7. Pull instrument cluster outward three inches, and disconnect speedometer

REMOVE

1. Remove ignition and dimmer switch.

2. Remove parts as shown.

3. For KEY RELEASE refer below.

INSTALL

1. For KEY RELEASE refer below.

2. Assemble rack so that first rack tooth engages between first and second tooth of sector.

3. Install parts as shown.

4. Install ignition and dimmer switch.

Fig. 4 Housing and wiper switch removal & installation. Standard steering column

Fig. 5 Cover and wiper switch removal & installation. Tilt steering column

cable from cluster by pushing retaining clip toward cluster and pulling cable away from speedometer.

8. Pull cluster out remainder of the way, then remove one screw retaining electrical connector, **Fig. 9.**

9. Reverse procedure to install.

1983–86 Mechanical Cluster

1. Disconnect battery ground cable.

2. Remove steering column opening filler, then the ash tray.

3. Remove seven left hand trim panel attaching screws.

4. Place gear shift lever into low position and pull trim panel straight forward to release two retaining clips in center of panel, then remove panel.

5. Remove 4 screws attaching cluster assembly to instrument panel, **Fig. 9.**

6. Disconnect speedometer cable from transmission. If two piece cable is used, disconnect in engine compartment to ensure there is cable slack.

7. Remove shift indicator clip and position gear selector in low.

8. Pull cluster assembly out far enough to reach behind and disconnect speedometer cable.

Fig. 6 Trim plate removal. 1982–86 Celebrity

Fig. 7   Trim pad removal. 1982–86 Celebrity

Fig. 8   Instrument cluster. 1982–86 Celebrity

Fig. 9   Instrument cluster removal. 1982–85 Century

NOTE: Shift indicator needle, spring and cable stay with tube and circuit board.

9. To ease removal of cluster on vehicles equipped with tilt wheel, lower wheel, then unscrew tilt lever.
10. On all models, tilt top side of cluster assembly downward and remove cluster.
11. Reverse procedure to install.

1983–86 Digital Cluster
1. Disconnect battery ground cable.
2. Remove steering column opening filler, then the ash tray.
3. Remove seven left hand trim panel attaching screws.
4. Place gear shift lever into low position and pull trim panel straight forward to release two retaining clips in center of panel, then remove panel.
5. Remove 4 screws attaching cluster assembly to instrument panel.
6. Disconnect speedometer cable from transmission. If two piece cable is used, disconnect in engine compartment to ensure there is cable slack.
7. Pull cluster assembly out far enough to disconnect optics head from vehicle speed sensor, then remove cluster assembly.
8. Disconnect 2 electrical connectors on printed circuit from the tube and circuit board assembly.

9. Remove cluster push buttons by pulling straight out.
10. Remove lens and bezel attaching screws, then lens and bezel.
11. Remove tube and circuit board to cluster attaching screws, then tube and circuit board.
12. Remove mechanical odometer from tube and circuit board.
13. Remove 2 telltale lenses and pads from face plate.

Fig. 10   Trim pad removal. 1982–84 Cutlass Ciera & Cruiser

14. Reverse procedure to install.

CUTLASS CIERA & CRUISER

1. Disconnect battery ground cable.
2. On 1982–84 models proceed as follows:
   a. Carefully insert a clean putty knife blade between the trim panel and left trim pad, then gently pry trim panel outward. Using same procedure, remove center trim cover.
   b. Remove three screws in steering column trim collar and remove collar, then remove ash tray.
   c. Remove six screws attaching trim pad to instrument panel, **Fig. 10.** Remove trim pad.
3. On 1985–86 models proceed as follows:
   a. Pry steering column collar rearward, using a suitable tool, and remove.
   b. Remove two outer ducts, then the two screws behind the ducts, **Fig. 11.**
   c. Remove screw from behind steering column collar.

1. TRIM PLATE
2. I.P.
3. SPEAKER OPENING
4. DUCT

VIEW A

Fig. 11   Trim plate removal. 1985–86 Cutlass Ciera & Cruiser

d. On models less console, open ash tray and remove two screws.
e. On models with console, remove two screws from ash tray cover and trim panel.
f. On all models, pull trim plate rearward to release clips, then remove trim plate.
4. On all models, remove screws attaching cluster trim cover to instrument panel, then remove cover.
5. Disconnect speedometer cable at transmission or cruise control transducer (if equipped).
6. Remove steering column trim cover.
7. Disconnect shift indicator clip from steering column shift bowl.
8. Remove 4 screws attaching cluster assembly to instrument panel.
9. Pull assembly out far enough to reach behind cluster and disconnect speedometer cable.
10. Remove cluster assembly.
11. Reverse procedure to install.

6000

1. Remove headlight rod knob assembly.
2. Using thin, flat tool carefully pry left side trim plate away from instrument panel.
3. Remove six screws attaching instrument cluster to instrument panel carrier.
4. Remove instrument panel cluster.
5. Reverse procedure to install.

RADIO
REPLACE

CENTURY

1. Disconnect battery ground cable.
2. On 1982–84 models, remove instrument panel trim plate.
3. On 1985–86 models, remove left hand trim cover.
4. On all models, remove right side instrument panel switch trim panel by removing three screws and gently rocking panel out.
5. Remove four radio assembly attaching screws.
6. Disconnect antenna cable, power and speaker electrical connections.
7. Pull radio outward through instrument panel carrier housing.

8. Reverse procedure to install.

EXCEPT CENTURY

1982–84
1. Disconnect battery ground cable.
2. Remove instrument panel trim plate, except Cutlass Ciera, on Cutlass Ciera left side trim pad.
3. Remove three screws at radio bracket, except Cutlass Ciera, on Cutlass Ciera four screws.
4. Pull radio rearward and disconnect electrical connectors and antenna lead.
5. Remove radio.
6. Reverse procedure to install.

1985–86
1. Disconnect battery ground cable.
2. Loosen instrument panel insulator panel attaching screws, then remove steering column trim cover.
3. Remove ash tray, ash tray assembly and fuse block, separate fuse block and ash tray and push forward to gain access to cigar lighter and rear defogger switch electrical connectors.
4. Disconnect electrical connectors, then remove cigar lighter and glove box.
5. Remove instrument panel center trim panel retaining nuts, then pull trim panel outward to gain access to radio attaching screws.
6. Remove attaching screws, disconnect electrical and antenna connections, then remove radio from vehicle.
7. Reverse procedure to install.

W/S WIPER MOTOR
REPLACE

1. Raise hood, then remove right and left wiper arm and blade assemblies.
2. Remove shroud grille to body attaching screws, then shroud grille.
3. Loosen, but do not remove nuts securing transmission drive link to motor crank arm, then disconnect drive link.
4. Disconnect wiring connectors and washer hoses.
5. Remove 3 screws attaching wiper motor to firewall.
6. Remove motor while guiding crank arm through hole.
7. Reverse procedure to install. Motor must be in "Park" position before

assembling transmission drive link to crank arm. Torque transmission drive link to 53–75 in. lbs.

W/S WIPER TRANSMISSION
REPLACE

1. Raise hood, then remove right and left wiper arm and blade assemblies.
2. Remove shroud grille to body attaching screws, then shroud grille.
3. Loosen, but do not remove nuts securing transmission drive link to motor crank arm, then disconnect drive link, **Fig.12.**
4. Remove 6 screws attaching wiper transmission to body, **Fig.11.**
5. Carefully guide transmission assembly through access hole in upper shroud panel to remove.
6. Reverse procedure to install. Torque transmission drive link nuts to 53–75 in. lbs.

HEATER CORE
REPLACE

LESS A/C

Exc. 1983–86 Century & Cutlass Ciera & 1984–86 Cutlass Cruiser

NOTE: For service procedures on 1983–86 Century and Cutlass Ciera, refer to models with A/C.

1. Drain cooling system.
2. Remove heater inlet and outlet hoses.
3. Remove radio noise supression strap.
4. Remove cover retaining screws and cover.
5. Remove heater core.
6. Reverse procedure to install.

WITH A/C

1. Drain cooling system.
2. On all except diesel engine models, disconnect heater inlet and outlet hoses. On diesel engine models, raise vehicle and disconnect heater inlet

and outlet hoses, then lower vehicle.
3. On diesel engine models, remove instrument panel lower sound absorber. On all models, working inside vehicle, remove the heater ducts, then the heater case side cover.
4. Remove heater lower outlet.
5. Remove 2 housing cover to air valve housing clips, then the housing cover.
6. Remove heater core retaining straps, core tubing retainers, then the core.
7. Reverse procedure to install.

BLOWER MOTOR
REPLACE

1. Disconnect battery ground cable.
2. Disconnect blower motor electrical connections.
3. Remove blower motor attaching screws and the blower motor.
4. Reverse procedure to install.

Fig.12 Windshield wiper transmission removal (typical)

CRUISE CONTROL
ADJUST

BRAKE RELEASE SWITCHES

Electrical & Vacuum Switches
Push switch fully into retaining clip, then pull brake pedal upward to adjust switch position. The electrical switch should break the electrical circuit when the brake pedal is depressed approximately .23–.51 inch.

SERVO, ADJUST

Models With Rod
Install pin retainer to provide minimum slack with throttle in slow idle position.

Models With Bead Chain
Assemble chain into swivel and install retainer so that slack in the chain is not greater than one half the diameter of the ball stud with the engine at normal operating temperature and idle speed solenoid, if equipped, de-energized.

Models With Cable
1. With cable installed in cable and servo brackets, rotate throttle lever so that stud aligns with hole in end of cable.
2. Engage cable with throttle lever stud, then release throttle lever.
3. Hold throttle lever position and pull cable taut from servo end.
4. Connect servo end of cable to servo actuator with pin, using hole which most closely aligns with cable end.

NOTE: Do not stretch cable or open throttle to align cable, as this will not allow engine to return to idle.

CRUISE SPEED, ADJUST

NOTE: On 1984–86 vehicles, cruise speed is controlled by the electronic controller and is not adjustable.

1980–83
The cruise speed adjustment can be set as follows:
1. If vehicle cruises below engagement speed, screw orifice tube on transducer outward.
2. If vehicle cruises above engagement speed, screw orifice tube inward.

NOTE: Each ¼ turn of the orifice tube will change cruise speed approximately one mile per hour. Tighten lock nut after each adjustment.

4-151 & V6-173 Engine Section

Fig. 1   Engine mounts. 1982–86 4-151

Fig. 2   Engine mounts. 1982–84 V6-173

ENGINE MOUNTS
REPLACE

4-151

1. Raise and support front of vehicle, then remove chassis to mount attaching nuts, **Fig. 1.**
2. On models equipped with A/C, remove forward torque rod attaching bolts at radiator support panel.
3. Raise engine slightly using a suitable engine lifting device. Raise engine only enough to provide clearance for mount removal.
4. Remove two upper mount to engine support bracket attaching nuts and remove engine mount.
5. Reverse procedure to install.

V6-173

1. Remove mount retaining nuts from below cradle mounting bracket.
2. Raise engine and remove mount to engine attaching nuts, then remove mount, **Figs. 2 and 3.** Raise engine only enough to provide clearance for mount removal.
3. Reverse procedure to install, then lower engine into position. Install retaining nuts and torque to 35 ft. lbs.

NOTE: After engine mount is properly installed, check both transaxle mounts for proper alignment. If window "A" is not properly located, **Fig. 4,** loosen mount to cradle retaining nuts and allow mount to reposition itself. If transaxle mount is allowed to remain out of position, damage to drive train components may result. Torque retaining nuts to 18 ft. lbs.

ENGINE
REPLACE

1981–86 4-151

Manual Transaxle
1. Disconnect cables from battery.
2. Raise and support vehicle.

3. Remove front engine mount-to-cradle attaching nuts.
4. Remove front exhaust pipe, then disconnect starter motor and position aside.
5. Remove flywheel inspection cover, then lower vehicle.
6. Remove air cleaner assembly.
7. Remove all bell housing attaching bolts.
8. Remove front torque reaction rod from engine and core support.
9. On models equipped with A/C, remove compressor drive belt, then disconnect compressor and position aside. Do not disconnect refrigerant lines from compressor.
10. Disconnect vacuum hoses from vapor canister.

11. On models equipped with power steering, disconnect power steering hose.
12. Disconnect all vacuum hoses and electrical connections needed for engine removal.
13. Remove heater blower motor as described under "Blower Motor, Replace" in the electrical section of this chapter.
14. Disconnect throttle cable.
15. Drain cooling system.
16. Disconnect heater hoses from engine and radiator hoses from radiator.
17. Disconnect engine electrical harness at bulkhead connector.
18. Install suitable engine lifting equipment and raise engine. Disconnect fuel line and the heater hose from

10–15

intake manifold, then remove engine from vehicle.
19. Reverse procedure to install.

Automatic Transaxle
1. Disconnect cables from battery, then drain cooling system.
2. Remove air cleaner assembly and pre-heat tube.
3. Disconnect engine electrical harness connector.
4. Disconnect all external vacuum hose connections.
5. Remove throttle and transaxle linkages at the throttle body assembly and intake manifold.
6. On models equipped with A/C, disconnect compressor and position aside. Do not disconnect refrigerant lines from compressor.
7. Remove upper radiator hose and front engine strut assembly.
8. Disconnect heater hose from intake manifold.
9. Remove all transaxle-to-engine attaching bolts except the top two bolts.
10. Remove front engine mount-to-cradle nuts.
11. Remove front exhaust pipe, then the flywheel inspection cover.
12. Remove starter motor.
13. Remove torque converter-to-flywheel attaching bolts.
14. On models equipped with power steering, remove power steering pump and bracket and position aside.
15. Disconnect heater hose and lower radiator hose.
16. Remove 2 rear transaxle support bracket bolts.
17. Disconnect fuel feed line at fuel filter.
18. Using a suitable jack and a block of wood placed under transaxle, raise engine and transaxle until engine front mount studs clear cradle bracket.
19. Attaching suitable lifting equipment to engine. Put tension on engine and remove 2 remaining transaxle-to-engine attaching bolts.
20. Slide engine assembly forward and lift from vehicle.
21. Reverse procedure to install.

1982–86 V6-173
1. Disconnect battery cables from battery and remove air cleaner.
2. Drain cooling system.
3. Remove engine strut bracket from radiator support and swing rearward.
4. Remove AIR pump and bracket, then remove A/C compressor from mounting bracket and place aside, if so equipped.
5. Disconnect vacuum hosing to all non-engine mounted components.
6. Disconnect accelerator cable and detent cable if so equipped.
7. Disconnect engine harness from ECM and pull connector through front of dash.
8. Disconnect engine harness from junction block at left side of dash panel.
9. Disconnect radiator and heater hoses from engine.
10. Remove power steering pump and

Fig. 3 Engine mounts. 1985–86 V6-173

ALLOW WINDOW ('A') TO CENTER IN INTERLOCK ('B') BEFORE TORQUING RETAINING NUTS

Fig. 4 Transaxle mount alignment. V6-173

bracket assembly from engine, if so equipped.
11. Disconnect fuel lines rubber hose connections at left side of engine compartment.
12. Raise vehicle, remove engine front mount-to-cradle and mount-to-engine bracket retaining nuts at right side of vehicle.
13. Disconnect battery cables from starter motor and transaxle case and remove starter.
14. Remove transaxle inspection cover and on automatic transaxle models, disconnect torque converter flex plate.
15. Remove crankshaft lower pulley and all belts.
16. Disconnect exhaust pipe.
17. Remove lower transaxle-to-engine bolt, located at back side of engine.
18. Disconnect power steering cut-off switch, if so equipped.
19. Remove exhaust cross over pipe, then lower vehicle.
20. Remove remaining transaxle-to-engine bolts. Make note of ground stud location.
21. Place a support under transaxle rear extension. Install suitable lifting device and remove engine.
22. Reverse procedure to install.

Fig. 5   Cylinder head tightening sequence. 4-151

TORQUE ALL BOLTS TO (34 N•m) 25 LB. FT. IN THE NUMERICAL SEQUENCE INDICATED

Fig. 6   Typical intake manifold tightening sequence. 4-151 engines

Fig. 7   Cylinder head tightening sequence. V6-173

CYLINDER HEAD
REPLACE

4-151

1. Raise and support front of vehicle, then drain cooling system and disconnect exhaust pipe from exhaust manifold.
2. Lower vehicle and remove oil dipstick tube and air cleaner.
3. Disconnect wire connectors and vacuum hoses from carburetor or TBI unit.
4. Remove EGR valve base plate from intake manifold, if applicable.
5. Disconnect heater hose from intake manifold, then remove AIR system discharge tube attaching bolt from intake manifold.
6. Remove ignition coil lower attaching bolt, then disconnect wiring from coil.
7. Disconnect all wiring from cylinder head and intake manifold, then remove engine upper support attaching bolt from engine strut.
8. Remove A/C compressor and position aside with refrigerant lines attached.
9. Remove alternator drive belt, then remove AIR pump bracket bolt from engine block, if equipped.
10. Disconnect throttle and throttle valve cables from throttle lever and intake manifold.
11. Disconnect upper radiator hose from cylinder head, then disconnect AIR hose from tube assembly, if equipped.
12. Remove rocker arm cover, then remove rocker arms and push rods.
13. Remove cylinder head attaching bolts, then lift cylinder head and intake and exhaust manifolds as an assembly from cylinder block.
14. Reverse procedure to install. Coat heads and threads of cylinder bolts with a suitable sealing compound, then install bolts finger tight. Tighten cylinder head bolts in sequence shown in **Fig. 5**. Tighten intake manifold bolts in sequence shown in **Fig. 6**, if necessary.

1982–86 V6-173
Right
1. Raise and support vehicle.
2. Drain cooling system.
3. Disconnect exhaust pipe, then lower vehicle.
4. On models equipped with cruise control, remove servo bracket.
5. Remove air management valve and hose.
6. Remove intake manifold, then disconnect exhaust crossover pipe.
7. Remove cover and loosen rocker arm stud nuts until push rods can be removed.
8. Remove cylinder head attaching bolts and the cylinder head.
9. Reverse procedure to install. Coat cylinder head bolt threads with a suitable sealing compound. Torque cylinder head attaching bolts to specifications in sequence shown in **Fig. 7**.

Left
1. Raise and support vehicle.
2. Drain cooling system.
3. Lower vehicle, then remove intake manifold and exhaust crossover pipe.
4. Remove alternator bracket, then the air injection pump and brackets.
5. Remove dipstick tube, then loosen rocker arm stud nuts until push rods can be removed.
6. Remove cylinder head attaching bolts and the cylinder head.
7. Reverse procedure to install. Coat cylinder head bolt threads with suitable sealing compound. Torque cylinder head attaching bolts to specifications in sequence shown in **Fig. 7**.

INTAKE MANIFOLD
REPLACE

4-151

1. Disconnect battery ground cable, then remove air cleaner and heat stove pipe.
2. Disconnect PCV valve and hose at TBI unit, then drain cooling system.
3. Disconnect fuel line and all vacuum hoses that will interfere with manifold removal.
4. Disconnect all electrical connections, then the throttle linkage from TBI unit.
5. Disconnect downshift and cruise control linkage, if applicable.
6. Disconnect throttle linkage and bellcrank and position aside.
7. Disconnect heater hose, then remove upper power steering pump bracket and ignition coil.
8. Remove intake manifold attaching bolts, then the intake manifold.
9. Reverse procedure to install. Torque bolts to specification in sequence shown in **Fig. 6**.

V6-173
Exc. EFI
1. Disconnect battery ground cable, drain cooling system and remove air cleaner.
2. Remove front engine strut, then the strut bracket from the cylinder head, if applicable.
3. Disconnect vacuum hoses and fuel lines as needed.
4. Disconnect wires from spark plugs and retainers on valve covers.
5. Disconnect electrical connectors from carburetor and manifold, as needed, then remove harness from clamps on valve cover.
6. Remove accelerator linkage and return springs from carburetor, and disconnect transmission detent cable, if equipped.
7. On models with cruise control, remove diaphragm actuator bracket.
8. On all models, remove both valve covers.
9. Remove AIR pump and bracket.
10. On all models, remove distributor cap and plug wire assembly.
11. Mark position of distributor rotor for installation, then remove distributor.
12. Disconnect heater, radiator and brake booster hoses from manifold.
13. On all models, remove manifold retaining bolts, manifold and gaskets.
14. Install replacement gaskets on cylinder heads, cutting gaskets only where needed to clear push rods. Hold gaskets in position by extending sealer bead approximately ¼ inch past end of block end rails.
15. Install manifold and torque bolts in sequence as shown in **Fig. 8**.
16. Reverse remaining procedure to complete installation.

With EFI
1. Disconnect battery ground cable, drain cooling system and remove air duct between throttle body and air cleaner.
2. Disconnect vacuum hoses from plenum.
3. Remove bolts securing EGR pipe and throttle body to plenum.
4. Remove throttle cable bracket bolts and bracket.
5. Remove 10 plenum retaining bolts and the plenum, **Fig. 9**.
6. Connect gauge J-34730-1 or equivalent to fuel pressure regulator and bleed off pressurized fuel into a suitable container.
7. Disconnect cold start valve and fuel

Apply 5 mm diameter bead of sealer (#1052366)

Fig. 8   Intake manifold installation. V6-173 exc. MFI

25 N·m (18 FT. LBS.)

21 N·m (15 FT. LBS.)

| 1 | INTAKE MANIFOLD | 3 | GASKET |
| 2 | FUEL RAIL ASSEMBLY | 4 | PLENUM |

Fig. 9   Intake manifold installation. V6-173 w/MFI

0.25 OS

Fig. 10   Oversize valve lifter marking. V6-173

V6-173	1982–86	.347	.394
V6-173 H.O.	1982–84	.394	.410
V6-173 EFI	1985–86	.393	.410

VALVE TIMING
INTAKE OPENS BEFORE TDC

Engine	Year	Degrees
4-151	1982–86	33
V6-173	1982–86	25
V6-173 H.O.	1982–84	31
V6-173 EFI	1985-86	31

VALVE GUIDES

Valve guides are an integral part of the cylinder head and are not removable. If valve stem clearance becomes excessive, the valve stem guide should be reamed to the next oversize and the appropriate oversize valves installed. Valves are available in .003 and .005 inch oversizes for 4-151 engine and .0035, .0155 and .0305 inch for V6-173 engines.

VALVE LIFTERS

NOTE: Some V6-173 engines will be equipped with both standard and .25 mm. oversize valve lifters. The cylinder case will be marked where the oversize valve lifters are installed with a daub of white paint and .25 mm. O.S. will be stamped on the valve lifter boss, **Fig. 10.**

Failure of a hydraulic valve lifter, **Fig. 11,** is generally caused by an inadequate oil supply or dirt. An air leak at the intake side of the oil pump or too much oil in the engine will cause air bubbles in the oil supply to the lifters causing them to collapse. This is a probable cause of trouble if several lifters fail to function, but air in oil is an unlikely cause of failure of a single unit.

On 4-151 engines, valve lifters can be removed after removing rocker arm cover, intake manifold, push rod cover and push rod retainer and guide, if applicable. Loosen rocker arm stud nut and rotate rocker arm so that push rod can be removed, then remove valve lifter. It may be necessary to use tool No. J-3049 to facilitate lifter removal.

On V6-173 engines, valve lifters can be removed after removing rocker arm covers, intake manifold, rocker stud nuts, rocker arm balls, rocker arms and push rods.

lines from fuel rail assembly.
8. Disconnect vacuum hose from regulator and electrical connectors from injectors.
9. Remove fuel rail retaining bolts and the fuel rail.
10. Remove intake manifold.
11. Reverse procedure to install, using new gaskets and injector seals.

ROCKER ARM STUDS
4-151

Rocker arm studs that are cracked or have damaged threads can be removed from the cylinder head using a deep well socket. Install and torque new rocker arm stud to 75 ft. lbs.

V6-173

Rocker arm studs that are cracked or have damaged threads can be replaced. If threads in cylinder head are damaged or stripped, the head can be retapped and a helical type insert added. When installing a new rocker arm stud, torque stud to 43 to 49 ft. lbs.

VALVES
ADJUST
V6-173

1. Crank engine until mark on torsional damper is aligned with TDC mark on timing tab. Check to ensure engine is in the No. 1 cylinder firing position by placing fingers on No. 1 cylinder rocker arms as mark on damper comes near TDC mark on timing tab. If valves are not moving, the engine is in the No. 1 firing position. If valves move as damper mark nears TDC mark on tim-

ing tab, engine is in the No. 4 cylinder firing position and should be rotated one revolution to reach the No. 1 cylinder firing position.
2. With engine in the No. 1 cylinder firing position, adjust the following valves: Exhaust–1, 2, 3; Intake–1, 5, 6. To adjust valves, back off adjusting nut until lash is felt at push rod, then tighten adjusting nut until all lash is removed. This can be determined by rotating the push rod while tightening the adjusting nut. When all lash has been eliminated, turn adjusting nut the additional number of turns listed in the Valve Specifications.
3. Crank engine one revolution until mark on torsional damper and TDC mark are again aligned. This is the No. 4 cylinder firing position. With engine in this position, the following valves can be adjusted: Exhaust–4, 5 & 6; Intake–2, 3 & 4.
4. Install rocker arm covers, then start engine and check timing and idle speed.

VALVE ARRANGEMENT
FRONT TO REAR

4-151	I-E-I-E-E-I-E-I
V6-173 Right	E-I-E-I-I-E
V6-173 Left	E-I-I-E-I-E

VALVE LIFT SPECS.

Engine	Year	Intake	Exhaust
4-151	1982–86	.406	.406

Fig. 11 Hydraulic lifter exploded view. Exc. 1985–86 4-151

Fig. 12 Engine front cover installation. 1982–83 V6-173

ENGINE FRONT COVER
REPLACE

4-151

1982–84

1. Remove drive belts, then remove right front inner fender splash shield.
2. Remove crankshaft pulley attaching bolt, then remove pulley and hub from shaft.
3. Remove alternator lower bracket.
4. Remove front engine mount to cradle nuts, then install suitable engine lifting equipment and raise engine.
5. Remove engine mount bracket to cylinder block bolts, then remove mount and bracket as an assembly.
6. Remove oil pan to front cover attaching screws. Pull front cover slightly forward to permit cutting of oil pan front seal.
7. Using a suitable cutting tool, cut oil pan front seal flush with cylinder block at both sides of cover.
8. Remove front cover and attached portion of oil pan front seal, then remove front cover gasket.
9. Clean gasket surfaces on cylinder block and front cover.
10. Cut tabs from a new oil pan front seal using a suitable cutting tool, then install seal to front cover, pressing tabs into holes provided on front cover.
11. Coat front cover gasket with gasket sealer, then position gasket on front cover.
12. Apply a ⅛ inch bead of RTV sealer to joint formed at oil pan and cylinder block.
13. Install centering tool No. J-23042 into front cover seal bore. It is important that the centering tool be used to align front cover, otherwise damage to seal may result when hub is installed.
14. Install front cover to block, then install and partially tighten the two oil pan to front cover screws.
15. Install front cover to cylinder block attaching screws. Torque all cover attaching screws to 90 inch lbs., then remove centering tool J-23042.

16. Install front mount bracket assembly and alternator lower mounting bracket.
17. Lower engine and remove engine lifting equipment.
18. Install lower mount to cradle nuts, crankshaft pulley and hub, right front fender inner splash shield and drive belts.

NOTE: Apply Drylock No. 299 or equivalent to threaded area of crankshaft pulley to hub bolts before installing bolts.

1985–86

1. Remove drive belts, then the right front inner fender splash shield.
2. Remove crankshaft pulley attaching bolt, then the pulley and hub assembly.
3. Remove lower alternator bracket, then install engine support fixture J28467 or equivalent.
4. Remove engine mount bracket to cylinder block attaching bolts, then the mount and bracket as an assembly.
5. Remove front cover attaching screws, then the front cover.
6. Position oil pan front seal onto cover.
7. Apply a ⅜ inch bead of RTV sealer to joint where front cover meets oil pan, then a ¼ inch bead of sealer to front cover to cylinder block mating surface.
8. Position centering tool J34995 into cover, then install and partially tighten two opposing cover screws.
9. Install remaining attaching screws, then torque all screws to 90 inch lbs.
10. Remove centering tool, then install engine mount and bracket.
11. Install alternator bracket, hub and pulley assembly and retaining bolt.

V6-173

1. Disconnect battery ground cable.
2. Remove accessory drive belts.
3. On 1983–86 models equipped with A/C, remove air injection pump and pump bracket.
4. On all models, remove water pump as described under "Water Pump, Replace."

5. On 1982 models equipped with A/C, remove compressor from mounting bracket and position compressor aside, then remove bracket.
6. On all models, raise and support vehicle.
7. Remove inner fender splash shield, then the accessory drive pulley and damper retaining bolt.
8. Remove damper using tool No. J-23523, or equivalent.
9. On 1982 models, disconnect lower radiator hose from front cover and heater hose from water pump.
10. On 1983–86 models, remove oil pan-to-cover attaching bolts, then lower vehicle.
11. On all models, remove remaining front cover attaching bolts and the cover.
12. Reverse procedure to install. Apply sealant to mating surfaces as shown in **Fig. 12.**

NOTE: On 1984–86 engines, it is only necessary to coat oil pan to front cover sealing surfaces since gasket is used in production.

TIMING GEARS
4-151 ENGINE

When necessary to install a new camshaft gear, the camshaft will have to be removed as the gear is a pressed fit on the camshaft. The camshaft is held in place by a thrust plate which is retained to the engine by two capscrews which are accessible through the two holes in the gear web.

To remove gear, use an arbor press and a suitable sleeve to properly support gear on its steel hub.

Before installing gear, assemble thrust plate and gear spacer ring, then press gear onto shaft until it bottoms against spacer ring. The thrust plate end clearance should be .0015–.0050 inch. If clearance is less than .0015 inch, the spacer ring should be

TIMING MARKS

Fig. 13   Valve timing marks.
4-151

1 CYLINDER
AT T.D.C.

4 CYLINDER
AT T.D.C.

Fig. 14   Valve timing marks.
V6-173

NOTCH TOWARD
FRONT OF ENGINE

DIMPLES
TOWARD REAR
OF ENGINE

Fig. 15   Piston & rod assembly.
4-151

replaced. If clearance is greater than .0050 inch, the thrust plate should be replaced.

The crankshaft gear can be removed using a puller and two bolts in the tapped holes of the gear.

When installing timing gears, make sure that the marks on the gears are properly aligned, **Fig. 13.**

NOTE: The valve timing marks, **Fig. 13,** do not indicate TDC, compression stroke for No. 1 cylinder for use during distributor installation. When installing the distributor, rotate engine until No. 1 cylinder is on compression stroke and the camshaft timing mark is 180° from the valve timing position shown in **Fig. 13.**

TIMING CHAIN
REPLACE

V6-173

1. Remove front cover as described under "Front Cover, Replace."
2. Place No. 1 piston at top dead center with marks on camshaft and crankshaft sprockets aligned, **Fig. 14.**
3. Remove camshaft sprocket bolts, then remove sprocket and timing chain. If sprocket does not come off easily, tap lower edge of sprocket with a plastic mallet.
4. If crankshaft sprocket is to be replaced, remove sprocket using a suitable puller. Install new sprocket, aligning key and keyway.
5. Install timing chain on camshaft sprocket. Hold sprocket vertically with chain hanging down and align marks on camshaft and crankshaft sprockets.
6. Align dowel pin hole in sprocket with dowel pin on camshaft, then install sprocket on camshaft.
7. Using camshaft sprocket attaching bolts, draw sprocket on camshaft. Torque bolts to 15 to 20 ft. lbs.
8. Lubricate timing chain with engine oil, then install front cover as outlined previously.

CAMSHAFT
REPLACE

4-151

1. Remove engine from vehicle as

described under "Engine, Replace."
2. Remove rocker arm cover, then loosen rocker arm stud nuts and pivot rocker arms clear of push rods.
3. Remove distributor and fuel pump or vacuum pump, if equipped.
4. Remove push rod cover, push rods and valve lifters.
5. Remove alternator, alternator lower mounting bracket and engine front mount bracket assembly.
6. Remove oil pump driveshaft and gear assembly.
7. Remove front pulley hub and front cover assembly.
8. Working through holes in camshaft sprocket, remove two camshaft thrust plate retaining screws.
9. Pull camshaft and gear assembly from engine block. Use care not to damage camshaft bearings.
10. Reverse procedure to install. When installing camshaft, align crankshaft and camshaft valve timing marks on gear teeth, **Fig. 13.**

NOTE: The valve timing marks, **Fig. 13,** does not indicate TDC compression stroke for No. 1 cylinder for use during distributor installation. When installing the distributor, rotate engine until No. 1 cylinder is on compression stroke and the camshaft timing mark is 180 degrees from valve timing position shown in **Fig. 13.**

V6-173

1. Remove engine from vehicle as described under "Engine, Replace."
2. Remove valve lifters and engine front cover as described previously.
3. Remove fuel pump and push rod.
4. Remove timing chain and sprocket as described under "Timing Chain, Replace."
5. Withdraw camshaft from engine, using care not to damage camshaft bearings.
6. Reverse procedure to install. When installing timing chain, align valve timing marks as shown in **Fig. 14.**

NOTE: The valve timing marks, **Fig. 14,** does not indicate TDC compression stroke for No. 1 cylinder for use during distributor

installation. When installing the distributor, rotate engine until No. 1 cylinder is on compression stroke and the camshaft timing mark is 180 degrees from valve timing position shown in **Fig. 14.**

PISTONS & RODS
ASSEMBLE

4-151

Assemble piston to rod with notch on piston facing toward front of engine and the raised notch side of rod at bearing end facing toward rear of engine, **Fig. 15.**

Upon installation, measure the connecting rod side clearance using a suitable feeler gauge. Clearance should be .006 to .022 inch.

V6-173

Assemble pistons to connecting rods as shown in **Fig. 16.**

Upon installation, measure the connecting rod side clearance using a suitable feeler gauge. Clearance should be .006 to .017 inch.

PISTONS, PINS & RINGS

4-151

Pistons and rings are available in standard and oversizes of .010, .020 and .030 inch. Piston pins are available in oversizes of .001 and .003 inch.

V6-173

Pistons and rings are available in standard size and oversizes of .05 and 1 mm.

NOTCHES TOWARD FRONT OF ENGINE

BEARING TANG SLOTS

RIGHT BANK NOS. 1·3·5

LEFT BANK NOS. 2·4·6

Fig. 16   Piston & rod assembly. V6-173

1—OIL PAN

2—APPLY A 3/8" WIDE BY 3/16" THICK BEAD OF RTV SEALER IN AREA INDICATED

3—APPLY A 3/16" WIDE BY 1/8" THICK BEAD OF RTV SEALER IN AREA INDICATED

4—ENGINE BLOCK ASSEMBLY

5—REAR BEARING

6—GROOVE IN MAIN BEARING CAP MUST BE FILLED FLUSH TO 1/8" ABOVE SURFACE WITH RTV

Fig. 17   Oil pan sealer application. 1984–86 V6-173

MAIN & ROD BEARINGS

Main and rod bearings are available in standard size and undersizes of .001, .002 and .010 inch for the 4-151 engine. Main bearings are available in standard size and undersizes of .013 and .026 mm and connecting rod bearings are available in standard size and undersizes of .016 and .032 mm. for the V6-173 engine.

OIL PAN
REPLACE
4-151

1. Raise vehicle and drain crankcase.
2. Remove engine front mount to cradle attaching nuts.
3. Disconnect exhaust pipe at manifold and rear transaxle mount or converter.
4. Remove starter motor and flywheel housing cover, then the splash shield, if applicable.
5. Remove alternator upper mounting bracket and if equipped with power steering, the power steering pump and bracket.
6. Install a suitable engine lifting device and raise engine.
7. Remove lower alternator mounting bracket and engine support bracket.
8. Remove oil pan attaching bolts and oil pan.
9. Clean engine block and oil pan gasket surfaces.
10. Reverse procedure to install, noting the following:
    a. On 1982–83 engines, apply a ⅛ inch by ¼ inch bead of RTV sealant at split lines of front and side oil pan gaskets. Also apply a small amount of sealant in depressions where rear oil pan gasket engages engine block.
    b. On 1984–86 engines, apply RTV sealant as shown in **Fig. 17**.

NOTE: When installing oil pan attaching bolts, the bolts attaching the oil pan to the front cover should be installed last. These bolts are installed at an angle and the bolt holes will only be aligned after the other oil pan bolts have been installed.

V6-173

1. Disconnect battery ground cable.
2. Raise and support vehicle.
3. Drain engine oil from crankcase.
4. On all models, remove flywheel housing shield or clutch housing cover as applicable.
5. Remove starter motor.
6. Attach suitable lifting equipment to engine. Remove engine mount bracket-to-engine attaching bolts and raise engine slightly.
7. On all models, remove oil pan attaching bolts and the oil pan.
8. Reverse procedure to install. Apply a ⅛ inch bead of RTV sealer to oil pan sealing flange.

OIL PUMP SERVICE
4-151
Removal

1. Drain crankcase, then remove oil pan as described under "Oil Pan, Replace."
2. Remove two oil pump mounting bolts and nuts from main cap bolt and remove oil pump and screen as an assembly.

Disassemble

1. Remove four pump cover to body attaching screws, then remove cover, idler and drive gears and shaft, **Fig. 18.**
2. Remove pin, retainer, spring and pressure regulator valve.

Inspection

Inspect pump components and should any of the following conditions be found, the oil pump assembly should be replaced.
    a. Inspect pump body for cracks and excessive wear.
    b. Inspect oil pump gears for damage, cracks or excessive wear.
    c. Check shaft for looseness in housing.
    d. Check cover for wear that would allow oil to leak past ends of

PUMP BODY   PICKUP TUBE   PICKUP SCREEN ASSEMBLY

DRIVE GEAR AND SHAFT

IDLER GEAR

COVER

COVER SCREWS

PRESSURE REGULATOR

PRESSURE REGULATOR SPRING

SPRING RETAINER

Fig. 18   Oil pump exploded view. 4-151

gears.
    e. Check oil pick screen for damage to screen or relief grommet. Also remove any debris from screen surface.
    f. Check pressure regulator valve for fit in body.

Assemble

1. Place drive gear and shaft in pump body, then install idler gear with smooth side of gear facing pump cover, **Fig. 18**.
2. Install and torque pump cover attaching screws to 105 inch lbs. Check to ensure that pump rotates freely.
3. Install pressure regulator valve, spring, retainer and pin.

Installation

1. Align oil pump shaft with tang on oil pump drive shaft, then install pump on block, positioning pump flange over oil pump drive shaft lower bushing.
2. Install oil pump mounting bolts and torque bolts to 20 ft. lbs., then install oil pan as described under "Oil Pan, Replace."

V6-173
Removal

1. Remove oil pan as described under "Oil Pan, Replace."
2. Remove pump to rear main bearing

Fig. 19 Oil pump exploded view. V6-173

Fig. 20 Rear main seal installation. 1982–84 V6-173

Fig. 21 Rear main bearing cap sealing areas. V6-173

cap bolt and remove pump and extension shaft.

Disassembly

1. Remove pump cover attaching bolts and pump cover, **Fig. 19.**
2. Mark drive and idler gear teeth so they can be installed in the same position, then remove idler and drive gear and shaft from pump body.
3. Remove pin, spring and pressure regulator valve from pump cover.
4. If pick-up tube and screen assembly are to be replaced, mount pump cover in a soft jawed vise and remove pick-up tube from cover. Do not remove screen from pick-up tube, these components are serviced as an assembly.

Inspection

1. Inspect pump body and cover for excessive wear and cracks.
2. Inspect pump gear for damage or excessive wear. If pump gears are damaged or worn, the entire pump assembly must be replaced.
3. Check drive gear shaft for looseness in pump body.
4. Inspect pump cover for wear that would allow oil to leak past gear teeth.
5. Inspect pick-up tube and screen assembly for damage.
6. Check pressure regulator valve for fit in pump cover.

Assembly

1. If pick-up tube and screen were removed, apply sealer to end of pick-up tube, then mount pump cover in a soft jawed vise and using tool No. J-8369, tap pick-up tube into position using a plastic mallet.

NOTE: Whenever the pick-up tube and screen assembly has been removed, a new pick-up tube and screen assembly should be installed. Use care when installing pick-up tube and screen assembly so that tube does not twist, shear or collapse. Loss of a press fit condition could result in an air leak and a loss of oil pressure.

2. Install pressure regulator valve, spring and pin, **Fig. 19.**
3. Install drive gear and shaft in pump body.

4. Align marks made during disassembly, then install idler gear.
5. Install pump cover gasket, cover and attaching bolts. Torque bolts to 6 to 9 ft. lbs.
6. Rotate pump drive shaft by hand and check pump for smooth operation.

Installation

1. Assemble pump and extension shaft with retainer to rear main bearing cap, aligning top end of hexagon extension shaft with hexagon socket on lower end of distributor shaft.
2. Install pump to rear main bearing cap bolt.
3. Install oil pan as described under Oil Pan, Replace.

CRANKSHAFT REAR OIL SEAL
REPLACE

4-151

NOTE: The rear main oil seal is a one piece unit and is replaced without removing the oil pan or crankshaft.

1. Remove transaxle and flywheel.
2. Using a suitable screwdriver, remove rear main bearing oil seal. Use care not to scratch crankshaft.
3. Lubricate inside and outside diameters of replacement seal with engine oil. Install seal by hand onto rear crankshaft flange with helical lip side facing toward engine. Ensure seal is firmly and evenly seated.
4. Install flywheel and transaxle.

REAR MAIN BEARING OIL SEAL REPAIR
V6-173

1982–84

SERVICE BULLETIN: When replacement of the rear main seal is necessary, the rope type seal used during engine assembly should be replace with rubber split seal No. 14069889, or equivalent using the following procedure. Disregard instructions furnished with the replacement seal that refer to Cavalier models.

1. Remove oil pan and oil pump.
2. Remove rear main bearing cap.
3. Remove upper and lower rope seals, taking care not to damage crankshaft, then clean seal remnants and oil from seal channels.

NOTE: It may be necessary to loosen No. 2 and 3 bearing cap bolts to allow removal of the rope type seal and installation of the upper split seal.

4. Apply a thin coating of gasket sealing compound 1050026 or equivalent to outer circumference of replacement seal, **Fig. 20,** keeping sealer off seal lips.
5. Use a piece of shim stock to guide seal into block channel and roll seal into block by turning crankshaft.

NOTE: Ensure that large seal lip is toward front of engine and that smaller dust lip faces the flywheel.

6. Apply sealer to lower half of seal as in step 4, then install seal into bearing cap.
7. Apply a thin bead of anaerobic sealant to bearing cap surface as shown in **Fig. 21.** Keep sealant off ends of seal, main bearing, and out of drain slot.
8. Apply a thin film of motor oil to seal lip, install bearing cap and torque cap bolts to specifications.

NOTE: If other main bearing cap bolts were loosened, retorque as needed.

9. Reinstall oil pump and pan as outlined.
10. Fill crankcase, start engine and check for leaks.

1985–86

Thin Seal

1. Remove engine as outlined under "Engine, Replace" procedure.
2. Remove oil pan and oil pump assembly.
3. Remove water pump and timing chain.
4. Remove connecting rod and main bearing caps, then the crankshaft and oil seal.

Fig. 22 Installing thin type seal. 1985–86 V6-173

POSITION J-29176 AGAINST TIMING COVER BOSS PRIOR TO REMOVING WATER PUMP BOLTS.

J-29176

TORQUE MOUNTING BOLT 12 N·m (10 FT. LBS.)

Fig. 24 Positioning tool J-29176 against timing cover boss. V6-173

5. Coat outer diameter of new seal with sealant 1052756 or equivalent.
6. Position seal/tool assembly on rear of crankshaft, ensuring arrows on tool face toward cylinder and case assembly, **Fig. 22.**
7. Install crankshaft, discard tool, then coat crankshaft journals with engine oil.
8. Apply a 1 millimeter bead of anaerobic sealant to bearing cap surface as shown in **Fig. 21.**
9. Reinstall rear main cap, main bearing caps and connecting rod caps and torque to specifications.
10. Reverse removal procedure to complete installation.

Thick Seal
1. Remove transaxle and flexplate.
2. Using a screwdriver or similar tool, pry out old seal. Use care to avoid damaging crankshaft. File all burrs or knicks as required.
3. Install new seal using tool J34686 as follows:
   a. Apply a light coat of engine oil to I.D. of oil seal.
   b. Slide seal over tool mandril until dust lip bottoms squarely against collar of tool.
   c. Align dowel pin of tool with dowel pin hole in crankshaft, **Fig. 23,** then

attach tool to crankshaft with screw provided.
   d. Turn handle of tool until seal is pushed into bore and collar is positioned firmly against case. Remove tool.
4. Install flywheel and transmission, then start engine and check for leaks.

BELT TENSION DATA

	New Lbs.	Used Lbs.
Air Cond.		
4-151	135–165	65①
V6-173	145	65–80
A.I.R. Pump		
V6-173	100	45①
Alternator		
4-151	120–150	55①
V6-173	145	65–80
Power Steer.		
4-151	120–150	55①
V6-173	135	65–80

①—Minimum.

WATER PUMP
REPLACE

4-151

Removal
1. Disconnect battery negative cable, then drain cooling syste.
2. Remove accessory drive belts.
3. Using tool J 25034, remove pulley.
4. Remove water pump attaching bolts and remove pump.

Installation
1. With sealing surfaces cleaned, place a ⅛ inch bead of sealant, part number 1052289 or equivalent, on water pump sealing surface.
2. With sealing surfaces still wet, install pump and attaching bolts. Coat threaded area of bolts with part number 1052080 sealer or equivalent and torque bolts to 6 ft. lbs. on 1982–84 models or 20 ft. lbs. for 1985–86.
3. Using tool J-25033, install pulley on pump.
4. Install accessory drive belts and adjust to specifications.
5. Connect battery negative cable.

V6-173

1. Disconnect battery ground cable, then drain cooling system.
2. Disconnect heater hose at water pump, then remove drive belts and water pump pulley.
3. Using the existing tapped hole in the cylinder head, install tool No. J-29167 and torque mounting bolt to 10 ft. lbs., **Fig. 24.**
4. Remove water pump attaching bolts, then remove pump assembly from engine.
5. Clean mating surfaces of water pump and cylinder block, then apply a bead of sealant 1052375 or equivalent to water pump mating surface, **Fig. 25.**

Fig. 23 Installing thick type seal. 1985–86 V6-173

2 mm DIAMETER BEAD OF ANAEROBIC SEALANT # 1052357 OR EQUIVALENT

Fig. 25 Applying sealer to water pump mating surfaces. V6-173

NOTE: On some engines a gasket is used to seal mating surfaces. On these engines, replace gasket instead of using sealant mentioned above.

6. Apply sealant 1052080 or equivalent to pump attaching bolt threads, then install water pump assembly. Torque M6x1.0 bolts to 8 ft. lbs., M8x1.25 bolts to 16 ft. lbs. and M10x1.5 bolts to 25 ft. lbs.
7. Remove tool J-29176, then install water pump pulley and drive belts and connect heater hose to pump.
8. Fill cooling system and connect battery ground cable, then start engine and check for leaks.

FUEL PUMP
REPLACE

V6-173 Less EFI

1. Disconnect fuel inlet and outlet lines from pump.
2. Disconnect vapor return hose if equipped.
3. Remove fuel pump attaching nuts and the fuel pump.
4. Reverse procedure to install, using a new gasket.
5. Start engine and check for leaks.

V6-181 & V6-231 Engine Section

Fig. 1 Engine mount removal

Fig. 3 Cylinder head bolt tightening sequence. 1982–83 models

ENGINE MOUNTS, REPLACE

1. Raise and support front of vehicle.
2. Attach suitable engine lifting fixture to engine.
3. Remove mount to engine mount bracket nuts. Raise engine slightly and remove mount to frame nuts. Remove mount, **Fig. 1**.
4. Reverse procedure to install.

ENGINE
REPLACE

1. Disconnect battery cables from battery and remove air cleaner.
2. Drain cooling system.
3. Disconnect vacuum hosing to all non-engine mounted components.
4. Disconnect detent cable from throttle lever.
5. Disconnect accelerator linkage.
6. Disconnect engine harness connector.
7. Remove alternator attaching bolts, then alternator.
8. Remove fan blower motor, then AIR pump and mounting bracket, if equipped.
9. Disconnect radiator hoses from radiator and heater hose from engine.
10. Remove power steering pump and bracket assembly from engine, if equipped.
11. Disconnect fuel lines at rubber hose connections.
12. Remove gas spring cylinder from hood, if equipped, then place hood in full open position.

13. Raise vehicle and disconnect exhaust pipe at manifold.
14. Remove engine front mount to cradle retaining nuts, located at right side of vehicle.
15. Disconnect battery cables from starter motor and transaxle case.
16. Remove flex plate cover, then disconnect torque converter form flex plate.
17. Remove transaxle case to cylinder case support bracket bolts, **Fig. 2**.
18. Lower vehicle. Place a support under transaxle rear extension.
19. Disconnect ground strap from engine at engine forward strut. Remove engine strut bracket from radiator support and swing rearward.
20. Remove transaxle to cylinder case retaining bolts. Make note of ground stud location.
21. If equipped with A/C, remove compressor and lay aside.
22. Using a suitable lifting device, remove engine.
23. Reverse procedure to install.

CYLINDER HEAD
REPLACE

1. Disconnect battery ground cable.
2. Remove intake manifold, then loosen and remove belts.
3. If left cylinder head is to be removed, remove dipstick, also remove air and vacuum pumps with mounting bracket if equipped, and position aside with hoses attached.
4. If right cylinder head is to be removed, remove alternator, also disconnect power steering gear pump and brackets attaching to cylinder head.
5. Disconnect wires from spark plugs, then remove spark plug wire clips from rocker arm cover studs.
6. Remove exhaust manifold bolts from head being removed.
7. Clean adjacent area to prevent dirt from entering engine, then remove intake manifold.
8. Remove rocker arm cover, then rocker arm and, if applicable, shaft assembly from cylinder head. Lift out push rods, keeping them in order to ensure proper installation.
9. Loosen all cylinder head bolts, then remove bolts and lift off cylinder head.
10. Reverse procedure to install. Torque cylinder head bolts to specifications in sequence shown in **Figs. 3 or 3A**. On fuel injected engines, torque intake manifold bolts to specifications in sequence shown in **Fig. 4**.

ROCKER ARMS
EXC. V6-231 SFI

A nylon retainer is used to retain the rocker arm. Break them below their heads with a chisel, or pry out with channel locks

Fig. 2 Transaxle to engine case support bracket removal

Fig. 3A Cylinder head bolt tightening sequence. 1984–86 models

Fig. 5. Production rocker arms can be installed in any sequence since the arms are identical.

Replacement rocker arms for all engines are identified with a stamping, right (R) and left (L), **Fig. 6** and must be installed as shown in **Fig. 7**.

To install rocker arms, position arm on rocker shaft, centering it over the ¼ inch hole in the rocker shaft. Then, install new rocker arm retainers in the holes using a ½ inch drift to seat them.

V6-231 SFI

Rocker arms are mounted to the cylinder head via individual iron pedestals and are retained by hardened steel bolts.

To install rocker arms, position pedestal retainer, rocker arm and pedestal onto cylinder head. Install retaining bolts and torque to specification.

VALVE ARRANGEMENT
FRONT TO REAR

V6-181 . . . . E-I-I-E-I-E
V6-231 . . . . E-I-I-E-I-E

VALVE GUIDES

The valve guides are an integral part of the cylinder head and cannot be replaced.

If valve stem clearance is excessive, the valve guide must be reamed and an oversize valve installed. On 1982–85 V6-181 and 1984–86 V6-231 engines, valves are available in oversize of .010 inch.

Fig. 4   Intake manifold tightening sequence V6-231 fuel injected engines

VALVE LIFTERS

Failure of an hydraulic valve lifter, **Fig. 8,** is generally caused by dirt or an inadequate oil supply. An air leak at the intake side of the oil pump or too much oil in the engine will cause air bubbles in the oil supply to the lifters, causing them to collapse. This is a probable cause of trouble if several lifters fail to function, but air in the oil is an unlikely cause of failure of a single unit.

The valve lifters may be lifted out of their bores after removing the rocker arms, push rods and intake manifold. Adjustable pliers with taped jaws may be used to remove lifters that are stuck due to varnish, carbon, etc. **Fig. 8** illustrates one type of lifter used. On V6-231 SFI engines, roller lifters are used to reduce friction and improve performance. The lifters are cylindrical with the exception of two parallel flats milled into the upper part of the body. Slotted guides which hold the lifters in pairs fit over the milled area to keep the lifters from turning in their bores.

ENGINE FRONT COVER
REPLACE

1. Drain engine coolant.

Fig. 7   Service rocker arm installation

Fig. 5   Removing nylon retainer

2. Disconnect upper and lower radiator hoses and heater return hose at water pump.
3. Remove nuts securing front engine mount to cradle, raise engine using suitable lifting device, then remove water pump pulley and drive belts.
4. Remove alternator bracket and alternator.
5. Remove distributor, if applicable. If timing chain and sprockets are not going to be disturbed, note position of distributor rotor for reinstallation in same position.
6. Remove balancer bolt and washer, then remove balancer assembly.
7. Remove bolts attaching engine front cover to cylinder block, **Fig. 9,** also remove two oil pan to engine front cover bolts.
8. Remove engine front cover assembly and gasket, **Fig. 9.**
9. Reverse procedure to install.

NOTE: Prior to reinstalling the engine front cover, remove the oil pump cover and pack the space around the oil pump drive gears completely full of petroleum jelly. Failure to do this may result in the pump losing its prime, causing a "dry" engine start.

When reinstalling engine front cover bolts, apply a suitable sealer to the threads to prevent leakage.

TIMING CHAIN
REPLACE

1. With front cover removed, as outlined in "ENGINE FRONT COVER, RE-PLACE", temporarily install balancer bolt and washer in end of crankshaft. Turn crankshaft so timing marks on

Fig. 6   Service rocker arm identification

sprockets are as close together as possible. Remove balancer bolt and washer using a sharp blow on wrench handle, so bolt can be removed without changing position of sprockets.
2. Remove crankshaft oil slinger and camshaft sprocket bolts.
3. Using two large screwdrivers, alternately pry off sprockets and chain.
4. Thoroughly clean all parts that are to be reused.
5. Assemble timing chain on sprockets and slide sprockets and chain assembly onto camshaft and crankshaft with timing marks aligned as shown in **Fig. 10.**
6. Install sprocket bolts and torque to 20 ft. lbs.
7. Install oil slinger, camshaft thrust button, timing chain dampener, if equipped, and engine front cover.

CAMSHAFT
REPLACE

1. Remove engine as outlined in "ENGINE, REPLACE".
2. Remove intake manifold.
3. Remove rocker arm covers.
4. Remove rocker arm and shaft assemblies, push rods and valve lifters.
5. Remove timing chain cover.
6. Align timing marks of camshaft and crankshaft sprocket. This avoids burring of camshaft journals by crankshaft during removal. Remove timing chain and sprocket.

1	LIFTER BODY	5	BALL CHECK	6	PLUNGER
2	PLUNGER SPRING	7	OIL METERING VALVE		
3	BALL CHECK RETAINER	8	PUSH ROD SEAT		
4	BALL CHECK SPRING	9	RETAINER RING		

Fig. 8   Exploded view of hydraulic valve lifter. Exc. V6-231 SFI engine

Fig. 9 Engine front cover removal & installation

Fig. 11 Piston and rod assembly

Fig. 10 Valve timing marks

Fig. 12 Oil pump cover and relief valve and spring installation

MAIN & ROD BEARINGS

Main bearings are available in standard sizes and undersizes of .001 and .002 inch. Rod bearings are available in standard sizes and in undersize of .008.

OIL PAN
REPLACE

1. Disconnect battery ground cable.
2. Raise and support vehicle.
3. Drain oil and remove flywheel cover.
4. Remove oil pan.
5. Reverse procedure to install. Apply RTV sealer to oil pan flange and torque oil pan bolts to 14 ft. lbs.

NOTE: Late model vehicles use a formed rubber gasket. When replacing oil pan, clean oil pan flange, then install pan using new gasket.

OIL PUMP SERVICE
Exc. Gerotor Type

Pump (V6-231 SFI)
REMOVAL & INSPECTION

1. Remove oil filter.
2. Remove screws attaching oil pump cover assembly to timing chain cover. Remove cover assembly and slide out oil pump gears.
3. Wash off gears and inspect for wear or scoring. Replace any gears not found serviceable.
4. Remove oil pressure relief valve cap, spring and valve, **Fig. 12**. Oil filter by-pass valve and spring are staked in place and should not be removed.
5. Wash parts thoroughly, inspect relief valve for wear or scoring. Check relief valve spring to see that it is not worn on its side or collapsed. Replace any

7. Slide camshaft forward out of bearing bores, using care so as not to damage bearing surfaces.
8. Reverse procedure to install. When installing camshaft, align crankshaft and camshaft timing marks as shown in **Fig. 10**.

PISTON & ROD
ASSEMBLE

Rods and pistons should be assembled and installed as shown in **Fig. 11**.

Measure connecting rod side clearance using a suitable feeler gauge. Clearance should be .0005–.0026 inch.

PISTONS, PINS & RINGS

Pistons are available in standard sizes and oversizes of .010 and .030 inch. Rings are available in standard sizes and oversizes of .010 and .030 inch. Piston pins are supplied with piston and available only in standard sizes.

relief valve spring that is questionable.
6. Check relief valve in its bore in cover. The valve should have no more clearance than an easy slip fit. If any excessive clearance can be felt, valve and/or cover should be replaced.
7. Check relief by-pass valve for cracks, or warping. Valve should be free of nicks or scratches.

ASSEMBLY & INSTALLATION

1. Lubricate and install pressure relief valve and spring in bore of oil pump cover, **Fig. 12**.
2. Install cap and gasket. Torque cap to 35 ft. lbs.
3. Install oil pump gears and shaft in oil pump body section of timing chain cover to check gear end clearance and side clearance.
4. Check oil pump end clearance by placing a straight edge over gears and measure clearance between straight edge and gasket surface, **Fig. 13**. Clearance should be between .002 and .006 inch. If clearance is less than .002 inch, measure gears and pocket to determine which is out of specifica-

Fig. 13 Checking oil pump gear end clearance

LENGTH OF GEAR
.8735" — .8720"

DIAMETER OF GEAR
1.666" — 1.664"

Fig. 14 Checking length and diameter of pump gear

DEPTH OF POCKET
.8697"—.8677"

DIAMETER OF POCKET
1.674"—1.671"

Fig. 15 Checking depth and diameter of gear pocket

1 CHECK CLEARANCE BETWEEN GEAR TEETH AND SIDE WALL, CLEARANCE SHOULD BE BETWEEN .002" & .005"

Fig. 16 Checking oil pump gear side clearance

tion, **Figs. 14 and 15.**

5. Check oil pump side clearance, **Fig. 16.** Clearance should be between .002 and .005 inch. If clearance is greater than .0050 inch, measure gears and pocket to determine which is out of specification, **Figs. 14 and 15.**
6. Check oil pump cover flatness by placing a straight edge across cover face, using feeler gauge between straight edge and pump cover. If clearance is .001 or more pump cover must be replaced.
7. If gear clearance and oil pump cover is flat and side clearance is satisfactory remove gears and pack gear pocket full of petroleum jelly.

NOTE: Never use chassis lube when reinstalling oil pump gears.

8. Reinstall gears so petroleum jelly fills entire gear pocket and between teeth of gears. Place gasket in position.

NOTE: Unless the pump is packed with petroleum jelly it may fail to prime itself when engine is started and damage to engine may result.

9. Install cover assembly screws. To ensure proper seal of gasket, torque screws alternately and evenly to 10 ft. lbs.
10. Install filter on nipple.

Gerotor Type Pump (V6-231 SFI)

REMOVAL & INSPECTION

1. Remove engine front cover, then the oil filter adapter, pressure regulator valve and valve spring.
2. Remove oil pump cover attaching screws, cover and gears, **Fig. 17.**
3. Inspect pump cover and housing for cracks, scoring, porosity and damaged threads, pressure regulator valve and spring for sticking, scoring or tension loss and gears for chipping, galling or excessive wear. Replace as necessary.
4. Check gear clearance as follows:
   a. Check inner gear tip clearance with feeler gauge as shown in **Fig. 18.** Maximum clearance should not exceed .006 inch.
   b. Check outer gear diameter clearance with feeler gauge as shown in **Fig. 19.** Clearance should be .008–.015 inch.
   c. Check gear end clearance(gear drop in housing)with suitable dial indicator as shown in **Fig. 20.** Clearance should be .001–.0035 inch.
5. Replace parts as necessary.

ASSEMBLY & INSTALLATION

1. Lubricate gears with motor oil, then install into oil pump housing.
2. Pack pump cavity with petroleum jelly, then install pump cover and attaching screws. Torque attaching screws to 88 inch lbs.
3. Install pressure regulator valve spring and valve.
4. Install oil filter adapter using new gasket. Torque adapter to 30 ft.lbs.
5. Reinstall front cover onto engine.

REAR MAIN BEARING OIL SEAL REPAIR

1. Remove oil pan and oil pump as described previously.
2. Remove rear main bearing cap.
3. Using suitable tool, gently drive upper

1 11 N·m (88 IN. LBS.)
2 OIL PUMP COVER
3 PUMP OUTER GEAR
4 PUMP INNER GEAR
5 FRONT COVER

Fig. 17 Oil pump and housing assembly. Gerotor pump

seal into groove approximately ¼ in.
4. Repeat step 3 for other end of seal.
5. Measure the amount that was driven in on one side and add ¹⁄₁₆ in. Using a suitable cutting tool, cut this length from the oil rear main bearing cap lower seal using the main bearing cap as a guide. Repeat this step for the other end of seal.
6. Place piece of cut seal into groove of seal installer tool guide and install tool guide onto engine block.
7. Using seal packing tool, drive piece of seal into block. Drive seal in until packing tool contacts machined stop.
8. Remove tool guide and repeat steps 6 and 7 for other end of seal.
9. Install new seal in bearing cap.
10. Install rear main bearing cap. Apply a thin film of sealant No. 1052357 or equivalent to rear main bearing cap and case interface. Use care not to allow sealant to contact crankshaft journal or main bearing.

ELECTRIC FUEL PUMP
REPLACE

1. Disconnect battery ground cable, then drain fuel tank.
2. Disconnect tank unit wire from connector in rear compartment.
3. Remove ground wire retaining screw from under body.
4. Disconnect hoses from tank unit.
5. Support fuel tank and disconnect the two fuel tank retaining straps.

Inner Gear Tip Clearance

Fig. 18 Checking inner gear tip clearance. Gerotor pump

Outer Gear Dia. Clearance

Fig. 19 Checking outer gear diameter clearance. Gerotor pump

Gear End Clearance

Fig. 20 Checking gear end clearance. Gerotor pump

30 N·m
(22 FT. LB.)

10 N·m
(7 FT. LBS.)

FRT

Fig. 21 Water pump removal & installation

6. Remove fuel tank from vehicle.
7. Remove fuel gage retaining cam, using tool J-24187, or other suitable tool.
8. Remove sending unit from tank.
9. Electric fuel pump can be unbolted from tank sending unit after sending unit has been removed.
10. Reverse procedure to install.

WATER PUMP
REPLACE

1982

1. Disconnect battery ground cable, then drain cooling system.
2. Remove accessory drive belts.
3. Remove water pump attaching bolts, **Fig. 21.**
4. Remove engine support strut.

5. Place jack under front crossmember and raise jack until vehicle just starts to raise.
6. Remove front two body mount bolts, (#1 and #3), **Fig. 22,** also remove lower cushions and retainers.
7. Thread body mount bolts with retainers a minimum of three turns into cage nuts so bolts restrain cradle movement.
8. Release floor jack slowly until crossmember contacts body mount bolt retainers. As jack is being lowered watch and correct any interference with hose, lines, pipes and cables.

NOTE: Do not lower the cradle without it being restrained as possible damage can occur to the body and underhood items

9. Remove water pump from engine.
10. Reverse procedure to install.

1983–86

1. Disconnect battery ground cable.
2. Drain cooling system, then remove accessory drive belts.
3. Remove lower radiator hose and heater hose at pump.
4. On 1983 models, remove two nuts from front engine mount at cradle, then raise engine using a suitable lifting device and remove water pump pulley attaching bolts.
5. On 1984–86 models, remove water pump pulley attaching bolts. Long bolt is removed through access hole located in the body side rail.

MOUNT #3

MOUNT #4

MOUNT #2

MOUNT #1

Fig. 22 Removing front body mounts

6. On all models, remove water pump pulley.
7. Remove water pump attaching bolts, then the water pump, **Fig. 21.**
8. Reverse procedure to install

BELT TENSION DATA

	New Lbs.	Used Lbs.
1982		
Air Cond.	145	65–80
Alternator	145	65–80
Power Steer.	135	65–80
Air Pump	100	45
1983–85		
Air Cond.	165	90
Alternator	145	70
Power Steer.	165	90
AIR or Vacuum Pump	75	45

V6-262 Diesel Engine Section

Fig. 1   Glow plug wiring schematic (part 1 of 2). 1982–83 models

DIESEL ENGINE DIAGNOSIS

For engine diagnosis, refer to "Section 20."

DIESEL ENGINE ELECTRICAL TROUBLESHOOTING

1982–83

Engine Runs Rough On Cold Start

1. With ignition switch in Run position and engine off, disconnect electrical connector from engine temperature switch, **Fig. 1.**
2. Connect jumper wire between terminals on engine temperature switch electrical connector, and note if fast idle solenoid extends.
3. If solenoid extends, proceed to step 4. If solenoid does not extend, check throttle linkage or solenoid plunger for binding. If linkage is satisfactory, replace solenoid.
4. Connect tachometer J-26925 or equivalent to engine, then start engine and leave jumper wire attached to the engine temperature switch.
5. Disconnect electrical connector from cold advance solenoid. Engine speed should vary 30 RPM when connector is removed.
6. If there is no change in RPM, check solenoid and pump for proper operation and repair or replace as necessary.
7. Turn engine off, then check continuity of engine temperature switch using suitable self-powered test lamp.
8. Test lamp should not light above 120° F. If not satisfactory, replace switch.
9. Using suitable test lamp, ground one lead and connect other lead to dark green wire terminal at diode module A. If test lamp lights and engine is cold, replace coolant temperature switch.
10. Turn ignition OFF, then disconnect all glow plug wire connectors. Connect suitable self-powered test lamp between rear post of glow plug relay and ground.
11. At each glow plug, momentarily connect glow plug wire connector to plug spade terminal. Observe test light.
12. If test lamp lights, glow plug and wire connector are satisfactory. If test lamp does not light, touch wire connector to engine block or other ground. If test lamp lights, replace glow plug. If lamp does not light, replace wire to glow plug.

Engine Stays On Fast Idle

1. With ignition switch in Run position and engine not running, disconnect electrical connector from engine temperature switch, **Fig. 1.**
2. Connect jumper wire between terminals on engine temperature switch and note if fast idle solenoid extends.
3. If solenoid extends, proceed to step 4. If solenoid does not extend, check throttle linkage or solenoid plunger for binding. If linkage is satisfactory, replace solenoid.
4. Check continuity of engine temperature switch with suitable self-powered test lamp.
5. Lamp should light below 120° F and shut off above 120° F. If not satisfactory, replace switch.

Engine Continues To Run With Ignition Off

1. With ignition turned off and engine running, disconnect electrical connector from diode module, **Fig. 1.**
2. If engine stops, diode "C" is shorted. Replace diode module.
3. If engine continues to run, disconnect fuel solenoid pink wire connector.
4. If engine stops, repair or replace fuel solenoid.
5. If engine continues to run, stop engine by crimping flexible fuel return line near fuel supply pump, then repair or replace fuel solenoid.

No Fast Idle W/ Cold Engine

1. With ignition switch in Run position and engine off, disconnect electrical connector from engine temperature switch, **Fig. 1.**
2. Connect jumper wire to both terminals on engine temperature switch connector.
3. Momentarily disconnect and connect fast idle solenoid electrical connector while noting if fast idle solenoid extends.
4. If solenoid does not extend, refer to step 5. If solenoid extends, readjust for correct fast idle operation.
5. Connect one end of suitable test lamp to ground and the other end to white/green lead on models without A/C, or black/pink lead at fast idle solenoid on models with A/C.
6. If test lamp lights, proceed as follows:
   a. Disconnect electrical connector from fast idle solenoid.
   b. Check continuity of fast idle solenoid using suitable self-powered test lamp.
   c. If lamp does not light, replace solenoid.
7. If test lamp does not light, proceed as follows:
   a. Momentarily connect test light lead to pink/black terminal of engine temperature switch.
   b. If test lamp lights, remove connector from switch and check switch for continuity using suitable self-powered test lamp.
   c. If test light shuts off below 120° F, replace engine temperature switch.

No Wait Lamp On Cold Engine

1. With ignition switch in Run position and engine off, observe "Charge" light, which should illuminate.
2. If "Charge" light is not lit, check condition of GAUGES fuse and replace if necessary.
3. If GAUGES fuse is satisfactory, confirm glow plug operation by listening for clicking noise from relay.
4. If relay operates, check pink/black wire between fuse block and splice S204 for a short or open and repair as necessary, **Fig. 1.** If wire is satisfactory, proceed to step 6.
5. If relay does not operate, check pink wires between ignition switch and fuse block for a short or open and repair as necessary. If wires are satisfactory, proceed to step 6.
6. Disconnect electrical connector from "Wait" lamp control relay. Connect jumper wire between ground and dark blue wire at connector, and observe "Wait" light, which should illuminate.
7. If "Wait" light is not lit, check condition of lamp bulb and replace if necessary.
8. If lamp bulb is satisfactory, check dark blue wire between "Wait" lamp control relay electrical connector and "Wait" lamp, and the pink/blue wire between "Wait" lamp and splice S204 for a short or open, and repair as necessary. If wires are satisfactory, proceed to step 9.

9. Using suitable test lamp, check ground connection at G104. Attach one end of test lamp to red wire terminal of Glow Plug Relay and the other end to the black wire lead of "Wait" lamp control relay.
10. If lamp does not light, circuit is satisfactory. If lamp lights, replace "Wait" lamp control relay.

Wait Lamp Pulses Slowly On & Off

1. With "Wait" lamp pulsing, connect suitable test lamp between white and yellow wires of wait lamp control relay, **Fig. 1.**
2. If test light is on when "Wait" lamp is off, and off when "Wait" lamp is on, replace "Wait" lamp control relay.
3. If test light does not turn on, connect test lamp between ground and orange or orange/black wires at thermal controller. With "Wait" lamp pulsing, confirm test light pulses on and off with "Wait" lamp.
4. If test lamp does not light, connect test lamp to front red wire and rear dark blue/black wire terminals of glow plug relay. Defect may be in red wire between battery and glow plug relay, or in black, dark blue, dark green, and orange or orange/black wires between relay and thermal controller or glow plug relay. Repair as necessary.
5. If test light flashes on and off with "Wait" lamp when connected to orange or orange/black wires at thermal controller, then connect test light between black wire at controller and ground.
6. If test lamp flashes on and off, repair black wire between controller and ground.
7. If test lamp does not light, replace controller.

Wait Lamp Stays On Longer Than 10 Seconds

1. Check glow plug relay operation. Disconnect connector at diesel diode module, **Fig. 1.** Connect one end of test lamp to ground and other end of test lamp to red (front) post of glow plug relay. Then touch test lamp to rear post (dark blue and black wires) of glow plug relay. Test lamp should light, indicating glow plug relay is operating properly.
2. If test lamp remains OFF, proceed as follows:
   a. Check ECM fuse and ground connection G104.
   b. Disconnect connector from thermal controller. Connect a suitable test lamp between pin 3 (pink/black wire) and pin 6 (yellow wire) of harness connector. If test lamp lights with ignition ON, check continuity between pins 3 and 6 of thermal controller. If test lamp remains ON, replace thermal controller.
   c. If test lamp remains OFF, connect a suitable ohmmeter to glow plug relay coil, and check resistance of coil. If ohmmeter indicates a high glow plug relay coil resistance, replace coil. Check continuity of pink/black, yellow and black wires.

3. If test lamp lights (glow plug relay is operating properly), proceed as follows:
   a. Disconnect "Wait" lamp control relay connector. "Wait" lamp should go OFF. Connect test lamp between white and yellow wires of connector. If test lamp lights, replace "Wait" lamp control relay.
   b. If test lamp remains OFF, turn ignition OFF. Connect a suitable ohmmeter to pins 4 and 5 of thermal controller, and check for 30 ohms resistance. If ohmmeter indicates more than 30 ohms, replace thermal controller. Check continuity of black, dark green, dark blue, orange or orange/black, white, yellow and black wires.

Engine Does Not Start When Cold (Wait Lamp OK-Goes On, Then Off)

1. If engine cranking speed is slow, turn ignition OFF, then, using a suitable voltmeter, check battery voltage. Voltmeter should indicate approximately 12.4 volts.
2. Using a suitable test lamp and with ignition in RUN position, check voltage at pink wire at fuel injection pump solenoid, **Fig. 1.** If test lamp remains OFF, repair pink wire. If test lamp lights, turn ignition OFF and check for continuity through fuel solenoid to ground using test lamp KD-125 or equivalent. If there is no continuity, replace fuel injection pump solenoid.
3. With ignition switch in RUN position and engine not operating, check glow plug relay operation. Glow plug should click ON and OFF.
4. If glow plug relay operates as described in step 3, proceed as follows:
   a. Turn ignition OFF.
   b. Disconnect all glow plug harness connectors from glow plugs.
   c. Connect test lamp KD-125 or equivalent between rear post (dark blue and black wires) of glow plug relay and ground.
   d. At each glow plug, touch harness connector to glow plug spade terminal. If test lamp lights, glow plug and harness are operating properly. Connect harness connector to glow plugs.

NOTE: Disconnect harness connector after testing each glow plug.

   e. If test lamp does not light, touch harness connector to engine block. If test lamp lights, replace glow plug. If test lamp remains OFF, replace wire(s) to glow plug(s).
   f. If test lamp remains OFF for each glow plug tested after replacement of wires, replace glow plugs and thermal controller, as required.
5. If glow plug relay does not operate as described in step 3, proceed as follows:
   a. If glow plug relay does not click ON and OFF, and "Wait" lamp comes ON then OFF, check thermal controller and glow plug relay circuit.
   b. Disconnect connector at thermal

Fig. 1   Glow plug wiring schematic (part 2 of 2). 1982–83 models

Fig. 1A   Glow plug wiring schematic. 1984 models

Fig. 1B   Glow plug wiring schematic. 1985 models

controller. Connect one end of suitable test lamp to ground and turn ignition to RUN position. Connect other end of test lamp to brown wire and check for voltage. If test lamp lights, check coolant temperature switch. If coolant temperature switch is closed, replace switch.

c. With one end of test lamp grounded, connect other end of test lamp to orange or orange/black wire. If test lamp lights, check for shorted glow plug relay wires (red to dark blue and black wires). Replace damaged wires as required. If test lamp remains OFF after replacement of wires, replace glow plugs and thermal controller as required.

d. Connect one end of test lamp to battery. With other end of test lamp touch yellow wire between thermal controller and glow plug relay. If test lamp remains OFF, repair yellow wire between thermal controller and glow plug relay. If test lamp lights, replace thermal controller.

1984–85

Refer to **Figs. 1A & 1B** for troubleshooting.

GLOW PLUG RESISTANCE TEST

1. In 1982–83 models, use a high impedence digital multimeter tool No. J-29125. On 1984–85 models, use high impedence digital multimeter tool No. J-29125A.
2. Position multimeter lefthand switch to "OHMS," turn righthand switch counterclockwise to "200 OHMS" and slide center switch to the left "D.C. LO."
3. Start engine, turn heater ON and allow engine to reach normal operating temperature. Remove all feed wires from glow plugs.
4. On 1983–85 models, disconnect electrical connector from alternator.
5. Using magnetic tachometer No. J-26925, turn idle speed screw located on the side of injection pump until the roughest engine idle is obtained. Do not exceed 900 rpm.
6. Allow engine to operate at its roughest idle speed for at least 1 minute. Thermostat must be open and upper radiator hose hot.
7. Connect a suitable clip to the black test lead of multimeter. The clip must be grounded to the fast idle solenoid and must remain grounded until all tests are completed.

8. With engine idling, probe each glow plug terminal and note resistance values on each cylinder in firing order. On 1982–83 models, reading will be between 1.8 and 3.4 ohms. If these readings are not obtained, turn engine OFF and check glow plugs. Resistance should be .7 or .8 ohms. If reading is not obtained, check multimeter for correct settings and for low or incorrect battery in multimeter. Check multimeter ground wire to engine. On 1984–85 models equipped with an electric cooling fan, note resistance values with cooling fan OFF. Do not disconnect electrical connector from fan.

NOTE: The resistance values are dependent on the temperature in each cylinder, and indicate the output of each cylinder.

9. If an ohm reading on any cylinder is approximately 1.2 or 1.3 ohms on 1982–83 models, or 1.3 or 1.4 ohms on 1984–85 models, check for engine mechanical problem. Check compression of the low reading cylinder and the cylinder which fires before and after the low cylinder reading.

NOTE: Correct the cause of the low compression cylinder before proceeding to the

1. 45 N·m (33 FT. LBS.)
2. Washers
3. Bracket
4. 48 N·m (35 FT. LBS.)
5. Washers
6. Mount
7. Part Of Frame (Cradle)

Fig. 1C   Front engine mount removal and installation

1. 41 N·m (30 FT. LBS.)
2. Bracket
3. Washers
4. 57 N·m (42 FT. LBS.)
5. Spacer
6. Strut
7. Nut (Torque No. 4)
8. Bracket
9. 23 N·m (17 FT. LBS.)
10. Brace
11. 48 N·m (35 FT. LBS.)

Fig. 2   Engine mount strut & bracket removal and installation. 1982—84 models

fuel system.

10. Compare glow plug resistance readings, checking for differences between cylinders. Rough idle engines will normally vary .3 ohms on 1982—83 models, and on 1984—85 models, .4 ohms or more between cylinders in firing order. To compensate, it will be necessary to raise or lower the reading on one or more cylinders by selecting nozzles.
11. Remove nozzles from cylinders with the high or low ohm reading. Determine nozzle pop off pressure and check nozzle for leakage and spray pattern.
12. Install nozzles with a higher pop off pressure to lower ohm reading and nozzles with a lower pop off pressure to raise ohm readings.

NOTE: A change of approximately 30 psi in pressure will change reading by .1 ohm.

13. During cleaning or replacement of nozzle and before installation of injection pipe, crank engine and check for air bubbles at nozzle inlet. If bubbles are present, clean or replace nozzles as required.
14. Install injection tube, start engine and check idle speed. If engine idle is rough, check and note glow plug resistance values of each cylinder firing order.
15. Compare glow plug resistance readings, noting differences of .3 ohms on 1982—83 models, and on 1984—85

models, .4 ohms between cylinders.

NOTE: It will be necessary to raise or lower resistance reading on one or more cylinders as described previously.

16. After additional nozzle changes have been performed, check engine idle.

NOTE: After completing two resistance checks and nozzle changes, correct engine idle can now be obtained.

17. Injection pump replacement may be necessary if the following occurs:
    a. Problem cylinder moves from cylinder to cylinder as nozzle changes are made.
    b. Cylinder ohm readings do not change when nozzles are changed (replaced).

NOTE: Always check cylinders at the same engine rpm. A nozzle with a tip leak can allow more fuel into the cylinder, which will raise glow plug ohm reading. This will rob fuel from the next nozzle in firing order, and will result in glow plug having a low ohm reading. Remove and check nozzle with a high reading. If nozzle is leaking, this could cause a rough engine idle. If a low glow plug resistance value is noted and it does not change with nozzle replacement, switch glow plugs between a known good cylinder and a bad cylinder. If resistance reading of each cylinder is not the same as before the switch, the glow plug cannot be used for rough engine idle diagnosis.

ENGINE MOUNTS
REPLACE

Refer to **Figs. 1C, 2, and 2A** for service procedures.

ENGINE
REPLACE

1. Drain cooling system. Remove serpentine drive belt, also remove vacuum pump drive belt if equipped.
2. Remove air cleaner and install a suitable cover.
3. Disconnect battery ground cable at battery (on vehicles equipped with heavy duty system there will be two batteries), ground wires at inner fender and engine ground strap.
4. Raise vehicle. Remove flywheel cover.
5. Remove flywheel to torque converter attaching bolts.
6. Disconnect exhaust pipe from rear exhaust manifold.
7. Remove engine to transaxle brace.
8. Remove engine mount to cradle retaining nuts and washers.
9. Disconnect leads to starter motor, No. 2 cylinder glow plug and battery ground cable at transaxle to engine bolt.
10. Disconnect lower oil cooler hose and plug openings.
11. Remove accessible power steering pump bracket fasteners and lower vehicle.

1. 50 N·m (37 LBS. FT.)
2. BRACKET
3. WASHERS
4. BOLT
5. SPACER
6. STRUT
7. 57 N·m (42 LBS. FT.)
8. BRACKET
9. 23 N·m (17 LBS. FT.)
10. REINFORCEMENT
11. BRACE (A/C ONLY)

MOVE ENGINE FORWARD 10mm (3/8″)
AND HOLD WHILE TIGHTENING NO. 7

Fig. 2A   Engine mount strut & bracket removal and installation. 1985 models

Fig. 3   Intake manifold drain tube removal & installation

Fig. 4   Removal & installation of intermediate adapter, pump adapter & seal

12. Remove remaining power steering pump bracket/brace.
13. Remove heater outlet pipe.
14. Disconnect all remaining glow plug leads at glow plugs.
15. Disconnect all other leads at engine, disconnect engine harness at cowl connector and body mounted relays and position engine harness aside.
16. If equipped with A/C, disconnect compressor with brackets and lines attached and position aside.
17. Disconnect fuel and vacuum hoses, plug all fuel line openings.
18. Disconnect throttle and T.V. cables at injection pump and cable bracket. Position cables aside.
19. Disconnect upper oil cooler hose and plug openings. Remove exhaust crossover pipe heat shield.
20. Disconnect and position aside trans-axle filler tube.
21. Remove exhaust crossover pipe.
22. Remove engine mounting strut and strut brackets.
23. Install a suitable engine lifting device.

NOTE: When installing lifting chains to cylinder heads, ensure that washers are used under the chains and bolt heads and the bolts are torqued to 20 ft. lbs.

24. Position a suitable support under transaxle rear extension. As engine is being removed it may be necessary to raise support. Remove engine to transaxle bolts, then engine.
25. Reverse procedure to install.

NOTE: Before installing the flex plate to converter bolts, ensure the weld nuts on

the converter are flush with the flex plate and converter rotates freely by hand in this position. Hand start the three bolts and finger tighten, then torque converter bolts to 35 ft. lbs. This ensures proper alignment of converter.

INTAKE MANIFOLD
REPLACE

REMOVAL

1. Disconnect battery ground cable(s), then remove air cleaner.
2. Drain radiator coolant, then disconnect upper radiator hose from water outlet, and heater hoses from intake manifold.
3. Remove fuel injection pump. Refer to "Injection Pump, Replace".
4. Disconnect wiring from engine accessories.
5. If equipped with cruise control, remove servo.
6. If equipped with A/C, remove compressor and braces. Position aside.
7. Remove alternator assembly.
8. Disconnect engine mounting strut.
9. Remove fuel lines, filter and brackets. Plug all openings.
10. Disconnect glow plug controller and sending units wire connectors.
11. Disconnect heat shield from exhaust pipe crossover.
12. Using a suitable back-up wrench, remove left (forward) injection lines and plug all openings.

13. Disconnect T.V. and throttle cables from bracket.
14. Remove intake manifold drain tube, **Fig. 3.**
15. Remove injection pump intermediate adapter, pump adapter and seal, **Fig. 4.**
16. Remove intake manifold.

INSTALLATION

1. Thoroughly clean machined surfaces of cylinder head and intake manifold, ensuring neither surface becomes gouged or scratched. Clean all bolts and bolt holes.
2. Using a suitable sealer, coat both sides of the manifold to head sealing gasket surface, and place in position, **Fig. 5.**
3. Install end seals, ensure ends are positioned under cylinder heads. Apply RTV sealer to each end of seal, **Fig. 5.**

NOTE: The end seals and mating surfaces must be dry to prevent gasket slippage.

4. Carefully position intake manifold on engine.
5. Lubricate intake manifold bolts entire length with lubricant 1052080 or equivalent.
6. Install bolts. Torque to specifications following sequence shown in **Fig. 6,** to 15 ft. lbs. Then retorque to specifications.

Fig. 5   Intake manifold installation

Fig. 8   Cylinder head bolt tightening sequence

Fig. 6   Intake manifold torquing sequence

Fig. 9   Exploded view of cylinder head

Fig. 7   Cylinder head pipe plug removal

Fig. 10   Rocker arm assembly

7. Reverse steps 1 through 15 of removal procedure to complete installation.

CYLINDER HEAD
REPLACE

1. Remove intake manifold and valve cover.
2. Remove or loosen any accessory bracket or pipe that interferes with removal of cylinder head.
3. Disconnect glow plug wiring and block heater lead (if equipped).
4. Remove ground strap from right cylinder head.
5. Remove rocker arm nuts, pivots, rocker arms and push rods. Scribe mark on pivots and separate so they may be easily identified and replaced in their original location.
6. Disconnect exhaust crossover pipe from exhaust manifold on side being removed and loosen it on opposite side.
7. Remove pipe plugs covering upper cylinder head bolts, **Fig. 7.**
8. Remove engine block drain plug, from side that is to be worked on.
9. Remove cylinder head bolts and cylinder head. If necessary to remove prechamber, remove glow plug and nozzle, then tap out with a small blunt ⅛

inch drift. Do not use tapered drift.
10. Reverse procedure to install. Refer to **Fig. 8** for correct torque sequence. Torque cylinder head bolts except bolts 5, 6, 11, 12, 13 and 14 to 100 ft. lbs. Torque bolts 5, 6, 11, 12, 13 and 14 to 41 ft. lbs. After original torquing, retorque bolts mentioned above to 142 and 59 ft.lbs respectively.

NOTE: The head gaskets used on this engine are composition type, and not to be used with a sealer of any kind. Any sealer applied may result in head gasket leakage.

ROCKER ARMS

NOTE: This engine uses valve rotators, **Fig. 9.** The rotator operates on a sprag clutch principle utilizing the collapsing action of a coil spring to give rotation to the rotor body which turns the valve.

1. Remove valve cover.
2. Remove flanged bolts, rocker arm pivot and rocker arms, **Fig. 10.**
3. When installing rocker arm assemblies, lubricate wear surfaces with suitable lubricant. Torque flanged

bolts to 28 ft. lbs.

VALVE ROTATORS

The rotator operates on a Sprag clutch principle utilizing the collapsing action of coil spring to give rotation to the rotor body which turns the valve, **Fig. 9.**

To check rotator action, draw a line across rotator body and down the collar. Operate engine at 1500 rpm, rotator body should move around collar. Rotator action can be in either direction. Replace rotator if no movement is noted.

When servicing valves, valve stem tips should be checked for improper wear pattern which could indicate a defective valve rotator, **Fig. 11.**

VALVE LIFT SPECS.

Engine	Year	Intake	Exhaust
V6-262 Diesel	1982–85	.375	.375

VALVE ARRANGEMENT

V6-262 Diesel . . . . I-E-E-I-E-I

Proper Tip Pattern | No Rotation Pattern | Partial Rotation Tip Pattern

Rotator Functioning Properly | Replace Rotator and check rotation | Replace Rotator and check rotation

Fig. 11 Inspecting valve stem for rotator malfunction

Fig. 14 Oversize valve lifter marking

Fig. 17 Front oil seal removal

Fig. 12 Measuring valve stem height

Fig. 15 Hydraulic roller lifter retainer and guide

Fig. 13 Measuring valve rotator height

Fig. 16 Exploded view of hydraulic roller lifter

Fig. 18 Front oil seal installation

VALVE TIMING

INTAKE OPENS BEFORE TDC

Engine	Year	Degrees
V6-262 Diesel	1982–85	16

VALVES

Whenever a new valve is installed or after grinding valves, it is necessary to measure the valve stem height with the special tool as shown in **Fig. 12.**

There should be at least .015 inch clearance between the gauge and end of valve stem. If clearance is less than .015 inch, remove valve and grind end of valve stem as required.

Check valve rotator height, **Fig. 13.** If valve stem end is less than .005 inch above rotator, the valve is too short and a new valve must be installed.

VALVE GUIDES

Valve stem guides are not replaceable, due to being cast in place. If valve guide bores are worn excessively, they can be reamed oversize.

If a standard valve guide bore is being reamed, use a .003 inch or .005 inch oversize reamer. For the .010 inch oversize valve guide bore, use a .013 inch oversize reamer. If too large a reamer is used and the spiraling is removed, it is possible that the valve will not receive the proper lubrication.

NOTE: Occasionally a valve guide will be oversize as manufactured. These are marked on the cylinder head. If no markings are present, the guide bores are standard. If oversize markings are present, any valve replacement will require an oversize valve. Service valves are available in standard diameters as well as .003 inch, .005 inch, .010 inch and .013 inch oversize.

VALVE LIFTER
REPLACE

NOTE: Some engines have both standard and .010 inch oversize valve lifters. The .010 inch oversize valve lifters are etched with a "0" on the side of the lifter. Also, the cylinder block will be marked if an oversize lifter is used, **Fig. 14.**

1. Remove intake manifold as outlined previously.
2. Remove valve covers, rocker arm assemblies and push rods. Note location of valve train components so they can be installed in original position.
3. Remove hydraulic lifter retainer bolts, then retainer, **Fig. 15.**
4. Remove valve lifters, then disassemble, **Fig. 16.**
5. If plunger and body appear satisfactory, blow off air to remove all particles of dirt. Install the plunger in the body without other parts and check for free movement. A simple test is to be sure that the plunger will drop of its own weight in the body, **Fig. 16.**
6. Reverse procedure to install.

Fig 19   Dowel pin chamfer

Trim 1/8" from each end of pan seal

Fig. 20   Trimming oil pan seal

NOTE: Before installation, prime new or reassembled lifters by working lifter plunger while submerged in kerosene or diesel fuel. Lifter could be damaged if installed dry when starting engine. When assembling lifters, do not interchange plungers, as they are specifically fitted to the bodies during manufacture.

FRONT OIL SEAL
REPLACE

1. Disconnect battery ground cables.
2. Remove accessory drive belts.
3. Remove crankshaft pulley and harmonic balancer.
4. Using tool BT-6406 or equivalent, remove front oil seal, **Fig. 17.**
5. Apply suitable sealant to outside diameter of new oil seal.
6. Using tool J-29659 or equivalent, install new oil seal, **Fig. 18.**
7. Install harmonic balancer and crankshaft pulley.
8. Install and tension accessory drive belts.

ENGINE FRONT COVER
REPLACE

1. Disconnect battery ground cables.
2. Drain cooling system and disconnect lower radiator and heater hoses.
3. Remove drive belts, crankshaft pulley, harmonic balancer and accessory brackets.
4. Remove timing indicator.
5. Remove front cover attaching bolts, then the front cover. Also, remove the dowel pins. It may be necessary to grind a flat on the dowel pin to provide a rough surface for gripping.
6. Grind a chamfer on one end of each dowel pin, **Fig. 19.**

1. CAMSHAFT
2. CRANKSHAFT
3. CAMSHAFT SPROCKET KEY
4. INJECTION PUMP DRIVE GEAR
5. CRANKSHAFT SPROCKET KEY
6. FRONT CAMSHAFT BEARING RETAINER
7. RETAINER BOLT
8. CRANKSHAFT SPROCKET
9. TIMING CHAIN
10. CAMSHAFT SPROCKET
11. WASHER
12. CAMSHAFT SPROCKET BOLT
13. SLINGER
14. GASKET
15. FRONT COVER
16. TIMING COVER BOLTS
17. WATER PUMP BOLTS
18. PROBE HOLDER (RPM COUNTER)
19. CRANKSHAFT BALANCER
20. WASHER
21. CRANKSHAFT BOLT
22. PULLEY ASSEMBLY
23. PULLEY BOLTS

Fig. 21   Engine front cover installation

7. Cut excess material from front end of oil pan gasket on each side of cylinder block.
8. Trim approximately 1/8 inch from each end of new front pan seal, **Fig. 20.**
9. Install new front cover gasket and apply suitable sealer to gasket around coolant holes.
10. Apply RTV sealer to mating surfaces of cylinder block, oil pan and front cover.
11. Place front cover on cylinder block and press downward to compress seal. Rotate cover right and left and guide oil pan seal into cavity with a small screwdriver.
12. Apply engine oil to bolts.
13. Install two bolts finger tight to retain cover.
14. Install the two dowel pins, chamfered end first.
15. Install timing indicator and remaining bolts, **Fig. 21.** Torque bolts as follows: water pump bolts, 21 ft. lbs.; timing cover bolts, 41–42 ft. lbs.

NOTE: Water pump and front cover to block attaching bolts must be coated with sealer 1052624 or equivalent, since coolant leaks and loss of bolt torque may result.

16. Install harmonic balancer and crankshaft pulley, **Fig. 21.** Torque crankshaft bolt to 160–350 ft. lbs. and pulley bolts to 30 ft. lbs.
17. Install accessory brackets.
18. Install drive belts.
19. Connect lower radiator and heater hoses.
20. Connect ground cables to batteries.

TIMING CHAIN & GEARS
REPLACE

1. Remove front cover as outlined previously. Loosen rocker arm pivot bolts evenly so that some lash is present between rocker arms and valves.

2. Remove oil slinger, cam gear, crank gear and timing chain.
3. Install key in crankshaft, if removed.
4. Install cam gear, crank gear and timing chain with timing marks aligned, **Fig. 22.** Torque cam gear bolt to 64 ft. lbs. on 1982 models, or 70 ft. lbs. on 1983–85 models.
5. Install oil slinger.
6. Install front cover.

CAMSHAFT & INJECTION PUMP DRIVE & DRIVEN GEARS
REPLACE

1. Remove engine assembly as previously outlined.
2. Remove intake manifold and gasket.
3. Remove oil pump drive assembly.
4. Remove front cover, then rotate crankshaft so that timing marks are in alignment.
5. Remove all rocker arms, pivots, push rods, and lifters. Note valve train component location for proper location upon installation.
6. Remove bolt securing camshaft sprocket, then remove both cam and crank sprocket. If crank sprocket is tight on shaft, remove with a suitable puller.
7. Remove bolts retaining front camshaft bearing retainer, then remove retainer.
8. Remove cam sprocket key.
9. Remove injection pump drive gear.
10. Remove intake manifold, intermediate pump adapter and pump adapter. Remove snap ring, selective washer, driven gear and spring, **Fig. 23.**
11. Install a long bolt into camshaft to act as a handle and carefully slide camshaft out of block.

NOTE: Do not force the camshaft out of the block. Damage to the bearings and or the camshaft can result.

Fig. 22 Valve timing marks

Fig. 23 Fuel injection pump driven gear removal and installation

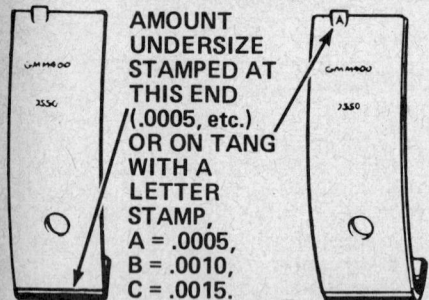

AMOUNT UNDERSIZE STAMPED AT THIS END (.0005, etc.) OR ON TANG WITH A LETTER STAMP, A = .0005, B = .0010, C = .0015.

Fig. 24 Main bearing identification

If the bearings are to be replaced, it will be necessary to remove the oil pan before removing the bearings.

12. Reverse procedure to install. Check injection pump driven gear end play. If end play is not .002–.006 inch, replace selective washer, **Fig. 23.** Selective washers are available from .080 to .115 inch in increments of .003 inch.

PISTON & ROD
ASSEMBLE

The pistons must be installed with the notch in the top facing the front of the engine.

Fig. 25 Packing upper rear main bearing seal

Measure the connecting rod side clearance using a suitable feeler gauge. Clearance should be .008–.021 inch.

PISTON & RINGS

Pistons are available in standard sizes and .010 oversizes. Rings are available in standard and oversizes of .010 and .030.

MAIN & ROD BEARINGS

Main bearings are available in standard sizes and undersizes of .0005, .0010 and .0015 inch. The amount of undersize is stamped on the bearing shell, **Fig. 24.**

Rod bearings are available in standard sizes and an undersize of .010 inch.

SERVICE BULLETIN: On 1982–84 vehicles, there are two different length main bearing cap-to-block bolts being used in production. Any given engine will use only one length cap bolt. A $3^{15}/_{16}$ inch (100mm) long bolt is used on engines that have main bearing caps that have their locations in the engine cast into the cap. A $4^{11}/_{32}$ inch (110mm) long bolt is used on engines that have main bearing caps that have their location in engine identified by the number of raised ribs cast into the cap. Use of improper bolts will cause the block threads to strip.

On 1985 vehicles, two distinct cylinder blocks are used in production. Type 1 blocks have two bolts retaining the No. 2 and 3 main bearing caps, while Type 2 blocks have four bolts retaining the caps. On Type 2 blocks, torque outer retaining bolts to 52 ft.lbs. and inner bolts to 89 ft.lbs.

REAR CRANKSHAFT SEAL SERVICE

Since the braided fabric seal used on these engines can be replaced only when the crankshaft is removed, the following repair procedure is recommended.

1. Remove oil pan and bearing cap.
2. Drive end of old seal gently into groove, using a suitable tool, until packed tight. This may vary between ¼ and ¾ inch depending on amount of pack required.
3. Repeat previous step for other end of seal.
4. Measure and note amount that seal was driven up on one side. Using the old seal removed from bearing cap, cut a length of seal the amount previously noted plus ¹⁄₁₆ inch.
5. Repeat previous step for other side of seal.
6. Pack cut lengths of seal into appropriate side of seal groove. A packing tool, BT-6433, **Fig. 25,** may be used since the tool has been machined to provide a built-in stop. Use tool BT-6436 to trim the seal flush with block, **Fig. 26.**
7. Install new seal in lower bearing cap.

Fig. 26 Trimming upper rear main bearing seal

Fig. 27 Oil pump removal

Fig. 28 Oil pump disassembled

OIL PAN
REPLACE

1. On 1983–85 models, rotate intermediate steering shaft until steering gear stub shaft clamp bolt is in the up position and remove clamp bolt, then disconnect the intermediate shaft from stub shaft. Install suitable engine lifting fixture on all models.
2. Raise vehicle but keep rear slightly lower than front.
3. Install suitable supports at front of body at forward lift points.
4. Drain engine oil.
5. Remove left side steering gear to cradle bolt, then loosen right side steering gear to cradle bolt.
6. Remove front stabilizer bar.
7. Using ½ inch drill bit, drill through spot weld located between rear holes at left hand front stabilizer bar mounting.
8. Remove engine and transaxle to cradle mount nuts.
9. Disconnect left lower ball joint from knuckle.
10. Position suitable support and block of wood under transaxle oil pan, then raise transaxle until mount stud clears cradle.
11. Remove bolts securing front crossmember to right side of cradle.
12. Remove left side body mount bolts.
13. Remove left side and front crossmember assembly, then lower rear crossmember below left side by careful use of a pry bar.
14. Remove flywheel cover, starter assembly and engine mount bracket.
15. Remove oil pan attaching bolts and oil pan.
16. Reverse procedure to install.

OIL PUMP
REPLACE & SERVICE

REPLACEMENT

1. Remove oil pan as outlined previously.
2. Remove oil pump to rear main bearing cap attaching bolts, **Fig. 27.**
3. Remove oil pump and drive shaft extension.
4. Reverse procedure to install. Torque attaching bolts to 18 ft. lbs.

SERVICE
Disassembly
1. Remove oil pump drive shaft extension, **Fig. 28.** Do not attempt to remove washers from drive shaft extension. The drive shaft extension and washers are serviced as an assembly.
2. Remove cotter pin, spring and pressure regulator valve, **Fig. 28.**

NOTE: Apply pressure on pressure regulator bore before removing cotter pin since the spring is under pressure.

3. Remove oil pump cover attaching screws, then oil pump cover and gasket.
4. Remove drive gear and idler gear from pump body.

Inspection
1. Check gears for scoring or other damage, replace if necessary.
2. Proper end clearance is .0005–.0075 inch.
3. Check pressure regulator valve, valve spring and bore for damage. Proper bore to valve clearance is .0025–.0050 inch.
4. Check extension shaft ends for wear.

Assembly
1. Install gears and shaft in oil pump body.
2. Check gear end clearance by placing a straight edge over the gears and measure the clearance between the straight edge and gasket surface. If end clearance is excessive, check for scores in cover that would bring the clearance over specified limits.
3. Install cover and torque attaching screws to 7 ft. lbs.
4. Install pressure regulator valve, closed end first, into bore, then the valve spring and cotter pin.

WATER PUMP
REPLACE

1. Disconnect battery ground cable.
2. Drain radiator.
3. Disconnect heater return hose at water pump, then remove bolt retaining heater water return pipe to intake manifold and position aside.
4. Remove vacuum pump drive belt, if equipped with A/C.

1 J-29785 REMOVAL

2 J-29786 INSTALL UNTIL FLUSH

Fig. 29 Water pump pulley removal & installation

5. Remove serpentine drive belt.
6. Remove alternator. Then, remove A/C compressor or vacuum pump brackets (if equipped).
7. Remove water pump attaching bolts and water pump assembly.
8. Remove water pump pulley, **Fig. 29.**
9. Reverse procedure to install.

FUEL PUMP
REPLACE

1. Ensure ignition switch is in "off" position.
2. Remove air cleaner and disconnect 12 volt lead wire from pump.
3. Use ¾ inch wrench to support the inlet fitting firmly, then with ⅝ inch wrench disconnect inlet tube and plug openings.
4. Repeat step three to disconnect outlet fitting. Place a suitable rag under pump outlet side to collect fuel since this line is slightly pressurized.

NOTE: Do not overtwist pump outlet fitting; otherwise cover crimp may be loosened.

5. Remove pump mounting bracket nut and pump.
6. Remove dust plugs from openings on new pump, then install pump and bracket assembly on engine. Torque pump mounting bracket nut to 18 ft. lbs. Torque inlet and outlet fuel line fittings to 19 ft. lbs.

NOTE: In some instances, it may be necessary to adjust pump location by loosening the bracket screw and turning the pump to get the exact alignment between pump fittings and fuel lines. Be sure to torque

bracket screw after the adjustment.

7. After pump is installed, disconnect fuel line at fuel filter and turn ignition switch "On" in order to prime and bleed lines. Use a suitable container to catch fuel. If pump runs with a clicking sound or there are air bubbles in fuel, check for leaks in line. Check all connections to see that they are dry and that no fuel is leaking. When clicking sound disappears, tighten fuel line at filter.

BELT TENSION DATA

NOTE: This engine is equipped with a serpentine drive belt that is self adjusting

DIESEL FUEL INJECTION SYSTEM DESCRIPTION

The V6-262 diesel engine may be

Fig. 30 Roosa-Master pump fuel flow schematic. 1982–83 shown, 1984–85 similar

Fig. 31 CAV pump fuel flow schematic

equipped with one of two fuel injection pumps: the Roosa Master which can be identified by a looped fuel inlet pipe, and CAV pump which can be identified by a straight fuel inlet pipe.

Injection timing is controlled by two pressure regulators. One regulator is the Housing Pressure Cold Advance (HPCA), located in the pump. The other pressure regulator, used on 1984 except California models and all 1985 models, is the Housing Pressure Altitude Advance (HPAA), located in the fuel return line. The HPCA is designed to advance injection timing about 4° during cold operation. The HPAA will regulate housing pressure according to altitude.

The Metering Valve Sensor (MVS), used on 1984 California models and all 1985 models with Diesel Electronic Control System, is a variable resistor which electronically signals the diesel ECM as to the position of the metering valve.

The injection pump is mounted on top of the engine. It is gear driven off the camshaft and turns at camshaft speed. It is a high pressure rotary pump that injects a metered amount of fuel to each cylinder at the proper time. The six high pressure

Fig. 31A Grounding ALCL diagnostic test ground terminal

1 JUMPER "B" TO "A" TO DISPLAY DIAGNOSTIC CODES

2 TEST TERMINAL

3 GROUND TERMINAL

Fig. 32 Roosa-Master pump pressure tap plug location

delivery pipes from the pump to the injection nozzle in each cylinder are the same length to prevent any difference in timing, cylinder-to-cylinder. The fuel injection pump provides the required timing advance under all operating conditions. Engine RPM is controlled by a rotary fuel metering valve. Pushing down on the accelerator pedal moves the throttle cable to open the metering valve and allow more fuel to be delivered. The injection pump also has a low pressure transfer pump to deliver fuel from the fuel line to the high pressure pump.

The fuel filter is located between the electric fuel pump and the injection pump.

The fuel tank is at the rear of the vehicle, connected by fuel pipes and hoses to the fuel pump. Excess fuel returns from the fuel injection pump to the fuel tank through pipes and hoses.

The fuel flow schematics, **Figs. 30 and 31,** show the major components and their relationships and also provides a means of determining the differences in the two systems.

INJECTION PUMP TIMING

USING TIMING METER J-33075

Checking
1. Block drive wheels and apply parking brake.

2. Start engine, allow to reach normal operating temperature, then shut off.
3. On 1985 models, proceed as follows:
   a. Ground the instrument panel mounted Assembly Line Communication Link (ALCL) diagnostic test ground terminal, **Fig. 31A.**
   b. Remove air cleaner cover, then remove MAP sensor retainer and position MAP sensor out of way with electrical connectors connected.
4. On all models, remove air cleaner assembly, then place suitable screen over intake manifold inlets. EGR valve hose must be disconnected.
5. Clean any dirt or oil from engine probe holder, crankshaft balancer rim, glow plug probe lens and lens in photoelectric pickup.

NOTE: Retarded reading will result if probe of injection pump timing meter is not clean.

6. Install RPM probe into crankshaft RPM counter.
7. Remove glow plug from number 1 cylinder, then install glow plug probe in glow plug opening. Torque probe to 8 ft. lbs.
8. Set timing meter selector to A (20), then connect meter battery leads.
9. Disconnect alternator electrical connector, then start engine and adjust engine RPM to specifications.
10. Observe timing reading at 2 minute intervals. When readings stabilize, compare to reading under "Tune-Up

Specifications" at beginning of chapter.
11. Disconnect timing meter, then apply suitable thread lubricant to glow plug.
12. Install glow plug and torque to 12 ft. lbs.
13. Connect alternator and install air cleaner.
14. On 1985 models, install MAP sensor and air cleaner cover, then remove jumper from ALCL.

Adjust
1. Loosen injection pump retaining nuts with tool J-25304.
2. Rotate pump to left to advance timing, and to right to retard timing.
3. Torque injection pump retaining nut to 35 ft. lbs.
4. Start engine and recheck timing as previously described. Reset as needed.

WITHOUT TIMING METER J-33075

NOTE: Alignment of timing marks may be used in situations where timing meter J-33075 is not available. However for optimum engine operation, the timing should be adjusted with the meter. For adjustment of timing marks use following procedure.

1. The mark on the injection pump adapter must be aligned with the mark on the injection pump flange.
2. To adjust:
   a. Loosen the injection pump retaining nuts with tool J-25304.
   b. Align the mark on the injection pump flange with the mark on the injection pump adapter.
   c. Torque injection pump retaining nuts to 35 ft. lbs.

FUEL INJECTION PUMP HOUSING FUEL PRESSURE CHECK

1982–83
1. Remove air crossover and install screen covers J-29657 or other suitable covers.
2. On Roosa-Master pumps, remove pressure tap plug. On CAV pumps, remove torque screw, **Figs. 32 and**

Fig. 33 CAV pump torque screw location

1. FAST IDLE SOLENOID.
2. HOUSING PRESSURE COLD ADVANCE SOLENOID.
3. FUEL SHUT OFF (SHUT DOWN) SOLENOID.
4. TORQUE CONVERTER CLUTCH SWITCH (PART OF VACUUM REGULATOR VALVE).

Fig. 34 Roosa Master pump solenoids and connectors location

Fig. 35 CAV pump solenoids and connectors location

33. If equipped with torque screw, to avoid disturbing adjustment add a second nut to lock nut, then back out screw with nuts attached.
3. Attach low pressure gage to adapters.
4. Connect magnetic pick-up tachometer.
5. With gear shift lever in park position and parking brake on, check pressure with engine running at 1000 RPM. Pressure should be between 8–12 psi with no more than 2 psi fluctuation.
6. If pressure is at 0, check operation of housing pressure cold advance as follows:
   a. Remove electrical connector from housing pressure cold advance terminal, **Figs. 34 and 35**. If pressure remains at 0, remove injection pump cover and check operation of advance solenoid. If it is binding, repair or replace parts as necessary.
   b. If pressure is as specified with housing cold pressure advance electrical connector disconnected, check operation of temperature switch located in cylinder head bolt.
7. If pressure is not within specifications, replace fuel return line connector assembly or check for restricted HPAA, if equipped.
8. Remove tachometer, pressure gauge and adapter.
9. Install a new pressure tap plug seal on pressure tap plug and install plug into pump housing.
10. Remove screened covers and install air crossover.

1984

1. Ensure that temperature switch is functioning properly.
2. Remove air cleaner and install protective cover J-26996-1 or equivalent.
3. Disconnect fuel return line from return line connector.
4. Remove return line connector from injection pump cover.
5. Push Housing Pressure Cold Advance (HPCA) solenoid plunger into solenoid.
6. Disconnect electrical connector at HPCA terminal and, using suitable jumper wire, apply 12 volts to HPCA solenoid.
7. If HPCA solenoid plunger does not extend fully, remove pump cover and repair or replace HPCA terminal.
8. Install suitable adapter in pump cover, connect return line to adapter, and attach low pressure gauge and suitable tachometer to adapter.
9. Apply parking brake, block drive wheels, place selector lever in "PARK" and check pressure at 1000 RPM. Pressure should be as shown, **Fig. 35A.**
10. If pressure is too low, replace fuel return line connector assembly.
11. If pressure is too high, remove return line at adapter pump and install a fitting with short piece of hose to allow return flow to empty into suitable container.
12. If pressure drops, clear restriction in fuel line.

13. If pressure does not drop in step 13, replace fuel return line connector assembly, then check timing, adjusting as necessary.
14. If pressure is still too high, repair or replace injection pump as necessary.
15. Remove tachometer, pressure gauge and adapter.
16. Using new O-ring, install fuel return line connector into pump cover.
17. Connect fuel return line to return line connector.
18. Start engine and check for leaks.
19. Remove protective cover and install air crossover.

1985

NOTE: Refer to diagnostic chart, **Fig. 35B,** to check housing fuel pressure. The following procedures are to be used in conjunction with letter references contained in the diagnostic chart.

Procedure "A"

1. Block drive wheels, apply parking brake and shift transaxle to Park.
2. Start engine and run until normal operating temperature is reached, then stop engine.
3. Remove air cleaner cover.
4. Remove Manifold Absolute Pressure (MAP) sensor retainer and position MAP sensor aside, leaving wiring and vacuum hose attached.
5. Remove air cleaner assembly, then the air crossover pipe.
6. On models equipped with external Ex-

	CONDITION		HPCA	HPAA	NOMINAL HOUSING PRESSURE kPa (psi)
	ALTITUDE	COOLANT			
FEDERAL PACKAGE	BELOW 1219m (4000 FT.)	COLD	ON	OFF	0
	BELOW 1219m (4000 FT.)	HOT	OFF	OFF	68.9 (10)
	ABOVE 1219m (4000 FT.)	COLD	ON	OFF	0
	ABOVE 1219m (4000 FT.)	HOT	ON	ON	48.3 (7)
ALTITUDE PACKAGE	ABOVE 1219m (4000 FT.)	COLD	ON	OFF	0
	ABOVE 1219m (4000 FT.)	HOT	OFF	OFF	68.9 (10)
	BELOW 1219m (4000 FT.)	COLD	ON	OFF	0
	BELOW 1219m (4000 FT.)	HOT	OFF	ON	89.6 (13)

HPCA = HOUSING PRESSURE COLD ADV.   HPAA = HOUSING PRESSURE ALTITUDE ADV.
TIMING RETARDS WITH HIGHER HOUSING PRESSURE

Fig. 35A Injection pump housing fuel pressure specifications. 1984 models

INJECTION PUMP HOUSING PRESSURE DIAGNOSIS

Fig. 35B   Injection pump housing fuel pressure diagnostic chart. 1985 models

Fig. 36   Air crossover removal & installation

3. Replace pressure regulator if operation is not satisfactory.

NOTE: If regulator is contaminated with foreign matter, remove injection pump cover to determine source of contamination.

4. Check HPCA solenoid as follows:
   a. Connect electrical connectors to HPCA solenoid.
   b. Turn ignition switch to Run position and ensure HPCA solenoid plunger is extended upward, then turn ignition switch to Off or Lock position.
   c. When ignition switch is turned Off, solenoid plunger should retract automatically or be able to be pushed back with light pressure applied. If not, remove injection pump cover and repair or replace HPCA solenoid as necessary.

Procedure "D"
1. Disconnect fuel return line from Housing Pressure Altitude Advance (HPAA) inlet.
2. Attach a suitable hose to pipe outlet and position opposite end of hose into a drain pan.
3. Start engine and observe pressure reading.
4. If housing pressure is now 9–11 psi, there is a restriction in HPAA solenoid assembly, hoses, tank unit, or other fuel return lines.

Procedure "E"
1. Reconnect injection pump fuel return line to Housing Pressure Altitude Advance (HPAA) solenoid inlet.
2. Disconnect fuel return line from HPAA solenoid outlet.
3. Attach a suitable hose to HPAA outlet and position opposite end of hose into a drain pan.
4. Start engine.

Procedure "F"
1. Remove Housing Pressure Altitude Advance (HPAA) solenoid assembly from engine.
2. Apply a maximum of 30 psi air pressure through both sides of solenoid (first from pump side, then from outlet side). If air does not flow freely in both directions, replace solenoid.
3. Remove pressure regulator from solenoid and check solenoid plunger. If plunger does not move freely, replace solenoid.
4. Install HPAA solenoid assembly, then disconnect electrical connector from Manifold Absolute Pressure (MAP) sensor.
5. Start engine and observe housing pressure, which should be 3–5 psi.
6. If housing pressure is not within specifications, adjust pressure regulator as follows:
   a. Remove HPAA assembly from engine.
   b. Remove line fitting from pressure regulator.
   c. Insert a ⅛ inch Allen wrench into pressure regulator and rotate adjustment screw as necessary to obtain 3–5 psi pressure.

Fig. 37   Offset on fuel injection pump

NOTE: Rotate the adjustment screw counterclockwise to decrease pressure or clockwise to increase pressure. One complete turn of the screw will alter pressure by approximately 3.2 psi.

INJECTION PUMP
REPLACE

REMOVAL

1. Remove air cleaner assembly.
2. Remove crankcase ventilation filter and pipes from valve cover and air crossover.
3. Remove air crossover, **Fig. 36,** and install suitable intake screen covers.
4. Remove fuel lines, filter and fuel pump as an assembly. Plug all openings.
5. Remove throttle and T.V. cables from intake manifold brackets and position aside.
6. Disconnect fuel return line from injection pump.
7. Disconnect injection line clamps that are closest to the pump.
8. Disconnect injection lines from pump and plug all openings. Then carefully reposition lines to gain enough clearance to remove pump.
9. Remove two bolts retaining injection pump.
10. Remove pump and discard pump to adapter "O"-ring.

INSTALLATION

1. Position No. 1 cylinder at firing position by aligning mark on balance with zero mark on indicator located at front of engine.
2. Align offset tang on pump drive shaft with pump driven gear, **Fig. 37.**
3. Install new pump to adapter "O"-ring, then install pump.
4. If a new intermediate adapter is installed, set injection pump at center of slots in pump mounting flange. If original intermediate adapter is being used, align pump timing mark with mark on intermediate adapter. Install two bolts and washers retaining pump and torque bolts to 35–37 ft. lbs.
5. Reverse steps 1 through 8 of removal procedure for remainder of installation. If necessary adjust T.V. cable, pump timing, vacuum regulator valve or idle speed.

haust Gas Recirculation (EGR), disconnect vacuum hose from EGR valve.
7. On all models, remove Metering Valve Sensor (MVS) adjustment hole plug.
8. Install washers onto tool No. J-28526, then attach a suitable pressure gauge to tool.
9. Disconnect electrical connectors from Housing Pressure Cold Advance (HPCA) solenoid.
10. Disconnect Housing Pressure Altitude Advance (HPAA) electrical connector from engine wiring harness.
11. Attach suitable tachometer to engine, then start engine.
12. Inspect for fuel leaks and correct as necessary.
13. Increase engine idle speed to 1000 RPM and note pressure reading.

Procedure "B"
1. Stop engine, then remove line fitting from pressure regulator.
2. Insert a ⅛ inch Allen wrench into pressure regulator and rotate adjustment screw as necessary to obtain 10 psi pressure.

NOTE: Rotate the adjustment screw counterclockwise to decrease pressure or clockwise to increase pressure. One complete turn of the screw will alter pressure by approximately 3.2 psi.

3. Check injection pump timing and adjust as necessary as described under "Injection Pump Timing."

Procedure "C"

NOTE: If housing pressure is very low, or cannot be brought to 9–11 psi by adjusting the regulator, the Housing Pressure Cold Advance (HPCA) pressure regulator or solenoid is defective.

1. Remove pressure regulator from pump.
2. Apply a maximum of 30 psi air pressure through regulator at both ends (first from pump side, then from outlet side). The check ball should seat when applying air from outlet side.

1. DIGITAL VOLT METER
2. ENGINE HARNESS
3. MVS TEST HARNESS (BT-8342 OR J-34678)
4. MVS HARNESS
5. METERING VALVE SENSOR
6. INJECTION PUMP

Fig. 38 MVS voltage check. 1984 models

1. **DIGITAL VOLTMETER**
2. **ENGINE HARNESS**
3. **MVS TEST HARNESS (BT-8342 OR J-34678)**
4. **MVS ADAPTER HARNESS (BT-8342-10 OR J-34678-50)**
5. **MVS HARNESS**
6. **METERING VALVE SENSOR (MVS)**
7. **INJECTION PUMP**

Fig. 38A MVS voltage check. 1985 models

METERING VALVE SENSOR (MVS)

CHECKING

1984

1. Block drive wheels and apply parking brake.
2. Start engine, allow it to reach normal operating temperature, then shut off.
3. Remove air cleaner and air crossover assembly, then place suitable screens over intake manifold openings, **Fig. 36.**
4. Disconnect MVS harness connector and install tool BT-8342 or T-34678 as shown, **Fig. 38.**
5. Install suitable tachometer.
6. Torque MVS assembly attaching bolts to 30 inch lbs. before attempting to check or adjust voltage.

7. Start engine in park, then raise engine speed to 1500 RPM for 10–20 seconds to stabilize fuel flow.
8. Return engine to idle and shift transmission to drive.
9. Set engine speed to 650 RPM.
10. Using suitable multi-meter set at 20 volt scale, measure V-REF voltage between terminals A and C, **Fig. 38.**
11. Measure MVS voltage between terminals B and C for given engine load.
12. Shift transmission into park, then compare voltage recorded in steps 10 and 11 with chart in **Fig. 39.**
13. Measure the voltage between terminals B and C as the throttle is moved from idle to wide open position. Voltage should range from zero to over 4 volts.
14. If MVS voltage is within specifications in steps 12 and 13, sensor is operating correctly. If not as specified, refer to

"Adjust" procedure.
15. Connect MVS connectors, then start engine and adjust idle speed to specifications.
16. Remove screens from intake manifold openings, then install air crossover and air cleaner assembly, **Fig. 36.**

1985

1. Perform steps 1 and 2 as described for 1984.
2. Remove air cleaner cover, then the MAP sensor retainer, and position MAP sensor out of way with electrical connectors and vacuum hose attached.
3. Remove air cleaner assembly and the air crossover, disconnect vacuum hose to EGR valve and install suitable screened covers in intake manifold openings.
4. Disconnect electrical connector at HPAA solenoid.
5. Connect MVS test harness as shown, **Fig. 38A.**
6. Install suitable tachometer.
7. Perform steps 7 through 14 as described for 1984, referring to **Fig. 38A** instead of **Fig. 38.**
8. Connect HPAA solenoid connector and MVS connectors, then install air crossover, MAP sensor and air cleaner and connect EGR vacuum hose.

ADJUST

1984

1. With engine shut off, remove MVS hole plug, **Fig. 40.**
2. Using a file, resize metering valve sensor adjuster tool J-24182-2 so it enters into the MVS.
3. Turn the MVS adjustment screw clockwise to increase the voltage reading and counterclockwise to decrease voltage reading.
4. Install MVS hole plug finger tight, then proceed to steps 7 through 12 in MVS "Checking."
5. If voltage reading is not within chart specifications, readjust the MVS as necessary.
6. When the MVS voltage reading is within specifications, install MVS hole plug using new "O" ring. Torque plug to 30 inch lbs.

1985

1. Shut off engine, then remove MVS adjusting hole plug, being careful not to move MVS assembly while removing cap nut.
2. Turn adjustment screw clockwise to increase voltage reading or counterclockwise to reduce voltage reading. Adjust in 1/8 turn increments.
3. Install adjusting hole plug finger tight.
4. Perform steps 7 through 12 in MVS "Checking", "1984".
5. If MVS voltage reading is not within

MVS VOLTAGE TABLE

V-REF →	4.5	4.6	4.7	4.8	4.9	5.0	5.1	5.2	5.3	5.4	5.5
MVS VOLTAGE → (IN "0" 650 RPM)	.53–.55	.54–.56	.55–.57	.57–.59	.58–.60	.59–.61	.60–.62	.61–.63	.63–.65	.64–.66	.65–.67

Fig. 39 MVS voltage chart

1. METERING VALVE SENSOR
2. ADJUSTMENT COVER
3. HARNESS CONNECTOR
4. INJECTION PUMP

Fig. 40   MVS assembly

Fig. 43   Roosa-Master pump with cover removed

specifications, readjust MVS as necessary.
6. When voltage reading is within specifications, install adjusting hole plug with new O-ring, torquing to 30 inch lbs.
7. Connect MVS connector, then start engine and check for leaks.
8. Install air crossover and air cleaner assembly.

INJECTION NOZZLES
REPLACE

1. Remove fuel lines, using a backup wrench on upper injection nozzle hex.
2. Plug nozzle and lines to prevent damage or contamination, then remove nozzles by applying torque to largest nozzle hex.
3. When working on rear bank, it may be necessary to perform the following procedures:
   a. Rotate the intermediate steering shaft so steering gear stub shaft clamp bolt is in up position, then remove clamp bolt.
   b. Disconnect intermediate shaft from stub shaft.
   c. Remove engine support strut.
   d. Place a floor jack under front crossmember of cradle and raise jack until it just starts to raise vehicle.
   e. Remove front two body mount bolts with lower cushions and retainers. Remove cushions from bolts.
   f. Thread body mount bolts with retainers a minimum of three turns

Fig. 41   Roosa-Master pump right side view

into cage nuts so that the bolts restrain cradle movement.
   g. Release floor jack slowly until crossmember contacts body mount bolt retainers. As jack is being lowered watch and correct any interference with hose, lines, pipes and cables.

NOTE: Do not lower cradle without it being restrained as possible damage may occur to the body and underhood items.

4. Remove copper nozzle gasket from cylinder head if gasket did not remain on nozzle.
5. Reverse procedure to install. Apply suitable lubricant to nozzle threads, then torque nozzles to 25 ft. lbs. When tightening nozzle, torque must be applied to largest nozzle hex. Torque fuel line to 25 ft. lbs. using a backup wrench on upper injection nozzle hex.

NOTE: Failure to apply the correct lubricant can cause engine damage. Use lubricant No. 9985462 or equivalent.

VACUUM REGULATOR VALVE
REPLACE

1. Note location of valve vacuum hoses, then disconnect vacuum hoses.
2. Remove two valve attaching bolts, then valve.
3. Reverse procedure to install.

ROOSA-MASTER PUMP ON VEHICLE SERVICE

THROTTLE SHAFT SEAL, REPLACE

1. Disconnect battery ground cable.
2. Remove air cleaner and air crossover, **Fig. 36,** then install air screens.
3. Disconnect injection pump fuel solenoid, housing pressure cold advance wires and fuel return pipe, **Fig. 41.**
4. Scribe an alignment mark on vacuum regulator valve and pump body, then

Fig. 42   Installation of tool J-29601 on injection pump. Roosa-Master pump

Fig. 44   Installation of pump cover. Roosa-Master pump

proceed as follows:
   a. On 1982 models, remove throttle rod, vacuum regulator valve, return spring and detent cable.
   b. On 1983–85 models, remove vacuum regulator valve, then disconnect throttle and T.V. cables and return springs.
5. Place tool J-29601 over throttle shaft and pin, then position spring clip of tool over throttle shaft advance cam and tighten wing nut. Without loosening wing nut, pull tool off shaft. This will provide proper alignment during reassembly, **Fig. 42.**
6. Drive pin from throttle shaft and remove shaft advance cam and fiber washer. Remove any burrs from shaft which may have resulted from pin removal.
7. Clean injection pump cover, upper portion of pump, throttle shaft and guide stud area. Position several shop cloths in engine valley area to absorb fuel.
8. On 1984 California models only, remove MVS.
9. On all models, remove injection pump cover screws, then cover.

CAUTION: Use care to avoid any foreign matter from entering pump when cover is removed. If any object or foreign matter enter pump, it must be removed before engine is started as injection pump damage or engine damage may occur.

10. Note position of metering valve spring before removal as its position must be duplicated exactly during reassembly, **Fig. 43.**
11. Remove guide stud and washer, not-

1. FUEL RETURN PIPE
2. CLIP
3. FULLY DRIVEN, SEATED & NOT STRIPPED
4. HOUSING PRESSURE ALTITUDE ADVANCE SOLENOID
5. 13 N·m (9.5 LBS. FT.)

Fig. 44A   HPAA removal & installation

Fig. 45   CAV pump fuel inlet pipe removal

ing parts before removal.

12. Rotate min-max governor assembly up for clearance then remove it, **Fig. 43.** If idle governor spring becomes disengaged from throttle block, it must be reinstalled with tightly wound coils toward throttle block.
13. Remove throttle shaft assembly and inspect shaft for unusual wear or damage, replace if necessary. It may be necessary to loosen nuts at injection pump mounting flange and rotate pump slightly to allow throttle shaft to clear intake manifold.
14. Inspect throttle shaft bushings in pump housing for damage or unusual wear. If replacement of bushings is necessary, it must be performed by a qualified repair facility.
15. Remove throttle shaft seals. Do not cut seals to remove, as any nicks in the seal seat will cause leakage.
16. Install new shaft seals, lubricated with chassis grease. Use care to avoid cutting seals on sharp edges of shaft.
17. Carefully slide throttle shaft into pump to point where min-max governor assembly will slide back onto throttle shaft, **Fig. 43.**
18. Rotate min-max governor assembly downward, then hold in position and slide throttle shaft and governor into position.
19. Install new fiber washer, throttle shaft advance cam (do not tighten screw at this time) and a new throttle shaft drive pin, **Fig. 41.**
20. Align throttle shaft advance cam so tool J-20601 can be installed over throttle shaft, pins in slots and spring clip over advance cam.
21. Insert a .005 inch feeler gauge between cam and fiber washer, then tighten cam screw and remove tool

J-29601.

22. Install guide stud with new washer, assuring that upper extension of metering valve spring slides on top of guide stud. Torque guide studs to 85 inch lbs.

CAUTION: Over torquing may strip the aluminum threads in the housing.

23. Hold throttle in idle position and install new pump cover seal. Making sure that screws are not in cover, position cover above ¼ inch forward toward shaft end and about ⅛ inch above pump, **Fig. 44.** Move cover rearward and downward into position, using care to avoid cutting seal, then reinstall cover screws. Each screw must have a flat washer and internal lock washer, with flat washer against pump cover. Torque screws to 33 inch lbs. and install vacuum regulator.
24. On 1984 California models only, install the MVS using a new "O" ring. Coat the threads using a suitable sealer and torque to 30 inch lbs.
25. On all models, reconnect both battery ground cables, then turn ignition switch to run position and touch pink solenoid wire to solenoid. A clicking noise should be heard as the wire is connected and disconnected. If not, the linkage may be jammed in the wide open position and the engine must not be started. Proceed to step 26. If clicking is heard, connect pump solenoid and housing pressure cold advance wires and proceed to step 26.
26. Remove cover, then ground solenoid lead (opposite hot lead) and connect pink wire. With ignition switch in run position, the solenoid in the cover

should move the linkage. If not, the solenoid must be replaced. Minimum voltage across solenoid terminals must be 12 volts. Reinstall cover and repeat step 25.

27. Install throttle cable bracket, throttle rod, throttle cable and return springs. Make sure timing marks on pump and adapter are aligned and make sure nuts retaining pump are tight. Install fuel return pipe.
28. Start engine and check for fuel leaks.

NOTE: Rough idle may be due to air in the pump. Allow sufficient time for air to purge by allowing engine to idle. It may be necessary to turn engine off to allow air bubbles to rise to top of pump where they will be purged.

29. Adjust Vacuum Regulator Valve or MVS if equipped, then remove intake manifold screens and install air crossover and air cleaner, **Fig. 36.**

PUMP COVER SEAL AND/OR GUIDE STUD, REPLACE

1. Disconnect battery ground cable.
2. Remove air cleaner and air crossover, **Fig. 36,** and install air screen J-29657.
3. Disconnect injection pump fuel solenoid, housing pressure cold advance wires and fuel return pipe.
4. Clean injection pump cover, upper portion of pump and guide stud area. Position shop cloths to absorb fuel.
5. Remove injection pump cover screws, then cover.

CAUTION: Use care to avoid any foreign matter from entering pump when cover is removed. If any object or foreign matter enter pump, it must be removed before starting engine as injection pump damage or engine damage may occur.

6. Note position of metering valve spring before removal as its position must be duplicated exactly during reassembly, **Fig. 43.**
7. Remove guide stud and washer, noting location of parts before removal.
8. Refer to steps 21 thru 27 under "Throttle Shaft Seal, Replace" procedure for reassembly of "Pump Cover Seal And/Or Guide Stud".

1. Rubber "O" ring		13. Locknut	
2. Back leakage connection		14. Tang drive hub	
3. Elbow connection		15. Snap ring	
4. Governor control cover		16. Rubber "O" ring	
5. Joint (Gasket)		17. Shakeproof washer	
6. Spring filter		18. Screw - dome headed	
7. Cold advance solenoid		19. Inspection cover	
8. Backing washer		20. Rubber sealing joint (Gasket)	
9. Rubber "O" ring		21. Stop solenoid	
10. Insulating washer		22. Throttle lever	
11. Plain washer		23. Shakeproof washer	
12. Nut		24. Hexagon socket screw	

Fig. 46 Exploded view of CAV pump

1. Rubber "O" ring	8. Light load advance cam
2. Idling adjuster screw	9. Pin
3. Thrust washer	10. Locknut and rubber "O" ring
4. "E" type circlip	11. Torque screw
5. Thrust washer	12. Throttle shaft
6. Rubber "O" ring	13. Maximum speed adjustment screw
7. Clamp screw	(Do not adjust)

Fig. 47 Throttle shaft and seals. CAV pump

1. Rubber "O" ring	7. Governor carrier assembly
2. Governor support rod	8. Idle spring
3. Locking pin	9. Governor arm
4. Sleeve	10. Throttle block
5. Throttle lever	11. Throttle shaft
6. Idling screw and spring	

Fig. 48 Governor assembly. CAV pump

METERING VALVE SENSOR (MVS), REPLACE

1. Remove air cleaner and air crossover, **Fig. 36,** then install cover J-29657.
2. Disconnect sensor electrical connector, then remove sensor from pump, **Fig. 40.**
3. Install new "O" ring on sensor, then coat threads with suitable sealer. Torque sensor to 30 inch lbs.
4. Remove cover J-29657, then install air cleaner and air crossover.

HOUSING PRESSURE COLD ADVANCE (HPCA) & SHUTDOWN SOLENOID, REPLACE

1. Remove pump cover.
2. Remove terminal contact nuts, then remove solenoid from cover noting position of any insulating washers.
3. Place solenoid in cover ensuring that shut-off solenoid linkage is free. Also, check that housing pressure cold advance solenoid plunger is centered so that it will contact fitting check ball, **Fig. 34.**
4. Place insulator washers on terminal studs and install terminal nuts. Torque nuts to 10–15 inch lbs. and replace pump cover.

HOUSING PRESSURE ALTITUDE ADVANCE (HPAA), REPLACE

Refer to **Fig. 44A** for removal and installation procedures.

ALTITUDE FUEL LIMITER (AFL), REPLACE

1. Disconnect battery ground cable.
2. Remove air cleaner assembly and air crossover, then install suitable screened covers on manifold.

3. Disconnect AFL electrical wiring harness from engine wiring harness.
4. Remove pump cover.
5. Remove sufficient amount of fuel so fuel level is below AFL opening.
6. Disconnect AFL shaft from linkage hook.
7. Loosen AFL lock nut while holding AFL assembly.
8. Mark AFL to facilitate assembly, then remove AFL, noting number of turns required for removal.
9. Remove O-ring and lock nut.
10. Reverse procedure to install, threading AFL in the same number of turns required for removal, and align mark made during disassembly. Torque lock nut to 85 inch lbs. while holding AFL in position.

CAV PUMP ON VEHICLE SERVICE

END PLATE ACCESS PLUG OR STOP PLUG WASHER, REPLACE

1. Remove air cleaner and install cover J-26996-1 or equivalent.
2. Clean any dirt from area.
3. Remove stop plug and/or end plate plug and discard washers.
4. Reverse procedure to install. Torque stop plug to 80 inch lbs. and end plate to 43 ft. lbs.

FUEL INLET CONNECTION WASHER, REPLACE

1. Remove air cleaner and install cover J-26996-1 or equivalent.
2. Clean any dirt from area.
3. Remove fuel inlet pipe, **Fig. 45.**
4. Remove inlet connection and discard washer.
5. Reverse procedure to install. Using new washer, install inlet to pump and torque to 33 ft. lbs.

GOVERNOR CONTROL COVER GASKET, REPLACE

1. Remove air crossover, **Fig. 36,** and install cover J-29657.
2. Clean any dirt from injection pump cover and upper area of pump.
3. Place several rags in engine valley to catch spilled fuel.
4. Remove fuel return pipe.
5. Remove control cover screws and cover, **Fig. 46,** discarding washers and gasket.

NOTE: Extreme care must be exercised to keep foreign material out of the pump when the cover is off. If any objects are dropped into the pump, they must be removed before the engine is started or injection pump or engine damage may occur.

6. Reverse procedure to install. Torque screws to 25 inch lbs.

HOUSING PRESSURE COLD ADVANCE SOLENOID, REPLACE

1. Remove governor control cover, see "Governor Control Cover Gasket, Replace".
2. Remove solenoid terminal nut, spring filter, insulating washers and solenoid, **Fig. 46.** Discard gasket.
3. Reverse procedure to install. Torque terminal nut to 20 in. lbs. and ensure solenoid is centered in cover.

INSPECTION COVER PLATE GASKET, REPLACE

1. Remove air cleaner and install cover J-26996-1.
2. Place several shop rags in engine valley to catch spilled fuel.
3. Scribe a line on the vacuum regulator valve and pump body so valve can be reinstalled without readjusting.
4. Remove vacuum regulator valve from pump, then clean dirt from inspection

plate area.

5. Remove inspection plate retaining screws, then inspection plate and gasket.
6. Reverse procedure to install. Using new gasket, torque inspection plate retaining screws to 20 inch lbs.

STOP SOLENOID, REPLACE

1. Remove air cleaner and install cover J-26996-1
2. Clean dirt from area around solenoid.
3. Remove electrical lead.
4. Remove solenoid and "O"-ring, **Fig. 46.** Discard "O"-ring.
5. Reverse procedure to install. Torque solenoid to 130 inch lbs.

THROTTLE SHAFT SEAL, REPLACE

1. Remove air crossover and install cover J-29657 or equivalent.
2. Disconnect fuel return pipe, then remove governor control cover screws and cover.
3. Remove fast idle solenoid and vacuum regulator valve.
4. Disconnect throttle cable and T.V. cable.
5. Disconnect throttle return spring.
6. Install tool J-29601 or equivalent over

throttle shaft with slots of tool engaging vacuum regulator valve lock pin. Place spring clip of tool over throttle shaft advance cam and tighten wing nut. Without loosening wing nut, pull tool off of shaft.

7. Remove lock pin from throttle shaft, **Fig. 47.**
8. Remove rollpin from pump housing and remove governor support rod.
9. Tilt governor carrier assembly by lifting end nearest drive end of pump and remove carrier from pump housing.
10. Remove clamping screw from light load cam, then remove cam.
11. Remove "E" clip from throttle shaft, then remove throttle shaft from pump.
12. Remove and discard "O" rings.
13. Check throttle shaft assembly and governor housing bores for damage and wear and replace as necessary.
14. Lubricate shaft and "O" rings with oil and assemble larger "O" rings onto shaft.
15. Install throttle shaft into housing until thrust washers can be installed onto shaft in original positions. Install smaller "O" ring onto shaft.
16. Assemble light load advance cam onto shaft and install but do not tighten clamping screw.
17. Install "E" clip into throttle shaft recess. If new throttle shaft is

installed, shaft end play must be checked and adjusted by selective fitting of thrust washers. Throttle shaft end play should be .006–.012 inch.

18. Install new pin onto head of shaft. Align throttle shaft advance cam until tool J-29601 or equivalent can be installed over throttle shaft. Tighten cam screw, then remove tool J-29601.
19. Rotate throttle lever forwards to the drive end of pump. Install governor carrier assembly onto pump housing and engage lug on underside of throttle block with cut away notch in throttle shaft.
20. Lubricate governor support rod and new "O" ring, then install "O" ring onto support rod using tool J-33096 or equivalent.
21. Insert plain end of rod through rear of governor housing and into carrier assembly sleeve.
22. Install support rod into housing and install new locking pin, **Fig. 48.**
23. Install governor cover and fuel return pipe.
24. Install throttle return springs and connect throttle cable.
25. Connect TV detent cable.
26. Install vacuum regulator valve and fast idle solenoid.
27. Start engine and check for leaks. Install air crossover and air cleaner.

Clutch & Manual Transaxle Section

CLUTCH PEDAL ADJUST

The clutch is automatically adjusted by a self-adjusting mechanism, **Fig. 1**, mounted to the clutch pedal and bracket assembly. The cable is a fixed length cable and cannot be shortened or lengthened, however, the position of the cable can be changed by adjusting the position of the quadrant in relation to the clutch pedal. The self-adjusting mechanism monitors clutch cable tension and adjusts the quadrant position, changing the effective cable length.

INSPECTION

1. With engine running and service and parking brakes applied, depress clutch pedal to approximately ½ inch from floor mat.

2. Move shift lever between "First" and "Reverse" gears several times. If no clashing of the gears occur when going into "Reverse", the clutch is releasing fully.
3. If the shifting in Step 2 is not smooth, the clutch is not releasing fully and the linkage should be inspected and corrected as necessary.
4. Check clutch pedal bushings for sticking or excessive wear.
5. Have an assistant depress the clutch pedal to the floor and observe clutch fork lever travel at transaxle. The end of the clutch fork lever should have a total travel of approximately 1.5–1.7 inches on 1982–86 models.
6. To check the self-adjusting mechanism, proceed as follows:
   a. Depress the clutch pedal and observe if the pawl firmly engages the teeth of the quadrant.
   b. Release the clutch pedal and observe if the pawl is lifted off the quadrant teeth by the stop on the bracket.

CLUTCH REPLACE

1. On 1982–86 models, disconnect clutch cable from clutch release lever and transaxle as follows:
   a. Support clutch pedal upward against bumper stop to release pawl from quadrant.

Fig. 1 Clutch self-adjusting mechanism

b. Disconnect cable from clutch release lever on transaxle. Use care to avoid cable from snapping toward rear of vehicle.

c. Disconnect cable from quadrant. Lift the locking pawl away from quadrant, then slide cable out on right side.

2. On all models, remove transaxle as described under "Manual Transaxle, Replace."
3. Mark position of pressure plate to flywheel to aid reassembly.
4. Gradually loosen pressure plate attaching bolts until spring pressure is relieved.
5. Support pressure plate and remove mounting bolts, pressure plate and driven disc, **Fig. 2.**
6. Clean pressure and flywheel mounting surfaces. Inspect bearing retainer outer surface of transaxle.
7. Place driven disc in relative installed position and support with a dummy shaft.

NOTE: The driven disc is installed with the damper springs offset toward the transaxle. Stamped letters found on the driven disc identify the "Flywheel Side."

8. Install and gradually tighten the pressure plate to flywheel bolts. Remove dummy shaft.
9. Lubricate the release bearing outside diameter groove and the inside diameter recess.
10. Install transaxle.

MANUAL TRANSAXLE SHIFT CABLE
ADJUST

1982–86

1. Disconnect battery ground cable.
2. Shift transaxle into first gear.
3. Loosen shift cable attaching nuts "E" on transaxle lever "D" and "F," **Fig. 3.**
4. Remove console trim plate, then slide shifter boot up shifter handle and remove console.
5. Insert a yoke clip to hold lever as shown in view "D," **Fig. 3.**
6. Insert 5/32 inch or No. 22 drill bit into alignment hole on side of shifter assembly, view "C," **Fig. 3.**
7. Rotate lever "D" in direction of arrow while tightening nut "E," **Fig. 3,** to remove lash from transaxle.
8. Tighten nut "E" on lever "F," **Fig. 3.**
9. Remove drill bit and yoke from shifter assembly.
10. Reconnect battery ground cable.
11. Check for proper operation. If "hang-up" is encountered when shifting in the 1–2 gear range and shift cables are adjusted properly, it may be necessary to change shifter shaft selective washer.
12. Perform the following procedure to obtain correct washer thickness:
    a. Remove reverse inhibitor fitting spring and washer from end of housing.

Fig. 2   Clutch assembly

SHIFT POSITIONS OF LEVERS
VIEW B

Fig. 3   Manual transaxle shift cable adjustment. 1982–86

MANUAL TRANSAXLE
REPLACE

APPLY
LOAD ON END OF SHAFT

SHIFTER SHAFT
(LEVERS NOT SHOWN)

Fig. 4   Manual transaxle shifter shaft selective washer measurement

b. Place shifter shaft in "Second" gear.
c. Measure dimension "A", **Fig. 4,** which is distance between end of housing and the shoulder just behind end of shaft.
d. Apply a 9–13 pound load on opposite end of shaft, then measure dimension "B", **Fig. 4,** which is distance between end of housing and end of shifter shaft major diameter.
e. Subtract dimension "B" from dimension "A" to obtain dimension "C".
f. Refer to the following chart to obtain correct thickness shim:

Dimension "C" Inch	Shim Part No.
.07	14008235
.08	476709
.09	476710
.11	476711
.12	476712
.13	476713
.14	476714
.15	476715
.16	476716

1982

1. Disconnect battery ground cable from transaxle case and attach to upper radiator hose with wire or tape.
2. Remove two transaxle strut bracket bolts at transaxle, on left side of engine compartment, if so equipped.
3. Remove exhaust crossover pipe, if equipped.
4. Remove top four engine to transaxle bolts and one to rear of vehicle near cowl. The bolt nearer cowl is installed from engine side, **Fig. 5.**
5. Loosen but do not remove transaxle bolt near starter, at front of vehicle.
6. Disconnect speedometer cable at transaxle. On vehicles equipped with cruise control, remove transaxle speedometer cable at cruise control transducer.
6. Remove retaining clip and washer from transaxle shift linkage at transaxle.
7. Remove clips securing shift cables to mounting bosses on transaxle case.
8. Disconnect clutch cable. Install engine support fixture, **Fig. 6.**
9. Remove left hand side and crossmember assembly using following procedures:
   a. Rotate steering wheel so that intermediate shaft to steering gear stub shaft attaching bolt is in up position and remove bolt.
   b. Raise vehicle.
   c. Position jack under engine to act as a support during removal and installation.
   d. Remove left front tire and wheel assembly.
   e. Remove power steering pressure and return line brackets.
   f. Disconnect drive line vibration absorber and disconnect front stabilizer bar from left hand lower control arm.
   g. Disconnect left lower ball joint at knuckle then remove both front stabilizer bar reinforcement.
   h. Using a ½ inch drill bit, drill through spot weld located between rear

Fig. 5   Transaxle to engine attachment

holes of left hand front stabilizer bar mounting.
   i. Disconnect engine and transaxle mounts from cradle.
   j. Remove side to crossmember bolts also bolts from left side body mounts.
   k. Remove left side and front crossmember assembly. It may be necessary to pull or gently pry crossmember loose.
10. Drain fluid from transaxle.
11. Install drive axle boot seal protectors. Disconnect drive axles from transaxle then swing left side drive axle outward from transaxle. Right side drive axle can be removed as transaxle is being removed from vehicle.
12. Remove flywheel and starter shield bolts. Remove shields.
13. Securely attach transaxle case to jack for removal.
14. Remove last transaxle to engine bolt.
15. Remove transaxle by sliding to left side, away from engine. Carefully lower jack, and move transaxle to bench.
16. Reverse procedure to install and note the following:
   a. When installing the transaxle, position the right side drive axle shaft into its bore as transaxle is being installed. The right hand driveshaft cannot be readily installed after the transaxle is attached to the engine.
   b. After the transaxle is attached to the engine, swing the cradle into position and immediately install the cradle to body bolts. When swinging the cradle into the installed position, guide the left side driveshaft into the case bore.

1983-86

1. Disconnect battery ground cable from transaxle and attach to upper radiator hose with wire or tape.
2. Disconnect electrical connector from horn, then remove horn attaching bolt.
3. Remove air cleaner assembly.
4. Disconnect clutch cable as follows:
   a. Support clutch pedal upward

SUPPORT J-22825-45
WIPER PIVOT   COWL
HOOK J-22825-48
SUPPORT BAR J-22825-1 OR BT-6603
FASTENERS TORQUE TO 67 N·m (50 FT. LBS.)
RADIATOR SUPPORT
SUPPORT J-22825-45

Fig. 6   Engine support tool installation

against bumper stop to release pawl from quadrant.

b. Disconnect cable from clutch release lever on transaxle. Use care to prevent cable from snapping toward rear of vehicle.

c. Disconnect cable from quadrant. Lift locking pawl away from quadrant, then slide cable out on right side.

d. Disconnect 2 upper nuts on engine side of cowl, holding cable retainer to upper studs.

e. Disconnect cable from bracket on transaxle.

5. On models with V6 engine, disconnect fuel lines and fuel line clamps from clutch cable bracket.

6. On all models, remove clutch cable bracket from transaxle.

7. On models with V6 engine, remove exhaust crossover pipe.

8. On all models, remove retaining clips and washers from transaxle shift linkage at transaxle.

9. Remove shift cable to mounting boss retaining clips from transaxle case.

10. Disconnect speedometer cable from transaxle.

11. Remove 5 upper engine-to-transaxle attaching bolts.

12. Install engine support fixture, **Fig. 6.**

13. Raise and support vehicle.

14. Drain fluid from transaxle.

15. Install suitable drive axle boot seal protectors on both inner and outer seals.

16. Remove left front wheel assembly.

17. Remove left side cradle and crossmember assembly as follows:

a. Position jack under engine to act as a support during removal and installation.

b. Disconnect front ball joint.

c. Disconnect front stabilizer bar from control arm.

d. Remove front stabilizer bar plate and bushing from sidemember.

e. Disconnect engine and transaxle mount from left sidemember.

f. Remove sidemember-to-crossmember attaching bolts.

g. Remove 2 left side body mount bolts.

h. Remove left side and crossmember assembly.

18. Disconnect drive axles from transaxle, then swing left side drive axle outward from transaxle. Right side drive axle can be removed as transaxle is being removed from vehicle.

19. Remove flywheel and starter motor shield attaching bolts.

20. Securely attach transaxle case to jack for removal.

21. Remove remaining transaxle-to-engine attaching bolt.

22. Remove transaxle by sliding to left side away from engine and carefully lowering assembly from vehicle.

23. Reverse procedure to install, noting the following:

a. When installing transaxle, position right side drive axle shaft into it's bore, as driveshaft cannot be installed after transaxle is attached to engine.

b. After transaxle is attached to engine, swing cradle into position and immediately install cradle-to-body attaching bolts.

Rear Axle, Rear Suspension & Brakes

DESCRIPTION

The rear suspension. **Fig. 1,** consists of a rear axle assembly, control arms, coil springs, shock absorbers and a track bar. The rear axle is trailing arm type design. A stabilizer bar is welded to the inside of the axle housing and is an integral part of the axle assembly. A single unit hub and bearing assembly is bolted to each end of the axle assembly. The hub and bearing assembly is a sealed unit and must be replaced as an assembly.

REAR AXLE
REPLACE

NOTE: When removing rear axle assembly, do not use twin-post type hoist. The swing arc tendency of this axle may cause it to slip from hoist. Perform axle removal on floor if necessary.

1. Raise rear of vehicle and support rear axle using a suitable jack.

2. Remove rear wheel assembly and brake drum. Do not hammer on brake drum since damage to bearings may result.

3. Disconnect parking brake cable at equalizer, then remove brake line brackets from frame.

4. Disconnect shock absorber from lower mountings on axle housing.

5. Remove track bar attaching nut and bolt and disconnect track bar.

NOTE: Do not suspend rear axle by brake hoses, otherwise damage to hoses may result.

1. UNDERBODY
2. INSULATOR UPPER
3. SPRING
4. LOWER INSULATOR ON A SERIES ONLY
5. TRACK BAR

Fig. 1 Rear axle and suspension

6. Carefully lower rear axle assembly and remove coil spring and insulators.

7. Disconnect brake lines from control arm attachments.

8. Remove parking brake cable from rear axle attachments.

9. Remove hub attaching bolts, then the hub and bearing assembly and position backing plate out of way.

10. Remove control arm bracket to underbody attaching bolts, then lower axle assembly and remove from vehicle.

11. Reverse procedure to install, noting the following:

a. If control arm brackets were removed from control arms, torque attaching nuts to 78 ft.lbs.

b. Install control arm bracket at a 40.5–44.5° angle as shown in **Fig. 2.**

c. Torque control arm-to-underbody attaching bolts to 28 ft.lbs.

d. Torque track bar attaching nut to 35 ft.lbs.

HUB & BEARING ASSEMBLY
REPLACE

1. Raise and support rear of vehicle, then remove wheel and tire assembly and brake drum.

NOTE: Do not hammer on brake drum since damage to bearing may result.

2. Remove four hub and bearing assembly to rear axle attaching bolts, then the hub and bearing assembly from axle.

3. Reverse procedure to install. Torque hub and bearing assembly to rear axle attaching bolts to 45 ft.lbs.

NOTE: Use care not to drop hub and bearing assembly since damage to bearing may result.

COIL SPRING
REPLACE

1. Raise rear of vehicle and support rear

REINFORCEMENT

CONTROL ARM

CONTROL ARM
BRACKET
(REF)

VIEW B
(TYPICAL BOTH SIDES)
POSITION CONTROL ARM BRACKETS
AS SHOWN PRIOR TO INSTALLING
AXLE ASM. TO UNDERBODY AND
TIGHTEN NUT TO SPECIFIED TORQUE

"FRONT"

AXLE ASM.

CONTROL ARM
(WELDED TO AXLE ASM.)

L.H. SIDE SHOWN (TYPICAL BOTH SIDES)

Fig. 2   Control arm bracket installation

UNDERBODY

± 15°

INSULATOR

SPRING

POSITION LEG OF UPPER
COIL ON SPRINGS PARALLEL
TO AXLE ASM. & TOWARDS
L.H. SIDE OF VEHICLE
WITHIN LIMITS SHOWN.

AXLE ASM.

± 15°

"FRONT"

LOWER SPRING
INSULATOR ON
"A" SERIES ONLY

Fig. 3   Coil spring & insulator installation

**Fig. 4   Control arm bushing
removal**

**Fig. 5   Control arm bushing
installation**

axle using a suitable jack.
2. Remove right and left brake line bracket attaching bolts from frame and allow brake lines to hang freely.
3. Remove track bar attaching nut and bolt, then disconnect track bar.
4. Disconnect shock absorbers at lower mountings.

NOTE: Do not suspend rear axle by brake hoses since damage to hoses may result.

5. Carefully lower rear axle assembly and remove springs and insulators.
6. Reverse procedure to install, **Fig. 3**.

CONTROL ARM BUSHING
REPLACE

1. Raise rear of vehicle and support rear axle under front side of spring seat using a suitable jack.
2. If right hand side bushing is to be replaced, disconnect parking brake cable from equalizer.
3. Remove parking brake cables from bracket attachment and position out of way.
4. Disconnect brake line bracket from frame.
5. Disconnect shock absorber from lower mounting, then pull spring out of way.
6. Remove four control arm to underbody attaching bolts and allow control arm to rotate downward.
7. Remove nut and bolt from bracket attachment and remove bracket.
8. The bushing can now be replaced using tools shown in **Figs. 4 and 5.** When installing bushing, press bushing in until end of bushing is aligned with scribed line on tool J-28685-2, **Fig. 5.**
9. Reverse procedure to install control arm. Install bracket to control arm as shown in **Fig. 2.**

TRACK BAR
REPLACE

1. Raise rear of vehicle and support rear axle using a suitable jack.
2. Remove nut and bolt attaching track bar at axle housing and underbody and remove track bar, **Fig. 6.**
3. Reverse procedure to install, **Fig. 6.** Open side of track bar must face rear of vehicle. Also nut must be at rear of attachments at both axle and underbody attachments.

SHOCK ABSORBER
REPLACE

1. Open deck lid and remove trim cover, then remove shock absorber upper attaching nut.
2. Raise rear of vehicle and support rear axle using a suitable jack.
3. Disconnect shock absorber at lower

attachment and remove shock absorber from vehicle.

4. Reverse procedure to install. Torque shock absorber lower attaching nut to 43 ft. lbs. Torque shock absorber upper attaching nut to 13 ft. lbs.

DRUM BRAKE ADJUSTMENTS

These brakes have self adjusting shoe mechanisms that assure correct lining-to-drum clearances at all times. The automatic adjusters operate only when the brakes are applied as the car is moving rearward.

Although the brakes are self-adjusting, an initial adjustment is necessary after the brake shoes have been relined or replaced, or when the length of the star wheel adjuster has been changed during some other service operation.

Frequent usage of an automatic transmission forward range to halt reverse vehicle motion may prevent the automatic adjusters from functioning, thereby inducing low pedal heights. Should low pedal heights be encountered, it is recommended that numerous forward and reverse stops be made until satisfactory pedal height is obtained.

NOTE: If a low pedal height condition cannot be corrected by making numerous reverse stops (provided the hydraulic system is free of air) it indicates that the self-adjusting mechanism is not functioning. Therefore, it will be necessary to remove the brake drum, clean, free up and lubricate the adjusting mechanism. Then adjust the brakes as follows, being sure the parking brake is fully released.

ADJUSTMENT

A lanced "knock out" area is provided in the web of the brake drum for servicing purposes on some models. When adjustment is required on models that do not have a lanced area on the brake drum, carefully drill a ½ in. hole into the round flat area on the backing plate opposite the parking brake cable. If lanced area of brake drum has been knocked out or if a hole was drilled in backing plate, ensure that all metal particles are removed from the brake compartment.

1. Turn brake adjusting screw to expand shoes until wheel can just be turned by hand.
2. Using a suitable tool to hold actuator

1—UNDERBODY BRACKET

2—47 N•m (35 FT. LB.)

3—AXLE ASSEMBLY

4—60 N•m (44 FT. LB.)

5—BRACE - "A" SERIES WAGON

6—BRACE HANGER

Fig. 6   Track bar installation

from adjuster, back off adjuster 30 notches. If shoes still drag, back off one or two additional notches.

NOTE: Brakes should be free of drag when adjuster has been backed off approximately 12 notches. Heavy drag at this point indicates tight parking brake cables.

3. Install adjusting hole cover on brake drum or backing plate.
4. Check parking brake adjustment.

PARKING BRAKE
ADJUST

Need for parking brake adjustment is indicated if the service brake operates with sufficient pedal reserve, but the parking brake pedal travel is less than 9 ratchet clicks or more than 16 ratchet clicks.

1. Depress parking brake pedal three ratchet clicks, then raise and support rear of vehicle.
2. Check to ensure that equalizer nut groove is sufficiently lubricated with grease, then tighten adjusting nut until right rear wheel can just be rotated rearward, but is locked when forward rotation is attempted.
3. Release parking brake lever. Both wheels should rotate freely in either direction with no brake drag.

MASTER CYLINDER
REPLACE

1. Disconnect master cylinder push rod from brake pedal.
2. Disconnect wire connector at brake warning pressure switch.
3. Disconnect brake lines from master cylinder, then remove two master cylinder mounting nuts and remove master cylinder.
4. Reverse procedure to install, then bleed brake system.

POWER BRAKE UNIT
REPLACE

1. Disconnect brake unit push rod from brake pedal.
2. Remove two master cylinder to power brake unit mounting nuts, then position master cylinder away from brake unit with brake lines attached.

NOTE: Use care not to bend or kink brake lines.

3. Disconnect vacuum hose from vacuum check valve. Plug vacuum hose to prevent entry of dirt.
4. Remove power brake unit to dash panel attaching nuts, then remove brake unit.
5. Reverse procedures to install.

Front Suspension & Steering Section

Fig. 1   Front suspension

Fig. 2   Front wheel bearing assembly & seal

Fig. 3   Removing front wheel bearing & hub assembly

DESCRIPTION

The front suspension, **Fig. 1,** on these vehicles is a MacPhereson strut design. The lower control arms pivot from the engine cradle. This engine cradle has isolation mounts to the body and conventional rubber bushings are used for the lower control arm pivots. The upper end of the strut is isolated by a rubber mount incorporating a bearing for wheel turning. The lower end of the steering knuckle pivots on a ball stud which is retained in the lower control arm with rivets and is clamped to the steering knuckle. Sealed wheel bearings are used and are bolted to the steering knuckle.

WHEEL ALIGNMENT

NOTE: Camber and toe-in are the only adjustments that can be performed on these vehicles.

CAMBER

The camber angle is adjusted by loosening the strut cam bolt and the through bolt and rotating the cam bolt to move the upper portion of the steering knuckle inboard or outboard. When correct camber angle is obtained, torque cam and through bolts to 140 ft. lbs.

NOTE: When performing this adjustment, the top through bolt must be loosened to prevent damage to the outer cam guide.

TOE-IN

Toe-in is controlled by tie-rod position. Adjustment is made by loosening the nuts at the steering knuckle end of the tie-rods and rotating the rods to obtain proper toe-in setting. When adjusting toe-in, the tie-rod boot clamps must be removed. After correct toe-in setting is obtained, torque tie-rod nuts to 45 ft. lbs.

WHEEL BEARING
REPLACE

REMOVAL

1. Loosen hub nut with vehicle on ground.
2. Raise and support vehicle and remove front wheel.
3. Install drive axle boot cover, tool J-28712.
4. Remove and discard hub nut.
5. Remove brake caliper from support and suspend caliper from frame with a length of wire. Do not suspend caliper by the brake hose.
6. Remove three hub and bearing attaching bolts. If the old bearing is being re-installed, mark attaching bolts and holes for re-installation, **Fig. 2.**
7. Using tool J-28733 or equivalent, remove bearing, **Fig. 3.**

NOTE: If excessive corrosion is present, ensure that the bearing is loose in the knuckle before using puller tool.

8. If installing new bearing, replace steering knuckle seal.

INSTALLATION

1. Clean and inspect bearing mating sur-

Fig. 4   Installing front wheel bearing seal

faces and steering knuckle bore for dirt, nicks and burrs.
2. If installing steering knuckle seal, use tool J-28671 or equivalent to install seal, **Fig. 4.** Apply grease to seal and knuckle bore.
3. Push bearing onto axle shaft.
4. Tighten hub nut to fully seat bearing.
5. Install bearing attaching bolts and torque to 63 ft. lbs, **Fig. 2.**
6. Install caliper assembly and the wheel.
7. Lower vehicle and torque hub nut to 225 ft. lbs. on 1982 models, 185 ft. lbs. on 1983–84 models, or 192 ft. lbs. on 1985–86 models.

LOWER BALL JOINT
REPLACE

SERVICE BULLETIN: When servicing lower ball joint, be sure to align broached notch in ball joint stud with clamp bolt hole during reassembly. This prevents interference between stud and clamp bolt. To ensure proper bolt torque, replace clamp bolt and nut each time ball joint stud is separated from steering knuckle.

For removal and installation procedures, refer to **Fig. 5.**

USING ⅛" DRILL, DRILL RIVETS APPROXIMATELY ¼" DEEP IN CENTER OF RIVET

DRILLING RIVETS

USING ½" DRILL, DRILL JUST DEEP ENOUGH TO REMOVE RIVET HEAD

DRILLING RIVETS

PUNCH

HAMMER

REMOVE RIVETS

BALL JOINT

18 N·m (13 FT. LBS.)

INSTALL BALL JOINT

REPLACE

BOLT SHOULD EASILY GO IN PLACE. IF NOT, CHECK STUD ALIGNMENT.

50 N·m (40 FT. LBS.) TORQUE APPLIED TO NUT

Fig. 5 Lower ball joint removal & installation

LOWER CONTROL ARM & BUSHINGS
REPLACE

For removal and installation procedures, refer to **Fig. 6.** Torque ball joint clamping bolt to 40 ft. lbs. and control arm attaching bolts to 66 ft.lbs.

STEERING KNUCKLE
REPLACE

For removal and installation procedures, refer to **Fig. 7.**

STABILIZER BAR & BUSHINGS
REPLACE

For removal and installation procedures, refer to **Fig. 8.**

STRUT ASSEMBLY
REPLACE

For removal and installation procedures, refer to **Fig. 9.**

STRUT ASSEMBLY SERVICE
DISASSEMBLY

1. Mount compressor J-26584 in suitable vise.
2. Mount strut in compressor using bottom adapter J-26584-4 on 1982 models, J-26584-89 on 1983 models, or J-26585-400 on 1984–86 models.
3. Ensure that strut is fully contained by bottom adapter and that locating pins are fully engaged.
4. Rotate strut to align lip of top mount with notch in compressor support.
5. On 1982–83 models, install both J-26584-40 top adapters ensuring that split lines are at 9 o'clock and 3 o'clock positions, **Fig. 10.**
6. On 1984–86, install top adapter J-26584-430, aligning studs with properly marked holes on adapter.
7. Rotate compressor screw clockwise until top support contacts strut/adapter assembly, then keep turning screw until spring is compressed to approximately ½ of its height on 1984–86 models or 4 turns on 1982–83 models.
8. Remove nut from damper shaft and install alignment rod J26584-27 on 1982–83 models, J-3414-27 on 1984 models, or J-34013-27 on 1985–86 models.
9. Gradually release spring tension, then remove and disassemble strut noting position of components for reassembly, **Fig. 11.**

ASSEMBLY

1. Perform steps 1 through 3 as outlined in the "Disassembly" procedure.
2. Rotate strut assembly until mounting flange is facing outward opposite compressor forcing screw.
3. Install spring and related components on strut. Ensure spring is properly seated on bottom spring plate.
4. Install strut spring seat assembly on top of spring. Ensure flat faces in same direction as lower flange.
5. Position top adapters over spring seat assembly.
6. Rotate compressor forcing screw until compressor top support makes contact with top adapters. Do not compress spring at this time.
7. Install strut alignment rod through top spring seat. Thread rod onto damper shaft hand tight, **Fig. 12.**

NOTE: Install shims between lower spring seat and bottom adapter to keep alignment rod centered in upper spring seat opening.

8. Compress spring by slowly rotating forcing screw. While rotating screw, observe position of damper shaft, as it must pass directly through center of opening in upper spring seat to provide proper operation. If spring is off-center, back off screw and proceed as follows:
   a. Reposition both top adapters in support fixture to provide proper spring seat-to-damper position.
   b. Install thin shim stock between lower spring seat and bottom adapter to tilt strut assembly into proper position.
   c. When damper shaft can be held in proper position, rotate screw until approximately 1½ inch of shaft can

BOLT SHOULD EASILY GO IN PLACE.
IF NOT, CHECK STUD ALIGNMENT.

CROSSMEMBER

LOWER CONTROL ARM

BEARING — J-21474-24 — J-21474-5

J-21474-18

J-21474-19

J-21474-25

REMOVE LOWER CONTROL ARM BUSHING

J-21474-19 — J-21474-5 — J-21474-20

J-21474-18

BEARING

J-21474-25

INSTALL LOWER CONTROL ARM BUSHING

Fig. 6   Lower control arm & bushing removal & installation

be pulled through upper spring seat. Do not compress spring beyond this point.
9. Remove alignment rod, place strut mounting assembly over damper shaft and install nut. Torque nut to 65 ft.lbs.
10. Rotate forcing screw counterclockwise and remove strut assembly from compressor.

STEERING GEAR
REPLACE

1982-86

Removal
1. On models equipped with power steering, remove air cleaner, then disconnect and cap hydraulic lines from steering gear.
2. Pull intermediate shaft seal upward, then remove intermediate shaft to steering gear stub shaft pinch bolt, **Fig. 13.**
3. Raise and support vehicle, then remove both front wheel and tire assemblies.
4. Using tool J6627 or equivalent, disconnect tie rod ends from steering knuckles.
5. Remove AIR pipe bracket to crossmember attaching bolt, if equipped.
6. Remove two rear frame cradle mounting bolts and lower rear of cradle 4 to 5 inches.

CAUTION: Do not lower cradle more than specified, as damage to engine components may result.

7. Remove steering gear heat shield from crossmember.

8. Remove steering gear assembly mounting bolts, then the steering gear assembly through the left wheel opening.

Installation
1. Place steering gear assembly into mounts on crossmember, then install and torque mounting bolts to 70 ft. lbs.
2. Install heat shield.
3. Raise frame cradle and install mounting bolts. Torque bolts to 75 ft. lbs.
4. Install AIR pipe bracket to crossmember, then connect tie rod ends to steering knuckles. Torque ball studs to 30 ft. lbs.
5. Install wheel and tire assemblies and lower vehicle.
6. Connect intermediate shaft to steering gear stub shaft, install pinch bolt and torque to 45 ft. lbs.
7. Check and adjust toe-in as required.

REMOVE

1. Refer to front wheel bearing removal.
2. Mark cam bolt.
3. Remove parts as shown.

INSTALL

1. Install knuckle to ball joint.
2. Loosely install knuckle to strut.
3. Refer to front wheel bearing installation.
4. Place jackstand under hub and rotor assembly and lower hoist to load control arm. Then place cam in position as noted and tighten nuts.
5. Install parts as shown.

KNUCKLE

MARK CAM BEFORE REMOVING BOLTS

BOLT SHOULD EASILY GO IN PLACE. IF NOT, CHECK STUD ALIGNMENT

190 N·m (140 FT. LBS.)

CAM BOLT

STRUT

KNUCKLE

54 N·m (40 FT. LBS.)

CONTROL ARM

TIE ROD

60 N·m (45 FT. LBS.)

J-6627 or BT-7101

J-22269-01

27mm or 1-1/8" SOCKET

TIE ROD END

REMOVE TIE ROD END

INSTALL TIE ROD END

Fig. 7 Steering knuckle removal & installation

Do not remove studs from control arm.

LOWER CONTROL ARM

CROSSMEMBER

BUSHING

End of stabilizer should be equal distance from bushing on both sides.

45 N·m (35 FT. LBS.)

CROSSMEMBER

BRACKET

BUSHING

FRONT STABILIZER

PLATE

55 N·m (40 FT. LBS.)

POWER STEERING PUMP
REPLACE

4-151

1. Raise and support vehicle, then remove radiator hose clamp bolt.
2. Disconnect and cap hydraulic lines at power steering pump.
3. Remove power steering pump to rear bracket attaching nut.
4. Remove front pump bracket to engine and front pump bracket to rear pump bracket attaching bolts, **Fig. 14.**
5. Remove pump and bracket assembly from vehicle.
6. Reverse procedure to install.

V6-173

1. Disconnect battery ground cable.

2. Disconnect electrical connector at blower motor, then remove blower motor from vehicle.
3. Disconnect heater hose from water pump and hydraulic lines from power steering pump. Cap lines to avoid fluid leakage.
4. Remove rear pump bracket to engine bracket attaching nut and front pump bracket to cylinder head attaching bolts, **Fig. 15.**
5. Remove pump and bracket assembly from vehicle.
6. Reverse procedure to install.

V6-181, 231

1. Disconnect battery ground cable, then remove air cleaner.
2. Remove alternator drive belt and alternator, then raise and support vehicle.

EXHAUST PIPE

20 N·m (15 FT. LBS.)

SEAL

FRONT PIPE

Fig. 8 Stabilizer bar & bushing removal & installation

USE J-28712 FOR DOUBLE-OFFSET JOINT

USE J-33162 FOR TRI-POT JOINT*

INSTALL DRIVE AXLE BOOT PROTECTOR

24 N•m (18 FT. LBS)

190 N•m (140 FT. LBS)

FWD

Fig. 9 Strut assembly removal & installation

REMOVE

1. Remove (3) top attaching nuts.
2. Loosen wheel lug nuts.
3. Raise car and support on frame.
4. Remove wheel-and-tire; remove brake line clip.
5. Install boot protectors as shown in upper panel.
   *Whenever a tri-pot design joint is used on a drive axle shaft, it is necessary to disconnect the axle shaft from the trans-axle BEFORE separating the knuckle from the strut. Use J-33008.
6. Scribe the parts.
7. Remove (2) bolts; separate the strut from the knuckle.
8. Remove the strut.

INSTALL

1. Install parts in reverse order of removal.
2. Place jack stand under hub and rotor assembly. Lower hoist and place car in position as noted in removal.
3. Raise hoist.
4. Install brake line clip.
5. Remove boot protectors.
6. Install wheel and lower car.

INSTALL TOP ADAPTERS WITH SPLIT LINE IN THIS POSITION

SUPPORT

ADAPTORS J-26584-40

BOTTOM ADAPTOR J-26584-89

DIRECTION OF LOWER STRUT FLANGE

Fig. 10 Strut disassembly. 1982-83, 1984-86 similar

MOUNT ASSY.

UPPER SPRING SEAT
• FLAT MUST BE FACING IN SAME DIRECTION AS LOWER FLANGE ON BOTTOM OF STRUT

BUMPER

SHIELD

UPPER SPRING INSULATOR

SPRING

LOWER SPRING SEAT

ABSORBER AND STRUT ASSEMBLY

LOWER SPRING INSULATOR

ALWAYS INSPECT BUMPER WHEN REPLACING SPRING. REPLACE AS REQUIRED.

THIS LIP SITS INSIDE THE SPRING SEAT

THIS LIP IS CAPTURED BY FOUR LARGE TANGS

SPRING TO BE INSTALLED WITH SMALLEST COIL AT LOWEST POSITION, AND PLACED RELATIVE TO THE LOWER SPRING SEAT AS SHOWN

LOWER SEAT

SPRING

14 MM + 6 MM

Fig. 11 Strut assembly exploded view. 1982-86

ALIGNMENT ROD J-26584-27

DAMPER SHAFT

INSTALL SHIM STOCK HERE

Fig. 12 Strut alignment rod installation (Typical)

Fig. 13   Steering gear replacement. 1982–86

Fig. 14   Power steering pump replacement. 4-151

1. POWER STEERING PUMP
2. REAR ADJ. BRACKET
3. BOLT — 50 N·m (38 LBS. FT.)
4. GENERATOR MOUNTING BRACKET
5. GENERATOR ADJUSTING BRACKET
6. PULLEY
7. ENG. LIFT BRACKET AND SHIELD
8. FRONT ADJ. BRACKET
9. NUT — 50 N·m (38 LBS. FT.)
10. REAR BRACKET SPACER
11. NUT — 27 N·m (20 LBS. FT.)
12. PROTECTOR

**Fig. 16 Power steering pump replacement.
V6-181, 231**

3. Remove rear adjustment bracket to pump retaining nut, **Fig. 16.**
4. Remove alternator adjustment bracket and power steering pump drive belt.
5. Remove double nut and two studs, then the alternator mounting bracket.
6. Remove rear pump adjustment bracket, then disconnect hydraulic lines from power steering pump. Cap lines to prevent spillage of fluid.
7. Remove pump and bracket assembly from vehicle.
8. Reverse procedure to install.

V6-262 DIESEL

1982
1. Remove drive belt, then drain power steering fluid from power steering pump reservoir.
2. Raise and support vehicle and disconnect pressure and return lines from power steering pump.
3. Working through access holes in pump pulley, remove three bolts from front of pump.
4. Remove two nuts holding lower brace to engine and remove bracket.
5. Remove pump and pulley assembly from vehicle.
6. Reverse procedure to install, **Fig. 17.**

1983–84
1. Remove drive belt, then drain power steering fluid from power steering pump reservoir.
2. Disconnect pressure and return lines from power steering pump.
3. Remove pulley using puller J-25034 or equivalent.
4. Remove two pump attaching bolts, then pump from vehicle.
5. Reverse procedure to install, **Fig. 18.**

1985
1. Rotate drive belt tensioner counterclockwise, remove serpentine drive belt, then slowly release tensioner.
2. Raise and support vehicle and remove right front wheel.
3. Place suitable drain pan under pump assembly, disconnect lines from pump, then plug lines and open ports.
4. Remove bolts and nut securing pump and the pump, **Fig. 19.**
5. Remove pulley using J-25034 or equivalent.
6. Install pulley on replacement pump using J-25033 or equivalent, then reverse remaining procedure to complete installation.

FRONT PUMP
BRACKET

34 N·m (25 FT. LBS.)

50 N·m (35 FT. LBS.)

REAR PUMP
BRACKET

PUMP
ASSEMBLY

PULLEY

34 N·m (25 FT. LBS.)

Fig. 15 Power steering pump replacement. V6-173

Fig. 17   Power steering pump removal & installation. 1982 V6-262 Diesel

Fig. 18   Power steering pump removal & installation. 1983-84 V6-262 Diesel

Fig. 19   Power steering pump removal & installation. 1985 V6-262 Diesel

INDEX OF SERVICE OPERATIONS

NOTE: Refer to the rear of this manual for vehicle manufacturer's special service tool suppliers.

Serial Number Location

On top of instrument panel, left front.

Engine Number Location

On V6-181 & V6-231 engines, the engine code stamping is located on vertical pad on engine to transmission mounting flange located on forward side of block.

On V8-250 engines, the engine code stamping is located on cylinder block behind left cylinder head.

On V6-262 diesel engines, the engine code stamping is located on vertical pad located on right side of engine front cover.

Engine V.I.N. Code

The eighth digit of the seventeen digit V.I.N. code denotes engine code.

Grille Identification

1985—86 Buick Electra

1985—86 Cadillac DeVille & Fleetwood

1985 Olds 98

1986 Buick LeSabre

1986 Olds Delta 88

1985 Olds 98

General Engine Specifications

Year	Engine CID①/Liter	V.I.N. Code②	Carburetor	Bore and Stroke	Compression Ratio	Net H.P. @ R.P.M.③	Maximum Torque Ft. Lbs. @ R.P.M.	Normal Oil Pressure Pounds
1985	V6-181, 3.0L	E	E2ME, 2 Bbl.⑤	3.80 × 2.666	8.4	110 @ 4800	145 @ 2600	37
	V6-231 MFI, 3.8L	3	Fuel Injection	3.80 × 3.40	8	125 @ 4400	195 @ 2000	37
	V6-262, 4.3L④	T	Fuel Injection	4.057 × 3.385	22.5	85 @ 3600	165 @ 1600	30–45
	V8-250, 4.1L	8	Fuel Injection	3.465 × 3.307	9	125 @ 4200	190 @ 2200	30
1986	V6-231, 3.8L	—	Fuel Injection	3.80 × 3.40	8.5	140 @ 4400	200 @ 2000	37
	V8-250, 4.1L	—	Fuel Injection	3.465 × 3.307	9.0	130 @ 4200	200 @ 2200	30

①—CID—Cubic inch displacement.
②—The eighth digit denotes engine code.
③—Ratings are net—as installed in vehicle.
④—Diesel engine.
⑤—Rochester.

Valve Specifications

Year	Engine/V.I.N.	Valve Lash Int.	Valve Lash Exh.	Valve Angles Seat	Valve Angles Face	Valve Spring Installed Height	Valve Spring Pressure Lbs. @ In.	Stem Clearance Intake	Stem Clearance Exhaust	Stem Diameter Intake	Stem Diameter Exhaust
1985	V6-181/E	Hydraulic②		45	45	1.727	200 @ 1.340	.0015–.0035	.0015–.0032	.3412–.3401	.3412–.3405
	V6-231/3	Hydraulic②		45	45	1.727	200 @ 1.340	.0015–.0035	.0015–.0032	.3412–.3401	.3412–.3405
	V6-262/T①	Hydraulic②		③	④	1.670	210 @ 1.220	.0010–.0027	.0015–.0032	.3425–.3432	.3420–.3428
	V8-250/8	Hydraulic②		45	44	1.73	182 @ 1.28	.001–.003	.001–.003	.3420–.3413	.3420–.3413
1986	V6-231	Hydraulic②		45	45	1.727	200 @ 1.340	.0015–.0035	.0015–.0032	.3412–.3401	.3412–.3405
	V8-250	Hydraulic②		45	44	1.73	182 @ 1.28	.001–.003	.001–.003	.3420–.3413	.3420–.3413

①—Diesel engine.
②—No adjustment.
③—Intake 45°; Exhaust 31°.
④—Intake 44°; Exhaust 30°.

Pistons, Pins, Rings, Crankshaft & Bearings

Year	Engine Model/V.I.N.	Piston Clearance	Ring Gap① Comp.	Ring Gap① Oil	Wrist-pin Diameter	Rod Bearings Shaft Diameter	Rod Bearings Bearing Clearance	Main Bearings Shaft Diameter	Main Bearings Bearing Clearance	Thrust on Bear. No.	Shaft End Play
1985	V6-181/E	.0008–.0020	.010	.015	.9392	2.2487–2.2495	.0005–.0026	2.4995	.0003–.0018	3	.003–.011
	V6-231/3	.0008–.0020	.010	.015	.9392	2.2487–2.2495	.0005–.0026	2.4995	.0003–.0018	3	.003–.011
	V6-262/T②	.0035–.0045	③	.010	1.095	2.2490–2.2500	.0005–.0025	2.9993–3.0003	④	3	.0035–.0135
	V8-250/8	.0010–.0018	.023	.010	.8658	1.929	.0005–.0028	2.64	.0004–.0027	3	.001–.007
1986	V6-231	.0008–.0020	.010	.015	.9392	2.2487–2.2495	.0005–.0026	2.4995	.0003–.0018	3	.003–.011
	V8-250	.0010–.0018	.023	.010	.8658	1.929	.0005–.0028	2.64	.0004–.0027	3	.001–.007

①—Fit rings in tapered bores for clearance given in tightest portion of ring travel. Clearances specified are minimum gaps.
②—Diesel engine.
③—Top ring, .019 inch; 2nd ring, .013 inch.
④—Nos. 1, 2 & 3, .0005–.0020 inch; No. 4, .0020–.0034 inch.

Engine Tightening Specifications★

★ Torque specifications are for clean and lightly lubricated threads only. Dry or dirty threads produce increased friction which prevents accurate measurement of tightness.

Year	Engine Model/V.I.N.	Spark Plugs Ft. Lbs.	Cylinder Head Bolts Ft. Lbs.	Intake Manifold Ft. Lbs.	Exhaust Manifold Ft. Lbs.	Rocker Arm Stud Ft. Lbs.	Rocker Arm Cover Ft. Lbs.	Connecting Rod Cap Bolts Ft. Lbs.	Main Bearing Cap Bolts Ft. Lbs.	Flywheel to Crankshaft Ft. Lbs.	Vibration Damper or Pulley Ft. Lbs.
1985	V6-181/E	15	72	47	25	25②	6	40	100	60	200
	V6-231/3	15	72	47	25	25②	6	40	100	60	200
	V6-262/T①	—	③④	41	31	⑤	⑥	42	89	76	203–350
	V8-250/8	11	⑦	④	18	22⑧	50⑨	22	85	63	18
1986	V6-231	15	72	47	25	25②	6	40	100	60	200
	V8-250	11	⑦	④	18	⑧	50⑨	22	85	63	18

①—Diesel engine.
②—Rocker arm shaft.
③—Clean & dip entire bolt in engine oil before tightening to obtain correct torque reading.
④—Refer to text for proper torque and sequence procedure.
⑤—Rocker arm pivot studs, 11 ft. lbs.; rocker arm nuts, 28 ft. lbs.
⑥—Fully driven, seated & not stripped.
⑦—Torque bolts to 45 ft. lbs., then retorque to 90 ft. lbs.
⑧—Rocker arm to support bolts, 22 ft. lbs.; support to cylinder head nuts, 37 ft. lbs.
⑨—Inch lbs.

Front Wheel Alignment Specifications

Year	Model	Caster Angle, Degrees		Camber Angle, Degrees				Toe-In Inch	Toe-Out on Turns, Deg.	
		Limits	Desired	Limits		Desired			Outer Wheel	Inner Wheel
				Left	Right	Left	Right			
1985–86	Exc. DeVille & Fleetwood	+1.8 to +2.8	+2.3	0 to +1①	0 to +1①	+.5①	+.5①	Zero	—	—
	DeVille & Fleetwood	—	—	−.1 to +1.1	−.1 to +1.1	+.6	+.6	②	—	—

①—Left and right side should be equal within 0.5°.
②—.125° toe-in.

Rear Wheel Alignment Specifications

Year	Model	Camber Angle, Degrees		Toe-In, Inches
		Limits	Desired	
1985–86	Exc. DeVille & Fleetwood	−.8 to +.2①	−.3①	②
	DeVille & Fleetwood	−.3 to +.5	+.10	³⁄₃₂

①—Left and right side should be equal within 0.5°.
②—0.1° toe-in.

Alternator Specifications

Year	Model	Rated Hot Output Amps.
1985	01100278	108
	01105086	108
	01105200	85
	01105428	94
	01105553	97
1986	—	108
	—	120

Starting Motor Applications

Year	Engine/V.I.N.	Starter Ident. No.
1985	V6-181/E	1998448
	V6-231 MFI/3	1998445
	V6-262 Diesel/T	22523207
	V8-250/8	1998476
1986	V6-231	—
	V8-250	—

Cooling System & Capacity Data

Year	Model or Engine/V.I.N.	Cooling Capacity, Qts.		Radiator Cap Relief Pressure, Lbs.	Thermo. Opening Temp.	Fuel Tank Gals.	Engine Oil Refill Qts.	Transaxle Oil	
		Less A/C	With A/C					Manual Transaxle Pts.	Auto. Transaxle Qts. ①
1985	V6-181/E	13.3②	13.3②	15	195	18	4①	—	6.5
	V6-231/3	13.1③	13.1③	15	195	18	4①	—	6.5
	V6-262/T④	13.3	13.3	17	185	18	6.5⑤	—	6.5
	V6-262/T⑥	13.3	13.3	17	185	18	6⑤	—	5.8
	V8-250/8	—	13.2	15	195	18	5	—	6
1986	V6-231	—	12.37⑦	26	180	18	4①	—	5.3
	V8-250	—	—	—	—	18	5	—	—

①—Approximate. Make final check with dipstick.
②—W/heavy duty cooling system, 13.6 qts.
③—W/heavy duty cooling system, 13.2 qts.
④—Exc. DeVille & Fleetwood.
⑤—Includes filter.
⑥—DeVille & Fleetwood.
⑦—W/heavy duty cooling system, 12.47 qts.

Electrical Section

STARTER
REPLACE

NOTE: When removing starter, note if any shims are used between the starter and mounting surface. If shims are found, reinstall in original locations.

If starter is noisy during cranking, remove one .015 inch double shim or add one .015 inch single shim to the outer bolt. If starter makes a high pitched whine after engine start, a high pitched whine after engine start, add .015 inch double shims until noise ceases.

EXC. V6-262 DIESEL

1. Disconnect battery ground cable and raise and support vehicle.
2. Remove starter braces, shields or other components that may hinder starter removal.
3. Support starter and remove mounting bolts.
4. Lower starter and disconnect solenoid wires and battery cable.
5. Remove starter from vehicle.
6. Reverse procedure to install. Refer to previous note.

V6-262 DIESEL

1. Disconnect battery ground cable. On

TO ASSEMBLE, ROTATE TO STOP WHILE HOLDING CYLINDER.

Fig. 1 Lock cylinder removal

vehicles with heavy duty option there are two batteries.
2. Install suitable engine lifting equipment.
3. Raise and support vehicle.
4. Remove left and center engine mount stud nuts, then the two front cradle mounting bolts and lower the cradle.
5. Remove flywheel cover.
6. Remove starter lower shield nut and starter flex shield.
7. Disconnect solenoid wires and battery cable from starter.

8. Remove starter mounting bolts and the starter from vehicle.
9. Reverse procedure to install.

STEERING WHEEL
REPLACE

STANDARD & TILT WHEEL

1. Disconnect battery ground cable.
2. Remove two steering wheel pad retaining screws.
3. Disconnect horn wire from cam tower.
4. Remove steering wheel nut retainer.
5. Remove steering wheel retaining nut.
6. Using a suitable puller, remove steering wheel.
7. Reverse procedure to install.

TILT & TELESCOPING WHEEL

Exc. Cadillac

1. Disconnect battery ground cable.
2. Remove two steering wheel pad retaining screws.
3. Disconnect horn wire from steering wheel pad.
4. Remove steering shaft lock knob bolt positioning screws, then the lock knob

REMOVE

1. Remove parts as shown.

INSTALL

1. Install parts as shown
2. Position rod in slider hole and install ignition switch. Install lower stud and tighten to 4.0 N·m.
3. Install dimmer switch and depress switch slightly to insert 3/32" drill. Force switch up to remove lash, then tighten screw, and nut to 4.0 N·m.
4. Place shifter in neutral and install shift lever.

Fig. 2 Ignition & dimmer switch removal & installation. Except tilt column

REMOVE

1. Remove parts as shown.

INSTALL

1. Install parts as shown.
2. Position rod in slider hole and install ignition switch. Install lower stud and tighten to 4.0 N·m.
3. Install dimmer switch and depress switch slightly to insert 3/32" drill. Force switch up to remove lash, then tighten screw, and nut to 4.0 N·m.
4. Place shifter in neutral and install shift lever.

Fig. 3   Ignition & dimmer switch removal & installation. Tilt column

bolt from steering shaft.

5. Remove steering wheel nut retainer and the steering wheel nut. Using a suitable puller, remove steering wheel.
6. Reverse procedure to install.

Cadillac

1. Disconnect battery ground cable.
2. Remove two steering wheel pad retaining screws.
3. Disconnect horn wire from steering wheel pad.
4. Remove three screws from telescoping adjusting lever.

5. Remove steering shaft lock knob from steering shaft.
6. Remove steering wheel nut.
7. Using a suitable puller, remove steering wheel.
8. Reverse procedure to install.

IGNITION LOCK
REPLACE

1. Remove steering wheel as outlined under "Steering Wheel, Replace" procedure.

2. Remove turn signal switch as outlined under "Turn Signal Switch, Replace" procedure.
3. Remove buzzer switch.
4. Turn lock cylinder to "Run" position, then remove lock cylinder retaining screw and the lock cylinder, **Fig. 1.**
5. To install, rotate lock cylinder to the stop while holding housing. Align cylinder key with keyway in housing, then push lock cylinder into housing until fully seated.
6. Install lock cylinder retaining screw.
7. Install buzzer switch, turn signal switch and steering wheel.

TIGHTEN NUT UNTIL TOOL SLIGHTLY
DEPRESSES SHAFT LOCK

Fig. 4   Compressing lock plate

IGNITION & DIMMER SWITCHES
REPLACE

1. Remove turn signal switch as outlined under "Turn Signal Switch, Replace" procedure.
2. Refer to **Figs. 2 and 3** to remove ignition and dimmer switches.
3. When installing dimmer switch, depress switch slightly to install a ³⁄₃₂ inch twist drill. Force switch upward to remove lash and tighten retaining screw.

TURN SIGNAL SWITCH
REPLACE

1. Disconnect battery ground cable.
2. Remove steering wheel as outlined previously.

Fig. 6   Cover & wiper switch removal & installation. Tilt steering column

REMOVE

1. Remove ignition and dimmer switch. Refer to step 5.
2. Remove parts as shown.
3. For KEY RELEASE refer below

INSTALL

1. For KEY RELEASE refer below.
2. Assemble rack so that first rack tooth engages between first and second tooth of sector.
3. Install parts as shown.
4. Install ignition and dimmer switch. Refer to step 5.

NOTE: Housing without bearing retainer and bushing has spun-in bearing. If repair is necessary, complete housing assembly replacement is necessary.

Fig. 5   Housing & wiper switch removal & installation. Standard steering column

Fig. 7   Mechanical neutral start system

1 I/P CARRIER   3 HEADLAMP SWITCH
2 INTERIOR LIGHT DIMMER   4 TWILIGHT SENTINEL SWITCH

Fig. 8   Headlamp switch removal. Electra & Park Avenue

Fig. 9   Headlamp switch removal. DeVille & Fleetwood

1. HEADLAMP SWITCH
2. FULLY DRIVEN, SEATED AND NOT STRIPPED
3. PLUG FIBER OPTIC INTO REAR OF SWITCH ASM.

Fig. 10   Headlamp switch removal. Ninety Eight

1 I/P TOP COVER (PAD)   3 A/C OUTLET SEALS
2 I/P CARRIER

Fig. 11   Removing instrument panel top cover pad. Electra & Park Avenue

1 INSTRUMENT PANEL   3 TRIM COVER
2 STEERING COLUMN   4 A/C OUTLET HOSE

Fig. 12   Removing steering column cover to disconnect shift cable. Electra & Park Avenue w/quartz cluster

1 CLUSTER HOUSING ASM.   2 I/P CARRIER

Fig. 13   Cluster removal. Electra & Park Avenue

1	CHART – PAD ASSEMBLY
2	SCREW
3	SCREW
4	NUT
5	GRILLE
6	NUT
23	OUTLET

Fig. 14 Upper trim pad assembly. DeVille & Fleetwood

3. Using a suitable screwdriver, pry cover from housing.
4. Using lock plate compressing tool J-23653, compress lock plate and pry snap ring from shaft groove, **Fig. 4.** Slowly release lock plate compressor and remove tool and lock plate from shaft end.
5. Slide cancelling cam and upper bearing preload spring from end of shaft.
6. Remove turn signal switch lever.
7. Remove hazard warning knob retaining screw, button, spring and knob.
8. Remove pivot arm.
9. Wrap upper portion of electrical connector with tape to prevent snagging of wires during switch removal.
10. Remove switch retaining screws and pull switch up from column, guiding wiring harness through column.
11. Reverse procedure to install.

37	CLUSTER ASSEMBLY
38	SCREW
39	NUT
87	PLATE
88	SCREW
89	NUT

Fig. 15 Cluster removal. DeVille & Fleetwood

1. CENTER TRIM PLATE
2. FULLY DRIVEN, SEATED AND NOT STRIPPED
3. NUT

Fig. 16 Center instrument panel trim plate. Ninety Eight

1. I.P. LOWER TRIM

TIGHTEN FASTENERS UNTIL THEY ARE FULLY
DRIVEN, SEATED AND NOT STRIPPED — 1.8 N•m
(16 LBS. IN.) MAXIMUM

**Fig. 17   Lower instrument panel trim plate.
Ninety Eight**

1. CLUSTER TRIM PLATE
2. NUT (3)
3. FULLY DRIVEN, SEATED AND NOT STRIPPED
4. WEDGE TRIM PLATE EXISTING CLIPS
   AND I.P. PAD ASSEMBLY

Fig. 18   Cluster removal. Ninety Eight

| 1 | RADIO | 3 | COVER IF NO RADIO | 4 | I/P CARRIER |
| 2 | BRACKET | | | | |

**Fig. 19   Radio installation. Electra & Park
Avenue**

1. RADIO ASSEMBLY
2. TRIM PLATE
3. SCREW

4. SCREW
5. CONNECTORS
6. ANTENNA LEAD-IN

Fig. 20   Radio installation. DeVille & Fleetwood

1. RADIO
2. L.H. BRACKET
3. BOLT/SCREW ASSEMBLY
4. FULLY DRIVEN, SEATED AND NOT STRIPPED
5. INSULATOR

Fig. 21   Radio replace. Ninety Eight

WIPER SWITCH
REPLACE

1. Remove turn signal switch as outlined under "Turn Signal Switch, Replace" procedure.
2. Refer to **Figs. 5 and 6** for wiper switch replacement.

MECHANICAL NEUTRAL START SYSTEM

Actuation of the ignition switch is prevented by a mechanical lockout system, **Fig. 7.** This prevents the lock cylinder from rotating when the transmission is out of the Park or Neutral position. When the selector lever is in the Park or Neutral position, the slots in the bowl plate and the finger on the actuator rod align, allowing the finger to pass through the bowl plate in turn actuating the ignition switch. If the transmission shift lever is in any other position, the finger contacts the bowl plate when the lock cylinder is rotated.

PARK/NEUTRAL & BACKUP LAMP SWITCH
REPLACE

NOTE: This switch is mounted on the transaxle.

1. Disconnect battery ground cable.
2. Disconnect shift cable from transaxle.
3. Disconnect electrical connector from switch.
4. Remove two switch mounting bolts and the switch.
5. Align flats on switch with flats on transaxle shaft and push switch over shaft and fully seat on transaxle.
6. Install and torque switch mounting bolts to 20 ft. lbs.

NOTE: If switch was rotated and the pin broken, the switch will be automatically reset to the neutral position as follows:
a. Place transaxle shaft in neutral position.
b. Install switch on transaxle as outlined previously and loosely install mounting bolts.

c. Insert a ³⁄₃₂ inch gauge pin into service adjustment hole of switch.
d. Rotate switch until pin drops to a depth of ²³⁄₆₄ inch.
e. Torque mounting bolts to 20 ft. lbs.

HEADLAMP SWITCH
REPLACE

BUICK

Refer to **Fig. 8** for switch replacement.

CADILLAC

Refer to **Fig. 9** for switch replacement.

OLDSMOBILE

Refer to **Fig. 10** for switch replacement.

INSTRUMENT CLUSTER
REPLACE

BUICK EXC. 1986 LESABRE

Refer to **Figs. 11, 12 and 13** for instrument cluster replacement.

CADILLAC

1. Disconnect battery ground cable.
2. Remove upper trim pad as follows:
   a. Remove A/C outlets from upper trim pad.
   b. Remove screws locations 2 and 3 from both side of pad, **Fig. 14.**
   c. Remove upper trim pad.
3. Remove screw (88) and plate (87), **Fig. 15.**
4. Remove cluster attaching screws.
5. Disconnect wiring from rear of cluster and remove cluster from vehicle.
6. Reverse procedure to install.

OLDSMOBILE

Refer to **Figs. 16, 17 and 18** for switch replacement.

BLOWER MOTOR
REPLACE

1. Disconnect battery ground cable.

2. Disconnect blower motor electrical connector.
3. Remove blower motor attaching screws and the blower motor.
4. Reverse procedure to install.

RADIO
REPLACE

BUICK

Refer to **Fig. 19** for radio replacement.

CADILLAC

1. Disconnect battery ground cable.
2. Remove radio trim plate, **Fig. 20.**
3. Remove screws from rear support bracket and front of radio. The ashtray must be opened for access.
4. Remove light bulb and socket.
5. Disconnect electrical connectors from radio.
6. Disconnect antenna lead from radio.
7. Remove radio from vehicle.
8. Reverse procedure to install.

OLDSMOBILE

Refer to **Fig. 21** for radio replacement.

HEATER CORE
REPLACE

1. Disconnect battery ground cable.
2. Drain cooling system.
3. Remove lower sound insulator.
4. Remove center and lower instrument panel trim plates.
5. Remove speaker grille and speaker for access to programmer attaching bolt.
6. Disconnect wiring and hoses from programmer.
7. Remove programmer linkage cover and disconnect linkage.
8. Remove programmer attaching bolt and the programmer.
9. Remove heater core cover and the splash cover for access to heater core.
10. Disconnect heater hoses from heater core.
11. Remove heater core from case.
12. Reverse procedure to install.

V6-181 & V6-231 Gasoline Engine Section

| 1 | ENGINE MOUNT | 2 | NUT 41 N·m (30 FT. LBS.) |

Fig. 1 Engine mount, Right side

ENGINE MOUNTS
REPLACE

1. Raise and support front of vehicle.
2. Attach suitable engine lifting equipment to engine.
3. Remove mount to engine bracket nuts. Raise engine slightly and remove mount to frame nuts.
4. Remove engine mount, **Figs. 1 and 2.**
5. Reverse procedure to install.

ENGINE
REPLACE

1. Disconnect battery cables.
2. Disconnect mass airflow sensor electrical connector.
3. Remove air intake duct.
4. Drain cooling system.
5. Raise and support vehicle.
6. Disconnect exhaust pipe from exhaust manifolds.
7. Remove engine mount bolts.
8. Remove driveline vibration absorber, **Fig. 3.**
9. Remove starter motor.
10. Remove A/C compressor from bracket and position aside.
11. Disconnect power steering hoses from steering gear.
12. Remove lower transaxle to engine bolts.

NOTE: One bolt is located between the transaxle case and the engine block and is installed in the opposite direction.

13. Remove flexplate cover, then the flexplate to torque converter bolts.

1	BOLT 50 N·m (37 FT. LBS.)	3	BOLT 95 N·m (70 FT. LBS.)
2	NEGATIVE BATTERY CABLE	4	NUT 35 N·m (25 FT. LBS.)
		5	ENGINE MOUNT

Fig. 2 Engine mount, Left side

14. Remove engine support bracket from transaxle.
15. Lower vehicle.
16. Disconnect radiator and heater hoses from engine.
17. Remove alternator from bracket and position aside.
18. Disconnect engine wiring harness.
19. Remove remaining transaxle to engine bolts.
20. Remove engine from vehicle.
21. Reverse procedure to install.

INTAKE MANIFOLD
REPLACE

1. Disconnect battery ground cable.

| 1 | DRIVELINE VIBRATION ABSORBER |

Fig. 3 Typical drive line vibration absorber

Fig. 4 Intake manifold bolt torque sequence

11–13

Fig. 5   Cylinder head bolt torque sequence

1 ROCKER ARM RETAINERS

Fig. 6   Removing nylon retainer. 1985

2. Drain cooling system.
3. Remove mass airflow sensor and air intake duct.
4. Disconnect accelerator, cruise control and throttle valve cables from throttle body.
5. Remove crankcase ventilation pipe.
6. Disconnect vacuum line from throttle body.
7. Disconnect upper radiator and heater hoses from engine.
8. Disconnect fuel line.
9. Disconnect the following electrical connectors: TPS switch, IAC connector at throttle body, water temperature switch, coolant temperature switch and fan control switch.
10. Remove fuel rail.
11. Remove alternator and bracket and position aside.
12. Remove distributor cap and rotor. This is for access to the torx head bolt.
13. Remove intake manifold bolts and the intake manifold.
14. Reverse procedure to install. Torque manifold bolts in sequence, **Fig. 4,** to 47 ft. lbs.

EXHAUST MANIFOLD
REPLACE

LEFT SIDE

1. Disconnect battery ground cable.
2. Remove mass airflow sensor, air intake duct and crankcase ventilation pipe.
3. Remove two bolts attaching exhaust crossover pipe to manifold.
4. Disconnect spark plug wires from spark plugs.
5. Remove exhaust manifold attaching bolts and the exhaust manifold.

NOTE: The dipstick and tube may be removed to provide additional clearance.

6. Reverse procedure to install. Torque manifold bolts to 25 ft. lbs.

RIGHT SIDE

1. Disconnect battery ground cable.
2. Remove mass airflow sensor, air

intake duct and crankcase ventilation pipe.
3. Disconnect IAC wiring connector from throttle body.
4. Remove two bolts attaching exhaust crossover pipe to manifold.
5. Disconnect spark plug wires from spark plugs.
6. Disconnect oxygen sensor electrical lead.
7. Remove heater inlet pipe from manifold studs.
8. Remove alternator support bracket.
9. Remove exhaust manifold bolts.
10. Raise and support vehicle.
11. Remove exhaust pipe to manifold bolts.
12. Remove front exhaust pipe.
13. Remove exhaust manifold.
14. Reverse procedure to install. Torque manifold bolts to 25 ft. lbs.

CYLINDER HEAD
REPLACE

1. Disconnect battery ground cable and

RIGHT AND LEFT MARKING

Fig. 7   Service rocker arm identification. 1985

R L R L R L

FRT

L R L R L R

Fig. 8   Service rocker arm installation. 1985

1 CYLINDER HEAD
2 PEDESTAL RETAINER
3 ROCKER ARM
4 PEDESTAL
5 DOUBLE ENDED BOLT
   60 N·m (45 FT. LBS.)
6 60 N·m (45 FT. LBS.)

Fig. 9 Rocker arm installation. 1986

1. RETAINER
2. PUSH ROD
3. GUIDE
4. LIFTER
5. 33 N·m (25 LBS. FT.)

Fig. 9A Hydraulic roller lifter installation

drain cooling system.

2. Remove mass airflow sensor and air intake duct.
3. Disconnect accelerator, cruise control and throttle valve cables from throttle body.
4. Remove crankcase ventilation pipe.
5. Disconnect vacuum hoses attached to throttle body and intake manifold.
6. Remove exhaust crossover pipe.
7. Disconnect heater hoses from engine.
8. Disconnect fuel line and electrical connector from throttle body.
9. Disconnect upper radiator hose.
10. Remove fuel rail.
11. Remove alternator and bracket and position aside.
12. Remove power steering pump and position aside.
13. Remove right side exhaust manifold.
14. Remove distributor cap and rotor.
15. Remove A/C compressor bracket bolt.
16. Remove left side exhaust manifold.
17. Remove valve covers.
18. Remove intake manifold.
19. Remove rocker arm shaft assemblies and push rods. All valve train parts must be installed in original locations.
20. Remove cylinder head bolts and the cylinder head.
21. Reverse procedure to install. Tighten cylinder head bolts in sequence, **Fig. 5.** Tighten bolts in three steps. Final torque is 72 ft. lbs. After 15 minutes, retorque bolts to 72 ft. lbs.

ROCKER ARMS
1985 MODELS

A nylon retainer is used to retain the rocker arm. Break them below their heads with a chisel or pry out with channel lock pliers, **Fig. 6.** Production rocker arms can be installed in any sequence since the rocker arms are identical.

Replacement rocker arms are identified with a stamping indicating right (R) or left (L), **Fig. 7,** and must be installed as shown in **Fig. 8.**

To install, position rocker arm on shaft and center over ¼ inch hole in shaft. Install new rocker arm retainers using a ½ inch drift. Torque rocker shaft bolts to 25 ft. lbs.

1986 MODELS

Rocker arms are pedestal mounted, over support plates, **Fig. 9.** To replace rocker arms, remove valve cover, pedestal retaining bolt(s), pedestal and the rocker arm, noting position of double ended bolts for assembly. Replace rocker arms and pedestals as an assembly if they are damaged or excessively worn. If rocker arms are to be reused, they should be installed in original position.

1 LIFTER BODY
2 PLUNGER SPRING
3 BALL CHECK RETAINER
4 BALL CHECK SPRING
5 BALL CHECK
6 PLUNGER
7 OIL METERING VALVE
8 PUSH ROD SEAT
9 RETAINER RING

Fig. 9B Hydraulic valve lifter exploded view (Typical)

FRONT COVER SCHEMATIC BOLT LOCATIONS

SEE SCHEMATIC FOR BOLT LOCATIONS

Fig. 10 Timing case cover removal & installation

Fig. 11   Timing chain & sprocket

1   NOTCH ON PISTON TOWARDS FRONT OF ENGINE

   LEFT BANK

2   NO. 1, 3 & 5 TWO BOSSES ON
    ROD TOWARDS REAR OF ENGINE (NOT SHOWN)

3   CHAMFERED CORNERS ON ROD CAP TOWARDS
    FRONT OF ENGINE

   RIGHT BANK

2   NO. 2, 4 & 6 TWO BOSSES ON
    ROD TOWARDS FRONT OF ENGINE (NOT SHOWN)

3   CHAMFERED CORNERS ON ROD CAP TOWARDS
    REAR OF ENGINE

Fig. 12   Piston & rod assembly

VALVE ARRANGEMENT
FRONT TO REAR

V6-181, 231 . . . . E-I-I-E-I-E

VALVE GUIDES

The valve guides are an integral part of the cylinder head and cannot be replaced. If excessive valve stem clearance is noted, the valve guide must be reamed and an oversize valve guide installed. Valves are available in an oversize of .010 inch.

VALVE LIFTERS

On 1985 models, valve lifters can be removed after removal of rocker arms, push rods and intake manifold. On 1986 models, roller hydraulic valve lifters are used, **Fig. 9A.** To remove lifters on these models, the retainer and support plates must also be removed. Pliers with taped jaws can be used to remove lifters that are stuck due to carbon varnish etc. Disassemble only one lifter at a time, **Fig. 9B,** keeping components for each lifter separate. Replace lifters as an assembly if housing plunger or valve seat is damaged or excessively worn.

TIMING CASE COVER
REPLACE

1. Disconnect battery ground cable and drain cooling system.
2. Disconnect all hoses from water pump.
3. Remove water pump pulley and drive belts.
4. Remove alternator and bracket and position aside.
5. Remove distributor.
6. Remove crankshaft damper bolt and washer, then the damper.
7. Remove bolts attaching bolts to cylinder block and the two oil pan to case cover bolts.
8. Remove timing case cover, **Fig. 10.**
9. Reverse procedure to install.

NOTE: Before installing the case cover, remove oil pump cover and pack oil pump with petroleum jelly. Failure to pack oil pump may result in the pump losing it's "Prime" when the engine is started.

Also, apply suitable sealer to case cover bolts.

TIMING CHAIN
REPLACE

1. Remove timing case cove as outlined under "Timing Case Cover, Replace" procedure.
2. Reinstall damper bolt and rotate crankshaft until the valve timing marks on camshaft sprocket and crankshaft sprocket are as close together as possible. Remove damper bolt without changing position of valve timing marks.
3. Remove crankshaft oil slinger and the camshaft sprocket bolt.
4. Pry off the two sprockets and timing chain assembly.
5. Assemble new chain on sprockets with timing marks aligned and slide assembly onto shafts. Be sure that marks are aligned, **Fig. 11.**

37   OIL PUMP COVER
40   A. PLUG
     B. WASHER
     C. SPRING
     D. RELIEF VALVE

Fig. 13   Oil pump cover

Fig. 14   Checking oil pump gear end clearance

Fig. 16 Checking depth & diameter of pump gear pocket

Fig. 15 Checking length & diameter of pump gear

6. Install camshaft sprocket bolt and torque to 31 ft. lbs.
7. Install crankshaft oil slinger and the timing case cover.

CAMSHAFT
REPLACE

1. Remove engine as outlined under "Engine, Replace" procedure.
2. Remove intake manifold, rocker arms, valve lifters, timing case cover and timing chain.
3. Slide camshaft out from engine with care not to damage bearings.
4. Reverse procedure to install.

PISTON & ROD ASSEMBLE

Pistons should be assembled to rods as shown in **Fig. 12**.

After piston and rod installation, measure connecting rod side clearance. Side clearance should be .003–.015 inch.

PISTONS, PINS & RINGS

Pistons and ring are available in standard sizes and oversizes of .010 and .030. Piston pins are supplied with the piston and are available in standard size only.

To check piston fit in bore, measure bore diameter using suitable telescoping gauges and record reading. Measure piston across skirt at a point ¾ inch below piston pin center line and record reading. Subtract piston diameter from bore diameter and compare to specified clearance.

MAIN & ROD BEARINGS

Main bearings are available in standard sizes and undersizes of .001 and .002 inch. Rod bearings are available in standard size and an undersize of .008 inch.

OIL PAN
REPLACE

1. Disconnect battery ground cable and raise and support vehicle.
2. Drain oil pan and remove flexplate cover.
3. Remove oil pan bolts, oil pan and gasket, as equipped

NOTE: Production engines with 14 bolt oil pan are produced using RTV sealer to seal pan, while models with 20 bolt pan use a formed rubber gasket. If oil pan must be removed for service, use replacement composition gasket for models with 14 bolt pan and new formed rubber gasket for models with 20 bolt pan.

4. Position replacement gasket on pan, insert 2 bolts to maintain position, then install pan and gasket assembly.
5. Install remaining bolts, then evenly torque bolts on 20 bolt pan to 88 inch lbs., or bolts on 11 bolt pan to 13 ft. lbs.

NOTE: Do not over tighten oil pan retaining bolts as pan may be damaged, resulting in oil leaks.

Fig. 17 Checking oil pump gear side clearance

6. Reverse remaining procedure to complete installation.

OIL PUMP SERVICE
REMOVAL & INSPECTION

1. Remove oil filter.
2. Remove oil pump cover attaching screws and the cover.
3. Slide oil pump gears from pump.
4. Inspect gears for wear and damage. Replace if necessary.
5. Remove oil pressure relief valve cap, spring and valve, **Fig. 13**. Oil filter bypass valve and spring is staked in place and should not be removed.
6. Inspect relief valve and spring. Replace if necessary.
7. Check fit of relief valve in cover bore. The clearance should be an easy slip fit. If excessive clearance is noted, replace valve and/or cover.
8. Check bypass valve for cracks and warping. Replace if necessary.

ASSEMBLY & INSTALLATION

1. Lubricate and install pressure relief valve and spring in cover bore, **Fig. 13**.
2. Install and torque cap to 35 ft. lbs.
3. Install pump gears and shaft in housing.
4. Check gear end clearance by placing a straightedge over gears and with a feeler gauge, measure clearance between straightedge and gears, **Fig. 14**. Clearance should be .002-inch, measure gears and pocket to determine which is out of specification, **Figs. 15 and 16**.
5. Check gear side clearance, **Fig. 17**. Clearance should be .002–.005 inch. If clearance is excessive, measure gears and pocket to determine which is out of specification, **Figs. 15 and 16**.
6. Check pump cover for flatness with a straightedge and feeler gauge. If clearance is greater than .001 inch, replace pump cover.
7. Remove gears and pack gear pocket with petroleum jelly and reinstall gears. The pump must be filled with petroleum jelly to prime the pump.

8. Place new gasket and cover on pump. Install and torque cover screws to 97 inch lbs.
9. Install new oil filter.

CRANKSHAFT OIL SEAL
REPLACE

1. Remove oil pan and oil pump.
2. Remove rear main bearing cap.
3. Using tool J-21526-2, drive upper seal into groove approximately ¼ inch.
4. Repeat step 3 for other end of seal.
5. Measure the amount that was driven in on one side and add ¹⁄₁₆ inch. Cut this length from lower seal removed from lower cap.
6. Repeat step 5 for other end of seal.
7. Place piece of cut seal into groove of seal installer tool J-21526-1 and install tool guide onto block.
8. Using seal packing tool J-21526-2, drive piece of seal into place. Drive seal in until tool contacts machined stop.
9. Remove tool guide and repeat steps 7 and 8 for other end of seal.
10. Install replacement seal in bearing cap as follows:
    a. Ensure that cap mating surfaces, seal grooves and side seal channels are clean and free from old seal material.
    b. Soak sealing strips in kerosene or light oil for 5 minutes and apply GM sealer 1052621, Loctite 414 or equivalent to seal groove in cap.
    c. Within 1 minute after applying sealer, roll seal into groove using installer J-28693, pressing seal into groove until seal projects no more than ¹⁄₁₆ inch above each mating surface of cap.
    d. Holding seal in place, cut seal flush with mating surfaces of cap using tool sharp enough to produce clean cut.
    e. Apply thin film of chassis grease to seal surface and thin film of suitable sealer to cap mating surfaces.

NOTE: Do not allow sealer to contact journal or bearing surfaces.

11. Install side seals in cap, position bearing cap in block ensuring that cap is properly seated, then torque cap bolts to specifications.
12. Reverse remaining procedure to complete installation.

FUEL PUMP
REPLACE

1. Disconnect battery ground cable.
2. Drain fuel tank and disconnect tank unit wire from connector in rear compartment.
3. Remove ground wire retaining screw from underbody.
4. Disconnect hoses from tank unit.
5. Support fuel tank and release the two retaining straps. Lower tank from vehicle.
6. Using tool J-24187 or equivalent, release retaining cam and remove sending unit and pump assembly from tank.
7. Remove pump from sending unit.
8. Reverse procedure to install.

WATER PUMP
REPLACE

1. Disconnect battery ground cable and drain cooling system.
2. Remove drive belts and disconnect radiator hoses and heater hoses from pump.
3. Remove water pump pulley attaching bolts. The long bolt is accessed through hole in body side rail. Remove pump pulley.
4. Remove water pump attaching bolts and the water pump.
5. Reverse procedure to install.

BELT TENSION DATA

	New Lbs.	Used Lbs.
1985–86		
Air Cond.	165	90
Alternator	145	70
Power Steer.	165	90
AIR or vacuum pump	75	45

V8-250 Gasoline Engine Section

Fig.1 Right side engine, brace & transaxle mount

ENGINE MOUNTS
REPLACE

RIGHT SIDE

1. Remove brace from engine bracket to engine, **Fig. 1.**
2. Remove two nuts securing engine bracket to mount.
3. Raise and support vehicle.
4. Remove two nuts securing engine mount to frame.
5. Remove two nuts securing transaxle bracket to frame.
6. Remove two nuts securing transaxle mount to frame bracket.
7. Attach suitable engine lifting equipment to engine and raise engine until bracket is free from engine mount and transaxle mount.
8. Remove stud and two bolts securing bracket to block.
9. Remove mount and bracket by pulling forward.
10. Remove transaxle mount bracket from transaxle.
11. Remove engine mount assembly.
12. Reverse procedure to install.

LEFT SIDE

1. Raise and support vehicle.
2. Remove one nut securing mount to transaxle bracket and two nuts securing mount to frame, **Fig. 2.**
3. Attach suitable engine lifting equipment to engine.
4. Remove three bolts securing bracket to transaxle.

Fig. 2 Left side engine & transaxle assembly mounts

5. Raise engine until brackets are free from mounts.
6. Remove mount and bracket by pulling upward.
7. Reverse procedure to install.

ENGINE
REPLACE

1. Disconnect battery ground cable.
2. Drain cooling system.
3. Remove air cleaner and hood.
4. Disconnect A/C hose strap from right side strut tower.
5. Remove A/C accumulator from bracket and position aside.
6. Remove canister hoses from A/C accumulator bracket.
7. Disconnect ground wire from A/C accumulator bracket.
8. Remove A/C accumulator bracket from wheel house.
9. Remove cooling fans.
10. Remove drive belts and disconnect heater hoses.
11. Disconnect electrical connectors from: oil pressure switch, coolant temperature sensor, distributor, EGR solenoid and engine temperature switch.
12. Disconnect cables from: accelerator, cruise control and transaxle throttle valve.
13. Remove cruise control diaphragm and position aside.
14. Disconnect vacuum supply hose.
15. Remove exhaust crossover pipe.
16. Disconnect oil cooler lines from oil filter adapter.
17. Remove oil cooler line bracket from transaxle and position aside.
18. Remove air cleaner mounting bracket.
19. Disconnect fuel lines from throttle body.

NOTE: Carefully bleed fuel pressure at fuel line schraeder valve using a suitable tool. Use a container or rag to catch fuel.

20. Remove fuel line bracket from transaxle and position fuel lines aside.
21. Disconnect small vacuum line from brake booster.
22. Disconnect AIR solenoid electrical and hose connections.
23. Remove AIR valves with bracket.
24. Disconnect electrical connectors from: ISC, TPS, fuel injectors, MAT sensor, oxygen sensor, throttle body base warmer and ground wires from alternator bracket.
25. Remove idler pulley.
26. Remove power steering hose strap from stud-headed bolt in front of right side cylinder head, then the stud-headed bolt.
27. Disconnect AIR pipe clip near number 2 spark plug.
28. Remove power steering pump with bracket and position aside.
29. Raise and support vehicle.
30. Disconnect electrical connectors from starter motor and ground wires from

31. Remove two flexplate covers and the starter motor.
32. Remove three flexplate to torque converter bolts.
33. Remove A/C compressor lower dust shield.
34. Remove right front wheel assembly.
35. Remove outer wheelhouse plastic shield.
36. Remove A/C compressor mounting bolts and position compressor aside.
37. Remove lower radiator hose.
38. Remove driveline dampener with brackets from lower right front of engine and cradle.
39. Remove three right front engine to transaxle bracket bolts.
40. Pull alternator wire with plastic cover down out of way.
41. Remove two exhaust pipe to manifold bolts and springs.
42. Disconnect AIR pipe to converter bracket from exhaust manifold stud.
43. Remove lower right hand transaxle bellhousing to engine bolt.
44. Attach suitable engine lifting equipment to engine and support engine.
45. Remove five upper transaxle bellhousing to engine bolts.
46. Remove three left front engine mount bracket to engine bolts.
47. Remove engine from vehicle.
48. Reverse procedure to install.

INTAKE MANIFOLD
REPLACE

1. Disconnect battery ground cable.
2. Drain cooling system.
3. Remove air cleaner.
4. Remove drive belts.
5. Disconnect spark plug wires from spark plugs.
6. Remove two upper power steering pump bracket bolts and loosen lower nuts.
7. Remove distributor cap, wires and conduit.
8. Disconnect heater hose from thermostat housing.
9. Disconnect electrical connectors from: distributor, oil pressure switch, coolant sensor and EGR solenoid.
10. Remove distributor.
11. Disconnect cables from: accelerator, cruise control and transaxle throttle valve.
12. Disconnect fuel lines from throttle body.

NOTE: Carefully bleed fuel pressure at fuel line schraeder valve using a suitable tool. Use a container or rag to catch fuel.

13. Disconnect upper radiator hose from thermostat housing.
14. Remove fuel line brackets from transaxle and position fuel lines aside.
15. Remove cruise control servo bracket from intake manifold.
16. Remove vacuum line bracket from engine lift brackets.
17. Disconnect vacuum supply line from throttle body.

FRONT OF ENGINE

BOLT TIGHTENING SEQUENCE

1. TIGHTEN BOLTS 1, 2, 3, & 4 IN SEQUENCE TO 20.0 N•m (15 FT-LBS).
2. TIGHTEN BOLTS 5 THRU 16 IN SEQUENCE TO 30.0 N•m (22 FT-LBS).
3. RETIGHTEN ALL BOLTS IN SEQUENCE TO 30.0 N•m (22 FT-LBS).
4. REPEAT STEP 3.

ACTUAL LENGTHS

A 30mm
B 40mm
C 60mm
D 55mm

Fig. 3   Intake manifold bolt size & bolt torque sequence

18. Disconnect transaxle modulator vacuum line.
19. Remove belt tensioner and power steering pump and bracket assembly and position aside.
20. Disconnect alternator electrical connectors and remove alternator.
21. Disconnect AIR management solenoid electrical connectors.
22. Remove AIR management valves and bracket assembly.
23. Disconnect electrical connectors from: ISC, TPS, fuel injectors, MAT sensor, oxygen sensor and throttle body base warmer.
24. Disconnect MAP hose.
25. Remove EGR solenoid and bracket assembly.
26. Remove rocker arm covers.
27. Remove rocker arm support assemblies.
28. Remove triangular seals.
29. Remove push rods.

NOTE: Push rods must be installed in original locations.

30. Remove idler pulley.
31. Remove power steering pipe and AIR pipe brackets from right side cylinder head.
32. Remove alternator mounting bracket.
33. Remove right front engine lift bracket bolt and position bracket aside.
34. Remove oil filter.
35. Remove right rear engine lift bracket.
36. Remove intake manifold bolts, noting position for installation.
37. Remove intake manifold from vehicle.
38. Reverse procedure to install. Install and torque manifold bolts to specifications in sequence shown in **Fig. 3**.

EXHAUST MANIFOLD
REPLACE

RIGHT SIDE

1. Disconnect battery ground cable.
2. Remove air cleaner and exhaust crossover pipe.
3. Disconnect oxygen sensor and coolant temperature sensor electrical connectors.
4. Remove catalytic converter air pipe to AIR pipe clip bolt.
5. Remove two forward, upper exhaust manifold to cylinder head bolts.
6. Raise and support vehicle.
7. Remove converter air pipe bracket from stud.
8. Remove manifold to converter exhaust pipe.
9. Remove five remaining exhaust manifold to cylinder head attaching bolts.
10. Disconnect AIR pipe from manifold.
11. Remove exhaust manifold from vehicle.
12. Reverse procedure to install.

LEFT SIDE

1. Disconnect ground cable.
2. Remove cooling fans.
3. Remove exhaust crossover pipe.
4. Remove drive belts.
5. Remove AIR pump pivot bolt.
6. Remove belt tensioner and power steering pump brace.
7. Disconnect AIR pipe from manifold.
8. Remove exhaust manifold from vehicle.
9. Reverse procedure to install.

CYLINDER HEAD
REPLACE

1. Disconnect battery ground cable.
2. Drain cooling system.
3. Remove intake manifold as outlined under "Intake Manifold, Replace" procedure.
4. If removing left side cylinder head, remove the two cooling fans.
5. Remove appropriate exhaust manifold as outlined under "Exhaust Manifold, Replace", procedure.

PUSHROD

ROCKER ARM PIVOT

ROCKER ARM SUPPORT

ROCKER ARM SUPPORT STUD (HEAD BOLT)

Fig. 5 Rocker arm support, rocker arms & pivots

| (6) | (3) | (1) | (4) | (5) | INBOARD |
| (10) | (7) | (2) | (8) | (9) | OUTBOARD |

Fig. 4 Cylinder head bolt torque sequence

6. Remove ten cylinder head bolts.
7. Reverse procedure to install, referring to **Fig. 4** for bolt tightening sequence. Torque cylinder head bolts in 3 steps as follows:
   a. Torque all bolts to 38 ft. lbs. in specified sequence.
   b. Torque all bolts to 74 ft. lbs. in specified sequence.
   c. Torque bolts 1, 3 and 4 to 90 ft. lbs.

VALVE ARRANGEMENTS
FRONT TO REAR

V8-250 .... I-E-I-E-E-I-E-I

VALVE LIFT SPECS

Engine	Year	Intake	Exhaust
V8-250	1985–86	.384	.396

VALVE TIMING
INTAKE OPENS BEFORE TDC

Engine	Year	Degrees
V8-250	1985–86	37

ROCKER ARM SUPPORT, ROCKER ARM & PIVOT
REPLACE

1. Remove rocker arm covers.
2. Remove five rocker arm support retaining nuts from stud headed cylinder head bolts, **Fig. 5.**

NOTE: Removing the rocker arm support with the rocker arms and pivots attached is recommended since the pivot assemblies may be damaged if pivot bolt torque is not removed evenly against valve spring pressure.

3. Secure support in a suitable vise and remove rocker arms and pivots.
4. Reverse procedure to install. Torque pivot bolts to 22 ft. lbs.

VALVE GUIDES

Check valve stem to valve guide clearance. Clearance should be .005 inch or less. Service valves are available in standard size (.343 inch) or oversizes of .003 and .006 inch. If clearance is excessive, ream valve guide to accommodate next oversize valve. Some engines are factory fitted with .003 inch oversize valve guides

ARRANGEMENT OF VALVES AND VALVE LIFTERS

LOCK RING
PUSH ROD CUP
METERING DISC
PLUNGER

BALL
SPRING
BALL RETAINER
SPRING

BODY

PLUNGER AND BODY ARE FITTED PAIRS AND MUST NOT BE MISMATED.

Fig. 6 Hydraulic valve lifter

FRONT OF ENGINE

EXTRA RTV

Fig. 7 RTV sealant application

Fig. 8 Timing case oil seal removal

DOWEL

WHEN PROPERLY TIMED, MARKS WILL LINE UP AS SHOWN.

KEYWAY

NOTE: ENGINE IS ON THE #1 FIRING STROKE IN THIS POSITION.

Fig. 9 Camshaft timing marks

and valves and are identified by a "3" stamped on the cylinder head gasket surface in-line with the oversize valve.

HYDRAULIC VALVE LIFTERS
REPLACE

Valve lifters may be removed from their bores after the intake manifold, rocker arms and push rods are removed. Adjustable pliers with taped jaws may be used to remove lifters that are stuck due to varnish, carbon, etc. **Fig. 6** illustrates the type of lifter used.

TIMING CASE COVER
REPLACE

1. Disconnect battery ground cable.
2. Drain cooling system.
3. Remove air cleaner.
4. Remove drive belt.
5. Remove alternator and position aside.
6. Remove A/C accumulator from bracket and position aside.
7. Remove idler pulley, water pump pulley and water pump.
8. Raise and support vehicle.
9. Remove crankshaft puller and hub.
10. Remove cover attaching bolts and the cover.
11. Reverse procedure to install. When

installing, place a bead of RTV sealer on the front cover lip on the oil pan sealing surface and a ¼ inch bead of RTV sealer on the oil pan where the oil pan, cylinder block and cover join together, **Fig. 7.** The ¼ inch bead is needed because the cover has a rounded corner instead of a square corner. If the extra RTV is not applied an oil leak may occur.

TIMING CASE OIL SEAL
REPLACE

1. Remove crankshaft pulley and vibration damper.
2. Remove oil seal with tools J-1859-03 and J-23129 or equivalents, **Fig. 8.**
3. Lubricate new oil seal with engine oil and install with tool J-29662 or equivalent.
4. Install crankshaft puller and vibration damper.

TIMING CHAIN
REPLACE

1. Remove timing case cover as outlined under "Timing Case Cover, Replace" procedure.
2. Remove oil slinger from crankshaft.
3. Rotate crankshaft to align camshaft and crankshaft sprocket timing marks, **Fig. 9.**
4. Remove screw attaching camshaft sprocket to camshaft, then the camshaft and crankshaft sprockets with the timing chain attached.
5. Reverse procedure to install. Ensure that timing marks are aligned, **Fig. 9.**

CAMSHAFT
REPLACE

1. Remove engine as outlined under "Engine, Replace" procedure.
2. Remove timing case cover and timing chain.
3. Remove intake manifold and valve lifters.

NOTCH TOWARD FRONT OF ENGINE

Fig. 10 Piston & rod assembly

MEASURE PISTON 3/16" BELOW CROSS SLOT- PERPENDICULAR TO PISTON PIN

CROSS SLOT

Fig. 11 Measuring piston diameter

1	OIL PAN	**4**	STUD
2	REINFORCEMENT	**5**	NUT
3	BOLT		

Fig. 12 Oil pan removal & installation

Fig. 13 Oil pump assembly

4. Slide camshaft forward carefully from engine.
5. Reverse procedure to install.

PISTON & RODS
ASSEMBLE

Assemble pistons to rods as shown in **Fig. 10.** Measure connecting rod side clearance with a suitable feeler gauge after installation. Clearance should be .008 to .020 inch.

PISTONS

When measuring piston diameter, place micrometer 3/16 inch below cross slot or 3/8 inch below oil ring groove, **Fig. 11.** Cylinder liner diameter is measured two inches down from top of liner and perpendicular to the cylinder centerline. The difference between the two readings should be .0010–.0018 inch. Cylinder bore out-of-round should not exceed .0005–.002 inch. If any reading is not within specifications, the piston and cylinder liner must be replaced. No attempt should be made to rebore or hone the cylinder liner. Refer to "Cylinder Liner, Replace" procedure.

PISTON RINGS

On these engines, replacement rings are available in standard size only. If piston ring clearance is excessive, the piston and cylinder liner must be replaced. Refer to "Cylinder Liner, Replace" procedure.

PISTON PINS

Piston pins are a matched fit with the piston and are not available for separate replacement. Piston pins are pressed into the connecting rods and will not become loose enough to cause a knock or tapping until after very high mileage.

CYLINDER LINER
REPLACE

NOTE: The cylinder heads, pistons and connecting rods must be removed before replacing cylinder liner. After removing cylinder heads, install tool J-29775 to retain the cylinder liners not being replaced.

1. If original liners are to be reinstalled, mark position of cylinder liner in cylinder block and keep piston with original liner for reference during installation.
2. Pull cylinder liner from cylinder block. Discard O-ring from base of liner.
3. Check cylinder liner and cylinder block mating surfaces.
4. If original cylinder liner is to be installed and engine has not experienced overheating, install new O-ring onto bottom of liner. Align reference marks made during removal and install liner into cylinder block.
5. If new liner is being installed or if original liner is being installed and the engine has experienced overheating, then cylinder liner height must be measured as follows:
   a. Place liner in cylinder block without O-ring.
   b. Place gauge J-29776 or equivalent on cylinder liner. Check that spring-loaded guide pins fit into liner with machined pads resting on edge of liner and dial indicator plunger contacting block deck face. Apply moderate pressure to gauge until dial indicator stops moving. Record this reading. If reading is on the + side of dial indicator, cylinder liner is higher than block face. If reading is on the − side, the liner is lower than the block face.
   c. Repeat step b at two other locations on the liner. Use average of the three readings as actual liner height.
   d. Cylinder liner height should be .0004 liner.
   e. Check liner-to-liner height with tool J-29766 or equivalent. Install adjacent liners with O-ring. Liner-to-liner height should be −.002 to +.002 inch. Mark liners in measured positions.
6. When installing liners into block, check alignment marks. Be sure to install O-ring onto liner.

MAIN & ROD BEARINGS

Main and rod bearings are supplied in standard sizes only.

CRANKSHAFT OIL SEAL
REPLACE

NOTE: Before replacing the crankshaft oil seal, be sure that the apparent oil seal leak is not actually a leak between the sides of the rear main cap and crankcase.

1. Remove transaxle, then the flex plate from crankshaft.

2. Remove old seal with tool J-26868 or equivalent.
3. Lubricate new seal lip with wheel bearing grease and place on crankshaft with spring facing inside of engine.
4. Press seal into position with tool J-34604 or equivalent. Seal is fully installed when flush with block or slightly below. The use of the tool is recommended since the seal must fit squarely on the crankshaft, otherwise an oil leak could result.

OIL PAN
REPLACE

1. Disconnect battery ground cable.
2. Raise and support vehicle.
3. Remove two flexplate covers.
4. Drain oil pan.
5. Remove oil pan attaching bolts and the two nuts from studs.
6. Remove oil pan, **Fig. 12.**
7. Reverse procedure to install. RTV sealer is used to seal the oil pan. Torque oil pan bolts and nuts to 22 ft. lbs.

OIL PUMP
REPLACE

1. Remove oil pan as outlined under "Oil Pan, Replace" procedure.
2. Remove bolts securing oil pump to engine, **Fig. 13.**
3. Remove oil pump.
4. Reverse procedure to install.

OIL PUMP SERVICE

1. Remove screws securing pump cover to housing, **Fig. 13.**
2. Remove driveshaft, drive gear and driven gear from housing.

FRONT OF CAR

1 DRIVE BELT TENSIONER

2 SERPENTINE DRIVE BELT

Fig. 14   Drive belt removal

3. Remove oil pressure regulator valve and spring from bore in housing. Inspect regulator for nicks and burrs.
4. Check regulator spring free length. Length should be 2.57 inches. Spring compressed length should be 1.46 inches under 9.3–10.5 pound load.
5. Check pump housing for wear and gears for nicks and burrs.
6. Install drive gear over driveshaft so that retaining ring is inside gear. Place drive gear over pump housing shaft closest to pressure regulator bore.
7. Place driven gear over remaining shaft in pump housing, meshing driven gear with drive gear.
8. Install pressure regulator spring and valve in housing bore.
9. Install pump cover over driveshaft. Install and torque retaining screws to 5 ft. lbs.

WATER PUMP
REPLACE

1. Disconnect battery ground cable and drain cooling system.
2. Remove A/C accumulator from bracket and position aside.
3. Remove A/C accumulator bracket from wheel house.
4. Remove right hand cross-car brace.
5. Remove drive belt.

NOTE: These engines use a serpentine drive belt, **Fig. 14.**

6. Remove drive belt idler puller and bracket.
7. Remove water pump pulley.
8. Remove water pump attaching bolts and the water pump.
9. Reverse procedure to install.

FUEL PUMP
REPLACE

1. Remove fuel tank.
2. Remove cam lock with tool J-24187 or equivalent.
3. Remove fuel sending unit and fuel pump assembly from tank.
4. Remove fuel pump from sending unit.
5. Reverse procedure to install.

V6-262 Diesel Engine Section

Refer to section 10 for service procedures not found in this section.

ENGINE MOUNT
REPLACE

Refer to **Fig. 1** for engine mount replacement.

ENGINE
REPLACE

1. Remove hood. Scribe locations of hinges for reassembly.
2. Disconnect battery cables and drain cooling system.
3. Remove serpentine drive belt and vacuum pump drive belt.
4. Remove air cleaner and install cover J-26996-1.
5. Disconnect ground wires at inner fender panel.
6. Disconnect engine ground strap.
7. Raise and support vehicle.
8. Remove engine to transaxle brace.
9. Remove flexplate cover and the flexplate to torque converter bolts.
10. Disconnect exhaust pipe from right side exhaust manifold.
11. Remove engine mount to cradle retaining nuts and washers.
12. Remove engine absorber assembly from frame bracket.
13. Disconnect wiring from starter motor.
14. Disconnect No. 2 cylinder glow plug wire.
15. Disconnect lower oil cooler hose and plug opening.
16. Remove accessible power steering pump bracket bolts.
17. Lower vehicle.
18. Remove remaining power steering pump bracket bolts and position assembly aside.
19. Disconnect radiator hoses and heater hoses from engine.
20. Disconnect remaining glow plug wires.
21. Disconnect all other electrical leads from engine and the engine harness connector at cowl connector and body mounted relays.
22. Remove A/C compressor bracket bolts and position assembly aside.
23. Disconnect fuel and vacuum hoses.
24. Disconnect accelerator and throttle valve cables from fuel injection pump.
25. Disconnect and plug upper oil cooler hose.
26. Remove exhaust crossover pipe heat shield.
27. Remove transaxle filler tube.
28. Install suitable engine lifting equipment to engine.
29. Place a suitable support under transaxle rear extension.
30. Remove engine to transaxle bolts and carefully lift engine from vehicle.
31. Reverse procedure to install.

OIL PAN
REPLACE

1. Disconnect battery ground cable.
2. Install engine support fixture J-28467 or equivalent.

NOTE: The engine must be properly supported, otherwise, personal injury could result.

3. Raise and support vehicle.
4. Support front of vehicle body at forward lift points.
5. Remove left front wheel assembly.
6. Drain oil pan.
7. Remove left side lower control arm to frame bolts and the left side stabilizer bar link. Position control arm out of way.

VIEW A

1. ABSORBER ASSEMBLY
2. BRACKET
3. 25 N·m (18 LBS. FT.)
4. 47 N·m (35 LBS. FT.)
5. 31 N·m (23 LBS. FT.)
6. RETAINER
7. INSULATOR
8. SPACER
9. BRACKET
10. 55 N·m (41 LBS. FT.)
11. P/S PUMP BRACKET
12. WASHER
13. ENGINE MOUNT
14. SHIELD
15. BRACKET

Fig. 1 Engine mounting

ROTATE TENSIONER IN DIRECTION OF ARROW TO REMOVE OR INSTALL BELT

Fig. 2   Serpentine drive belt installation

1. TENSIONER ASM.
2. 105 N•m (77 LBS. FT.)

LOCATE PROJECTION ON BRACKET IN REAR HOLE OF TENSIONER ASSEMBLY

Fig. 3   Belt tensioner installation

8. Remove engine splash shield.
9. Remove engine mount to frame nuts and the front transaxle to frame nuts.
10. Raise transaxle until mount studs clear cradle.
11. Disconnect wiring harness from front frame crossmember.
12. Remove left side rear crossmember to frame attaching bolts.
13. Remove right side front crossmember to frame attaching bolts.
14. Remove left side front body mount bolts.
15. Remove left and front crossmember assembly.
16. Remove flexplate cover and starter motor.
17. Remove engine mount bracket.
18. Remove engine absorber assembly.
19. Remove oil pan attaching bolts and the oil pan.
20. Reverse procedure to install. Apply sealer No. 1050026 or equivalent to both sides of pan gaskets. Torque oil pan attaching bolts to 10 ft. lbs.

SERPENTINE DRIVE BELT

A single serpentine drive belt is used to drive all engine accessories except the vacuum pump, **Fig. 2**. Tension is maintained by a spring loaded tensioner. To replace belt, refer to **Fig. 3**. The tensioner has provisions for a visual check to verify belt tension is in the operating range, **Fig. 4**.

LIFT

OPERATING RANGE

POINTER

POINTER MUST BE POINTING TO SHADED AREA WITH BELT INSTALLED

Fig. 4   Belt tensioner operating range indicator

Rear Suspension & Brake Section

Fig. 1   Rear suspension

DESCRIPTION

These vehicles use an independent rear suspension consisting of lower control arms, coil springs, toe links, suspension knuckles, superlift struts and stabilizer bar, **Fig. 1.** The hub and wheel bearing is an assembly and does not require periodic lubrication.

HUB & BEARING ASSEMBLY
REPLACE

1. Raise and support rear of vehicle.

Fig. 2   Hub & bearing assembly

Remove wheel assembly and brake drum.

NOTE: Do not hammer on drum since damage to bearing may occur.

2. Remove four hub and bearing assembly to axle attaching bolts and the assembly from axle, **Fig. 2.**

3. Reverse procedure to install. Torque attaching bolts to 51 ft. lbs.

COIL SPRING
REPLACE

1. Support vehicle so the rear wheel and control arm hang free. Remove rear wheel.

Fig. 3   Installing tool J-23028-01

Fig. 4   Coil spring replacement

2. Disconnect rear stabilizer bar from knuckle bracket.
3. Disconnect electronic level control height sensor link if removing right control arm.
4. Disconnect parking brake cable clip from frame if removing left control arm.
5. Place tool J-23028-01 in position to cradle control arm bushings, **Fig. 3.**

NOTE: Tool J-23028-01 should be secured to a suitable jack, otherwise, personal injury could result.

6. Raise jack to relieve tension from control arm pivot bolts.
7. Place a chain around spring and control arm for safety.
8. Remove rear control arm pivot bolt and nut, **Fig. 4.**
9. Slowly lower jack until front bolt and nut can be removed.
10. Remove coil spring.

NOTE: Do not apply force on lower arm and ball joint to remove spring. Maneuver spring to remove.

11. Reverse procedure to install, noting the following:
    a. Replace spring insulators that are damaged or if vehicle has been in service for more than 50,000 miles
    b. Install springs so that upper pigtail end of left spring faces rear of vehi-

5	REAR CONTROL ARM	**39**	LINK RETAINING NUT (85 N·m/63 FT. LB.)
24	KNUCKLE	**40**	LINK RETAINER
36	COTTER PIN	**41**	SUSPENSION ADJUSTMENT LINK ASSEMBLY
37	CASTELLATED NUT (50 N·m/37 FT. LB.)		
38	OUTER SUSPENSION ADJUSTMENT LINK		

Fig. 5   Tie rod/adjustment link installation

PLACE J 29330 INTO POSITION AS SHOWN. LOOSEN NUT AND BACK OFF UNTIL . . .

KNUCKLE

. . . THE NUT CONTACTS THE TOOL. CONTINUE BACKING OFF THE NUT UNTIL THE NUT FORCES THE BALL STUD OUT OF THE KNUCKLE.

VIEW A

J-9519-03

J-9519-7

VIEW B

39

38

24

40

42

J-9519-03

J-9519-9

VIEW C

Fig. 6 Ball joint replacement

Fig. 7 Stabilizer bar & bushing

Fig. 8 Stabilizer bar mounting bracket

cle, or upper pigtail end of right spring faces front of vehicle when vehicle is at normal ride height. c.Y

Tighten suspension fasteners sufficiently to retain position of components, lower vehicle so that it rests on the wheels at normal ride height, then torque fasteners as follows: 1-Torque control arm pivot nuts to 85 ft. lbs. 2-Torque control arm pivot bolts to 125 ft. lbs. 2-Torque stabilizer support bolt to 160 inch lbs.

NOTE: Failure to torque fasteners to specifications in listed sequence may adversely affect ride and handling.

REAR TIE ROD/ ADJUSTMENT LINK
REPLACE

1. Raise and support vehicle.
2. Remove wheel assembly, cotter key and castle nut, **Fig. 5.**
3. Using tool J-24319-01, disconnect outer tie rod/adjustment from knuckle.

NOTE: When disconnecting the tie rod/adjustment from knuckle, do not use a wedge since seal damage will occur.

4. Remove rod/link assembly retaining nut and retainer.
5. Remove rod/link assembly from lower

control arm.
6. Reverse procedure to install. Torque link retaining nut to 63 ft. lbs. and castellated nut securing ball stud to 37 ft. lbs. Install cotter pin retaining castellated nut, tightening nut as needed to insert pin through hole in stud. Do not loosen nut to align slots with hole.

LOWER CONTROL ARM BALL JOINT
REPLACE

1. Raise and support vehicle.
2. Remove wheel assembly, cotter key and castle nut.
3. Disconnect outer tie rod/adjustment link from knuckle as outlined previously.
4. Disconnect electronic level control height sensor link from right side control arm.
5. Support control arm with a suitable jack.
6. Remove ball joint cotter pin and nut.
7. Using tool J-29330, disconnect ball joint from knuckle, **Fig. 6.**
8. Using tool J-9519-7, remove ball joint from control arm.
9. Reverse procedure to install.

STABILIZER BAR
REPLACE

Refer to **Figs. 7 and 8** for replacement

3	COIL SPRING
30	CONTROL ARM PIVOT BOLT-REAR (170 N·m/125 FT. LB.)
31	CONTROL ARM PIVOT NUTS (115 N·m/85 FT. LB.)
32	CONTROL ARM PIVOT BOLT-FRONT (170 N·m/125 FT. LB.)
33	LOWER COIL SPRING INSULATOR
34	UPPER COIL SPRING INSULATOR

Fig. 9   Control arm installation

1	SUPERLIFT STRUT	27	STRUT ANCHOR BOLTS
10	KNUCKLE BRACKET	28	STRUT ANCHOR WASHERS
24	KNUCKLE	29	STRUT ANCHOR NUTS (195 N·m/ 144 FT. LBS.)
25	ELC AIR LINE		
26	STRUT MOUNTING NUTS (25 N·m/ 19 FT. LBS.)		

Fig. 10   Strut assembly

LOWER CONTROL ARM
REPLACE

1. Remove coil spring as outlined under "Coil Spring, Replace" procedure.
2. Remove control arm front pivot bolt, **Fig. 9.**
3. Remove control arm from vehicle.
4. Reverse procedure to install.

REAR STRUT
REPLACE

1. Raise and support vehicle.
2. Remove trunk side cover.
3. Remove wheel assembly.
4. Disconnect air tube from superlift strut, **Fig. 10.**
5. Remove two strut tower mount nuts.
6. Remove two strut anchor bolts, washers and nuts from knuckle, then the knuckle bracket.
7. Remove strut from vehicle.
8. Reverse procedure to install.

REAR WHEEL ALIGNMENT

NOTE: When checking rear wheel alignment, the electronic leveling system must have the superlift struts inflated with residual pressure only.

Place a weight in trunk and turn ignition on and move transmission selector from Park to Reverse position and back. This will activate the compressor. Turn ignition off and remove weight from trunk. Wait 30 seconds for the system to exhaust. Roll vehicle forward one complete wheel rotation. Jounce vehicle before checking alignment.

CAMBER ADJUSTMENT

1. Loosen strut to knuckle attaching nuts.
2. Install camber adjusting tool J-29862, **Fig. 11.**
3. Move strut to set camber to specifications.
4. Remove camber adjusting tool and torque strut to knuckle nuts to 144 ft. lbs.
5. Recheck camber setting.

TOE ADJUSTMENT

Toe adjustment is made by loosening the lock nut at tie rod end and turning inner tie rod to set toe to specifications, **Fig. 11.**

SERVICE BRAKE ADJUSTMENT

The rear brakes are self-adjusting and require no periodic adjustment. Self-adjustment is made when the vehicle stops in reverse.

PARKING BRAKE ADJUSTMENT

1. Depress parking brake pedal 1.33 inches.

2. Raise and support vehicle.
3. Tighten adjusting nut until left rear wheel can just be rotated in reverse direction by hand and is locked when forward rotation is attempted.
4. Release parking brake. Both rear wheel should be able to rotate freely with no brake drag.

1. TURN TIE ROD TO ADJUST TOE
2. LOCK NUT, TORQUE TO 65 N•m (48 LBS. FT.)
3. J-29862
4. WASHERS
5. NUT 195 N•m (144 LBS. FT.)

Fig. 11   Rear camber & toe adjustments

MASTER CYLINDER
REPLACE

1. Disconnect master cylinder push rod from brake pedal.
2. Disconnect electrical connector from brake warning pressure switch.
3. Disconnect brake lines from master cylinder.
4. Remove master cylinder attaching nuts and the master cylinder.
5. Reverse procedure to install. Bleed master cylinder and brake system.

POWER BRAKE UNIT
REPLACE

1. Remove master cylinder as outlined previously with brake lines attached and position aside.

NOTE: Use care not to kink or bend brake lines.

3. Disconnect vacuum hose from check valve and plug hose to prevent entry of dirt.
4. Remove power brake unit attaching nuts and the power brake unit.
5. Reverse procedure to install.

Front Suspension & Steering Section

DESCRIPTION

The front suspension is of the MacPherson design, **Fig. 1.** The control arm pivots from the cradle and is mounted in rubber bushings. The upper end of the strut is isolated by a rubber mount and contains a non-serviceable bearing to allow for rotation. The lower end of the steering knuckle pivots on a ball joint riveted to the control arm. The ball joint is fastened to the steering knuckle with a castle nut and cotter pin.

WHEEL ALIGNMENT

NOTE: Camber and toe are the only adjustments normally required. After checking settings, perform adjustments in the following order: caster, camber and toe in.

CASTER, ADJUST

1. Loosen, but do not remove, two of the three top strut mounting nuts covering the slotted mounting holes, **Fig. 2.**
2. Remove the third nut over the oval strut mounting hole and move the washer away from the mounting hole.

3. Raise vehicle by the body to separate the strut from inner wheel house.
4. Drill 11/32 inch holes at front and rear of oval strut mounting hole and file excess metal, **Fig. 2.**
5. Lower body and insert strut into proper position.
6. Set caster to specifications by moving top of strut forward or backward as needed.
7. Install mounting nut and washer. Torque all mounting nuts to 18 ft. lbs.
8. Recheck caster.

CAMBER, ADJUST

1. Loosen both strut to knuckle attaching nuts, **Fig. 3.**
2. Install camber adjusting tool J-29862.
3. Set camber to specifications.
4. Remove adjusting tool and torque strut to knuckle attaching nuts to 144 ft. lbs.
5. Recheck camber.

TOE, ADJUST

1. Loosen lock nuts on both inner tie rods, **Fig. 4.**
2. Adjust toe to specifications by rotating inner tie rod.
3. Torque lock nuts to 50 ft. lbs.
4. Recheck toe setting.

HUB & BEARING
REPLACE

1. Raise and support vehicle and remove wheel assembly.
2. Install drive axle boot protector tool J-28712 on outer joints and J-34754 on inner joints.
3. Insert a suitable drift through opening in caliper into rotor cooling fins to prevent assembly from rotating, then remove hub nut and washer.
4. Remove caliper bracket mounting bolts and the caliper and bracket assembly, then secure assembly aside taking care not to stretch brake hose. Use care not to damage brake hose.
5. Remove rotor, then press drive axle from hub using J-28733 or equivalent, **Fig. 5.**
6. Remove hub assembly retaining bolts, shield, hub and bearing assembly, and O-ring, **Fig. 6**
7. Reverse procedure to install. Torque hub attaching bolts to 70 ft. lbs., caliper bolts to 28 ft. lbs. and hub nut to 180 ft. lbs.

BALL JOINT
REPLACE

1. Raise and support vehicle and place

MANDATORY COTTER PIN
INSTALLATION

Fig. 1   Front suspension

1. NUT 24 N•m (18 LBS. FT.)
2. WASHER
3. STRUT ASSY.
4. COVER
5. DRILL 8.731mm (11/32″) HOLES
6. FILE HERE

Fig. 2 Caster adjustment

1. INNER TIE ROD - TURN TO ADJUST TOE
2. NUT 70 N•m (50 LBS. FT.) LOOSEN TO ADJUST TOE
3. BOOT - READJUST AFTER SETTING TOE
4. NUT 195 N•m (144 LBS. FT.)
5. J-29862
6. STRUT ASSEMBLY
7. KNUCKLE
8. WASHER

Fig. 3 Camber adjustment

1. TURN TO ADJUST TOE
2. RE-ADJUST BOOTS
3. LOOSEN NUT TO ADJUST TOE, RE-TIGHTEN TO 70 N•m (50 LBS. FT.)

Fig. 4 Toe adjustment

Fig. 5 Separating drive axle from hub

jackstands under cradle. Vehicle weight should not be placed on the control arms.
2. Remove wheel assembly.
3. Install drive axle boot protectors.
4. Remove cotter key from ball joint nut and, using tool J-34505, separate ball joint from steering knuckle, **Fig. 7.**
5. Drill out ball joint retaining rivets.

6. Remove stabilizer bar bushing to control arm bolt.
7. Pull control arm downward and remove ball joint from steering knuckle and control arm.
8. Reverse procedure to install. Torque new ball joint attaching nuts to 50 ft. lbs., **Fig. 8,** and ball joint castle nut to 81 ft. lbs.

CONTROL ARM
REPLACE

1. Raise and support vehicle and place jackstands under cradle. Vehicle weight should not be placed on the control arms.
2. Remove wheel assembly.
3. Install drive axle boot protectors.

1. HUB AND BEARING ASSEMBLY
2. STEERING KNUCKLE
3. SHIELD
4. WASHER
5. HUB NUT 245 N•m (180 LBS. FT.)
6. SEAL
7. HUB AND BEARING RETAINING BOLT (55 TORX) 95 N•m (70 LBS. FT.)
8. "O" RING

Fig. 6 Hub & bearing assembly

1. BALL JOINT
2. STEERING KNUCKLE
3. BALL JOINT SEPERATOR J-34505
4. ROTOR

Fig. 7 Separating ball joint from steering knuckle

BC

1. SERVICE BALL JOINT
2. BALL JOINT MOUNTING BOLTS MUST FACE DOWN
3. STEERING KNUCKLE
4. CONTROL ARM
5. BALL JOINT MOUNTING NUTS 68 N·m (50 LBS. FT.)
6. BALL JOINT TO STEERING KNUCKLE NUT 110 N·m (81 LBS. FT.) BEFORE COTTER PIN INSTALLATION
7. COTTER PIN

Fig. 8 Service ball joint attachment

1. Control Arm
2. Cradle
3. Cradle Mounted Bushing
4. Control Arm Mounted Bushing
5. Cradle Mounted Bushing Nut 190 N·m (140 LBS. FT.)
6. Control Arm Mounted Bushing Nut 123 N·m (90 LBS. FT.)
7. Washer

Fig. 9 Control arm assembly

1. Stabilizer Bar
2. Control Arm
3. Insulator (4)
4. Retainer (4)
5. Bolt
6. Nut 17 N·m (13 LBS. FT.)

Fig. 10 Stabilizer bar bushing assembly

1. Stabilizer Bar
2. Stabilizer Bar Mounting Bracket
3. Stabilizer Bar Mounting Bushing
4. 50 N·m (37 LBS. FT.)
5. Frame Welded Nuts
6. Cradle

VIEW A

FRT

Fig. 11 Stabilizer bar mounting

1. STABILIZER BAR
2. STEERING KNUCKLE
3. TIE ROD

383101543

Fig. 12 Stabilizer bar replacement

4. Remove cotter key from ball joint nut and, using tool J-34505, separate ball joint from steering knuckle.
5. Remove stabilizer bar bushing to control arm bolt.
6. Remove control arm mounting bolts and the control arm, **Fig. 9.**
7. Reverse procedure to install. When installing control arms, install but do not torque control arm mounting bolts. Sufficiently tighten bolts to assure security but final torque is applied when vehicle weight is supported by control arms. Torque rear arm bolt to 90 ft. lbs. and front bolt to 140 ft. lbs.

STABILIZER BAR
REPLACE

1. Raise and support vehicle and place jackstands under cradle. Vehicle weight should not be placed on the control arms.
2. Remove wheel assembly.
3. Install drive axle boot protectors.

4. Remove nuts, washers, bushings and bolt securing stabilizer shaft to each control arm, **Fig. 10.**
5. Remove stabilizer bar mounting bolts, two bolts from each side, **Fig. 11.**
6. Disconnect tie rods from steering knuckles.
7. Remove exhaust pipe between exhaust manifold and catalytic converter. Remove intermediate pipe on diesel models.
8. On vehicles with V6-181 and V8-250 engines, remove air pipe to exhaust pipe bolt.
9. Rotate right side strut assembly completely to the right.
10. Slide stabilizer bar to the right over the steering knuckle and pull downward on left side until stabilizer bar clears the cradle, **Fig. 12.**
11. Reverse procedure to install.

STRUT ASSEMBLY
REPLACE

1. Remove three nuts attaching top of

strut to body, **Fig. 13.**
2. Raise and support vehicle and place jackstands under cradle. Vehicle weight should not be placed on the control arms.
3. Remove wheel assembly.
4. Install drive axle boot protectors.
5. Remove brake line bracket bolt from strut assembly.
6. Remove strut to steering knuckle attaching bolts.
7. Remove strut assembly from vehicle.
8. Reverse procedure to install. Torque strut mounting bolts to 144 ft. lbs.

STRUT SERVICE

1. Remove strut as outlined under "Strut Assembly, Replace" procedure.
2. Mount strut in compressor tool J-34013 and holding fixture J-3289-20, **Fig. 14.**
3. Rotate compressor forcing screw until spring compresses slightly.
4. Hold damper shaft from rotating and remove nut from top of strut assembly.
5. Use tool J-34013-30 to guide damper shaft from assembly.
6. Loosen compressor forcing screw while guiding damper shaft from assembly. Continue to loosen nut until strut damper and spring can be removed.
7. Reverse procedure to assemble. When assembling spring, the flat on upper spring seat must face outward 90 degrees from centerline of vehicle or when mounted in the strut compressor, the seat faces in the same direction as the steering knuckle mounting flange.

POWER STEERING GEAR
REPLACE

1. Raise and support vehicle with weight

1. STRUT ASSEMBLY
2. STRUT TO BODY NUTS 24 N•m (18 LBS.FT.)
3. BRAKE LINE BRACKET BOLT 17 N•m (13 LBS. FT.)
4. STRUT TO STEERING KNUCKLE NUTS 195 N•m (144 LBS. FT.)
5. RETAIN STEERING KNUCKLE WITH WIRE ONCE STRUT ASSEMBLY IS REMOVED

Fig. 13   Strut assembly

resting on suspension.
2. Remove front wheel assemblies.
3. Disconnect intermediate shaft from steering gear stub shaft.
4. Disconnect both tie rod ends from steering knuckles.
5. Remove line retainers and disconnect hydraulic lines from steering gear.
6. Remove five steering gear attaching bolts, **Fig. 15.**
7. Remove steering gear from vehicle by sliding out to the side.
8. Reverse procedure to install. Torque steering gear attaching bolts to 50 ft. lbs.

POWER STEERING PUMP
REPLACE

V6-181, 231 GASOLINE ENGINES

1. Disconnect battery ground cable.
2. Remove air cleaner on V6-181 engine.
3. Remove alternator drive belt and alternator.
4. Raise and support vehicle.
5. Disconnect hydraulic lines from pump.
6. Remove rear pump adjustment bracket to pump nut.
7. Remove pump drive belt.
8. Lower vehicle.
9. Remove pump rear adjustment bracket.
10. Remove power steering pump from vehicle.
11. Reverse procedure to install.

V8-250 GASOLINE ENGINE

1. Disconnect battery ground cable.
2. Remove pump drive belt and the pulley.
3. Disconnect hydraulic lines from pump.
4. Remove two pump mounting bolts.
5. Remove power steering pump from vehicle.
6. Reverse procedure to install.

V6-262 DIESEL ENGINE

1. Disconnect battery ground cable.
2. Remove pump drive belt.
3. Raise and support vehicle.
4. Remove engine splash shield and crankshaft pulley.
5. Remove engine absorber.
6. Disconnect reservoir hose from pump and drain pump.
7. Remove high pressure support and disconnect high pressure hose from pump.
8. Remove two front bracket nuts.
9. Remove one rear bracket bolt.
10. Remove power steering pump with brackets attached.
11. Remove brackets from pump assembly.
12. Reverse procedure to install.

1. STRUT ASSEMBLY
2. STRUT COMPRESSOR J-34013
3. INSTALL LOCKING PINS THROUGH STRUT ASSEMBLY
4. TIGHTEN NUTS TILL FLUSH WITH STRUT COMPRESSOR
5. COMPRESSOR FORCING SCREW

Fig. 14 Spring compressor installation

1. BOLT 68 N·m (50 LBS. FT.) AFTER SECOND REUSE OF BOLT, LOCTITE THREAD LOCKING KIT, # 1052624 MUST BE USED
2. STEERING GEAR
3. FRAME
4. 50 N·m (35 LBS. FT.), 70 N·m (52 LBS. FT.) MAXIMUM PERMISSIBLE TORQUE TO ALIGN COTTER PIN SLOT. (1/6 TURN MAXIMUM) DO NOT BACK OFF FOR COTTER PIN INSERTION
5. RETAINER
6. WASHER
7. STEERING KNUCKLE

VIEW A

Fig. 15 Steering gear replacement

1986 BUICK RIVIERA • CADILLAC ELDORADO & SEVILLE • OLDS. TORONADO

INDEX OF SERVICE OPERATIONS

Refer to the rear of this manual for vehicle manufacturer's special service tool suppliers.

General Engine Specifications

Year	Engine CID①/Liter	Engine V.I.N. Code②	Fuel Injection System	Bore and Stroke	Compression Ratio	Net H.P. @ R.P.M.③	Maximum Torque Ft. Lbs. @ R.P.M.	Normal Oil Pressure Pounds
1986	V6-231/3.8L	B	S.F.I.④	3.80 × 3.40	8.0	142 @ 4000	200 @ 2000	37
	V8-250/4.1L	—	D.F.I.⑤	3.465 × 3.307				

①—CID—Cubic inch displacement.
②—The eighth digit denotes engine code.
③—Ratings are net—as installed in vehicle.
④—Sequential-port Fuel Injection.
⑤—Digital Fuel Injection.

Alternator Specifications

Year	Ident. No.	Rated Hot Output Amps.
1986	—	108

Starting Motor Specifications

Year	Engine/V.I.N.	Starter Ident. No.
1986	V6-231/B	1998521
	V8-250/	—

Valve Specifications

Year	Engine/V.I.N.	Valve Lash Int.	Valve Lash Ex.	Valve Angles Seat	Valve Angles Face	Valve Spring Installed Height	Valve Spring Pressure Lbs. @ In.	Stem Clearance Intake	Stem Clearance Exhaust	Stem Diameter Intake	Stem Diameter Exhaust
1986	V6-231/B	Hydraulic①		45°	45°	1.727	185 @ 1.34	.0015–.0035	.0015–.0032	.3401–.3412	.3405–.3412
	V8-250/	Hydraulic①		45°	44°	1.730	181 @ 1.28	.0010–.0030	.0010–.0030	.3413–.3420	.3413–.3420

①—No adjustment.

continued

Pistons, Pins, Rings, Crankshaft & Bearings

| Year | Engine/ V.I.N. | Piston Clearance | Ring Gap① | | Wristpin Diameter | Rod Bearings | | Main Bearings | | | Shaft End Play |
			Comp.	Oil		Shaft Diameter	Bearing Clearance	Shaft Diameter	Bearing Clearance	Thrust on Bear. No.	
1986	V6-231/B	.0008–.0020	.010	.015	.9392	2.2487–2.2495	.0005–.0026	2.4995	.0003–.0018	3	.003–.011
	V8-250	.0010–.0018	.023	.010	.8663	1.929	.0005–.0028	2.6400	.0004–.0027	3	.001–.007

①—Fit rings in tapered bores for clearance given in tightest portion of ring travel. Clearances specified are minimum gaps.

Engine Tightening Specifications★

★ Torque specifications are for clean and lightly lubricated threads only. Dry or dirty threads produce increased friction which prevents accurate measurement of tightness.

Year	Engine/ V.I.N.	Spark Plugs Ft. Lbs.	Cylinder Head Bolts Ft. Lbs.	Intake Manifold Ft. Lbs.	Exhaust Manifold Ft. Lbs.	Rocker Arm to Cylinder Head Ft. Lbs.	Rocker Arm Cover Ft. Lbs.	Connecting Rod Cap Bolts Ft. Lbs.	Main Bearing Cap Bolts Ft. Lbs.	Flywheel to Crankshaft Ft. Lbs.	Vibration Damper or Pulley Ft. Lbs.
1986	V6-231/B	20	—	32	37	43	88①	40	100	60	200
	V8-250/	—	—	—	—	—	—	—	—	—	—

①—Inch Lbs.

Front Wheel Alignment Specifications

| Year | Model | Caster Angle, Degrees | | Camber Angle, Degrees | | | | Toe-In Degree |
| | | Limits | Desired | Limits | | Desired | | |
				Left	Right	Left	Right	
1986	All	+1.7° to +3.3°	+2.5°	−.5° to +.5°	−.5° to +.5°	0°	0°	0°

Rear Wheel Alignment Specifications

| Year | Model | Camber Angle, Degrees | | Toe-In, Degrees |
		Limits	Desired	
1986	All	−1° to −.4°	−.7°	+.1°

Cooling System & Capacity Data

| Year | Model or Engine/V.I.N. | Cooling Capacity, Qts. | | Radiator Cap Relief Pressure, Lbs. | Thermo. Opening Temp. | Fuel Tank Gals. | Engine Oil Refill Qts. | Transaxle Oil | |
		Less A/C	With A/C					Manual Transaxle Pts.	Auto. Transaxle Qts.①
1986	V6-231/B	12	12	15	195	18	4②	—	11
	V8-250/	—	—	15	195	18	—	—	11

①—Approximate make final check with dipstick.   ②—Additional oil will be necessary when changing filter.

continued

Grille Identification

1986 Buick Riviera **1986 Cadillac Eldorado** **1986 Cadillac Seville**

1986 Toronado

Engine Section

Refer to Section 11 for service procedures on V6-231 and V8-250 engines.

Rear Suspension & Brake Section

DESCRIPTION

An assembled view and an exploded view of the left side of the rear suspension is shown in **Fig. 1.**

REAR WHEEL ALIGNMENT

Rear wheel toe is the only adjustable angle. If camber is not within specifications, inspect for bent struts.

Before checking rear trim height or measuring rear alignment angles, the following procedure should be performed to ensure that the rear air-adjustable struts are filled with residual pressure only.

1. Place a weight of at least 300 lbs. in vehicle trunk.
2. Turn ignition on.
3. Turn ignition off and remove weight from trunk.
4. Wait 30 seconds for ELC system to exhaust.
5. Roll car forward or backward at least 25 ft. to eliminate the effects of tire camber side thrust.
6. Jounce front and rear bumpers 3 times to normalize suspension prior to measuring angles.

1 UNDERBODY ASSEMBLY
2 SUSPENSION CROSSMEMBER INSULATORS
3 UPPER STRUT MOUNTING NUT
4 STRUT MOUNT INSULATORS
5 STRUT
6 KNUCKLE
7 HUB AND BEARING ASSEMBLY
8 CONTROL ARM
9 SPRING RETAINER
10 SPRING INSULATORS
11 SINGLE LEAF SPRING
12 STABILIZER BAR AND BRACKET
13 SUSPENSION CROSSMEMBER ASSEMBLY

Fig. 1 Rear suspension exploded view. Left side shown

12-3

REAR TOE ADJUSTMENT

1. Loosen front and rear inside control arm mounting bolts, **Fig. 2.**
2. Insert a screwdriver or pry bar between the inside rear control arm mounting bolt and rear support assembly, then move control arm to set toe to specifications.
3. Torque inside front control arm mounting bolt to 66 ft. lbs.

STRUT
REPLACE

When replacing strut, refer to **Fig. 3.**

LOWER CONTROL ARM
REPLACE

When replacing lower control arm, refer to **Figs. 4 through 8.**

LOWER CONTROL ARM BUSHINGS
REPLACE

When replacing lower control arm bushings, refer to **Fig. 9.**

SPRING
REPLACE

When replacing spring, refer to **Figs. 10 and 11.**

VIBRATION DAMPER
REPLACE

When replacing vibration damper, refer to **Fig. 12.**

CROSSMEMBER INSULATORS
REPLACE

When replacing upper or lower crossmember insulator, refer to **Fig. 13.**

DISC BRAKE COMPONENTS
REPLACE

REAR BRAKES

When replacing components of rear brakes, refer to **Fig. 5.**

MASTER CYLINDER
REPLACE

1. Disconnect electrical connector from

INCREASE TOE   **DECREASE TOE**

VIEW A

1	BOLT
2	CONTROL ARM
3	SCREW DRIVER OR PRY BAR
4	SLOTTED HOLE

Fig. 2   Adjusting rear toe

fluid level sensor switch.
2. Disconnect hydraulic lines at master cylinder, plugging lines and openings.
3. Remove master cylinder attaching nuts and the master cylinder.
4. Reverse procedure to install, torquing master cylinder attaching nuts to 26 ft. lbs and hydraulic lines to 150 inch lbs.

BRAKE BOOSTER
REPLACE

1. Remove master cylinder.
2. Remove booster attaching nuts.
3. Disengage booster pushrod at brake pedal and remove booster.
4. Reverse procedure to install, torquing booster attaching nuts to 28 ft. lbs.

FRONT

1 STRUT	4 NUTS (58 N•m/43 FT. LBS.)	7 BRACKET BOLT (58 N•m/43 FT. LBS.)
2 STRUT BRACKET	5 STABILIZER BAR	8 STABILIZER BRACKET
3 BOLT	6 INSULATOR	9 SUSPENSION CROSSMEMBER ASSEMBLY

Fig. 3   Replacing rear strut

FRONT

1 WIRE	3 ROTOR
2 CALIPER ASSEMBLY	4 STRUT

Fig. 4   Securing caliper out of way

1 CALIPER MOUNTING BOLTS (113 N•m/83 FT. LBS.)

2 SPLASH SHIELD

3 CALIPER ASSEMBLY

4 HUB AND BEARING ASSEMBLY

5 ROTOR

6 ROTOR RETAINER

7 HUB MOUNTING BOLTS (70 N•m/52 FT. LBS.)

8 KNUCKLE

9 CONTROL ARM

10 BOLT (50 N•m/37 FT. LBS.)

Fig. 5   Removing rear disc brake components

1 STRUT ROD CAP	**7** STRUT
2 NUT (88 N•m/65 FT. LBS.)	**8** LOWER PINCH BOLT (55 N•m/40 FT. LBS.)
3 RETAINER	**9** KNUCKLE
4 UPPER INSULATOR	**10** LOCATING SLOT
5 SUSPENSION CROSSMEMBER ASSEMBLY	**11** CONTROL ARM
6 LOWER INSULATOR	**12** SPRING

Fig. 6   Spring, strut & control arm assembly

VIEW A

1 KNUCKLE
2 NUT (80 N•m/59 FT. LBS.)
3 RETAINER
4 PIVOT BOLT
5 CONTROL ARM

Fig. 7   Removing knuckle from lower control arm

1 SUSPENSION CROSSMEMBER ASSEMBLY
2 INNER CONTROL ARM BOLTS
3 CONTROL ARM
4 NUTS (90 N•m/66 FT. LBS.)

Fig. 8   Removing lower control arm

Fig. 9 Replacing lower control arm bushings

1. J-21474-18 NUT
2. J-21474-19 BOLT
3. BEARING (PART OF J-21474-19)
4. J-21474-5
5. J-21474-23
6. J-28576-1
7. J-35739-3
8. J-35739-1 SPACER — USE WIDER SIDE ON OUTER BUSHINGS, NARROW SIDE ON INNER BUSHINGS
9. J-35739-2

1	SPRING
2	SPRING RETAINER
3	SUSPENSION CROSSMEMBER ASSEMBLY
4	RETAINER BOLTS (28 N•m/21 FT. LBS.)
5	LOWER OUTBOARD INSULATOR
6	JACKSTAND

Fig. 11   Removing spring

1	CENTER INSULATOR
2	CENTER INSULATOR NUTS (28 N•m/21 FT. LBS.)
3	OUTBOARD INSULATOR NUTS (28 N•m/21 FT. LBS.)
4	SUSPENSION CROSSMEMBER ASSEMBLY
5	UPPER OUTBOARD INSULATOR
6	OUTBOARD INSULATOR LOCATING BAND
7	SPRING
8	SPRING RETAINER
9	RETAINER BOLTS (28 N•m/21 FT. LBS.)
10	LOWER OUTBOARD INSULATOR
11	CENTER INSULATOR LOCATING BAND

Fig. 10   Exploded view of spring installation

1	NUT (28 N•m/21 FT. LBS.)
2	VIBRATION DAMPENER
3	CROSSMEMBER ASSEMBLY
4	STUD
5	TAB — MUST ENGAGE FLANGE ON CROSSMEMBER

Fig. 12   Replacing vibration dampener

1. UNDERBODY
2. UPPER CROSSMEMBER INSULATOR
3. CROSSMEMBER FORWARD ARM BOLT (90 N•m/66 FT. LBS.)
4. LOWER CROSSMEMBER INSULATOR
5. UPPER MOUNTING BOLT (90 N•m/66 FT. LBS.)
6. SUSPENSION CROSSMEMBER ASSEMBLY
7. NUT
8. WASHER — USED ON LEFT SIDE ONLY

Fig. 13 Replacing crossmember insulators

Front Suspension & Steering

WHEEL ALIGNMENT

Steering and vibration complaints are not always the result of improper alignment. Another possibility is tire "lead" due to worn or improperly manufactured tires. "Lead" is the vehicles's deviation from a straight path on a level road without pressure on the steering wheel.

Before making any adjustment affecting wheel alignment, make the following checks to ensure correct alignment readings and alignment adjustments.

1. Check all tires for proper inflation pressures and ensure that all tires have approximately equal tread wear.
2. Check hub and bearing assemblies for excessive wear, correcting as necessary.
3. Check ball joints and tie rod ends. If they are excessively loose, correct before making adjustment.
4. Check run out of wheels and tires.
5. Check vehicle trim height, correcting as necessary before adjusting alignment.
6. Check strut dampers for proper operation.
7. Check control arms for loose bushings.
8. Check stabilizer bar for loose or missing parts.

Consideration must also be given to excess loads, such as tool boxes or sample cases. If these items are normally carried in the vehicle, they should remain in the vehicle during alignment adjustments. Consideration should be given to condition of equipment being used to adjust alignment. Be sure to follow equipment manufacturer's instructions. Regardless of equipment being used, vehicle must be on level surface, both fore and aft and sideways.

MEASURING FRONT ALIGNMENT ANGLES

Install alignment equipment following equipment manufacturer's instructions. Measure alignment angles, **Fig. 1,** and record the readings. If adjustments are necessary, they must be made in order; caster first, camber second and toe third. Jounce front and rear bumpers 3 times to normalize suspension prior to measuring angles.

FRONT CASTER ADJUSTMENT

1. Loosen but do not remove, 2 of 3 top strut attaching nuts covering slotted mounting holes, **Fig. 2,** then remove nut over remaining oval strut mounting hole.
2. Move washer away from oval strut mounting hole.
3. Lift front of vehicle by body to separate strut from inner wheel house.
4. Drill two 11/32 inch holes at front and rear of oval strut mounting hole, then file away excess metal.
5. Lower front of vehicle and install washer and nut.
6. Adjust caster by moving top of strut forward or rearward.
7. Torque top strut attaching nuts to 18 ft. lbs.

FRONT CAMBER ADJUSTMENT

1. Loosen both strut to knuckle bolts just enough to allow movement.
2. Adjust camber by turning camber adjustment bolt, **Fig. 3.**
3. Torque strut to knuckle nuts to 140 ft. lbs.
4. Torque camber adjustment bolt to 7 ft. lbs.

FRONT TOE ADJUSTMENT

1. Loosen lock nut on inner tie rods, **Fig. 4.**
2. Adjust toe by turning inner tie rods.
3. Adjust boots so that they are not twisted.
4. Torque lock nuts to 45 ft. lbs.

STABILIZER SHAFT, REPLACE

When replacing stabilizer shaft, refer to **Fig. 5.**

CONTROL ARM
REPLACE

When replacing control arm, refer to **Fig. 6.**

BALL JOINT
REPLACE

When replacing ball joint, refer to **Fig. 7.**

Fig. 1   Front end alignment angles

1. NUT 24 N·m (18 LBS. FT.)
2. WASHER
3. STRUT ASSY.
4. COVER
5. DRILL 8.731mm (11/32") HOLES
6. FILE HERE THEN PAINT WITH PRIMER

Fig. 2   Adjusting front wheel caster

LOWER CONTROL ARM BUSHINGS
REPLACE

When replacing lower control arm bushings, refer to **Fig. 8.**

HUB & BEARING ASSEMBLY
REPLACE

When replacing hub and bearing assembly, refer to **Fig. 9.**

STRUT ASSEMBLY
REPLACE

When replacing strut assembly, refer to **Fig. 10.**

STRUT SERVICE

1. Place strut assembly in strut compressor J-34013, **Fig. 11.**
2. Turn compressor forcing screw until spring compresses slightly.
3. Keep dampener shaft from turning with socket and remove 24mm nut on top of dampener shaft.
4. Using tool J-34013-38 or equivalent, guide dampener shaft out of assembly.
5. Loosen compressor screw while guiding dampener shaft out of assembly, continually loosening compressor screw till strut dampener and spring can be removed.

NOTE: Be careful to avoid chipping or cracking the spring coating when handling the front suspension coil spring.

6. Install strut dampener in strut compressor J-34013 with clamp J-34013-

1. NUT 185 N·m (145 LBS. FT.)
2. BOLT
3. WASHER
4. CAMBER ADJUSTMENT BOLT

Fig. 3   Adjusting front wheel caster

1. INNER TIE ROD
2. LOCK NUT — 60 N·m (45 LBS. FT.)
3. BOOT — READJUST AFTER SETTING TOE

Fig. 4   Adjusting front wheel toe

1. STABILIZER SHAFT
2. BRACKET
3. BOLT – 45 N·m (33 LBS. FT.)
4. INSULATOR – INSTALL WITH SLIT TO REAR OF CAR
5. NUT 17 N·m (13 LBS. FT.) OBTAIN TORQUE BY RUNNING NUT TO UNTHREADED PORTION OF BOLT
6. RETAINER
7. INSULATOR
8. SPACER
9. BOLT – INSTALL IN DIRECTION SHOWN
10. FRAME

Fig. 5   Replacing stabilizer shaft

1. CONTROL ARM
2. BOLT – 140 N·m (100 LBS. FT.) TIGHTEN WITH CAR AT PROPER TRIM HEIGHT
3. NUT – 123 N·m (91 LBS. FT.) TIGHTEN WITH CAR AT PROPER TRIM HEIGHT
4. INSULATOR
5. RETAINER
6. NUT – 70 N·m (52 LBS. FT.)
7. PIN
8. NUT – TIGHTEN NUT TO 10 N·m (88 LBS. IN.). CONTINUE TIGHTENING BY ROTATING NUT AN ADDITIONAL 120°, DURING WHICH A MINIMUM TORQUE OF 50 N·m (37 LBS. FT.) MUST BE OBTAINED. INSTALL COTTER PIN
9. KNUCKLE
10. BALL JOINT ATTACHMENT RIVETS
11. BUSHING

Fig. 6   Replacing lower control arm

20 clamped on dampener shaft.
7. Install spring over strut in correct position and move assembly upright in strut compressor and install upper locking pin.

CAUTION: Flat on upper spring seat must face out from centerline of vehicle, **Fig. 12**, or when mounted in strut compressor spring seat faces same direction as steering knuckle mounting flange.

8. Install rod J-34013-38 or equivalent into strut assembly to guide dampener shaft on reassembly of strut.
9. Start turning compressor screw clockwise on J-34013 while guiding J-34013-38 which will center dampener shaft in the assembly.
10. Continue turning compressor screw until dampener shaft threads are visible through top of strut assembly.
11. Install washer and nut, then remove J-34013-20 from dampener shaft.
12. Using 24mm crowsfoot line wrench while holding dampener shaft with socket, torque dampener shaft nut to 44 ft. lbs.
13. Remove three nuts securing strut assembly to strut compressor, the two locking pins at bottom of strut compressor and the strut assembly.

POWER STEERING PUMP
REPLACE

When replacing power steering pump, refer to **Fig. 13**.

1. SERVICE BALL JOINT
2. BALL JOINT MOUNTING BOLTS MUST FACE UP
3. STEERING KNUCKLE
4. CONTROL ARM
5. BALL JOINT MOUNTING NUTS 68 N·m (50 LBS. FT.)

Fig. 7   Replacing ball joint

1. J-35561-1
2. J-35561-2
3. J-35561-3
4. BUSHING
5. LOWER CONTROL ARM
6. PRESS

REMOVE BUSHING

INSTALL BUSHING

Fig. 8 Replacing lower control arm bushings

POWER STEERING GEAR
REPLACE

When replacing power steering gear, refer to **Fig. 14.**

1. HUB AND BEARING ASSEMBLY
2. STEERING KNUCKLE
3. SHIELD
4. WASHER
5. HUB NUT 245 N·m (180 LBS. FT.)
6. SEAL
7. HUB AND BEARING RETAINING BOLT (55 TORX) 95 N·m (70 LBS. FT.)
8. "O" RING

Fig. 9   Replacing hub & bearing assembly

1. COVER
2. NUT 24 N·m (18 LBS. FT.)
3. WASHER
4. STRUT AND SPRING ASSEMBLY
5. NUT 196 N·m (145 LBS. FT.)
6. BOLT – INSTALL IN DIRECTION SHOWN
7. KNUCKLE

Fig. 10   Replacing strut assembly

1. STRUT ASSEMBLY
2. STRUT COMPRESSOR J-34013
3. INSTALL LOCKING PINS THROUGH STRUT ASSEMBLY
4. TIGHTEN NUTS TILL FLUSH WITH STRUT COMPRESSOR
5. COMPRESSOR FORCING SCREW

Fig. 11   Installing strut assembly in strut compressor

1. ROD J-34013-38 INSTALLED
2. CLAMP J-34013-20 INSTALLED
3. FLAT ON SPRING SEAT MUST FACE SAME DIRECTION AS STEERING KNUCKLE FLANGE
4. BOTH LOCKING PINS INSTALLED
5. COMPRESSOR FORCING SCREW

Fig. 12   Aligning flat on upper spring seat

1. POWER STEERING PUMP
2. BOLT – 27 N·m (20 LBS. FT.) – 2 BOLTS USED ON VIN L
3. PULLEY
4. BOLT – 27 N·m (20 LBS. FT.) – VIN 8 AND 3 ONLY

Fig. 13   Replacing power steering pump

1. STEERING GEAR
2. BOLT – 68 N·m (50 LBS. FT.) AFTER SECOND REUSE OF BOLT, LOCKTITE THREAD LOCKING KIT NO. 1052624 MUST BE USED.
3. WASHER
4. RETAINER
5. NUT – TIGHTEN NUT TO 10 N·m (7 LBS. FT.) THEN TIGHTEN NUT AN ADDITIONAL 120 DEGREES (2 FLATS) DURING WHICH A MINIMUM TORQUE OF 45 N·m (33 LBS. FT.) IS TO BE OBTAINED. IF 45 N·m (33 LBS. FT.) IS NOT OBTAINED, INSPECT FOR STRIPPED THREADS. IF THREADS ARE SATISFACTORY, REPLACE KNUCKLE.
6. PIN
7. KNUCKLE
8. FRAME
9. RTV SEALER AROUND INSERTS

Fig. 14   Replacing power steering gear

BUICK SKYLARK (1980-85) • CHEVROLET CITATION • OLDSMOBILE OMEGA • PONTIAC PHOENIX

INDEX OF SERVICE OPERATIONS

NOTE: Refer to the rear of this manual for vehicle manufacturer's special service tool suppliers.

CITATION • OMEGA • PHOENIX • 1980–85 SKYLARK

SERIAL NUMBER LOCATION

On top of instrument panel, left front.

ENGINE NUMBER LOCATION

On 4-151 engine, the engine code stamping is located on pad at left front of cylinder block below cylinder head. On V6-173, the engine code label is located at front and rear of left rocker arm cover.

ENGINE V.I.N. CODE

On 1980 vehicles, the fifth digit in the V.I.N. denotes engine code. On 1981–85 vehicles, the eighth digit in the V.I.N. denotes engine code.

Engine Identification Code

4-151 engine are identified by code letters on pad. V6-173 are identified by code letters immediately following the engine number.

Year	Engine	V.I.N. Code	Code
1980	4-151	5	WA, WB
	4-151	5	XA, XB
	4-151	5	AC, AU
	4-151	5	Z4, Z6, Z9
	V6-173	7	CNF, CNH
	V6-173	7	CNJ, CNK
	V6-173	7	CNL, CNM
	V6-173	7	CNR, CNS
	V6-173	7	DDB, DCZ
1981	4-151	5	WAN, WAO
	4-151	5	WAL, WAM
	V6-173	X	DBB, DBD
	V6-173	X	DBA, DBC
	V6-173	X	DBN, DBS
	V6-173	Z	DJD, DJF
	V6-173	Z	DBU, DBX
1982	4-151	R	3L, 3M
	4-151	R	3P, 3S
	4-151	R	3J, 3K
	V6-173	X	CAY, CAZ
	V6-173	X	CBA, CBB
	V6-173	X	CBC, CBD
	V6-173	X	CBF, CBH
	V6-173	X	CBJ, CBK
	V6-173	X	CMC, CMF

Year	Engine	V.I.N. Code	Code
	V6-173	X	CMH, CNJ
	V6-173	X	CMM, CMS
	V6-173	X	C7N, C7R
	V6-173	X	C7S, C7T
	V6-173	X	C7U, C7W
	V6-173	X	D2A, D2B
	V6-173	X	D2C, D2D
	V6-173	X	D2F, D2H
	V6-173	Z	CAM, CAN
	V6-173	Z	CAR, CAU
	V6-173	Z	CJJ, CJK
	V6-173	Z	CJM, CJS
	V6-173	Z	CMK, CMN
	V6-173	Z	CMR, CMT
	V6-173	Z	CMU, CMW
	V6-173	Z	CMX, CMY
1983	4-151	R	YAA, YAL
	4-151	R	YAP
	V6-173	X	DCA, DCB
	V6-173	X	DCC, DCD
	V6-173	X	DCF, DCH
	V6-173	X	DCJ, DCK
	V6-173	X	DCM, DCN
	V6-173	X	DCR, DCS
	V6-173	X	DCT, DCV
	V6-173	X	DCW, DCX
	V6-173	X	DMC, DMD
	V6-173	X	DMF, DMH
	V6-173	X	D2J, D2K
	V6-173	X	D2M, D2N
	V6-173	X	D2R, D2S
	V6-173	Z	DFA, DFB
	V6-173	Z	DFC, DFB
	V6-173	Z	DFF, DFH

Year	Engine	V.I.N. Code	Code
	V6-173	Z	DGK, DTA
	V6-173	Z	DTB, DTC
	V6-173	Z	DTJ, DTK
1984	4-151	R	Z3J, Z3K
	4-151	R	Z3K, Z5C
	4-151	R	Z5L, Z5M
	V6-173	X	C4F, C4H
	V6-173	X	C4J, C4K
	V6-173	X	C4M, C4X
	V6-173	X	C4Y, C4Z
	V6-173	X	C5C, C5F
	V6-173	X	C5H, C5J
	V6-173	X	C5K, C5M
	V6-173	X	C5N, SCC
	V6-173	X	SCH, SCK
	V6-173	X	SCM, SCS
	V6-173	X	SCT, SCU
	V6-173	X	SCW
	V6-173	Z	SFA, SFB
	V6-173	Z	SFC, SFF
	V6-173	Z	SFM, SFN
	V6-173	Z	SFR, SFS
1985	4-151	R	AAF, ABY
	4-151	R	ACC, ACM
	4-151	R	ADJ, ADK
	V6-173	W	CAA, CAB
	V6-173	W	CAC, CAH
	V6-173	W	CAK, CAL
	V6-173	X	CAS, CAX
	V6-173	X	CBT, CDA
	V6-173	X	CDB, CDC
	V6-173	X	C5R, C5S
	V6-173	X	C5T, C8R
	V6-173	X	C8S, C8

Grille Identification

1980 Buick Skylark

1980 Buick Skylark Sport Coupe

1980 Chevrolet Citation

1980 Oldsmobile Omega

1980 Pontiac Phoenix

1981 Buick Skylark

GRILLE IDENTIFICATION—Continued

1981 Buick Skylark Sport Coupe

1981—85 Chevrolet Citation "X-11"

1981—83 Oldsmobile Omega "ES"

1981 Pontiac Phoenix

1981—83 Chevrolet Citation Exc. "X-11"

1982 Oldsmobile Omega Exc. "ES"

1982—83 Buick Skylark Exc. "T" Type

1983 Buick Skylark "T" Type

1983 Oldsmobile Omega Exc. "ES"

1983 Pontiac Phoenix

1984 Buick Skylark Exc. "T" Type

1984 Buick Skylark "T" Type

1984—85 Chevrolet Citation Exc. "X-11"

1984 Oldsmobile Omega Exc. "ES"

1984 Oldsmobile Omega "ES"

1984 Pontiac Phoenix "LE"

1985 Buick Skylark

General Engine Specifications

Year	Engine CID①/Liter	Engine V.I.N. Code②	Carburetor	Bore and Stroke	Compression Ratio	Net H. P. @ R.P.M.③	Maximum Torque Lbs. Ft. @ R.P.M.	Normal Oil Pressure Pounds
1980	4-151, 2.5L	5	2SE, 2 Bbl.④⑤	4.0 × 3.0	8.3	90 @ 4000	134 @ 2400	36–41
	V6-173, 2.8L	7	2SE, 2 Bbl.④⑤	3.5 × 3.0	8.6	115 @ 4800	150 @ 2000	30–45
1981	4-151, 2.5L	5	2 Bbl.④	4.0 × 3.0	8.2	84 @ 3600	125 @ 2400	30–45
	V6-173, 2.8L	X	2 Bbl.④	3.5 × 3.0	8.5	110 @ 4800	145 @ 2400	30–45
	V6-173, 2.8L	Z	2 Bbl.④	3.5 × 3.0	8.9	135 @ 5400	142 @ 2400	30–45
1982	4-151, 2.5L	R	T.B.I.⑥	4.0 × 3.0	8.2	90 @ 4000	134 @ 2400	37.5
	V6-173, 2.8L	X	E2SE, 2 Bbl.④	3.5 × 3.0	8.5	112 @ 5100	148 @ 2400	50–65
	V6-173, 2.8L H.O.	Z	E2SE, 2 Bbl.④	3.5 × 3.0	8.9	135 @ 5400	142 @ 2400	50–65
1983	4-151, 2.5L	R	T.B.I.⑥	4.0 × 3.0	8.2	90 @ 4000	134 @ 2800	37.5
	V6-173, 2.8L	X	E2SE, 2 Bbl.④	3.5 × 3.0	8.5	112 @ 4800	145 @ 2100	50–65
	V6-173, 2.8L H.O.	Z	E2SE, 2 Bbl.④	3.5 × 3.0	8.9	130 @ 5400	145 @ 2400	50–65
1984	4-151, 2.5L	R	T.B.I.⑥	4.0 × 3.0	8.2	92 @ 4400	132 @ 2800	37.5
	V6-173, 2.8L	X	E2SE, 2 Bbl.④	3.5 × 3.0	8.5	112 @ 4800	145 @ 2100	50–65
	V6-173, 2.8L H.O.	Z	E2SE, 2 Bbl.④	3.5 × 3.0	8.9	130 @ 5400	145 @ 2400	50–65
1985	4-151, 2.5L	R	T.B.I.⑥	4.0 × 3.0	9.0	92 @ 4400	134 @ 2800	37.5
	V6-173, 2.8L	W	M.F.I.⑦	3.5 × 3.0	8.9	130 @ 4800	160 @ 3600	50–65
	V6-173, 2.8L	X	E2SE, 2 Bbl.④	3.5 × 3.0	8.5	112 @ 4800	145 @ 2100	30–45

①—CID—cubic inch displacement.
②—On 1980 vehicles the fifth digit in the VIN denotes engine code. On 1981–85 vehicles the eighth digit denotes engine code.
③—Ratings are net—as installed in vehicle.
④—Rochester.
⑤—Model E2SE used on vehicles equipped with C-4 system.
⑥—Throttle body injection.
⑦—Multi-point Fuel Injection.

Alternator Specifications

Year	Model	Rated Hot Output Amps.	Year	Model	Rated Hot Output Amps.	Year	Model	Rated Hot Output Amps.
1980	1103043	42	1984	1100231	42		1100257	78
	1103078	42		1100233	42		1100260	78
	—	63		1100235	42		1105028	78
	—	70		1100208	66		1105441	94
1981–82	11100115	42		1100252	66		1105443	94
	1103187	42		1100254	66		1105444	94
	1103197	63		1100217	78		1105446	94
	1101067	70		1100268	78		1105447	94
1983	1100231	42		1100272	78		1105493	94
	1100233	42		1105441	94		1105494	78
	1100235	42		1105443	94		1105562	66
	1100208	63		1105542	94		1105588	78
	1100252	63	1985	1100200	78		1105590	56
	1100254	63		1100206	56		1105592	94
	1100217	78		1100208	66		1105600	66
	1100260	78		1100217	78		1105607	42
	1100272	78		1100231	42		1105617	94
	1105199	85		1100247	66			

Starting Motor Applications

Year	Engine/V.I.N.	Starter Ident. No.	Year	Engine/V.I.N.	Starter Ident. No.
1980	4-151/5, V6-173/7	1109526		V6-173/X,Z	1109564
1981	4-151/5, V6-173/X,Z	1109530	1984	4-151/R	1998450
1982	4-151/R, V6-173/X,Z	1109530		V6-173/X,Z	1109564
1983	4-151/R	1109556	1985	4-151/R	1998450
	4-151/R	1998556		V6-173/W,X	1109564
	V6-173/X,Z	1109533			

Valve Specifications

Year	Engine/V.I.N.	Valve Lash Int.	Valve Lash Exh.	Valve Angles Seat	Valve Angles Face	Valve Spring Installed Height	Valve Spring Pressure Lbs. @ In.	Stem Clearance Intake	Stem Clearance Exhaust	Stem Diameter Intake	Stem Diameter Exhaust
1980	4-151/5	Hydraulic①		46	45	1.69	151 @ 1.254	.0010–.0027	.0010–.0027	.3418–.3425	.3418–.3425
	V6-173/7	1½ Turn②		46	45	1.57	195 @ 1.181	.0010–.0027	.0010–.0027	.3409–.3417	.3409–.3417
1981	4-151/5	Hydraulic①		46	45	1.69	151 @ 1.254	.0010–.0027	.0010–.0027	.3418–.3425	.3418–.3425
	V6-173/X,Z	1½ Turn②		46	45	1.57	195 @ 1.181	.0010–.0027	.0010–.0027	.3410–.3417	.3410–.3417
1982–84	4-151/R	Hydraulic①		46	45	1.69	151 @ 1.254	.0010–.0027	.0010–.0027	.3418–.3425	.3418–.3425
	V6-173/X,Z	1½ Turn②		46	45	1.57	195 @ 1.181	.0010–.0027	.0010–.0027	.3410–.3417	.3410–.3417
1985	4-151/R	Hydraulic①		46	45	1.66	151 @ 1.254	.0010–.0027	.0010–.0032	.3418–.3425	.3418–.3425
	V6-173/W	1½ Turn②		46	45	1.57	195 @ 1.181	.0010–.0027	.0010–.0027	.3410–.3417	.3410–.3417

①—No adjustment.
②—Turn rocker arm stud nut until all lash is eliminated, then tighten nut the additional turn listed.

Pistons, Pins, Rings, Crankshaft & Bearings

Year	Engine Model/V.I.N.	Piston Clearance	Ring Gap① Comp.	Ring Gap① Oil	Wristpin Diameter	Rod Bearings Shaft Diameter	Rod Bearings Bearing Clearance	Main Bearings Shaft Diameter	Main Bearings Bearing Clearance	Thrust on Bear. No.	Shaft End Play
1980	4-151/5	.0017–.0041	②	.015	.9400	2.000	.0005–.0026	2.300	.0005–.0022	5	.0035–.0085
	V6-173/7	.0017–.0027	.010	.020	.9054	1.9983–1.9994	.0014–.0035	2.4937–2.4946	.0017–.0030	3	.0020–.0079
1981	4-151/5	.0017–.0041	.010	.015	.9400	2.000	.0005–.0026	2.300	.0005–.0022	5	.0035–.0085
	V6-173/X,Z	.0017–.0027	.010	.020	.9054	1.9983–1.9994	.0014–.0035	2.4937–2.4946	.0017–.0030	3	.0020–.0067
1982	4-151/R	.0017–.0041	.010	.015	.9400	2.000	.0005–.0026	2.300	.0005–.0022	5	.0035–.0085
	V6-173/X,Z	.0017–.0027	.010	.020	.9054	1.9983–1.9994	.0014–.0035	2.4937–2.4946	.0017–.0030	3	.0020–.0067
1983	4-151/R	.0017–.0041	.010	.015	.9400	2.000	.0005–.0026	2.300	.0005–.0022	5	.0035–.0085
	V6-173/X,Z	.0007–.0017	.010	.020	.9054	1.9983–1.9994	.0014–.0037	③	.0016–.0032	3	.0024–.0083
1984	4-151/R	.0017–.0041	.010	.015	.9400	2.000	.0005–.0026	2.300	.0005–.0022	5	.0035–.0085
	V6-173/X,Z	.0007–.0017	.010	.020	.9054	1.9983–1.9994	.0014–.0037	③	.0016–.0032	3	.0024–.0083
1985	4-151/R	.0017–.0041	.010	.015	.9400	2.000	.0005–.0026	2.300	.0005–.0022	5	.0035–.0085
	V6-173/W	.0007–.0017	.010	.020	.9054	1.9983–1.9994	.0014–.0037	2.6472–2.6482	.0016–.0032	3	.0024–.0083
	V6-173/X	.0007–.0017	.010	.020	.9054	1.9983–1.9994	.0014–.0037	③	.0016–.0032	3	.0024–.0083

①—Fit rings in tapered bores for clearance given in tightest portion of ring travel. Clearances specified are minimum gaps.
②—Upper, .015"; lower, .009".
③—Nos. 1, 2, & 4, 2.4937–2.4946 inch; No. 3, 2.4931–2.4941 inch.

Engine Tightening Specifications★

★ Torque specifications are for clean and lightly lubricated threads only. Dry or dirty threads produce increased friction which prevents accurate measurement of tightness.

Year	Engine Model/V.I.N.	Spark Plugs Ft. Lbs.	Cylinder Head Bolts Ft. Lbs.	Intake Manifold Ft. Lbs.	Exhaust Manifold Ft. Lbs.	Rocker Arm Stud Ft. Lbs.	Rocker Arm Cover	Connecting Rod Cap Bolts Ft. Lbs.	Main Bearing Cap Bolts Ft. Lbs.	Flywheel to Crankshaft Ft. Lbs.	Vibration Damper or Pulley Ft. Lbs.
1980	4-151/5	7–15	90③	29	44	75①	6	32	70	44	200
	V6-173/7	7–15	65–75	20–25	22–28	43–49	6–9	34–40	63–74	④	66–84
1981	4-151/5	7–15	90③	29	44	20②	6	32	70	44	200
	V6-173/X,Z	7–15	65–75	20–25	22–28	43–49	6–9	34–40	63–74	④	66–84
1982–83	4-151/R	7–15	85③	29	44	20②	6	32	70	44	200
	V6-173/X,Z	7–15	65–75	20–25	22–28	43–49	6–9	34–40	63–74	④	66–84
1984	4-151/R	7–15	92③	29	44	20②	6	32	70	44	200
	V6-173/X,Z	7–15	65–75	20–25	22–28	43–49	6–9	34–40	63–74	④	66–84
1985	4-151/R	7–15	92③	29	44	20②	6	32	70	44	200
	V6-173/W,X	7–15	65–75	20–25	22–28	43–49	6–9	34–40	63–74	④	66–84

①—Rocker arm nut, 20 ft. lbs.
②—Rocker arm bolt.
③—Requires thread sealer on bolt head & threads.
④—Auto. trans., 25–35 ft. lbs.; manual trans., 45–55 ft. lbs.

Wheel Alignment Specifications

Year	Model	Caster Angle, Degrees		Camber Angle Degrees				Toe-In Inch	Toe-Out on Turns, Deg.	
		Limits	Desired	Limits		Desired			Outer Wheel	Inner Wheel
				Left	Right	Left	Right			
1980–81	All	−2° to +2°	Zero	+½° to +1½°	+½° to +1½°	+1°	+1°	①	—	—
1982–85	All	—	—	−½° to +½°	−½° to +½°	Zero	Zero	Zero	—	—

①—2.5 mm.

Cooling System & Capacity Data

Year	Model or Engine/V.I.N.	Cooling Capacity, Qts.		Radiator Cap Relief Pressure, Lbs.	Thermo. Opening Temp.	Fuel Tank Gals.	Engine Oil Refill Qts.	Transaxle Oil	
		Less A/C	With A/C					Manual Transaxle Pts.	Auto. Transaxle Qts.①
1980	Citation 4-151/5	9½	9¾	15	195	14	3②	6	③
	Omega 4-151/5	8½	8¾	15	195	14	3②	6	③
	Phoenix 4-151/5	8.3④	8.6④	15	195	14	3②	6	③
	Skylark 4-151/5	8.3⑤	8.6⑤	15	195	14	3②	6	③
	Citation V6-173/7	11½	11¾	15	195	15	4②	6	③
	Omega V6-173/7	10¼⑥	10¾⑥	15	195	14	4②	6	③
	Phoenix V6-173/7⑦	10.2⑧	10.6⑧	15	195	14	4②	6	③
	Phoenix V6-173/7⑨	10.5⑧	10.8	15	195	14	4②	6	③
	Skylark V6-173/7	10.2⑧	10.6⑧	15	195	14	4②	6	③
1981	Citation 4-151/5	9½	9¾	15	195	14	3②	6	③
	Omega 4-151/5	8.4⑩	8.6⑩	15	195	14	3②	6	③
	Phoenix 4-151/5	8.3④	8.6④	15	195	14	3②	6	③
	Skylark 4-151/5	8.3⑤	8.6⑤	15	195	14	3②	6	③
	Citation V6-173/X,Z	11½	11¾	15	195	14	4②	6	③
	Omega V6-173/X	10	10.1	15	195	14	4②	6	③
	Phoenix V6-173/X⑦	10.2⑧	10.6⑧	15	195	14	4②	6	③
	Phoenix V6-173/X⑨	10.5⑧	10.8	15	195	14	4②	6	③
	Skylark V6-173/X	10.2	10.6	15	195	14	4②	6	③

COOLING SYSTEM & CAPACITY DATA—Continued

Year	Model or Engine/V.I.N.	Cooling Capacity, Qts.		Radiator Cap Relief Pressure, Lbs.	Thermo. Opening Temp.	Fuel Tank Gals.	Engine Oil Refill Qts.	Transaxle Oil	
		Less A/C	With A/C					Manual Transaxle Pts.	Auto. Transaxle Qts.①
1982	Citation 4-151/R	9.5	9.75	15	195	14	3②	5.9	⑪
	Omega 4-151/R	9.5	9.75	15	195	14	3②	5.9	⑪
	Phoenix 4-151/R	8.3④	8.6④	15	195	14	3②	5.9	⑪
	Skylark 4-151/R	9.4⑬	9.8⑬	15	195	14	3②	5.9	⑪
	Citation V6-173/X,Z	11.5	11.75	15	195	14	4②	5.9	⑪
	Omega V6-173/X,Z	11.5	11.75	15	195	14	4②	5.9	⑪
	Phoenix V6-173/X,Z⑦	10.2⑧	10.6⑧	15	195	14	4②	5.9	⑪
	Phoenix V6-173/X,Z⑨	10.5⑧	10.8	15	195	14	4②	5.9	⑪
	Skylark V6-173/X,Z	11.4	11.8	15	195	14	4②	5.9	⑪
1983	Citation 4-151/R	8.5	9	15	195	14.6	3②	5.9	⑪
	Omega 4-151/R	9.5⑬	9.75⑬	15	195	14.6	3②	5.9	⑪
	Phoenix 4-151/R	9.5⑭	9.8⑭	15	195	14.6	3②	5.9	⑪
	Skylark 4-151/R	9.5	9.7	15	195	14.6	3②	5.9	⑪
	Citation V6-173/X,Z	10.5	11	15	195	15.1	4②	5.9	⑪
	Omega V6-173/X,Z	10.25⑧	10.5⑧	15	195	15.1	4②	5.9	⑪
	Phoenix V6-173/X,Z	11.4⑫	11.8⑫	15	195	15.1	4②	5.9	⑪
	Skylark V6-173/X,Z	11.4⑫	11.8⑫	15	195	15.1	4②	5.9	⑪
1984	Citation 4-151/R	8.7⑮	9	15	195	14.6	3②	5.9	⑪
	Omega 4-151/R	9.3⑬	9.6⑬	15	195	14.2	3②	5.9	⑪
	Phoenix 4-151/R	9.5	10.4	15	195	14.6	3②	5.9	⑪
	Skylark 4-151/R	9.5⑫	9.7⑫	15	195	14.6	3②	5.9	⑪
	Citation V6-173/X,Z	10.7⑥	11	15	195	15.1	4②	5.9	⑪
	Omega V6-173/X,Z	⑯⑧	10.5⑧	15	195	15.1	4②	5.9	⑪
	Phoenix V6-173/X,Z	11.1	11.8	15	195	15.1	4②	5.9	⑪
	Skylark V6-173/X,Z	11.4	11.8	15	195	15.1	4②	5.9	⑪
1985	Citation 4-151/R	8.75	9.0	15	195	14.6	3②	5.9	⑪
	Citation V6-173/W	10.5	11.0	15	195	14.6	4②	5.9	⑪
	Citation V6-173/X	10.5	11.0	15	195	15.1	4②	5.9	⑪
	Skylark 4-151/R	9.5	9.7	15	195	14.6	3②	5.9	⑪
	Skylark V6-173/W	11.4	11.8	15	195	14.6	4②	5.9	⑪
	Skylark V6-173/X	11.4	11.8	15	195	15.1	4②	5.9	⑪

①—Approximate make final check with dipstick.
②—Additional oil may be required when changing filter.
③—Oil pan capacity, 4 qts.; total capacity, 9 qts.
④—With heavy duty cooling system, man. trans. 8.7 qts., auto. trans., 9.3 qts.
⑤—With heavy duty cooling system, man. trans., 8.7 qts.; auto. trans., 10.8 qts.
⑥—With heavy duty cooling system, 11 qts.
⑦—Exc. Calif.
⑧—Heavy duty cooling system, 10.8 qts.
⑨—California.
⑩—With heavy duty cooling system, 8.9 qts.
⑪—Oil pan capacity, 4 qts.; total capacity, 6 qts.
⑫—Heavy duty cooling system, 12 qts.
⑬—Heavy duty cooling system, 10 qts.
⑭—Heavy duty cooling system, 10.4 qts.
⑮—Heavy duty cooling system, 9 qts.
⑯—Auto. trans., 9.9 qts.; man. trans., 10.5 qts.

Electrical Section

STARTER
REPLACE

EXC. 1983-84 PHOENIX

1. Disconnect battery ground cable.
2. Raise and support vehicle.
3. Remove the starter to engine brace, if equipped.
4. Remove starter mounting bolts and lower starter. Note position of shims, if used.
5. Disconnect solenoid wires and the battery cable.
6. Remove starter from vehicle.
7. Reverse procedure to install.

1983-84 PHOENIX

1. Disconnect battery ground cable.
2. Raise and support vehicle.
3. Remove three dust cover attaching bolts.
4. Pull dust cover back to gain access to front starter attaching bolt, then remove bolt.
5. Pull rear of dust cover backward and remove rear starter attaching bolt.
6. Push dust cover back into position, then pull starter back and out.
7. Disconnect solenoid wires and battery cable, then remove starter from vehicle.
8. Reverse procedure to install. Replace any shims that were removed.

IGNITION LOCK
REPLACE

1. Remove steering wheel as outlined under "Steering Wheel, Replace" procedure.
2. Remove turn signal switch as outlined under "Turn Signal Switch, Replace" procedure.
3. Remove the buzzer switch and spring clip.
4. Turn lock cylinder to "Run" position, then remove the lock cylinder retaining screw and the lock cylinder, **Fig. 1.**
5. To install, rotate lock cylinder to the stop while holding housing. Align cylinder key with keyway in housing, then push lock cylinder into housing until fully seated.
6. Install lock cylinder retaining screw.
7. Install buzzer switch, turn signal switch and steering wheel.

IGNITION & DIMMER SWITCHES
REPLACE

1. Remove turn signal switch as outlined under "Turn Signal Switch, Replace" procedure.
2. Refer to **Figs. 2 and 3** to remove ignition and dimmer switches.
3. When installing dimmer switch, depress switch slightly to install a $\frac{3}{32}$ inch twist drill. Force switch upward to re-

move lash and tighten retaining screw.

W/S WIPER SWITCH
REPLACE

1. Disconnect battery ground cable.
2. Remove turn signal switch and ignition lock as outlined.
3. Remove lower steering column trim covers and bolts securing steering column bracket, then lower column and disconnect electrical connector to wiper switch.
4. Remove steering column housing screws and the housing, **Figs. 4 and 5.**
5. Remove housing cover screw and the cover.
6. Remove wiper switch pivot and the switch.
7. Reverse procedure to install.

PULSE W/S WIPER SWITCH
REPLACE

NOTE: On models where pulse wipers are controlled at turn signal lever, a malfunction may be caused by a faulty pulse wiper module. The module is located behind left hand side of instrument panel.

CITATION

1. Disconnect battery ground cable.
2. Remove radio knobs and nuts and the clock knob.
3. Remove instrument cluster bezel to instrument panel carrier retaining screws and pull bezel rearward.
4. Depress headlamp switch shaft retaining button and pull knob and shaft assembly from switch.
5. Disconnect accessory switch wiring connectors.
6. Remove controller knob and ferrule nut attaching controller to bezel.
7. Disconnect wiring connector at steering column.
8. Remove switch from vehicle.
9. Reverse procedure to install.

To assemble, rotate to stop while holding cylinder.

LOCK CYLINDER

LOCK RETAINING SCREW

CLIP

KEY WARNING SWITCH

HOUSING

Fig. 1   Lock cylinder removal

1981-84 OMEGA

Refer to "W/S Wiper Switch, Replace" for pulse wiper switch replacement procedure on these models.

1980 OMEGA

1. Disconnect battery ground cable.
2. Remove headlamp switch knob by depressing retaining clip behind knob and pulling knob from shaft.
3. Remove left hand trim cover attaching screws and the trim cover.
4. Remove two screws retaining controller switch to adapter assembly.
5. Disconnect wiring connector at steering column.
6. Remove switch from instrument panel.
7. Reverse procedure to install.

1981-84 PHOENIX

Refer to "W/S Wiper Switch, Replace" for pulse wiper switch replacement procedure on these models.

1980 PHOENIX

1. Disconnect battery ground cable.
2. Remove the switch knob and the four screws securing the trim plate.
3. Pull trim plate rearward and rotate for clearance for switch.
4. Remove light guide and the switch retaining screws.
5. Remove screws securing steering column trim cover to instrument panel and the trim cover.
6. Disconnect switch harness connector.
7. Cut both ends of pulse wiring harness as close to the steering column as possible. Remove the switch end and wiring harness end.
8. Install new switch in instrument panel and make electrical connection at instrument panel wiring harness. Route the new controller wiring under steering column and secure wiring so as not to fall in the driver's foot area.
9. Reverse Steps 1 through 5 to complete installation.

1981-85 SKYLARK

Refer to "W/S Wiper Switch, Replace" for pulse wiper switch replacement procedure on these models.

1980 SKYLARK

1. Disconnect battery ground cable.
2. Remove the knobs from the following: W/S wiper switch, rear window defogger switch and radio.
3. Remove headlamp switch knob by depressing retaining clip behind knob and pulling knob from shaft.
4. Remove radio retaining nuts.
5. Remove three screws at bottom of instrument panel trim plate.
6. Place transmission shift lever in "Low" and remove instrument panel trim

plate.

7. Remove switch retaining screws.
8. Pull switch rearward and cut the five wire harness at rear of switch.
9. Feed new wiring harness through switch cavity and pull through bottom of instrument panel.
10. Connect wiring harness between column mounted switch and related junction block.
11. Reverse Steps 1 through 7 to complete installation.

STOPLAMP SWITCH
ADJUST

Insert switch into tubular clip until the switch body seats on the tube clip. Pull the brake pedal rearward against internal pedal stop. The switch will be properly positioned in the tubular clip.

NEUTRAL SAFETY SWITCH
REPLACE

1981–82 MODELS W/ AUTO. TRANS. & CONSOLE SHIFT & ALL 1983–85 MODELS W/AUTO. TRANS.& KEY RELEASE

1. Disconnect battery ground cable.
2. Place gear selector in Neutral.
3. Gently rock switch out of steering column, **Fig. 6.**
4. Disconnect electrical connectors, then remove switch from vehicle.
5. Connect electrical connectors to new switch.
6. Align switch actuator with hole in shift tube.

7. Position connector side of switch into lower jacket cutout.
8. Push down front of switch, ensuring switch tangs snap into holes in steering column jacket.
9. Adjust switch by replacing gear selector in Park position. The switch main housing and housing back should ratchet, providing proper adjustment.
10. If readjustment is needed, move housing as far as possible toward Low gear position, then repeat step 9.

ALL 1980 MODELS W/AUTO. TRANS. & 1981–85 MODELS W/AUTO. TRANS. LESS KEY RELEASE

These vehicles do not use a neutral safety switch. A mechanical block on the transmission gear selector, **Fig. 7,** prevents starting the engine when the trans-

REMOVE

1. Remove parts as shown.

INSTALL

1. Install parts as shown.
2. Position rod in slider hole and install ignition switch. Install lower stud and tighten to 3.9 N•m (35 in. lbs.)
3. Install dimmer switch and depress switch slightly to insert 3/32" drill. Force switch up to remove lash, then tighten screw, and nut to 3.9 N•m (35 in. lbs.).
4. Place shifter in neutral and install shift lever.

IGNITION SWITCH — STUD — SCREW — SHIFT LEVER — PIN — RACK ASSEMBLY — WASHER — SPRING AND BOLT — SPRING — BOWL — SHROUD — BEARING — ACTUATOR ROD — NUT — JACKET — DIMMER SWITCH

3/32" Drill — DIMMER SWITCH — ACTUATOR ROD

ADJUST DIMMER SWITCH

EXC. KEY RELEASE

MOVE SWITCH SLIDER TO EXTREME LEFT (ACC.) POSITION. THEN MOVE SLIDER TWO DETENTS TO THE RIGHT TO "OFF UNLOCK" POSITION.

KEY RELEASE

MOVE SWITCH SLIDER TO EXTREME LEFT (ACC.) POSITION THEN

INSTALL IGNITION SWITCH

Fig. 2   Ignition & dimmer switch removal & installation. Except tilt column

REMOVE

1. Remove parts as shown.

INSTALL

1. Install parts as shown.

2. Position rod in slider hole and install ignition switch. Install lower stud and tighten to 3.9 N•m (35 in. lbs.)

3. Install dimmer switch and depress switch slightly to insert 3/32" drill. Force switch up to remove lash, then tighten screw, and nut to 3.9 N•m (35 in. lbs.).

4. Place shifter in neutral and install shift lever.

SHIFT LEVER

SHROUD

BOWL

PIN

SPRING

PLATE

LOCK PLATE

SCREW

PIN

SCREW

IGNITION SWITCH
ACTUATOR ROD

STUD

SCREW

IGNITION SWITCH

THRUST WASHER

WAVE WASHER

RETAINING RING

SUPPORT

BACK-UP LIGHT SWITCH

JACKET

NUT

RETAINER

SCREW

ADAPTER AND RETAINER

SHIFT TUBE (COLUMN SHIFT ONLY)

DIMMER SWITCH

ACTUATOR ROD

J-23074

STEERING COLUMN HOLDING FIXTURE

EXC. KEY RELEASE

MOVE SWITCH SLIDER TO EXTREME RIGHT POSITION (ACC).

KEY RELEASE

MOVE SLIDER TO EXTREME RIGHT POSITION (ACC.) THEN MOVE SLIDER TWO DETENTS TO THE LEFT TO "OFF-UNLOCK" POSITION.

INSTALL IGNITION SWITCH

DIMMER SWITCH

3/32" DRILL

ACTUATOR ROD

ADJUST DIMMER SWITCH

LEVER

SPRING

J-23072

REMOVE SHIFT TUBE FROM BOWL

J-23073

INSTALL SHIFT TUBE

KEY RELEASE LEVER

Fig. 3   Ignition & dimmer switch removal & installation. Tilt column

REMOVE
1. Remove ignition and dimmer switch.
2. Remove parts as shown.
3. For KEY RELEASE

INSTALL
1. For KEY RELEASE refer below.
2. Assemble rack so that first rack tooth engages between first and second tooth of sector.

Fig. 4 Windshield wiper switch removal & installation. Except tilt column

mission is in any gear other than Park or Neutral.

TURN SIGNAL SWITCH
REPLACE

1. Disconnect battery ground cable.
2. Remove steering wheel as outlined under "Steering Wheel, Replace" procedure.
3. Using a screwdriver, pry cover from housing.

Fig. 6 Neutral safety switch removal. 1981–82 models with auto. trans. & console shift & all 1983–85 models with auto. trans. & key release

4. Using lock plate compressing tool J-23653, compress lock plate and pry snap ring from groove on shaft, **Fig. 8.** Slowly release lock plate compressing tool, remove tool and lock plate from shaft end.
5. Slide canceling cam and upper bearing preload spring from end of shaft.
6. Remove turn signal (multi-function) lever.
7. Remove hazard warning knob retaining screw, button, spring and knob.
8. Remove pivot arm.
9. Wrap upper part of electrical connector with tape to prevent snagging of wires during switch removal.
10. Remove switch retaining screws and pull switch up from column, guiding wire harness through column.
11. Reverse procedure to install.

STEERING WHEEL
REPLACE

1. Disconnect battery ground cable.
2. Remove horn button or pad.
3. Remove retainer and steering wheel retaining nut.
4. Remove steering wheel with a suitable puller (tool No. J-1859-03 or BT-61-9).
5. Reverse procedure to install.

HEADLAMP SWITCH
REPLACE

CITATION

1. Disconnect battery ground cable.
2. Pull switch knob to full "On" position.
3. On 1980 models, proceed as follows:
   a. Remove instrument panel bezel-to-panel carrier attaching screws.

Fig. 5 Windshield wiper switch removal & installation. Tilt column

   b. Remove radio knobs and nuts and the clock knob.
   c. Pull bezel rearward, then depress headlamp switch shaft release button and pull knob and shaft assembly from switch.
4. On 1981–85 models, remove spring clip retainer from knob shaft, then slide shaft out of switch housing.
5. On all models, disconnect accessory switch electrical connectors.
6. Remove switch ferrule nut, then push switch forward out from mounting hole.
7. Lift switch up and out through opening above switch mounting, then disconnect electrical connector.
8. Remove switch from instrument panel.
9. Reverse procedure to install.

OMEGA

1. On 1980–82 models disconnect battery ground cable.
2. Remove headlamp switch knob by depressing retaining clip behind knob and pulling knob from shaft.
3. On all models, remove left hand trim cover attaching screws and the trim cover.
4. Remove switch attaching screws and pull switch from panel.

NOTE: The switch plugs directly into a terminal plug in the switch mounting cavity.

5. Reverse procedure to install.

PHOENIX

1. Disconnect battery ground cable.
2. Remove steering column trim cover attaching screws and the trim cover.
3. Pull headlamp switch to full "On" posi-

Fig. 7   Mechanical neutral start system. All 1980 models with auto. trans. & 1981-85 models with auto. trans. less key release

Tighten nut until tool slightly depresses lock plate

Fig. 8   Compressing lock plate

tion, depress knob release button on switch and remove rod and knob assembly.
4. Remove left hand trim plate attaching screws and the trim plate.
5. Remove switch escutcheon, disconnect electrical connector from switch and remove switch from instrument panel.
6. Reverse procedure to install.

1983-85 SKYLARK

1. Disconnect battery ground cable.
2. Remove headlamp switch knob by using a small screwdriver through slot to depress retainer while pulling knob out.
3. Remove switch bezel.
4. Remove rear window defogger switch knob, if equipped, by pulling straight off.
5. Remove 3 attaching screws from lower edge of left hand trim panel.
6. Pull left hand trim panel straight forward and remove from vehicle.
7. Remove 2 headlamp switch attaching screws and the switch.

NOTE: Pulling switch straight out of dash will also disconnect the electrical connector.

8. Reverse procedure to install.

Fig. 9   Instrument cluster trim cover. 1980-85 Citation

1980-82 SKYLARK

1. Disconnect battery ground cable.
2. Remove headlamp switch knob by depressing retaining clip behind knob and pulling knob from shaft.
3. Remove escutcheon from switch and shaft.
4. Remove the knobs from the following: W/S wiper switch, rear window defogger switch and radio.
5. Remove radio retaining nuts.
6. Remove three screws from bottom of instrument panel trim plate.
7. Place transmission shift lever in "Low", then remove instrument panel trim plate.

8. Remove headlamp switch retaining screws and pull switch from panel.

NOTE: The switch plugs directly into a terminal plug in the switch mounting cavity.

9. Reverse procedure to install.

INSTRUMENT CLUSTER
REPLACE
CITATION

1. Disconnect battery ground cable.

Fig. 10   Instrument cluster. 1980-85 Citation

PRY AT LOCATIONS INDICATED BY ARROWS TO UNLOCK

PULL CONNECTOR OUT, TURN CLOCKWISE AND PUSH THROUGH HOLE IN ADAPTER ASSEMBLY TO REMOVE
USE SAME PROCEDURE FOR L.H. CONNECTOR

Fig. 11   Instrument cluster. 1980-84 Omega

Fig. 12   Instrument cluster. 1980–84 Phoenix

2. Remove radio knobs and nuts and the clock knob.
3. Remove instrument cluster bezel to panel carrier attaching screws, then pull bezel rearward for access, **Fig. 9.**
4. On 1980 models, depress headlamp switch shaft release button and pull knob and shaft assembly from switch.
5. On 1981–85 models, remove spring clip retainer from knob shaft, then slide shaft out of switch housing.
6. On all models, pull bezel rearward and disconnect accessory switch electrical connectors.
7. Remove instrument cluster bezel.
8. Remove four screws securing cluster assembly to instrument panel pad.
9. Disconnect shift indicator cable from steering column shift bowl.
10. Pull cluster rearward and disconnect speedometer cable and electrical connectors.
11. Remove instrument cluster from vehicle, **Fig. 10.**
12. Reverse procedure to install.

1983–84 OMEGA

1. Disconnect battery ground cable.

Fig. 13   Instrument cluster trim cover. 1980–85 Skylark

2. Remove 4 steering column lower trim pad attaching screws and the pad.
3. Remove 6 center instrument panel trim cover attaching screws and the cover.
4. Disconnect shift indicator from steering column shift bowl.
5. Remove 4 instrument cluster-to-instrument panel attaching screws.
6. Disconnect speedometer cable from transaxle, or from transducer on models equipped with cruise control.
7. Pull cluster rearward and disconnect speedometer cable.
8. Remove vehicle speed sensor L.E.D./photo cell attaching screw from rear of speedometer head.
9. Remove instrument cluster from vehicle, **Fig. 11.**
10. Reverse procedure to install.

1980–82 OMEGA

1. Disconnect battery ground cable.
2. Remove the 2 screws attaching assembly line communication link connector bracket to steering column trim cover if so equipped. Remove the 2 screws attaching steering column trim cover to instrument panel and remove trim cover.

3. Mark location of shift indicator clip on steering column shift bowl for proper reassembly. Remove shift indicator clip. Remove the 2 bolts holding steering column to support and lower steering column, resting steering wheel on front seat.
4. Remove four screws attaching center instrument panel trim cover to instrument panel pad.
5. Pull trim cover rearward and disconnect accessory switch wiring and remote control mirror cable, if equipped. Remove trim cover.
6. Remove four screws attaching instrument cluster assembly to instrument panel pad.
7. Disconnect shift indicator cable from steering column shift bowl.
8. Pull cluster rearward and disconnect speedometer cable and electrical connections.
9. Remove instrument cluster from vehicle, **Fig. 11.**
10. Reverse procedure to install.

PHOENIX

1. Disconnect battery ground cable.
2. Remove four speedometer cluster trim plate attaching screws and the trim plate.
3. Remove steering column trim cover attaching screws and the trim cover.
4. Remove speedometer cluster attaching screws.
5. Disconnect shift indicator detent cable, marking the cable location on steering column shift bowl.
6. Disconnect speedometer cable and pull cluster from panel.
7. Disconnect wiring harness from cluster and remove cluster from vehicle, **Fig. 12.**
8. Reverse procedure to install.

SKYLARK

1. Disconnect battery ground cable.
2. Disconnect speedometer cable at cruise control transducer, if equipped, or at upper and lower cable connections.
3. Remove trip meter reset knob retaining screw and pull knob from meter.
4. Remove knobs from the following: W/S wiper switch, rear window defogger switch and radio.
5. Remove headlamp switch knob by depressing retaining clip behind knob and pulling knob from shaft. Remove switch escutcheon.
6. Remove radio retaining nuts.
7. Remove three screws from bottom of instrument panel trim plate, **Fig. 13.**
8. Place transmission shift lever in "Low" and remove instrument panel trim plate.
9. Remove four instrument cluster lens plate screws and the lens plate.
10. Remove four instrument cluster cover plate screws and the cover plate.
11. Disconnect shift indicator spring below speedometer and slide indicator needle toward the right side and out from cluster housing.
12. Pull instrument cluster rearward and disconnect speedometer cable and

Fig. 14 Instrument cluster. 1980—85 Skylark

electrical connections.
13. Remove screw securing vehicle speed sensor head, if equipped, then disconnect sensor and remove cluster housing, **Fig. 14.**
14. Reverse procedure to install.

RADIO
REPLACE

CITATION

1. Disconnect battery ground cable.
2. Remove radio knob and nuts and the clock knob.
3. Remove instrument cluster bezel to panel carrier attaching screws, then pull bezel rearward.
4. On 1980 models, depress headlamp switch shaft release button and pull knob and shaft assembly from switch.
5. On 1981—85 models, remove spring clip retainer from knob shaft, then slide shaft out of switch housing.
6. On all models, pull bezel rearward and disconnect accessory switch wiring connectors.
7. Remove instrument cluster bezel.
8. Remove two screws securing radio bracket to instrument panel.
9. Pull radio rearward while twisting slightly toward left side and disconnect electrical connections. Remove lamp socket.
10. Remove radio from instrument panel.
11. Reverse procedure to install.

1983—84 OMEGA

1. Disconnect battery ground cable.
2. Remove 4 steering column lower trim pad attaching screws and the pad.
3. Remove 6 center instrument panel attaching screws and the cover.
4. Remove 4 radio-to-instrument panel attaching screws.
5. Pull radio rearward, then disconnect all electrical connections from radio.
6. Remove radio from vehicle.
7. Reverse procedure to install.

1980—82 OMEGA

1. Disconnect battery ground cable.
2. Remove radio knobs.
3. Pull out glove box switches and disconnect the wiring connectors.
4. Remove two screws securing glove box stop arm to door.

Fig. 15 Heater core & blower motor, less A/C

5. Remove two screws from instrument panel molding and pull molding rearward to remove. Note that the molding is retained by five clips.
6. Remove ash tray assembly, then the lamp and socket assembly from lamp housing.
7. Pull radio and ash tray retainer out from panel and disconnect all electrical connections.
8. Remove radio from panel.
9. Reverse procedure to install.

PHOENIX

1. Disconnect battery ground cable.
2. Remove eight screws attaching center instrument panel trim plate and the trim plate.
3. Remove two radio attaching screws and pull radio from panel, then disconnect all electrical connectors from radio. Remove radio from panel.
4. Remove radio knobs and separate face plate from radio.
5. Reverse procedure to install.

1983—85 SKYLARK

1. Disconnect battery ground cable.
2. Remove steering column opening cover plate.
3. Remove headlamp switch knob by using a small screwdriver through slot to depress retainer while pulling knob out.
4. Remove headlamp switch bezel.
5. Remove rear window defogger switch knob, if equipped, by pulling straight off.
6. Remove 3 attaching screws from lower edge of left hand trim panel.
7. Pull left hand trim straight forward and remove from vehicle.
8. Remove 2 attaching screws from left

side of radio and 1 nut from lower right side of radio.
9. Pull radio out through instrument panel opening and disconnect all electrical connectors.
10. Remove radio from vehicle.
11. Reverse procedure to install.

1980—82 SKYLARK

1. Disconnect battery ground cable.
2. Remove the knobs from the following: W/S wiper switch, rear window defogger switch and radio.
3. Remove headlamp switch knob by depressing retaining clip behind knob and pulling knob from shaft. Remove the switch escutcheon.
4. Remove radio retaining nuts.
5. Remove three screws at bottom of instrument panel trim plate.
6. Place transmission shift lever in "Low" and remove instrument panel trim plate.
7. Remove radio mounting plate screws.
8. Disconnect all electrical connection from radio.
9. Pull radio out through instrument panel opening.
10. Reverse procedure to install.

W/S WIPER MOTOR
REPLACE

1. Remove wiper arms as outlined previously.
2. Remove the lower windshield reveal molding, front cowl panel and cowl screen. Disconnect washer hose.

NOTE: Prior to removing the front cowl screen, mask the corners of the hood to prevent damage to paint.

3. Loosen but do not remove transmission drive link to motor crank arm attaching nuts. Then, disconnect drive link from motor crank arm.
4. Disconnect wiper motor electrical leads.
5. Remove wiper motor attaching bolts.
6. On models equipped with A/C, support motor assembly and remove motor crank arm. Use a suitable pair of locking pliers and wrench, remove crank arm nut and the crank arm.
7. On all models, rotate motor assembly upward and outward to remove.
8. Reverse procedure to install.

W/S WIPER TRANSMISSION
REPLACE

1. Remove lower windshield reveal molding, wiper arms and front cowl panel.
2. Loosen but do not remove drive link to motor crank arm attaching nuts.
3. Remove transmission to cowl panel attaching screws and the transmission.
4. Reverse procedure to install.

BLOWER MOTOR
REPLACE

1. Disconnect battery ground cable.
2. Disconnect blower motor electrical connections.
3. Remove blower motor attaching screws and the blower motor, **Fig. 15.**
4. Reverse procedure to install.

HEATER CORE
REPLACE

LESS AIR CONDITIONING

1. Disconnect battery ground cable and drain cooling system.

2. Disconnect the heater hoses from heater core.
3. Remove radio noise supression strap.
4. Remove heater core cover retaining screws and the cover, **Fig. 15.**
5. Remove heater core from vehicle.
6. Reverse procedure to install.

WITH AIR CONDITIONING

1. Disconnect battery ground cable and drain cooling system.
2. Disconnect heater hoses from heater core.
3. Remove right side hush panel and open the glove box.
4. Remove heater duct retaining screw and the duct.
5. Remove instrument panel support bracket.
6. Remove heater case side cover retainers and the cover.
7. Remove heater core retaining clamps and the inlet and outlet tube support clamps.
8. Remove heater core from case.
9. Reverse procedure to install.

CRUISE CONTROL
ADJUST

BRAKE RELEASE SWITCHES

Electrical & Vacuum Switches
Push the switch fully into the retaining clip, then pull the brake pedal upward to adjust switch position. The electrical switch should break the electrical circuit when the brake pedal is depressed approximately .23–.51 inch.

SERVO, ADJUST

Models With Rod
Install the pin retainer to provide minimum slack with carburetor in slow idle position.

Models With Bead Chain
Assemble the chain into swivel and install retainer so that slack in the chain is not greater than one-half the diameter of the ball stud with the engine at operating temperature and the idle solenoid de-energized.

Models With Cable
1. With cable installed in cable and servo brackets, rotate throttle lever so that stud aligns with hole in end of cable.
2. Engage cable with throttle lever stud, then release throttle lever.
3. Hold throttle lever position and pull cable taut from servo end.
4. Connect servo end of cable to servo actuator with pin, using hole which most closely aligns with cable end.

NOTE: Do not stretch cable or open throttle to align cable, as this will not allow engine to return to idle.

CRUISE SPEED, ADJUST

NOTE: On 1984–85 vehicles, cruise speed is controlled by the electronic controller and is not adjustable.

1980–83
The cruise speed adjustment can be set as follows:
1. If car cruises below engagement speed, screw orifice tube on transducer outward.
2. If car cruises above engagement speed, screw orifice tube inward.

NOTE: Each ¼ turn of the orifice tube will change cruise speed about one mile per hour. Snug up lock nut after each adjustment.

Engine Section

NOTE: Refer to section 10 for service procedures not covered in this section.

ENGINE MOUNTS
REPLACE

4-151

1. Raise and support front of vehicle, then remove chassis to mount attaching nuts, **Figs. 1 and 2.**
2. On models equipped with A/C, remove forward torque rod attaching bolts at radiator support panel.
3. Raise engine slightly using a suitable engine lifting device. Raise engine only enough to provide clearance for mount removal.
4. Remove two upper mount to engine support bracket attaching nuts and remove engine mount.
5. Reverse procedure to install.

V6-173

1. Remove mount retaining nuts from below cradle mounting bracket.
2. Raise engine and remove mount to engine attaching nuts, then remove mount, **Figs. 3 through 5.** Raise engine only enough to provide clearance for mount removal.
3. Reverse procedure to install, then lower engine into position. Install retaining nuts and torque to 35 ft. lbs.

NOTE: After engine mount is properly installed, check both transaxle mounts for proper alignment. If window "A" is not properly located, **Fig. 3,** loosen mount to cradle retaining nuts and allow mount to reposition itself. If transaxle mount is

Fig. 1 Engine mounts. 1980–81 4-151

allowed to remain out of position, damage to drive train components may result. Torque retaining nuts to 18 ft. lbs.

ENGINE
REPLACE

1980 4-151

1. Disconnect battery ground cable.
2. Drain cooling system, then remove air cleaner.
3. Disconnect distributor, starter, alternator, oil pressure and engine temperature sender wiring and all other electrical connections that will interfere with engine removal. Also disconnect engine to body ground cable.
4. Disconnect and tag all vacuum hose connections that will interfere with engine removal.
5. Disconnect throttle and transaxle linkage at carburetor, then remove upper radiator hose.
6. On models equipped with A/C, remove A/C compressor from mounting bracket and position aside. Do not disconnect hoses.
7. Remove front engine strut assembly.
8. Disconnect heater hose at intake manifold.
9. Remove transaxle to engine attaching bolts, leaving the upper two bolts in place.
10. Remove front mount to cradle bracket attaching nuts.
11. Remove forward exhaust pipe, then remove flywheel inspection cover and starter motor.
12. On models equipped with automatic transmission, remove torque converter to flywheel attaching bolts.
13. Remove power steering pump and bracket and position aside, if equipped.
14. Remove heater hose and lower radiator hose.
15. Remove two rear transaxle support bracket bolts.
16. Disconnect fuel line at fuel pump.
17. Using a suitable jack and a block of wood placed under the transaxle, raise engine and transaxle until engine front mount studs clear cradle bracket.
18. Using suitable engine lifting equipment, put tension on engine, then remove the two remaining transaxle bolts.
19. Slide engine forward and lift engine from vehicle.
20. Install engine using suitable engine lifting equipment. Align engine with transaxle bell housing.

NOTE: Do not completely lower engine into chassis while jack is supporting trans-

axle.

21. With engine lifting equipment supporting engine, install two upper bell housing to engine attaching bolts.
22. Remove jack supporting transaxle, then lower engine onto chassis mounts and remove engine lifting equipment.
23. Raise and support front of vehicle, then install front mount to chassis attaching nuts.
24. To complete installation, reverse procedure following steps 1 through 16.

1981–85 4-151
Manual Transaxle

1. Disconnect cables from battery.
2. Raise and support vehicle.
3. Remove front engine mount-to-cradle attaching nuts.
4. Remove front exhaust pipe, then disconnect starter motor and position aside.
5. Remove flywheel inspection cover, then lower vehicle.
6. Remove air cleaner assembly.
7. Remove all bell housing attaching bolts.
8. Remove front torque reaction rod from engine and core support.
9. On models equipped with A/C, remove compressor drive belt, then disconnect compressor and position aside. Do not disconnect refrigerant lines from compressor.
10. Disconnect vacuum hoses from vapor canister.
11. On models equipped with power steering, disconnect power steering hose.
12. Disconnect all vacuum hoses and electrical connections needed for engine removal.
13. Remove heater blower motor as described under "Blower Motor, Replace" in the electrical section of this chapter.
14. Disconnect throttle cable.

Fig. 2 Engine mounts. 1982–85 4-151

Mount must be installed with tab in forward position.

MOUNT BRACKET

VIEW A

FRONT ENGINE MOUNT

RADIATOR SUPPORT

STRUT

STRUT BRACKETS

STRUT BRACKET

STRUT

STRUT

WITH A/C

WITHOUT A/C

ENGINE STRUT

Fig. 3   Engine mounts. 1980–81 V6-173

15. Drain cooling system.
16. Disconnect heater hoses from engine and radiator hoses from radiator.
17. Disconnect engine electrical harness at bulkhead connector.
18. Install suitable engine lifting equipment and raise engine. Disconnect fuel line and the heater hose from intake manifold, then remove engine from vehicle.
19. Reverse procedure to install.

Automatic Transaxle
1. Disconnect cables from battery, then drain cooling system.
2. Remove air cleaner assembly and pre-heat tube.
3. Disconnect engine electrical harness connector.
4. Disconnect all external vacuum hose connections.
5. Remove throttle and transaxle link-

ages at the throttle body assembly and intake manifold.
6. On models equipped with A/C, disconnect compressor and position aside. Do not disconnect refrigerant lines from compressor.
7. Remove upper radiator hose and front engine strut assembly.
8. Disconnect heater hose from intake manifold.
9. Remove all transaxle-to-engine attaching bolts except the top two bolts.
10. Remove front engine mount-to-cradle nuts.
11. Remove front exhaust pipe, then the flywheel inspection cover.
12. Remove starter motor.
13. Remove torque converter-to-flywheel attaching bolts.
14. On models equipped with power steering, remove power steering pump and bracket and position

aside.
15. Disconnect heater hose and lower radiator hose.
16. Remove 2 rear transaxle support bracket bolts.
17. Disconnect fuel feed line at fuel filter.
18. Using a suitable jack and a block of wood placed under transaxle, raise engine and transaxle until engine front mount studs clear cradle bracket.
19. Attaching suitable lifting equipment to engine. Put tension on engine and remove 2 remaining transaxle-to-engine attaching bolts.
20. Slide engine assembly forward and lift from vehicle.
21. Reverse procedure to install.

1980–81 V6-173
Manual Transaxle
1. Disconnect battery cables from battery, then remove air cleaner.

Fig. 4 Engine mounts. 1982–85 V6-173

2. Drain cooling system, then disconnect and tag all vacuum hoses that will interfere with engine removal.
3. Disconnect throttle linkage from carburetor.
4. Disconnect engine wiring harness connector.
5. Disconnect radiator hoses from radiator and heater hoses from engine.
6. Remove power steering pump and bracket from engine, if equipped.
7. Disconnect clutch cable from transaxle and shift linkage from transaxle shift levers. Remove cables from transaxle bosses.
8. Disconnect speedometer cable from transaxle, then lower vehicle.
9. Install engine support fixture J-22825 between cowl and radiator support, locate support hook into engine rear lifting eye, **Fig. 7.** Raise engine until weight is relieved from mount assemblies.
10. Remove all but one transaxle to engine attaching bolts.
11. Unlock steering column and raise vehicle.
12. Remove stabilizer bar to lower control arm attaching nuts.
13. Remove side and crossmember plate to side and crossmember assembly attaching bolts and remove plate assembly on lefthand side. Loosen plate bolts on right side.
14. Remove crossover pipe, then remove front, rear and side powertrain mount to cradle attaching bolts.
15. Remove left front wheel and tire assembly.
16. Remove front crossmember to right side member attaching bolts.
17. Using tool No. J-28468, pull both driveshafts from transaxle assembly.
18. Remove lefthand side cradle to body mount attaching bolts.
19. Swing side and crossmember assembly to left and secure to fender well.
20. Lower left side of engine by loosening

engine support fixture J-22825, then position a suitable jack under transaxle.
21. Remove the one remaining transaxle to engine attaching bolt, then separate transaxle from engine and lower transaxle from vehicle.
22. Install suitable engine lifting equipment.
23. If equipped with A/C, remove A/C compressor from mounting bracket and position aside. Do not disconnect hoses.
24. Disconnect forward strut bracket from radiator support and position out of way.
25. Raise engine and remove from vehicle.
26. Reverse procedure to install.

Automatic Transaxle
1. Disconnect battery ground cable and remove air cleaner.
2. Drain cooling system, then disconnect

Fig. 5 Engine mounts. 1985 V6-173

ALLOW WINDOW ('A') TO CENTER IN INTERLOCK ('B')
BEFORE TORQUING RETAINING NUTS

REAR MOUNT   FRONT MOUNT

Fig. 6 Transaxle mount alignment. V6-173

all vacuum hoses that will interfere with engine removal.

3. Disconnect detent cable and throttle cable from carburetor.
4. Disconnect engine wiring harness connector and engine to body ground strap at engine forward strut.
5. Disconnect radiator hoses from radiator and heater hoses from engine.
6. Remove power steering pump and bracket from engine and position aside.
7. Raise vehicle and remove crossover pipe.
8. Disconnect fuel lines at hose connects on right hand side of engine.
9. Remove engine front mount to cradle attaching nuts.
10. Disconnect battery cables from starter motor and transaxle case.
11. Remove torque converter housing cover and disconnect torque converter from flex plate.
12. Remove transaxle to engine block support bracket bolts.
13. Lower vehicle and support transaxle by positioning a suitable jack under transaxle rear extension.

14. Remove engine strut bracket from radiator support and position out of way.
15. Remove transaxle to engine retaining bolts. Note location of ground stud.
16. If equipped with A/C, remove A/C compressor from mounting bracket and position aside.
17. Install suitable engine lifting equipment, then raise engine and remove from vehicle.
18. Reverse procedure to install.

1982–85 V6-173

1. Disconnect battery cables from battery and remove air cleaner.
2. Drain cooling system.
3. Remove engine strut bracket from radiator support and swing rearward.
4. Remove AIR pump and bracket, then remove A/C compressor from mounting bracket and place aside, if so equipped.
5. Disconnect vacuum hosing to all non-engine mounted components.
6. Disconnect accelerator cable and detent cable if so equipped.
7. Disconnect engine harness from ECM and pull connector through front of dash.
8. Disconnect engine harness from junction block at left side of dash panel.
9. Disconnect radiator and heater hoses from engine.
10. Remove power steering pump and bracket assembly from engine, if so equipped.
11. Disconnect fuel lines rubber hose connections at left side of engine compartment.
12. Raise vehicle, remove engine front mount-to-cradle and mount-to-engine bracket retaining nuts at right side of vehicle.
13. Disconnect battery cables from starter motor and transaxle case and remove starter.
14. Remove transaxle inspection cover and on automatic transaxle models, disconnect torque converter flex plate.
15. Remove crankshaft lower pulley and all belts.
16. Disconnect exhaust pipe.
17. Remove lower transaxle-to-engine bolt, located at back side of engine.
18. Disconnect power steering cut-off switch, if so equipped.
19. Remove exhaust cross over pipe, then lower vehicle.
20. Remove remaining transaxle-to-engine bolts. Make note of ground stud location.
21. Place a support under transaxle rear extension. Install suitable lifting device and remove engine.
22. Reverse procedure to install. plate retaining screws.

OIL PAN
REPLACE

4-151

1. Raise vehicle and drain crankcase.
2. Remove engine front mount to cradle

Fig. 7 Engine support fixture

Fig. 8 Oil pump exploded view. 4-151

attaching nuts.
3. Disconnect exhaust pipe at manifold and rear transaxle mount.
4. Remove starter motor and flywheel housing cover.
5. Remove alternator upper mounting bracket.
6. Install a suitable engine lifting device and raise engine.
7. Remove lower alternator mounting bracket and engine support bracket.
8. Remove oil pan attaching bolts and oil pan.
9. Clean engine block and oil pan gasket surfaces.
10. Reverse procedure to install. Apply a ⅛ in. by ¼ in. long bead of RTV sealer at split lines of front and side oil pan gaskets. Also apply a small amount of RTV sealer in depressions where rear oil pan gasket engages engine block.

NOTE: When installing oil pan attaching bolts, the bolts attaching the oil pan to the front cover should be installed last. These bolts are installed at an angle and the bolt holes will only be aligned after the other oil pan bolts have been installed.

V6-173

1. Disconnect battery ground cable.
2. Raise and support vehicle.
3. Drain engine oil from crankcase.
4. On 1980–81 models, disconnect crossover pipe from exhaust manifold.
5. On all models, remove flywheel housing shield or clutch housing cover as applicable.
6. Remove starter motor.
7. On 1980–81 models with manual transmission and all 1982–85 models, attach suitable lifting equipment to engine. Remove engine mount bracket-to-engine attaching bolts and raise engine slightly.
8. On all models, remove oil pan attaching bolts and the oil pan.

9. Reverse procedure to install. Apply a ⅛ inch bead of RTV sealer to oil pan sealing flange.

OIL PUMP SERVICE
4-151
Removal
1. Drain crankcase, then remove oil pan as described under "Oil Pan, Replace."
2. Remove two oil pump mounting bolts and nuts from main cap bolt and remove oil pump and screen as an assembly.

Disassemble
1. Remove four pump cover to body attaching screws, then remove cover, idler and drive gears and shaft, **Fig. 8.**
2. Remove pin, retainer, spring and pressure regulator valve.

Inspection
Inspect pump components and should any of the following conditions be found, the oil pump assembly should be replaced.
 a. Inspect pump body for cracks and excessive wear.
 b. Inspect oil pump gears for damage, cracks or excessive wear.
 c. Check shaft for looseness in housing.
 d. Check cover for wear that would allow oil to leak past ends of gears.
 e. Check oil pick screen for damage to screen or relief grommet. Also remove any debris from screen surface.
 f. Check pressure regulator valve for fit in body.

Assemble
1. Place drive gear and shaft in pump body, then install idler gear with smooth side of gear facing pump cover, **Fig. 8.**

2. Install and torque pump cover attaching screws to 105 inch lbs. Check to ensure that pump rotates freely.
3. Install pressure regulator valve, spring, retainer and pin.

Installation
1. Align oil pump shaft with tang on oil pump drive shaft, then install pump on block, positioning pump flange over oil pump drive shaft lower bushing.
2. Install oil pump mounting bolts and torque bolts to 20 ft. lbs., then install oil pan as described under "Oil Pan, Replace."

V6-173
Removal
1. Remove oil pan as described under "Oil Pan, Replace."
2. Remove pump to rear main bearing cap bolt and remove pump and extension shaft.

Disassembly
1. Remove pump cover attaching bolts and pump cover, **Fig. 9.**
2. Mark drive and idler gear teeth so they can be installed in the same position, then remove idler and drive gear and shaft from pump body.
3. Remove pin, spring and pressure regulator valve from pump cover.
4. If pick-up tube and screen assembly are to be replaced, mount pump cover in a soft jawed vise and remove pick-up tube from cover. Do not remove screen from pick-up tube, these components are serviced as an assembly.

Inspection
1. Inspect pump body and cover for excessive wear and cracks.
2. Inspect pump gear for damage or excessive wear. If pump gears are damaged or worn, the entire pump assembly must be replaced.
3. Check drive gear shaft for looseness in pump body.
4. Inspect pump cover for wear that would allow oil to leak past gear teeth.

Fig. 9 Oil pump exploded view. V6-173

Fig. 10 Rear main seal installation. V6-173

Fig. 11 Rear main bearing cap sealing areas. V6-173

5. Inspect pick-up tube and screen assembly for damage.
6. Check pressure regulator valve for fit in pump cover.

Assembly

1. If pick-up tube and screen were removed, apply sealer to end of pick-up tube, then mount pump cover in a soft jawed vise and using tool No. J-8369, tap pick-up tube into position using a plastic mallet.

NOTE: Whenever the pick-up tube and screen assembly has been removed, a new pick-up tube and screen assembly should be installed. Use care when installing pick-up tube and screen assembly so that tube does not twist, shear or collapse. Loss of a press fit condition could result in an air leak and a loss of oil pressure.

2. Install pressure regulator valve, spring and pin, **Fig. 9.**
3. Install drive gear and shaft in pump body.
4. Align marks made during disassembly, then install idler gear.
5. Install pump cover gasket, cover and attaching bolts. Torque bolts to 6 to 9 ft. lbs.
6. Rotate pump drive shaft by hand and check pump for smooth operation.

Installation

1. Assemble pump and extension shaft with retainer to rear main bearing cap, aligning top end of hexagon extension shaft with hexagon socket on lower end of distributor shaft.
2. Install pump to rear main bearing cap bolt.
3. Install oil pan as described under Oil Pan, Replace.

CRANKSHAFT REAR OIL SEAL
REPLACE

4-151

NOTE: The rear main oil seal is a one piece unit and is replaced without removing the oil pan or crankshaft.

1. Remove transaxle and flywheel.
2. Using a suitable screwdriver, remove rear main bearing oil seal. Use care not to scratch crankshaft.
3. Lubricate inside and outside diameters of replacement seal with engine oil. Install seal by hand onto rear crankshaft flange with helical lip side facing toward engine. Ensure seal is firmly and evenly seated.
4. Install flywheel and transaxle.

REAR MAIN BEARING OIL SEAL REPAIR
V6-173

SERVICE NOTE: When replacement of the rear main seal is necessary, the rope type seal used during engine assembly should be replace with rubber split seal No. 14069889, or equivalent using the following procedure. Disregard instructions furnished with the replacement seal that refer to Cavalier models.

1. Remove oil pan and oil pump.
2. Remove rear main bearing cap.
3. Remove upper and lower rope seals, taking care not to damage crankshaft,

then clean seal remnants and oil from seal channels.

NOTE: It may be necessary to loosen No. 2 and 4 bearing cap bolts to allow removal of the rope type seal and installation of the upper split seal.

4. Apply a thin coating of gasket sealing compound 1050026 or equivalent to outer circumference of replacement seal, **Fig. 10,** keeping sealer off seal lips.
5. Use a piece of shim stock to guide seal into block channel and roll seal into block by turning crankshaft.

NOTE: Ensure that large seal lip is toward front of engine and that smaller dust lip faces the flywheel.

6. Apply sealer to lower half of seal as in step 4, then install seal into bearing cap.
7. Apply a thin bead of anaerobic sealant to bearing cap surface as shown in **Fig. 11.** Keep sealant off ends of seal, main bearing, and out of drain slot.
8. Apply a thin film of motor oil to seal lip, install bearing cap and torque cap bolts to specifications.

NOTE: If other main bearing cap bolts were loosened, retorque as needed.

9. Reinstall oil pump and pan as outlined.
10. Fill crankcase, start engine and check for leaks.

Clutch & Manual Transaxle Section

NOTE: Refer to section 10, "CLUTCH & TRANSAXLE SECTION" for service procedures.

Rear Axle, Rear Suspension & Brakes

NOTE: Refer to section 10, "REAR AXLE, REAR SUSPENSION & BRAKES" Section for service procedures.

Front Suspension & Steering Section

NOTE: Refer to section 10, "FRONT SUSPENSION & STEERING SECTION" for service procedures.

1985-86 BUICK SOMERSET REGAL, OLDSMOBILE CALAIS & PONTIAC GRAND AM • 1986 BUICK SKYLARK

INDEX OF SERVICE OPERATIONS

NOTE: Refer to the rear of this manual for vehicle manufacturer's special service tool suppliers.

Vehicle Identification Number Location

On top of instrument panel, left front.

Engine Number Location

The engine code stamping is located on vertical pad on engine to transmission mounting flange located on forward side of block.

Engine V.I.N. Code

The eighth digit of the seventeen digit V.I.N. code denotes engine code.

Engine Identification Codes

Year	Engine	V.I.N. Code	Engine Code
1985—86	4-151①	U	ADS, ADT
	V6-181②	L	WAC

①—Pontiac built engine.
②—Buick built engine.

Grille Identification

1985 Buick Somerset Regal Limited   1985 Oldsmobile Calais Supreme   1985—86 Pontiac Grand Am

1985—86 Pontiac Grand Am w/optional running lights   1986 Buick Skylark & Somerset

General Engine Specifications

Year	Engine CID①/Liter	Engine V.I.N. Code②	Carburetor	Bore and Stroke	Compression Ratio	Net H.P. @ R.P.M.③	Maximum Torque Ft. Lbs. @ R.P.M.	Normal Oil Pressure Pounds
1985—86	4-151/2.5L	U	Fuel Injection	4.00 × 3.00	9	92 @ 4400	132 @ 2800	37
	V6-181/3.0L	L	Fuel Injection	3.80 × 2.70	9	125 @ 4900	150 @ 2400	37

①—CID—Cubic inch displacement.   ②—The eighth digit denotes engine code.   ③—Ratings are net—as installed in vehicle.

Alternator Specifications

Year	Model	Rated Hot Output Amps.	Year	Model	Rated Hot Output Amps.
1985	1100257	78	1986	1105669	85
	1105494	78		1105670	100
	1105495	94		1105671	85
	1105496	94		1105672	100
	1105497	108			

Starting Motor Applications

Year	Engine/V.I.N.	Starter Ident. No.
1985	4-151/U	1998447
	V6-181/L	1998445
1986	4-151/U	1109564
	V6-181/L	1998521

Engine Tightening Specifications ★

★ Torque specifications are for clean and lightly lubricated threads only. Dry or dirty threads produce increased friction which prevents accurate measurement of tightness.

Year	Engine Model/ V.I.N.	Spark Plugs Ft. Lbs.	Cylinder Head Bolts Ft. Lbs.	Intake Manifold Ft. Lbs.	Exhaust Manifold Ft. Lbs.	Rocker Arm Stud Ft. Lbs.	Rocker Arm Cover Ft. Lbs.	Connecting Rod Cap Bolts Ft. Lbs.	Main Bearing Cap Bolts Ft. Lbs.	Flywheel to Crankshaft Ft. Lbs.	Vibration Damper or Pulley Ft. Lbs.
1985	V6-181/L	15	80	45	25	45	7	40	100	60	200
1985-86	4-151/U	20	92①	29	44	20	4	32	70	44	200
1986	V6-181/L	20	—	32	37	43	7	40	100	60	200

①—Requires thread sealer on bolt head and threads.

Pistons, Pins, Rings, Crankshaft & Bearings

Year	Engine Model/ V.I.N.	Piston Clearance	Ring Gap① Comp.	Ring Gap① Oil	Wrist-pin Diam-eter	Rod Bearings Shaft Diameter	Rod Bearings Bearing Clearance	Main Bearings Shaft Diameter	Main Bearings Bearing Clearance	Thrust on Bear. No.	Shaft End Play
1985-86	4-151/U	.0014–.0022	.010	.020	.9400	2.0000	.0005–.0026	2.3000	.0005–.0022	5	.0035–.0085
	V6-181/L	.0008–.0020	.010	.015	.9393	2.2487–2.2495	.0005–.0026	2.4995	.0003–.0018	3	.0030–.0110

①—Fit rings in tapered bores for clearances given in tightest portion of ring travel. Clearances specified are minimum gaps.

Valve Specifications

Year	Engine/V.I.N.	Valve Lash		Valve Angles		Valve Spring Installed Height	Valve Spring Pressure Lbs. @ In.	Stem Clearance		Stem Diameter	
		Int.	Exh.	Seat	Face			Intake	Exhaust	Intake	Exhaust
1985–86	4-151/U	Hydraulic①		45	45	1.69	175 @ 1.26	.0010–.0027	.0010–.0027	.3420–.3430	.3420–.3430
	V6-181/L	Hydraulic①		45	45	1.73	220 @ 1.34	.0015–.0035	.0015–.0032	.3401–.3412	.3405–.3412

①—No adjustment.

Cooling System & Capacity Data

Year	Model or Engine/V.I.N.	Cooling Capacity, Qts.		Radiator Cap Relief Pressure, Lbs.	Thermo. Opening Temp.	Fuel Tank Gals.	Engine Oil Refill Qts.	Transaxle Oil	
		Less A/C	With A/C					Manual Transaxle Pts.	Auto. Transaxle Qts. ①
1985	4-151/U	9½	9¾②	15	195	13½	3③	6	④
	V6-181/L	12¾	12¼②	15	195	13½	4③	6	④
1986	4-151/U	8	8	15	195	13½	3③	6	⑤
	V6-181/L	10.3	11	15	195	13½	4③	6	⑤

①—Approximate; make final check with dipstick.
②—With heavy duty cooling, 10 qts.
③—Additional oil may be required.
④—THM 125C, oil pan only, 4 qts.; total capacity, 6 qts. THM 440-T4, oil pan only, 6¼ qts.; total capacity, 10 qts.
⑤—THM 125C, oil pan only, 4 qts.; total capacity, 11 qts. THM 440-T4, oil pan only, 6 qts.; total capacity, 11 qts.

Wheel Alignment Specifications

Year	Model	Caster Angle, Degrees		Camber Angle, Degrees				Toe-In Inch	Toe-Out on Turns, Deg.	
		Limits	Desired	Limits		Desired			Outer Wheel	Inner Wheel
				Left	Right	Left	Right			
1985	All	+.7° to +2.7°	+1.7°	+.25° to +1.5°	+.25° to +1.5°	+.85°	+.85°	①	—	—
1986	All	+.7° to +2.7°	+1.7°	+.2° to +1.4°	+.2° to +1.4°	+.8°	+.8°	①	—	—

①—.13° toe-out total (.6° per wheel).

Electrical Section

Refer to section 15 'Electrical Section' for service procedures not covered in this section.

STARTER
REPLACE

1. Disconnect battery ground cable.
2. Raise and support vehicle, if necessary.
3. Remove rear starter motor support bracket bolts, then the bracket.
4. Remove A/C compressor support rod, if equipped.
5. Remove starter motor mounting bolts, then the starter motor.
6. Reverse procedure to install.

SATELLITE SWITCHES
REPLACE

NOTE: The headlamp, hazard flasher, rear defogger and windshield wiper/washer controls are incorporated into switch modules mounted on either side of the instrument cluster

1. Disconnect battery ground cable.
2. Remove steering column collar, if equipped, then the steering column filler plate screws and filler plate or lap duct assembly.
3. Remove instrument cluster trim plate attaching screws, then the trim plate.
4. On Somerset Regal and 1986 Skylark, remove switch bezel retaining screws and the bezels.
5. On all models, remove switch retaining screws, pull switch assembly away from instrument panel, **Figs. 1 and 2**, and disconnect electrical connectors as needed to complete removal.
7. Reverse procedure to install.

INSTRUMENT CLUSTER
REPLACE

1. Disconnect battery ground cable.

2. Remove steering column collar, if equipped and the steering column opening filler plate or lap duct assembly
3. Remove instrument cluster trim plate attaching screws, then the trim plate.
4. Remove screws attaching steering column support to lower steering column assembly.
5. Remove instrument cluster to instrument panel attaching screws, then pull cluster assembly rearward, **Figs. 3, 4 and 5.**

NOTE: On models with electronic instrument cluster, note warning printed on front of cluster and do not touch electronic components as static electricity may damage components. Transfer NVM chip from rear of cluster, **Fig. 6,** and the odometer to replacement cluster.

6. Reverse procedure to install.

REAR WINDOW DEFROSTER RELAY
REPLACE

1. Disconnect battery ground cable.
2. Remove glove compartment door and door stop strap.
3. Disconnect electrical connector from relay assembly.
4. Remove relay mounting screw, then the rear window defroster relay.
5. Reverse procedure to install.

RADIO
REPLACE

CALAIS

Models W/Auto Calculator
1. Disconnect battery ground cable.

2. Remove radio trim plate attaching screws, then the trim plate.
3. Remove radio mounting bracket attaching screws, then disconnect antenna lead and electrical connector(s) from radio.
4. Remove radio.
5. Reverse procedure to install.

Models Less Auto Calculator
1. Disconnect battery ground cable, then open ash tray and remove insert.
2. Depress tab on each ash tray locking tang, pull ash tray out to second stop, depress tabs again and remove ash tray.

NOTE: There is a locking tang on each side of ash tray and each tang has a tab on the right side, **Fig. 7.**

3. Remove 2 screws securing upper ash tray bracket and the bracket and trim plate assembly
4. Remove radio mounting screws and withdraw radio.
5. Disconnect antenna lead and electrical connectors, then remove radio.
6. Reverse procedure to install.

GRAND AM

1. Disconnect battery ground cable.
2. Remove right console extension panel and rear main plate.
3. Remove radio mounting screws.
4. Disconnect antenna lead and electrical connectors, then remove radio.
5. Reverse procedure to install

SOMERSET REGAL & 1986 SKYLARK

1. Disconnect battery ground cable.
2. Remove console extensions, lower instrument panel trim and face plates, as needed, to gain access to components and mounting hardware.

Fig. 1   Satellite switch removal. Somerset Regal

1. HEADLIGHT SWITCH
2. HEADLIGHT SWITCH CONNECTORS
3. FULLY DRIVEN, SEATED AND NOT STRIPPED

Fig. 2   Typical satellite switch removal. Calais & Grand Am

1. CLUSTER ASSEMBLY
2. CLUSTER CONNECTORS
3. FULLY DRIVEN, SEATED AND NOT STRIPPED

Fig. 3   Instrument cluster removal. Calais

1—INSTRUMENT PANEL
2—CLUSTER ASM.
3—TRIM PLATE
4—BOLT/SCREW—USE TORQUE
   CONTROL TOOL 800 RPM MAX.

Fig. 4   Instrument cluster installation. Grand Am

* WHEN CLUSTER IS
REPLACED, ODOMETER
MUST BE TRANSFERRED
TO NEW CLUSTER
(IF SO EQUIPPED)

1	CLUSTER FACE PLATE
2	INSTRUMENT CLUSTER
3	ODOMETER
4	BULB COVER

Fig. 5   Instrument cluster installation. Somerset Regal & 1986 Skylark

NVM CHIP

Fig. 6   NVN chip installation. Models w/electronic instrument cluster

1. TRIM PLATE
2. LOWER ASHTRAY HOUSING
3. RADIO
4. FULLY DRIVEN, SEATED AND NOT STRIPPED
5. LOCKING TANG
6. TAB
7. UPPER ASHTRAY HOUSING

Fig. 7   Radio Installation. Calais

3. Remove necessary screws and nuts, **Fig. 8**, disconnect electrical connectors and antenna lead if necessary, then remove components.
4. Reverse procedure to install.

HEATER CORE
REPLACE

1. Disconnect battery ground cable.
2. Drain cooling system.
3. Raise and support vehicle.
4. Disconnect heater hoses from heater core assembly.
5. Remove drain tube.
6. Lower vehicle.
7. Remove instrument panel sound insulator.
8. Remove heater duct and hose assembly and position aside.
9. Remove 2 heater core cover attaching screws, then the covers.
10. Remove heater core from vehicle.
11. Reverse procedure to install.

BLOWER MOTOR
REPLACE

1. Disconnect battery ground cable.
2. Remove blower motor mounting screws.
3. Disconnect electrical connectors from blower motor.
4. Remove blower motor assembly.
5. Reverse procedure to install.

Fig. 8   Radio installation. Somerset Regal & 1986 Skylark

4-151 Engine Section

ENGINE MOUNTS
REPLACE

1. Support engine using fixture No. J-28467 or equivalent.
2. Raise and support vehicle.
3. Remove engine mount-to-chassis attaching bolts from front mount, **Fig. 1**, and engine mount-to-bracket nuts from rear mount, **Fig. 2**.
4. Remove engine mount-to-bracket nuts from front mount and engine mount-to-chassis attaching bolts from rear mount.
5. Remove engine mounts.
6. Reverse procedure to install.

ENGINE
REPLACE

1. Disconnect battery cables, then drain cooling system and remove air cleaner assembly.
2. Disconnect ECM electrical connectors. Route electrical harness through bulkhead and position aside.

3. Disconnect engine wiring harness and position aside.
4. Disconnect all vacuum and coolant hoses necessary for engine removal.
5. On models equipped with A/C, unfasten A/C compressor and position aside, leaving refrigerant lines attached.
6. On models equipped with power steering, unfasten power steering pump and position aside, leaving hoses attached.
7. On all models, remove front transaxle mount.
8. Disconnect fuel lines from injection pump.
9. On models equipped with automatic transaxle, disconnect transaxle cooler lines, then the transaxle shift linkage and downshift cable.
10. On all models, disconnect throttle cable from injection pump.
11. Disconnect redundant ground wire, then remove multi-relay bracket.
12. Raise and support vehicle.
13. On models equipped with power steering, remove power steering line bracket from engine.
14. On all models, remove front wheels.

15. Remove brake calipers and rotors.
16. Remove 2 steering knuckle-to-strut attaching bolts from each side.
17. Disconnect exhaust pipe from exhaust manifold and position aside.
18. Remove 2 body-to-cradle attaching bolts from lower control arm on each side.
19. Loosen 8 remaining body-to-cradle attaching bolts.
20. Remove one bolt from each end of cradle side, leaving one bolt per corner.
21. Position suitable jack stands under front of body, then move hoist back to body pan with a 4 × 4 inch block of wood between hoist and vehicle.
22. Raise hoist and remove jack stands, then place dolly under engine with wooden blocks to maintain position on dolly.
23. Lower vehicle, allowing engine to rest on dolly, then remove engine mount bolts and right front bracket.
24. Remove 4 remaining cradle-to-body bolts, then slide engine/transaxle assembly out from under vehicle.
25. Separate engine from transaxle.
26. Reverse procedure to install.

Fig. 1 Front engine mount

1—R.H. RAIL ASM.

2—COWL ASM.

3—ENGINE ASM.

4—DEFLECTOR

5—ENGINE ASM.

6—DEFLECTOR

7—TRANSAXLE ASM.

Fig. 2 Rear engine mount

ROCKER ARM STUDS

Rocker arm studs that are cracked or have damaged threads can be removed from the cylinder head using a deep well socket. Install and torque new rocker arm stud to 75 ft. lbs.

VALVE ARRANGEMENT
FRONT TO REAR

4-151 . . . . I-E-I-E-E-I-E-I

VALVE LIFT SPECS.

Engine	Year	Intake	Exhaust
4-151	1985–86	.398	.398

VALVE TIMING
INTAKE OPENS BEFORE TDC

Engine	Year	Degrees
4-151	1985–86	33

VALVE GUIDES

Valve guides are an integral part of the cylinder head and are not removable. If valve stem clearance becomes excessive, the valve guide should be reamed to the next oversize and the appropriate oversize valves installed. Valves are available in .003 and .005 inch oversizes.

VALVE LIFTERS

Hydraulic roller valve lifters are used on these engines. Lifter retainers and guide plates are used to keep the lifter from rotating on the camshaft. Failure of a hydraulic valve lifter, **Fig. 3,** is generally caused by an inadequate oil supply or dirt. An air leak at the intake side of the oil pump or too much oil in the engine will cause air bubbles in the oil supply to the lifters causing them to collapse. This is a probable cause of trouble if several lifters fail to function, but air in oil is an unlikely cause of failure of a single unit.

Valve lifters can be removed after removing rocker arm cover and push rod cover. Loosen rocker arm stud nut and rotate rocker arm so that push rod can be removed, then remove lifter guide, retainer and the valve lifter. It may be necessary to use tool No. J-3049 to facilitate lifter removal.

ENGINE FRONT COVER
REPLACE

1. Remove drive belts, then the inner

1 RETAINER SPRING

2 PUSH ROD SEAT

3 ROCKER FEED METERING VALVE

4 PLUNGER

5 BALL CHECK VALVE

6 BALL CHECK VALVE SPRING (HIGH BALL LIFTER ONLY)

7 BALL CHECK VALVE RETAINER

8 PLUNGER SPRING

9 LIFTER BODY

Fig. 3 Hydraulic valve lifter components

TIMING MARKS

Fig. 4 Valve timing marks

Fig. 5   Piston & rod assembly

1—OIL PAN

2—APPLY A 3/8" WIDE BY 3/16" THICK BEAD OF RTV SEALER IN AREA INDICATED

3—APPLY A 3/16" WIDE BY 1/8" THICK BEAD OF RTV SEALER IN AREA INDICATED

4—ENGINE BLOCK ASSEMBLY

5—REAR BEARING

6—GROOVE IN MAIN BEARING CAP MUST BE FILLED FLUSH TO 1/8" ABOVE SURFACE WITH RTV

Fig. 6   Oil pan sealant application

fender splash shield.

2. Remove crankshaft pulley attaching bolts, then slide pulley and hub from shaft.
3. Remove front cover attaching bolts and the front cover.
4. Clean gasket surfaces on cylinder block and front cover.
5. Install oil pan front seal in front cover, then apply a ⅜ inch bead of RTV sealant (³⁄₁₆ inch thick) to joint at oil pan and front cover.
6. Apply a ¼ inch bead of RTV sealant (⅛ inch thick) to front cover and cylinder block mating surfaces.
7. Install centering tool No. J-34995 or equivalent in front cover oil seal bore.
8. Install and partially tighten 2 opposing front cover screws with centering tool in place.
9. Install remaining cover-to-block screws and torque to 90 inch lbs.
10. Install hub, pulley and splash shield.

TIMING GEARS

When necessary to install a new camshaft gear, the camshaft will have to be removed as the gear is a pressed fit on the camshaft. The camshaft is held in place by a thrust plate which is retained to the engine by two capscrews which are accessible through the two holes in the gear web.

To remove gear, use an arbor press and a suitable sleeve to properly support gear on its steel hub.

Before installing gear, assemble thrust plate and gear spacer ring, then press gear onto shaft until it bottoms against spacer ring. The thrust plate end clearance should be .0015–.0050 inch. If clearance is less

than .0015 inch, the spacer ring should be replaced. If clearance is greater than .0050 inch, the thrust plate should be replaced.

The crankshaft gear can be removed using a puller and two bolts in the tapped holes of the gear.

When installing timing gears, make sure that the marks on the gears are properly aligned, Fig. 4.

NOTE: The valve timing marks, Fig. 4, do not indicate TDC, compression stroke for No. 1 cylinder for use during distributor installation. When installing the distributor, rotate engine until No. 1 cylinder is on compression stroke and the camshaft timing mark is 180° from the valve timing position shown in Fig. 4.

CAMSHAFT
REPLACE

1. Remove engine from vehicle as de-

Fig. 7   Oil pump exploded view

scribed under "Engine, Replace."

2. Remove rocker arm cover, push rods, push rod cover and valve lifters.
3. Remove distributor, then the oil pump drive shaft.
4. Remove front cover as described under "Engine Front Cover, Replace."
5. Remove camshaft thrust plate screws, then slide camshaft and gear out through front of block. Use care not to damage camshaft bearings.
6. Reverse procedure to install. When installing camshaft, align crankshaft and camshaft valve timing marks on gear teeth, Fig. 4.

PISTONS & RODS
ASSEMBLE

Assemble piston to rod with notch on piston facing toward front of engine and the raised notch side of rod at bearing end facing toward rear of engine, Fig. 5.

Upon installation, measure the connecting rod side clearance using a suitable feeler gauge. Clearance should be .006 to .022 inch.

PISTONS, PINS & RINGS

Pistons and rings are available in standard and oversizes of .010, .020 and .030 inch. Piston pins are available in oversizes of .001 and .003 inch.

MAIN & ROD BEARINGS

Main and rod bearings are available in standard size and undersizes of .001, .002 and .010 inch.

OIL PAN
REPLACE

1. Disconnect battery ground cable.
2. Raise and support vehicle.
3. Drain engine oil, then disconnect exhaust pipe from exhaust manifold.
4. Remove starter and flywheel inspection cover, then the starter motor.
5. Remove oil pan attaching bolts and the oil pan.
6. Reverse procedure to install. Apply RTV sealant to locations shown in **Fig. 6.**

OIL PUMP SERVICE
REMOVAL

1. Drain crankcase, then remove oil pan as described under "Oil Pan, Replace."
2. Remove two oil pump mounting bolts and nuts from main cap bolt and remove oil pump and screen as an assembly.

DISASSEMBLE

1. Remove four pump cover to body attaching screws, then remove cover, idler and drive gears and shaft, **Fig. 7.**
2. Remove pin, retainer, spring and pressure regular valve.

INSPECTION

Inspect pump components and should any of the following conditions be found, the oil pump assembly should be replaced.
a. Inspect pump body for cracks and excessive wear.
b. Inspect oil pump gears for damage, cracks or excessive wear.
c. Check shaft for looseness in housing.
d. Check cover for wear that would allow oil to leak past ends of gears.
e. Check oil pick screen for damage to screen or relief grommet. Also remove any debris from screen surface.
f. Check pressure regulator valve for fit in body.

ASSEMBLE

1. Place drive gear and shaft in pump body, then install idler gear with smooth side of gear facing pump cover, **Fig. 7.**
2. Install and torque pump cover attaching screws to 105 inch lbs. Check to ensure that pump rotates freely.
3. Install pressure regulator valve, spring, retainer and pin.

INSTALLATION

1. Align oil pump shaft with tang on oil pump drive shaft, then install pump on block, positioning pump flange over oil pump drive shaft lower bushing.
2. Install oil pump mounting bolts and torque bolts to 20 ft. lbs., then install oil pan as described under "Oil Pan, Replace."

V6-181 Engine Section

ENGINE MOUNTS
REPLACE

1. Support engine using fixture No. J-28467 or equivalent.
2. Raise and support vehicle.
3. Remove engine mount-to-bracket attaching nuts.
4. Raise engine slightly, then remove engine mount-to-frame attaching nuts and the mount.
5. Reverse procedure to install.

ENGINE
REPLACE

1. Disconnect battery ground cable.
2. Scribe hood hinge locations and remove hood.
3. Raise and support vehicle.
4. Disconnect electrical connectors from starter motor and remove starter.

5. Remove flexplate cover, then mark relationship between flexplate and torque converter and remove 3 torque converter bolts.
6. On models equipped with A/C, unfasten A/C compressor and position aside.
7. On all models, drain cooling system, then disconnect lower radiator hose.
8. Remove right front engine mount attaching bolts.
9. Remove right inner fender splash shield.
10. Remove transaxle-to-engine mount attaching bolt located between cylinder block and transaxle.
11. Remove right rear engine mount attaching nuts.
12. Disconnect exhaust pipe from exhaust manifold.

13. Disconnect heater hoses from engine, then lower vehicle.
14. Remove serpentine drive belt.
15. Remove alternator.
16. On models equipped with power steering, unfasten power steering pump and position aside.
17. On all models, remove mass air flow sensor and air intake duct.
18. Disconnect electrical connector from cooling fan and remove the fan.
19. Disconnect upper radiator hose and remove the radiator.
20. Attach suitable lifting equipment to engine, then remove left upper transaxle mount.
21. Remove master cylinder, then disconnect fuel lines from fuel rail.
22. Disconnect throttle, throttle valve and cruise control (if equipped) cables

Fig. 1   Cylinder head bolt tightening sequence

Fig. 2   Intake manifold bolt tightening sequence

Fig. 3   Rocker arm installation

1	CYLINDER HEAD
2	PEDESTAL RETAINER
3	ROCKER ARM
4	PEDESTAL
5	DOUBLE ENDED BOLT 60 N·m (45 FT. LBS.)
6	60 N·m (45 FT. LBS.)

Fig. 4 Hydraulic valve lifter exploded view

from throttle body.
23. Remove remaining engine-to-transaxle attaching bolts, then lift engine from vehicle.
24. Reverse procedure to install.

CYLINDER HEAD
REPLACE

1. Disconnect battery ground cable.
2. Remove mass air flow sensor and air intake duct.
3. Remove serpentine drive belt.
4. Remove alternator.
5. Remove ignition module complete with wiring.
6. Disconnect vacuum lines and electrical connectors necessary for cylinder head removal.
7. Disconnect throttle, throttle valve and cruise control (if equipped) cables from throttle body.
8. Remove fuel lines and fuel rail.
9. Disconnect throttle body and intake manifold heater and radiator hoses and drain coolant.
10. Disconnect ignition wires from spark plugs, then remove intake manifold and valve covers.

Fig. 7 Valve timing marks

Fig. 5 Engine front cover replacement

11. Remove radiator and cooling fan.
12. Remove left exhaust manifold, then the rocker arms, pedestals and pushrods.
13. On models equipped with power steering, remove power steering pump.
14. On all models, remove engine oil level indicator and tube.
15. Remove left cylinder head attaching bolts and the cylinder head.
16. Raise and support vehicle.
17. Disconnect exhaust pipe from exhaust manifold, then lower vehicle.
18. Remove right cylinder head attaching bolts and the cylinder head.
19. Install cylinder head(s) noting the following:
    a. If steel replacement gasket is used, coat both sides of gasket with suitable sealer.
    b. Use new head bolts when installing cylinder head.
    c. Torque bolts to specifications in sequence shown in **Fig. 1**: First, torque bolts to 25 ft. lbs. Second, tighten each bolt 90 degrees in sequence shown. Third, tighten each bolt an additional 90 degrees in sequence shown.
20. Reverse remaining procedure to complete installation, torquing intake manifold bolts to specifications in sequence shown in **Fig. 2**.

ROCKER ARMS

1. Remove valve cover.
2. Remove rocker arm pedestal retaining bolt, noting position of double ended bolts for assembly.
3. Remove rocker arm and pedestal, and the pedestal support plates, **Fig. 3**.

NOTE: Keep rocker arms and pedestals together and note installation position. Components that are to be reused should be installed in original position.

4. Reverse procedure to install, torquing pedestal retaining bolts to 45 ft. lbs.

VALVE ARRANGEMENT
Front to Rear

V6-181 . . . . E-I-I-E-I-E

Fig. 6 Timing chain replacement

VALVE LIFT SPECS

Engine	Year	Intake	Exhaust
V6-181	1985	—	—

VALVE TIMING

Engine	Year	Degrees
V6-181	1985	—

VALVE GUIDES

The valve guides are an integral part of the cylinder head and cannot be replaced.

If the valve stem clearance is excessive, the valve guide must be reamed and an oversize valve installed. Valves are available in oversize of .010 inch.

VALVE LIFTERS

Failure of an hydraulic valve lifter, **Fig. 6,** is generally caused by dirt or an inadequate oil supply. An air leak at the intake side of the oil pump or too much oil in the engine will cause air bubbles in the oil supply to the lifters, causing them to collapse. This is a probable cause of trouble if several lifters fail to function, but air in the oil is an unlikely cause of failure of a single unit.

The valve lifters may be lifted out of their bores after removing the rocker arms, push rods and intake manifold. Adjustable pliers with taped jaws may be used to remove lifters that are stuck due to varnish, carbon, etc.

1. NOTCH ON PISTON TOWARDS FRONT OF ENGINE
LEFT BANK
2. NO. 1, 3 & 5 TWO BOSSES ON ROD TOWARDS REAR OF ENGINE (NOT SHOWN)
3. CHAMFERED CORNERS ON ROD CAP TOWARDS FRONT OF ENGINE
RIGHT BANK
2. NO. 2, 4 & 6 TWO BOSSES ON ROD TOWARDS FRONT OF ENGINE (NOT SHOWN)
3. CHAMFERED CORNERS ON ROD CAP TOWARDS REAR OF ENGINE

Fig. 8 Piston & rod assembly

ENGINE FRONT COVER
REPLACE

1. Drain engine coolant.
2. Disconnect upper and lower radiator hoses and heater return hose at water pump.
3. Remove water pump pulley and belts.
4. Remove alternator bracket and alternator.
5. Remove balancer bolt and washer, then remove balancer assembly.
6. Remove bolts attaching engine front cover to cylinder block, **Fig. 7**, also remove two oil pan to engine front cover bolts.
7. Remove engine front cover assembly and gasket, **Fig. 7**.
8. Reverse procedure to install.

NOTE: Prior to reinstalling the engine front cover, remove the oil pump cover and pack the space around the oil pump drive gears completely full of petroleum jelly. Failure to do this may result in the pump losing its prime, causing a "dry" engine start. When reinstalling engine front cover bolts, apply a suitable sealer to the threads to prevent leakage.

TIMING CHAIN
REPLACE

1. Remove engine front cover as described under 'Engine Front Cover, Replace'.
2. Align timing marks on sprockets so they are as close together as possible.

3. Remove camshaft sprocket attaching bolts, then the camshaft sprocket, chain and crankshaft sprocket, **Fig. 8.**
4. Reverse procedure to install. Install chain with No. 1 piston at TDC, timing mark on camshaft sprocket facing straight down and timing marks on sprockets as close together as possible.

CAMSHAFT
REPLACE

1. Remove engine as outlined in "Engine, Replace".
2. Remove intake manifold.
3. Remove rocker arm covers.
4. Remove rocker arm and shaft assemblies, push rods and valve lifters.
5. Remove timing chain cover.
6. Align timing marks of camshaft and crankshaft sprocket. This avoids burring of camshaft journals by crankshaft during removal. Remove timing chain and sprocket.
7. Slide camshaft forward out of bearing bores, using care so as not to damage bearing surfaces.
8. Reverse procedure to install. When installing camshaft, align crankshaft and camshaft timing marks as shown in **Fig. 9.**

PISTON & ROD, ASSEMBLE

Rods and pistons should be assembled and installed as shown in **Fig. 10.**

Measure connecting rod side clearance using a suitable feeler gauge. Clearance should be .0005—.0026 inch.

PISTONS, PINS & RINGS

Pistons are available in standard sizes and oversizes of .010 and .030 inch. Rings are available in standard sizes and oversizes of .010 and .030 inch. Piston pins are supplied with piston and available only in standard sizes.

MAIN & ROD BEARINGS

Main bearings are available in standard sizes and undersizes of .001 and .002 inch. Rod bearings are available in standard sizes and in undersize of .008.

OIL PAN
REPLACE

1. Disconnect battery ground cable.
2. Raise and support vehicle.
3. Drain oil and remove flywheel cover.
4. Remove oil pan.
5. Reverse procedure to install. Apply RTV sealer to oil pan flange and torque oil pan bolts to 8 ft. lbs.

BELT TENSION DATA

A self-adjusting serpentine drive belt is used to drive accessories in place of the usual v-type belt arrangement.

Clutch & Manual Transaxle Section

Refer to section 15, 'Clutch & Transaxle Section' for service procedures.

Rear Axle, Rear Suspension & Brakes Section

Refer to section 15, 'Rear Suspension & Brakes Section' for service procedures.

Front Suspension & Steering Section

Refer to section 15, 'Front Suspension & Steering Section' for service procedures not covered in this section.

POWER STEERING PUMP, REPLACE

Refer to **Figs. 1 and 2** when replacing the power steering pump.

1. REAR ADJ. BRACKET
2. POWER STEERING PUMP
3. FRONT ADJ. BRACKET
4. BOLT – 50 N·m (38 LBS. FT.)
5. BOLT – 27 N·m (20 LBS. FT.)
6. PULLEY
7. SPACER
8. WASHER

Fig. 1   Power steering pump replacement. 4-151 engine

1. POWER STEERING PUMP
2. BOLT – 27 N·m (20 LBS. FT.)
3. PULLEY
4. BELT TENSIONER

Fig. 2   Power steering pump replacement. V6-181 engine

1982-86 CHEV. CAVALIER • BUICK SKYHAWK • CAD. CIMARRON • OLDS. FIRENZA • PONT. SUNBIRD & 2000

INDEX OF SERVICE OPERATIONS

NOTE: Refer to the rear of this manual for vehicle manufacturer's special service tool suppliers.

Vehicle Identification Number Location

On top of instrument panel, left front.

Engine Number Location

When facing vehicle, on pad on right side
of engine block below cylinder head.

Engine V.I.N. Code

The eighth digit in the V.I.N. denotes
engine code.

Engine Identification Code

Year	Engine	V.I.N. Code	Engine Code	Year	Engine	V.I.N. Code	Engine Code
1982	4-112①	G	CXA, CXC, CXD		4-121	P	DSD, DSF, DSH
	4-112①	G	CYA, CYB, CYC		4-121	P	DSJ, DSK, DSM
	4-112①	G	CYD, CYF, CYH		4-121	P	DSN, DSR, DSS
	4-112①	G	CYJ, CYK, CYM		4-121	P	DST, DSU, DSW
	4-112①	G	CYN, CYR, CYS		4-121	P	DSX, DSY, DSZ
	4-112①	G	CYT, CYU		4-121	P	DXL, DXN, DXR
	4-112①	G	CYX, CYY, CYZ		4-121	P	DXS, DXT, DXU
	4-112①	G	CZF, CZJ, CZK		4-121	P	DXW, DXX, DXY, DXZ
	4-112①	G	CZY, CZZ	1984	4-110②	O	Z3A, Z3C
	4-112①	G	C8A, C8B, C8C		4-110③	J	Z5P, Z5T
	4-112①	G	C8D, C8F, C8H		4-121	P	SRB, SRC, SRD
	4-112①	G	C8J, C8K, C8M		4-121	P	SRF, SRH, SRJ
	4-110②	O	UHJ, UHK, UHL		4-121	P	SRK, SRM, SRN
	4-110②	O	UHP, UHS, UHT		4-121	P	SRR, SRS, SRT
	4-110②	O	UHY, UHZ		4-121	P	SRW, SRX
	4-121	B	CSA, CSB, CSC	1985	4-110②	O	AAS, AAT
1983	4-110②	O	YCP, YDD, YDF		4-110③	J	ADL, ADP
	4-110②	O	YDH, YDJ, YDK		4-121	P	CAJ, CHA, CSB
	4-110②	O	YDT, YDY, YLL, YLM		4-121	P	CSH, C2L, CSD
	4-121	P	DJN, DJR, DJS		4-121	P	C2N, CSF, CSC
	4-121	P	DJT, DJU, DJW		V6-173	W	CAA, CAB, CAC
	4-121	P	DJX, DJY, DJM		V6-173	W	CAH, CAK, CAL
	4-121	P	DMN, DMR, DMS	1986	4-110②	O	
	4-121	P	DMT, DMU, DMW		4-110③	J	
	4-121	P	DMX, DMY, DMZ		4-121	P	
	4-121	P	DSA, DSB, DSC		V6-173	W	

①—Overhead valve engine.
②—Overhead cam engine.
③—Turbocharged overhead cam engine.

continued

Grille Identification

1982–85 Buick Skyhawk Exc. "T" Type

1982 Cadillac Cimarron

1982–83 Chevrolet Cavalier Except Hatchback

1982–83 Chevrolet Cavalier Hatchback

1982–83 Olds Firenza

1982–83 Pontiac 2000

1983–85 Buick Skyhawk "T" Type

1983 Cadillac Cimarron

1984–85 Cadillac Cimarron

1984–86 Chevrolet Cavalier Exc. Convertible & Z24

1984 Chevrolet Cavalier Convertible

1984–86 Olds Firenza

1984–85 Pontiac 2000 Sunbird Exc. LE, SE & Convertible Less Driving Lamps

1984–85 Pontiac 2000 Sunbird LE, SE & Convertible Less Driving Lamps

1984–86 Pontiac 2000 Sunbird w/Driving Lamps

1985–86 Chevrolet Cavalier Z24

1985 Olds Firenza GT

1986 Buick Skyhawk Exc. "T" Type

1986 Buick Skyhawk "T" Type

1986 Cadillac Cimarron

continued

General Engine Specifications

Year	Engine CID①/Liter	Engine V.I.N. Code②	Carburetor	Bore and Stroke	Com- pression Ratio	Net H.P. @ R.P.M.③	Maximum Torque Ft. Lbs. @ R.P.M.	Normal Oil Pressure Pounds
1982	4-112/1.8L⑤	G	E2SE, 2 Bbl.④	3.50 × 2.90	9.0	85 @ 5100	100 @ 2800	45
	4-110/1.8L⑥	O	E.F.I.⑦	3.34 × 3.12	9.0	84 @ 5200	102 @ 2800	65
	4-121/2.0L	B	E2SE, 2 Bbl.④	3.50 × 3.14	9.0	90 @ 5100	111 @ 2700	45
1983	4-110/1.8L⑥	O	E.F.I.⑦	3.34 × 3.12	9.0	84 @ 5200	102 @ 2800	45
	4-121/2.0L	P	E.F.I.⑦	3.50 × 3.15	9.3	86 @ 4900	110 @ 3000	63–77
1984	4-110/1.8L⑥	O	E.F.I.⑦	3.34 × 3.12	9.0	84 @ 5200	102 @ 2800	65
	4-110/1.8L⑥⑧	J	E.F.I.⑦	3.34 × 3.12	8.0	150 @ 5600	150 @ 2800	65
	4-121/2.0L	P	E.F.I.⑦	3.50 × 3.15	9.3	86 @ 4900	110 @ 2400	63–77
1985–86	4-110/1.8L⑥	O	E.F.I.⑦	3.34 × 3.12	9.0	84 @ 5200	102 @ 2800	65
	4-110/1.8L⑥⑧	J	E.F.I.⑦	3.34 × 3.12	8.0	150 @ 5600	150 @ 2800	65
	4-121/2.0L	P	E.F.I.⑦	3.50 × 3.15	9.3	86 @ 4900	110 @ 2400	63–77
	V6-173/2.8L	W	E.F.I.⑦	3.50 × 2.99	8.9	130 @ 4800	160 @ 3600	50–55

①—CID—cubic inch displacement.
②—The eighth digit denotes engine code.
③—Ratings are net as installed in vehicle.
④—Rochester.
⑤—Overhead valve engine.
⑥—Overhead cam engine.
⑦—Electronic Fuel Injection.
⑧—Turbocharged engine.

Alternator Specifications

Year	Model	Rated Hot Output Amps.
1982	1100169①	63
	1100220①	63
	1101438②	70
1983	1105249②	85
	1105331②	85
	1105335③	63
1983–85	1100288③	78
	1100289③	78
	1100290③	56

Year	Model	Rated Hot Output Amps.
	1100291③	56
	1105091③	66
	1105092③	66
	1105446	94
	1105447	94
	1105508	78
	1105541	94
1983–86	1100258③	78
	1105329	85

Year	Model	Rated Hot Output Amps.
	1105354①	42
	1105439③	78
	1105440③	66
	1105541	94
	1105599③	56
	1105602③	94
	1105610③	78
	1105611①	66

①—10 SI.   ②—15 SI.   ③—12 SI.

Starting Motor Applications

Year	Engine/V.I.N.	Starter Ident. No.
1982	4-112/G①	1109537
	4-110/O②	—
	4-121/B①	1109562
1983	4-110/O②	1109551
	4-121/P①	1109562

Year	Engine/V.I.N.	Starter Ident. No.
1984–86	4-110/O②	1998447
	4-110 Turbo/J②	1998447
	4-121/P①	1998429
	V6-173/W	1109564

①—Overhead valve engine.   ②—Overhead cam engine.

Valve Specifications

Year	Engine/V.I.N.	Valve Lash Int.	Valve Lash Exh.	Valve Angles Seat	Valve Angles Face	Valve Spring Installed Height	Valve Spring Pressure Lbs. @ In.	Stem Clearance Intake	Stem Clearance Exhaust	Stem Diameter Intake	Stem Diameter Exhaust
1982	4-112/G②	1½ Turn①		46	45	1.598	182 @ 1.33	.0011–.0026	.0014–.0031	.3139–.3144	.3129–.3136
1982–83	4-110/O③	Hydraulic④		45	46	—	—	.0006–.0016	.0012–.0024	—	—
	4-121/B,P	1½ Turn①		46	45	1.598	182 @ 1.33	.0011–.0026	.0014–.0031	.3139–.3144	.3129–.3136
1984–86	4-110/O③	Hydraulic④		45	46	—	—	.0006–.0020	.0010–.0024	—	—
	4-110 Turbo/J③	Hydraulic④		45	46	—	—	.0006–.0020	.0010–.0024	—	—
	4-121/P	1½ Turn①		46	45	1.62	180 @ 1.33	.0011–.0026	.0014–.003	—	—
1985–86	V6-173/W	1½ Turn①		46	45	1.57	195 @ 1.18	.0010–.0027	.0010–.0027	—	—

continued

VALVE SPECIFICATIONS—Continued

①—Turn rocker arm adjusting nut until all lash is eliminated, then tighten nut an additional one and one-half turn to center plunger.
②—Overhead valve engine.
③—Overhead cam engine.
④—Hydraulic valve compensator, no adjustment.

Pistons, Pins, Rings, Crankshaft & Bearings

Year	Engine Model/V.I.N.	Piston Clearance	Ring Gap① Comp.	Oil	Wrist-pin Diameter②	Rod Bearings Shaft Diameter	Bearing Clearance	Main Bearings Shaft Diameter	Bearing Clearance	Thrust on Bear. No.	Shaft End Play
1982	4-112/G③	.0008–.0018	.010	—	.9054	1.9983–1.9993	.0010–.0031	④	⑤	4	.002–.007
1982–83	4-110/O⑥	.0008⑧	.012	.016	—	1.9280–1.9286	.0007–.0024	⑦	.0006–.0016	3	.002–.012
	4-121/B,P	.0008–.0018	.010	—	.9054	1.9983–1.9993	.0010–.0031	④	⑤	4	.002–.007
1984–85	4-110/O⑥	.0008⑧	.012	.016	—	1.9278–1.9286	.0007–.0025	⑦	.0006–.0016	3	.003–.012
	4-110 Turbo/J⑥	.0004–.0012	.012	.016	—	1.9278–1.9286	.0007–.0025	⑦	.0006–.0016	3	.003–.012
	4-121/P	.0007–.0017	.010	.020	.9385	1.9983–1.9994	.0010–.0031	④	⑤	4	.002–.007
1985–86	V6-173/W	.0007–.0017	.010	.020	.9054	1.9983–1.9994	.0014–.0037	2.6473–2.6482	.0016–.0032	3	.0024–.0083
1986	4-110/O⑥	.0008⑧	.012	.016	—	1.9278–1.9286	.0007–.0025	⑦	.0006–.0016	3	.003–.012
	4-110 Turbo/J⑥	.0004–.0012	.012	.016	—	1.9278–1.9286	.0007–.0025	⑦	.0006–.0016	3	.003–.012
	4-121/P	.0007–.0017	.010	.020	.8001	1.9983–1.9994	.0010–.0031	④	⑤	4	.002–.007

①—Fit rings in tapered bores for clearance given in tightest portion of ring travel. Clearances specified are minimum gaps.
②—Minimum diameter.
③—Overhead valve engine.
④—Nos. 1, 2, 3, 4, 2.4945–2.4954 inch; No. 5, 2.4937–2.4946 inch.
⑤—Nos. 1, 2, 3, 4, .0006–.0018 inch; No. 5, .0014–.0026 inch.
⑥—Overhead cam engine.
⑦—Brown color code, 2.2830–2.2833 inch; green color code, 2.2827–2.2830 inch.
⑧—Maximum.

Engine Tightening Specifications★

★ Torque specifications are for clean and lightly lubricated threads only. Dry or dirty threads produce increased friction which prevents accurate measurement of tightness.

Year	Engine Model/V.I.N.	Spark Plugs Ft. Lbs.	Cylinder Head Bolts Ft. Lbs.	Intake Manifold Ft. Lbs.	Exhaust Manifold Ft. Lbs.	Rocker Arm Stud Ft. Lbs.	Rocker Arm Cover Ft. Lbs.	Connecting Rod Cap Bolts Ft. Lbs.	Main Bearing Cap Bolts Ft. Lbs.	Flywheel to Crankshaft Ft. Lbs.	Vibration Damper or Pulley Ft. Lbs.
1982	4-112/G①	7–15	65–75	20–25	22–28	43–49	6–9	34–40	63–74	45–55	66–84
1982–83	4-110/O②	15	③	16	19	—	5	39	57	45	20
	4-121/B,P	7–15	65–75	20–25	22–28	43–49	6–9	34–40	63–74	45–55	66–84
1984	4-121/P	7–20	65–75	18–25	20–30	43–49	4–9	34–43	63–77	⑤	66–89
1984–85	4-110/J,O②	15	③	25	16	—	5	39	57	45	20
1985	4-121/P	7–20	73–85	18–25	34–44	43–49	4–9	34–43	63–77	⑤	66–89
	V6-173/W	17–33	65–90	13–25	19–31	—	7–15	34–45	63–83	—	67–85

①—Overhead valve engine.
②—Overhead cam engine.
③—Torque cylinder head & camshaft carrier bolts to 18 ft. lbs., then tighten bolts an additional 180° in 60° increments. Start engine & allow to reach operating temperature, then tighten bolts an additional 30° to 50°.
④—Auto. trans., 45 to 59 ft. lbs.; man. trans., 45–63 ft. lbs.

Wheel Alignment Specifications

Year	Model	Caster Angle, Degrees Limits	Desired	Camber Angle, Degrees Limits Left	Right	Desired Left	Right	Toe-Out Inch	Toe-Out on Turns, Deg. Outer Wheel	Inner Wheel
1982	All	—	—	+.1 to +1.1	+.1 to +1.1	+.6	+.6	①	—	—
1983–86	③	+.7 to +2.7	+1.7	+.2 to +1.2	+.2 to +1.2	+.7	+.7	②	—	—
1984–86	Cavalier	+.7 to +2.7	+1.7	+.2 to +1.5	+.2 to +1.2	+.85	+.85	②	—	—

①—.25° toe-out.
②—.13° toe-out.
③—Exc. 1984–86 Cavalier.

continued

15–5

Cooling System & Capacity Data

Year	Model or Engine/V.I.N.	Cooling Capacity, Qts.		Radiator Cap Relief Pressure, Lbs.	Thermo. Opening Temp.	Fuel Tank Gals.	Engine Oil Refill Qts.	Transaxle Oil	
		Less A/C	With A/C					Manual Transaxle Pts.	Auto. Transaxle Qts.①
1982	Cavalier 4-112/G	9.0	9.3⓪	15	195	14	4②	6	③
	Cimarron 4-112/G	—	8.28	15	195	14	4②	6	③
	Firenza 4-112/G	8.0	8.0	15	195	14	4②	6	③
	J2000 4-112/G	8.3	8.3	15	195	14	4②	6	③
	Skyhawk 4-112/G	8.0	8.0	15	195	14	4②	6	③
	All 4-110/O	7.8	7.9	15	195	14	3②	6	③
	All 4-121/B	8.0	8.0	15	195	14	4②	6	③
1983	Cavalier 4-110/O	9.6	9.6⑥	15	195	13.6	3②	5.4	③
	Firenza 4-110/O	8.0	8.0	15	195	13.6	3②	5.4	③
	2000 4-110/O	7.8	7.9	15	195	13.6	3②	⑤	③
	Skyhawk 4-110/O	7.8	7.8	15	195	13.6	3②	5.4	③
	Cavalier 4-121/P	9.6⑥	9.6⑥	15	195	13.6	4②	5.4	③
	Cimarron 4-121/P	④	④	15	195	13.6	4②	5.4	③
	Firenza 4-121/P	8.0	8.0	15	195	13.6	4②	5.4	③
	2000 4-121/P	7.8	7.9	15	195	13.6	4②	⑤	③
	Skyhawk 4-121/P	9.7	9.75	15	195	13.6	4②	5.4	③
1984	Cavalier 4-121/P	9.6⑥	9.6⑥	15	195	13.6	4②	6	③
	Cimarron 4-121/P	④	④	15	195	13.6	4②	6	③
	Firenza 4-110/O	8.0	8.0	15	195	13.6	3②	6	③
	Firenza 4-121/P	9.5	9.75	15	195	13.6	4②	6	③
	Skyhawk 4-110/O	7.8	7.8	15	195	13.6	3②	6	③
	Skyhawk 4-110 Turbo/J	7.8	7.8	15	195	13.6	4②⑦	6	③
	Skyhawk 4-121/P	9.5	9.75	15	195	13.6	4②	6	③
	Sunbird 4-110/O	7.8	7.9	15	195	13.6	3②	⑤	③
	Sunbird 4-110 Turbo/J	7.8	7.9	15	195	13.6	4②⑦	⑤	③
	Sunbird 4-121/P	7.8	7.9	15	195	13.6	4②	⑤	③
1985	Cavalier 4-121/P	9.6	9.8	15	195	14	4②	6	③
	Cavalier V6-173/W	11	11.1	15	195	14	4②	6	③
	Cimarron 4-121/P	9.6	9.8	15	195	14	4②	6	③
	Cimarron V6-173/W	11	11.1	15	195	14	4②	6	③
	Firenza 4-110/O	8	8	15	195	13.6	4②	6	③
	Firenza 4-121/P	9.5	9.7	15	195	13.6	4②	6	③
	Firenza V6-173/W	10.7	11.1	15	195	13.6	4②	6	③
	Skyhawk 4-110/O	7.8	7.8	15	195	13.6	4②	6	③
	Skyhawk 4-110 Turbo/J	7.8	7.8	15	195	13.6	4②⑦	6	③
	Skyhawk 4-121/P	9.5	9.7	15	195	13.6	4②	6	③
	Sunbird 4-110/O	7.9	7.9	15	195	13.6	4②	6	③
	Sunbird 4-110 Turbo/J	7.9	7.9	15	195	13.6	4②⑦	6	③
1986	Cavalier 4-121	8.8	8.8	15	195	13.6	4②	6	③
	Cavalier V6-173	11.3	11.3	15	195	13.6	4②	6	③
	Cimarron 4-121	—	—	15	195	13.6	4②	6	③
	Cimarron V6-173	—	—	15	195	13.6	4②	6	③
	Firenza 4-110	7.8	7.9	15	195	13.6	4②	6	③
	Firenza 4-121	7.8	7.9	15	195	13.6	4②	6	③
	Firenza V6-173	10.7	11.1	15	195	13.6	4②	6	③
	Skyhawk 4-110	—	—	15	195	13.6	4②	6	③
	Skyhawk 4-110 Turbo	—	—	15	195	13.6	4②⑦	6	③
	Skyhawk 4-121	—	—	15	195	13.6	4②	6	③
	Sunbird 4-110	—	—	15	195	13.6	4②	6	③
	Sunbird 4-110 Turbo	—	—	15	195	13.6	4②⑦	6	③

①—Approximate, make final check with dipstick.
②—With or without filter change.
③—Oil pan only, 4 qts. After overhaul, less torque canverter drain, 6 qts.; with torque converter drain, 9 qts.
④—Man. trans., 8.7 qts.; auto. trans., 9.3 qts.
⑤—4 spd., 5.9 pts.; 5 spd., 5.3 pts.
⑥—With heavy duty cooling system, 9.8 qts.
⑦—Before allowing engine to start after oil change, crank engine over until a steady oil pressure reading is obtained to prime engine and turbocharger lubrication system.

Electrical Section

Fig. 1   Lock cylinder removal

Fig. 2   Ignition & dimmer switch removal. Models less tilt column

STARTER
REPLACE

4-112 & 4-121 OVERHEAD VALVE ENGINES

1. Disconnect battery ground cable.
2. Raise and support front of vehicle.
3. Disconnect solenoid wires and battery cable at starter.
4. Remove rear engine mount support bracket, then the A/C compressor support rod (if equipped).
5. Remove starter to engine mounting bolts and lower starter. Note position of shims if used.
6. Reverse procedure to install.

1982-84 4-110 OVERHEAD CAM ENGINE EXC. TURBOCHARGED

Models W/ Manual Transaxle
1. Disconnect battery ground cable.
2. Remove upper starter to engine block bolt.
3. Raise and support front of vehicle.
4. Remove rear starter brace attaching bolt from engine block and nut from starter, then the brace.
5. Remove lower starter to engine mounting bolt.
6. Disconnect battery positive cable and solenoid leads from starter motor, then lower starter from engine.
7. Reverse procedure to install.

Models W/ Automatic Transaxle
1. Disconnect battery ground cable.
2. Remove air cleaner from engine.
3. Remove lower starter to engine block bolt.
4. Remove rear starter brace attaching bolt from engine block and nut from starter, then the brace.
5. Disconnect battery positive cable and solenoid leads from starter motor.
6. Remove starter to engine block bolt, then raise and support front of vehicle.
7. Disconnect speedometer cable.

8. While pushing upward on shift cable, lower armature end of starter motor down between stabilizer bar and engine, then remove starter motor from engine.

NOTE: It may be necessary to pry engine block forward to provide clearance for starter motor removal.

9. Reverse procedure to install.

1985 4-110 OVERHEAD CAM ENGINE EXC. TURBOCHARGED

1. Disconnect battery ground cable, then remove wiring harness clamp at motor mount.
2. Remove upper starter-to-engine block bolt.
3. Raise and support vehicle.
4. On automatic transaxle equipped models, disconnect speedometer cable, then remove rear transaxle strut.
5. On all models, remove throttle cable bracket, rear starter brace bolts and brace.
6. Remove lower starter-to-engine block bolt, then disconnect starter wiring.
7. Position starter nose down between transaxle and sway bar and attempt to remove. If necessary, pry engine forward or detach sway bar.
8. Reverse procedure to install.

4-110 OVERHEAD CAM TURBOCHARGED ENGINE

1. Disconnect battery ground cable.
2. Remove intake manifold support brace.
3. On 1982-84 models, disconnect lead at coil and MAT electrical connector at intake manifold.
4. Remove upper starter to engine block bolt.
5. Remove engine harness bracket to intake manifold bolt.
6. Raise and support front of vehicle,

then remove transmission strut.
7. Remove fuel line to support bracket bolt, then loosen fuel lines ½ turn to gain access to the starter motor.
8. Remove fuel line support bracket.
9. Remove rear starter support bracket. Do not bend turbocharger oil supply line.
10. Disconnect battery positive cable and solenoid leads from starter motor.
11. Remove lower starter bolt, then starter from engine.
12. Reverse procedure to install.

V6-173 ENGINES

1. Disconnect battery ground cable, then raise and support vehicle.
2. Remove nuts and washers securing electrical connectors to starter solenoid, then disconnect connectors noting position for installation.
3. Remove starter mounting bolts, then the starter motor, noting installation position of starter shims if equipped.
4. Reverse procedure to install.

IGNITION LOCK
REPLACE

1. Remove steering wheel as outlined under "Steering Wheel, Replace" procedure.
2. Remove turn signal switch as outlined under "Turn Signal Switch, Replace" procedure.
3. Remove buzzer switch.
4. Turn lock cylinder to "Run" position, then remove the lock cylinder retaining screw and lock cylinder, **Fig. 1.**
5. To install, rotate lock cylinder to stop while holding housing. Align cylinder key with keyway in housing, then push cylinder into housing until fully seated.
6. Install lock cylinder retaining screw.
7. Install buzzer switch, turn signal switch and steering wheel.

IGNITION & DIMMER SWITCHES
REPLACE

1. Remove steering wheel as outlined under "Steering Wheel, Replace" procedure, then the turn signal switch and lock cylinder as previously described.
2. Refer to **Figs. 2 and 3** to remove ignition and dimmer switches.
3. When installing dimmer switch, depress switch slightly and install a ³⁄₃₂ drill into switch. Force switch upward to remove lash and tighten retaining screw.

W/S WIPER SWITCH
REPLACE

1. Remove turn signal switch as outlined under "Turn Signal Switch, Replace" procedure.
2. Refer to **Figs. 4 and 5** for wiper switch replacement.

PULSE W/S WIPER MODULE
REPLACE

1982–83 2000; 1982–86 CAVALIER, CIMARRON & 1984–86 SUNBIRD

1. Disconnect battery ground cable.
2. Remove headlamp switch knob by depressing retaining clip behind knob and pulling knob from shaft.
3. Remove left hand trimplate attaching screws and the trimplate.
4. Remove screws retaining module to adapter assembly.

Fig. 3   Ignition & dimmer switch removal. Models with tilt column

Fig. 4   W/S wiper switch removal. Models less tilt column

Fig. 5   W/S wiper switch removal. Models with tilt column

5. Disconnect wire connectors from module.
6. Remove module from instrument panel.
7. Reverse procedure to install.

1982–86 FIRENZA & SKYHAWK

1. Disconnect battery ground cable.
2. Remove six screws attaching steering column trim cover to instrument panel and two screws attaching cover to left hand instrument panel insulator, then remove trim cover.
3. Disengage retaining clip and remove pulse wiper module from cover.
4. Remove screw attaching module ground wire to instrument panel lower brace, then disconnect wire connector and remove module.
5. Reverse procedure to install.

REAR WINDOW DEFROSTER OR WASHER/WIPER SWITCH
REPLACE

1. Disconnect battery ground cable.
2. Remove lower trimplate and disconnect switch wiring connector.
3. Depress switch retaining tabs and remove switch from dash.
4. Reverse procedure to install.

STOPLIGHT SWITCH
ADJUST

Insert stoplight switch into tubular clip until switch body seats fully into clip. Pull brake pedal rearward against internal pedal stop. The switch will be properly positioned in the tubular clip automatically.

NOTE: Rotate switch ½ turn counterclockwise to be sure that switch does not hold brake pedal down after adjustment.

BACKUP LIGHT/NEUTRAL START SWITCH
REPLACE

NOTE: On vehicles equipped with automatic transmission, the neutral start and backup light switches are combined into one unit and must be replaced as an assembly.

Man. Trans.

1. Disconnect battery ground cable.
2. Apply parking brake and block wheels, then place gear shift lever in Neutral position.
3. Remove front ash tray, then remove two console attaching screws through ash tray opening.

Fig. 6 Compressing lock plate

4. Remove retaining screw, then remove gear shift knob.
5. On 1982–83 2000, 1982–86 Cavalier, Cimarron and 1984–86 Sunbird, proceed as follows:
   a. Remove console attaching screw located under parking brake handle.
   b. Toward rear of console, remove one screw from each side, retaining console to rear bracket.
6. On 1982–86 Firenza and Skyhawk, proceed as follows:
   a. Pull upward on front of console trim cover, then lift cover from console and disconnect wire connector.
   b. Remove three screws attaching console to front mounting bracket.
   c. Remove rear ash tray, then remove screw attaching console to rear mounting bracket.
7. On all models, remove console assembly.

NOTE: On models equipped with arm rest, it may be necessary to remove arm rest assembly to provide clearance for console removal.

8. Disconnect wire connector from backup light switch.
9. Remove retaining clip, then remove backup light switch from side of shifter.
10. Reverse procedure to install.

Auto. Trans.

1. Disconnect battery ground cable.
2. Apply parking brake and block wheels, then place gear shift lever in Neutral position.
3. Remove front ash tray, then remove two console attaching screws through ash tray opening.
4. Carefully pry button from center of shift lever knob, then remove snap ring retaining knob.
5. Pull front of console trim cover upward, then lift trim cover from console and disconnect wire connector.
6. Remove three screws attaching front of console to mounting bracket.
7. Remove rear ash tray, then remove screw attaching console to rear support.
8. Remove console assembly.

NOTE: On models equipped with arm rest, it may be necessary to remove arm rest assembly to provide clearance for console removal.

9. Disconnect wire connector from Neutral Safety/Backup light switch.
10. Remove screws attaching switch to shifter lever, then remove switch.
11. If the same switch is to be reinstalled, proceed as follows:
    a. Place shift lever in Neutral position.
    b. Position switch to shift lever and loosely install attaching screws.
    c. Rotate switch on shifter to align adjustment hole with carrier tang, then insert a 2.34 mm diameter pin into hole to a depth of 5 mm.
    d. Torque switch attaching screws to 20 inch lbs., then remove gauge pin.
12. If a new replacement switch is to be installed, proceed as follows:
    a. Position shift lever in the Neutral position.
    b. Insert switch carrier tang into hole on shift lever, then install switch and torque attaching screws to 20 inch lbs.

NOTE: Replacement switches are held in the Neutral position by an internal plastic pin.

    c. Move shift lever out of Neutral position to shear switch internal plastic pin.
13. Install console and connect battery ground cable.
14. Check to ensure that vehicle will not start in any shift lever position except Neutral and Park.

CLUTCH START SWITCH
REPLACE

1. Remove lower left hush panel.
2. Disconnect wiring connector from switch.
3. Disconnect switch link from pedal, then remove switch retaining screw and switch.
4. Reverse procedure to install.

TURN SIGNAL SWITCH
REPLACE

1. Disconnect battery ground cable.
2. Remove steering wheel as outlined under "Steering Wheel, Replace" procedure.
3. Using a suitable screwdriver, pry cover from housing.
4. Using lock plate compressing tool J-23653-4, compress lock plate and pry snap ring from groove on steering shaft, **Fig. 6.** Slowly release compressing tool, then remove tool and lock plate from shaft.
5. Slide canceling cam and bearing preload spring from steering shaft.
6. Remove turn signal (multi-function) lever.
7. Remove hazard warning knob retaining screw, button, spring and knob.
8. Remove actuator arm screw and actuator arm.
9. Remove switch retaining screws and

pull switch upward from column, guiding wire harness through column.
10. Reverse procedure to install.

STEERING WHEEL
REPLACE

1. Disconnect battery ground cable.
2. Remove steering wheel center pad.
3. Remove steering wheel retaining nut and retainer.
4. Scribe alignment marks on steering wheel and shaft to aid installation.
5. Using tool J-1859-03 or equivalent, remove steering wheel from shaft.
6. Reverse procedure to install.

INSTRUMENT CLUSTER
REPLACE

1982–83 2000, 1982–86 CAVALIER, CIMARRON & 1984–86 SUNBIRD

1. Disconnect battery ground cable.
2. Remove six screws attaching instrument panel trimplate to instrument panel.
3. Pull top of trimplate outward and remove trimplate from instrument panel.
4. Remove four screws securing instrument cluster to instrument panel, **Fig. 7.**
5. Remove screws attaching steering column cover to instrument panel, then the lower column cover.
6. Remove two steering column retaining bolts and lower steering column to floor.
7. Pull instrument cluster out slightly and disconnect speedometer cable.
8. On automatic transmission equipped vehicles, disconnect vehicle speed sensor (VSS) connector from rear of cluster.
9. Remove cluster and disconnect instrument panel harness connector from printed circuit located at rear of cluster.
10. Reverse procedure to install.

1982–85 FIRENZA & SKYHAWK

1. Disconnect battery ground cable.
2. Remove six screws attaching steering column trim cover to instrument panel and two screws attaching trim cover to left hand instrument panel trim cover, then remove trim cover.
3. Remove screw attaching right end of left hand trim cover to instrument panel, then pull trim cover rearward to disengage retaining clips and remove cover.
4. Remove screw attaching left end of right hand trim cover to instrument panel, then remove two screws from under center trim cover and four screws from front of glove compartment. Pull right hand trim cover rearward to disengage retaining clips, then

Fig. 7 Instrument cluster. 1982–83 2000, 1982–86 Cavalier, Cimarron & 1984–86 Sunbird

1. INSTRUMENT PANEL   3. CLUSTER HOUSING   5. I. P. HARNESS   7. L. H. CLUSTER LEAD
2. CLUSTER CARRIER   4. SCREW   6. RETAINER   8. R. H. CLUSTER LEAD

Fig. 8 Instrument cluster. 1982–86 Firenza & Skyhawk

disconnect wire connectors and remove trim cover.
5. Remove seven screws attaching cluster trim cover to instrument cluster pad, then remove trim cover.
6. Remove five screws attaching bezel and lens to instrument cluster carrier, then remove bezel and lens.
7. Loosen two upper steering column mounting bolts, then lower steering column slightly to provide clearance for cluster removal.
8. Remove four screws attaching cluster housing to cluster carrier, then pull housing slightly outward and disconnect speedometer cable and remove cluster housing, **Fig. 8.**
9. Reverse procedure to install.

HEADLIGHT SWITCH
REPLACE

1982–83 2000, 1982–86 CAVALIER, CIMARRON & 1984–86 SUNBIRD

1. Disconnect battery ground cable.
2. Remove headlight switch knob by pulling knob to full "ON" position, depressing retaining clip behind knob and pulling knob from shaft.
3. Gently pry left hand side trimplate out of instrument panel.
4. Remove switch retaining nut, rotate and tilt switch forward and pull switch from instrument panel.

5. Disconnect wiring connector and remove switch.
6. Reverse procedure to install.

1982–86 FIRENZA & SKYHAWK

1. Disconnect battery ground cable.
2. Remove six screws attaching steering column lower cover to instrument panel, then remove lower cover.
3. Remove one screw attaching right end of left hand trim cover to instrument panel, then pull cover rearward to detach retaining clips.
4. Remove four screws attaching headlamp switch to instrument panel, then pull switch rearward and disconnect wire connector.
5. Reverse procedure to install.

RADIO
REPLACE

1982–83 2000, 1982–86 CAVALIER, CIMARRON & 1984–86 SUNBIRD

1. Disconnect battery ground cable.
2. Loosen six instrument panel trimplate to instrument panel attaching screws and remove trimplate.

NOTE: Determine whether right side of radio is retained with nut or rubber stud.

1	HEATER CASE AIR INLET ASM.
2	STUD DASH PANEL
3	LOCATING STUDS DASH PANEL
4	HEATER CORE
5	HEATER MODULE ASM.
6	MODULE COVER

Fig. 9 Heater core & blower motor. (Typical) Models less A/C

3. On vehicles equipped with radio side retainer nut:
   a. Without A/C, remove right lower hush panel then loosen side retainer nut. Disconnect wire and antenna connections and remove radio from instrument panel.
   b. With A/C, remove right lower hush panel, A/C duct and A/C control head, then loosen side retainer nut. Disconnect wiring and antenna connections and remove radio from instrument panel.
4. On vehicles equipped with radio side retainer rubber stud, remove two radio bracket to instrument panel attaching screws, then pull radio forward and disconnect wiring and antenna connections. Remove radio from instrument panel.
5. Reverse procedures to install.

1982–86 FIRENZA & SKYHAWK

1. Disconnect battery ground cable.
2. Remove six screws attaching steering column trim cover to instrument panel, then lower trim cover.
3. Remove screw attaching left end of right hand trim cover to instrument panel.
4. Remove two screws from under center trim cover and four screws from front of glove compartment, then pull trim cover rearward to disengage retaining clips and disconnect wire connectors.
5. Remove four screws attaching upper and lower radio mounting brackets to instrument panel.
6. Pull radio out just enough to disconnect wire connector and antenna lead, then remove radio.
7. Reverse procedure to install.

W/S WIPER MOTOR
REPLACE

1. Disconnect battery ground cable.

2. Remove wiper arms from transmission spindle shafts.
3. Remove shroud top vent grille panel and screen.
4. Loosen, but do not remove, transmission drive link to motor crank arm attaching nuts, then pull drive link out of motor crank arm.
5. Disconnect wiper motor electrical connections and remove wiper motor attaching bolts.
6. Rotate wiper motor upward and outward, and remove from vehicle.
7. Reverse procedure to install.

W/S WIPER TRANSMISSION ASSEMBLY
REPLACE

1. Remove wiper arms from transmission spindle shafts.
2. Remove shroud top vent grille panel and screen.
3. Loosen, but do not remove, transmission drive link to motor crank arm attaching nuts then pull drive link from motor crankarm.
4. Remove transmission to cowl panel attaching screws and the transmission assembly.
5. Reverse procedure to install.

BLOWER MOTOR
REPLACE

1. Disconnect battery ground cable.
2. Disconnect blower motor electrical connections.
3. Remove plastic water shield from right side of cowl.
4. Remove blower motor retaining screws and blower motor.
5. Reverse procedure to install.

HEATER CORE
REPLACE

LESS AIR CONDITIONING

1. Disconnect battery ground cable and drain cooling system.
2. Disconnect heater hoses from heater core.
3. Remove heater outlet deflector.
4. Remove heater core module cover retaining screws and module cover, **Fig. 9.**
5. Remove heater core retaining straps and heater core.
6. Reverse procedure to install.

WITH AIR CONDITIONING

1. Disconnect battery ground cable and drain cooling system.
2. Raise and support vehicle and disconnect drain tube from heater and evaporator assembly.
3. Lower vehicle and remove right and left hush panels, steering column trim cover and glovebox.
4. Remove heater duct retaining screw and heater duct.
5. Remove heater core cover attaching screws, then gently pull cover rearward and out of vehicle, **Fig. 10.**

CAUTION: When removing heater core assembly, pull assembly straight toward interior of vehicle until plastic drain tube clears cowl. If assembly is tilted in any direction before tube clears cowl, the drain tube may break.

---

6. Remove heater core retaining clamps and heater core from case.
7. Reverse procedure to install.

CRUISE CONTROL
RELEASE SWITCHES

Automatic Transmission
Both the electrical and vacuum release switches are located at the brake pedal. To adjust, depress brake pedal and insert switch fully into tubular clip. Pull pedal rearward until clicking sounds are no longer audible. The switch is now automatically adjusted.

Manual Transmission
On manual transmission equipped vehicles, the electrical release switch is located at the clutch pedal, while the vacuum release switch is found at the brake pedal. Adjustment procedures for these switches are the same as for those under automatic transmission equipped vehicles.

SERVO, ADJUST
With engine off and carburetor in slow

Fig. 10 Heater core & blower motor. (Typical) Models with A/C

Legend in figure:
1 HEATER & EVAPORATOR
2 DRAIN TUBE
3 BLOWER ASSEMBLY

NOTICE: WHEN REMOVING THE HEATER & EVAPORATOR ASSEMBLY, PULL ASSEMBLY STRAIGHT TOWARD INTERIOR OF CAR UNTIL PLASTIC DRAIN TUBE CLEARS COWL. IF ASSEMBLY IS TILTED IN ANY DIRECTION BEFORE THE TUBE CLEARS THE COWL, THE TUBE MAY BREAK.

Fig. 11 Aspirated assisted vacuum system schematic

idle position, connect cable swivel to third ball on servo chain. Adjust cable nuts until chain has a slight amount of slack, then tighten lock nut securely.

CRUISE SPEED, ADJUST

1982–83
The cruise speed adjustment can be set as follows:
1. If cruise speed is lower than engagement speed, loosen orifice tube locknut and turn orifice tube counterclockwise.
2. If cruise speed is higher than engagement speed, loosen orifice tube locknut and turn orifice tube clockwise.

NOTE: Each ¼ turn of orifice tube will change cruise speed approximately one mile per hour. Tighten locknut after adjustment is completed.

1984–86
On these models, the cruise speed cannot be adjusted. If cruise speed is lower or higher than engagement speed, the cruise control module should be replaced.

ASPIRATOR ASSISTED VACUUM SYSTEM

The aspirator assisted vacuum system supplements engine vacuum when engine vacuum is low. The system, **Fig. 11**, consists of an aspirator, 3-port check valve, 2-port check valve and related components such as the air pump and air management valve. The air for the aspirator is tapped off the air line that connects the air pump to the air management valve. Aspirator vacuum and manifold vacuum (after passing through the 2-port check valve) supply the two upper ports of the 3-port check valve. The lower of the 3-port check valve supplies air to the cruise control transducer. The aspirator assisted vacuum system operates as follows:

1. Under normal vacuum conditions, air is bled into the system from the transducer resume valve to the lower "T" of the 3-port check valve, then to the 2-port check valve and finally into the intake manifold, **Fig. 11**.
2. Also during normal operation, as the air pump is pumping air into the air management valve, a small amount of air is diverted through the aspirator to the atmosphere. As air passes through the aspirator, a venturi action inside the aspirator assembly develops a vacuum. This vacuum is used to provide the vacuum assist needed under high cruise conditions.
3. Should manifold vacuum fall below aspirator vacuum, the 2-port check valve is designed to close while the 3-port check valve is designed to open. Opening of the 3-port check valve exposes the higher vacuum at the aspirator, providing the needed vacuum for proper cruise operation.

To check the aspirator system for correct operation, note the following information:
1. Ensure all hoses and connections are secure and check valves are correctly installed.

NOTE: The check valves are arrowhead shaped in the direction of air flow.

2. Connect a suitable vacuum gauge to the aspirator output at point A, **Fig. 11**.
3. Start and operate engine at 2500 RPM.

NOTE: Engine should be thoroughly warmed up to ensure that the computer command control system (CCC) is operating in closed loop.

4. Check vacuum gauge. A minimum of 6 inches should be indicated. If vacuum reading is not within specified amount, clean aspirator using a suitable solvent and recheck. Also check air pump for air output. If there is no air output from the air pump, check air pump for damage. If air pump is not damaged, proceed to step a.
   a. Disconnect vacuum gauge at port A, **Fig. 11**. Disconnect and plug 2-port check valve at port B. Blow air into the resume valve hose at port C. Air should flow through and exit at port A.
   b. Remove plug from 2-port check valve at port B and plug hose at port A. Blow air into cruise resume valve at port C. Air should flow and exit at port B.

NOTE: Steps a & b determine if the hoses and check valves are operating in one direction. To check for operation in the opposite direction, proceed to step c.

   c. Blow air into hose at port A while port B is plugged, then into port B while hose at port A is plugged.

NOTE: No air should exist at port C in either case.

4-110 Overhead Cam Engine Section

Fig. 1 Front engine mounts. 1982—84

Fig. 2 Right hand front engine mount brackets. 1982—84

1—BOLT/SCREW 54 N·m (40 LB.FT.)
2—SIDE FRAME
3—BRACKET
4—MOUNT ASM.
5—NUT

Fig. 3 Front engine mounts. 1985—86

ENGINE MOUNTS
REPLACE

FRONT ENGINE MOUNT

1982—84
1. Disconnect battery ground cable.
2. Remove engine mount nuts, then raise and support vehicle.
3. Remove inner fender shield attaching bolts, then the shield.
4. Support engine and remove and discard engine mount attaching bolts, **Figs. 1 and 2.**
5. Remove engine mount from vehicle.

CAUTION: Whenever engine mount is removed, alignment bolt M6X1X65 must be used during installation to prevent power train misalignment.

6. Reverse procedure to install, using new engine mount bolts. Remove alignment bolt.

NOTE: If excessive effort is required to remove alignment bolt, loosen transaxle adjusting bolts to align powertrain components.

1985—86
1. Disconnect battery ground cable.
2. Support engine, then remove two mount to bracket attaching bolts, **Fig. 3.**
3. Remove two top mount attaching bolts, then raise and suppot vehicle.
4. Remove lower mount attaching bolt, then the engine mount.
5. Reverse procedure to install.

REAR ENGINE MOUNT

1982—84
1. Disconnect battery ground cable.
2. Raise and support vehicle.
3. If equipped with manual transaxle, remove oil filter.
4. Support engine and remove engine mount nuts, **Fig. 4.**
5. Remove and discard engine mount to engine attaching bolts.
6. Remove engine mount from vehicle.
7. Reverse procedure to install.

1985—86
1. Disconnect battery ground cable.
2. Support engine, then remove two mount to bracket attaching bolts, **Fig. 5.**
3. Raise and support vehicle.
4. Remove two lower mount attaching nuts and reinforcement, then the engine mount.
5. Reverse procedure to install.

ENGINE
REPLACE

1. Disconnect battery ground cable, then drain cooling system.

Disassembled view of engine

Fig. 4 Right hand rear engine mount brackets. 1982–84

2. Remove air cleaner, then disconnect engine electrical harness connector at bulkhead and electrical connector at brake cylinder.
3. Disconnect throttle cable from bracket and throttle body assembly.
4. Disconnect vacuum hoses from throttle body assembly, then disconnect power steering high pressure hose at cut-off switch.
5. Disconnect vacuum hoses at map sensor and canister, then disconnect air conditioning relay cluster switches.
6. Disconnect power steering return hose at power steering pump.
7. Disconnect ECM electrical connectors, then pull harness through bulkhead and position harness over engine.
8. Disconnect upper and lower radiator hoses from engine, then disconnect wire connector at temperature switch on thermostat housing.
9. Disconnect transmission shift cable at transmission, then raise and support

vehicle.
10. Disconnect speedometer cable at transmission and bracket.
11. Disconnect exhaust pipe at exhaust manifold and remove exhaust pipe from converter.
12. Remove heater hoses from heater core, fuel lines at flex hoses and transmission cooler lines at flex hoses.
13. Remove front wheels, right hand spoiler section and splash shield.
14. Remove and support right and left brake calipers.
15. Using tool No. J-24319-1 or equivalent, remove right and left tie rod ends.
16. Disconnect electrical connectors at A/C compressor, then remove A/C compressor and mounting brackets. Using a piece of wire, support compressor in wheel opening.
17. Remove six front suspension support attachment bolts.
18. Lower vehicle and support front end by placing jack stands under core support.
19. Using a suitable hoist, position front post of hoist to rear of cowl.
20. Using a suitable piece of wood (4 inch × 4 inch × 6′), position onto front post of hoist.
21. Raise vehicle slightly and remove jack stands from front end.
22. Position a suitable dolly under engine and transaxle assembly.
23. Position three pieces of wood (4 inch × 4 inch × 12 inch) under engine and transaxle assembly only, allowing support rails to hang free.
24. Slightly lower vehicle onto dolly and remove two rear transaxle mount attaching bolts.
25. Remove three left front engine mount attaching bolts and two engine support to body attaching bolts behind right hand inner axle U-joint.
26. Remove one bolt and nut from right hand chassis side rail to engine mount bracket.
27. Remove six strut attaching nuts, then raise vehicle, allowing engine, transaxle and suspension assemblies to rest onto dolly.
28. Remove engine and transaxle as an assembly.
29. Position engine and transaxle assembly into vehicle.
30. Loosely install transaxle and left front mounts to side rail bolts.
31. To prevent powertrain misalignment, install bolt No. M6X1X65 into left front mount, on 1982–84 models.
32. Torque transaxle mount bolts to 40 ft. lbs. and left front mount bolts to 18 ft. lbs. on 1982–84 models or 40 ft. lbs. on 1985–86 models.
33. Install right rear mount to body bolts and torque to approximately 38 ft. lbs.
34. Position a suitable jack under control arms and raise struts into position, then install retaining nuts.
35. Raise vehicle, then using suitable lifting equipment, raise control arms and install tie rod ends.
36. Reverse procedure to complete installation.

1—BOLT/SCREW 54 N·m (40 LB.FT.)

2—R.H. RAIL

3—MOUNT ASM.

4—COWL ASM.

5—REINFORCEMENT

6—NUT 24 N·m (18 LB.FT.)

7—NUT 54 N·m (40 LB. FT.)

8—BRACKET ASM.

9—GENERATOR BRACKET

10—STUD (LA5)

11—BOLT (LH8)

12—BRACE

Fig. 5 Rear engine mounts. 1985–86

Fig. 6 Cylinder head & camshaft carrier bolt loosening sequence

Fig. 7 Cylinder head & camshaft carrier bolt tightening sequence

Fig. 8 Using tool No. 33302 to compress valve spring

CYLINDER HEAD
REPLACE

1. Disconnect battery ground cable, remove air cleaner and drain cooling system.
2. Remove alternator and pivot bracket from camshaft carrier housing.
3. Remove power steering pump and bracket and position aside.
4. Disconnect ignition coil electrical connectors, then remove coil.
5. Disconnect spark plug wires from distributor cap.
6. Remove throttle cable from bracket on intake manifold.
7. Disconnect accelerator cable, downshift cable and throttle valve cable from throttle body assembly.
8. Disconnect ECM connectors from throttle body assembly.
9. Disconnect vacuum brake hose from filter, then disconnect inlet and return fuel lines from flex joints.
10. Remove water pump bypass hose from intake manifold and water pump.
11. Disconnect ECM harness connectors and heater hose from intake manifold.
12. Disconnect exhaust pipe from exhaust manifold and breather hose from camshaft carrier.
13. Disconnect upper radiator hose, then disconnect engine electrical harness and wires from thermostat housing.
14. Remove timing cover and timing probe holder.
15. Loosen water pump bolts and remove timing belt.
16. Loosen camshaft carrier and cylinder head bolts a little at a time in sequence shown in **Fig. 6.**

NOTE: Camshaft carrier and cylinder head bolts should only be removed when engine is cold.

17. Remove camshaft carrier assembly.
18. Remove cylinder head, intake manifold and exhaust manifold as an assembly.
19. Remove all carbon deposits from combustion chambers and valve ports. Check cylinder head for cracks in the exhaust ports and combustion chambers. Remove water jacket plugs and clean, if necessary.
20. Reverse procedure to install. Torque cylinder head bolts a little at a time in sequence shown in **Fig. 7** to 18 ft. lbs. Tighten each bolt in the proper se-

quence an additional 180° in 60° increments.
21. After installation is completed (with the exception of brackets that install onto carrier), start engine and let engine idle until thermostat opens. Turn engine off and torque all bolts an additional 30 to 50° in the proper sequence.

ROCKER ARM & HYDRAULIC VALVE LASH COMPENSATORS
REPLACE

1. Disconnect battery ground cable.
2. Remove camshaft carrier cover.
3. Using tool No. J-33302 or equivalent, **Fig. 8,** compress valve springs and remove rocker arms. Place rocker arms in a suitable rack so they can be installed in the same location.
4. Remove hydraulic lash compensators and place them in a rack so they can be installed in the same location.
5. Reverse procedure to install.

NOTE: No adjustment of valve lash is required. The preload of the hydraulic valve lash compensator is automatic and servicing of the compensator requires only care and cleanliness be exercised in the handling of these components.

VALVE SPRING & VALVE STEM OIL SEAL
REPLACE

REMOVAL

1. Disconnect battery ground cable.
2. Remove rocker arms and spark plugs.
3. Install air line adapter tool No. J-23590 or equivalent, into spark plug port and apply compressed air to hold valves in place.
4. Using tool No. J-33302 or equivalent, **Fig. 8,** compress valve spring and remove rocker guides, valve locks, caps and valve spring.
5. Remove valve stem oil seal.

INSTALLATION

1. Using clean engine oil, lubricate valve stem and install new valve stem oil seal over valve stem and seat onto valve guide.
2. Position valve spring and cap over valve stem. Using tool No. J-33302 or equivalent, compress valve spring and install valve locks.
3. Install rocker guides and rocker arms, then remove tool No. J-33302.
4. Remove air line adapter tool and install spark plugs.
5. Install camshaft carrier cover. Torque bolts to 5 ft. lbs.

VALVE SEAT SERVICE

Using a suitable dial indicator measure valve seat concentricity. Valve seat should be concentric to within .002 inch of total indicator reading. Ensure valve guide bores are free from carbon or dirt to allow proper seating of the pilot in the valve guide. When reconditioning the valve seats, use a 45° stone to rough the valve seat and another stone with the same angle to finish the valve seat. Narrow down the valve seats to the proper width, .051–.055 inch for intake valves and .067–.071 for exhaust valves.

VALVE GUIDES

Valve guides are an integral part of the cylinder head. If valve stem to guide clearance is excessive, the guide should be reamed to the next oversize and the appropriate oversize valve installed. Valves are available in standard size and oversize of .010 inch (.25 mm).

CRANKSHAFT PULLEY
REMOVAL

1. Disconnect battery ground cable.
2. Loosen alternator and power steering bracket bolt, then remove drive belt.
3. Remove inner fender splash shield, then remove crankshaft pulley bolts and pulley.

Fig. 9 Timing belt tension adjustment

INSTALLATION

1. Position pulley onto crankshaft sprocket. Using a suitable sealer, coat threads of pulley bolts and install onto pulley. Torque bolts to 15 ft. lbs.
2. Install splash shield.
3. Install alternator and power steering belt, then connect battery ground cable.

TIMING BELT
REPLACE

1. Disconnect battery ground cable.
2. Remove timing belt front cover, then rotate crankshaft until timing mark on crankshaft pulley aligns with 10° BTDC mark on indicator tab. The mark on the camshaft sprocket must align with mark on camshaft carrier.
3. Remove crankshaft pulley as previously described.
4. Remove timing probe holder.
5. Loosen water pump bolts, then rotate water pump to loosen and remove timing belt.
6. Reverse procedure to install. Note the following information:
   a. Ensure mark on camshaft sprocket aligns with mark on camshaft carrier. The timing mark on the crankshaft pulley should align with the 10° BTDC mark on the indicator tab.
   b. Using tool No. J-33039 or equivalent, **Fig. 9,** rotate water pump clockwise until all slack is removed from timing belt. Install tool No. J-26486 or equivalent, **Fig. 9,** between water pump and camshaft sprockets so pointer is midway between sprockets.
7. To adjust timing belt tension, refer to **Fig. 9** and note the following information:

Belt Size . . . . 748 inch
Initial Adjustment
New Belt . . . . 74 ft. lbs.
Used Belt . . . . 59 ft. lbs.

Checking
New Belt . . . . 59–88 ft. lbs.
Used Belt . . . . 44–74 ft. lbs.

NOTE: These values are for a cold engine.

   a. If timing belt tension is incorrect, loosen and using tool No. J-33039 or equivalent, rotate water pump until proper tension is obtained.
   b. Torque water pump bolts to 19 ft. lbs. Ensure water pump does not shift when torquing bolts.

TIMING BELT REAR COVER
REPLACE

1. Disconnect battery ground cable.
2. Remove timing belt as described under "TIMING BELT, REPLACE".
3. Remove timing belt rear cover bolts and cover.
4. Reverse procedure to install. Torque cover bolts to 19 ft. lbs.

CAMSHAFT CARRIER COVER
REPLACE

1. Remove air cleaner and disconnect breather hoses.
2. Remove cover bolts and cover.
3. Reverse procedure to install. Torque camshaft carrier cover bolts to 5 ft. lbs.

CAMSHAFT SPROCKET
REPLACE

1. Disconnect battery ground cable.
2. Remove timing belt front cover and align mark on camshaft sprocket with mark on camshaft carrier cover.
3. Remove timing probe holder.
4. Loosen water pump bolts and remove timing belt from camshaft sprocket.
5. Remove camshaft carrier cover.
6. Using a suitable tool, secure camshaft and remove camshaft sprocket bolt, washer and sprocket, **Fig. 10.**
7. Reverse procedure to install. Torque camshaft sprocket bolt to 34 ft. lbs, timing probe holder to 19 ft. lbs and camshaft carrier cover bolts to 5 ft. lbs.

CAMSHAFT
REMOVAL

1. Disconnect battery ground cable.
2. Remove camshaft carrier cover.
3. Using tool No. J-33302 or equivalent, **Fig. 8,** compress valve springs and remove rocker arms.
4. Remove timing belt front cover and timing belt as described under "TIMING BELT, REPLACE".

Fig. 10 Camshaft sprocket removal

5. Remove camshaft sprocket as described under "CAMSHAFT SPROCKET, REPLACE".
6. Disconnect spark plug wires from spark plugs, then remove distributor from engine.
7. Remove camshaft thrust plate from rear of camshaft carrier.
8. Slide camshaft rearward and remove camshaft from carrier.

INSTALLATION

1. Using tool No. J-33085 or equivalent, install new front oil seal onto camshaft carrier.
2. Position camshaft into carrier.

NOTE: Ensure not to damage front oil seal when installing camshaft.

3. Install camshaft thrust plate and bolts. Torque bolts to 70 inch lbs.
4. Check camshaft end play. End play should be within .016 to .064 inch.
5. Install distributor, camshaft sprocket, timing belt and timing belt front cover.
6. Using tool No. J-33302 or equivalent, **Fig. 8,** compress valve springs and install rocker arms.
7. Install camshaft carrier cover. Torque bolts to 5 ft. lbs.

CRANKSHAFT SPROCKET
REPLACE

1. Disconnect battery ground cable.
2. Remove timing belt as described under "TIMING BELT, REPLACE".
3. Remove crankshaft sprocket bolt, washer and sprocket.
4. Reverse procedure to install. Refer to step 7 under "TIMING BELT, REPLACE" and adjust belt tension. Torque crankshaft sprocket bolt to 115 ft. lbs. on 1982–84 models or 107 ft. lbs. on 1985–86 models.

CRANKSHAFT FRONT OIL SEAL
REPLACE

1. Disconnect battery ground cable.

Fig. 11 Crankshaft front oil seal installation

2. Remove crankshaft sprocket as described under "CRANKSHAFT SPROCKET, REPLACE".
3. Remove key and rear thrust washer from end of crankshaft.
4. Using a suitable tool, remove crankshaft front oil seal.
5. During installation of crankshaft front oil seal, position tool No. J-33083 or equivalent, **Fig. 11,** onto crankshaft. Lubricate front oil seal lip and install onto crankshaft.
6. Reverse procedure to complete installation.

PISTON & ROD ASSEMBLE

Assemble piston to rod, with arrow on piston facing toward front of engine and numbered side toward intake manifold side of engine, **Fig. 12.** Upon installation, measure connecting rod side clearance using a suitable feeler gauge. Side clearance should be .0027 to .0095 inch.

PISTONS, PINS & RINGS

Pistons and rings are available in standard size and oversize of .020 inch (.5 mm). Piston pins are available in standard size only.

MAIN & ROD BEARINGS

Main and rod bearings are available in standard sizes and undersizes of .010 inch (.25 mm) and .020 inch (.5 mm).

REAR MAIN BEARING OIL SEAL
REPLACE

1. Remove engine from vehicle as described under "ENGINE, REPLACE".
2. On vehicles equipped with automatic transaxle, remove flywheel dust cover and flex plate to torque converter bolts.
3. Remove bell housing bolts and separate engine from transaxle assembly.
4. On vehicles equipped with automatic transaxle, remove flex plate.
5. On vehicles equipped with manual

Fig. 12 Piston & rod assembly

transaxle, remove pressure plate, clutch disc and flywheel.
6. Using a suitable tool, remove rear main bearing oil seal.
7. Reverse procedure to install. During installation of seal, position seal over seal pilot tool No. J-33004 or equivalent, **Fig. 13.** Using clean engine oil, lubricate new rear oil seal and position onto crankshaft by turning starter bolts on tool No. J-33004 in rotational sequence until rear oil seal bottoms in engine block.

OIL PAN
REPLACE

1. Disconnect battery ground cable.
2. Raise and support vehicle.
3. Remove right front wheel and right hand splash shield.
4. Remove lower A/C bracket strut rod bolt and swing aside.
5. Remove flywheel dust cover.
6. Disconnect exhaust pipe from exhaust manifold.
7. Drain engine oil, remove oil pan bolts and oil pan.
8. Reverse procedure to install. Using a suitable sealer, coat threads of oil pan bolts. Torque bolts to 4 ft. lbs.

OIL PUMP SCREEN & PICK-UP TUBE
REPLACE

1. Disconnect battery ground cable.
2. Remove oil pan as described under "OIL PAN, REPLACE".
3. Remove pick-up tube support bolts, pick-up tube to oil pump bolts, pick-up tube and "O" ring.

Fig. 13 Rear main bearing oil seal installation

4. Reverse procedure to install. Torque pick-up tube to oil pump bolts to 5 ft. lbs. Torque pick-up tube support bolts to 5 ft. lbs.

OIL PUMP
REMOVAL

1. Disconnect battery ground cable.
2. Remove crankshaft sprocket and timing belt rear cover.
3. Disconnect engine oil pressure switch electrical connector from the switch.
4. Remove oil pan and oil filter.
5. Remove pick-up tube to engine block bolts, pick-up tube and oil pump.

DISASSEMBLE

1. Remove five screws and rear cover from oil pump, **Fig. 14.**
2. Remove gears, plug, pressure regulator valve plunger and spring.
3. If necessary, remove pick-up tube and "O" ring from oil pump body.

INSPECTION

NOTE: After disassembling the oil pump, thoroughly clean all oil pump components and check them for excessive wear and damage.

1. Using a suitable straight edge and feeler gauge, **Fig. 15,** check oil pump clearances.
2. Check clearances for the following oil pump components:
   a. Clearance between idler gear and oil pump body should be .004–.007 inch.
   b. Clearance between drive gear and oil pump body should be .014–.018 inch.
   c. Clearance between gears and oil pump cover should be .002–.004 inch.
3. If clearances obtained are not within specified limits, replace worn or damaged oil pump components.

ASSEMBLE

1. Install valve plunger and spring.
2. Using a suitable sealer, coat threads of pressure regulator valve plunger plug and install. Torque plug to 15 ft. lbs.
3. Install oil pump gears into oil pump body.

Engine oiling system. 4-110 overhead cam engine

Fig. 14 Disassembled view of oil pump

Fig. 15 Checking drive gear to oil pump housing clearance

INSTALLATION

1. Install gasket and oil pump onto engine. Torque oil pump bolts to 5 ft. lbs.
2. Install pick-up tube and bolts. Torque bolts to 5 ft. lbs.
3. Install oil pan and oil filter.
4. Connect engine oil pressure switch electrical connector to switch.
5. Install timing belt rear covers and crankshaft sprocket.

WATER PUMP
REPLACE

1. Drain cooling system, then remove timing belt. Refer to "Timing Belt, Replace" for procedure.
2. Remove timing belt rear protective covers.
3. Remove lower radiator hose from water pump.
4. Remove water pump attaching bolts then the water pump and sealing ring.
5. Clean engine block and water pump sealing surfaces, then apply a ³⁄₃₂ inch of RTV sealant to sealing surfaces. While RTV sealant is still wet, install water pump. Tighten attaching bolts finger tight.
6. Install lower radiator hose on water pump, then timing belt rear protective covers.
7. Install timing belt. Refer to "Timing Belt, Replace" for procedure.

ELECTRIC FUEL PUMP
REPLACE

1. Depressurize fuel system as follows:
   a. Remove fuel pump fuse from fuse panel.
   b. Start engine and operate until fuel supply remaining in fuel lines is consumed. Engage starter for approximately 3 seconds to ensure fuel pressure has been relieved.
   c. With ignition switch in the "OFF" position, install fuel pump fuse.

NOTE: Unless this procedure is followed before servicing fuel system, fuel spray could occur.

2. Disconnect battery ground cable.
3. Raise and support vehicle.
4. Remove fuel tank.
5. Remove fuel meter pump assembly by turning cam lock ring counterclockwise.
6. Remove fuel meter pump assembly from fuel tank and fuel pump from fuel meter.
7. Pull fuel pump upward into fuel hose while pulling outward away from bottom support.

NOTE: Do not damage rubber insulator and strainer during fuel pump removal.

8. After fuel pump assembly is clear of bottom support, pull pump assembly out of rubber connector and from vehicle.
9. Reverse procedure to install.

TURBOCHARGER

The turbocharger is used to increase power on a demand basis. As engine load increases and the throttle is opened, more air/fuel mixture is drawn into the combustion chambers. As this increased volume is burned, a larger volume of high energy exhaust gasses enters the engine exhaust system and is directed through the turbocharger turbine housing. Some of the exhaust gas energy is used to increase the speed of the turbine wheel which is connected to the compressor wheel. The increased speed of the compressor wheel compresses the air/fuel mixture and delivers it to the intake manifold. The high pressure in the intake manifold allows a denser charge to enter the combustion chambers, in turn developing more engine power during the combustion cycle. The intake manifold pressure (boost) is controlled to a maximum value by an exhaust gas bypass valve (wastegate). The wastegate allows a portion of the exhaust gas to bypass the turbine wheel, thereby not increasing turbine speed. The wastegate is operated by a spring-loaded diaphragm device sensing the pressure differential across the compressor. When intake manifold pressure reaches a predetermined value above ambient pressure, the wastegate begins to bypass the exhaust gas.

4-112 & 121 Overhead Valve Engine Section

TRANSAXLE MOUNT

SIDE FRAME

FRT

FRT

ALIGNMENT BOLT

SIDE FRAME

ENGINE MOUNT

Fig. 1   Engine front mount

ENGINE MOUNTS
REPLACE

FRONT ENGINE MOUNT

1. Disconnect battery ground cable.
2. Remove engine mount nuts, then raise and support vehicle.
3. Remove inner fender shield attaching bolts, then the shield.
4. Support engine and remove and discard engine mount attaching bolts, **Fig. 1.**
5. Remove engine mount from vehicle.

CAUTION: Whenever engine mount is removed, alignment bolt M6.0 x 1 x 65 must be used during installation to prevent power train misalignment.

6. Reverse procedure to install, using new engine mount bolts. Remove alignment bolt and torque engine mount to side frame bolts to 35–45 ft. lbs. Torque all other nuts and bolts to 25–35 ft. lbs.

NOTE: If excessive effort is required to remove alignment bolt, loosen transaxle adjusting bolts to align powertrain components.

REAR ENGINE MOUNT

1. Disconnect battery ground cable.
2. Raise and support vehicle.
3. If equipped with manual transaxle, remove oil filter.
4. Support engine and remove engine mount nuts, **Fig. 2.**

5. Remove and discard engine mount to engine attaching bolts.
6. Remove engine mount from vehicle.
7. Reverse procedure to install. Check oil level and torque nuts to 15–20 ft. lbs. and bolts to 25–35 ft. lbs.

ENGINE
REPLACE

1. Disconnect battery and drain cooling system.
2. Remove air cleaner.
3. Disconnect accelerator and, if so equipped, TV cables.
4. Disconnect ECM wiring on engine.
5. Disconnect any vacuum hoses interfering with engine removal.
6. Disconnect radiator and heater hoses at engine.
7. Remove exhaust heat shield, if equipped.
8. On vehicles equipped with A/C, remove adjustment bolt at engine mount.
9. On all vehicles, disconnect engine wiring harness at firewall.

P/S BRACKET

Fig. 2   Engine rear mount

10. Remove windshield washer reservoir.
11. Remove alternator drive belt.
12. Remove power steering belt.
13. Disconnect fuel lines.
14. Raise and support vehicle.
15. On vehicles equipped with A/C, remove A/C brace.
16. On all vehicles, remove inner fender splash shield.

Cylinder head assembly & related components

1. Distributor Assembly
2. Oil Filter
3. Fuel Pump
4. Dipstick
5. Cam Sprocket
6. Thrust Plate
7. Camshaft and Bearings
8. Cylinder Block
9. Engine Lift Hook
10. Water Pump Pulley
11. Water Pump
12. Water Inlet
13. Dampener
14. Tensioner
15. Piston Rings
16. Piston
17. Starter
18. Accessory Drive Pulley
19. Hub
20. Seal

21. Front Cover
22. Timing Chain
23. Cranksprocket
24. Connecting Rod Bearings
25. Connecting Rod Bearing Cap
26. Main Bearings
27. Crankshaft

28. Main Thrust Bearing
29. Rope Seal
30. Main Bearing Caps
31. Flywheel and Flex Plate
32. Oil Pump
33. Oil Pan
34. Seal

Cylinder block assembly & components

FRONT OF ENGINE

CYLINDER HEAD BOLT TIGHTENING SEQUENCE

Fig. 3   Cylinder head bolt tightening sequence

PULLEY

TIMING NOTCH

NOTE: PULLEY CONTAINS TWO SETS OF NOTCHES 180° APART. USE NOTCH CUT ACROSS ENTIRE LENGTH OF PULLEY FOR #1 TDC.

Fig. 4   Aligning crankshaft pulley timing marks

17. On vehicles equipped with A/C, remove A/C compressor.
18. Remove flywheel splash shield and disconnect starter wiring.
19. Disconnect front starter brace and remove starter.
20. On vehicles with automatic transaxles, remove torque converter bolts.
21. Remove crankshaft pulley using tool J-24420 or equivalent.
22. Remove oil filter.
23. Disconnect engine to transmission bracket and right rear engine mount.
24. Disconnect exhaust at manifold and center hanger. Loosen muffler hanger.
25. On vehicles with automatic transaxles, disconnect TV and shift cable bracket.
26. Remove 2 lower bellhousing bolts.
27. Lower vehicle.
28. Remove right front engine mount nuts.
29. Remove alternator and adjusting bracket.
30. Disconnect master cylinder and position aside.
31. Attach suitable lifting device to engine.
32. Remove right front engine mount bracket.
33. Remove upper bellhousing bolts.
34. Lift engine and remove power steering pump, if so equipped.
35. Remove engine.
36. Install engine mount alignment bolt M6.0 x 1 x 65, **Fig. 1,** to ensure proper powertrain alignment.
37. Lower engine into vehicle.
38. Install upper bellhousing bolts and left front engine mount nuts.
39. Reverse removal procedure to install. On 1982-83 models, once engine is installed, check alignment bolt. If excessive effort is required to remove bolt, loosen transaxle mount adjusting bolts and realign powertrain.

CYLINDER HEAD
REPLACE

NOTE: The cylinder head, carburetor or TBI (Throttle Body Injection) unit and the intake and exhaust manifolds are removed as an assembly.

1. Disconnect battery ground cable, drain cooling system and remove air cleaner.
2. Raise and support vehicle, then remove exhaust manifold shield, if equipped.
3. Disconnect exhaust pipe at exhaust manifold and heater hose at intake manifold.
4. Lower vehicle, then remove engine lift bracket and distributor.
5. Disconnect vacuum manifold from alternator bracket.
6. Disconnect and tag all vacuum lines that will interfere with cylinder head removal, then disconnect AIR pipe at exhaust check valve.
7. Disconnect accelerator linkage at carburetor or TBI unit, then remove accel-

erator linkage bracket bolt and the bracket.
8. Disconnect all electrical wires that will interfere with cylinder head removal, then remove upper radiator hose from cylinder head.
9. Remove dipstick tube bracket bolt and the hot water tube bracket.
10. Remove idler pulley assembly and AIR/power steering belt, if equipped.
11. Remove power steering pump, if equipped, and position aside.
12. Remove AIR bracket to intake manifold bolt, if equipped.
13. On power steering equipped vehicles, remove AIR pump pulley, AIR pump through bolt and power steering pump adjusting bracket.
14. Loosen AIR bracket lower bolt and rotate bracket aside, if equipped.
15. Disconnect fuel line from carburetor or TBI unit.
16. Remove alternator and position aside. Do not remove wires.
17. Remove alternator upper support bracket and brace.
18. Remove rocker arm cover and rocker arms, then the push rods.
19. Remove cylinder head bolts and the cylinder head assembly.
20. Reverse procedure to install. Coat cylinder head and cylinder head bolts with sealer and install bolts finger tight. Torque cylinder head bolts to specification in sequence shown in **Fig. 3.**

ROCKER ARM STUDS

Rocker arm studs that have stress cracks or damaged threads can be replaced. If threads in cylinder head are damaged or stripped, the head can be retapped and a helical type insert added. When installing a new rocker arm stud, torque stud to 43–49 ft. lbs.

VALVES
ADJUST

1. Crank engine until mark on crankshaft pulley is aligned with TDC mark on timing tab. Check to ensure engine is in the No. 1 cylinder firing position by placing fingers on No. 1 cylinder rocker arms as mark on pulley comes near TDC mark on timing tab. If valves are not moving, the engine is in the No. 1 firing position. If valves move as pulley nears TDC mark on timing tab, engine is in No. 4 cylinder firing position and

Fig. 5 Valve adjustment

Fig. 8 Removing crankshaft pulley & hub

NOTE: AT TIME OF INSTALLATION, FLANGES MUST BE FREE OF OIL. A 2.0-3.0 BEAD OF SEALANT MUST BE APPLIED TO FLANGES AND SEALANT MUST BE WET TO TOUCH WHEN BOLTS ARE TORQUED.

Fig. 6 Rocker arms & rocker arm cover

1. Lifter Body	6. Push Rod Seat Retainer
2. Push Rod Seat	7. Plunger
3. Metering Valve	8. Check Ball Spring
4. Check Ball	9. Plunger Spring
5. Check Ball Retainer	

Fig. 7 Sectional view of hydraulic valve lifter

Fig. 9 Installing front cover

VALVE LIFT SPECS.

Engine	Year	Int.	Exh.
4-112 & 121	1982	.393	.393
4-121	1983–86	.393	.393

VALVE TIMING
INTAKE OPENS BEFORE TDC

Year	Engine	Degrees
1982	4-112 & 121	32

VALVE GUIDES

Valve guides are an integral part of the cylinder head and are not removable. If valve stem clearance becomes excessive, the valve guide should be reamed to the next oversize and the appropriate oversize valves installed. Valves are available in .003, .006, and .012 inch oversizes.

VALVE LIFTERS
REPLACE

SERVICE BULLETIN: Some 4-121 engines have been manufactured with 0.26mm oversize lifter bores. An oversize lifter bore can be identified by a vertical stripe of white paint on both sides of the lifter bore inside the lifter cavity. In addition, these engines can also be identified buy a .26 OS stamp on the top right front cylinder block machining pad.

1. Remove rocker arm cover attaching bolts and rocker arm cover, **Fig. 6.**
2. Loosen rocker arm stud nut and rotate rocker arm so that pushrod can be removed. Remove pushrod.

should be rotated one revolution to reach the No. 1 cylinder firing position.

NOTE: The crankshaft pulley contains two sets of marks 180° apart. Use those marks which cut across entire length of pulley to find No. 1 cylinder firing position, **Fig. 4.**

2. With engine in No. 1 cylinder firing position, adjust the following valves: Exhaust: 1, 3; Intake: 1, 2. To adjust valves, back off adjusting nut until lash is felt at push rod, then tighten adjusting nut until all lash is removed, **Fig. 5.** This can be determined by rotating the push rod while tightening the adjusting nut. When all lash has been eliminated, the push rod will no longer rotate, **Fig. 5.** Turn the adjusting nut the additional number of turns listed in the Valve Specifications Chart.
3. Crank engine one full revolution until mark on crankshaft pulley and TDC mark are again aligned. This is the No. 4 cylinder firing position. With engine in this position, the following valves can be adjusted: Exhaust 2, 4; Intake 3, 4.
4. Install rocker arm cover, then start engine and check timing and idle speed.

VALVE ARRANGEMENT
FRONT TO REAR

4-112 & 121 . . . . E-I-I-E-E-I-I-E

3. Using tool J-29834, remove valve lifter from lifter bore.
4. Coat base of new lifter, **Fig. 7,** with "Molykote", or equivalent, and install lifter into lifter bore.
5. Reverse procedure to install and adjust valves as outlined under "VALVES, ADJUST" procedure.

ENGINE FRONT COVER
REPLACE

1. Disconnect battery ground cable.
2. Remove accessory drive belts, then raise and support vehicle.
3. Remove right front wheel and tire.
4. Remove right inner fender splash shield attaching bolts and the shield.
5. Remove A/C drive belt, if equipped.
6. Remove crankshaft pulley retaining bolts and crankshaft pulley, **Fig. 8.**
7. Using tool J-24420, remove crankshaft hub from crankshaft.
8. Remove engine front cover retaining bolts and front cover.
9. Clean sealing surface of front cover and engine block. Apply a 2 mm bead of RTV sealant to front cover sealing surface.
10. Position front cover to engine block. Using centering tool J-23042, install front retaining bolts and torque bolts to 6-9 ft. lbs. Remove centering tool, **Fig. 9.**
11. Reverse procedure to install.

Fig. 11 Timing chain tensioner. 1982 4-112 & 4-121

Fig. 10 Valve timing marks

Fig. 12 Compressing timing chain tensioner spring. 1983—84 4-121

TIMING CHAIN
REPLACE

1. Remove engine front cover as previously described.
2. Place No. 1 cylinder at TDC and align timing marks on crankshaft and camshaft sprockets, **Fig. 10.**
3. On 1982 models, remove timing chain upper attaching bolts, then loosen nut as far as possible without removing. On 1983—86 models, remove timing chain tensioner as described under Timing Chain Tensioner, Replace.
4. Remove camshaft sprocket retaining bolt. Tap lower edge of sprocket with plastic mallet and remove sprocket and timing chain.
5. If crankshaft sprocket is to be replaced, remove sprocket using a suitable puller.
6. To install crankshaft sprocket, align keyway on sprocket with key on crankshaft.
7. Align timing marks, **Fig. 10,** and install timing chain on sprockets.
8. Align dowel on camshaft with dowel hole on camshaft sprocket, then install sprocket to camshaft, using retaining bolt to draw sprocket fully to camshaft. Torque bolt to 66—85 ft. lbs.
9. Lubricate timing chain with engine oil, then install timing chain tensioner.
10. Install engine front cover as outlined previously.

TIMING CHAIN TENSIONER
REPLACE

1982 4-112 & 121

1. Remove engine front cover as described under Engine Front Cover, Replace.
2. Remove attaching bolt (1), **Fig. 11,** and lower nut.

NOTE: Use a suitable tool, such as a loop of wire, to prevent nut from falling into oil pan.

3. Remove timing chain tensioner.
4. Position timing chain tensioner to engine.
5. Using a suitable tool, such as a wire loop around nut, position nut on stud.
6. Install bolt (1), **Fig. 11,** finger tight.
7. Torque nut to 15 to 22 ft. lbs. and bolt to 13 to 18 ft. lbs.

1983—84 4-121

1. Remove engine front cover as described under Engine Front Cover, Replace.
2. Remove tensioner attaching bolts, then remove tensioner.
3. Position tangs of tool No. J33875 under tensioner sliding blocks, then pull tool to compress tensioner spring.
4. While compressing tensioner spring, insert a cotter pin or other suitable tool into hole (A), **Fig. 12,** to hold spring in the compressed position, then remove tool No. J33875.
5. Position tensioner to engine, then install attaching bolts and remove cotter pin holding tensioner spring in the compressed position.

1985-86 4-121

1. Remove front cover as described previously.
2. Remove attaching bolts.
3. Remove tensioner and damper.
4. Compress spring in direction of arrow, **Fig. 13.**
5. While compressing spring, use a cotter pin and insert into hole A shown.
6. Install chain tensioner.
7. Remove cotter pin from tensioner.

CAMSHAFT
REPLACE

1. Remove engine from vehicle as previously described.
2. Remove valve lifters and engine front cover as described previously.
3. Mark position of rotor to distributor body, then remove distributor from engine.
4. Remove fuel pump and fuel pump push rod from engine block.
5. Remove timing chain and camshaft sprocket as previously described.
6. Remove camshaft thrust plate to engine block retaining bolts and the thrust plate, **Fig. 10.**
7. Remove camshaft from engine block.
8. Reverse removal procedure to install. When installing camshaft, align crankshaft and camshaft sprocket timing marks, **Fig. 10.**

PISTON & ROD
ASSEMBLE

Install piston to rod with notch or arrow and hole on piston facing toward front of engine and rod bearing tang slot opposite camshaft, **Figs. 14 and 15** Upon installation, measure the connecting rod side clearance using a suitable feeler gauge. Measurement taken should be as follows:

Engine	Year	Clearance in inch
4-112	1982	.004—.024
4-121	1982—86	.004—.024

PISTONS, PINS & RINGS

Pistons and rings are available in standard and oversizes of .020 and .040 inch. Oversize piston pins are not available due to the press fit design.

MAIN & ROD BEARINGS

NOTE: When removing No. 1 main bearing cap, it will be necessary to remove the timing chain tensioner, refer to Timing Chain Tensioner, Replace.

Main bearings are available in standard size and undersizes of .0013 inch, and connecting rod bearings are available in standard size and undersizes of .0010 inch.

OIL PAN
REPLACE

1. Disconnect battery ground cable, then

Fig. 13 Compressing timing chain tensioner spring. 1985-86 4-121

DIRECTION OF TENSION TO BE APPLIED

NOTCH AND HOLE TO FRONT OF ENGINE

Fig. 14 Piston & rod assembly. Exc. 1985-86

NOTCH TOWARDS FRONT OF ENGINE

Fig. 15 Piston & rod assembly. 1985-86

DISTRIBUTOR

OIL PUMP

SEAL

Fig. 16 Removing oil pan & pump

1. PICK UP TUBE AND SCREEN.
2. PUMP COVER.
3. DRIVE GEAR AND SHAFT.
4. IDLER GEAR.
5. PUMP BODY.
6. PRESSURE REGULATOR SPRING.
7. PRESSURE REGULATOR VALVE.
8. RETAINING PIN.
9. GASKET.
10. ATTACHING BOLTS.

Fig. 17 Sectional view of oil pump assembly

remove exhaust pipe shield.
2. Raise and support front of vehicle, then drain crankcase.
3. Disconnect exhaust pipe at exhaust manifold.
4. Detach A/C compressor brace at starter motor and A/C compressor bracket.
5. Remove flywheel cover and starter motor bracket, then remove starter motor and position aside.
6. Remove A/C compressor mounting bracket.
7. Remove four right hand suspension support bolts, then lower suspension support slightly to provide clearance for oil pan removal.
8. On models equipped with auto. transaxle, remove oil filter adapter.
9. Remove oil pan attaching bolts and oil pan.
10. Reverse procedure to install. Before installing oil pan, apply a thin coat of RTV sealer to both ends of oil pan rear seal, then seat seal firmly into rear main bearing cap. Do not allow sealer to extend beyond oil pan rear seal tabs. Apply a continuous 2 mm bead of RTV sealer along oil pan side rails in line with bolt holes, circling inward

around each bolt hole location. Also apply RTV sealer to oil pan surface which contacts engine front cover. This bead of sealer must meet the bead at each oil pan side rail. Do not apply any RTV sealer to oil pan rear seal mating surface. Carefully install oil pan and torque attaching bolts alternately and evenly to 6 to 9 ft. lbs., then to a final torque of 13 to 18 ft. lbs. Torque attaching bolts while RTV sealer is still wet to touch.

OIL PUMP SERVICE
REMOVAL

1. Drain crankcase, then remove oil pan as previously described.
2. Remove pump to rear main bearing attaching bolt, then remove pump, extension shaft and retainer, **Fig. 16.**

DISASSEMBLE

1. Remove four pump cover to body attaching bolts, then remove cover, idler and drive gears and shaft, **Fig. 17.**

NOTE: Place align mark on oil pump drive and idler gear teeth so they can be installed in the same position.

2. Remove pressure regulator valve retaining pin, spring and the valve from pump body.

INSPECTION

Inspect pump components and should any of the following conditions exist, the oil pump assembly should be replaced.
1. Inspect pump body, gears and cover for cracks or excessive wear.
2. Check drive gear shaft for looseness in housing.
3. Check inside of pump cover for wear that would allow oil to leak past ends of gears.
4. Check oil pickup screen assembly for damage to screen or pickup tube.
5. Check pressure regulator valve for fit in pump body.

ASSEMBLE

1. Install a replacement pickup screen and tube assembly, if removed. Position pump in a soft jawed vise, then

Engine Oiling System

COATED AREA INDICATED WITH #1052357 SEALER OR EQUIVALENT.

Fig. 18   Replacing crankshaft rear main bearing oil seal

OVAL MARKING IN THIS LOCATION INDICATES "THICK REAR MAIN SEAL"

Fig. 19   Thick seal identification mark location. 1984 4-121

apply sealer to end of tube and tap into position using tool No. J8369 and a plastic hammer. Use care not to damage inlet screen and tube assembly when installing on pump housing.

2. Place pressure regulator valve, spring and retaining pin into pump body, then install drive gear and shaft.
3. Install idler gear into pump body, then the pump cover gasket. **Fig. 17.**
4. Install pump cover and cover retaining bolts, then torque bolts to 6–9 ft. lbs.

INSTALLATION

1. Align oil pump extension shaft to distributor drive gear socket and pump housing with dowels on cap, then install shaft retainer and pump assembly.
2. Install oil pump assembly retaining bolt to rear main bearing cap and torque bolt to 26–35 ft. lbs.
3. Install oil pan as previously described.

REAR MAIN BEARING OIL SEAL
REPLACE
4-112

SERVICE NOTE: 4-112 engines use a rope type rear main bearing oil seal. When service replacement of seal is indicated, a new rubber split seal, Part No. 14069889, should be used. Refer to procedure below when replacing rope type seal with rubber split design.

1. Remove oil pan and oil pump as described previously.
2. Remove rear main bearing cap.
3. Remove upper and lower seal, then clean seal channel of oil.

NOTE: Loosening No. 2, 3 & 4 main bearing caps may be helpful when removing and replacing upper seal.

4. Apply a thin coat of sealing compound 1050026, or equivalent, to outer diameter of upper seal. Roll seal into position in block, turning crankshaft to ease installation.
5. Apply sealer to lower seal as described above, and position into main bearing cap.
6. Position a piece of Plastigage onto main journal or bearing, install main bearing cap and torque to specifications.
7. Remove bearing cap and measure Plastigage for proper bearing clearance. If clearance is not within specifications, correct as necessary.
8. Clean Plastigage from journal and bearing, then lubricate bearing lightly.
9. Apply a 1 mm bead of sealant 1052357 or equivalent to the bearing cap between the rear main seal end and the oil pan rear seal groove as shown, **Fig. 18.** Keep sealant off main seal and out of drain slot in bearing cap.
10. Apply light coat of engine oil to crankshaft to seal contact surface.
11. Install rear main bearing cap, then torque all bolts to specifications.
12. Install oil pump and oil pan, then start engine and check for leaks.

SERVICE NOTE: A new 1-piece rear crankshaft oil seal is available to replace the 2-piece seal previously used on 1983 and some 1984 engines. Some 1984 and all 1985–86 engines are assembled with the 1-piece seal. The new seal should be used on early models if replacement is necessary. Before replacing a rear oil seal, make absolutely sure it is the exact source of leakage. On 1984 models, once it has been determined that the seal must be replaced, it is necessary to determine the type of seal (thin or thick) installed in the engine, **Fig. 19.** Refer to the appropriate following procedures.

THIN SEAL

1. Drain coolant and oil from engine.
2. Remove engine and mount on engine stand in inverted position. Remove oil pan and pump.
3. Remove timing chain cover, then lock chain tensioner with pin.
4. Rotate crankshaft so crankshaft and camshaft sprocket timing marks line up.

5. Remove camshaft sprocket and timing chain.
6. Rotate crankshaft to horizontal position.
7. Remove connecting rod caps and bearings, taking care not to mix caps and bearings.
8. Remove main bearing caps and bearings, taking care not to mix caps and bearings.
9. Remove crankshaft.
10. Remove old oil seal and clean sealant from grooves in block and cap.
11. Using solvent, clean crankshaft seal area to remove excess solvent, taking care not to damage surface.
12. Inspect sealing and mating surfaces and crankshaft journal, checking for nicks, scratches, or machining defects.
13. Apply a 1 mm bead of anaerobic sealant 1052357 or equivalent to outside circumference of seal.
14. Place seal and tool assembly on rear of crankshaft.
15. Position seal tool so arrow points toward engine block, **Fig. 20.**
16. Position crankshaft in engine block with seal tool in place.
17. Remove seal tool and discard.
18. Lightly oil crankshaft journals.
19. Apply sealant 1052357 or equivalent to rear journal mating surfaces and install main bearing and cap.
20. Install remaining bearings and caps. Torque cap bolts to 63–75 ft. lbs.
21. Install connecting rod bearings and caps. Torque cap bolts to 34–40 ft. lbs.
22. Install oil pump, making sure that mating surface is clean. Torque oil pump to 26–35 ft. lbs.
23. Align crankshaft sprocket timing mark and install camshaft sprocket and timing chain. Torque sprocket bolt to 66–84 ft. lbs.
24. Clean, seal and install oil pan.

THICK SEAL

NOTE: Some 1984 and all 1985-86 models use the thick seal.

1. Support engine and remove transaxle.
2. Remove flywheel and check that rear seal is leaking.

**Fig. 20   Installing thin seal.
4-121**

**Fig. 21   Installing thick seal.
4-121**

**Fig. 22   Replacing water pump
assembly**

3. Remove seal by carefully inserting screwdriver in through dust lip and prying towards end of crankshaft pilot. Repeat as necessary around circumference of seal until seal is removed, taking care not to damage crankshaft circumference.
4. Check inside of seal bore for nicks or burrs and correct as necessary. Inspect crankshaft for burrs or nicks on seal contact surface. Repair or replace crankshaft as necessary.
5. Install new seal using tool J-34686.
6. Place seal on mandril, making sure that dust lip on seal bottoms squarely against collar of tool, **Fig. 21.**
7. After aligning dowel pin with dowel pin hole in crankshaft, attach tool to crankshaft and torque screws to 2–5 ft. lbs.
8. Turn T-handle of tool until collar is tight against engine block to ensure that seal is seated properly in block.
9. Loosen T-handle of tool until it comes to a stop. Remove attaching screws.
10. Check that seal is seated squarely in bore.

11. Install flywheel and engine.
12. Start engine and check for leaks.

WATER PUMP
REPLACE

1. Disconnect battery ground cable and drain cooling system.
2. Remove accessory drive belts.
3. Remove alternator to alternator bracket retaining bolts and position alternator aside.
4. Remove water pump pulley to water pump attaching bolts, then the pulley from water pump.
5. Remove four water pump to block attaching bolts and the water pump, **Fig. 22.**
6. Clean sealing surfaces of pump and engine block and place a 1/8 inch bead of sealant 1052289, or equivalent, to sealing surfaces. Install pump. Coat threaded area of pump bolts with sealant 1052080, install torque bolts to 13–18 ft. lbs.
7. Reverse removal procedures to complete installation.

BELT TENSION DATA

	New Lbs.	Used Lbs.
Air Cond.	168②	90①
Alternator	145②	70①
Power Steer.	145②	70①
Air Pump	145②	70①

①—Minimum.
②—Maximum.

FUEL PUMP
REPLACE

1. Disconnect battery ground cable.
2. Raise and support vehicle.
3. Disconnect inlet hose and outlet pipe from fuel pump.
4. Remove two fuel pump retaining nuts and rotate pump upward to clear studs in block. Remove fuel pump from vehicle.
5. Clean block to pump mating surface and install new gasket over studs in block.
6. Install pump and pump retaining nuts and torque nuts to 15–22 ft. lbs.
7. Reverse procedure to complete installation.

V6-173 Engine Section

Fig. 1 Front engine mount

Fig. 2 Rear engine mount

ENGINE MOUNTS
REPLACE

FRONT MOUNT

1. Disconnect battery ground cable.
2. Remove engine mount nuts, then raise and support vehicle.
3. Support engine with suitable jack.
4. Remove inner fender shield.
5. Remove and discard engine mount bolts, **Fig. 1.**
6. Remove engine mount from vehicle.
7. Reverse procedure to install, using new engine mount bolts. Remove alignment bolt.

NOTE: If excessive force is required to remove alignment bolt, loosen transaxle adjusting bolts to align powertrain components.

REAR MOUNT

1. Disconnect battery ground cable, then raise and support vehicle.
2. Support engine with suitable jack.
3. Remove motor mount nuts and attach-

ing bolts, **Fig. 2.**
4. Reverse procedure to install.

ENGINE
REPLACE

1. Disconnect battery ground cable and drain cooling system.
2. Remove air cleaner and the mass air flow meter.
3. Remove exhaust crossover heat shield and the exhaust crossover pipe.
4. Remove accessory drive belt and the tensioner.
5. Remove power steering pump mounting bracket and disconnect heater pipe at power steering pump mounting bracket.
6. Disconnect radiator hose at engine.
7. Disconnect accelerator and T.V. cables at throttle valve.
8. Remove alternator and disconnect wiring harness at engine.
9. Disconnect fuel hoses and the coolant bypass and overflow hoses at engine.
10. Disconnect canister purge hose at canister and remove vacuum hoses as necessary.
11. Raise and support vehicle, then

remove right inner fender splash shield.
12. Remove harmonic balance and the flywheel cover.
13. Remove starter attaching bolts, disconnect electrical connectors at starter and remove starter.
14. Disconnect electrical connector at oil sending unit.
15. Remove A/C compressor and its mounting bracket(s).
16. Disconnect exhaust pipe at rear of manifold.
17. Remove flex plate to torque converter attaching bolts and the transaxle to engine brace bolts.
18. Remove engine rear mount to frame nuts.
19. Disconnect shift cable bracket at transaxle.
20. Remove lower bellhousing bolts and lower vehicle.
21. Disconnect heater hoses at engine.
22. Install suitable engine lifting device and support transaxle with suitable jack.
23. Remove upper bellhousing and front mount attaching bolts.
24. Remove brake master cylinder and position out of way.
25. Remove engine from vehicle.
26. Reverse procedure to install.

Fig. 3   Installing cylinder head

Head Torque Sequence

CUT TOP AS NECESSARY

THIS SIDE UP

Fig. 4   Installing intake manifold gasket

CYLINDER HEAD
REPLACE

REMOVAL

1. Disconnect battery ground cable.
2. Remove intake manifold as described under "Intake Manifold, Replace".
3. Remove exhaust manifold as described under "Exhaust Manifold, Replace".
4. Disconnect wiring harness at cylinder head.
5. Remove spark plug wires and the spark plugs.
6. Remove rocker arm covers, rocker arm nuts, rocker arm balls, rocker arms and pushrods.
7. Remove cylinder head attaching bolts and the cylinder head.

INSTALLATION

NOTE: Gasket surfaces on cylinder head and case must be clean and free of nicks or heavy scratches. Cylinder bolt threads in case and threads on cylinder head bolts must be clean to obtain true torque.

1. Place gasket in position over dowel pins with note "This Side Up" showing and install cylinder head.
2. Coat cylinder head bolt threads with suitable sealant and install bolts.
3. Torque bolts to 70 ft. lbs. in proper sequence, **Fig. 3**.
4. Install pushrods and loosely retain with rocker arms, ensuring lower ends of push rods are in lifter seats.
5. Install spark plugs and wires.
6. Install intake and exhaust manifolds, then adjust valves as necessary.

INTAKE MANIFOLD
REPLACE

1. Disconnect battery ground cable.
2. Disconnect accelerator and T. V. cable bracket at plenum.
3. Disconnect throttle body at plenum.
4. Disconnect E.G.R. pipe at E.G.R. valve, then remove plenum.
5. Disconnect fuel inlet and return pipes at fuel rail.
6. Disconnect serpentine belt, then remove power steering pump mounting bracket.
7. Disconnect heater pipe at power steering pump bracket.
8. Disconnect electrical connectors at alternator and remove alternator.
9. Disconnect electrical connector at cold start injector and remove injector.
10. Disconnect idle air vacuum hose at throttle body and the electrical connectors at injectors.
11. Remove fuel rail, breather tube and the runners.
12. Disconnect coil wires at bracket.
13. Remove both rocker arm covers and drain cooling system.
14. Disconnect radiator hose at thermostat outlet and the heater pipe at thermostat housing.
15. Disconnect electrical connectors at thermostat housing.
16. Remove distributor, thermostat housing, intake manifold attaching bolts and the intake manifold.
17. Reverse procedure to install, noting the following:
    a. When installing gaskets, install only on right or left side as marked.
    b. Clean cylinder case sealing surface front and rear ridges and apply a ³⁄₁₆ inch bead of suitable sealant on each ridge.
    c. Install new intake gaskets on cylinder heads, holding in place by extending ridge sealant bead up 6mm onto onto gasket ends. The new intake gaskets will have to be cut where indicated, **Fig. 4**, to install behind push rods. Cut only those areas that are necessary.
    d. When installing intake manifold, ensure areas between case ridges and manifold are completely sealed.
    e. Install manifold retaining bolts and nuts, torquing to 23 ft. lbs. in proper sequence, **Fig. 5**.
    f. After completing installation, start engine and set initial timing, torque distributor hold down clamp bolt to 25 ft. lbs. and recheck timing.

EXHAUST MANIFOLD
REPLACE

LEFT SIDE

1. Disconnect battery ground cable and remove air cleaner.
2. Remove mass air flow sensor and the heat shield.
3. Disconnect crossover pipe at manifold, then remove manifold attaching bolts and the manifold.
4. Reverse procedure to install, torquing bolts to 25 ft. lbs.

RIGHT SIDE

1. Disconnect battery ground cable and remove air cleaner.
2. Remove mass air flow sensor and the heat shield.
3. Disconnect crossover pipe at manifold.
4. Disconnect accelerator and T. V. cable at throttle lever.
5. Remove accelerator and T. V. cable bracket at plenum and position out of way.
6. Disconnect power steering line at pump.
7. Remove E.G.R. valve and related parts.
8. Raise and support vehicle.
9. Disconnect exhaust pipe at exhaust manifold, then lower vehicle.
10. Remove manifold attaching bolts and the manifold.
11. Reverse procedure to install.

VALVES
ADJUST

1. Remove rocker arm covers.
2. Crank engine until mark on torsional damper lines up with O mark on timing tab. The engine should also be in the No. 1 firing position. This can be determined by placing fingers on No. 1

rocker arms as mark on damper approaches O mark.

3. If valves are not moving, engine is in No. 1 firing position. If valves move as the mark comes up to the timing tab, engine is in No. 4 firing position and should be rotated one revolution to reach No. 1 position.

4. With engine in No. 1 firing position, adjust exhaust valves 1, 2 and 3 and intake valves 1, 5 and 6, as follows:

   a. Back out adjusting nut until lash is felt at push rod, then turn in adjusting nut until all lash is removed.

   b. When lash has been removed, turn adjusting nut in additional 1½ turns to center lifter plunger.

5. Crank engine one revolution until timing tab O mark and torsional damper mark are again in alignment.

6. With the engine in this, the No. 4 firing position. adjust exhaust valves 4, 5 and 6 and intake valves 2, 3 and 4 as previously described.

7. Install rocker arm covers, then start engine and check timing and idle speed.

VALVE ARRANGEMENT
Front to Rear

Right ....E-I-E-I-I-E
Left.........................E-I-I-E-I-E

VALVE LIFT SPECS.

Engine	Intake	Exhaust
V6-173	.394	.410

VALVE STEM OIL SEAL & VALVE SPRING
REPLACE
Removal

1. Remove rocker arm cover, then the spark plug, rocker arm and push rod on cylinder(s) being serviced.

2. Install air line adapter tool J-23590 or equivalent to spark plug port and apply compressed air to hold valves in place.

3. Using tool J-5892 or equivalent to compress valve spring, remove valve locks, valve caps, oil shedder and valve spring and damper.

4. Remove valve stem oil seal.

INSTALLATION

1. Set valve spring and damper around valve guide boss.

2. Install a valve stem seal over the valve stem and valve guide base-inlet only.

3. Drop an oil shedder and valve rotator over the exhaust, and a valve spring cap over the valve spring.

4. Compress spring with tool J-5892 and install oil seal in lower groove of stem, ensuring seal is flat and not twisted.

5. Install valve locks and release compressor tool, ensuring locks seat properly in upper groove of valve stem. Use suitable grease as necessary to hold locks in place while releasing compressor tool.

6. Using tool J-23994 or equivalent, apply vacuum to valve cap to ensure no air leaks past seal.

7. Install spark plug, torquing to 11 ft. lbs.

8. Install and adjust valve mechanism.

VALVE GUIDES

Valve guides are an integral part of the cylinder head and are not removable. If valve stem clearance becomes excessive, the valve guide should be reamed to the next oversize and the appropriate oversize valves installed. Valves are available in .003, .015 and .030 inch oversizes.

VALVE LIFTERS
REPLACE

1. Remove intake manifold as previously decribed

2. Remove valve mechanism, then the valve lifters.

3. Install valve lifters. When installing new lifters, coat foot of valve lifters with "Molykote" or equivalent, ensuring lifter foot is convex.

4. Install intake manifold as previously described.

5. Install and adjust valve mechanism.

TORQUE TO
18 to 34 N·m
(13-25 FT. LBS.)

INLET MANIFOLD BOLT/SCREW
& NUT TIGHTENING SEQUENCE

NOTE APPLY A SMOOTH CONTINUOUS BEAD APPROX. 2.0-3.0 WIDE AND 3.0-5.0 THICK ON BOTH SURFACES. BEAD CONFIGURATION MUST INSURE COMPLETE SEALING OF WATER AND OIL. SURFACE MUST BE FREE OF OIL AND DIRT TO INSURE ADEQUATE SEAL.

Fig. 5   Installing intake manifold

1   26-32 N•M (19-24 FT.LBS.)

2   27-41 N•M (20-30 FT.LBS.)

Fig. 6   Installing front cover

Fig. 7 Valve timing marks

Fig. 8 Piston & rod assembly

Fig. 9 Removing oil seal

FRONT COVER
REPLACE

1. Disconnect battery ground cable and drain cooling system.
2. Disconnect M.A.P. sensor and E.G.R. solenoid.
3. Remove coolant recovery tank and the serpentine belt adjusting pulley.
4. Remove alternator and disconnect electrical connectors.
5. Remove power steering pump bracket and disconnect heater pipe at bracket.
6. Raise and support vehicle, then remove inner splash shield.
7. Remove A/C compressor belt and the flywheel cover at transaxle.
8. Using tool J-23523-1 or equivalent, remove harmonic balance.
9. Remove serpentine belt idler pulley.
10. Remove pan to front cover attaching bolts and the lower attaching bolts.
11. Lower vehicle, then disconnect radiator hose at water pump.
12. Remove heater pipe at goose neck.
13. Disconnect bypass and overflow hoses.
14. Disconnect canister purge hose.
15. Remove upper front cover attaching bolts and the front cover.
16. Reverse procedure to install, noting the following:
    a. With a clean sealing surface on both the front cover and oil pan, apply a continuous 3mm bead of suitable sealant to oil pan surface of front cover.
    b. Torque bolts to specifications, **Fig. 6.**

FRONT COVER OIL SEAL
REPLACE

1. Remove inner splash shield and tortional damper, then pry seal from cover using a suitable screwdriver.

NOTE: Use caution not to damage crankshaft surface during seal removal.

2. Install new seal so open end faces toward inside of cover, then drive seal into position using suitable tool.

TIMING CHAIN & SPROCKET
REPLACE

1. Remove crankcase front cover, refer to "Front Cover, Replace" procedure.
2. Place No. 1 cylinder at TDC and align timing marks on crankshaft and camshaft sprockets, **Fig. 7.**
3. Remove camshaft sprocket attaching bolts. Tap lower edge of sprocket with plastic mallet and remove sprocket and timing chain.
4. Align timing marks, **Fig. 7,** and install timing chain on sprockets.
5. Align dowel on camshaft with dowel hole on camshaft sprocket, then install sprocket to camshaft, using attaching bolts to to draw sprocket fully to camshaft. Torque attaching bolts to 15–20 ft. lbs.
6. Lubricate timing chain with engine oil, then install front cover.

CAMSHAFT
REPLACE

1. Remove engine from vehicle, refer to "Engine, Replace" procedure.
2. Remove valve lifters, refer to "Valve Lifter, Replace" procedure.
3. Remove crankcase front cover, refer to "Front Cover, Replace" procedure.
4. Remove fuel pump and push rod, then the timing chain and sprocket. Refer to "Timing Chain & Sprocket, Replace" procedure.
5. Remove camshaft.

NOTE: Use caution not to damage bearings during camshaft removal.

6. Reverse procedure to install. Coat camshaft lobes with suitable grease before installation.

PISTON & ROD ASSEMBLE

There is a machined hole or cast notch in the top of all pistons. The piston assemblies should always be installed with the hole or notch toward front of engine, **Fig. 8.**

PISTONS, PINS & RINGS

Pistons and rings are available in standard and oversize. Piston pins are available in standard size only.

MAIN & ROD BEARINGS

Main and rod bearing are available in standard sizes and undersizes.

REAR MAIN BEARING OIL SEAL
REPLACE

1. Support engine, then remove transaxle assembly.
2. Remove flywheel assembly.
3. Remove oil seal as shown in **Fig. 9.** Use caution not to damage crankshaft surface with removal tool.
4. Check inside diameter of bore and crankshaft for nicks or burrs. Repair as required.
5. Apply oil to inside diameter of new seal, then install seal on mandrell of tool No. J-34686 until back of seal bottoms squarely against collar of tool, **Fig. 10.**
6. Align dowel pin of tool with dowel pin of crankshaft, then attach tool to crankshaft. Torque attaching screws to 2–5 ft. lbs.
7. Turn "T" handle of tool so collar pushes seal into bore. Ensure seal is properly seated.
8. Loosen "T" handle of tool until it

Fig. 10   Installing oil seal

Fig. 11   Oil pump assembly

comes to a stop, then remove tool attaching screws. Ensure seal is seated squarely in bore.

9. Install flywheel and transaxle assembly.

OIL PAN
REPLACE

1. Disconnect battery ground cable.
2. Raise and support vehicle, then drain crankcase.
3. Remove flywheel dust cover, then the starter motor.
4. Remove oil pan attaching bolts, then the oil pan.
5. Reverse procedure to install. Apply suitable sealer to oil pan mating surfaces, then torque 6mm bolts to 6–15 ft. lbs. and 8mm bolts to 15–30 ft. lbs.

OIL PUMP
REMOVAL

1. Remove oil pan, refer to "Oil Pan, Replace" procedure.
2. Remove pump to rear main bearing attaching bolt, then the pump and extension shaft.

DISASSEMBLY

1. Remove pump cover attaching bolts (7), **Fig. 11,** and pump cover (3).

NOTE: Mark gear teeth to ensure correct position during assembly.

2. Remove idler gear and drive gear (2), then the shaft from pump body (1).
3. Remove pressure regulator valve retaining pin (6), pressure regulator spring (5) and valve (4).
4. If pickup screen and pipe assembly need to be replaced, mount pump in a suitable vise, then remove pipe from pump cover.

NOTE: Do not remove pickup screen from pipe, this is serviced as an assembly.

CLEANING & INSPECTION

1. Wash all parts in suitable cleaning solvent, then dry with compressed air.
2. Inspect pump body and cover for cracks or excessive wear.
3. Inspect pump gears for damage or excessive wear. Pump gears and body are not serviced separately. If pump gears are defective, replace entire oil pump assembly.
4. Check drive gear shaft for looseness in the pump body.
5. Inspect inside of pump cover for wear that would permit oil to leak past ends of gears.
6. Inspect pickup screen and pipe assembly for looseness or damage.
7. Check pressure regulator valve for damage and proper fit.

Assembly

1. If pickup screen and pipe assembly was removed, it should be replaced with a new part. Mount pump in suitable vise and apply suitable sealer to outside diameter of swaged end of pipe, then tap pipe in place using a suitable tool.

NOTE: Loss of press fit condition could result in an air leak and loss of oil pressure. Also use caution not to twist, shear or collapse pipe during installation.

2. Install pressure regulator valve assembly.
3. Install drive gear and shaft in pump body.
4. Align idler gear installation marks, then install gear in pump body.
5. Install cover gasket, then the pump cover and attaching bolts.
6. Turn drive shaft by hand to ensure smooth operation.

INSTALLATION

1. Install pump and extension shaft with retainer to rear main bearing cap, aligning top end of hexagon extension shaft with hexagon socket of distributor drive gear.

2. Install pump to rear bearing cap bolt and tighten securely.
3. Install oil pan, refer to "Oil Pan, Replace" procedure.

WATER PUMP
REPLACE

1. Disconnect battery ground cable, then drain cooling system.
2. Disconnect serpentine belt at the water pump pulley.
3. Disconnect A/C pressure cycling switch electrical connectors, then remove pressure cycling switch.
4. Remove water pump pulley, then the water pump.
5. Reverse procedure to install.

BELT TENSION DATA

	New Lbs.	Used Lbs.
Air. Cond.	160	100
Alternator	①	①
Power Steer.	①	①

①—Serpentine belt.

FUEL PUMP
REPLACE

1. Relieve fuel system pressure, then disconnect battery ground cable.
2. Raise and support vehicle, then remove fuel tank.
3. Remove fuel lever sending unit and pump assembly by turning cam lock ring counterclockwise. Lift assembly from fuel tank, then remove fuel pump from fuel lever sending unit.
4. Pull fuel pump up to attaching hose or pulsator while pulling outward away from bottom support. After pump assembly is clear of bottom support, remove assembly from rubber connector or pulsator.

NOTE: Use caution not to damage rubber insulator and strainer during removal.

5. Reverse procedure to install.

Clutch & Transaxle Section

Fig. 1   Clutch self-adjusting mechanism. 1982–84 Models

Fig. 2   Hydraulic clutch assembly. 1985–86 Models

pedal to the floor and observe clutch fork lever travel at transaxle. The end of the clutch fork lever should have a total travel of approximately 1.5 to 1.7 inches.

6. To check the self-adjusting mechanism, depress the clutch pedal and observe if the pawl firmly engages the teeth of the detent.

1985–86 Models

On these models, a hydraulic clutch system is used, **Fig. 2**. The system consists of a dash mounted master cylinder with integral reservoir, a transmission mounted slave cylinder and high pressure tubing to connect the two components.

The hydraulic clutch system provides automatic clutch adjustment, therefore, there is no provision for adjustment.

Inspection

1. While observing clutch slave cylinder push rod travel, have an assistant depress clutch pedal.
2. If slave cylinder push rod moves .433 inch or more, hydraulic system is operating properly.
3. If slave cylinder push rod did not move .433 inch, proceed as follows:
   a. Check clutch master cylinder fluid level. The clutch slave cylinder must be installed during this operation. Refill as necessary.
   b. If master cylinder requires fluid, check hydraulic system components for leakage. Remove rubber boots from cylinders and check for leakage past pistons. A slight wetting of piston and wall surfaces is acceptable.
   c. If excessive leakage is indicated, entire hydraulic system must be replaced.

CLUTCH
REPLACE

1. Disconnect battery ground cable.
2. On 1985–86 models, remove hush panel from driver's footwell, then disconnect clutch master cylinder push rod from clutch pedal.
3. Remove transaxle as outlined under "Manual Transaxle, Replace" procedure.
4. Mark position of pressure plate to flywheel to aid reassembly.
5. Gradually loosen pressure plate to flywheel attaching bolts until spring tension is relieved.
6. Support pressure plate and remove attaching bolts, pressure plate and driven disc, **Fig. 3**.
7. Clean pressure plate and flywheel mounting surfaces. Inspect bearing outer surface of the transaxle.
8. Place pressure plate and driven disc in position and support with tool No. J-29074, **Fig. 4**.

CLUTCH PEDAL
ADJUST

1982–84 Models

The clutch is automatically adjusted by a self-adjusting mechanism, **Fig. 1**, mounted to the clutch pedal and bracket assembly. The clutch cable is a fixed length and cannot be shortened or lengthened, however, the position of the cable can be changed by adjusting the position of the detent in relation to the clutch pedal. This is accomplished by pulling the clutch pedal upward to the rubber bumper. This action forces the pawl against the stop and causes the pawl to be out of mesh with the detent

teeth, allowing the cable to play out until the detent spring load is balanced against the load applied by the release bearing.

Inspection

1. With engine running and parking brake applied, depress clutch pedal to approximately ½ inch from floor mat.
2. Move shift lever between "First" and "Reverse" gears several times. If no gear clashing occurs when shifting into "Reverse", the clutch is releasing fully.
3. If the shifting in Step 2 is not smooth, the clutch is not releasing fully and the linkage should be inspected.
4. Check clutch pedal bushings for sticking or excessive wear.
5. Have an assistant depress the clutch

Fig. 3 Clutch assembly

Fig. 4 Aligning clutch disc & pressure plate

Fig. 5 Four speed manual transaxle shift cable adjustment

Fig. 6 Four speed manual transaxle shifter shaft selective washer measurement

NOTE: The driven disc is installed with the damper springs offset toward the transaxle. Stamped letters found on the driven disc identify the "Flywheel Side".

9. Install and gradually torque the pressure plate to flywheel attaching bolts to 15 ft. lbs. Remove support tool.
10. Lubricate the release bearing outside diameter groove and inside diameter recess.
11. Install transaxle.

MANUAL TRANSAXLE SHIFT CABLE
ADJUST

4 SPEED MANUAL TRANSAXLE

Shift Cable Adjustment
1. Disconnect battery ground cable.
2. Place shift lever into first gear position, then loosen shift cable nuts (E) at levers (D) and (F), **Fig. 5.**
3. Remove console trim plate, then slide shift lever boot upward on shift lever.
4. Remove console assembly.
5. With shift lever in the first gear position and held against stop, insert a suitable yoke type clip to hold lever in position, **Fig. 5.**
6. Insert a 5/32 inch drill bit into alignment hole on side of shifter assembly, **Fig. 5.**
7. Rotate lever (D), **Fig. 5,** in direction of arrow while tightening cable retaining nut.
8. Tighten cable retaining nut at lever (F), **Fig. 5.**
9. Remove drill bit and yoke clip, then install console and connect battery ground cable.
10. Check shift lever for proper operation and readjust as necessary.

Shifter Shaft Washer Selection
    When shift cables are properly adjusted,

but improper first and second gear shifts are encountered, it may be necessary to check the shifter shaft selective thrust washer. This washer helps position the shifter shaft for proper shifter operation. Proceed as follows to determine the correct selective thrust washer thickness:
1. Remove reverse inhibitor fitting, spring and washer from end housing, then position shifter shaft into second gear.
2. Measure distance from end of housing to shifter shaft shoulder, dimension A, **Fig. 6.**
3. Apply a load of 9 to 13 lbs. to opposite end of shifter shaft, then measure distance from end of housing to shifter shaft shoulder, dimension B, **Fig. 6.**
4. Subtract measurement obtained in step 2 from measurement obtained in step 3, which will equal the thickness of the selective thrust washer to be installed, dimension C, **Fig. 6.** When selecting a thrust washer, refer to **Fig. 7.**

5 SPEED MANUAL TRANSAXLE

1. Disconnect battery ground cable.
2. Place shift lever in third gear position, then remove lock pin (H), **Fig. 8,** and

Dimension "C" Fig. 6 Inch (mm)	Ident. Color & No. of Stripes	Shim Part No.
.0708 (1.8)	3 White	14008235
.0827 (2.1)	1 Orange	476709
.0945 (2.4)	2 Orange	476710
.1063 (2.7)	3 Orange	476711
.1181 (3.0)	1 Blue	476712
.1299 (3.3)	2 Blue	476713
.1417 (3.6)	3 Blue	476714
.1535 (3.9)	1 White	476715
.1654	2 White	476716

Fig. 7   Shifter shaft selective thrust washer identification chart. Four speed manual transaxle

Fig. 8   Five speed manual transaxle shift cable adjustment

MODIFY THIS LEG BY DRILLING ⅛" HOLE AS SHOWN.

ENGINE SUPPORT FIXTURE

TOOL MOUNTING ON ENGINE

Fig. 9   Engine support fixture installation

reinstall with tapered end of pin facing downward to lock transaxle in third gear.

3. Loosen shift cable retaining nuts (E) at levers (G) and (F), **Fig. 8.**
4. Remove console trim plate and pull shifter boot upward on shift lever.
5. Remove console assembly from vehicle.
6. Insert a ⁵⁄₃₂ inch drill bit into align hole on side of shifter assembly, **Fig. 8.**
7. Align shifter lever slot with slot in shifter plate, then insert a ¹³⁄₁₆ inch drill bit.
8. Tighten nuts (E) at levers (G) and (F), **Fig. 8,** then remove drill bits from alignment holes.
9. Remove lock pin (H), **Fig. 8,** and reinstall with tapered end facing upward.
10. Install console assembly and connect battery ground cable.
11. Check shifter for proper operation and readjust as necessary.

MANUAL TRANSAXLE
REPLACE

4 SPEED MANUAL TRANSAXLE

1. Disconnect battery ground cable.
2. Install engine support fixture so that one end is supported on cowl tray over the wiper motor and the other end rests on the radiator support. Connect fixture hook to engine lift ring and raise engine to relieve weight from engine mounts, **Fig. 9.**

CAUTION: The engine support fixture must be positioned in the center of the cowl and the attaching parts properly tightened before supporting engine. This fixture is not intended to support entire weight of engine and transaxle. Personal injury may result from improper use of support fixture.

3. Remove heater hose clamp at transaxle mount bracket, then disconnect horn wires and remove horn assembly.

NOTE: Whenever the transaxle mount is removed, alignment bolt M6.0 x 1 x 65 must be installed in right front engine mount to prevent powertrain misalignment.

4. Remove transaxle mount attaching bolts. Discard mount to sideframe attaching bolts.
5. On 1985–86 models, remove clutch slave cylinder from support assembly. On 1982–84 models, disconnect clutch cable at clutch release lever, then remove transaxle mount bracket attaching bolts and nuts.
6. Disconnect shift cables and remove retaining clips at transaxle.
7. Disconnect ground cable at transaxle mounting stud, then remove air management valve attaching bolts (if equipped) to provide clearance for removal of upper right hand transaxle to engine attaching bolt. Remove four upper transaxle to engine mounting bolts.

8. Raise and support vehicle, then remove left front wheel.
9. Remove left front inner splash shield retaining screws and the splash shield.
10. Remove transaxle strut to transaxle bracket and crossmember attaching bolts and remove strut from vehicle.
11. Remove transaxle strut bracket attaching bolts and the strut bracket.
12. Remove clutch housing cover attaching bolts, then disconnect speedometer cable at transaxle.
13. Disconnect stabilizer bar at the left suspension support and control arm.
14. Using tool J-29330, separate left ball joint from steering knuckle.
15. Remove left suspension support to chassis attaching bolts, then remove the support and lower control arm as an assembly.
16. Install boot protectors at drive axles, then disengage both drive axles at transaxle. Remove left drive axle from transaxle housing bore.
17. Attach the transaxle case to a suitable jack, then remove two lower transaxle to engine mounting bolts.
18. Slide transaxle away from engine, lower jack and guide right drive axle from transaxle housing bore. Remove transaxle from vehicle.
19. Reverse removal procedure to install.

NOTE: When installing transaxle, guide the right drive axle into transaxle bore as transaxle is being raised. The right drive axle cannot be installed after the transaxle is connected to engine.

5 SPEED MANUAL TRANSAXLE

1. Disconnect battery ground cable.
2. Support engine using suitable engine holding fixture. Position holding fixture so that one end is supported by the cowl tray and the other end is resting

15–35

on the radiator support, **Fig. 9.** Attach holding fixture hook to engine lifting bracket and raise engine just enough to relieve weight from engine mounts.

NOTE: The engine holding fixture must be located in center of cowl and fixture attachments properly tightened before supporting engine. This support is not designed to support the entire weight of the engine and transaxle assembly.

3. Remove transaxle mount attaching bolts.

NOTE: When removing transaxle mount, alignment bolt M6.0 x 1 x 65 must be installed in right front engine mount to ensure proper powertrain alignment.

4. On 1985–86 models, remove clutch slave cylinder from support assembly. On 1982–84 models, disconnect clutch cable at clutch fork, then remove transaxle mount bracket retaining bolts and nuts.
5. Disconnect shift cables and remove retaining clips at transaxle.
6. Disconnect ground cables at transaxle mounting stud, then remove air management valve attaching bolts to provide clearance for upper right hand transaxle to engine attaching bolt.
7. Raise and support front of vehicle, then drain transaxle fluid.
8. Remove left hand front wheel and tire assembly, then remove front inner splash shield.
9. Remove transaxle strut and strut bracket.
10. Remove clutch cover attaching bolts, then disconnect speedometer cable at transaxle.
11. Disconnect stabilizer bar at left hand suspension support and control arm.
12. Detach ball joint from steering knuckle.

13. Remove left hand front suspension support attaching bolts, then remove support and control arm as an assembly.
14. Install boot protectors, then disengage drive axle shafts at transaxle using tool Nos. J28468, J29794 and a suitable screwdriver. Remove left hand drive axle shaft from transaxle.
15. Secure transaxle to a suitable transaxle jack, then remove transaxle to engine attaching bolts.
16. Remove transaxle by sliding toward drivers side of vehicle (away from engine), then carefully lower jack while guiding right hand drive axle shaft out of transaxle.
17. Reverse procedure to install. When installing transaxle, carefully guide right hand drive axle shaft into transaxle bore as transaxle is being raised. The right hand drive axle shaft cannot be installed once the transaxle has been connected to the engine.

Rear Axle, Rear Suspension & Brakes Section

DESCRIPTION

The rear suspension, **Fig. 1,** is a semi-independent type suspension consisting of an axle assembly with trailing arms and twisting cross beam, coil springs and double action shock absorbers. A stabilizer bar is available and is attached to the inside of the axle beam and to the lower end of the control arms. A single unit hub and bearing assembly is bolted to each end of the axle assembly. The hub and bearing assembly is a sealed, non-serviceable unit and must be replaced as an assembly.

REAR AXLE
REPLACE

1. Raise vehicle and support vehicle. Support rear suspension with suitable jack.

2. Disconnect stabilizer bar at axle assembly, if equipped, **Fig. 2.**
3. Remove rear wheel assembly and brake drum. Do not hammer on brake drum since damage to bearings may result.
4. Remove shock absorber to lower mounting bracket attaching bolts, then

disconnect shock absorbers from axle assembly, **Figs. 2 and 2A.**
5. Disconnect parking brake cable and brake lines at axle brackets.
6. Carefully lower rear axle assembly and remove coil springs and insulators.
7. Remove control arm to underbody

1	CONTROL ARM BUSHING
2	AXLE ASSEMBLY
3	SPRING INSULATOR
4	SHOCK ABSORBER

Fig. 1   Rear suspension

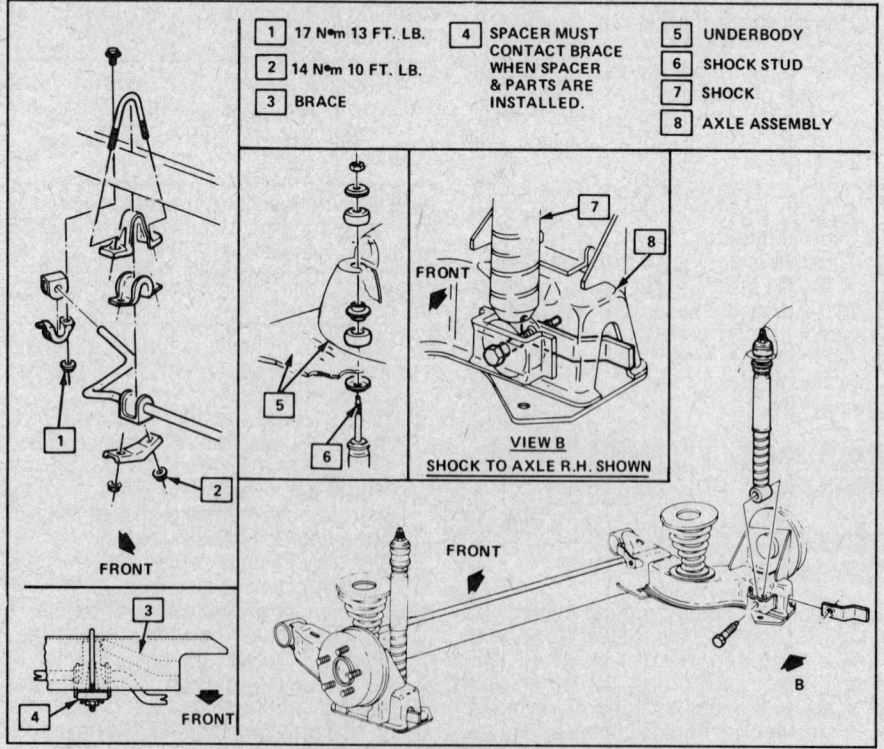

1	17 N•m 13 FT. LB.	4	SPACER MUST CONTACT BRACE WHEN SPACER & PARTS ARE INSTALLED.	5	UNDERBODY
2	14 N•m 10 FT. LB.			6	SHOCK STUD
3	BRACE			7	SHOCK
				8	AXLE ASSEMBLY

VIEW B
SHOCK TO AXLE R.H. SHOWN

Fig. 2   Rear shock absorber upper attachment components

Fig. 2A Stabilizer bar & shock absorber removal

Fig. 3 Coil spring installation

bracket bolts, then lower the axle assembly and remove from vehicle.

8. Remove hub to rear axle attaching bolts, then the hubs, bearings and backing plates from rear axle assembly.

9. Reverse procedure to install and bleed brake system.

HUB & BEARING ASSEMBLY
REPLACE

1. Raise and support vehicle, then remove wheel and tire assembly and brake drum.

NOTE: Do not hammer brake drum since damage to bearing may result.

2. Remove four hub/bearing assembly to rear axle attaching bolts, then the hub/bearing assembly from axle.

NOTE: The upper rear hub attaching bolt may not clear brake shoe when removing hub and bearing assembly. Partially remove hub and bearing assembly prior to removing this bolt.

3. Reverse procedure to install. Torque hub to axle attaching bolts to 37 ft. lbs.

CAUTION: Use care not to drop hub/bearing assembly since damage to bearing may result.

SHOCK ABSORBER
REPLACE

1. Open deck lid, then remove trim cover and shock absorber upper retaining nut.
2. Raise rear of vehicle and support rear axle using a suitable jack.
3. Remove shock absorber lower attaching bolt, then disconnect shock absorber from mounting bracket, **Fig. 2.** Remove shock absorber from vehicle.
4. Reverse procedure to install. Torque lower attaching bolt to 41 ft. lbs. and upper attaching nut to 13 ft. lbs.

NOTE: When installing upper shock absorber attachment components, refer to **Fig. 2A,** for proper installation order.

COIL SPRING
REPLACE

1. Raise and support rear of vehicle. Support rear axle using a suitable jack.
2. Remove wheel and tire assemblies.
3. Remove brake line bracket attaching bolts from frame, **Fig. 2,** and allow brake lines to hang freely.
4. Remove shock absorber to lower mounting bracket bolts, then disconnect shock absorbers from axle assembly.

CAUTION: Do not suspend rear axle by brake hoses since damage to hoses may result.

5. Carefully lower rear axle assembly and remove springs and insulators.
6. Reverse procedure to install. Position ends of upper coil in seat of body and within limits shown in **Fig. 3.**

Fig. 4 Control bushing removal

Fig. 5 Control arm bushing installation

J-21177

Fig. 6 Measuring brake drum inside diameter

CONTROL ARM BUSHING
REPLACE

1. Raise rear of vehicle and support rear axle under front side of spring seat using a suitable jack.
2. Remove wheel and tire assembly.
3. If right hand side bushing is to be replaced, disconnect brake line bracket from body. If left hand side bushing is to be replaced, disconnect brake line bracket from frame and parking brake cable at hook guide.
4. Remove control arm to mounting bracket attaching nut, bolt and washer, then allow control arm to rotate downward.
5. The bushing can now be replaced using tools shown in **Figs. 4 and 5.** When installing bushing, the arrow on the installer must align with arrow on the receiver, **Fig. 4.**
6. Reverse procedure to complete installation.

NOTE: The control arm attaching bolt must be torqued after vehicle is lowered to

floor and is in its standing height position. Torque attaching bolt to 67 ft. lbs.

DRUM BRAKE ADJUSTMENTS

The rear drum brakes, have self-adjusting shoe mechanisms that assure correct lining-to-drum clearances at all times. The automatic adjusters operate only when the brakes are applied as the vehicle is moving rearward.

Although the brakes are self-adjusting, an initial adjustment is necessary after the brake shoes have been replaced, or when the length of the star wheel adjuster has been changed during some other service operation.

ADJUSTMENT

1. Raise and support vehicle, then remove rear wheels and brake drums.
2. Check to make sure that parking brake cable linkage and levers on secondary brake shoe are in "free" position.
3. Using tool J-21177, measure brake drum inside diameter, **Fig. 6.**
4. Turn brake adjusting screw to expand shoes to diameter obtained on outside caliper portion of tool J-21177, **Fig. 7.**
5. Adjust parking brake.

NOTE: Whenever rear drum brakes are serviced, the parking brake linkage cable at the equalizer must always be readjusted to prevent possible damage to brake shoes.

6. Install brake drums, wheels and tires and lower vehicle to floor.
7. Drive vehicle alternately forward and backward, applying brakes moderately, to obtain satisfactory pedal height.

PARKING BRAKE
ADJUST

1. Lift parking brake lever five ratchet

J-21177

Fig. 7 Adjusting brake shoe clearance

clicks, then raise and support rear of vehicle.
2. Tighten adjusting nut until right rear wheel can be rotated backward, but is locked when forward rotation is attempted.
3. Release parking brake lever. Both wheels should rotate freely with no brake drag.

MASTER CYLINDER
REPLACE

1. Disconnect electrical connector and four brake lines at master cylinder.
2. Remove two master cylinder to brake booster attaching nuts, then the master cylinder from vehicle.
3. Reverse procedure to install. Bleed brake system.

POWER BRAKE UNIT
REPLACE

1. Remove master cylinder as previously described.
2. Disconnect power brake unit pushrod at brake pedal.
3. Disconnect vacuum hose from vacuum check valve. Plug vacuum hose to prevent entry of dirt.
4. Remove four power brake unit to dash panel attaching nuts, then the power brake unit from vehicle.
5. Reverse procedure to install. Torque attaching bolts to 22–33 ft. lbs.

Front Suspension & Steering Section

Fig. 2 Modifying strut bracket to adjust camber

Fig. 1 Front suspension

Fig. 3 Front hub & wheel bearing assembly

DESCRIPTION

The front suspension, **Fig. 1,** on these vehicles is of the MacPherson strut design. The lower control arms pivot from the lower side rails through rubber bushings. The upper end of the strut is isolated by a rubber mount incorporating a non-serviceable bearing for wheel turning. The tie rods connect to the steering arm on the strut, below the spring seat. The lower end of the steering knuckle pivots on a ball stud which is retained to the lower control arm by rivets and is secured to the steering knuckle with a nut and cotter pin. The sealed wheel bearings are integral with the hub and are serviced as an assembly.

WHEEL ALIGNMENT

NOTE: Toe setting is the only adjustment normally required. However, in special circumstances, such as damage due to road hazard or collision, camber may be adjusted by modifying the strut assembly.

CAMBER ADJUSTMENT

1. Secure bottom of strut assembly in a suitable vise.
2. Enlarge bottom holes in outer flanges with a round file until holes in outer flanges match slots in inner flanges, **Fig. 2.**
3. Connect strut to steering knuckle and install bolts finger tight.
4. Grasp top of tire firmly, then move tire inboard or outboard until correct camber reading is obtained. Tighten retaining bolts enough to secure camber setting.
5. Remove wheel and tire and torque strut to steering knuckle retaining bolts to 140 ft. lbs.

TOE-OUT

Toe-Out is controlled by tie rod position. Adjustment is made by loosening the clamp bolts at the steering knuckle end of the tie rods and rotating the rods to obtain proper toe setting. After correct toe setting is obtained, torque clamp bolts to 14 ft. lbs.

WHEEL BEARING
REPLACE

REMOVAL

1. Loosen hub nut with vehicle on ground.
2. Raise and support vehicle, then remove front wheel.
3. Install drive axle protective boot cover J-28712.
4. Remove hub nut.
5. Remove brake caliper from support and suspend caliper from flame with a length of wire. Do not suspend caliper by brake hose.
6. Remove three hub and bearing attaching bolts. If the old bearing is being reinstalled, mark attaching bolts and corresponding holes for reinstallation, **Fig. 3.**
7. Using tool J-28733 or equivalent, remove bearing from steering knuckle, **Fig. 4.**

NOTE: If excessive corrosion is present, ensure that bearing is loose in the knuckle

TOOL J-28733

Fig. 4   Front hub & bearing assembly removal

TEMPORARILY INSTALL LONG BOLT

Fig. 5   Hub nut installation

BOLT MUST BE INSTALLED IN DIRECTION SHOWN

Fig. 6   Assembling lower ball joint to lower control arm

---

before using puller tool.

8. If installing new bearing, replace steering knuckle seal.

NOTE: Do not move drive axle until hub nut is installed and torqued to specifications.

INSTALLATION

1. Clean and inspect bearing mating surfaces and steering knuckle bore for dirt, nicks and burrs.
2. If installing new steering knuckle seal, apply grease to seal and knuckle bore, then press seal into steering knuckle.
3. Push bearing onto axle shaft and install two hub to steering knuckle attaching bolts. Install a longer bolt into third mounting hole and through hub cutout. Install hub to axle retaining nut and torque to 70 ft. lbs., **Fig. 5.**
4. Remove long bolt and replace with original bolt. Torque hub to steering knuckle attaching bolts to 63 ft. lbs. on 1982–83 models, or 40 ft. lbs. on 1984–86 models.
5. Install brake caliper and wheel assembly.
6. Lower vehicle and torque hub to axle nut to 185 ft. lbs.

LOWER BALL JOINT
REPLACE

1. Raise and support vehicle, then remove wheel and tire.
2. Locate center of rivet body and mark with a center punch.
3. Using a ⅛ inch drill, drill pilot holes completely through the rivets. Using a ½ inch drill, drill final holes through rivets to ensure fitting of new ball joint.
4. Remove ball joint stud retaining nut, then, using tool J-29330, separate ball joint from steering knuckle. Remove ball joint from lower control arm.
5. Assemble new ball joint to lower control arm with bolts provided in service package, **Fig. 6.** Torque bolts to 50 ft. lbs.
6. Insert ball joint stud into steering knuckle and torque nut to 55 ft. lbs.
7. Install wheel and tire, check toe setting and adjust as required.

LOWER CONTROL ARM & BUSHING
REPLACE

1. Raise and support vehicle, then remove wheel and tire.

2. Disconnect stabilizer bar at lower control arm and control arm support.
3. Using tool J-29330, separate ball joint from steering knuckle.
4. Remove control arm support to chassis retaining bolts and remove control arm support and control arm as an assembly.
5. Separate control arm from support, then using tools shown in **Fig. 7,** remove bushings from control arm.
6. Lubricate new bushings and install into control arm using tools shown in **Fig. 7.**
7. Attach lower control arm to control arm support and torque pivot bolts to 67 ft. lbs.
8. Install control arm support to chassis, using attaching bolt tightening sequence shown in **Fig. 8.** Torque bolts to 63 ft. lbs.
9. Reverse procedure to complete installation. Check toe setting and adjust as required.

STEERING KNUCKLE
REPLACE

1. Raise and support vehicle, then remove wheel and tire.
2. Remove front hub and bearing as outlined under "WHEEL BEARING, REPLACE" procedure.

CONTROL ARM

J 29792-1

J 29797-2

SUPPORT PLATE

TO REMOVE, INSERT J 29792-1 INTO BUSHING, SUPPORT CONTROL ARM ON J 29792-2, AND PRESS AS SHOWN.

CONTROL ARM

J 29792-2

J 29792-3

SUPPORT PLATE

TO INSTALL, SUPPORT CONTROL ARM ON J 29792-3, PLACE BUSHING INTO J 29792-2, AND PRESS BUSING INTO CONTROL ARM USING J 29792-1. LUBRICATE BUSHING.

Fig. 7   Replacing lower control arm bushing

1. LOOSELY INSTALL CENTER BOLT INTO HOLE (A).
2. LOOSELY INSTALL TIE BAR BOLT INTO OUTBOARD HOLE (B).
3. INSTALL BOTH REAR BOLTS INTO HOLES (C) TORQUE REAR BOLTS.
4. INSTALL BOLT INTO CENTER HOLE (D), THEN TORQUE.
5. TORQUE BOLT IN HOLE (A).
6. INSTALL BOLT INTO FRONT HOLE (E), THEN TORQUE.
7. TORQUE BOLT IN HOLE (B).

Fig. 8 Replacing lower control arm

INSTALL STABILIZER SHAFT INSULATOR WITH SLIT TOWARD FRONT OF VEHICLE AS SHOWN.

INSULATOR

SUPPORT

28 N·m (20 FT. LBS.)

Fig. 9 Stabilizer bar installation

3. Using tool J-29330, separate ball joint from steering knuckle.
4. Remove strut to steering knuckle attaching bolts, then disconnect strut from steering knuckle.
5. Assemble strut to new steering knuckle and install attaching bolts finger tight.
6. Insert ball joint stud into steering knuckle and torque stud nut to 55 ft. lbs.
7. Torque strut to steering knuckle attaching bolts to 140 ft. lbs.
8. Reverse removal procedure to complete installation.

STABILIZER BAR & BUSHINGS
REPLACE

1. Raise and support vehicle, allowing control arms to hang freely.
2. Remove left front wheel and tire.
3. Disconnect stabilizer bar at control arms and control arm supports.
4. Remove rear and center control arm support bolts, lower support assembly

and remove stabilizer bar through left side of vehicle.
5. Install stabilizer bar bushing with slit facing toward front of vehicle, **Fig. 9.**
6. Holding stabilizer bar approximately 2¼ inches above support assembly, torque stabilizer bar to control arm support attaching bolts to 20 ft. lbs, **Fig. 9.**
7. Install stabilizer bar to lower control arm and torque attaching bolts to 15 ft. lbs, **Fig. 9.**

STRUT ASSEMBLY
REPLACE

1. Raise hood and remove strut protective cap and three strut to body attaching nuts.
2. Raise and support vehicle, allowing suspension to hang freely.
3. Remove wheel and tire, then install drive axle protective cover, J-28712.
4. Using tool J-24319, disconnect tie rod from strut assembly.
5. Remove strut to steering knuckle attaching bolts, then remove strut from

vehicle.
6. Reverse procedure to install. Position flats of strut mounting bolts as shown in **Fig. 10.** Torque all nuts and bolts to specifications.

STRUT ASSEMBLY SERVICE
DISASSEMBLY

1. Clamp strut compressor tool J-26584 in a suitable vise.
2. Place strut assembly in compressor tool and install bottom adapter J-26584-86, making sure that adapter captures strut and locating pins are fully engaged, **Fig. 11.**
3. Rotate strut assembly to align top mounting assembly lip with strut compressor support notch.
4. Insert J-26584-88 top adapters between top mounting assembly and top spring seat. Position top adapters so that split line is perpendicular to spring compressor, **Fig. 11.**
5. Rotate compressor forcing screw

Fig. 10 Installing strut assembly

Fig. 11 Removing damper & coil spring from strut

clockwise until top support flange contacts top adapters. Continue rotating forcing screws until strut spring is compressed approximately ½ inch.

CAUTION: Do not bottom the spring or strut damper rod.

6. Remove damper top nut, then remove strut mounting assembly from damper shaft.
7. Rotate forcing screw counterclockwise to relieve spring tension, then remove spring from strut assembly.

STRUT CARTRIDGE REPLACEMENT

1. Clamp strut assembly firmly in a suitable vise. Do not overtighten.
2. Install pipe cutter at cut line groove located at top of strut damper. Cut around groove until reservoir tube is cut completely through, **Fig. 12.**
3. Remove and discard end cap, cylinder and piston rod assembly.
4. Place flaring cup tool, provided in service package, onto open end of reservoir tube and strike with hammer until cup flat outer surface rests on reservoir tube.
5. Install strut carriage into reservoir tube and align grooves on cartridge base with pads at bottom of reservoir tube.
6. Using tool J-29778, torque cartridge retaining hex nut to 140–170 ft. lbs.

ASSEMBLY

1. Perform Steps 1 & 2 as outlined in the "Disassembly" procedure.
2. Rotate strut assembly until mounting flange is facing outward, opposite compressor forcing screw.
3. Position spring on strut, making sure spring is properly seated on bottom spring plate, **Fig. 13.**
4. Install strut spring seat assembly and J26584-88 top adapters over strut spring.
5. Turn compressor forcing screw until compressor top support contacts top adapters.
6. Install a long extension and socket onto hex on damper shaft to align components during installation, **Fig. 14.**
7. Compress spring until approximately 1½ inch of damper shaft extends through spring plate.
8. Remove extension and socket, then position top mounting assembly over damper shaft and install retaining nut. Torque retaining nut to 68 ft. lbs.
9. Turn forcing screw counterclockwise and remove strut assembly from compressor.

MANUAL STEERING GEAR
REPLACE

1. Disconnect battery ground cable.

2. Remove left hand sound insulator.
3. From under instrument panel, pull downward on steering column seal, then remove upper pinch bolt from flexible coupling.
4. Remove air cleaner, then remove windshield washer reservoir attaching screws and position reservoir aside.
5. Raise and support front of vehicle, then remove both front wheel and tire assemblies.
6. Disconnect tie rods from struts using tool No. J24319-01, then lower vehicle.
7. Remove steering gear mounting clamps, **Fig. 15.**
8. Move steering gear assembly slightly forward, then remove lower pinch bolt from flexible coupling and detach coupling from steering gear stub shaft.
9. Remove dash panel seal from steering gear.
10. Raise and support front of vehicle, then remove splash shield from left inner fender.
11. Place left hand knuckle and hub assembly in the full left turn position, then remove steering gear through access hole in left hand inner fender.
12. Reverse procedure to install. If steering gear mounting clamp studs have backed out during removal, install double nuts on stud and torque stud to 15 ft. lbs. Torque coupling to stub shaft pinch bolt to 29 ft. lbs. and coupling to steering column shaft pinch bolt to 30 ft. lbs. Torque steering gear mounting

CUT LINE
GROOVE

STEERING ARM

VISE

PIPE
CUTTER

**Fig. 12   Strut reservoir tube
removal**

90 N·m
(68 FT. LBS.)

STRUT
MOUNTING
ASSEMBLY

SPRING SEAT

℄ OF
SPINDLE

FLAT ℄

SPRING SEAT
MUST BE
INSTALLED
WITH FLAT 10°
FORWARD OF
CENTERLINE
OF STRUT
ASM SPINDLE.

SPRING
INSULATOR

BUMPER

SHIELD

SPRING

STRUT

FRT

**Fig. 13   Strut coil spring & upper
mounting installation**

LONG EXTENSION
AND SOCKET
TO FIT HEX ON
DAMPER SHAFT

DAMPER
SHAFT

Fig. 14   Aligning strut assembly

clamp attaching nuts to 28 ft. lbs. Torque tie rod to strut attaching nuts to 35 ft. lbs. The tie rod to strut attaching nuts can be tightened up to an additional ⅛ turn to allow installation of cotter pin.

POWER STEERING GEAR
REPLACE

1. Disconnect battery ground cable.
2. Remove left hand sound insulator.
3. From under instrument panel, pull downward on steering column seal, then remove upper pinch bolt from flexible coupling.
4. Remove air cleaner, then remove windshield washer reservoir attaching screws and position reservoir aside.
5. Disconnect pressure line from steering gear and remove screw attaching line bracket to cowl.
6. Raise and support front of vehicle, then remove both front wheel and tire assemblies.
7. Disconnect tie rods from struts using tool No. J24319-01, then lower vehicle.
8. Remove steering gear mounting clamps, **Fig. 15.**
9. Move steering gear slightly forward, then disconnect return line from gear and drain power steering fluid.
10. Remove lower pinch bolt from flexible coupling, then detach coupling from steering gear stub shaft and remove dash seal.

50 N·m (35 FT. LBS.) AFTER REACHING TORQUE REQUIRED, NUT MUST ALWAYS BE TIGHTENED (UP TO 1/6 TURN) FURTHER. NEVER BACK OFF TO INSERT COTTER PIN.

Fig. 15 Power rack & pinion steering gear removal

Fig. 16 Power steering pump removal

11. Raise and support front of vehicle, then remove splash shield from left inner fender.
12. Place steering knuckle and hub assembly into the full left turn position, then remove steering gear through access hole in left hand inner fender.
13. Reverse procedure to install. If steering gear mounting clamps have backed out during removal, install double nuts on stud and torque to 15 ft. lbs. Torque coupling to stub shaft pinch bolt to 37 ft. lbs. and coupling to steering column shaft pinch bolts to 30 ft. lbs. Torque steering gear mounting clamp attaching nuts to 28 ft. lbs.

Torque pressure and return line fittings to 20 ft. lbs. Torque tie rod to strut attaching nuts to 35 ft. lbs. The tie rod to strut attaching nuts can be tightened up to an additional 1/6 turn to allow installation of cotter pin.

POWER STEERING PUMP
REPLACE

1. Remove air cleaner assembly.
2. Disconnect reservoir to pump hose and pressure line from pump.

3. Remove clip attaching pressure line to pump.
4. Loosen pump pivot and adjusting bolts, then remove pump drive belt.
5. Remove three pump to bracket attaching bolts, **Fig. 16.**

NOTE: On some models, the pump may be attached to bracket by special bolts. To remove these special bolts, use tool No. T-45 or equivalent.

6. Remove pump from mounting bracket.
7. Reverse procedure to install.

NOTE: Refer to the rear of this manual for vehicle manufacturer's special service tool suppliers.

Serial Number Location

On top of instrument panel, left front.

Engine Number Location

On all engines except V6-252, V8-250 and V8-350, engine unit number is located on cylinder block behind left cylinder head. V.I.N. derivative is located on cylinder block behind intake manifold.

The engine identification number on V6-252 engines is stamped on the left rear of cylinder block.

On 1980—82 V8-350, engine code label is located on top of left hand valve cover and engine unit number label is located on top of right hand valve cover. On 1983—86 V8-250, engine code label is located on front left side of crankcase below the cylinder head.

On 1982—86 V8-250 engines, the engine identification plate is located on a pad at the lower left side of the crankcase.

Engine Identification

Year	Engine	V.I.N. Code	Engine Code
1980	V6-252⑥	4	MF, MZ
	V8-350③④	N	VCJ, VCS, VBW
	V8-350③⑤⑥	N	VBK, VCK
	V8-350①⑤⑥	8	HFA, VBX
	V8-368②④	6	HAA, HBA, KA
	V8-368①⑤	9	HDA
	V8-368①⑥	9	HHA
1981	V6-252⑦	4	SA, SB, SC, SD, SF, SG, SJ, SK, SL, SM, SN, SP, SQ
1982	V6-252⑦	4	FA, FB, FC, FD, FE, FF, FG, FH, FJ, FK
	V8-250①	8	AA, AB, AD, AF
	V8-350③	N	VKB, VKC, VKH, VKJ, VKN, VKR, VKU, VKY, VLA, VLC, VLD, VLK, VLL, VLN, VLP, VL8, VLY, VMJ, VMT, VMX, VMY, VNA, VNB, VNC, VND, VNE, VPB, VPC, VPD, VPF
	V8-368①	9	AA, BA, CA, DA, FA, HA, RA, SA, TA

Year	Engine	V.I.N. Code	Engine Code
	V8-350③	N	VAB, VAC, VAD, VAK, VAL, VAM, VAN, VAP, VAS, VAU, VAW, VAX, VAY, VAZ, VBA, VBB, VBC, VBP, VBU, VBW
1983	V8-250①	8	HLA, HMA, HNA, HOA, HPA, HQA, HRA
	V8-350③	N	VKB, VKC, VKD, VKK, VKL, VKR, VKS, VKT, VKZ, VLA, VLB, VLP, VLS, VLT, VLW
1984	V8-250①	8	....
	V8-350③	N	....
1985	V8-250①	8	....
	V8-350③	N	....
1986	V8-250		

①—Fuel injected engine.
②—Carbureted engine.
③—Oldsmobile built diesel engine.
④—Brougham & DeVille.
⑤—Eldorado.
⑥—Seville.
⑦—Buick built engine.

Grille Identification

1980 Exc. Eldorado & Seville	1980 Eldorado	1980—81 Seville
1981 Exc. Eldorado & Seville	**1981 Eldorado**	**1982 Exc. Eldorado & Seville**

GRILLE IDENTIFICATION—Continued

1982 Eldorado	1982 Seville	1983 Exc. Eldorado & Seville
1983 Eldorado	1983 Seville	1984 Exc. Eldorado & Seville 1985–86 Fleetwood Brougham
1984–85 Eldorado	1984 Seville	1985 Seville

General Engine Specifications

Year	Engine CID①/Liter	Engine VIN Code②	Carburetor	Bore and Stroke	Compression Ratio	Net H.P. @ R.P.M.③	Maximum Torque Ft. Lbs. @ R.P.M.	Normal Oil Pressure Pounds
1980	V6-252, 4.1L⑦	4	M4ME, 4 Bbl④	3.96 × 3.40	8.0	125 @ 4000	205 @ 2000	37
	V8-350, 5.7L⑤	N	Fuel Injection	4.057 × 3.385	22.5	105 @ 3200	205 @ 1600	30–45
	V8-350, 5.7L	8	Fuel Injection	4.057 × 3.385	8.0	160 @ 4400	265 @ 1600	30–45
	V8-368, 6.0L	9	Fuel Injection	3.800 × 4.060	8.2	145 @ 3600	270 @ 2000	30–45
	V8-368, 6.0L	6	M4ME, 4 Bbl④⑥	3.800 × 4.060	8.2	150 @ 3800	265 @ 1600	30–45
1981	V6-252, 4.1L⑦	4	E4ME, 4 Bbl④	3.96 × 3.40	8.0	125 @ 3800	210 @ 2000	37
	V8-350, 5.7L⑤	N	Fuel Injection	4.06 × 3.38	22.5	105 @ 3200	200 @ 1600	30–45
	V8-368, 6.0L	9	Fuel Injection	3.80 × 4.06	8.2	140 @ 3800	265 @ 1400	30–45
1982	V6-252, 4.1L⑦	4	E4ME, 4 Bbl.④	3.96 × 3.40	8.0	125 @ 4000	205 @ 2000	37
	V8-250, 4.1L	8	Fuel Injection	3.465 × 3.307	8.5	135 @ 4600	200 @ 1600	30
	V8-350, 5.7L⑤	N	Fuel Injection	4.06 × 3.38	22.5	105 @ 3200	200 @ 1600	30–45
1983	V8-250, 4.1L	8	Fuel Injection	3.465 × 3.307	8.5	135 @ 4200	200 @ 2200	30
	V8-350, 5.7L⑤	N	Fuel Injection	4.06 × 3.38	22.5	105 @ 3200	200 @ 1600	30–45
1984–85	V8-250, 4.1L	8	Fuel Injection	3.465 × 3.307	8.5	135 @ 4400	200 @ 2200	30
	V8-350, 5.7L⑤	N	Fuel Injection	4.06 × 3.38	22.7	105 @ 3200	200 @ 1600	30–45
1986	V8-250, 4.1L	8	Fuel Injection	3.465 × 3.307	8.5	135 @ 4400	200 @ 2200	30

①—CID—Cubic inch displacement.
②—On 1980 vehicles, the fifth digit in the VIN denotes the engine code. On 1981–86 vehicles, the eighth digit in the VIN denotes the engine code.
③—Net rating—as installed in the vehicle.
④—Rochester.
⑤—Oldsmobile built diesel engine.
⑥—DeVille and all vehicles with C-4 system, E4ME.
⑦—Buick built engine.

Alternator Specifications

Year	Alternator		
	Model	Rated Hot Output Amps.	Field Current 12 Volts @ 80° F.
1980—81	1101040	70	4.0—4.5
	1101050	100	4.4—4.9
	1101061	80	4.0—4.6
1982—85	1101044	70	4.0—4.6
	1101046	80	4.4—4.9
	1101050	100	4.4—4.9
1986	—	—	—

Starting Motor Applications

Year	Engine/V.I.N.	Starter Number	Year	Engine/V.I.N.	Starter Number
1980	V8-350/N④⑥	1109216		V8-350/N⑥	1109216
	V8-350/N③⑤⑥	1109218	1983	V8-250/8②④	1109531
	V8-350/8②③⑤	1998205		V8-250/8②③⑤	1998233
	V8-368/5①④	1109062		V8-350/N④⑥	1109216
	V8-368/T②③⑤	1998205		V8-350/N③⑤⑥	1109495
1981	V6-252/4①	1109062	1984—85	V8-250/8②④	—
	V8-350/N⑥	1109216		V8-250/8②③⑤	—
	V8-368/T②	1109062		V8-350/N④⑥	—
1982	V8-250/8②	1109531		V8-350/N③⑤⑥	—
	V6-252/4①	1109062	1986	V8-250/8④	—

①—4 Bbl.
②—Fuel injected.
③—Seville.
④—Exc. Eldorado & Seville.
⑤—Eldorado.
⑥—Diesel engine.

Engine Tightening Specifications★

★ Torque specifications are for clean and lightly lubricated threads only. Dry or dirty threads produce increased friction which prevents accurate measurement of tightness.

Year & Engine/V.I.N.	Spark Plugs Ft. Lbs.	Cylinder Head Bolts Ft. Lbs.	Intake Manifold Ft. Lbs.	Exhaust Manifold Ft. Lbs.	Rocker Arm Shaft Bracket Ft. Lbs.	Rocker Arm Cover Ft. Lbs.	Connecting Rod Cap Bolts Ft. Lbs.	Main Bearing Cap Bolts Ft. Lbs.	Flex Plate to Crankshaft Ft. Lbs.	Vibration Damper or Pulley Ft. Lbs.
1980 V8-350/B,8	25	130⑤	40⑤	25⑦	25⑥	7	42	②	60	310
1980—85 V8-350/N④	—	130⑤	40⑤	25	28⑥	3	42	120	60	200—310
1980—82 V6-252/4⑦	15	80	45	25	30	4	40	100	60	225
1980—81 V8-368/6,9	25	95	30	③	⑥⑩	71①	40	90	75	17
1982—85 V8-250/8	10	⑧	⑨	20	20⑥	50①	20	85	35	20
1986 V8-250/8	—	—	—	—	—	—	—	—	—	—

①—Inch pounds. Retorque after engine has been run.
②—Exc. No. 5, 80 ft. lbs.; No. 5, 120 ft. lbs.
③—Long screws, 35 ft. lbs. Short screw, 12 ft. lbs.
④—Diesel engine.
⑤—Clean and dip entire bolt in engine oil before tightening.
⑥—Rocker arm pivot bolt to head.
⑦—Buick built engine.
⑧—Torque bolts to 45 ft. lbs., then retorque to 90 ft. lbs.
⑨—Refer to text for procedure.
⑩—70 ft. lbs. on 1980 models; 22 ft. lbs. on 1981 models.

Valve Specifications

Year	Engine/V.I.N.	Valve Lash	Valve Angles		Valve Spring Installed Height	Valve Spring Pressure Lbs. @ In.	Stem Clearance		Stem Diameter	
			Seat	Face			Intake	Exhaust	Intake	Exhaust
1980	V8-350/8	Hydraulic①	②	③	1.670	187 @ 1.27	.0010–.0027	.0015–.0032	.3425–.3432	.3420–.3427
1980-81	V6-252/4⑤	Hydraulic①	45	45	1.727	⑥	.0015–.0035	.0015–.0032	.3401–.3412	.3405–.3412
	V8-350/N④	Hydraulic①	②	③	1.670	210 @ 1.3	.0010–.0027	.0015–.0032	.3425–.3432	.3420–.3427
	V8-368/6,9	Hydraulic①	45	44	1.946	160 @ 1.496	.0010–.0027	.0010–.0027	.3413–.3420	.3413–.3420
1982	V8-250/8	Hydraulic①	45	44	1.73	182 @ 1.28	.001–.003	.001–.003	.3413–.3420	.3411–.3418
	V6-252/4⑤	Hydraulic①	45	45	1.727	220 @ 1.34	.0015–.0035	.0015–.0032	.3401–.3412	.3405–.3412
	V6-350/N④	Hydraulic①	②	③	1.670	210 @ 1.22	.0010–.0027	.0015–.0032	.3425–.3432	.3420–.3427
1983-85	V8-250/8	Hydraulic①	45	44	1.73	182 @ 1.28	.001–.003	.001–.003	.3413–.3420	.3411–.3418
	V8-350/N④	Hydraulic①	②	③	1.670	210 @ 1.22	.0010–.0027	.0015–.0032	.3425–.3432	.3420–.3427
1986	V8-250/8	Hydraulic①	45	44	1.73	182 @ 1.28	.001–.003	.001–.003	.3413–.3420	.3411–.3418

①—No adjustment.
②—Intake 45°; exhaust 31°.
③—Intake 44°; exhaust 30°.
④—Diesel engine.
⑤—Buick built engine.
⑥—Intake, 164 @ 1.34; Exhaust, 182 @ 1.34.

Pistons, Pins, Rings, Crankshaft & Bearings

Year	Model/ V.I.N.	Piston Clearance	Ring End Gap①		Wrist-pin Diameter	Rod Bearings		Main Bearings			
			Comp.	Oil		Shaft Diameter	Bearing Clearance	Shaft Diameter	Bearing Clearance	Thrust on Bear. No.	Shaft End Play
1980	V8-350/8	.0010–.0020	.010②	.015②	.9805	2.1238–2.1248	.0004–.0033	④	⑤	3	.0035–.0135
1980-81	V6-252/4⑦	.0008–.0020	.013	.015	.9394	2.2495	.0005–.0026	2.4995	.0003–.0018	2	.003–.009
	V8-350/N⑥	.0050–.0060	.015	.015	1.0951	1.877–1.887	.0005–.0026	2.9993–3.0003	⑤	3	.0035–.0135
	V8-368/6,9	.0006–.0014	.013	.015	.9997	2.500	.0005–.0028	3.250	.0005–.0026	3	.002–.013
1982	V6-252/4⑦	.0008–.0020	.013	.015	.9393	2.2487–2.2495	③	2.4995	.0003–.0018	2	.003–.009
1982-85	V8-250/8	.0010–.0018	.009	.010	.8658	1.93	.0005–.0028	2.64	.0004–.003	—	.001–.007
	V8-350/N⑥	.0030–.0040	.015	.015	1.0951	2.1238–2.1248	.0005–.0026	2.9993–3.0003	⑤	3	.0035–.0135
1986	V8-250/8	.0010–.0018	.009	.010	.8658	1.93	.0005–.0028	2.64	.0004–.003	—	.001–.007

①—Fit rings in tapered bores for clearance given in tightest portion of ring travel.
②—See text.
③—No. 1, .0005–.0025 inch; Nos. 2, 3, 4, .0005–.0035 inch.
④—Exc. No. 1, 2.4985–2.4995; No. 1, 2.4988–2.4998.
⑤—Exc. No. 5, .0005–.0021; No. 5 .0015–.0031.
⑥—Diesel engine.
⑦—Buick built engine.

Wheel Alignment Specifications

Year	Model	Caster Angle, Degrees		Camber Angle, Degrees				Toe-In. Inch	Toe-Out on Turns, Deg.	
		Limits	Desired	Limits		Desired			Outer Wheel	Inner Wheel
				Left	Right	Left	Right			
1980-85	Eldorado & Seville	+2 to +3	+2½	−½ to +½	−½ to +½	Zero	Zero	−1/16 to +1/16	—	—
	Others	+2½ to +3½	+3	+.1 to +.9	+.1 to +.9	+½	+½	⅛	—	—
1986	Brougham	+2½ to +3½	+3	+.1 to +.9	+.1 to +.9	+½	+½	⅛	—	—

Drive Axle Specifications

Year	Model	Carrier Type	Ring Gear Pinion Backlash		Pinion Bearing Preload			Differential Bearing Preload		
			Method	Adjustment	Method	Adjustment New Bearings Inch-Lbs.	Adjustment Used Bearings Inch-Lbs.	Method	Adjustment New Bearings Inch-Lbs.	Adjustment Used Bearings Inch-Lbs.
1980–82	Exc. Eldorado & Seville	Integral	Shims	.005–.009①	Shims	24–32	8–12	Shims	②	②
	Eldorado & Seville	Integral	Shims	.005–.009①	Shims	18–24	5	Shims	③	③
1983–85	Exc. Eldorado & Seville	Integral	Shims	.006–.008①	Shims	20–25	10–15	Shims	②	②
	Eldorado & Seville	Integral	Shims	.005–.009①	Shims	18–24	5	Shims	③	③
1986	Eldorado & Seville	—	—	—	—	—	—	—	—	—
	Exc. Eldorado & Seville	—	—	—	—	—	—	—	—	—

①—New gears. ②—Slip fit plus .008". ③—Slip fit plus .006".

Cooling System & Capacity Data

Year	Model or Engine/V.I.N.	Cooling Capacity, Qts. Less A/C	With A/C	Radiator Cap Relief Pressure, Lbs.	Thermo. Opening Temp.	Fuel Tank Gals.	Engine Oil Refill Qts. ①	3 Speed Pints	4 Speed Pints	Auto. Trans. Qts. ②	Rear Axle Oil Pints
1980	Eldorado V8-350 E.F.I./8	—	15.2	15	178	20.6	4	—	—	⑧	3⅛⑦
	Eldorado V8-368 D.E.F.I./9	—	22.4	15	178	20.6	5	—	—	⑧	3⅛⑦
	Eldorado V8-350 Diesel/N	—	18.5	15	195	23	7⑩	—	—	⑧	3⅛⑦
	Seville V8-350 E.F.I./8	—	15.2	15	178	20.6	4	—	—	⑧	3⅛⑦
	Seville V8-368 D.E.F.I./9	—	22.4	15	178	20.6	5	—	—	⑧	3⅛⑦
	Seville V8-350 Diesel/N	—	18.5	15	195	23	7⑩	—	—	⑧	3⅛⑦
	Others V6-252/4	—	13	15	195	25	4	—	—	4③	4¼
	Others V8-368/6	—	21.4	15	195	20.7	4	—	—	4③	4¼
	Others V8-350 Diesel/N	—	23.7	15	195	26	7⑩	—	—	⑨	4¼
1981	Eldorado V6-252/4	—	13.1	15	195	21.1	4	—	—	⑧	3⅛⑦
	Eldorado V8-368 D.E.F.I./9	—	22.4	15	178	20.3	4	—	—	⑧	3⅛⑦
	Eldorado V8-350 Diesel/N	—	18.4	15	195	22.8	7⑪	—	—	⑧	3⅛⑦
	Seville V6-252/4	—	13.1	15	195	21.1	4	—	—	⑧	3⅛⑦
	Seville V8-368 D.E.F.I./9	—	22.4	15	178	20.3	4	—	—	⑧	3⅛⑦
	Seville V8-350 Diesel/N	—	18.4	15	195	22.8	7⑪	—	—	⑧	3⅛⑦
	Others V6-252/4	—	18.2	15	195	25	4	—	—	⑬	4¼
	Others V8-368/9	—	21.4	15	195	25	4	—	—	⑬	4¼
	Others V8-350 Diesel/N	—	23.7	15	195	27	7⑪	—	—	⑬	4¼
1982	Eldorado V6-252/4	—	13.1	15	195	21.1	4	—	—	⑥	3⅛⑦
	Seville V6-252/4	—	13.1	15	195	21.1	4	—	—	⑥	3⅛⑦
	Others V6-252/4	—	18.2	15	195	25	4	—	—	⑫	4¼
	Eldorado V8-250/8	—	11.8	15	195	20.3	5④	—	—	⑥	3⅛⑦
	Seville V8-250/8	—	11.8	15	195	20.3	5④	—	—	⑥	3⅛⑦
	Others V8-250/8	—	10.8	15	195	25	4④	—	—	⑫	4¼
	Eldorado V8-350 Diesel/N	—	18.4	15	195	22.8	7⑪	—	—	⑥	3⅛⑦
	Seville V8-350 Diesel/N	—	18.4	15	195	22.8	7⑪	—	—	⑥	3⅛⑦
	Others V8-350 Diesel/N	—	23.7	15	195	27	7⑪	—	—	⑫	4¼

continued

COOLING SYSTEM & CAPACITY DATA—Continued

Year	Model or Engine/V.I.N.	Cooling Capacity, Qts.		Radiator Cap Relief Pressure, Lbs.	Thermo. Opening Temp.	Fuel Tank Gals.	Engine Oil Refill Qts. ①	Transmission Oil			Rear Axle Oil Pints
		Less A/C	With A/C					3 Speed Pints	4 Speed Pints	Auto. Trans. Qts. ②	
1983	Eldorado V8-250/8	—	10.9	15	195	20.3	5④	—	—	⑤	3⅕⑦
	Seville V8-250/8	—	10.9	15	195	20.3	5④	—	—	⑤	3⅕⑦
	Others V8-250/8	—	11.0	15	195	24.5	4④	—	—	⑭	4¼
	Eldorado Diesel/N	—	18.4	15	195	22.8	7⑪	—	—	⑤	3⅕⑦
	Seville Diesel/N	—	18.4	15	195	22.8	7⑪	—	—	⑤	3⅕⑦
	Others Diesel/N	—	23.7	15	195	26	7⑪	—	—	⑭	4¼
1984–85	Eldorado V8-250/8	—	—	15	195	20.3	5④	—	—	—	3⅕⑦
	Seville V8-250/8	—	—	15	195	20.3	5④	—	—	—	3⅕⑦
	Others V8-250/8	—	—	15	195	24.5	4④	—	—	—	4¼
	Eldorado Diesel/N	—	—	15	195	22.8	7⑪	—	—	—	3⅕⑦
	Seville Diesel/N	—	—	15	195	22.8	7⑪	—	—	—	3⅕⑦
	Others Diesel/N	—	—	15	195	26	7⑪	—	—	—	4¼
1986	Brougham	—	—	15	195	24.5	4④	—	—	—	4¼

①—Add one quart with filter change.
②—Approximate. Make final check with dipstick.
③—Oil pan only.
④—Includes filter.
⑤—Oil pan 5 qts. Total capacity 13 qts.
⑥—Oil pan 5 qts. Total capacity 11¾ qts.
⑦—Front drive axle.
⑧—Oil pan 5 qts. Total capacity 12 qts.

⑨—Oil pan 3 qts. Total capacity 9 qts.
⑩—Includes filter. Recommended diesel engine oil—1980, use oil designated SE/CC.
⑪—Includes oil filter. Recommended diesel engine oil—use oil designated SF/CD, SF/CC or SE/CC on all except 1982–85 models or SF/CD, SF/CC on

1982–85 models.
⑫—Oil pan 3½ qts. Total capacity 11 qts.
⑬—THM 200C—oil pan 3½ qts., total capacity 11 qts.; THM 350 & 350C—oil pan 3.15 qts., total capacity 10 qts.; THM 400—oil pan 3 qts., total capacity 10 qts.
⑭—Oil pan, 5 qts. Total capacity, 11 qts.

Electrical Section

Fig. 1 Ignition lock removal. 1980–86 models

Fig. 2 Ignition switch. 1980–86

STARTER
REPLACE

1980–86

1. Disconnect battery ground cable (two ground cables on diesel engines).
2. Raise and support front of vehicle.
3. Remove starter braces, shields, brackets and clips that may interfere with starter removal.
4. Remove starter attaching bolts, then lower starter.
5. Disconnect wiring harness from starter and remove starter.
6. Reverse procedure to install.

IGNITION LOCK
REPLACE

1980–86

1. Remove steering wheel as described under Horn Sounder and Steering Wheel.
2. Remove turn signal switch as described under Turn Signal Switch, Replace, then remove buzzer switch.
3. Place ignition switch in Run position, then remove lock cylinder retaining screw and lock cylinder.
4. To install, rotate lock cylinder to stop while holding housing, **Fig. 1.** Align cylinder key with keyway in housing, then push lock cylinder assembly into housing until fully seated.
5. Install lock cylinder retaining screw. Torque screw to 40 in. lbs. for standard columns. On adjustable columns, torque retaining screw to 22 in. lbs.
6. Install buzzer switch, turn signal switch and steering wheel.

IGNITION SWITCH
REPLACE

1980–86

1. Disconnect battery cable and position ignition key in "Lock".
2. Remove steering column lower cover.
3. Loosen two upper column support nuts and allow column to drop as far as possible without removing the nuts.

NOTE: Do not remove nuts as column may bend under its own weight.

4. Disconnect switch connector and remove switch, **Fig. 2.**
5. When reassembling, make sure the ignition key is in the "Lock" position. Assemble switch on actuator rod. Hold rod stationary and move switch towards bottom of column, then back off one detent on standard steering column models. On models with tilt column, move switch toward upper end of column, then back off one detent.

LIGHT SWITCH
REPLACE

1980–85 ELDORADO & SEVILLE

1. Disconnect battery ground cable.
2. Remove instrument cluster trim panel.
3. Remove two screws attaching switch to cluster carrier, then pull switch rearward to remove.
4. Reverse procedure to install.

1980–86 EXCEPT ELDORADO & SEVILLE

1. Disconnect battery ground cable.
2. Remove left hand instrument panel insert.
3. Remove three screws attaching light switch to instrument panel.
4. On vehicles equipped with Cruise Control and Twilight Sentinel, remove two screws retaining Cruise Control switch to instrument panel.
5. Slide Cruise Control switch forward to remove headlamp switch.
6. Disconnect electrical connector from headlamp switch, then if used, disconnect Guidematic connector from under instrument panel.
7. Remove switch.
8. Reverse procedure to install.

STOP LIGHT SWITCH
1980–86

The stoplight switch is retained to the brake pedal bracket. To adjust, pull the brake pedal fully up to its stop. This action automatically adjusts the switch.

NEUTRAL START SWITCH
1980–86 MODELS

Actuation of the ignition switch is prevented by a mechanical lockout system, **Figs. 3 and 4,** which prevents the lock cylinder from rotating when the selector lever is out of Park or Neutral. When the selector lever is in Park or Neutral, the slots in the bowl plate and the finger on the actuator rod align allowing the finger to pass through the bowl plate in turn actuating the ignition switch, **Fig. 5.** If the selector lever is in any position other than Park or Neutral, the finger contacts the bowl plate when the lock cylinder is rotated,

Fig. 3 Mechanical neutral switch system with Tilt-Telescope column. 1980–86

Fig. 4 Mechanical neutral start system with standard column. 1980–86 models

Fig. 5 Mechanical neutral start system in Park position

Fig. 6 Compressing lock plate & removing snap ring

Fig. 7 Taping turn signal connector & wiring

thereby preventing full travel of the lock cylinder.

NOTE: On all models incorporating an electric neutral start switch, this switch plus the back-up light switch and parking brake vacuum release valve are combined into one unit. This unit is mounted on the steering column under the instrument panel.

TURN SIGNAL SWITCH
REPLACE

1980–86

Standard Column

1. Disconnect battery ground cable, then remove steering wheel.
2. Remove lock plate cover.
3. Using tool J-23653 or equivalent, compress lock plate and spring, then remove snap ring from groove in steering shaft, **Fig. 6.**
4. Remove lock plate, turn signal cancelling cam, upper bearing preload spring and thrust washer from steering shaft.

CAUTION: At this point steering shaft is free. Do not slide shaft out of steering column.

5. Remove turn signal lever attaching screw, then signal lever.

6. On vehicles equipped with cruise control, proceed as follows:
   a. Attach a long piece of piano wire to cruise control switch harness connector.
   b. Pull cruise control harness up through and out of column.
   c. Remove piano wire from harness connector. Do not remove wire from column.
7. On all models, remove turn signal switch attaching screws, then slide switch wire connector off bracket.
8. Remove mounting bracket to steering column attaching bolts, then bracket.
9. Disconnect switch connector from wire harness.
10. Wrap a piece of tape around switch connector and harness to facilitate removal, **Fig. 7.**
11. Pull turn signal straight up with wire protector attached, and remove switch harness and connector from column.
12. Reverse procedure to install.

Tilt & Telescope Wheel
1. Disconnect battery cable.
2. Remove steering wheel and slide rubber sleeve from steering shaft.
3. Remove plastic retainer from C-ring.
4. With a suitable compressor, thread bolt into steering shaft lock hole.
5. Compress preload spring and remove C-ring, **Fig. 6.**
6. Remove compressor and remove lock plate, horn contact carrier and preload spring.
7. Remove steering column lower cover and the signal lever.
8. On cars equipped with cruise control proceed as follows:
   a. Disconnect cruise control wire from harness.
   b. Remove harness protector from cruise control.
   c. Wrap wire around turn signal lever until lever is disconnected. Do not remove wire from column.
9. On all models remove bolts at upper support.
10. Remove four screws securing upper mounting bracket to column and remove bracket.
11. Disconnect turn signal harness and remove wires from plastic protector. Wrap a piece of tape around connector and harness to facilitate removal, **Fig. 7.**

12. Remove screw securing turn signal switch to column and pull switch out.
13. Reverse procedure to install.

HORN SOUNDER & STEERING WHEEL
REPLACE

1980–86

1. Disconnect battery ground cable.
2. Remove attaching screws from back of spokes and lift pad assembly from wheel.
3. Remove horn contact wire from plastic tower.
4. On tilt and telescope models, remove three screws securing lever assembly to adjuster, then adjuster from steering shaft.
5. On standard models, remove locking lever assembly.
6. On all models, scribe an alignment mark on wheel hub in line with slash mark on steering shaft to be used upon installation.
7. Loosen steering shaft nut, then using a suitable puller, remove nut and wheel.
8. Reverse procedure to install.

INSTRUMENT CLUSTER
REPLACE

1980–85 ELDORADO & SEVILLE

1. Disconnect battery ground cable.
2. Remove instrument cluster trim panel.
3. Remove headlamp and windshield wiper switches.
4. Unlock headlamp, windshield wiper and cruise control wire connectors from cluster carrier.
5. Disconnect speedometer cable and instrument cluster wiring.
6. Remove instrument cluster attaching screws and remove cluster assembly.
7. Reverse procedure to install.

1980–86 EXCEPT SEVILLE & ELDORADO

1. Disconnect battery ground cable.
2. Remove cluster bezel, then with shift lever in "Park" remove screw securing shift indicator cable to steering column.
3. Remove four screws securing cluster to instrument horizontal support, **Fig. 8.**

NOTE: On vehicles equipped with speed control sensor, disconnect sensor from cluster before completely removing cluster assembly. This will prevent connector from damaging cluster during removal.

4. Disengage speedometer cable at neck by pulling cluster straight out and depressing retaining spring.

NOTE: To remove cluster, place shift lever in low range and on cars with tilt wheel, place wheel in lowest position.

5. Rotate cluster downward, disconnect printed circuit connector and remove cluster.
6. Reverse procedure to install.

RADIO
REPLACE

NOTE: When installing radio, be sure to adjust antenna trimmer for peak performance.

1980–85 ELDORADO & SEVILLE

1. Disconnect battery ground cable.
2. Remove center applique retaining screws, radio knobs, and hex nuts, then remove center applique.
3. Remove rear window defogger switch on 1980–81 Eldorado and Seville.
4. Remove radio mounting screws, then pull radio rearward. Disconnect electrical connectors and antenna lead

Fig. 8   Instrument cluster. 1980–86 Exc. Eldorado & Seville

from radio, then remove radio.
5. Reverse procedure to install.

1980–86 EXCEPT ELDORADO & SEVILLE

1. Remove center instrument panel insert.
2. Remove screws retaining radio to lower instrument panel.
3. Disconnect electrical connectors and antenna leads(s) and remove radio.

W/S WIPER MOTOR
1980–86

1. Raise hood and remove cowl screen. On 1980–85 Eldorado and Seville, remove cowl panel prior to removing cowl screen.
2. Loosen transmission drive link to crank arm attaching nuts.
3. Remove transmission drive link from motor crank arm.
4. Disconnect motor electrical connectors and hoses.
5. Remove motor attaching screws, then remove motor while guiding crank arm through hole.
6. Reverse procedure to install.

NOTE: Check to ensure wiper motor is in

Park position before assembling crank arm to transmission drive link.

W/S WIPER TRANSMISSION
1980–86

1. Raise hood and remove cowl vent screen. On Seville it is first necessary to remove cowl panel.
2. Loosen attaching nuts securing transmission drive link to motor crank arm.
3. Disconnect transmission drive link from crank arm.
4. Remove attaching screws securing transmission to body.
5. Remove transmission and linkage assembly through plenum chamber opening.

W/S WIPER SWITCH
1980–85 ELDORADO & SEVILLE

1. Disconnect battery ground cable.
2. Remove instrument cluster trim panel.
3. Remove two screws attaching switch

Fig. 9 Heater core. 1980–85 Eldorado & Seville

Fig. 10 Blower motor. 1980–86 (Typical)

to cluster carrier, then pull switch rearward to remove.
4. Reverse procedure to install.

EXCEPT 1980–86 ELDORADO & SEVILLE

1. Disconnect battery ground cable.
2. Remove left hand climate control outlet grille.
3. Remove screw securing switch to instrument panel.
4. Pull control switch and electrical connector out and disconnect from panel.

HEATER CORE
REPLACE

After draining radiator and disconnecting heater hoses and battery ground cable proceed as follows:

1980–85 ELDORADO & SEVILLE

1. Plug heater core outlets to prevent spillage when removing heater core.
2. Remove instrument panel sound absorbers, then lower steering column.
3. Remove instrument cluster trim panel and instrument cluster as described under Instrument Cluster, Replace.
4. Remove radio front speakers.
5. Remove screws attaching manifold to heater case.
6. Remove instrument panel upper and lower attaching screws, then disconnect parking brake release cable.
7. Disconnect instrument panel wiring harness from dash wiring assembly.
8. Disconnect right hand remote control mirror cable from instrument panel pad.
9. Disconnect speedometer cable from clip and temperature control cable from heater case.
10. Disconnect radio and A/C wiring, vacuum lines and all necessary wiring to remove instrument panel. If equipped with pulse wipers, remove wiper switch, and then disconnect wire connector from instrument cluster carrier and separate pulse wiper jumper harness from wiper switch wire connector.

11. Remove instrument panel and wiring harness assembly.
12. Remove four screws retaining defroster nozzle to cowl and one screw at heater case, then remove defroster nozzle.
13. Disconnect vacuum hoses to programmer and vacuum actuators.
14. Disconnect wire connector from programmer.
15. From engine side of dash, remove four nuts retaining heater case to cowl, **Fig. 9.**
16. From passenger compartment side of dash, remove one screw retaining heater case to cowl, and remove heater case.
17. Remove four screws securing heater core to case and remove heater core.
18. Reverse procedure to install.

1980–86 EXCEPT ELDORADO & SEVILLE

1. Disconnect electrical connectors from blower motor, blower resistors and thermostatic cycling switch.
2. Remove right hand windshield washer nozzle and remove right hand air inlet screen from plenum and cover plate at center of plenum opening.
3. On 1983–85 models, remove blower motor.
4. On all models, remove screws retaining thermostatic cycling switch and position switch aside.
5. Remove the 16 fasteners retaining cover and remove cover.
6. Remove one screw and retainer holding heater core to frame at top.
7. Place temperature door in the max. heat position and reach through temperature housing and push lower forward corner of heater core away from housing, then rotate core parallel to housing. This will cause core to snap out of lower clamp. Remove heater core from temperature housing.
8. Reverse procedure to install.

BLOWER MOTOR
REPLACE

1980 ELDORADO & SEVILLE & 1981–86 ALL MODELS

1. Disconnect battery ground cable.
2. Disconnect wire connector and cooling hose.
3. Remove five blower motor attaching screws and remove blower motor.
4. Reverse procedure to install.

1980 EXCEPT ELDORADO & SEVILLE

1. Disconnect battery ground cable.
2. Remove cooling hose from nipple and blower.
3. Disconnect electrical connector at lead to motor.
4. Unfasten and remove motor, **Fig. 10.**
5. Reverse procedure to install.

SPEED CONTROL
ADJUST

Bead Chain Adjustment

On 1980–81 Eldorado, install the bead chain with second ball on the inboard slot of the throttle plate clip. This will provide the proper adjustment.

On 1980–81 Seville models, install bead chain to throttle plate clip, and adjust chain in clip to provide a minimum of sag without holding the throttle open. Inboard to outboard slot on the clip will provide a ½ ball adjustment.

On 1980–81 models except Eldorado and Seville, a control cable is used in place of the bead chain. With cable installed in throttle bracket and throttle lever, pull power unit end of cable as far as it will go. If one of four holes in power unit tab is aligned with cable pin, connect pin to tab with retainer. If tab does not align, move cable away from tab until the next closest hole in tab aligns with cable pin and connect pin to tab with retainer.

On 1982 V6-252 models except Eldorado and Seville, a bead chain is used. Install bead chain into throttle lever clip and lock into position. With throttle lever in hot idle position and idle control solenoid de-energized, place bead chain into swivel cavity. The ball swivel must be installed on the inboard side of lever. Chain slack should not exceed one half the diameter of ball stud. Cut off excess chain.

On 1982–86 V8-250 DFI models except Eldorado and Seville, a combination cable and bead chain is used. Install cable into throttle clip and lock into position. Chain should be taut with throttle body lever in hot idle position and idle speed solenoid fully retracted. Place bead into swivel, then install retainer and lock into place. Chain slack should not exceed one half the diameter of ball stud. Cut off excess chain.

On 1982–85 Eldorado and Seville models, a rod assembly is used. Install rod into servo assembly bushing, then assemble plastic end of rod to ball stud on throttle body lever. Adjust by rotating rod assembly to obtain minimum slack with idle speed control screw fully retracted and engine stopped.

Brake Release Switch Adjustment, 1980–86

With brake pedal depressed, push cruise control/stoplight switch fully into retainer and pull brake pedal fully back to rest position. Switch will back out of retainer and adjust automatically.

Vacuum Dump Valve Adjustment

With brake pedal depressed, push vacuum valve switch all the way into the retaining clip. Pull the brake pedal to the stop to automatically adjust the valve.

Engine Section

Refer to Section 9 for Service Procedures on V6-252 Engine not included in this Section. Refer to Section 20 for Service Procedures on V8-350 Diesel Engine.

Fig. 1 Modulated displacement engine valve selector operation. 1981 V8-368

Fig. 2 Vacuum pump installation. 1981 V8-368 modulated displacement engine

1981 V8-368 MODULATED DISPLACEMENT ENGINE

DESCRIPTION

The 1981 V8-368 engine is of a modulated displacement design which deactivates select cylinders to reduce engine displacement from eight cylinders to six cylinders to four cylinders as necessary. Reducing the number of operating cylinders is accomplished through the use of valve selectors, **Fig. 1.** At low power requirements, the valve selectors deactivate both intake and exhaust valves on two or four cylinders. For full power output, normal valve operation is restored. In each of the deactivated cylinders, the piston continues to travel, but the intake and exhaust valves are closed. By closing both valves, the cylinders are not allowed to cool and there is a smooth flow of power when the valves are reactivated and the cylinders return to power operation.

Since this engine does not supply adequate vacuum, a belt-driven vacuum pump, **Fig. 2,** is installed. The vacuum pump supplies vacuum for proper operation of the various vacuum operated accessories.

SYSTEM COMPONENTS

Certain engine operating conditions are monitored by the sensors used in the Digital Electronic Fuel Injection System's (DEFI) Electronic Control Module (ECM). This information includes engine speed, coolant temperature, throttle position and intake manifold absolute pressure. The ECM processes the input data and, based on data and programming, determines the number of operating cylinders required. The ECM then energizes the electrical solenoids in the valve selectors. Each selector controls both the intake and exhaust valve on one cylinder. Valve selectors are installed on cylinders 1, 4, 6 and 7. In the 6 cylinder mode of operation, cylinders 1 and 4 are deactivated. In the 4 cylinder mode of operation, cylinders 6 and 7 are also deactivated. Other engine system components that have been changed or modified to accommodate the Modulated Displacement engine are the ECM, rocker arm covers, rocker arm supports on modulated cylinders and the necessary wiring harnesses. Also, due to the decreased engine vacuum levels during the 6 and 4 cylinder modes of operation, an auxiliary vacuum pump is used to allow normal operation of vacuum operated systems. A belt driven vacuum pump attached to the power steering pump is used.

SYSTEM OPERATION

The operating principle of the valve selectors is to control the pivot point of the rocker arm assembly, and by so doing cause the rocker arm to open the valve or allow the valve to remain closed while the remainder of the valve train operates normally. During active operation, the rocker arm pivots near the center of the rocker arm fulcrum point. As the cam lobe reaches its high point the valve is opened,

Fig. 3   Engine mounts. 1982—86 models with V8-250 engine

Fig. 4   Front engine mounts. 1980—82 models with V6-252 engine

Fig. 5   Front engine mounts. 1981 Eldorado & Seville V8-368

allowing the air/fuel mixture to enter the cylinder. When the valve selector is activated and the engine is operating in either the 4 or 6 cylinder mode, and the cam lobe is on its highest point, the valve will not open because the rocker arm does not pivot at the center of its fulcrum point. The selector will shift the rocker arm pivot point and allow the rocker arm to slide up and down its mounting stud. This shifts the fulcrum point to the tip of the now stationary valve. With the valve held closed by its spring, the cylinder is inactive. The valve selectors are mounted on the intake and exhaust valve rocker arms above the rocker arm fulcrums. When the solenoid is not energized, view A, **Fig. 2**, the selector body is prevented from moving upward by contact between the body projections and the blocking plate above it. The rocker arm pivots near its center, the valves operate normally and the cylinder is active. When the selector is energized, view B, **Fig. 2**, the blocking plate is rotated by the solenoid to align the windows in the blocking plate with the body projections. As the rocker arm is lifted by the push rod, the rocker arm and body ride up the stud since the body is no longer restrained by the blocking plate. The rocker arm now pivots at the tip of the valve and the valve remains closed. The body is spring loaded downward by an internal spring. This spring provides valve train action and normal hydraulic lifter function when the valve train is deactivated by

providing tension in the valve body and maintaining zero valve lash. The solenoid force is less than that required to overcome blocking plate/body friction when the valve is lifted. This prevents deactivation of the valve while it is lifted, which would cause abrupt valve seating. The valve selector, if defective, must be replaced as an assembly.

ENGINE MOUNTS
REPLACE

1982—86 V8-250

Engine Mount, Replace
1. Open hood, then remove screws securing strut support rod and position rods aside, **Fig. 3**.
2. Position upper radiator shroud so that it will not be damaged when engine is raised.
3. Raise and support vehicle, then remove engine mount through bolt.
4. Raise engine slightly using suitable jack until engine mount bracket is free from mount.
5. Remove nuts securing engine mount, then remove engine mount.

1980—82 V6-252
Removal
1. Remove front engine mount to cylinder block bolts, **Fig. 4**.
2. Raise and support vehicle.
3. Using a suitable jack, raise and support engine weight at front edge of oil pan.
4. Remove rear engine mount to cylinder block bolts.
5. Raise engine slightly and remove engine mount through-bolts.
6. Remove mount.

Installation
1. Install rear engine mount to cylinder block bolts and torque to 55 ft. lbs.
2. Lower engine until mounts rest on cross-member bracket.
3. Install and tighten engine mount through-bolts.
4. Lower vehicle. Install front engine mount bolts and torque to 55 ft. lbs.

Fig. 6   Front engine mounts. 1980 Eldorado & Seville V8-368

Fig. 7   Front engine mounts. 1980–81 V8 Exc. Eldorado & Seville

1980–81 ALL V8-368 ENGINES

1. Open hood.
2. Remove two screws on each side securing radiator cover to strut support rods. Loosen one screw on each side and position support rods aside.
3. Remove two screws securing upper radiator shroud to radiator cover and one screw securing upper radiator hose bracket to shroud. Drill out the rivets securing upper shroud to lower shroud and remove the upper shroud.
4. Raise and support vehicle.
5. Remove through bolt from mount being replaced, **Figs. 5, 6 and 7.**
6. Loosen the through bolt on the mount on the opposite side.
7. Using a suitable jack under the oil pan, raise engine until the bracket is free from the engine mount. Remove three flanged locking nuts and bolts, then the engine mount.
8. Reverse procedure to install.

1980 ELDORADO & SEVILLE V8-350

1. Raise and support vehicle.
2. Remove front splash shield, then two screws from engine bracket to engine mount on each side, **Fig. 8.**
3. Remove nut and washer from each mount.
4. Using a suitable jack and block of wood under harmonic balancer, raise engine until each mount can be removed from vehicle.
5. Reverse procedure to install.

ENGINE
REPLACE

1982–86 V8-250

1. Disconnect battery ground cable and drain cooling system.
2. Remove screws securing strut support rods and position rods aside.
3. Remove radiator shroud to radiator support screws. Remove staples securing upper and lower fan shrouds.
4. Remove radiator cover from radiator support.
5. Remove power steering reservoir from upper fan shroud, then position reservoir aside and remove fan shroud.
6. Mark hood hinge outlines on hood, then remove hood.
7. Remove air cleaner and duct assembly.
8. Disconnect upper radiator hose from thermostat housing.
9. Disconnect following electrical connectors:
   a. Coolant temperature sensor.
   b. Engine metal temperature switch.
   c. MAT sensor.
   d. Idle speed control motor.
   e. Throttle position sensor.
   f. EGR solenoid.
   g. AIR management valve.
   h. Oxygen sensor.
   i. Ignition timing connector.
   j. Distributor and A/C compressor.
   k. Alternator, cruise control servo and right side cylinder head ground wires.
10. Disconnect wiring harness support clips and position harness aside.

11. Disconnect brake vacuum hose from pipe, throttle linkage, and vapor canister hose.
12. Remove clutch fan assembly, then disconnect lower radiator hose.
13. Remove A/C compresor mounting bolts and position compressor aside with all lines attached.
14. Disconnect coolant reservoir hose and remove water nipple from rear of intake manifold.
15. Disconnect fuel inlet and return lines.
16. On Brougham and DeVille models, raise and support vehicle, then proceed as follows:
    a. Disconnect oil cooler lines from filter adapter, then remove filter adapter.
    b. Remove strut rods connecting engine mounts to flywheel cover.
    c. Remove flywheel cover.
    d. Remove six engine to transmission screws, then remove motor mount through bolts.
    e. Remove screws securing flywheel to converter.
    f. Disconnect starter motor electrical connectors, then disconnect exhaust pipes from exhaust manifold.
    g. Lower vehicle to ground, then support transmission with suitable jack.
    h. Attach suitable lifting equipment to engine lift brackets, then raise engine slowly and position forward to disengage from transmission.
    i. Remove engine from vehicle.
    j. Reverse procedure to install.
7. On Eldorado and Seville models, raise and support vehicle, then proceed as follows:
    a. Disconnect oil cooler lines from junction at right hand side of engine compartment.
    b. Remove six engine to transaxle screws, then remove nuts securing engine mount brackets to transmission.
    c. Remove flywheel cover and screws securing flywheel to converter.
    d. Disconnect starter motor electrical connectors, then disconnect exhaust pipes from exhaust manifold.
    e. Lower vehicle, then support transaxle with suitable jack.
    f. Attach suitable lifting equipment to engine lift brackets, then raise engine slowly and pull forward to disengage from transmission.
    g. Remove engine from vehicle.
    h. Reverse procedure to install.

MOUNTING ASSEMBLY TAB MUST BE INSTALLED INTO SLOT IN RESTRICTOR.

RH ENGINE MOUNTING BRACKET

RESTRICTOR

STEERING PUMP BRACKET

BOLT

BOLT

LH ENGINE MOUNTING BRACKET

ENGINE MOUNTING ASSEMBLY

POSITIONING TAB ON MOUNTING ASSEMBLY MUST BE INSTALLED INTO HOLE/SLOT LOCATED ON FRAME ASSEMBLY.

NUT

FRAME

Fig. 8   Front engine mounts. 1980 Eldorado & 1980 Seville V8-350

1980—82 V6-252, EXCEPT ELDORADO & SEVILLE

Removal

1. Mark hood hinge and hinge bracket for installation alignment, then remove hood.
2. Remove battery ground cable.
3. Drain engine coolant, remove air cleaner, then disconnect A/C compressor ground wire from mounting bracket.
4. Disconnect compressor clutch connector.
5. Remove compressor from mounting bracket and position out of the way.
6. Remove fan, pulley and belts.
7. Disconnect radiator and heater hoses and position aside, then remove radiator and fan shroud.
8. Remove power steering pump from bracket and position aside.
9. Disconnect and plug fuel pump hose.
10. Disconnect vacuum feed hose from carburetor, then the vacuum modulator and power brake vacuum hoses from engine.
11. Disconnect the three evaporative canister to carburetor hoses.
12. Disconnect throttle and TV cable from carburetor.
13. Disconnect Cruise Control servo cable at mounting bracket, if equipped.
14. Disconnect all sending unit switch connections from engine. Remove alternator, then disconnect engine wiring harness at engine.
15. Raise and support vehicle, then disconnect engine wiring harness at starter and remove starter.
16. Disconnect exhaust pipes from exhaust manifold.
17. Remove lower flywheel cover, then mark flywheel and converter for reassembly alignment. Remove converter to flywheel bolts.
18. Remove engine to transmission bolts and engine mount through-bolts.
19. Lower vehicle and support transmission. Using a suitable lifting device, raise engine. Ensure wiring harness, vacuum hoses and other parts are clear of engine before removal.
20. Lift engine just enough to clear engine

mounts, then lift transmission support evenly and alternately until engine is separated from transmission and can be removed.

Installation

1. Lower engine into vehicle, engaging transmission. Align flywheel and converter marks, then install and torque flywheel bolts to 35 ft. lbs.
2. Install and tighten engine mount through-bolts and nuts.
3. Raise and support vehicle, then install transmission to engine bolts and torque to 35 ft. lbs.
4. Install starter, then install flywheel cover. Connect starter electrical leads.
5. Connect exhaust pipes to exhaust manifolds.
6. Lower vehicle, then connect engine wiring harness, throttle cable, vacuum and water hoses, emission control line from canister to air cleaner and the transmission cooler line clip to exhaust manifold stud.
7. Connect battery ground cable to A/C compressor bracket.
8. Connect fuel line to fuel pump.
9. Install power steering pump into bracket. Adjust power steering belt tension.
10. Install fan shroud and radiator assembly. Attach radiator hoses and transmission cooler lines.
11. Install pulley, fan and belts. Adjust belt tension.
12. Install A/C compressor into bracket and connect wiring.
13. Install alternator to bracket and connect wiring.
14. Install air cleaner.
15. Install engine coolant; ensure proper level is attained after engine reaches operating temperature.
16. Connect negative battery cable to battery.
17. Install hood, aligning marks made at removal.

1980—81 ELDORADO & SEVILLE

1. Mark hood hinge location on hood, then remove hood.

2. Disconnect battery cables and remove battery from vehicle.
3. Remove battery ground cable ground screw from right hand fender.
4. Drain cooling system, then remove air cleaner assembly.
5. Relieve fuel presure from E.F.I. lines by loosely installing valve depressor J-5420 on pressure fitting. Position shop towels or a suitable container under fitting, then slowly tighten valve depressor until pressure is relieved.
6. Raise vehicle and remove crossover pipe from vehicle.
7. Disconnect shift linkage from transmission.
8. Remove clamp and disconnect fuel hose from fuel pipe.
9. Remove left and right drive axle to output shaft attaching screws.
10. Remove nuts from left and right hand engine mounts and nut and washer from left and right hand transmission mounts.
11. Remove two fan shroud lower attaching screws and disconnect lower radiator hose from radiator, then lower vehicle.
12. Disconnect upper radiator hose and transmission cooler lines from radiator, then remove radiator upper cover and slide radiator out of vehicle.
13. Remove clutch fan and radiator shroud.
14. Disconnect power steering hoses at steering gear and cap hoses.
15. Remove clamp and disconnect fuel return hose from presure regulator fuel return pipe.
16. Disconnect M.A.P. hose at throttle body, then pull hose out of tie straps and position aside.
17. If equipped with cruise control, disconnect vacuum hose from power unit, then pull hose out of tie strap and position on top of cowl.
18. Disconnect canister hose, vacuum supply hose and throttle cable from throttle body and position out of way.
19. Disconnect heater hoses at water valve and water pump.
20. Disconnect power brake unit vacuum hose.
21. Disconnect speedometer cable from transmission.
22. Disconnect engine wiring harness from bulkhead connector, E.S.S. connector from distributor, heater wire from water valve, wiring from wiper motor and washer bottle and ground strap from cowl.
23. Remove coolant reservoir and disconnect wiring from A/C compressor clutch.
24. Remove A/C compressor and A.I.R. pump drive belts.
25. Remove compressor to mounting bracket attaching bolts and position compressor on right hand fender skirt. Use care not to damage refrigerant hoses.
26. Install a suitable engine lifting fixture.
27. Carefully raise engine and pull forward until transmission clears front of dash.
28. Remove engine, transmission and drive as an assembly.
29. Reverse procedure to install.

1980—81 BROUGHAM & DEVILLE EXCEPT V6-252

1. Disconnect battery ground cable.
2. Drain cooling system.
3. Remove self-tapping screw and washer securing each wheelhouse strut to radiator cover and position struts aside.
4. Remove two screws securing top radiator shroud to cradle and one screw securing upper radiator hose to shroud. Drill out nine rivets securing upper shroud to lower shroud. Remove two screws securing radiator cover to cradle and the cover.
5. On all models, scribe hood hinge locations and remove hood.
6. Remove air cleaner and inlet duct.
7. Disconnect upper radiator hose from thermostat housing.
8. Disconnect wiring at the following locations: coolant temperature sender, ignition coil or H.E.I. distributor, downshift switch, engine metal temperature switch, anti-dieseling solenoid, oil pressure switch, heater turn-on switch and A/C compressor.
9. On vehicles equipped with Electronic Fuel Injection, disconnect EFI wiring harness and position aside.
10. On all models, bend back clips on rocker cover and position harness aside.
11. Disconnect brake hose from brake pipe.
12. Remove Cruise Control servo and disconnect bead chain at carburetor.
13. Disconnect throttle linkage from carburetor and position aside.
14. Disconnect vapor canister hose.
15. Disconnect power steering pump and position aside with hoses attached.
16. Remove fan and spacer.
17. Remove right side spark plug wires and position aside.
18. Remove A/C compressor and position aside with refrigerant line attached.
19. Disconnect alternator wiring and bend back clips securing harness to right valve cover and position harness aside.
20. Disconnect PCV vacuum line and the automatic level control vacuum line, if equipped.
21. Disconnect modulator line from carburetor.
22. Remove hot water valve hose from rear of right cylinder head.
23. Remove two nuts securing each cowl to wheelhouse tie strut to wheelhousing. Loosen nuts securing each strut to cowl and swing the struts outboard.
24. Remove two top screws securing engine to transmission.
25. Raise and support vehicle.
26. Remove nut and washer securing each engine mount to frame.
27. Remove starter motor.
28. Remove flywheel inspection cover.
29. Remove screws securing converter to flywheel.
30. Support the exhaust system and disconnect exhaust pipes from exhaust manifolds.
31. Disconnect fuel line and vapor return line from fuel pump.

◀ FRONT OF ENGINE

BOLT TIGHTENING SEQUENCE

1. TIGHTEN BOLTS 1, 2, 3, & 4 IN SEQUENCE TO 15.0-20.0 N·m (11-15 FT-LBS).
2. TIGHTEN BOLTS 5 THRU 16 IN SEQUENCE TO 24.5-30.0 N·m (18-22 FT-LBS).
3. RETIGHTEN ALL BOLTS IN SEQUENCE TO 24.5-30.0 N·m (18-22 FT-LBS).

Fig. 9 Intake manifold bolt tightening sequence. V8-250

32. Support transmission with a suitable jack. Remove remaining engine to transmission bolts.
33. Attach suitable engine lifting equipment to engine.
34. Remove engine from vehicle.
35. Reverse procedure to install.

INTAKE MANIFOLD
REPLACE

WITH E.F.I.

V8-250

1. Drain coolant from radiator, then disconnect radiator hose from thermostat housing.
2. Disconnect electrical connectors from coolant sensor, MAT sensor, throttle position sensor, distributor, ISC motor and fuel injectors.
3. Disconnect heater hoses from manifold.
4. Disconnect fuel lines from throttle body and remove distributor.
5. Remove both rocker arm covers.
6. Remove rocker arm support and rocker arms as an assembly.
7. Remove bolts securing A/C compressor, then position compressor aside with all hoses and lines attached.
8. Remove vacuum harness connectors from rear of manifold.
9. Remove intake manifold bolts and lower thermostat housing to front cover bolts.

NOTE: Engine lift brackets must be bent or

positioned aside for intake manifold removal.

10. Remove intake manifold by lifting straight up off dowels.
11. Reverse procedure to install. Refer to **Fig. 9** for intake manifold bolt tightening sequence and torque procedure.

SERVICE BULLETIN: The V8-250 engine uses three different intake manifolds, all using different intake manifold to cylinder head bolts. To determine which manifold and bolts are used, an identification mark is located next to the manifold air temperature sensor.

The first type manifold has no identification mark. Bolt location, **Fig. 9,** and size are as follows: locations 1, 2, 3, 4, 12, 13 and 16; 1.57 inch (40 mm) bolts; locations 5, 6, 7, 8, 9, 10, 11 and 14; 1.18 inch (30 mm) bolts; and location 15; 2.36 inch (60 mm) bolt.

The second type manifold is identified by an X. Bolt location, **Fig. 9,** and sizes are as follows: locations 1, 2, 3 and 4; 2.16 inch (55 mm) bolts; locations 5, 6, 7, 8, 9, 10, 11 and 14; 1.18 inch (30 mm) bolts; locations 12, 13 and 16; 1.57 inch (40 mm) bolts; and location 15, 2.36 inch (60 mm) bolt.

The third type manifold is identified by an Ⓧ. This manifold uses the same bolts in the same location as the manifold with the X identification mark, with the exception of bolt 12. In this manifold a 2.16 inch (55 mm) bolt is used, **Fig. 9.**

V8-350

1. Disconnect battery ground cable and drain cooling system.
2. Remove air cleaner and crankcase filter.
3. Disconnect throttle and Cruise Control linkage from throttle body. Remove cable from bracket and position aside.
4. Disconnect coolant temperature telltale switch, H.E.I. lead wire, speed sensor connector and injector valve wiring.
5. Disconnect EGR solenoid leads, throttle position switch, fast idle valve, air temperature sensor connector and MAP sensor hose.
6. Disconnect the two ground wires from A/C compressor bracket.
7. Disconnect the two vacuum hoses from throttle body to TVS switch.
8. Disconnect vacuum hoses and power brake pipe from rear of throttle body.
9. Disconnect fuel line from fuel rail.
10. Remove PCV valve from rocker cover.
11. Disconnect spark plug leads and position aside.
12. Disconnect upper radiator hose, bypass hose and the heater hose, located at the rear of the manifold.
13. Remove A/C compressor and position aside with refrigerant hoses attached.
14. Remove fuel return hose from pressure regulator.
15. On 1980—82 models, remove oil pressure switch and oil fill tube.
16. Remove intake manifold bolts and the intake manifold.

Fig. 10   Intake manifold tightening sequence. V8-350

LESS E.F.I.

Except V6-252
1. Disconnect battery ground cable and remove air cleaner.
2. Disconnect throttle linkage and Cruise Control linkage, if equipped.
3. Disconnect coil wires at H.E.I. connector, then remove distributor cap and disconnect right hand spark plug wires at spark plugs and place aside.
4. Disconnect wire connectors from temperature sender, down shift switch and anti-dieseling solenoid.
5. Remove coil, anti-dieseling solenoid and solenoid bracket.
6. Disconnect vacuum lines from carburetor, remove Cruise Control servo top mounting bolt and position brake hose aside, if equipped.
7. Disconnect wiring connector from A/C compressor, if equipped.
8. Disconnect fuel line at carburetor and remove vacuum lines from intake manifold.
9. Loosen power steering mounting bolts and pivot pump toward engine. Remove A/C compressor drive belt, then the screws attaching compressor rear mounting to engine and the screws attaching compressor mounting flange to front mounting bracket. Position compressor aside.
10. Remove PCV valve from rocker cover.
11. Remove manifold to cylinder head bolts, intake manifold, manifold shield and gaskets.
12. Reverse procedure to install.

V6-252
1. Disconnect battery ground cable, then drain cooling system.
2. Remove air cleaner.
3. Disconnect the following:
   a. Upper radiator hose and heater hose at manifold.
   b. Accelerator linkage at carburetor, linkage bracket at manifold and cruise control chain if equipped.
   c. Booster vacuum pipe at manifold.
   d. Fuel line at carburetor.
   e. Transmission vacuum modulator line.
   f. Idle stop solenoid wire, if equipped.
   g. Distributor wires and temperature sending unit wire.
   h. Vacuum hoses from, distributor TVS and EFE valve pipe, from carburetor to vacuum manifold.
   i. Fuel economy and load leveler hose, if equipped.
   j. Coolant by-pass hose at manifold.
4. Remove distributor cap and rotor to gain access to left intake manifold torx head bolt. Use Tool J-24394 or equivalent to remove torx head bolt.
5. Remove accelerator linkage springs.
6. Remove compressor upper bracket, if equipped.
7. Remove intake manifold.
8. Reverse procedure to install.

17. Reverse procedure to install. Torque intake manifold bolts in sequence, **Fig. 10**, to 40 ft. lbs.

V8-368 & 425
1. Disconnect battery ground cable and remove air cleaner and crankcase filter.
2. Disconnect throttle cable and cruise control linkage, if equipped, from throttle body. Remove cable from bracket and position aside.
3. Working on engine left side, disconnect coolant temperature tell-tale switch wire, HEI lead wire, speed sensor connector, downshift switch and injector wires. Disconnect harness from fuel rail brackets and position aside.
4. Disconnect two vacuum hoses from throttle body to TVS switch.
5. Disconnect vacuum hoses and power brake pipe from throttle body.

NOTE: Use a back-up wrench when removing power brake pipe to prevent damage to fitting.

6. Disconnect fuel line from fuel rail.

NOTE: Use a back-up wrench on fuel rail to prevent damage to fitting.

7. Working on engine right side, disconnect injector wires, EGR solenoid leads, air temperature sensor connector and MAP sensor hose. Disconnect harness from fuel rail brackets and position aside.
8. Remove PCV valve from rocker cover and position aside.
9. Remove spark plug leads and distributor cap.
10. Remove front fuel rail.
11. Position A/C compressor aside, do not disconnect refrigerant lines.
12. Remove fuel return hose from pressure regulator.
13. Remove manifold bolts and lift manifold from engine. Do not pry or lift manifold by the fuel rails or the mounting brackets.
14. Reverse procedure to install. Torque manifold bolts to 30 ft. lbs.

Fig. 11   Cylinder head bolt hole locations. V8-250

CYLINDER HEAD
REPLACE

V8-250

NOTE: Some V8-250 engine blocks may exhibit casting porosity, indicated by oil leakage around the threads of cylinder head bolts. This leakage is caused by porosity between a pressurized oil passage and the threaded bolt hole. This condition occurs between an oil gallery and holes #11, 12, 13, 14, 17, 18, 19 or 20, **Fig. 11.** An internal oil leak will occur around these bolts and will rarely be detected. However, when this condition is experienced at bolt holes #1, 2, 3, 4, 5, 6, 7, 8, 9, 10, 15, or 16, **Fig. 11,** an external oil leak may result. To provide a permanent repair for this condition, remove the bolt and clean both the bolt and hole with a suitable cleaner. With compressed air, blow out the bolt hole and apply a suitable two-part epoxy to the lower 5 or 6 threads of the bolt. Install the bolt and torque to 90 ft. lbs.

1. Remove valve covers, then remove intake manifold as described under "Intake Manifold, Replace".
2. On right hand side cylinder head removal, remove alternator and AIR pump.
3. For left hand side cylinder head removal, remove vacuum pump and bracket. Remove bolts and position power steering pump aside.
4. Remove exhaust manifold from cylinder head, then bolt securing AIR pipe to cylinder head.
5. Remove cylinder head bolts, then remove cylinder head.
6. Reverse procedure to install. refer to **Fig. 12** for cylinder head bolt tightening sequence.

V8-350
1. Drain cooling system and remove intake manifold as described under "Intake Manifold Replace".
2. Remove exhaust manifolds.

Fig. 12 Cylinder head bolt tightening sequence. V8-250

Bolt Location	Length
A (Bolt)	2.96 (Short)
B (Bolt)	4.16 (Long)
C (Bolt/Stud Head)	2.96 (Short)
D (Bolt/Stud Head)	4.16 (Long)
E (Bolt-Special)*	4.16 (Long)*

* This special bolt has an extra thick hex head which is drilled and tapped to accept the temperature switch.

Fig. 13 Location and length of cylinder head bolts. V8-350

Fig. 14 Cylinder head tightening sequence. V8-350

3. Remove rocker cover, rocker arm bolts, pivots, rocker arms and push rods.

NOTE: Note location of rocker arms and pivots to ensure installation in original position.

4. Remove cylinder head bolts and the cylinder head.
5. When installing cylinder head it is important that cylinder head bolts are installed in the correct position, refer to **Fig. 13.** Torque cylinder head bolts in sequence, **Fig. 14.** Torque intake manifold bolts in sequence shown in **Fig. 10.**

V8-368 & 425

NOTE: Engine rocker arm covers on 1980–81 V8-368 engines are made of a nylon material and are sealed to the cylinder head with RTV sealer. Use caution when removing covers. Do not pry the cover off. If cover removal is difficult, use a rubber mallet and tap gently in an upward direction on lower surface and only at ribbed areas of the cover. When installing covers, clean off all old sealant thoroughly, including sealing groove in cover face. Apply a new bead of sealer, P/N 1051435 or equivalent and torque attaching screws to 30 inch pounds.

1. Drain coolant from radiator.
2. Remove intake manifold.
3. Disconnect ground strap at rear of cylinder heads from cowl where used.
4. Disconnect wiring connector for high engine temperature warning system from sending unit at rear of left cylinder head.
5. Remove alternator if working on right cylinder head, or partially remove power steering pump if working on left cylinder head.
6. Remove A.I.R. manifold from both cylinder heads if equipped.
7. Disconnect wiring harness from cylinder head and and position out of the way.
8. Remove exhaust manifold from cylinder head.

NOTE: On early production V8-368 D.E.F.I. engine, with non-locking bolts and

lock tabs, exhaust manifold leaks may be corrected by replacing lock tabs and bolts with prevailing torque bolts. The prevailing torque bolts should be torqued to 15 ft. lbs. Later production V8-368 D.E.F.I. engines are equipped with prevailing torque bolts.

9. Remove rocker arm cover.
10. Remove rocker arm asemblies and lift out push rods.
11. Remove cylinder head bolts, remove head.
12. After carefully removing all gasket material from mating surfaces of head and block, position new gasket over

Fig. 15 Location and length of cylinder head screws. V8-368 & 425

Bolt Location	Length
A (Bolt)	4.36'' (Medium)
B (Bolt)	4.77'' (Long)
C (Bolt)	3.02'' (Short)
D (Bolt/stud)	4.77'' (Long)

dowels and install cylinder head in reverse order of removal, being sure to install the bolts as indicated in **Fig. 15.**

NOTE: When installing cylinder head bolts no torque sequence is required, start at center and work from side to side outwards and towards the ends.

VALVE ARRANGEMENT
FRONT TO REAR

Engine	Arrangement
V6-252	E-I-I-E-I-E
V8-368, 425	
Left	E-I-E-I-E-I-E-I
Right	I-E-I-E-I-E-I-E
V8-250, 350	I-E-I-E-E-I-E-I

VALVE LIFT SPECS

Engine	Year	Intake	Exhaust
V8-350	1980	.400	.400
V8-368	1980–81	.457	.473
V6-252①	1980–82	.357	.366
V8-250	1982–86	.384	.396

①—Refer to Buick Chapter for service procedures.

VALVE TIMING
INTAKE OPENS BEFORE TDC

Engine	Year	Degrees
V6-252①	1980–82	16
V8-250	1982–86	37
V8-350	1980	22
V8-368	1980–81	11

①—Refer to Buick Chapter for service procedures.

ROCKER ARMS
REPLACE

V8-250

1. Remove valve cover.
2. Remove nuts from stud headed cylinder head bolts, then remove valve train support with rocker arms and pivots as an assembly, **Fig. 16.**

NOTE: Pivot assemblies may be damaged unless rocker arms and pivots are removed as an assembly.

Fig. 16 Rocker arm assembly exploded view. V8-250

Fig. 17 Rocker arm components disassembled. V8-350

3. Position rocker arm support in suitable vise and remove rocker arms and pivots.
4. Install rocker arms and pivots into valve train support and tighten pivot bolts.
5. Position valve train support over mounting studs and snug tighten retaining nuts.
6. Check push rods for correct positioning, then tighten nuts alternately and evenly.

V8-350

1. Remove rocker cover, rocker arm bolts, pivot and rocker arms.

NOTE: Remove each set as a unit.

2. Position rocker arms on cylinder head, apply lubricant 1050169 or equivalent to wear points on pivot, then install pivot.
3. Install rocker arm bolts, tighten alternately, torque to 25 ft. lbs., **Fig. 17.**

1981 V8-368

On V8-368 modulated displacement engines, refer to **Fig. 18** for rocker arm replacement.

1980 V8-368

When disassembling the rocker arm assembly, be sure to keep the supports and rocker arms in order so they can be installed in the exact same position.

Install rocker arms on supports and place supports in retainers as shown in **Fig. 19.**

Place capscrews through the reinforcements, supports and retainers and position assemblies on cylinder head. Make sure

Fig. 18 Rocker arm assembly. V8-368 modulated displacement engine.

Fig. 19 Rocker arm components

Fig. 20 Hydraulic valve lifter

Fig. 21 New design valve lifter.
V8-250

Fig. 22 Engine front cover
attaching screws V8-350

that push rods are properly seated in the lifter seats and in the rocker arms. Lubricate rocker arm bearing surfaces before assembling in order to prevent wear. Torque rocker arm support bolts to 70 ft. lbs.

VALVE GUIDES
V8-350

Valve stem to guide clearance should be .001–.003 inch. Service valves are available in standard (.343 inch) and .003, .005, .010, .013 inch oversizes. If stem to guide clearance is excessive, ream valve guide bore to the next oversize using appropriate reamer. Install proper oversize valve and valve seal. Valve seals can be identified as follows:

Intake
Std.–.005 O.S. ....Gray Colored
.010–.013 O.S. ...... Orange Colored
Exhaust
Std.–005 O.S. ....Ivory Colored
.010–.013 O.S. .... Blue Colored

On occasion an engine will be manufactured with an oversize valve and valve guide bore. A number stamped on the inboard side of the head will indicate which valve and valve guide bore are oversize. The number 10 would indicate that a .010 inch oversize valve is installed in the adjacent valve guide bore.

V8-250, 368, 425

Check valve stem to valve guide clearance, clearance should be no more than .005 inch. Service valves are available in standard (.343 inch) and .003, .006 and .013 inch oversizes. If clearance is found to be excessive, valve guide should be reamed out to next oversize using appropriate reamer, and a corresponding oversize valve installed. On some engines, valves with a .003 inch oversize diameter and .003 inch oversize valve guides are installed at the factory. Engines so fitted will be identified by a "3" stamped on the cylinder head gasket surface inline with the oversize valve.

HYDRAULIC VALVE LIFTERS
REPLACE

The valve lifters may be lifted out of their

bores after removing the rocker arms, push rods and intake manifold. Adjustable pliers with taped jaws may be used to remove lifters that are stuck due to varnish, carbon, etc. **Fig. 20** illustrates the type of lifter used.

SERVICE NOTE: On 1982–83 V8-250 engines, if valve lifter replacement is required, replacement should be made with the new design type. The new design type lifter foot is more convex in shape and is identified by two machined grooves on the lifter body, **Fig. 21.** If camshaft replacement is necessary, all 16 lifters should be replaced with the new design type.

Key	No.	Size	Torque
V8-368			
A	4	3/8–16 × 1–3/8	22 ft. lbs.
C	3	5/16–18 × 1–1/4	10 ft. lbs.
D	1	5/16–18 × 5/8	10 ft. lbs.
E	2	3/8–16 × 5/8	22 ft. lbs.
V8-425			
A	4	3/8–16 × 1–3/8	25 ft. lbs.
C	3	5/16–18 × 1–1/4	15 ft. lbs.
D	1	5/16–18 × 5/8	15 ft. lbs.
E	2	3/8–16 × 5/8	25 ft. lbs.

Fig. 23 Engine front cover
attaching screws. V8-368, 425

TIMING CASE COVER
REPLACE

V8-250

1. Disconnect battery ground cable and drain cooling system.
2. On Brougham and DeVille models, position support rods aside.
3. Disconnect wiring harness from upper fan shroud clamps.
4. Remove power steering pump reservoir from upper fan shroud, then remove upper fan shroud.
5. Remove clutch fan, then loosen alternator and AIR pump mounting bolts and remove drive belts.
6. Loosen power steering pump retaining bolts and remove vacuum pump drive belts.
7. Remove A/C compressor mounting bolts, then remove drive belt and position compressor aside with all hoses and lines attached.
8. Remove alternator and support bracket, then disconnect coolant reservoir hose at water pump.
9. Disconnect hoses from water pump.
10. Remove water pump and crankshaft pulleys.
11. Remove A/C compressor bracket from engine.
12. Remove timing mark tab from front cover, then remove crankshaft vibration damper.
13. Remove bolts securing front cover to cylinder block, then remove cover, water pump and lower thermostat housing as an assembly.
14. Reverse procedure to install. Coat oil pan front lip with suitable sealer.

V8-350

1. Drain cooling system, disconnect radiator hoses, heater hose and bypass hose.
2. Remove radiator upper support and radiator.

Fig. 24   Timing gear locating marks. V8-368, 425

Fig. 25   Timing gear locating marks. V8-350

Fig. 26   Timing gear location marks. V8-250

3. Remove belts, fan, fan pulley, crankshaft pulley and harmonic balancer.
4. Remove oil pan, front cover attaching bolts, front cover and water pump.
5. Reverse procedure to install, refer to **Fig. 22.**

V8-368, 425

1. Remove harmonic balancer.
2. Loosen starter sufficiently to gain access to oil pan screws and lower front of oil pan until it clears front studs.
3. Drain radiator and remove lower hose from water pump.
4. Remove the 10 screws securing front cover to the cylinder block and remove cover with water pump as an assembly.
5. Reverse removal procedure, to install, referring to **Fig. 23.**

TIMING CASE COVER OIL SEAL
REPLACE

V8-250

1. Remove crankshaft pulley and vibration damper.
2. Remove front cover oil seal using tools J-1859-03 and J-23129 or equivalents.
3. Lubricate new seal with engine oil, then install using tool J-29662 or equivalent.
4. Install vibration damper and crankshaft pulley.

V8-350

1. Remove drive belts, crankshaft pulley and harmonic balancer.
2. Using tool J-1859-03 or a suitable puller, remove front cover oil seal.
3. Apply sealer to outside diameter of seal.
4. Position seal on front cover, then using tools No. J-25264 and J-21150, drive seal into place.
5. Install harmonic balancer and crankshaft pulley, install and adjust drive belts.

V8-368 & 425

1. Remove vibration damper.
2. With a thin blade screw driver or similar tool, pry out front cover oil seal.
3. Lubricate new seal and fill cavity with wheel bearing grease. Position seal on end of crankshaft with garter spring side toward engine.
4. Using a suitable installer, drive seal into cover until it bottoms against cover.

TIMING CHAIN
REPLACE

V8-368 & 425

1. Remove engine timing case cover as described under "Timing Case Cover, Replace".
2. Remove distributor, oil pump and crankshaft oil slinger.
3. On models less fuel injection, remove fuel pump, then remove fuel pump slinger from camshaft.
4. Rotate crankshaft to align camshaft and crankshaft sprocket timing marks, **Fig. 24.**
5. Remove two screws attaching camshaft sprocket to camshaft, then remove camshaft sprocket and timing chain.
6. If necessary, remove crankshaft sprocket using a suitable puller.
7. Reverse procedure to install. Ensure that timing marks are aligned as shown in **Fig. 24.**

NOTE: The valve timing marks, **Fig. 24,** do not indicate TDC compression stroke for No. 1 cylinder, which is used during distributor installation. Rotate engine until No. 1 cylinder is on compression stroke and camshaft timing mark is 180° from the valve timing position shown in **Fig. 24,** then install distributor.

V8-350

1. Remove engine timing case cover as described under "Timing Case Cover, Replace".
2. Remove oil slinger from crankshaft.

3. Rotate crankshaft to align camshaft and crankshaft sprocket timing marks, **Fig. 25.**
4. Remove screw attaching camshaft sprocket to camshaft, then remove camshaft sprocket and timing chain.
5. If necessary, remove crankshaft sprocket using a suitable puller.
6. Reverse procedure to install. Ensure that timing marks are aligned as shown in **Fig. 25.**

NOTE: The valve timing marks, **Fig. 25,** do not indicate TDC compression stroke for No. 1 cylinder, which is used during distributor installation. If distributor was removed, rotate engine until No. 1 cylinder is on compression stroke and camshaft timing mark is 180° from the valve timing position shown in **Fig. 25,** then install distributor.

V8-250

1. Remove engine timing case cover as described under "Timing Case Cover, Replace".
2. Remove oil slinger from crankshaft.
3. Rotate crankshaft to align camshaft and crankshaft sprocket timing marks, **Fig. 26.**
4. Remove screw attaching camshaft sprocket to camshaft, then remove camshaft and crankshaft sprockets with timing chain attached.
5. Reverse procedure to install. Ensure that timing marks are aligned as shown in **Fig. 26.**

CAMSHAFT
REPLACE

V8-250

1. Remove timing chain as described previously.
2. Remove valve lifters as described under "Valve Lifters, Replace".
3. Remove radiator, then remove camshaft from engine. Use caution not to damage camshaft bearings when removing camshaft.
4. Reverse procedure to install.

Fig. 27   Piston & rod assembly. V8-250

Fig. 30   Measuring piston diameter

Fig. 28   Piston & rod assembly. V8-350

Fig. 29   Piston & rod assembly. V8-368, 425

Fig. 31   Off centered piston pin. V8-250

Letter	Cylinder Size (Diameter in inches)	Piston Size (Diameter in inches)
A	4.0560-4.0565	4.05475-4.05525
B	4.0565-4.0570	4.05525-4.05575
C	4.0570-4.0575	4.05575-4.05625
D	4.0575-4.0580	4.05625-4.05675
J	4.0660-4.0665	4.06475-4.06525
K	4.0665-4.0670	4.06525-4.06575
L	4.0670-4.0675	4.06575-4.06625
M	4.0675-4.0680	4.06625-4.06675

Fig. 32   Cylinder and piston sizes. V8-350

V8-350

1. Disconnect battery, then remove air cleaner.
2. Drain cooling system and remove radiator, four bolts attaching A/C condenser to radiator and position condenser aside.
3. Remove crankshaft pulley and balancer, then the front cover.
4. Remove A/C compressor from engine and position aside.

NOTE: Do not disconnect refrigerant hoses from compressor.

5. Remove intake manifold as described under "Intake Manifold Replace".
6. Remove rocker covers, rocker arms, push rods and lifters.

NOTE: Note position of rocker arms, pivots, push rods and lifers to ensure installation in original position.

7. Remove camshaft.
8. Reverse procedure to install.

V8-368, 425

1. Remove engine front cover.
2. Remove distributor and oil pump.
3. Remove oil slinger from crankshaft.
4. Remove fuel pump and fuel pump eccentric.
5. Unfasten and remove camshaft sprocket with chain attached.
6. Remove valve lifters as previously

outlined.

7. Remove radiator.
8. Carefully slide camshaft forward until it is out of engine.
9. Reverse procedure to install.

PISTONS & RODS ASSEMBLE

On all engines, assemble and install the piston and rod assemblies as shown in **Figs. 27, 28 and 29.**

Measure connecting rod side clearance using a suitable feeler gauge. Clearances should be .008–.020 inch on Cadillac built engines, .006–.020 inch on Oldsmobile built engines and .006–.023 inch on Buick built engines.

PISTONS
V8-250

When measuring piston diameter, place micrometer ³⁄₁₆ inch below cross slot or ³⁄₈ inch below oil ring groove, **Fig. 30.** Cylinder liner diameter is measured by placing a micrometer two inches down from top of liner and perpendicular to cylinder center-

line. The difference between the two readings should be .0010–.0018 inch. Cylinder bore out-of-round should not exceed .0008 inch and piston bore taper should not exceed .0005–.002 inch. If any reading is not as specified, piston and cylinder liner assembly must be replaced. No attempt should be made to rebore or hone cylinder liners. Refer to "Cylinder Liner, Replace" for procedure.

SERVICE BULLETIN: On some 1982 V8-250 engines a minor to severe internal metallic knock may be encountered. This may be caused by close piston to counterbalance tolerance on cylinder Nos. 1, 2, 3, 6, 7 and 8 and is usually heard when engine is at operating temperature between 800–1400 RPM.

The following procedure should be used to correct this problem:

1. Remove engine oil pan and cylinder heads as previously described.
2. Inspect all pistons for correct installation.
3. Using a wax pencil, mark right and left sides of outboard piston skirts which rotate next to crankshaft counterbalance weights on piston Nos. 1, 2, 3, 6, 7 and 8.
4. Remove and inspect all pistons for off-centered piston wrist pins, **Fig. 31.** If off-centered piston pins are encountered, replace piston and liner assembly.

LETTER	CYLINDER SIZE (DIAMETER IN INCHES)	PISTON SIZE (DIAMETER IN INCHES)
A	3.8000 - 3.8004	3.7990 - 3.7994
B	3.8004 - 3.8008	3.7994 - 3.7998
C	3.8008 - 38012	3.7998 - 3.8002
D	3.8012 - 3.8016	3.8002 - 3.8006
E	3.8016 - 3.8020	3.8006 - 3.8010

Fig. 33   Cylinder & piston sizes. V8-368

Letter	Cylinder Size (Diameter in Inches)	Piston Size (Diameter in Inches)
A	4.0820-4.0824	4.0810-4.0814
B	4.0824-4.0828	4.0814-4.0818
C	4.0828-4.0832	4.0818-4.0822
D	4.0832-4.0836	4.0822-4.0826
E	4.0836-4.0840	4.0826-4.0830
AA	4.0920-4.0924	4.0910-4.0914
BB	4.0924-4.0928	4.0914-4.0918
CC	4.0928-4.0932	4.0918-4.0922
DD	4.0932-4.0936	4.0922-4.0926
EE	4.0936-4.0940	4.0926-4.0930

Fig. 34   Cylinder & piston sizes. V8-425

PERFECT CIRCLE — TOP & SECOND

SEALED POWER — TOP & SECOND

MUSKEGON — TOP & SECOND

Fig. 35   Piston ring identification. 1980 V8-350 gasoline engine

CYLINDER HEAD — HEAD GASKET

CRANKCASE — ENGINE COOLANT

CYLINDER — "O" RING SEAL

Fig. 36   Cylinder liner assembly. V8-250

5. Using a suitable file, remove a small amount of material from piston skirt edges marked in step 3. All surfaces must be smooth and free of all file marks after reworking. If interference marks are evident in the piston skirts and filing does not remove marks, replace piston and liner assembly.
6. Reinstall pistons into block.
7. Check piston skirt to crankshaft counterweight clearance by placing an index card between skirts and counterweights while rotating crankshaft. No drag should be felt on card. If drag is felt, crankshaft should be replaced.
8. Reinstall cylinder heads and oil pan.

V8-350

Measure pistons for size, **Fig. 30.** Measure cylinder bore, piston to cylinder bore clearance should be .00075–.00175 inch. Measure piston for taper, the largest reading must be at the bottom of the skirt. Allowable taper is .000–.0001 inch.

Cylinder and piston sizes are indicated by a letter stamped on the cylinder gasket surface of the block. The letters that denote cylinder and piston sizes are listed in **Fig. 32.**

V8-368, 425

Pistons should be measured for size as shown in **Fig. 30.** Cylinders should be measured 1⅛ inch from the top, crosswise to the cylinder block. The clearance should be .0006–.0014 for V8-368, 425 engines in

this position at room temperature (70°F). Subtract .0001 inch from measurement for every 6° above 70°.

On V8-368, 425 engines an identification letter is stamped on the cylinder head face of cylinder block located directly below cylinder bore. The letters are in groups of two for adjacent cylinders (such as "A" "B") midway between the two cylinders. This letter denotes the cylinder size as shown in **Figs. 33 and 34.** The table indicates piston sizes to match corresponding bore sizes. This makes it possible to maintain the proper clearance between block and piston.

If double letters (such a "AA" "BB") appear, it indicates that the cylinder has been bored .010 inch over the diameter indicated by the single letter in the chart.

Cylinder bores must not be reconditioned to more than .0100 inch oversize, as pistons are not available over this range.

PISTON RINGS

NOTE: On 1980 V8-350 engines except diesel, when measuring compression ring gap clearance, refer to **Fig. 35** for piston ring identification. For Muskegon and Perfect Circle piston rings, ring gap should be .013 to .023 in. For Sealed Power piston rings, ring gap should be .010 to .020 in.

Replacement rings are available on all except V8-250 engines in standard size and .010 inch oversize. On V8-250 engine, replacement rings are available in standard size only. If piston ring clearance is

excessive on this engine, new piston and cylinder liner must be installed. Refer to "Cylinder Liner, Replace".

PISTON PINS

V8-350

Piston pin to piston clearance should be .0003–.0005 inch. If clearance is more than .0005 inch, a new piston pin should be installed. Piston pin to connecting rod is a press fit and clearance should be .0008–.0018 inch tight fit.

V8-250, 368, 425

Piston pins are a matched fit with the piston and are not available separately. Piston pins are pressed in the connecting rods and will not become loose enough to cause a knock or tapping until after very high mileages. In such cases a new piston and pin assembly should be installed.

CYLINDER LINER
REPLACE

V8-250

NOTE: The cylinder heads, pistons, connecting rods, bearings and crankshaft must be removed from engine before replacing cylinder liners.

1. If original liners, **Fig. 36,** are to be reinstalled, mark position of liner in cylinder block and keep piston with original liner for reference during installation.
2 Use tool J-29775 or equivalent to remove liners from cylinder block. Discard O ring from bottom of cylinder liner.
3. Check cylinder liner and block mating surfaces to ensure they are free of nicks and burrs.
4. If original liners are to be installed into original block, it is not necessary to gauge their height. Install new O ring seal onto liner, align reference marks made during removal, then install liner into block using tool J-29775 or equivalent.

16–23

Fig. 37 Measuring liner to liner height. V8-250

NO. LETTER · STD
LETTER 'A' · .0005
LETTER 'B' · .0010
LETTER 'C' · .0015

Fig. 38 Main bearing identification. V8-350

After Correctly Positioning Seal, Rotate Tool Slightly And Cut Off Each End Of Seal Flush With Block

Fig. 39 Rear main bearing oil seal installation. V8-350

Fig. 40 Main bearing oil seal tool. V8-250, 368, 425

5. If new liner and piston assembly is to be installed, or if original block experienced overheating, then cylinder liner height must be gauged.
6. Position new liner into block without O ring.
7. Position gauge J-29776 or equivalent onto cylinder liner. Check to ensure that spring loaded guide pins fit into liner with machined pads resting on edge of liner and dial indicator contacting block deck face. Apply moderate pressure to gauge until dial indicator stops moving.
8. Record this reading. If reading is on + side of dial indicator, cylinder liner is higher than block face by indicated amount. If reading is on − side, cylinder liner is below block face.
9. Repeat steps 7 and 8 at two other locations. Take average of three readings as actual liner height.
10. Specified liner height is .01–.08 mm above block deck face. If specified height cannot be obtained, replace liner with new one. Liners may be rotated in block to obtain specified height.
11. If liner height is satisfactory, then liner-to-liner height must be checked. Install adjacent liners into cylinder block without O ring. Using gauge J-29766 or equivalent, measure height between liners while second liner is held firmly in place, **Fig. 37**. Liner-to-liner height should be ±.05 mm. Mark liners in this position.

12. When installing liners into block, check to ensure that liners are installed in marked position. Install O ring onto liner, then install liner into block using tool J-29775 or equivalent.

MAIN & ROD BEARINGS

V8-350

Main bearing clearance should not exceed .0035 inch. If clearance is more than .0035 inch replace both bearing shells. Main bearings are available in undersizes, **Fig. 38**.

Rod bearing clearance should not exceed .0035 inch. If clearance is more than .0035 inch replace both bearing shells and recheck clearance.

V8-250, 368, 425

Main and rod bearings are supplied by Cadillac in standard sizes only.

CRANKSHAFT OIL SEAL
REPLACE

V8-350

To replace upper rear main bearing seal, the crankshaft must be removed. After removing crankshaft use tool No. J-25285 to install seal, **Fig. 39**.

Lower rear main bearing seal can be installed with crankshaft in place and engine in vehicle. Remove oil pan, then the rear main bearing cap. Remove bearing and seal from cap. Position new seal in groove in bearing cap. Using tool J-25285, hammer seal into groove. Rotate tool slightly, then cut seal ends flush with bearing cap surface. Pack seal end fibers away from edges, using a screw driver. Install bearing in cap, then install cap, lubricate bolt threads and torque to 120 ft. lbs. Install oil pan and lower flywheel cover.

Fig. 41 Installing rear main bearing oil seal. V8-250, 368 & 425

V8-250, 368, 425

Rear main bearing installation tool can be made from shim stock or a metal banding strap using dimensions in **Fig. 40**.

The two seal halves are identical and can be used in either the lower or upper location. However, both seal halves are pre-lubricated with a film of wax for break-in. Do not remove or damage this film.

To install the lower half of the seal into the bearing cap, slide either end of seal into position at one end of bearing cap and place tool on seal land at other end of bearing. Make sure seal is positioned over bearing ridge and lip of seal is facing forward (car position).

Hold thumb over end of seal that is flush with split line to prevent it from slipping upward, and push seal into seated position by applying pressure to the other end. Make sure seal is pressed down firmly and is flush on each side to avoid possibility of a leak at seal split line. Avoid pressing on lip as damage to sealing edge could result.

To install upper half of seal in cylinder block (with crankshaft in car), position "shoehorn" tool on land of block, **Fig. 41**. Start seal into groove in block with lip facing forward and rotate seal into position. Do not press on lip or sealing edge may be

Engine oiling system. V8-350

Engine oiling system. V8-368, 425

damaged. Both ends of seal must be flush at seal split line to avoid leaks. If necessary, Lubriplate or its equivalent may be used to facilitate installation of both upper and lower seal halves. Do not use silicone or a leak may result.

OIL PAN
REPLACE

NOTE: Some 1981 V8 engines might exhibit an oil leak at the second oil pan bolt from front of the engine, on the left hand side. The hole for the bolt in the block may have been drilled through into the crankcase. A leak can be corrected by removing and cleaning the bolt and hole. Coat the bolt with a suitable sealer and reinstall.

1982–86 V8-250 EXCEPT ELDORADO & SEVILLE

1. Disconnect battery ground cable, then raise and support vehicle.
2. Drain engine oil and remove oil filter.
3. Remove flywheel cover and support struts.
4. Disconnect exhaust pipe from manifold and remove catalytic converter bracket bolt.
5. Remove oil pan nuts and bolts, then lower exhaust pipe and remove oil pan from vehicle.
6. Reverse procedure to install. Use suitable RTV sealer in sufficient quantities when installing pan. Torque pan attaching bolts and nuts to 11 ft. lbs. on 1982 models and 15 ft. lbs. on 1983–86 models.

1982–85 V8-250 ELDORADO & SEVILLE

1. Raise and support vehicle and drain engine oil. Remove oil filter.
2. Remove flywheel cover, then remove final drive assembly.
3. Disconnect exhaust pipe from manifold, then remove front suspension stone shield.
4. Remove bolts securing engine mount to frame crossmember.
5. Remove oil pan bolts and nuts, then lower exhaust pipe and remove oil pan from vehicle.

NOTE: To facilitate oil pan removal, place suitable jack under cylinder head ledge of crankcase or against cylinder head, and raise engine just enough to remove oil pan.

6. Reverse procedure to install. Use suitable RTV sealer in sufficient quantities when installing pan. Torque pan attaching bolts to 10 to 11 ft. lbs.

1980–82 V6-252 EXCEPT 1982 ELDORADO & SEVILLE
Removal
1. Raise and support vehicle. Drain oil.
2. Remove flywheel cover.
3. Remove exhaust crossover pipe.
4. Remove oil pan attaching bolts and the oil pan.

Installation
1. Reverse procedure to install. Ensure oil pan and cylinder block mating surfaces are clean.

NOTE: 1981–82 V6-252 engines use RTV silicone sealer in place of a cork gasket for oil pan to crankcase sealing. If replacement of the oil pan or gasket is necessary, either RTV sealer or a cork gasket may be used for reassembly. If RTV sealer is used, the pan rail and block mating surfaces should be thoroughly cleaned and a ¼ inch bead of sealant applied evenly to the pan rail. Use caution to avoid any breaks or gaps in the sealer during application.

2. Torque oil pan bolts to 14 ft. lbs.
3. Torque flywheel cover bolts to 4 ft. lbs.
4. Lower vehicle and add oil.

1982 V6-252 ELDORADO & SEVILLE

1. Disconnect battery ground cable.
2. Remove one final drive to transmission bolt.
3. Install engine support and hoist car, then install jack stands and lower hoist.
4. Disconnect idler arm bracket at frame.
5. Lock steering wheel in full left position.
6. Disconnect drive axles from output shafts and disconnect battery cable bracket from output shaft support, then disconnect shaft support from engine block.
7. Remove remaining final drive to transmission bolts and place transmission jack under final drive.
8. Remove final drive cover and final drive unit.
9. Remove splash shield, then disconnect starter wires and remove starter.
10. Remove flywheel cover and drain oil pan.
11. Remove oil pan attaching bolts and remove oil pan.
12. Reverse procedure to install. Apply suitable RTV sealer when installing pan.

Fig. 42 Water pump attaching screws. V8-368, 425

1980-82 EXCEPT V6-252 & ELDORADO & SEVILLE

1. Disconnect battery ground cable.
2. Remove two screws on each side securing radiator cover to strut rods, support rods and loosen two screws at strut. Position support rods aside.
3. Remove two screws securing upper radiator shroud to radiator and one screw securing upper radiator hose clamp to shroud.
4. Drill out the six rivets securing the upper shroud to the lower shroud and remove shroud.
5. Loosen drive belts and remove crankshaft pulleys.
6. Raise vehicle and drain oil pan.
7. Remove exhaust "Y" pipe at exhaust manifold and converter.
8. Remove through bolts from engine mounts.
9. Remove starter motor.
10. Remove transmission lower cover.
11. Using a suitable jack, raise engine to gain clearance for oil pan removal.
12. Remove nuts and screws securing oil pan to cylinder block.
13. Reverse procedure to install.

1980 V8-350 SEVILLE

1. Remove wheel housing struts from both fenders.
2. Remove fan shroud.
3. Remove front motor mount through bolts, disconnect crossover pipe at manifold.
4. Remove starter, then remove converter cover.
5. Remove oil pan attaching bolts, raise engine until pan can be removed.
6. Reverse procedure to install.

1980 ELDORADO V8-350

1. Remove final drive assembly with output shafts attached. Refer to main index, "GM Front Wheel Drive".
2. Disconnect starter motor electrical connectors, then remove starter.
3. Drain oil from crankcase, then remove

Key	No.	Size	Torque
C	(2)	5/16·18× 1·1/2	22 foot/ lbs.
D	(1)	5/16·18× 2·1/2	22 foot/ lbs.
E	(4)	1/4·20× 1·1/4	13 foot/ lbs.
G	(1)	5/16·18× 1·1/2 (Stud On Head)	22 foot/ lbs.

Fig. 43 Water pump attaching screws. V8-350

oil pan attaching screws and the oil pan.
4. Reverse procedure to install.

OIL PUMP
REPLACE

1982-86 V8-250

1. Remove oil pan as described previously.
2. Remove bolts securing oil pump to engine, then remove pump.
3. Reverse procedure to install.

V8-350

1. Remove oil pan, then remove pump to rear main bearing attaching screws, remove pump.

V8-368, 425

1. Raise car and remove oil filter.
2. Remove five screws securing pump to engine. The screw nearest the pressure regulator should be removed last, allowing the pump to come down with the screw.
3. Remove pump drive shaft.
4. Reverse procedure to install, being sure to pack the pump with petrolatum.

OIL PUMP
SERVICE

V8-250

1. Remove screws securing pump cover to housing.

KEY	NO.	SIZE	TORQUE	
			N·M	FT. LBS.
A	4	M10 X 1.50 X 45	40	30
B	1	M8 X 1.25 X 35	20	15
C	3	M6 X 1.0 (NUT)	7	5
D	1	(1620262)	10	7
E	1	M10 X 1.50 (NUT)	40	30
F	1	M10 X 1.50 X 50 (STUD HEAD)	40	30

Fig. 44 Water pump attaching screws. V8-250

2. Remove drive shaft, drive gear and driven gear from pump housing.
3. Remove oil pressure regulator valve and spring from bore in housing assembly. Inspect oil pressure regulator for nicks and burrs.
4. Check for free length of 2.57 inches on regulator spring. Check that spring can be compressed to 1.46 inches under 9.3-10.5 lbs. load.
5. Inspect drive gear and driven gear for nicks and burrs.
6. Inspect pump housing for excessive wear.
7. Check pump cover interior surface for scoring. Check pump housing cover surface for wear.
8. Check drive shaft for damage and wear.
9. To assemble, install pump drive gear over drive shaft so that retaining ring is inside gear. Position drive gear over pump housing shaft closest to pressure regulator bore.
10. Position driven gear over remaining shaft in pump housing, meshing driven gear with drive gear.
11. Install oil pressure regulator spring and valve in bore of housing.
12. Install pump cover over drive shaft and install retaining screws. Torque to 5 ft. lbs.

V8-350

1. Remove oil pump as described previously.
2. Remove oil pump driveshaft extension.

NOTE: Do not attempt to remove washers from drive shaft extension. The drive shaft extension and washers must be serviced as an assembly if washers are not 1¹¹/₃₂ inch from end of shaft.

3. Remove cotter pin, spring and pressure regulator valve.

NOTE: Place finger over pressure regulator bore before removing cotter pin, as the spring is under pressure.

4. Remove oil pump cover screws, then remove cover and washer.
5. Remove drive gear and idler gear.
6. Check gears for scoring or other damage. If damaged, install new gears.
7. Check pressure regulator valve, valve spring and bore for damage. Check valve to bore clearance which should be .0025–.0050 inch.
8. Install gears and shaft in pump body and check gear end clearance by placing a straight edge over the gears and measure the clearance between the straight edge and gasket surface. The end clearance should be .0015–.0025 inch. If end clearance is near the excessive clearance, check for scores in the cover that would bring the clearance over the specified limit.
9. Reverse procedure to assemble.

V8-368, 425

1. Remove oil pump.
2. Slide drive shaft, drive gear and driven gear out of pump housing.
3. Using a 5/16 inch hex head wrench, remove plug from pump housing assembly and remove oil pressure regulator valve and spring from bore in housing assembly.
4. Inspect oil pressure regulator valve for nicks and burrs that might cause a leak or binding condition in bore of pump housing.
5. Check free length of regulator valve spring. It should be about 2.57 inches to 2.69 inches. A force of 9.3 to 10.5 pounds should be required to compress spring to a length of 1.46 inches.
6. Inspect drive gear and driven gear for nicks and burrs.
7. Inspect pump housing for wear and score marks.
8. Check pump mating surfaces for wear and score marks.
9. Reverse procedure to assemble.

BELT TENSION DATA

	New Lbs.	Used Lbs.
1980		
All	110–140	60–120
1981–82 Exc. V8-250		
Air Conditioning	168	67
A.I.R. Pump	78	45
Generator	145	90
Power Steering	168	67
1982 V8-250		
Air Conditioning/ Steering Pump	202	90
A.I.R. Pump	180	67
Generator	147	56
Vacuum Pump	49	25
1983–86 V8-250		
Air Conditioning/ Steering Pump	191	146
A.I.R. Pump	169	135
Generator	135	90
Vacuum Pump	45	34

WATER PUMP
REPLACE
1980

1. Disconnect battery ground cable, then drain cooling system.
2. On DeVille models, remove two screws, one from each side at radiator end of support rods. Loosen screws at strut end of support rods and move support rods aside.
3. Remove screws from upper fan shroud and remove screw securing upper radiator hose brace.
4. Drill out seven rivets securing upper fan shroud to lower fan shroud, then remove upper shroud.
5. Remove fan assembly.
6. Remove generator drive belt.
7. Remove power steering pump belt.
8. Remove water pump pulley.
9. Disconnect water inlet hose from water pump.
10. Disconnect fuel line at carburetor inlet and fuel pump. Remove fuel line.
11. Loosen screws securing crankshaft pulley to hub approximately half way and move pulley out slightly.
12. Remove screws securing water pump to engine front cover, then remove pump, **Figs. 42 and 43.** Discard gasket and clean gasket surfaces.
13. Remove studs from pump flange.
14. Reverse procedure to install.

1981–86

1. Disconnect battery ground cable, then drain cooling system.
2. On DeVille and Brougham models, remove two screws, one from each side at radiator end of support rods. Loosen screws at strut end of support rods and move support rods aside.
3. Remove screws from upper fan shroud, then remove wiring harness from upper fan shroud clamps.
4. Remove screws securing power steering pump reservoir to upper fan shroud, then remove reservoir.
5. Remove staples securing upper fan shroud to lower shroud and remove upper shroud.
6. Remove fan assembly.
7. Loosen generator mounting screws and remove drive belt.
8. Remove A.I.R. pump drive belt.
9. Remove lower power steering pump mounting bolt and loosen the remaining bolt. Remove the vacuum pump drive belt.
10. Remove A/C compressor drive belt.
11. Remove air conditioning compressor from engine mounting brackets and position aside. Do not remove high and low pressure lines from compressor.
12. Remove generator and support bracket from engine.
13. Loosen clamp and disconnect coolant reservoir to water pump hose at pump.
14. Loosen clamps and disconnect water pump inlet and outlet hoses at pump.
15. Remove water pump and crankshaft pulleys.

16. Remove A/C compressor bracket.
17. Remove timing mark tab.
18. Remove screws and nuts securing water pump, **Fig. 44,** to engine front cover and remove pump. Discard gasket and clean gasket surfaces.
19. Reverse procedure to install.

FUEL PUMP
REPLACE

WITH FUEL INJECTION

NOTE: On 1980 models with EFI, two fuel pumps are used; one in-tank unit and a chassis mounted unit. All other models use an in-tank fuel pump.

In-Tank Fuel Pump
1. Drain and remove fuel tank.
2. Remove locknut(s) securing wiring to fuel gauge pump unit, then fuel pump feed and gauge wires to tank unit.
3. Using tool J-24187, disengage lock ring from fuel tank. Remove tool, then lift gauge pump unit from tank and separate components.
4. On 1980 Eldorado and Seville models, proceed as follows:
   a. Remove filter screen from pump.
   b. Cut off rubber coupler, then remove fuel pump from bracket.
   c. Disconnect electrical wiring.
   d. Lubricate fuel tube and fuel pump outlet tube with suitable lubricant. Slide new rubber coupler into fuel tube.
   e. Connect wiring to fuel pump, then install new rubber isolator and pump on to mounting bracket. Align fuel pump outlet with fuel tube and slide rubber coupler into position.

NOTE: Support pump bracket to prevent it from bending during coupler installation.

   f. Position new in-tank filter.
5. Reverse procedure to install.

Chassis Mounted Fuel Pump
1. Remove fuel inlet and outlet hoses.
2. Pull back rubber boot and remove nuts from electrical terminals, then electrical leads.
3. Remove fuel pump to mounting bracket screws, then fuel pump assembly.
4. Reverse procedure to install. Torque fuel pump mounting screws to 25 inch lbs. Connect 14 dark green wire to positive terminal and 14 black wire to negative terminal.

1980–82 Less Fuel Injection
1. Raise vehicle and disconnect fuel inlet line at pump and plug line.
2. Disconnect fuel outlet pipe at pump.
3. Disconnect vapor return hoses.
4. Remove upper pump flange mounting screws.
5. Remove nut from mounting stud at lower pump flange.
6. Tipping pump upward, pull pump straight out from engine and remove.
7. Reverse procedure to install.

Rear Axle, Propeller Shaft & Brakes

Fig. 1   Rear wheel spindle disassembled. 1980–85 Eldorado & Seville

Fig. 2   Checking wheel bearing for looseness. 1980–85 Eldorado & Seville

REAR AXLE

1980–85 ELDORADO & SEVILLE

The spindle and wheel bearing is a unitized assembly which eliminates the need for periodic maintenance and adjustments. The spindle and wheel bearing assembly is bolted to the rear suspension control arm, **Fig. 1.**

Wheel Bearing Inspection

1. Raise and support rear of vehicle, then remove wheel and tire assembly.
2. Free disc brake shoes from disc or remove calipers, then reinstall two wheel nuts to secure disc to bearing.
3. Mount dial indicator as shown in **Fig. 2,** then grasp rotor and check inward and outward movement of spindle assembly. Movement should be less than .020 in.
4. Remove dial indicator and rotate spindle by hand to check for roughness or grinding within the spindle.
5. Replace spindle and bearing assembly if out of specifications or roughness or grinding is present.

Spindle & Bearing Assembly, Replace

1. Raise vehicle and remove wheel and tire assembly.
2. Remove brake caliper assembly.
3. Mark wheel stud and corresponding place on rotor for use during installation, then remove rotor.
4. Remove four nuts and bolts attaching spindle and bearing assembly to control arm, **Fig. 1.**
5. Reverse procedure to install. Torque spindle to lower control arm attaching bolts to 34 ft. lbs.

1980–84 DEVILLE & 1980–86 BROUGHAM

In this axle, **Fig. 3,** the rear axle housing and differential carrier are cast into an integral assembly. The drive pinion assembly is mounted in two opposed tapered roller bearings. The pinion bearings are preloaded by a spacer behind the front bearing. The pinion is positioned by a washer between the head of the pinion and the rear bearing.

The differential is supported in the carrier by two tapered roller side bearings. These bearings are preloaded by spacers located between the bearings and carrier housing. The differential assembly is positioned for proper ring gear and pinion backlash by varying these spacers. The differential case houses two side gears in mesh with two pinions mounted on a pinion shaft which is held in place by a lock pin. The side gears and pinions are backed by thrust washers.

REAR AXLE, REPLACE

1. Raise vehicle and support rear axle and frame, then remove rear wheels and drums.
2. Disconnect overtravel lever from link, if equipped.
3. Remove shock absorbers from lower mount.
4. Place jack under front differential to relieve tension on lower control arm.
5. Remove upper and lower control arms as outlined under "Control Arms and Bushings, Replace" procedure in Rear Suspension Section.
6. Remove propeller shaft and support with wire.
7. Remove brake hose at differential housing and plug.

CAUTION: If axle is allowed to wind up as it is lowered, springs may snap from their seats and could cause injury or damage. Use extreme caution to prevent wind-up condition.

8. Lower axle shaft and remove springs from vehicle.
9. Reverse procedure to install.

DIFFERENTIAL, REPLACE

1. Raise vehicle and support so axle can be raised and lowered.
2. Disconnect leveling control lever from link and hold lever down until shock absorbers are deflated.
3. Remove shock absorber lower mounting bolts and position shock aside.
4. Mark propeller shaft flange and pinion flange to ensure installation in original position. Remove attaching screws and position propeller shaft aside.
5. Remove stabilizer bar link nuts, retainer and bushings.
6. Remove nut from parking brake equalizer, then disconnect cables at connectors.
7. Remove clips securing brake tubing to axle, then lower axle slightly.
8. Position drain pan under axle, loosen rear cover bolts and allow axle to drain, then remove cover.
9. Remove wheel and brake drum.
10. Remove differential cross shaft through bolt, then the shaft. Push in on axle shafts, then remove "C" locks and pull axle shafts out about 1 inch.
11. Install cross shaft and bolt, then remove side bearing cap and bearing.

NOTE: Mark bearing caps to ensure installation in original position

12. Remove one ring gear attaching bolt, position tools, **Fig. 4,** and pull differential case from housing until side shims can be removed, then remove differential.

NOTE: Mark shims to ensure installation in original position.

13. Reverse procedure to install.

Fig. 3   Rear axle assembly. 1980–84 Deville & 1980–86 Brougham (Typical)

AXLE SHAFT, REPLACE

1. Raise vehicle and remove wheel and brake drum.
2. Place drain pan under differential and remove cover.
3. Remove differential cross shaft.
4. Push axle shaft toward center of vehicle and remove "C" lock from butt end of axle shaft.
5. Remove axle shaft from housing.
6. Reverse procedure to install.

BEARING REPLACE

1. Remove axle shaft.

2. Position tool J-22813-01 or J-23689 on bearing, attach slide hammer J-2619, then remove bearing and seal, **Fig. 5.**
3. Lubricate bearing and seal with bearing lubricant.
4. Position bearing on tool J-23690 and drive bearing in until tool bottoms against tube, **Fig. 6.**
5. Using suitable tool, tap seal in until flush with axle tube.

PROPELLER SHAFT
REPLACE

1. Raise vehicle on hoist with transmission in neutral.

NOTE: Mark propeller shaft relationship to axle pinion flange to maintain balance.

2. Remove propeller shaft flange retaining bolts.

Fig. 4 Removing differential. & 1980—84 DeVille & 1980—86 Brougham

Fig. 5 Removing axle bearing

Fig. 6 Installing axle bearing

Fig. 7 Measuring brake drum inner diameter

CAUTION: Do not allow propeller shaft to be supported by front or center universal joint, as damage to universal joint may result. Rear of propeller shaft must be supported to underbody of vehicle.

3. Pull propeller shaft forward to clear pinion flange and support rear end of shaft.

NOTE: Place a suitable container under transmission, to catch any fluid which may leak when slip joint is removed.

4. On two piece type propeller shafts, remove the two center bearing supports to frame bolts and nuts.
5. On all types, slide propeller shaft rearward until slip yoke comes off transmission output shaft.

NOTE: Place a protective device such as a cardboard shipping cover, over yoke. This will prevent damage to yoke when shaft is removed.

6. Remove shaft and install a spare yoke into transmission extension housing to prevent loss of oil.
7. Reverse procedure to install. Torque flange attaching bolts to 70 ft. lbs.
8. Check transmission oil.

DRUM BRAKE ADJUSTMENTS
SELF-ADJUSTING BRAKES

These brakes have self-adjusting shoe mechanisms that assure correct lining-to-drum clearances at all times. The automatic adjusters operate only when the brakes are applied as the car is moving rearward.

Although the brakes are self-adjusting, an initial adjustment is necessary after the brake shoes have been relined or replaced, or when the length of the star wheel adjuster has been changed during some other service operation.

Frequent usage of an automatic transmission forward range to halt reverse vehicle motion may prevent the automatic adjusters from functioning, thereby inducing low pedal heights. Should low pedal heights be encountered, it is recommended that numerous forward and reverse stops be made with a moderate pedal effort until satisfactory pedal height is obtained.

NOTE: If a low pedal height condition cannot be corrected by making numerous reverse stops (provided the hydraulic system is free of air) it indicates that the self-adjusting mechanism is not functioning. Therefore, it will be necessary to remove the brake drum, clean, free up and lubricate the adjusting mechanism. Then adjust the brakes, being sure the parking brake is fully released.

The recommended method of adjusting the brakes is by using the Drum-to-Brake Shoe Clearance Gauge to check the diameter of the brake drum inner surface, **Fig. 7.** Turn the tool to the opposite side and fit over the brake shoes by turning the star wheel until the gauge just slides over the linings, **Fig. 8.** Rotate the gauge around the brake shoe lining surface to assure proper clearance.

PARKING BRAKE
ADJUST

1980—86 W/REAR DISC BRAKES

1. Lubricate parking brake cables at equalizer and underbody rub points.

Check all cables for freedom of operation.
2. Fully release parking brake and raise vehicle.
3. Hold cable stud from turning and tighten equalizer nut until cable slack is removed and levers are against stops on caliper housing. If levers are off stops, loosen cable until levers return to stop.
4. Operate parking brake several times to check adjustment. When properly adjusted, the parking brake pedal should move 5¼-6¾ inches on 1980—86 all except Seville and Eldorado, 4-5½ inches on 1980-85 Eldorado and 1980—85 Seville.

1980—86 W/REAR DRUM BRAKES

1. With service brakes properly adjusted, lubricate parking brake linkage at equalizer and cable stud with heat-resistant lubricant, and check for free movement of cables.
2. Depress parking brake pedal about 1½ inch from full released position.
3. Raise rear wheels off floor.
4. Hold brake cable and stud from turning and tighten equalizer nut until a slight drag is felt on either wheel (going forward). After each turn of equalizer nut, check to see if either wheel begins to drag.
5. Release parking brake. No brake drag should be felt at either rear wheel. Operate several times to check adjustment. When properly adjusted, the parking brake pedal should move 5¼ to 6¾ inches.

VACUUM RELEASE PARKING BRAKE
1980—86

The foot-operated parking brake is mounted on the cowl to the left of the steering column. It incorporates a vacuum release, **Fig. 9,** operated by a vacuum diaphragm that is connected to the parking brake mechanism. When the transmission

Fig. 8 Checking brake shoe lining clearance

Fig. 9 Parking brake linkage. 1980—86 drum brake (typical)

selector is moved into any Drive position, a vacuum valve in the neutral safety switch opens, allowing diaphragm to be actuated by engine vacuum.

The diaphragm is connected by a link to a release mechanism on the parking brake. Vacuum acting on the diaphragm unlocks the parking brake pedal, permitting it to return to the release position by spring action. Any abnormal leaks in the vacuum release system will prevent proper brake release. A manual release is provided and may be used if the automatic release is inoperative or if manual release is desired at any time.

NOTE: Under some conditions, aided by cold weather, the parking brake vacuum release valve (integral with the back-up light switch on steering column) may not release the parking brake automatically. Although when the brake is applied, the "Brake" indicator light will go on, brake can be released manually. If this condition is present the back-up light switch must be replaced.

TESTING VACUUM RELEASE

1. If the mechanism is inoperative, first check for damaged or kinked vacuum hoses and for loose hose connections at the diaphragm, vacuum release valve at neutral safety switch, and at engine manifold connection.
2. Check adjustment of neutral safety switch and operation of vacuum release valve.
3. Check diaphragm piston travel by running engine and moving transmission selector lever from drive to neutral. The manual release lever should move up and down as vacuum is applied and released. If no movement is observed, or if movement is slow (more than 1 or 2 seconds to complete the full stroke) diaphragm is leaking and should be replaced.
4. Check brake release with vacuum applied. If diaphragm piston completes full stroke but does not release brake, a malfunction of the pedal assembly is indicated, and the complete parking brake assembly should be replaced.
5. Check operation of parking brake with engine off. Parking brake should remain engaged regardless of transmission selector lever position. If not, replace parking brake assembly.

MASTER CYLINDER
REPLACE

1. Remove brake lines from master cylinder. Plug lines and ports.
2. Remove booster to master cylinder attaching nuts, then remove master cylinder.
3. Reverse procedure to install. On 1980 models, torque master cylinder attaching nuts to 20 ft. lbs., 1981 models to 22–30 ft. lbs. and 1982–86 models to 28 ft. lbs. On 1980 models, torque brake line to master cylinder nuts to 20 ft. lbs., on 1981 models to 10–15 ft. lbs. and on 1982–86 models to 18 ft. lbs.

POWER BRAKE UNIT
REPLACE

Service Bulletin: A sign of brake fluid dampness below the master cylinder at the power brake unit or on wheel cylinders at the bottom of the boot, does not necessarily indicate that these cylinders are leaking.

A small amount of fluid leakage at these areas can occur due to the creeping action of a very light film of fluid on the cylinder bores around the seals. This action provides proper seal lubrication. In addition, normal brake heat will produce a slight escape of lubricant from the impregnated, porous-metal wheel cylinder pistons.

Normal dampness at the master cylinder or wheel cylinders is not easily distinguishable from a definite leak. Therefore, this condition must be checked carefully.

If there is sufficient dampness to form a "teardrop" of fluid at the bottom of the master cylinder or on the bottom of the wheel cylinders at the boot area, the rate of fluid seepage is too high and the cause should be determined and corrected.

HYDRO-BOOST
1980—86

1. With engine off pump brake pedal several times to empty accumulator of fluid.
2. Remove master cylinder to booster attaching nuts, then move master cylinder away from booster with brakes lines attached.
3. Remove three hydraulic lines from booster, cap all ports and lines to prevent entry of dirt and loss of fluid.
4. Remove retainer and washer securing booster pedal rod to brake pedal arm.
5. Remove four booster to firewall attaching nuts.
6. Loosen booster from firewall and move booster pedal rod inboard until it disconnects from brake arm.
7. Remove spring washer from brake pedal arm and remove booster.
8. Reverse procedure to install. To purge system, disconnect feed wire from injection pump. Fill power steering pump reservoir, then crank engine for several seconds without starting and recheck power steering pump fluid level. Connect injection pump feed wire and start engine, then cycle steering gear wheel from stop to stop twice and turn off engine. Discharge accumulator by depressing brake pedal several times, then check fluid level. Start engine, then turn steering wheel from stop to stop and turn off engine. Check fluid level and add fluid if necessary. If foaming occurs, turn off engine and wait for approximately one hour for foam to dissipate, then recheck fluid level.

VACUUM BOOSTER

1. Remove master cylinder to booster attaching nuts, then move master cylinder away from booster with brake lines attached.

NOTE: On some models, it may be necessary to remove brake lines from master cylinder. If lines must be removed, cover exposed ends of brake lines to prevent contamination.

2. Remove vacuum hose from check valve on booster.
3. Remove nuts attaching brake unit to cowl and pedal support bracket.
4. From inside of vehicle, disconnect power brake push rod from brake pedal and remove vacuum booster.
5. Reverse procedure to install.

Rear Suspension

Fig. 1   1980–85 Eldorado & Seville rear suspension

POSITIONING DIMPLES

Fig. 2   Coil spring installation.
1980–85 Eldorado & Seville

SHOCK ABSORBER
REPLACE

1980–86

1. If equipped with Automatic Level Control, disconnect air lines from shock absorber fittings.
2. With the rear axle supported properly disconnect shock absorber at upper and lower mountings.

NOTE: Use care not to damage brake hoses or lines when removing shock absorber.

3. Reverse procedure to install, noting the following:
   a. When installing shocks equipped with automatic level control, air ports should face front of vehicle.
   b. Extend shocks completely before installation.

COIL SPRINGS
REPLACE

1980–85 ELDORADO & SEVILLE

1. Raise and support rear of vehicle, then remove wheel and tire assembly.
2. Remove stabilizer bar as described under Stabilizer Bar, Replace.
3. Using a suitable jack support lower control arm.
4. Disconnect automatic level air line at shock absorber. If removing left hand spring from vehicle, disconnect automatic level control link from ball pivot at control arm.

5. Disconnect shock absorber from upper and lower mountings and remove shock absorber.
6. Carefully lower control arm until spring tension is relieved, then remove spring and insulator, **Fig. 1.**
7. Reverse procedure to install. Locate bottom end of spring between dimples on lower control arm assembly, **Fig. 2.**

1980–86 EXCEPT ELDORADO & SEVILLE

1. Support vehicle at frame and support rear axle using a suitable jack.
2. Remove shock absorbers.
3. If equipped with Automatic Level Control, remove bolts attaching stabilizer bar to lower control arms and remove stabilizer bar.
4. Remove bolt attaching brake line junction block to rear axle housing, then disconnect brake lines from clips on rear axle housing.
5. If equipped with Automatic Level Control, disconnect link from leveling valve arm.
6. Position a jack stand under nose of differential carrier to relieve tension on lower control arm to axle housing bolts, then remove bolts, **Fig. 3.**
7. Disconnect drive shaft from pinion flange and support from frame with wire.
8. Remove jack stand from under nose of differential carrier, then remove upper control arm pivot bolts at rear axle housing.
9. Disconnect left hand parking brake cable at equalizer and cable at frame by removing clip.
10. Disconnect parking brake cable from clip at center of rear cross member

and cable at "C" connector located at left hand side of frame.
11. Lower axle assembly to a point where springs can be pried out, using care not to stretch brake lines or parking brake cables.

NOTE: When lowering axle and prying out springs, use care to prevent axle assembly from rotating, as springs may snap from seats.

12. Reverse procedure to install. Note spring positions, **Fig. 4.**

CONTROL ARMS & BUSHINGS
REPLACE

NOTE: Replace one control arm at a time as axle assembly may slip sideways, making installation difficult.

UPPER CONTROL ARMS

1980–86 Except Eldorado & Seville

1. Support vehicle at frame and support rear axle using a suitable jack.
2. If vehicle is equipped with Automatic Level Control, remove bolt attaching height control link to right upper control arm. Position overtravel lever in center position.
3. Position a jack stand under differential pinion retainer.
4. Remove both control arm pivot bolts and control arm.
5. Reverse procedure to install. Tighten control arm pivot bolts with vehicle curb weight applied to axle.

Fig. 3   1980–86 rear suspension (typical). Except Eldorado & Seville

Fig. 4   Coil spring installation. 1980–86 Except Eldorado & Seville

4. Position a suitable jack under front of differential carrier to relieve tension on lower control arm bolts.
5. Remove front and rear lower control arm bolts and lower control arm.

NOTE: Lower control arm bushings are not serviceable.

6. Reverse procedure to install. Tighten control arm bolts with vehicle at curb height.

LOWER CONTROL ARMS

1980–85 Eldorado & Seville

1. Raise and support rear of vehicle, then remove wheel and tire assembly.
2. Remove stabilizer bar as described under Stabilizer Bar, Replace.
3. Disconnect brake line bracket from control arm, then remove caliper assembly.
4. Mark a wheel stud and a corresponding point on the rotor for alignment, then remove rotor.
5. If left hand control arm is to be removed, disconnect automatic level control link from ball pivot on control arm.
6. Using a suitable jack support control arm.
7. Disconnect air line from shock absorber, then disconnect shock absorber from upper and lower mountings and remove shock absorber.
8. Carefully lower the control arm until spring tension is relieved, then remove spring and insulator.
9. Remove two bolts mounting control arm to frame and remove control arm, **Fig. 1.**
10. Reverse procedure to install. Torque control arm to frame mounting bolts to 75 ft. lbs.

1980–86 Except Eldorado & Seville

1. Support vehicle at frame and support rear axle using a suitable jack.
2. If equipped with Automatic Level Control, remove two bolts securing stabilizer bar to control arm being removed.
3. Remove front and rear lower control arm nuts.

STABILIZER BAR
REPLACE

1980–85 ELDORADO & SEVILLE

1. Raise and support rear of vehicle.
2. Remove nuts and bolts securing front of stabilizer bar to control arms.
3. Remove inside nut and bolt from each side of stabilizer bar link, then loosen outside nut and bolt on the stabilizer link.
4. Rotate bottom parts of link to one side and slip stabilizer out of bushings.

1980–86 EXCEPT ELDORADO & SEVILLE

1. Raise and support rear of vehicle.
2. Remove bolts securing stabilizer bar to lower control arms, then remove stabilizer bar from vehicle.

Front End & Steering Section

Refer to Section 32 for Front Drive Axle Service

1980–86 BROUGHAM & 1980–84 DEVILLE FRONT SUSPENSION

The front suspension consist of two upper and lower control arm assemblies, steel coil springs, shock absorbers, stabilizer bar, two integral steering arms, and knuckles, **Fig. 1.**

Ball joints are used at outer ends of upper and lower control arms. The upper ball joints is riveted to the upper control arm. The lower ball joint is pressed into the lower control arm.

A stabilizer bar is mounted in rubber bushings to the front frame side rails and is attached to the lower control arms by means of steel links.

WHEEL ALIGNMENT

Caster and camber are adjusted by adding or removing shims from between the upper control arm and frame bracket, **Fig. 2.** Caster is adjusted by transfering shims from front to rear and rear to front. Transfering shims from front bolt to rear bolt will increase positive caster, from rear bolt to front bolt will increase negative caster.

Camber is adjusted by adding or removing an equal number of shims from the front and rear bolts. To increase positive camber remove an equal amount of shims from front and rear bolts, to increase negative camber add an equal amount of shims to front and rear bolts.

After adjusting caster and camber torque nut to 70–80 ft. lbs. Tighten bolt with the least amount of shims first. After adjusting caster and camber toe-in must be adjusted.

NOTE: The difference in thickness between front and rear shim packs should not exceed .40 inch. If difference is greater than .40 inch check arms, frame and related parts for damage.

TOE-IN, ADJUST

Toe-in can be adjusted by loosening the clamp bolts at each end of each tie rod and turning each tie rod to increase or decrease its length as necessary until proper toe-in is secured and the steering gear is on the high point for straight-ahead driving.

WHEEL BEARINGS, ADJUST

SERVICE BULLETIN: Looseness at a front wheel does not necessarily indicate worn bearings or a loose spindle nut, since the tapered roller bearings used on front wheels of all standard Cadillacs should not be preloaded and normally can have up to .004 inch end play.

Fig. 1   Front suspension disassembled. 1980–86 Brougham & 1980–84 DeVille

1. While rotating wheel and tire assembly, tighten spindle nut to 12 ft. lbs. for 1980–86 vehicles making certain that hub is fully seated on spindle.
2. Back off spindle nut until free, and tighten nut finger tight.
3. Install new cotter pin. If pin cannot be installed, back off nut to next hole and install pin.

NOTE: Cotter pin must be tight after installation, as vibration can break pin.

WHEEL BEARINGS, REPLACE

1. Remove caliper retaining bolts, then slide caliper off disc and using a length of wire, attach caliper to upper control arm.

NOTE: Never allow caliper to hang from brake hose.

2. Remove dust cap, cotter pin, spindle

Fig. 2   Caster and camber adjustment. 1980–86 Brougham & 1980–84 DeVille

FRONT SUSPENSION BALL JOINT WEAR INDICATOR

WORN   NEW

SINTERED IRON BEARING

WEAR SURFACES

HOUSING SOCKET

.050 INCH

RUBBER PRESSURE RING

WEAR INDICATOR

WHEN BALL JOINT WEAR CAUSES WEAR INDICATOR SHOULDER TO RECEDE WITHIN THE SOCKET HOUSING REPLACEMENT IS REQUIRED

Fig. 3 Ball joint wear indicator

Remove Upper   Remove Lower

Heavy Flat Washer

J·23742   J·23742

Fig. 4 Removing ball joint studs from steering knuckle. 1980–86 Brougham & 1980–84 DeVille

2 × 4

J- 9519-10

J- 9519-7

Fig. 5 Removing ball joint from lower control arm. 1980–86 Brougham & 1980–84 DeVille

nut, washer and outer bearing assembly.
3. Remove hub and disc assembly, being careful to avoid damage to spindle threads or grease seal.
4. Remove inner bearing grease seal and bearing assembly.

NOTE: Inner and outer bearing cups are press fit in hub and can be driven out from the opposite side using a brass drift. Tap alternately on opposite sides to prevent cocking cup and damaging hub.

CHECKING BALL JOINTS FOR WEAR

Upper Ball Joint

If ball joint has any noticeable lateral movement or can be twisted within its socket using finger pressure, the joint must be replaced.

Lower Ball Joint

A wear indicator is built in the ball joint. Remove dirt deposits around service plug and observe position of nipple. Refer to **Fig. 3,** for wear tolerance.

UPPER BALL JOINT, REPLACE

1. Raise vehicle and remove wheel.
2. Remove cotter pin from upper ball joint stud.
3. Remove caliper and position aside.

NOTE: When removing caliper use care not to damage brake tubing or hose. Secure caliper to frame with wire.

4. Loosen stud nut, however, not more than one turn.
5. Using tool No. J-23742, free ball joint stud from steering knuckle, **Fig. 4.**

NOTE: The lower control arm must be supported so spring can not force arm down.

6. Remove upper ball joint stud nut, allow steering knuckle to swing out of way and place block of wood between frame and upper control arm.
7. To remove rivets securing ball joint to upper control arm, grind rivet heads off, then, using a punch, drive rivets out.

NOTE: Use care not to damage ball joint seat or upper control arm when removing rivets.

8. Remove ball joint.
9. Install new ball joint in control arm and attach with bolt and nut assembly provided with new joint. Install bolts from bottom and torque nuts to 25 ft. lbs. on 1980–81 models, and 20 ft. lbs. on 1982–86 models.
10. Remove block of wood from between frame and upper control arm, position upper ball stud to steering knuckle, install and torque nut to 60 to 61 ft. lbs. Install cotter pin.

NOTE: If cotter pin hole is not aligned do not back nut off. Nut may be torqued to a maximum of 100 ft. lbs. (⅙ additional turn) to align cotter pin hole.

11. Install caliper, lubricate ball joint and install wheel.
12. Check wheel alignment.

LOWER BALL JOINT, REPLACE

1. Raise vehicle and remove wheel.
2. Remove cotter pin from lower ball joint stud and loosen nut one turn.

3. Using tool No. J-23742, free ball joint stud from steering knuckle, **Fig. 4.**

NOTE: Lower control arm must be supported so spring cannot force arm down.

4. Remove lower stud nut and pull upward and outward on bottom of brake disc to free ball joint stud from steering knuckle.
5. Lift upper control arm up with steering knuckle and hub attached and place a block of wood between frame and upper control arm.

NOTE: It may be necessary to remove tie rod from steering knuckle.

6. Using tools J-9519-10 and J-9519-7 or equivalent, remove ball joint from lower control arm, **Fig. 5.**
7. Install ball joint in lower control arm using tools J-9519-9 and J-9519-10 or equivalent.

NOTE: Position bleed vent in ball joint rubber boot to face inward and the stud cotter pin hole to face forward.

8. Remove block of wood from between frame and upper control arm, then install lower ball joint stud in steering

Fig. 6 Removing and installing front spring. 1980–86 Brougham & 1980–84 DeVille

knuckle. Install and torque nut to 80 to 83 ft. lbs. and install cotter pin.

NOTE: Some models are equipped with prevailing torque fasteners, and therefore no cotter pins are used. On models with fasteners that use cotter pins as locking devices, nut may be torqued to a maximum of 125 ft. lbs. on 1980–81 models or a maximum of 92 ft. lbs. on 1982–86 models to align cotter pin holes.

9. Lubricate ball joint and install tie rod, if removed. Torque tie rod nut to 35 ft. lbs. for 1980 and 1981 models, 40 ft. lbs. for 1980 and 1982 models, and 30 ft. lbs. for 1983–86 models.

NOTE: Some models are equipped with prevailing torque fasteners, and therefore no cotter pins are used.

10. Install wheel and check wheel alignment.

SHOCK ABSORBER, REPLACE

The shock absorbers are removed through the bottom of the lower control arm after unfastening it at the top and bottom.

To install, place the retainer and rubber grommet on the upper stem and fully extend the shock absorber rod. Insert the shock absorber up into the coil spring and guide the stem through the tower in the crossmember. Then place the lower end in position on the lower control arm. Install bolts and torque to 20 to 22 ft. lbs. on all except Seville or 19 ft. lbs. on Seville. On all models, install shock stud retaining nut and tighten to end of threads on stud (about 1⅛ inch).

COIL SPRING, REPLACE

1. Raise vehicle on hoist, remove shock absorber lower mounting bolts and push shock through control arm up into spring.
2. Support vehicle so control arms hang free and disconnect stabilizer bar from lower control arm.
3. Secure tool No. J-23028-01 to a suitable jack, position tool so lower control arm is supported by inner bushings, **Fig. 6.**

Fig. 7 Front suspension disassembled. 1980–85 Eldorado & Seville

4. Raise jack to relieve spring tension from lower control arm pivot and install a safety chain around spring and through lower control arm.
5. Remove bolt from rear of lower control arm, then remove other bolt and slowly lower control arm until all spring tension is relieved.
6. Remove safety chain, spring and spring insulator.
7. Reverse procedure to install.

NOTE: When installing spring, bottom coil must cover all or part of one inspection hole on the lower control arm. The other inspection hole must be fully or partially uncovered.

Fig. 8 Checking standing height 1980–85 Eldorado & Seville

1980–85 ELDORADO & 1980–85 SEVILLE FRONT SUSPENSION

The front suspension consists of two upper and two lower control arms, a stabilizer bar, shock absorbers and a right and left torsion bar, **Fig. 7.** Torsion bars are used instead of the conventional coil springs. The front end of the torsion bar is attached to the lower control arm. The rear of the torsion bar is mounted into an adjustable arm in the torsion bar crossmember. The standing height of the car is controlled by this adjustment.

STANDING HEIGHT, ADJUST

NOTE: Before standing height adjustment is performed, vehicle should be on a flat, level surface, with front seat all the way back, fuel tank full and tires inflated to proper pressure. Air lines must be loosened at shock absorbers, if equipped with electronic level control, and system must be depressurized.

The standing height must be checked and adjusted if necessary before checking and adjusting front wheel alignment. The standing height is controlled by the adjustment setting of the torsion bar adjusting bolt, **Fig. 7.** Clockwise rotation of the bolt increases standing height: counterclockwise rotation decreases standing height.

Fig. 9 Caster-camber cam locations. 1980—85 Eldorado & Seville

Fig. 10 Tie rod clamp and sleeve positioning

Fig. 11 Sealed wheel bearing assembly. 1980—85 Eldorado & Seville

To check vehicle height, measure from lower edge of front shock absorber dust tube (A) to centerline of lower attachment (B), **Fig. 8.** This dimension between (A) and (B) should be 5½—6 inch on 1980—85 vehicles.

WHEEL ALIGNMENT, ADJUST

1980—84 Eldorado & Seville

Caster

Record camber reading, then hold front cam bolt and loosen nut, **Fig. 9.** Turn front cam bolt to obtain ¼ of the desired caster change. At front cam bolt a positive camber change produces a positive caster change and a negative camber change produces a negative caster change. Hold cam bolt in position and tighten nut. Loosen rear cam bolt nut and rotate cam bolt to return camber to setting recorded previously, **Fig. 9.** When adjustment has been completed hold rear cam bolt and torque nut to 90 ft. lbs. on 1980—81 models and 70 ft. lbs. on 1982—85 models.

Camber

While holding cam bolt in position, loosen cam bolt nut, **Fig. 9.** Rotate cam bolt to

obtain a change in camber equal to ½ the needed correction. Hold cam bolt in position and tighten cam bolt nut. To obtain the remaining ½ of needed correction apply the above procedue to the other cam bolt.

TOE-IN, ADJUST

Toe-in is adjusted by turning the tie rod adjusting tubes at outer ends of each tie rod after loosening clamp bolts. Readings should be taken only when front wheels are straight ahead and steering gear is on its high spot.

1980—85 Eldorado & Seville

1. Loosen clamp bolts at each end of tie rod adjusting sleeve.
2. Turn tie rod adjusting sleeve to obtain the proper toe-in adjustment.
3. After completing adjustment, check to ensure that the number of threads at each end of sleeve are equal and tie rod end housings and clamps are properly positioned, **Fig. 10.** Torque clamp bolt to 14 to 15 ft. lbs.

WHEEL BEARING INSPECTION

1980—85 Eldorado & Seville

The front wheel bearing is a sealed unit bearing. The bearing can not be adjusted or repacked. There are darkened areas on the bearing assembly. These darkened areas are from a heat treatment process and do not indicate need for bearing replacement, **Fig. 11.**

To check wheel bearing assembly for looseness, free brake pads from disc or remove calipers. Install two lug nuts to secure disc to bearing. Mount dial indicator as shown in **Fig. 12,** then rock disc and note indicator reading. If looseness exceeds .005 in. replace hub and bearing assembly.

WHEEL BEARING & STEERING KNUCKLE, REPLACE

1980—85 Eldorado & Seville

1. Raise and support vehicle under lower control arms.
2. Remove drive axle nut and washer and remove wheel and tire assembly.
3. Remove brake hose clip from ball joint and replace nut, then remove brake caliper off disc, and using a length of wire support caliper on suspension.

NOTE: Do not allow caliper to hang from brake hose as this could cause damage and premature failure of hose.

4. Mark hub and disc assembly for alignment during assembly and remove disc, then strike steering knuckle in

Fig. 12 Checking wheel bearing for looseness. 1980—85 Eldorado & Seville

Fig. 13 Wheel bearing & steering knuckle assembly. 1980—85 Eldorado & Seville

Fig. 14   Checking ball joints for wear. 1980–85 Eldorado & Seville

Fig. 15   Torsion bar removal. 1980–85 Eldorado & Seville

area of upper ball joint until upper ball joint is loose.

CAUTION: Use extreme care to prevent striking and damaging brake hose or ball joint seal.

5. Place a short length of rubber hose over lower control arm torsion bar connector to avoid damage to inboard tripot joint seal when hub and knuckle are removed.
6. Using appropriate puller, disconnect tie rod end, upper and lower ball joints and remove steering knuckle and hub assembly, **Fig. 13.**
7. Reverse procedure to install, noting the following torque values: drive axle nut to hub and bearing, 175 ft. lbs. on 1980–85 models; lower ball joint nut, 65 ft. lbs. on 1980–81 models or 83 ft. lbs. on 1982–85 models; upper ball joint nut, 90 ft. lbs. on 1980–81 models or 61 ft. lbs. on 1982–85 models; tie rod to steering knuckle nut, 35 ft. lbs. on 1980–81 models or 40 ft. lbs. on 1982–85 models; hub and bearing to knuckle bolts, 75 ft. lbs. on 1980–85 models.

CHECKING BALL JOINTS FOR WEAR

1. Raise car and position jack stands under lower control arms as near as possible to each ball joint.
2. Clamp vise grips on end of drive axle and position a dial indicator so that dial indicator ball rests on vise grip, **Fig. 14.**
3. Place a pry bar between lower control arm and outer race and pry down on bar. Reading must not exceed ⅛ inch.

UPPER BALL JOINT, REPLACE

1980–85 Eldorado & Seville
1. Raise vehicle and support under lower control arms.

2. Remove wheel and tire assembly.
3. Remove cotter pin and nut from upper ball joint stud, then disconnect brake hose clip from stud.
4. Using a hammer and brass drift, disengage ball joint stud from steering knuckle.
5. Place a block of wood between control arm and frame, then drill rivets with a ⅛ in. drill bit ¼ in. deep from top side of control arm.
6. Drill rivet heads off using a ½ inch drill bit. Do not drill into control arm.
7. Using a hammer and punch, drive rivets out and remove ball joint.
8. Install ball joint into control arm and torque nuts and bolts to 8 ft. lbs. for 1980–81 models, or 3 ft. lbs. for 1982–85 models.

LOWER BALL JOINT, REPLACE

1980–85 Eldorado & Seville
1. Remove knuckle.
2. Using ⅛ in. drill bit, drill center of rivets ¼ in. deep, then using ½ in. drill bit,

drill deep enough to remove rivet heads.
3. Using a hammer and punch, drive rivets out and remove ball joint.
4. Install ball joint into control arm and torque nuts and bolts to 8 ft. lbs. for 1980–81 models, or 3 ft. lbs. for 1982–85 models.

TORSION BAR, REPLACE

1980–85 ELDORADO & SEVILLE
1. Raise and support vehicle, then remove parts as shown in **Fig. 15.**
2. Remove torsion bar adjusting screw as shown in **Fig. 15.**

NOTE: Count number of turns when removing screw. When installing, turn screw in the same number of turns to return vehicle to proper height.

3. Slide torsion bar forward in lower control arm until torsion bar clears support, then pull down on bar and remove from control arm.

27 N·m
(20 FT. LBS.)

34 N·m
(25 FT. LBS.)

37 N·m
(27 FT. LBS.)

PUMP
ASSEMBLY

34 N·m
(25 FT. LBS.)

BRACKET

PULLEY

LIMOUSINE

BRACKET

PUMP
ASSEMBLY

SPACER

41 N·m
(30 FT. LBS.)

27 N·m
(20 FT. LBS.)

41 N·m
(30 FT. LBS.)

90 N·m
(66 FT. LBS.)

BRACKET

41 N·m
(30 FT. LBS.)

PULLEY

27 N·m
(20 FT. LBS.)

DEVILLE AND BROUGHAM-DIESEL

LH CYLINDER
HEAD

47 N·m
(35 FT. LBS.)

41 N·m
(30 FT. LBS.)

BRACKET

47 N·m
(35 FT. LBS.)

47 N·m
(35 FT. LBS.)

PULLEY

PUMP ASSEMBLY

60 N·m
(44 FT. LBS.)

V-6 ENGINE—ALL

BRACKET

PUMP
ASSEMBLY

41 N·m
(30 FT. LBS.)

41 N·m
(30 FT. LBS.)

27 N·m
(20 FT. LBS.)

PULLEY

BRACKET

95 N·m
(70 FT. LBS.)

27 N·m
(20 FT. LBS.)

41 N·m
(30 FT. LBS.)

ELDORADO AND SEVILLE—DIESEL

Fig. 16 Power steering pump installation. Except V8-250 (Typical)

4. Reverse procedure to install. Torque torsion bar support retainer bolts to 35 ft. lbs. for 1980–81 models or 20 ft. lbs. for 1982–85 models.

POWER STEERING GEAR
REPLACE

1. Disconnect pressure and return lines from gear and plug all lines and openings.
2. Remove stone shield, if equipped.
3. Remove pinch bolt, then flex coupling from gear.
4. Raise and support vehicle.
5. On all models except 1983–85 Eldorado and Seville, remove pitman arm nut and lock washer, then using a suitable puller remove pitman arm from steering gear.
6. Remove steering gear to side rail retaining bolts, then steering gear.
7. On 1983–85 Eldorado and Seville, remove pitman arm from steering shaft.
8. Reverse procedure to install, noting the following torque values: steering gear to side rail retaining bolts, 70 ft. lbs.; pitman arm to pitman shaft nut, 185 ft. lbs.; flex coupling pinch bolt, 30 ft. lbs.; steering gear pressure lines, 30 ft. lbs. on 1980 models or 20 ft. lbs. on 1981–86 models.

1	24 N•m (18 FT. LBS.)	5	VACUUM PUMP
2	44 N•m (33 FT. LBS.)	6	PULLEY
3	BRACE	7	39 N•m (29 FT. LBS.)
4	BRACKET	8	STEERING PUMP

Fig. 17 Power steering pump installation. V8-250

POWER STEERING PUMP
REPLACE

1980

Except Seville
1. Disconnect pressure and return lines from pump and filter inlet.
2. Remove nut securing pump mounting bracket to cylinder head stud.
3. Remove adjusting screw securing mounting bracket to front of cylinder block.
4. Remove drive belts from pulley.
5. Remove bottom pivot screw and steering pump with bracket and filter attached.
6. Reverse procedure to install.

Seville
1. Remove alternator and alternator adjusting bracket.
2. Disconnect pressure and return lines at pump.
3. Loosen pump adjusting bolt, pivot bolt and pivot nut. Remove belt from pulley.
4. Remove nuts and spacer securing pump mounting bracket to water pump and timing chain cover.
5. Remove bracket connecting bolt, then remove pump and bracket as an assembly.

1981–86

V6-252
1. Disconnect pressure and return lines from pump.
2. Loosen adjusting screws on front and rear bracket, then remove drive belt.
3. Remove adjusting screws securing front of mounting bracket, **Fig. 16.**
4. Remove adjusting nut securing pump to rear mounting bracket.
5. Remove pivot screw, then remove steering pump and bracket as an assembly.
6. Reverse procedure to install.

V8-350
1. Remove cruise control servo as necessary, if equipped.
2. Loosen generator adjusting bolt, then remove alternator belt. Pivot alternator aside with wiring attached.
3. Remove alternator adjusting bracket, then disconnect pressure and return hoses from pump.
4. Loosen pump adjusting bolt, pivot bolt and pivot nut, **Fig. 16.** Remove belt from pulley.
5. Remove nuts and spacer securing pump mounting bracket to water pump and timing chain cover. Remove bracket connecting bolt, then remove

steering pump and bracket as an assembly.
6. Reverse procedure to install.

V8-368
1. Disconnect pressure and return lines from steering pump.
2. Loosen vacuum pump adjusting screw, **Fig. 16,** then remove drive belt.
3. Remove nut securing pump mounting bracket to cylinder head stud.
4. Remove adjusting screw and nuts securing mounting bracket.
5. Remove drive belts from pulley.
6. Remove nut and bolt securing vacuum pump brace, then remove brace.
7. Remove pivot bolt, then remove pump and bracket as an assembly.
8. Reverse procedure to install.

1981–86

V8-250
1. Loosen A/C mounting bracket and vacuum pump bracket, then remove belts from pulley.
2. Disconnect pressure and return lines from pump and plug all openings.
3. Remove two bolts holding pump to engine block through access holes in pulley, then remove pump, **Fig. 17.**
4. Reverse procedure to install.

CAMARO • CHEVROLET • CORVETTE • MALIBU • MONTE CARLO

INDEX OF SERVICE OPERATIONS

NOTE: Refer to the rear of this manual for vehicle manufacturer's special service tool suppliers.

Serial Number Location

Plate on left front door pillar or top of left
side instrument panel.

Engine Number Location

Buick built engines have the distributor located at the front of the engine.

On 1980–84 engines, the code is stamped on the left side of the bell housing flange.

On Chevrolet built 6-250 engines, the identification code is located on the cylinder block next to the distributor. On Chevrolet built V6 and V8 except V6-173 engines, the code is stamped on the block in front of the right cylinder head. On V6-173 engines, the code is stamped on the left side of the bell housing flange.

On Oldsmobile built diesel engines, the code is stamped on the left front of the engine.

Pontiac built 4-151 engine, stamped on engine flange at left rear of engine above drive end of starter motor.

Engine Identification Code

Engines are identified in the following table by the code letter or letters immediately following the engine serial number.

Engine V.I.N. Code

On 1980 vehicles, the fifth digit in the V.I.N. denotes engine code. On 1981–85 vehicles, the eighth digit in the V.I.N. denotes engine code.

Camaro

Code	Engine	V.I.N. Code	Year	Code	Engine	V.I.N. Code	Year	Code	Engine	V.I.N. Code	Year
CRA	V6-229	K	1980	X3C	4-151③	2	1982	CFZ	V8-305	H	1982
CRC	V6-229	K	1980	X3F	4-151③	2	1982	CRA	V8-305	H	1982
OM	V6-231①	A	1980	X3H	4-151③	2	1982	C2R	V8-305	H	1982
ON	V6-231①	A	1980	X5A	4-151③	2	1982	C2S	V8-305	H	1982
C8X	8-267	J	1980	X5F	4-151③	2	1982	C2T	V8-305	H	1982
CPD	8-267	J	1980	X5H	4-151③	2	1982	C2U	V8-305	H	1982
D9B	8-305	H	1980	CBT	V6-173	1	1982	C2W	V8-305	H	1982
CEJ	8-305	H	1980	CBU	V6-173	1	1982	C2X	V8-305	H	1982
CEL	8-305	H	1980	CBW	V6-173	1	1982	CFJ	V8-305	7	1982
CEM	8-305	H	1980	CBX	V6-173	1	1982	CFK	V8-305	7	1982
CET	8-305	H	1980	CBZ	V6-173	1	1982	CFM	V8-305	7	1982
CML	8-305	H	1980	CJB	V6-173	1	1982	CFN	V8-305	7	1982
CHA	8-350	L	1980	CKA	V6-173	1	1982	YMM	4-151③	2	1983
CEU	8-350	L	1980	CKB	V6-173	1	1982	YMT	4-151③	2	1983
DAH	V6-229	K	1981	C7A	V6-173	1	1982	DAF	V6-173	1	1983
DAJ	V6-229	K	1981	C7B	V6-173	1	1982	DAJ	V6-173	1	1983
RA	V6-231①	A	1981	C7C	V6-173	1	1982	DAK	V6-173	1	1983
DFH	V8-267	J	1981	C7D	V6-173	1	1982	DAA	V6-173	1	1983
D8H	V8-267	J	1981	CFA	V8-305	H	1982	DAB	V6-173	1	1983
DHJ	V8-305	H	1981	CFB	V8-305	H	1982	DAC	V6-173	1	1983
DHK	V8-305	H	1981	CFC	V8-305	H	1982	DAD	V6-173	1	1983
D6D	V8-305	H	1981	CFD	V8-305	H	1982	D6A	V6-173	1	1983
DHZ	V8-305	H	1981	CFF	V8-305	H	1982	D6B	V6-173	1	1983
DKB	V8-305	H	1981	CFH	V8-305	H	1982	D6C	V6-173	1	1983
DMA	V8-350	L	1981	CFR	V8-305	H	1982	D6D	V6-173	1	1983
D5A	V8-350	L	1981	CFT	V8-305	H	1982	D5B	V8-305	H	1983
D5B	V8-350	L	1981	CFW	V8-305	H	1982	DDB	V8-305	H	1983
X3A	4-151③	2	1982	CFY	V8-305	H	1982	DDC	V8-305	H	1983

continued

CAMARO—Continued

Code	Engine	V.I.N. Code	Year	Code	Engine	V.I.N. Code	Year	Code	Engine	V.I.N. Code	Year
DDD	V8-305	H	1983	SUF	V8-305	G	1984	CDM	V8-305	G	1985
DDF	V8-305	H	1983	SUH	V8-305	G	1984	CFF	V8-305	G	1985
DDH	V8-305	H	1983	SUJ	V8-305	G	1984	CFH	V8-305	G	1985
DDJ	V8-305	H	1983	SXA	V8-305	G	1984	CFA	V8-305	F	1985
DDK	V8-305	H	1983	SDA	V8-305	H	1984	CFB	V8-305	F	1985
D5C	V8-305	H	1983	SDH	V8-305	H	1984	CDN	V8-305	F	1985
DDN	V8-305	H	1983	SDJ	V8-305	H	1984	CDR	V8-305	F	1985
D5F	V8-305	H	1983	SDN	V8-305	H	1984	CDD	V8-305	H	1985
D5H	V8-305	H	1983	SDR	V8-305	H	1984	CDF	V8-305	H	1985
DGN	V8-305	H	1983	SDS	V8-305	H	1984	CDH	V8-305	H	1985
DDA	V8-305	S	1983	SDU	V8-305	H	1984	CDJ	V8-305	H	1985
DUA	V8-305	S	1983	C4A	V8-305	H	1984	C4P	V8-305	H	1985
Z3F	4-151③	2	1984	C4B	V8-305	H	1984	CKA	V8-305	H	1985
Z3H	4-151③	2	1984	C4C	V8-305	H	1984	C4R	V8-305	H	1985
Z5F	4-151③	2	1984	C4D	V8-305	H	1984	CDL	V8-305	H	1985
SAC	V6-173	1	1984	C4W	V8-305	H	1984	C7A	V8-305	H	1985
SAD	V6-173	1	1984	AAM	4-151③	2	1985	T9R	V8-305	H	1985
C3A	V6-173	1	1984	AAP	4-151③	2	1985	T9S	V8-305	H	1985
C3B	V6-173	1	1984	CAD	V6-173	S	1985	T9N	V8-305	H	1985
C3C	V6-173	1	1984	CAF	V6-173	S	1985	T9P	V8-305	H	1985
C3D	V6-173	1	1984	CDK	V8-305	G	1985				

Chevrolet

Code	Engine	V.I.N. Code	Year	Code	Engine	V.I.N. Code	Year	Code	Engine	V.I.N. Code	Year
CLC	V6-229	K	1980	CCK	V6-229	K	1982	VAD	V8-350②	N	1982
ES	V6-231①	A	1980	CCM	V6-229	K	1982	VAK	V8-350②	N	1982
ET	V6-231①	A	1980	CCN	V6-229	K	1982	VAL	V8-350②	N	1982
CPC	8-267	J	1980	CCR	V6-229	K	1982	VAM	V8-350②	N	1982
CPH	8-267	J	1980	CCS	V6-229	K	1982	VAN	V8-350②	N	1982
CED	8-305	H	1980	MA	V6-231①	A	1982	VAP	V8-350②	N	1982
CEH	8-305	H	1980	MC	V6-231①	A	1982	VAS	V8-350②	N	1982
CMH	8-305	H	1980	MG	V6-231①	A	1982	VAU	V8-350②	N	1982
CMJ	8-305	H	1980	MK	V6-231①	A	1982	VAW	V8-350②	N	1982
CMR	8-305	H	1980	ML	V6-231①	A	1982	VAX	V8-350②	N	1982
CMS	8-305	H	1980	MM	V6-231①	A	1982	VAY	V8-350②	N	1982
CMT	8-305	H	1980	CDB	V8-267	J	1982	VAZ	V8-350②	N	1982
CHC	8-350	L	1980	CDC	V8-267	J	1982	VBA	V8-350②	N	1982
VBS	8-350 Diesel②	N	1980	CDD	V8-267	J	1982	VBL	V8-350②	N	1982
VBT	8-350 Diesel②	N	1980	CDJ	V8-267	J	1982	VBP	V8-350②	N	1982
DAD	V6-229	K	1981	C4N	V8-267	J	1982	VBW	V8-350②	N	1982
NL	V6-231①	A	1981	C4R	V8-267	J	1982	VB4	V8-350②	N	1982
RL	V6-231①	A	1981	C4S	V8-267	J	1982	DBA	V6-229	9	1983
RK	V6-231①	A	1981	C4T	V8-267	J	1982	DBB	V6-229	9	1983
DFD	V8-267	J	1981	C4U	V8-267	J	1982	DBC	V6-229	9	1983
DFF	V8-267	J	1981	C4W	V8-267	J	1982	NJ	V6-231①	A	1983
D8D	V8-267	J	1981	CFA	V8-305	H	1982	ND	V6-231①	A	1983
D8F	V8-267	J	1981	CFB	V8-305	H	1982	NG	V6-231①	A	1983
DHD	V8-305	H	1981	CFC	V8-305	H	1982	NH	V6-231①	A	1983
DHF	V8-305	H	1981	CFD	V8-305	H	1982	NL	V6-231①	A	1983
DHH	V8-305	H	1981	CFF	V8-305	H	1982	D5B	V8-305	H	1983
DHR	V8-305	H	1981	CFH	V8-305	H	1982	DDB	V8-305	H	1983
DHS	V8-305	H	1981	CFR	V8-305	H	1982	DDC	V8-305	H	1983
DHT	V8-305	H	1981	CFT	V8-305	H	1982	DDD	V8-305	H	1983
D6B	V8-305	H	1981	CFW	V8-305	H	1982	DDF	V8-305	H	1983
D6C	V8-305	H	1981	CFY	V8-305	H	1982	DDH	V8-305	H	1983
DMD	V8-350	L	1981	CFZ	V8-305	H	1982	DDJ	V8-305	H	1983
VKH	V8-350②	N	1981	CRA	V8-305	H	1982	DDK	V8-305	H	1983
VKJ	V8-350②	N	1981	C2R	V8-305	H	1982	D5C	V8-305	H	1983
VKK	V8-350②	N	1981	C2S	V8-305	H	1982	DDN	V8-305	H	1983
VKN	V8-350②	N	1981	C2T	V8-305	H	1982	D5F	V8-305	H	1983
VKP	V8-350②	N	1981	C2U	V8-305	H	1982	D5H	V8-305	H	1983
CCA	V6-229	K	1982	C2W	V8-305	H	1982	DGN	V8-305	H	1983
CCC	V6-229	K	1982	C2X	V8-305	H	1982	D5N	V8-350	6	1983
CCF	V6-229	K	1982	VAB	V8-350②	N	1982	DUC	V8-350	6	1983
CCH	V6-229	K	1982	VAC	V8-350②	N	1982	VKB	V8-350②	N	1983

continued

CHEVROLET—Continued

Code	Engine	V.I.N. Code	Year	Code	Engine	V.I.N. Code	Year	Code	Engine	V.I.N. Code	Year
VKC	V8-350②	N	1983	C4A	V8-305	H	1984	RCH	V8-350②	N	1984
VKD	V8-350②	N	1983	C4B	V8-305	H	1984	RCJ	V8-350②	N	1984
VKK	V8-350②	N	1983	C4C	V8-305	H	1984	NFA	V6-231①	A	1985
VKL	V8-350②	N	1983	C4D	V8-305	H	1984	N4A	V6-231①	A	1985
VKR	V8-350②	N	1983	RAA	V8-350②	N	1984	CCB	V6-262	Z	1985
VKS	V8-350②	N	1983	RAB	V8-350②	N	1984	CLB	V6-262	Z	1985
VKT	V8-350②	N	1983	RAF	V8-350②	N	1984	CLC	V6-262	Z	1985
VKZ	V8-350②	N	1983	RAH	V8-350②	N	1984	CLD	V6-262	Z	1985
VLA	V8-350②	N	1983	RAJ	V8-350②	N	1984	CLF	V6-262	Z	1985
VLB	V8-350②	N	1983	RAM	V8-350②	N	1984	CLH	V6-262	Z	1985
VLP	V8-350②	N	1983	RAN	V8-350②	N	1984	CDD	V8-305	H	1985
VLS	V8-350②	N	1983	RAP	V8-350②	N	1984	CDF	V8-305	H	1985
VLT	V8-350②	N	1983	RAT	V8-350②	N	1984	CDH	V8-305	H	1985
VLW	V8-350②	N	1983	RAU	V8-350②	N	1984	CDJ	V8-305	H	1985
SBA	V6-229	9	1984	RAX	V8-350②	N	1984	C4P	V8-305	H	1985
SBC	V6-229	9	1984	RAY	V8-350②	N	1984	CKA	V8-305	H	1985
SBF	V6-229	9	1984	RAZ	V8-350②	N	1984	C4R	V8-305	H	1985
SBJ	V6-229	9	1984	RBL	V8-350②	N	1984	CDL	V8-305	H	1985
FRA	V6-231①	A	1984	RBM	V8-350②	N	1984	C7A	V8-305	H	1985
FSA	V6-231①	A	1984	RBR	V8-350②	N	1984	C7B	V8-305	H	1985
FUA	V6-231①	A	1984	RBS	V8-350②	N	1984	RLA	V8-350②	N	1985
FWA	V6-231①	A	1984	RBT	V8-350②	N	1984	RLB	V8-350②	N	1985
FXA	V6-231①	A	1984	RBU	V8-350②	N	1984	RLD	V8-350②	N	1985
FYA	V6-231①	A	1984	RBW	V8-350②	N	1984	RLF	V8-350②	N	1985
FZA	V6-231①	A	1984	RBX	V8-350②	N	1984	RLH	V8-350②	N	1985
SDA	V8-305	H	1984	RBY	V8-350②	N	1984	RLJ	V8-350②	N	1985
SDH	V8-305	H	1984	RBZ	V8-350②	N	1984	RLM	V8-350②	N	1985
SDJ	V8-305	H	1984	RCA	V8-350②	N	1984	RLL	V8-350②	N	1985
SDN	V8-305	H	1984	RCB	V8-350②	N	1984	RLP	V8-350②	N	1985
SDR	V8-305	H	1984	RCC	V8-350②	N	1984	RLS	V8-350②	N	1985
SDS	V8-305	H	1984	RCD	V8-350②	N	1984				
SDU	V8-305	H	1984	RCF	V8-350②	N	1984				

Malibu & Monte Carlo

Code	Engine	V.I.N. Code	Year	Code	Engine	V.I.N. Code	Year	Code	Engine	V.I.N. Code	Year
CLA	V6-229	K	1980	D8A	V8-267	J	1981	CDJ	V8-267	J	1982
CLB	V6-229	K	1980	D8B	V8-267	J	1981	C4N	V8-267	J	1982
CRC	V6-229	K	1980	D8C	V8-267	J	1981	C4R	V8-267	J	1982
ED	V6-231①	A	1980	DHA	V8-305	H	1981	C4S	V8-267	J	1982
EF	V6-231①	A	1980	DHB	V8-305	H	1981	C4T	V8-267	J	1982
EG	V6-231①	A	1980	DHC	V8-305	H	1981	C4U	V8-267	J	1982
EH	V6-231①	3	1980	DHM	V8-305	H	1981	C4W	V8-267	J	1982
OP	V6-231①	A	1980	DHN	V8-305	H	1981	CFA	V8-305	H	1982
OR	V6-231①	A	1980	D6A	V8-305	H	1981	CFB	V8-305	H	1982
CPA	8-267	J	1980	DMC	V8-350	L	1981	CFC	V8-305	H	1982
CPB	8-267	J	1980	CCA	V6-229	K	1982	CFD	V8-305	H	1982
CEA	8-305	H	1980	CCC	V6-229	K	1982	CFF	V8-305	H	1982
CEC	8-305	H	1980	CCF	V6-229	K	1982	CFH	V8-305	H	1982
CER	8-305	H	1980	CCH	V6-229	K	1982	CFR	V8-305	H	1982
CMC	8-305	H	1980	CCK	V6-229	K	1982	CFT	V8-305	H	1982
CMD	8-305	H	1980	CCM	V6-229	K	1982	CFW	V8-305	H	1982
CMF	8-305	H	1980	CCN	V6-229	K	1982	CFY	V8-305	H	1982
CMM	8-305	H	1980	CCR	V6-229	K	1982	CFZ	V8-305	H	1982
CHB	8-350	L	1980	CCS	V6-229	K	1982	CRA	V8-305	H	1982
DAA	V6-229	K	1981	MA	V6-231①	A	1982	C2R	V8-305	H	1982
DAB	V6-229	K	1981	MC	V6-231①	A	1982	C2S	V8-305	H	1982
DAC	V6-229	K	1981	MG	V6-231①	A	1982	C2T	V8-305	H	1982
D7A	V6-229	K	1981	MK	V6-231①	A	1982	C2U	V8-305	H	1982
D7B	V6-229	K	1981	ML	V6-231①	A	1982	C2W	V8-305	H	1982
DAK	V6-229	K	1981	MM	V6-231①	A	1982	C2X	V8-305	H	1982
NB	V6-231①	A	1981	UAA	V6-262②	V	1982	DBA	V6-229	9	1983
NE	V6-231①	3	1981	UAD	V6-262②	V	1982	DBB	V6-229	9	1983
RO	V6-231①	3	1981	UAJ	V6-262②	V	1982	DBC	V6-229	9	1983
DFA	V8-267	J	1981	CDB	V8-267	J	1982	NJ	V6-231①	A	1983
DFB	V8-267	J	1981	CDC	V8-267	J	1982	ND	V6-231①	A	1983
DFC	V8-267	J	1981	CDD	V8-267	J	1982	NG	V6-231①	A	1983

continued

MALIBU & MONTE CARLO—Continued

Code	Engine	V.I.N. Code	Year
NH	V6-231①	A	1983
NL	V6-231①	A	1983
UKA	V6-262②	V	1983
UKB	V6-262②	V	1983
UKC	V6-262②	V	1983
UKJ	V6-262②	V	1983
UKK	V6-262②	V	1983
ULP	V6-262②	V	1983
UMF	V6-262②	V	1983
UMH	V6-262②	V	1983
UMP	V6-262②	V	1983
UMR	V6-262②	V	1983
UMS	V6-262②	V	1983
UMT	V6-262②	V	1983
UMU	V6-262②	V	1983
UMW	V6-262②	V	1983
UMX	V6-262②	V	1983
UMZ	V6-262②	V	1983
UNH	V6-262②	V	1983
UNJ	V6-262②	V	1983
UNK	V6-262②	V	1983
UNL	V6-262②	V	1983
UNM	V6-262②	V	1983
UNN	V6-262②	V	1983
UNP	V6-262②	V	1983
D5B	V8-305	H	1983
DDB	V8-305	H	1983
DDC	V8-305	H	1983
DDD	V8-305	H	1983
DDF	V8-305	H	1983
DDH	V8-305	H	1983
DDJ	V8-305	H	1983
DDK	V8-305	H	1983
D5C	V8-305	H	1983
DDN	V8-305	H	1983
D5F	V8-305	H	1983
D5H	V8-305	H	1983
DGN	V8-305	H	1983
VKB	V8-350②	N	1983
VKC	V8-350②	N	1983
VKD	V8-350②	N	1983
VKK	V8-350②	N	1983
VKL	V8-350②	N	1983
VKR	V8-350②	N	1983
VKS	V8-350②	N	1983
VKT	V8-350②	N	1983
VKZ	V8-350②	N	1983
VLA	V8-350②	N	1983
VLB	V8-350②	N	1983
VLP	V8-350②	N	1983
VLS	V8-350②	N	1983
VLT	V8-350②	N	1983
VLW	V8-350②	N	1983
SBA	V6-229	9	1984
SBC	V6-229	9	1984
SBF	V6-229	9	1984
SBJ	V6-229	9	1984
FRA	V6-231①	A	1984
FSA	V6-231①	A	1984
FUA	V6-231①	A	1984
FWA	V6-231①	A	1984
FXA	V6-231①	A	1984
FYA	V6-231①	A	1984
FZA	V6-231①	A	1984
SUF	V8-305	G	1984
SUH	V8-305	G	1984
SUJ	V8-305	G	1984
SXA	V8-305	G	1984
SDA	V8-305	H	1984
SDH	V8-305	H	1984
SDJ	V8-305	H	1984
SDN	V8-305	H	1984
SDR	V8-305	H	1984
SDS	V8-305	H	1984
C4A	V8-305	H	1984
C4B	V8-305	H	1984
C4C	V8-305	H	1984
C4D	V8-305	H	1984
RAA	V8-350②	N	1984
RAB	V8-350②	N	1984
RAF	V8-350②	N	1984
RAH	V8-350②	N	1984
RAJ	V8-350②	N	1984
RAM	V8-350②	N	1984
RAN	V8-350②	N	1984
RAP	V8-350②	N	1984
RAT	V8-350②	N	1984
RAU	V8-350②	N	1984
RAX	V8-350②	N	1984
RAY	V8-350②	N	1984
RAZ	V8-350②	N	1984
RBL	V8-350②	N	1984
RBM	V8-350②	N	1984
RBR	V8-350②	N	1984
RBS	V8-350②	N	1984
RBT	V8-350②	N	1984
RBU	V8-350②	N	1984
RBW	V8-350②	N	1984
RBX	V8-350②	N	1984
RBY	V8-350②	N	1984
RBZ	V8-350②	N	1984
RCA	V8-350②	N	1984
RCB	V8-350②	N	1984
RCC	V8-350②	N	1984
RCD	V8-350②	N	1984
RCF	V8-350②	N	1984
RCH	V8-350②	N	1984
RCJ	V8-350②	N	1984
NFA	V6-231	A	1985
N4A	V6-231	A	1985
CCB	V6-262	Z	1985
CLB	V6-262	Z	1985
CLC	V6-262	Z	1985
CLD	V6-262	Z	1985
CLF	V6-262	Z	1985
CLH	V6-262	Z	1985
CDD	V8-305	H	1985
CDF	V8-305	H	1985
CDH	V8-305	H	1985
CDJ	V8-305	H	1985
C4P	V8-305	H	1985
CKA	V8-305	H	1985
C4R	V8-305	H	1985
CDL	V8-305	H	1985
C7A	V8-305	H	1985
C7B	V8-305	H	1985
CDK	V8-305	G	1985
CDM	V8-305	G	1985
CFF	V8-305	G	1985
CFH	V8-305	G	1985

Corvette

Code	Engine	V.I.N. Code	Year
ZCA	8-305	H	1980
ZAK	V8-350	8	1980
ZBC	V8-350	6	1980
ZAM	V8-350	8	1980
ZBD	V8-350	6	1980
ZDA	V8-350	6	1981
ZDB	V8-350	6	1981
ZDC	V8-350	6	1981
ZDD	V8-350	6	1981
ZBA	V8-350	8	1982
ZBC	V8-350	8	1982
ZFN	V8-350	8	1982
ZFC	V8-350	8	1984
ZFF	V8-350	8	1984
ZFM	V8-350	8	1984
ZFN	V8-350	8	1984
ZDF	V8-350	8	1984
ZJB	V8-350	8	1984
ZJC	V8-350	8	1984
ZJJ	V8-350	8	1984
ZJK	V8-350	8	1984
ZDF	V8-350	8	1985
ZJB	V8-350	8	1985
ZJC	V8-350	8	1985
ZJJ	V8-350	8	1985
ZJK	V8-350	8	1985

①—Buick built engine. ②—Oldsmobile built diesel engine. ③—Pontiac built engine.

continued

Grille Identification

1980 Malibu Classic

1980 Caprice Classic

1980 Impala

1980 Monte Carlo

1980—81 Camaro Sport Coupe

1980—81 Camaro Berlinetta

1980—81 Camaro Z28

1980—82 Corvette

1981 Malibu

1981 Monte Carlo

1981—85 Caprice

1982 Malibu

1982 Monte Carlo

1982—85 Camaro Exc. Z28 & 1985 IROC-Z

1982—84 Camaro Z28

1983 Malibu

1983—85 Monte Carlo Exc. 1984—85 Monte Carlo SS

1984—86 Corvette

1984—86 Monte Carlo SS

1985—86 Camaro IROC-Z

1985—86 Camaro Z28 & 1986 Camaro

continued

1986 Camaro Berlinetta   **1986 Caprice**   **1986 Monte Carlo**

General Engine Specifications

Year	Engine CID①/Liter	V.I.N. Code②	Carburetor	Bore and Stroke	Compression Ratio	Net Brake H.P. @ R.P.M.③	Maximum Torque Ft. Lbs. @ R.P.M.	Normal Oil Pressure Pounds
1980	V6-229, 3.8L	K	M2ME, 2 Bbl.④	3.736 × 3.48	8.6	115 @ 4000	175 @ 2000	45
	V6-231, 3.8L⑤	A	M2ME, 2 Bbl.⑥④	3.80 × 3.40	8.0	110 @ 3800	190 @ 1600	45
	V6-231, 3.8L⑤⑦	3	M4ME, 4 Bbl.④⑧	3.80 × 3.40	8.0	170 @ 4000	265 @ 2400	37
	V8-267, 4.4L	J	M2ME, 2 Bbl.④	3.50 × 3.48	8.5	120 @ 3600	215 @ 2000	45
	V8-305, 5.0L	8	M4ME, 4 Bbl.④⑧	3.736 × 3.48	8.6	155 @ 4000	240 @ 1600	45
	V8-305⑫	H	M4ME④	3.736 × 3.48	8.5	180 @ 4200	255 @ 2000	45
	V8-350, 5.7L⑬	L	M4ME, 4 Bbl.④	4.00 × 3.48	8.5	190 @ 4200	280 @ 2400	45
	V8-350, 5.7L⑫	6	M4ME, 4 Bbl.④	4.00 × 3.48	9.0	230 @ 5200	275 @ 3600	45
	V8-350, 5.7L⑫	8	M4ME, 4 Bbl.④	4.00 × 3.48	8.5	190 @ 4400	280 @ 2400	45
	V8-350, 5.7L⑨⑩	N	Fuel Injected	4.057 × 3.385	22.5	105 @ 3200	205 @ 1600	30–45
1981	V6-229, 3.8L⑪	K	E2ME, 2 Bbl.④	3.736 × 3.48	8.6	110 @ 4200	170 @ 2000	45
	V6-231, 3.8L⑤	A	E2ME, 2 Bbl.④	3.80 × 3.40	8.0	110 @ 3800	190 @ 1600	45
	V6-231, 3.8L⑤⑦	3	E4ME, 4 Bbl.④	3.80 × 3.40	8.0	170 @ 4000	275 @ 2400	45
	V8-267, 4.4L⑪	J	E2ME, 2 Bbl.④	3.50 × 3.48	8.3	115 @ 4000	200 @ 2400	45
	V8-305, 5.0L	H	E4ME, 4 Bbl.④	3.736 × 3.48	8.6	150 @ 3800	240 @ 2400	45
	V8-305⑬	H	M4ME④	3.736 × 3.48	8.6	165 @ 4000	180 @ 4200	45
	V8-350, 5.7L	L	E4ME, 4 Bbl.④	4.00 × 3.48	8.2	175 @ 4000	275 @ 2400	45
	V8-350, 5.7L⑫	6	E4ME, 4 Bbl.④	4.00 × 3.48	8.2	190 @ 4200	280 @ 1600	45
	V8-350, 5.7L⑨⑩	N	Fuel Injection	4.057 × 3.385	22.5	105 @ 3200	200 @ 1600	45
1982	4-151, 2.5L⑭	2	Fuel Injection	4.00 × 3.00	8.2	90 @ 4000	132 @ 2800	37.5
	V6-173, 2.8L	1	E2SE, 2 Bbl.④	3.50 × 2.99	8.5	102 @ 4800	142 @ 2400	50–65
	V6-229, 3.8L⑪	K	E2ME, 2 Bbl.④	3.736 × 3.480	8.6	110 @ 4200	170 @ 2000	50–65
	V6-231, 3.8L⑤	A	E2ME, 2 Bbl.④	3.80 × 3.40	8.0	110 @ 3800	190 @ 1600	50–65
	V8-262, 4.3L⑨⑩	V	Fuel Injection	4.057 × 3.385	22.5	85 @ 3600	165 @ 1600	30–45
	V8-267, 4.4L⑪	J	E2ME, 2 Bbl.④	3.50 × 3.48	8.3	115 @ 4000	200 @ 2400	45
	V8-305, 5.0L	H	E4ME, 4 Bbl.④	3.736 × 3.480	8.6	145 @ 4000	240 @ 2400	50–65
	V8-305, 5.0L	7	Fuel Injection	3.736 × 3.480	9.5	165 @ 4200	240 @ 2400	50–65
	V8-350, 5.7L	6	Fuel Injection	4.00 × 3.48	9.0	200 @ 4200	285 @ 2800	45
	V8-350, 5.7L⑨⑩	N	Fuel Injection	4.057 × 3.385	22.5	105 @ 3200	200 @ 1600	30–45
1983	4-151, 2.5L⑭	2	Fuel Injection	4.00 × 3.00	8.2	92 @ 4000	134 @ 2800	37.5
	V6-173, 2.8L	1	E2SE, 2 Bbl.④	3.50 × 2.99	8.5	107 @ 4800	145 @ 2100	50–65
	V6-229, 3.8L	9	E2ME, 2 Bbl.④	3.736 × 3.480	8.6	110 @ 4200	170 @ 2000	50–65
	V6-231, 3.8L⑤	A	E2ME, 2 Bbl.④	3.80 × 3.40	8.0	110 @ 3800	190 @ 1600	45
	V6-262, 4.3L⑨⑩	V	Fuel Injection	4.057 × 3.385	21.6	85 @ 3600	165 @ 1600	30–45
	V8-305, 5.0L	H	E4ME, 4 Bbl.④	3.736 × 3.480	8.6	150 @ 3800	240 @ 2400	50–65
	V8-305, 5.0L	S	Fuel Injection	3.736 × 3.480	9.5	175 @ 4200	250 @ 2800	45
	V8-350, 5.7L⑨⑩	N	Fuel Injection	4.057 × 3.385	21.6	105 @ 3200	200 @ 1600	30–45
1984	4-151, 2.5L⑭	2	Fuel Injection	4.00 × 3.00	9.0	90 @ 4000	132 @ 2800	37.5
	V6-173, 2.8L	1	E2SE, 2 Bbl.④	3.50 × 2.99	8.5	112 @ 5100	148 @ 2400	50–65
	V6-229, 3.8L	9	E2ME, 2 Bbl.④	3.736 × 3.480	8.6	110 @ 4200	170 @ 2000	50–65
	V6-231, 3.8L⑤	A	E2ME, 2 Bbl.④	3.80 × 3.40	8.0	110 @ 3800	190 @ 1600	45
	V6-262, 4.3L⑨⑩	V	Fuel Injection	4.057 × 3.385	21.6	85 @ 3600	165 @ 1600	30–45
	V8-305, 5.0L	H	E4ME, 4 Bbl.④	3.736 × 3.480	8.6	150 @ 3800	240 @ 2400	50–65
	V8-305 H.O. 5.0L	G	E4ME, 4 Bbl.④	3.736 × 3.480	9.5	190 @ 4800	240 @ 3200	50–65
	V8-350, 5.7L	8	Fuel Injection	4.00 × 3.48	9.0	205 @ 4300	290 @ 2800	50–65
	V8-350, 5.7L⑨⑩	N	Fuel Injection	4.057 × 3.385	21.6	105 @ 4200	200 @ 1600	30–45

continued

GENERAL ENGINE SPECIFICATIONS—Continued

Year	Engine CID①/Liter	Engine V.I.N. Code②	Carburetor	Bore and Stroke	Compression Ratio	Net Brake H.P. @ R.P.M.③	Maximum Torque Ft. Lbs. @ R.P.M.	Normal Oil Pressure Pounds
1985	4-151/2.5L⑭	2	Fuel Injection	4.00 × 3.00	9.0	88 @ 4400	132 @ 2800	37.5
	V6-173/2.8	S	Fuel Injection	3.50 × 2.99	8.9	135 @ 5100	165 @ 3600	50—65
	V6-262/4.3L	Z	Fuel Injection	4.00 × 3.48	9.3	130 @ 3600	210 @ 2000	50—65
	V8-305/5.0L	F	Fuel Injection	3.74 × 3.48	9.5	215 @ 4400	275 @ 3200	—
	V8-305/5.0L⑮	G	E4ME, 4 Bbl.④	3.74 × 3.48	9.5	190 @ 4800	240 @ 3200	50—65
	V8-305/5.0L⑯	G	E4ME, 4 Bbl.④	3.74 × 3.48	9.5	180 @ 4800	235 @ 3200	50—65
	V8-305/5.0L⑮	H	E4ME, 4 Bbl.④	3.74 × 3.48	8.6	165 @ 4400	250 @ 2000	50—65
	V8-305/5.0L⑯	H	E4ME, 4 Bbl.④	3.74 × 3.48	8.6	150 @ 4000	240 @ 2000	50—65
	V8-305/5.0L⑰	H	E4ME, 4 Bbl.④	3.74 × 3.48	8.6	165 @ 4200	245 @ 2400	50—65
	V8-350/5.7L⑫	8	Fuel Injection	4.00 × 3.48	9.0	230 @ 4000	330 @ 3200	50—65
	V8-350/5.7L	N	Fuel Injection	4.00 × 3.39	22.1	105 @ 3200	200 @ 1600	30—45
1986	4-151/2.5L⑭	2	Fuel Injection	4.00 × 3.00	9.0	88 @ 4400	132 @ 2800	37.5
	V6-173/2.8	S	Fuel Injection	3.50 × 2.99	8.9	135 @ 5100	165 @ 3600	50—65
	V6-262/4.3L	Z	Fuel Injection	4.00 × 3.48	9.3	130 @ 3600	210 @ 2000	50—65
	V8-305/5.0L	F	Fuel Injection	3.74 × 3.48	9.5	215 @ 4400	275 @ 3200	—
	V8-305/5.0L	G	E4ME, 4 Bbl.④	3.74 × 3.48	9.5	190 @	240 @	50—65
	V8-305/5.0L	H	E4ME, 4 Bbl.④	3.74 × 3.48	8.6	155 @	245 @	50—65
	V8-350/5.7L⑫	8	Fuel Injection	4.00 × 3.48	9.0	230 @	335 @	50—65

①—CID—Cubic inch displacement.
②—V.I.N.—On 1979–80 vehicles, the fifth digit in the V.I.N. denotes engine code. On 1981–85 vehicles, the 8th digit in the V.I.N. denotes engine code.
③—Ratings are net—As installed in the vehicle.
④—Rochester.
⑤—For service procedures on this engine, see Buick chapter.
⑥—Calif. V6-231 with Electronic Fuel Control E2ME.
⑦—Turbocharged.
⑧—Calif. V8 with Electronic Fuel Control, E4ME.
⑨—For service procedures on this engine, see Oldsmobile chapter.
⑩—Diesel.
⑪—Exc. Calif.
⑫—Corvette.
⑬—Camaro Z28.
⑭—For service procedures on this engine, refer to Pontiac chapter.
⑮—Camaro.
⑯—Monte Carlo.
⑰—Caprice/Impala.

Starting Motor Applications

Year	Model/V.I.N.	Starter Number	Year	Model/V.I.N.	Starter Number	Year	Model/V.I.N.	Starter Number
1980	V6-229/K	1109524		V8-350/L⑤	1109065		V8-305/H,G	1109534
	V6-231/A	1109061		V8-350 Diesel/N	1109213		V8-305/S	1109534
	V8-267/J⑧	1109524	1982	4-151/F⑬	1109533		V8-350 Diesel/N	1998554
	V8-267/J⑤	1109064		V6-173/1	1109535	1984	4-151/2⑬	1109556
	V8-305/H⑥	1109524		V6-229/K⑨	1109524		V6-173/1	1109535
	V8-305/H③⑤	1109064		V6-229/K⑩	1109534		V6-229/9	1998236
	V8-305/H④⑤	1109074		V6-231/A	1109524		V6-231/A	1981109
	V8-305/H①	1998217		V6-262 Diesel/V	1998552		V6-262 Diesel/V	1981104
	V8-350⑫①③	1109052		V8-267/J⑨	1109064		V8-305/H⑧	1981102
	V8-350⑫①④	1109059		V8-267/J⑩	1109534		V8-305/S & H⑤	1109534
	V8-350/L③	1109067		V8-305/H⑨	1109064		V8-350/8①	1998435
	V8-350/L④	119065		V8-305/H⑩	1109534		V8-350 Diesel/N	1981104⑭
1980–81	V8-350 Diesel/N	1109213		V8-350/8①	1998241	1985–86	4-151/2	1998450
1981	V6-229/K	1109524		V8-350 Diesel/N	1998552		V6-173/S	1998427
	V6-231/A⑦	1109061	1983	4-151/2⑯	1109556		V6-262/Z	1998435
	V8-267/J②	1109064		V6-173/1	1109535		V8-305/H③	1998435
	V8-267/J⑦	1109524		V6-229/9	1998236		V8-305/G,H④	1998466
	V8-305/L③	1109064		V6-231/A	1998236		V8-305/F	1998452
	V8-305/L④⑤	1109074		V6-262 Diesel/V	1998554		V8-350/8	1998435

①—Corvette.
②—Exc. Malibu & Malibu Classic.
③—With auto. trans.
④—With manual trans.
⑤—Camaro.
⑥—Except Camaro & Corvette.
⑦—Malibu & Malibu Classic.
⑧—Exc. Camaro.
⑨—Malibu & Monte Carlo.
⑩—Exc. Malibu & Monte Carlo.
⑪—Exc. Corvette.
⑫—1980 V.I.N. code is 8 or 6 (high performance).
⑬—Refer to Pontiac chapter for service procedures.
⑭—With heavy duty battery, 1981106.

continued

Alternator Specifications

Year	Model	Rated Hot Output Amps	Field Current 12 Volts @ 80°F.	Year	Model	Rated Hot Output Amps	Field Current 12 Volts @ 80°F.	Year	Model	Rated Hot Output Amps	Field Current 12 Volts @ 80°F.
1980	1101044	70	4–4.5		1103122	63	4–4.5		1105022	78	4–4.5
	1101066	70	4–4.5		1103161	37	4–4.5		1105025	63	4–4.5
	1101071	70	4–4.5		1103162	37	4–4.5		1105041	78	4–4.5
	1102474	61	4–4.5		1103169	63	4–4.5		1105513	97	4–4.5
	1102484	42	4–4.5	1982	1103060	42	4–4.5	1985	1100200	78	4.5–5.0
	1103043	42	4–4.5		1101040	70	4–4.5		1100226	37	4.0–5.0
	1103044	63	4–4.5		1100195	70	4–4.5		1100237	56	4.5–5.0
	1103085	55	4–4.5		1100294	63	4–4.5		1100239	56	4.5–5.0
	1103088	55	4–4.5		1101097	85	4–4.5		1100246	66	4.5–5.0
	1103091	63	4–4.5		1100285	85	4–4.5		1100260	78	4.5–5.0
	1103092	55	4–4.5	1983	1105360	42	4–4.5		1100270	78	4.5–5.0
	1103100	55	4–4.5		1100250	63	4–4.5		1105521	78	4.5–5.0
	1103102	63	4–4.5		1101040	70	4–4.5		1105522	37	4.0–5.0
	1103118	37	4–4.5		1103061	42	4–4.5		1105523	56	4.5–5.0
	1103122	63	4–4.5		1105357	63	4–4.5		1105555	66	4.5–5.0
	1103161	37	4–4.5	1984	1100200	78	4–4.5		1105564	66	4.5–5.0
	1103162	37	4–4.5		1100226	37	4–4.5		1105565	78	4.5–5.0
1981	1101044	70	4–4.5		1100228	37	4–4.5		1105566	66	4.5–5.0
	1101066	70	4–4.5		1100230	40	4–4.5		1105567	78	4.5–5.0
	1101071	70	4–4.5		1100237	55	4–4.5	1986	1100254	66	—
	1103043	42	4–4.5		1100239	55	4–4.5		1100272	78	—
	1103044	63	4–4.5		1100246	63	4–4.5		1105521	78	—
	1103085	55	4–5		1100247	63	4–4.5		1105545	94	—
	1103088	55	4–4.5		1100260	78	4–4.5		110555	66	—
	1103091	63	4–4.5		1100263	78	4–4.5		110556	42	—
	1103092	55	4–4.5		1100264	78	4–4.5		1105587	97	—
	1103100	55	4–4.5		1100270	78	4–4.5		1105588	78	—
	1103102	63	4–4.5		1100297	42	4–4.5		1105600	66	—
	1103103	63	4–4.5		1100300	63	4–4.5		1105639	108	—
	1103118	37	4–4.5								

Engine Tightening Specifications★

★ Torque specifications are for clean and lightly lubricated threads only. Dry or dirty threads produce increased friction which prevents accurate measurement of tightness.

Year	Engine Model/V.I.N.	Spark Plugs Ft. Lbs.	Cylinder Head Bolts Ft. Lbs.	Intake Manifold Ft. Lbs.	Exhaust Manifold Ft. Lbs.	Rocker Arm Stud Ft. Lbs.	Rocker Arm Cover Ft. Lbs.	Connecting Rod Cap Bolts Ft. Lbs.	Main Bearing Cap Bolts Ft. Lbs.	Flywheel to Crankshaft Ft. Lbs.	Vibration Damper or Pulley Ft. Lbs.
1982–83	4-151/[13][18]	7–15	85	29	44	20[7]	6	32	70	44	160
1984–85	4-151/[13][18]	7–15	92	29	44	20[7]	7.5	32	70	44	160
1986	4-151/2	7–15	92[19]	[20]	[21]	20[7]	6	32	70	55	162
1982–85	V6-173/[18]	7–15	70	23	25	46	8	37	69	[2]	75
1986	V6-173/S	7–15	65–90	13–25	19–31	—	7–15	34–45	63–83	—	67–85
1980–84	V6-229/[18]	22	65	30	20	—	45[3]	45	70	60	60
1980–84	V6-231/A[10]	15	80	45	25	30[4]	4	40	100	60	225
1982–83	V6-262/V[14][15]	15[5]	[16][17]	41[16]	29	28[7]	9	42	107	48	160–350
1985	V6-262/Z	22	65	30	20	—	45[3]	45	70	60	60
1980–82	8-267/J	22	65	30	20	—	45[3]	45	70	60	60
1980–85	8-305/[18]	22	65	30	20	—	45[3]	45	70	60	60
1986	V8-305/F,G,H	22	60–75	25–45	[22]	—	[23]	42–47	60–75	50–70	—
1980–85	V8-350/[18][12]	22	65	30	20[1]	[11]	45[3]	45	70	60	60
1980–85	V8-350/N[14][15]	12[5]	130[16]	40[16]	25	28[7]	70[3]	42	120	60	200–310

continued

ENGINE TIGHTENING SPECIFICATIONS NOTES—Continued

①—Inside bolts 30 ft. lbs.
②—Auto. trans., 25–35 ft. lbs.; manual trans., 45–55 ft. lbs.
③—Inch lbs.
④—Rocker arm shaft to cylinder head bolts.
⑤—Glow plug torque.
⑥—Integral Intake Manifold.
⑦—Rocker arm pivot bolt.
⑧—Left hand front head bolt 85 ft. lbs.
⑨—Fully driven, seated, not stripped.
⑩—Refer to Buick Chapter for service procedures on this engine.
⑪—Corvette, 50 ft. lbs.

⑫—Gasoline engine.
⑬—Refer to Pontiac chapter for service procedures.
⑭—Diesel engine.
⑮—Refer to Oldsmobile Section for service procedures on this engine.
⑯—Clean & dip bolt in engine oil before tightening to obtain correct torque reading.
⑰—Bolts 5, 6, 11, 12, 13 & 14, 59 ft. lbs.; All others, 142 ft. lbs.
⑱—For V.I.N. code, refer to the "General Engine Specifications" at the beginning of the chapter.

⑲—Requires thread sealer.
⑳—Torque stud bolts except front upper to 25 ft. lbs.; torque front upper stud bolt to 37 ft. lbs. Torque hex bolts to 28 ft. lbs.
㉑—Torque four outer manifold attaching bolts to 31 ft. lbs.; torque three center manifold attaching bolts to 37 ft. lbs.
㉒—Outer four bolts, 14–26 ft. lbs.; inner two bolts, 20–32 ft. lbs.
㉓—Studs 10 inch lbs. min.; nuts, 50–65 inch lbs.

Pistons, Pins, Rings, Crankshaft & Bearings

Year	Engine Model/V.I.N. Code	Piston Clearance	Ring End Gap ① Comp. ②	Ring End Gap ① Oil ②	Wrist-pin Diameter	Rod Bearings Shaft Diameter	Rod Bearings Bearing Clearance	Main Bearings Shaft Diameter	Main Bearings Bearing Clearance	Thrust on Bear. No.	Shaft End Play
1982–85	4-151/2⑭	.0017–.0041	.010	.015	.9400	2.0000	.0005–.0026	2.3000	.0005–.0022	5	.0035–.0085
1986	4-151/2⑭	.0014–.0022	.010	.020	.9400	2.0000	.0005–.0026	2.3000	.0005–.0022	5	.0035–.0085
1982	V6-173/1	.0016–.0027	.010	.020	.9054	1.9983–1.9993	.0014–.0035	2.4936–2.4946	.0017–.0029	3	.002–.007
1983–85	V6-173/⑬	.0006–.0016	.010	.020	.9054	1.9983–1.9993	.0014–.0037	⑮	.0016–.0032	3	.002–.007
1986	V6-173/S	.0007–.0017	.010	.020	.9199	2.0303–2.0314	.0016–.0032	2.6896–2.6906	.0014–.0038	3	.002–.008
1980–84	V6-229/⑬	.0007–.0017	.010	.015	.9272	2.0986–2.0998	.0013–.0035	③	④	4	.002–.006
1980–82	V6-231/A⑨	.0008–.0020	.010	.015	.9392	2.2487–2.2495	.0005–.0026	2.4995	.0004–.0015	2	.004–.008
1983–84	V6-231/A⑨	.0008–.0020	.010	.015	.9393	2.2487–2.2495	.0005–.0026	2.4995	.0003–.0018	2	.006–.015
1982	V6-262/V⑤⑪	.0030–.0040	.015	.015	1.0952	2.3742–2.3750	.0003–.0025	2.9993–3.0003	⑫	3	.0035–.0135
1983	V6-262/V⑤⑪	.0035–.0045	⑯	.015	1.0951	2.3742–2.3750	.0003–.0025	2.9993–3.0003	⑫	3	.0035–.0135
1985–86	V6-262/Z	.0007–.0017	.010	.015	.9272	2.2487–2.2498	.0013–.0035	③	④	4	.002–.006
1980–82	V8-267/J	.0007–.0017	.010	.015	.9272	2.0986–2.0998	.0013–.0035	③	④	5	.002–.006
1980–81	8-305⑬	.0007–.0017	.010	.015	.9272	2.0986–2.0998	.0013–.0035	③	④	5	.002–.006
1982–86	V8-305/⑬⑯	.0007–.0017	.010	.015	.9272	2.0986–2.0998	.0013–.0035	③	④	5	.002–.006
1982–86	V8-305/⑬⑱	.0007–.0017	.010	.015	.9272	2.0986–2.0998	.0018–.0039	③	④	5	.002–.006
1980	8-350/L⑥	.0007–.0017	.010	.015	.9272	2.0986–2.0998	.0013–.0035	③	④	5	.002–.006
	8-350/L⑦	.0046–.0056	.010	.015	.9272	2.0986–2.0998	.0013–.0035	③	④	5	.002–.006
1981–82	V8-350/L⑥	.0007–.0017	.015	.020	.9272	2.099–2.100	.0013–.0035	③	④	5	.002–.007
	V8-350/L⑦	.0046–.0056	.010	.015	.9272	2.0986–2.0998	.0013–.0035	③	④	5	.002–.006
	V8-350/6⑦	.0025–.0035	.010	.015	.9272	2.0988–2.0998	.0013–.0035	③	④	5	.002–.006
1984–86	V8-350/8	.0025–.0045	.010	.015	.9272	2.0988–2.0998	.0013–.0035	③	④	5	.002–.006
1980–82	8-350/N⑤⑪	.0050–.0060	.015	.015	1.0951	2.1238–2.1248	.0005–.0026	2.9993–3.0003	⑧	3	.0035–.0135
1983–84	V8-350/N⑤ ⑪	.0035–.0045	⑯	.015	1.0951	2.2495–2.2500	.0005–.0026	2.9993–3.0003	⑧	3	.0035–.0135
1985	V8-350/N⑤ ⑪	.0035–.0045	.015	.015	1.0951	2.1238–2.1248	.0005–.0026	2.9993–3.0003	⑧	3	.0035–.0135

①—Fit rings tapered bores to the clearance listed in tightest portion of ring travel.
②—Clearances specified are minimum gaps.
③—Front: 2.4484–2.4493; intermediate: 2.4481–2.4490; rear: 2.4479–2.4488.
④—Front: .0008–.0020; intermediate: .0011–.0023; rear: .0017–.0032.
⑤—Refer to Oldsmobile Chapter for service procedures on this engine.
⑥—Except Corvette High Performance engine.

⑦—Corvette High Performance engine.
⑧—No. 1, 2, 3, 4: .0005–.0021; 1980–82 No. 5: .0015–.0031; 1983–84 No. 5: .0020–.0034.
⑨—Refer to Buick Chapter for service procedures on this engine.
⑩—Nos. 1–6; .0010–.0024. Nos. 7; .0016–.0035.
⑪—Diesel engine.
⑫—No. 1, 2, 3: .0005–.0021; No. 4: .0020–.0034.

⑬—For V.I.N. code, refer to the "General Engine Specifications" at the beginning of the chapter.
⑭—Refer to the Pontiac chapter for service procedures on this engine.
⑮—Nos. 1, 2, 4, 2.4937–2.4946 inch; No. 3, 2.4932–2.4941 inch.
⑯—Top, 0.019 inch; 2nd, 0.013 inch.
⑰—Exc. Camaro.
⑱—Camaro.

continued

Rear Axle Specifications

Year	Model	Carrier Type	Ring Gear Pinion Backlash		Pinion Bearing Preload			Differential Bearing Preload		
			Method	Adjustment	Method	New Bearings Inch-Lbs.	Used Bearings Inch-Lbs.	Method	New Bearings	Used Bearings
1980–81	Exc. Corvette	Integral	Shims	.005–.008	Spacer	15–30①	10–15①	Shims	.008②	.008②
1982	③	Integral	Shims	.005–.008	Spacer	20–25①	10–15①	Shims	.008②④	.008②④
	Camaro	Integral	Shims	.005–.009	Spacer	24–32①	8–12①	Shims	.008	.008
1980–82	Corvette	Integral	Shims	.005–.009	Shims	15–35①	—	Shims	.008②	.008②
1983–85	Exc. Corvette	Integral	Shims	.005–.008	Spacer	24–32①	8–12①	Shims	.008②	.008②
1984–86	Corvette	Integral	Shims	.005–.008	Shims	15–35	—	Shims	.008②	.008②

①—Use inch-pound torque wrench on pinion shaft nut.
②—Slip fit plus 0.004 inch additional preload per side.
③—Exc. Camaro & Corvette.
④—Total preload measured with torque wrench at pinion flange nut with new seal installed. 35–40 inch lbs., new bearings; 20–25 inch lbs., used bearings.

Valve Specifications

Year	Engine/V.I.N.	Valve Lash		Valve Angles		Valve Spring Installed Height	Valve Spring Pressure Lbs. @ In.	Stem Clearance		Stem Diameter	
		Int.	Exh.	Seat	Face			Intake	Exhaust	Intake	Exhaust
1980	V6-229/K	1 Turn⑤		46	45	1²³⁄₃₂	200 @ 1.25	.0010–.0027	.0010–.0027	.3410–.3417	.3410–.3417
	V6-231/A④	Hydraulic③		45	45	1.727	182 @ 1.34	.0015–.0035	.0015–.0032	.3402–.3412	.3405–.3412
	V8-267/J	1 Turn⑤		46	45	1²³⁄₃₂	200 @ 1.25	.0010–.0027	.0010–.0027	.3410–.3417	.3410–.3417
	V8-305/H	1 Turn⑤		46	45	1²³⁄₃₂	200 @ 1.25	.0010–.0027	.0010–.0027	.3410–.3417	.3410–.3417
	V8-350/L⑦	1 Turn⑤		46	45	1²³⁄₃₂	200 @ 1.25	.0010–.0027	.0010–.0027	.3410–.3417	.3410–.3412
	V8-350/L⑥	1 Turn⑤		46	45	②	①	.0010–.0027	.0010–.0027	.3410–.3417	.3410–.3412
	V8-350 Diesel/N⑧	Hydraulic③		⑨	⑩	1.67	151 @ 1.30	.0010–.0027	.0015–.0032	.3425–.3432	.3420–.3427
1981	V6-229/K	1 Turn⑤		46	45	1.70	175 @ 1.25	.0010–.0027	.0010–.0027	.3410–.3417	.3410–.3417
	V6-231/A④	Hydraulic③		45	45	1.727	182 @ 1.34	.0015–.0035	.0015–.0032	.3402–.3412	.3405–.3412
	V8-267/J	1 Turn⑤		46	45	1.70	175 @ 1.25	.0010–.0027	.0010–.0027	.3410–.3417	.3410–.3417
	V8-305/H	1 Turn⑤		46	45	1.70	175 @ 1.25	.0010–.0027	.0010–.0027	.3410–.3417	.3410–.3417
	V8-350/L⑦	1 Turn⑤		46	45	1.70	⑪	.0010–.0027	.0010–.0027	.3410–.3417	.3410–.3417
	V8-350/L⑥	1 Turn⑤		46	45	②	①	.0010–.0027	.0010–.0027	.3410–.3417	.3410–.3417
	V8-350 Diesel/N⑧	Hydraulic③		⑨	⑩	1.67	155 @ 1.30	.0010–.0027	.0015–.0032	.3425–3432	.3420–.3427
1982	4-151/F⑫	Hydraulic③		46	45	1.66	151 @ 1.254	.0010–.0027	.0010–.0027	.3418–.3425	.3418–.3425
	V6-173/1	1½ Turn⑤		46	45	1.57	195 @ 1.1811	.0010–.0027	.0010–.0027	.3410–.3420	.3410–.3420
	V6-229/K	1 Turn⑤		46	45	1²³⁄₃₂	200 @ 1.25	.0010–.0027	.0010–.0027	.3410–.3417	.3410–.3417
	V6-231/A④	Hydraulic③		45	45	1.727	220 @ 1.34	.0015–.0035	.0015–.0032	.3401–.3412	.3405–.3412
	V6-262 Diesel/V⑧	Hydraulic③		⑨	⑩	1.67	210 @ 1.22	.0010–.0027	.0015–.0032	.3425–.3432	.3420–.3427
	V8-267/J	1 Turn⑤		46	45	1²³⁄₃₂	200 @ 1.25	.0010–.0027	.0010–.0027	.3410–.3417	.3410–.3417
	V8-305/H & 7	1 Turn⑤		46	45	1²³⁄₃₂	200 @ 1.25	.0010–.0027	.0010–.0027	.3410–.3417	.3410–.3417
	V8-350/6⑥	1 Turn⑤		46	45	②	①	.0010–.0027	.0010–.0027	.3410–.3417	.3410–.3417
	V8-350 Diesel/N⑧	Hydraulic③		⑨	⑩	1.67	210 @ 1.22	.0010–.0027	.0015–.0032	.3425–3432	.3420–.3427
1983	4-151/2⑫	Hydraulic③		46	45	1.69	151 @ 1.254	.0010–.0027	.0010–.0027	.3425–.3418	.3425–.3418
	V6-173/1	1½ Turns⑤		46	45	1.57	195 @ 1.1811	.0010–.0027	.0010–.0027	.3410–.3420	.3410–.3420
	V6-229/9	1 Turn⑤		46	45	1²³⁄₃₂	200 @ 1.25	.0010–.0027	.0010–.0027	.3410–.3417	.3410–.3420
	V6-231/A④	Hydraulic③		45	45	1.727	182 @ 1.340	.0015–.0035	.0015–.0032	.3401–.3412	.3405–.3412
	V6-262 Diesel/V⑧	Hydraulic③		⑨	⑩	1.67	210 @ 1.22	.0010–.0027	.0015–.0032	.3425–.3432	.3420–.3427
	V8-305/H, G & S	1 Turn⑤		46	45	1²³⁄₃₂	200 @ 1.25	.0010–.0027	.0010–.0027	.3410–.3417	.3410–.3420
	V8-350 Diesel/N⑧	Hydraulic③		⑨	⑩	1.67	210 @ 1.22	.0010–.0027	.0015–.0032	.3425–3432	.3420–.3427

continued

VALVE SPECIFICATIONS—Continued

Year	Engine/V.I.N.	Valve Lash Int.	Valve Lash Exh.	Valve Angles Seat	Valve Angles Face	Valve Spring Installed Height	Valve Spring Pressure Lbs. @ In.	Stem Clearance Intake	Stem Clearance Exhaust	Stem Diameter Intake	Stem Diameter Exhaust
1984	4-151/2⑫	Hydraulic③		46	45	1.66	151 @ 1.254	.0010–.0027	.0010–.0027	.3425–.3418	.3425–.3418
	V6-173/1	1½ Turns⑤		46	45	1.57	195 @ 1.1811	.0010–.0027	.0010–.0027	.3410–.3420	.3410–.3420
	V6-229/9	1 Turn⑤		46	45	1²³⁄₃₂	200 @ 1.25	.0010–.0027	.0010–.0027	.3410–.3417	.3410–.3420
	V6-231/A④	Hydraulic③		45	45	1.727	182 @ 1.340	.0015–.0035	.0015–.0032	.3401–.3412	.3405–.3412
	V8-305/H & G	1 Turn⑤		46	45	1²³⁄₃₂	200 @ 1.25	.0010–.0027	.0010–.0027	.3410–.3417	.3410–.3420
	V8-350/8⑥	1 Turn⑤		46	45	②	①	.0010–.0027	.0010–.0027	.3410–.3417	.3410–.3417
	V8-350/N⑧	Hydraulic③		⑨	⑩	1.67	210 @ 1.22	.0010–.0027	.0015–.0032	.3425–3432	.3420–.3427
1985	4-151/2⑫	Hydraulic③		45	45	1.69	180 @ 1.26	—	—	.3420–3430	.3420–.3430
	V6-173/S	1½ Turns③		46	45	1.57	195 @ 1.1811	.0010–.0027	.0010–.0027	.3410–.3420	.3410–.3420
	V6-262/Z	1 Turn⑤		46	45	1²³⁄₃₂	200 @ 1.25	.0010–.0027	.0010–.0027	.3410–.3417	.3410–.3417
	V8-305/F	1 Turn⑤		46	45	1²³⁄₃₂	200 @ 1.25	.0010–.0027	.0010–.0027	—	—
	V8-305/G, H	1 Turn⑤		46	45	1²³⁄₃₂	200 @ 1.25	.0010–.0027	.0010–.0027	.3410–.3417	.3410–.3417
	V8-350/8	1 Turn⑤		46	45	②	200 @ 1.25	.0010–.0027	.0010–.0027	—	—
	V8-350 Diesel/N⑧	Hydraulic③		⑨	⑩	1.67	210 @ 1.22	.0010–.0027	.0015–.0032	.3424–3432	.3420–.3428
1986	4-151/2	Hydraulic③		45	45	1.69	180 @ 1.26	.0010–.0027	.0010–.0027	.3420–3430	.3420–.3430
	V6-173/S	1 Turn⑤		46	45	1.57	198 @ 1.1811	.0010–.0027	.0010–.0027	.3410–.3420	.3410–.3420
	V6-262/Z	1 Turn⑤		46	45	1²³⁄₃₂	200 @ 1.25	.0010–.0027	.0010–.0027	.3410–.3417	.3410–.3417
	V8-305/F	1 Turn⑤		46	45	1²³⁄₃₂	200 @ 1.25	.0010–.0027	.0010–.0027	—	—
	V8-305/G, H	1 Turn⑤		46	45	1²³⁄₃₂	200 @ 1.25	.0010–.0027	.0010–.0027	.3410–.3417	.3410–.3417
	V8-350/8	1 Turn⑤		46	45	1²³⁄₃₂	200 @ 1.25	.0010–.0027	.0010–.0027	—	—

①—Intake 200 @ 1.25; Exhaust 200 @ 1.16.
②—Intake, 1²³⁄₃₂. Exhaust 1¹⁹⁄₃₂.
③—No Adjustment.
④—Refer to Buick Chapter for service procedures on this engine.
⑤—Turn rocker arm stud nut until all lash is eliminated, then tighten nut the additional turn listed.
⑥—Corvette.
⑦—Except Corvette.
⑧—Refer to Oldsmobile Chapter for service procedures on this engine.
⑨—Intake, 45°; Exhaust, 31°.
⑩—Intake, 44°; Exhaust, 30°.
⑪—Intake, 184 @ 1.70; Exhaust, 190 @ 1.16.
⑫—Refer to Pontiac chapter for service procedures.

Wheel Alignment Specifications

Year	Model	Caster Angle, Degrees Limits	Caster Angle, Degrees Desired	Camber Angle, Degrees Limits Left	Camber Angle, Degrees Limits Right	Camber Angle, Degrees Desired Left	Camber Angle, Degrees Desired Right	Toe-In Inch	Toe-Out on Turns, Deg.① Outer Wheel	Toe-Out on Turns, Deg.① Inner Wheel
CAMARO										
1980–81	All	0 to +2	+1	+.2 to +1.8	+.2 to +1.8	+.5	+.5	+¹⁄₁₆ to +¼	—	—
1982–84	All	+2 to +4	+3	+.2 to +1.8	+.2 to +1.8	+1	+1	①	—	—
1985	Exc. IROC-Z	+2 to +4	+3	+.2 to +1.8	+.2 to +1.8	+1	+1	①	—	—
	IROC-Z	+3 to +5	+4	+.2 to +1.8	+.2 to +1.8	+1	+1	+.05 to +.25②	—	—
1986	Exc. Z-28	+2½ to +3½	+3	+½ to +1½	+½ to +1½	+1	+1	④	—	—
	Z-28	+3 to +4	+3½	+½ to +1½	+½ to +1½	+1	+1	④	—	—
MALIBU & MONTE CARLO										
1980–86	Manual Steering	0 to +2	+1	−.3 to +1.3	−.3 to +1.3	+.5	+.5	+¹⁄₁₆ to +¼	—	—
	Power Steering	+2 to +4	+3	−.3 to +1.3	−.3 to +1.3	+.5	+.5	+¹⁄₁₆ to +¼	—	—
CHEVROLET										
1980–86	Caprice, Impala	+2 to +4	+3	0 to +1.6	0 to +1.6	+.8	+.8	+¹⁄₁₆ to +¼	—	—
CORVETTE										
1980–82	Front Whl. Align.	+1¼ to +3¼	+2¼	0 to +1½	0 to +1½	+¾	+¾	+⅛ to +⅜	—	—
	Rear Whl. Align.	—	—	−½ to +½	−½ to +½	0	0	+.06②	—	—
1984	Front Whl. Align.	+2.2 to +3.8	+3	+.3 to +1.3	+.3 to +1.3	+.8	+.8	0 to +.3②	—	—
	Rear Whl. Align.	—	—	−.5 to +.5	−.5 to +.5	0	0	+.15②	—	—
1985–86	Front Whl. Align.	+2.2 to +3.8	+3	+.3 to +1.3	+.3 to +1.3	+.8	+.8	0 to +.15	—	—
	Rear Whl. Align.	—	—	+.1 to +.9	+.1 to +.9	+.4	+.4	+.15	—	—

①—Exc. Z-28, +.1 to +.3 degrees per wheel; Z-28, +.05 to +.25 degrees per wheel.
②—Degrees per wheel.
③—Inches per wheel.
④—Toe-in .15°.

continued

Cooling System & Capacity Data

Year	Model or Engine/V.I.N.	Cooling Capacity, Qts.		Radiator Cap Relief Pressure, Lbs.	Thermo. Opening Temp.	Fuel Tank Gals.	Engine Oil Refill Qts. [1]	Transmission Oil			Rear Axle Oil Pints
		Less A/C	With A/C					3 Speed Pints	4 Speed Pints	Auto. Trans. Qts. [2]	
CAMARO											
1980	V6-229/K	14.5	14.5	15	195	21	4[16]	3	—	[20]	4¼
	V6-231/A	12	12	15	195	21	4	—	—	[20]	4¼
	V8-267/J, V8-305/H	15	15	15	195	21	4	—	—	[20]	4¼
	V8-350/L	16	16	15	195	21	4	—	3	[20]	4¼
1981	V6-229/K	14½	14½	15	195	20.8	4[16]	3½	—	[11]	[3]
	V6-231/A	12	12	15	195	20.8	4	—	—	[11]	[3]
	V8-267/J, V8-305/H	15	15	15	195	20.8	4	—	3½	[11]	[3]
	V8-350/L	16	16	15	195	20.8	4	—	—	[11]	[3]
1982	4-151/2	8.8	9.1	15	195	16	3[16]	—	3½	[27]	3½
	V6-173/I	12½	12½	15	195	16	4[16]	—	3½	[27]	3½
	V8-305/H,7	15	15	15	195	16	4	—	3½	[27]	3½
1983	4-151/2	8.8	9.1	15	195	16	3[16]	—	[30]	[28]	3½
	V6-173/I	12½	12½	15	195	16	4[16]	—	[30]	[28]	3½
	V8-305/H, G	15	15	15	195	16	4	—	[30]	[28]	3½
	V8-305 E.F.I./7	15	15	15	195	16	4	—	[30]	[28]	3½
1984	4-151/2	8.8	9.1	15	195	16	3[16]	—	[30]	[29]	3½
	V6-173/1	12.5	12.5	15	195	16	4[16]	—	[30]	[29]	3½
	V8-305/H, G	15	15	15	195	16	4	—	[30]	[29]	3½
1985	4-151/2	[5]	[5]	15	195	15.5	3[16]	—	[6]	[29]	3.5
	V6-173/S	[21]	[22]	15	195	15.5	4[16]	—	6.9	[29]	3.5
	V8-305/F	—	—	15	195	15.5	4	—	—	[29]	3.5
	V8-305/G	15.8	16.8	15	195	16.2	4	—	6.9	—	3.5
	V8-305/H	15.2[9]	15.7[9]	15	195	16.2	4	—	6.9	[29]	3.5
1986	4-151/2	9.8	9.8	15	195	15.5	3[16]	—	3.5	[29]	3.5
	V6-173/S	12½	12.5	15	195	15.5	4[16]	—	3.5	[29]	3.5
	V8-305/F	17	17	15	195	15.5	4	—	3.5	[29]	3.5
	V8-305/G	15.6	15.6	15	195	16.2	4	—	3.5	[29]	3.5
	V8-305/H	15.3	15.6	15	195	16.2	4	—	3.5	[29]	3.5

continued

Year	Model or Engine/V.I.N.	Cooling Capacity, Qts.		Radiator Cap Relief Pressure, Lbs.	Thermo. Opening Temp.	Fuel Tank Gals.	Engine Oil Refill Qts. ①	Transmission Oil			Rear Axle Oil Pints
		Less A/C	With A/C					3 Speed Pints	4 Speed Pints	Auto. Trans. Qts. ②	

MALIBU & MONTE CARLO

Year	Model or Engine/V.I.N.	Less A/C	With A/C	Radiator Cap Relief	Thermo.	Fuel Tank	Engine Oil ①	3 Speed	4 Speed	Auto. Trans. ②	Rear Axle
1980	V6-229/K	18.5	18.5	15	195	18.1	4⑯	3	—	⑳	③
	V6-231/A	15.5	15.5	15	195	18.1	4	—	—	⑳	③
	V8-267/J	21.0	21.0	15	195	18.1	4	—	—	⑳	③
	V8-305/H	19.0	19.0	15	195	18.1	4	—	3	⑳	③
1981	V6-229/K	18½	18½	15	195	18.1	4⑯	3½	—	⑪	③
	V6-231/A	15½	15½	15	195	18.1	4	—	—	⑪	③
	V8-267/J	21	21	15	195	18.1	4	—	—	⑪	③
	V8-305/H	19	19	15	195	18.1	4	—	3½	⑪	③
1982	V6-229/K	18½	18½	15	195	18.1	4⑯	—	—	⑪	③
	V6-231/A	15½	15½	15	195	18.1	4⑯	—	—	⑪	③
	V8-267/J	21	21	15	195	18.1	4	—	—	⑪	③
	V8-305/H	19	19	15	195	18.1	4	—	—	⑪	③
1983	V6-229/9	18½	18½	15	195	18.1	4⑯	—	—	⑪	3½
	V6-231/A	15½	15½	15	195	18.1	4⑯	—	—	⑪	3½
	V6-262/V	13.4	13.4	15	195	19.8	6⑫	—	—	⑪	3½
	V8-305/H	19	19	15	195	18.1	4	—	—	⑪	3½
	V8-350/N⑱	18.3	18.4	15	195	19.8	7⑫	—	—	⑪	3½
1984	V6-229/9	14¼	14¼	15	195	25⑮	4⑯	—	—	㉛	③
	V6-231/A	11¾	11¾	15	195	25⑮	4⑯	—	—	㉛	③
	V8-305/H, G	⑰	⑰	15	195	25⑮	4	—	—	㉛	③
	V8-350/N⑱	18.3	18.3	15	195	27⑮	7⑫	—	—	㉛	③
1985	V6-262/Z	13.0㉓	13.1㉓	15	195	17.6	—	—	—	㉔	㉕
	V8-305/G	15.9	16.7	15	195	18.1	4	—	—	㉔	㉕
	V8-305/H	16.4	15.9	15	195	18.1	4	—	—	㉔	㉕
1986	V6-262/Z	12	12	15	195	17.6	4⑯	—	—	㉔	㉕
	V8-305/H	16.3	16.3	15	195	18.1	4	—	—	㉔	㉕
	V8-305/G	16.6	16.6	15	195	18.1	4	—	—	㉔	㉕

COOLING SYSTEM & CAPACITY DATA—Continued

Year	Model or Engine/V.I.N.	Cooling Capacity, Qts. Less A/C	Cooling Capacity, Qts. With A/C	Radiator Cap Relief Pressure, Lbs.	Thermo. Opening Temp.	Fuel Tank Gals.	Engine Oil Refill Qts. ①	3 Speed Pints	4 Speed Pints	Auto. Trans. Qts. ②	Rear Axle Oil Pints
CHEVROLET											
1980	V6-229/K	14.25	14.25	15	195	25⑮	4⑯	—	—	⑳	③
	V6-231/A	11.75	11.75	15	195	25⑮	4	—	—	⑳	③
	V8-267/J	⑰	⑰	15	195	25⑮	4	—	—	⑳	③
	V8-305/H	15.5	15.5	15	195	25⑮	4	—	—	⑳	③
	V8-350/L	16.25	16.25	15	195	25⑮	4	—	—	⑳	③
	V8-350/N⑱	18.3	18	15	195	25⑮	7④	—	—	⑳	③
1981–82	V6-229/K	14¼	14¼	15	195	25⑮	4⑯	—	—	⑪	③
	V6-231/A	11¾	11¾	15	195	25⑮	4⑯	—	—	⑪	③
	V8-267/J	⑰	⑰	15	195	25⑮	4	—	—	⑪	③
	V8-305/H	15½	15½	15	195	25⑮	4	—	—	⑪	③
	V8-350/N⑱	18.3	18	15	195	25⑮	7④	—	—	⑪	③
1983	V6-229/K	14¼	14¼	15	195	25⑮	4⑯	—	—	㉛	③
	V6-231/A	11¾	11¾	15	195	25⑮	4⑯	—	—	㉛	③
	V8-305/H	15½	15½	15	195	25⑮	4	—	—	㉛	③
	V8-350/N⑱	18.3	18.3	15	195	27⑮	7⑫	—	—	㉛	③
1984	V6-229/K	18½	18½	15	195	25⑮	4⑯	—	—	㉛	③
	V6-231/A	15½	15½	15	195	25⑮	4⑯	—	—	㉛	③
	V8-305/H	19	19	15	195	25⑮	4	—	—	㉛	③
	V8-350/N⑱	18.1㉖	18.2㉖	15	195	25⑮	7.0⑫	—	—	㉛	③
1985	V6-262/Z	12	12	15	195	25	—	—	—	㉔	㉕
	V8-305/H	16.5	16.5	15	195	25⑮	4	—	—	㉔	㉕
	V8-350/N	18	18	15	195	25⑮	7.0⑫	—	—	㉔	㉕
1986	V6-262/Z	12	12	15	195	25⑮	4⑯	—	—	㉔	㉕
	V8-305/H	16½	16½	15	195	25⑮	4	—	—	㉔	㉕
CORVETTE											
1980	V8-305/H	17½	18½	15	195	20	3¼	—	—	⑦	3¾
	V8-350/8, 6	17½	18½	15	195	20	3¼	—	3½	⑦	3¾
1981	V8-350/6	21	22	15	195	23.7	4	—	3.4	4⑧	3¾
1982	V8-350/6	21	21	15	195	23.7	4	—	3	10	4
1984	V8-350/8	14.5㉜	14.5㉜	15	195	20	4	—	⑲	10	4
1985	V8-350 TPI/8	14	14	15	195	20	4	—	⑲	㉙	4
1986	V8-350 TPI/8	—	—	15	195	—	—	—	—	—	—

COOLING SYSTEM & CAPACITY DATA NOTES—Continued

①—Add one quart with filter change.
②—Approximate. Make final check with dipstick.
③—7½" ring gear, 3½ pts.; 8½" ring gear, 4¼ pts.; 8¾" ring gear, 5.4 pts.
④—Includes filter. Use recommended diesel engine oil, designated SF/CC, SF/CD or SE/CC.
⑤—Std. cooling: auto. trans., 9.1 qts.; manual trans., 9.3 qts. Heavy duty cooling, 9.25 qts.
⑥—4 spd., 2.4 pts.; 5 spd., 6.9 pts.
⑦—Oil pan only, 3 qts. Total capacity, 10 qts.
⑧—Oil pan only.
⑨—Heavy duty cooling, 15.8 qts.
⑩—3¼ pts. for 7½" ring gear. 4 pts. for 8½" and 8¾" ring gears.
⑪—THM 200 oil pan only, 3½ qts. Total capacity, 5 qts., THM 350 oil pan only, 3 qts. Total capacity, 10 qts.
⑫—Includes filter. Use recommended diesel engine oil, designated SF/CC or SF/CD.

⑬—With heavy duty cooling system, add 1 qt.
⑭—With auto. trans., add 1 qt.
⑮—Sta. Wag., 22 gals.
⑯—With or without filter change.
⑰—Exc. Sta. Wag. Standard cooling, 16.75 qts.; Sta. Wag. with standard cooling, 15.5 qts.
⑱—Diesel.
⑲—4 spd., 2 pts.; over drive, 4 pts.
⑳—THM 200, oil pan only 3½ qts., total capacity 5 qts. THM 250, oil pan 4 qts., total capacity 10¾ qts. THM 350, oil pan only 3 qts., total capacity 10 qts.
㉑—Auto. trans., 12.3 qts.; manual trans., 12.4 qts.
㉒—Std. cooling: auto. trans., 12.2 qts; manual trans., 12.3 qts. Heavy duty cooling: auto. trans., 12.3 qts.; manual trans., 12.4 qts.
㉓—Heavy duty cooling, 13.2 qts.
㉔—THM 200C, pan only 3½ qts.; total capacity, 9½ qts. THM 200-4R, pan only 3½ qts.; total capacity, 11 qts.

THM 700-4R, pan only 4.95 qts.; total capacity, 11.5 qts.
㉕—7¼ & 7⅝ inch ring gear, 3₁₋₂ pts.; 8½ inch ring gear, 4¼ pts.
㉖—Heavy duty cooling, 18.3 qts.
㉗—Oil pan only, 3½ qts.; total capacity, 5 qts.
㉘—T.H.M. 200c, oil pan only, 3½ qts.; total capacity 5 qts. T.H.M. 700-R4, oil pan only, 4.95 qts.; total capacity, 11½ qts.
㉙—Oil pan only, 4.95 qts.; total capacity, 11½ qts.
㉚—4 spd. trans., 4.3 pts.; 5 spd. trans., 5.3 pts.
㉛—T.H.M. 200C, oil pan only 3½ qts.; total capacity, 9½ qts.; T.H.M. 200-4R, oil pan only, 3.48 qts.; total capacity, 11.05 qts. T.H.M. 250C & 350C, oil pan only, 3.15 qts.; total capacity, 10 qts. T.H.M. 700-R4, oil pan only, 4.95 qts.; total capacity, 11½ qts.
㉜—Heavy duty cooling, 14.8 qts.

Electrical Section

Fig. 1   Ignition lock installation

Fig. 2   Ignition switch

STARTER
REPLACE

NOTE: If shims are used between starter and engine block, they should be placed in their original location during installation. If starter is noisy during cranking, remove one .015 inch double shim or add one .015 single shim to the outer bolt. If starter makes a high pitched whine after firing, add .015 inch double shims until noise ceases.

1. Disconnect battery ground cable.
2. Raise and support vehicle.
3. Remove starter to engine brace and starter heat shields, if equipped.
4. Remove starter mounting bolts and lower starter. Note position of shims, if used.
5. Disconnect solenoid wires and the battery cable.
6. Remove starter from vehicle.
7. Reverse procedure to install.

IGNITION LOCK
REPLACE

1. Remove steering wheel as described under Horn Sounder and Steering Wheel.
2. Remove turn signal switch as described under Turn Signal Switch, Replace, then remove buzzer switch.
3. Place ignition switch in "Run" position, then remove lock cylinder retaining screw and lock cylinder.
4. To install, rotate lock cylinder to stop while holding housing, **Fig. 1**. Align cylinder key with keyway in housing, then push lock cylinder assembly into housing until fully seated.
5. Install lock cylinder retaining screw. Torque screw to 35 in. lbs. for standard columns. On adjustable columns, torque retaining screw to 35 in. lbs.
6. Install buzzer switch, turn signal switch and steering wheel.

IGNITION SWITCH
REPLACE

The ignition switch is mounted on top of the mast jacket inside the brake pedal support and is actuated by a rod and rack assembly.
1. Disconnect battery cable.
2. Disconnect and lower steering column.

NOTE: It may be necessary, on some models, to remove the upper column mounting bracket if it hinders servicing of switch.

CAUTION: Use extreme care when lowering steering column to prevent damage to column assembly. Only lower steering column a sufficient distance to perform ignition switch service.

3. Rotate ignition lock to "Off" unlocked position.
4. If lock cylinder has been removed, pull switch actuator rod up to stop, then push rod down to second detent to place switch in "Off" unlocked position, **Fig. 2**.
5. Remove column mounted dimmer switch, if equipped, then remove switch retaining screws and switch.
6. Reverse procedure to install, noting the following:

Fig. 3   Headlamp switch knob removal

a. Place gear shift lever in neutral.
b. Place lock cylinder and switch in "Off" unlocked position, **Fig. 2**.
c. Fit actuator rod into hole in switch slider and secure switch with retaining screws, ensuring switch does not move out of detent.
d. Install and adjust dimmer switch, if removed, as outlined in "Dimmer Switch, Replace."
e. Torque retaining screws to 35 inch lbs., then check switch operation.

LIGHT SWITCH
REPLACE

MALIBU & MONTE CARLO

1. Disconnect battery ground cable.
2. Remove instrument panel bezel.
3. Pull switch knob to "On" position.
4. Remove three screws attaching windshield wiper/light switch mounting plate to cluster and pull assembly rearward.
5. Depress shaft retainer button on switch and pull knob and shaft assembly from switch, **Fig. 3**.
6. Remove ferrule nut and switch assembly from mounting plate.
7. Reverse procedure to install.

CORVETTE

1980–82
1. Disconnect battery ground cable.
2. Remove left air distribution duct.
3. Remove instrument cluster to instrument panel attaching screws and pull cluster rearward.
4. Disconnect speedometer cable and electrical connectors and remove cluster.
5. Remove two instrument panel to left door pillar attaching screws and pull left side of instrument panel slightly rearward.
6. Pull switch knob to "On" position, depress release button on switch and

remove shaft and knob assembly, **Fig. 3.** Remove bezel nut securing switch to instrument panel.
7. Disconnect vacuum hoses from switch and the electrical connector.
8. Remove light switch from vehicle.
9. Reverse procedure to install.

1984–86
1. Disconnect battery ground cable.
2. Remove hush panel from under left side of instrument panel.
3. Pull switch knob to "On" position, reach up under dash and depress release button on switch, and remove shaft and knob assembly, **Fig. 3.**
4. Remove cluster bezel and nut securing switch to instrument panel and lower switch.
5. Disconnect electrical connectors and remove switch.
6. Reverse procedure to install.

CHEVROLET
1. Disconnect battery ground cable.
2. Pull switch knob to "On" position, reach up under instrument panel and depress switch shaft retainer, then pull knob and shaft assembly from switch, **Fig. 3.**
3. Remove windshield wiper switch.
4. Remove light switch ferrule nut and remove switch from panel.
5. Disconnect electrical connector from switch and remove switch from vehicle.
6. Reverse procedure to install.

CAMARO
1980–81
1. Disconnect battery ground cable.
2. Remove steering column lower cover.
3. Pull switch knob to "On" position, depress release button on switch and remove shaft and knob assembly, **Fig. 3.**
4. Remove nut securing switch to carrier.
5. Remove cluster carrier screws and tilt right side of cluster out.
6. Unplug connector and remove switch.

1982–84 Exc. 1984–86 Berlinetta
1. Disconnect battery ground cable.
2. Remove left and right lower instrument panel trim plates.
3. Pull light switch to on position, depress release button on switch frame, then remove knob and stem from switch, **Fig. 3.**
4. Remove switch bezel and retaining nut.
5. Depress switch retaining tabs, if equipped, pull switch from instrument cluster and disconnect electrical connector.
6. Reverse procedure to install

1984–86 Berlinetta
1. Disconnect battery ground cable.
2. Remove instrument panel close-out panel and lower steering column cover.
3. Remove bottom front screw securing left control pod, then release pod retainer.

Fig. 4 Left control pod removal. 1984–86 Berlinetta

4. Disconnect left control pod electrical connector below instrument panel, **Fig. 4.**
5. Remove pod housing and screw securing control assembly to track.
6. Slide control assembly from track.
7. Reverse procedure to install.

1985–86 Exc. Berlinetta
1. Disconnect battery ground cable.
2. Remove right and left hand lower trim plates and the instrument panel cluster trim plate.
3. Remove 2 switch attaching screws, then depress side tangs and remove switch from instrument panel.
4. Reverse procedure to install.

STOP LIGHT SWITCH
REPLACE

EXC. CORVETTE

NOTE: On 1982–86 Camaro, remove hush panel.

1. Disconnect wiring connector at switch.
2. Remove retaining nut, if so equipped, and unscrew switch from bracket.
3. To install: Depress brake pedal and push new switch into clip until shoulder bottoms out.
4. Plug connector onto switch and check operation. Electrical contact should be made when pedal is depressed $3/8$ to $5/8$ from fully released position.

CORVETTE
1980–82
1. Disconnect wiring connector at switch.
2. Remove retaining nut and unscrew switch from bracket.
3. Upon installation, check for proper operation. Electrical contact should be made when pedal is depressed $1/4$ to $5/8$. Switch bracket has a slotted screw hole for adjustment.

1984–86
1. Remove hush panel from under left side of instrument panel.
2. Disconnect electrical connectors from switch and pull switch out of retaining clip on brake pedal support.
3. Depress brake pedal and push replacement switch into retainer until switch shoulder is bottomed against bracket.
4. Adjust switch by pulling brake pedal back against stop.
5. Ensure switch has continuity when pedal is depressed .53 inch from normal rest position, and pedal fully returns to rest position.
6. Reconnect electrical connectors and install hush panel.

CLUTCH START SWITCH
REPLACE

1982–86 CAMARO
1. Disconnect wire connector at switch.
2. Remove retaining nut, if so equipped and unscrew switch from bracket.
3. To install: depress clutch pedal, then insert and push switch into clip until shoulder bottoms out.
4. Plug connector on switch and check for proper operation.

CORVETTE
1980–82
1. Disconnect wiring connector from switch.
2. Remove retainer from pins or link on clutch pedal arm.
3. Remove retaining screw and switch.

1984–86
1. Disconnect battery ground cable and set parking brake.
2. Remove retaining screw and switch from clutch pedal bracket, rotate switch slightly, and pull switch actuating lever from hole in pedal arm.
3. Disconnect electrical connector and remove switch.
4. Position replacement switch with actuating lever installed in hole in pedal arm, then secure switch to bracket with retaining screw.
5. Connect electrical connector to switch and adjust by fully depressing clutch pedal.

NOTE: If readjustment is necessary, depress detent on switch adjusting block and slide block fully forward on switch rod. Fully depress clutch pedal to complete adjustment.

EXC. CORVETTE & 1982–86 CAMARO
1. Disconnect wiring connector from switch.
2. Compress switch actuating shaft retainer and remove shaft with switch attached from switch bracket.

Fig. 5   Mechanical neutral start system. Chevrolet, Malibu & Monte Carlo

Fig. 6   Lock plate retaining ring removal

Fig. 7   Turn signal switch assembly

Fig. 8   Turn signal switch removal

NEUTRAL SAFETY SWITCH
REPLACE

CHEVROLET MALIBU & MONTE CARLO

Actuation of the ignition switch is prevented by a mechanical lockout system, **Fig. 5,** which prevents the lock cylinder from rotating when the selector lever is out of Park or Neutral. When the selector lever is in Park or Neutral, the slots in the bowl plate and the finger on the actuator rod align allowing the finger to pass through the bowl plate in turn actuating the ignition switch, **Fig. 5.** If the selector lever is in any position other than Park or Neutral, the finger contacts the bowl plate when the lock cylinder is rotated, thereby preventing full travel of the lock cylinder.

1980–81 CAMARO

1. Disconnect wiring connector at switch terminals.
2. Unfasten and remove switch from mast jacket.
3. To install: position shift lever against "Park" gate on models with floor shift, or "Neutral" gate on models with column shift, by rotating lower lever counterclockwise as viewed from drivers seat.
4. Assemble switch to column by insert-

ing actuating tang in shifter tube slot.
5. Tighten screws, connect wiring connector and move selector lever out of "Park" on models with floor shift or "Neutral" on models with column shift to shear pin which is part of new switch.

1980–82 CORVETTE

1. Disconnect shift control lever arm from transmission control rod.
2. Remove shift control knob.
3. Remove trim plate.
4. Remove control assembly from seal and disconnect switch wiring.
5. Remove switch from control assembly.
6. To install, position gearshift in Drive position, align hole in contact support with hole in switch and insert a pin (3/32 inch) to hold support in place.
7. Place contact support drive slot over drive tang and tighten switch mounting screws.
8. Connect wiring harness to switch wiring.
9. Install trim plate control knob and connect shift lever arm to transmission control rod.

1982–86 CAMARO & 1984–86 CORVETTE

1. Remove floor console cover, then disconnect electrical connectors from switch.
2. Place shift lever in "Neutral" position of detent plate, then remove switch attaching screws and switch.
3. To install, ensure that the shift lever is in "Neutral", then position switch on shift lever making sure pin on shaft is in slot of switch.
4. Install attaching screws and torque to 16 inch lbs.
5. Move shift lever out of "Neutral" to shear pin which is part of new switch.
6. Reconnect electrical connectors to switch, then apply parking brake and start engine. Check backup lights and seat belt warning system for proper operation and ensure that engine will start only in "Park" or "Neutral".
7. Turn ignition off and install floor console.

Fig. 9   Column mounted dimmer switch installation

TURN SIGNAL SWITCH
REPLACE

1. Disconnect battery cable, then remove steering wheel and column to instrument panel trim cover.
2. On models with telescoping column, remove bumper spacer and snap ring retainer. On all other models, remove cover from lockplate.
3. Using a suitable tool, compress lock plate (horn contact carrier on tilt models) and remove snap ring ("C" ring on tilt models), **Fig. 6.**

NOTE: On 1980–82 Corvette models with tilt-telescopic column, place a 5/16 inch nut under each leg of puller.

4. Remove lock plate, cancelling cam, upper bearing preload spring, thrust washer and signal lever.
5. Remove turn signal lever or actuating arm screw, if equipped, or on models with column mounted wiper switch, pull lever straight out of detent. Depress hazard warning button, then unscrew button.
6. Pull connector from bracket and wrap upper part of connector with tape to prevent snagging the wires during removal. On Tilt models, position shifter housing in "Low" position. Remove harness cover.
7. Remove retaining screws and remove switch, **Figs. 7 and 8.**
8. Reverse procedure to install.

Fig. 10   Steering wheel and horn contact (Typical). Standard wheel

Fig. 11   Instrument cluster bezel removal (Typical). Malibu & Monte Carlo

COLUMN-MOUNTED DIMMER SWITCH
REPLACE

1. Disconnect battery ground cable.
2. Remove instrument panel lower trim and on models with A/C, remove A/C duct extension at column.
3. Disconnect shift indicator from column and remove toe-plate cover screws.
4. Remove two nuts from instrument panel support bracket studs and lower steering column, resting steering wheel on front seat.
5. Remove dimmer switch retaining screws and the switch. Tape actuator rod to column and separate switch from rod.
6. Reverse procedure to install. To adjust switch, depress dimmer switch slightly and install a 3/32 inch twist drill to lock the switch to the body, **Fig. 9.** Force switch upward to remove lash between switch and pivot. Torque switch retaining screw to 35 inch lbs. and remove tape from actuator rod. Remove twist drill and check for proper operation.

HORN SOUNDER & STEERING WHEEL
REPLACE

NOTE: Mark position of steering wheel in relation to shaft prior to removal to ensure correct installation.

CUSHIONED RIM WHEEL

1. Disconnect battery ground cable.
2. Pry off horn button cap.
3. Remove three spacer screws, spacer, plate and belleville spring.
4. Remove steering wheel nut, washer and snap ring.
5. Using a suitable puller, remove steering wheel.
6. Reverse procedure to install.

STANDARD WHEEL

1. Disconnect battery ground cable.
2. Remove attaching screws on underside of the steering wheel, **Fig. 10.**
3. Lift steering wheel shroud and pull horn wires from cancelling cam tower.
4. Remove steering wheel nut, washer and snap ring.
5. Using a suitable puller, remove steering wheel.
6. Reverse procedure to install.

1980–82 CORVETTE

1. Disconnect battery ground cable.
2. Remove horn button cap, 3 screws securing upper horn contact, and upper contact.
3. Remove shim, if used, then the screw securing the center star screw and the star screw and lever.
4. Remove snap ring and nut from shaft.
5. Using a suitable puller, remove steering wheel assembly.
6. To disassemble the steering wheel assembly, remove three screws securing wheel and separate, then remove four screws retaining extension to wheel and separate.
7. Reverse procedure to install.

1984–86 CORVETTE

1. Disconnect battery ground cable.
2. Pry up horn button cap, disconnect contact from steering wheel, and remove cap.
3. Remove screws securing center star screw, star screw, and adjusting lever.
4. Remove snap ring and nut from steering shaft.
5. Remove steering wheel using a suitable puller.
6. Reverse procedure to install.

INSTRUMENT CLUSTER
REPLACE

NOTE: On some 1980 models, a yellow flag with the word "emissions" will rotate into the odometer window at 30,000 mile intervals indicating either a catalyst or oxygen sensor change is required. After performing the required maintenance, the emissions flag can be reset after removing the instrument cluster lens. Using a pointed tool inserted at an angle to engage flag wheel detents, rotate flag wheel downward. When flag wheel is reset, the alignment mark will be in center of odometer window.

1980–81 MALIBU STANDARD CLUSTER

1. Disconnect battery ground cable.
2. Remove clock set stem knob, if equipped.
3. Remove instrument bezel retaining screws, **Fig. 11.**
4. Pull bezel from panel slightly and disconnect rear defogger switch, if equipped.
5. Remove bezel, **Fig. 11.**
6. Remove two screws at transmission selector indicator and lower indicator assembly to disconnect cable.
7. Remove three screws at windshield wiper/light switch mounting plate and pull assembly rearward for access to lower left cluster attaching bolt and nut.
8. Remove nuts attaching cluster to instrument panel.
9. Pull cluster rearward and disconnect the speedometer cable and all wiring and cables.
10. Remove cluster from vehicle, **Fig. 12.**
11. Reverse procedure to install.

Fig. 12 Instrument cluster removal (Typical). Malibu & Monte Carlo

Fig. 13 Instrument cluster, exploded view. Chevrolet Full Size

Fig. 14 Instrument cluster, exploded view. 1980-81 Camaro

Fig. 15 Instrument cluster, exploded view. 1982-86 Camaro exc. 1984-86 Berlinetta

1980-81 MALIBU OPTIONAL CLUSTER & 1980-86 MONTE CARLO & 1982-83 MALIBU

1. Disconnect battery ground cable.
2. Remove radio knobs and clock set stem knob.
3. Remove instrument bezel retaining screws, **Fig. 11.**
4. Pull bezel rearward slightly and disconnect the rear defogger switch and remote control mirror control, if equipped.
5. Remove bezel, **Fig. 11.**
6. Remove speedometer retaining screws, pull speedometer from cluster slightly, disconnect speedometer cable and remove speedometer.
7. Remove fuel gauge or tachometer retaining screws, disconnect electrical connectors and remove fuel gauge or tachometer.
8. Remove clock or voltmeter retaining screws, disconnect electrical connectors and remove clock or voltmeter.
9. Disconnect transmission shift indicator cable from steering column.
10. Disconnect all wiring connectors and remove cluster case, **Fig. 12.**
11. Reverse procedure to install.

CHEVROLET

1. Disconnect battery ground cable.
2. Remove four steering column lower cover screws and the cover.
3. If equipped with automatic transmission, disconnect shift indicator cable from steering column.
4. Remove two steering column to instrument panel screws and lower steering column.

CAUTION: Use extreme care when lowering steering to prevent damage to column assembly.

5. Remove six screws and the three snap-in fasteners from perimeter of instrument cluster lens, **Fig. 13.**
6. Remove two screws from upper surface of grey sheet metal trim plate.
7. Remove two stud nuts from lower corner of cluster.
8. Disconnect speedometer cable and

pull cluster from instrument panel.
9. Disconnect electrical connectors from cluster and remove from vehicle.
10. Reverse procedure to install.

CAMARO

1980-81
1. Disconnect battery ground cable.
2. Remove 6 screws securing trim cover beneath steering column. Two of these screws are located above the ash tray.
3. Remove headlamp switch retaining nut.
4. From behind panel, disconnect cigar lighter and unscrew retainer. Note grounding ring.
5. From under lower edge of cluster, remove screw on either side of column, **Fig. 14.**
6. Remove 4 screws visible on front of carrier.
7. Remove screw retaining ground wire for wiper switch. Screw is fastened under top left corner of switch.
8. Carefully tilt carrier out of access to the connectors on headlamp and wiper switches.
9. Remove lens screws then cluster screws.
10. Disconnect shift indicator from steering column.
11. Disconnect speedometer cable and tilt cluster forward and remove remaining

Fig. 16   Instrument cluster removal. 1984–86 Berlinetta

connectors.
12. Lift cluster out.
13. Reverse procedure to install.

1982–86 Exc. 1984–86 Berlinetta

1. Disconnect battery ground cable.
2. Remove instrument cluster bezel, **Fig. 15.**
3. Remove 6 cluster retaining screws, then pull cluster back and disconnect speedometer cable and electrical connectors.
4. Reverse procedure to install.

1984–86 BERLINETTA

1. Disconnect battery ground cable.
2. Remove close out panel, 8 screws securing steering column cover and the cover, **Fig. 16.**
3. Remove right control pod as outlined in "Wiper Switch, Replace," and left pod as outlined in "Headlamp Switch, Replace."
4. Remove 3 cluster bezel retaining screws and the bezel; 5 cluster lens retaining screws and the lens.
5. Remove nuts securing steering column bracket and lower steering column.
6. Pull cluster away from carrier, disconnect electrical connectors and remove cluster.
7. Reverse procedure to install.

CORVETTE

1980–82

Left Hand Side

1. Disconnect battery ground cable.
2. Remove left air distribution duct.
3. Remove lens to bezel attaching screws and the lens.
4. Remove cluster to instrument panel attaching screws.
5. Pull cluster rearward slightly, then disconnect speedometer cable and electrical connectors.
6. Remove cluster from vehicle.
7. Reverse procedure to install.

Center Cluster

1. Disconnect battery ground cable.
2. Remove console tunnel side panels.

Fig. 17   Center cluster bezel removal. 1980–82 Corvette

3. Remove radio knobs.
4. Remove two screws securing console trim plate to instrument cluster, **Fig. 17.**
5. Remove rear window defogger switch, if equipped, from console trim plate.
6. Remove five screws from upper perimeter of instrument cluster.
7. Pull instrument cluster outward slightly and disconnect electrical connectors.
8. Remove cluster from vehicle.
9. Reverse procedure to install.

CORVETTE

1984–86

1. Disconnect battery ground cable.
2. Remove left hush panel, lower instrument panel pad, and steering column cover.
3. Remove light switch knob and shaft, and bezel nut securing switch
4. Remove nuts securing steering column to instrument panel brace and lower column.
5. Remove cluster bezel retaining screws and bezel.
6. Remove cluster retaining screws and pull cluster away from dash.
7. Release metal retainers securing electrical connectors, disconnect electrical connectors from cluster, and remove cluster assembly.

FRONT WIPER MOTOR
REPLACE

EXC. CORVETTE

1. Raise hood and remove cowl screen or grille.
2. Disconnect wiring and washer hoses.
3. Reaching through cowl opening, loosen transmission drive link attaching nuts to motor crankarm.
4. Disconnect drive link from motor crankarm.
5. Remove motor attaching screws.
6. Remove motor while guiding crankarm through hole.
7. Reverse procedure to install.

CORVETTE

1980–82

1. Make sure wiper motor is in "Park" position.
2. Disconnect washer hoses and electrical connectors from assembly.
3. Remove the air intake screen.
4. Remove the nut which retains the crank arm to the motor.
5. Remove the ignition shield and distributor cap to gain access to the motor retaining screws or nuts.

NOTE: Remove left bank spark plug wires from the cap and mark both cap and wires for aid in reinstallation.

6. Remove three motor retaining screws or nuts and remove motor.

CAUTION: Wiper motor must be in the "Park" position prior to installation on the cowl. Do not install a motor that was dropped or hung by the drive link.

1984–86

1. Open hood, then remove wiper arms and air inlet screen.
2. Turn ignition on and operate motor.

Stop motor with crank arm pointing to a position between 4 and 5 o'clock (viewed from passenger compartment) by turning ignition off.
3. Disconnect battery ground cable.
4. Disconnect upper electrical connector from wiper motor.
5. Remove motor retaining bolts, and remove motor after disconnecting lower electrical connector and linkage.
6. Reverse procedure to install.

REAR WIPER MOTOR
REPLACE

1982–86 CAMARO

1. Remove wiper arm using tool No. J-8966 or equivalent.
2. Remove nut and spacer from wiper motor shaft, then raise lid and remove lift window trim panel.
3. Disconnect wire connectors from motor, then remove rivets securing motor support to trim panel and remove assembly from vehicle.
4. Remove motor attaching screws and motor.
5. Reverse procedure to install.

FRONT WIPER TRANSMISSION
REPLACE

1980 w/RECTANGULAR MOTOR

1. Remove wiper arms and blades.
2. Raise hood and remove cowl vent screen or grille.
3. Disconnect wiring from motor.
4. Loosen, but do not remove, transmission drive link to motor crankarm attaching nuts and disconnect drive link from crankarm.
5. Remove right and left transmission to body attaching screws and guide transmission and linkage through cowl opening.

NOTE: When installing, motor must be in "Park" position.

6. Reverse procedure to install.

1980–83 w/ROUND MOTOR EXC. CORVETTE & 1984–86 CAMARO

1. Ensure that motor is in park position.
2. Raise hood and remove wiper arm assemblies.
3. Remove cowl vent screen.
4. Loosen nuts securing pivot at motor crankarm, then disconnect transmission rod from crankarm.
5. Remove retaining nuts or screws securing transmission to body, then withdraw transmission assembly through cowl opening.
6. Reverse procedure to install.

1980–82 CORVETTE

1. Make sure motor is in "Park" position.
2. Disconnect battery ground cable.
3. Open hood and remove chamber screen.
4. Loosen nuts retaining ball sockets to crankarm and detach drive rod from crankarm.
5. Remove transmission nuts, then lift rod assemblies from chamber.
6. Remove transmission linkage from chamber.
7. Reverse procedure to install.

1984–86 CHEVROLET & MONTE CARLO

1. Raise hood and remove wiper arm assemblies.
2. Remove lower windshield reveal molding and cowl vent screen.
3. Place suitable lever between drive link and motor crankarm, then pry drive link from crankarm.
4. Remove screws securing transmission pivot retainers to body, then withdraw transmission assembly through plenum opening.
5. Reverse procedure to install.

REAR WIPER TRANSMISSION
REPLACE

1982–86 CAMARO

1. Remove three mounting grommets from transmission housing cover and cover.
2. Remove drive link retainer, then disengage drive link from cam drive pin and position so that cam retainer is accessible.

NOTE: When reassembling drive link to cam, a new retainer must be used.

3. Remove cam retainer and washer, then cam from shaft.

NOTE: During assembly, if cam does not seat fully when pushed onto drive shaft, rotate cam 180 degrees.

4. Drill out three rivets attaching housing to wiper gearbox, and remove transmission.
5. Reverse procedure to install.

NOTE: A service kit is available for installation of the transmission. The kit includes screw, nuts and washers to replace the rivets.

WINDSHIELD WIPER SWITCH
REPLACE

CORVETTE

1980–82
1. Disconnect battery ground cable.
2. Remove left air distribution duct.
3. Remove instrument cluster attaching screws and pull cluster rearward.
4. Disconnect speedometer cable and all electrical connectors, then remove cluster.
5. Remove two instrument panel to left door pillar attaching screws and pull left side of instrument panel rearward for access.
6. Remove wiper switch to mounting plate screws, disconnect electrical connector and remove switch.
7. Reverse procedure to install.

1984–86
1. Disconnect battery ground cable.
2. Remove 2 screws securing left armrest, push inward to release armrest from door trim and remove armrest.
3. Remove screws securing accessory trim plate to door panel, including screw behind handle, and remove lock button.
4. Pull accessory plate away from door panel and disconnect electrical connectors to panel switches.
5. Remove wiper switch from trim plate.
6. Reverse procedure to install.

1980–82 MALIBU & MONTE CARLO

1. Disconnect battery ground cable.
2. Remove instrument panel bezel.
3. Remove screws securing wiper switch mounting plate to cluster and pull assembly rearward.
4. Disconnect electrical connector and remove wiper switch.
5. Reverse procedure to install.

1980–83 CHEVROLET

1. Disconnect battery ground cable.
2. Remove screws securing control shroud on instrument panel. (One screw is hidden above headlight switch shaft and one is hidden above cigarette lighter knob.)
3. Lift off shroud and remove remaining screws.
4. Unplug wiper switch and remove.
5. Reverse procedure to install.

1980–81 CAMARO

1. Disconnect battery ground cable.
2. Remove trim plate and A/C outlet from below steering column if so equipped.
3. Remove light switch.
4. Remove 6 screws securing instrument carrier. Two of these are behind the cluster on either side of steering column.

NOTE: Cigar lighter grounding ring may

Fig. 18 Column mounted wiper switch removal. 1982–86 w/standard column

Fig. 19 Column mounted wiper switch removal. 1982–86 w/tilt column

Fig. 20 Wiper switch pivot removal. Models w/column mounted switch

Fig. 21 Right control pod removal. 1984–86 Berlinetta

have to be removed with lighter housing to gain access to left side of carrier.

5. Disconnect wiper switch wiring.
6. Tilting carrier forward, reach behind and remove 3 switch retaining screws and lift out switch.
7. Reverse procedure to install.

1982–86 CAMARO EXC. 1984–86 BERLINETTA, 1983 MALIBU, 1983–86 MONTE CARLO & 1984–86 CHEVROLET

1. Disconnect battery ground cable and remove turn signal switch as outlined.
2. Remove ignition lock, ignition switch and dimmer switch as outlined.
3. Remove ignition lock housing retaining screws and housing, **Figs. 18 and 19.**
4. Remove pivot bolt and wiper switch from lock housing, **Fig. 20.**
5. Reverse procedure to install.

1984–86 BERLINETTA

1. Disconnect battery ground cable.
2. Remove retaining screw from bottom front of right control pod housing, then release retaining tab.
3. Disconnect electrical connector, then slide right pod assembly from track, **Fig. 21.**
4. Reverse procedure to install.

RADIO
REPLACE

NOTE: When installing radio, be sure to adjust antenna trimmer for peak reception.

Also, be sure to connect speaker before applying power to radio.

MALIBU & MONTE CARLO

1. Disconnect battery ground cable.
2. Remove control knobs from control shafts.
3. Remove trim plate attaching screws and trim plate.
4. Disconnect antenna lead and wire connector from radio.
5. Remove stud nut at right side of bracket attachment.
6. Remove control shaft nuts and washers.
7. Remove instrument panel bracket screws and bracket.
8. Remove radio through opening in instrument panel.
9. Reverse procedure to install.

CHEVROLET
1980–84

1. Disconnect battery ground cable.
2. Remove control knobs from control shafts.
3. Remove three radio trim plate attaching screws.
4. Remove two screws and bottom nut attaching radio bracket to instrument panel.
5. Disconnect antenna lead and wire connector from radio.
6. Remove radio with mounting bracket attached from instrument panel.
7. Remove bracket from radio.
8. Reverse procedure to install.

1985–86

1. Disconnect battery ground cable.
2. Remove glove box to provide access to temperature control cable.

3. Disconnect temperature cable from temperature door.
4. Remove radio/heater A/C control panel fasteners.
5. Pull control panel out of dash and disconnect vacuum and electrical connectors.
6. Remove A/C control trimplate with knobs, then the radio from bracket.
7. Reverse procedure to install.

CORVETTE
1980–82

1. Disconnect battery ground cable.
2. Remove control knobs from control shafts.
3. Remove instrument cluster as described under Instrument Cluster, Replace.
4. Remove screw attaching radio mounting bracket to reinforcement on floor pan.
5. Pull radio outward and disconnect antenna lead and wire connector from rear of radio.
6. Remove mounting bracket from radio.
7. Reverse procedure to install.

1984–86

1. Disconnect battery ground cable and remove instrument cluster as outlined.
2. Remove accessory trim plate retaining screws and trim plate.
3. Remove screws securing radio and bracket, and pull radio away from dash.
4. Disconnect electrical connectors and antenna lead, then remove radio.
5. Reverse procedure to install, ensuring A/C center outlet seal is properly positioned.

Fig. 22 Blower motor & heater core. Malibu & Monte Carlo less A/C

Legend text (diagram):
HEATER MODULE
R&R GLOVE BOX
R&R HEATER AIR DISTRIBUTOR OUTLET & UPPER LEVEL VENT DUCT
R&R DEFROSTER OUTLET ATTACH. SCREW
D&C ELECTRICAL HARNESS AT MODULE
D&C PASS. COMPT. CABLES & GROUND AT MODULE
D&C BLOWER MOTOR & RESISTOR CONNECTORS
D-R RADIATOR COOLANT
R&R R.H. W/SHLD. WIPER ARM
R&R MODULE LEAF SCREEN & SEAL
D&C HEATER HOSES
R&R MODULE TO COWL SCREWS
TRANSFER PARTS
APPLY NEW STRIP-CAULK TYPE SEALING MATERIAL

SEAL PULL OFF

MODULE LEAF SCREEN R&R SCREWS

BLOWER MOTOR
D&C ELECTRICAL CONNECTORS
R&R MOTOR SCREWS

HEATER CORE
R&R HEATER HOSES
D&C ELECTRICAL CONNECTORS
R&R FRONT MODULE COVER SCREWS
R&R CORE

APPLY TO TOP AND SIDES ONLY
EXTEND COVERAGE BELOW LOWER SCREW ON BOTH VERTICAL FLANGES.
*SCREW ATTACHING SEQUENCE AS FOLLOWS: ①,②, THEN CLOCKWISE AROUND MODULE.

SECTION SHOWING SCREEN IN RELATION TO REVEAL MOULDING

CAMARO

1980-81
1. Disconnect battery ground cable.
2. Pull off radio control knobs and bezels.
3. Remove control shaft nuts and washers.
4. Remove screws or nuts from radio brackets.
5. Push radio forward until shafts clear instrument panel and lower unit enough to remove electrical connections.
6. Disconnect antenna, speaker and power leads and remove radio.
7. Reverse procedure to install.

1982-86 Exc. 1984-86 Berlinetta
1. Disconnect battery ground cable.
2. Remove three console bezel and four radio to console attaching screws.
3. Pull radio outward and disconnect electrical connector, then remove radio.
4. Reverse procedure to install.

1984-86 Berlinetta
1. Disconnect battery ground cable.
2. Remove 4 retaining screws from console trim plate, raise shift lever trim panel and position aside, leaving electrical connectors connected.
3. Remove 4 screws securing radio control head to bracket.
4. Remove control head, pulling back on spring pawl while lifting control, then disconnect electrical connector to control.
5. Remove screws securing radio receiver.
6. Disconnect antenna and electrical connectors, then remove receiver.
7. Reverse procedure to install.

BLOWER MOTOR
REPLACE

1980-83 MALIBU, 1980-86 MONTE CARLO & CHEVROLET & 1980-81 CAMARO
1. Disconnect battery ground cable.
2. Disconnect blower motor lead wire. On models with A/C, disconnect cooling tube.
3. Remove blower motor to case attaching screws, then remove blower motor, **Figs. 22 through 26.**
4. Reverse procedure to install.

1982-86 CAMARO
1. Disconnect battery ground cable.
2. Disconnect blower motor and resistor wires.
3. Disconnect cooling tube, if equipped.
4. Remove blower motor retaining screws and motor/cage assembly from case.
5. While holding blower motor cage, remove cage retaining screw and slide cage from motor shaft.
6. Reverse procedure to install.

CORVETTE

1980-82
1. Disconnect battery ground cable.
2. Remove A/C compressor mounting bolts and position compressor aside with refrigerant lines attached.
3. Remove air cleaner from front and right side inlet ducts, then position air cleaner out of way.
4. Remove engine coolant recovery bottle.

5. Disconnect hose and electrical connections from blower motor.
6. Remove blower motor mounting flange attaching screws, then remove blower with impeller from vehicle, **Fig. 26.**

1984-86
1. Disconnect battery ground cable.
2. Remove right front wheel housing rear panel, and push housing aside.
3. Remove motor cooling tube and screws securing relay, and set relay aside.
4. Remove motor retaining screws, motor and impeller.
5. Reverse procedure to install.

HEATER CORE
REPLACE

LESS AIR COND.

1982-86 Camaro
1. Disconnect battery ground cable and drain cooling system.
2. Remove right lower hush panel and instrument panel trim panel.
3. Remove ESC module, if equipped.
4. Remove lower right instrument panel carrier to cowl screw.
5. Remove heater case cover attaching screws and cover.

NOTE: To gain access to the upper left screw, position a long ⅜ inch socket extension through the opening exposed by removal of the trim panel. Carefully lift lower right corner of instrument panel to align socket extension.

6. Remove support plate and baffle screws, then heater core, support plate and baffle from case.

Malibu & Monte Carlo
1. Disconnect battery ground cable and drain cooling system.
2. Disconnect heater hoses from heater core. Plug core outlets to prevent coolant spillage.
3. Disconnect wire connectors, then remove front module cover attaching screws and cover.
4. Remove heater core from module, **Fig. 22.**
5. Reverse procedure to install.

Chevrolet
1. Disconnect battery ground cable and drain cooling system.
2. Disconnect heater hoses from heater core. Plug core outlets to prevent coolant spillage.
3. Remove attaching screws from around perimeter of heater core cover on engine side of dash panel.
4. Pull heater core cover from dash panel mounting.
5. Remove heater core from module assembly, **Fig. 24.**
6. Reverse procedure to install.

1980-81 Camaro & 1980-82 Corvette
1. Disconnect battery ground cable.
2. Drain radiator, disconnect heater hos-

Fig. 23 Blower motor & heater core. Malibu & Monte Carlo with A/C

es at core and plug openings to prevent spillage of water.

3. Remove nuts from air distributor duct studs on engine side of firewall, **Figs. 27 and 28.**
4. On Camaro, remove glove box, radio, and defroster duct to distributor duct screw.
5. On Corvette, remove right instrument panel pad, right hand dash braces, center dash console duct and floor outlet duct, radio and center dash console.
6. On all models, pull distributor duct from firewall being careful not to bend cable.
7. On Camaro, disconnect cable and resistor wires and remove distributor and core.
8. On all other models, remove core assembly from duct.
9. Reverse procedure to install.

WITH AIR COND.

CAMARO

1980—81

1. Disconnect battery ground cable.

2. Drain radiator and disconnect heater hoses from core. Plug openings to prevent spillage of coolant.
3. Remove nuts from distributor studs on engine side of firewall, **Fig. 27.**
4. Remove glove box and radio.
5. Remove defroster duct to distributor duct screw. With radio removed, the defroster duct can be pulled rearward to gain clearance for distributor duct removal.
6. Carefully pull distributor from firewall and disconnect wiring and cables. Remove duct and core from vehicle.
7. Reverse procedure to install.

1982—86

For removal procedure, refer to "Heater Core, Replace" less air conditioning.

MALIBU & MONTE CARLO

1. Disconnect battery ground cable and drain cooling system.
2. Disconnect heater hoses at heater core.
3. Remove retaining bracket and ground strap.
4. Remove module rubber seal and module screen, **Fig. 23.**

5. Remove right hand w/s wiper arm.
6. Remove high blower relay and thermostatic switch mounting screws.
7. Disconnect wire connector at top of module, then remove module top cover.
8. Remove heater core from module.
9. Reverse procedure to install.

CHEVROLET

1. Disconnect battery ground cable and drain cooling system.
2. Disconnect heater hoses at heater core. Cap core outlets to prevent coolant spillage.
3. Remove diagnosis connector to upper case attaching screws.
4. Disconnect wire connectors from blower motor, resistor, blower relay and thermostatic switch.
5. Remove wiring harness retainer from blower case shroud.
6. Remove module screen to cowl attaching screws and remove screen.
7. Remove upper case to lower case attaching screws.

NOTE: Two screws are located inside air

X APPLY TO TOP AND SIDES ONLY. EXTEND COVERAGE BELOW LOWER SCREW ON BOTH VERTICAL FLANGES.

Y SEALER MUST NOT CONTACT THE WATER DRAIN VALVE, EVAPORATOR DRAIN HOLE OR MODULE AIR INLET AREA.

Z ASSEMBLE UPPER OUTBOARD SCREW FIRST, UPPER INBOARD SCREW NEXT AND BALANCE OF SCREWS CLOCKWISE AROUND MODULE.

Fig. 24   Blower motor & heater core. Chevrolet Full Size less A/C

intake area at case separation point.

8. Disconnect wire connector from thermostatic switch, then remove screws attaching switch to evaporator case. Carefully remove insulation and loosen two clamps enough to pull formed end of switch capillary tube from under clamps attaching tube to evaporator inlet pipe for installation.
9. Remove evaporator inlet pipe support bracket to case attaching screws and remove bracket.
10. Remove heater-evaporator core case cover, using care not to damage sealer.
11. Remove heater core to case attaching screws at top of heater core, then remove heater core, **Fig. 25.**

NOTE: The heater core is held in position at bottom by a spring clip. Pull up firmly on heater core to disengage from clip. When installing, position core base in alignment with clip before lowering core into case. Upper retaining bracket will line up with hole at top of core when core is properly seated.

12. Reverse procedure to install.

CORVETTE

1980
1. Disconnect battery ground cable. Drain radiator and disconnect heater hoses from core. Plug openings to prevent spillage of coolant.

2. Remove nuts from engine side distributor duct, **Fig. 28.**
3. Remove right hand dash pad and center instrument cluster. Remove dash braces.
4. Disconnect right dash outlet duct from center duct. Remove screws attaching center duct to selector duct and remove center duct.
5. Remove screws attaching selector duct to firewall and pull selector rearward and to the right. Disconnect cables and wiring.
6. Remove selector duct from car. Remove temperature door camming plate from duct and remove core and housing.
7. Reverse procedure to install.

1981—82
1. Disconnect battery ground cable and drain radiator.
2. Disconnect heater hoses from core and plug hoses and core openings.
3. Remove heater case retaining nut from top of blower case.
4. Remove glove box.
5. Remove console side panels retaining screw and swing both sides out.
6. Remove center gauge cluster assembly and radio.
7. Remove right windshield pillar trim panel.
8. Remove right side dash panel retaining screws and pull panel rearward to release upper retaining clip.
9. Remove right side vent, main vent dis-

tribution, and lower heater deflector ducts.
10. Remove heater-defroster distribution duct assembly, then disconnect temperature cable and vacuum hose from heater housing.
11. Remove heater housing assembly from vehicle and heater core from housing.
12. Reverse procedure to install.

1984—86
1. Disconnect battery ground cable, place heater control in warm position, and drain cooling system.
2. Remove instrument cluster bezel and tilt wheel control lever.
3. Remove instrument panel upper trim pad retaining screws and trim pad, then remove A/C distribution ducts and disconnect flex hoses.
4. Remove right lower hush panel and side defroster flex hose.
5. Remove screws securing side defroster outlet to heater cover, and disconnect extension.
6. Remove temperature control cable and bracket from heater cover and disconnect heater door control shaft.
7. Remove electronic control module and disconnect electrical connectors to module.
8. Remove support brace between door pillar and instrument panel reinforcement brace.
9. Remove screws securing heater core cover, heater pipe bracket and water

EVAPORATOR CORE
D-E-C A/C SYSTEM
D&C MODULE RUBBER SEAL
R&R MODULE SCREEN
R&R R.H. W/SHLD. WIPER ARM
R&R DIAG. CONN., HI-BLOWER RELAY, THERM. SWITCH MNTG. SCREWS
D&C AIR ELECTRICAL CONNECTORS AT MODULE TOP
R&R MODULE TOP COVER
R&R ACCUMULATOR BRACKET SCREWS
D&C REFRIGERANT LINES AT ACCUMULATOR & LIQUID LINE
R&R CORE
APPLY NEW SEALING MATERIAL

SEAL
PULL OFF

MODULE LEAF SCREEN
R&R SCREWS

HEATER CORE
**D-R RADIATOR COOLANT
D&C HOSES AT CORE PIPES
R&R RET. BRACKET & GROUND STRAP
D&C MODULE RUBBER SEAL
R&R MODULE SCREEN
R&R R.H. W/SHIELD. WIPER ARM
R&R DIAG. CONN., HI-BLOWER RELAY, THERM. SWITCH MNTG. SCREWS
D&C ALL ELECTRICAL CONNECTORS AT MODULE TOP
R&R MODULE TOP COVER
R&R CORE
APPLY NEW SEALING MATERIAL

BLOWER MOTOR
D&C COOLING TUBE
D&C ELECTRICAL CONNECTORS
R&R MOTOR SCREWS
R & R IMPELLER

A/C MODULE
D&C NEG. BATTERY CABLE
D-E-C A/C SYSTEM
R&R HOOD
R&R R.H. W/SHLD. WIPER ARM
R&R MODULE LEAF, SCREEN, SEAL, TOP COVER/BLOWER MOTOR AS ASM.
R&R EVAPORATOR CORE
R&R HEATER CORE
R&R PASS. SIDE HUSH PANEL
R&R GLOVE BOX
D&C TEMP. CABLE AT MODULE
R&R A/C DUCTWORK & HEATER DISTRIBUTOR OUTLET
R&R A/C CONTROL (LEAVING HARNESSES, CABLES, ETC. ATTACHED TO MODULE)
D&C COMPRESSOR & PRESSURE CUT-OUT SWITCH WIRING
R&R VACUUM RESERVE TANK
R&R ACCUMULATOR BRACKET
R&R MODULE TO COWL SCREWS
TRANSFER PARTS
PPLY NEW STRIP – CAULK
PE SEALING MATERIAL

SUPPORT & BAFFLE ASM

SUPPORT & BAFFLE ASM

SUPPORT & BAFFLE ASM

VIEW A

VIEW B

B SERIES CONDENSER MOUNTING 231 (V-6)

Fig. 25 Blower motor & heater core. Chevrolet Full Size with A/C

SEALER

VIEW A

Fig. 26 Typical blower motor installation. 1980—81 Camaro & 1980—82 Corvette

Fig. 27 Heater core installation. 1980—81 Camaro

FWD

Fig. 28 Heater core installation. 1980—82 Corvette

control valve bracket.
10. Cut heater hoses at core pipes and remove heater core.

NOTE: Measure and install replacement heater hose links during reassembly.

11. Reverse procedure to install. Refill cooling system and check for leaks.

SPEED CONTROLS
1980—83 CRUISE MASTER
Servo Unit Adjustment

Adjust the bead chain cable or rod so that it is as tight as possible without holding the throttle open when the carburetor is set at its lowest idle throttle position. The cable is adjusted by turning the hex portion of servo. The bead chain or cable is adjusted so there is 1/16 inch of lost motion in servo cable. The rod is adjusted by turning link onto rod. With rod hooked through tab, on power unit, turn link onto rod until dimension in **Fig. 29** is obtained, then install link and retainer. This adjustment should be made with ignition off and fast idle cam in off position with throttle completely closed.

When connecting the bead chain or cable (engine stopped) manually set the fast idle cam at its lowest step and connect the chain so that it does not hold the idle screw off the cam. If the chain needs to be cut, cut it three beads beyond the bead that pulls the linkage.

Regulator Unit Adjustment

To remove any difference between engagement and cruising speed, one adjustment is possible. However, no adjustment should be made until the following items have been checked or serviced.
1. Bead chain or cable properly adjusted.
2. All hoses in good condition, properly attached, not leaking, pinched or cracked.

Fig. 29   Servo unit rod adjustment. 1980–83

Fig. 30   Typical release switch installation. 1980–83

3. Regulator air filter cleaned and properly oiled.
4. Electric and vacuum switches properly adjusted.

Engagement—Cruising Speed Zeroing

If the cruising speed is lower than the engagement speed, loosen the orifice tube locknut and turn the tube outward; if higher turn the tube inward. Each ¼ turn will alter the engagement-cruising speed difference one mph. Tighten locknut after adjustment and check the system operation at 50 mph.

Brake Release Switch

The electric brake switch is actuated when the brake pedal is depressed .38–.64 inch, **Fig. 30.** The vacuum release switch is actuated when brake pedal is moved 5/16 inch on all units.

1984–86

Cruise Set Speed Too High Or Low

1. Check vacuum hoses for restrictions, leaks and proper routing, and repair as needed.
2. Check servo linkage, and adjust or

repair as needed.
3. If all other components are satisfactory, replace electronic controller assembly.

Servo Adjustment

1. With servo cable installed on bracket, place second ball of cable chain on cable end.
2. With throttle completely closed (ignition and fast idle control off), adjust cable housing jam nuts until cable is tight, but not holding throttle open.
3. Tighten jam nuts and check system operation.

Gasoline Engine Section

Refer to Section 21 for service procedures on 4-151 engines. Refer to Section 9 for service procedures on V6-231 engines.

ENGINE MOUNTS
REPLACE

1982–86 V6-173

1. Disconnect battery ground cable.
2. Remove upper half of fan shroud.
3. Raise and support vehicle.
4. Remove engine mount through bolt, then raise front of engine to release weight from mount.
5. Remove mount to engine bolts and mount.

NOTE: Raise engine only enough to provide sufficient clearance for mount removal. Check for interference between rear of engine and cowl panel which could result in distributor damage.

6. Reverse procedure to install.

ALL V-8 EXC. 1984–86 CORVETTE, 1980–84 V6-229 & 1985–86 V6-262

1. Remove mount retaining bolt from below frame mounting bracket, **Figs. 1 and 2.**
2. Raise front of engine and remove mount to engine bolts and mount. On

Fig. 1   Engine mounts. V6-229, 262 & V8 engines exc. Corvette

models equipped with V6 engines, the right hand mount may be removed by loosening the through bolt.

NOTE: Raise engine only enough to provide sufficient clearance for mount remov-

al. Check for interference between rear of engine and cowl panel which could result in distributor damage.

3. Reverse procedure to install.

Fig. 2   Engine mounts. 1980–82 Corvette

1984–86 CORVETTE

1. Disconnect battery ground cable, then raise and support vehicle.
2. Support engine and remove mount through bolt, **Fig. 3.**
3. Disconnect AIR injection pipe at manifold, exhaust pipe and catalytic converter.
4. Raise engine sufficiently to provide clearance for mount bolt removal.
5. Remove bolts securing engine mount to block and the mount.
6. Position replacement mount on engine, lower engine into position and install retaining bolts.
7. Reverse procedure to install.

ENGINE
REPLACE

EXC. 1982–86 CAMARO & 1984–86 CORVETTE

1. Disconnect battery ground cable and remove air cleaner.
2. Mark position of hinges for reassembly, then remove hood.
3. Drain cooling system, remove radiator hoses, and disconnect heater hoses from engine.
4. On models with A/C, disconnect electrical connector from compressor clutch and ground wire from bracket, remove compressor and secure aside.
5. On V6-231 engines, remove fan blade, pulleys and shroud. On all other

engines, remove fan shroud and radiator.

NOTE: On models with automatic transmission, disconnect and plug cooler lines.

6. Remove power steering pump retaining bolts, if equipped, and secure pump aside.
7. Disconnect accelerator linkage at throttle lever and bracket. Disconnect vacuum hoses to body mounted accessories and fuel hoses at fuel pump, then plug fuel hoses.
8. Disconnect battery and chassis ground straps from engine.
9. Disconnect electrical connectors from alternator, distributor or remote mounted coil and all engine mounted switches and accessories.
10. Remove engine harness from retaining clips and secure aside.
11. Raise and support vehicle and drain crankcase.
12. Disconnect exhaust pipes and AIR pipe from manifolds, and remove front exhaust and cruise control brackets, if equipped.
13. Disconnect electrical connectors and battery cable from starter, or remove starter.
14. Remove flywheel shield and remove bolts securing torque converter to flex plate, if equipped.

NOTE: Mark position of converter in relation to flex plate for reassembly.

15. Remove motor mount through bolts and bolts securing bell housing to engine.
16. Lower vehicle and support transmission with suitable floor jack.
17. Attach suitable lifting equipment to engine lifting brackets, raise engine and transmission, and remove motor mount to engine brackets.
18. Separate engine and transmission while supporting transmission with jack.

NOTE: On automatic transmission models, ensure converter remains with transmission during engine removal and is properly seated prior to engine installation.

19. Lift and remove engine after disconnecting any remaining harness connectors.
20. Reverse procedure to install.

1982–86 CAMARO

1. Disconnect battery ground cable and remove air cleaner and fresh air hoses.
2. Disconnect electrical connectors from hood lamp or air door, if equipped, mark position of hood hinges for reassembly, and remove hood.
3. Drain cooling system, remove radiator hoses, and disconnect heater hoses from engine.
4. If equipped with A/C, disconnect electrical connector from compressor clutch and ground wire from bracket,

28-34 N•m (21-25 ft. lbs)

40-60 N•m (30-44 ft. lbs.)

Fig. 3   Engine mounts. 1984–86 Corvette

remove compressor and secure aside.

5. Disconnect and plug transmission cooler lines at radiator, if equipped, then remove fan blade, shroud and radiator.

NOTE: On 4-151 engines with manual transmission, only fan blade and upper shroud should be removed.

6. On V6 and V8 engines, remove power steering pump retaining bolts and secure pump aside. On 4-151 engines, disconnect and plug power steering hoses at pump.
7. Disconnect accelerator and cruise control linkage at throttle and brackets, then the vacuum hoses from all body mounted accessories, and secure cables and hoses.
8. Disconnect and plug fuel supply and return hoses.

NOTE: On models with EFI, relieve fuel system pressure before disconnecting hoses.

9. On V6 and V8 engines, proceed as follows:
   a. Remove distributor cap and lay wiring aside.
   b. Disconnect electrical connectors to alternator, distributor and all other engine mounted switches and accessories.
   c. Release engine harness from retaining clips and secure harness aside.
10. On 4-151 engines, proceed as follows:
   a. Disconnect engine electrical harness at bulkhead connector.
   b. From inside vehicle, lower right hush panel and remove ECM harness from main ECM connector.
   c. Remove splash shield from right inner fender and carefully pull ECM harness into engine compartment.
   d. Secure harnesses to engine.
11. Disconnect battery and chassis ground straps from engine, then raise and support vehicle.
12. Disconnect exhaust pipes from manifolds, and on 4-151 engines, remove exhaust pipe assembly.
13. On V6 and V8 engines, disconnect electrical connectors and battery cable from starter and remove wiring shields. On 4-151 engines, disconnect

13. electrical connectors from transmission and remove starter.
14. Remove flywheel shield and bolts securing converter to flex plate, if equipped.

NOTE: Mark position of converter in relation to flex plate for reassembly.

15. On models with manual transmission, remove clutch linkage.
16. Remove motor mount through bolts and bolts securing bell housing to engine.
17. Lower vehicle and support transmission with suitable floor jack.
18. Attach suitable lifting equipment to engine lifting brackets, remove bracket securing AIR injection pipe, then raise engine and transmission assembly.
19. Separate engine and transmission, and lift engine from vehicle after removing bracket from rear of left cylinder head (V6 and V8).

NOTE: On automatic transmission models, ensure that converter remains with transmission during engine removal, and that it is properly seated prior to engine installation.

20. Reverse procedure to install.

1984 CORVETTE

1. Disconnect battery ground cable, remove air cleaner and fresh air ducts, and drain cooling system.
2. Disconnect AIR pump inlet and outlet hoses at check valves.
3. Rotate belt tensioner counterclockwise to release tension, then remove drive belt.
4. Remove A/C compressor rear brackets and disconnect electrical connectors to compressor.
5. Remove pulley and air management valves from AIR pump, then remove pump.
6. Remove upper radiator hose and bolt securing power steering reservoir brace to thermostat housing.
7. Disconnect electrical connectors to alternator, then remove alternator and brace.
8. Remove bolt securing AIR pipe and steering reservoir bracket to intake manifold.
9. Disconnect power steering hoses at rack and plug open fittings, remove power steering pump lower bracket, then secure pump, reservoir and A/C harness toward front of vehicle.
10. Disconnect and plug fuel supply and return lines.

NOTE: Relieve fuel system pressure before disconnecting hoses.

11. Remove nuts securing A/C bracket to water pump and lower compressor mounting bolt, move bracket forward and remove upper mounting bolt, then secure compressor aside.
12. Remove fuel line, detent cable and idler pulley brackets, disconnect hoses from water pump and secure hoses and fuel lines aside.

13. Disconnect accelerator, cruise control and downshift cables from TBI and brackets.
14. Disconnect brake booster and PCV hoses from intake cover and vacuum hoses between engine and body mounted components.
15. Disconnect electrical connectors from TBI, front ground stud, coolant sensor and EGR solenoid.
16. Release clips securing wiring to valve cover, then move harness, AIR pipe and air management valves toward rear of engine.
17. Remove tach filter and ground wire from intake stud, and disconnect electrical connectors to distributor.
18. Remove distributor cap and spark plug wires after removing shields, then disconnect heater hose from manifold.
19. Mark and remove distributor, then remove oil pressure sensor and bolt securing ground strap to engine.
20. Remove crankshaft damper, raise and support vehicle.
21. Disconnect crossover pipe and AIR pipe from manifolds and converter, and remove crossover pipe brace.
22. Disconnect electrical connectors from block, coolant, oil, and oxygen sensors and starter, remove wiring shields and release harness clips, and secure harness aside.
23. Disconnect battery and chassis ground straps from above oil filter.
24. Remove flywheel shield and bolts securing converter to flex plate, if equipped.

NOTE: Mark position of converter in relation to flex plate for reassembly.

25. Remove right lower and upper bell housing bolts, then remove right center and left side bolts.
26. Support engine and remove bolts securing right and left motor mounts to block.
27. Lower vehicle and support transmission with suitable floor jack.
28. Attach suitable lifting equipment to engine lifting brackets, then separate engine and transmission.
29. Lift and remove engine assembly after disconnecting wiring from rear of left cylinder head.

NOTE: On automatic transmission models, ensure that converter remains with transmission during engine removal, and that it is properly seated prior to engine installation.

30. Reverse procedure to install.

1985-86 CORVETTE

1. Disconnect battery ground cable.
2. Drain cooling system, then remove air cleaner assembly.
3. Remove serpentine drive belt.
4. Remove rear A/C compressor brackets, then disconnect electrical connectors from compressor.
5. Relieve fuel system pressure, then disconnect and plug fuel supply and return lines.

6. Remove A/C compressor mounting bracket nuts and bolts.
7. Disconnect heater hoses, then the upper radiator hose from thermostat outlet.
8. Disconnect fuel line clip from fuel pump cover plate.
9. Unfasten A/C compressor from mounting bracket, then position compressor aside and remove bracket.
10. Disconnect fuel injection wiring harness from engine.
11. Disconnect cruise, detent and accelerator cables, then remove distributor shield and cap.
12. Disconnect electrical connector from distributor.
13. Disconnect detent cable bracket from intake manifold, then remove distributor.
14. Disconnect electrical connector from oil pressure sending unit, then remove the sending unit.
15. Disconnect all vacuum lines necessary for engine removal.
16. Disconnect power steering hoses from rack and pinion.
17. Remove crankshaft pulley.
18. Disconnect bulkhead connector and all other electrical connectors necessary for engine removal.
19. Disconnect air injection hose from converter check valve.
20. Position fuel lines aside as necessary.
21. Disconnect radiator hose from water pump and the upper radiator hose from power steering reservoir bracket.
22. Raise and support vehicle.
23. Disconnect air injection pipe from exhaust manifold, then remove converter air pipe.
24. Disconnect exhaust pipe hanger, then remove heat shields from exhaust pipe and converter.
25. Disconnect oxygen sensor electrical connector, then remove exhaust pipe.
26. Remove flywheel cover, then the torque converter attaching bolts.
27. Loosen motor mount thru bolts and remove motor mount-to-engine bolts.
28. REmove bell housing bolts, then lower vehicle.
29. Disconnect knock sensor electrical connector
30. Disconnect ground cable from block, then the positive battery cable from battery and harness.
31. Remove right rear intake manifold bolt and install suitable lifting hook.
32. Support transmission with suitable jack, then attach lifting equipment to engine and lift engine from vehicle after disconnect wires from rear of left cylinder head.
33. Reverse procedure to install.

CYLINDER HEAD
REPLACE

1982-86 V6-173

1. Remove intake manifold.
2. Raise and support vehicle.

Fig. 4 Cylinder head tightening sequence. V6-173

Fig. 6 Cylinder head tightening sequence. V8 engines

Fig. 7 Cylinder head tightening sequence. V6-229 & 262

Fig. 5 Intake manifold tightening sequence. V6-173

Fig. 8 Intake manifold tightening sequence. V6- 229, 262 & all V8 engines exc. 1982 & 1984—86 Corvette & 1985—86 V8-305 w/EFI

3. Disconnect exhaust pipe from manifold, then drain engine block.
4. If left hand cylinder head is to be removed, remove dipstick tube attachment.
5. Lower vehicle.
6. Loosen rocker arms until push rods can be removed.
7. If right hand cylinder head is to be removed, remove alternator bracket.
8. Remove cylinder head bolts and cylinder head.
9. Reverse procedure to install. Coat cylinder head bolts with sealer. Torque cylinder bolts in sequence shown in **Fig. 4** and intake manifold bolts in sequence shown in **Fig. 5**.

V6-229, 262 & ALL V8s EXC. 1984—86 CORVETTE & 1985—86 V8-305 w/EFI

1. Drain cooling system and engine block.
2. Remove intake and exhaust manifolds.
3. Remove alternator lower mounting bolt and position alternator aside.
4. If equipped with A/C, remove compressor and forward mounting bracket and position aside.
5. Remove rocker arm cover, rocker arms and push rods.

NOTE: Keep rocker arm, rocker arm balls and push rods in order so they can be installed in the same position.

6. On all 1981—86 models, except Corvette, remove diverter valve.
7. Remove cylinder head bolts and cylinder head.
8. Reverse procedure to install. Tighten cylinder head and intake manifold bolts in sequence shown in **Figs. 6 through 9**.

1984—86 CORVETTE

1. Disconnect battery ground cable and remove air cleaner.

TORQUE SEQUENCE

Fig. 9 Intake manifold installation. 1982 & 1984—86 Corvette

2. Drain cooling system and remove intake manifold as follows:
   a. Disconnect and plug fuel supply and return lines.

NOTE: Relieve fuel system pressure before disconnecting fuel hoses.

   b. Disconnect electrical connectors and vacuum hoses as needed, and secure wiring and hoses aside.
   c. Disconnect accelerator, cruise control and downshift cables from TBI unit and brackets.
   d. Rotate belt tensioner counterclockwise to release tension, and remove drive belt.

e. Remove AIR pump pulley, air management valve adapter and AIR pump.
f. Disconnect upper radiator and heater hoses, and remove bolts securing accessory mounting brackets to manifold.
g. Disconnect spark plug wires from cylinder head to be removed, remove distributor cap, and lay cap and wire assembly aside.
h. Mark position of distributor rotor and remove distributor.
i. Remove intake cover and TBI assembly.
j. Remove intake manifold bolts and manifold.

3. Disconnect AIR hose from exhaust manifold check valve, and if right cylinder head is to be removed, disconnect AIR hose from converter pipe.
4. If right cylinder head is to be removed, remove A/C compressor as follows:
   a. Remove lower compressor mounting bolt and nuts securing bracket to water pump.
   b. Move compressor assembly forward, remove upper mounting bolt and disconnect electrical connector, and secure compressor aside.
   c. Disconnect electrical connectors to high pressure switch, then remove high pressure switch and EGR solenoid.
   d. Disconnect EFI harness from rocker cover clamp.
5. If left cylinder head is to be removed, remove alternator and brace.
6. Remove valve cover retaining bolts, bend plug wire bracket away from cover for clearance, and remove cover.
7. Remove spark plugs and temperature sending unit from cylinder head.
8. Raise and support vehicle, and disconnect exhaust pipe from manifold. If right cylinder head is to be replaced, remove 2 rear manifold bolts and dipstick tube bolt.

Fig. 10   Rocker arm stud removal. Press type studs

9. Lower vehicle and remove exhaust manifold.
10. If left cylinder head is to be removed, remove AIR pump upper bracket and power steering reservoir, and set aside.
11. Remove spark plug wire bracket and bolts securing ground straps to cylinder head.
12. Loosen rocker arm nuts and remove pushrods.
13. Remove head bolts and cylinder head.
14. Reverse procedure to install, noting the following:
   a. Ensure gasket surfaces are clean and free of nicks or deep scratches, and bolt and block threads are clean.
   b. Coat both sides of head gasket with a thin even coat of sealer, and ensure gasket is properly positioned over dowel pins.
   c. Coat cylinder head bolt threads with GM sealer No. 1052080 or equivalent, then install all bolts finger tight.
   d. Torque cylinder head bolts to specifications in sequence shown in **Fig. 6.**
   e. Install intake manifold gaskets on head with blocked openings toward rear, bend gasket tabs flush with rear face of cylinder head, and apply a ³⁄₁₆ inch bead of RTV sealer on front and rear cylinder block ridges, **Fig. 9.**
   f. Install manifold, apply Locktite No. 1052624 or equivalent to manifold bolts, and torque bolts to 30 ft. lbs. in sequence shown in **Fig. 9.**

VALVES
ADJUST

NOTE: After the engine has been thoroughly warmed up the valves may be adjusted with the engine shut off as follows: With engine in position to fire No. 1 cylinder the following valves may be adjusted: V6-173, Exhaust 1-2-3, intake 1-5-6. V6-229 and 262, Exhaust 1-5-6, intake 1-2-3. V8's, Exhaust 1-3-4-8, intake 1-2-5-7. Then crank the engine one more complete revolution which will bring No. 4 cylinder on V6-173, V6-229 and 262, engine and No. 6

cylinder on V8 engines, to the firing position at which time the following valves may be adjusted: V6-173, Exhaust 4-5-6, intake 2-3-4. V6-229 and 262, Exhaust 2-3-4, intake 4-5-6. V8's, Exhaust 2-5-6-7, intake 3-4-6-8.

The following procedure, performed with the engine running should be done only in case readjustment is required.
1. After engine has been warmed up to operating temperature, remove valve cover and install a new valve cover gasket.
2. With engine running at idle speed, back off valve rocker arm nut until rocker arm starts to clatter.
3. Turn rocker arm nut down slowly until the clatter just stops. This is the zero lash position.
4. Turn nut down ¼ additional turn and pause 10 seconds until engine runs smoothly. Repeat additional ¼ turns, pausing 10 seconds each time, until nut has been turned down the number of turns listed in the Valve Specifications Chart from the zero lash position.

NOTE: This preload adjustment must be done slowly to allow the lifter to adjust itself to prevent the possibility of interference between the intake valve head and top of piston, which might result in internal damage and/or bent push rods. Noisy lifters should be replaced.

ROCKER ARM STUDS
REPLACE

Damaged rocker arm studs can be replaced using the following procedure. If studs are loose in cylinder head, .003 inch or .013 inch oversize studs may be installed on all engines with pressed-in type studs, after reaming holes with a proper size reamer. On engines with threaded rocker studs, looseness can be corrected by installing the proper size Heli-Coil insert, or by replacing cylinder head.
1. Remove the old stud by placing a suitable spacer, **Fig. 10,** over stud. Install nut and flat washer and remove stud by turning nut.
2. Ream hole for oversize stud.
3. Coat press-fit area of stud with rear axle lube. Then install new stud, **Fig. 11.** If tool shown is used, it should bottom on the head.

PUSH RODS

On engines that use push rods with a hardened insert at one end, the hardened end is identified by a color stripe and should always be installed toward the rocker arm during assembly.

VALVE GUIDES

On all engines valves operate in guide holes bored in the head. If clearance becomes excessive, use the next oversize

valve and ream the bore to fit. Valves with oversize stems are available in .003, .015 and .030 inch.

Fig. 11   Rocker arm stud installation. Press type studs

VALVE ARRANGEMENT
FRONT TO REAR

V6 engines . . . . E-I-I-E-I-E
Small V8 . . . . E-I-I-E-I-I-E

VALVE LIFT SPECS

Engine	Year	Intake	Exhaust
V6-173	1982–84	.3466	.3938
V6-173	1985–86	.3500	.3850
V6-229	1980–82	.5355	.5355
V6-229	1983–84	.3510	.3855
V6-262	1985–86	.3500	.3850
V8-267	1980–82	.3570	.3900
V8-305	1980–81	.3726	.4000
V8-305①	1982	.3726	.4000
V8-305②③	1982	.3570	.3900
V8-305④	1982	.3900	.4095
V8-305③	1983–84	.3510	.3855
V8-305④	1983–84	.3855	.4035
V8-305③	1985–86	.3510	.3855
V8-305③⑨	1985–86	.4035	.4140
V8-350⑤	1980–82	.3900	.4100
V8-350⑥	1980–81	.4500	.4600
V8-350⑦	1982 & 84	.4100	.4230
V8-350⑧	1983–84	.3855	.4035
V8-350⑦	1985–86	.4040	.4150

① —Exc. Camaro.
② —Camaro.
③ —Exc. EFI.
④ —EFI.
⑤ —Exc. Corvette high performance.
⑥ —Corvette high performance.
⑦ —Corvette.
⑧ —Exc. Corvette.
⑨ —High performance VIN code G.

Fig. 12 Hydraulic lifter exploded view

Fig. 13 Timing gear locating marks. V6 & V8 engines

Fig. 14 Piston & rod assembly. V8 engines exc. V8-350 high performance

VALVE TIMING

INTAKE OPENS BEFORE TDC

Engine	Year	Degrees
4-151⑥	1982	33
V6-173	1982	25
V6-229	1980–82	42
V6-231①	1980–82	16
V6-262④⑤	1982	16
V8-267	1981–82	44
V8-267	1980	28
V8-305⑦	1982	38
V8-305	1981–82	44
V8-305	1980	28
V8-350	1981	38
V8-350②	1980	28
V8-350③	1980	52
	1982	32
V8-350④⑤	1980–82	16

①—Refer to Buick Chapter for service procedures on this engine.
②—Except Corvette high performance engine.
③—Corvette high performance engine.
④—Diesel engine.
⑤—Refer to Oldsmobile Chapter for service procedures on this engine.
⑥—Refer to Pontiac Chapter for service procedures on this engine.
⑦—Fuel injected engine.

HYDRAULIC LIFTERS
REPLACE

Valve lifters can be lifted from their bores after removing rocker arms and push rods. On V6 and V8 engines, intake manifold must be removed, and on L-4 and L-6 engines, engine side covers must be removed in order to gain access to lifers. Adjustable pliers with protected jaws may be used to remove lifters which are stuck due to carbon or varnish deposits. Fig. 12 illustrates the type of valve lifter used.

TIMING CASE COVER
REPLACE

NOTE: On all engines the cover oil seal may be replaced without taking off the timing gear cover. After removing the vibration damper, pry out the old seal with a screw-driver. Install the new seal with the lip or open end toward inside of cover and drive it into position.

V6-173

1. Remove water pump, then, on vehicles equipped with A/C, remove compressor and mounting bracket and position aside.
2. Remove vibration damper, then disconnect lower radiator hose from cover and heater hose from water pump.
3. Remove cover retaining bolts and cover.
4. Thoroughly clean sealing surfaces of front cover and engine block, then apply a continuous bead of anerobic sealant #1052357 or equivalent to front cover sealing surface.
5. Install front cover and water pump on engine, then install retaining bolts and nut and torque to specifications.

NOTE: Final torquing of bolts must be completed within five minutes of installing the cover.

6. Reconnect hoses and install vibration damper.
7. Install A/C compressor and mounting bracket.
8. Service cooling system as required.

V6 & V8 ENGINES EXC. V6-173

1. Remove vibration damper and water pump.
2. Remove cover retaining screws and cover.
3. Clean gasket surface of block and timing case cover.
4. Remove any excess oil pan gasket material that may be protruding at the oil pan to engine block junction.
5. Apply a thin bead of RTV #1052366 sealer or equivalent to the joint formed at oil pan and block.
6. Coat new gasket with sealer and position it on cover, then install cover to oil pan seal on cover and coat bottom of seal with engine oil.
7. Position cover on engine and loosely install the upper bolts.

8. Tighten screws alternately and evenly while pressing downward on cover so that dowels are aligned with holes in cover. Do not force cover over dowels as cover can be distorted.
9. Install remaining cover screws, vibration damper and water pump.

TIMING CHAIN
REPLACE

V6 & V8 ENGINES

1. Remove timing chain cover as outlined previously.
2. Remove crankshaft oil slinger.
3. Crank engine until timing marks on sprockets are in alignment, **Fig. 13.**
4. Remove three camshaft-to-sprocket bolts.
5. Remove camshaft sprocket and timing chain together. Sprocket is a light press fit on camshaft for approximately ⅛ inch. If sprocket does not come off easily, a light blow with a plastic hammer on the lower edge of the sprocket should dislodge it.
6. If crankshaft sprocket is to be replaced, remove it with a suitable gear puller. Install new sprocket, aligning key and keyway.
7. Install chain on camshaft sprocket. Hold sprocket vertical with chain hanging below and shift around to align the timing marks on sprockets.
8. Align dowel in camshaft with dowel hole in sprocket and install sprocket on camshaft. Do not attempt to drive sprocket on camshaft as welch plug at rear of engine can be dislodged.
9. Draw sprocket onto camshaft, using the three mounting bolts. Tighten to 20 ft. lb. torque.
10. Lubricate timing chain and install cover.

Fig. 15   Piston & rod assembly. V8-350 high performance

Fig. 16   Piston & rod assembly. V6-229 & 262

Fig. 17   Piston & rod assembly. V6-173

CAMSHAFT
REPLACE

1. Remove valve lifters and engine front cover.
2. Remove grille, radiator and condenser.
3. On all models, remove fuel pump and the push rod, if equipped.
4. Remove timing chain as outlined previously.
5. On all except V6-173, install two 5/16–18×4 bolts in camshaft bolt holes, then remove camshaft.
6. Reverse procedure to install.

PISTONS & RODS
ASSEMBLE

Assemble pistons to connecting rods as shown in **Figs. 14 through 17.**

Upon installation, measure the connecting rod side clearance using a suitable feeler gauge. Clearance should be as follows:

Engine	Year	Clearance
4-151	1982–86	.006–.022
V6-173	1982–86	.006–.017
V6-229	1980–84	.006–.014
V6-231	1980–82	.006–.027
V6-231	1983–84	.005–.015
V6-262①	1982–83	.0062–.021
V6-262	1985–86	.006–.014
V8-267	1980–82	.006–.016
V8-305	1980–86	.006–.014
V8-350②	1980–84	.006–.014
V8-350③	1980–82 & 1984–86	.008–.014
V8-350①	1980–85	.006–.020

①—Diesel.
②—Exc. Corvette & Diesel.
③—Corvette.

Fig. 18   Rear main seal installation tool

PISTONS, PINS & RINGS

Pistons are available in standard and oversizes of .010 and .030 inch. Piston rings are available in standard and oversizes of .030 inch.

MAIN & ROD BEARINGS

Connecting rod bearings are available in standard and undersizes of .001, .002, .010 and .020 inch.

Main bearings are available in standard and undersizes of .001, .002, .009, .010 and .020 inch.

CRANKSHAFT REAR OIL SEAL
REPLACE

EXC. V6-173

NOTE: These engines are equipped with helix type rear seal. A seal starting tool, **Fig. 18,** must be used to prevent the upper seal half from coming into contact with the sharp edge of the block.

When necessary to correct an oil leak due to a defective seal, always replace the upper and lower seal halves as a unit. When installing either half, lubricate the lip portion only with engine oil, keeping oil off the parting line surface as this is treated with glue. Always clean crankshaft surface before installing a new seal.

1. To replace the lower seal, remove seal from groove in bearing cap, using a small screwdriver to pry it out.
2. Insert new seal and roll it in place with finger and thumb.
3. To replace the upper seal (with engine in car) use a small hammer and tap a brass pin punch on one end of the seal until it protrudes far enough to be removed with pliers.
4. Position tip of tool, **Fig. 18,** between crankshaft and seal seat in cylinder block.
5. Position seal between crankshaft and tip of tool with seal bead contacting tip of tool. Ensure oil seal lip is facing toward front of engine.
6. Roll seal around crankshaft, using tool as a "Shoehorn" to protect seal bead from sharp corner of seal seat surface in cylinder block.

NOTE: Tool must remain in position until seal is properly seated with both ends flush with block.

7. Remove tool, using care not to dislodge seal.
8. Install new seal into bearing cap with tool as outlined previously.
9. Install bearing cap with sealant applied to the cap to case interface, **Fig. 19.** Do not apply sealant to seal ends. Torque rear main bearing cap bolts to specifications as listed in the "Engine Tightening Specification Chart".

V6-173

SERVICE NOTE: When replacement of

COAT AREA INDICATED WITH #1052357 SEALER OR EQUIVALENT.

SEALER

Fig. 19   Rear main bearing cap sealing areas

the rear main seal is necessary, the rope type seal used during engine assembly should be replaced with rubber split seal No. 14069889 or equivalent using the following procedure. Disregard instructions furnished with the replacement seal that refer to Cavalier models.

1. Remove oil pan and oil pump.
2. Remove rear main bearing cap.
3. Remove upper and lower rope seals, taking care not to damage crankshaft, then clean seal remnants and oil from seal channels.

NOTE: It may be necessary to loosen No. 2 and 3 bearing cap bolts to allow removal of the rope type seal and installation of the upper split seal.

4. Apply a thin coating of gasket sealing compound 1050026 or equivalent to outer circumference of replacement seal, **Fig. 20**, keeping sealer off seal lips.
5. Use a piece of shim stock to guide seal into block channel and roll seal into block by turning crankshaft.

NOTE: Ensure that large seal lip toward front of engine and that smaller dust lip faces the flywheel.

6. Apply sealer to lower half of seal as in step 4, then install seal into bearing cap.
7. Apply a thin bead of anaerobic sealant to bearing cap surface as shown in **Fig. 19.** Keep sealant off ends of seal, main bearing, and out of drain slot.
8. Apply a thin film of motor oil to seal lip. Install bearing cap and torque cap bolts to specifications.

NOTE: If other main bearing cap bolts were loosened, retorque as needed.

9. Reinstall oil pump and pan as outlined.
10. Fill crankcase, start engine and check for leaks.

OIL PAN
REPLACE

1982–86 CAMARO V6-173 & V8-305

1. Disconnect battery ground cable, then remove fan shroud.
2. Raise and support vehicle, then drain crankcase.
3. Remove A.I.R. pipe and hanger bolts from catalytic converter.
4. Remove starter motor attaching bolts and position starter motor aside.
5. Remove engine mount through bolts, then raise engine.
6. Remove oil pan attaching bolts and oil pan.

NOTE: If oil pan removal is hampered by the forward crankshaft throw and/or counterweight extending downward, turn crankshaft as needed to put throw in a horizontal position.

7. Reverse procedure to install, using a new gasket and seals, if equipped. If RTV sealer is used to seal pan, apply a ⅛ inch wide bead of sealant 1052366 or equivalent to pan sealing flange.

NOTE: If M6 x 1.0 bolts are used, torque to 8 ft. lbs. If M8 x 1.25 bolts are used, torque to 18 ft. lbs.

1980–84 V6-229

1. Disconnect battery ground cable, then remove upper half of fan shroud.
2. On 1981–83 models equipped with cruise control, remove cruise control servo bracket.
3. Raise vehicle and drain crankcase.
4. Disconnect exhaust crossover pipe from exhaust manifold.
5. Remove torque converter cover, if equipped.
6. Remove starter motor attaching bolts and position starter motor aside.
7. Remove left hand engine mount through bolt, then lossen right hand engine mount through bolt.
8. Raise engine and reinstall through bolt. Do not tighten through bolt.
9. Remove oil pan attaching bolts and remove oil pan.
10. Reverse procedure to install. Torque oil pan attaching bolts to 80 inch lbs. Torque engine mount attaching bolts to 50 ft. lbs.

1980–86 V8 EXC. CORVETTE & 1982–86 CAMARO

1. Disconnect battery ground cable.
2. Remove air cleaner and snorkle.
3. On models with 2 piece fan shroud, remove upper half of shroud. On models with one piece shroud, remove retaining screws and release shroud from lower retaining clips.
4. Remove distributor cap to prevent breakage and lay cap aside, leaving spark plug wires connected.

◀ FRONT ENGINE   FLYWHEEL SIDE ▶

DUST LIP

APPLY GASKET SEALING COMPOUND TO THIS AREA

END VIEW OF SEAL

Fig. 20   Rear main seal installation. V6-173

5. On 1981–86 models equipped with cruise control, remove cruise control servo bracket.
6. On all models, raise and support vehicle, then drain oil pan.
7. Disconnect exhaust crossover pipe at exhaust manifold and catalytic converter.
8. Remove flywheel cover or torque converter cover.

NOTE: If equipped with manual transmission, remove starter motor before the flywheel cover.

9. Support engine with a suitable jack and remove engine mount through bolts.
10. Remove oil pan bolts and lower oil pan. Check that the forward crankshaft throw and/or counterweight is not extending downward as to block removal of oil pan. Rotate crankshaft as necessary to position crankshaft to permit pan removal.
11. Raise engine and install engine mount through bolts.
12. Remove oil pan.
13. Reverse procedure to install. Torque oil pan bolts to 80 inch lbs.

CORVETTE

1980–82
1. Disconnect battery ground cable.
2. Raise and support vehicle, then drain oil pan.
3. Remove engine oil dipstick and tube.
4. Disconnect idler arm and lower steering linkage.
5. Remove flywheel splash shield.
6. On 1980 models, disconnect exhaust pipe from exhaust manifold and catalytic converter.
7. Remove oil pan bolts and oil pan.
8. Reverse procedure to install. Torque oil pan bolts to 80 inch lbs.

1984–86
1. Disconnect battery ground cable.
2. Raise and support vehicle, then drain crankcase.

Fig. 21 Oil pump exploded view V6 & V8 engines

Fig. 22 Typical serpentine drive belt installation. 1984–86 Corvette

Engine oiling system. V8 engines

3. Remove starter brace and retaining bolts, and secure starter aside.
4. Remove flywheel cover.
5. Remove oil pan bolts and oil pan.
6. Reverse procedure to install. Torque oil pan retaining bolts to 80 inch lbs.

OIL PUMP

OIL PUMP, REPLACE

1. Remove oil pan as described previously.
2. Remove pump to rear main bearing cap bolt and remove pump and extension shaft.
3. Reverse procedure to install. Make sure that installed position of oil pump screen is with bottom edge parallel to oil pan rails.

OIL PUMP SERVICE

1. Remove oil pump as described previously.
2. Remove pump cover screws and pump cover, **Fig. 21.**
3. Mark gear teeth so they can be reassembled with same teeth indexing, then remove drive gear, idler gear and shaft.
4. Remove pressure regulator valve retaining pin, pressure regulator valve and related parts.
5. If pickup screen and pipe require replacement, mount pump in a soft-jawed vise and extract pipe from pump.
6. Wash all parts in cleaning solvent and dry with compressed air.
7. Inspect pump body and cover for cracks and excessive wear.
8. Inspect pump gears for damage or excessive wear.
9. Check drive gear shaft for looseness in pump body.
10. Inspect inside of pump cover for wear that would allow oil to leak past the ends of the gears.
11. Inspect pickup screen and pipe assembly for damage to screen, pipe or relief grommet.
12. Check pressure regulator valve for fit in pump housing.
13. Reverse procedure to assemble. Turn drive shaft by hand to check for smooth operation.

NOTE: The pump gears and body are not serviced separately. If the pump gears or body are damaged or worn, the pump assembly should be replaced. Also, if the pick-up screen and pump assembly was removed, it should be replaced with a new one as loss of the press fit condition could result in an air leak and loss of oil pressure.

BELT TENSION DATA

	New Lbs.	Used Lbs.
1980–81		
A/C Compressor Exc. V6-231 & V8-350 Diesel	135–145	85–95
V6-231	165	100
V8-350 Diesel	135–165	85–95
AIR Pump	120–130	70–80
Alternator Exc. V6-231 & V8-350 Diesel	120–130	70–80
V6-231	145	80
1982–83		
V8-350 Diesel	110–140	70–80
Power Steering Pump Exc. V6-231 & V8-350 Diesel	120–130	70–80
V6-231	165	100
V8-350 Diesel	110–140	70–80
A/C Compressor 4-151	135–165	65
V6-133 & 229; V8-267, 305, 350	145	65–80
V6-231	165	100
V6-262 Diesel & V8-350 Diesel	135–165	85–95
AIR Pump 4-151	120–150	55
V6-173	100	45
V6-229, V8-267, 305 & 350	130	65–80
Alternator 4-151	120–150	55
V6-173	145	65–80
V6-229, V8-267, 305 & 350	130	65–80
V6-231	145	80
V6-262 Diesel & V8-350 Diesel	110–140	70–80
Power Steering Pump 4-151	120–150	55
V6-173 & 229; V8-267, 305 & 350	135	65–80
V6-231	165	100
V6-262 Diesel & V8-350 Diesel	110–140	70–80
1984 Exc. Corvette		
A/C Compressor 4-151	135–165	65
V6-173 & 229; V8-305 & 350	135–145	85–95
V6-231	165	100
V8-350 Diesel	135–165	85–95
AIR Pump 4-151	120–150	55
V6-173	100	45
V6-229, V8-305 & 350	120–130	70–80
Alternator 4-151	120–150	55
V6-173	145	65–80
V6-229, V8-305 & V8-350	120–130	70–80
V6-231	145	80
V8-350 Diesel	110–140	70–80
Power Steering Pump 4-151	120–150	55
V6-173	135	65–80
V6-229, V8-305 & V8-350	120–130	70–80
V8-350 Diesel	110–140	70–80
1984–86 Corvette		
Serpentine Drive Belt	120–140①	120–140①
1985–86 Exc. Corvette		
A/C Compressor V6-262 & V8-305	135–145	85–95
V8-350 Diesel	135–165	85–95
AIR Pump, Alternator & Power Steering Pump V6-262 & V8-305	120–130	70–80
V8-350 Diesel	110–140	70–80

①—Checked between alternator & AIR Pump.

WATER PUMP

REPLACE

EXC. 1984–86 CORVETTE

1. Disconnect battery ground cable and drain cooling system.
2. Remove fan shroud or upper radiator support, as applicable, then remove accessory drive belts.

3. Remove fan and pulley from water pump hub.
4. Remove upper and lower alternator brackets. On 1982–86 Camaro, remove AIR brace and bracket.
5. If equipped with power steering, remove power steering lower bracket from water pump and position aside.
6. Remove radiator lower hose and heater hose from water pump.
7. Remove water pump attaching bolts and pump, noting position of bolts for assembly.
8. Reverse procedure to install.

1984–86 CORVETTE

1. Disconnect battery ground cable, and drain cooling system.
2. Rotate belt tensioner counterclockwise to release tension, and remove drive belt, **Fig. 22.**

3. Remove water pump and AIR pump pulleys, and disconnect air management valve adapter from AIR pump.
4. Remove AIR pump, then disconnect fuel supply and return lines.

NOTE: Relieve fuel system pressure before disconnecting fuel hoses.

5. Remove A/C compressor rear braces and lower mounting bolt.
6. Remove nuts securing A/C compressor and idler pulley bracket to water pump and disconnect electrical connector from compressor.
7. Move compressor bracket forward, remove upper mounting bolt and compressor, and secure aside.
8. Disconnect AIR hoses at check valves and AIR pipe at intake manifold and power steering bracket.
9. Remove power steering reservoir

bracket and upper alternator mounting bolt.
10. Remove lower AIR pump bracket, then disconnect hoses from water pump.
11. Remove mounting bolts and water pump.
12. Reverse procedure to install.

FUEL PUMP
REPLACE

CARBURETED ENGINES

1. Disconnect fuel lines from pump.
2. Disconnect vapor return line, if so equipped.
3. Remove fuel pump attaching bolts and pump.
4. Reverse procedure to install.

Diesel Engine Section

Refer to Section 20 for service procedures on the V6-262 and V8-350 Diesel engines.

Clutch & Manual Transmission Section

Fig. 1   Clutch linkage adjustment. 1980–81 Exc. Corvette

CLUTCH PEDAL
ADJUST

1980–83 EXCEPT CORVETTE

1. Disconnect return spring at clutch fork.
2. Rotate clutch lever and shaft assembly until pedal is against rubber bumper on dash brace.
3. Push outer end of clutch fork rearward until throwout bearing lightly contacts pressure plate fingers.
4. Install push rod in gauge hole and increase length until all lash is removed, **Figs. 1 and 2.**

Fig. 2   Clutch linkage adjustment. 1982–83 Camaro

5. Remove swivel or rod from gauge hole and insert into lower hole on lever. Install retainer and tighten lock nut being careful not to change rod length.
6. Reinstall return spring and check pedal free travel:
   1982–83 Camaro ...... ½ to 1 inch
   1980–81 Camaro .. ⅞ to 1⁷⁄₁₆ inches
   1980–81 Malibu .. 1¹⁄₁₆ to 1¼ inches

1984–86 CAMARO

The hydraulic clutch release mechanism on these models consists of a clutch master cylinder, slave cylinder and connecting hose which is serviced as a complete assembly. The hydraulic system is supplied filled with fluid, and no adjustment or bleeding is required. Before removing release mechanism for service, verify that a malfunction exists as follows:

1. Remove clutch housing dust shield and note position of slave cylinder plunger.
2. Depress clutch pedal fully and measure slave cylinder plunger travel.
3. If plunger moves release lever a minimum of .57 inch, check clutch disc, pressure plate, release fork and bearing for damage and repair as needed.
4. If plunger does not move lever at least .57 inches, check fluid level in clutch master cylinder with pedal depressed, and fill to step in reservoir.

NOTE: Do not overfill. Upper portion of reservoir must be open to accept fluid displaced in slave cylinder due to clutch wear.

5. Recheck plunger travel and check hydraulic components for leaks.
6. If plunger travel is still less than .57 inch, or if excessive leakage is noted, replace hydraulic system as an assembly.

1980–81 CORVETTE

1. Disconnect return spring between toe pan brace and cross shaft lever, **Fig. 3.**
2. Rotate clutch lever and shaft assembly until pedal is against dash brace rubber bumper.
3. Install swivel (C) into clutch lever hole and install retainer.
4. Loosen nuts (A) and (B), then apply a 5 pound load in direction of arrow (F) until bearing lightly contacts plate fingers.
5. Rotate nut (B) toward swivel until dimension "X" is approximately ⅜ to ⁷⁄₁₆ inch, then tighten nut (A) to lock swivel against nut (B).
6. Reinstall return spring and adjust clutch pedal free travel which should be 1 to 1½ inch.

1984–86 CORVETTE

The clutch release mechanism on these models is hydraulically operated, and is not adjustable. When the clutch pedal is depressed, the pedal push rod contacts a plunger in the clutch master cylinder bore.

Fig. 3   Clutch linkage adjustment. 1980–81 Corvette

The plunger first closes off the master cylinder fluid return port, then when moved further, forces fluid under pressure into the clutch slave cylinder. As pressure is applied to the slave cylinder, the slave cylinder piston is forced outward activating the clutch release fork. To diagnose malfunctions in the clutch release system, proceed as follows:

Inspection

1. With engine running at normal operating temperature and brakes applied, hold clutch pedal approximately ½ inch from fully depressed position and move transmission selector between 1st and reverse several times.
2. If transmission selector can be moved without binding or gear clash, clutch is releasing properly.
3. If shifter cannot be moved or if gear clash is evident, inspect linkage, fork and ball stud for damage and wear, and replace as needed.
4. If linkage is satisfactory, check clutch pedal and slave cylinder travel.
5. Clutch pedal travel should be 7⅜ inch, and slave cylinder plunger travel should be .70 inch, measured at the clutch fork.
6. If pedal travel is not within specifications, repair as needed. If plunger travel is not as specified, bleed or repair hydraulic system.

Bleeding

1. Fill master cylinder reservoir with specified fluid.
2. Raise and support vehicle.
3. Remove slave cylinder attaching bolts and secure cylinder at 45° angle with bleeder screw at highest point.
4. Fully depress and hold clutch pedal, then open bleeder.
5. Close bleeder then release clutch pedal.
6. Repeat steps 4 and 5 until all air has been purged from system, remount slave cylinder and repeat inspection.

NOTE: Check and fill master cylinder reservoir, as needed, to ensure that no air is drawn into system during bleeding.

CLUTCH
REPLACE

1. Support engine and remove transmission as outlined further on.
2. On all except 1984–86 Camaro and Corvette, disconnect clutch fork push rod and return spring. On 1984–86 Camaro and Corvette, remove slave cylinder heat shield and cylinder from flywheel housing.

NOTE: Prior to removing slave cylinder on 1984–86 Camaro and Corvette, disconnect push rod from clutch master cylinder.

3. Remove flywheel housing.
4. Slide clutch fork from ball stud and remove fork from dust boot.

NOTE: Look for "X" mark on flywheel and on clutch cover. If "X" mark is not evident, prick punch marks on flywheel and clutch cover for indexing purposes during installation.

5. Loosen clutch-to-flywheel attaching bolts evenly one turn at a time until spring pressure is released. Then remove bolts and clutch assembly.
6. Reverse procedure to install, using suitable pilot tool to center clutch disc. Tighten clutch cover bolts evenly and gradually to avoid distorting cover.

MANUAL TRANSMISSION
REPLACE

NOTE: It may be necessary to remove the catalytic converter and its support bracket to facilitate transmission removal.

1982–86 CAMARO
Four Speed
1. Raise and support vehicle, then drain transmission fluid.
2. Remove torque arm and propeller shaft.
3. Disconnect speedometer cable and all electrical connectors at transmission, then remove exhaust brace.
4. Remove shifter support attaching bolts from transmission and disconnect shift linkage from shifter.
5. Support transmission with a suitable jack, then remove crossmember and

transmission mount attaching bolts and the crossmember and mount.
6. Remove transmission attaching bolts and the transmission.
7. Reverse procedure to install.

Five Speed
1. Disconnect battery ground cable, remove shifter boot retaining screws and slide boot up lever.
2. Remove shift lever retaining bolts and lever, then raise and support vehicle.
3. Remove torque arm and propeller shaft, and on 1983 models disconnect clutch cable.
4. Disconnect speedometer cable and electrical connectors from transmission.
5. Support transmission and remove transmission mount retaining bolts and catalytic converter bracket.
6. Remove crossmember retaining bolts, crossmember and bolts securing flywheel cover.
7. Remove bolts securing transmission to engine, transmission and flywheel cover.
8. Reverse procedure to install.

1980–81 EXC. CORVETTE

1. Disconnect battery ground cable.
2. Remove shift lever knob and, on four speed models, the spring and "T" handle.
3. Raise and support vehicle.
4. Disconnect speedometer cable and TCS wiring at transmission.
5. Remove propeller shaft.
6. Remove transmission mount to crossmember bolts and the crossmember to frame bolts.
7. Remove shift lever attaching bolts and shift levers from transmission. Disconnect back drive rod at bell housing crank on floor shift models.
8. On floor shift models, remove bolts attaching shift control assembly to support on transmission. Carefully pull unit downward until shift lever clears rubber boot and remove assembly from vehicle.
9. On all models, remove transmission to clutch housing upper retaining bolts and install guide pins in holes and remove the lower retaining bolts.
10. Slide transmission rearward until clutch drive gear clears the clutch assembly and remove transmission from vehicle.
11. Reverse procedure to install.

1980–81 CORVETTE

1. Disconnect battery ground cable.
2. Remove shifter ball spring and "T" handle.
3. Remove console trim plate.
4. Raise and support vehicle.
5. Remove right and left exhaust pipes from vehicle.
6. Disconnect propeller shaft from transmission slip yoke. Lower the propeller shaft and remove slip yoke from transmission.
7. Remove transmission rear mount to rear mount bracket.
8. With a suitable jack, raise engine slightly to lift transmission off rear

mount bracket.
9. Remove bolts retaining transmission linkage mounting bracket to frame.
10. Disconnect shifter rods from levers at transmission cover.
11. Remove bolts attaching shift control to mounting bracket, then the mounting bracket. Remove shifter mechanism with rods and levers attached.
12. Remove shift levers from transmission and disconnect the speedometer cable and TCS switch wiring.
13. Remove transmission mount bracket to crossmember bolts, then the mount bracket. Remove bolts retaining rear mount cushion and exhaust pipe yoke.
14. Remove transmission to clutch housing bolts and the lower left extension bolt.
15. Pull transmission rearward until clear of clutch housing, rotating transmission clockwise while pulling rearward. To allow clearance for transmission removal, slowly lower rear of engine until tachometer drive cable at distributor clears horizontal ledge across front of dash.
16. Remove transmission from vehicle.
17. Reverse procedure to install.

1984–86 CORVETTE

1. Disconnect battery ground cable and remove air cleaner assembly.
2. Disconnect overdrive throttle valve cable from throttle linkage.
3. Remove distributor cap to prevent damage and lay cap aside, leaving plug wires connected.
4. Raise and support vehicle.
5. Remove complete exhaust system as follows:
   a. Disconnect AIR pipe from converter and remove AIR pipe clamps from manifold.
   b. Disconnect electrical connector to oxygen sensor.
   c. Remove bolts securing exhaust hangers to mufflers and hanger bracket from converter.
   d. Disconnect exhaust system from manifolds and remove system as an assembly.

Fig. 4 Three speed column shift linkage adjustment

e. Remove exhaust hanger from transmission.
6. Support transmission with suitable jack.
7. Remove bolts securing driveline beam to transmission and axle housings, then the driveline beam.
8. Mark installation position of propeller shaft, then remove shaft assembly.

NOTE: Tape bearing cups to universal joints to prevent loss of needle bearings.

9. Disconnect oil cooler lines and throttle valve cable from overdrive unit.
10. Disconnect shift linkage at transmission side cover, noting position for installation.
11. Disconnect electrical connectors from transmission and overdrive unit.
12. Lower transmission and support engine.
13. Remove bolts securing transmission to bell housing, slide transmission rearward until input shaft clears housing, then lower transmission from vehicle.

THREE SPEED SHIFT LINKAGE
ADJUST

COLUMN SHIFT

1. Place shift lever in "Reverse" position and ignition switch in "Lock".
2. Raise vehicle on a hoist.
3. Loosen shift control rod swivel lock nuts. Pull down slightly on 1/R rod attached to column lever to remove any slack and then tighten clevis lock nut at transmission lever, **Fig. 4**.
4. Unlock ignition switch and shift column lever to "Neutral". Position column lower levers in "Neutral", align gauge holes in levers and insert gauge pin.
5. Support rod and swivel to prevent movement and tighten ⅔ shift control rod lock nut.
6. Remove alignment tool from column

Fig. 5   Three speed floor shift linkage adjustment. 1980—81 Malibu & Monte Carlo

lower levers and check operation. Then place column lever in "Reverse" and check interlock control.

FLOOR SHIFT

1. Place ignition switch in "Off" position and raise vehicle.
2. Loosen lock nuts at shift rod swivels, **Figs. 5 and 6.** The rods should pass freely through the swivels.
3. Place transmission shift levers in neutral position.
4. Move shift control lever into the neutral detent position, align control assembly levers and insert locating pin into lever alignment slot.
5. Tighten lock nuts at shift rod swivels and remove locating pin.
6. Place transmission control lever in reverse position and the ignition switch in "Lock" position. Loosen lock nut at backdrive control rod swivel, then pull

rod downward slightly to remove slack in the column mechanism, then tighten the lock nut.
7. Check interlock control. The ignition switch should move freely to and from the "Lock" position.
8. Check transmission shift operation and if satisfactory, lower vehicle.

FOUR SPEED SHIFT LINKAGE
ADJUST

1982—84 CAMARO

1. Place levers (L), (M) and (N) in neutral position, **Fig. 7.** To obtain neutral position, move levers counter-clockwise to forward detent, then clockwise one detent.
2. Move lever (F) to neutral position. Align holes of levers (E), (H) and (J) with notch in lever and bracket assembly, then insert Gauge J-33195 or equivalent to secure levers in neutral position.
3. Attach rod (C) to lever (N) with washer (A) and retainer (B).
4. Loosely assemble nuts (R) and (T) and swivel (S) on rod (C).
5. Insert swivel (S) into lever (E), then attach washer (Q) and secure with retainer (P). Apply a load on lever (N) in direction of arrow (Z). At the same time, finger tighten nuts (T) and (R) against swivel, then torque nuts to 25 ft. lbs.
6. Repeat steps 3, 4 and 5 for rod (D) and levers (J) and (M).
7. Repeat steps 3, 4 and 5 for rod (K) and levers (H) and (L).
8. Remove gauge and check that centerlines of shift levers are aligned to provide free crossover motion.

Fig. 6   Three speed floor shift linkage adjustment. Exc. 1980—81 Malibu & Monte Carlo

1980—81

Exc. Corvette

The procedure, **Fig. 8,** is the same as that for Three Speed transmissions described previously.

Corvette

1. Place levers (K), (M), and (P) in neutral position, **Fig. 9.** To obtain neutral position, move levers counter-clockwise to forward detent, then clockwise one detent.
2. Move lever (E) to neutral position. Align levers (C), (D) and (F) with notch in lever and bracket assembly, then insert a suitable tool to secure levers in neutral position.

Fig. 7   Four speed shift linkage adjustment. 1982—84 Camaro

Fig. 8   Four speed shift linkage adjustment. 1980—81 exc. Corvette

Fig. 9 Four speed shift linkage adjustment. 1980–81 Corvette

Fig. 10 Four speed shift linkage adjustment. 1984–86 Corvette

3. Attach rod (N) to lever (C) with retainer (G).
4. Loosen assembly nuts (Q) and (S) and swivel (R) on rod (N).
5. Insert swivel (R) into lever (P), attach washer (B) and secure retaining (A). Apply a load on lever (P) in direction of arrow (Z). Tighten nut (S) against swivel, then nut (Q) against swivel.
6. Repeat steps 3, 4 and 5 for rod (J) and levers (F) and (K).
7. Repeat steps 3, 4 and 5 for rod (L) and levers (D) and (M).

8. Remove alignment tool from levers. The centerlines of shift levers must be aligned to provide free crossover motion.
9. Check for proper operation. Be sure all cables have adequate clearance around control rods.

1984–86 CORVETTE

1. Disconnect battery ground cable.
2. Remove left seat, disconnecting electrical connectors as needed.
3. Remove shift knob, console cover and glove box lock.
4. Remove left console side panel and shifter cover.

5. Loosen front and rear adjuster nut on each shift rod.
6. Ensure that transmission is in neutral, align shifter levers in neutral position, then insert gauge pin through lever alignment holes, **Fig. 10.**
7. Equalize swivels on each shift rod, hand tightening front and rear adjuster nuts simultaneously.
8. Simultaneously torque front and rear adjuster nuts on each shift rod to 20–30 ft. lbs.
9. Remove gauge pin and check shifter operation.
10. Reinstall components removed to gain access to shifter.

Rear Axle, Propeller Shaft & Brakes

REAR AXLE

Figs. 1 and 2 illustrate the rear axle assemblies used. When necessary to overhaul any of these units, refer to the Rear Axle Specifications table in this chapter.

CORVETTE

NOTE: These models are equipped with Positraction differentials.

In this axle, the drive pinion is mounted in two tapered roller bearings that are preloaded by a spacer. The pinion is positioned by a shim located between the head of the drive pinion and the rear pinion bearing. The front bearing is held in place by a large washer and a locking pinion nut.

The differential is supported in the carrier by two tapered roller side bearings. The differential side bearings are preloaded by shims between the bearings and carrier housing, **Fig. 2.** The differential assembly is positioned for proper ring gear and pinion backlash by varying the position and thickness of these shims.

The ring gear is bolted to the case. The case houses two side gears in mesh with two pinions mounted on a pinion shaft which is held in place by a lock screw. The side gears are backed by thrust washers.

The differential side gears drive two splined yokes which are retained by snap rings located on the yoke splined end. The yokes are supported on caged needle bearings pressed into the carrier, adjacent to the differential bearings. A lip seal, pressed into the carrier outboard of the bearing, prevents oil leakage and dirt entry.

REMOVE & REPLACE

1984–86

1. Remove air cleaner and distributor shields, then disconnect cap from distributor.
2. Raise and support vehicle, and remove spare and tire cover.
3. Remove exhaust system assembly as follows:
   a. Disconnect AIR pipe at converter and AIR pipe clamps at manifold.
   b. Disconnect electrical connector

from oxygen sensor.
   c. Support exhaust system, remove bolts securing mufflers to hangers, and remove converter bracket.
   d. Disconnect exhaust pipes at manifolds and remove exhaust system.
4. Disconnect leaf spring from spindle support knuckles, then remove bolts securing spring to differential carrier and spring as outlined in "Rear Suspension Section."
5. Scribe mark between cam bolts and brackets, then remove cam bolts and mounting bracket from carrier.
6. Disconnect tie rods from left and right spindle support knuckles.
7. Remove straps securing driveshaft universal joints to differential side yokes, push wheel and tire assemblies outward, and disconnect drive shafts from side yokes.

NOTE: Tape bearing cups to universal joint yokes to prevent loss of needle bearings.

Fig. 1 Rear axle cutaway view (Typical of C, G, K, M & P types; B & O Type similar). Exc. Corvette

Fig. 2 Rear axle cutaway view. Corvette

8. Remove straps securing propeller shaft universal joint to pinion flange, push propeller shaft forward into transmission and tie shaft to support beam.
9. Support transmission and remove bolts securing differential carrier beam to frame brackets, **Fig. 3.**
10. Remove mounting bolts at front of differential carrier and carrier assembly.
11. Reverse procedure to install, then check rear suspension alignment.

1980–82
1. Raise vehicle and remove spare tire.
2. Remove spare tire cover by removing support hooks attached to carrier cover.
3. Remove exhaust system, then position jack stands under front control arms to support vehicle.
4. Remove heat shield.
5. Using a suitable jack and C-clamp, raise spring to relieve tension, then disconnect spring from spindle support.
6. Remove rear spring cover plate.
7. Place alignment marks on cam bolt for reassembly, then remove cam bolt from bracket.
8. Remove bolts attaching strut bracket to carrier, then lower strut rods by pushing outward on wheel and tire assembly.
9. Mark propeller shaft and pinion flange, then disconnect propeller shaft
10. Remove differential carrier to frame crossmember mount bolt, **Fig. 3A.**
11. Position jack stand under carrier, then remove carrier to body attaching bolts, **Fig. 3A.**
12. Lower differential to gain access to cover bolts.
13. Drain differential and remove cover.
14. Disconnect drive shaft at spindle at companion flange.
15. Lower and remove differential assembly.
16. Remove drive shafts from side yokes.
17. Reverse procedure to install.

EXC. CORVETTE

In these rear axles, **Fig. 1,** the rear axle housing and differential carrier are cast into an integral assembly. The drive pinion assembly is mounted in two opposed tapered roller bearings. The pinion bearings are preloaded by a spacer behind the front bearing. The pinion is positioned by a washer between the head of the pinion and the rear bearing.

The differential is supported in the carrier by two tapered roller side bearings. These bearings are preloaded by spacers located between the bearings and carrier housing. The differential assembly is positioned for proper ring gear and pinion backlash by varying these spacers. The differential case houses two side gears in mesh with two pinions mounted on a pinion shaft which is held in place by a lock pin. The side gears and pinions are backed by thrust washers.

A limited slip rear axle, available on most models, uses disc or cone type clutches

COVER TO BODY ATTACHMENT CARRIER TO SUPPORT BEAM

Fig. 3   Rear axle assembly mounting. 1984—86 Corvette

Fig. 3A   Rear axle assembly mounting. 1980—82 Corvette

Fig. 4   Rear axle identification. exc. Corvette

which are splined to the side gears to "lock" the axle shafts to the case, or in effect to each other. Therefore, if one drive wheel is on a slippery surface, the other wheel must develop more torque than on a standard type differential before the differential case will allow wheel spin. However, axle shaft torques produced during cornering are sufficient to overcome the clutch action, allowing axles to rotate at different speeds.

Remove & Replace

Construction of the axle assembly is such that service operations may be performed with the housing installed in the vehicle or with the housing removed and installed in a holding fixture. The following procedure is necessary only when the housing requires replacement.

1. Raise and support vehicle, then support rear axle with a suitable jack.
2. Disconnect shock absorbers from lower mountings.
3. Remove propeller shaft.
4. Disconnect upper control arms from axle housing attachments, if equipped with coil springs.
5. Disconnect brake line from axle housing junction block and the parking brake cable.
6. Disconnect lower control arms from axle housing attachments, if equipped with coil springs.
7. On models equipped with coil springs, lower axle slowly until springs can be moved. Roll axle assembly out from under vehicle.
8. On models equipped with leaf springs, remove leaf springs as outlined under "Leaf Springs & Bushings, Replace" in Rear Suspension Section. Roll axle assembly out from under vehicle.
9. Reverse procedure to install.

AXLE SHAFT
REPLACE

NOTE: Refer to manufacturer's code to determine rear axle service procedures. Codes are stamped on the left or right axle tube, **Fig. 4**, or on a tag attached to the housing.

C, G, K, M, & P TYPE

1. Raise vehicle and remove wheel and brake drum.
2. Drain lube from carrier and remove cover.
3. Remove differential pinion shaft lock screw and remove differential pinion shaft.
4. Pull flanged end of axle shaft toward center of vehicle and remove "C" lock from button end of axle.
5. Remove axle shaft from housing, being careful not to damage seal.
6. Reverse procedure to install the axle shaft.

1980—82 CORVETTE

1. Raise and support vehicle.
2. Disconnect inboard driveshaft trunnion from side gear yoke.
3. On 1982 models, remove plastic splash shields attaching screws and the shields.
4. Remove bolts securing shaft flange to spindle drive flange.
5. Scribe a mark on the camber adjusting cam and mounting bracket for alignment during assembly.
6. Loosen camber adjusting nut and rotate cam so the high point of the cam faces inboard. This pushes the control arm outboard providing spindle-driveshaft clearance.
7. Remove driveshaft by withdrawing outboard end first.
8. Reverse procedure to install, then check rear suspension alignment.

1984—86 CORVETTE

1. Remove center cap from wheel.
2. Remove cotter pin, spindle nut and washer from spindle, **Fig. 5**.
3. Raise and support vehicle, and remove wheel and tire.
4. Disconnect tie rod and spring from

Fig. 5   Rear hub & spindle assembly, exploded view. 1984—86 Corvette

spindle support knuckle as outlined in "Rear Suspension Section."
5. Scribe a reference mark between cam bolt and bracket, remove cam bolt and separate spindle support rod from bracket.
6. Remove straps securing inner universal joint to drive yoke, pull knuckle assembly outward, and disconnect driveshaft from yoke.

NOTE: Tape bearing cups to universal joint yoke to prevent loss of needle bearings.

7. Pull spindle out of hub and remove driveshaft.
8. Reverse procedure to install, torquing cam bolt to 158—213 ft. lbs. and spindle nut to 151—177 ft. lbs., then check rear suspension alignment.

REAR SPINDLE & BEARINGS
REPLACE

1980—82 CORVETTE

1. Raise and support vehicle, and remove wheel and tire.

Fig. 6   Rear hub & spindle assembly, exploded view. 1980–82 Corvette

Fig. 7   Spindle removal. 1980–82 Corvette

Fig. 8   Parking brake shoe adjustment. Corvette

2. Remove axle driveshaft as outlined in "Drive Axle, Replace."
3. Set parking brake to prevent spindle from turning, and remove cotter pin and nut from spindle, **Fig. 6.**
4. Release parking brake and remove spindle flange and deflector.
5. Remove 2 brake caliper mounting bolts and secure caliper assembly aside.
6. Disconnect shock absorber and strut rod from spindle support.
7. Install thread protector over end of spindle, and puller J-22602 or equivalent on strut rod stud, **Fig. 7.**

NOTE: Ensure puller is installed vertically on spindle support before tightening puller screw.

8. Tighten puller screw and remove spindle and outer bearing.
9. Remove outer bearing from spindle using a suitable puller, then the outer seal.
10. Remove spacer tube, end play shim, inner bearing, race, seal and outer bearing race from spindle support.
11. Clean and inspect all components, and replace as needed.
12. Install bearing races in spindle support using driver J-7827 or equivalent, and pack bearings with EPB-2 bearing lube or equivalent.
13. Check end play prior to spindle installation as follows:
    a. Mount outer bearing, spacer and end play shim on gauging tool J-24626, and insert assembly into spindle support.
    b. Install inner bearing, washer and nut on gauging tool, ensure bearings are properly seated in races, and torque nut to 100 ft. lbs.
    c. Mount dial indicator on control arm with pointer bearing on outer end of gauging tool.
    d. Move gauging tool in and out while observing end play on indicator.
    e. End play should be .001 to .008 inch. If end play is not within spec-

ifications, replace shim as needed to provide proper clearance.

NOTE: If gauging tool is not available, install spindle and bearings as outlined, then check end play at spindle flange. If end play is not within specifications, note dial indicator reading, press out spindle, and replace shim with one which will provide .001 to .008 inch clearance.

14. Remove gauging tool, bearings, spacer and shim.
15. Install outer bearing in race, then seat outer seal in bore of spindle support using a suitable driver.
16. Insert spindle through outer seal and bearing, taking care not to damage seal.
17. Install spacer, shim and inner bearing over end of spindle.
18. Install threaded shaft J-24490-1 on end of spindle.
19. Install sleeve J-24490-2, washer and nut on threaded shaft, then tighten nut to draw spindle into final installed position.
20. Remove installation tool, install inner seal and reverse remaining procedure to complete installation. Torque spindle nut to 100 ft. lbs., and check rear suspension alignment.

NOTE: If specified nut does not allow insertion of cotter pin, tighten spindle flange nut to next flat, then install pin.

1984–86 CORVETTE

1. Remove drive shaft assembly as outlined in "Drive Axle, Replace."
2. Remove 2 bolts securing brake caliper bracket to support knuckle, secure caliper aside, then remove brake rotor.
3. Remove hub and bearing retaining bolts using a No. 45 Torx driver, **Fig. 5.**
4. Remove hub and bearing assembly.
5. Reverse procedure to install, torquing hub retaining bolts to 59–73 ft. lbs.,

then check rear suspension alignment.

PROPELLER SHAFT
REPLACE

EXC. 1984–86 CORVETTE

1. With transmission in neutral and parking brake released, raise and support vehicle.
2. Mark position of shaft in relation to pinion flange for reassembly.
3. Remove straps securing universal joint to pinion flange, then disconnect shaft from flange.

NOTE: Tape bearing cups to universal joint to prevent loss of needle bearings.

4. Slide yoke out of transmission and remove propeller shaft. Insert suitable plug in transmission to prevent fluid loss.
5. Reverse procedure to install.

1984–86 CORVETTE

1. With transmission in neutral and parking brake released, raise and support vehicle.
2. Remove exhaust system as follows:
   a. Disconnect AIR pipe from catalytic converter and exhaust pipe.
   b. Disconnect electrical connector to oxygen sensor.

c. Remove bolts securing muffler to hangers, disconnect exhaust pipes from manifolds and remove exhaust system as an assembly.
3. Support transmission, remove support beam retaining bolts and support beam.
4. Mark position of shaft in relation to pinion flange for installation.
5. Remove straps securing universal joint to pinion flange, then disconnect shaft from flange.

NOTE: Tape bearing cups to universal joint to prevent loss of needle bearings.

6. Slide yoke out of transmission and remove propeller shaft. Insert suitable plug in transmission to prevent fluid loss.
7. Reverse procedure to install.

BRAKE ADJUSTMENTS
SELF-ADJUSTING BRAKES

These brakes, have self-adjusting shoe mechanisms that assure correct lining-to-drum clearances at all times. The automatic adjusters operate only when the brakes are applied as the car is moving rearward or when the car comes to an uphill stop.

Although the brakes are self-adjusting, an initial adjustment is necessary after the brake shoes have been relined or replaced, or when the length of the adjusting screw has been changed during some other service operation.

Frequent usage of an automatic transmission forward range to halt reverse vehicle motion may prevent the automatic adjusters from functioning, thereby inducing low pedal heights. Should low pedal heights be encountered, it is recommended that numerous forward and reverse stops be made until satisfactory pedal height is obtained.

NOTE: If a low pedal condition cannot be corrected by making numerous reverse stops (provided the hydraulic system is free of air) it indicates that the self-adjusting mechanism is not functioning. Therefore it will be necessary to remove the brake drum, clean, free up and lubricate the adjusting mechanism. Then adjust the brakes, being sure the parking brake is fully released.

1. Using a suitable punch, knock out lanced area in backing plate or drum. If drum is installed on vehicle when this is done, remove drum and clean brake compartment of all metal.

NOTE: When adjustment is completed, a new hole cover must be installed in the backing plate.

2. Using Tool J-6166 or equivalent, turn brake adjusting screw to expand brake shoes at each wheel until wheel can just be turned by hand. Drag should be equal on all wheels.
3. On all except 1982–85 Camaro, back off adjusting screw at each wheel 30 notches.
4. On 1982–85 Camaro, back off screw 12 notches.
5. If shoe still drags slightly on drum, back off adjusting screw an additional one or two notches.
6. When adjusting screw has been backed off approximately 12 notches, brakes should be free of drag. Heavy drag at this point indicates tight parking brake cables.
7. Install adjusting hole cover in brake backing plate.
8. Check parking brake for proper adjustment.

PARKING BRAKE
ADJUST

EXC. CORVETTE & 1982–86 CAMARO w/REAR DISC BRAKES

1. Jack up both rear wheels.
2. Apply parking brake exactly two notches on all except 1980–81 Chevrolet, and 1 notch on 1980–81 Chevrolet.
3. Tighten adjusting nut until left rear wheel can just be rotated rearward but is locked when forward rotation is attempted.
4. Release parking brake and check to ensure that rear wheels rotate freely in either direction with no brake drag.

1982–86 CAMARO w/ REAR DISC BRAKES

1. Lubricate parking brake cables at underbody rub points and at equalizer hooks and ensure free movement of all cables.
2. With parking brake fully released, jack up both rear wheels.
3. Remove slack from cable by holding brake cable stud and tightening equalizer nut.

NOTE: After tightening nut, check that caliper levers are against stops on caliper housing. If not, loosen cable until levers return to stops.

4. Actuate parking brake several times to check adjustment.

1980–82 CORVETTE

1. Release parking brake lever, then raise and support vehicle.
2. Loosen parking brake cable adjusting nut at equalizer until brake shoe actuating levers move freely to the released position with slack in cables.
3. Remove rear wheels and turn each brake rotor until parking brake shoe star adjuster is visible through hole in rotor hub.
4. Insert a suitable adjusting tool through hole in rotor, and tighten adjusters by moving hand away from floor, **Fig. 8.**
5. Adjust one side at a time, tightening adjuster until rotor cannot be turned by

hand, then backing star wheel off 6 to 8 notches.
6. Install rear wheels and pull parking brake lever up 13 notches to the applied position.
7. Tighten cable adjusting nut at equalizer until 80 lbs. pull is required to lift parking brake lever to the 14th notch, then secure adjustment with lock nut.
8. Release parking brake lever and check adjustment. Rear wheels should turn freely in both directions with no brake drag.

1984–86 CORVETTE

1. Release parking brake lever, then raise and support vehicle.
2. Remove rear wheels, then install lug nuts on 2 opposite wheel studs to hold brake rotor in position.
3. Back caliper pistons into bores.
4. Loosen parking brake cable adjusting nut until there is no tension on parking brake shoes.
5. Turn each brake rotor until parking brake shoe star adjuster is visible through hole in rotor.
6. Adjusting one side at a time, tighten adjuster until rotor cannot be turned by hand, then back star wheel off 5 to 7 notches.

NOTE: Adjust parking brake shoes by inserting a suitable tool through hole in rotor. On driver's side, tighten adjuster by moving handle of tool upwards. On passenger side, tighten adjuster by moving handle of tool downwards.

7. Install rear wheels and pull parking brake lever up 2 notches.
8. Tighten cable adjusting nut at equalizer until there is drag on wheels.
9. Release parking brake lever and check adjustment. No drag should be felt when rotating wheels.

MASTER CYLINDER
REPLACE

1. Disconnect brake pipes from master cylinder. Plug lines and master cylinder ports to prevent entry of foreign material.
2. Disconnect brake pedal from master cylinder push rod, if equipped with manual brakes.
3. Remove master cylinder attaching nuts and the master cylinder.
4. Reverse procedure to install.

POWER BRAKE UNIT
HYDRO-BOOST

NOTE: Pump brake pedal several times with engine off to deplete accumulator of fluid.

1. Remove two nuts attaching master cylinder to booster, then move master cylinder away from booster with brake lines attached.

2. Remove three hydraulic lines from booster. Plug and cap all lines and outlets.
3. Remove retainer and washer securing booster push rod to brake pedal arm.
4. Remove four nuts attaching booster unit to dash panel.
5. From engine compartment, loosen booster from dash panel and move booster push rod inboard until it disconnects from brake pedal arm. Remove spring washer from brake pedal arm.
6. Remove booster unit from vehicle.
7. Reverse procedure to install. To purge

system, disconnect feed wire from injection pump. Fill power steering pump reservoir, then crank engine for several seconds and recheck power steering pump fluid level. Connect injection pump feed wire and start engine, then cycle steering wheel from stop to stop twice and stop engine. Discharge accumulator by depressing brake pedal several times, then check fluid level. Start engine, then turn steering wheel from stop to stop and turn engine off. Check fluid level and add fluid as necessary. If foaming occurs, stop engine and wait for approximately one hour for foam to dissipate,

then recheck fluid level.

EXC. HYDRO-BOOST

1. Remove vacuum hose from check valve and master cylinder retaining nuts.
2. Pull master cylinder forward so it clears mounting studs and move to one side. Support cylinder to avoid stress on hydraulic lines.
3. Remove power unit to dash nuts.
4. Remove brake pedal push rod retainer and disconnect push rod from pin.
5. Remove power unit from vehicle.
6. Reverse procedure to install.

Rear Suspension

SHOCK ABSORBER
REPLACE

1. If equipped with Superlift shock absorbers, disconnect air lines from shock absorber fittings.
2. With rear axle properly supported, disconnect shock absorber from upper and lower mountings, **Figs. 1 through 5.**
3. Reverse procedure to install.

COIL SPRINGS
REPLACE

CHEVROLET, MALIBU & MONTE CARLO

1. Support vehicle at frame and rear axle.
2. Disconnect shock absorbers at lower mountings.
3. Disconnect upper control arms from axle housing.
4. If equipped with a stabilizer bar, disconnect bar from either right or left hand side of control arm.
5. On all models, remove brake hose support bolt and support without disconnecting the brake lines.
6. Lower axle until it reaches end of its travel and using a suitable tool, pry lower pigtail over retainer on axle bracket. Remove spring and insulator.
7. Reverse procedure to install. Springs must be installed with an insulator between upper seat and spring and positioned properly, **Fig. 6.**

1982–86 CAMARO

1. Raise and support vehicle and support rear axle with a suitable adjustable jack.
2. Remove track bar mounting bolt from axle and loosen track bar bolt at body brace.
3. Disconnect rear brake hose clip at underbody, then disconnect shock absorbers at lower mountings.
4. On models equipped with 4-151 engine, remove propeller shaft.

Fig. 1   Typical rear suspension. Exc. Camaro & Corvette

Fig. 2   Rear suspension. 1980–81 Camaro

1 RAIL	8 TORQUE ARM
2 JOUNCE BUMPER	9 PROP SHAFT
3 SPRING INSULATOR ASM.	10 DAMPER ASM. WITH 4 CYC. ENGINE
4 COIL SPRING	11 SHOCK ABSORBER
5 OPTIONAL STABILIZER BAR	12 TRACK BAR
6 LOWER CONTROL ARM	13 TRACK BAR BRACE
7 UNDERBODY	

WITH RR DISC BRAKES

Fig. 3   Rear suspension. 1982–86 Camaro

Fig. 4   Typical rear suspension. 1980–82 Corvette

Fig. 5   Rear suspension. 1984–86 Corvette

Fig. 6   Coil spring installation

Fig. 7   Leaf spring bushing removal. 1980–81 Camaro

Fig. 8   Leaf spring bushing installation. 1980–81 Camaro

Fig. 9   Supporting leaf spring. 1980–82 Corvette

5. Lower rear axle and remove springs and insulators.
6. Reverse procedure to install.

LEAF SPRINGS & BUSHINGS
REPLACE

1980–81 CAMARO

1. Support vehicle at frame and rear axle, removing tension from spring.
2. Disconnect shock absorber from lower mounting.
3. Loosen spring front mount bolt.
4. Remove spring front mounting bracket attaching screws, lower axle and remove bracket.
5. Disconnect parking brake cable from spring plate bracket.
6. Remove spring plate by removing axle bracket nuts on single leaf models and the "U" bolts on multi-leaf models.
7. Support spring, remove front mount bolt and disassemble rear shackle.
8. Replace rear shackle and spring eye bushings as necessary, **Figs. 7 and 8.**
9. Reverse procedure to install.

1980–82 CORVETTE

1. Support vehicle at frame and remove rear wheels.
2. Install a "C" clamp approximately 9 inches from end of spring.
3. Place a suitable jack under spring, **Fig. 9,** and place a wooden block between "C" clamp and jack pad.
4. Raise jack until load is off spring link, then remove cotter pin, link nut and spring cushion, **Figs. 10 and 11.** Lower jack, removing tension from spring.
5. Repeat steps 2, 3 and 4 on opposite side of spring.
6. Remove bolts from spring center clamp plate, then remove clamp plate.
7. Remove spring from vehicle.
8. Reverse procedure to install.

1984–86 CORVETTE

1. Raise and support vehicle and remove one wheel and tire assembly.
2. Remove cotter pin, retaining nuts, bushings and link bolts securing spring to spindle support knuckles, **Fig. 12.**
3. Remove bolts securing spring to cover beam, spacers, insulators and spring, **Fig. 13.**
4. Reverse procedure to install. Torque bolts securing spring to cover beam to 29–44 ft. lbs.

Fig. 10 Transverse leaf spring mounting. 1980 Corvette

Fig. 11 Transverse leaf spring mounting. 1981—82 Corvette

Fig. 12 Transverse leaf spring link assembly. 1984—86 Corvette

Fig. 13 Transverse leaf spring mounting. 1984—86 Corvette

Year	Model	Upper		Lower	
		F	R	F	R
1980—83	Malibu & Monte Carlo	70	73	70	73①
1980—86	Chevrolet	92	70	92	92
1982—86	Camaro	—	—	68	68
1984	Monte Carlo	70	73	70	73①

①—Bolt torque.

Fig. 14 Control arm retaining nut torque specifications

LEAF SPRING SERVICE

NOTE: The spring leaves are not serviced separately, however, the spring leaf inserts may be replaced.

1. Clamp spring in a vise and remove spring clips.
2. File peened end of center bolt to permit nut removal, remove nut and open vise slowly, allowing spring to expand.
3. Replace spring leaves or leaf inserts.
4. On 1980—81 Corvette, to replace main leaf cushion retainers, chisel flared portion until retainer can be removed from leaf. Install new retainers and flare over with a hammer.
5. On all models use a drift to align center bolt holes, compress spring in vise and install new center bolt and nut. Peen end of bolt to retain nut.
6. Align springs and bend spring clips into position.

NOTE: Overtightening of spring clips will cause spring binding.

CONTROL ARMS & BUSHINGS
REPLACE

EXC. CORVETTE

NOTE: If more than one control arm is being replaced, remove and install one arm at a time to prevent axle assembly from slipping or twisting out of position.

CONTROL ARMS, REPLACE
1. Raise vehicle and support at frame pads. Support nose of axle housing to prevent assembly from twisting when control arm is removed.
2. If lower control arm is being replaced, remove bolts securing stabilizer bar to control arm, if equipped.
3. Remove bolts securing control arm to chassis and rear axle, and the control arm.
4. Reverse procedure to install, lower vehicle and torque control arm bolts to specifications, **Fig. 14,** with vehicle at normal ride height.

NOTE: All torque prevailing type fasteners must be torqued at the nut, not at the bolt, to ensure proper clamping force.

BUSHING REPLACEMENT

Differential Carrier Bushings (Upper Control Arm Rear Bushing)
The upper control arm rear bushing, which is pressed into the differential carrier, can be replaced using the following procedure:
1. Raise vehicle and support at frame pads, and support nose of axle housing to prevent assembly from twisting.
2. Lower rear axle to obtain clearance, disconnect upper control arm from axle and position aside.
3. Install suitable bushing removal tool as shown in **Fig. 15,** tighten puller screw and press bushing out of housing.
4. To install replacement bushing, reverse position of removal tool and pull bushing into position by tightening screw, **Fig. 16.**

Control Arm Bushings
1. Raise and support vehicle and remove control arm as outlined previously.
2. Press bushings out of control arm using suitable tools as shown in **Fig. 17.**
3. Reverse procedure to install, ensuring bushing is properly seated in control arm, **Fig. 18.**

NOTE: If replacement bushing fits loosely in control arm, or if mounting areas are damaged or deformed, control arm must be replaced.

1984—86 CORVETTE

Control Arms, Replace
1. Raise and support vehicle, and remove wheel and tire assembly.
2. Remove shock absorber. Use a back-up wrench on lower mounting stud when removing retaining nut.
3. Remove bolts securing control arm to spindle support knuckle.
4. Remove control arm bolt at mounting bracket and control arm.
5. Reverse procedure to install. Torque control arm to bracket bolt to 55—70 ft. lbs., and control arm to knuckle bolt to 125—154 ft. lbs.

Fig. 15 Upper control arm rear bushing (differential carrier bushing) removal

Fig. 16 Upper control arm rear bushing (differential carrier bushing) installation

Fig. 17 Control arm bushing removal. Exc. Corvette

Fig. 18 Control arm bushing installation. Exc. Corvette

Fig. 19 Stabilizer bar installation. Chevrolet, Malibu & Monte Carlo

Fig. 20 Stabilizer bar installation. 1980–81 Camaro

STABILIZER BAR
REPLACE

CHEVROLET, MALIBU & MONTE CARLO

1. Support vehicle at rear axle.
2. Remove bolts securing stabilizer bar to lower control arms, **Fig. 19**.
3. Reverse procedure to install. Use spacer shims, if needed, placed equally on each side of stabilizer bar. Tighten attaching bolts with vehicle at curb height.

1980–81 CAMARO

1. Support vehicle at rear axle.
2. Disconnect stabilizer bar from spring plate brackets, **Fig. 20**.
3. Disconnect stabilizer bar from body brackets.
4. Reverse procedure to install. Tighten attaching bolts with vehicle at curb height.

1982–86 CAMARO

1. Raise and support vehicle.
2. Remove link bolt nuts, washers, bushings, spacers and link bolts securing stabilizer to chassis, **Fig. 21**.
3. Remove clamps securing stabilizer shaft to rear axle and stabilizer shaft.
4. Reverse procedure to install. Torque link bolts to 12 ft. lbs., and U-bolt nuts to 20 ft. lbs.

Fig. 21 Stabilizer link assembly. 1982–86 Camaro

1980–82 CORVETTE

1. Disconnect stabilizer bar from torque control arms and remove stabilizer bar frame brackets, **Fig. 22**.
2. Replace bushings as necessary, **Fig. 22**.
3. Reverse procedure to install.

1984–86 CORVETTE

1. Raise and support vehicle.
2. Remove spare tire and carrier.
3. Disconnect stabilizer links from spindle support knuckles.
4. Remove retainers securing shaft bushings to crossmember, bushings and stabilizer shaft.
5. Reverse procedure to install. Torque bushing retaining nuts and bolts securing stabilizer links to knuckles to 14–22 ft. lbs., and bolts securing links to stabilizer bar to 25–35 ft. lbs.

TRACK BAR & BRACE
REPLACE

1982–86 CAMARO

1. Raise vehicle and support rear axle at curb height.

Fig. 22   Stabilizer bar installation. 1980–82 Corvette

Fig. 23   Track bar & brace installation. 1982–86 Camaro

MARK CAM AND BRACKET

Fig. 24   Indexing adjustment cam bolt & bracket (Typical). Corvette

Fig. 25   Strut rod bushing replacement. 1980–82 Corvette

2. Remove track bar mounting bolt and nut from rear axle and from body bracket, then remove track bar, **Fig. 23.**
3. Remove heat shield attaching screws from track bar brace.
4. Remove three track bar brace to body brace screws.
5. Remove nut and bolt from body bracket, then remove track bar brace.
6. Reverse procedure to install.

STRUT ROD, SPINDLE SUPPORT ROD & TIE ROD
REPLACE

1980–82 CORVETTE

Strut Rod
1. Support vehicle at frame.
2. Disconnect shock frame from lower mounting.
3. Remove cotter pin and nut from strut rod shaft. Pull shaft toward front of vehicle and remove from bracket.
4. Mark position of camber adjusting cam to ensure proper installation, **Fig. 24** and loosen camber bolt nut.
5. Remove bolts securing strut rod bracket to carrier.

6. Remove camber bolt and nut, pull strut rod out of bracket and remove bushing caps.
7. Replace bushings as necessary, **Fig. 25.**
8. Reverse procedure to install.

1984–86 CORVETTE

Spindle Support Rod
1. Raise and support vehicle, and remove wheel and tire.
2. Scribe mark between cam bolt and bracket for reassembly, **Fig. 24.**
3. Remove cam bolt and disconnect support rod from bracket.
4. Remove bolt securing spindle support rod to knuckle and rod.
5. Reverse procedure to install, then check rear suspension alignment. Torque retaining bolt at knuckle to 95–118 ft. lbs., and cam bolt to 158–213 ft. lbs.

Tie Rod
1. Raise and support vehicle, and remove wheel and tire.
2. Remove cotter pin and nut securing tie rod to spindle support knuckle.
3. Press tie rod from knuckle using tool J-24319-01 or equivalent.
4. Remove tie rod from adjusting sleeve, counting number of turns necessary.
5. Reverse procedure to install, then check rear suspension alignment.

Torque tie rod nut 29–36 ft. lbs., and locking nut to 39–53 ft. lbs.

SPINDLE SUPPORT KNUCKLE
REPLACE

1984–86 CORVETTE

1. Remove center cap from wheel, cotter pin and spindle nut.
2. Raise and support vehicle, and remove wheel and tire.
3. Remove 2 bolts securing brake caliper to knuckle, brake caliper assembly and brake rotor.
4. Disconnect tie rod, leaf spring and stabilizer shaft from knuckle as outlined previously.
5. Disconnect parking brake cable from backing plate and bracket.
6. Disconnect shock absorber and support rod from knuckle, using a back-up wrench on shock mounting stud.
7. Remove bolts securing control arms to knuckle, lower knuckle assembly and slide spindle out of hub and bearing.

Fig. 26 Torque control arm installation. 1980—82 Corvette

Fig. 27 Torque control arm bushing removal. 1980—82 Corvette

Fig. 28 Torque control arm bushing installation. 1980—82 Corvette

Fig. 29 Flaring tool back-up plate

8. Remove hub and bearing and parking brake assembly from knuckle, using a No. 45 Torx bit to remove hub retaining bolts, then remove splash shield.
9. Reverse procedure to install, then check rear suspension alignment. Torque all bolts to specifications given in individual component replacement procedures.

Fig. 30 Flaring torque control arm bushing retainer. 1980—82 Corvette

Fig. 31 Crossmember isolation mount installation. 1980—82 Corvette

TORQUE CONTROL ARMS & BUSHINGS
REPLACE

1980—82 CORVETTE

1. Perform steps 1 thru 4 as outlined under "Leaf Spring Replace" 1980—82 Corvette procedure.
2. If equipped with a stabilizer shaft, disconnect shaft at torque arms.
3. Disconnect shock absorber at lower mounting.
4. Disconnect and lower strut rod shaft.
5. Disconnect axle drive shaft from spindle flange by removing attaching bolts.

NOTE: It may be necessary to force torque arm outboard providing clearance to lower axle drive shaft.

6. Disconnect brake line from caliper and from torque arm. Disconnect parking brake cable.
7. Remove torque arm forward mounting bolt and toe-in shims, **Fig. 26,** and pull torque arm out of frame attachment.
8. Replace bushings if necessary as described under "Torque Control Arm Bushing Service."
9. Reverse procedure to install.

Torque Control Arm Bushing Service

1. Using an $^{11}/_{16}$ inch twist drill, drill out flared end of bushing retainer, remove retainer plate and retainer from bushing.
2. Spread bushing with a chisel, **Fig. 27,** and tap bushing from arm.

NOTE: If bushing is rusted in torque arm, torque arm may spread during bushing removal. Install a "C" clamp torque arm, preventing torque arm spreading.

3. Oil steel portion of new bushing and press bushing into arm, **Fig. 28.**
4. Place retainer plate over flared portion of bushing retainer and insert retainer into bushing.
5. Make a flaring tool back-up plate, **Fig. 29,** with ½ inch bolt holes.
6. Place back-up plate on flared end of bushing retainer and assemble tool to plate, **Fig. 30,** with ½ × 5 inch bolts. Center threaded hole in tool # J-8111-23 over unflared end of bushing retainer. Also center chamfered retainer plate over retainer tube.
7. Lubricate end of tool # J-8880-5 and thread screw into tool, flaring retainer.

REAR WHEEL ALIGNMENT

CORVETTE

Rear wheel alignment should be checked and adjusted periodically, when rear tires indicate abnormal wear, or when suspension components are replaced. Prior to rear wheel alignment, check suspension components for damage or excessive wear and repair as needed. Also ensure tires are properly inflated, and wheel bearing end play is within specifications.

Camber, Adjust

Wheel camber is adjusted by rotating the eccentric cam and bolt located at the inboard end of the strut rod or spindle support rod, **Figs. 4 and 5.** To check and adjust camber, proceed as follows:

1. Place rear wheels of vehicle on suitable alignment equipment following manufacturer's instructions, then check camber reading.
2. If wheel camber is not within specifications, loosen cam bolt retaining nut.
3. Rotate cam bolt until camber reading is within specifications listed at the front of this chapter.
4. Torque cam bolt nut to specifications while holding position of bolt, then recheck camber reading.

TOE-IN ADJUST

1980–82

Rear wheel toe-in is adjusted by inserting slotted shims of varying thickness inside the frame side member on both sides of the torque control arm pivot bushing. Shims are available in thicknesses of ¹⁄₆₄ inch, ¹⁄₃₂ inch, ⅛ inch and ¼ inch.

To adjust, loosen torque arm pivot bolts until shims are free enough to remove. Position torque arm assembly until toe-in is within specifications listed in the front of this chapter. Shim gap toward vehicle centerline between end of control arm bushing and frame side inner wall.

1984–86

Toe-in is adjusted by loosening lock nuts on tie rod ends and rotating adjuster sleeves until desired setting is obtained. Refer to front of this chapter for toe-in specifications.

Front Suspension & Steering Section

Fig. 1 Typical front suspension. Exc. 1982–86 Camaro & 1984–86 Corvette

Fig. 2 Front suspension exploded view. 1982–86 Camaro

Fig. 3 Front suspension. 1984–86 Corvette

FRONT SUSPENSION

All models except 1982–86 Camaro and 1984–86 Corvette use a Short-Long Arm (SLA) type front suspension with independent coil springs riding on lower control arms, **Fig. 1.** Ball joints link upper and lower control arms to a spindle assembly, and tubular shock absorbers are used to dampen spring action. On some models, a spring steel stabilizer shaft is connected between the chassis and lower control arms to control side roll.

A modified strut type suspension is used on 1982–86 Camaro, **Fig. 2.** Each wheel is independently connected to the chassis by a lower control arm, spindle and a strut assembly which locates the spindle and controls ride by dampening spring action. Coil springs are mounted between the lower control arm and crossmember, and a stabilizer shaft is connected between the chassis and control arms to control side roll.

The front suspension used on 1984–85 Corvette consists of forged aluminum upper and lower control arms and steering knuckle, a fiberglass mono-leaf spring, shock absorbers and stabilizer bar, **Fig. 3.** The front spring is transverse mounted on the crossmember and bears against lower control arms. The stabilizer bar and shock absorbers are connected between the chassis and lower control arms, and control side roll and dampen spring action respectively. Upper and lower control arms are connected through the knuckle, which is specially designed to move the wheel centerline rearward of the conventional ball joint centerline.

WHEEL ALIGNMENT

NOTE: Prior to checking or adjusting front suspension alignment, inspect suspension components for damage or excessive wear, and replace as needed. Ensure tire pressures and wheel bearings are properly adjusted, then raise and release front bumper several times to allow vehicle to assume normal ride height.

EXC. 1982–86 CAMARO

Caster and camber adjustments are made by means of shims between the upper control arm inner support shaft and the support bracket attached to the frame. Shims may be added, subtracted or transferred to change the readings as follows:

Caster, Adjust

Transfer shims from front to rear or rear to front. The transfer of one shim to the

Fig. 4 Camber and caster adjustment. 1982–86 Camaro

Fig. 5 Lower ball joint wear indicator.

front bolt from the rear bolt will decrease positive caster. One shim (1/32 inch) transferred from the rear bolt to the front bolt will change caster about 1/2 degree.

Camber, Adjust

Change shims at both the front and rear of the shaft. Adding an equal number of shims at both front and rear of the support shaft will decrease positive camber. One shim (1/32 inch) at each location will move camber approximately 1/5 degree on 1980–81 Camaro. On Chevrolet and Corvette the change will be about 1/6 degree.

1982–86 CAMARO

Caster and camber adjustments are made by moving the position of the upper strut mount assembly. To make adjustment, remove dust cap and fender bolt and attach tool J-29724 to original fender bolt, **Fig. 4.** Tighten the turnbuckle and loosen the three strut mount attaching nuts.

Adjust camber by rotating the turnbuckle to move mount assembly inward or outward. Move mount inboard to decrease camber, or outboard to increase camber.

Adjust caster by lightly tapping the mount assembly forward or rearward. Move mount forward to decrease caster, or rearward to increase caster.

When adjustments are completed, torque the three strut mount attaching nuts to 20 ft. lbs.

TOE-IN
ADJUST

Toe-in can be adjusted by loosening the clamp bolts at each end of each tie rod and turning each tie rod to increase or decrease its length as necessary until proper toe-in is secured and the steering gear is on the high point for straight-ahead driving.

WHEEL BEARINGS
ADJUST

EXC. 1984–86 CORVETTE

1. While rotating wheel forward, torque spindle nut to 12 ft. lbs.
2. Back off nut until "just loose" then hand tighten nut and back it off again until either hole in spindle lines up with hole in nut.

NOTE: Do not back off nut more than 1/2 flat.

3. Install new cotter pin. With wheel bearing properly adjusted, there will be .001–.005 inch end play.

WHEEL BEARINGS
REPLACE

EXC. 1984–86 CORVETTE

1. Raise car and remove front wheels.
2. Remove bolts holding brake caliper to its mounting and insert a fabricated block (1 1/16 × 1 1/16 × 2 inches in length) between the brake pads as the caliper is being removed. Once removed, the caliper can be wired or secured in some manner away from the disc.
3. Remove spindle nut and hub and disc assembly. Grease retainer and inner wheel bearing can now be removed.
4. Reverse procedure to install.

1984–86 CORVETTE

NOTE: The wheel bearing and hub assembly is a sealed unit. If end play exceeds .005 inch, or if noise or roughness is detected, unit must be replaced as an assembly.

1. Raise and support vehicle, and remove wheel and tire.
2. Remove 2 bolts securing brake caliper bracket to steering knuckle, and secure caliper assembly aside.
3. Remove brake rotor, bolts securing hub to knuckle and hub assembly.
4. Reverse procedure to install.

CHECKING BALL JOINTS FOR WEAR

Upper Ball Joint

1. Raise front of vehicle with jacks placed between the coil spring pocket and ball joint of lower control arm.
2. Shake top of wheel in and out. Observe steering knuckle for any movement relative to the control arm.
3. Replace upper ball joint if looseness is indicated.

Lower Ball Joint

Raise car and support lower control arm so spring is compressed in the same manner as if the wheels were on the ground and check axial (up and down) play at ball joint. If play exceeds 1/8 inch, replace the joint.

Another indication of lower ball joint excessive wear is when difficulty is experienced when lubricating the joint. If the liner has worn to the point where the lubrication grooves in the liner have been worn away, then abnormal pressure is required to force lubricant through the joint. Should this condition be evident, replace both lower ball joints.

NOTE: All models except 1980–82 Corvette and 1982–86 Camaro have a wear indicator built into the lower ball joint, **Fig. 5.** When inspecting wear indicator, vehicle must be supported normally on wheels to properly load ball joint.

SUSPENSION & STEERING LINKAGE CHECK

1. Raise vehicle with jack placed under frame torque box behind front wheel.
2. Lock steering wheel with wheels in straight ahead position, then mount

CHECKING STEERING LINKAGE WEAR
AS VIEWED FROM ABOVE

POSITION DIAL INDICATOR
TO CHECK MOVEMENT
AT THIS POINT

MOVE WHEEL IN AND OUT
AT FRONT AND BACK

Fig. 6   Suspension & steering linkage check

Fig. 7   Disconnecting ball joints from steering knuckle. Exc. 1980—82 Corvette & 1982—86 Camaro

Fig. 8   Pressing ball joint from lower control arm (Typical)

dial indicator on a suitable stand with pointer bearing against outer rim of wheel, **Fig. 6.**

3. Move wheel in and out at front and rear, without moving steering wheel, while observing gauge.
4. If gauge reading exceeds .108 inches, check steering linkage and suspension for excessive wear or damage.

UPPER BALL JOINT
REPLACE

EXC. 1980—82 CORVETTE

1. Raise vehicle and support with stands at outer ends of lower control arms.
2. Remove wheel and tire.
3. Remove cotter pin and retaining nut, then separate ball joint stud from knuckle using a suitable tool, **Fig. 7.**
4. Support upper control arm in a raised position.
5. Remove heads of rivets securing joint to arm, then drive out rivets to remove joint.
6. Position replacement joint on top of control arm, insert retaining bolts supplied with joint from under arm, install nuts and torque to 13 ft. lbs.
7. Remove upper control arm support, assemble ball joint to steering knuckle, install washer, if equipped, and retaining nut.

NOTE: On 1980—82 models, seat ball joint stud in knuckle before installing nut. Install tool J-29293 on stud, torque tool to 40 ft. lbs., then remove tool and install nut.

8. Torque retaining nut to 60 ft. lbs. on 1980—82 models, 65 ft. lbs. on 1983—86 models except Corvette, and 32 ft. lbs. on 1984—86 Corvette.
9. Tighten retaining nut up to an additional 1/16 turn, if necessary, to align hole in ball stud with nut, then install cotter pin.

NOTE: On 1980—82 Malibu and Monte Carlo, install cotter pin from rear.

1980—82 CORVETTE

1. Raise and support vehicle, and remove wheel and tire.
2. Remove cotter pin and loosen but do not remove ball joint retaining nut.

NOTE: Nut should not be loosened more than one full turn.

3. To release ball stud from knuckle, tap on boss of knuckle with hammer using another heavy hammer or similar tool as a drift.
4. Support lower control arm at outer end to release spring tension on upper control arm, remove retaining nut and support upper control arm in raised position.
5. Remove heads of rivets securing joint to arm, then drive out rivets to remove joint.
6. Position replacement joint on top of control arm, insert retaining bolts supplied with joint from under arm, install nuts and torque to 25 ft. lbs.
7. Remove upper control arm support, assemble ball joint to steering knuckle, install retaining nut and torque to 50 ft. lbs.
8. Tighten nut up to an additional 1/16 of a turn, if necessary, to align hole in ball stud with nut, then install cotter pin.

LOWER BALL JOINT
REPLACE

EXC. 1980—82 CORVETTE

1. Raise vehicle and support at frame, and remove wheel and tire.
2. Position a suitable jack under lower control arm spring seat, and raise jack to compress coil spring.

NOTE: Jack must remain in place during ball joint replacement to hold spring and lower control arm in position.

3. Remove cotter pin and nut securing ball joint stud to steering knuckle, then disconnect joint from knuckle using a suitable tool, **Fig. 7.**
4. Lift knuckle assembly from ball stud, guiding control arm out of splash shield, then support knuckle aside to allow clearance for joint removal.
5. Remove grease fitting, then press ball joint assembly out of lower control arm using a suitable tool, **Fig. 8.**
6. Press replacement joint into arm by

reversing removal tools, fit spindle over ball stud, install washer, if equipped, and retaining nut.

NOTE: On 1980—82 models except 1982 Camaro, seat ball stud in steering knuckle before installing nut. Install tool J-29194 over stud, torque tool to 40 ft. lbs., then remove tool and install nut.

7. Torque retaining nut to 90 ft. lbs. on 1980—86 models except 1984—86 Corvette and 48 ft. lbs. on 1984—86 Corvette.
8. Tighten nut up to an additional 1/16 turn, if necessary, to align hole in ball stud with nut, then install cotter pin.

NOTE: On 1980—82 Malibu and Monte Carlo, install cotter pin from rear.

1980—82 CORVETTE

1. Raise vehicle and support at frame, and remove wheel and tire.
2. Remove cotter pins from upper and lower joints and loosen but do not remove retaining nuts.

NOTE: Do not loosen nuts more than one full turn.

3. To release ball studs from knuckle, tap on boss of knuckle with a hammer, using another heavy hammer or similar tool as a drift.
4. Place a suitable floor jack under lower control arm, and raise jack to compress coil spring. Position jack as close to outer end of arm as possible, while leaving clearance for ball joint removal.
5. Remove ball joint retaining nuts and secure spindle assembly aside, taking care not to stretch brake hose.

Fig. 9 Coil spring removal (Typical)

NOTE: PIVOT PINS ARE REMOVED SO THAT THE BRACKET MAY BE PLACED OVER THE TOP OF THE SPRING.

Fig. 10   Leaf spring removal. 1984—86 Corvette

6. Remove rivets securing ball joint to control arm and ball joint.
7. Position replacement joint on control arm, install retaining bolts and nuts, and torque to 25 ft. lbs.
8. Install spindle assembly and ball joint retaining nuts, then torque upper nut to 50 ft. lbs. and lower nut to 80 ft. lbs.
9. Tighten nuts up to an additional 1/16 turn, if necessary, to align holes in ball studs with nuts, then install cotter pins.

SHOCK ABSORBER
REPLACE

NOTE: On 1982—86 Camaro, refer to "Strut, Replace" procedure.

1. Raise and support vehicle as needed, and remove wheel and tire.
2. Hold shock absorber shaft with a suitable wrench and remove upper retaining nut, washer and bushing.
3. Remove lower retaining bolts and shock absorber. On 1984—86 Corvette, remove shock mounting bracket, if necessary, to provide clearance for shock absorber removal.
4. Reverse procedure to install. Torque upper retaining nut to 90 inch lbs. on 1980—82 Corvette; 8 ft. lbs. on all 1980—86 models except Corvette, and 19 ft. lbs. on 1984—86 Corvette. Torque lower mounting bolts to 20 ft. lbs. on all models except Corvette; 150 inch lbs. on 1980—82 Corvette, and 22 ft. lbs. on 1984—86 Corvette.

STRUT
REPLACE

1982—86 CAMARO

1. Raise and support vehicle.
2. Remove wheel and support lower control arm with a suitable jack.
3. Remove brake hose bracket and two strut to knuckle bolts, **Fig. 2.**
4. Remove upper mounting assembly cover.
5. Remove nut from upper end of strut,

then the strut and shield.
6. Reverse procedure to install. Tighten strut to knuckle bolts to 195 ft. lbs., and strut to upper mount nut to 50 ft. lbs.

COIL SPRING
REPLACE

EXC. 1982—86 CAMARO

1. Disconnect shock absorber from lower mounting, push shock absorber through hole in lower control arm and compress into spring.
2. Support vehicle by frame so control arms hang free.
3. Install a safety chain through spring and lower control arm.
4. Install tool J-23028 onto a suitable jack and position jack so control arm is supported by bushings seated in grooves of tool, **Fig. 9.**
5. Remove stabilizer to lower control arm attachment.
6. Raise jack to relieve tension on control arm bolts and remove bolts.
7. Lower jack until tension is removed from spring, remove chain and spring from vehicle.
8. Reverse procedure to install, installing front pivot bolt first.

NOTE: To ensure adequate suspension clearance, install front pivot bolt from front, with nut toward rear of vehicle. Rear bolt can be installed from either direction.

9. Torque pivot bolts to specifications:
1980—82 Corvette front ... 70 ft. lbs.
                   rear ... 95 ft. lbs.
1980—81 Camaro .... 90 ft. lbs.
1980—83 Malibu .... 65 ft. lbs.
1980—86 Chevrolet .... 90 ft. lbs.
1980—86 Monte Carlo .... 65 ft. lbs.

1982—86 CAMARO

1. Raise and support vehicle and remove wheel.
2. Remove stabilizer link and bushings from lower control arm.
3. Remove pivot bolt nuts, leaving the bolts installed.
4. Install tool J-23028 onto a suitable

jack and position so that tool supports bushings, **Fig. 9.**
5. Raise jack to relieve tension on pivot bolts and remove bolts.
6. Carefully lower jack until tension is removed from spring and remove spring from vehicle.
7. Reverse procedure to install. Torque pivot bolt nuts to 65 ft. lbs. and stabilizer link nut to 20 ft. lbs.

CAUTION: The spring force under compression is very great. Exercise every safety precaution when performing this operation to see that individuals and materials subject to damage are removed from the path of the spring when the control arm is being lowered. Also, the compressed spring should be relaxed immediately after lowering the control arm to reduce the time of exposure to the great compressive force.

LEAF SPRING
REPLACE

1984—86 CORVETTE

1. Raise and support vehicle, and remove front wheels.
2. Remove both spring protectors.
3. Install spring compressor J-33432 or equivalent, **Fig. 10.**
4. Disconnect lower ball joints from steering knuckles.
5. Compress spring by rotating turnbuckle on spring compressor.
6. Remove bolts securing shock brackets to lower control arms and spring mounting bolts.
7. Release tension on spring compressor and remove compressor.
8. Remove spring.
9. Reverse procedure to install. Torque spring mounting bolts to 46 ft. lbs. with vehicle on ground.

Fig. 11 Power steering control valve and adapter, exploded view. 1980—82 Corvette

Fig. 12 Control valve ball stud seal replacement. 1980—82 Corvette

MANUAL STEERING GEAR
REPLACE

NOTE: On models where shield is installed, remove shield from coupling.

1. Remove nuts, washers and bolts at steering coupling.
2. Remove pitman arm nut and washer from sector shaft and mark relation of arm position to shaft.
3. Use a suitable puller to remove pitman arm.
4. Unfasten gear from frame and remove assembly.
5. Reverse procedure to install. Torque gear mounting bolts to 30 ft. lbs. on 1980—82 Corvette, 70 ft. lbs. on 1980—81 and 1983—86 models except Corvette, or 80 ft. lbs. on 1982 models except Corvette. Torque shaft coupling nuts to 30 ft. lbs. Torque pitman arm retaining nut to 185 ft. lbs. on all except 1980—81 or 180 ft. lbs. on all 1980—81 models.

INTEGRAL POWER STEERING
REPLACE

EXC. CORVETTE

To remove gear assembly, disconnect pressure and return hoses from gear housing and cap both hoses and steering gear outlets to prevent foreign material from entering system, then follow procedure as outlined under Steering Gear, Replace.

LINKAGE TYPE POWER STEERING

1980—82 CORVETTE

Power steering equipment consists of a recirculating ball type steering gear and linkage to which a hydraulic power mechanism has been added as part of the steering linkage. The hydraulic mechanism furnishes additional power to assist the man-

ual operation so that the turning effort at the steering wheel is greatly reduced. The hydraulic mechanism consists of three basic units: a hydraulic pump and reservoir, a control valve, and a power cylinder.

Control Valve, Adjust

1. Disconnect cylinder rod from frame bracket.
2. With car on a hoist, start the engine. One of the following two conditions will exist:
    a. If piston rod remains retracted, turn the adjusting nut clockwise until the rod begins to move out. Then turn the nut counterclockwise until the rod just begins to move in. Now turn the nut clockwise to exactly one half the rotation needed to change the direction of shaft movement.
    b. If the rod extends upon starting the pump, move the nut counter-clockwise until the rod begins to retract, then clockwise until the rod begins to move out again. Now turn the rod to exactly one half the rotation needed to change the direction of shaft movement.

NOTE: Do not turn the nut back and forth more than is absolutely necessary to balance the valve.

3. Restart engine. Front wheels should not turn from center if valve has been properly balanced.

POWER CYLINDER REPAIRS
Removal

1. Disconnect two hydraulic lines at power cylinder.
2. Unfasten power cylinder rod from brace at frame.
3. Unfasten power cylinder from relay rod bracket.
4. Remove power cylinder from car.

Inspection

1. Inspect seals for leaks around cylinder rod and if leaks are present, replace seals as follows:
2. Use a hook tool to remove retaining ring. Remove wiper ring, back-up washer, back-up ring and seal. Piston rod seal should not be removed unless there are signs of leakage

along the piston shaft at shaft seal.
3. Examine brass fitting hose connection seats for cracks or damage and replace if necessary.
4. For service other than seat or seal replacement, replace the power cylinder.

Installation

1. Install power cylinder on car by reversing removal procedure. Torque the frame bracket to rod nut to 23 ft lbs. and the relay rod bracket nut to 45 ft. lbs. Additional torque may be applied to align castellation with hole in stud, not to exceed 30 ft. lbs. on frame bracket to rod nut and 50 ft. lbs. on relay rod bracket nut.
2. Reconnect two hoses, fill system with fluid and bleed system as outlined below.

Filling & Bleeding System

1. Fill reservoir to proper level with Automatic Transmission Fluid and let fluid remain undisturbed for about two minutes.
2. Raise front wheels off floor.
3. Run engine at idle for two minutes.
4. Increase engine speed to about 1500 rpm.
5. Turn wheels from one extreme to the other, lightly contacting stops.
6. Lower wheels to floor and turn wheels right and left.
7. Recheck for leaks.
8. Check oil level and refill as required. Pump pressure should be 870 lbs.

CONTROL VALVE REPAIRS
Replace

1. Loosen relay rod-to-control valve clamp.
2. Disconnect hose connections at control valve.
3. Disconnect control valve from pitman arm.
4. Unscrew control valve from relay rod, **Fig. 11.**
5. Remove control valve from car.
6. Reverse procedure to install. Torque relay rod clamp bolt to 25 ft. lbs. Torque pitman arm nut to 45 ft. lbs. plus additional torque required to align castellation with hole in stud not to exceed 50 ft. lbs.

Ball Stud Seal, Replace

In servicing the control valve, refer to **Fig. 11**. To replace the ball stud seal, refer to **Fig. 12** and proceed as follows:

1. Remove pitman arm with a suitable puller.
2. Remove clamp by removing nut, bolt and spacer. If crimped type clamp is used, straighten clamp end and pull clamp and seal off end of stud.
3. Install new seal and clamp over stud so lips on seal mate with clamp. (A nut and bolt attachment type clamp replaces the crimped type for service, **Fig. 11**).
4. Center the ball stud, seal and clamp in opening in adapter housing, then install spacer, bolt and nut.

RACK & PINION STEERING GEAR
REPLACE

1984–86 CORVETTE

1. Raise and support vehicle, and remove left wheel and tire.

2. Disconnect hoses at steering gear, and plug lines and open ports.
3. Disconnect outer tie rods from steering knuckles.
4. Remove upper and lower mounting bolts on right side and single mounting bolt on left side.
5. Disconnect intermediate shaft universal joint from steering gear.
6. Remove stabilizer shaft and electric fan to provide clearance.
7. Remove steering gear.
8. Reverse procedure to install. Torque bolts securing right bracket to 18 ft. lbs., and bolt securing gear to crossmember to 25 ft. lbs.
9. Top off fluid reservoir, bleed system and check for leaks.

POWER STEERING PUMP
REPLACE

EXC. 1984–86 CORVETTE

1. Disconnect hoses at power steering pump, then plug pump parts and hoses.
2. Loosen pump adjusting bolt and remove pump drive belt.
3. Remove pump to support bracket attaching bolts and the pump.
4. Reverse procedure to install. Torque attaching bolts to the following specifications: 1980–82 Corvette, 25 ft. lbs., 1980–86 all except Corvette, 35 ft. lbs.

1984–86 CORVETTE

1. Rotate belt tensioner counterclockwise, and remove serpentine drive belt.
2. Remove AIR pump pulley.
3. Remove bolts securing power steering reservoir bracket and bolts securing reservoir brace to intake manifold.
4. Disconnect power steering hoses between pump and steering gear, then plug hoses and open fittings.
5. Remove pump mounting bolts, pump and reservoir.
6. Reverse procedure to install, torquing pump and bracket bolts to 18 ft. lbs.

NOTE: Refer to the rear of this manual for vehicle manufacturer's special service tool suppliers.

Vehicle Identification Number Location

On top of instrument panel, left front.

Engine Number Location

On right side of cylinder block, below No. 1 spark plug on gasoline models; at left rear of engine on diesel models.

Engine V.I.N. Code

On 1980 vehicles, the fifth digit in the V.I.N. denotes engine code. On 1981–86 vehicles, the eighth digit in the V.I.N. denotes engine code.

Engine Identification Code

Engines are identified in the following table by the code letter or letters immediately following the engine serial number.

Year	Engine	V.I.N. Code	Code
1980	4-97	9	CKA, CKB, CKC
	4-97	9	CKD, CKF, CKH
	4-97	9	CKJ, CKK
	4-97	O	CKL, CKM, CKR, CKS
1981	4-97	9	DCA, DCB, DCC
	4-97	9	DCD, DCF, DCH
	4-97	9	DCJ, DCU, DCW
	4-97	9	DCX, DCY, DCZ
	4-110	D	DCX, DCY, DCZ
1982	4-97①②	C	CHA, CHF, CHR
	4-97①③	C	CHT, CHW, CHX
	4-97②④	C	CUA, CUB
	4-97③④	C	CUC, CUD, CUF
	4-110①②⑤	D	CWA
	4-110①③⑤	D	CWB
1983	4-97	C	DAB, DAT
	4-97	C	DWA, DWB, DWC
	4-97	C	DWD, DWF, DWH
	4-97	C	DWK, DWM, DWN
	4-97	C	DWR, DWT, DWU
	4-97	C	DWW, DWX
	4-97	C	DWY, DWZ
	4-97	C	DZA, DZD, DZJ
	4-97	C	DZK, DZR, DZS
	4-97	C	DZW, DZX
	4-97	C	D8A, D8C
	4-97	C	D8D, D8F
	4-110①②⑤	D	DJB, DJD
	4-110①③⑤	D	DJA, DJC, DMR, DMT
	4-110②④⑤	D	DJC
	4-110③④⑤	D	DJD
1984	4-97	C	SWJ, SWK, SWM
	4-97	C	SWN, SWR
	4-97	C	SWS, SWT
	4-97	C	T4A, T4B, T4C
	4-97	C	T4D, TF4
	4-110⑤	D	—
1985	4-97	C	CAT, CTB, CTC
	4-97	C	CTD, CTF, CTH
	4-97	C	CTJ, CTM, T4J
	4-97	C	T4K, T4L, T4M
	4-97	C	T4N
	4-110	D⑤	—
1986	4-97	C	—
	4-110	D⑤	—

①—Except Calif.
②—Manual Trans.
③—Auto. Trans.
④—California.
⑤—Diesel engine.

Grille Identification

1980 Chevette

1981–82 Chevette

1981 1000

1982–86 1000

1983–84 Chevette

1985–86 Chevette

General Engine Specifications

Year	Engine CID①/Liter	Engine VIN Code	Carburetor	Bore and Stroke	Compression Ratio	Net H.P. @ R.P.M.②	Maximum Torque Lbs. Ft. @ R.P.M.	Normal Oil Pressure Pounds
1980	4-97, 1.6 Liter⑤	9③	6510C, 2 Bbl⑦	3.228 × 2.980 / 82.0 × 75.7 mm.	8.5	70 @ 5200	82 @ 2400	55
	4-97, 1.6 Liter⑤⑥	O③	5210C, 2 Bbl⑦	3.228 × 2.980 / 82.0 × 75.7 mm.	8.6	74 @ 5200	88 @ 2800	55
1981	4-97, 1.6 Liter⑤	9⑧	5210C, 2 Bbl⑦	3.228 × 2.980 / 82.0 × 75.7 mm.	8.6	70 @ 5200	82 @ 2400	55
	4-110, 1.8 Liter④	D⑧	Fuel Injection	3.310 × 3.230 / 84.0 × 82.0 mm.	22.0	51 @ 5000	72 @ 2000	64
1982–84	4-97, 1.6 Liter⑤	C⑧	6510C, 2 Bbl.⑦	3.228 × 2.980 / 82.0 × 75.7 mm.	9.2	65 @ 5200	80 @ 3200	55
	4-110, 1.8 Liter④	D⑧	Fuel Injection	3.310 × 3.230 / 84.0 × 82.0 mm.	22.0	51 @ 5000	72 @ 2000	64
1985–86	4-97, 1.6 Liter⑤	C⑧	6510C, 2 Bbl.⑦	3.228 × 2.980 / 82.0 × 75.7 mm.	9.0	65 @ 5200	80 @ 3200	55
	4-110, 1.8 Liter④	D⑧	Fuel Injection	3.310 × 3.230 / 84.0 × 82.0 mm.	22.0	51 @ 5000	72 @ 2000	64

①—CID—Cubic inch displacement.
②—Ratings are net as installed in vehicle.
③—Fifth digit in the VIN denotes engine code.
④—Diesel engine.
⑤—1600 cc engine.
⑥—High output engine.
⑦—Holley.
⑧—Eighth digit in the VIN denotes engine code.

Pistons, Pins, Rings, Crankshaft & Bearings

Year	Engine/ V.I.N.	Piston Clearance Top of Skirt	Ring End Gap① Comp.	Ring End Gap① Oil	Wrist-pin Diameter	Rod Bearings Shaft Diameter	Rod Bearings Bearing Clearance	Main Bearings Shaft Diameter	Main Bearings Bearing Clearance	Thrust on Bear. No.	Shaft End Play
1980	All	.0008–.0016 / .020–.040 mm	⑤	.015 / .381 mm	.9052 / 22.992 mm	1.8093–1.8103 / 45.958–45.984 mm	.0014–.0031 / .036–.078 mm	2.0078–2.0088 / 51.0–51.024 mm	②	5	.004–.008 / .100–.202 mm
1981–83	4-97④	.0007–.0015 / .020–.040 mm	⑤	.015 / .381 mm	.9052 / 22.994 mm	1.8093–1.8103 / 45.958–45.984 mm	.0014–.0031 / .036–.078 mm	2.0078–2.0088 / 51.0–51.024 mm	②	5	.004–.008 / .100–.202 mm
1984–86	4-97④	.0007–.0015 / .020–.040 mm	⑤	.015 / .381 mm	.9052 / 22.994 mm	1.8093–1.8103 / 45.958–45.984 mm	.0014–.0031 / .036–.078 mm	⑥	②	5	.004–.008 / .100–.202 mm
1981–82	4-110/D ③	.0060–.0070 / .143–.167 mm	.0078 / .200 mm	.0078 / .200 mm	.984 / 25.0 mm	1.925–1.926 / 48.895–48.920 mm	.0016–.0032 / .040–.081 mm	2.201–2.202 / 55.920–55.935 mm	.0015–.0027 / .039–.080 mm	3	.002–.009 / .06–.24 mm
1983–86	4-110/D ③	.0060–.0070 / .143–.167 mm	.0078 / .200 mm	.0078 / .200 mm	.984 / 25.0 mm	1.925–1.926 / 48.895–48.920 mm	.0016–.0027 / .040–.070 mm	2.201–2.202 / 55.920–55.935 mm	.0015–.0027 / .039–.080 mm	3	.002–.009 / .06–.24 mm

①—Fit ring in tapered bore for clearance listed in tightest portion of ring travel.
②—No. 1, 2, 3 & 4, .0006–.0018 (.014–046 mm); No. 5, .0009–.0026 (.024–.066 mm).
③—Diesel Engine.
④—For V.I.N. code, refer to the "General Engine Specifications" at the front of the chapter.
⑤—Top ring, .011 inch (.229 mm); 2nd ring, .008 inch (.203 mm).
⑥—Nos. 1, 2, 3, 4—2.0078–2.0088 inch (51.0–51.025 mm); No. 5, 2.0395–2.0405 inch (50.987–51.013 mm).

18–3

Valve Specifications

Year	Engine/ V.I.N.	Valve Lash Int.	Valve Lash Exh.	Valve Angles Seat	Valve Angles Face	Valve Spring Installed Height	Valve Spring Pressure Lbs. @ In.	Stem Clearance Intake	Stem Clearance Exhaust	Stem Diameter Intake	Stem Diameter Exhaust
1980–81	4-97.6/9	Hydraulic		45	46	1.26 32 mm.	173 @ .886 770N @ 22.5 mm.	.0006–.0017 .015–.045 mm.	.0014–.0025 .035–.065 mm.	.3138–.3144 7.970–7.986 mm.	.3130–.3136 7.950–7.965 mm.
1981–82	4-110/D③	.010④ .25 mm.	.014④ .35 mm.	45	45	①	②	.0015–.0028 .039–.071 mm.	.0018–.0030 .045–.077 mm.	.3128–.3124 7.946–7.961 mm.	.3126–.3132 7.940–7.955 mm.
1982–86	4-97.6/C	Hydraulic		45	46	1.30 33.1 mm.	170 @ .917 756N @ 23.3 mm.	.0006–.0017 .015–.045 mm.	.0014–.0025 .035–.065 mm.	.3138–.3144 7.970–7.986 mm.	.3130–.3136 7.950–7.965 mm.
1983–86	4-110/D③	.010④ .25 mm.	.014④ .35 mm.	45	45	①	②	.0015–.0028 .039–.071 mm.	.0018–.0030 .045–.077 mm.	.310–.314 7.88–8.0 mm.	.310–.314 7.88–8.0 mm.

①—Free length, inner 1.783 inch; outer 1.846 inch.
②—Inner, 19–22 lbs. @ 1.516 inch; outer, 32–37 lbs. @ 1.614 inch.
③—Diesel Engine.
④—Hot or Cold.

Engine Tightening Specifications★

★ Torque specifications are for clean and lightly lubricated threads only. Dry or dirty threads produce increased friction which prevents accurate measurement of tightness.

Year	Engine/ V.I.N.	Spark Plugs Ft. Lbs.	Camshaft Carrier Bolts Ft. Lbs.	Intake Manifold Ft. Lbs.	Exhaust Manifold Ft. Lbs.	Camshaft Sprocket Bolt Ft. Lbs.	Cam Cover In. Lbs.	Connecting Rod Cap Bolts Ft. Lbs.	Main Bearing Cap Bolts Ft. Lbs.	Flywheel to Crankshaft Ft. Lbs.	Vibration Damper or Pulley Ft. Lbs.
1980–82	4-97⑧	18.4 25 N-m	75 100 N-m	15 20 N-m	①	75 100 N-m	14 1.6 N-m	40 54 N-m	50 68 N-m	50 68 N-m	75 100 N-m
1981	4-110/D②	③	④	28 40 N-m	15 20 N-m	47 64 N-m	⑤	65 88 N-m	75 100 N-m	40⑥ 54 N-m	110 149 N-m
1982	4-110/D②	③	⑦	30	—	45	⑤	65	65–72	40⑥	110
1983–86	4-97⑧	18.4 25 N-m	75	18	25	75	14	40	50	50	100
	4-110②	③	⑦	30	—	55	⑤	65	65–72	40⑥	110

①—Center bolts, 15 ft. lbs. (22 Newton-meters); end legs, 22 ft. lbs. (30 Newton-meters).
②—Diesel engine.
③—Glow Plugs—54 ft. lbs., 73 N-m.
④—Cylinder head bolts—105 ft. lbs., 142 N-m.
⑤—Rocker arm cover—7 ft. lbs., 10 N-m.
⑥—Apply loctite to threads, do not lubricate bolts.
⑦—Cylinder head bolts; new, 83–98 ft. lbs.; used, 90–105 ft. lbs.
⑧—For V.I.N. code, refer to the "General Engine Specifications" at the beginning of the chapter.

Starting Motor Applications

Year	Model	Starter Number
1980	All	1109522
1981–83	4-97/9,C	1109532
1981–85	4-110 Diesel/D	9438758
1984	4-97/C	1998428
1985	4-97/C	1998525

Wheel Alignment Specifications

Year	Model	Caster Angle, Degrees Limits	Caster Angle, Degrees Desired	Camber Angle, Degrees Limits Left	Camber Angle, Degrees Limits Right	Camber Angle, Degrees Desired Left	Camber Angle, Degrees Desired Right	Toe-In Inch	Toe-Out on Turns, Deg. Outer Wheel	Toe-Out on Turns, Deg. Inner Wheel
1980–81	All	+3½° to +5½°	+4½°	−.2° to +.6°	−.2° to +.6°	+.2°	+.2°	①	—	—
1982–86	All	+4° to +6°	+5°	−.2° to +.6°	−.2° to +.6°	+.2°	+.2°	②	—	—

①—1981, 1/64 to 7/64 inch (.5 to 2.5 mm); 1980, ⅛ to 9/64 inch (1.3 to 3.7 mm).
②—+.06° ± .04° (+1.5 mm ± 1.0 mm).

Cooling System & Capacity Data

Year	Model or Engine/V.I.N.	Cooling Capacity, Qts.		Radiator Cap Relief Pressure, Lbs.	Thermo. Opening Temp.	Fuel Tank Gals.	Engine Oil Refill Qts.	Transmission Oil			Rear Axle Oils Pints
		Less A/C	With A/C					4 Speed Pints	5 Speed Pints	Auto. Trans. Qts. ①	
1980	All	9 8.5 ltr.	9.25 8.8 ltr.	15	190	12.5 47.3 ltr.	4 3.8 ltr.	3.4 1.6 ltr.	—	③	1.75 .83 ltr.
1981	All	9 8.5 ltr.	9.25 8.8 ltr.	15	190	12.5 47.3 ltr.	4 3.8 ltr.	3.4 1.6 ltr.	—	③	1.75 .83 ltr.
1981–82	4-110/D④	9 8.5 ltr.	—	15	180	12.5 47.3 ltr.	6⑤ 5.8 ltr.	3.25 1.5 ltr.	4 1.9 ltr.	⑥	1.75 .81 ltr.
1982	4-97/C	9 8.5 ltr.	9.25 8.6 ltr.	15	190	12.5 47.3 ltr.	4⑤ 3.8 ltr.	3.5	4 1.9 ltr.	②	1.75 .81 ltr.
1983–85	4-97/C	9 8.5 ltr.	9.25 8.6 ltr.	15	190	12.5 47.3 ltr.	4⑤ 3.8 ltr.	3.4 1.6 ltr.	4 1.9 ltr.	⑥	1.75 .81 ltr.
	4-110/D④	9 8.5 ltr.	—	15	180	12.5 47.3 ltr.	6⑤ 5.8 ltr.	3.3 1.55 ltr.	4 1.9 ltr.	⑥	1.75 .81 ltr.
1986	4-97/C	9 8.5 ltr.	9.26 8.7 ltr.	15	190	12.2 46.2 ltr.	4⑦ 3.8 ltr.	3.4 1.6 ltr.	4.5 2.13 ltr.	⑧	1.75 .81 ltr.
	4-110/D④	9 8.5 ltr.	—	15	180	12.2 46.2 ltr.	5⑦ 4.7 ltr.	—	3.3 1.55 ltr.		1.75 .81 ltr.

①—Approximate. Make final check with dipstick.
②—After overhaul, 4.9 qts.; oil pan only, 3 qts.
③—Drain and refill, 3 qts. (2.7 ltrs.).
④—Diesel engine.
⑤—Includes filter.
⑥—After overhaul, 5 qts.; oil pan only, 3.5 qts.
⑦—Less filter.
⑧—Drain and refill, 2.43 qts. (2.30 ltrs.).

Rear Axle Specifications

Year	Model	Carrier Type	Ring Gear & Pinion Backlash		Pinion Bearing Preload			Differential Bearing Preload		
			Method	Adjustment	Method	New Bearings Inch-Lbs.	Used Bearings Inch-Lbs.	Method	New Bearings Inch-Lbs.	Used Bearings Inch-Lbs.
1980–81	All	Integral	Shims	—	Spacer	15–25 1.7–2.82 N-m	5–10 .056–1.13 N-m	Shims	—	—
1982–86	All	Integral	Shims	—	Spacer	①	5–10 .056–1.13 mm	Shims	—	—

①—With NDH bearings, 10–20 inch lbs.; with Timken bearings, 5–15 inch lbs.

Alternator Specifications

Year	Model	Alternator	
		Rated Hot Output Amps.	Field Current 12 Volts @ 80° F.
1980	1102845	32	4.0–4.5
	1103080	32	4–5
1981–82	1100138②	42	4–5
	LR155-12B①	55	—
1983–85	1100234②	42	4–5
	1100253②	66	4.5–5.0
	1100261②	78	4.5–5.0
	94234987①	55	—

①—Diesel engine.
②—Exc. diesel engine.

Electrical Section

STARTER
REPLACE

DIESEL ENGINE

Refer to **Fig. 1** for starter removal and installation.

GASOLINE ENGINE

1980—86 Less Power Brakes

1. Disconnect battery ground cable, then remove air cleaner.
2. Disconnect fuel line at carburetor and position aside.
3. Disconnect vacuum hoses at carburetor.
4. Remove splash shield from distributor coil and position aside.
5. Remove upper and lower starter retaining bolts.
6. Disconnect electrical leads from starter and position starter aside for access.
7. Remove master cylinder mounting nuts to gain access for removing starter. It will be necessary to move the master cylinder aside to remove the starter.
8. Remove starter.
9. Reverse procedure to install.

1980—86 With Power Brakes

1. Disconnect battery ground cable, then remove air cleaner.
2. Disconnect fuel line at carburetor and position aside.
3. Remove splash shield from distributor coil and position aside.
4. Remove upper starter retaining bolt.

NOTE: To remove the upper starter retaining bolt on models equipped with A/C, use a 15mm short socket with short extension, universal 12 inch extension and a ratchet or speed handle. Access to the bolt is gained through the intake manifold 3rd and 4th runners. After completely loosening the bolt, remove it with a magnet.

5. Remove steering column cover screws and cover.
6. Remove steering column upper mounting nuts and toe pan screw.
7. Raise and support front of vehicle.
8. Remove steering shaft from steering coupling. Lower vehicle and move steering column from inside vehicle for access to starter.
9. Disconnect electrical leads from starter.
10. Remove lower starter retaining bolt and remove starter.
11. Reverse procedure to install.

IGNITION LOCK
REPLACE

1980—86

1. Remove steering wheel as described under Horn Sounder and Steering Wheel.
2. Remove turn signal switch as described under Turn Signal Switch, Replace, then remove buzzer switch.
3. Place ignition switch in Run position, then remove lock cylinder retaining screw and lock cylinder.
4. To install, rotate lock cylinder to stop while holding housing, **Fig. 2.** Align cylinder key with keyway in housing, then push lock cylinder assembly into housing until fully seated.
5. Install lock cylinder retaining screw. Torque screw to 40 in. lbs. for standard columns. On adjustable columns, torque retaining screw to 22 in. lbs.
6. Install buzzer switch, turn signal switch and steering wheel.

LIGHT SWITCH
REPLACE

1. Disconnect battery ground cable.
2. Pull headlamp switch knob to "ON" position, **Fig. 3.**
3. Reach under instrument panel and depress switch shaft retainer button while pulling on the switch control shaft knob.
4. With a large bladed screwdriver, remove the light switch ferrule nut from front of instrument panel.
5. Disconnect the multi-contact connector from side of switch and remove switch.
6. Reverse procedure to install.

STOP LIGHT SWITCH
REPLACE

1. Reach under right side of instrument panel at brake pedal support and release wiring harness connector at switch.
2. Pull switch from mounting bracket.
3. When installing switch, adjust by bringing brake pedal to normal position. Electrical contact should be made when pedal is depressed .53 inch (13.5 mm). To adjust, the switch may be rotated or pulled in the clip.

CLUTCH START SWITCH
REPLACE

NOTE: The clutch pedal must be fully depressed and the ignition switch in START position for the vehicle to start.

The clutch switch assembly mounts with two tangs to the clutch pedal brace switch pivot bracket and the clutch pedal arm, **Fig. 4.**

1. Under the instrument panel on the clutch pedal support remove the multi-contact connector from switch.
2. Compress switch assembly actuating shaft barb retainer and push out of clutch pedal.
3. Compress switch assembly pivot bracket barb and lift off switch.
4. When installing new switch, no adjustments are necessary as the switch is self aligning.

Fig. 1   Starter removal & installation. 1981—86 Diesel engine models

Fig. 2   Ignition lock removal & installation. 1980—86

Fig. 3   Light switch replacement

NEUTRAL SAFETY SWITCH
REPLACE

1. Remove floor console cover.
2. Disconnect electrical plugs on backup contacts, seat belt warning contacts and neutral start contacts of switch assembly, **Fig. 5**.
3. Place shift lever in Neutral.
4. Remove two screws securing switch to lever assembly.
5. When installing switch, make sure it is in Neutral position. When switch is installed, shifting out of Neutral will shear the switch plastic locating pin.

A/C COMPRESSOR CUT-OUT SWITCH

Vehicles equipped with automatic transmission and air conditioning utilize a full throttle A/C compressor cut-out switch, **Fig. 6,** which de-energizes the A/C compressor clutch during full throttle acceleration. A pressure sensitive switch, located in the transmission, overrides the cut-out

Fig. 5   Neutral start switch replacement

switch when the transmission is in third gear during full throttle acceleration.

TURN SIGNAL SWITCH
REPLACE

1. Remove steering wheel as described under "Horn Sounder & Steering Wheel" procedure.
2. Using a screw driver pry up and out to free cover from lock, **Fig. 7**.
3. Position lock plate compressing tool No. J-23653 on end of steering shaft and compress lock plate, **Fig. 8**.
4. Pry snap ring out of groove and discard, then remove tool J-23653 and lift lock plate off end of shaft.
5. Slide canceling cam, upper bearing preload spring and thrust washer off end of shaft.
6. Rotate multi-function lever to off position, then pull lever straight out to disengage.
7. Depress hazard warning knob and unscrew knob.
8. Remove two screws, pivot arm and spacer, **Fig. 9**.
9. Wrap upper part of connector with tape to prevent snagging of wires during switch removal, **Fig. 10**.
10. Remove three switch attaching screws and pull switch straight up guiding wires through column housing.

HORN SOUNDER & STEERING WHEEL
REPLACE

1. Disconnect battery ground cable.
2. Pry off horn button cap and retainer.
3. Remove steering wheel nut retainer and nut.

NOTE: Do not over expand retainer.

4. Using a suitable puller remove steering wheel.

W/S WIPER, DIMMER OR IGNITION SWITCHES
REMOVAL

1. Disconnect battery ground cable.
2. Remove steering column mounting bracket and unsnap switch connector from jacket.
3. Remove steering wheel.
4. Remove lock plate cover with a suitable screwdriver, **Fig. 7**.
5. Remove ring and lock plate. Use caution to prevent shaft from sliding out bottom of column. Slide upper bearing preload spring and turn signal cancelling cam off upper steering shaft, then the thrust washer off shaft.
6. Rotate turn signal lever-W/S switch assembly counter-clockwise to stop (off position) and pull straight out to disengage.
7. Remove two screws, pivot arm and

Fig. 4   Clutch start switch replacement

spacer, **Fig. 9**. Note that pivot arm retains spacer.
8. Lower steering column, then remove turn signal switch mounting screws and the switch.
9. Pull actuator rod to the stop to place ignition switch in "Off-Unlock". Remove upper attaching screw, releasing dimmer switch and actuator. The switches may now be removed, **Figs. 11 and 12**.
10. Remove remaining ignition switch retaining screw and the ignition switch.

INSTALLATION

1. Assemble windshield wiper switch and pivot assembly onto housing.
2. Assemble buzzer switch and lock cylinder, then turn lock cylinder clockwise to stop and then counter-clockwise to other stop (OFF-UNLOCK) position. Position ignition switch, **Fig. 13,** then move slider to extreme left (ACC) and slide back two positions to the right to OFF-UNLOCK position. Install actuator rod into slider and install the bottom screw only, to retain the ignition switch. Do not move switch out of detent.
3. Install washer, spring and cancelling cam on steering shaft. Position can-

Fig. 6   A/C compressor cut-out switch

Key No.	Part Name
1 —	NUT, HEXAGON JAM
2 —	COVER ASSEMBLY, SHAFT LOCK
3 —	RING, RETAINING
4 —	LOCK, STEERING SHAFT
5 —	CAM ASSEMBLY, TURN SIGNAL CANCELLING
6 —	SPRING, UPPER BEARING
7 —	SCREW, PAN HEAD CROSS RECESS
8 —	SCREW, FLAT HEAD CROSS RECESS
9 —	SCREW, ROUND HEAD CROSS RECESS
10 —	ARM, PIVOT
11 —	SPACER, TURN SIGNAL SCREW
12 —	SWITCH ASSEMBLY, TURN SIGNAL
13 —	SWITCH ASSEMBLY, PIVOT &
14 —	SCREW HEX WASHER HEAD TAPPING
15 —	WASHER, THRUST
16 —	SWITCH ASSEMBLY, BUZZER

Key No.	Part Name
17 —	CLIP, BUZZER SWITCH RETAINING
18 —	HOUSING, STEERING COLUMN
19 —	BEARING ASSEMBLY
20 —	RETAINER, BEARING
21 —	SECTOR, SWITCH ACTUATOR
22 —	SPRING, RACK PRELOAD
23 —	RACK, SWITCH ACTUATOR
24 —	BOLT ASSEMBLY, SPRING &
25 —	WASHER, SPRING THRUST
26 —	WASHER, WAVE
27 —	LEVER, KEY RELEASE

Key No.	Part Name
28 —	SPRING, LOCK INHIBITER
29 —	HOUSING ASSEMBLY, SHROUD &
30 —	SCREW, PAN HEAD CROSS RECESS
31 —	ROD, SWITCH ACTUATOR

Key No.	Part Name
32 —	ROD, DIMMER SWITCH ACTUATOR
33 —	SWITCH ASSEMBLY, DIMMER
34 —	SWITCH ASSEMBLY, IGNITION
35 —	SCREW, WASHER HEAD
36 —	JACKET ASSEMBLY, STEERING COLUMN
37 —	SEAL, STEERING SHAFT
38 —	BUSHING, STEERING COLUMN JACKET
39 —	SHAFT ASSEMBLY, STEERING
40 —	RETAINER

Service Kits

201 — BOLT ASSEMBLY, SPRING &
202 — HOUSING ASSEMBLY, BEARING, SHAFT, SECTOR &
203 — SECTOR SERVICE UNIT, IGNITION SWITCH ACTUATOR
204 — SHAFT REPAIR KIT, INJECTION STEERING

Fig. 7 Steering column, disassembled

celling cam lobes in relation to signal switch springs and assemble shaft lock and install new retaining ring, **Fig. 7.**

4. Install cover and snap ring, then install multi-function switch lever. Align lever pin with switch slot and push lever until it seats.

5. Install pinched end of dimmer switch actuator rod into dimmer switch, then install other end of rod into pivot switch. Install but do not tighten upper ignition switch screw. Depress dimmer switch and insert a 3/32 inch drill to lock switch body, **Fig. 13.**

6. Move dimmer switch up, removing lash between both switches and rod, then install and tighten upper ignition switch screw. Remove drill and check dimmer switch for proper operation.

7. Snap electrical connector into place and raise steering column, then install mounting nuts and torque to 22 ft. lbs. (30 Nm) and install steering wheel.

INSTRUMENT CLUSTER
REPLACE

1. Disconnect battery ground cable.
2. Remove clock stem knob.
3. Remove cluster bezel and lens retaining screws, then the bezel and lens, **Fig. 14.**
4. Remove instrument cluster to instrument panel retaining nuts and pull cluster toward vehicle rear.
5. Disconnect all electrical connectors and speedometer cable from cluster, then remove cluster.
6. Reverse procedure to install.

Fig. 8 Compressing lock plate and removing retaining ring

Fig. 9 Removing pivot arm

Fig. 10 Taping turn signal switch and wires

Fig. 11 Ignition switch

Fig. 12 Dimmer & ignition switch replacement

Fig. 13 Dimmer switch alignment

RADIO
REPLACE

1. Disconnect battery ground cable.
2. Remove mounting stud nut from bottom of radio, and the control knobs from shafts.
3. Remove screws from center trim panel and pull panel and radio toward the rear of the vehicle.
4. Disconnect all electrical connectors from radio.
5. Remove radio retaining nuts from radio control shafts.
6. Remove radio from vehicle.
7. Reverse procedure to install.

HEATER CORE
REPLACE

1. Disconnect battery ground cable and drain cooling system.
2. Disconnect heater hoses from core and plug openings in core.
3. Remove heater core housing to dash panel attaching screws, then the housing.
4. Remove core from housing.

BLOWER MOTOR
REPLACE

1. Disconnect battery ground cable.
2. Disconnect blower lead wire.
3. Remove blower motor to case attaching screws then the blower and wheel as an assembly.

NOTE: Scribe mark on blower motor and case so motor is installed in original posi-

Fig. 14 Instrument cluster

tion.

4. Remove nut and separate motor from wheel.
5. Reverse procedure to install.

NOTE: At assembly position open end of blower wheel away from blower motor. Replace sealer at blower motor flange if necessary.

W/S WIPER MOTOR, REPLACE

1. Reach under instrument panel above steering column and loosen transmission drive link to motor crank arm attaching nuts.
2. Disengage transmission drive link from motor crank arm.
3. Raise hood and disconnect electrical connectors.
4. Remove motor attaching bolts.

5. Remove motor while guiding crank arm through hole.
6. To install, align sealing gasket to base of motor assembly and reverse remaining removal procedure.

NOTE: If the wiper motor to dash panel sealing gasket is damaged during removal, it should be replaced to prevent possible water leaks.

W/S WIPER TRANSMISSION
REPLACE

1. Remove instrument panel pad and cluster housing.
2. On models with A/C, remove left A/C duct attaching screws and position duct aside.
3. On all models, remove left side air duct.
4. Remove speedometer cable shield and left side instrument brace.
5. From under instrument panel, loosen transmission drive link to motor crank arm attaching nuts and disengage drive link.
6. Remove wiper arms and blades, then remove transmission to dash panel attaching bolts.
7. Move transmission assembly to left, then while rotating assembly, work out through instrument panel access hole at right upper center of instrument panel.

NOTE: When installing, ensure motor is in park position.

Gasoline Engine Section

ENGINE MOUNT
REPLACE

FRONT

1. Remove heater assembly and position on top of engine.
2. Remove radiator upper support.
3. Remove engine mount nuts and the restraint cable.
4. Raise vehicle, install engine lifting device and raise engine to relieve weight from mounts.
5. Remove mount to engine bracket, then using tool J-25510, remove mount.

REAR

1. Raise vehicle and remove crossmember to mount bolts.
2. Raise transmission at extension housing to relieve weight from mount.
3. Remove mount to transmission bolts and the mount.

ENGINE
REPLACE

1. Remove hood.
2. Disconnect battery cables and remove clips securing battery cable to right side frame rail.
3. Drain cooling system and disconnect radiator and heater hoses.
4. Disconnect engine wiring harness.
5. Remove radiator upper support, radiator and fan.
6. Remove air cleaner.
7. Disconnect fuel line at rubber hose located along left side frame rail.
8. Disconnect accelerator and automatic transmission throttle valve linkage, if equipped.
9. Remove A/C compressor from mounting bracket and position aside, if equipped.
10. Raise vehicle and disconnect exhaust pipe at manifold.
11. Remove flywheel dust cover.
12. On models with automatic transmission, remove converter to flywheel bolts.
13. Remove converter housing to engine bolts on automatic transmission models or flywheel housing to engine bolt on manual transmission models, then lower vehicle.

![Cylinder tightening sequence diagram showing numbers: top row FRONT 7 3 2 6 10, bottom row 8 4 1 5 9]

Fig. 1   Cylinder tightening sequence

14. Support transmission using a suitable jack.
15. Remove safety straps from engine mounts, then remove engine mount bolts.
16. Install engine lifting device, raise engine slowly, pull engine forward to clear transmission and remove engine from vehicle.

INTAKE MANIFOLD
REPLACE

1. Disconnect battery ground cable and drain cooling system.
2. Remove air cleaner and disconnect upper radiator hose and heater hoses from intake manifold.
3. Remove EGR valve.
4. Disconnect fuel line, wiring, vacuum hoses and linkage from carburetor.
5. If equipped with A/C, perform the following:
   a. Remove radiator upper support, alternator and A/C drive belts.
   b. Remove fan, pulley and timing belt cover.
   c. Position A/C compressor aside.
   d. Raise vehicle and remove the lower A/C compressor bracket.
   e. Lower vehicle and remove the upper A/C compressor bracket.
6. On all models, remove ignition coil and position aside.
7. Remove intake manifold attaching bolts and the intake manifold.
8. Reverse procedure to install.

CYLINDER HEAD
REPLACE

1. Remove timing belt.
2. Drain cooling system, remove upper radiator hose and heater hose at intake manifold.
3. Remove air cleaner, then remove accelerator support bracket.
4. Disconnect spark plug wires.
5. Disconnect wiring harnesses at idle solenoid, choke, temperature sending switch and alternator.
6. Raise vehicle and disconnect exhaust pipe at manifold.
7. Lower vehicle and remove bolt retaining dipstick bracket to manifold.
8. Disconnect fuel line at carburetor.
9. Remove coil bracket bolts and position coil aside.
10. Remove camshaft covers, then remove camshaft cover to housing attaching studs.
11. Remove rocker arms, guides and lash adjusters.

NOTE: Rocker arms, guides and lash adjusters must be installed in original location during assembly.

12. Remove camshaft carrier from cylinder head.

NOTE: It may be necessary to use a wedge to separate camshaft carrier from cylinder head.

13. Remove cylinder head and manifold as an assembly.
14. Reverse procedure to install, tighten cylinder bolts in the sequence, **Fig. 1**.

HYDRAULIC VALVE LASH ADJUSTERS

Failure of an hydraulic valve lash adjuster is generally caused by an inadequate oil supply or dirt. An air leak at the intake side of the oil pump or too much oil in the engine will cause air bubbles in the oil supply to the lash adjusters, causing them to collapse. This is a probable cause of trouble if several lash adjusters fail to function, but air in the oil is an unlikely cause of failure of a single unit.

ROCKER ARMS
REPLACE

1. Remove camshaft covers.
2. On 1980–86 models, remove carburetor.
3. Using tool J-25477, depress valve spring and remove rocker arm, guide and lash adjuster, **Fig. 2**.

NOTE: Rocker arms, guides and lash adjusters must be installed in the same location during assembly.

VALVE GUIDES

Valve guides are an integral part of the cylinder head. If stem to guide clearance is excessive, the guide should be reamed to the next oversize and the appropriate oversize valve installed. Valves are available in standard size and oversizes of .003 in. (.075mm), .006 in. (.150mm), and .012 in. (.300mm).

Fig. 2   Depressing valve spring

CAMSHAFT COVER
REPLACE

1. Raise hood to fully open position.
2. Disconnect battery ground cable.
3. Remove air cleaner, PCV valve, air cleaner snorkle and heat tube assembly.
4. Remove spark plug wires from retainer on camshaft cover.
5. Remove accelerator cable support and position aside.
6. Remove nut and gasket from stud and the camshaft cover.

CAMSHAFT SPROCKET
REPLACE

1. Remove drive belts, then the fan and pulley.
2. Remove timing belt front cover.
3. Loosen idler pulley and remove timing belt from camshaft sprocket.
4. Remove camshaft sprocket bolt and washer, remove camshaft sprocket.

CAMSHAFT
REPLACE

1. Remove camshaft sprocket as described under "Camshaft Sprocket" procedure.
2. Remove rocker arms.
3. Remove heater assembly and position aside.
4. Remove camshaft carrier rear cover.
5. Remove camshaft thrust plate bolts, slide camshaft rearward and remove thrust plate.
6. Raise engine, then carefully slide camshaft from carrier.

CAM LOBE LIFT SPECS.

Year	Intake	Exhaust
All 1980–86	.2407 (6.1163mm)	.2407 (6.1163mm)

VALVE TIMING
INTAKE OPEN BEFORE TDC

Engine	Year	Degrees
Hi Output	1980	31
All	1981–86	28

TIMING BELT FRONT COVER
REPLACE

UPPER COVER

1. Raise hood and disconnect battery ground cable.
2. Remove fan.
3. Remove upper cover retaining screw and the upper cover.

LOWER COVER

1. Remove crankshaft pulley.
2. Remove upper front cover.
3. Remove lower cover attaching nut and the lower cover.

UPPER REAR TIMING BELT COVER
REPLACE

1. Remove timing belt front cover, timing belt and camshaft sprocket.
2. Remove three upper rear timing belt cover to camshaft carrier attaching screws.
3. Inspect camshaft seal and replace, if necessary.

TIMING BELT
REPLACE

NOTE: To verify camshaft timing, position crankshaft so that No. 1 cylinder is at top dead center compression stroke. With No. 1 cylinder at top dead center compression stroke, a ⅛ inch drill bit can be inserted through a hole in rear cover and hole in camshaft sprocket, if timing is correct, **Fig. 3.**

1. Remove timing belt front upper and lower covers and crankshaft pulley.
2. Loosen idler pulley bolt and remove timing belt from camshaft and crankshaft sprockets.
3. Position timing belt over crankshaft sprocket, then install crankshaft pulley.
4. Position crankshaft at TDC number 1 cylinder.
5. Align timing mark on camshaft sprock-

et with hole in upper rear cover, **Fig. 3.**
6. Install timing belt on crankshaft and camshaft sprockets, then adjust belt tension.

TIMING BELT TENSION
ADJUST

1. Remove fan, drive belt, pulley and upper timing belt cover.
2. Rotate crankshaft at least one revolution and position No. 1 piston at top dead center.
3. Install belt tension gauge, Tool J-26486, **Fig. 4,** on timing belt midway between the cam sprocket and idler pulley. Ensure the gauge center finger engages in a notch on the belt.
4. Correct belt tension is 70 ft. lbs. To adjust, loosen idler pulley attaching bolt, **Fig. 5.** Then, using a ¼ inch allen wrench, rotate the pulley counterclockwise on the attaching bolt until correct belt tension is obtained and torque attaching bolt to 13–18 ft. lbs. (18–24 N-m).
5. Remove gauge and install upper timing belt cover, pulley, drive belt and fan.

CRANKSHAFT SPROCKET
REPLACE

1. Remove timing belt front cover, crankshaft pulley and timing belt.
2. Remove crankshaft sprocket.

PISTON & ROD ASSEMBLE

Assemble pistons and rods as indicated in **Fig. 6.** Measure connecting rod side

Quick Check Hole (In Sprocket) should align with hole in Timing Belt Upper Cover (A) when #1 Cyl. is at T.D.C.

A
TIMING BELT UPPER COVER
Tension Checking Area
CAM SPROCKET
TIMING BELT
IDLER
CRANK SPROCKET
TIMING TAB

Pulley timing mark should align with 0° mark on timing tab.

Fig. 3 Camshaft & crankshaft sprocket alignment marks

Fig. 4 Adjusting timing belt tension

Fig. 5 Timing belt idler arm and pulley

clearance with a feeler gauge. Side clearance should be .004–.012 inch.

PISTONS & RINGS

Pistons and rings are available in standard size, .001 and .030 in. (.750mm) oversize.

MAIN & ROD BEARINGS

Main bearings are available in standard size and undersizes of .001 in. (.026mm), .002 in. (.050mm), .010 in. (.250mm) and .020 in. (.500mm).

Rod bearings are available in standard size and undersizes of .001 in. (.026mm), .010 in. (.250mm) and .020 in. (.500mm).

OIL PAN
REPLACE

1980–86 LESS TURBO HYDRA-MATIC 200 AUTOMATIC TRANSMISSION

NOTE: This procedure applies only to 1980–86 models equipped with manual transmission or Turbo Hydra-Matic 180 automatic transmission. The Turbo Hydra-Matic 180 automatic transmission is equipped with a full converter housing, while the Turbo Hydra-Matic 200 automatic transmission has a partial converter housing and splash shield.

1. Disconnect battery ground cable, then drain cooling system.
2. Remove upper radiator support. On models equipped with A/C, remove upper half of fan shroud.
3. On models equipped with automatic transmission, disconnect transmission oil cooler lines from radiator.
4. On all models, disconnect radiator hoses, then remove radiator from vehicle.

5. If equipped with A/C, remove condenser to radiator support attaching nuts and position on top of engine.
6. Remove heater core housing and position on top of engine.
7. Remove engine mount retaining nuts and clips.
8. Raise and support front of vehicle, then drain crankcase.
9. Disconnect exhaust pipe at exhaust manifold, then remove body to cross-member braces.
10. Remove rack and pinion steering gear unit from cross member and steering shaft, then pull unit down and out of way.
11. Remove stabilizer bar from body.
12. Install a suitable engine lifting device and raise engine sufficiently to permit oil pan removal.
13. Remove oil pan attaching screws, then pull pan down and remove oil pump pick-up tube and screen assembly.
14. Remove oil pan through from of vehicle.
15. Reverse procedure to install. When installing oil pump pick-up tube and screen assembly, use a new seal. Torque oil pan attaching screws to 55 inch lbs.

1980–86 WITH TURBO HYDRA-MATIC 200 AUTOMATIC TRANSMISSION

NOTE: This procedure applies only to models equipped with Turbo Hydra-Matic 200 automatic transmission. The Turbo Hydra-Matic 200 automatic transmission is equipped with a partial converter housing and splash shield, while the Turbo Hydra-Matic 180 automatic transmission has a full converter housing.

1. Disconnect battery ground cable, then remove air cleaner.
2. Remove heater housing assembly from front of dash panel and position on top of engine.
3. Pull back on motor mount wire restraints and remove mount nuts.
4. Remove radiator upper support or fan shroud, as necessary.
5. Raise and support front of vehicle, then drain crankcase.
6. Remove converter housing splash shield.
7. Remove rack and pinion steering gear unit from front crossmember.
8. Loosen catalytic converter to rear exhaust pipe clamp bolts.
9. Install a suitable engine lifting device and raise engine sufficiently to permit oil pan removal.
10. Remove oil pan attaching screws, then remove oil pan.
11. Reverse procedure to install. Torque oil pan attaching screws to 55 inch lbs.

OIL PUMP
REPLACE

1. Remove coil bracket attaching bolts

Fig. 6 Piston and rod assembly

and position coil aside.
2. Remove fuel pump and push rod.
3. Remove distributor.
4. Remove oil pan.
5. Remove oil pump screen and pipe assembly.
6. Remove oil pump.
7. Reverse procedure to install.

CRANKSHAFT REAR OIL SEAL
REPLACE

1. Disconnect battery ground cable.
2. Remove transmission, as described under "TRANSMISSION, REPLACE".
3. Remove flywheel.
4. Remove rack and pinion bracket bolts.
5. Remove left side strut assembly.
6. Disconnect flex coupling and pull steering gear down.
7. Drain engine oil, then remove oil pan mounting bolts.
8. With oil pan pulled down away from engine block, remove oil pump suction pipe and screen.
9. With engine mounts attached, raise engine slightly with suitable jack and block of wood and remove oil pan from vehicle.
10. Remove rear main bearing cap and oil seal.
11. Clean bearing cap, case and crankshaft seal surface, then inspect crankshaft seal surface for excessive wear and nicks. If excessive wear or nicks exist, replace crankshaft.
12. Install new seal in case, then install bearing cap, but do not tighten bolts.

NOTE: When installing seal in case, ensure seal is seated against rear main bearing bulkhead.

13. Torque main bearing cap bolts to 11 ft. lbs., then using suitable soft-faced hammer, tap end of crankshaft rearward, then forward. Retorque main bearing cap to specifications.
14. Using 2 part RTV sealer or equivalent, pack sealer into vertical grooves until

Fig. 7   Fabricating crankcase front cover to oil pan seal

Fig. 8   Installing crankcase front cover

excess flows from slots adjacent to rear seal. Clean excess sealer.
15. Reverse steps 1 through 9 to install.

CRANKCASE FRONT COVER
REPLACE

1. Remove timing belt upper and lower front covers, crankshaft pulley, timing belt and crankshaft sprocket.
2. Remove three crankcase front cover to oil pan attaching bolts, then the crankcase cover to engine attaching bolts.
3. Remove crankcase front cover, cover gasket and front portion of oil pan gasket.

NOTE: To fabricate a replacement crankcase front cover to oil pan gasket, position crankcase cover over a new oil pan gasket as shown in **Fig. 7.** When installing gasket apply sealer to cut off portion of gasket.

4. Inspect crankshaft oil seal, replace if necessary.
5. Install crankcase front cover using tool J-26434, **Fig. 8.**

BELT TENSION DATA

	New Lbs.	Used Lbs.
1980–81		
A/C Compressor	135–145	90–100
Timing Belt		
15 mm	55	
19 mm	70	
All other belts	120–130	70–80
1982–86		
A/C Compressor	168	90
Timing Belt	70	
All other belts	146	70

FUEL PUMP
REPLACE

1980–86

1. Disconnect battery ground cable.
2. Remove distributor cap.
3. Remove spark plug wire retaining clips.
4. Remove coil wire and coil assembly.
5. Remove air cleaner assembly.
6. Disconnect fuel pump inlet and outlet hoses.
7. Remove fuel pump and gasket.
8. Reverse procedure to install.

WATER PUMP
REPLACE

1. Position No. 1 cylinder at top dead center.

NOTE: When No. 1 cylinder is at top dead center, a ⅛ in. drill rod may be inserted through the hole in the rear timing belt cover into the hole located on camshaft sprocket.

2. Disconnect battery ground cable, then drain cooling system.
3. Loosen alternator and A/C drive belts, then remove crankshaft pulley.
4. On models equipped with A/C, remove upper portion of fan shroud, if equipped.
5. On models less A/C, remove radiator upper mounting panel, if equipped.
6. On all models, remove engine fan.
7. Remove timing belt cover attaching bolts and nuts, then remove timing belt cover.
8. Loosen idler pulley mounting bolts and allow pulley to rotate clockwise.
9. Remove timing belt from camshaft and crankshaft pulleys.
10. Disconnect lower radiator hose and heater hose from water pump.
11. Remove water pump to cylinder block attaching bolts, then remove water pump.
12. Reverse procedure to install. Before installing timing belt cover, adjust timing belt tension as described under "Timing Belt Tension Adjust."

Diesel Engine Section

DIESEL ENGINE TROUBLESHOOTING

HARD STARTING

1. Check fuel level, replenish if necessary.
2. Check notched line on injection pump flange, reset timing as necessary.
3. Check to ensure fuel is reaching injection nozzles. If fuel is reaching injectors:
   a. Check connections of fuse, glow plugs, Q.S.S.I. controller and glow plug relays.
   b. Check fuel spray pattern, and ensure injection starting pressure is approximately 1707 p.s.i.
   c. Check to ensure valve clearances are satisfactory. Refer to specifications.
   d. Check compression pressure in each cylinder. Standard value should be 441 psi.
   e. Check to ensure proper installation of timing belt and camshaft.
4. If fuel is not reaching injectors:
   a. Check for air in fuel filter.
   b. Check if air is being drawn into fuel line through leakage in the pipe joints.
   c. Check operation of fuel cut out solenoid.
   d. Check fuel filter for restrictions.
   e. Check fuel pipes for restrictions.
   f. Check delivery valve for possible sticking.
5. Replace or readjust setting of injection pump.

ENGINE IDLING ROUGH

1. Check if idle speed is within specifications.
2. Check to ensure accelerator control cable is not binding or twisting.
3. Check accelerator lever setting for looseness.
4. Check for air or water in fuel filter.
5. Check for proper alignment on injection pump flange.
6. Check engine mounting for cracks or looseness.
7. Check fuel spray pattern, and ensure injection starting pressure is 1707 p.s.i.
8. Check to ensure intake clearances are satisfactory. Refer to specifications.
9. Check compression pressure in each cylinder. Standard value should be 441 p.s.i.
10. Check to ensure proper installation of timing belt and camshaft.
11. Check delivery valve for sticking.
12. Replace or readjust setting of injection pump.

ENGINE LACKS POWER

1. Check air cleaner for restrictions.
2. Check to ensure accelerator control cable is not binding or twisting.
3. Check seals on full load adjustment bolt and maximum speed stop bolt.
4. Check to ensure accelerator control lever is in full contact with maximum speed stop bolt.
5. Check exhaust system for restrictions.
6. Check for air in fuel filter.
7. Check notched line on injection pump flange, repair as necessary.
8. Check engine mounting for cracks or looseness.
9. Check fuel spray pattern, and ensure injection starting pressure is 1707 p.s.i.
10. Check to ensure valve clearances are satisfactory. Refer to specifications.
11. Check compression pressure in each cylinder. Standard value should be 441 p.s.i.
12. Check to ensure proper installation of timing belt and camshaft.
13. Check delivery valve for sticking.
14. Replace or readjust setting of injection pump.

ENGINE OVERHEATING

1. Check coolant level in radiator.
2. Check condition of coolant for contamination, ratio of anti-freeze to water, and leakage of oil into coolant.
3. Check for leakage in hoses, and clamps.
4. Check water pump and thermostat housing for leakage.
5. Check for damaged cylinder head gasket.
6. Check fan belt tension. Deflection of fan belt should be no more than .4 inch.
7. Check operation of fan clutch.
8. Check for proper operation of radiator cap.
9. Check thermostat operation. Thermostat opening temperature is 180° F.
10. Check injection timing.
11. Check condition of water pump impeller.

12. Check to ensure proper level of engine oil.
13. Replace or readjust setting of injection pump.

ENGINE KNOCKING

1. Check if engine has been thoroughly warmed up.
2. Check injection timing.
3. Check fuel spray pattern, and ensure injection starting pressure is 1707 p.s.i.
4. Check compression pressure in each cylinder. Standard value should be 441 p.s.i.
5. Check to ensure proper quality of fuel.
6. Replace or readjust setting of injection pump.

NOISE INDICATING ABNORMAL LEAKAGE

1. Check exhaust system for loose connections or leakage.
2. Check to ensure proper installation of nozzles and glow plugs.
3. Check for damaged cylinder head gasket.
4. Check to ensure valve clearances are satisfactory. Refer to specifications.
5. Check compression pressure in each cylinder. Standard value should be 441 p.s.i.

CONTINUOUS NOISE

1. Check fan belt tension. Deflection of fan belt should be no more than .4 inch.
2. Check to ensure cooling fan is secure.
3. Check water pump bearing for wear and damage.
4. Check operation of generator and vacuum pump.
5. Check to ensure valve clearances are satisfactory. Refer to specifications.

Fig. 1 Controller, dropping resistor & glow plug relay locations

CONTROLLER

Position to which connector terminal is connected

1. Starter switch (ON position)
2. Sensing resistor
3. Thermo switch
4. Starter switch (ST position)
5. Sensing resistor
6. Glow plug relay No. 1
7. Ground
8. Glow indicator lamp
9. Not used

Fig. 1A   Controller wiring connections

Fig. 2   Dropping resistor test connections

Fig. 3   Testing glow plug

Fig. 4   Glow plug relay test connections

Fig. 5   Fusible link test connections

Fig. 5A   Sensing resistor location

Fig. 6   Testing thermo switch

SLAPPING NOISE

1. Check valve retainers for damage.
2. Check to ensure valve clearances are satisfactory. Refer to specifications.
3. Check rocker arms for damage.
4. Check camshaft for seizure.
5. Check to ensure flywheel bolts are secure.
6. Check crankshaft and thrust bearing for wear and damage.
7. Check main bearing oil clearances.
8. Check connecting rod bearing and bushing oil clearances.
9. Check to ensure clearance between pistons and cylinder walls is satisfactory. Refer to specifications.

EXCESSIVE OIL CONSUMPTION

1. If oil is leaking:
   a. Check engine oil level.
   b. Check to ensure drain plug is secure.
   c. Check oil pipes for leakage.
   d. Check cooler seat gasket, oil filter and oil seal retainer for leakage.
   e. Check cylinder head cover, oil pan and oil pump gaskets for leakage.
   f. Check cylinder head gasket for leakage.
   g. Check oil seals for leakage.
   h. Check function of P.C.V.
   i. Check to ensure flywheel bolts are secure.
2. If oil is burning:
   a. Check to ensure quality of oil.
   b. Check valve stem oil seals.
   c. Check valve guides and valve stems for wear and damage.
   d. Check for damaged cylinder head gasket.
   e. Check to ensure proper setting of piston rings.
   f. Check piston rings for wear and damage.
   g. Check cylinder walls for wear and damage.

EXCESSIVE FUEL CONSUMPTION

1. Check air cleaner for restrictions.
2. Check fuel lead adjustment bolt seal for leakage.
3. Check fuel pipes for leakage.
4. Check exhaust system for restrictions.
5. Check if idle speed is within specifications.
6. Check to ensure proper quality of fuel.
7. Check injection timing.
8. Check fuel spray pattern, and ensure injection starting pressure is 1707 p.s.i.
9. Check to ensure valve clearances are satisfactory. Refer to specifications.
10. Check compression pressure in each cylinder. Standard valve should be 441 p.s.i.
11. Check delivery valve for sticking.
12. Replace or readjust setting of injection pump.

Fig. 7 Cylinder head tightening sequence

Fig. 8 Removing valve guides

Fig. 9 Installing valve guides

DIESEL ENGINE ELECTRICAL TROUBLESHOOTING

NOTE: In a normally operating quick start system, when coolant temperature is below 122° F. and the key is in the "On" position, the glow plug indicator turns on for about 3.5 seconds and No. 1 Relay turns on for a few seconds.

RELAY NO. 1 AND GLOW INDICATOR ARE BOTH INOPERATIVE

1. Starter circuit fuse is burnt out or fusible link wire is open.
2. Starter wire circuit is open or not properly connected.
3. Controller defective or not properly connected.
4. Starter switch is inoperative.

RELAY NO. 1 INOPERATIVE

1. Relay No. 1 is open.
2. Relay coil in relay No. 1 is open.
3. Controller to No. 1 relay circuitry is open or not properly connected.
4. Grounding circuit for No. 1 relay is open or not properly connected.
5. Controller is inoperative.
6. Circuit from controller to signal feed wire of sensing resistor is open or not properly connected.
7. Terminals of sensing resistor are not connected.
8. Main terminal of No. 1 relay not connected.
9. Main contact open in No. 1 relay.
10. Terminals in quick preheat circuit not connected.
11. Engine harness ground not properly connected.
12. Quick preheating wiring not properly connected or circuit open.

GLOW INDICATOR LIGHT INOPERATIVE

1. Controller damaged.
2. Indicator circuit not properly connected or open.
3. Light bulb burnt out.

RELAY NO. 1 TURNS OFF WITHIN 2 SECONDS

1. Controller damaged.
2. One or more glow plugs defective.
3. Wiring at connector poorly connected.

RELAY NO. 1 WILL NOT TURN OFF AFTER A FEW SECONDS

1. Controller damaged.

RELAY NO. 1 OPERATES WHEN COOLANT TEMPERATURE IS ABOVE 122° F.

1. Thermostat switch is inoperative.
2. Short in circuit.

NOTE: In a normally operating quick start system, when coolant temperature is below 122° F. and, the key held in the "Start" position, the glow plug indicator and the No. 2 relay will remain on until key is moved to "On" position.

RELAY NO. 2 AND GLOW INDICATOR INOPERATIVE

1. Starter switch "R" circuit not properly connected or open.

RELAY NO. 2 INOPERATIVE

1. Relay No. 2 terminals not connected.
2. Circuit between R terminal and No. 2 relay not properly connected or open.
3. No. 2 relay coil is open.

GLOW INDICATOR LIGHT INOPERATIVE

1. Controller damaged.

Fig. 10 Timing mark locations on damper pulley

Fig. 11 Injection pump pulley alignment

Fig. 12 Fixing injection pump pulley with lock bolt

Fig. 13   Fixing camshaft in place with tool No. J-29761

Fig. 14   Timing belt holder

Fig. 15   Timing belt installation sequence

NOTE: In a normally operating quick start system, when coolant temperature is above 122° F. and the key is in the "On" position the glow plug indicator light will turn on for about 0.3 seconds.

GLOW PLUG LIGHT REMAINS ON FOR 3.5 SECONDS AND CAUSES RELAY NO. 1 TO TURN ON

1. Thermo-switch circuit not properly connected or open.
2. Thermostat switch is inoperative.

DIESEL ENGINE ELECTRICAL DIAGNOSIS & TESTING

CONTROLLER

Controller in this system has four functions. As engine coolant temperature changes, it controls the glow plug relay. For determining glow plug heating requirements, it monitors differences between sensing resistance and glow plug resistance. It controls rapid preheat circuit to 1652° F. of glow plug temperature and, during pre-heat cycle, controls glow plug pre-heat indicator lamp (3.5 sec.). Refer to **Figs. 1 and 1A** for wiring connections.

DROPPING RESISTOR

During stabilized heating, this fixed value resistor is used to lower voltage of glow plugs. Check dropping resistor by performing continuity check across the terminals. Replace resistor if no continuity is found. Refer to **Figs. 1 and 2.**

GLOW PLUGS

The glow plugs used in this system are the fast warm up type. Check glow plugs by performing continuity test across plug terminals and body. If no continuity is found, heater wire is damaged and glow plug should be replaced. Refer to **Fig. 3.**

GLOW PLUG RELAY

This relay is main relay for stabilized heating circuit and rapid pre-heat cycle. Check glow relay by performing continuity test across terminals C and D while battery voltage is applied to terminals A and B. If no continuity is found, replace glow plug relay. Refer to **Fig. 4.**

GLOW PLUG RELAY 2

During starting, this relay is used to provide stabilized heating. To check this relay, use same procedure as for glow plug relay 1.

FUSIBLE LINKS

These two in-line fusible links are used to protect the glow plug electrical wiring. To check fusible links, perform continuity check across terminals. If no continuity is found, fusible link should be replaced. Refer to **Fig. 5.**

SENSING RESISTOR

Used in series with the glow plugs, this shunt type sensing resistor causes a small voltage drop which is monitored by the controller, **Fig. 5A.**

THERMO SWITCH

This thermo switch is used to provide a ground circuit to controller circuitry when engine temperature is above 122° F. To check thermo switch, perform continuity check across terminal and body while end of thermal switch is submerged in water. Gradually bring temperature of water to 122° F. Replace thermal switch if continuity is not found at this temperature. Refer to **Fig. 6.**

Fig. 16   Semi-tightening sequence of tension pulley

Fig. 17   Torquing tension pulley bolt sequence

Fig. 18   Static timing gauge, J-29763 installed

Fig. 19   Injection pump flange nuts

Fig. 20   Injection pump rear bracket tightening sequence

Fig. 21   Rocker arm bracket bolt tightening sequence

ENGINE
REPLACE

1. Remove hood.
2. Disconnect battery ground cable and drain cooling system.
3. Disconnect radiator hoses and remove radiator.
4. Disconnect engine wiring harnesses.
5. Remove air cleaner.
6. Disconnect accelerator and automatic transmission throttle valve linkage, if equipped.
7. Disconnect fuel lines and heater hoses.
8. Remove A/C compressor from mounting bracket and position aside, if equipped.
9. Remove power steering pump and bracket and position aside, if equipped.
10. Disconnect vacuum hose to master cylinder.
11. Remove engine mount nuts.
12. Raise vehicle and disconnect exhaust pipe at manifold.
13. Remove engine strut (shock type).
14. Remove flywheel dust cover.
15. On models with automatic transmission, remove converter to flywheel bolts.
16. Remove transmission rear crossmember to body bolts and bellhousing bolts.
17. Reinstall crossmember bolts.
18. Lower vehicle.
19. Remove oil filter.
20. Install engine lifting device, raise and

FRONT MARK

CYLINDER NUMBER

Fig. 22   Piston & connecting rod assembly

remove engine.
21. Reverse procedure to install.

CYLINDER HEAD
REPLACE

1. Disconnect battery ground cable and drain cooling system.
2. Remove cam cover.
3. Remove timing belt. It will not be necessary to remove lower cover and damper.
4. Remove camshaft.
5. Remove glow plug resistor wires and injector lines.
6. Remove fuel return line hose.
7. Raise vehicle and disconnect exhaust pipe at manifold.
8. Lower vehicle and remove oil feed pipe at rear of cylinder head.
9. Disconnect upper radiator hose.
10. Remove cylinder head bolts. Remove cylinder head and gasket.
11. Reverse procedure to install, tighten cylinder head bolts in sequence shown in **Fig. 7.**

VALVE TIMING
INTAKE OPENS BEFORE TDC

Engine	Year	Degrees
4-110.8	1981–86	32°

VALVES
ADJUST

1. Remove cam cover.
2. Inspect the rocker arm shaft bracket bolts for looseness, retorque as necessary.
3. Bring No. 1 cylinder to TDC on compression stroke.
4. Adjust valve clearances of cylinder No. 1, intake valve of No. 2 and exhaust valve of No. 3. Turn crankshaft one full revolution to bring cylinder No. 4 TDC on compression stroke. Adjust clearances of cylinder No. 4, exhaust valve of No. 2 and intake valve of No. 3.
5. Reinstall cam cover.

VALVE GUIDE
REPLACE

1. Using tool No. J-26512 drive out the valve guide from the lower face of the cylinder head, **Fig. 8.**
2. Apply engine oil to outer circumference of valve guide, using tool No. J-26512 drive the guide into position from the upper face of the cylinder head, **Fig. 9.**

NOTE: Always replace valve guide and valve as a set.

TIMING BELT
REPLACE

1. Disconnect battery ground cable.
2. Remove undercover and drain coolant.
3. Remove fan shroud, alternator belt, cooling fan and water pump pulley.
4. Remove ten bolts securing upper dust cover, remove dust cover.
5. Remove bypass hose.
6. Bring cylinder No. 1 to TDC, **Fig 10,** ensure that setting mark on injection pump pulley is in alignment with front plate, then fix the pulley with 8 mm 1.25 pitch bolt, **Fig. 11 and Fig. 12.**
7. Remove cam cover and loosen valve adjustment screws so rocker arms are in a free state. Fix the camshaft by installing fixing plate, tool No. J-29761 into the slit in rear end of the camshaft, **Fig. 13.**
8. Remove crankshaft damper pulley, lower dust cover and timing belt hold-

Fig. 23   Removing oil pump

Fig. 24 Oil pump, disassembled

er, **Fig. 14.**

NOTE: Under no circumstances should he crankshaft be disturbed from TDC.

9. Remove tension pulley spring then loosen tension pulley and plate bolts, remove timing belt.
10. Remove camshaft pulley bolt, using a suitable puller remove camshaft pulley, then reinstall pulley and bolt. Tighten bolt just enough to allow the pulley to be turned smoothly by hand.
11. Install new timing belt using sequence shown in **Fig. 15.** Ensure that belt cogs are properly installed in pulleys. Do not disturb crankshaft setting.
12. Concentrate belt looseness on tension pulley, depress tension pulley with finger and install tension spring. Semitighten bolts in numerical sequence 1 and 2 to prevent movement of tension pulley, **Fig. 16.**
13. Tighten camshaft pulley bolt.
14. Remove injection pump pulley lock bolt and camshaft fixing plate.
15. Install crankshaft damper pulley, ensure No. 1 cylinder is at TDC.
16. Ensure injection pump pulley mark is in alignment with mark on plate and fixing plate should fit smoothly into the rear slit of the camshaft. Remove plate.
17. Loosen tensioner plate bolts and pulley. Concentrate looseness of belt on tensioner, then tighten the bolts in numerical sequence 1, 2, and 3. **Fig. 17.** Torque bolts 1 and 2, 11 to 18 ft. lbs. Bolt 3, 47 to 61 ft. lbs.
18. Using a belt tension gauge, check tension between camshaft pulley and injection pump pulley. Tension should be 47 to 64 lbs.
19. Remove crankshaft damper and install timing belt holder.
20. Adjust valves. Refer to "Valves, Adjust" for procedure.
21. Reverse steps 1 through 8 to reassemble.

INJECTION TIMING
ADJUST

1. Check that alignment mark on injection pump flange is aligned with alignment mark on front plate.

2. Bring cylinder No. 1 to TDC on compression stroke by turning crankshaft until timing mark on pulley aligns with pointer, **Fig. 10.**

NOTE: The damper pulley has eleven notched lines as shown in **Fig. 10.** Four lines on one side, seven elsewhere. The four lines are intended for service use while the other seven are for factory use only.

3. Remove upper dust cover, ensure the injection pump belt is properly tensioned and the timing marks are aligned. See "Timing Belt, Replace".
4. Remove the cam cover and rear plug, ensure that the fixing plate fits smoothly into the camshaft rear slit, then remove the fixing plate. See "Timing Belt, Replace".
5. Disconnect the injection pipe from the injection pump, remove distributor head screw and gasket, install static timing gauge J-29763, **Fig. 18.** Set the lift approximately .040 inch (1 mm) from the plunger.
6. Bring No. 1 piston to a point 45–60 degrees BTDC by turning the crankshaft, set dial indicator to zero. Turn crankshaft slightly in both directions, ensuring gauge indication is stable.
7. Turn crankshaft in normal direction of rotation until the 18 degree mark on the damper is aligned with the timing pointer, **Fig. 10.** Note reading of dial indicator, if reading is not .020 inch (.5 mm), hold crankshaft at 18 degrees and loosen the two nuts on injection pump flange, **Fig. 19.** Move pump until reading on dial indicator is .020 inch (.5 mm), then tighten nuts.

INJECTION PUMP
REPLACE

1. Remove timing belt. See "Timing Belt, Replace".
2. To prevent rotation of injection pump pulley during disassembly, thread a 8 mm 1.25 pitch bolt through the pulley into the housing, **Fig. 12.**
3. Remove injection pump pulley bolt.
4. Remove bolt installed in step two, then using a suitable puller remove injection pump pulley.
5. Disconnect fuel cut solenoid valve switch wiring and tachometer pick up sensor wiring at connector.
6. Disconnect accelerator cable from pump lever. If equipped with automatic transmission, remove throttle valve control cable.
7. Disconnect vacuum hose from fast idle actuator.
8. Disconnect fuel hoses from injection pump.
9. Remove six screws attaching injection pipe clips and remove.
10. Remove injection pipes.
11. Remove injection pump rear bracket then control lever spring.
12. Remove attaching nuts and pump with fast idle device installed.
13. Install injection pump with fast idle device installed by aligning notched line on pump flange with the line on

Fig. 25 Oil cooler assembly

the front plate.
14. Install rear bracket bolts following sequence in **Fig. 20.**
15. Install the injection pump pulley by aligning it with key groove, torque nut to 43 to 50 ft. lbs. Hold pulley from rotating by installing a bolt as described in step 2.
16. Refer to "Timing Belt, Replace" for reassembly procedures.

ROCKER ARM SHAFT ASSEMBLY
REPLACE

1. Remove cam cover.
2. Remove rocker arm shaft bracket bolts and nuts, then remove rocker arm shaft and rocker arm assembly.
3. Prior to installation, apply a generous amount of engine oil to the rocker arm shaft, rocker arms and valve stem end caps.
4. Install rocker arm shaft assembly and tighten bolts in sequence as shown in **Fig. 21.**
5. Adjust valves. Refer to "Valves, Adjust" for procedure.

CAMSHAFT
REPLACE

1. Remove cam cover.
2. Remove timing belt as described in "Timing Belt, Replace".
3. Remove camshaft gear as described in "Timing Belt, Replace".
4. Remove rocker arm shaft assembly as described in "Rocker Arm Shaft Assembly, Replace".
5. Remove bolts attaching front head plate and remove.
6. Remove the camshaft bearing cap bolts, then remove bearing caps with cap side bearing.
7. Remove camshaft oil seal followed by the camshaft.
8. Install camshaft oil seal, camshaft and rocker arm shaft assembly. Loosen rocker arm adjustment screws so the

rocker arms are in a free state. Reverse procedure from step five to reinstall.

CRANKSHAFT FRONT OIL SEAL
REPLACE

1. Remove timing belt. Refer to 'Timing Belt, Replace".
2. Remove crankshaft hub center bolt and washer.
3. Using a suitable puller, remove hub from crankshaft.
4. Using puller No. J-29752, remove crankshaft timing belt pulley.
5. Pry out front oil seal using a suitable screwdriver.
6. Apply clean engine oil to inner and outer surfaces of new seal, using a suitable seal installer, install the oil seal.
7. Position crankshaft timing belt pulley flange into seal, align pulley groove with crankshaft key. Drive pulley onto crankshaft using installer tool No. J-26587.
8. Align crankshaft hub keyway with crankshaft key, install center bolt. Torque to 98 to 119 ft. lbs.
9. Reinstall timing belt. Refer to 'Timing Belt, Replace".

CRANKSHAFT REAR OIL SEAL
REPLACE

1. Remove the clutch pressure plate assembly.
2. Remove the six flywheel attaching bolts, then the flywheel.
3. Using a suitable screwdriver, pry out the rear seal.
4. Apply clean engine oil to all sides of new seal.
5. Install the oil seal in the oil seal retainer using tool No. J-29818.
6. Position flywheel on crankshaft hub. Using new bolts, apply loctite to threads and install flywheel. Torque bolts 36 to 43 ft. lbs.
7. Reverse procedure to install remain-

ing parts.

PISTON & CONNECTING ROD

Install the piston on the connecting rod, so that the combustion chamber on piston head is on the same side with the cylinder mark side (side with bearing stopper) of the connecting rod big end. The front of the piston should be on same side as the "Isuzu" mark on the connecting rod, **Fig. 22.** Pistons are available in oversizes of .010 and .030 in.

Check connecting rod side clearance with a feeler gauge. Clearance should be .003–.024 inch.

OIL PAN
REPLACE

1. Remove engine assembly. Refer to "Engine, Replace" for procedure.
2. Remove fourteen bolts and four nuts attaching oil pan and remove.
3. Discard old gasket, clean mounting surfaces. Install new gasket using a suitable sealing compound on oil pan, and install.
4. Torque bolts 4–6 ft. lbs.

OIL PUMP
REPLACE

1. Remove timing belt. Refer to "Timing Belt, Replace".
2. Remove four allen bolts securing oil pump, remove oil pump and pulley as an assembly, see **Fig. 23.**
3. Refer to "Oil Pump, Inspection & Service".
4. Prior to installation apply a generous amount of clean engine oil to vane, install with taper side towards the cylinder body.
5. Install new pump O-ring, lubricate with motor oil and install in the housing groove. Lubricate oil pump rotor and install pump body together with pulley.
6. Reverse procedure to install.

OIL PUMP, INSPECTION & SERVICE
DISASSEMBLY

1. Inspect all parts for any signs of abnormal wear, or damage, **Fig. 24.**
2. Measure outside diameter of pulley flange. Diameter should be 1.1–1.1035 inch (27.94–28.03 mm).
3. Using a straightedge and feeler gauge, check clearance between vane and cylinder body in direction of thrust. Clearance should be .0011–.0027 inch (.03–.07 mm).
4. Check clearance between vane and cylinder body. Clearance should be .0094–.0141 inch (.24–.36 mm).
5. Check clearance between vane and rotor. Clearance should be .0051–.0059 (.13–.15).
6. Reassemble as shown in **Fig. 24.**

OIL COOLER
REPLACE

1. Disconnect battery ground cable.
2. Remove oil cooler drain plug, allow cooler to drain.
3. Remove rubber hoses.
4. Remove two joint bolts securing cooler, **Fig. 25.** Remove cooler.
5. Install new joint bolt gaskets and install cooler.
6. Reverse steps 1 to 3 to install.

WATER PUMP
REPLACE

1. Disconnect battery ground cable.
2. Drain cooling system.
3. Remove four nuts securing cooling fan and pulley assembly and remove. Remove fan belt.
4. Remove crankshaft damper pulley.
5. Remove front engine dust covers.
6. Remove by-pass hose.
7. Remove five water pump attaching bolts and remove pump.
8. Reverse procedure to install.

Clutch & Transmission Section

CLUTCH
ADJUST

INITIAL BALL STUD ADJUSTMENT

1. Place gauge J-28449 with flat end against clutch housing front face and the hooked end positioned in the bottom depression of the clutch fork, **Fig. 1.**
2. Turn ball inward until clutch release bearing contacts clutch spring.
3. Install and torque lock nut to 25 ft. lbs. (33 N-m).
4. Remove gauge.

CLUTCH CABLE ATTACHMENT & ADJUSTMENT

1. Install clutch cable through hole in clutch fork and seat, then install return spring.
2. From engine compartment, pull cable until clutch pedal is firmly against pedal stop and hold in position, **Fig. 2.**
3. Install snap ring in first fully visible groove in cable from sleeve, then release cable.
4. Clutch pedal lash should be .58 to 1.08 in. (15–27 mm), if not, adjust clutch pedal as described under Clutch Pedal Adjustment.

CLUTCH PEDAL ADJUSTMENT

1. If clutch pedal lash is insufficient, remove snap ring from cable and allow cable to move into dash by one cable notch, then reinstall snap ring, **Fig. 2.**
2. If clutch pedal lash is excessive, remove snap ring from cable, and pull cable out of dash by one cable notch, then reinstall snap ring, **Fig. 2.**

3. Check to ensure clutch pedal lash is .58–1.08 in. (15–27 mm).

CLUTCH
REPLACE

1. Raise vehicle and remove transmission as outlined under "Manual Transmission, Replace" procedure.
2. Remove release bearing from the clutch fork and sleeve by sliding lever off ball stud and against spring force. If ball stud is to be replaced, remove cap, lock nut and stud from housing.
3. Make sure alignment marks on clutch assembly and flywheel are distinguishable.
4. Loosen clutch cover to flywheel bolts one turn at a time until spring pressure is released, to avoid bending the clutch cover flange.
5. Support the pressure plate and cover assembly while removing bolts and clutch assembly.

NOTE: Do not disassemble the clutch cover, spring and pressure plate for repairs. If defective replace complete assembly.

6. Reverse procedure to install making sure to index alignment marks.

CAUTION: Check position of engine in front mounts and realign as necessary.

MANUAL TRANSMISSION
REPLACE

1. Remove shifter assembly.
2. Raise vehicle and drain transmission lubricant.
3. Remove propeller shaft.
4. Disconnect speedometer cable and the back-up lamp switch.
5. Disconnect return spring and clutch cable from clutch fork.
6. Remove transmission to crossmember bolts.
7. Remove exhaust manifold nuts and the catalytic converter to transmission bracket bolts.
8. Remove crossmember to frame bolts, then the crossmember from vehicle.
9. Remove dust cover.
10. Remove clutch housing to engine retaining bolts, slide transmission rearward and remove from vehicle.
11. Reverse procedure to install.

Fig. 1 Ball stud adjustment

Fig. 2 Clutch cable adjustment

Rear Axle, Propeller Shaft & Brakes

REAR AXLE
DESCRIPTION

The rear axle, **Fig. 1,** is a semi-floating type consisting of a cast carrier and large bosses on each end into which two welded steel tubes are fitted. The carrier contains an overhung hypoid pinion and ring gear. The differential is a two pinion arrangment.

The overhung hypoid drive pinion, is supported by two preloaded tapered roller bearings. The pinion shaft is sealed by means of a molded, spring loaded, rubber seal. The seal is mounted on the pinion shaft flange which is splined and bolts to the hypoid pinion shaft.

The ring gear is bolted to a one piece differential case and is supported by two preloaded tapered roller bearings.

A rear axle extension housing is bolted to the axle housing and is attached to the underbody by a center bearing support. An extension shaft inside the housing is splined to the drive pinion at the rear end and to the companion flange at the forward end.

REMOVAL

1. Raise vehicle on a hoist.
2. Place adjustable lifting device under axle.
3. Disconnect rear shock absorbers from axle and remove propeller shaft and extension housing, **Fig. 2.**
4. Remove both rear wheels.
5. Retract shoes and remove right and left brake drums, **Fig. 3.**
6. Disconnect brake lines from clips on axle tubes.
7. Disconnect track and stabilizer bars from axle tube.
8. Remove differential cover and drain lubricant.
9. Unscrew differential lock screw, remove pinion shaft and axle shaft "C" locks. Reinstall pinion shaft and tighten lock screw to retain differential gears.
10. Remove both axle shafts.
11. Remove brake backing plate retaining nuts and remove backing plates, with shoes and brake lines attached, and wire to frame.
12. Remove right and left lower control arm pivot bolts at axle.
13. Lower axle assembly slowly until coil spring tension is released, then remove axle.

AXLE SHAFT
REPLACE

1. Raise vehicle on a hoist and remove wheel and tire assembly and brake drum.
2. Drain lubricant from axle by removing carrier cover.
3. Unscrew pinion shaft lock screw and

remove pinion shaft.
4. Push flanged end of axle shaft toward center of car and remove "C" lock from button end of shaft.
5. Remove axle shaft from housing being careful not to damage seal.

OIL SEAL &/OR BEARING REPLACEMENT

1. If replacing seal only, remove the seal by using the button end of axle shaft. Insert the button end of shaft behind the steel case of the seal and pry seal out of bore being careful not to damage housing.
2. If replacing bearings, insert tool J-25593 into bore so tool head grasps behind bearing. Slide washer against seal, or bearing, and turn nut against washer. Attach slide hammer J-2619 and remove bearing.
3. Lubricate bearing with rear axle lubricant, then install bearing into housing bore with tool J-25594 and slide hammer J-8092. Make sure tool contacts end of axle housing to insure proper bearing depth.
4. Pack cavity between seal lips with a high melting point wheel bearing lubricant. Position seal on tool J-22922 and position seal in axle housing bore, tap seal in bore until flush with end of axle housing.

REAR AXLE EXTENSION
REPLACE

1. Raise vehicle and support rear axle.
2. Disconnect propeller shaft from the rear yoke and remove from transmission, **Fig. 2.**
3. Support front end of rear axle carrier housing. Ensure the rear axle extension is also supported.
4. Disconnect center support bracket from underbody and the extension housing flange from axle housing.
5. Remove axle extension housing from vehicle. Pry extension housing from axle housing with a suitable screwdriver, if necessary.
6. Reverse procedure to install.

SERVICE

1. Remove bolt securing extension housing to center support bracket.
2. Mount companion flange in a vise and loosen lock nut.
3. Drive splined companion flange off shaft by tapping on lock nut end of shaft.
4. Remove lock nut, companion flange and thrust washer, then pull shaft from housing. If centering bearing, located in the rubber cushion, remains on ex-

Fig. 1   Rear axle cross section

Fig. 2   Rear axle assembly

Rotate Adjuster Bolts In Direction Of Arrows To Retract Shoes

Fig. 3   Retracting brake shoes

Fig. 4   Rear drum brake

tension shaft, drive off shaft with a suitable drift.
5. Note position of bearing in rubber cushion and the cushion in center support. Then, using a suitable screwdriver, separate rubber cushion from center support bracket and remove bearing from cushion.
6. Clean, inspect and replace components, if necessary.
7. Install rubber cushion into center support bracket and place center support assembly over extension housing.
8. Press bearing onto extension shaft and insert shaft into housing through rubber cushion. Install thrust washer with circular cavity facing toward bearing, then the companion flange, using the lock nut to press flange onto shaft splines.
9. Install bolts retaining bracket to housing.

PROPELLER SHAFT
REPLACE

1. Raise vehicle on a hoist. Mark relationship of shaft to companion flange and disconnect the rear universal joint by removing trunnion bearing "U" bolts. Tape bearing cups to trunnion to prevent dropping and loss of bearing rollers.
2. Withdraw propeller shaft front yoke from transmission.
3. When installing, be sure to align

marks made in removal to prevent driveline vibration.

BRAKE ADJUSTMENTS

NOTE: If manual adjustment or shoe retraction is necessary refer to **Fig. 3.**

Disc brakes are used on front wheels and drum brakes are use on rear wheels. Rear brake adjustment is automatic. Adjustment takes place whenever brakes are applied. An adjuster is attached to each brake shoe by means of a pin, **Fig. 4.** This pin is smaller than the slot in the brake shoe. When brakes are applied and brake shoes move outward the automatic adjuster follows. When brakes are released the brake shoe moves inward until it contacts the automatic adjuster pin. The space between adjuster pin and slot in brake shoe provides shoe to drum clearance.

PARKING BRAKE
ADJUST

1. Raise vehicle.
2. Apply parking brake three notches from fully released position.
3. Tighten equalizer adjusting nut until a light drag is felt when rear wheels are rotated in a forward direction.
4. Release parking brake and rotate rear wheels. No drag should be felt.

MASTER CYLINDER
REPLACE

1. Disconnect push rod from brake pedal and remove push rod boot.
2. Remove air cleaner.
3. Disconnect brake lines from master cylinder. Cap ends of lines to prevent entry of dirt.
4. Remove master cylinder to dash attaching nuts and the master cylinder.

POWER BRAKE UNIT
REPLACE

1. Remove air cleaner, then disconnect vacuum hose from check valve.
2. Remove master cylinder brace rod.
3. Remove remaining master cylinder to brake unit attaching nuts, then pull master forward until it clears brake unit mounting studs. Carefully move master cylinder aside with brake lines attached.

NOTE: Support master cylinder to avoid stress on brake lines. Move master cylinder only enough to provide clearance for brake unit removal.

4. Remove nuts attaching brake unit to dash panel.
5. Remove push rod to pedal retainer and slide push rod off pedal pin.
6. Remove power brake unit from vehicle.

Rear Suspension Section

DESCRIPTION

This suspension system, **Fig. 1,** incorporates two tubular lower control arms, a straight track rod, two shock absorbers, two coil springs and a stabilizer bar.

SHOCK ABSORBER
REPLACE

1. Raise vehicle and support rear axle with a suitable jack.
2. Disconnect shock absorber from upper and lower mounting.
3. Reverse procedure to install.

COIL SPRING
REPLACE

1. Raise vehicle and support rear axle with a suitable jack.
2. Disconnect both shock absorbers from lower brackets.
3. Disconnect rear axle extension bracket.

NOTE: Ensure axle is properly supported before disconnecting extension bracket.

4. Slowly lower axle until springs and insulators can be removed.

NOTE: When lower axle ensure that brake hoses do not stretch or become damaged.

5. Reverse procedure to install.

TRACK ROD
REPLACE

1. Raise vehicle and support rear axle with a suitable jack.
2. Disconnect stabilizer bar, if equipped, **Fig. 2.**
3. Remove control arm front and rear attaching bolts and control arm, **Fig. 3.**
4. Remove attaching bolts and track rod.
5. Reverse procedure to install.

NOTE: Vehicle must be at curb height when tightening pivot bolts.

LOWER CONTROL ARMS
REPLACE

1. Raise vehicle and support rear axle.
2. Disconnect stabilizer bar, if equipped, **Fig. 2.**
3. Disconnect the front and rear control arm attaching bolts and remove control arm from vehicle, **Fig. 3.**

NOTE: Replace one control arm at a time to prevent axle from rolling or slipping sideways.

4. Reverse procedure to install.

STABILIZER BAR
REPLACE

1. Raise vehicle and support rear axle.
2. Disconnect stabilizer bar from underbody and axle tube connections, **Fig. 2,** then remove stabilizer bar from vehicle.
3. Reverse procedure to install.

Fig. 1   Rear suspension

Fig. 2   Stabilizer bar installation

Fig. 3   Track rod and lower control arm

Front Suspension & Steering Section

DESCRIPTION

This front suspension system, **Fig. 1**, uses long and short control arms with coil springs mounted between the lower control arms and front suspension crossmember.

WHEEL ALIGNMENT

Caster

Caster angle is adjusted by rearranging washers located at both ends of the upper control arm, **Fig. 2**. A kit consisting of two washers, one of 3 mm thickness and one of 9 mm thickness, must be used when adjusting caster angle.

Camber

Camber is adjusted by removing the upper ball joint, rotating it ½ turn and reinstalling it with flat of upper flange on inboard side of control arm, **Fig. 3**. This will increase positive camber by approximately 1°.

TOE-IN ADJUST

To adjust toe-in, loosen tie rod jam nuts at tie rod ends and loosen clamp at rubber bellows. Turn each tie rod to increase or decrease its length until proper toe-in is obtained. Torque jam nut to 50 ft. lbs.

WHEEL BEARINGS
ADJUST

1. While rotating wheel in the forward direction, torque spindle nut to 12 ft. lbs.
2. Back spindle nut off to the just loose position.
3. Hand tighten spindle nut, then loosen until cotter holes are aligned, install cotter pin.

NOTE: Do not loosen nut more than ½ flat to align cotter pin holes.

4. With bearings properly adjusted, end play must be .001–.005 inch.

WHEEL BEARINGS
REPLACE

1. Raise vehicle, remove wheel and tire assembly.
2. Remove two caliper mounting bracket to steering knuckle attaching bolts, remove caliper.
3. Remove hub dust cap, cotter pin, spindle nut, washer, outer wheel bearing and hub.
4. Pry out grease seal, then remove inner bearing from hub.

SHOCK ABSORBER
REPLACE

1. Hold upper stem of shock absorber, and remove nut, retainer and grommet.
2. Raise vehicle and remove lower shock absorber retaining bolts.
3. Lower shock absorber from vehicle.
4. Reverse procedure to install. Torque shock absorber lower retaining bolts to 35–50 ft. lbs. on 1980–84 models or 29 ft. lbs. on 1985-86 models and the upper retaining nut to 60–120 in. lbs. on 1980-84 models or 13 ft. lbs. on 1985-86 models.

BALL JOINTS
REPLACE

UPPER BALL JOINT

1. Raise vehicle and remove wheel and tire assembly.
2. Support lower control arm using a suitable jack.
3. Loosen upper ball joint stud nut, however, do not remove nut.
4. Position tool J-26407 with cupped end over lower ball joint stud and turn threaded end of tool until upper ball joint stud is free of steering knuckle, **Fig. 4**.
5. Remove tool, then the upper stud nut.

NOTE: Discard the stud nut. The stud nut is of special design and must be replaced whenever removed or loosened.

6. Remove two nuts securing ball joint to upper control arm and the ball joint.

NOTE: Inspect tapered hole in steering knuckle. If out of round or damaged, the knuckle must be replaced.

7. Install ball joint on upper control arm and torque bolts to 29 ft. lbs.
8. Position upper ball joint stud on steering knuckle, then install a standard nut to draw ball joint into position on knuckle. Torque standard nut to 35 ft. lbs., then remove standard nut. Install special nut for final assembly and torque to 29–36 ft. lbs.
9. Install wheel and tire assembly and lower vehicle.

LOWER BALL JOINT

1. Raise vehicle and remove wheel and tire assembly.
2. Support lower control arm using a suitable jack.
3. Loosen lower ball joint stud nut, however, do not remove nut.
4. Position tool J-26407 with cupped end of tool over upper ball joint stud and turn threaded end of tool until lower ball joint stud is free of steering knuckle, **Fig. 4**.
5. Remove tool, then the lower ball joint stud nut.

NOTE: Discard the stud nut. The stud nut is of special design and must be replaced whenever removed or loosened.

6. Remove ball joint from lower control arm.

NOTE: Inspect tapered hole in steering knuckle, if out of round or damaged, the knuckle must be replaced.

7. Insert ball joint through lower control arm and into steering knuckle.
8. Install a standard nut to draw ball joint into position on knuckle. Torque standard nut to 35 ft. lbs., then remove

Fig. 1   Front suspension

FRONT WASHER
REAR WASHER
LOCATING TUBE (LOCATES UPPER CONTROL ARM-TO-FRONT SUSPENSION UNIT)

Fig. 2   Caster adjustment

NOTE: TO INCREASE CAMBER, DISCONNECT UPPER BALL JOINT, ROTATE 180° TO POSITION "FLAT" OF FLANGE INBOARD, THEN RECONNECT BALLJOINT.

Fig. 3   Camber adjustment

Fig. 4 Separating ball joint studs from steering knuckle

standard nut. Install special nut for final assembly and torque to 41–54 ft. lbs.
9. Install wheel and tire assembly and lower vehicle.

COIL SPRING
REPLACE

1. Support vehicle by frame, remove wheel and tire assembly.
2. Disconnect stabilizer bar from lower control arm and tie rod from steering knuckle.
3. Support lower control arm using a suitable jack.
4. Loosen lower ball joint stud nut, then use tool J-26407 to free stud from steering knuckle, position knuckle and hub out of way. Remove stud nut.

NOTE: Discard stud nut. The stud nut is of special design and must be replaced whenever removed or loosened.

5. Loosen lower control arm pivot bolts.
6. Install a safety chain around spring and through lower control arm.
7. Slowly lower control arm until spring is extended as far as possible, then use pry bar to carefully lift spring over lower control arm spring seat.

LOWER CONTROL ARM
REPLACE

1. Remove coil spring as described in "Coil Spring, Replace".
2. Remove control arm pivot bolts, and then remove arm.
3. Reverse procedure to install. Torque lower control arm pivot bolts to 49 ft. lbs.

UPPER CONTROL ARM
REPLACE

1. Support vehicle by frame, remove tire and wheel assembly.
2. Position jack to support lower control arm.
3. Disconnect upper ball joint as described in "Ball Joints, Replace".
4. Remove upper control arm pivot bolts, then remove control arm from vehicle.
5. Reverse procedure to install. Torque upper control arm pivot bolts to 47 ft. lbs.

MANUAL STEERING GEAR
REPLACE

1. Raise vehicle and remove bolts and shield.
2. Remove tie rod cotter pins and nuts from tie rod ends and separate tie rods from steering knuckles.
3. Remove flexible coupling pinch bolt.
4. Remove steering gear clamp bolts, then the steering gear assembly from vehicle.
5. Reverse procedure to install. Torque steering knuckle to tie rod nut to 30 ft.

Fig. 5 Power steering pump installation (Typical)

lbs., flex coupling pinch bolt to 30 ft. lbs. and steering gear clamp bolt to 14 ft. lbs.

POWER STEERING GEAR
REPLACE

The procedure for power steering gear, **Fig. 5,** replacement is identical to manual type gear replacement. In addition, it is necessary to disconnect and connect the two hydraulic lines at the steering gear.

POWER STEERING PUMP
REPLACE

1. Remove pump adjusting bolt.
2. Remove lower brace to pump bracket attaching bolt.
3. Remove crossmember to frame support brace, then disconnect hydraulic lines at pump.
4. Remove rear pump adjusting bracket, then the front pivot bolt.
5. Remove front pump bracket to engine attaching bolt, then the pump and bracket.
6. Reverse procedure to install.

CHEVROLET NOVA

INDEX OF SERVICE OPERATIONS

NOTE: Refer to rear of this manual for vehicle manufacturer's special service tool suppliers.

Engine Number & V.I.N. Code

The engine identification number is stamped on the right side of the engine next to the bell housing flange.

The eighth digit in the V.I.N. denotes engine code.

Grille Identification

1985—86 Nova

General Engine Specifications

Year	Engine CID①/Liter	Engine V.I.N. Code②	Carburetor	Bore and Stroke	Compression Ratio	Net H.P. @ R.P.M.③	Maximum Torque Ft. Lbs. @ R.P.M.	Normal Oil Pressure Pounds
1985	4-97/1.6L	4	2 Bbl.④	3.19 × 3.08	9.0	70 @	—	34
1986	4-97/1.6L	4	2 Bbl.④	3.19 × 3.08	9.0	74 @ 5200	86 @ 2800	34

①—CID—Cubic inch displacement.
②—The eighth digit of the V.I.N. denotes engine code.
③—Ratings are net—as installed in vehicle.
④—Aisan carburetor.

Alternator Specifications

Year	Model	Rated Hot Output Amps.	Field Current 12 Volts @ 80°F
1985—86	—	60	—

Starting Motor Applications

Year	Engine/V.I.N.	Starter Number
1985—86	4-97/4	—

Valve Specifications

Year	Engine/V.I.N.	Valve Lash Int.	Valve Lash Exh.	Valve Angles Seat	Valve Angles Face	Valve Spring Installed Height	Valve Spring Pressure Lbs. @ In.	Stem Clearance Intake	Stem Clearance Exhaust	Stem Diameter Intake	Stem Diameter Exhaust
1985—86	4-97/4	.008H	.012H	45	44.5	1.52	43.6 @ 1.52	.0010–.0024	.0012–.0026	.2744–.2750	.2742–.2748

Pistons, Pins, Rings, Crankshaft & Bearings

Year	Engine/ V.I.N.	Piston Clearance	Ring Gap①		Wristpin Diam- eter	Rod Bearings		Main Bearings			Shaft End Play
			Comp.	Oil		Shaft Diameter	Bearing Clearance	Shaft Diameter	Bearing Clearance	Thrust on Bear. No.	
1985–86	4-97/4	.0039–.0047	②	.0118	—	1.5742–1.5748	.0008–.0020	1.8892–1.8898	.0005–.0019	3	.0008–.0073

①—Fit rings in tapered bores for clearance given in tightest portion of ring travel. Clearances listed are minimum gaps.

②—No. 1 comp. ring, .0098 inch; No. 2 comp. ring, .0059 inch.

Engine Tightening Specifications★

★ Torque specifications are for clean and lightly lubricated threads only. Dry or dirty threads produce increased friction which prevents accurate measurement of tightness.

Year	Engine/ V.I.N.	Spark Plugs Ft. Lbs.	Cylinder Head Bolts Ft. Lbs.	Intake Manifold Ft. Lbs.	Exhaust Manifold Ft. Lbs.	Rocker Arm Support Bolts Ft. Lbs.	Rocker Arm Cover Ft. Lbs.	Connecting Rod Cap Bolts Ft. Lbs.	Main Bearing Cap Bolts Ft. Lbs.	Flywheel to Crankshaft Ft. Lbs.	Vibration Damper or Pulley Ft. Lbs.
1985–86	4-97/4	13	43	18	18	18	—	29	43	58	87

Wheel Alignment Specifications

Year	Model	Caster Angle, Degrees		Camber Angle, Degrees				Toe-In Inch	Toe-Out on Turns, Deg.	
		Limits	Desired	Limits		Desired			Outer Wheel	Inner Wheel
				Left	Right	Left	Right			
1985	Front	+²⁄₁₅° to +1¹⁹⁄₃₀°	+⁵³⁄₆₀°	0° to −1°	0° to −1°	−½°	−½°	0	—	—
	Rear	—	—	0° to −1¹⁄₆₀°	0° to −1¹⁄₆₀°	−³¹⁄₆₀°	−³¹⁄₆₀°	⁵⁄₃₂°	—	—
1986	Front	+²³⁄₆₀° to +1²³⁄₆₀°	+⁵³⁄₆₀°	−¾° to +¼°	−¾° to +¼°	−¼°	−¼°	0	—	—
	Rear	—	—	0° to −1¹⁄₆₀°	0° to −1¹⁄₆₀°	−³¹⁄₆₀°	−³¹⁄₆₀°	⁵⁄₃₂°	—	—

Cooling System & Capacity Data

Year	Model or Engine/V.I.N.	Cooling Capacity, Qts.		Radiator Cap Relief Pressure, Lbs.	Thermo. Opening Temp.	Fuel Tank Gals.	Engine Oil Refill Qts.	Transaxle Oil	
		Less A/C	With A/C					Manual Transaxle Pts.	Auto. Transaxle Qts.①
1985–86	4-97 (1.6L)/4	6.3	6.3	10.7–14.9	180	13.2	3.2②	5.4	5.8

①—Approximate make final check with dipstick.

②—With filter change add .3 qt.

Electrical Section

1. SIDE DEFROSTER NOZZLE	13. NO. 1 HEATER DUCT	25. CENTER CLUSTER FINISH PANEL
2. SIDE DEFROSTER DUCT	14. COLUMN HOUSING	26. RETAINER
3. DEFROSTER NOZZLE	15. GLOVE COMPARTMENT DOOR	27. ASH RECEPTACLE
4. SAFETY PAD	16. DOOR LOCK STRIKER	28. NO. 1 PANEL UNDER COVER
5. END FINISH PANEL	17. SPEAKER BRACKET	29. ENGINE HOOD RELEASE LEVER
6. NO. 1 REGISTER	18. SPEAKER	30. NO. 1 SPEAKER PANEL
7. NO. 2 REGISTER	19. NO. 2 SPEAKER PANEL	31. SPEAKER
8. CENTER REGISTER	20. HINGE	32. LOWER FINISH PANEL
9. SIDE REGISTER	21. HEATER CONTROL PANEL	33. FINISH PANEL
10. NO. 3 HEATER DUCT	22. RADIO	34. STEERING WHEEL
11. DUCT	23. NO. 2 PANEL UNDER COVER	35. COMBINATION METER
12. NO. 2 HEATER DUCT	24. LOWER CENTER CLUSTER FINISH PANEL	36. METER HOOD

Fig. 1   Instrument panel & related components

IGNITION LOCK
REPLACE

1. Remove steering wheel assembly.
2. Remove instrument lower finish panel, air duct and column lower cover.
3. Disconnect ignition and turn signal switch electrical connector.
4. Remove switch assembly from column upper cover.
5. Remove three screws from and retainer from upper bracket.
6. Remove snap ring, insert key into ignition and release steering lock.
7. Tap out tapered head bolt.
8. Remove lock cylinder and retaining

screw.
9. Reverse procedure to install.

STARTER
REPLACE

1. Disconnect battery ground cable.
2. Disconnect electrical connectors from starter motor.
3. Remove transmission cable and bracket at transmission.
4. Remove starter motor attaching bolts.
5. Remove starter motor.
6. Reverse procedure to install.

IGNITION SWITCH/TURN SIGNAL SWITCH
REPLACE

1. Disconnect battery ground cable.
2. Remove steering wheel cover and steering wheel.
3. Remove instrument lower finish panel, air duct and column lower cover.
4. Disconnect electrical connector from ignition/turn signal switch.
5. Remove switch assembly with steering column upper cover.
6. Reverse procedure to install.

RADIO
REPLACE

Refer to "Instrument Panel Pad/Cluster, Replace" for radio removal procedure.

BLOWER ASSEMBLY
REPLACE

1. Disconnect battery ground cable.
2. Remove evaporator assembly, if equipped.
3. Disconnect electrical connector from blower motor.
4. Disconnect air source selector control cable from blower assembly side.
5. Loosen nuts and bolts, then remove blower assembly.

6. Reverse procedure to install.

INSTRUMENT PANEL PAD/CLUSTER
REPLACE

1. Disconnect battery ground cable.
2. Remove steering wheel assembly.
3. Remove left speaker grille.
4. Remove steering column lower trim cover.
5. Remove hood release lever.
6. Remove heater duct.
7. Remove meter hood, A/C registers and register hood, **Fig. 1.**
8. Remove combination meter, disconnect speedometer cable and electrical connectors. Remove meter from instrument panel.
9. Remove end finish panel.
10. Remove panel under cover.
11. Remove right side speaker grille.
12. Remove speaker bracket and speaker.
13. Remove glove compartment door and hinge.
14. Remove glove compartment door lock striker.
15. Remove center cluster finish panel.
16. Remove radio equipment assembly.
17. Remove lower center cluster finsh panel.
18. Disconnect vacuum lines and electrical connectors, then remove heater control panel.
19. Remove side defroster nozzle.
20. Remove instrument panel pad assembly.
21. Reverse procedure to install.

Engine Section

ENGINE MOUNT
REPLACE

1. Disconnect battery ground cable.
2. Raise and support vehicle.
3. Loosen center engine mount.
4. Lower vehicle.
5. Support engine assembly.
6. Disconnect engine mount at engine assembly.
7. Raise engine assembly.
8. Remove engine mount.
9. Reverse procedure to install.

ENGINE
REPLACE

1. Disconnect battery ground cable.
2. Drain coolant and engine oil.
3. Drain transmission fluid.
4. Mark hood hinges, then remove hood.
5. Remove air cleaner assembly.
6. Disconnect upper radiator hose at outlet and overflow hose.
7. Disconnect coolant hose at cylinder head rear coolant pipe.
8. Disconnect coolant hose at thermostat housing.
9. Disconnect fuel lines from fuel pump.
10. Mark, then disconnect all vacuum lines and electrical connectors from engine assembly.
11. Remove drive belts.
12. Disconnect speedometer cable from transaxle assembly.
13. Raise and support vehicle.
14. Disconnect exhaust pipe from exhaust manifold.
15. Disconnect air hose from converter pipe.
16. Disconnect transaxle cooler lines from radiator.
17. Remove left and righthand under covers.
18. Remove power steering pump and A/C compressor, if equipped and position aside.

19. Disconnect cable and bracket from transaxle.
20. Disconnect steering knuckles from lower control arms.
21. Disconnect driveshafts from transaxle.
22. Remove flywheel cover.
23. Remove flex plate to torque converter attaching bolts.
24. Disconnect front and rear mounting from center crossmember.
25. Disconnect cable and remove center member.
26. Lower vehicle.
27. Remove radiator and fan assembly.
28. Install suitable engine lifting equipment on to engine lifting eyes.
29. Remove righthand motor mount through bolt.
30. Remove lefthand transaxle mount bolt and mount.
31. Remove engine and transaxle as an assembly.
32. Reverse procedure to install.

CYLINDER HEAD
REPLACE

1. Disconnect battery ground cable.
2. Drain cooling system.
3. Remove air cleaner assembly.
4. Raise and support vehicle.
5. Drain engine oil.
6. Disconnect exhaust pipe from exhaust manifold.
7. Disconnect air hose from converter pipe.
8. Loosen power steering pivot bolt, if equipped.
9. Lower vehicle.
10. Disconnect accelerator and throttle cable from carburetor and bracket.
11. Mark, then disconnect all vacuum lines and electrical connectors from cylinder head assembly.
12. Disconnect fuel lines from fuel pump.
13. Disconnect upper radiator hose, water outlet and heater hose.
14. Remove power steering bracket, if equipped.
15. Place No. 1 cylinder at TDC of compression stroke, then disconnect spark plug wires and remove distributor assembly.
16. Remove PCV valve and wiring harness.
17. Remove No. 1 (upper) timing belt cover bolts.
18. Remove cylinder head cover and gasket.
19. Remove alternator drive belt and water pump pulley bolts.
20. Remove No. 1 (upper) timing cover and gasket.
21. Mark camshaft timing pulley position and timing belt rotational direction.
22. Loosen idler pulley and move aside slightly to release timing belt tension, then snug down pulley bolt.
23. Pull timing belt away from camshaft timing pulley.
24. Loosen and remove cylinder head bolts gradually in three steps and in sequence shown in **Fig. 1.**
25. Remove cylinder head with intake and exhaust manifolds attached.
26. Reverse procedure to install, noting the following:
   a. Install cylinder head, then gradually tighten cylinder head bolts in three steps and in sequence shown in **Fig. 2,** to 43 ft. lbs.
   b. Install camshaft timing pulley and timing belt in original (marked) position as removed.

Fig. 1 Cylinder head bolt loosening sequence

CHEVROLET NOVA

INTAKE & EXHAUST MANIFOLDS
REPLACE

1. Disconnect battery ground cable.
2. Remove air cleaner assembly.
3. Disconnect vacuum lines.
4. Disconnect throttle valve cable.
5. Disconnect accelerator cable.
6. Disconnect electrical connector from carburetor.
7. Disconnect fuel line from fuel pump.
8. Disconnect all necessary vacuum lines to remove carburetor assembly.
9. Remove early fuel evaporation (EFE) gasket.
10. Disconnect vacuum line, then remove dashpot bracket.
11. Remove heat shield.
12. Raise and support vehicle.
13. Disconnect exhaust pipe from exhaust manifold.
14. Remove exhaust bracket from engine.
15. Disconnect air hose from converter pipe.
16. Lower vehicle.
17. Disconnect brake vacuum hose.
18. Remove accelerator and throttle cable bracket.
19. Remove intake and exhaust manifolds and gaskets.
20. Reverse procedure to install.

ROCKER ARM SHAFT & ROCKER ARMS
REPLACE

1. Remove cylinder head cover attaching bolts, then the cylinder head cover.
2. Loosen each rocker support bolt a little at a time and in sequence shown in **Fig. 3.**
3. During installation, proceed as follows:
   a. Loosen adjusting screw lock nuts.
   b. Assemble rocker arm assembly and face the oil holes of the rocker shaft to the right, left and bottom as shown in **Fig. 4.**
   c. Install and tighten rocker support bolts gradually in three steps in sequence shown in **Fig. 5.**

VALVES
ADJUST

1. Position No. 1 cylinder to TDC of compression stroke.
2. Turn crankshaft in normal direction of rotation to align timing marks at TDC, then set groove on pulley to the 0 position.
3. Ensure rocker arms on No. 1 cylinder are loose and rockers on No. 4 are tight. If not, turn crankshaft one complete revolution and align marks.
4. Adjust valve clearances of the valves shown in **Fig. 6,** to specification.
5. Turn crankshaft one revolution and align the timing marks.

1. CYLINDER HEAD COVER
2. CYLINDER HEAD COVER GASKET
3. EXHAUST MANIFOLD
4. CAMSHAFT TIMING PULLEY
5. 47 N·m (34 FT.LBS)
6. TIMING BELT UPPER COVER AND GASKET
7. TIMING BELT LOWER COVER
8. TIMING BELT
9. HEAD GASKET
10. 59 N·m (43 FT.LBS)
11. VALVE
12. CYLINDER HEAD

13 VALVE KEEPER
14 VALVE SPRING RETAINER
15 VALVE SPRING
16 VALVE STEM OIL SEAL
17 VALVE SPRING SEAT
18 CAMSHAFT
19 CAMSHAFT OIL SEAL
20 DRIVE GEAR
21 29 N·m (22 FT.LBS)
22 CAMSHAFT BEARING CAP
23 13 N·m (9 FT.LBS)
24 ROCKER ARM ASSEMBLY
25 PCV VALVE

Cylinder head & related components

Fig. 2 Cylinder head bolt tightening sequence

Fig. 3 Rocker arm support loosening sequence

CUTAWAY VIEW
TOP

OIL HOLE

BOTTOM

FRONT

PROJECTED VIEW

Fig. 4 Rocker shaft oil holes

Fig. 5 Rocker arm torque sequence

VALVE CLEARNACE (HOT):
INTAKE   0.20mm (0.008 in.)
EXHAUST 0.30mm (0.012 in.)

FIRST

FRONT

IN   EX   IN   EX

Fig. 6 First valve clearance adjustment

6. Adjust remaining valves as shown in **Fig. 7**, to specification.

NO. 1 TIMING BELT COVER
REPLACE

1. Disconnect battery ground cable.
2. Loosen coolant pump pulley bolts.
3. Remove alternator drive belt.
4. Remove power steering pump drive belt, if equipped.
5. Remove water pump pulley.
6. Drain cooling system.
7. Disconnect upper radiator hose at outlet.
8. Disconnect all necessary vacuum lines.
9. Remove upper No. 1 timing cover attaching bolts.
10. Raise and support vehicle.
11. Remove lower cover attaching bolts.
12. Lower vehicle, then remove No. 1 timing cover.
13. Reverse procedure to install.

NO. 2 TIMING BELT COVER
REPLACE

1. Disconnect battery ground cable.
2. Remove alternator belt.
3. Remove A/C drive belt, if equipped.
4. Raise and support vehicle.
5. Remove righthand under cover.
6. Remove flywheel cover.
7. Remove crankshaft pulley.
8. Remove No. 2 timing cover and gasket.
9. Reverse procedure to install.

NO. 3 TIMING BELT COVER
REPLACE

1. Remove No. 1 timing belt cover as described previously.
2. Loosen A/C idler pulley mount nut and adjusting bolt, then remove A/C belt, if equipped.
3. Remove A/C idler pulley and adjusting bolt, if equipped.
4. Remove alternator and position aside.
5. Remove No. 3 timing belt cover and gasket.
6. Reverse procedure to install.

TIMING BELT & CAMSHAFT TIMING PULLEY
REPLACE

1. Disconnect battery ground cable.
2. Drain cooling system.
3. Loosen coolant pump pulley bolts.
4. Remove alternator drive belt.
5. Remove power steering pump belt, if equipped.
6. Remove water pump pulley.
7. Loosen A/C idler pulley mount nut and adjusting bolt, if equipped.
8. Remove A/C idler pulley and adjusting bolt, if equipped.
9. Raise and support vehicle.
10. Remove righthand under cover.
11. Remove flywheel cover and crankshaft pulley.

12. Remove No. 2 timing belt cover with gasket.
13. Disconnect engine mounting center member.
14. Lower vehicle.
15. Disconnect upper radiator hose at outlet.
16. Disconnect all necessary vacuum hoses.
17. Remove No. 1 timing belt cover and gasket.
18. Remove alternator and position aside.
19. Remove No. 3 timing belt cover.
20. Support engine with a suitable jack.
21. Position No. 1 cylinder at TDC of compression stroke, then turn crankshaft until the timing mark is aligned with the TDC mark. The rocker arms on the No. 1 cylinder should be loose. If not, turn crankshaft one complete turn.
22. Disconnect righthand engine mount.
23. Loosen idler pulley to relieve belt tension.
24. Lower engine and remove timing belt.

NOTE: If reusing the timing belt, draw a direction arrow on the belt (in direction of engine rotation) and place alignment marks on the pulleys and belt as shown in **Fig. 8**.

25. Remove idler pulley bolt, pulley and return spring.
26. Remove camshaft timing pulley.
27. During installation of belt and timing pulley, proceed as follows:
   a. Align camshaft knock pin and camshaft timing pulley. Torque bolt to 34 ft. lbs.
   b. Align bearing cap mark and the center of the small hole on the

SECOND

FRONT

EX   IN EX   IN

Fig. 7 Second valve clearance adjustment

Fig. 8 Belt & pulley alignment

ALIGNMENT MARK

Fig. 9 Camshaft timing pulley alignment

Fig. 10   Crankshaft timing pulley alignment

Fig. 11   Timing mark alignment

FRONT

ALIGN

Fig. 12   Piston & rod assembly

camshaft timing pulley as shown in **Fig. 9.**

c. Align TDC marks on the oil pump body and crankshaft timing pulley as shown in **Fig. 10.**

d. Remove any oil or water on the crankshaft timing pulley and keep it clean.

e. Install timing belt idler pulley and tension spring. Pry timing belt idler pulley toward the left as far as it will go and temporarily tighten it.

f. Install timing belt. If reusing the original timing belt, align the points marked during removal and install the belt with the arrow pointing in the direction of engine rotation.

g. Raise engine slightly, then loosen timing belt idler pulley mounting bolt. Temporarily install the crank pulley bolt and turn the crankshaft two revolutions from TDC to TDC.

h. Check valve timing. Ensure each pulley aligns with the marks as shown in **Fig. 11.**

i. Reverse remaining removal procedure to complete installation procedure.

CAMSHAFT
REPLACE

1. Disconnect battery ground cable.
2. Remove cylinder head cover.
3. Drain cooling system.
4. Loosen water pump pulley bolts and alternator drive belt.
5. Raise and support vehicle.
6. Remove power steering pivot bolt, if equipped.
7. Remove bolt that goes through both the No. 1 and No. 2 timing covers.
8. Lower vehicle.
9. Remove power steering drive belt, if equipped.
10. Remove water pump pulley.
11. Disconnect upper radiator hose at outlet.
12. Disconnect all necessary vacuum lines.
13. Remove No. 1 timing belt cover and gasket.
14. Disconnect spark plug wires and electrical connectors.
15. Remove distributor.
16. Disconnect fuel lines, then remove fuel pump.
17. Remove distributor gear bolt.
18. Remove rocker arm assembly.
19. Turn crankshaft clockwise and position No. 1 cylinder to TDC of compression stroke.
20. Place alignment marks on the camshaft timing pulley and belt.
21. Loosen idler pulley mount bolt and push idler pulley toward the left as far as it will go and temporarily tighten it. Remove belt.
22. Support belt so that the meshing of the crankshaft timing pulley and timing belt does not shift.
23. Do not allow belt to contact oil, water or dust.
24. Remove camshaft bearing caps and camshaft.
25. Reverse procedure to install, noting the following:
    a. Install camshaft bearing caps with the arrows on caps facing toward the front.
    b. Ensure timing belt and timing pulley alignment marks align properly.

PISTONS & RODS
ASSEMBLE

Assemble pistons to connecting rods as shown in **Fig. 12.**

Fig. 13   Oil pump body clearance check

MAXIMUM CLEARANCE: 0.35 mm (0.0138 in.)

Fig. 14   Oil pump gear tip clearance check

MAXIMUM CLEARANCE: 0.1 mm (0.004 in.)

Fig. 15   Oil pump side clearance check

MAIN & ROD BEARINGS

Connecting rod service bearings are available in 3 standard sizes, marked either 1, 2 or 3. Replace the bearing with one having the same mark on the bearing cap. Main bearings are available in 3 standard sizes marked 1, 2 or 3. If replacing the bearing, replace with one having the same number as marked on the cylinder block.

CRANKSHAFT REAR OIL SEAL
REPLACE

1. Remove transaxle and flywheel assembly.
2. Remove rear end plate.
3. Carefully pry oil seal from groove.
4. Reverse procedure to install.

OIL PAN
REPLACE

1. Disconnect battery ground cable.
2. Raise and support vehicle.
3. Drain engine oil.
4. Remove righthand under cover.
5. Remove oil pan bolts.
6. Remove oil pan.
7. Reverse procedure to install.

OIL PUMP
REPLACE

1. Remove Nos. 1, 2 and 3 timing belt covers as described previously.
2. Remove oil pan attaching bolts, then the oil pan.
3. Remove righthand under cover.
4. Remove flywheel cover and crankshaft pulley.
5. Mark position of camshaft and crankshaft timing pulleys and timing belt rotational direction.
6. Loosen idler pulley bolt, move pulley over to relieve belt tension and tighten bolt.
7. Pull timing belt off of crankshaft timing pulley.
8. Remove dipstick tube.
9. Remove timing belt idler pulley.
10. Remove oil pump bolts and oil pump.
11. Reverse procedure to install, noting the following:
    a. Using a feeler gauge, measure clearance between the driven gear and body, **Fig. 13.**
    b. If clearance is greater than .008 inch, replace gear and/or body.
    c. Using a feeler gauge, measure clearance between both gear tips and crescent as shown in **Fig. 14.**
    d. If clearance is greater than .0138 inch, replace gear and/or body.
    e. Using a feeler gauge and flat block, measure side clearance as shown in **Fig. 15.**
    f. If clearance is greater than .004 inch, replace gear and/or body.

WATER PUMP
REPLACE

1. Disconnect battery ground cable.
2. Remove No. 1 timing belt cover.
3. Remove inlet pipe mount bolt, nuts and inlet pipe.
4. Remove inlet pipe from water inlet housing.
5. Remove inlet pipe from water pump.
6. Remove oil level gauge guide.
7. Remove righthand under cover.
8. Remove power steering adjusting bracket, if equipped.
9. Remove water pump attaching bolts, then the water pump.
10. Reverse procedure to install.

FUEL PUMP
REPLACE

1. Disconnect battery ground cable.
2. Disconnect fuel hoses from fuel pump.
3. Remove mounting bolts.
4. Remove fuel pump and heat insulator assembly.
5. Remove fuel pump.
6. Reverse procedure to install.

Clutch & Manual Transmission Section

CLUTCH PEDAL
ADJUST

1. Check height as shown in **Fig. 1.**
2. If it is necessary to adjust pedal height, remove instrument lower finish panel and air duct.
3. Loosen lock nut and turn stopper bolt until the height is correct, then tighten lock nut.

CLUTCH
REPLACE

1. Remove transaxle assembly from vehicle.
2. Loosen each set bolt one turn at a time until spring tension is released.
3. Remove attaching bolts and pull off clutch assembly.
4. Remove release bearing fork and boot from the transaxle.
5. Reverse procedure to install.

PUSH ROD PLAY AND FREEPLAY ADJUST POINT

PEDAL HEIGHT ADJUST POINT

1.0-5.0mm (0.039-0.197 in.) PUSH ROD PLAY

PEDAL HEIGHT

Fig. 1 Clutch pedal adjustment

MANUAL TRANSAXLE
REPLACE

Refer to "Engine Section" under "Engine, Replace" for transaxle replace procedure. The engine and transaxle assembly is removed as an assembly.

SHIFT LEVER FREE-PLAY
ADJUST

1. Remove shift lever cover.
2. Using a feeler gauge measure clearance between shim and shift lever retainer through slot provided at side of shift lever cap.
3. Select a shim that will allow a 0–.004 inch clearance between adjusting shim and retainer.
4. Shims are aviable in .020, .024, .028, .031, .035, .039, .043 and .047 inch thicknesses.

Rear Axle, Rear Suspension & Brakes

REAR AXLE
REPLACE

1. Remove rear axle hub.
2. Disconnect brake line from wheel cylinder.
3. Remove bolt and nut holding axle carrier to strut rod.
4. Remove bolt and nut holding axle carrier to the front suspension arm.
5. Remove bolt and nut holding axle carrier to the rear suspension arm.
6. Remove bolts and nuts holding axle carrier to the strut, then the axle carrier assembly.
7. Reverse procedure to install.

REAR AXLE HUB
REPLACE

1. Raise and support vehicle.
2. Remove wheel and tire assembly.
3. Remove brake drum, **Fig. 1.**
4. Remove four bolts attaching axle hub and rear brake assembly.
5. Remove hub, brake assembly and O-ring.
6. Reverse procedure to install.

STRUT/COIL SPRING ASSEMBLY
REPLACE

1. Remove quarter window garnish molding and back window panel.
2. Raise and support vehicle, then remove tire and wheel assembly.
3. Remove brake line at flex hose on strut, **Fig. 2.**
4. Disconnect flexible hose from shock absorber.
5. Remove bolts attaching strut to axle carrier.
6. Reverse procedure to install.

REAR SUSPENSION ARM
REPLACE

1. Raise and support vehicle.
2. Remove bolt and nut attaching rear suspension arm to axle carrier.
3. Remove cam and bolt attaching rear suspension arm to body, then the rear suspension arm.
4. Note location of cam plate mark before removing bolt and cam.
5. Reverse procedure to install.

FRONT SUSPENSION ARM
REPLACE

1. Raise and support vehicle.

2. Remove bolt and nut attaching front suspension arm to axle carrier.
3. Remove bolt and nut attaching front suspension arm to the body, then the front suspension arm.
4. Reverse procedure to install.

STRUT ROD
REPLACE

1. Raise and support vehicle.
2. Remove bolt and nut attaching strut rod to axle carrier.
3. Remove bolt and nut attaching strut rod to body, then the strut rod assembly from the vehicle.
4. Reverse procedure to install.

PARKING BRAKE
ADJUST

1. Check that parking brake lever travel is correct by pulling parking brake lever all the way up and counting the number of clicks.
2. Parking brake lever travel should be 4–7 clicks. If not, loosen lock nut and turn adjusting nut until travel is correct.

MASTER CYLINDER
REPLACE

1. Clean area around reservoir and brake pipes at master cylinder.
2. Disconnect level warning switch electrical connector.
3. Remove brake fluid from master cylinder.
4. Disconnect, then cap brake lines.
5. Remove two attaching nuts.
6. Remove master cylinder and gasket from booster.
7. Reverse procedure to install.

1. STRUT
2. CARRIER ASSEMBLY
3. REAR BRAKE ASSEMBLY
4. REAR AXLE HUB ASSEMBLY
5. BRAKE DRUM
6. REAR SUSPENSION ARM
7. FRONT SUSPENSION ARM
8. STRUT ROD
9. BOLT 142 N·M (105 FT. LBS.)
10. 87 N·M (64 FT. LBS.)
11. 80 N·M (50 FT. LBS.)

1. NUT 123 N·M (90 FT. LBS)
2. INNER BEARING INNER RACE
3. BEARING OUTER RACE WITH BEARINGS INSTALLED
4. REAR AXLE HUB (BEARING CASE)
5. OUTER BEARING INNER RACE
6. AXLE SEAL
7. AXLE

Fig. 1 Rear hub assembly

VIEW A

1. DUST COVER
2. STRUT PISTON ROD NUT
3. SUSPENSION SUPPORT
4. UPPER INSULATOR
5. COIL SPRING
6. BUMPER
7. LOWER INSULATOR
8. STRUT ASSEMBLY
9. BRAKE LINE
10. RETAINING CLIP
11. FLEXIBLE BRAKE HOSE
12. NUT 142 N·M (105 FT. LBS.)
13. BOLT
14. CARRIER, HUB, AND DRUM ASSEMBLY
15. STRUT ROD
16. BOLT 87 N·M (64 FT. LBS.)
17. NUT
18. REAR SUSPENSION ARM
19. FRONT SUSPENSION ARM
20. NUT
21. BOLT 87 N·M (64 FT. LBS.)
22. BUSHING
23. TOE-IN ADJUSTING CAM NUT
24. TOE-IN INDICATOR
25. BOLT 87 N•m (64 FT. LBS.)
26. BODY (SUSPENSION ARM ATTACHMENTS)

FWD

Fig. 2   Rear suspension assembly

CHEVROLET NOVA
Front Suspension & Steering Section

DESCRIPTION

The front suspension, **Fig. 1**, on this vehicle is a MacPherson strut design. The upper end of the strut is anchored to the body by a strut support. The strut and strut support are isolated by a rubber mount. The lower end of the strut is connected to the upper end of the steering knuckle. The lower end of the knuckle is attached to the ball joint, which is attached to the suspension control arm assembly. Movement of the steering wheel is transmitted to the tie-rod end and then to the knuckle, turning the wheel and tire assembly.

WHEEL ALIGNMENT
Caster & Camber

Camber is adjusted by first loosening the upper and lower strut to knuckle nuts and bolts, then rotating cam to obtain correct specification.

Caster cannot be adjusted. Should caster be found out of specification, locate cause first. If components are damaged, bent, loose, dented or worn, they should be replaced. To prevent an incorrect reading of camber or caster, jounce the bumper three times before checking.

After adjustment, tighten nuts to specification.

Toe-in

Toe-in is adjusted by changing tie-rod lenght. Loosen boot clamps and slide from the boot assembly. Loosen right and left tie-rod end lock nuts, then turn right and left tie-rods to align toe-in to specification. Right and left tie-rods must be equal in lenght.

After adjustment, install boot clamps, tighten nuts to specification and ensure rack boots are not twisted.

NOTE: Torque strut-to-knuckle nut to 105 ft. lbs., and tie-rod locking nut to 35 ft. lbs.

STRUT
REPLACE

1. Open hood, then remove strut to body attaching nuts.
2. Loosen wheel lug nuts. Loosen axle shaft nut if knuckle will be removed.
3. Raise and support vehicle until wheels are clear from ground.
4. Remove tire and wheel assembly.
5. Disconnect brake flex hose clip at strut bracket.
6. Disconnect brake flex hose to brake pipe connection. Remove brake hose clip.
7. Pull brake hose back through strut bracket opening, then tape or cap brake hose and caliper.
8. Remove two brake caliper mounting bracket bolts, then the caliper.

1. COVER, DUST
2. NUT, ABSORBER SHAFT
3. NUT, STRUT SUPPORT
4. SUPPORT, STRUT
5. SEAL, SUPPORT
6. SEAT, SPRING
7. BUMPER, SPRING
8. INSULATOR, UPPER
9. SPRING, COIL
10. INSULATOR, LOWER
11. ABSORBER, SHOCK/STRUT
12. NUT, STRUT TO KNUCKLE
13. CAM, CAMBER ADJUST
14. BOLT, STRUT TO KNUCKLE
15. KNUCKLE, STEERING
16. NUT, BALL JOINT TO KNUCKLE
17. JOINT, LOWER BALL
18. DEFLECTOR, DUST
19. SEAL, INNER HUB
20. RING, SNAP
21. BEARING, FRONT AXLE HUB
22. SEAL OUTER HUB
23. STUD, WHEEL
24. HUB, FRONT AXLE
25. DISC, FRONT BRAKE
26. WASHER, FRONT HUB
27. NUT, FRONT HUB
28. CAP, FRONT HUB
29. PIN, COTTER
30. NUT, CONTROL ARM
31. RETAINER, BUSHING
32. BRACKET, BUSHING
33. BOLT, BUSHING BRACKET
34. BUSHING, CONTROL ARM
35. RETAINER, BUSHING
36. ARM, LOWER CONTROL
37. BOLT, CONTROL ARM
38. BOLT, BALL JOINT
39. NUT, BALL JOINT

Fig. 1   Disassembled view of front suspension (Part 1 of 2)

9. Mark adjusting cam, then remove both strut to knuckle attaching nuts and bolts.
10. Remove strut assembly and chamber adjusting cam from knuckle.
11. Reverse procedure to install. Torque strut to knuckle attaching nuts and bolts to 105 ft. lbs., upper mount bolts to 13 ft. lbs.,and wheel nuts to 76 ft. lbs.

LOWER CONTOL ARM
REPLACE

1. Raise and support vehicle.
2. Remove lower control arm to steering knuckle attaching nuts and bolts.
3. Remove control arm from vehicle.
4. Reverse procedure to install. Torque control arm to body front nuts and bolts to 83 ft. lbs., and rear nuts and bolts to 64 ft. lbs.

LOWER CONTROL ARM BUSHING
REPLACE

1. Remove control arm.
2. Using a suitable tool, remove lower control arm bushing from lower control arm.
3. Reverse procedure to install. Torque bushing nut to 76 ft. lbs.

LOWER BALL JOINT
REPLACE

1. Loosen wheel lug nuts.
2. Raise and support vehicle.
3. Remove tire and wheel assembly.
4. Using tool J-35413 or equivalent, separate ball joint from knuckle assembly.
5. Remove two nuts and bolts attaching ball joint and control arm.
6. Remove ball joint.
7. Reverse procedure to install. Torque knuckle to ball joint nut to 82 ft. lbs. and control arm attaching nuts to 47 ft. lbs. During installation, always replace a self-locking nut with a new one.

STEERING KNUCKLE
REPLACE

1. Loosen wheel and hub nuts.
2. Raise and support vehicle.
3. Remove tire and wheel assembly.
4. Remove brake hose retaining clip at strut.
5. Disconnect flex hose from brake line.
6. Remove caliper bracket to knuckle mounting bolts, then support caliper.
7. Remove disc assembly.
8. Remove drive axle unit. Use tool J-25287 or equivalent, to push out drive axle assembly.
9. Remove cotter pin and tie-rod to knuckle attaching nut. Use tool J-24319-01 or equivalent to separate the tie-rod assembly.
10. Remove ball joint to control arm

Fig. 1 Disassembled view of front suspension (Part 2 of 2)

attaching nuts and bolt.
11. Mark chamber relationship for installation, then remove two strut to knuckle attaching nuts and bolts, then the knuckle.
12. Reverse procedure to install. Torque contol arm nuts and bolts to 47 ft. lbs, ball joint to knuckle, 14 ft. lbs., strut to lower bracket bolts to 105 ft. lbs., tie-rod to knuckle 38 ft. lbs. and brake caliper bracket to knuckle attaching bolts to 65 ft. lbs.

HUB
REPLACE

1. Remove knuckle from vehicle and mount into a suitable vise.
2. Using a suitable screwdriver, remove dust deflector.
3. Using tool J-26941 or equivalent, remove inner grease seal from knuckle, **Fig. 2.**
4. Remove inner bearing snap ring and disc brake dust shield.

5. Push out hub using tool J-25287 and J-35378 or equivalents.
6. Using tools mentioned in step 5, remove outer bearing race from hub.
7. Using tool J-26941 or equivalent, remove outer grease seal.
8. Using tools J35399 and J-35379 or equivalents, remove bearing assembly.
9. Reverse procedure to install. Use tool J-8092 and J-35411 to install hub bearing assembly. Use tool J-35737 to install outer grease seal. Install hub using tool J-8092 and J-35399. Use tool J-35737 to install inner grease seal. Use tool J-35379 to install dust deflector ring. Ensure dust deflector ring faces down (open end down).

MANUAL STEERING GEAR
REPLACE

1. Disconnect battery ground cable.

2. Remove intermediate shaft cover.
3. Loosen upper pinch bolt. Remove lower pinch bolt from pinion shaft.
4. Loosen wheel lug nuts.
5. Raise and support vehicle.
6. Remove both front wheel and tire assemblies.
7. Remove cotter pins from tie-rod ends.
8. Disconnect both tie-rod ends from steering knuckles. Use tool J-24319-01 or equivalent only, to separate tie-rod joints.
9. Remove steering gear to body mounting nuts and bolts.
10. Remove steering assembly from vehicle.
11. Reverse procedure to install. Torque intermediate shaft pinch bolts to 26 ft. lbs., torque tie-rod to knuckle nuts to 36 ft. lbs., gear housing to mounting nuts and bolts to 43 ft. lbs., tie-rod end locking nut to 35 ft.lbs., inner tie-rod to rack nuts to 61 ft. lbs., and wheel nuts to 76 ft. lbs.

1 DEFLECTOR DUST   3 RACE, INNER BEARING   5 BEARING, AXLE HUB   7 SHIELD DUST   9 RACE, OUTER BEARING
2 SEAL INNER GREASE   4 RING, SNAP   6 KNUCKLE, STEERING FRONT   8 SEAL OUTER GREASE   10 HUB, DRIVE AXLE

Fig. 2   Disassembled view of hub & bearing assembly

POWER STEERING GEAR
REPLACE

1. Remove intermediate steering shaft protector.
2. Loosen upper, and remove lower intermediate shaft pinch bolts.
3. Open hood and place drain pan under gear assembly.
4. Loosen wheel lug nuts.
5. Raise and support vehicle.
6. Remove both front wheel and tire assemblies.
7. Using tool J-24319-01 or equivalent, remove both tie-rod ends from knuckles.
8. Support transaxle with a suitable jack.
9. Remove rear center engine mounting member to body mounting bolts.
10. Remove rear engine mount to mount bracket attaching nut and bolt. Raise and lower rear of transaxle to gain access to steering gear to body attaching nuts and bolts.
11. Disconnect pressure and return lines at steering gear.
12. Remove four gear to body mounting nuts and bolts.
13. Remove gear through access opening.
14. Reverse procedure to install.

POWER STEERING PUMP
REPLACE

1. Remove air cleaner assembly.
2. Remove return hose clamp.
3. Disconnect and cap pressure and return lines from pump.
4. Loosen pump pulley.
5. Remove adjusting bolt, pivot bolt and drive belt.
6. Remove pump assembly.
7. Reverse procedure to install.

OLDSMOBILE—REAR WHEEL DRIVE & 1980–85 TORONADO

INDEX OF SERVICE OPERATIONS

NOTE: Refer to the rear of this manual for vehicle manufacturer's special service tool suppliers.

Vehicle Identification Plate

On left upper dash.

Engine Number Location

Buick built engines have the distributor located at the front of the engine. The engine production code is located on front of right hand valve cover and top of left hand valve cover. Chevrolet built V8 engines have the distributor located at the rear of the engine with clockwise rotor rotation. On 1980 V8 engines, the engine production code is located front of right hand valve cover.

Oldsmobile built engines have the distributor located at the rear of the engine with counterclockwise rotor rotation and right side mounted fuel pump. The engine production code is located on the left side valve cover.

Pontiac built V8 engines have the distributor located at the rear of the engine with counter-clockwise rotor rotation and left side mounted fuel pump.

Engine Identification Codes

Engine	Engine Code	V.I.N. Code
1980		
V6-231 Man. Tr.①⑪	EA	A
V6-231 Auto. Tr.①⑪	EB, EC, EO, EP	A
V6-231 Auto. Tr.②⑪	OV, OW	A
V6-231 Auto. Tr.⑪	OX, OY	A
V8-260 Auto. Tr.①	QAC, QAD, QAF, QAH	F
V8-260 Auto. Tr.①	QBB, QBC, QBD	F
V8-260 Auto. Tr.①	QBF, QBH, QBJ	F
V8-305 Auto. Tr.①⑥	CEA, CMC, CMD, CMF	H
V8-305 Auto. Tr.②⑥	CEC, CMM	H
V8-307 Auto. Tr.①⑲	TAA, TAB, TAR, TAS	Y
V8-307 Auto. Tr.①⑲	TAT, TAU, TAX, TAW	Y
V8-307 Auto. Tr.①⑲	TAJ, TAK, TAY, TAZ	Y
V8-307 Auto. Tr.①⑦	TBA, TAN	Y
V8-307 Auto. Tr.①⑯	TBB, TAN	Y
V8-350 Auto. Tr.①⑩	UAN, UAR	R
V8-350 Auto. Tr.①⑲	UAA, UAB, UAX, UAY	R
V8-350 Auto. Tr.①⑦⑯	UAC, UAN, UAZ, UBA	R
V8-350 Auto. Tr.②⑦⑲	UAD, UAF	R
V8-350 Auto. Tr.②⑯	UAH	R
V8-350 Auto. Tr.①⑩⑱	VBP, VBR	N
V8-350 Auto. Tr.①⑦⑱⑲	VBM, VBN, VCL, VCM	N
V8-350 Auto. Tr.①⑱⑲	VBS, VBT	N
V8-350 Auto. Tr.①⑯⑱	VBU	N
V8-350 Auto. Tr.②⑩⑱	VCF	N
V8-350 Auto. Tr.②⑦⑱⑲	VCD	N
V8-350 Auto. Tr.②⑯⑱	VCH	N
1981		
V6-231 Man. Tr.①⑩⑪	NA	A
V6-231 Auto. Tr.①⑩⑪	NB	A
V6-231 Auto. Tr.①⑲⑪	NL	A
V6-231 Auto. Tr.②⑩⑪	NF, NT	A
V6-231 Auto. Tr.②⑲⑪	NC	A
V6-252 Auto. Tr.⑯⑪		4
V8-260 Auto. Tr.①⑩	QKA, QKB, QKH, QKJ	F
V8-260 Auto. Tr.①⑲	OKJ, OKH, QKM	F
V8-260 Auto. Tr.②⑩	QKC, QKK	F
V8-260 Auto. Tr.②⑲	QKN	F
V8-307 Auto. Tr.①⑩	TKA, TKB, TKJ, TKU	Y
V8-307 Auto. Tr.①⑦⑩⑲	TKL, TLR	Y
V8-307 Auto. Tr.①⑯	TKP, TLK	Y
V8-307 Auto. Tr.②⑩	TKB	Y
V8-307 Auto. Tr.②⑲	TKU	Y
V8-307 Auto. Tr.①⑲		Y
V8-350 Auto. Tr.①⑩⑱	VKB, VKC, VNJ, VNK	N
V8-350 Auto. Tr.①⑩⑱	VLM, VLN, VLP, VLN	N
V8-350 Auto. Tr.①⑱⑲	VKH, VKJ, VLL, VLM, VLN, VNN, VNP, VNR, VNT	N
V8-350 Auto. Tr.①⑫⑱	VNH, VNK, VNW, VNX	N
V8-350 Auto. Tr.①⑦⑱	VKN, VLS, VNX, VNY	N
V8-350 Auto. Tr.①⑯⑱	VKU, VNX	N
V8-350 Auto. Tr.②⑩⑱	VLY, VNL	N
V8-350 Auto. Tr.②⑦⑫⑱⑲	VMJ, VNU	N
V8-350 Auto. Tr.②⑯⑱	VMT, VPA	N
1982		
V6-231 Auto. Tr.①⑩⑬	MA	A
V6-231 Auto. Tr.①⑲	MK	A
V6-231 Auto. Tr.②⑩⑬	ML	A
V6-231 Auto. Tr.②⑲	MM	A
V6-252 Auto. Tr.①⑦	FT	4
V6-252 Auto. Tr.①⑯	FV	4
V6-252 Auto. Tr.②⑦	FT	4
V6-252 Auto. Tr.②⑯	FW	4
V8-260 Auto. Tr.①⑩	QAD, QAF	8
V8-260 Auto. Tr.①⑬⑲	QAA, QAH	8
V8-260 Auto. Tr.②⑩	QAH	8
V8-260 Auto. Tr.②⑬⑲	QAC	8
V8-307 Auto. Tr.①⑬	TAD, TAF	Y
V8-307 Auto. Tr.①⑦⑫⑲	TAA, TAB, TAF, TAK, TAM	Y
V8-307 Auto. Tr.①⑯	TBB	Y
V8-307 Auto. Tr.②⑬	TAF	Y
V8-307 Auto. Tr.②⑦⑫⑲	TAB, TAF, TAK, TAM, TMR	Y
V8-307 Auto. Tr.②⑯	TBB	Y
V6-262 Auto. Tr.④⑱	UAA, UAD	V
V6-262 Auto. Tr.②⑱	UAA, UAD	V
V6-262 Auto. Tr.③⑱	UAJ	V
V8-350 Auto. Tr.④⑩⑬⑱	VAY, VAZ, VBA, VBB	N
V8-350 Auto. Tr.④⑱⑲	VAB, VAC, VAD	N
V8-350 Auto. Tr.④⑫⑱	VAK, VAL, VAM	N
V8-350 Auto. Tr.④⑦⑱	VAN, VAP	N
V8-350 Auto. Tr.④⑯⑱	VAW, VBP	N
V8-350 Auto. Tr.②⑩⑬⑱	VAY, VAZ, VBA, VBB	N
V8-350 Auto. Tr.②⑱⑲	VAB, VAC, VAD	N
V8-350 Auto. Tr.②⑫⑱	VAK, VAM	N
V8-350 Auto. Tr.②⑦⑱	VAN, VAP	N
V8-350 Auto. Tr.②⑯⑱	VAW, VBP	N
V8-350 Auto. Tr.③⑩⑬⑱	VBC	N
V8-350 Auto. Tr.③⑱⑲	VAZ	N
V8-350 Auto. Tr.③⑫⑱	VAU	N
V8-350 Auto. Tr.③⑯⑱	VAX	N
1983		
V6-231 Auto. Tr.①⑩⑪	NR	A
V6-231 Auto. Tr.②⑩⑪⑬	NP, NH	A
V6-231 Auto. Tr.①⑪⑫⑲	NO	A
V6-231 Auto. Tr.②⑪⑫⑲	NS	A
V6-252 Auto. Tr.⑦	SO	4
V6-252 Auto. Tr.①⑯	SN	4

continued

ENGINE IDENTIFICATION CODES—Continued

Engine	Engine Code	V.I.N. Code
1983—Continued		
V6-252 Auto. Tr.②⑯	SR	4
V6-262 Auto. Tr.④⑩⑬⑱	UKA, UKB, UNH, UNJ	V
V6-262 Auto. Tr.②⑩⑬⑱	UKA, UKB, UNH, UNJ	V
V6-262 Auto. Tr.③⑩⑬⑱	UKC, UNK	V
V8-307 Auto. Tr.①⑮	TKN, TKP, TKY	Y
V8-307 Auto. Tr.②⑮	TKN, TKP, TKY	Y
V8-307 Auto. Tr.①⑯	TKH	Y
V8-307 Auto. Tr.②⑯	TKH	Y
V8-307 Auto. Tr.⑭	TLA	9
V8-350 Auto. Tr.④⑩⑬⑱	VKZ, VLA, vNA, VNB, VNC	N
V8-350 Auto. Tr.②⑩⑬⑱	VKZ, VLA, VNA, VNB, VNC	N
V8-350 Auto. Tr.③⑩⑬⑱	VLB, VNC	N
V8-350 Auto. Tr.④⑦⑱⑲	VKB, VKC, VKK, VKL, VMR, VMT	N
V8-350 Auto. Tr.②⑦⑱⑲	VKB, VKC, VKK, VKL, VMR, VMT	N
V8-350 Auto. Tr.③⑦⑱⑲	VKD, VKK, VMW	N
V8-350 Auto. Tr.⑫⑱	VMA, VMB, VMS, VMU, VMW	N
V8-350 Auto. Tr.⑤⑯	VKR, VKS, VMX, VMY	N
V8-350 Auto. Tr.③⑯	VKT, VMZ	N
1984		
V6-231 Auto. Tr.①⑩	FRC, FWC	A
V6-231 Auto. Tr.②⑩	FRB, FRC, FRC, FWC	A
V6-231 Auto. Tr.⑫⑲	FWC	A
V6-252 Auto. Tr.⑯	HDD	4
V6-262 Auto. Tr.④⑱	UAM, UBA, UBB, UBD, UCN, UCP, UCR, UDW, UDY, ULX, ULY	T
V6-262 Auto. Tr.③⑱	UBF, UCS, UFA, UFF, ULZ	T
V6-262 Auto. Tr.②⑱	UAC, UCB, UCD, UDN, UDP, UDR, UDS, UFC, UFJ, UFK, UKX, UMB	T
V6-262 Auto. Tr.⑤⑱	ULR, ULS	V
V6-262 Auto. Tr.③⑱	ULT	V
V8-307 Auto. Tr.⑭	PAT	9
V8-307 Auto. Tr.①⑮	PAA, PAB, PAC, PBB	Y
V8-307 Auto. Tr.②⑮	PAC	Y
V8-307 Auto. Tr.①⑯	PAB, PAC, PBA, PBB	Y
V8-307 Auto. Tr.②⑯	PAH	Y
V8-350 Auto. Tr.⑤⑩⑱	RAN, RAP	N
V8-350 Auto. Tr.③⑩⑱	RAT	N
V8-350 Auto. Tr.⑤⑦⑱⑲	RAA, RAB	N
V8-350 Auto. Tr.③⑦⑱⑲	RAF	N
V8-350 Auto. Tr.⑤⑫⑱	RBL, RBM	N
V8-350 Auto. Tr.③⑫⑱	RAF	N
V8-350 Auto. Tr.⑤⑯⑱	RAH, RAJ	N
V8-350 Auto. Tr.③⑯⑱	RAM	N
1985		
V6-231 Auto. Tr.	NFA	A
V8-307 Auto. Tr.⑭	PKS	9
V8-307 Auto. Tr.①⑩⑫⑲	PKH, PKJ, PLA, PLB, PLL, PLM	Y
V8-307 Auto. Tr.②⑩⑫⑲	PKJ, PKR, PLB, PLM, PLP, PLU	Y
V8-307 Auto. Tr.①⑯	PKD, PLF, PLJ	Y
V8-307 Auto. Tr.②⑯	PKP, PLH, PLK	Y
V8-350 Auto. Tr.⑩⑱	RLH, RLJ	N
V8-350 Auto. Tr.⑱⑲	RLA, RLB	N
V8-350 Auto. Tr.⑫⑱	RLD, RLF	N
V8-350 Auto. Tr.⑯⑱	RLL, RLM	N

①—Except California.
②—California.
③—High altitude.
④—Exc. Calif. & High altitude.
⑤—Exc. high altitude.
⑥—Chevrolet built engine.
⑦—98.
⑧—Early production.
⑨—Late production.
⑩—Cutlass.
⑪—Buick built.
⑫—Custom Cruiser.
⑬—Cutlass Cruiser.
⑭—Hurst option.
⑮—Except Toronado.
⑯—Toronado.
⑰—Exc. even fire engine.
⑱—Diesel engine.
⑲—88.

Grille Identification

1980 Cutlass Supreme   1980 Cutlass Supreme LS   1980 Cutlass Salon

1980 Cutlass "442"   1980 Delta 88 Royale   1980–82 Toronado

continued

1980 98 Regency

1981 Cutlass Supreme

1981 88 & Custom Cruiser

1981 Cutlass Cruiser & Brougham

1981 Cutlass Calais

1981 98 Regency

1982 Cutlass Brougham

1982 Cutlass Supreme

1982 88

1982 98

1982 Cutlass Calais

1982 Toronado

1983 Cutlass Supreme

1983 Cutlass Cruiser

1983 Hurst/Olds

1983 88

1983-84 98

1983 Toronado

1984 Olds Cutlass Supreme

1984 Hurst/Olds

1984 Olds Delta 88 & Custom Cruiser

continued

1984 Olds Toronado

1985 Cutlass Supreme Coupe

1985 Cutlass Supreme Sedan

1985 Cutlass Supreme "442"

1985 Toronado

1985 Toronado Caliente

1985 88

1985 88 Royal Brougham

1986 Cutlass Salon

1986 Cutlass Supreme

1986 Cutlass "442"

1986 Custom Cruiser

General Engine Specifications

Year	Engine CID①/Liter	Engine V.I.N. Code②	Carburetor	Bore and Stroke	Compression Ratio	Net H.P. @ R.P.M.③	Maximum Torque Ft. Lbs. @ R.P.M.	Normal Oil Pressure Pounds
1980	V6-231, 3.8L⑦	A	M2ME, 2 Bbl.⑤	3.80 × 3.40	8.0	110 @ 3800	190 @ 1600	37
	V8-260, 4.3L	F	M2MC, 2 Bbl.⑤	3.50 × 3.385	7.5	105 @ 3400	195 @ 1600	30–45
	V8-305, 5.0L④⑪	H	M4MC, 4 Bbl.⑤	3.736 × 3.48	8.6	155 @ 4000	240 @ 1600	45
	V8-305, 5.0L④⑥	H	E4MC, 4 Bbl.⑤	3.736 × 3.48	8.6	155 @ 4000	230 @ 1600	45
	V8-307, 5.0L	Y	M4MC, 4 Bbl.⑤	3.80 × 3.385	7.9	150 @ 3600	245 @ 1600	30–45
	V8-350, 5.7L⑩	N	Fuel Injection	4.057 × 3.385	22.5	105 @ 3200	205 @ 1600	30–45
	V8-350, 5.7L	R	E4MC, 4 Bbl.⑤	4.057 × 3.385	8.0	160 @ 3600	270 @ 2000	30–45
1981	V6-231, 3.8L⑦	A	2ME, 2 Bbl.⑤	3.80 × 3.40	8.0	110 @ 3800	190 @ 1600	30–45
	V8-252, 4.1L⑦	4	M4MC, 4 Bbl.⑤	3.96 × 3.40	8.0	125 @ 4000	205 @ 2000	30–45
	V8-260, 4.3L	F	2MC, 2 Bbl.⑤	3.50 × 3.38	7.5	100 @ 3600	190 @ 1600	30–45
	V8-307, 5.0L	Y	2ME, 2 Bbl.⑤	3.80 × 3.38	8.0	140 @ 3600	240 @ 1600	30–45
	V8-307, 5.0L	Y	M4MC, 4 Bbl.⑤	3.80 × 3.38	8.0	140 @ 3600	240 @ 1600	30–45
	V8-350⑩	N	Fuel Injection	4.05 × 3.38	22.5	105 @ 3200	200 @ 1600	30–45
1982	V6-231, 3.8L⑦	A	E2ME, 2 Bbl.⑤	3.80 × 3.40	8.0	110 @ 3800	190 @ 1600	37
	V6-252, 4.1L⑦	4	E4ME, 4 Bbl.⑤	3.96 × 3.40	8.0	125 @ 4000	205 @ 1600	37
	V6-262, 4.3L⑩	V	Fuel Injection	4.05 × 3.38	21.6	85 @ 3600	165 @ 1600	30–45
	V8-260, 4.3L	8	E2ME, 2 Bbl.⑤	3.50 × 3.38	7.5	100 @ 3600	190 @ 1600	35
	V8-307, 5.0L	Y	E4ME, 4 Bbl.⑤	3.80 × 3.38	8.0	140 @ 3600	240 @ 1600	35
	V8-350, 5.7L⑩	N	Fuel Injection	4.05 × 3.38	22.5	105 @ 3200	200 @ 1600	30–45
1983	V6-231, 3.8L⑦	A	2 Bbl.⑤	3.80 × 3.40	8.0	110 @ 3800	190 @ 1600	37
	V6-252, 4.1L⑦	4	4 Bbl.⑤	3.96 × 3.40	8.0	125 @ 4000	205 @ 2000	37
	V6-262, 4.3L⑩	V	Fuel Injection	4.05 × 3.38	22.5	85 @ 3600	165 @ 1600	30–45
	V8-307, 5.0L⑧	Y	4 Bbl.⑤	3.80 × 3.38	8.0	140 @ 3600	240 @ 1600	30–45
	V8-307, 5.0L⑨	9	E4MC, 4 Bbl.⑤	3.80 × 3.38	—	180	245	30–45
	V8-350, 5.7L⑩	N	Fuel Injection	4.05 × 3.38	22.5	105 @ 3200	200 @ 1600	30–45
1984	V6-231, 3.8L⑦	A	E2ME, 2 Bbl.⑤	3.80 × 3.40	8.0	110 @ 4000	190 @ 1600	37
	V6-252, 4.1L⑦	4	E4ME, 4 Bbl.⑤	3.96 × 3.40	8.0	125 @ 4000	205 @ 2000	37
	V6-262, 4.3L⑩	V	Fuel Injection	4.05 × 3.38	22.8	85 @ 3600	165 @ 1600	30–45
	V8-307, 5.0L⑧	Y	E4MC, 4 Bbl.⑤	3.80 × 3.38	8.0	140 @ 3600	240 @ 1600	30–45
	V8-307, 5.0L⑨	9	4 Bbl.	3.80 × 3.38	—	180 @ 4000	245 @ 3200	30–45
	V8-350, 5.7L⑩	N	Fuel Injection	4.05 × 3.38	22.7	105 @ 3200	200 @ 1600	30–45
1985	V6-231, 3.8L⑦	A	E2ME, 2 Bbl.⑤	3.80 × 3.40	8.0	110 @ 3800	190 @ 1600	—
	V6-262, 4.3L⑩	V	Fuel Injection	4.05 × 3.38	22.8	85 @ 3600	165 @ 1600	30–45
	V8-307, 5.0L	Y	E4MC, 4 Bbl.⑤	3.80 × 3.38	8.0	140 @ 3200	255 @ 2000⑫	30–45
	V8-350, 5.7L⑩	N	Fuel Injection	4.05 × 3.38	22.7	105 @ 3200	200 @ 1600	30–45
1986	V6-231, 3.8L⑦	—	E2ME, 2 Bbl.⑤	3.80 × 3.40	8.0	—	—	37
	V8-307, 5.0L	—	E4MC, 4 Bbl.⑤	3.80 × 3.38	8.0	—	—	30–45

①—CID—cubic inch displacement.
②—On 1980 vehicles, the fifth digit in the VIN denotes engine code. On 1981–86 vehicles, the eighth digit in the VIN denotes engine code.
③—All ratings are net—as installed in vehicle.
④—Chevrolet built engine. Distributor located at rear of engine, clockwise rotation.
⑤—Rochester.
⑥—Calif.
⑦—Buick built engine. Distributor located at front of engine.
⑧—Exc. Hurst option.
⑨—Hurst option.
⑩—Diesel.
⑪—Exc. Calif.
⑫—88 & Custom Cruiser 240 @ 1600.

continued

Pistons, Pins, Rings, Crankshaft & Bearings

Year	Model/V.I.N.	Piston Clearance	Ring End Gap①		Wrist-pin Diameter	Rod Bearings		Main Bearings			Shaft End Play
			Comp.	Oil		Shaft Diameter	Bearing Clearance	Shaft Diameter	Bearing Clearance	Thrust on Bear. No.	
1980	V6-231/A⑫	.0011-.0023	.013	.015	.9392	2.2487-2.2495	.0004-.0033	2.4995	.0003-.0018	2	.003-.009
	V8-260/F	.00075-.00175	.010	.015	.9805	2.1238-2.1248	.0004-.0033	②	⑪	3	.0035-.0135
	V8-305/H⑧	.0007-.0042	⑦	.010	.9272	2.099-2.100	.0013-.0035	⑬	⑭	5	.002-.007
	V8-307/Y	.0005-.0015	.010	.015	.9805	2.1238-2.1248	.0004-.0033	②	⑪	3	.0035-.0135
	V8-350/L	.00075-.00175	.010	.015	.9805	2.1238-2.1248	.0005-.0026	②	⑪	3	.0035-.0135
	V8-350/N⑥	.0050-.0060	.015	.015	1.0951	2.1238-2.1248	.0005-.0026	3.00	⑪	3	.0035-.0135
1981	V6-231/A, 252/4⑫	.0008-.0020	.013	.015	.9392	2.2487-2.2495	.0005-.0026	2.4995	.0003-.0018	2	.003-.009
	V8-260/F	.00075-.00175	.010	.015	.9805	2.1238-2.1248	.0004-.0033	⑯	⑪	3	.0035-.0135
	V8-307/Y	.00075-.00175	.010	.015	.9805	2.1238-2.1248	.0005-.0026	⑯	⑪	3	.0035-.0135
	V8-350/N⑥	.005-.006	.015	.015	1.0951	2.1238-2.1248	.0005-.0026	3.00	⑪	3	.0035-.0135
1982-83	V6-231/A, 252/4⑫	.0008-.0020	.013	.015	.9392	2.2487-2.2495	.0005-.0026	2.4995	.0003-.0018	2	.003-.009
	V6-262/V⑥	.0035-.0045	⑰	⑯	1.0951	2.2490-2.2510	.0003-.0025	2.9993-3.0003	④	3	.0035-.0135
	V8-260/8	.00075-.00175	.010	.015	.9805	2.1238-2.1248	.0004-.0033	⑮	⑪	3	.0035-.0135
	V8-307/Y,9	.00075-.00175	.010	.015	.9805	2.1238-2.1248	.0004-.0033	②	⑪	3	.0035-.0135
	V8-350/N⑥	.003-.004	⑰	.015	1.0951	2.1238-2.1248	.0005-.0026	2.9993-3.0003	⑨	3	.0035-.0135
1984	V6-231/A, 252/4⑫	.0008-.0020	.010	.015	.9392	2.2487-2.2495	.0005-.0026	2.4995	.0003-.0018	2	.0030-.0110
	V6-262/V⑥	.0035-.0045	⑰	.010	1.0951	2.2490-2.2510	.0005-.0025	2.9993-3.0003	④	3	.0035-.0135
	V8-307/Y,9	.00075-.00175	.010	.015	.9805	2.1238-2.1248	.0004-.0033	②	⑪	3	.0035-.0135
	V8-350/N⑥	.0035-.0045	⑰	.010	1.0951	2.1238-2.1248	.0005-.0026	2.9993-3.0003	⑨	3	.0035-.0135
1985	V6-231/A⑫	.0008-.0020	.010	.015	.9392	2.2487-2.2495	.0005-.0026	2.4995	.0003-.0018	2	.0030-.0110
	V6-262/V⑥	.0035-.0045	⑰	.015	1.0951	2.2490-2.2498	.0004-.0026	2.9993-3.0003	④	3	.0035-.0135
	V8-307/Y	.00075-.00175	.009	.015	.9805	2.1238-2.1248	.0004-.0033	③	⑤	3	.0035-.0135
	V8-350/N⑥	.0035-.0045	.015	.015	1.0951	2.1238-2.1248	.0005-.0026	2.9993-3.0003	⑨	3	.0035-.0085
1986	V6-231	.0008-.0020	.010	.015	.9392	2.2487-2.2495	.0005-.0026	2.4995	.0003-.0018	2	.0030-.0110
	V8-307	.00075-.00175	.009	.015	.9805	2.1238-2.1248	.0004-.0033	③	⑤	3	.0035-.0135

①—Fit rings in tapered bores for clearance listed in tightest portion of ring travel.
②—No. 2-3-4-5, 2.4990-2.4995; No. 1, 2.4993-2.4998.
③—No. 2-3-4-5, 2.4985-2.4995; No. 1, 2.4988-2.4998.
④—Nos. 1, 2 & 3, .0005-.0021; No 4, .0020-.0034.
⑤—No. 1-2-3-4, .0005-.0021; No. 5, .0016-.0032.
⑥—Diesel.
⑦—Pontiac built engine. Distributor located at rear of engine, clockwise rotation.
⑧—Chevrolet built engine. Distributor located at rear of engine, clockwise rotation.
⑨—Nos. 1, 2, 3 & 4, .0005-.0021; No. 5, .0020-.0034.
⑩—Top—.010"; No. 2—.013".
⑪—No. 1, 2, 3, 4: .0015-.0021; No. 5: .0015-.0031.
⑫—Buick built engine.
⑬—No. 1: 2.4484-2.4493; No. 2, 3, 4: 2.4481-2.4490; No. 5: 2.4479-2.4488.
⑭—No. 1: .0008-.0020; No. 2, 3, 4: .0011-.0023; No. 5: .0017-.0032.
⑮—No. 2-3-4-5, 2.4990-2.4995; No. 1, 2.4993-2.4998.
⑯—.015"-.055".
⑰—Top—.019"-.027"; No. 2—.013"-.021".

continued

Valve Specifications

Year	Model/V.I.N.	Valve Lash		Valve Angles		Valve Spring Installed Height	Valve Spring Pressure Lbs. @ In.	Stem Clearance		Stem Diameter	
		Int.	Exh.	Seat	Face			Intake	Exhaust	Intake	Exhaust
1980	V6-231/A⑦	Hydraulic⑤		45	45	1.727	168 @ 1.34	.0015–.0035	.0015–.0032	.3402–.3412	.3405–.3412
	V8-260/F	Hydraulic⑤		②	⑧	1.67	187 @ 1.27	.0010–.0027	.0015–.0032	.3425–.3432	.3420–.3427
	V8-305/H⑥	1 Turn③		46	45	1.70	④	.0010–.0027	.0010–.0027	.3410–.3417	.3410–.3417
	V8-307/Y	Hydraulic⑤		②	⑧	1.67	187 @ 1.27	.0010–.0027	.0015–.0032	.3425–.3432	.3420–.3427
	V8-350/R	Hydraulic⑤		②	⑧	1.67	187 @ 1.27	.0010–.0027	.0015–.0032	.3425–.3432	.3420–.3427
	V8-350/N①	Hydraulic⑤		②	⑧	1.67	151 @ 1.30	.0010–.0027	.0015–.0032	.3425–.3432	.3420–.3427
1981	V6-231/A⑦	Hydraulic⑤		45	45	1.727	⑩	.0015–.0035	.0015–.0032	.3401–.3412	.3405–.3412
	V6-252/4⑦	Hydraulic⑤		45	45	1.727	⑩	.0015–.0035	.0015–.0032	.3401–.3412	.3405–.3412
	V8-260/F	Hydraulic⑤		②	⑧	1.67	187 @ 1.27	.0010–.0027	.0015–.0032	.3425–.3432	.3420–.3427
	V8-307/Y	Hydraulic⑤		②	⑧	1.67	187 @ 1.27	.0010–.0027	.0015–.0032	.3425–.3432	.3420–.3427
	V8-350/N①	Hydraulic⑤		②	⑧	1.67	210 @ 1.22	.0010–.0027	.0015–.0032	.3425–.3432	.3420–.3427
1982–83	V6-231/A⑦	Hydraulic⑤		45	45	1.727	⑫	.0015–.0035	.0015–.0032	.3401–.3412	.3405–.3412
	V6-252/4⑦	Hydraulic⑤		45	45	1.727	⑫	.0015–.0035	.0015–.0032	.3401–.3412	.3405–.3412
	V6-262/V①	Hydraulic⑤		②	⑧	1.67	210 @ 1.22	.0010–.0027	.0015–.0032	.3425–.3432	.3420–.3427
	V8-260/8	Hydraulic⑤		②	⑧	1.67	187 @ 1.27	.0010–.0027	.0015–.0032	.3425–.3432	.3420–.3427
	V8-307/Y	Hydraulic⑤		②	⑧	1.67	187 @ 1.27	.0010–.0027	.0015–.0032	.3425–.3432	.3420–.3427
	V8-307/9	Hydraulic⑤		②	⑧	1.67	210 @ 1.22	.0010–.0027	.0015–.0032	.3425–.3432	.3420–.3427
	V8-350/N①	Hydraulic⑤		②	⑧	1.67	210 @ 1.22	.0010–.0027	.0015–.0032	.3425–.3432	.3420–.3427
1984	V6-231/A⑦	Hydraulic⑤		45	45	1.727	182 @ 1.34	.0015–.0035	.0015–.0032	.3401–.3412	.3405–.3412
	V6-252/4⑦	Hydraulic⑤		45	45	1.727	182 @ 1.34	.0015–.0035	.0015–.0032	.3401–.3412	.3405–.3412
	V6-262/V①	Hydraulic⑤		②	⑧	1.67	210 @ 1.22	.0010–.0027	.0015–.0032	.3425–.3432	.3420–.3428
	V8-307/Y	Hydraulic⑤		②	⑧	1.67	187 @ 1.27	.0010–.0027	.0015–.0032	.3425–.3432	.3420–.3427
	V8-307/9	Hydraulic⑤		②	⑧	1.67	210 @ 1.22	.0010–.0027	.0015–.0032	.3425–.3432	.3420–.3427
	V8-350/N①	Hydraulic⑤		②	⑧	1.67	210 @ 1.22	.0010–.0027	.0015–.0032	.3425–.3432	.3420–.3427
1985	V6-231/A	Hydraulic⑤		45	45	1.727	182 @ 1.34	.0015–.0035	.0015–.0032	.3401–.3412	.3405–.3412
	V6-262/V①	Hydraulic⑤		②	⑧	1.67	210 @ 1.22	.0010–.0027	.0015–.0032	.3425–.3432	.3420–.3428
	V8-307/Y	Hydraulic⑤		⑪	⑫	1.67	187 @ 1.27	.0010–.0027	.0015–.0032	.3425–.3432	.3420–.3427
	V8-350/N①	Hydraulic⑤		②	⑧	1.67	210 @ 1.22	.0010–.0027	.0015–.0032	.3424–.3432	.3420–.3428
1986	V6-231	Hydraulic⑤		45	45	1.727	182 @ 1.34	.0015–.0035	.0015–.0032	.3401–.3412	.3405–.3412
	V8-307	Hydraulic⑤		⑪	⑫	1.67	187 @ 1.27	.0010–.0027	.0015–.0032	.3425–.3432	.3420–.3427

①—Oldsmobile built diesel engine.
②—Intake 45°, exhaust 31°.
③—Tighten rocker arm adjusting screw to eliminate all push rod end clearance. Then tighten screw the number of turns listed.
④—Intake, 180 @ 1.25; exhaust, 190 @ 1.16.
⑤—No adjustment.
⑥—Chevrolet built engine. Distributor located at rear of engine, clockwise rotation.
⑦—Buick built engine.
⑧—Intake 44°, exhaust 30°.
⑨—Intake, 220 @ 1.34; exhaust 177 @ 1.450.
⑩—Intake, 164 @ 1.34; exhaust, 182 @ 1.34.
⑪—Intake, 45°; exhaust, 59°.
⑫—Intake, 46°; exhaust, 60°.

continued

Engine Tightening Specifications★

★ Torque specifications are for clean and lightly lubricated threads only. Dry or dirty threads produce increased friction which prevents accurate measurement of tightness.

Year	Engine Model/V.I.N.	Spark Plugs Ft. Lbs.	Cylinder Head Bolts Ft. Lbs.	Intake Manifold Ft. Lbs.	Exhaust Manifold Ft. Lbs.	Rocker Arm Shaft Bracket Ft. Lbs.	Rocker Arm Cover Ft. Lbs.	Connecting Rod Cap Bolts Ft. Lbs.	Main Bearing Cap Bolts Ft. Lbs.	Flywheel to Crankshaft Ft. Lbs.	Vibration Damper or Pulley Ft. Lbs.
1980	V6-231/A⑨	15	80	45	25	30	4	40	100	60	225
	V8-260/F	25	85④	40④	25	28①	—	42	80⑧	60	200–310
	V8-305/H②	22	65	30	20	—	45⑤	45	70	60	60
	V8-307/Y	25	130④	40④	25	28①	—	42	70⑧	60	200–310
	V8-350/R	25	130④	40④	25	28①	—	42	80⑧	60	200–310
	V8-350/N⑦	—	130④	40④	25	28①	—	42	120	60	200–310
1981	V6-231/A⑨	15	80	45	25	30	4	40	100	60	225
	V6-252/4⑨	15	80	45	25	30	4	40	100	60	225
	V8-260/F	25	85④	40④	25	28①	—	42	80⑧	60	200–310
	V8-307/Y	25	130④	40④	25	28①	—	42	80⑧	60	200–310
	V8-350/N⑦	—	130④	40④	25	28①	—	42	120	60	200–310
1982–83	V6-231/A⑨	15	80	45	25	30	4	40	100	60	225
	V6-252/4⑨	15	80	45	25	30	4	40	100	60	225
	V6-262/V⑦	—	③	41	29	28①	—	42	⑥	48	160–350
	V8-260/8	25	85④	40④	25	28①	—	42	80⑥	60⑩	200–310
	V8-307/Y,9	25	125④	40④	25	28①	—	42	80⑥	60⑩	200–310
	V8-350/N⑦	—	130④	40④	25	28①	—	42	120	60	210–300
1984	V6-231/A⑨	15	80	45	25	30	4	40	100	60	225
	V6-252/4⑨	15	80	45	25	30	4	40	100	60	225
	V6-262/V⑦	—	③	41	31	28①	—	42	89	57	203–350
	V8-307/Y,9	25	125④	40④	25	28①	—	42	80⑧	60	200–310
	V8-350/N⑦	—	130④	40④	25	28①	—	42	120	60	200–310
1985	V6-231/A⑨	15	80	45	25	30	4	40	100	60	225
	V6-262/V⑦	—	③	41	28	28①	—	42	89⑪	57	203–350
	V8-307/Y	25	125④	40④	25	28①	—	42	80⑧	60	200–310
	V8-350/N⑦	—	130④	40④	25	28①	—	42	120	60	200–310
1986	V6-231	15	80	45	25	30	4	40	100	60	225
	V8-307	25	125④	40④	25	28①	—	42	80⑧	60	200–310

① —Rocker arm pivot bolt to head.
② —Chevrolet built engine. Distributor located at rear of engine, clockwise rotation.
③ —See text for procedure.
④ —Clean and dip entire bolt in engine oil before tightening.
⑤ —Inch lbs.
⑥ —1982, 107 ft. lbs.; 1983, 89 ft. lbs.
⑦ —Oldsmobile built diesel engine.
⑧ —Rear 120 ft. lbs.
⑨ —Buick built engine.
⑩ —With automatic transmission.
⑪ —Type II bolts at Nos. 2 and 3 outer positions.

continued

Drive Axle Specifications

Year	Model	Carrier Type	Ring Gear & Pinion Backlash		Pinion Bearing Preload			Differential Bearing Preload		
			Method	Adjustment	Method	New Bearings Inch-Lbs.	Used Bearings Inch-Lbs.	Method	New Bearings Inch-Lbs.	Used Bearings Inch-Lbs.
1980-85	Exc. Toronado	Integral	Shims	.005-.009	Spacer	24-32	8-12	Shims	①	①
	Toronado	Integral	Shims	.005-.007	Spacer	22	5	Shims	①	①

①—Slip fit plus .004 inch clearance on each side.

Alternator Specifications

Year	Model	Rated Hot Output Amps.	Field Current 12 Volts @ 80° F.	Year	Model	Rated Hot Output Amps.	Field Current 12 Volts @ 80° F.	Year	Model	Rated Hot Output Amps.	Field Current 12 Volts @ 80° F.
1980	1100111	63	4-5	1982	1100164	55	4-5		1105250	70	4.0-4.6
	1100122	63	4-5		1100165	63	4-5		1105343	85	4.0-4.6
	1100124	63	4-5		1100190	85	4.0-4.6	1984	1100200	78	4.5-5.0
	1101038	70	4.0-4.6		1100194	70	4.0-4.6		1100239	55	4.5-5.0
	1101044	70	4.0-4.6		1100195	85	4.0-4.6		1100260	78	4.5-5.0
	1101065	70	4.0-4.6		1100198	42	4-5		1105025	66	4.5-5.0
	1101068	70	4.0-4.6	1983	1100200	78	4.5-5.0		1105028	78	4.5-5.0
	1101071	70	4.0-4.6		1100230	42	4-5		1105041	78	4.5-5.0
	1101074	70	4.0-4.6		1100239	55	4.5-5.0		1105197	70	4.0-4.6
	1103103	63	4-5		1100247	63	4.5-5.0		1105548	70	4.0-4.6
	1103104	42	4-5		1100260	78	4.5-5.0		1105564	66	4.5-5.0
	1103112	63	4-5		1100263	78	4.5-5.0		1105565	78	4.5-5.0
	1103186	63	4-5		1100297	42	4-5		1105566	66	4.5-5.0
1980-82	1100110	42	4-5		1100298	55	4.5-5.0		1105567	78	4.5-5.0
	1100121	63	4-5		1100300	63	4.5-5.0		1105568	78	4.5-5.0
	1103151	63	4-5		1101264	78	—		1105569	78	4.5-5.0
1981	1100110	42	4-5		1105022	78	4.5-5.0	1985	1100200	78	4.5-5.0
	1100121	63	4-5		1105025	63	4.5-5.0		1100239	55	4.5-5.0
	1100156	55	4-5		1105027	63	4.5-5.0		1100260	78	4.5-5.0
	1101068	70	4.0-4.6		1105029	63	4.5-5.0		1105197	70	4.0-4.6
1981-82	1100164	55	4-5		1105032	78	4.5-5.0		1105562	94	—
	1101037	70	4.0-4.6		1105041	78	4.5-5.0		1105565	78	4.5-5.0
	1101045	85	4.0-4.6		1105042	78	4.5-5.0		1105569	78	4.5-5.0
	1101084	85	4.0-4.6		1105194	78	4.5-5.0				
	1101088	70	4.0-4.6		1105198	85	4.0-4.6				

continued

Starting Motor Applications

Year	Model/V.I.N.	Starter Number	Year	Model/V.I.N.	Starter Number	Year	Model/V.I.N.	Starter Number
1980	V6-231/A	1109061	1982	V6-231/A	1998236		V6-262 Diesel/V	1998556
	V8-260/F	1109523		V6-252/4②	1998234			22511854
	V8-265/S	1109523		V6-252/4③	1998237		V8-307/Y,9①②	1109544
	V8-305/H	1109524		V6-262 Diesel/V	1998552		V8-307/Y③	1998237
	V8-307/Y②	1109523		V8-260/8	1109544		V8-350 Diesel/N①②	1998553
	V8-307/Y③	1998205		V8-307/Y①②	1109544			22511854
	V8-350/L②	1109072		V8-307/Y③	1998237		V8-350 Diesel/N③	1109495
	V8-350/L③	1998205		V8-350 Diesel/N①②	1998552	1985	V6-231/A	1998236
	V8-350 Diesel/N②	1109215		V8-350 Diesel/N③	1109495		V6-262 Diesel/V	1998556
	V8-350 Diesel/N②	1109216	1983	V6-231/A	1998236			22511854
	V8-350 Diesel/N③	1109214		V6-252/4②	1998234		V8-307/Y①④	1109544
	V8-350 Diesel/N③	1109218		V6-252/4③	1998237		V8-307/Y③	1998237
1981	V6-231/A	1109061		V6-262 Diesel/V	1998554		V8-350 Diesel/N①④	1998553
	V6-252/4②	1998227		V8-307/Y,9①②	1109544			22523207
	V6-252/4	1998205		V8-307/Y③	1998237		V8-350 Diesel/N③	1109495
	V8-260/F, V8-307/Y③	1109523		V8-350 Diesel/N①②	1998554	1986	V6-231	—
	V8-307/Y①②	1998205		V8-350 Diesel/N③	1109495		V8-307	—
	V8-350 Diesel/N①②	1109216	1984	V6-231/A	1998236			
	V8-350 Diesel/N③	1109218		V6-252/4	1998237			

①—Cutlass.
②—88 & 98.
③—Toronado.
④—88.

Wheel Alignment Specifications

Year	Model	Caster Angle, Degrees		Camber Angle, Degrees					Toe-In. Inch
		Limits	Desired	Limits		Desired			
				Left	Right	Left	Right		
1980–83	Cutlass②	+½ to +1½	+1	0 to +1	0 to +1	+½	+½		+1/16 to +3/16
	Cutlass①	+2½ to +3½	+3	0 to +1	0 to +1	+½	+½		+1/16 to +3/16
	88, 98	+2½ to +3½	+3	+¼ to +1¼	+¼ to +1¼	+¾	+¾		+1/16 to +3/16
	Toronado	+2 to +3	+2½	−½ to +½	−½ to +½	0	0		−1/16 to +1/16
1984–85	Cutlass	+2½ to +3½	+3	0 to +1	0 to +1	+½	+½		+1/10 to +2/10
	88, 98	+2½ to +3½	+3	+3/10 to +13/10	+3/10 to +13/10	+4/5	+4/5		+1/10 to +2/10
	Custom Cruiser	+2½ to +3½	+3	+3/10 to +13/10	+3/10 to +13/10	+4/5	+4/5		+1/10 to +2/10
	Toronado	+2 to +3	+2½	−½ to +½	−½ to +½	0	0		−1/20 to +1/20
1986	Cutlass	+2 to +4	+3	−3/10 to +13/10	−3/10 to +13/10	+½	+½		+1/16 to +¼
	Custom Cruiser	—	—	—	—	—	—		—

①—Power Steering.
②—Manual Steering.

continued

Cooling System & Capacity Data

Year	Model or Engine/V.I.N.	Cooling Capacity, Qts. Less A/C	Cooling Capacity, Qts. With A/C	Radiator Cap Relief Pressure, Lbs.	Thermo. Opening Temp.	Fuel Tank Gals.	Engine Oil Refill Qts. ①	Transmission Oil 3 Speed Pints	Transmission Oil 4 Speed Pints	Transmission Oil 5 Speed Pints	Auto. Trans. Qts. ②	Rear Axle Oil Pints
1980	V6-231/A Cutlass⑦	13	13	15	195	18⑯	4	3	—	—	㉖	4½
	V6-231/A 88⑦	13	13	15	195	25	4	—	—	—	㉖	⑲
	V8-260/F Cutlass	16⑰	16⑰	15	195	18⑯	4	—	—	—	㉖	4¼
	V8-305/H Cutlass	15¼㉗	15¼㉗	15	195	18⑯	4	—	—	—	⑧	4¼
	V8-307/Y 88 & 98	15½㉘	15½㉘	15	195	25⑨	4	—	—	—	⑧	⑲
	V8-307/Y Toronado	16¼	16¼	15	195	21	4	—	—	—	㉕	3¼③
	V8-350/R Cutlass	15	15	15	195	18⑯	4	—	—	—	㉖	4¼
	V8-350/R 88 & 98	14½㉔	14½㉔	15	195	25⑨	4	—	—	—	⑧	⑲
	V8-350/R Toronado	15½㉒	15½㉒	15	195	21	4	—	—	—	㉕	3¼③
	V8-350/N Cutlass⑭	17¼	17¼	15	195	19¾⑯	7⑥⑱	—	—	—	㉙	4¼
	V8-350/N 88 & 98⑭	18¼	18	15	195	27⑨	7⑥⑱	—	—	—	㉖	⑲
	V8-350/N Toronado⑭	18	18	15	195	23	7⑥⑱	—	—	—	㉕	3¼③
1981	V6-231/A Cutlass⑦	13㉚	13㉚	15	195	18	4	3	—	—	㉛	4¼
	V6-231/A 88⑦	13	13	15	195	25	4	—	—	—	㉛	4¼
	V6-252/4 98	12.8	12.8	15	195	25	4	—	—	—	⑪	4¼
	V6-252/4 Toronado	13.1	13.1	15	195	21	4	—	—	—	⑪	3¼③
	V8-260/F Cutlass	15.9⑰	15.5⑰	15	195	18	4	—	—	—	㉛	4¼
	V8-260/F 88	16.5⑫	16.2⑫	15	195	25⑨	4	—	—	—	㉛	4¼
	V8-307/Y Cutlass	14.9㉓	15.6	15	195	18	4	—	—	—	㉛	4¼
	V8-307/Y 88 & Cust. Cruiser	15.6⑬	15.3⑬	15	195	25⑨	4	—	—	—	㉑	4¼
	V8-307/Y 98	16.2	16.2	15	195	25	4	—	—	—	⑪	4¼
	V8-307/Y Toronado	16.5	16.5	15	195	21	4	—	—	—	⑳	3¼③
	V8-350/N Cutlass⑭	17.4	17.3	15	195	19¾④	7⑥⑱	—	—	—	㉑	4¼
	V8-350/N 88 & 98⑭	18.3	18	15	195	27⑨	7⑥⑱	—	—	—	㉛	4¼
	V8-350/N Toronado⑭	18	18	15	195	23	7⑥⑱	—	—	—	⑳	3¾③
1982	V6-231/A Cutlass⑦	13㉚	13㉚	15	195	18	4	—	—	—	⑤	④
	V6-231/A 88⑦	13	13	15	195	25⑨	4	—	—	—	⑤	④
	V6-252/4 98	12.8	12.8	15	195	25	4	—	—	—	⑤	④
	V6-252/4 Toronado	13.1	13.1	15	195	21	4	—	—	—	⑤	3¼③
	V6-262/V⑭	14.5	15.3	15	195	19.75	7⑥⑱	—	—	—	⑤	④
	V8-260/8	16.5⑫	16.2⑫	15	195	25⑨	4	—	—	—	⑤	④
	V8-307/Y Cutlass	14.9㉓	15.6	15	195	25⑨	4	—	—	—	⑤	④
	V8-307/Y 88 & Custom Cruiser	15.6⑬	15.3⑬	15	195	25⑨	4	—	—	—	⑤	④
	V8-307/Y 98	16.2	16.2	15	195	25	4	—	—	—	⑤	④
	V8-307/Y Toronado	16.5	16.5	15	195	21	4	—	—	—	⑤	3¼③
	V8-350/N Cutlass⑭	17.4	17.3	15	195	19.75⑯	7⑥⑱	—	—	—	⑤	④
	V8-350/N 88 & 98⑭	18	18	15	195	26.5⑨	7⑥⑱	—	—	—	⑤	④
	V8-350/N Toronado⑭	18.1	18.1	15	195	22.75	7⑥⑱	—	—	—	⑤	3¼③
1983	V6-231/A Cutlass	13⑩	13⑩	15	195	18	4	—	—	—	⑤	④
	V6-231/A 88	13	13	15	195	25⑨	4	—	—	—	⑤	④
	V6-252/4 98	12.5	12.5	15	195	25	4	—	—	—	⑤	④
	V6-252/4 Toronado	13.25	13.25	15	195	21	4	—	—	—	⑤	3¼③
	V6-262/V⑭	13.75	14.25	15	195	19.8	6⑥⑱	—	—	—	⑤	④
	V8-307/Y Cutlass	14.75	15.5	15	195	18	4	—	—	—	⑤	④
	V8-307/Y 88	15.5⑮	15.3⑮	15	195	25	4	—	—	—	⑤	④
	V8-307/Y 98	15.25⑮	15.25⑮	15	195	25	4	—	—	—	⑤	④
	V8-307/Y Toronado	16.25	16.25	15	195	21	4	—	—	—	⑤	3¼③
	V8-350/N Cutlass	17.5	17.5	15	195	19.8	7⑥⑱	—	—	—	⑤	④
	V8-350/N 88 & 98	18.25	18	15	195	26	7⑥⑱	—	—	—	⑤	④
	V8-350/N Toronado	18.25	18.25	15	195	22.8	7⑥⑱	—	—	—	⑤	3¼③

continued

COOLING SYSTEM & CAPACITY DATA—Continued

Year	Model or Engine/V.I.N.	Cooling Capacity, Qts.		Radiator Cap Relief Pressure, Lbs.	Thermo. Opening Temp.	Fuel Tank Gals.	Engine Oil Refill Qts. ①	Transmission Oil				Rear Axle Oil Pints
		Less A/C	With A/C					3 Speed Pints	4 Speed Pints	5 Speed Pints	Auto. Trans. Qts. ②	
1984	V6-231/A Cutlass	13[10]	13[10]	15	195	18.2	4	—	—	—	[5]	[4]
	V6-231/A 88	13	13	15	195	25[9]	4	—	—	—	[5]	[4]
	V6-252/4 Toronado	—	12.5	15	195	21	4	—	—	—	[5]	3⅓[3]
	V6-262/V[14] Cutlass	13.6	14.4	15	195	19.8	6[6][18]	—	—	—	[5]	[4]
	V8-307/Y Cutlass	14.9	15.6	15	195	18.2	4	—	—	—	[5]	[4]
	V8-307/Y 88 & 98	15.6[15]	15.3[15]	15	195	25	4	—	—	—	[5]	[4]
	V8-307/Y Toronado	—	16.4	15	195	21	4	—	—	—	[5]	3⅓[3]
	V8-350/N Cutlass	17.4	17.3	15	195	19.8	7[6][18]	—	—	—	[5]	[4]
	V8-350/N 88 & 98	18.3	18	15	195	27[9]	7[6][18]	—	—	—	[5]	[4]
	V8-350/N Toronado	—	18.2	15	195	22.8	7[6][18]	—	—	—	[5]	3⅓[3]
1985	V6-231/A Cutlass	13	13.5	15	195	18	4	—	—	—	[34]	[4]
	V6-231/A 88	13	13	15	195	25[9]	4	—	—	—	[34]	[4]
	V6-262/V[14] Cutlass	13.6	14.4	15	195	19.8	6[6][18]	—	—	—	[34]	[4]
	V8-307/Y Cutlass	14.9	15.5	15	195	18	4	—	—	—	[34]	[4]
	V8-307/Y 88	15.5	15.3[15]	15	195	25[9]	4	—	—	—	[34]	[4]
	V8-307/Y Toronado	—	16.5[32]	15	195	21	4	—	—	—	[33]	3½[3]
	V8-350/N[14] Cutlass	17.4	17.4	15	195	19.8	4	—	—	—	[34]	[4]
	V8-350/N[14] 88	18.3	18	15	195	26[9]	7[6][18]	—	—	—	[34]	[4]
	V8-350/N[14] Toronado	—	18.3	15	195	22.8	7[6][18]	—	—	—	[33]	3½[3]
1986	V6-231 Cutlass	13	13.5	15	195	18	4	—	—	—	4.2	3.5[3]
	V8-307 Cutlass	14.9	15.6	15	195	18	4	—	—	—	4.2	3.5[3]
	V8-307 Custom Cruiser	—	—	—	—	—	—	—	—	—	—	—

①—Add one quart with filter change.
②—Approximate; make final check with dipstick.
③—Final drive.
④—7.5 inch ring gear, 3.5 pints; 8.5 inch ring gear, 4.25 pints.
⑤—T.H.M. 200C, oil pan 4⅛ qts.; total capacity, 10½ qts. T.H.M. 2004R, oil pan 5 qts.; total capacity, 11 qts. T.H.M. 250C & 350C, oil pan 3⅛ qts.; total capacity 10 qts. T.H.M. 325-4L, oil pan 5½ qts.; total capacity 13 qts.
⑥—Recommended diesel engine oil—1980, use oil designation SE/CC; 1981, use oil designation SF/CC, SF/CD or SE/CC; 1982–85 use oil designation SF/CC or SF/CD.
⑦—Buick built engine.
⑧—T.H.M. 200 & 200C, oil pan 3½ qts.; after overhaul 9½ qts.; T.H.M. 250C, oil pan 4 qts., after overhaul 10 qts.; T.H.M. 350 & 350C, oil pan 3¼ qts., after overhaul 12¼ qts.; T.H.M. 400, oil pan 3 qts., after overhaul 10 qts.
⑨—Custom Cruiser, 22 gals.

⑩—With high capacity cooling, 13.25 qts.
⑪—Oil pan, 3½ qts.; after overhaul, 11¼ qts.
⑫—Trailer towing, 17.0 qts.; Heavy duty, 17.25 qts.
⑬—Heavy duty & trailer towing, 16.25 qts.
⑭—Diesel engine.
⑮—High capacity cooling, 16.25 qts.; heavy duty trailer tow, 16 qts.
⑯—Cutlass Cruiser, 18.25 gals.
⑰—Heavy duty cooling system & trailer tow, 16½ qts.
⑱—Includes filter.
⑲—Exc. 7.5″ ring gear, 4.25 pts.; 7.5″ ring gear, 3.5 pts.
⑳—Oil pan, 5¼ qts.; after overhaul, 13½ qts.
㉑—T.H.M. 200-4R, oil pan 3½ qts., after overhaul 11¼ qts.; T.H.M. 250C, oil pan 3¼ qts., after overhaul 10 qts.
㉒—Trailer towing, 15.25 qts.
㉓—Heavy duty & trailer towing, 15.5 qts.
㉔—Heavy duty, 16 qts.; trailer towing 15.5 qts.

㉕—Oil pan, 5 qts.; after overhaul, 12 qts.
㉖—T.H.M. 200 & 200C, oil pan 3½ qts., after overhaul 9½ qts.; T.H.M. 350 & 350C, oil pan 3¼ qts., after overhaul 12¼ qts.
㉗—With heavy duty cooling system, 16 qts.
㉘—High capacity, 16¼ qts., heavy duty trailer tow, 16 qts.
㉙—Oil pan, 3½ qts.; after overhaul, 9½ qts.
㉚—With heavy duty or trailer tow, 13.6 qts.
㉛—T.H.M. 200C, oil pan 4¼ qts., after overhaul 10½ qts.; T.H.M. 250C & 350C, oil pan 3¼ qts., after overhaul 10 qts.
㉜—Trailer Towing, 18.5 qts.
㉝—Oil pan only, 4.25 qts.; total capacity, 10 qts.
㉞—T.H.M. 200C, oil pan only, 3.5 qts.; total capacity 9.5 qts. T.H.M. 250-4R, oil pan only, 3.5 qts.; total capacity, 11 qts. T.H.M. 325-4L, oil pan only, 3.25 qts.; total capacity, 10 qts.

Electrical Section

IGNITION LOCK
REPLACE

1. Remove steering wheel as described under Horn Sounder and Steering Wheel, Replace.
2. Remove turn signal switch as described under Turn Signal Switch. Replace, then remove buzzer switch.
3. Place ignition switch in Run position, then remove lock cylinder retaining screw and lock cylinder.
4. To install, rotate lock cylinder to stop while holding housing, **Fig. 1**. Align cylinder key with keyway in housing, then push lock cylinder assembly into housing until fully seated.
5. Install lock cylinder retaining screw. Torque screw to 40 in. lbs. for standard columns. On adjustable columns, torque retaining screw to 22 in. lbs.
6. Install buzzer switch, turn signal switch and steering wheel.

STARTER
REPLACE

NOTE: Upon removal of starter, note if any shims are used. If shims are used, they should be reinstalled in their original location during installation.

If starter is noisy during cranking, remove one .015 inch double shim or add one .015 inch single shim to the outer bolt. If starter makes a high pitched whine after firing, add .015 inch double shims until noise ceases.

V6-231 & 252

1. Disconnect battery ground cable, then raise and support vehicle.
2. On vehicles with automatic transmis-

Fig. 1   Ignition lock removal

sion, disconnect exhaust crossover pipe and disconnect oil cooler lines at transmission, then remove flywheel housing cover.
3. On vehicles with manual transmission, remove front crossmember to body bolts, right and left brace to crossmember bolts, then remove crossmember.
4. Remove starter bolts, then lower the starter, disconnect electrical leads and remove starter.
5. Reverse procedure to install.

EXC. TORONADO, V6-231 & 252 & V8-260 DIESEL WITH MAN. TRANS.

1. Disconnect battery ground cable, then raise and support vehicle.
2. On all except V8-305 and 350 Chev. built engine:
   a. Remove upper support retaining bolts.
   b. On V8 engines, remove flywheel housing cover.
3. On V8-305 and 350 Chev. built

engine, disconnect starter brace, then remove the wire guide retaining bolts.
4. Remove starter retaining bolts, then lower starter, disconnect electrical leads and remove starter.
5. Reverse procedure to install.

TORONADO

1. Disconnect battery ground cable, then raise and support vehicle.
2. Remove starter attaching bolts and position starter so that starter wiring can be disconnected.
3. Disconnect starter wiring, then lower starter from vehicle.
4. Reverse procedure to install. If shims were removed, they must be installed in their original location.

IGNITION SWITCH
REPLACE

1. Disconnect battery ground cable.

Fig. 2   Headlight switch. Toronado

Fig. 3   Headlight switch. 1980—81 Cutlass

Fig. 4   Headlight switch. 1982–86 Cutlass

Fig. 5   Brake switch installation.

Fig. 6   Back-up light or neutral start/back-up light switch adjustment

2. On models with regular steering column, turn ignition lock to "Off-Unlock" position. On models with tilt and telescope steering column, turn ignition lock to "Accessory" position.
3. Remove cover attaching bolts, loosen toe pan clamp bolts and remove trim cap from lower part of panel.
4. Remove bracket retaining nuts and lower steering column to the seat.
5. Disconnect and remove switch.
6. On models equipped with column mounted dimmer switch, remove two switch attaching screws, then remove switch and disconnect wire connector.
7. Be sure that lock is in same position as when switch was removed then install switch onto actuator and column.
8. Connect wiring and reinstall column. On models with column mounted dimmer switch, install and adjust dimmer switch as described under "Column Mounted Dimmer Switch."

LIGHT SWITCH
REPLACE

TORONADO

1. Disconnect battery ground cable.
2. Remove headlamp switch knob, radio knobs and steering column trim cover.
3. Remove four screws from underside of left hand trim cover, **Fig. 2.**
4. Remove left hand sound absorber, then carefully pull left hand trim cover from instrument panel.

NOTE: It may be necessary to disconnect shift indicator cable clip and lower steering column slightly to remove left hand trim cover.

5. Remove two screws attaching switch to instrument cluster carrier, then pull switch rearward to remove.
6. To disconnect wire connector, remove two connector attaching screws, then pry connector at locations shown in **Fig. 2.**
7. Reverse procedure to install.

CUTLASS

1. Disconnect battery ground cable.

2. Remove cluster pad assembly.
3. Remove two headlight switch mounting screws, then pull switch away from panel adapter.
4. To disconnect wire connector, pry connector at locations indicated by arrows as shown in **Figs. 3 and 4.** Pull connector out, then slide to left and push forward to remove.
5. Reverse procedure to install. Refer to **Figs. 3 and 4,** to install wire connector.

88, 98 & CUSTOM CRUISER

1980–81
1. Disconnect battery ground cable.
2. Rotate headlight switch so notch on switch faces downward. Bend a ⅛ inch hook on a piece of stiff wire. Use the wire hook in the notch to pull the knob retainer clip and pull knob off shaft.
3. Remove twilight sentinel knob.
4. Position steering column collar upward and remove column lower trim cover.
5. Remove two screws securing trim cover to cluster carrier.
6. Pull trim cover from clips.
7. Remove light switch mounting plate screws.
8. Pull switch through opening and disconnect electrical connector.
9. Remove nut and switch from mounting plate.
10. Reverse procedure to install.

1982–86
1. Disconnect battery ground cable.
2. Remove steering column trim cover, gauge cluster and headlamp switch knob.
3. Remove two screws attaching left side trim cover to cluster carrier, then remove trim cover by pulling rearward.
4. Remove two screws attaching mounting plate to cluster carrier.
5. Pull switch and mounting plate rearward and disconnect electrical connector.
6. Remove nut and separate mounting plate from switch.
7. Reverse procedure to install.

STOP LIGHT SWITCH

The stop light switch is attached to the brake pedal bracket and is actuated by the brake pedal arm, **Fig. 4.** When installing the switch, insert switch into tubular clip until switch body seats on tube clip. Pull brake pedal rearward until it contacts brake pedal stop. This moves the switch in the tubular clip providing proper adjustment.

CLUTCH START SWITCH
1980–81

All cars equipped with a manual transmission use a clutch start switch which is mounted on the pedal bracket. The switch closes when the clutch is depressed and completes solenoid connection. When installing switch, no adjustment is necessary.

BACK-UP LIGHT SWITCH
REPLACE

1980–81 MODELS EXC. 1981 V8 TORONADO

1. On 1980 models and 1981 models with column shift, place gear selector in "Neutral". On 1981 models with console shift, place gear selector in "Park".
2. Remove screws attaching switch to steering column, then remove switch.
3. Disconnect wiring connectors. Connect wiring connectors to new switch.
4. Position new switch on steering column and loosely install screws.
5. Install .096 inch gauge pin in switch as shown in **Fig. 6.**
6. Rotate switch until gauge pin aligns with the alignment hole in inner plastic slide.
7. On 1981 models with console shift, rotate shift bowl clockwise to remove free play, then lightly hold against stop.
8. Tighten attaching screws and remove

Fig. 7 Back-up light switch installation. 1981 V-8 Toronado & 1982–86 models

Fig. 8 Mechanical neutral start system with standard column

Fig. 9 Mechanical neutral start system with tilt column

gauge pin.

9. Ensure vehicle will start in "Park" and "Neutral" only. If not, repeat procedure.

1981 V8 TORONADO & 1982–86 MODELS

1. Place gear selector in "Neutral".
2. Gently rock back-up light switch out of steering column.
3. Disconnect wiring connectors. Connect wiring connectors to new switch.
4. Align switch actuator with hole in shift tube, **Fig. 7.**
5. Position connector side of switch into lower jacket cut out.
6. Push down front of switch, ensuring switch tangs snap into holes in steering column jacket.
7. Adjust switch by placing gear selector in "Park" position. The switch main housing and housing back should ratchet, providing proper adjustment.

NEUTRAL START SYSTEM

Actuation of the ignition switch is prevented by a mechanical lockout system, **Figs. 8 and 9,** which prevents the lock cylinder from rotating when the selector lever is out of Park or Neutral. When the selector lever is in Park or Neutral, the slots in the bowl plate and the finger on the actuator rod align allowing the finger to pass through the bowl plate in turn actuating the ignition switch, **Fig. 10.** If the selector lever is in any position other than Park or Neutral, the finger contacts the bowl plate when the lock cylinder is rotated, thereby preventing full travel of the lock cylinder.

TURN SIGNAL SWITCH
REPLACE

TILT & TELESCOPE

1. Disconnect battery ground cable and remove steering wheel.
2. Remove instrument panel lower trim panel, then disconnect turn signal harness connector. Remove connector from packet mounting bracket and wrap tape around connector and wires to prevent wires from snagging when removing switch, **Fig. 11.**
3. Remove four bolts securing column bracket assembly to mast jacket.
4. Disconnect shift indicator.
5. Hold column in position and remove two nuts securing column bracket assembly. Then, remove bracket and

turn signal wiring connector. Loosely re-install bracket to hold column in place.
6. Remove rubber bumper and plastic retainer.
7. Using a suitable compressor, **Fig. 12,** depress lock plate far enough to remove "C" ring from shaft.

NOTE: Compressor must be positioned on large lips of cancelling cam.

8. Remove lock plate and carrier assembly, then the upper bearing spring.
9. On models less column mounted dimmer switch, place turn signal lever in right turn position and unscrew lever. Lift tilt lever and position in center position.
10. On models with column mounted dimmer switch, remove actuator arm screw and actuator arm, then remove turn signal lever by pulling straight out to disengage.
11. Push in hazard warning knob, then remove screw and hazard warning knob.
12. Remove turn signal switch attaching screws, then pull switch and wiring from top of column.

EXC. TILT & TELESCOPE

1. Disconnect battery ground cable.
2. Remove steering wheel.
3. Remove cover screws and cover.
4. Using suitable compressor, depress lock plate far enough to remove the "C" ring from shaft.
5. Remove lock plate, cancelling cam,

Fig. 10 Mechanical neutral start system in Park position

Fig. 11 Taping turn signal connector & wires

Fig. 12 Compressing lock plate & removing retaining ring

Fig. 13   Instrument cluster. Toronado

spring and signal lever.
6. Depress hazard warning knob then unscrew knob and remove.
7. On models less column mounted dimmer switch, position lever in right turn position and remove three switch attaching screws.
8. On models with column mounted dimmer switch, remove actuator arm screw and actuator arm, then remove turn signal lever by pulling straight out to disengage.
9. Remove panel lower trim cap, disconnect switch harness and remove bolts attaching bracket to column jacket.
10. Disconnect shift indicator if equipped.
11. Remove two nuts holding column in position, remove bracket and wire protector while holding column in position then loosely install bracket to hold column in place.
12. Tape switch wires at connector keeping wires flat, then carefully remove wires and switch.

COLUMN-MOUNTED DIMMER SWITCH
REPLACE

1. Disconnect battery ground cable.
2. Remove instrument panel lower trim and on models with A/C, remove A/C duct extension at column.
3. Disconnect shift indicator from column and remove toe-plate cover screws.
4. Remove two nuts from instrument panel support bracket studs and lower steering column, resting steering wheel on front seat.
5. Remove dimmer switch retaining screw and the switch. Tape actuator rod to column and separate switch from rod.

NOTE: Two screws are used to retain dimmer switch to steering column.

6. Reverse procedure to install. To adjust switch, depress dimmer switch slightly and install a 3/32 inch twist drill to lock the switch to the body. Force switch upward to remove lash

between switch and pivot. Torque switch retaining screw to 35 inch lbs. and remove tape from actuator rod. Remove twist drill and check for proper operation.

HORN SOUNDER & STEERING WHEEL
REPLACE

1. Disconnect battery ground cable.
2. For tilt and telescope steering column proceed as follows:
   a. Remove pad assembly retaining screws, disconnect connector and remove pad assembly.
   b. Move locking lever counterclockwise until full release is obtained. Scribe a mark on the plate assembly where the two screws attach plate assembly to locking lever (for ease of installation) and remove the two screws.
   c. Unscrew and remove plate assembly.
3. For standard wheel, pull up on horn cap retainer assembly and disconnect horn contacts.
4. For deluxe wheel, remove three screws from pad assembly and disconnect connectors.
5. On sport wheel, pull up on and remove emblem and horn contact assembly from wheel.
6. On wood grain wheel, carefully pry horn cap assembly from wheel.
7. On all models, remove steering wheel nut and using a suitable puller, remove steering wheel.

NOTE: Some vehicles have a snap ring on the end of the steering shaft which must be removed before removing steering wheel nut.

8. Reverse procedure to install.

INSTRUMENT CLUSTER
REPLACE

NOTE: On some models, a yellow flag with the word emissions will rotate into the odometer window at 30,000 mile intervals indicating either a catalyst or oxygen sensor change is required. After performing the required maintenance, reset the emissions flag as follows:
   a. On Cutlass models, remove cluster pad assembly. On 88, 98, Custom Cruiser and Toronado, remove left hand trim cover.
   b. On all models, remove trip odometer reset knob, if equipped.
   c. Remove screws attaching cluster lens to cluster assembly and remove lens.
   d. Using a pointed tool inserted at an angle to engage flag wheel detents, rotate flag wheel downward. When flag wheel is reset, the alignment mark will be in center of odometer window.

Fig. 14   Instrument panel cluster pad. Cutlass

Fig. 15 Instrument cluster. 88, 98 & Custom Cruiser

Fig. 16 W/S wiper switch removal & installation. 1982-86 models w/ standard steering column

TORONADO

1. Disconnect battery ground cable.
2. Remove headlamp switch knob, radio knobs and steering column trim cover.
3. Remove four screws from underside of left hand trim cover.
4. Remove left hand sound absorber, then pull left hand trim cover from instrument panel.

NOTE: It may be necessary to disconnect shift indicator cable clip and lower steering column slightly to remove left hand trim cover.

5. Remove two screws attaching headlamp switch to cluster carrier, then pull switch from carrier.
6. Remove windshield wiper switch, then remove radio from instrument panel.
7. Remove four screws attaching heater-A/C control to cluster. Pull control out of cluster and disconnect wiring, vacuum lines and temperature control cable, then remove control assembly.

8. Unlock headlamp switch, windshield wiper, cruise control and defogger switch connectors from cluster carrier, then disconnect speedometer cable.
9. Remove nine cluster carrier attaching screws, then remove cluster carrier, **Fig. 13.**

CUTLASS

1. Disconnect battery ground cable.
2. Remove right hand and left hand trim panels, **Fig. 14.**
3. Remove the 7 screws retaining cluster pad to panel adapter.
4. Pull panel pad to disengage it from retaining clips and remove pad assembly, **Fig. 14.**
5. Remove steering column trim cover, then disconnect shift indicator clip from shift bowl.
6. Remove the 4 screws retaining cluster assembly, then disconnect speedometer cable and electrical connectors and remove cluster assembly.
7. Reverse procedure to install.

88, 98 & Custom Cruiser

1. Disconnect battery ground cable.
2. Rotate headlight switch so notch on switch faces downward. Bend a 1/8 inch hook on a piece of stiff wire. Use the wire hook in the notch to pull the knob retainer clip and pull knob off shaft.
3. Remove twilight sentinel knob.
4. Position steering column collar upward and remove column lower trim cover.
5. Remove two screws securing trim cover to cluster carrier, **Fig. 15.**
6. Pull trim cover from clips.
7. Remove radio knobs and cigar lighter.
8. Remove two screws securing to panel, **Fig. 15.**
9. Pull trim cover from panel clips.
10. Remove radio as outlined under "Radio, Removal."
11. Remove A/C-heater control attaching screws, pull control outward and disconnect control cables and electrical connectors.
12. Remove switches, clock and disconnect ash tray lamp.
13. Remove right hand outside remote mirror control screws.

Fig. 17 W/S wiper switch removal & installation. 1982-86 models w/ tilt steering column

Fig. 18 Windshield wiper switch. 1980-81 Toronado

PRY AT LOCATIONS INDICATED BY ARROWS TO UNLOCK

WIPER SWITCHES   LENS

PULL CONNECTOR OUT THEN SLIDE TO RIGHT AND PUSH FORWARD TO REMOVE

PANEL ADAPTER

INSTALL CONNECTOR TO PANEL ADAPTER IN NUMBERED SEQUENCE & DIRECTION OF ARROWS

INSERT CONNECTOR IN PANEL ADAPTER IN DIRECTION OF ARROW 1 BY ALIGNING CONNECTOR SLOTS WITH ADAPTER TABS

ALIGN CONNECTOR LOCKING TABS BY SLIDING THE CONNECTOR SIDEWAYS IN DIRECTION OF ARROW 2.

LOCK CONNECTOR TO PANEL ADAPTER BY PULLING OUT IN DIRECTION OF ARROW 3. BOTH LOCKING TABS MUST BE ENGAGED.

PULSE WIPER CONNECTOR MUST BE IN PLACE PRIOR TO ADAPTER INSTALLATION.

WINDSHIELD WIPER SWITCH CONNECTOR

PULSE WIPER JUMPER

Fig. 19   Windshield wiper switch. 1980-81 Cutlass

ASPIRATOR HOSE

ASPIRATOR

VIEW B

DIESEL ENGINE ONLY

A/C DISTRIBUTOR CLIP

VIEW A

Fig. 20   Heater core. Toronado

14. Disconnect shift indicator cable clip.
15. Remove steering column bolts at floor pan and the nuts from the steering column bracket. Then, lower the steering column and rest steering wheel on seat.
16. Disconnect speedometer cable.
17. Remove instrument panel cluster carrier bolts and the two instrument panel screws, **Fig. 15.**
18. Remove center air duct screws.
19. Pull cluster outward to disconnect electrical connectors.
20. Remove cluster carrier, **Fig. 15.**

W/S WIPER MOTOR
REPLACE

1. Raise hood and remove cowl screen or grille.
2. Reach through cowl opening and loosen transmission drive link attaching nuts to motor crankarm.
3. Disconnect wiring and washer hoses.
4. Disconnect transmission drive link from motor arm.
5. Remove motor attaching screws.
6. Remove motor while guiding crankarm through opening.

W/S WIPER TRANSMISSION
REPLACE

RECTANGULAR MOTOR

1. Remove wiper arms and blades.
2. Raise hood and remove cowl vent screen or grille.
3. Disconnect wiring from motor.
4. Loosen, do not remove, transmission drive link to motor crankarm attaching nuts and disconnect drive link from crankarm.
5. Remove right and left transmission to body attaching screws and guide transmission and linkage out through cowl opening.

ROUND MOTOR

1. Raise hood and remove cowl vent screen.
2. On all except Toronado, remove right and left wiper arm and blade assemblies. On Toronado, remove arm and blade only from transmission to be removed.
3. Loosen, do not remove, attaching nuts securing transmission drive link to motor crankarm.

NOTE: On Toronado, if only the left transmission is to be removed, it will not be necessary to loosen attaching nuts securing the right transmission drive link to the motor.

4. Disconnect drive link from motor crankarm.
5. On all except Toronado, remove right and left transmission to body attaching screws. On Toronado, remove the attaching screws securing only the transmission to be removed.
6. Remove transmission and linkage by guiding it through opening.

W/S WIPER SWITCH
REPLACE

1982-86 ALL

1. Remove steering wheel as described under "Horn Sounder and Steering Wheel, Replace."
2. Remove turn signal switch as described under "Turn Signal Switch, Replace."
3. Remove ignition lock as described under "Ignition Lock, Replace."
4. Remove and install cover and wiper switch as shown in **Figs. 16 and 17.**
5. Reverse steps 1 through 3 to install.

1980-81 TORONADO

1. Disconnect battery ground cable.
2. Remove headlamp switch knob, radio knobs and steering column trim cover.

3. Remove four screws from under side of left hand trim cover.
4. Remove left hand sound absorber, then carefully pull left hand trim cover from instrument panel.

NOTE: It may be necessary to disconnect shift indicator cable clip and lower steering column slightly to remove left hand trim cover.

5. Remove two screws attaching switch to cluster, then pull switch rearward to remove, **Fig. 18.**

1980-81 CUTLASS

1. Disconnect battery ground cable.
2. Remove cluster pad assembly.
3. Remove switch retaining screws, then pull switch out to remove, **Fig. 20.**
4. Reverse procedure to install.

1980-81 88, 98 & Custom Cruiser

1. Disconnect battery ground cable.
2. Rotate headlight switch knob so that notch on back of switch knob is down. Bend a ⅛ in. hook on paper clip wire and use in notch to pull knob retainer clip while pulling knob off shaft.
3. Remove twilight sentinel knob, if equipped.
4. Move steering column collar up and snap out lower trim cover.
5. Remove two trim cover attaching screws, then pull trim cover out of clips.
6. Remove switch mounting plate screws, then pull switch through opening, disconnect wire connector and remove switch.

RADIO
REPLACE

NOTE: When installing radio, be sure to adjust antenna trimmer for peak performance.

TORONADO

1. Disconnect battery ground cable.
2. Remove headlamp switch knob, radio knobs and steering column trim cover.

Fig. 21 Heater core and blower motor (less air conditioning). 88, 98 & Custom Cruiser

Fig. 22 Heater core and blower motor (with air conditioning). 88, 98 & Custom Cruiser

3. Remove four screws from underside of left hand trim cover.
4. Remove left hand sound absorber, then pull left hand trim cover from instrument panel.

NOTE: It may be necessary to disconnect shift indicator cable clip and lower steering column slightly to remove left hand trim cover.

5. Remove right hand sound absorber.
6. Remove screw attaching instrument panel wiring harness to radio bracket and screw attaching radio to tie bar. Move tone generator aside, if equipped.
7. Remove four screws attaching radio mounting plate to cluster carrier.
8. Disconnect antenna lead and radio wiring.
9. Pull radio and mounting plate rearward to remove.

CUTLASS

1. Disconnect battery ground cable.
2. Remove instrument panel lower trim cover.
3. Remove the 4 radio mounting plate screws, and the screw from radio support bracket on lower instrument panel tie bar.
4. Pull radio outward, then disconnect antenna and electrical connectors and remove radio.
5. Reverse procedure to install.

88, 98 & Custom Cruiser

1. Disconnect battery ground cable.
2. Remove radio knobs, cigar lighter and right hand trim panel cover.
3. Remove radio bracket to lower tie bar screw and the four mounting plate screws.
4. Pull radio out, then disconnect the electrical connectors and antenna lead, and remove radio.
5. Reverse procedure to install.

HEATER CORE
REPLACE

TORONADO

1. Disconnect battery ground cable, then drain cooling system.
2. Disconnect heater hoses at heater core, then install plugs in core outlets to prevent spillage.
3. Remove instrument panel sound absorbers, then lower steering column.
4. Remove instrument cluster as described under "Instrument Cluster, Replace".
5. Remove radio front speakers.
6. Remove three screws attaching manifold to heater case.
7. Remove four upper and three lower instrument panel attaching screws.
8. Disconnect parking brake release cable.
9. Disconnect instrument wiring harness from dash wiring assembly.
10. Disconnect right hand remote control mirror cable from instrument panel pad.
11. Disconnect speedometer cable from clip and temperate control cable at heater case.
12. Disconnect radio and A/C wiring, vacuum lines and all wiring necessary to remove instrument panel assembly. If equipped with pulse wiper, remove wiper switch and unlock wire connector from cluster carrier, then separate pulse wiper jumper harness from wiper switch wire connector.
13. Remove instrument panel and wiring harness assembly.
14. Remove defroster ducts, then disconnect lines from actuators.
15. Remove blower motor resistor.
16. From engine side of dash panel, remove three heater and A/C case retaining nuts.
17. From passenger compartment, remove screws and clip retaining heater and A/C case to dash panel.
18. Remove heater and A/C case, then remove heater core from case, **Fig. 20.**

88, 98 & Custom Cruiser

Less A/C

1. Disconnect battery ground cable.
2. Disconnect blower resistor and blower motor wiring.
3. Drain cooling system into a suitable container, then remove heater hoses from heater core.
4. Remove seven screws attaching heater and blower case to plenum case, then remove case.

NOTE: The heater temperature air valve can be removed at this time by disconnecting valve cable and tapping hinge pin down until it clears the upper pivot, then lift valve and hinge pin out of lower pivot, **Fig. 21.**

5. Remove four screws securing heater core shroud, then shroud and core, **Fig. 22.**
6. Remove core mounting screws and clamps, then separate core from shroud.
7. Reverse procedure to install. Replace sealer as necessary during installation to prevent air and water leaks.

With A/C

1. Disconnect battery ground cable.
2. Disconnect blower resistor and blower motor wiring.
3. Disconnect A/C wiring, then heater core ground strap.
4. Remove thermostatic switch and diagnostic connector (if equipped).
5. Remove right half of hood seal, then seven screws attaching air inlet screen. Remove screen.
6. Remove five bolts attaching case to dash, nine upper to lower case attaching screws around flange and two upper to lower case attaching screws located inside plenum.

7. Remove upper case by lifting straight up, then off, **Fig. 22.**
8. Remove accumulator bracket, then lift evaporator out of case.
9. Remove heater hoses, then lift heater core out of case.
10. Reverse procedure to install. Replace sealer as necessary during installation to prevent air and water leaks.

CUTLASS

Less A/C
1. Disconnect battery ground cable and drain cooling system.
2. Disconnect heater hoses.
3. Disconnect electrical connectors from heater module.
4. Remove module front cover screws.
5. Remove heater core from module.
6. Reverse procedure to install.

With A/C
1. Disconnect battery ground cable and drain cooling system.
2. Disconnect heater hoses from core.
3. Remove retention bracket and ground strap.
4. Remove module rubber seal and screen.
5. Remove right hand W/S wiper arm.
6. Remove attaching screws from the diagnostic connector, hi-blower relay and thermostatic switch.
7. Disconnect all electrical connectors from top of module.
8. Remove top cover from module.
9. Remove heater core from module.
10. Reverse procedure to install.

BLOWER MOTOR
REPLACE

TORONADO
1. Disconnect battery ground cable.
2. Disconnect hi blower relay electrical

connectors, then remove relay.
3. Remove screws securing blower motor, then remove blower motor.
4. Reverse procedure to install. Apply continuous bead of suitable sealer to blower motor mounting.

88, 98 & Custom Cruiser
1. Disconnect battery ground cable.
2. Disconnect blower motor ground and feed wires.
3. Remove six blower motor attaching screws and blower motor, **Figs. 21 and 22.**

CUTLASS
1. Disconnect battery ground cable.
2. If equipped with air conditioning, disconnect cooling tube from blower motor, if necessary.
3. On all models, disconnect electrical connector from blower motor.
4. Remove blower motor retaining screws and the blower motor.
5. Reverse procedure to install.

CRUISE CONTROL
ADJUST

SYSTEM RELEASE SWITCHES, ADJUST
Insert switches into tubular clip until the switch seats on clip. Then, pull brake pedal rearward against stop. The switches will be moved in the clip, thereby providing the proper adjustment.

SERVO LINKAGE, ADJUST
UNITS WITH SERVO ROD

Except 1980 V8-305
With curb idle speed properly adjusted and the carburetor in curb idle position with the engine off, install servo rod retainer in hole that provides clearance between retainer and servo bushing. Some clearance is required, however, do not exceed the width of one hole.

1980 V8-305
Screw rod into link with ignition "Off" and fast idle cam off and throttle closed. Hook rod through tab on servo. Adjust length so link assembles over end of stud, then install retainer.

UNITS WITH BEAD CHAIN
Assemble chain to be taut with carburetor in hot idle position and the idle solenoid deenergized. Place chain into swivel cavities which permits chain to have slight slack. Place retainer over swivel and chain assembly. Retainer must be made to rest between balls. Cut off chain flush with side of swivel to remove excess length. Chain slack should not exceed one half diameter of ball stud, .150 inch, when measured at hot idle position.

UNITS WITH CABLE
With throttle closed, ignition and fast idle cam off, adjust cable jam nuts until free play is removed from cable sleeve at carburetor without holding throttle open. Torque jam nuts to 50 in. lbs. Ensure servo boot is over cable washer.

ORIFICE TUBE ADJUSTMENT
MODELS WITH TRANSDUCER REGULATOR
If the cruising speed is lower than the engagement speed, loosen the orifice tube locknut and turn the tube outward; if higher turn the tube inward. Each ¼ turn will alter the engagement-cruising speed difference one mph. Tighten locknut after adjustment and check the system operation.

Gasoline Engine Section

See chapter 17 for service procedures on V8-305 engines. See chapter 9 for service procedures on V6-231 & V6-252 engines.

ENGINE MOUNTS

TORONADO

1. Raise and support vehicle.
2. Remove front splash shield.
3. Remove two screws from engine mount bracket to engine mount on each side, **Fig. 1.**
4. Place a suitable lifting device under the harmonic balancer and raise engine only enough to remove each mount.
5. Reverse procedure to install.

V8 EXC. TORONADO

Removal or replacement of a motor mount can be accomplished by supporting the weight of the engine at the area of the mount to be replaced, **Figs. 2 and 3.**

ENGINE
REPLACE

V8 EXC. TORONADO

1. Mark hood hinge before removing to aid in proper alignment upon reassembly.
2. Drain radiator and disconnect battery.
3. Disconnect radiator hoses, heater hoses, vacuum hoses, power steering pump hoses (if necessary), starter cable at junction block, engine-to-body ground strap, fuel hose from fuel line, wiring and accelerator linkage.
4. Remove fan blade and pulley, coil, upper radiator support and radiator, as necessary.
5. Raise car.
6. Disconnect exhaust pipes at manifolds.
7. Remove torque converter cover and the three bolts securing converter to flywheel.
8. Remove engine mount bolts, then three transmission to engine bolts on right side.
9. Remove starter with wiring attached and position aside.
10. Lower vehicle and support engine with suitable lifting equipment.
11. Support transmission with a suitable jack and remove three left hand transmission to engine bolts.
12. Remove engine from vehicle.

TORONADO

1. Disconnect battery ground cable and drain cooling system.
2. Remove radiator upper support.
3. Remove air cleaner assembly.

Fig. 1   Front engine mounts. Toronado

4. Scribe hood hinge locations and remove hood.
5. Disconnect engine ground strap.
6. Disconnect upper and lower radiator hoses from engine.
7. Disconnect transmission oil cooler lines from radiator.
8. Disconnect heater hoses from water pump and water control valve.
9. Remove radiator, fan and the shroud.
10. Disconnect power steering pump bracket from engine and position aside without disconnecting lines.
11. Disconnect A/C compressor bracket from engine and position aside without disconnecting lines.
12. Disconnect fuel lines.

Fig. 2   Engine mounts. Cutlass

Fig. 3 Engine mounts. 88, 98 & Custom Cruiser

Fig. 4 Cylinder head tightening sequence. V8-260, 307, 350

Fig. 5   Intake manifold tightening sequence. V8-260, 307, 350

13. Disconnect throttle cable, vacuum hoses and electrical connections.
14. Disconnect left hand exhaust pipe from manifold.
15. On left side of engine, remove through bolt and bracket securing final drive to engine.
16. Raise and support vehicle.
17. Remove flywheel shield.
18. Disconnect right hand exhaust pipe from manifold.
19. Disconnect starter motor wiring and remove starter motor.
20. Remove converter to flywheel bolts. Mark location of converter on flywheel for alignment during installation.
21. Remove splash shield.
22. Remove engine front mounting attaching nuts.
23. Remove two bolts securing right hand output shaft support brackets. Using a sharp tool, scribe a mark around the washers as far as possible. Use these scribe marks to position bracket upon installation.
24. Remove lower right hand transmission to engine attaching bolts. One bolt retains the modulator line clip.
25. Use a suitable length of chain to retain final drive in vehicle.
26. Lower vehicle and attach suitable engine lifting equipment to engine.
27. Remove the remaining transmission to engine bolts. It may be necessary to raise or lower transmission with a suitable jack to facilitate bolt removal.
28. Raise engine and remove from vehicle.
29. Reverse procedure to install.

CYLINDER HEAD
REPLACE

Head gaskets used on these engines are of a special composition material that is not to be used with a sealer.

Prior to installation, clean the head bolts and dip in engine oil. Tighten head bolts in steps and in the sequence shown in **Fig. 4**. Final torquing should be to the specifications listed in "Engine Tightening Specifications".

V8-260, 307, 350

1. Disconnect battery ground cable.
2. Drain radiator and cylinder block.
3. Remove intake and exhaust manifolds.
4. Remove ground strap from left cylinder head.
5. Remove rocker arm bolts, pivots, rocker arms and push rods. Keep rocker arms, pivots and push rods in order so they can be installed in the same position.
6. Remove cylinder head attaching bolts and remove cylinder head.
7. Reverse procedure to install. Torque cylinder head bolts in sequence shown in **Fig. 7** and torque intake manifold bolts in sequence shown in **Fig. 5**.

ROCKER ARMS

NOTE: V8 engines use valve rotators, **Fig. 6**. The rotator operates on a sprag clutch principle utilizing the collapsing action of a coil spring to give rotation to the rotor body which turns the valve.

V8-260, 307, 350

1. Remove valve cover.
2. Remove flanged bolts, rocker arm piv-

ot and rocker arms, **Fig. 6**.
3. When installing rocker arm assemblies, lubricate wear surfaces with suitable lubricant. Torque flanged bolts to 25 ft. lbs.

VALVE ROTATORS

The rotator operates on a Sprag clutch principle utilizing the collapsing action of coil spring to give rotation to the rotor body which turns the valve, **Fig. 6**.

To check rotator action, draw a line across rotator body and down the collar. Operate engine at 1500 rpm, rotator body should move around collar. Rotator action can be in either direction. Replace rotator if no movement is noted.

When servicing valves, valve stem tips should be checked for improper wear pattern which could indicate a defective valve rotator, **Fig. 7**.

VALVES

Whenever a new valve is installed or after grinding valves, it will be necessary to measure valve stem height using the Special Tool shown in **Figs. 8 and 9**.

On V8-260, 307, 350 and 403 engines, there should be a minimum clearance of .015 inch between gauge surface and the valve stem, **Fig. 8**.

Check valve rotator height, **Fig. 9**. If valve stem tip extends less than .005 inch above rotator, replace the valve.

Lacking this tool the only alternative is to lay flat feeler gauges on the retainer and check the distance between the retainer and valve stem tip.

Fig. 6   Cylinder head exploded. V8

Fig. 7   Checking valve stems for rotator malfunction

Fig. 8   Measuring valve stem height. V8-260, 307, 350

Fig. 9   Measuring valve retainer or valve rotator height. V8-260, 307, 350

Fig. 10   Valve guide bore marking. V8-260, 307, 350

V8-260, 307, 350③ ...... I-E-I-E-E-I-E-I
V8-305, 350② .... E-I-I-E-E-I-I-E
①—Refer to Buick chapter for service procedures.
②—Refer to Chevrolet chapter for service procedures.
③—Oldsmobile engine.

VALVE GUIDES
V8-260, 307, 350

Valve stem guides are not replaceable, due to being cast in place. If valve guide bores are worn excessively, they can be reamed oversize.

If a standard valve guide bore is being reamed, use a .003 inch or .005 inch oversize reamer. For the .010 inch oversize valve guide bore, use a .013 inch oversize reamer. If too large a reamer is used and the spiraling is removed, it is possible that the valve will not receive the proper lubrication.

NOTE: Occasionally a valve guide will be oversize as manufactured. These are marked on the cylinder head as shown in **Fig. 10.** If no markings are present, the guide bores are standard. If oversize markings are present, any valve replacement will require an oversize valve. Service valves are available in standard diameters as well as .003 inch, .005 inch, .010 inch and .013 inch oversize.

VALVE LIFTERS

Valve lifters are available in standard size and an oversize of .010 inch. An "O" is etched on the side of the .010 inch oversize lifter for identification. Also, the cylinder block near the valve lifter bore is marked with an "O". Ensure valve lifters are re-installed in original bores.

Plungers are not interchangeable because they are selectively fitted to the bodies at the factory.

If plunger and body appear satisfactory blow off with air to remove all particles of dirt. Install the plunger in the body without other parts and check for free movement. A simple test is to be sure that the plunger will drop of its own weight in the body, **Fig. 11.**

VALVE ARRANGEMENT
FRONT TO REAR

V6-231① .... E-I-I-E-I-E
V6-252① .... E-I-I-E-I-E

VALVE TIMING
INTAKE OPENS BEFORE TDC

Engine	Year	Degrees
V6-231②	1980–84	16
V6-252②	1981–84	16
V8-260	1980–82	14
V8-305①	1980	28
V8-307	1980–84	20
V8-350	1980	16

①—Refer to Chevrolet chapter for service procedures.
②—Refer to Buick chapter for service procedures.

VALVE LIFT SPECS.

Engine	Year	Intake	Exhaust
V6-231②	1980–86	.357	.366
V6-252②	1981–84	.357	.366
V8-260	1980–82	.395	.400
V8-305①	1980	.357	.390
V8-307③	1981–86	.400	.400
V8-307④	1983–85	.440	.440
V8-350	1980	.400	.400
V8-350①	1980	.390	.410

1 LIFTER BODY	**5** BALL CHECK	**6** PLUNGER	
2 PLUNGER SPRING	**7** OIL METERING VALVE		
3 BALL CHECK RETAINER	**8** PUSH ROD SEAT		
4 BALL CHECK SPRING	**9** RETAINER RING		

Fig. 11 Hydraulic valve lifter (typical)

Fig. 12 Engine front cover bolts. V8-260, 307, 350

Fig. 13   Timing chain position. V8-260, 307, 350

①—Refer to Chevrolet chapter for service procedures.
②—Refer to Buick chapter for service procedures.
③—Exc. Hurst Olds.
④—Hurst Olds.

TIMING CASE COVER
REPLACE

NOTE: When it becomes necessary to replace the cover oil seal, the cover need not be removed.

V8-260, 307, 350

1. Disconnect battery ground cable.
2. Drain cooling system and disconnect radiator hoses and bypass hose.
3. Remove all drive belts, fan and pulley, crankshaft pulley and harmonic balancer, and accessory brackets.
4. Remove timing indicator and water pump.
5. Remove remaining front cover attaching bolts and the front cover. Also, remove the dowel pins. It may be necessary to grind a flat on the dowel pin to provide a rough surface for gripping.
6. Grind a chamfer on one end of each dowel pin.
7. Cut excess material from front end of oil pan gasket on each side of cylinder block.

8. Trim approximately ⅛ inch from each end of new front pan seal.
9. Install new front cover gasket and apply suitable sealer to gasket around coolant holes.
10. Apply RTV sealer to mating surfaces of cylinder block, oil pan and front cover.
11. Place front cover on cylinder block and press downward to compress seal. Rotate cover right and left and guide oil pan seal into cavity with a small screwdriver.
12. Apply engine oil to bolts.
13. Install two bolts finger tight to retain cover.
14. Install the two dowel pins, chamfered end first.
15. Install timing indicator and water pump and torque bolts as shown in **Figs. 12.**
16. Install harmonic balancer and crankshaft pulley.
17. Install accessory brackets.
18. Install fan and pulley and drive belts.
19. Connect radiator hoses and bypass hose.
20. Connect battery ground cable.

TIMING CHAIN
REPLACE

V8-260, 307, 350

1. After removing front cover, remove fuel pump eccentric, oil slinger, crankshaft sprocket, chain and camshaft sprocket.
2. Install camshaft sprocket, crankshaft sprocket and timing chain together, aligning timing marks as shown in **Fig. 13.**
3. Install fuel pump eccentric with flat side rearward, **Fig. 14.** Then install oil slinger and replace front cover.

NOTE: The valve timing marks, **Figs. 13 and 14,** do not indicate TDC compression stroke for No. 1 cylinder, which is used for distributor installation. If distributor was removed, install timing chain and sprockets, aligning timing marks, **Figs. 13 and 14,** then rotate engine until No. 1 cylinder is on compression stroke and camshaft timing mark is 180° from valve timing position

Fig. 14   Fuel pump eccentric. V8-260, 307, 350

shown in illustrations, then install distributor.

CAMSHAFT
REPLACE

V8-260, 307, 350

1. Disconnect battery ground cable and drain radiator.
2. Remove upper radiator baffle and disconnect upper radiator hose from water outlet.
3. Disconnect transmission oil cooler lines at radiator.
4. Remove radiator fan shroud, then the radiator.
5. Disconnect fuel lines from fuel pump.
6. Remove air cleaner and disconnect throttle cable.
7. Remove all drive belts and position alternator, power steering pump and air conditioning compressor aside.
8. Disconnect by-pass hose from water pump and all electrical and vacuum connections from engine.

20-25

Fig. 15   Assembly of piston to rod. V8-260, 307 & 350

Fig. 16   Piston compression ring identification. V8-260, 307 & 350

Fig. 17   Main bearing size location. V8-260, 307, 350

Fig. 18   Packing upper rear main bearing oil seal

Fig. 19   Trimming upper rear main bearing oil seal

21. Slide camshaft from front of engine.
22. Reverse procedure to install.

NOTE: To insure proper camshaft installation, and to provide initial lubrication, it is extremely important that the camshaft be coated with GM Concentrate (Part No. 1051396).

PISTON & ROD ASSEMBLE

Lubricate the piston pin hole and piston pin to facilitate installation of pin, then position the connecting rod with its respective piston as shown in **Fig. 15**. Measure connecting rod side clearance using a suitable feeler gauge, clearance should be .006—.020 inch.

PISTONS, RINGS & PINS

NOTE: Different types of piston compression rings are used, refer to **Fig. 16** for piston ring identification. On V8-260 engines, piston ring end gap should be .009—.019 in. for Sealed Power piston rings and .010—.020 in. for Perfect Circle and Muskegon piston rings. On V8-307 engines, piston ring end gap should be .009—.019 in. for Sealed Power piston rings and .010—.020 in. for TRW piston rings. On V8-350 engines, piston ring end gap should be .010—.020 in. for Sealed Power piston rings and .013—.023 in. for Perfect Circle and Muskegon piston rings.

Pistons are available in standard sizes and oversizes of .010 and .030 inch. Rings are available in standard sizes and oversizes of .010 and .030 inch.

MAIN & ROD BEARINGS

Main bearings are available in standard sizes and undersizes of .0005, .001, .0015, .002, .010 and .020 inch.

Rod bearings are available in standard sizes and undersizes of .001, .002, .005, .010, .012 and .020 inch.

NOTE: Main bearing clearances not within specifications must be corrected by the use of selective upper and lower shells. **Fig. 17** illustrate the undersize identification marking on the bearing tang.

REAR CRANKSHAFT SEAL SERVICE

Since the braided fabric seal used on these engines can be replaced only when the crankshaft is removed, the following repair procedure is recommended.

1. Remove oil pan and bearing cap.
2. Drive end of old seal gently into groove, using a suitable tool, until packed tight. This may vary between ¼ and ¾ inch depending on amount of pack required.

9. Remove distributor.
10. Raise vehicle and drain oil pan.
11. Remove exhaust cross-over pipe and the starter.
12. Disconnect exhaust pipe from manifold.
13. Install engine support bar.
14. Remove engine mount to bracket bolts, raise engine and remove engine mounts.
15. Remove flywheel cover and engine oil pan.
16. Place wood blocks between exhaust manifolds and cross-member to support engine, then remove engine support bar.
17. Remove crankshaft pulley and balancer, then the engine front cover.
18. Lower vehicle and remove valve covers, intake manifold, rocker arms, push rods and valve lifters.

NOTE: Note position of the valve train components to ensure installation in original location.

19. If equipped with A/C, discharge refrigerant and remove condenser.
20. Remove fuel pump eccentric, camshaft sprocket, oil slinger and timing chain.

Fig. 20 Oil pump disassembled. V8-260, 307, 350, Typical)

Engine lubrication. V8-260, 307, 350, 403 (Typical)

remove clutch fan assembly and pulley.
3. Remove pump from front cover.

BELT TENSION DATA

	New Lbs.	Used Lbs.
1981–86		
V6 All		
Air Conditioning	145	80
A.I.R. Pump	80	45
Alternator	145	70
Power Steering	170	90
Vacuum Pump	80	45
V8 All		
Air Conditioning	170	90
A.I.R. Pump	80③	45③
Alternator	160④	80④
Power Steering	170	90
Vacuum Pump	125	55
1980		
5/16 inch Belts	80	50
3/8 inch Belts①	140	70
3/8 inch Belts②	140	60
15/32 inch Belts	165	90

①—Except cogged belts.
②—Cogged belts.
③—3/8 inch belts; new, 145; used, 70.
④—Cogged belts; new, 145; used, 55.

FUEL PUMP
REPLACE

1. Disconnect fuel line fron fuel pump.
2. Remove fuel pump mounting bolts and the fuel pump.
3. Remove all gasket material from the pump and block gasket surfaces. Apply sealer to both sides of new gasket.
4. Position gasket on pump flange and hold pump in position against its mounting surface. Make sure rocker arm is riding on camshaft eccentric.
5. Press pump tight against its mounting. Install retaining screws and tighten them alternately.
6. Connect fuel lines. Then operate engine and check for leaks.

3. Repeat previous step for other end of seal.
4. Measure and note amount that seal was driven up on one side. Using the old seal removed from bearing cap, cut a length of seal the amount previously noted plus 1/16 inch.
5. Repeat previous step for other side of seal.
6. Pack cut lengths of seal into appropriate side of seal groove. A packing tool, BT-6433, **Fig. 18,** may be used since the tool has been machined to provide a built-in stop. Use tool BT-6436 to trim the seal flush with block, **Fig. 19.**
7. Install new seal in lower bearing cap.

OIL PAN
REPLACE

EXC. TORONADO

1. Remove distributor cap and align rotor with No. 1 firing position.
2. Disconnect ground cable, remove dip stick and drain oil pan.
3. Remove upper radiator support and fan shroud attaching screws.
4. Remove flywheel cover and starter.
5. Disconnect exhaust pipes and crossover pipe on single exhaust models.
6. Disconnect engine mounts and raise engine.
7. Remove oil pan bolts and oil pan.
8. Reverse procedure to install. Torque oil pan bolts to 10 ft. lbs.

TORONADO

1. Disconnect battery ground cable.
2. Raise and support vehicle, then remove three final drive to transmission bolts.

3. Disconnect frame braces, then disconnect idler arm and pitman arm from relay rod.
4. Separate drive axles from output shafts.
5. Remove battery cable bracket from output shaft support.
6. Disconnect output shaft support from engine block.
7. Support transmission with suitable jack, then remove final drive assembly.
8. Remove splash shield and starter motor.
9. Drain engine oil and remove oil pan.
10. Reverse procedure to install.

OIL PUMP REPAIRS
V8-260, 307, 350

1. Remove oil pan and pump baffle. Remove attaching screws and remove pump and drive shaft extension.
2. To service the pump, refer to **Fig. 20.**
3. To install, insert the drive shaft extension through the opening in the block until the shaft mates into the distributor drive gear. Position pump onto rear main bearing cap and torque the attaching bolts to 35 ft-lbs.
4. Install oil pump baffle and pan.

WATER PUMP
REPLACE

V8-260, 307, 350

1. Drain cooling system and remove heater and lower hoses from pump.
2. Loosen pulley belts and remove fan and pulley. On air conditioned cars,

Diesel Engine Section

INDEX

DESCRIPTION

ENGINE CONSTRUCTION

The Oldsmobile four stroke cycle diesel engine is basically the same in construction as the Oldsmobile gasoline engine. The cylinders are numbered 1,3,5,7 on the left bank and 2,4,6,8 on the right bank on 8 cylinder engines or 1, 3 and 5 on the left bank and 2, 4 and 6 on the right bank on 6 cylinder engines. The firing order is 1-8-4-3-6-5-7-2 on 8 cylinder engines or 1-6-5-4-3-2 on 6 cylinder engines. The major differences between the diesel and gasoline versions is in the cylinder heads, combustion chamber, fuel distribution system, air intake manifold and method of ignition. The cylinder block, crankshaft, main bearings, connecting rods, pistons and pins are of heavy construction due to the high compression ratio required to ignite the diesel fuel. The diesel fuel is ignited when the heat developed in the combustion chamber during the compression stroke reaches a certain temperature.

The valve train operates the same as in the gasoline engine, but are of special design and material for diesel operation. The stainless steel pre-chamber inserts in the cylinder head combustion chambers are serviced separately from the cylinder head. With the cylinder head removed, these pre-chamber inserts can be driven from the cylinder head after removing the glow plugs or injection nozzles. The glow plugs are threaded into the cylinder head and the injection nozzles are retained by a bolt and clamp. The injection nozzles are spring loaded and calibrated to open at a specified fuel pressure.

FUEL SYSTEM

The fuel injection pump is mounted on top of the engine and is gear driven by the camshaft and rotates at camshaft speed. This high pressure rotary pump injects a metered amount of fuel to each cylinder at the proper time. Six or eight high pressure fuel delivery pipes from the injection pump to the injection nozzles, **Fig. 1,** are the same length to prevent any difference in timing from cylinder to cylinder. The fuel injection pump provides the required timing advance under all operating conditions. Engine speed is controlled by a rotary fuel metering valve, **Figs. 2 and 3.** When the accelerator is depressed, the throttle cable opens the metering valve and allows more fuel to be delivered to the engine. The injection pump also incorporates a low pressure transfer pump to deliver fuel to the fuel line to the high pressure pump, **Figs. 2 and 3.**

The fuel filter is located between the mechanical fuel pump and the injection pump on 8 cylinder engines, or between the electric fuel pump and the injection pump on 6 cylinder engines. The diaphragm type mechanical fuel pump used on 8 cylinder engines is mounted on the right hand side of the engine and is driven by a cam on the crankshaft. The electric fuel pump used on 6 cylinder engines is mounted on the engine. The fuel tank at the rear of the vehicle is connected by fuel pipes to the mechanical fuel pump.

"WATER IN FUEL" SYSTEM

This system is available on some 1980 and all 1981—85 models. These vehicles

Fig. 1   Fuel injection nozzle

INLET FITTING

NOZZLE GASKET   NOZZLE BODY

Fig. 2   Fuel injection pump circuit, V8 engine

METERING VALVE — GOVERNOR SPRING — HOUSING PRESSURE REGULATOR — VENT WIRE ASSEMBLY — HEAD PRESSURE — CAM RING — TRANSFER PRESSURE TAP HOLE PLUG — BALL CHECK ASSEMBLY — AUTOMATIC ADVANCE MECHANISM — GOVERNOR HOUSING LUBE — CHARGING PASSAGE — ROTOR — PRES. REG. — FILTER — FUEL PUMP — FUEL TANK — FILTER — DELIVERY VALVE — TRANSFER PUMP — NOZZLE

■ HIGH PRESSURE DISCHARGE CIRCUIT
▨ TRANSFER PUMP PRESSURE CIRCUIT
▨ HOUSING PRESSURE CIRCUIT
▨ INLET PRESSURE AND RETURN OIL CIRCUIT

1. OIL PICK-UP
2. LIFTER FEED
3. ROCKER ARM VALVE TIP FEED
4. SPLASH LUBE TO TIMING CHAIN FUEL PUMP CAM & DIST. & OIL PUMP DRIVE
5. LEFT MAIN GALLERY FEED
6. CAM BEARING FEED
7. MAIN BEARING FEED
8. ROD BEARING FEED
9. INJECTION PUMP DRIVE BEARING FEED

RIGHT MAIN GALLERY
VACUUM PUMP AND OIL PUMP DRIVE
LEFT MAIN GALLERY
OIL PUMP

Fig. 4   Engine lubricating system. Typical. (V6 engine similar)

TRANSFER PRESSURE
FEED PRESSURE
METERING PRESSURE
INJECTION PRESSURE
HOUSING PRESSURE

1. Head & Rotor
2. Auto-advance Unit
3. Charging Passage
4. Transfer Pump
5. Pressure Regulator
6. Metering
7. H.P.C.A.
8. Light Load Advance Arm

Fig. 3   Fuel injection pump circuit. V6 engine

have a "Water in Fuel" light mounted in the instrument panel. The "Water in Fuel" light has a bulb check feature and should light for 2 to 2½ seconds when the ignition is turned on. If not, the bulb is burned out or there is an open in the wiring circuit. When there is water in the fuel, the light will come back on and remain on after a 15 to 20 second delay.

A water sensing probe, mounted on the fuel sender, actuates the instrument panel light when it is partially covered with water. About 1 to 2½ gallons of water must be present in the fuel tank to cause the sensor light to activate.

If the "Water in Fuel" lamp goes on while the vehicle is being driven, the fuel system should be checked for water. If the lamp goes on immediately after refueling and before the vehicle is moved, there is a large quantity of water in the tank and should be removed immediately.

The water may be removed from the tank with a pump or by siphoning. The pump or siphon hose should be connected to the quarter inch fuel return hose (the smaller of the two hoses), located under the hood near the fuel pump. Refer to "Purging Water From Fuel Tank" procedure.

HOUSING PRESSURE COLD ADVANCE (HPCA)

This feature is used on all 1981–85 engines and advances the injection timing 3° during cold operation. This circuit is actuated by a temperature switch calibrated to open the circuit at 125° F. Below the switching point, housing pressure is decreased from 10 to 0 psi which advances the injection timing 3°. Above the switching point, the switch opens, de-energizing the solenoid and the housing pressure is returned to 10 psi. The fast idle solenoid is energized by the same switch and closes when the temperature falls below 95° F.

HOUSING PRESSURE ALTITUDE ADVANCE (HPAA)

Used on 1984–85 engines (exc. Calif.), the HPAA is used to meet emission standards at both low and high altitudes. Altitude compensation is achieved through timing changes and EGR modification and is controlled by an altitude sensitive switch.

Timing is controlled by two pressure regulators, the Housing Pressure Cold Advance, located in the injection pump, and the Housing Pressure Altitude Advance solenoid in the fuel return line.

The HPAA solenoid regulates housing pressure according to altitude. When the solenoid is activated, the glass check ball seats, regulating pressure at its calibrated value. When the solenoid is de-activated, the check ball moves off its seat, opening the fuel return line and preventing pressure regulation. It is possible for both the HPCA and the HPAA to regulate housing pressure at the same time. Likewise, it is also possible to have just the HPCA or the HPAA regulate pressure singularly. The HPCA must be energized and not regulating to allow the HPAA solenoid to regulate at its calibrated value.

ENGINE LUBRICATION SYSTEM

NOTE: On 1980 engines, the recommended diesel engine oil designation is SE/CC. On 1981 engines, the recommended diesel engine oil is SF/CC, SF/CD or SE/CC. On 1982–85 engines the recommended diesel engine oil is SF/CC or SF/CD.

The diesel engine lubrication system is basically the same as the gasoline engine. The fuel injection pump driven gear is lubricated by oil directed through a passage from the top of the camshaft bearing, **Fig. 4.** An angled passage in the shaft portion of the driven gear directs the oil to the rear driven gear bearing. At the front of the right oil gallery, a small orifice sprays oil to lubricate the fuel pump eccentric cam on the crankshaft and timing chain.

ENGINE COOLING SYSTEM

The diesel engine cooling system is the same as the gasoline engine except the radiator incorporates two oil coolers. One cooler is used to cool the transmission fluid and the other cooler is used to cool the engine oil.

ENGINE ELECTRICAL SYSTEM

1980-83

Eight glow plugs are used to pre-heat the pre-chamber to aid in starting. The type 1 glow plugs are 12 volt heaters and are activated when the ignition switch is turned to the "Run" position. The type 1 system uses steady current applied to 12 volt glow plugs. The type 2 glow plug system uses 6 volt glow plugs with a controlled pulsating current applied to them for starting. The type 2 glow plug system uses an electro-mechanical controller to control glow plug temperature, preglow time, wait/start lights and after glow time. The Cutlass Electronic Glow Plug Control System uses an electronic module and a control sensor to control glow plug temperature, the glow plug relay and the wait light. On this system a coolant temperature switch controls the fast idle solenoid through a fast idle relay. The 6 volt and 12 volt glow plugs are not interchangeable and can be identified by the wire connector spade. The 6 volt glow plugs have a 5/16 in. wire connector spade, while the 12 volt glow plugs have a ¼ in. wire connector spade. The glow plugs remain activated for a short time after starting then are automatically turned "Off". Two 12 volt batteries connected in parallel are required for the higher electrical load due to the glow plugs and starter motor. The diesel starter motor is larger than the gasoline engine starter and is designed to crank the engine at least the 100 RPM required for starting. An alternator supplies charging current to both batteries at the same time and there are no switches or relays in the charging circuit.

1. WEATHER PACK SEAL
2. RELAY ASSEMBLY
3. GASKET
4. TIMER MODULE
5. COVER PLATE

Fig. 5 Glow plug control module. 1984

1984

The glow plug system used on 1984 diesel engines features a self-limiting feature that regulates maximum temperature, while the glow plugs are programmed to shut off automatically should the vehicle not be started within the specified time period.

System Components

The glow plug control module, **Fig. 5**, is an integral assembly that includes the timer functions, lamp switch and glow plug relay. The control module serves the following functions:

1. Controls wait lamp operation, which varies according to system voltage and/or ambient temperature.
2. Controls system shutdown timing depending on voltage and ambient temperature.
3. An overvoltage function that protects the glow plugs from failure, should higher than normal voltages be incurred.
4. A thermal cutout function that disengages the glow plug system when module temperatures are greater than 113° F.
5. A power relay function that switches the voltage applied to the glow plugs.
6. A quick reset function that permits the module to recycle quickly, after initial shutdown time.

This control module can only be used with glow plugs that regulate their own temperature. The new glow plugs used have positive temperature coefficient properties, which mean they have low resistance values at low temperatures and high resistance values at high temperatures. The new plugs offer a fast temperature rise similar to past fixed resistance plugs, plus improved and simpler glow plug control.

System Operation

The glow plug control circuit, **Fig. 6**, operates the glow plug system in three steps: pre-glow, after-glow and off. During pre-glow, the circuit activates the wait lamp and heats the glow plugs until they are sufficiently warm to start the engine. During after-glow, the circuit deactivates the wait lamp, but continues to apply power to the glow plugs. During the Off cycle, the circuit removes power from the glow plugs and keeps it off until the engine is restarted.

As stated previously, the glow plug control module controls all circuit functions. The thermal controls open the pre-glow and after-glow switches to end the respective cycles, and are responsive to engine

Fig. 6 Glow plug control circuit schematic. 1984

temperature. When the system is energized with the engine cold, both switches are in the "Cold" position. As time passes, current flow heats the thermal controls, moving both switches toward their "HOT" position. The time needed for each switch to reach its "HOT" position is dependent upon how cold the engine and control module were when the system was first energized. As the pre-glow switch reaches the "HOT" position, the wait lamp deactivates and the engine may now be started. The control module continues to operate, whether the engine is started or not, since the after-glow switch has not yet reached its "HOT" position. Current flow continues to heat the thermal control. When the thermal control reaches full temperature, the after-glow switch moves to "HOT", opening the path to ground from the coil of the glow plug relay. This allows current flow to bypass the coil of the reset relay. With the path to ground now open, current must flow to bypass the coil of the reset relay. With the path to ground now open, current must flow to ground through the reset relay coil. The glow plug relay de-energizes, removing power to the glow plugs. The reset relay now energizes, opening the contact of the relay and locking off the thermal controls. When the ignition switch is turned off, the reset relay contact closes, and the glow plug module is ready to repeat the cycle. If the engine is above 140° F. when restarted, the thermal controls will be "HOT", energizing the reset relay and preventing glow plug operation.

The over-voltage protector protects the glow plugs should battery voltage rise above 14 volts. When the protector senses over 14 volts, it opens the circuit to the glow plug relay coil and prevents current from flowing to the glow plugs. After a short time, the protector closes the circuit. If battery voltage is still above 14 volts, it will reopen the circuit again. The protector continues to cycle in this way as long as the over-voltage condition exists and as long as glow plug operation is needed.

1985

A glow plug relay in the glow plug controller regulates the hearing of the glow plugs. The relay is operated by the thermal controls in the controller. these thermal controls respond to engine temperature as well as the heating coil inside the thermal control unit.

When the ignition switch is turned to the Run position, battery voltage is applied to the "Wait" lamp. The "Wait" lamp switched is closed when cold and open when hot. When the lamp is on, battery voltage is applied to the glow plugs and they begin to heat. After approximately six seconds, when the glow plugs and engine are sufficiently heated, the "Wait" lamp goes out and the engine can be started. At this time, the glow plug relay remains closed continue heating the glow plugs to reduce exhaust smoke and improve cold driveability.

After approximately one minute of engine operation, the glow plug relay is opened and heating of the glow plugs is stopped. If the engine is restarted when hot, the thermal controller keeps both the lamp switch and relay open to prevent any further plug heating.

When the engine cools, the "Wait" lamp switch returns to the closed position and the glow plug relay remains open until battery voltage is applied to the thermal controls.

The thermal controls provide protection from overvoltage conditions by automatically de-energizing and energizing the glow plug relay. If the overvoltage surge remains present, voltage is cycled on and off to the glow plugs without damaging them.

DIESEL ENGINE ELECTRICAL DIAGNOSIS

1980-84

Refer to **Figs. 8 through 12** for diesel engine electrical diagnosis.

1985

Glow Plug Controller Diagnosis

1. If there is no voltage at the glow plugs, or a "Wait" lamp malfunction, disconnect electrical connector from glow plug controller.
2. Place ignition switch in Run position and check for voltage at connector terminals as well as controller relay stud terminals. Ensure terminal C (black) is grounded.

Fig. 7 Glow plug controller test connections. 1985

3. Battery voltage should be indicated at terminals A (dark blue) and B (pink/black) and the red relay terminal. No voltage should be indicated at terminal D (purple) or the green relay terminal.
4. If voltage is not present at terminal A, check "Wait" lamp bulb and associated wiring for an open. If voltage at any other terminal is incorrect, check circuit to that terminal.
5. If voltages at connector and relay terminals are correct, replace glow plug controller.

Glow Plug Controller Bench Test
1. Remove glow plug controller from vehicle and allow to cool below 122° F.
2. Connect test equipment to controller as shown in **Fig. 7.**
3. Close test switch and observe test lamps. Both lamps should immediately go on when test switch is closed. After 5–7 seconds, "Wait" lamp should go off, followed by the "Glow Plug" lamp in 35–55 seconds. After 2 minutes, both lamps should remain off.
4. Open test switch, wait several seconds, then close switch. Both test lamps should immediately go on.
5. Replace controller if operation is not as described.

ROUGH IDLE DIAGNOSIS

Check for mechanical malfunctions such as incorrect idle speed or injection pump timing, or leaking nozzles or high pressure lines. If rough idle is still evident, refer to "Glow Plug Resistance Check".

GLOW PLUG RESISTANCE CHECK

1981–85
1. Using multi-meter J-29125 (1981–83) or J-29125A (1984–85) set left selector switch to "OHMS", right selector switch to 200 ohms and center slide switch to "D.C. LO".

NOTE: If another ohmmeter is used, different values will result. Tools J-29125 and J-29125A were used in the development of this procedure. Their use is required if similar readings are to be obtained.

2. Start engine, allow it to reach normal operating temperature, then disconnect all feed wires from glow plugs. Turn heater to "On" position.
3. Disconnect alternator two wire connector.
4. Using tachometer J-26925, or equivalent, adjust idle speed screw to obtain worst engine idle roughness condition.

Do not exceed 900 RPM.
5. Allow engine to run at worst idle speed for approximately one minute, then attach an alligator clip to black test lead of meter. Ground black test lead to fast idle solenoid (1983–85) or engine lift strap (1981–82).
6. Write down the engine firing order on a piece of paper, then with engine idling, probe each glow plug terminal and record the resistance values on each cylinder in the firing sequence.

NOTE: If vehicle is equipped with an electric cooling fan, record resistance values with cooling fan inoperative. Do not disconnect cooling fan circuitry. The resistance values are dependent on the temperature in each cylinder, and therefore, can indicate cylinder output.

7. If a resistance reading on any cylinder is 1.3–1.4 ohms for 1984–85 vehicles, or 1.2–1.3 for 1981–83 vehicles, check engine for a mechanical problem. Make a compression check of the lowest reading cylinder and the cylinders which fire before and after. Correct cause of low compression before proceeding to fuel system.
8. On 1984–85 vehicles, install glow plug luminosity probe, from tool J-33075, into cylinder with lowest resistance value. Observe combustion light flashes of probe. The flashes will usually be erratic and in sequence with the misfire. If not, move to the next lowest reading cylinder, until the misfire is found.
9. On all vehicles, observe the results of all glow plug resistance readings, looking for differences between cylinders. Rough engines will normally have a difference of .4 ohms or more between cylinders in the firing sequence. To correct rough engine idle, it will be necessary to raise or lower the resistance values on one or more of the offending cylinders by replacing the injection nozzles.
10. Remove nozzle from the cylinder(s) affecting idle performance. Determine the pop off pressure of the nozzle and check the nozzle for leakage and spray pattern. Refer to tool manufacturer for proper testing procedures. Install nozzles with higher pop off pressures to lower resistance values, and nozzles with lower pop off pressures to raise values. A change of 30 psi nozzle pressure will result in a .1 ohm difference in resistance. Use new nozzles on new vehicles and broken in nozzles on vehicles with 1500 or more miles, if possible.

NOTE: Whenever a nozzle is cleaned or replaced, crank the engine and watch for air bubbles at the nozzle inlet before connecting the injection pipe. If bubbles are evident, clean or replace the nozzle.

11. Connect injection pipe, restart engine and check idle quality. If idle quality is still not acceptable, repeat steps 6 through 10.
12. After making additional nozzle changes, check idle quality again.

DIESEL ENGINE DIAGNOSIS

Condition	Possible Cause	Correction
ENGINE WILL NOT CRANK	1. Loose or corroded battery cables 2. Discharged batteries 3. Starter Inoperative	1. Check connections at battery, engine block and starter solenoid. 2. Check charging system. 3. Check starting system.
ENGINE CRANKS SLOWLY—WILL NOT START (Minimum Engine Crank Speed—100 RPM)	1. Battery cable connections loose or corroded 2. Batteries undercharged 3. Wrong engine oil	1. Check connections at battery, engine block and starter. 2. Check charging system. 3. Drain and refill with recommended oil.
ENGINE CRANKS NORMALLY—WILL NOT START	1. Incorrect starting procedure 2. Incorrect or contaminated fuel 3. No fuel to nozzles	1. Use recommended starting procedure. 2. Flush fuel system and install correct fuel. 3. Loosen injection line at a nozzle. Do not disconnect. Use care to direct fuel away from sources of ignition. Wipe connection to be sure it is dry. Crank 5 seconds. Fuel should flow from injection line. Tighten connection. If fuel does not flow, check fuel solenoid operation as follows: Connect a 12 volt test lamp from wire at injection pump solenoid to ground. Turn ignition to "ON". Lamp should light. If lamp does not light, check wiring to solenoid.
	4. No fuel to injection pump	4. Remove line at inlet to injection pump fuel filter. Connect hose from line to metal container. Crank engine. If no fuel is discharged, test the fuel supply pump. If the pump is OK, check the injection pump fuel filter and replace if plugged. If filter and inlet line to injection pump are OK, replace injection pump.
	5. Plugged fuel return system	5. Disconnect fuel return line at injection pump and route hose to a metal container. Connect a hose to the injection pump connection and route it to the metal container. Crank the engine; if engine starts and runs, correct restriction in fuel return system.
	6. Pump timing incorrect 7. Glow plug control system inoperative 8. Glow plugs inoperative 9. Internal engine problems 10. No voltage to fuel solenoid	6. Make certain that pump timing mark is aligned with mark on adapter. 7. Refer to Diesel Engine Electrical System Diagnosis. 8. Refer to Diesel Engine Electrical System Diagnosis. 9. Correct as necessary. 10. Connect a 12 volt test lamp from injection pump solenoid to ground. Turn ignition to "On", lamp should light. If lamp lights, remove test lamp and connect and disconnect solenoid connector and listen for solenoid operation. If solenoid does not operate, remove injection pump for repairs. If lamp does not light, refer to Diesel Engine Electrical System Diagnosis.
	11. Restricted fuel tank filter.	11. Remove fuel tank and check filter.

DIESEL ENGINE DIAGNOSIS—Continued

Condition	Possible Cause	Correction
ENGINE STARTS BUT WILL NOT CONTINUE TO RUN AT IDLE	1. No fuel in tank	1. Install correct fuel in tank.
	2. Incorrect or contaminated fuel	2. Flush fuel system and install correct fuel.
	3. Limited fuel to injection pump	3. Test the fuel supply pump. Replace as necessary.
	4. Fuel solenoid disengaged with ignition switch in the "ON" position	4. Connect a 12 volt test lamp from wire at injection pump solenoid to ground. Turn ignition to "ON". Lamp should light. Turn ignition to "START". Lamp should light. If lamp does not light in both positions, check wiring to solenoid.
	5. Restricted fuel return system	5. Disconnect fuel return line at injection pump and route hose to a metal container. Connect a hose to injection pump connection and route to metal container. Crank engine; if engine starts and runs, correct restriction in fuel return system.
	6. Fast idle solenoid inoperative	6. With engine cold, start car; solenoid should move to support injection pump lever in "fast idle position" for about 5 seconds. If solenoid does not move, refer to Electrical System Diagnosis.
	7. Low idle incorrectly adjusted	7. Adjust idle screw to specification.
	8. Pump timing incorrect	8. Make certain that timing mark, on injection pump, is aligned with mark on adapter.
	9. Glow plug control system malfunction	9. Refer to Diesel Engine Electrical System Diagnosis.
	10. Injection pump malfunction	10. Install replacement pump.
	11. Internal engine problems	11. Correct as necessary.
ENGINE STARTS, IDLES ROUGH, WITHOUT ABNORMAL NOISE OR SMOKE	1. Low idle incorrectly adjusted	1. Adjust idle screw to specification.
	2. Injection line leaks	2. Wipe off injection lines and connections. Run engine and check for leaks. Correct leaks.
	3. Restricted fuel return system	3. Disconnect fuel return line at injection pump and route hose to a metal container. Connect a hose to the injection pump connection and route it to the metal container. Crank the engine; if engine starts and runs, correct restriction in fuel return system.
	4. Incorrect or contaminated fuel	4. Flush fuel system and install correct fuel.
	5. Nozzle(s) inoperative	5. With engine running, loosen injection line fitting at each nozzle in turn. Use care to direct fuel away from sources of ignition. Each nozzle should contribute to rough running. If nozzle is found that does not change idle quality, it should be replaced.
	6. Internal fuel leak at nozzle(s)	6. Disconnect fuel return system from nozzles on one bank at a time. With the engine running, observe the normal fuel seepage at the nozzles. Replace any nozzle with excessive fuel leakage.
	7. Fuel supply pump malfunctions	7. Test the fuel supply pump. Replace if necessary.
	8. Uneven fuel distribution to cylinders	8. Install new or reconditioned nozzles, one at a time, until condition is corrected as indicated by normal idle.

DIESEL ENGINE DIAGNOSIS—Continued

Condition	Possible Cause	Correction
ENGINE STARTS AND IDLES ROUGH WITH EXCESSIVE NOISE AND/OR SMOKE	1. Injection pump timing incorrect	1. Be sure timing mark on injection pump is aligned with mark on adapter.
	2. Nozzle(s) inoperative	2. With engine running, crack injection line at each nozzle, one at a time. Use care to direct fuel away from sources of ignition. Each nozzle should contribute to rough running. If a nozzle is found that does not affect idle quality or changes noise and/or smoke, it should be replaced.
	3. High pressure lines incorrectly installed	3. Check routing of each line. Correct as required.
ENGINE COLD, STARTS AND IDLES ROUGH WITH EXCESSIVE NOISE AND/OR SMOKE, BUT CLEARS UP AFTER WARM-UP	1. Incorrect starting procedure	1. Advise operator on correct procedure. (See owners manual.)
	2. Injection pump timing incorrect	2. Check timing with J-33075 timing meter and reset if needed.
	3. Insufficient engine break-in time	3. Break in engine 2000 miles or more.
	4. Air in system	4. Install a section of clear plastic tubing on the fuel return fitting from the engine. Evidence of bubbles in fuel when cranking or running indicates the presence of an air leak in the suction fuel line.
	5. Inoperative glow plug	5. Replace faulty glow plug.
	6. Nozzle(s) malfunction	6. Remove and clean or replace.
	7. Housing pressure cold advance inoperative	7. Check operation and repair.
ENGINE MISFIRES BUT IDLES CORRECTLY	1. Plugged fuel filter	1. Replace filter.
	2. Incorrect injection pump timing	2. Be sure that timing mark on injection pump and adapter are aligned.
	3. Incorrect or contaminated fuel	3. Flush fuel system and install correct fuel.
ENGINE WILL NOT RETURN TO IDLE	1. External linkage misadjustment or failure	1. Reset linkage or replace as required.
	2. Internal injection pump malfunction	2. Install replacement injection pump.
FUEL LEAKS ON GROUND—NO ENGINE MALFUNCTION	1. Loose or broken fuel line or connection	1. Examine complete fuel system, including tank, supply, injection and return system. Determine source and cause of leak and repair.
	2. Internal injection pump failure	2. Install replacement injection pump.
SIGNIFICANT LOSS OF POWER	1. Incorrect or contaminated fuel	1. Flush fuel system and install correct fuel.
	2. Pinched or otherwise restricted return system	2. Examine system for restriction and correct as required.
	3. Plugged fuel tank vent	3. Remove fuel cap. If "hissing" noise is heard, vent is plugged and should be cleaned.
	4. Restricted supply	4. Examine fuel supply system to determine cause of restriction. Repair as required.
	5. Plugged fuel filter	5. Remove and replace filter.
	6. External compression leaks	6. Check for compression leaks at all nozzles and glow plugs, using "Leak-Tec" or equivalent. If leak is found, tighten nozzle clamp or glow plug. If leak persists at a nozzle, remove it and reinstall with a new carbon stop seal and compression seal.
	7. Plugged nozzle(s)	7. Remove nozzles, check for plugging and have repaired or replaced.
	8. Internal engine problem	8. Correct as necessary.

DIESEL ENGINE DIAGNOSIS—Continued

Condition	Possible Cause	Correction
NOISE—"RAP" FROM ONE OR MORE CYLINDERS	1. Air in fuel system 2. Air in high pressure line(s)	1. Check for leaks and correct. 2. Crack line at nozzle(s) and bleed air at each cylinder determined to be causing noise. Use care to direct fuel away from sources of ignition and be sure to carefully retighten lines.
	3. Nozzle(s) sticking open or with very low blowoff pressure 4. Internal engine problem	3. Replace the nozzle(s) causing the problem. 4. Correct as necessary.
NOISE—SIGNIFICANT OVERALL COMBUSTION NOISE INCREASE WITH EXCESSIVE BLACK SMOKE	1. Timing not set to specification 2. Internal engine problem 3. Injection pump housing pressure out of specifications. 4. Internal injection pump problem	1. Align timing marks on adapter and injection pump. 2. Check for presence of oil in the air crossover. If present, determine cause and correct. 3. Check housing pressure. If incorrect, replace fuel return line connector assembly. 4. Replace pump.
NOISE—INTERNAL OR EXTERNAL	1. Fuel supply pump, alternator, water pump, valve train, vacuum pump, bearings etc.	1. Inspect and correct as necessary.
ENGINE OVERHEATS	1. Coolant system leak or oil cooler system leak 2. Belt failure 3. Thermostat malfunction, head gasket failure or internal engine problem	1. Check for leaks and correct as required. 2. Replace. 3. Inspect and correct as necessary.
INSTRUMENT PANEL OIL WARNING LAMP "ON" AT IDLE	1. Oil cooler or oil cooler line restricted 2. Internal engine problem	1. Remove restriction in cooler or cooler line. 2. Correct as necessary.
ODOR OR SMOKE—EXCESSIVE AND NOT PREVIOUSLY COVERED	1. Same as Gasoline Engines	1. Correct as necessary. Refer to Trouble-Shooting Chapter.
ENGINE WILL NOT SHUT OFF WITH KEY	1. Injection pump solenoid does not drop out 2. Injection pump solenoid return spring failed	1. Refer to electrical diagnosis. If problem is determined to be internal with the injection pump, replace the injection pump. 2. Replace injection pump.

NOTE: With engine at idle, pinch the fuel return line at the injection pump to shut off engine.

13. If problem moves from cylinder to cylinder and resistance values do not change as nozzles are changed, the injection pump may be defective.

NOTE: Always recheck cylinders at same engine RPM. Sometimes cylinder readings may not indicate that an improvement has been made, even though the engine may idle better. A nozzle with a tip leak can allow more fuel than required into a cylinder, raising the glow plug resistance value. This will steal fuel from the next nozzle in the firing order and will result in that glow plug having a lower resistance value. If this is evident, remove and check the nozzle with the high reading. If it is leaking, it may be responsible for the rough idle. If low readings are evident on a glow plug and it does not change with a nozzle change, switch glow plugs between the good and bad cylinder. If the reading of each cylinder is not the same as before the switch, then the glow plug cannot be used for rough idle diagnosis.

WATER IN FUEL SYSTEM DIAGNOSIS

WATER IN FUEL LAMP DOES NOT GO ON

If the likelihood of water in the fuel tank exists and the Water In Fuel lamp is off, siphon the fuel tank to check for water by connecting a pump to the fuel return line. If at least 3 gallons of water are siphoned from the tank, proceed as follows:
1. Disconnect Water In Fuel electrical lead at fuel tank and ground the lead. If lamp does not go on, proceed to step 4. If it does, check for at least 8 volts at the electrical lead. If no voltage is present, replace the Water In Tank light bulb.
2. Ground the Water In Tank electrical lead. If lamp does not go on, check for open circuit in wiring, **Fig. 13**.
3. Remove fuel level sender and Water in Fuel detector unit from fuel tank.
4. Check connections to "Water In Fuel".

If satisfactory, check detector unit as follows:
a. Remove detector from fuel sender unit, **Fig. 14**.
b. Connect the detector to a bulb and power source as shown in **Fig. 15**. The lamp should go on when the detector probe is lowered into the container of water ⅜ inch or less. Make sure water is grounded to negative side of battery.

WATER IN FUEL LAMP STAYS ON

Under this condition, siphon the tank to check for water by connecting a pump to the fuel return line. If no water is present, proceed as follows:
1. Disconnect the Water In Fuel electrical lead near the fuel tank. If lamp does not go off, proceed to step 2. If lamp goes off, remove fuel level sender and check detector as described previously under "Water In Fuel Lamp Does Not Go On".

Fig. 8   Diesel engine electrical system, part 1 of 2. 1980—83 88, 98 & Toronado Type 2

Fig. 8   Diesel engine electrical system, part 2 of 2. 1980—83 88, 98 & Toronado Type 2

Fig. 9   Diesel engine electrical diagnosis, part 1 of 4. 1980–83 Type 2 exc. Cutlass

NO FAST IDLE WITH A/C ON. OK WITH COLD ENGINE

With ignition switch on and engine at operating temperature, turn A/C on. Connect a 12-volt test light to ground and touch the dark green wire on fast idle relay.

LIGHT ON → Replace relay.

LIGHT OFF → Repair open circuit in lt. grn. wire from fast idle relay to A/C harness.

WAIT LIGHT STAYS ON GLOW PLUGS OPERATE OK

Connect 12-volt test light to ground and touch yellow wire terminal at lamp control relay.

LAMP ON → Replace lamp control relay.

LAMP OFF → Repair open circuit in yellow wire from lamp control relay to glow plug relay.

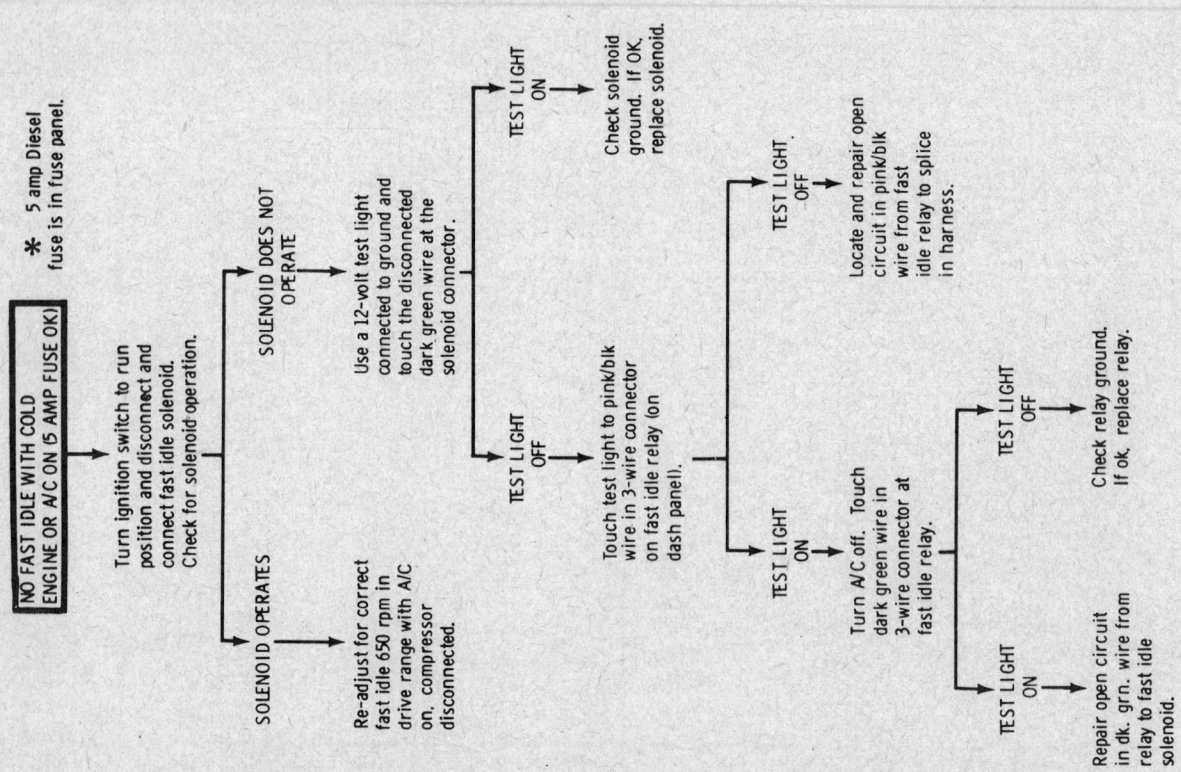

NO FAST IDLE WITH COLD ENGINE OR A/C ON (5 AMP FUSE OK)

* 5 amp Diesel fuse is in fuse panel.

Turn ignition switch to run position and disconnect and connect fast idle solenoid. Check for solenoid operation.

SOLENOID DOES NOT OPERATE

Use a 12-volt test light connected to ground and touch the disconnected dark green wire at the solenoid connector.

SOLENOID OPERATES

Re-adjust for correct fast idle 650 rpm in drive range with A/C on, compressor disconnected.

TEST LIGHT ON → Check solenoid ground. If OK, replace solenoid.

TEST LIGHT OFF → Touch test light to pink/blk wire in 3-wire connector on fast idle relay (on dash panel).

TEST LIGHT OFF → Locate and repair open circuit in pink/blk wire from fast idle relay to splice in harness.

TEST LIGHT ON → Turn A/C off. Touch dark green wire in 3-wire connector at fast idle relay.

TEST LIGHT OFF → Check relay ground. If ok, replace relay.

TEST LIGHT ON → Repair open circuit in dk. grn. wire from relay to fast idle solenoid.

Fig. 9   Diesel engine electrical diagnosis, part 2 of 4. 1980—83 Type 2 exc. Cutlass

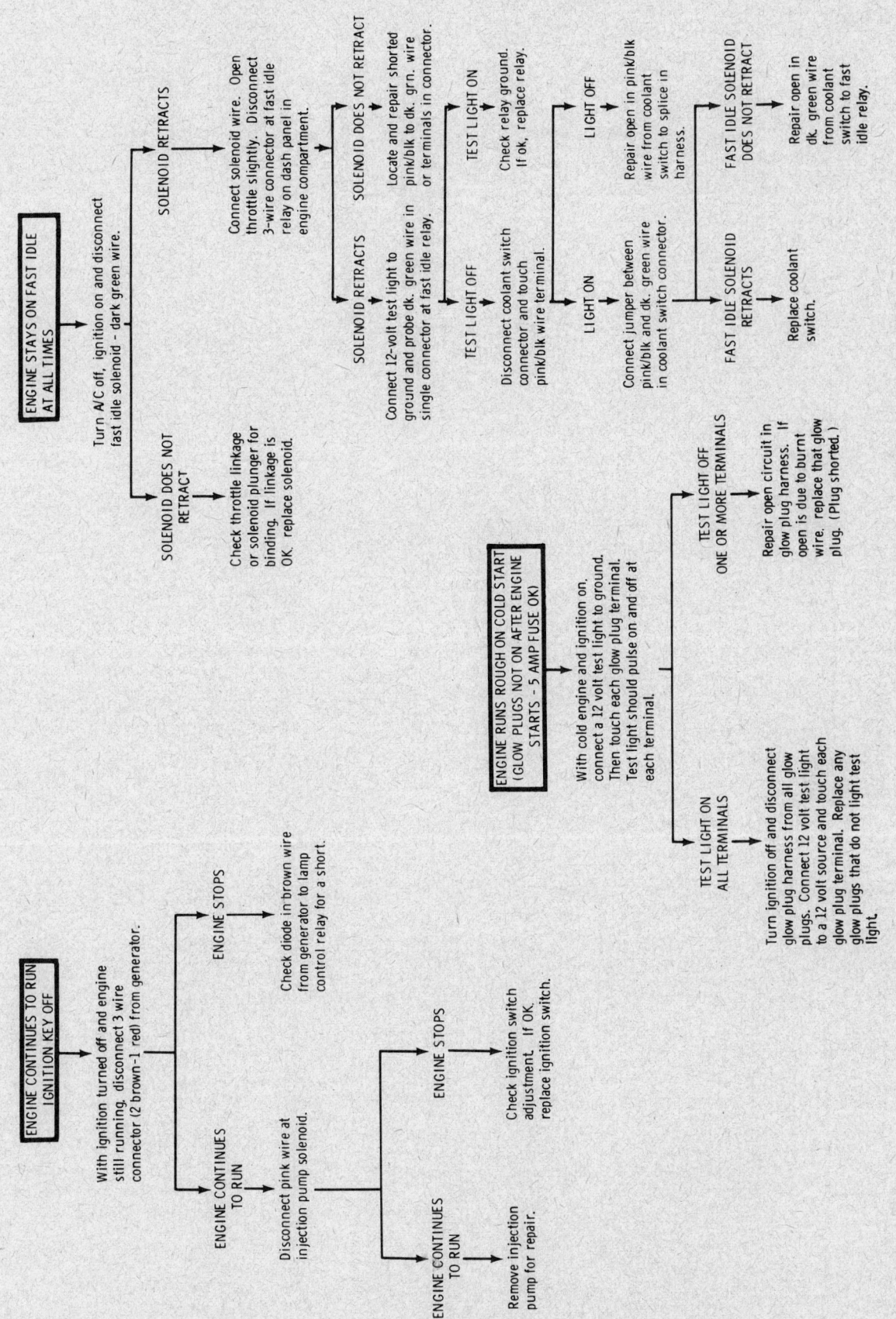

Fig. 9   Diesel engine electrical diagnosis, part 3 of 4. 1980–83 Type 2 exc. Cutlass

NORMAL OPERATION: Turn ignition to run. Wait light will come on while glow plugs are coming up to operating temperature. When glow plugs reach temperature the first time, the wait light will go out to indicate the engine is ready to start. No wait light with cold engine, or a continuous wait light after the engine starts are indications to the driver of a problem with the glow plug control systems. In many cases the engine may still be started cold, but the glow plug system should be repaired.

NO WAIT LIGHT - COLD ENGINE

With ignition on, disconnect connector with dk. blue wire at control relay and ground dk. blue wire terminal with a grounded jumper wire.

- WAIT LIGHT OFF → Check wait light bulb. If ok, locate and repair open circuit in dk. blu wire from control relay to wait light bulb.
- WAIT LIGHT ON → Replace control relay.

Use a 12 volt test light connected to ground except where instructed otherwise. Turn ignition on.

WAIT LIGHT STAYS ON AFTER ENGINE STARTS

NOTICE: USE VOLTMETER ONLY WHEN MAKING THIS TEST.

Connect voltmeter between white wire terminal at control relay and pink wire terminal at fast idle relay.

- BAT. VOLTAGE → Check for voltage at battery terminal of glow plug relay.
- 0 VOLTS → Connect voltmeter between the yellow and white wire terminal of the control relay.
  - BAT. VOLTAGE → Replace lamp control relay.
  - 0 VOLTS → Repair open in white wire to controller or yellow wire to glow plug relay.

Check for voltage at battery terminal of glow plug relay.

- BAT. VOLTAGE → Disconnect harness connector at controller. Connect voltmeter to 12 volt source and touch #4 terminal (orange) in connector.
- 0 VOLTS → Repair open circuit in wire from glow plug relay to battery.

Disconnect harness connector at controller. Connect voltmeter to 12 volt source and touch #4 terminal (orange) in connector.

- BAT. VOLTAGE → Touch voltmeter to yellow terminal at glow plug relay.
- 0 VOLTS → Check for open circuit in orange wire and/or fusible link. Repair or replace as required.

Touch voltmeter to yellow terminal at glow plug relay.

- LESS THAN BAT. VOLTAGE OR 0 VOLTS → Check yellow wire from glow plug relay to controller. If ok, replace controller.
- BAT. VOLTAGE → Check glow plug relay ground. If ok, replace relay.

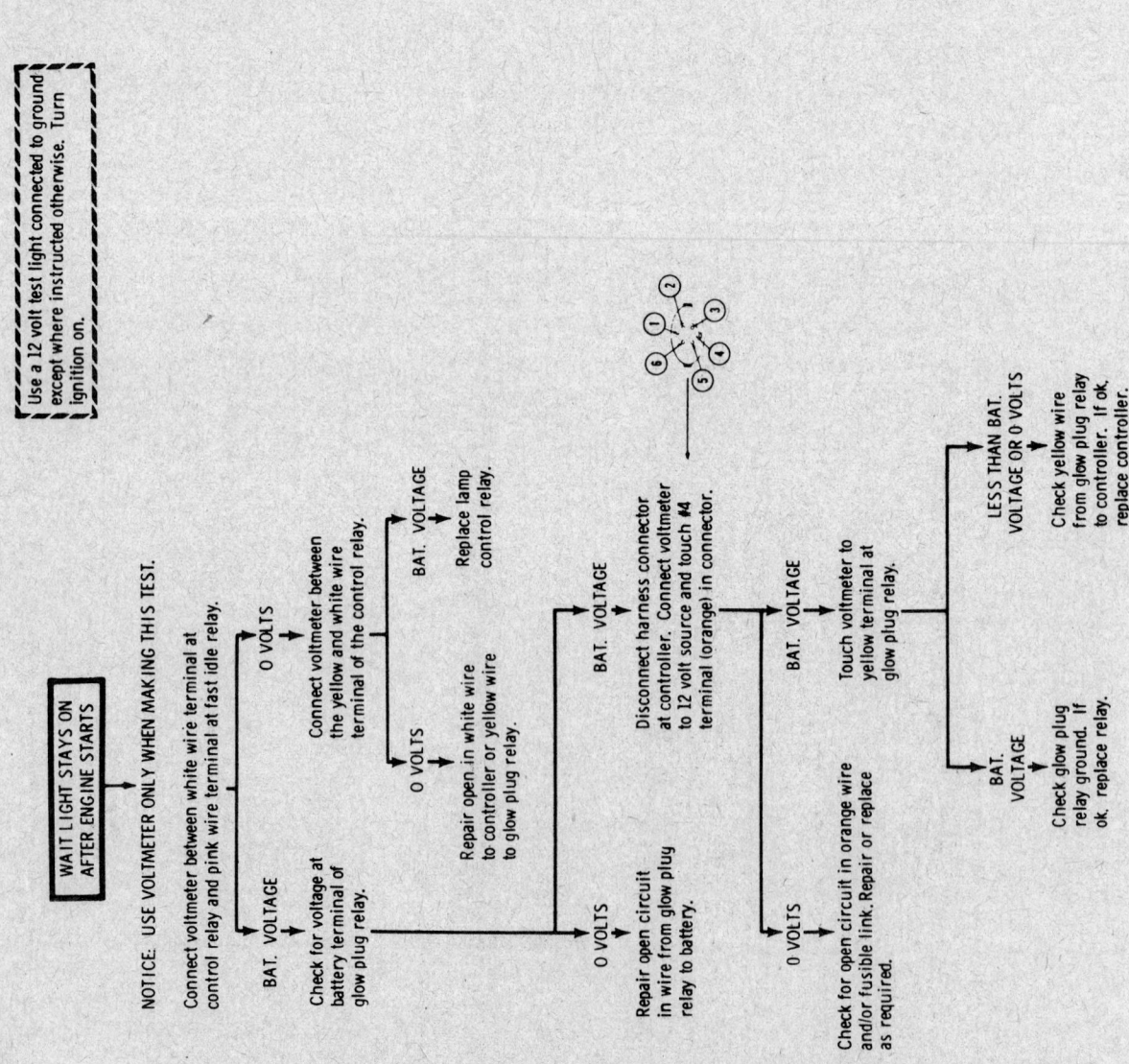

Fig. 9 Diesel engine electrical diagnosis, part 4 of 4. 1980–83 Type 2 exc. Cutlass

Fig. 10   Diesel engine electrical system. 1980–83 Cutlass with V8 engine

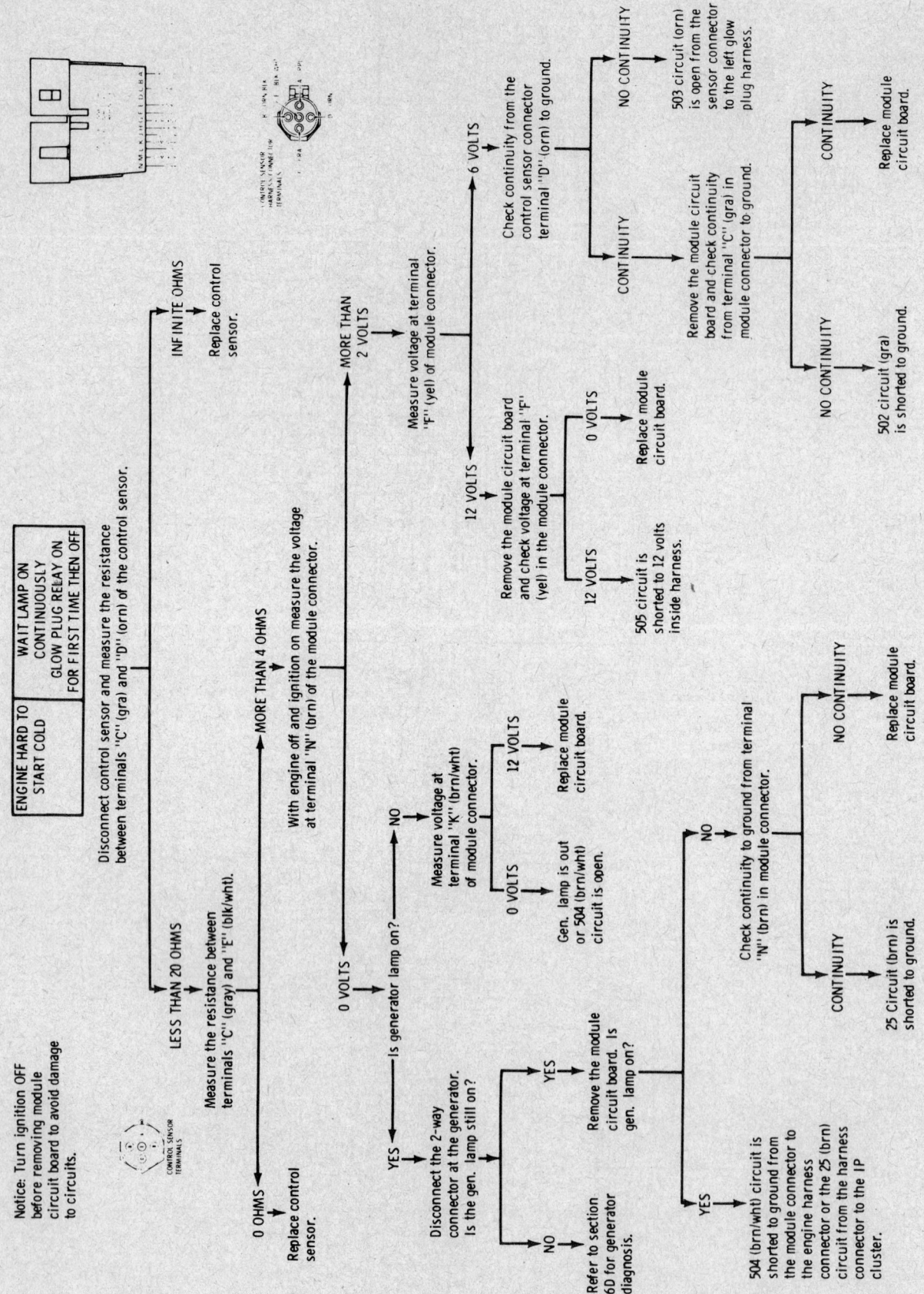

Fig. 11   Diesel engine electrical diagnosis, part 1 of 10. 1980–83 Cutlass with V8 engine

Fig. 11   Diesel engine electrical diagnosis, part 2 of 10. 1980–83 Cutlass with V8 engine

Fig. 11 Diesel engine electrical diagnosis, part 3 of 10. 1980—83 Cutlass with V8 engine

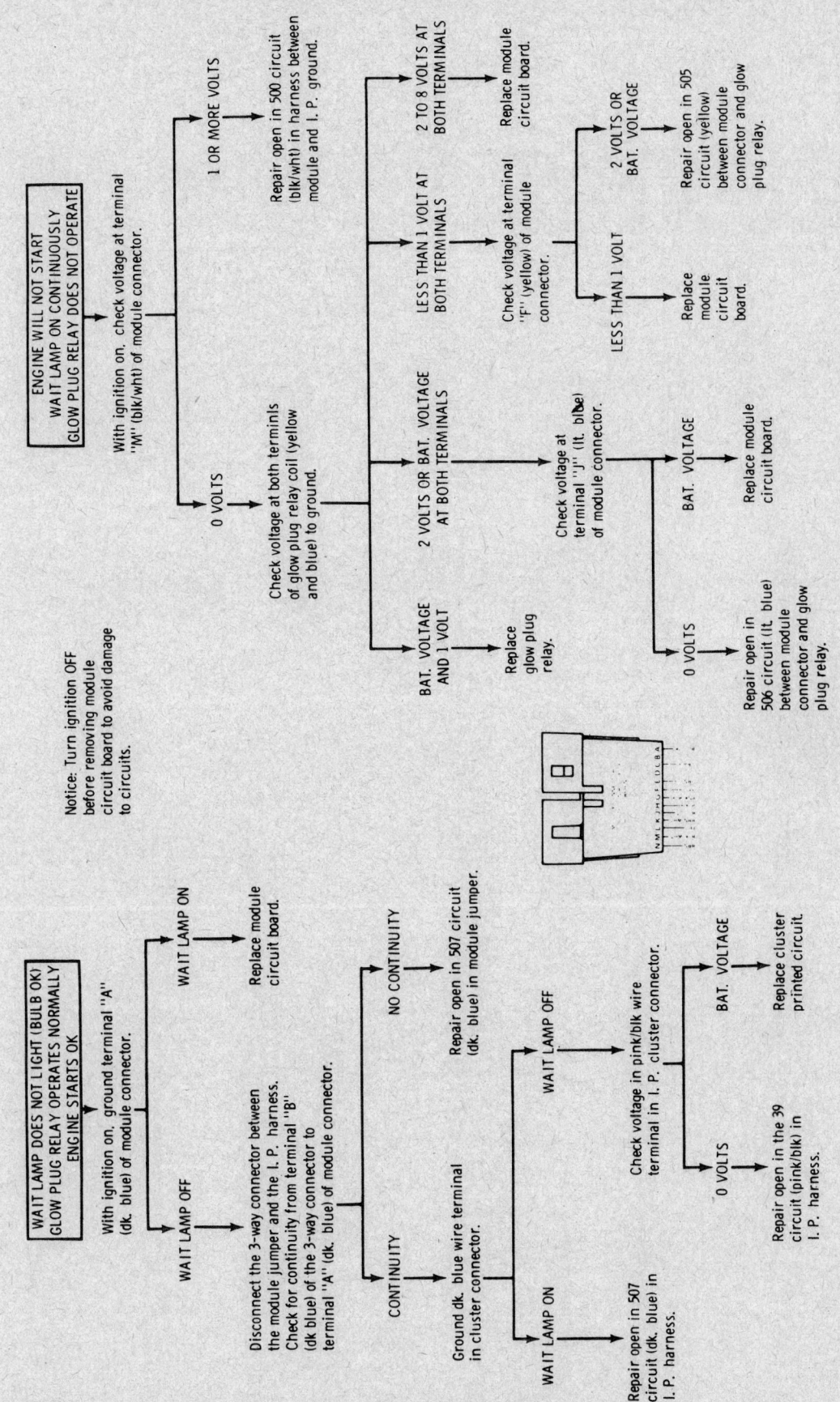

Fig. 11   **Diesel engine electrical diagnosis, part 4 of 10. 1980–83 Cutlass with V8 engine**

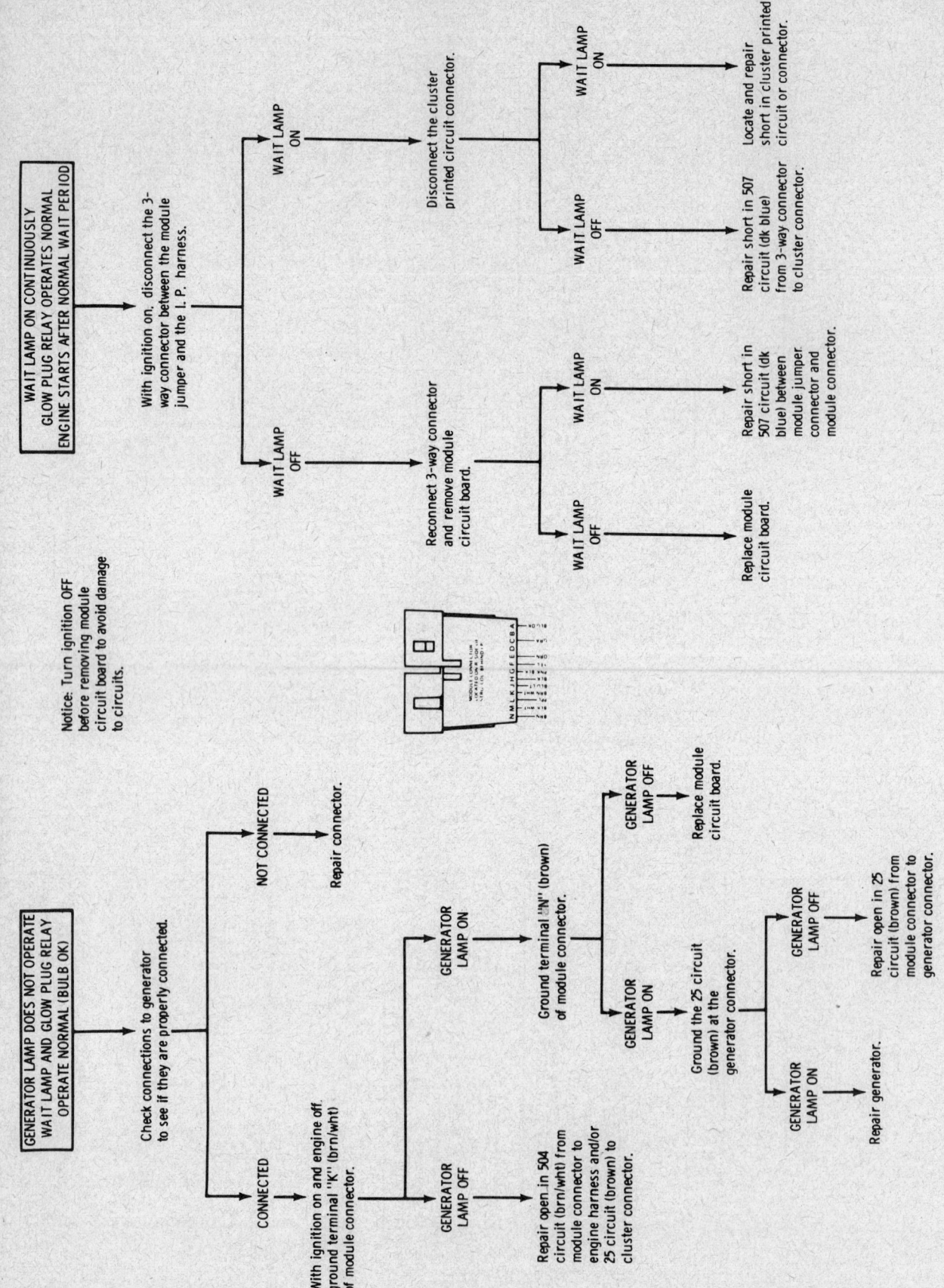

WAIT LAMP ON CONTINUOUSLY GLOW PLUG RELAY OPERATES NORMAL ENGINE STARTS AFTER NORMAL WAIT PERIOD

With ignition on, disconnect the 3-way connector between the module jumper and the I.P. harness.

WAIT LAMP ON → Disconnect the cluster printed circuit connector.

WAIT LAMP ON → Locate and repair short in cluster printed circuit or connector.

WAIT LAMP OFF → Repair short in 507 circuit (dk blue) from 3-way connector to cluster connector.

WAIT LAMP OFF → Reconnect 3-way connector and remove module circuit board.

WAIT LAMP ON → Repair short in 507 circuit (dk blue) between module jumper connector and module connector.

WAIT LAMP OFF → Replace module circuit board.

Notice: Turn ignition OFF before removing module circuit board to avoid damage to circuits.

GENERATOR LAMP DOES NOT OPERATE WAIT LAMP AND GLOW PLUG RELAY OPERATE NORMAL (BULB OK)

Check connections to generator to see if they are properly connected.

NOT CONNECTED → Repair connector.

CONNECTED → With ignition on and engine off, ground terminal "K" (brn/wht) of module connector.

GENERATOR LAMP ON → Ground terminal "N" (brown) of module connector.

GENERATOR LAMP OFF → Repair open in 504 circuit (brn/wht) from module connector to engine harness and/or 25 circuit (brown) to cluster connector.

GENERATOR LAMP OFF → Replace module circuit board.

GENERATOR LAMP ON → Ground the 25 circuit (brown) at the generator connector.

GENERATOR LAMP OFF → Repair open in 25 circuit (brown) from module connector to generator connector.

GENERATOR LAMP ON → Repair generator.

Fig. 11   Diesel engine electrical diagnosis, part 5 of 10. 1980–83 Cutlass with V8 engine

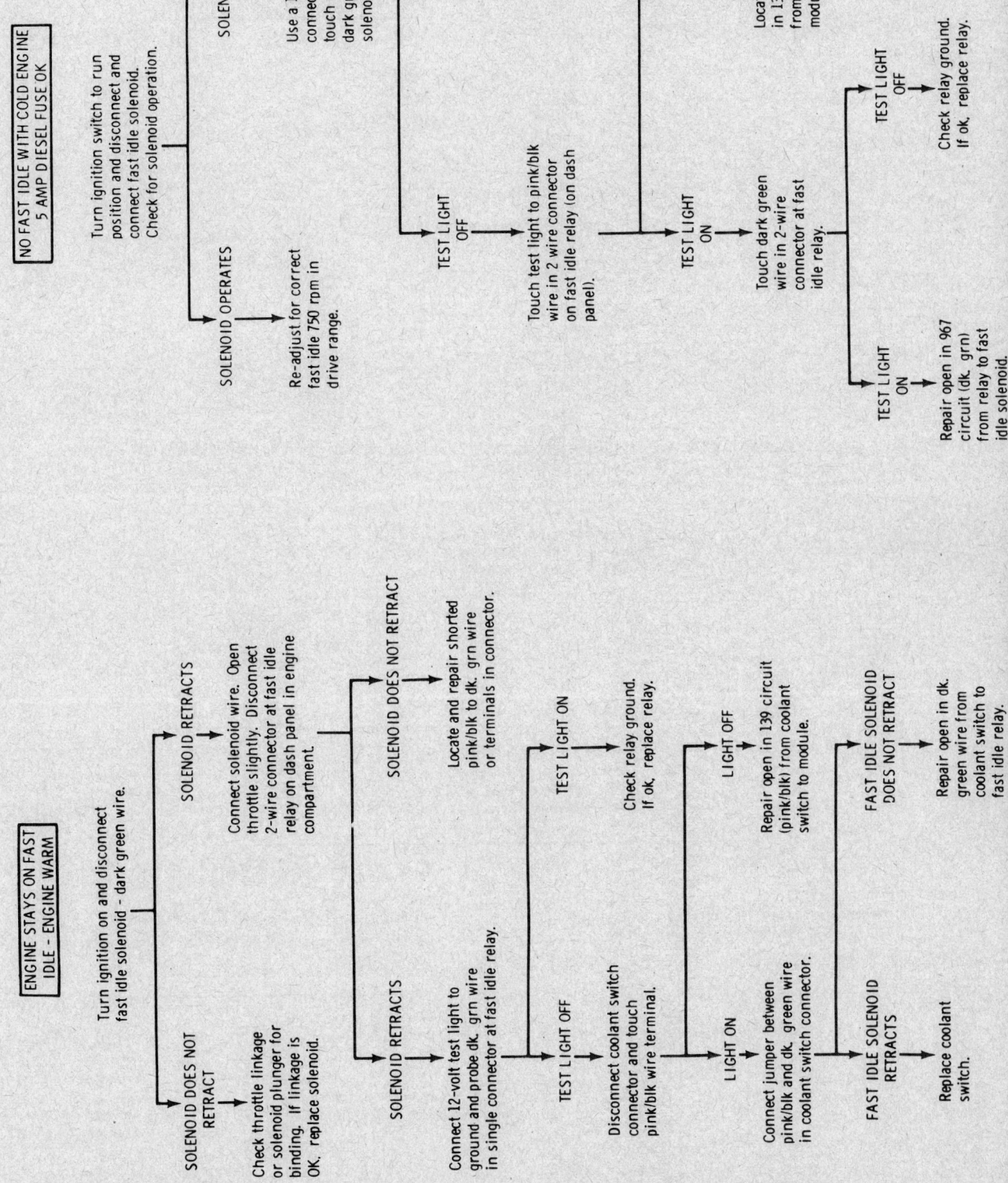

Fig. 11   Diesel engine electrical diagnosis, part 6 of 10. 1980—83 Cutlass with V8 engine

GLOW PLUG RELAY BUZZING

Notice: Turn ignition OFF before removing module circuit board to avoid damage to circuits.

WAIT LAMP AND GLOW PLUG RELAY NORMAL, CAR WON'T START

Disconnect the 3-way connector between control sensor harness and module jumper harness. Check for continuity between terminal "E" (orange) of module connector and terminal "C" (orange) of jumper connector.

Disconnect connector from each glow plug and check continuity to ground from glow plug terminal.

CONTINUITY — Replace module circuit board.

NO CONTINUITY — Repair open in 503 circuit (orange) between module connector and jumper connector.

NO CONTINUITY — Replace bad glow plugs.

CONTINUITY — Measure continuity from glow plug relay output to each glow plug connector.

CONTINUITY — Check fuel system.

NO CONTINUITY — Repair or replace glow plug harness.

NMLKJHGFEDCBA

Fig. 11 Diesel engine electrical diagnosis, part 7 of 10. 1980–83 Cutlass with V8 engine

ENGINE STAYS ON FAST IDLE ENGINE WARM - A/C OFF

MAKE ALL CHECKS WITH AIR CONDITIONING OFF

With engine warm, turn ignition switch to run position. With 12V test light connected to ground, probe fast idle solenoid wire at solenoid.

TEST LIGHT OFF — Check and make idle and fast idle adjustments as necessary. (Refer to emission label.) If fast idle solenoid will not adjust properly, replace solenoid.

TEST LIGHT ON — Use a 12V test light connected to ground and probe the dark green wire (967) at the fast idle relay. Ignition switch in run.

TEST LIGHT ON — With one test light lead grounded, probe lt. grn/blk (936) wire at fast idle relay. Ignition switch in run.

TEST LIGHT OFF — Check for short in dark grn. Wire (967) from fast idle solenoid to fast idle relay.

TEST LIGHT OFF — With one test light lead grounded, probe lt. green wire (66) at fast idle relay. Ignition switch in run.

TEST LIGHT ON — With one test light lead grounded, probe lt. green/blk wire (139) at engine temperature switch (left rear head bolt). Ignition in run.

TEST LIGHT OFF — Replace fast idle relay.

TEST LIGHT ON — Check to make sure air conditioning is in off. If off, refer to air conditioning electrical schematics. Lt. green wire (66) has voltage applied only with A/C on.

TEST LIGHT OFF — Check for short in lt. green/blk wire (936) between engine temperature switch and fast idle relay.

TEST LIGHT ON — Check terminals of engine temperature switch for shorted connection. If OK, replace engine temperature switch.

Fig. 11 Diesel engine electrical diagnosis, part 8 of 10. 1982–83 Cutlass V6 engine

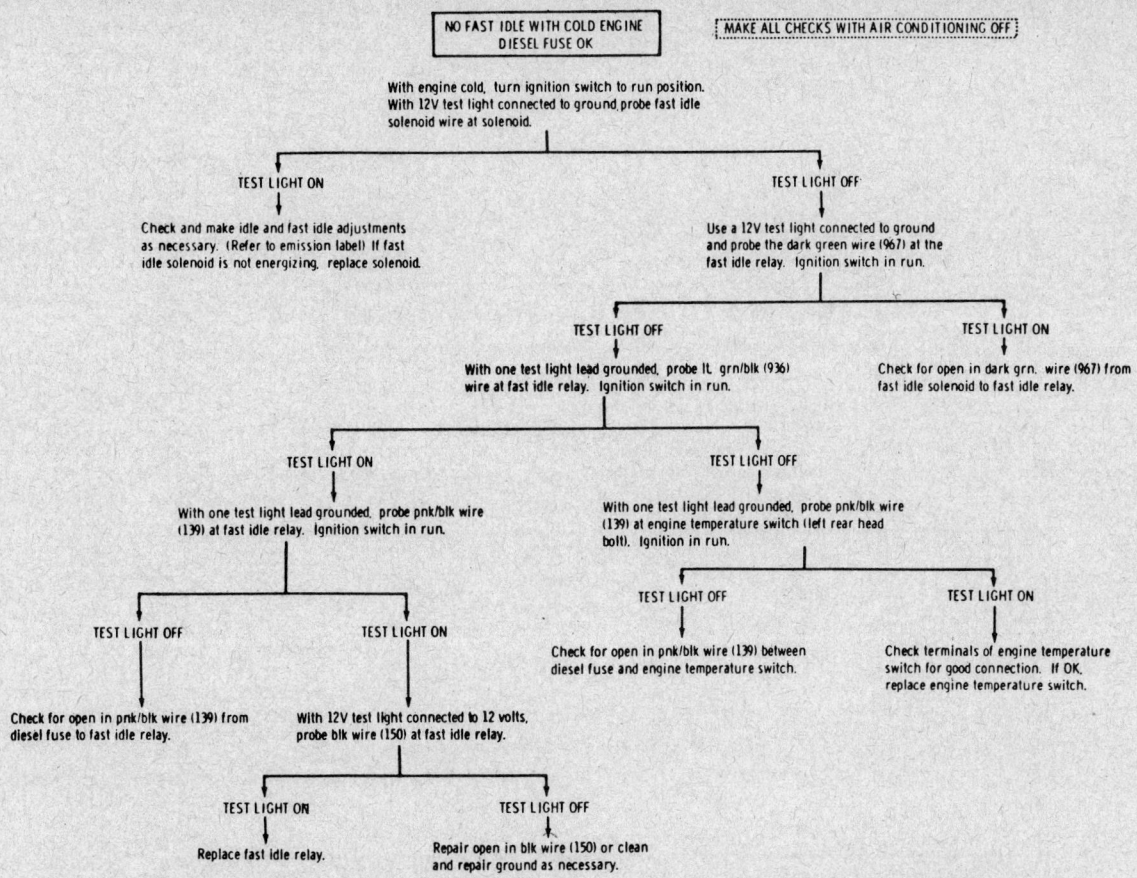

Fig. 11 Diesel engine electrical diagnosis, part 9 of 10. 1982–83 Cutlass V6 engine

Fig. 11 Diesel engine electrical diagnosis, part 10 of 10. 1982–83 Cutlass V6 engine

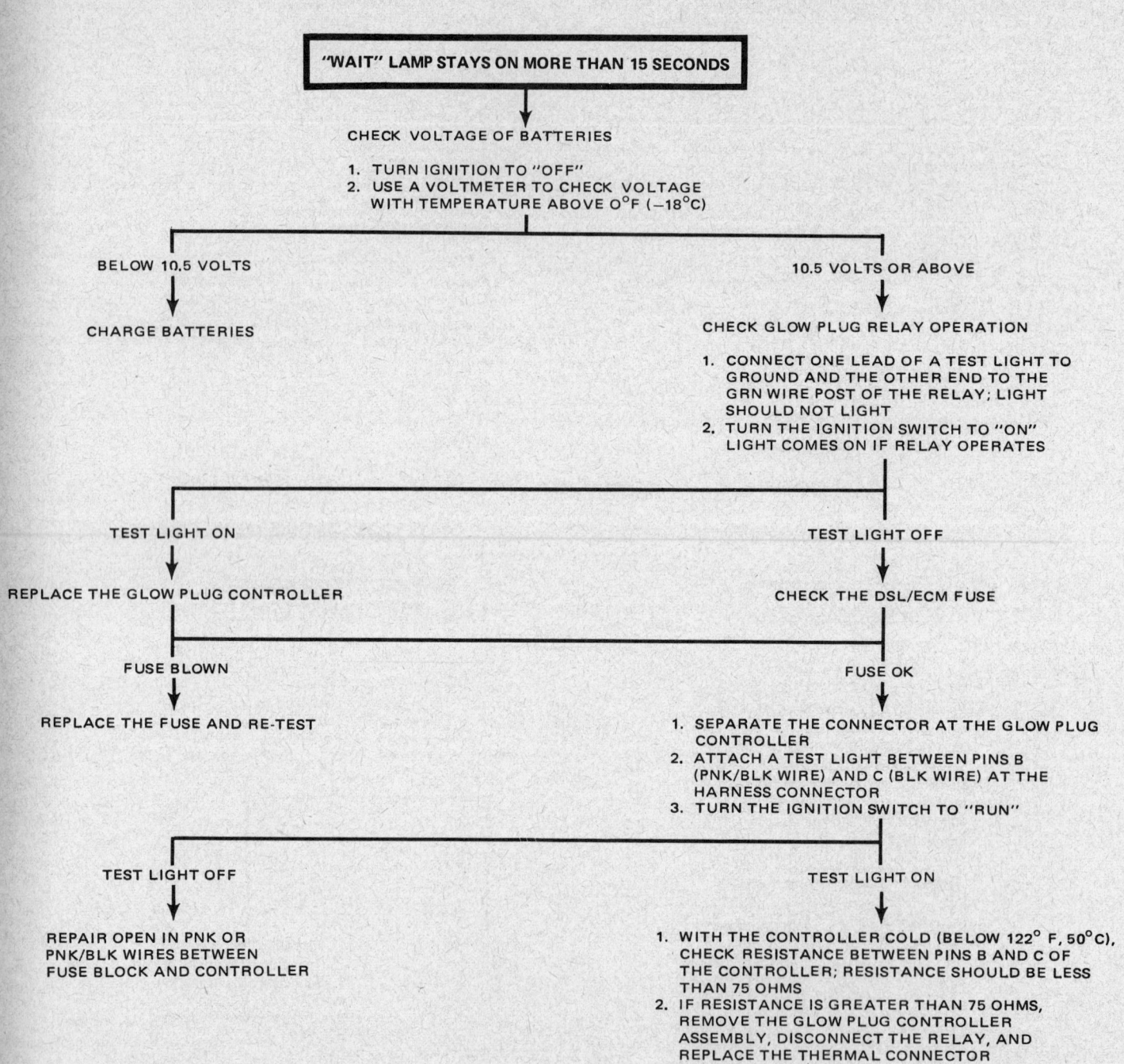

"WAIT" LAMP STAYS ON MORE THAN 15 SECONDS

CHECK VOLTAGE OF BATTERIES

1. TURN IGNITION TO "OFF"
2. USE A VOLTMETER TO CHECK VOLTAGE
   WITH TEMPERATURE ABOVE 0°F (−18°C)

BELOW 10.5 VOLTS

CHARGE BATTERIES

10.5 VOLTS OR ABOVE

CHECK GLOW PLUG RELAY OPERATION

1. CONNECT ONE LEAD OF A TEST LIGHT TO
   GROUND AND THE OTHER END TO THE
   GRN WIRE POST OF THE RELAY; LIGHT
   SHOULD NOT LIGHT
2. TURN THE IGNITION SWITCH TO "ON"
   LIGHT COMES ON IF RELAY OPERATES

TEST LIGHT ON

REPLACE THE GLOW PLUG CONTROLLER

TEST LIGHT OFF

CHECK THE DSL/ECM FUSE

FUSE BLOWN

REPLACE THE FUSE AND RE-TEST

FUSE OK

1. SEPARATE THE CONNECTOR AT THE GLOW PLUG
   CONTROLLER
2. ATTACH A TEST LIGHT BETWEEN PINS B
   (PNK/BLK WIRE) AND C (BLK WIRE) AT THE
   HARNESS CONNECTOR
3. TURN THE IGNITION SWITCH TO "RUN"

TEST LIGHT OFF

REPAIR OPEN IN PNK OR
PNK/BLK WIRES BETWEEN
FUSE BLOCK AND CONTROLLER

TEST LIGHT ON

1. WITH THE CONTROLLER COLD (BELOW 122° F, 50°C),
   CHECK RESISTANCE BETWEEN PINS B AND C OF
   THE CONTROLLER; RESISTANCE SHOULD BE LESS
   THAN 75 OHMS
2. IF RESISTANCE IS GREATER THAN 75 OHMS,
   REMOVE THE GLOW PLUG CONTROLLER
   ASSEMBLY, DISCONNECT THE RELAY, AND
   REPLACE THE THERMAL CONNECTOR

Fig. 12   Diesel engine electrical diagnosis, part 1 of 3. 1984

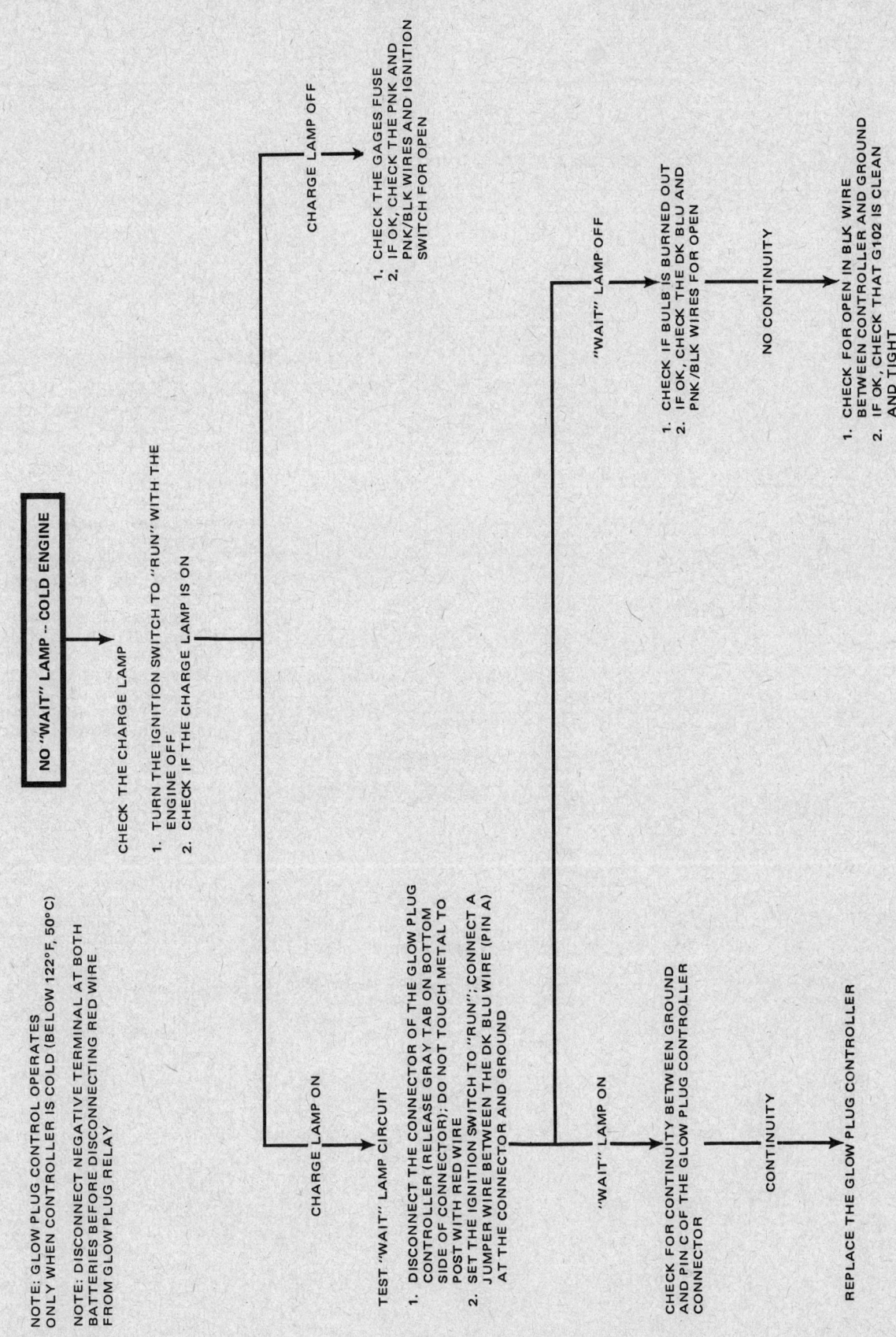

Fig. 12   Diesel engine electrical diagnosis, part 2 of 3. 1984

Fig. 12   Diesel engine electrical diagnosis, part 3 of 3. 1984

Fig. 13   Water In Fuel System wiring circuit

2. Check for short circuit in wire between the "Water In Fuel" connection at the fuel tank and the dash indicator lamp, **Fig. 13.**

ENGINE MOUNTS

Refer to **Figs. 16 through 19** for engine mount installation.

ENGINE
REPLACE

EXC. TORONADO

1. Disconnect ground cable from batteries and drain cooling system.

2. Remove air cleaner.
3. Scribe hood hinge locations and remove hood.
4. Disconnect ground wires at inner fender and the engine ground strap at right cylinder head.
5. Disconnect radiator hoses, oil cooler lines, heater hoses, vacuum hoses, power steering hoses from gear, A/C compressor with brackets and hoses attached, fuel pump hose from fuel pump and the wiring.
6. Remove hairpin clip from bellcrank, on all except 6 cylinder engine.
7. Remove throttle and throttle valve cables from intake manifold brackets and position cables aside.
8. Remove upper radiator support and the radiator on all except 6 cylinder engine.
9. Raise and support vehicle.
10. Disconnect exhaust pipes from exhaust manifold.
11. Remove torque converter cover and the three bolts securing torque converter to flywheel.
12. Remove engine mount bolts or nuts.
13. Remove three engine to transmission bolts on the right side.
14. Disconnect starter wiring and remove starter.
15. Lower vehicle.
16. Attach suitable engine lifting equipment to engine. Support transmission with a suitable jack.

Fig. 14   Water in Fuel System fuel level sender & water detector

Fig. 15   Checking water detector operation

Fig. 16   Diesel engine mount. 88, 98 & Custom Cruiser

Fig. 17   Diesel engine mount. Cutlass w/V8 engine

17. Remove the three engine to transmission bolts on the left side.
18. Remove engine from vehicle.
19. Reverse procedure to install.

TORONADO

1. Disconnect battery ground cable and drain cooling system.
2. Remove radiator upper support.
3. Remove air cleaner assembly.
4. Scribe hood hinge locations and remove hood.
5. Disconnect engine ground strap.
6. Disconnect upper and lower radiator hoses from engine.
7. Disconnect transmission oil cooler lines from radiator.
8. Disconnect heater hoses from water pump and water control valve.
9. Remove radiator, fan and the shroud.
10. Disconnect power steering pump bracket from engine and position aside without disconnecting lines.
11. Disconnect A/C compressor bracket from engine and position aside without disconnecting lines.
12. Disconnect fuel lines.
13. Disconnect throttle cable, vacuum hoses and electrical connections.
14. Disconnect left hand exhaust pipe from manifold.
15. On left side of engine, remove through bolt and bracket securing final drive to engine.
16. Raise and support vehicle.
17. Remove flywheel shield.
18. Disconnect right hand exhaust pipe from manifold.
19. Disconnect starter motor wiring and remove starter motor.
20. Remove converter to flywheel bolts. Mark location of converter on flywheel for alignment during installation.
21. Remove splash shield.
22. Remove engine front mounting attaching nuts.
23. Remove two bolts securing right hand output shaft support brackets. Using a sharp tool, scribe a mark around the washers as far as possible. Use these scribe marks to position bracket upon installation.
24. Remove lower right hand transmission to engine attaching bolts. One bolt retains the modulator line clip.
25. Use a suitable length of chain to retain final drive in vehicle.
26. Lower vehicle and attaching suitable engine lifting equipment to engine.
27. Remove the remaining transmission to engine bolts. It may be necessary to raise or lower transmission with a suitable jack to facilitate bolt removal.
28. Raise engine and remove from vehicle.
29. Reverse procedure to install.

INTAKE MANIFOLD
REPLACE

V8 ENGINE

1. Disconnect ground cables from batteries.

MOUNTING ASSEMBLY TAB MUST BE INSTALLED INTO SLOT IN RESTRICTOR.

LOCK PLATE

R. H. ENGINE MOUNTING BRACKET

RESTRICTOR

61 N·m ★ (45 FT. LBS.)

APPLY 1051343 LOC-TITE #242 OR EQUIVALENT TO THESE BOLTS

47 N·m ★ (35 FT. LBS.)

STEERING PUMP BRACKET

70 N·m (51 FT. LBS.)

60 N·m (44 FT. LBS.)

L. H. ENGINE MOUNTING BRACKET

61 N·m ★ (45 FT. LBS.)

ENGINE MOUNTING ASSEMBLY

POSITIONING TAB ON MOUNTING ASSEMBLY MUST BE INSTALLED INTO HOLE/SLOT LOCATED ON FRAME ASSEMBLY

100 N·m (74 FT. LBS.)

FRAME

FRONT OF CAR   ENGINE MOUNTS

Fig. 18   Diesel engine mount. 1980 Toronado. 1981-85 Toronado similar

2. Remove air cleaner assembly.
3. Drain cooling system, then disconnect upper radiator hose and thermostat bypass hose from water pump outlet. Disconnect heater hose and vacuum hose from water control valve.
4. Remove breather pipes from valve covers and air crossover, **Fig. 20.**
5. Remove air crossover and cap intake manifold, **Fig. 21.**
6. Disconnect throttle rod and return spring. If equipped with Cruise Control, remove servo.
7. Remove hairpin clip from bellcrank and disconnect the cables. Remove throttle and throttle valve cables from intake manifold brackets and position cables aside.
8. Disconnect wiring as necessary.

9. Disconnect or remove alternator and A/C compressor brackets as necessary.
10. Disconnect fuel line from fuel pump and filter and remove fuel filter and bracket.
11. Disconnect lines from injector nozzles and remove injection pump, refer to "Injection Nozzle Replace, Injection Pump & Lines". Cap all open fuel line lines and fittings.
12. Disconnect fuel return line from injection pump.

13. Disconnect vacuum lines at vacuum pump. Remove vacuum pump, if equipped with A/C, or oil pump drive assembly, if less A/C, **Fig. 22.**
14. Remove intake manifold drain tube, **Fig. 23.**
15. Remove intake manifold bolts and the intake manifold.
16. Remove adapter seal and injection pump adapter.
17. Reverse procedure to install. Torque intake manifold bolts in sequence, **Fig. 24,** to specifications.

BREATHER CAP AND VALVE ASSY.

FLOW CONTROL VALVE

VENT PIPE TO NIPPLE CONNECTOR

VENTILATION PIPE

VENTILATION ELBOW

VENTILATION FILTER ASSEMBLY

75 N·m (55 FT. LBS.)

52 N·m 38 FT. LBS.

FRONT MOUNT

BRACKET

WASHER

50 N·m (37 FT. LBS.)

Fig. 19   Motor mounts. 1982-84 Cutlass V6 engine

Fig. 20   Crankcase ventilation system. V8 engine

Fig. 21 Air crossover installation. Typical

Fig. 24 Intake manifold tightening sequence. V8 engine

Fig. 27 Intake manifold bolt tightening sequence. V6 engine

V6 ENGINE

1. Disconnect battery ground cable and remove air cleaner.
2. Drain cooling system, then disconnect upper radiator hose and thermostat bypass hose from water outlet.
3. Disconnect heater inlet hose and on models equipped with air conditioning, the water valve vacuum line.

Fig. 22 Vacuum pump & oil pump drive assembly

Fig. 25 Crankcase ventilation system. V6 engine

4. Disconnect crankcase ventilation pipe from air crossover, **Fig. 25.** Remove air crossover.
5. Remove fuel pump and plug all open lines and fittings.
6. Remove fuel injection pump as described under "Injection Pump, Replace".
7. Disconnect electrical connectors as necessary.
8. Remove cruise control servo, if equipped.
9. Disconnect fuel lines and position aside. Disconnect vacuum lines as necessary.
10. Remove drain tube, then remove intermediate pump adapter, **Fig. 26.**
11. Remove intake manifold bolts and the intake manifold.
12. Reverse procedure to install. Lubricate intake manifold bolts with engine oil before installing, then torque bolts as specified in sequence shown in **Fig. 27.** Apply chassis grease to seal area of intake manifold and pump adapter and to inside and outside diameter of seal and seal area of tool J-28425 or equivalent. Install seal onto tool, then install seal.

Fig. 23 Intake manifold drain tube installation

Fig. 26 Removing intermediate pump adapter. V6 engine

Fig. 28 Cylinder head bolt markings

CYLINDER HEAD
REPLACE

SERVICE NOTE:

V8-350

New head bolts with increased torque capacity were introduced into production during March 1980 and are now available, **Fig. 28.**

When replacing a cylinder head, it is recommended new head bolts be used if they have not already been installed in the engine. When installing later production model head bolts, be sure to clean and oil the threads. Before installation of the cylinder head, ensure bolt holes are tapped deep enough into the block. Blow out any chips or liquid in the bolt holes. Then position cylinder head on cylinder block without the cylinder head gasket. Install bolt and tighten by hand until bolt head contacts the cylinder head. This will indicate that the holes are tapped deep enough into the block, allowing for proper torque. For cylinder head bolt location, part number and size, refer to **Fig. 29.**

New design head gaskets are available for service and will supersede previous gaskets used on V8-350 diesel engines.

LOCATION NUMBER		PART NUMBER	SIZE
1		22510580	1/2 - 13 x 3.10
2		22510582	1/2-13 x 3.10 stud end
3		22510579	1/2 - 13 x 4.30
4		22510585	1/2 - 13 x 4.30 stud end

Fig. 29 Pre-chamber installation

Fig. 30 Cylinder head bolt identification

Fig. 31 Cylinder head tightening sequence. V8 engine

TORQUE ALL BOLTS (EXCEPT 5, 6, 11, 12, 13 & 14) TO 193 N·m (142 FT. LBS.). NUMBERS 5, 6, 11, 12, 13 & 14 TORQUE TO 80 N·m (59 FT. LBS.).

Fig. 32 Cylinder head bolt tightening sequence. V6 engine

Fig. 33 Cylinder head exploded view

Fig. 34 Type 1 rocker arm pivot. 1980–83 V8-350 diesel

These gaskets are the same gaskets recommended for use on engines using .030 inch oversize pistons and will now be used for all applications. The use of these gaskets on standard engines should prevent loss of compression due to the gasket sealing ring falling into the combustion chamber. On 1980 and 1983 engines, use new gasket, Part No. 22519416. This gasket is evident by the grey seal located on the gasket face. On 1981–82 engines, use new gasket, Part No. 22510719, evident by the purple seal on the gasket face. No gasket sealer should be used on either gasket during installation.

When servicing cylinder head, ensure that prechambers are not recessed into cylinder head or protrude out of cylinder head more than .004 inch, since head gasket leakage may result. Measure the difference between flat or prechamber and the flat surface of cylinder head at two or more points around circumference of prechamber, using a straight edge and feeler gauge. If prechamber is recessed more than specified, replace prechamber or cylinder head, depending on which is at fault. If prechamber protrudes more than specified, grind top of prechamber for a flush fit, or replace as necessary.

1. Remove intake manifold as outlined previously.
2. Remove valve cover. It may be necessary to remove any interfering accessory brackets.

3. Disconnect glow plug wiring.
4. Remove ground strap from right cylinder head, if removing.
5. Remove rocker arm bolts, pivots, rocker arms and push rod. Note locations of valve train components so they can be installed in original locations.
6. Remove fuel return lines from injection nozzles if equipped.
7. Remove exhaust manifold.
8. Remove engine block drain plug on side of block that cylinder head is being removed.
9. Remove cylinder head bolts and cylinder head. On 1982 V8 diesel remove TCC temperature switch located on exposed right rear cylinder head bolt.
10. If necessary to remove pre-chamber, remove a glow plug or injection nozzle, then tap out pre-chamber with a suitable drift, **Fig. 30.**
11. Reverse procedure to install. Do not use any sealing compound on cylinder head gasket. On 8 cylinder engines, torque cylinder head bolts in sequence, **Fig. 31,** to 100 ft. lbs., then to 130 ft. lbs. On 6 cylinder engines, torque cylinder head bolts except bolts 5, 6, 11, 12, 13 and 14, **Fig. 32,** to 142 ft. lbs. Torque bolts 5, 6, 11, 12, 13 and 14 to 59 ft. lbs.

ROCKER ARMS

NOTE: This engine uses valve rotators, **Fig. 33.** The rotator operates on a sprag clutch principle utilizing the collapsing action of a coil spring to give rotation to the rotor body which turns the valve.

SERVICE NOTE: Some 1980–83 V8-350 diesel engines may experience valve train ticking noise and/or exhaust backfire. This condition may be caused by premature wear of the rocker arm pivots. Two types of rocker arm pivots were used on these engines. Type 1 pivot assemblies, **Fig. 34,** are the only ones showing premature wear. It is therefore recommended that only Type 2 pivot assemblies, **Fig. 35,** be used when servicing the engine for the above mentioned condition.

1. Remove valve cover.
2. Remove flanged bolts, rocker arm pivot and rocker arms, **Fig. 33.**
3. When installing rocker arm assemblies, lubricate wear surfaces with suitable lubricant. Torque flanged bolts to 25 ft. lbs. On 8 cylinder engines or 28 ft. lbs. on 6 cylinder engines.

VALVE ROTATORS

The rotator operates on a sprag clutch principle utilizing the collapsing action of coil spring to give rotation to the rotor body which turns the valve, **Fig. 33.**

To check rotator action, draw a line across rotator body and down the collar. Operate engine at 1500 rpm, rotator body should move around collar. Rotator action can be in either direction. Replace rotator if no movement is noted.

Fig. 35 Type 2 rocker arm pivot. 1980—83 V8-350 diesel

Fig. 36 Checking valve stem for rotator malfunction

Fig. 37 Measuring valve stem height

Fig. 38 Measuring valve rotator height

When servicing valves, valve stem tips should be checked for improper wear pattern which could indicate a defective valve rotator, **Fig. 36.**

VALVE LIFT SPECS.

Engine	Year	Intake	Exhaust
V8-260, 350 Diesel	1980–85	.375	.376
V6-262 Diesel	1982–84	.375	.375

VALVE ARRANGEMENT

V8-260, 350 Diesel . . . . I-E-I-E-I-E-I
V6-262 Diesel . . . . I-E-E-I-E-I

VALVE TIMING

INTAKE OPENS BEFORE TDC

Engine	Year	Degrees
V8-260, 350 Diesel	1980–85	16
V6-262 Diesel	1982–84	16

VALVES

Whenever a new valve is installed or after grinding valves, it is necessary to measure the valve stem height with the special tool as shown in **Fig. 37.**

There should be at least .015 inch clearance between the gauge and end of valve stem. If clearance is less than .015 inch, remove valve and grind end of valve stem as required.

Check valve rotator height, **Fig. 38.** If valve stem end is less than .005 inch above rotator, the valve is too short and a new valve must be installed.

VALVE GUIDES

Valve stem guides are not replaceable, due to being cast in place. If valve guide bores are worn excessively, they can be reamed oversize.

If a standard valve guide bore is being reamed, use a .003 inch or .005 inch oversize reamer. For the .010 inch oversize valve guide bore, use a .013 inch oversize reamer. If too large a reamer is used and the spiraling is removed, it is possible that the valve will not receive the proper lubrication.

NOTE: Occasionally a valve guide will be oversize as manufactured. These are marked on the cylinder head as shown in **Fig. 39.** If no markings are present, the guide bores are standard. If oversize markings are present, any valve replacement will require an oversize valve. Service valves are available in standard diameters as well as .003 inch, .005 inch, .010 inch and .013 inch oversize.

VALVE LIFTERS
REPLACE

NOTE: Some engines have both standard and .010 inch oversize valve lifters. The .010 inch oversize valve lifters are etched with a "0" on the side of the lifter. Also, the cylinder block will be marked if an oversize lifter is used, **Fig. 40.**

1. Remove intake manifold as outlined previously.
2. Remove valve covers, rocker arm assemblies and push rods. Note location of valve train components so they can be installed in original position.
3. On 1981–85 models, remove the hydraulic lifter retainer bolts, **Fig. 41.**
4. Remove valve lifters.
5. Reverse procedure to install.

NOTE: Plungers are not interchangeable because they are selectively fitted to the bodies at the factory.

Fig. 39 Valve guide bore marking

Fig. 40 Oversize valve lifter bore marking

Fig. 41 Hydraulic roller lifter retainer and guide. 1981–85 (Typical)

Fig. 42 Valve lifter exploded view. 1980

Fig. 43 Hydraulic roller lifter assembly exploded view. 1981–85

Fig. 44 Front oil seal removal

VALVE LIFTERS
SERVICE

1. Remove valve lifters, refer to "Valve Lifters, Replace."
2. Using a small screwdriver, remove retainer ring, **Figs. 42 and 43.**
3. Remove pushrod seat, oil metering valve, plunger, and plunger spring.
4. Remove check ball retainer from plunger, then remove ball and spring.
5. Clean parts in a suitable solvent.

NOTE: Do not interchange parts between lifters. If any parts are worn, replace lifter.

6. Inspect all parts for nicks, burrs or scoring. If any parts are defective, replace lifter.
7. On 1981–85 roller lifters, inspect roller. It should rotate freely, but without excessive play, also check for missing or broken needle bearing. If any parts are defective, replace lifter.
8. Apply a coating of light engine oil to all lifter surfaces.
9. Install ball check spring and retainer into plunger. Ensure retainer flange is pressed tight against bottom of recess in plunger.
10. Install plunger spring over check retainer.
11. Hold plunger with spring up and insert in lifter body. Hold plunger vertically to prevent cocking spring.
12. Submerge lifter assembly in clean diesel fuel or kerosene, then install oil metering valve and push rod seat into lifter and install retaining ring.

VALVE LIFTER BLEED DOWN

If the intake manifold has been removed and if any rocker arms have been removed or loosened, it will be necessary to remove those lifters, disassemble them, drain the oil from them and reassemble. Refer to "Valve Lifters, Service."

If the intake manifold has not been removed, but rocker arms have been loosened or removed, the valve lifters must be bled down to prevent possible valve to piston interference by using the following procedure:

1. Prior to installing rocker arms, rotate crankshaft pulley to a position 32° BTDC (before top dead center). This is approximately 2 inches counterclockwise from 0° pointer.
2. If the right side valve cover was removed only, remove cylinder No. 1 glow plug and determine if No. 1 piston is in the correct position, this can be determined by compression pressure.
3. If the left side valve cover was removed only, rotate crankshaft until No. 5 cylinder intake valve push rod is .28 inch above the No. 5 cylinder exhaust valve push rod.
4. If removed, install cylinder No. 5 pivot and rocker arms. Alternately torque the bolts until the intake valve begins to open and stop tightening.

NOTE: When torquing rocker arms, use only hand wrenches to prevent engine damage.

5. Install remaining rocker arms except No. 3 exhaust valve. Torque bolt to 25 ft. lbs. on 1980 models and 28 ft. lbs. on 1981–85.
6. If removed, install No. 3 exhaust rocker arm and pivot, but do not torque beyond the point that the valve would be fully opened. This is indicated by a strong resistance while turning the pivot retaining bolt. Going beyond this point would bend the push rod.

NOTE: While performing step 6, torque bolt slowly allowing the lifter to bleed down.

7. Finish torquing No. 5 rocker arm pivot bolt slowly, allowing valve lifter to bleed down. Do not torque beyond the point that the valve would be fully opened. This is indicated by a strong resistance while turning the pivot retaining bolt. Going beyond this point would bend the push rod.
8. Do not turn the crankshaft for at least 45 minutes while lifters bleed down.

NOTE: Do not rotate the engine until the valve lifters have bled down, otherwise engine damage might occur.

FRONT OIL SEAL
REPLACE

1. Disconnect ground cables from batteries.
2. Remove accessory drive belts.

Fig. 45 Modifying tool for front oil seal installation

Fig. 46 Front oil seal installation

Fig. 47 Dowel pin chamfer

Fig. 49 Valve timing marks

Fig. 48 Engine front cover installation. Typical

3. Remove crankshaft pulley and harmonic balancer.
4. Using tool BT-6406, remove front oil seal, **Fig. 44.**
5. Apply suitable sealer to outside diameter of new oil seal.
6. File .020 inch from flange of tool No. J-25264, **Fig. 45,** to prevent tool from contacting oil slinger before seal is properly seated in front cover.
7. Using tool BT-6611, install new oil seal, **Fig. 46.**
8. Install harmonic balancer and crankshaft pulley.
9. Install and tension accessory drive belts.

ENGINE FRONT COVER
REPLACE

1. Disconnect ground cables from batteries.
2. Drain cooling system and disconnect radiator hoses and bypass hose.
3. Remove all drive belts, fan and pulley, crankshaft pulley and harmonic balancer, and accessory brackets.
4. Remove timing indicator and water pump.
5. Remove remaining front cover attaching bolts and the front cover. Also, remove the dowel pins. It may be nec-

essary to grind a flat on the dowel pin to provide a rough surface for gripping.
6. Grind a chamfer on one end of each dowel pin, **Fig. 47.**
7. Cut excess material from front end of oil pan gasket on each side of cylinder block.
8. Trim approximately ⅛ inch from each end of new front pan seal.
9. Install new front cover gasket and apply suitable sealer to gasket around coolant holes.
10. Apply RTV sealer to mating surfaces of cylinder block, oil pan and front cover.
11. Place front cover on cylinder block and press downward to compress seal. Rotate cover right and left and guide oil pan seal into cavity with a small screwdriver.
12. Apply engine oil to bolts.
13. Install two bolts finger tight to retain cover.
14. Install the two dowel pins, chamfered end first.
15. Install timing indicator and water pump and torque bolts as shown in **Fig. 48.**
16. Install harmonic balancer and crankshaft pulley.
17. Install accessory brackets.
18. Install fan and pulley and drive belts.
19. Connect radiator hoses and bypass hose.
20. Connect ground cables to batteries.

TIMING CHAIN & GEARS
REPLACE

1. Remove front cover as outlined previously. On 6 cylinder engines, loosen rocker arm pivot bolts evenly so that some lash is present between rocker arms and valves.
2. Remove oil slinger, cam gear, crank gear and timing chain.
3. Remove fuel pump eccentric from crankshaft.
4. Install key in crankshaft, if removed.
5. Install fuel pump eccentric, if removed.
6. Install cam gear, crank gear and timing chain with timing marks aligned, **Fig. 49.**

NOTE: With the timing marks aligned in **Fig. 49,** No. 6 cylinder is in the firing position. To place No. 1 cylinder in the firing position, rotate crankshaft one complete revolution. This will bring the camshaft gear mark to top and No. 1 cylinder will be in the firing position.

7. Install oil slinger.
8. Install front cover.

CAMSHAFT & INJECTION PUMP DRIVE & DRIVEN GEARS
REPLACE

1. Disconnect ground cables from batter-

Fig. 50 Fuel injection pump driven gear installation

NOTCH TOWARD FRONT OF ENGINE

Fig. 52 Piston & rod assembly. 1982-85 V6-262 & V8-350

ies.
2. Drain cooling system.
3. Remove radiator upper baffle.
4. Disconnect upper radiator hose at water outlet and hose support clamp.
5. Disconnect cooler lines at radiator.
6. Remove fan shroud and radiator.
7. Remove intake manifold as outlined previously.
8. Remove engine front cover as outlined previously.
9. Remove valve covers.
10. Remove rocker arm bolts, pivots, rocker arms and push rod. Note valve train component locations to install components in original locations.
11. If equipped with A/C, discharge refrigerant system and remove condenser.
12. On all models, remove timing chain and gears as outlined previously.
13. Position camshaft dowel pin at 3 o'clock position.
14. While holding the camshaft rearward and rocking the injection pump driven gear slide, slide the injection pump drive gear from camshaft.
15. Remove injection pump adapter, snap ring, selective washer, injection pump driven gear and spring, **Fig. 50.**

NOTE: On some 1980 vehicles, the fuel injection pump shaft spring, **Fig. 50,** may be missing. The absence of this spring could affect the idle characteristics of the engine. The spring is available as part No. 22502241.

16. Slide camshaft from front of engine.
17. Reverse procedure to install. Check injection pump driven gear end play. If

end play is not .002–.006 inch, replace selective washer, **Fig. 50.** Selective washers are available from .080 to .115 inch in increments of .003 inch.

PISTON & ROD ASSEMBLE

1980-81 V8

Assemble piston to rod and install in cylinder block. On 8 cylinder engines, the piston is installed with the valve depression facing toward the crankshaft. Also, there are two different pistons used in this engine. In cylinder numbers 1, 2, 3 and 4, the large valve depression faces the front of the engine, **Fig. 51.** In cylinder numbers 5, 6, 7 and 8 the large valve depression faces the rear of the engine, **Fig. 51.** The pistons are interchangeable between cylinder numbers 1, 3, 6 and 8 and 2, 4, 5 and 7. Check connecting rod side clearance. Clearance should be .006–.020 inch.

1982-85 V6 & V8

Install piston and rod assembly so that notch at top of piston is facing toward front of engine, **Fig. 52.** Check connecting rod side clearance. Clearance should be .006–.020 inch on V8 engines or .008–.021 on V6 engines.

PISTONS, RINGS & PINS

SERVICE NOTE: Some V8-350 diesel engines may exhibit excessive oil consumption, low compression and/or excessive blowby. These conditions may be caused by stuck or frozen piston rings. To correct the above mentioned problem, proceed as follows:
1. With engine warm, remove all glow plugs from cylinders.
2. Using top engine cleaner Part No. 1050002, or equivalent, divide contents of can equally into each cylinder. Allow engine to soak for 24 hours.
3. Crank engine with glow plugs removed to expel excess cleaner.
4. Install glow plugs and start engine.

Pistons are available in standard sizes and oversizes of .010 and .030 inch on 8 cylinder engines or in standard size and oversize of .010 inch on 6 cylinder engines.
Rings are available in standard sizes and oversizes of .010 and .030 inch.

MAIN & ROD BEARINGS

SERVICE NOTE: Beginning with 1981 production engines, a new ¼ inch longer main bearing cap bolt is used on V8-350 engines. To accommodate the longer bolts, all holes in the cylinder block have a ¼ inch deeper tap and counter bore.

Fig. 51 Piston & rod installation. 1980-81 V8 engine

Fig. 53 Main bearing identification

Main bearings are available in standard sizes and undersizes of .0005, .0010 and .0015 inch. The amount of undersize and part number is stamped on the bearing shell, **Fig. 53.**
Rod bearings are available in standard sizes and an undersize of .010 inch.

REAR CRANKSHAFT SEAL SERVICE

Since the braided fabric seal used on these engines can be replaced only when the crankshaft is removed, the following repair procedure is recommended.
1. Remove oil pan and bearing cap.
2. Drive end of old seal gently into groove, using a suitable tool, until packed tight. This may vary between ¼ and ¾ inch depending on amount of pack required.
3. Repeat previous step for other end of seal.
4. Measure and note amount that seal was driven up on one side. Using the old seal removed from bearing cap, cut a length of seal the amount previously noted plus 1/16 inch.
5. Repeat previous step for other side of seal.
6. Pack cut lengths of seal into appropriate side of seal groove. A packing tool,

Fig. 54 Packing upper rear main bearing seal

BT-6433, **Fig. 54,** may be used since the tool has been machined to provide a built-in stop. Use tool BT-6436 to trim the seal flush with block, **Fig. 55.**

7. Install new seal in lower bearing cap.

OIL PAN
REPLACE

NOTE: On 1980 engines, the recommended diesel engine oil designation is SE/CC. On 1981 engines, the recommended diesel engine oil is SF/CC, SF/CD and SE/CC. On 1982–85 engines the recommended diesel engine oil is SF/CC or SF/CD.

88, 98 & Custom Cruiser

1. Disconnect ground cables from batteries.
2. Remove oil pump drive and vacuum pump, if equipped with A/C, or oil pump drive, if less A/C.
3. Remove oil dipstick.
4. Remove radiator upper support and fan shroud attaching screws.
5. Raise and support vehicle and drain oil pan.
6. Remove flywheel cover.
7. Disconnect exhaust and crossover pipes from exhaust manifold.
8. Remove oil cooler lines at filter base.
9. Disconnect starter wiring and remove starter.
10. Remove engine mounts from engine block, then raise front of engine with suitable equipment.
11. Remove oil pan attaching bolts and the oil pan.
12. Reverse procedure to install. Torque oil pan attaching bolts to 10 ft. lbs.

TORONADO

1. Disconnect battery ground cables.
2. Remove three final drive to transmission bolts, then raise and support vehicle.
3. Disconnect frame brace retaining

Fig. 55 Trimming upper rear main bearing seal

bolts. Disconnect idler arm and pitman arm from relay rod.
4. Disconnect drive axles from output shafts.
5. Disconnect battery cable bracket from output shaft support.
6. Disconnect output shaft support from engine block.
7. Position suitable jack under final drive, then remove final drive.
8. Remove splash shield and starter motor.
9. Drain oil, then remove oil pan.

NOTE: To remove oil pan on 1982–85 models, engine must be raised 1–1½ inch using tool No. BT-6501, or equivalent.

10. Reverse procedure to install.

OIL PUMP
REPLACE & SERVICE

REPLACEMENT

1. Remove oil pan as outlined previously.
2. Remove oil pump to rear main bearing cap attaching bolts, **Fig. 56.**
3. Remove oil pump and drive shaft extension.
4. Reverse procedure to install. Torque attaching bolts to 35 ft. lbs.

SERVICE
Disassembly

1. Remove oil pump drive shaft extension, **Fig. 57.** Do not attempt to remove washers from drive shaft extension. The drive shaft extension and washers is serviced as an assembly.
2. Remove cotter pin, spring and pressure regulator valve.

NOTE: Apply pressure on pressure regulator bore before removing cotter pin since the spring is under pressure.

Fig. 56 Oil pump installation. Typical

3. Remove oil pump cover attaching screws and the oil pump cover and gasket.
4. Remove drive gear and idler gear from pump body.

Inspection

1. Check gears for scoring or other damage, replace if necessary.
2. Proper end clearance is .0005–.0075 inch.
3. Check pressure regulator valve, valve spring and bore for damage. Proper bore to valve clearance is .0025–.0050 inch.
4. Check extension shaft ends for wear, **Fig. 58.**

Assembly

1. Install gears and shaft in oil pump body.
2. Check gear end clearance by placing a straight edge over the gears and measure the clearance between the straight edge and gasket surface. If end clearance is excessive, check for scores in cover that would bring the clearance over specified limits.
3. Install cover and torque attaching screws to 8 ft. lbs.
4. Install pressure regulator valve, closed end first, into bore, then the valve spring and cotter pin.

BELT TENSION DATA

	New Lbs.	Used Lbs.
1982–85③		
⅜ inch①	160	80
⅜ inch②	145	55
⁷⁄₁₆ inch	170	90
1980–81		
⁵⁄₁₆ inch Belts	80	50
⅜ inch Belts①	140	70
⅜ inch Belts②	140	60
¹⁵⁄₃₂ inch Belts	165	90

①—Except cogged belts.
②—Cogged belts.
③—V8 engine only. V6 engine serpentine drive belt is self adjusting.

WATER PUMP
REPLACE

V6-262

1. Disconnect battery ground cables and drain cooling system.

Fig. 57   Oil pump disassembled

Fig. 58   Oil pump driveshaft extension. V8 engines

Fig. 60   Fuel injection pump timing marks. Typical

Fig. 59   Installing fuel line stud & clip assembly

2. Remove fan clutch and fan, then disconnect radiator inlet hose at radiator.
3. Remove upper radiator support.
4. Remove drive belt and water pump pulley.
5. Remove vacuum pump and bracket assembly, then the cruise control servo mounting bracket, if equipped.
6. Remove power steering pump and brackets and position aside. Do not disconnect hoses from pump.
7. Disconnect heater and radiator outlet hoses at water pump, then loosen thermostat bypass hose clamp.
8. Remove water pump to front cover and water pump and front cover to block retaining bolts.
9. Remove water pump from front cover.
10. Reverse procedure to install. Coat gaskets with suitable sealer and water pump and front cover to block retaining bolts with primer and adhesive, Part No. 1052624, or equivalent.

NOTE: Failure to use the above mentioned primer and adhesive may cause coolant leaks and/or loss of bolt torque.

V8-350

1. Disconnect ground cables from batteries.
2. Drain cooling system.
3. Loosen drive belts and remove fan and pulley assembly.
4. Disconnect all hoses from water pump.
5. Remove water pump attaching screws and the water pump, **Fig. 48.**
6. Reverse procedure to install.

MECHANICAL FUEL PUMP
REPLACE

SERVICE NOTE: Some diesel engines may exhibit a condition of hard cold starts. If this condition exists, check the fuel pump housing for a crack in the area where the fuel line is connected to the fuel pump, which may allow air to enter the system. The cracked fuel pump housing could be caused by the fuel line vibrating.

To correct this condition, remove the right hand thermostat housing bolt and install stud, part No. 6270979. Disconnect fuel line at the fuel pump and install clip, part No. 343463 onto fuel line as shown in **Fig. 59.** Install washer face nut, part No. 10008001. Replace the fuel pump and connect the fuel line.

1. Disconnect fuel lines and electrical connectors from pump.
2. Remove fuel pump mounting bolts and the fuel pump.
3. Remove all gasket material from the pump and block gasket surfaces. Apply sealer to both sides of new gasket.
4. Position gasket on pump flange and hold pump in position against its mounting surface. Make sure rocker arm is riding on crankshaft eccentric.
5. Press pump tight against its mounting. Install retaining screws and tighten them alternately.
6. Connect fuel lines. Then operate engine and check for leaks.

NOTE: Before installing the pump, it is good practice to crank the engine so that the nose of the crankshaft eccentric is out of the way of the fuel pump rocker arm when the pump is installed. In this way there will be the least amount of tension on the rocker arm, thereby easing the installation of the pump.

INJECTION PUMP TIMING
LESS TIMING METER

1. The mark on the injection pump adapter must be aligned with the mark on the injection pump flange, **Fig. 60.**
2. To adjust:
   a. Loosen the injection pump retaining nuts with tool J-26987.
   b. Align the mark on the injection pump flange with the mark on the injection pump adapter, **Fig. 60.**
   c. Torque injection pump retaining nuts to 35 ft. lbs. (V6) or 18 ft. lbs. (V8).

Fig. 61   Fuel injection pump connections. 1980

Fig. 62   Fuel injection pump connections. 1981–83 V8 engine

Fig. 63   Fuel injection pump housing torque screw. 1982–83 V6 engine

WITH TIMING METER J-33075

NOTE: Certain engine malfunctions can cause inaccurate timing readings. Engine malfunctions should be corrected before adjusting pump timing. The marks on the pump and pump adapter will normally be aligned within .030 (V8) or .050 (V6) inch.

1. Place transmission in Park, apply parking brake and block drive wheels.
2. Start engine and allow to reach normal operating temperature.
3. Shut engine off.
4. Remove air cleaner assembly, install cover J-26996-1 then disconnect EGR valve hose.
5. Clean dirt from engine probe holder and crankshaft balancer rim.
6. Clean lens on both ends of glow plug probe. Look through probe to ensure that it is clean.
7. Remove glow plug from No. 1 (V6) or No. 3 (V8) cylinder. Insert glow plug probe into glow plug opening and torque probe to 8 ft. lbs.
8. Set timing meter selector to A (V6) or B (V8), then connect meter battery leads.
9. Disconnect generator two lead connector, then start engine and adjust idle speed to specifications.
10. Observe timing meter, wait approximately two minutes, then observe timing meter again. When meter stabilizes, compare timing reading to specifications. If timing is as specified, proceed to step 16. If timing is not as specified, proceed to next step.
11. Turn engine off and note relative position of marks on pump flange and adapter.
12. Loosen nuts or bolts holding pump to adapter, then rotate pump to the left (advance) or right (retard) as necessary. Torque retaining nuts or bolts to 18 (V8) or 35 (V6 and 1985 V8) ft. lbs.

NOTE: Move pump gradually when adjusting timing. On V8 engines, the width of the adapter timing mark is equal to approximately 1 degree. On V6 and 1985 V8 engines, the width of the mark is equal to approximately ⅔ of a degree.

13. Start engine and recheck timing. Reset timing, if necessary.
14. On V8 engines, adjust pump rod.
15. On all engines, reset curb and fast idle speeds.
16. Disconnect timing meter and install removed glow plug. Torque glow plug to 12 (V8) or 15 (V6) ft. lbs.
17. Connect generator two lead connector, install air cleaner assembly and reconnect EGR valve hose.

SERVICE NOTE: The timing marks on the injection pump and adapter should be close to being lined up after timing the engine. If they are not, and the engine still exhibits poor performance, the timing may still be incorrect. A misfiring cylinder can result in incorrect timing. When this occurs, it is necessary that timing be checked in an alternate cylinder. Timing can be checked in cylinders 2 or 3 on V8 engines, or 1 or 4 on V6 engines. If a difference exists between cylinders, try both positions to determine which timing performs best.

If the engine continues to run poorly and excessive exhaust smoke is evident, check the housing pressure cold advance (1981–85) for proper operation. If the advance is operating properly, a stuck or frozen injection pump advance piston may be at fault. This piston is used on 1980–85 vehicles and can be checked by pushing in on the bottom of the face cam lever on the right side of the injection pump. If the piston is free, the timing will retard and cause the engine to run roughly. If no change is evident, the piston is sticking and must be repaired.

FUEL INJECTION PUMP HOUSING FUEL PRESSURE CHECK

1980–83

1. Remove air crossover and install screened covers J-29657 (V6 engines) or J-26996-10 (V8 engines) or equivalent.
2. Remove fuel return pressure tap plug or torque screw, **Figs. 61, 62 and 63.** If equipped with torque screw, add second nut to lock nut and back out screw with nuts attached to avoid disturbing the adjustment.

3. Install the seal from the pressure tap plug on the pressure tap adapter, tool J-28526, then install the adapter into pump housing.
4. Connect a low pressure gauge to the adapter.
5. Connect pick-up tachometer, tool J-26925, to the engine.
6. Check pressure with engine operating at 1000 RPM in Park. The pressure should be 8–12 PSI with no more than a 2 PSI fluctuation.
7. If pressure reading is zero on 1981–83 models, check operation of housing pressure cold advance as follows:
   a. Disconnect housing cold pressure advance electrical connector.
   b. If pressure reading is still zero, remove injection pump cover and check operation of advance solenoid. Repair or replace as necessary.
   c. If pressure is as specified with housing cold pressure advance electrical connector disconnected, check operation of temperature switch located on cylinder head bolt.
8. If pressure is still low, replace fuel return line connector assembly. If pressure is too high, fuel return system or HPAA may be restricted. Remove return line at injection pump. Install fitting and short piece of hose to allow return flow to empty into a small container.
9. If pressure is lower than before, correct restriction in fuel line.
10. If pressure is still too high, replace fuel return line connector assembly. If assembly is replaced check injection pump timing and adjust if necessary.
11. If pressure remains too high, remove injection pump for repair.
12. Remove tachometer, pressure gauge and adapter.
13. Install a new pressure tap plug seal on the pressure tap plug and install plug into housing.
14. Remove screened covers and install air crossover.

1984

1. Ensure proper operation of temperature switch on EGR thermostatic vacuum switch.
2. Remove air cleaner and install screened cover No. J-26996-1, or equivalent.

Fig. 64 Fuel injection pump connections. 1984

1. 3 MM (3/32")
2. PART NO. 561888 OR EQUIVALENT
3. FLAT WASHERS
4. J-28526
5. FITTING

Fig. 66 Housing pressure checking tool adapter. 1985

	CONDITION		HPCA	HPAA	NOMINAL HOUSING PRESSURE kPa (psi)
	ALTITUDE	COOLANT			
FEDERAL PACKAGE	BELOW 1219m (4000 FT.)	COLD	ON	OFF	0
	BELOW 1219m (4000 FT.)	HOT	OFF	OFF	68.9 (10)
	ABOVE 1219m (4000 FT.)	COLD	ON	OFF	0
	ABOVE 1219m (4000 FT.)	HOT	ON	ON	48.3 (7)
ALTITUDE PACKAGE	ABOVE 1219m (4000 FT.)	COLD	ON	OFF	0
	ABOVE 1219m (4000 FT.)	HOT	OFF	OFF	68.9 (10)
	BELOW 1219m (4000 FT.)	COLD	ON	OFF	0
	BELOW 1219m (4000 FT.)	HOT	OFF	OFF	89.6 (13)

HPCA = HOUSING PRESSURE COLD ADV.   HPAA = HOUSING PRESSURE ALTITUDE ADV.
TIMING RETARDS WITH HIGHER HOUSING PRESSURE

Fig. 65 Injection pump housing pressure specifications. 1984

11. Remove tachometer, pressure gauge and adapter.
12. Install fuel return line connector into pump cover, using a new O-ring.
13. Connect fuel return line to return line connector.
14. Start engine and check for leaks.
15. Remove screened covers and reinstall air cleaner.

1985
1. Block drive wheels, apply parking brake and shift transmission to Park.
2. Start engine and run until normal operating temperature is reached, then stop engine.
3. Remove air cleaner cover.
4. Remove MAP sensor retainer, then position vacuum sensor aside with leads and vacuum hose connected.
5. Remove air cleaner assembly and the air crossover.
6. Remove MVS adjustment hole plug.
7. Install washers onto adapter No. J-28526, **Fig. 66,** then attach a suitable pressure gauge to adapter.
8. Disconnect electrical connector from HPCA solenoid and the HPAA solenoid connector from engine harness.
9. Connect suitable tachometer to engine, then start engine. Check for fuel leaks and correct if necessary.
10. Raise engine speed to 1000 RPM and check housing pressure reading.
11. If pressure reading in step 10 is below 5 psi, proceed as follows:
   a. Remove pressure regulator from injection pump.
   b. Apply a minimum of 30 psi air pressure to regulator, first from pump side, then from outlet side. The check ball should seat when air is applied to outlet side.
   c. Replace pressure regulator if operation is not as described.
   d. Reconnect electrical connector to HPCA solenoid, ensuring wire colors are properly matched.
   e. Turn ignition switch to Run position and ensure solenoid plunger extends upward.
   f. Turn ignition switch to Off or Lock position and ensure plunger retracts automatically or can be made to do so with a light pressure applied.
   g. Replace HPCA solenoid if operation is not as described.
12. If pressure reading in step 10 is 5–9 psi, proceed as follows:
   a. Stop engine, then remove line fitting from pressure regulator.
   b. Insert a suitable hex head key into pressure regulator and rotate

1. METERING VALVE SENSOR
2. ADJUSTMENT COVER
3. HARNESS CONNECTOR
4. INJECTION PUMP

Fig. 67 Metering valve sensor. 1984 V6-262 (Calif.)

adjustment screw as necessary to obtain 10 psi pressure reading.
   c. Check injection timing and adjust as necessary.
   d. Check operation of pressure regulator and HPCA solenoid as described in step 11.
13. If pressure reading in step 10 is 9–11 psi, proceed as follows:
   a. Reconnect HPCA and HPAA electrical connectors and recheck pressure. If pressure reading rises, proceed to step 13b. If pressure reading drops to below 6 psi or above 8 psi, proceed to step 13c. If pressure reading does not change, either the HPCA or HPAA is defective.
   b. Disconnect HPPA electrical connector. If pressure reading is now 9–11 psi, the HPCA is defective. If pressure reading drops to zero, check and adjust HPAA as described in steps 15 and 16.
   c. Disconnect HPAA electrical connector. If pressure drops or does not change, check and adjust HPAA as described in steps 15 and 16.
14. If pressure reading in step 10 is above 11 psi, proceed as follows:
   a. Disconnect fuel return line from HPAA inlet. Install a suitable hose over pipe outlet and position opposite end of hose in a small container.
   b. Start engine and observe pressure reading.
   c. If pressure reading does not change, perform step 12 above.
   d. If pressure reading si 9–11 psi, check for restriction in return line or HPAA and correct as necessary. If no restriction is found, proceed to step 14e.

3. Disconnect fuel return line from return line connector, then remove the connector from injection pump cover.
4. Push HPCA solenoid plunger into the solenoid, then disconnect electrical connector from HPCA terminal, **Fig. 64.**
5. Apply 12 volts to HPCA terminal ,using a suitable jumper, and observe solenoid plunger. If plunger does not extend fully, remove pump cover and repair or replace solenoid as necessary.
6. Install adapter No. J-34151 into pump cover and attach return line to adapter.
7. Attach a low pressure gauge to adapter, then install magnetic pickup tachometer No. J-26925 or equivalent.
8. Check housing pressure at 1000 RPM with transmission in Park, parking brake applied and drive wheels blocked. Compare recorded pressure to specifications in chart, **Fig. 65.**
9. If pressure is low, replace fuel return line connector assembly.
10. If pressure is high, proceed as follows:
   a. Disconnect return line from adapter pump.
   b. Install a suitable fitting and length of hose to allow return fuel flow to to drain into a small container, then recheck pressure.
   c. If pressure is lower than original reading, locate and correct restriction in fuel line.
   d. If pressure is still high, replace fuel return line connector assembly.
   e. If pressure remains high, remove injection pump and repair or replace as necessary.

1. SLOW IDLE ADJUSTMENT SCREW
2. FUEL SHUT-OFF SOLENOID (HIDDEN)
3. TO FUEL RETURN LINE
4. FUEL RETURN LINE CONNECTOR
5. HOUSING PRESSURE COLD ADVANCE LEADS
6. PINK-BLACK
7. GREEN-BLACK
8. ALTITUDE FUEL LIMITER
9. METERING VALVE SENSOR (MVS)
10. THROTTLE LEVER
11. DO NOT ADJUST
12. MVS ADJ. HOLE PLUG
13. STRAP
14. PROTECTOR SLEEVE

Fig. 68 Metering valve sensor. 1985

e. Reconnect pump return line to HPAA solenoid inlet and disconnect return line from HPAA solenoid outlet. Install a suitable hose over outlet and position opposite end of hose in a small container.
f. Start engine and observe pressure. If pressure is still high, check and adjust HPAA as described in steps 15 and 16.
15. Check HPAA solenoid and pressure regulator operation as follows:
   a. Remove HPAA solenoid from engine.
   b. Apply a minimum of 30 psi air pressure to assembly, first from pump side, then from outlet side.
   c. If air does not flow freely in both directions, replace solenoid.
   d. Remove pressure regulator from solenoid. If solenoid plunger does not move freely, the solenoid must be replaced.
16. To adjust HPAA solenoid, proceed as follows:
   a. Install HPAA solenoid assembly.
   b. Disconnect electrical connector from MAP sensor.
   c. Start engine and note housing pressure, which should now read 6–8 psi.

MVS VOLTAGE TABLE

V-REF →	4.5	4.6	4.7	4.8	4.9	5.0	5.1	5.2	5.3	5.4	5.5
MVS VOLTAGE → (In "D" 650 RPM)	.53-.55	.54-.56	.55-.57	.57-.59	.58-.60	.59-.61	.60-.62	.61-.63	.63-.65	.64-.66	.65-.67

Fig. 70 Metering valve sensor voltage chart. 1984

d. If pressure reading is not within specifications, remove HPAA assembly from engine and the line fitting from pressure regulator. Insert a suitable hex key into regulator and turn adjustment screw as necessary to bring reading within specifications.
e. Install HPAA assembly and recheck housing pressure.

METERING VALVE SENSOR

Used on 1984 California V6-262 and 1985 V8-350 engines with Diesel Electronic Control System, the metering valve sensor, **Figs. 67 and 68,** is a variable type resistor that electrically signals the diesel ECM as to metering valve position.

TESTING

1984

1. Block drive wheels, apply parking brake and place transmission in Park.
2. Start engine, allow it to reach normal operating temperature, then shut engine off.
3. Remove air cleaner.
4. Remove air crossover, then install cover J-29657, or equivalent.
5. Disconnect metering valve sensor harness and attach test harness J-34678 or BT-8342 as shown, **Fig. 69.**
6. Install tachometer J-26925, or equivalent, then torque metering valve sensor to pump attaching bolts to 30 inch lbs.
7. Start engine, accelerate to 1500 RPM for 10–20 seconds to stabilize fuel flow, then return engine to idle.
8. Place transmission in Drive and set idle speed to 650 RPM.
9. Using voltmeter J-29124, or equivalent, set meter at 20V scale and measure voltage between terminals A and C of test harness, **Fig. 69.** Observe and record voltage (V-REF) reading.
10. Measure voltage between terminals B and C of test harness. Observe and record MVS voltage reading.
11. Shift transmission into Park, then compare voltages recorded in steps 9 and 10 with specifications in chart, **Fig. 70.** Voltages should be within ranges shown.
12. With gear selector in Park, measure voltage between terminals B and C as throttle is quickly opened to wide open throttle position. Voltage should range from less than 1 volt at idle to over 4 volts as throttle approaches wide open position.
13. If MVS voltage is as specified in steps 11 and 12, the sensor is operating properly. If voltage is not as specified, proceed to "Adjustment" procedure.
14. Connect sensor harness, start engine and adjust idle speed to specifications.
15. Install air crossover, then the air cleaner.

1985

1. Block drive wheels, apply parking brake and shift transmission to Park.
2. Start engine and run until normal operating temperature is reached, then stop engine.
3. Remove air cleaner cover and MAP sensor retainer.
4. Position MAP sensor aside, leaving electrical connectors and vacuum line connected, then remove air cleaner assembly.
5. Remove air crossover and install screened covers No. J-26996-10.
6. Disconnect electrical connector from HPAA solenoid.
7. Disconnect MVS harness and install harness adapter, **Fig. 71.**
8. Connect suitable tachometer to engine.
9. Start engine and run at 1500 RPM for 10–20 seconds, then return to idle.
10. Ensure parking brake is still applied and drive wheels are blocked, then shift transmission to Drive.

1	DIGITAL VOLT METER
2	ENGINE HARNESS
3	MVS TEST HARNESS (BT-8342 OR J-34678)
4	MVS HARNESS
5	METERING VALVE SENSOR
6	INJECTION PUMP

Fig. 69 Metering valve sensor test connections. 1984

1. DIGITAL VOLTMETER
2. ENGINE HARNESS
3. MVS TEST HARNESS (BT-8342 OR J-34678)
4. MVS ADAPTER HARNESS (BT-8342-10 OR J-34678-50)
5. MVS HARNESS
6. METERING VALVE SENSOR (MVS)
7. INJECTION PUMP

Fig. 71   Metering valve sensor test connections. 1985

MVS VOLTAGE TABLE								
V-REF	4.0	4.1	4.2	4.3	4.4	4.5	4.6	4.7
MVS VOLTAGE	.47 - .49	.48 - .50	.49 - .51	.50 - .52	.51 - .54	.53 - .55	.54 - .56	.55 - .57
V-REF	4.8	4.9	5.0	5.1	5.2	5.3	5.4	5.5
MVS VOLTAGE	.57 - .59	.58 - .60	.59 - .61	.60 - .62	.61 - .63	.63 - .65	.64 - .66	.65 - .67

Fig. 72   Metering valve sensor voltage chart. 1985

Fig. 73   Fuel filter & lines. V8 engine

Fig. 74   Fuel filter & lines. V6 engine

11. Adjust idle speed to 600 RPM.
12. Measure and record voltage between terminals A and C, **Fig. 71.** This will be considered the V-Ref voltage.
13. Measure and record voltage between terminals B and C, **Fig. 71.** This is the MVS voltage.
14. Compare voltages recorded in steps 12 and 13 to specifications in chart, **Fig. 72.**
15. Shift transmission to Park and measure voltage between terminals B and C while quickly moving throttle between idle and wide open positions. Voltage should go from less than 1 volt at idle to more than 4 volts at wide open throttle.
16. If MVS voltages are within specifications, the sensor is operating properly. If voltages are not within specifications, proceed to adjustment procedure.
17. Reconnect HPAA solenoid connector and the MVS electrical connectors.
18. Install air crossover, MAP sensor and air cleaner assembly.

ADJUSTMENT

1984
1. With engine off, hold metering valve sensor assembly and carefully remove hole plug. Use caution to prevent sensor assembly from moving.
2. Using tool J-24182-2, or equivalent, turn adjustment screw clockwise to increase voltage reading, or counterclockwise to decrease reading. Turn adjustment screw in 1/8 turn increments.

NOTE: It may be necessary to file tool J-24182-2, to enable it to enter sensor assembly.

3. Install hole plug finger tight, then perform steps 7 through 11 of testing procedure. If voltages are not within chart specifications, readjust sensor as necessary.
4. Install hole plug using a new "O" ring

seal, then hold sensor assembly and torque hole plug to 30 inch lbs.
5. Connect sensor harness, start engine and check for fuel leaks.
6. Adjust idle speed to specifications, then install air crossover and air cleaner.

1985
1. With engine not running, remove MVS adjusting hole plug.
2. Using tool No. 34829, turn MVS adjustment screw clockwise to increase voltage reading or counterclockwise to decrease voltage reading. Turn adjustment screw in 1/8 turn increments.
3. Install adjusting hole plug finger tight, then recheck voltages as described previously.
4. If voltages are not within specifications, readjust sensor as necessary.
5. Install hole plug using a new O-ring, then torque plug to 30 inch lbs.
6. Reconnect MVS electrical connector, then start engine and check for fuel leaks.
7. Install air crossover and air cleaner.

INJECTION PUMP
REPLACE

INJECTION PUMP & LINES

Removal
1. Disconnect ground cables from batteries.
2. Remove air cleaner.
3. Remove filters and pipes from valve covers and air crossover, **Figs. 20 and 25.**
4. Remove air crossover and plug intake manifold, **Fig. 21.**
5. Disconnect throttle rod and return spring on V8 engines or throttle cable and TV detent cable from pump throttle lever.

6. Remove bellcrank.
7. Remove throttle and throttle valve cables from intake manifold brackets and position cables aside.
8. Remove fuel lines to fuel filter, then the fuel filter, **Figs. 73 and 74.**
9. Disconnect fuel line at fuel pump and remove fuel line. If equipped with A/C, remove rear compressor brace.
10. Disconnect fuel return line from injection pump, **Figs. 74 and 75.**
11. Slide clamp from fuel return lines at injector nozzles and remove fuel return lines from each bank.
12. Disconnect injection pump lines at injector nozzles, **Fig. 76.** It is necessary to use two wrenches.
13. Remove nuts retaining injection pump with tool No. J-26987.
14. Remove injection pump and cap all lines and fittings.

Installation
1. Align offset tang on pump drive shaft with pump driven gear, **Fig. 77,** and install injector pump.
2. Loosely install the injector pump retaining nuts and lock washers. Connect fuel lines to injector pump and torque line fittings to 25 ft. lbs., **Fig. 76.**
3. Connect fuel return lines to injector nozzles and injector pump.
4. Align mark on injection pump with line on adapter and torque retaining nuts to 18 ft. lbs. on V8 engines or 35 ft. lbs. on V6 engines.
5. Adjust throttle rod.
6. Install fuel line from fuel pump to fuel filter, **Figs. 73 and 74.** If equipped with A/C, install rear compressor brace.
7. Install bellcrank and hairpin clip.
8. Install throttle and throttle valve cables, to intake manifold brackets

Fig. 75 Fuel return line

Fig. 76 Injection nozzle installation

Fig. 77 Offset on fuel injection pump driven gear

Fig. 78 Fuel injection pump adapter installation

Fig. 79 Fuel injection pump adapter seal installation

Fig. 80 Marking fuel injection pump adapter with new timing mark

and attach to bellcrank. Adjust throttle valve cable.
9. Connect throttle rod and return spring on V8 engines or throttle cable and TV cable on V6 engines.
10. Crank engine and check for fuel leaks.
11. Remove plugs from intake manifold and install air crossover, **Fig. 21.**
12. Install tubes in flow control valve in air crossover and ventilation filters in valve covers, **Figs. 20 and 25.**
13. Install air cleaner.

INJECTION PUMP

Removal
1. Disconnect battery ground cable and remove air cleaner assembly.
2. Remove crankcase ventilation filters and pipes from the valve covers and air crossover.
3. Remove the air crossover, **Fig. 21,** and install intake manifold screened covers J-26996-10.
4. Disconnect the throttle rod and throttle return spring.
5. Remove bellcrank.
6. Remove throttle and TV detent cables from intake manifold brackets and position cables aside.
7. Remove fuel lines to fuel filter, then the fuel filter, **Figs. 73 & 74.**
8. Disconnect fuel line at fuel pump and remove fuel line. If equipped with A/C remove rear compressor brace.
9. Disconnect fuel return line from injection pump, **Figs. 74 and 75.**

10. Disconnect the injection line clamps closest to pump.
11. Disconnect the injection lines from pump and cap all openings.
12. Remove three nuts retaining injection pump, using tool No. J-26987.
13. Remove pump and discard the pump to adapter O-ring.

Installation
1. Align offset tang on pump drive shaft with pump driven gear, **Fig. 77.**
2. Install new pump to adapter O-ring, then install the pump fully seating pump by hand.
3. Align mark on injection pump with line on adapter and torque retaining nuts to 18 ft. lbs.
4. Remove caps from the openings and connect the injection lines to the pump.
5. Install injection line clamps.
6. Connect the fuel return line.
7. Reconnect the fuel line at the fuel pump. If equipped with A/C, install the rear compressor brace.
8. Install the fuel filter and fuel filter to injection pump line.
9. Install throttle and TV detent cables on intake manifold.
10. Install bellcrank.
11. Install throttle rod and throttle return spring.
12. Remove screened covers from intake manifold, then install air crossover.
13. Install pipes and hoses in the air crossover and ventilation filters in valve covers.

14. Install air cleaner assembly and connect battery ground cable.

INJECTION PUMP ADAPTER, ADAPTER SEAL & NEW TIMING MARK

1. Remove injection pump as outlined previously.
2. Remove injection pump adapter, **Fig. 78.**
3. Remove seal from injection pump adapter.
4. File mark off injection pump adapter. Do not file mark from injection pump.
5. Position engine to No. 1 cylinder firing position. Align marks on balancer with zero mark on indicator. The injection pump driven gear should be offset to the right when No. 1 cylinder is at top dead center.
6. Loosely install injection pump adapter.
7. Install seal in injection pump adapter with tool J-28425, **Fig. 79.**
8. Torque injection pump adapter bolts to 25 ft. lbs.
9. Install timing tool J-26896 into injection pump adapter. Rotate torque wrench counterclockwise to obtain a 50 ft. lbs. reading, then mark injection pump adapter, **Fig. 80.**
10. Install injection pump as outlined previously.

Fig. 81 Injection nozzle identification

Fig. 82 Injection pump right side view. 1981-85. V8 engine

Fig. 83 Installing tool J-29601 on injection pump. 1981-85. V8 engine

Fig. 84 Injection pump with cover removed. 1981-85. V8 engine

Fig. 85 Installing injection pump cover. 1981-85. V8 engine

INJECTION NOZZLE
REPLACE

SERVICE NOTE: Injection nozzle body leaks may be corrected by loosening the inlet fitting and retorquing to 45 ft. lbs. on DED type injection nozzles, and 19 ft. lbs. on CAV type injection nozzles, **Fig. 81.** In the event this does not correct the leak, remove the inlet fitting. Using a piece of crocus cloth, press and rotate the end of the inlet fitting against the crocus cloth back and forth about six times. After polishing has been performed, flush inlet fitting using diesel fuel and install fitting onto pump.

1. Remove fuel lines, using a backup wrench on upper injection nozzle hex.
2. Remove nozzle by applying torque to largest nozzle hex, **Fig. 76.**
3. Cap nozzle and lines to prevent entry of dirt. Also remove copper gasket from cylinder head if gasket did not remain with nozzle.
4. Reverse procedure to install. Torque nozzle to 25 ft. lbs. When tightening nozzle, torque must be applied to largest nozzle hex. Torque fuel line to 25 ft. lbs. using a backup wrench on upper injection nozzle hex.

TRANSMISSION VACUUM VALVE
REPLACE

1. Note location of the valve vacuum

hoses, then disconnect the vacuum hoses.
2. Remove the two valve attaching bolts and the valve.
3. Reverse procedure to install.

THROTTLE SHAFT SEAL
REPLACE

1981-85

V8 Engine
1. Disconnect both battery ground cables.
2. Remove air cleaner and air crossover and install air screens J-26996-2 or J-26996-10.
3. Disconnect injection pump fuel solenoid, housing pressure cold advance wires and fuel return pipe, **Fig. 82.**
4. Remove throttle rod, vacuum regulator valve, return spring and throttle cable bracket.
5. Place tool J-29601 over throttle shaft and pin, then position spring clip of tool over throttle shaft advance cam and tighten wing nut. Without loosening wing nut, pull tool off shaft. This will provide proper alignment during reassembly, **Fig. 83.**
6. Drive pin from throttle shaft and remove shaft advance cam and fiber washer. Remove any burrs from shaft which may have resulted from pin removal.
7. Clean injection pump cover, upper portion of pump, throttle shaft and guide stud area. Position several shop cloths in engine valley area to absorb fuel.
8. Remove injection pump cover and screws.

CAUTION: Use care to avoid any foreign matter from entering pump when cover is removed. If any object or foreign matter enter pump, it must be removed before engine is started as injection pump damage or engine damage may occur.

9. Note position of metering valve spring before removal as its position must be duplicated exactly during reassembly,

Fig. 84.
10. Remove guide stud and washer, noting parts before removal.
11. Rotate min-max governor assembly up for clearance then remove it, **Fig. 84.** If idle governor spring becomes disengaged from throttle block, it must be reinstalled with tightly wound coils toward throttle block.
12. Remove throttle shaft assembly and inspect shaft for unusual wear or damage, replace if necessary. It may be necessary to loosen nuts at injection pump mounting flange and rotate pump slightly to allow throttle shaft to clear intake manifold.
13. Inspect throttle shaft bushings in pump housing for damage or unusual wear. If replacement of bushings is necessary, it must be performed by a qualified repair facility.
14. Remove throttle shaft seals. Do not cut seals to remove, as any nicks in the seal seat will cause leakage.
15. Install new shaft seals, lubricated with chassis grease. Use care to avoid cutting seals on sharp edges of shaft.
16. Carefully slide throttle shaft into pump to point where min-max governor assembly will slide back onto throttle shaft, **Fig. 84.**
17. Rotate min-max governor assembly downward, then hold in position and slide throttle shaft and governor into position.
18. Install new fiber washer, throttle shaft advance cam (do not tighten screw at this time) and a new throttle shaft drive pin, **Fig. 82.**

1. Rubber "O" ring
2. Idling adjuster screw
3. Thrust washer
4. "E" type circlip
5. Thrust washer
6. Rubber "O" ring
7. Clamp screw
8. Light load advance cam
9. Pin
10. Locknut and rubber "O" ring
11. Torque screw
12. Throttle shaft
13. Maximum speed adjustment screw (Do not adjust)

Fig. 86 Throttle shaft & seals. V6 engine

1. Rubber "O" ring
2. Governor support rod
3. Locking pin
4. Sleeve
5. Throttle lever
6. Idling screw and spring
7. Governor carrier assembly
8. Idle spring
9. Governor arm
10. Throttle block
11. Throttle shaft

Fig. 87 Governor assembly. V6 engine

19. Align throttle shaft advance cam so tool J-20601 can be installed over throttle shaft, pins in slots and spring clip over advance cam.
20. Insert a .005 inch feeler gauge between cam and fiber washer, then tighten cam screw and remove tool J-29601.
21. Install guide stud with new washer, assuring that upper extension of metering valve spring slides on top of guide stud. Torque guide studs to 85 inch lbs.

CAUTION: Over torquing may strip the aluminum threads in the housing.

22. Hold throttle in idle position and install new pump cover seal. Making sure that screws are not in cover, position cover about ¼ inch forward toward shaft end and above ⅛ inch above pump, **Fig. 85.** Move cover rearward and downward into position, using care to avoid cutting seal, then reinstall cover screws. Each screw must have a flat washer and internal lock washer, with flat washer against pump cover. Torque screws to 37 inch lbs. and install vacuum regulator.
23. Reconnect both battery ground cables, then turn ignition switch to run position and touch pink solenoid wire to solenoid. A clicking noise should be heard as the wire is connected and disconnected. If not, the linkage may be jammed in the wide open position and the engine must not be started. Proceed to step 24. If clicking is heard, connect pump solenoid and housing pressure cold advance wires and proceed to step 25.
24. Remove cover, then ground solenoid lead (opposite hot lead) and connect pink wire. With ignition switch in run position, the solenoid in the cover should move the linkage. If not, the solenoid must be replaced. Minimum voltage across solenoid terminals must be 12 volts. Reinstall cover and repeat step 23.
25. Install throttle cable bracket, throttle rod, throttle cable and return springs. Make sure timing marks on pump and adapter are aligned and make sure nuts retaining pump are tight. Install fuel return pipe.
26. Start engine and check for fuel leaks.

NOTE: Rough idle may be due to air in the pump. Allow sufficient time for air to purge by allowing engine to idle. It may be necessary to turn engine off to allow air bubbles to rise to top of pump where they will be purged.

27. Adjust Transmission Vacuum Valve as described further on, then remove intake manifold screens and install air crossover and air cleaner.

V6 Engine
1. Remove air crossover and install cover J-29657 or equivalent.
2. Disconnect fuel return pipe, **Fig. 74,** then remove governor control cover screws and the cover.
3. Remove fast idle solenoid and vacuum regulator valve.
4. Disconnect throttle cable and TC detent cable.
5. Disconnect throttle return spring.
6. Install tool J-29601 or equivalent over throttle shaft with slots of tool engaging vacuum regulator valve lock pin. Place spring clip of tool over throttle shaft advance cam and tighten wing nut. Without loosening wing nut, pull tool off of shaft.
7. Remove lock pin from throttle shaft, **Fig. 86.**
8. Remove rollpin from pump housing and remove governor support rod.
9. Tilt governor carrier assembly by lifting end nearest drive end of pump and remove carrier from pump housing.
10. Remove clamping screw from light load cam, then remove cam.
11. Remove E clip from throttle shaft, then remove throttle shaft from pump.
12. Remove and discard O rings.
13. Check throttle shaft assembly and governor housing bores for damage and wear and replace as necessary.
14. Lubricate shaft and O rings with oil and assemble larger O rings onto shaft.
15. Install throttle shaft onto housing until thrust washers can be installed onto shaft in original positions. Install smaller O ring onto shaft.
16. Assemble light load advance cam onto shaft and install but do not tighten clamping screw.
17. Install E clip into throttle shaft recess. If new throttle shaft is installed, shaft end play must be checked and adjusted by selective fitting of thrust washers. Throttle shaft end play should be .006–.012 inch.
18. Install new pin onto head of shaft.

Fig. 88 Throttle linkage. V8 engine

Fig. 89 Throttle valve or detent cable adjustment

Fig. 90 Transmission vacuum valve adjustment. (Typical)

Align throttle shaft advance cam until tool J-29601 or equivalent can be installed over throttle shaft. Tighten cam screw, then remove tool J-29601.

19. Rotate throttle lever forward to the drive end of pump. Install governor carrier assembly onto pump housing and engage lug on underside of throttle block with cut away notch in throttle shaft.
20. Lubricate governor support rod and new O ring, then install O ring onto support rod using tool J-33096 or equivalent.
21. Insert plain end of rod through rear of governor housing and into carrier assembly sleeve.
22. Install support rod into housing and install new new locking pin, **Fig. 87.**
23. Install governor cover and fuel return pipe.
24. Install throttle return springs and connect throttle cable.
25. Connect TV detent cable.
26. Install vacuum regulator valve and fast idle solenoid.
27. Start engine and check for leaks. Install air crossover and air cleaner.

PUMP COVER SEAL AND/OR GUIDE STUD
REPLACE
1981–85

1. Disconnect both battery ground cables.
2. Remove air cleaner and air crossover and install air screens J-26996-2 or J-26996-10.
3. Disconnect injection pump fuel solenoid, housing pressure cold advance wires and fuel return pipe.
4. Clean injection pump cover, upper portion of pump and guide stud area. Position shop cloths to absorb fuel.
5. Remove injection pump cover, then remove screws from cover.

CAUTION: Use care to avoid any foreign matter from entering pump when cover is removed. If any object or foreign matter enter pump, it must be removed before

starting engine as injection pump damage or engine damage may occur.

6. Note position of metering valve spring before removal as its position must be duplicated exactly during reassembly, **Fig. 84.**
7. Remove guide stud and washer, noting location of parts before removal.
8. Refer to steps 21 thru 27 under "Throttle Shaft Seal, Replace" procedure for reassembly of "Pump Cover Seal And/Or Guide Stud".

THROTTLE ROD
ADJUST

1. If equipped with Cruise Control, remove clip from Cruise Control rod, then the rod from bellcrank.
2. Remove throttle valve cable from bellcrank, **Fig. 88.**
3. Loosen the throttle rod locknut and shorten the rod several turns.
4. Rotate the bellcrank to the full throttle stop, then lengthen the throttle rod until the injection pump lever contacts the injection pump full throttle stop. Release the bellcrank.
5. Tighten the throttle rod locknut.
6. Connect the throttle valve cable and Cruise Control rod, if equipped, to bellcrank.

THROTTLE VALVE OR DETENT CABLE
ADJUST

1. Remove throttle rod from bellcrank, **Fig. 89.**
2. Push snap lock to disengaged position.
3. Rotate bellcrank to full throttle stop position and push in snap lock until flush with cable end fitting. Release bellcrank.
4. Connect the throttle rod.

TRANSMISSION VACUUM VALVE
ADJUST

1. Remove air crossover, then install screened covers J26996-2.
2. Remove throttle rod from throttle lever

on V8 models or disconnect throttle cable and TV detent cable on V6 models, then loosen transmission vacuum valve injection pump bolts.
3. Install carburetor angle gauge J26701-15 and adapter on injection pump throttle lever, **Fig. 90.**
4. Rotate throttle lever to the wide open position and set angle gauge to zero degrees.
5. Center bubble in level, then set angle gauge to 50 degrees on 1980 units, 58 degrees on 1981–85 V8 engines or 49° on V6 engines.
6. Rotate throttle lever so level bubble is centered.
7. Attach a suitable vacuum pump to center port of vacuum valve and install a vacuum gauge to outside port of vacuum valve, then apply 18–22 inches of vacuum.
8. Rotate vacuum valve clockwise to obtain 7 to 8 inches of vacuum on 1980 units, 8.6 to 9.2 inches of vacuum on 1981 units and 10.6 inches of vacuum on 1982–85 units, then tighten vacuum valve bolts. Remove vacuum gauge and vacuum pump.
9. Install throttle rod to bellcrank, on V8 models or connect throttle cable and TV detent cable on V6 models, then remove screened covers and install air crossover.

PURGING WATER FROM FUEL TANK
MODELS w/ WATER IN FUEL DETECTOR

On these vehicles, any water in the fuel tank may be purged by siphoning or using a pump. The pump or siphon hose should be connected to the ¼ inch fuel return hose (smaller of the two hoses) under the hood near the fuel pump. Purging should continue until all water is removed from the fuel tank. Also, remove fuel filler cap while purging, and replace cap when completed.

CAUTION: Use all safety precautions while handling the fuel/water mixture.

Clutch & Transmission Section

Fig. 1   Clutch linkage. 1980—81 Cutlass

Fig. 2   Three speed shift linkage (typical)

CLUTCH PEDAL
ADJUST

1980—81 CUTLASS

1. Disconnect clutch return spring.
2. Rotate clutch lever and shaft assembly until clutch pedal firmly contacts rubber bumper on bracket.
3. Push outer end of clutch fork rearward until release bearing lightly contacts clutch plate.
4. Install lower push rod "A", **Fig. 1**, in clutch fork and rod "B", **Fig. 1**, in gauge (Upper) hole.
5. Increase length of push rod "A" until all lash is removed.
6. Install rod "B" in lower hole of lever and shaft, then the retaining clip.
7. Tighten lock nut "C" against rod "B", **Fig. 1**. Do not change rod length.
8. Connect return spring.
9. Free pedal play should be $^{11}\!/_{16}$ to $^{5}\!/_{8}$ inch.

CLUTCH
REPLACE

1980—81

1. Remove transmission.
2. Disconnect clutch release spring and clutch rod.
3. Remove clutch release bearing.
4. Remove flywheel housing, leaving starter attached to engine. Release yoke and ball stud will remain in housing.
5. Scribe mark on clutch cover to flywheel for correct assembly.
6. Unfasten and remove clutch cover

and disc.

NOTE: Loosen pressure plate bolts alternately, one turn at a time.

7. Reverse removal procedure to install clutch and adjust clutch pedal free play.

THREE SPEED
MANUAL TRANS.
REPLACE

1980—81

1. On models with floor shift, remove shift lever from shifter assembly.
2. Raise car and remove driveshaft.
3. Disconnect shift rods from shift levers and the TCS switch wiring, if equipped.
4. Support rear of engine.
5. Remove cross support bar-to-rear transmission mount attaching bolts.
6. Remove catalytic converter support bracket.
7. Disconnect parking brake cables from cross support and remove cross support bar.
8. If equipped with dual exhaust it may be necessary to disconnect left-hand exhaust pipe at exhaust manifold to provide clearance.
9. Disconnect speedometer cable.
10. Remove transmission upper attaching bolts and install aligning studs in the bolt holes.
11. Remove lower bolts and remove transmission.
12. Reverse procedure to install.

3 SPEED SHIFT
LINKAGE
ADJUST

1980 COLUMN SHIFT

1. Place transmission in reverse and raise vehicle.
2. Loosen swivel bolts on shift rods at transmission, ensuring rods are free to move in swivels.
3. Hold 1st-reverse column relay lever in position, push up on shift rod until detent in column is felt, then torque swivel bolt to 20 ft. lbs.
4. Place transmission in Neutral, insert $^{3}\!/_{16}$ inch rod through column relay lever into alignment hole and torque swivel nut to 20 ft. lbs.
5. Lower vehicle and check shift operation.
6. Place transmission in reverse, turn ignition switch to lock position and ensure that the key can be removed, steering wheel will not turn and transmission will not shift out of reverse.
7. Place ignition switch in run position, shift transmission to second gear, ensure that steering wheel will turn and key can not be removed from ignition switch.

1980—81 FLOOR SHIFT

1. Place ignition switch in "Off" position, then raise vehicle.
2. Remove retainers from shift rods, then place transmission shift levers in neutral.
3. Place control lever in neutral position. Align levers and insert gauge pin into levers and bracket, **Fig. 2**.
4. Loosen nuts on 1st-reverse shift rod and adjust trunion and pin assembly, then tighten nuts.
5. Loosen nuts on 2nd-3rd shift rod and adjust trunion and pin assembly, then tighten nuts.
6. Remove gauge pin, then check linkage for proper operation.

4 SPEED TRANS.
REPLACE

1980

1. Raise vehicle and drain transmission.
2. Remove propeller shaft.
3. Disconnect speedometer cable and backup light switch from transmission.
4. Disconnect transmission control rod and lever assemblies from shifter shafts. Position rods aside.
5. Remove crossmember to transmission mount bolts.
6. Remove catalytic converter support bracket.
7. Support engine with a suitable jack and remove crossmember to frame bolts, then the crossmember.
8. Remove transmission to clutch housing upper retaining bolts and install guide pins in holes.
9. Remove the transmission to clutch housing lower retaining bolts, slide transmission rearward and remove from vehicle.
10. Reverse procedure to install.

4 SPEED SHIFT LINKAGE
ADJUST

1980

1. Turn ignition switch to "Off" position

Fig. 3 Four speed shift linkage. 1980

and raise vehicle.
2. Loosen lock nuts on shift rod swivels, **Fig. 3.** The rods should pass freely through the swivels.
3. Place transmission shift levers in neutral.
4. Place shift control lever in neutral. Align control levers and install a suitable pin into levers and bracket.
5. Tighten 1st.-2nd. shift rod nut against swivel.
6. Tighten 3rd.-4th. shift rod nut against swivel.
7. Tighten reverse shift control rod nut.
8. Remove pin from control lever assembly and check for proper operation.

Rear Axle, Propeller Shaft & Brakes

REAR AXLE

Toronado

On these models the hub and wheel bearing is incorporated into one assembly which eliminates the need for wheel bearing adjustment and does not require periodic maintenance.

WHEEL BEARING & SPINDLE, REPLACE

REAR DISC BRAKES
Removal

1. Raise and support rear of vehicle.
2. Remove tire and wheel assembly.
3. Mark a wheel stud and a corresponding place on the rotor to assist in installation if bearing is not replaced.
4. Disconnect brake line at bracket on control arm.
5. Remove caliper and rotor assembly.
6. Remove four nut and bolts securing the spindle to the control arm and remove bearing assembly **Fig. 1.**

Fig. 1 Wheel bearing and hub assembly removal. Toronado

Fig. 2   Integral carrier type rear axle. Type B & O (Except 7½ inch) axle

Installation

NOTE: Before installing bearing, remove all rust and corrosion from bearing mounting surfaces. Lack of a flat surface may result in early bearing failure. A slip fit must exist between the bearing and the control arm assembly.

1. Install rear spindle, shield and plate to lower control arm with four nut and bolt assemblies. Tighten to 32 ft. lbs. **Fig. 1.**
2. If bearing was not replaced install rotor using reference marks made at time of removal.
3. Install brake caliper assembly.
4. Connect brake line at bracket on con-

trol arm, tighten and bleed brake system.
5. Install wheel and tire assembly. Tighten to 100 ft. lbs.
6. Remove support and lower car.

REAR DRUM BRAKES
Removal

1. Raise and support rear of vehicle.
2. Remove tire and wheel assembly.
3. Remove brake drum.
4. Remove four nuts attaching rear wheel bearing assembly to control arm.
5. Remove wheel bearing and four attaching bolts, **Fig. 1.**

Installation

NOTE: Before installing bearing, remove all rust and corrosion from bearing mounting surfaces. Lack of a flat surface for any reason may result in early bearing failure. A slip fit must exist between the bearing and the control arm assembly.

1. Install four nuts and bolts attaching wheel bearing to rear control arm assembly, **Fig. 1.**
2. Install brake drum.
3. Install wheel and tire assembly, tighten to 100 ft. lbs.
4. Remove supports and lower car.

Exc. Toronado

Figs. 2 and 3 illustrate the rear axle assemblies used on conventional models. When necessary to overhaul any of these units, refer to the Rear Axle Specifications table in this chapter.

INTEGRAL CARRIER TYPE "B" & "O" (EXCEPT 7½ inch)

As shown in **Fig. 2,** the drive pinion is mounted on two tapered roller bearings that are preloaded by two selected spacers. The drive pinion is positioned by shims located between a shoulder on the pinion and the rear bearing. The front bearing is held in place by a large nut.

The differential is supported in the carrier by two tapered roller side bearings. These are preloaded by inserting shims between the bearings and the pedestals. The differential assembly is positioned for ring gear and pinion backlash by varying these shims.

TYPE C, G, K, M, O (7½ inch) & P

In these rear axles, **Fig. 3,** the rear axle housing and differential carrier are cast into an integral assembly. The drive pinion assembly is mounted in two opposed tapered roller bearings. The pinion bearings are preloaded by a spacer behind the front bearing. The pinion is positioned by a washer between the head of the pinion and the rear bearing.

The differential is supported in the carrier by two tapered roller side bearings. These bearings are preloaded by spacers located between the bearings and carrier

Fig. 3   Integral carrier type differential. Types C, G, K, M, O (7½ inch) & P axle

Fig. 4 Removing axle shaft bearing retainer

CHISEL RETAINER BUT DO NOT MARK SHAFT ON BEARING SURFACE

RETAINER (OUTER)

SHAFT SEAL BEARING

Fig. 5 Propeller shaft installation (Typical)

SPIDER AND BEARINGS

STRAP

SPIDER AND BEARINGS

STRAP

SLIP YOKE

housing. The differential assembly is positioned for proper ring gear and pinion backlash by varying these spacers. The differential case houses two side gears in mesh with two pinions mounted on a pinion shaft which is held in place by a lock pin. The side gears and pinions are backed by thrust washers.

REAR AXLE, REPLACE

Construction of the axle assembly is such that service operations may be performed with the housing installed in the vehicle or with the housing removed and installed in a holding fixture. The following procedure is necessary only when the housing requires replacement.

1. Raise car and remove rear wheels, drums and axle shafts.
2. Disconnect brake line from wheel cylinders.
3. Unfasten and support backing plates with wire hooks to frame kickup.
4. Disconnect shock absorbers at housing.
5. Position jack stands under frame rear torque boxes, then disconnect upper control arms and slowly lower axle housing to stands.
6. Remove springs.
7. Remove propeller shaft and support front of axle housing at companion flange to prevent assembly from rotating when the lower control arms are disconnected.
8. Remove lower control arm bolts at axle housing.
9. Remove support at companion flange and lower axle housing.
10. Remove assembly to bench and transfer parts to new axle housing.
11. Reverse procedure to install.

AXLE SHAFT, REPLACE

Type C, G, K, M, O (7½ inch) & P

1. Raise vehicle and remove wheel and brake drum.
2. Clean all dirt from area of carrier cover.
3. Drain lubricant from carrier by removing cover.
4. Remove differential pinion shaft lock screw and shaft.
5. Push flanged end of axle shaft toward center of vehicle and remove "C" lock from button end of shaft.

6. Remove axle shaft from housing, being careful not to damage oil seal.
7. Reverse procedure to install.

Type B & O (Except 7½ inch)

1. Remove wheel and brake drum.
2. Remove axle bearing retainer (4 nuts).

NOTE: On 1980–81 8½ inch axles, new retainers are used and can be identified by a raised area around the axle shaft opening. This raised area provides proper seating of the seal and bearing.

3. Pull axle shaft from housing. If bearing is a tight fit in housing, use a slide hammer-type puller. Do not drag shaft over seal as this may damage seal.
4. Attach one axle bearing retainer nut to hold brake backing plate in position.
5. Before installing axle shaft, examine oil seal. The seals have feathered edges which form a tight seal around the shaft. If these edges are damaged in any way, seal must be replaced. Examine seal surface on shaft; if it is not smooth, dress it down with very fine emery cloth.
6. Reverse removal procedure to install axle shaft, being sure to grease outside of axle bearing, seal surface on axle shaft and bore of axle housing with differential lubricant. Place new gasket and bearing retainer over studs, install nuts and tighten to 35 ft. lbs.
7. Bearings should be replaced if found to be rough or have greater than .020 inch end play. Remove bearing only when new bearing is to be installed; once removed it must not be reused.
8. With axle shaft removed from housing, split bearing retainer with a chisel, **Fig. 4.**
9. Press bearing off shaft.
10. Press new bearing on shaft up against shoulder on shaft.
11. Press retainer on shaft up against bearing.
12. Reverse removal procedure to install axle shaft.

PROPELLER SHAFT

The propeller shaft is of one or two piece construction with a single or double U-joint securing the shaft to the companion flange, **Fig. 5.**

1. Mark propeller shaft and companion flange so they can be installed in the same position.
2. Remove strap bolts, **Fig. 5.** Use a piece of tape or wire to hold universal joint bearing caps in place.
3. Lower rear of shaft and slide rearward.
4. Reverse procedure to install. If drive shaft yokes do not have vent holes, lubricate internal splines with engine oil. If drive shaft yokes have vent holes apply lubricant No. 1050169 or equivalent to internal splines prior to installation. Torque strap bolts to 14–16 ft. lbs.

BRAKE ADJUSTMENTS

These brakes have self adjusting shoe mechanisms that assure correct lining-to-drum clearances at all times. The automatic adjusters operate only when the brakes are applied as the car is moving rearward.

Although the brakes are self-adjusting, an initial adjustment is necessary after the brake shoes have been relined or replaced, or when the length of the star wheel adjuster has been changed during some other service operation.

Frequent usage of an automatic transmission forward range to halt reverse vehicle motion may prevent the automatic adjusters from functioning, thereby inducing low pedal heights. Should low pedal heights be encountered, it is recommended that numerous forward and reverse stops be made until satisfactory pedal height is obtained.

Fig. 6   Brake shoe gauge measuring inside diameter of brake drum.

Fig. 7   Brake shoe gauge measuring outside diameter of brake shoes.

Fig. 8   Backing off brake shoe adjustment

NOTE: If a low pedal height condition cannot be corrected by making numerous reverse stops (provided the hydraulic system is free of air) it indicates that the self-adjusting mechanism is not functioning. Therefore, it will be necessary to remove the brake drum, clean, free up and lubricate the adjusting mechanism. Then adjust the brakes as follows, being sure the parking brake is fully released.

ADJUSTMENT

NOTE: Inasmuch as there is no way to adjust these brakes with the drums installed, the following procedure is mandatory after new linings are installed or if it becomes necessary to change the length of the brake shoe adjusting screw.

1. With brake drums removed, position the caliper shown in **Fig. 6** to the inside diameter of the drum and tighten the clamp screw.
2. Next position brake shoe end of the caliper tool over the brake shoes as shown in **Fig. 7**.
3. Rotate the gauge slightly around the shoes to insure that the gauge contacts the linings at the largest diameter.
4. Adjust brake shoes until the gauge is a snug fit on the linings at the point of largest lining diameter.

NOTE: If it is necessary to back off the brake shoe adjustment, it will be necessary to hold the adjuster lever away from the adjuster screw, **Fig. 8**.

PARKING BRAKE
ADJUST

EXC. MODELS w/REAR WHEEL DISC BRAKES

Depress parking brake pedal 2 clicks. Tighten adjusting nut until left rear wheel can just be rotated rearward using both hands and cannot be rotated forward. Release parking brake, rear wheels should turn freely in either direction with no brake drag.

MODELS w/REAR WHEEL DISC BRAKES

1. Lubricate parking brake cables at underbody contact points and equalizer hooks.
2. Raise and support rear of vehicle with parking brakes fully released.
3. Prevent cable stud from turning and tighten equalizer nut until cable slack is removed. Ensure caliper levers are against stops on caliper housing after tightening equalizer nut, otherwise, loosen cable until levers return to stops.
4. Operate parking brake several times to check adjustment. Pedal should travel 4–5½ inches with approximately 120 lbs. force applied to pedal.
5. Lower vehicle and ensure levers remain on caliper stops. If not, back off parking brake adjuster as necessary.

POWER BRAKE UNIT
REPLACE

HYDRO-BOOST

NOTE: Pump brake pedal several times with engine off to deplete accumulator of fluid.

1. Remove two nuts attaching master cylinder to booster, then move master cylinder away from booster with brake lines attached.
2. Remove three hydraulic lines from booster. Plug and cap all lines and outlets.
3. Remove retainer and washer securing booster push rod to brake pedal arm.
4. Remove four nuts attaching booster unit to dash panel.
5. From engine compartment, loosen booster from dash panel and move booster push rod inboard until it disconnects from brake pedal arm. Remove spring washer from brake pedal arm.
6. Remove booster unit from vehicle.
7. Reverse procedure to install. To purge system, disconnect feed wire from injection pump. Fill power steering pump reservoir, then crank engine for several seconds and recheck power steering pump fluid level. Connect injection pump feed wire and start engine, then cycle steering wheel from stop to stop twice and stop engine. Discharge accumulator by depressing brake pedal several times, then check fluid level. Start engine, then turn steering wheel from stop to stop and turn engine off. Check fluid level and add fluid as necessary. If foaming occurs, stop engine and wait for approximately one hour for foam to dissipate, then recheck fluid level.

VACUUM BOOSTER

1. Disconnect vacuum hose from vacuum cylinder and cover openings to prevent entrance of dirt.
2. Disconnect pipes from master cylinder outlets and cover openings in master cylinder and end of pipes to prevent entrance of dirt.
3. Disconnect push rod from brake pedal.
4. Unfasten and remove power brake unit.
5. Reverse procedure to install.

BRAKE MASTER CYLINDER
REPLACE

1. Be sure area around master cylinder is clean, then disconnect the hydraulic lines at master cylinder. Plug or tape end of line to prevent entrance of dirt or loss of brake fluid.
2. On Cutlass models with manual brakes, remove push rod to brake pedal pin.
3. Remove master cylinder retaining nuts and the master cylinder.
4. Reverse procedure to install.

Rear Suspension

Fig. 1   Rear suspension. Toronado

Fig. 2   Upper control arm axle bracket bushing removal

Fig. 3   Upper control arm axle bracket bushing installation

SHOCK ABSORBER
REPLACE

1. With rear axle properly supported, disconnect shock absorber from upper mounting.
2. Disconnect shock absorber from lower mounting.
3. Reverse procedure to install.

COIL SPRING
REPLACE
EXC. TORONADO

1. Position a suitable jack under rear axle housing and raise rear of vehicle, then support frame side rails with support stands. Do not lower jack.
2. Disconnect brake line at axle housing.
3. Disconnect upper control arms at axle housing.
4. Disconnect shock absorber at lower mounting, then carefully lower rear axle assembly.

NOTE: Use care not to stretch or kink brake hoses.

5. Remove coil spring from vehicle.

TORONADO

1. Raise and support rear of vehicle, then remove wheel and tire assembly.
2. Remove stabilizer bar as described under Stabilizer Bar, Replace.
3. Using a suitable jack support lower control arm.
4. Disconnect automatic level air line at shock absorber. If removing left hand spring from vehicle, disconnect automatic level control link from ball pivot at control arm.
5. Disconnect shock absorber from upper and lower mountings and remove shock absorber.
6. Carefully lower control arm until spring tension is relieved, then remove spring and insulator, **Fig. 1.**
7. Reverse procedure to install. Locate bottom end of spring between dimples on lower control arm assembly.

Fig. 4   All front & lower control arm rear bushing removal

Fig. 5   All front & lower control arm rear bushing installation

Fig. 6   Stabilizer bar installation (typical)

STABILIZER BAR
REPLACE

EXC. TORONADO

1. Support vehicle at rear axle.
2. Remove bolts attaching stabilizer bar to the lower control arms, **Fig. 6.**
3. Reverse procedure to install

TORONADO

1. Raise and support rear of vehicle.
2. Remove nuts and bolts securing front of stabilizer bar to control arms.
3. Remove inside nut and bolt from each side of stabilizer bar link, then loosen outside nut and bolt on the stabilizer link.
4. Rotate bottom parts of link to one side and slip stabilizer out of bushings.

CONTROL ARMS & BUSHINGS
REPLACE

NOTE: Replace control arms one at a time

to prevent axle assembly misalignment, making installation difficult.

UPPER CONTROL ARMS

Exc. Toronado

1. Support vehicle at frame and rear axle.
2. Remove control arm front and rear mount bolts.
3. Remove bushings as necessary, **Figs. 2 and 3.**

LOWER CONTROL ARMS

Exc. Toronado

Follow "Upper Control Arms" procedure for replacement of lower control arms. Replace control arm bushings as shown in **Figs. 4 and 5.**

TORONADO

1. Raise and support rear of vehicle,

then remove wheel and tire assembly.
2. Remove stabilizer bar as described under Stabilizer Bar, Replace.
3. Disconnect brake line bracket from control arm, then remove caliper assembly.
4. Mark a wheel stud and a corresponding point of the rotor for alignment, then remove rotor.
5. If left hand control arm is to be removed, disconnect automatic level control link from ball pivot on control arm.
6. Using a suitable jack support control arm.
7. Disconnect air line from shock absorber, then disconnect shock absorber from upper and lower mountings and remove shock absorber.
8. Carefully lower the control arm until spring tension is relieved, then remove spring and insulator.
9. Remove two bolts mounting control arm to frame and remove control arm.
10. Reverse procedure to install.

Front Suspension & Steering Section

For service procedures on Toronado, refer to chapter 16–1, "Front Suspension & Steering." Follow procedures pertaining to Eldorado & Seville.

FRONT SUSPENSION

As shown in **Figs. 1 and 2,** the front suspension is of the conventional "A" frame design with ball joints. Double acting shock absorbers are mounted within the coil springs. Caster and camber are controlled by shims.

WHEEL ALIGNMENT

Camber and caster are adjusted by shims placed between the upper pivot shafts and the frame. In order to remove or install shims, do not remove weight from front wheels. Loosen pivot shaft-to-frame bolts. To gain access to these bolts, loosen top and rear fasteners on fender filler plate aprons.

To decrease positive caster, add shim at the front bolt. To increase positive caster, remove shim at the front bolt.

To increase camber, remove shims at both front and rear bolt. To decrease camber, add shims at both bolts.

By adding or subtracting an equal amount of shims from both front and rear bolts, camber will change without affecting caster adjustment.

TOE-IN
ADJUST

To adjust the toe-in, loosen the clamps at both ends of the adjustable tubes at each tie rod. Then turn the tubes an equal

amount until the toe-in is correct. When the tie rods are mounted ahead of the steering knuckle, they must be decreased in length to increase toe-in. When the tie rods are mounted behind the steering knuckle, they must be increased in length to increase toe-in.

NOTE: The steering knuckle and steering arm "rock" or tilt as front wheel rises and falls. Therefore, it is vitally important to position the bottom face of the tie rod end parallel with the machined surface at the outer end of the steering arm when tie rod length is adjusted. Severe damage and possible failure can result unless this precaution is taken. The tie rod sleeve clamps must be straight down to provide clearance.

Fig. 1 Front suspension. Full Size (Typical)

Fig. 2 Front suspension. Exc. Full Size

Fig. 3 Checking ball joints for wear

FRONT SUSPENSION BALL JOINT WEAR INDICATOR

WORN

NEW

SINTERED IRON BEARING

WEAR SURFACES

HOUSING SOCKET

.050 INCH

RUBBER PRESSURE RING

WEAR INDICATOR

WHEN BALL JOINT WEAR CAUSES WEAR INDICATOR SHOULDER TO RECEDE WITHIN THE SOCKET HOUSING REPLACEMENT IS REQUIRED

Fig. 4 Ball joint wear indicator

CHECKING BALL JOINTS FOR WEAR

If loose ball joints are suspected, first be sure the front wheel bearings are properly adjusted and that the control arms are tight. Then check ball joints for wear as follows:

Referring to **Fig. 3**, raise wheel with a jack placed under the lower control arm as shown. Then test by moving the wheel up and down to check axial play, and rocking it at the top and bottom to measure radial play.

CUTLASS

1. Upper ball joint should be replaced if looseness exceeds .125 inch.

NOTE: A wear indicator is built into the lower ball joint, **Fig. 4**.

FULL SIZE CARS

1. Upper ball joint should be replaced if looseness exceeds .125 inch.

NOTE: A wear indicator is built into the lower ball joint. Refer to **Fig. 4**.

BALL JOINTS
REPLACE

On some models the ball joints are riv-eted to the control arms. All service ball joints, however, are provided with bolt, nut and washer assemblies for replacement purposes.

Some ball joints are pressed into the control arms, in which case they may be pressed out and new ones installed.

LOWER BALL JOINT

1. Raise vehicle and support at frame. Remove wheel.
2. Support lower control arm with a suitable jack.
3. Remove cotter pin and loosen stud nut 2–3 turns. Using tool No. J-8806 or equivalent, break ball joint loose from the knuckle, **Fig. 5**.
4. Remove stud nut and lower the control arm. Position knuckle assembly aside.
5. Pry ball joint seal retainer from joint and remove seal.
6. Press ball joint from lower control arm with suitable tools.
7. Reverse procedure to install. Torque ball joint stud nut to the following specifications:

Year	Model	Ft. Lbs.
1982–86	All	70
1981	All	90
1980	All	90①

①—Before installing stud nut, tool No. J-29194 must be used to seat the stud on the steering knuckle. Torque tool to 40 ft. lbs., then remove tool and install and torque stud nut.

UPPER BALL JOINT

1. Raise vehicle and support at frame. Remove wheel.
2. Support lower control arm with suit-able jack or jack stand.
3. Remove cotter pin and loosen stud nut 2–3 turns. Using tool No. J-8806 or equivalent, break ball joint loose from the knuckle, **Fig. 6**.
4. Remove stud nut and support knuckle assembly to prevent damage to brake hose.
5. Using a ⅛ inch twist drill, drill the 4 ball joint rivets approximately ¼ inch. Then drill off rivets heads using a ½ inch twist drill.
6. Punch out rivets and remove lower ball joint.
7. Install new ball joint in lower control arm and torque attaching bolts to 8 ft. lbs.
8. Reverse procedure to assemble. Torque ball joint stud nut to the following specifications:

Year	Model	Ft. Lbs.
1982–86	All	50
1981	All	65
1980	All	65①

①—Before installing stud nut, tool No. J-29193 must be used to seat the stud on the steering knuckle. Torque tool to 40 ft. lbs., then remove tool and install and torque stud nut.

WHEEL BEARINGS
REPLACE

1. Raise car and remove front wheels.
2. Remove brake pads and caliper assembly but do not disconnect brake line. Suspend caliper from a wire loop or hook to avoid strain on the brake hose.
3. Remove grease cap, cotter pin and nut. Pull off hub and disc assembly. Grease retainer and inner bearing can now be removed.

Fig. 5 Removing lower ball joint stud from knuckle

Fig. 6 Removing upper ball joint stud from knuckle

WHEEL BEARINGS
ADJUST

1. While rotating hub assembly, tighten spindle nut to 12 ft. lbs. to insure bearings are properly seated.
2. Back off nut to the just loose position.
3. Hand tighten spindle nut, then loosen nut until either hole in spindle aligns with slot in nut. Do not back off more than ½ flat.
4. Install cotter pin, then measure hub assembly end play. There will be .001 to .005 in. end play when bearings are properly adjusted.

SHOCK ABSORBER
REPLACE

1. Remove upper attaching nut, retainer and grommet from shock absorber.
2. Remove two bolts and washers attaching shock absorber to lower control arm and remove shock absorber.
3. To install, position grommet and retainer over shock and slide shock up through spring and frame. Install and tighten attaching nut and lower capscrews.

COIL SPRING
REPLACE

IMPORTANT: Left and right coil springs should not be interchanged. Spring part number is stamped on outer side of end coil.

1. Place transmission in Neutral.
2. Disconnect shock absorber from upper mounting.
3. Raise vehicle and support at frame. Remove wheel.
4. Disconnect stabilizer bar from lower control arm.
5. Remove shock absorber.
6. Install lower plate BT-7408-1A or 1B, **Fig. 7,** with pivot ball seat facing downward into spring coils. Rotate plate to fully seat it in lower control arm spring seat.
7. Install upper plate BT-7408-1A or 1B, **Fig. 7,** with pivot ball seat facing upward into spring coils. Insert ball nut BT-7408-4 through spring coils and onto upper plate.
8. Install rod BT-7408-5 through shock absorber opening in lower control arm and through the upper and lower plates. Depress lock pin on shaft and thread into upper ball nut BT-7408-4. Ensure lock pin is fully extended above ball nut upper surface.
9. With ball nut tang engaged in slot in upper plate, rotate upper plate until it contacts upper spring seat.
10. Install lower pivot ball, thrust bearing and nut on rod and rotate nut until coil spring is compressed enough to be free in the seat.
11. Remove lower control arm pivot bolts. Move control arm rearward and remove coil spring.
12. Reverse procedure to install.

MANUAL STEERING GEAR
REPLACE

1. Remove two flex coupling flange nuts.

NOTE: Remove coupling shield.

2. Hoist and support car with stands under outer ends of lower control arms.
3. Remove nut and use a puller to remove pitman arm.
4. Remove gear-to frame bolts.
5. Position steering linkage out of the way and withdraw gear assembly from under car.
6. Reverse procedure to install unit.

POWER STEERING GEAR
REPLACE

1. Remove coupling flange hub bolt.

NOTE: Remove coupling shield.

2. Disconnect hoses from gear and cap gear and hose fittings.
3. Remove pitman arm nut and, using a suitable puller, remove pitman arm.
4. Remove gear-to-frame bolts. Permit lower shaft to slide free of coupling flange, then remove gear with hoses attached.

Fig. 7 Replacing coil spring

POWER STEERING PUMP
REPLACE

To replace the power steering pump, loosen pump adjusting bolts and position pump so that drive belt can be removed from pump pulley. Disconnect hydraulic lines from pump and plug all lines and openings to prevent entry of dirt. Remove bolts securing pump or pump and bracket to engine and remove pump from vehicle. It may be necessary, depending on engine and vehicle model, to remove other accessories and components from front of engine to facilitate steering pump removal.

PONTIAC
EXC. FIERO, SUNBIRD, 1000 &
FRONT WHEEL DRIVE

INDEX OF SERVICE OPERATIONS

NOTE: Refer to the rear of this manual for vehicle manufacturer's special service tool suppliers.

Serial Number Location

1980–86: On plate fastened to upper left instrument panel area, visible through windshield.

On 1980, the 5th digit represents engine identification code. On 1981–86 the 8th digit represents engine identification code.

Engine Identification

Buick built engines have the distributor located at the front of the engine. On 1980–82 V6-231 engines, the engine identification code is located on the front of the left rocker arm cover. On 1983–86 V6-231 engines, the engine identification code is located on the left side engine to transmission mounting flange below the cylinder head. On 1982 V6-252 engines, the engine identification code is located on the left rear engine block. On V8-350 engines, the engine identification code is located on the front of the left rocker arm cover.

Chevrolet built engines have the distributor located at the rear of the engine, with clockwise rotor rotation. On V6-173 and 229, V8-305 and V8-350 engines, the engine identification code is located on a machined surface on the front of the block below the right cylinder head.

Oldsmobile built engines have the distributor located at the rear of the engine with counter clockwise rotor rotation and right side mounted fuel pump. On 1981 V8-307 engine, the engine identification code is located on the right side valve cover. On 1980 V8-350 and engines, the engine identification code is located on the front of the left rocker arm cover. On 1980–82 V8-350 diesel engines, the engine identification code is located on the right side valve cover. On 1983–86 V8-350 diesel engines, the engine identification code is located on the left front of the engine below the cylinder head.

Pontiac built V8 engines have the distributor located at the rear of the engine with counter clockwise rotor rotation and left side mounted fuel pump. On 1982–86 4-151 engines, the engine identification code is located on the left side engine to transmission mounting flange above the starter. On 1980–81 V8-265 engines, the engine identification code is located on the front of the left and right hand valve covers. On V8-301, V8-350 and V8-400 engines, the engine identification code is located on a machined surface on the front of the engine block below the right cylinder head.

Engine Codes

Code	Trans.	V.I.N. Code ①	Engine
1980			
CLA	②	K	V6-229④⑤
CLB,CLC	③	K	V6-229④⑤
EA,EX,OJ	②	A	V6-231④⑥
EB,EC,EO,EP	③	A	V6-231④⑥
EZ,OA,OK,OL	③	A	V6-231④⑥
EF,EG,ES,ET	③	A	V6-231⑥⑦
OB,OC,OM,ON	③	A	V6-231⑥⑦
XH,XR,X6	③	S	V8-301④
XT,XW,X3,X9	③	W	V8-301④
XN,YN,YR	③	W	V8-301④
YL	③	T	V8-301⑧
CEC,CEL,CEM	③	H	V8-305⑤⑦
ML,MV	③	X	V8-350④⑥
UAD,UAF	③	R	V8-350⑦⑨
VBN,VBT,VCD,VCP	③	N	V8-350⑩
1981			
NA,NZ	②	A	V6-231④⑥
NB,NL,RA	③	A	V6-231④⑥
NC,ND,RB	③	A	V6-231⑥⑦
RK,RL,RC,RD	③	A	V6-231⑥
AU,AW,AZ	③	S	V8-265
BA,DB,DC	③	S	V8-265
DH,DJ	③	S	V8-265
WAV	③	S	V8-265
WDB	③	S	V8-265④
WDH	③	S	V8-265⑦
WBD,WBJ	③	W	V8-301
WBO	③	T	V8-301⑧
DHA,DHB,DHC	③⑪	H	V8-305⑤
DHD,DHF,DHH	③⑪	H	V8-305⑤
DHJ,DHK,DHU	③⑪	H	V8-305⑤
DHZ	②	H	V8-305④⑤
DHZ	③	H	V8-305⑤⑦
DKB,D6A,D6B	③⑪	H	V8-305⑤
D6C,D6D	③⑪	H	V8-305⑤
TKA,TKB,TKC	③	Y	V8-307⑨
TKJ,TKM	③	Y	V8-307④⑨
TKL,TKR	③	Y	V8-307⑦⑨
TKP,TKT,TKU	③	Y	V8-307⑨
TKX,TKY,TKZ	③	Y	V8-307⑨
TLA,TLB,TLD	③	Y	V8-307⑨
TLF,TLH,TLJ	③	Y	V8-307⑨
TLK,TLL,TLM,TLN	③	Y	V8-307⑨
VKB,VKC,VKH	③	N	V8-350⑨⑩
VKJ,VKN,VKR	③	N	V8-350⑨⑩
VKU,VKY,VLA	③	N	V8-350⑨⑩
VLC,VLD,VLK	③	N	V8-350⑨⑩
VLL,VLN,VLP	③	N	V8-350⑨⑩
VL8,VLY,VMJ	③	N	V8-350⑨⑩
VMT,VMX,VMY	③	N	V8-350⑨⑩
VNA,VNB,VNC	③	N	V8-350⑨⑩
VND,VNE	③	N	V8-350⑨⑩
1982			
X3A,X3C,X3F	②	2	4-151
X3H,X5A,X5F,X5H	③	2	4-151
CBT,CBU,CBW	③⑪	1	V6-173⑤
CBX,CB2,CJB	③	1	V6-173⑤
C7A,C7B,C7C,C7D	③	1	V6-173⑤
MA,MG,MC	③	A	V6-231⑥
MK,ML,MM	③	A	V6-231⑥
FA,FB,FC	③	4	V6-252⑥
FD,FE,FF	③	4	V6-252⑥
FG,FH,FJ,FK	③	4	V6-252⑥
CFA,CFB,CFC,CFD	③	H	V8-305⑤
CFF,CFH,CFR,C2R	③	H	V8-305⑤
C2S,C2T,C2U,C2W	③	H	V8-305⑤
CFT,CFW,CFY,CF2,CRA	③	H	V8-305⑤
CEJ,CFK,CFM,CFN	③	7	V8-305⑤
VAB,VAC,VAD,VAK	③	N	V8-350⑨⑩
VAL,VAM,VAN,VAP	③	N	V8-350⑨⑩
VAS,VAU,VAW,VAX	③	N	V8-350⑨⑩
VAY,VAZ,VBA,VBB	③	N	V8-350⑨⑩
VBC,VBP,VBU,VBW	③	N	V8-350⑨⑩
1983			
YMM,YMT		2	4-151
DAA,DAB,DAC,DAD		2	4-151

continued

ENGINE CODES—Continued

Code	Trans.	V.I.N. Code ①	Engine
1983—Continued			
DAF,DAJ,DAK,D6A	2		4-151
D6B,D6C,D6D	1		V6-173⑤
—	L		V6-173 H.O.⑤
DBA,DBB,DBC,DBD	9		V6-229⑤
DBF,DBH	9		V6-229⑤
ND,NG,NH,NJ,NL	A		V6-231⑥
DDB,DDC,DDD,DDF	H		V8-305⑤
DDH,DDJ,DDK,DDM	H		V8-305⑤
DDN,DDS,DDW,DDY	H		V8-305⑤
DDZ,DGN,DRA,DSC	H		V8-305⑤
DUK,DVA,D5B,D5C	H		V8-305⑤
D5D,D5F,D5H,D5N	H		V8-305⑤
D5R	H		V8-305⑤
DDA,DUA	S		V8-305TBI⑤
VKB,VKC,VKD,VKK	N		V8-350⑨⑩
VKL,VKR,VKS,VKT	N		V8-350⑨⑩
VKZ,VLA,VLB,VLP	N		V8-350⑨⑩
VLS,VLT,VLW,VMR	N		V8350⑨⑩
VMS,VMT,VMU,VMW	N		V8-350⑨⑩
VMX,VMY,VMZ,VNA	N		V8-350⑨⑩
VNB,VNC,VND,VNF	N		V8-350⑨⑩
VNH,VNJ	N		V8-350⑨⑩
1984			
Z3F,Z3H,Z5F	2		4-151
C3A,C3B,C3C,C3D	1		V6-173⑤
SAN,SAR	L		V6-173⑤
FRA,FSA,FUA,FWA	A		V6-231⑥
FXA,FYA,FZA	A		V6-231⑥
C4A,C4B,C4C	H		V8-305⑤
C4D,C4W	H		V8-305⑤
SDA,SDH,SDJ	H		V8-305⑤
SDN,SDR,SDS,SDU	H		V8-305⑤
SUF,SUH,SUJ,SXA	G		V8-305⑤
RAA,RAB,RAF,RAH	N		V8-350⑨⑩
RAJ,RAM,RAN,RAP	N		V8-350⑨⑩

Code	Trans.	V.I.N. Code ①	Engine
RAT,RAU,RAX,RAY	N		V8-350⑨⑩
RAZ,RBL,RBM,RBR	N		V8-350⑨⑩
RBS,RBT,RBU,RBW	N		V8-350⑨⑩
1985			
RBX,RBY,RBZ,RCA	N		V8-350⑨⑩
RCB,RCC,RCD,RCF	N		V8-350⑨⑩
RCH,RCJ	N		V8-350⑨⑩
NFA,F4A	A		V6-231⑥
CCB,CLB,CLC	Z		V6-262TBI⑤
CLD,CLF,CLH	Z		V6-262TBI⑤
CDD,CDF,CDH	H		V8-305⑤
CDJ,CDL,CKA	H		V8-305⑤
C4P,C7A,C7B	H		V8-305⑤
T9N,T9P,T9R,T9S	H		V8-305⑤
RLA,RLB,RLD,RLF	N		V8-350⑨⑩
RLH,RLJ,RLL,RLM	N		V8-350⑨⑩
RLP,RLS	N		V8-350⑨⑩
C5P	6		V8-350⑨⑩

①—On 1980 vehicles, the fifth digit in the V.I.N. denotes engine code. On 1981–86 vehicles, the eighth digit in the V.I.N. denotes engine code.
②—Man. trans.
③—Auto. trans.
④—Except California.
⑤—See Chevrolet chapter for service procedures.
⑥—See Buick chapter for service procedures.
⑦—California.
⑧—Turbocharged engine.
⑨—See Oldsmobile chapter for service procedures.
⑩—Diesel.
⑪—Four speed man. trans.

Grille Identification

1980–81 Firebird Formula

1980–81 Firebird Trans Am

1980 Grand Am

1980 Grand LeMans

1980 Grand Prix

1980 Bonneville & Catalina

1981 Bonneville

1981 LeMans

1981 Grand Prix

continued

1982 Bonneville

1982 Grand Prix

1982–83 Firebird; 1984 Firebird Exc. Trans Am

1983–86 Bonneville

1983–84 Grand Prix

1983–84 Pontiac Parisienne

1985–86 Grand Prix

1985–86 Pontiac Parisienne

1985–86 Firebird

1985–86 Firebird Trans Am

General Engine Specifications

Year	Engine CID①/Liter	V.I.N. Code②	Carburetor	Bore and Stroke	Compression Ratio	Net H.P. @ R.P.M.③	Maximum Torque Ft. Lbs. @ R.P.M.	Normal Oil Pressure Pounds
1980	V6-229, 3.8L④	K	M2ME, 2 Bbl.⑤	3.376 × 3.48	8.6	115 @ 4000	175 @ 2000	45
	V6-231, 3.8L⑦	A	M2ME, 2 Bbl.⑤	3.80 × 3.40	8.0	115 @ 3800	188 @ 2000	37
	V8-265, 4.3L	S	M2ME, 2 Bbl.⑤	3.75 × 3.00	8.3	120 @ 3600	210 @ 1600	35–40
	V8-301, 4.9L	W	M4ME, 4 Bbl.⑤	4.00 × 3.00	8.2	150 @ 4000	240 @ 2000	35–40
	V8-301, 4.9L⑩	W	M4ME, 4 Bbl.⑤	4.00 × 3.00	8.2	170 @ 4400	240 @ 2200	55–60
	V8-301, 4.9L⑨	T	M4ME, 4 Bbl.⑤	4.00 × 3.00	7.5	205 @ 4000	310 @ 2800	55–60
	V8-305, 5.0L④	H	E4ME, 4 Bbl.⑤	3.736 × 3.48	8.4	150 @ 3800	230 @ 2400	45
	V8-350, 5.7L⑦	X	M4MC, 4 Bbl.⑤	3.80 × 3.85	—	—	—	37
	V8-350, 5.7L⑥	R	E4MC, 4 Bbl.⑤	4.057 × 3.385	—	160 @ 3600	270 @ 2000	30–45
	V8-350, 5.7L⑥⑧	N	Fuel Injection	4.057 × 3.385	22.5	105 @ 3200	205 @ 1600	30–45
1981	V6-231, 3.8L⑥	A	E2ME, 2 Bbl.⑤	4.00 × 3.00	8.0	110 @ 3800	190 @ 1600	35–40
	V8-265, 4.3L	S	E2ME, 2 Bbl.⑤	3.75 × 3.00	8.3	120 @ 4000	205 @ 2000	35–40
	V8-301, 4.9L⑩	W	E4ME, 4 Bbl.⑤	4.00 × 3.00	8.1	135 @ 3600	235 @ 3600	35–40
	V8-301, 4.9L⑨	T	E4ME, 4 Bbl.⑤	4.00 × 3.00	7.5	200 @ 4000	340 @ 2000	55–60
	V8-305, 5.0L④	H	E4ME, 4 Bbl.⑤	3.736 × 3.48	8.6	145 @ 3800	240 @ 2400	30–45
	V8-307, 5.0L⑥	Y	E4ME, 4 Bbl.⑤	3.80 × 3.385	8.5	145 @ 3800	240 @ 2000	30–45
	V8-350, 5.7L⑥⑧	N	Fuel Injection	4.057 × 3.385	22.5	105 @ 3200	205 @ 1600	37

continued

GENERAL ENGINE SPECIFICATIONS—Continued

Year	Engine CID①/Liter	V.I.N. Code②	Carburetor	Bore and Stroke	Compression Ratio	Net H.P. @ R.P.M.③	Maximum Torque Ft. Lbs. @ R.P.M.	Normal Oil Pressure Pounds
1982	4-151, 2.5L	2	T.B.I.	4.00 × 3.00	8.2	90 @ 4000	132 @ 2800	36–41
	V6-173, 2.8L④	1	E2SE, 2 Bbl.⑤	3.50 × 3.00	8.5	102 @ 4800	142 @ 2400	50–65
	V6-231, 3.8L⑦	A	E2ME, 2 Bbl.⑤	3.80 × 3.40	8.0	110 @ 3800	190 @ 1600	37
	V6-252, 4.1L⑦	4	E4ME, 4 Bbl.⑤	3.965 × 3.40	8.0	125 @ 3800	210 @ 2000	37
	V8-305, 5.0L④	H	E4ME, 4 Bbl.⑤	3.736 × 3.48	8.6	145 @ 4000	240 @ 2000	50–65
	V8-305, 5.0L④	7	T.B.I.	3.736 × 3.48	9.5	165 @ 4200	240 @ 2400	50–65
	V8-350, 5.7L⑥⑧	N	Fuel Injection	4.057 × 3.385	22.5	105 @ 3200	200 @ 1600	35
1983	4-151, 2.5L	2	T.B.I.	4.00 × 3.00	8.2	92 @ 4000	134 @ 2800	36–41
	V6-173, 2.8L④	1	E2SE, 2 Bbl.⑤	3.50 × 3.00	8.5	107 @ 4800	145 @ 2100	50–65
	V6-173 H.O., 2.8L④	L	E2SE, 2 Bbl.⑤	3.50 × 3.00	8.9	135 @ 5400	145 @ 2400	50–65
	V6-229, 3.8L④	9	E2ME, 2 Bbl.⑤	3.736 × 3.48	8.6	110 @ 4200	170 @ 2000	50–65
	V6-231, 3.8L⑦	A	E2ME, 2 Bbl.⑤	3.80 × 3.40	8.0	110 @ 3800	190 @ 1600	37
	V8-305, 5.0L④	H	E4ME, 4 Bbl.⑤	3.736 × 3.48	8.6	150 @ 4000	240 @ 2400	50–65
	V8-305, 5.0L④	S	T.B.I.	3.736 × 3.48	9.5	175 @ 4200	250 @ 2800	50–65
	V8-305 H.O., 5.0L④	G	E4ME, 4 Bbl.⑤	3.736 × 3.48	9.5	190 @ 4800	240 @ 3200	50–65
	V8-350, 5.7L⑥⑧	N	Fuel Injection	4.057 × 3.385	22.5	105 @ 3200	200 @ 1600	30–45
1984	4-151, 2.5L	2	T.B.I.	4.00 × 3.00	9.0	92 @ 4400	132 @ 2800	36–41
	V6-173, 2.8L④	1	E2SE, 2 Bbl.⑤	3.50 × 3.00	8.5	107 @ 4800	145 @ 2100	50–65
	V6-173 H.O. 2.8L④	L	E2SE, 2 Bbl.⑤	3.50 × 3.00	8.9	125 @ 5400	145 @ 2400	50–65
	V6-231, 3.8L⑦	A	E2ME, 2 Bbl.⑤	3.80 × 3.40	8.0	110 @ 3800	190 @ 1600	37
	V8-305, 5.0L④	H	E4ME, 4 Bbl.⑤	3.736 × 3.48	8.6	150 @ 4000	240 @ 2400	50–65
	V8-305, H.O., 5.0L④	G	E4ME, 4 Bbl.⑤	3.736 × 3.48	9.5	190 @ 4800	240 @ 3200	50–65
	V8-350, 5.7L⑥⑧	N	Fuel Injection	4.057 × 3.385	22.5	105 @ 3200	200 @ 1600	30–45
1985	4-151, 2.5L	—	T.B.I.	4.00 × 3.00	8.2	—	—	37.5
	V6-173, 2.8L④	—	M.F.I.	3.50 × 3.00	8.9	135 @ 5100	165 @ 3600	50–65
	V6-231, 3.8L⑦	A	E2ME, 2 Bbl.⑤	3.80 × 3.40	8.0	110 @ 3800	190 @ 1600	37
	V6-262, 4.3L⑤	Z	T.B.I.	4.00 × 3.48	9.3	130 @ 3600	210 @ 2000	50–65
	V8-305, 5.0L④	H	E4ME, 4 Bbl.⑤	3.736 × 3.48	9.5	165 @ 4200	245 @ 2400	50–65
	V8-305, H.O., 5.0L④	G	E4ME, 4 Bbl.⑤	3.736 × 3.48	9.5	—	—	50–65
	V8-305, TPI, 5.0L④	6	T.P.I.	3.736 × 3.48	9.5	215 @ 4400	275 @ 3200	—
	V8-350, 5.7L⑥⑧	N	Fuel Injection	4.057 × 3.385	21.6	105 @ 3200	200 @ 1600	30–45
1986	4-151, 2.5L	2	T.B.I.	4.00 × 3.00	9.0	—	—	37.5
	V6-173, 2.8L④	S	M.F.I.	3.50 × 3.00	8.9	—	—	50–65
	V6-231, 3.8L⑦	A	E2ME, 2 Bbl.⑤	3.80 × 3.40	—	—	—	37.5
	V6-262, 4.3L④	Z	T.B.I.	4.00 × 3.48	9.3	—	—	50–65
	V8-305, 5.0L④	H	E4ME, 4 Bbl.⑤	3.736 × 3.48	9.5	—	—	50–65
	V8-305, H.O. 5.0L④	G	E4ME, 4 Bbl.⑤	3.736 × 3.48	9.5	—	—	50–65
	V8-305, TPI, 5.0L④	F	T.P.I.	3.736 × 3.48	9.5	—	—	50–65

①—CID—Cubic Inch displacement.
②—VIN Code—On 1980 vehicles the fifth digit in the VIN denotes engine code. On 1981–86 vehicles the eighth digit in the VIN denotes engine code.
③—Ratings are net—as installed in vehicle.
④—See Chevrolet chapter for service procedures on this engine.
⑤—Rochester.
⑥—See Oldsmobile chapter for service procedures on this engine.
⑦—See Buick chapter for service procedures on this engine.
⑧—Diesel engine.
⑨—Turbocharged engine.
⑩—E/C (electronic engine control).

Rear Axle Specifications

Year	Model	Carrier Type	Ring Gear & Pinion Backlash		Pinion Bearing Preload			Differential Bearing Preload		
			Method	Adjustment	Method	New Bearings Inch-Lbs.	Used Bearings Inch-Lbs.	Method	New Bearings Inch-Lbs.	Used Bearings Inch-Lbs.
1980–86	Exc. 1983–86 Parisienne	Integral	Shims	.006–.008	①	20–25	10–15	Shims	35–40	20–25
1983–86	Parisienne	Integral	Shims	.005–.008	Spacer	15–30②	10–15②	Shims	—	—

①—Tighten pinion shaft nut with inch-pound torque wrench.
②—Use inch-pound torque wrench on pinion shaft nut.

Starting Motor Applications

Year	Model/V.I.N.	Starter Number	Year	Model/V.I.N.	Starter Number
1980	V6-229/K	1109524	1983	4-151/2	1109556
	V6-231/A	1109061		V6-173/L,1	1109535
	V8-305/H	1109524		V6-229/9	1998236
	V8-350/X	1109061		V6-231/A	1998236
	V8-350/R②	1109072		V8-305/G,H,S	1109534⑤
	V8-350 Diesel/N	1109213		V8-350 Diesel/N	1998554
1981	V6-231/A	1109061	1984	4-151/2	1998450
	V8-265/S, 301/T,W	1109523		V6-173/L,1	1998427
	V8-305/H①	1109524		V6-231/A⑥	1998236
	V8-305/H④	1109074		V6-231/A⑦	1998452
	V8-307/Y	1998205		V8-305/G,H	1998430⑤
	V8-350 Diesel/N	1109216		V8-350 Diesel/N	1998554
1982	4-151/2	1109533		V6-231/A	1998236
	V6-173/1	1109535	1985	V6-262/Z	1998435
	V6-231/A	1998236		V8-305/H	1998435
	V6-252/4	1998234		V8-350 Diesel/N	22522853
	V8-305/H,7	④	1986	V6-231/A	1998516
	V8-350 Diesel/N	1998552		V8-305/H	1998557

①—Except Firebird.
②—Distributor located rear of engine, rotor rotation counter clockwise. Fuel pump located right side of engine.
③—Firebird.
④—Models less 4 spd. man. trans., #1109534; models w/4 spd. man. trans., #1998240.
⑤—With high output option, 1998466.
⑥—Exc. Parisienne.
⑦—Parisienne.

Alternator Specifications

Year	Model	Rated Hot Output Amps	Field Current 12 Volts @ 80°F.	Year	Model	Rated Hot Output Amps	Field Current 12 Volts @ 80°F.	Year	Model	Rated Hot Output Amps	Field Current 12 Volts @ 80°F.
1980	1101038	70	4.0–4.6		1100226	37	4.0–5.0		1105569	78	4.5–5.0
	1103043	42	4.0–5.0		1100230	42	4.0–5.0		1105548	85	4.0–4.6
	1103103	63	4.0–5.0		1100239	55	4.5–5.0		1105444	94	4.5–5.0
	1103104	42	4.0–5.0		1100246	63	4.0–4.5		1105523	56	4.5–5.0
	1103112	63	4.0–5.0		1100247	55	4.0–4.5		1105606	94	4.5–5.0
1981	1101037	70	4.0–4.6		1100263	78	4.0–4.5		1100237	56	4.5–5.0
	1101038	70	4.0–4.6		1100270	78	4.0–4.5		1100260	78	4.5–5.0
	1103088	55	4.0–5.0		1100300	63	4.5–5.0		1105521	78	4.5–5.0
	1103091	63	4.0–5.0		1105022	78	4.0–4.5		1100200	78	4.5–5.0
	1103103	63	4.0–5.0		1105798	63	4.0–4.6	1986	1105548	85	—
1982	1100110	42	4.0–5.0		1105343	85	—		1100246	66	—
	1100179	42	4.0–5.0	1984	1100200	78	4.5–5.0		1105651	94	—
	1103187	42	4.0–5.0		1100239	56	4.5–5.0		1105523	56	—
	1100121	63	4.0–5.0		1100260	78	4.5–5.0		1105444	94	—
	1103197	63	4.0–5.0		1105197	70	4.0–4.6		1105569	78	—
	1100199	63	4.0–5.0		1105443	94	4.5–5.0		1105676	56	—
	1101037	70	4.0–4.6		1105444	94	4.5–5.0		1105650	78	—
	1101088	70	4.0–4.6		1105493	94	4.5–5.0		1100237	56	—
	1100187	70	4.0–4.6		1105548	85	4.0–4.6		1105652	78	—
	1101449	70	—		1105565	78	4.5–5.0		1105673	56	—
	1101045	85	4.0–4.6	1985	1105555	66	4.5–5.0		1100239	56	—
	1101443	85	4.0–4.6		1100239	56	4.5–5.0		1100200	78	—
1983	1100200	78	4.5–5.0		1100270	78	4.5–5.0				

①—At 5500 RPM.

continued

Valve Specifications

Year	Model/V.I.N.	Valve Lash		Valve Angles		Valve Spring Installed Height	Valve Spring Pressure Lbs. @ In.	Stem Clearance		Stem Diameter	
		Int.	Exh.	Seat	Face			Intake	Exhaust	Intake	Exhaust
1980	V6-229/K①	1 Turn②		46	45	1.70	200 @ 1.25	.0010–.0027	.0010–.0027	.3410–.3417	.3410–.3417
	V6-231/A④	Hydraulic⑨		45	45	1.727	③	.0015–.0035	.0015–.0032	.3401–.3412	.3405–.3412
	V8-265/S	Hydraulic⑤		46	45	1.66	175 @ 1.29	.0010–.0027	.0010–.0027	.3418–.3425	.3418–.3425
	V8-301/T,W	Hydraulic⑤		46	45	1.66	175 @ 1.29	.0010–.0027	.0010–.0027	.3418–.3425	.3418–.3425
	V8-305/L①	1 Turn②		46	45	1.70	200 @ 1.25	.0010–.0027	.0010–.0027	.3410–.3417	.3410–.3417
	V8-350/X④⑩	Hydraulic⑨		45	45	1.727	182 @ 1.34	.0015–.0035	.0015–.0032	.3401–.3412	.3405–.3412
	V8-350/R⑧⑪	Hydraulic⑨		⑥	⑦	1.67	187 @ 1.27	.0010–.0027	.0015–.0032	.3425–.3432	.3420–.3427
	V8-350 Diesel/N⑪	Hydraulic⑨		⑥	⑦	1.67	151 @ 1.30	.0010–.0027	.0015–.0032	.3425–.3432	.3420–.3427
1981	V6-231/A④	Hydraulic⑨		45	45	1.727	③	.0015–.0035	.0015–.0032	.3401–.3412	.3405–.3412
	V8-265/S	Hydraulic⑤		46	45	1.66	175 @ 1.29	.0010–.0027	.0010–.0027	.3425	.3425
	V8-301/T,W	Hydraulic⑤		46	45	1.66	175 @ 1.29	.0010–.0027	.0010–.0027	.3425	.3425
	V8-305/L①	1 Turn②		46	45	1.70	200 @ 1.25	.0010–.0027	.0010–.0027	.3425–.3432	.3420–.3427
	V8-307/Y⑪	Hydraulic⑨		⑥	⑦	1.67	189 @ 1.27	.0010–.0027	.0015–.0032	.3425–.3432	.3420–.3427
	V8-350 Diesel/N⑪	Hydraulic⑨		⑥	⑦	1.67	210 @ 1.3	.0010–.0027	.0015–.0032	.3425–.3432	.3420–.3427
1982	4-151/2	Hydraulic⑨		46	45	1.69	160 @ 1.25	.0010–.0027	.0010–.0027	.3418–.3425	.3418–.3425
	V6-173/1①	1½ Turns②		46	45	1.57	195 @ 1.18	.0010–.0027	.0010–.0027	.3409–.3417	.3409–.3417
	V6-231/A④	Hydraulic⑨		45	45	1.727	182 @ 1.34	.0015–.0035	.0015–.0032	.3401–.3412	.3405–.3412
	V6-252/4④	Hydraulic⑨		45	44	1.727	182 @ 1.34	.0015–.0035	.0015–.0032	.3401–.3412	.3405–.3412
	V8-305/H,7①	1 Turn②		46	45	1.70	200 @ 1.25	.0010–.0027	.0010–.0027	.3425–.3432	.3420–.3427
	V8-350 Diesel/N⑪	Hydraulic⑨		⑥	⑦	1.67	210 @ 1.22	.0010–.0027	.0015–.0032	.3425–.3432	.3420–.3427
1983–84	V6-229/9	1 Turn②		46	45	1.17	200 @ 1.25	.0010–.0027	.0010–.0027	.3410–.3417	.3410–.3417
1983–86	4-151/2	Hydraulic⑨		46	45	1.69	160 @ 1.25	.0010–.0027	.0010–.0027	.3418–.3425	.3418–.3425
	V6-173/1,L①	1½ Turns②		46	45	1.57	195 @ 1.18	.0010–.0027	.0010–.0027	.3409–.3417	.3409–.3417
	V6-231/A④	Hydraulic⑨		45	45	1.72	182 @ 1.34	.0015–.0035	.0015–.0032	.3410–.3412	.3405–.3412
	V8-305/①	1 Turn②		46	45	1.70	200 @ 1.25	.0010–.0027	.0010–.0027	.3425–.3432	.3420–.3427
	V8-350 Diesel/N	Hydraulic⑨		⑥	⑦	1.67	210 @ 1.22	.0010–.0027	.0015–.0032	.3425–.3432	.3420–.3427
1985–86	V6-262/Z	1 Turn②		46	45	1.70	200 @ 1.25	.0110–.0027	.0010–.0027	.3410–.3417	.3410–.3417

①—For service on this engine, see Chevrolet Chapter.
②—Turn rocker arm stud nut until all lash is eliminated, then tighten nut the additional turns listed.
③—Intake 164 ± 5 @ 1.340; Exhaust 182 ± 8 @ 1.340.
④—See Buick chapter for service procedures.
⑤—No adjustment. On V8's, rocker arms are correctly positioned when ball retainer nuts are tightened to 20 ft. lbs.
⑥—Intake, 45°; exhaust, 31°.
⑦—Intake, 44°; exhaust, 30°.
⑧—Distributor located at rear of engine, counterclockwise rotor rotation. Fuel pump located right side of engine.
⑨—No adjustment.
⑩—Distributor located at front of engine.
⑪—See Oldsmobile Chapter for service procedures.

continued

Pistons, Pins, Rings, Crankshaft & Bearings

Year	Model/V.I.N.	Piston Skirt Clearance	Ring End Gap① Comp.⑱	Ring End Gap① Oil⑱	Wrist-pin Diameter	Rod Bearings Shaft Diameter	Rod Bearings Bearing Clearance	Main Bearings Shaft Diameter	Main Bearings Bearing Clearance	Main Bearings Thrust on Bear. No.	Shaft End Play
1980	V6-229/K⑦	.0007–.0017	.010	.015	.9271	2.0986–2.0998	.0013–.0035	②	③	4	.002–.006
	V6-231/A⑧	.0008–.0020	.013	.015	.9392	2.2487–2.2495	.0005–.0026	2.4995	.0003–.0018	2	.003–.009
	V8-265/S	.0025–.0033	.010	.035	.927	2.00	.0005–.0026	3.000	.0002–.0018	4	.0035–.0085
	V8-301/W⑨	.0025–.0033	.010	.035	.927	2.25	.0005–.0026	3.000	.0004–.0020	4	.006–.022
	V8-301/T⑪	.0017–.0025	.010	.035	—	2.25	.0005–.0026	3.000	.0004–.0020	4	.006–.022
	V8-305/H⑦	.0007–.0017	.010	.015	.9271	2.0986–2.0998	.0013–.0035	②	③	5	.002–.006
	V8-350/X⑤⑧	.0008–.0020	.013	.015	.9392	1.991–2.000	.0005–.0026	3.000	.0004–.0015	3	.003–.009
	V8-350/R⑥⑩	.00075–.00175	.010	.015	.9805	2.1238–2.1248	.0005–.0026	2.4985–2.4995	④	3	.0035–.0135
	V8-350/N⑩	.005–.006	.015	.015	1.0951	2.1238–2.1248	.0005–.0026	2.9993–3.0003	⑬	3	.0035–.0135
1981	V6-231/A⑧	.008–.0020	.013	.015	.9392	2.2487–2.2495	.0005–.0026	2.4995	.0003–.0018	2	.003–.009
	V8-265/S	.0017–.0025	.010	.035	.940	2.00	.0005–.0026	3.00	.0002–.0018	4	.003–.009
	V8-301/T,W	.0017–.0025	.010	.035	.940	2.00	.0005–.0026	3.00	.0002–.0018	4	.003–.009
	V8-305/H⑦	.0007–.0017	.010	.015	.9271	2.090–2.100	.0013–.0035	②	③	5	.002–.007
	V8-307/Y⑩	.0005–.0015	.009	.015	.9805	2.1238–2.1248	.0004–.0033	⑫	④	3	.0035–.0135
	V8-350/N⑩	.0005–.0006	.015	.015	1.0951	2.1238–2.1248	.0005–.0026	3.00	⑬	3	.0035–.0135
1982	4-151/2	⑮	.010	.015	.940	2.000	.0005–.0026	2.300	.0005–.0022	5	.0035–.0085
	V6-173/1⑦	.0017–.003	.010	.020	.905	2.0303–2.031	.0014–.0037	⑯	.002–.003	3	.002–.007
	V6-231/A⑧	.0008–.0020	.013	.015	.9392	2.2487–2.2495	.0005–.0026	2.4995	.0003–.0018	2	.003–.009
	V6-252/4⑧	.0008–.0020	.013	.015	.9392	2.2487–2.2495	.0005–.0026	2.4995	.0003–.0018	2	.003–.009
	V8-305/H,7⑦	.0007–.0017	.010	.015	.9271	2.0986–2.0998	.0018–.0039	②	③	5	.002–.007
	V8-350/N⑩	.005–.006	.015	.015	1.0946	2.1238–2.1248	.0005–.0026	2.9993–3.0003	⑬	3	.0035–.0135
1983–84	V6-229/9⑦	.0007–.0017	.010	.015	.927	2.0986–2.0998	.0013–.0035	②	③	4	.004–.008
1983–86	4-151/2	⑮	.010	.015	.940	2.000	.0005–.0026	2.300	.0005–.0022	5	.0035–.0085
	V6-173/1,L⑦	.0017–.003	.010	.020	.905	2.0303–2.031	.0014–.0037	⑯	.002–.003	3	.002–.007
	V6-231/A⑧	.0008–.0020	.010	.015	.939	2.2487–2.2495	.0005–.0026	2.4995	.0003–.0018	2	.003–.009
	V8-305/⑦	.0007–.0017	.010	.015	.927	2.0986–2.0998	.0018–.0039	②	④	5	.002–.006
	V8-350/N⑩	.005–.006	.015	.015	1.094	2.1238–2.1248	.0005–.0026	2.993–3.0003	⑬	3	.0035–.0135
1985–86	V6-262/Z	.0007–.0017	.010	.015	.927	2.0986–2.0998	.0013–.0035	②	④	4	.002–.006

①—Fit rings in tapered bores for clearance listed in tightest portion of ring travel.
②—Front 2.4484–2.4493; Intermediate 2.4481–2.4490; Rear 2.4479–2.4488.
③—Front .0008–.0020; Intermediate .0011–.0023; Rear .0017–.0032.
④—No. 1, 2, 3, 4, .0005–.0021; No. 5, .0015–.0031.
⑤—Distributor located at rear of engine, counter clockwise rotor rotation. Fuel pump located right side of engine.
⑥—Distributor located at front of engine.
⑦—For service on this engine, see Chevrolet Chapter.
⑧—See Buick chapter for service procedures.
⑨—Except turbocharged engine.
⑩—See Oldsmobile Chapter for service procedures.
⑪—Turbocharged engine.
⑫—No. 1—2.4988–2.4998; No. 2, 3, 4, 5; 2.4985–2.4995.
⑬—Distributor located at rear of engine, counter clockwise rotor rotation. Fuel pump located left side of engine.
⑭—No. 1, 2, 3 & 4; .0005–.0021; No. 5, .0020–.0034.
⑮—Clearances specified are minimum gaps.
⑯—Top of bore, .0025–.0033; bottom of bore, .0017–.0041.
⑰—Nos. 1, 2 & 4, 2.5336–2.5345; No. 3, 2.5328–2.534.

continued

Engine Tightening Specifications★

★ Torque specifications are for clean and lightly lubricated threads only. Dry or dirty threads produce increased friction which prevents accurate measurement of thickness.

Year	Model/V.I.N.	Spark Plugs Ft. Lbs.	Cylinder Head Bolts Ft. Lbs.	Intake Manifold Ft. Lbs.	Exhaust Manifold Ft. Lbs.	Rocker Arm Ft. Lbs.	Rocker Arm Cover Ft. Lbs.	Connecting Rod Cap Bolts Ft. Lbs.	Main Bearing Cap Bolts Ft. Lbs.	Flywheel to Crankshaft Ft. Lbs.	Vibration Damper or Pulley Ft. Lbs.
1980–81	V6-229/K③	22	65	30	20	—	45④	45	70	60	60
	V6-231/A⑨	15	80	45	25	30⑧	4	40	100	60	225
	V8-265/S	15	95	35	40	20	6	30	70①	95	160
	V8-301/W⑫	15	95	35	40	20	6	30	70①	95	160
	V8-301/T⑬	20	93	37	40	20	7	28	100①	—	163
	V8-305/H③	22	65	30	20⑤	—	45④	45	70	60	60
	V8-350/X⑨⑪	15	80	45	25	30⑧	4	40	100	60	225
	V8-350/R⑥⑩	25	130⑦	40⑦	25	28	—	42	80②	60	200–310
	V8-350 Diesel/N⑥	—	130⑦	40⑦	25	28	—	42	120	60	200–310
1981	V8-307/Y⑥	25	130⑦	40⑦	25	28	—	42	80②	60	200–310
1982	4-151/2	15	85⑯	29	44	20	6	32	70	44	160
	V6-173/1③	7–15	65–75	20–25	22–28	43–49⑮	6–9	34–40	63–74	45–55	75
	V6-231/A⑨	15	80	45	25	30⑧	4	40	100	60	225
	V6-252/4⑨	15	80	45	20	30⑧	4	40	100	60	225
	V8-305/H,7③	22	65	30	20⑤	—	4	45	70	60	60
	V8-350 Diesel/N⑥	—	130⑦	40⑦	25	28	—	42	120	60	200–310
1983	4-151/2	15	85⑯	29	44	20	6	32	70	⑭	200
	V6-173/1, L③	7–15	70	23	25	46⑮	8	37	69	50	75
	V6-229/9③	22	65	30	20	—	45④	45	70	60	60
	V6-231/A⑨	15	80	45	25	30⑧	4	40	100	60	225
	V8-305/G,H,S③	22	65	30	20⑤	—	45④	45	70	60	60
	V8-350/N⑥	—	130⑦	40⑦	25	28	—	42	120	60	200–310
1984	4-151/2	15	92⑯	29	44	20	6	32	70	44	200
	V6-173/1,L③	7–15	70	23	25	46⑮	8	37	69	50	66–84
	V6-231/A⑨	15	80	45	25	30⑧	4	40	100	60	225
	V8-305/G,H③	22	65	30	20⑤	—	45④	45	70	60	60
	V8-350/N⑥	—	130⑦	40⑦	25	28	—	42	120	60	200–310
1985–86	4-151/	15	92⑯	29	44	20	45④	32	70	44	200
	V6-173/③	7–15	70	23	25	46⑮	8	37	69	50	66–84
	V6-231/A⑨	15	80	45	25	30⑧	4	40	100	60	225
	V6-262/2③	22	65	30	20	—	45④	45	70	60	60
	V8-305/G,H,6③	22	65	30	20	—	45④	45	70	60	60
	V8-350/N⑥	—	130⑦	40⑦	25	28	8	42	120	60	200–310

①—Rear, 100.
②—Rear, 120.
③—For service on this engine, see Chevrolet Chapter.
④—Inch pounds.
⑤—Inside bolts 30 ft. lbs.
⑥—For service on this engine, see Oldsmobile Chapter.

⑦—Clean & dip entire bolt in engine oil before tightening.
⑧—Rocker arm shaft to cylinder head.
⑨—See Buick chapter for service procedures.
⑩—Distributor located at rear of engine, counter clockwise rotor rotation. Fuel pump located right side of engine.

⑪—Distributor located front of engine.
⑫—Except turbocharged engine.
⑬—Turbocharged engine.
⑭—Automatic transmission, 63; Manual transmission, 77.
⑮—Rocker arm stud.
⑯—Requires thread sealer on bolt heads & threads.

continued

Cooling System & Capacity Data

Year	Model or Engine/V.I.N.	Cooling Capacity, Qts. Less A/C	With A/C	Radiator Cap Relief Pressure, Lbs.	Thermo. Opening Temp.	Fuel Tank Gals.	Engine Oil Refill Qts. [1]	Transmission Oil 3 Speed Pints	4 Speed Pints	5 Speed Pints	Auto Trans. Qts. [2]	Rear Axle Oil Pints
1980	V6-229/K LeMans	18.5	18.5	15	195	18.1	4	3.5	—	—	[3]	3.5
	V6-231/A LeMans	13.3	13.3	15	195	18.1	4	3.5	—	—	[3]	3.4
	V6-231/A Firebird	14	14	15	195	20.8	4	3.5	—	—	[3]	4¼
	V6-231/A Grand Prix	13.3	13.3	15	195	18.1	4	—	—	—	[3]	3.5
	V6-231/A Pontiac	13.3	13.3	15	195	25[8]	4	—	—	—	[3]	[9]
	V8-265/S LeMans	20.3	20.3	15	195	18.1	4[14]	—	—	—	[3]	3.5
	V8-265/S Firebird	21.6	21.6	15	195	20.8	4[14]	—	—	—	[3]	4¼
	V8-265/S Grand Prix	20.3	20.3	15	195	18.1	4[14]	—	—	—	[3]	3.5
	V8-265/S Pontiac	21.1	21.1	15	195	25[8]	4[14]	—	—	—	[3]	[9]
1980	V8-301/T LeMans	20.3	20.3	15	195	18.1	4[14]	—	—	—	[3]	3.5
	V8-301/T Firebird	21.6	21.6	15	195	20.8	4[14]	—	—	—	[3]	4¼
	V8-301/T Grand Prix	20.3	20.3	15	195	18.1	4[14]	—	—	—	[3]	3.5
	V8-301/T Pontiac	21.1	21.1	15	195	25[8]	4[14]	—	—	—	[3]	[9]
	V8-305/H LeMans	18.5	18.5	15	195	18.1	4	—	—	—	[3]	3.5
	V8-305/H Firebird	17.3	17.3	15	195	20.8	4	—	—	—	[3]	4¼
	V8-305/H Grand Prix	18.2	18.2	15	195	18.1	4	—	—	—	[3]	3.4
	V8-305/H Pontiac	20.1	20.1	15	195	25[8]	4	—	—	—	[3]	[9]
	V8-350/X Pontiac[10]	14.8	14.8	15	195	25[8]	4	—	—	—	[3]	[9]
	V8-350/R Pontiac[11]	16.4	16.4	15	195	25[8]	5[14]	—	—	—	[3]	[9]
	V8-350 Diesel/N Pontiac	18.2	18.2	15	195	27[8]	7[15]	—	—	—	[3]	[9]
1981	V6-231/A LeMans	13.1	13.1	15	195	18.1	4	3½	—	—	[5]	3.5
	V6-231/A Firebird	13.1	13.1	15	195	20.8	4	3½	—	—	[5]	4.2
	V6-231/A Grand Prix	13.1	13.1	15	195	18.1	4	—	—	—	[6]	3.5
	V6-231/A Pontiac	13.1	13.3	15	195	25	4	—	—	—	[7]	[9]
	V8-265/S LeMans	20.3	20.3	15	195	18.1	4[14]	—	—	—	[5]	3.5
	V8-265/S Firebird	20.9[16]	20.9[16]	15	195	20.8	4[14]	—	—	—	[5]	4.2
	V8-265/S Grand Prix	20.3	20.3	15	195	18.1	4[14]	—	—	—	[6]	3.5
	V8-265/S Pontiac	19	19	15	195	25	4[14]	—	—	—	[7]	[9]
	V8-301/W LeMans	20.3[12]	21	15	195	18.1	4[14]	—	—	—	[5]	3.5
	V8-301/W Firebird	20.9[16]	20.9[16]	15	195	20.8	4[14]	—	—	—	[5]	4.2
	V8-301/T Firebird	23	23	15	195	20.8	5[22]	—	—	—	[5]	4.2
	V8-305/H Firebird	17.2	17.2	15	195	20.8	4	—	—	—	[5]	4.2
	V8-307/Y Pontiac	15.6	15.3[13]	15	195	25[8]	4	—	—	—	[7]	[9]
	V8-350/N Grand Prix	17	17	15	195	19.8	7[15]	—	—	—	[6]	3.5
	V8-350/N Pontiac	17	17	15	195	27[8]	7[15]	—	—	—	[7]	[9]
1982	4-151/2 Firebird	12.8	13	15	195	16	3[14]	—	3.5	—	[18]	3.5
	V6-173/1 Firebird	12.5	12.5	15	195	16	4[14]	—	3.5	—	[18]	3.5
	V6-231/A Bonneville	13	13	15	195	18	4	—	—	—	[19]	3.5
	V6-231/A Grand Prix	13	13	15	195	18	4	—	—	—	[19]	3.5
	V6-252/4 Bonneville	13	13	15	195	18	4	—	—	—	[19]	3.5
	V6-252/4 Grand Prix	13	13	15	195	18	4	—	—	—	[19]	3.5
	V8-305/H Firebird	15	15	15	195	16	4	—	—	—	[18]	3.5
	V8-305 E.F.I./7 Firebird	15	15	15	195	16	4	—	—	—	[18]	3.5
	V8-350 Diesel/N Bonneville	17.3	17.3	15	195	19.8[4]	7[17]	—	—	—	[19]	3.5
	V8-350 Diesel/N Grand Prix	17.3	17.3	15	195	19.8	7[17]	—	—	—	[19]	3.5
1983	4-151/2 Firebird	12.8	13	15	195	16	3[14]	—	4.3	5.3	[21]	3.5
	V6-173/1 Firebird	12.5	12.5	15	195	16	4[14]	—	—	5.3	[21]	3.5
	V6-173/L H.O. Firebird	12.5	12.5	15	195	16	4[14]	—	—	5.3	[21]	3.5
	V6-229/9 Parisienne	14.3	14.3	15	195	25[8]	4[14]	—	—	—	[24]	[23]
	V6-231/A Bonneville	13	13	15	195	17.5[4]	4	—	—	—	[20]	3.5
	V6-231/A Grand Prix	13	13	15	195	17.5	4	—	—	—	[20]	3.5
	V8-305/H Bonneville	15.3	15.9	15	195	17.5	4	—	—	—	[20]	3.5

continued

COOLING SYSTEM & CAPACITY DATA—Continued

Year	Model or Engine/V.I.N.	Cooling Capacity, Qts.		Radiator Cap Relief Pressure, Lbs.	Thermo. Opening Temp.	Fuel Tank Gals.	Engine Oil Refill Qts. ①	Transmission Oil				Rear Axle Oil Pints
		Less A/C	With A/C					3 Speed Pints	4 Speed Pints	5 Speed Pints	Auto Trans. Qts. ②	
1983 cont'd	V8-305/G,H Firebird	15	15	15	195	16	4	—	—	5.3	㉑	3.5
	V8-305/H Grand Prix	15.3	15.9	15	195	17.5	4	—	—	—	⑳	3.5
	V8-305 TBI/S Firebird	15	15	15	195	16	4	—	—	—	㉑	3.5
	V8-305/H Parisienne	15.5	15.5	15	195	25⑧	4	—	—	—	㉔	㉓
	V8-350 Diesel/N Bonneville	17.3	17.3	15	195	19.8	7⑰	—	—	—	⑳	3.5
	V8-350 Diesel/N Grand Prix	17.3	17.3	15	195	19.8	7⑰	—	—	—	⑳	3.5
	V8-350 Diesel/N Parisienne	18.3	18.3	15	195	27⑧	7⑰	—	—	—	㉔	㉓
1984–85	4-151/2 Firebird	12.8	13	15	195	15.9	3⑭	—	4.3	5.3	㉑	3.5
	V6-173/1,L Firebird	12.5	12.5	15	195	15.9	4⑭	—	—	5.3	㉑	3.5
	V6-231/A Bonneville	13	13	15	195	18.1	4	—	—	—	㉒	3.5
	V6-231/A Grand Prix	13	13	15	195	18.1	4	—	—	—	㉒	3.5
	V6-231/A Parisienne	11.75	11.75	15	195	25⑧	4	—	—	—	㉒	㉓
	V8-305/H Bonneville	15.25	15.25	15	195	18.1	4	—	—	—	㉒	3.5
	V8-305/H Firebird	17.2	17.2	15	195	15.9	4	—	—	5.3	㉑	㉓
	V8-305/H Grand Prix	15.3	16.1	15	195	18.1	4	—	—	—	㉒	3.5
	V8-305/H Parisienne	15.25	15.25	15	195	25⑧	4	—	—	—	㉒	㉓
	V8-305 H.O./G Firebird	17.2	17.2	15	195	15.9	7⑰	—	—	5.3	㉑	3.5
	V8-350 Diesel/N Bonneville	17.2	17.2	15	195	19.8	7⑰	—	—	—	㉒	3.5
	V8-350 Diesel/N Grand Prix	17.2	17.2	15	195	19.8	7⑰	—	—	—	㉒	3.5
	V8-350 Diesel/N Parisienne	18.3	18.3	15	195	27⑧	7⑰	—	—	—	㉒	㉓
1986	4-151/2	—	—	15	195	15.5	3㉒	—	—	6.87	—	3.5
	V6-173/S	—	—	15	195	15.5	4㉒	—	—	6.87	㉚	3.5
	V6-231/A	—	—	—	—	—	—	—	—	—	—	—
	V6-262/Z	12.2	12.2	15	195	24.5	4㉒	—	—	—	㉛	㉜
	V8-305/H	—	—	15	195	—	—	—	—	—	—	—
	V8-305/G	—	—	15	195	—	—	—	—	—	—	—
	V8-305/F	16.9	16.9	15	195	15.5	5	—	—	—	㉚	3.5

①—Add one quart with filter change.
②—Approximate. Make final check with dipstick.
③—THM 200—oil pan, 3.5 qts.; after overhaul, 9½ qts. THM 250 & 350—oil pan, 2¾ qts., after overhaul, 10¼ qts.
④—Station Wagons, 18 gals.
⑤—T.H.M. 200/C, oil pan 4.15 qts., after overhaul 10.55 qts.; T.H.M. 250/C, oil pan 2¾ qts., after overhaul 10.25 qts.; T.H.M. 350/C, oil pan 3.15 qts., after overhaul 10 qts.; T.H.M. 350/O, oil pan 3.15 qts. after overhaul 11.45 qts.
⑥—T.H.M. 200/C, oil pan 4.25 qts., after overhaul 10.55 qts.; T.H.M. 250/C, oil pan 2.75 qts., after overhaul, 10.25 qts.; T.H.M. 350/C, oil pan 3.15 qts., after overhaul 10 qts.
⑦—T.H.M. 200/C, oil pan 4.25 qts., after overhaul 10.55 qts.; T.H.M. 250/C, oil pan 2.75 qts., after overhaul 10.25 qts.; T.H.M. 350/C, oil pan 3.15 qts., after overhaul 10 qts.; T.H.M. 200-4R, oil pan 5.05 qts., after overhaul 11 qts.

⑧—Station Wagons, 22 gals.
⑨—7½ inch axle 3½ pints. 8½ & 8¾ inch axle 4¼ pints.
⑩—With fuel pump located on driver side of engine.
⑪—With fuel pump located on passenger side of engine.
⑫—With heavy duty cooling system, 21 qts.
⑬—With heavy duty cooling system, 16.2 qts.
⑭—With or without filter change.
⑮—Includes filter. Recommended diesel engine oil—on 1980 units, use oil designated SE/CC; on 1981 units, use engine oil designated SF/CC, SF/CD or SE/CC.
⑯—With heavy duty cooling system, 21.6 qts.
⑰—Includes filter. Recommended diesel engine oil—on 1982-84 units, use oil designated SF/CD or SF/CC.
⑱—Oil pan only, 3.5 qts.; after overhaul, 5 qts.
⑲—T.H.M. 250C, oil pan only, 2.75 qts.;

after overhaul, 10.25 qts. T.H.M. 350C, oil pan only, 3.15 qts.; after overhaul, 10.15 qts.
⑳—T.H.M. 250C, oil pan only, 2.75 qts.; after overhaul, 10.25 qts. T.H.M. 350C, oil pan only, 3.25 qts.; after overhaul, 10.15 qts.
㉑—T.H.M. 200C, oil pan only, 4¼ qts.; after overhaul, 10½ qts.; T.H.M. 700-4R, oil pan only, 4.7 qts.; total capacity, 11½ qts.
㉒—T.H.M. 200C, oil pan only, 4¼ qts.; after overhaul, 10½ qts.; T.H.M. 200-4R, oil pan only, 3.48 qts.; after overhaul, 11.05 qts.; T.H.M. 250C, oil pan only, 3.15 qts.; after overhaul, 10.0 qts. T.H.M. 700-4R, oil pan only, 4.7 qts; after overhaul 11.5
㉓—7½ inch axle, 3.5 pints; 8½ inch axle, 4.3 pints; 8¾ inch axle, 5.4 pints.
㉔—T.H.M. 200C, oil pan, 3.5 qts.; after overhaul, 5 qts. T.H.M. 350C, oil pan, 3 qts.; after overhaul, 10 qts.

continued

Wheel Alignment Specifications

| Year | Model | Caster Angle, Degrees | | Camber Angle, Degrees | | | | Toe-In. Inch | Toe-Out on Turns, Deg. | |
| | | Limits | Desired | Limits | | Desired | | | Outer Wheel | Inner Wheel |
				Left	Right	Left	Right			
1980	Firebird	+.5 to +1.5	+1	+.5 to +1.5	+.5 to +1.5	+1	+1	1/16 to 3/16	—	—
	LeMans①	+.5 to +1.5	+1	0 to +1	0 to +1	+.5	+.5	1/16 to 3/16	—	—
	LeMans②	+2.5 to +3.5	+3	0 to +1	0 to +1	+.5	+.5	1/16 to 3/16	—	—
	Grand Prix	+2.5 to +3.5	+3	0 to +1	0 to +1	+.5	+.5	1/16 to 3/16	—	—
	Pontiac	+2.5 to +3.5	+3	+.3 to +1.3	+.3 to +1.3	+.8	+.8	1/16 to 3/16	—	—
1981	Firebird	+.5 to +1.5	+1	+.5 to +1.5	+.5 to +1.5	+1	+1	1/16 to 3/16	—	—
	LeMans	+2.5 to +3.5	+3	−.4 to +.6	−.4 to +.6	+.1	+.1	1/16 to 3/16	—	—
	Grand Prix	+2.5 to +3.5	+3	−.4 to +.6	−.4 to +.6	+.1	+.1	1/16 to 3/16	—	—
	Pontiac	+.5 to +1.5	+1	+.3 to +1.3	+.3 to +1.3	+.8	+.8	1/16 to 3/16	—	—
1982	Firebird	+2.5 to +3.5	+3	+1/2 to +1 1/2	+1/2 to +1 1/2	+1	+1	1/8 to 1/4	—	—
	Grand Prix	+2.5 to +3.5	+3	0 to +1	0 to +1	+.5	+.5	1/16 to 3/16	—	—
	Bonneville	+2.5 to +3.5	+3	0 to +1	0 to +1	+.5	+.5	1/16 to 3/16	—	—
1983–86	Firebird④	+2.5 to +3.5	+3	+.5 to +1.5	+.5 to +1.5	+1	+1	③	—	—
	Grand Prix	+2.5 to +3.5	+3	0 to +1	0 to +1	+5	+5	1/16 to 3/16	—	—
	Bonneville	+2.5 to +3.5	+3	0 to +1	0 to +1	+5	+5	1/16 to 3/16	—	—
	Parisienne	+2.5 to +3.5	+3	+.3 to +1.3	+.3 to +1.3	+.8	+.8	1/16 to 3/16	—	—
1986	Firebird⑤	—	—	—	—	—	—	—	—	—

①—Manual Steering.
②—Power Steering.
③—Toe-in degrees per wheel, −.3° to +.7°.
④—Less WS6 suspension package.
⑤—With WS6 suspension package.

Electrical Section

Fig. 1   Ignition lock replacement. 1980—86 models

Fig. 2   Ignition switch. 1980—86 (typical)

STARTER
REPLACE

NOTE: Upon removal of starter, note if any shims are used. If shims are used, they should be reinstalled in their original location during installation.

If starter is noisy during cranking, remove one .015 inch double shim or add one .015 inch single shim to the outer bolt. If starter makes a high pitched whine after firing, add .015 inch double shims until noise ceases.

1. Disconnect battery ground cable.
2. Disconnect brace from starter and swing brace forward, then remove heat shields, if used.
3. On 4-151, disconnect wiring from starter, then remove retaining bolts and starter.
4. On all other engines, remove starter retaining bolts, then lower starter, disconnect wiring and remove starter.
5. Reverse procedure to install.

IGNITION LOCK
REPLACE

1. Remove steering wheel as described under Horn Sounder and Steering Wheel.
2. Remove turn signal switch as described under Turn Signal Switch, Replace, then remove buzzer switch.
3. Place ignition switch in "Run" position, then, remove lock cylinder retaining screw and lock cylinder.
4. To install, rotate lock cylinder to stop while holding housing, **Fig. 1.** Align cylinder key with keyway in housing, then push lock cylinder assembly into housing until fully seated.
5. Install lock cylinder retaining screw. Torque screw to 40 in. lbs. for standard columns. On adjustable columns, torque retaining screw to 22 in. lbs.
6. Install buzzer switch, turn signal switch and steering wheel.

IGNITION SWITCH
REPLACE

1. Disconnect battery ground cable.
2. Position ignition key in off-unlock position on standard columns, or ACC on tilt columns.
3. Remove lower portion of instrument panel, then toe-pan trim cover.
4. Remove shift indicator cable clip from shift bowl, if equipped with column shift.
5. Loosen toe-pan clamp bolts, then remove switch attaching screws.
6. Disconnect electrical wiring from switch, then remove switch from steering column.
7. Position new switch slider in same position as old switch slider, **Fig. 2.**
8. Install new switch.

LIGHT SWITCH
REPLACE

1980—81 & 1983—86 FULL SIZE

1. Disconnect battery ground cable.
2. Pull headlight knob to "ON" position, then reach under instrument panel, depress switch shaft release button and pull knob and shaft assembly from switch.
3. Remove switch retaining nut, wire connector and switch.
4. Reverse procedure to install.

1980—86 INTERMEDIATE SIZE

1. Disconnect battery ground cable.
2. Remove left side lower trim panel.
3. Remove instrument panel bezel attaching screws, then bezel.
4. Pull headlight knob to "ON" position, then remove light switch mounting plate to cluster attaching screws and pull assembly rearward.
5. Depress switch shaft retainer and pull out knob and shaft assembly.

6. Remove wiring connector from switch, then switch.
7. Disassemble light switch from bracket.
8. Reverse procedure to install.

1980—81 FIREBIRD

1. Disconnect battery ground cable.
2. Remove lower cover from steering column.
3. Reach up under left side of instrument cluster and depress light switch shaft retainer while pulling on shaft.
4. Remove switch to carrier retaining nut.
5. Remove instrument cluster retaining screws, and tilt right side of cluster out.
6. Disconnect electrical connectors from switch, then remove switch.
7. Reverse procedure to install.

1982—86 FIREBIRD

1. Remove right and left lower trim plates.
2. Remove instrument panel cluster trim plate.
3. Remove two retaining screws from switch assembly.
4. Depress side tangs and pull switch assembly from instrument panel.
5. Reverse procedure to install.

STOP LIGHT SWITCH
REPLACE

EXCEPT 1982—86 FIREBIRD

The stop light switch has a slip fit in the mounting sleeve which permits positive adjustment by pulling the brake pedal up firmly against the stop. The pedal arm forces the switch body to slip in the mounting sleeve bushing to position the switch properly.

1. Disconnect wires from switch and remove switch from bracket.
2. Position new switch in bracket and push in to maximum distance. Brake pedal arm moves switch to correct distance on rebound. Check if pedal is in full return position by lifting slightly by hand.
3. Connect switch wires by inserting plug on switch.

Fig. 3 Self-adjusting type neutral safety switch (typical)

Fig. 6 Neutral safety switch. 1982–86 Firebird

1982–86 FIREBIRD

1. Remove left hand side hush panel.
2. Located under instrument panel, disconnect wire connector from switch at brake pedal support.
3. Remove switch from mounting bracket.
4. Depress brake pedal and install new switch into clip, until shoulder on switch bottoms out against clip.
5. If adjustment of the switch is necessary, the switch may be rotated or pulled in the clip. Electrical contact should be made when brake pedal is depressed .053 inch from its fully released position.

NEUTRAL SAFETY SWITCH
REPLACE

NOTE: Some models use a combination neutral start and back-up light switch, while others use a separate back-up light switch. Both switches are serviced in the following manner.

1982–86 SELF-ADJUSTING TYPE

1. Place gear selector in "Neutral."

Fig. 4 Manual adjust type neutral safety switch. Manual transmission (typical)

2. Gently rock switch out of steering column.
3. Disconnect wiring connectors. Connect wiring connectors to new switch.
4. Align switch actuator with hole in shift tube, **Fig. 3.**
5. Position connector side of switch into lower jacket cut out.
6. Push down front of switch, ensuring switch tangs snap into holes in steering column jacket.
7. Adjust switch by placing gear selector in "Park" position. Switch main housing and housing back should ratchet, providing proper adjustment.

MANUAL ADJUST TYPE, EXC. 1982–86 FIREBIRD

1. Lock steering column in "Park" position for automatic transmissions and "Reverse" for manual transmissions, then remove screws attaching switch to steering column.
2. Remove switch electrical connectors, then switch.
3. Connect wiring connector to new switch.
4. Position new switch on steering column, aligning switch carrier tang in shift selector tube slot.
5. Install attaching screws and tighten.

NOTE: The switch is held in the proper position with a plastic sheer pin. No additional pinning is required.

6. Adjust switch by loosening attaching screws, then inserting a .096 inch gauge pin in gauge hole of switch, **Figs. 4 and 5.**
7. Rotate switch in clockwise direction until freeplay is eliminated and gauge pin slides in gauge hole to a depth of ⅜ inch.
8. Tighten attaching screws and remove gauge pin.

1982–86 FIREBIRD

1. Remove floor console cover.
2. Disconnect wire connectors from backup lamp/neutral start switch.
3. Position gear shift lever into Neutral position.

Fig. 5 Manual adjust type neutral safety switch. Automatic transmission (typical)

Fig. 7 Mechanical neutral start system with standard column. 1980–81 Full size models, 1980–81 Grand Am, Grand Prix and LeMans & 1982–86 Bonneville & Grand Prix & 1983–86 Parisienne

4. Remove two screws securing neutral starter switch, then remove switch.
5. Ensure gear shift lever is in Neutral position before installing switch.
6. Install new switch in position on gear shift lever. Ensure pin on gear shift lever is in slot of switch. Tighten switch and torque to 14–19 inch lbs., **Fig. 6.**
7. Move gear shift lever out of Neutral position to break plastic shear pin.
8. Connect electrical connectors to switch. Apply parking brake and start vehicle. Ensure vehicle starts only in Park or Neutral positions.
9. Turn ignition off and install floor console cover.

MECHANICAL NEUTRAL START SYSTEM

1980–81 FULL SIZE, 1980–81 GRAND AM, GRAND PRIX & LEMANS & 1982–86 BONNEVILLE & GRAND PRIX & 1983–86 PARISIENNE

Actuation of the ignition switch is prevented by a mechanical lockout system,

Fig. 8   Mechanical neutral start system with tilt column. 1980– 81 Full size models, 1980–81 Grand Am, Grand Prix and LeMans & 1982–86 Bonneville & Grand Prix & 1983–86 Parisienne

Fig. 9   Mechanical neutral start system in Park position. 1980–81 Full size models, 1980–81 Grand Am, Grand Prix and LeMans & 1982–86 Bonneville & Grand Prix & 1983–86 Parisienne

Fig. 10   Compressing lock plate and removing retaining ring

Fig. 11   Taping turn signal connector & wires

Fig. 12   Instrument panel. 1980–81 Firebird

Figs. 7 and 8, which prevents the lock cylinder from rotating when the selector lever is out of Park or Neutral. When the selector lever is in Park or Neutral, the slots in the bowl plate and the finger on the actuator rod align allowing the finger to pass through the bowl plate in turn actuating the ignition switch, **Fig. 9.** If the selector lever is in any position other than Park or Neutral, the finger contacts the bowl plate when the lock cylinder is rotated, thereby preventing full travel of the lock cylinder.

CLUTCH START SWITCH

All cars equipped with a manual transmission use a clutch start switch which is mounted on the pedal bracket. The switch closes when the clutch is depressed and completes solenoid connection. When installing switch, no adjustment is necessary.

TURN SIGNAL SWITCH
REPLACE

1980–86

NOTE: On tilt column, the column must first be lowered from panel.

1. Disconnect battery ground cable, then remove steering wheel using puller.

Caution: Do not hammer on end of shaft as hammering could collapse shaft or loosen plastic injections which maintain column rigidity.

2. Remove cover by prying out with a screwdriver at slots provided in cover for this purpose.
3. Depress lock plate and pry round wire lock ring out of shaft groove, **Fig. 10.** Remove lock plate.
4. Slide upper bearing preload spring and turn signal cancelling cam off shaft.
5. Remove turn signal lever.

NOTE: On models with column mounted dimmer switch, remove actuator arm screw and actuator arm before removing turn signal lever.

6. Push hazard warning switch in and unscrew knob.
7. Pull turn signal wiring connector out of bracket on jacket and disconnect.
8. Remove three turn signal switch screws.
9. Remove shift indicator cable, if equipped.
10. Lower steering column from instrument panel and remove wire protector, then pull switch straight up with wire protector and remove housing.

NOTE: Place tape around upper part of connector and wires to prevent snagging when switch is being removed, **Fig. 12.**

COLUMN-MOUNTED DIMMER SWITCH
REPLACE

1980–81 FULL SIZE, 1980– 81 GRAND PRIX & LEMANS & 1982–86 BONNEVILLE, GRAND PRIX & FIREBIRD & 1983–86 PARISIENNE

1. Disconnect battery ground cable.
2. Remove instrument panel lower trim and on models with A/C, remove A/C duct extension at column.
3. Remove toe-plate cover screws.
4. Remove two nuts from instrument panel support bracket studs and lower steering column, resting steering wheel on front seat.
5. Remove dimmer switch retaining screw(s) and the switch. Tape actuator rod to column and separate switch from rod.
6. Reverse procedure to install. To adjust switch, depress dimmer switch slightly and install a 3/32 inch twist drill to lock the switch to the body. Force switch upward to remove lash. Torque retaining screws to 35 inch lbs. and remove tape from actuator rod. Remove twist drill and check for proper operation.

HORN SOUNDER & STEERING WHEEL
REPLACE

EXCEPT 1982–86 FIREBIRD

1. Disconnect battery ground cable.
2. Remove screws attaching horn pad assembly to steering wheel.
3. Disconnect horn contact from steering wheel.
4. Remove steering wheel nut retainer and attaching nut.
5. Using suitable steering wheel puller, remove steering wheel. Note position of steering wheel to shaft.
6. Reverse procedure to install.

1982–86 FIREBIRD

1. Disconnect battery ground cable.
2. Remove steering wheel shroud screws on underside of steering wheel.
3. Remove steering wheel shroud and horn contact lead assembly from the steering wheel.
4. Remove snap ring and steering wheel nut.
5. Using steering wheel puller tool No. J-2927 or equivalent, remove steering wheel. Note position of steering wheel to shaft.
6. Reverse procedure to install.

INSTRUMENT CLUSTER
REPLACE

1980–86 MODELS EXC. 1982–86 FIREBIRD & 1983–86 PARISIENNE

1. Disconnect battery ground cable.
2. Remove upper and lower instrument panel trim plates, **Figs. 12 through 14.**
3. Remove instrument panel bezel attaching screws and bezel, if equipped.
4. On column mounted shift models, remove shift indicator cable.
5. On Firebird, loosen steering column nuts and lower column approximately ½ inch.
6. On all models, remove cluster retaining screws, pull cluster outward and disconnect speedometer cable and printed circuit connector, if equipped.
7. Remove lower bezel anti-rattle clips, if equipped, then instrument cluster, **Figs. 14 through 16.**
8. Reverse procedure to install.

1983–86 PARISIENNE

1. Disconnect battery ground cable.
2. Remove four steering column lower cover screws and cover.
3. If equipped with automatic transmission, disconnect shift indicator cable from steering column.
4. Remove two steering column to instrument panel screws and lower steering column.

Fig. 13 Instrument panel. 1980 Grand Am, 1980–81 LeMans, 1980–86 Grand Prix & 1982–86 Bonneville

Fig. 14 Instrument panel and cluster. 1980–81 Full Size

Fig. 15 Instrument cluster. 1980–81 Firebird

Fig. 16   Instrument cluster. 1980 Grand Am, 1980–81 LeMans, 1980–86 Grand Prix & 1982–86 Bonneville

Fig. 17   Instrument cluster. 1983–86 Parisienne

1	TRIM PLATE ASM.-CLUSTER
2	BOLT/SCREW
3	COVER, LOWER R.H.
4	COVER, LOWER L.H.
5	LOWER TRIM PLATE ASM. (LH)
6	LOWER TRIM PLATE ASM. (RH)
7	HEATER ONLY
8	I.P. LOWER REINF.
9	BRACKET
10	CONVENIENCE CENTER MOUNTING BRACKET

VIEW A
(HEATER ONLY)

Fig. 18   Instrument cluster. 1982–86 Firebird

CAUTION: Use extreme care when lowering steering to prevent damage to column assembly.

5. Remove six screws and three snap-in fasteners from perimeter of instrument cluster lens, **Fig. 17.**
6. Remove two screws from upper surface of grey sheet metal trim plate.
7. Remove two stud nuts from lower corner of cluster.
8. Disconnect speedometer cable and pull cluster from instrument panel.
9. Disconnect electrical connectors from cluster and remove from vehicle.
10. Reverse procedure to install.

1982–86 FIREBIRD

1. Disconnect battery ground cable, then remove right and left lower trim plates, **Fig. 18.**
2. Remove instrument cluster trim plate.
3. Remove six cluster attachment screws, pull cluster back and disconnect speedometer cable.
4. Disconnect necessary electrical connections.
5. Remove trip odometer and cluster lens.
6. Reverse procedure to install.

W/S WIPER MOTOR
REPLACE

1. Raise hood and remove cowl screen or grille.
2. Disconnect wiring and washer hoses.
3. Reaching through opening, loosen transmission drive link to crankarm attaching nuts.
4. Remove drive link from motor crankarm.
5. Remove three motor attaching screws and remove motor while guiding crankarm through opening.
6. Reverse procedure to install.

W/S WIPER TRANSMISSION
REPLACE

WITH RECTANGULAR MOTOR
1. Remove wiper arms and blades.
2. Raise hood and remove cowl vent screen or grille.
3. Disconnect wiring from motor.
4. Loosen, but do not remove, transmission drive link to motor crankarm attaching nuts and disconnect drive link from crankarm.
5. Remove right and left transmission to body attaching screws and guide transmission and linkage assembly out through opening.

NOTE: When installing, motor must be in Park position.

With Round Motor
1. Raise hood and remove cowl vent screen.

Fig. 19 Windshield wiper switch removal & installation. 1982–86 models less tilt wheel

Fig. 20 Windshield wiper switch removal & installation. 1982–86 models less tilt wheel

2. On Intermediates and full size models, remove right and left wiper arm and blade assemblies.
3. Loosen, but do not remove, attaching nuts securing transmission drive link to motor crankarm.
4. Disconnect transmission drive link from motor crankarm.
5. On Intermediate and full size models, remove right and left transmission to body attaching screws.
6. Remove transmission and linkage assembly by guiding it through opening.

NOTE: When installing, motor must be in Park position.

W/S WIPER SWITCH
REPLACE

1982–86 EXC. 1983–86 PARISIENNE

1. Remove steering wheel as described under Horn Sounder and Steering Wheel, Replace.
2. Remove turn signal switch as described under Turn Signal Switch, Replace.
3. Remove ignition lock and buzzer as described under Ignition Lock, Replace.
4. Remove and install cover and wiper switch as shown in **Fig. 19 & 20.**
5. Reverse remaining procedure to install.

1983–86 PARISIENNE

1. Disconnect battery ground cable.
2. Pull headlight switch knob to ON position.
3. Reach up under instrument panel and depress headlight switch shaft release

button, then pull out switch shaft and knob assembly.
4. Remove four screws securing control shroud to instrument panel.

NOTE: When removing control shroud to instrument panel screws, one screw is hidden above cigar lighter knob while another is hidden above headlamp switch shaft location.

4. Remove control shroud, then two remaining screws.
5. Remove wiper switch electrical connector, then light bulb and socket from rear of switch.
6. Remove switch.
7. Reverse procedure to install.

1980–81

1. Disconnect battery ground cable. Remove upper and lower instrument panel trimplates.
2. Remove switch mounting plate and disconnect connector.
3. Remove switch retaining screws and remove switch.

RADIO
REPLACE

NOTE: When installing radio, be sure to adjust antenna trimmer for peak performance.

1983–86 PARISIENNE

1. Disconnect battery ground cable.
2. Remove control knobs from control shafts.
3. Remove three radio trim plate attaching screws.
4. Remove two screws and bottom nut attaching radio bracket to instrument panel.
5. Disconnect antenna lead and wire connector from radio.
6. Remove radio with mounting bracket attached from instrument panel.
7. Remove bracket from radio.
8. Reverse procedure to install.

1980–81 GRAND AM, GRAND LEMANS, GRAND PRIX, LEMANS & 1982–86 BONNEVILLE & GRAND PRIX

1. Disconnect battery ground cable.
2. Remove upper and lower trim plates.
3. If equipped with console, move shift lever fully rearward.
4. On all models, remove four radio attaching screws from front of radio.
5. Open glove box door and lower by releasing spring clip.
6. Loosen radio rear attaching nut and pull radio outward slightly.
7. Disconnect electrical leads from radio and remove radio from vehicle.
8. Reverse procedure to install.

1980–81 FULL SIZE

1. Disconnect battery ground cable.
2. Remove upper trim plate.
3. Remove radio trim plate by removing the two top screws and ash tray assembly, then disconnect cigar lighter electrical connector and remove the two small screws and large screw retaining ash tray bracket.
4. Remove two screws securing radio.
5. Pull radio from instrument panel opening and disconnect electrical leads from radio.
6. Remove radio from vehicle. Remove bezel nuts from front of radio to remove front trim plate if new radio is installed.
7. Reverse procedure to install.

1982–86 FIREBIRD

1. Disconnect battery ground cable.
2. Remove radio and A/C heater console trim plate.
3. Remove four radio to console attaching screws, then pull radio outward and disconnect wire connectors and antenna lead.
4. Reverse procedure to install.

1980–81 FIREBIRD

1. Disconnect battery ground cable.
2. Remove glove box and door and right lower A/C duct if equipped.

Fig. 21 Heater core & blower motor (less air conditioning). 1980–81 Full size

3. Remove radio knobs and hex nuts and trim plate.
4. Disconnect all leads to radio.
5. Remove radio bracket and radio from passenger side of instrument panel through glove box opening.

HEATER CORE
REPLACE

WITHOUT AIR COND.

Parisienne
1. Disconnect battery ground cable and drain cooling system.
2. Disconnect heater hoses from heater core. Plug core outlets to prevent coolant spillage.
3. Disconnect wire connectors from module cover, then remove front module cover attaching screws and cover.
4. Remove heater core from module.
5. Reverse procedure to install.

1982–86 Firebird
1. Disconnect battery ground cable.
2. Drain radiator and remover heater hoses from heater core.
3. Remove right lower hush panel.
4. Remove right lower instrument trim panel.
5. Vehicles equipped with the V8-305 EFI engine, remove ESC module.
6. Remove lower right instrument panel carrier to cowl screw.
7. Remove four heater case cover screws.
8. Remove heater case cover.
9. Remove core support plate and baffle screws.
10. Remove heater core, support plate and baffle from case.
11. Reverse procedure to install.

1980–81 Grand Am, Grand LeMans, Grand Prix, LeMans & 1982–86 Bonneville & Grand Prix
1. Disconnect battery ground cable and drain cooling system.
2. Disconnect heater hoses.
3. Disconnect electrical connectors from heater module.
4. Remove module front cover screws.
5. Remove heater core from module.
6. Reverse procedure to install.

1980–81 Full Size
1. Disconnect battery ground cable.
2. Disconnect hoses from heater core and plug core tubes to prevent spilling coolant.
3. Remove retaining screws from around heater core cover.
4. Remove heater core cover, then heater core from module, **Fig. 21.**
5. Reverse procedure to install.

1980–81 Firebird
1. Drain radiator and disconnect heater hoses from core.
2. Remove retaining nuts from core case studs on engine side of dash.
3. Inside car, remove glove box and door on Firebird and heater outlet from case on Firebird.
4. Remove defroster duct retaining screw from heater case and pull entire heater assembly from firewall.
5. Disconnect control cables and wiring and remove assembly.
6. Remove core tube seal and core retaining strips and remove core.

WITH AIR COND.

1983–86 Parisienne
1. Disconnect battery ground cable and drain cooling system.
2. Disconnect heater hoses from heater core. Plug core outlets to prevent coolant spillage.
3. Remove heater core retainer bracket and ground strap.
4. Remove module rubber seal and module screen.
5. Remove right hand windshield wiper arm.
6. Remove high blower relay, then thermostatic switch mounting screws.
7. Disconnect wire connector at top of module, then remove module top cover.
8. Remove heater core from module.
9. Reverse procedure to install.

1982–86 Bonneville & Grand Prix
1. Disconnect negative battery cable.
2. Discharge air conditioning system and drain cooling system.
3. Remove both windshield wipers and wiper stops.
4. Remove cover windshield molding and leaf screens.
5. Remove lower windshield molding brackets, bolts from upper half of module case, all electrical connections and module cover.
6. Remove heater core clamp bolt and remove heater core.
7. Reverse procedure to install.

1982–86 Firebird
1. Disconnect battery ground cable.
2. Drain radiator and remove heater hoses from heater core.
3. Remove right lower hush panel.
4. Remove right lower instrument trim panel.
5. Vehicles equipped with the V8-305 TBI engine, remove ESC module.
6. Remove lower right instrument panel carrier to cowl screw.
7. Remove four heater case cover screws.
8. Remove heater case cover.
9. Remove core support plate and baffle screws.
10. Remove heater core, support plate and baffle from case.

Fig. 22 Heater core & blower motor (with air conditioning). 1980–81 Full size

11. Reverse procedure to install.

1980–81 Grand Am, Grand LeMans, Grand Prix & LeMans
1. Disconnect battery ground cable.
2. Remove right hand windshield wiper arm and blade assembly.
3. Drain cooling system, then disconnect heater hoses at heater core and plug core openings.
4. Remove bracket and ground strap.
5. Remove module cover as follows:
   a. Remove seals and screens, then disconnect wire connector.
   b. Loosen and move up lower windshield reveal moulding, then remove reveal moulding cowl brackets.
   c. Tape a strip of wood below lower edge of windshield over module to prevent damage to windshield.
   d. Remove all cover attaching screws, then cut through sealing material along cowl.
   e. Carefully pry cover off from side, then lift cover away from flange of fender cowl brace.
   f. Remove heater core and seal from module.

1980–81 Full Size
1. Disconnect battery ground cable.
2. Remove right half of hood seal from air inlet screen.
3. Remove air inlet screen.
4. Remove screws securing top of module, then disconnect electrical connectors from electrical components on top of module.
5. Remove thermostatic switch mounting screws from top of module.
6. Remove A/C diagnostic connector mounting screws and position aside.
7. Remove top of module.
8. Disconnect and remove heater core from module.
9. Reverse procedure to install.

1980–81 Firebird
1. Drain radiator.
2. Remove glove box and door.
3. Remove cold air duct (lower right hand duct) and remove left and center lower A/C ducts.
4. Jack right front area of car and place on safety stand.
5. Remove rocker panel trim on right side and remove screws holding forward portion of rocker panel trim attaching bracket.
6. Remove three lower fender bolts at rear of fender.

Fig. 23 Centering spring adjustment. Early model flyweight type regulator

7. Remove four fender to skirt bolts at rear of wheel opening.
8. Remove two fender skirt bolts near blower motor area.
9. Pry rear portion of fender out at bottom to gain access to hose clamp on lower core hose and disconnect hose.
10. Disconnect water pump to core hose at core.
11. Remove heater case retaining nuts under hood at dash.
12. Remove two heater case retaining bolts (inside car).
13. Remove console, if equipped. If equipped with tape player, remove console with tape player intact. If equipped with tape player and no console, remove tape player.
14. Disconnect temperature cable at heater case.
15. Remove heater outlet duct.
16. Remove lower defroster duct screw at heater case.
17. Remove right kick panel.
18. Remove heater core and case.
19. Disconnect vacuum hoses from heater case.
20. Remove core from case.

BLOWER MOTOR
REPLACE

1980—81 Grand Am, Grand Lemans, Grand Prix, Lemans & 1982—86 Bonneville and Grand Prix & 1983—86 Parisienne
1. Disconnect battery ground cable.
2. If equipped with air conditioning, disconnect cooling tube from blower motor.
3. On all models, disconnect electrical connector from blower motor.
4. Remove blower motor retaining screws and the blower motor.
5. Reverse procedure to install.

1980—81 Full Size Without Air Cond.
1. Disconnect battery ground cable.
2. Disconnect blower motor electrical lead.
3. Remove blower motor retaining screws and remove blower motor, **Fig. 21.**
4. Reverse procedure to install.

1980—81 Full Size With Air Cond.
1. Disconnect battery ground cable.
2. Remove right half of hood seal from air inlet screen.
3. Remove air inlet screen.
4. Remove screws securing top of module, then disconnect electrical connec-

tors from electrical components on top of module.
5. Remove thermostatic switch mounting screws from top of module.
6. Remove A/C diagnostic connector mounting screws and position aside.
7. Remove top of module.
8. Disconnect and remove blower motor from module, **Fig. 22.**
9. Reverse procedure to install.

1980—86 Firebird
1. Disconnect battery ground cable.
2. Disconnect wire connector. On models with A/C, disconnect cooling tube.
3. Remove motor attaching screws and nuts, then remove blower motor assembly from case.
4. Reverse procedure to install.

SPEED CONTROLS
1980—84 CRUISE CONTROL

Brake Release Switches, Adjust
Apply brake pedal and push both switches forward as far as possible. Pull pedal forcibly rearward to adjust switches.

Centering Spring Adjustment Exc. Cruise Master Units
If speed control holds speed three or more mph higher than selected speed, turn centering screw (C) clockwise ⅛ turn or less, **Fig. 23.**
If speed control holds speed three or more mph below selected speed, turn centering adjustment screw (C) counterclockwise ⅛ turn or less. Do not move adjustment screw (R).

Orifice Tube Adjustment, Cruise Master Units
To check engagement speed, engage the system at 55 mph. If vehicle cruises below the engagement speed, loosen the locknut and screw the orifice tube outward. If vehicle cruises above the engagement speed, loosen the locknut and screw the orifice tube inward, **Fig. 24.**

NOTE: Approximately ¼ turn of the orifice tube will change the cruise speed about 1 mph. Also, do not remove orifice tube as it cannot be reinstalled once removed.

Bead Chain Adjustment, Buick Built Engines
Assemble chain to be taut with carburetor in hot idle position and the idle solenoid deenergized. Place chain into swivel cavities which permits chain to have slight slack. Place retainer over swivel and chain assembly. Retainer must be made to rest between balls. Cut off chain flush with side of swivel to remove excess length. Chain slack should not exceed one half diameter of ball stud, .150 inch, when measured at hot idle position.

Cable Adjustment, Pontiac Built Engines
1. Set carburetor choke to hot idle position.
2. With cable connected to vacuum servo, pull steel tube of servo as far as it will go and check if one of the cross holes in the steel tube aligns with car-

Fig. 24 Orifice tube adjustment. Late model transducer type regulator

buretor lever pin.
3. If one of the cross holes in the steel tube aligns with carburetor lever pin, install the tube, washer and cotter pin.
4. If none of the cross holes in the steel aligns with carburetor lever pin, move tube rearward to align the next closest hole and install cable, washer and cotter pin.

CAUTION: Do not stretch cable to make adjustment, as this will prevent carburetor from returning to normal idle.

Cable Adjustment, Chevrolet Built Engines Less Electronic Fuel Injection
1. Assemble cable to cable bracket and throttle lever.
2. Install cable assembly onto servo bracket.
3. Place throttle in fully closed position. Attach servo chain to cable assembly with first two beads of servo chain hanging loose outside cable assembly clip.
4. Adjust cable assembly jam nuts until there is a .03 inch clearance between throttle lever stud pin and end of slot on throttle cable assembly. Torque jam nuts to 35—48 inch lbs. Pull rubber boot over washer on cable.

Cable Adjustment, Chevrolet Built Engines With Electronic Fuel Injection
1. Assemble cable to cable bracket and TBI lever and servo bracket.
2. Place throttle in fully closed position. Attach servo chain to cable assembly with first two beads of servo chain hanging loosely outside cable assembly clip.
3. Adjust cable jam nuts until cable sleeve at TBI unit is tight but not holding throttle open. Torque jam nuts to 35—48 inch lbs. Pull rubber boot over washer on cable.

Rod Adjustment, Oldsmobile Built Engines
Adjust length of rod to minimum slack with carburetor in hot idle position and the engine static.

Rod Adjustment, Chevrolet Built Engines
Screw rod into link with ignition "Off" and fast idle cam off and throttle closed. Hook rod through tab on servo. Adjust length so link assemblies over end of stud, then install retainer.

For service on V6-231, 252 & 1980 V8-350 engines with distributor located at front of engine, refer to Section 9.

For service on V6-173, V6-229, V8-305 & all 1980 V8-350 engines with distributor located at rear of engine and fuel pump located on right side of engine, refer to Section 17.

For service on all V8-307 & 350 gasoline engines with distributor located at rear of engine, fuel pump located on right side of engine and oil filler tube located on engine front cover & diesel engines refer to Section 20.

LEFT HAND VIEW

RIGHT HAND VIEW

Fig. 1 Engine mounts. 1982–86 4-151

ENGINE MOUNTS
REPLACE

4-151
1982–86
1. Disconnect battery ground cable.
2. Raise and support front of vehicle.
3. Remove mount through bolts on left and right hand side, **Fig. 1.**
4. Raise front of engine and remove mount to engine attaching bolts, then remove mounts.
5. Reverse procedure to install.

1980–81 V8-265, 301, 350 & 400
1. Disconnect battery ground cable.
2. Raise engine to release weight off front mounts.
3. Remove bolts fastening engine insulators to engine, **Fig. 2.**
4. Raise engine just clear of insulator.
5. Remove insulator.

ENGINE
REPLACE

1980–81
1. Disconnect battery cables at battery and drain cooling system.

2. Scribe alignment marks on hood and remove hood from hinges.
3. Disconnect all wiring, ground straps, fuel lines and vacuum hoses from engine.

NOTE: On V8 engines, remove thermal feed switch, located on rear of left cylinder head on all models except Ventura. On Venture models, switch is located on the right cylinder head.

4. Remove air cleaner and upper radiator shield assembly.
5. Disconnect radiator hoses and heater hoses at engine.
6. Remove fan and disconnect accelerator linkage.
7. If equipped with power steering or air conditioning, remove pump and/or compressor from mountings and set aside. Do not disconnect hoses.
8. On V8, disconnect transmission vacuum modulator line and power brake vacuum line at carburetor and fold back out of way.
9. Raise vehicle on hoist and drain crankcase.
10. Disconnect exhaust pipe from manifold and remove starter.
11. If equipped with automatic transmission, remove converter cover and three converter retaining bolts and slide converter to rear.
12. With manual transmission, disconnect clutch linkage and remove clutch cross shaft.

13. Remove four lower bell housing bolts.
14. Disconnect transmission filler tube support and starter wire harness shield from cylinder head.
15. Remove two front motor mount to frame bracket bolts.
16. Lower vehicle and using a jack and block of wood, support transmission.
17. Support weight of engine with suitable lifting device.
18. Remove two remaining bell housing bolts.
19. Raise transmission slightly.
20. Position engine forward to free it from transmission and remove from car by tilting front of engine up.

1982–86 4-151
1. Disconnect battery ground cable.
2. Drain cooling system.
3. Scribe alignment marks on hood, then remove hood from hinges.
4. Remove A/C compressor, brackets and position aside.
5. Remove upper and lower radiator hoses from engine.
6. Remove fan assembly.
7. On models with auto. trans., remove radiator and shroud assembly. On models with manual transmission, remove upper half of radiator shroud.
8. Disconnect power steering hoses, then remove power steering pump from mounting brackets.
9. Disconnect engine wiring at bulkhead connection.
10. Disconnect inlet and return fuel lines at flex hoses.
11. Remove vacuum brake hose from filter.
12. Disconnect engine to body ground strap from rear of cylinder head.
13. From inside of vehicle, remove right hand hush panel, then disconnect E.C.M. harness from E.C.M. unit.
14. Remove splash shield from right fender and feed E.C.M. harness from inside of vehicle.
15. Disconnect heater hoses from heater core.
16. Disconnect throttle linkage and canister hose from E.F.I. assembly.
17. Raise and support vehicle.
18. Disconnect electrical connectors from transmission.
19. Remove flywheel dust cover.
20. On models equipped with automatic transmission, remove torque converter to flywheel bolts.

Fig. 2   Engine mounts (typical). V8-265, 301 & 350

Fig. 3   Cylinder head tightening sequence. 1982—86 4-151

TORQUE ALL BOLTS TO 50 N•m (37 LB. FT.) IN THE NUMERICAL SEQUENCE INDICATED

EXHAUST MANIFOLD GASKET

HEAT SHIELD

RIVET

BOLT LOCATIONS

Fig. 5   Exhaust manifold tightening sequence. 1982—86 4-151

| 1 | 34 N.M. (25 LB. FT.) |
| 2 | 50 N.M. (37 LB. FT.) |

FRT

TORQUE ALL BOLTS IN THE NUMERICAL SEQ. INDICATED.

Fig. 4   Intake manifold tightening sequence. 1982—86 4-151

21. Remove bell housing to engine bolts.
22. Disconnect exhaust pipe at manifold, then remove exhaust pipe support at bell housing.
23. Disconnect catalytic converter at tail pipe joint, then remove converter and exhaust pipe assembly.
24. Disconnect starter wiring, then remove starter assembly.
25. On models equipped with manual transmission, remove clutch fork return spring.
26. Remove motor mount through bolts.
27. Lower vehicle, then using a suitable jack and block of wood, support transmission.
28. Support weight of engine with suitable lifting device.
29. Remove engine from vehicle. On models equipped with manual transmission, swing engine slightly to the right to remove clutch swing arm from ball.

CYLINDER HEAD
REPLACE

4-151

1. Drain cooling system and remove air cleaner.
2. Disconnect accelerator and fuel and vacuum lines at carburetor.
3. Remove intake and exhaust manifolds.
4. Remove bolts attaching alternator bracket to cylinder head.
5. If equipped with power steering or A/C, remove right side front bracket.
6. Disconnect temperature sending unit wiring harness, battery ground cable and radiator and heater hoses.
7. Disconnect spark plug wires and remove spark plugs.
8. Remove rocker cover, then back off rocker arm nuts.

9. Pivot rocker arms to clear push rods and remove push rods.
10. Remove cylinder head attaching bolts and cylinder head.
11. Reverse procedure to install. Coat cylinder head bolts with sealer. Torque bolts in sequence as shown in **Fig. 3**. When installing intake and exhaust manifolds, refer to **Figs. 4 and 5** for bolt tightening sequence.

V8-265, 301, 350

1. Drain cooling system and remove air cleaner.
2. Remove intake manifold, push rod cover and rocker arm cover.
3. Loosen all rocker arm nuts and move rocker arms off push rods.
4. Remove push rods, keeping them in order so they may be installed in their original locations.
5. Detach exhaust crossover pipe from manifolds.
6. Remove battery ground strap and engine ground strap on left head or engine ground strap.
7. Unfasten and remove head with exhaust manifold attached.

CAUTION: Use extreme care when handling heads as the rocker arm studs are hardened and may crack if struck.

NOTE: If left head is being removed, it will be necessary to raise head off dowel pins, move it forward and maneuver it in order to clear power steering and power brake equipment if so equipped.

Fig. 6 Cylinder head tightening sequence. V8-265, 301 & 350

①—Refer to Oldsmobile Chapter for service procedures.
②—Refer to Buick Chapter for service procedures.
③—Distributor located at rear of engine, counter-clockwise distributor rotor rotation. Fuel pump located at right side of engine.
④—Diesel.
⑤—Distributor located at front of engine.
⑥—Except E/C (Electronic control) engine.
⑦—E/C (Electronic control) engine.
⑧—Refer to Chevrolet Chapter for service procedures.

Fig. 7 Hydraulic valve lifter

8. Reverse procedure to install. On V8-301, coat cylinder head bolts with sealer.
9. On 1980–82 engines, torque cylinder heads to specifications in sequence shown in **Fig. 6**.

ROCKER ARM STUDS
REPLACE

WITH SCREW IN STUDS

1. On V8-301, drain cooling system.
2. Remove rocker arm cover.
3. Remove rocker arm and nut.
4. Using a deep socket, remove rocker stud.
5. Install new stud and tighten to 50 ft. lbs.

NOTE: On V8-301, coat lower rocker arm stud threads with sealer.

6. Install rocker arm and tighten nut to 20 ft. lbs.
7. Install rocker cover using new gasket.

VALVE ARRANGEMENT
FRONT TO REAR

Four Cyl................... E-I-I-E-E-I-I-E
V8s .... E-I-I-E-E-I-I-E

VALVE LIFT SPECS.

Year	Engine	Intake	Exhaust
1980–82	V6-231②	.383	.366
1980	V6-229⑧	.373	.410
	V8-350①③	.400	.400
	V8-350②⑤	.357	.366
1980–82	V6-231②	.357	.366
	V8-265	.364	.364
	V8-301⑥	.350	.350
	V8-301⑦	.364	.364
	V8-305⑧	.357	.390
	V8-350①④	.376	.376
1981	V8-307①	.400	.400
1982–85	4-151	.398	.398
	V6-173⑧	.231	.262
	V6-252②	.358	.366

VALVE TIMING
INTAKE OPENS BEFORE TDC

Engine	Year	Degrees
4-151	1980–82	33
V6-229⑥	1980	42
V6-231⑥	1980–82	16
8-265	1980	27
8-265	1981	16
	1981③	16
	1981④	17
8-305⑤	1980	28
8-305⑤	1981–82	44
8-307②	1981	20
8-350①②	1980–82	16
	1980	16

①—Distributor located at rear of engine, counter clockwise distributor rotor rotation. Fuel pump located at right side of engine.
②—Refer to Oldsmobile Chapter for service procedures.
③—Except E/C (Electronic Control) engine.
④—E/C (Electronic Control) engine.
⑤—Refer to Chevrolet Chapter for service procedures.
⑥—Refer to Buick Chapter for service procedures.

VALVE GUIDES

Valve guides are cast integral with the cylinder head. Valves with oversize stems are available in .001 inch, .003 inch and .005 inch larger than standard.

Oversize reamers are required to enlarge valve guide holes to fit the oversize stems. best results when installing .005 inch oversize valve stem use a .003 inch oversize reamer first and then ream to .005 inch oversize. Always reface the valve and valve seat after reaming valve guide. Valves are marked .001, .003 or .005 with colored ink.

VALVE LIFTERS
REPLACE

1. Remove intake manifold.
2. Remove push rod cover and valve cover.
3. Loosen rocker arm, then rotate rocker arm off push rod and remove push rod.
4. Remove lifter, **Fig. 7**.

NOTE: If more than one lifter is to be removed, identify lifters and push rods, so they can be reinstalled in their original locations.

5. Reverse procedure to install. Torque rocker arm ball nut to 20 ft. lbs.

TIMING CASE COVER
REPLACE

NOTE: If necessary to replace the cover oil seal it can be accomplished without removing the timing chain cover.

V8s

1. Drain cooling system.
2. Loosen alternator adjusting bolts.
3. Remove fan and accessory drive belts.
4. Remove fan and pulley.
5. Remove water pump.
6. Disconnect radiator hoses.
7. Remove fuel pump.
8. Remove vibration damper.
9. Remove front four oil pan-to-timing chain cover screws.
10. Remove cover attaching screws.
11. Pull cover forward to clear studs and remove.

4-151

1. Disconnect battery ground cable.
2. Remove torsional damper and the two oil pan to front cover screws.
3. Remove front cover retaining screws.
4. Pull cover forward just enough to permit cutting of oil pan front seal, then cut oil pan front seal flush with cylinder block at both sides and remove front cover.
5. Reverse procedure to install.

TIMING CHAIN
REPLACE

V8 ENGINES

1. Remove timing chain cover.
2. Remove fuel pump eccentric, bushing and timing chain cover oil seal, **Fig. 8**.
3. Align timing marks to simplify proper

Fig. 8   Front of engine with timing case cover removed. V8 engines

Fig. 9   Valve timing marks. V-8 engines

Fig. 10   Camshaft thrust plate screw removal. 4-151

Fig. 11   Camshaft gear removal. 4-151

Fig. 12   Camshaft gear installation & thrust plate clearance check. 4-151

CAMSHAFT
REPLACE

4-151

1. Disconnect battery ground cable.
2. Drain oil pan and radiator.
3. Remove radiator, fan and water pump pulley.
4. Remove distributor, spark plugs and fuel pump.
5. Remove push rod cover and valve cover, then loosen rocker arms and rotate rocker arms off push rods.
6. Remove push rods and valve lifters.

NOTE: Identify push rods and lifters so they can be reinstalled in their original locations.

7. Remove harmonic balancer and timing gear cover.
8. Remove camshaft thrust plate retaining screws, **Fig. 10,** and carefully pull camshaft out of engine.

NOTE: Use care to avoid damaging camshaft bearings.

9. To remove gear, proceed as follows:
   a. Support gear on press using a suitable sleeve, **Fig. 11,** then press camshaft out of gear using a socket or other suitable tool.

NOTE: Thrust plate must be positioned so that woodruff key in shaft does not damage thrust plate when camshaft is pressed out.

   b. To install gear, firmly support camshaft at back of front journal in press using plate adapters.
   c. Place gear spacer ring and thrust plate over end of shaft and install woodruff key.
   d. Press gear until it bottoms against the gear spacer ring. Check end clearance which should be .0015 to .0050 inch, **Fig. 12.** If clearance is less than specified, the spacer ring should be replaced. If clearance is greater than specified, the thrust plate should be replaced.

10. Carefully install camshaft making sure that marks are aligned as shown in **Fig. 13.** Torque thrust plate retaining screws to 75 inch lbs.

NOTE: The valve timing marks shown in **Fig. 13** do not indicate TDC compression stroke for No. 1 cylinder for use during distributor installation. Before installing distributor, turn crankshaft one complete revolution to firing position of No. 1 cylinder (TDC compression stroke), then install distributor in its original position and align shaft so that rotor points toward No. 1 cylinder in distributor cap.

11. Reverse procedure to install remaining components.

ALL V8s

The camshaft and camshaft bearings can be replaced with the engine installed in the car or with engine removed and disassembled for overhaul. However, to replace the rear camshaft bearing without removing and completely disassembling the engine, the propeller shaft, transmission and clutch housing must first be removed. The procedure for removing the camshaft is as follows:

1. Drain cooling system and remove air cleaner.
2. Disconnect radiator and heater hoses, distributor vacuum hose and spark plug wires.

positioning of sprockets during assembly, **Fig. 9.**

NOTE: The valve timing marks, **Fig. 9,** does not indicate TDC, compression stroke for No. 1 cylinder for use during distributor installation. When installing the distributor, rotate engine until No. 1 cylinder is on compression stroke and the camshaft timing mark is 180° from the valve timing position shown in **Fig. 9.**

4. Slide off chain and sprockets.
5. Install new chain and sprockets, making sure timing marks are aligned exactly on a straight line passing through the shaft centers, **Fig. 9.** Camshaft should extend through sprocket so that hole in fuel pump eccentric will locate on shaft.
6. Install fuel pump eccentric and bushing, indexing tab on eccentric with keyway cutout in sprocket. Install retainer bolt with washer and tighten securely.
7. Making sure hollow dowels are in place in block, place timing chain cover gasket over studs and dowels.
8. Install cover, making sure O-ring seal is in place.

Fig. 13 Valve timing marks. 4-151

Fig. 14 Piston & rod assembly. 4-151, V8-265 & 301 less turbo

Fig. 15 Piston & rod assembly. V8-301 turbo

3. Disconnect carburetor linkage, fuel lines and wire connector from temperature sending unit.
4. Remove hood latch brace.
5. Remove radiator, fan and pulleys.
6. On air conditioned cars, remove alternator and its mounting bracket.
7. Remove crankcase ventilator hose or outlet pipe.
8. Remove distributor.
9. Remove rocker arm covers.
10. Remove intake manifold. Make certain O-ring seal between intake manifold and timing chain cover is retained and installed during assembly.
11. Remove push rod cover.
12. Loosen rocker arm ball retaining nuts so that rocker arms can be disengaged from push rods and turned sideways.
13. Remove push rods and hydraulic lifters, keeping them in proper sequence so that they may be returned to their original locations.
14. Remove vibration damper.
15. Remove fuel pump.
16. Remove timing chain cover.
17. Remove fuel pump eccentric and fuel pump bushing.
18. Remove chain and sprockets.
19. Remove camshaft thrust plate and carefully pull camshaft from engine. Clearance for camshaft removal is very limited and, in cases where engine mounts are worn excessively, it may be necessary to raise the front of the engine to permit removal.

PISTON & ROD
ASSEMBLE

Assemble pistons and rods as indicated in **Figs. 14 & 15**.

When installing connecting rod and piston assemblies into V8-301 engines, the raised notches at bearing end of each connecting rod must all face toward the rear of the engine. When installing connecting rod and piston assemblies in V8-350 engines, the raised notches at the bearing end of each connecting rod in the right bank cylinders (2, 4, 6 and 8) must face front of engine. Connecting rods installed in the left bank cylinders (1, 3, 5 and 7) must have all the raised notches facing toward the rear of the engine.

On all engines, the notch cast in the piston heads must face the front of the engine when the piston and connecting rod assemblies are installed.

Fig. 16 Rear main bearing oil seal tool V8-301 & 350

Correct piston and connecting rod assembly installation is extremely important as incorrect installation could cause an engine knock.

Upon installation, measure the connecting rod side clearance using a suitable feeler gauge. Measurement obtained should be .006–.022 inch for 4-151, V8-265, 301 & 350.

PISTONS, PINS & RINGS

Pistons and rings are available in standard sizes and oversizes of .005, .010, .020 and .030 inch.

Piston pins are available in oversizes of .001 and .003 inch.

MAIN & ROD BEARINGS

Main bearings are available in standard sizes and undersizes of .001 and .002 inch.

Rod bearings are available in standard sizes and undersizes of .001 and .002 inch.

CRANKSHAFT REAR OIL SEAL
REPLACE

V8S

1. Remove oil pan, oil pump and pump drive shaft.
2. Remove oil baffle and cylinder block-to-oil baffle tube.
3. Remove rear main bearing cap.
4. Use tool shown in **Fig. 16** made from brass bar stock to pack upper seal as follows:
   a. Insert tool against one end of oil seal in cylinder block and drive seal gently into groove until tool bottoms.
   b. Remove tool and repeat at other end of seal in cylinder block.
5. Clean block and bearing cap parting line thoroughly.
6. Form a new seal in cap.
7. Remove newly formed seal from cap and cut four pieces about ⅜ inch long from this seal.
8. Work two ⅜ inch pieces into each end of the gaps which have been made at the end of seal in cylinder block. Without cutting off the ends, work these seal pieces in until flush with parting line, being sure that no fibers are protruding over the metal adjacent to the groove.
9. Form another new seal in the cap, **Fig. 17**.
10. Assemble the cap to the block and torque to specifications.
11. Remove cap and inspect parting line to insure that no seal material has been compressed between the block and cap.
12. Apply a 1/16 inch bead of sealer from the center of the seal to the external cork groove.
13. Reassemble the cap and torque to specifications.

21—25

Fig. 17 Installing rear main bearing oil seal. V8-265, 301 & 350

Fig. 20 Rear oil pan gasket positioned in oil pan. V8-265, 301 & 350

4-151

1. Disconnect battery ground cable.
2. Remove transmission.
3. Remove flywheel retaining bolts, then flywheel.
4. On all models, remove seal using suitable screwdriver.
5. Reverse procedure to install.

NOTE: To facilitate installation, apply a light coat of engine oil to outside sealing surface of new seal, then evenly press seal into place.

OIL PAN
REPLACE

4-151

1. Disconnect battery ground cable and remove engine fan.
2. Raise vehicle and drain oil pan.
3. Disconnect exhaust pipe at manifold and loosen hanger bracket.
4. Remove starter and place aside, then remove flywheel housing inspection cover.
5. Raise engine slightly to remove weight from engine mounts and remove both brackets to engine mount bolts.

Fig. 18 Installing oil pan gasket retainers. V8-265, 301 & 350

6. Remove oil pan bolts, then raise engine to allow oil pan removal and remove oil pan.
7. Reverse procedure to install.

V8-265, 301, 350 PONTIAC BUILT ENGINES

1. Disconnect battery ground cable and remove fan.
2. Make sure that all hoses and wiring are properly routed to avoid binding or stretching when engine is raised.
3. On some air conditioned vehicles, it will be necessary to remove A/C compressor from mounting brackets and place aside for clearance.
4. Remove distributors cap, then raise vehicle and drain engine oil.
5. Disconnect exhaust pipes from manifolds, then remove starter and flywheel housing cover.
6. Rotate crankshaft until number on cylinder is at bottom dead center.
7. Remove engine mount through bolts.
8. Remove oil pan bolts, then raise engine just enough to allow oil pan removal and remove oil pan.
9. Reverse procedure to install. Install gasket as shown in **Figs. 18, 19 and 20.**

OIL PUMP
REPLACE

4-151

Remove oil pan. Remove the two flange mounting bolts and nut and remove pump.

Remove the four cover retaining screws, cover, gears and shaft and regulator parts, **Fig. 21.**

CAUTION: Do not attempt to remove or disturb oil pick-up tube.

Clean and inspect pump. If any of the following conditions are found, the oil pump should be replaced:
1. Inspect pump body for cracks or wear.
2. Inspect gears for excessive wear or damage.
3. Inspect shaft for looseness in housing.
4. Inspect inside of cover for wear which may permit oil to leak past the ends of the gears.
5. Inspect oil pick-up screen.

Fig. 19 Front oil pan gasket overlapping side gasket, V8-265, 301 & 350

Fig. 21 Oil pump disassembled. 4-151

To assemble, install drive gear and shaft in housing, then install idler gear with smooth side facing cover. Install cover and screws and torque screws to 105 inch lbs. Make sure that shaft turns freely. Install regulatory valve spring, retainer and pin.

To install pump, align drive shaft with distributor tang, then position pump on engine and install retaining bolts and nut. On 1982–84 models torque bolts and nuts to 20 to 22 ft. lbs.

V8 ENGINES

Remove oil pan. While holding pump in place, remove attaching screws. Lower the pump away from the block with one hand while removing the oil pump drive shaft with the other.

Remove oil screen and pressure regulator parts. Detach cover from pump body and take out gears, **Fig. 22.**

Examine all parts for damage and assemble. Do not attempt to change oil pressure by varying length of pressure regulator spring.

Position drive shaft in distributor and oil pump drive gear. Place pump in position in the block, indexing the drive shaft with pump drive gear shaft. Install attaching screws with lock washers and tighten securely.

Fig. 22   Oil pump disassembled. V8 Pontiac engines

Fig. 23   Turbocharger assembly installation

Engine oiling system. V8s

BELT TENSION DATA

	New Lbs.	Used Lbs.
1980–81		
Air Conditioning		
Exc. 4-151	135–145	90–100
4-151	120–130	70–80
Air Pump		
Exc. V6-231	120–130	70–80
V6-231	65–75	45–55
Alternator		
All	120–130	70–80
Power Steering		
Exc. 4-151	135–145	90–100
4-151	120–130	70–80
1982		
5/16 inch Wide	80	50
3/8 inch Wide	140	70
15/32 inch Wide	165	90
7/16 inch Wide	165	90
1983–85		
Air Conditioning		
4-151	165	90
Generator		
4-151		
With A/C	165	90
Without A/C	145	70
Power Steering		
4-151	145	70

WATER PUMP
REPLACE

NOTE: Water pump is serviced as an assembly only.

1. Disconnect battery cable and drain cooling system.
2. Loosen alternator adjusting bolt and remove fan belt.
3. Remove fan and pulley.
4. Disconnect radiator and heater hose at pump, then remove water pump retaining bolts and pump.
5. Reverse procedure to install. Torque water pump retaining bolts to 15 ft. lbs.

FUEL PUMP
REPLACE

1. Disconnect fuel lines from pump.
2. Remove pump retaining bolts and pump.
3. Remove all gasket material from the pump and block gasket surfaces. Apply sealer on both sides of new gasket.
4. Position gasket on pump flange and hold pump in position against its mounting surface. Make sure rocker arm is riding on camshaft eccentric.
5. Press pump tight against its mounting. Install retaining screws and tighten them alternately.
6. Connect fuel lines. Then operate engine and check for leaks.

SERVICE NOTE: Before installing the pump, it is good practice to crank the engine so that the nose of the camshaft eccentric is out of the way of the fuel pump rocker arm when the pump is installed. In this way there will be the least amount of tension on the rocker arm, thereby easing the installation of the pump.

Fig. 24 Sectional view of turbocharger assembly

NORMAL OPERATING MODE

Fig. 25 Turbocharger operating schematic

TURBOCHARGER

The turbocharger, **Figs. 23 and 24,** is used to increase engine power on demand, while maintaining the capability of good fuel economy.

As engine load increases and the throttle opens, more air-fuel mixture flows into the combustion chambers. As the increased flow is burned, a larger volume of high energy exhaust gasses enters the engine exhaust system and is directed through the turbocharger turbine housing, **Fig. 25.** Some of the exhaust gas energy is used to increase the speed of the turbine wheel

which is connected to the compressor wheel. The increased speed of the compressor wheel compresses the air-fuel mixture from the carburetor and delivers the compressed air-fuel mixture to the intake manifold, **Fig. 25.** The high pressure in the intake manifold allows a denser charge to enter the combustion chambers, in turn developing more engine power during the combustion cycle.

The intake manifold pressure (Boost) is controlled to a maximum value by an exhaust gas bypass valve (Wastegate), **Fig. 25.** The wastegate allows a portion of the exhaust gas to bypass the turbine

wheel, thereby not increasing turbine speed. The wastegate is operated by a spring loaded diaphragm device sensing the pressure differential across the compressor. When intake manifold pressure reaches a set value above ambient pressure, the wastegate begins to bypass the exhaust gas.

An Electronic Spark Control System is used to retard ignition timing up to 18°–22° to minimize detonation. The power enrichment vacuum regulator (PEVR) is used to control vacuum flow to the carburetor power piston.

NOTE: Engine oil on turbocharged engines must be changed every 3000 miles since turbocharger bearing damage may occur from oil contamination. Before starting engine after changing oil and filter, disconnect ignition switch wire connector (pink wire) from distributor. Crank engine several times, not to exceed 30 seconds for each interval, until oil light goes out, then reconnect ignition switch wire connector to distributor.

Diesel Engine Section

Refer to Section 20 for service procedures on this engine.

Clutch & Transmission Section

CLUTCH PEDAL
ADJUST

1. Disconnect return spring from clutch fork.
2. Rotate clutch lever and shaft assembly until clutch pedal is firmly seated against rubber bumper on dash brace.
3. Push outer end of clutch fork rearward until release bearing lightly contacts diaphragm spring fingers.
4. Disconnect lower push rod from lever and shaft assembly and install it in gauge hole.
5. Rotate fork rod finger tight until all lash has been removed from linkage.
6. Remove swivel from gauge hole and install it in hole furthest from lever and shaft assembly.
7. Install washers and retainer, then tighten lock nut being careful not to change length of rod.
8. Reconnect return spring and check pedal free travel. Free travel should be approximately 1.0 inch.

CLUTCH
REPLACE

1. Remove transmission as described under "Transmission, Replace."
2. Disconnect clutch fork push rod and spring.
3. Remove flywheel housing from engine.
4. Slide clutch fork from ball stud and remove fork from dust boot.
5. Install a dummy shaft to support clutch assembly during removal.
6. Mark clutch plate and flywheel to ensure reassembly in the same position.
7. Loosen clutch cover to flywheel bolts one turn at a time until spring pressure is relieved, then remove mounting bolts and clutch cover and disc.

THREE-SPEED MANUAL TRANS.
REPLACE

1. Disconnect battery ground cable.
2. Raise vehicle and drain lubricant from transmission.
3. Scribe mark on companion flange and drive shaft yoke, then remove drive shaft.
4. Disconnect speedometer cable and backup light switch wire connector.
5. On models with column shift, disconnect transmission shift levers from transmission shifter shafts. On models with floor shift, it will also be necessary to remove shifter assembly to shifter support bolts and remove shifter assembly from transmission.
6. Remove crossmember to transmission mount bolts and catalytic converter to transmission bracket, if equipped, then remove crossmember to frame bolts.
7. Raise transmission and remove crossmember.
8. Remove transmission to clutch housing upper attaching bolts and install guide pins.
9. Remove transmission to clutch housing lower attaching bolts, then slide transmission straight back on guide pins until main drive splines are clear of clutch plate and remove transmission from vehicle.
10. Reverse procedure to install.

SHIFT LINKAGE 3 SPEED TRANS.
ADJUST

Column Shift

1. Place shift lever in reverse position and ignition switch in Lock position.
2. Raise vehicle and loosen shift control rod swivel lock nuts.
3. Pull down slightly on 1st–reverse control rod attached to column lever to remove slack in column mechanism, then tighten lock nut at transmission.
4. Unlock ignition switch and position shift lever in neutral position. Position column lower levers in neutral, then align gauge holes in levers and insert ³⁄₁₆ in. gauge pin.

NOTE: Alignment holes are located on lower side of levers.

5. Support rod and swivel to prevent movement of assembly and tighten 2nd–3rd control rod lock nut.
6. Remove alignment tool from column levers and check shifter operation. Place shift lever in reverse and check interlock control.

NOTE: With shift lever in reverse, ignition key must move freely to Lock position. It must not be possible to obtain Lock position in any other selector position than reverse.

Floor Shift

1. Place ignition switch in off position, then raise vehicle.
2. Loosen lock nuts at swivels on shift rods. Rods should pass freely through swivels.
3. Shift shift levers into neutral at transmission.
4. Place shift control lever in neutral detent, then align control assembly levers and insert a ³⁄₁₆ in. gauge pin into lever alignment slot.
5. Tighten locknuts at shift rod swivels and remove gauge pin.
6. Place shift control lever in reverse position and ignition switch in Lock position. Loosen lock nut at back drive control rod swivel, then pull down on rod slightly to remove slack in column mechanism and tighten clevis jam nut.

7. Check interlock control, ignition key should move freely to and from Lock position.
8. Lower vehicle and check adjustment.

4 SPEED TRANS.
REPLACE

Follow procedure outlined for three-speed model.

NOTE: For 1982–86 Firebird, torque arm must be removed after step 2 of removal procedure. Refer to "Rear Axle, Propeller Shaft and Brake Section" of this chapter for torque arm removal procedure.

SHIFT LINKAGE 4 SPEED TRANS
ADJUST

1. Place selector lever in neutral.
2. Loosen trunnion nuts on transmission control rod.
3. Place transmission lever and bracket assembly in neutral and install a gauge pin through hole and slot provided in bracket.
4. Position lever on transmission in neutral.
5. Tighten trunnion nuts and remove gauge pin.
6. Position shift lever in Reverse, set steering column lever in Lock position and lock ignition. Push up on control rod to remove clearance and tighten nut of adjusting swivel.

5 SPEED TRANS.
REPLACE

1. Disconnect battery ground cable.
2. From inside vehicle, remove screws attaching bezel to tunnel, then remove bezel by slipping over boot and shift lever.
3. With shift lever in neutral, hold boot out of way and remove four bolts attaching shift lever to transmission, then remove shift lever assembly.
4. Raise vehicle and scribe a mark on companion flange and drive shaft yoke, then remove drive shaft.
5. Remove bolts attaching catalytic converter support bracket to transmission.
6. Remove two bolts attaching transmission mount to support.
7. Raise transmission and remove two long end bolts, then remove transmission support.
8. Disconnect speedometer cable and backup light switch wire connector.
9. Remove transmission to clutch housing upper attaching bolts and install guide pins.
10. Remove transmission to clutch housing lower attaching bolts, then slide transmission back on guide pins until main drive gear splines clear clutch plate and remove transmission from vehicle.

Rear Axle, Propeller Shaft & Brake Section

REAR AXLES

Figs. 1 and 2 illustrate the rear axle assemblies used on 1980–86 conventional models. When necessary to overhaul either of these units, refer to the Rear Axle Specifications table in this chapter.

1980–86

In this rear axle, **Fig. 1,** the rear axle housing and differential carrier are cast into an integral assembly. The drive pinion assembly is mounted in two opposed tapered roller bearings. The pinion bearings are preloaded by a spacer behind the front bearings. The pinion is positioned by a shim between the head of the pinion and the rear bearing.

The differential is supported in the carrier by two tapered roller side bearings. These bearings are preloaded by shims located between the bearings and carrier housing. The differential assembly is positioned for proper ring gear and pinion backlash by varying these shims. The differential case houses two side gears in mesh with two pinions mounted on a pinion shaft which is held in place by a lock screw. The side gears and pinions are backed by thrust washers.

Fig. 1   Rear Axle assembly exploded. Except "C" lock axle retention

REAR AXLE, REPLACE

Except 1982–86 Firebird

It is not necessary to remove rear axle assembly from vehicle to perform any normal service operation. However, if any part of housing is damaged, rear axle assembly may be removed and installed using the following procedure.

1. Raise car and place a floor jack under center of axle housing so it starts to raise rear axle assembly. Place jack stands solidly under frame members on both sides.
2. Disconnect rear U-joint from drive pinion flange and support propeller shaft out of the way.
3. Remove both axle shafts.
4. Support both brake backing plates out of the way.
5. Disconnect rear brake hose bracket by removing top cover bolt. Remove brake line from housing by bending back tabs.
6. Loosen remaining cover bolts, break loose cover about ⅛ inch and allow lube to drain.
7. Disconnect shock absorbers at axle housing.
8. On models with coil springs:
   a. Disconnect upper control arms at axle housing.
   b. Slowly lower jack until all spring tension is relieved and remove springs.
   c. Disconnect lower control arms and remove axle assembly.
9. On models with leaf springs,
   a. While supporting spring, remove rear shackle from spring.

b. Lower spring and remove nut and bolt from spring front bushing, remove spring.
c. Remove axle assembly.

1982–86 Firebird

1. Hoist car and support at frame and under rear axle housing.
2. Disconnect both shock absorbers and remove bolt from left side of track bar to axle.
3. Remove bolt from brake line junction block at axle housing and disconnect brake lines from junction block.

4. Lower rear axle assembly and remove springs.
5. Remove rear wheels and drums and remove rear axle cover and drain lube.
6. Disconnect brake lines from axle housing clips.
7. Remove axle shafts, brake backing plates, lower control arms and torque arm from axle housing.
8. Disconnect drive shaft from rear axle flange and place aside after marking for reinstallation.

Fig. 2   Rear Axle assembly exploded. With "C" lock retention

Fig. 3 Removing axle shaft with slide hammer-type puller

PULLER J-21579

9. Remove rear axle housing.
10. Reverse procedure to install.

AXLE SHAFT, REPLACE

NOTE: Design allows for axle shaft end play of .032 inches max. on 1980–81 "P" (8¾ inch) axles; and .002–.020 inches max. on 1980–81 "C", "G", "K", "O" and "P" (7½ and 8½ inch) axles. The axle type identification marks for 1980–86 except 1980–81 "B" axles will be stamped on right rear axle tube, on forward side. 1980–81 "B" axles will have a tag attached by a cover bolt at the seven o'clock position. This end play can be checked with wheel and brake drum removed by measuring difference between end of housing and axle shaft flange while moving the axle shaft in and out by hand.

TYPE "B & O" (EXCEPT 7½ inch)

1. To remove, take off wheels and brake drums.
2. Remove nuts holding retainer plates and brake backing plates. Pull retainers clear of bolts and reinstall two lower nuts finger tight to hold backing plate in position.
3. Use a slide hammer-type puller to remove axle shaft, **Fig. 3.**

Axle Shaft Bearing
1. Press axle shaft bearing off shaft.
2. Press new bearing against shoulder on shaft.

CAUTION: Outer retainer plate which retains bearing in housing must be on axle shaft before bearing is installed. A new outer retainer gasket can be installed after bearing. Use care not to wedge outer retainer between bearing and shoulder of shaft. Do not press bearing and inner retainer on in one operation.

3. Press new inner retainer ring against bearing.

Axle Shaft Seal
1. Insert suitable tongs behind seal and pull straight out to remove seal.
2. Apply sealer to outside diameter of new seal.
3. Position seal over a suitable installer and drive straight into axle housing until tool bottoms on bearing shoulder in housing.

Axle Shaft, Install
1. Apply a coat of wheel bearing grease in bearing recess of housing. Also lightly lubricate the axle shaft with rear axle lube from the sealing surface to about 6 inch inboard.
2. Install new axle housing-to-brake backing plate gasket.
3. Install brake assembly with backing plate in proper position.
4. With a new outer retainer gasket in proper position, insert axle shaft until splines engage differential. Do not allow shaft to drag on seal.
5. Drive axle shaft into position.
6. Place new outer retainer gasket and retainer over studs and install nuts.
7. Install brake drums and wheels.

TYPE "C", "G", "K", "O" (7½ inch) & "P" AXLE

1. Raise and support car leaving the rear wheels and differential suspended.
2. Remove rear wheels and brake drums.
3. Remove differential cover and drain lubricant.
4. Remove pinion shaft lock bolt and pinion shaft.
5. Push axle shaft inward to permit removal of "C" locks then remove axle shaft.
6. Install axle shaft bearing and seal remover and remove the bearing and seal.

PROPELLER SHAFT
REPLACE

One type of propeller shaft is used on all vehicles. The type being used is a one-piece shaft with two single cardan type U-joints.

Two methods of retention are used at the rear of the propeller shaft. The first method uses a pair of straps retained by bolts, while the second method uses a set of bolted flanges.
1. Raise and properly support vehicle, then mark relationship of propeller shaft to companion flange in order to insure correct alignment during reassembly.
2. Disconnect rear U-joint by removing strap bolts of flange bolts.

NOTE: If U-joint bearing cups are loose, tape them together to avoid dropping and losing needle rollers.

3. Remove propeller shaft by pulling rearward.

CAUTION: Support propeller shaft during removal. Do not allow propeller shaft to drop or allow universal joints to bend to an extreme angle.

4. Reverse procedure to install, making sure that alignment marks are properly aligned. Torque strap retaining bolts to 15 ft. lbs. Torque flange bolts to 45 ft. lbs.

BACKING PLATE
TOOL J-4735

INSERT SMALL SCREW DRIVER OR AWL THROUGH BACKING PLATE SLOT AND HOLD ADJUSTER LEVER AWAY FROM SPROCKET BEFORE BACKING OFF BRAKE SHOE ADJUSTMENT

Fig. 4 Backing off adjusting screw

BRAKE ADJUSTMENTS
1980–86 SELF-ADJUSTING BRAKES

These brakes have self-adjusting shoe mechanisms that assure correct lining-to-drum clearances at all times. The automatic adjusters operate only when the brakes are applied as the car is moving rearward.

Although the brakes are self-adjusting, an initial adjustment is necessary after the brake shoes have been relined or replaced, or when the length of the star wheel adjuster has been changed during some other service operation.

Frequent usage of an automatic transmission forward range to half reverse vehicle motion may prevent the automatic adjusters from functioning, thereby inducing low pedal heights. Should low pedal heights be encountered, it is recommended that numerous forward and reverse stops be made until satisfactory pedal height is obtained.

If a low pedal height condition cannot be corrected by making numerous reverse stops (provided the hydraulic system is free of air) it indicates that the self-adjusting mechanism is not functioning. Therefore, it will be necessary to remove the drum, clean, free up and lubricate the adjusting mechanism. Then adjust the brakes as follows, being sure the parking brake is fully released.

ADJUSTMENT

1. Knock out lanced area from brake backing plate with a suitable punch.

NOTE: If this is done with drum installed on car, drum must be removed and brake area cleaned of all metal particles.

2. Turn brake adjusting screw with tool J6166 or equivalent until brake shoes are expanded to where wheel can just be turned by hand. Amount of effort to turn wheels should be same at all four wheels.
3. While holding adjusting lever out of engagement with a suitable screw driver, **Fig. 4,** back off adjusting screw

Fig. 5 Measuring brake drum inside diameter

several notches and check for drag. If brakes still drag, back off adjusting screw one or two more notches.

NOTE: Brakes should be free of drag when screw has been backed off approximately 12 notches. Heavy drag at this point indicates tight parking brake cables.

4. Install new adjusting hole cover in brake backing plate cover.
5. Check parking brake adjustment.

NOTE: The recommended method of adjusting the brakes is by using the Drum-to-Brake Shoe Clearance Gauge shown in **Fig. 5** to check the diameter of the brake drum inner surface. Turn the tool to the opposite side and fit over the brake shoes by turning the star wheel until the gauge just slides over the linings, **Fig. 6**. Rotate the gauge around the brake shoe lining surface to assure proper clearance.

PARKING BRAKE
ADJUST

CAUTION: Adjustment of parking brake cable is necessary whenever rear brake cables are disconnected. The need for parking brake adjustment is indicated if parking brake pedal travel is less than 9 ratchet clicks or more than 17 ratchet clicks. It is also important that parking brake cables are not adjusted too tightly as brake drag will occur. Incorrect cable tension can damage brake system and cause premature wear to brake linings.

1980–86, LESS REAR DISC BRAKES

1. Raise and support rear of vehicle.
2. Apply parking brake pedal two to three ratchet clicks on all except 1979–81 full size models, and six ratchet clicks on 1980–81 full size models.
3. Tighten adjusting nut until left rear

wheel can just be rotated rearward but is locked when forward rotation is attempted.
4. Release parking brake and check to ensure that rear wheels rotate freely in either direction with no brake drag.

1980–86 FIREBIRD WITH REAR DISC BRAKES

1. Lubricate parking brake cables at underbody rub points and at equalizer hooks. Check for free movement of all cables.
2. Ensure parking brake hand lever is in fully released position.
3. Raise and support rear of vehicle.
4. Hold brake cable stud from turning and tighten equalizer nut until cable slack is removed.
5. Ensure caliper levers are against stops on caliper housing after tightening equalizer nut.
6. If levers are off the stops, loosen cable until levers return to stops.
7. Operate parking brake lever several times to check adjustment. After cable adjustment is performed, parking brake lever should travel 14 clicks with approximately 150 ± 20 pounds force of handle effort using tool J-28662.
8. Lower vehicle and ensure levers are against caliper stops. If necessary back off parking brake adjuster to keep levers against stops.

POWER BRAKE UNIT
REPLACE

HYDRO-BOOST

NOTE: Pump brake pedal several times with engine off to deplete accumulator of fluid.

1. Remove two nuts attaching master cylinder to booster, then move master cylinder away from booster with brake lines attached.
2. Remove three hydraulic lines from booster. Plug and cap all lines and outlets.
3. Remove retainer and washer securing booster push rod to brake pedal arm.
4. Remove four nuts attaching booster unit to dash panel.
5. From engine compartment, loosen booster from dash panel and move booster push rod inboard until it disconnects from brake pedal arm. Remove spring washer from brake pedal arm.
6. Remove booster unit from vehicle.
7. Reverse procedure to install. To purge system, disconnect feed wire from injection pump. Fill power steering pump reservoir, then crank engine for

Fig. 6 Checking brake shoe lining clearance

several seconds and recheck power steering pump fluid level. Connect injection pump feed wire and start engine, then cycle steering wheel from stop to stop twice and stop engine. Discharge accumulator by depressing brake pedal several times, then check fluid level. Start engine, then turn steering wheel from stop to stop and turn engine off. Check fluid level and add fluid as necessary. If foaming occurs, stop engine and wait for approximately one hour for foam to dissipate, then recheck fluid level.

VACUUM BOOSTER

1. Remove vacuum check valve.
2. If brake booster and master cylinder are being removed as an assembly, disconnect hydraulic lines and cover openings in master cylinder and lines to avoid entry of dirt. If only brake booster is to be removed, remove master cylinder retaining nuts and position master cylinder aside.

CAUTION: Be careful not to bend or kink hydraulic lines.

3. Remove clevis pin retainer from brake pedal.
4. Remove brake booster retaining nuts and remove brake booster.
5. Reverse procedure to install.

BRAKE MASTER CYLINDER
REPLACE

1980–86

1. Disconnect brake lines from two outlets on master cylinder and tape end of lines to prevent entrance of dirt.
2. On models less power brakes, disconnect master cylinder push rod from brake pedal.
3. Remove two nuts attaching master cylinder to dash or power brake unit and remove master cylinder from vehicle.

Rear Suspension

Fig. 1   Leaf spring front bushing removal

Fig. 2   Leaf spring front bushing installation

Fig. 3   Coil spring suspension (typical) Except 1982–86 Firebird

LEAF SPRING SERVICE

NOTE: The main leaf may be serviced separately, however, if any of the smaller leaves require replacement, the entire assembly must be replaced.

1. Clamp spring in a vise, remove spring clips and center bolt, then carefully open vise, allowing spring to expand.
2. Replace main leaf and use a drift to align center bolt holes, compress spring in a vise, remove drift and install new center bolt.
3. Align spring leaves and bend spring clips into position.

NOTE: Overtightening spring clips will bind spring action.

SHOCK ABSORBER
REPLACE

NOTE: If vehicle is equipped with Superlift shock absorbers, bleed system air pressure through service valve before disconnecting lines at shock absorber fittings.

1. With rear axle supported properly, disconnect shock absorber from lower mounting nut. Use a wrench to prevent mounting stud rotation.
2. Disconnect shock absorber from upper mounting nut.
3. Reverse procedure to install.

LEAF SPRING & BUSHINGS
REPLACE

1980–81 FIREBIRD

1. Raise and support vehicle so that axle can be raised and lowered.
2. Lower axle assembly to relieve tension from spring.
3. Disconnect shock absorber from lower mounting.
4. Loosen spring eye to bracket retaining bolt.
5. Remove bolts attaching spring retainer bracket to under body.
6. Lower axle assembly to permit access to spring retainer bracket, and remove bracket from spring.
7. Pry parking brake cable out of retainer bracket mounted on anchor plate.
8. Remove lower spring plate to axle bracket retaining nuts.
9. Remove upper and lower cushions and anchor plate.
10. Support spring, then remove lower bolt from spring rear shackle. Separate shackle and remove spring from vehicle.
11. To replace bushings, refer to **Figs. 1 and 2**.
12. Reverse procedure to install.

COIL SPRING
REPLACE

1980–86 ALL EXC. FIREBIRD

1. Support vehicle at frame rails and support rear axle with a suitable jack.
2. Remove brake line connector block bolt at axle housing.
3. Release brake line from clips on axle housing as necessary.
4. Disconnect upper control arms from axle housing, **Fig. 3.**
5. Disconnect shock absorbers from lower mountings.
6. Lower rear axle. Do not permit the rear brake hose to kink or stretch.
7. When the axle has been lowered sufficiently to provide clearance for coil spring removal, remove coil spring.
8. Reverse procedure to install. Ensure that coil springs are properly indexed, **Fig. 4.**

1982–86 FIREBIRD

1. Raise car on suitable hoist and support rear axle on adjustable type lifting device.

Fig. 4 Indexing coil springs. 1980—81 & 1983—86 Full Size and 1980—86 Intermediates

Fig. 5 Coil spring suspension. 1982—86 Firebird

Fig. 6 All front & lower control arm rear bushing removal. 1980—86 models

Fig. 7 All front & lower control arm rear bushing installation. 1980—86 models

Fig. 8 Upper control arm rear bushing removal. 1980—86 models

2. Loosen track bar bolt at body brace and remove track bar mounting bolt at axle assembly, **Fig. 5.**
3. Disconnect rear brake hose clip at underbody and remove both shock absorber lower attaching nuts.
4. Remove prop shaft from vehicles with four cylinder engines.
5. Lower rear axle and remove coil spring and insulators.
6. Reverse procedure to install.

CONTROL ARMS & BUSHINGS
REPLACE

NOTE: Replace control arms one at a time to prevent axle misalignment, making installation difficult.

UPPER CONTROL ARMS

NOTE: 1982—86 Firebird uses a single torque arm in place of upper control arms. Refer to "Torque Arm, Replace" & **Fig. 5.**

1. Support vehicle at frame and rear axle.
2. Remove control arm front and rear mounting bolts.

NOTE: On some vehicles, disconnect the shock absorber lower mounting stud to provide clearance. Also, use a suitable jack under the nose of differential housing to aid bolt removal.

3. Replace bushings as necessary, **Figs. 6 thru 9.**
4. Reverse procedure to install. Tighten control arm bolts with vehicle at curb height.

LOWER CONTROL ARMS

Follow "Upper Control Arms" procedure for replacement of lower control arms. Lower control arm bushings are serviceable, **Figs. 6 & 7.**

NOTE: On models equipped with a stabilizer bar, remove stabilizer bar outlined under "Stabilizer Bar & Bushings, Replace" procedure before removing low-

er control arm mounting bolts.

TORQUE ARM
REPLACE

1. Raise vehicle on suitable hoist and support rear axle assembly with adjustable jack.
2. Loosen track bar bolt at body brace and remove track bar bolt at axle assembly.
3. Disconnect rear brake hose clip at underbody and remove both shock absorber lower attaching nuts.
4. Remove prop shaft from vehicles with four cylinder engine.
5. Lower rear axle and remove coil springs.

NOTE: Coil springs must be removed before removing torque arm to avoid rear axle forward twist which may cause vehicle damage.

6. Remove torque arm rear attaching bolts, front torque arm outer bracket and remove torque arm.

Fig. 9 Upper control arm rear bushing installation. 1980—86 models

Fig. 10 Stabilizer bar installation. 1980—86 intermediates

1	(UNDERBODY PAN ASM.)
2	47NM (35 FT. LB.)
3	17NM (12 FT. LB.)
4	AXLE ASM.
5	SADDLE
6	27NM (20 FT. LB.)

(R.H. SHOWN L.H. OPPOSITE)

Fig. 11 Stabilizer bar installation. 1982—86 Firebird

7. Reverse procedure to install. Torque track bar mounting nut at axle to 93 ft. lbs. and torque track bar to body bracket nut to 58 ft. lbs.

STABILIZER BAR
REPLACE

MODELS WITH COIL SPRINGS

Exc. 1982—86 Firebird

1. With vehicle supported at rear axle, remove bolts attaching stabilizer bar to lower control arms, **Fig. 10.**
2. If equipped with shims, note number and location.
3. Reverse procedure to install. Tighten attaching bolts with vehicle at curb height.

1982—86 Firebird

Refer to **Fig. 11** for removal and installation procedures.

Fig. 12 Stabilizer bar installation. 1980—81 Firebird

MODELS WITH LEAF SPRINGS

1. Raise and support rear of vehicle.
2. Remove clamping bolts to disconnect lower end of each support assembly from stabilizer shaft, **Fig. 12.**
3. Remove insulator and bracket from below each spring and shock absorber anchor plate.
4. Reverse procedure to install making sure that slit in insulators are positioned toward front of vehicle.

Front Suspension & Steering Section

FRONT SUSPENSION

EXC. 1982—86 FIREBIRD

The front suspension is of the conventional "A" frame design with coil springs and ball joints. The ball joints have a "fixed boot" grease seal for protection against the entry of dirt and water. The steering knuckles and spindles are of integral design.

On most models, an integral steering knuckle which is a combination steering knuckle, brake caliper support and steering arm is used. On other models, the steering knuckle is of the conventional type with a separate steering arm.

Rubber bushings at the inner ends of the upper control arms pivot on shafts attached to the car frame. Caster and camber adjustments are made with shims at this point, **Fig. 1.** Direct acting shock absorbers operate within the coil springs.

1982—85 FIREBIRD

The front suspension is designed to allow each wheel to compensate for changes in the road surface level without appreciably affecting the opposite wheel. Each wheel is independently connected to the frame by a steering knuckle, strut assembly, ball joint, and lower control arm. The steering knuckles move in a prescribed three dimensional arc. The front wheels are held in proper relationship to each other by two tie rods which are connected to the steering knuckles and to a relay rod assembly.

Coil springs are mounted between the spring housings on the front crossmember and the lower control arms. The upper portion of each strut assembly extends through the fender well and attaches to the upper mount assembly with a nut, **Fig. 2.**

The inner ends of the lower control arm have pressed in bushings. Bolts, passing through the bushings, attach the arm to the suspension crossmember. The lower ball joint assembly is a press fit in the arm and attaches to the steering knuckle with a torque prevailing nut.

WHEEL ALIGNMENT

EXC. 1982—86 FIREBIRD

Caster and camber adjustments are made by placing shims between the upper pivot shafts and frame, **Fig. 3.** Both adjustments can be made at the same time. In order to remove or install shims, raise car to remove weight from front wheel, then loosen control arm shaft-to-frame bolts.

NOTE: Shim pack thickness should not exceed .40 inch maximum on 1980—86 models. Also, difference between front and rear shim packs should not exceed ⅜ inch maximum.

1. To increase negative caster, add shims to front bolt or remove shims from rear bolt.

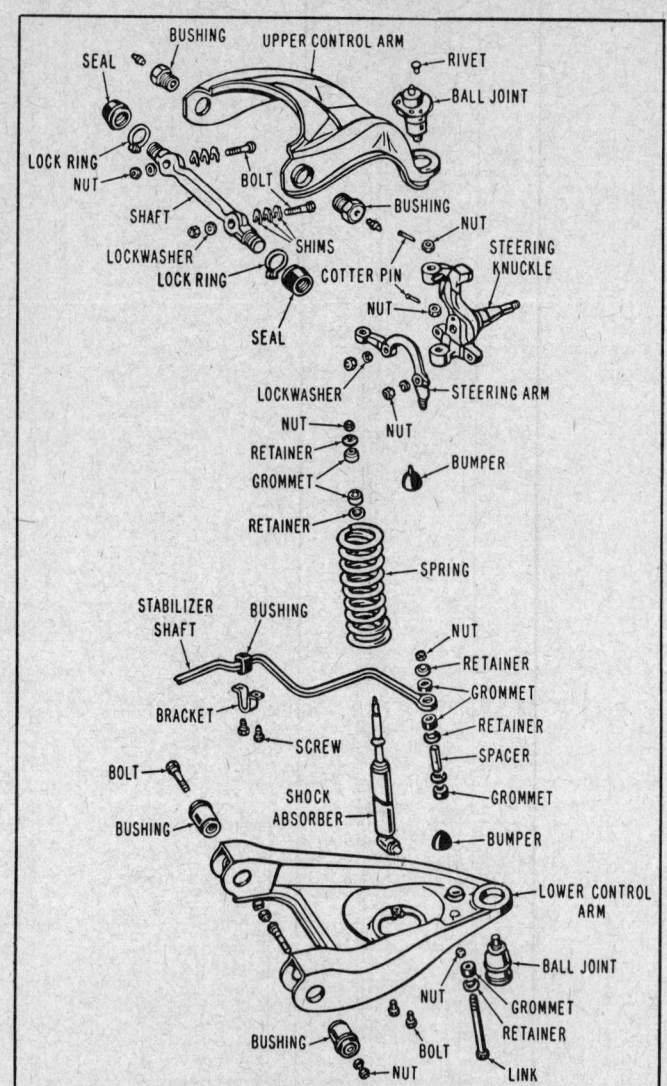

Fig. 1   Disassembled view of front suspension. 1980—86 (typical), Exc. 1982—86 Firebird

Fig. 2   Disassembled view of front suspension. 1982—86 Firebird

PIVOT SHAFT INBOARD OF FRAME

Fig. 4   Installing tool J-29724, for caster and camber adjustment. 1982—86 Firebird

Fig. 3   Caster and camber shim location

Fig. 5   Camber adjustment. 1982—86 Firebird

Fig. 6   Caster adjustment. 1982—86 Firebird

2. To decrease negative caster (increase positive caster), remove shims from front bolt or add shims to rear bolt.
3. To increase positive camber, remove shims from both front and rear bolts.
4. To decrease positive camber (increase negative camber), add shims to both front and rear bolts.

NOTE: By adding or subtracting an equal amount of shims from front and rear bolts, camber will be changed without affecting caster.

5. After proper shim pack has been installed, torque pivot shaft mounting bolts to 70 to 75 ft. lbs. on all models except 1981—86 Intermediates, and 45 ft. lbs. on 1981—86 Intermediates.

1982—86 FIREBIRD

Caster and camber can be adjusted by moving the position of the upper strut mount assembly.
1. Remove dust cap and fender bolt.
2. Attach J-29724, using original fender bolt and tighten the turnbuckle, **Fig. 4.**
3. Loosen three nuts attaching mount assembly.
4. Adjust camber by rotating the turnbuckle to allow the mount assembly to move inboard or outboard, **Fig. 5.**
5. Adjust the caster by lightly tapping the mount assembly forward or rearward, **Fig. 6.**
6. When correct camber and caster readings have been obtained to specifications, tighten the three nuts attaching the mount assembly to 20 ft. lbs.

7. Remove tool J-29724, and install fender bolt and dust cap.

TOE-IN
ADJUST

1. Remove steering wheel trim cover or horn button and set gear on high point by turning steering wheel until mark on end of shaft is exactly at top. This mark locates high point or middle travel of steering gear.
2. Loosen tie rod clamp bolts and turn both adjuster sleeves an equal amount until toe-in is set to specifications. To increase toe-in, turn left tie rod adjuster sleeve in direction of forward rotation of wheels. Turn right tie rod adjuster sleeve in opposite direction.
3. Make sure front wheels are straight ahead by measuring from a reference point at same place on each side of frame center to front of wheel rims. If measurements are unequal, turn both tie rod adjuster sleeves in same direction (so as not to change toe-in) until measurements become equal. Recheck toe-in and re-adjust as necessary.
4. Torque tie rod clamp bolts to 15 ft. lbs.

NOTE: Open end clamps should be located to a vertical down position. Refer to **Figs. 7 and 8.**

WHEEL BEARINGS
ADJUST

1. While rotating wheel, torque spindle nut to 12 ft. lbs.
2. Back off spindle nut until just loose, then retighten by hand.
3. Loosen spindle nut until cotter pin can be inserted, however, do not loosen spindle nut more than ½ flat.
4. With bearing properly adjusted, there should be .001–.005 inch end play.

WHEEL BEARINGS
REPLACE

(DISC BRAKES)

1. Raise vehicle and remove front wheels.
2. Remove brake hose support to caliper mounting bracket screw.
3. Remove caliper to mounting bracket bolts.

NOTE: Do not place strain on brake hose.

4. Remove spindle nut, and disc and hub assembly. Grease retainer and inner bearing can now be removed.

CHECKING BALL JOINTS FOR WEAR
EXCEPT 1982—86 FIREBIRD

Before checking ball joints for wear, make sure the front wheel bearings are properly adjusted and that the control arms are tight.

Referring to **Fig. 9,** raise wheel with a jack placed under the lower control at the point Shown. Then test by moving the wheel up and down to check axial play, and rocking it at the top and bottom to measure radial play.
1. Upper ball joint should be replaced if there is any noticeable looseness at this joint. If the ball joint is the type using a built in rubber pre-load cushion it will be necessary to remove the ball stud from the knuckle. Then replace the ball joint retaining nut on the ball stud. Using a socket and

Fig. 7 Tie rod clamp and sleeve positioning. Except 1982-86 Firebird

Fig. 8 Tie rod clamp and sleeve positioning. 1982-86 Firebird & 1983-86 Parisienne

Fig. 9 Checking ball joints for wear

torque wrench, measure amount of torque required to turn the ball stud in its socket. If any torque is required, the ball joint is satisfactory. If no torque is required, the ball joint must be replaced.

2. A visual wear indicator is built into the lower ball joint on all models, **Fig. 10.**

CHECKING FRONT SUSPENSION FOR WEAR

1982-86 FIREBIRD

1. Raise vehicle with floor jack placed under frame torque box, located behind front wheel.
2. Place steering wheel in locked position, then place suitable dial indicator on outside perimeter of wheel.
3. Test by moving wheel back and forth without moving steering wheel. Gauge reading should not exceed .108 inch.
4. If gauge reading is not within specifications, A thorough front end inspection should be performed and parts replaced as necessary.

BALL JOINTS
REPLACE

EXCEPT 1982-86 FIREBIRD

On all models the upper ball joint is riveted to the control arm. All service ball joints, however, are provided with bolt, nut and washer assemblies for replacement purposes.

The lower ball joint is pressed into the control arm. They may be pressed out and new joints pressed in.

Upper Ball Joint

1. Raise vehicle and support lower control arm.
2. Remove wheel assembly.
3. Remove upper ball joint stud from steering knuckle, **Fig. 11.**
4. Drill or chisel rivet heads from ball joint rivets. Then, drive rivets from control arm with a suitable punch.

5. Install new ball joint and torque retaining bolts to 9 ft. lbs. except on 1983–86 Parisienne, and 13 ft. lbs. for 1983–86 Parisienne.
6. Install ball joint stud into steering knuckle and torque to 88 ft. lbs. for 1980 models and 65 for 1981–86 models.
7. Install cotter pin.
8. Install wheel assembly and lower vehicle.

Lower Ball Joint

1. Raise vehicle and support lower control arm under spring seats.
2. Remove brake drum and backing plate or caliper.
3. Remove lower ball joint stud from steering knuckle, **Fig. 11.**
4. With a screwdriver, pry ball joint seal and retainer from ball joint.
5. Press lower ball joint from control arm.
6. Press new ball joint into lower control arm.
7. Install ball joint stud into steering knuckle and torque nut to 83 ft. lbs. for 1980 models, and 90 ft. lbs. for 1981–86 models.
8. Install cotter pin.
9. Install brake backing plate and drum or caliper, then the wheel assembly.

1982-86 FIREBIRD

1. Raise and support vehicle.
2. Remove tire and wheel assembly.
3. Place a suitable floor jack under control arm spring seat.

CAUTION: Floor jack must remain under control arm spring seat during removal and installation to retain spring and control arm in position.

Fig. 10 Lower ball joint wear indicator. 1980—86 Exc. 1982—86 Firebird

Fig. 11 Removing ball joint studs from steering knuckle.

Fig. 12 Removing & installing ball joint. 1982—86 Firebird

4. Remove cotter pin and loosen nut. Use tool J-24292A to break ball joint loose from steering knuckle.
5. Remove tool and separate joint from knuckle.
6. Guide lower control arm out of opening in splash shield with a suitable tool.
7. Remove grease fittings, and install special tools as shown in **Fig. 12.**
8. Reverse procedure to install. Torque ball stud nut to 90 ft. lbs.

SHOCK ABSORBER
REPLACE

EXCEPT 1982—86 FIREBIRD

Hold the shock absorber upper stem from turning with a suitable wrench and remove the nut and grommet. Remove the lower shock absorber pivot from the lower control arm and pull the shock absorber and mounting out at the bottom of the spring housing.

To install, reverse the removal procedure. Torque upper retaining nut to 10 ft. lbs. Torque shock absorber lower retaining bolts to 20 ft. lbs.

STRUT
REPLACE

1982—86 FIREBIRD

1. Raise and support vehicle.
2. Remove tire and wheel assembly.
3. Support lower control arm with jack-stand.
4. Remove brake hose bracket.
5. Remove two strut-to-knuckle bolts.
6. Remove cover from upper mount assembly.
7. Remove nut from upper end of strut assembly.
8. Remove strut and shield.
9. Reverse procedure to install. Torque nuts to 52 ft. lbs.

COIL SPRING
REPLACE

1980—86, EXCEPT 1982—86 FIREBIRD

1. Support vehicle at frame and remove wheel.
2. Disconnect shock absorber from lower

control arm and push shock absorber through hole in lower control arm up into spring.
3. Remove stabilizer link nut, link, spacer, grommets and retainer.
4. Support lower control arm with tool J-23028 bolted onto a suitable jack.
5. Install a safety chain through spring and lower control arm, remove the two lower control arm to frame crossmember pivot bolts. Lower jack, allowing spring to expand and remove spring.
6. Reverse procedure to install. Torque lower control arm to frame attaching nuts, with weight of vehicle on wheels, to specifications listed below:

Year	Nuts, Ft. Lbs.
1980	
Grand Prix & LeMans	70
Full Size	124
Firebird	90
1981	
Grand Prix & LeMans	65
Full Size	95
Firebird	95
1982—86	
Intermediates	65
1983—86	
Parisienne	90

1982—86 FIREBIRD

1. Raise and support vehicle.
2. Remove tire and wheel assembly.
3. Remove stabilizer link and bushings at lower control arm.
4. Remove pivot bolt nuts.

NOTE: Do not remove pivot bolts at this time.

5. Install adapter tool No. J-23028 or equivalent adapter to floor jack and place into position with supporting bushings.
6. Install jackstand under outside frame on opposite side of vehicle.
7. Raise tool No. J-23028 enough to remove both pivot bolts.
8. Lower tool No. J-23028 carefully and remove spring.
9. Remove ball joint from steering knuckle using tool No. J-24292A or equivalent as outlined under "Ball Joint, Replace".
10. Replace bushings in lower control arm.

11. Reverse procedure to install. Torque nut to 70 ft. lbs.

STEERING GEAR
REPLACE

1. Use puller to remove pitman arm from steering gear shaft.
2. Remove flex coupling shield, if equipped, then scribe a mark on worm shaft flange and steering shaft and disconnect lower flange from steering shaft.
3. Unfasten gear housing from frame (3 bolts) and remove from car.

POWER STEERING GEAR
REPLACE

1. Remove flex coupling shield if equipped, then scribe mark on worm shaft flange and steering shaft and disconnect lower flange from steering shaft.
2. Disconnect pressure and return hoses from gear housing.
3. Raise vehicle and disconnect pitman arm from shaft.
4. Remove gear housing to frame bolts and remove steering gear assembly.
5. Reverse procedure to install.

POWER STEERING PUMP
REPLACE

1. Disconnect battery ground cable.
2. Remove power steering pump belt drive, then remove pulley from pump.
3. Disconnect pressure and return line from power steering pump. Cap lines and fittings to prevent entry of dirt.
4. Remove pump and bracket from engine as an assembly, then remove bracket from pump.
5. Reverse procedure to install.

PONTIAC FIERO
INDEX OF SERVICE OPERATIONS

NOTE: Refer to the rear of this manual for vehicle manufacturer's special service tool suppliers.

Vehicle Identification Number Location

The vehicle identification number is located on top of instrument panel, lower left.

Engine Number Location

The engine code stamping is located on vertical pad on front of block below cylinder head.

Engine V.I.N. Code

The eighth digit of the seventeen digit V.I.N. code denotes engine code.

Engine Identification Code

Year	Engine	V.I.N. Code	Engine Code
1984	4-151	R	Z3J, Z3K, Z3L, Z5C, Z5L, Z5M
1985	4-151	R	AAF, ABY, ACC, ACM, ADJ, ADK
	V6-173	8	CBX, CBY

Grille Identification

1984–86 Pontiac Fiero Exc. GT

1986 Fiero GT

General Engine Specifications

Year	Engine CID①/Liter	V.I.N. Code	Carburetor	Bore and Stroke	Compression Ratio	Net H.P. @ R.P.M.②	Maximum Torque Ft. Lbs. @ R.P.M.	Normal Oil Pressure Pounds
1984	4-151, 2.5L	R	E.F.I.③	4.00 × 3.00	9.0	92 @ 4000	134 @ 2800	36–41
1985	4-151, 2.5L	R	E.F.I.③	4.00 × 3.00	9.0	65 @ 5200	80 @ 3200	36–41
	V6-173, 2.8L	9	MPFI④	3.50 × 2.99	8.5	140 @ 5200	170 @ 3600	30–45
1986	4-151, 2.5L	—		4.00 × 3.00	—	—	—	—
	V6-173, 2.8L	—		3.50 × 2.99	—	—	—	—

①—CID—Cubic inch displacement.
②—Ratings are net as installed in vehicle.
③—Electronic fuel injection.
④—Multi-point fuel injection.

Valve Specifications

Year	Engine/V.I.N.	Valve Lash Int.	Valve Lash Exh.	Valve Angles Seat	Valve Angles Face	Valve Spring Installed Height	Valve Spring Pressure Lbs. @ In.	Stem Clearance Intake	Stem Clearance Exhaust	Stem Diameter Intake	Stem Diameter Exhaust
1984	4-151/R	Hydraulic①		46	45	1.69	151 @ 1.254	.0010–.0027	.0010–.0027	.3420–.3430	.3420–.3430
1985–86	4-151/	②		46	45	1.69	175 @ 1.26	.0010–.0027	.0010–.0027	.3420–.3430	.3420–.3430
	V6-173/9	1½ Turn③		46	45	1.57	195 @ 1.181	.0010–.0027	.0010–.0027	.3410–.3417	.3410–.3417

①—No adjustment.
②—Uses hydraulic roller lifter valve train.
③—Turn rocker arm stud nut until all lash is eliminated, then tighten nut the additional turn listed.

Wheel Alignment Specifications

Year	Model	Caster Angle, Degrees Limits	Caster Angle, Degrees Desired	Camber Angle, Degrees Limits Left	Camber Angle, Degrees Limits Right	Camber Angle, Degrees Desired Left	Camber Angle, Degrees Desired Right	Toe-In mm	Toe-Out on Turns, Deg.① Outer Wheel	Toe-Out on Turns, Deg.① Inner Wheel
1984–85	All①	+3°–+7°②	+5°	–.3°–+1.3°	–.3°–+1.3°	+.5°	+.5°	1.6	—	—
	All③	—	—	–1.5°––.5°	–1.5°––.5°	–1°	–1°	1.6	—	—
1986	—	—	—	—	—	—	—	—	—	—

①—Front wheel alignment.
②—Left & right side should be equal within 2°.
③—Rear wheel alignment.

Pistons, Pins, Rings, Crankshaft & Bearings

Year	Engine V.I.N.	Piston Clearance Top of Skirt	Ring Gap① Comp.	Ring Gap① Oil	Wristpin Diameter	Rod Bearings Shaft Diameter	Rod Bearings Bearing Clearance	Main Bearings Shaft Diameter	Main Bearings Bearing Clearance	Thrust on Bear. No.	Shaft End Play
1984	4-151/R	.0025–.0030	.010	.020	.940	2.000	.0005–.0026	2.300	.0005–.0022	5	.0035–.0085
1985–86	4-151/R	.0014–.0022②	.010	.020	.9400	2.000	.0005–.0026	2.300	.0005–.0022	5	.0035–.0085
	V6-173/9	.0007–.0017	.010	.020	.9054	1.9983–1.9993	.0014–.0038	2.6477	.0016–.0032	3	.0024–.0084

①—Fit rings in tapered bores for clearance given in tightest portion of ring travel. Clearances specified are minimum gaps.
②—Measured 1.8 inch below top of piston.

Alternator Specifications

Year	Model	Rated Hot Output Amps.
1984–85	—	66①
1986	—	

continued

Starting Motor Applications

Year	Model	Starter Number
1984	All	1109564
	All	1998429
1985	All	1998503
1986	—	—

Engine Tightening Specifications★

★ Torque specifications are for clean and lightly lubricated threads only. Dry or dirty threads produce increased friction which prevents accurate measurement of tightness.

Year	Engine Model/ V.I.N.	Spark Plugs Ft. Lbs.	Cylinder Head Bolts Ft. Lbs.	Intake Manifold Ft. Lbs.	Exhaust Manifold Ft. Lbs.	Rocker Arm Stud Ft. Lbs.	Rocker Arm Cover Ft. Lbs.	Connecting Rod Cap Bolts Ft. Lbs.	Main Bearing Cap Bolts Ft. Lbs.	Flywheel to Crank-shaft Ft. Lbs.	Vibration Damper or Pulley Ft. Lbs.
1984–86	4-151/R	7–15	92①	29	44	20②	③	32	70	44	200
1985–86	V6-173	7–15	65–75	20–25	22–28	43–49	6–9	34–40	63–74	45–55	66–84

①—Requires thread sealer on bolt heads & threads.
②—Rocker arm bolt.
③—1984, 6 ft. lbs.; 1985–86 .45 inch lbs.

Cooling System & Capacity Data

Year	Model or Engine/V.I.N.	Cooling Capacity, Qts. Less A/C	Cooling Capacity, Qts. With A/C	Radiator Cap Relief Pressure, Lbs.	Thermo. Opening Temp.	Fuel Tank Gals.	Engine Oil Refill Qts.	Transaxle Oil Manual Transaxle Pts.	Transaxle Oil Auto. Transaxle Qts.①
1984	4-151	13.0	13.4	15	195	10.5	3②	5.9	③
1985	4-151	13.8	⑥	15	195	10.3	3	④	⑤
	V6-173	13.8	13.8	15	195	10.3	4	④	⑤
1986	4-151	—	—	—	—	—	—	—	—
	V6-173	—	—	—	—	—	—	—	—

①—Approximate; make final check with dipstick.
②—With or without filter change.
③—Oil pan capacity, 4 qts.; total capacity, 6 qts.
④—4 speed, 5.9 pts.; 5 speed, 5.3 pts.
⑤—Oil pan capacity, 4 qts.; total capacity, 5 qts.
⑥—Auto. trans., 13.8 qts.; man. trans., 14.1 qts.

Electrical Section

To assemble, rotate to stop while holding cylinder.

LOCK CYLINDER
LOCK RETAINING SCREW
CLIP
KEY WARNING BUZZER SWITCH
COVER

Fig. 1   Lock cylinder replacement

REMOVE
1. Remove parts as shown.

INSTALL
1. Install parts as shown
2. Position rod in slider hole and install ignition switch. Install lower stud and tighten to 4.0 N·m.
3. Install dimmer switch and depress switch slightly to insert 3/32" drill. Force switch up to remove lash, then tighten screw, and nut to 4.0 N·m.

SCREWS (2)
STUD
SCREW
IGNITION SWITCH ASSEMBLY
IGN. SWITCH INHIBITOR HOUSING ASSEMBLY
PARK LOCK
STEERING COLUMN JACKET
NUT
DIMMER SWITCH
DIMMER SWITCH ACTUATOR ROD

• KEY RELEASE
  Leave slider at extreme left
• PARK LOCK
  Move slider one detent to the right (off lock)
• ALL OTHER COLUMNS
  Move slider two detents to the right (off unlock)

MOVE SWITCH SLIDER TO EXTREME LEFT POSITION
INSTALL IGNITION SWITCH

DIMMER SWITCH
DIMMER SWITCH ACTUATOR ROD
3/32" Drill
ADJUST DIMMER SWITCH

Fig. 2   Ignition & dimmer switch replacement. Except tilt column

REMOVE
1. Remove parts as shown.

INSTALL
1. Install parts as shown.
2. Position rod in slider hole and install ignition switch. Install lower stud and tighten to 4.0 N·m.
3. Install dimmer switch and depress switch slightly to insert 3/32" drill. Force switch up to remove lash, then tighten screw, and nut to 4.0 N·m.
4. Place shifter in neutral.

STUD
IGNITION SWITCH
SCREW WITH WASHER HEAD
STEERING COLUMN JACKET ASSY.
HEX NUT
DIMMER SWITCH ASSY.
DIMMER SWITCH ACTUATOR ROD

J-23074
STEERING COLUMN HOLDING FIXTURE

MOVE SWITCH SLIDER TO EXTREME RIGHT POSITION
• KEY RELEASE
  Leave slider at extreme right
• PARK LOCK
  Move slider one detent to the left (off lock)
• ALL OTHER COLUMNS
  Move slider two detents to the left (off unlock)
INSTALL IGNITION SWITCH ASSEMBLY

DIMMER SWITCH ASSEMBLY
3/32" Drill
DIMMER SWITCH ROD
ADJUST DIMMER SWITCH ASSEMBLY

J-23072
REMOVE SHIFT TUBE ASSEMBLY FROM BOWL

J-23073
INSTALL SHIFT TUBE ASSEMBLY

KEY RELEASE LEVER
KEY RELEASE SPRING
KEY RELEASE LEVER

Fig. 3   Ignition & dimmer switch replacement. Tilt column

STARTER, REPLACE

1. Disconnect battery ground cable.
2. Disconnect solenoid wires from starter motor.
3. Raise and support vehicle.
4. Remove heat shield, if equipped.
5. On models with 4-151 engine, remove rear starter bracket attaching bolts.
6. On all models, remove the 2 starter motor-to-engine bolts.
7. Remove starter motor through front of converter toward front of engine.
8. Reverse procedure to install.

IGNITION LOCK
REPLACE

1. Remove turn signal switch as described under "Turn Signal Switch, Replace."
2. Remove key warning buzzer switch.
3. Turn lock cylinder to Run position, then remove retaining screw and the lock cylinder, **Fig. 1.**
4. Reverse procedure to install. Turn lock cylinder to Run position before installing key warning buzzer switch.

IGNITION & DIMMER SWITCHES
REPLACE

1. Remove turn signal switch as described under "Turn Signal Switch, Replace."
2. Refer to **Figs. 2 and 3** to replace ignition and dimmer switches.

TURN SIGNAL SWITCH
REPLACE

1. Disconnect battery ground cable.

PONTIAC FIERO

REMOVE
1. Remove parts as shown.

INSTALL
1. Install parts as shown.

SHAFT LOCK COVER
RETAINING RING
SHAFT LOCK
CANCELLING CAM ASSEMBLY
SPRING
COVER
SHAFT LOCK RETAINER
CARRIER SNAP RING RETAINER SPACERS
RETRACTED STRG SHAFT BUMPER
*ON TELESCOPE STEERING ONLY

Pry out at these locations to remove cover
Screwdriver
J-23653
J-23653-4
RETAINING RING
Tighten nut until tool slightly depresses shaft lock
REMOVE SHAFT LOCK COVER
REMOVE AND INSTALL RETAINING RING

REMOVE
1. Remove parts as shown.

INSTALL
1. Install parts as shown.

SIGNAL SWITCH ARM
SCREW
SCREW
TURN SIGNAL SWITCH
COVER
BOWL
WIRE PROTECTOR

Fig. 4   Turn signal switch replacement

2. Remove steering wheel as described under "Steering Wheel, Replace."
3. Refer to **Fig. 4** to replace turn signal switch.

STEERING WHEEL
REPLACE

1. Disconnect battery ground cable.
2. Remove horn button.
3. Remove retainer and steering wheel retaining nut.
4. Remove steering wheel using puller J-1859-03 or equivalent.
5. Reverse procedure to install.

W/S WIPER SWITCH
REPLACE

1. Remove ignition lock as described under "Ignition Lock, Replace."
2. Refer to **Figs. 5 and 6** to replace wiper switch.

22-6

REMOVE
1. Remove ignition and dimmer switch.
2. Remove parts as shown.

INSTALL
1. Assemble rack so that first rack tooth engages between first and second tooth of sector.
2. Install parts as shown.
3. Install ignition and dimmer switch.

HOUSING
WASHER
PIVOT AND SWITCH ASSY.
BEARING
PIVOT PIN
BOWL
CAP SCREW
SCREW
PIN SECTOR
HORN CONTACT
BUSHING
RETAINER
GATE
Punch
Punch
REMOVE AND INSTALL SECTOR
INSTALL BEARING
WAVE WASHER
LEVER
SPRING
LEVER SPRING
REMOVE LEVER AND SPRING
INSTALL LEVER AND RETURN SPRING

Fig. 5   Windshield wiper switch replacement. Except tilt column

W/S WIPER PULSE MODULE
REPLACE

NOTE: The pulse module is located under the instrument panel on the right hand steering column support bracket.

1. Disconnect battery ground cable.
2. Remove instrument panel steering column cover.
3. Disconnect electrical connectors from module.
4. Disconnect module ground wire.
5. Remove module attaching bolt and the module.
6. Reverse procedure to install.

STOP LAMP SWITCH
ADJUST

Insert switch into retainer until switch body seats on retainer. Pull brake pedal rearward until clicks are no longer audible.

BACKUP LIGHT/NEUTRAL START SWITCH
REPLACE

NOTE: On vehicles equipped with automatic transmission, the neutral start and backup light switches are combined into one unit and must be replaced as an assembly.

REMOVE
1. Remove parts as shown

INSTALL
1. Install parts as shown.

SCREW
COVER
ACTUATOR
SHIELD
SPRING
PIVOT OR PIVOT SWITCH ASSEMBLY
SWITCH ACTUATOR PIVOT PIN
CAP
TILT LEVER
Punch
SWITCH ACTUATOR PIVOT PIN
REMOVE AND INSTALL PIVOT AND SWITCH ASSEMBLY

Fig. 6   Windshield wiper switch replacement. Tilt column

MANUAL TRANSMISSION

1. Disconnect battery ground cable.
2. Remove shift trim plate cover.
3. Disconnect electrical connector from switch, **Fig. 7.**
4. Remove switch retainer and the switch.
5. Reverse procedure to install.

AUTOMATIC TRANSMISSION

1. Disconnect battery ground cable.
2. Open deck lid, then open retaining clip and disconnect electrical connector from switch.
3. Pry cable from pivot pin at bottom of shift lever, then remove lever-to-transmission shaft attaching nut.
4. Remove 2 switch-to-transaxle attaching bolts and the switch, **Fig. 8.**
5. Reverse procedure to install, noting the following:
   a. Transmission must be in Neutral when installing switch.
   b. Torque switch attaching bolts to 20 ft. lbs.
   c. Torque lever attaching nut to 20 ft. lbs. while holding lever out of Park.

BACKUP LIGHT/NEUTRAL START SWITCH
ADJUST

AUTOMATIC TRANSMISSION

1. Shift transmission into Neutral.
2. Align flats in switch insert with flats on transmission shaft, and slide switch over shaft.

1—RETAINER CLIP
2—BACK-UP LAMP SWITCH ASSEMBLY
3—MANUAL TRANSMISSION CONTROL ASSEMBLY
4—MAIN HARNESS ASSEMBLY
5—BACK-UP LAMP SWITCH CONNECTOR

Fig. 7   Backup light switch replacement. Manual transmission

3. Install attaching bolts hand tight.
4. Insert a 2.34 inch diameter gauge pin into adjustment hole, then rotate switch until pin drops to .354 inch.
5. Torque attaching bolts to 20 ft. lbs. and remove gauge pin.

CLUTCH START SWITCH
REPLACE

1. Disconnect battery ground cable.
2. Disconnect electrical connector from switch.
3. Remove switch attaching bolt. Rotate switch to disconnect shaft from clutch pedal hole, then remove switch from vehicle, **Fig. 9.**
4. Reverse procedure to install.

HEADLAMP SWITCH
REPLACE

1. Disconnect battery ground cable.
2. Remove 4 switch attaching screws.
3. Pull switch out of panel and disconnect electrical connectors, then remove switch from vehicle.
4. Reverse procedure to install.

NOTE: When replacing switch, install lower attaching screws first.

INSTRUMENT CLUSTER
REPLACE

1. Disconnect battery ground cable.
2. Remove rear cluster cover, front trim plate and steering column cover.
3. Remove instrument cluster attaching screws.

1 – NUT/CABLE ASSY.	8 – BRACKET
2 – NUT/SHIFTING LEVER	9 – CABLE ASSY.
3 – LEVER/SHIFTING	10 – RETAINER ASSY.
4 – SWITCH/NEUTRAL START AND BACK-UP	11 – T HANDLE
5 – BOLT/NEUTRAL START SWITCH (2)	12 – SNAP SECURELY ONTO PIN
6 – TRANSAXLE	13 – GEAR SHIFT SUPPORT
7 – BOLT/BRACKET	14 – NUT 23 N·M (17 FT. LB.)

Fig. 8   Backup light/neutral start switch replacement. Automatic transmission

4. Pull cluster rearward and disconnect all electrical connectors, then remove cluster from vehicle, **Fig. 10.**
5. Reverse procedure to install.

RADIO
REPLACE

1. Disconnect battery ground cable.
2. Remove shift knob and both ash trays.
3. Remove 4 shift plate attaching bolts and the plate.
4. Remove front trim plate, then the front pad attaching screws and front pad.
5. Remove radio attaching screws.
6. Pull radio rearward and disconnect all electrical connectors, then remove radio from vehicle.
7. Reverse procedure to install.

1—NEUTRAL START SWITCH ASSEMBLY (MANUAL TRANSMISSION)   3—BOLT
2—PEDAL ASSEMBLY

Fig. 9   Clutch start switch replacement

W/S WIPER MOTOR
REPLACE

1984

1. Disconnect battery ground cable.
2. Remove both wiper arms using tool No. J-8966 or equivalent.
3. Remove cowl top vent screen.
4. Remove drive link from crank arm.
5. Disconnect electrical connectors from wiper motor.
6. Remove wiper motor attaching screws and the motor.
7. Reverse procedure to install. Torque motor attaching screws to 40–58 inch lbs. and drive link attaching nuts to 49–80 inch lbs.

1985–86

1. Disconnect battery ground cable.
2. Loosen transmission drive link-to-motor attaching nuts, then disconnect drive link from motor crank arm.
3. Disconnect electrical connectors from wiper motor.
4. Rotate motor up and remove from vehicle.
5. Reverse procedure to install.

W/S WIPER TRANSMISSION
REPLACE

1. Remove both wiper arms using tool No. J-8966 or equivalent.
2. Remove cowl top vent screen.
3. Remove drive link from crank arm.
4. Remove 6 cowl panel attaching screws and the cowl panel.
5. Remove transmission assembly from vehicle.
6. Reverse procedure to install. Torque cowl attaching screws and drive link attaching nuts to 49–80 inch lbs.

1 — CLUSTER ASM.
2 — REAR CLUSTER COVER
3 — CLUSTER HOUSING ASM.
4 — I/P
5 — STEERING COL. SUPT.

A — INSTALL THIS BOLT/SCREW FIRST
B — INSTALL THIS BOLT/SCREW SECOND
C — INSTALL THIS BOLT/SCREWS THIRD
D — INSTALL THIS BOLT/SCREWS FOURTH
E — INSTALL THIS BOLT/SCREW FIFTH
F — INSTALL THIS BOLT/SCREW SIXTH
G — INSTALL THIS BOLT/SCREWS SEVENTH
H — INSTALL THIS BOLT/SCREWS EIGHTH
I — INSTALL THESE BOLT/SCREWS LAST

Fig. 10 Instrument cluster

BLOWER MOTOR
REPLACE

1. Disconnect battery ground cable.
2. Remove cooling tube from blower motor.
3. Disconnect blower motor electrical connections.
4. Remove 5 blower motor attaching screws and the blower motor assembly, **Fig. 11**.
5. Remove fan cage attaching screw and slide cage off motor shaft.
6. Reverse procedure to install.

HEATER CORE
REPLACE

LESS AIR CONDITIONING

1. Disconnect battery ground cable.
2. Disconnect all electrical connectors from rear of heater case.
3. Remove forward courtesy lamp bulb socket, if equipped.
4. Remove windshield washer fluid tank.
5. Disconnect heater hoses from heater core, then remove heater core grommets. Plug hoses to prevent spillage.
6. Remove heater case cover attaching screws and the cover, **Fig. 11**.
7. Remove heater core retainer and the heater core.
8. Reverse procedure to install.

WITH AIR CONDITIONING

1. Disconnect battery ground cable.
2. Disconnect heater hoses from heater core. Plug hoses to prevent spillage.
3. Remove speaker grille and the speaker.
4. Remove heater core cover, then the heater core retainers and heater core.
5. Reverse procedure to install.

CRUISE CONTROL
ADJUST

SERVO CABLE, ADJUST

1. Install cable assembly end onto throttle body unit lever stud, with cable installed in bracket, and secure with retainer.
2. Pull servo end of cable toward servo without moving injector lever.
3. Connect pin to tab with retainer.

NOTE: If a tab hole does not line up with pin, move cable away from servo until the next closest hole aligns, then connect pin to tab.

1 — COVER, AIR INL & DIST
2 — VALVE, VENT
3 — VALVE, DEFR
4 — SHAFT, W/LVR, TEMP VLV
5 — RIVET, TRUSS HD
     (9/16" x 1/4")
6 — BRACKET, CBL MTG
7 — SEAL, HTR & BLO CASE
8 — CASE, HTR
9 — SCREW, HWH TAP
     (M4.2 x 1.41 x 13)
10 — BAFFLE, AIR

11 — VALVE, TEMP
12 — FAN, BLO
13 — SCREW, HWH TAP
     (M4.2 x 1.41 x 14)
14 — TERMINAL, BLO MTR GRD
15 — TUBE, MTR CLG
16 — WASHER, FAN SUPT
17 — NUT, BLO FAN
18 — COVER, BLO
19 — SEAL, HTR CORE TUBE
20 — BRACKET, MT

21 — CLAMP, CORE MT
22 — SEAL, HTR CORE
23 — CORE, HTR
24 — SEAL, HTR CORE CASE
25 — CLIP, HTR CORE MT
26 — BRACKET, CBL MT
27 — CASE, AIR INL & DISTR
28 — BRACKET, CBL MT
29 — SHAFT, W/LVR, DEFR VLV
30 — SHAFT, W/LVR, VENT VLV

Fig. 11 Heater core & blower motor. Models less A/C

4-151 Engine Section

Fig. 1 Engine mounts

INSULATOR TO SUPPORT BRACKET STUDS
ENGINE INSULATOR
FRONT
56 N·m (41 LB. FT.)
INSULATOR TO CHASSIS ATTACHING NUT

APPLY SEALING COMPOUND PART NUMBER 1052080 OR EQUIVALENT TO THREADS ON BOLTS SHOWN.

MOUNTING SURFACES OF BLOCK ASM., HEAD ASM. AND BOTH SIDES OF GASKET MUST BE FREE OF OIL AND FOREIGN MATERIAL.

NUMBERS SHOWN DESIGNATE BOLT POSITIONS AND BOLT TIGHTENING SEQUENCE.

FRONT

LOCATING PINS

Fig. 2 Cylinder head bolt tightening sequence

ENGINE MOUNTS
REPLACE

1. Raise and support vehicle.
2. Remove engine mount-to-chassis attaching nuts, **Fig. 1.**
3. On 1984 models equipped with A/C, and all 1985-86 models, remove forward torque reaction rod attaching bolts.
4. On all models, raise engine slightly using a suitable engine lifting device. Raise engine only enough to provide clearance for mount removal.
5. Removal 2 upper mount-to-engine support bracket attaching nuts and the engine mount.
6. Reverse procedure to install.

ENGINE
REPLACE

1. Disconnect battery cables, then drain cooling system.
2. Remove rear compartment lid.

NOTE: Do not remove torsion rod retaining bolts.

3. Remove air cleaner, then disconnect throttle and transaxle cables.
4. Disconnect all necessary vacuum hoses from non-engine components.
5. Disconnect heater hose from intake manifold.
6. Disconnect fuel lines and remove fuel filter.
7. Disconnect fuel pump relay and oxygen sensor electrical connectors.
8. On models equipped with automatic transaxle, disconnect transaxle cooler lines.
9. On models equipped with manual transaxle, remove slave cylinder.
10. On all models, disconnect engine ground strap.
11. Disconnect radiator and heater hoses.
12. Disconnect engine harness connector from bulkhead.
13. On models equipped with A/C, discharge refrigerant from system, then disconnect and cap lines from A/C compressor.
14. Remove rear console.
15. Disconnect electronic control module

(ECM) electrical connector through bulkhead panel.
16. Install engine support fixture, tool No. J-28467 or equivalent to engine.
17. Mark the engine strut bracket and attaching bolt for assembly reference, then remove bolt and bracket.
18. Raise and support vehicle.
19. Remove rear wheels.
20. On models equipped with automatic transaxle, remove torque converter attaching bolts.
21. Disconnect parking brake cable.
22. Remove brake calipers and suspend from frame with a piece of wire. Do not suspend calipers by brake hoses.
23. Mark struts for proper realignment as described under "Strut Assembly, Replace" in the "Rear Axle, Rear Suspension & Brakes" section, then remove strut attaching bolts.
24. Disconnect any remaining electrical connectors interfering with engine removal.
25. Remove engine cradle attaching bolts.
26. Release parking brake cables from cradle using tool No. J-34065 or equivalent.
27. Support engine, transaxle and cradle assembly with a suitably dolly, then lower vehicle and remove engine support fixture.

NOTE: When lowering vehicle, ensure outboard ends of lower control arms are properly supported.

28. Raise vehicle and slide engine, transaxle and cradle assembly out from under vehicle.
29. Separate engine from transaxle.
30. Reverse procedure to install.

CYLINDER HEAD
REPLACE

1. Disconnect battery ground cable.
2. Drain cooling system.
3. Raise and support vehicle.
4. Disconnect exhaust pipe from exhaust manifold, then lower vehicle.
5. Remove oil dipstick tube and air cleaner.
6. On 1984 models, disconnect throttle body injection unit electrical connectors and vacuum hoses.
7. On 1985-86 models, disconnect electrical connectors and throttle linkage from throttle body injection unit.
8. On 1984 models, remove EGR base plate, then disconnect heater hose from intake manifold. Remove ignition coil lower attaching bolt, then disconnect wiring from coil.
9. On 1985-86 models, disconnect heater hose from intake manifold, then remove ignition coil.
10. On all models, disconnect all electrical connectors from cylinder head and intake manifold.
11. Remove engine strut attaching bolt from upper engine support.
12. On 1984 models, remove alternator drive belt, then disconnect throttle and throttle valve cables from intake manifold.
13. On 1985-86 models, remove or reposition accessory brackets as necessary.
14. On all models, disconnect upper radiator hose from cylinder head.
15. Remove rocker arm cover, then the rocker arms and push rods.
16. Remove cylinder head attaching bolts, then lift cylinder head and intake and exhaust manifolds as an assembly

1	LIFTER BODY	5	BALL CHECK	6	PLUNGER
2	PLUNGER SPRING	7	OIL METERING VALVE		
3	BALL CHECK RETAINER	8	PUSH ROD SEAT		
4	BALL CHECK SPRING	9	RETAINER RING		

Fig. 3 Hydraulic valve lifter

TIMING MARKS

Fig. 4 Engine front cover installation

from cylinder block.

17. Reverse procedure to install. Coat threads of cylinder head bolts with a suitable sealing compound, then install bolts finger tight. Torque cylinder head bolts to specifications in sequence shown, **Fig. 2.**

ROCKER ARM STUDS

Rocker arm studs which are cracked or have damaged threads can be removed from the cylinder head using a deep well socket. Install and torque new rocker arm stud to 75 ft. lbs.

VALVE ARRANGEMENT
FRONT TO REAR

I-E-I-E-E-I-E-I

VALVE LIFT SPECS.

Year	Intake	Exhaust
1984–86	.398	.398

VALVE TIMING
INTAKE OPENS BEFORE TDC

Year	Degrees
1984–86	33

VALVE GUIDES

Valve guides are an integral part of the cylinder head and are not removable. If valve stem clearance becomes excessive, the valve guide should be reamed to the next oversize and the appropriate oversize valves installed. Valves are available in oversizes of .003 and .005 inch.

VALVE LIFTERS

Failure of a hydraulic valve lifter, **Fig. 3,** is generally caused by an inadequate oil supply or dirt. An air leak at the intake side of the oil pump or excessive oil in the engine will produce air bubbles in the oil supply to the lifters, causing them to collapse. This is a probable cause of trouble when several lifters fail to function, but air in oil is not likely to cause failure of a single unit.

Valve lifters can be removed after removing rocker arm cover, intake manifold and push rod cover. Loosen rocker arm stud nut and rotate rocker arm so push rod can be removed, then remove valve lifter. It may be necessary to use tool No. J-3049 to facilitate lifter removal.

ENGINE FRONT COVER
REPLACE

1. Remove drive belts, then the right rear inner splash shield.
2. Remove pulley attaching bolt, then the pulley and hub from shaft.
3. On 1984 models, remove oil pan-to-front cover attaching screws and the front cover.
4. On 1985–86 models, support engine using fixture No. J-28467, then remove engine mount and bracket as an assembly. REmove front cover attaching screws and the front cover.
5. Clean cylinder block and front cover sealing surfaces, then position oil pan front seal on front cover.
6. Apply a ⅜ inch wide by 3/16 inch thick bead of RTV sealer to joint formed at oil pan and front cover.
7. Apply a ¼ inch wide by ⅛ inch thick bead of RTV sealer on front cover to block mating surface.
8. Install centering tool No. J-23042 in front cover seal.
9. Install front cover. Install 2 attaching screws finger tight, then install remaining screws and torque all screws to 90 inch lbs.
10. Remove centering tool and install pulley, hub, splash shield and drive belts.

TIMING GEARS

When necessary to install a new camshaft gear, the camshaft will have to be removed as the gear is a pressed fit on the camshaft. The camshaft is held in place by a thrust plate retained to the engine by two capscrews which are accessible through the two holes in the gear web.

To remove gear, use an arbor press and a suitable sleeve to properly support gear on its steel hub.

CENTERING TOOL INSTALLED

Fig. 5 Valve timing marks

NOTCH TOWARD FRONT OF ENGINE

DIMPLES TOWARD REAR OF ENGINE

Fig. 6 Piston & rod assembly

Before installing gear, assemble thrust plate and gear spacer ring, then press gear onto shaft until it bottoms against spacer ring. The thrust plate end clearance should be .0015–.0050 inch. If clearance is less than .0015 inch, the spacer ring should be replaced. If clearance is greater than .0050 inch, the thrust plate should be replaced.

The crankshaft gear can be replaced using a puller and two bolts in the tapped holes of the gear.

When installing timing gears, ensure marks on gears are properly aligned, **Fig. 5.**

NOTE: The valve timing marks, **Fig. 5,** do not indicate TDC compression for No. 1 cylinder for use during distributor installation. When installing the distributor, rotate engine until No. 1 cylinder is on compression stroke and the camshaft timing mark is 180° from the valve timing position shown in **Fig. 5.**

CAMSHAFT
REPLACE

1. Remove engine as described under "Engine, Replace." Do not separate engine from transaxle.
2. Remove rocker arm cover, then loosen rocker arm stud nuts. Pivot rocker

arms clear of push rods and remove the rods.

3. Remove distributor, then, on 1984 models, the alternator and mounting brackets.
4. Remove front engine mount and bracket assembly.
5. Remove oil pump drive shaft.
6. Remove front cover as described under "Engine Front Cover, Replace."
7. Remove camshaft thrust plate attaching screws.
8. Carefully remove camshaft and gear through front of block.
9. Reverse procedure to install. When installing camshaft, align crankshaft and camshaft timing marks on gear teeth, **Fig. 5.**

PISTONS & RODS
ASSEMBLE

Assemble piston to rod with notch on piston facing toward front of engine and the raised notch side of rod at bearing end facing toward rear of engine, **Fig. 6.**

Upon installation, measure connecting rod side clearance using a suitable feeler gauge. Clearance should be .006–.022 inch.

PISTONS, PINS & RINGS

Pistons and rings are available in standard size and oversizes of .010, .020 and .030 inch. Piston pins are available in oversizes of .001 and .003 inch.

MAIN & ROD BEARINGS

Main and rod bearings are available in standard size and oversizes of .001, .002 and .010 inch.

OIL PAN
REPLACE

1984

1. Install engine support fixture, tool No. J-28467 or equivalent, and raise engine slightly to relieve tension from cradle mounts, **Fig. 7.**
2. Raise and support vehicle.
3. Disconnect exhaust pipe from exhaust manifold, then remove rear wheels.
4. Disconnect both lower control arms and toe link rods from knuckle.
5. Disconnect parking brake cable from cradle.
6. Remove engine and transmission attaching bolts.
7. Remove cradle attaching bolts and the cradle.
8. Drain engine oil, then remove front engine mount-to-support bracket attaching nuts.
9. Disconnect exhaust pipe from rear transaxle mount.

Fig. 7   Engine support fixture

1—OIL PAN

2—APPLY A 3/8" WIDE BY 3/16" THICK BEAD OF RTV SEALER IN AREA INDICATED

3—APPLY A 3/16" WIDE BY 1/8" THICK BEAD OF RTV SEALER IN AREA INDICATED

4—ENGINE BLOCK ASSEMBLY

5—REAR BEARING

6—GROOVE IN MAIN BEARING CAP MUST BE FILLED FLUSH TO 1/8" ABOVE SURFACE WITH RTV

Fig. 8   Oil pan installation

10. Remove starter and flywheel cover, then the upper alternator bracket.
11. Remove lower alternator and engine support brackets.
12. Remove oil pan retaining bolts and the oil pan.
13. Reverse procedure to install, noting the following:
    a. Apply RTV sealer as shown in **Fig. 8.**
    b. Install 2 bolts in front cover after all other pan attaching bolts have been torqued to 75 inch lbs. Torque front cover bolts to 90 inch lbs.
    c. When installing cradle, first install front cradle attaching bolts and nuts finger tight, then note the following torques: rear cradle bolts, 76 ft. lbs.; front cradle nut, 67 ft. lbs.; engine mount bolts, 42 ft. lbs.; rear mount bolts, 18 ft. lbs.; front mount bolts, 36 ft. lbs.; lower control arm-to-knuckle bolts, 33 ft. lbs.; lower control arm-to-cradle bolts, 69 ft. lbs.; tow rod-to-knuckle bolts, 35 ft. lbs.; exhaust pipe-to-manifold bolts, 25 ft. lbs.

1985–86

1. Disconnect battery cables.
2. Remove engine compartment lid and side panels.
3. Raise and support vehicle.
4. Drain engine oil, then remove front engine mount-to-cradle nuts.
5. Remove flywheel cover, then the starter motor, splash shield and alternator.
6. Lower vehicle, then remove engine strut.
7. Install engine support fixture tool No. J-28467 or equivalent.
8. Raise and support vehicle.
9. Remove engine front support brackets.
10. Remove oil pan attaching bolts and the oil pan.
11. Reverse procedure to install, noting the following:
    a. Apply RTV sealant as as shown in **Fig. 8.**
    b. Install 2 bolts in front cover after all other pan attaching bolts have been torqued to 54 inch lbs.

1	PUMP BODY	6	SPRING RETAINER
2	PICKUP TUBE	7	COVER SCREWS
3	PICKUP SCREW ASSEMBLY	8	COVER
4	PRESSURE REGULATOR VALVE	9	IDLER GEAR
5	PRESSURE REGULATOR SPRING	10	DRIVE GEAR AND SHAFT

Fig. 9   Exploded view of oil pump

Fig. 12   Measuring oil pump gears

Fig. 10   Measuring oil pump gear backlash

Fig. 13   Measuring oil pump gear side clearance

Fig. 11   Measuring oil pump gear pocket

Fig. 14   Measuring oil pump gear end clearance

OIL PUMP SERVICE

REMOVAL

1. Remove oil pan as described under "Oil Pan, Replace."
2. Remove oil pump attaching bolts and nuts, then the oil pump and screen as an assembly.

DISASSEMBLY

1. Drain residual oil from pump.
2. Remove suction pipe and screen assembly from pump.
3. Remove pump cover attaching screws, then the pump cover and gears, **Fig. 9.**
4. Remove pump regulator valve. Remove plug, spring and ball from valve.

INSPECTION

1. Inspect pump housing and cover for wear or damage, and replace if necessary.
2. Inspect pressure regulator valve for scoring or sticking. Burrs may be removed with a fine oil stone, however more extensive damage requires replacement of valve.
3. Inspect idler gear shaft for wear or damage, and replace if necessary.
4. Inspect pressure regulator spring for lack of tension or distortion, and replace if necessary.
5. Inspect suction pipe and screen, and clean or replace as necessary.

NOTE: If suction pipe is permanently pressed into the pump body, and if it is loose or has been removed, a new pipe must be installed.

6. Inspect gears and driveshaft for wear or damage and replace as necessary.
7. Install gears into housing and measure gear backlash, **Fig. 10.** Backlash should measure .009–.015 inch.
8. Measure pump housing gear pocket depth and diameter, **Fig. 11.** Depth should measure .995–.998 inch and diameter 1.503–1.506 inches.
9. Measure length and diameter of gears, **Fig. 12.** Length of both gears should be .999–1.002 inch and diameter should be 1.496–1.500 inches.
10. Measure gear side clearance, **Fig. 13.** Side clearance should measure no more than .004 inch.

11. Measure gear end clearance, **Fig. 14.** End clearance should be .002–.005 inch.
12. If any measurements taken in steps 7 through 11 are not within specifications, replace oil pump components as necessary.

ASSEMBLY

1. Lubricate all internal components with clean engine oil and pack all pump cavities with petroleum jelly.
2. Install pump gears into housing.
3. Install pump cover, pressure regulator valve and spring. Torque cover attaching bolts to 10 ft. lbs. and the pressure regulator valve plug to 15 ft. lbs.
4. Apply suitable sealer to new pipe, then tap pipe into position using a plastic hammer and tool No. J-8369.

INSTALLATION

1. Align oil pump shaft with tang on oil pump drive shaft, then install pump on block, positioning pump flange over oil pump drive shaft lower bushing.
2. Install pump attaching bolts and torque to 20 ft. lbs.
3. Install oil pan.

CRANKSHAFT REAR OIL SEAL
REPLACE

NOTE: The rear main oil seal is a one-piece seal which can be replaced without removing the oil pan or crankshaft.

1. Remove transaxle and flywheel.
2. On models equipped with manual transaxle, remove pressure plate and disc.
3. On all models, remove rear main bearing oil seal using a suitable screwdriver. Use care not to scratch crankshaft.
4. Reverse procedure to install. Lubricate outside of seal to ease assembly.

WATER PUMP
REPLACE

1. Disconnect battery ground cable and drain cooling system.
2. Remove accessory drive belts.
3. Disconnect lower radiator hose from water pump.
4. Remove water pump attaching bolts and the pump.
5. Reverse procedure to install. Apply a ⅛ inch bead of suitable sealer to pump sealing surface, and install pump before sealer dries.

FUEL PUMP
REPLACE

1. Release pressure from fuel system as follows:
   a. Remove fuel pump fuse from fuse block, then start and run engine until engine stalls from fuel starvation.
   b. Energize starter for approximately 3 seconds to release any residual pressure from system.
   c. Turn ignition off and replace fuel pump fuse.
2. Disconnect battery ground cable.
3. Raise and support vehicle.
4. Remove fuel tank from vehicle.
5. Remove fuel meter/pump assembly. Turn cam lock ring counterclockwise, then lift assembly from fuel tank and remove pump from meter.
6. Lift pump up into attaching hose while pulling away from bottom support. When pump is clear of lower support, remove assembly from rubber connector.

NOTE: Use care to avoid damage to rubber insulator and strainer during removal.

7. Reverse procedure to install.

V6-173 Engine Section

ENGINE MOUNTS
REPLACE

ENGINE MOUNT

1. Disconnect battery ground cable.
2. Remove engine compartment lid and side cover panels.
3. Support engine with tools J-28467 and J-35563.
4. Remove torque reaction rod bolt.
5. Raise and support vehicle.
6. Remove engine mount to chassis attaching nuts, **Fig.1**
7. Remove engine mount to support bracket upper nuts.
8. Remove engine mount from vehicle.
9. Reverse procedure to install.

TRANSAXLE MOUNTS

1. Disconnect battery ground cable.
2. Remove engine compartment lid and side cover panels. **Do not** remove torsion rod retaining bolts.
3. Support engine and transaxle with tools J-28467 and J-35563.
4. Remove mount to cradle and support bracket attaching nuts, **Fig. 2.**
5. Remove transaxle mount and shield, if equipped.
6. Reverse procedure to install.

ENGINE
REPLACE

1. Disconnect battery ground cable and drain cooling system.
2. Remove engine compartment lid and side cover panels. **Do not** remove torsion rod retaining bolts.
3. Remove intake flex duct.
4. Disconnect throttle and shift cable.
5. Disconnect heater hoses from engine.
6. Disconnect vacuum hoses to components **not** engine mounted.
7. Disconnect fuel lines from engine and remove fuel pump relay.
8. On automatic transaxle models, disconnect transaxle cooler lines.
9. On manual transaxle models, remove slave cylinder and shield from transaxle.
10. Disconnect ground strap from engine.
11. Remove radiator hoses.
12. Disconnect engine harness at junction block.
13. Remove rear heat shield.
14. If equipped, discharge air conditioning system. Disconnect A/C lines and wiring from compressor. **Plug A/C lines.**
15. Remove rear console.
16. Disconnect ECM harness through bulkhead panel.
17. Remove engine strut front bolt.
18. Install engine support fixture and bracket.
19. Raise and support vehicle.
20. Remove rear wheels.
21. Remove brake calipers and position aside. **Do not** disconnect brake hoses.
22. Remove two strut bolts on each side.

NOTE: Scribe alignment marks on bolts to retain camber setting.

23. Loosen four cradle bolts.
24. Lower vehicle.
25. Support engine and transaxle assembly on a suitable dolly.
26. Remove four cradle bolts.
27. Raise vehicle, leaving engine and transaxle assembly on dolly.
28. Reverse procedure to install. Torque rear cradle bolts to 76 ft. lbs. and front cradle bolts to 66 ft. lbs.

INTAKE MANIFOLD
REPLACE

1. Disconnect battery ground cable. Drain cooling system.
2. Remove rocker arm covers.
3. Remove intake duct.
4. Remove distributor. Mark location of distributor on engine and rotor on distributor body.
5. Disconnect throttle body from upper plenum.
6. Remove radiator hose and radiator fill inlet.
7. Disconnect heater hoses and the pipe to throttle body.
8. Disconnect wiring harness.
9. Remove heater hoses and disconnect vacuum hoses.
10. Remove brake booster pipe and bracket.
11. Disconnect EGR pipe.
12. Remove upper manifold plenum and gaskets, **Fig. 3.**
13. Remove intermediate intake manifold and gasket.
14. Remove lower intake manifold and gaskets.
15. Reverse procedure to install. Refer to **Fig. 3** for torque sequence. Torque lower intake manifold bolts to 19 ft. lbs. Torque intermediate intake manifold bolts to 15 ft. lbs. Torque upper manifold plenum bolts to 19 ft.lbs.

EXHAUST MANIFOLD
REPLACE

FRONT

1. Disconnect battery ground cable.

1–CRADLE

2–DRAIN HOLE–AWAY FROM CRADLE

3–GENERATOR BRACKET

4–ENGINE MOUNT

5–BRACKET

6–BRACKET ENGINE FRONT

7–BRACKET, STRUT

8–SUPPORT STRUT

9–STRUT

NOTE: TO POSITION STRUT IN SUPPORT, PUSH ENGINE REARWARD WITH A HORIZONTAL LOAD OF 200-250 NEWTONS. LOAD IS APPLIED ON A LINE DIRECTLY THROUGH CENTER OF SUPPORT SLOTS. TIGHTEN BOLT WITH LOAD APPLIED.

Fig. 1   Engine mount installation

1—MOUNT ASM. (REAR)

2—SHIELD

3—MOUNT ASM. (FRONT)

4—BRACKET

Fig. 2   Transaxle mount installation

1—MANIFOLD, UPPER PLENUM
2—GASKET
3—INTAKE MANIFOLD, INTERMEDIATE
4—BOLT 21 N·m (15 LB.FT.)
5—INTAKE MANIFOLD, LOWER
6—NUT 26 N·m (19 LB.FT.)
7—BOLT 26 N·m (19 LB.FT.)
8—APPLY A SMOOTH—CONTINUOUS
    BEAD APPROX. 2.0-3.0 mm WIDE
    AND 3.0-3.5mm THICK ON BOTH
    SURFACES. BEAD CONFIGURATION
    MUST INSURE COMPLETE SEALING
    OF WATER AND OIL. SURFACE
    MUST BE FREE OF OIL AND DIRT
    TO INSURE ADEQUATE SEAL.

Fig. 3   Intake manifold installation

2. Remove engine compartment lid. **Do not** remove torsion rod retaining bolts.
3. Disconnect brake vacuum hose.
4. Remove manifold heat shield.
5. Remove front crossover bolts, **Fig. 4.**
6. Raise and support vehicle.
7. Remove front converter heat shield.
8. Remove lower manifold bolts.
9. Lower vehicle.
10. Remove upper manifold bolts and the manifold.
11. Reverse procedure to install. Torque manifold bolts to 18 ft. lbs. Torque crossover bolts to 22 ft. lbs.

REAR

1. Remove manifold to crossover bolts, **Fig. 4.**
2. Remove manifold bolts and the manifold.
3. Reverse procedure to install. Torque manifold bolts to 18 ft. lbs. Torque crossover bolts to 22 ft. lbs.

CYLINDER HEAD
REPLACE

LEFT SIDE

1. Disconnect battery ground cable and drain cooling system.
2. Remove intake manifold and exhaust crossover pipe.
3. Remove alternator bracket and oil dipstick tube.
4. Remove rocker arm cover, rocker arms and push rods.
5. Remove cylinder head bolts and cylinder head.
6. Reverse procedure to install. Torque cylinder head bolts **in sequence, Fig. 5,** to 66 ft. lbs.

RIGHT SIDE

1. Disconnect battery ground cable and

1—BOLT/STUD LOCKWASHER ASM.(L.H. ONLY) 24 N·m (18 LB.FT.)
2—EXHAUST MANIFOLD ASM. R.H.
3—BOLT—30 N·m (22 LB.FT.)
4—CROSSOVER PIPE
5—SEAL
6—MUFFLER
7—SPRING
8—BOLT—20 N·m (15LB.FT.)
9—BOLT & LOCKWASHER ASM. 24 N·m (18 LB.FT.)
10—EXHAUST MANIFOLD ASM. L.H.
11—GASKET

Fig. 4   Exhaust manifold installation

drain cooling system.
2. Raise and support vehicle.
3. Disconnect exhaust pipe from manifold.
4. Remove cruise control servo bracket.
5. Remove intake manifold and exhaust crossover pipe.
6. Remove rocker arm cover, rocker arms and push rods.
7. Remove cylinder head bolts and cylinder head.
8. Reverse procedure to install. Torque cylinder head bolts **in sequence, Fig. 5,** to 66 ft. lbs.

ROCKER ARM COVER
REPLACE

FRONT

1. Disconnect battery ground cable.
2. Remove engine compartment lid. **Do not** remove torsion rod retaining bolts.
3. Remove vacuum boost line and tube.
4. Disconnect throttle and downshift cables and remove bracket.
5. Disconnect cruise control cable, if equipped.
6. Remove ground cable.
7. Remove PCV valve from rocker arm cover.
8. Remove oil dipstick tube.
9. Disconnect spark plug wires and remove bracket.
10. Remove engine lift hook.
11. Remove rocker arm cover bolts and the cover.

NOTE: If cover adheres to cylinder head, shear the adhesion by tapping the end of the cover with a rubber mallet. If cover will not release, pry **carefully** until loose. **Do not distort** the sealing flange.

12. Reverse procedure to install. Torque cover bolts to 90 inch lbs.

Head Torque Sequence

Fig. 5   Cylinder head installation & torque sequence

Fig. 6   Adjusting valves

Fig. 7   Oversize valve lifter marking

1	LIFTER BODY	5	BALL CHECK	6	PLUNGER
2	PLUNGER SPRING	7	OIL METERING VALVE
3	BALL CHECK RETAINER	8	PUSH ROD SEAT
4	BALL CHECK SPRING	9	RETAINER RING

Fig. 8   Valve lifter. Exploded view

Fig. 9   Engine front cover installation

VALVE ARRANGEMENT
Front to Rear
Right . . . . E-I-E-I-I-E
Left . . . . E-I-I-E-I-E

VALVE LIFT SPECS

Engine	Year	Intake	Exhaust
V6-173	1985	.394	.410

VALVE TIMING
Intake Opens Before TDC

Engine	Year	Degrees
V6-173	1985	31

ROCKER ARM STUDS

Rocker arm studs that are cracked or have damaged threads can be replaced. If threads in cylinder head are damaged or stripped, the head can be retapped and a helical type insert added. When installing a new rocker arm stud, torque to 43–49 ft. lbs.

VALVES
ADJUST

1. Crank engine until mark on torsional damper is aligned with "0" mark on timing tab. Check to ensure engine is in the No. 1 cylinder firing position by placing fingers on No. 1 cylinder rocker arms as mark on damper comes near "0" mark on timing tab. If valves are not moving, the engine is in the No. 1 firing position. If valves move as damper mark nears "0" mark on timing tab, engine is in the No. 4 cylinder firing position and should be rotated one revolution to reach the No. 1 cylinder firing position.
2. With engine in the No. 1 cylinder firing position, adjust the following valves: Exhaust- 1, 2, 3; Intake- 1, 5, 6. To adjust valves, back off adjusting nut until lash is felt at push rod, then tighten adjusting nut until all lash is removed, Fig. 6. This can be determined by rotating the push rod while tightening the adjusting nut. When all lash has been eliminated, turn adjusting nut the additional number of turns listed in the Valve Specifications.
3. Crank engine one revolution until mark on torsional damper and TDC mark are again aligned. This is the No. 4 cylinder firing position. With engine in this position, the following valves can be adjusted: Exhaust- 4, 5 & 6; Intake- 2, 3 & 4.
4. Install rocker arm covers, then start engine and check timing and idle speed.

VALVE GUIDES

Valve guides are an integral part of the cylinder head and are not removable. If valve stem clearance becomes excessive, the valve guide should be reamed to the next oversize and the appropriate oversize valves installed. Valves are available in of oversizes .0035, .0155 and .0305 inch.

VALVE LIFTERS

NOTE: Some V6-173 engines will be equipped with both standard and .25 mm. oversize valve lifters. The cylinder case will be marked where the oversize valve lifters are installed with a daub of white paint and .25 mm. O.S. will be stamped on the valve lifter boss, **Fig. 7.**

Failure of a hydraulic valve lifter, **Fig. 8,** is generally caused by an inadequate oil supply or dirt. An air leak at the intake side of the oil pump or too much oil in the engine will cause air bubbles in the oil supply to the lifters causing them to collapse. This is a probable cause of trouble if several lifters fail to function, but air in oil is an unlikely cause of failure of a single unit.

Valve lifters can be removed after removing rocker arm covers, intake manifold, rocker stud nuts, rocker arm balls, rocker arms and push rods.

ENGINE FRONT COVER
REPLACE

1. Disconnect battery ground cable.
2. Remove accessory drive belts.
3. On models equipped with air conditioning, remove A/C compressor and bracket.
4. On all models, remove water pump as described under "Water Pump, Replace."
5. On all models, raise and support vehicle.
6. Remove torsional damper and the oil pan to cover bolts.
7. Lower vehicle.
8. Remove front cover bolts and the cover, **Fig. 9.**

GASKET

3mm BEAD OF RTV SEALANT
#1052366 OR EQUIVALENT

Fig. 10   Engine front cover sealant location

1 CYLINDER
AT T.D.C.

4 CYLINDER
AT T.D.C.

Fig. 11   Valve timing marks

SEAL WITH RTV

Fig. 12   Camshaft rear cover installation

9. Reverse procedure to install. Apply sealant to mating surfaces as shown in **Fig. 10.**

NOTE: It is only necessary to coat oil pan to front cover sealing surfaces since gasket is used in production.

TIMING CHAIN
REPLACE

1. Remove front cover as described under "Engine Front Cover, Replace."
2. Place No. 1 piston at top dead center with marks on camshaft and crankshaft sprockets aligned, **Fig. 11.**

NOTE: The valve timing marks, **Fig. 11,** does not indicate TDC compression stroke for No. 1 cylinder for use during distributor installation. When installing the distributor, rotate engine until No. 1 cylinder is on compression stroke and the camshaft timing mark is 180 degrees from valve timing position shown in **Fig. 11.**

3. Remove camshaft sprocket bolts, then remove sprocket and timing chain. If sprocket does not come off easily, tap lower edge of sprocket with a plastic mallet.
4. If crankshaft sprocket is to be replaced, remove sprocket using a suitable puller or tool J-5825. Install new sprocket, aligning key and keyway.
5. Install timing chain on camshaft sprocket. Hold sprocket vertically with chain hanging down and align marks on camshaft and crankshaft sprockets.

6. Align dowel pin hole in sprocket with dowl pin on camshaft, then install sprocket on camshaft.
7. Using camshaft sprocket attaching bolts, draw sprocket onto camshaft. Torque bolts to 15 to 20 ft. lbs.
8. Lubricate timing chain with engine oil, then install front cover as outlined previously.

CAMSHAFT
REPLACE

1. Remove engine from vehicle as described under "Engine, Replace."
2. Remove valve lifters and engine front cover as described previously.
3. Remove timing chain and sprocket as described under "Timing Chain, Replace."
4. Remove camshft rear cover, **Fig. 12.**
5. Withdraw camshaft from engine, using care not to damage camshaft bearings.
6. Reverse procedure to install. When installing timing chain, align valve timing marks as shown in **Fig. 11.**

NOTE: The valve timing marks, **Fig. 11,** does not indicate TDC compression stroke for No. 1 cylinder for use during distributor installation. When installing the distributor, rotate engine until No. 1 cylinder is on compression stroke and the camshaft timing mark is 180 degrees from valve timing position shown in **Fig. 11.**

PISTONS & RODS
ASSEMBLE

Assemble pistons to connecting rods as shown in **Fig. 13.**
Upon installation, measure the connecting rod side clearance using a suitable feeler gauge. Clearance should be .006 to .017 inch.

PISTONS, PINS & RINGS

Pistons and rings are available in standard size and oversizes of .05 and 1 mm.

NOTCHES TOWARD FRONT OF ENGINE

BEARING TANG SLOTS

RIGHT BANK NOS. 1·3·5

LEFT BANK NOS. 2·4·6

Fig. 13   Piston & rod assembly

Fig. 14   Oil pump. Exploded view

CRANKSHAFT

BOTTOM FACE CYLINDER & CASE

SEAL

FRT

REAR FACE OF CYLINDER & CASE

CYLINDER & CASE

CAUTION RETAINER SPRING SIDE OF SEAL MUST FACE TOWARD FRONT OF CYLINDER & CASE.

Fig. 15   Rear main bearing oil seal installation. Thin seal

MAIN & ROD BEARINGS

Main bearings are available in standard size and undersizes of .013 and .026 mm and connecting rod bearings are available in standard size and undersizes of .016 and .032 mm.

OIL PAN
REPLACE

1. Disconnect battery ground cable.
2. Raise and support vehicle.
3. Drain engine oil from crankcase.
4. Remove flywheel housing shield or clutch housing cover as applicable.
5. Remove starter motor.
6. Remove oil pan attaching bolts and the oil pan.
7. Reverse procedure to install. Apply a ⅛ inch bead of RTV sealer to oil pan sealing flange.

OIL PUMP SERVICE
REMOVAL

1. Remove oil pan as described under "Oil Pan, Replace."
2. Remove pump to rear main bearing cap bolt and remove pump and extension shaft.

DISASSEMBLY

1. Remove pump cover attaching bolts and pump cover, **Fig. 14.**
2. Mark drive and idler gear teeth so they can be installed in the same position, then remove idler and drive gear and shaft from pump body.
3. Remove pin, spring and pressure regulator valve from pump cover.
4. If pick-up tube and screen assembly are to be replaced, mount pump cover in a soft jawed vise and remove pick-up tube from cover. Do not remove

screen from pick-up tube, these components are serviced as an assembly.

INSPECTION

1. Inspect pump body and cover for excessive wear and cracks.
2. Inspect pump gear for damage or excessive wear. If pump gears are damaged or worn, the entire pump assembly must be replaced.
3. Check drive gear shaft for looseness in pump body.
4. Inspect pump cover for wear that would allow oil to leak past gear teeth.
5. Inspect pick-up tube and screen assembly for damage.
6. Check pressure regulator valve for fit in pump cover.

ASSEMBLY

1. If pick-up tube and screen were removed, apply sealer to end of pick-up tube, then mount pump cover in a soft jawed vise and using tool No. J-8369, tap pick-up tube into position using a plastic mallet.

NOTE: Whenever the pick-up tube and screen assembly has been removed, a new pick-up tube and screen assembly should be installed. Use care when installing pick-up tube and screen assembly so that tube does not twist, shear or collapse. Loss of a press fit condition could result in an air leak and a loss of oil pressure.

2. Install pressure regulator valve, spring and pin, **Fig. 14.**
3. Install drive gear and shaft in pump body.
4. Align marks made during disassembly, then install idler gear.
5. Install pump cover gasket, cover and attaching bolts. Torque bolts to 6 to 9 ft. lbs.
6. Rotate pump drive shaft by hand and check pump for smooth operation.

INSTALLATION

1. Assemble pump and extension shaft

SPRING SIDE   DUST LIP SIDE

J-34686

SEAL BORE TO SEAL SURFACE
TO BE LUBRICATED
WITH ENGINE OIL BEFORE
ASSEMBLY

**Fig. 16   Rear main bearing oil seal installation.
Thick seal**

| 1— | 30 N•m (22 FT-LBS) | 2— | 30 N•m (22 FT-LBS) | 3— | 10 N•m (7 FT-LBS) |

Fig. 17   Water pump installation

with retainer to rear main bearing cap, aligning top end of hexagon extension shaft with hexagon socket on lower end of distributor shaft.
2. Install pump to rear main bearing cap bolt.
3. Install oil pan as described under Oil Pan, Replace.

REAR MAIN BEARING OIL SEAL REPAIR

THIN SEAL

1. Remove engine as outlined under "Engine, Replace" procedure.
2. Remove oil pan and oil pump assembly.
3. Remove water pump and timing chain.
4. Remove connecting rod and main bearing caps, then the crankshaft and oil seal.
5. Coat outer diameter of new seal with sealant 1052756 or equivalent.
6. Position seal/tool assembly on rear of crankshaft, ensuring arrows on tool face toward cylinder and case assembly, **Fig. 14.**

7. Install crankshaft, discard tool, then coat crankshaft journals with engine oil.
8. Apply a 1 millimeter bead of anaerobic sealant to bearing cap surface.
9. Reinstall rear main cap, main bearing caps and connecting rod caps and torque to specifications.
10. Reverse removal procedure to complete installation.

THICK SEAL

1. Remove transaxle and flexplate.
2. Using a screwdriver or similar tool, pry out old seal. Use care to avoid damaging crankshaft. File all burrs or knicks as required.
3. Install new seal using tool J34686, **Fig. 16,** as follows:
   a. Apply a light coat of engine oil to I.D. of oil seal.
   b. Slide seal over tool mandril until dust lip bottoms squarely against collar of tool.
   c. Align dowel pin of tool with dowel pin hole in crankshaft, **Fig. 16,** then attach tool to crankshaft with screw provided.
   d. Turn handle of tool until seal is pushed into bore and collar is posi-

tioned firmly against case. Remove tool.
4. Install flywheel and transmission, then start engine and check for leaks.

WATER PUMP
REPLACE

1. Disconnect battery ground cable, then drain cooling system.
2. Remove right hand louvered outer cover.
3. Remove plastic battery cover.
4. Disconnect wires from junction block.
5. Remove EVRV and bracket.
6. Raise and support vwehicle.
7. Remove right rear wheel and inner fender splash shield.
8. Remove alternator drive belt.
9. Remove water pump attaching bolts, **Fig. 17.**
10. Lower vehicle.
11. Remove water pump.
12. Reverse procedure to install. Apply a 2mm bead of suitable sealer to water pump sealing surface.

Clutch & Transaxle Section

FLYWHEEL

DRIVEN PLATE ASSEMBLY

PRESSURE PLATE AND COVER ASSEMBLY

CLUTCH RELEASE BEARING

TRANSAXLE

Fig. 1   Clutch assembly

HYDRAULIC CLUTCH
BLEED

NOTE: Extreme cleanliness must be maintained while bleeding the clutch system. Do not use linty rags, and ensure no dirt enters the system, particularly at the supply tank. Never add previously used fluid to the supply tank as it may be contaminated or have an excessive moisture content.

1. Fill supply tank with suitable brake fluid.
2. Remove floormat or any other object which may impede full travel of clutch pedal.
3. Back out bleed screw on slave cylinder until fluid can be pumped out (approximately ½ turn).
4. Depress clutch pedal fully, then apply three short, rapid strokes.
5. Release pressure to allow clutch pedal to return quickly to its stop.
6. Repeat steps 2 and 3 until all air has been released from bleed screw.
7. Close bleed screw immediately following last downward stroke of pedal when air bubbles no longer appear.

CLUTCH
REPLACE

1984

1. Remove transaxle as described under "Manual Transaxle, Replace."
2. Mark position of pressure plate to flywheel for assembly reference.
3. Gradually loosen pressure plate attaching bolts until spring pressure is relieved.
4. Support pressure plate and remove mounting bolts, pressure plate and driven disc, **Fig. 1.**

MANUAL TRANSAXLE SHIFT CABLE
ADJUST

1. Disconnect battery ground cable.
2. Shift transaxle into first gear.
3. Loosen shift cable attaching nuts "E" on transaxle levers "D" and "F", **Fig. 2.**
4. Remove console and trim plates to provide access to shifter.
5. With transaxle in first gear, insert a yoke clip to retain lever, **Fig. 2**, view "D."
6. Insert a No. 22 or ⁵⁄₃₂ inch drill bit into alignment hole at side of shifter assembly, **Fig. 2**, view "C."
7. Remove backlash from transaxle by rotating lever "D" in direction of arrow while torquing nut "E" on lever "F" to 20 ft. lbs., **Fig. 2.**
8. Remove drill bit and yoke from shifter.
9. Install console and trim pads.
10. Connect battery ground cable, then road test vehicle and check shifter for proper operation. If "hang-up" is encountered when shifting in the 1–2 gear range, and the shift cables are properly adjusted, it may be necessary to change the shifter shaft selective washer. Perform the following procedure to determine correct washer thickness:
    a. Remove reverse inhibitor fitting spring and washer from end of housing, then place shifter shaft in second gear.
    b. Measure dimension "A," **Fig. 3**, which is the distance between end of housing and shoulder just behind end of shaft.
    c. Apply a 9–13 lb. load on opposite end of shaft, then measure dimension "B," **Fig. 3**, which is distance between end of housing and end of

shifter shaft major diameter.
    d. Subtract dimension "B" from dimension "A" to obtain dimension "C."
    e. Refer to chart, **Fig. 4,** to determine correct thickness shim.

1985–86

1. Disconnect battery ground cable.
2. Shift transaxle into first gear.
3. Loosen shift cable attaching nuts "E" on transaxle levers "D" and "F", **Fig. 5.**
4. Remove console and trim plates to provide access to shifter.
5. With transaxle in first gear, insert alignment pins "F" and "G", view "C", **Fig. 5.**
6. Remove backlash from transaxle by rotating lever "D" in direction of arrow while tightening nut "A" to 20 ft. lbs. Repeat procedure for nut "E" on lever "F".

NOTE: Levers "D" and "F" must remain stationary while tightening nuts.

7. Ensure reverse inhibit cam is against roller and align if necessary.
8. Remove alignment pins from shifter assembly.
9. Install console trim plate and reconnect battery ground cable.
10. Road test vehicle and check shifter for proper operation. If "hang-up" is encountered when shifting in the 1-2 gear range and the shift cables are properly adjusted, it may be necessary to replace the shifter shaft selective washer. Refer to step 10 under "1984" for procedure.

MANUAL TRANSAXLE
REPLACE

1984

1. Disconnect battery ground cable, then remove air cleaner.
2. Disconnect ground cable from transaxle.
3. Disconnect shift and select cables from transaxle.
4. Remove upper transaxle-to-engine attaching bolts.
5. Install engine support fixture, tool No. J-28467 or equivalent, **Fig. 6.**
6. Raise and support vehicle.
7. Remove rear wheels, then disconnect axle shafts from transaxle as described in the "Drive Axle, Rear Suspension & Brakes" section under "Drive Axle, Replace."
8. Remove heat shield from catalytic converter, then disconnect exhaust pipe from exhaust manifold.
9. Remove engine mount and transaxle mount-to-cradle attaching nuts.
10. Support cradle with a suitable jack, then remove front and rear cradle-to-body attaching bolts.
11. Lower cradle from vehicle and position

1 — CABLE A	9 — 1ST, 2D
2 — CABLE B	10 — R
3 — DRILL BIT	11 — R, 3RD, 1ST
4 — LEVER D	12 — 2ND, 4TH
5 — NUT E	13 — LEVER F
6 — P. WASHER	14 — 5/32" DRILL BIT
7 — PIN	15 — YOKE
8 — 4TH, 3D	

Fig. 2 Manual transaxle shift cable adjustment. 1984

APPLY
LOAD ON END OF SHAFT

SHIFTER SHAFT
(LEVERS NOT SHOWN)

Dimension "C" Fig. 3 Inch (mm)	Ident. Color & No. of Stripes	Shim Part No.
.0708 (1.8)	3 White	14008235
.0827 (2.1)	1 Orange	476709
.0945 (2.4)	2 Orange	476710
.1063 (2.7)	3 Orange	476711
.1181 (3.0)	1 Blue	476712
.1299 (3.3)	2 Blue	476713
.1417 (3.6)	3 Blue	476714
.1535 (3.9)	1 White	476715
.1654 (4.2)	2 White	476716

Fig. 4   Shifter shaft selective washer identification

Fig. 3   Manual transaxle shifter shaft selective washer measurement

aside.
12. Remove starter and inspection cover shields, then the starter motor.
13. Remove flywheel-to-converter attaching bolts.
14. Support transaxle with a suitable jack, then remove lower transaxle-to-engine attaching bolts and lower transaxle assembly from vehicle.
15. Reverse procedure to install.

NOTE: When installing cradle, work into position on rear mounts, then raise front into position.

1985

1. Disconnect battery ground cable.
2. Remove deck lid and louvered panels.
3. Remove upper rear engine support bolt.
4. Install engine support fixture tool No. J-28467 or equivalent, **Fig. 6.**
5. Raise and support vehicle.
6. Unfasten slave cylinder from clutch, leaving hydraulic line connected.

7. Disconnect shift cables from transaxle.
8. Disconnect EGR valve output pipe from exhaust manifold.
9. Remove both wheel and tire assemblies.
10. Disconnect parking brake cable from brake calipers and body brackets.
11. Remove lower ball joints, then disconnect tie rods.
12. REmove axle shafts from transaxle.
13. Remove rubber boots from splash shield cradle retainers.
14. Remove rear transaxle bracket mount attaching bolts.
15. Remove motor mount nuts from cradle and from engine mount shock.
16. Remove crossover pipe-to-converter attaching bolts.
17. Support cradle with a suitable jack, then remove cradle attaching bolts and lower cradle from vehicle.
18. Disconnect electrical connector from oxygen sensor.
19. Remove crossover pipe heat shields, then the exhaust crossover pipe.
20. Support transaxle with a suitable jack.
21. Remove upper transaxle-to-engine attaching bolts, then the clutch inspection plate cover.
22. Remove lower engine blot studs, then the coolant pipe from stud and nut.
23. Lower transaxle assembly from vehicle.
24. Reverse procedure to install.

Fig. 5   Manual transaxle shift cable adjustment. 1985–86

Fig. 6   Engine support fixture

1 – STRUT ASM.   4 – REAR CONTROL ARM

2 – TOE LINK RODS   5 – DRIVE AXLES

3 – SPRING

Fig. 1   Rear suspension

DESCRIPTION

The drive axles are completely flexible assemblies which consist of an inner and outer constant velocity joint connected by an axle shaft. The inner constant velocity joint has the capability of moving in and out, whereas the outer joint does not.

The rear suspension, **Fig. 1,** is a Mac-Pherson strut design. The lower control arms pivot from the engine cradle. The cradle uses isolation mounts to the body and conventional rubber bushings at the lower control arm pivots. A rubber mount isolates the upper end of the strut.

DRIVE AXLE
REPLACE

NOTE: It is important that the axle not be overextended. When one or both ends of the shaft are disconnected, over-extending the joint may cause separation of internal components, which could lead to failure of the joint.

1. Remove and discard hub nut.
2. Raise and support vehicle.
3. Remove wheel and tire assembly.
4. Install axle shaft boot seal protector J-27812 on outer seal and J-33162 on inner seal, **Fig. 2.**

Fig. 2   Drive axle removal

1 — RACE, C.V. JOINT OUTER	13 — BALL, TRI-POT JOINT (3)
2 — CAGE, C.V. JOINT	14 — THIS NO. NOT USED
3 — RACE, C.V. JOINT INNER	15 — HOUSING ASSY, TRI-POT (LH)
4 — RING, SHAFT RETAINING	16 — HOUSING ASSY, TRI-POT (RH)
5 — BALL (6)	17 — SHAFT, AXLE (RH)
6 — RETAINER, SEAL	18 — RING, SPACER
7 — SEAL, C.V. JOINT	19 — RING, RACE RETAINING
8 — CLAMP, SEAL RETAINING	20 — CLAMP, SEAL RETAINING
9 — SHAFT, AXLE (LH)	21 — RETAINER, NEEDLE
10 — SEAL, TRI-POT JOINT	22 — RING, NEEDLE RETAINER
11 — SPIDER, TRI-POT JOINT	23 — RING, JOINT RETAINING
12 — ROLLER, NEEDLE	

Fig. 3   Exploded view of drive axle

REMOVE AND INSTALL OUTER JOINT SEAL.

REMOVE

1. Remove parts as shown.

INSTALL

1. Flush grease from joint and repack joint with approx. half of grease provided.
2. Put remainder of grease in seal.
3. Install parts as shown. Use tool J-22610 to secure seal retaining clamp.

- Seal groove
- AXLE SHAFT
- SEAL RETAINING CLAMP
- OUTBOARD SEAL
- SEAL RETAINER
- Coat inside of seal lip with grease
- RACE RETAINING RING
- JOINT ASSEMBLY

- Side cutter — Cut off clamp
- SEAL RETAINER
- Brass drift — Lightly tap evenly all around retainer
- REMOVE CLAMP AND RETAINER

- Snap Ring Pliers J-8059 Spread retaining ring ears apart and pull shaft out
- RACE RETAINING RING

REMOVE JOINT ASSEMBLY

- Push assembly onto shaft until retaining ring is seated in groove

INSTALL JOINT ASSEMBLY

- Arbor press
- SEAL RETAINER

INSTALL SEAL RETAINER

DISASSEMBLE AND ASSEMBLE OUTER JOINT ASSEMBLY.

REMOVE

1. Remove parts as shown.

INSTALL

1. Put a light coat of recommended grease on ball grooves of inner and outer races.
2. Install parts as shown.
   NOTICE: Be sure retaining ring side of inner race faces axle shaft.
3. Pack joint with recommended grease.

- BALLS (6)
- INNER RACE
- CAGE
- OUTER RACE

- OUTER RACE
- Remove ball
- INNER RACE
- Brass drift gently tap on cage until tilted enough to remove first ball Remove other balls in similar manner.
- CAGE

DISASSEMBLE AND ASSEMBLE BALLS

- Pivot cage and inner race at 90° to center line of outer race with cage windows aligned with lands of outer race, lift out cage and inner race.
- CAGE
- Land
- Land
- Windows
- OUTER RACE

DISASSEMBLE AND ASSEMBLE CAGE AND INNER RACE TO OUTER RACE

- Rotate up and out of cage
- INNER RACE
- CAGE
- Land
- Cage window

DISASSEMBLE AND ASSEMBLE INNER RACE AND CAGE

Fig. 4   Outer constant velocity joint & seal service

REMOVE AND INSTALL INNER TRI-POT SEAL

REMOVE
1. Remove parts as shown.

INSTALL
1. Flush grease from housing and repack housing with approx. half of grease furnished with new seal.
2. Put remainder of grease in seal.
3. Install parts as shown. Use tool J-22610 to secure seal retaining clamp.

SEAL RETAINING CLAMP

Side cutters

Brass drift – Lightly tap evenly all around retainer

REMOVE AND INSTALL CLAMP & SEAL RETAINER

TRI-POT HOUSING

SHAFT RETAINING RING

SPIDER ASSEMBLY

SEAL RETAINER

TRI-POT JOINT SEAL

SPACER RING

Coat inside seal lip with grease

SEAL RETAINING CLAMP

AXLE

Seal groove

SPACER RING
Slide ring back on axle shaft
NOTICE: Be sure spacer ring is seated in groove at reassembly

SHAFT RETAINING RING
Remove from axle shaft then slide spider assembly off axle

SPIDER ASSEMBLY

SPACER RING

Counter bore in spider assembly must face this end of axle

Snap ring pliers J-8059

REMOVE AND INSTALL SPIDER ASSEMBLY

Fig. 5   Inner tri-pot seal replacement

5. Disconnect toe link rod from knuckle assembly.
6. Disconnect parking brake cables from engine cradle.
7. Remove brake line bracket from underbody in inner wheel house opening.
8. Remove axle shaft from hub and bearing assembly using tool No. J-28733 or equivalent.
9. Support axle shaft and remove clamp bolt from lower control arm ball stud.
10. Separate knuckle from lower control arm.
11. Move strut, knuckle and caliper assembly away from body, and secure in this position.
12. Disengage snap rings retaining drive axle using tools J-33008 and J-2619-01, then carefully pull drive axles from transaxle.
13. Reverse procedure to install. Torque hub nut to 70 ft. lbs., toe link rod nut to 15 ft. lbs., and lower control arm ball stud nut to 33 ft. lbs.

DRIVE AXLE SERVICE

Refer to **Figs. 3, 4 and 5** for service procedures on drive axle assembly.

WHEEL ALIGNMENT
CAMBER
1. Loosen both strut-to-knuckle attaching bolts sufficiently to allow movement between strut and knuckle.
2. Move top of tire inboard or outboard until camber is within specifications, then torque both strut-to-knuckle bolts to 140 ft. lbs.

NOTE: If complete torque cannot be applied to bolts due to inaccessibility, tighten bolts just enough to hold camber position, then remove wheel and wire and apply final torque.

TOE-IN
1. Loosen jam nuts on toe link rod, then rotate rods until toe-in is within specifications, **Fig. 6**.
2. Torque jam nuts to 47 ft. lbs.

NOTE: Use care not to twist or damage rubber boots.

WHEEL BEARING
REPLACE
REMOVAL
1. On vehicles equipped with steel wheels, remove hub cap and loosen hub nut, then raise and support vehi-

ADJUST TOE-IN BY ROTATING

LOOSEN NUT TO ADJUST TOE-IN

Fig. 6   Toe-in adjustment

1 – SHIELD
2 – HUB AND BEARING ASM.
3 – KNUCKLE
4 – KNUCKLE SEAL ASM.
5 – FILL HUB BEARING CAVITY BETWEEN SEALING LIPS WITH .8 GRAMS OF CHASSIS LUBRICANT.
6 – BOLT 75-95 N·m (55-70 FT. LB.)

Fig. 7   Rear wheel hub & bearing assembly

TOOL J-28733

Fig. 8   Hub & bearing assembly removal

Fig. 9 Lower ball joint replacement

Fig. 10 Lower control arm & bushing replacement

cle and remove wheel and tire assembly.

2. On vehicles equipped with 14 inch aluminum wheels, set parking brake, then raise and support vehicle and remove wheel and tire assembly.

3. On all models, install drive axle boot protector J-33162.

4. Remove and discard hub nut.

5. Remove brake caliper and rotor. Suspend caliper from frame with a piece of wire.

6. Remove hub and bearing attaching bolts.

NOTE: If the old bearing is being reinstalled, mark attaching bolts and corresponding holes for installation reference, **Fig. 7.**

7. Remove hub and bearing assembly using tool No. J-28671 or equivalent, **Fig. 8.**

NOTE: If assembly is heavily corroded, ensure hub and bearing are loose in knuckle before using puller tool.

8. Replace knuckle seal if installing new bearing.

CAUTION: Do not move drive axle until hub nut is installed and torqued to specifications.

INSTALLATION

1. Clean and inspect knuckle bore and bearing mating surfaces for dirt, nicks and burrs.

2. If installing new knuckle seal, apply suitable grease to seal and knuckle bore, then press seal into knuckle using tool No. J-28671 or equivalent.

3. Install hub and bearing assembly onto axle shaft. Torque attaching bolts to 55–70 ft. lbs.

4. Install hub nut and torque to 74 ft. lbs.

5. Install brake rotor and caliper.

6. Install wheel and tire assembly, then

lower vehicle and torque hub nut to 200 ft. lbs.

LOWER BALL JOINT
REPLACE

1. Raise and support vehicle.

2. Remove wheel and tire assembly, then the ball stud clamp bolt.

3. Disconnect ball joint from knuckle by tapping with a mallet.

4. Replace ball joint as shown in **Fig. 9.**

LOWER CONTROL ARM & BUSHINGS
REPLACE

1. Raise and support vehicle.

2. Remove wheel and tire assembly, then the ball joint clamp bolt.

3. Disconnect ball joint from knuckle by tapping with a mallet.

4. Remove lower control arm pivot bolts from frame.

5. Replace lower control arm and bushings as shown in **Fig. 10.**

REAR KNUCKLE
REPLACE

Refer to **Fig. 11** for removal and installation procedures.

STRUT ASSEMBLY
REPLACE

1. Remove engine compartment cover.

2. Remove three upper strut nuts and washers, **Fig. 12.**

3. Loosen wheel lug nuts, then raise vehicle and support at rear control arm.

4. Remove wheel and tire assembly, then the brake line retaining clip.

5. Scribe strut and knuckle, **Fig. 13,** for assembly reference.

NOTE: When servicing the jounce bumper, strut mount, strut shield, spring seal or spring insulator, the strut and knuckle must be scribed as shown in **Fig. 13** to maintain the original camber setting. However, it will be necessary to check toe-in setting and adjust as necessary.

When servicing the strut damper, knuckle or rear ride spring, the scribe marks should not be made. However, it will be necessary to check both toe-in and camber settings and correct as necessary.

6. Remove strut attaching nuts and bolts, then the strut assembly and spacer plate.

7. Reverse procedure to install. Torque knuckle attaching nuts to 140 ft. lbs., and upper strut attaching nuts to 18 ft. lbs.

STRUT ASSEMBLY
SERVICE

DISASSEMBLY

1. Clamp strut compressor, tool No. J-26854, in a suitable vise.

2. Install strut assembly into bottom adapter of compressor and install bottom adapter, **Fig. 14.** Ensure strut and locating pins are fully engaged.

3. Rotate strut assembly until top mounting assembly lip is aligned with compressor support notch.

4. Install upper adapter onto top spring

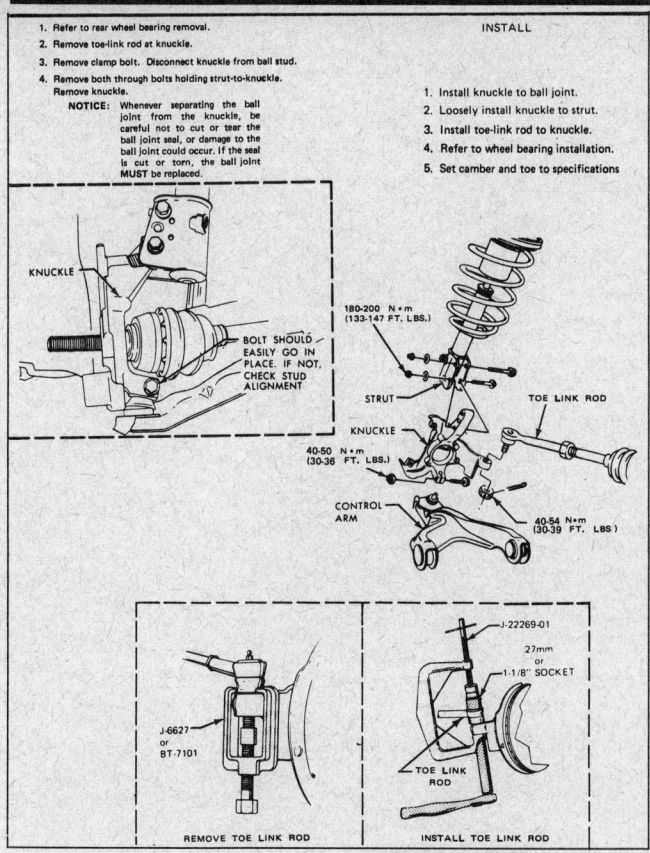

1. Refer to rear wheel bearing removal.
2. Remove toe-link rod at knuckle.
3. Remove clamp bolt. Disconnect knuckle from ball stud.
4. Remove both through bolts holding strut-to-knuckle. Remove knuckle.
   NOTICE: Whenever separating the ball joint from the knuckle, be careful not to cut or tear the ball joint seal, or damage to the ball joint could occur. If the seal is cut or torn, the ball joint MUST be replaced.

INSTALL

1. Install knuckle to ball joint.
2. Loosely install knuckle to strut.
3. Install toe-link rod to knuckle.
4. Refer to wheel bearing installation.
5. Set camber and toe to specifications

Fig. 11 Rear knuckle replacement

1 – NUT, MOUNT
2 – MOUNT ASM.
3 – WASHER, SEAT
4 – INSULATOR, UPPER SPRING
5 – SHIELD
6 – INSULATOR LOWER SPRING
7 – LOWER SPRING SEAT
8 – SPRING
9 – BUMPER
10 – SEAT ASM.
11 – WASHER, MOUNT UPPER
12 – STRUT ASM. RR. SUSP.
13 – MOUNTING BOLTS STRUT
14 – KNUCKLE & HUB ASM.
15 – CRADLE ASM.

16 – MOUNTING NUTS, STRUT
17 – WASHERS, STRUT LOWER
18 – WASHERS, STRUT UPPER
19 – NUTS, STRUT UPPER
20 – MOUNT ASM.-RR. STRUT
21 – ASM. REAR SUSPENSION
22 – BRAKE LINE CLIP
23 – BOLT, BRAKE LINE CLIP
24 – HOSE ASM. RR BRAKE LH. & RH.
25 – CALIPER ASM.

Fig. 12 Strut assembly replacement

seal, **Fig. 14,** so long stud is at high location to strut flange.
5. Rotate compressor forcing screw clockwise until top support flange contacts top adapter, and continue turning screw to compress strut spring.
6. Install second upper adapter over spring seat assembly, then rotate forcing screw counterclockwise until strut spring tension is relieved.
7. Remove top adapters, bottom adapter and strut.

1. USING A SHARP TOOL, SCRIBE THE KNUCKLE ALONG THE LOWER OUTBOARD STRUT RADIUS, AS IN VIEW A.
2. SCRIBE THE STRUT FLANGE ON THE INBOARD SIDE, ALONG THE CURVE OF THE KNUCKLE, AS IN VIEW B.
3. MAKE A CHISEL MARK ACROSS THE STRUT/KNUCKLE INTERFACE, AS IN VIEW C.
4. ON REASSEMBLY, CAREFULLY MATCH THE MARKS TO THE COMPONENTS.

Fig. 13 Scribing strut & knuckle

ASSEMBLY

1. Perform steps 1 and 2 as outlined in the "Disassembly" procedure.
2. Rotate strut assembly until mounting flange is facing outward, opposite compressor forcing screw.
3. Install strut components, **Fig. 15.** Ensure spring is properly seated on bottom spring plate.
4. Install strut spring seat assembly on top of spring with long stud positioned 180° from strut mounting flange.
5. Install top adapter over spring seat assembly.
6. Rotate compressor forcing screw until compressor top support just contacts top adapter. Do not compress spring.
7. Install strut alignment rod through top spring seat and thread onto damper shaft hand tight, **Fig. 15.**
8. Rotate compressor forcing screw clockwise to compress spring until damper shaft is exposed enough so nut can be threaded securely, then install the nut. Ensure damper shaft comes through center of spring seat opening to prevent damage.

NOTE: Do not compress spring until bottomed.

9. Remove alignment rod, then install mount and torque nut to 65 ft. lbs.
10. Rotate compressor forcing screw counterclockwise and remove strut assembly from compressor.

Fig. 14 Removing damper & coil spring from strut

SPECIAL TOOL J-26584-430
LONG STUD 180° FROM STRUT FLANGE
SUPPORT
ADAPTER J-26584-430
BOTTOM ADAPTER J-26584-89
DIRECTION OF LOWER STRUT FLANGE

WASHER

NUT 85 N·m
(65 FT. LB.)

MOUNT
ASM.

SEAT
ASM.

WASHER

INSULATOR

BUMPER

SHIELD

SPRING

SPRING TO BE INSTALLED
WITH SMALLEST COIL AT
LOWEST POSITION, AND
PLACED RELATIVE TO THE
LOWER SPRING SEAT AS
SHOWN

INSULATOR

LOWER
SPRING
SEAT

ABSORBER & STRUT ASM.

ALIGNMENT ROD
J-26584-27

DAMPER
SHAFT

LOWER
SEAT

SPRING

14 MM + 6 MM

Fig. 15   Strut assembly alignment & components

PARKING BRAKE
ADJUST

1. Jack up both rear wheels with parking brake fully released.
2. Apply suitable lubricant to groove in equalizer nut.
3. Remove slack from cable by tightening equalizer nut while preventing brake cable stud from turning.

NOTE: After tightening nut, ensure caliper levers are against stops on caliper housing. If levers are not against stops, loosen cable until they return.

4. Activate parking brake several times to check adjustment. The parking brake lever should move 5–8 notches when a force is applied perpendicularly at a midway point on handle grip.
5. Lower rear wheels and ensure levers are on caliper stops. If necessary, back off parking brake adjuster to keep levers on stops.

MASTER CYLINDER
REPLACE

1. Disconnect both brake lines from master cylinder.
2. Remove 2 master cylinder attaching nuts and the master cylinder.

3. Reverse procedure to install. Torque master cylinder attaching nuts to 22–30 ft. lbs., and brake line nuts to 120–180 inch lbs.

POWER BRAKE UNIT
REPLACE

1. Remove 2 master cylinder-to-power brake unit attaching nuts, and position master cylinder aside with brake lines attached.
2. Disconnect power brake unit pushrod from brake pedal.
3. Remove power brake unit attaching nuts and the power brake unit.
4. Reverse procedure to install. Torque attaching nuts to 22–30 ft. lbs.

Front Suspension & Steering Section

DESCRIPTION

The front suspension, **Fig. 1,** is a conventional short and long arm design with coil springs. The control arms are attached with bolts and bushings at the inner pivot points, and are attached to the steering knuckle/front wheel spindle assembly at the outer pivot points.

WHEEL ALIGNMENT
CAMBER

1. Remove upper ball joint as described under "Upper Ball Joint, Replace."
2. Camber may be increased approximately 1° by rotating ½ turn and reinstalling with flat of upper flange on inboard side of control arm, **Fig. 2.**

CASTER

1. Remove upper control arm as described under "Upper Control Arm, Replace."
2. Adjust caster by installing washers between legs of upper control arm, **Fig. 3.**

NOTE: When caster is adjusted, two washers totalling .472 inch (12mm) must be installed, with one at each end of locating tube.

TOE-IN

1. Loosen jam nuts on toe link rod, then rotate rods until toe-in is within specifications, **Fig. 4.**
2. Torque jam nuts to 47 ft. lbs.

NOTE: Use care not to twist or damage rubber boots.

WHEEL BEARING
ADJUST

1. Raise and support vehicle.
2. Remove wheel and tire assembly.
3. Remove dust cap from hub, then the cotter pin from spindle and spindle nut.
4. Torque spindle nut to 12 ft. lbs. while rotating wheel forward by hand.
5. Back off spindle nut until just loose, then hand tighten nut and back off again until either hole in spindle lines up with hole in nut.

NOTE: Do not back off nut more than ½ flat.

6. Install new cotter pin, then measure hub end play. With bearing properly adjusted, end play should measure .001–.005 inch.

WHEEL BEARING
REPLACE

REMOVAL

1. Raise and support vehicle.
2. Remove wheel and tire assembly, then disconnect brake caliper from steering knuckle and suspend from frame with a piece of wire. Do not let brake lines support weight of caliper.
3. Remove hub dust cap, cotter pin, spindle nut and washer.
4. Remove hub and bearing from spindle.
5. Remove outer bearing from hub, then pry out grease seal and remove inner bearing. Discard seal.

INSTALLATION

1. Clean all grease from hub, spindle and bearing.
2. Apply a thin film of suitable grease to spindle at outer bearing seat and the inner bearing seat, shoulder and seal seat.
3. Apply grease inboard of each bearing race in hub.
4. Completely fill bearing cone and roller assemblies with grease.
5. Install inner bearing into hub and apply additional grease outboard of bearing.
6. Install new grease seal flush with hub and lubricate seal lip with a thin coating of grease.
7. Install hub and rotor assembly onto spindle, then position outer bearing in race.
8. Install washer and nut, then adjust bearing as previously described.
9. Install brake caliper, then the wheel and tire assembly.

UPPER BALL JOINT
REPLACE

1. Raise and support vehicle.
2. Remove wheel and tire assembly, then support lower control arm with a suitable jack.
3. Remove upper ball joint stud nut, then reinstall nut finger tight.
4. Install tool No. J-26407 with cup end over lower ball joint stud nut. Rotate threaded end of tool until upper stud is free of steering knuckle, then remove tool and nut from stud, **Fig. 5.**
5. Remove 2 ball joint-to-upper control arm attaching bolts and nuts.
6. Note position of flat on ball joint for proper installation, then remove ball joint from vehicle.
7. Reverse procedure to install. Torque ball joint-to-upper control arm attaching bolts to 28 ft. lbs. Torque stud nut to 35 ft. lbs., then tighten nut up to an additional ⅙ turn to align cotter pin hole.

LOWER BALL JOINT
REPLACE

The lower ball joint is permanently attached to the lower control arm and cannot be serviced separately. If the lower ball joint requires replacement, the entire lower control arm must be replaced.

SHOCK ABSORBER
REPLACE

1. Raise and support vehicle.
2. Remove wheel and tire assembly, then the 2 shock absorber upper attaching bolts.
3. Remove shock absorber lower attaching bolts and nut, **Fig. 1.**
4. Remove shock absorber from vehicle.
5. Reverse procedure to install. Torque upper attaching bolts to 20 ft. lbs., and lower attaching bolt to 35 ft. lbs.

STABILIZER BAR
REPLACE

1. Raise and support vehicle.
2. Remove stabilizer bar attaching bolt and nut and associated components from lower control arms, **Fig. 1.**
3. Remove stabilizer bar clamp and the stabilizer bar from vehicle.
4. Reverse procedure to install. Torque clamp attaching bolts to 15 ft. lbs., and stabilizer bar attaching bolt to 16 ft. lbs.

LOWER CONTROL ARM & COIL SPRING
REPLACE

1. Raise vehicle and support at frame crossmember.
2. Remove wheel and tire assembly, then disconnect stabilizer bar from lower control arm.
3. Disconnect tie rod from steering knuckle, then the shock absorber from lower control arm.
4. Support lower control arm with a suitable jack, then remove lower ball joint stud nut and press ball joint out of steering knuckle, using tool No. J-26407, **Fig. 6.** Position steering knuckle and hub aside.
5. Loosen lower control arm pivot bolts.
6. Install a safety chain through coil spring, then slowly lower jack and remove spring, **Fig. 1.**
7. Remove lower control arm attaching bolts and the lower control arm.

NOTE: It may be necessary to loosen or remove steering gear attaching bolts to gain access to the control arm attaching bolt at the crossmember.

FRONT SPRING

FRONT SUSPENSION ASM.

FRONT STABILIZER ASSEMBLY

VIEW A

VIEW B

VIEW C

FRONT SHOCK ABSORBER ASSEMBLY

1—SPRING

2—WELD NUTS

3—BOLT/SCREW TORQUE 18-24 N•m (13-17 FT. LB.)

4—CLAMP

5—BUSHING

6—FRONT RAIL

7—NOTE: TIGHTEN UNTIL NUT BOTTOMS ON END OF BOLT THREAD

8—WASHER

9—GROMMET

10—SHAFT FRONT STABILIZER NOTE PROTRUDING SHAPE ON LEFT-HAND END

11—SPACER

12—BOLT NOTE: TORQUE FROM THIS END 17-26 N•m (13-20 FT. LBS.)

13—SHOCK ABSORBER

14—SUPPORT SHOCK ABSORBER

15—BOLT

16—CONTROL ARM

17—NUT

18—BOLT

Fig. 1   Front suspension

NOTE: TO INCREASE CAMBER, DISCONNECT UPPER BALL JOINT, ROTATE 180° TO POSITION "FLAT" OF FLANGE INBOARD, THEN RECONNECT BALLJOINT.

Fig. 2   Camber adjustment

ADJUST TOE-IN BY ROTATING

LOOSEN NUT TO ADJUST TOE-IN

Fig. 4   Toe-in adjustment

8. Reverse procedure to install, noting the following:
   a. Install control arm attaching bolts finger tight. Do not torque bolts until all other components have been assembled and torqued to specifications.
   b. Torque ball joint stud nut to 55 ft. lbs.
   c. Torque stabilizer bar attaching bolt to 16 ft. lbs.
   d. Torque tie rod attaching nut to 29 ft. lbs.
   e. Torque shock absorber lower attaching bolt to 35 ft. lbs.
   f. If steering gear attaching bolts have been loosened or removed, install new bolts and torque to 21 ft. lbs.
   g. Torque control arm-to-body attaching bolt to 62 ft. lbs. and control arm-to-crossmember nut to 52 ft. lbs.

1 —	FRONT WASHER	SERVICE CHANGE		
2 —	REAR WASHER			NET
3 —	UPPER CONTROL	FRONT	REAR	CHANGE
	ARM SUPPORT	3MM	9MM	+1°
	BRACKET	9MM	3MM	−1°

Fig. 3   Caster adjustment

UPPER CONTROL ARM
REPLACE

1. Raise and support vehicle.
2. Remove wheel and tire assembly, then the rivet securing brake line clip to upper control arm.
3. Support lower control arm with a suitable jack, then remove upper ball joint as described under "Upper Ball Joint, Replace."
4. Remove control arm attaching bolt and the control arm from vehicle.
5. Reverse procedure to install. Torque control arm attaching bolt to 66 ft. lbs.

NOTE: Washers and shims, **Fig. 3**, must be installed in their original positions unless a change in caster angle is desired.

CROSSMEMBER BUMPER
REPLACE

1. Remove coil spring as described under "Lower Control Arm & Coil Spring, Replace."
2. Remove crossmember bumper from vehicle.
3. Reverse procedure to install.

STEERING KNUCKLE
REPLACE

1. Raise and support vehicle. Support lower control arm with a suitable jack.
2. Remove wheel and tire assembly, then disconnect brake caliper from steering knuckle and suspend from frame with a piece of wire. Do not let brake lines support weight of caliper.

J-26407

Fig. 5   Upper ball joint removal

HEAVY FLAT WASHER

J-26407

Fig. 6   Lower ball joint removal

STEERING GEAR TO CROSS MEMBER

1—BOLT

2—STEERING ASSEMBLY

3—CROSS MEMBER

4—NUT 43 N•m (32 FT. LBS.)

5—WASHER

6—STUD ASSEMBLY 48 N•m (36 FT. LBS.)

7—DAMPER, STEERING LINK

STEERING LINKAGE DAMPER ASM.

Fig. 7   Steering gear replacement

NOTE: Install a block of wood between brake shoes to hold piston in caliper bore.

3. Remove hub, disc and splash shield.
4. Remove both ball joint studs as previously described.
5. Disconnect tie rod end from steering knuckle.
6. Press both ball joint studs from steering knuckle using tool No. J-26407 or equivalent.
7. Remove ball joint stud nuts, then the steering knuckle.

8. Reverse procedure to install, noting the following torques: lower ball joint stud nut, 55 ft. lbs.; upper ball joint stud nut, 35 ft. lbs.; splash shield bolts, 7 ft. lbs.; tie rod nut, 29 ft. lbs.

MANUAL STEERING GEAR
REPLACE

1. Raise and support vehicle.
2. Remove both front crossmember braces.

3. Remove flex coupling pinch bolt from shaft.
4. Remove outer tie rod cotter pins and nuts on both sides, and disconnect tie rods from steering knuckles.
5. Remove 4 steering gear attaching bolts and the steering gear, **Fig. 7.**
6. Reverse procedure to install, noting the following torques: flex coupling bolt, 46 ft. lbs.; steering gear bolts, 21 ft. lbs.; tie rod nuts, 29 ft. lbs., plus up to an additional ⅛ turn to align cotter pin hole; front crossmember brace bolts, 20 ft. lbs.

AIR CONDITIONING

TABLE OF CONTENTS

American Motors Corp. System Testing

INDEX

Evaporator Pressure Gauge Reading	Evaporator Temperature F°	High Pressure Gauge Reading	Ambient Temperature
0	-21°	45	20°
0.6	-20°	55	30°
2.4	-15°	72	40°
4.5	-10°	86	50°
6.8	-5°	105	60°
9.2	0°	126	70°
11.8	5°	140	75°
14.7	10°	160	80°
17.1	15°	185	90°
21.1	20°	195	95°
22.5	22°	220	100°
23.9	24°	240	105°
25.4	26°	260	110°
26.9	28°	275	115°
28.5	30°	290	120°
37.0	40°	305	125°
46.7	50°	325	130°
57.7	60°		
70.1	70°		
84.1	80°		
99.6	90°		
116.9	100°		
136.0	110°		
157.1	120°		
179.0	130°		

Fig. 1   Pressure-temperature relationship (Typical). Conditions equivalent to 30 mph or 1750 engine rpm

GENERAL PRECAUTIONS

The Freon refrigerant used is also known as R-12 or F-12. It is colorless and odorless both as a gas and a liquid. Since it boils (vaporizes) at −21.7°F., it will usually be in a vapor state when being handled in a repair shop. But if a portion of the liquid coolant should come in contact with the hands or face, note that its temperature momentarily will be at least 22° below zero.

Protective goggles should be worn when opening any refrigerant lines. If liquid coolant does touch the eyes, bathe the eyes quickly in cold water, then apply a bland disinfectant oil to the eyes. See an eye doctor.

When checking a system for leaks with a torch type leak detector, do not breathe the vapors coming from the flame. Do not discharge refrigerant in the area of a live flame. A poisonous phosgene gas is produced when R-12 or F-12 is burned. While the small amount of this gas produced by a leak detector is not harmful unless inhaled directly at the flame, the quantity of refrigerant released into the air when a system is purged can be extremely dangerous if allowed to come in contact with an open flame. Thus, when purging a system, be sure that the discharge hose is routed to a well ventilated place where no flame is present. Under these conditions the refrigerant will be quickly dissipated into the surrounding air.

Never allow the temperature of refrigerant drums to exceed 125°F. The resultant increase in temperature will cause a corresponding increase in pressure which may cause the safety plug to release or the drum to burst.

AIR CONDITIONING

If it is necessary to heat a drum of refrigerant when charging a system, the drum should be placed in water that is no hotter than 125°F. Never use a blow torch or other open flame. If possible, a pressure release mechanism should be attached before the drum is heated.

When connecting and disconnecting service gauges on A/C system, ensure that gauge hand valves are fully closed and that compressor service valves, if equipped, are in the back-seated (fully counterclockwise) position. Do not disconnect gauge hoses from service port adapters, if used, while gauges are connected to A/C system. To disconnect hoses, always remove adapter from service port. Do not disconnect hoses from gauge manifold while connected to A/C system, as refrigerant will be rapidly discharged.

After disconnecting gauge lines, check the valve areas to be sure service valves are correctly seated and Schraeder valves, if used, are not leaking.

EXERCISE SYSTEM

An important fact most owners ignore is that A/C units must be used periodically. Manufacturers caution that when the air conditioner is not used regularly, particularly during cold months, it should be turned on for a few minutes once every two or three weeks while the engine is running. This keeps the system in good operating condition.

Checking out the system for the effects of disuse before the onset of summer is one of the most important aspects of A/C servicing.

First clean out the condenser core, mounted in all cases at the front of the radiator. All obstructions, such as leaves, bugs and dirt, must be removed, as they will reduce heat transfer and impair the efficiency of the system. Make sure the space between the condenser and the radiator also is free of foreign matter.

Make certain the evaporator water drain is open. The evaporator cools and dehumidifies the air before it enters the passenger compartment: there, the refrigerant is changed from a liquid to a vapor. As the core cools the air, moisture condenses on it but is prevented from collecting in the evaporator by the water vane.

PERFORMANCE TEST

The system should be operated for at least 15 minutes to allow sufficient time for all parts to become completely stabilized. Determine if the system is fully charged by the use of test gauges and sight glass if one is installed on system. Head pressure will read from 180 psi to 220 psi or higher, depending upon ambient temperature and the type unit being tested. The sight glass should be free of bubbles if a glass is used in the system. Low side pressures should read approximately 15 psi to 30 psi, again

1 — TO SERVICE PORT
2 — TO HOSE
3 — TO COMPRESSOR

VIEW A — FRONT-SEATED

VIEW B — BACK-SEATED

VIEW C — MID POSITIONED

Fig. 2   Service valve positions (Typical).

depending on the ambient temperature and the unit being tested. It is not feasible to give a definite reading for all types of systems used, as the type control and component installation used on a particular system will directly influence the pressure readings on the high and low sides, **Fig. 1.**

The high side pressure will definitely be affected by the ambient or outside air temperature. A system that is operating normally will indicate a high side gauge reading between 150–170 psi with an 80°F ambient temperature. The same system will register 210–230 psi with an ambient temperature of 100°F. No two systems will register exactly the same, which requires that allowance for variations in head pressures must be considered. Following are the most important normal readings likely to be encountered during the season.

Ambient Temp.	High Side Pressure
80	150–170
90	175–195
95	185–205
100	210–230
105	230–250
110	250–270

RELATIVE TEMPERATURE OF HIGH AND LOW SIDES

The high side of the system should be uniformly hot to the touch throughout. A difference in temperature will indicate a partial blockage of liquid or gas at this point.

The low side of the system should be uniformly cool to the touch with no excessive sweating of the suction line or low side service valve. Excessive sweating or frosting of the low side service valve usually indicates an expansion valve is allowing an excessive amount of refrigerant into the evaporator.

EVAPORATOR OUTPUT

At this point, provided all other inspection tests have been performed, and components have been found to operate as they should, a rapid cooling down of the interior of the vehicle should result. The use of a thermometer is not necessary to determine evaporator output. Bringing all units to the correct operating specifications will insure that the evaporator performs as intended.

DISCHARGING & EVACUATING SYSTEM

SERVICE NOTE: On all models equipped with the York 2 cylinder compressor, 1981 California models equipped with 6-258 engine and Sankyo 5 cylinder rotary compressor and all 1982–85 models, it is not necessary to discharge refrigerant system for compressor removal. The compressor can be isolated from the system, eliminating need for recharging when performing compressor service or oil level check. Proceed as follows:

Isolating Compressor From System
1. Connect pressure gauge and manifold set, then close both gauge hand valves and crack (mid-position) both service valves, **Fig. 2.**
2. Start engine and operate air conditioning.
3. Slowly turn suction service valve clockwise toward the front seated position, **Fig. 2.** When pressure reading drops to zero or less stop engine and finish front-seating suction service valve, then front-seat discharge service valve, **Fig. 2.**
4. Slowly loosen oil sump filler plug to relieve any internal pressures in the compressor.

NOTE: A face shield should be worn when loosening the oil filler plug.

5. Compressor is now isolated from system, service valve can be removed from compressor. Plug all openings to prevent entry of dirt and moisture.

Purging Compressor of Air
The compressor must be purged of air whenever it has been isolated from the system for oil level check or compressor service.
1. Connect service valve and lines to compressor, then cap service gauge ports on both service valves.
2. Back-seat suction valve to allow refrigerant to enter compressor.
3. Place discharge service valve in mid-

Fig. 3   Manifold gauge set hose connections (Typical).

position, then loosen discharge service valve gauge port cap to allow refrigerant to force air from compressor.
4. Back-seat discharge service valve and tighten gauge port cap.
5. Remove manifold and gauge set.

DISCHARGING SYSTEM

1. Connect gauges into system, **Fig. 3**, and adjust controls for maximum cooling. This is necessary when the system has not been operating to return excess oil to the compressor.
2. Operate engine for 10 to 15 minutes to stabilize the system at 1500–1750 rpm.
3. Adjust engine speed to slow idle, then shut off engine and controls.
4. Open low side hand manifold valve slightly, using a container to catch oil and refrigerant. Do not discharge the refrigerant near an open flame as a toxic gas (phosgene) can result.
5. Open high side manifold valve slightly.

NOTE: Open hand valve(s) only enough to bleed refrigerant from system. Too rapid purging will draw excessive oil from compressor and system.

6. Close gauge manifold hand valves when refrigerant ceases to bleed from discharge hose and manifold gauges read zero.

EVACUATE SYSTEM WITH VACUUM PUMP

Vacuum pumps suitable for removing air and moisture from A/C systems are commercially available. A specification for system pump-down used here is 28 to 29½ inches vacuum. This reading can be attained at or near sea level only. For each 1000 feet of altitude this operation is being

performed, the reading will be 1 inch vacuum lower. As an example, at 5000 feet elevation, only 23–24½ inches of vacuum can be obtained.

CAUTION: The system must be completely discharged before it can be evacuated. Damage to vacuum pump may result if pressurized refrigerant is allowed to enter.

1. With gauges connected into system, remove cap from vacuum hose connector. Install center hose from gauge manifold to vacuum pump connector. Mid-position high and low side compressor service valves (if used). Open high and low side gauge manifold hand valves.
2. Operate vacuum pump a minimum of 30 minutes for air and moisture removal. Watch compound gauge that system pumps down into a vacuum. System will reach 28–29½ inches vacuum in not over 5 minutes. If system does not pump down, check all connections and leak-test if necessary.
3. Close gauge manifold hand valves and shut off vacuum pump.
4. Check ability of system to hold vacuum. Watch compound gauge to see that gauge does not rise at a faster rate than 1 inch vacuum every 4 or 5 minutes. If compound gauge rises at too rapid a rate, install partial charge and leak-test. Then evacuate system as outlined above.
5. If system holds vacuum, charge system with refrigerant.

EVACUATE SYSTEM USING CHARGING STATION

A vacuum pump is built into the charging station and is constructed to withstand repeated and prolonged use without damage. Complete moisture removal from the

system is possible only with a vacuum pump constructed for the purpose.

CAUTION: The system must be completely discharged before it can be evacuated. Damage to the vacuum pump may result if pressurized refrigerant is allowed to enter.

1. Connect hose to vacuum pump if system was discharged through charging station.
2. Open high and low side gauge valves of charging station.
3. Connect station into 110-volt current.
4. Engage "Off-On" switch to vacuum pump according to directions of specific station being used.
5. System should pump down into a 28–29½ inch vacuum in not more than 5 minutes. If system fails to meet this specification, repair as necessary.
6. Operate pump a minimum of 30 minutes to remove all air and moisture.
7. Close high and low side gauge valves. Open switch to turn off pump.
8. Check ability of system to hold vacuum by watching compound gauge to see that it does not rise at a rate higher than 1 inch of vacuum every 4 or 5 minutes: If rise rate is not within specifications, repair system as necessary. If rise rate is within specifications, charge system with refrigerant.

CHARGING THE SYSTEM
Charging Procedure
Using Multi-Refrigerant Can Opener

1. Connect pressure gauge and manifold assembly J-23575 or equivalent. Keep both service valves in mid-position.
2. Close both gauge hand valves and disconnect service hose from vacuum pump.
3. Connect service hose to center of refrigerant can opener. Close valves on dispenser.
4. Attach refrigerant cans to opener. Refer to A/C Data Table for proper weight of refrigerant for vehicle being serviced.
5. Open one petcock valve and loosen center service hose at gauge to allow refrigerant to purge air from hose. Tighten hose and close petcock valve.
6. Open suction gauge hand valve and one petcock valve. Do not open high pressure gauge hand valve.
7. Start engine and set A/C system controls to maximum cooling position. Compressor will help pull refrigerant gas into suction side of system.

NOTE: Refrigerant cans can be placed in pan of water no hotter than 125°F to aid charging process.

8. When first can is empty, open next valve to continue charging until specified amount of refrigerant is in system.

Frost line on can may be used as a guide when specifications call for using part of full can. If a scale is available, weigh cans before and during charging procedure to ensure accurate filling.

9. When system is fully charged, close suction gauge hand valve and all petcock valves.

10. Operate system for 5–10 minutes to allow it to stabilize and to determine if system cycles properly.

11. After checking operation of system, backseat suction and discharge service valves to normal operating position by turning valves fully counterclockwise.

12. Loosen pressure gauge and manifold assembly service hoses to release refrigerant trapped in hoses. Remove pressure gauge and manifold assembly and install dust caps on fittings.

Using Charging Station J-23500-01

1. After discharging and evacuating system, close low pressure valve on charging station. Fully open left hand refrigerant control valve at base of cylinder and high pressure valve on charging station and allow required charge of refrigerant to enter high side of system. When full charge has entered system, close refrigerant control valve and high pressure valve on charging station.

NOTE: If bubbles appear in the sight glass, tilt the charging station back momentarily.

CAUTION: Do not permit level of liquid to drop below zero mark on cylinder sight glass.

2. After charging is completed, close manifold gauges and check high and low pressures and system operation.

CAUTION: Read gauges with high and low pressure valves closed on charging station. Low pressure gauge can be damaged if both high and low pressure valves are opened.

3. Close all valves on charging station and close refrigerant drum valve when all operations are finished.

4. After completing operational check, back-seat suction and discharge service valves to their normal operating position by turning them fully counterclockwise.

5. Disconnect high and low pressure charging hoses from compressor.

6. Open valve on top of cylinder to remove remaining refrigerant as charging cylinder is not designed to store refrigerant.

7. Replace quick seal caps on compressor service valves.

LEAK TEST SYSTEM

The propane torch Halide Leak Detector is the most widely used of the detection devices. Therefore, only the procedure for this device will be given. The procedure is the same for any electronic detector, except that the pick-up device registers the presence of refrigerant by a flashing light or high pitched squeal instead of changing the color of the flame. All other steps in preparing the system and leak testing are the same and can be followed as outlined below:

1. Stabilize system at 1500–1750 rpm. If system is empty of refrigerant, it will be necessary to install a partial charge before continuing. With gauges connected into system, adjust A/C controls for maximum cooling. Operate for 10 to 15 minutes, then shut off car engine.

2. Light leak detector. Open valve to a low flame that will not blow itself out. Warm up until copper element turns cherry red. Lower flame until flame tip is even with or slightly below center of element. For electronic tester, follow preparation procedure as given in operating instructions.

3. Move leak detector pick-up under hoses, joints, seals, and any possible place for a leak to occur.

NOTE: Freon 12 refrigerant is heavier than air and will move downward. If concentration of refrigerant is located, move pick-up upward to locate leak. Do not inhale fumes produced by burning refrigerant.

4. Watch for color change of flame: Pale blue, no refrigerant; yellow, small amount of refrigerant; purplish-blue, large amount of refrigerant. Repair system as necessary if leaks are located.

5. Check sensitivity of reaction plate: Pass pick-up hose over empty can or crack open refrigerant container; flame should show violent reaction. If no color change, replace reaction plate, following instructions accompanying leak detector. Too high a flame will result in short life to reaction plate and poor reaction and will soon burn out element.

6. Charge system if repairs were necessary.

American Motors Corp. System Servicing

INDEX

OIL CHARGE

DELCO AIR 4 CYLINDER RADIAL COMPRESSOR

Oil Charge-Component Replacement

If there are no signs of excessive leakage, add the following amount of oil depending on component to be replaced.

Evaporator .... 3 ounces
Condenser .... 1 ounce

If accumulator or compressor are to be replaced, drain oil from component to be replaced and measure, then add same amount of new oil to replacement compo-

nent plus one additional ounce.

NOTE: The radial 4 cylinder compressor does not have an oil sump.

Oil Charge-Leak Condition

On models with radial 4 cylinder compressor, it will only be necessary to remove and drain and measure oil from accumulator assembly in cases of excessive oil leakage. The radial 4 cylinder compressor does not have an oil sump, therefore it is not necessary to remove compressor in cases of oil leakage. If amount of oil recovered is 2 ounces or more, add same amount of new refrigerant oil to system. If

amount of oil recovered is less than 2 ounces, add two ounces of new refrigerant oil to system.

NOTE: If accumulator is replaced one additional ounce of oil must be added to replace amount captured by dessicant in old accumulator.

OIL LEVEL CHECK

NOTE: The oil level of these compressors should be checked whenever refrigerant has been lost due to leakage or through

A/C Data Table

Year	Model	Refrigerant Capacity, Lbs.	Refrigeration Oil			Compressor Clutch Air Gap Inch
			Viscosity	Total System Capacity, Ounces	Compressor Oil Level Check, Inches	
AMERICAN MOTORS						
1980	York 2 Cyl. Comp.	①	②	7	③	—
	Delco Air 4 Cyl. Comp.	①	525	6	④	.020–.040
1981	York 2 Cyl. Comp.	2	②	7	③	—
	Delco Air 4 Cyl. Comp.	2	525	6	④	.020–.040
	Sankyo 5 Cyl. Comp.	2	500	7–8	④	.016–.031
1982–83	All	2	500	7–8	④	.016–.031
1984–85	All	2	500	4–6	④	.016–.031

①—AMX, Concord & Spirit, 2; Pacer 2⅛.
②—Suniso 5G or Capella E.
③—York Comp.—Vertical mount., ⅞–1⅛; horizontal mount., 13/16–1 3/16. Tecumseh Comp.—Vertical mount., ⅞–1⅜; horizontal mount., ⅞–1⅝.
④—Note that "Oil level inches" cannot be checked. Refer to total capacity in ounces. See text for procedure.

normal system servicing.

SANKYO 5 CYL. ROTARY COMPRESSOR

1981 California Models W/6-258 Engine & All 1982–85

When installing a replacement compressor, proceed as follows:

1. Isolate compressor from system, then remove compressor.
2. Remove oil plug from compressor, then drain refrigerant oil into a calibrated container.
3. Drain refrigerant oil from compressor to be installed.
4. Add the same amount of refrigerant oil removed from compressor to be replaced plus 1 ounce to the compressor to be installed.

5. Install drain plug, then install and purge air from compressor.

YORK

1. Connect manifold gauge set, then operate system for approximately 10 minutes or until system pressures stabilize. This will allow oil in the system to return to compressor sump.
2. Isolate compressor as outlined earlier.
3. Slowly loosen compressor oil filler plug to relieve any internal pressures in compressor.

NOTE: A face shield should be worn when loosening or removing oil filler plug.

4. Insert clean dipstick into filler plug hole until it bottoms in sump, **Fig. 1**.

NOTE: Ensure keyway in shaft faces head of compressor before checking oil level.

5. Remove dipstick and measure oil level. Refer to "A/C Data Table" and add refrigerant oil as necessary. Install filler plug and O-ring.
6. Purge air from compressor.

CHARGING VALVE LOCATION

On models with 6 cylinder engine, the high and low pressure service ports are located on the compressor; On models with 4 cylinder engine, the high and low pressure service ports are located on service valve adapter.

Fig. 1 York compressor oil level dipstick fabrication.

Chrysler Corp. System Testing

INDEX

GENERAL PRECAUTIONS

The Freon refrigerant used is also known as R-12 or F-12. It is odorless and colorless both as a gas and a liquid. Since it boils (vaporizes) at −21.7°F., it will usually be in a vapor state when being handled in a repair shop. But if a portion of the liquid coolant should come in contact with the hands or face, note that its temperature momentarily will be at least 22° below zero.

Protective goggles should be worn when opening any refrigerant lines. If liquid coolant does touch the eyes, bathe the eyes quickly in cold water, then apply a bland disinfectant oil to the eyes. See an eye doctor.

When checking a system for leaks with a torch type leak detector, do not breathe the vapors coming from the flame. Do not discharge refrigerant in the area of a live flame. A poisonous phosgene gas is produced when R-12 or F-12 is burned. While the small amount of gas produced by a leak detector is not harmful unless inhaled directly at the flame, the quantity of refrigerant released into the air when a system is purged can be extremely dangerous if allowed to come in contact with an open flame. Thus, when purging a system, be sure that the discharge hose is routed to a well ventilated place where no flame is present. Under these conditions the refrigerant will be quickly dissipated into the surrounding air.

Never allow the temperature of refrigerant drums to exceed 125°F. The resultant increase in temperature will cause a corresponding increase in pressure which may cause the safety plug to release or the drum to burst.

If it is necessary to heat a drum of refrigerant when charging a system, the drum should be placed in water that is no hotter than 125°F. Never use a blow torch or other open flame. If possible, a pressure release mechanism should be attached before the drum is heated.

When connecting and disconnecting service gauges on A/C system, ensure that gauge hand valves are fully closed and that compressor service valves, if equipped, are in the back-seated (fully counterclockwise) position. Do not disconnect gauge hoses from service port adapters, if used, while gauges are connected to

Evaporator Pressure Gauge Reading	Evaporator Temperature F°	High Pressure Gauge Reading	Ambient Temperature
0	−21°	45	20°
0.6	−20°	55	30°
2.4	−15°	72	40°
4.5	−10°	86	50°
6.8	− 5°	105	60°
9.2	0°	126	70°
11.8	5°	140	75°
14.7	10°	160	80°
17.1	15°	185	90°
21.1	20°	195	95°
22.5	22°	220	100°
23.9	24°	240	105°
25.4	26°	260	110°
26.9	28°	275	115°
28.5	30°	290	120°
37.0	40°	305	125°
46.7	50°	325	130°
57.7	60°		
70.1	70°		
84.1	80°		
99.6	90°		
116.9	100°		
136.0	110°		
157.1	120°		
179.0	130°		

Fig. 1 Pressure-temperature relationship (Typical). Conditions equivalent to 30 mph or 1750 engine rpm

A/C system. To disconnect hoses, always remove adapter from service port. Do not disconnect hoses from gauge manifold while connected to A/C system, as refrigerant will be rapidly discharged.

After disconnecting gauge lines, check the valve areas to be sure service valves are correctly seated and Schraeder valves, if used, are not leaking.

EXERCISE SYSTEM

An important fact most owners ignore is that A/C units must be used periodically. Manufacturers caution that when the air conditioner is not used regularly, particularly during cold months, it should be turned on for a few minutes once every two or three weeks while the engine is running. This keeps the system in good operating condition.

Checking out the system for effects of disuse before the onset of summer is one of the most important aspects of A/C servicing.

First clean out the condenser core, mounted in all cases in front of the radiator. All obstructions, such as leaves, bugs and dirt, must be removed, as they will reduce heat transfer and impair the efficiency of the system. Make sure the space between the condenser and the radiator is also free of foreign matter.

Make certain the evaporator water drain is open. The evaporator cools and dehu-

Fig. 2 Manifold gauge set connections. Chrysler Airtemp RV2 compressor

midifies the air before it enters the passenger compartment; there, the refrigerant is changed from a liquid to a vapor. As the core cools the air, moisture condenses on it but is prevented from collecting in the evaporator by the water drain.

PERFORMANCE TEST

The system should be operated for at least 15 minutes to allow sufficient time for all parts to become completely stabilized. Determine if the system is fully charged by the use of test gauges and sight glass if one is installed on system. Head pressure will read from 180 psi to 220 psi or higher, depending upon ambient temperature and the type unit being tested. The sight glass should be free of bubbles if a glass is used in the system. Low side pressures should read approximately 15 psi to 30 psi, again depending on the ambient temperature and the unit being tested. It is not feasible to give a definite reading for all types of systems used, as the type control and component installation used on a particular system will directly influence the pressure readings on the high and low sides, **Fig. 1.**

The high side pressure will definitely be affected by the ambient or outside air temperature. A system that is operating normally will indicate a high side gauge reading between 150–170 psi with an 80°F ambient temperature. The same system will register 210–230 psi with an ambient temperature of 100°F. No two systems will register exactly the same, which requires that allowance for variations in head pressures must be considered. Following are the most important normal readings likely to be encountered during the season.

Ambient Temp.	High Side Pressure
80	150–170
90	175–195
95	185–205
100	210–230
105	230–250
110	250–270

RELATIVE TEMPERATURE OF HIGH AND LOW SIDES

The high side of the system should be uniformly hot to the touch throughout. A difference in temperature will indicate a partial blockage of liquid or gas at this point.

The low side of the system should be uniformly cool to the touch with no excessive sweating of the suction line or low side service valve. Excessive sweating or frosting of the low side service valve usually indicates an expansion valve is allowing an excessive amount of refrigerant into the evaporator.

EVAPORATOR OUTPUT

At this point, provided all other inspection tests have been performed, and components have been found to operate as they should, a rapid cooling down of the interior of the vehicle should result. The use of a thermometer is not necessary to determine evaporator output. Bringing all units to the correct operating specifications will insure that the evaporator performs as intended.

DISCHARGING & EVACUATING SYSTEM

DISCHARGING SYSTEM

1. Connect gauges into system, **Figs. 2 and 3,** and adjust controls for maximum cooling. This is necessary when the system has not been operating to return excess oil to the compressor.
2. Operate engine for 10 to 15 minutes to stabilize the system at 1500–1750 rpm.
3. Adjust engine speed to slow idle, then shut off engine and controls.
4. Open low side hand manifold valve slightly, using a container to catch oil and refrigerant. Do not discharge the refrigerant near an open flame as a toxic gas (phosgene) can result.

5. Open high side manifold valve slightly.

NOTE: Open hand valve(s) only enough to bleed refrigerant from system. Too rapid purging will draw excessive oil from compressor and system.

6. Close gauge manifold hand valves when refrigerant ceases to bleed from discharge hose and manifold gauges read zero.

EVACUATE SYSTEM WITH VACUUM PUMP

Vacuum pumps suitable for removing air and moisture from A/C systems are commercially available. A specification for system pump-down used here is 28 to 29½ inches vacuum. This reading can be attained at or near sea level only. For each 1000 feet of altitude this operation is being performed, the reading will be 1 inch vacuum lower. As an example, at 5000 feet elevation, only 23–24½ inches of vacuum can be obtained.

CAUTION: The system must be completely discharged before it can be evacuated. Damage to vacuum pump may result if pressurized refrigerant is allowed to enter.

1. With gauges connected into system, remove cap from vacuum hose connector. Install center hose from gauge manifold to vacuum pump connector. Mid-position high and low side compressor service valves (if used). Open high and low side gauge manifold hand valves.
2. Operate vacuum pump a minimum of 30 minutes for air and moisture removal. Watch compound gauge that system pumps down into a vacuum. System will reach 28–29½ inches vacuum in not over 5 minutes. If system does not pump down, check all connections and leak-test if necessary.
3. Close gauge manifold hand valves and shut off vacuum pump.
4. Check ability of system to hold vacuum. Watch compound gauge to see that gauge does not rise at a faster rate than 1 inch vacuum every 4 or 5 minutes. If compound gauge rises at too rapid a rate, install partial charge and leak-test. Then evacuate system as outlined above.
5. If system holds vacuum, charge system with refrigerant.

EVACUATE SYSTEM USING CHARGING STATION

A vacuum pump is built into the charging station and is constructed to withstand repeated and prolonged use without damage. Complete moisture removal from the system is possible only with a vacuum pump constructed for the purpose.

AIR CONDITIONING

CAUTION: The system must be completely discharged before it can be evacuated. Damage to the vacuum pump may result if pressurized refrigerant is allowed to enter.

1. Connect hose to vacuum pump if system was discharged through charging station.
2. Open high and low side gauge valves of charging station.
3. Connect station into 110-volt current.
4. Engage "Off-On" switch to vacuum pump according to directions of specific station being used.
5. System should pump down into a 28–29½ inches vacuum in not more than 5 minutes. If system fails to meet this specification, repair as necessary.
6. Operate pump a minimum of 30 minutes to remove all air and moisture.
7. Close high and low side gauge valves. Open switch to turn off pump.
8. Check ability of system to hold vacuum by watching compound gauge to see that it does not rise at a rate higher than 1 inch of vacuum every 4 or 5 minutes: If rise rate is not within specifications, repair system as necessary. If rise rate is within specifications, charge system with refrigerant.

CHARGING THE SYSTEM

CHARGING WITH 14 OUNCE CANS

CAUTION: Never use cans to charge into high pressure side of system (compressor discharge port) or into system at high temperature, as high system pressure transferred into charging can may cause it to explode.

1. Attach center hose from manifold gauge set to refrigerant dispensing manifold. Turn refrigerant manifold valves completely counterclockwise to open fully, and remove protective caps from refrigerant manifold.
2. Screw refrigerant cans into manifold, ensuring gasket is in place and in good condition. Torque can and manifold nuts to 6–8 ft. lbs.
3. Turn refrigerant manifold valves clockwise to puncture cans, and close manifold valves, **Fig. 4.**
4. Loosen charging hose at gauge set manifold and turn a refrigerant valve counterclockwise to release refrigerant and purge air from charging hose. When refrigerant gas escapes from loose connection, retighten hose.
5. Fully open all refrigerant manifold valves being used and place refrigerant cans into pan of hot water at 125°F to aid transfer of refrigerant gas.

CAUTION: Do not heat refrigerant cans over 125°F as they may explode.

Fig. 3   Manifold gauge set hose connections (Typical). Except Chrysler Airtemp RV2 compressor

Place water pan and refrigerant cans on scale and note weight.
6. Connect a jumper wire across cycling clutch switch terminals located on suction line near H valve so clutch will remain engaged.
7. Start engine and set controls to A/C low blower position. Low pressure cutout switch will prevent clutch from engaging until refrigerant is added to system. If clutch does engage, replace switch before continuing.
8. Charge through suction side of system by slowly opening suction manifold valve. Adjust valve so charging pressure does not exceed 50 psig.
9. Adjust engine speed to fast idle of 1400 RPM.
10. After specified refrigerant charge has entered system, close gauge set manifold valves, refrigerant manifold valves, and reconnect wiring.

CHARGING WITH BULK REFRIGERANT SUPPLY

CAUTION: Only a charging bottle may be used to charge liquid refrigerant through the compressor discharge muffler. Never charge with liquid through compressor inlet or suction line ports, as damage to compressor is likely to occur. Do not run compressor while adding liquid refrigerant.

NOTE: Beginning with 1984 models, charging system with liquid on compressor discharge side is no longer recommended due to safety reasons.

1. Warm charging bottle in pan of 125°F water. Do not heat R-12 with a torch, as it may explode.
2. Loosen charging hose at gauge set manifold and slowly open refrigerant supply valve until refrigerant has purged air from hose. Retighten the hose.
3. Place refrigerant container upside down on scale and note weight.
4. Open refrigerant supply valve and compressor discharge gauge valve to charge system. When scale indicates proper amount of charge has entered system, close valves.

If required amount of refrigerant does not enter system, close compressor discharge valve on manifold gauge set. Turn charging bottle right side up so gas, not liquid, will enter system. Start engine and set A/C control in A/C position. Slowly open suction line valve on manifold gauge set. The compressor will draw refrigerant into system. Charging line valve should be set so suction pressure does not exceed 50 psig.

LEAK TEST SYSTEM

The propane torch Halide Leak Detector is the most widely used of the detection devices. Therefore, only the procedure for this device will be given. The procedure is the same for any electronic detector, except that the pick-up device registers the presence of refrigerant by a flashing light or high pitched squeal instead of changing the color of the flame. All other steps in preparing the system and leak testing are the same and can be followed as outlined below:

1. Stabilize system at 1500–1750 rpm. If system is empty of refrigerant, it will be necessary to install a partial charge before continuing. With gauges connected into system, adjust A/C controls for maximum cooling. Operate for 10 to 15 minutes, then shut off car engine.
2. Light leak detector. Open valve to a low flame that will not blow itself out. Warm up until copper element turns

Fig. 4 Complete charging of system.

cherry red. Lower flame until flame tip is even with or slightly below center of element. For electronic tester, follow preparation procedure as given in operating instructions.

3. Move leak detector pick-up under hoses, joints, seals, and any possible place for a leak to occur.

NOTE: Freon 12 refrigerant is heavier than air and will move downward. If concentra- tion of refrigerant is located, move pick-up upward to locate leak. Do not inhale fumes produced by burning refrigerant.

4. Watch for color change of flame: Pale blue, no refrigerant; yellow, small amount of refrigerant; purplish-blue, large amount of refrigerant. Repair system as necessary if leaks are located.
5. Check sensitivity of reaction plate:

Pass pick-up hose over empty can or crack open refrigerant container; flame should show violent reaction. If no color change, replace reaction plate, following instructions accompanying leak detector. Too high a flame will result in short life to reaction plate and poor reaction and will soon burn out element.

6. Charge system if repairs were necessary.

Chrysler Corp. System Servicing

INDEX

OIL CHARGE

C-171

1. Discharge system and remove suction and discharge lines from compressor.
2. Remove compressor assembly from vehicle, then drain compressor oil from suction and discharge ports.
3. Add 5 fl. oz. of refrigerant oil to compressor through suction port.
4. Install compressor assembly and, using new gaskets, attach suction and discharge lines.
5. Evacuate and charge system. If any of the following components are to be replaced, oil must be added to the system:
   Evaporator . . . . 2 ounces
   Condenser . . . . 1 ounce
   Filter-Drier . . . . 1 ounce

OIL LEVEL CHECK

NOTE: The oil level of these compressors should be checked whenever refrigerant has been lost due to leakage or through normal system servicing.

CHRYSLER AIR TEMP COMPRESSORS

RV2 Compressor

1. Connect gauge and manifold assembly and slowly discharge refrigerant system. Near completion of discharge, flush dipstick with existing freon. This will ensure dipstick is clean and at approximately the same temperature as refrigerant oil in compressor sump.
2. Carefully remove compressor oil sump filler plug, then insert dipstick into hole until it bottoms in sump, **Fig. 1.**

NOTE: When removing compressor oil sump filler plug a face shield should be worn. Refrigerant dissolved in compressor oil could cause oil to purcolate out through filler plug opening.

3. Remove dipstick and measure oil level, refer to A/C Specification Tables. Add refrigerant oil as necessary to bring oil level within limits.

NOTE: Oil level should be checked only after refrigerant has boiled off and oil surface has stabilized.

4. If any of the following components are to be replaced, it will be necessary to add additional oil to system.
   Evaporator . . . . 2 ounces
   Condenser . . . . 1 ounce
   Filter Drier . . . . 1 ounce
5. On all models, install filler plug, then evacuate and recharge system.

A/C Data Table

Year	Model	Refrigerant Capacity, Lbs.	Refrigerant Oil			Compressor Clutch Air Gap Inch
			Viscosity	Total System Capacity, Ounces	Compressor Oil Level Check, Inches	
CHRYSLER						
1980	Gran Fury, Newport, New Yorker & St. Regis	2⅞	500	①	②	.020–.035
	Rear Wheel Drive Exc. Gran Fury, Newport, New Yorker & St. Regis	2⅝	500	①	②	.020–.035
1980–81	Horizon & Omni	2⅛	500	①	③	.020–.035
1981	Aries & Reliant	2⅜	500	①	③	.020–.035
	Rear Wheel Drive	2⅝	500	①	②	.020–.035
1982–85	Horizon, Omni, Charger, Turismo, 024 & TC3	2⅛	500	9–10	③	.020–.035
	Front Wheel Drive Exc. Horizon, Omni, Charger, Turismo, 024 & TC3	2⅜	500	9–10	③	.020–.035
	Rear Wheel Drive	2⅝	500	9–10	③	.020–.035

①—With RV2 compressor, 10–12 ounces. With Sankyo compressor, 7–8 ounces. With C-171 compressor, 9 ounces.

②—RV2 compressor, 2⅜ inches. On Sankyo compressors, the oil level should be at the third to fourth increment on the dipstick which represents 3 to 4 ounces of oil. Refer to text for procedure. On C-171 compressor refer to text.

③—Refer to text for C-171 compressor.

C-171 Compressor

1. Discharge refrigerant from system.
2. Remove compressor from vehicle, then invert compressor and allow oil to drain from suction and discharge ports.
3. Add 5 fluid ounces of clean refrigerant oil through suction port, then install compressor and connect suction and discharge lines using new gaskets.
4. Evacuate and recharge system.

NOTE: The C-171 compressor contains 9 to 10 ounces of refrigerant oil. While the A/C system is in operation, the oil is carried through the entire system by the refrigerant. Some of the oil will be retained in the various components of the system. If a replacement evaporator coil is installed, add 2 ounces of refrigerant oil to system. If a replacement condenser coil or filter-drier is installed, add one additional ounce of refrigerant oil to system. This additional oil must be added to compensate for oil removed with the component. Replacement compressors are charged with 9 to 10 ounces of refrigerant oil, therefore before installing a replacement compressor, approximately 4 ounces of refrigerant oil should be drained from the compressor.

Fig. 1 Air Temp compressor oil level dipstick fabrication and filler plug location

CHARGING VALVE LOCATION

All charging valves are located on the compressor except the high pressure valve for the C-171 compressor, which is located on the muffler.

Ford Motor Co. System Testing

INDEX

Evaporator Pressure Gauge Reading	Evaporator Temperature F°	High Pressure Gauge Reading	Ambient Temperature
0	-21°	45	20°
0.6	-20°	55	30°
2.4	-15°	72	40°
4.5	-10°	86	50°
6.8	-5°	105	60°
9.2	0°	126	70°
11.8	5°	140	75°
14.7	10°	160	80°
17.1	15°	185	90°
21.1	20°	195	95°
22.5	22°	220	100°
23.9	24°	240	105°
25.4	26°	260	110°
26.9	28°	275	115°
28.5	30°	290	120°
37.0	40°	305	125°
46.7	50°	325	130°
57.7	60°		
70.1	70°		
84.1	80°		
99.6	90°		
116.9	100°		
136.0	110°		
157.1	120°		
179.0	130°		

Fig. 1 Pressure-temperature relationship (Typical). Conditions equivalent to 30 mph or 1750 engine rpm

GENERAL PRECAUTIONS

The Freon refrigerant used is also known as R-12 or F-12. It is colorless and odorless both as a gas and a liquid. Since it boils (vaporizes) at −21.7°F., it will usually be in a vapor state when being handled in a repair shop. But if a portion of the liquid coolant should come in contact with the hands or face, note that its temperature momentarily will be at least 22° below zero.

Protective goggles should be worn when opening any refrigerant lines. If liquid coolant does touch the eyes, bathe the eyes quickly in cold water, then apply a bland disinfectant oil to the eyes. See an eye doctor.

When checking a system for leaks with a torch type leak detector, do not breathe the vapors coming from the flame. Do not discharge refrigerant in the area of a live flame. A poisonous phosgene gas is produced when R-12 or F-12 is burned. While the small amount of this gas produced by a leak detector is not harmful unless inhaled directly at the flame, the quantity of refrigerant released into the air when a system is purged can be extremely dangerous if allowed to come in contact with an open flame. Thus, when purging a system, be sure that the discharge hose is routed to a well ventilated place where no flame is present. Under these conditions the refrigerant will be quickly dissipated into the surrounding air.

Never allow the temperature of refrigerant drums to exceed 125°F. The resultant increase in temperature will cause a corresponding increase in pressure which may cause the safety plug to release or the drum to burst.

If it is necessary to heat a drum of refrigerant when charging a system, the drum should be placed in water no hotter than 125°F. Never use a blow torch or other open flame. If possible, a pressure release mechanism should be attached before the drum is heated.

When connecting and disconnecting service gauges on A/C system, ensure that gauge hand valves are fully closed and that compressor service valves, if equipped, are in the back-seated (fully counterclockwise) position. Do not disconnect gauge hoses from service port adapters, if used, while gauges are connected to A/C system. To disconnect hoses, always remove adapter from service port. Do not disconnect hoses from gauge manifold while connected to A/C system, as refrigerant will be rapidly discharged.

After disconnecting gauge lines, check the valve areas to be sure service valves are correctly seated and Schraeder valves, if used, are not leaking.

EXERCISE SYSTEM

An important fact most owners ignore is that A/C units must be used periodically. Manufacturers caution that when the air conditioner is not used regularly, particularly during cold months, it should be turned on for a few minutes once every two or three weeks while the engine is running. This keeps the system in good operating condition.

Checking out the system for the effects of disuse before the onset of summer is one of the most important aspects of A/C servicing.

First clean out the condenser core, mounted in all cases at the front of the radiator. All obstructions, such as leaves, bugs and dirt, must be removed, as they will reduce heat transfer and impair the efficiency of the system. Make sure the space between the condenser and the radiator also is free of foreign matter.

AIR CONDITIONING

Make certain the evaporator water drain is open. The evaporator cools and dehumidifies the air before it enters the passenger compartment; there, the refrigerant is changed from a liquid to a vapor. As the core cools the air, moisture condenses on it but is prevented from collecting in the evaporator by the water drain.

PERFORMANCE TEST

The system should be operated for at least 15 minutes to allow sufficient time for all parts to become completely stabilized. Determine if the system is fully charged by the use of test gauges and sight glass if one is installed on system. Head pressure will read from 180 psi to 220 psi or higher, depending upon ambient temperature and the type unit being tested. The sight glass should be free of bubbles if a glass is used in the system. Low side pressures should read approximately 15 psi to 30 psi, again depending on the ambient temperature and the unit being tested. It is not feasible to give a definite reading for all types of systems used, as the type control and component installation used on a particular system will directly influence the pressure readings on the high and low sides, **Fig. 1.**

The high side pressure will definitely be affected by the ambient or outside air temperature. A system that is operating normally will indicate a high side gauge reading between 150–170 psi with an 80°F ambient temperature. The same system will register 210–230 psi with an ambient temperature of 100°F. No two systems will register exactly the same, which requires that allowance for variations in head pressures must be considered. Following are the most important normal readings likely to be encountered during the season.

Ambient Temp.	High Side Pressure
80	150–170
90	175–195
95	185–205
100	210–230
105	230–250
110	250–270

RELATIVE TEMPERATURE OF HIGH AND LOW SIDES

The high side of the system should be uniformly hot to the touch throughout. A difference in temperature will indicate a partial blockage of liquid or gas at this point.

The low side of the system should be uniformly cool to the touch with no excessive sweating of the suction line or low side service valve. Excessive sweating or frosting of the low side service valve usually indicates an expansion valve is allowing an excessive amount of refrigerant into the evaporator.

EVAPORATOR OUTPUT

At this point, provided all other inspection tests have been performed, and components have been found to operate as they should, a rapid cooling down of the

Fig. 2   Manifold gauge set hose connections (Typical).

interior of the vehicle should result. The use of a thermometer is not necessary to determine evaporator output. Bringing all units to the correct operating specifications will insure that the evaporator performs as intended.

DISCHARGING & EVACUATING SYSTEM
DISCHARGING SYSTEM

1. Connect gauges into system, **Fig. 2,** and adjust controls for maximum cooling. This is necessary when the system has not been operating to return excess oil to the compressor.
2. Operate engine for 10 to 15 minutes to stabilize the system at 1500–1750 rpm.
3. Adjust engine speed to slow idle, then shut off engine and controls.
4. Open low side hand manifold valve slightly, using a container to catch oil and refrigerant. Do not discharge the refrigerant near an open flame as a toxic gas (phosgene) can result.
5. On Ford full size models, open high side manifold valve slightly. On Ford except full size models, allow all refrigerant to discharge through the low side fitting only.

NOTE: Open hand valve(s) only enough to bleed refrigerant from system. Too rapid purging will draw excessive oil from compressor and system.

6. On Ford full size models, close gauge manifold hand valves when refrigerant ceases to bleed from discharge hose and manifold gauges read zero. On Ford except full size models, when refrigerant ceases to bleed from the discharge hose on the low side, crack open the high side hand valve to check for any remaining pressure. If

pressure does exist, allow high side to discharge slowly. This condition indicates a high side restriction, and it must be diagnosed and corrected before evacuating and charging the system.

EVACUATE SYSTEM WITH VACUUM PUMP

Vacuum pumps suitable for removing air and moisture from A/C systems are commercially available. A specification for system pump-down used here is 28 to 29½ inches vacuum. This reading can be attained at or near sea level only. For each 1000 feet of altitude this operation is being performed, the reading will be 1 inch vacuum lower. As an example, at 5000 feet elevation, only 23–24½ inch of vacuum can be obtained.

CAUTION: The system must be completely discharged before it can be evacuated. Damage to vacuum pump may result if pressurized refrigerant is allowed to enter.

Ford Full Size Models
1. With gauges connected into system, remove cap from vacuum hose connector. Install center hose from gauge manifold to vacuum pump connector. Mid-position high and low side compressor service valves (if used). Open high and low side gauge manifold hand valves.
2. Operate vacuum pump a minimum of 30 minutes for air and moisture removal. Watch compound gauge that system pumps down into a vacuum. System will reach 28–29½ inches vacuum in not over 5 minutes. If system does not pump down, check all connections and leak-test if necessary.
3. Close gauge manifold hand valves and shut off vacuum pump.

CHARGING THE SYSTEM

Fig. 3   Service connections for systems with mini-combination valve. 1981 Ford

4. Check ability of system to hold vacuum. Watch compound gauge to see that gauge does not rise at a faster rate than 1 inch vacuum every 4 or 5 minutes. If compound gauge rises at too rapid a rate, install partial charge and leak-test. Then evacuate system as outlined above.
5. If system holds vacuum, charge system with refrigerant.

Ford Except Full Size

1. With hand gauges connected into system, remove cap from vacuum hose connector. Install hand gauge manifold center hose to vacuum pump connector. Open low side gauge manifold hand valve only.
2. Ensure low side gauge is calibrated correctly. It should be reading zero. If not, adjust calibration.
3. Evacuate system with the vacuum pump until the low pressure gauge reads at least 28 inches of vacuum. Continue evacuating system for an additional 15 minutes for routine system servicing or 20 to 30 minutes, if any parts have been replaced.
4. When system evacuation is complete, close low side gauge manifold hand valve, then turn vacuum pump off.
5. Check ability of system to hold vacuum. Watch low side gauge to see that gauge does not rise at a faster rate than 1 inch vacuum every 4 to 5 minutes. if low side gauge rises at too rapid a rate, install partial charge and leak test. Evacuate system again.
6. If system holds vacuum, charge system with refrigerant.

EVACUATE SYSTEM USING CHARGING STATION

A vacuum pump is built into the charging station and is constructed to withstand repeated and prolonged use without damage. Complete moisture removal from the system is possible only with a vacuum pump constructed for the purpose.

CAUTION: The system must be completely discharged before it can be evacuated. Damage to the vacuum pump may result if pressurized refrigerant is allowed to enter.

Ford Full Size Models

1. Connect hose to vacuum pump if system was discharged through charging station.
2. Open high and low side gauge valves of charging station.
3. Connect station into 110-volt current.
4. Engage "Off-On" switch to vacuum pump according to directions of specific station being used.
5. System should pump down into a 28–29½ inch vacuum in not more than 5 minutes. If system fails to meet this specification, repair as necessary.
6. Operate pump a minimum of 30 minutes to remove all air and moisture.
7. Close high and low side gauge valves. Open switch to turn off pump.
8. Check ability of system to hold vacuum by watching compound gauge to see that it does not rise at a rate higher than 1 inch of vacuum every 4 or 5 minutes: If rise rate is not within specifications, repair system as necessary. If rise rate is within specifications, charge system with refrigerant.

Ford Except Full Size Models

1. Connect hose to vacuum pump, if system was discharged through charging station.
2. Open low side gauge hand valve of charging station.
3. Connect station into 110 volt current.
4. Engage "Off-On" switch to vacuum pump according to instructions for specific station being used.
5. Evacuate system with the vacuum pump until the low pressure gauge reads at least 28 inches of vacuum. Continue evacuating system for an additional 15 minutes for routine system servicing or 20 to 30 minutes, if any parts have been replaced.
6. Close low side gauge hand valve, then turn vacuum pump off.
7. Check ability of system to hold vacuum. Watch low side gauge to see that gauge does not rise at a faster rate than 1 inch vacuum every 4 to 5 minutes. If low side gauge rises at too rapid a rate, install partial charge and leak test. Then evacuate system again.
8. If system holds vacuum, charge system with refrigerant.

CHARGING FROM SMALL CONTAINERS

When charging from small cans, do not open manifold gauge set high pressure (discharge) gauge valve, as this can cause containers to explode.

1. Connect a suitable refrigerant dispensing valve and valve retainer such as Motorcraft tool YT-280 or equivalent to the refrigerant can.
2. Connect manifold gauge set to system, **Figs. 3 and 4.** Connect hose normally connected to R-12 tank to special valve on small can adaptor. Make sure valve is closed (full clockwise position).
3. When can is connected, charge system according to procedure under "Charging From Drum." When can is empty, close valve and remove can. Connect new can open valve and continue charging until correct weight of refrigerant has entered system. Note capacity of refrigerant cans. When specifications require use of a portion of a can, weigh it to ensure proper amount of refrigerant is installed.

CHARGING FROM DRUM

1. With manifold gauge set valves closed to center hose, disconnect vacuum pump from manifold gauge set.
2. Connect center hose of manifold gauge set to refrigerant drum.
3. Purge air from center hose by loosening hose at manifold gauge set and open refrigerant drum valve. When refrigerant escapes from hose, tighten center hose connection at manifold gauge set.
4. On vehicles so equipped, disconnect wire harness connector at clutch cycling pressure switch. Install jumper wire across terminals of connector.
5. On all models, open manifold gauge set low side valve and allow refrigerant to enter system. Refrigerant can must be kept upright if vehicle low pressure service gauge port is not on suction accumulator/drier or suction accumulator fitting.
6. When system stops drawing refrigerant in, start engine and set control lever to A/C position and blower switch to "HI" position to draw remaining refrigerant into system.
7. When specified weight of refrigerant is in system, close gauge set low pressure valve and refrigerant supply valve.
8. On vehicles so equipped, remove jumper wire from clutch cycling pressure switch connector and connect connector to pressure switch.
9. On all models, operate system until pressures stabilize to check operation and system pressures. During high ambient temperatures, a high volume

fan may be necessary to blow air through the radiator and condensor to cool engine and prevent excessive refrigerant system pressures.

10. When charging is complete and system operating pressures are normal, disconnect manifold gauge set from vehicle and install protective caps on service gauge port valves.

LEAK TEST SYSTEM

The propane torch Halide Leak Detector is the most widely used of the detection devices. Therefore, only the procedure for this device will be given. The procedure is the same for any electronic detector, except that the pick-up device registers the presence of refrigerant by a flashing light or high pitched squeal instead of changing the color of the flame. All other steps in preparing the system and leak testing are the same and can be followed as outlined below:

1. Stabilize system at 1500–1750 rpm. If system is empty of refrigerant, it will be necessary to install a partial charge before continuing. With gauges connected into system, adjust A/C controls for maximum cooling. Operate for 10 to 15 minutes, then shut off car engine.
2. Light leak detector. Open valve to a low flame that will not blow itself out. Warm up until copper element turns cherry red. Lower flame until flame tip is even with or slightly below center of

Fig. 4   Refrigerant system service connections. Ford fixed orifice systems

element. For electronic tester, follow preparation procedure as given in operating instructions.
3. Move leak detector pick-up under hoses, joints, seals, and any possible place for a leak to occur.

NOTE: Freon 12 refrigerant is heavier than air and will move downward. If concentration of refrigerant is located, move pick-up upward to locate leak. Do not inhale fumes produced by burning refrigerant.

---

4. Watch for color change of flame: Pale blue, no refrigerant; yellow, small amount of refrigerant; purplish-blue, large amount of refrigerant. Repair system as necessary if leaks are located.
5. Check sensitivity of reaction plate: Pass pick-up hose over empty can or crack open refrigerant container; flame should show violent reaction. If no color change, replace reaction plate, following instructions accompanying leak detector. Too high a flame will result in short life to reaction plate and poor reaction and will soon burn out element.
6. Charge system if repairs were necessary.

Ford Motor Co. System Servicing

INDEX

OIL CHARGE

MOTORCRAFT AXIAL 6 CYL. COMPRESSOR

Compressor Replacement

1. Idle engine for 10 minutes at approximately 1250 rpm at maximum cooling and high blower speed to distribute oil in system.
2. Remove compressor from vehicle.
3. Remove plug and allow oil to drain from compressor into a container calibrated in ounces.
4. Drain oil from new compressor.
5. If amount drained from original compressor is more than four ounces, add the same amount of new refrigerant oil to the new compressor plus amount lost during discharge.
6. If amount of oil drained from original compressor is less than 4 ounces, add 6 ounces of new refrigerant oil to the new compressor plus amount lost during discharge.

Component Replacement

Whenever a component of the A/C system is replaced, if not pre-charged by factory, measured quantities of refrigeration oil should be added to the component to assure that the total oil charge in the system is correct before the unit is placed into operation.

The oil is poured directly into the replacement component. If an evaporator is installed, pour oil into the inlet pipe with the pipe held vertically so the oil will drain into the evaporator core. No additional oil is required if valves and hoses are replaced.

Add additional oil as specified if any of the following components are replaced.

Evaporator	3 ounces
Condenser	1 ounce
Receiver	1 ounce
Condenser & Receiver Assembly	2 ounces

FORD FS6 COMPRESSOR

1. If compressor is not seized, operate engine at 1000 to 1500 RPM with A/C on maximum cooling and high blower for approximately 10 minutes.
2. Discharge refrigerant system, then remove compressor from vehicle.
3. Remove drain plug from compressor and pour refrigerant oil into a calibrated container.

4. If oil drained is less than 3 ounces, add 6 ounces of new refrigerant oil to compressor.
5. If oil drained is between 3 and 6 ounces, add the same amount of new refrigerant oil to the compressor.
6. If oil drained is more than 6 ounces, only add six ounces to compressor.

NOTE: Replacement compressors are charged with 10 ounces of refrigerant oil. Before installing a replacement compressor, the oil must be drained and only 6 ounces of oil reinstalled into the replacement compressor. When certain other refrigerant system components are replaced, the oil level must be adjusted to compensate for oil retained in these components. When installing a replacement evaporator core, add 3 ounces of oil to evaporator. When installing a replacement condenser or accumulator, add 1 ounce of oil to the component.

FORD HR-980 RADIAL 4 CYLINDER & 6P148 AXIAL 6 CYLINDER COMPRESSORS

A new service replacement 4 cylinder compressor contains 8 fluid ounces of refrigerant oil. Before installing replacement compressor, drain 4 fluid ounces of oil from compressor in order to maintain total system oil charge within specified limits, and a 6 cylinder compressor contains 10 ounces of oil.

When other air conditioning system components are replaced, measured amounts of 500 viscosity oil should be added to the component to ensure total oil charge is correct. Clean refrigerant oil should be added as follows:

Evaporator core	3 fluid ounces
Condenser	1 fluid ounce

Accumulator: Drain oil from accumulator through pressure switch fitting and measure. Add equal amount plus 1 ounce clean refrigerant oil to new accumulator.

Replacement of other components such as valves or hoses does not require the addition of any refrigerant oil.

OIL LEVEL CHECK

NOTE: The oil level of these compressors should be checked whenever refrigerant

has been lost due to leakage or through normal system servicing.

TECUMSEH & YORK

1. Connect manifold gauge set, then operate system for approximately 10 minutes or until system pressures stabilize. This will allow oil in the system to return to compressor sump.
2. Discharge entire refrigerant system.
3. Slowly loosen compressor oil filler plug to relieve any internal pressures in compressor.

NOTE: A face shield should be worn when loosening or removing oil filler plug.

4. Insert clean dipstick into filler plug hole until it bottoms in sump, **Figs. 1 and 2.**

NOTE: On York compressors ensure keyway in shaft faces head of compressor before checking oil level.

5. Remove dipstick and measure oil level. Refer to "A/C Data Table" and add refrigerant oil as necessary. Install filler plug and O-ring.
6. Evacuate and recharge system.

NIPPONDENSO

1. Operate compressor for 10 to 15 minutes at maximum cooling to stabilize system.
2. Discharge system and remove compressor from vehicle. Remove drain plug and measure amount of oil drained from compressor.
3. If less than three ounces of oil were drained from compressor, add six ounces of refrigerant oil to drained service replacement compressor.
4. If between three and six ounces of oil were drained from compressor, oil is properly distributed throughout system. Add an equal amount of refrigerant oil to drained service replacement compressor.
5. Never add more than six ounces of refrigerant oil to a replacement compressor and never install a replacement compressor containing more than six ounces of refrigerant oil. Clean refrigerant oil should be added to the following replacement components:

Evaporator	3 ounces
Condenser	1 ounce
Accumulator	1 ounce

A/C Data Table

Year	Model	Refrigerant Capacity, Lbs.	Refrigeration Oil			Compressor Clutch Air Gap Inch
			Viscosity	Total System Capacity, Ounces	Compressor Oil Level Check, Inches	
FORD & MERCURY FULL SIZE						
1980	All	3¼	①	②	③	④
1981–82	All	3¼	500	13	③	.021–.036
1983–85	All	3¼	500	10	③	.021–.036
FORD & MERCURY COMPACT & INTERMEDIATE (EXC. BOBCAT, CAPRI, MUSTANG & PINTO)						
1980	Granada & Monarch	4	525	10½	③	.022–.057
1980–81	York Comp.	3½	⑤	10	⑥⑦	—
	Tecumseh Comp.	3½	⑤	11	⑥⑦	—
1982	Ford FS-6 Comp.	2½	500	13	③	.021–.036
1982–83	York Comp.	2½	⑤	10	⑥⑦	—
	Tecumseh 2 Cyl. Comp.	2½	⑤	11	⑥⑦	—
1983–85	Ford FS-6 Comp.	2½	500	10	③	.021–.036
	Tecumseh HR-980 Comp.	2½	500	8	③	.021–.036
FORD ESCORT, EXP & TEMPO; MERCURY LYNX, LN7 & TOPAZ						
1981	Escort & Lynx	2½	500	13	③	.021–.036
1982	All	2⁹⁄₁₆	500	10	③	.021–.036
1983	Escort & Lynx	2⁹⁄₁₆	500	10	③	.021–.036
	EXP & LN7	2⁵⁄₁₆	500	10	③	.021–.036
1984	All	2⁹⁄₁₆	500	10	③	.021–.036
1985	Exc. EXP	2⁹⁄₁₆	500	10	③	.021–.056
	EXP	2⁵⁄₁₆	500	10	③	.021–.036
FORD MUSTANG & MERCURY CAPRI						
1980–81	York Comp.	3½	⑤	10	③	—
	Tecumseh Comp.	3½	⑤	11	③	—
1982–83	York Comp.	2½	⑤	10	③	—
	Tecumseh 2 Cyl. Comp.	2½	⑤	11	③	—
1983–85	Nippondenso 6P148 Comp.	2½	500	10	③	.021–.036
	Tecumseh HR-980 Comp.	2½	500	8	③	.021–.036
	FS-6 Comp.	2½	500	10	③	—
FORD PINTO & MERCURY BOBCAT						
1980	York Comp.	2¼	⑤	10	⑥⑦	—
	Tecumseh Comp.	2¼	⑤	11	⑥⑦	—
LINCOLN						
1980	Exc. Versailles	4¼	①	②	③	④
	Versailles	4	①	②	③	.022–.057
1981–82	All exc. 1982 Continental	3	500	13	③	.021–.036
1982	Continental	2½	500	13	③	.021–.036
1983	Continental	2½	500	10	③	.021–.036
	Exc. Continental	3	500	10	③	.021–.036
1984–85	Continental & Mark VII	2½	500	10	③	.021–.036
	Town Car	3	500	10	③	.021–.036

① —Motorcraft compressor, 525 viscosity; Nippondenso compressor, 500 viscosity.

② —Motorcraft compressor, 10½ ounces; Nippondenso compressor, 13 ounces.

③ —Note that "Oil level inches" cannot be checked. Refer to total capacity in ounces. See text for procedure.

④ —Motorcraft compressor, .022–.057"; Nippondenso compressor, .021–.036".

⑤ —Suniso 5G or Capella E.

⑥ —Dipstick reading with compressor installed.

⑦ —York Comp.—Vertical mount., ⅞–1⅛; horizontal mount., ¹³⁄₁₆–1³⁄₁₆. Tecumseh Comp.—Vertical mount., ⅞–1⅜; horizontal mount., ⅞–1⅝.

Charging Valve Location

Year	Model	High Pressure Fitting	Low Pressure Fitting
1980	Versailles	High Pressure Line From Compressor	Combination Valve
1980–81	Ford & Mercury w/2 Cyl. Compressor	Liquid Line At Combination Valve	Combination Valve
	Ford & Mercury w/6 Cyl. Compressor	High Pressure Line From Compressor	Accumulator
	Lincoln Exc. Versailles	High Pressure Line From Compressor	Accumulator
1982–85	Ford & Mercury Exc. Full Size	High Pressure Line From Compressor	Low Pressure Line From Compressor
	Ford & Mercury Full Size	High Pressure Line From Compressor	Accumulator
	Lincoln Exc. Continental	High Pressure Line From Compressor	Accumulator
	Continental	High Pressure Line From Compressor	Low Pressure Line From Compressor

Fig. 1   York compressor oil level dipstick fabrication. Ford Motor Co. models

Fig. 2   Tecumseh compressor oil level dipstick fabrication. Ford Motor Co. models

General Motors Corp. System Testing

INDEX

GENERAL PRECAUTIONS

The Freon refrigerant used is also known as R-12 or F-12. It is colorless and odorless both as a gas and a liquid. Since it boils (vaporizes) at −21.7°F., it will usually be in a vapor state when being handled in a repair shop. But if a portion of the liquid coolant should come in contact with the hands or face, note that its temperature momentarily will be at least 22° below zero.

Protective goggles should be worn when opening any refrigerant lines. If liquid coolant does touch the eyes, bathe the eyes quickly in cold water, then apply a bland disinfectant oil to the eyes. See an eye doctor.

When checking a system for leaks with a torch type leak detector, do not breathe the vapors coming from the flame. Do not discharge refrigerant in the area of a live flame. A poisonous phosgene gas is produced when R-12 or F-12 is burned. While the small amount of gas produced by a leak detector is not harmful unless inhaled directly at the flame, the quantity of refrigerant released into the air when a system is purged can be extremely dangerous if allowed to come into contact with an open flame. Thus, when purging a system, be sure that the discharge hose is routed to a well ventilated area where no flame is present. Under these conditions the refrigerant will be quickly dissipated into the surrounding air.

Never allow the temperature of refrigerant drums to exceed 125°F. The resultant increase in temperature will cause a corresponding increase in pressure which may cause the safety plug to release or the drum to burst.

If it is necessary to heat a drum of refrigerant when charging a system, the drum should be placed in water no hotter than 125°F. Never use a blow torch or other open flame. If possible, a pressure release mechanism should be attached before the drum is heated.

When connecting and disconnecting service gauges on an A/C system, ensure that gauge hand valves are fully closed and that compressor service valves, if equipped, are in the back-seated (fully counterclockwise) position. Do not disconnect gauge hoses from service port adapters, if used, while gauges are connected to A/C system. To disconnect hoses, always remove adapter from service port. Do not

Evaporator Pressure Gauge Reading	Evaporator Temperature F°	High Pressure Gauge Reading	Ambient Temperature
0	-21°	45	20°
0.6	-20°	55	30°
2.4	-15°	72	40°
4.5	-10°	86	50°
6.8	- 5°	105	60°
9.2	0°	126	70°
11.8	5°	140	75°
14.7	10°	160	80°
17.1	15°	185	90°
21.1	20°	195	95°
22.5	22°	220	100°
23.9	24°	240	105°
25.4	26°	260	110°
26.9	28°	275	115°
28.5	30°	290	120°
37.0	40°	305	125°
46.7	50°	325	130°
57.7	60°		
70.1	70°		
84.1	80°		
99.6	90°		
116.9	100°		
136.0	110°		
157.1	120°		
179.0	130°		

Fig. 1 Pressure-temperature relationship (Typical). Conditions equivalent to 30 mph or 1750 engine rpm

disconnect hoses from gauge manifold while connected to A/C system, as refrigerant will be rapidly discharged.

After disconnecting gauge lines, check the valve areas to be sure service valves are correctly seated and Schraeder valves, if used, are not leaking.

EXERCISE SYSTEM

An important fact most owners ignore is that A/C units must be used periodically. Manufacturers caution that when the air conditioner is not used regularly, particularly during the cold months, it should be turned on for a few minutes once every two or three weeks while the engine is running. This keeps the system in good operating condition.

Checking out the system for the effects of disuse before the onset of summer is one of the most important aspects of A/C servicing.

First clean out the condenser core, mounted in all cases at the front of the radiator. All obstructions, such as leaves, bugs or dirt, must be removed, as they will reduce heat transfer and impair the efficiency of the system. Make sure the space between the condenser and the radiator also is free of foreign matter.

Make certain the evaporator water drain is open. The evaporator cools and dehu-

LOW PRESSURE GAUGE

HIGH PRESSURE GAUGE

TO LOW PRESSURE CHARGING VALVE

TO HIGH PRESSURE CHARGING VALVE

TO REFRIGERANT SUPPLY TANK

TO VACUUM PUMP

Fig. 2   Manifold gauge set hose connections (Typical).

4. Open low side hand manifold valve slightly, using a container to catch oil and refrigerant. Do not discharge the refrigerant near an open flame as a toxic gas (phosgene) can result.
5. Allow all refrigerant to discharge through the low side fitting only.

NOTE: Open hand valve(s) only enough to bleed refrigerant from system. Too rapid purging will draw excessive oil from compressor and system.

6. When refrigerant ceases to bleed from the discharge hose on the low side, crack open the high side hand valve to check for any remaining pressure. If pressure does exist, allow high side to discharge slowly. This condition indicates a high side restriction, and it must be diagnosed and corrected before evacuating and charging the system.

midifies the air before it enters the passenger compartment; there, the refrigerant is changed from a liquid to a vapor. As the core cools the air, moisture condenses on it but is prevented from collecting in the evaporator by the water drain.

PERFORMANCE TEST

The system should be operated for at least 15 minutes to allow sufficient time for all parts to become completely stabilized. Determine if the system is fully charged by the use of test gauges and sight glass if one is installed on system. Head pressure will read from 180 psi to 220 psi or higher, depending upon ambient temperature and the type unit being tested. The sight glass should be free of bubbles if a glass is used in the system. Low side pressures should read approximately 15 psi to 30 psi, again depending on the ambient temperature and the unit being tested. It is not feasible to give a definite reading for all types of systems used, as the type control and component installation used on a particular system will directly influence the pressure readings on the high and low sides, **Fig. 1.**

The high side pressure will definitely be affected by the ambient or outside air temperature. A system that is operating normally will indicate a high side gauge reading between 150–170 psi with an 80°F ambient temperature. The same system will register 210–230 psi with an ambient temperature of 100°F. No two systems will register exactly the same, which requires that allowance for variations in head pressures must be considered. Following are the most important normal readings likely to be encountered during the season.

Ambient Temp.	High Side Pressure
80	150–170
90	175–195
95	185–205
100	210–230
105	230–250
110	250–270

RELATIVE TEMPERATURE OF HIGH AND LOW SIDES

The high side of the system should be uniformly hot to the touch throughout. A difference in temperature will indicate a partial blockage of liquid or gas at this point.

The low side of the system should be uniformly cool to the touch with no excessive sweating of the suction line or low side service valve. Excessive sweating or frosting of the low side service valve usually indicates an expansion valve is allowing an excessive amount of refrigerant into the evaporator.

EVAPORATOR OUTPUT

At this point, provided all other inspection tests have been performed, and components have been found to operate as they should, a rapid cooling down of the interior of the vehicle should result. The use of a thermometer is not necessary to determine evaporator output. Bringing all units to the correct operating specifications will insure that the evaporator performs as intended.

DISCHARGING & EVACUATING SYSTEM

DISCHARGING SYSTEM

1. Connect gauges into system, **Fig. 2,** and adjust controls for maximum cooling. This is necessary when the system has not been operating to return excess oil to the compressor.
2. Operate engine for 10 to 15 minutes to stabilize the system at 1500–1750 rpm.
3. Adjust engine speed to slow idle, then shut off engine and controls.

EVACUATE SYSTEM WITH VACUUM PUMP

Vacuum pumps suitable for removing air and moisture from A/C systems are commercially available. A specification for system pump-down used here is 28 to 29½ inches vacuum. This reading can be attained at or near sea level only. For each 1000 feet of altitude this operation is being performed, the reading will be 1 inch vacuum lower. As an example, at 5000 feet elevation, only 23–24½ inch of vacuum can be obtained.

CAUTION: The system must be completely discharged before it can be evacuated. Damage to vacuum pump may result if pressurized refrigerant is allowed to enter.

1. With hand gauges connected into system, remove cap from vacuum hose connector. Install hand gauge manifold center hose to vacuum pump connector. Open low side gauge manifold hand valve only.
2. Ensure low side gauge is calibrated correctly. It should be reading zero. If not, adjust calibration.
3. Evacuate system with the vacuum pump until the low pressure gauge reads at least 28 inches of vacuum. Continue evacuating system for an additional 15 minutes for routine system servicing or 20 to 30 minutes, if any parts have been replaced.
4. When system evacuation is complete, close low side gauge manifold hand valve, then turn vacuum pump off.
5. Check ability of system to hold vacuum. Watch low side gauge to see that gauge does not rise at a faster rate than 1 inch vacuum every 4 to 5 minutes. If low side gauge rises at too rapid a rate, install partial charge and leak test. Evacuate system again.
6. If system holds vacuum, charge system with refrigerant.

EVACUATE SYSTEM USING CHARGING STATION

A vacuum pump is built into the charging station and is constructed to withstand repeated and prolonged use without damage. Complete moisture removal from the system is possible only with a vacuum pump constructed for the purpose.

CAUTION: The system must be completely discharged before it can be evacuated. Damage to the vacuum pump may result if pressurized refrigerant is allowed to enter.

1. Connect hose to vacuum pump, if system was discharged through charging station.
2. Open low side gauge hand valve of charging station.
3. Connect station into 110 volt current.
4. Engage "Off-On" switch to vacuum pump according to instructions for specific station being used.
5. Evacuate system with the vacuum pump until the low pressure gauge reads at least 28 inches of vacuum. Continue evacuating system for an additional 15 minutes for routine system servicing or 20 to 30 minutes, if any parts have been replaced.
6. Close low side gauge hand valve, then turn vacuum pump off.
7. Check ability of system to hold vacuum. Watch low side gauge to see that gauge does not rise at a faster rate than 1 inch vacuum every 4 to 5 minutes. If low side gauge rises at too rapid a rate, install partial charge and leak test. Then evacuate system again.
8. If system holds vacuum, charge system with refrigerant.

CHARGING THE SYSTEM

J 23500-01 CHARGING STATION METHOD

Use instructions provided with charging station with the following exceptions:
1. Do not connect high pressure line to A/C system.
2. Always keep high pressure valve closed on charging station.
3. Perform all evacuation and charging through accumulator low-side pressure service fitting.

Use of these procedures will prevent charging station from being accidentally exposed to high-side vehicle system pressure.

DISPOSABLE CAN OR REFRIGERANT DRUM METHOD

CAUTION: Never use these cans to charge into the high pressure side of the

Fig. 3 Charging C.C.O.T. A/C system.

system (compressor discharge port) or into a system that is at high temperature, because the high system pressures could be transfered into the charging can causing it to explode.

If R-12 drum is used, place on scale and note total weight before charging. During charging, watch scale to determine amount of R-12 used.

If 14 ounce R-12 cans are used, close tapping valve, then attach cans following instructions included with manifold adaptor.

Charging Of System

1. Start engine and allow to warm up (choke off, normal idle). Set A/C control lever to OFF.
2. With R-12 drum or cans inverted, open R-12 supply valve and allow 1 lb. of liquid R-12 to flow into system through low-side service fitting on accumulator, **Fig. 3.**
3. When 1 lb. of refrigerant has entered system, engage compressor by setting A/C lever to NORM and blower switch to HI to draw in remainder of charge. Cooling condenser with a large fan will speed up charging procedure by maintaining condenser temperature below charging cylinder temperature.
4. Close refrigerant supply valve and run engine for 30 seconds to clear lines and gauges.
5. With engine running, remove charging low-side hose adapter from accumulator service fitting. Unscrew rapidly to avoid excessive refrigerant loss.

CAUTION: Do not remove a gauge line from its adapter when line is connected to A/C system. To disconnect line, always remove line adapter from service fitting. Do not remove charging hose at gauge set while attached to accumulator, as system

will be discharged due to depressed Schraeder valve.

6. Replace protective cap on accumulator fitting and turn engine off.
7. Check system for leaks.
8. Start engine and check for proper system pressures.

LEAK TEST SYSTEM

The propane torch Halide Leak Detector is the most widely used of the detection devices. Therefore, only the procedure for this device will be given. The procedure is the same for any electronic detector, except that the pick-up device registers the presence of refrigerant by a flashing light or high pitched squeal instead of changing the color of the flame. All other steps in preparing the system and leak testing are the same and can be followed as outlined below:

1. Stabilize system at 1500–1750 rpm. If system is empty of refrigerant, it will be necessary to install a partial charge before continuing. With gauges connected into system, adjust A/C controls for maximum cooling. Operate for 10 to 15 minutes, then shut off car engine.
2. Light leak detector. Open valve to a low flame that will not blow itself out. Warm up until copper element turns cherry red. Lower flame until flame tip is even with or slightly below center of element. For electronic tester, follow preparation procedure as given in operating instructions.
3. Move leak detector pick-up under hoses, joints, seals, and any possible place for a leak to occur.

NOTE: Freon 12 refrigerant is heavier than

air and will move downward. If concentration of refrigerant is located, move pick-up upward to locate leak. Do not inhale fumes produced by burning refrigerant.

4. Watch for color change of flame: Pale blue, no refrigerant; yellow, small amount of refrigerant; purplish-blue, large amount of refrigerant. Repair system as necessary if leaks are located.

5. Check sensitivity of reaction plate: Pass pick-up hose over empty can or crack open refrigerant container; flame should show violent reaction. If no color change, replace reaction plate, following instructions accompanying leak detector. Too high a flame will result in short life to reaction plate and poor reaction and will soon burn out element.

6. Charge system if repairs were necessary.

General Motors Corp.
System Servicing

INDEX

OIL CHARGE
Delco Air & Harrison Radiator Division
COMPRESSOR MODELS WITH CYCLING CLUTCH

Oil Charge-Component Replacement

If there are no signs of excessive leakage, add the following amount of oil depending on component to be replaced.
Evaporator .... 3 ounces
Condenser .... 1 ounce

If accumulator or compressor are to be replaced, drain oil from component to be replaced and measure, then add same amount of new oil to replacement component plus one additional ounce.

CAUTION: On 1981–85 units, if accumulator is replaced, two additional ounces of oil must be added to replace amount captured by desiccant in old accumulator.

NOTE: The radial 4 cylinder compressor does not have an oil sump.

Oil Charge-Leak Condition

On models with axial 6 cylinder compressor, both accumulator and compressor must be removed and oil drained and measured in cases of excessive oil leakage. If oil recovered is 4 ounces or more, add same amount of new refrigerant oil to system. If amount of oil recovered is less than 4 ounces, add 6 ounces of new refrigerant oil to system.

On models with radial 4 cylinder compressor, it will only be necessary to remove, drain and measure oil from accumulator assembly in cases of excessive oil leakage. The radial 4 cylinder compressor does not have an oil sump, therefore it is not necessary to remove compressor in

cases of oil leakage. On 1980 units, if amount of oil recovered is 2 ounces or more, add same amount of new refrigerant oil to system. If amount of oil recovered is less than 2 ounces, add two ounces of new refrigerant oil to system. On 1981–85 units, if amount of oil recovered is 3 ounces or more, add the same amount of new refrigerant oil to system. If amount recovered is less than 3 ounces, add 3 ounces of new refrigerant oil to system.

NOTE: On 1980 units, if accumulator is replaced one additional ounce of oil must be added to replace amount captured by desiccant in old accumulator. On 1981–85 units, if accumulator is replaced two additional ounces of oil must be added to replace amount captured by desiccant in old accumulator.

MODELS LESS CYCLING CLUTCH

RADIAL 4 CYLINDER COMPRESSOR

Component Replacement

When replacing a system component, oil should be added to the system as follows. If compressor is operating, idle engine for 10 minutes with A/C controls set for maximum cooling and high blower prior to discharging system.

Add additional oil as specified if any of components are replaced.
Condenser .... 1 ounce
Evaporator .... 1 ounce
VIR .... 3 ounce
Accumulator .... 1 ounce

Compressor Replacement

1. Discharge system and remove compressor from vehicle.
2. Position compressor with shaft end up and allow oil to drain from suction and discharge ports into a container calibrated in ounces.

3. Drain oil from new compressor, then add same amount of new refrigerant oil to new compressor as was drained from original compressor.

NOTE: If system was flushed the total oil capacity must be added to the compressor as specified in the A/C Data Table.

4. Install new compressor and charge system.

Component Rupture, Fast Discharge

1. Repair leak and flush system.
2. Remove compressor and drain oil.
3. Add total capacity as specified in A/C Data Table of new refrigerant oil to suction port of compressor.
4. Install compressor, charge system and perform leak check.

Slow Leak

1. If refrigerant loss has occurred over an extended period of time, add 3 ounces of refrigerant oil to system.
2. Recharge system.

System Performance Evaluation

When system performance, efficiency and proper oil charge are in doubt, the system should be flushed and the total capacity, as specified in the A/C Data Table, of new refrigerant oil be added to the compressor prior to any further checks of the system.

AXIAL 6 CYLINDER COMPRESSOR

Oil Charge

1. Idle engine for 10 minutes at 1250 rpm with system controls set for maximum cooling and high blower speed.
2. Stop engine, discharge system and remove compressor.
3. With compressor in a horizontal position and drain plug down, remove plug and drain oil into a measured container.

A/C Data Table

Year	Model	Refrigerant Capacity, Lbs.	Refrigeration Oil			Compressor Clutch Air Gap Inch
			Viscosity	Total System Capacity, Ounces	Compressor Oil Level Check, Inches	
BUICK—EXC. SKYHAWK, 1980–84 SKYLARK, 1982–84 CENTURY & 1985 ELECTRA, PARK AVENUE						
1980	Century, Regal, Riviera	3½	525	②	①	③
	Electra & LeSabre	3¾	525	②	①	③
1981	Century, Regal, Riviera	3¼	525	②	①	③
	Electra & LeSabre	3½	525	②	①	③
1982–85	Regal & Riviera	3¼	525	6	①	.020–.040
	Electra & LeSabre	3½	525	6	①	.020–.040
1985 BUICK ELECTRA & PARK AVENUE, CAD. DEVILLE & FLEETWOOD & OLDS. 98						
1985	All	2¾	525	④	①	⑤
CADILLAC—EXC. CIMARRON & 1985 DEVILLE & FLEETWOOD						
1980–81	All	3¾	525	6	①	③
1982	All	3¼	525	6	①	.020–.040
1983	All	3½	525	6	①	.020–.040
1984–85	All	3½	525	④	①	⑤
CHEVROLET—CAMARO, CHEVROLET, MALIBU, MONTE CARLO & NOVA						
1980	Exc. Camaro	3¾	525	②	①	③
1980–81	Camaro	3¼	525	②	①	③
1981–82	Caprice, Impala	3½	525	②	①	③
	Malibu, Monte Carlo	3¼	525	②	①	③
1982–83	Camaro	3	525	6	①	.020–.040
1983–85	Caprice, Impala	3½	525	6	①	.020–.040
	Malibu, Monte Carlo	3¼	525	6	①	.020–.040
1984–85	Camaro	3	525	④	①	⑤
1982–85 CHEV. CAVALIER, BUICK SKYHAWK, CAD. CIMARRON, OLDS. FIRENZA & PONT. 2000						
1982–83	All	2¾	525	6	①	.020–.040
1984–85	All	2¾	525	④	①	⑤
1982–85 CHEV. CELEBRITY, BUICK CENTURY, OLDS. CUTLASS CIERA & PONT. 6000						
1982	All	2¾	525	6	①	.020–.040
1983–85	All	2¾	525	④	①	⑤
CHEVROLET CHEVETTE & PONTIAC 1000						
1980–81	All	2¼	525	②	①	③
1982–84	All	2¼	525	6	①	.020–.040
1980–85 CHEVROLET CITATION, BUICK SKYLARK, OLDS OMEGA & PONTIAC PHOENIX						
1980–85	All	2¾	525	④	①	⑤
1980 CHEVROLET MONZA, BUICK SKYHAWK, OLDS STARFIRE & PONTIAC SUNBIRD						
1980	Monza	2¹³⁄₁₆	525	②	①	③
1980	Skyhawk	2½	525	6	①	.020–.040
	Sunbird	2½	525	6	①	.020–.040
1980	Starfire	⑨	525	6	①	.020–.040
CHEVROLET CORVETTE						
1980–81	All	3	525	②	①	③
1982	All	3	525	6	①	.020–.040
1984–85	All	2¾	525	6	①	.015–.025
OLDSMOBILE—88, 98 (1980–84), TORONADO & CUTLASS EXC. CIERA						
1980	All	3¾	525	②	①	③
1981	Cutlass	3¼	525	②	①	③
1981	All exc. Cutlass	3½	525	②	①	③
1982–85	Cutlass	3¼	525	6	①	.020–.040
1982–85	All exc. Cutlass & 1985 98	3½	525	6	①	.020–.040

A/C DATA TABLE—Continued

Year	Model	Refrigerant Capacity, Lbs.	Refrigeration Oil			Compressor Clutch Air Gap Inch
			Viscosity	Total System Capacity, Ounces	Compressor Oil Level Check, Inches	
PONTIAC—EXC. FIERO, SUNBIRD, 1000 & FRONT WHEEL DRIVE						
1980	Firebird	3¼	525	②	①	③
1980	Gran Prix & LeMans	3¾	525	②	①	③
1980–81	All exc. Gran Prix & LeMans	3½	525	②	①	③
1981	Gran Prix & LeMans	3¼	525	②	①	③
1982–85	All exc. Firebird & Parisienne	3¼	525	6	①	.020–.040
1982–85	Firebird	3	525	④	①	⑤
1983–85	Parisienne	3½	525	6	①	.020–.040
PONTIAC FIERO						
1984–85	All	—	525	8	①	.015–.025

①—Note that "Oil level inches" cannot be checked. Refer to total capacity in ounces. See text for procedure.
②—Axial compressor, 10 ounces; radial compressor, 6 ounces.
③—R-4 compressor, .020–.040 inch; A-6 compressor, .022–.057 inch.
④—Axial compressor, 8 ounces; radial compressor, 5 ounces.
⑤—Axial compressor, .015–.025 inch; radial compressor, .020–.040 inch.

4. If 4 ounces or more of oil was drained, add the same amount to the compressor. If less than 4 ounces of oil was drained, add 6 ounces of oil to compressor.

Compressor Replacement
1. Idle engine for 10 minutes at approximately 1250 rpm at maximum cooling and high blower speed to distribute oil in system.
2. Remove compressor from vehicle.
3. Remove plug and allow oil to drain from compressor into a container calibrated in ounces.
4. Drain oil from new compressor.
5. If amount drained from original compressor is more than four ounces, add the same amount of new refrigerant oil to the new compressor plus amount lost during discharge.
6. If amount of oil drained from original compressor is less than 4 ounces, add 6 ounces of new refrigerant oil to the new compressor plus amount lost during discharge.

Component Replacement
Whenever a component of the A/C system is replaced, if not pre-charged by factory, measured quantities of refrigeration oil should be added to the component to assure that the total oil charge in the system is correct before the unit is placed into operation.

The oil is poured directly into the replacement component. If an evaporator is installed, pour oil into the inlet pipe with the pipe held vertically so the oil will drain into the evaporator core. No additional oil is required if valves and hoses are replaced.

Add additional oil as specified if any of the following components are replaced.

Evaporator .... 3 ounces
Condenser .... 1 ounce
VIR .... 1 ounce
Accumulator .... 1 ounce
Receiver .... 1 ounce

NOTE: If the system is flushed with sufficient of a flushing agent that would remove oil from the system, install the full amount specified in the A/C Data Table. On a newly installed system, install the full capacity of oil prior to operation. On systems containing metal particles in the oil, replace or overhaul the compressor, replace the receiver-dehydrator or VIR dessicant and install a high capacity, low pressure drop filter in the liquid line to the filter to protect the expansion valve and new compressor from damage due to foreign particles.

CHARGING VALVE LOCATION

The high pressure charging valve is located on either the high pressure vapor line or the muffler. The low pressure charging valve is located on the accumulator.

DASH GAUGES

TABLE OF CONTENTS

American Motors Corp.

INDEX

TESTING

Gauge failures are often caused by defective wiring or grounds. The first step in locating trouble should be a thorough inspection of all wiring, terminals and printed circuits. If wiring is secured by clamps, check to see whether the insulation has been severed thereby grounding the wire. In the case of a fuel gauge installation, rust may cause failure by corrosion at the ground connection of the tank unit.

CONSTANT VOLTAGE REGULATOR TYPE (CVR)

The Constant Voltage Regulator (CVR) type indicator is a bimetal-resistance type system consisting of an Instrument Voltage Regulator (IVR), an indicator gauge, and a variable resistance sending unit. Current to the system is applied to the gauge terminals by the IVR, which maintains an average-pulsating value of 5 volts.

The indicator gauge consists of a pointer which is attached to a wire-wound bimetal strip. Current passing through the coil heats the bimetal strip, causing the pointer to move. As more current passes through the coil, heat increases, moving the pointer farther.

The circuit is completed through a sending unit which contains a variable resistor. When resistance is high, less current is allowed to pass through the gauge, and the pointer moves very little. As resistance decreases due to changing conditions in system being monitored, more current passes through gauge coil, causing pointer to move farther.

Fig. 1 Conventional type ammeter (typical)

OPERATIONAL TEST

1. Disconnect wiring harness connector at sending unit. Connect a test lamp or voltmeter between terminal in wiring harness connector and ground.
2. With ignition switch in ON position, light should pulse or meter reading should fluctuate.
3. If lamp lights but does not pulse, or if meter reading remains steady, check ground to IVR. If ground is satisfactory, IVR is defective.
4. If lamp fails to light, or if meter reads 0 volts, check for open circuit across IVR terminals, indicator gauge terminals, or open circuit in wiring harness and printed circuit between components.
5. Connect test lamp or voltmeter ground lead to ground terminal in sending unit wiring harness connector. Light should pulse or meter reading should fluctuate as in step 2. If not, locate open in ground circuit.

NOTE: Do not apply battery voltage to system or ground output terminals of IVR,

as damage to system components or wiring circuits may result.

SENDING UNIT TESTS

Fuel Tank Gauge

1. Disconnect wiring harness connector at sending unit and connect ohmmeter between ground terminal and resistor terminal on sending unit.
2. Meter should read 11–61 ohms on Pacer or 31–248 ohms on others. If reading shows no continuity (infinite reading), check ground connection to tank gauge.
3. If ground is satisfactory, but reading is not within specification, tank unit is defective.
4. If reading is within specification, remove fuel tank gauge from vehicle and connect ohmmeter between resistor terminal and ground terminal (metal housing on single terminal units).
5. Observe meter while slowly moving float rod between empty and full stops. Meter should read 61 ohms on Pacer or 248 ohms on others at empty stop and 11 ohms on Pacer or 31 ohms on others at full stop. Change in readings should be smooth, without hesitation or jumping.
6. If tank unit fails to operate as outlined, unit is defective.

NOTE: Before installing fuel tank gauge, connect wiring harness connector to gauge and move float rod from empty to full position with ignition key in ON position. If dash gauge reading is incorrect, check IVR and dash gauge. If system tests prove satisfactory, but system still does not operate correctly, check that tank gauge rod is not bent or binding and that float is not damaged, loose or filled with fuel.

Oil & Temperature Sending Units

1. Test dash gauge and IVR as outlined above.
2. If system is satisfactory, start engine and allow it to reach operating temperature.
3. If no reading is indicated on the gauge, check the sending unit-to-gauge wire by removing the wire from the sending unit and momentarily ground this wire to a clean, unpainted portion of the engine.
4. If the gauge still does not indicate, the wire is defective. Repair or replace the wire.
5. If grounding the new or repaired wire causes the dash gauge to indicate, the sending unit is faulty.

Fig. 2 Charge indicator lamp wiring. Delco SI type charging system

VARIABLE VOLTAGE TYPE

The variable voltage type dash gauge consists of two magnetic coils to which battery voltage is applied. The coils act on the gauge pointer and pull in opposite directions. One coil is grounded directly to the chassis, while the other coil is grounded through a variable resistor within the sending unit. Resistance through the sending unit determines current flow through its coil, and therefore pointer position.

When resistance is high in the sending unit, less current is allowed to flow through its coil, causing the gauge pointer to move toward the directly grounded coil. When resistance in the sending unit decreases, more current is allowed to pass through its coil, increasing the magnetic field. The gauge pointer is then attracted toward the coil which is grounded through the sending unit.

A special tester is required to diagnosis this type gauge. Follow instructions included with the tester.

AMMETERS

The ammeter is an instrument used to indicate current flow into and out of the battery. When electrical accessories in the vehicle draw more current than the alternator can supply, current flows from the battery and the ammeter indicates a discharge (−) condition. When electrical loads of the vehicle are less than alternator output, current is available to charge the battery, and the ammeter indicates a charge (+) condition. If battery is fully charged, the voltage regulator reduces alternator output to meet only immediate vehicle electrical loads. When this happens, ammeter reads zero.

CONVENTIONAL AMMETER

A conventional ammeter must be connected between the battery and alternator in order to indicate current flow. This type ammeter, **Fig. 1**, consists of a frame to which a permanent magnet is attached. The frame also supports an armature and

pointer assembly. Current in this system flows from the alternator through the ammeter, then to the battery or from the battery through the ammeter into the vehicle electrical system, depending on vehicle operating conditions.

When no current flows through the ammeter, the magnet holds the pointer armature so that the pointer stands at the center of the dial. When current passes in either direction through the ammeter, the resulting magnetic field attracts the armature away from the effect of the permanent magnet, thus giving a reading proportional to the strength of the current flowing.

Troubleshooting

When the ammeter apparently fails to register correctly, there may be trouble in the wiring which connects the ammeter to the alternator and battery or in the alternator or battery itself.

To check the connections, first tighten the two terminal posts on the back of the ammeter. Then, following each wire from the ammeter, tighten all connections on the ignition switch, battery and alternator. Chafed, burned or broken insulation can be found by following each ammeter wire from end to end.

All wires with chafed, burned or broken insulation should be repaired or replaced. After this is done, and all connections are tightened, connect the battery cable and turn on the ignition switch. The needle should point slightly to the discharge (−) side.

Start the engine and speed it up a little above idling speed. The needle should then move to the charge side (+), and its movement should be smooth.

If the pointer does not behave correctly, the ammeter itself is out of order and a new one should be installed.

SHUNT TYPE AMMETER

The shunt type ammeter is actually a specially calibrated voltmeter. It is con-

nected to read voltage drop across a resistance wire (shunt) between the battery and alternator. The shunt is located either in the vehicle wiring or within the ammeter itself.

When voltage is higher at the alternator end of the shunt, the meter indicates a charge (+) condition. When voltage is higher at the battery end of the shunt, the meter indicates a discharge (−) condition. When voltage is equal at both ends of the shunt, the meter reads zero.

Troubleshooting

Ammeter accuracy can be determined by comparing reading with an ammeter of known accuracy.

1. With engine stopped and ignition switch in RUN position, switch on headlamps and heater fan. Meter should indicate a discharge (−) condition.
2. If ammeter pointer does not move, check ammeter terminals for proper connection and check for open circuit in wiring harness. If connections and wiring harness are satisfactory, ammeter is defective.
3. If ammeter indicates a charge (+) condition, wiring harness connections are reversed at ammeter.

ALTERNATOR INDICATOR LIGHT

DELCOTRON SI INTEGRAL CHARGING SYSTEM

This system features an integral solid state regulator mounted inside the alternator slip ring end frame. The alternator indicator lamp is installed in the field wire circuit connected between the ignition "Ign." terminal and alternator No. 1 terminal, **Fig. 2**. The resistance provided by the alternator warning light circuit is needed to protect the diode trio. The alternator indicator lamp should light when the ignition switch is turned on before engine is started. If lamp does not light, either lamp is burned out or indicator lamp wiring has an open circuit. After engine is started, the indicator lamp should be out at all times. If indicator lamp comes on, alternator belt may be loose, alternator or regulator may be defective, charging circuit may be defective or fuse may be blown.

Troubleshooting

1. Switch Off, Lamp On:
   a. Disconnect electrical connector from alternator terminals 1 and 2.
   b. If indicator light remains lit, repair short circuit between leads.
   c. If indicator light goes out, replace alternator rectifier bridge.
2. Switch On, lamp Off, engine not running:
   a. Perform tests described in step 1.
   b. If problem still exists, there may be an open circuit.
   c. To locate open circuit, check for blown fuse or fusible link, burned out bulb, defective bulb socket or an open in No. 1 lead circuit between alternator and ignition switch.
   d. If no faults are found, check charging system for proper operation.
3. Switch On, lamp On, engine running:
   a. On models so equipped, check condition of fuse between indicator light and ignition switch and fuse in A/C circuit.
   b. Check charging system for proper operation.

Fig. 3 Typical vacuum gauge

VOLTMETER

The voltmeter is a gauge which measures the electrical flow from the battery to indicate whether the battery output is within tolerances. The voltmeter reading can range from 13.5–14.0 volts under normal operating conditions. If an undercharge or overcharge condition is indicated for an extended period, the battery and charging system should be checked.

TROUBLESHOOTING

To check voltmeter, turn key and headlights on with engine off. Pointer should move to 12.5 volts. If no needle movement is observed, check connections from battery to circuit breaker. If connections are tight and meter shows no movement, check wire continuity. If wire continuity is satisfactory, the meter is inoperative and must be replaced.

ELECTRICAL TEMPERATURE GAUGES

This temperature indicating system consists of a sending unit, located on the cylinder head, electrical temperature gauge and an instrument voltage regulator. As engine temperature increases or decreases, the resistance of the sending unit changes, in turn controlling current flow to the gauge. When engine temperature is low, the resistance of the sending unit is high, restricting current flow to the gauge, in turn indicating low engine temperature. As engine temperature increases, the resistance of the sending unit decreases, permitting an increased current flow to the gauge, resulting in an increased temperature reading.

TROUBLESHOOTING

Troubleshooting for the electrical temperature indicating system is the same as for the electrical oil pressure indicating system.

ELECTRICAL OIL PRESSURE GAUGES

This oil pressure indicating system incorporates an instrument voltage regulator, electrical oil pressure gauge and a sending unit which are connected in series. The sending unit consists of a diaphragm, contact and a variable resistor. As oil pressure increases or decreases, the diaphragm actuated the contact on the variable resistor, in turn controlling current flow to the gauge. When oil pressure is low, the resistance of the variable resistor is high, restricting current flow to the gauge, in turn indicating low oil pressure. As oil pressure increases, the resistance of the variable resistor is lowered, permitting an increased current flow to the gauge, resulting in an increased gauge reading.

TROUBLESHOOTING

Disconnect the oil pressure gauge lead from the sending unit, connect a 12 volt test lamp between the gauge lead and the ground and turn ignition ON. If test lamp flashes, the instrument voltage regulator is functioning properly and the gauge circuit is not broken. If the test lamp remains lit, the instrument voltage regulator is defective and must be replaced. If the test lamp does not light, check the instrument voltage regulator for proper ground or an open circuit. Also, check for an open in the instrument voltage regulator to oil pressure gauge wire or in the gauge itself.

NOTE: If test lamp flashes and gauge is not accurate, the gauge may be out of calibration, requiring replacement.

OIL PRESSURE INDICATOR LIGHT

Many cars utilize a warning light on the instrument panel in place of the conventional dash indicating gauge to warn the driver when the oil pressure is dangerously low. The warning light is wired in series with the ignition switch and the engine unit—which is an oil pressure switch.

The oil pressure switch contains a diaphragm and a set of contacts. When the ignition switch is turned on, the warning light circuit is energized and the circuit is completed through the closed contacts in the pressure switch. When the engine is started, build-up of oil pressure compresses the diaphragm, opening the contacts, thereby breaking the circuit and putting out the light.

TROUBLESHOOTING

The oil pressure warning light should go on when the ignition is turned on. If it does not light, disconnect the wire from the engine unit and ground the wire to the frame or cylinder block. Then if the warning light still does not go on with the ignition switch on, replace the bulb.

If the warning light goes on when the wire is grounded to the frame or cylinder block, the engine unit should be checked for being loose or poorly grounded. If the unit is found to be tight and properly grounded, it should be removed and a new one installed. (The presence of sealing compound on the threads of the engine unit will cause a poor ground).

If the warning light remains lit when it normally should be out, replace the engine unit before proceeding further to determine the cause for a low pressure indication.

The warning light sometimes will light up or will flicker when the engine is idling, even though the oil pressure is adequate. However the light should go out when the engine speed is increased.

TEMPERATURE INDICATOR LIGHT

The temperature indicator light illuminates whenever engine coolant temperature exceeds a predetermined value. The sending unit is an On-Off switch, and is normally in the "Off" position. Whenever coolant temperature is above the predetermined value of the switch, the switch

DASH GAUGES

closes and provides a ground circuit for the indicator light.

TROUBLESHOOTING

If the red light is not lit when the engine is being cranked, check for a burned out bulb, an open in the light circuit, or a defective ignition switch.

If the red light is lit when the engine is running, check the wiring between light and switch for a ground, temperature switch defective, or overheated cooling system.

NOTE: As a test circuit to check whether the red bulb is functioning properly, a wire which is connected to the ground terminal of the ignition switch is tapped into its circuit. When the ignition is in the "Start" (engine cranking) position, the ground terminal is grounded inside the switch and the red bulb will be lit. When the engine is started and the ignition switch is in the "On" position, the test circuit is opened and the bulb is then controlled by the temperature switch.

SPEEDOMETERS

The following material covers only that service on speedometers which can be performed by the average service man. Repairs on the units themselves are not included as they require special tools and extreme care when making repairs and adjustments and only an experienced speedometer mechanic should attempt such servicing.

The speedometer has two main parts—the indicator head and the speedometer drive cable. When the speedometer fails to indicate speed or mileage, the cable or housing is probably broken.

SPEEDOMETER CABLE

Most cables are broken due to lack of lubrication or a sharp bend or kink in the housing.

A cable might break because the speedometer head mechanism binds. If such is the case, the speedometer head should be repaired or replaced before a new cable or housing is installed.

A "jumpy" pointer condition, together with a sort of scraping noise, is due, in most instances, to a dry or kinked speedometer cable. The kinked cable rubs on the housing and winds up, slowing down the pointer. The cable then unwinds and the pointer "jumps".

To check for kinks, remove the cable, lay it on a flat surface and twist one end with the fingers. If it turns over smoothly the cable is not kinked. But if part of the cable flops over as it is twisted, the cable is kinked and should be replaced.

LUBRICATION

The speedometer cable should be lubricated with special cable lubricant every 10,000 miles.

Fill the ferrule on the upper end of the housing with the cable lubricant. Insert the cable in the housing, starting at the upper end. Turn the cable around carefully while feeding it into the housing. Repeat filling the ferrule except for the last six inches of cable. Too much lubricant at this point may cause the lubricant to work into the indicating hand.

INSTALLING CABLE

During installation, if the cable sticks when inserted in the housing and will not go through, the housing is damaged inside or kinked. Be sure to check the housing from one end to the other. Straighten any sharp bends by relocating clamps or elbows. Replace housing if it is badly kinked or broken. Position the cable and housing so that they lead into the head as straight as possible.

Check the new cable for kinks before installing it. Use wide, sweeping, gradual curves when the cable comes out of the transmission and connects to the head so the cable will not be damaged during its installation.

If inspection indicates that the cable and housing are in good condition, yet pointer action is erratic, check the speedometer head for possible binding.

The speedometer drive pinion should also be checked. If the pinion is dry or its teeth are stripped, the speedometer may not register properly.

The transmission mainshaft nut must be tight or the speedometer drive gear may slip on the mainshaft and cause slow speed readings.

ELECTRIC CLOCKS

Regulation of electric clocks used on automobiles is accomplished automatically by merely resetting the time. If the clock is running fast, the action of turning the hands back to correct the time will automatically cause the clock to run slightly slower. If the clock is running slow, the action of turning the hands forward to correct the time will automatically cause the clock to run slightly faster (10 to 15 seconds day).

A lock-out feature prevents the clock regulator mechanism from being reset more than once per wind cycle, regardless of the number of times the time is reset. After the clock rewinds, if the time is then reset, automatic regulation will take place. If a clock varies over 10 minutes per day, it will never adjust sufficiently, and must be repaired or replaced.

WINDING CLOCK WHEN CONNECTING BATTERY OR CLOCK WIRING

The clock requires special attention when reconnecting a battery that has been disconnected for any reason, a clock that has been disconnected, or when replacing a blown clock fuse. It is very important that the initial wind be fully made. The procedure is as follows:

1. Make sure that all other instruments and lights are turned off.
2. Connect positive cable to battery.
3. Before connecting the negative cable, press the terminal to its post on the battery. Immediately afterward strike the terminal against the battery post to see if there is a spark. If there is a spark, allow the clock to run down until it stops ticking, and repeat as above until there is no spark. Then immediately make the permanent connection before the clock can again run down. The clock will run down in approximately two minutes.
4. Reset clock after all connections have been made. This procedure should also be followed when reconnecting the clock after it has been disconnected, or if it has stopped because of a blown fuse. Be sure to disconnect battery before installing a new fuse.

TROUBLESHOOTING

If clock does not run, check for blown "clock" fuse. If fuse is blown check for short in wiring. If fuse is not blown check for open circuit.

With an electric clock, the most frequent cause of clock fuse blowing is voltage at the clock which will prevent a complete wind and allow clock contacts to remain closed. This may be caused by any of the following: discharged battery, corrosion on contact surface of battery terminals, loose connections at battery terminals, at junction block, at fuse clips, or at terminal connection of clock. Therefore, if in reconnecting battery or clock it is noted that the clock is not ticking, always check for blown fuse, or examine the circuits at the points indicated above to determine and correct the cause.

VACUUM GAUGE

This gauge, **Fig. 3** measures intake manifold vacuum. The intake manifold vacuum varies with engine operating conditions, carburetor adjustments, valve timing, ignition timing and general engine condition.

Since the optimum fuel economy is directly proportional to a properly functioning engine, a high vacuum reading on the gauge relates to fuel economy. For this reason some manufacturers call the vacuum gauge a "Fuel Economy Indicator." Most gauges have colored sectors the green sector being the "Economy" range and red the "Power" range. Therefore, the vehicle should be operated with gauge registering in the green sector or a high numerical number, **Fig. 3,** for maximum economy.

TROUBLESHOOTING

The vacuum gauge is a nonadjustable mechanical gauge. Accuracy may be tested by connecting a test vacuum gauge of known accuracy with the existing gauge using a T-fitting. Compare the vacuum readings of the gauges and replace defective gauge as required.

Chrysler Corp.

INDEX

GAUGES

Gauge failures are often caused by defective wiring or grounds. The first step in locating trouble should be a thorough inspection of all wiring, terminals and printed circuits. If wiring is secured by clamps, check to see whether the insulation has been severed thereby grounding the wire. In the case of a fuel gauge installation, rust may cause failure by corrosion at the ground connection of the tank unit.

VOLTAGE LIMITER TYPE

The voltage limiter type indicator is a bimetal-resistance type system consisting of a voltage limiter, an indicator gauge, and a variable resistance sending unit. Current to the system is applied to the gauge terminals by the voltage limiter, which maintains an average-pulsating value of 5 volts.

The indicator gauge consists of a pointer which is attached to a wire-wound bimetal strip. Current passing through the coil heats the bimetal strip, causing the pointer to move. As more current passes through the coil, heat increases, moving the pointer farther.

The circuit is completed through a sending unit which contains a variable resistor. When resistance is high, less current is allowed to pass through the gauge, and the pointer moves very little. As resistance decreases due to changing conditions in system being monitored, more current passes through gauge coil, causing pointer to move farther.

Voltage Limiter Test

1. Connect one lead of a suitable voltmeter to temperature sending unit and other lead to a good ground. Do not disconnect sending unit lead from sending unit.
2. Turn ignition switch to the "On" position and observe voltmeter.
3. A fluctuating voltmeter indicates that voltage limiter is operating.

AMMETERS

The ammeter is an instrument used to

Fig. 1   Conventional type ammeter (typical)

indicate current flow into and out of the battery. When electrical accessories in the vehicle draw more current than the alternator can supply, current flows from the battery and the ammeter indicates a discharge (−) condition. When electrical loads of the vehicle are less than alternator output, current is available to charge the battery, and the ammeter indicates a charge (+) condition. If battery is fully charged, the voltage regulator reduces alternator output to meet only immediate vehicle electrical loads. When this happens, ammeter reads zero.

CONVENTIONAL AMMETER

A conventional ammeter must be connected between the battery and alternator in order to indicate current flow. This type ammeter, **Fig. 1**, consists of a frame to which a permanent magnet is attached. The frame also supports an armature and pointer assembly. Current in this system flows from the alternator through the ammeter, then to the battery or from the battery through the ammeter into the vehicle electrical system, depending on vehicle operating conditions.

When no current flows through the ammeter, the magnet holds the pointer armature so that the pointer stands at the center of the dial. When current passes in either direction through the ammeter, the resulting magnetic field attracts the armature away from the effect of the permanent magnet, thus giving a reading proportional to the strength of the current flowing.

Troubleshooting

When the ammeter apparently fails to register correctly, there may be trouble in the wiring which connects the ammeter to the alternator and battery or in the alternator or battery itself.

To check the connections, first tighten the two terminal posts on the back of the ammeter. Then, following each wire from the ammeter, tighten all connections on the ignition switch, battery and alternator. Chafed, burned or broken insulation can be found by following each ammeter wire from end to end.

All wires with chafed, burned or broken insulation should be repaired or replaced. After this is done, and all connections are tightened, connect the battery cable and turn on the ignition switch. The needle should point slightly to the discharge (−) side.

Start the engine and speed it up a little above idling speed. The needle should then move to the charge side (+), and its movement should be smooth.

If the pointer does not behave correctly, the ammeter itself is out of order and a new one should be installed.

SHUNT TYPE AMMETER

The shunt type ammeter is actually a specially calibrated voltmeter. It is connected to read voltage drop across a resistance wire (shunt) between the battery and alternator. The shunt is located either in the vehicle wiring or within the ammeter itself.

When voltage is higher at the alternator end of the shunt, the meter indicates a charge (+) condition. When voltage is higher at the battery end of the shunt, the meter indicates a discharge (−) condition. When voltage is equal at both ends of the shunt, the meter reads zero.

Troubleshooting

Ammeter accuracy can be determined by comparing reading with an ammeter of known accuracy.

1. With engine stopped and ignition switch in RUN position, switch on headlamps and heater fan. Meter should indicate a discharge (−) condition.
2. If ammeter pointer does not move,

check ammeter terminals for proper connection and check for open circuit in wiring harness. If connections and wiring harness are satisfactory, ammeter is defective.

3. If ammeter indicates a charge (+) condition, wiring harness connections are reversed at ammeter.

VOLTMETER

The voltmeter is a gauge which measures the electrical flow from the battery to indicate whether the battery output is within tolerances. The voltmeter reading can range from 13.5–14.0 volts under normal operating conditions. If an undercharge or overcharge condition is indicated for an extended period, the battery and charging system should be checked.

TROUBLESHOOTING

To check voltmeter, turn key and headlights on with engine off. Pointer should move to 12.5 volts. If no needle movement is observed, check connections from battery to circuit breaker. If connections are tight and meter shows no movement, check wire continuity. If wire continuity is satisfactory, the meter is inoperative and must be replaced.

ELECTRICAL TEMPERATURE GAUGES

This temperature indicating system consists of a sending unit, located on the cylinder head, electrical temperature gauge and an instrument voltage regulator. As engine temperature increases or decreases, the resistance of the sending unit changes, in turn controlling current flow to the gauge. When engine temperature is low, the resistance of the sending unit is high, restricting current flow to the gauge, in turn indicating low engine temperature. As engine temperature increases, the resistance of the sending unit decreases, permitting an increased current flow to the gauge, resulting in an increased temperature reading.

TROUBLESHOOTING

A special tester is required to diagnosis this type of gauge. Follow instructions included with the tester.

ELECTRICAL OIL PRESSURE GAUGES

This oil pressure indicating system incorporates an instrument voltage regulator, electrical oil pressure gauge and a sending unit which are connected in series. The sending unit consists of a diaphragm, contact and a variable resistor. As oil pres-

Fig. 2 Gauges incorporating the L.E.D. system

sure increases or decreases, the diaphragm actuated the contact on the variable resistor, in turn controlling current flow to the gauge. When oil pressure is low, the resistance of the variable resistor is high, restricting current flow to the gauge, in turn indicating low oil pressure. As oil pressure increases, the resistance of the variable resistor is lowered, permitting an increased current flow to the gauge, resulting in an increased gauge reading.

TROUBLESHOOTING

A special tester is required to diagnosis this type of gauge. Follow instructions included with the tester.

OIL PRESSURE INDICATOR LIGHT

Many cars utilize a warning light on the instrument panel in place of the conventional dash indicating gauge to warn the driver when the oil pressure is dangerously low. The warning light is wired in series with the ignition switch and the engine unit—which is an oil pressure switch.

The oil pressure switch contains a diaphragm and a set of contacts. When the ignition switch is turned on, the warning light circuit is energized and the circuit is completed through the closed contacts in the pressure switch. When the engine is started, build-up of oil pressure compresses the diaphragm, opening the contacts, thereby breaking the circuit and putting out the light.

TROUBLESHOOTING

The oil pressure warning light should go on when the ignition is turned on. If it does not light, disconnect the wire from the engine unit and ground the wire to the frame or cylinder block. Then if the warning light still does not go on with the ignition switch on, replace the bulb.

If the warning light goes on when the wire is grounded to the frame or cylinder

block, the engine unit should be checked for being loose or poorly grounded. If the unit is found to be tight and properly grounded, it should be removed and a new one installed. (The presence of sealing compound on the threads of the engine unit will cause a poor ground).

If the warning light remains lit when it normally should be out, replace the engine unit before proceeding further to determine the cause for a low pressure indication.

The warning light sometimes will light up or will flicker when the engine is idling, even though the oil pressure is adequate. However, the light should go out when the engine is speeded up. There is no cause for alarm in such cases; it simply means that the pressure switch is not calibrated precisely correct.

TEMPERATURE INDICATOR LIGHT

A bimetal temperature switch located in the cylinder head control the operation of a temperature indicator light with a red lens. If the engine cooling system is not functioning properly and coolant temperature exceeds a predetermined value, the warning light will illuminate.

TROUBLESHOOTING

If the red light is not lit when the engine is being cranked, check for a burned out bulb, an open in the light circuit, or a defective ignition switch.

If the red light is lit when the engine is running, check the wiring between light and switch for a ground, temperature switch defective, or overheated cooling system.

NOTE: As a test circuit to check whether the red bulb is functioning properly, a wire which is connected to the ground terminal of the ignition switch is tapped into its circuit. When the ignition is in the "Start" (engine cranking) position, the ground terminal is grounded inside the switch and the red bulb will be lit. When the engine is started and the ignition switch is in the "On" position, the test circuit is opened and the bulb is then controlled by the temperature switch.

GAUGE ALERT SYSTEM

L.E.D. (LIGHT EMITTING DIODE)

The fuel, temperature and ammeter gauges are equipped with a L.E.D. (Light Emitting Diode) mounted in each of the gauge dials, **Fig. 2**. This diode will illuminate and alert the driver that the system the gauge is monitoring is malfunctioning. The electronic sensor circuit is mounted on the gauge housing. The printed circuit board is permanently attached and is not serviceable. If the L.E.D. is malfunctioning, the gauge and the printed circuit board must be replaced as an assembly.

OPERATION

Fuel Gauge

When gauge indicator shows approximately ⅛ of a tank of fuel remaining, the L.E.D. will light alerting the driver of a low fuel situation.

Temperature Gauge

When gauge indicator shows engine temperature approximately 240 to 260 degrees F. the L.E.D. will light alerting the driver of an overheat condition.

Ammeter Gauge

This L.E.D. operates independently of the gauge indicator and monitors system voltage. The L.E.D. will alert the driver of three charging system potential malfunctions.

1. A discharging condition, caused by excessive electrical demand on charging system, (engine at idle rpm).
2. A weak or defective battery with ignition switch in the "ON" position, (before the ignition switch is moved to the "START" position).
3. A weak or defective battery with minimum demand on charging system, while vehicle is being used in stop and go driving (intermittent L.E.D. illumination occurring).

TESTING

Fuel and Temperature L.E.D.

Use tester C-3826 for diagnosing systems.

Ammeter L.E.D.

NOTE: Only if battery and charging system are functioning properly can the following test be performed.

Turn ignition switch to the "ON" position and turn on headlights, windshield wipers and stoplights. This will cause excessive

Fig. 3   Typical vacuum gauge

demand on charging system activating the L.E.D. immediately or within approximately one minute. If the L.E.D. does not light there is a malfunction in the system. If L.E.D. lights, run engine at approximately 2000 rpm, L.E.D. should stop emitting light, if the L.E.D. continues to emit light there is a malfunction in the system.

NOTE: In all cases of system malfunctions the complete gauge must be replaced.

SPEEDOMETERS

The following material covers only that service on speedometers which can be performed by the average service man. Repairs on the units themselves are not included as they require special tools and extreme care when making repairs and adjustments and only an experienced speedometer mechanic should attempt such servicing.

The speedometer has two main parts—the indicator head and the speedometer drive cable. When the speedometer fails to indicate speed or mileage, the cable or housing is probably broken.

SPEEDOMETER CABLE

Most cables are broken due to lack of lubrication or a sharp bend or kink in the housing.

A cable might break because the speedometer head mechanism binds. If such is the case, the speedometer head should be repaired or replaced before a new cable or housing is installed.

A "jumpy" pointer condition, together with a sort of scraping noise, is due, in most instances, to a dry or kinked speedometer cable. The kinked cable rubs on the housing and winds up, slowing down the pointer. The cable then unwinds and the pointer "jumps".

To check for kinks, remove the cable, lay it on a flat surface and twist one end with

the fingers. If it turns over smoothly the cable is not kinked. But if part of the cable flops over as it is twisted, the cable is kinked and should be replaced.

LUBRICATION

The speedometer cable should be lubricated with special cable lubricant every 10,000 miles.

Fill the ferrule on the upper end of the housing with the cable lubricant. Insert the cable in the housing, starting at the upper end. Turn the cable around carefully while feeding it into the housing. Repeat filling the ferrule except for the last six inches of cable. Too much lubricant at this point may cause the lubricant to work into the indicating hand.

INSTALLING CABLE

During installation, if the cable sticks when inserted in the housing and will not go through, the housing is damaged inside or kinked. Be sure to check the housing from one end to the other. Straighten any sharp bends by relocating clamps or elbows. Replace housing if it is badly kinked or broken. Position the cable and housing so that they lead into the head as straight as possible.

Check the new cable for kinks before installing it. Use wide, sweeping, gradual curves when the cable comes out of the transmission and connects to the head so the cable will not be damaged during its installation.

If inspection indicates that the cable and housing are in good condition, yet pointer action is erratic, check the speedometer head for possible binding.

The speedometer drive pinion should also be checked. If the pinion is dry or its teeth are stripped, the speedometer may not register properly.

The transmission mainshaft nut must be tight or the speedometer drive gear may slip on the mainshaft and cause slow speed readings.

ELECTRIC CLOCKS

Regulation of electric clocks used on automobiles is accomplished automatically by merely resetting the time. If the clock is running fast, the action of turning the hands back to correct the time will automatically cause the clock to run slightly slower. If the clock is running slow, the action of turning the hands forward to correct the time will automatically cause the clock to run slightly faster (10 to 15 seconds day).

A lock-out feature prevents the clock regulator mechanism from being reset more than once per wind cycle, regardless of the number of times the time is reset. After the clock rewinds, if the time is then reset, automatic regulation will take place. If a clock varies over 10 minutes per day, it will never adjust sufficiently, and must be repaired or replaced.

DASH GAUGES

WINDING CLOCK WHEN CONNECTING BATTERY OR CLOCK WIRING

The clock requires special attention when reconnecting a battery that has been disconnected for any reason, a clock that has been disconnected, or when replacing a blown clock fuse. It is very important that the initial wind be fully made. The procedure is as follows:

1. Make sure that all other instruments and lights are turned off.
2. Connect positive cable to battery.
3. Before connecting the negative cable, press the terminal to its post on the battery. Immediately afterward strike the terminal against the battery post to see if there is a spark. If there is a spark, allow the clock to run down until it stops ticking, and repeat as above until there is no spark. Then immediately make the permanent connection before the clock can again run down. The clock will run down in approximately two minutes.

4. Reset clock after all connections have been made. The foregoing procedure should also be followed when reconnecting the clock after it has been disconnected, or if it has stopped because of a blown fuse. Be sure to disconnect battery before installing a new fuse.

TROUBLESHOOTING

If clock does not run, check for blown "clock" fuse. If fuse is blown check for short in wiring. If fuse is not blown check for open circuit.

With an electric clock, the most frequent cause of clock fuse blowing is voltage at the clock which will prevent a complete wind and allow clock contacts to remain closed. This may be caused by any of the following: discharged battery, corrosion on contact surface of battery terminals, loose connections at battery terminals, at junction block, at fuse clips, or at terminal connection of clock. Therefore, if in reconnecting battery or clock it is noted that the clock is not ticking, always check for blown fuse, or examine the circuits at the points indicated above to determine and correct the cause.

VACUUM GAUGE

This gauge, **Fig. 3**, measures intake manifold vacuum. The intake manifold vacuum varies with engine operating conditions, carburetor adjustments, valve timing, ignition timing and general engine condition.

Since the optimum fuel economy is directly proportional to a properly functioning engine, a high vacuum reading on the gauge relates to fuel economy. For this reason some manufacturers call the vacuum gauge a "Fuel Economy Indicator." Most gauges have colored sectors the green sector being the "Economy" range and red the "Power" range. Therefore, the vehicle should be operated with gauge registering in the green sector or a high numerical number, **Fig. 3**, for maximum economy.

Ford Motor Co.

INDEX

TESTING

Gauge failures are often caused by defective wiring or grounds. The first step in locating trouble should be a thorough inspection of all wiring, terminals and printed circuits. If wiring is secured by clamps, check to see whether the insulation has been severed thereby grounding the wire. In the case of a fuel gauge installation, rust may cause failure by corrosion at the ground connection of the tank unit.

CONSTANT VOLTAGE REGULATOR TYPE (CVR)

The Constant Voltage Regulator (CVR) type indicator is a bimetal-resistance type system consisting of an Instrument Voltage Regulator (IVR), an indicator gauge, and a variable resistance sending unit. Current to the system is applied to the gauge terminals by the IVR, which maintains an average-pulsating value of 5 volts.

The indicator gauge consists of a pointer which is attached to a wire-wound bimetal strip. Current passing through the coil heats the bimetal strip, causing the pointer to move. As more current passes through the coil, heat increases, moving the pointer farther.

The circuit is completed through a sending unit which contains a variable resistor. When resistance is high, less current is allowed to pass through the gauge, and the pointer moves very little. As resistance decreases due to changing conditions in system being monitored, more current passes through gauge coil, causing pointer to move farther.

OPERATIONAL TEST

1. Disconnect wiring harness connector at sending unit. Connect a test lamp or voltmeter between terminal in wiring harness connector and ground.
2. With ignition switch in ON position, light should pulse or meter reading should fluctuate.
3. If lamp lights but does not pulse, or if meter reading remains steady, check ground to IVR. If ground is satisfactory, IVR is defective.
4. If lamp fails to light, or if meter reads 0 volts, check for open circuit across IVR terminals, indicator gauge terminals, or open circuit in wiring harness and printed circuit between components.
5. Connect test lamp or voltmeter ground lead to ground terminal in sending unit wiring harness connector. Light should pulse or meter reading should fluctuate as in step 2. If not, locate open in ground circuit.

NOTE: Do not apply battery voltage to system or ground output terminals of IVR, as damage to system components or wiring circuits may result.

DASH GAUGE TEST

1. Disconnect battery ground cable and remove gauge from vehicle.
2. Connect ohmmeter between gauge terminals and read coil winding resistance.
3. An upward movement of ohmmeter needle from 10 ohms to 14 ohms is normal, as test current of ohmmeter causes a temperature rise in gauge coil windings.
4. If ohmmeter reads below 10 ohms or above 14 ohms, gauge is defective.

SENDING UNIT TESTS

Fuel Tank Gauge
1. Disconnect wiring harness connector at sending unit and connect ohmmeter between ground terminal and resistor terminal on sending unit.
2. Meter should read 8–86 ohms. If reading shows no continuity (infinite reading), check ground connection to tank gauge.

Fig. 1 Conventional type ammeter (typical)

Fig. 2 Typical vacuum gauge

CONDITION	POSSIBLE SOURCE	ACTION	LOCATION
• Taillamp L.E.D. Illuminated/False Indication	• Bad Bulb • Open Wire	• Replace Bulb • Check Cir. 14/102	• Rear Running Lamps • 14401 Connector to Module
• Headlamp L.E.D. Illuminated or False Indications	• Bad Headlamp Bulb • Non-Halogen Bulb • Open Wire	• Replace Headlamp • Replace with Halogen Bulb • Check Cir. 13 or 108	• Headlamp • 14401 Connector to Module
• Brake Lamp L.E.D. Illuminated or False Indication	• Bad Bulb • Open Wire	• Replace Bulb • Check Cir. 5 and 105, 9 and 104	• Tail lamp • Console
• Low Fuel L.E.D. Illuminated or False Indication	• Low Fuel • Warning Switch (Inoperative)	• Fill Gas Tank • Replace	• Console • Washer Reservoir
• Washer Fluid L.E.D. Illuminated or False Indication	• Low Washer Fluid • Warning Switch (Inoperative)	• Fill Washer Reservoir • Replace	• Under Hood • 14401 Connector to Module
• (Test) No L.E.D.'s Will Illuminate	• No Voltage • Open Wire	• Check Fuse • Check Cir. 296-57D	• Fuse Panel • 14401 Connector to Module
• (Test) One or More L.E.D.'s Will Not Illuminate	• Bad L.E.D.s	• Replace Indicator	• Console

Fig. 3   Graphic display warning indicator diagnosis chart

3. If ground is satisfactory, but reading is not within specification, tank unit is defective.
4. If reading is within specification, remove fuel tank gauge from vehicle and connect ohmmeter between resistor terminal and ground terminal (metal housing on single terminal units).
5. Observe meter while slowly moving float rod between empty and full stops. Meter should read 60–86 ohms at empty stop and 8–12 ohms at full stop. Change in readings should be smooth, without hesitation or jumping.
6. If tank unit fails to operate as outlined, unit is defective.

NOTE: Before installing fuel tank gauge, connect wiring harness connector to gauge and move float rod from empty to full position with ignition key in ON position. If dash gauge reading is incorrect, check IVR and dash gauge. If system tests prove satisfactory, but system still does not operate correctly, check that tank gauge rod is not bent or binding and that float is not damaged, loose or filled with fuel.

Oil & Temperature Sending Units
1. Test dash gauge and IVR as outlined above.
2. If system is satisfactory, start engine and allow it to reach operating temperature.
3. If no reading is indicated on the gauge, check the sending unit-to-gauge wire by removing the wire from the sending unit and momentarily ground this wire to a clean, unpainted portion of the engine.

4. If the gauge still does not indicate, the wire is defective. Repair or replace the wire.
5. If grounding the new or repaired wire causes the dash gauge to indicate, the sending unit is faulty.

AMMETERS

The ammeter is an instrument used to indicate current flow into and out of the battery. When electrical accessories in the vehicle draw more current than the alternator can supply, current flows from the battery and the ammeter indicates a discharge (−) condition. When electrical loads of the vehicle are less than alternator output, current is available to charge the battery, and the ammeter indicates a charge (+) condition. If battery is fully charged, the voltage regulator reduces alternator output to meet only immediate vehicle electrical loads. When this happens, ammeter reads zero.

CONVENTIONAL AMMETER

A conventional ammeter must be connected between the battery and alternator in order to indicate current flow. This type ammeter, **Fig. 1,** consists of a frame to which a permanent magnet is attached. The frame also supports an armature and pointer assembly. Current in this system flows from the alternator through the ammeter, then to the battery or from the battery through the ammeter into the vehicle electrical system, depending on vehicle operating conditions.

When no current flows through the ammeter, the magnet holds the pointer arma-

ture so that the pointer stands at the center of the dial. When current passes in either direction through the ammeter, the resulting magnetic field attracts the armature away from the effect of the permanent magnet, thus giving a reading proportional to the strength of the current flowing.

Troubleshooting

When the ammeter apparently fails to register correctly, there may be trouble in the wiring which connects the ammeter to the alternator and battery or in the alternator or battery itself.

To check the connections, first tighten the two terminal posts on the back of the ammeter. Then, following each wire from the ammeter, tighten all connections on the ignition switch, battery and alternator. Chafed, burned or broken insulation can be found by following each ammeter wire from end to end.

All wires with chafed, burned or broken insulation should be repaired or replaced. After this is done, and all connections are tightened, connect the battery cable and turn on the ignition switch. The needle should point slightly to the discharge (−) side.

Start the engine and speed it up a little above idling speed. The needle should then move to the charge side (+), and its movement should be smooth.

If the pointer does not behave correctly, the ammeter itself is out of order and a new one should be installed.

SHUNT TYPE AMMETER

The shunt type ammeter is actually a specially calibrated voltmeter. It is connected to read voltage drop across a resistance wire (shunt) between the battery and alternator. The shunt is located either in the vehicle wiring or within the ammeter itself.

When voltage is higher at the alternator end of the shunt, the meter indicates a charge (+) condition. When voltage is higher at the battery end of the shunt, the meter indicates a discharge (−) condition. When voltage is equal at both ends of the shunt, the meter reads zero.

Troubleshooting

Ammeter accuracy can be determined by comparing reading with an ammeter of known accuracy.

1. With engine stopped and ignition switch in RUN position, switch on headlamps and heater fan. Meter should indicate a discharge (−) condition.
2. If ammeter pointer does not move, check ammeter terminals for proper connection and check for open circuit in wiring harness. If connections and wiring harness are satisfactory, ammeter is defective.
3. If ammeter indicates a charge (+) condition, wiring harness connections are reversed at ammeter.

ALTERNATOR INDICATOR LIGHT

The indicator lamp glows when field relay fails to close. When ignition is in the On position, battery current flows through the charge indicator lamp and a parallel resistor, and through regulator to field, and the lamp comes on. Vehicles with electronic voltage regulator have a 500 ohm resistor. On all others the resistor is 15 ohms. When the alternator builds up enough voltage to close the field relay the charge indicator lamp will go out. Place ignition switch in the Run position with the engine stopped. The lamp should light. If not, the bulb is burned out or indicator lamp has an open circuit.

On vehicles with electro-mechanical or transistorized regulators, an open resistor wire in the alternator charging circuit will usually cause the indicator lamp to remain on until engine speed is increased to approximately 2000 rpm. In some cases the lamp will remain on above 2000 rpm. The charge indicator lamp may be tested using a test light containing a No. 67 or 1155 bulb. Disconnect regulator wire connector from regulator, then place ignition switch in the Run position. Place one test lamp lead on regulator wire connector "I" terminal and other lead on regulator base. Test lamp will light if circuit is in proper working order. If 15 ohm resistor or circuit is open, indicator lamp will operate at full brightness and test lamp will not light.

VOLTMETER

The voltmeter is a gauge which mea-

sures the electrical flow from the battery to indicate whether the battery output is within tolerances. The voltmeter reading can range from 13.5–14.0 volts under normal operating conditions. If an undercharge or overcharge condition is indicated for an extended period, the battery and charging system should be checked.

TROUBLESHOOTING

To check voltmeter, turn key and headlights on with engine off. Pointer should move to 12.5 volts. If no needle movement is observed, check connections from battery to circuit breaker. If connections are tight and meter shows no movement, check wire continuity. If wire continuity is satisfactory, the meter is inoperative and must be replaced.

ELECTRICAL TEMPERATURE GAUGES

This temperature indicating system consists of a sending unit, located on the cylinder head, electrical temperature gauge and an instrument voltage regulator. As engine temperature increases or decreases, the resistance of the sending unit changes, in turn controlling current flow to the gauge. When engine temperature is low, the resistance of the sending unit is high, restricting current flow to the gauge, in turn indicating low engine temperature. As engine temperature increases, the resistance of the sending unit decreases, permitting an increased current flow to the gauge, resulting in an increased temperature reading.

TROUBLESHOOTING

Troubleshooting for the electrical temperature indicating system is the same as for the electrical oil pressure indicating system.

ELECTRICAL OIL PRESSURE GAUGES

This oil pressure indicating system incorporates an instrument voltage regulator, electrical oil pressure gauge and a sending unit which are connected in series. The sending unit consists of a diaphragm, contact and a variable resistor. As oil pressure increases or decreases, the diaphragm actuated the contact on the variable resistor, in turn controlling current flow to the gauge. When oil pressure is low, the resistance of the variable resistor is high, restricting current flow to the gauge, in turn indicating low oil pressure. As oil pressure increases, the resistance of the variable resistor is lowered, permitting an increased current flow to the gauge, resulting in an increased gauge reading.

TROUBLESHOOTING

Disconnect the oil pressure gauge lead from the sending unit, connect a 12 volt test lamp between the gauge lead and the ground and turn ignition ON. If test lamp flashes, the instrument voltage regulator is functioning properly and the gauge circuit is not broken. If the test lamp remains lit, the instrument voltage regulator is defective and must be replaced. If the test lamp does not light, check the instrument voltage regulator for proper ground or an open circuit. Also, check for an open in the instrument voltage regulator to oil pressure gauge wire or in the gauge itself.

NOTE: If test lamp flashes and gauge is not accurate, the gauge may be out of calibration, requiring replacement.

OIL PRESSURE INDICATOR LIGHT

Many cars utilize a warning light on the instrument panel in place of the conventional dash indicating gauge to warn the driver when the oil pressure is dangerously low. The warning light is wired in series with the ignition switch and the engine unit—which is an oil pressure switch.

The oil pressure switch contains a diaphragm and a set of contacts. When the ignition switch is turned on, the warning light circuit is energized and the circuit is completed through the closed contacts in the pressure switch. When the engine is started, build-up of oil pressure compresses the diaphragm, opening the contacts, thereby breaking the circuit and putting out the light.

TROUBLESHOOTING

The oil pressure warning light should go on when the ignition is turned on. If it does not light, disconnect the wire from the engine unit and ground the wire to the frame or cylinder block. Then if the warning light still does not go on with the ignition switch on, replace the bulb.

If the warning light goes on when the wire is grounded to the frame or cylinder block, the engine unit should be checked for being loose or poorly grounded. If the unit is found to be tight and properly grounded, it should be removed and a new one installed. (The presence of sealing compound on the threads of the engine unit will cause a poor ground).

If the warning light remains lit when it normally should be out, replace the engine unit before proceeding further to determine the cause for a low pressure indication.

The warning light sometimes will light up or will flicker when the engine is idling, even though the oil pressure is adequate. However, the light should go out when the engine is speeded up. There is no cause for alarm in such cases; it simply means that the pressure switch is not calibrated precisely correct.

Fig. 4 Graphic display warning indicator wiring diagram. 1980—81 Ford & Mercury Exc. Escort & Lynx (Mustang/Capri & Fairmont/Zephyr sedan shown, typical of other models)

Fig. 5 Graphic display warning indicator wiring diagram. 1982–85 Ford & Mercury Exc. Escort & Lynx (Mustang/Capri & Fairmont/Zephyr sedan shown, typical of other models)

TEMPERATURE INDICATOR LIGHT

TROUBLESHOOTING

If the red light is not lit when the engine is being cranked, check for a burned out bulb, an open in the light circuit, or a defective ignition switch.

If the red light is lit when the engine is running, check the wiring between light and switch for a ground, temperature switch defective, or overheated cooling system.

NOTE: As a test circuit to check whether the red bulb is functioning properly, a wire which is connected to the ground terminal of the ignition switch is tapped into its circuit. When the ignition is in the "Start" (engine cranking) position, the ground terminal is grounded inside the switch and the red bulb will be lit. When the engine is started and the ignition switch is in the "On" position, the test circuit is opened and the bulb is then controlled by the temperature switch.

BOOST/OVERBOOST WARNING SYSTEM

1980 CAPRI & MUSTANG, W/TURBOCHARGED 4-140 ENGINE

Two calibrated pressure switches provide the driver visual indication that turbo boost pressure is satisfactory and visual and audible indication when turbo boost pressure is unsatisfactory. One switch will illuminate the green Turbo lamp located on the instrument panel when turbo boost pressure levels are within satisfactory limits. The second pressure switch will turn off the green Turbo lamp and illuminate the red engine warning lamp and sound the audible buzzer when excessive turbo boost pressure or high engine oil temperatures are encountered. When the red engine lamp is constant and buzzer sounds, the turbocharger is in an overboost condition, reduce engine speed immediately until buzzer ceases and warning lamp goes off. When the red engine warning light flashes on and off with no buzzer, this indicates excessive engine oil temperature, reduce engine speed to approximately 2500 RPM. The engine warning lamp should go out within 5 minutes. When the red engine warning lamp flashes on and off and buzzer sounds simultaneously, excessive turbo overboost and/or high engine oil temperatures are occuring, reduce engine speed immediately.

NOTE: Whenever the engine warning lamp has illuminated or the audible buzzer sounds, the vehicle should be inspected as soon as possible to determine the cause.

With ignition switch in start position and engine not operating, the warning lamps should glow and the buzzer should sound to indicate the electrical circuits are operating properly. If warning lamps do not glow or if buzzer does not sound, the boost/overboost electrical system should be checked as soon as possible.

SPEEDOMETERS

The following material covers only that service on speedometers which can be performed by the average service man. Repairs on the units themselves are not included as they require special tools and extreme care when making repairs and adjustments and only an experienced speedometer mechanic should attempt such servicing.

The speedometer has two main parts—the indicator head and the speedometer drive cable. When the speedometer fails to indicate speed or mileage, the cable or housing is probably broken.

SPEEDOMETER CABLE

Most cables are broken due to lack of lubrication or a sharp bend or kink in the housing.

A cable might break because the speedometer head mechanism binds. If such is the case, the speedometer head should be repaired or replaced before a new cable or housing is installed.

A "jumpy" pointer condition, together with a sort of scraping noise, is due, in most instances, to a dry or kinked speedometer cable. The kinked cable rubs on the housing and winds up, slowing down the pointer. The cable then unwinds and the pointer "jumps".

To check for kinks, remove the cable, lay it on a flat surface and twist one end with the fingers. If it turns over smoothly the cable is not kinked. But if part of the cable flops over as it is twisted, the cable is kinked and should be replaced.

LUBRICATION

The speedometer cable should be lubricated with special cable lubricant every 10,000 miles.

Fill the ferrule on the upper end of the housing with the cable lubricant. Insert the cable in the housing, starting at the upper end. Turn the cable around carefully while feeding it into the housing. Repeat filling the ferrule except for the last six inches of cable. Too much lubricant at this point may cause the lubricant to work into the indicating hand.

INSTALLING CABLE

During installation, if the cable sticks when inserted in the housing and will not go through, the housing is damaged inside or kinked. Be sure to check the housing from one end to the other. Straighten any sharp bends by relocating clamps or elbows. Replace housing if it is badly kinked or broken. Position the cable and housing so that they lead into the head as straight as possible.

Check the new cable for kinks before installing it. Use wide, sweeping, gradual curves when the cable comes out of the transmission and connects to the head so the cable will not be damaged during its installation.

If inspection indicates that the cable and housing are in good condition, yet pointer action is erratic, check the speedometer head for possible binding.

The speedometer drive pinion should also be checked. If the pinion is dry or its teeth are stripped, the speedometer may not register properly.

The transmission mainshaft nut must be tight or the speedometer drive gear may slip on the mainshaft and cause slow speed readings.

ELECTRIC CLOCKS

Regulation of electric clocks used on automobiles is accomplished automatically by merely resetting the time. If the clock is running fast, the action of turning the hands back to correct the time will automatically cause the clock to run slightly slower. If the clock is running slow, the action of turning the hands forward to correct the time will automatically cause the clock to run slightly faster (10 to 15 seconds day).

A lock-out feature prevents the clock regulator mechanism from being reset more than once per wind cycle, regardless of the number of times the time is reset. After the clock rewinds, if the time is then reset, automatic regulation will take place. If a clock varies over 10 minutes per day, it will never adjust sufficiently, and must be repaired or replaced.

WINDING CLOCK WHEN CONNECTING BATTERY OR CLOCK WIRING

The clock requires special attention when reconnecting a battery that has been disconnected for any reason, a clock that has been disconnected, or when replacing a blown clock fuse. It is very important that the initial wind be fully made. The procedure is as follows:

1. Make sure that all other instruments and lights are turned off.
2. Connect positive cable to battery.
3. Before connecting the negative cable, press the terminal to its post on the battery. Immediately afterward strike the terminal against the battery post to see if there is a spark. If there is a spark, allow the clock to run down until it stops ticking, and repeat as above until there is no spark. Then immediately make the permanent connection before the clock can again run down. The clock will run down in approximately two minutes.
4. Reset clock after all connections have been made. The foregoing procedure should also be followed when reconnecting the clock after it has been dis-

connected, or if it has stopped because of a blown fuse. Be sure to disconnect battery before installing a new fuse.

TROUBLESHOOTING

If clock does not run, check for blown "clock" fuse. If fuse is blown check for short in wiring. If fuse is not blown check for open circuit.

With an electric clock, the most frequent cause of clock fuse blowing is voltage at the clock which will prevent a complete wind and allow clock contacts to remain closed. This may be caused by any of the following: discharged battery, corrosion on contact surface of battery terminals, loose connections at battery terminals, at junction block, at fuse clips, or at terminal connection of clock. Therefore, if in reconnecting battery or clock it is noted that the clock is not ticking, always check for blown fuse, or examine the circuits at the points indicated above to determine and correct the cause.

FIBER OPTIC MONITORING SYSTEM

Fiber optics are non-electric light conductors made up of coated strands which, when exposed to a light source at one end, will reflect the light through their entire length, thereby illuminating a monitoring lens on the instrument panel or fender without the use of a bulb when the exterior lights are turned on.

LOW FUEL WARNING SYSTEM

The switch type consists of an indicator light and a low fuel warning switch located on the instrument panel.

The warning switch contacts are closed by the difference in voltage potential between the fuel gauge terminals. This voltage differential will activate the warning switch when the fuel tank is less than ¼ full and, in turn, cause the indicator to light.

TROUBLESHOOTING

This system incorporates an indicator light. With ignition switch turned to "ON", the indicator should light. If not, check bulb and all electrical connections.

Improper operation of the warning switch will be indicated when the light remains "ON" when tank is more than ¼ full. To test system, disconnect connector on warning switch and turn ignition "ON". Starting with the terminal on the end opposite the blank position, connect a jumper wire between the battery positive terminal and connector terminal. The indicator on instrument panel should light. If not, replace warning switch. Skip the next connector terminal and connect a test lamp between the battery positive terminal and connector terminal. The test lamp should

light. If not, trace wire from ignition switch for an open circuit. Test the remaining connector terminals with the test lamp making connections between ground and terminal connectors. If lamp fails to light, trace particular wire for an incomplete circuit.

VACUUM GAUGE

This gauge, **Fig. 2,** measures intake manifold vacuum. The intake manifold vacuum varies with engine operating conditions, carburetor adjustments, valve timing, ignition timing and general engine condition.

Since the optimum fuel economy is directly proportional to a properly functioning engine, a high vacuum reading on the gauge relates to fuel economy. For this reason some manufacturers call the vacuum gauge a "Fuel Economy Indicator." Most gauges have colored sectors the green sector being the "Economy" range and red the "Power" range. Therefore, the vehicle should be operated with gauge registering in the green sector or a high numerical number, **Fig. 2,** for maximum economy.

GRAPHIC DISPLAY WARNING INDICATOR SYSTEM
1980—85 FORD/MERCURY
Operation

This system is equipped with five L.E.D. (light emitting diodes) located on console, which will indicate running lamp failure, headlamp failure, brake lamp or low w/s washer fluid or fuel level. If lamp is burned out, L.E.D. will illuminate, indicating bulb failure. Application of emergency flasher or rear turn signal when turn signal/stop lamp bulb is burned out will cause L.E.D. to flash. When w/s washer fluid or fuel is below a predetermined level, corresponding L.E.D. will illuminate.

Troubleshooting, Fig. 3
1. Depress graphic indicator button with ignition switch in ACC or Run position. All of L.E.D. should illuminate. If not, check fuse.
2. Check to ensure that indicator module wire connector is properly installed.
3. Visually check vehicle for lamp outage, low w/s washer fluid level and low fuel indicator on instrument panel.
4. If any of the above components are not operating properly, repair inoperative circuit and recheck operation, **Figs. 4 through 8.**

LAMP-OUT WARNING SYSTEM
1981—85 THUNDERBIRD, COUGAR & XR-7; 1982 LINCOLN CONTINENTAL; 1983—85 LTD & MARQUIS

The lamp-out warning system monitors

low-beam headlamps, tail lamps and brake lamps. The system consists of a warning module, a wiring harness and a set of three indicator lamps located on the upper tier of the instrument panel.

The wiring harness used with the system uses special resistance wire to ensure proper system operation. To prevent malfunctioning of the system, the lengths of these wires should never be altered.

The warning module contains a printed circuit board and logic circuitry. Normal operating voltage is 10–15 volts, however the unit will withstand up to 24 volts for a period of 15 minutes.

The lamp-out warning system operates when the ignition is in ACC or RUN position.

If one or more low beam lamps are burned out when headlamps are energized in low beam mode, the low beam Out indicator will illuminate. The tail lamp Out indicator will illuminate when running lamps are energized and one or more tail lamps are burned out. The brake lamp Out indicator will light when brake lights are energized and one or more brake lamps are burned out.

When ignition key is in START position, all three warning lights should illuminate.

1981—85 LINCOLN TOWN CAR & 1981—83 MARK VI

The lamp-out warning system monitors low beam headlamps, tail lamps and brake lamps. Each assembly is equipped with three outputs connected to the electronic message center module which displays the appropriate warning message.

Lamp outages are sensed by measuring change in voltage drop across a section of wiring harness by a transistor-diode bridge which provides logic level signals to external message center.

The lamp-out warning module contains a printed circuit board and logic circuitry. Normal operating voltage is 10–15 volts, however the unit will withstand up to 24 volts for a period of 15 minutes.

The lamp-out warning system operates when ignition is in ACC or RUN position.

If one or more low beam lamps are burned out when headlamps are energized in low beam mode, the headlamp outage message will flash. The tail lamp outage indicator will flash when headlamp switch is energized and one or more tail lamps are burned out. The brake lamp outage indicator will flash when brake or turn signal is applied and one or more brake lamps are burned out. The brake lamp indicator will also be illuminated if turn signal or emergency flasher is activated with message center on and one or more lamps burned out.

When the "check out" button on message center is depressed with ignition in ACC or RUN position, all lamp-out warning displays should illuminate.

1983 LINCOLN CONTINENTAL

The lamp-out warning system monitors

Fig. 6   Graphic display warning indicator wiring diagram. 1981—83 Escort & Lynx base model

Fig. 7 Graphic display warning indicator wiring diagram. 1981–83 Escort & Lynx exc. base model

Fig. 8   Graphic display warning indicator wiring diagram. 1984—85 Escort, Lynx, Tempo & Topaz

rear lamps and headlamps by measuring change in voltage across a section of wiring harness with a transistor-bridge diode. Warning indicators are located on either side of the tripminder.

The lamp-out warning system operates when ignition is in ACC or RUN position.

The rear outage light will illuminate when headlamp switch is energized and one or more tail lamps are burned out, or when one or more brake lamps are burned out and brake or turn signal is applied. The rear lamp indicator will also light if turn signal or emergency flasher is applied with one or more brake lamps out.

When the headlamp switch is energized in low beam mode and one or more low beam lamps are burned out, headlamp outage light will illuminate.

When the ignition key is in START position, both warning lights should illuminate.

1984—85 LINCOLN CONTINENTAL & MARK VII

The lamp-out warning system monitors low beam headlamps, tail lamps and brake lamps. Lamp outages are sensed by measuring change in voltage drop across a section of wiring harness by a transistor-diode bridge. The warning lights are located on the roof console.

The lamp-out warning system operates when ignition is in ACC or RUN position.

If one or more low beam lamps are burned out when headlamps are energized in low beam mode, the headlamp warning lamp will light. The tail lamp warning lamp will light when the headlamp switch is energized and one or more tail lamps are burned out. The brake lamp warning lamp will light when brakes are applied or the turn signal or emergency flashers are activated and one or more brake lamps are burned out.

General Motors Corp.

INDEX

TESTING

Gauge failures are often caused by defective wiring or grounds. The first step in locating trouble should be a thorough inspection of all wiring, terminals and printed circuits. If wiring is secured by clamps, check to see whether the insulation has been severed thereby grounding the wire. In the case of a fuel gauge installation, rust may cause failure by corrosion at the ground connection of the tank unit.

VARIABLE VOLTAGE TYPE

The variable voltage type dash gauge consists of two magnetic coils to which battery voltage is applied. The coils act on the gauge pointer and pull in opposite directions. One coil is grounded directly to the chassis, while the other coil is grounded through a variable resistor within the sending unit. Resistance through the sending unit determines current flow through its coil, and therefore pointer position.

When resistance is high in the sending unit, less current is allowed to flow through its coil, causing the gauge pointer to move toward the directly grounded coil. When resistance in the sending unit decreases, more current is allowed to pass through its coil, increasing the magnetic field. The gauge pointer is then attracted toward the coil which is grounded through the sending unit.

A special tester is required to diagnose this type gauge. Follow instructions included with the tester.

AMMETERS

The ammeter is an instrument used to indicate current flow into and out of the battery. When electrical accessories in the vehicle draw more current than the alterna-

Fig. 1 Conventional type ammeter (typical)

POINTER

PERMANENT MAGNET

ARMATURE

tor can supply, current flows from the battery and the ammeter indicates a discharge (−) condition. When electrical loads of the vehicle are less than alternator output, current is available to charge the battery, and the ammeter indicates a charge (+) condition. If battery is fully charged, the voltage regulator reduces alternator output to meet only immediate vehicle electrical loads. When this happens, ammeter reads zero.

A conventional ammeter must be connected between the battery and alternator in order to indicate current flow. This type ammeter, **Fig. 1,** consists of a frame to which a permanent magnet is attached. The frame also supports an armature and pointer assembly. Current in this system flows from the alternator through the ammeter, then to the battery or from the battery through the ammeter into the vehicle electrical system, depending on vehicle operating conditions.

When no current flows through the ammeter, the magnet holds the pointer armature so that the pointer stands at the center of the dial. When current passes in either direction through the ammeter, the resulting magnetic field attracts the armature away from the effect of the permanent magnet, thus giving a reading proportional to the strength of the current flowing.

TROUBLESHOOTING

When the ammeter apparently fails to register correctly, there may be trouble in the wiring which connects the ammeter to the alternator and battery or in the alternator or battery itself.

To check the connections, first tighten the two terminal posts on the back of the ammeter. Then, following each wire from the ammeter, tighten all connections on the ignition switch, battery and alternator. Chafed, burned or broken insulation can be found by following each ammeter wire from end to end.

All wires with chafed, burned or broken insulation should be repaired or replaced. After this is done, and all connections are tightened, connect the battery cable and turn on the ignition switch. The needle should point slightly to the discharge (−) side.

Start the engine and speed it up a little above idling speed. The needle should then move to the charge side (+), and its movement should be smooth.

If the pointer does not behave correctly, the ammeter itself is out of order and a new one should be installed.

ALTERNATOR INDICATOR LIGHT

DELCOTRON SI INTEGRAL CHARGING SYSTEM

This system features an integral solid state regulator mounted inside the alternator slip ring end frame. The alternator indicator lamp is installed in the field wire circuit connected between the ignition "Ign." terminal and alternator No. 1 terminal, **Fig. 2.** The resistance provided by the alternator warning light circuit is needed to protect the diode trio. The alternator indicator lamp should light when the ignition switch is turned on before engine is started. If lamp does not light, either lamp is burned out or

Fig. 2 Charge indicator lamp wiring. Delco SI type charging system

indicator lamp wiring has an open circuit. After engine is started, the indicator lamp should be out at all times. If indicator lamp comes on, alternator belt may be loose, alternator or regulator may be defective, charging circuit may be defective or fuse may be blown.

Troubleshooting

1. Switch Off, Lamp On:
   a. Disconnect electrical connector from alternator terminals 1 and 2.
   b. If indicator light remains lit, repair short circuit between leads.
   c. If indicator light goes out, replace alternator rectifier bridge.
2. Switch On, lamp Off, engine not running:
   a. Perform tests described in step 1.
   b. If problem still exists, there may be an open circuit.
   c. To locate open circuit, check for blown fuse or fusible link, burned out bulb, defective bulb socket or an open in No. 1 lead circuit between alternator and ignition switch.
   d. If no faults are found, check charging system for proper operation.
3. Switch On, lamp On, engine running:
   a. On models so equipped, check condition of fuse between indicator light and ignition switch and fuse in A/C circuit.
   b. Check charging system for proper operation.

VOLTMETER

The voltmeter is a gauge which measures the electrical flow from the battery to indicate whether the battery output is within tolerances. The voltmeter reading can range from 13.5–14.0 volts under normal operating conditions. If an undercharge or overcharge condition is indicated for an extended period, the battery and charging system should be checked.

TROUBLESHOOTING

To check voltmeter, turn key and headlights on with engine off. Pointer should move to 12.5 volts. If no needle movement is observed, check connections from battery to circuit breaker. If connections are tight and meter shows no movement, check wire continuity. If wire continuity is satisfactory, the meter is inoperative and must be replaced.

ELECTRICAL TEMPERATURE GAUGES

This temperature indicating system consists of a sending unit, located on the cylinder head, electrical temperature gauge and an instrument voltage regulator. As engine temperature increases or decreases, the resistance of the sending unit changes, in turn controlling current flow to the gauge. When engine temperature is low, the resistance of the sending unit is high, restricting current flow to the gauge, in turn indicating low engine temperature. As engine temperature increases, the resistance of the sending unit decreases, permitting an increased current flow to the gauge, resulting in an increased temperature reading.

TROUBLESHOOTING

Troubleshooting for the electrical temperature indicating system is the same as for the electrical oil pressure indicating system.

ELECTRICAL OIL PRESSURE GAUGES

This oil pressure indicating system incorporates an instrument voltage regulator, electrical oil pressure gauge and a

sending unit which are connected in series. The sending unit consists of a diaphragm, contact and a variable resistor. As oil pressure increases or decreases, the diaphragm actuated the contact on the variable resistor, in turn controlling current flow to the gauge. When oil pressure is low, the resistance of the variable resistor is high, restricting current flow to the gauge, in turn indicating low oil pressure. As oil pressure increases, the resistance of the variable resistor is lowered, permitting an increased current flow to the gauge, resulting in an increased gauge reading.

TROUBLESHOOTING

Disconnect the oil pressure gauge lead from the sending unit, connect a 12 volt test lamp between the gauge lead and the ground and turn ignition ON. If test lamp flashes, the instrument voltage regulator is functioning properly and the gauge circuit is not broken. If the test lamp remains lit, the instrument voltage regulator is defective and must be replaced. If the test lamp does not light, check the instrument voltage regulator for proper ground or an open circuit. Also, check for an open in the instrument voltage regulator to oil pressure gauge wire or in the gauge itself.

NOTE: If test lamp flashes and gauge is not accurate, the gauge may be out of calibration, requiring replacement.

OIL PRESSURE INDICATOR LIGHT

Many cars utilize a warning light on the instrument panel in place of the conventional dash indicating gauge to warn the driver when the oil pressure is dangerously low. The warning light is wired in series with the ignition switch and the engine unit—which is an oil pressure switch.

The oil pressure switch contains a diaphragm and a set of contacts. When the ignition switch is turned on, the warning light circuit is energized and the circuit is completed through the closed contacts in the pressure switch. When the engine is started, build-up of oil pressure compresses the diaphragm, opening the contacts, thereby breaking the circuit and putting out the light.

TROUBLESHOOTING

NOTE: On some models, the oil pressure indicator light also serves as the electric choke defect indicator. If Oil or Eng. indicator light does not light, check to ensure electric choke is not disconnected at carburetor. Also check for defect in electric choke heater, blown gauge fuse or defect in lamp or wiring circuit. If indicator light stays on with engine running possible causes are: oil pressure is low, switch to indicator light wiring has an open circuit, oil pressure switch wire connector has disconnected or on some models, gauge or radio fuse has blown.

The oil pressure warning light should go on when the ignition is turned on. If it does not light, disconnect the wire from the engine unit and ground the wire to the frame or cylinder block. Then if the warning light still does not go on with the ignition switch on, replace the bulb.

If the warning light goes on when the wire is grounded to the frame or cylinder block, the engine unit should be checked for being loose or poorly grounded. If the unit is found to be tight and properly grounded, it should be removed and a new one installed. (The presence of sealing compound on the threads of the engine unit will cause a poor ground).

If the warning light remains lit when it normally should be out, replace the engine unit before proceeding further to determine the cause for a low pressure indication.

The warning light sometimes will light up or will flicker when the engine is idling, even though the oil pressure is adequate. However, the light should go out when the engine is speeded up. There is no cause for alarm in such cases; it simply means that the pressure switch is not calibrated precisely correct.

TEMPERATURE INDICATOR LIGHT
TROUBLESHOOTING

If the red light is not lit when the engine is being cranked, check for a burned out bulb, an open in the light circuit, or a defective ignition switch.

If the red light is lit when the engine is running, check the wiring between light and switch for a ground, temperature switch defective, or overheated cooling system.

NOTE: As a test circuit to check whether the red bulb is functioning properly, a wire which is connected to the ground terminal of the ignition switch is tapped into its circuit. When the ignition is in the "Start" (engine cranking) position, the ground terminal is grounded inside the switch and the red bulb will be lit. When the engine is started and the ignition switch is in the "On" position, the test circuit is opened and the bulb is then controlled by the temperature switch.

SPEEDOMETERS

The following material covers only that service on speedometers which can be performed by the average service man. Repairs on the units themselves are not included as they require special tools and extreme care when making repairs and adjustments and only an experienced speedometer mechanic should attempt such servicing.

The speedometer has two main parts—the indicator head and the speedometer drive cable. When the speedometer fails to

Fig. 3 Typical vacuum gauge

indicate speed or mileage, the cable or housing is probably broken.

SPEEDOMETER CABLE

Most cables are broken due to lack of lubrication or a sharp bend or kink in the housing.

A cable might break because the speedometer head mechanism binds. If such is the case, the speedometer head should be repaired or replaced before a new cable or housing is installed.

A "jumpy" pointer condition, together with a sort of scraping noise, is due, in most instances, to a dry or kinked speedometer cable. The kinked cable rubs on the housing and winds up, slowing down the pointer. The cable then unwinds and the pointer "jumps".

To check for kinks, remove the cable, lay it on a flat surface and twist one end with the fingers. If it turns over smoothly the cable is not kinked. But if part of the cable flops over as it is twisted, the cable is kinked and should be replaced.

LUBRICATION

The speedometer cable should be lubricated with special cable lubricant every 10,000 miles.

Fill the ferrule on the upper end of the housing with the cable lubricant. Insert the cable in the housing, starting at the upper end. Turn the cable around carefully while feeding it into the housing. Repeat filling the ferrule except for the last six inches of cable. Too much lubricant at this point may cause the lubricant to work into the indicating hand.

INSTALLING CABLE

During installation, if the cable sticks when inserted in the housing and will not go through, the housing is damaged inside or kinked. Be sure to check the housing from one end to the other. Straighten any sharp bends by relocating clamps or elbows. Replace housing if it is badly kinked or broken. Position the cable and

housing so that they lead into the head as straight as possible.

Check the new cable for kinks before installing it. Use wide, sweeping, gradual curves when the cable comes out of the transmission and connects to the head so the cable will not be damaged during its installation.

If inspection indicates that the cable and housing are in good condition, yet pointer action is erratic, check the speedometer head for possible binding.

The speedometer drive pinion should also be checked. If the pinion is dry or its teeth are stripped, the speedometer may not register properly.

The transmission mainshaft nut must be tight or the speedometer drive gear may slip on the mainshaft and cause slow speed readings.

ELECTRIC CLOCKS

Regulation of electric clocks used on automobiles is accomplished automatically by merely resetting the time. If the clock is running fast, the action of turning the hands back to correct the time will automatically cause the clock to run slightly slower. If the clock is running slow, the action of turning the hands forward to correct the time will automatically cause the clock to run slightly faster (10 to 15 seconds day).

A lock-out feature prevents the clock regulator mechanism from being reset more than once per wind cycle, regardless of the number of times the time is reset. After the clock rewinds, if the time is then reset, automatic regulation will take place. If a clock varies over 10 minutes per day, it will never adjust sufficiently, and must be repaired or replaced.

WINDING CLOCK WHEN CONNECTING BATTERY OR CLOCK WIRING

The clock requires special attention when reconnecting a battery that has been disconnected for any reason, a clock that has been disconnected, or when replacing a blown clock fuse. It is very important that the initial wind be fully made. The procedure is as follows:

1. Make sure that all other instruments and lights are turned off.
2. Connect positive cable to battery.
3. Before connecting the negative cable, press the terminal to its post on the battery. Immediately afterward strike the terminal against the battery post to see if there is a spark. If there is a spark, allow the clock to run down until it stops ticking, and repeat as above until there is no spark. Then immediately make the permanent connection before the clock can again run down. The clock will run down in approximately two minutes.
4. Reset clock after all connections have been made. The foregoing procedure should also be followed when reconnecting the clock after it has been dis-

DASH GAUGES

connected, or if it has stopped because of a blown fuse. Be sure to disconnect battery before installing a new fuse.

TROUBLESHOOTING

If clock does not run, check for blown "clock" fuse. If fuse is blown check for short in wiring. If fuse is not blown check for open circuit.

With an electric clock, the most frequent cause of clock fuse blowing is voltage at the clock which will prevent a complete wind and allow clock contacts to remain closed. This may be caused by any of the following: discharged battery, corrosion on contact surface of battery terminals, loose connections at battery terminals, at junction block, at fuse clips, or at terminal connection of clock. Therefore, if in reconnecting battery or clock it is noted that the clock is not ticking, always check for blown fuse, or examine the circuits at the points indicated above to determine and correct the cause.

FIBER OPTIC MONITORING SYSTEM

Fiber optics are non-electric light conductors made up of coated strands which, when exposed to a light source at one end, will reflect the light through their entire length, thereby illuminating a monitoring lens on the instrument panel or fender without the use of a bulb when the exterior lights are turned on.

LOW FUEL WARNING SYSTEM

The switch type consists of an indicator light and a low fuel warning switch located on the instrument panel.

The warning switch contacts are closed by the difference in voltage potential between the fuel gauge terminals. This voltage differential will activate the warning switch when the fuel tank is less than ¼ full and, in turn, cause the indicator to light.

TROUBLESHOOTING

This system incorporates an indicator light. With ignition switch turned to "ON", the indicator should light. If not, check bulb and all electrical connections. Replace warning switch if bulb and connections prove satisfactory.

LOW WASHER FLUID INDICATOR

There are two types of low washer fluid indicating systems. They are the mechanical type and electrically controlled type. The mechanical type consists of a float and rod assembly, sending unit and a fiber

Fig. 4 Water in fuel indicator & tank purge procedure. 1981–84 GM with diesel engine

FUEL TANK PURGE PROCEDURE

Cars which have a "Water in Fuel" light may have the water removed from the fuel tank with a pump or by siphoning. The pump or siphon hose should be hooked up to the 1/4 inch fuel return hose (smaller of the two fuel hoses) above the rear axle or under the hood near the fuel pump. Siphoning should continue until all water is removed from the fuel tank. Use a clear plastic line or observe filter bowl on draining equipment to determine when clear fuel begins to flow. Be sure to remove the cap on fuel tank while using this purge procedure. Replace the cap when finished. The same precautions for handling gasoline should be observed when purging diesel fuel tanks.

optic. The electrically controlled type consists of a float, magnet, contact points and a resistor.

On the mechanical type, the upper end of the rod extends into the sending unit and has colored red and green portions. When the windshield wipers are activated, a lamp bulb in the sending unit lights either the red or green sections of the rod. The colored light is then picked up by the fiber optic and is transmitted through it to the tell tale lens. The lens will show red or green depending upon washer fluid level.

The electrically controlled indicator is activated when the windshield wipers are engaged. A slight amount of current flows from the wiper motor to the washer bottle float unit. This current will either pass through the contact points or the resistor which is in parallel with the points. When the washer fluid level is high, the magnet holds the contact points open. The current will now flow through the resistor where it is reduced so the indicator will not light. When the washer fluid level is low, the float drops and the magnet will separate from the cap assembly allowing the current to pass through the contact points and activate the indicator light.

TROUBLESHOOTING

On the mechanical indicating system, if the tell tale lens fails to glow when the windshield wipers are activated, check lamp bulb in sending unit and see that fiber optic is not broken.

On the electrically controlled system, the first item to check is the indicator bulb. With the windshield wipers "ON", connect a jumper wire between the two terminals on the washer bottle cap. The indicator should then light. If not, replace bulb. If the bulb is found to be satisfactory, remove cap and float assembly from washer bottle. Float should be able to move to the bottom of the stem and the magnet should separate from the cap. If not, replace float and cap assembly.

VACUUM GAUGE

This gauge, **Fig. 3,** measures intake manifold vacuum. The intake manifold vacuum varies with engine operating conditions, carburetor adjustments, valve timing, ignition timing and general engine condition.

Since the optimum fuel economy is directly proportional to a properly functioning engine, a high vacuum reading on the gauge relates to fuel economy. For this reason some manufacturers call the vacuum gauge a "Fuel Economy Indicator." Most gauges have colored sectors the green sector being the "Economy" range and red the "Power" range. Therefore, the vehicle should be operated with gauge registering in the green sector or a high numerical number, **Fig. 3,** for maximum economy.

LOW COOLANT LEVEL INDICATOR

Some vehicles use a buzzer or indicator lamp to indicate a low coolant level condition. The buzzer or lamp is activated by a sensor, located in the radiator, when the coolant level becomes one quart or more low.

FUEL USAGE GAUGE
1980–85 BUICK & CADILLAC
Operation

This system consists of green and amber indicator lights located on the fuel gauge or telltale lamp cluster, a switch mounted on the instrument panel behind the gauges and an interconnecting vacuum hose and tee. The system operates on engine vacuum through a dual contact vacuum sensing switch. When the accelerator is operated slowly and smoothly, engine vacuum remains high and the switch passes current to the green indicator light which indicates economical fuel consumption. When the accelerator pedal is depressed rapidly, vacuum decreases and the switch passes current to the amber indicator light, which indicates high fuel consumption. The amber indicator light will glow when the ignition switch is in the "On" position with the engine stopped.

Functional Test

1. With ignition switch in the "On" position, ground each terminal at the economy switch. Both green and amber indicator lights should glow. If not check for burned out bulbs.
2. With ignition switch in "On" position, amber indicator light should glow. If not, check for loose or disconnected wires at fuel economy switch or for poor ground. If amber indicator light still does not glow replace switch.
3. Start engine and allow to idle, the green indicator light should glow. If not, check for leaking, plugged or kinked vacuum hose between vacuum source and fuel economy switch. Check for loose or disconnected wires at economy switch or poor ground. If green indicator lamp still does not glow, replace switch.

TURBO-POWER INDICATOR

1980–85 BUICK V6-231 TURBOCHARGED ENGINE

Century, Regal and Riviera models utilize two lights located in the lower right hand gauge area. The yellow light indicates moderate acceleration and the orange light indicates power or heavy acceleration. When neither light is illuminated, the indication visible is a green paint band signifying economy. LeSabre models utilize three lights located at the bottom of the fuel gauge. On light acceleration or cruising, a green light indicates economy. Moderate acceleration activates a yellow indicator light. The orange light is activated during heavy acceleration.

WATER IN FUEL INDICATOR

DESCRIPTION & OPERATION

1981–84 Models W/Diesel Engine

The Water In Fuel warning system employs an electronic water detector, mounted inside the fuel tank, on the fuel gauge sending unit. The detector provides a warning when a predetermined amount of water is present in the fuel tank by lighting a warning lamp on the instrument pan-

el. The sending unit assembly also contains a provision for siphoning-off water in the tank through the fuel return line, **Fig. 4.**

The water in fuel lamp will come on for 2–5 seconds each time ignition is switched to RUN position to insure that the lamp is operating. If there is water in the fuel, the warning lamp will come back on after a 15–20 second delay and remain on.

1985 Models W/Diesel Engine

The Water In Fuel warning system employs a fuel detector integral with the fuel filter and fuel heater, and mounted on the engine. When more than 2.2 ounces of water has been collected in the filter, the Water In Fuel lamp on the instrument panel will light. After the light comes on, the filter should be drained as soon as possible to prevent fuel injection system failure or damage.

TROUBLESHOOTING

1980–84

If warning indicator fails to light during bulb check, disconnect wiring harness connector at fuel gauge sending unit, containing a yellow/black stripe wire. With ignition switch in RUN position, connect yellow/black stripe wire to ground, using a suitable jumper wire. If lamp lights, problem is in water detector. If lamp fails to light, check for open circuit between sender and warning lamp, a burned out bulb, or a blown fuse.

If warning lamp remains on at all times, disconnect wiring harness connector at fuel tank sending unit with ignition switch in RUN position. If warning lamp remains on, check for short circuit to ground between sender and warning lamp. If warning lamp goes out when harness is disconnected, first purge water in fuel tank, **Fig. 4,** then recheck circuit. If lamp remains on with harness connected to sending unit, water detector is defective.

1985

1. If warning lamp lights intermittently, drain water in fuel filter.
2. If warning lamp remains light lit with engine running and ambient temperature above 32° F, drain fuel filter immediately. If lamp remains light, replace filter.
3. If warning lamp remains lit with engine running and ambient temperature 32° F or below, drain fuel filter immediately. If water is frozen and cannot be drained, open air bleed to check for fuel pressure. If no fuel pressure is present, replace filter.

4. If warning lamp lights at high speed or under heavy acceleration, the fuel filter is plugged and must be replaced.
5. If warning lamp remains light and engine stalls and will not restart after initial start-up, then fuel filter or fuel lines may be plugged. Repair or replace as required.
6. If warning lamp remains lit and engine stalls and will not restart immediately after refueling, a large quantity of water has likely been pumped into the fuel tank and should be purged.

DRIVER REMINDER PACKAGE

1983–85 CUTLASS, TORONADO, 88 & 98

The driver reminder package incorporates several warning and reminder features into one system. The system uses three distinct sounds, and warning and reminder lights on the center instrument cluster.

If engine coolant level is 3 quarts or more low, a red LOW COOLANT warning light will illuminate and a fast-pulsed tone will be heard. The light will remain lit and the tone will be heard until coolant is added to the cooling system. The light will also illuminate during engine starting as a bulb check.

When the headlight switch is in the ON position and the ignition is off, a red LIGHTS ON warning light will illuminate and a fast-pulsed tone will be heard. Turning the headlight switch to the right will dim the instrument panel lights and shut off the tone.

When there is less than approximately 3 gallons of fuel in the tank, an amber LOW FUEL warning light will illuminate and a steady 5 second tone will be heard, however the lamp may not light until fuel level is diminished to as low as ½ gallon. The light will remain lit until fuel is added to the tank. This warning light will also illuminate during engine starting as a bulb check.

The amber LOW WASH FLUID reminder light will illuminate while the windshield wipers are operated if the washer fluid reservoir is less than approximately ⅓ full. This light will remain lit during wiper operation until fluid is added.

Additional tones used to warn operator of potential problems are: engine overheating, fast-pulsed tone; malfunction in the charging system, fast-pulsed tone; seat belt reminder, slow-pulsed tone; key reminder, steady tone.

STARTER MOTORS & SWITCHES

TABLE OF CONTENTS

American Motors Corp.

INDEX

General Information

STARTER TROUBLE CHECK-OUT

When trouble develops in the starting motor circuit, and the starter cranks the engine slowly or not at all, several preliminary checks can be made to determine whether the trouble lies in the battery, in the starter, in the wiring between them, or elsewhere. Many conditions besides defects in the starter itself can result in poor cranking performance.

To make a quick check of the starter system, turn on the headlights. They should burn with normal brilliance. If they do not, the battery may be run down and it should be checked with a hydrometer.

If the battery is in a charged condition so that lights burn brightly, operate the starting motor. Any one of three things will happen to the lights: (1) They will go out, (2) dim considerably or (3) stay bright without any cranking action taking place.

IF LIGHTS GO OUT

If the lights go out as the starter switch is closed, it indicates that there is a poor connection between the battery and starting motor. This poor connection will most often be found at the battery terminals. Correction is made by removing the cable clamps from the terminals, cleaning the terminals and clamps, replacing the clamps and tightening them securely. A coating of corrosion inhibitor (vaseline will do) may be applied to the clamps and terminals to retard the formation of corrosion.

IF LIGHTS DIM

If the lights dim considerably as the starter switch is closed and the starter operates

slowly or not at all, the battery may be run down, or there may be some mechanical condition in the engine or starting motor that is throwing a heavy burden on the starting motor. This imposes a high discharge rate on the battery which causes noticeable dimming of the lights.

Check the battery with a hydrometer. If it is charged, the trouble probably lies in either the engine or starting motor itself. In the engine, tight bearings or pistons or heavy oil place an added burden on the starting motor. Low temperatures also hamper starting motor performance since it thickens engine oil and makes the engine considerably harder to crank and start. Also, a battery is less efficient at low temperatures.

In the starting motor, a bent armature, loose pole shoe screws or worn bearings, any of which may allow the armature to drag, will reduce cranking performance and increase current draw.

In addition, more serious internal damage is sometimes found. Thrown armature windings or commutator bars, which sometimes occur on over-running clutch drive starting motors, are usually caused by excessive overrunning after starting. This is the result of such conditions as the driver keeping the starting switch closed too long after the engine has started, the driver opening the throttle too wide in starting, or improper carburetor fast idle adjustment. Any of these subject the over-running clutch to extra strain so it tends to seize, spinning the armature at high speed with resulting armature damage.

Another cause may be engine backfire during cranking which may result, among other things, from ignition timing being too far advanced.

To avoid such failures, the driver should pause a few seconds after a false start to make sure the engine has come complete-

ly to rest before another start is attempted. In addition, the ignition timing should be reset if engine backfiring has caused the trouble.

LIGHTS STAY BRIGHT, NO CRANKING ACTION

This condition indicates an open circuit at some point, either in the starter itself, the starter switch or control circuit. The solenoid control circuit can be eliminated momentarily by placing a heavy jumper lead across the solenoid main terminals to see if the starter will operate. This connects the starter directly to the battery and, if it operates, it indicates that the control circuit is not functioning normally. The wiring and control units must be checked to locate the trouble.

If the starter does not operate with the jumper attached, it will probably have to be removed from the engine so it can be examined in detail.

CHECKING CIRCUIT WITH VOLTMETER

Excessive resistance in the circuit between the battery and starter will reduce cranking performance. The resistance can be checked by using a voltmeter to measure voltage drop in the circuits while the starter is operated. There are three checks to be made:

1. Voltage drop between car frame and grounded battery terminal post (not cable clamp).
2. Voltage drop between car frame and starting motor field frame.
3. Voltage drop between insulated battery terminal post and starting motor terminal stud (or the battery terminal stud of the solenoid).

STARTER MOTORS & SWITCHES—American Motors

Each of these should show no more than one-tenth (0.1) volt drop when the starting motor is cranking the engine. Do not use the starter for more than 30 seconds at a time to avoid overheating it.

If excessive voltage drop is found in any of these circuits, make correction by disconnecting the cables, cleaning the connections carefully, and then reconnecting the cables firmly in place. A coating of vaseline on the battery cables and terminal clamps will retard corrosion.

NOTE: On some cars, extra long battery cables may be required due to the location of the battery and starter. This may result in somewhat higher voltage drop than the above recommended 0.1 volt. The only means of determining the normal voltage drop in such cases is to check several of these vehicles. Then when the voltage drop is well above the normal figure for all cars checked, abnormal resistance will be indicated and correction can be made as already explained.

SOLENOID SWITCHES

The solenoid switch on a cranking motor not only closes the circuit between the battery and the cranking motor but also shifts the drive pinion into mesh with the engine flywheel ring gear. This is done by means of a linkage between the solenoid switch plunger and the shift lever on the cranking motor.

There are two windings in the solenoid; a pull-in winding and a hold-in winding. Both windings are energized when the external control switch is closed. They produce a magnetic field which pulls the plunger in so that the drive pinion is shifted into mesh, and the main contacts in the solenoid switch are closed to connect the battery directly to the cranking motor. Closing the main switch contacts shorts out the pull-in winding since this winding is connected across the main contacts. The magnetism produced by the hold-in winding is sufficient to hold the plunger in, and shorting out the pull-in winding reduces drain on the battery. When the control switch is opened, it disconnects the hold-in winding from the battery. When the hold-in winding is disconnected from the battery, the shift lever spring withdraws the plunger from the solenoid, opening the solenoid switch contacts and at the same time withdrawing the drive pinion from mesh. Proper operation of the switch depends on maintaining a definite balance between the magnetic strength of the pull-in and hold-in windings.

This balance is established in the design by the size of the wire and the number of turns specified. An open circuit in the hold-in winding or attempts to crank with a discharged battery will cause the switch to chatter.

STARTING MOTOR SERVICE

To obtain full performance data on a starting motor or to determine the cause of abnormal operation, the starting motor should be submitted to a no-load and torque test. These tests are best performed on a starter bench tester with the starter mounted on it.

From a practical standpoint, however, a simple torque test may be made quickly with the starter in the car. Make sure the battery is fully charged and that the starter circuit wires and terminals are in good condition. Then operate the starter to see if the engine turns over normally. If it does not, the torque developed is below standard and the starter should be removed for further checking.

STARTER DRIVE TROUBLES

Starter drive troubles are easy to diagnose and they usually cannot be confused with ordinary starter difficulties. If the starter does not turn over at all or if it drags, look for trouble in the starter or electrical supply system. Concentrate on the starter drive or ring gear if the starter is noisy, if it turns but does not engage the engine, or if the starter won't disengage after the engine is started. After the starter is removed, the trouble can usually be located quickly.

Worn or chipped ring gear or starter pinion are the usual causes of noisy operation. Before replacing either or both of these parts try to find out what caused the damage. With the Bendix type drive, incomplete engagement of the pinion with the ring gear is a common cause of tooth damage. The wrong pinion clearance on starter drives of the over-running clutch type leads to poor meshing of the pinion and ring gear and too rapid tooth wear.

A less common cause of noise with either type of drive is a bent starter armature shaft. When this shaft is bent, the pinion gear alternately binds and then only partly meshes with the ring gear. Most manufacturers specify a maximum of .003 inch radial run-out on the armature shaft.

WHEN CLUTCH DRIVE FAILS

The over-running clutch type drive seldom becomes so worn that it fails to engage since it is directly activated by a fork

and lever. The only thing that is likely to happen is that, once engaged, it will not turn the engine because the clutch itself is worn out. A much more frequent difficulty and one that rapidly wears ring gear and teeth is partial engagement. Proper meshing of the pinion is controlled by the end clearance between the pinion gear and the starter housing or pinion stop, if used.

On some starters, the solenoids are completely enclosed in the starter housing and the pinion clearance is not adjustable. If the clearance is not correct, the starter must be disassembled and checked for excessive wear of solenoid linkage, shift lever mechanism, or improper assembly of parts.

Failure of the over-running clutch drive to disengage is usually caused by binding between the armature shaft and the drive. If the drive, particularly the clutch, shows signs of overheating it indicates that it is not disengaging immediately after the engine starts. If the clutch is forced to over-run too long, it overheats and turns a bluish color. For the cause of the binding, look for rust or gum between the armature shaft and the drive, or for burred splines. Excess oil on the drive will lead to gumming, and inadequate air circulation in the flywheel housing will cause rust.

Over-running clutch drives cannot be overhauled in the field so they must be replaced. In cleaning, never soak them in a solvent because the solvent may enter the clutch and dissolve the sealed-in lubricant. Wipe them off lightly with kerosene and lubricate them sparingly with SAE 10 or 10W oil.

WHEN BENDIX DRIVE FAILS

When a Bendix type drive doesn't engage the cause usually is one of three things: either the drive spring is broken, one of the drive spring bolts has sheared off, or the screwshaft threads won't allow the pinion to travel toward the flywheel. In the first two cases, remove the drive by unscrewing the set screw under the last coil of the drive spring and replace the broken parts. Gummed or rusty screwshaft threads are fairly common causes of Bendix drive failure and are easily cleaned with a little kerosene or steel wool, depending on the trouble. Here again, as in the case of over-running clutch drives, use light oil sparingly, and be sure the flywheel housing has adequate ventilation. There is usually a breather hole in the bottom of the flywheel housing which should be open.

The failure of a Bendix drive to disengage or to mesh properly is most often caused by gummed or rusty screwshaft threads. When this is not true, look for mechanical failure within the drive itself.

Delco-Remy Starters

NOTE: For service procedures on this starter, refer to "Delco-Remy Starters" in "General Motors" section.

Ford Motorcraft Starters

NOTE: For description, diagnosis, and starter overhaul procedures on these starters, refer to "Ford Motorcraft Starters" in "Ford" section. For testing, refer to this section.

INDEX

IN-VEHICLE TESTING

SOLENOID GROUND TEST

1. Connect one ohmmeter test probe to battery negative post and other probe to sheet metal adjacent to solenoid on manual transmission, or ground terminal on automatic transmission, and note resistance.
2. Move test probe to solenoid S terminal. If resistance increases by more than 5 ohms, check solenoid ground.

SOLENOID PULL-IN COIL WINDING TEST

1. Disconnect S terminal wire from solenoid.
2. Connect ohmmeter leads to S terminal and the mounting bracket on manual transmission, or ground terminal on automatic transmission.
3. If there is no continuity, replace solenoid.

STARTER MOTOR FULL LOAD CURRENT TEST

1. Ensure that battery is fully charged, then disconnect and ground ignition coil secondary wire.
2. Connect remote control starter switch between positive battery terminal and S terminal on starter.
3. Connect circuit tester, **Fig. 1,** then actuate remote starter switch and note voltmeter reading.

NOTE: Note voltage after starter has reached maximum RPM.

4. Turn off remote starter switch, then turn load control knob clockwise until indicated voltage is exactly the same as when starter was running.
5. If ammeter does not read 180-220 amps, bench test starter.

OFF-VEHICLE TESTING

ARMATURE BALANCE TEST

1. Place armature in growler and turn power switch to "GROWLER" position.
2. Place contact fingers of meter test probe across adjacent commutator bars, then adjust voltage control until pointer indicates highest voltage on scale.
3. Test each commutator bar with adjacent bar. If any reading of zero volts is obtained, replace armature.

ARMATURE GROUND TEST

1. Place armature in growler and turn power switch to "TEST" position.
2. Place one lead of test lamp on armature core and other lead to each commutator bar.
3. If test lamp lights at any time, replace armature.

ARMATURE SHORT TEST

1. Place armature in growler and turn power switch to "GROWLER" position.
2. Hold steel blade parallel to and touching armature core, then slowly rotate armature at least one full turn.
3. If steel blade vibrates, replace armature.

FIELD WINDING TERMINAL-TO-BRUSH CONTINUITY TEST

1. Insert a piece of paper between contact points.
2. Touch ohmmeter leads to field winding terminal and insulated brush.
3. If resistance is greater than zero ohms, determine which solder joints have excessive resistance and repair with 600 watt soldering iron.

HOLD-IN COIL WINDING RESISTANCE TEST

1. Insert a piece of paper between contact points.
2. Using ohmmeter, measure resistance between S terminal and starter motor frame.
3. If resistance is not 2.0–3.5 ohms, replace field winding assembly.

INSULATED BRUSH CONNECTION TEST

1. Using ohmmeter, test resistance

Fig. 1 Full-load current test connections.

through solder joint by touching leads to brush and the copper bus bar.

2. If resistance is more than zero ohms, resolder joint with 600 watt soldering iron.

NO-LOAD CURRENT TEST

1. Connect test equipment as shown, **Fig. 2**, and turn tester load control knob fully counterclockwise, then operate starter and note voltage.
2. Using mechanical tachometer, determine exact motor RPM. Connect tachometer by removing seal from end of drive end housing and clean grease from end of armature shaft.
3. Disconnect battery cable from starter.
4. Turn load control knob clockwise until voltage reading is exactly that obtained in step 1.
5. If ammeter does not read 67 amps with a starter motor RPM of 7380–9356, repair or replace starter as necessary.

SOLENOID CONTACT POINT TEST

1. Using ohmmeter, test resistance through solder joint.
2. If resistance is more than zero ohms, resolder joint using 600 watt soldering iron.

TERMINAL BRACKET INSULATION TEST

1. Using ohmmeter, test resistance between terminal bracket and end cap.
2. If resistance is less than infinite, replace end cap.

Fig. 2 No-load current test connections

Chrysler Corp.

TABLE OF CONTENTS

General Information

INDEX

STARTER TROUBLE CHECK-OUT

When trouble develops in the starting motor circuit, and the starter cranks the engine slowly or not at all, several preliminary checks can be made to determine whether the trouble lies in the battery, in the starter, in the wiring between them, or elsewhere. Many conditions besides defects in the starter itself can result in poor cranking performance.

To make a quick check of the starter system, turn on the headlights. They should burn with normal brilliance. If they do not, the battery may be run down and it should be checked with a hydrometer.

If the battery is in a charged condition so that lights burn brightly, operate the starting motor. Any one of three things will happen to the lights: (1) They will go out, (2) dim considerably or (3) stay bright without any cranking action taking place.

IF LIGHTS GO OUT

If the lights go out as the starter switch is closed, it indicates that there is a poor connection between the battery and starting motor. This poor connection will most often be found at the battery terminals. Correction is made by removing the cable clamps from the terminals, cleaning the terminals and clamps, replacing the clamps and tightening them securely. A coating of corrosion inhibitor (vaseline will do) may be applied to the clamps and terminals to retard the formation of corrosion.

IF LIGHTS DIM

If the lights dim considerably as the start-

er switch is closed and the starter operates slowly or not at all, the battery may be run down, or there may be some mechanical condition in the engine or starting motor that is throwing a heavy burden on the starting motor. This imposes a high discharge rate on the battery which causes noticeable dimming of the lights.

Check the battery with a hydrometer. If it is charged, the trouble probably lies in either the engine or starting motor itself. In the engine, tight bearings or pistons or heavy oil place an added burden on the starting motor. Low temperatures also hamper starting motor performance since it thickens engine oil and makes the engine considerably harder to crank and start. Also, a battery is less efficient at low temperatures.

In the starting motor, a bent armature, loose pole shoe screws or worn bearings, any of which may allow the armature to drag, will reduce cranking performance and increase current draw.

In addition, more serious internal damage is sometimes found. Thrown armature windings or commutator bars, which sometimes occur on over-running clutch drive starting motors, are usually caused by excessive overrunning after starting. This is the result of such conditions as the driver keeping the starting switch closed too long after the engine has started, the driver opening the throttle too wide in starting, or improper carburetor fast idle adjustment. Any of these subject the over-running clutch to extra strain so it tends to seize, spinning the armature at high speed with resulting armature damage.

Another cause may be engine backfire during cranking which may result, among other things, from ignition timing being too far advanced.

To avoid such failures, the driver should

pause a few seconds after a false start to make sure the engine has come completely to rest before another start is attempted. In addition, the ignition timing should be reset if engine backfiring has caused the trouble.

LIGHTS STAY BRIGHT, NO CRANKING ACTION

This condition indicates an open circuit at some point, either in the starter itself, the starter switch or control circuit. The solenoid control circuit can be eliminated momentarily by placing a heavy jumper lead across the solenoid main terminals to see if the starter will operate. This connects the starter directly to the battery and, if it operates, it indicates that the control circuit is not functioning normally. The wiring and control units must be checked to locate the trouble.

If the starter does not operate with the jumper attached, it will probably have to be removed from the engine so it can be examined in detail.

CHECKING CIRCUIT WITH VOLTMETER

Excessive resistance in the circuit between the battery and starter will reduce cranking performance. The resistance can be checked by using a voltmeter to measure voltage drop in the circuits while the starter is operated. There are three checks to be made:

1. Voltage drop between car frame and grounded battery terminal post (not cable clamp).
2. Voltage drop between car frame and starting motor field frame.
3. Voltage drop between insulated bat-

tery terminal post and starting motor terminal stud (or the battery terminal stud of the solenoid).

Each of these should show no more than one-tenth (0.1) volt drop when the starting motor is cranking the engine. Do not use the starter for more than 30 seconds at a time to avoid overheating it.

If excessive voltage drop is found in any of these circuits, make correction by disconnecting the cables, cleaning the connections carefully, and then reconnecting the cables firmly in place. A coating of vaseline on the battery cables and terminal clamps will retard corrosion.

NOTE: On some cars, extra long battery cables may be required due to the location of the battery and starter. This may result in somewhat higher voltage drop than the above recommended 0.1 volt. The only means of determining the normal voltage drop in such cases is to check several of these vehicles. Then when the voltage drop is well above the normal figure for all cars checked, abnormal resistance will be indicated and correction can be made as already explained.

SOLENOID SWITCHES

The solenoid switch on a cranking motor not only closes the circuit between the battery and the cranking motor but also shifts the drive pinion into mesh with the engine flywheel ring gear. This is done by means of a linkage between the solenoid switch plunger and the shift lever on the cranking motor.

There are two windings in the solenoid; a pull-in winding and a hold-in winding. Both windings are energized when the external control switch is closed. They produce a magnetic field which pulls the plunger in so that the drive pinion is shifted into mesh, and the main contacts in the solenoid switch are closed to connect the battery directly to the cranking motor. Closing the main switch contacts shorts out the pull-in winding since this winding is connected across the main contacts. The magnetism produced by the hold-in winding is sufficient to hold the plunger in, and shorting out the pull-in winding reduces drain on the battery. When the control switch is opened, it disconnects the hold-in winding from the battery. When the hold-in winding is disconnected from the battery, the shift lever spring withdraws the plunger from the solenoid, opening the solenoid switch contacts and at the same time withdrawing the drive pinion from mesh. Proper operation of the switch depends on maintaining a definite balance between the magnetic strength of the pull-in and hold-in windings.

This balance is established in the design by the size of the wire and the number of turns specified. An open circuit in the hold-in winding or attempts to crank with a discharged battery will cause the switch to chatter.

STARTING MOTOR SERVICE

To obtain full performance data on a starting motor or to determine the cause of abnormal operation, the starting motor should be submitted to a no-load and torque test. These tests are best performed on a starter bench tester with the starter mounted on it.

From a practical standpoint, however, a simple torque test may be made quickly with the starter in the car. Make sure the battery is fully charged and that the starter circuit wires and terminals are in good condition. Then operate the starter to see if the engine turns over normally. If it does not, the torque developed is below standard and the starter should be removed for further checking.

STARTER DRIVE TROUBLES

Starter drive troubles are easy to diagnose and they usually cannot be confused with ordinary starter difficulties. If the starter does not turn over at all or if it drags, look for trouble in the starter or electrical supply system. Concentrate on the starter drive or ring gear if the starter is noisy, if it turns but does not engage the engine, or if the starter won't disengage after the engine is started. After the starter is removed, the trouble can usually be located quickly.

Worn or chipped ring gear or starter pinion are the usual causes of noisy operation. Before replacing either or both of these parts try to find out what caused the damage. With the Bendix type drive, incomplete engagement of the pinion with the ring gear is a common cause of tooth damage. The wrong pinion clearance on starter drives of the over-running clutch type leads to poor meshing of the pinion and ring gear and too rapid tooth wear.

A less common cause of noise with either type of drive is a bent starter armature shaft. When this shaft is bent, the pinion gear alternately binds and then only partly meshes with the ring gear. Most manufacturers specify a maximum of .003 inch radial run-out on the armature shaft.

WHEN CLUTCH DRIVE FAILS

The over-running clutch type drive seldom becomes so worn that it fails to engage since it is directly activated by a fork and lever. The only thing that is likely to happen is that, once engaged, it will not turn the engine because the clutch itself is worn out. A much more frequent difficulty and one that rapidly wears ring gear and teeth is partial engagement. Proper meshing of the pinion is controlled by the end clearance between the pinion gear and the starter housing or pinion stop, if used.

On some starters, the solenoids are completely enclosed in the starter housing and the pinion clearance is not adjustable. If the clearance is not correct, the starter must be disassembled and checked for excessive wear of solenoid linkage, shift lever mechanism, or improper assembly of parts.

Failure of the over-running clutch drive to disengage is usually caused by binding between the armature shaft and the drive. If the drive, particularly the clutch, shows signs of overheating it indicates that it is not disengaging immediately after the engine starts. If the clutch is forced to over-run too long, it overheats and turns a bluish color. For the cause of the binding, look for rust or gum between the armature shaft and the drive, or for burred splines. Excess oil on the drive will lead to gumming, and inadequate air circulation in the flywheel housing will cause rust.

Over-running clutch drives cannot be overhauled in the field so they must be replaced. In cleaning, never soak them in a solvent because the solvent may enter the clutch and dissolve the sealed-in lubricant. Wipe them off lightly with kerosene and lubricate them sparingly with SAE 10 or 10W oil.

WHEN BENDIX DRIVE FAILS

When a Bendix type drive doesn't engage the cause usually is one of three things: either the drive spring is broken, one of the drive spring bolts has sheared off, or the screwshaft threads won't allow the pinion to travel toward the flywheel. In the first two cases, remove the drive by unscrewing the set screw under the last coil of the drive spring and replace the broken parts. Gummed or rusty screwshaft threads are fairly common causes of Bendix drive failure and are easily cleaned with a little kerosene or steel wool, depending on the trouble. Here again, as in the case of over-running clutch drives, use light oil sparingly, and be sure the flywheel housing has adequate ventilation. There is usually a breather hole in the bottom of the flywheel housing which should be open.

The failure of a Bendix drive to disengage or to mesh properly is most often caused by gummed or rusty screwshaft threads. When this is not true, look for mechanical failure within the drive itself.

Bosch Starter Motors

INDEX

DESCRIPTION

The Bosch starter is a direct drive starter motor with an overrunning clutch type starter drive. A solenoid switch is mounted on the starter motor.

DIAGNOSIS

Refer to **Fig. 1** when diagnosing starter.

IN-VEHICLE TESTING

NOTE: Before starting any tests, ensure that battery is fully charged and that all connections are good.

AMPERAGE DRAW TEST

1. Run engine until it reaches operating temperature, then turn engine off.
2. Connect a suitable battery-starter tester according to manufacturer's instructions.
3. Turn battery-starter tester control knob to "OFF" position.
4. Turn voltmeter selector knob to "16 VOLT" position.
5. Turn battery-starter function selector to "STARTER SYSTEM TEST" (0–500 amp scale).
6. Connect red positive ammeter lead to positive battery terminal and the black negative ammeter lead to negative battery terminal.
7. Connect red positive voltmeter lead to positive battery terminal and the black negative voltmeter lead to the negative battery terminal.
8. Connect a remote starter jumper according to manufacturer's instructions.

CAUTION: Do not crank engine excessively during testing.

9. Disconnect coil wire from distributor cap center tower and secure to good ground.
10. Crank engine with remote starter switch and observe exact voltmeter reading, then stop cranking engine.

11. Turn tester control knob clockwise until voltmeter reads exactly the same as when engine was being cranked. Ammeter should read 120–160 amps.

STARTER RESISTANCE TEST

1. Disconnect positive battery cable and connect 0–300 scale ammeter between disconnected lead and battery terminal post.
2. Connect a voltmeter, graduated in tenths, between positive post on battery and starter relay terminal on starter solenoid.
3. Crank engine while observing reading on voltmeter and ammeter. A voltage reading exceeding .3 volts indicates high resistance caused by loose circuit connections, a faulty cable, burned starter relay or solenoid switch contacts. A high current combined with slow cranking speed indicates need for starter repair.
4. Reconnect positive battery lead to battery.

INSULATED CIRCUIT TEST

1. Turn voltmeter selector knob to 4 volt position.
2. Disconnect ignition coil secondary cable.
3. Connect voltmeter positive lead to battery positive post and voltmeter negative lead to solenoid connector that connects to starter field coils.

NOTE: It may be necessary to peel back rubber boot on solenoid to reach solenoid connection.

4. Connect remote control starter switch to battery solenoid terminal of starter relay.
5. Crank engine with remote control starter switch while observing voltmeter reading. If voltmeter reading exceeds .3 volt, there is high resistance in starter insulated coil, proceed as follows:
   a. Remove voltmeter lead from solenoid connector and connect to following points, repeating test at each connection. Starter terminal of solenoid, battery terminal of solenoid, battery cable terminal at solenoid, starter relay and cable clamp at battery.
   b. A small change will occur each time a normal portion of the circuit is removed from test. A definite change in voltmeter reading indicates that last part eliminated in test is at fault.

STARTER GROUND TEST

1. Connect voltmeter positive lead to starter through bolt and negative voltmeter lead to battery negative post.
2. Crank engine with remote control starter switch and observe voltmeter reading.
3. If voltmeter reading exceeds .2 volt, make following tests to isolate points of excessive voltage loss, repeating test at each connection; starter drive housing, cable terminal at engine, cable clamp at battery.
4. A small change will occur each time a normal portion of circuit is removed from test. A definite change in voltmeter reading indicates last part eliminated in test is at fault.

STARTER SOLENOID TEST

1. Connect heavy jumper wire on starter relay between battery and solenoid terminals. If engine cranks, perform starter relay test.
2. If engine does not crank or solenoid chatters, check wiring and connectors from relay to starter for loose or corroded connections.
3. Repeat test and, if engine still does not crank properly, repair or replace starter as necessary.

STARTER SOLENOID BENCH TEST

1. Disconnect field coil wire from field coil terminal.
2. Check for continuity between solenoid terminal and field coil terminal. There should be continuity.
3. Check for continuity between solenoid terminal and solenoid housing. There should be continuity.
4. If there is no continuity in either test, replace solenoid assembly.

Fig. 1 Starter motor diagnosis

Fig. 2 Disconnecting coil wire from solenoid (typical). Bosch units

Fig. 3 Solenoid plunger removal. Bosch units for A-404 auto. transaxle or 1983 A-460 man. transaxle

Fig. 4 "C" washer & bearing washer removal. Bosch units

Fig. 5 Brush plate removal. Bosch units

Fig. 6 Metal plate & rubber gasket removal. Bosch units

Fig. 7 Shift lever bolt removal. Bosch units

2. Check for battery voltage between starter relay battery terminal and ground.
3. Connect jumper wire on starter relay between battery and ignition terminals.
4. If engine does not crank, connect a second jumper wire to starter relay between ground terminal and good ground and repeat test.
5. If engine cranks in step 4, transmission linkage is misadjusted or neutral safety switch is defective.
6. If engine does not crank in step 4, starter relay is defective.

Fig. 8 Armature assembly & shift fork. Bosch units for A-404 auto. transaxle or 1983 A-460 man. transaxle

5. Connect field coil wire to field coil terminal.

STARTER RELAY TEST

1. Place transmission in Neutral and apply parking brake.

STARTER OVERHAUL

1.7 L Engine W/A-404 AUTO. TRANSAXLE OR A-412 OR 1983 A-460 MAN. TRANSAXLE

1. Disconnect field coil wire from solenoid terminal, Fig. 2.
2. Remove solenoid mounting screws and the solenoid. On automatic transaxle, or 1983 A-460 manual transaxle units, remove solenoid plunger from shift fork, Fig. 3.
3. Remove end shield bearing cap, then the "C" washer and bearing washer, Fig. 4.
4. Remove through bolts and the end shield.
5. Remove both field brushes and the brush plate, Fig. 5.
6. Remove field frame from starter.
7. Remove rubber gasket and metal plate, Fig. 6.

Fig. 9 Pressing stop collar from snap ring. Bosch units except models w/A-412 man. transaxle

8. Remove clutch lever pivot bolt, Fig. 7.
9. On automatic transaxle, or 1983 A-460 manual transaxle units, remove armature assembly and shift lever from drive end housing, Fig. 8.
10. On all models, press stop collar off snap ring, Figs. 9 and 10, and remove snap ring.
11. Remove stop collar and clutch, Fig. 11.
12. On A-412 manual transaxle units, remove drive end housing from armature, Fig. 12.
13. Reverse procedure to assemble.

Fig. 10 Pressing stop collar from snap ring. Bosch units for A-412 man. transaxle

Fig. 11 Clutch removal (Typical). Bosch units

Fig. 12 Drive end housing removal. Bosch units for A-412 man. transaxle

1981—82 1.7 L ENGINE W/A-460 MAN. TRANSAXLE; 1981—83 2.2 L ENGINE W/A-413 AUTO. TRANSAXLE OR A-460 OR A-465 MAN. TRANSAXLE & ALL 1984—85 W/2.2 L ENGINE

1. Remove nut from solenoid field coil terminal, then remove field coil strap from terminal, **Fig. 2.**
2. Remove three solenoid attaching screws, then work solenoid from shift fork and remove solenoid.
3. Remove two starter motor end shield bearing cap attaching screws and remove end shield cap, C-washer and bearing washer, **Fig. 4.**
4. Remove starter motor through bolts, then remove starter motor brush end shield.
5. Remove two starter motor brushes by prying the brush retaining springs back, then remove brush plate, **Fig. 5.**
6. Slide field frame from armature, then remove armature and clutch assembly from drive end housing.
7. Remove rubber seal and clutch lever bolt from drive end frame, then remove clutch lever.
8. Position armature in a suitable vise, then using a socket, press collar from pinion gear stop snap ring, **Fig. 9.** Remove snap ring from armature shaft using snap ring pliers.
9. Remove stop collar and clutch assembly from armature shaft, **Fig. 11.**
10. Reverse procedure to assemble.

Chrysler Reduction Gear Starter

INDEX

DESCRIPTION

This reduction gear starting motor, **Fig. 1,** has an armature-to-engine crankshaft ratio of 2 to 1 or a 3½ to 1 reduction gear set is built into the motor assembly. The starter utilizes a solenoid shift. The housing of the solenoid is integral with the starter drive end housing.

DIAGNOSIS

Refer to **Fig. 2** when diagnosing starter.

IN-VEHICLE TESTING

AMPERAGE DRAW TEST

1980—82 Models
1. Run engine until it reaches operating temperature, then turn engine off.
2. Connect battery-starter tester following manufacturer's instructions.
3. Turn variable resistor control knob on tester to zero or off position.
4. Connect remote starter switch following manufacturer's instructions.
5. Crank engine just long enough to read cranking voltage on voltmeter.
6. Turn variable resistor control knob on tester until voltmeter reads cranking voltage previously noted. Amperage should be 165-180 amps on 225 and 318 cubic inch engines, or 180-200 amps on 225 (equipped with 1.8 horsepower starter) and 360 cubic inch engines.

1983—85 Models
When performing this test on these vehicles refer to amperage draw test for Bosch starters.

CIRCUIT RESISTANCE TEST

1. Connect voltmeter leads across each connection shown in circuit resistance chart, **Fig. 3.**
2. If readings are higher than specified, clean or repair connection, then repeat test.

STARTER SOLENOID TEST

1. Connect heavy jumper wire on starter relay between battery and solenoid terminals.
2. If starter does not crank, or solenoid chatters, check wiring and connectors from relay to starter for loose or corroded connections, then repeat test.
3. If engine still will not crank, repair or replace starter as necessary.

STARTER SOLENOID BENCH TEST

1. Remove solenoid assembly.
2. Connect solenoid to 6 volt DC power supply with an ammeter in series. Connect positive lead of power supply to solenoid terminal, positive lead of ammeter to solenoid sleeve and negative lead of power supply to other ammeter terminal.
3. Turn on circuit and check current draw for hold-in coil.
4. Transfer positive ammeter lead to solenoid lead terminal and check cur-

PIN
GEAR HOUSING
CORE
RING
SOLENOID
SOLENOID TERMINAL
SEAL
FORK
SPRING
SOLENOID LEAD
CONTACT AND PLUNGER
RING
SPRING
CLUTCH
RING
SHAFT
WASHER
DUST COVER
ACTUATOR
RING
GEAR
WASHER
BEARING
WASHER
NUT
WASHER
NUT
BRUSH HOLDER PLATE
SCREW AND WASHER
SPRING
SCREW
BATTERY TERMINAL
BRUSH
INSULATOR
SPRING
FIELD FRAME ASSEMBLY
WASHER
ARMATURE
WASHER
END HEAD
THROUGH BOLTS

Fig. 1   Chrysler built reduction gear starting motor

STARTER MOTOR DIAGNOSIS

DIAGRAM OF STARTER RELAY:
TO BALLAST RESISTOR
FROM BATTERY
TO EGR TIMER
TO SOLENOID
BAL   BATT
IGN   SOL
FROM IGNITION SWITCH
TO NEUTRAL START OR CLUTCH START SWITCH

CAUTION: BEFORE TESTING STARTER, PLACE TRANSMISSION IN PARK OR NEUTRAL POSITION. SET BRAKES AND DISCONNECT COIL WIRE FROM DISTRIBUTOR AND SECURE TO A GOOD GROUND TO PREVENT ENGINE FROM STARTING.

TEST BATTERY. SEE BATTERY GROUP FOR PROCEDURE

CONDITION 1 STARTER FAILS TO OPERATE (NO STARTER RELAY CLICK)

TEST SOLENOID AND STARTER. CONNECT REMOTE STARTER SWITCH BETWEEN RELAY TERMINALS "B" AND "SOL" ACTUATE SWITCH (STARTER SHOULD OPERATE)

STARTER DOES NOT OPERATE

STARTER OPERATION NORMAL

SOLENOID DOES NOT OPERATE

SOLENOID OPERATES OR CHATTERS STARTER MOTOR DOES NOT OPERATE

TEST RELAY CIRCUIT. CONNECT REMOTE STARTER SWITCH BETWEEN RELAY TERMINALS "B" AND "I". ACTUATE SWITCH (STARTER SHOULD OPERATE)

LOOSE OR CORRODED BATTERY TERMINALS, CABLES, OR CONNECTIONS

LOOSE OR CORRODED BATTERY TERMINALS, CABLES, OR CONNECTIONS

STARTER DOES NOT OPERATE

STARTER OPERATION NORMAL

LOOSE OR DISCONNECTED WIRE FROM RELAY "SOL" TERMINAL TO SOLENOID

SOLENOID SWITCH CONTACTS BURNED

CONNECT JUMPER WIRE BETWEEN RELAY "G" TERMINAL AND GROUND

LOOSE BULKHEAD CONNECTOR

FAULTY SOLENOID

FAULTY STARTER

REPEAT RELAY CIRCUIT TEST (STARTER SHOULD OPERATE)

OPEN WIRE FROM RELAY "B" TERMINAL TO IGNITION SWITCH "BAT" TERMINAL

STARTER OPERATES

STARTER DOES NOT OPERATE

OPEN WIRE FROM IGNITION SWITCH TO RELAY "I" TERMINAL

AUTOMATIC TRANSMISSION: FAULTY TRANSMISSION LINKAGE ADJUSTMENT. FAULTY NEUTRAL START SWITCH OR WIRING

MANUAL TRANSMISSION: FAULTY CLUTCH START SWITCH, ADJUSTMENT OR WIRING

FAULTY RELAY

IGNITION SWITCH CONTACTS BURNED OR CORRODED

CONDITION 2 STARTER CRANKS TOO SLOW

CONDITION 3 STARTER OPERATES BUT DOES NOT ENGAGE ENGINE

CONDITION 4 STARTER OPERATES BUT ENGAGES ENGINE ONLY MOMENTARILY

CONDITION 5 STARTER OPERATES BUT WILL NOT DISENGAGE WHEN IGNITION STARTER SWITCH IS RELEASED

OVERHEATED ENGINE OR CRANKCASE OIL TOO HEAVY

OVERRUNNING CLUTCH MALFUNCTION

ENGINE TIMING TOO FAR ADVANCED

STARTER RELAY CONTACT STICKING

TEST STARTER AMPERAGE DRAW

BROKEN STARTER CLUTCH HOUSING

STARTER OVERRUNNING CLUTCH NOT OPERATING

SOLENOID SWITCH STICKING

AMPERAGE BELOW SPECIFICATION

AMPERAGE ABOVE SPECIFICATION

HIGH RESISTANCE BATTERY TO STARTER CABLE

GROUNDED STARTER CABLE

BROKEN TEETH ON ENGINE RING GEAR

BROKEN STARTER CLUTCH HOUSING

STARTER CLUTCH NOT DISENGAGING

FAULTY ENGINE GROUND

FAULTY STARTER

STARTER ARMATURE SHAFT SHEARED OR REDUCTION GEAR TEETH STRIPPED

BROKEN TEETH ON ENGINE RING GEAR

IGNITION STARTER SWITCH CONTACTS STICKING

BURNED (HIGH RESISTANCE) SOLENOID CONTACTS

STEERING COLUMN IGNITION LINKAGE HANGING UP

FAULTY STARTER

Fig. 2   Starter motor diagnosis (Part 1 of 2)

Fig. 2   Starter motor diagnosis (Part 2 of 2)

CIRCUIT RESISTANCE CHART			
Connection	Voltmeter Lead Connection		Voltmeter Reading
	Positive	Negative	
Positive post on battery to cable clamp	To post	To clamp	0
Negative post on battery to cable clamp	To post	To clamp	0
Battery ground cable to engine block	To bolt	To cable connector	Not to exceed 0.2 volts
Battery Cable to Starter	To Battery Positive Post	To Battery Terminal on Starter	Not to exceed 0.2 volts
Starter housing to ground	To starter housing	To negative post on battery	Not to exceed 0.2 volts

Fig. 3   Circuit resistance chart

Fig. 5   Unwinding solenoid lead wire

Fig. 6   Solenoid contact & plunger

Fig. 4   Terminal screw replacement

Fig. 7   Dust cover removal, all (Typical)

Fig. 8   Driven gear snap ring replacement, all (Typical)

Fig. 9   Pinion shaft "C" clip replacement

rent draw for pull-in coil.
5. If current draw for hold-in coil is not 8–9 amps @ 77°F., current draw for pull-in coil is not 13–15 amps @ 77°F. or winding appears burnt or damaged, replace solenoid assembly.

STARTER RELAY TEST

Vehicles w/Automatic Transmission

1. Place shift lever in Neutral, then connect jumper wire on starter relay between battery and ignition terminals.
2. If engine does not crank, connect a second jumper wire on starter relay between ground terminal and good ground. If engine now cranks, transmission linkage is misadjusted or neutral safety switch is defective.
3. If engine still does not crank, replace starter relay.

Vehicles w/Manual Transmission

1. Have assistant depress clutch pedal.
2. Connect jumper wire on starter relay

between battery and ignition terminals.
3. If engine does not crank, connect second jumper wire on starter relay between ground terminal and good ground.
4. If engine cranks, clutch neutral start switch is misadjusted or defective. If engine does not crank, replace starter relay.

STARTER OVERHAUL

DISASSEMBLY

1. Place gear housing of starter in a vise with soft jaws. Use vise as a support fixture only; do not clamp.
2. Remove through bolts and starter end head assembly.
3. Carefully remove armature from gear housing and field frame assembly.
4. Pull field frame assembly from gear housing to expose terminal screw.
5. Support terminal screw with a finger, then remove terminal screw, **Fig. 4.**

6. Remove field frame assembly.
7. Remove nuts attaching solenoid and brush holder plate assembly to gear housing, then remove the solenoid and brush plate assembly.
8. Remove nut, steel washer and insulating washer from solenoid terminal.
9. Unwind solenoid lead wire from brush terminal, **Fig. 5,** and remove screws securing solenoid to brush plate, then remove the solenoid from brush plate.
10. Remove nut from battery terminal on brush plate, then the battery terminal.
11. Remove solenoid contact and plunger assembly from solenoid, **Fig. 6,** then the return spring from the solenoid moving core.
12. Remove dust cover from gear housing, **Fig. 7.**
13. Release retainer clip positioning driven gear on pinion shaft, **Fig. 8.**

NOTE: The retainer clip is under tension. Therefore, it is recommended that a cloth be placed over the retainer clip when released, preventing it from springing away.

Fig. 10 Removing pinion shaft

Fig. 11 Clutch assembly replacement (Typical)

Fig. 12 Solenoid core replacement (Typical)

Fig. 13 Shifter fork pin replacement, all (Typical)

Fig. 14 Shifter fork assembly (Typical)

Fig. 15 Shifter fork & clutch assembly (Typical)

Fig. 16 Solenoid to brush holder plate assembly (Typical)

14. Remove pinion shaft "C" clip, **Fig. 9.**
15. Push pinion shaft toward rear of housing, **Fig. 10,** and remove retainer ring and thrust washers, clutch and pinion assembly, with the two shift fork nylon actuators as an assembly, **Fig. 11.**
16. Remove driven gear and thrust washer.
17. Pull shifting fork forward and remove solenoid moving core, **Fig. 12.**
18. Remove shifting fork retainer pin, **Fig. 13,** and remove clutch shifting fork assembly.

REASSEMBLY

NOTE: The shifter fork consists of two spring steel plates assembled with two rivets, **Fig. 14.** There should be about 1/16 inch side movement to insure proper pinion gear engagement. Lubricate between plates sparingly with SAE 10 engine oil.

1. Position shift fork in drive housing and install fork retaining pin, **Fig. 13.** One tip of pin should be straight, the other tip should be bent at a 15 degree angle away from housing. Fork and pin should operate freely after bending tip of pin.
2. Install solenoid moving core and engage shifting fork, **Fig. 12.**
3. Enter pinion shaft in drive housing and install friction washer and driven gear.
4. Install clutch and pinion assembly, **Fig. 11,** thrust washer, retaining ring, and thrust washer.
5. Complete installation of pinion shaft, engaging fork with clutch actuators, **Fig. 15.** Friction washer must be positioned on shoulder of splines of pinion shaft before driven gear is positioned.
6. Install driven gear snap ring, **Fig. 8,** then the pinion shaft retaining ring or "C" clip, **Fig. 9.**

7. Install starter solenoid return spring into movable core bore.

NOTE: Inspect starter solenoid switch contacting washer. If top of washer is burned, disassemble contact switch plunger assembly and reverse the washer.

8. Install solenoid contact plunger assembly into solenoid, **Fig. 6.** Ensure contact spring is properly positioned on shaft of solenoid contact plunger assembly.
9. Install battery terminal stud in brush holder.

NOTE: Inspect contacts in brush holder. If contacts are badly burned, replace brush holder with brushes and contacts as an assembly.

Fig. 17 Solenoid & brush holder installation (Typical)

Fig. 18 Installing brushes & armature thrust washer (Typical)

Fig. 19 Armature installation (Typical)

10. Position seal on brush holder plate.
11. Install solenoid lead wire through hole in brush holder, **Fig. 16,** then the solenoid stud, insulating washer, flat washer and nut.
12. Wrap solenoid lead wire around brush terminal post, **Fig. 5,** and solder with a high temperature resin core solder and resin flux.
13. Install brush holder attaching screws.

14. Install solenoid coil and brush plate assembly into gear housing bore and position brush plate assembly into starter gear housing, **Fig. 17.** Then, install and tighten housing attaching nuts.
15. Install brushes with armature thrust washer, **Fig. 18.** This holds brushes out and facilitates proper armature installation.
16. Install brush terminal screw, **Fig. 4.**

17. Position field frame on gear housing and install armature into field frame and starter gear housing, **Fig. 19,** carefully engaging splines of shaft with reduction gear by rotating armature slightly to engage splines.
18. Install thrust washer on armature shaft.
19. Install starter end head assembly, then the through bolts.

Mitsubishi Starters

INDEX

Fig. 1 Mitsubishi starter exploded view

Fig. 2 Field coil terminal identification

Fig. 4 Rubber gasket & metal plate removal

DESCRIPTION

The Mitsubishi starter, **Fig. 1,** is a direct drive starter motor with an overrunning clutch type starter drive. A solenoid switch is mounted on the starter motor.

DIAGNOSIS

For diagnosis of this starter, refer to "Bosch Starters".

IN-VEHICLE TESTING

When testing this starter, refer to "Bosch Starters".

STARTER OVERHAUL

1. Disconnect field coil wire from solenoid terminal, **Fig. 2.**
2. Remove solenoid mounting screws and the solenoid.
3. Remove through bolts and the starter support bracket.
4. Remove brush plate mounting screws and the starter end shield, **Fig. 3.**
5. Remove both field brushes and the brush plate.
6. Slide field frame over armature, then remove rubber seal and spring from drive end housing, **Fig. 4.**
7. Remove armature and clutch assembly from drive end housing.
8. Remove shift lever assembly from drive end housing. Remove bushings from shift lever.
9. Press stop collar off snap ring using a suitable socket, **Fig. 5,** then remove snap ring and stop collar.
10. Remove clutch assembly from armature shaft.
11. Reverse procedure to assemble.

Fig. 3 Starter end plate removal

Fig. 5 Stop collar, snap ring & clutch assembly

Nippondenso Starters

INDEX

DESCRIPTION

Nippondenso starters, **Figs. 1 and 2,** are either direct drive or reduction gear types. The direct drive starter has an overrunning clutch type starter drive and a solenoid switch is mounted on the starter motor. The structure of the reduction gear type starter differs from that of the direct drive type, but the electrical wiring is the same for both types.

DIAGNOSIS & TESTING

When diagnosing or testing Nippondenso starters, refer to "Bosch Starters".

STARTER OVERHAUL

1983 1.6 L ENGINE W/A-460 MAN. TRANSAXLE

1. Remove nut from solenoid field coil terminal, then disconnect field coil wire from solenoid terminal, **Fig. 3.**
2. Remove solenoid attaching screws, then remove solenoid.
3. Remove starter motor through bolts, then remove front support bracket.
4. Remove brush plate attaching screws, then remove end plate, **Fig. 4.**
5. Pry brush plate springs back, then remove the two brushes from their holders.
6. Remove brush plate, then slide field frame off armature.
7. Remove rubber seal and spring from drive end housing, **Fig. 5.**
8. Remove armature and clutch assembly from drive end housing.
9. Remove shift lever assembly from drive end housing. Remove bushings from shift lever.
10. Using a suitable socket, press stop collar off snap ring, **Fig. 6,** then remove snap ring and stop collar.
11. Remove clutch assembly from armature shaft.
12. Reverse procedure to assemble.

Fig. 1 Nippondenso direct drive starter exploded view

Fig. 2 Nippondenso reduction gear starter exploded view

Fig. 5 Rubber seal & spring removal. Nippondenso units for 1983 1.6 L engine W/A-460 man. transaxle

Fig. 6 Stop collar, snap ring & clutch assembly. Nippondenso units except 2.6 L engine

Fig. 3 Field coil terminal identification. Nippondenso units except 2.6 L engine

Fig. 4 Starter end plate removal. Nippondenso units for 1983 1.6 L engine W/A-460 man. transaxle

Fig. 7 Rubber gasket & metal plate removal. Nippondenso units for A-404 auto. transaxle & A-412 & 1983 A-460 man. transaxle

1.7 L ENGINE W/A-404 AUTO. TRANSAXLE OR A-412 OR 1983 A-460 MAN. TRANSAXLE

1. Disconnect field coil wire from solenoid terminal, **Fig. 3.**
2. Remove solenoid mounting screws and the solenoid.
3. Remove rubber gasket and metal plate, **Fig. 7.**
4. Remove bearing cover mounting screws and the bearing cover.
5. Remove armature shaft lock, washer, spring and seal, **Fig. 8.**
6. Remove through bolts and the commutator end frame cover.
7. Remove field brushes and the brush plate, **Fig. 9.**

1981–82 1.7 L ENGINE W/A-460 MAN. TRANSAXLE; 1981–85 2.2 L ENGINE W/A-413 AUTO. TRANSAXLE OR A-460 OR A-465 MAN. TRANSAXLE

1. Remove nut from solenoid field coil

8. Remove field frame from starter.
9. Remove shift lever pivot bolt, **Fig. 10.**
10. Remove armature assembly and shift lever from drive end housing, **Fig. 11.**
11. Press stop collar off snap ring, **Fig. 6.**
12. Remove snap ring, stop collar and clutch, **Fig. 6.**
13. Reverse procedure to assemble.

terminal, then remove field coil strap, **Fig. 3.**
2. Remove two nuts attaching solenoid to starter housing, then work solenoid from shift fork and remove solenoid.
3. Remove two attaching screws end shield bearing cap, then remove end shield cap, C-washer, bearing spring and bearing washer, **Fig. 12.**
4. Remove two starter motor through bolts, then remove starter motor brush end shield.
5. Pry back on brush spring and remove field brushes, then remove brush plate, **Fig. 9.**
6. Remove field frame from armature, then remove rubber seal from drive end housing, **Fig. 13.**
7. Remove armature and clutch assembly from drive end frame, **Fig. 14.**
8. Remove clutch lever retainer from drive end frame, then remove clutch lever, **Fig. 15.**
9. Press stop collar from snap ring, then

Fig. 8 Armature shaft lock, washer & spring removal. Nippondenso units for A-404 auto. transaxle & A-412 & 1983 A-460 man. transaxle

Fig. 9 Brush plate removal. Nippondenso units except 2.6 L engine

Fig. 10 Shift lever pivot removal. Nippondenso units for 1.7 L engine w/A-404 auto. transaxle & A-412 & 1983 A-460 man. transaxle

Fig. 11 Armature assembly removal. Nippondenso units for A-404 auto. transaxle & A-412 man. transaxle

Fig. 12 C-washer removal. Nippondenso units for A-413 auto. transaxle & A-460 or A-465 man. transaxle. Exc. 1983 1.7 L W/A-460

Fig. 13 Rubber seal removal. Nippondenso units for A-413 auto. transaxle & A-460 or A-465 man. transaxle. Exc. 1983—85 1.6 L & 1983 1.7 L W/A-460

Fig. 14 Armature & clutch assembly removal. Nippondenso units for A-413 auto. transaxle & A-460 or A-465 man. transaxle. Exc. 1983—85 1.6 L & 1983 1.7 L W/A-460

Fig. 15 Clutch shift lever retainer. Nippondenso units for A-413 auto. transaxle & A-460 or A-465 man. transaxle. Exc. 1983—85 1.6 L & 1983 1.7 L W/A-460

Fig. 16 Field coil terminal nut removal. Nippondenso units for 2.6 L engine

Fig. 17 Field brush removal. Nippondenso units for 2.6 L engine

Fig. 18 Separating solenoid from gear and housing. Nippondenso units for 2.6 L engine

Fig. 19 Pinion roller retainer removal. Nippondenso units for 2.6 L engine

Fig. 20   Reduction gear & clutch assembly removal. Nippondenso units for 2.6 L engine

Fig. 21   Solenoid ball & spring removal. Nippondenso units for 2.6 L engine

Fig. 22   Solenoid plunger removal. Nippondenso units for 2.6 L engine

remove snap ring, stop collar and clutch, **Fig. 6.**

10. Reverse procedure to assemble.

2.6 L ENGINE

1. Pull rubber boot from field coil terminal, then remove nut from field coil terminal stud, **Fig. 16.**
2. Remove field coil lead from field coil terminal stud.
3. Remove two starter motor through bolts, then remove two screws from starter motor end shield.
4. Remove upper left solenoid attaching screw retaining field coil lead retainer, then remove field coil lead retainer.
5. Remove starter motor brush end shield.
6. Pry back on brush retaining springs and remove brushes, then remove brush plate, **Fig. 17.**
7. Slide armature from field frame, then remove field frame from gear end frame.
8. Remove two gear end frame to solenoid attaching screws, then using a soft faced mallet separate solenoid from end frame, **Fig. 18.**
9. Remove reduction gear pinion roller retainer from gear end frame, **Fig. 19.**
10. Remove reduction gear and clutch assembly from gear end frame, **Fig. 20.**
11. Remove pinion gear from gear end frame, then remove pinion gear rollers.
12. Remove solenoid ball and spring, **Fig. 21,** then remove two remaining solenoid cover screws from solenoid and remove solenoid cover.
13. Remove solenoid plunger from solenoid housing, **Fig. 22.**
14. Reverse procedure to assemble.

Ford Motor Co.

TABLE OF CONTENTS

General Information

INDEX

STARTER TROUBLE CHECK-OUT

When trouble develops in the starting motor circuit, and the starter cranks the engine slowly or not at all, several preliminary checks can be made to determine whether the trouble lies in the battery, in the starter, in the wiring between them, or elsewhere. Many conditions besides defects in the starter itself can result in poor cranking performance.

To make a quick check of the starter system, turn on the headlights. They should burn with normal brilliance. If they do not, the battery may be run down and it should be checked with a hydrometer.

If the battery is in a charged condition so that lights burn brightly, operate the starting motor. Any one of three things will happen to the lights: (1) They will go out, (2) dim considerably or (3) stay bright without any cranking action taking place.

IF LIGHTS GO OUT

If the lights go out as the starter switch is closed, it indicates that there is a poor connection between the battery and starting motor. This poor connection will most often be found at the battery terminals. Correction is made by removing the cable clamps from the terminals, cleaning the terminals and clamps, replacing the clamps and tightening them securely. A coating of corrosion inhibitor (vaseline will do) may be applied to the clamps and terminals to retard the formation of corrosion.

IF LIGHTS DIM

If the lights dim considerably as the starter switch is closed and the starter operates slowly or not at all, the battery may be run down, or there may be some mechanical condition in the engine or starting motor that is throwing a heavy burden on the starting motor. This imposes a high discharge rate on the battery which causes noticeable dimming of the lights.

Check the battery with a hydrometer. If it is charged, the trouble probably lies in either the engine or starting motor itself. In the engine, tight bearings or pistons or heavy oil place an added burden on the starting motor. Low temperatures also hamper starting motor performance since it thickens engine oil and makes the engine considerably harder to crank and start. Also, a battery is less efficient at low temperatures.

In the starting motor, a bent armature, loose pole shoe screws or worn bearings, any of which may allow the armature to drag, will reduce cranking performance and increase current draw.

In addition, more serious internal damage is sometimes found. Thrown armature windings or commutator bars, which sometimes occur on over-running clutch drive starting motors, are usually caused by excessive overrunning after starting. This is the result of such conditions as the driver keeping the starting switch closed too long after the engine has started, the driver opening the throttle too wide in starting, or improper carburetor fast idle adjustment. Any of these subject the over-running clutch to extra strain so it tends to seize, spinning the armature at high speed with resulting armature damage.

Another cause may be engine backfire during cranking which may result, among other things, from ignition timing being too far advanced.

To avoid such failures, the driver should pause a few seconds after a false start to make sure the engine has come completely to rest before another start is attempted. In addition, the ignition timing should be reset if engine backfiring has caused the trouble.

LIGHTS STAY BRIGHT, NO CRANKING ACTION

This condition indicates an open circuit at some point, either in the starter itself, the starter switch or control circuit. The solenoid control circuit can be eliminated momentarily by placing a heavy jumper lead across the solenoid main terminals to see if the starter will operate. This connects the starter directly to the battery and, if it operates, it indicates that the control circuit is not functioning normally. The wiring and control units must be checked to locate the trouble.

If the starter does not operate with the jumper attached, it will probably have to be removed from the engine so it can be examined in detail.

CHECKING CIRCUIT WITH VOLTMETER

Excessive resistance in the circuit between the battery and starter will reduce cranking performance. The resistance can be checked by using a voltmeter to measure voltage drop in the circuits while the starter is operated. There are three checks to be made:
1. Voltage drop between car frame and grounded battery terminal post (not cable clamp).
2. Voltage drop between car frame and starting motor field frame.
3. Voltage drop between insulated battery terminal post and starting motor terminal stud (or the battery terminal stud of the solenoid).

Each of these should show no more than one-tenth (0.1) volt drop when the starting motor is cranking the engine. Do not use the starter for more than 30 seconds at a time to avoid overheating it.

If excessive voltage drop is found in any of these circuits, make correction by disconnecting the cables, cleaning the connections carefully, and then reconnecting the cables firmly in place. A coating of vaseline on the battery cables and terminal clamps will retard corrosion.

NOTE: On some cars, extra long battery cables may be required due to the location of the battery and starter. This may result in somewhat higher voltage drop than the above recommended 0.1 volt. The only means of determining the normal voltage drop in such cases is to check several of these vehicles. Then when the voltage drop is well above the normal figure for all cars checked, abnormal resistance will be indicated and correction can be made as already explained.

SOLENOID SWITCHES

The solenoid switch on a cranking motor not only closes the circuit between the battery and the cranking motor but also shifts the drive pinion into mesh with the engine flywheel ring gear. This is done by means of a linkage between the solenoid switch plunger and the shift lever on the cranking motor.

There are two windings in the solenoid; a pull-in winding and a hold-in winding. Both windings are energized when the external control switch is closed. They produce a magnetic field which pulls the plunger in so that the drive pinion is shifted into mesh, and the main contacts in the solenoid switch are closed to connect the battery directly to the cranking motor. Closing the main switch contacts shorts out the pull-in winding since this winding is connected across the main contacts. The magnetism produced by the hold-in winding is sufficient to hold the plunger in, and shorting out the pull-in winding reduces drain on the battery. When the control switch is opened, it disconnects the hold-in winding from the battery. When the hold-in winding is disconnected from the battery, the shift lever spring withdraws the plunger from the solenoid, opening the solenoid switch contacts and at the same time withdrawing the drive pinion from mesh. Proper operation of the switch depends on maintaining a definite balance between the magnetic strength of the pull-in and hold-in windings.

This balance is established in the design by the size of the wire and the number of turns specified. An open circuit in the hold-in winding or attempts to crank with a discharged battery will cause the switch to chatter.

STARTING MOTOR SERVICE

To obtain full performance data on a starting motor or to determine the cause of abnormal operation, the starting motor should be submitted to a no-load and torque test. These tests are best performed on a starter bench tester with the starter mounted on it.

From a practical standpoint, however, a simple torque test may be made quickly with the starter in the car. Make sure the battery is fully charged and that the starter circuit wires and terminals are in good condition. Then operate the starter to see if the engine turns over normally. If it does not, the torque developed is below standard and the starter should be removed for further checking.

STARTER DRIVE TROUBLES

Starter drive troubles are easy to diagnose and they usually cannot be confused with ordinary starter difficulties. If the starter does not turn over at all or if it drags, look for trouble in the starter or electrical supply system. Concentrate on the starter drive or ring gear if the starter is noisy, if it turns but does not engage the engine, or if the starter won't disengage after the engine is started. After the starter is removed, the trouble can usually be located quickly.

Worn or chipped ring gear or starter pinion are the usual causes of noisy operation. Before replacing either or both of these parts try to find out what caused the damage. With the Bendix type drive, incomplete engagement of the pinion with the ring gear is a common cause of tooth damage. The wrong pinion clearance on starter drives of the over-running clutch type leads to poor meshing of the pinion and ring gear and too rapid tooth wear.

A less common cause of noise with either type of drive is a bent starter armature shaft. When this shaft is bent, the pinion gear alternately binds and then only partly meshes with the ring gear. Most manufacturers specify a maximum of .003 inch radial run-out on the armature shaft.

WHEN CLUTCH DRIVE FAILS

The over-running clutch type drive seldom becomes so worn that it fails to engage since it is directly activated by a fork and lever. The only thing that is likely to happen is that, once engaged, it will not turn the engine because the clutch itself is worn out. A much more frequent difficulty and one that rapidly wears ring gear and teeth is partial engagement. Proper meshing of the pinion is controlled by the end clearance between the pinion gear and the starter housing or pinion stop, if used.

On some starters, the solenoids are completely enclosed in the starter housing and the pinion clearance is not adjustable. If the clearance is not correct, the starter must be disassembled and checked for excessive wear of solenoid linkage, shift lever mechanism, or improper assembly of parts.

Failure of the over-running clutch drive to disengage is usually caused by binding between the armature shaft and the drive. If the drive, particularly the clutch, shows signs of overheating it indicates that it is not disengaging immediately after the engine starts. If the clutch is forced to over-run too long, it overheats and turns a bluish color. For the cause of the binding, look for rust or gum between the armature shaft and the drive, or for burred splines. Excess oil on the drive will lead to gumming, and inadequate air circulation in the flywheel housing will cause rust.

Over-running clutch drives cannot be overhauled in the field so they must be replaced. In cleaning, never soak them in a solvent because the solvent may enter the clutch and dissolve the sealed-in lubricant. Wipe them off lightly with kerosene and lubricate them sparingly with SAE 10 or 10W oil.

WHEN BENDIX DRIVE FAILS

When a Bendix type drive doesn't engage the cause usually is one of three things: either the drive spring is broken, one of the drive spring bolts has sheared off, or the screwshaft threads won't allow the pinion to travel toward the flywheel. In the first two cases, remove the drive by unscrewing the set screw under the last coil of the drive spring and replace the broken parts. Gummed or rusty screwshaft threads are fairly common causes of Bendix drive failure and are easily cleaned with a little kerosene or steel wool, depending on the trouble. Here again, as in the case of over-running clutch drives, use light oil sparingly, and be sure the flywheel housing has adequate ventilation. There is usually a breather hole in the bottom of the flywheel housing which should be open.

The failure of a Bendix drive to disengage or to mesh properly is most often caused by gummed or rusty screwshaft threads. When this is not true, look for mechanical failure within the drive itself.

Ford Motorcraft Starters

INDEX

FORD MOTORCRAFT STARTER WITH INTEGRAL POSITIVE ENGAGEMENT DRIVE

DESCRIPTION

This type starting motor, **Figs. 1 and 2**, is a four pole, series parallel unit with a positive engagement drive built into the starter. The drive mechanism is engaged with the flywheel by lever action before the motor is energized.

When the ignition switch is turned on to the start position, the starter relay is energized and supplies current to the motor. The current flows through one field coil and a set of contact points to ground. The magnetic field given off by the field coil pulls the moveable pole, which is part of the lever, downward to its seat. When the pole is pulled down, the lever moves the drive assembly into the engine flywheel, **Fig. 3**.

When the moveable pole is seated, it functions as a normal field pole and opens the contact points. With the points open, current flows through the starter field coils, energizing the starter. At the same time, current also flows through a holding coil to hold the movable pole in its seated position.

When the ignition switch is released from the start position, the starter relay opens the circuit to the starting motor. This allows the return spring to force the lever back, disengaging the drive from the flywheel and returning the movable pole to its normal position.

DIAGNOSIS

When diagnosing this starter motor, refer to **Fig. 4**.

IN-VEHICLE TESTING

NOTE: Disconnect vacuum line to thermactor bypass valve before performing any cranking tests. After tests, run engine 3 minutes before connecting vacuum line.

Starter Cranking Circuit Test
1. Make test connections as shown in **Fig. 5.**
2. Disconnect ignition coil and crank engine.
3. Connect remote control starter switch from battery terminal of starter relay to S terminal of relay.
4. Maximum allowable voltage drop should be as follows:
   a. .5 volt with voltmeter negative lead connected to starter terminal and positive lead connected to battery positive terminal.
   b. .1 volt with voltmeter negative lead

Fig. 1   Ford Motorcraft positive engagement starting motor. 1984 4-2300cc & 1982–85 1600cc engines (Typical)

Fig. 2   Ford Motorcraft positive engagement starting motor. 1980—85 except 4-1600cc & 4-2300cc (Typical)

connected to starter relay (battery side) and positive lead connected to positive terminal of battery.

c. .3 volt with voltmeter negative lead connected to starter relay (starter side) and positive lead connected to positive terminal of battery.

d. .3 volt with voltmeter negative lead connected to negative terminal of battery and positive lead connected to engine ground.

Starter Load Test
1. Connect test equipment as shown in **Fig. 6.**

2. Ensure that no current is flowing through ammeter and heavy duty carbon pile rheostat portion of circuit.
3. Crank engine with ignition off and determine exact reading on voltmeter. This test is accomplished by disconnecting push-on connector S at starter relay and by connecting a remote control starter switch from positive battery terminal to S terminal of starter relay.
4. Stop cranking engine and reduce resistance of carbon pile until voltmeter indicates same reading as that obtained while starter cranked engine. Ammeter should read 150-250 amps.

STARTER OVERHAUL
Disassembly
1. Remove cover screw, cover, through bolts, starter drive end housing and starter drive plunger lever return spring, **Figs. 1 & 2.**
2. Remove plunger lever retaining pin, then remove lever and armature.
3. Remove stop ring retainer from armature shaft, then remove stop ring and starter drive gear assembly.
4. Remove brush end plate and insulator assembly.
5. Remove brushes from brush holder, then remove brush holder. Note position of brush holder to end terminal.

Fig. 3   Starter drive engaged

CONDITION	POSSIBLE CAUSE	RESOLUTION
Engine will not crank — starter spins.	1. Starter motor.	1. Remove starter, inspect for broken or worn starter drive components. Repair or replace as required.
	2. Flywheel ring gear.	2. Inspect ring gear teeth. Replace flywheel and ring gear if necessary.
Engine will not crank.	1. Loose or corroded battery cables.	1. Clean and tighten cable connections.
	2. Undercharged battery.	2. Check battery. Charge or replace.
	3. Burned fusible link in main wire feed to ignition switch.	3. Check fusible link — correct wiring problem.
	4. Starter relay.	4. Replace starter relay.
	5. Loose or broken cables.	5. Tighten or replace cable.
	6. Loose or open wiring through neutral switch to relay.	6. Repair, adjust or replace as required.
	7. Starter motor.	7. Repair or replace as required.
Engine cranks slowly.	1. Loose connections or corroded battery cables.	1. Clean and tighten cable connections.
	2. Undercharged battery.	2. Check battery. Charge or replace.
	3. Starter motor.	3. Repair or replace as required.

Fig. 4   Diagnosis chart

Fig. 5 Starter cranking circuit test connections

6. Remove two screws retaining ground brushes to frame.
7. Bend up edges of sleeve inserted in frame, then remove sleeve and retainer.
8. Detach field coil ground wire from copper tab on frame.
9. Using tool No. 10044-A, remove three coil retaining screws, **Fig. 7.** Cut field coil connection at switch post lead and pole shoes and coils from frame.
10. Cut positive brush leads from field coils, as close to field connection as possible.

Assembly
1. Position pole pieces and coils in frame, **Figs. 1 & 2,** then install retaining screws using tool No. 10044-A, **Fig. 7.** As pole shoes are tightened, strike frame several times with a soft faced mallet to seat and align pole shoes, then stake screws.
2. Install plunger coil sleeve and retainer, then bend tabs to retain coils to frame.

3. Position grommet on end terminal, then insert terminal and grommet into notch on frame.
4. Solder field coil to starter terminal post strap.

NOTE: Use 300 watt soldering iron and rosin core solder.

5. Check coils for continuity and grounds.
6. Position brushes to starter frame and install retaining screws.
7. Apply a thin coat of Lubriplate 777 or equivalent to armature shaft splines.
8. Install drive gear assembly on armature shaft, then install stop ring and stop ring retainer.
9. Install armature into starter frame.
10. Position starter drive gear plunger to frame and starter drive assembly, then install pivot assembly. Fill end housing bearing bore approximately ¼ full with grease, then position drive end housing to frame.

11. Install brush holder, then insert brushes into holder and install brush springs.

NOTE: Ensure positive brush leads are properly positioned in slots on brush holder.

12. Install brush end plate. Ensure brush end plate insulator is properly positioned.
13. Install through bolts, then install starter drive plunger lever cover and tighten retaining screw.

FORD MOTORCRAFT 2.0 & 2.4 L DIESEL STARTER

Description

This type starting motor has the solenoid

Fig. 6 Starter load test connection. Positive engagement starter

Fig. 7 Removing field coil pole shoe screws

Fig. 8   Starter load test connections. Diesel starter

mounted on the starter housing. When the starter relay contacts are closed, the solenoid is energized and the starter drive is engaged to start the engine. During the engine starting, the starter is protected from excessive speed by an overrunning clutch in the drive. Current flows through the solenoid energizing coil until the solenoid plunger reaches the end of its travel, at which time the plunger closes a set of contacts that bypass the energizing coil. The holding coil keeps the starter drive engaged and passes current to the starting motor.

DIAGNOSIS

When diagnosing this starter motor, refer to **Fig. 4.**

IN-VEHICLE TESTING

Starter Load Test
1. Connect test equipmemt as shown in **Fig. 8.**
2. Ensure that no current is flowing through ammeter and heavy duty carbon pile rheostat portion of circuit.
3. Crank engine with ignition off and determine exact reading on voltmeter.

Fig. 9   Exploded view of Ford Motorcraft diesel engine starting motor

This test is accomplished by disconnecting push on connectors at starter relay and by connecting remote control starter switch from positive battery terminal to S terminal on starter relay.

4. Stop cranking engine, then reduce resistance at carbon pile until voltmeter indicates the same reading as that obtained while starter cranked engine. Ammeter should read less than 375 amps.

STARTER OVERHAUL

Disassembly

1. Disconnect field coil connection from solenoid motor terminal.
2. Remove solenoid attaching screws, then rotate solenoid 90° and remove solenoid and plunger return spring, **Fig. 9.**
3. Remove field frame through bolts and the brush end plate.
4. Remove brush springs and brushes, then the brush holder. Note position of brush holder for assembly reference.
5. Remove frame and armature assemblies.
6. Remove gear housing attaching bolt and the gear housing.
7. Remove plunger and lever assembly attaching bolt and the assembly.
8. Remove gear, output shaft and drive assembly.
9. Remove thrust washer, retainer and drive stop ring, then slide drive assembly off output shaft.

Inspection

1. Clean drive assembly, field coils, armature, gear and housing using compressed air or a brush.
2. Inspect armature windings for burned or broken insulation or open connections at commutator.
3. Measure commutator runout. If commutator is more than .005 inch out of round, repair or replace as necessary.
4. Inspect brush holder for damage and replace as necessary.
5. Measure brush length and replace if worn to .25 inch or less.
6. Inspect field coils and insulators for damage or burns and replace as necessary.
7. Check continuity of coil and brush connections and repair or replace as necessary.
8. Inspect gears, output shaft spline and drive pinion for damage and replace as necessary.

Assembly

1. Apply a thin coat of Lubriplate 777 or equivalent on output shaft spline.
2. Slide drive assembly onto shaft, then install a new stop ring, retainer and thrust washer.
3. Install shaft and drive assembly into drive end housing.
4. Install plunger and lever assembly and torque attaching bolt to 7–11 ft. lbs. Ensure notches in lever engage flange ears of starter drive.
5. Install lubricated gear and washer on end of output shaft.
6. Install gear housing and torque attaching bolt to 5–7 ft. lbs.
7. Lubricate pinion, then install armature and washer on end of shaft.
8. Position grommet around field lead and press into notch in starter frame.
9. Install frame assembly to gear housing, ensuring grommet is properly positioned.
10. Install brush holder, then the brush springs and brushes.

NOTE: Ensure positive brush leads are installed in correct slots to prevent grounding.

11. Install brush end plate and through bolts. Torque through bolts to 5–7 ft. lbs.

NOTE: Threaded hole in brush plate must be properly positioned to accommodate vacuum pump support bracket installation.

12. Install return spring on solenoid plunger.
13. Install solenoid and torque attaching bolts to 5–7 ft. lbs. Apply suitable sealer to mating surface of solenoid case flange, gear and drive end housings.
14. Connect motor field terminal to solenoid M terminal and torque to 20–30 inch lbs.

General Motors Corp.

TABLE OF CONTENTS

General Information

INDEX

STARTER TROUBLE CHECK-OUT

When trouble develops in the starting motor circuit, and the starter cranks the engine slowly or not at all, several preliminary checks can be made to determine whether the trouble lies in the battery, in the starter, in the wiring between them, or elsewhere. Many conditions besides defects in the starter itself can result in poor cranking performance.

To make a quick check of the starter system, turn on the headlights. They should burn with normal brilliance. If they do not, the battery may be run down and it should be checked with a hydrometer.

If the battery is in a charged condition so that lights burn brightly, operate the starting motor. Any one of three things will happen to the lights: (1) They will go out, (2) dim considerably or (3) stay bright without any cranking action taking place.

IF LIGHTS GO OUT

If the lights go out as the starter switch is closed, it indicates that there is a poor connection between the battery and starting motor. This poor connection will most often be found at the battery terminals. Correction is made by removing the cable clamps from the terminals, cleaning the terminals and clamps, replacing the clamps and tightening them securely. A coating of corrosion inhibitor (vaseline will do) may be applied to the clamps and terminals to retard the formation of corrosion.

IF LIGHTS DIM

If the lights dim considerably as the start-

er switch is closed and the starter operates slowly or not at all, the battery may be run down, or there may be some mechanical condition in the engine or starting motor that is throwing a heavy burden on the starting motor. This imposes a high discharge rate on the battery which causes noticeable dimming of the lights.

Check the battery with a hydrometer. If it is charged, the trouble probably lies in either the engine or starting motor itself. In the engine, tight bearings or pistons or heavy oil place an added burden on the starting motor. Low temperatures also hamper starting motor performance since it thickens engine oil and makes the engine considerably harder to crank and start. Also, a battery is less efficient at low temperatures.

In the starting motor, a bent armature, loose pole shoe screws or worn bearings, any of which may allow the armature to drag, will reduce cranking performance and increase current draw.

In addition, more serious internal damage is sometimes found. Thrown armature windings or commutator bars, which sometimes occur on over-running clutch drive starting motors, are usually caused by excessive overrunning after starting. This is the result of such conditions as the driver keeping the starting switch closed too long after the engine has started, the driver opening the throttle too wide in starting, or improper carburetor fast idle adjustment. Any of these subject the over-running clutch to extra strain so it tends to seize, spinning the armature at high speed with resulting armature damage.

Another cause may be engine backfire during cranking which may result, among other things, from ignition timing being too far advanced.

To avoid such failures, the driver should

pause a few seconds after a false start to make sure the engine has come completely to rest before another start is attempted. In addition, the ignition timing should be reset if engine backfiring has caused the trouble.

LIGHTS STAY BRIGHT, NO CRANKING ACTION

This condition indicates an open circuit at some point, either in the starter itself, the starter switch or control circuit. The solenoid control circuit can be eliminated momentarily by placing a heavy jumper lead across the solenoid main terminals to see if the starter will operate. This connects the starter directly to the battery and, if it operates, it indicates that the control circuit is not functioning normally. The wiring and control units must be checked to locate the trouble.

If the starter does not operate with the jumper attached, it will probably have to be removed from the engine so it can be examined in detail.

CHECKING CIRCUIT WITH VOLTMETER

Excessive resistance in the circuit between the battery and starter will reduce cranking performance. The resistance can be checked by using a voltmeter to measure voltage drop in the circuits while the starter is operated. There are three checks to be made:
1. Voltage drop between car frame and grounded battery terminal post (not cable clamp).
2. Voltage drop between car frame and starting motor field frame.
3. Voltage drop between insulated battery terminal post and starting motor

terminal stud (or the battery terminal stud of the solenoid).

Each of these should show no more than one-tenth (0.1) volt drop when the starting motor is cranking the engine. Do not use the starter for more than 30 seconds at a time to avoid overheating it.

If excessive voltage drop is found in any of these circuits, make correction by disconnecting the cables, cleaning the connections carefully, and then reconnecting the cables firmly in place. A coating of vaseline on the battery cables and terminal clamps will retard corrosion.

NOTE: On some cars, extra long battery cables may be required due to the location of the battery and starter. This may result in somewhat higher voltage drop than the above recommended 0.1 volt. The only means of determining the normal voltage drop in such cases is to check several of these vehicles. Then when the voltage drop is well above the normal figure for all cars checked, abnormal resistance will be indicated and correction can be made as already explained.

SOLENOID SWITCHES

The solenoid switch on a cranking motor not only closes the circuit between the battery and the cranking motor but also shifts the drive pinion into mesh with the engine flywheel ring gear. This is done by means of a linkage between the solenoid switch plunger and the shift lever on the cranking motor.

There are two windings in the solenoid; a pull-in winding and a hold-in winding. Both windings are energized when the external control switch is closed. They produce a magnetic field which pulls the plunger in so that the drive pinion is shifted into mesh, and the main contacts in the solenoid switch are closed to connect the battery directly to the cranking motor. Closing the main switch contacts shorts out the pull-in winding since this winding is connected across the main contacts. The magnetism produced by the hold-in winding is sufficient to hold the plunger in, and shorting out the pull-in winding reduces drain on the battery. When the control switch is opened, it disconnects the hold-in winding from the battery. When the hold-in winding is disconnected from the battery, the shift lever spring withdraws the plunger from the solenoid, opening the solenoid switch contacts and at the same time withdrawing the drive pinion from mesh. Proper operation of the switch depends on maintaining a definite balance between the magnetic strength of the pull-in and hold-in windings.

This balance is established in the design by the size of the wire and the number of turns specified. An open circuit in the hold-in winding or attempts to crank with a discharged battery will cause the switch to chatter.

STARTING MOTOR SERVICE

To obtain full performance data on a starting motor or to determine the cause of abnormal operation, the starting motor should be submitted to a no-load and torque test. These tests are best performed on a starter bench tester with the starter mounted on it.

From a practical standpoint, however, a simple torque test may be made quickly with the starter in the car. Make sure the battery is fully charged and that the starter circuit wires and terminals are in good condition. Then operate the starter to see if the engine turns over normally. If it does not, the torque developed is below standard and the starter should be removed for further checking.

STARTER DRIVE TROUBLES

Starter drive troubles are easy to diagnose and they usually cannot be confused with ordinary starter difficulties. If the starter does not turn over at all or if it drags, look for trouble in the starter or electrical supply system. Concentrate on the starter drive or ring gear if the starter is noisy, if it turns but does not engage the engine, or if the starter won't disengage after the engine is started. After the starter is removed, the trouble can usually be located quickly.

Worn or chipped ring gear or starter pinion are the usual causes of noisy operation. Before replacing either or both of these parts try to find out what caused the damage. With the Bendix type drive, incomplete engagement of the pinion with the ring gear is a common cause of tooth damage. The wrong pinion clearance on starter drives of the over-running clutch type leads to poor meshing of the pinion and ring gear and too rapid tooth wear.

A less common cause of noise with either type of drive is a bent starter armature shaft. When this shaft is bent, the pinion gear alternately binds and then only partly meshes with the ring gear. Most manufacturers specify a maximum of .003 inch radial run-out on the armature shaft.

WHEN CLUTCH DRIVE FAILS

The over-running clutch type drive sel-

dom becomes so worn that it fails to engage since it is directly activated by a fork and lever. The only thing that is likely to happen is that, once engaged, it will not turn the engine because the clutch itself is worn out. A much more frequent difficulty and one that rapidly wears ring gear and teeth is partial engagement. Proper meshing of the pinion is controlled by the end clearance between the pinion gear and the starter housing or pinion stop, if used.

On some starters, the solenoids are completely enclosed in the starter housing and the pinion clearance is not adjustable. If the clearance is not correct, the starter must be disassembled and checked for excessive wear of solenoid linkage, shift lever mechanism, or improper assembly of parts.

Failure of the over-running clutch drive to disengage is usually caused by binding between the armature shaft and the drive. If the drive, particularly the clutch, shows signs of overheating it indicates that it is not disengaging immediately after the engine starts. If the clutch is forced to over-run too long, it overheats and turns a bluish color. For the cause of the binding, look for rust or gum between the armature shaft and the drive, or for burred splines. Excess oil on the drive will lead to gumming, and inadequate air circulation in the flywheel housing will cause rust.

Over-running clutch drives cannot be overhauled in the field so they must be replaced. In cleaning, never soak them in a solvent because the solvent may enter the clutch and dissolve the sealed-in lubricant. Wipe them off lightly with kerosene and lubricate them sparingly with SAE 10 or 10W oil.

WHEN BENDIX DRIVE FAILS

When a Bendix type drive doesn't engage the cause usually is one of three things: either the drive spring is broken, one of the drive spring bolts has sheared off, or the screwshaft threads won't allow the pinion to travel toward the flywheel. In the first two cases, remove the drive by unscrewing the set screw under the last coil of the drive spring and replace the broken parts. Gummed or rusty screwshaft threads are fairly common causes of Bendix drive failure and are easily cleaned with a little kerosene or steel wool, depending on the trouble. Here again, as in the case of over-running clutch drives, use light oil sparingly, and be sure the flywheel housing has adequate ventilation. There is usually a breather hole in the bottom of the flywheel housing which should be open.

The failure of a Bendix drive to disengage or to mesh properly is most often caused by gummed or rusty screwshaft threads. When this is not true, look for mechanical failure within the drive itself.

Delco-Remy Starters

INDEX

DESCRIPTION

The Delco-Remy starter, **Figs. 1 through 5,** has the solenoid shift lever mechanism and the solenoid plunger enclosed in the drive housing to protect them from exoposure to road dirt, icing conditions and splash. They have an extruded field frame and an overrunning clutch type drive. The overrunning clutch is operated by a solenoid switch mounted to a flange on the drive housing. The diesel starters, 25MT and 27MT, have a center bearing.

The solenoid, **Fig. 6,** is attached to the drive end housing by two screws. The cover can be removed to inspect the contacts and contact disc, but the switch is serviced as assembly only.

Most motors of this type have graphite and oil impregnated bronze bearings which ordinarily require no added lubrication except at time of overhaul when a few drops of light engine oil should be placed on each bearing before reassembly.

DIAGNOSIS

When diagnosing Delco-Remy starters, refer to **Fig. 7.**

IN-VEHICLE TESTING

FREE SPEED TEST

With the circuit connected as shown in **Fig. 8,** use a tachometer to measure armature revolutions per minute. Failure of the motor to perform to specifications may be due to tight or dry bearings, or high resistance connections.

PINION CLEARANCE

There is no provision for adjusting pinion clearance on this type motor. When the shift lever mechanism is correctly assembled, the pinion clearance should fall within the limits of .010 to .140 inch. When the clearance is not within these limits, it may indicate excessive wear of the solenoid linkage or shift lever yoke buttons.

Pinion clearance should be checked after the motor has been disassembled and reassembled. To check, disconnect motor field coil connector from solenoid terminal and insulate end. Connect one battery lead to solenoid switch terminal and the other lead to the solenoid frame, **Fig. 9.** Using a jumper lead connected to the solenoid motor terminal, momentarily flash the lead to the solenoid frame. This will shift the pinion into the cranking position until the battery is disconnected.

After energizing the solenoid with the clutch shifted toward the pinion stop retainer, push the pinion back toward the commutator end as far as possible to take up any slack movement; then check the clearance with feeler gauge, **Fig. 10.**

Fig. 1 Delco-Remy starter with enclosed shift lever

STARTER OVERHAUL
5MT & 10MT MOTORS

Disassembly

NOTE: The 5 MT series starting motor will be used on some models. On this type starting motor, the field coils and pole shoes are permanently bonded to the motor frame. The frame and field coils must be replaced as an assembly.

Normally the motor should be disassembled only so far as necessary to repair or replace defective parts.

1. Disconnect field coil connectors from solenoid "motor" terminal.
2. Remove thru bolts.
3. Remove commutator end frame and field frame assembly.
4. Remove armature assembly from drive housing. On some models it may be necessary to remove solenoid and shift lever assembly from the drive housing before removing the armature assembly. Important: When solenoid is installed, apply sealing compound between field frame and solenoid flange, **Fig. 11.**
5. Remove overrunning clutch from armature shaft as follows:
   a) Slide thrust collar off end of armature shaft, **Fig. 12.**
   b) Slide a standard ½ inch pipe coupling, a ⅝ inch deep socket or other metal cylinder of suitable size onto shaft so end of coupling or cylinder butts against edge of retainer. Tap end of coupling with hammer, driving retainer toward armature and off snap ring, **Fig. 13.**
   c) Remove snap ring from groove in shaft. If snap ring is too badly distorted during removal, use a new one when reassembling the clutch.
   d) Slide retainer, clutch and assist spring from armature shaft.

Reassembly

1. Lubricate drive end and splines of armature shaft with lubricant 1960954 or equivalent.
2. Place "assist" spring on drive end of shaft next to armature, with small end against lamination stack.
3. Slide clutch assembly onto armature shaft with pinion outward.
4. Slide retainer onto shaft with cupped surface facing end of shaft.
5. Stand armature on end on wood surface with commutator down. Position snap ring on upper end of shaft and hold in place with a block of wood. Hit wood block with a hammer forcing snap ring over end of shaft, **Fig. 14.** Slide snap ring into groove, squeezing it to ensure a good fit in groove.
6. Assemble thrust collar on shaft with shoulder next to snap ring.
7. Position retainer and thrust collar next to snap ring. With clutch pressed against assist spring, for clearance next to retainer, use two pairs of pliers

1. FRAME—COMMUTATOR END	10. PLUNGER	19. THRU BOLT
2. BRUSH AND HOLDER PKG.	11. SHIFT LEVER	20. BUSHING—COMMUTATOR END
3. BRUSH	12. PLUNGER RETURN SPRINGER	21. BUSHING—DRIVE END
4. BRUSH HOLDER	13. SHIFT LEVER SHAFT	22. PINION STOP COLLAR
5. HOUSING—DRIVE END	14. LOCK WASHER	23. THRUST COLLAR
6. FRAME AND FIELD ASM.	15. SCREW—BRUSH ATTACHING	24. GROMMET
7. SOLENOID SWITCH	16. SCREW—FIELD LEAD TO SWITCH	25. GROMMET
8. ARMATURE	17. SCREW—SWITCH ATTACHING	26. PLUNGER PIN
9. DRIVE ASM.	18. WASHER—BRAKE	27. PINION STOP RETAINER RING
		28. LEVER SHAFT RETAINING RING

Fig. 2 Disassembled view of Delco-Remy 5MT series starting motor

Fig. 3 Disassembled view of Delco-Remy 10MT series starting motor

at the same time (one pair on either side of shaft) to grip retainer and thrust collar. Then squeeze until snap ring is forced into retainer, **Fig. 15.**

8. Lubricate drive end housing bushing with lubricant 1960954 or equivalent. Make sure thrust collar is in place against snap ring and retainer; then slide armature and clutch assembly into place in drive housing.
9. Attach solenoid and shift lever assembly to drive housing. Be sure lever buttons are located between sides of clutch collar.
10. Position field frame over armature,

applying sealing compound between frame and solenoid flange (Fig. 11). Position frame against drive housing, using care to prevent damage to brushes.

11. Lubricate commutator end frame bushing with lubricant 1960954 or equivalent. Make sure leather brake washer is on armature shaft; then slide commutator end frame onto shaft.
12. Install thru bolts and tighten securely.
13. Reconnect field coil connectors to solenoid "motor" terminal.

Fig. 4   Disassembled view of Delco-Remy 25 MT & 27 MT series starting motor. Olds built diesel.

25 & 27 MT SERIES

Disassembly

1. Remove screw from field coil connector and solenoid mounting screws, then rotate solenoid 90° and remove solenoid with plunger return spring.
2. Remove two through bolts, then commutator end frame with washer.
3. Remove end frame assembly from drive gear housing.
4. Remove shift lever pivot bolt.
5. Remove center bearing screws, then remove drive gear housing from armature shaft. Shift lever and plunger assembly, should fall from starter clutch.
6. Remove thrust washer or collar from armature shaft.

7. Position a ⅝ in. deep socket over shaft against retainer, then tap socket to move retainer off snap ring.
8. Remove snap ring from groove in shaft, then remove retainer, clutch assembly, fiber washer and center bearing from armature shaft.
9. Remove roll pin and separate shift lever and plunger.
10. Remove brush pivot pin and brush spring, then replace brushes as necessary.

Assembly

1. Lubricate drive end of armature with lubricant 1960954 or equivalent.
2. Install center bearing with bearing facing toward armature winding, then install fiber washer on armature shaft.

3. Position clutch assembly on armature shaft with pinion facing away from armature.
4. Position retainer on armature shaft with cupped side facing end of shaft.
5. Install snap ring into groove on armature shaft, then install thrust washer.
6. Using two pliers, grip retainer and thrust washer or collar and squeeze until snap ring is forced into retainer and is held securely in groove on armature shaft.
7. Lubricate drive end housing bushing with lubricant 1960954 or equivalent.
8. Engage shift lever yoke with clutch and slide complete assembly into drive gear housing.
9. Install center bearing attaching screws and shift lever pivot bolt.
10. Install solenoid on drive gear housing.
11. Apply sealer No. 1050026 or equivalent to solenoid flange where field frame contacts solenoid.
12. Position field frame against drive gear housing on alignment pin, using care to prevent damage to brushes.

NOTE: Brush Assembly Parts Not Shown

Fig. 5   Disassembled view of 15MT/GR starting motor. Olds built diesel.

Fig. 6   Solenoid contact assembly

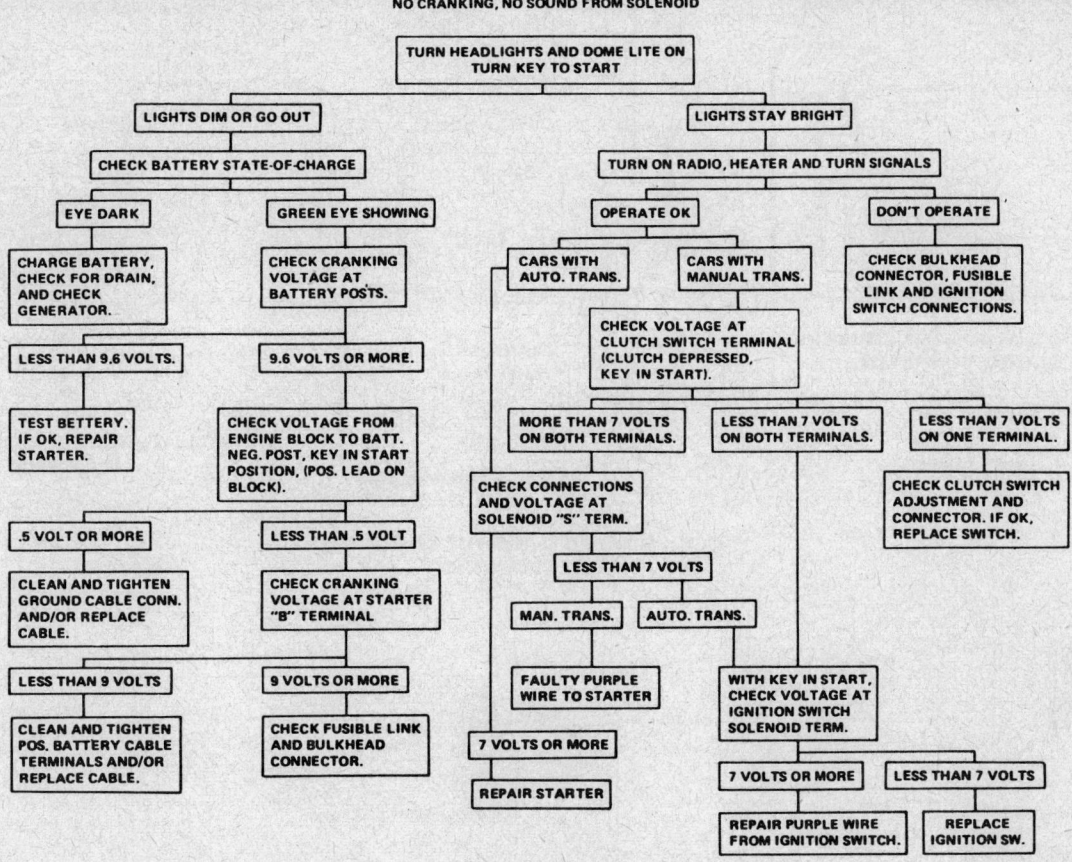

Fig. 7 Diagnosis chart (Part 1 of 2)

13. Lubricate commutator end frame bushing with lubricant 1960954 or equivalent.
14. Install washer on armature shaft and slide end frame onto shaft, then install and tighten through bolts.
15. Connect field coil connector to solenoid terminal, then check pinion clearance.

15 MT/GR SERIES

Disassembly

1. Remove screw from field coil connector and field frame thru bolts.
2. Separate field frame and drive gear assemblies, then remove armature and commutator end frame from field frame.
3. Remove solenoid attaching screws and solenoid from drive housing.
4. Remove retaining ring, shift lever shaft and housing thru bolts, then separate drive assembly, drive housing and gear housing.
5. Remove overrunning clutch from drive shaft as follows:
   a. Remove thrust washer from drive shaft.
   b. Slide a ⅝ inch deep socket or a piece of pipe of suitable size over shaft and butt it against retainer. Lightly tap tool to move retainer off snap ring.

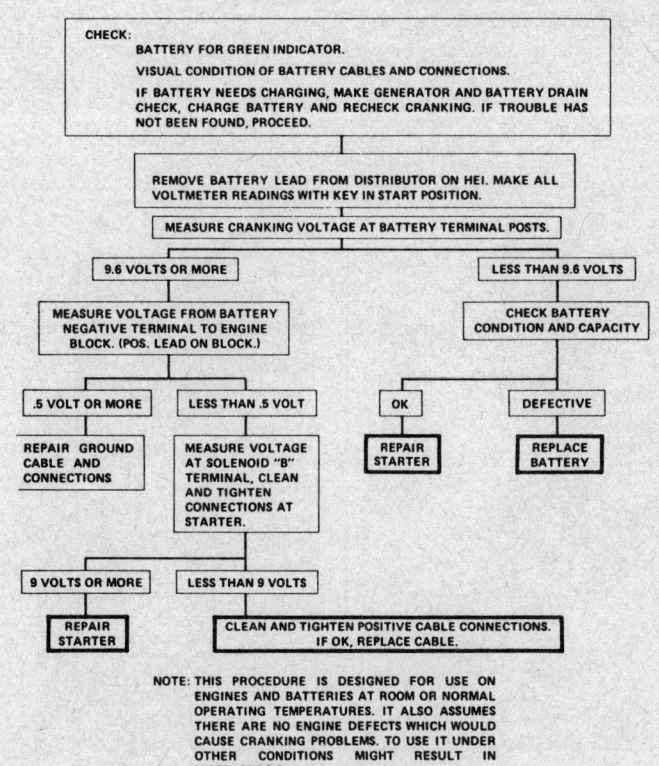

Fig. 7 Diagnosis chart (Part 2 of 2)

Fig. 8   Connections for checking free speed of motor

Fig. 9   Connections for checking pinion clearance

Fig. 10   Checking pinion clearance

Fig. 11   Sealing solenoid housing to frame

Fig. 12   View of armature and over-running clutch

Fig. 13   Removing over-running clutch snap ring retainer

Fig. 14   Installing snap ring onto armature shaft

Fig. 15   Installing snap ring onto retainer

c. Remove snap ring from groove in shaft. If snap ring is too badly distorted, a new one must be used when reassembling the clutch.
d. Remove retainer and clutch assembly from drive shaft.

Assemble

NOTE: The roller bearings are pre-lubricated and must not be lubricated during assembly of starter motor.

1. Slide clutch assembly onto drive shaft and position retainer with cupped side toward end of shaft, snap ring and washer.
2. Using two pairs of pliers, force snap ring into retainer and groove, in shaft, **Fig. 15.**
3. Install plunger and shift lever into drive housing with lever shaft and retaining ring.
4. Place washer over drive shaft on side of gear opposite drive assembly, then lubricate gear teeth with lubricant

1960954, or equivalent.
5. Assemble gear housing with attaching screws and attach solenoid to drive housing.
6. Lubricate bushing in commutator end frame with lubricant 1960954, or equivalent, then slide washer on commutator end of armature shaft.
7. Assemble armature, field frame and commutator end frame to gear housing with thru bolts.
8. Attach field coil connector to solenoid terminal.

Hitachi Starter

INDEX

DESCRIPTION

In this starter, **Fig. 1,** the solenoid windings are energized when the switch is closed. The resulting plunger and shift lever movement causes the pinion to engage the engine flywheel ring gear and the solenoid main contacts to close, and cranking takes place. When the engine starts, pinion overrun protects the armature from excessive speed until the switch is opened, at which time the return spring causes the pinion to disengage. To prevent excessive overrun, the switch should be opened immediately when the engine starts.

DIAGNOSIS

When diagnosing this starter, refer to **Fig. 2.**

STARTER OVERHAUL

DISASSEMBLY

1. Disconnect solenoid lead wire.
2. Remove solenoid to starter attaching bolts and remove the solenoid from the shift lever, **Fig. 1.**
3. Remove the solenoid torsion spring.
4. Remove starter through bolts and separate the rear cover.
5. Using long-nose pliers, remove brushes and brush holder from the armature.
6. Remove the frame and armature together as an assembly from the gear case.
7. Remove two screws from gear drive housing and separate drive housing and solenoid.
8. Remove two pinions from gear case, then remove the overrunning clutch and retainer.
9. Remove the solenoid return spring.

10. Remove the steel ball from the overrunning clutch.

ASSEMBLE

1. Reverse disassembly procedure to assemble, noting the following:
   a. Be sure to install the steel ball and solenoid return spring.
   b. Use caution not to get oil or other contaminants on brushes or armature.
   c. Always replace O-rings with new ones.
   d. Lubricate all necessary parts prior to assembly.

DISASSEMBLY ORDER

1	Lead wire	14	Armature
2	Bolt	15	Screw
3	Solenoid assembly	16	Bearing retainer
4	Torsion spring	17	Pinion assembly
5	Plunger	18	Pinion stop retainer
6	Adjusting plates	19	Pinion stop retainer clip
7	Solenoid	20	Return spring
8	Screw	21	Pinion shaft
9	Through bolt	22	Clutch
10	Rear cover	23	Dust cover
11	Motor assembly	24	Shift lever
12	Brush holder	25	Gear case
13	Yoke		

Fig. 1 Hitachi S13-62A starter

Complaint	Faulty parts	Cause	Correction
Pinion does not jump out when starter switch is turned on	Wiring	Circuit open, battery or switch terminals loosened, or poor connections at connector	Correct and retighten
	Starter switch	Current not flowing due to poor contact	Correct or replace
	Starter	1. Helical splines on pinion shaft damaged preventing smooth movement of pinion	Correct or replace
		2. Torsion spring or shift lever broken	Replace
	Solenoid	Plunger operation sluggish, coil open or shorted	Correct or replace
	Battery	Under-charged	Recharge
Pinion engages ring gear but starter does not turn over	Wiring	1. Cable connecting solenoid to battery broken	Correct, retighten or replace
		2. Lead wire between solenoid and motor poorly connected.	
	Starter	1. Incorrectly installed.	Remove and reinstall correctly
		2. Brushes worn beyond limit	Replace
		3. Commutator face fouled	Correct
		4. Armature or field coil(s) shorted	Replace
		5. Brushes not properly connected to field coils	Correct
		6. Ball bearing locked	Replace
	Solenoid	Contact points defective	Replace
Motor operates before pinion engages ring gear	Starter	1. Torsion spring weakened or shift lever distorted	Replace
		2. Pinion shaft sticking or binding	Replace
		3. Pinion gear teeth worn	Correct
		4. Pinion setting incorrect	Replace
	Engine	Ring gear worn	Replace
Pinion engages ring gear and motor operates but power is not carried to engine	Starter	1. Clutch defective	Replace
		2. Reduction gear broken	Replace
Motor continues to spin even when starter switch is turned off after engine starting.	Starter switch	Contact point returning action poor	Replace
	Solenoid	Contact point returning action poor	Replace

Fig. 2   Diagnosis chart

Mitsubishi Starter

INDEX

STARTER OVERHAUL

DISASSEMBLY

1. Remove nut from field coil connector, solenoid switch mounting screws and solenoid switch, **Fig. 1.**

NOTE: Some starters may have shims between solenoid switch and drive end housing, used to set drive pinion position.

2. Remove thru bolts and brush holder retaining screws.

3. Remove commutator end frame from armature and bearing assembly.
4. Remove field frame assembly and armature from center housing.
5. Bend back each brush spring so that each brush can be backed away from armature approximately ¼ inch, then release spring to hold brushes in backed out position, **Fig. 2.**
6. Remove armature from field frame and brush holder.
7. Remove pinion shaft cover on center housing by removing two screws, C-washer and plate, **Fig. 3.**

8. Remove center housing retaining bolts, center housing and shim thrust washer(s).
9. Remove reduction gear, spring holder and lever springs.
10. Slide a ⅝ inch socket, or piece of pipe of suitable size, over shaft against stopper, then tap tool to move stopper off ring, **Fig. 4.**
11. Remove ring, stopper and drive pinion. If ring is distorted, a new one must be used on reassembly.
12. Remove pinion shaft and lever assembly, noting direction of levers and lever holders.

Fig. 1   Disassembled view of diesel aluminum starter. (Mitsubishi)

Fig. 2   Brush holder assembly

Fig. 3   Disassembled view of pinion shaft (overrunning clutch) assembly

Fig. 4   Removing pinion shaft ring

Fig. 5   Installing lever assembly on overrunning clutch

ASSEMBLY

1. Lubricate bearing surfaces and splines of pinion shaft assembly, nylon lever holders, and both ends of lever with lubricant 2960954, or equivalent.
2. Install lever assembly on overrunning clutch, **Fig. 5.**

NOTE: If lever is not positioned properly, pinion travel will be incorrect, causing a lock-up in the clutch mechanism.

3. Install pinion shaft and lever assembly into drive end housing.
4. Slide spring, drive pinion and stopper ring over pinion shaft with cupped surface of stopper facing end of shaft.
5. Install ring into groove on pinion shaft while forcing drive pinion and stopper down against drive end housing.

6. Force stopper over ring with tool J-22888, **Fig. 6.**
7. Install the two lever springs and spring holder into drive end housing.
8. Lubricate reduction gear teeth with lubricant 1960954, or equivalent.
9. Install gear and shim thrust washers onto pinion shaft assembly.
10. Assemble center housing to drive end housing, then install and tighten the two attaching bolts.
11. If the drive end housing, pinion shaft, reduction gear, shim washer(s), or center housing were replaced, pinion shaft end play must be checked as follows:
    a. Install plate and C-washer onto end of pinion shaft, then mount drive end housing in a suitable holding fixture.
    b. Insert feeler gauge between C-washer and cover plate, rotate

pinion shaft with a screwdriver and measure end play, **Fig. 7.** Proper end play is .004–.020 inch.
    c. If end play does not fall within limits, remove plate, C-washer and center bracket, add or remove shim thrust washers as needed, and recheck clearance.
    d. Fill cap one-half full with lubricant 1960954, or equivalent, and install the cap. Install and tighten the two attaching bolts.
12. Install armature, carefully engaging splines of shaft with reduction gear by slightly rotating armature to engage splines.
13. Install field frame and brush holder assembly on center housing.

NOTE: The rubber grommet for the field coil lead must be installed in the locating ribs, **Fig. 8.**

14. Install brushes by prying back on springs to allow brushes to seat against commutator bars.
15. Install commutator end frame onto field frame with alignment marks lined up, **Fig. 9.**
16. Install and tighten brush holder screws and thru bolts.
17. Install solenoid switch and shims on drive end housing, ensuring that slot in plunger engages with top of lever, then install and tighten the two bolts.

Fig. 6   Installing stopper on overrunning clutch

Fig. 7   Checking pinion shaft end play

Fig. 8   Installing field frame and brush holder assembly

Fig. 9   Installing commutator end frame on field frame

18. Connect field coil connector to solenoid switch terminal.

PINION CLEARANCE CHECK

1. Disconnect field coil connector from solenoid terminal and insulate carefully.

2. Connect one 12 volt battery lead to solenoid switch terminal and other lead to starter motor frame.

3. Flash a jumper lead momentarily from solenoid motor terminal to starter motor frame. This will shift pinion into cranking position until battery is disconnected.

4. Push pinion back as far as possible to take up any movement, then check pinion clearance using a feeler gauge. Pinion clearance should be .010–.140 in. On V6 diesel aluminum starter, clearance should be .020–.080 inch. If clearance is not within limits, check for improper installation or worn parts and replace as necessary.

NOTE: On diesel aluminum starter, clearance may be adjusted by adding or removing shims located between the switch and front bracket. Adding shims decreases amount of movement. Shims are available in thicknesses of .010 and .020 inch.

Starting Motor Specifications

Starter Make	Starter Model Number	Brush Spring Tension, Ounces	Free Speed Test			Solenoid	
			Amps	Volts	RPM	Hold-In Windings	Pull-In Windings
Bosch	5206255	—	47	11	6600	—	—
	5206260	—	47	11	6600	—	—
	5213045	—	47	11	6600	—	—
	5213080	—	47	11	6600	—	—
	5213395	—	47	11	6600	—	—
	5213450	—	47	11	6600	—	—
Chrysler	3755250	32–36	90	11	5700	13–15	8–9
	3755900	32–36	90	11	3700	13–15	8–9
	4111855	32–36	90	11	5700	13–15	8–9
	4111860	32–36	91	11	5700	13–15	8–11
Delco-Remy	1100214	—	—	—	—	—	—
	1100215	—	—	—	—	—	—
	1100534	35①	45–70	10	7000–11900	—	—
	1100941	—	—	—	—	—	—
	1102844	35①	60–85②	9	6800–10300	—	—
	1103519	—	—	—	—	—	—
	1108415	35①	35–75②	9	6000–9000	—	—
	1108758	35①	55–80②	9	3500–6000	14.5–16.5	13–15.5
	1108759	35①	65–95②	9	7500–10500	—	—
	1108762	35①	55–80②	9	3500–6000	14.5–16.5	13–15.5
	1108764	35①	65–95②	9	7500–10000	—	—
	1108765	35①	55–80②	9	3500–6000	14.5–16.5	13–15.5
	1108771	35①	50–75②	9	6500–10000	—	—
	1108772	35①	50–75②	9	6500–10000	—	—
	1108774	35①	60–88②	9	6500–10100	—	—
	1108779	35①	50–80②	9	5500–10000	—	—
	1108790	35①	55–80②	9	3500–6000	—	—
	1108794	35①	65–95②	9	7500–10000	14.5–16.5	13–15.5
	1108795	35①	65–95②	9	7500–10000	—	—
	1108796	35①	65–95②	9	7500–10000	—	—
	1108797	35①	55–80②	9	5500–10000	14.5–16.5	13–15.5
	1108799	35①	50–80②	9	5500–10500	14.5–16.5	13–15.5
	1109038	35①	65–95②	9	7000–10500	—	—
	1109039	35①	65–95②	9	7000–10500	—	—
	1109052	35①	65–95②	9	7500–10500	14.5–16.5	13–16.5
	1109056	35①	50–80②	9	5500–10500	14.5–16.5	13–15.5
	1109059	35①	65–95②	9	7500–10500	—	—
	1109061	35①	65–85②	9	6800–10300	17–19	24–27
	1109062	35①	65–95②	9	7500–10500	17–19	24–27
	1109063	—	70–110②	10	6500–10700	—	—
	1109064	35①	60–85②	9	6800–10300	17–19	24–27
	1109065	35①	65–95②	9	7500–10500	17–19	24–27
	1109067	35①	65–95②	9	7500–10500	—	—
	1109070	35①	65–95②	9	7500–10500	—	—
	1109072	35①	65–95②	9	7500–10500	17–19	24–27
	1109074	35①	60–85②	9	6800–10300	15–20	20–30
	1109213	35①	40–140②	9	8000–13000	—	—
	1109214	35①	40–140②	9	8000–13000	—	—
	1109215	35①	40–140②	9	8000–13000	—	—
	1109216	35①	120–210②	10.6	9000–13400	15–20	20–30
	1109218	35①	120–210②	10.6	9000–13400	—	—
	1109412	35①	50–75②	9	6500–10500	—	—
	1109414	35①	50–75②	9	6500	—	—
	1109495	35①	120–210	11	9000–13400	—	—
	1109521	35①	45–75②	9	6500–9700	—	—
	1109522	—	55–85②	10	6000–12000	—	—

continued

Starter Make	Starter Model Number	Brush Spring Tension, Ounces	Free Speed Test			Solenoid	
			Amps	Volts	RPM	Hold-In Windings	Pull-In Windings
Delco-Remy cont'd	1109523	35①	45–70②	9	7000–11900	17–23	16–18
	1109524	35①	45–70②	9	7000–11900	17–23	16–18
	1109526	35①	45–70②	9	7000–11900	15–20	20–30
	1109530	35①	85⑥	9	6800–10300	15–20	20–30
	1109531	—	50–75②	10	6000–11900	—	—
	1109532	—	55–85②	10	6000–12000	—	—
	1109533	35①	45–70②	9	7000–11900	13–19	23–30
	1109534	35①	45–70	9	7000–11900	—	—
	1109535	35①	45–70②	9	7000–11900	13–19	26–38
	1109537	35①	45–75②	9	6500–9700	13–19	46–60
	1109544⑮	35①	45–70	9	7000–11900	—	—
	1109544⑦	—	50–75	10	6000–11900	—	—
	1109551	35①	55–85②	10	6000–12000	13–19	23–30
	1109556⑯	35①	55–85	10	6000–12000	—	—
	1109556⑰	35①	60–90	10	6500–10500	—	—
	1109560	35①	50–75	10	6000–11900	—	—
	1109562	35①	45–70②	9	7000–11900	13–19	23–30
	1109564	35①	50–74	10	6000–11900	—	—
	1998204	35①	60–85②	9	6800–10300	17–19	24–27
	1998205	35①	65–95②	9	7500–10500	17–19	24–27
	1998217	—	70–110②	10	6500–10700	—	—
	1998227	35①	65–95②	9	7500–10500	—	—
	1998233	—	60–90②	10	6500–10500	—	—
	1998234	35①	65–95②	9	7500–10500	—	—
	1998236⑮	35①	60–85②	9	6800–10300	—	—
	1998236⑯	—	60–90	10	6500–10500	—	—
	1998237⑮	35①	65–95②	9	7500–10500	—	—
	1998237⑦	—	70–110②	10	6500–10700	—	—
	1998240	35①	60–85②	9	6800–10300	—	—
	1998241	35①	70–110②	9	6500–10700	—	—
	1998400	—	70–110②	10.6	6500–10700	—	—
	1998428	—	55–85②	10	6000–12000	—	—
	1998429	—	50–75②	10	6000–11900	—	—
	1998430	—	50–75②	10	6000–11900	—	—
	1998435	—	70–110②	10.6	6500–10700	—	—
	1998435	—	50–75	10	6000–11900	—	—
	1998436	—	70–110②	10	6500–10700	—	—
	1998445	—	52–76②	10	6000–12000	—	—
	1998447	—	55–85②	10	6000–12000	—	—
	1998448	—	50–75②	10	6000–11900	—	—
	1998450	—	50–75②	10	6000–11900	—	—
	1998452	—	50–75②	10	6000–11900	—	—
	1998466	—	52–76②	10	6000–12000	—	—
	1998552	35①	160–220	9	4000–5500	—	—
	1998553⑮	35①	160–220	9	4000–5500	15–20	30–40
	1998553⑦	—	160–220	10	4400–6300⑤	—	—
	1998554	35①	160–240	10	4400–6300⑤	—	—
	1998556⑮	35①	55–85	9	6000–12000	13–19	23–30
	1998556⑦	—	160–240	10	4400–6300⑤	—	—
	3236659	—	45–70	9	7000–11900	—	—
Hitachi	94238754	—	—	—	—	—	—
	94238758	—	—	—	—	—	—
Mitsubishi	22511854	—	125–170	10	3200–4100⑤	—	—
	22515863	—	125–170	10	3200–4100⑤	—	—
	22523207	—	125–170	10	3200–4100⑤	—	—
	5213301	—	120–160	11	6600	—	—

continued

STARTING MOTOR SPECIFICATIONS—Continued

Starter Make	Starter Model Number	Brush Spring Tension, Ounces	Free Speed Test			Solenoid	
			Amps	Volts	RPM	Hold-In Windings	Pull-In Windings
Motorcraft	D5AF-EA	80	80	12	—	—	—
	D6AF-AA	40	70	12	—	—	—
	D6BF-AA	80	80	12	—	—	—
	D6BF-BA	80	80	12	—	—	—
	D6DF-AA	80	80	12	—	—	—
	D6EF-AA	40①	70	12	—	—	—
	D6EF-BA	40①	70	12	—	—	—
	D6OF-AA	80	80	12	—	—	—
	D8AF-AA	80	80	12	—	—	—
	D8AF-BA	80	80	12	—	—	—
	D8BF-AA	40	70	12	—	—	—
	D8BF-AA⑧	40–80	85	12	—	—	—
	D8BF-CA⑧	40–80	85	12	—	—	—
	D8DF-AA	80	80	12	—	—	—
	D8EF-AA⑨	40	80	12	—	—	—
	D8EF-AA⑩	80	80	12	—	—	—
	D8OF-AA⑪	40–80	85	12	—	—	—
	D8ZF-AA	40①	70	12	—	—	—
	E1AF-BA	40–80	85	12	—	—	—
	E1BF-AA	40–80	85	12	—	—	—
	E1BF-BA	40–80	85	12	—	—	—
	E1EF-AB	80	80	12	—	—	—
	E1EF-AD	80	80	12	—	—	—
	E1EF-11001-BA	—	67	12	7380–9356	—	—
	E1ZF-AA	80	80	12	—	—	—
	E1ZF-BA	80	80	12	—	—	—
	E2BF-AA	80	80	12	—	—	—
	E25F-AA	40–80	85	12	—	—	—
	⑫	80	80	12	—	—	—
	⑬	40–80	85	12	—	—	—
	⑭	208	190⑥	12	—	—	—
	3212235	40	65	12	9250	—	—
	3229844	40	65	12	9250	—	—
	3231371	—	77	12	8900–9600	—	—
	3231372	—	67	12	7380–9356	—	—
	3238665	—	67	12	7380–9356	—	—
	3250032	—	69	12	6709–10843	—	—
Nippondenso	5206265	—	47	11	6600	—	—
	5206270	—	47	11	6600	—	—
	5213085	—	47	11	6600	—	—
	5213190	—	85	11	3700	—	—
	5213235	—	47③	11	6600④	—	—
	5213295	—	47	11	6600	—	—
	5213301	—	47	11	6600	—	—
	5213645	—	47	11	6600	—	—

①—Minimum.
②—Includes solenoid.
③—1984–85, 85 amps.
④—1984–85, 3700 RPM.
⑤—Pinion speed.
⑥—Maximum.
⑦—1984–85 models.
⑧—1980.
⑨—1980 Mustang, Capri, Pinto and Bobcat.
⑩—1980 Exc. Mustang, Capri, Pinto and Bobcat.
⑪—1980–81.
⑫—1983–85 four cylinder Ford models.
⑬—1983–85 six and eight cylinder Ford models.
⑭—1984–85 diesel Ford models.
⑮—Except 1984–85 models.
⑯—Except 1985 models.
⑰—1985 models.

ALTERNATOR SYSTEMS

TABLE OF CONTENTS

American Motors Corp.

TABLE OF CONTENTS

General Information

INTRODUCTION

Alternators are composed of the same functional parts as the conventional D.C. generator but they operate differently: The field is called a rotor and is the turning portion of the unit. A generating part, called a stator, is the stationary member, comparable to the armature in a D.C. generator. The regulator, similar to those used in a D.C. system, regulates the output of the alternator-rectifier system.

The power source of the system is the alternator. Current is transmitted from the field terminal of the regulator through a slip ring to the field coil and back to ground through another slip ring. The strength of the field regulates the output of the alternating current. This alternating current is then transmitted from the alternator to the rectifier where it is converted to direct current.

These alternators employ a three-phase stator winding in which the phase windings are electrically 120 degrees apart. The rotor consists of a field coil encased between interleaved sections producing a magnetic field with alternate north and south poles. By rotating the rotor inside the stator the alternating current is induced in the stator windings. This alternating current is rectified (changed to D.C.) by silicon diodes and brought out to the output terminal of the alternator.

DIODE RECTIFIERS

Six silicon diode rectifiers are used and act as electrical one-way-valves. Three of the diodes have ground polarity and are pressed or screwed into a heat sink which is grounded. The other three diodes (ungrounded) are pressed or screwed into and insulated from the end head; these diodes are connected to the alternator output terminal.

Since the diodes have a high resistance to the flow of current in one direction and a low resistance in the opposite direction, they may be connected in a manner which allows current to flow from the alternator to the battery in the low resistance direction. The high resistance in the opposite direction prevents the flow of current from the battery to the alternator. Because of this feature no circuit breaker is required between the alternator and battery.

SERVICE PRECAUTIONS

1. Be certain that battery polarity is correct when servicing units. Reversed battery polarity will damage rectifiers and regulators.
2. If booster battery is used for starting, be sure to use correct polarity in hook up.
3. When a fast charger is used to charge a vehicle battery, the vehicle battery cables should be disconnected unless the fast charger is equipped with a special Alternator Protector, in which case the vehicle battery cables need not be disconnected. Also the fast charger should never be used to start a vehicle as damage to rectifiers will result.
4. Lead connections to the grounded rectifiers (negative) should never be soldered as the excessive heat may damage the rectifiers.
5. Unless the system includes a load relay or field relay, grounding the alternator output terminal will damage the alternator and/or circuits. This is true even when the system is not in operation since no circuit breaker is used and the battery is applied to the alternator output terminal at all times. The field or load relay acts as a circuit breaker in that it is controlled by the ignition switch.
6. When adjusting the voltage regulator, do not short the adjusting tool to the regulator base as the regulator may be damaged. The tool should be insulated by taping or by installing a plastic sleeve.
7. Before making any "on vehicle" tests of the alternator or regulator, the battery should be checked and the circuit inspected for faulty wiring or insulation, loose or corroded connections and poor ground circuits.
8. Check alternator belt tension to be sure the belt is tight enough to prevent slipping under load.
9. The ignition switch should be off and the battery ground cable disconnected before making any test connections to prevent damage to the system.
10. The vehicle battery must be fully charged or a fully charged battery may be installed for test purposes.

Bosch Type K1 Alternator

INDEX

Fig. 1   Bosch Type K1 alternator with integral regulator

DESCRIPTION

The main components of the Bosch type K1 alternator, **Fig. 1,** are the front and rear housings, stator windings, rotor and rectifying diodes. Current is supplied to the rotor through slip rings and two brushes which are built into the voltage regulator positioned on the rear housing. The rotor is supported in the front and rear housings by ball bearings. The stator windings are assembled inside a laminated core which forms part of the alternator frame. A diode plate containing three positive and three negative diodes is soldered to the stator winding leads. Alternator field current is supplied through a diode trio which is also connected to the stator windings. A capacitor which is mounted to the rear housing, protects the diode plate assembly from high voltages and suppresses radio noises. The voltage regulator is solid state, which is not serviceable or adjustable. The voltage regulator can be replaced without disassembling the alternator.

IN-VEHICLE TESTING

INDICATOR LAMP DIAGNOSIS

NOTE: If indicator lamp lights with engine operating, indicating a no charge condition

perform the following test.

1. Check alternator belt tension and adjust as necessary.
2. Start engine and measure battery voltage using a suitable voltmeter.
3. Raise engine speed to fast idle.
4. Ground the metal sleeve on the voltage regulator to the alternator housing and check voltage reading, **Fig. 2.** If voltage reading is higher than reading obtained in step 2, the regulator is defective and should be replaced. If voltage reading is lower or remains the same, the alternator must be removed and repaired.

UNDERCHARGED BATTERY

Refer to diagnosis charts, **Figs. 3 and 4** for test procedure.

OVERCHARGED BATTERY

Refer to diagnosis chart, **Fig. 5** for test procedure.

ALTERNATOR DISASSEMBLY

1. Scribe marks on alternator front and rear housings for use during reassembly.
2. Remove regulator and brush holder retaining screws and washers, then tilt regulator and brush holder assembly and remove from rear housing, **Fig. 6.**
3. Disconnect condenser wire, then remove retaining screws, washer and condenser.
4. Remove through bolts, then separate front housing and rotor assembly from stator and rear housing assembly. Remove wave washer from rear housing.

NOTE: Place a piece of tape over rear housing bearing and slip ring end of rotor shaft to prevent entry of dirt. Do not use tape which will leave a gummy deposit on rotor shaft. If brushes are to be reused, clean with a soft dry cloth.

Fig. 2   Voltage regulator grounding sleeve.

5. Remove battery terminal nuts and washers. Note positioning of components for reassembly.
6. Position rotor assembly in a vise, then remove shaft nut, lockwasher, pulley, key and fan from rotor shaft.

NOTE: When positioning rotor in vise, tighten vise only enough to permit loosening of shaft nut. Overtightening may cause damage to rotor.

7. Remove bearing retainer attaching screws from front housing, then remove rotor assembly.
8. Remove stator and diode assembly from rear housing.
9. Unsolder stator leads from diode plate assembly.
10. Separate drive housing from rotor shaft.
11. Press rear bearing from rotor shaft using a suitable press and support.

NOTE: The rear rotor shaft bearing must be replaced if it is found to be insufficiently lubricated. Do not attempt to lubricate or reuse a dry bearing.

12. Press front bearing from rotor shaft.

STEP   SEQUENCE   RESULT

1 CHECK ALTERNATOR BELT

ADJUST TENSION TO 90-115 LBS. REPLACE IF NECESSARY

MAKE SURE NO ACCESSORIES ARE ON, IGNITION OFF, DOORS CLOSED, UNDER HOOD LIGHTS DIS-CONNECTED

DISCONNECT NEGATIVE CABLE

(+)
(-)

CONNECT TEST LIGHT BETWEEN CABLE AND BATTERY POST

TEST LIGHT ON → **2**

TEST LIGHT OFF—NO DRAIN ON BATTERY → **3**

2 TRACE AND CORRECT CONTINUOUS DRAIN ON BATTERY

CONNECT TEST LIGHT BETWEEN CABLE AND BATTERY POST

(+)
(-)

TEST LIGHT OFF → STOP

TEST LIGHT ON → **3**

3 RECONNECT NEGATIVE CABLE

CONNECT JUMPER (-) TERMINAL AND GROUND

CONNECT VOLTMETER (+) TERMINAL AND GROUND

CRANK ENGINE LONG ENOUGH FOR STABILIZED READING

NEEDLE ABOVE 9.0V → **6**

NEEDLE BELOW 9.0V → **4**

4 CHECK VOLTAGE ACROSS POST WHILE CRANKING

IF READING IS WITHIN .5 VOLT OF VOLTAGE AT ALTERNATOR

IF READING IS NOT WITHIN .5 VOLT OF READING AT ALTERNATOR, CHECK FOR BATTERY-TO-ALTERNATOR CIRCUIT RESISTANCE

TEST BATTERY USING BATTERY LOAD TEST PROCEDURE

BATTERY OK. CHARGE AS SPECIFIED BY TEST → **6**

BATTERY NOT OK → **5**

Fig. 3 Bosch K1 alternator with integral regulator undercharged battery test chart. Part 1 of 2

Fig. 4   Bosch K1 alternator with integral regulator undercharged battery test chart. Part 2 of 2

Fig. 5   Bosch K1 alternator with integral regulator overcharged battery test chart.

BENCH TESTS
ROTOR & SLIP RING TEST

To test rotor for grounds, set ohmmeter to 1000 scale, then place one ohmmeter lead on rotor shaft and contact other ohmmeter lead to slip ring, **Fig. 7.** Repeat test with other slip ring. The ohmmeter should indicate an infinite reading. If ohmmeter indicates other than infinite reading, a short to ground exists. Inspect soldered connections at slip rings to ensure they are not grounded against the rotor coil. Inspect rotor coil and replace if damaged.

To test rotor for an open circuit, set ohmmeter to 1 scale, then contact ohmmeter leads to slip rings, **Fig. 8.** Ohmmeter reading should be 3.0 to 3.7 ohms. If an infinite reading is obtained, rotor winding has an open circuit.

To check rotor for short circuit, connect a 12 volt battery and ammeter in series with slip rings, **Fig. 9.** Field current at 12 volts and 80 degrees F should be between 3.5 and 5 amps. If reading is above 5 amps, shorted windings are indicated. Winding resistance and ammeter readings will vary with temperatures. A reading below the specified value indicates excessive resistance. This test can also be performed by connecting an ohmmeter between the two slip rings. If resistance is below 3 ohms, at 80 degrees F, the winding is shorted. If reading is above 3.7 ohms at 80 degrees F, winding has excessive resistance.

STATOR WINDING TEST

To test stator for short circuit, set ohmmeter to 1000 scale, then connect one ohmmeter lead to stator core and the other ohmmeter lead to one of the three stator leads, **Fig. 10.** The ohmmeter should indi-

cate an infinite reading. If ohmmeter indicates other than infinite reading, the stator is grounded and should be replaced.

To test stator for continuity, set ohmmeter to 1 scale, then contact ohmmeter leads to two of the stator leads, **Fig. 11.** Test all three stator leads in this manner. Equal readings should be obtained for each pair. An infinite reading would indicate an open stator winding. Check junction splice for poor solder connection and resolder as necessary. Recheck stator continuity, if an open still exists replace stator. A reading of more than one ohm indicates a poor solder splice, check junction splice.

NOTE: Shorted stator windings are difficult to locate without special equipment. If other tests indicate normal, but alternator fails to supply rated output, shorted stator windings are indicated.

1. PULLEY NUT	9. THROUGH-SCREW	17. REAR HOUSING
2. LOCKWASHER	10. WASHER	18. COMPRESSION SPRING
3. BEARING	11. PULLEY	19. CARBON BRUSH SET
4. COVER PLATE	12. FAN	20. REGULATOR
5. COLLAR	13. FRONT HOUSING	21. SPRING WASHER AND SCREW
6. ROTOR	14. STATOR	22. SUPPRESSION CAPACITOR
7. COLLECTOR RING	15. WASHER AND SCREW ASSEMBLY	23. SPRING WASHER AND SCREW
8. BEARING	16. RECTIFIER	24. BATTERY TERMINAL NUTS AND WASHERS

Fig. 6   Exploded view of Bosch Type K1 alternator with integral regulator.

Fig. 7   Rotor short to ground test

Fig. 8   Rotor open circuit test

Fig. 9   Rotor internal short test.

Fig. 10   Stator short to ground test

Fig. 11   Stator continuity test

DIODE TEST

Unsolder stator winding leads at junctions. Bend lead wires as little as possible to avoid damaging wires. Set ohmmeter to 1 scale, then contact one ohmmeter lead to diode plate and the other ohmmeter lead to the individual diode junctions, **Fig. 12.** Each combination of terminals tested should give one high reading and one low reading. High and low readings will vary slightly with temperature. If one high and one low reading is not observed for all diodes, replace diode plate assembly.

ALTERNATOR ASSEMBLY

1. Fill cavity between retainer plate and bearing one quarter full with Bosch lubricant FT1v34 or equivalent. Do not overfill.
2. Install front bearing, retainer and collar into front housing. Press rear bearing

Fig. 12   Diode test

onto rotor shaft. Install wave washer into rear housing, **Fig. 6.**

NOTE: Use care not to misalign bearings.

3. Install rotor into front housing.
4. Solder stator leads to diode plate assembly, then install stator assembly on rear housing.
5. Remove tape from rear housing bearing and rotor shaft, then position front and rear housings together, aligning scribe marks made during disassembly.
6. Install and tighten through bolts.
7. Position key, fan, pulley and washer on rotor shaft, then install pulley nut.
8. Place rotor in a vise and tighten pulley nut. Tighten vise only enough to permit tightening of pulley nut.
9. Install nuts and washer on battery terminal.
10. Install condenser on rear housing and connect condenser lead.
11. Install voltage regulator and brush assembly on rear housing.

Delcotron Type SI Integral Charging System

NOTE: For service procedures on these alternators, refer to the "General Motors Alternators Systems" chapter.

CHRYSLER CORP. ALTERNATOR SYSTEMS

TABLE OF CONTENTS

General Information

INDEX

INTRODUCTION

Alternators are composed of the same functional parts as the conventional D.C. generator but they operate differently: The field is called a rotor and is the turning portion of the unit. A generating part, called a stator, is the stationary member, comparable to the armature in a D.C. generator. The regulator, similar to those used in a D.C. system, regulates the output of the alternator-rectifier system.

The power source of the system is the alternator. Current is transmitted from the field terminal of the regulator through a slip ring to the field coil and back to ground through another slip ring. The strength of the field regulates the output of the alternating current. This alternating current is then transmitted from the alternator to the rectifier where it is converted to direct current.

These alternators employ a three-phase stator winding in which the phase windings are electrically 120 degrees apart. The rotor consists of a field coil encased between interleaved sections producing a magnetic field with alternate north and south poles. By rotating the rotor inside the stator the alternating current is induced in the stator windings. This alternating current is rectified (changed to D.C.) by silicon diodes and brought out to the output terminal of the alternator.

DIODE RECTIFIERS

Six silicon diode rectifiers are used and act as electrical one-way-valves. Three of the diodes have ground polarity and are pressed or screwed into a heat sink which is grounded. The other three diodes (ungrounded) are pressed or screwed into and insulated from the end head; these diodes are connected to the alternator output terminal.

Since the diodes have a high resistance to the flow of current in one direction and a low resistance in the opposite direction, they may be connected in a manner which allows current to flow from the alternator to the battery in the low resistance direction. The high resistance in the opposite direction prevents the flow of current from the battery to the alternator. Because of this feature no circuit breaker is required between the alternator and battery.

SERVICE PRECAUTIONS

1. Be certain that battery polarity is correct when servicing units. Reversed battery polarity will damage rectifiers and regulators.
2. If booster battery is used for starting, be sure to use correct polarity in hook up.
3. When a fast charger is used to charge a vehicle battery, the vehicle battery cables should be disconnected unless the fast charger is equipped with a special Alternator Protector, in which case the vehicle battery cables need not be disconnected. Also the fast charger should never be used to start a vehicle as damage to rectifiers will result.
4. Lead connections to the grounded rectifiers (negative) should never be soldered as the excessive heat may damage the rectifiers.
5. Unless the system includes a load relay or field relay, grounding the alternator output terminal will damage the alternator and/or circuits. This is true even when the system is not in operation since no circuit breaker is used and the battery is applied to the alternator output terminal at all times. The field or load relay acts as a circuit breaker in that it is controlled by the ignition switch.
6. Before making any "on vehicle" tests of the alternator or regulator, the battery should be checked and the circuit inspected for faulty wiring or insulation. loose or corroded connections and poor ground circuits.
7. Check alternator belt tension to be sure the belt is tight enough to prevent slipping under load.
8. The ignition switch should be off and the battery ground cable disconnected before making any test connections to prevent damage to the system.
9. The vehicle battery must be fully charged or a fully charged battery may be installed for test purposes.

Bosch Type K1 Alternator

INDEX

Fig. 1   Bosch Type K1 alternator w/integral regulator

Fig. 2   Rear view of Bosch Type K1 alternator w/external regulator

Fig. 3   Rear view of Bosch Type alternator w/regulator in engine electronics

DESCRIPTION

The main components of the Bosch type K1 alternator, **Figs. 1 through 3,** are the front and rear housings, stator windings, rotor and rectifying diodes. Current is supplied to the rotor through slip rings and two brushes which, on integral regulator units, are built into the voltage regulator positioned on the rear housing. The rotor is supported in the front and rear housings by ball bearings. The stator windings are assembled inside a laminated core which forms part of the alternator frame. A diode plate containing three positive and three negative diodes is soldered to the stator winding leads. Alternator field current is supplied through a diode trio which is also connected to the stator windings. A capacitor which is mounted to the rear housing, protects the diode plate assembly from high voltages and suppresses radio noises. On all units, the voltage regulator is solid state, which is not serviceable or adjustable. On integral regulator units, the voltage regulator can be replaced without disassembling the alternator. On units with voltage regulator in engine electronics, the electronic voltage regulator is contained within engine electronics Power Module and Logic Module.

IN-VEHICLE TESTING
INTEGRAL REGULATOR UNITS
Charging Circuit Resistance Test
1. Disconnect ground cable from battery and the "Bat" lead from alternator output terminal.
2. Complete test connections as shown in **Fig. 4.**
3. Connect battery ground cable, then start engine and operate at idle.
4. Adjust engine speed and carbon pile rheostat to obtain 20 amps in the circuit and check voltmeter reading. Reading should not exceed .5 volts. If a higher voltage drop is indicated, inspect, clean and tighten all connections in the circuit. A voltage drop test at each connection can be performed to isolate the problem.

Current Output Test
1. Disconnect ground cable from battery and the "Bat" lead from alternator output terminal.
2. Complete test connections as shown in **Fig. 5.**
3. Connect battery ground cable, then start engine and operate at idle.
4. Adjust carbon pile rheostat and engine speed to obtain 28–35 amps at 13.5 volts at 500 RPM, 75–85 amps at 13.5 volts at 1000 RPM and 89 amps at 13.5 volts at 2000 RPM.

NOTE: While increasing engine speed, do not allow voltage to exceed 16 volts.

5. If amperage does not meet specifications, remove alternator from vehicle and perform bench tests.

Voltage Regulator Test
1. Disconnect ground cable from battery and the "Bat" lead from alternator output terminal.
2. Complete test connections as shown in **Fig. 6.**

Fig. 4 Charging circuit resistance test. Models w/integral regulator

3. Ensure voltmeter reads zero. Any other voltage reading indicates a defective alternator.
4. Turn ignition switch to On position and ensure voltmeter reads within one-half volt of battery voltage.
5. Connect a suitable tachometer to engine, then start engine with a jumper wire connected between test ammeter terminals.
6. Remove jumper wire from ammeter terminals and immediately increase engine speed to 2000–3000 RPM while noting ammeter reading.
7. If ammeter reading is 10 amps or less, recheck voltmeter reading without changing engine speed to obtain a correct charging voltage reading. Charging voltage should be 13.9–14.2 volts at 77°F, with an allowance of .05–.09 volt for each 18°F variation of temperature.
8. If ammeter reading is more than 10 amps, continue charging battery until amperage falls below 10 amps, or replace battery with a fully charged one.

EXC. INTEGERAL REGULATOR UNITS

CHARGING CIRCUIT RESISTANCE TEST
1. Disconnect battery ground cable and the "Bat" lead from alternator output terminal.
2. Complete test connections as shown in **Figs. 7 and 8.**
3. On units with external regulator, disconnect wiring harness electrical connector from the electronic voltage regulator.

Fig. 5 Current output test. Models w/integral regulator

Fig. 6 Voltage regulator test. Models w/integral regulator

4. On units with regulator in engine electronics, remove air hose between power module and air cleaner, then the wiring harness electrical connector.
5. On all models, connect a suitable jumper wire from wiring harness connector green wire terminal to ground.

NOTE: Do not connect blue J2 lead of wiring electrical connector to ground.

6. Connect battery ground cable, then start engine and operate at idle.
7. Adjust engine speed and carbon pile rheostat to obtain 20 amps in the circuit and check voltmeter reading.

Reading should not exceed .5 volts. If a higher voltage drop is indicated, inspect, clean and tighten all connections in the circuit. A voltage drop test at each connection can be performed to isolate the problem.

CURRENT OUTPUT TEST

1. Disconnect battery ground cable and "Bat" lead from alternator output terminal.
2. Complete test connections as shown in **Figs. 9 and 10.**
3. On units with external regulator, disconnect wiring harness electrical connector from the electronic voltage regulator.

4. On units with regulator in engine electronics, remove air hose between power module and air cleaner, then the wiring harness electrical connector.
5. On all models, connect a suitable jumper wire from wiring harness connector green wire terminal to ground.

NOTE: Do not connect blue J2 lead of wiring electrical connector to ground.

6. Connect battery ground cable, then start engine and operate at idle.
7. Adjust carbon pile rheostat and engine speed to obtain 15 volts at 1250 RPM.

Fig. 7 Charging circuit resistance test. Models w/external regulator

Fig. 8 Charging circuit resistance test. Models w/regulator in engine electronics

NOTE: While increasing engine speed, do not allow voltage to exceed 16 volts.

8. If ammeter reading is not approximately 87 amps, proceed to "Bench Tests."

VOLTAGE REGULATOR TEST

Units W/External Regulator

1. Disconnect battery ground cable and connect suitable tachometer.
2. Complete test connections as shown in **Fig. 11.**
3. Connect battery ground cable, then start engine and operate at 1250 RPM

with all lights and accessories turned off.
4. Check voltmeter. If voltage readings are as specified in **Fig. 12,** regulator is satisfactory. If voltage readings are below limits or fluctuate, perform steps 5 through 7. If voltage readings are above limits, proceed to step 8 through 10.
5. Ensure voltage regulator is properly grounded through the regulator case, then turn ignition switch to the "Off" position and disconnect voltage regulator wiring harness connector.

NOTE: Ensure terminals of connector

have not spread open to cause open or intermittant connection.

6. Turn ignition switch to the "On" position, then check battery voltage at voltage regulator wiring harness connector terminals. Both blue and green terminals should read battery voltage.
7. If steps 5 and 6 are satisfactory, replace regulator and repeat test.
8. Turn ignition switch to the "Off" position and disconnect voltage regulator wiring harness connector.

NOTE: Ensure terminals of connector have not spread open to cause open or

Fig. 9 Current output test. Models w/external regulator

Fig. 10 Current output test. Models w/regulator in engine electronics

Fig. 11 Voltage regulator test. Models w/external regulator

VOLTAGE CHART	
AMBIENT TEMPERATURE NEAR VOLTAGE REGULATOR	VOLTAGE RANGE
−30°C −20°F	14.9 to 15.8
27°C 80°F	13.9 to 14.4
60°C 140°F	13.0 to 13.7
Above 60°C Above 140°F	Less than 13.60

Fig. 12 Voltage regulator test chart. Models w/external regulator

intermittant connection.

9. Turn ignition switch to the "On" position, then check battery voltage at voltage regulator wiring harness connector terminals. Both blue and green terminals should read battery voltage.

10 If steps 8 and 9 are satisfactory, replace regulator and repeat test.

Units W/Regulator In Engine Electronics

Voltage regulator is controlled by Electronic Control Unit.

ALTERNATOR DISASSEMBLY

INTEGRAL REGULATOR UNITS

1. Mount alternator in a suitable vise using mounting lug as a clamping point.

2. Remove pulley nut, lockwasher, pulley, spacer, fan and key, **Fig. 13.**

3. Disconnect capacitor lead from terminal, then remove capacitor attaching

Fig. 13 Exploded view of Bosch Type K1 alternator w/integral regulator.

screw and the capacitor.

4. Remove voltage regulator and brush holder attaching screw, then the regulator and brush holder.
5. Remove "D+" stud nut, lockwasher, flat washer and insulators.
6. Remove "B+" stud nut, lockwasher, flat washer and insulators.
7. Remove alternator through bolts, then pry between stator and drive end shield with a suitable screwdriver. Carefully separate rotor and housing assembly from stator and rectifier

housing assembly.

8. Press rotor from drive end housing then remove pulley fan spacer.
9. Remove front bearing retainer attaching screws, then the retainer and bearing.
10. Remove front drive bearing from front drive end housing.
11. Unsolder stator-to-rectifier leads, using needle nose pliers as a heat sink.
12. Scribe an alignment mark on stator and housing assembly for assembly

reference, then remove stator from rear housing.

13. Remove rectifier assembly mounting screws and the rectifier assembly.
14. Remove inner "B+" stud insulator.
15. Remove inner "D+" stud insulator, nut and washers.
16. Remove rear bearing oil and dust seal.
17. Remove rear bearing using a suitable puller.

Fig. 14 Exploded view of Bosch Type K1 alternator w/external regulator

Fig. 15   Rotor short to ground test

Fig. 16   Rotor open circuit test

Fig. 17   Stator short to ground test

EXC. INTEGRAL REGULATOR UNITS

1. Mount alternator in a suitable vise using mounting lug as a clamping point.
2. Remove pulley nut, lockwasher, pulley, spacer, fan and key, **Fig. 14.**
3. Remove brush holder mounting screw, then brush holder.
4. Disconnect capacitor lead from terminal, then remove capacitor mounting screw and capacitor.
5. Remove ground stud nut and washer. Scribe alignment marks on alternator housings to aid in reassembly.
6. Remove alternator through bolts, then pry between stator and drive end shield with a suitable screwdriver. Carefully separate rotor and housing assembly from stator and rectifier housing assembly.
7. Using a suitable press, press rotor from drive end housing, then remove front bearing retaining screws and press out front bearing.
8. Remove battery terminal stud nut, lockwasher, flat washer and insulators from rear end housing.
9. Remove rectifier assembly mounting screws, then remove rectifier and stator assembly.
10. Using a suitable soldering gun and a pair of long nosed pliers as a heat sink, unsolder stator to rectifier leads.

11. Remove inner battery terminal stud insulator, then remove rear housing bearing dust and oil seal.
12. Using a suitable puller, remove rear bearing from rotor assembly.

BENCH TESTS
ROTOR & SLIP RING TEST

To test rotor for grounds, set ohmmeter to 1000 scale, then place one ohmmeter lead on rotor shaft and contact other ohmmeter lead to slip ring, **Fig. 15.** Repeat test with other slip ring. The ohmmeter should indicate an infinite reading. If ohmmeter indicates other than infinite reading, a short to ground exists. Inspect soldered connections at slip rings to ensure they are not grounded against the rotor coil. Inspect rotor coil and replace if damaged.

To test rotor for an open circuit, check for continuity across slip rings, **Fig. 16.** If continuity does not exist, field coil is defective and rotor should be replaced.

STATOR WINDING TEST

To test stator for short circuit, set ohmmeter to 1000 scale, then connect one ohmmeter lead to stator core and the other ohmmeter lead to one of the three stator leads, **Fig. 17** The ohmmeter should indicate an infinite reading. If ohmmeter indicates other than infinite reading, the stator is grounded and should be replaced.

To test stator for continuity, set ohmmeter to 1 scale, then contact ohmmeter leads to two of the stator leads, **Fig. 18.** Test all three stator leads in this manner. Equal readings should be obtained for each pair. An infinite reading would indicate an open stator winding. Check junction splice for poor solder connection and resolder as necessary. Recheck stator continuity, if an open still exists replace stator. A reading of more than one ohm indicates a poor solder splice, check junction splice.

NOTE: Shorted stator windings are difficult to locate without special equipment. If other tests indicate normal, but alternator fails to supply rated output, shorted stator windings are indicated.

DIODE TEST

Unsolder stator winding leads at junctions. Bend lead wires as little as possible to avoid damaging wires. Set ohmmeter to 1 scale, then contact one ohmmeter lead to diode plate and the other ohmmeter lead to the individual diode junctions, **Fig. 19.** Each combination of terminals tested should give one high reading and one low reading. High and low readings will vary slightly with temperature. If one high and one low reading is not observed for all diodes, replace diode plate assembly.

ALTERNATOR ASSEMBLY
INTEGRAL REGULATOR UNITS

1. Install rear bearing on rotor assembly, **Fig. 13,** using a suitable press.
2. Install rear bearing oil and dust seal.
3. Install inner "B+" stud insulator.
4. Install inner "D+" stud washers, nut and insulator.
5. Install rectifier assembly and secure with mounting screws.
6. Positon stator into rear housing with scribe marks aligned, then solder stator leads to rectifier assembly.

Fig. 18   Stator continuity test

Fig. 19   Diode test

7. Install "B+" stud insulators, washers and stud nut.
8. Install "D+" stud insulators, washers and stud nut.
9. Press front bearing into drive end housing.
10. Install front bearing retainer and retainer attaching screws.
11. Install pulley fan spacer, then press drive end housing onto rotor.
12. Install recifier end housing over drive end housing.
13. Install and tighten alternator through bolts.
14. Install brush holder and voltage regulator and secure with mounting screws.
15. Install capacitor and capacitor attaching screw, then reconnect capacitor electrical connector.
16. Install key into rotor shaft.
17. Install pulley spacer, pulley and lock-

washer, then install and tighten pulley nut.

EXC. INTEGRAL REGULATOR UNITS

1. Using a suitable press, install rear bearing on rotor assembly until bearing bottoms, **Fig. 14**
2. Install rear housing bearing dust and oil seal, then inner battery terminal stud insulator.
3. Using long nosed pliers as a heat sink, solder stator leads to rectifier assembly, then install stator and rectifier assembly in rear end housing. Tighten screws securely.
4. Install battery terminal stud insulators, flat washer, lock washer and stud nut.

5. Using a suitable press, install drive end housing bearing, then install bearing retainer and attaching screws.
6. Using a suitable press, install drive end housing onto rotor.
7. Align marks made previously, then install stator and rectifier housing assembly over rotor and housing assembly.
8. Install alternator through bolts and tighten securely.
9. Install ground stud washer and nut, then install capacitor to rear end housing.
10. Position brush holder in rear end housing, then install attaching screws and tighten securely.
11. Install rotor fan key, fan, spacer, pulley, lockwasher and nut. Tighten pulley nut securely.

Chrysler Alternators

INDEX

All Chrysler alternators except the 100 and 114 amp units are equipped with six silicon rectifiers, **Figs. 1, 2 and 3.** The 100 and 114 amp alternators are equipped with twelve silicon rectifiers, **Figs. 4 and 5.**

IN-VEHICLE TESTING

NOTE: When testing alternators except 100 and 114 amp units, use a 0–100 amp ammeter. When testing 100 and 114 amp alternators, use a 0–150 amp ammeter.

CHARGING CIRCUIT RESISTANCE TEST

Exc. Units W/Regulators In Engine Electronics

1. Disconnect battery ground cable. Dis-

connect "Batt" lead at the alternator.
2. Complete test connections as per **Figs. 6 and 7.**
3. Connect battery ground cable, start engine and operate at idle.
4. Adjust engine speed and carbon pile to obtain 20 amps in the circuit and check voltmeter reading. Reading should not exceed .7 volts. (.5 volts on 1984–85 models). If a voltage drop is indicated, inspect, clean and tighten all connections in the circuit. A voltage drop test at each connection can be performed to isolate the trouble.

Units W/Regulator In Engine Electronics

1. Disconnect battery ground cable and the "Bat" lead from alternator output terminal.
2. Complete test connections as shown in **Fig. 8.**

3. Remove air hose between power module and air cleaner, then the wiring harness electrical connector.
4. Connect a suitable jumper wire from wiring harness connector green wire terminal to ground.

NOTE: Do not connect blue J2 lead of wiring electrical connector to ground.

5. Connect battery ground cable, then start engine and operate at idle.
6. Adjust engine speed and carbon pile rheostat to obtain 20 amps in the circuit and check voltmeter reading. Reading should not exceed .5 volts. If a higher voltage drop is indicated, inspect, clean and tighten all connections in the circuit. A voltage drop test at each connection can be performed to isolate the problem.

Fig. 1 Alternator assembly exc. 100 & 114 amp units & units w/regulator in engine electronics

CURRENT OUTPUT TEST

Exc. Units W/Regulator In Engine Electronics

1. Disconnect battery ground cable, complete test connections as per **Figs. 9 and 10** and start engine and operate at idle. Immediately after starting, reduce engine speed to idle.
2. Adjust the carbon pile and engine speed in increments until a speed of 1250 RPM and 15 volts are obtained on all units except 100 and 114 amp alternators. On 100 and 114 amp alternators, obtain engine speed of 900 RPM and 13 volts.

CAUTION: While increasing speed, do not allow voltage to exceed 16 volts.

3. Check ammeter reading. Output current should be within specifications.

Units W/Regulator In Engine Electronics

1. Disconnect battery ground cable and "Bat" lead from alternator output terminal.
2. Complete test connections as shown in **Fig. 11**.
3. Remove air hose between power module and air cleaner, then the wiring harness electrical connector.
4. Connect a suitable jumper wire from wiring harness connector green wire terminal to ground.

NOTE: Do not connect blue J2 lead of wiring electrical connector to ground.

5. Connect battery ground cable, then start engine and operate at idle.
6. Adjust carbon pile rheostat and engine speed to obtain 15 volts at 1250 RPM.

NOTE: While increasing engine speed, do not allow voltage to exceed 16 volts.

7. If ammeter reading is not approximately 96 amps, proceed to "Bench Tests."

VOLTAGE REGULATOR TEST

NOTE: Battery must be fully charged for test to be accurate.

Exc. Units W/Regulator Controlled By Engine Electronics

1. Connect test equipment, **Figs. 12 and 13.**
2. Start and run engine at 1250 RPM with all lights and accessories turned "Off." Voltage should be as specified in **Fig. 14.**
3. It is normal for the vehicle ammeter to indicate an immediate charge, then gradually return to the normal position.
4. If voltage is below limits or is fluctuating, proceed with the following:
   a. Check voltage regulator for proper ground. The ground is obtained through the regulator case to mounting screws, then to the vehicle sheet metal.
   b. With ignition switch "Off", disconnect voltage regulator connector. Turn ignition "On" and check for battery voltage at the wiring harness terminal. Both green and blue leads should have battery voltage.
   c. If voltage regulator was grounded properly and battery voltage was present at the green and blue leads, replace voltage regulator except on systems incorporating a field-loads relay. On systems with a field-loads relay, test the relay as outlined under "Field-Loads Relay Test." If relay tests satisfactory, replace voltage regulator. On all systems, repeat test.
5. If voltage is above limits, refer to Steps 4b and 4c.

Units W/Regulator In Engine Electronics

Voltage regulator is controlled by Electronic Control Unit.

BENCH TESTS

If the alternator performance does not meet current output specification limits, it will have to be disassembled for further tests and servicing.

To remove the alternator, disconnect the battery ground cable and the leads at the alternator. Then unfasten and remove the

Fig. 2 Alternator disassembled exc. 100 & 114 amp units & units w/regulator in engine electronics (typical)

Fig. 3 Alternator assembly. Units w/regulator in engine electronics

Fig. 4   100 & 114 amp alternator assembly

alternator from the vehicle.

FIELD COIL DRAW

1. Place alternator on an insulated surface.
2. On all units, connect a jumper wire between one alternator field terminal and the negative terminal of a fully charged battery.
3. Connect test ammeter positive lead to the other alternator field terminal and the ammeter negative lead to the positive battery terminal.
4. On 1980–83 units except 100 and 114 amp, connect a jumper wire between alternator end shield and negative terminal of battery.
5. On all units, slowly rotate rotor by hand and note ammeter reading. On units except 100 and 114 amp, field current at 12 volts should be 4.5 to 6.5 amps (1984–85, 2.5–5.0 amps). On 100 and 114 amp units, field current should be 4.75 to 6.0 amps.
6. A low rotor coil draw is an indication of high resistance in the field coil circuit, (brushes, slip rings or rotor coil). A high rotor coil draw indicates shorted rotor coil or grounded rotor. No reading indicates an open rotor or defective brushes.

ALTERNATOR REPAIRS EXCEPT 100 & 114 AMP UNITS
DISASSEMBLY
Exc. Units W/Regulator In Engine Electronics

To prevent possible damage to the brush assemblies, they should be removed before disassembling the alternator. Both brushes are insulated and mounted in plastic holders.

1. Remove both brush screws, insulating nylon washers and remove brush assemblies, **Fig. 2.**

NOTE: The stator is laminated; do not burr it or the end shield.

2. Remove through bolts and pry between stator and drive end shield with a screwdriver. Carefully separate drive end shield, pulley and rotor from stator and diode rectifier shield, **Fig. 15.**
3. The pulley is an interference fit on the rotor shaft; therefore, a suitable puller must be used to remove it, **Fig. 16.**
4. Pry drive end bearing spring retainer from end shield with a screwdriver, **Fig. 17.**
5. Support end shield and tap rotor shaft with a plastic hammer to separate rotor from end shield.
6. The drive end ball bearing is an interference fit with the rotor shaft; therefore, a suitable pulley must be used to remove it, **Fig. 18.**
7. To remove rectifiers and heat sinks, loosen screws securing negative rectifier and heat sink assembly to end shield, remove the two outer screws and lift assembly from end shield. Remove nuts securing positive rectifier and heat sink assembly to insulated terminals in end shield. Then, remove capacitor ground screw and lift insulated washer, capacitor and positive rectifier and heat sink assembly from end shield.
8. The needle roller bearing in the rectifier end shield is a press fit. If it is necessary to remove the rectifier end

frame needle bearing, protect the end shield by supporting the shield when pressing out the bearing as shown in **Fig. 19.**

Units W/Regulator In Engine Electronics

1. Remove dust cover attaching nuts, then the dust cover.
2. Remove two brush holder attaching screws, then the brush holder.
3. Remove three stator to rectifier attaching screws.
4. Remove rectifier assembly attaching screws, then the rectifier insulator.
5. Remove condensor attaching screw, then the rectifier assembly.
6. Remove four through bolts, then carefully pry between stator and drive end shield with two screwdrivers to separate end shields.
7. Position drive end over bosses of suitable holding fixture, Fig. 20, then secure to fixture using mounting nuts.

NOTE: Do not position alternator motor plastic insulators over fixture bosses or damage may result.

8. Remove pulley attaching nut, pulley washer, pulley and fan.
9. Remove bearing spacer, then press rotor out of drive end shield.
10. Remove inner bearing spacer.
11. Remove bearing assembly from rotor using a suitable puller.
12. Position rotor into fixture C-4885 and position new bearing onto rotor, then drive bearing onto rotor with tool No. C-4894 until tool bottoms.

Fig. 5   100 & 114 amp alternator disassembled

NOTE: Bearing position is critical and should be installed with specified tools.

13. Remove four front bearing attaching screws, then press front bearing out of drive end housing.
14. Install new front bearing in drive end housing using a suitable press.
15. Remove stator from drive end shield.

TESTING DIODE RECTIFIERS

A special Rectifier Tester Tool C-3829 provides a quick, simple and accurate method to test the rectifiers without the necessity of disconnecting the soldered rectifier leads. This instrument is commercially available and full instructions for its use are provided. Lacking this tool, the rectifiers may be tested with a 12 volt battery and a test lamp having a No. 67 bulb. The procedure is as follows:

1. Remove nuts securing stator windings, positive and negative rectifier straps to terminal block. Remove stator winding terminals and pry stator from end shield.
2. Connect one side of test lamp to positive battery post and the other side of the test lamp to a test probe. Connect another test probe to the negative battery post, **Fig. 21.**
3. Contact heat sink with one probe and strap on top of rectifier with the other probe.
4. Reverse position of probes. If test lamp lights in one direction only, the rectifier is satisfactory. If test lamp lights in both directions, the rectifier is shorted. If test lamp lights in neither direction, the rectifier is open.

NOTE: Possible cause of an open or a blown rectifier is a faulty capacitor or a battery that has been installed on reverse polarity. If the battery is installed properly and the rectifiers are open, test the capacitor capacity, which should be .50 microfarad plus or minus 20%.

TESTING STATOR

1. Separate stator from end shields.
2. Using a 12 volt test lamp, **Fig. 22,** test stator for grounds. Contact one test probe to any pin on stator frame and the other to each stator lead. If lamp lights, stator is grounded.

NOTE: Remove varnish from stator frame pin to ensure proper electrical connection.

Fig. 6   Charging circuit resistance test. 1980–83 alternators

3. Use a 12-volt test lamp to test stator for continuity. Contact one stator lead with one probe and the remaining two leads with the other probe, **Fig. 23.** If test lamp does not light, the stator has an open circuit.
4. Install new stator if one tested is defective.

TESTING ROTOR

The rotor may be tested electrically for grounded, open or shorted field coils as follows:
Grounded Field Coil Test: Connect an ohmmeter between each slip ring and the rotor shaft. The ohmmeter should indicate infinite resistance. If reading is zero or higher, rotor is grounded.

Open or Shorted Field Coil Test: Connect an ohmmeter between slip rings and note reading. Ohmmeter reading should be between 1.5 and 2 ohms at room temperature. A reading of 2.5 to 3 ohms, would indicate that the alternator was operated at high underhood temperature, however the rotor is still satisfactory. A reading above 3.5 ohms would indicate a high resistance in rotor coils and further testing or replacement of rotor is required. If resistance is below 1.5 ohms, the field coil is shorted.

REPLACING SLIP RINGS

NOTE: Slip rings are not serviced as a separate item. Rotor replacement is re-

quired when the slip rings are defective.

ALTERNATOR ASSEMBLE

Exc. Units W/Regulator In Engine Electronics
1. Press grease retainer onto rotor shaft using tool No. C-3921, **Fig. 24.** The grease retainer is properly positioned when the inner bore of the installed tool bottoms on the rotor shaft.
2. Install diode end shield bearing, **Fig. 25.**
3. Install drive end bearing in end shield with bearing retainer plate to hold bearing in position. Place assembly on rotor shaft and press into position, **Fig. 26.**

Fig. 7   Charging circuit resistance test. 1984–85 exc. units w/regulator in engine electronics

Fig. 8 Charging circuit resistance test. 1985 units w/regulator in engine electronics

4. Press pulley onto rotor shaft until it contacts inner race of bearing, **Fig. 27.**

NOTE: Do not exceed 6800 lbs.

5. Install output terminal stud and insulator through end shield. Then place positive heat sink assembly over studs, guiding rectifier straps over studs.
6. Place capacitor terminal over capacitator end stud and install capacitor shoulder insulator. Ground the capacitor bracket to end shield with a metal screw. Install and tighten positive heat sink lockwashers and nuts.
7. Slide negative rectifier and heat sink assembly into place, position straps on terminal block studs, then install and tighten attaching screws.
8. Position stator on diode end shield.
9. Position rotor end shield on stator and diode end shield.
10. Align through bolt holes in stator, diode end shield and drive end shield.
11. Compress stator and both end shields by hand and install through bolts, washers and nuts.
12. Install field brush into vertical and horizontal holders. Place an insulating washer on each field brush terminal and install lock-washers and attaching screws.

NOTE: Ensure brushes are not grounded.

13. Rotate pulley slowly by hand to be sure rotor fans do not touch diodes, capacitor lead and stator connections.
14. Install alternator and adjust drive belt.
15. Connect leads to alternator.
16. Connect battery ground cable.
17. Start and operate engine and observe alternator operation.
18. If necessary, test current output and

Fig. 9 Current output test. 1980–83 alternators

Fig. 10 Current output test. 1984–85 exc. units w/regulator in engine electronics

regulator voltage setting.

Units W/Regulator in Engine Electronics

1. Install inner bearing spacer, then position rotor onto suitable mounting fixture.
2. Install drive end shield on rotor, then press shield onto rotor using a suitable tool.
3. Position drive end on mounting fixture so fixture bosses do not contact rotor insulators, then secure with mounting nuts.
4. Install front pulley spacer, alternator fan, pulley and pulley washer.
5. Install pulley nut and torque to 80–105 ft. lbs.
6. Remove drive end assembly from mounting fixture, then install drive end assembly to rectifier end housing.
7. Install four through bolts, then the rectifier assembly.
8. Install condensor attaching screws, then the rectifier assembly insulator.
9. Install rectifier assembly attaching screws.
10. Install three stator to rectifier attaching screws.
11. Slide brushes into position, then install brush holder and brush holder attaching screws.
12. Install dust cover and dust cover attaching screws.

ALTERNATOR REPAIRS 100 & 114 AMP UNITS

DISASSEMBLY & TESTING

Separating End Shields

1. Remove brush holder screw and insulating washer, then lift brush holder from end shield.
2. Remove the through bolts, then using a screwdriver, pry between the stator and end shield in the slot provided to separate end shields, **Fig. 28.**

Fig. 11 Current output test. 1985 units w/regulator in engine electronics

Fig. 12 Voltage regulator test. 1980—83 alternators

Fig. 13 Voltage regulator test. 1984—85 exc. units w/regulator in engine electronics

Ambient Temperature Near Regulator	−20°F	80°F	140°F	Above 140°F
1980—83	14.9–15.9	13.9–14.6	13.3–13.9	Less than 13.6
1984—85	14.6–15.8	13.9–14.4	13.0–13.7	Less than 13.6

Fig. 14 Voltage regulator test specifications

Fig. 15   Separating drive end shield from stator

Fig. 16   Removing pulley

Fig. 17   Disengaging bearing retainer from end shield

Fig. 18   Removing bearing from rotor shaft

Fig. 19   Removing rectifier end shield bearing

Fig. 20   Positioning drive end of alternator on mounting fixture. 1985 units w/regulator in engine electronics

Fig. 23   Testing stator windings for continuity (typical)

Fig. 21   Testing diodes with a test lamp

Fig. 22   Testing stator for grounds

Fig. 24   Installing bearing grease retainer

Fig. 25 Installing diode end shield bearing

Fig. 26 Installing drive end shield and bearing

Fig. 27 Installing pulley

Rectifier Testing

1. Remove stator winding leads to terminal block stud nuts, **Fig. 29.**
2. Lift stator winding leads and pry stator from end shield.
3. Using a 12 volt battery and a test lamp equipped with a #67 bulb, test rectifiers as follows:
   a. Connect one test probe to rectifier heat sink and the other test probe to the metal strap on top of rectifier, **Fig. 30.** Reverse the probes.
   b. If test lamp lights in one direction and does not light in the other, rectifier is satisfactory. If test lamp lights in both directions, rectifier is shorted. If test lamp does not light in either direction, rectifier is open.

Rectifier & Heat Sink Assembly Removal

1. Remove nut and insulator securing positive heat sink assembly to end shield stud.
2. Remove capacitor attaching screw.
3. Remove nut and insulator securing positive heat sink assembly stud to end shield, then remove positive heat sink assembly, **Fig. 31,** noting location of the insulators.
4. Remove screws securing negative heat sink assembly to end shield, then

the negative heat sink assembly, **Fig. 32.**
5. Remove terminal block, then the capacitor and insulator.

Stator Testing

1. Contact one test lamp probe to outer diameter of stator frame and the other probe to each of the stator lead terminals, one at a time, **Fig. 33.**
2. If test lamp lights, the stator lead is grounded, requiring replacement.

NOTE: The stator windings are Delta Wound, therefore the windings cannot be tested for opens or shorts using a test lamp. If the stator is not grounded, and all other electrical circuits and alternator components test satisfactory, the stator may be open or shorted.

Pulley & Bearing Removal

1. Remove pulley with a suitable puller, **Fig. 34.**
2. Remove bearing retainer to drive end shield attaching screws.
3. Support end shield and using a mallet, tap rotor from end shield.
4. Remove bearing with a suitable puller, **Fig. 35.**
5. If necessary to remove needle roller bearing in rectifier end shield, use tool C-4330, **Fig. 36.**

Rotor Testing

Grounded Field Coil Test: Connect a test lamp between each slip ring and the rotor shaft, **Fig. 37.** If test lamp lights, the rotor is grounded, requiring replacement.

Open Field Coil Test: Connect a test lamp between the slip rings, **Fig. 38.** If test lamp does not light, the rotor is open, requiring replacement.

Shorted Field Coil Test: Connect an ohmmeter between the slip rings, **Fig. 38.** If reading is below 1.7 ohms, the rotor is shorted.

High Resistance Test: with an ohmmeter connected across the slip rings, reading should be between 1.7 and 2.1 ohms at 80°F. If not, replace rotor.

ASSEMBLY

1. Press grease retainer onto rotor shaft, **Fig. 36** (Omit tool C-4330-3).
2. Place rectifier end shield bearing on base of tool C-4330-1, **Fig. 36** (Omit tool C-4330-3), then place rectifier end shield on top of bearing. Using tool C-4330-2, press end shield onto bearing until end shield contacts press base.
3. Install drive end bearing and retainer in drive end shield.
4. Position bearing and drive end shield on rotor and while supporting base of rotor shaft, press end shield onto shaft. Ensure rotor spacer is in place before pressing bearing and end shield on shaft.
5. Press pulley onto rotor shaft until it contacts inner race of bearing.

NOTE: Do not exceed 6800 lbs.

6. Place insulator and capacitor on positive heat sink mounting stud, then install capacitor mounting screw.
7. Place terminal block into position in rectifier end shield and install mounting screws.

Fig. 28 Separating end shields. 100 & 114 amp units

Fig. 29 Removing stator winding leads. 100 & 114 amp units

Fig. 30 Testing rectifiers with a test lamp. 100 & 114 amp units

Fig. 31   Positive rectifier assembly. 100 & 114 amp units

Fig. 32   Negative rectifier assembly. 100 & 114 amp units

Fig. 33   Testing stator. 100 & 114 amp units

Fig. 34   Removing pulley. 100 & 114 amp units

Fig. 35   Removing bearing from rotor shaft. 100 & 114 amp units

Fig. 36   Removing rectifier end shield bearing. 100 & 114 amp units

8. Place negative heat sink into position, ensuring metal straps are properly located over studs on terminal block, then install negative heat sink mounting screws.
9. Place insulator over positive heat sink stud and install positive heat sink assembly into position in end shield, ensuring metal straps are properly located over terminal block studs. From inside end shield, place insulator on positive heat sink mounting stud, then install mounting nut. From outside end shield, place insulator on positive heat sink stud, then install mounting nut.

10. Place stator over rectifier end shield and install terminals on terminal block. Then, press stator pins into end shield and install terminal nuts.

NOTE: Route leads to avoid contact with rotor or sharp edge of negative heat sink.

11. Place rotor and drive end shield assembly over stator and rectifier end shield assembly, aligning bolt holes. Compress stator and both end shields, then install and torque through bolts to 40–60 inch lbs.
12. Install field brushes into brush holder with long terminal on bottom and the short terminal on top, **Fig. 39.** Then, install insulators and mounting screw.
13. Place brush holder on end shield, ensure it is properly seated and tighten mounting screw.
14. Slowly rotate pulley to ensure rotor poles do not contact stator winding leads.

Fig. 37   Testing rotor for opens or shorts 100 & 114 amp units

Fig. 38   Testing rotor for grounds 100 & 114 amp units

Fig. 39   Assembling field brushes. 100 & 114 amp units

Mitsubishi Alternator

INDEX

DESCRIPTION

On these units the regulator is incorporated into the alternator rear housing, **Figs. 1, 2 and 3.** The electronic voltage regulator has the ability to vary regulated system voltage upward or downward as temperature changes. No voltage regulated adjustments are required on these units.

IN-VEHICLE TESTS

VOLTAGE REGULATOR TEST

1. With ignition switch in the Off position, disconnect battery positive cable and connect an ammeter between battery positive post and battery cable, **Figs. 4 and 5.**
2. Connect a voltmeter between alternator L terminal and ground, **Figs. 4 and**

5. Voltmeter should indicate zero voltage. If voltage is present, the alternator or charging system wiring is defective.
3. Place ignition switch in the On position and note voltmeter reading. Voltmeter reading should be 1 volt or less, if a higher reading is indicated, the alternator should be removed for bench tests.
4. Connect a tachometer to engine, then start and operate engine at approximately 2000 to 3000 RPM and note ammeter reading.

NOTE: When starting engine, ensure that no starting current is applied to ammeter.

5. If ammeter reading is 5 amps or less on 1981–83 models, or 10 amps or less on 1984-85 models, check voltmeter reading with engine operating at

2000–3000 RPM. The charging voltage should be 14.4 volts at 68°F.
6. If ammeter reading is above 5 amps on 1981–83 models, or above 10 amps on 1984-85 models, continue to charge battery until reading drops below this value and check voltmeter reading at 2000–3000 RPM. If voltage is not within limits, remove alternator for bench tests.

CURRENT OUTPUT TEST

1. With ignition switch in the Off position, disconnect battery ground cable, then disconnect battery lead from alternator output terminal.
2. Connect an ammeter set at the 0 to 100 amp scale between alternator output terminal and the disconnected battery lead, **Figs. 6 and 7.**
3. Connect positive lead of voltmeter to alternator output terminal and nega-

Fig. 1   Disassembled view of Mitsubishi alternator

Fig. 2   Wiring diagram of Mitsubishi charging system. 1981—83

Fig. 3   Wiring diagram of Mitsubishi charging system. 1984—85

Fig. 4 Voltage regulator test connections. 1981—83

Fig. 5 Voltage regulator test connections. 1984—85

Fig. 6 Current output test connections. 1981—83

Engine RPM	Alternator Current Output Hot or Cold At 13.5 Volts
500	17—25 Amps
1000	63—70 Amps
2000	74 Amps

Fig. 8 Alternator output test specifications

Fig. 7 Current output test connections. 1984—85

tive lead to ground, **Figs. 6 and 7.**

4. Connect suitable tachometer to engine and reconnect battery ground cable.
5. Connect a variable carbon pile regulator between battery terminals. When installing carbon pile regulator, ensure that regulator is in the Open or Off position.
6. Adjust carbon pile regulator and accelerate engine to the specified RPM, noting ammeter and voltmeter readings, **Fig. 8.**
7. If ammeter reading is less than specified, the alternator should be removed for bench tests.

and the "Bat" lead from alternator output terminal.

2. Complete test connections as shown in **Fig. 9.**
3. Connect battery ground cable, then start engine and operate at idle.
4. Adjust engine speed and carbon pile rheostat to obtain 20 amps in the circuit and observe voltmeter reading, which should not exceed .5 volt.
5. If a higher voltage drop is indicated, inspect, clean and tighten all connections in the circuit. A voltage drop test at each connection can be performed to isolate the problem.

in a soft jawed vise, then remove three alternator through bolts, **Fig. 1.**

2. Using a screwdriver, pry between stator and drive end frame, then carefully separate drive end frame and rotor from stator and rectifier end frame.
3. Remove pulley nut, pulley, fan and pulley spacer from rotor shaft, then lift drive end housing from rotor.
4. Remove front and rear dust shields from drive end housing.
5. Remove drive end housing bearing retainer, then using a suitable socket, tap bearing from drive end housing.
6. Unsolder six stator leads from rectifier terminals, then remove stator assembly from rectifier end housing.
7. Remove four screws attaching rectifiers to end housing, then remove brush holder and screw attaching regulator to end housing.
8. Remove nut from alternator B terminal and disconnect capacitor lead.
9. Remove rectifier and regulator assembly from end housing.
10. Unsolder joint attaching one of the rectifiers to the regulator, then remove the other rectifier by sliding the battery stud out of the regulator.

CHARGING CIRCUIT RESISTANCE TEST

1984-85

1. Disconnect ground cable from battery

ALTERNATOR
DISASSEMBLE

1. Position alternator with mounting lug

BENCH TESTS
ROTOR TEST

Check for continuity between field coil and slip rings. If continuity does not exist, the rotor assembly must be replaced. Check for continuity between slip rings and rotor shaft. If continuity exists, the rotor assembly should be replaced.

STATOR COIL TEST

Using an ohmmeter, check for continuity between stator leads. If continuity does not exist, replace stator.

RECTIFIER TEST

Using an ohmmeter, check for continuity

Fig. 9 Charging circuit resistance test connections. 1984—85

Fig. 10 Positioning brushes for rotor installation

between stator coil lead terminal and heat sink, then reverse ohmmeter leads. Continuity should exist with only one connection. If continuity exists with both connections, the diode is short circuited and the rectifier assembly should be replaced.

Using an ohmmeter, check rectifier diodes for continuity, then reverse ohmmeter leads. If continuity or an open circuit is indicated with both connections, the diode

is defective and rectifier assembly must be replaced.

BRUSH & BRUSH SPRING INSPECTION

Check brush length, a brush worn to .315 inch or less should be replaced. Check brush spring tension, brush spring tension should be .7 to 1 lb.

ALTERNATOR
ASSEMBLE

Refer to "Alternator, Disassemble" and reverse procedure to assemble. When installing rotor, push brushes into holder and insert a suitable piece of wire, **Fig. 10.** After rotor has been installed, remove wire from brushes.

Ford Motor Co.

TABLE OF CONTENTS

General Information

INDEX

INTRODUCTION

Alternators are composed of the same functional parts as the conventional D.C. generator but they operate differently: The field is called a rotor and is the turning portion of the unit. A generating part, called a stator, is the stationary member, comparable to the armature in a D.C. generator. The regulator, similar to those used in a D.C. system, regulates the output of the alternator-rectifier system.

The power source of the system is the alternator. Current is transmitted from the field terminal of the regulator through a slip ring to the field coil and back to ground through another slip ring. The strength of the field regulates the output of the alternating current. This alternating current is then transmitted from the alternator to the rectifier where it is converted to direct current.

These alternators employ a three-phase stator winding in which the phase windings are electrically 120 degrees apart. The rotor consists of a field coil encased between interleaved sections producing a magnetic field with alternate north and south poles. By rotating the rotor inside the stator the alternating current is induced in the stator windings. This alternating current is rectified (changed to D.C.) by silicon diodes and brought out to the output terminal of the alternator.

DIODE RECTIFIERS

Six silicon diode rectifiers are used and act as electrical one-way-valves. Three of the diodes have ground polarity and are pressed or screwed into a heat sink which is grounded. The other three diodes (ungrounded) are pressed or screwed into and insulated from the end head; these diodes are connected to the alternator output terminal.

Since the diodes have a high resistance to the flow of current in one direction and a low resistance in the opposite direction, they may be connected in a manner which allows current to flow from the alternator to the battery in the low resistance direction. The high resistance in the opposite direction prevents the flow of current from battery to the alternator. Because of this feature no circuit breaker is required between the alternator and battery.

SERVICE PRECAUTIONS

1. Be certain that battery polarity is correct when servicing units. Reversed battery polarity will damage rectifiers and regulators.
2. If booster battery is used for starting, be sure to use correct polarity in hook up.
3. When a fast charger is used to charge a vehicle battery, the vehicle battery cables should be disconnected unless the fast charger is equipped with a special Alternator Protector, in which case the vehicle battery cables need not be disconnected. Also the fast charger should never be used to start a vehicle as damage to rectifiers will result.
4. Unless the system includes a load relay or field relay, grounding the alternator output terminal will damage the alternator and/or circuits. This is true even when the system is not in operation since no circuit breaker is used and the battery is applied to the alternator output terminal at all times. The field or load relay acts as a circuit breaker in that it is controlled by the ignition switch.
5. When adjusting the voltage regulator, do not short the adjusting tool to the regulator base as the regulator may be damaged. The tool should be insulated by taping or by installing a plastic sleeve.
6. Before making any "on vehicle" tests of the alternator or regulator, the battery should be checked and the circuit inspected for faulty wiring or insulation. loose or corroded connections and poor ground circuits.
7. Check alternator belt tension to be sure the belt is tight enough to prevent slipping under load.
8. The ignition switch should be off and the battery ground cable disconnected before making any test connections to prevent damage to the system.
9. The vehicle battery must be fully charged or a fully charged battery may be installed for test purposes.

Ford Motorcraft Alternator

INDEX

GENERAL DESCRIPTION

A charge indicator lamp or ammeter can be used in charging system.

If a charge indicator lamp is used in the charging system, **Figs. 1 and 2**, the system operation is as follows: when the ignition switch is turned ON, a small electrical current flows through the lamp filament (turning the lamp on) and through the alternator regulator to the alternator field. When the engine is started, the alternator field rotates and produces a voltage in the stator winding. When the voltage at the alternator stator terminal reaches about 3 volts, the regulator field relay closes. This puts the same voltage potential on both sides of the charge indicator lamp causing it to go out. When the field relay has closed, current passes through the regulator A terminal and is metered to the alternator field.

If an ammeter is used in the charging system, **Figs. 2 and 3**, the regulator 1 terminal and the alternator stator terminal are not used. When the ignition switch is turned ON, the field relay closes and electrical current passes through the regulator A terminal and is metered to the alternator field. When the engine is started, the alternator field rotates causing the alternator to operate.

All vehicles except 1985 Tempo and Topaz are equipped with electronic voltage regulators. These solid state regulators are used in conjunction with other components in the charging system such as an alternator with a high field current requirement, a warning indicator lamp shunt resistor (500 ohms) and a wiring harness with a regulator connector. 1985 Tempo and Topaz are equipped with Integral Alternator/Regulator (IAR) charging system. This system has a solid state voltage regulator located in the rear of the alternator.

When replacing system components, note the following precautions:
1. Always use the proper alternator in the system.
2. Do not use an electro-mechanical regulator in the system since the wiring harness connector will not index properly with this type of regulator.
3. On models with external voltage regulator, the electronic regulators are color coded for proper installation. The black color coded unit is installed in systems equipped with a warning indicator lamp. The blue color coded regulator is installed in systems equipped with an ammeter.
4. The systems use a 500 ohm resistor on the rear of the instrument cluster on vehicles equipped with a warning indicator lamp.

On systems with an indicator lamp, closing the ignition switch energizes the warning lamp and turns on the regulator output stage. The alternator receives maximum field current and is ready to generate an output voltage. As the alternator rotor speed increases, the output and stator terminal voltages increase from zero to the system regulation level determined by the regulator setting. When the ignition switch is turned off, the solid state relay circuit turns the output stage off, interrupting current flow through the regulator so there is not a current drain on the battery.

On vehicles equipped with an ammeter, the operating principle is similar.

NOTE: The ammeter indicates current flow into (charge) or out of (discharge) the vehicle battery.

Fig. 1   Typical indicator light charging circuit. 1980-85 exc. 1985 alternator w/integral regulator

Fig. 2   Alternator charging circuit. 1985 alternator w/integral regulator

Fig. 3 Ammeter charging circuit. 1980-85 exc. 1985 alternator w/integral regulator

Fig. 4 Voltmeter test scale

IN-VEHICLE TESTING

NOTE: The operations and on vehicle test procedures for the side terminal alternator are same as for rear terminal alternator. However, the internal wiring and bench test procedures differ.

CHARGING SYSTEM TEST

NOTE: All lights and electrical systems in the off position, parking brake applied, transmission in neutral and a charged battery (at least 1.200 specific gravity).

1. Connect the negative lead of the voltmeter to the negative battery cable clamp (not bolt or nut).
2. Connect the positive lead of the voltmeter to the positive battery cable clamp (not bolt or nut).
3. Record the battery voltage reading shown on the voltmeter scale.
4. Connect the red lead of a tachometer to the distributor terminal of the coil and the black tachometer lead to a good ground.

5. Then, start and operate the engine at approximately 1500 rpm. With no other electrical load (foot off brake pedal and car doors closed), the voltmeter reading should increase but not exceed (2 volts) above the first recorded battery voltage reading. The reading should be taken when the voltmeter needles stops moving.
6. With the engine running, turn on the heater and/or air conditioner blower motor to high speed and headlights to high beam.
7. Increase the engine speed to 2000 rpm. The voltmeter should indicate a minimum reading of 0.5 volts above the battery voltage, **Fig. 4.**

NOTE: If the above tests indicate proper voltage readings, the charging system is operating normally. Proceed to "Test Results" if a problem still exists.

TEST RESULTS

Exc. Alternators W/Integral Regulators

1. If voltmeter reading indicates 2 volts over battery voltage (over voltage), proceed as follows:
   a. Stop the engine and check the ground connections between the regulator and alternator and/or regulator to engine. Clean and tighten connections securely and repeat the Charging System Test Procedures.
   b. If over voltage condition still exists, disconnect regulator wiring plug from regulator and repeat the Charging System Test Procedures.
   c. If over voltage still exists with the regulator wiring plug disconnected, repair the short in the wiring harness between the alternator and regulator. Then, replace the regulator and connect the regulator wiring plug to the regulator and repeat the Charging System Test Procedures.
2. If voltmeter does not indicate more

USE JUMPER WIRE TO CONNECT "A" TO "F" TERMINALS AT REGULATOR PLUG

Fig. 5 Regulator plug jumper wire connection

JUMPER WIRE CONNECTED TO ALTERNATOR "BAT" AND "FLD" TERMINALS

TESTING ALTERNATOR FOR DEFECTIVE WIRING BETWEEN ALTERNATOR AND REGULATOR

Fig. 6 Rear terminal alternator. Typical jumper wire connection

JUMPER WIRE CONNECTED TO ALTERNATOR "BAT" AND "FLD" TERMINALS

REGULATOR PLUG REMOVED FROM REGULATOR

Fig. 7 Side terminal alternator. Typical jumper wire connection.

Fig. 8 Charging circuit test points. Alternator w/integral regulator

Fig. 9 Regulator plug voltage test

Fig. 10 Side terminal alternator rectifier short or grounded & stator grounded test

than ½ volt above battery voltage, proceed as follows:

a. Disconnect voltage regulator wire connector and connect an ohmmeter between wire connector "F" terminal and ground. If reading is less than 3 ohms on 1980–83 models, or 2.4 ohms on 1984–85 models, repair grounded field circuit and repeat Charging System Test procedure.

b. If ohmmeter reading is more than 3 ohms on 1980–83 models, or 2.4 ohms on 1984-85 models, connect a jumper wire between voltage regulator wire connector terminals A and F, **Fig. 5,** then repeat Charging System Test procedure. If voltmeter reading is now no more than ½ volt above battery voltage, the voltage regulator or wiring is defective, refer to Regulator Test.

c. If voltmeter still indicates less than ½ volt, disconnect jumper wire from voltage regulator wire connector and leave connector disconnected from regulator. Connect a jumper wire between alternator FLD and BAT terminals, **Figs. 6 and 7,** then repeat Charging System Test procedures.

d. If voltmeter reading now indicates ½ volt or more above battery voltage, repair alternator to regulator wiring harness.

e. If voltmeter still indicates less than ½ volt above battery voltage, stop engine and move voltmeter positive lead to alternator BAT terminal.

f. If voltmeter now indicates battery voltage, the alternator should be removed, inspected and repaired. If zero volts is indicated, repair BAT terminal wiring.

Alternators W/Integral Regulators

1. If voltmeter reading indicates 2 volts or

over battery voltage (over voltage), proceed as follows:

a. Stop engine and place ignition switch in the "On" position. then connect voltmeter negative lead to the alternator rear housing.

b. Connect voltmeter positive lead first to the alternator output connection at the starter solenoid, then to the regulator "A" screw head, **Fig. 8.**

c. If the voltage difference between the two locations is greater than .5 volts, repair the "A" wiring circuit to eliminate the high resistance condition indicated by the excessive voltage drop.

d. If over voltage condition still exists, check for loose regulator to alternator grounding screws. Torque regulator grounding screws to 15–26 inch lbs.

e. If over voltage condition still exists, connect voltmeter negative lead to the alternator rear housing.

f. Place ignition switch in the "Off" position, then connect voltmeter positive lead first to the regulator "A" screw head and then to the regulator "F" screw head, **Fig. 8.**

g. Different voltage readings at the two screw heads in step 1f indicates a defective regulator, grounded brush lead or grounded rotor coil. Repair or replace as required.

h. If battery voltage is obtained at both screw heads in step 1f, replace regulator.

2. If voltmeter does not indicate more than .5 volts over battery voltage, proceed as follows:

a. Disconnect wiring plug from regulator, then connect an ohmmeter between regulator "A" and "F" terminal screws, **Fig. 8.** Meter should indicate more than 2.4 ohms.

b. If meter indicates less than 2.4

ohms in step 2a, check integral alternator/regulator unit for a defective regulator, then check the alternator for a shorted rotor or field circuit. Perform Charging System Test procedure after servicing alternator.

NOTE: Do not replace the regulator until a shorted rotor coil or field circuit has been serviced.

c. If meter indicates greater than 2.4 ohms in step 2a, reconnect regulator wiring plug. Connect voltmeter ground lead to the alternator rear housing and voltmeter positive lead to the regulator "A" terminal screw.

d. Meter should read battery voltage. If battery voltage is not present, repair "A" wiring circuit, then perform Charging Circuit Test procedure. If battery voltage is present, connect the voltmeter ground lead to the alternator rear housing.

e. Place ignition switch in the "Off" position, then connect voltmeter positive lead to the regulator "F" terminal screw. Meter should indicate battery voltage.

f. If voltage is not present, check integral altenator/regulator unit for an open field circuit. Repair as required, then perform Charging Circuit Test procedure. If voltmeter indicates battery voltage, connect voltmeter negative ground lead to alternator rear housing.

g. Turn ignition switch to the "On" position and connect voltmeter positive probe lead to the regulator "F" terminal screw. Voltmeter should indicate 1.5 volts or less.

h. If more than 1.5 volts is present, proceed to "I Circuit Test." If "I Circuit" is satisfactory, replace the

Fig. 11 Rear terminal alternator rectifier short or grounded & stator grounded test

Fig. 12 Alternator w/integral regulator rectifier short or grounded & stator grounded test

Fig. 13 Side terminal alternator field open or short circuit test

regulator and preform Charging Circuit Test procedure. If 1.5 volts or less is present, disconnect alternator wiring plug and connect suitable jumper wires between the alternator B(+) terminal and mating wiring connector terminals.

i. Perform Charging System Test procedure, but connect voltmeter positive terminal to one of the B(+) jumper wire terminals.

j. If voltage rises more than .5 volts above battery voltage, check alternator and starter relay wiring, then repeat Charging System Test procedure, measuring voltage at battery cable clamps.

k. If voltage does not rise more than .5 volts above battery voltage, connect jumper wire from alternator rear housing to the regulator "F" terminal.

l. Repeat Charging System Tests procedure with voltmeter positive lead connected to one of the jumper wire terminals.

m. If voltage rises more than .5 volts, replace regulator. If voltage does not rise more than .5 volts, service the alternator.

DIODE TEST
1980

Test Procedure

1. Disconnect electric choke, if equipped.
2. Disconnect voltage regulator wiring connector.
3. Connect a jumper wire between the "A" and "F" terminals of the voltage regulator wiring connector, **Fig. 5.**
4. Connect voltmeter to battery clamps. Then, start and idle engine.
5. Observe and note voltmeter reading.
6. Move the voltmeter positive lead to the alternator "S" terminal and note voltage reading.

Test Results

1. If voltmeter reading is within ½ of battery voltage, the diodes are satisfactory.

2. If voltmeter reading is approximately 1.5 volts, the alternator has a shorted negative diode or a grounded stator winding.
3. If voltmeter reading is approximately 1.5 volts less than battery voltage, the alternator has a shorted positive diode.
4. If voltage reading is approximately 1 to

Fig. 14 Rear terminal alternator field open or short circuit test

Fig. 15 Alternator w/integral regulator field open or short circuit test

Fig. 16 Rear terminal diode test

1.5 volts less than ½ battery voltage, the alternator has an open positive diode.

5. If voltage reading is 1 to 1.5 volts above ½ battery voltage, the alternator has an open negative diode.

6. Reconnect electric choke into circuit after tests are completed, if equipped.

REGULATOR TESTS

S CIRCUIT TEST—WITH AMMETER

Exc. Alternators W/Integral Regulator

1. Connect the positive lead of the voltmeter to the S terminal of the regulator wiring plug **Fig. 9**. Turn the ignition switch to the "ON" position. Do not start the engine.
2. The voltmeter reading should indicate battery voltage.
3. If there is no voltage reading, disconnect the positive voltmeter lead from the positive battery clamp and repair the S wire lead from the ignition switch to the regulator wiring plug.
4. Connect the positive voltmeter lead to the positive battery cable terminal and repeat the Charging System Test Procedures.

Alternators W/Integral Regulator

For test procedures, refer to "S and I Circuit Test-With Indicator Light."

S AND I CIRCUIT TEST—WITH INDICATOR LIGHT

Exc. Alternators W/Integral Regulator

1. Disconnect regulator wiring plug, then install a suitable jumper wire between connector "A" and "F" terminals, **Fig. 5.**
2. With the engine idling, connect the positive lead of the voltmeter to the S terminal and then to the I terminal of the regulator wiring plug. **Fig. 9**. The voltage of the S circuit should read approximately ½ of the I circuit.
3. If no voltage is present, repair the alternator or the wiring circuit at fault. Reconnect the positive voltmeter lead to the positive battery cable terminal and repeat the Charging System Test Procedures.
4. If the above tests are satisfactory, install a new regulator.
5. Then, remove the jumper wire from the regulator wiring plug and connect the wiring plug to the regulator. Repeat the Charging System Test Procedures.

Alternators W/Integral Regulator

1. Disconnect wiring plug from regulator, then connect voltmeter negative lead to the battery ground terminal and positive lead to wiring plug I terminal. No voltage should be present with ignition switch in "Off" position.
2. If voltage is present, repair circuit between the I circuit and ignition switch.

OHMMETER ARE 27-42

Contact Each Terminal

Contact Diode Plate

Contact Terminal Screw

Fig. 17   Side terminal alternator diode test

3. Turn ignition switch to the "On" position. Battery voltage should be present at wiring plug I terminal.
4. If no voltage reading is present, repair the I lead circuit from the ignition switch to the regulator.
5. If voltage readings in steps 1 through 3 were satisfactory, check resistance value of the 500 ohm resistor. Replace resistor if its value is off by more than 50 ohms.

NOTE: Make resistance check with the regulator wiring plug disconnected and bulb removed, if equipped.

6. Connect wiring plug to the regulator and replace bulb, if equipped.

FIELD CIRCUIT DRAIN TEST

Alternators W/Integral Regulator

NOTE: Connect voltmeter negative lead to the alternator rear housing for all of the following voltage readings.

1. Turn ignition switch to the "Off" position, then connect voltmeter positive lead to the regulator "F" terminal screw. Battery voltage should be present.
2. If less than battery voltage is present, disconnect regulator electrical connector and connect voltmeter positive lead to connector I terminal. No volt-

age should be present.

3. If voltage is present, repair circuit between I lead and ignition switch. If no voltage is present, proceed to step 4.
4. Connect voltmeter positive lead to the connector S terminal.
5. If no voltage is present, replace regulator. If voltage is present, disconnect alternator electrical connector. Again, connect voltmeter positive lead to the regulator connector S terminal.
6. If voltage is still present, repair circuit between S lead and alternator connector. If no voltage is present, replace alternator rectifier assembly.

BENCH TESTS

RECTIFIER SHORT OR GROUNDED AND STATOR GROUNDED TEST

Using a suitable ohmmeter, connect one probe to the alternator BAT or B+ terminal, **Figs. 10, 11 and 12,** the other probe to the STA terminal (rear blade terminal). Then, reverse the ohmmeter probes and repeat the test. A reading of about 6–6.5 ohms should be obtained in one direction and no needle movement with the probes reversed. A reading in both directions indicates a bad positive diode, a grounded positive diode plate, grounded BAT or B+ terminal or a shorted radio suppression capacitor, if equipped.

Perform the same test using the STA and GND (ground) terminals of the alternator. A reading in both directions indicates either a bad negative diode, a grounded stator winding, a grounded stator terminal, a grounded positive diode plate, or a shorted radio capacitor, if equipped.

Infinite readings (no needle movement) in all four probe positions in the proceeding tests indicates an open terminal lead connection inside the alternator.

FIELD OPEN OR SHORT CIRCUIT TEST

Exc. Alternators W/Integral Regulators

Using a suitable ohmmeter, connect the alternator field terminal with one probe and the ground terminal with the other probe, **Figs. 13 and 14.** Then, spin the alternator pulley. The ohmmeter reading should be between 2.4 and 25 ohms on 1980 units 2.4 and 100 ohms on 1981–85 units, and should fluctuate while the pulley is turning. An infinite reading (no meter movement) indicates an open brush lead, worn or stuck brushes, or a bad rotor assembly. An ohmmeter reading less than 2.4 ohms indicates a grounded brush assembly, a grounded field terminal or a bad rotor.

Regulators W/Integral Regulator

1. Using a suitable ohmmeter, connect regulator A blade terminal with one probe and the regulator "F" screw head with the other probe, **Fig. 15.**

2. Spin the alternator pulley and note meter reading, then reverse probes and repeat step 1. In one probe direction ohmmeter reading should be between 2.2 and 100 ohms and may fluctuate while pulley is turning. In the other direction, reading should fluctuate between 2.2 and approximately 9 ohms.

3. An infinite reading, no meter movement, in one direction and approximately 9 ohms in the other, indicates an open brush lead, worn or stuck brushes, defective rotor or a loose regulator to brush holder attaching screw.

4. An ohmmeter reading less than 2.2 ohms in both directions indicates a shorted or defective regulator.

5. An ohmmeter reading significantly over 9 ohms in both directions indicates a defective regulator or loose "F" terminal screw.

6. Connect alternator rear housing with one ohmmeter probe and touch the other probe first to regulator "A" blade terminal and then to the regulator "F" screw head.

7. If ohmmeter reads less than infinite at either point, a grounded brush lead, grounded rotor or defective regulator is indicated.

DIODE TEST

Exc. Alternators W/Integral Regulator

To test one set of diodes, contact one probe of a suitable ohmmeter to the terminal bolt, **Figs. 16 and 17** and contact each of the three stator lead terminals with the other probe. Reverse the probes and repeat the test. All diodes should show a low reading of about 60 ohms on 1980–82 models or 6 ohms on 1983–85 models in one direction, and an infinite reading (no needle movement) with the probes reversed. Repeat the preceding tests for the other set of diodes except that the other terminal screw is used.

If the meter readings are not as specified, replace the rectifier assembly.

Alternator W/Integral Regulators

NOTE: Digital meter should not be used to perform the following test.

1. Using a suitable ohmmeter, connect one probe to one of the rectifier assembly B+ blade terminals and contact each of the three stator terminals with the other probe, **Fig. 18.** Reverse probes and repeat test. All diodes should show a low reading of approximately 7 ohms in one direction and an infinite reading with the probes reversed.

2. Repeat step 1 for the negative diodes by connecting the diode assembly base plate and the three stator terminals.

3. If steps 1 and 2 are not satisfactory, replace diode assembly.

Fig. 18   Alternator w/integral regulator diode test

STATOR COIL OPEN OR GROUNDED TEST

Disassemble stator from alternator, then set a suitable ohmmeter to read up to 1000 ohms. Connect ohmmeter probes to stator leads and to stator laminated core, ensuring probe makes good electrical connection with stator core. Ohmmeter should indicate infinite resistance. If ohmmeter does not read infinity, stator winding is shorted to core and must be replaced. Repeat test for each stator lead.

ROTOR OPEN OR SHORT CIRCUIT TEST

Disassemble the front housing and rotor from the rear housing and stator.

Contact each ohmmeter probe to a rotor slip ring. The meter reading should be 2.4 to 4.9 ohms on 1980 units, and 2.0 to 3.9 ohms on 1981–85 units. A higher reading indicates a damaged slip ring solder connection or a broken wire. A lower reading indicates a shorted wire or slip ring.

Contact one ohmmeter probe to a slip ring and the other probe to the rotor shaft. The meter reading should be infinite (no deflection). A reading other than infinite indicates the rotor is shorted to the shaft. Inspect the slip ring soldered terminals to be sure they are not bent and touching the rotor shaft, or that excess solder is not grounding the rotor coil connections to the shaft. Replace the rotor if it is shorted and cannot be repaired.

RADIO SUPPRESSION CAPACITOR OPEN OR SHORT TEST

NOTE: The radio suppression capacitor is built into the diode assembly and cannot be serviced by itself.

1. Using a suitable ohmmeter, connect

one probe to the diode assembly B+ blade terminal and the other probe to the diode assembly base plate. Reverse probes and repeat test.

2. If meter indicates infinite reading in one direction, proceed to step 3. If meter indicates same reading in both directions, replace diode assembly.

3. Connect ohmmeter probes to diode assembly B+ terminal and base plate so an infinite reading is present. Reverse probes and observe meter indicator needle movement. The indicator needle should jump slightly, then return to its original position.

REGULATOR ADJUSTMENTS

These regulators are factory calibrated and sealed and no adjustment is possible. If regulator calibration values are not within specifications, the regulator must be replaced.

ALTERNATOR REPAIRS

Rear Terminal Alternator

NOTE: Use a 100 watt soldering iron.

DISASSEMBLY

1. Mark both end housings and the stator with a scribe mark for assembly, **Fig. 19.**

2. Remove the three housing through bolts.

3. Separate the front housing and rotor from the stator and rear housing.

4. Remove all the nuts and insulators from the rear housing and remove the rear housing from the stator and rectifier assembly.

5. Remove the brush holder mounting screws and remove the holder, brushes, brush springs, insulator and terminal.

6. If replacement is necessary, press the bearing from the rear housing, supporting the housing on the inner boss.

7. If the rectifier assembly is being replaced, unsolder the stator leads from the printed-circuit board terminals, and separate the stator from the rectifier assembly.

8. Original production alternators will have one of two types of rectifier assembly circuit boards, **Fig. 20**, one has the circuit board spaced away from the diode plates with the diodes exposed. Another type is a single circuit board with built-in diodes.

If the alternator rectifier has an exposed diode circuit board, remove the screws from the rectifier by rotating the bolt heads ¼ turn clockwise to

Fig. 19 Disassembled rear terminal alternator

unlock them and then remove the screws, **Fig. 20.** Push the stator terminal screw straight out on a rectifier with the diodes built into the circuit board, **Fig. 20.** Avoid turning the screw while removing to make certain that the straight knurl will engage the insulators when installing. Do not remove the grounded screw, **Fig. 21.**

9. Remove the drive pulley nut, **Fig. 22,** then, pull the lockwasher, pulley, fan, fan spacer, front housing and rotor stop from the rotor shaft.

10. Remove the three screws that hold the front end bearing retainer, and remove the retainer. If the bearing is damaged or has lost its lubricant, support the housing close to the bearing boss and press out the old bearing from the housing.

11. Perform a diode test and a field open or short circuit test.

ASSEMBLY

NOTE: Refer to "Cleaning and Inspection" procedures before reassembly.

1. The rotor, stator and bearings must not be cleaned with solvent. Wipe these parts off with a clean cloth.

2. Press the front bearing in the front housing bearing boss (put pressure on the outer race only), and install the bearing retainer, **Fig. 19.**

3. If the stop-ring on the rotor drive shaft was damaged, install a new stop-ring. Push the new ring on the shaft and into the groove.

NOTE: Do not open the ring with snap ring pliers as permanent damage will result.

4. Position the rotor stop on the drive shaft with the recessed side against the stop-ring.

5. Position the front housing, fan spacer, fan, pulley and lock washer on the drive shaft and install the retaining nut. Torque the retaining nut, **Fig. 22,** to 60–100 ft lbs.

6. If the rear housing bearing was removed, support the housing on the inner boss and press in a new bearing flush with the outer end surface.

7. Place the brush springs, brushes,

brush terminal and terminal insulator in the brush holder and hold the brushes in position by inserting a piece of stiff wire in the brush holder, **Fig. 23.**

8. Position the brush holder assembly in the rear housing and install the mounting screws. Position the brush leads in the brush holder, **Fig. 24.**

9. Wrap the three stator winding leads around the circuit board terminals and solder them. Position the stator neutral lead eyelet on the stator terminal screw and install the screw in the rectifier assembly, **Fig. 25.**

10. For a rectifier with the diodes exposed insert the special screws through the wire lug, dished washers and circuit board, **Fig. 20.** Turn them ¼ turn counterclockwise to lock them. For single circuit boards with built in diodes, insert the screws straight through the wire lug, insulating washer and rectifier into the insulator, **Fig. 21.**

NOTE: The dished washers are to be used only on the circuit board with exposed diodes, **Fig. 20.** If they are used on the single circuit board, a short circuit will occur. A flat insulating washer is to be used between the stator terminal and the board when a single circuit board is used, **Fig. 21.**

11. Position the radio noise suppression capacitor on the rectifier terminals. On the circuit board with exposed diodes, install the STA and BAT terminal insulators, **Fig. 25.** On the single circuit board, position the square stator-terminal insulator in the square hole in the rectifier assembly, **Fig. 21.** Position the BAT terminal insulator, **Fig. 26.**

Position the stator and rectifier assembly in the rear housing. Make certain that all terminal insulators are seated properly in the recesses, **Fig. 25.** Position the STA (black), BAT (red) and FLD (orange) insulators on the terminal bolts, and install the retaining nuts, **Fig. 27.**

12. Wipe the rear end bearing surface of the rotor shaft with a clean lint-free rag.

13. Position the rear housing and stator assembly over the rotor and align the scribe marks made during disassembly. Seat the machined portion of the stator core into the step in both end housings. Install the housing through bolts. Remove the brush retracting wire, and put a daub of water-proof cement over the hole to seal it.

Fig. 20 Rectifier assembly

Side Terminal Alternator

DISASSEMBLY

NOTE: Use a 200 watt soldering iron.

Fig. 21   Stator terminal installation.
Integral rectifier circuit board

Fig. 22   Typical pulley removal &
installation

1. Mark both end housings and the stator with a scribe mark for use during assembly, **Fig. 28.**
2. Remove the four housing through bolts, and separate the front housing and rotor from the rear housing and stator. Slots are provided in the front housing to aid in disassembly. Do not separate the rear housing from the stator at this time.
3. Remove the drive pulley nut, **Fig. 22.** Remove the lockwasher, pulley, fan and fan spacer from the rotor shaft.
4. Pull the rotor and shaft from the front housing, and remove the spacer from the rotor shaft, **Fig. 28.**
5. Remove three screws retaining the bearing to the front housing. If the bearing is damaged or has lost its

lubricant, remove the bearing from the housing. To remove the bearing, support the housing close to the bearing boss and press the bearing from the housing.
6. Unsolder and disengage the three stator leads from the rectifier, **Fig. 29.**
7. Lift the stator from the rear housing.
8. Unsolder and disengage the brush holder lead from the rectifier.
9. Remove the screw attaching the capacitor lead to the rectifier.
10. Remove four screws attaching the rectifier to the rear housing, **Fig. 29.**
11. Remove the two terminal nuts and insulator from outside the housing, and remove the rectifier from the housing.
12. Remove two screws attaching the brush holder to the housing and remove the brushes and holder.
13. Remove sealing compound from rear housing and brush holder.
14. Remove one screw attaching the capacitor to the rear housing and remove the capacitor.
15. If bearing replacement is necessary, support the rear housing close to the bearing boss and press the bearing out of the housing from the inside.

ASSEMBLY

NOTE: Refer to "Cleaning and Inspection" procedures before reassembly.

1. If the front housing bearing is being replaced, press the new bearing in the housing.

NOTE: Put pressure on the bearing outer race only. Then, install the bearing retaining screws.

2. Place the inner spacer on the rotor shaft and insert the rotor shaft into the front housing and bearing.
3. Install the fan spacer, fan, pulley, lockwasher and nut on the rotor shaft, **Fig. 22.**
4. If the rear bearing is being replaced, press a new bearing in from inside the housing until it is flush with the boss outer surface.
5. Position the brush terminal on the brush holder, **Fig. 30.** Install the springs and brushes in the brush holder, and insert a piece of stiff wire to hold the brushes in place, **Fig. 30.**
6. Position the brush holder in the rear housing and install the attaching screws. Push the brush holder toward the rotor shaft opening and tighten the brush holder attaching screws.
7. Position the capacitor to the rear housing and install the attaching screw.
8. Place the two cup shaped (rectifier) insulators on the bosses inside the housing, **Fig. 31.**
9. Place the insulator on the BAT (large) terminal of the rectifier, and position the rectifier in the rear housing. Place

Fig. 23   Brush holder assembly

Fig. 24   Typical brush lead
positions

Fig. 25 Stator lead connections. Rear terminal alternator

the outside insulator on the BAT terminal, and install the nuts on the BAT and GRD terminals finger tight.

10. Install but do not tighten the four rectifier attaching screws.
11. Tighten the BAT and GRD terminal nuts on the outside of the rear housing. Then, tighten the four rectifier attaching screws.
12. Position the capacitor lead to the rectifier and install the attaching screw.
13. Press the brush holder lead on the rectifier pin and solder securely, **Fig. 29.**
14. Position the stator in the rear housing and align the scribe marks. Press the three stator leads on the rectifier pins and solder securely, **Fig. 29.**
15. Position the rotor and front housing into the stator and rear housing. Align the scribe marks and install the four through bolts. Tighten two opposing bolts and then the two remaining bolts.
16. Spin the fan and pulley to be sure

nothing is binding within the alternator.
17. Remove the wire retracting the brushes, and place a daub of waterproof cement over the hole to seal it.

BRUSH REPLACEMENT
Removal
1. Mark both end housings and the stator with a scribe mark for use during assembly.
2. Remove the four housing through bolts, and separate the front housing and rotor from the rear housing and stator. Slots are provided in the front housing to aid in disassembly.

NOTE: Do not separate the rear housing and stator.

3. Unsolder and disengage the brush holder lead from the rectifier.
4. Remove the two brush holder attaching screws and lift the brush holder

from the rear housing.
5. Remove the brushes from the brush holder.

Installation
1. Insert the brushes into the brush holder and position the terminal on the brush holder.
2. Depress the brushes and insert a 1½ inch piece of stiff wire, **Fig. 30,** to hold the brushes in the retracted position.
3. Position the brush holder to the rear housing, inserting the wire used to retract the brushes through the hole in the rear housing.
4. Install the brush holder attaching screws. Push the brush holder toward the rotor shaft opening and tighten the attaching screws.
5. Press the brush holder lead on the rectifier pin and solder securely.
6. Position the rotor and front housing into the stator and rear housing. Align the scribe marks and install the four through bolts. Tighten two opposing bolts and then the two remaining bolts.
7. Spin the fan and pulley to be sure nothing is binding within the alternator.
8. Remove the wire retracting the brushes, and place a daub of waterproof cement over the hole to seal it.

RECTIFIER REPLACEMENT
Removal
1. Mark both end housings and the stator with a scribe mark for use during assembly, **Fig. 28.**
2. Remove the four housing through bolts, and separate the front housing and rotor from the rear housing and stator. Slots are provided in the front housing to aid in disassembly.

NOTE: Do not separate the rear housing and stator at this time.

3. Unsolder and disengage the three stator leads from the rectifier, **Fig. 29.** Lift the stator from the rear housing.
4. Unsolder and disengage the brush holder lead from the rectifier.
5. Remove the screw attaching the capacitor lead to the rectifier.

Fig. 26 Fiberglass circuit board terminal insulators

Fig. 27 Alternator terminal locations

Fig. 28 Disassembled side terminal alternator

Fig. 29 Stator lead connections. Side terminal alternator

6. Remove four screws attaching the rectifier to the rear housing, **Fig. 29.**
7. Remove two terminal nuts and insulator from outside the housing, and remove the rectifier from the housing.

Installation

1. Insert a piece of wire through the hole in the rear housing to hold the brushes in the retracted position.
2. Place the two cup shaped (rectifier) insulators on the bosses inside the housing, **Fig. 31.**
3. Place the insulator on the BAT (large) terminal of the rectifier, and position the rectifier in the rear housing. Place the outside insulator on the BAT terminal, and install the nuts on the BAT and GRD terminals finger tight.
4. Install but do not tighten the four rectifier attaching screws.
5. Tighten the BAT and GRD terminal nuts on the outside of the rear housing. Then, tighten the four rectifier attaching screws.
6. Position the capacitor lead to the rectifier and install the attaching screw.
7. Press the brush holder lead on the rectifier pin and solder securely, **Fig. 29.**
8. Position the stator in the rear housing

and align the scribe marks. Press the three stator leads on the rectifier pins and solder securely, **Fig. 29.**
9. Position the rotor and front housing into the stator and rear housing. Align the scribe marks and install the four through bolts. Partially tighten all four through bolts. Then, tighten two opposing bolts and then the two remaining bolts.
10. Spin the fan and pulley to be sure nothing is binding within the alternator.
11. Remove the wire retracting the brushes in the brush holder, and place a daub of waterproof cement over the hole in the rear housing to seal it.

Alternator W/Integral Regulator

DISASSEMBLY

1. On models equipped with fan shield, remove attaching clip, then the fan shield.
2. On all models, remove four regulator to alternator rear housing attaching screws, then the regulator with brush holder attached, **Fig. 32.**
3. Remove two regulator to brush holder attaching screws, then separate regulator, attaching nuts, brushes and brush springs from brush holder.
4. Scribe a line across the end housings and stator laminated core for reference during assembly.
5. Remove three through bolts, then separate front housing and rotor assembly from stator and rear housing.

NOTE: It may be necessary to tap front housing with a plastic hammer to loosen housing from stator core.

6. Remove three stator lead terminals from the rectifier assembly using a 100 watt soldering iron and needle

nose pliers, **Fig. 33.**

NOTE: Do not allow soldering iron to overheat rectifier.

7. Remove rectifier assembly attaching screws, then the rectifier assembly from housing.
8. Remove bearing from rear housing using a suitable press. Support housing close to bearing boss to prevent housing damage.
9. Clamp front housing in suitable vise, then remove drive pulley attaching nut from rotor using a suitable tool.
10. Remove flat washer, drive pulley, fan and fan spacer from the rotor shaft.
11. Remove rotor from housing, then the housing from vise.
12. Remove front rotor stop from rotor shaft.

NOTE: Do not remove stop ring from rotor shaft unless it is damaged.

13. Remove bearing retainer to front housing attaching screws, then the bearing retainer.
14. Remove bearing from front housing using a suitable press.

Fig. 30 Brush replacement. Exc. alternator w/integral regulator

Fig. 31 Brush holder and rectifier insulators installed

Fig. 32 Disassembled alternator w/integral regulator

ASSEMBLY

NOTE: Refer to "Cleaning and Inspection" procedure before assembly.

1. Install bearing in front housing using a suitable press, **Fig. 32.**
2. Install bearing retainer in front housing, then the bearing retainer attaching screws. Torque attaching screws to 25–40 inch lbs.
3. If stop ring was removed from rotor shaft, install new ring by sliding it over end of shaft and into groove.

NOTE: Do not open ring with snap ring pliers as permanent damage to ring may result.

4. Install rotor stop on rotor shaft with recessed side against stop ring.
5. Install rotor in front housing, then clamp housing in a suitable vise.

6. Install fan spacer, fan, drive pulley, flat washer and nut on rotor shaft. Torque nut to 60–100 ft. lbs. using suitable tool.
7. Remove rotor and housing assembly from vise. Ensure rotor rotates freely in housing.
8. Install bearing in rear housing using a suitable press. Press bearing into bore until it is flush with outside rear surface of housing.
9. Wipe rectifier assembly base plate with clean cloth, then apply ³⁄₃₂ inch wide by ¼ inch long strip of suitable heat sink compound lengthwise across rectifier assembly base plate.
10. Wipe rectifier mounting surface of rear housing with clean cloth, then seat rectifier into recessed mounting area.

NOTE: Failure to remove foreign material from mounting surfaces or failure to apply heat sink compound may cause rectifier

overheating.

11. Install four rectifier assembly attaching screws. Torque screws to 25–35 inch lbs.
12. Install stator assembly in rear housing and align scribe marks made during disassembly.
13. Solder stator terminals onto rectifier blade terminals using suitable resin core solder. Use caution not to overheat rectifier.
14. Install rear housing and stator assembly over rotor and align scribe marks made during disassembly.
15. Seat machined portion of stator core in recess in both end housings, then install housing through bolts. Torque bolts to 35–60 inch lbs. Spin rotor to ensure free movement.
16. Install springs and brushes in brush holder. Hold brushes in position by inserting a 1 ⅜ inch piece of suitable wire into brush holder pin hole, **Fig. 34.**
17. Install nut and washer assemblies into retaining slots in brush holder. Tip holder back slightly so nut and washer assemblies fall to nut side of slot, then insert brush terminals past washers and into the slots, **Fig. 35.**
18. Position regulator against brush holder, then install regulator to brush holder attaching screws. Torque screws to 20–30 inch lbs.

NOTE: Loop brush leads toward brush end of brush holder.

19. Install regulator and brush holder assembly onto alternator rear housing, then the regulator attaching screws. Torque screws to 25–35 inch lbs.
20. Remove wire holding brushes, then place a daub of suitable waterproof sealer over the brush pin to prevent water entry.

NOTE: Do not use silicone sealer on brush pin hole.

Cleaning and Inspection Procedures

NOTE: When rebuilding a high tempera-

Fig. 33 Removing stator terminals from rectifier

Fig. 34 Brush replacement. Alternator w/integral regulator

Fig. 35 Brush terminal installation. Alternator w/integral regulator

ture alternator, use only high temperature rectifier assembly and bearings. If standard parts are used, alternator failure will occur.

1. The rotor, stator, and bearings must not be cleaned with solvent. Wipe these parts off with a clean cloth.
2. Rotate the front bearing on the drive end of the rotor drive shaft. Check for any scraping noise, looseness or roughness that will indicate that the bearing is excessively worn. Look for excessive lubricant leakage. If any of these conditions exist, replace the bearing.
3. Inspect the rotor shaft at the rear bearing surface for roughness or severe chatter marks. Replace the rotor assembly if the shaft is not smooth.
4. Place the rear end bearing on the slip ring end of the shaft and rotate the bearing on the shaft. Make the same check for noise, looseness or roughness as was made for the front bearing. Inspect the rollers and cage for damage. Replace the bearing if these conditions exist, or if the lubricant is lost or contaminated.
5. Check the pulley and fan for excessive looseness on the rotor shaft. Replace any pulley or fan that is loose or bent out of shape. Check the rotor shaft for stripped or damaged threads. Inspect the hex hole in the end of the shaft for damage.
6. Check both the front and rear housing for cracks. Check the front housings for stripped threads in the mounting gear. Replace defective housings.
7. Check all wire leads on both the stator and rotor assemblies for loose soldered connections, and for burned insulation. Resolder poor connections. Replace parts that show burned insulation.
8. Check the slip rings for nicks and surface roughness. If the slip rings are badly damaged, the entire rotor will have to be replaced, as it is serviced as a complete assembly.
9. Replace any parts that are burned or cracked. Replace brushes and brush springs that are not to specifications.

General Motors Corp.

TABLE OF CONTENTS

General Information

INDEX

INTRODUCTION

Alternators are composed of the same functional parts as the conventional D.C. generator but they operate differently: The field is called a rotor and is the turning portion of the unit. A generating part, called a stator, is the stationary member, comparable to the armature in a D.C. generator. The regulator, similar to those used in a D.C. system, regulates the output of the alternator-rectifier system.

The power source of the system is the alternator. Current is transmitted from the field terminal of the regulator through a slip ring to the field coil and back to ground through another slip ring. The strength of the field regulates the output of the alternating current. This alternating current is then transmitted from the alternator to the rectifier where it is converted to direct current.

These alternators employ a three-phase stator winding in which the phase windings are electrically 120 degrees apart. The rotor consists of a field coil encased between interleaved sections producing a magnetic field with alternate north and south poles. By rotating the rotor inside the stator the alternating current is induced in the stator windings. This alternating current is rectified (changed to D.C.) by silicon diodes and brought out to the output terminal of the alternator.

DIODE RECTIFIERS

Six silicon diode rectifiers are used and act as electrical one-way-valves. Three of the diodes have ground polarity and are pressed or screwed into a heat sink which is grounded. The other three diodes (ungrounded) are pressed or screwed into and insulated from the end head; these diodes are connected to the alternator output terminal.

Since the diodes have a high resistance to the flow of current in one direction and a low resistance in the opposite direction, they may be connected in a manner which allows current to flow from the alternator to the battery in the low resistance direction. The high resistance in the opposite direction prevents the flow of current from the battery to the alternator. Because of this feature no circuit breaker is required between the alternator and battery.

SERVICE PRECAUTIONS

1. Be certain that battery polarity is correct when servicing units. Reversed battery polarity will damage rectifiers and regulators.
2. If booster battery is used for starting, be sure to use correct polarity in hook up.
3. When a fast charger is used to charge a vehicle battery, the vehicle battery cables should be disconnected unless the fast charger is equipped with a special Alternator Protector, in which case the vehicle battery cables need not be disconnected. Also the fast charger should never be used to start a vehicle as damage to rectifiers will result.
4. Unless the system includes a load relay or field relay, grounding the alternator output terminal will damage the alternator and/or circuits. This is true even when the system is not in operation since no circuit breaker is used and the battery is applied to the alternator output terminal at all times. The field or load relay acts as a circuit breaker in that it is controlled by the ignition switch.
5. When adjusting the voltage regulator, do not short the adjusting tool to the regulator base as the regulator may be damaged. The tool should be insulated by taping or by installing a plastic sleeve.
6. Before making any "on vehicle" tests

of the alternator or regulator, the battery should be checked and the circuit inspected for faulty wiring or insulation. loose or corroded connections and poor ground circuits.

7. Check alternator belt tension to be sure the belt is tight enough to prevent slipping under load.
8. The ignition switch should be off and the battery ground cable disconnected

before making any test connections to prevent damage to the system.
10. The vehicle battery must be fully charged or a fully charged battery may be installed for test purposes.

Delcotron Type SI Integral Charging System

INDEX

DESCRIPTION

These units, **Figs. 1 thru 6,** feature a solid state regulator mounted inside the alternator slip ring end frame, along with the brush holder assembly. All regulator components are enclosed in a solid mold with no need or provision for adjustment of the regulator. A rectifier bridge, containing six diodes and connected to the stator windings, changes A.C. voltage to D.C. voltage which is available at the output terminal. Generator field current is supplied through a diode trio which is also connected to the stator windings. The diodes and rectifiers are protected by a capacitor which is also mounted in the end frame.

NOTE: General Motors units incorporate a resistor in the warning indicator circuit. **Fig. 7.**

Some alternators used on diesel engines are equipped with an R terminal for the tachometer. On these units, if the alternator pulley is to be replaced, a pulley of

the same diameter as the one removed must be installed, otherwise tachometer may provide inaccurate readings.

No maintenance or adjustments of any kind are required on this unit.

TROUBLESHOOTING

SERVICE NOTE: If a condition of a dimly lit "No Charge" indicator lamp occurs under heavy electrical load on 1982 and some 1983 Cadillac Brougham and Deville models with Digital Fuel Injection, it may be caused by insufficient filtering of the "No Charge" indicator bulb.

This condition is not caused by a low charging rate but, by the alternator charging at near maximum capacity, with alternator voltage output in excess of battery voltage. This causes a voltage potential difference across the indicator lamp termi-

nals, resulting in a dim bulb glow.

This condition can be checked by thoroughly testing the charging system. If all systems are satisfactory, the indicator lamp should be removed and a filter (GM part No. 25076102) installed over the bulb. The bulb should then be reinstalled.

UNDERCHARGED BATTERY

1. Disconnect battery ground cable.
2. Disconnect wire at "BAT" terminal of alternator, connect ammeter, positive lead to "BAT" terminal and negative lead to wire.
3. Connect battery ground cable.
4. Turn on all accessories, then connect a carbon pile regulator across battery.
5. Operate engine at moderate speed, adjust carbon pile regulator to obtain maximum current output.

Fig. 1 Delcotron type 10 SI alternator (typical)

Fig. 2 Cross-sectional view of 10 SI alternator

Fig. 3 Delcotron type 12 SI alternator

Fig. 4 Delcotron type 15 SI alternator

Fig. 5 Delcotron type 27 SI alternator

6. If ammeter reading is within 10 amps of rated output, alternator is not at fault.

NOTE: Alternator rated output is stamped on alternator frame.

7. If ammeter reading is not within 10 amps of rated output, ground field winding by inserting screwdriver in end frame hole, contacting tab, **Fig. 8.**

NOTE: Do not insert screwdriver deeper than one inch since tab is usually located within ¾ inch of casing surface.

8. If reading is within 10 amps of rated output, regulator must be replaced. If reading is not within limits, check field winding, diode trio, rectifier bridge and stator.
9. Turn off all accessories and disconnect ammeter and carbon pile regulator.

OVERCHARGING BATTERY

1. Remove alternator from vehicle and separate end frames as outlined under "Alternator Disassembly."
2. Check field winding, if shorted replace rotor and regulator.
3. Connect ohmmeter from brush clip to end frame, set meter on low scale and note reading. **Fig. 9.**
4. Reverse leads, if both readings are zero remove screw from brush clip and inspect sleeve and insulator.
5. If sleeve and insulator are in good condition, then regulator is at fault and must be replaced.

ALTERNATOR DISASSEMBLY

NOTE: When pressing bearings or seals from end frames, support frames from inside.

1. Scribe mark across end frames and stator ring so parts can be installed in same position.
2. Remove four through bolts, then using screw driver in stator slot pry end frames apart. **Fig. 10.**

NOTE: Brushes may fall from holders and become contaminated with bearing grease, if so they must be cleaned prior to assembly.

3. Place tape over slip ring end frame bearing and shaft at slip ring end.
4. Remove nut, washer, pulley, fan and collar from rotor shaft, then slide drive end frame from shaft.
5. Remove bearing, retainer and seal from drive and frame.
6. Remove stator lead attaching nuts, then pry stator from slip ring end frame.

Fig. 6 Sectional view of Delcotron type SI alternator (typical)

Fig. 7 Typical Wiring diagram of charging circuit. 1980–85 G.M. vehicles

Fig. 8 Grounding field windings

7. Remove capacitor, diode trio, rectifier bridge and battery terminal stud.

NOTE: On diesel engine alternators equipped with R terminal for tachometer, the R terminal nut and jumper strap must be removed, before removing the rectifier bridge and battery terminal.

8. Remove resistor (if equipped), brush holder and regulator.
9. Remove bearing and seal from slip ring end frame.

BENCH TESTS
ROTOR & SLIP RING TEST

NOTE: Ohmmeter must be at low scale setting during this test.

1. Inspect rotor for wear or damage.
2. Touch ohmmeter leads to slip rings, **Fig. 11.**
3. If no reading is obtained an open circuit exists in windings.
4. If reading below 2.4 ohms on G.M., or 2.2 ohms on A.M.C. vehicles, is obtained, winding is shorted.
5. If a reading above 3 ohms, or 3.5 ohms on 1982–85 G.M. vehicles, is obtained, excessive resistance exists in windings.
6. Connect one ohmmeter lead to rotor shaft and touch slip rings with other lead, if any reading is obtained there is a ground in the circuit, **Fig. 11.**

NOTE: If any of the above problems are present the rotor assembly must be replaced.

STATOR WINDING TEST

1. Inspect stator for discolored windings, loose connections and damage.
2. Connect an ohmmeter from stator lead to frame, if any reading is obtained windings are grounded, **Fig. 12.**
3. On 10 SI and 12 SI units, connect ohmmeter between stator leads, if reading is high when connected between each pair of leads, an open circuit exists in windings. The stator windings on 15 SI and 27 SI units cannot be checked for open circuits.

NOTE: Shorted windings are difficult to locate without special equipment. If other tests indicate normal, but rated alternator output cannot be obtained the windings are probably shorted.

DIODE TRIO

1. With diode unit removed, connect an ohmmeter to the single connector and to one of the three connectors, **Fig. 13.**
2. Observe the reading. Reverse ohmmeter leads.

Fig. 9   Testing brush clip

3. Reading should be high with one connection and low with the other. If both readings are the same, unit must be replaced.
4. Repeat between the single connector and each of the three connectors.

NOTE: There are two diode units differing in appearance. These are completely interchangeable.

The diode unit can be checked for a grounded brush lead while still installed in the end frame by connecting an ohmmeter from the brush lead clip to the end frame as in Steps 1 and 2 above. If both readings are zero, check for a grounded brush or brush lead.

RECTIFIER BRIDGE TEST

1. Connect a suitable ohmmeter between grounded heat sink and one of the three flat metal clips surrounding the studs, **Fig. 14.**
2. Observe the reading then reverse leads.
3. Reading should be high with one connection and low with the other. If both readings are the same, unit must be replaced.
4. Repeat test for each of the other terminals.
5. Repeat entire test between insulated heat sink and three flat metal clips surrounding the studs.

VOLTAGE REGULATOR/ BRUSH LEAD TEST

Connect an ohmmeter from the brush lead clip to the end frame, note reading, then reverse connections. If both readings are zero, either the brush lead clip is grounded or the regulator is defective.

ALTERNATOR ASSEMBLY

NOTE: When pressing bearings or seals, end frames must be supported from inside.

1. Lightly lubricate seal and position on slip ring end frame with lip facing toward rotor. **Fig. 10.**
2. Press seal part way into housing.
3. On 10 S, 12 SI and 27 SI units, position bearing and end plug on slip ring end frame, press bearing and plug in until flush with end frame. On 15 SI units, refer to **Fig. 15,** when installing slip ring end frame bearing.
4. Place regulator in end frame, install brushes and springs in brush holder, use pin to hold brushes in compressed position.

NOTE: Insulating washers are installed under two of the attaching screws, **Fig. 16.**

Regulator

Brush unit

Insulating washer

Terminal assembly

Spring

Brush assembly

Ring end seal

Roller bearing

Through bolt

Slip ring end frame

Diode

Capacitor bracket

Rotor

Stator

Diode bridge

Capacitor

Drive end frame

Fan

Pulley

Pulley nut

Plate assembly

Bearing spacer

Washer

Roller bearing

Bearing spacer

Wave washer

Fig. 10   Alternator disassembled

Fig. 11   Testing rotor & slip rings

Fig. 12   Testing stator winding

Fig. 13   Testing diode trio

Fig. 14 Testing rectifier bridge diodes

Fig. 15 Installing slip ring end frame bearing. 10 SI, 12 SI & 15 SI units

5. Install rectifier bridge and battery terminal stud.
6. On diesel engine alternators equipped with R terminal for tachometer, install plastic insulating washer on R terminal stud, then position terminal stud into end frame. Install fiber insulating washer, jumper strap and nut on R terminal stud. Position jumper strap on rectifier bridge, then tighten R terminal stud.
7. Install diode trio, ensure current only flows one way through single connector.
8. Install capacitor.

NOTE: On 15 SI units, the capacitor lead uses a push clip connector to attach to the rectifier bridge instead of a screw, **Fig. 17.**

9. Install stator, check the three leads for continuity, ensure stator is not grounded against case or holder.
10. On 1980–82 10 SI and 27 SI units, position slinger on drive end frame, then press ball bearing into end frame, **Fig. 18.** On 1980–82 and early production 1983–85 15 SI and 27 SI units, refer to **Fig. 19,** when installing drive end bearing. On late production 1983–85 15 SI and 27 SI units and all 1983–85 10 SI and 12 SI units, refer to **Fig. 20.**
11. Fill seal cavity ¼ full with special alternator lubricant, then install retainer.
12. Install rotor in drive end frame, then install collar, fan, pulley, washer and nut.
13. Align scribe marks on end frames and stator plate, install through bolts and remove brush retaining pins.

Fig. 16 Brush holder & regulator installation

Fig. 17 Slip ring end frame. 15 SI units

Fig. 18 Drive end frame bearing & slinger installed. 1980–82 10 SI & 27 SI units

Fig. 19 Drive end frame bearing. 1980–82 15 SI & 1983–85 early production 15 SI & 27 SI units

Fig. 20 Drive end frame bearing. 1983–85 10 SI & 12 SI & late production 15 SI & 27 SI

Hitachi LR155-12B Alternator

INDEX

DESCRIPTION

This alternator is a solid state unit which incorporates an integral regulator. A vacuum pump is attached to the rear cover and is driven off the alternator shaft.

ALTERNATOR
DISASSEMBLE

1. Scribe reference marks on front and rear covers, **Fig. 1,** for use during reassembly.
2. Remove bolts securing vacuum pump. Holding the center plate, remove pump in direction in line with rotor shaft, **Fig. 1.**
3. Remove brush cover, then remove the screws securing the brushes and remove.
4. Remove through bolts, and carefully separate the alternator body into front and rear sections. Ensure the stator coils remain with the rear section.

NOTE: When separating sections care must be taken not to damage the oil seal in the rear section. Taping the vacuum pump drive splines will provide some protection.

5. Clamp the rotor assembly in a suitable vise, then remove the pulley nut, pulley, front cover and rotor.
6. Remove front cover bearing retainer screws, then remove the bearing.
7. Remove nuts securing "B" terminal and diode holder, then remove the screw inside the stator.

NOTE: Use care to note the position of any insulating washers to ensure correct installation.

8. Using long-nose pliers as a heatsink, separate diodes from the stator by melting away solder on stator coils, diodes and "L" terminal leads.
9. Unsolder connections on IC regulator holder plate terminal, and remove regulator.
10. Inspect all parts for wear or abnormal damage and replace or repair as necessary.

BENCH TESTS
ROTOR & SLIP RING TEST

1. Visually inspect slip rings for contamination or roughness. If rings are roughened, dress with fine sandpaper.

If rings are contaminated, they may be cleaned with an alcohol saturated cloth.
2. Measure outside diameter of rings. Minimum diameter is 1.181 inches.
3. Check resistance of rotor coil across slip rings, **Fig. 2.** Ohmmeter should read 4.2 ohms at 68 degrees F.
4. Check for continuity across slip ring and rotor core or shaft, **Fig. 3.** If continuity exists, replace parts as necessary.
5. Check front and rear ball bearings for binding or abnormal noise and replace as necessary.

STATOR WINDING TEST

1. Check for continuity across stator coils, **Fig. 4.** If there is no continuity, replace coils.
2. Measure resistance across coil and terminal N. Ohmmeter should read .05 ohms at 68 degrees F.
3. Check for continuity across one of the stator coils and stator core, **Fig. 5.** If continuity exists, replace coil.

BRUSHES, INSPECT

Measure length of brushes. Standard brush length is .787 inch and minimum

Fig. 2 Testing rotor & slip rings for open circuit

Fig. 3 Testing rotor & slip rings for grounds

Disassembly order

1. Vacuum pump
2. Cover
3. Brush
4. Through bolt
5. Pulley assembly
6. Pulley nut
7. Pulley
8. Fan
9. Rotor assembly
10. Spacer
11. Ball bearing
12. Rotor
13. Front cover assembly

14. Front cover
15. Ball bearing
16. Bearing retainer
17. Screw
18. Terminal bolt and nut
19. Condenser
20. Rear cover
21. Stator
22. Diode
23. Holder plate
24. Brush holder
25. IC regulator assembly
26. Lead wire

▲ See disassembly procedures for details.

Fig. 1 Hitachi LR155-12B alternator

length is .551 inch. Brushes are marked with a line to indicate wear limit.

DIODE TEST

1. Check for continuity across terminals, **Fig. 6**. If continuity exists, diode is satisfactory. If there is no continuity, replace diode.
2. Check for continuity with polarities reversed. If there is no continuity, diode is satisfactory. If there is continuity at any point, replace diode.

NOTE: Auxiliary diodes are not provided with terminal and a continuity test should be made across terminals of conventional diodes.

REGULATOR TEST

NOTE: To perform regulator tests, the following measuring instruments will be needed: resistor (10 ohms, 3 watts). . . . R1, variable resistor (0–300 ohms, 3 watts). . . . Rv, battery (12 volts, 2 pieces). . . . BAT1, BAT2, DC voltmeter (0–30 volts).

1. Connect instruments as shown in **Fig. 7.**
2. Measure voltage at BAT1 (V1). Voltmeter reading should be 10–13 volts.
3. Measure voltage between terminals F and E (V2). Voltmeter reading should be approximately 2 volts.
4. Measure voltage between BAT1 and BAT2 (V3) with terminal S disconnected. Voltmeter reading should be 20–26 volts.
5. Measure voltage between terminals E and F while varying resistance gradually with variable resistor. Voltage should increase from 2 volts to 10–13 volts without any interruption. If voltage increase is interrupted, replace regulator.

U.V.W. INDICATES STATOR COIL LEAD TERMINALS

Fig. 4 Testing stator coils for open circuit

Fig. 5 Testing stator coils for grounds

Fig. 6 Testing diodes

Fig. 7   Testing IC regulator

Fig. 8   Testing IC regulator

Fig. 9   Replacing vacuum pump oil seal

6. Measure voltage between intermediate tap on variable resistor and terminal E (V4) without actuating variable resistor. Voltmeter should read 14.0–14.6 volts, or regulator must be replaced.
7. Connect instruments as shown in **Fig. 8.**
8. Measure voltage between terminals B and E while gradually increasing voltage with variable resistor. Voltage should increase from approximately 2 volts to 10–13 volts. If voltage does not vary, replace regulator.
9. Check voltage between intermediate tap of variable resistor and terminal E without actuating variable resistor. Voltmeter should read 14.5–16.6 volts, or regulator must be replaced.

VACUUM PUMP, INSPECT

1. Measure length of vanes. Vanes should measure .511–.531 inch, or must be replaced.
2. Measure inside diameter of pump

housing. Diameter should be 2.2440–2.2441 inches.
3. Apply light pressure to check valve with a screwdriver and ensure smooth operation of valve.
4. Inspect inner face of rear cover for signs of oil leakage and inspect oil seal for excessive wear or damage.
5. If rear seal requires replacement, remove old seal from rear cover side with a screwdriver and install new seal with seal installer, **Fig. 9.**

ALTERNATOR
ASSEMBLE

1. Solder the IC regulator wires to the IC regulator, **Fig. 1.**
2. Using long-nose pliers as a heatsink and working as quickly as possible,

solder stator coil leads and diode leads.
3. Clamp the rotor in a suitable vise, install front cover, pulley and pulley nut.
4. Install rear cover over rotor, remove tape on splines. Insert and tighten through bolts.
5. Install brushes into brush holder, and install brush cover.
6. Install vacuum pump. Torque bolts to 4–5 ft. lbs. If necessary, pour approximately 5 cc of engine oil into the vacuum pump filler port.

Nippondenso Alternator

INDEX

DESCRIPTION

This alternator has an IC integral solid state regulator. All regulator components are enclosed into a solid mold and are attached to the slip ring end frame along with the brush holder assembly. The alternator voltage setting cannot be adjusted.

The alternator rotor bearing contain enough grease to eliminate the need for periodic lubrication. Two brushes carry current through the two slip rings to the field coil mounted on the rotor.

The stator windings are assembled on the inside of a laminated core that form part of the alternator frame. The rectifier bridge contains six diodes which electrically change stator A.C. voltage into D.C. voltage. The neutral diodes serve to con-

vert the voltage fluctuation at the neutral point to direct current for increasing generator output.

IN-VEHICLE TESTING

1. Connect suitable ammeter and voltmeter as follows:
   a. Disconnect wire from "B" terminal of alternator, then connect ammeter negative probe to the wire.
   b. Connect ammeter positive probe to "B" terminal of alternator.
   c. Connect voltmeter positive probe to "B" terminal of alternator and the negative probe to ground.
2. Start engine and allow to run at 2,000 RPM, then check reading of ammeter and voltmeter. Ammeter should read

less than 10 amps. Voltmeter should read 13.9–15.1 volts at 77° F.
3. If voltage reading is greater than specified voltage, replace IC regulator. If voltage reading is less than specified voltage, check the IC regulator and alternator as follows:
   a. With engine running and "F" terminal grounded, check voltage reading at "B" terminal.
   b. If voltage reading is greater than specified voltage, replace IC regulator. If voltage reading is less than specified voltage, check alternator.
4. With engine running at 2,000 RPM, turn on high beam headlights and place heater fan control switch in the "HI" position.
5. Check ammeter reading. If reading is less than 30 amps, repair alternator.

Fig. 1   Nippondenso alternator

Fig. 2   Pulley nut removal

Less than 3 Ω

Fig. 3   Checking rotor for open circuit

No Continuity

Fig. 4   Checking for grounded rotor

SERVICE
Disassembly

1. Remove terminal insulator nut, then the terminal insulator, **Fig. 1.**
2. Remove end cover attaching nuts, then the end cover.
3. Remove five screws, brush holder and IC regulator.
4. Remove four rectifier holder attaching screws, then the rubber insulators.
5. Remove pulley using tool No. J-35452

and a suitable breaker bar as shown, **Fig. 2.**

INSPECTION & REPAIR
Rotor Assembly

1. Inspect rotor for open circuit using a suitable ohmmeter, by checking for continuity between slip rings, **Fig. 3.** If no continuity exists, replace rotor.
2. Check for continuity between slip rings and rotor, **Fig. 4.** If continuity exists,

replace rotor.
3. Inspect rotor for rough or scored surface and replace as necessary.

Stator Assembly

1. Inspect stator for open circuit using a suitable ohmmeter, by checking leads of open circuit, **Fig. 5.** If no continuity exists, replace drive end assembly
2. Check for continuity between coil leads and drive end frame, **Fig. 6.** If no continuity exists, replace drive end

Fig. 5   Checking stator for open circuit

Fig. 6   Checking stator for grounded circuit

10.5mm (0.413 in.)

Fig. 7   Brush replacement

frame assembly

Brush & Brush Holder

1. Check brush length. If brush length is less than .177 inch, replace as follows:
   a. Unsolder and remove brush and spring assembly.
   b. Place brush wire through spring, then insert brush holder.
   c. Solder wire to brush holder, **Fig. 7**, then ensure freedom of movement of new brush.

d. Remove excess wire.

Bearings

1. Inspect for rough or worn bearings and replace as necessary.
2. If front bearing is to be replaced, remove four bearing retainer attaching screws, then the bearing retainer. Install new bearing, then reinstall bearing retainer.
3. If rear bearing is to be replaced, remove bearing and cover from rotor shaft using suitable pullers. Install new rear bear and bearing cover onto rotor shaft using suitable puller.

ASSEMBLY

Reverse disassembly procedures to assembly, noting the following:
1. Install pulley onto rotor shaft, then finger tighten pulley nut.
2. Hold tool No. J-35452 with a suitable breaker bar, then torque nut counterclockwise to 69–94 ft. lbs.

ENGINE COOLING FANS

TABLE OF CONTENTS

Variable Speed Fans

INDEX

DESCRIPTION

The fan drive clutch, **Fig. 1,** is a fluid coupling containing silicone oil. Fan speed is regulated by the torque-carrying capacity of the silicone oil. The more silicone oil in the coupling the greater the fan speed, and the less silicone oil the slower the fan speed.

Two types of fan drive clutches are in use. On one, **Fig. 2,** a bi-metallic strip and control piston on the front of the fluid coupling regulates the amount of silicone oil entering the coupling. The bi-metallic strip bows outward with an increase in surrounding temperature and allows a piston to move outward. The piston opens a valve regulating the flow of silicone oil into the coupling from a reserve chamber. The silicone oil is returned to the reserve chamber through a bleed hole when the valve is closed.

On the other type of fan drive clutch, **Fig. 3,** a heat-sensitive, bi-metal spring connected to an opening plate brings about a similar result. Both units cause the fan speed to increase with a rise in tempera-ture and to decrease as the temperature goes down.

In some cases a Flex-Fan is used instead of a Fan Drive Clutch. Flexible blades vary the volume of air being drawn through the radiator, automatically increasing the pitch at low engine speeds.

FAN DRIVE CLUTCH TEST

CAUTION: Do not operate the engine until the fan has been first checked for possible cracks and separations.

Run the engine at a fast idle speed (1000 RPM) until normal operating temperature is reached. This process can be speeded up by blocking off the front of the radiator with cardboard. Regardless of temperatures, the unit must be operated for at least five minutes immediately before being tested.

Stop the engine and, using a glove or a cloth to protect the hand, immediately check the effort required to turn the fan. If considerable effort is required, it can be assumed that the coupling is operating satisfactorily. If very little effort is required to turn the fan, it is an indication that the coupling is not operating properly and should be replaced.

If the clutch fan is the coiled bi-metal spring type, it may be tested while the vehicle is being driven. To check, disconnect the bi-metal spring, **Fig. 4,** and rotate 90° counterclockwise. This disables the temperature-controlled free-wheeling feature and the clutch performs like a conventional fan. If this cures the overheating condition, replace the clutch fan.

SERVICE PROCEDURE

CAUTION: To prevent silicone fluid from draining into fan drive bearing, do not store or place drive unit on bench with rear of shaft pointing downward.

The removal procedure for either type of fan clutch assembly is generally the same for all cars. Merely unfasten the unit from

Fig. 1   Typical variable-speed fan installed

Fig. 2   Variable-speed fan with flat bi-metal thermostatic spring

27-1

Fig. 3   Variable-speed fan with coiled bi-metal thermostatic spring

Fig. 4   Disconnecting bi-metal spring

the water pump and remove the assembly from the car.

The type of unit shown in **Fig. 2** may be partially disassembled for inspection and cleaning. Take off the capscrews that hold the assembly together and separate the fan from the drive clutch. Next remove the metal strip on the front by pushing one end of it toward the fan clutch body so it clears the retaining bracket. Then push the strip to the side so that its opposite end will spring out of place. Now remove the small control piston underneath it.

Check the piston for free movement of the coupling device. If the piston sticks, clean it with emery cloth. If the bi-metal strip is damaged, replace the entire unit. These strips are not interchangeable.

When reassembling, install the control piston so that the projection on the end of it will contact the metal strip. Then install the metal strip. After reassembly, clean the clutch drive with a cloth soaked in solvent. Avoid dipping the clutch assembly in any type of liquid. Install the assembly in the reverse order of removal.

The coil spring type of fan clutch cannot be disassembled, serviced or repaired. If it does not function properly it must be replaced with a new unit.

Chrysler Corp. Electric Cooling Fans

INDEX

CAUTION: On models equipped with electric engine cooling fans, the battery ground cable should be disconnected whenever underhood service is performed.

Fig. 1   Electric engine cooling fan (typical)

DESCRIPTION

On all models except 1985 equipped with 4-135 engine, the fan is controlled by a fan switch which is located on the radiator, **Fig. 1,** The switch will automatically turn on when coolant temperature reaches 193 to 207 degrees F. On models with A/C, when the A/C system is in operation, the fan motor will operate continually regardless of engine coolant temperature. When the ignition switch is turned off the fan motor will stop operating, except on 1981–82 models equipped with 2.6 L engine and air conditioning. On 1981–82 models equipped with 2.6 L engines and air conditioning, the fan will remain operating with ignition off for approximately 5 minutes if ambient temperature at radiator is above a predetermined level.

On 1985 models equipped with 4-135 engine, the fan is controlled by the on-board computer. The computer shuts off the fan motor automatically when it is not needed on vehicles less air conditioning, or when the A/C is shut off on vehicles with air conditioning. The fan motor is always on when the air conditioning compressor is running. With A/C off or on models less A/C, the fan runs with vehicle speed above 40 mph only if coolant temperature reaches 230°F and will turn off when temperature drops to 220°F. At speeds below 40 mph, the fan switches on at 210°F. and off at 200°F. The fan motor does not operate when the ignition is turned off.

RADIATOR FAN SWITCH

The radiator fan switch is located on left hand radiator tank. The switch is normally open and incorporates a bimetal disc which pushes the plunger when coolant temperature reaches approximately 200 degrees F. If the fan motor turns on and off at the appropriate temperature, the switch is operating properly.

To check switch continuity, drain coolant until level is below switch. The switch can be viewed by looking downward through the radiator filler neck. Disconnect electrical connector from switch and remove switch from radiator. Dip switch into an oil bath which has achieved a temperature of 208 degrees F or higher and check switch for continuity using a test lamp or ohmmeter. If continuity is not indicated, replace switch.

AMBIENT TEMPERATURE SWITCH

The ambient temperature switch is used on air conditioned 1981–82 2.6 L engines only. The switch is located on the radiator cooling fan mounting bracket and is used in conjunction with the time delay relay to activate the radiator cooling fan for approximately 5 minutes with engine off during periods of radiator ambient temperature of 105° F. or above.

The switch is tested using a suitable ohmmeter. When the switch is cold, continuity should not exist. When the switch is warmed to 105° F. or above, continuity should be present. Replace if defective.

ELECTRIC FAN MOTOR

DIAGNOSIS

Disconnect wire connector from fan motor terminal, then connect a 14 gauge jumper wire from battery to fan motor terminal. If fan motor does not operate properly, replace fan motor.

ENGINE COOLING FANS

FAN MOTOR, REPLACE

1980–82 Models

1. Disconnect wire connectors from fan motor and fan switch, then drain cooling system.
2. Disconnect upper and lower radiator hoses from radiator. On models equipped with automatic transmission, disconnect fluid cooling hoses from radiator, if necessary.
3. Remove upper fan shroud attaching screws, then lift shroud upward and out of bottom shroud retaining clips, separating shroud from radiator.

NOTE: When removing shroud from radiator, use care not to damage fan or radiator cooling fans.

4. Remove fan motor to shroud attaching screws, then while supporting fan motor and shaft, remove fan motor retaining clip and fan motor.
5. Reverse procedure to install.

1983–85 Models

1. Disconnect fan motor electrical connector.
2. Remove fan motor, fan and fan shroud or support as an assembly from radiator support.
3. To remove fan blade from motor, support motor and shaft assembly on work bench, then remove fan blade retaining clip. Use caution to prevent bending motor shaft.

NOTE: Do not allow fan blades to become bent or damaged in any way.

4. Reverse procedure to install.

ELECTRIC FAN MOTOR RELAY

The fan motor relay is used on models equipped with A/C, except for 1985 models with 4-135 engine. The relay is located on the left hand shock absorber housing. If radiator fan switch and fan motor test results are satisfactory, but fan motor will not operate the fan motor relay is then suspected. After replacing relay, disconnect wire connector from radiator fan switch and connect a 14 gauge jumper wire between wire connector terminals. Place ignition switch in the Accessory position. Fan motor should operate.

On 1981–82 models equipped with 2.6 L engines, the electric engine cooling fan relay also contains the time delay, which operates the cooling fan when ignition is off and the radiator ambient temperature is 105° F. or above.

Ford Motor Co. Electric Cooling Fans

INDEX

CAUTION: On models equipped with electric engine cooling fans, the battery ground cable should be disconnected whenever underhood service is performed.

1980 FAIRMONT & ZEPHYR & 1980–81 CAPRI & MUSTANG W/4-140 TURBO ENGINE

DESCRIPTION

Two thermal switches are used to activate the cooling fan motor. When engine temperature reaches 221 degrees F, the coolant temperature switch will close, thus activating the normally open coolant relay which supplies current to the fan motor. After engine has been turned off, extreme underhood temperatures may develop, causing fuel vaporization in the carburetor, which could cause a no start or hard starting condition. When carburetor temperature reaches 155 degrees F, the carburetor switch closes providing battery voltage to the fan motor relay which operates the fan motor. When the carburetor temperature switch closes, it also activates a timer which allows the fan motor to operate for a period of approximately 15 to 20 minutes. On models equipped with A/C, the engine cooling fan will operate whenever the compressor clutch is in operation.

DIAGNOSIS, FIGS. 1 & 2

Fan Motor Check

Disconnect fan motor wire connector, then connect jumper wires between battery and motor connector terminal with brown yellow wire and motor connector terminal with black wire to ground. If motor fails to operate, replace fan motor. If fan motor operates, proceed to next test.

Coolant Relay Check

Disconnect delay relay wire connector, then place ignition switch in the On position and connect a jumper wire from coolant temperature switch to ground. If fan motor operates, replace coolant temperature switch. If motor fails to operate, disconnect coolant relay wire connector and check for battery voltage at connector terminals A and B. If battery voltage is not indicated, trace circuit to ignition switch and battery and repair as necessary. If battery voltage is indicated, check for continuity between coolant relay wire connector terminals C and D, with coolant temperature switch connected to ground. If continuity does not exist, repair circuit. If continuity does exist, replace coolant relay.

Delay Relay Check

Disconnect coolant relay wire connector, then place ignition switch in the On position and connect a jumper wire from carburetor temperature switch to ground. If fan motor operates, replace carburetor temperature switch. If fan motor fails to operate, disconnect delay relay wire connector and check for battery voltage at connector terminals E and F. If battery voltage is not indicated, trace circuits and repair as necessary. If battery voltage is indicated, check for continuity between delay relay connector terminals G and H. If continuity does not exist, trace circuit and repair as necessary. If continuity does exist, replace delay relay.

A/C Relay Check

Disconnect A/C compressor clutch lead and connect a jumper wire from battery to compressor clutch. If compressor clutch does not click, replace clutch. If compressor clutch clicks, disconnect coolant and delay relay wire connectors, then disconnect ambient temperature switch wire connector and connect a jumper wire between ambient temperature switch connector terminals. Place ignition switch in the On position and turn on A/C controls. The fan motor should be operating and the compressor clutch should click. If neither occurs, disconnect A/C relay wire connector and check for battery voltage at connector terminals N, J and K. If battery voltage is not indicated, check circuit and repair as necessary. If A/C fuse continues to blow, check for short in circuit, otherwise replace relay. If when jumper wire was connected between ambient switch wire connector terminals only the fan motor operated or only the A/C clutch clicked, or if neither occurred and battery voltage was indicated at A/C relay terminals N, J and K, check for continuity between A/C relay connector terminals L and M. If continuity does not exist, trace circuit and repair as necessary. If continuity does exist, replace A/C relay.

Fan Will Not Stop Operating

With ignition switch and A/C controls in the off position, disconnect A/C relay wire

Fig. 1 Electric engine cooling fan wiring diagram. 1980 Fairmont, Zephyr & 1980–81 Capri & Mustang less A/C

ENGINE COOLING FANS

connector, then disconnect coolant relay. If fan stops operating, replace relay that was disconnected at time fan stopped operating. If fan continues to operate, connect a jumper wire from carburetor temperature switch to ground and cycle ignition switch on and off. If fan does not stop operating after approximately 20 minutes, replace delay relay.

FAN MOTOR, REPLACE

1. Detach wiring harness retainer from fan shroud, and disconnect fan motor wire connector.
2. Remove four fan shroud and fan motor assembly to radiator attaching screws, then remove shroud and motor assembly.
3. Remove retainer clip from end of fan motor shaft and remove fan blade.
4. Remove three nuts attaching fan motor to shroud, then remove fan motor.
5. Reverse procedure to install.

FORD & MERCURY EXC. 1980 FAIRMONT & ZEPHYR & 1980–81 CAPRI & MUSTANG W/4-140 TURBO ENGINE

DESCRIPTION

Exc. 1985 Continental & Mark VII w/6-146 Diesel Engine

The cooling fan is activated by the thermal switch when engine coolant temperature reaches approximately 210–220 degrees F. The fan will continue to operate until coolant temperature drops to approximately 185 to 193 degrees F, at which time the thermal switch opens, releasing the relay contacts which supply current to the fan motor. On models equipped with A/C, the fan motor will continue to operate whenever the compressor clutch is operating regardless of coolant temperature. On some models, two fuses are used to protect the fan motor and thermal switch. A 16 amp fuse is located in the fan motor relay at the left hand dash panel near the steering column. There is also an 8 amp fuse located in the fuse panel. Cycling of the cooling fan will cause the temperature gauge to read between mid and upper range of the gauge range.

1985 Continental & Mark VII w/6-146 Diesel Engine

These vehicles have an electric pusher fan mounted behind the grill, in addition to the belt driven engine cooling fan attached to the water pump.

The electric cooling fan system consists of a fan and an electric motor mounted on the fan shroud, an ambient temperature switch and a cooling fan relay.

The electric cooling fan is wired to operate only when the A/C compressor is oper-

Fig. 2 Electric engine cooling fan wiring diagram. 1980 Fairmont, Zephyr & 1980–81 Capri & Mustang 4-140 Turbo with A/C

ating and the ambient temperature is above 70°F. The cooling fan relay is energized by power from the A/C blower motor speed controller which then allows battery current to flow to the electric cooling fan. The cooling fan relay is energized only when the A/C compressor clutch field coil is engaged and the ambient temperature switch, located on the hood lock support, is closed. The electric cooling fan will only operate when the ignition switch is in the "Run" position, since the A/C system can only operate when the ignition switch is in "Run".

The A/C clutch field coil is powered through the A/C cutout relay, which is energized to turn off power to the clutch field coil in one of two ways.

With EGR vacuum below 7 inches Hg. and turbo boost pressure below 2 psi the A/C cutout switch and the A/C turbo boost switch are closed, providing a ground to energize the A/C cutout relay. With the

relay energized, the current to the A/C clutch field coil is turned off.

With engine coolant temperature above 233°F., the coolant temperature switch closes, providing the ground to energize the A/C cutout relay.

TROUBLESHOOTING

For troubleshooting procedures on Ford and Mercury models except 1980 Fairmont and Zephyr and 1980–81 Capri and Mustang with 4-140 turbocharged engine, refer to **Fig. 3,** to determine which Electric Engine Cooling Fan system applies to a particular model.

TYPE 1 & 2, FIGS. 4 & 5

1. Check cooling fan fusible link. If fusible link is not blown, go to step 2. If blown, repair and retest.
2. Disconnect fan motor electrical connector, then connect a jumper wire from motor ground connection to a

Year	Engine	Models	With Fuel Economy Package	With Auto. Trans.	With Power Brakes	With Air Conditioning	With High Output Engine	With Fuel Injection	System Type
1981	1.6L	Escort & Lynx	—	—	—	No	—	—	1
	1.6L	Escort & Lynx	—	—	—	Yes	—	—	8
1982	1.6L	Escort, EXP, LN7 & Lynx	—	—	—	No	—	—	1
	1.6L	Escort, EXP, LN7 & Lynx	—	—	No	Yes	—	—	3
	1.6L	Escort, EXP, LN7 & Lynx	—	—	Yes	Yes	—	—	4
	2.3L	Fairmont & Zephyr	Yes	—	—	No	—	—	1
	2.3L	Capri & Mustang	—	—	—	—	—	—	5
	2.3L	Cougar, Fairmont, Granada & Zephyr	No	—	—	Yes	—	—	5
1983	1.6L	Escort, EXP, LN7 & Lynx	No	Yes	—	No	No	No	1
	1.6L	Escort, EXP, LN7 & Lynx	Yes	No	—	No	No	No	2
	1.6L	Escort, EXP, LN7 & Lynx	No	Yes	Yes	Yes	—	No	9
	1.6L	Escort, EXP, LN7 & Lynx	No	No	—	Yes	No	No	11
	1.6L	Escort, EXP, LN7 & Lynx	No	No	—	Yes	Yes	No	13
	1.6L	Escort, EXP, LN7 & Lynx	No	—	—	Yes	No	Yes	10
	2.3L	All	Yes	—	—	No	—	—	2
	2.3L	All	No	—	—	No	—	—	1
	2.3L, 3.3L	All	No	—	—	Yes	—	—	6
	3.8L	Exc. Capri & Mustang	No	—	—	Yes	—	—	6
	3.8L	Capri & Mustang	No	—	—	Yes	—	—	5
1984	1.6L①	Escort, EXP & Lynx	—	No	—	Yes	No	No	14
	1.6L①	Escort, EXP & Lynx	—	No	—	Yes	Yes	No	15
	1.6L①	Escort, EXP & Lynx	—	Yes	—	Yes	No	No	17
	1.6L①	Escort, EXP & Lynx	—	—	—	Yes	No	Yes	18
	1.6L①	Escort, EXP & Lynx	—	—	—	No	No	No	26
	1.6L②	Escort, EXP & Lynx	—	—	—	Yes	Yes	Yes	20
	2.0L③	Escort, EXP, Lynx, Tempo & Topaz	—	—	—	Yes	—	Yes	19
	2.3L①	Exc. Tempo & Topaz	—	—	—	Yes	—	—	7
	2.3L②	Exc. Tempo & Topaz	—	—	—	Yes	Yes	Yes	5
	—	Tempo & Topaz	—	—	—	—	—	—	25
	2.3L	Tempo & Topaz	Yes	—	—	—	No	—	2
	2.3L	Tempo & Topaz	No	—	—	—	Yes	—	12
1985	1.6L	Escort, EXP & Lynx	Yes	No	—	Yes	No	—	14
	1.6L	Escort, EXP & Lynx	No	No	—	Yes	Yes	—	16
	1.6L	Escort, EXP & Lynx	—	Yes	—	Yes	—	No	21
	1.6L	Escort, EXP & Lynx	—	—	—	Yes	—	Yes	22
	1.6L	Escort, EXP & Lynx	—	—	—	No	—	—	26
	2.0L③	Escort, EXP, Lynx, Tempo & Topaz	—	—	—	Yes	—	Yes	23
	2.3L	Tempo & Topaz	—	—	—	Yes	—	—	24
	2.3L	Tempo & Topaz	—	—	—	No	—	—	27
	2.3L	Exc. Tempo & Topaz	—	—	—	—	—	—	28
	2.4L③	Continental & Mark VII	—	—	—	Yes	—	Yes	29

①—Exc. Turbocharged.   ②—Turbocharged.   ③—Diesel.

Fig. 3   Electric engine cooling fan system application chart

known good ground and a jumper wire from battery positive to motor B+ connection. If motor does not run, replace motor. If motor runs, reconnect electrical connector and proceed to step 3.
3. On type 2 systems, turn ignition "On." On both systems disconnect coolant temperature switch connector, then connect a jumper wire from connector to ground. If motor runs, check switch ground. If ground is satisfactory, re-

place coolant temperature switch. If motor does not run, proceed to step 4.
4. Using an ohmmeter, check continuity of wire 197 from temperature switch to fan relay. If no continuity exists, check circuit 197 for opens. If continuity exists, connect a jumper wire from coolant temperature switch connector to ground and proceed to step 5.
5. Disconnect fan relay wire connector

then, connect a jumper wire from wire terminal 37 to 228. If motor runs, replace fan relay. If motor does not run, check circuit 37 for opens.
TYPE 3, FIG. 6
1. Check cooling fan fusible link. If fusible link is not blown, go to step 2. If blown, repair and retest.
2. Disconnect coolant temperature switch connector, then connect a jumper wire from connector to ground

COOLING FAN
COOLANT FAN RELAY
228
N.O.
BATTERY
FUSIBLE LINK (IN 14401 HARNESS)
37
37
COOLANT TEMPERATURE SWITCH
197

COLOR CODES

CIRCUIT NUMBER	COLOR
37	Y
197	T/O HASH
228	BR/Y

Fig. 4 Electric engine cooling fan wiring diagram. Type 1

and turn ignition "On." If fan motor does not run, proceed to step 3. If fan motor does run, primary system is operating satisfactory. If complaint is overheating, replace coolant temperature switch.

3. Reconnnect coolant temperature switch connector. Set A/C controls on maximum and turn ignition "On." If fan motor does not run, proceed to step 4. If fan motor runs, system is satisfactory.

4. Disconnect fan motor electrical connector, then connect a jumper wire from motor ground connection to a known good ground and a jumper wire from battery positive to motor B+ connection, **Fig. 7** If motor does not run, replace motor. If motor runs, reconnect electrical connection and proceed to step 5.

5. Disconnect cooling fan relay connector and turn ignition "On." Using a test light, check for voltage at terminals 37 and 354, **Fig. 8.** If there is no voltage at one or both terminals, service relay feed circuits. If voltage at both terminals, proceed to step 6.

6. Connect jumper wire between terminals 354 and 228, **Fig. 8.** If fan motor does not run, repair wiring from relay connector to motor connector. If motor runs, disconnect jumper wire and proceed to step 7.

7. Using an ohmmeter, check continuity of wire 228 from relay connector to coolant temperature switch connector. If no continuity exists, repair wires and/or connectors. If continuity exists, replace cooling fan relay and recheck step 2.

8. Disconnect A/C relay connector. Using an ohmmeter, check continuity of wire 228 from relay to motor. If no continuity exists, repair wires and/or connectors. If continuity exists, proceed to step 9.

9. Reconnect fan motor connector, then disconnect A/C relay connector. Set A/C controls on maximum and turn ignition "On." Using a test light, check for voltage at terminals 37 and 321, **Fig. 9.** If there is no voltage at one or

both terminals, service relay feed circuits or A/C control and recheck step 3. If there is voltage at both terminals, go to step 10.

10. Connect jumper wire to base of relay and connect to known good ground. If fan motor does not run, replace relay and recheck step 3. If fan motor runs, clean relay ground.

TYPE 4, FIG. 10

1. Check cooling fan fuse and fusible link. If fuse or fusible link is not blown, proceed to step 2. If fuse or fusible link is blown, repair or replace as necessary and retest.

2. Disconnect coolant temperature switch connector, then connect a jumper wire from connector to ground and turn ignition "On." If fan motor does not run, proceed to step 5. If fan motor runs, primary system is operating satisfactory. If complaint is overheating, replace coolant temperature switch.

3. Reconnect coolant temperature switch connector. Set A/C controls on maximum and turn ignition "On." If fan motor does not run, proceed to step 10. If fan motor does run, secondary system is operating satisfactorily, except possibly the coolant temperature switch. If complaint is overheating, proceed to step 4.

4. Using an ohmmeter, check coolant temperature switch body to thermostat housing for continuity. If no continuity exists, tighten switch until continuity exists. Start engine and allow to warm up thoroughly. If fan motor runs, system is satisfactory. If fan motor does not run, replace coolant temperature switch.

COOLING FAN
228
COOLANT FAN RELAY
37
37
N.O.
FUSIBLE LINK (IN 14401 HARNESS)
COOLANT TEMPERATURE SWITCH
197

COLOR CODES

CIRCUIT NUMBER	COLOR
37	Y
197	T/O HASH
228	BR/Y

Fig. 5 Electric engine cooling fan wiring diagram. Type 2

5. Disconnect cooling fan motor connector, then connect a jumper wire from motor ground connection to a known good ground and a jumper wire from battery positive to motor B+ connection, **Fig. 7.** If fan motor does not run, replace motor. If fan motor runs, proceed to step 6.

6. Using an ohmmeter, check fan motor ground. If continuity exists, proceed to step 7. If continuity does not exist, repair ground.

7. Remove jumper wires, then reconnect fan motor connector. Disconnect cooling fan relay connector and switch ignition "On." Using a test light, check for voltage at terminals 37 and 354, **Fig. 11.** If there is no voltage at one or both terminals, repair relay feed circuits. If there is voltage at both termi-

COLOR CODE

CIRCUIT NO.	COLOR	CIRCUIT NO.	COLOR
37	Y	197	T/O HASH
198	T/Y DOT	175	B/Y DOT
228	B/Y	330	Y/LG
E321	G/W	640	R/YHASH
57	B	347	B/YHASH
354	LG/Y		

NOTE:
CIRCUIT SHOWN IN NORMAL VEHICLE RUN MODE, WITH A/C OFF & COOLANT TEMP. SWITCH OPEN

Fig. 6 Electric engine cooling fan wiring diagram. Type 3

POSITIVE

CONNECTOR
AT BACK OF
MOTOR

Fig. 7 Fan motor terminal identification

Fig. 8 Cooling fan relay wire connector terminal identification. Exc. type 4 & 8

Fig. 9 A/C relay wire connector terminal identification

nals, proceed to step 8.

8. Jump terminals 37 to 228 of cooling fan relay connector, **Fig. 11.** If fan motor does not run, repair wiring from relay connector to fan motor connector. (Check capacitor, if equipped.) If fan motor runs, proceed to step 9.

9. Remove jumper wires. Using an ohmmeter, check continuity of wire 354 from relay connector to coolant temperature switch connector, **Fig. 11.** If continuity does not exist, repair wires and/or connectors. If continuity does exist, replace cooling fan relay and retest.

10. Disconnect A/C relay connector. Using an ohmmeter, check continuity of wire 228 from relay to motor. If continuity does not exist, repair wires and/or connectors. If continuity does exist, proceed to step 11.

11. Reconnect fan motor connector, then disconnect A/C relay connector. Set A/C controls on maximum and turn ignition "On." Using a test light, check for voltage at terminals 37 and 321, **Fig. 9.** If there is no voltage at terminal 37, repair relay connector feed circuit. If there is no voltage at terminal 321, proceed to step 13. If there is voltage at both terminals, proceed to step 12.

12. Reconnect A/C relay connector. Connect jumper wire to base of relay to a known good ground. If fan motor does not run, replace relay and retest step 4. If fan motor runs, clean relay ground.

13. Using a test light, test for voltage at circuit 296 of A/C function control harness. If voltage exists, proceed to step 14. If no voltage exists, repair feed wire from fuse box.

14. Using an ohmmeter, check continuity of terminals 296 to 321 in A/C function control. Continuity should only exist in the following positions: A/C Max., A/C

Norm. and Defrost. If continuity is not satisfactory, replace A/C function control. If continuity is satisfactory, proceed to step 15.

15. Using an ohmmeter, check continuity of circuit 321 from A/C function control to A/C relay. If continuity does not exist, repair wiring and/or connectors. If continuity does exist, repeat step 11.

TYPE 5, 6 & 7, FIGS. 12, 13 & 14

Fan Motor Inoperative

1. Check cooling fan fuses and fusible link. If fuses or fusible link are not blown, proceed to step 2. If fuses or fusible link are blown, repair or replace as necessary, and retest.

2. Disconnect fan motor electrical connector, then connect a jumper wire from motor ground connection to a known good ground and a jumper wire from battery positive to motor B+ connection. If motor does not run, replace motor. If motor runs, reconnect electrical connector and proceed to step 3.

3. Disconnect coolant temperature switch connector, then connect a jumper wire from connector to ground and turn ignition "On." If fan motor does not run, proceed to step 4. If motor does run, check switch ground, and if satisfactory, replace coolant temperature switch.

4. Turn ignition "Off," then remove jumper wire installed in step 3. Using an ohmmeter, check continuity of circuit 45 from cooling fan controller terminal #1 to coolant temperature switch. The controller, **Fig. 15,** is located under instrument panel. If continuity does not exist, check wire circuit 45 for opens. If continuity does exist, jump coolant temperature switch to ground and proceed to step 5.

5. Without disconnecting wiring connector from controller, **Fig. 15,** connect battery positive to circuit 68 at controller (terminal #8). If fan motor runs, check ignition feed circuits for opens.

Fig. 10 Electric engine cooling fan wiring diagram. Type 4

NOTE: ① TIMER RELAY TURNS OFF A/C FOR 3-5 SEC. EACH TIME IT IS PULSED BY STOPLAMP SWITCH, COOLANT FAN REMAINS ON.
② CIRCUIT SHOWN IN NORMAL VEHICLE RUN MODE, WITH A/C OFF & COOLENT TEMP. SWITCH OPEN

Fig. 11 Cooling fan relay connector terminal identification. Type 4 & 8

Fig. 12 Electric engine cooling fan wiring diagram. Type 5

If fan motor does not run, remove jumper wire and proceed to step 6.
6. Disconnect cooling fan wiring connector at controller, **Fig. 15.** Using a jumper wire, connect battery positive current to circuit 228 (terminal #5). If fan motor does not run, check circuit 228 for opens. If motor runs, remove jumper and proceed to step 7.
7. Using a jumper wire, connect circuit 175 to 228 (terminals #2 & 5) at the cooling fan motor controller connector. If motor does not run, check circuit 175 for opens. If motor does run, replace cooling fan controller, then remove jumper wire from temperature switch and reconnect connector.

Fan Motor Operates When Engine Overheats, Does Not Operate With A/C On
1. Set A/C controls selector lever in A/C position and turn ignition "On." If A/C clutch does not engage, proceed to step 2. If A/C clutch does engage, proceed to step 7.
2. Check fuse in fuse panel. If blown, replace. If fuse is not blown, proceed to step 3.
3. Disconnect A/C clutch cycle pressure switch. Use a jumper wire to jump

across connector. If A/C clutch does not engage, proceed to step 5. If A/C clutch does engage, proceed to step 4.
4. Check A/C system for low refrigerant charge. If charge is insufficient, leak test, service and charge system. If charge is satisfactory, replace clutch cycling pressure switch.
5. Using a test light, check for voltage on 348 circuit at clutch cycling pressure switch. If there is no voltage, proceed to step 6. If there is voltage, repair open 347 circuit to A/C clutch.
6. Using a test light, test for voltage on 296 and 348 circuits at A/C function selector switch in instrument panel. If there is voltage on 296 but not on 348, replace A/C control assembly. If there is no voltage on 296 circuit, trace circuits 296 and 297 toward ignition switch.
7. Using a test light, check for voltage on 347 or 883 circuit (terminal #6) of cooling fan controller, **Fig. 15.** If there is no voltage, repair open 347 or 883 circuit. If voltage does exist, proceed to step 8.
8. Leaving connector attached to controller, ground 57 circuit (terminal #4) of controller. If fan motor runs, repair

ground circuit. If fan does not run, replace controller.

TYPE 8, FIG. 16
1. Check cooling fan fuses located in the fuse panel and fan motor relay. If fuse is not blown, proceed to step 2. If fuse is blown, replace and retest.
2. Disconnect wire connector at coolant temperature switch, then connect a jumper wire between connector terminal and ground and place ignition switch in the Run position. If fan motor operates, proceed to step 3. If fan motor fails to operate, proceed to step 5.
3. If vehicle is equipped with A/C, proceed to step 4. On models less A/C, the system is operating properly and if overheating has occured, replace coolant temperature switch.
4. Connect wire connector to coolant temperature switch, then place A/C control at Max. A/C and ignition switch in Run position. If fan motor operates, system is satisfactory. If fan motor fails to operate, proceed to step 9.
5. Disconnect wire connector at fan motor, then connect a jumper wire between fan motor positive terminal and battery and fan motor negative

Fig. 13   Electric engine cooling fan wiring diagram. Type 6

terminal and ground, **Fig. 7.** If fan motor operates, proceed to step 6. If fan motor fails to operate, replace fan motor.

6. Disconnect jumper wires and reconnect fan motor wire connector. Disconnect wire connector at fan motor relay, then place ignition switch in the run position and check for voltage at connector terminals 37 and 197, **Fig. 11.** If no voltage is indicated at one or both terminals, trace circuit and repair as necessary. If voltage is indicated at both circuits, proceed to step 7.

7. Connect a jumper wire between relay wire connector terminals 37 and 228, **Fig. 11.** If fan motor operates, proceed to step 8. If fan motor fails to operate, trace circuit from wire connector to motor connector and repair as necessary.

8. Disconnect jumper wire from relay wire connector, then check for continuity of circuit 354 from relay wire connector, **Fig. 11,** to coolant temperature switch wire connector. If continuity exists, replace fan relay and perform step 2. If continuity does not exist, check circuit and repair as necessary.

9. Disconnect wire connector at A/C

relay and check circuit 228 from relay wire connector, **Fig. 11,** to fan motor wire connector. If continuity exists, proceed to step 10. If continuity does not exist, trace circuit and repair as necessary.

10. Connect fan motor relay and disconnect wire connector at A/C relay, then place A/C control on Max. A/C and ignition switch in Run position. Check for voltage at wire connector terminals 37 and 321, **Fig. 9.** If voltage is available at both terminals, proceed to step 11. If voltage is not available at one or both terminals, trace circuit and repair as necessary. If problem is not found in circuit, check A/C control and repair as necessary. Proceed to step 4.

11. Connect a jumper wire from A/C relay base to ground. If fan motor operates, clean relay ground surfaces. If fan motor fails to operate, replace relay and proceed to step 4.

TYPE 9, 10, 11 & 12, FIGS. 17, 18, 19 & 20

1. Check cooling fan fuse and fusible link. If satisfactory, proceed to step 2. If fuse or fusible link is blown, repair or replace as necessary and retest.

2. Bring engine to operating temperature and above while operating A/C to determine when cooling fan does or does not operate. If cooling fan operates during A/C operation only, proceed to step 3. If cooling fan does not operate at any time, proceed to step 13. If cooling fan operates only during high engine temperature, proceed to step 6.

3. Disconnect coolant temperature switch connector, then connect a jumper wire from connector to ground. If fan motor operates, proceed to step 4. If fan motor does not operate, proceed to step 5.

4. Using a suitable ohmmeter, check temperature switch body to thermostat housing continuity. If continuity does not exist (poor ground), tighten switch until continuity exists, then recheck operation. If continuity does exist between switch and thermostat housing, replace temperature switch.

5. Disconnect cooling fan controller connector, then using a suitable ohmmeter, check continuity of 197 circuit from controller to temperature switch. If continuity exists, replace controller. If no continuity exists, service 197 circuit.

Fig. 14 Electric engine cooling fan wiring diagram. Type 7

COLOR CODES	
CIRCUIT NUMBER	COLOR
687	GY/Y
68 AND 302	ORG/BR
687	GY/Y
181	BR/O
348	LG/P
347	BK/Y HASH
57	BK
45	Y/R
228	BR/Y
175	BK/Y DOT
297	BK/LG
296	W/P

6. With engine running, engage A/C clutch. If clutch engages, proceed to step 7. If clutch does not engage, check fuse. If satisfactory, proceed to step 9.

7. Inspect wide open throttle switch to determine position. If switch is open, replace or adjust as necessary. If switch is closed, proceed to step 8.

8. Disconnect cooling fan controller connector, then check for voltage at 354 circuit. If no voltage exists, service 354 circuit as necessary. If voltage exists, replace cooling fan controller.

9. Disconnect cooling fan controller connector, then turn ignition and A/C "On." Check for voltage at 198 circuit. If voltage exists, replace cooling fan controller. If voltage does not exist, proceed to step 10.

10. Disconnect A/C clutch cycling pressure switch, then using a suitable jumper wire, jump across connector. Check again for voltage at 198 circuit. If voltage exists, proceed to step 11. If voltage does not exist, proceed to step 12.

11. Check A/C system for sufficient charge. If charge is sufficient, replace clutch cycling pressure switch.

12. Disconnect A/C control assembly connector, then jump 296 circuit to 321 circuit and check for voltage at 198 and 348 circuits at cooling fan controller connector. If voltage exists at both circuits, replace function selector switch. If voltage exists at 198 circuit only, service 348 circuit.

13. Disconnect fan motor electrical connector, then connect a jumper wire from motor ground connection to a known good ground and a jumper wire from battery positive to motor B+ connection. If fan motor does not run, replace motor. If fan motor runs, proceed to step 14.

14. Remove jumper wire, then reconnect fan motor connector. Disconnect fan motor controller connector. With ignition "On," check for voltage at controller connector 37 and 354 circuits. If voltage exists at both circuits, proceed to step 15. If no voltage exists at one or both circuits, service circuit(s).

15. Using a jumper wire, jump circuit 37 to 228 circuit at cooling fan controller connector. If fan motor runs, replace cooling fan controller. If fan motor does not run, service motor ground.

TYPE 13, FIG. 21

1. Refer to steps 1 through 5 of Type 9, 10, 11 & 12 electric engine cooling fan systems, then continue using the following procedures.

Fig. 15 Cooling fan controller terminal identification. Type 5, 6 & 7

Fig. 16 Electric engine cooling fan wiring circuit. Type 8

2. With engine running, engage A/C clutch. If clutch engages, proceed to step 3. If clutch does not engage, check fuse. If satisfactory, proceed to step 4.
3. Disconnect cooling fan controller connector, then check for voltage at 640 and 37 circuits. If voltage exists at both circuits, replace controller. If voltage does not exist at one or both circuits, service circuits as necessary.
4. Disconnect A/C clutch cycling pressure switch, then using a suitable jumper wire, jump across connector. Check to see if A/C clutch engages. If clutch engages, proceed to step 5. If clutch does not engage, proceed to step 6.
5. Check A/C system for sufficient charge. If charge is insufficient, leak test, repair and recharge system, then retest. If charge is sufficient, replace clutch cycling pressure switch.
6. Disconnect A/C control assembly connector, then jump 296 circuit to 321 circuit and check for voltage at black/yellow wire of clutch connector. If voltage exists, replace function selector switch. If voltage does not exist, service 321, 347 or 348 circuit.
7. Remove jumper wire from A/C clutch cycling pressure switch connector and connect to pressure switch.

TYPE 14, 15 & 16, FIGS. 22, 23 & 24
1. Check fuse and fusible link. If satisfactory, proceed to step 2. If not satisfactory, repair or replace as required.
2. Bring engine to operating temperature while operating A/C to determine when cooling fan does or does not operate. If cooling fan operates only during A/C operation, proceed to step 3. If cooling fan does not operate at any time, proceed to step 11. If cooling fan operates only during high engine temperature, proceed to step 6.
3. With A/C off and ignition on, disconnect coolant temperature switch connector. Connect a jumper wire from

Fig. 17 Electric engine cooling fan wiring circuit. Type 9

connector to ground. If fan motor oper- ates, proceed to step 4. If fan motor does not operate, proceed to step 5.

4. Using a suitable ohmmeter, check temperature switch body to thermostat housing continuity. If continuity does not exist (poor ground), tighten switch until continuity exists, then recheck operation. If continuity does exist between switch and thermostat hous- ing, replace temperature switch.

5. Disconnect cooling fan controller con- nector, then using a suitable ohmme- ter, check continuity of 197 circuit from controller to temperature switch. If continuity exists, replace controller. If no continuity exists, service 197 cir- cuit.

6. With engine running, engage A/C clutch. If clutch engages, proceed to step 7. If clutch does not engage, check fuse. If satisfactory, proceed to step 8.

7. Disconnect cooling fan controller con- nector, then check for voltage at 37 and 640 circuits on type 14 or 37 and 354 circuits on type 15. If no voltage exists at one or both circuits, service circuit(s) as necessary. If voltage exists at both circuits, replace control- ler.

8. Disconnect A/C clutch cycling pres- sure switch, then using a suitable jumper wire, jump across connector. If clutch engages, proceed to step 9. If clutch does not engage, proceed to step 10.

9. Check A/C system for sufficient charge. If charge is insufficient, leak test, repair and recharge system, then retest. If charge is sufficient, replace clutch cycling pressure switch.

10. Disconnect A/C control connector. Using a jumper wire, connect 321 cir- cuit to 296 circuit, then check for volt- age at yellow/black A/C connector.

11. If voltage exists, replace A/C function selector switch. If voltage does not exist, service 321, 347 or 348 circuits as necessary. Reconnect all removed wiring.

12. Disconnect fan motor electrical con- nector, then connect a jumper wire from motor ground connection to a known good ground and a jumper wire from motor B+ connection to battery positive terminal. If fan motor does not run, replace motor. If fan motor runs, proceed to step 13.

13. Remove jumper wires, then reconnect fan motor electrical connector to fan motor. Disconnect cooling fan control- ler connector and turn ignition On. Check for voltage at 37 and 640 cir- cuits on type 14 and 16, or 37 and 354 circuits on type 15. If no voltage exists at one or both circuits, service circuit(s) as necessary. If voltage exists at both circuits, proceed to step 14.

14. Using a jumper wire connect circuit 37 to circuit 228 at cooling fan controller. If fan motor runs, replace cooling fan controller. If fan motor does not run, service motor ground.

TYPE 17, 18, 19, 20, 21, 22, 23 & 24 FIGS. 25, 26, 27, 28, 29, 30, 31 & 32

1. Check fuse and fusible link. If satisfac-

Fig. 18 Electric engine cooling fan wiring diagram. Type 10

tory, proceed to step 2. If not satisfac- tory, repair or replace as required.

2. Bring engine to operating temperature while operating A/C to determine when cooling fan does or does not operate. If cooling fan operates only during A/C operation, proceed to step 3. If cooling fan does not operate at any time, proceed to step 13. If cooling fan operates only during high engine temperature, proceed to step 6.

3. With A/C off and ignition on, discon- nect coolant temperature switch con- nector. Connect a jumper wire from connector to ground. If fan motor oper- ates, proceed to step 4. If fan motor does not operate, proceed to step 5.

4. Using a suitable ohmmeter, check

temperature switch body to thermostat housing continuity. If continuity does not exist (poor ground), tighten switch until continuity exists, then recheck operation. If continuity does exist between switch and thermostat hous- ing, replace temperature switch.

5. Disconnect cooling fan controller con- nector, then using a suitable ohmme- ter, check continuity of 197 circuit from controller to temperature switch. If continuity exists, replace controller. If no continuity exists, service 197 cir- cuit.

6. With engine running, engage A/C clutch. If clutch engages, proceed to step 7. If clutch does not engage, check fuse. if satisfactory, proceed to

Fig. 19 Electric engine cooling fan wiring diagram. Type 11

Fig. 20 Electric engine cooling fan wiring circuit. Type 12

circuit.

13. Disconnect fan motor electrical connector, then connect a jumper wire from motor ground connection to a known good ground and a jumper wire from motor B+ connection to battery positive terminal. If fan motor runs, proceed to step 14. If fan motor does not run, replace motor.

14. Remove jumper wires, then reconnect fan motor electrical connector to fan motor. Disconnect cooling fan controller connector and turn ignition On. Check for voltage at 37 circuit and 354 circuit. If no voltage exists at one or both circuits, service circuit(s) as necessary. If voltage exists at both circuits, proceed to step 15.

15. Using a jumper wire connect circuit 37 to circuit 228 at cooling fan controller. If fan motor runs, replace cooling fan controller. If fan motor does not run, service motor ground.

TYPE 25, FIG. 33

1. Check cooling fan fusible link, if satisfactory, proceed to step 2. If not satisfactory, repair and retest.

2. With ignition On, disconnect coolant temperature switch connector, then jump both connector terminals to ground. If fan motor runs, service fan motor ground circuit. If fan motor does not run, proceed to step 3.

3. Disconnect fan motor electrical connector, then connect a jumper wire from motor ground connection to a known good ground and a jumper wire from battery positive terminal to motor B+ connection, **Fig. 7.** If fan motor runs, proceed to step 4. If fan motor does not run, replace motor.

4. Remove jumper wires and reconnect fan motor connector. Disconnect cooling fan relay connector, then turn ignition On. Check for voltage at relay connector terminals 37 and 197, **Fig. 8.** If no voltage exists at either terminal, service feed circuits. If voltage exists at both terminals, proceed to step 5.

5. Jump terminals 37 and 228 of cooling fan relay connector, **Fig. 8.** If fan motor runs, proceed to step 6. If fan motor does not run, service wiring from relay connector to motor connector 228.

6. Reconnect cooling fan relay connector. Turn ignition On, then jump terminal 354 to ground (with connector attached to relay). If fan motor runs, service 354 circuit. If fan motor does not run, replace relay.

TYPE 26 & 27, FIGS. 34 & 35

1. Disconnect fan motor electrical connector, then connect a jumper wire from motor ground connection to a known good ground and a jumper wire from battery positive terminal to motor B+ connection. If fan motor runs, proceed to step 2. If fan motor does not run, replace motor.

2. Disconnect cooling fan temperature switch connector, then check for battery voltage on 37 (Y) circuit for Type 26 or 197 (T/OH) circuit for Type 27. If battery voltage exists, proceed to step

---

step 9.

7. Check wide open throttle switch to determine if switch is opened or closed. If switch is open, adjust or replace switch as necessary. If switch is closed, proceed to step 8.

8. Disconnect cooling fan controller connector, then check for voltage at 354 circuit. If no voltage exists, service circuit as necessary. If voltage exists, replace controller.

9. With cooling fan controller connector disconnected and A/C on, check for voltage at 198 circuit. If no voltage exists, proceed to step 10. If voltage exists, replace cooling fan controller.

10. Disconnect A/C clutch cyling pressure switch, then using a suitable jumper wire, jump across connector. Again check for voltage at 198 circuit. If voltage exists, proceed to step 11. If voltage does not exist, proceed to step 12.

11. Check A/C system for sufficient charge. If charge is insufficient, leak test, repair and recharge system. If charge is sufficient, replace clutch cycling pressure switch.

12. Disconnect A/C control connector. Using a jumper wire, connect 321 circuit to 296 circuit. Check for voltage at 198 circuit and 348 circuit at cooling fan controller connector. If voltage exists at both circuits, replace A/C function selector switch. If voltage exists at 198 circuit only, service 348

Fig. 21 Electric engine cooling fan wiring diagram. Type 13

Fig. 22 Electric engine cooling fan wiring diagram. Type 14

Fig. 23 Electric engine cooling fan wiring diagram. Type 15

Fig. 24 Electric engine cooling fan wiring diagram. Type 16

3. If battery voltage does not exist, check for opens or shorts in 37 or 197 circuits.

3. Jump cooling fan temperature switch connector pins together. If fan motor runs, replace temperature switch. If fan motor does not run, proceed to step 4.

4. Disconnect fan motor connector, then check for voltage at 228 (BR/Y) terminal with cooling fan temperature switch jumped. If battery voltage is indicated, proceed to step 5. If battery voltage is not indicated, check 228 and 182 circuits for opens and repair as necessary. Recheck cooling fan operation.

5. Check ground circuit (57) for continuity. If continuity exists, replace cooling fan motor and recheck cooling fan operation. If continuity does not exist, service open in ground circuit (57) and recheck cooling fan operation.

TYPE 28 & 29, FIGS. 36 & 37

Fan Motor Inoperative

1. Disconnect electrical connector at fan motor and connect jumper wires between negative terminal and ground and between positive terminal and B+ at motor. If motor does not run, replace motor. If motor runs, connect electrical connector at motor and proceed to step 2.

2. Disconnect electrical connector at coolant temperature switch, connect jumper wire between connector and ground on circuit 45 and turn ignition switch to "Run". If motor runs, check switch ground. If ground is satisfactory, replace coolant temperature switch. If motor does not run, proceed to step 3.

3. Turn ignition switch to "Off" and remove jumper wire installed in step 2, then check continuity of circuit 45 from cooling fan controller (terminal 1) to coolant temperature switch. If there is no continuity, check for open in circuit 45. If there is continuity, connect jumper wire between coolant temperature switch connector to ground and proceed to step 4.

4. Connect jumper wire between B+ and circuit 687 at cooling fan controller (terminal 8) without disconnecting electrical connector from controller. If motor runs, check for open in ignition feed circuits 68 and 687. If motor does not run, remove jumper wire and proceed to step 5.

5. Disconnect electrical connector at cooling fan controller, then connect jumper wire between B+ and circuit 228 (terminal 5). If motor does not run, check for open in circuit 228. If motor runs, remove jumper wire and proceed to step 6.

6. Connect jumper wire between circuits 68 and 228 (terminals 2 and 5) at the cooling fan controller connector. If motor does not run, check for open in circuit 68. If motor runs, replace cooling fan controller and remove jumper wire from temperature switch electrical connector.

Fig. 25   Electric engine cooling fan wiring diagram. Type 17

Fig. 26   Electric engine cooling fan wiring diagram. Type 18

Fig. 27   Electric engine cooling fan wiring diagram. Type 19

Fig. 28   Electric engine cooling fan wiring diagram. Type 20

Fan Motor Operates When Engine Overheats But Does Not Operate With The A/C Compressor Clutch

1. Place selector switch in A/C position and turn ignition switch "On". If A/C clutch does not engage, proceed to step 2. If A/C clutch engages, proceed to step 8.
2. Check 20 amp fuse in fuse panel. If fuse is not blown, proceed to step 3.
3. Disconnect A/C clutch cycle pressure switch and connect jumper wire across connector terminals. If A/C clutch engages, proceed to step 4. If A/C clutch does not engage, proceed to step 6.
4. Check A/C system for loss of refrigerant charge. If there is no refrigerant charge, leak test, repair and charge system. If refrigerant system has

charge with low pressure above 50 psi, proceed to step 5.
5. Check wide open throttle signal from EEC. If there is no continuity, repair linkage or EEC signal. If there is continuity, replace clutch cycling pressure switch.
6. Check for voltage in circuit 348 at A/C clutch cycling pressure switch. If there is voltage, repair open in circuit 347 to A/C clutch. If there is no voltage, proceed to step 7.
7. Check for voltage in circuits 296 and 348 at function selector switch in instrument panel. If there is voltage in circuit 296 but not in circuit 348, replace A/C control assembly. If there is no voltage in circuit 296, trace circuits 296 and 297 toward ignition switch.

8. Check for voltage in circuit 883 at pin 6 of cooling fan controller. If there is voltage, proceed to step 9. If there is no voltage, repair open in circuit 883 to controller.
9. Ground circuit 57 at pin 4 of controller without disconnecting controller electrical connector. If fan runs, repair ground circuit. If fan does not run, replace controller.

FAN MOTOR, REPLACE

1981–83 ESCORT & LYNX & 1982–83 EXP & LN7

1. Disconnect battery ground cable, then disconnect fan motor wire connector and detach wire loom clip from fan shroud.
2. Remove two nuts attaching fan motor

Fig. 29   Electric engine cooling fan wiring diagram. Type 21

Fig. 30 Electric engine cooling fan wiring diagram. Type 22

Fig. 31 Electric engine cooling fan wiring diagram. Type 23

Fig. 32   Electric engine cooling fan wiring diagram. Type 24

and shroud, then remove fan motor and shroud assembly from vehicle.
3. Remove nut or clip retaining fan blade to fan motor shaft, then remove fan blade.

NOTE: The nut retaining the fan blade to the motor shaft has a left handed thread. The nut should be rotated clockwise to loosen and counterclockwise to tighten.

4. Remove three nuts and washers attaching fan motor to shroud, then remove fan motor.
5. Reverse procedure to install. Torque fan motor to fan shroud attaching nuts to 6.6 to 9.6 ft. lbs., fan blade to fan motor retaining nut to 30 to 40 inch lbs.

and fan shroud to radiator attaching nuts to 80 to 100 inch lbs.

1981–83 EXC. ESCORT, EXP, LN7 & LYNX & 1984-85 EXC. ESCORT, EXP, LYNX, TEMPO & TOPAZ
1. Disconnect battery ground cable, then remove wiring from routing clip.
2. Disconnect fan motor wiring connector.
3. Remove four screws securing mounting bracket and remove fan assembly from vehicle.
4. Remove fan blade retaining clip, then remove fan.
5. Remove nuts securing fan motor to mounting bracket.
6. Reverse procedure to install. Torque fan motor attaching nuts to 70–95 in. lbs., fan shroud to radiator attaching bolts, 70–95 in. lbs.

1984–85 ESCORT, EXP, LYNX, TEMPO & TOPAZ
1. Disconnect battery ground cable.
2. Disconnect electrical connector at fan motor, then disconnect wire loom from clip on shroud.
3. Remove two nuts retaining fan motor and shroud assembly and remove from vehicle.
4. Remove retaining clip from motor shaft and remove fan.
5. Remove three nuts and washers and withdraw fan motor from shroud.
6. Reverse procedure to install, torquing motor to shroud attaching nuts and washers to 44–66 inch lbs. and the fan, motor, shroud assembly retaining nuts to 35–45 inch lbs. on Escort, EXP and Lynx, or 23–33 inch lbs. on Tempo and Topaz.

COLOR CODES

CIRCUIT NUMBER	COLOR
354	BR/Y
37	Y
197	T/O HASH
228	BR/Y

Fig. 33   Electric engine cooling fan wiring diagram. Type 25

Fig. 34   Electric engine cooling fan wiring diagram. Type 26

Fig. 35   Electric engine cooling fan wiring diagram. Type 27

Fig. 36 Electric engine cooling fan wiring diagram. Type 28

Fig. 37 Electric engine cooling fan wiring diagram. Type 29

ENGINE COOLING FANS

ELECTRO-DRIVE COOLING FAN REPLACE

1985 Continental & Mark VII w/6-146 Diesel Engine

NOTE: The cooling fan and motor are replaced as an assembly on these vehicles.

1. Disconnect battery ground cable, then raise and support vehicle.
2. Remove nuts and bolts attaching mounting brackets to radiator support.
3. Disconnect electrical connector at fan.
4. Remove bolts attaching hood latch to radiator support and position latch out of way.
5. Remove nuts and bolts attaching mounting brackets to fan and motor assembly, then remove fan and motor assembly from vehicle.
6. Reverse procedure to install, torquing all nuts and bolts to 4–5 ft. lbs.

General Motors Corp.
Electric Cooling Fans
INDEX

> **CAUTION:** On models equipped with electric engine cooling fans, the battery ground cable should be disconnected whenever underhood service is performed.

1980–82 CORVETTE AUXILIARY FAN

DESCRIPTION

Current is supplied to the auxiliary fan motor through a 30 amp. circuit breaker located in the fuse panel. The fan motor is controlled by an engine temperature switch located at the rear of the right hand cylinder head. When engine temperature reaches approximately 238 degrees F, the engine temperature switch will close and the fan motor will operate to provide supplementary air flow in addition to that supplied by the engine cooling fan. When engine temperature decreases to approximately 201 degrees F, the engine temperature switch will open and current will no longer be supplied to the fan motor. The fan motor will only operate when the ignition switch is in the "Run" position.

FAN MOTOR, REPLACE

1. Disconnect battery ground cable, then remove fresh air scoop.
2. Remove engine cooling fan, then disconnect fan motor wire connector from

Fig. 1   Electric engine cooling fan wiring diagram. 1984 Corvette

vehicle wire connector. Remove retainer securing fan motor wiring to chassis, if equipped.
3. Remove upper fan shroud mounting bolts, then remove fan shroud and auxiliary fan motor as an assembly.
4. Remove nuts attaching auxiliary fan motor to fan shroud, then disconnect wiring from fan motor and remove motor.
5. Reverse procedure to install.

1984 CORVETTE COOLING FAN

DESCRIPTION

Current is supplied to the engine cooling fan relay through an ignition switch controlled 3 amp fuse. When engine temperature reaches approximately 238 degrees F, the engine coolant temperature switch closes, which completes the fan motor circuit to ground. The fan motor frame serves as the fan motor ground and is insulated from the engine ground by plastic shroud surrounding it. When engine temperature decreases to approximately 201 degrees F, the engine coolant temperature switch opens the fan ground circuit, shutting off the fan. The fan motor will only operate when the ignition switch is in the "Run" position.

TROUBLESHOOTING

1. Check fan fuse. If fuse is satisfactory, proceed to step 2. If fuse is not satisfactory, replace fuse and retest.
2. Check voltage to relay, Fig. 1. If voltage is satisfactory, proceed to step 3. If voltage is not satisfactory, repair wiring as necessary.
3. Check relay operation. If satisfactory, proceed to step 4. If unsatisfactory, replace relay.
4. Check coolant temperature switch. If satisfactory, proceed to step 5. If not satisfactory, replace switch.
5. With ignition switch in the "Run" position, ground circuit 335 (dark green wire), Fig. 1, at relay. If fan motor does not operate, check circuit 2, Fig. 1, for power at relay. Repair as required.

1984 FIERO

DESCRIPTION

A single speed electric cooling fan is used on models less air conditioning, while air conditioned models use a two speed electric cooling fan. On all models, a single relay is used to control the electric fan, Figs. 2 and 3. On single speed models, when coolant temperature exceeds 235° F, the coolant temperature switch closes. On two speed models, when coolant temperature exceeds 221° F, the low speed coolant temperature switch closes, and at 246° F, the high speed coolant temperature switch closes. When the coolant temperature switch closes, it allows current to pass through the choke heater fuse and coolant

Fig. 2 Electric engine cooling fan wiring diagram. 1984 Fiero less A/C

fan relay to ground, thus closing the relay contacts. When the contacts are closed, current flows through a fusible link and into the fan motor.

TROUBLESHOOTING

1. If fan motor does not operate, check the following:
   a. Check for blown fuse.
   b. Check fusible link.
   c. Disconnect wire connector from engine coolant temperature switch. With ignition "On", ground end of wire. Fan motor should operate.
2. If cooling fan operates whenever the ignition switch is in the Run position, check the following:
   a. Check cooling fan temperature switch, compressor pressure switch, if equipped and other related mechanical components.
   b. Check cooling fan relay.

FAN MOTOR, REPLACE

1. Disconnect battery ground cable.
2. Disconnect wiring harness from fan motor and frame.
3. Remove fan frame to radiator support attaching bolts.

4. Remove fan motor and frame assembly.
5. Reverse procedure to install. Torque fan frame to radiator support attaching bolts to 85 inch lbs.

1980–84 GM FRONT WHEEL DRIVE MODELS EQUIPPED WITH TRANSVERSE MOUNTED ENGINES

DESCRIPTION

The single speed electric cooling fan is used on all models except those equipped with V6 gasoline engines with heavy duty cooling systems and all diesel engines, which use a two-speed electric motor. The fan motor is operated by the cooling fan relay on single speed models or cooling fan relay and cooling fan speed control on two speed models. On single speed models, when coolant temperature exceeds 230 degrees F, the cooling fan temperature switch closes. On two-speed models, when the coolant temperature reaches approximately 226 (diesel 223) degrees F, the low speed cooling fan temperature switch closes, and at approximately 239 (diesel 246) degrees F, the high speed cooling fan temperature switch closes. On all models, when the cooling fan temperature switch closes on single speed models, or the low speed cooling fan temperature switch closes on two speed models, it allows current to pass through the fuse and cooling fan relay coil to ground, thus closing the relay contacts. On single speed models, when the relay contacts are closed, current flows through a fusible link to the fan motor. On two speed models when the relay contacts are closed, current flows through a fusible link, then cooling fan speed control low speed contacts, and into the fan motor. On two speed models, when the high speed cooling fan temperature switch closes, the solid state circuitry of the cooling fan speed control is grounded, causing cooling fan speed control high speed contacts to close and cooling fan motor to operate at high speed. On single speed models, when coolant temperature falls below a predetermined level, the cooling fan temperature switch opens and current is no longer supplied to the fan motor. On two speed models, when coolant temperature falls below the high speed cooling fan temperature switch predetermined level, the contacts open, opening the ground circuit to the cooling fan speed control and causing the fan motor to operate at low speed. When the coolant temperature falls below the low speed cooling fan temperature switch predetermined level, the contacts open, causing the cooling fan relay to open and shut off current to the cooling fan speed control and the cooling fan motor. On 1980 models and 1982–85 diesel engine models with A/C, a second switch (diesel engine models use two switches) which senses compressor head pressure to the condenser, is used to activate the fan motor when the A/C compressor is

Fig. 3 Electric engine cooling fan wiring diagram. 1984 Fiero with A/C

dual cooling fans are used.

On models equipped with dual cooling fans, the left side fan has two speeds while the right side has one speed and only operates when the left side is running in the high speed mode.

The on and off operation of the cooling fan(s) is controlled by the Electronic control Module (ECM), while the fan speed and mode of operation are controlled by vehicle speed, engine temperature, A/C head pressure and transmission converter clutch operation.

TROUBLESHOOTING

Gasoline Engines

1. Check fuse No. 21. If satisfactory, proceed to step 2. If not satisfactory, replace fuse and retest.
2. Check all system grounds, **Figs. 4 and 6.** If satisfactory, proceed to step 3. If not satisfactory, repair grounds as necessary.
3. Check fusible link. If satisfactory, proceed to step 4. If not satisfactory, repair fusible link, then inspect electrical system for short circuits.
4. Check red wire between fusible link and relay(s) for opens. If satisfactory, proceed to step 5. If not satisfactory, repair opens.
5. If large cooling fan (if equipped) does not run, proceed as follows:
   a. Disconnect coolant temperature switch connector, then connect to a suitable ground.
   b. Using a suitable test light, check for battery voltage at the B terminal (white wire) of the high speed cooling fan relay, **Figs. 4 and 5.** If voltage is present, proceed to step c. If voltage is not present, check the high speed relay and replace as necessary.
   c. If voltage is present, check for an open in the white wire between high speed cooling fan relay and large cooling fan and repair as necessary. If cooling fan still does not run, check common ground between large and small fans and repair as necessary.
6. If small cooling fan does not run at high speed, proceed as follows:
   a. Disconnect coolant temperature switch connector, then connect to a suitable ground.
   b. Using a suitable test light, check for battery voltage at the A terminal (2 white wires) of the high speed cooling fan relay, **Figs. 4 and 5.** If voltage is present, proceed to step c. If voltage is not present, check the high speed relay and replace as necessary.
   c. If voltage is present, check for an open in the white wire between high speed cooling fan relay and small cooling fan and repair as necessary. If cooling fan still does not run, check fan motor ground and repair as necessary.
7. If small cooling fan does not run at low speed, proceed as follows:
   a. Start engine, then place A/C selector switch in "Norm" position.

operating. On all other models equipped with A/C, the cooling fan relay is grounded whenever the A/C selector switch is in the Max., Normal or Bi-Level position, causing the cooling fan to operate. On some automatic transmission models with gasoline V6 engines, the electric engine cooling fan operates when the torque converter clutch is engaged.

TROUBLESHOOTING

1. If fan motor does not operate, check the following:
   a. Check for blown fuse.
   b. Check fusible link.
   c. Disconnect wire connector from engine coolant temperature switch. With ignition "On", ground end of wire. Fan motor should operate.
2. If cooling fan operates whenever the ignition switch is in the Run position, check the following:
   a. Check cooling fan temperature switch, compressor pressure switch, if equipped and other related mechanical components.
   b. Check cooling fan relay.

FAN MOTOR, REPLACE

1. Disconnect battery ground cable, then disconnect wire connector from fan motor.
2. Detach front lamp wiring harness from fan motor, then remove harness from fan motor frame.
3. Remove fan motor frame to radiator support attaching bolts, then remove fan motor.
4. Reverse procedure to install. Torque fan to radiator support attaching bolts to 85 inch lbs.

1985 BUICK ELECTRA, PARK AVENUE & OLDSMOBILE NINETY-EIGHT

DESCRIPTION

On gasoline engine equipped models less heavy duty cooling, a single two speed fan is used for cooling purposes. On gasoline engine models equipped with heavy duty cooling and all diesel engine models,

Fig. 4   Electric engine cooling fan wiring diagram. 1985 Buick Electra, Park Avenue & Oldsmobile Ninety-Eight with V6-181 gasoline engine

b. Connect a suitable jumper wire across the coolant fan resistor. If cooling fan runs, replace coolant fan resistor.
c. With engine still running and A/C operating, use a suitable test light to test for voltage at terminal B (red wire) of low speed cooling fan relay, **Figs. 4 and 5.** If voltage is not present, check for opens in red wire between fusible link and low speed cooling fan relay.
d. Using test light, check for voltage at terminal A of low speed cooling fan relay, **Figs. 4 and 5.** If voltage is not present, check wiring connected to terminal A for opens.
e. On models equipped with V6-181 engine, connect suitable jumper wire from black wire terminal of low speed cooling fan relay to ground.

If relay operates, repair open circuit in black wire between relay and ground. If relay does not operate, check relay.
f. On models equipped with V6-231 engine, disconnect A/C pressure switch connector, then connect a jumper wire from dark green wire of connector to ground. If cooling fan runs, check connector ground wire for opens. If satisfactory, replace A/C pressure switch.

Diesel Engine Models

1. If fan motor does not operate, check the following:
   a. Check for blown fuse, **Fig. 6.**
   b. Check for blown fusible link.
   c. Connect jumper wire from one of the cooling fan relay coils to ground. Cooling fan should run.

2. If fan motor operates whenever the ignition switch is in the Run, Bulb Test or Start position, check the following:
   a. Dual temperature switch and A/C high pressure switch to see if any contacts are closed at all times.
   b. Coolant fan relay for stuck contacts.

1985 CADILLAC DEVILLE & FLEETWOOD

DESCRIPTION

The radiator cooling system is comprised of two electric motor driven cooling fans. The electric motors are controlled electronically by the Body Control Module

Fig. 5 Electric engine cooling fan wiring diagram. 1985 Buick Electra, Park Avenue & Oldsmobile Ninety-Eight with V6-231 gasoline engine

(BCM) which monitors engine temperature and the A/C high pressure refrigerant temperature. The BCM determines the proper fan speed and varies the speed as necessary through pulse width modulation to the cooling fan control module, **Fig. 7.**

Both cooling fans are turned on at half power when engine coolant temperature or A/C high pressure refrigerant temperature reaches a predetermined level. As engine coolant temperature or A/C high pressure refrigerant temperature increases, fan power also increases until full power is reached. On then Off operation of the fans is eliminated due to utilizing turn off temperatures lower than turn on temperatures.

1985 BUICK SKYLARK & CHEVROLET CITATION

SYSTEM DESCRIPTION

The cooling fan located between radiator and condenser cools both engine coolant and A/C refrigerant. The fan is controlled by the cooling fan relay (located on LH side of engine compartment) which in turn is controlled by the coolant temperature fan switch (located on front of engine left of exhaust manifold on 4-151 engines; top of engine left of carburetor on V6-173 VIN X engines). The coolant switch closes at temperatures above 230° F.

On vehicles equipped with air conditioning, the relay is energized when the A/C is operating in certain modes. The relay is also energized under certain conditions when the A/C high pressure switch (located on compressor) closes at pressures above 280 psi. The switch then re-opens when pressure drops below 180 psi.

Models Less A/C

With ignition switch in RUN position voltage is applied through C-H fuse to cooling fan relay coil. Voltage is applied at all times through fusible link C (located at front of engine at starter solenoid) to cooling fan relay contacts.

When coolant temperature fan switch is closed, circuit through C-H fuse, relay coil, and switch is completed to ground. This causes relay contacts to close, thus completing circuit through fusible link C, relay

ENGINE COOLING FANS

Fig. 6   Electric engine cooling fan wiring diagram. 1985 Buick Electra, Park Avenue & Oldsmobile Ninety-Eight with V6-260 diesel engine

contacts, and cooling fan motor to ground, causing fan to run.

Models W/4-151 & A/C

When vehicle speed is below 35 mph, the ECM (Electronic Control Module, located behind RH side of instrument panel) grounds fan relay circuit. Current can flow in this circuit under either 1 of 2 conditions:

1. When high refrigerant pressure causes the A/C high pressure switch to close, the circuit is completed through C-H fuse, relay coil, A/C high pressure switch, and ECM to ground. This causes relay contacts to close and fan to run.

2. When A/C selector lever is set to MAX, NORM, or BI-LEVEL, circuit is completed through C-H fuse, relay coil, dk grn/wht wire, A/C selector switch, and ECM to ground. This causes relay contacts to close and fan to run.

Models W/V6-173 VIN X & A/C

With ignition switch in RUN, voltage is applied through C-H fuse to cooling fan relay coil. Voltage is always applied through fusible link C (located at front of engine, at starter solenoid) to cooling fan relay (located at front side of LH strut tower) contacts. Current can flow in this circuit under 2 conditions:

1. When coolant temperature fan switch closes, it completes circuit through C-H fuse, cooling fan relay coil, and coolant temperature fan switch to ground. This causes relay contacts to close and fan to run.

2. When A/C high pressure switch closes at pressures above 280 psi, circuit is completed through C-H fuse, relay coil, dk grn/wht wire, and A/C high pressure switch to ground. This causes relay contacts to close and fan to run. When refrigerant pressure drops below 180 psi, switch

reopens and relay de-energizes.

Models W/V6-173 VIN W & A/C

With ignition switch in RUN position, voltage is applied through C-H fuse to cooling fan relay coil. Voltage is always applied from battery junction block to cooling fan relay contacts.

Cooling fan relay is switched on by ECM which provides a ground path for relay coil to energize relay and close relay contacts.

When refrigerant pressure exceeds 240 psi, cooling fan pressure switch grounds ECM input causing ECM to switch on cooling fan.

TROUBLESHOOTING

Cooling Fan Does Not Operate

1. Check C-H fuse.
2. Check fusible link C, located at front of engine at starter solenoid.

Fig. 7 Electric engine cooling fan wiring diagram. 1985 Cadillac DeVille & Fleetwood

3. Connect wire from cooling fan relay coil (dk grn/wht wire) to ground-cooling fan should run.

Cooling Fan Runs Whenever Ignition Is In RUN Position

1. Check temperature switch, pressure switch, and related mechanical systems.
2. Check cooling fan relay.

COOLING FAN, REPLACE

1. Disconnect battery ground cable.
2. Disconnect wiring from fan motor and frame.
3. Remove fan assembly from radiator support.
4. Reverse procedure to install.

1985 BUICK SOMERSET REGAL & OLDSMOBILE CALAIS

SYSTEM DESCRIPTION

4-151 Engines

A cooling fan relay is used to control the cooling fan. When coolant temperature is high, the cooling fan temperature switch closes and provides a path to ground for the relay coil. The contacts close applying battery voltage to the fan.

On vehicles equipped with A/C, the cooling fan runs when the compressor is on. The coil of a separate A/C cooling fan relay receives battery voltage through the A/C mode selector and the pressure cycling switch and is grounded through the ECM. When the compressor clutch is on, the ECM grounds the coil of the separate A/C cooling fan relay whose contacts close to ground the cooling fan relay coil. The cooling fan relay is energized and battery voltage is applied to the cooling fan causing it to run. A diode is connected across the cooling fan relay coil to absorb voltage spikes.

V6-183 Engines

These vehicles use a 2-speed heavy duty cooling fan which is controlled by a cooling fan relay having 2 coils and 2 independent sets of contacts.

During low speed cooling fan operation, the low speed relay is grounded through either the ECM or the low speed contacts of the A/C high pressure switch. The ECM grounds the coil when vehicle speed is less than 45 mph and the engine coolant is at normal operating temperature. The low speed contacts of the A/C high pressure switch close when high refrigerant pressure is present at the compressor.

With the low speed relay coil grounded, the appropriate contacts close thus applying voltage through the cooling fan resistor to the cooling fan motor. The resistor drops part of the battery voltage so the fan runs at low speed.

During high speed cooling fan operation, the high speed relay coil is grounded through the high speed contacts in the A/C high pressure switch or through the cooling fan temperature switch. The fan the runs at high speed.

SYSTEM CHECK

4-151 Less A/C

1. Run engine at fast idle for several minutes. Cooling fan should turn on before coolant temperature indicator on instrument panel comes on.

4-151 With A/C

1. With engine at normal operating tem-

ENGINE COOLING FANS

perature and running at slow idle, set A/C mode selector to NORM position. Cooling fan should turn on.
2. Set A/C mode selector to OFF position. Run engine at fast idle for several minutes. Cooling fan should turn on before coolant temperature indicator on instrument panel comes on.

V6-183

1. With engine cold and at idle, set A/C mode selector to NORM position and blower to HI position. Set temperature selector to COLD position. Leave vehicle doors open. Cooling fan should run first at low speed, then at high speed.
2. Set A/C mode selector to OFF position, and run engine at fast idle. After a few minutes, cooling fan should run at low speed. Cooling fan should run at high speed before coolant temperature indicator on instrument panel comes on.

TROUBLESHOOTING

1. On models with 4-151 engine, operate A/C blower to check fuse 22 on Calais; HTR-A/C fuse on Somerset.
2. On all models, visually check fuse 21 on Calais; ENG/FAN fuse on Somerset.
3. If cooling fan operates only with compressor on and not for hot engine, install new cooling fan temperature switch.
4. Connect a fused jumper wire from battery to cooling fan terminal B, blu/blk wire on Calais; red/blk wire on Somerset.
   a. If fan runs, ECM diagnosis must be performed.
   b. If fan does not run, check that blk wire terminal E on Calais; terminal A on Somerset, is grounded. If ground is good, cooling fan is defective.

COOLING FAN, REPLACE

1. Disconnect battery ground cable.
2. Disconnect wiring from fan motor and frame.
3. Remove fan assembly from radiator support.
4. Reverse procedure to install.

1985 BUICK SKYHAWK, OLDSMOBILE FIRENZA & PONTIAC SUNBIRD

SYSTEM DESCRIPTION

The cooling fan cools both engine coolant and A/C system refrigerant.

4-110 Turbo VIN J

The cooling fan can be switched on by either the cooling fan relay (located on front of dash, left of master cylinder) or the 5 minute turbo fan relay (located on LH

front fender, forward of shock tower). Both relay contacts always have voltage available from fusible link C (located at starter). With ignition switch in RUN position, voltage is available from C-H fuse to cooling fan relay coil and to solid state control in 5 minute turbo fan relay.

When engine coolant temperature exceeds 238° F, cooling fan switch (located on RH front of engine, on coolant outlet) closes, signalling solid state control in 5 minute turbo fan relay to close contact which provides path for current to cooling fan.

When ignition switch is turned off, contacts in 5 minute turbo fan relay close and set 5 minute timer, allowing cooling fan to run for 5 minutes.

4-110 VIN O

When coolant temperature exceeds 238°, cooling fan switch (located on front RH side of engine, bottom of thermostat housing) provides ground for cooling fan relay (located on front of dash, left of master cylinder). The relay energizes and current flows from fusible link C to cooling fan.

When A/C mode selector lever is in MAX, NORM, or BI-LEVEL position, and vehicle speed is below 35 mph, ECM will provide path to ground for cooling fan relay so A/C refrigerant can be cooled. At speeds above 35 mph, ECM shuts off cooling fan.

At high refrigerant pressures, A/C high pressure fan switch (located on RH front of engine, near LH end of compressor) sends voltage to ECM, which then switches on fan.

4-121 VIN P

Cooling fan relay is activated by ECM when engine coolant sensed by coolant temperature sensor is above 238° F and vehicle speed is below 35 mph. ECM also activates cooling fan relay when A/C mode selector sends voltage to ECM.

Cooling fan will also run if cooling fan switch and A/C high pressure switch are closed, such as when A/C mode selector is in DEF position and ambient temperature is above 32° F and A/C system is properly charged.

SYSTEM CHECK

With A/C

1. When engine at normal operating temperature and idle speed, set A/C mode selector to NORM. Cooling fan should turn on.
2. Set mode selector off. Allow engine to run at fast idle for several minutes. Cooling fan should turn on before coolant temperature indicator in instrument panel comes on or before coolant temperature gauge reaches H.
3. On models with 4-110 Turbo VIN J engine, turn engine off when at normal operating temperature. Cooling fan should run for 5 minutes.

Less A/C

1. Run engine at fast idle for several minutes. Coolant fan should turn on before coolant temperature indicator

in instrument panel comes on or before coolant temperature gauge reaches H.
2. On models with 4-110 Turbo VIN J engine, turn engine off when at normal operating temperature. Cooling fan should run for 5 minutes.

TROUBLESHOOTING

1. If cooling fan only comes on with A/C compressor and not for a hot engine, install new cooling fan switch.
2. Connect a fused jumper wire from positive terminal of battery to terminal B (blk/red) on all Buick Skyhawk engines and on Oldsmobile Firenza and Pontiac Sunbird with 4-121 VIN P engine; to terminal B (red/wht) on Pontiac Sunbird with 4-110 Turbo VIN J engine; to terminal A (red/wht) on Oldsmobile Firenza and Pontiac Sunbird with 4-110 VIN O engine.
   a. If fan runs, ECM diagnosis must be performed since circuit is controlled by ECM.
   b. If fan does not run, check continuity to ground at terminal B on Oldsmobile Firenza and Pontiac Sunbird with 4-110 VIN O engine; terminal A on models exc. Oldsmobile Firenza and Pontiac Sunbird with 4-110 VIN O engine.
3. If a cooling fan relay has failed, test cooling fan switch for intermittent operation as follows:
   a. Warm up engine until cooling fan comes on.
   b. Remove connector from cooling fan switch.
   c. Connect self-powered test lamp to switch and to ground. Test lamp should light steadily. If test lamp flickers, install new cooling fan switch.
   d. Test both high speed and low speed switches if vehicle is so equipped.

COOLING FAN, REPLACE

1. Disconnect battery ground cable.
2. Disconnect wiring from fan motor and frame.
3. Remove fan assembly from radiator support.
4. Reverse procedure to install.

1985 CADILLAC CIMARRON

SYSTEM DESCRIPTION

The cooling fan is controlled by the cooling fan relay whose contacts have voltage available at all times. The relay coil has voltage through the C-H fuse when ignition switch is in RUN position.

The cooling fan relay is activated by any of the following conditions:
   a. When engine coolant temperature exceeds 234° F, coolant temperature sender signals ECM. The ECM in turn activates cooling fan relay which receives voltage

27-30

through C-H fuse. The cooling fan relay contacts close, allowing current to flow through fusible link C and operate cooling fan.

b. On 4-121 VIN P engine, ECM will activate cooling fan relay when A/C is on and vehicle speed is below 40 mph. With vehicle speed above 40 mph, engine temperature determines operation of cooling fan relay. When A/C is off, and vehicle speed is above 40 mph, ECM will deactivate cooling fan relay at 225° F.

c. On V6-173 VIN W engine, ECM activates cooling fan relay when A/C high side pressure exceeds 240 psi.

TROUBLESHOOTING

Cooling Fan Does Not Run
1. Check C-H fuse.
2. Check fusible link C.
3. Check cooling fan relay by listening for click when grounding dk grn/wht wire at cooling fan relay.

Cooling Fan Runs Constantly With Ignition Switch In RUN
1. Check cooling fan relay.
2. Disconnect dk grn/wht wire at cooling fan relay. If fan stops, check ECM.

COOLING FAN, REPLACE
1. Disconnect battery ground cable.
2. Disconnect wiring from fan motor and frame.
3. Remove fan assembly from radiator support.
4. Reverse procedure to install.

1985 CHEVROLET CAVALIER
SYSTEM DESCRIPTION

The cooling fan is operated by a cooling fan relay. The relay contacts have voltage at all times, while coil has voltage through C-H fuse on 4 door models; or fuse 17 on 2 door models when ignition switch is in RUN position.

When engine coolant temperature exceeds 238° F, coolant temperature sensor sends a signal to ECM which controls cooling fan relay. By acting as a ground, ECM allows cooling fan relay coil to energize, causing relay contacts to close, allowing current to flow through fusible link C to operate cooling fan.

When coolant temperature decreases to below 214° F, ECM no longer acts as ground, de-energizing cooling fan relay. The cooling fan relay contacts open and cooling fan stops.

TROUBLESHOOTING

Cooling Fan Runs Constantly With Ignition Switch In RUN
1. Check dk grn/wht wire for short to ground.
2. Check cooling fan relay.

Cooling Fan Does Not Run At All
1. Check dk grn/wht wire for open.
2. Check blk wire for continuity to ground.
3. Check blk/red wire for continuity.
4. Check cooling fan relay.
5. With ignition switch in RUN position, check cooling fan relay for 12 volts at red wire and at brn/wht wire.

COOLING FAN, REPLACE
1. Disconnect battery ground cable.
2. Disconnect wiring from fan motor and frame.
3. Remove fan assembly from radiator support.
4. Reverse procedure to install.

1985 CHEVROLET CAMARO
SYSTEM DESCRIPTION

V6-173 VIN S
Voltage is always available through fusible link E to cooling fan relay contacts. With ignition switch in RUN position, voltage is available through C-H fan fuse on Berlinetta; or FP fan fuse on Sport Coupe to cooling fan relay coil.

With fan pressure switch contacts closed, current flows through C-H fan fuse on Berlinetta; FP fan fuse on Sport Coupe, then through cooling fan relay coil, ECM, and fan pressure switch contacts to ground causing cooling fan relay contacts to close. Current flows through fusible link E, cooling fan relay contacts, and cooling fan to ground causing cooling fan to run.

V8-305 VIN F
Voltage is always available through fusible link D to cooling fan relay contacts. With ignition switch in RUN position, voltage is available through FP fan fuse to cooling fan relay coil.

With fan pressure switch contact closed, current flows through FP fan fuse, cooling fan relay coil, ECM, and fan pressure switch contacts to ground, causing cooling fan relay contacts to close. Current then flows through fusible link E, cooling fan relay contacts, and cooling fan to ground, causing cooling fan to operate.

On vehicles with A/C, cooling fan also runs when A/C mode selector is in MAX, NORM, or BI-LEVEL positions.

V8-305 VIN G
Voltage is always available through fusible link B to cooling fan relay contacts. With ignition switch in RUN position, voltage is available through C-H fuse, and throttle kicker relay to cooling fan relay coil.

With cooling fan switch contact closed, current flows through C-H fan fuse, throttle kicker relay, cooling fan relay coil, and cooling fan switch contact to ground, causing cooling fan relay contacts to close. Current flows through fusible link B, cooling fan relay contacts, and cooling fan to ground, causing cooling fan to operate.

TROUBLESHOOTING

V6-173 VIN S

Cooling Fan Does Not Run
1. Check C-H fan fuse on Berlinetta; FP fuse on Sport Coupe.
2. Check fusible link E located at junction block.
3. Check that grounds are clean and tight.
4. Connect jumper wire from cooling fan relay coil (dk grn/wht wire) to ground. Cooling fan should run.

Cooling Fan Runs Constantly With Ignition Switch In RUN
1. Check that fan pressure switch is closed at all times.
2. Check cooling fan relay for stuck contacts.

V8-305 VIN F

Cooling Fan Does Not Run
1. Check FP fan fuse.
2. Check fusible link D located at battery.
3. Check that grounds are clean and tight.
4. Connect jumper wire from cooling fan relay coil (dk grn/wht wire) to ground. Cooling fan should run.

Cooling Fan Runs Constantly With Ignition Switch In RUN
1. Check that fan pressure switch is closed at all times.
2. Check cooling fan relay for stuck contacts.

V8-305 VIN G

Cooling Fan Does Not Run
1. Check C-H fuse.
2. Check fusible link B located at lower RH side of engine, near starter.
3. Check that grounds are clean and tight.
4. Connect jumper wire from cooling fan relay coil (dk grn wire) to ground. Cooling fan should run.

Cooling Fan Runs Constantly With Ignition Switch In RUN
1. Check that cooling fan switch is closed.
2. Check that A/C control head is grounded at all times.
3. Check cooling fan relay for stuck contacts.

COOLING FAN, REPLACE
1. Disconnect battery ground cable.
2. Disconnect wiring from fan motor and frame.
3. Remove fan assembly from radiator support.
4. Reverse procedure to install.

1985 PONTIAC FIREBIRD
SYSTEM DESCRIPTION

V6-173 VIN S & V8-305 VIN F
The cooling fan is controlled by a cooling

ENGINE COOLING FANS

fan relay whose coil is controlled by the redundant cooling fan switch and by the ECM which closes when coolant temperature exceeds 228° F. The relay is then energized and its contacts close to supply battery voltage to cooling fan.

V8-305 VIN G

The cooling fan is controlled by a cooling fan relay whose coil is grounded by the cooling fan switch (which closes when coolant temperature is above 228° F) and also through the A/C control head. The relay is then energized and its contacts close to supply battery voltage to cooling fan.

TROUBLESHOOTING

V6-173 VIN S & V8-305 VIN F

If cooling fan relay has failed, test redundant cooling fan switch for intermittent operation as follows:
1. Warm up engine until cooling fan comes on.
2. Disconnect connector from redundant cooling fan switch.
3. Connect self-powered test lamp to switch and to ground. Test lamp should light steadily.
4. If test lamp flickers at all, install new redundant cooling fan switch.

V8-305 VIN G

If cooling fan relay has failed, test cooling fan switch for intermittent operation as follows:
1. Warm up engine until cooling fan comes on.
2. Disconnect connector from cooling fan switch.
3. Connect self-powered test lamp to switch and to ground. Test lamp should light steadily.
4. If test lamp flickers at all, install new cooling fan switch.

SYSTEM DIAGNOSIS

V6-173 VIN S & V8-305 VIN F

Fan Runs When Jumped; Does Not Operate In Normal Use
1. Disconnect connectors from cooling fan relay (located at upper LH side of front of dash, V6-173 VIN S; RH side of radiator support, V8-305 VIN F) and check voltage to ground at connectors with ignition switch in RUN. Battery voltage should be at terminal E, red wire, V6-173 VIN S; orn wire V8-305 VIN F, and at terminal, C brn wire.
2. If battery voltage is not available at terminals, check circuit that supplies terminal. If voltage is available, proceed to step 3.
3. Reconnect connector to cooling fan relay. Disconnect dk grn/wht wire from redundant cooling fan switch (located rear of engine, near distributor, V6-173 VIN S; lower RH rear of engine, V8-305 VIN F). Connect fused jumper from wire to ground.
4. With ignition switch in RUN, check that fan runs.
5. If fan runs, relay and wiring are OK. Install new redundant cooling fan switch.

6. If cooling fan does not run, check dk grn/wht wire to relay and blk/red wire to fan. If wiring is OK, install new cooling fan relay.

V8-305 VIN G

Fan Runs When Jumped; Does Not Run In Normal Use.
1. Disconnect connectors from cooling fan relay (located on engine harness, LH front of dash) and measure voltage to ground at connectors with ignition switch in RUN. Battery voltage should be available at terminal D, red wire, and terminal C, brn/wht wire.
2. If battery voltage is not available at terminal, check circuit that supplies terminal. If voltage is correct, proceed to step 3.
3. Reconnect connector to cooling fan relay. Disconnect dk grn wire from cooling fan switch (located at RH side of engine, above rear of starter solenoid).
4. Connect fused jumper wire from dk grn wire to ground. With ignition switch in RUN, cooling fan should run and battery voltage should be available at terminal D, red wire.
5. If cooling fan runs, relay and wiring are OK. Cooling fan switch should be replaced.
6. If cooling fan does not run, check dk grn wire to relay and blk/red wire to fan. If OK, install new cooling fan relay.

COOLING FAN, REPLACE

1. Disconnect battery ground cable.
2. Disconnect wiring from fan motor and frame.
3. Remove fan assembly from radiator support.
4. Reverse procedure to install.

1985 PONTIAC FIERO
SYSTEM DESCRIPTION

Single Speed Fan

A cooling fan relay controls operation of the cooling fan. Voltage is always available to relay contacts through fusible link A (located at RH front of engine compartment, at battery junction block). With ignition switch in RUN position, voltage is available through C-H fuse to relay coil.

At coolant temperatures above 235° F, coolant temperature switch closes. Current flows through the C-H fuse, through cooling fan relay coil, and through the closed coolant temperature switch to ground, causing relay contacts to close. Current then flows through fusible link A, through closed relay contacts, through cooling fan to ground, causing cooling fan to run.

On vehicles equipped with A/C, cooling fan relay is also operated by A/C high pressure switch when closed, or by A/C mode selector when in MAX, NORM, or BI-LEVEL positions.

Two Speed Fan

Voltage is always available through fusible link A (located at RH front of engine

compartment, at battery junction block), to low and high speed contacts of cooling fan relay. With ignition switch in RUN position, voltage is available through C-H fuse to low and high speed coils of cooling fan relay.

With A/C mode selector in MAX, NORM, or BI-LEVEL position and with either A/C high pressure switch closed or low temperature side of coolant temperature switch closed, current flows through C-H fuse, through low speed relay coil to ground.

The low speed contacts then close. Current then flows through fusible link A, through low speed relay contact to terminal C of cooling fan, through an internal resistor, through fan motor and to ground. Cooling fan then operates at low speed.

With high temperature side of coolant temperature switch closed, current flows through C-H fuse and high speed relay coil to ground, causing high speed contacts of cooling fan relay to close. Current then flows through fusible link A and the high speed cooling fan contacts to terminal B of cooling fan. Current then flows directly through fan motor to ground, causing cooling fan to operate at high speed.

TROUBLESHOOTING

Cooling Fan Does Not Run
1. Check C-H fuse.
2. Check fusible link A.
3. On vehicles with single speed fan, connect jumper wire from Low Speed cooling fan relay coil (dk grn/wht wire) to ground. Cooling fan should run.
4. Vehicles with two speed fan:
   a. Connect jumper wire from low speed cooling fan relay coil (dk grn/wht wire) to ground. Cooling fan should run at low speed.
   b. Connect jumper wire from high speed cooling fan relay coil (lt grn/wht wire) to ground. Cooling fan should run at high speed.

Cooling Fan Runs Constantly With Ignition In RUN
1. Check that coolant temperature switch contacts are open with engine cold.
2. Check that cooling fan relay contacts are open with ignition off.

1985 CHEVROLET CORVETTE
SYSTEM DESCRIPTION

SINGLE FAN

With ignition switch in RUN, voltage is applied through cooling fan fuse, through cooling fan relay, and then through cooling fan temperature switch which closes when coolant temperature exceeds 238° F.

This energizes cooling fan relay and completes circuit to cooling fan motor. Voltage from fusible link D (located near LH rear of engine compartment, near battery) is applied through cooling fan relay to operate cooling fan motor.

The ECM also controls the cooling fan motor by grounding the cooling fan relay coil.

DUAL FANS

With ignition switch in RUN, voltage is applied through cooling fan fuse, through either cooling fan relay or auxiliary cooling fan relay.

When coolant temperature exceeds 238° F, auxiliary cooling fan temperature switch closes, thus energizing relay which closes switch to auxiliary cooling fan motor. Current flows through fusible link E (located at LH rear of engine compartment, near battery) through auxiliary cooling fan relay to auxiliary cooling fan motor.

The cooling fan motor is operated by the ECM.

TROUBLESHOOTING

Single Fan

1. Check cooling fan fuse.
2. Disconnect connector from cooling fan relay and connect a fused jumper wire from terminal A to D. Cooling fan should run.
3. If cooling fan does not run, check fusible link D and wiring to cooling fan motor. Check that ground G117 (located at LH side of engine compartment) is clean and tight. If wiring and fusible link D are OK, replace cooling fan motor.
4. If cooling fan runs, ECM diagnosis must be performed.

Dual Fan

1. Check cooling fan fuse.
2. If auxiliary cooling fan does not run with hot engine, check temperature switch as follows:
   a. Disconnect connector from auxiliary cooling fan temperature switch. Using fused jumper wire, ground dk grn wire. Auxiliary cooling fan should run.
   b. If fan runs, replace temperature switch.
   c. If fan does not run, disconnect connector at auxiliary cooling fan relay and measure voltage at relay connector. Battery voltage should be available at terminal C (dk blu wire) and terminal D (red wire).
   d. If either terminal does not have battery voltage, check circuit supplying that terminal.
   e. If battery voltage is available at both terminals, connect a fused jumper wire between terminals A and D.
   f. If fan does not run, check ground and blk/red wire to fan. If OK, install new auxiliary cooling fan motor.
   g. If fan runs with jumper wire, relay may be defective. Check dk grn/wht wire to temperature switch for an open. If wire is OK, install new auxiliary cooling fan relay.
3. If cooling fan does not run, check if motor is OK as follows:
   a. Connect fused jumper wire from battery positive terminal to terminal B of cooling fan motor (blk/red wire).
   b. If cooling fan motor does nut run, check ground at terminal A. If ground is OK, replace cooling fan motor.

c. If motor does run with jumper, ECM diagnosis must be performed.

COOLING FAN, REPLACE

1. Disconnect battery ground cable.
2. Disconnect wiring from fan motor and frame.
3. Remove fan assembly from radiator support.
4. Reverse procedure to install.

1985 BUICK CENTURY & OLDSMOBILE CUTLASS CIERA

System Description

The cooling fan is controlled by a cooling fan relay whose coil is grounded by the cooling fan switch when coolant temperature exceeds 228° F. The cooling fan relay is energized and its contacts close to supply battery voltage to cooling fan.

The cooling fan delay relay operates cooling fan for short time after engine is turned off. A solid state timer removes ground from cooling fan delay relay coil to switch off cooling fan.

4-151 VIN R

The cooling fan is controlled by the following:
1. Coolant temperature fan switch.
2. ECM and A/C mode selector switch.
3. ECM and A/C high pressure switch.

These switch combinations complete circuit to ground through cooling fan relay coil. With coil energized and relay contacts closed, battery voltage is applied to cooling fan.

On vehicles equipped with A/C, cooling fan also runs when compressor is on. With A/C mode selector is in MAX, NORM, or BI-LEVEL position, a path to ground exists through mode selector switch and ECM.

A suppression resistor is connected across cooling fan relay coil to absorb voltage spikes. An A/C high pressure switch is included in A/C relay grounding circuit to ensure grounding of cooling fan relay coil and cooling fan operation when mode selector is in DEF position and ambient temperature is above 32° F.

V6-183 VIN E

Three types of cooling fans are used with V6-183 VIN E engines:
a. Single speed.
b. Two speed (internal resistor).
c. Heavy Duty Two Speed (external resistor).

On vehicles with single speed fan, cooling fan relay coil is grounded through cooling fan switch, which closes when coolant temperature exceeds 228° F. With relay coil grounded, cooling fan relay contacts close and battery voltage is applied to cooling fan causing it to run.

On vehicles with 2 speed cooling fan, the fan is controlled by low speed and high speed cooling fan relays. A resistor is connected in series with the cooling fan for low speed operation.

On vehicles less A/C, two separate cooling fan switches are combined in a single unit. During low speed operation low speed cooling fan relay coil is grounded through low speed contacts of cooling fan switch.

On vehicles with A/C, low speed cooling fan relay coil is grounded through solid state relay and A/C mode selector. The circuit to ground is completed when A/C mode selector in MAX, NORM, or BI-LEVEL position. When vehicle speed exceeds 35 mph and torque converter clutch is energized, ECM breaks connection to ground causing fan to stop. When vehicle speed is above 35 mph, ECM applies a ground to low speed cooling fan relay to energize solid state relay coil. (Same ground is applied to torque converter clutch and assembly line communications link connector.) The solid state relay contacts open to interrupt current flow through a second relay coil, whose contacts open to switch off low speed fan operation.

When coolant temperature is above 228° F, cooling fan switch closes to energize high speed cooling fan relay whose contacts close to apply battery voltage directly to cooling fan causing it to run at high speed.

V6-231 VIN 3

Three types of cooling fans are used with V6-231 VIN 3 engines:
a. Single speed.
b. Two speed (internal resistor).
c. Heavy Duty Two Speed (external resistor).

On vehicles with single speed cooling fans, cooling fan relay coil is grounded through cooling fan switch. At coolant temperatures exceeding 228° F, switch contacts close and ground relay coil causing relay contacts to close, thus applying battery voltage to cooling fan.

On vehicles with two speed cooling fans, low speed cooling fan relay coil is grounded through low speed contacts of A/C high pressure switch (with A/C on) or through ground provided by ECM. On vehicles with Heavy Duty Two Speed cooling fan less A/C, ground is only provided by ECM with vehicle speed below 35 mph.

With low speed cooling fan relay coil grounded, relay contacts close, applying battery voltage through cooling fan resistor to heavy duty fan or directly to two speed fan. The resistor which is external with heavy duty cooling fan; internal with two speed fan, drops part of voltage so fan runs at low speed.

During high speed operation, high speed cooling fan relay coil is grounded through high speed contacts of A/C high pressure switch (with A/C on) or cooling fan switch.

With high speed cooling fan relay coil grounded, relay contacts close. Battery voltage is applied directly to cooling fan causing it to run at high speed.

ENGINE COOLING FANS

V6-262 DIESEL VIN T

Two types of cooling fans are used: a single speed or a two speed cooling fan.

The two speed cooling fan is controlled by a cooling fan relay that has two coils and two independent sets of contacts.

During low speed operation, either low speed switch in cooling fan switch closes to ground or low speed switch in A/C high pressure switch closes to ground. The low speed coil of cooling fan relay is energized, causing contacts to apply battery voltage to resistor in two speed fan so fan runs at low speed.

During high speed operation, either high speed cooling fan switch or high speed A/C high pressure switch closes. Circuit is then completed through high speed coil of cooling fan relay, causing battery voltage to be applied directly to cooling fan so it runs at high speed.

The single speed cooling fan uses same relay and switch circuits without a resistor. It runs only at high speed controlled by low speed relay contacts (blk/red wire), while high speed relay contacts (blk/pnk wire) are unused.

System Check
BUICK CENTURY

Less A/C
1. Run engine at fast idle for several minutes.
2. Cooling fan should turn on before coolant temperature indicator in instrument panel comes on.

With A/C
1. With engine at normal operating temperature, and running at curb idle, set A/C mode selector to NORM position. Cooling fan should turn on.
2. Set A/C mode selector to OFF. Run engine at fast idle for several minutes. Cooling fan should come on before coolant temperature indicator on instrument panel comes on.

OLDSMOBILE CUTLASS CIERA

4-151 VIN R Less A/C
1. Run engine at fast idle for several minutes. Cooling fan should turn on before coolant temperature indicator comes on.

4-151 VIN R With A/C
1. With engine at normal operating temperature and running at curb idle, move A/C selector switch to NORM position. Cooling fan should go on.
2. Move A/C selector switch to OFF position. Allow engine to run at fast idle for several minutes. Cooling fan should turn on before coolant temperature indicator goes on.

Troubleshooting
BUICK CENTURY

If cooling fan relay has failed, replace it

and check cooling fan switch for intermittent operation as flows:
1. Warm up engine until cooling fan turns on.
2. Disconnect connector from cooling fan switch.
3. Connect self-powered test lamp to switch and to ground. Test lamp should light steadily.
4. If test lamp flickers, replace cooling fan switch.
5. Perform test on both high and low speed switches, if equipped.

Cooling Fan Does Not Operate
1. Check C-H fuse or F-P fuse. On V6-231 VIN 3, check ECM/ERLS fuse.
2. On all models, check for loose connections on fan and relays.
3. If OK, connect fused jumper wire from positive battery terminal to cooling fan blk/red and/or pnk/blk wires.
4. If fan does not run, check that blk wire is grounded and that fan mounting bolts are clean and tight. If fan is properly grounded and does not run, replace cooling fan.
5. If cooling fan runs in step 3, problem is in control switches or wiring:
   a. On vehicles with 4-151 VIN R, V6-183 VIN E with A/C, V6-231 VIN 3, perform ECM diagnosis.
   b. On vehicles with V6-183 VIN E less A/C, or V6-262 Diesel VIN T, refer to "System Diagnosis."

OLDSMOBILE CUTLASS CIERA W/4-151 VIN R

1. If cooling fan comes on only with A/C compressor and not for hot engine, install new cooling fan switch.
2. If cooling fan does not come on with A/C compressor, check for continuity to ground at terminal A (dk grn/yel wire) of A/C selector switch. If ground is good, check for continuity between terminal B of A/C selector switch and terminal B of coolant fan relay (dk grn/wht wire) with relay disconnected. If good, replace A/C selector switch.

System Diagnosis
BUICK CENTURY W/V6-231 VIN E LESS A/C

SINGLE SPEED FAN
Fan Runs When Jumped; Does Not Run In Normal Use
1. Disconnect connectors from cooling fan relay. With ignition switch in RUN position, check for battery voltage at terminal A (brn wire), and at terminal B (red wire).
2. If battery voltage is not available at a terminal, check circuit that supplies terminal. If voltages are correct, proceed to step 3.
3. Re-connect connector to cooling fan relay.
4. Disconnect dk grn/yel wire from cooling fan switch. Connect fused jumper wire from connector on dk grn/yel wire to ground.

5. With ignition switch in RUN, fan should run.
6. If fan runs, relay and wiring are good, install new cooling fan switch.
7. If fan does not run in step 5, check dk grn/yel wire to relay and blk/red wire to fan. If OK, install new cooling fan relay.

TWO SPEED FAN
Fan Runs At Both Speeds When Jumped; Does Not Run In Normal Use
1. Disconnect connector from high speed cooling fan relay.
2. With ignition in RUN position, measure voltage to ground at connector. Battery voltage should be available at terminal 1 (red wire) and at terminal 5 (brn wire).
3. If any terminal does not have battery voltage, check circuit supplying terminal.
4. If voltages are correct, re-connect connector to high speed cooling fan relay.
5. Disconnect connector form cooling fan switch. Connect fused jumper from connector to ground.
6. With ignition switch in RUN, fan should run at high speed.
7. If fan runs, relay and wiring are OK. Install new high speed cooling fan relay.
8. Disconnect connectors from low speed cooling fan relay. With ignition switch in RUN, check voltage to ground.
9. Battery voltage should be available at terminal A (brn wire) and at terminal C (dk grn/yel wire).
10. If any terminal does not have battery voltage, check circuit supplying terminal.
11. If voltages in step 9 are OK, re-connect connector to low speed cooling fan relay.
12. Disconnect connector from cooling fan switch.
13. Connect a fused jumper from terminal A to ground. With ignition switch in RUN, cooling fan should run at low speed.
14. If cooling fan runs at low speed, relay, cooling fan resistor, and wiring are good. Install new cooling fan switch.
15. If cooling fan does not run, check dk grn/yel wire to relay. Check blk/red and blk/pnk wires and cooling fan resistor. If OK, install new low speed cooling fan relay.

BUICK CENTURY V6-262 DIESEL VIN T

Fan Runs At Both Speeds When Jumped; Does Not Run In Normal Use
1. Disconnect connector from cooling fan relay. With ignition in RUN, measure voltage to ground at connector. Battery voltage should be available at terminal C (brn/wht wire) and terminal G (red wire).
2. If any terminal does not have battery

voltage, check circuit supplying terminal. If voltages are correct, proceed to step 3.

3. Re-connect connector to cooling fan relay. Disconnect connector from cooling fan switch and connect fused jumper from connector to ground.
4. With ignition switch in RUN, check that cooling fan runs at low speed when grounding dk grn/wht wire. Check that fan runs at high speed when grounding lt grn/blk wire.
5. If an does not run at one speed or both, check wires to fan motor and to cooling fan switch from relay. If wiring is OK, install new cooling fan relay.
6. With connector still disconnected from cooling fan switch, start engine. Turn A/C mode selector switch to NORM, and blower to HI, and leave vehicle doors open. Cooling fan should run at low speed, then at high speed. If not, install new A/C high pressure switch.
7. Re-connect connector to cooling fan switch and disconnect connector from A/C high pressure switch.
8. Turn A/C mode selector to OFF. Run engine at fast idle. Cooling fan should run at low speed and then at high speed, before temperature indicator comes on. Install new cooling fan switch if fan does not run at both speeds.

NOTE: If engine temperature is high enough that cooling fan is running at high speed, turn engine off. The cooling fan will switch to low speed as engine cools down.

OLDSMOBILE CUTLASS CIERA

4-151 VIN R

Cooling Fan Does Not Run
1. Check that cooling fan case ground is clean and tight.
2. Check F-P fuse.
3. Turn ignition switch to RUN without starting engine. Disconnect cooling fan switch connector (dk grn/wht wire). Connect jumper wire from dk grn/wht wire to ground and leave connected for duration of test.
4. If fan runs, replace cooling fan switch.
5. If fan does not run in step 3, connect test lamp to ground and check for voltage at terminal C (brn/wht wire) of coolant fan relay.
6. If test lamp does not light, repair open in brn/wht or brn wire between relay and fuse block.
7. If test lamp lights in step 5, check for voltage at terminal D (red wire).
8. If test lamp does not light, check and, if necessary, repair red wire between relay and fusible link C. Check and, if necessary, repair fusible link C.
9. If test lamp lights in step 7, check for voltage at terminal B (dk grn/wht wire) of relay.
10. If test lamp lights, repair open in dk grn/wht wire between relay and cooling fan switch.

11. If test lamp does not light, check for voltage at terminal A (blk/red wire) of relay.
12. If test lamp does not light, replace cooling fan relay.
13. If test lamp lights in step 11, check for voltage at cooling fan connector (blk/red wire).
14. If test lamp does not light, repair open in blk/red wire between relay and cooling fan.
15. If test lamp lights in step 13, repair or replace cooling fan.

V6-183 VIN E WITH SINGLE SPEED FAN LESS A/C

Cooling Fan Does Not Run
1. Check F-P and C-H fuse.
2. Check that cooling fan housing ground is clean and tight.
3. Turn ignition to RUN without starting engine.
4. Disconnect cooling fan switch connector (single dk grn/yel wire). Connect jumper wire from dk grn/yel wire to ground and leave connected for duration of test.
5. If fan runs, replace cooling fan switch.
6. If fan does not run in step 4, connect test lamp to ground and check for voltage at terminal B (red wire) of connector C2 on cooling fan relay.
7. If test lamp does not light, check, and if necessary, repair open in red wire between relay and fusible link C. Check, and if necessary, repair open in fusible link C.
8. If test lamp lights in step 6, connect test lamp to ground and check for voltage at terminal A (brn wire) of connector C1 on relay.
9. If test lamp does not light, repair open in brn wire between relay and fuse block.
10. If test lamp lights in step 8, check for voltage at terminal C (dk grn/yel wire) of connector C1 on relay.
11. If test lamp lights, repair open in dk grn/yel wire between relay and cooling fan switch.
12. If test lamp does not light in step 10, check for voltage at terminal B (blk/red wire) of connector C1 on relay.
13. If test lamp does not light, replace cooling fan relay.
14. If test lamp lights in step 12, check for voltage at cooling fan connector (single blk/red wire).
15. If test lamp does not light, repair open in blk/red wire between relay and cooling fan.
16. If test lamp lights in step 14, repair or replace cooling fan.

V6-183 VIN E WITH 2 SPEED FAN LESS A/C

Cooling Fan Does Not Run At Any Speed
1. Check F-P and C-H fuse.
2. Turn ignition switch to RUN without starting engine.
3. Connect test lamp to ground and check for voltage at terminal E (brn wire) of high speed cooling fan relay.

4. If test lamp does not light, repair open between splice S129 (engine harness, front of LH shock tower) and fuse block.
5. If test lamp lights in step 3, check for voltage at terminal A (red wire) of high speed relay.
6. If test lamp does not light, check, and if necessary, repair red wire. Check, and if necessary, repair fusible link C (located at starter solenoid).
7. If test lamp lights in step 5, disconnect cooling fan connector and check for voltage at terminal B (blk/pnk wire) of cooling fan.
8. If test lamp does not light, repair open in blk/pnk wire between cooling fan harness connector and splice S154 (located in engine harness, LH front of engine).
9. If test lamp lights in step 7, re-connect cooling fan connector and check for voltage at terminal A (blk wire) or cooling fan.
10. If test lamp does not light, repair or replace cooling fan.
11. If test lamp lights in step 9, repair open in blk wire between cooling fan and ground G104 (located on top LH side of engine).

V6-183 VIN E WITH A/C

Cooling Fan Does Not Run At Any Speed
1. Check F-P and C-H fuse.
2. Turn A/C mode selector to Norm.
3. Set ignition switch to RUN without starting engine.
4. Connect test lamp to ground and check for voltage at terminal E (brn wire) of high speed cooling fan relay.
5. If test lamp does not light, repair open in brn wire between splice S129 (located in engine harness, front of LH shock tower) and fuse block.
6. If test lamp lights in step 4, check for voltage at terminal A (red wire) of high speed relay.
7. If test lamp does not light, check and, if necessary, repair red wire. Also. check and, if necessary, repair fusible link C.
8. If test lamp lights in step 6, disconnect cooling fan connector and check for voltage at terminal B (blk/pnk wire) of cooling fan.
9. If test lamp does not light, repair open in blk/pnk wire between cooling fan harness connector and terminal D of high speed relay.
10. If test lamp lights in step 8, re-connect cooling fan connector. Check for voltage at terminal A (black wire) of heavy duty cooling fan or terminal C (black wire) of two speed cooling fan.
11. If test lamp does not light, repair or replace cooling fan.
12. If test lamp lights in step 10, repair open in black wire between cooling fan and ground G104 (located top LH side of engine).

Two Speed Cooling Fan Does Not Run At Low Speed
1. Turn ignition switch to RUN without starting engine.

2. Turn A/C mode selector to NORM position.
3. Connect test lamp to ground and check for voltage at terminal A of connector C1 (brn wire) on low speed cooling fan relay.
4. If test lamp does not light, repair open in brn wire between low speed relay and splice S129.
5. If test lamp lights in step 3, check for voltage at terminal B of connector C2 (red wire) on low speed relay.
6. If test lamp does not light, repair open in red wire between fusible link C and low speed relay.
7. If test lamp lights in step 5, check for voltage at terminal B of connector C1 (blk/red wire) on low speed relay.
8. If test lamp lights, check for voltage at terminal A (blk/red wire) of cooling fan connector.
   a. If test lamp lights, replace cooling fan.
   b. If test lamp does not light, repair open in blk/red wire between relay and of cooling fan connector.
9. If test lamp does not light in step 7, check for voltage at terminal B of connector C2 (red wire) on low speed relay.
10. If test lamp does not light, disconnect connector C2 from relay. Remove terminal C from connector C2 and reconnect C2 to relay.
    a. If fan runs, check for short to ground in tan/blk wires. If no short is found, ECM diagnosis must be performed.
    b. If fan does not run, replace low speed relay.
11. If test lamp lights in step 9, connect jumper wire from terminal A of C2 (lt grn wire) to ground.
    a. If fan does not run, replace low speed relay.
    b. If fan runs, check for open in lt grn or dk grn/wht wire between low speed relay and A/C mode selector. Also check for open in A/C mode selector and in blk wire between A/C mode selector and ground G104.

Heavy Duty Fan Does Not Run At Low Speed

1. Turn ignition switch to RUN position without starting engine.
2. Set A/C mode selector to NORM.
3. Connect test lamp to ground and check for voltage at terminal A of connector C1 (brn wire) on low speed coolant fan relay.
4. If test lamp does not light, repair open in brn wire between low speed relay and splice S129.
5. If test lamp lights in step 3, check for voltage at terminal B of connector C2 (red wire).
6. If test lamp does not light, repair open in red wire between fusible link C and low speed relay.
7. If test lamp lights in step 5, check for voltage at terminal B of connector C1 (blk/red wire) on low speed relay.
8. If test lamp lights, disconnect cooling fan resistor connector. Connect jumper wire in place of resistor.

a. If fan runs, replace cooling fan resistor.
b. If fan does not run, check for open in blk/red wire between relay and connector C141 (LH front of engine). Also check for open in blk/pnk wire between connector C141 and splice S154 (engine harness, LH front of engine).
9. If test lamp does not light in step 7, check for voltage at terminal B of connector C2 (red wire) on low speed relay.
10. If test lamp does not light, disconnect connector C2 from relay. Remove terminal C from C2 and reconnect C2 to relay.
    a. If fan runs, check for short to ground in tan/blk wires. If not short is found, refer to ECM diagnosis.
    b. If fan does not run, replace low speed relay.
11. If test lamp lights in step 9, connect jumper wire from terminal A of C2 (lt grn wire) to ground.
    a. If fan does not run, replace low speed relay.
    b. If fan runs, check for open in lt grn or dk grn/wht wire between low speed relay and A/C mode selector. Also check for open in A/C mode selector and in blk wire between A/C mode selector and ground G104 located on top LH side of engine.

Cooling Fan Does Not Run At High Speed

1. Turn ignition switch to RUN without starting engine.
2. Disconnect cooling fan switch connector (single dk grn/yel wire) and connect a jumper wire from dk grn/yel wire to ground and leave connected for duration of test.
3. If fan runs, replace cooling fan switch.
4. If cooling fan does not run in step 2, connect test lamp to ground and check for voltage at terminal E (brn wire) of high speed cooling fan relay.
5. Connect test lamp to ground and check for voltage at terminal E (brn wire) of high speed cooling fan relay.
6. If test lamp does not light, repair open in brn wire between high speed cooling fan relay and splice S129.
7. If test lamp lights in step 5, check for voltage at terminal A (red wire) of high speed cooling fan relay.
8. If test lamp does not light, repair open in red wire between fusible link C and high speed relay.
9. If test lamp lights in step 7, check for voltage at terminal D (blk wire) of high speed relay.
10. If test lamp does not light, replace high speed relay.
11. If test lamp lights in step 9, repair open in blk/pnk wire between high speed relay and cooling fan.

V6-231 VIN 3 WITH SINGLE SPEED FAN

Cooling Fan Does Not Run

1. Check crank/fan fuse.

2. Check that cooling fan case ground is clean and tight.
3. Turn ignition switch to RUN without starting engine.
4. Disconnect cooling fan switch connector (single dk grn/yel wire) and connect a jumper wire from dk grn/yel wire to ground and leave connected for duration of test.
5. If fan runs in step 4, replace cooling fan switch.
6. If cooling fan does not run in step 4, connect test lamp to ground and check for voltage at terminal A (red wire) of connector on cooling fan relay.
7. If test lamp does not light, check, and if necessary, repair open in red wire between relay and fusible link C. Check, and if necessary, repair open in fusible link C (at starter solenoid).
8. If test lamp lights in step 6, check for voltage at terminal E (brn wire) of connector on relay.
9. If test lamp does not light, repair open in brn wire between relay and fuse block.
10. If test lamp lights in step 8, check for voltage at terminal B (dk grn/yel wire) of connector on relay.
11. If test lamp lights, repair open in dk grn/yel wire between relay and cooling fan switch.
12. If test lamp does not light in step 10, check for voltage at terminal D (blk/red wire) of connector on relay.
13. If test lamp does not light, replace cooling fan relay.
14. If test lamp lights in step 12, check for voltage at cooling fan connector (single blk/red wire).
15. If test lamp does not light, repair open in blk/red wire between relay and cooling fan.
16. If test lamp lights, repair or replace cooling fan.

Cooling Fan Does Not Run For Delay Period After Engine Is Shut Off With Coolant Hot

1. Check ECM/ERLS fuse.
2. Connect test lamp to ground and check for voltage at terminal A (red wire) of connector C1 on cooling fan delay relay.
3. If test lamp lights, check, and if necessary, repair open in red wire between coolant fan delay relay and fusible link C.
4. If test lamp lights, check for voltage at terminal A (red wire) of connector C2 on cooling fan delay relay.
5. If test lamp does not light, check, and if necessary, repair red wire between delay relay and fusible link F.
6. If test lamp lights in step 4, check for voltage at terminal C (blk/pnk wire) of connector C1 on delay relay.
7. If test lamp lights, repair open in blk/pnk wire between delay relay and splice S181 (engine harness, front of LH shock tower).
8. If test lamp does not light, disconnect cooling fan switch connector (single dk grn/yel wire) and connect a jumper

from dk grn/yel wire to ground. Turn ignition switch to RUN then off.
9. If fan runs, replace cooling fan switch.
10. If fan does not run in step 8, check for voltage at terminal B (dk grn/yel wire) of connector C1 on delay relay.
11. If test lamp does not light, replace cooling fan delay relay.
12. If test lamp lights, repair open in dk grn/yel wire between delay relay and splice S182 (engine harness, top RH end of engine).

V6-231 VIN 3 WITH 2 SPEED FAN

Coolant Fan Does Not Run At Any Speed
1. Check crank/fan fuse.
2. Connect test lamp to ground and check for voltage at terminal E (brn wire) of high speed cooling fan relay.
3. If test lamp does not light, repair open in brn wire between high speed cooling fan relay (LH side of radiator on bracket) and fuse block.
4. If test lamp lights, check for voltage at terminal E (brn wire) of low speed cooling fan relay.
5. If test lamp does not light, check, and if necessary, repair brn wire between low speed cooling fan relay (LH side of radiator on bracket) and high speed cooling fan relay.
6. If test lamp does not light in step 4, check for voltage at terminal A (red wire) of high speed cooling fan relay.
7. If test lamp does not light, check, and if necessary, repair red wire between high speed cooling fan relay and fusible link C. Check, and if necessary, repair fusible link C.
8. If test lamp lights, check for voltage at terminal A (red wire) of low speed cooling fan relay.
9. If test lamp does not light, check, and if necessary, repair red wire between low speed cooling fan relay and high speed cooling fan relay.
10. If test lamp lights in step 8, disconnect cooling fan switch connector (single dk grn/yel wire) and connect jumper wire from dk grn/yel wire to ground. Check for voltage at terminal D (blk/pnk wire) of high speed cooling fan relay.
11. If test lamp does not light, replace high speed cooling fan relay.
12. If test lamp lights in step 10, check for voltage at terminal B (blk/pnk wire) of cooling fan.
13. If test lamp does not light, repair open in blk/pnk wire between cooling fan and high speed cooling fan relay.
14. If test lamp lights, replace cooling fan.

Cooling Fan Does Not Run At Low Speed
1. Turn ignition switch to RUN without starting engine.
2. Connect test lamp to ground and check for voltage at terminal D (blk/red wire) on low speed cooling fan.

3. If test lamp does not light, check for voltage at terminal B (dk grn wire) of low speed cooling fan relay.
   a. If lamp does not light, replace low speed cooling fan relay.
   b. If test lamp lights, check, and repair, if necessary, open dk grn wire between relay and splice S175. Also check, and if necessary, repair open in blk/wht wire between splice S166 and ground G104.
4. If test lamp lights in step 2, proceed as follows:
   a. On vehicles with internal cooling fan resistor, check for voltage at terminal A of cooling fan. If test lamp lights, replace cooling fan. If test lamp does not light, repair open in blk/red wire between low speed cooling fan relay and cooling fan.
   b. On vehicles with external cooling fan resistor (heavy duty fan), disconnect cooling fan resistor connector and connect jumper wire in place of cooling fan resistor. If fan runs, replace cooling fan resistor. If fan does not run, repair open in blk/red wire between low speed relay and connector C141 (LH front of engine) or in blk/pnk wire between connector C141 and splice S154.

Cooling Fan Does Not Run At High Speed
1. Turn ignition switch to RUN without starting engine.
2. Disconnect cooling fan switch connector (single dk grn/yel wire) and connect a jumper wire from dk grn/yel wire to ground.
3. If cooling fan runs, replace cooling fan switch.
4. If cooling fan does not run in step 2, leave jumper connected. Connect test lamp to ground and check for voltage at terminal D (blk/pnk wire) of high speed cooling fan relay.
5. If test lamp lights, repair open in blk/pnk wire between relay and splice S154.
6. If test lamp does not light, check for voltage at terminal B (dk grn/yel wire) of high speed cooling fan relay.
7. If test lamp lights, reconnect cooling fan switch connector. Repair dk grn/yel wire between high speed relay and splice S155 (engine harness, top RH end of engine.
8. If test lamp does not light, reconnect cooling fan switch connector and replace high speed cooling fan relay.

Cooling fan Does Not Run At Low And/Or High Speed With A/C On
1. Start engine and set A/C mode selector to NORM and blower to HI.
2. Disconnect cooling fan switch connector (single dk grn/yel wire) and connect test lamp to ground. Check voltage at terminal B (dk grn wire) on A/C high pressure switch connector.

3. If test lamp does not light, repair open in dk grn wire between pressure switch connector and splice S175 (engine harness, front of LH shock tower).
4. If test lamp lights in step 2, check for voltage at terminal C (blk/wht wire) of A/C high pressure switch.
5. If test lamp does not light, replace A/C high pressure switch.
6. If test lamp lights in step 4, repair open in blk/wht wire between pressure switch connector and splice S166 (EFI harness, behind I/P near grommet. Run engine at fast idle with A/C on and check for voltage at terminal A (dk grn/yel wire) of A/C high pressure switch.
7. If test lamp lights, replace A/C high pressure switch.
8. If test lamp does not light in step 6, repair open in dk grn/yel wire between pressure switch connector and splice S155.

Cooling Fan Does Not Run For Delay Period After Engine Is Shut Off With Coolant Hot
1. Check ECM/ERLS fuse.
2. Connect test lamp to ground and check for voltage at terminal A (red wire) of connector C1 on cooling fan delay relay.
3. If test lamp does not light, check/repair open in red wire between cooling fan delay relay and fusible link C (at starter solenoid).
4. If test lamp lights in step 2, check for voltage at terminal A (red wire) of connector C2 on cooling fan delay relay.
5. If test lamp does not light, check/repair open in red wire between delay relay and fusible link F.
6. If test lamp lights in step 4, check for voltage at terminal C (blk/pnk wire of connector C1 on delay relay.
7. If test lamp lights, repair open in blk/pnk wire between delay relay and splice S154.
8. If test lamp lights in step 6, disconnect cooling fan switch connector (single dk grn/yel wire). Connect jumper wire from dk grn/yel wire to ground. Turn ignition switch to RUN, then turn switch off.
9. If cooling fan runs, replace cooling fan switch.
10. If cooling fan does not run in step 8, check for voltage at terminal B (dk grn/yel wire) of connector C1 on delay relay.
11. If test lamp lights, replace cooling fan delay relay.
12. If test lamp lights in step 10, repair open in dk grn/yel wire between delay relay and splice S155 (engine harness, top of RH end of engine).

V6-262 DIESEL VIN T

Cooling Fan Does Not Run At Any Speed
1. Check that cooling fan case ground is clean and tight.
2. Check F-P and C-H fuse.

3. Turn ignition switch to RUN without starting engine.
4. Disconnect cooling fan switch connector and connect a jumper wire from either terminal on cooling fan switch to ground and leave connected for duration of test.
5. If fan runs, replace cooling fan switch.
6. If fan does not run in step 4, connect teat lamp to ground and check for voltage at terminal C (brn/wht wire) of cooling fan relay.
7. If test lamp does not light, repair open in brn/wht or brn wire between fuse block and relay.
8. If test lamp lights in step 6, check voltage at terminal G (red wire) of relay.
9. If test lamp does not light, check/repair open in red wire between relay and fusible link C. Check/repair fusible link C.
10. If test lamp lights in step 8, check voltage at terminal A (blk/pnk wire) of relay or terminal B (blk/red wire) of relay.
11. If test lamp does not light on either terminal, replace cooling fan relay.
12. If test lamp lights on either terminal in step 10, check voltage at terminal B of cooling fan or terminal C of connector C108.
13. If test lamp does not light, repair open in blk/pnk wire or blk/red wire between relay and cooling fan.
14. If test lamp lights in step 12, repair or replace cooling fan.

Cooling Fan Does Not Run At Low Speed

1. Turn ignition switch to RUN without starting engine.
2. Disconnect cooling fan switch connector and connect jumper from terminal A (dk grn/wht wire) to ground and leave connected for duration of test.
3. If cooling fan runs, replace cooling fan switch.
4. If cooling fan does not run in step 2, connect test lamp to ground and check for voltage at terminal B (blk/red wire) of cooling fan relay.
5. If test lamp does not light, replace cooling fan relay.
6. If test lamp lights in step 4, check for voltage at terminal C (blk/red wire) of cooling fan.
7. If test lamp does not light, repair open in blk/red wire between relay and cooling fan.
8. If test lamp lights in step 6, replace cooling fan.

Cooling Fan Does Not Run At High Speed

1. Turn ignition switch to RUN without starting engine.
2. Disconnect cooling fan switch connector and connect a jumper wire from terminal B (lt grn/blk wire) to ground and leave connected for duration of test.
3. If fan runs, replace cooling fan switch.

4. If cooling fan does not run in step 2, connect test lamp to ground and check for voltage at terminal A (blk/pnk wire) of cooling fan relay. If test lamp does not light, replace cooling fan relay.
5. If test lamp does not light, check for voltage at terminal B (blk/pnk wire) of cooling fan.
6. If test lamp lights, replace cooling fan.
7. If test lamp does not light in step 5, repair open in blk/pnk wire between cooling fan and relay.

Cooling Fan, Replace

1. Disconnect battery ground cable.
2. Disconnect wiring from fan motor and frame.
3. Remove fan assembly from radiator support.
4. Reverse procedure to install.

1985 CHEVROLET CELEBRITY

SYSTEM DESCRIPTION

4-151 VIN R & V6-173 VIN X

Less A/C

Voltage is always available through fusible link C (located at front of engine, near starter) to cooling fan relay contacts. With ignition switch in RUN, voltage is available through C-H fuse to cooling fan relay coil.

When high coolant temperatures close cooling fan switch contacts, current flows through C-H fuse, cooling fan relay coil, and cooling fan switch contact to ground. This causes cooling fan relay contacts to close, which allows current to flow through fusible link C, cooling fan relay contacts, and cooling fan to ground.

With A/C

Voltage is always available through fusible link C to cooling fan relay contacts. With ignition switch in RUN, voltage is available through C-H fuse to cooling fan relay coil.

With cooling fan switch contacts closed at high temperatures, current flows through C-H fuse, cooling fan relay coil, and cooling fan switch contacts to ground. The cooling fan relay contacts then close, allowing current to flow through fusible link C, cooling fan relay contacts, and cooling fan to ground.

To ensure adequate air flow over condenser, cooling fan runs with A/C compressor.

In vehicles with 4-151 VIN R, cooling fan runs when A/C mode selector is in MAX, NORM, or BI-LEVEL positions, or when A/C high pressure switch closes and ECM completes current path to ground.

In vehicles with V6-173 VIN X, cooling fan also runs when A/C high pressure switch closes.

V6-173 VIN W

Voltage is always available through battery junction block to cooling fan relay contacts. With ignition switch in RUN, voltage is available through C-H fuse to cooling fan relay coil.

When ECM receives signal from coolant temperature sensor, it provides a ground for cooling fan relay between ECM's cooling fan control terminal and ground terminal. Current then flows through C-H fuse, cooling fan relay coil, and ECM to ground, causing cooling fan relay contacts to close. Current then flows through battery junction block, cooling fan relay contacts, and cooling fan to ground, causing cooling fan to operate.

To ensure adequate air flow over A/C condenser, cooling fan runs with A/C compressor on.

The cooling fan runs when A/C high pressure switch closes and ECM provides ground.

V6-262 DIESEL VIN T

This circuit provides automatic 2-speed operation of cooling fan.

Voltage is always available through fusible link C (located behind LH battery, near bracket) to cooling fan relay contacts. With ignition switch in RUN position, voltage is available through C-H fuse to cooling fan relay coils.

With cooling fan switch low speed contacts closed, current flows through C-H fuse, cooling fan relay low speed coil, and cooling fan switch low speed contact to ground. This causes cooling fan low speed contacts to close. Current then flows through fusible link C, cooling fan relay contacts, and cooling fan to ground, causing cooling fan to run at low speed. Operation of the high speed circuit is similar.

On vehicles equipped with A/C, cooling fan runs when contacts of either A/C high pressure switch are closed to ensure adequate air flow over A/C condenser.

TROUBLESHOOTING

Cooling Fan Does Not Run

1. Check C-H fuse.
2. Check fusible link C.
3. Connect jumper from cooling fan relay coil to ground. Cooling fan should run.

Cooling Fan Runs Constantly With Ignition On

1. Check if cooling fan switch contacts are closed at all times.
2. Check cooling fan relay for stuck contacts.
3. On vehicles with A/C, check if A/C high pressure switch contacts are constantly closed.
4. On vehicles with 4-151 VIN R, check if A/C mode selector is grounded at all times.

COOLING FAN, REPLACE

1. Disconnect battery ground cable.
2. Disconnect wiring from fan motor and frame.

3. Remove fan assembly from radiator support.
4. Reverse procedure to install.

1985 PONTIAC 6000

SYSTEM DESCRIPTION

The cooling fan is controlled by a cooling fan relay whose coil is grounded by cooling fan switch which closes when coolant temperature exceeds 228° F. The relay is then energized, causing its contacts to close to supply battery voltage to fan.

Exc. Diesel Engine

On vehicles equipped with 4-151 VIN R engine with A/C, cooling fan is controlled by the following:
a. Coolant temperature fan switch.
b. ECM and A/C mode selector.
c. ECM and A/C high pressure switch.
On vehicles equipped with V6-173 VIN X engine with A/C, cooling fan is controlled by the following:
a. Coolant temperature switch.
b. A/C mode selector.
c. A/C high pressure switch.
Any of these switch combinations will complete circuit to ground through coil of cooling fan relay. The relay then energizes causing contacts to close and to apply battery voltage to cooling fan.
On vehicles equipped with V6-VIN W, the cooling fan is also controlled by the ECM. The ECM provides a ground path for relay coil to energize relay and close relay contacts. The A/C high pressure switch closes when refrigerant pressure exceeds 280 psi. This grounds an ECM input, causing ECM to turn on cooling fan.

V6-262 Diesel VIN T

Two types of cooling fans are used: a single speed or a two speed cooling fan.
The two speed cooling fan is controlled by a cooling fan relay that has two coils and two independent sets of contacts.
During low speed operation, either low speed switch in cooling fan switch closes to ground or low speed switch in A/C high pressure switch closes to ground. The low speed coil of cooling fan relay is energized, causing contacts to apply battery voltage to resistor in two speed fan so fan runs at low speed.
During high speed operation, either high speed cooling fan switch or high speed A/C high pressure switch closes. Circuit is then completed through high speed coil of cooling fan relay, causing battery voltage to be applied directly to cooling fan so it runs at high speed.
The single speed cooling fan uses same relay and switch circuits without a resistor. It runs only at high speed controlled by low speed relay contacts (blk/red wire), while high speed relay contacts (blk/pnk wire) are unused.

TROUBLESHOOTING

Exc. V6-162 DIESEL VIN T

Cooling Fan Does Not Operate
1. Check C-H or Fan/Elec fuse.
2. Check for loose connectors on fan and relays.
3. If fuses and connectors are OK, connect fused jumper wire from positive battery terminal to cooling fan blk/red and/or pnk/blk wires.
4. If fan does not run, check that blk wire is grounded and that mounting bolts are clean and tight. If fan is grounded and does not run, install new cooling fan.
5. If fan does not run in step 3, problem is in control switches or wiring. Proceed as follows:
   a. Vehicles with 4-151 VIN R less A/C or V6-173 VIN X, perform system diagnosis.
   b. Vehicles with 4-151 VIN R with A/C or V6-173 VIN W, perform ECM diagnosis.

SYSTEM CHECK

V6-262 DIESEL VIN T LESS A/C
1. Run engine at fast idle for several minutes. Cooling fan should turn on before coolant temperature indicator on instrument panel comes on.

V6-262 Diesel VIN T with A/C
1. With engine idling, set A/C mode selector to NORM and blower to HI. Set temperature selector to COLD. Cooling fan should turn on and run at low speed, before coolant temperature indicator comes on. Fan will run at low speed as long as coolant temperature remains below 246° F.
2. Increase engine speed from idle. Run engine for several minutes. Cooling fan should switch to high speed before coolant temperature indicator comes on.

SYSTEM DIAGNOSIS

4-151 VIN R & V6 173 VIN X LESS A/C

Fan Runs When Jumped, Does Not Run In Normal Use
1. Disconnect connector from cooling fan relay. With ignition is RUN position, check for battery voltage at terminal C (brn/wht wire) and at terminal D (red wire) and terminal E (red wire).
2. If any terminal does not have battery voltage, check circuit that supplies terminal. If voltages are correct, proceed to step 3.
3. Reconnect connector to cooling fan relay. Disconnect dk grn/wht wire from cooling fan switch. Connect fused jumper from wire to ground. Turn ignition switch to RUN.
4. If fan runs, relay and wiring are OK. Install new cooling fan switch.
5. If fan does not run, check dk grn/wht

wire to relay and blk/red wire to fan. If OK, install new cooling fan relay.
6. If cooling fan relay has failed, cooling fan switch should be checked for intermittent operation as follows:
   a. Warm up engine until cooling fan runs.
   b. Disconnect connector from cooling fan switch.
   c. Connect self-powered test lamp to switch and ground. Test lamp should light steadily.
   d. If test lamp flickers at all, install new cooling fan switch.
   e. Test both high speed and low speed switches, if so equipped.
7. On vehicles with V6-173 VIN X with A/C, check operation of A/C high pressure switch and A/C mode selector as follows:
   a. Disconnect connector from A/C high pressure switch. With engine idling, turn mode selector to NORM. A/C compressor will run and cooling fan come on.
   b. If cooling fan does not run, connect jumper wire from dk grn/wht wire at terminal B on mode selector to ground.
   c. If fan runs, check that blk wire at A is grounded. If ground is OK, install new A/C mode selector.
   d. With A/C compressor running, and connector disconnected from A/C high pressure switch, test switch terminals for continuity to ground using self-powered test lamp. If both terminals are not grounded, install new A/C high pressure switch.

V6-262 DIESEL VIN T

Fan Runs At Both Speeds When Jumped, But Does Not Run In Normal Service
1. Disconnect connector from cooling fan relay and measure voltage to ground at connector. With ignition switch in RUN position, battery voltage should be available at terminal C (brn/wht wire) and at terminal G (red wire).
2. If any terminal does not have battery voltage, check circuit supplying terminal. If voltages are correct, proceed to next step.
3. Reconnect connector to cooling fan relay. Disconnect connector from cooling fan switch and connect fused jumper wire from connector to ground. With ignition switch in RUN position, cooling fan should run at low speed when dk grn/wht wire is grounded; high speed when lt grn/wht wire is grounded.
4. If fan does not run at one or both speeds, check wires to motor and to cooling fan switch from relay. If wiring is OK, install new cooling fan relay.
5. With connector still disconnected from cooling fan switch, start engine. Turn

ENGINE COOLING FANS

A/C mode selector to NORM and blower to HI, and leave vehicle doors open. Cooling fan should run at low speed, then at high speed. Install new A/C high pressure switch if not.

6. Reconnect connector to cooling fan switch and remove connector from A/C high pressure switch. Turn A/C mode selector off. Run engine at fast idle. Cooling fan should run at low speed, then at high speed, before temperature indicator comes on. Install new cooling fan switch if fan does not run at both speeds. Note that if engine has warmed up enough for fan to run at high speed, turn engine off. As engine cools off, fan will switch to low speed.

COOLING FAN, REPLACE

1. Disconnect battery ground cable.
2. Disconnect wiring from fan motor and frame.
3. Remove fan assembly from radiator support.
4. Reverse procedure to install.

UNIVERSAL JOINTS

INDEX

SERVICE NOTES

Before disassembling any universal joint, examine the assembly carefully and note the position of the grease fitting (if used). Also, be sure to mark the yokes with relation to the propeller shaft so they may be reassembled in the same relative position. Failure to observe these precautions may produce rough car operation which results in rapid wear and failure of parts, and place an unbalanced load on transmission, engine and rear axle.

When universal joints are disassembled for lubrication or inspection, and the old parts are to be reinstalled, special care must be exercised to avoid damage to universal joint spider or cross and bearing cups.

NOTE: Some late model cars use an injected nylon retainer on the universal joint bearings. When service is necessary, pressing the bearings out will sheer the nylon retainer. Replacement with the conventional steel snap ring type is then necessary.

CROSS & ROLLER TYPE

Figs. 1 and 2 illustrate typical examples of universal joints of this type. They all operate on the same principle and similar service and replacement procedures may be applied to all.

DISASSEMBLY

1. Remove snap rings (or retainer plates) that retain bearings in yoke and drive shaft.
2. Place U-joint in a vise.
3. Select a wrench socket with an outside diameter slightly smaller than the U-joint bearings. Select another wrench socket with an inside diameter slightly larger than the U-joint bearings.
4. Place the sockets at opposite bearings in the yoke so that the smaller socket becomes a bearing pusher and the larger socket becomes a bearing receiver when the vise jaws come together, **Fig. 3.** Close vise jaws until both bearings are free of yoke and remove bearings from the cross or spider.
5. If bearings will not come all the way out, close vise until bearing in receiver socket protrudes from yoke as much as possible without using excessive force. Then remove from vise and place that portion of bearing which protrudes from yoke between vise jaws. Tighten vise to hold bearing and drive yoke off with a soft hammer.
6. To remove opposite bearing from yoke, replace in vise with pusher socket on exposed cross journal with receiver socket over bearing cup. Then tighten vise jaws to press bearing back through yoke into receiving socket.
7. Remove yoke from drive shaft and again place protruding portion of bearing between vise jaws. Then tighten vise to hold bearing while driving yoke off bearing with soft hammer.
8. Turn spider or cross ¼ turn and use the same procedure to press bearings out of drive shaft.

ASSEMBLY

1. If old parts are to be reassembled, pack bearing cups with universal joint grease. Do not fill cups completely or use excessive amounts as over-lubrication may damage seals during reassembly. Use new seals.
2. If new parts are being installed, check new bearings for adequate grease before assembling.
3. With the pusher (smaller) socket, press one bearing part way into drive shaft. Position spider into the partially installed bearing. Place second bearing into drive shaft. Fasten drive shaft in vise so that bearings are in contact with faces of vise jaws, **Fig. 4.** Some spiders are provided with locating lugs which must face toward drive shaft when installed, **Fig. 5.**
4. Press bearings all the way into position and install snap rings or retainer plates.
5. Install bearings in yoke in same manner. When installation is completed, check U-joint for binding or roughness. If free movement is impeded, correct the condition before installation in vehicle.

Fig. 1 Cross & roller type universal joint. Chrysler-built cars

UNIVERSAL JOINTS

Fig. 2 Cross & roller universal joints (single Cardan type) & propeller shaft (Typical)

Fig. 3 Removing bearings from yoke using small & large wrench sockets as pusher & receiver tools, respectively

Fig. 4 Installing bearings into drive shaft yoke

Fig. 5 Some units have locating lugs which must face propeller shaft when installed

Fig. 6 Cross-section of typical GM constant velocity U-joint

Fig. 7 Production type universal joints

Fig. 8 Removing bearing using cross press

Fig. 9 Installing spacer J-9522-5

1	BEARING CUP	4	NEEDLE BEARINGS	7	SEAL
2	SNAP RING	5	FLAT DELRIN WASHER	8	SHIELD
3	ROUND DELRIN WASHER	6	SPIDER		

Fig. 10 Service universal joint kit

Fig. 11 Partially installed bearing cap

CONSTANT VELOCITY TYPE

G.M. MODELS

This type of U-joint, **Fig. 6,** is composed of two conventional cross and roller joints connected with a special link yoke. Because the two joint angles are the same, even though the usual U-joint fluctuation is present within the unit, the acceleration of the front joint (within the yoke) is always neutralized by the deceleration of the rear joint (within the yoke) and vice versa. The end result is the front and rear propeller shafts always turn at a constant velocity.

Disassembly

NOTE: During disassembly, two types of univeral joints may be found, **Fig. 7.**

1. Support propeller shaft horizontally, in line with base plate of a suitable press.
2. Position universal joint so that lower ear of shaft yoke is supported on a 1⅛ inch socket.
3. Position universal joint bearing separator tool No. J-2522-3 or equivalent, onto open portion of horizontal bearing cups, then press lower bearing cup out of yoke ear, **Fig. 8.** This will shear the plastic retaining ring on the lower bearing cup. If the bearing cup is not completely removed, lift bearing separator and insert spacer remover tool No. J-9522-5 or equivalent, between

the seal and bearing cup, **Fig. 9.** Complete removal of bearing cup by pressing out from yoke.
4. Rotate propeller shaft, shear the opposite plastic retainer, and press opposite bearing cup out from yoke.

NOTE: There are no bearing retainer grooves in production type bearing cups, and cannot be reused.

5. If the front universal joint is being replaced, remove bearing cup from the slip yoke in the same manner described in steps 2, 3 and 4.

Assembly

NOTE: During assembly of universal joint, always install a complete universal service kit. This kit includes, one pregreased cross assembly, four service bearing cup assemblies with seals, needle roller bearings, washers, bearing retainers and grease, **Fig. 10.** Ensure seals are in place on the service bearing cups.

1. Install one bearing cup partially into one side of the yoke, then turn yoke ear toward bottom.
2. Insert universal joint bearing separator tool No. J-9522-3 or equivalent, so that trunnion seats freely into bearing cup, **Fig. 11.**
3. Partially install opposite bearing cup. Ensure both truunions are installed straight into both bearing cups.
4. Press against opposite bearing cups, moving the cross to ensure free movement of the trunnions in the bearings. If the bearing cups bind, check needle roller bearings.
5. When one bearing retainer groove clears the inside of the yoke, stop pressing and insert bearing retainer into position, **Fig. 12.**
6. Continue pressing bearing cup until opposite bearing retainer, can be installed into postiton.
7. If opposite bearing retainer cannot be installed, firmly tap yoke and install bearing retainer, **Fig. 13.**
8. Install other half of the universal joint in the same manner.

1980 VERSAILLES

These models use a one-piece driveshaft with a constant velocity universal joint

between the driveshaft and companion flange, **Fig. 14.**

Disassembly

1. Mark relative positions of the spiders, center yoke and centering socket yoke to the companion flange.
2. Install tool CJ91B, **Fig. 15.** Thread tool clockwise until bearing protrudes approximately ⅜ inch from yoke.
3. Remove driveshaft from vise.
4. Tighten the bearing in a vise and tap on yoke to free bearing from center yoke, **Fig. 16.** Do not tap on driveshaft tube.
5. Repeat steps 2 through 4 on remaining bearings.
6. Remove spider from center yoke.
7. Remove bearings from driveshaft yoke as outlined in steps 2 through 4. Remove spider from yoke.
8. Insert a screwdriver into centering ball socket, located in companion flange, and pry out rubber seal. Remove retainer, three piece ball seat, washer and spring from ball socket.

Assembly

1. Inspect centering ball socket assembly for worn or damaged components and replace the assembly if necessary.
2. Insert spring, washer, three piece ball seat and retainer into ball socket.
3. With a suitable tool, install centering ball socket seal.
4. Place spider in driveshaft yoke. Ensure that spider bosses are in the

Fig. 12 Installing retaining ring

Fig. 13 Taping yoke with hammer to seat retaining ring

Fig. 14   Constant velocity universal joint (double Cardan type). 1980 Versailles

Fig. 15   Partially pressing bearing from center yoke

original position. Press in bearing cups with tool CJ91B. Install snap rings.

5. Place center yoke over spider ends and press in bearing cups. Install snap rings.
6. Install spider in companion flange yoke. Ensure that spider bosses are in original positions. Press on bearing cups and install snap rings.
7. Place center yoke over spider ends and press in bearing cups. Install snap rings.

1980–82 COUGAR XR7 & THUNDERBIRD & 1982–85 CONTINENTAL & MARK VII

NOTE: When rear U-joint disassembly is required, new U-joints should be installed.

Disassembly

1. Mark position of all yokes so that original position can be maintained during assembly.

2. Support driveshaft in suitable vise.
3. Remove two snap rings that secure rear spider bearing to center yoke.
4. Install tool T74P-4635-C onto joint. Tighten tool until bearing cup extends approximately ⅜ inch from yoke.
5. Remove driveshaft from vise and grip bearing cup in vise. Tap on center yoke to free bearing from yoke, **Fig. 17.**
6. Repeat steps 2 through 5 on opposite bearing.
7. Pull flanged center socket yoke off center stud.
8. Remove spider from flanged center socket yoke following steps 2 through 5.
9. Remove snap rings from center yoke and studs. Install tool T74P-4635-C on driveshaft stud yoke and press bearing cup outward until inside of center yoke almost contacts slinger ring attached to stud yoke. Grip protruding bearing cup in vise and tap on yoke center to remove. Repeat this step on opposite bearing.

Assembly

1. Install front spider in driveshaft stud

yoke. Press in bearing cups using tool T74P-4635-C and install snap rings.
2. Install center yoke over spider ends and press in bearing cup assemblies using tool T74P-4635-C. Install snap rings.
3. Install rear spider in flanged center socket yoke and press in bearing cup assemblies using tool T74P-4635-C. Install snap rings.
4. Pack inside of ball with ESW-MIC147-A and place centering spring inside ball stud yoke.
5. Assemble flanged center socket yoke to ball stud and center yoke by guiding ball onto stud while flexing spider in flange. Press in center yoke bearing cup assemblies using tool T74P-4635-C. Install snap rings.
6. Rap center yoke to free joint.
7. Remove grease plug from each spider and lubricate all U-joints with ESW-M1C147-A. Install plugs.

NOTE: Flush type grease fittings are required to insure proper clearance during normal vehicle operation.

Fig. 16   Removing bearing from center yoke

Fig. 17   Drive shaft & universal joint (double Cardan type) exploded view. 1980–82 Cougar XR7, Thunderbird, 1982–85 Continental & Mark VII

DRUM BRAKES

TABLE OF CONTENTS

American Motors Corp.

NOTE: Refer to "Brake Usage Chart" to determine which type brakes are used on vehicle being serviced.

TABLE OF CONTENTS

Brake Usage Chart

	Type No.		Type No.
1980 AMX	2	1980 Pacer	2
1980-83 Concord Exc. Station Wagon w/6 Cylinder Engine	1	1980-83 Spirit Exc. GT Models w/Rally Tuned Suspension	1
1980-83 Concord Station Wagon w/6 Cylinder Engine	2	1980-83 Spirit w/V8 Engine Or Rally Tuned Suspension	2
1980-85 Eagle	2		

General Information

SERVICE PRECAUTIONS

When working on or around brake assemblies, care must be taken to prevent breathing asbestos dust, as many manufacturers incorporate asbestos fibers in the production of brake linings. During routine service operations the amount of asbestos dust from brake lining wear is at a low level, due to a chemical breakdown during use and a few precautions will minimize exposure.

CAUTION: Do not sand or grind brake linings unless suitable local exhaust ventilation equipment is used to prevent excessive asbestos exposure.

1. Wear a suitable respirator approved for asbestos dust use during all repair procedures.
2. When cleaning brake dust from brake parts, use a vacuum cleaner with a highly efficient filter system. If a suitable vacuum cleaner is not available, use a water soaked rag.

NOTE: Do not use compressed air or dry brush to clean brake parts.

3. Keep work area clean using same equipment as for cleaning brake parts.
4. Properly dispose of rags and vacuum cleaner bags by placing them in plastic bags.
5. Do not smoke or eat while working on brake systems.

NOTE: Never use gasoline, kerosene, alcohol, motor oil, transmission fluid, or any fluid containing mineral oil to clean brake system components. These fluids will damage the rubber caps and seals. If system contamination is suspected, check brake fluid in the reservoir for dirt, discoloration, or separation (breakdown) of the brake fluid into distinct layers. Drain and flush the hydraulic system with clean brake fluid if contamination is suspected.

GENERAL INSPECTION

BRAKE DRUMS

Any time the brake drums are removed for brake service, the braking surface diameter should be checked with a suitable brake drum micrometer at several points to determine if they are within the safe oversize limit stamped on the brake drum outer surface. If the braking surface diameter exceeds specifications, the drum must be replaced. If the braking surface diameter is within specifications, drums should be cleaned and inspected for cracks, scores, deep grooves, taper, out of round and heat spotting. If drums are cracked or heat spotted, they must be replaced. Minor scores should be removed with sandpaper. Grooves and large scores can only be removed by machining with special equipment, as long as the braking surface is within specifications stamped on brake drum outer surface. Any brake drum sufficiently out of round to cause vehicle vibration or noise while braking or showing taper should also be machined, removing only enough stock to true up the brake drum.

After a brake drum is machined, wipe the braking surface diameter with a denatured alcohol soaked cloth. If one brake drum is machined, the other should also be machined to the same diameter to maintain equal braking forces.

BRAKE LININGS & SPRINGS

Inspect brake linings for excessive wear, damage, oil, grease or brake fluid contamination. If any of the above conditions exists, brake linings should be replaced. Do not attempt to replace only one set of brake shoes; they should be replaced as an axle set only to maintain equal braking forces. Examine brake shoe webbing, hold down and return springs for signs of overheating indicated by a slight blue color. If any component exhibits overheating signs, replace hold down and return springs with new ones. Overheated springs lose their pull and could cause brake linings to wear out prematurely. Inspect all springs for sags, bends and external damage and replace as necessary.

Inspect hold down retainers and pins for bends, rust and corrosion. If any of the above is found, replace as required.

BACKING PLATE

Inspect backing plate shoe contact surface for grooves that may restrict shoe movement and cannot be removed by lightly sanding with emery cloth or other suitable abrasive. If backing plate exhibits above condition, it should be replaced. Also inspect for signs of cracks, warpage and excessive rust, indicating need for replacement.

ADJUSTER MECHANISM

Inspect all components for rust, corrosion, bends and fatigue. Replace as necessary. On adjuster mechanism equipped with adjuster cable, inspect cable for kinks, fraying or elongation of eyelet and replace as necessary.

PARKING BRAKE CABLE

Inspect parking brake cable end for kinks, fraying and elongation and replace as necessary. Use a small hose clamp to compress clamp where it enters backing plate to remove.

Types 1 & 2

INDEX

REMOVAL

1. Raise and support rear of vehicle, then remove tire and wheel assembly.
2. Remove brake drum. If brake lining is dragging on brake drum, back off brake adjustment by rotating adjustment screw. Refer to individual car chapter for procedure.

NOTE: If brake drum is rusted or corroded to axle flange and cannot be removed, lightly tap axle flange to drum mounting surface with a suitable hammer.

3. Install suitable wheel cylinder clamp over ends of wheel cylinder to retain pistons in bore.
4. Remove parking brake lever retaining clip, **Figs. 1 and 2.**
5. On type 2, **Fig. 2,** remove adjuster lever spring, primary and secondary shoe return springs using a suitable pair of brake spring pliers. On type 1, **Fig. 1,** remove adjuster lever spring, secondary shoe return spring, adjuster cable eyelet and primary shoe return spring.
6. On all types, remove shoe guide plate (if equipped), and adjuster cable and guide plate.
7. Using suitable tool, compress hold down springs, then remove spring retainers, hold down springs and pins.
8. Separate springs and remove from backing plate.
9. Remove parking brake lever from cable.
10. Separate all components from brake shoes.
11. Clean dirt from brake drum, backing plate and all other components.

CAUTION: Do not use compressed air or dry brush to clean brake parts. Many brake parts contain asbestos fibers which, if inhaled, can cause serious injury. Clean brake parts with a water soaked rag or a suitable vacuum cleaner to minimize airborne dust.

INSPECTION

1. Inspect components for damage and unusual wear. Replace as necessary.
2. Inspect wheel cylinders. Boots which are torn, cut, or heat damaged indicate need for wheel cylinder replacement. Fluid spilling from boot center hole, or wetness around wheel cylinder ends indicates cup leakage and need for wheel cylinder replacement.

NOTE: A small amount of fluid is always present and is considered normal, acting as a lubricant for the cylinder pistons.

3. Inspect backing plate for evidence of seal leakage. If leakage exists, refer to individual car chapters for axle seal replacement procedure.
4. Inspect backing plate attaching bolts and ensure they are tight.
5. Check adjuster screw operation. If satisfactory, lightly lubricate adjusting screw and washer with suitable brake lube. If operation is unsatisfactory, replace.
6. Using fine emery cloth or other suitable abrasive, clean rust and dirt from shoe contact surfaces on backing plate.

INSTALLATION

1. Lightly lubricate backing plate shoe contact surfaces with suitable brake lube.
2. Assemble parking brake lever to secondary shoe and secure with spring washer and retaining clip. Crimp ends of clip with suitable pliers.
3. Position brake shoes on backing plate, primary (short lining) shoe facing front of vehicle and secondary (long lining) facing rear. Secure brake shoes with hold down springs, pins and retainers.
4. Install parking brake link and spring between shoes.

Fig. 1   Drum brake assembly. Type 1

5. Loosen parking brake adjustment nut, then install parking brake cable on parking brake lever.
6. On type 1, proceed as follows:
   a. Using suitable brake spring pliers, install primary return spring from brake shoe to anchor.
   b. Install adjuster cable eyelet on anchor pin with crimp facing out.
   c. Position adjuster cable guide on secondary shoe, then using suitable brake spring pliers, install secondary return spring from brake shoe to anchor.
7. On types 2, proceed as follows:
   a. Install shoe guide plate and adjuster cable eyelet on anchor. Ensure adjuster cable crimp faces out.
   b. Ensure parking brake link is properly positioned between brake shoes and wheel cylinder links are engaged in shoe web.
   c. Using suitable brake spring pliers, install primary return spring from brake shoe to anchor, then secondary return spring from brake shoe to anchor.
8. On all types, remove wheel cylinder clamp installed during removal of brake shoes.
9. Tighten adjuster screw assembly to thread limit and back off one-half turn.
10. Install adjuster screw assembly between shoes. Ensure toothed wheel is on secondary shoe side.

NOTE: Adjuster screw assemblies are stamped R (right) and L (left). To ensure proper adjuster operation, they must be installed on their respective sides.

11. Hook adjuster cable hook into adjuster lever hole, then position adjuster spring hook in large hole in primary shoe web. Using suitable brake spring pliers, install adjuster spring in adjuster lever hole.
12. Ensure adjuster cable is properly seated in cable guide, then pull adjuster lever, cable and adjuster spring down and towards the rear, engaging lever pivot hook in the large hole of secondary shoe web.
13. After installation, check adjuster operation by pulling adjuster cable between cable guide and adjuster lever towards secondary shoe sufficiently to lift adjuster lever past one tooth on adjuster screw assembly. The adjuster lever should snap into position behind the next tooth, then upon release of adjuster cable, rotate toothed wheel one notch. If operation is not satisfactory, recheck installation.

Fig. 2   Drum brake assembly. Type 2

Fig. 3   Measuring brake drum inside diameter

14. Ensure brake shoe upper ends are seated against anchor pin and shoe assemblies are centered on backing plate. If not, back off parking brake adjustment.
15. Using suitable brake drum to shoe gauge, **Fig. 3,** measure brake drum inside diameter. Adjust brake shoes to dimension obtained on outside portion of gauge using adjuster screw.
16. Install brake drum, wheel and tire assembly.

17. If any hydraulic brake connections have been opened, bleed brake system.
18. Adjust parking brake. Refer to individual car chapter for procedures.
19. Inspect all hydraulic lines and connections for leakage and repair as necessary.
20. Check master cylinder fluid level and replenish as necessary.
21. Check brake pedal for proper feel and return.

22. Lower vehicle and road test.

NOTE: Do not severely apply brakes immediately after installation of new brake linings or permanent damage may occur to linings, and/or brake drums may become scored. Brakes must be used moderately during first several hundred miles of operation to ensure proper burnishing of linings.

Specifications

Year	Model	Brake Drum Inside Dia. In.
1980–83	Exc. Concord & Spirit	10
	Concord	9①
	Spirit	9②
1984–85	Eagle	10

①—Concord sta. wag. w/6 cyl. engine, 10".
②—Spirit GT models w/rally tuned suspension, 10".

Chrysler Corp.

NOTE: Refer to "Brake Usage Chart" to determine which type brakes are used on vehicle being serviced.

TABLE OF CONTENTS

Brake Usage Chart

	Type No.
1980–82 Front Wheel Drive	2
1983–85 Front Wheel Drive	3
Rear Wheel Drive	1

General Information

INDEX

SERVICE PRECAUTIONS

When working on or around brake assemblies, care must be taken to prevent breathing asbestos dust, as many manufacturers incorporate asbestos fibers in the production of brake linings. During routine service operations the amount of asbestos dust from brake lining wear is at a low level, due to a chemical breakdown during use and a few precautions will minimize exposure.

CAUTION: Do not sand or grind brake linings unless suitable local exhaust ventilation equipment is used to prevent excessive asbestos exposure.

1. Wear a suitable respirator approved for asbestos dust use during all repair procedures.
2. When cleaning brake dust from brake parts, use a vacuum cleaner with a highly efficient filter system. If a suitable vacuum cleaner is not available, use a water soaked rag.

NOTE: Do not use compressed air or dry brush to clean brake parts.

3. Keep work area clean using same equipment as for cleaning brake parts.
4. Properly dispose of rags and vacuum cleaner bags by placing them in plastic bags.
5. Do not smoke or eat while working on brake systems.

NOTE: Never use gasoline, kerosene, alcohol, motor oil, transmission fluid, or any fluid containing mineral oil to clean brake system components. These fluids will damage the rubber caps and seals. If system contamination is suspected, check brake fluid in the reservoir for dirt, discoloration, or separation (breakdown) of the brake fluid into distinct layers. Drain and flush the hydraulic system with clean brake fluid if contamination is suspected.

GENERAL INSPECTION

BRAKE DRUMS

Any time the brake drums are removed for brake service, the braking surface diameter should be checked with a suitable brake drum micrometer at several points to determine if they are within the safe oversize limit stamped on the brake drum outer surface. If the braking surface diameter exceeds specifications, the drum must be replaced. If the braking surface diameter is within specifications, drums should be cleaned and inspected for cracks, scores, deep grooves, taper, out of round and heat spotting. If drums are cracked or heat spotted, they must be replaced. Minor scores should be removed with sandpaper. Grooves and large scores can only be removed by machining with special equipment, as long as the braking surface is within specifications stamped on brake drum outer surface. Any brake drum sufficiently out of round to cause vehicle vibration or noise while braking or showing taper should also be machined, removing only enough stock to true up the brake drum.

After a brake drum is machined, wipe the braking surface diameter with a denatured alcohol soaked cloth. If one brake drum is machined, the other should also be machined to the same diameter to maintain equal braking forces.

BRAKE LININGS & SPRINGS

Inspect brake linings for excessive wear, damage, oil, grease or brake fluid contamination. If any of the above conditions exists, brake linings should be replaced. Do not attempt to replace only one set of brake shoes; they should be replaced as an axle set only to maintain equal braking forces. Examine brake shoe webbing, hold down and return springs for signs of overheating indicated by a slight blue color. If any component exhibits overheating signs, replace hold down and return springs with new ones. Overheated springs lose their pull and could cause brake linings to wear out prematurely. Inspect all springs for sags, bends and external damage and replace as necessary.

Inspect hold down retainers and pins for bends, rust and corrosion. If any of the above is found, replace as required.

BACKING PLATE

Inspect backing plate shoe contact surface for grooves that may restrict shoe movement and cannot be removed by lightly sanding with emery cloth or other suitable abrasive. If backing plate exhibits above condition, it should be replaced. Also inspect for signs of cracks, warpage and excessive rust, indicating need for replacement.

ADJUSTER MECHANISM

Inspect all components for rust, corrosion, bends and fatigue. Replace as necessary. On adjuster mechanism equipped with adjuster cable, inspect cable for kinks, fraying or elongation of eyelet and replace as necessary.

PARKING BRAKE CABLE

Inspect parking brake cable end for kinks, fraying and elongation and replace as necessary. Use a small hose clamp to compress clamp where it enters backing plate to remove.

Type 1

INDEX

REMOVAL

1. Raise and support rear of vehicle, then remove tire and wheel assembly.
2. Remove brake drum. If brake lining is dragging on brake drum, back off brake adjustment by rotating adjustment screw.

NOTE: If brake drum is rusted or corroded to axle flange and cannot be removed, lightly tap axle flange to drum mounting surface with a suitable hammer.

3. Using brake spring pliers or equivalent, remove primary and secondary shoe return springs, **Fig. 1.**
4. Remove automatic adjuster cable from anchor plate, then unhook from adjuster lever.
5. Remove adjuster cable, overload spring, cable guide and anchor plate.
6. Unhook adjuster lever spring from lever, then remove spring and lever.
7. Remove shoe to shoe spring from secondary shoe web, then primary shoe.
8. Spread shoes apart and remove parking brake strut and spring.
9. Using suitable tool, remove shoe retainers, then springs and nails.
10. Disconnect parking brake cable from lever, then remove brake shoes.
11. Remove parking brake lever from secondary shoe.
12. Clean dirt from brake drum, backing plate and all other components.

CAUTION: Do not use compressed air or dry brush to clean brake parts. Many brake parts contain asbestos fibers which, if inhaled, can cause serious injury. To clean brake parts, use a water soaked rag or a suitable vacuum cleaner to minimize airborne dust.

Fig. 1 Drum brake assembly. Type 1

INSPECTION

1. Inspect components for damage and unusual wear. Replace as necessary.
2. Inspect wheel cylinders. Boots which are torn, cut or heat damaged indicate

need for wheel cylinder replacement. Peel back lower edge of boot. If fluid spills out, cup leakage is indicated and wheel cylinder should be replaced.

NOTE: A slight amount of fluid is always present and considered normal, acting as a lubricant for the cylinder pistons.

3. Inspect backing plate for evidence of seal leakage. If leakage exists, refer to individual car chapter for axle seal replacement procedure.
4. Inspect backing plate attaching bolts, and ensure they are tight.
5. Inspect adjuster screw operation. If satisfactory, lightly lubricate adjusting screw and washer with suitable brake lube. If operation is unsatisfactory, replace.
6. Using fine emery cloth or other suitable abrasive, clean rust and dirt from shoe contact surfaces on backing plate.

INSTALLATION

1. Lubricate parking brake lever fulcrum with suitable brake lube, then attach lever to secondary brake shoe. Ensure lever operates smoothly.
2. Lightly lubricate backing plate shoe contact surfaces with suitable brake lube.
3. Connect parking brake lever to cable, then slide secondary brake shoe into position.
4. Connect wheel cylinder link to brake shoe (if equipped).
5. Slide parking brake lever strut behind axle flange and into parking brake lever slot, then place parking brake anti-rattle spring over strut.
6. Position primary brake shoe on backing plate, then connect wheel cylinder link (if equipped) and parking brake strut.
7. Install anchor plate, then position adjuster cable eye over anchor pin.
8. Install primary shoe return spring using brake spring pliers or equivalent.
9. Place protruding hole rim of cable guide in secondary shoe web hole, then holding guide in position, install secondary shoe return spring through cable guide and secondary shoe. Install spring on anchor pin using brake spring pliers or equivalent.

NOTE: Ensure cable guide remains flat against secondary shoe web during and after return spring installation. Also ensure secondary spring end overlaps primary spring end on anchor pin.

10. Using suitable pliers, squeeze spring ends around anchor pin until parallel.
11. Install adjuster screw assembly between primary and secondary brake shoes with star wheel on secondary shoe side.

NOTE: The left side adjuster assembly stud is stamped "L" and is cadmium-plated. The right side adjuster assembly is not stamped and is colored black.

12. Install shoe to shoe spring, then position adjusting lever spring over pivot pin on shoe web.
13. Install adjusting lever under spring and over pivot pin, then slide lever slightly rearward.
14. Install nails, springs and retainers.
15. Thread adjuster cable over guide and hook end of overload spring in lever. Ensure eye of cable is pulled tight against anchor and in a straight line with guide.
16. Install brake drum, tire and wheel assembly.
17. Adjust brakes. Refer to individual car chapters for procedure.
18. If any hydraulic connections have been opened, bleed brake system.
19. Check master cylinder fluid level, and replenish as necessary.
20. Check brake pedal for proper feel and return.
21. Lower vehicle and road test.

NOTE: Do not severely apply brakes immediately after installation of new brake linings or permanent damage may occur to linings, and/or brake drums may become scored. Brakes must be used moderately during first several hundred miles of operation to ensure proper burnishing of linings.

Type 2

INDEX

REMOVAL

1. Raise and support rear of vehicle, then remove tire and wheel assembly.
2. Remove brake drum. If brake lining is dragging on brake drum, back off brake adjustment by rotating adjustment screw.
3. Disconnect parking brake cable from parking brake lever, **Fig. 1.**
4. Using suitable pliers, remove brake shoe to anchor springs and hold down springs.
5. Fully seat adjuster nut, then spread shoes apart and remove adjuster screw assembly.
6. Raise parking brake lever, then pull trailing shoe away from support to ease return spring tension and disengage spring end from support. Remove trailing shoe.
7. Pull leading shoe away from support to ease return spring tension and disengage spring end from support. Remove leading shoe.
8. Remove parking brake lever from trailing shoe.
9. Clean dirt from brake drum, support plate and all other components.

CAUTION: Do not use compressed air or dry brush to clean brake parts. Many brake parts contain asbestos fibers which, if inhaled, can cause serious injury. To clean brake parts, use a water soaked rag or a suitable vacuum cleaner to minimize airborne dust.

INSPECTION

1. Inspect components for damage and unusual wear. Replace as necessary.
2. Inspect wheel cylinders. Any torn, cut or heat damaged boots indicates need for wheel cylinder replacement. Peel back lower edge of boot. If fluid spills out, cup leakage is indicated and wheel cylinder should be replaced.

NOTE: A slight amount of fluid is always present and is considered normal. Fluid acts as a lubricant for the cylinder pistons.

Fig. 1 Drum brake assembly. Type 2

3. Inspect support plate attaching bolts, and ensure they are tight.
4. Inspect adjuster screw assembly operation. If satisfactory, lightly lubricate threads with suitable brake lube. If operation is unsatisfactory, replace.
5. Using fine emery cloth or other suitable abrasive, clean rust and dirt from shoe contact surfaces on support plate.

INSTALLATION

1. Lightly lubricate support plate shoe contact surfaces with suitable brake lube.
2. Remove brake drum hub grease seal and bearings, then clean and repack bearings and reinstall. Install new grease seal.
3. Position leading shoe return spring on shoe, then while holding shoe away from support, engage return spring in support plate, **Fig. 2,** and swing shoe end into position under anchor.
4. Install parking brake lever on trailing shoe.
5. Install trailing shoe return spring on shoe, then while holding shoe away from support, engage return spring in support plate, **Fig. 3,** and swing shoe end into position under anchor.
6. Spread shoes apart and install adjuster screw assembly. Ensure forked end enters the leading shoe with curved tines facing down, **Fig. 1.**
7. Using a suitable pair of pliers, install hold down springs and shoe to anchor springs.
8. Pull back parking brake cable return spring slightly to expose cable, then slide parking brake cable into parking brake lever and release spring.
9. Install brake drum and bearings. Refer to individual car chapter for wheel bearing adjustment procedure.
10. Adjust brakes. Refer to individual car chapter for procedure.
11. Install tire and wheel assembly.
12. If any hydraulic connections have been opened, bleed brake system.
13. Check master cylinder level, replenish as necessary.
14. Check brake pedal for proper feel and return.
15. Lower vehicle and road test.

NOTE: Do not severely apply brakes immediately after installation of new brake linings or permanent damage may occur to linings and/or brake drums may become scored. Brakes must be used moderately during first several hundred miles of operation to ensure proper burnishing of linings.

Fig. 2 Installing leading brake shoe. Type 2

Fig. 3 Installing trailing brake shoe. Type 2

Type 3

INDEX

REMOVAL

1. Raise and support rear of vehicle, then remove tire and wheel assembly.
2. Remove brake drum. If brake lining is dragging on brake drum, back off brake adjustment by rotating adjustment screw.
3. Using suitable pliers, remove adjuster lever spring, **Fig. 1.**
4. Remove adjuster lever.
5. Turn automatic adjuster screw out to expand shoes past wheel cylinder boot.
6. Using suitable tool, remove hold down springs.
7. Pull brake shoe assembly down and away from anchor plate.
8. Remove "C" clip retaining parking brake lever to trailing brake shoe webbing.
9. Disassemble shoe assembly.
10. Clean dirt from brake drum, anchor plate and all other components.

CAUTION: Do not use compressed air or dry brush to clean brake parts. Many brake parts contain asbestos fibers, which, if inhaled, can cause serious injury. To clean brake parts, use a water soaked rag or a suitable vacuum cleaner to minimize airborne dust.

INSPECTION

1. Inspect components for damage and unusual wear. Replace as necessary.
2. Inspect wheel cylinders. Any torn, cut or heat damaged boot indicates need of wheel cylinder replacement. Peel back lower edge of boot. If fluid spills out, cup leakage is indicated and wheel cylinder should be replaced.

NOTE: A slight amount of fluid is always present and is considered normal. Fluid acts as a lubricant for the cylinder pistons.

3. Inspect anchor plate attaching bolts, and ensure they are tight.
4. Inspect automatic adjuster screw assembly operation. If satisfactory, lightly lubricate threads with suitable brake lube. If operation is unsatisfactory, replace.
5. Using fine emery cloth or other suitable abrasive, clean rust and dirt from shoe contact surfaces on anchor plate.

INSTALLATION

1. Lightly lubricate anchor plate shoe contact surfaces with suitable brake lube.
2. Remove brake drum hub grease seal and bearings, then clean and repack bearings and reinstall. Install new grease seal.
3. Assemble automatic adjuster screw assembly, return spring and shoe-to-shoe spring to brake shoe assembly.
4. Position lining assembly near anchor plate, then assemble parking brake

Fig. 1   Drum brake assembly. Type 3

lever to trailing shoe webbing. Secure with "C" clip.
5. Install lining assembly onto anchor plate. When positioned, back off adjuster nut to seat brake shoe ends in wheel cylinder.
6. Install hold down springs.
7. Position adjuster lever, then using suitable pliers, install adjuster lever spring.
8. Install brake drum and bearings. Refer

to individual car chapter for wheel bearing adjustment procedure.
9. Adjust brakes. Refer to individual car chapter for procedure.
10. Install tire and wheel assembly.
11. If any hydraulic connections have been opened, bleed brake system.
12. Check master cylinder level, and replenish as necessary.
13. Check brake pedal for proper feel and return.

14. Lower vehicle and road test.

NOTE: Do not severely apply brakes immediately after installation of new brake linings or permanent damage may occur to linings and/or brake drums may become scored. Brakes must be used moderately during first several hundred miles of operation to ensure proper burnishing.

Specifications

Year	Model	Brake Drum Inside Dia. In.
FRONT WHEEL DRIVE MODELS		
1980–82	All	7.87
1983–84	Exc. E-Class, New Yorker & 600	7.87
	E-Class, New Yorker & 600	8.66
1985	Horizon, Lancer, LeBaron, & Omni; Aries & Reliant Exc. Station Wagon; Standard Brakes	7.87
	Daytona, Laser, New Yorker & 600; Aries, Reliant & Town & Country Station Wagon; Heavy Duty Brakes	8.66
REAR WHEEL DRIVE MODELS		
1980	Exc. LeBaron	①
	LeBaron	10
1981	Cordoba, Imperial, Mirada	10
	Chrysler, St. Regis, Gran Fury	10②
	Diplomat & LeBaron	10②③
1982–85	All	10②

①—Exc. taxi & police, 10"; taxi & police, 11".
②—Heavy duty, 11".
③—Wagon, 11".

FORD MOTOR CO. DRUM BRAKES

NOTE: Refer to "Brake Usage Chart" to determine which type brakes are used on vehicle being serviced.

TABLE OF CONTENTS

Brake Usage Chart

	Type No.		Type No.		Type No.
Ford & Mercury Full Size & Lincoln	1	1982-85 EXP	4	Styled Steel Wheels	4
1980 Bobcat	2	1980-81 Fairmont Exc. Station Wagon	2	1983-84 Marquis Exc. Station Wagon	2
1980-85 Capri	2	1980-81 Fairmont Station Wagon	1	1983-84 Marquis Station Wagon	1
1981 Cougar Less V8 Engine	2	1982-83 Fairmont	2	1985 Marquis Exc. Station Wagon & Touring Sedan	2
1981 Cougar w/V8 Engine	1	1980 Granada	1	1985 Marquis Station Wagon & Touring Sedan	1
1982 Cougar Exc. Station Wagon	2	1981 Granada Less V8 Engine	2	1980 Monarch	1
1982 Cougar Station Wagon	1	1981 Granada w/V8 Engine	1	1980-85 Mustang	2
1983-84 Cougar	2	1981 Granada Exc. Station Wagon	2	1980 Pinto	2
1985 Cougar Less Heavy Duty Brakes	2	1982 Granada Station Wagon	1	1984-85 Tempo	4
1985 Cougar w/Heavy Duty Brakes	1	1982-83 LN7	4	1984-85 Topaz	4
1980-81 Cougar XR-7	2	1983-84 LTD Exc. Station Wagon	2	1980-81 Thunderbird	2
1982 Cougar XR-7 Less V8 Engine	2	1983-84 LTD Station Wagon	1	1982 Thunderbird Less V8 Engine	2
1982 Cougar XR-7 w/V8 Engine	1	1985 LTD Exc. Station Wagon & Touring Sedan	2	1982 Thunderbird w/V8 Engine	1
1981-84 Escort 2 & 3 Door Hatchback	3	1985 LTD Station Wagon & Touring Sedan	1	1983-84 Thunderbird	2
1981-84 Escort Exc. 2 & 3 Door Hatchback	4	1981-84 Lynx 2 & 3 Door Hatchback	3	1985 Thunderbird Less Heavy Duty Brakes	2
1985 Escort 3 Door Less Styled Steel Wheels	3	1981-84 Lynx Exc. 2 & 3 Door Hatchback	4	1985 Thunderbird w/Heavy Duty Brakes	1
1985 Escort Exc. 3 Door Less Styled Steel Wheels	4	1985 Lynx 3 Door Less Styled Steel Wheels	3	1980-81 Zephyr Exc. Station Wagon	2
		1985 Lynx Exc. 3 Door Less		1980-81 Zephyr Station Wagon	1
				1982-83 Zephyr	2

General Information

INDEX

SERVICE PRECAUTIONS

When working on or around brake assemblies, care must be taken to prevent breathing asbestos dust, as many manufacturers incorporate asbestos fibers in the production of brake linings. During routine service operations the amount of asbestos dust from brake lining wear is at a low level, due to a chemical breakdown during use and a few precautions will minimize exposure.

CAUTION: Do not sand or grind brake linings unless suitable local exhaust ventilation equipment is used to prevent excessive asbestos exposure.

1. Wear a suitable respirator approved for asbestos dust use during all repair procedures.

2. When cleaning brake dust from brake parts, use a vacuum cleaner with a highly efficient filter system. If a suitable vacuum cleaner is not available, use a water soaked rag.

NOTE: Do not use compressed air or dry brush to clean brake parts.

3. Keep work area clean using same

equipment as for cleaning brake parts.

4. Properly dispose of rags and vacuum cleaner bags by placing them in plastic bags.
5. Do not smoke or eat while working on brake systems.

NOTE: Never use gasoline, kerosene, alcohol, motor oil, transmission fluid, or any fluid containing mineral oil to clean brake system components. These fluids will damage the rubber caps and seals. If system contamination is suspected, check brake fluid in the reservoir for dirt, discoloration, or separation (breakdown) of the brake fluid into distinct layers. Drain and flush the hydraulic system with clean brake fluid if contamination is suspected.

GENERAL INSPECTION

BRAKE DRUMS

Any time the brake drums are removed for brake service, the braking surface diameter should be checked with a suitable brake drum micrometer at several points to determine if they are within the safe oversize limit stamped on the brake drum outer surface. If the braking surface diameter exceeds specifications, the drum must be replaced. If the braking surface diameter is within specifications, drums should be cleaned and inspected for cracks, scores, deep grooves, taper, out of round and heat spotting. If drums are cracked or heat spotted, they must be replaced. Minor scores should be removed with sandpaper. Grooves and large scores can only be removed by machining with special equipment, as long as the braking surface is within specifications stamped on brake drum outer surface. Any brake drum sufficiently out of round to cause vehicle vibration or noise while braking or showing taper should also be machined, removing only enough stock to true up the brake drum.

After a brake drum is machined, wipe the braking surface diameter with a denatured alcohol soaked cloth. If one brake drum is machined, the other should also be machined to the same diameter to maintain equal braking forces.

BRAKE LININGS & SPRINGS

Inspect brake linings for excessive wear, damage, oil, grease or brake fluid contamination. If any of the above conditions exists, brake linings should be replaced. Do not attempt to replace only one set of brake shoes; they should be replaced as an axle set only to maintain equal braking forces. Examine brake shoe webbing, hold down and return springs for signs of overheating indicated by a slight blue color. If any component exhibits overheating signs, replace hold down and return springs with new ones. Overheated springs lose their pull and could cause brake linings to wear out prematurely. Inspect all springs for sags, bends and external damage and replace as necessary.

Inspect hold down retainers and pins for bends, rust and corrosion. If any of the above is found, replace as required.

BACKING PLATE

Inspect backing plate shoe contact surface for grooves that may restrict shoe movement and cannot be removed by lightly sanding with emery cloth or other suitable abrasive. If backing plate exhibits above condition, it should be replaced. Also inspect for signs of cracks, warpage and excessive rust, indicating need for replacement.

ADJUSTER MECHANISM

Inspect all components for rust, corrosion, bends and fatique. Replace as necessary. On adjuster mechanism equipped with adjuster cable, inspect cable for kinks, fraying or elongation of eyelet and replace as necessary.

PARKING BRAKE CABLE

Inspect parking brake cable end for kinks, fraying and elongation and replace as necessary. Use a small hose clamp to compress clamp where it enters backing plate to remove.

Types 1 & 2

INDEX

REMOVAL

1. Raise and support rear of vehicle, then remove tire and wheel assembly.
2. Remove brake drum. If brake lining is dragging on brake drum, back off brake adjustment by rotating adjustment screw. Refer to individual car chapter for procedure.

NOTE: If brake drum is rusted or corroded to axle flange and cannot be removed, lightly tap axle flange to drum mounting surface with a suitable hammer.

3. Install suitable wheel cylinder clamp over ends of wheel cylinder to retain pistons in bore.
4. On type 1, **Fig 1**, remove parking brake lever retaining clip.
5. On both types, **Figs. 1 and 2**, remove adjuster lever spring, primary and secondary shoe return springs using a suitable pair of brake spring pliers.
6. Remove shoe guide plate (if equipped), and adjuster cable and guide plate.
7. Using suitable tool, compress hold down springs, then remove spring retainers, hold down springs and pins.
8. Separate springs and remove from backing plate.
9. On type 2 brake, disengage parking brake lever from secondary shoe.
10. On all types, remove parking brake lever from cable.
11. Separate all components from brake shoes.
12. Clean dirt from brake drum, backing plate and all other components.

CAUTION: Do not use compressed air or dry brush to clean brake parts. Many brake parts contain asbestos fibers which, if inhaled, can cause serious injury. Clean brake parts with a water soaked rag or a suitable vacuum cleaner to minimize airborne dust.

INSPECTION

1. Inspect components for damage and

Fig. 1   Drum brake assembly. Type 1

Fig. 2   Drum brake assembly. Type 2

unusual wear. Replace as necessary.

2. Inspect wheel cylinders. Boots which are torn, cut, or heat damaged indicate need for wheel cylinder replacement. Fluid spilling from boot center hole, or wetness around wheel cylinder ends indicates cup leakage and need for wheel cylinder replacement.

NOTE: A small amount of fluid is always present and is considered normal, acting as a lubricant for the cylinder pistons.

3. Inspect backing plate for evidence of seal leakage. If leakage exists, refer to individual car chapters for axle seal replacement procedure.
4. Inspect backing plate attaching bolts and ensure they are tight.
5. Check adjuster screw operation. If satisfactory, lightly lubricate adjusting screw and washer with suitable brake lube. If operation is unsatisfactory, replace.
6. Using fine emery cloth or other suitable abrasive, clean rust and dirt from shoe contact surfaces on backing plate.

INSTALLATION

1. Lightly lubricate backing plate shoe contact surfaces with suitable brake lube.
2. On type 1, assemble parking brake lever to secondary shoe and secure with spring washer and retaining clip. Crimp ends of clip with suitable pliers. On type 2, engage parking brake lever tang with secondary shoe.
3. Position brake shoes on backing plate, primary (short lining) shoe facing front of vehicle and secondary (long lining) facing rear. Secure brake shoes with hold down springs, pins and retainers.

4. Install parking brake link and spring between shoes.
5. Loosen parking brake adjustment nut, then install parking brake cable on parking brake lever.
6. Install shoe guide plate and adjuster cable eyelet on anchor. Ensure adjuster cable crimp faces out.
7. Ensure parking brake link is properly positioned between brake shoes and wheel cylinder links are engaged in shoe web.
8. Using suitable brake spring pliers, install primary return spring from brake shoe to anchor, then secondary return spring from brake shoe to anchor.
9. On all types, remove wheel cylinder clamp installed during removal of brake shoes.

Fig. 3   Measuring brake drum inside diameter

10. Tighten adjuster screw assembly to thread limit and back off one-half turn.
11. Install adjuster screw assembly between shoes. Ensure toothed wheel is on secondary shoe side.

NOTE: Adjuster screw assemblies are stamped R (right) and L (left). To ensure proper adjuster operation, they must be installed on their respective sides.

12. Hook adjuster cable hook into adjuster lever hole, then position adjuster spring hook in large hole in primary shoe web. Using suitable brake spring pliers, install adjuster spring in adjuster lever hole.
13. Ensure adjuster cable is properly seated in cable guide, then pull adjuster lever, cable and adjuster spring down and towards the rear, engaging lever pivot hook in the large hole of secondary shoe web.
14. After installation, check adjuster operation by pulling adjuster cable between cable guide and adjuster lever towards secondary shoe sufficiently to lift adjuster lever past one tooth on adjuster screw assembly. The adjuster lever should snap into position behind the next tooth, then upon release of adjuster cable, rotate toothed wheel one notch. If operation is not satisfactory, recheck installation.
15. Ensure brake shoe upper ends are seated against anchor pin and shoe assemblies are centered on backing plate. If not, back off parking brake adjustment.
16. Using suitable brake drum to shoe gauge, **Fig. 3**, measure brake drum

inside diameter. Adjust brake shoes to dimension obtained on outside portion of gauge using adjuster screw.

17. Install brake drum, wheel and tire assembly.
18. If any hydraulic brake connections have been opened, bleed brake system.
19. Adjust parking brake. Refer to individual car chapter for procedures.
20. Inspect all hydraulic lines and connections for leakage and repair as necessary.
21. Check master cylinder fluid level and replenish as necessary.
22. Check brake pedal for proper feel and return.
23. Lower vehicle and road test.

NOTE: Do not severely apply brakes immediately after installation of new brake linings or permanent damage may occur to linings, and/or brake drums may become scored. Brakes must be used moderately during first several hundred miles of operation to ensure proper burnishing of linings.

Type 3

INDEX

REMOVAL

1. Raise and support rear of vehicle, then remove tire and wheel assembly.
2. Remove brake drum. If brake lining is dragging on brake drum, back off brake adjustment. Refer to individual car chapters for procedure.
3. Using suitable tool, remove hold down retainers, springs and pins, **Fig. 1.**
4. Remove brake shoe and adjuster assemblies from backing plate by lifting up and away from anchor block and shoe guide, **Fig. 2.**

NOTE: When removing brake shoe and adjuster assemblies, use care not to damage wheel cylinder boots.

5. Remove parking brake cable from parking brake lever.
6. Remove lower retracting spring from leading and trailing shoes.
7. While holding brake shoe and adjuster assemblies, remove leading shoe upper retracting spring by rotating leading shoe over adjuster quadrant until spring is slack, then remove spring. Remove leading shoe from adjuster assembly.

8. Remove parking brake strut from trailing shoe by pulling strut outward from shoe assembly, then twisting strut downward until spring tension is released. Unhook brake shoe strut spring, then remove parking brake strut and adjuster assembly from trailing shoe.
9. If adjuster disassembly is required, pull adjuster quadrant away from knurled pin in parking brake strut and rotate quadrant in either direction until quadrant teeth are disengaged from strut pin. Remove spring and slide quadrant out of strut.

NOTE: Do not overstress quadrant spring during removal.

10. Remove parking brake lever retaining clip and spring washer, then the parking brake lever.
11. Clean dirt from brake drum, backing plate and all other components.

CAUTION: Do not use compressed air or dry brush to clean brake parts. Many brake

Fig. 1   Drum brake assembly. Type 3

Fig. 2   Removing brake shoe and adjuster assemblies. Type 3

parts contain asbestos fibers which, if inhaled, can cause serious injury. Clean brake parts with a water soaked rag or a suitable vacuum cleaner to minimize airborne dust.

INSPECTION

1. Inspect components for damage and unusual wear. Replace as necessary.
2. Inspect wheel cylinders. Boots which are torn, cut or heat damaged indicate need for wheel cylinder replacement. Peel back lower edge of boot. If fluid spills out, cup leakage is indicated and wheel cylinder should be replaced.

NOTE: A slight amount of fluid is always present and is considered normal, acting as a lubricant for the cylinder pistons.

3. Inspect backing plate attaching bolts and ensure they are tight.
4. Using fine emery cloth or other suitable abrasive, clean rust and dirt from shoe contact surfaces on backing plate.

INSTALLATION

1. Lightly lubricate backing plate shoe contact surfaces with suitable brake lube.
2. Remove brake drum hub grease seal and bearings, then clean and repack bearings and reinstall. Install new grease seal.
3. Lightly lubricate strut to adjuster quadrant contact surfaces with suitable brake lube.
4. Position adjuster quadrant pin in strut slot and install quadrant spring, then pivot quadrant until it engages with

Fig. 3   Adjusting brake shoes to brake drum inside diameter

strut knurled pin in third or fourth notch of outboard end of quadrant.
5. Assemble parking brake lever to trailing shoe, then install spring washer and retaining clip. Using suitable pliers, crimp retaining clip until securely fastened.
6. Assemble parking brake strut to trailing shoe by attaching brake shoe strut spring to slots in shoe web and strut, and pivoting strut into position, tensioning spring and holding assembly in place.

NOTE: Ensure end of spring with hook parallel to the center line of spring coils is installed in shoe web hole. Installed spring should be flat against shoe web and parallel to parking brake strut.

7. Install lower retracting spring between shoes. Ensure spring hook with longest straight piece fits into trailing shoe hole, **Fig. 1.**
8. Install upper retracting spring by installing hooks in leading shoe web

and other end in parking brake strut, then pivot leading shoe over adjuster quadrant and into position.
9. Spread shoe and strut assemblies sufficiently to fit over anchor plate and wheel cylinder piston inserts, and install onto backing plate.

NOTE: When installing brake shoe and adjuster assemblies, use care not to damage wheel cylinder boots.

10. Connect parking brake cable to parking brake lever.
11. Using suitable tool, install hold down springs, retainers and pins.
12. Using suitable brake drum to shoe gauge, measure brake drum inside diameter. Adjust brake shoes to dimension obtained on outside portion of gauge, **Fig. 3.**
13. Install brake drum. Refer to individual car chapters for wheel bearing adjustment procedure.
14. Install tire and wheel assembly.
15. If any hydraulic connections have been opened, bleed brake system.
16. Adjust parking brake. Refer to individual car chapters for procedure.
17. Inspect all hydraulic lines and connections for leakage and repair as necessary.
18. Check master cylinder fluid level and replenish as necessary.
19. Check brake pedal for proper feel and return.
20. Lower vehicle and road test.

NOTE: Do not severely apply brakes immediately after installation of new brake linings or permanent damage may occur to lining, and/or brake drums may become scored. Brakes must be used moderately during first several hundred miles of operation to ensure proper burnishing of linings.

Type 4

INDEX

REMOVAL

1. Raise and support rear of vehicle, then remove tire and wheel assembly.
2. Remove brake drum. If brake lining is dragging on brake drum, back off brake adjustment. Refer to individual car chapters for procedure.
3. Using suitable tool, remove hold down

retainers, springs and pins, **Fig. 1.**
4. Remove brake shoes and adjuster assemblies from backing plate by lifting up and away from wheel cylinder assembly.

NOTE: When removing brake shoe and adjuster assemblies, use care not to bend adjusting lever.

5. Remove parking brake cable from

parking brake lever.
6. Remove lower retracting spring, adjuster screw retracting spring and adjuster lever.
7. Separate brake shoes, then remove parking brake lever retaining clip and spring washer and slide lever off parking brake lever pin on the trailing shoe.
8. Clean dirt from brake drum, backing plate and all other components.

DRUM BRAKES—Ford Motor Co.

Fig. 1 Drum brake assembly. Type 4

CAUTION: Do not use compressed air or dry brush to clean brake parts. Many brake parts contain asbestos fibers which, if inhaled, can cause serious injury. Clean brake parts with a water soaked rag or a suitable vacuum cleaner to minimize airborne dust.

INSPECTION

1. Inspect components for damage and unusual wear. Replace as necessary.
2. Inspect wheel cylinders. Boots which are torn, cut or heat damaged indicate need for wheel cylinder replacement. Peel back lower edge of boot. If fluid spills out, cup leakage is indicated and wheel cylinder should be replaced.

NOTE: A small amount of fluid is always present and is considered normal, acting as a lubricant for the cylinder pistons.

3. Inspect backing plate attaching bolts and ensure they are tight.

4. Using fine emery cloth or other suitable abrasive, clean rust and dirt from shoe contact surfaces on backing plate.
5. Check adjuster screw operation. If satisfactory, lightly lubricate adjusting screw and washer with suitable brake lube. If operation is unsatisfactory, replace.

INSTALLATION

1. Lightly lubricate backing plate shoe contact surfaces with suitable brake lube.
2. Remove brake drum hub grease seal and bearings, then clean and repack bearings and reinstall. Install new grease seal.
3. Assemble parking brake lever to trailing shoe, then install spring washer and retaining clip. Using suitable pliers, crimp retaining clip until securely fastened.
4. Attach parking brake cable to parking brake lever.
5. Assemble lower retracting spring to leading and trailing shoe assemblies, then spread lower part of shoes and install on backing plate.
6. Using suitable tool, install hold down springs.
7. Tighten adjuster assembly, then back off one-half turn. Install adjuster assembly between leading shoe slot and trailing shoe/parking brake lever slot. The adjuster socket end slot must fit into trailing shoe/parking brake lever.

NOTE: Adjuster assemblies are stamped R (right) and L (left). To ensure proper adjuster operation, they must be installed on their respective sides. The letter must be installed in the upright position, facing wheel cylinder to ensure the deeper of the two slots in the adjuster socket fits in the parking brake lever.

8. Install adjuster lever in the parking brake lever groove and into the adjuster socket slot.
9. Using suitable brake spring pliers, install adjusting screw retracting spring from leading shoe slot to adjuster lever notch.
10. Using suitable brake drum to shoe gauge, **Fig. 3,** measure brake drum inside diameter. Adjust brake shoes to dimension obtained on outside portion of gauge, **Fig. 6.**
11. Install brake drum. Refer to individual car chapters for wheel bearing adjustment procedure.
12. Install tire and wheel assembly.
13. If any hydraulic connections have been opened, bleed brake system.
14. Adjust parking brake. Refer to individual car chapters for procedure.
15. Inspect all hydraulic lines and connection for leakage, and repair as necessary.
16. Check master cylinder fluid level and replenish as necessary.
17. Check brake pedal for proper feel and return.
18. Lower vehicle and road test.

NOTE: Do not severely apply brakes immediately after installation of new brake linings or permanent damage may occur to linings, and/or brake drums may become scored. Brakes must be used moderately during first several hundred miles of operation to ensure proper burnishing of linings.

Specifications

Year	Model	Brake Drum Inside Dia. In.
FORD & MERCURY—Full Size Models		
1980–84	All①	10.00
	All②③	11.03
1985	All①	10.00
	All②	11.03
FORD & MERCURY—Compact & Intermediate Models		
1980	Cougar XR-7 & Thunderbird	9.00
	Fairmont & Zephyr	④
	Granada & Monarch	10.00
1981	Cougar & Granada	⑤
	Cougar XR-7 & Thunderbird	9.00
	Fairmont & Zephyr	④
1982	Cougar & Granada	④
	Cougar XR-7 & Thunderbird	③
	Fairmont & Zephyr	9
1983	Cougar & Thunderbird	9
	Fairmont & Zephyr	9
	LTD & Marquis	④
1984	Cougar & Thunderbird	9.0
	LTD & Marquis	④
1985	Cougar & Thunderbird	⑥
	LTD & Marquis	⑦

Year	Model	Brake Drum Inside Dia. In.
FORD MUSTANG & PINTO • MERCURY BOBCAT & CAPRI		
1980–85	All	9.0
FORD ESCORT, EXP & TEMPO • MERCURY LN7, LYNX & TOPAZ		
1981	All	⑧
1982–83	Escort & Lynx	⑧
	EXP & LN7	8
1984	Tempo & Topaz	8
	Escort, Lynx & EXP	⑧
1985	EXP, Tempo & Topaz	8
	Escort & Lynx	⑨
LINCOLN		
1980	Lincoln & Mark VI	⑩
1981–83	All	10.00
1984	Continental & Mark VII	⑪
1985	Lincoln	10.00

①—Station wagon, police, taxi & trailer tow.
②—Sedan exc. police, taxi & trailer tow.
③—With 6 cyl. engine, 9"; w/V8 engine 10".
④—Exc. sta. wag., 9"; sta. wag., 10".
⑤—Models w/4 or 6 cyl. engine, 9"; models w/V8 engine, 10".
⑥—Standard brakes, 9"; heavy duty brakes, 10".
⑦—Exc. Touring Sedan & sta. wag., 9"; Touring Sedan & sta. wag., 10".
⑧—Exc. 2 & 3 door hatchback, 8"; 2 & 3 door hatchback, 7".
⑨—3 door models less styled steel wheels, 7"; exc. 3 door models less styled steel wheels, 8".
⑩—V8-302, 10"; V8-351W, 11.03".
⑪—With 4¾" bolt circle, 9.5"; w/5" bolt circle, 11".

General Motors Corp.

NOTE: Refer to "Brake Usage Chart" to determine which type brakes are used on vehicle being serviced.

TABLE OF CONTENTS

Brake Usage Chart

	Type No.		Type No.		Type No.
1980-81 Bonneville	1	1980-84 Citation	4	1980-83 Malibu	3
1982-85 Bonneville	3	1985 Citation	5	1980-85 Monte Carlo	3
1980-85 Cadillac Exc. Cimarron &		1985 Custom Cruiser	1	1985 98	5
1985 Deville & Fleetwood	1	1980-85 Cutlass	3	1980-84 Omega	4
1985 Calais	5	1982-84 Cutlass Ciera	4	1980-85 1000	4
1980-81 Camaro	1	1985 Cutlass Ciera	5	1983-85 Parisienne	1
1982-85 Camaro	3	1984 Cutlass Cruiser	4	1985 Park Avenue	5
1980-81 Catalina	1	1985 DeVille	5	1980-84 Phoenix	4
1982-84 Cavalier	4	1980-85 88	1	1980-85 Regal	3
1985 Cavalier	5	1980-84 Electra	1	1980-84 Riviera	2
1982-84 Celebrity	4	1985 Electra Exc. Estate Wagon	5	1985 Riviera	1
1985 Celebrity	5	1985 Electra Estate Wagon	1	1982-84 6000	4
1980-81 Century	3	1980-81 Firebird	1	1985 6000	5
1982-84 Century	4	1982-85 Firebird	3	1982-84 Skyhawk	4
1985 Century	5	1982-84 Firenza	4	1985 Skyhawk	5
1980-84 Chevette	4	1985 Firenza	5	1980-84 Skylark	4
1985 Chevette	5	1985 Fleetwood	5	1985 Skylark	5
1980-81 Chevrolet	1	1980 Grand Am	3	1985 Somerset Regal	5
1982-84 Chevrolet	3	1985 Grand Am	5	1982-84 Sunbird	4
1985 Chevrolet	1	1980-85 Grand Prix	3	1980-83 Toronado	2
1982-84 Cimarron	4	1980-81 LeMans	3	1982-84 2000	4
1985 Cimarron	5	1980-85 LeSabre	1		

General Information

INDEX

SERVICE PRECAUTIONS

When working on or around brake assemblies, care must be taken to prevent breathing asbestos dust, as many manufacturers incorporate asbestos fibers in the production of brake linings. During routine service operations the amount of asbestos dust from brake lining wear is at a low level, due to a chemical breakdown during use and a few precautions will minimize exposure.

CAUTION: Do not sand or grind brake linings unless suitable local exhaust ventilation equipment is used to prevent excessive asbestos exposure.

1. Wear a suitable respirator approved for asbestos dust use during all repair procedures.
2. When cleaning brake dust from brake parts, use a vacuum cleaner with a highly efficient filter system. If a suitable vacuum cleaner is not available, use a water soaked rag.

NOTE: Do not use compressed air or dry

brush to clean brake parts.

3. Keep work area clean using same equipment as for cleaning brake parts.
4. Properly dispose of rags and vacuum cleaner bags by placing them in plastic bags.
5. Do not smoke or eat while working on brake systems.

NOTE: Never use gasoline, kerosene, alcohol, motor oil, transmission fluid, or any fluid containing mineral oil to clean brake system components. These fluids will damage the rubber caps and seals. If system contamination is suspected, check brake fluid in the reservoir for dirt, discoloration, or separation (breakdown) of the brake fluid into distinct layers. Drain and flush the hydraulic system with clean brake fluid if contamination is suspected.

GENERAL INSPECTION

BRAKE DRUMS

Any time the brake drums are removed for brake service, the braking surface diameter should be checked with a suitable brake drum micrometer at several points to determine if they are within the safe oversize limit stamped on the brake drum outer surface. If the braking surface diameter exceeds specifications, the drum must be replaced. If the braking surface diameter is within specifications, drums should be cleaned and inspected for cracks, scores, deep grooves, taper, out of round and heat spotting. If drums are cracked or heat spotted, they must be replaced. Minor scores should be removed with sandpaper. Grooves and large scores can only be removed by machining with special equipment, as long as the braking surface is within specifications stamped on brake drum outer surface. Any brake drum sufficiently out of round to cause vehicle vibration or noise while braking or showing taper should also be machined, removing only enough stock to true up the brake drum.

After a brake drum is machined, wipe the braking surface diameter with a denatured alcohol soaked cloth. If one brake drum is machined, the other should also be machined to the same diameter to maintain equal braking forces.

BRAKE LININGS & SPRINGS

Inspect brake linings for excessive wear, damage, oil, grease or brake fluid contamination. If any of the above conditions exists, brake linings should be replaced. Do not attempt to replace only one set of brake shoes; they should be replaced as an axle set only to maintain equal braking forces. Examine brake shoe webbing, hold down and return springs for signs of overheating indicated by a slight blue color. If any component exhibits overheating signs, replace hold down and return springs with new ones. Overheated springs lose their pull and could cause brake linings to wear out prematurely. Inspect all springs for sags, bends and external damage and replace as necessary.

Inspect hold down retainers and pins for bends, rust and corrosion. If any of the above is found, replace as required.

BACKING PLATE

Inspect backing plate shoe contact surface for grooves that may restrict shoe movement and cannot be removed by lightly sanding with emery cloth or other suitable abrasive. If backing plate exhibits above condition, it should be replaced. Also inspect for signs of cracks, warpage and excessive rust, indicating need for replacement.

ADJUSTER MECHANISM

Inspect all components for rust, corrosion, bends and fatigue. Replace as necessary. On adjuster mechanism equipped with adjuster cable, inspect cable for kinks, fraying or elongation of eyelet and replace as necessary.

PARKING BRAKE CABLE

Inspect parking brake cable end for kinks, fraying and elongation and replace as necessary. Use a small hose clamp to compress clamp where it enters backing plate to remove.

Types 1, 2 & 3

INDEX

REMOVAL

1. Raise and support rear of vehicle, then remove tire and wheel assembly.
2. Remove brake drum. If brake lining is dragging on brake drum, back off brake adjustment by rotating adjustment screw. Refer to individual car chapter for procedure.

NOTE: If brake drum is rusted or corroded to axle flange and cannot be removed, lightly tap axle flange to drum mounting surface with a suitable hammer.

3. Using brake spring pliers or equivalent, unhook primary and secondary return springs, **Figs. 1, 2 and 3.**

NOTE: Observe location of brake parts being removed to aid during installation.

4. Remove brake hold down springs with suitable tool.
5. Lift actuating lever, then unhook actuating link from anchor pin and remove.
6. Remove actuating lever(s) and return spring.
7. Spread shoes apart and remove parking brake strut and spring.
8. Disconnect parking brake cable from lever, then remove brake shoes from backing plate.
9. Separate brake shoes by removing adjusting screw and spring, then unhook parking brake lever from shoe assembly.

10. Clean dirt from brake drum, backing plate and all other components.

CAUTION: Do not use compressed air or dry brush to clean brake parts. Many brake parts contain asbestos fibers which, if inhaled, can cause serious injury. Clean brake parts with a water soaked rag or a suitable vacuum cleaner to minimize airborne dust.

INSPECTION

1. Inspect components for damage and unusual wear. Replace as necessary.
2. Inspect wheel cylinders. Boots which

Fig. 1   Drum brake assembly. Type 1 typical

Fig. 2   Drum brake assembly. Type 2 typical

Fig. 3   Drum brake assembly. Type 3

Fig. 4   Measuring brake drum inside diameter

are torn, cut or heat damaged indicate need for wheel cylinder replacement. On type 1 brakes, remove wheel cylinder links. Fluid spill from boot center hole indicates cup leakage and need for wheel cylinder replacement. On type 2 and 3 brakes, use a small screwdriver to pry center hole of boot away from piston. If fluid spills from center hole, cup leakage is indicated and wheel cylinder should be replaced. On all types, light fluid coatings on piston within cylinder is considered normal.

3. Inspect backing plate for evidence of axle seal leakage. If leakage exists, refer to individual car chapters for axle seal replacement procedures.
4. Inspect backing plate attaching bolts, and ensure they are tight.
5. Using fine emery cloth or other suitable abrasive, clean rust and dirt from shoe contact surface on backing plate.

INSTALLATION

1. Lubricate parking brake lever fulcrum

with suitable brake lube, then attach lever to brake shoe. Ensure lever operates smoothly.
2. Connect brake shoes with adjusting screw spring, then position adjusting screw.

NOTE: Ensure adjusting screw star wheel does not contact adjusting screw spring after installation and also ensure right hand

Fig. 5   Adjusting brake shoes to brake drum inside diameter

thread adjusting screw is installed on left side of vehicle and left hand thread adjusting screw is installed on right side of vehicle. When brake shoe installation is completed, ensure starwheel lines up with adjusting hole in backing plate.

3. Lightly lubricate backing plate shoe contact surfaces with suitable brake lube, then the area where parking brake cable contacts backing plate.
4. Install brake shoes on backing plate while engaging wheel cylinder links (if equipped) with shoe webbing. Connect parking brake cable to parking brake lever.

NOTE: The primary shoe (short lining) faces towards front of vehicle.

5. Install actuating levers, actuating link and return spring, **Figs. 1, 2 and 3.**
6. Install hold down springs with suitable tool.
7. Install primary and secondary shoe return springs using brake spring pliers or equivalent.
8. Using suitable brake drum to shoe gauge, **Fig. 4,** measure brake drum

inside diameter. Adjust brake shoes to dimension obtained on outside portion of gauge, **Fig. 5.**
9. Install brake drum, wheel and tire assembly.
10. If any hydraulic connections have been opened, bleed brake system.
11. Adjust parking brake. Refer to individual car chapters for procedures.

12. Inspect all hydraulic lines and connections for leakage and repair as necessary.
13. Check master cylinder fluid level and replenish as necessary.
14. Check brake pedal for proper feel and return.
15. Lower vehicle and road test.

NOTE: Do not severely apply brakes immediately after installation of new brake linings or permanent damage may occur to linings, and/or brake drums may become scored. Brakes must be used moderately during first several hundred miles of operation to ensure proper burnishing of linings.

Type 4

INDEX

REMOVAL

1. Raise and support rear of vehicle, then remove tire and wheel assembly.
2. Remove brake drum. If brake lining is dragging on brake drum, back off brake adjustment by rotating adjustment screw.

NOTE: If brake drum is rusted or corroded to axle flange and cannot be removed, lightly tap axle flange to drum mounting surface with a suitable hammer.

3. Using brake spring pliers or equivalent, unhook primary and secondary return springs, **Fig. 1.**
4. Remove hold down springs with suitable tool, then lift off lever pivot.
5. Remove hold down pins, then lift actuator lever and remove actuator link.
6. Remove actuator lever, pivot and return spring.
7. Spread shoes apart and remove parking brake strut and spring.
8. With brake shoes spread, disconnect parking brake spring from lever, then lift brake shoes, adjusting screw and spring from backing plate.
9. Note position of adjusting screw and spring, then remove from shoe assemblies.
10. Remove parking brake lever from secondary shoe.
11. Clean dirt from brake drum, backing plate and all other components.

CAUTION: Do not use compressed air or dry brush to clean brake parts. Many brake parts contain asbestos fibers which, if inhaled, can cause serious injury. Clean brake parts with a water soaked rag or a suitable vacuum cleaner to minimize airborne dust.

INSPECTION

1. Inspect components for damage or unusual wear. Replace as necessary.
2. On Chevette and 1000 models, inspect backing plate for evidence of axle seal leakage. If leakage exists, refer to individual car chapter for axle seal replacement procedure.
3. Inspect backing plate attaching bolts, and ensure they are tight.
4. Inspect wheel cylinders. Excessive fluid indicates cup leakage and need for wheel cylinder replacement.

NOTE: A slight amount of fluid is always present and is considered normal, acting as a lubricant for the cylinder pistons.

5. Check adjuster screw operation. If satisfactory, lightly lubricate adjusting screw and washer with suitable brake lube. If operation is unsatisfactory, replace.
6. Using fine emery cloth or other suitable abrasive, clean rust and dirt from shoe contact surfaces on backing plate, **Fig. 1.**

INSTALLATION

1. Lightly lubricate backing plate shoe contact surfaces with suitable brake lube.
2. Install parking brake lever on secondary shoe.
3. Connect primary and secondary brake

Fig. 1 Drum brake assembly. Type 4

Fig. 2   Measuring brake drum inside diameter

shoes with adjusting screw spring, then position adjusting screw in same position from which it was removed.

NOTE: Ensure adjusting screw spring starwheel does not contact adjusting screw spring after installation, and also ensure right hand thread adjusting screw is installed on left side of vehicle and left hand thread adjusting screw is installed on right side of vehicle.

4. Spread brake shoes apart to clear axle flange, then install parking brake cable on lever. Position brake assembly on backing plate.
5. Spread brake shoes slightly, then install parking brake strut and spring. Spring end of strut engages the primary shoe, while the other end engages the parking brake lever and secondary shoe.
6. Install actuator lever, pivot and return spring, then hook actuating link in shoe retainer.
7. Lift actuator lever and hook actuating link to lever.
8. Install hold down pins, lever pivot and hold down springs.
9. Install primary and secondary return springs using suitable brake spring pliers.
10. Using suitable brake drum to shoe gauge, **Fig. 2,** measure brake drum inside diameter. Adjust brake shoes to dimension obtained on outside portion of gauge, **Fig. 3.**
11. Install brake drum, tire and wheel assembly.
12. If any hydraulic connections have been opened, bleed brake system.
13. Adjust parking brake. Refer to individual car chapters for procedures.
14. Inspect all hydraulic lines and connections for leakage, and repair as necessary.

Fig. 3   Adjusting brake shoes to brake drum inside diameter

15. Check master cylinder fluid level, and replenish as necessary.
16. Check brake pedal for proper feel and return.
17. Lower vehicle and road test.

NOTE: Do not severely apply brakes immediately after installation of new brake linings or permanent damage may occur to linings, and/or brake drums may become scored. Brakes must be used moderately during first several hundred miles of operation to ensure proper burnishing of linings.

Type 5

INDEX

REMOVAL

1. Raise and support rear of vehicle, then remove tire and wheel assembly.
2. Remove brake drum. If brake lining is dragging on brake drum, back off brake adjustment by rotating adjusting screw. Refer to individual car chapter for procedure.

NOTE: If brake drum is rusted or corroded to axle flange and cannot be removed, lightly tap axle flange to drum mounting surface with a suitable hammer.

3. Using tool No. J-8049 or equivalent, remove brake return springs, **Fig. 7.**
4. Using suitable pliers, remove hold down springs and lever pivot.
5. While lifting up on actuator lever, disconnect actuating link.
6. Remove actuator lever and return spring.
7. Remove parking brake strut and spring.
8. Disconnect parking brake cable, then remove brake shoe and lining assembly.
9. Remove adjusting screw assembly and spring as follows:
   a. Note position of adjusting spring.
   b. Remove retaining ring, pin, and parking brake lever from secondary shoe.
   c. Remove adjusting screw and spring.

NOTE: Do not interchange adjusting screws from right and lefthand brake assemblies.

INSPECTION

1. Inspect brake components for damage and/or wear. Replace as necessary.
2. Inspect wheel cylinders. Excessive fluid indicates cup leakage and need for wheel cylinder replacement.
3. Inspect backing plate for evidence of axle seal leakage.
4. Inspect backing plate attaching bolts. Ensure bolts are tight.
5. Check adjuster operation. If adjusters are worn, frozen or loose, replace adjuster and backing plate assembly as required.
6. Using fine emery cloth or other suitable abrasive, clean rust and/or dirt from shoe contact surface on backing plate.

INSTALLATION

1. Install parking brake lever, pin and retaining ring onto secondary shoe.
2. Apply silicone brake lubricant onto adjuster screw threads, inside diameter of socket and socket face. Adequate lubrication is achieved when a continuous bead of lubricant is at open end of pivot nut and socket when adjuster threads are completely engaged.
3. Install adjusting screw assembly and spring.

NOTE: Spring coils must not overlap star wheel. Do not interchange right and left-hand springs.

4. Connect parking brake cable, then install shoe and lining assembly.
5. Using a suitable tool, spread brake shoes apart, then install parking brake strut and spring.

NOTE: Ensure parking brake strut is properly positioned. Ensure strut end without spring engages parking brake lever. Ensure strut end with spring engages primary brake shoe.

6. Install actuator lever and return spring.
7. Install actuator link onto anchor pin.
8. While holding up on actuator lever, install link onto lever.
9. Install hold down pins, lever pivot and hold down springs.
10. Install shoe return springs.
11. Install brake drum, tire and wheel assembly.
12. If any hydraulic connections have been opened, bleed brake system.
13. Adjust brakes. Refer to individual car chapters for procedure.

*LUBRICATE WITH THIN COATING OF 5450032 LUBRICANT (OR EQUIVALENT)

1.	RETURN SPRING
2.	RETURN SPRING
3.	HOLD-DOWN SPRING
4.	LEVER PIVOT
5.	HOLD-DOWN PIN
6.	ACTUATOR LINK
7.	ACTUATOR LEVER
8.	LEVER RETURN SPRING
9.	PARKING BRAKE STRUT
10.	STRUT SPRING
11.	PRIMARY SHOE & LINING
12.	SECONDARY SHOE & LINING
13.	ADJUSTING SCREW SPRING
17.	RETAINING RING
18.	PIN
19.	PARKING BRAKE LEVER
27.	BACKING PLATE
29.	ADJUSTING SCREW ASSEMBLY
30.	SHOE RETAINER
32.	ANCHOR PIN
33.	SHOE PADS (6 PLACES)

Fig. 1   Drum brake assembly. Type 5

Specifications

Year	Model	Brake Drum Inside Dia. In.
BUICK (EXC. SKYHAWK, SKYLARK, 1982–85 CENTURY & 1985 ELECTRA & PARK AVENUE)		
1980	Century, Regal	9.45
	LeSabre①	9.5
	LeSabre, LeSabre Estate Wagon②	11
	Electra, Electra Estate Wagon	11
	Riviera	9.45
1981	Century, Regal	9.5
	LeSabre①	9.5
	LeSabre, LeSabre Estate Wagon②	11
	Electra, Electra Estate Wagon	11
	Riviera	9.5
1982	Regal, LeSabre	9.5
	LeSabre Estate Wagon	11
	Electra	11
	Riviera	9.5
1983	Regal & LeSabre	9.5
	LeSabre Estate Wagon	11
	Electra	11
	Riviera	9.5
1984	Regal & LeSabre	9.5
	LeSabre Estate Wagon	11
	Electra	11
	Riviera	9.5

Year	Model	Brake Drum Inside Dia. In.
1985	Somerset Regal	7.87
	Riviera	9.5
	LeSabre Exc. Estate Wagon & Regal	9.5
	LeSabre Estate Wagon	11
1985 BUICK ELECTRA, PARK AVENUE, CAD. DEVILLE, FLEETWOOD & OLDS. 98		
1985	All Exc. Estate Wagon	8.86
	Electra Estate Wagon	11
CADILLAC (EXC. CIMMARON & 1985 DEVILLE & FLEETWOOD)		
1980–85	Brougham & DeVille	11
CHEVROLET (CAMARO, CHEVROLET, MALIBU, MONTE CARLO & NOVA)		
1980–85	All	9½③
1982–84 CHEV. CAVALIER • BUICK SKYHAWK • CAD. CIMMARON • OLDS. FIRENZA • PONT. 2000 & SUNBIRD		
1982–85	All	7.87
CHEVROLET CHEVETTE • PONTIAC 1000		
1980–85	All	7.88

continued

SPECIFICATIONS—Continued

1980–85 CHEV. CITATION, BUICK SKYLARK, OLDS. OMEGA, PONT. PHOENIX • 1982–85 CHEV. CELEBRITY, BUICK CENTURY, OLDS. CUTLASS CIERA & PONT. 6000 • 1984–85 OLDS. CUTLASS CRUISER

Year	Model	Brake Drum Inside Dia. In.
1980–83	All	7.87
1984	Citation & Celebrity	7.87
	Skylark	7.87
	Century	8.86
	Omega	7.87
	Cutlass Ciera	8.86
	Phoenix	7.87
	6000	8.86
1985	Celebrity	8.86
	Century	8.86
	Ciera	8.86
	Citation	7.87
	Cutlass	9.5
	Skylark	7.87
	6000	8.86

OLDSMOBILE (EXC. FIRENZA, STARFIRE, 1980–84 OMEGA, 1982–83 CUTLASS CIERA, 1984–85 CUTLASS CRUISER & 1985 98)

Year	Model	Brake Drum Inside Dia. In.
1980–84	Exc. 98 & Custom Cruiser	9½
	98 & Custom Cruiser	11
1985	Calais	7.87
	88	9.5

PONTIAC (EXC. SUNBIRD, 1000 & FRONT WHEEL DRIVE)

Year	Model	Brake Drum Inside Dia. In.
1980–81	Exc. Pontiac	9.5
	Pontiac	④
1982–84	Exc. Bonneville	9.5
	Bonneville	④
1985	Grand Am	7.87
	Firebird	9.5
	Bonneville, Grand Prix & Parisienne	⑤

①—Models w/V6 engine.
②—Models w/V8 engine.
③—On Chevrolet sta. wagon, 11".
④—With 4¾" bolt circle, 9.5"; w/5" bolt circle, 11".
⑤—Standard brakes, 9.5"; heavy duty brakes, 11".

DISC BRAKES

TABLE OF CONTENTS

American Motors Corp.

TABLE OF CONTENTS

NOTE: Refer to "Brake Usage Chart" to determine which type brakes are used on vehicle being serviced.

General Information

BRAKE SHOES, LININGS & CALIPERS

Remove wheels and inspect brake disc, caliper and linings. The wheel bearings should be inspected at this time and repacked if necessary. Do not get any grease on the linings.

The brake shoe and lining assemblies should be replaced if the lining is worn to within 1/32 inch of rivet heads (riveted linings) or brake shoe (bonded linings). It is recommended that both front and/or rear wheel sets be replaced whenever a respective shoe and lining assembly is replaced.

If a visual inspection does not adequately determine the condition of the linings, the brake shoe and lining assemblies should be removed and inspected. If shoes do not require replacement, reinstall them in their original positions. Brake shoes and linings should also be replaced if cracked or damaged.

If the caliper is cracked or fluid leakage through the casting is evident, it must be replaced as a unit.

BRAKE ROUGHNESS

The most common cause of brake chatter on disc brakes is a variation in thickness of the disc. If roughness or vibration is encountered during highway operation or if pedal pumping is experienced at low speeds, the disc may have excessive thickness variation. To check for this condition, measure the disc at 12 points with a micrometer at a radius approximately one inch from edge of disc. If thickness measurements vary by more than .0005 inch, the disc should be replaced with a new one.

Excessive lateral runout of braking disc may cause a "knocking back" of the pistons, possibly creating increased pedal travel and vibration when brakes are applied.

Before checking the runout, wheel bearings should be adjusted. The readjustment is very important and will be required at the completion of the test to prevent bearing failure. Be sure to make the adjustment according to the recommendations given under Front Wheel Bearings, Adjust, in the car chapters.

BRAKE DISC SERVICE

Servicing of disc brakes is extremely critical due to the close tolerances required in machining the brake disc to insure proper brake operation.

The maintenance of these close controls of the shape of the rubbing surfaces is necessary to prevent brake roughness. In addition, the surface finish must be non-directional and maintained at a micro inch finish. This close control of the rubbing surface finish is necessary to avoid pulls and erratic performance and promote long lining life and equal lining wear of both left and right brakes.

In light of the foregoing remarks, refinishing of the rubbing surfaces should not be attempted unless precision equipment, capable of measuring in micro inches (millionths of an inch) is available.

To check lateral runout of a disc, mount a dial indicator on a convenient part (steering knuckle, tie rod, disc brake caliper housing) so that the plunger of the dial indicator contacts the disc at a point one inch from the outer edge, **Fig. 1.** If the total indicated runout exceeds specifications, install a new disc.

To check parallelism (thickness variation), mount dial indicators, **Fig. 2,** so the plunger contacts rotor approximately 1 inch from outer edge. If parellelism exceeds specifications, replace rotor.

GENERAL PRECAUTIONS

1. Grease or any other foreign material must be kept off the caliper, surfaces of the disc and external surfaces of the hub, during service procedures. Handling the brake disc and caliper should be done in a way to avoid deformation of the disc and nicking or scratching brake linings.
2. If inspection reveals rubber piston

Fig. 1   Checking rotor for lateral runout

be honed, provided the diameter of the bore is not increased more than .002 inch. If the bore does not clean up within this specification, a new caliper housing should be installed (black stains on the bore walls are caused by piston seals and will do no harm).

When using a hone, **Fig. 3,** be sure to install the hone baffle before honing bore. The baffle is used to protect the hone stones from damage. Use extreme care in cleaning the caliper after honing. Remove all dust and grit by flushing the caliper with alcohol. Wipe dry with clean lint-less cloth and then clean a second time in the same manner.

Fig. 2   Checking rotor parallelism (Thickness variation)

seals are worn or damaged, they should be replaced immediately.

3. During removal and installation of a wheel assembly, exercise care so as not to interfere with or damage the caliper splash shield, or bleeder screw.
4. Front wheel bearings should be adjusted to specifications.
5. Be sure vehicle is centered on hoist before servicing any of the front end components to avoid bending or damaging the disc splash shield on full right or left wheel turns.
6. Before the vehicle is moved after any brake service work, be sure to obtain a firm brake pedal.
7. The assembly bolts of the two caliper housings should not be disturbed unless the caliper requires service.

INSPECTION OF CALIPER

Should it become necessary to remove the caliper for installation of new parts, clean all parts in alcohol, wipe dry using lint-free cloths. Using an air hose, blow out drilled passages and bores. Check dust boots for punctures or tears. If punctures or tears are evident, new boots should be installed upon reassembly.

Inspect piston bores in both housings for scoring or pitting. Bores that show light scratches or corrosion can usually be cleaned with crocus cloth. However, bores that have deep scratches or scoring may

BLEEDING DISC BRAKES

NOTE: Pressure bleeding is recommended for all hydraulic disc brake systems.

The disc brake hydraulic system can be bled manually or with pressure bleeding equipment. On vehicles with disc brakes the brake pedal will require more pumping and frequent checking of fluid level in master cylinder during bleeding operation.

Never use brake fluid that has been drained from hydraulic system when bleeding the brakes. Be sure the disc brake pistons are returned to their normal positions and that the shoe and lining assemblies are properly seated. Before driving the vehicle, check brake operation to be sure that a firm pedal has been obtained.

PROPORTIONING VALVE

The proportioning valve (when used), **Fig. 4,** provides balanced braking action between front and rear brakes under a wide range of braking conditions. The valve regulates the hydraulic pressure applied to the rear wheel cylinders, thus limiting rear braking action when high pressures are required at the front brakes. In

this manner, premature rear wheel skid is prevented.

TESTING PROPORTIONING VALVE

When a premature rear wheel slide is obtained on a brake application, it usually is an indication that the fluid pressure to the rear wheels is above the 50% reduction ratio for the rear line pressure and that malfunction has occurred within the proportioning valve.

To test the valve, install gauge set shown in **Fig. 4** in brake line between master cylinder and proportioning valve, and at output end of proportioning valve and brake line as shown. Be sure all joints are fluid tight.

Have a helper exert pressure on brake pedal (holding pressure). Obtain a reading on master cylinder output of approximately 700 psi. While pressure is being held as above, reading on valve outlet should be 550–610 psi. If the pressure readings do not meet these specifications, the valve should be removed and a new valve installed.

Fig. 3   Honing caliper piston bore

Fig. 4   Gauge hook-up for testing proportioning valve (typical)

Bendix Sliding Caliper

INDEX

This sliding caliper disc brake assembly incorporates a hub and rotor assembly, caliper, brake shoes and linings, caliper anchor plate and a splash shield, **Fig. 1.**

Cooling fins are cast into the rotor between the two braking surfaces to ventilate and cool the rotor. The sliding caliper is positioned in, and slides on, the abutment surfaces on the leading and trailing edges of the caliper anchor plate. A caliper support key, located between the forward edge of the caliper and abutment surface, is secured with a retaining screw. A support spring is installed between the support key and caliper to maintain tension on the support key.

The caliper is a one-piece casting containing the piston, piston seal and dust seal, **Fig. 2.** The hydraulic seal between the caliper piston and piston bore is achieved by a square cut piston seal, located in a machined groove in the piston bore. The dust seal seats in a recess machined on the edge of the piston bore and into a groove in the caliper piston.

CALIPER REMOVAL

1. Siphon two-thirds of brake fluid from master cylinder reservoir serving front disc brakes.
2. Raise vehicle, support on jackstands and remove front wheels.

3. Bottom the caliper piston in bore. Insert a screwdriver between inboard shoe and piston, then pry piston back into bore. The piston can also be bottomed in the bore with a large C-clamp.
4. Using a ¼ inch allen wrench, remove support key retaining screw, **Fig. 3.**
5. Drive caliper support key and spring from anchor plate with a suitable drift and hammer, **Fig. 4.**
6. Lift caliper from anchor plate and off rotor, **Fig. 5.** Hang caliper from coil spring with wire. Do not allow caliper to hang from brake hose.
7. Remove inboard brake shoe from anchor plate, then the anti-rattle spring from the brake shoe, **Fig. 6.** Remove teflon slipper plate from leading anchor abutment surface, if equipped.
8. Remove outboard brake shoe from caliper, **Fig. 7.** It may be necessary to loosen the brake shoe with a hammer to permit shoe removal.

CALIPER DISASSEMBLY

1. Drain brake fluid from caliper.
2. Position caliper with shop cloths, **Fig. 8,** and apply compressed air to fluid inlet port to ease piston from bore.

NOTE: Do not attempt to catch piston or to protect it when applying compressed air since personal injury is possible.

3. Remove dust seal from piston, then the piston seal from bore, **Fig. 2.** Use wooden or plastic tool to remove piston seal since metal tools may damage piston.
4. Remove bleeder screw.

CALIPER ASSEMBLY

1. Coat square cut piston seal with clean brake fluid, then install seal into piston bore. Work seal into groove with clean fingers.
2. Install bleeder screw and plastic cap.
3. Lubricate dust seal and tool J-24387 with clean brake fluid, then place dust seal on tool, allowing ¼ inch of tool to extend past small lip of dust seal, **Fig. 9.**
4. Place dust seal and tool over piston bore, then work large lip of dust seal into seal groove, **Fig. 10.** Ensure dust seal is fully seated.
5. Lubricate caliper piston and insert through tool. Center piston in bore and use a hammer handle to apply pressure to install piston halfway into bore, **Fig. 10.**

Fig. 1 Bendix sliding caliper disc brake (Typical)

Fig. 2   Caliper assembly

Fig. 3   Removing support key retaining screw

Fig. 4   Removing support key

Fig. 5   Removing or installing caliper

Fig. 6   Removing or installing inboard brake shoe

Fig. 7   Removing or installing outboard brake shoe

Fig. 8   Removing piston from caliper

Fig. 9.   Dust seal & installer tool assembly

PRESS SEAL LIP FIRMLY INTO GROOVE

TOOL J24837

DUST SEAL

VIEW A

Fig. 11 Lubricating caliper piston bore

CLEAN & LUBE SURFACE

CLEAN & LUBE SURFACE

Fig. 12 Caliper & anchor plate abutment surfaces

INSERT PISTON THROUGH INSTALLER TOOL

CALIPER PISTON

DUST SEAL

TOOL J24837

VIEW B

Fig. 10 Installing dust seal & caliper piston

ANTI-RATTLE SPRING

Fig. 13 Installing inboard brake shoe anti-rattle spring

NOTE: On some models, disc brake caliper pistons may develop a light coating of rust under the dust seal and outboard of the piston seal. This rust may cause the piston to not fully retract. Before installing piston, apply a light coating of dielectric compound 8126688, or equivalent, to caliper piston bore, **Fig. 11.**

6. Remove tool J-24387 and seat small lip of dust seal in caliper piston groove, then bottom piston in bore.

BRAKE SHOE & LINING, REPLACE

The procedures to remove & install the brake shoe and lining assemblies are outlined under "Caliper Removal" and "Caliper Installation". It is not necessary to dis-

connect the brake hose, however, use caution not to twist or kink hose.

CALIPER INSTALLATION

1. Clean and lubricate abutment surfaces of caliper and the anchor plate with a suitable molydisulfide grease, **Fig. 12.**
2. Install inboard brake shoe anti-rattle spring on brake shoe rear flange, ensure looped section of clip is facing away from rotor, **Fig. 13.** Install teflon slipper plate on leading anchor abutment surface, if equipped.
3. Install inboard brake shoe on caliper anchor plate, **Fig. 6.**
4. Install outboard brake shoe in caliper,

Fig. 7. Ensure the shoe flange is seated fully into outboard arms or caliper. It may be necessary to use a hammer to seat the shoe.
5. Place caliper assembly over rotor and position in caliper anchor plate. Ensure dust boot is not torn or mispositioned by inboard brake shoe during caliper installation.
6. Align caliper with anchor plate abutment surfaces, then insert support key and spring between abutment surfaces, then insert support key and spring between abutment surfaces at the trailing end of caliper and anchor plate. With a hammer and brass drift, drive caliper support key and spring into position, then install and torque support key retaining screw to 15 ft. lbs.
7. Refill master cylinder to within ¼ inch of rim. Press brake pedal several times to seat shoes.
8. Install front wheels and lower vehicle.

American Motors Dual Pin Sliding Caliper

INDEX

OPERATION

This dual pin sliding caliper assembly incorporates a hub and rotor assembly, a caliper, brake shoes and linings, caliper anchor plate, adapter bracket and splash shield on Spirit and Concord models, **Fig. 1.** On Eagle models, the caliper assembly incorporates a rotor which mounts to the hub assembly, a caliper, brake shoes and linings, caliper anchor plate and splash shield, **Fig. 2.**

The caliper used on all models has a 2.6 inch diameter piston. The caliper is positioned over the rotor and slides on two mounting pins which maintain caliper position relative to the rotor and caliper anchor plate. The caliper is a one-piece casting with a groove machined in the bore to hold the square cut piston seal to maintain a hydraulic seal between the piston and bore wall. The dust boot is seated in a machined recess in the top of the piston bore and a groove in the piston exterior surface.

The inner and outer brakeshoes are positioned by the caliper anchor plate. The brakeshoe anti-rattle clip is positioned between the brakeshoe and caliper anchor plate. The brake linings are riveted to the shoes and the inner and outer brake shoes are not interchangeable.

BRAKE SHOE & LININGS, REPLACE

Removal

1. Drain and discard approximately ⅔ of the brake fluid from the larger brake fluid reservoir.
2. Raise and support vehicle, then remove tire and wheel assembly.
3. Using a suitable screwdriver, pry piston fully into caliper bore.

NOTE: If piston cannot be bottomed in cylinder bore using a screwdriver, use a C-clamp.

4. Using a 7 mm Allen wrench, remove caliper mounting pins.
5. Lift caliper from anchor plate and off rotor.
6. Suspend caliper from coil spring with suitable wire to prevent damaging brake hose.
7. Hold anti-rattle clip against caliper anchor plate and remove outer brake shoe.

NOTE: Note position of anti-rattle clip for assembly reference.

8. Remove inner brake shoe from caliper anchor plate, then anti-rattle clip.
9. Wipe inside of caliper with dry, clean cloth and inspect piston bore for leakage. If leakage is present, refer to "Caliper Overhaul".

NOTE: Do not clean caliper with com-

Fig. 1   American Motors dual pin slider disc brake assembly. 1982–83 Spirit & Concord

Fig. 2   American Motors dual pin slider disc brake assembly. 1982–85 Eagle

pressed air as damage to the dust boot may result.

Installation

1. Inspect caliper and anchor plate abutment surfaces for rust and corrosion. If rust and corrosion are evident, clean surfaces with wire brush.
2. Lightly lubricate caliper and anchor plate abutment surfaces with Molydisulfide grease.
3. Install anti-rattle clip on trailing end of anchor plate. Ensure split end of clip faces away from rotor.
4. While holding anti-rattle clip in position, install inner and outer brake shoes.
5. Install caliper over rotor and into position on adapter.
6. Install caliper mounting pins. Torque to 26 ft. lbs. on 1982-84 models, or 30 ft. lbs. on 1985 models.
7. Fill master cylinder with clean brake fluid, then pump brake pedal several times to position caliper piston and brake shoes.
8. Install tire and wheel assembly, then lower vehicle.
9. Check brake fluid and refill as necessary.

NOTE: Before moving vehicle, ensure a firm brake pedal is obtained.

CALIPER OVERHAUL

Removal

1. Follow steps 1 through 3 of Removal procedure under "Brake Shoe and Linings, Replace."
2. Clean dirt from brake hose fittings.
3. Disconnect brake hose from caliper, then cap open lines to prevent entry of dirt.
4. Discard hose fitting washer.
5. Remove caliper following steps 4 through 8 of Removal procedure under "Brake Shoe and Linings, Replace."

Disassembly

1. Clean caliper exterior with suitable brake cleaning solvent.
2. Drain caliper, then place on clean

Fig. 3   Disassembled view of disc brake caliper. 1982–85 American Motors (typical)

work surface.
3. Pad caliper interior with clean shop cloths, then using compressed air, gently apply just enough air pressure into caliper fluid inlet hole to ease piston out of bore.

NOTE: Do not place fingers in front of piston in an attempt to catch or protect it when applying compressed air. This could result in serious injury.

4. Using a suitable screwdriver, pry dust boot from bore using care not to damage piston bore, **Fig. 3.**
5. Using a pencil or other suitable wooden object, remove piston seal.

Inspection

1. Clean all parts in brake cleaning solvent or brake fluid, then blow out caliper fluid passages with filtered compressed air.
2. Inspect caliper mounting pins for corrosion, replace as necessary.

NOTE: Do not attempt to clean or polish caliper mounting pins with abrasives as protective plating will be removed.

3. Inspect caliper piston. If nicked, scratched, corroded or protective plating is worn off, replace.

NOTE: Do not attempt to refinish piston in any way as protective plating will be removed, leading to corrosion and eventual failure.

4. Inspect caliper bore. If nicked, scratched, worn, cracked, or badly corroded, replace caliper.

NOTE: Minor corrosion and stains can be removed from caliper bore with crocus cloth. Do not attempt to clean caliper bore with any other abrasives.

Assembly

1. Lubricate piston bore and seal with brake fluid, then work seal into piston groove using fingers only.
2. Lubricate piston with brake fluid, then slide metal portion of dust seal over open end of piston and pull rearwards until seal boot seats in piston groove, then push metal portion of seal forward until retainer is flush with rim and seal fold snaps into position.
3. Insert piston and seal assembly into bore. Do not unseat piston seal.
4. Using a hammer handle, press piston in bore.
5. Using tool No. J-33028, install dust seal in caliper housing.
6. Install bleeder screw and tighten securely.
7. Install replacement plastic sleeves and rubber bushings in caliper ears.

Installation

1. Follow steps 1 through 6 of Installation procedures under "Brake Shoe and Linings, Replace."
2. Install replacement hose fitting washer on brake hose, then install hose in caliper and torque to 25 ft. lbs.
3. Fill master cylinder with clean brake fluid and bleed brakes.
4. Install tire and wheel assembly, then lower vehicle.
5. Check brake fluid and refill as necessary.

NOTE: Before moving vehicle, ensure a firm rake pedal is obtained.

Rotor Specifications

CAR	Year	Nominal Thickness	Minimum Refinish Thickness	Thickness Variation Parallelism	Lateral Runout (T.I.R.)	Finish (Micro-In.)
All	1980	.880	.810	.0005	.003	15–80
Exc. Eagle	1981–83	—	.815	.0005	.003	15–80
Eagle	1981–85	—	.815	.0005	.004	15–80

Caliper Specifications

Year	Model	Caliper Bore Dia. In.
1980–85	All	2.6

Chrysler Corp.

NOTE: Refer to "Brake Usage Chart" to determine which type brakes are used on vehicle being serviced.

TABLE OF CONTENTS

Brake Usage Chart

General Information

BRAKE SHOES, LININGS & CALIPERS

Remove wheels and inspect brake disc, caliper and linings. The wheel bearings should be inspected at this time and repacked if necessary. Do not get any grease on the linings.

On rear wheel drive models, the brake shoe and lining assemblies should be replaced if the lining is worn to within 1/32 inch of rivet heads (riveted linings) or brake shoe (bonded linings). On front wheel drive models, the brake shoe and lining assemblies should be replaced when the combined thickness of the shoe and lining is 5/16 inch or less. It is recommended that both front and/or rear wheel sets be replaced whenever a respective shoe and lining assembly is replaced.

If a visual inspection does not adequately determine the condition of the linings, the brake shoe and lining assemblies should be removed and inspected. If shoes do not require replacement, reinstall them in their original positions. Brake shoes and linings should also be replaced if cracked or damaged.

If the caliper is cracked or fluid leakage through the casting is evident, it must be replaced as a unit.

BRAKE ROUGHNESS

The most common cause of brake chatter on disc brakes is a variation in thickness of the disc. If roughness or vibration is encountered during highway operation or if pedal pumping is experienced at low speeds, the disc may have excessive thickness variation. To check for this condition, measure the disc at 12 points with a micrometer at a radius approximately one inch from edge of disc. If thickness measurements vary by more than .0005", the disc should be replaced with a new one.

Excessive lateral runout of braking disc may cause a "knocking back" of the pistons, possibly creating increased pedal travel and vibration when brakes are applied.

Before checking the runout, wheel bearings should be adjusted. The readjustment is very important and will be required at the completion of the test to prevent bearing failure. Be sure to make the adjustment according to the recommendations given under Front Wheel Bearings, Adjust in the car chapters.

BRAKE DISC SERVICE

Servicing of disc brakes is extremely critical due to the close tolerances required in machining the brake disc to insure proper brake operation.

The maintenance of these close controls of the shape of the rubbing surfaces is necessary to prevent brake roughness. In addition, the surface finish must be non-directional and maintained at a micro inch finish. This close control of the rubbing surface finish is necessary to avoid pulls and erratic performance and promote long lining life and equal lining wear of both left

Fig. 1   Checking rotor for lateral runout

Fig. 2   Checking rotor parallelism (Thickness variation)

and right brakes.

In light of the foregoing remarks, refinishing of the rubbing surfaces should not be attempted unless precision equipment, capable of measuring in micro inches (millionths of an inch) is available.

To check lateral runout of a disc, mount a dial indicator on a convenient part (steering knuckle, tie rod, disc brake caliper housing) so that the plunger of the dial indicator contacts the disc at a point one inch from the outer edge, **Fig. 1.** If the total indicated runout exceeds specifications, install a new disc.

To check parallelism (thickness variation), mount dial indicators, **Fig. 2,** so the plunger contacts rotor approximately 1 inch from outer edge. If parellelism exceeds specifications, replace rotor.

GENERAL PRECAUTIONS

1. Grease or any other foreign material must be kept off the caliper, surfaces of the disc and external surfaces of the hub, during service procedures. Handling the brake disc and caliper should be done in a way to avoid deformation of the disc and nicking or scratching brake linings.
2. If inspection reveals rubber piston seals are worn or damaged, they should be replaced immediately.
3. During removal and installation of a wheel assembly, exercise care so as not to interfere with or damage the caliper splash shield, or bleeder screw.
4. Front wheel bearings should be adjusted to specifications.
5. Be sure vehicle is centered on hoist

before servicing any of the front end components to avoid bending or damaging the disc splash shield on full right or left wheel turns.
6. Before the vehicle is moved after any brake service work, be sure to obtain a firm brake pedal.
7. The assembly bolts of the two caliper housings should not be disturbed unless the caliper requires service.

INSPECTION OF CALIPER

Should it become necessary to remove the caliper for installation of new parts, clean all parts in alcohol, wipe dry using lint-free cloths. Using an air hose, blow out drilled passages and bores. Check dust boots for punctures or tears. If punctures or tears are evident, new boots should be installed upon reassembly.

Inspect piston bores in both housings for scoring or pitting. Bores that show light scratches or corrosion can usually be cleaned with crocus cloth. However, bores that have deep scratches or scoring may be honed, provided the diameter of the bore is not increased more than .002″. If the bore does not clean up within this specification, a new caliper housing should be installed (black stains on the bore walls are

caused by piston seals and will do no harm).

When using a hone, **Fig. 3,** be sure to install the hone baffle before honing bore. The baffle is used to protect the hone stones from damage. Use extreme care in cleaning the caliper after honing. Remove all dust and grit by flushing the caliper with alcohol. Wipe dry with clean lint-less cloth and then clean a second time in the same manner.

BLEEDING DISC BRAKES

NOTE: Pressure bleeding is recommended for all hydraulic disc brake systems.

The disc brake hydraulic system can be bled manually or with pressure bleeding equipment. On vehicles with disc brakes the brake pedal will require more pumping and frequent checking of fluid level in master cylinder during bleeding operation.

Never use brake fluid that has been drained from hydraulic system when bleeding the brakes. Be sure the disc brake pistons are returned to their normal positions and that the shoe and lining assemblies are properly seated. Before driving the vehicle, check brake operation to be sure that a firm pedal has been obtained.

Fig. 3   Honing caliper piston bore

Fig. 4   Gauge hook-up for testing proportioning valve (typical)

PROPORTIONING VALVE

The proportioning valve (when used), **Fig. 4,** provides balanced braking action between front and rear brakes under a wide range of braking conditions. The valve regulates the hydraulic pressure applied to the rear wheel cylinders, thus limiting rear braking action when high pressures are required at the front brakes. In this manner, premature rear wheel skid is prevented.

TESTING PROPORTIONING VALVE

When a premature rear wheel slide is obtained on a brake application, it usually is an indication that the fluid pressure to the rear wheels is above the 50% reduction ratio for the rear line pressure and that malfunction has occured within the proportioning valve.

To test the valve, install gauge set shown in **Fig. 4** in brake line between master cylinder and proportioning valve, and at output end of proportioning valve and brake line as shown. Be sure all joints are fluid tight.

Have a helper exert pressure on brake pedal (holding pressure). Obtain a reading on master cylinder output of approximately 700 psi. While pressure is being held as above, reading on valve outlet should be 550–610 psi. If the pressure readings do not meet these specifications, the valve should be removed and a new valve installed

Kelsey-Hayes Sliding Caliper

INDEX

OPERATION

This sliding caliper single piston system uses a one piece hub and is actuated by the hydraulic system and disc assembly, **Fig. 1.** Alignment and positioning of the caliper is achieved by two machined guides or "ways" on the adaptor, while caliper retaining clips allow lateral movement of the caliper, **Fig. 2.** Outboard shoe flanges are used to position and locate the shoe on the caliper fingers, **Fig. 3,** while the inboard shoe is retained by the adaptor, **Fig. 4.** Braking force applied onto the outboard shoe is transferred to the caliper, while braking force applied onto the inboard shoe is transferred directly to the adaptor.

A square cut piston seal provides a hydraulic seal between the piston and the cylinder bore, **Fig. 1.** A dust boot with a wiping lip installed in a groove in the cylinder bore and piston, prevents contamination in the piston and cylinder bore area. Adjustment between the disc and the shoe is obtained automatihcally by the outward relocation of the piston as the inboard lining wears and inward movement of the caliper as the outboard lining wears.

CALIPER REMOVAL

1. Raise the vehicle and remove front wheel.
2. Remove caliper retaining clips and anti-rattle springs, **Fig. 2.**
3. Remove caliper from disc by slowly sliding caliper assembly out and away from disc.

NOTE: Use some means to support caliper. Do not let caliper hang from hydraulic line.

BRAKE SHOE REMOVAL

1. Remove caliper assembly as outlined above.
2. Remove outboard shoe by prying between the shoe and the caliper fingers, **Fig. 5,** since flanges on outboard shoe retain caliper firmly.

NOTE: Caliper should be supported to avoid damage to the flexible brake hose.

3. Remove inboard brake shoe from the adaptor, **Fig. 4.**

BRAKE SHOE INSTALLATION

NOTE: Remove approximately ⅓ of the brake fluid out of the reservoir to prevent overflow when pistons are pushed back into the bore.

1. With care, push piston back into bore until bottomed.
2. Install new outboard shoe in recess of caliper.

NOTE: No free play should exist between brake shoe flanges and caliper fingers, **Fig. 6.**

If up and down movement of the shoe shows free play, shoe must be removed and flanges bent to provide a slight interference fit, **Fig. 3.** Reinstall shoe after modification, if shoe can not be finger snapped into place, use light "C" clamp pressure, **Fig. 7.**

3. Position inboard shoe with flanges inserted in adaptor "ways," **Fig. 4.**
4. Carefully slide caliper assembly into adaptor and over the disc while aligning caliper on machined "ways" of adaptor.

NOTE: Make sure dust boot is not pulled out from groove when piston and boot slide over the inboard shoe.

5. Install anti-rattle springs and retaining clips and torque retaining screws to 180 inch-pounds.

NOTE: The inboard shoe anti-rattle spring is to be installed on top of the retainer spring plate, **Fig. 2.**

CALIPER DISASSEMBLY

1. With caliper and shoes removed as described previously, place caliper onto the upper control arm and slowly depress brake pedal, in turn hydraulically pushing piston out of bore.

NOTE: Pedal will fall when piston passes bore opening.

2. Support pedal below first inch of pedal travel to prevent excessive fluid loss.
3. To remove piston from the opposite caliper, disconnect flexible brake line at frame bracket, from vehicle side where piston has been removed previously and plug tube to prevent pressure loss. By depressing brake pedal this piston can also be hydraulically pushed out.
4. Mount caliper in a vise equipped with protector jaws.

NOTE: Excessive vise pressure will distort caliper bore.

5. Remove the dust boot, **Fig. 8.**
6. Insert a suitable tool such as a small, pointed wooden or plastic object between the cylinder bore and the seal and work seal out of the groove in the piston bore.

NOTE: A metal tool such as a screwdriver should not be used since it can cause damage to the piston bore or burr the edges of the seal groove.

CALIPER ASSEMBLY

1. Dip new piston seals in clean brake

DISC BRAKES

WHEEL

CALIPER

BOOT

SEAL

PISTON

SHOE AND LINING

WHEEL STUD

INNER BEARING

SEAL

MOUNTING BOLT

SPINDLE

ADAPTOR

MOUNTING BOLT

OUTER BEARING

STEERING KNUCKLE

BRAKING DISC AND HUB

SPLASH SHIELD

Fig. 1   Sectional view of Kelsey-Hayes sliding caliper front disc brake

STEEL BAR OR ANVIL

OUTBOARD SHOE RETAINER FLANGE

Fig. 3   Fitting outboard shoe retaining flange

WIRE SUPPORT FOR CALIPER

INBOARD SHOE

ADAPTER

"O" RINGS

BRAKING DISC

CALIPER

ADAPTER "WAYS"

Fig. 4   Replacing inboard shoe

ANTI-RATTLE SPRING

RETAINER CLIP

INBOARD SHOE FLANGE

CALIPER (MACHINED "WAYS")

ADAPTOR (MACHINED "WAYS")

RETAINER CLIP

ANTI-RATTLE SPRING

OUTBOARD SHOE FLANGE

Fig. 2   Caliper machined "ways" and assembly retention

ADAPTER

CALIPER

CALIPER FINGER

OUTBOARD SHOE REACTION FLANGE

OUTBOARD BRAKE SHOE RETENTION FLANGES

Fig. 5   Removing outboard shoe

Fig. 6 Positioning outboard shoe onto caliper finger machined retainer ledge

fluid. Work seal gently into the groove (using clean fingers) until seal is properly seated, make sure that seal is not twisted or rolled.

NOTE: Old seals should never be re-used.

2. On 1981–85 models, install piston into bore and push past seal until piston bottoms in bore.
3. Lubricate piston boot generously with clean brake fluid. On 1980 models, using finger pressure, install into caliper by pushing into outer groove of the caliper bore. When properly positioned in groove boot will snap into place. Double check to make sure boot is properly installed and seated by running finger around the inside of the boot. On 1981–85 models, install piston boot with tool C-4689 and handle C-4171, **Fig. 9.**
4. On 1980 models, plug high pressure inlet to caliper and bleeder screw hole and coat piston with a generous amount of lubricant. Spread boot with finger and work piston into boot while pressing down on piston. As piston is depressed, entrapped air below piston will force boot around piston and into its groove.
5. On 1980 models, remove the plug and apply uniform force to the piston (avoid cocking piston) until piston bottoms in bore.

Fig. 7 Installing outboard shoe using "C" clamp

6. Install brake hose to caliper using new seal washers.
7. Install caliper and shoes as described under "Brake Shoe Installation."

Fig. 8 Exploded view of Kelsey-Hayes sliding caliper disc brake

Fig. 9 Installing piston dust boot. 1981–85 models

Chrysler Corp. Front Wheel Drive A.T.E. Dual Pin Floating Caliper Disc Brake

INDEX

OPERATION

The single piston floating caliper disc brake assembly consists of the hub and disc brake rotor assembly, caliper, shoes and linings, splash shield and adapter, **Fig. 1.**

The caliper assembly floats on two rubber bushings riding on two steel guide pins threaded into the adapter. The bushings are inserted on the inboard portion of the caliper. Two machined abutments on the adapter position and align the caliper fore and aft. Guide pins and bushings control caliper and piston seal movement to assist in maintaining proper shoe clearance.

All braking force is taken directly by the adapter. The steel piston used on 1980—82 Horizon & Omni models is 1.89 inches in diameter. The plastic piston used on 1981—82 Aries & Reliant, 1982 LeBaron and 400 and the phenolic piston used on 1983—84 Omni, Horizon, Reliant, 400, 600, Aries, LeBaron, E-Class, New Yorker & all 1985 models are 2.13 inches in diameter.

BRAKE SHOE & LINING, REPLACE

Omni, Horizon & 1983—84 Charger & Turismo

1. Raise and support front of vehicle, then remove wheel and tire assembly.
2. Remove caliper guide pins and anti-rattle spring, **Fig. 2.**
3. Carefully slide caliper assembly away from disc, **Fig. 3.** Support caliper assembly to prevent damage to brake hose.
4. Remove outboard shoe and lining assembly from adapter, **Fig. 4.**
5. Remove rotor from drive axle flange and studs, **Fig. 5.**
6. Remove inboard shoe and lining assembly from adapter, **Fig. 6.**
7. Carefully push piston into caliper bore.

NOTE: Remove some brake fluid from reservoir to prevent overflowing when pushing piston into caliper bore.

8. Position inboard shoe and lining on adapter. Ensure metal portion of shoe is properly positioned in recess of adapter.
9. Install rotor over studs and drive flange.
10. While holding outboard shoe in position on adapter, carefully position adapter over disc brake rotor.
11. Carefully lower caliper over disc brake rotor and adapter.
12. Install guide pins through bushings, caliper and adapter.

13. Press in on guide pins and thread pin into adapter. Torque pins to 25 to 40 ft. lbs.
14. Install wheel and tire assembly, then lower vehicle.

1981—84 Aries, Reliant, 1982—84 LeBaron & 400, 1983—84 E-Class, New Yorker, 600 And All 1985 Models

1. Raise and support vehicle, then remove wheel and tire assemblies.
2. Remove hold down spring from caliper assembly by pressing spring outward.
3. Loosen, but do not remove, caliper guide pins, then remove caliper from disc. Inboard shoe will remain inside caliper. Support caliper assembly to prevent damage to hydraulic brake hose.

NOTE: Remove caliper guide pins only if bushings or sleeves are to be replaced.

4. Remove inboard shoe from caliper and outboard shoe from adapter.
5. Push caliper piston into bore.

NOTE: Remove some brake fluid from master cylinder reservoir to prevent overflowing when piston is pushed into bore.

Fig. 1   Dual pin floating caliper disc brake. Chrysler front wheel drive models

Fig. 2   Removing caliper guide pins

Fig. 3   Removing caliper

Fig. 4   Removing outboard pad & lining assembly

Fig. 5   Removing disc brake rotor from hub

Fig. 6   Removing inboard pad & lining assemblies

Fig. 7   Disassembled view of disc brake caliper. Omni, Horizon & 1983—84 Charger & Turismo

Fig. 8   Disassembled view of disc brake caliper. 1981—84 Aries, Reliant, 1982—84 LeBaron & 400, 1983—84 E-Class, New Yorker, 600 & all 1985 models

Fig. 9   Installing piston seal

Fig. 10   Installing piston dust boot

4. Disconnect brake hose from caliper.
5. Mount caliper in a soft jawed vise.
6. Support caliper and remove dust boot and discard.
7. Using a small wooden or plastic stick, remove seal from groove in piston bore and discard.
8. Using a suitable tool, remove bushings from caliper.

Inspection

1. Clean all components using alcohol or other suitable cleaning solvent, then blow dry using compressed air. With compressed air blow out drilled passages and bores.
2. Inspect piston bore for pitting or scoring. Light scratches or corrosion can usually be cleared with crocus cloth. Bores that have deep scratches or scoring should be honed with tool No. C-4095, providing bore diameter is not increased by more than .001 in. If scratches or scoring cannot be cleared up, or if caliper bore is increased by more than .001 in., replace caliper housing.

NOTE: When using hone C-4095, coat hone and caliper bore with clean brake fluid. After honing carefully clean boot and seal grooves with a stiff non-metallic brush. Flush caliper with clean brake fluid and wipe dry with a clean lintless cloth, then flush and wipe caliper dry again.

3. Replace piston if found to be scored, pitted or if plating is severely worn or if caliper bore was honed. Black stains on steel piston are caused by piston seal and are not cause for replacing piston.

Assemble

1. Mount caliper in a soft jawed vise.
2. Lubricate piston seal with clean brake fluid and install seal in caliper bore groove, **Fig. 9.** Ensure seal is properly seated, **Fig. 7 & 8.**
3. Lubricate piston boot with clean brake fluid and install boot in caliper bore groove, **Fig. 10.**
4. Using a hammer and small steel plate or a suitable C-clamp, drive into caliper until seated, **Fig. 11.** Ensure boot is properly seated in caliper bore.

Fig. 11   Installing caliper piston

5. Plug brake hose inlet boss and bleeder screw hole, then lubricate piston with clean brake fluid.
6. Spread boot with finger and work piston into boot, then press down on piston.
7. Remove plug and carefully push piston down in bore until bottomed.
8. Compress flanges of guide pin bushings and install bushings on caliper housing. Ensure that bushing flanges extend evenly over caliper housing on both sides.

NOTE: On 1981–84 Aries, Reliant, 1982–84 LeBaron, 400, 1983–84 E-Class, New Yorker, 600 and all 1985 models, remove teflon sleeves from guide pin bushings prior to installing bushings into caliper. After bushings are installed into caliper, reinstall teflon sleeves into bushings.

9. Connect brake hose to brake line at frame bracket.
10. Install caliper on vehicle as described under Brake Shoe & Lining, Replace.
11. Check brake fluid level of master cylinder reservoir, then open caliper bleed screw and bleed brake system. Continue bleeding procedure until firm pedal is obtained.

6. Install new inboard shoe into caliper with retainer positioned in piston bore.
7. Install outboard shoe onto adapter.
8. Position caliper over brake disc and adapter, then torque guide pins to 18–22 ft. lbs.
9. Install hold down spring, then install tire and wheel assemblies and lower vehicle to ground.
10. Check master cylinder reservoir for proper level of brake fluid and add as necessary.

CALIPER OVERHAUL

Disassemble

1. Remove caliper assembly as described under Brake Shoe & Lining, Replace.
2. With brake hose attached to caliper, **Figs. 7 & 8,** carefully depress brake pedal to push piston out of caliper bore. Prop brake pedal to any position below first inch of brake pedal travel to prevent brake fluid loss.
3. If pistons are to be removed from both calipers, disconnect brake hose at frame bracket after removing piston, then cap brake line and repeat procedure to remove piston from other caliper.

Kelsey-Hayes Single Pin Floating Caliper Disc Brake

INDEX

Fig. 1 Disassembled view of Kelsey-Hayes single pin floating caliper

Fig. 2 Anti-rattle spring location

Operation

The caliper assembly consists of a rotor, caliper, shoes and linings, and adapter, **Fig. 1.** The single piston caliper assembly floats through a rubber bushing on a single pin, threaded into the adapter. The bushing is inserted into the inboard portion of the caliper. Two machined abutments on the adapter, position and align the caliper fore and aft. The guide pin and bushing controls the movement of the caliper and the piston seal, to assist in maintaining proper shoe clearance.

This assembly has three anti-rattle clips. One is on top of the inboard shoe, one clip is on the bottom of the outboard shoe, and one clip is on top of the caliper, **Fig. 2.**

All of the braking force is taken directly by the adapter. The caliper is a one piece casting with the inboard side containing a single piston cylinder bore. The phenolic piston is 2.13 inches in diameter.

A square cut rubber piston seal is located in a machined groove in the caliper bore and provides a seal between piston and caliper bore, **Fig. 3.**

A molded rubber dust boot installed in a groove in the cylinder bore and piston keeps contamination from the caliper bore and piston. The boot mounts in the caliper bore and in a groove in the piston, **Fig. 3.**

BRAKE SHOE & LINING, REPLACE

Removal

1. Remove brake fluid until reservoir is half full.
2. Raise and support front of vehicle, then remove wheel and tire assembly.
3. Remove caliper guide pin and anti-rattle clips.

4. Remove caliper from disc by sliding caliper assembly out and away from braking disc, **Fig. 4.** Suspend caliper with wire so as not to damage flexible brake hose.
5. Remove outboard brake lining, then lift off rotor and remove inboard brake lining.

Installation

1. Push piston back into cylinder bore with uniform pressure until it is bottomed, **Fig. 5.**
2. Position inboard shoe and lining on adapter, then install rotor.
3. While holding outboard shoe in position on adapter, carefully position caliper over disc brake rotor.

Fig. 3 Sectional view of piston seal & dust boot

Fig. 4 Removing caliper

Fig. 5 Piston installation

4. Lower caliper over rotor and adapter.
5. Install guide pin through bushing, caliper and adapter.
6. Press in on guide pin and thread pin into adapter. Torque pin to 25 to 40 ft. lbs.
7. Install wheel and tire assembly, then lower vehicle.

CALIPER OVERHAUL

Refer to Caliper Overhaul under "Chrysler Corp. Front Wheel Drive Dual Pin Floating Caliper Disc Brake" for procedure.

Rotor Specifications

CAR	Year	Nominal Thickness	Minimum Refinish Thickness	Thickness Variation Parallelism	Lateral Runout (T.I.R.)	Finish (Micro-In.)
CHRYSLER, DODGE & PLYMOUTH						
Full Size	1980–85	1.010	.940	.0005	.004	15–80
Imperial	1981–83	1.010	.940	.0005	.004	15–80
Intermediate (Exc. Below)	1980–85	1.010	.940	.0005	.004	15–80
Aspen, Valiant & Volare	1980	1.010	.940	.0005	.004	15–80
Omni & Horizon	1980	.490	.431	.0005	①	15–80
	1981–85	.498	.431	.0005	.005	15–80
Charger & Turismo	1983–85	.498	.431	.0005	.005	15–80
Aries & Reliant	1981–85	.935	.882	.0005	.005	15–80
400 & LeBaron	1982–85	.935	.882	.0005	.005	15–80
600, E-Class & New Yorker	1983–84	.935	.882	.0005	.005	15–80
Daytona & Laser	1984–85	.935	.882	.0005	.005	15–80
600 & New Yorker	1985	.935	.882	.0005	.005	15–80

①—1980, .005.

Caliper Specifications

Year	Model	Caliper Bore Dia. In.
CHRYSLER CORP. FRONT WHEEL DRIVE		
1980	All	1.89
1981–82	Omni & Horizon	1.894
	Exc. Omni & Horizon	2.130
1983–85	All	2.130
CHRYSLER CORP. REAR WHEEL DRIVE		
1979–85	All	2.755

Ford Motor CO.

NOTE: Refer to "Brake Usage Chart" to determine which type brakes are used on vehicle being serviced.

TABLE OF CONTENTS

Brake Usage Chart

Page No.   Page No.   Page No.

FORD Rear Wheel Disc Brake .... 30—25

Lincoln, 1982—85
Mark VII, 1984—85
Mustang SVO, 1984—85
Versailles, 1980

FORD Sliding Caliper .. 30—21

Bobcat, 1980
Granada, 1980
Monarch, 1980
Pinto, 1980
Versailles, 1980

KELSEY-HAYES Pin Slider Caliper .... 30—23

Capri, 1980—85
Cougar, 1981—82
Cougar, 1980—85
Escort, 1981—85
EXP, 1982—85
Fairmount, 1980—83
Ford Full Size, 1980—85
Granada, 1981—82

Lincoln Continental, 1980—85
LN7, 1982—83
LTD, 1983—85
Lynx, 1981—85
Mark VI, 1980—83
Mark VII, 1984—85
Marquis, 1983—85
Mercury Full Size, 1980—85
Mustang, 1980—85
Mustang SVO, 1984—85
Tempo, 1984—85
Topaz, 1984—85
Thunderbird, 1980—85
Zephyr, 1980—83

General Information

INDEX

BRAKE SHOES, LININGS & CALIPERS

Remove wheels and inspect brake disc, caliper and linings. The wheel bearings should be inspected at this time and repacked if necessary. Do not get any grease on the linings.

The brake shoe and lining assemblies should be replaced if the lining is worn to within 1/32 inch of rivet heads (riveted linings) or brake shoe (bonded linings). It is recommended that both front and/or rear wheel sets be replaced whenever a respective shoe and lining assembly is replaced.

If a visual inspection does not adequately determine the condition of the linings, the brake shoe and lining assemblies should be removed and inspected. If shoes do not require replacement, reinstall them in their original positions. Brake shoes and linings should also be replaced if cracked or damaged.

If the caliper is cracked or fluid leakage through the casting is evident, it must be replaced as a unit.

BRAKE ROUGHNESS

The most common cause of brake chatter on disc brakes is a variation in thickness of the disc. If roughness or vibration is encountered during highway operation or if pedal pumping is experienced at low speeds, the disc may have excessive thickness variation. To check for this condition, measure the disc at 12 points with a micrometer at a radius approximately one inch from edge of disc. If thickness measurements vary by more than .0005 inch, the disc should be replaced with a new one.

Excessive lateral runout of braking disc may cause a "knocking back" of the pistons, possibly creating increased pedal travel and vibration when brakes are applied.

Before checking the runout, wheel bearings should be adjusted. The readjustment is very important and will be required at the completion of the test to prevent bearing failure. Be sure to make the adjustment according to the recommendations given under "Front Wheel Bearings, Adjust" in the car chapters.

BRAKE DISC SERVICE

Servicing of disc brakes is extremely crit-

DISC BRAKES

Fig. 1 Checking rotor for lateral runout

Fig. 2 Checking rotor parallelism (thickness variation)

ical due to the close tolerances required in machining the brake disc to insure proper brake operation.

The maintenance of these close controls of the shape of the rubbing surfaces is necessary to prevent brake roughness. In addition, the surface finish must be non-directional and maintained at a micro inch finish. This close control of the rubbing surface finish is necessary to avoid pulls and erratic performance and promote long lining life and equal lining wear of both left and right brakes.

In light of the foregoing remarks, refinishing of the rubbing surfaces should not be attempted unless precision equipment, capable of measuring in micro inches (millionths of an inch) is available.

To check lateral runout of a disc, mount a dial indicator on a convenient part (steering knuckle, tie rod, disc brake caliper housing) so that the plunger of the dial indicator contacts the disc at a point one inch from the outer edge, **Fig. 1.** If the total indicated runout exceeds specifications, install a new disc.

To check parallelism (thickness variation), mount dial indicators, **Fig. 2,** so the plunger contacts rotor approximately 1 inch from outer edge. If parellelism exceeds specifications, replace rotor.

hub, during service procedures. Handling the brake disc and caliper should be done in a way to avoid deformation of the disc and nicking or scratching brake linings.

2. If inspection reveals rubber piston seals are worn or damaged, they should be replaced immediately.

3. During removal and installation of a wheel assembly, exercise care so as not to interfere with or damage the caliper splash shield, or bleeder screw.

4. Front wheel bearings should be adjusted to specifications.

5. Be sure vehicle is centered on hoist before servicing any of the front end components to avoid bending or damaging the disc splash shield on full right or left wheel turns.

6. Before the vehicle is moved after any brake service work, be sure to obtain a firm brake pedal.

7. The assembly bolts of the two caliper housings should not be disturbed unless the caliper requires service.

INSPECTION OF CALIPER

Should it become necessary to remove the caliper for installation of new parts, clean all parts in alcohol, wipe dry using lint-free cloths. Using an air hose, blow out drilled passages and bores. Check dust boots for punctures or tears. If punctures or tears are evident, new boots should be installed upon reassembly.

Inspect piston bores in both housings for scoring or pitting. Bores that show light scratches or corrosion can usually be cleaned with crocus cloth. However, bores that have deep scratches or scoring may be honed, provided the diameter of the bore is not increased more than .002 inch. If the bore does not clean up within this specification, a new caliper housing should be installed (black stains on the bore walls are caused by piston seals and will do no harm).

When using a hone, **Fig. 3,** be sure to install the hone baffle before honing bore.

The baffle is used to protect the hone stones from damage. Use extreme care in cleaning the caliper after honing. Remove all dust and grit by flushing the caliper with alcohol. Wipe dry with clean lint-less cloth and then clean a second time in the same manner.

BLEEDING DISC BRAKES

NOTE: Pressure bleeding is recommended for all hydraulic disc brake systems.

The disc brake hydraulic system can be bled manually or with pressure bleeding equipment. On vehicles with disc brakes the brake pedal will require more pumping and frequent checking of fluid level in master cylinder during bleeding operation.

Never use brake fluid that has been drained from hydraulic system when bleeding the brakes. Be sure the disc brake pistons are returned to their normal positions and that the shoe and lining assemblies are properly seated. Before driving the vehicle, check brake operation to be sure that a firm pedal has been obtained.

GENERAL PRECAUTIONS

1. Grease or any other foreign material must be kept off the caliper, surfaces of the disc and external surfaces of the

Fig. 3 Honing caliper piston bore

Fig. 4 Gauge hook-up for testing proportioning valve (typical)

PROPORTIONING VALVE

The proportioning valve (when used), **Fig. 4,** provides balanced braking action between front and rear brakes under a wide range of braking conditions. The valve regulates the hydraulic pressure applied to the rear wheel cylinders, thus limiting rear braking action when high pressures are required at the front brakes. In this manner, premature rear wheel skid is prevented.

TESTING PROPORTIONING VALVE

When a premature rear wheel slide is obtained on a brake application, it usually is an indication that the fluid pressure to the rear wheels is above the 50% reduction ratio for the rear line pressure and that malfunction has occured within the proportioning valve.

To test the valve, install gauge set shown in **Fig. 4** in brake line between master cylinder and proportioning valve, and at output end of proportioning valve and brake line as shown. Be sure all joints are fluid tight.

Have a helper exert pressure on brake pedal (holding pressure). Obtain a reading on master cylinder output of approximately 700 psi. While pressure is being held as above, reading on valve outlet should be 550-610 psi. If the pressure readings do not meet these specifications, the valve should be removed and a new valve installed.

Ford Sliding Caliper

INDEX

OPERATION

The caliper assembly is made up of a sliding caliper housing assembly and an anchor plate, **Fig. 1.**

The anchor plate is bolted to the wheel spindle arm. Two angular machined surfaces on the upper end of the caliper housing contact mating machined surfaces of the anchor plate. A steel, plated key and a caliper support spring are fitted between the angular machined surfaces of the lower end of the caliper and the machined surface of the anchor plate. The key is held in position with a retaining screw. The caliper is held in position against the mating surfaces of the anchor plate by means of the caliper support spring. A brake shoe anti-rattle spring clip is provided on the anchor plate at the lower end of the inner brake shoe and lining assembly. The inner and outer brake shoe assemblies are not interchangeable.

The sliding caliper contains a single cylinder and a piston with a molded dust boot to seal the cylinder bore from contamination. A square section rubber piston seal is positioned in a groove in cylinder bore to provide sealing between cylinder and piston.

CALIPER REMOVAL

1. Raise car and support with safety stands. Block both rear wheels if a jack is used.
2. Remove wheel and tire assembly from hub.
3. Disconnect brake hose from caliper.
4. Remove retaining screw from caliper retaining key, **Fig. 1.**
5. Slide caliper retaining key and support spring either inward or outward from anchor plate. Use hammer and drift, if necessary, to remove the key and caliper support spring. Use care to avoid damaging the key.
6. Lift caliper assembly away from anchor plate by pushing caliper down against anchor plate and rotate upper end upward out of anchor plate, **Fig. 2.**
7. Remove inner shoe and lining from anchor plate. The brake shoe anti-rattle clip (inner shoe only) may become displaced at this time and if so, reposi-

Fig. 1 Ford sliding caliper disc brake

Fig. 2 Removing caliper assembly

DISC BRAKES

Fig. 3 Caliper and outer shoe removed from anchor plate

Fig. 4 Removing piston from caliper

tion it on anchor plate, **Fig. 3.** Tap lightly on outer shoe and lining to free it from caliper.

8. Clean caliper, anchor plate and rotor assemblies and inspect them for signs of fluid leakage, wear or damage. If either lining is worn to within 1/32 inch of any rivet head, both shoe and lining assemblies must be replaced. Also, if necessary to replace shoes and lining on one wheel, they must be replaced on both wheels to maintain equal brake action.

CALIPER DISASSEMBLY

1. With caliper removed as described previously, disconnect brake hose. Cap hose and plug caliper inlet to prevent fluid loss.
2. With caliper on work bench, remove inlet plug and drain fluid from housing.
3. Place a wooden block or an old brake pad into the caliper, then place a shop cloth between wooden block and piston.
4. Apply air pressure slowly to caliper inlet port to remove piston, **Fig. 4.**

NOTE: If high pressure is applied quickly, piston may pop out and cause injury. A cocked or seized piston can be eased out by rapping sharply on piston end with a soft brass hammer.

5. Remove boot from piston and seal from caliper cylinder bore.

CALIPER ASSEMBLY

1. Lubricate piston seal with clean brake fluid and piston seal in its cylinder bore groove.
2. Assemble dust boot on caliper housing by seating boot flange in the outer groove of cylinder bore, making sure it is fully seated.
3. Coat piston with clean brake fluid and install in cylinder bore.
4. Spread dust boot over piston as piston is installed and then bottom piston in the bore. Seat dust boot in its piston groove.

CALIPER INSTALLATION

1. If new shoe and lining assemblies are to be installed, use a 4 inch C-clamp and a block of wood 1¾ inch × 1 inch and about ¾ inch thick to seat the caliper piston in its bore. This must be done to provide clearance for the caliper to fit over new shoes when installed.

2. Be sure brake shoe anti-rattle clip is in place on lower inner brake shoe support on anchor plate with pigtail of clip toward inside of anchor plate. Position inner shoe and lining on anchor plate with lining toward rotor, **Fig. 3.**
3. Install outer shoe and lining with lower flange ends against the caliper leg abutments and the brake shoe upper flanges over the shoulders on caliper legs. The shoe upper flanges fit tightly against the shoulder machined sur-

Fig. 5 Installing caliper assembly

faces. If the same brake shoes and linings are to be used, be sure they are installed in their original positions.

4. Remove C-clamp if used, from the caliper (the piston will remain seated in its bore).
5. Position caliper housing lower V groove on anchor plate lower abutment surface, **Fig. 5**. Refer to **Figs. 5 and 6** to complete assembly following steps shown. Connect brake hose, bleed brakes and replace wheel.
6. Install key retaining screw and torque to 12–20 ft. lbs.

BRAKE SHOE & LINING
REPLACE

The procedure to replace the shoe and lining assemblies is the same as the caliper removal discussed previously with the exception that it is not necessary to discon-

Fig. 6 Installing caliper support spring and retaining key

ANCHOR PLATE

CALIPER SUPPORT SPRING AND KEY

nect the brake hose. Use care to avoid twisting or stretching the brake hose.

HUB & ROTOR REMOVAL

1. Remove caliper and shoes as previously described. If no repairs are necessary on the caliper it is not necessary to disconnect the brake hose. The caliper can be temporarily secured to the upper suspension arm. Do not remove the anchor plate and be careful not to stretch or twist the brake hose.
2. Remove grease cap from wheel spindle and remove cotter pin and nut lock from wheel bearing adjustment nut.
3. Remove wheel bearing adjusting nut and grasp the hub and rotor and pull it out far enough to loosen the washer and outer wheel bearing, then push it back in and remove the washer, outer wheel bearing and the hub and rotor.

Kelsey-Hayes Pin Slider Disc Brake

INDEX

OPERATION

The caliper assembly consists of a pin slider caliper housing, inner and outer shoe and lining assemblies and a single piston, **Fig. 1**. The caliper slides on two pins which also act as attaching bolts between caliper and the combination anchor plate and spindle. The outer brake shoe and lining assembly is longer than the inner brake shoe and lining assembly. Inner and outer shoe and lining assemblies are attached to the caliper by spring clips riveted to the shoe surfaces. The inner shoe is attached to the caliper by installing the spring clip to the inside of the caliper piston. The outer shoe clips directly to the caliper housing. A wear indicator is incorporated which emits a noise when the lining is worn to a point when replacement is necessary. Inner and

outer shoes are of left and right hand and are not interchangeable.

NOTE: The inner shoe and lining on Capri, Fairmont, Mustang, and Zephyr with V8-302 engine has a replaceable single finger anti-rattle clip and an insulator held in position by the clip. The shoe is slotted to accept the snap on clip which loads the assembly against the caliper bridge. The inner shoe on the Capri and Mustang with 2300cc and 2800cc has a single finger anti-rattle clip similar to the Fairmont and Zephyr inner shoe, holding the shoe down against the spindle ledge. The clip does not lock into the piston. The insulator is also riveted to the shoe and is not replaceable.

BRAKE SHOE & LINING
REPLACE

REMOVAL

1. Remove brake fluid until reservoir is half full.
2. Raise and support front of vehicle, then remove wheel and tire assembly.
3. Remove caliper locating pins.
4. Lift caliper assembly from spindle and adapter plate, then remove outer shoe from caliper assembly.

CALIPER ASSY. 2B119 L.H. 2B118 R.H.

PISTON SEAL 2B115

PISTON 2196

DUST BOOT 2207

INSULATOR 2B299

PLASTIC SLEEVE 2B393

LOCATING PIN 2B296

INNER SHOE 2019 R.H. 2C046 L.H.

OUTER SHOE 2018 R.H. 2C088 L.H.

WEAR INDICATOR

Fig. 1 Kelsey-Hayes pin slider disc brake caliper (Typical)

Fig. 2   Installing inner brake shoe on caliper

NOTE: On 1982–85 Lincoln Continental, 1984 Mark VII & Mustang SVO models, slip shoe down caliper leg until clip is disengaged.

5. Remove inner shoe and lining assembly.

NOTE: On 1982–85 Lincoln Continental, 1984 Mark VII & Mustang SVO models, pull shoe straight out of piston. This could require a force as high as 20–30 lbs.

6. Suspend caliper from inner fender housing with wire to avoid damaging brake hose.
7. Remove and discard locating pin insulators and plastic sleeves.

INSTALLATION

1. Using a 4 in. C-clamp and a block of wood 2¾ × 1 in. and approximately ¾ in. thick, seat caliper piston in bore, then remove C-clamp and wooden block.

NOTE: On 1982–85 Lincoln Continental, 1984–85 Mark VII & Mustang SVO, late 1983 and 1984–85 Escort, EXP, LN7 and Lynx and 1984–85 Tempo and Topaz models, the piston is made of phenolic material. Do not seat piston in bore by applying C-clamp directly to piston. Extra care must be taken during this procedure to prevent damage to the piston. Metal or sharp objects cannot come into direct contact with the piston or damage may result.

2. Install locating pin insulators and plastic sleeves on caliper housing. Ensure insulators and sleeves are properly positioned.
3. Install inner shoe and lining assembly on caliper piston, **Fig. 2.**

NOTE: Inner brake shoes are marked LH (left hand) and RH (right hand) and must be installed on the proper caliper. Use care to not bend spring clips too far during installation in piston, otherwise distortion and rattles may result.

4. Install outer brake shoe and lining assembly, **Fig. 3.** Ensure that shoes are installed on proper caliper. Make sure that clip and buttons on shoe are properly seated.

NOTE: The outer shoe can be identified as left hand and right hand by the wear indicator which must be installed toward front of vehicle.

5. Install locating pins and torque to 30–40 ft. lbs.

NOTE: On 1982–85 Lincoln Continental, 1984–85 Mark VII & Mustang SVO and 1980–85 Ford and Mercury full size and Lincoln models, torque locating pins to 40–60 ft. lbs. On 1981–85 Escort, EXP, LN7 and Lynx and 1984–85 Tempo and Topaz, torque to 18–25 ft. lbs.

CAUTION: On 1982–85 models except Lincoln Continental, 1984–85 Mark VII & Mustang SVO ensure that two round torque buttons are firmly seated in the two holes of outer caliper leg and that shoe is held tightly against housing by spring clip. A temporary loss of brakes may occur if buttons are not properly seated.

6. Refill master cylinder, then install wheel and tire assembly and lower vehicle.
7. Pump brake pedal several times to position brake linings before moving vehicle.

CALIPER
REPLACE
REMOVAL

NOTE: Before removing calipers, mark left and right hand calipers so they can be installed in the same position.

1. Raise and support front of vehicle, then remove wheel and tire assembly.
2. Loosen brake tube fitting which connects brake tube to fitting on frame and plug brake tube. Remove retaining clip from brake hose and bracket, then disconnect brake hose from caliper.
3. Remove caliper locating pins.
4. Lift caliper from rotor and spindle anchor plate assembly.

NOTE: On late 1983–85 Escort, EXP, LN7, and Lynx and 1984–85 Tempo and Topaz with phenolic caliper piston, do not pry directly against the piston or damage may result.

INSTALLATION

1. Install caliper assembly over rotor with outer shoe against rotor braking surface during installation on spindle and anchor plate to prevent pinching of piston boot between inner brake shoe and piston.

NOTE: Ensure calipers are installed in the correct position.

2. Install locating pins. Torque locating pins to 30–40 ft. lbs.

NOTE: On 1982–85 Lincoln Continental, 1984–85 Mark VII & Mustang SVO and 1980–85 Ford and Mercury full size and

Fig. 3   Installing outer brake shoe on caliper

Lincoln models, torque locating pins to 40–60 ft. lbs. On 1981–85 Escort, EXP LN7 and Lynx and 1984–85 Tempo and Topaz, torque to 18–25 ft. lbs.

3. Connect brake hose to caliper and tighten hose fitting.
4. Position upper end of brake hose in bracket and install retaining clip. Remove plug from brake line, then connect brake hose fitting to brake line. Torque fitting to 10–18 ft. lbs.
5. Bleed brake system and centralize pressure differential valve.
6. Install wheel and tire assembly, then lower vehicle.
7. Pump brake pedal several times to position brake shoes before moving vehicle.

CALIPER OVERHAUL
DISASSEMBLE

1. Remove caliper assembly from vehicle as described under "Caliper, Replace".
2. Position fiber block and shop towels between caliper piston and caliper housing, then apply compressed air to caliper brake line fitting bore to force piston from caliper.
3. Remove dust boot from caliper assembly, **Fig. 1.**
4. Remove pistol seal from cylinder and discard.

INSPECTION

Clean all metal parts with isopropyl alcohol, then clean and dry passages and grooves with compressed air. Check caliper and piston for damage and wear and replace as necessary.

ASSEMBLE

1. Lubricate piston seal with clean brake fluid, then install seal in caliper bore.

NOTE: Ensure seal is firmly seated in groove.

2. Install dust boot in outer groove of caliper bore, **Fig. 1.**
3. Coat piston with clean brake fluid and install piston in caliper bore. Spread dust boot over piston as it is installed. Seat dust boot in piston groove.
4. Install caliper assembly as described under "Caliper, Replace."

Ford Rear Wheel Disc Brake & Parking Brake

INDEX

OPERATION

Sliding caliper rear disc brakes are used on some 1980 models and on the 1982-85 Lincoln Continental, 1984-85 Mark VII & Mustang SVO **Fig. 1.** The caliper is basically the same as the larger front wheel caliper, however, a parking brake mechanism and a larger inner brake shoe anti-rattle spring have been added, **Fig. 2.** A hydraulically powered brake booster (Hydroboost) provides the power assist for this four wheel disc brake system.

The parking brake lever, located at the rear of the caliper, is actuated by a cable system similar to rear drum brake applications. When the parking brake is applied, the cable rotates the lever and operating shaft. Three steel balls, placed in pockets between the opposing heads of the operating shaft and thrust screw, roll between ramps formed in the pockets and force the thrust screw away from the operating shaft, in turn, driving the caliper piston and brake shoe assembly against the rotor. An automatic adjuster in the assembly compensates for lining wear and maintains proper clearance in the parking brake mechanism.

The cast iron rotors are ventilated by curved fins located between the braking surfaces and are designed to cause the rotor to act as an air pump when the vehicle is traveling forward. The rotors are not interchangeable and are identified by a Right or Left marking cast inside the hat section of the rotor. The rotor is secured to the axle flange in the same manner as a rear brake drum. A splash shield is bolted to a forged axle adapter to protect the inboard rotor surface.

NOTE: The 1984 Mustang SVO four wheel disc brake system is the same as the Continental and Mark VII brake system, except that the Mustang SVO incorparates a vacuum booster.

CALIPER REMOVAL

NOTE: After performing any service work, obtain a firm brake pedal before moving vehicle.

1. Raise vehicle and support on safety stands, then remove tire and wheel assemblies.
2. Disconnect fitting on rear brake tube from hose end fitting at frame mounted bracket and plug end of brake tube to prevent loss of fluid and entry of dirt. Remove horseshoe retaining clip from hose fitting and disengage hose from bracket.

NOTE: On Versailles models, disconnect hose bracket from axle spring seat, then remove hollow retaining bolt, connecting hose fitting to caliper.

3. Disconnect parking cable from lever, **Fig. 3,** using care to avoid kinking or cutting cable or return spring, then remove retaining screw from caliper retaining key, **Fig. 4.** On 1982-85 Lincoln Continental, 1984-85 Mark VII & Mustang SVO, remove caliper locating pins.
4. Slide caliper retaining key and support spring from anchor plate, **Fig. 4.** If necessary, use a hammer and brass drift, being careful to avoid damaging key on sliding ways or hitting parking brake lever.

NOTE: If caliper cannot be removed due to rust build-up on outer edge of rotor, scrape off loose scale, being careful not to damage braking surfaces. If rotor wear or scoring prevents removal of caliper, it will be necessary to loosen caliper end retainer ½ turn maximum, to allow piston to be forced

Fig. 1 Rear disc brake

Fig. 2 Caliper housing cutaway to show parking brake mechanism

DISC BRAKES

Fig. 3   Parking lever & cable installation

Fig. 4   Removing rear caliper assembly

Fig. 5   Adjusting piston depth for lining installation

back into its bore. To loosen end retainer, remove parking brake lever and mark or scribe end retainer and caliper housing to be sure that end retainer is not loosened more than ½ turn, then force piston back in its bore, **Fig. 2,** and move caliper back and forth to center rotor and remove caliper. If retainer must be loosened more than ½ turn, use caution, as the seal between the thrust screw and housing may be broken and brake fluid will enter parking brake mechanism chamber. In this case, the end retainer must be removed and the internal parts cleaned and lubricated.

5. On all except 1982–85 Lincoln Continental, 1984–85 Mark VII & Mustang SVO, remove inner shoe and lining assembly from anchor plate, then tap lightly on outer shoe and lining assembly to free it from caliper. Mark each shoe for identification if they are to be reused.

6. On 1982–85 Lincoln Continental, 1984–85 Mark VII & Mustang SVO, proceed as follows:
   a. Remove outer shoe and lining assembly from anchor plate, then remove rotor retainer nuts and rotor from axle shaft.
   b. Remove inner brake shoe and lining assembly from anchor plate and mark each shoe for identification if they are to be reused.
   c. Remove anti-rattle clip from anchor plate, then remove flexible hose from caliper by removing hollow retaining bolt.

CLEANING & INSPECTION

Clean caliper, anchor plate and rotor assembly and inspect for signs of brake fluid leakage, excessive wear or damage. The caliper must be inspected for leakage both in piston boot area and operating shaft seal area. Lightly sand or wire brush any rust or corrosion from caliper and anchor plate sliding surfaces and inner brake shoe abutment surfaces in anchor plate. Inspect brake shoes for wear. If either lining is within 1/32 inch of any rivet head, replace both shoe and lining assemblies from both wheels in order to maintain equal brake action.

NOTE: On 1982–85 Lincoln Continental, 1984–85 Mark VII & Mustang SVO models, linings must not be worn to within less than 1/8 inch of shoe surface.

CALIPER INSTALLATION

1. If end retainer has been loosened only ½ turn, reinstall caliper in anchor plate using key. Do not install shoe and lining assembly. Torque end retainer to 75–95 ft. lbs. and install parking brake actuating lever on its keyed spline. Lever arm must point down and rearward so that parking brake cable will pass freely under axle. Torque retainer screw to 16–22 ft. lbs.

NOTE: Parking brake lever must rotate feely after torquing retainer screw.

2. Remove caliper from anchor plate. If new shoe and lining assemblies are to be installed, the piston must be bottomed in caliper bore using tool T75P-2588-B to provide clearance. Remove rotor and install caliper without lining and shoe assemblies in anchor plate using key only. Install tool and while holding shaft, rotate tool handle counterclockwise until the tool seats firmly against piston, **Fig. 5.** Loosen handle about ¼ turn, and while holding handle rotate tool shaft clockwise until piston is fully bottomed in bore (piston will continue to turn even after it is bottomed). Turn tool handle until there is no further inward movement of piston and there is a firm seating force, then remove caliper from mounting plate and reinstall rotor.

NOTE: For use on 1982–85 Lincoln Continental, 1984–85 Mark VII & Mustang SVO models, tool T75P-2588-B must be slightly modified, **Fig. 6.**

3. Making certain that brake shoe anti-rattle clip is in place in lower inner brake shoe support on anchor plate with loop of clip toward inside of anchor plate, **Fig. 4,** position inner brake shoe and lining assembly on anchor plate. On 1982–85 Lincoln Continental, 1984–85 Mark VII & Mustang SVO models, install rotor and two retaining nuts.

4. Install outer brake shoe with lower flange ends against caliper abutments and brake shoe upper flanges over shoulders on caliper legs. The shoe upper flanges fit tightly against machined shoulder surfaces.

NOTE: If old brake shoes and lining assemblies are re-used, be certain the shoes are installed in their original positions as marked for identification during removal.

5. Lubricate caliper and anchor sliding ways with M1C-167-A (LPS-ESA-100) grease, using care to prevent lubricant from getting on braking surfaces, then position caliper housing lower V-groove on anchor plate lower abutment surfaces. On 1982–85 Lincoln Continental, 1984–85 Mark VII & Mustang SVO models, use D7AE-019590, or equivalent grease.

6. Rotate caliper until it is completely over rotor, being careful not to damage piston dust boot, then pull caliper outboard until inner shoe and lining is firmly seated against rotor. Measure clearance between outer lining and rotor which should be 1/16 inch or less, **Fig. 7.** On 1982–85 Lincoln Continental, 1984–85 Mark VII & Mustang SVO models, clearance must be between 1/32 and 3/32 inch. If it is greater, remove caliper and move piston outward to narrow gap. Follow procedure in step 2 and note that ¼ turn of the shaft counterclockwise, moves piston about 1/16 inch.

CAUTION: A clearance greater than specified limit may allow adjuster to be pulled out of piston when service brake is applied, causing parking brake to fail to adjust. It will then be necessary to replace piston/adjuster assembly.

7. While holding caliper against anchor plate upper abutment surfaces, center

EXISTING TOOL T75P-2588-A
DISC BRAKE PISTON REMOVER
(DOES NOT REQUIRE MODIFICATION)

EXISTING TOOL T75P-2588-B
BRAKE PISTON TURNING TOOL

1-3/8"

1-1/4"

MODIFY TOOL BY REMOVING
METAL AS INDICATED BY
DOTTED LINES

Fig. 6   Disc brake tool modification

BOOT - 2207
PISTON AND ADJUSTER
ASSY. - 2B588

PISTON SEAL - 2B115

BLEEDER SCREW

CALIPER HOUSING

SEAL 386062

BALL 380243

ACTUATING LEVER 2B597

SEAL 386073

THRUST BEARING 2B598

SEAL 2B595

INLET PORT THUNDERBIRD AND MARK IV

INLET PORT MERCURY AND LINCOLN

PIN 2K329

PARKING BRAKE THRUST
SCREW - 2A873-4

PARKING BRAKE
OPERATING
SHAFT
2A870-1

PARKING BRAKE END
RETAINER - 2A872

BOLT 386065-S100

Fig. 8   Rear disc brake caliper assembly

Silicone Lube

Magnet Or Tweezers

Anti-Rotating Pin

End Retainer Removed

Removing Anti-Rotating Pin

Allen Wrench

Tool T75P-2588-A

Removing Thrust Screw

Pressing Out Piston

Fig. 9   Disassembling rear disc brake caliper

1/16" OR LESS

Fig. 7   Checking lining clearance

caliper over lower anchor plate abutment, then position caliper support spring and key in slot and slide them into opening between lower end of caliper and lower anchor plate abutment until key semi-circular slot is centered over retaining screw threaded hole in anchor plate.

8. Install key retaining screw and torque to 12–16 ft. lbs., then reinstall brake hose on caliper. Place a new gasket on each side of the fitting outlet, then install the attaching bolt through the washers and fitting and torque to 17–25 ft. lbs. (20–30 ft. lbs. on 1982–85 Lincoln Continental, 1984–85 Mark VII & Mustang SVO models).

NOTE: On Versailles models, ensure the pin in the hose fitting engages the mating hole in the caliper before torquing the bolt.

9. On all except 1982–85 Lincoln Continental, 1984–85 Mark VII & Mustang SVO models, position upper end of flexible hose in bracket and install retaining clip, then connect brake tube to hose and torque fitting to 10–15 ft. lbs.

NOTE: Do not twist or coil brake hose, the stripe on the hose must be kept straight.

10. On 1982–85 Lincoln Continental, 1984–85 Mark VII & Mustang SVO models, lubricate pins and inside of insulator with D7AZ-19A331-A or equivalent silicone grease and add one drop of Loctite EOAC-19554-A, or equivalent, to locating pin threads. Install locating pins through caliper insulators and into anchor plate and torque to 29–37 ft. lbs.

11. Connect parking brake lever to lever on caliper.

12. Bleed brake system, then with engine running pump brake pedal lightly about 40 times allowing 1 second between pedal applications. An alternate with engine off is to pump brake pedal lightly about 10 times to discharge accumulator, then pump brake pedal firmly about 30 times. Check parking brake for excessive travel or very light effort, if so, repeat pumping brake pedal, and if necessary check parking brake cable tension.

13. Install wheel and torque nuts to 70–115 ft. lbs.

NOTE: Before moving vehicle, make certain that a firm brake pedal has been obtained.

Fig. 10 Checking parking brake adjuster operation

Fig. 11 Filling piston/adjuster assembly

Fig. 12 Bottoming piston in caliper

SHOE & LINING REMOVAL & INSTALLATION

To remove shoe and lining assemblies, follow "Caliper Removal" procedure and omit step 2 as it is not necessary to disconnect brake hose. After removing caliper, support it with a length of wire to avoid damaging brake hose. To install shoe and lining assemblies, follow "Caliper Installation" procedure, making certain that proper parking brake adjustment is obtained.

CALIPER OVERHAUL

DISASSEMBLE

1. Remove caliper assembly as described previously.
2. Remove caliper end retainer, operating shaft, thrust bearing and balls, **Fig. 8.**
3. Remove thrust screw anti-rotation pin with a magnet or tweezers. If pin cannot be removed with a magnet or tweezers, proceed with the following procedure:
   a. With tool T75P-2588B, force piston approximately one inch from caliper bore.
   b. Push piston back into caliper housing with tool, then with tool in position, hold tool shaft in place and rotate handle counter-clockwise until thrust screw clears anti-rotation pin. Remove thrust screw and anti-rotation pin.
4. Remove thrust screw by rotating with ¼ inch allen wrench.
5. Install tool T75P-2588-A through back of caliper housing and remove piston assembly, **Fig. 9.**

CAUTION: Use care not to damage polished surface in thrust screw bore and do not attempt to remove or press adjuster can, as it is a press fit in piston.

6. Remove and discard piston seal, boot, thrust O-ring seal, end retainer, O-ring and end retainer lip seal.

CLEANING & INSPECTION

1. Clean all metal parts with alcohol, then using clean, dry compressed air, blow out and dry all grooves and passages making sure the caliper bore and component parts are free of any foreign material.
2. Inspect caliper bore for damage or excessive wear. The thrust screw must be smooth and free of pits. If piston is pitted, scored or chrome plating is worn, replace piston and adjuster assembly.
3. Adjuster can be bottomed in piston to be properly seated and provide consistent brake operation. If adjuster can is loose, appears high in piston, is damaged, or if brake adjustment is usually too tight, too loose or not functioning, replace piston/adjuster assembly. Check adjuster operation by assembling thrust screw into piston/ adjuster assembly, then pull the two parts apart about ¼ inch and release them, **Fig. 10.** When pulling on the two parts, the brass drive ring must remain stationary causing the nut to rotate. When releasing the two parts, the nut must remain stationary and drive ring must rotate. If action does not follow this pattern, replace piston/adjuster assembly.
4. Inspect ball pockets, threads, grooves, bearing surfaces of thrust screw, operating shaft, balls and anti rotation pin for wear, brinnelling or pitting. Replace operating shaft, balls, thrust screw and anti rotation pin if any of these parts are worn or damaged. A polished appearance on the ball paths is acceptable if there is no sign of wear into the surface.
5. Inspect thrust bearing for corrosion, pitting or wear and replace as necessary.
6. Inspect end plug bearing surface for wear or brinnelling and replace as necessary. A polished appearance on bearing surface is acceptable if there is no sign of wear into surface.
7. Inspect operating lever for damage and replace as necessary.

ASSEMBLE

1. Coat new caliper piston seal with clean brake fluid and install it in caliper making certain that seal is not twisted and is fully seated in groove.
2. Install new dust boot by seating flange squarely in outer groove of caliper bore, then coat piston/adjuster assembly with clean brake fluid and install it in caliper bore. Spread dust boot over piston as it is installed and seat dust boot in piston groove.
3. Install caliper in vise, **Fig. 11,** and fill piston/adjuster assembly with clean brake fluid.
4. Coat new thrust screw O-ring with clean brake fluid and install it in thrust screw groove, then install thrust screw into piston adjuster assembly until top surface of thrust screw is flush with bottom of threaded bore, being careful to avoid cutting O-ring seal. Index notches on thrust screw and caliper housing and install anti-rotation pin.

NOTE: The thrust screw and operating shafts are not interchangeable from side to side since the ramp direction in the ball pockets are different. The pocket surfaces of the operating shaft and thrust screws are stamped "R" (Right) and "L" (Left).

5. Place a ball in each of three pockets of thrust screw and apply a liberal amount of silicone grease M1C-169-A on parking brake components, then install operating shaft on balls.
6. Coat thrust bearing with silicone grease and install it on operating shaft, then install a new lip seal and O-ring on end retainer.
7. Lightly coat O-ring seal and lip seal with silicone grease and install end retainer in caliper. Firmly hold operating shaft against internal mechanism while installing end retainer to prevent mislocation of balls. If lip seal moves out of position, reseat seal. Torque end retainer to 75–95 ft. lbs.

NOTE: Parking brake lever must rotate freely after torquing.

8. Install parking brake lever on keyed spline facing down and rearward. Torque retaining screw to 16–22 ft. lbs.
9. Bottom piston using tool T75P-2588-B, **Fig. 12,** and install caliper as described previously.

Rotor Specifications

CAR	Year	Nominal Thick-ness	Minimum Refinish Thick-ness	Thickness Variation Parallelism	Lateral Runout (T.I.R.)	Finish (Micro-In.)
FORD MOTOR CO.						
Ford & Mercury Full Size	1980–85	1.030	.972	.0005	.003	10–80
Ford & Mercury Intermediate	1980①	.870	.810	.0005	.003	15–80
	1981–85①	.870	.810	.0005⑧	.003	15–125⑨
Granada, Monarch & Versailles	1980	.870④	.810⑤	.0005	.003⑥	15–80
	1981–82	.870	.810	.0005	.003	15–125
Lincoln Continental, Mark V, VI, VII, Mustang SVO & Town Car	1980–85②	1.030	.972	.0005	.003	10–80
	1982–85③	1.030④	.972⑤	.0005	.003⑥	15–125⑦
Capri, Mustang, (Exc. SVO), Pinto & Bobcat	1980	.870	.810	.0005	.003	15–80
	1981–83	.870	.810	.0005	.003	15–125
	1984	.945	.895	.0005	.004	15–80
Fairmont & Zephyr	1980	.870	.810	.0005	.003	15–80
	1981–83	.870	.810	.0005	.003	15–125
Escort, EXP, LN7 & Lynx	1981–84	.945	.882	.0004	.003⑧	16–79
	1985	.945	.882	.0004	.002	20–140
Tempo & Topaz	1984	.945	.882	.0005	.003	15–80
	1985	.945	.882	.0005	.003	10–80

① —Cougar, Cougar XR-7, Thunderbird & 1983–85 LTD & Marquis.
② —Mark VI & Town Car.
③ —Continental, Mark VII & Mustang SVO.
④ —Rear disc, .945.
⑤ —Rear disc, .895.
⑥ —Rear disc, .004.
⑦ —Rear disc, 15–80.
⑧ —1984–85 LTD & Marquis, .0003.
⑨ —1984–85, 10–81.

Caliper Specifications

Year	Model	Caliper Bore Dia. In.
FORD & MERCURY—Full Size Models		
1980–85	All	2.88①
FORD & MERCURY—Compact & Intermediate Models		
1980	Cougar, XR-7 & Thunderbird	2.36
	Fairmont & Zephyr	2.36
	Granada & Monarch	2.60
1981–85	All	2.36
FORD MUSTANG, MUSTANG SVO & PINTO • MERCURY BOBCAT & CAPRI		
1980	Bobcat & Pinto	2.6
1981–85	Capri & Mustang	2.36②
FORD ESCORT, EXP & TEMPO • MERCURY LN7, LYNX & TOPAZ		
1981–83	All	2.125
1984–85	All	2.36
LINCOLN		
1980	Exc. Versailles	2.88
	Versailles	2.6②
1981	Lincoln & Mark VI	2.88
1982–83	Exc. Continental	2.88
	Continental	2.38②
1984–85	Continental & Mark VII	2.87②
	Town Car	2.88

①—Rear disc brake caliper bore, 2.6".   ②—Rear disc brake caliper bore, 2.1".

General Motors Corp.

NOTE: Refer to "Brake Usage Chart" to determine which type brakes are used on vehicle being serviced.

TABLE OF CONTENTS

Brake Usage Chart

DELCO MORAINE Single Piston Single Mounting Bolt ... 30–34

Chevrolet Chevette, 1980–82
Pontiac 1000, 1981–82

DELCO MORAINE Opposed Piston ... 30–36

Chevrolet Corvette, 1980–82 (4 Wheel Disc Brakes)

DELCO MORAINE Single Piston Dual Mounting Bolt ... 30–38

TYPE 1
Buick Century, 1980–81
Buick Electra, 1980–84
Buick Electra (RWD), 1985
Buick LeSabre, 1980–85
Buick Regal, 1980–85
Buick Riviera, 1980–85
Cadillac Brougham, 1980–8?
Cadillac Deville, 1980–84
Cadillac Eldorado, 1980–85
Cadillac Seville, 1980–85
Chevrolet Camaro, 1980–85
Chevrolet Caprice, 1980–85
Chevrolet Impala, 1980–85
Chevrolet Malibu, 1980–83
Chevrolet Monte Carlo, 1980–85
Oldsmobile Cutlass

Exc. Ciera, 1980–85
Oldsmobile Toronado, 1980–85
Oldsmobile 88, 1980–85
Oldsmobile 98, 1980–84
Oldsmobile 98 (RWD), 1985
Pontiac Bonneville, 1980–85
Pontiac Catalina, 1980–81
Pontiac Firebird, 1980–85
Pontiac Grand Am, 1980
Pontiac Grand LeMans, 1980–81
Pontiac Gran Prix, 1980–85
Pontiac Parisienne, 1983–85
TYPE 2
Buick Century, 1982–85
Buick Electra (FWD), 1985
Buick Skyhawk, 1982–85
Buick Skylark, 1980–85
Buick Somerset Regal, 1985
Cadillac Cimarron, 1982–85
Cadillac Deville, 1985
Cadillac Fleetwood Brougham (FWD), 1985
Chevrolet Cavalier, 1982–85
Chevrolet Celebrity, 1982–85
Chevrolet Chevette, 1982–85
Chevrolet Citation, 1980–85
Oldmobile Calais, 1985
Oldmobile Cutlass Ciera, 1982–85
Oldmobile Firenza, 1982–85
Oldmobile Omega, 1980–84
Oldmobile 98 (FWD), 1985

Pontiac Grand Am, 1985
Pontiac Phoenix, 1980–84
Pontiac 1000, 1982–85
Pontiac 2000 Sunbird, 1982–85
Pontiac 6000, 1982–85
TYPE 3
Pontiac Fiero, 1984–85 (4 Wheel Disc Brakes)

DELCO MORAINE Rear Wheel Disc Brake ... 30–46

Buick Electra, 1980
Buick Riviera, 1980–85
Cadillac Eldorado, 1980–85
Cadillac Fleetwood Brougham, 1980
Cadillac Seville, 1980–85
Chevrolet Camaro, 1982–85
Oldsmobile Toronado, 1980–85
Pontiac Firebird, 1980–85

GIRLOCK Single Piston Caliper ... 30–49

Chevrolet Corvette, 1984–85 (4 Wheel Disc Brakes)

TOYOTA/GM Single Piston Caliper ... 30–50

Chevrolet Nova, 1985

General Information

INDEX

Fig. 1 Checking rotor for lateral runout

BRAKE SHOES, LININGS & CALIPERS

Remove wheels and inspect brake disc, caliper and linings. The wheel bearings should be inspected at this time and repacked if necessary. Do not get any grease on the linings.

On all models except Chevrolet Corvette, the brake shoe and lining assemblies should be replaced if the lining is worn to within 1/32 inch of rivet heads (riveted linings) or brake shoe (bonded linings). On Chevrolet Corvette, the brake shoe and lining assemblies should be replaced when the lining is the approximate thickness of the brake shoe. On Pontiac Fiero rear brake shoes, note that a 1/10 inch thick thermal insulation is included between the brake pad friction material and shoe, and that this thickness should not be considered as usable lining material. It is recommended that brake linings always be replaced as axle sets. Do not replace individual pads or replace pads on one wheel of an axle set alone, as braking performance will be adversely affected.

If a visual inspection does not adequately determine the condition of the linings, the brake shoe and lining assemblies should be removed and inspected. If shoes do not require replacement, reinstall them in their original positions. Brake shoes and linings should also be replaced if cracked or damaged.

If the caliper is cracked or fluid leakage through the casting is evident, it must be replaced as a unit.

BRAKE ROUGHNESS

The most common cause of brake chatter on disc brakes is a variation in thickness of the disc. If roughness or vibration is encountered during highway operation or if pedal pumping is experienced at low speeds, the disc may have excessive thickness variation. To check for this condition, measure the disc at 12 points with a micrometer at a radius approximately one inch from edge of disc. If thickness measurements vary by more than .0005 inch, the disc should be replaced with a new one.

Excessive lateral runout of braking disc may cause a "knocking back" of the pistons, possibly creating increased pedal travel and vibration when brakes are applied.

Before checking the runout, wheel bearings should be adjusted. The readjustment is very important and will be required at the completion of the test to prevent bearing failure. Be sure to make the adjustment according to the recommendations given under "Front Wheel Bearings, Adjust" in the car chapters.

BRAKE DISC SERVICE

Servicing of disc brakes is extremely critical due to the close tolerances required in machining the brake disc to insure proper brake operation.

The maintenance of these close controls of the shape of the rubbing surfaces is necessary to prevent brake roughness. In addition, the surface finish must be non-directional and maintained at a micro inch finish. This close control of the rubbing surface finish is necessary to avoid pulls and erratic performance, and to promote long lining life and equal lining wear of both left and right brakes.

In light of the foregoing remarks, refinishing of the rubbing surfaces should not be attempted unless precision equipment, capable of measuring in micro inches (millionths of an inch) is available.

To check lateral runout of a disc, mount a dial indicator on a convenient part (steering knuckle, tie rod, disc brake caliper housing) so that the plunger of the dial indicator contacts the disc at a point one inch from the outer edge, **Fig. 1.** If the total indicated runout exceeds specifications, install a new disc.

To check parallelism (thickness variation), mount dial indicators, **Fig. 2,** so the plunger contacts rotor approximately 1 inch from outer edge. If parallelism exceeds specifications, replace rotor.

GENERAL PRECAUTIONS

1. Grease or any other foreign material

Fig. 2 Checking rotor parallelism (Thickness variation)

must be kept off the brake linings, caliper, surfaces of the disc and external surfaces of the hub, during service procedures. Handling the brake disc and caliper should be done in a way to avoid deformation of the disc and nicking or scratching brake linings.

2. If inspection reveals rubber piston seals are worn or damaged, they should be replaced immediately.
3. During removal and installation of a wheel assembly, exercise care so as not to interfere with or damage the caliper splash shield, or bleeder screw.
4. Front wheel bearings should be adjusted to specifications.
5. Be sure vehicle is centered on hoist before servicing any of the front end components to avoid bending or damaging the disc splash shield on full right or left wheel turns.
6. Before the vehicle is moved after any brake service work, be sure to obtain a firm brake pedal.
7. The assembly bolts of two piece caliper housings should not be disturbed unless the caliper requires service.

INSPECTION OF CALIPER

Should it become necessary to remove the caliper for installation of new parts, clean all parts in alcohol, wipe dry using lint-free cloths, using an air hose to blow out drilled passages and bores. Check dust boots for punctures or tears. If punctures or tears are evident, new boots should be installed upon reassembly.

Inspect piston bores in both housings for scoring or pitting. Bores that show light

Fig. 3   Honing caliper piston bore

Fig. 4   Gauge hook-up for testing proportioning valve (typical)

scratches or corrosion can usually be cleaned with crocus cloth. However, bores that have deep scratches or scoring may be honed, provided the diameter of the bore is not increased more than .002 inches. If the bore does not clean up within this specification, a new caliper housing should be installed (black stains on the bore walls are caused by piston seals and will do no harm).

When using a hone, **Fig. 3,** be sure to install the hone baffle before honing bore. The baffle is used to protect the hone stones from damage. Use extreme care in cleaning the caliper after honing. Remove all dust and grit by flushing the caliper with alcohol. Wipe dry with clean lint-less cloth and then clean a second time in the same manner.

BLEEDING DISC BRAKES

NOTE: Pressure bleeding is recommended for all hydraulic disc brake systems.

The disc brake hydraulic system can be bled manually or with pressure bleeding equipment. On vehicles with disc brakes the brake pedal will require more pumping and frequent checking of fluid level in master cylinder during bleeding operation.

Never use brake fluid that has been drained from hydraulic system when bleeding the brakes. Be sure the disc brake pistons are returned to their normal positions and that the shoe and lining assemblies are properly seated. Before driving the vehicle, check brake operation to be sure that a firm pedal has been obtained.

PROPORTIONING VALVE

The proportioning valve (when used), **Fig. 4,** provides balanced braking action between front and rear brakes under a wide range of braking conditions. The valve regulates the hydraulic pressure applied to the rear wheel cylinders, thus limiting rear braking action when high pressures are required at the front brakes. In this manner, premature rear wheel skid is prevented.

TESTING PROPORTIONING VALVE

When a premature rear wheel slide is obtained on a brake application, it usually is an indication that the fluid pressure to the rear wheels is above the 50% reduction ratio for the rear line pressure and that malfunction has occurred within the proportioning valve.

To test the valve, install gauge set shown in **Fig. 4** in brake line between master cylinder and proportioning valve, and at output end of proportioning valve and brake line as shown. Be sure all joints are fluid tight.

Have a helper exert pressure on brake pedal (holding pressure). Obtain a reading on master cylinder output of approximately 700 psi. While pressure is being held as above, reading on valve outlet should be 550–610 psi. If the pressure readings do not meet these specifications, the valve should be removed and a new valve installed.

DISC BRAKES

Delco-Moraine Single Piston W/Single Mounting Bolt

INDEX

Fig. 1   Single piston disc brake assembly cross-sectional view

DESCRIPTION

This single piston sliding caliper assembly, **Figs. 1 and 2,** incorporates a one piece housing with the inboard side of the housing bored for the piston. A seal within the housing bore provides a hydraulic seal between the piston and housing wall.

A spring steel scraper (wear sensor) is incorporated on each inboard shoe. When shoe lining has worn to within .030 inch of the shoe, the sensor scrapes the rotor and emits an audible high frequency sound indicating that the linings should be replaced.

The caliper assembly slides on a mounting sleeve which is secured by a mounting bolt. Upon brake application fluid pressure against the piston forces the inboard shoe against the inboard side of the rotor. This action causes the caliper to slide until the outboard shoe comes in contact with the rotor.

CALIPER REMOVAL

1. Siphon brake fluid from master cylinder to bring level to ⅓ full, discard brake fluid removed.
2. Raise vehicle and remove wheel and tire assembly.
3. Install a 7 inch C-clamp on caliper with solid end of clamp on caliper housing and screw end on metal portion of outboard brake shoe. Tighten clamp until piston bottoms in caliper bore, then remove clamp.
4. Disconnect brake hose from caliper and remove copper gaskets, cap end of brake hose.

Fig. 2   Delco-Moraine single piston disc brake with single mounting bolt

NOTE: If only brake shoes are to be replaced do not disconnect brake hose.

5. Remove the two mounting brackets to steering knuckle bolts, **Fig. 3.**

Fig. 3   Removing mounting bracket from steering knuckle

NOTE: Do not remove socket head retaining bolt. Support caliper when removing second bolt to prevent caliper from falling.

6. Slide caliper from rotor.

NOTE: If only brake shoes are to be replaced support caliper from suspension using wire. Do not stretch or kink brake hose.

BRAKE SHOE REMOVAL

1. Remove caliper as described under "Caliper Removal".
2. Remove brake shoes, if retaining spring does not come off with inboard shoe remove it from piston.

CALIPER DISASSEMBLY

1. Using clean brake fluid clean exterior

Fig. 4 Bracket assembly installed on caliper

Fig. 6 Removing piston boot

of caliper.
2. Drain brake fluid from caliper.
3. Remove caliper mounting bracket bolt and slide bracket from caliper, **Fig. 4**, then remove sleeve and bushing from bolt and bushing from caliper mounting hole, **Fig. 2**.
4. Remove clips if still in place, then remove cushions, **Fig. 5**.
5. Pad interior of caliper with clean shop towels, then direct compressed air through caliper inlet hole to remove piston.

NOTE: Use only enough air pressure to ease piston out of bore.

CAUTION: Do not place fingers in front of piston for any reason when applying compressed air. This could result in serious personal injury.

6. Using a screwdriver carefully pry boot from caliper, **Fig. 6**.
7. Remove piston seal from caliper bore using a piece of wood or plastic.

NOTE: Do not use metal tool to remove piston seal as it may damage caliper bore.

8. Remove bleeder valve.
   boot.

CALIPER ASSEMBLY

1. Lubricate caliper bore and piston seal with clean brake fluid, then position seal in caliper bore groove.

2. Lubricate piston with clean brake fluid and install boot into piston groove with fold facing the open end of piston, **Fig. 2**.
3. Insert piston into caliper, then using care to avoid unseating seal, force piston into caliper.

NOTE: To force piston into caliper a force of 50–100 pounds will be required.

4. Position outside diameter of boot into caliper counterbore and seat with suitable boot installer. **Fig. 7**.

CAUTION: Ensure that retaining ring molded into boot is not bent and that boot is installed fully and evenly below and around the caliper, as dirt and moisture may enter caliper and cause damage and corrosion.

5. Install bleeder screw.
6. Position and stretch cushions over caliper lugs, fitting the heavy section in the lug recess and saw-tooth edges of cushions facing out, **Fig. 5**.
7. Using silicone lubricant, liberally lubricate sleeve and bushings and the unthreaded portion of the retainer bolt. Install the larger bushing in the caliper hole groove and install the sleeve. Install the smaller bushing in the retainer bolt groove.
8. With caliper clamped in a vise, position clips over cushions and squeeze mounting bracket over clips, aligning the bolt hole. Move bracket against retainer boss on caliper and install retainer bolt. Torque bolt to 28 ft. lbs., (38 N-m).

NOTE: Considerable force may be required to squeeze bracket over cushions and clips on caliper. Start open end of bracket over ends of clips near the boot and move the bracket toward the closed end of caliper.

BRAKE SHOE INSTALLATION

1. Position retaining spring on inboard shoe, place single leg in brake shoe hole, then snap two other legs over notch in shoe.

NOTE: Some inboard replacement brake pads incorporate wear sensors and have a specific left and right hand assembly. Properly installed, the wear sensor will face toward the rear of caliper.

2. Install shoe in caliper.
3. Position caliper over rotor, align mounting holes, install and torque bolts to 70 ft. lbs., (95 N-m).
4. Using suitable pliers clinch outboard shoe to caliper, place lower jaw of pliers on bottom edge of shoe, place upper jaw of pliers on shoe tab, squeeze pliers and bend tab. Clinch other end of shoe in same manner.

Fig. 5 Removing and installing cushions

Fig. 7 Installing boot on caliper

Outboard end play should be zero to .005 inch., (zero to 0.127 mm).
5. Install wheel and tire assembly and lower vehicle.
6. Add brake fluid to within ¼ inch from top of master cylinder.

NOTE: Pump brake pedal several times to ensure it is firm before moving vehicle.

CALIPER INSTALLATION

1. Install caliper as described under "Brake Shoe Installation", then install brake hose with new copper gaskets, torque fitting to 21 ft. lbs., (29 N-m), if removed, bleed brake system.

NOTE: Brake hose fitting must be against machined surface on caliper to ensure proper hose positioning.

Delco Moraine W/ Opposed Pistons

INDEX

Fig. 1 Delco-Moraine opposed piston disc brake assembly

Fig. 2 Delco-Moraine parking brake components

DESCRIPTION

These brakes are used on all four wheels. The components of the disc brake system are shown in **Fig. 1**. The caliper assemblies replace the conventional wheel cylinder, brake shoes and linings, and the disc replaces the brake drum.

The caliper assembly contains four pistons, two acting on each shoe with one shoe on each side of the disc.

The brake disc is riveted to the hub flange at the front wheel and to the spindle flange at the rear wheel. The disc rotates through the caliper assembly, which is bolted to a support that is attached to the steering knuckle at the front wheel and the spindle support bolts at the rear wheel. The disc has cooling fins between the two shoe reacting surfaces. When a disc must be replaced, the rivets can be drilled out and then the wheel studs will be used for disc retention purposes.

A miniature set of brake shoes, mounted on a flange plate and shield assembly attached to the rear wheel spindle support bolts, are used for vehicle parking, **Fig. 2.**

REMOVING LINING

1. To prevent overflow, remove two thirds of brake fluid from master cylinder.
2. Support vehicle on hoist and remove wheel.
3. Remove cotter pin from inboard end of retaining pin.
4. Remove inboard and outboard shoe by pulling up.

INSTALLING LINING

1. Install inboard and outboard shoe one at a time. Use two screwdrivers to push pistons back as shoes are inserted, **Fig. 3.**
2. Install retaining pin through outboard caliper half, outboard shoe, inboard shoe and inboard caliper half. Insert a new $\frac{3}{32} \times \frac{5}{8}$ inch plated cotter pin through retaining pin.
3. Repeat above procedure at each wheel where shoes are to be replaced.
4. Refill master cylinder, then install wheel and lower vehicle.

CAUTION: Do not move vehicle until a firm brake pedal has been obtained.

CALIPERS

The caliper assembly, **Fig. 4,** incorporates two halves retained by bolts at the flange end. The two halves contain fluid crossover passages from one to the other, sealed with O-rings.

The bleeder screw is threaded into a passage drilled to intersect the fluid crossover passage. The bleeder screws are located at the front of each caliper. There are two bleeder screws, one inboard, one outboard at the rear wheels, and one bleeder screw at the inboard side at the front wheel. It is necessary, therefore, to remove the rear wheel when bleeding the rear caliper.

REMOVING CALIPER

1. Support vehicle on hoist and remove wheel.
2. On front caliper, disconnect brake hose from support bracket. On rear caliper, disconnect tubing from inboard caliper. Tape open tube or line end to prevent entry of dirt.
3. Remove caliper mounting bolts and remove caliper.

DISASSEMBLING CALIPER

1. Remove brake hose from front caliper.
2. Remove cotter pin from retaining pin, then remove pin and shoe assembly from caliper.
3. Remove caliper retaining bolts and separate caliper halves, then remove the two O-rings from fluid transfer cavities in ends of caliper halves.
4. Push piston into caliper as far as it will move, then insert a screwdriver under inner edge of steel ring in boot and using piston as a fulcrum, pry piston boot from its seat in caliper half.

CAUTION: Use care not to puncture seal when removing pistons from caliper.

Fig. 3   Installing Delco Moraine disc brake shoes

Fig. 4   Delco-Moraine disc brake caliper components

Fig. 5   Installing piston in caliper

5. Remove pistons and springs from caliper half, then remove boot and seal from piston.

CLEANING & INSPECTION

1. Clean all metal parts using clean brake fluid, removing all traces of dirt and grease.

CAUTION: Never use mineral base cleaning solvents as they can cause deterioration of rubber parts or make them soft and swollen.

2. Using air pressure, blow out all fluid passages in caliper halves, making sure that these passages are not obstructed.
3. Discard all rubber parts and replace with new service kit parts.
4. Inspect piston bores. They must be free of scores and pits. A damaged bore will cause leaks and unsatisfactory brake operation. If either caliper half is damaged to the extent that polishing with fine crocus cloth will not restore to satisfactory condition, replace the caliper half.
5. Check fit of piston in bore using a feeler gauge. Clearance should be as follows:
   1⅞ inch bore   .0045–.010
   1⅜ inch bore   .0035–.009
If bore is not damaged and clearance exceeds specifications, only a new piston will be required.

ASSEMBLING CALIPER

1. Install seal in piston groove which is closest to flat end of piston. The seal lip must face toward large end of piston.

NOTE: Make certain seal lips are in piston groove and do not extend over step in end of groove.

2. Place spring in piston bore, then lubricate seal with brake fluid.
3. Install piston assembly in bore using tool J-22591, 22629 or 22639, **Fig. 5.** Use care not to damage seal lip as piston is pressed past edge of bore.
4. Install piston boot in groove closest to concave end of piston with fold in boot facing toward end of piston with seal attached.

NOTE: Apply a bead of suitable sealer (GM 1052366 or equivalent) into piston boot groove, then install boot into groove.

5. Make certain that piston slides smoothly into bore until end of piston is flush with end of bore. If not, recheck piston assembly and position of piston spring and seal.
6. Using boot seal installer tool J-22592, J-22628 or J-22638, **Fig. 6,** over piston, seat steel boot retaining ring evenly into counterbore.

NOTE: Boot retaining ring must be flush or below machined face of caliper. Any distortion or uneven seating could allow corrosive elements to enter bore. Push pistons into bore fully and hold in place. Apply a bead of suitable sealer (GM 1052366 or equivalent) onto outer edge of boot retaining ring to form a seal between retaining ring and caliper housing.

7. Install O-rings in cavities around brake fluid transfer holes at both ends of outboard caliper halves. Lubricate caliper bolts with Delco Brake Lube

Fig. 6   Installing boot seal in caliper

#540032 (or equivalent) or clean brake fluid, then secure caliper halves together and torque front caliper housing bolts to 130 ft. lbs. and rear caliper housing bolts to 68 ft. lbs.

INSTALLING CALIPER

1. Mount caliper over disc, then using two screwdrivers, depress pistons so that caliper can be lowered into place.

NOTE: Use care not to damage boots on edge of disc as caliper is installed.

2. Install mounting bolts and torque to 70 ft. lbs.

CAUTION: If reusing old shoe assemblies, be sure to install shoes in same location from which removed.

3. Install disc pads as outlined previously.
4. Place a new copper gasket on male end of front wheel brake hose and install brake hose in calipers. With wheels straight ahead, pass female end of hose through support bracket, then making certain that tube seat is clean, connect brake line tube nut to caliper and tighten securely.
5. Allowing hose to seek a normal position, without twist, insert hose fitting in support bracket and secure with "U" shaped retainer, then while turning steering geometry from stop to stop, check that hose does not contact other parts at anytime. If contact does occur, remove "U" shaped retainer and twist hose in a direction that will eliminate hose contact. Reinstall retainer and recheck for hose contact. If satisfactory, place steel tube connecter in hose fitting and tighten securely.
6. If rear caliper is being serviced, connect brake line to caliper.
7. Bleed brakes and install wheels.

CAUTION: Do not move vehicle until a firm pedal has been obtained.

SERVICE SUMMARY

1. There is no brake shoe adjustment on the disc brakes.
2. The groove in the brake shoe is an indicator of brake wear. When the groove is just about gone it is time for shoe replacement.
3. When replacing shoes it is necessary to siphon fluid from master cylinder reservoir to make room for fluid to return to the reservoir when pushing the caliper pistons back into their bores to make room for the thickness of the new shoes.
4. The shoes have a directional arrow on the back of the shoe plate. This arrow points to the forward rotation of the disc, and the purpose is for aligning the grain of the lining material in relation to the disc.
5. When bleeding the calipers, the rear

wheel must be removed to reach the outboard bleeder screw.
6. A retaining clip of thin metal is used to hold the pistons into the bores while installing the new brake shoes.
7. The caliper assembly is removable, after disconnecting the brake line, by removing the two mounting bolts and lifting the assembly off the disc.
8. The disc is riveted to the spindle flange in production. However, the rivets may be drilled out and the wheel studs and nuts are sufficient to hold the new disc in place when replacing the disc.
9. The rear wheel spindle must be removed to gain access to the parking brake shoes. It is necessary then to remove the caliper, the axle drive shaft, the spindle drive shaft yoke and remove the spindle and disc as an assembly from the wheel support. You now have access to the parking brake shoes the same as any other conventional bendix type brake shoe, **Fig. 2.**

Delco-Moraine Single Piston W/Dual Mounting Bolts (Type 1)

INDEX

DESCRIPTION

This single piston sliding caliper assembly, **Fig. 1,** incorporates a one piece housing with the inboard side of the housing bored for the piston. A seal within the housing bore provides a hydraulic seal between the piston and housing wall.

A spring steel scraper (wear sensor) is incorporated on each inboard shoe. When the shoe lining has worn to within .030 inch of the shoe, the sensor scrapes the rotor and emits an audible high frequency sound indicating that the linings should be replaced.

The caliper assembly slides on the mounting bolts. Upon brake application, fluid pressure against the piston forces the inboard shoe and lining assembly against the inboard side of the disc. This action causes the caliper assembly to slide until the outboard lining comes into contact with the disc. As pressure builds up, the linings are pressed against the disc with increased force.

CALIPER REMOVAL

1. Siphon enough brake fluid out of the

master cylinder to bring fluid level to 1/3 full to avoid fluid overflow when the caliper piston is pushed back into its bore.
2. Raise vehicle and remove front wheels.
3. Using a "C" clamp, as illustrated in **Fig. 2,** push piston back into its bore.
4. Remove two mounting bolts, **Fig. 3,** and lift caliper away from disc.

BRAKE SHOE REMOVAL

1. Remove caliper assembly as outlined above.
2. Remove inboard shoe. Dislodge outboard shoe and position caliper on the front suspension so the brake hose will not support the weight of the caliper.
3. Remove shoe support spring from piston.
4. Remove two sleeves from inboard ears of the caliper.
5. Remove four rubber bushings from the grooves in each of the caliper ears.

BRAKE SHOE INSTALLATION

1. Lubricate new sleeves, rubber bushings, bushing grooves and mounting bolt ends with Delco Silicone Lube or its equivalent.
2. Install new bushings and sleeves in caliper ears.

NOTE: Position the sleeve so that the end toward the shoe is flush with the machined surface of the ear.

3. Install shoe support spring by positioning single tang end of spring into notch cut at top of inboard shoe. Press remaining end of spring over bottom edge of shoe until shoe is engaged securely, **Fig. 4.**
4. Position inboard shoe with spring attached into caliper with ear end facing downward and bottom end facing upward with spring resting on inside diameter of piston. Press downward on both ends of shoe until shoe contacts piston and support spring contacts piston inside diameter.

NOTE: Some inboard replacement brake

CALIPER ASSEMBLY

MOUNTING BOLTS

OUTBOARD BRAKE SHOE

SLEEVES

BUSHINGS

SEAL

PISTON

DUST BOOT

SPRING

INBOARD BRAKE SHOE

Fig. 1   Exploded view of caliper assembly (Typical). Delco Moraine single piston w/dual bolt mounting (Type 1)

pads incorporate wear sensors and have a specific left and right hand assembly. Properly installed, the wear sensor will face toward the rear of caliper.

5. Position outboard shoe in caliper with shoe ears over caliper ears and tab at bottom of shoe engaged in caliper cut-out.
6. With shoes installed, lift caliper and rest bottom edge of outboard lining on outer edge of brake disc to be sure there is no clearance between outboard shoe tab and caliper abutment.
7. Install caliper and torque mounting bolts to 30–40 ft. lbs. on 1980 models. On 1981–85 vehicles, torque to 28 ft. lbs.
8. Clinch upper ears of outboard shoe by positioning pliers with one jaw on top of upper ear and one jaw in notch on bottom shoe opposite ear, **Fig. 5.** Ears are to be flat against caliper housing with no radial clearance. If clearance exists, repeat clinching procedure.

NOTE: Before moving vehicle, pump brake pedal several times to be sure it is firm. Do not move vehicle until a firm pedal

is obtained. On 1981–85 models with low drag calipers, apply approximately 175 pounds of pressure to the brake pedal three times to properly seat the caliper and related components.

Fig. 2   Compressing piston and shoes with "C" clamp

SLEEVE

CALIPER

RETAINING EARS INBOARD SHOE

MOUNTING BOLTS

SLEEVE

ROTOR

Fig. 3   Caliper & mounting bolts

30-39

Fig. 4 Installing support spring

CLINCHING LOOP EARED SHOE

CHANNEL LOCK PLIERS (12")

UPPER SHOE EAR

SMALL NOTCH

Fig. 5 Clinching loop eared brake shoe

Fig. 6 Removing piston from caliper

remove piston, **Fig. 6.**

NOTE: Use just enough air pressure to ease piston out of bore. Do not blow piston out of bore.

CAUTION: Do not place fingers in front of piston in an attempt to catch or protect it when applying compressed air. This could result in serious injury.

6. Carefully pry dust boot out of bore.
7. Using a small piece of wood or plastic, remove piston seal from bore.

NOTE: Do not use a metal tool of any kind to remove seal as it may damage bore.

8. Remove bleeder valve.

ASSEMBLING CALIPER

1. Lubricate caliper piston bore and new piston seal with clean brake fluid. Position seal in bore groove.
2. Lubricate piston with clean brake fluid and assemble a new boot into the groove in the piston so the fold faces the open end of the piston, **Fig. 7.**
3. Using care not to unseat the seal, insert piston into bore and force the piston to the bottom of the bore.
4. Position dust boot in caliper counter-bore and install, using suitable seal installer, **Fig. 8.**

NOTE: Check the boot installation to be sure the retaining ring molded into the boot is not bent and that the boot is installed below the caliper face and evenly all around. If the boot is not fully installed, dirt and moisture may enter the bore and cause corrosion.

5. Install the brake hose in the caliper using a new copper gasket.
6. Install shoes and re-install caliper assembly.

DUST BOOT

PISTON

END OF GROOVE

Fig. 7 Installing boot to piston

BOOT INSTALLER

DUST BOOT

Fig. 8 Installing boot to caliper

DISASSEMBLING CALIPER

1. Remove caliper as outlined above.
2. Disconnect hose from steel line, remove U shaped retainer and withdraw hose from frame support bracket.
3. After cleaning outside of caliper, remove brake hose and discard copper gasket.
4. Drain brake fluid from caliper.
5. Pad caliper interior with clean shop towels and use compressed air to

.012 MAX.
.005 MIN.

CALIPER

.012 MAX.
.005 MIN.

THE DIMENSION BETWEEN EACH CALIPER STOP AND THE CALIPER SHOULD BE .005"-.012"

FILE TO OBTAIN CLEARANCE

Fig. 9 Checking clearance between caliper & stops

CALIPER INSTALLATION

1. Position caliper over disc, lining up holes in caliper with holes in mounting bracket. If brake hose was not disconnected during removal, be sure not to kink it during installation.
2. Start mounting bolts through sleeves in inboard caliper ears and the mounting bracket, making sure ends of bolts pass under ears on inboard shoe.

NOTE: Right and left calipers must not be interchanged.

3. Push mounting bolts through to engage holes in the outboard ears. Then thread mounting bolts into bracket.
4. Torque mounting bolts to 30–40 ft. lbs. on 1980 models. On 1981–85 vehicles, torque to 28 ft. lbs.
5. Check the dimensions between each caliper stop and caliper, **Fig. 9.**
6. If brake hose was removed, reconnect

it and bleed the calipers.
7. Replace front wheels, lower vehicle and add brake fluid to master cylinder to bring level to ¼ inch from top.

NOTE: Before moving vehicle, pump brake pedal several times to be sure it is firm. Do not move vehicle until a firm pedal is obtained. On 1981–85 models with low drag calipers, apply approximately 175 pounds of pressure to the brake pedal three times to properly seat the caliper and related components.

Delco-Moraine Single Piston W/Dual Bolt Mounting (Type 2)

INDEX

DESCRIPTION

The caliper has a single piston and is mounted to the support bracket by two mounting bolts, **Fig. 1.** The caliper assembly slides on the two mounting bolts. Upon brake application, fluid pressure against the piston forces the inboard shoe and lining assembly against the inboard side of the disc. This action causes the caliper assembly to slide until the outboard lining comes into contact with the disc. As pressure builds up the linings are pressed against the disc with increased force.

CALIPER REMOVAL

1. Remove approximately ⅔ of brake flu-

id from master cylinder.
2. Raise and support front of vehicle, then remove wheel and tire assembly.
3. Position C-clamp as shown in **Fig. 2**, tighten C-clamp until piston bottoms in piston bore, then remove C-clamp.
4. If caliper assembly is being removed for service, remove brake line fitting mounting bolt, **Fig. 3.** If only shoe and lining assemblies are to be replaced, do not disconnect brake line fitting from caliper.
5. Remove allen head caliper mounting bolts, **Fig. 4.** If bolts show signs of corrosion, use new bolts when installing caliper assembly.
6. Remove caliper assembly from disc. If only shoe and lining assemblies are to

be replaced, using a length of wire suspend caliper from spring coil. Never allow caliper to hang from brake hose.

SHOE & LINING REMOVAL

1. Remove caliper assembly as described under Caliper Removal.
2. Remove shoe and lining assemblies from caliper, **Fig. 1.**
3. Remove sleeves and bushings from grooves in caliper mounting bolt holes, **Fig. 1.**

CALIPER DISASSEMBLE

1. Use clean shop towels to pad interior

Fig. 1   Exploded view of caliper assembly. Delco Moraine single piston w/dual bolt mounting (Type 2)

Fig. 2   Compressing piston & shoes with C-clamp

DISC BRAKES

Fig. 3 Disconnecting brake line fitting from caliper

Fig. 6 Removing dust boot

of caliper assembly, then remove piston by directing compressed air into caliper brake line inlet hole, **Fig. 5.**

NOTE: Use just enough air pressure to ease piston out of bore.

CAUTION: Do not place fingers in front of piston for any reason when applying compressed air. This could result in serious personal injury.

2. Remove bleeder screw from caliper body.
3. Using a suitable screwdriver, remove dust boot from caliper bore, **Fig. 6.**
4. Using a piece of wood or plastic, remove piston seal from groove in caliper bore.

NOTE: Do not use any type of metal tool to remove piston seal, since damage to caliper bore may result.

5. Inspect piston for corrosion, scoring, nicks, wear and damage to chrome plating. If any of the above defects are found, replace piston.
6. Inspect caliper bore for corrosion, scoring, nicks, and wear. Light corrosion can be polished out using crocus cloth. If crocus cloth fails to remove corrosion, the caliper housing must be replaced.

CALIPER ASSEMBLE

1. Lubricate piston seal with clean brake fluid, then install piston seal into caliper bore groove. Check to ensure that piston seal is not twisted.
2. Lubricate caliper bore with clean brake fluid.

Fig. 4 Removing caliper mounting bolts

Fig. 7 Seating dust boot in caliper

3. Insert piston into caliper bore, then force piston down until piston bottoms in bore.
4. Position outer diameter of dust boot in caliper housing counterbore, then seat boot as shown in **Fig. 7.**
5. Install bleeder screw on caliper housing.

SHOE & LINING INSTALLATION

1. Install outboard shoe and lining assembly into caliper housing.
2. Install retaining spring onto inboard shoe and lining assembly, **Fig. 8,** then install inboard shoe into caliper housing.
3. On 1980–81 models, clinch outboard shoe and lining assembly ears to caliper housing using suitable pliers, **Fig. 9.**

Fig. 5 Applying compressed air to caliper line port

Fig. 8 Installing retainer spring on inboard shoe

Fig. 9 Clinching outboard shoe to caliper

4. On 1982–85 models, to clinch caliper to brake outboard shoe proceed as follows:
   a. To seat shoe flange to caliper, tightly position a large flat blade screwdriver between outboard shoe flange and hat section of rotor, **Fig. 10.**
   b. Pressurize the hydraulic system by moderately applying brake pedal, then using suitable tool, clamp the outboard shoe tightly to the caliper.
   c. Position a ball peen hammer on outboard shoe tab, **Fig. 11,** then using a larger brass hammer, lightly tap the ball peen hammer to bend the outboard shoe tab. Tabs must be bent around casting to approximately 45 degrees.

30-42

Fig. 10   Screwdriver in position between outboard shoe flange & hat section of rotor

Fig. 11   Ball peen hammer in position on outboard shoe tab

d. After both tabs have been bent pressure should be released and outboard shoe should be locked into position. If shoe is loose, repeat steps a. through d.

NOTE: If an outboard shoe is removed from the caliper, or the tabs unclinched for any reason, then it will be necessary to replace the disc shoe and lining assem-

blies. Do not re-clinch outboard shoe locking tabs after having removed shoe from caliper.

CALIPER INSTALLATION

1. Position caliper assembly over disc

and align mounting bolt holes. If brake hoses were not disconnected during removal, use care not to kink hoses during installation.
2. Install mounting bolts and torque to 21 to 35 ft. lbs., **Fig. 4.**
3. If brake line fitting was disconnected during removal, install brake line fitting and torque retaining bolt to 18 to 30 ft. lbs., **Fig. 3.**
4. Fill master cylinder. Bleed brake system if brake line was disconnected and recheck master cylinder fluid level.
5. Install wheel and tire assembly on vehicle, then lower vehicle and check brake system operation.

Delco-Moraine Single Piston W/Dual Mounting Bolts (Type 3)

INDEX

DESCRIPTION

This caliper, **Figs. 1 and 2,** has a single bore and is mounted to the support bracket with two mounting bolts. Hydraulic force, created by applying force to the brake pedal, is converted by the caliper into friction. The hydraulic force is applied equally against the piston and the bottom of the caliper bore moving the piston outward, resulting in a clamping action on the brake rotor.

FRONT BRAKE ASSEMBLY

CALIPER REMOVAL

1. Drain approximately ⅔ of brake fluid

from master cylinder assembly.
2. Raise and support vehicle, then remove tire and wheel assembly.
3. If caliper is to be serviced or replaced, remove bolt securing inlet fitting, then disconnect brake hose and secure in raised position.

NOTE: If only shoe and lining assemblies are being replaced, do not disconnect brake hose from caliper.

4. Remove caliper retaining bolts and boots, **Fig. 1.**
5. Compress piston, placing suitable adjustable pliers over inboard surface of caliper housing and support bracket as shown in **Fig.3.**
6. Remove caliper from disc. If shoe and lining assemblies are to be replaced, use a length of wire to suspend cali-

per. Do not allow caliper to hang from brake line.

SHOE & LINING REMOVAL

1. Remove caliper ...
   "Caliper R...
2. To re... shoe and lining assem... a suitable screwdriver to disengage shoe buttons from caliper holes.
3. Remove inboard shoe and lining assembly from caliper.
4. Remove sleeves from mounting bolt holes.
5. Remove bushings from mounting bolt hole grooves.

CALIPER DISASSEMBLY

1. Position a clean shop towel on inside

of caliper, then using compressed air, remove piston from caliper.
2. Remove piston protector from piston.
3. Inspect piston for wear, corrosion or damage. Replace piston, if necessary.
4. Inspect caliper housing for corrosion. If corrosion exists, use a crocus cloth to remove light surface corrosion. If corrosion cannot be removed with crocus cloth, replace caliper.
5. Remove bleeder valve protector.

CALIPER ASSEMBLY

1. Clean all brake components in clean denatured alcohol. Use dry, filtered compressed air to dry components and blow out caliper housing passages.
2. Install bleeder valve onto caliper. Torque valve to 80–140 inch lbs.
3. Using clean brake fluid, lubricate caliper housing bore and bore seals.
4. Install piston seal into caliper bore groove. Ensure seal is not twisted in groove.
5. Install boot and piston protector onto piston.
6. Install piston into caliper bore and push piston completely to the bottom.
7. Using tool No. J-29077 or equivalent, install boot into caliper housing counterbore.

SHOE & LINING INSTALLATION

1. Lubricate, then install bushings into mounting bolt hole grooves.

1. MOUNTING BOLT
2. SLEEVE
3. BOLT BOOT
4. BUSHING
5. OUTBOARD SHOE & LINING
6. INBOARD SHOE & LINING
7. CALIPER BOOT
8. PISTON PROTECTOR
9. PISTON
10. PISTON SEAL
11. PROTECTOR
12. BLEEDER VALVE
13. CALIPER HOUSING
18. WEAR SENSOR

Fig. 1 Exploded view of front caliper assembly. Delco-Moraine single piston W/dual mounting (Type 3)

2. Lubricate, then install sleeves into mounting bolt holes.
3. Install inboard shoe and lining onto caliper.

NOTE: Ensure that tabs on inboard shoe are positioned so that they fit into corresponding holes in face of piston

4. Install outboard shoe and lining onto caliper. Ensure wear sensor is positioned at leading edge of brake shoe.

CALIPER INSTALLATION

1. Install caliper onto brake rotor mounting bracket.

1. NUT
2. LEVER
3. RETURN SPRING
4. BOLT
5. BRACKET
6. LEVER SEAL
7. ANTI-FRICTION WASHER
8. MOUNTING BOLT
9. SLEEVE
10. BOLT BOOT
11. BUSHING
12. OUTBOARD SHOE & LINING
13. INBOARD SHOE & LINING
14. SHOE DAMPENING SPRING
15. CALIPER BOOT
16. TWO WAY CHECK VALVE
17. PISTON ASSEMBLY
18. PISTON SEAL
19. ACTUATOR SCREW
20. BALANCE SPRING
21. THRUST WASHER
22. SHAFT SEAL
23. PROTECTOR
24. BLEEDER VALVE
25. CALIPER HOUSING
26. WEAR SENSOR

Fig. 2 Exploded view of rear caliper assembly. Delco-Moraine single piston W/dual mounting (Type 3)

25. CALIPER HOUSING
28. PLIERS

Fig. 3 Compressing front caliper piston for caliper removal

1. NUT
2. LEVER
3. RETURN SPRING
6. LEVER SEAL
7. ANTI-FRICTION WASHER
27. CABLE

Fig. 4 Parking brake lever assembly

2. Using silicone grease or equivalent, liberally coat shoulder and mounting bolt threads so caliper cavity will be filled.
3. Install caliper mounting bolts. Torque bolts to 21–35 ft. lbs.

REAR BRAKE ASSEMBLY

CALIPER REMOVAL

1. Drain approximately ⅔ of brake fluid from master cylinder assembly.
2. Raise and support vehicle, then remove tire and wheel assembly.
3. Loosen tension on parking brake cable at equalizer, remove cable and spring from parking brake lever, **Fig. 4**
4. While holding parking brake lever, remove locknut, parking brake lever, lever seal and anti-friction washer, **Fig. 4.**

NOTE: Parking brake lever assembly must be removed to provide clearance for compressing caliper piston. Failure to remove lever will cause piston to be damaged when it is bottomed in bore.

5. Remove brake line fittings from caliper if caliper is to be removed for service or replacement.

NOTE: If only the shoes and linings are to be replaced, do not disconnect brake hose from caliper.

6. Remove caliper mounting bolts, then position C-clamp onto caliper as shown in **Fig. 5,** and tighten clamp until piston bottoms in piston bore.

7. Lift caliper off rotor and mounting bracket and support caliper, as needed, to prevent stretching brake hose.

SHOE & LINING REMOVAL

1. Remove caliper as described under "Caliper Removal."
2. Remove inboard shoe and lining assembly from caliper.
3. To remove outboard shoe and lining assembly, use a suitable screwdriver to disengage shoe buttons from caliper holes.
4. Remove sleeves from mounting bolt holes.
5. Remove bolt boots and bushings from caliper.
6. Using a suitable screwdriver, remove two-way check valve from piston end.

CALIPER DISASSEMBLY

1. Remove dampening spring from piston end, **Fig. 2.**
2. Remove nut and lever assembly.
3. Remove lever seal and anti-friction washer.
4. Place caliper into a soft jaw vise. Place a clean shop towel on inside of caliper, then using compressed air, remove piston from caliper.
5. Press on threaded end of actuator screw, then remove screw.
6. Remove shaft seal and thrust washer.
7. Remove boot from caliper housing bore. Do not use a sharp tool to remove boot from caliper.
8. Inspect piston for wear and damage. Replace caliper, if necessary.
9. If surface corrosion exists on caliper, use crocus cloth to remove corrosion from caliper.
10. Remove bleeder valve and protector.
11. Inspect caliper mounting bracket. If mounting bracket is damaged, replace as required.

CALIPER ASSEMBLY

1. Install bleeder valve. Torque valve to 80–140 inch lbs.
2. Install protector onto bleeder valve.
3. Install mounting bracket, if removed. Torque bracket bolt to 24–38 ft. lbs.
4. Using clean brake fluid, lubricate caliper housing bore seals.
5. Install piston seal into caliper bore groove.
6. Ensure caliper seal is not twisted in groove.
7. Install boot onto piston with inside lip of boot in piston groove and boot fold toward end of piston.
8. Install thrust washer onto actuator screw with bearing surface toward caliper housing.
9. Lubricate shaft seal with clean brake fluid, then install seal onto actuator screw.
10. Lubricate actuator screw, then install screw into piston.
11. Install balance spring into piston.
12. Lubricate piston with clean brake fluid, then install piston into caliper bore.

CAUTION: DO NOT ALLOW C-CLAMP TO CONTACT ACTUATOR SCREW.

1 ACTUATOR SCREW
2 CALIPER HOUSING
3 C-CLAMP

Fig. 5 Positioning C-clamp to compress rear caliper piston

Use tool No. J-23072 or equivalent to push piston completely down into bore.
13. Install anti-friction washer and lever seal onto actuator screw. ensure sealing bead on lever is against housing. Install lever onto actuator screw. Rotate lever away from stop slightly and hold while install nut. Torque nut to 30–40 ft. lbs. After nut is torqued, rotate lever back to the stop.
14. Install boot into caliper housing counterbore. Using tool No. J-28678, seat boot into counterbore.
15. Install dampening spring into groove end of piston. It may be necessary to move parking brake lever off the stop to extend piston and make spring groove accessible.

SHOE & LINING INSTALLATION

1. Lubricate, then install bushings into mounting bolt hole grooves.
2. Lubricate, then install bolt boots into mounting bolt holes.
3. Lubricate, then install sleeves into mounting bolt holes.
4. Install two-way check valve into piston end.
5. Install inboard shoe and lining into caliper. Note the following:
   a. Ensure D shaped tab on shoe engages D shaped notch in piston.
   b. If tab and notch do not align, use tool J-7624 or equivalent to turn piston.
   c. Brake wear sensor must be at leading edge of shoe during forward wheel rotation.
   d. Slide edge of metal shoe under ends of dampening spring and snap shoe into position, flat against the piston.
6. Install outboard shoe and lining assembly into piston. Ensure spring ends on outboard shoe snap into piston recess.

7. After installation of caliper assembly, apply brakes slowly and firmly three times to seat linings.

CALIPER INSTALLATION

1. Install caliper onto brake rotor mounting bracket.
2. Torque caliper mounting bolts to 30–45 ft. lbs.
3. Install brake line fitting onto caliper.

Torque fitting to 30 ft. lbs.
4. Install anti-friction washer.
5. Lubricate seal, then install into caliper housing. Ensure sealing bead on seal contacts housing.
6. Install lever onto actuator screw.
7. While holding lever, install nut. Torque nut to 30–40 ft. lbs.
8. Rotate lever back against caliper stop, then install spring.

9. Install parking brake cable. Tighten cable at equalizer until lever starts to move off caliper stop. Loosen adjustment until lever moves back against caliper stop.
10. Install tire and wheel assembly, then lower vehicle.
11. Fill master cylinder with brake fluid.
12. Bleed brake system, if necessary.

Delco-Moraine Single Piston Rear Disc Brake

INDEX

OPERATION

Upon application of brake, **Figs. 1, 2 & 3,** the cone and piston move out as one part. The nut remains stationary on the high lead screw and a gap develops between the cone and nut. When lining wear occurs, the cone and piston do not return to their original position, thereby leaving a small gap equal to the lining wear between the nut and cone. The adjusting spring causes the nut to rotate on the high lead screw to close the gap and adjust the caliper.

Upon application of parking brake, the lever rotation causes the high lead screw to turn and the nut to move down the screw, thereby loading through the cone and the cone-clutch interface of the piston, resulting in a clamp load on the linings. When the parking brake is released, the cone rotates on the clutch interface to adjust the caliper. The clutch interface prevents the cone from turning when the parking brake is applied.

CALIPER REMOVAL

CAUTION: Do not mix power steering fluid with brake fluid. If brake seals contact steering fluid or steering seals contact brake fluid, damage will result.

1. Remove two thirds of the total brake fluid capacity from the master cylinder front reservoir, to prevent overflow of brake fluid.
2. Support vehicle on a hoist and remove tire and wheel assembly.
3. Install one nut with flat side facing rotor to prevent rotor from falling out when caliper is removed.
4. Loosen parking brake cable tension at equalizer, then remove cable from parking brake lever and remove return spring, lock nut, lever, lever seal and anti-friction washer.

NOTE: Lever must be held in place while removing nut.

5. Clean surface in area of lever seal, then using a 7 inch (or larger) C-clamp, with the solid end on lever stop and screw end on back of outboard lining, turn clamp until piston is bottomed in caliper.

NOTE: Do not position C-clamp on actuator screw.

6. Before removing clamp, lubricate housing surface under lever seal with silicone lubricant.
7. Install a new anti-friction washer, a new lever seal and lever.

NOTE: Install lever on hex with arm pointing downward.

8. Rotate lever toward front of vehicle and while holding in this position, install nut and torque to 25 ft. lbs. and rotate lever back to stop.
9. Install lever return spring and remove C-clamp.

NOTE: On Cadillac springs are color coded, red for the right hand caliper and black for the left hand caliper.

10. Disconnect brake line from caliper and plug openings to prevent loss of fluid and entry of dirt.
11. On all calipers except Eldorado and right hand Brougham remove the brass bolt from the block.

NOTE: If brake line nut is seized, brass bolt and block can be removed with brake line attached by removing bolt. Plug open-

Fig. 1 Typical Delco-Moraine rear disc brake cross-sectional view

Fig. 2   Rear disc brake caliper exploded view. 1980 Electra

Fig. 3   Rear disc brake caliper exploded view. Eldorado, Firebird, Riviera, Seville, Toronado & 1982—84 Camaro

DISC BRAKES

Fig. 4 Removing piston from bore

Fig. 7 Driving boot into caliper

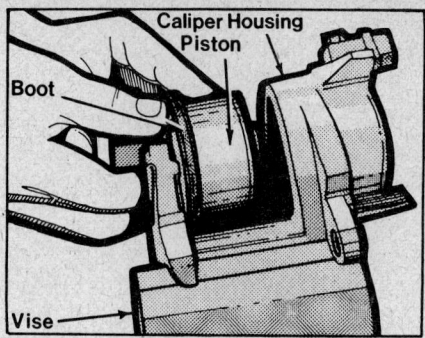

Fig. 5 Positioning piston in caliper

Fig. 8 Removing piston check valve

Fig. 6 Installing piston into caliper

Fig. 9 Rotating piston in bore

ings to prevent loss of fluid and entry of dirt.

12. Remove caliper mounting bolts and remove caliper.
13. Reverse procedure to install and torque caliper mounting bolts to 30 ft. lbs.

NOTE: When installing brass bolt and block, use two new copper gaskets. Torque bolt or connector to 30 ft. lbs.

INSPECTION

1. Clean corrosion and dirt from face of piston. Inspect piston and check valve area for fluid leakage, indicated by excessive moisture around boot area
2. Inspect dust boot for cuts, cracks or other damage which may affect its sealing ability. If leaks are present, replace dust boot.

NOTE: Do not use compressed air to clean caliper as it may unseat the dust boot.

3. Inspect piston boot seal. Replace boot seal if leakage is indicated.
4. Inspect for leaks at threaded end of actuator screw. Replace seal if leakage is indicated. If bore is nicked or scratched, replace caliper.

CALIPER OVERHAUL
DISASSEMBLY

1. Clamp caliper in a vise and remove the two mounting sleeves and four bushings, **Fig. 2 and 3.**
2. Remove brake shoes and lever return spring.
3. Rotate parking brake lever back and forth to remove piston from housing, **Fig. 4.** If piston will not move from housing, remove lock nut, lever and anti-friction washer. With a 9/16 inch wrench, rotate screw clockwise on right hand caliper or counter-clockwise on left hand caliper until the piston moves from housing.

NOTE: Pad caliper with shop cloths when removing piston.

4. Remove piston assembly and balance spring.
5. Remove lock nut, lever, lever seal and anti-friction washer if not removed previously.
6. Push screw from housing, then remove piston seal and boot.

ASSEMBLY

1. Install new piston seal.
2. Install new boot onto piston assembly with lip of boot located in piston groove.
3. Install new thrust washer and seal on actuator screw.
4. Install actuator screw into piston

assembly. The piston assemblies are identified by a stamped letter on the adjuster nut end. "L" denote left hand and "R" denotes right hand. The caliper housing is also marked with a letter. The parking brake will not function if the caliper and actuator screw are located on the wrong side of vehicle.

5. Coat piston seal with clean brake fluid. Install balance spring into piston and install assembly into caliper housing, **Fig. 5.**
6. With tool J-23072, push piston fully into caliper housing, **Fig. 6.**

NOTE: The piston must be pushed straight into caliper to prevent damage to the actuator screw seal as it passes through hole in rear of piston bore.

7. Before removing tool J-23072, install lubricated anti-friction washer, new lever seal, lever and lock nut. Position lever away from stop, rotate forward and hold lever in position, then torque nut to 25 ft. lbs.
8. Remove tool J-23072, rotate lever back to stop and install return spring.

NOTE: On Cadillac the return springs are color coded red for right hand and black for left hand.

9. With tool J-26296, drive boot until seal bottoms in caliper housing, **Fig. 7.**

SHOE & LINING REPLACEMENT

1. Remove caliper as described previously and remove shoe and lining.
2. Remove and discard the two caliper mounting sleeves and the four bushings. Using silicone lubricant, install new bushings and seals.

NOTE: Sleeves are installed in inner bushings.

3. Remove and discard piston check valve and install a new one, **Fig. 8.**

CAUTION: Front brake shoes must not be installed on rear calipers.

4. Position new inboard shoe assembly on piston. The D-shaped tab must fit into indentation in piston. If piston requires rotation, use tool J-7642 to rotate it, **Fig. 9.**

NOTE: Install new spring retainers on all exc. Eldorado outboard shoe assembly.

5. Install new outboard shoe assembly onto caliper. Install caliper and torque mounting bolts to 30 ft. lbs.

Girlock Single Piston Caliper

INDEX

DESCRIPTION

This caliper, **Fig. 1,** has a single piston in an aluminum housing suspended in the mounting bracket on two slide pins. Hydraulic pressure, created by applying force to the brake pedal, acts equally against the piston and the bottom of the caliper bore to move the piston outward and to slide the caliper inward resulting in a clamping action on the brake rotor.

BRAKE SHOE & LINING REMOVAL

1. Drain approximately ⅔ of brake fluid from master cylinder.
2. Raise and support vehicle.
3. Mark relationship of wheel to axle assembly, then remove wheel(s).
4. Position a suitable C-clamp into caliper, with one end of clamp against inlet fitting bolt head and other end of clamp against outboard shoe.
5. Tighten clamp screw until caliper piston bottoms in piston bore.
6. Remove and discard upper caliper self locking bolt.
7. Rotate caliper until shoe and lining assemblies are exposed.
8. Remove shoe and lining assemblies.

BRAKE SHOE & LINING INSTALLATION

1. Install new shoe and lining assemblies onto mounting bracket.
2. Rotate caliper into position and install a new self locking bolt. Torque bolt to 22–25 ft. lbs.
3. Install wheel(s) and lower vehicle. Bleed brake system, if necessary.

CALIPER DISASSEMBLY

1. Remove caliper as described under "Brake Shoe & Caliper Removal."
2. If caliper requires machining, remove inlet fitting.
3. Remove and discard self locking bolts.
4. Remove bracket bolts.

NOTE: Remove brake shoe and lining assemblies only if they are to be replaced or if the mounting bracket is being removed for rotor machining.

5. Position a clean shop towel on the inside of the caliper housing, then using compressed air, apply air to brake hose port and remove piston.
6. Inspect piston for wear and/or damage. Replace, if necessary.
7. Remove piston boot from housing.
8. Remove piston seal from caliper bore groove.

NOTE: Do not use a sharp tool to remove piston seal.

Fig. 1 Girlock single piston caliper exploded view

DISC BRAKES

9. Inspect caliper bore for scoring or corrosion. If scoring or corrosion exists, replace caliper as required.
10. Remove bleeder screw and rubber cap from bleeder screw.
11. Inspect guide pins for corrosion. If corrosion exists, replace guide pins as required.

CALIPER ASSEMBLY

1. Clean all brake components in clean denatured alcohol. Use dry, filtered compressed air to dry components and blow out caliper housing passages.
2. Check piston to bore fit, by sliding piston in and out of piston bore. Piston should slide in and out smoothly.
3. Install rubber cap onto bleeder screw, then insert bleeder screw into caliper.
4. Using clean brake fluid, lubricate piston seal, then install seal into caliper bore groove. Ensure seal is not twisted in piston bore groove.
5. Using clean brake fluid, lubricate caliper bore and piston assembly.
6. Install boot over end of piston. Place piston into caliper bore. Push piston completely down into caliper bore. Ensure boot is properly seated into groove around piston and into groove in caliper bore.
7. Using silicone grease or equivalent, lubricate caliper guide pins.
8. Install new guide pin boots over guide pins.
9. Install guide pins into mounting bracket.
10. Install caliper over rotor and into mounting bracket. Ensure brake shoe springs are positioned properly.
11. Install new self locking bolts. Torque bolts to 26–40 ft. lbs.
12. Pump brake pedal firmly and slowly three times to bring pads into contact with brake rotor.
13. Bleed brake system, if necessary.

Toyota/GM Single Piston Caliper

INDEX

1. MOUNTING BOLT
2. DUST BOOT
3. COLLAR
4. SLIDE BUSHING
5. CALIPER HOUSING
6. PISTON
7. PISTON SEAL
8. BOOT
9. SET RING
10. CAP
11. BLEEDER SCREW
12. ANTI-RATTLE SPRING
13. ANTI-SQUEAL SHIM
14. PAD
15. PAD SUPPORT PLATE
16. PAD WEAR INDICATOR PLATE
17. MOUNTING BRACKET

Fig. 1   Toyota/GM front brake caliper exploded view

Fig. 2   Caliper support installation

1. ANTI-RATTLE SPRINGS
2. BRAKE PADS
3. WEAR INDICATOR
4. ANTI-SQUEAL SHIMS
5. SUPPORT PLATES

Fig. 3   Brake pad assembly

Fig. 4   Lubrication points for caliper assembly

CALIPER
REPLACE

REMOVAL

1. Siphon ⅔ of the brake fluid from master cylinder, raise and support vehicle, and remove wheels.
2. Reinstall 2 wheel nuts to retain rotor, then remove caliper mounting bolts, **Fig. 1.**
3. Remove union nut securing brake hose to caliper and drain fluid into suitable container.

NOTE: If caliper is only being removed for brake pad replacement, do not disconnect brake hose.

4. Compress piston as needed, then remove caliper. If brake hose remains connected, secure caliper aside to prevent hose from being stretched.

INSTALLATION

1. Seat piston in caliper bore, taking care not to damage piston.
2. Ensure that support plates, **Fig. 2,** and anti-rattle springs are properly positioned, then mount caliper over rotor onto mounting bracket.
3. Install caliper mounting bolts and torque bolts to 18 ft. lbs.
4. Install brake hose and mounting bolts, using new copper gaskets, then torque bolt to 17 ft. lbs.
5. Refill master cylinder and bleed brake system.

BRAKE PADS
REPLACE

NOTE: Replace brake pads on one wheel at a time to prevent opposite side caliper piston from being forced out of bore.

REMOVAL

1. Remove caliper as outlined, leaving brake hose connected, and secure caliper aside.
2. Remove 2 anti rattle clips, then the brake brake pads, **Fig. 3.**
3. Remove pad wear indicator plates and anti-squeal shims.
4. Remove support plates.

INSTALLATION

1. Install new support plates on caliper mounting bracket, **Fig. 2.**
2. Install new wear indicators and anti-squeal shims on each pad, **Fig. 3,** then position pads in caliper mounting bracket.

NOTE: Ensure that arrow on wear indicator is pointing in rotating direction of rotor.

3. Install anti-rattle springs.
4. Seat piston in caliper bore, then install caliper and mounting bolts, and torque bolts to 18. ft lbs.
5. Refill master cylinder and bleed brakes as needed.

CALIPER OVERHAUL
DISASSEMBLY

1. Remove 2 caliper slide bushings, 4

dust boots and spacer collars, **Fig. 1.**
2. Pry out caliper dust boot retaining ring and remove dust boot.
3. Place clean shop towels in caliper web to protect piston, then apply compressed air to caliper fluid inlet to force piston from bore.

CAUTION: Keep fingers clear of caliper web when removing piston. Use only enough air pressure to ease piston out of bore, or piston may be damaged.

4. Remove piston seal from caliper bore, taking care not to mar machined surface of caliper.
5. Remove bleeder valve.
6. Clean components with alcohol and wipe dry with clean, lint-free shop towels. Blow out caliper body and fluid passages with clean, filtered compressed air.
7. Inspect caliper and piston for damage, distortion, excessive wear and pitting, and replace as needed.
8. Replace mounting bolts, collars and caliper slides if they are damaged or worn.

ASSEMBLY

1. Apply lithium soap base glycol grease to components shown in **Fig. 4.**
2. Install piston seal in caliper, ensuring that seal is squarely seated in groove.
3. Press piston into bore, ensuring that piston enters bore straight.
4. Seat piston dust boot in caliper groove, then install retaining ring.
5. Install 2 collars and 4 slide bushing dust boots, **Fig. 1,** rotating boots as they are pressed in to ensure that they are fully seated.
6. Install slide bushings through dust boots, ensuring that boots remain seated in caliper grooves.

Disc Brake Rotor Specifications

CAR	Year	Nominal Thickness	Minimum Refinish Thickness	Thickness Variation Parallelism	Lateral Runout (T.I.R.)	Finish (Micro-In.)
BUICK (EXC. SKYHAWK, SKYLARK, 1982–84 CENTURY & 1985 ELECTRA FWD)						
Full Size	1980–83①	1.040	.980	.0005	.004②	④
	1980–83③	.974	.921	.0005	.004②	④
	1984–85	1.043	.980	.0005	.004	④
Intermediate	1980–83	1.040	.980	.0005	.004	30–80
	1984–85	1.043	.980	.0005	.004	—
CADILLAC (EXC. CIMARRON & 1985 DEVILLE & FLEETWOOD FWD)						
Exc. Eldorado & Seville①	1980–81	1.037	—	.0005	.005	—
Eldorado & Seville①	1980–81	1.036	—	.0005	.005	—
Eldorado & Seville③	1980–81	1.036	—	.0005	.005	—
All	1982–84	1.000	—	.0005	.004	—
1985 BUICK ELECTRA, CAD. DEVILLE, FLEETWOOD & OLDS. 98 FRONT WHEEL DRIVE						
All	1985	.885	.830	.0005	.004	—
CHEVROLET (CAMARO, CHEVROLET, CORVETTE, MALIBU & MONTE CARLO)						
Corvette	1980–82	1.250	1.230	.0005	.005	20–60
All exc. Corvette	1980–83	1.030	.980	.0005	.004	20–60
Corvette	1984	—	.724	.0005	.006	—
All exc. Corvette	1984	—	.980	.0005	.004	30–80
CHEV. CAVALIER • BUICK SKYHAWK • CAD. CIMARRON • OLDS FIRENZA • PONT. 2000 • SUNBIRD						
All	1982–85	.885	.830	.0005	.002	—
CHEVROLET CHEVETTE • PONTIAC 1000						
All	1980–85	.4334 (11 mm)	.390 (9.9 mm)	.0005 (.013 mm)	.005 (.13 mm)	20–60 (.5–1.6 micro/m)
CHEV. CITATION, BUICK SKYLARK, OLDS. OMEGA & PONT. PHOENIX • 1982–85 CHEV. CELEBRITY, BUICK CENTURY, OLDS CUTLASS CIERA & CRUISER (1984) & PONT. 6000						
All	1980	1.040	.980	.0005	.005	30–80
All	1981–85	.885	.830	.0005	.004	12–50
OLDSMOBILE (EXC. FIRENZA, OMEGA, CUTLASS CIERA & 1984–85 CRUISER & 1985 98 FWD)						
88, 98 & Custom Cruiser	1980–81	1.040	.965	.0005	⑪	30–50
	1982	1.020	.984	.0005	.004	—
	1984–85	1.035	1.020	.0005	.004	—
Intermediate	1980–81	1.040	.980	.0005	.004	30–50
	1982–85	1.020	.984	.0005	.004	—
Toronado	1980	1.040	1.020	.0005	.005	19–80
	1981	1.020	.960	.0005	.005	19–80
	1982–85	1.020	.984	.0005	.004	19–80

continued

DISC BRAKE ROTOR SPECIFICATIONS—Continued

CAR	Year	Nominal Thick-ness	Minimum Refinish Thick-ness	Thickness Variation Parallelism	Lateral Runout (T.I.R.)	Finish (Micro-In.)
PONTIAC (EXC. 1000 & FRONT WHEEL DRIVE)						
Bonneville & Catalina	1980	1.040	.980	.0005	.005	20–60
	1981–84	1.030	.980	.0005	.005	20–60
Grand Am, Grand Prix & LeMans	1980	1.040	.980	.0005	.005	20–60
	1981–85	1.030	.980	.0005	.005	30–80
Firebird	1980–84	1.030	.980	.0005	.004	30–80
Parisienne	1983–85	1.030	.980	.0005	.004	20–60

①—Front.
②—Riviera, .005 inch.
③—Rear.
④—Exc. Riviera, 30–80; Riviera, 19–80.

Disc Brake Caliper Specifications

Year	Model	Caliper Bore Dia. In.
BUICK (EXC. SKYHAWK, SKYLARK, 1982–84 CENTURY & 1985 ELECTRA FWD)		
1980–81	Century & Regal	2⁷⁄₁₆
	Riviera	2½
	Exc. Century, Regal & Riviera	2¹⁵⁄₁₆
1982–85	Regal & Riviera	2½
	Exc. Regal & Riviera	2¹⁵⁄₁₆
1985 BUICK ELECTRA, CAD. DEVILLE, FLEETWOOD & OLDS. 98 FRONT WHEEL DRIVE		
1985	All	2.52
CHEVROLET (CAMARO, CHEVROLET, CORVETTE, MALIBU & MONTE CARLO)		
1980–81	Exc. Malibu, Monte Carlo & Corvette	2¹⁵⁄₁₆
	Malibu & Monte Carlo	2½
	Corvette	①
1982	Camaro	②
	Malibu & Monte Carlo	2½
	Chevrolet	2¹⁵⁄₁₆
	Corvette	①
1983	Camaro	②
	Malibu & Monte Carlo	2½
	Chevrolet	2¹⁵⁄₁₆
1984–85	Camaro	⑥
	Malibu & Monte Carlo	2.5
	Chevrolet	2¹⁵⁄₁₆
	Corvette	③

continued

DISC BRAKE CALIPER SPECIFICATIONS—Continued

Year	Model	Caliper Bore Dia. In.
CHEV. CAVALIER • BUICK SKYHAWK • CAD. CIMARRON • OLDS FIRENZA • PONTIAC 2000 & SUNBIRD		
1982–85	All	2.24
CHEVROLET CHEVETTE • PONTIAC 1000		
1980–82	All	1⅞
1983–85	All	2.05
CHEV. CITATION • BUICK SKYLARK • OLDS OMEGA • PONT. PHOENIX		
1980–85	All	2.24
1982–84 CHEV. CELEBRITY • BUICK CENTURY • OLDS. CUTLASS CIERA & CRUISER (1984) • PONT. 6000		
1982–85	All	2.24
OLDSMOBILE (EXC. FIRENZA, OMEGA, CUTLASS CIERA & 1984–85 CRUISER & 1985 98 FWD)		
1980–81	Exc. Cutlass	2¹⁵⁄₁₆
	Cutlass	2½
1982–85	Cutlass & Toronado	2½
	88, 98 & Custom Cruiser	2¹⁵⁄₁₆
PONTIAC (EXC. 1000 & FRONT WHEEL DRIVE)		
1980–81	Exc. Grand Prix & LeMans	2.9375
	Grand Prix & LeMans	2.5
1982–85	Exc. Firebird	2.9375
	Firebird	⑥
1984–85	Fiero	2.52

①—Front, 1⅞"; Rear, 1⅜".
②—Front, 2½"; Rear, 1⁵⁷⁄₆₄".
③—Front, 2.1"; Rear, 1.6".
④—If equipped with rear disk brakes, rear disc brake caliper bore, 2.6".
⑤—Rear disc brake caliper bore, 2.1".
⑥—Front, 2.5"; Rear, 1.89".

AUTOMATIC TRANSMISSIONS/TRANSAXLES
TABLE OF CONTENTS

Torque-Command Transmission
INDEX

IDENTIFICATION

The transmission identification markings, 904 on 4-151 engines or 904 or 998 on 6-258 engines, are cast in raised letters and numerals on the lower left side of the bell housing.

There are sufficient variations to make it necessary to service transmission by serial number, a stamped 7 digit number appearing on the oil pan side rail.

DESCRIPTION

These transmissions, **Fig. 1**, combine a torque converter with a fully automatic three-speed gear system. The converter housing and transmission case are an integral aluminum casting. The transmission consists of two multiple disc clutches, an overrunning (one-way) clutch, two servos and bands and two planetary gear sets to provide three forward speeds and reverse.

The common sun gear of the planetary gear sets is connected to the front clutch by a driving shell that is splined to the sun gear and to the front clutch retainer.

The hydraulic system consists of a single oil pump and a valve body that contains all the valves except the governor valve.

Venting of the transmission is accomplished by a drilled passage through the upper part of the front pump housing.

The torque converter is attached to the engine crankshaft through a flexible driving plate. The converter is cooled by circulating the transmission fluid through an oil-to-water type cooler located in the radiator lower tank. The converter is a sealed assembly that cannot be disassembled. On 1980–83 models with 6 cyl. engine, the lock-up torque converter is used.

TROUBLESHOOTING GUIDE

When troubleshooting this transmission, refer to "Torqueflite Automatic Transmission" in Chrysler section.

MAINTENANCE
CHECKING OIL LEVEL

To check the oil level, apply the parking brake and operate the engine at idle speed with the transmission in Neutral position.

CHANGING OIL

Fluid and filter changes or band adjustments are not required for average passenger car use. Severe usage such as police, taxi, trailer towing or prolonged operation in city traffic, requires that fluid and filter be changed and bands adjusted every 15,000 miles.

Whenever the factory fill fluid is changed, only fluids of the type labeled DEXRON should be used.
1. Remove drain plug (if equipped) from transmission oil pan and drain oil.

NOTE: If the oil pan does not have a drain plug, loosen pan bolts and tap pan with a soft mallet to break it loose, permitting fluid to drain.

2. Remove transmission oil pan, replace filter or clean intake screen and pan, adjust bands and reinstall.

3. Add 4 quarts of automatic transmission fluid through filler tube.
4. Start engine.
5. Allow engine to idle for about two minutes. With parking brake applied, move selector lever momentarily to each position and place in neutral.

BANDS
ADJUST

KICKDOWN BAND

The kickdown band adjusting screw is located on the left side of the transmission case near the throttle lever shaft.
1. Loosen lock nut and back off approximately five turns. Check adjusting screw for free turning in transmission case.
2. Using an inch-pound torque wrench, tighten the band adjusting screw to a reading of 72 inch lbs.
3. Back off adjusting screw 2 turns on all 1980–81 models and 1982–85 models with 904 transmission and 6 cylinder engine, 2½ turns on 1982–85 models with 904 transmission and 4 cylinder engine or 3 turns on models with 998 transmission.
4. Hold adjusting screw in backed off position and tighten locknut.

LOW AND REVERSE BAND

1. Raise vehicle, drain transmission and remove oil pan.
2. Inspect fluid for friction material or metal particles which indicate damaged or worn parts.
3. Loosen adjusting screw lock nut and

31–1

Fig. 1   Series 904 Torqueflite transmission (typical). 998 model is similar

back off nut approximately five turns. Check adjusting screw for free turning in lever.

4. Using an inch pound torque wrench, tighten band adjusting screw to 72 in. lbs. on all except 904 and 1980–81 998 series transmissions. On 904 and 1980–81 998 series transmissions, tighten adjusting screw to 41 in. lbs.
5. Back off adjusting screw 4 turns on 998 transmission or 7 turns on 904 transmission.
6. Hold adjusting screw and tighten lock nut to 35 ft. lbs., then install oil pan and refill transmission.

GEARSHIFT CONTROL LINKAGE
ADJUST

Place the selector lever in the Park position and place the transmission shift lever in the Park detent. Adjust the shift rod to obtain a "free pin" fit. Check steering column lock for ease of operation. Move selector lever to Neutral position and check safety switch operation.

THROTTLE LINKAGE
ADJUST

1. Disconnect throttle control spring, then use spring to hold transmission throttle control lever forward against stop, **Fig. 2.**
2. Block choke open and set throttle off fast idle.

NOTE: On carburetors equipped with a throttle solenoid, energize solenoid and open throttle part way to allow solenoid to lock and return carburetor to idle.

3. Loosen retaining bolt on throttle control adjusting link. Do not remove spring clip and nylon washer.
4. Pull on end of link to eliminate lash and tighten retaining bolt, **Fig. 3.**
5. Reconnect throttle control rod spring.

EXTENSION HOUSING & PARKING LOCK CONTROL ROD

NOTE: On 1982–85 models, unload both

torsion bars, then remove the left torsion bar and lower one side of the torsion bar crossmember for clearance.

1. Mark parts for reassembly and remove propeller shaft.
2. Remove speedometer pinion and adapter assembly, then drain about two quarts of fluid from transmission.
3. Remove extension housing to crossmember bolts, then raise transmission with jack and remove crossmember.
4. Remove extension housing to transmission bolts. On console shift models, remove torque shaft lower bracket to extension housing bolts.

NOTE: In the following step, the gearshift must be in "low" therefore positioning the parking lock control rod rearward so it can be disengaged or engaged with the parking lock sprag.

5. Remove two screws, plate and gasket from bottom of extension housing mounting pad, then spread snap ring from output shaft bearing, **Fig. 4,** and carefully tap extension housing off output shaft bearing.
6. Slide extension housing off shaft to re-

Fig. 2   Install spring on lever.

Fig. 3   Six cylinder throttle linkage (Typical)

Fig. 4   Removing or installing extension housing snap ring

move parking sprag and spring, then remove snap ring and slide reaction plug and pin assembly out of housing, **Fig. 5.**

7. To replace parking lock control rod, refer to "Valve Body".

OUTPUT SHAFT OIL SEAL

1. Mark propeller shaft to aid in reassembly and remove propeller shaft being careful not to scratch or nick surface on sliding spline yoke.
2. Using a screwdriver and hammer, drive between extension housing and seal and remove seal.
3. Position new seal and drive it into extension housing using tool C-3995 or C-3972.
4. Carefully install yoke into housing, then align marks made at removal and install propeller shaft.

GOVERNOR

1. Remove extension housing, then remove output shaft bearing rear snap ring and remove bearing.
2. Remove snap ring, **Fig. 6,** from weight end of governor valve shaft and remove valve shaft from governor body.
3. Remove large snap ring from weight end of governor housing, and lift out weight assembly.
4. Remove snap ring from inside governor weight and remove inner weight and spring from outer weight.
5. Remove snap ring from behind governor housing, then slide governor housing and parking brake sprag assembly off output shaft. If necessary, separate governor housing from sprag (4 screws).
6. The primary cause of governor operating failure is due to a sticking governor valve or weights. Rough surfaces may be removed with crocus cloth. Thoroughly clean all parts and check for free movement before assembly.
7. Reverse above operations to assemble and install governor.

VALVE BODY

1. Drain transmission and remove oil pan.
2. Loosen clamp bolts and remove throttle and gear selector levers from manual lever, **Fig. 7.**
3. Remove neutral safety switch and oil filter.
4. Place a drain pan under transmission and remove the ten valve body to transmission bolts. Hold valve body in place while removing bolts.
5. Carefully lower valve body while pulling it forward to disengage parking control rod.

NOTE: It may be necessary to rotate output shaft to permit parking control rod to clear sprag.

6. Remove accumulator piston and spring from transmission case. Inspect piston for nicks, scores and wear. Inspect spring for distortion. Inspect rings for freedom in piston grooves and wear or breakage. Replace parts as necessary.

TRANSMISSION
REPLACE

CAUTION: The hood must be open to prevent damage to hood and air cleaner when removing rear crossmember.

1. Disconnect fan shroud. Remove front cover from bell housing.
2. Drain fluid from transmission as described in "Changing Oil". Remove filler tube and starter.

Fig. 5   Parking lock components

Fig. 6   Governor disassembled

3. Mark rear universal joint and yoke for alignment purposes during installation. Then remove propeller shaft.

NOTE: Disconnect catalytic converter, if equipped, and front exhaust pipes for clearance.

4. Disconnect speedometer cable, throttle and shift linkages, neutral safety switch and transmission controlled spark switch wires. Remove transmission oil cooler lines.
5. Mark converter and drive plate for alignment purposes during installation. Remove converter to drive plate bolts.
6. Install a suitable jack under transmission and remove crossmember from side sill and rear support cushion.
7. Remove support cushion and adapter from extension housing.
8. Remove transmission to engine attaching bolts and move transmission an adequate distance to the rear to clear crankshaft.
9. Lower transmission, maintaining pressure against converter, until transmission clears engine.
10. Reverse procedure to install.

Fig. 7 Valve body external parts

TABLE OF CONTENTS

Torqueflite Automatic Transmission

INDEX

IDENTIFICATION

Transmission Identification markings shown in the following application chart are cast in raised letters and numerals on the lower left side of the bell housing.

NOTE: There are sufficient variations within each of the main categories listed below to make it necessary to service them by serial number—a stamped 7-digit number appearing on the oil pan side rail.

	Code
1984–85 V8-318	A-904LA
1981–83 6-225	A-904, A-904 HD①
V8-318 Federal & California	A-904 LA
V8-318 Federal & California	A-727 HD①
1980 6-225	A-904
6-225 Police & Taxi	A-904-HD
V8-318 Aspen, Volare, Diplomat & LeBaron	A-904-LA
V8-318 Exc. Aspen & Volare	A-727

V8-360 Aspen & Volare	A-904-LA
V8-360 Exc. Aspen & Volare	A-727
V8-360 H.P.	A-727

① —HD—Heavy duty.

DESCRIPTION

These transmissions, **Figs. 1 and 2**, combine a torque converter with a fully automatic three speed gear system. The converter housing and transmission case are an integral aluminum casting. The transmission consists of two multiple disc clutches, an overrunning (one-way) clutch, two servos and bands and two planetary gear sets to provide three forward speeds and reverse.

The common sun gear of the planetary gear sets is connected to the front clutch by a driving shell that is splined to the sun gear and to the front clutch retainer.

The hydraulic system consists of a single oil pump and a valve body that contains all the valves except the governor valve.

Venting of the transmission is accomplished by a drilled passage through the upper part of the front pump housing.

The torque converter is attached to the engine crankshaft through a flexible driving plate. The converter is cooled by circulating the transmission fluid through an oil-to-water type cooler located in the radiator lower tank. The converter is a sealed assembly that cannot be disassembled. On Chrysler Corp., the lock-up torque converter is used on all vehicles except 6-225 California, and heavy duty applications.

TROUBLESHOOTING GUIDE

HARSH ENGAGEMENT IN D-1-2-R

1. Engine idle speed too high.

Fig. 1 Series 904 Torqueflite transmission (typical). 998 model is similar

2. Hydraulic pressures too high or too low.
3. Low-reverse band out of adjustment.
4. Accumulator sticking, broken rings or spring.
5. Low-reverse servo, band or linkage malfunction.
6. Worn or faulty front and/or rear clutch.
7. Valve body malfunction or leakage.
8. Throttle linkage sticking or incorrect adjustment.
9. Accumulator broken seal rings, scratched bore, broken or collapsed spring, cracked piston.

DELAYED ENGAGEMENT IN D-1-2-R

1. Low fluid level.
2. Incorrect manual linkage adjustment.
3. Oil filter clogged.
4. Hydraulic pressures too high or low.
5. Valve body malfunction or leakage.
6. Accumulator sticking, broken rings or spring.
7. Clutches or servos sticking or not operating.
8. Faulty front oil pump.

9. Worn or faulty front and/or rear clutch.
10. Worn or broken input shaft and/or reaction shaft support seal rings.
11. Aerated fluid.
12. Incorrect idle adjustment.
13. Incorrect low and reverse band adjustment.

RUNAWAY OR HARSH UPSHIFT AND 3-2 KICKDOWN

1. Low fluid level.
2. Incorrect throttle linkage adjustment.
3. Hydraulic pressures too high or low.
4. Kickdown band out of adjustment.
5. Valve body malfunction or leakage.
6. Governor malfunction.
7. Accumulator sticking, broken rings or spring.
8. Clutches or servos sticking or not operating.
9. Kickdown servo, band or linkage malfunction.
10. Worn or faulty front clutch.
11. Worn or broken input shaft and/or reaction shaft support seal rings.
12. Aerated oil.
13. Clogged oil filter.

NO UPSHIFT

1. Low fluid level.
2. Incorrect throttle linkage adjustment.
3. Kickdown band out of adjustment.
4. Hydraulic pressures too high or low.
5. Governor sticking.
6. Valve body malfunction or leakage.
7. Accumulator sticking, broken rings or spring.
8. Clutches or servos sticking or not operating.
9. Faulty oil pump.
10. Kickdown servo, band or linkage malfunction.
11. Worn or faulty front clutch.
12. Worn or broken input shaft and/or reaction shaft support seal rings.
13. Incorrect gearshift linkage adjustment.
14. Governor support seal rings broken or worn.

DELAYED UPSHIFT

1. Incorrect throttle linkage adjustment.
2. Kickdown band out of adjustment.
3. Governor support seal rings broken or worn.

Fig. 2   Series 727 Torqueflite transmission (typical)

4. Worn or broken reaction shaft support seal rings.
5. Governor malfunction.
6. Kickdown servo band or linkage malfunction.
7. Worn or faulty front clutch.

NO KICKDOWN OR NORMAL DOWNSHIFT

1. Incorrect throttle linkage adjustment.
2. Incorrect gearshift linkage adjustment.
3. Kickdown band out of adjustment.
4. Hydraulic pressure too high or low.
5. Governor sticking.
6. Valve body malfunction or leakage.
7. Accumulator sticking, broken rings or spring.

8. Clutches or servos sticking or not operating.
9. Kickdown servo, band or linkage malfunction.
10. Overrunning clutch not holding.
11. Low fluid level.

ERRATIC SHIFTS

1. Low fluid level.
2. Aerated fluid.
3. Incorrect throttle linkage adjustment.
4. Incorrect gearshift control linkage adjustment.

5. Hydraulic pressures too high or low.
6. Governor sticking.
7. Oil filter clogged.
8. Valve body malfunction or leakage.
9. Clutches or servos sticking or not operating.
10. Faulty oil pump.
11. Worn or broken input shaft and/or reaction shaft support rings.
12. Governor support seal rings broken or worn.
13. Kickdown servo band or linkage malfunction.
14. Worn or faulty front clutch.

Fig. 3   Console gearshift linkage.

Fig. 4   Column gearshift linkage. 1980–81 except Aspen, Diplomat, LeBaron & Volare, 1980–81 Cordoba & Mirada & 1981 Imperial

Fig. 6 Throttle linkage adjustment.

Fig. 5 Column gearshift linkage. 1980 Aspen, & Volare, 1980–81 Cordoba, Diplomat, LeBaron & Mirada, 1981 Imperial & all 1982–85 models

SLIPS IN FORWARD DRIVE POSITIONS

1. Low oil level.
2. Aerated fluid.
3. Incorrect throttle linkage adjustment.
4. Incorrect gearshift control linkage adjustment.
5. Hydraulic pressures too low.
6. Valve body malfunction or leakage.
7. Accumulator sticking, broken rings or springs.
8. Clutches or servos sticking or not operating.
9. Worn or faulty front and/or rear clutch.
10. Overrunning clutch not holding.
11. Worn or broken input shaft and/or reaction shaft support seal rings.
12. Clogged oil filter.
13. Faulty oil pump.
14. Overrunning clutch worn, broken or seized.
15. Incorrect kickdown band adjustment.

SLIPS IN REVERSE ONLY

1. Low fluid level.
2. Aerated fluid.
3. Incorrect gearshift control linkage adjustment.
4. Hydraulic pressures too high or low.
5. Low-reverse band out of adjustment.
6. Valve body malfunction or leakage.
7. Front clutch or rear servo sticking or not operating.
8. Low-reverse servo, band or linkage malfunction.
9. Faulty oil pump.
10. Worn or broken reaction shaft support seal rings.
11. Worn or faulty front clutch.

SLIPS IN ALL POSITIONS

1. Low fluid level.
2. Hydraulic pressures too low.
3. Valve body malfunction or leakage.
4. Faulty oil pump.
5. Clutches or servos sticking or not operating.
6. Worn or broken input shaft and/or reaction shaft support seal rings.
7. Oil filter clogged.
8. Aerated oil.

NO DRIVE IN ANY POSITION

1. Low fluid level.
2. Hydraulic pressures too low.
3. Oil filter clogged.
4. Valve body malfunction or leakage.
5. Faulty oil pump.
6. Clutches or servos sticking or not operating.
7. Planetary gear sets broken or seized.
8. Torque converter failure.
9. Incorrect gearshift linkage adjustment.

NO DRIVE IN FORWARD DRIVE POSITIONS

1. Hydraulic pressures too low.
2. Valve body malfunction or leakage.
3. Accumulator sticking, broken rings or spring.
4. Clutches or servos sticking or not operating.
5. Worn or faulty rear clutch.
6. Overrunning clutch not holding.
7. Worn or broken input shaft and/or reaction shaft support seal rings.
8. Low fluid level.
9. Planetary gear sets broken or seized.
10. Overrunning clutch worn, broken or seized.
11. Incorrect gearshift linkage adjustment.

Fig. 7 Removing or installing extension housing snap ring

Fig. 8 Parking lock components

Fig. 9 Governor disassembled

Fig. 10 Valve body external parts

NO DRIVE IN REVERSE

1. Incorrect gearshift control linkage adjustment.
2. Hydraulic pressures too low.
3. Low-reverse band out of adjustment.
4. Valve body malfunction or leakage.
5. Front clutch or rear servo sticking or not operating.
6. Low-reverse servo, band or linkage malfunction.
7. Worn or faulty front and/or rear clutch.
8. Worn or broken reaction shaft support seal rings.
9. Planetary gear sets broken or seized.

DRIVES IN NEUTRAL

1. Incorrect gearshift control linkage adjustment.
2. Valve body malfunction or leakage.
3. Rear clutch worn, faulty, dragging or inoperative.
4. Insufficient clutch plate clearance.

DRAGS OR LOCKS

1. Kickdown band out of adjustment.
2. Low-reverse band out of adjustment.
3. Kickdown and/or low-reverse servo, band or linkage malfunction.
4. Front and/or rear clutch faulty.
5. Planetary gear sets broken or seized.
6. Overrunning clutch worn, broken or seized.
7. Hydraulic pressure too low.
8. Valve body: nicks, scratches and burrs on valve and plugs. Rounded edges on valve lands. Scratches on bores, collapsed springs. Nicked or warped mating surfaces.
9. Accumulator, broken seal rings, scratched bore, broken or collapsed spring, cracked piston.

GRATING, SCRAPING OR GROWLING NOISE

1. Kickdown band out of adjustment.
2. Low-reverse band out of adjustment.
3. Output shaft bearing and/or bushing damaged.
4. Governor support binding or broken seal rings.
5. Oil pump scored or binding.
6. Front and/or rear clutch faulty.

7. Planetary gear sets broken or seized.
8. Overrunning clutch worn, broken or seized.
9. Low fluid level.
10. Clogged oil filter.

BUZZING NOISE

1. Low fluid level.
2. Pump sucking air.
3. Valve body malfunction.
4. Overrunning clutch inner race damaged.
5. Aerated oil.
6. Governor valve: burrs, nicks, scores or binding on weights, shaft and valve.
7. Collapsed or distorted springs or distorted snap ring. Cracked or warped body. Dirty filter.

HARD TO FILL, OIL FLOWS OUT FILLER TUBE

1. High fluid level.
2. Breather clogged.
3. Oil filter clogged.
4. Aerated fluid.
5. Clogged lines to cooler.

TRANSMISSION OVERHEATS

1. Low fluid level.
2. Kickdown band adjustment too tight.
3. Low-reverse band adjustment too tight.
4. Faulty cooling system.
5. Cracked or restricted oil cooler line or fitting.
6. Faulty oil pump.
7. Insufficient clutch plate clearance in front and/or rear clutches.
8. Engine idle too low.
9. Hydraulic pressures too low.
10. Incorrect gearshift linkage adjustment.
11. Kickdown band adjustment too tight.
12. Clogged oil filter.
13. Valve body: Nicks, scratches and burrs on valve and plugs. Rounded edges on tralve lands. Scratches on bores, collapsed springs. Nicked or warped mating surfaces.

STARTER WILL NOT ENERGIZE IN NEUTRAL OR PARK

1. Incorrect gearshift control linkage adjustment.
2. Faulty or incorrectly adjusted neutral starting switch.
3. Broken lead to neutral switch.

SLUGGISH ACCELERATION, EXCESSIVE THROTTLE NEEDED TO MAINTAIN SPEED

1. Low fluid level.
2. Sticking or incorrect throttle linkage adjustment.
3. Faulty torque converter or clutches.
4. Incorrect hydraulic pressures.

NO LOCK-UP

1. Faulty input shaft, seal ring, locking clutch or torque converter.
2. Sticking failsafe switch, lock-up valve or switch valve.
3. Faulty oil pump.

WILL NOT UNLOCK

1. Sticking failsafe valve, lock-up valve, switch valve or governor valve.
2. Valve body malfunctioning.

REMAINS LOCKED-UP AT TOO LOW A SPEED IN DRIVE

1. Sticking failsafe valve, lock-up valve or governor valve.

LOCKS UP OR DRAGS IN LOW OR SECOND

1. Sticking failsafe valve.
2. Faulty oil pump.

ENGINE STALLS OR IS SLUGGISH IN REVERSE

1. Plugged cooler lines or fittings.
2. Valve body malfunctioning or, faulty oil pump.

LOUD CHATTER WHILE LOCKING-UP WHEN COLD

1. Leaking turbine hub seal.
2. Faulty torque converter.

VIBRATIONS AFTER LOCK-UP

1. Throttle linkage misadjusted, or sticking governor valve.
2. Engine requires tune-up, or otherwise not performing properly.
3. Exhaust system contacting vehicle.

VIBRATION WHEN VEHICLE IS ACCELERATED IN NEUTRAL

1. Unbalanced torque converter.

OVERHEATING (OIL BLOWING OUT OF DIPSTICK OR PUMP SEAL)

1. Sticking switch valve.
2. Plugged cooler lines or fittings.

MAINTENANCE
CHECKING OIL LEVEL

To check the oil level, apply the parking brake and operate the engine at idle speed with the transmission in Neutral position.

CHANGING OIL

Fluid and filter changes or band adjustments are not required for average passenger car use. Severe usage such as police, taxi, trailer towing or prolonged operation in city traffic, requires that fluid and filter be changed and bands adjusted every 15,000 miles.

Whenever the factory fill fluid is changed, only fluids of the type labeled DEXRON should be used.

1. Remove drain plug (if equipped) from transmission oil pan and drain oil.

NOTE: If the oil pan does not have a drain plug, loosen pan bolts and tap pan with a soft mallet to break it loose, permitting fluid to drain.

2. Remove transmission oil pan, replace filter or clean intake screen and pan, adjust bands and reinstall.
3. Add 4 quarts of automatic transmission fluid through filler tube.
4. Start engine.
5. Allow engine to idle for about two minutes. With parking brake applied, move selector lever momentarily to each position and place in neutral.

BANDS
ADJUST

KICKDOWN BAND

The kickdown band adjusting screw is located on the left side of the transmission case near the throttle lever shaft.

1. Loosen lock nut and back off approximately five turns. Check adjusting screw for free turning in transmission case.
2. Using an inch-pound torque wrench, tighten the band adjusting screw to a reading of 72 inch lbs.
3. Back off adjusting screw 2½ turns.
4. Hold adjusting screw in this position and tighten locknut.

LOW AND REVERSE BAND

1. Raise vehicle, drain transmission and remove oil pan.
2. Inspect fluid for friction material or metal particles which indicate damaged or worn parts.
3. Loosen adjusting screw lock nut and back off nut approximately five turns. Check adjusting screw for free turning in lever.
4. Using an inch pound torque wrench, tighten band adjusting screw to 72 in. lbs. on all except 904 and 1980–81 998 series transmissions. On 904 and 1980–81 998 series transmissions, tighten adjusting screw to 41 in. lbs.
5. Back off adjusting screw the number of turns indicated:
   A-904 .... 7 turns
   A-904-LA .... 4 turns
   A-727 .... 2 turns
6. Hold adjusting screw and tighten lock nut to 35 ft. lbs., then install oil pan and refill transmission.

GEARSHIFT CONTROL LINKAGE
ADJUST

1. Referring to **Figs. 3 to 5,** place selector lever in Park and loosen control rod swivel clamp screw a few turns.
2. Move transmission control lever all the way to rear (in Park detent).
3. With both levers still in Park position, tighten swivel clamp screw securely. On all 1981–85 models, torque swivel clamp screw to 90 inch lbs.

THROTTLE LINKAGE
ADJUST

NOTE: Before proceeding with the adjustment, disconnect the choke rod at the carburetor or block the choke valve wide open. Open the throttle slightly to release the fast idle cam, then return carburetor to the hot idle position.

Hold or fasten the transmission lever firmly forward against the stop while performing the adjustment to insure a proper adjustment.

1. Support vehicle on hoist and loosen swivel lock screw, **Fig. 6.**

NOTE: To insure correct adjustment, swivel must be free to slide along flat end of throttle rod so that preload spring action is not restricted. If necessary, disassemble and clean or repair parts to assure free action.

2. Hold transmission lever firmly forward against its internal stop and tighten swivel lock screw to 100 inch lbs.

NOTE: Adjustment is now finished. Linkage backlash was automatically removed by the preload spring.

3. Lower vehicle and test linkage operation by moving throttle rod rearward and slowly releasing it making certain that it returns fully.

EXTENSION HOUSING & PARKING LOCK CONTROL ROD

NOTE: On models except Aspen, Volare, Diplomat, LeBaron and all 1982–85 models, unload both torsion bars, then remove the left torsion bar and lower one side of the torsion bar crossmember for clearance.

1. Mark parts for reassembly and remove propeller shaft.
2. Remove speedometer pinion and adapter assembly, then drain about two quarts of fluid from transmission.
3. Remove extension housing to crossmember bolts, then raise transmission with jack and remove crossmember.
4. Remove extension housing to transmission bolts. On console shift models, remove torque shaft lower bracket to extension housing bolts.

NOTE: In the following step, the gearshift must be in "low" therefore positioning the parking lock control rod rearward so it can be disengaged or engaged with the parking lock sprag.

5. Remove two screws, plate and gasket from bottom of extension housing mounting pad, then spread snap ring from output shaft bearing, **Fig. 7,** and carefully tap extension housing off output shaft bearing.
6. Slide extension housing off shaft to remove parking sprag and spring, then remove snap ring and slide reaction plug and pin assembly out of housing, **Fig. 8.**
7. To replace parking lock control rod, refer to "Valve Body".

OUTPUT SHAFT OIL SEAL

1. Mark propeller shaft to aid in reassembly and remove propeller shaft being careful not to scratch or nick surface on sliding spline yoke.
2. Using a screwdriver and hammer, drive between extension housing and seal and remove seal.
3. Position new seal and drive it into extension housing using tool C-3995 or C-3972.
4. Carefully install yoke into housing, then align marks made at removal and install propeller shaft.

GOVERNOR

1. Remove extension housing, then remove output shaft bearing rear snap ring and remove bearing. On 727 Series, remove remaining snap ring from shaft.
2. Remove snap ring, **Fig. 9,** from weight end of governor valve shaft and remove valve shaft from governor body.
3. Remove large snap ring from weight end of governor housing, and lift out weight assembly.
4. Remove snap ring from inside governor weight and remove inner weight and spring from outer weight.
5. Remove snap ring from behind governor housing, then slide governor housing and parking brake sprag assembly off output shaft. If necessary, separate governor housing from sprag (4 screws).
6. The primary cause of governor operating failure is due to a sticking governor valve or weights. Rough surfaces may be removed with crocus cloth. Thoroughly clean all parts and check for free movement before assembly.
7. Reverse above operations to assemble and install governor.

VALVE BODY

1. Drain transmission and remove oil pan.
2. Loosen clamp bolts and remove throttle and gear selector levers from manual lever, **Fig. 10.**
3. Remove neutral safety switch and oil filter.
4. Place a drain pan under transmission and remove the ten valve body to transmission bolts. Hold valve body in place while removing bolts.
5. Carefully lower valve body while pulling it forward to disengage parking control rod.

NOTE: It may be necessary to rotate output shaft to permit parking control rod to clear sprag.

6. Remove accumulator piston and spring from transmission case. Inspect piston for nicks, scores and wear. Inspect spring for distortion. Inspect rings for freedom in piston grooves and wear or breakage. Replace parts as necessary.

TRANSMISSION
REPLACE

CAUTION: The transmission and converter must be removed as an assembly, otherwise, the converter drive plate, front pump bushing and oil seal will be damaged. The drive plate will not support the load; therefore, none of the weight of the transmission should be allowed to rest on the plate during removal.

1. Disconnect battery ground cable.

NOTE: Some models will require that the exhaust system be lowered for clearance.

2. Remove engine to transmission struts (if equipped), then disconnect transmission cooler lines and remove starter motor, cooler line bracket and converter access cover.
3. Drain fluid from transmission as described in "Changing Oil".
4. Mark converter and drive plate to aid in reassembly. The crankshaft flange bolt circle, inner and outer circle of holes in the drive plate, and the four tapped holes in front face of converter all have one hole offset so these parts will be installed in the original position. This maintains balance of the engine and converter.
5. Remove converter to drive plate bolts. Rotate engine clockwise using socket wrench to gain access to all bolts.

CAUTION: Do not rotate converter or drive plate by prying with a screwdriver or similar tool as the drive plate might become distorted. Also, the starter should never be engaged if the drive plate is not attached to the converter with at least one bolt or if the transmission case-to-engine bolts have been loosened.

6. Mark driveshaft to aid in reassembly and remove driveshaft.
7. Disconnect neutral and back-up light switch and gearshift and torque shaft assembly from transmission.

NOTE: When disassembling linkage rods from levers which use plastic grommets as retainers, the grommets should be replaced with new ones.

8. Disconnect throttle rod from lever at left side of transmission, then remove linkage bellcrank from transmission, if so equipped.
9. Install a suitable fixture or jack that will support engine, then raise transmission slightly with a jack to relieve the load on the supports, and remove the crossmember.

NOTE: Some models have a torsion bar anchor crossmember that remains in place and requires a careful downward tilt on front of transmission as it is being lowered. If these models have a vibration dampening weight bolted to rear of extension housing, it must be removed.

10. Remove transmission to engine bolts and carefully work transmission and converter assembly rearward off engine block dowels and disengage converter hub from end of crankshaft. Using a small C-clamp on edge of bell housing, hold converter in place during transmission removal.
11. Remove transmission assembly from under vehicle.
12. Reverse procedure to install.

Torqueflite Automatic Transaxle

INDEX

IDENTIFICATION

A seven digit part number is stamped on a pad located at the rear of the transaxle on the transmission oil pan flange. This number must be referred to when servicing the transmission due to differences in some internal components.

CHRYSLER CORP. FRONT WHEEL DRIVE

	Code
1980 4-105	A-404
1981–82 4-105, 4-135 & 4-156	A-404, A-413, & A-470
1983 4-97, 4-105, 4-135 & 4-156	A-404, A-413, A-415 & A-470
1984–85 4-97, 4-135 & 4-156	A-413, A-415 & A-470

DESCRIPTION

These transaxles combine a torque converter, automatic 3 speed transmission, final drive gearing and differential combined into one unit. The torque converter, transaxle and differential assemblies are housed in an integral aluminum die cast housing, **Fig. 1.**

NOTE: The differential oil sump is separate from the transaxle pump. Ensure differential oil lever is ⅛ to ⅜ inch below the oil filler hole on the differential cover.

The torque converter is connected to the crankshaft through a flexible drive plate. Converter cooling is accomplished by an oil to water type cooler, located in the radiator side tank. The torque converter cannot be disassembled.

The transaxle consists of two multiple disc clutches, an overrunning clutch, two servos, a hydraulic accumulator, two bands and two planetary gear assemblies to provide three forward and one reverse gear. The sun gear is connected to the front clutch retainer. The hydraulic system consists of an oil pump, and a single valve body which contains all of the valves except the governor valves. Output torque from the main drive gears is transferred through helical gears to the transfer shaft. An integral ring gear on the transfer shaft drives the differential ring gear.

TROUBLESHOOTING GUIDE

HARSH ENGAGEMENT FROM N TO D OR R

1. High idle speed.
2. Defective or leaking valve body.
3. High hydraulic pressure.
4. Worn or damaged rear clutch.

DELAYED ENGAGEMENT FROM N TO D OR R

1. Low hydraulic pressure.
2. Defective or leaking valve body.
3. Low-reverse servo, band or linkage malfunction.
4. Low fluid level.
5. Incorrect gearshift linkage adjustment.
6. Clogged transmission oil filter.
7. Faulty oil pump.
8. Worn or damaged input shaft seal rings.
9. Aerated fluid.
10. Low idle speed.
11. Worn or damaged reaction shaft support seal rings.
12. Worn or defective front clutch.
13. Worn or defective rear clutch.

RUNAWAY UPSHIFTS

1. Low hydraulic pressure.
2. Defective or leaking valve body.
3. Low fluid level.
4. Clogged transmission oil filter.
5. Aerated fluid.
6. Incorrect throttle linkage adjustment.
7. Worn or damaged reaction shaft support seal rings.

8. Kickdown servo, band or linkage malfunction.
9. Worn or faulty front clutch.

NO UPSHIFT

1. Low hydraulic pressure.
2. Defective or leaking valve body.
3. Low fluid level.
4. Incorrect gearshift linkage adjustment.
5. Incorrect throttle linkage adjustment.
6. Worn or damaged governor support seal rings.
8. Faulty governor.
9. Kickdown servo, band or linkage malfunction.
10. Worn or faulty front clutch.

3-2 KICKDOWN RUNAWAY

1. Low hydraulic pressure.
2. Defective or leaking valve body.
3. Low fluid level.
4. Aerated fluid.
5. Incorrect throttle linkage adjustment.
6. Kickdown band adjustment.
7. Worn or damaged reaction shaft support seal rings.
8. Kickdown servo, band or linkage malfunction.
9. Worn or faulty from clutch.

NO KICKDOWN OR NORMAL DOWNSHIFT

1. Defective or leaking valve body.
2. Incorrect throttle linkage adjustment.
3. Faulty governor.
4. Kickdown servo, band or linkage malfunction.

ERRATIC SHIFTS

1. Low hydraulic pressure.
2. Defective or leaking valve body.
3. Low fluid level.
4. Incorrect gearshift linkage adjustment.
5. Clogged transmission oil filter.
6. Faulty oil pump.
7. Aerated fluid.
8. Incorrect throttle linkage adjustment.

Fig. 1 Sectional view of automatic transaxle. Typical

Fig. 2 Kickdown band adjusting screw location

Fig. 3 Loosening transfer shaft gear retaining nut

Fig. 4 Removing transfer shaft gear

9. Worn or damaged governor support seal rings.
10. Worn or damaged reaction shaft support seal rings.
11. Faulty governor.
12. Kickdown servo, band or linkage malfunction.
13. Worn or faulty front clutch.

SLIPS IN 1, 2 OR D

1. Low hydraulic pressure.
2. Defective or leaking valve body.
3. Low fluid level.
4. Incorrect gearshift linkage adjustment.
5. Clogged transmission oil filter.
6. Faulty oil pump.
7. Worn or damaged input shaft seal rings.
8. Aerated fluid.
9. Incorrect throttle linkage adjustment.
10. Overrunning clutch not holding.
11. Worn or faulty rear clutch.
12. Overrunning clutch worn damaged or seized.

SLIPS IN R ONLY

1. Low hydraulic pressure.
1. Low-reverse band adjustment.
3. Defective or leaking valve body.
4. Low-reverse servo, band or linkage malfunction.
5. Low fluid level.
6. Incorrect gearshift linkage adjustment.
7. Faulty oil pump.
8. Aerated fluid.
9. Worn or damaged reaction shaft seal rings.
10. Worn or faulty front clutch.

SLIPS IN ALL RANGES

1. Low hydraulic pressure.
2. Defective or leaking valve body.
3. Low fluid level.
4. Clogged transmission oil filter.
5. Faulty oil pump.
6. Worn or damaged input shaft seal rings.
7. Aerated fluid.

NO DRIVE IN ANY RANGE

1. Low hydraulic pressure.
2. Defective or leaking valve body.
3. Low fluid level.
4. Clogged transmission oil filter.

5. Faulty oil pump.
6. Planetary gear sets damaged or seized.

NO DRIVE IN 1, 2 OR D

1. Low hydraulic pressure.
2. Defective or leaking valve body.
3. Low fluid level.
4. Worn or damaged input shaft seal rings.
5. Overrunning clutch not holding.
6. Worn or faulty rear clutch.
7. Planetary gear sets damaged or seized.
8. Overrunning clutch worn, damaged or seized.

NO DRIVE IN R

1. Low hydraulic pressure.
2. Low-reverse band adjustment.
3. Defective or leaking valve body.
4. Low-reverse servo, band or linkage malfunction.
5. Incorrect gearshift linkage adjustment.
6. Worn or damaged reaction shaft support seal rings.
7. Worn or faulty front clutch.
8. Worn or faulty rear clutch.
9. Planetary gear sets damaged or seized.

DRIVE IN NEUTRAL

1. Defective or leaking valve body.
2. Incorrect gearshift linkage adjustment.
3. Insufficient clutch plate clearance.
4. Worn or faulty rear clutch.
5. Rear clutch dragging.

DRAGS OR LOCKS

1. Low-reverse band adjustment.
2. Kickdown band adjustment.
3. Planetary gear sets damaged or seized.
4. Overrunning clutch worn, damaged or seized.

HARD TO FILL (OIL BLOWS OUT FILLER TUBE)

1. Clogged transmission oil filter.
2. Aerated fluid.
3. High fluid level.
4. Breather clogged.

TRANSMISSION OVERHEATS

1. Stuck switch valve.
2. High idle speed.
3. Low hydraulic pressure.
4. Low fluid level.
5. Incorrect gearshift adjustment.
6. Faulty oil pump.
7. Kickdown band adjustment too tight.
8. Faulty cooling system.
9. Insufficient clutch plate clearance.

HARSH UPSHIFTS

1. Low hydraulic pressure.
2. Incorrect throttle linkage adjustment.
3. Kickdown band adjustment.
4. High hydraulic pressure.

DELAYED UPSHIFT

1. Incorrect throttle linkage adjustment.
2. Kickdown band adjustment.
3. Worn or damaged governor support seal rings.
4. Worn or damaged reaction shaft support seal rings.
5. Faulty governor.
6. Kickdown servo, band or linkage malfunction.
7. Worn or faulty front clutch.

GRATING, SCRAPING OR GROWLING NOISE

1. Low-reverse band out of adjustment.
2. Kickdown band adjustment.
3. Output shaft bearing or bushing damaged.
4. Planetary gear sets damaged or seized.
5. Overrunning clutch worn, damaged or seized.

BUZZING NOISE

1. Defective or leaking valve body.
2. Low fluid level.
3. Aerated fluid.
4. Overrunning clutch inner race damaged.

MAINTENANCE

ADDING OIL

To check fluid level, apply the parking brake and operate engine at idle speed

Fig. 5 Removing governor assembly

Fig. 6 Installing transfer shaft oil seal

Fig. 7 Prying drive shaft out of side gear

with transmission in Neutral or Park position. Add fluid as necessary.

CHANGING OIL

Fluid and filter changes are not required for average passenger car use. Severe usage such as commercial type usage or prolonged operation in city traffic, requires that fluid be changed and bands adjusted every 15,000 miles.

Whenever factory fill fluid is changed, only fluid of the type labeled Dexron should be used.

1. Raise vehicle and place a suitable drain pan under transmission oil pan.
2. Loosen transmission oil pan attaching bolts and allow fluid to drain, then remove oil pan.
3. Replace oil filter and adjust bands if necessary, then install oil pan and gasket.
4. Add four quarts of approved automatic transmission fluid through the filler tube.
5. Start engine and allow to idle for at least two minutes, then with parking brake applied move selector lever momentarily to each position. Place selector lever in Neutral or Park and check fluid level. Add fluid to bring level to Add mark.
6. Recheck fluid level after transmission has reached operating temperature. The level should be between Add and Full marks.

BANDS
ADJUST

KICKDOWN BAND

1. Loosen lock nut and back off nut approximately five turns, **Fig. 2**.
2. Using tool No. C-3380-A and adapter C-3705, tighten band adjusting screw to 47 to 50 inch lbs. If adapter C-3705 is not used, tighten adjusting screw to 72 inch lbs.
3. Back off adjusting screw 2½ turns on all 1980 models and 1981 404 models, and 1984–85 A-413 & A-470 models, 3 turns on 1981 413 and 470 models, 1982–83 404 models and 1983–84 415 models, or 2¾ turns on 1982–83 413 and 470 models. Torque lock nut to 35 ft. lbs. while preventing adjusting screw from turning.

LOW REVERSE BAND, ADJUST

The low reverse band is adjustable on 413 and 470 models only.
1. Loosen locknut and back off nut approximately five turns.
2. Torque adjusting nut to 41 inch lbs.
3. Back off adjusting nut 3½ turns, then torque locknut to 20 ft. lbs. on 1980–82 models, or 10 ft. lbs. on 1983–85 models.

GEARSHIFT LINKAGE
ADJUST

1. Place selector lever in Park position.
2. Raise vehicle, then loosen swivel lock bolt.
3. Move transmission lever to PARK position.
4. Torque swivel lock bolt to 90 inch lbs., then check adjustment.

NOTE: On 1981–84 models with column shift, apply a 10 pound forward load on the cable housing insulator while torquing swivel lock bolt. On models with console shift, apply a minimum forward load of 10 pounds on the console shift lever knob while torquing swivel lock bolt. On some models, it may be necessary to apply the forward load to the transaxle lever while tightening lock bolt.

THROTTLE CABLE
ADJUST

1. Perform adjustment with engine at operating temperature, otherwise ensure carburetor is not on fast idle cam by disconnecting choke.
2. Loosen adjusting bracket lock screw.
3. Hold transmission lever rearward against internal stop and tighten adjusting bracket lock screw to 105 inch lbs.

VALVE BODY
REPLACE

1. Loosen transmission oil pan attaching bolts and allow transmission to drain, then remove oil pan.
2. Remove oil filter attaching screws and oil filter.
3. Using a screwdriver, remove E-clip, then remove parking rod.
4. Remove seven valve body attaching bolts, then remove valve body and governor oil tubes.

GOVERNOR & TRANSFER SHAFT OIL SEAL
REPLACE

1. Remove rear cover attaching bolts and rear cover.
2. Using tool No. L-4434, remove transfer shaft gear retaining nut, **Fig. 3**.
3. Using tool No. L-4407, remove transfer shaft gear and shim, **Fig. 4**.
4. Remove governor support retainer, then remove low-reverse band anchor pin.
5. Remove governor assembly, **Fig. 5**.
6. Remove transfer shaft retainer snap ring, then using tool No. L-4512 and a suitable puller, remove transfer shaft and retainer assembly.
7. Remove transfer shaft retainer from shaft.
8. Using a screwdriver, remove oil seal from transfer shaft retainer.
9. Using tool No. L-4520 and C-4171, tap oil seal into shaft retainer, **Fig. 6**.
10. Reverse procedure to install. Torque transfer shaft gear retaining nut to 200 ft. lbs.

TRANSMISSION
REPLACE

NOTE: The transaxle and converter must be removed as an assembly.

1. Disconnect battery cables.
2. Disconnect transaxle shift control and throttle cables from transaxle and position aside.
3. Remove upper cooler tube, then support engine with suitable engine lifting equipment.

4. Remove three upper bell housing bolts.
5. Remove wheel hub nut and left splash shield.
6. Drain fluid from differential, then remove cover.
7. Remove speedometer adapter, cable and pinion as an assembly.
8. Remove sway bar and both lower ball joint to steering knuckle bolts.
9. Pry lower ball joint from steering knuckle, then remove drive shaft from hub.
10. Rotate both drive shafts until circlip ends are visible in the opening, then while squeezing circlip ends together, remove drive shaft from side gear, **Fig. 7.**
11. Mark position of torque converter to drive plate and remove torque converter retaining bolts.
12. Remove access plug in right splash shield to rotate engine.
13. Remove lower cooler tube and neutral/park safety switch wire.
14. Remove engine mount bracket from front crossmember.
15. Remove front engine mount insulator through bolt and bell housing bolts.
16. Support transaxle with a suitable jack.
17. Remove left engine mount and long through bolt.
18. Remove lower bell housing bolts.
19. Move transaxle away from engine and lower from vehicle.

NOTE: It may be necessary to pry transaxle away from vehicle between the extension housing and engine block for proper clearance.

20. Reverse procedure to install. Use RTV sealant when installing differential cover.

Ford Automatic Overdrive Transmission

INDEX

TRANSMISSION IDENTIFICATION

Car Model	Trans. Code	Engine Model
1980		
Cougar	PKA-Y, 1, 2, 3	V8-302
Ford	PKA-E, 1, 2, 3	V8-302
	PKA-C, 1, 2, 3	V8-351
	PKA-R, 1, 2, 3	V8-351
	PKA-T, 1, 2, 3	V8-351
	PKA-Z, 1, 2, 3	V8-351
Lincoln	PKA-M, 1, 2, 3	V8-302
	PKA-D, 1, 2, 3	V8-351
	PKA-U, 1, 2, 3	V8-351
Mercury	PKA-W, 1, 2, 3	V8-302
	PKA-C, 1, 2, 3	V8-351
	PKA-R, 1, 2, 3	V8-351
	PKA-T, 1, 2, 3	V8-351
	PKA-Z, 1, 2, 3	V8-351
Mark VI	PKA-M, 1, 2, 3	V8-302
	PKA-D, 1, 2, 3	V8-351
	PKA-U, 1, 2, 3	V8-351
Thunderbird	PKA-Y, 1, 2, 3	V8-302
1981		
Cougar & XR7	PKA-AH	V8-255
	PKA-Y8	V8-302
Ford & Mercury	PKA-AF, AT	V8-255
	RPA-E6, AG, AL	V8-302
	PKA-C6, C8, R8, T8, Z8, AR, AS	V8-351

Car Model	Trans. Code	Engine Model
Lincoln	PKA-M8	V8-302
Mark VI	PKA-M8	V8-302
Thunderbird	PKA-AH	V8-255
	PKA-Y8	V8-302
1982		
Continental	PKA-BF, 1, 2	V6-232
	PKA-BD, 1, 2	V8-302
Cougar & XR7	PKA-BH, 1	V6-232
	PKA-AH5, 6	V8-255
Ford	PKA-AT5	V8-255
	PKA-AG5, AU5	V8-302
	PKA-AY, BB	V8-302
	PKA-Cl3, AS5	V8-351
Mark VI	PKA-M13, BC	V8-302
Mercury	PKA-AF5, 6	V8-255
	PKA-AT5, 6	V8-255
	PKA-AG	V8-302
	PKA-AG5, 6	V8-302
	PKA-AU5, 6	V8-302
	PKA-AY1	V8-302
	PKA-BB, 1	V8-302
	PKA-C13, 14	V8-351
	PKA-AS5, 6	V8-351
Thunderbird	PKA-BH	V6-232
	PKA-AH5	V8-255
Town Car	PKA-M13, 14, 15	V8-302
	PKA-BC, 1, 2	V8-302

Car Model	Trans. Code	Engine Model
1983		
Continental	PKA-BD12	V8-302
Cougar/ Thunderbird	PKA-BR, BT	V6-232
	PKA-K	V8-302
Ford/Mercury	PKA-AU17	V8-302
	PKA-AG17	V8-302
	PKA-AY12	V8-302
	PKA-BB12	V8-302
	PKA-C25	V8-351
	PKA-AS17	V8-351
LTD/Marquis	PKA-BR, BT	V6-232
Mark VI	PKA-M25	V8-302
	PKA-BC5	V8-302
1984		
Capri	PKA-BZ1, 2	V6-232
	PKA-CD1, 2	V6-232
	PKA-BW1	V8-302
Continental	PKA-BD18, 19, 20	V8-302
Cougar	PKA-BT6, 7, 8	V6-232
Cougar	PKA-CB6, 7, 8	V6-232
	PKA-K6, 7, 8	V8-302
Ford	PKA-AG23, 24, 25, 26, 27	V8-302
	PKA-AU23, 24, 25, 26, 27	V8-302
	PKA-AY18, 19, 20, 21, 22	V8-302
	PKA-BB18, 19, 20, 21, 22	V8-302
LTD	PKA-BT6, 7, 8, 9, 10	V6-232
	PKA-CB6, 7, 8, 9, 10	V6-232
Mark VII	PKA-BV1, 2	V8-302
Marquis	PKA-BT6, 7, 8	V6-232
	PKA-CB6, 7, 8	V6-232
Mercury	PKA-AG23, 24, 25	V8-302
	PKA-AU23, 24, 25	V8-302
	PKA-AY18, 19, 20	V8-302
	PKA-BB18, 19, 20	V8-302
Mustang	PKA-BZ1, 2, 3, 4	V6-232
	PKA-CD1, 2, 3, 4	V6-232
	PKA-BW1, 2, 3	V8-302

Car Model	Trans. Code	Engine Model
Thunderbird	PKA-BT6, 7, 8, 9, 10	V6-232
	PKA-CB6, 7, 8, 9, 10	V6-232
	PKA-K6, 7, 8, 9, 10	V8-302
Town Car	PKA-BC12, 13, 14	V8-302
	PKA-M31, 32, 33	V8-302
1985		
Capri	PKA-CD7	V6-232
	PKA-BW17	V8-302
Cougar	PKA-CB13	V6-232
	PKA-K13	V8-302
	PKA-CJ	V8-302
Ford	PKA-AG30	V8-302
	PKA-AU30	V8-302
	PKA-AY25	V8-302
	PKA-BB25	V8-302
	PKA-C38	V8-351
	PKA-AS30	V8-351
LTD	PKA-CB13	V6-232
	PKA-BW7	V8-302
	PKA-CE6	V8-302
	PKA-CF6	V8-302
Marquis	PKA-CB13	V6-232
	PKA-BW7	V8-302
	PKA-CE6	V8-302
	PKA-CF6	V8-302
Mercury	PKA-AG30	V8-302
	PKA-AU30	V8-302
	PKA-AY25	V8-302
	PKA-BB25	V8-302
	PKA-C38	V8-351
	PKA-AS30	V8-351
Mustang	PKA-CD7	V6-232
	PKA-BW7	V8-302
Thunderbird	PKA-CB13	V6-232
	PKA-K13	V8-302
	PKA-CJ	V8-302

DESCRIPTION

This unit is a 4 speed automatic transmission incorporating an integral overdrive feature. With selector lever in 1 position, the transmission will start and remain in first gear until the selector lever is moved to another position. In 3 position, the transmission will automatically shift through 1-2-3 range, but will not engage overdrive. In D position, the transmission will automatically select the appropriate time to shift into overdrive (4th gear). The design of the transmission features a split torque path in third gear, where 40% of the engine torque is transmitted hydraulically through the torque converter and 60% is transmitted mechanically through solid connections (direct drive input shaft) to the driveshaft. When transmission is in overdrive (4th gear), 100% of engine torque is transmitted through the direct drive input shaft.

The transmission consists essentially of a torque converter assembly, compound planetary gear train and a hydraulic control system, **Fig. 1.** For gear control the transmission has four friction clutches, two one-way roller clutches and two bands. Overdrive is accomplished by the addition of a band to lock the reverse sun gear while driving the planet carrier. The torque converter operation is similar to other types of automatic transmission, but has an added damper assembly and input shaft for 3rd gear and overdrive. The direct drive input shaft couples the engine directly to the direct clutch. This shaft is driven by the torque converter cover through the damper assembly which cushions engine shock to the transmission.

TROUBLESHOOTING GUIDE

ROUGH INITIAL ENGAGEMENT IN FORWARD OR REVERSE

1. Improper fluid level.
2. High engine idle.
3. Loose driveshaft, engine mounts or U-joints.
4. Sticking or dirty valve body.
5. Improper clutch or band application, or low oil control pressure.

SLOW INITIAL ENGAGEMENT

1. Improper fluid level.

2. Damaged or improperly adjusted linkage.
3. Contaminated fluid.
4. Low main control pressure or improper clutch and band application.

HARSH ENGAGEMENTS WITH WARM ENGINE

1. Improper fluid level.
2. Damaged or improperly adjusted linkage.
3. High engine idle.
4. Sticking or dirty valve body.

SLOW FORWARD ENGAGEMENT

1. Improper fluid level.
2. Damaged or improperly adjusted linkage.
3. Low main control pressure.
4. Sticking or dirty valve body.
5. Blocked filter.
6. Damaged pump.

SLOW REVERSE ENGAGEMENT

1. Improper fluid level.

Fig. 1 Sectional view of Ford Automatic Overdrive Transmission

2. Damaged or improperly adjusted linkage.
3. Low main control pressure.
4. Damaged forward clutch assembly.
5. Sticking or dirty valve body.
6. Blocked filter.
7. Damaged pump.

NO ENGINE BRAKING IN MANUAL LOW

1. Improper fluid level.
2. Damaged or improperly adjusted linkage.
3. Damaged low reverse servo piston band.
4. Damaged planetary low one-way clutch.

NO ENGINE BRAKING IN MANUAL 2ND

1. Improper fluid level.
2. Damaged or improperly adjusted linkage.
3. Improper clutch or band application.

4. Improper control system pressure.
5. Leaking intermediate servo.
6. Damaged intermediate one-way clutch.

SLIPS OR CHATTERS IN DRIVE

1. Improper fluid level.
2. Improper throttle valve rod adjustment.
3. Damaged or improperly adjusted linkage.
4. Low main control pressure.
5. Sticking or dirty valve body.
6. Open forward clutch check valve.
7. Damaged forward clutch piston seal.
8. Blocked forward clutch feed hole.
9. Damaged planetary low one-way clutch.

SLIPS OR CHATTERS IN REVERSE

1. Improper fluid level.
2. Low main control pressure in reverse.

3. Damaged reverse servo bore.
4. Damaged planetary low one-way clutch.
5. Damaged reverse clutch drum bushing.
6. Worn reverse clutch stator support seal rings or grooves.
7. Reverse clutch piston seal.
8. Reverse band adjustment.
9. Loosen driveshaft, engine mounts or U-joints.

NO DRIVE OR SLIPS OR CHATTERS IN D2

1. Improper fluid level.
2. Damaged or improperly adjusted linkage.
3. Intermediate friction or one-way clutch.
4. Blocked intermediate bleed hole or bleed hole not at 12 o'clock position.
5. Sticking or dirty valve body.
6. Damaged or worn servo.

AUTOMATIC TRANSMISSIONS/TRANSAXLES

NO DRIVE OR SLIPS OR CHATTERS IN D1

1. Damaged planetary low one-way clutch.

STARTS IN 2ND OR 3RD

1. Improper fluid level.
2. Damaged or improperly adjusted linkage.
3. Improper clutch or band application.
4. Improper control system pressure.
5. Sticking governor valve.
6. Sticking or dirty valve body.
7. Leaking valve body mating surface.

IMPROPER SHIFT POINTS

1. Improper fluid level.
2. Damaged or improperly adjusted linkage.
3. Improper speedometer gear installed.
4. Improper clutch or band application.
5. Improper control system pressure.
6. Damaged or worn governor.
7. Sticking or dirty valve body.

HARSH, DELAYED OR NO UPSHIFTS

1. Improper fluid level.
2. Damaged or improperly adjusted linkage.
3. Governor sticking.
4. High main control pressure.
5. Sticking or dirty valve body.

ALL UPSHIFTS EARLY

1. Improper fluid level.
2. Damaged or improperly adjusted linkage.
3. Low main control pressure.
4. Sticking throttle control valve or valve body.
5. Sticking governor valve.

NO 1-2 UPSHIFTS

1. Improper fluid level.
2. Damaged or improperly adjusted linkage.
3. Low main control pressure to intermediate friction clutch.
4. Sticking, leaking or bent diaphragm unit.
5. Sticking or dirty valve body.
6. Burnt intermediate clutch, band or servo.

EARLY OR SLIPPING UPSHIFT IN 1-2

1. Improper fluid level.
2. Improperly tuned engine.
3. Damaged or improperly adjusted linkage.
4. High main control pressure.
5. Sticking governor valve.

NO 2-3 UPSHIFT

1. Improper fluid level.
2. Damaged or improperly adjusted linkage.
3. Low main control pressure to direct clutch.
4. Sticking or dirty valve body.
5. Burnt or worn direct clutch.
6. Broken weld on converter damper hub.

EARLY OR SLIPPING 2-3 UPSHIFT

1. Improper fluid level.
2. Improperly tuned engine.
3. Damaged or improperly adjusted linkage.
4. Cut or worn 2-3 accumulator piston seals.
5. Plugged 2-3 accumulator piston drain hole.
6. Damaged accumulator.
7. Dirty or sticking valve body.
8. Leaking vacuum diaphragm.

NO 3-4 UPSHIFT

1. Low fluid level.
2. Damaged or improperly adjusted linkage.
3. Low pressure to overdrive band servo.
4. Sticking or dirty valve body.
5. Burnt or worn overdrive band assembly.
6. Blocked case passage.
7. Broken converter damper hub.

EARLY OR SLIPPING 3-4

1. Improper fluid level.
2. Damaged or improperly adjusted linkage.
3. Low main control pressure to overdrive band servo.
4. Sticking or dirty valve body.
5. Burnt overdrive band assembly.
6. Damaged or glazed reverse clutch drum or overdrive band.

ERRATIC SHIFTS

1. Improper fluid level.
2. Improperly tuned engine.
3. Damaged or improperly adjusted linkage.
4. Dirty or sticking valve body.
5. Sticking governor valve.
6. Damaged output shaft collector body seal rings.

SHIFTS 1-3 IN D

1. Improper fluid level.
2. Damaged or burnt intermediate friction clutch.
3. Damaged intermediate one-way clutch.
4. Improper control system pressure or clutch application.
5. Sticking or dirty valve body.
6. Sticking governor valve.

LATE 2-3 SHIFTING

1. Improper fluid level.
2. Damaged or improperly adjusted linkage.
3. Improper control system pressure or clutch application.
4. Damaged or worn high clutch or intermediate servo.
5. Sticking or dirty valve body.
6. Broken converter damper hub.

SHIFT HUNTING 3-4 OR 4-3

1. Improperly tuned engine.
2. Damaged or improperly adjusted linkage.

NO FORCED DOWNSHIFTS

1. Improper fluid level.
2. Damaged or improperly adjusted linkage.
3. Improper control system pressure or clutch application.
4. Sticking or dirty valve body.
5. Sticking or dirty governor.

3-1 SHIFT AT CLOSED THROTTLE IN D

1. Improper fluid level.
2. Improperly tuned engine.
3. Damaged or improperly adjusted linkage.
4. Improper control system pressure or clutch application.
5. Improper governor operation.
6. Sticking or dirty valve body.

HARSH OR SLIPPING 4-2 OR 3-1 SHIFT

1. Improper fluid level.
2. Improperly tuned engine.
3. Damaged or improperly adjusted linkage.
4. Improper application of intermediate friction and one-way clutch.
5. Sticking or dirty valve body.

HIGH SHIFT EFFORT

1. Damaged or improperly adjusted linkage.
2. Loose manual lever nut.
3. Damaged manual lever retainer pin.

TRANSMISSION OVERHEATS

1. Improper fluid level.
2. Improperly tuned engine.
3. Improper control system pressure or clutch application.
4. Restricted cooler or lines.
5. Seized converter one-way clutch.
6. Sticking or dirty valve body.

CLUNK OR SQUAWK IN 1-2 OR 2-3

1. Blocked intermediate bleed hole or bleed hole not at 12 o'clock position.
2. Misaligned anti-clunk spring.

HARSH DOWNSHIFT COASTING CLUNK

1. Improperly seated anti-clunk spring.
2. Damaged or improperly adjusted linkage.

POOR VEHICLE ACCELERATION

1. Improperly tuned engine.
2. Seized torque converter one-way clutch.

SLIPPING SHIFT FOLLOWED BY SUDDEN ENGAGEMENT

1. Throttle valve linkage set too short.

TRANSMISSION NOISY (VALVE RESONANCE)

1. Improper fluid level.
2. Damaged or improperly adjusted linkage.
3. Improper control system pressure or clutch application.
4. Cooler lines contacting frame, floor pan or other components.
5. Sticking or dirty valve body.
6. Internal leakage or pump cavitation.

TRANSMISSION NOISY (OTHER THAN VALVE RESONANCE)

1. Improper fluid level.
2. Damaged or improperly adjusted linkage.
3. Contaminated fluid.
4. Loose converter to flywheel housing bolts or nuts.
5. Loose or worn speedometer driven gear.
6. Damaged or worn extension housing bushing seal or driveshaft.
7. Damaged or worn front or rear planetary and/or one-way clutch.

THROTTLE VALVE LINKAGE DIAGNOSIS

Refer to the following for TV linkage conditions and subsequent shift troubles.

TV CONTROL LINKAGE ADJUSTED TOO SHORT

1. Early or soft up-shifts.
2. Harsh light throttle shift into and out of overdrive.
3. No forced downshift at proper speeds.

TV LINKAGE ADJUSTED TOO LONG

1. Harsh idle engagement after engine warm up.
2. Clunking when throttle is released after heavy acceleration.
3. Harsh coasting downshifts out of overdrive.

INTERFERENCE PREVENTING RETURN OF TV CONTROL ROD

1. Delayed or harsh upshifts.
2. Harsh idle engagement.

BINDING GROMMETS PREVENTING TV LINKAGE RETURN

1. Delayed or harsh upshifts.
2. Harsh idle engagement.

TV CONTROL ROD DISCONNECTED

1. Delayed or harsh upshifts.
2. Harsh idle engagement.

CLAMPING BOLT ON TRUNNION AT LOWER END OF TV CONTROL ROD LOOSE.

1. Delayed or harsh upshifts.
2. Harsh idle engagement.

LINKAGE LEVER RETURN SPRING BROKEN OR DISCONNECTED.

1. Delayed or harsh upshifts.
2. Harsh idle engagements.

MAINTENANCE
CHECKING OIL LEVEL

1. With transmission at operating temperature, park vehicle on level surface.
2. Operate engine at idle speed with parking brake applied and move selector lever through each detent position. Return selector lever to Park.
3. With engine idling, remove dipstick and check fluid level. Fluid level should be between arrows on dipstick.
4. Add fluid as necessary to bring fluid to proper level. Use only fluid meeting Ford Qualification No. M2C-138-CJ or Dexron II.

MANUAL LINKAGE
ADJUST

1. Position selector lever against D detent stop. It is recommended that an 8 pound weight be suspended from the selector lever to hold the lever against the D stop.
2. Position transmission lever in D detent. The D detent is the third detent from the front of the transmission.
3. Tighten adjusting nut, **Figs. 2 through 5,** and check transmission for proper operation.

THROTTLE VALVE LINKAGE
ADJUST

TRANSMISSION

1. Position screw at linkage lever at midpoint, ensure that throttle is against idle stop. Set parking brake and place transmission lever in Neutral.
2. Loosen bolt on control rod trunnion block, **Fig. 6.** Clean rod and trunnion so that trunnion slides freely on rod.
3. Push up on lower end of rod to ensure that carburetor linkage lever is held firmly against throttle lever.

4. Release rod and check to ensure that rod stays in position.
5. Push transmission lever against its internal stop and tighten bolt on trunnion.
6. Check to ensure throttle lever is against idle stop.

AT CARBURETOR

1. Position throttle lever at idle stop, place shift lever in neutral and set parking brake (engine off).
2. Turn linkage lever adjusting screw counterclockwise until end of screw is flush with throttle lever face.
3. Turn adjusting screw clockwise to provide .005 inch clearance between end of screw and throttle lever. Continue turning adjusting screw an additional three turns. If screw travel is limited, one turn is acceptable.
4. If adjusting screw cannot be turned at least one turn, refer to the "At Transmission" procedure.

NOTE: Whenever idle speed is adjusted by more than 50 RPM, the adjustment screw on the linkage lever at the carburetor should also be adjusted as listed in the "Idle Speed/Throttle Valve Linkage Adjustment Chart", **Fig. 7.** If idle speed was adjusted, ensure that .005 inch clearance exists between linkage lever adjusting screw and the throttle lever. The throttle lever should be at the idle stop and the shift lever in Neutral.

THROTTLE VALVE PRESSURE ADJUSTMENT
1980–83

1. Connect an 0–100 psi pressure gauge to throttle valve limit pressure tap, **Fig. 8.** Use a gauge hose long enough so that gauge can be viewed from under hood.
2. Check to ensure that throttle lever is against idle stop. Operate engine at idle speed in Neutral with parking brake applied.
3. Place a 1/16 inch drill between linkage lever adjusting screw and throttle lever, **Fig. 9.** Pressure gauge reading should be 5 psi or lower. If pressure gauge reading is above 5 psi linkage is set too long. Back linkage lever adjusting screw out as necessary to reduce pressure.
4. Remove 1/16 inch drill and insert a 5/16 inch drill. With engine idling in Neutral, pressure gauge reading should be at least 22 psi. If pressure gauge reading is below 22 psi, linkage is set too short. Turn linkage lever adjusting screw as necessary to bring pressure to 22 psi.

NOTE: If correct pressure cannot be obtained by turning linkage lever adjusting screw, it may be necessary to adjust control rod length at transmission.

Fig. 2   Manual linkage. 1980—82 Cougar, XR-7, 1980—85 Thunderbird, 1982—85 Continental, 1983—85 Cougar, LTD & Marquis

Fig. 3   Manual linkage. 1980 Lincoln Continental & 1980—81 Ford, Mercury & Mark VI

TRANSMISSION PARK GEAR
LOCK-OUT RETURN SPRING

KNOB ASSEMBLY

TRANSMISSION CONTROL
SELECTOR DIAL BEZEL
ASSEMBLY

HEX HEAD SCREW
4.2 X 13mm - 4 REQ'D

TRANSMISSION CONTROL
SELECTOR ROD

PARKING BRAKE
RELEASE SWITCH
ASSEMBLY

HEX HEAD SCREW
4.2 X 13mm

CLIP

STEERING COLUMN
IGNITION LOCK
CABLE ASSEMBLY

DIESEL
BRACKET

PAN HEAD SCREW
NO. 8 X 18 X .50

HEX NUT—M5

SELF-LOCKING
PIN

HEX HEAD
SCREW
4.2 X 23mm
2 REQ'D

TRANSMISSION SHIFT
CONTROL MOUNTING
PLATE ASSEMBLY

BRACKET

TRANSMISSION CONTROL
SHIFTER TO
TRANSMISSION CABLE
ASSEMBLY

TRANSMISSION
CONTROL HOUSING
AND LEVER
ASSEMBLY

HEX HEAD BOLT
M6 X 12mm
4 REQ'D

J-NUT
M6 X 1
2 REQ'D

Fig. 4 Manual linkage. 1984–85 Mark VII

ADJUSTING NUT
N801087-S2
(14-23 LB-FT)

7200 ASSY.

7B125

7326

7C431 ASSY.

W611633-S2
2 REQ'D.
12-24 N·m
(9-18 LB-FT)

7A024

381673-S2
20-34 N·m
(15-25 LB-FT)

7C324 ASSY.

2 EXTRUDED HOLES
IN INNER FRAME RAIL

*LUBRICATE WITH ESE-M2C96-E ENGINE OIL
★LUBRICATE I.D. OF BEARING LIBERALLY WITH ESA-MIC75-B

**Fig. 5   Manual linkage. 1982–85 Ford,
Lincoln Town Car, Mark VI & Mercury**

T.V. LEVER ADJ.
SCREW FOR IDLE

INSULATOR ASSY.
REF.

SLIDING INNER MEMBER

Y.

VIEW V

Fig. 6   Throttle valve linkage adjustment

Change on Linkage Lever Adj. Screw	Idle Speed Change
No change.	Less than 50 RPM
1½ turns counterclockwise	50–100 RPM increase
1½ turns clockwise	50–100 RPM decrease
2½ turns counterclockwise	100–150 RPM increase
2½ turns clockwise	100–150 RPM decrease

Fig. 7   Idle Speed/Throttle Valve Linkage Adjustment Chart

Fig. 8 Gauge connections to throttle valve pressure tap

Fig. 9 Positioning throttle lever

1984—85

1. Check curb idle speed, adjusting as necessary. If equipped, ensure curb idle speed is within specifications with and without throttle solenoid positioner (anti-diesel solenoid) energized.
2. Attach 0—100 psi pressure gauge to TV port on transmission, using enough flexible hose so that gauge can be read while operating engine.
3. Run engine until it reaches normal operating temperature and throttle lever is off fast idle or the idle speed control plunger, if equipped, is at normal idle position.
4. Apply parking brake, place shift selector in Neutral, remove air cleaner and turn off air conditioner. On vehicles equipped with vacuum operated throttle modulator, disconnect and plug vacuum line to modulator. If equipped with throttle solenoid positioner or idle speed control, do not disconnect these components.
5. With engine idling in Neutral, insert .397 inch drill shank between carburetor throttle lever and adjusting screw on transmission linkage lever. TV pressure should be 30—40 psi. For optimum operation, use adjusting screw to set pressure as close to 35 psi as possible. Turning screw in will raise pressure 1.5 psi per turn. Backing out screw will lower pressure. On vehicles equipped with idle speed control, some "hunting" may occur and an average pressure reading will have to be determined. If adjusting screw does not have enough adjustment range, first adjust rod at transmission.
6. Remove drill shank, allowing TV lever to return to idle. With engine still idling in Neutral, TV pressure must be less than 5 psi. If not, back out adjusting screw until TV pressure is less than 5 psi, then install drill shank and ensure that TV pressure is still 30—40 psi.

IN-VEHICLE REPAIRS
CONTROL VALVE BODY

1. Raise and support vehicle, drain transmission fluid, then remove transmission pan, gasket and filter.
2. Remove detent spring attaching bolt, then the spring.
3. Remove valve body to case attaching bolts, then the valve body.
4. Reverse procedure to install. Use suitable guide pins to align valve body to case.

OVERDRIVE SERVO ASSEMBLY

1. Remove valve body as previously described.
2. Compress overdrive servo piston cover with a suitable tool, then remove snap ring retainer.
3. Apply compressed air to servo piston release passage and remove the overdrive servo piston cover and spring. Remove piston from cover, then the rubber seal from piston and cover.
4. Install new servo piston and cover seals on the servo piston and cover.
5. Lubricate all seals, piston and piston bore with transmission fluid.
6. Install servo piston into cover, then the return spring into servo piston.
7. Install overdrive piston assembly into overdrive servo bore.
8. Compress overdrive piston using suitable tool, then install snap ring retainer.
9. Install valve body, filter, pan and gasket. Refill transmission to proper fluid level.

REVERSE SERVO ASSEMBLY

1. Refer to "Overdrive Servo Assembly" procedure for replacement. Apply compressed air to the servo piston release passage to remove servo piston from case.

NOTE: Reverse servo piston is under spring pressure. Use caution when removing servo piston cover.

3-4 ACCUMULATOR PISTON

1. Remove valve body as previously described.
2. Compress 3-4 accumulator piston cover, then remove snap ring retainer.
3. Release cover slowly, then remove piston cover, return spring and piston. Some models do not use a spring.
4. Remove seal from 3-4 accumulator cover and piston and inspect for damage and wear.
5. Install new seals on 3-4 accumulator cover, if necessary. Lubricate cover pocket of case with transmission fluid.
6. Install 3-4 accumulator piston and return spring into case, then the cover.
7. Compress cover using suitable tool, then install snap ring. Ensure cover is reseated snugly against snap ring.
8. Install valve body, filter, pan and gasket. Refill transmission pan to proper fluid level.

2-3 ACCUMULATOR PISTON

1. Refer to "3-4 Accumulator Piston" procedure for replacement.

EXTENSION HOUSING

1. Raise and support vehicle.
2. Disconnect parking brake cable from equalizer, if necessary. On Lincoln Continental remove equalizer.
3. Disconnect driveshaft from rear axle flange, then remove driveshaft from transmission.
4. Disconnect speedometer cable from extension housing.
5. Remove engine rear support to extension housing attaching bolts. On Lincoln Continental, remove reinforcement plate.
6. Support transmission with suitable jack and raise transmission enough to remove weight from rear engine support.
7. Remove engine rear support from crossmember, then lower transmission and remove extension housing

1. MANUAL VALVE
2. THROTTLE SYSTEM VALVES
3. 2-3 BACKOUT VALVE
4. ORIFICE CONTROL VALVE/2-3 CAPACITY
   MODULATOR VALVE (FUNCTIONS ARE
   SEPARATED BY A SPRING RETAINING PLATE)
5. 3-4 SHIFT AND 3-4 TV MODULATOR VALVES
6. TV LIMIT VALVE
7. 1-2 SHIFT VALVE

8. O.D. SERVO REGULATOR VALVE
9. 3-4 SHUTTLE VALVE
10. 1-2 ACCUMULATOR VALVE
11. 1-2 CAPACITY MODULATOR VALVE
12. MAIN REGULATOR AND PRESSURE BOOST VALVES
13. 2-1 SCHEDULING VALVE/LOW SERVO MODULATOR
    VALVE (FUNCTIONS ARE SEPARATED BY A SPRING
    RETAINING PLATE)
14. 3-4 BACKOUT VALVE
15. 2-3 SHIFT AND 2-3 TV MODULATOR VALVES

Fig. 10 Control valve body assembly

Fig. 11   Internal transmission linkage

attaching bolts. Slide extension housing from output shaft and allow fluid to drain.
8. Reverse procedure to install.

GOVERNOR

1. Remove extension housing as described above.

NOTE: If governor body only is being removed, proceed to step 4.

2. Remove governor to output shaft retaining snap ring.
3. Remove governor assembly from output shaft using suitable tool. Remove governor driveball.
4. Remove governor to counterweight attaching screws. Remove governor from counterweight.
5. Reverse procedure to install.

INTERNAL & EXTERNAL SHIFT LINKAGE

1. Raise and support vehicle.
2. Drain transmission fluid from pan, then remove pan and gasket.
3. Disconnect shift rod at transmission manual lever, then the throttle valve linkage at transmission.
4. Disconnect inner throttle lever spring.

Remove detent spring, **Fig. 11.**
5. Hold outer throttle lever, then loosen outer throttle lever attaching nut. Remove attaching nut and lock washer.
6. Remove outer throttle lever seal, then the manual lever roll pin.
7. Remove outer manual lever attaching bolt, then the outer manual lever.
8. Remove inner throttle lever and spring.
9. Remove inner manual lever and park pawl actuating rod.
10. Remove manual lever oil seal.
11. Reverse procedure to install. Adjust transmission manual linkage and throttle linkage as outlined previously.

TRANSMISSION
REPLACE

1. Raise and support vehicle.
2. Drain transmission fluid from pan. After fluid is drained, install pan.
3. Remove converter access cover from lower end of converter housing. Rotate engine to gain access to converter drain plug. Remove drain plug, drain fluid from converter, then replace drain plug.

4. Remove converter to flywheel attaching nuts, then the driveshaft from vehicle.
5. Disconnect battery cable from starter motor, then remove starter motor. Disconnect neutral start switch electrical connector.
6. Remove rear mount to crossmember bolts and crossmember to frame bolts.
7. Remove engine rear support to extension housing bolts.
8. Disconnect manual linkage from transmission, then remove bolts securing bellcrank bracket to converter housing.
9. Raise transmission with suitable jack and remove crossmember.
10. Lower transmission slightly and disconnect oil cooler lines and speedometer cable from transmission.
11. Remove filler tube and dipstick from transmission.
12. With transmission secured to jack, remove converter housing to cylinder block attaching bolts. Move transmission and converter assembly rearward, then lower transmission and remove from under vehicle.
13. Reverse procedure to install. On Lincoln Continental and Mark VI, align yellow balancing marks on converter and flywheel. Lubricate pilot.

Ford C3 & C4 Automatic Transmission

INDEX

TRANSMISSION IDENTIFICATION

Each transmission may be identified by the tag attached to the low-reverse servo cover bolt. The tag includes the model prefix and suffix, a service identification number and a build date code. The service identification number indicates changes to service details which affect interchangeability when the transmission model is not changed. For interpretation of this number the Ford Master Parts Catalog should be consulted.

C3 Transmission

Year	Car Model	Trans. Code	Engine Model	Year	Car Model	Trans. Code	Engine Model
1980	Bobcat	80DT-AA, AB	4-140			81DT-DAA, AB, DA, DB, EA, EB, GA, GB	6-200
	Capri①	80DT-CA, CB	4-140		Granada	81DT-CFA, HA, KA, MA	4-140
	Capri②	80DT-CDA, CDB	4-140			81DT-DAA, AB, DA, DB, EA, EB, GA, GB	6-200
	Capri	80DT-EA, EB	6-200		Mustang	81DT-CFA, HA	4-140
	Cougar	80DT-LB	6-200			81DT-DAA, AB, EA, EB	6-200
	Fairmont①	80DT-CA, CB, HA, HB	4-140		Thunderbird	81DT-DDA, DB, GA, GB	6-200
	Fairmont②	80DT-CDA, CDB	4-140		Zephyr	81DT-CFA, HA, KA, MA	4-140
	Fairmont	80DT-EA, EB, LA, LB, CEB	6-200			81DT-DAA, AB, DA, DB, EA, EB, GA, GB	6-200
	Mustang①	80DT-CA, CB	4-140	1982	Capri	82DT-AAA, ACA	4-140
	Mustang②	80DT-CDA, CDB	4-140			82DT-BBA	6-200
	Mustang	80DT-EA, EB	6-200		Cougar	82DT-AAA, ABA	4-140
	Pinto	80DT-AA, AB	4-140			82DT-ACA, ADA	4-140
	Thunderbird	80DT-LB	6-200		Fairmont	82DT-AAA, ABA	4-140
	Zephyr①	80DT-CA, CB, HA, HB	4-140			82DT-ACA, ADA	4-140
	Zephyr②	80DT-CDA, CDB	4-140			82DT-BAA, BBA	6-200
	Zephyr	80DT-EA, EB, LA, LB, CEB	6-200		Granada	82DT-AAA, ABA	4-140
1981	Capri	81DT-CFA, HA	4-140			82DT-ACA, ADA	4-140
		81DT-DAA, AB, EA, EB	6-200		Mustang	82DT-AAA, ACA	4-140
	Cougar & XR7	81DT-CFA, HA, KA, MA	4-140			82DT-BBA	6-200
		81DT-DAA, AB, DA, DB	6-200		Zephyr	82DT-AAA, ABA	4-140
		81DT-DEA, EB, GA, GB	6-200				
	Fairmont	81DT-CFA, HA, KA, MA	4-140				

C3 Transmission—continued

Year	Car Model	Trans. Code	Engine Model
		82DT-ACA, ADA	4-140
		82DT-BAA, BBA	6-200
1983	Capri	83DT-AAB	4-140
	Fairmont	83DT-AAB, ABB	4-140
		82DT-BAA	6-200
	LTD/Marquis	83DT-AAB, ABB, AGB, AHB	4-140
	Mustang	83DT-AAB	4-140
	Zephyr	83DT-AAB, ABB	4-140
		82DT-BAA, BBA	6-200
1984	Capri	84DT-AAA, ACA, AJA	4-140
	Cougar	84DT-AEA, AFA	4-140
	LTD/Marquis	83DT-AGB, AHG; 84DT-ABA,	

Year	Car Model	Trans. Code	Engine Model
		ACA, ADA, AKA	4-140
	Mustang	84DT-AAA, ACA, AJA	4-140
	Thunderbird	84DT-AEA, AFA	4-140
1985	Capri	85DT-AAA, EAA	4-140
		85DT-JAA	4-140
	Cougar	85DT-KAAA, LAA	4-140
	LTD	85DT-BAA, DAA	4-140
		85DT-FAA	4-140
	Marquis	85DT-BAA, DAA	4-140
		85DT-FAA	4-140
	Thunderbird	85DT-AEA, AFA	4-140

C4 Transmission

Year	Car Model	Trans. Code	Engine Model
1980	Bobcat	PEJ-Z, 1,2	4-140
	Capri	PEJ-AC, 1, 2	4-140
		PEB-P, 4, 5, 6	6-200
		PEM-B, E, N, 1, 2	V8-255
	Cougar	PEB-T3	6-200
		PEM-D, L	V8-255
		PEE-FL, FN	V8-302
	Fairmont	PEJ-AC, AD, 1	4-140
		PEB-N, 6, 7, 8	6-200
		PEB-P, 4, 5, 6	6-200
		PEB-S, 3, 4	6-200
		PEB-T, 1, 2, 3	6-200
		PEB-U, 1, 2	6-200
		PEM-C, 1, 2, D, 1, 2, E, 1, 2	V8-255
		PEM-G, 1, H, 1, 2, M, 1, 2	V8-255
		PEM-L, 1, 2, N, 1, 2	V8-255
	Ford	PEE-D, Z, 3, 4, 5	V8-302
		PEE-FA, 3, 4, 5	V8-302
		PEE-EM, 3, 4	V8-302
		PEE-FC1, 2	V8-302
		PEE-FE1, 2, 3	V8-302
	Granada	PEL-A1, 2, B1, 2, C1	6-250
		PEL-D1	6-250
		PEM-J1, K1, P, R	V8-255
		PEE-CW5, 6, 7	V8-302
		PEE-FP, 1, 2	V8-302
		PEE-FR1, 2	V8-302
	Mercury	PEE-DZ3, 4, 5	V8-302
		PEE-EA3, 4, 5	V8-302
		PEE-EM3, 4	V8-302
		PEE-FC1, 2	V8-302
		PEE-FE1, 2, 3	V8-302
	Monarch	PEL-A1, 2, B1, 2, C1, D1	6-250
		PEL, J1, K1, P, R	V8-255
	Mustang	PEJ-AC1	4-140
		PEB-P4, 5, 6	6-200
		PEM-B1, 2, E1, 2, N1, 2	V8-255
	Pinto	PEJ-Z1, 2	4-140
	Thunderbird	PEB-T3	6-200
		PEM-D1, 2, L1, 2	V8-255
		PEE-FL, FN1, 2	V8-302
	Versailles	PEE-EY2	V8-302
		PEE-FV1, 2	V8-302
	Zephyr	PEJ-AC1, 2, AD1, 2	4-140
		PEB-N6, 7, 8	6-200
		PEB-P4, 5, 6	6-200
		PEB-S3, 4	6-200
		PEB-T1, 2, 3, U1, 2	6-200
		PEM-C1, 2, D1, 2, E1, 2	V8-255
		PEM-G1, H1, 2, L1, 2	V8-255

Year	Car Model	Trans. Code	Engine Model
		PEM-M1, 2, N1, 2	V8-255
1981	Capri	PEB-P8, P9	6-200
		PEJ-AC3	4-140
		PEJ-AC4	6-200
		PEM-E5, E6, W, W1	V8-255
		PEM-AD, D1, AK	V8-255
		PEM-A1, B1	6-200
	Cougar & XR7	PEB-N10, 11, P8, P9	6-200
		PEB-Z, Z1	6-200
		PEJ-AC3	4-140
		PEJ-AC4	6-200
		PEJ-AD3, D4	4-140
		PEM-C5, C6, D5, D6, E5, E6, AC, AC1	V8-255
		PEM-AD, AD1, AE, AE1, AL, AL1	V8-255
		PEM-AM, AM1, AN, AN1	V8-255
		PEN-A, A1, B, B1	6-200
	Fairmont	PEB-N10, N11	6-200
		PEB-P8, P9, U4, U5, Z, Z1	6-200
		PEJ-AC3, AC4, AD3, AD4	4-140
		PEM-C5, C6, D5, D6, E5, E6	V8-255
		PEM-AC, AC1, AD, AD1	V8-255
		PEM-AL, AL1, AM, AM1, AN, AN1	V8-255
		PEN-A, A1, B, B1	6-200
	Granada	PEB-N10, N11	6-200
		PEB-P8, P9	6-200
		PEJ-AC3, AC4, AD3, AD4	4-140
		PEN-A, A1, B, B1	6-200
		PEM-C5, C6, E5, E6	V8-255
		PEM-AC, AC1, AD, AD1	V8-255
		PEM-AL, AL1, AM, AM1, AN, AN1	V8-255
	Mustang	PEB-P8, P9	6-200
		PEJ-AC3, AC4	4-140
		PEM-E5, E6, W, W1, AD, AD1, AK, AK1	V8-255
	Thunderbird	PEB-Z, Z1	6-200
		PEM-D5, D6, AC, AC1, AE, AE1	V8-255
	Zephyr	PEB-N10, N11, P8, P9, U4, U5	6-200
		PEB-Z, Z1	6-200
		PEJ-AC3, D3, D4	4-140
		PEM-C5, C6, D5, D6, E5, E6	V8-255
		PEM-AC, C1, AD, D1	V8-255
		PEM-AL, L1, AM, M1, AN, N1	V8-255
		PEN-A, A1, B, B1	6-200

①—Without turbocharger.
②—With turbocharger.

Fig. 1   C3 Dual Range Automatic

DESCRIPTION

The main control incorporates a manually selective first and second gear range. The transmission features a drive range that provides for fully automatic upshifts and downshifts, and manually selected low and second gears.

The transmission consists essentially of a torque converter, a compound planetary gear train, two multiple disc clutches, a one-way clutch and a hydraulic control system, **Figs. 1 and 2.**

For all normal driving the selector lever is moved to the green dot under "Drive" on the selector quadrant on the steering column or on the floor console. As the throttle is advanced from the idle position, the transmission will upshift automatically to intermediate gear and then to high.

The driver can force downshift the transmission from high to intermediate at speeds up to 65 mph. A detent on the downshift linkage warns the driver when the carburetor is wide open. Accelerator pedal depression through the detent will bring in the downshift.

With the throttle closed the transmission will downshift automatically as the car speed drops to about 10 mph. With the throttle open at any position up to the detent, the downshifts will come in automatically at speeds above 10 mph and in proportion to throttle opening. This prevents engine lugging on steep hill climbing, for example.

When the selector lever is moved to "L" with the transmission in high, the transmission will downshift to intermediate or to low

depending on the road speed. At speed above 25 mph, the downshift will be from high to intermediate. At speeds below 25 mph, the downshift will be from high to low. With the selector lever in the "L" position the transmission cannot upshift.

TROUBLESHOOTING GUIDE

ROUGH INITIAL ENGAGEMENT IN D1 OR D2

1. Engine idle speed.
2. Vacuum diaphragm unit or tubes restricted, leaking or maladjusted.
3. Check control pressure.
4. Pressure regulator.
5. Valve body.
6. Forward clutch.

1-2 OR 2-3 SHIFT POINTS ERRATIC

1. Check fluid level.
2. Vacuum diaphragm unit or tubes restricted, leaking or maladjusted.
3. Immediate servo.
4. Manual linkage adjustment.
5. Governor.
6. Check control pressure.
7. Valve body.
8. Make air pressure check.

ROUGH 1-2 UPSHIFTS

1. Vacuum diaphragm unit or tubes restricted, leaking or maladjusted.

2. Intermediate servo.
3. Intermediate band.
4. Check control pressure.
5. Valve body.
6. Pressure regulator.

ROUGH 2-3 UPSHIFTS

1. Vacuum diaphragm unit or tubes restricted, leaking or maladjusted.
2. Intermediate servo.
3. Check control pressure.
4. Pressure regulator.
5. Intermediate band.
6. Valve body.
7. Make air pressure check.
8. Reverse-high clutch.
9. Reverse-high clutch piston air bleed valve.

DRAGGED OUT 1-2 SHIFT

1. Check fluid level.
2. Vacuum diaphragm unit or tubes restricted, leaking or maladjusted.
3. Intermediate servo.
4. Check control pressure.
5. Intermediate band.
6. Valve body.
7. Pressure regulator.
8. Make air pressure check.
9. Leakage in hydraulic system.

ENGINE OVERSPEEDS ON 2-3 SHIFT

1. Manual linkage.
2. Check fluid level.
3. Vacuum diaphragm unit or tubes re-

Fig. 2   C4 Dual Range Automatic

stricted, leaking or maladjusted.
4. Reverse servo.
5. Check control pressure.
6. Valve body.
7. Pressure regulator.
8. Intermediate band.
9. Reverse-high clutch.
10. Reverse-high clutch piston air bleed valve.

NO 1-2 OR 2-3 SHIFT

1. Manual linkage.
2. Downshift linkage, including inner lever position.
3. Vacuum diaphragm unit or tubes restricted, leaking or maladjusted.
4. Governor.
5. Check control pressure.
6. Valve body.
7. Intermediate band.
8. Intermediate servo.
9. Reverse-high clutch.
10. Reverse-high clutch piston air bleed valve.

NO 3-1 SHIFT IN D1 OR 3-2 Shift IN D2

1. Governor.
2. Valve body.

NO FORCED DOWNSHIFTS

1. Downshift linkage, including inner lever position.

2. Valve body.
3. Vacuum diaphragm unit or tubes restricted, leaking or maladjusted.

RUNAWAY ENGINE ON FORCED 3-2 DOWNSHIFT

1. Check control pressure.
2. Intermediate servo.
3. Intermediate band.
4. Pressure regulator.
5. Valve body.
6. Vacuum diaphragm unit or tubes restricted, leaking or maladjusted.
7. Leakage in hydraulic system.

ROUGH 3-2 OR 3-1 SHIFT AT CLOSED THROTTLE

1. Engine idle speed.
2. Vacuum diaphragm unit or tubes restricted, leaking or maladjusted.
3. Intermediate servo.
4. Valve body.
5. Pressure regulator.

SHIFTS 1-3 IN D1 AND D2

1. Intermediate band.
2. Intermediate servo.
3. Vacuum diaphragm unit or tubes restricted, leaking or maladjusted.
4. Valve body.
5. Governor.
6. Make air pressure check.

NO ENGINE BRAKING IN 1ST GEAR—MANUAL LOW

1. Manual linkage.
2. Reverse band.
3. Reverse servo.
4. Valve body.
5. Governor.
6. Make air pressure check.

SLIPS OR CHATTERS IN 1ST GEAR—D1

1. Check fluid level.
2. Vacuum diaphragm unit or tubes restricted, leaking or maladjusted.
3. Check control pressure.
4. Pressure regulator.
5. Valve body.
6. Forward clutch.
7. Leakage in hydraulic system.
8. Planetary one-way clutch.

SLIPS OR CHATTERS IN 2ND GEAR

1. Check fluid level.
2. Vacuum diaphragm unit or tubes restricted, leaking or maladjusted.
3. Intermediate servo.
4. Intermediate band.
5. Check control pressure.
6. Pressure regulator.
7. Valve body.
8. Make air pressure check.
9. Forward clutch.

10. Leakage in hydraulic system.

SLIPS OR CHATTERS IN R

1. Check fluid level.
2. Vacuum diaphragm unit or tubes restricted, leaking or maladjusted.
3. Reverse band.
4. Check control pressure.
5. Reverse servo.
6. Pressure regulator.
7. Valve body.
8. Make air pressure check.
9. Reverse-high clutch.
10. Leakage in hydraulic system.
11. Reverse-high piston air bleed valve.

NO DRIVE IN D1 ONLY

1. Check fluid level.
2. Manual linkage.
3. Check control pressure.
4. Valve body.
5. Make air pressure check.
6. Planetary one-way clutch.

NO DRIVE IN D2 ONLY

1. Check fluid level.
2. Manual linkage.
3. Check control pressure.
4. Intermediate servo.
5. Valve body.
6. Make air pressure check.
7. Leakage in hydraulic system.
8. Planetary one-way clutch.

NO DRIVE IN L ONLY

1. Check fluid level.
2. Manual linkage.
3. Check control pressure.
4. Valve body.
5. Reverse servo.
6. Make air pressure check.
7. Leakage in hydraulic system.
8. Planetary one-way clutch

NO DRIVE IN R ONLY

1. Check fluid level.
2. Manual linkage.
3. Reverse band.
4. Check control pressure.
5. Reverse servo.
6. Valve body.
7. Make air pressure check.
8. Reverse-high clutch.
9. Leakage in hydraulic system.
10. Reverse-high clutch piston air bleed valve.

NO DRIVE IN ANY SELECTOR POSITION

1. Check fluid level.
2. Manual linkage.
3. Check control pressure.
4. Pressure regulator.
5. Valve body.
6. Make air pressure check.
7. Leakage in hydraulic system.
8. Front pump.

LOCKUP IN D1 ONLY

1. Reverse-high clutch.
2. Parking linkage.

3. Leakage in hydraulic system.

LOCKUP IN D2 ONLY

1. Reverse band.
2. Reverse servo.
3. Reverse-high clutch.
4. Parking linkage.
5. Leakage in hydraulic system.
6. Planetary one-way clutch.

LOCKUP IN L ONLY

1. Intermediate band.
2. Intermediate servo.
3. Reverse-high clutch.
4. Parking linkage.
5. Leakage in hydraulic system.

LOCKUP IN R ONLY

1. Intermediate band.
2. Intermediate servo.
3. Forward clutch.
4. Parking linkage.
5. Leakage in hydraulic system.

PARKING LOCK BINDS OR WON'T HOLD

1. Manual linkage.
2. Parking linkage.

MAXIMUM SPEED TOO LOW, POOR ACCELERATION

1. Engine performance.
2. Brakes bind.
3. Converter one-way clutch.

NOISY IN N OR P

1. Check fluid level.
2. Pressure regulator.
3. Front pump.
4. Planetary assembly.

NOISY IN ALL GEARS

1. Check fluid level.
2. Pressure regulator.
3. Planetary assembly.
4. Forward clutch.
5. Front pump.
6. Planetary one-way clutch.

CAR MOVES FORWARD IN N

1. Manual linkage.
2. Forward clutch.

MAINTENANCE

NOTE: Ford Motor Company recommends the use of an automatic transmission fluid with the specification No. ESW-M2C33-F (Type F) for 1980 C3 units. On 1980–81 C4 and 1981–85 C3 units, it is recommended that an automatic transmission fluid meeting specification No. ESP-MC138-CJ or Dextron II series D be used. Use of a fluid other than specified above may result in transmission malfunction or failure.

CHECKING OIL LEVEL

1. With transmission at operating temperature, park vehicle on a level surface.
2. Run engine at idle speed with service and parking brakes applied and move selector lever through each range. Return selector lever to Park.
3. With engine idling, remove dipstick and check fluid level. Fluid level should be between the Add and Full marks.
4. Add specified fluid as required to bring the fluid to the proper level.

DRAIN & REFILL

NOTE: Normal maintenance and lubrication requirements do not necessitate periodic fluid changes. If a major failure has occurred in the transmission, it will have to be removed for service. At this time the converter must be thoroughly flushed to remove any foreign matter.

When filling a dry transmission and converter, install five quarts of specified fluid. Start engine, shift the selector lever through all ranges and place it at P position. Check fluid level and add enough to raise the level in the transmission to the "F" (full) mark on the dipstick. When a partial drain and refill is required due to front band adjustment or minor repair, proceed as follows:

1. Loosen and remove all but two oil pan bolts and drop one edge of the pan to drain the oil.

NOTE: Some models of the C4 transmission can be drained by removing the filler tube from the pan.

2. Remove and clean pan and screen.
3. Place a new gasket on pan and install pan and screen.
4. Add three quarts of specified fluid to transmission.
5. Run engine at idle speed for about two minutes.
6. Check oil level and add oil as necessary.
7. Run engine at a fast idle until it reaches normal operating temperature.
8. Shift selector lever through all ranges and then place it in P position.
9. Add fluid as required to bring the level to the full mark.

MANUAL LINKAGE
ADJUST

FLOOR SHIFT

1. Place transmission selector lever in D position.
2. Raise vehicle and loosen shift rod retaining nut, **Figs. 3 and 4.**

NOTE: On some models, shift linkage adjustment is done at the transmission end of shift rod.

Fig. 3 Floorshift linkage adjustment. Rod type (Typical). Column lock rod is used on some models

Fig. 4 Floorshift linkage adjustment. Cable type

Fig. 7 Column shift manual linkage. 1982 Cougar & Granada, 1982–83 Fairmont & Zephyr, 1983–85 LTD & Marquis

Fig. 5 1980–81 Cougar XR-7 & Thunderbird manual linkage, adjust.

Fig. 6 Column shift linkage adjustment. 1980–81 Fairmont & Zephyr & 1981 Cougar & Granada

Fig. 8 Manual linkage, column shift. 1980 Ford & Mercury

3. Move transmission manual lever to D position.
4. Torque attaching nut to 10 to 15 ft. lbs.

COLUMN SHIFT

1. Place selector lever in "D" position. Use suitable force on the lever to keep it against the "D" stop during adjustment.
2. Raise vehicle and loosen shift rod adjusting nut at point A, **Figs. 5 through 9.**
3. Shift transmission manual lever into drive position, second detent from the full counter clockwise position.
4. On models equipped with shift cable, place cable end on transmission manual lever stud. Align flats on stud with flats on cable, then install adjustment nut.
5. On all models, tighten adjustment at point A. Ensure selector lever is against D stop when tightening adjustment nut.
6. Check transmission for proper operation in all selector lever detent positions.

THROTTLE & DOWNSHIFT LINKAGE ADJUST

1. Apply parking brake and place selector lever in "N".
2. Run engine at normal idle speed.
3. Connect tachometer to engine.
4. Adjust engine idle speed to specified RPM with selector lever in either Drive position.

NOTE: The carburetor throttle lever must be against the hot idle speed adjusting screw at specified idle speed.

5. Proceed with adjustments as outlined below.

1983–85

Refer to **Figs. 10 through 13** for adjustment procedure.

1982 ALL WITH 4-140

1. Remove downshift retracting spring and hold throttle in wide open position.

2. Depress downshift rod with 6 lbs. weight positioned against through detent stop.
3. Turn downshift adjusting screw to obtain .01–.08 inch clearance between screw and throttle arm.
4. Return system to idle and install downshift retracting spring.

1980 CAPRI, FAIRMONT, MUSTANG, ZEPHYR, EXC. V8-255

1. Remove downshift retracting spring and hold throttle in wide open position.
2. Depress downshift rod with 4.25 lb. weight positioned against through detent stop.
3. Turn downshift adjusting screw to obtain .05–.08 inch clearance between screw and throttle arm.
4. Return system to idle and install downshift retracting spring.

Fig. 9   Manual linkage. 1980 Versailles column shift, Granada & Monarch

Fig. 10   Throttle & downshift linkage adjustment. Capri & Mustang w/4-140 engine

* KICK-DOWN CONTROL ADJUSTMENT
A. ASSEMBLE ALL COMPONENTS OF K/D CONTROLS.
B. WITH CARBURETOR HELD AT W.O.T. POSITION AND THE KICKDOWN ROD 7A186 HELD DOWNWARD WITH THE SPECIFIED 1.93Kg WEIGHT AGAINST THE "THROUGH DETENT" STOP, ADJUST THE KICKDOWN ADJUSTING SCREW TO OBTAIN 0.25 TO 2.03 - CLEARANCE BETWEEN SCREW HEAD AND THROTTLE ARM.
C. RETURN SYSTEM TO HOLE.

Fig. 11   Throttle & downshift linkage adjust. Capri & Mustang w/V6-232 engine

*ADJUSTMENT OF THE TRANSMISSION K.D. CONTROL

1. TRANSMISSION KICKDOWN CONTROLS
A. ASSEMBLE ALL COMPONENTS OF KICKDOWN CONTROLS.
B. WITH CARBURETOR HELD AT W.O.T. POSITION AND THE KICKDOWN ROD (7A186) HELD DOWNWITH THE SPECIFIED 2.72 Kg WEIGHT AGAINST THE "THROUGH DETENT" STOP, ADJUST THE KICKDOWN ADJUSTING SCREW TO OBTAIN 0.25 TO 2.03mm CLEARANCE BETWEEN SCREW AND THROTTLE ARM.
C. RETURN SYSTEM TO IDLE.
D. INSTALL K.D. 7B146 RETRACTING SPRING.

Fig. 12   Throttle & downshift linkage adjust. Fairmont Futura & Zephyr w/4-140 engine

Fig. 13 Throttle & downshift linkage adjust. Fairmont Futura & Zephyr w/6-200 engine

1980—81 COUGAR, FORD, LTD II, MERCURY, THUNDERBIRD, & 1982 CAPRI, FAIRMONT, MUSTANG, ZEPHYR, WITH V8-255

1. Hold throttle in wide open position.
2. Depress downshift rod with 4.25 lb. weight positioned against through detent stop.
3. Turn downshift adjusting screw to obtain .01—.08 inch clearance between screw and throttle arm.
4. Return system to idle.

1980, ALL WITH V8-255, EXC. COUGAR & THUNDERBIRD, VERSAILLES, GRANADA & MONARCH; 1981, ALL EXC. FORD, MERCURY, THUNDERBIRD, XR-7; 1982 ALL WITH 6-200

1. Remove downshift retracting spring and hold throttle in wide open position.
2. Depress downshift rod with 4.25 lb. weight positioned against through detent stop, **Figs. 14 and 15.**

3. Turn downshift adjusting screw to obtain .01—.08 inch clearance between screw and throttle arm.
4. Return system to idle and install downshift retracting spring.

1980 BOBCAT, CAPRI, FAIRMONT, MUSTANG, PINTO & ZEPHYR WITH 4-140

1. Hold throttle in wide open position.
2. Depress downshift rod with 6 lb. weight positioned against through detent stop.
3. Turn downshift adjusting screw to obtain .01—.08 inch clearance between screw and throttle arm.
4. Return system to idle, **Fig. 16.**

Fig. 14   Downshift linkage 6-cyl. (typical). 1980–81 Cougar & Thunderbird & 1980-82 Capri, Fairmont, Granada, Monarch, Mustang & Zephyr

Fig. 15   Throttle & downshift linkage V8 (typical). 1980-81 Cougar, Fairmont, Granada, LTD II, Monarch, Thunderbird, Versailles & Zephyr & 1980-82 Capri & Mustang

Fig. 16 Throttle & downshift linkage 9 (typical). 1980 Bobcat, Capri, Fairmont, Mustang, Pinto & Zephyr & 1981–82 w/4-140 engine, all

BANDS
ADJUST

NOTE: The intermediate and low-reverse bands adjusting screw locknut must be discarded and a new one installed each time a band is adjusted.

INTERMEDIATE BAND

1. On C3 units, disconnect downshift linkage from transmission lever.
2. On all units, discard adjusting screw locknut and install a new locknut.
3. With tools shown in **Figs. 17 and 18**, tighten adjusting screw until tool handle clicks. This tool is a pre-set torque wrench which clicks and overruns when the torque on the adjusting screw reaches 10 ft-lbs.
4. On 1980 C3 units, back off adjusting screw 1½ turns or 2 turns on 1981–85 units. On C4 units back screw off 1¾ turns for coarse pitch threads or 3 turns for fine pitch threads. Torque locknut to 35–45 ft. lbs.
5. Hold adjusting screw from turning and tighten locknut.
6. On C3 units, connect downshift linkage to transmission lever.

C4 LOW-REVERSE BAND

1. Loosen lock nut several turns.
2. Tighten adjusting screw until tool handle clicks, **Fig. 19**. Tool shown is a pre-set torque wrench which clicks and overruns when the torque on the adjusting screw reaches 10 ft-lbs.
3. Back off adjusting screw exactly 3 full turns.
4. Hold adjusting screw from turning and tighten lock nut.

CONTROL VALVE

NOTE: All fasteners used on C3 transmissions are designed to metric specifications.

1. Support vehicle on jack stands.
2. Drain transmission fluid, then remove oil pan, fluid screen, gasket and on early C3 units, remove three spacers.

Fig. 17 Intermediate band adjustment. C4

NOTE: If fluid is to be reused, filter it through a 100 mesh screen.

3. On C3 units:
   a. Remove rear servo cover and gasket.
   b. Remove control valve attaching bolts. Note the different length and location of each bolt.
   b. Carefully remove control valve while unlocking and detaching selector lever connecting rod.
4. On C4 units:
   a. Shift selector lever into PARK and remove the two detent spring to control valve and case bolts.
   b. Remove remaining control valve to case bolts, then while holding manual valve inward, remove control valve.

NOTE: Failure to hold manual valve inward, while removing control valve, could cause manual valve to become damaged.

5. After installing valve, torque attaching bolts to 84–108 in. lbs. on C3 units and 80–120 in. lbs. on C4 units.

SERVO REPAIR
C4 INTERMEDIATE SERVO

1. Support vehicle on jack stands.
2. On some models, it is necessary to remove crossmember to gain access to the servo.
3. Remove servo cover attaching screws, servo cover, gasket, piston and piston return spring.
4. Replace piston seals. Lubricate new seals with transmission fluid before installation.
5. Reverse procedure to install.

C4 LOW-REVERSE SERVO

1. Support vehicle on jack stands.

Fig. 18 Intermediate band adjustment. C3

2. Loosen reverse band adjusting screw locknut and torque adjusting screw to 10 ft. lbs. With adjusting screw torqued, the band strut is forced against case, preventing the strut from falling out of position when removing servo piston.
3. Remove servo cover retaining bolts, servo cover, seal and servo piston from case.
4. On some models, the piston seal is bonded to the piston, requiring piston replacement. To remove piston from stem, insert a small screwdriver through hole in stem and remove piston from stem, insert a small screwdriver through hole in stem and remove piston retaining nut, piston, accumulator spring and spacer.
5. On all other models, replace piston seals. Lubricate new seals with transmission fluid before installation.
6. Reverse procedure to install making sure to readjust low-reverse band.

NOTE: If the band cannot be adjusted, the low-reverse band struts are not in position. Remove the fluid pan and valve body to install the struts into position. Adjust the band.

C3 REAR SERVO

1. Support vehicle on jack stands, then drain transmission.
2. Remove oil filter screws, gasket and on early models, three spacers.
3. Remove servo cover retaining screws, servo cover, piston and spring, **Fig. 20.**
4. Reverse procedure to install.

EXTENSION HOUSING

1. Support vehicle on jack stands and remove driveshaft.

NOTE: Scribe marks on driveshaft yoke and companion flange, to insure proper positioning of driveshaft during assembly.

2. Support transmission with suitable jack and disconnect speedometer cable.

Fig. 19   Low-reverse band adjustment. C4

NOTE: On some models, it will be necessary to disconnect the exhaust system from the exhaust manifolds to perform the following step.

3. Remove engine rear support to crossmember attaching bolts or nuts, then raise transmission slightly and remove rear support from extension housing.

NOTE: On some models, it will be necessary to remove crossmember in order to remove rear support from extension housing.

4. Loosen extension housing bolts and allow transmission fluid to drain and remove extension housing.

GOVERNOR

1. Remove extension housing as described previously.
2. Remove governor to governor housing retaining bolts and slide governor off output shaft.

3. Reverse procedure to install. Torque governor retaining bolts to 7 to 10 ft. lbs.

TRANSMISSION
REPLACE

ALL MODELS

1. Support vehicle on jack stands and remove converter housing lower cover.
2. Drain transmission oil pan and the converter. Use a wrench on crankshaft pulley nut to rotate crankshaft and converter to gain access to drain plug.

NOTE: Do not rotate overhead camshaft engines in opposite direction of normal rotation.

3. Remove converter to flywheel bolts or nuts.
4. Remove propeller shaft.
5. Remove vacuum line hose from transmission vacuum unit. Disconnect vacuum line from clip.
6. If equipped, disconnect TRS switch wire.
7. Remove two extension housing to crossmember bolts.
8. Remove speedometer cable from extension housing.
9. Disconnect exhaust system if necessary.

NOTE: On some models with C3 transmission, remove rear engine support.

10. On all models, disconnect oil cooler lines from transmission.
11. Remove the manual and kickdown linkage rods from transmission shift levers.
12. Where necessary disconnect the neu-

Fig. 20   Rear servo removal C3

tral start switch wires.
13. Remove starter.
14. Remove transmission fluid filler tube.
15. Support transmission with suitable jack and remove cross-member.
16. Remove converter housing to engine bolts and lower transmission from vehicle.
17. Reverse procedure to install.

NOTE: Flywheel assemblies used with C3 transmissions have a pilot hole to ensure proper flywheel to converter alignment. During installation, the flywheel must be indexed with the pilot hole in the six o'clock position. Because the flywheel has only one converter drain plug access hole, it is necessary to rotate the converter so the drain plug is located at 4 o'clock position with a 2.3 Litre engine, and 8 o'clock position with a 2.8 Litre engine. On some models with C4 transmission, align dyed converter drive stud into painted flywheel hole to maintain initial engine to transmission balance.

Ford C5 Automatic Transmission

INDEX

TRANSMISSION IDENTIFICATION

Each transmission is identified by a tag, **Fig. 1,** located under the lower front intermediate servo cover bolt. The tag indicates model prefix and suffix, assembly part numbers, and the build date code. The service identification number indicates changes to service details which affect interchangeability within the same transmission model line.

Fig. 1   C5 identification tag

C5 Transmission

Year	Car Model	Trans. Code	Engine Model
1982	Mustang/Capri	PEN-G	6-200
		PEM-AM3	V8-255
	Fairmont/Zephyr	PEN-C	6-200
		PEN-G	6-200
	Zephyr	PEN-P	6-200
	Fairmont/Zephyr	PEM-AL3	V8-255
	Granada/Cougar & XR7	PEN-C	6-200
		PEN-G	6-200
		PEN-J	6-200
		PEN-K	6-200
		PEN-P	6-200
		PEP-B	V6-232
		PEP-D	V6-232
		PEP-E	V6-232
		PEP-F	V6-232
		PEP-G	V6-232
		PEP-H	V6-232
		PEP-N	V6-232
		PEP-P	V6-232
	Thunderbird	PEN-K	6-200
		PEB-Z2	6-200
		PEN-S	6-200
1983	Mustang/Capri	PEP-B1	V6-232
		PEP-R	V6-232

Year	Car Model	Trans. Code	Engine Model
	Fairmont/Zephyr	PEN-G1	6-200
		PEN-P1	6-200
		PEN-AA	6-200
		PEN-AB	6-200
		PEN-BA	6-200
		PEN-CA	6-200
	LTD/Marquis	PEN-S1	6-200
		PEN-U	6-200
		PEN-Y	6-200
		PEN-Z	6-200
		PEP-R	V6-232
		PEP-W	V6-232
	Thunderbird/Cougar	PEP-V	V6-232
		PEP-W	V6-232
1984	Mustang/Capri	PEP-AF	V6-232
	LTD	PEP-AK	V6-232
	LTD/Marquis	PEP-AC	V6-232
		PEP-AE	V6-232
		PEP-Z	V6-232
	Thunderbird/Cougar	PEP-AD	V6-232
		PEP-AE	V6-232
1985	LTD/Marquis	PEP-Z1, AC1, AE1	V6-232
	Mustang/Capri	PEP-AF1, AG1	V6-232
	Thunderbird/Cougar	PEP-AD1, AE1	V6-232

Fig. 2   Ford C5 transmission

DESCRIPTION

The C5 transmission, **Fig. 2,** is a three-speed fully automatic unit. First and second gear can be selected manually. The transmission consists of a welded torque converter assembly, a two-unit planetary gear train, and a hydraulic system which controls gear selection and automatic shifts. Larger displacement engines use a 12-inch torque converter which has a converter clutch. The planetary gear train, which is the same as that used in the C4 with minor changes, is a Simpson design with two gear sets in series and common sun gear. Gear operation is controlled by two friction clutches and two bands.

In spite of some similarities to the C4, the C5 incorporates major differences in the hydraulic system. The valve body is different and the converter relief valve has been moved from the reactor support in the pump assembly to the timing valve body. As a result C4 oil pump assemblies cannot be used when servicing the C5.

With the selector in P (Park) position the transmission is in neutral and the output shaft is locked to the case by the parking pawl. In R (Reverse) the transmission is in reverse gear. In N (Neutral) the engine is in neutral and the output shaft is not locked to the case. D (Drive) is the normal driving range in which the vehicle starts in low with automatic upshifts to second (intermediate) and high (direct drive). With throttle closed, the transmission downshifts from high to low, when vehicle speed drops to 10 mph. In 2 (intermediate), the transmis-

sion shifts to second gear and remains there regardless of speed. In 1 (low), the transmission stays in low and does not upshift. If placed in 1 above 25 mph, the transmission will shift to second and downshift to low, once vehicle speed has dropped below 25 mph. At speeds below 25 mph, the transmission shifts to low immediately.

TROUBLESHOOTING GUIDE

SLOW INITIAL ENGAGEMENT

1. Improper fluid level.
2. Damaged or improperly adjusted linkage.
3. Contaminated fluid.
4. Improper clutch and band application or low main control pressure.

ROUGH INITIAL ENGAGEMENTS IN EITHER FORWARD OR REVERSE

1. Improper fluid level.
2. High engine idle.
3. Automatic choke on (warm temp.).
4. Looseness in the driveshaft U-joint or engine mount.
5. Incorrect linkage adjustment.
6. Improper clutch or band application, or oil control pressure.

NO OR DELAYED FORWARD ENGAGEMENT

1. Improper fluid level.
2. Manual linkage, misadjusted or damaged.
3. Low main control pressure.
4. Valve body bolts, loose or too tight.
5. Valve body, dirty or sticking valve.
6. Forward clutch assembly burnt or damaged.
7. Forward clutch assembly piston seals worn or cut.
8. Forward clutch assembly cylinder ball check not seating.
9. Forward clutch assembly stator support seal ring grooves, damaged or worn.

NO OR DELAYED REVERSE ENGAGEMENT

1. Improper fluid level.
2. Low main control pressure in reverse.
3. Manual linkage misadjusted or damaged.
4. Valve body, dirty or sticking valve.
5. Valve body bolts loose or too tight.
6. Reverse clutch assembly, burnt or worn.
7. Reverse clutch assembly piston seals, worn or cut.
8. Reverse clutch assembly piston ball not seating.
9. Reverse clutch assembly stator support seal rings or ring grooves, worn or damaged.

AUTOMATIC TRANSMISSIONS/TRANSAXLES

NO OR DELAYED REVERSE ENGAGEMENT AND/OR NO ENGINE BRAKING IN MANUAL LOW (1)

1. Low reverse band or servo piston burnt or worn.
2. Low reverse servo seal worn or cut.
3. Low reverse servo bore damaged.
4. Low reverse servo piston sticking in bore.
5. Low reverse band, line pressure low.
6. Low reverse bands out of adjustment.
7. Polished or glazed band or drum.

NO ENGINE BRAKING IN MANUAL SECOND GEAR

1. Improper fluid level.
2. Linkage out of adjustment.
3. Intermediate band out of adjustment.
4. Improper band or clutch application, or oil pressure control system.
5. Intermediate servo leaking.
6. Polished or glazed band or drum.

NO ENGAGEMENT FORWARD AND REVERSE

1. Pump gear damaged.
2. Output shaft broken.
3. Turbine shaft or input shaft broken.

FORWARD ENGAGEMENT SLIP, SHUDDERS OR CHATTERS

1. Improper fluid level.
2. Manual linkage misadjusted or damaged.
3. Low main control pressure.
4. Valve body bolts, loose or too tight.
5. Valve body dirty or sticking valve.
6. Forward clutch piston ball check not sealing.
7. Forward clutch piston seal cut or worn.
8. Contamination blocking forward clutch feed hole.
9. Low (planetary) one way clutch damaged.

REVERSE ENGAGEMENT SLIP, SHUDDERS OR CHATTERS

1. Improper fluid level.
2. Low main control pressure in reverse.
3. Reverse servo or servo bore damaged.
4. Low (planetary) one-way clutch damaged.
5. Reverse clutch drum bushing damaged.
6. Reverse clutch stator support seal rings or ring grooves worn or damaged.
7. Reverse clutch piston seal cut or worn.
8. Reverse band out of adjustment or damaged.
9. Looseness in the driveshaft U-joints or engine mounts.

NO DRIVE, SLIPS OR CHATTERS IN FIRST GEAR "D"

1. Damaged or worn one-way clutch.

NO DRIVE, SLIPS OR CHATTERS IN SECOND

1. Improper fluid level.
2. Damaged or improperly adjusted linkage.
3. Intermediate band out of adjustment.
4. Improper band or clutch application, or oil pressure control.
5. Damaged or worn servo and/or internal leaks.
6. Dirty or sticking valve body.
7. Polished or glazed intermediate band or drum.

START UP IN SECOND OR THIRD

1. Improper fluid level.
2. Damaged or improperly adjusted linkage.
3. Improper band and/or clutch application, or oil pressure control system.
4. Damaged or worn governor, governor sticking.
5. Valve body loose.
6. Dirty or sticking valve body.
7. Cross leaks between valve body and case mating surface.

SHIFT POINTS INCORRECT

1. Improper fluid level.
2. Improper vacuum hose routing or leaks.
3. Improper operation of EGR system.
4. Throttle out of adjustment.
5. Improper clutch or band application, or oil pressure control system.
6. Damaged or worn governor.
7. Dirty or sticking valve body.

ALL UPSHIFTS HARSH, DELAYED OR NO UPSHIFTS

1. Improper fluid level.
2. Manual linkage misadjusted or damaged.
3. Governor sticking.
4. Main control pressure too high.
5. Valve body bolts loose or too tight.
6. Valve body dirty or valves sticking.
7. Vacuum leak to diaphragm unit.

ALL UPSHIFTS EARLY OR SLUGGISH

1. Improper fluid level.
2. Low main control pressure.
3. Valve body loose or too tight.
4. Valve body valve sticking.
5. Governor valve sticking.

NO LOW TO SECOND UPSHIFT

1. Improper fluid level.
2. Manual linkage misadjusted or damaged.
3. Governor valve sticking.
4. Valve body bolts loose or too tight.

5. Valve body dirty or sticking valves.
6. Intermediate clutch or band and/or servo assembly burnt.
7. Intermediate piston seals worn or cut.
8. Intermediate piston not positioned properly.
9. Intermediate clutch in improper stack up.
10. Low line pressure in intermediate clutch or band.

ROUGH, HARSH, OR DELAYED UPSHIFT LOW TO SECOND

1. Governor valve sticking.
2. Improper fluid level.
3. Poor engine performance.
4. Main control pressure too high.
5. Valve body bolts loose or too tight.
6. Valve body dirty or valves sticking.
7. Intermediate band out of adjustment.
8. Damaged intermediate servo.
9. Engine vacuum leak.

EARLY, SOFT OR SLIPPING LOW TO SECOND UPSHIFT

1. Improper fluid level.
2. Low main control.
3. Valve body bolts loose or too tight.
4. Valve body dirty or valves sticking.
5. Governor valve sticking.
6. Incorrect engine performance.
7. Intermediate band out of adjustment.
8. Damaged intermediate servo or band.
9. Polished or glazed band or drum.

NO SECOND TO THIRD UPSHIFT

1. Low fluid level.
2. Low main control pressure to direct clutch.
3. Valve body bolts too loose or too tight.
4. Valve body dirty or valves sticking.
5. Converter damper hub weld broken.

HARSH OR DELAYED SECOND TO THIRD UPSHIFT

1. Low fluid level.
2. Valve body bolts loose or too tight.
3. Valve body dirty or valves sticking.
4. Damaged or worn intermediate servo release and high clutch piston check ball.
5. Incorrect engine performance.
6. Engine vacuum leak.

EARLY OR SOFT SECOND TO THIRD UPSHIFT

1. Improper fluid level.
2. Valve body bolts loose or too tight.
3. Valve body dirty or valves sticking.

ERRATIC SHIFTS

1. Improper fluid level.
2. Throttle linkage binding or sticking.
3. Valve body bolts loose or too tight.
4. Valve body dirty or valves sticking.
5. Governor valve sticking.

6. Output shaft collector body seal rings (large cast iron) worn or cut.

SHIFTS FROM LOW TO THIRD IN "D"

1. Improper fluid level.
2. Intermediate band out of adjustment.
3. Damaged intermediate servo and/or internal leaks.
4. Polished or glazed band or drum.
5. Improper band or clutch application, or oil pressure control system.
6. Valve body dirty or valves sticking.

ENGINE OVER SPEEDS ON SECOND TO THIRD UPSHIFT

1. Improper fluid level.
2. Linkage out of adjustment.
3. Improper band or clutch application, or oil pressure control system.
4. Damaged or worn high clutch and/or intermediate servo.
5. Valve body dirty or valves sticking.

ROUGH OR SHUDDER THIRD TO LOW SHIFT AT CLOSED THROTTLE

1. Improper fluid level.
2. Incorrect engine idle or performance.
3. Improper linkage adjustment.
4. Improper clutch or band application, or oil pressure control system.
5. Improper governor operation.
6. Valve body dirty or valves sticking.

NO FORCED DOWNSHIFT

1. Improper fluid level.
2. Kickdown linkage out of adjustment.
3. Damaged internal kickdown linkage.
4. Damaged or misadjusted (short) throttle linkage.
5. Valve body dirty or valves sticking.
6. Dirty or sticking governor.

ENGINE RUNAWAY ON THIRD TO SECOND SHIFT

1. Improper fluid level.
2. Linkage out of adjustment.
3. Intermediate band out of adjustment.
4. Improper band or clutch application, or oil pressure control system.
5. Damaged or worn intermediate servo.
6. Polished or glazed band or drum.
7. Valve body dirty or valves sticking.

SHIFT EFFORTS HIGH

1. Manual shift linkage damaged or misadjusted.
2. Inner manual lever nut loose.
3. Manual level retainer pin damaged.

NO START IN "P"

1. Manual linkage misadjusted.
2. Plug connector for the neutral start switch does not fit properly.
3. Neutral start switch plunger travel, inadequate.

NO START IN "P" AND "N"

1. Plug connector for the neutral start switch does not fit properly.

TRANSMISSION OVERHEATS

1. Improper fluid level.
2. Incorrect engine idle or performance.
3. Improper band or clutch application, or oil pressure control system.
4. Restriction in cooler or lines.
5. Seized converter one-way clutch.
6. Valve body dirty or valves sticking.

MAINTENANCE

CHECKING OIL LEVEL

1. With engine idling, foot brake applied and vehicle on level surface, move selector lever through each range, pausing in each position.
2. Place selector in Park and apply parking brake. Leave engine running during fluid level check.
3. Clean dirt from transmission fluid dipstick cap and remove dipstick. Wipe dipstick and push back into tube making sure it is fully seated.
4. Pull dipstick out and check fluid level. With transmission at operating temperature, fluid level should be between arrows. With transmission cool, fluid level should read between inner holes. Use only Type H fluid, Ford spec. ESP M2C166-H. Do not overfill.
5. Insert dipstick, making sure it is fully seated.

MANUAL LINKAGE
ADJUST

1. Locate slotted rod in linkage and loosen nut or screw, **Figs. 3, 4 & 5.**
2. Place selector in "D" firmly against gate stop.
3. Move manual shift lever on transmission to "D" position, three detents away from Park.
4. Tighten nut securely.
5. Move shift lever through all ranges. Check to see that detents agree with markings on shift lever. Make sure that lever cannot be moved from "D" position to 2, without ungating lever.

DOWNSHIFT LINKAGE
ADJUST
1982

1. Hold throttle lever wide open against stop.
2. Push rod down so down shift valve is forced to bottom in valve body.
3. Measure clearance between tip of adjusting screw and throttle lever, **Fig. 6.** Clearance should be .050–.070 inch.

4. Turn screw, if necessary, to obtain this clearance.

1983–85

Refer to **Fig. 7** for adjustment procedure on 1983 models or **Fig. 8** for adjustment procedures on 1984–85 models.

BANDS
ADJUST

To determine the need for adjustments, the bands can be checked as follows:

Make sure oil level is correct. Then shift selector to "R" and 2, checking for firm engagement. If engagement in "R" is delayed or mushy, adjust rear band, **Fig. 9.** If engagement in 2 is delayed or mushy, adjust front band, **Fig. 10.** Adjust bands as follows:

1. Loosen adjuster stop, remove and discard locknut. Install new locknut loosely.
2. Torque screw to 10 ft. lbs.
3. Back screw off exactly 4¼ turns for the front (intermediate) band; 3 turns for the rear (low-reverse) band.
4. Hold adjustment and torque new locknut to 35–45 ft. lbs.

VALVE BODY
REPLACE

1. Raise and support vehicle.
2. Loosen pan bolts and drain transmission fluid.
3. Remove oil pan bolts, pan, and gasket.
4. Shift transmission lever to Park, and remove two bolts attaching detent spring to valve body and case.
5. Remove filter.
6. Remove remaining valve body bolts. Hold manual valve in valve body and remove valve body from case. Manual valve must be held to prevent it from being bent or damaged.
7. Clean and remove all gasket material from pan and pan mounting face. Remove and discard nylon shipping plug, if found in pan.
8. Position valve body in case. Make sure inner downshift lever is between downshift lever stop and downshift valve. The two lands on end of manual valve must engage actuating pin on manual detect lever. Install seven valve body bolts.
9. Position detent spring on lower valve body and install spring-to-case bolt.
10. Hold detent spring roller in center of manual detent lever and install detent spring-to-lower valve body bolt. Torque bolt to 80–120 inch lbs.
11. Torque valve body bolts to 80–120 inch lbs.
12. Position filter and torque bolt to 30 inch lbs.
13. Install pan using new gasket and torque bolts to 12–16 ft. lbs.
14. Lower vehicle and fill transmission with fluid. Check pan area for leakage.

Fig. 3 Column shift manual linkage. 1982 Cougar & Granada, 1982—83 Fairmont & Zephyr, 1983—84 Cougar, LTD, Marquis & Thunderbird

Fig. 4 Floor shift manual linkage. Exc. V8-255

Fig. 5   Floor shift manual linkage. V8-255

EXTENSION HOUSING
REPLACE

1. Raise and support vehicle and remove driveshaft.
2. Using suitable jack, support transmission.
3. Remove speedometer cable from extension housing.
4. Remove engine rear support to crossmember nuts.
5. Raise transmission and remove rear support bolts. Remove crossmember.
6. Loosen extension housing bolts and let transmission drain.
7. Remove the six extension housing bolts and vacuum tube clip and remove extension housing.
8. Reverse procedure to install, noting the following torques: extension housing bolts, 28–40 ft. lbs; crossmember nuts, 35–50 ft. lbs.; rear support bolts, 25–35 ft. lbs.

GOVERNOR
REPLACE

1. Refer to "Extension Housing, Replace" and remove extension housing.
2. Remove bolts holding governor housing to governor distributor.
3. Slide governor away from distributor body and off output shaft.

4. Reverse procedure to install. Torque governor bolts to 80–120 inch lbs.

LOW-REVERSE SERVO
REPLACE

EXC. 1982 MUSTANG & CAPRI WITH V8-255 ENGINE & 1983–85 MUSTANG & CAPRI WITH V6-232 ENGINE

1. Raise and support vehicle.
2. Loosen low-reverse band adjusting screw lock nut. Torque band adjusting screw to 10 ft. lbs. to prevent band

Fig. 6   Downshift rod adjustment

strut from falling when reverse servo piston assembly is removed.
3. Disengage neutral switch harness from clips on servo cover.
4. Remove servo cover bolts, servo cover, and seal from case.
5. Remove servo piston from case. If seal is bad, piston must be replaced.
6. Install piston in case. Install cover with new seal. Use two 5/16-18×1 1/4 bolts to position cover against case. Install two cover bolts, remove two locating bolts and install remaining bolts. Torque to 12–20 ft. lbs.
7. Position neutral switch harness in clips.
8. Adjust low-reverse band. Refer to "Bands, Adjust" procedure.

NOTE: If band cannot be adjusted properly, low-reverse band struts are not in position. Remove oil pan and valve body. Position struts and install valve body and pan. Adjust band.

9. Lower vehicle and check transmission fluid level.

1982 MUSTANG & CAPRI WITH V8-255 ENGINE & 1983–85 MUSTANG & CAPRI WITH V6-232 ENGINE

1. Disconnect fan shroud and position against engine.
2. Raise and support vehicle and position suitable transmission jack under

Fig. 7 Throttle & downshift linkage adjustment. 1983 LTD & Marquis w/6-200 engine

Fig. 8 Throttle & downshift linkage adjustment. 1984–85 Cougar & Thunderbird w/V6-232 engine

TOOL T7IP-77370·H

TOOL T7IP-77370-D

Fig. 9   Low-Reverse band adjustment

transmission.
3. Remove transmission crossmember bolts.
4. Lower transmission.
5. Loosen low-reverse band adjusting screw lock nut. Torque band adjusting screw to 10 ft. lbs. to prevent band strut from falling down.
6. Disengage neutral switch wiring harness from clips on servo cover.
7. Remove servo cover bolts, servo cover, and seal from case.
8. Remove servo cover piston and spring from case. If piston seal is bad, piston must be replaced.
9. Install piston and return spring in case. Install cover with new seal. Use two 5/16-18×1¼ bolts to position cover. Install two cover bolts, remove two locating bolts and install remaining two cover bolts. Torque bolts to 12–20 ft. lbs.
10. Position neutral start switch wiring harness in clips.
11. Refer to "Bands, Adjust" procedure to adjust low-reverse band.

NOTE: If band cannot be adjusted properly, low-reverse band struts are not in position. Remove oil pan and valve body. Position struts and install valve body and pan. Adjust band.

12. Raise transmission into position and install crossmember bolts. Torque nuts to 35–50 ft. lbs.
13. Remove transmission jack and lower vehicle.
14. Install fan shroud and check transmission fluid.

INTERMEDIATE SERVO
REPLACE

1. Disconnect fan shroud from radiator

and push shroud back against engine.
2. Raise and support vehicle.
3. Support transmission with suitbable jack and remove crossmember bolts.
4. Lower transmission.
5. On models with V6-232 engine, except 1982 Thunderbird and XR7, disconnect oil cooler line.
6. On all models, remove servo cover bolts.
7. Remove servo cover/piston assembly and return spring from case.
8. Remove and discard servo cover gasket.
9. Position new gasket on servo cover so notch aligns with fluid passage in case.
10. Install piston return spring and servo cover/piston assembly in case. Use two 5/16-18×1¼ bolts to position cover against case. Install two cover bolts, remove locating bolts and install remaining cover bolts. Torque bolts to 12–20 ft. lbs.
11. Refer to "Bands, Adjust" and adjust intermediate band.

NOTE: If band cannot be adjusted properly, intermediate band strut is not in position. Remove oil pan and valve body. Position struts and install valve body and oil pan. Adjust band.

12. On Granada and Cougar models with V6-232 engine, connect transmission oil cooler line.
13. On all models, raise transmission into position and install crossmember bolts. Torque nuts to 35–50 ft. lbs.
14. Remove jack and lower vehicle.
15. Position fan shroud bolt to radiator. Check transmission fluid level.

TRANSMISSION
REPLACE

1. Disconnect battery ground cable.
2. On Granada and Cougar models with V6-232 engine, except 1982 Thunderbird, remove air cleaner assembly.
3. On all models, remove fan shroud bolts and position shroud back over fan.
4. On 1982 Granada and Cougar models with V6-232 and Mustang and Capri models with V8-255 and all 1983–85 models with V6-232, loosen clamp and disconnect thermactor air injection hose at catalytic converter check valve.
5. On models with V6-232 engine, except 1982 Thunderbird and XR7, remove the top two engine-to-transmission bolts.
6. On all models, remove driveshaft after raising vehicle.
7. Disconnect muffler inlet pipe from catalytic converter outlet pipe. Support muffler pipe assembly.

TOOL T7IP-77370-H

TOOL T7IP-77370-D

Fig. 10   Intermediate band adjustment

8. Disconnect exhaust pipes from exhaust manifolds.
9. Release catalytic converter hangers from bracket by pulling back on converter.
10. Remove speedometer cable clamp bolt and pull cable out of extension housing.
11. Disconnect neutral start switch harness connector.
12. Disconnect kick down rod at transmission lever.
13. Disconnect shift linkage at bellcrank. On vehicles with floor shifts, remove shift cable routing bracket bolts and disconnect cable at transmission lever.
14. Remove converter dust shield.
15. Remove torque converter drive plate nuts. Crankshaft can be turned by using socket and ratchet handle on crankshaft pulley bolt.
16. Remove starter.
17. Loosen nuts attaching rear support to No. 3 crossmember.
18. Position suitable jack under transmission oil pan.
19. Remove bolt attaching No. 3 crossmember to body brackets.
20. Lower transmission enough to allow access to cooler line fittings. Disconnect cooler lines.
21. Remove all transmission-to-engine bolts.
22. Pull transmission back to clear converter studs. Lower transmission.
23. Reverse procedure to install. Note the following torque values: engine-to-transmission bolts, 40–50 ft. lbs.; no. 3 crossmember bolts, 20–30 ft. lbs.; rear support nuts, 30–50 ft. lbs.; torque converter-to-drive-plate nuts, 20–30 ft. lbs.; linkage bellcrank bracket, 12–16 ft. lbs.; speedometer cable clamp, 36–54 inch lbs.

Ford C6 Automatic Transmission

INDEX

TRANSMISSION IDENTIFICATION

An identification tag attached to the servo cover bolt, includes the model prefix and suffix

Year	Car Model	Trans. Code	Engine Model
1980	Ford	PGD-BH5, CU5	V8-302
		PGD-DD, DE, DG	V8-351
	Mercury	PGD-BH5, CU5	V8-302
		PGD-DD, DE, DG	V8-351

①—Police or fleet

DESCRIPTION

As shown in **Fig. 1,** the transmission consists essentially of a torque converter, a compound planetary gear train controlled by one band, three disc clutches and a one-way clutch, and a hydraulic control system. The transmission is made so that a system of manual and automatic shifting is provided.

AUTOMATIC & MANUAL SHIFTING

This unit has a shift pattern which is indicated on the selector as P-R-N-D-2-1. This refers respectively to Park, Reverse, Neutral, Full Automatic, Second Gear (manual), Low Gear (manual). In this unit an overriding control is provided which enables the driver to exercise his own judgement with regard to the gear ratios to be selected and an understanding of what is possible greatly enhances the pleasure to be derived from driving the car. No automatic mechanism has the power of anticipation, but the driver can see ahead and has the means for over-riding the automatic mechanism.

Automatic Shift

In "D" position the shift sequence is fully automatic in that the transmission starts in low gear and upshifts through second gear to third or high gear.

Manual Shifting

The shift to 2 or 1 is done manually by shifting the lever from neutral to either position. In "1" position, the transmission starts in 1st (low gear) and is retained. In "2" position it starts in 2nd gear and remains in 2nd gear, regardless of road speed.

Manual Shift To "1"

Manual shifting from "D" to "1" can also be accomplished any time. Here the transmission immediately shifts to second and remains in second until the predetermined governor control speed allows it to shift down to low gear where it remains. The governor speed control at this point eliminates the possibility of a direct down shift to low gear until the road speed is reduced.

Shift Lever Controls

A shift lever button control is used to shift from neutral to reverse or park, also when shifting from "D" to "2" or "1" position. However, the button control function is not required when shifting from neutral to "D", or to shift forward from "1" to "2" position.

PARKING PAWL

The transmission gear train is in neutral in both P and N positions. There is no pressure to any clutch and only the transmission input shaft turns. In park, a pawl engages a parking gear which is splined to the transmission output shaft, **Fig. 1,** to lock the rear wheels to the transmission main case.

A neutral start switch, mounted on the transmission and operated by the selector linkage, completes the engine cranking circuit in P and N only so that the engine cannot be started in any drive gear.

FORCED DOWNSHIFTS

Forced downshifts (kickdown shifts) from high to second gear are possible at speeds as high as 65 mph. In D1 it is possible to force a downshift to 1st gear up to 30 mph.

The carburetor is at full throttle before the accelerator is floored. Up to full throttle, a "torque demand" downshift to 2nd is possible up to 40 mph. "Kickdown" shifts require depressing the accelerator to the floor to actuate the downshift valve in the transmission.

TROUBLESHOOTING GUIDE

NO DRIVE IN FORWARD SPEEDS

1. Manual linkage adjustment.
2. Check control pressure.
3. Valve body.
4. Make air pressure check.
5. Forward clutch.
6. Leakage in hydraulic system.

STATOR SUPPORT · CASE · FRONT PUMP · FORWARD CLUTCH HUB AND RING GEAR · LOW-REVERSE CLUTCH · PARKING GEAR · GOVERNOR DISTRIBUTOR SLEEVE · GOVERNOR · SPLINE SEAL · OUTPUT SHAFT · INPUT SHELL · REVERSE RING GEAR · ONE-WAY CLUTCH · INTERMEDIATE BAND · EXTENSION HOUSING SEAL · EXTENSION HOUSING · SPEEDOMETER DRIVE GEAR · GOVERNOR DISTRIBUTOR · INPUT SHAFT · PARKING PAWL · REVERSE PLANET CARRIER · FRONT PLANET CARRIER · CONVERTER · PARK TOGGLE ROD · FORWARD CLUTCH · CONTROL LEVERS · CONVERTER ONE-WAY CLUTCH · TURBINE · STATOR · IMPELLER · CONTROL VALVE BODY · REVERSE-HIGH CLUTCH

Fig. 1   Sectional view of C6 transmission

ROUGH INITIAL ENGAGEMENT IN D, D1, D2 OR 2

1. Engine idle speed too high.
2. Vacuum diaphragm unit or tubes restricted, leaking or maladjusted.
3. Check control pressure.
4. Valve body.
5. Forward clutch.

1-2 OR 2-3 SHIFT POINTS INCORRECT OR ERRATIC

1. Check fluid level.
2. Vacuum diaphragm unit or tubes restricted, leaking or maladjusted.
3. Downshift linkage, including inner lever position.
4. Manual linkage adjustment.
5. Governor defective.
6. Check control pressure.
7. Valve body.
8. Make air pressure check.

ROUGH 1-2 UPSHIFTS

1. Vacuum diaphragm unit or tubes restricted, leaking or maladjusted.
2. Intermediate servo.
3. Intermediate band.
4. Check control pressure.
5. Valve body.

ROUGH 2-3 SHIFTS

1. Vacuum diaphragm or tubes restricted, leaking or maladjusted.
2. Intermediate servo.
3. Check control pressure.
4. Intermediate band.
5. Valve body.
6. Make air pressure check.
7. Reverse-high clutch.
8. Reverse-high clutch piston air bleed valve.

DRAGGED OUT 1-2 SHIFT

1. Check fluid level.
2. Vacuum diaphragm unit or tubes restricted, leaking or maladjusted.
3. Intermediate servo.
4. Check control pressure.
5. Intermediate band.
6. Valve body.
7. Make air pressure check.
8. Leakage in hydraulic system.

ENGINE OVERSPEEDS ON 2-3 SHIFT

1. Manual linkage adjustment.
2. Check fluid level.
3. Vacuum diaphragm unit or tubes restricted, leaking or maladjusted.
4. Intermediate servo.
5. Check control pressure.
6. Valve body.
7. Intermediate band.
8. Reverse-high clutch.
9. Reverse-high clutch piston air bleed valve.

NO 1-2 OR 2-3 SHIFT

1. Manual linkage adjustment.
2. Downshift linkage including inner lever position.
3. Vacuum diaphragm unit or tubes restricted, leaking or maladjusted.
4. Governor.
5. Check control pressure.
6. Valve body.
7. Intermediate band.
8. Intermediate servo.
9. Reverse-high clutch.
10. Leakage in hydraulic system.

NO 3-1 SHIFT IN D1, 2 OR 3-2 SHIFT IN D2 OR D

1. Governor.
2. Valve body.

NO FORCED DOWNSHIFTS

1. Downshift linkage, including inner lever position.
2. Check control pressure.
3. Valve body.

RUNAWAY ENGINE ON FORCED 3-2 SHIFT

1. Check control pressure.
2. Intermediate servo.
3. Intermediate band.
4. Valve body.

5. Vacuum diaphragm unit or tubes restricted, leaking or maladjusted.
6. Leakage in hydraulic system.

ROUGH 3-2 SHIFT OR 3-1 SHIFT AT CLOSED THROTTLE

1. Engine idle speed.
2. Vacuum diaphragm unit or tubes restricted, leaking or maladjusted.
3. Intermediate servo.
4. Check control pressure.
5. Valve body.

SHIFTS 1-3 IN D, D1, 2, D2

1. Intermediate band.
2. Intermediate servo.
3. Valve body.
4. Governor.
5. Make air pressure check.

NO ENGINE BRAKING IN 1ST GEAR—MANUAL LOW RANGE

1. Manual linkage adjustment.
2. Low-reverse clutch.
3. Valve body.
4. Governor.
5. Make air pressure check.
6. Leakage in hydraulic system.

CREEPS EXCESSIVELY

1. Engine idle speed too high.

SLIPS OR CHATTERS IN 1ST GEAR, D1

1. Check fluid level.
2. Vacuum diaphragm unit or tubes restricted, leaking or maladjusted.
3. Check control pressure.
4. Valve body.
5. Forward clutch.
6. Leakage in hydraulic system.
7. Planetary one-way clutch.

SLIPS OR CHATTERS IN 2ND GEAR

1. Check fluid level.
2. Vacuum diaphragm unit or tubes restricted, leaking or maladjusted.
3. Intermediate servo.
4. Intermediate band.
5. Check control pressure.
6. Valve body.
7. Make air pressure check.
8. Forward clutch.
9. Leakage in hydraulic system.

SLIPS OR CHATTERS IN REVERSE

1. Check fluid level.
2. Vacuum diaphragm unit or tubes restricted, leaking or maladjusted.
3. Manual linkage adjustment.
4. Low-reverse clutch.
5. Check control pressure.
6. Valve body.
7. Make air pressure check.
8. Reverse-high clutch.
9. Leakage in hydraulic system.
10. Reverse-high clutch piston air bleed

valve.

NO DRIVE IN D1 OR 2

1. Manual linkage adjustment.
2. Check control pressure.
3. Valve body.
4. Planetary one-way clutch.

NO DRIVE IN D, D2

1. Check fluid level.
2. Manual linkage adjustment.
3. Check control pressure.
4. Intermediate servo.
5. Valve body.
6. Make air pressure check.
7. Leakage in hydraulic system.

NO DRIVE IN L OR 1

1. Check fluid level.
2. Check control pressure.
3. Valve body.
4. Make air pressure check.
5. Leakage in hydraulic system.

NO DRIVE IN R ONLY

1. Check fluid level.
2. Manual linkage adjustment.
3. Low-reverse clutch.
4. Check control pressure.
5. Valve body.
6. Make air pressure check.
7. Reverse-high clutch.
8. Leakage in hydraulic system.
9. Reverse-high clutch piston air bleed valve.

NO DRIVE IN ANY SELECTOR POSITION

1. Check fluid level.
2. Manual linkage adjustment.
3. Check control pressure.
4. Valve body.
5. Make air pressure check.
6. Leakage in hydraulic system.
7. Front pump.

LOCKUP IN D1 OR 2

1. Valve body.
2. Parking linkage.
3. Leakage in hydraulic system.

LOCKUP IN D2 OR D

1. Low-reverse clutch.
2. Valve body.
3. Reverse-high clutch.
4. Parking linkage.
5. Leakage in hydraulic system.
6. Planetary one-way clutch.

LOCKUP IN L OR 1

1. Valve body.
2. Parking linkage.
3. Leakage in hydraulic system.

LOCKUP IN R ONLY

1. Valve body.
2. Forward clutch.
3. Parking linkage.
4. Leakage in hydraulic system.

PARKING LOCK BINDS OR DOES NOT HOLD

1. Manual linkage adjustment.
2. Parking linkage.

TRANSMISSION OVERHEATS

1. Oil cooler and connections.
2. Valve body.
3. Vacuum diaphragm unit or tubes restricted, leaking or maladjusted.
4. Check control pressure.
5. Converter one-way clutch.
6. Converter pressure check valves.

MAXIMUM SPEED TOO LOW, POOR ACCELERATION

1. Engine performance.
2. Car brakes.
3. Forward clutch.

TRANSMISSION NOISY IN N AND P

1. Check fluid level.
2. Valve body.
3. Front pump.

NOISY IN 1ST, 2ND, 3RD OR REVERSE

1. Check fluid level.
2. Valve body.
3. Planetary assembly.
4. Forward clutch.
5. Reverse-high clutch.
6. Planetary one-way clutch.

CAR MOVES FORWARD IN N

1. Manual linkage adjustment.
2. Forward clutch.

FLUID LEAK

1. Check fluid level.
2. Converter drain plugs.
3. Oil pan gasket, filler tube or seal.
4. Oil cooler and connections.
5. Manual or downshift lever shaft seal.
6. ⅛" pipe plugs in case.
7. Extension housing-to-case gasket.
8. Extension housing rear oil seal.
9. Speedometer driven gear adapter seal.
10. Vacuum diaphragm unit or tubes.
11. Intermediate servo.
12. Engine rear oil seal.

MAINTENANCE

CHECKING OIL LEVEL

1. Make sure car is on a level floor.
2. Apply parking brake firmly.
3. Run engine at normal idle speed. If transmission fluid is cold, run engine at a fast idle until fluid reaches normal operating temperature. When fluid is warm, slow engine to normal idle speed.
4. Shift selector lever through all positions, then place lever at "P". Do not

Fig. 2 Column shift linkage. 1980 Ford & Mercury

Fig. 3 Manual linkage, floor shift. Typical. Column lock rod is used on some models

shut down engine during fluid level checks.

5. Clean all dirt from dipstick cap before removing dipstick from filler tube.
6. Pull dipstick out of tube, wipe it clean and push it all the way back in tube.
7. Pull dipstick out of tube again and check fluid level. If necessary, add enough fluid to raise the level to the "F" mark on dipstick. Do not overfill.

DRAIN & REFILL

NOTE: The Ford Motor Company recommends the use of an automatic transmission fluid with Qualification No. M2C-138-CJ. The recommended fluid is said to have a greater coefficient of friction and greater ability to handle maximum engine torques without band or clutch slippage.

Normal maintenance and lubrication requirements do not necessitate periodic fluid changes. If a major failure has occurred in the transmission, it will have to be removed for service. At this time the con-

verter and transmission cooler must be thoroughly flushed to remove any foreign matter.

1. To drain the fluid, loosen pan attaching bolts and allow fluid to drain.
2. After fluid has drained to the level of the pan flange, remove pan bolts working from rear and both sides of pan to allow it to drop and drain slowly.
3. When fluid has stopped draining, remove and clean pan and screen. Discard pan gasket.
4. Using a new gasket, install pan.
5. Add 3 quarts of recommended fluid to transmission through filler tube.
6. Run engine at idle speed for 2 minutes, and then run it at a fast idle until it reaches normal operating temperature.
7. Shift selector lever through all positions, place it at "P" and check fluid level.
8. If necessary, add enough fluid to

transmission to bring it to the "F" mark on the dipstick.

MANUAL LINKAGE
ADJUST

ALL MODELS

Column Shift
1. Place selector lever into "D" position using suitable force to hold it tight against the stop.
2. Loosen shift rod adjusting nut, point A in **Fig. 2**.
3. Shift transmission manual lever to D.
4. Make sure selector lever has not moved from D position then tighten adjusting nut to 10–20 ft. lbs.

Floor Shift
1. Place transmission selector lever in D position.
2. Raise car and loosen shift rod retaining nut, **Fig. 3**.
3. Move transmission manual lever to D position.
4. Tighten retaining nut to 10–20 ft. lbs.

THROTTLE & DOWNSHIFT LINKAGE

Adjusting the throttle linkage is important to be certain the throttle and kickdown systems are properly adjusted. The kickdown system should come in when the accelerator is pressed through detent, and not before detent. See **Fig. 4.**

ALL MODELS

1. Hold carburetor lever in the wide open throttle position.
2. Hold downshift rod against through

Fig. 4 Throttle & downshift linkage. 1980 Ford, Mercury & Lincoln Continental (typical)

Fig. 5 Band adjustment

Fig. 6 Intermediate servo disassembled

detent stop.
3. On all models except Versailles, adjust downshift screw to provide 0.01–0.08 inch clearance between throttle arm and screw. On Versailles models, adjust screw for 0.01–0.03 inch clearance.
4. Connect downshift lever return spring.

BAND ADJUSTMENT

NOTE: When making the intermediate band adjustment, the lock nut must be discarded and a new one installed each time the band is adjusted.

1. Loosen the locknut on the adjusting screw several turns, **Fig. 5**.
2. Torque the screw to 10 ft. lbs, or until the adjuster wrench overruns.
3. Back the screw off exactly 1½ turns.
4. Hold the adjustment and torque the locknut to the 35–45 ft. lbs.

OIL PAN & CONTROL VALVE

REMOVAL

1. Raise car on hoist or jack stands.
2. Loosen and remove all but two oil pan bolts from front of case and drop rear edge of pan to drain fluid. Remove and clean pan and screen.
3. Unfasten and remove valve body.

INSTALLATION

1. Position valve body to case, making sure that selector and downshift levers are engaged, then install and torque attaching bolts to specifications.
2. Using a new pan gasket, secure pan to case and torque bolts to specifications.
3. Lower car and fill transmission to the correct level with specified fluid.

Fig. 7 Governor installed

INTERMEDIATE SERVO

REMOVAL, EXC. CONTINENTAL

1. Raise car and remove engine rear support-to-extension housing bolts.
2. Raise transmission high enough to relieve weight from support.
3. Remove support (1 bolt).
4. Lower transmission.
5. Place drain pan beneath servo.
6. Remove servo cover-to-case bolts.
7. Loosen band adjusting screw locknut.
8. Remove servo cover, piston, spring and gasket from case, screwing band adjusting screw inward as piston is removed. This insures that there will be enough tension on the band to keep the struts properly engaged in the band end notches while the piston is removed.

REMOVAL, CONTINENTAL

1. Raise vehicle and remove servo cover retaining bolts.
2. Remove manual and downshift control rod splash shield from frame side rail and reinforcement plate from beneath transmission oil pan.
3. Loosen band adjusting screw locknut.
4. Remove engine rear mount to crossmember nuts and with a suitable jack,

raise transmission to remove weight from crossmember.
5. Remove engine rear support to extension housing bolts, then the support.
6. Remove servo cover, piston, spring and gasket from case, turning adjusting screw inward as piston is removed. This places enough tension on the band to keep struts properly engaged in band end notches as piston is withdrawn.

INSTALLATION, ALL

NOTE: If piston or piston sealing lips are damaged, replace complete piston and rod assembly, **Fig. 6**.

1. Coat piston and servo cover seal with transmission fluid. Coat a new servo cover gasket with petroleum jelly and install on cover.
2. Install piston into servo cover and spring onto piston stem.
3. Insert piston stem in case. Secure cover with bolts, taking care to back off band adjusting screw while tightening cover bolts. Make sure that vent tube retaining clip is in place.
4. Raise transmission high enough to install engine rear support. Secure support to extension housing. Lower transmission as required to install support-to-cross-member bolt.
5. On Continental models, secure manual and downshift rod splash shield to frame side rail.
6. Remove jack supporting transmission and adjust the band as outlined previously.
7. Lower car and replenish fluid as required.

EXTENSION HOUSING & GOVERNOR

REMOVAL

1. Raise vehicle and disconnect parking brake cable from equalizer and on Continental models, remove the equalizer.
2. Disconnect drive shaft from rear axle flange and remove from transmission.

3. Disconnect speedometer cable from extension housing.
4. Remove engine rear support to extension housing bolts and on Continental models, remove reinforcement plate from beneath oil pan.
5. Raise transmission slightly with a suitable jack to remove weight from engine rear support.
6. Remove engine rear support to crossmember bolt and the support.
7. Lower transmission to permit access to extension housing bolts. Remove bolts and slide housing off output shaft.
8. Disconnect governor from distributor (4 bolts) and slide governor off output shaft.

INSTALLATION FIG. 7

1. Secure governor to distributor flange.
2. Position new gasket on transmission.
3. Secure extension housing to case.
4. Raise transmission to position engine rear support on crossmember and install the support attaching bolt.
5. Lower transmission and remove jack.

Install engine rear support to extension housing bolts and on Continental models, oil pan reinforcement plate.
6. Install speedometer cable.
7. On Continental models, install parking brake cable equalizer and on all models, connect parking brake cable to equalizer. Adjust parking brake.
8. Install drive shaft.
9. Correct transmission fluid level.

TRANSMISSION
REPLACE

NOTE: On models with the neutral safety switch wire harness connected at the dash panel, disconnect the harness before raising the vehicle.

NOTE: On Mark V models, disconnect fan shroud from radiator.

1. Raise vehicle and drain transmission and converter.

NOTE: On Continental models, disconnect idler arm from frame side rail.

2. Remove drive shaft and starter.
3. Remove four converter to flywheel attaching bolts.
4. Disconnect parking brake front cable from equalizer.
5. Disconnect speedometer cable and transmission linkage.
6. Disconnect TRS switch wire, if equipped.
7. Where necessary, disconnect muffler inlet pipes from exhaust manifold.
8. Support the transmission with a suitable jack, remove parking brake rear cables from the equalizer and remove the crossmember.
9. Lower transmission and remove oil cooler lines, vacuum line and transmission oil filler tube.
10. Secure the transmission to the jack with the chain, remove the converter housing to cylinder block bolts and carefully move the transmission away from the engine, at the same time lowering it to clear the underside of the vehicle.
11. Reverse procedure to install.

Ford FMX Automatic Transmission

INDEX

TRANSMISSION IDENTIFICATION

The identification tag is on the lower right hand extension housing-to-case bolt.

FORD MODELS

Year	Engine	Trans. Code
1980	8-351	PHB-BK, 1
	8-351	PHB-BP, 1
	8-351	PHB-BT, 1
	8-351	PHB-BU, 1

MERCURY MODELS

Year	Engine	Trans. Code
1980	8-302	PHB-BH2, 3
	8-351	PHB-BK, 1
	8-351	PHB-BP, 1
	8-351	PHB-BT, 1
	8-351	PHB-BT, 1

①—Windsor engine.
②—Modified engine.

DESCRIPTION

This transmission, **Fig. 1,** features a drive range that provides for fully automatic upshifts and downshifts, and manually selected low and second gears. The six selector lever positions provided are P (park), R (reverse), N (neutral), D (automatic drive range), 2 (second gear hold) and 1 (low gear hold).

D is a fully automatic range providing for a first gear start with automatic upshifts to second and high gear occurring at appropriate intervals.

Second gear (2) is a manually selected second gear hold. When the selector lever is moved to 2, the transmission will engage and remain in second gear, regardless of throttle opening or road speed.

Fig. 1 FMX three speed dual range unit with cast iron case

Low gear (1) is a manually selected first gear hold. When the selector lever is moved to this position the transmission will remain in first gear. To provide engine braking, moving the lever to this position will cause the transmission to downshift from 2nd when the car speed reaches about 22 to 39 mph depending on axle ratio and tire size.

D—Drive

The normal automatic driving range is indicated by D. In this range the car starts off in first gear and gives the best combination of automatic gear shifts to provide for economy and full power starts. As the accelerator is depressed and the car picks up speed, automatic shifts to second and high gears will occur. The transmission will automatically downshift as speed decreases. Forced downshifts in D are made by pressing the accelerator pedal all the way to the floor.

2—Second Gear Hold

When the car is started and the shift lever is moved to 2, the car will start off and remain in second gear, regardless of throttle opening or road speed. This range is especially useful for starting the car on icy pavements or other slippery surfaces. Similarly, when engine braking is required and the shift lever is moved from D to 2, the

transmission will engage and remain in second gear.

Selector lever position 2 is not a cruising range in the usual sense of the term. While the transmission is capable of limited cruising in second gear, maximum fuel economy and best all-around performance are realized in D range.

1—Low Gear Hold

This range is identical in operation to manual low range except that when the shift lever is moved to 1 to provide engine braking, the automatic shift from second to low gear will occur between 22 and 39 mph (exact shift point will vary with axle ratio and tire size).

TROUBLESHOOTING GUIDE

ROUGH INITIAL ENGAGEMENT

1. Idle speed.
2. Vacuum unit or tubes.
3. Front band.
4. Check control pressure.
5. Pressure regulator.
6. Valve body.

SHIFT POINTS HIGH, LOW OR ERRATIC

1. Fluid level.
2. Vacuum unit or tubes.
3. Manual linkage.
4. Governor.
5. Check control pressure.
6. Valve body.
7. Downshift linkage.

ROUGH 2-3 SHIFT

1. Manual linkage.
2. Front band.
3. Vacuum unit or tubes.
4. Pressure regulator.
5. Valve body.
6. Front servo.

ENGINE OVERSPEEDS, 2-3 SHIFT

1. Vacuum unit or tubes.
2. Front band.
3. Valve body.
4. Pressure regulator.

NO 1-2 OR 2-3 SHIFTS

1. Governor.
2. Valve body.

3. Manual linkage.
4. Rear clutch.
5. Front band.
6. Front servo.
7. Leakage in hydraulic system.
8. Pressure regulator.

NO FORCED DOWNSHIFTS

1. Downshift linkage.
2. Check control pressure.
3. Valve body.

ROUGH 3-2 OR 3-1 SHIFTS

1. Engine idle speed.
2. Vacuum unit or tubes.
3. Valve body.

SLIPS OR CHATTERS IN 2ND

1. Fluid level.
2. Vacuum unit or tubes.
3. Front band.
4. Check control pressure.
5. Pressure regulator.
6. Valve body.
7. Front servo.
8. Front clutch.
9. Leakage in hydraulic system.

SLIPS OR CHATTERS IN 1ST

1. Fluid level.
2. Vacuum unit or tubes.
3. Check control pressure.
4. Pressure regulator.
5. Valve body.
6. Front clutch.
7. Leakage in hydraulic system.
8. Fluid distributor sleeve in output shaft.
9. Planetary one-way clutch.

SLIPS OR CHATTERS IN REVERSE

1. Fluid level.
2. Rear band.
3. Check control pressure.
4. Pressure regulator.
5. Valve body.
6. Rear servo.
7. Rear clutch.
8. Vacuum unit or tubes.
9. Leakage in hydraulic system.
10. Fluid distributor sleeve in output shaft.

NO DRIVE IN D OR D2

1. Valve body.
2. Make air pressure check.
3. Manual linkage.
4. Front clutch.
5. Leak in hydraulic system.
6. Fluid distributor sleeve in output shaft.

NO DRIVE IN D1

1. Manual linkage.
2. Valve body.
3. Planetary one-way clutch.

NO DRIVE IN L

1. Manual linkage.
2. Front clutch.
3. Valve body.
4. Make air pressure check.
5. Leak in hydraulic system.
6. Fluid distributor sleeve in output shaft.

NO DRIVE IN R

1. Rear band.
2. Rear servo.
3. Valve body.
4. Make air pressure check.
5. Rear clutch.
6. Leak in hydraulic system.
7. Fluid distributor sleeve in output shaft.

NO DRIVE IN ANY RANGE

1. Fluid level.
2. Manual linkage.
3. Check control pressure.
4. Pressure regulator.
5. Valve body.
6. Make air pressure check.
7. Leak in hydraulic system.

LOCKUP IN D OR D1

1. Manual linkage.
2. Rear servo.
3. Front servo.
4. Rear clutch.
5. Parking linkage.
6. Leak in hydraulic system.

LOCKUP IN D2

1. Manual linkage.
2. Rear band.
3. Rear servo.
4. Rear clutch.
5. Parking linkage.
6. Leak in hydraulic system.
7. Planetary one-way clutch.

LOCKUP IN R

1. Front band.
2. Front servo.
3. Front clutch.
4. Parking linkage.
5. Leak in hydraulic system.

LOCKUP IN L

1. Front band.
2. Pressure regulator.
3. Valve body.
4. Rear clutch.
5. Parking linkage.
6. Leak in hydraulic system.

PARKING LOCK BINDS OR WON'T HOLD

1. Manual linkage.
2. Parking linkage.

TRANSMISSION OVERHEATS

1. Oil cooler and connections.
2. Pressure regulator.
3. Converter one-way clutch.

ENGINE RUNAWAY ON FORCED DOWNSHIFT

1. Front band.
2. Pressure regulator.
3. Valve body.
4. Front servo.
5. Vacuum unit or tubes.
6. Leak in hydraulic system.

MAXIMUM SPEED BELOW NORMAL, ACCELERATION POOR

1. Converter one-way clutch.

NO 3-1 DOWNSHIFT

1. Engine idle speed.
2. Vacuum unit or tubes.
3. Valve body.

NOISE IN NEUTRAL

1. Pressure regulator.
2. Front clutch.
3. Front pump.

NOISE IN 1-2-3 OR R

1. Pressure regulator.
2. Planetary assembly.
3. Front clutch.
4. Rear clutch.
5. Front pump.

NOISE IN REVERSE

1. Pressure regulator.
2. Front pump.

NOISE ON COAST IN NEUTRAL

1. Rear pump.

MAINTENANCE

ADDING FLUID

The fluid level in the transmission should be checked at 1000-mile intervals. Make sure that the car is standing level, and firmly apply the parking brake.

Run the engine at normal idle speed. If the transmission fluid is cold, run the engine at fast idle speed until the fluid reaches normal operating temperature. When the fluid is warm, slow the engine down to normal idle speed, shift the transmission through all ranges and then place the lever at P.

Clean all dirt from the transmission fluid dipstick cap before removing the dipstick from the filler tube. Pull the dipstick out of

Fig. 2 Manual linkage. Floor shift (typical)

Fig. 4 Throttle & Downshift linkage. 1980 Ford & Mercury (typical)

Fig. 3 Manual linkage. 1980 Ford & Mercury column shift

the tube, wipe it clean and push it all the way back into the tube.

Pull the dipstick out again and check the fluid level. If necessary, add enough Type F Automatic Transmission Fluid to the transmission to raise the fluid level to the F (full mark) on the dipstick.

CHANGING FLUID

NOTE: Normal maintenance and lubrication does not require periodic transmission fluid changes. However, a major transmission repair will require that the fluid be drained and be replaced with type F "lifetime" fluid.

1. Raise and support vehicle on hoist, then place a drain pan under transmission.
2. Loosen pan bolts and drain fluid until it has reached level of pan flange, then remove bolts working from rear and both sides of pan allowing to drop and drain slowly.
3. When fluid has completely drained, remove and thoroughly clean pan and filter.
4. Install filter, then using a new gasket install oil pan and add three quarts of fluid.
5. With transmission at operating temperature and parking brake applied, move shift lever through each range, allowing time for transmission to engage, then return shift lever to Park.
6. Check fluid level and add fluid as necessary to bring level between ADD and FULL mark.

MANUAL LINKAGE
ADJUST

COUGAR, FORD, LTD II, MERCURY, & THUNDERBIRD

Floor Shift
1. Place selector lever in D.
2. Raise vehicle and loosen manual shift rod retaining nut, **Fig. 2.**
3. Move transmission manual lever to D position.
4. Torque nut to 10–20 ft-lbs.

Column Shift
1. Place selector lever in D position.
2. Raise vehicle and loosen shift rod adjusting nut at point A, **Fig. 3.**
3. Shift transmission manual lever into drive position, second detent from the full counter clockwise position.
4. On models equipped with shift cable, place cable end on transmission manual lever stud. Align flats on stud with flats on cable, then install adjustment nut.
5. On all models, tighten adjustment at point A. Ensure selector lever is against D stop when tightening adjustment nut.
6. Check transmission for proper operation in all selector lever detent positions.

THROTTLE LINKAGE
ADJUST

ALL MODELS
1. Disconnect downshift lever return spring and hold throttle lever in wide open position and the downshift rod against the through detent stop, **Fig. 4.**
2. Hold downshift rod against the through detent stop.
3. Adjust downshift screw to provide .01 to .08 inch clearance between screw.
4. Connect downshift lever return spring and throttle arm.

BAND ADJUSTMENTS
FRONT BAND

1. Drain fluid from transmission, remove and clean oil pan and screen.
2. Loosen front servo adjusting screw locknut.
3. Pull back on actuating rod and insert a ¼ inch spacer between adjusting screw and servo piston stem, **Fig. 5.**
4. Tighten adjusting screw to 10 inch-lbs torque. Remove spacer and tighten adjusting screw an additional ¾ turn. Hold adjusting screw stationary and tighten locknut securely.
5. Install oil pan with new gasket and add fluid to transmission.

REAR BAND

NOTE: There is no access hole in the floor pan to adjust the rear band. With the use of special tools this band can be adjusted externally as follows.

1. Loosen rear band adjusting screw locknut, **Figs. 9 and 10.** A special tool is required to gain access in limited space.
2. Tighten adjusting screw until special tool clicks. It is preset to overrun when torque reaches 10 ft. lbs.

NOTE: If screw is found to be tighter than 10 ft. lbs., loosen screw and tighten until wrench clicks and overruns.

3. Back off adjusting screw 1½ turns.

NOTE: Severe damage may result if adjusting screw is not backed off the exact amount of turns indicated.

4. Hold adjusting screw stationary and tighten locknut securely.

CONTROL VALVE BODY

1. Support vehicle on hoist, then drain transmission fluid and remove pan.

NOTE: If fluid is to be reused, filter it through a 100-mesh screen before replacing it in transmission.

2. Disconnect hoses from vacuum diaphragm unit, then using Snap-On tool S8696-A, remove vacuum diaphragm and push rod.
3. Remove fluid screen retaining clip and small compensator pressure tube.
4. Remove main pressure oil tube, by gently prying up end that connects to main control valve, then remove other end of tube from pressure regulator.

NOTE: Tube must be removed in this manner. Failure to do so, could kink or bend tube causing excessive internal transmission leakage.

5. Loosen front servo bolts three turns, then remove the three control valve body screws, and lower valve body while pulling it off front servo tubes, being careful not to damage valve body or tubes.
6. Before installing control valve, check for bent manual valve by rolling it on a flat surface.

NOTE: Before torquing control valve attaching bolts, move valve toward center of case until clearance is less than .050 inch between manual valve and actuating pin.

7. After installing control valve, torque control valve attaching bolts to 8–10 ft. lbs., front servo bolts to 30–35 ft. lbs. and vacuum diaphragm to 15–23 ft. lbs.
8. After completing assembly, adjust front and rear bands. If valve body was replaced, adjust control linkage.

FRONT & REAR SERVOS

1. Drain transmission fluid and remove oil pan and screen.
2. Remove vacuum diaphragm, then loosen control valve body attaching bolts.
3. Remove retaining bolts from servo, then hold actuating strut and remove servo.
4. After installation, if front servo was serviced, torque front servo attaching bolts to 30–35 ft. lbs. and adjust front band. If rear servo was serviced, torque rear servo attaching bolts to 40–45 ft. lbs., adjust rear bands and check for less than .050 inch clearance between manual lever actuating pin and manual lever as outlined under "Control Valve."

EXTENSION HOUSING BUSHING & REAR SEAL

Proper removal and installation of extension housing bushing and rear seal will necessitate the use of five specialty tools.

Fig. 5 Front band adjustment. Ford, Mercury and Thunderbird

When removing bushing and rear seal, the vehicle will have to be raised and driveshaft removed.

EXTENSION HOUSING

1. Drain transmission fluid and remove driveshaft.
2. Disconnect speedometer cable from housing and remove engine rear supports to crossmember nuts.
3. Raise transmission slightly with suitable jack, then remove crossmember to side rail bolts and position the crossmember out of way.
4. Remove the two engine rear support-to-extension housing bolts and remove support.
5. Remove extension housing attaching bolts, then slide housing off output shaft and remove gasket.

NOTE: Hold output shaft and rear support from moving rearward to prevent needle bearing and race from dropping out.

GOVERNOR

1. Remove extension housing as outlined previously.
2. Remove governor to counterweight screws and lift governor from counterweight.

NOTE: When removing governor, hold output shaft and rear support from moving rearward to prevent needle bearing and race from dropping out.

3. When installing governor torque attaching bolts to 50–60 in. lbs.

PRESSURE REGULATOR

1. Drain transmission fluid and remove oil pan and fluid screen.
2. Remove small compensator pressure tube from control valve body and pressure regulator.
3. Remove main pressure oil tube by gently prying up end that connects to main control valve assembly, then remove other end of tube from pressure regulator.

NOTE: Tube must be removed in this manner. Failure to do so, could kink or bend tube, causing excessive internal transmission leakage.

4. Remove pressure regulator spring retainer, springs and spacer.

NOTE: Maintain pressure on retainer to prevent springs from falling out.

5. Remove regulator attaching bolts and remove regulator.
6. After installing regulator, torque attaching bolts to 17–22 ft. lbs.

PARKING PAWL

1. Drain transmission fluid and remove driveshaft.
2. Support rear of transmission and remove crossmember, then remove the two engine rear support-to-extension housing bolts and remove support.
3. Disconnect speedometer cable and remove oil pan and screen.
4. Loosen rear band adjusting screw locknut and tighten adjusting screw to 24 in. lbs.

NOTE: This will hold planetary carrier and clutch assemblies in place during parking pawl removal.

5. Remove small compensator pressure tube from pressure regulator and control valve body.
6. Remove main pressure oil tube by gently prying up end that connects to main valve body assembly, then remove other end of tube from pressure regulator.

NOTE: Tube must be removed in this manner. Failure to do so could kink or bend tube, causing excessive internal transmission leakage.

7. Remove vacuum diaphragm and loosen front servo attaching bolts, then remove valve body attaching bolts and lower valve body while pulling it off servo tubes, being careful not to damage valve body or tubes.
8. Remove rear servo bolts and remove servo and struts.

9. Remove extension housing and output shaft rear support.
10. Using a magnet, remove parking pawl pin from case, then working from inside of case, drive on shoulder of toggle lever pin with a small punch to move retaining plug part way out of case. Using a pair of pliers, remove plug.
11. Slide toggle lever toward front of case. Cock lever to one side to apply pressure on pin, then move toggle to rear of case to move pin outward.
12. Remove pawl and toggle lever as an assembly.
13. During assembly refer to "Control Valve Body" and "Front & Rear Servos" for installation. After assembly, adjust front and rear bands as outlined previously.

TRANSMISSION
REPLACE

NOTE: On some models, it is necessary to remove the two upper converter housing to engine bolts before raising vehicle.

1. Raise vehicle and place on jack stands, then drain transmission oil pan.
2. Remove converter access cover and remove converter drain plug.
3. Remove converter to flywheel attaching nuts, reinstall converter drain plugs and converter housing access cover to hold converter in place when transmission is removed.
4. Remove starter and propeller shaft.
5. Where necessary, disconnect exhaust pipes from manifold.
6. Disconnect oil cooler lines, speedometer cable, vacuum hose and manual downshift linkage.
7. Disconnect TRS switch wire, if equipped.
8. Support transmission with suitable jack and remove crossmember.

NOTE: On some models, it is necessary to remove the engine rear support to transmission bolts before crossmember removal.

9. Lower transmission and remove filler tube and dipstick.
10. Remove converter housing-to-engine bolts. Move transmission and jack rearward and lower away from vehicle.
11. Reverse procedure to install.

Ford (Jatco) Automatic Transmission

INDEX

Fig. 1 Ford (Jatco) transmission

TRANSMISSION IDENTIFICATION

GRANADA & MONARCH

1980 6-250 . . . . PLA

DESCRIPTION

The Jatco transmission, **Fig. 1,** is a three speed unit capable of providing automatic upshifts and downshifts through the three forward gear ranges, also manual selection of first and second gears. This transmission consists of a torque converter, planetary gear train, two multiple disc clutches, one multiple disc brake, a one-way clutch and a hydraulic control system.

MAINTENANCE

NOTE: Use only fluid that meets Ford Motor Company specification ESP-M2C138-CJ. Use of a fluid other than specified may result in transmission malfunction or failure.

CHECKING OIL LEVEL

1. With transmission at operating temperature, park vehicle on level surface.
2. Run engine at idle speed with service and parking brakes applied and move selector lever through all ranges and return to Park position.
3. With engine idling, remove dipstick and check fluid level. Fluid level should be between Add and Full marks.
4. Add specified fluid to bring fluid to proper level.

DRAIN & REFILL

NOTE: Normal maintenance and lubrication requirements do not necessitate periodic fluid changes.

When filling a dry transmission and converter, add five quarts of specified fluid. Start engine, move selector lever through all ranges and return to Park position. Check fluid level and add fluid to bring level to Full mark.

When a partial drain and refill is required due to a minor repair, proceed as follows:

1. Loosen and remove all but two oil pan bolts and drop one edge of the pan to drain oil.
2. Remove and clean oil pan and screen.
3. Place a new gasket on pan and install pan and screen.
4. Add three quarts of specified fluid to transmission.
5. Operate engine at idle speed for approximately two minutes, then run at fast idle until transmission reaches operating temperature.
6. Move selector lever through all ranges and return to Park position, recheck oil

Fig. 2   Intermediate band adjustment

level and add fluid, if necessary, to bring level to between Add and Full marks.

INTERMEDIATE BAND ADJUST

1. Raise and support vehicle.
2. Remove servo cover retaining bolts and cover, **Fig. 2.**
3. Loosen adjusting screw locknut and torque adjusting screw to 10 ft. lbs.
4. Back off adjusting screw two turns, then while holding adjusting screw stationary, torque adjusting screw locknut to 22–29 ft. lbs.
5. Install servo cover, gasket and bolts. Torque servo cover bolts to 5 ft. lbs.

IN VEHICLE REPAIRS

CONTROL VALVE BODY

1. Raise vehicle, drain transmission and remove oil pan.
2. Remove downshift solenoid, vacuum diaphragm, vacuum diaphragm rod and O-rings.
3. Remove valve body to case attaching bolts. Hold manual valve to keep it from sliding out of the valve body, then remove valve body from the case.

NOTE: Failure to hold the manual valve while removing control assembly may result in valve damage.

4. Reverse procedure to install.

SERVO

1. Raise and support vehicle.
2. Drain transmission fluid and remove oil pan.
3. Remove control valve body.
4. Remove servo cover bolts and cover.
5. Remove servo retainer to case bolts and remove retainer and servo piston as an assembly.

6. Remove return spring and apply strut.
7. Reverse procedure to install. Make sure to torque control valve body bolts to 5 ft. lbs.
8. Adjust intermediate band as described previously.

EXTENSION HOUSING SEAL

1. Raise vehicle and disconnect drive shaft.
2. Using a sharp chisel, remove seal from extension housing.
3. Install seal with a suitable tool.
4. Connect drive shaft.

EXTENSION HOUSING

1. Raise vehicle and disconnect drive shaft from rear axle.
2. Disconnect speedometer cable from extension housing.
3. Remove transmission rear support to crossmember bolts, raise transmission slightly with a suitable jack and loosen extension housing bolts to drain transmission fluid.
4. Remove extension housing to case bolts, then the extension housing.

CAUTION: Do not lose washer from parking panel shaft.

5. Reverse procedure to install.

GOVERNOR

1. Remove the extension housing as outlined previously.
2. Remove governor housing to oil distributor bolts, then the governor housing from distributor.
3. Reverse procedure to install.

TRANSMISSION
REPLACE

1. Disconnect battery ground cable.
2. Raise and support vehicle.
3. Drain transmission fluid and remove driveshaft.
4. Disconnect speedometer cable, shift cable, vacuum diaphragm line, downshift solenoid wire and oil cooler lines.
5. Remove converter housing cover, then the converter to flywheel nuts.
6. Remove transmission rear support to crossmember nuts.
7. Support transmission with a suitable jack and remove crossmember.
8. Secure transmission to jack with a safety chain, then lower transmission and remove starter motor.
9. Remove transmission to engine bolts and oil filler tube.
10. Using a pry bar, exert pressure between flex plate and converter to prevent converter from disengaging transmission when assembly is removed.
11. Lower transmission and converter as an assembly and remove from vehicle.
12. Reverse procedure to install.

ZF 4HP-22 Automatic Transmission

INDEX

TRANSMISSION IDENTIFICATION

The ZF automatic transmission is used on Continental and Mark VII models equipped with 2.4 liter diesel engines, and can be identified by a tag attached to the housing adjacent to the manual shift lever, Fig. 1.

DESCRIPTION

The 4HP-22 is a 4 speed transmission that provides automatic upshifts and downshifts through 4 forward gear ratios. While selector lever positions are the same as for the Automatic Overdrive (AOD) units, the 4HP-22 uses an entirely different gear train and includes a torque converter lockup feature.

The drivetrain consists of a front compound planetary gear set that operates in first, second, third and reverse speeds, and a separate overdrive gear set which provides fourth gear and remains locked for direct (through) drive in all other operating ranges. Drive train operation and gear selection is controlled by seven disc clutches and 3 one-way clutches. The output shaft is housed in a conventional Ford type extension housing which is fitted with a bushing and slip yoke seal common with C-3 transmissions.

The torque converter operates as a conventional torque multiplier and fluid coupling in all gears except fourth (overdrive). When fourth gear is engaged, a specific combination of road speed and accelerator position will signal the converter to lockup to mechanical drive. When converter lockup is signaled, the valve body applies fluid pressure to a hydraulic clutch in the converter, locking the impeller to the turbine.

The valve body is controlled by the manual selector, a centrifugal governor on the output shaft and a cable operated throttle valve which signals throttle lever position. The throttle valve (kickdown) cable is attached to a bracket and operated by the injection pump control lever.

Shift Selector Positions & Operation

The 4HP-22 is fully automatic when the selector lever is in either the overdrive or overdrive lockout position. Manual upshift-

ZF 4HP22 AUTOMATIC TRANSMISSION IDENTIFICATION TAG (ADJACENT TO MANUAL LEVER)

Fig. 1   Typical transmission identification tag

ing and downshifting is available through all forward drive ranges.

Overdrive

This is the selector lever position for normal operating conditions. In this range, the transmission starts in first gear and automatically upshifts to second, third and fourth gears as the vehicle accelerates; and the transmission automatically downshifts as vehicle speed decreases. When the transmission is operating in fourth gear and load and road speed are within specified limits, the torque converter clutch will be engaged and the converter will be locked. However, the transmission will not shift into or remain in fourth gear when the accelerator is fully depressed.

Overdrive Lockout

With the selector in this position, the transmission operates as in the overdrive mode except there is no shift into fourth (overdrive) gear and no converter clutch lockup. This position is used to provide increased performance and greater engine braking than is available in the overdrive position. The transmission can be shifted between overdrive and overdrive lockout positions at any vehicle speed.

Low (L Or 1)

This selector position is used when maximum engine braking is desired. At vehicle speeds above 20 mph, moving the selector to the low position will cause the transmission to shift to second gear until vehicle speed drops below 20 mph, then shift into and remain in first gear. When the low position is selected for initial driveaway, the transmission will remain in the selected range until the selector is moved to another

gear position. Upshifts from the low position can be made manually by moving the selector to the overdrive or overdrive lockout positions.

Reverse Inhibitor

The transmission operates in a conventional manner when the selector lever is placed in reverse position during normal operation. However, a reverse inhibitor is used which prevents reverse gear from being engaged when the vehicle is moving forward at speeds greater than 19 mph.

Forced Downshifts

Normal transmission shifting can be altered by changes in accelerator (throttle lever) position as follows:
1. At vehicle speeds of 20–50 mph when the selector lever is in overdrive or overdrive lockout, the transmission will downshift to second gear when the accelerator pedal is fully depressed.
2. At vehicle speeds below 20 mph, the transmission will downshift into first gear when the accelerator pedal is fully depressed.
3. When the selector is in overdrive range, the transmission will downshift from fourth to third gear at most vehicle speeds when the accelerator pedal is depressed to provide moderate to heavy acceleration.

MAINTENANCE
Fluid Level Check

NOTE: Transmission fluid level should be checked with unit at normal operating tem-

CONDITION	POSSIBLE SOURCE	ACTION
1. Position P		
1.1 Transmission does not engage Park	• Improperly adjusted linkage	• Adjust linkage
	• Excessive friction in Park mechanism	• Replace parts (cam and connection rod, eventually pawl)
1.2 Transmission does not hold Park	• Improperly adjusted linkage	• Adjust linkage
1.3 Engine cannot be started	• Improperly adjusted linkage	• Adjust linkage
	• Neutral start switch malfunctioning	• Replace switch
2. Position R		
2.1 No or delayed Reverse gear engagement	• Improperly adjusted linkage	• Adjust linkage
	• Transmission filter plugged	• Replace filter
	• Body dirty/sticking valves	• Replace valve body
	• Clutch burnt/worn, in this case no 3rd gear	• Replace transmission
	• Clutch burnt/worn, no engine braking in Position 1, 1st gear	• Replace transmission
	• Clutch burnt/worn, no engine braking in 2nd + 3rd gear, also in Position 1, 1st gear	• Replace transmission
2.2 Slipping or chatter at start in Reverse gear	• Clutches damaged, burnt or worn	• Replace transmission
2.3 Harsh engagement P-R or N-R, or distinct double jerk at P-R or N-R (below 1500 rpm engine speed)	• Valve body malfunction (will give the same symptoms when changing from 2nd to 3rd gear)	• Replace valve body
2.4 Backup lamp does not illuminate (bulbs, fuses and cables OK)	• Go to 1.3	• Go to 1.3
3. Position N		
3.1 Engine cannot be started	• Go to 1.3	• Go to 1.3
3.2 Vehicle moves in Position N	• Improperly adjusted linkage	• Adjust linkage
	• Clutch seized	• Replace transmission
4. Position Ⓓ		
4.1 No Drive	• Improperly adjusted linkage	• Adjust linkage
	• Transmission filter plugged	• Replace filter
	• Clutch burnt/worn	• Replace transmission
	• One way clutch 1st gear slips	• Replace transmission
4.2 Slipping or chatter at driveaway	• Clutch burnt/worn	• Replace transmission
4.3 Stroke jerk N-D (below 1500 rpm engine speed)	• Clutch damper malfunction	• Replace valve body
	• Clutch burnt/worn	• Replace transmission

Fig. 4 Transmission troubleshooting chart (Part 1 of 4)

perature of 150–170° F. (dipstick hot to touch). Normal operating temperature may be obtained by operating vehicle for 15–20 miles of city type driving with ambient temperatures above 50° F.

1. Start engine, set parking brake securely and ensure that curb idle speed is within specifications.
2. Firmly apply service brakes and move transmission selector through all ranges, allowing transmission time to engage in each range, then return selector to park.
3. Clean dirt from around transmission dipstick cap, withdraw dipstick and wipe it clean, then push dipstick back into tube ensuring that it is fully seated.
4. With engine running at normal curb idle speed, withdraw dipstick from tube and check fluid level against reference marks on dipstick.
5. If transmission is at normal operating temperature (150–170° F.), fluid level should be within cross-hatched area on dipstick. If fluid is at room temperature (70–90° F.), fluid level should be between middle and top holes in dipstick.
6. If fluid level is not within specifications, add a sufficient quantity of Dexron II type fluid through dipstick tube to bring fluid to specified level.

CAUTION: Do not overfill transmission as this may cause foaming and loss of fluid through vent. If transmission is overfilled, remove sufficient fluid to lower level using suitable suction pump.

TROUBLESHOOTING

Refer to **Fig. 2** when troublshooting this transmission.

ADJUSTMENTS
KICK DOWN (THROTTLE VALVE) CABLE, ADJUST

1. Ensure that injection pump linkage is properly adjusted.
2. Set injection pump top lever in full throttle position.
3. Loosen cable lock nut, then tighten adjusting nut, **Fig. 3**, until gap between end of cable housing and bead on cable is 1.54–1.57 inches.
4. Torque lock nut to 80–106 inch lbs., ensure that gap between end of housing and bead on cable is still within specifications, then release injection pump lever.

Manual Shift Linkage, Adjust
Column Shift
1. Place selector lever on column in overdrive position, ensuring that lever is tight against stop.

NOTE: Hang an 8 lb. weight from column shift lever to ensure that lever remains against stop during adjustment.

2. Raise and support vehicle as needed, then loosen adjusting stud nut securing slotted end of transmission control rod, **Fig. 4.**
3. Rotate manual lever on transmission fully rearward, then return lever to third detent position from the rear.
4. Ensure that flats on adjusting stud are aligned with slot in rod and that column shift lever is still tight against stop, then torque adjusting stud nut to 10–20 ft. lbs.
5. Remove weight from shift lever and check transmission operation in all selector lever detent positions.

Console Shift
1. Position console selector lever in overdrive position and secure so that lever is held rearward against stop during adjustment.
2. Raise and support vehicle as needed, then loosen nut securing slotted end of shift cable to manual lever on transmission.
3. Position transmission lever in third detent position from rear (overdrive position), then torque cable retaining nut to 10–18 ft. lbs.
4. Check operation of transmission in all selector lever positions.

IN-VEHICLE SERVICE
VALVE BODY, REPLACE
Removal
1. Raise and support vehicle, place suitable drain pan under transmission oil pan and drain transmission.
2. Disconnect oil filler tube from oil pan.
3. Remove bolts and clamps securing oil pan, the oil pan and gasket.
4. Remove bolts securing filter screen and O-ring.
5. Support valve body and remove

CONDITION	POSSIBLE SOURCE	ACTION
4.4 No or erratic shifts		
— No 1-2/2-1	• Governor valve sticking	• Replace governor
	• Shift valve 1-2 sticking	• Replace valve body
— No 1-2	• Clutches burnt/worn	• Replace transmission
— No 2-3/3-2	• Governor valve sticking	• Replace governor
	• Shift valve 2-3 sticking	• Replace valve body
— No 2-3	• Clutch burnt/worn	• Replace transmission
— No 3-4/4-3	• Governor valve sticking	• Replace governor
	• Shift valve 3-4 sticking	• Replace valve body
— No 3-4	• Clutch burnt/worn	• Replace transmission
4.5 Vehicle starts in 2nd gear	• Sticking governor	• Replace governor
	• 1-2 Shift valve sticking	• Replace valve body
Vehicle starts in 3rd gear	• Sticking governor	• Replace governor
	• 1-2, 2-3 Shift valves sticking	• Replace valve body
Shifts 1-3 in Ⓓ, D ranges	• 2-3 Shift valve sticking	• Replace valve body
4.6 Shift Speeds		
— No upshifts	• Stuck governor	• Replace governor
	• Shift valves sticking	• Replace valve body
— Shift points incorrect at full throttle	• Throttle cable setting incorrect	• Re-adjust throttle cable
— No 1-2/2-1 shift at kickdown	• Throttle cable setting incorrect	• Re-adjust throttle cable
— No 2-3/3-2 shift at kickdown	• Throttle cable setting incorrect	• Re-adjust throttle cable
— No 4-3 shift at kickdown	• 4-3 Kickdown valve sticking	• Replace valve body
4.7 Shift quality		
— Harsh shifts at light throttle	• Valve body malfunction	• Replace valve body
— Harsh shifts at full throttle and kickdown	• Valve body malfunction	• Replace valve body
— Soft shifts at full throttle and kickdown	• Clutch plates burnt/worn	• Replace transmission
	• Valve body malfunction	• Replace valve body
	• Clutch plates burnt/worn	• Replace transmission
5. Position D		
3rd Gear		
5.1 No engine braking	• Clutch burnt/worn	• Replace transmission
6. **Position L**		
6.1 No manual 2-1 downshift	• Dirty/sticking valve body	• Replace valve body
	• Governor sticking	• Replace governor
6.2 No engine braking	• Clutch burnt/worn	• Replace transmission

Fig. 4   Transmission troubleshooting chart (Part 2 of 4)

CONDITION	POSSIBLE SOURCE	ACTION
7. Torque Converter Lockup Clutch		
7.1 Lockup points incorrect	• Valve body malfunction	• Replace valve body
	• Governor pressure incorrect	• Replace governor
7.2 Shift too harsh	• Damper malfunction	• Replace valve body
	• Torque converter malfunction	• Replace transmission
7.3 No lockup	• Valve body malfunction	• Replace valve body
	• Torque converter malfunction	• Replace transmission
8. General		
8.1 Throttle cable sticking	• Too much friction in sleeve of throttle cable	• Replace cable
	• Throttle pressure valve sticking	• Replace valve body
8.2 Noisy and no Drive after long journey	• Oil filter on valve body dirty	• If there is no burnt clutch plate lining in oil sump, then replace filter, otherwise replace transmission
8.3 Very noisy and no Drive	• Flex plate is damaged	• Replace flex plate or transmission
	• Pump drive worn	• Replace transmission
9. Oil Leaks		
9.1 Oil dripping from converter housing	• Seal ring in pump housing damaged	• Replace seal
	• Pump housing porous	• Replace transmission
	• Converter leaking from welded seam	• Replace transmission
9.2 Leakage between transmission and oil pan	• Incorrect torque of bolts	• Tighten bolts
	• Pan gasket damaged	• Replace gasket
9.3 Leakage between intermediate plate and main housing (especially at pump pressure point)	• Converter housing bolts have worked loose	• Tighten bolts
9.4 Oil loss at speedo	• Damaged O-ring on speedo	• Replace O-ring
9.5 Oil leak at throttle connection cable	• O-ring connection damaged	• Replace O-ring or complete cable
9.6 Oil leak at extension housing	• Output oil seal damaged	• Replace seal
9.7 Loss of oil through breather	• Oil level too high	• Check and correct oil level
	• No breather cap	• Replace cap or change breather
	• O-ring breather damaged	• Remove extension housing and replace O-ring
	• Securing clip broken/damaged	• Replace clip

Fig. 4   Transmission troubleshooting chart (Part 3 of 4)

CONDITION	POSSIBLE SOURCE	ACTION
9.8 Leakage in cooler lines	• Loose connections	• Re-tighten
9.9 Oil leak at intermediate plate	• Plugs loose	• Tighten plugs • Replace washers
9.10 Leakage between main case and extension housing	• Loose bolts • Gasket damaged	• Re-tighten • Replace gasket
10. Noises 10.1 High pitched noise in all positions, especially if oil is cold	• Low oil level • Leaking valve body	• Top off as required • Replace valve body
10.2 High-pitched squeaking noise (dependent on engine rpm) in all gears when oil is warm, accompanied by intermittent no drive after long journey	• Dirty filter	• If no debris in sump, just replace filter, otherwise replace transmission
10.3 Loud noise when in lockup	• Torsional damper malfunction	• Replace transmission
10.4 Torsional vibrations from engine when in lockup	• Engine rpm is too low; lockup shift point incorrect	• Replace valve body

Fig. 4 Transmission troubleshooting chart (Part 4 of 4)

remaining 13 retaining bolts, **Fig. 5**, then lower valve body from case. Note position of bolts for installation.

NOTE: Remove only large head retaining bolts, Using Torx drive D79P-2100-T27 or equivalent.

6. Clean case and valve body mating surfaces, then inspect for burrs or distortion of surfaces.

Installation

1. Position valve body under case mounting surface and engage inner manual lever pin with manual valve (A), **Fig. 6**.
2. Pull down on kickdown cable to position accelerator cam so that roller on throttle lever clears cam (B), **Fig. 6**.
3. Support valve body against case and install 13 retaining bolts in proper positions, **Fig. 5**, then tighten bolts finger

tight.

4. Align valve body by inserting gauge T84P-77003-A or equivalent between throttle lever pin and valve body housing, **Fig. 7**.

NOTE: If throttle valve pin position interferes with alignment gauge, use notch on gauge handle to grip pin and draw throttle valve further from its bore.

5. Push valve body forward toward converter until alignment gauge is held snug, then tighten bolt, **Fig. 7**, firmly to hold valve body in position.
6. Torque valve body bolts to 71 inch lbs., then recheck position with gauge. Light pressure should be required to move gauge up and down.
7. Clean filter screen, insert new O-ring into screen inlet, install screen assembly on valve body and torque retaining bolts to 71 inch lbs.

8. Install oil pan, new gasket retaining bolts and clamps, installing long radiused clamps on corners, and torque retaining bolts to 53 inch lbs.
9. Lower vehicle and fill transmission to specified level with Dexron II type transmission fluid.
10. Road test transmission in all operating ranges and check for leaks.

KICKDOWN (THROTTLE VALVE) CABLE, REPLACE

Removal

1. Disconnect cable from injection pump lever and bracket, **Fig. 2**.
2. Raise and support vehicle and remove valve body as outlined.
3. Pry cable casing from transmission housing using suitable levers.
4. Disconnect "T" end of cable from accelerator cam, **Fig. 8**, then remove cable from transmission.

Fig. 2 Kickdown (throttle lever) cable installation at injection pump

Fig. 3 Manual shift linkage assembly. Models w/column shift

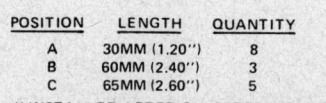

FRONT OF TRANSMISSION

POSITION	LENGTH	QUANTITY
A	30MM (1.20'')	8
B	60MM (2.40'')	3
C	65MM (2.60'')	5

INSTALLED AFTER OIL SCREEN IS IN PLACE

Fig. 5   Valve body retaining bolt identification

Fig. 6   Valve body installation

Installation

1. Push cable housing into bore in transmission case.
2. Rotate accelerator cam one revolution to load spring, then engage "T" end of cable in slot in cam.
3. Reinstall valve body and oil pan as outlined, lower vehicle and fill transmission to specified level with Dexron II type transmission fluid.
4. If new cable is being installed, spin rear adjusting nut back to end of housing and insert cable housing into slot in cable bracket, **Fig. 2.** If used cable is being installed, proceed to step 9.
5. Pull cable housing into bracket, install front lock nut and set adjusting nuts so that threaded barrel of cable housing is centered in bracket.
6. Pull cable out of housing just until detent step is felt (approximately 0.25 inch before maximum cable travel) and hold in position.
7. Slide bead stop along cable until bead is 1.54—1.57 inches from end of cable housing, then crimp bead to cable to secure position.
8. Remove cable and housing assembly from bracket.
9. Slip cable through slot in injection pump lever insert with "T" head toward trunion side and pull cable through insert.
10. Snap "T" head into insert trunions, thread cable through slot in injection pump lever and snap insert into rectangular hole in lever.
11. Spin cable adjusting nuts to opposite ends of threaded portion on cable housing, then mount cable housing in bracket.
12. Adjust cable as outlined in "Kickdown (Throttle Lever) Cable, Adjust."

EXTENSION HOUSING, BUSHING & SEAL, REPLACE

Removal

1. Place transmission selector lever in Neutral, then raise and support vehicle.
2. Mark position of propeller shaft yoke and rear axle companion flange, disconnect shaft from companion flange and remove propeller shaft.
3. If only seal and/or bushing is to be replaced, proceed as follows:
   a. Remove seal and bushing as needed, using suitable pullers, taking care not to damage extension housing or output shaft.
   b. Inspect counterbores in extension housing for burrs and damage, removing burrs as needed with crocus cloth.
   c. Install replacement bushing and/or seal using suitable drivers.
   d. Inspect propeller shaft yoke for damage and scoring, and replace as needed.
   e. Reinstall driveshaft as outlined under "Installation."
4. Disconnect speed sensor electrical connector from extension housing.
5. Remove position sensor from converter housing.
6. Remove bolts securing rear mount to extension housing, then raise and support transmission just enough to remove weight from rear mount.
7. Remove nuts securing rear mount to crossmember, then the rear mount.
8. Lower transmission to gain clearance, remove 9 bolts securing extension housing, then remove extension housing and gasket.

Installation

1. Position new extension housing gasket on transmission housing.
2. Ensure that alignment pins are properly seated in extension housing, slide housing over output shaft and position against case, then install retaining bolts.
3. Evenly torque extension housing bolts to 17 ft. lbs.

Fig. 7   Valve body alignment

4. Raise transmission and install rear support on extension housing.
5. Lower transmission, install nuts securing rear mount to crossmember, then remove support.
6. Insert propeller shaft into transmission, align matching marks between propeller shaft yoke and companion flange, then secure yoke to companion flange.
7. Install position sensor in converter housing and connect speed sensor electrical connector.
8. Lower vehicle and ensure that transmission is filled to specified level, then road test vehicle and check for leaks.

Fig. 8 Kickdown (throttle valve) cable installation at transmission

GOVERNOR, REPLACE

Removal & Disassembly

1. Remove extension housing as outlined.
2. Remove interlocking snap ring from output shaft, **Fig. 9.**
3. Remove parking gear, governor assembly and split drive rings from output shaft.
4. Remove 2 bolts securing governor housing to governor hub.
5. Remove 2 bolts securing governor hub to parking gear.
6. Remove counterweight and clamp from governor hub, noting installation position.
7. Remove O-ring, snap ring and seal rings.

Assembly & Installation

1. Lubricate and install seal rings, snap ring and new O-ring, **Fig. 9.**
2. Insert counterweight into governor hub and secure with clamp.
3. Install governor housing on hub and torque bolts to 7 ft. lbs.
4. Install parking gear on governor hub and torque bolts to 7 ft. lbs.
5. Lubricate O-ring on output shaft and slide parking gear with split drive ring and governor assembly onto shaft until assembly reaches stop.
6. Install interlocking snap ring onto output shaft.
7. Reinstall extension housing assembly as outlined.
8. Road test vehicle and check for leaks.

TRANSMISSION
REPLACE

REMOVAL

1. Disconnect kickdown cable from bracket and injection pump lever.
2. Place transmission selector lever in Neutral, then raise and support vehicle.
3. Remove nut securing outer manual lever and lever from manual lever shaft.
4. Remove position sensor from converter housing.
5. Disconnect brace from lower end of converter housing and engine block and remove brace.
6. Place suitable jack under transmission.
7. Rotate engine as needed using crankshaft pulley nut and remove nuts securing torque converter to flex plate.
8. Mark position of propeller shaft yoke and rear axle companion flange, then remove propeller shaft.
9. Disconnect neutral start switch electrical connector and remove extension housing damper.
10. Support transmission and remove rear support to crossmember nuts and two crossmember to side support bolts.
11. Remove bolts securing rear support to extension housing, the rear exhaust system support and the crossmember assembly.

NOTE: It may be necesasary to remove exhaust system components to facillitate crossmember and transmission removal.

12. On models with column shift, remove bolts securing linkage bellcrank bracket to the engine/transmission brace.
13. On all models, disconnect oil cooler lines from transmission using push connect tool T82L-9500-AH or equivalent.
14. Disconnect electrical connector to speed sensor and remove bolts securing starter motor to converter housing.
15. Ensure that transmission is properly secured to jack, then lower jack slightly.
16. Remove 4 bolts securing converter housing to engine block.
17. Disconnect and remove filler tube and dipstick assembly, draining fluid into suitable container.
18. Move transmission and torque converter assembly away from engine, lowering jack as needed to provide clearance.

INSTALLATION

1. Mount transmission and converter assembly on suitable jack and secure transmission with safety chain.
2. Position transmission assembly under vehicle, and rotate converter until converter studs are aligned with holes in flex plate, ensuring that converter is properly seated.

Fig. 9 Governor assembly exploded view

3. Mount transmission assembly on rear of engine, ensuring that converter face is seated squarely against face plate.
4. Install filler tube and dipstick assembly and insert converter housing retaining bolt through tube bracket and converter housing flange.
5. Install 3 remaining converter housing bolts, then torque bolts to 38–48 ft. lbs.
6. Remove chain from around transmission.
7. Connect oil cooler lines by pushing them into fittings located on intermediate shaft.
8. Connect speed sensor electrical connector, then install extension housing damper, torquing retaining bolts to 18–25 ft. lbs.

9. Install rear support on exhaust system.
10. Raise transmission assembly as needed, then install crossmember assembly and side mounting bolts.
11. Align extension housing with rear support, install bolts securing rear mount to extension housing and ensure that all crossmember and mount bolts are properly tightened. Install exhaust system components, if removed.
12. Insert nuts securing torque converter to flex plate and torque nuts to 20–34 ft. lbs.
13. Install brace between engine block and lower end of converter housing, torquing bolts to 15–18 ft. lbs.
14. On models equipped with column shift, mount linkage bellcrank bracket on engine/transmission brace and

torque retaining bolts to 10–20 ft. lbs.
15. On all models, lower and remove transmission jack.
16. Guide kickdown cable up into engine compartment, mount transmission manual lever on manual shaft, ensuring that linkage is properly aligned and torque retaining nut to 10–20 ft. lbs.
17. Connect neutral start switch harness and install position sensor in converter housing.
18. Insert propeller shaft yoke into transmission, align rear yoke with rear axle companion flange and secure yoke to flange.
19. Lower vehicle, fill transmission to specified level with Dexron II type fluid, adjust manual linkage and kickdown cable, then road test vehicle.

Ford Automatic Transaxle

INDEX

TRANSAXLE IDENTIFICATION

Year	Car Model	Trans. Code	Engine Model
1981	Escort & Lynx	PMA-A1, 2	4-98
	EXP & LN-7	PMA-K, 1	4-98
1982	Escort & Lynx	PMA-A3	4-98
		PMA-K2	4-98
		PMA-K2	4-98
	EXP & LN-7	PMA-K2	4-98
		PMA-R	4-98
1983	Escort & Lynx	PMA-K3	4-98
		PPMA-K4	4-98
		PMB-A1	4-98
		PMA-P	4-98 EFI
		PMA-P1	4-98 EFI
		PMA-R1	4-98 H.O.
		PMA-R2	4-98 H.O.
		PMA-T	4-98
		PMA-U	4-98 H.O.
		PMA-V	4-98 EFI
	EXP & LN-7	PMA-K3	4-98
		PMB-A1	4-98
		PMA-P	4-98 EFI
		PMA-R1	4-98 H.O.
		PMA-T	4-98
		PMA-T1	4-98
		PMB-B	4-98

Year	Car Model	Trans. Code	Engine Model
		PMA-U	4-98 EFI
		PMA-U1	4-98 EFI
		PMA-V	4-98 H.O.
		PMA-V1	4-98 H.O.
		PMA-V2	4-98 H.O.
1984	Escort & Lynx	PMA-V3	4-98 H.O.
		PMB-C2	4-98 H.O.
		PMA-U1	4-98 EFI
		PMA-U2	4-98 EFI
		PMB-D	4-98 EFI
	EXP	PMA-V3	4-98 H.O.
		PMB-C2	4-98 H.O.
		PMA-U1	4-98 EFI
		PMA-U2	4-98 EFI
		PMB-D	4-98 EFI
	Tempo & Topaz	PMA-N	4-140
		PMA-N1	4-140
		PMA-N2	4-140
		PMA-N3	4-140
1985	Escort & Lynx	PMA-U4	4-98
		PMA-V5	4-98
	EXP	PMA-U4	4-98 H.O.
		PMA-V5	4-98 EFI
	Tempo & Topaz	PMA-N5	4-140

AUTOMATIC TRANSMISSIONS/TRANSAXLES

Fig. 1   Transaxle identification tag

The transmission identification tag, **Fig. 1**, is located near the valve body (upper) cover.

DESCRIPTION

The transaxle combines an automatic transmission and differential into a front drive unit, **Fig. 2**. The components are housed in a one piece case and when bolted to the engine and installed in the vehicle, the engine/transaxle assembly is mounted transversely with the transaxle on the left side of the engine compartment. The transaxle consists of three friction clutches, one band and a single one way clutch. When applied as necessary, these components transmit engine torque through a compound planetary gearset which provides three forward and one reverse gear ratios. The planetary transmits engine torque to the input gear which meshes with the differential idler gear. The differential gear, riveted to the differential case, is in mesh with the idler gear. When the powerflow reaches the differential, engine torque flows outward to the wheels through the differential gears.

Fig. 2   Automatic transaxle. Sectional view

TROUBLESHOOTING GUIDE

SLOW INITIAL ENGAGEMENT

1. Improper fluid level.
2. Damaged or improperly adjusted manual linkage.
3. Incorrect throttle valve linkage adjustment.
4. Contaminated fluid.
5. Improper clutch or band application or oil control pressure.
6. Dirt in valve body.

ROUGH INITIAL ENGAGEMENT IN FORWARD OR REVERSE

1. Improper fluid level.
2. Engine idle too high.
3. Automatic choke closed on warm engine.
4. Play in halfshafts, constant velocity joints or engine mounts.
5. Improper clutch or band application or oil control pressure.
6. Incorrect throttle valve linkage adjustment.
7. Dirt in valve body.

NO DRIVE, ANY GEAR

1. Improper fluid level.
2. Damaged or improperly adjusted manual linkage.
3. Improper clutch or band application or oil control pressure.
4. Internal leak.
5. Loose valve body.
6. Damaged or worn clutches or bands.
7. Valve body sticking or dirty.

NO DRIVE IN 1, 2 OR D

1. Improper fluid level.
2. Damaged or improperly adjusted manual linkage.
3. Improper one way clutch or band application.
4. Incorrect oil pressure.
5. Damaged or worn band, servo or clutches.
6. Loose valve body.
7. Valve body sticking or dirty.

NO REVERSE OR SLIPS IN REVERSE

1. Improper fluid level.
2. Damaged or improperly adjusted manual linkage.
3. Play in halfshafts, constant velocity joints or engine mounts.

4. Improper oil pressure control.
5. Damaged or worn reverse clutch.
6. Loose valve body.
7. Valve body sticking or dirty.

NO START IN PARK OR NEUTRAL

1. Neutral start switch improperly adjusted.
2. Neutral start wire damaged.
3. Manual linkage improperly adjusted.

NO DRIVE OR SLIPS IN D

1. Damaged or worn one way clutch.
2. Improper fluid level.
3. Damaged or worn band.
4. Incorrect throttle valve linkage adjustment.

NO DRIVE OR SLIPS IN 2

1. Improper fluid level.
2. Incorrect throttle valve linkage adjustment.
3. Damaged or worn intermediate friction clutch.
4. Improper clutch application.
5. Internal leakage.
6. Valve body dirty or sticking.
7. Band or drum glazed.

TAKE OFF IN 2ND OR 3RD

1. Improper fluid level.
2. Damaged or improperly adjusted manual linkage.
3. Improper band or clutch application.
4. Damaged or worn governor.
5. Loose valve body.
6. Valve body sticking or dirty.
7. Leaks between valve body and case mating surface.

INCORRECT SHIFT POINTS

1. Improper fluid level.
2. Throttle valve linkage improperly adjusted.
3. Improper clutch or band application.
4. Improper oil control pressure.
5. Damaged or worn governor.
6. Valve body dirty or sticking.

NO UPSHIFT IN D

1. Improper fluid level.
2. Throttle valve linkage improperly adjusted.
3. Improper band or clutch application.
4. Improper oil control pressure.
5. Damaged or worn governor.
6. Valve body sticking or dirty.

SHIFT 1-3 IN D

1. Improper fluid level.
2. Damaged or worn intermediate friction clutch.
3. Improper clutch application.
4. Improper oil control pressure.
5. Valve body sticking or dirty.

RUNAWAY UPSHIFTS

1. Improper fluid level.
2. Improper band or clutch application.
3. Improper oil pressure.
4. Damaged or worn direct clutch or servo.
5. Valve body sticking or dirty.

DELAYED 1-2 SHIFT

1. Improper fluid level.
2. Improper engine performance.
3. Improper throttle valve linkage adjustment.
4. Improper intermediate clutch application.
5. Improper oil control pressure.
6. Damaged intermediate clutch.
7. Valve body sticking or dirty.

ROUGH 1-2 UPSHIFT

1. Improper fluid level.
2. Improper throttle valve linkage adjustment.
3. Incorrect engine idle or performance.
4. Improper intermediate clutch application.
5. Improper oil control pressure.
6. Valve body sticking or dirty.

ROUGH 2-3 UPSHIFT

1. Improper fluid level.
2. Incorrect engine performance.
3. Improper band release or direct clutch application.
4. Improper oil control pressure.
5. Valve body sticking or dirty.
6. Damaged or worn servo release and direct clutch piston check ball.
7. Improper throttle valve linkage adjustment.

ROUGH 3-2 DOWNSHIFT AT CLOSED THROTTLE IN D

1. Improper fluid level.
2. Incorrect engine idle or performance.
3. Improper throttle valve linkage adjustment.
4. Improper band or clutch application.
5. Improper oil control pressure.
6. Improper governor operation.
7. Valve body sticking or dirty.

NO FORCED DOWNSHIFTS

1. Improper fluid level.
2. Improper clutch or band application.
3. Improper oil control pressure.
4. Damaged internal kickdown linkage.
5. Throttle valve linkage improperly adjusted.
6. Valve body sticking or dirty.
7. Dirty or sticking governor.

DOWNSHIFT RUNAWAY

1. Improper fluid level.
2. Throttle valve linkage improperly adjusted.
3. Band improperly adjusted.
4. Improper band or clutch application.
5. Improper oil control pressure.
6. Damaged or worn servo.
7. Glazed band or drum.
8. Valve body sticking or dirty.

NO ENGINE BRAKING IN 1

1. Improper fluid level.
2. Throttle valve linkage improperly adjusted.
3. Damaged or improperly adjusted manual linkage.
4. Improperly adjusted band or clutch.
5. Improper oil control pressure.
6. Glazed band or drum.
7. Valve body sticking or dirty.

NO ENGINE BRAKING IN 2

1. Improper fluid level.
2. Throttle valve linkage improperly adjusted.
3. Manual linkage improperly adjusted.
4. Improper band or clutch application.
5. Improper oil control system.
6. Leaking servo.
7. Glazed band or drum.

MAINTENANCE
ADDING OIL

To check fluid level, apply parking brake, operate engine at idle speed with vehicle on level surface and transmission in Park position. Add fluid as necessary to bring mark on dipstick between "Add" and "Full" marks.

CHANGING OIL

Fluid and filter changes are not required for average passenger car use. Severe usage such as commercial use or prolonged periods of idling require fluid and filter be changed every 20,000 miles. Whenever fluid is changed only fluid labeled Dexron II should be used.

1. Raise and support vehicle.
2. Loosen transaxle oil pan attaching bolts and allow fluid to drain.
3. Remove oil pan and clean thoroughly.
4. Install new gasket onto pan, then the pan onto transaxle.
5. Fill transaxle to correct fluid level, then operate engine at idle. With parking brake applied, move selector lever to each position. Place lever in Park position and check fluid level with engine at operating temperature. Add fluid as necessary.

IN-VEHICLE ADJUSTMENTS
GEARSHIFT LINKAGE

1. Position selector lever in Drive position against rearward stop.
2. Raise and support vehicle, then loosen manual lever to control cable retaining nut.
3. Position transmission manual lever at second detent from most rearward position. This is Drive position.
4. Torque attaching nut to 10-15 ft. lbs. (14-20 Nm).
5. Lower vehicle and check for proper operation of transmission in each selector lever position.

THROTTLE VALVE LINKAGE

1981-82

1. Operate engine at curb idle speed, then turn engine Off. Ensure that carburetor throttle lever is against hot engine curb idle stop with choke off.

NOTE: Ensure throttle lever is not on choke fast idle cam.

2. Position coupling lever adjustment screw at its midpoint, then ensure throttle valve linkage shaft assembly is seated fully upward into coupling lever, **Fig. 3.**
3. Loosen sliding trunnion block bolt on throttle valve control rod assembly at least one turn.
4. Rotate transaxle throttle valve control lever upward to ensure throttle valve lever is against its internal idle stop. Maintain force on throttle control lever, then torque bolt on trunnion block to 24-36 in. lbs. (2.7-4.1 Nm).
5. Check that carburetor throttle lever is still against hot engine curb idle stop. If not, repeat steps 1 through 6.

1983-84 All & 1985 Exc. CFI Engines

1. Operate engine until normal operating temperature is reached, then turn engine off. Ensure carburetor throttle lever is against hot engine curb idle stop with choke off.

NOTE: Ensure throttle lever is not on choke fast idle cam.

2. Loosen sliding trunnion block bolt on throttle valve control rod assembly at least one turn. Ensure control rod is corrosion free so trunnion block is free to slide.
3. Idle engine in park. With light force, rotate throttle valve control lever upward against its internal idle stop. Maintain about a 1 lb. force on throttle control lever and torque bolt on trunnion block to 24–36 in. lbs.

1985 CFI Engines

1. Simultaneously hold throttle open to maintain 1000 RPM while pressing lightly on the ISC motor shaft.
2. After the shaft retracts completely, release throttle and quickly disconnect ISC motor electrical connector.
3. Loosen bolt on sliding trunion block on TV control rod assembly. A minimum of one turn is necessary.
4. Remove any surface corrosion from the control rod and ensure trunion block moves freely on control rod assembly.
5. With ISC plunger retracted and trunion block loosened, rotate transaxle TV control lever upward, using approximately a one lb. force to ensure TV control lever is completely against its internal idle stop. Without releasing force on TV control lever, tighten trunion block attaching bolt to 7–11 ft. lbs.

IN-VEHICLE REPAIRS

VALVE BODY, REPLACE

1. Remove battery and battery tray.
2. Remove ignition coil and transaxle dipstick.
3. Disconnect all hoses and lines from air management valve.
4. Remove remote air cleaner, if equipped.
5. Remove air management valve from transaxle valve body cover.
6. On 1981–83 models, disconnect neutral safety switch electrical connector and the fuel evaporator hose from frame rail. Also, disconnect fan motor and temperature sending unit electrical connectors.
7. On all models, remove valve body cover bolts, then the cover and gasket.
8. Remove valve body bolts, then the valve body and gasket.
9. Reverse procedure to install. Install guide pins to properly align valve body before tightening attaching bolts. One alignment pin may have to be temporarily removed to allow attachment of manual valve. Ensure roller on end of throttle valve plunger engages cam on end of throttle lever shaft. Torque valve body bolts to 6–8 ft. lbs. (8–11 Nm) and valve body cover bolts to 7–9 ft. lbs. (9–12 Nm).

GOVERNOR

1. Disconnect battery ground cable, and

Fig. 3 Adjusting throttle valve control linkage

all hoses and lines from air management valve.
2. Remove managed air valve supply hose band to intermediate shift control bracket attaching screw.
3. Remove air cleaner, then using a long screwdriver, remove governor cover retaining clip.
4. Remove governor cover, and governor.
5. Reverse procedure to install.

SERVO

1. Disconnect battery ground cable.
2. Disconnect electrical connectors from fan motor and temperature sending unit.
3. Disconnect FM capacitor wiring, if equipped.
4. Remove two fan shroud to radiator attaching nuts, then the fan and fan shroud.
5. Remove filler tube to case attaching bolt, then the filler tube and dipstick.
6. Remove lower left side mount to case attaching bolt.
7. Remove servo cap and snap ring using tool T81P-70027A or equivalent.
8. Reverse procedure to install.

TRANSAXLE, REPLACE

EXC. TEMPO & TOPAZ

1. Disconnect battery ground cable, then raise and support vehicle.
2. Remove bolts attaching managed air valve to valve body cover.
3. Disconnect electrical connector from neutral safety switch.
4. Disconnect throttle valve linkage and manual cable at their levers.
5. Remove two transaxle to engine upper attaching bolts.
6. Raise and support vehicle.
7. Remove nut from control arm to steering knuckle attaching bolt, then remove bolt using suitable punch and hammer. Repeat procedure on other side of vehicle. Nuts and bolts must be discarded.
8. Using a pry bar, disengage control arms from steering knuckles.

NOTE: Do not hammer on knuckles. Plastic shield installed behind rotor contains a molded pocket which accepts lower control arm ball joint. When separating control arm from knuckle, clearance for ball joint may be obtained by bending shield backwards towards rotor. Failure to provide clearance for the ball joint may result in damage to the shield.

9. Remove bolts attaching stabilizer bar brackets to frame rails and discard bolts.
10. Remove stabilizer bar to control arm attaching nuts and washers. Remove stabilizer bar. Discard nut.
11. Remove bolts securing brake hose routing clips to suspension strut brackets.
12. Remove steering gear tie rods from steering knuckles.
13. Remove halfshaft from right side of transaxle, then position halfshaft on transaxle housing.
14. Disengage left side halfshaft from differential side gear by inserting tool T81P-4026A or equivalent into right side halfshaft opening and driving out inner constant velocity joint.
15. Pull left side halfshaft from transaxle and wire to underbody. Do not allow shaft to hang unsupported.
16. Install seal plugs T81P-1177B or equivalent into differential seals.
17. Remove starter support bracket, then disconnect starter cable from starter.
18. Remove starter, then the transaxle support bracket.
19. Remove dust cover from torque converter housing. Remove torque converter to flywheel attaching nuts.
20. Remove left side front mounts to body bracket attaching nut. Remove bracket to body attaching bolts and bracket.
21. Remove left rear insulator attaching nut, and disconnect oil cooler lines.
22. Remove manual lever bracket to transaxle case attaching bolts.
23. Support transaxle with suitable jack, then remove four remaining transaxle to engine attaching bolts.
24. Using a screwdriver inserted between flywheel and torque converter, position transaxle and converter away from engine until torque converter studs clear flywheel.
25. Lower transaxle two to three inches and disconnect speedometer cable.
26. Lower transaxle and remove from vehicle.
27. Reverse procedure to install. Before installing halfshafts, replace circlip on constant velocity joint stub shaft. When installing halfshafts, ensure splines of constant velocity joint align with splines in differential.

TEMPO & TOPAZ

NOTE: On these models, the engine and transaxle is removed as an assembly.

1. Mark position of hood hinges, then remove hood.
2. Disconnect battery ground cable, then remove air cleaner assembly.

3. Remove lower radiator hose and drain coolant from engine. Remove upper radiator hose from engine.
4. Disconnect transaxle cooler lines from rubber hoses below radiator.
5. Remove coil assembly from cylinder head. Disconnect coolant fan electrical connector.
6. Remove radiator shroud, cooling fan and radiator.
7. Carefully discharge refrigerant from air conditioning system, if equipped. Remove inlet and outlet lines from compressor.
8. Mark and disconnect all electrical and vacuum lines from engine.
9. Disconnect TV linkage from transaxle.
10. Disconnect accelerator linkage, fuel supply and return lines from engine.
11. Disconnect air pump discharge hose.
12. Disconnect power steering pressure and return lines from pump, if equipped. Remove power steering line bracket from cylinder head.
13. Install engine support tool No. D79P-6000-A or equivalent, to engine lifting eye.
14. Raise and support vehicle.
15. Remove starter cable from starter.
16. Remove air hose from catalytic converter.
17. Remove bolt securing exhaust pipe bracket to oil pan. Remove two exhaust pipes to exhaust manifold nuts, then pull exhaust pipe out of rubber insulating grommets and position aside.
18. Disconnect speedo cable from transaxle.
19. Remove water pump inlet hose from engine.
20. Remove bolts securing control arms to body. Remove stabilizer bar bracket bolts and brackets.
21. Remove halfshaft assembly from transaxle.
22. Disconnect manual shift cable clip from transaxle shift lever. Remove manual shift linkage bracket bolts and bracket from transaxle.
23. Remove nuts and left hand rear No. 4 insulator mount bracket from body bracket.
24. Lower vehicle and install suitable lifting hoist to engine.

NOTE: Do not allow front wheels to touch floor.

25. Remove engine support tool No. D79L-6000-A or equivalent from engine.
26. Remove right hand No. 3 insulator intermediate bracket to engine bracket bolts and intermediate bracket to insulator nuts. Remove nut on the bottom of double ended stud which secures intermediate bracket to engine bracket. Remove bracket.
27. Carefully lower engine and transaxle assembly from vehicle.

Aisan Warner A131L Automatic Transaxle Section

INDEX

TROUBLESHOOTING

FLUID DISCOLORED OR SMELLS BURNT

1. Contaminated fluid.
2. Faulty torque converter.
3. Faulty transaxle.

VEHICLE DOES NOT MOVE IN ANY DRIVE GEAR

1. Misadjusted transaxle control cable.
2. Faulty valve body or primary regulator.
3. Faulty transaxle.

VEHICLE DOES NOT MOVE IN ANY RANGE

1. Faulty park lock pawl.
2. Faulty valve body or Primary regulator.
3. Faulty torque converter.
4. Broken converter drive plate.
5. Blocked oil pump intake strainer.
6. Faulty transmission.

INCORRECT SHIFT LEVER POSITION

1. Misadjusted transaxle control cable.
2. Faulty manual valve and lever.
3. Faulty transaxle.

HARSH ENGAGEMENT INTO ANY DRIVE RANGE

1. Misadjusted transaxle control cable.
2. Faulty valve body or primary regulator.
3. Faulty accumulator pistons.
4. Faulty transaxle.

DELAYED UPSHIFTS & DOWNSHIFTS

1. Misadjusted throttle cable.
2. Faulty governors.
3. Faulty valve body.

Fig. 1 Manual shift linkage adjustment

SWIVEL NUT

SLIPS ON UPSHIFTS OR SHUDDERS ON TAKEOFF

1. Misadjusted transaxle control cable.
2. Misadjusted throttle cable.
3. Faulty valve body.
4. Faulty transaxle.

DRAG OR BINDING ON UPSHIFT

1. Misadjusted transmission control cable.
2. Faulty valve body.
3. Faulty transaxle.

HARSH DOWNSHIFT

1. Misadjusted throttle cable.
2. Faulty accumulator pistons.
3. Faulty valve body.
4. Faulty transaxle.

NO DOWNSHIFT WHEN COASTING

1. Faulty governor.
2. Faulty valve body.

INCORRECT DOWNSHIFT

1. Misadjusted throttle cable.
2. Faulty governor.
3. Faulty valve body.
4. Faulty transaxle.

NO KICKDOWN

1. Misadjusted throttle cable.
2. Faulty governor.
3. Faulty valve body.

NO ENGINE BRAKING

1. Faulty valve body.
2. Faulty transaxle.

NO HOLD IN P

1. Misadjusted transaxle control cable.
2. Faulty parking lock pawl and rod.

ADJUSTMENTS

MANUAL SHIFT LINKAGE

1. Loosen swivel nut on lever, then push manual lever fully toward right side of vehicle. **Fig. 1.**
2. Return lever two notches to Neutral position, then place selector lever in Neutral position.
3. Manually hold lever lightly toward R range, then tighten swivel nut.

THROTTLE CABLE

1. Hold accelerator pedal in fully depressed position, then loosen cable adjusting nuts. **Fig. 2.**
2. Adjust cable to obtain .04 inch between end of boot and stopper on cable, then tighten adjusting nut.
3. Fully depress accelerator pedal and recheck adjustment, then road test vehicle.

NEUTRAL SAFETY SWITCH

1. Loosen neutral start switch attaching bolts, then place selector lever in Neutral position.
2. Disconnect Electrical connector, then connect a suitable ohmmeter between terminals.
3. Rotate switch until meter indicates

Fig. 2   Throttle cable adjustment

1. ADJUSTING NUTS
2. RUBBER BOOT
3. CABLE STOP
4. 0-1 MM (0-0.04 IN.)

Fig. 3   Valve body bolt identification

Fig. 4   Manual valve body bolt identification

continuity, then torque switch retaining bolts to 48 inch lbs. to secure adjustment.

4. Reconnect electrical connector to switch then ensure engine starts with selector lever in "N" and "P" only.

MAINTENANCE
CHANGING FLUID

1. Raise and support vehicle, then place a suitable container under transaxle drain plug.
2. Remove drain plug and drain fluid, then reinstall and tighten drain plug.
3. With ignition off, add 2.4 quarts of Dexron II type transmission fluid.
4. Start engine, then move selector lever through all ranges and end in "P."
5. With engine idling, check fluid level, then if necessary, add fluid as necessary to bring fluid to "Cool" level on dipstick.

IN-VEHICLE SERVICE
VALVE BODY, REPLACE
Removal

1. Clean area around pan, then Drain transmission fluid.
2. Remove oil pan and gasket, then the oil strainer.
3. Remove apply tube bracket attaching bolts, then the apply tube.
4. Remove oil tubes using a suitable screwdriver, then the manual detent spring.
5. Remove manual valve, then the manual valve body.
6. Remove valve body, then disconnect throttle cable.
7. Remove valve body, then the governor, apply gasket and governor oil gasket.

Installation

1. Install governor oil gasket, then the governor and governor apply gasket.
2. Hold valve body in place, then manually retain cam in downward position and slip cable end into slot.
3. Position valve body in installation position, then insert and finger tighten 14 attaching bolts. Torque bolts to 7 ft. lbs.

NOTE: Attaching bolt lengths (mm) are indicated in, **Fig. 3.**

4. Align manual valve with pin on manual valve lever, then install manual valve body.
5. Insert and finger tighten attaching bolts, then torque to 7 ft. lbs.

NOTE: Attaching bolt lengths (mm) are indicated in **Fig. 4.**

6. Install detent spring, then insert and finger tighten attaching bolts. Torque attaching bolts to 7 ft. lbs.
7. Ensure manual lever is in contact with center of roller at tip of detent spring, then install oil tubes.
8. Install apply tube bracket, then the oil strainer.
9. Insert magnet into pan, then install oil pan with new gasket.
10. Insert oil pan attaching bolts, then torque to 43 inch lbs.
11. Install drain plug with new gasket, then torque to 36 ft. lbs.
12. Fill transaxle to specifications, then ensure proper fluid level.

THROTTLE CABLE, REPLACE
Removal

1. Disconnect throttle cable from engine, then the transaxle control cable from manual shift lever.
2. Remove manual shift lever, then the neutral start switch.
3. Remove valve body as previously described, then the retaining plate bolt and retaining plate.
4. Pull cable from transaxle case.

Installation

1. Insert cable into transaxle case, then install retaining plate and bolt.
2. Install valve body as previously described, then position cable stop for adjustment reference as follows:

NOTE: Cable stop is not staked in place on replacement cable.

a. Bend cable to a radius of approximately 7.87 inches as shown, **Fig. 5.**
b. Lightly pull inner cable from housing until a slight resistance is felt, then hold in position.
c. Stake stopper onto inner cable so that .031–.059 inch clearance exists between stop and cable housing.
3. Connect throttle cable to throttle linkage, then adjust cable as previously

described.

4. Install neutral safety switch, then the manual shift lever. Adjust switch as previously described.
5. Ensure transaxle fluid level is to specifications, then road test vehicle.

GOVERNOR VALVE, REPLACE
Removal

1. Remove transaxle cover, then the LH driveshaft.
2. Remove governor cover, then the O-ring.
3. Remove governor body with thrust washer.
4. Remove washer, then the governor body adapter.

Installation

1. Install governor body adapter, then the governor body with thrust washer.
2. Install governor cover with O-ring, then the LH driveshaft.
3. Install transaxle dust cover, then ensure transaxle fluid level is to specifications.
4. Road test vehicle.

SECOND BRAKE SERVO ASSEMBLY, REPLACE
Removal

1. Raise and support vehicle, then remove shift cable bracket at transaxle.
2. Remove snap ring.
3. Remove cover.
4. Remove piston, then the outer spring.

Installation

1. Insert piston, less outer spring, then install snap ring.
2. Install tool No. J-35679, then observe groove on plunger of tool.
3. Push button on tool, **Fig. 6.** This allows tool to push brake apply rod into case. If groove is visible, piston stroke is correct (.059–.118 inch). If stroke is greater than specified, replace piston rod with 2.870 inch or 2.811 inch rod as needed.
4. Remove snap ring, then install piston and outer spring.
5. Install tool No. J-35549 to compress spring, then insert snap ring.
6. Install cover, then the shift cable bracket.
7. Lower vehicle.

Fig. 5 Positioning throttle cable for stopper installation

TRANSAXLE
REPLACE

1. Disconnect battery ground cable.
2. Remove air intake tube, then disconnect speedometer cable at transaxle.
3. Disconnect thermostat housing and ground cable at transaxle, then remove upper mount to bracket attaching bolt.
4. Disconnect transaxle electrical connectors, then the T.V. cable at carburetor.
5. Remove 2 upper bellhousing attach-

ing bolts, then support engine using a suitable support tool.
6. Raise and support vehicle, then remove left wheel assembly.
7. Remove left and right splash shields, then the center splash shield.
8. Remove center beam, then disconnect shift cable at transaxle.
9. Remove shift cable bracket, then the cooler bracket.
10. Disconnect cooler lines at outlets, then remove inspection cover.
11. Remove torque converter attaching bolts, then the left control arm at ball joint.
12. Remove right and left axle shafts at transaxle, then the starter attaching bolts.
13. Remove 3 rear transaxle attaching bolts, then support transaxle, using a suitable jack.
14. Remove remaining transaxle attaching bolts, then the remaining bellhousing attaching bolts.
15. Remove transaxle from vehicle.
16. Reverse procedure to install, noting the following:
    a. Torque transaxle housing attaching bolts to 47 ft. lbs. for 12mm

Fig. 6 Second brake servo plunger installation

bolts or 34 ft. lbs. for 10mm bolts.
b. Torque LH engine mount bolts to 38 ft. lbs.
c. Install white torque converter bolt first, then the five yellow bolts. Torque bolts evenly to 13 ft. lbs.
d. Torque engine mount center support bolts to 29 ft. lbs.
e. Torque front and rear mount bolts to 29 ft. lbs.

GM Turbo Hydra-Matic 125, 125C Automatic Transaxle

INDEX

IDENTIFICATION

These transaxles may be identified by a model tag attached to the oil pan flange pad to the right of the oil dipstick at the rear of the transaxle.

Citation, Omega, Phoenix & Skylark

1980	CV, PZ
1981	CD, CT, CV, PZ
1982	CT, PZ
1983	CC, CE, CL, CT, PD, PW
1984	CC, CE, CT, HS, PD, PW
1985	CE, CT, CX, PD, PW

Cavalier, Cimarron, Firenza, 2000 & Skyhawk

1982	CF, CJ, PG, P3
1983	CA, CB, CF, PG, P3

1984	CA, CB, CF, PE, PG, PJ
1985	CA, CB, CC, CI, CJ, PE, PG, PJ

Celebrity, Century, Ciera, 6000

1982	OP
1983	BF, BL, CC, CL, CT, OP, PD, PW
1984	BF, BL, CC, CL, OP, PD, PW
1985	BF, BL, CL, CT, CW, CX, OP, PD, PW

Fiero

1984	PF
1985	CD, PF

Calais, Somerset Regal

1985	BP, PN

DESCRIPTION

NOTE: The 125 and 125C automatic transaxles are identical, except the 125C incorporates a pressure plate and damper assembly.

These automatic transaxles, **Figs. 1 and 2**, are designed for use as a transverse mounted front wheel drive unit. The unit consists primarily of a 3 element torque converter, compound planetary gear set and dual sprocket and drive link assembly. A differential and final drive gear set is also incorporated in the transaxle case. Three multiple disc clutches, a roller clutch and a band provide the friction elements required to obtain the desired functions of the planetary gearset. Hydraulic pressure required to operate the friction elements and automatic control is provided by a vane type pump.

Fig. 1 Cross-sectional view of Turbo Hydra-Matic 125 automatic transaxle

TROUBLESHOOTING

NO DRIVE IN D RANGE

1. Low fluid level.
2. Manual linkage improperly adjusted.
3. Restricted or plugged screen or damaged screen O-ring.
4. Pressure regulator valve sticking.
5. Damaged pump rotor splines.
6. Manual valve disconnected.
7. Case cover gaskets mispositioned.
8. Forward clutch worn or damaged.
9. Roller clutch worn or damaged.

NO DRIVE IN D OR INTERMEDIATE RANGE

Hunts 1-2-1 At Low Speed
1. Governor springs distorted and/or weights binding.

Firm, Harsh Or Delayed Shifts
1. Disconnected or binding T.V. cable.
2. High oil pressure. Check oil pressure in neutral at minimum T.V.
3. Compare 1-2 shift feel at part throttle in Drive range to 1-2 shift feel at part throttle in intermediate range. If intermediate range is firmer, follow steps 2 through 12 under "Slow, Early or Drawn Out Shifts With End Bump." If shift feels the same for both ranges, proceed to next step.
4. Intermediate servo piston, piston seal or piston bore damaged.
5. Missing servo orifice bleed cup plug.
6. Leak between servo apply pin and and case or wrong apply pin.
7. Incorrect T.V. link.
8. T.V. plunger, T.V. shift valve or 1-2 accumulator valve binding.
9. 1-2 accumulator piston piston, seal spring or bore damaged.
10. Incorrect or leaking spacer plate and/or gaskets.

Fig. 2 Exploded view of torque converter clutch. 125C transaxle

11. Leaking 2nd oil passage in case or case cover.

2-3 SHIFT COMPLAINTS

NOTE: Before diagnosing 2-3 shift problems, check transmission fluid level and adjust T.V. cable and manual linkage as required.

Delayed Harsh Upshift
1. High oil pressure.
2. Direct clutch accumulator exhaust hole plugged or not drilled.
3. Direct clutch exhaust valve check ball (#1) missing, mislocated or leaking.
4. Valve body throttle valve and plunger binding.
5. T.V. shift valve binding.

Slow, Early Or Drawn Out Shifts With End Bump
1. Low oil pressure.
2. Intermediate servo piston to case seal ring missing or damaged.
3. Servo piston or bore (case) damaged.
4. Orifice plug missing from case servo bore area.
5. Accumulator exhaust check valve not seated.
6. Direct clutch feed orifice in spacer plate restricted.
7. Spacer plate or gaskets leaking or incorrectly installed.
8. Check ball #5 not seated.
9. Direct clutch case cover passages porous or incorrect cover gasket.
10. Driven sprocket support passages interconnected, leaking or restricted.
11. Driven sprocket support oil seal rings damaged or missing. Support inner sleeve loose or out of position.
12. Direct clutch piston or housing cracked, apply ring missing or incorrect number of clutch plates.

FAILS TO SHIFT 2-3 OR DELAYED 2-3 SHIFT

NOTE: Check transmission fluid level, set T.V. cable to specifications and check manual linkage before diagnosing shift problems.

1. Incorrect, broken, disconnected or binding T.V. cable.
2. Worn governor cover.
3. Governor thrust washer and seal worn or missing.
4. Governor spring unseated, weights binding or exhaust check balls missing.
5. Governor driven gear stripped or missing.
6. Intermediate servo piston, bore or seal ring damaged.
7. Intermediate servo orifice bleed cup in case missing or case porous in servo bore area.
8. Direct clutch accumulator cup plug or accumulator exhaust check valve leaking or missing.
9. Binding throttle lever and bracket assembly or wrong or disconnected T.V. link.
10. 2-3 shift valve, 2-3 T.V. valve or shift T.V. valve sticking or binding.
11. Governor feed to 2-3 T.V. valve or direct clutch feed orifice restricted.
12. Valve body spacer plate or gaskets leaking, damaged or incorrectly installed.
13. Missing or mislocated #5 check ball.
14. Governor shaft case sleeve or driven sprocket support oil seal damaged or missing.
15. Direct clutch piston, piston housing or seals damaged.
16. Direct clutch plates or check ball capsule damaged. Backing plate snap ring out of groove.
17. Leaking case center gasket or loose case cover bolts.
18. Leaking, interconnected or restricted driven sprocket support passages.
19. Driven sprocket support oil seal rings missing or damaged.
20. Driven sprocket support sleeve loose or out of position.

DELAY IN DRIVE & REVERSE
1. Low fluid level.
2. Low line pressures.

NOTE: A 3-5 second delay in Drive or reverse with engine off for 60 minutes or longer indicates converter drainback.

3. Damaged turbine shaft teflon seals. Replace with solid seals.

2ND SPEED START, MISSES 1ST
1. Governor springs distorted or out of place. Governor weights binding.
2. 1-2 Shift or throttle valves stuck in upshift position.

SHIFTS 2-1 AT HIGH SPEEDS, PASSING GEAR
1. Damaged governor assembly.
2. Sticking intermediate servo.
3. Direct clutch orifice controlled by #2 check ball restricted.
4. 1-2 accumulator piston or seal missing or leaking.

SLIPS OR CHATTERS IN 1ST
1. Low fluid level.
2. Wrong or Incorrectly adjusted T.V. cable.
3. Low oil pressure.
4. Restricted feed to forward clutch.
5. Burned forward clutch.
6. Rough machined surface on driven sprocket support.
7. Incorrect case cover gaskets.

SHIFTS 1-3 (MISSES 2ND)

1. Intermediate servo sticking, leaking or damaged.
2. Stuck or unseated accumulator exhaust check valve.
3. 1-2 valve sticking in control valve pump assembly.
4. Wrong or incorrectly installed spacer plate or gasket.
5. Governor feed passage to 1-2 valve blocked.
6. Intermediate band apply feed orifice blocked.
7. Case or case cover intermediate servo apply passage blocked.
8. Burned, improperly installed or broken intermediate band.

NO FULL THROTTLE 3-2 DOWNSHIFT

1. Wrong, improperly adjusted or binding T.V. cable or link.
2. Accelerator pedal and/or linkage will not open carburetor to wide open position.
3. Binding shift T.V. or throttle valve.
4. Spacer plate holes plugged and/or gaskets damaged or mispositioned.

NO INTERMEDIATE RANGE (2ND GEAR)

1. Intermediate servo oil seal ring missing or damaged.
2. Intermediate band broken, burned or mispositioned.
3. 1-2 accumulator piston or pin damaged or missing.

NO OVERRUN BRAKING IN LO, REVERSE OK

1. Manual linkage improperly adjusted.
2. Lo-reverse pipe or piston seals leaking.
3. Damaged lo blow off valve assembly.

TRANSAXLE NOISY

1. Low fluid level.
2. Screen plugged or screen O-ring damaged.
3. Coolant in fluid.
4. Transaxle grounded to body.
5. Roller bearing damaged or worn.
6. If noisy in 3rd gear or on turns only, check differential and final drive unit.

HIGH OR LOW FLUID PRESSURE

1. Throttle valve cable improperly adjusted or binding.
2. Throttle lever and bracket assembly binding or damaged.
3. Throttle valve or plunger binding.
4. Shift throttle valve binding.
5. Line boost valve binding.
6. Throttle valve boost valve or reverse boost valve binding.
7. Pressure regulator valve and spring binding.
8. Pressure relief valve damaged.

9. Manual valve disconnected.
10. Pump damaged.

NO DRIVE IN FORWARD RANGE, REVERSE TIES UP

1. Driven sprocket support sleeve turned.

NO FORWARD OR REVERSE IN ANY RANGE

Ties Up
1. Internal mechanical damage.
2. Broken differential.
3. Object between link and sprocket locking link assembly.

Slippage
1. Low fluid level.
2. Converter to flex plate bolts missing.
3. Low line pressure in drive.
4. Manual linkage binding.
5. Input shaft to forward clutch drum broken loose.
6. Reaction carrier broken at lo roller clutch cam.
7. Broken chain assembly.

NO DRIVE IN FORWARD RANGES, REVERSE OK

1. Low line pressure in Drive.
2. Binding manual linkage.
3. Driven sprocket support drive oil passage or case cover gasket restricted.
4. Drive oil passage leak in case cover.
5. Driven sprocket support sleeve loose or mislocated.
6. Burned forward clutch.
7. Leaking valve body pipe in control valve assembly.

NO REVERSE, ALL FORWARD RANGES OK

Ties Up
1. Forward clutch not releasing due to burned clutch plates, piston seal ring missing or sticking exhaust check ball.

Slippage
1. Low Line Pressure in reverse.
2. Restricted case to lo and reverse clutch housing cup plug assembly.
3. Lo and reverse clutch piston or seal leakage.
4. Lo and reverse pipe O-ring or washer damaged or missing.
5. Incorrect gasket for driven sprocket support height.
6. Lo 1st orifice in spacer plate plugged or missing.
7. Burned direct clutch.
8. Burned lo and reverse clutch.

MAINTENANCE

To check fluid, drive vehicle for at least 15 minutes to bring fluid to operating temperature (200° F). With vehicle on a level surface and engine idling in Park and parking brake applied, the level on the dipstick should be at the "Full" mark. To bring the fluid level from the ADD mark to the FULL mark requires one pint of fluid. If vehicle cannot be driven sufficiently to bring fluid to operating temperature, the level on the dipstick should be between the two dimples on the dipstick with fluid temperature at 70° F. Note that the two dimples are located above the FULL mark.

If additional fluid is required, use only Dexron II automatic transmission fluid.

NOTE: An early change to a darker color from the usual red color and or a strong odor that is usually associated with overheated fluid is normal and should not be considered as a positive sign of required maintenance or unit failure.

CAUTION: When adding fluid, do not over fill, as foaming and loss of fluid through the vent may occur as the fluid heats up. Also, if fluid level is too low, complete loss of drive may occur especially when cold, which can cause transmission failure.

Every 100,000 miles, the oil should be drained, the oil pan removed, the screen cleaned and fresh fluid added. For vehicles subjected to more severe use such as heavy city traffic especially in hot weather, prolonged periods of idling or towing, this maintenance should be performed every 15,000 miles.

CHANGING FLUID

1. Raise and support vehicle, then position drain pan under oil pan.
2. Remove front and side oil pan attaching bolts, then loosen rear pan attaching bolts.
3. Carefully pry oil pan loose from transaxle case and allow fluid to drain.
4. Remove remaining attaching bolt, oil pan and gasket. Thoroughly clean pan before reinstalling.
5. Remove and discard screen and O-ring seal.
6. Install replacement screen and O-ring seal, locating screen against dipstick stop.
7. Install gasket on oil pan, then install pan and torque attaching bolts to 12 ft. lbs.
8. Lower vehicle and add approximately 4 qts. of fluid.
9. With selector in park, parking brake applied and engine at idle speed and operating temperature, check fluid level and add fluid as necessary.

NOTE: Do not race engine or move shift lever through ranges.

IN-VEHICLE ADJUSTMENTS

MANUAL LINKAGE, ADJUST

Exc. Fiero
1. Place transaxle shift lever in "Neutral" position.
2. Place transaxle lever in "Neutral" position by moving transaxle lever clockwise to the "L" detent, then move lever counter clockwise through three detent positions to "Neutral".

Fig. 3 Manual cable mounting. 1980–81 models

1 CABLE ASM.	**7** 21 N·m (15 FT. LB.)	**12** GROMMET CABLE ASM.
2 PIN	**8** LEVER	**13** TRANSMISSION ASM.
3 2 N·m (32.4 IN. LB.)	**9** BRACKET	**14** FLOOR PAN
4 COVER	**10** 50 N·m (37 FT. LB.)	**15** SHIFTER ASM. (7A-P1)
5 NUT	**11** 24 N·m (18 FT. LB.)	
6 27 N·m (20 FT. LB.)		

Fig. 4 Manual cable mounting. 1982–85 Cavalier, Cimmarron, Firenza, Skyhawk & 2000

Fig. 5 Manual cable mounting. 1982–85 Celebrity, Century, Ciera, Citation, Omega, Phoenix, Skylark & 6000

3. On 1980–81 vehicles, attach shift cable to pin, **Fig. 3**, then torque attaching nut to specifications.
4. On 1982–85 vehicles, loosely assemble retainer, bushing and shift cable to pin, **Figs. 4 and 5**, then torque attaching nut to specifications.

Fiero
1. Place transaxle shift lever in "Neutral" position.
2. Place transaxle lever in "Neutral" position by rotating transaxle lever clockwise from "Park", through "Reverse" and into "Neutral."
3. Insert shift cable threaded pin through slotted hole in lever and hand start nut, **Fig. 6**.
4. Torque nut to 15–25 ft. lbs. while holding lever out of "Park" position.

T.V. OR DOWNSHIFT CABLE, ADJUST

1. Disengage snap lock so that cable is free to slide, **Fig. 7**.

2. Ensure cable housing is fully seated into control cable bracket and is secured to the transmission. Also ensure cable is attached to the carburetor idler lever.
3. Rotate carburetor idler lever to its full travel stop and hold in this position.
4. Keeping idler lever firmly against stop, push snap lock until it is flush with downshift cable fitting.
5. Release carburetor idler lever.

IN-VEHICLE, REPAIRS
VALVE BODY, REPLACE

1. Remove valve body cover and gasket.
2. On THM 125C transaxles, remove solenoid retaining bolt and the solenoid, then disconnect converter clutch wires from 3rd gear pressure switch.
3. Remove screws attaching throttle lever and bracket assembly, then

remove throttle lever and bracket assembly with T.V. cable link.
4. On THM 125 transaxles, remove pump cover screws except for one screw shown in **Fig. 8**. Loosen, but do not remove this screw.
5. On THM 125C transaxles, remove the auxiliary valve body screws except for the one screw shown in **Fig. 9**. Loosen, but do not remove, this screw.
6. Remove remaining valve body retaining screws, then the valve body and pump assembly.
7. On THM 125C transaxles, separate valve body from auxiliary valve body.
8. Reverse procedure to install. On THM 125 transaxles, torque 1 × 25mm., 1 × 45mm., and 1 × 65mm. valve body attaching bolts to 8 ft. lbs. Torque 1.25 × 65mm. and 1.25 × 85mm. bolts to 18 ft. lbs. On THM 125C transaxles, torque 1 × 20mm., 1 × 45mm., 1 × 65mm., and 1 × 90mm. valve body attaching bolts to 8 ft. lbs. Torque 1.25 × 85mm. and 1.25 × 130mm. bolts to 18 ft. lbs.
9. Using new gasket, install valve body cover to transaxle and torque bolts to 12 ft. lbs.

NOTE: THM 125C transaxle valve body covers and oil pans can have a raised rib, depressed rib or flat sealing flange. RTV sealant should be used on all oil pans and valve body covers that have a flat sealing flange. Gaskets should be used on all oil

Fig. 7   Downshift cable adjustment

1 – NUT/CABLE ASSY.	8 – BRACKET
2 – NUT/SHIFTING LEVER	9 – CABLE ASSY.
3 – LEVER/SHIFTING	10 – RETAINER ASSY.
4 – SWITCH/NEUTRAL START AND BACK-UP	11 – T HANDLE
5 – BOLT/NEUTRAL START SWITCH (2)	12 – SNAP SECURELY ONTO PIN
6 – TRANSAXLE	13 – GEAR SHIFT SUPPORT
7 – BOLT/BRACKET	14 – NUT 23 N·M (17 FT. LB.)

Fig. 6   Manual linkage. 1984—85 Fiero

Fig. 8   Pump cover & valve body assembly attaching bolts. THM 125

pans and valve body covers that have either depressed or raised rib sealing flanges.

INTERMEDIATE SERVO, REPLACE

1. Remove oil pan and gasket, then remove screen and O-ring.
2. Remove reverse oil pipe retaining brackets, intermediate servo cover and gasket.
3. Remove intermediate servo assembly.
4. Reverse procedure to install. Torque intermediate servo cover screws to 8 ft. lbs.

Fig. 9   Valve body & auxiliary valve body retaining screws. THM 125C

Fig. 10 Removing & installing governor assembly

Fig. 11 Drilling cradle spot weld

GOVERNOR, REPLACE

1. Remove speedometer driven gear and sleeve.
2. Remove governor cover and O-ring.
3. Remove speedometer drive gear thrust washer and gear, then remove governor assembly, **Fig. 10.**
4. Reverse procedure to install. Torque governor cover attaching bolts to 9 ft. lbs.

TRANSAXLE
REPLACE

1980–81 CITATION, OMEGA, PHOENIX & SKYLARK

1. Disconnect battery ground cable at transaxle and attach cable to upper radiator hose with tape.
2. Disconnect detent cable at carburetor, then remove detent cable attaching screw at transaxle. Pull up on detent cable cover at transaxle, until cable is exposed, then disconnect cable from rod.
3. Remove two transaxle strut bracket bolts at transaxle, if equipped.
4. Remove all engine to transaxle bolts except the one bolt near the starter motor. The bolt nearest the cowl is installed from the engine side.
5. Loosen the engine to transaxle bolt nearest the starter, but do not remove bolt.
6. Disconnect speedometer cable at upper and lower cable coupling. On models equipped with cruise control, disconnect speedometer cable at transducer.
7. Remove clip and washer and disconnect transaxle linkage at transaxle, then remove two shift linkage bracket bolts.
8. Disconnect transaxle oil cooler lines at transaxle.
9. Install engine holding fixture J-22825-1 and J-22825-20 and raise engine slightly to relieve weight from engine mounts.
10. Unlock steering column, then raise and support vehicle.
11. Remove two nuts attaching stabilizer bar left hand side lower control arm.
12. Remove four bolts attaching the plate that retains stabilizer to left hand side of cradle.
13. Loosen four bolts attaching stabilizer bar bracket to right hand side of cradle, then pull stabilizer bar down from left hand side of vehicle.
14. Disconnect front and rear transaxle mounts at cradle.
15. Remove two rear center crossmember bolts.
16. Remove right hand side front cradle attaching bolts. To gain access to attaching nuts, pull back on splash shield next to frame rail.
17. Remove upper bolt from lower front transaxle damper, if equipped.
18. Remove left hand side front and rear cradle to body attaching bolts.
19. Remove left front wheel and tire assembly.
20. Place tool No. J-28468 behind axle shaft cones and pull cones out away from transaxle. Position axle shafts out of way and plug bores to prevent fluid leakage.
21. Swing partial cradle toward left hand side of vehicle and secure to fender well with wire.
22. Remove four converter shield attaching bolts and shield.
23. Remove two transaxle extension bolts from engine to transaxle bracket.
24. Secure a suitable transaxle jack to transaxle case, then remove three converter to flywheel attaching bolts.
25. Remove the remaining transaxle to engine bolt located near starter motor.
26. Remove transaxle by sliding toward left hand side of vehicle away from engine.
27. Reverse procedure to install. Note the following when installing transaxle:
    a. Slide right axle shaft into case as transaxle is being installed.
    b. Install cradle to body bolts before installing stabilizer bar attachments.
    c. Use pry hole located on cradle to aid in stabilizer bar installation.

1982–85 CELEBRITY, CENTURY, CUTLASS CIERA, CITATION, OMEGA, PHOENIX, SKYLARK & 6000

1. Disconnect battery ground cable, then remove air cleaner.
2. Disconnect T.V. cable from transaxle and carburetor, then remove strut shock bracket bolts from transaxle.
3. Remove oil cooler lines from strut bracket.
4. Remove all transaxle to engine attaching bolts except the one nearest the starter. Loosen, but do not remove this bolt.
5. Disconnect speedometer cable at upper and lower couplings, then remove shift linkage retaining clip, washer and bracket bolts.
6. Disconnect oil cooler lines at transaxle.
7. Remove front and left sections of cradle as follows:
    a. Install engine support fixture J-22825-1 and J-22825-45 and torque fasteners to 30 ft. lbs.
    b. Position support hook into lifting bracket and tighten coupling nut only enough to remove slack from hook.

CAUTION: Engine support fixture must be located in center of cowl for 4 cylinder engines and on strut towers for 6 cylinder engines. Support fixture is not designed to support entire weight of engine and transaxle. Improper use may result in vehicle damage and/or personal injury.

c. Remove intermediate shaft to steering gear stub shaft attaching bolt, then raise and support vehicle.

FRONT SUSPENSION SUPPORT ATTACHING BOLT/SCREW SEQUENCE

1. INSTALL LOOSELY, THE CENTER SCREW INTO HOLE Ⓐ.
2. INSTALL LOOSELY, THE TIE BAR SCREW INTO THE SMALL SLOTTED OUTBOARD HOLE.
3. INSTALL AND TORQUE BOTH BOLTS IN THE REAR HOLES.
4. INSTALL AND TORQUE 2ND CENTER HOLE Ⓓ BOLT/SCREW.
5. TORQUE CENTER HOLE Ⓐ BOLT.
6. INSTALL OTHER TIE BAR BOLT (FRONT HOLE Ⓔ) AND TORQUE.
7. TORQUE 2ND BOLT/SCREW IN THE (FRONT HOLE Ⓑ).

FRONT SUSPENSION SUPPORT

88 N·m (65 FT. LBS.)

LOWER CONTROL ARM

88 N·m (65 FT. LBS.)

FRONT OF CAR

88 N·m (65 FT. LBS.)

88 N·m (65 FT. LBS.)

Fig. 12   Front suspension support attaching bolt sequence

d. Support engine with suitable jack, then remove left front wheel/tire assembly.
e. Remove power steering line brackets and steering gear mounting bolts.
f. Disconnect drive line vibration absorber, if equipped.
g. Disconnect left lower ball joint at steering knuckle, then remove both front stabilizer bar reinforcements and bushings.
h. Using a ½ inch drill bit, drill through spot weld located between rear holes of left stabilizer bar mounting, **Fig. 10.**
i. Disconnect engine and transaxle mounts from cradle, then remove side crossmember bolts.
j. Remove left side body mount bolts, then the left and front cradle assembly.

8. Install axle shaft boot protectors, then position axle shaft puller behind axle shaft cones and pull cones away from transaxle.
9. Remove left axle shaft and plug bore in transaxle to avoid fluid leakage.
10. Remove starter, then the converter shield.
11. Remove the three flywheel to converter attaching bolts.
12. Remove engine to transaxle bracket extension bolts, then the rear transaxle mount bracket assembly. Raise transaxle if necessary.
13. Remove the one remaining engine to transaxle bolt located near the starter.
14. Slide transaxle towards drivers side and remove from vehicle.
15. Reverse procedure to install. Note the following when installing transaxle:
    a. Position a ½ inch drill bit into drilled hole, **Fig. 11,** before tightening cradle bolts.
    b. Slide right axle shaft into case as transaxle is being installed.
    c. Check front suspension alignment after transaxle installation.
    d. Check and adjust T. V. cable if necessary.

1982–85 CAVALIER, CIMARRON, FIRENZA, 2000 & SKYHAWK

1. Disconnect battery ground cable from transaxle.
2. Insert a ¼ × 2 inch bolt into hole in right front motor mount to prevent mislocation of mount during transaxle removal.
3. Remove air cleaner, then disconnect T.V. cable from carburetor.
4. Remove T.V. cable retaining bolt from transaxle, pull up cable cover and disconnect cable from transaxle rod.
5. Remove engine wire harness retaining bolt, disconnect air management hose, then position harness aside.
6. Raise and support engine with a suitable lifting device so that weight is taken off motor mounts.
7. Remove top transaxle mount and bracket assembly, then disconnect shift control linkage from transaxle.
8. Remove top engine to transaxle attaching bolts and loosen, but do not remove, the bolt nearest the starter.
9. Raise and support vehicle, unlock steering column and remove both front wheel/tire assemblies.
10. Remove cotter pin and ball joint retaining nut, then separate ball joint from control arm. Repeat procedure for other side.
11. Remove stabilizer bar to left lower control arm attaching bolt.
12. Remove the six left front suspension support to body attaching bolts, then position axle shaft removal tools J-28468 and J-23907 behind axle shaft cones and pull cones away from transaxle.
13. Remove axle shrafts and plug transaxle bores to prevent fluid leakage.

14. Remove transaxle control cable bracket retaining nut, then the transaxle to engine attaching stud.
15. Disconnect speedometer cable and transaxle mounting strut.
16. Remove the four torque converter shield to transaxle attaching bolts, then the shield.
17. Remove the torque converter to flex plate retaining bolts, then disconnect and plug the transaxle cooler lines.
18. Remove starter.
19. Remove brake and fuel line brackets from left side of underbody and position aside.
20. Remove the last engine to transaxle attaching bolt, separate transaxle from engine by sliding away from engine and remove transaxle from vehicle.
21. Reverse procedure to install, making sure:
    a. Axle shafts are installed after transaxle is in place.
    b. To follow the tightening sequence shown in **Fig. 12** when installing the front suspension support assembly.
    c. To readjust throttle valve (T.V.) cable.
    d. To check front suspension alignment.

1984–85 FIERO

1. Disconnect battery ground cable.
2. Remove air cleaner assembly, then disconnect all electrical connectors from transaxle.
3. Disconnect shift cable and T.V. cable from transaxle.
4. Remove transaxle cooler line supports.
5. Remove upper transaxle-to-engine attaching bolts.
6. Install suitable engine support fixture (tool No. J-28467 or equivalent).
7. Raise and support vehicle.
8. Remove both rear wheels, then disconnect axle shafts from transaxle.
9. Remove heat shield from catalytic converter.
10. Disconnect exhaust pipe from exhaust manifold.
11. Remove engine mount-to-cradle nuts.
12. Support cradle with a suitable jack, then remove rear cradle-to-body attaching bolts.
13. Remove forward cradle-to-body through bolts, then lower cradle and position aside.
14. Remove shields from starter motor and inspection cover.
15. Remove starter motor.
16. Mark relationship of flywheel to converter, then remove flywheel attaching bolts.
17. Disconnect cooler lines from transaxle, then support transaxle with a suitable jack.
18. Remove right side transaxle support bracket bolts.
19. Remove lower transaxle-to-engine attaching bolts, then carefully lower transaxle from vehicle.
20. Reverse procedure to install.

GM Turbo Hydra-Matic 440-T4 Automatic Transaxle

INDEX

IDENTIFICATION

These transaxles may be identified by the following codes stamped into the horizontal cast rib on the right rear side of the transaxle housing.

BUICK

1984 V6-173 Century	CW
V6-231 Century	BC
1985 V6-181 Electra & Park Avenue	BS
V6-231 Electra & Park Avenue	BA
V6-262 Diesel Electra & Park Avenue	OB

CADILLAC

1985 V6-262 Diesel DeVille & Fleetwood	OB
V8-250 DeVille & Fleetwood	AY

CHEVROLET

1984 V6-173 Celebrity	CW

OLDSMOBILE

1984 V6-231 Cutlass Ciera	BC
1985 V6-181 98	BS
V6-231 98	BA
V6-262 Diesel 98	OB

DESCRIPTION

This transaxle, **Fig. 1,** is a fully automatic front wheel drive unit which provides four forward ranges including overdrive. A variable vane type oil pump supplies oil pressure, which is regulated by vacuum modulation. Shift points are controlled by throttle opening by a throttle valve cable.

TROUBLESHOOTING

OIL LEAK

1. Side cover distorted.
2. Oil pan attaching bolts loose.
3. Oil pan gaskets damaged.
4. T.V. cable, fill tube and/or electrical connector seal damaged.
5. Manual shaft seal assembly damaged.
6. Governor cover and/or servo covers O-rings damaged.
7. Cooler fittings and/or pressure taps insufficiently tightened, or threads stripped.
8. Converter seal damaged, or garter spring missing.
9. Axle seals damaged, or garter spring missing.
10. Modulator O-ring damaged.
11. Parking plunger guide O-ring damaged.
12. Speedometer O-ring damaged.

OIL COMING OUT OF VENT

1. High fluid level.
2. Coolant in transmission fluid or engine overheating.
3. Drive sprocket support drain holes blocked.
4. Thermo element in case remaining open when hot.
5. Oil filter O-ring damaged.

OIL PRESSURE HIGH OR LOW

1. Incorrect fluid level.
2. Vacuum line leaking.
3. Modulator leaking or modulator diaphragm damaged.
4. Modulator valve damaged or restricted.
5. Pressure regulator valve or spring damaged.
6. Pressure relief valve spring damaged or ball missing.
7. Oil pump damaged or restricted.

NO DRIVE IN D RANGE

1. Low fluid level.
2. Low oil pressure.
3. Manual linkage improperly adjusted.
4. Torque converter stator roller clutch sluggish or converter not properly attached to flex plate.
5. Oil pump damaged.
6. Check ball No. 13 improperly assembled.
7. Drive link assembly damaged.
8. Input clutch plates burned or missing.
9. Input clutch piston or piston seal damaged, or housing check ball missing.
10. Input shaft seals damaged.
11. Input shaft feed passages blocked.
12. Input sprag and sun gear improperly assembled or sprag damaged.
13. Input carrier and reaction carrier pinions, internal gear and/or sun gear damaged.
14. 1-2 band assembly burned.
15. 1-2 servo assembly piston or seal damaged or incorrect apply pin installed.
16. Final drive assembly or final drive sun gear shaft damaged.
17. Parking pawl spring broken.
18. Output shaft damaged or improperly assembled with axles.

NO 1-2 UPSHIFT, 1ST SPEED ONLY

1. Governor weights binding.
2. Governor springs or gear damaged.
3. Accumulator cover leaking or exhaust

Fig. 1   GM Turbo Hydra-Matic 440-T4 automatic transaxle

check balls missing or damaged.
4. Oil pipes leaking or governor screen blocked.
5. Orifice cup plug blocked or governor retainer leaking.
6. Check ball No. 14 missing.
7. Control valve 1–2 shift valve binding.
8. 2nd clutch assembly clutch plates, pistons or seals damaged, or components improperly assembled.
9. Driven sprocket support oil rings damaged.
10. Reverse reaction drum splines damaged, or drum plate missing.

HARSH OR SOFT 1–2 SHIFT

1. Incorrect oil pressure.
2. Accumulator cover bolts improperly tightened.
3. Accumulator pistons, seals or springs damaged.
4. Control valve assembly accumulator valve binding.
5. Check ball No. 8 missing or improperly installed.

HIGH OR LOW 1–2 SHIFT

1. T.V. cable disconnected or improperly adjusted.
2. T.V. link, lever or bracket damaged.
3. T.V. valve and plunger binding.
4. Governor pressure incorrect.

NO 2–3 UPSHIFT, 1ST & 2ND SPEEDS ONLY

1. Incorrect apply pin installed in 1–2 servo assembly.
2. 1–2 servo assembly check ball No. 7 damaged or missing.
3. 1–2 servo assembly bore orifice cup plug missing.
4. Control valve assembly 2–3 shift valve stuck.
5. Control valve assembly bolts improperly torqued or No. 11 check ball not seating.
6. 3rd clutch assembly clutch plates burned.
7. 3rd clutch assembly piston, seals or check ball assembly damaged.

8. 3rd roller clutch assembly cage or springs damaged, or assembly improperly installed on input sun gear shaft.
9. Control valve assembly check ball No. 5 or 6 damaged or missing.
10. Control valve assembly 2–3 accumulator valve binding.

HARSH OR SOFT 2–3 SHIFT

1. Incorrect oil pressure.
2. Check ball No. 12 mislocated.

HIGH OR LOW 2–3 SHIFT

1. Refer to "High or Low 1–2 Shift."

NO 3–4 UPSHIFT

1. Governor weights binding.
2. Governor springs or gear damaged.
3. Control valve assembly 3–4 shift valve binding.
4. 4th clutch assembly clutch plates burned or improperly installed.
5. 4th clutch assembly pistons or seals

damaged or piston improperly installed.

6. 4th clutch shaft spline damaged.

HARSH OR SOFT 3—4 SHIFT

1. Incorrect oil pressure.
2. Accumulator cover and pistons seal damaged or cover bolts improperly tightened.
3. Check ball No. 1 mislocated.

HIGH OR LOW 3—4 SHIFT

1. Refer to "High or Low 1—2 Shift."

NO CONVERTER CLUTCH OPERATION

Models w/ECM

1. ECM malfunction.
2. Transaxle electrical connector damaged or wires pinched.
3. 3rd clutch switch or solenoid inoperative.
4. Control valve assembly converter clutch apply valve stuck, or check ball No. 10 missing.
5. Channel plate converter clutch blow off check ball damaged or not seating.
6. Turbine shaft seals damaged.
7. Oil pump driveshaft seal damaged.

Models Less ECM

1. Transaxle electrical connector damaged or wires pinched.
2. Governor pressure switch or solenoid inoperative.
3. 3rd or 4th clutch switch inoperative.
4. Converter clutch shift apply valve or shift valve stuck.
5. Check ball No. 10 missing.
6. Channel plate converter clutch blow off check ball damaged or not seating.
7. Turbine shaft seals damaged.
8. Oil pump driveshaft seal damaged.

CONVERTER CLUTCH DOES NOT RELEASE

1. Converter clutch apply valve stuck in apply position.

ROUGH CONVERTER CLUTCH OPERATION

1. Converter clutch regulator valve stuck.
2. Channel plate converter clutch accumulator piston, seal or spring damaged.
3. Turbine shaft seals damaged.

HARSH 4—3 DOWNSHIFT

1. Control valve assembly check ball No. 1 missing.

HARSH 3—2 DOWNSHIFT

1. Control valve assembly 1—2 servo control valve, 3—2 control valve or 3—2 coast valve stuck.
2. Control valve assembly check ball No. 4 and/or No. 12 missing.
3. Channel plate input clutch accumulator piston or seal damaged.

Fig. 2 Manual linkage adjustment

HARSH 2—1 DOWNSHIFT

1. Control valve assembly check ball No. 8 missing.

NO REVERSE IN R RANGE

1. Incorrect oil pressure.
2. Oil pump damaged.
3. Drive link assembly damaged.
4. Reverse band burned or damaged.
5. Input clutch plates burned or missing.
6. Input clutch piston or piston seal damaged, or housing check ball missing.
7. Input shaft seals damaged.
8. Input shaft feed passages blocked.
9. Input sprag and sun gear improperly assembled or sprag damaged.
10. Reverse servo piston or seal damaged, or incorrect apply pin installed.
11. Input and reaction carrier pinions, internal gear and/or sun gear damaged.

NO PARK IN P RANGE

1. Final drive internal gear park pawl spring, park pawl or parking gear damaged.
2. Manual linkage damaged or disconnected.

HARSH N—D OR N—D SHIFT

1. Control valve assembly check ball No. 9 or No. 12 missing.
2. Spacer plate thermal plates remaining open when warm.

NO VISCOUS CLUTCH OPERATION

Models w/ECM

1. ECM thermistor or temperature switch damaged.

MAINTENANCE

To check fluid, drive vehicle for at least 15 minutes to bring fluid to operating temperature (200° F). With vehicle on a level surface and engine idling in Park and parking brake applied, the level on the dipstick should be at the "Full" mark. To bring the fluid level from the ADD mark to the FULL mark requires one pint of fluid. If vehicle cannot be driven sufficiently to bring fluid to operating temperature, the level on the dipstick should be between the two dimples on the dipstick with fluid temperature at 70° F. Note that the two dimples are located above the FULL mark.

If additional fluid is required, use only Dexron II automatic transmission fluid.

NOTE: An early change to a darker color from the usual red color and/or a strong odor that is usually associated with overheated fluid is normal and should not be considered as a positive sign of required maintenance or unit failure.

CAUTION: When adding fluid, do not over fill, as foaming and loss of fluid through the vent may occur as the fluid heats up. Also, if fluid level is too low, complete loss of drive may occur especially when cold, which can cause transmission failure.

Every 100,000 miles, the oil should be drained, the oil pan removed, the screen cleaned and fresh fluid added. For vehicles subjected to more severe use such as heavy city traffic especially in hot weather, prolonged periods of idling or towing, this maintenance should be performed every 15,000 miles.

CHANGING FLUID

1. Raise and support vehicle, then position drain pan under oil pan.

Fig. 3   T.V. cable adjustment

2. Remove front and side oil pan attaching bolts, then loosen rear pan attaching bolts.
3. Carefully pry oil pan loose from transaxle case and allow fluid to drain.
4. Remove remaining attaching bolt, oil pan and gasket. Thoroughly clean pan before reinstalling.
5. Remove and discard screen and O-ring seal.
6. Install replacement screen and O-ring seal, locating screen against dipstick stop.
7. Install gasket on oil pan, then install pan and torque attaching bolts to 10 ft. lbs.
8. Lower vehicle and add approximately 6 qts. of fluid.
9. With selector in park, parking brake applied and engine at idle speed and operating temperature, check fluid level and add fluid as necessary.

NOTE: Do not race engine or move shift lever through ranges.

IN-VEHICLE ADJUSTMENTS
MANUAL LINKAGE, ADJUST

1. Place transaxle shift lever in Neutral position.
2. Loosely assemble nut to cable through transaxle lever, **Fig. 2,** with cable attached to steering column bracket and installed at transaxle control cable bracket.
3. Torque nut to 20 ft. lbs. while holding lever out of Park position.

T.V. CABLE, ADJUST

1. Depress re-adjust tab and move slider back through fitting until slider stops, **Fig. 3.**
2. Release re-adjust tab and open carburetor or pump lever to "full throttle stop" position to automatically adjust cable.
3. Check cable for sticking or binding and road test vehicle.

IN-VEHICLE REPAIRS
VALVE BODY, REPLACE

1. Disconnect battery ground cable.
2. Remove air cleaner, then install engine support tool No. J-28467 or equivalent.

Fig. 4   Valve body replacement

3. Remove upper case side cover bolts.
4. Raise and support vehicle.
5. Remove left front wheel.
6. On Celebrity, Century and Cutlass Ciera, remove brake clip from underbody.
7. On all models, remove lower ball joint from left steering knuckle.
8. Remove stabilizer bar attaching bolt from left control arm.
9. Remove left front cradle assembly, then lower vehicle.
10. On Celebrity, Century and Cutlass Ciera, disconnect A.I.R. pipe.
11. On all models, lower transaxle by adjusting engine support tool, then raise and support vehicle.
12. Remove remaining transaxle case side cover pan bolts, then the drive axle and nuts around flange at channel plate.
13. Remove case side cover pan and gaskets.
14. Remove valve body attaching bolts, then the valve body and pump as an assembly, **Fig. 4.**

NOTE: Do not remove 3 pump cover-to-valve body attaching bolts.

15. Reverse procedure to install.

GOVERNOR, REPLACE

1. Raise and support vehicle.
2. Remove speed sensor assembly.
3. Remove governor cover attaching bolts, then the cover and seal.
4. Remove governor complete with sleeve and speedometer drive gear, **Fig. 5.**
5. Reverse procedure to install.

ACCUMULATOR, REPLACE

1. Raise and support vehicle.
2. Drain transaxle fluid and remove oil pan.

3. Remove oil filter and seal, then the accumulator cover attaching bolts and cover.
4. Remove accumulator piston, oil seal and spring.
5. Reverse procedure to install.

REVERSE SERVO, REPLACE

1. Disconnect exhaust crossover pipe.
2. Depress servo cover, then remove snap ring and servo cover.
3. Remove servo piston, sealing ring, apply pin and servo spring, **Fig. 6.**
4. Reverse procedure to install.

1–2 SERVO, REPLACE

1. Depress servo cover, then remove snap ring and servo cover.
2. Remove servo piston, sealing ring, apply pin and servo spring, **Fig. 7.**
3. Reverse procedure to install.

TRANSAXLE
REPLACE

1984 CELEBRITY, CENTURY & CUTLASS CIERA

1. Disconnect battery ground cable.
2. Remove air cleaner assembly, then disconnect T.V. cable at both ends.
3. Disconnect shift linkage from transaxle.
4. Install engine support fixture, then disconnect converter clutch electrical connector.
5. Remove 3 transaxle-to-engine attaching bolts.
6. Disconnect vacuum line from modulator.
7. Raise and support vehicle.
8. Remove left front wheel, then the lower ball joint pinch nut.
9. Remove brake line bracket from strut, then disconnect drive axles from transaxle.

Fig. 5 Governor replacement

Fig. 7 1—2 servo replacement

Fig. 6 Reverse servo replacement

10. Remove cradle-to-stabilizer attaching bolts.
11. Remove stabilizer-to-control arm attaching bolts, then the left front cradle assembly.
12. Disconnect speedometer cable from transaxle, then remove extension housing-to-engine block support bracket.
13. Disconnect cooler lines from trans-

axle, then remove right and left insulator attaching bolts.
14. Remove flywheel splash shield.
15. Mark relationship of flywheel to converter, then remove flywheel attaching bolts.
16. Remove all remaining transaxle-to-engine attaching bolts except one.
17. Support transaxle with a suitable jack, then remove remaining bolt and carefully lower transaxle from vehicle.
18. Reverse procedure to install.

1985 ELECTRA, PARK AVENUE & 98

V6-181 & V6-231 Engines
1. Disconnect battery ground cable.
2. Disconnect electrical connector from mass air flow sensor.
3. Loosen two hose clamps at air intake duct, then remove intake duct and mass air flow sensor as an assembly.
4. Disconnect T.V. cable at both ends.
5. On models equipped with cruise control, disconnect cable from throttle body and the vacuum hoses from servo, then remove servo assembly.
6. On all models, disconnect shift control linkage from transaxle.
7. Disconnect electrical connectors from park/neutral switch, torque converter clutch and vehicle speed sensor.
8. Disconnect vacuum modulator hose from modulator.
9. Remove 3 upper transaxle-to-engine attaching bolts, then install suitable engine support fixture.
10. Turn steering wheel to the full left position, then remove both front wheels.
11. Remove right front ball joint nut and separate control arm from steering knuckle.
12. Remove right drive axle from case, using care to avoid damaging the seal.
13. Remove left drive axle, using a suitable pry bar with axle boot seal protectors installed.
14. Disconnect electrical connector from

aspirator, then remove left front transaxle mount.
15. Remove right front transaxle mount attaching nuts.
16. Remove left rear transaxle mount-to-transaxle attaching bolts, then the right rear transaxle mount.
17. Remove engine support bracket-to-transaxle case attaching bolts.
18. Remove stabilizer link-to-control arm bolt.
19. Remove flywheel cover attaching bolts and the cover.
20. Mark relationship of flywheel to converter, then remove flywheel attaching bolts.
21. Remove rear cradle-to-front cradle attaching bolts.
22. Install suitable transaxle support fixture, then cradle assembly by swinging to one side and supporting with a suitable stand.
23. Disconnect cooler lines from transaxle, then remove remaining lower transaxle-to-engine attaching bolts.
24. Carefully lower transaxle from vehicle.
25. Reverse procedure to install.

V6-262 Diesel Engine
1. Disconnect battery ground cable.
2. Disconnect T.V. cable at both ends.
3. Remove crossover pipe shield, then disconnect shift control linkage from transaxle.
4. Disconnect electrical connectors from park/neutral switch, torque converter clutch and vehicle speed sensor.
5. Disconnect vacuum modulator hose from modulator.
6. Remove 3 upper transaxle-to-engine attaching bolts, then loosen transaxle-to-engine bolt at starter.
7. Install suitable engine support fixture, then turn steering wheel to the full left position.
8. Raise and support vehicle.
9. Remove both front wheels.
10. Remove right front ball joint from steering knuckle.
11. Remove right drive axle from trans-

Fig. 8   Transaxle bolt identification. 1985 DeVille

12. Remove left front and rear transaxle-to-cradle mounts, then the transaxle brace and brackets.
13. Disconnect speedometer cable from transaxle, then remove right rear transaxle mount, left stabilizer link and flywheel cover.
14. Mark relationship of flywheel to converter, then remove flywheel attaching bolts.
15. Remove rear cradle-to-front cradle attaching bolts.
16. Remove one stabilizer brace and loosen the opposite brace.

17. Remove front cradle-to-body attaching bolt.
18. Remove right front motor mount, then unfasten wiring harness cover from cradle and position aside.
19. Install suitable transaxle support fixture, then shift cradle assembly to one side and support.
20. Disconnect cooler lines, exhaust connector pipe and rear exhaust manifold.
21. Remove remaining transaxle-to-engine attaching bolts, then carefully lower transaxle from vehicle.
22. Reverse procedure to install.

1985 DEVILLE & FLEETWOOD

1. Disconnect battery ground cable.
2. Remove air cleaner assembly, then disconnect T.V. cable at both ends.
3. Disconnect all electrical connectors from transaxle.
4. Install suitable engine support fixture, then remove upper transaxle-to-engine attaching bolts.
5. Disconnect vacuum line from modulator.
6. Raise and support vehicle.
7. Remove both front wheels.
8. Disconnect lower ball joint from left steering knuckle, then remove both drive axles from transaxle.
9. Remove stabilizer bolt from left control arm.
10. Remove left front cradle assembly, then the extension housing-to-engine block support bracket.
11. Disconnect cooler lines from transaxle, then remove transaxle mount attachments from both sides of case.
12. Remove flywheel splash shield, then mark relationship of flywheel to converter and remove flywheel attaching bolts.
13. Remove all lower transaxle-to-engine attaching bolts, except bolt No. 6, **Fig. 8.**
14. Support transaxle with a suitable jack, then remove remaining bolt and lower transaxle assembly from vehicle.
15. Reverse procedure to install.

Turbo Hydra-Matic 180, 180C Automatic Transmission

INDEX

TRANSMISSION IDENTIFICATION

This transmission may be identified by the following codes located on the tag attached to the right side of the transmission.

Chevette & 1000

1980 4-98		MD
1981 4-98		ST
1982 4-98		VQ
1983 4-98		TN
1984 4-98		TP
1985 4-98		PR

GENERAL DESCRIPTION

This transmission is a fully automatic unit consisting of a three-element hydraulic torque converter on the 180 series or a four-element hydraulic torque converter on the 180C series, and a planetary gear set, **Fig. 1.** Three multiple disc clutches, a roller clutch and a band provide the friction elements required to obtain the desired function of the compound planetary gear set. The compound planetary gear set provides three forward speeds and reverse.

The torque converter couples the engine to the planetary gears through oil and provides torque multiplication. It consists of s pump or driving member, a turbine or driven member and a stator assembly. The stator is mounted on a one-way roller clutch which allows the stator to turn clockwise but not counterclockwise.

The torque converter housing is filled with oil and rotates at engine speed. The converter pump is an integral part of the converter housing, therefore the pump blades rotating at engine speed set the oil within the converter into motion and direct it to the turbine causing the turbine to rotate. As the oil passes through the turbine it travels in such a direction that if it were not redirected by the stator it would strike the rear of the converter pump blades and impede its pumping action. Therefore at low turbine speeds, the oil is redirected by the stator to the converter pump in such a manner that it actually assists the converter pump to deliver power or multiply engine torque. As turbine speed increases, the direction of the oil leaving the turbine changes and flows against the rear side of the stator vanes in a clockwise direction. Since the stator is now impeding the smooth flow of oil, its roller clutch releases and it revolves freely on its shaft. Once the stator becomes inactive, there is no further multiplication of torque within the converter. At this point the converter is acting as a fluid coupling since the converter pump and turbine are being driven at about the same speed, or at a one-to-one ratio.

The hydraulic system in this transmission is pressurized by a gear type pump to provide the working pressures required to operate the friction elements and automatic controls.

TROUBLESHOOTING

LOW FLUID LEVEL

1. Fluid coming out of filler tube.
2. External fluid leak.
3. Defective vacuum modulator.

FLUID COMING OUT OF FILLER TUBE

1. High fluid level.
2. Engine coolant in transmission fluid.
3. Clogged external vent.
4. Leak in pump suction circuit.

TORQUE CONVERTER HOUSING LEAK

1. Converter housing seal.
2. Converter to case seal.
3. Loose transmission attaching bolts.

TRANSMISSION CASE EXTERNAL LEAK

1. Shifter shaft seal.
2. Extension seal.
3. Oil pan gasket.
4. Extension to case gasket.
5. Vacuum modulator gasket.
6. Drain plug gasket.
7. Cooler line fittings.
8. Fluid tube seal ring.
9. Detent cable seal ring.
10. Pressure gauge fitting.
11. Electrical connector seal.

Fig. 1   Turbo Hydra-Matic 180 transmission

LOW FLUID PRESSURE

1. Low fluid level.
2. Clogged screen.
3. Leak in oil pump suction or pressure circuit.
4. Stuck priming valve.
5. Faulty pressure regulator valve.
6. Missing sealing ball in valve body.

HIGH FLUID PRESSURE

1. Modulator vacuum line leaking.
2. Defective vacuum modulator.
3. Leak in vacuum system.
4. Defective pressure regulator valve.

NO DRIVE

1. Low fluid level.
2. Clogged screen.
3. Manual valve linkage or inner transmission selector lever disconnected.
4. Broken input shaft.
5. Pressure regulator valve stuck in open position.
6. Defective oil pump.

DELAYED ENGAGEMENT

1. Manual valve position does not coincide with valve body channels.
   a. Missing selector lever shaft retaining pin.
   b. Loose connecting rod to manual valve connection.
   c. Loose selector lever shaft nut.

NO DRIVE WHEN SHIFTING FROM P TO D, L2 OR L1

1. Parking pawl does not engage.

HARSH ENGAGEMENT

1. Band servo piston jamming.
2. Low fluid level.
3. Defective oil pump.
4. Missing screen.
5. Missing sealing ball in valve body.

SHUDDER ON ACCELERATION

1. Low fluid pressure.
2. Wrong modulator valve installed.
3. Stuck pressure regulator valve.
4. Missing sealing ball in valve body.

DRIVE IN L1 & R BUT NOT IN D OR L2

1. Input sprag installed backwards.
2. Failed input sprag.

DRIVE IN R BUT NOT IN D, L2 OR L1

1. Worn band, slipping.
2. Band servo piston jamming.
3. Excessive leak in band servo.
4. Parking pawl does not disengage.

DRIVE IN D, L2 & L1 BUT NOT IN R

1. Failed reverse clutch.

DRIVE IN NEUTRAL POSITION

1. Linkage improperly adjusted.
2. Broken planetary gear set.
3. Band improperly adjusted.

NO 1-2 UPSHIFT IN D & L2

1. Stuck governor valves.
2. 1-2 shift valve stuck in first gear position.
3. Leaking seal rings in oil pump hub.
4. Excessive leak in governor pressure circuit.
5. Clogged governor screen.

NO 2-3 UPSHIFT IN D

1. 2-3 shift valve stuck.
2. Excessive leak in governor pressure circuit.

UPSHIFTS IN D & L2 ONLY AT FULL THROTTLE

1. Faulty vacuum modulator.
2. Modulator vacuum line leaking.
3. Leak in vacuum system.
4. Stuck detent valve or cable.

UPSHIFTS IN D OR L2 ONLY AT PART THROTTLE NO DETENT UPSHIFT

1. Stuck detent regulator valve.
2. Detent cable broken or adjusted improperly.

AUTOMATIC TRANSMISSIONS/TRANSAXLES

DRIVE IN 1ST GEAR OF D OR L2

1. L1 and R control valve stuck in L1 or R position.

NO PART THROTTLE 3-2 DOWNSHIFT AT LOW SPEEDS

1. Stuck 3-2 downshift control valve.

NO FORCED DOWNSHIFTS

1. Detent cable broken or improperly adjusted.
2. Stuck detent pressure regulator valve.

IMMEDIATE DOWNSHIFT AFTER FULL THROTTLE UPSHIFT & RELEASING ACCELERATOR

1. Detent valve stuck in open position.
2. Detent cable stuck.
3. Clogged or leaking vacuum modulator line.

TRANSMISSION DOWNSHIFTS AT HIGH VEHICLE SPEEDS

1. Missing selector lever shaft retaining pin.
2. Loose selector lever linkage to manual valve connection.
3. Pressure leak at governor.

HARD DISENGAGEMENT FROM PARK POSITION

1. Missing steel guide bushing from parking pawl actuating rod.
2. Stuck manual valve selector lever.

SLIPPING 1-2 SHIFT

1. Low fluid pressure.
2. Missing sealing ball in valve body.
3. Leaking second clutch piston seals.
4. Second clutch piston centrifugal ball stuck open.
5. Second clutch piston cracked or broken.
6. Second clutch plates worn.
7. Leaking oil pump hub sealing rings.

SLIPPING 2-3 SHIFT

1. Low fluid pressure.
2. Improper band adjustment.
3. Third clutch piston seals leaking.
4. Third clutch piston centrifugal ball stuck open.
5. Third clutch piston cracked or broken.
6. Worn input shaft bushing.
7. Missing sealing ball in valve body.

HARSH 1-2 SHIFT

1. High fluid pressure.
2. 1-2 accumulator valve stuck.
3. Second clutch spring cushion broken.
4. Second gear ball valve missing.

HARSH 2-3 SHIFT

1. High fluid pressure.
2. Improper band adjustment.

HARSH 3-2 DETENT DOWNSHIFT AT HIGH VEHICLE SPEEDS

1. High speed downshift valve stuck open.
2. Improper band adjustment.

HARSH 3-2 COAST DOWNSHIFT

1. Low speed downshift timing valve stuck open.

ENGINE FLARE ON HIGH SPEED FORCED DOWNSHIFT

1. Low fluid pressure.
2. Loose band adjustment.

ENGINE FLARE ON LOW SPEED FORCED DOWNSHIFT

1. Low fluid pressure.
2. Loose band adjustment.
3. High speed downshift timing valve stuck in closed position.
4. Sprag race does not engage on 3-1 downshift.

NO ENGINE BRAKING IN L1

1. Selector level linkage improperly adjusted.
2. Stuck low manual control valve.

NO ENGINE BRAKING IN L2

1. Selector lever linkage improperly adjusted.

NO PARK

1. Selector lever linkage improperly adjusted.
2. Parking lock actuator spring broken.
3. Parking pawl.
4. Governor hub.

EXCESSIVE NOISES IN ALL DRIVE RANGES

1. Excessive backlash between sun gear and planetary gears.
2. Lock plate on planetary carrier loose.
3. Defective thrust bearing.
4. Worn bearing bushings.
5. Excessive transmission axial play.
6. Unhooked parking pawl spring contacting governor hub.
7. Converter balancing weights loose.
8. Converter housing attaching bolts loose and contacting converter.

SCREECHING NOISE ON ACCELERATION

1. Converter failure.

SHORT VIBRATING HISSING NOISE BEFORE 1-2 UPSHIFT

1. Reverse clutch dampening cushion wearing into transmission case.

MAINTENANCE

To check fluid, drive vehicle for at least 15 minutes to bring fluid to operating temperature (200° F). With vehicle on a level surface and engine idling in Park and parking brake applied, the level on the dipstick should be at the "F" mark. To bring the fluid level from the ADD mark to the FULL mark requires one pint of fluid. If vehicle cannot be driven sufficiently to bring fluid to operating temperature, the level on the dipstick should be between the two dimples on the dipstick with fluid temperature at 70° F.

If additional fluid is required, use only Dexron II automatic transmission fluid.

NOTE: An early change to a darker color from the usual red color and or a strong odor that is usually associated with overheated fluid is normal and should not be considered as a positive sign of required maintenance or unit failure.

CAUTION: When adding fluid, do not over fill, as foaming and loss of fluid through the vent may occur as the fluid heats up. Also, if fluid level is too low, complete loss of drive may occur especially when cold, which can cause transmission failure.

Every 100,000 miles, the oil should be drained, the oil pan removed, the screen cleaned and fresh fluid added. For vehicles subjected to more severe use such as heavy city traffic especially in hot weather, prolonged periods of idling or towing, this maintenance should be performed every 15,000 miles.

DRAINING BOTTOM PAN

1. Raise vehicle, then remove drain plug and allow fluid to drain for at least 5 minutes.
2. If oil screen is to be serviced, remove oil pan bolts, oil pan and gasket.
3. Remove oil screen to valve body bolts, screen and gasket.
4. Thoroughly clean oil screen and oil pan with solvent.
5. Install oil screen using a new gasket and torque attaching bolts to 13–15 ft. lbs., then install oil pan using a new gasket and torque attaching bolts to 13–15 ft. lbs.
6. Add three quarts of fluid, then with engine idling and parking brake applied, move selector lever through each range and return selector lever to PARK.
7. Check fluid level and add fluid as required to bring level between the two dimples on the dipstick.

ADDING FLUID TO DRY TRANSMISSION

1. Add 4.9 quarts of fluid.
2. With transmission in PARK and parking brake applied, start engine and place carburetor on fast idle cam.
3. Move shifter lever through each range then with transmission in PARK, add additional fluid as required to bring the level between the two dimples on the dipstick.

31–88

Fig. 2 Manual linkage adjustment. 1980—82 Turbo Hydra-Matic 180

Fig. 3 Manual linkage adjustment. 1983 & 1985 Turbo Hydra-Matic 180

Fig. 4 Manual linkage adjustment. 1984 Turbo Hydra-Matic 180

IN-VEHICLE ADJUSTMENTS

MANUAL LINKAGE, ADJUST

NOTE: The following procedures must be followed exactly, since any inaccuracies may result in premature failure of the transmission due to operation without control in full detent.

1980—82
1. Place shifter assembly (A) in Neutral position, **Fig. 2.**
2. With link (B) loosely assembled to rod (F) and rod (F) attached to lever (G), place lever (G) in Neutral position. To obtain Neutral position, move lever (G) clockwise to maximum detent position (Park), then counterclockwise two detents to Neutral position.
3. While holding lever (G) in Neutral position, adjust link (B) until hole aligns with shifter assembly pin (C), then install link onto pin.
4. Install shim (D) and retainer (E).

1983
1. Place shifter assembly (A) in Park position, **Fig. 3.**
2. With link (B) loosely attached to lever (G), place lever (G) in Park position. To obtain Park position, move lever (G) clockwise to maximum detent position (Park).

3. Maintain lever (G) in Park position and adjust link (B) until hole aligns with shifter assembly pin (C), then install link onto pin.
4. Install washer (D) and retainer (E).

1984
1. Snap cable (1) into bracket (2), **Fig. 4.**
2. Turn ignition switch to Lock position.
3. Snap end of cable (1) onto sliding pin (3).
4. Place shifter lever (4) in Park position.
5. Install cable (1) onto shifter lever pin (5).
6. Attach cable (1) to shifter mounting bracket (7) by pressing lock assembly against spring (9) and dropping cable through slot in bracket.
7. Depress lock button (10) to complete adjustment.

1985
1. Position shifter assembly (A), **Fig. 3,** into Neutral position of detent plate.
2. With link (B) loosely assembled to rod (F), and rod attached to lever, place lever (G) into Neutral position.
3. Obtain Neutral position by moving lever (G) clockwise to maximum detent position (Park), then counterclockwise two detents to Neutral.
4. Retain lever (G) in neutral, then adjust link until hole aligns with shifter assembly pin (C).
5. Install link onto pin, install washer (D), then insert clip (E).

T.V. OR DETENT CABLE, ADJUST

1980—1981
1. Disengage cable "Snap Lock" from support, **Fig 5.**

NOTE: Cable should be free to slide through "Snap Lock".

2. With cable installed in support and attached to transmission and carburetor lever, move carburetor lever to wide open throttle position.
3. Push "Snap Lock" flush and return carburetor lever to closed position.

1982—85
1. Depress re-adjust tab and move slider back through fitting away from throttle body until slider stops against fitting, **Fig. 6.**
2. Release re-adjust tab and open carburetor or pump lever to "full throttle stop" position to automatically adjust cable. Release carburetor or pump lever.
3. Check cable for sticking or binding and road test vehicle. If delayed or only full throttle shifts still occur, proceed as follows:
   a. Remove oil pan and inspect throttle lever and bracket assembly, **Fig. 7.**
   b. Check T.V. exhaust valve lifter rod for distortion or binding in control valve assembly or spacer plate.

Fig. 5 Detent cable adjustment. 1980–81 Turbo Hydra-Matic 180

Fig. 7 Throttle lever and bracket assembly. 1982–85 Turbo Hydra-Matic 180

c. Check that the lifter spring holds lifter rod up against bottom of control valve assembly.
d. Check that T.V. plunger is not binding, and inspect transmission for proper throttle lever to cable link.

IN-VEHICLE REPAIRS

VALVE BODY, REPLACE

1. Drain transmission and remove oil pan and screen.
2. Remove screw and retainer securing detent cable to transmission, then disconnect detent cable.
3. Remove throttle lever and bracket assembly. Use caution not to bend the throttle lever link.
4. Remove manual detent roller and spring assembly
5. Remove transfer plate reinforcement attaching bolts and the reinforcement.
6. Remove servo cover and gasket.
7. Remove valve body attaching bolts, then the valve body and transfer plate.

NOTE: The two check balls in the case may fall out when removing the valve body.

8. Remove transfer plate to valve body bolts, then the plate from valve body.
9. Reverse procedure to install.

SERVO ASSEMBLY, REPLACE

1. Remove valve body from transmission as outlined previously.
2. Compress servo piston with tool J-23075.

3. With suitable pliers, remove servo piston snap ring and slowly loosen the tool. Remove tool, servo piston return spring and apply rod from transmission.
4. Install apply rod, return spring and piston into case.
5. Use tool J-23075 to compress spring and install snap ring. Remove tool.
6. With a 3/16 inch wrench on servo adjusting bolt, adjust apply rod by torquing bolt to 40 inch lbs, then back off bolt exactly 5 turns. Tighten lock nut while holding apply rod in position.
7. Install valve body.

SPEEDOMETER DRIVEN GEAR, REPLACE

1. Remove bolt securing driven gear housing retainer, then the retainer.
2. Pull speedometer driven gear from housing.
3. Install speedometer driven gear into housing, then the retainer into slot of driven gear housing.
4. Install retainer attaching bolt

REAR EXTENSION OIL SEAL

1. Remove propeller shaft.
2. Remove oil seal with a screwdriver or suitable tool.
3. Lubricate new seal lip with transmission fluid and install seal into extension housing with tool J-21426.
4. Install propeller shaft.

Fig. 6 Detent cable adjustment. 1982–85 Turbo Hydra-Matic 180

TRANSMISSION
REPLACE

1. Disconnect battery ground cable then disconnect detent downshift cable from bracket.
2. Remove air cleaner and dipstick, then on vehicles with air conditioning remove the 5 heater core retaining screws, disconnect connector and place heater core assembly aside.
3. Raise and support vehicle and remove propeller shaft.
4. Disconnect speedometer cable, electrical lead, oil cooler lines, and shift control linkage.
5. Support transmission with suitable jack and remove the crossmember re-

taining bolts.
6. Remove converter to bracket retaining nuts, then disconnect exhaust pipes from rear of catalytic converter and from exhaust manifolds and remove catalytic converter and converter bracket as an assembly.
7. Remove converter dust shield and remove converter to flywheel bolts.
8. Lower transmission until it is barely supported by jack and remove transmission to engine bolts.
9. Raise transmission to its normal position, then support engine with jack and lower and remove transmission from vehicle.

NOTE: Use converter holding tool J-5384,

or keep rear of transmission lower than the front to prevent the converter from sliding out.

10. Before installing transmission, place two inch blocks between rack and pinion housing assembly and oil pan to permit correct alignment of engine and transmission. Before installing flexplate to converter bolts, make sure than converter pilot hub is installed in crankshaft and that welded brackets on converter are flush with flexplate and converter rotates freely in this position.
11. Reverse the remaining procedure to install and torque converter to flexplate bolts to 20–30 ft. lbs. (27–41 Nm).

Turbo Hydra-Matic 200, 200C
Automatic Transmission

INDEX

TRANSMISSION IDENTIFICATION

This transmission may be identified by the following codes located on the serial number plate attached to the right side of the transmission.

Code

BUICK

1980 V8-265 Century & Regal .... BZ, PG, PW
V8-350 Electra & LeSabre.. BA, OT
1981 V6-231 Century & Regal ..... BZ
V6-252 Electra & LeSabre . BM, BY
V6-265 Century & Regal ...... PG
V8-307 Electra & LeSabre .... OG
V8-350 Century, Regal, Electra & LeSabre ..... OT
1982 V6-260 Century Sport Diesel .... OR
1983 V6-231 Electra Estate Wagon, LeSabre & Regal ... BH
V6-260 Regal Diesel .... OR
V8-350 Regal Diesel .... OU

1984 V6-231 Electra Estate Wagon, LeSabre & Regal ... BH
V8-307 Electra Estate Wagon & LeSabre .... OI
V8-350 Electra Estate Wagon & LeSabre Diesel.... OU
1985 V6-231 Electra Estate Wagon, LeSabre & Regal ... BH
V6-260 Regal Diesel .... OR

CADILLAC

1981 V8-350 Fleetwood & DeVille Diesels .... AS

CHEVROLET

1980 4-98 Chevette .... CN
4-151 Monza Except Calif...... PY
4-151 Monza Calif. .... PB
V6-229 Malibu, El Camino & Monte Carlo .... CA
V6-229 Malibu, El Camino, Monte Carlo, Impala, Caprice & Camaro .... CK

1981 4-98 Chevette................. CN
4-110 Chevette Diesel .... CY
V6-231 Malibu & El Camino ... BZ
V8-267 Malibu, El Camino, Impala & Caprice .... CE
V8-305 Malibu & El Camino ... CC
V8-350 Impala & Caprice Diesels .... OT
1982 Chevette .... JY
4-119 S/T 10 .... CZ
V6-173 S/T 10 Exc. Calif. .... CB
V6-173 S/T 10 Calif. .... CW
1983 4-110 Chevette Diesel ...... JY
4-151 Camaro .... PS
V6-173 Camaro .... CN, CS
V6-173 S/T 10 .... JH
V6-260 El Camino, Malibu & Monte Carlo Diesel ...... OR
V8-305 Camaro C7
1984 4-110 Chevette Diesel ...... JY
V6-173 S/T 10 .... JY
V6-231 Caprice, El Camino, Impala & Monte Carlo .... BH
V8-350 Caprice, El Camino, Impala & Monte Carlo Diesel .... OU

TORQUE CONVERTER — **PUMP** — **INTERMEDIATE BAND** — **DIRECT CLUTCH** — **FORWARD CLUTCH** — **ROLLER CLUTCH** — **LO AND REVERSE CLUTCH** — **CONTROL VALVE ASSEMBLY** — **COMPOUND PLANETARY GEAR SET**

Fig. 1 Turbo Hydra-Matic 200 transmission

1985 V6-231 Caprice, El Camino,
Impala & Monte Carlo...... HH
V6-260 Caprice, El Camino,
Impala & Monte Carlo
Diesel .... CS
V8-305 Monte Carlo CV

OLDSMOBILE

1980 4-151 Starfire Except Calif. .... PY
4-151 Starfire Calif. .... PB
V6-231 Cutlass................ BZ
V6-260 Delta 88 & Custom
Cruiser .... OW
V8-350 Delta 88 & Custom
Cruiser Except Calif. .... OS
1981 V6-231 Cutlass &
Custom Cruiser .... BZ
V6-260 Cutlass Custom
Cruiser & Delta 88 .... OW
V8-350 Cutlass, Custom
Cruiser, Delta 88 &
Ninety Eight .... OT
1982 V6-260 Cutlass Diesel .... OR
1983 V6-231 Cutlass............ BH
V6-260 Cutlass Diesel .... OR
V8-350 Cutlass & Delta 88
Diesel .... OU
1984 V6-231 Custom Cruiser &
Delta 88 .... BH
V6-260 Cutlass Diesel .... OR
V8-307 Delta 88, Custom
Cruiser & Cutlass .... OI

V8-350 Delta 88, Custom
Cruiser & Cutlass Diesel ....OU

PONTIAC

1980 4-151 Sunbird Except Calif. .... PY
4-151 Sunbird Calif. .... PB
V6-229 LeMans .... CA, CK
V6-231 LeMans & Grand
Prix .... BZ
V6-260 LeMans, Catalina,
Bonneville & Grand Prix ..... PG
V8-301 LeMans & Grand
Prix .... PW
V8-301 Firebird .... PD
V8-350 Catalina &
Bonneville .... BA
1981 V6-231 LeMans & Grand
Prix .... BZ
V6-260 LeMans, Catalina,
Bonneville &
Grand Prix .... DW, PG
V8-301 Firebird .... PE, PF
V8-350 LeMans, Grand
Prix, Catalina &
Bonneville Diesels .... OT
1983 4-110 1000 Diesel .... JY
4-151 Firebird .... PS
V6-173 Firebird .... CN, CS
V8-305 Firebird C7
V8-350 Bonneville, Grand
Prix & Parisienne Diesel .....OU
1984 4-110 1000 Diesel .... JY
V6-231 Bonneville, Grand
Prix & Parisienne .... BH

V8-350 Bonneville, Grand
Prix & Parisienne Diesel.....OU
1985 V6-231 Bonneville, Grand
Prix .... BH
V6-260 Parisienne Diesel...... CS
V8-305 Bonneville, Grand
Prix CV
V8-350 Bonneville, Grand
Prix & Parisienne Diesel.....OU

DESCRIPTION

The Turbo Hydra-Matic 200 and 200C transmissions, **Figs. 1 and 2,** are fully automatic and consist of a three element torque converter and a compound planetary gear set. Three multiple disc clutches, a roller clutch and a band provide the required friction elements to obtain the desired function of the planetary gear set. In addition, the 200C transmission is equipped with a locking torque converter. The converter clutch assembly consists of a three element torque converter with a converter clutch. The converter clutch is splined to the turbine assembly and, when operated, applies against the converter cover, providing a mechanical direct drive coupling of the engine to the planetary gears. When the converter clutch is released the assembly operates as a normal torque converter.

Fig. 2 Torque converter clutch, 200C transmission

TROUBLESHOOTING GUIDE

NO DRIVE IN DRIVE RANGE

1. Low oil level.
2. Manual linkage maladjusted.
3. Low oil pressure due to:
   a. Restricted or plugged oil screen.
   b. Oil screen gasket improperly installed.
   c. Oil pump pressure regulator.
   d. Pump drive gear tangs damaged by converter.
   e. Case porosity in intake bore.
4. Forward clutch malfunctioning due to:
   a. Forward clutch not applying due to cracked piston, damaged or missing seals, burned clutch plates, snap ring not in groove.
   b. Forward clutch seal rings damaged or missing on turbine shaft, leaking feed circuits due to damaged or mispositioned gasket.
   c. Clutch housing check ball stuck or missing
   d. Cup plug leaking or missing from rear of turbine shaft in clutch apply passage.
   e. Incorrect forward clutch piston assembly or incorrect number of clutch plates.
5. Roller clutch malfunctioning due to missing rollers or springs or possibly galled rollers.

OIL PRESSURE HIGH OR LOW

1. Throttle valve cable maladjusted, binding, disconnected or broken.
2. Throttle lever and bracket improperly installed, disconnected or binding.
3. Throttle valve shift valve, throttle valve or plunger binding.
4. Pressure regulator valve and spring malfunctioning due to:
   a. Binding valve.
   b. Incorrect spring.
   c. Oil pressure control orifice in pump cover plugged, causing high oil pressure.
   d. Pressure regulator bore plug leaking.
5. Manual valve disconnected.

6. Intermediate boost valve binding, causing oil pressures to be incorrect in 2nd and low ranges.
7. Orifice in spacer plate at end of intermediate boost valve plugged.
8. Reverse boost valve binding, causing pressure to be incorrect in reverse only.
9. Orifice in spacer plate at end of reverse boost valve plugged.

1-2 SHIFT AT FULL THROTTLE ONLY

1. Throttle valve cable maladjusted, binding, disconnected or broken.
2. Throttle lever and bracket assembly binding or disconnected.
3. Throttle valve exhaust ball lifter or number 5 check ball binding, mispositioned or disconnected.

NOTE: If number 5 ball is fully seated, it will cause full throttle valve pressure regardless of throttle valve position.

4. Throttle valve and plunger binding.
5. Valve body gaskets leaking, damaged or incorrectly installed.
6. Porous control valve assembly.

FIRST SPEED ONLY, NO 1-2 SHIFT

1. Due to governor and governor feed passages:
   a. Plugged governor oil feed orifice in spacer plate.
   b. Plugged orifice in spacer plate that feeds governor oil to the shift valves.
   c. Balls missing in governor assembly.
   d. Governor cover O-ring missing or leaking. If governor cover O-ring leaks, an external oil leak will be present and there will be no upshift.
   e. Governor shaft seal missing or damaged.
   f. Governor driven gear stripped.
   g. Governor weights binding.
   h. Governor assembly missing.
2. Control valve assembly 1-2 shift valve or 1-2 throttle valve stuck in downshift

position.
3. Porosity in case channels or undrilled 2nd speed feed holes.
4. Excessive leakage between case bore and intermediate band apply ring.
5. Intermediate band anchor pin missing or disconnected from band.
6. Missing or broken intermediate band.
7. Due to intermediate servo assembly:
   a. Servo to cover oil seal ring damaged or missing.
   b. Porous servo cover or piston.
   c. Incorrect intermediate band apply pin.
   d. Incorrect cover and piston.

1ST & 2ND ONLY, NO 2-3 SHIFT

1. 2-3 shift valve or 2-3 throttle valve stuck in downshift position.
2. Direct clutch feed orifice in spacer plate plugged.
3. Valve body gaskets leaking, damaged or incorrectly installed.
4. Porosity between case passages.
5. Pump passages plugged or leaking.
6. Pump gasket incorrectly installed.
7. Rear seal on pump cover leaking or missing.
8. Direct clutch oil seals missing or damaged.
9. Direct clutch piston or housing cracked.
10. Direct clutch plates damaged or missing.
11. Direct clutch backing plate snap ring out of groove.
12. Intermediate servo to case oil seal broken or missing on intermediate servo piston.
13. Intermediate servo exhaust hole in case between servo piston seals plugged or undrilled.

MOVES FORWARD IN NEUTRAL

1. Manual linkage maladjusted.
2. Forward clutch does not release.
3. Cross leakage between pump passages.
4. Cross leakage to forward clutch through clutch passages.

AUTOMATIC TRANSMISSIONS/TRANSAXLES

NO DRIVE IN REVERSE OR SLIPS IN REVERSE

1. Throttle valve cable binding or maladjusted.
2. Manual linkage maladjusted.
3. Throttle valve binding.
4. Reverse boost valve binding in bore.
5. Low overrun clutch valve binding in bore.
6. Reverse clutch piston cracked, broken or has missing seals.
7. Reverse clutch plates burned.
8. Reverse clutch has incorrect selective spacer ring.
9. Porosity in passages to direct clutch.
10. Pump to case gasket improperly installed or missing.
11. Pump passages cross leaking or restricted.
12. Pump cover seals damaged or missing.
13. Direct clutch piston or housing cracked.
14. Direct clutch piston seals cut or missing.
15. Direct clutch housing ball check, stuck, leaking or missing.
16. Direct clutch plates burned.
17. Incorrect direct clutch piston.
18. Direct clutch orifices plugged in spacer plate.
19. Intermediate servo to case seal cut or missing.

SLIPS 1-2 SHIFT

1. Aerated oil due to low level.
2. 2nd speed feed orifice in spacer plate partially blocked.
3. Improperly installed or missing spacer plate gasket.
4. 1-2 accumulator valve stuck, causing low 1-2 accumulator pressure.
5. Weak or missing 1-2 accumulator valve spring.
6. 1-2 accumulator piston seal leaking or spring missing or broken.
7. Leakage between 1-2 accumulator piston and pin.
8. Incorrect intermediate band apply pin.
9. Excessive leakage between intermediate band apply pin and case.
10. Porous intermediate servo piston.
11. Servo cover to servo seal damaged or missing.
12. Incorrect servo and cover.
13. Throttle valve cable improperly adjusted.
14. Shift throttle valve or throttle valve binding.
15. Intermediate band worn or burned.
16. Case porosity in 2nd clutch passages.

ROUGH 1-2 SHIFT

1. Throttle valve cable improperly adjusted or binding.
2. Throttle valve or plunger binding.
3. Shift throttle or 1-2 accumulator valve binding.
4. Incorrect intermediate servo pin.
5. Autemediate servo piston to case seal damaged or missing.
6. 1-2 accumulator oil ring damaged, pis-

ton stuck, bore damaged or spring broken or missing.

SLIPS 2-3 SHIFT

1. Low oil level.
2. Throttle valve cable improperly adjusted.
3. Throttle valve binding.
4. Direct clutch orifice in spacer plate partially blocked.
5. Spacer plate gaskets improperly installed or missing.
6. Intermediate servo to case seal damaged.
7. Porous direct clutch feed passages in case.
8. Pump to case gasket improperly installed or missing.
9. Pump passages cross feeding, leaking or restricted.
10. Pump cover oil seal rings damaged or missing.
11. Direct clutch piston or housing cracked.
12. Direct clutch piston seals cut or missing.
13. Direct clutch plates burned.

ROUGH 2-3 SHIFT

1. Throttle valve cable improperly installed or missing.
2. Throttle valve or throttle valve plunger binding.
3. Shift throttle valve binding.
4. Intermediate servo exhaust hole undrilled or plugged between intermediate servo piston seals.
5. Direct clutch exhaust valve number 4 check ball missing or improperly installed.

NO ENGINE BRAKING IN 2ND SPEED

1. Intermediate boost valve binding in valve body.
2. Intermediate-Reverse number 3 check ball improperly installed or missing.
3. Shift throttle valve number 3 check ball improperly installed or missing.
4. Intermediate servo to cover seal missing or damaged.
5. Intermediate band off anchor pin, broken or burned.

NO ENGINE BRAKING IN 1ST SPEED

1. Low overrun clutch valve binding in valve body.

NOTE: The following conditions will also cause no reverse.

2. Low-reverse clutch piston seals broken or missing.
3. Porosity in low-reverse piston or housing.
4. Low-reverse clutch housing snap ring out of case.
5. Cup plug or rubber seal missing or damaged between case and low-reverse clutch housing.

NO PART THROTTLE DOWNSHIFT

1. Throttle plunger bushing passages obstructed.
2. 2-3 throttle valve bushing passages obstructed.
3. Valve body gaskets improperly installed or damaged.
4. Spacer plate hole obstructed or undrilled.
5. Throttle valve cable maladjusted.
6. Throttle valve or shift throttle valve binding.

LOW OR HIGH SHIFT POINTS

1. Throttle valve cable binding or disconnected.
2. Throttle valve or shift throttle valve binding.
3. Number 1 throttle shift check ball improperly installed or missing.
4. Throttle valve plunger, 1-2 or 2-3 throttle valves binding.
5. Valve body gaskets improperly installed or missing.
6. Pressure regulator valve binding.
7. Throttle valve exhaust number 5 check ball and lifter, improperly installed, disconnected or missing.
8. Throttle lever binding, disconnected or loose at valve body mounting bolt or not positioned at the throttle valve plunger bushing pin locator.
9. Governor shaft to cover seal broken or missing.
10. Governor cover O-rings broken or missing.

NOTE: Outer ring will leak externally and the inner ring will leak internally.

11. Case porosity.

WILL NOT HOLD IN PARK

1. Manual linkage maladjusted.
2. Parking pawl binding in case.
3. Actuator rod or plunger damaged.
4. Parking pawl damaged.
5. Parking bracket loose or damaged.
6. Detent lever nut loose.
7. Detent lever hole worn or damaged.
8. Detent roller to valve body bolt loose.
9. Detent roller or pin damaged, incorrectly installed or missing.

CONVERTER CLUTCH APPLIED IN ALL RANGES, ENGINE STALLS WHEN TRANSMISSION PUT IN GEAR

1. Converter clutch valve stuck in apply position.

CONVERTER CLUTCH APPLIES ERRATICALLY

1. Vacuum hose leak.
2. Vacuum switch malfunction.
3. Release oil exhaust orifice at pump blocked or restricted.

Fig. 3 Console shift manual linkage adjustment. 1980—83 Chevette & 1000

Fig. 4 Console shift manual linkage adjustment. 1984 Chevette & 1000

4. Turbine shaft O-ring damaged.
5. Converter malfunction, clutch pressure plate warped.
6. O-ring damaged at solenoid.
7. Solenoid bolts loose.
8. Governor pressure switch malfunction.

MAINTENANCE

To check fluid, drive vehicle for at least 15 minutes to bring fluid to operating temperature (200° F.). With vehicle on a level surface and engine idling in Park and parking brake applied, the level on the dipstick should be at the "F" mark. To bring the fluid level from the ADD mark to the FULL mark requires 1 pint of fluid. If vehicle cannot be driven sufficiently to bring fluid to operating temperature, the level on the dipstick should be between the two dimples on the dipstick with fluid temperature at 70° F.

If additional fluid is required, use only Dexron or Dexron II automatic transmission fluid.

NOTE: An early change to a darker color from the usual red color and or a strong odor that is usually associated with overheated fluid is normal and should not be considered as a positive sign of required maintenance or unit failure.

CAUTION: When adding fluid, do not overfill, as foaming and loss of fluid through the vent may occur as the fluid heats up. Also, if fluid level is too low, complete loss of drive may occur especially when cold, which can cause transmission failure.

Every 100,000 the oil should be drained, the oil pan removed, the screen cleaned and fresh fluid added. For vehicles subjected to more severe use such as heavy city traffic, especially in hot weather, and prolonged periods of idling or towing, this maintenance should be performed every 15,000 miles.

DRAINING BOTTOM PAN

1. Remove front and side oil pan attaching bolts, then loosen the rear oil pan attaching bolts.

2. Carefully pry oil pan loose and allow fluid to drain into a suitable container.
3. Remove the oil pan and gasket, then remove the screen attaching bolts and remove screen.
4. Thoroughly clean oil screen and oil pan with solvent.
5. Install oil screen using a new gasket and torque attaching bolts to 6—10 ft. lbs., then install oil pan using a new gasket and torque attaching bolts to 10—13 ft. lbs.
6. Add 3 quarts of fluid, then with engine idling and parking brake applied, move selector lever through each range and return selector lever to PARK.
7. Check fluid level and add fluid as required to bring level between the two dimples on the dipstick.

ADDING FLUID TO DRY TRANSMISSION & CONVERTER

1. Add 4½ quarts of fluid.
2. With transmission in PARK and parking brake applied, start engine and place carburetor on fast idle cam.
3. Move shifter lever through each range, then with transmission in PARK, add additional fluid as required to bring the level between the two dimples on the dipstick.

MANUAL LINKAGE
ADJUST

CONSOLE SHIFT

1980—1983 Chevette & 1000
1. Place shift lever (A) in neutral position, Fig. 3.
2. Move lever (E) clockwise to maximum detent to PARK, then move lever counterclockwise two detent positions to NEUTRAL.
3. With lever (E) in NEUTRAL, insert pin (F) on fork (G). Adjust rod (H) until hole in rod aligns with shifter assembly pin (B) and install rod on pin.

1984 Chevette & 1000
1. Snap cable (1) into bracket (2), **Fig. 4.**

2. Turn ignition switch to Lock position.
3. Snap end of cable (1) onto sliding pin (3).
4. Place shifter lever (4) in Park position.
5. Install cable (1) onto shifter lever pin (5).
6. Attach cable (1) to shifter mounting bracket (7) by pressing lock assembly against spring (9) and dropping cable through slot in bracket.
7. Depress lock button (10) to complete adjustment.

1980—81 Century, Grand Prix, LeMans, 1980—83 Cutlass, Malibu, Monte Carlo & Regal, 1984—85 Cutlass, Grand Prix, Monte Carlo & Regal
1. Loosen shift rod clamp screw, then the pin in transmission manual lever, **Figs. 5 and 6.**
2. Place shift lever and manual lever in Park position and ignition key in Lock position.
3. Torque cable pin nut to 20 ft. lbs., then rotate manual lever fully against Park stop and release lever.
4. Pull shift rod downward against lock stop, then torque clamp screw to 20 ft. lbs.

COLUMN SHIFT

Intermediate Models
1. Place shift lever and transmission lever in Neutral position, **Figs. 7, 8 and 9.**
2. Assemble clamp, spring washer and screw to equalizer lever and control rod.
3. Hold clamp flush against equalizer lever and lightly tighten clamping screw against rod.
4. On all models except 1980—81 DeVille and Brougham with diesel engine, torque clamp screw to 20 ft. lbs. On 1980—81 DeVille and Brougham with diesel engine, torque clamp screw to 23 ft. lbs.

NOTE Do not exert force in either direction on rod or equalizer rod while tightening screw.

Fig. 5   Console shift manual linkage adjustment. 1980 Century, Cutlass, Grand Prix, LeMans, Malibu, Monte Carlo & Regal

Fig. 6   Console shift manual linkage adjustment. 1981 Century, Grand Prix, LeMans, 1981–83 Cutlass, Malibu, Monte Carlo & Regal, 1984–85 Cutlass, Grand Prix, Monte Carlo & Regal

All Full Size Models Except Grand Prix

1. Position shift lever and transmission lever in Neutral position, **Fig. 10**
2. Hold clamp flush against equalizer lever and lightly tighten.
3. Torque bolt to 20 ft. lbs.

NOTE: Do not exert force in either direction on rod or equalizer rod while tightening screw.

Fig. 7   Column shift manual linkage adjustments. 1980 Century, Cutlass, Grand Prix, LeMans, Monte Carlo & Regal

Fig. 8   Column shift manual linkage adjustment. 1980–81 DeVille & Brougham with diesel engine

Fig. 9 Column shift manual linkage adjustment. 1981—85 intermediate models (typical)

Fig. 11 Detent downshift cable adjust. 1980—81 Chevette & 1981 1000

DETENT CABLE ADJUSTMENT

Exc. 1980—81 Chevette, 1981 1000 & All 1982—85 Models
1. Disengage snap lock. Cable should be free to slide through snap lock.
2. Place carburetor in the wide open position.
3. Engage snap lock and position flush with cable fitting.

1980—81 Chevette & 1981 1000
1. Disconnect cable from support, **Fig. 11,** and check that cable is free to slide through snap lock.
2. With cable installed in support and connected to transmission and carburetor lever, move throttle valve to wide open position.
3. Push snap lock until flush with support and throttle valve.

1982—84 Chevette & 1000 Equipped With Diesel Engine
1. Remove cruise control rod on vehicles equipped with cruise control.
2. Disconnect throttle valve linkage from throttle assembly.
3. Loosen lock nut on pump rod, then shorten rod by rotating several turns.
4. Secure throttle lever assembly in full throttle position.
5. Lengthen pump rod by rotating in opposite direction as described in step 3 until injection pump lever contacts full throttle stop.
6. Release throttle lever assembly and tighten pump rod lock nut.
7. Disconnect pump rod from throttle lever.
8. Connect throttle valve linkage to throttle assembly.
9. Depress metal locking tab on upper end of cable and hold in this position.
10. Position slider through fitting and away from lever assembly until slider contacts metal fitting.
11. Release metal tab, then rotate throttle lever assembly to full throttle position and release.
12. Connect pump rod to lever assembly, then connect cruise control throttle rod, if equipped.
13. On models equipped with cruise control, adjust servo throttle rod until minimum amount of slack is present. Install clip into first hole closest to bellcrank that is within servo bail.

All 1982—85 Models Equipped With Gasoline Engine
1. With engine off, depress locking tab and move slider rearward through fitting until slider contacts fitting, **Fig. 9A.**
2. Release locking tab, then move carburetor throttle lever to wide open position and release.
3. On 1982—83 Camaro and Firebird with 4-151 engine, rotate idler lever to the maximum travel stop position. The cable will ratchet through its slider and automatically adjust itself. Release throttle idler lever. Do not adjust using the TBI or carburetor lever.
4. On all models, check cable for sticking or binding, then test vehicle for proper operation.
5. If transmission does not shift properly, raise and support vehicle and remove transmission oil pan. Inspect throttle lever and bracket assembly on valve body for damage. Check to ensure that throttle valve exhaust valve rod is not worn or damaged. Check to ensure that lifter spring holds lifter rod against bottom of valve body and that throttle valve plunger is not sticking.

T.H.M. 200C TORQUE CONVERTER CLUTCH SWITCH ADJUSTMENTS

LOW VACUUM SWITCH
1. Disconnect vacuum and electrical connectors from low vacuum switch, **Fig. 13.**
2. Connect a suitable test light to either terminal of vacuum switch. Connect a suitable jumper cable from the other

Fig. 10 Column shift linkage adjustment. All full size models except Grand Prix

Fig. 12 Self-adjusting throttle valve cable

terminal to a good ground.
3. Connect remaining lead of test light to power side of removed vacuum switch connector.
4. Attach suitable vacuum pump to vacuum port of switch.
5. Turn ignition on, then actuate vacuum pump. On V6-231 and 252 engines, test light should remain off until vacuum pump gauge reads 5.5—6.5 in. Hg. On V8-265 and 301 engines the test light should remain off until vacuum gauge reads 6.5—7.5 in. Hg. On V8-307 engines, the test light should remain off until vacuum gauge reads 8 in. Hg. On V8-350 gas engines, light should remain off until vacuum gauge reads 7.5—8.5 in. Hg. On V8-350 diesel engines, test light should remain off until vacuum gauge reads 5—6 in. Hg.
6. Decrease vacuum slowly. Light should remain on until vacuum drops to .3—1.3 in. Hg. on V6-231 and 252 engines, 1.2—2.2 in. Hg. on V8-265 and 301 engines, 1.5—2.5 in. Hg. on V8-307 and 350 gas engines and 3.5—4.5 in. Hg. on V8-350 diesel engines. Decreasing vacuum beyond above values should cause light to go out.
7. If above results cannot be obtained, switch is defective.
8. The point at which light comes on and the point at which light goes out must have at least 4 in. of vacuum difference.

HIGH VACUUM SWITCH

NOTE: The high vacuum switch must be adjusted anytime the throttle rod, transmission vacuum valve and high idle speed adjustments are changed.

IF AIR CLEANER IS REMOVED WHEN MAKING SWITCH ADJUSTMENT, THE EGR SOLENOID PORT TO THE EGR VALVE MUST BE PLUGGED TO PREVENT A VACUUM LEAK AT THE EGR SOLENOID.

LOW VACUUM SWITCH   HIGH VACUUM SWITCH

5/64" HEX WRENCH   EGR SWITCH ASSEMBLY

HIGH VACUUM SWITCH ELECTRICAL CONNECTOR

R. H. VALVE COVER

SELF-POWERED TEST LIGHT

Fig. 13   Vacuum switch location

1. Disconnect high vacuum switch electrical connector, **Fig. 13.**
2. Connect suitable test light across the terminals of the high vacuum switch.
3. Energize fast idle solenoid by disconnecting pink and green wire from coolant switch and operate engine at high idle speed, then remove cap from back of high vacuum switch.
4. Before adjustment is performed, the test light must be on, indicating that the switch contacts are closed. If test light is off, close the switch contacts by turning switch adjusting screw clockwise until contacts close.
5. Adjust vacuum switch by turning adjusting screw counterclockwise until switch contact just opens and test light goes off. Turn adjusting screw counterclockwise an additional 1/8–3/16 turn.
6. Reinstall cap on back of vacuum switch and reconnect high vacuum switch and coolant switch electrical connectors.

IN VEHICLE REPAIRS

VALVE BODY ASSEMBLY

1. Drain transmission fluid, then remove oil pan and screen.
2. Remove detent cable retaining bolt and disconnect cable.
3. Remove throttle lever and bracket assembly. Use care to avoid bending throttle lever link.
4. Remove detent roller and spring.
5. Support valve body and remove retaining bolts, then while holding manual valve, remove valve assembly, spacer plate and gaskets as an assembly to prevent dropping the five check balls.

NOTE: After removing valve body assembly, the intermediate band anchor band pin, and reverse cup plug may be removed.

6. To install control valve, reverse removal procedure and torque all valve body bolts to 8 ft. lbs.

CAUTION: Ensure that intermediate band anchor pin is located on intermediate band prior to installation of valve body, as damage will result.

GOVERNOR

Exc. 1982–83 Camaro & Firebird

1. Disconnect battery ground cable and remove air cleaner.
2. On Chevrolet models with air conditioning, remove the five heater core cover screws, then disconnect the electrical connectors and position heater core cover aside.
3. Disconnect exhaust pipe and allow to hang down.
4. Support transmission, then remove transmission rear support bolts and propeller shaft and lower transmission until enough clearance is obtained to remove governor.
5. Remove governor retainer ring and cover, then remove governor and washer.

NOTE: If governor to case washer falls into transmission, use a small magnet to remove it. If it cannot be easily removed, replace the washer with a new one.

6. To install governor, reverse removal procedure.

CAUTION: Do not attempt to hammer governor assembly into case, as damage to governor, case or cover may result.

1982–83 Camaro & Firebird

1. Raise and support vehicle.
2. Remove governor retaining ring and cover and the two seal rings.
3. Remove governor from case.
4. Reverse procedure to install.

PRESSURE REGULATOR VALVE

1. Drain transmission fluid, then remove oil pan and screen.
2. Using a small screwdriver or tool J-24684, **Fig. 14,** compress regulator spring.

Fig. 14   Removing or installing pressure regulator

3. Remove retaining ring and slowly release spring tension.
4. Remove pressure regulator bore plug, valve, spring and guide.
5. To assemble, install pressure regulator spring, guide and valve with stem end first and bore plug with hole side out.
6. Using a small screwdriver or tool J-24684, **Fig. 14,** compress regulator spring and install retaining ring.

GOVERNOR PRESSURE SWITCH

1. Drain transmission fluid from pan, then remove pan.
2. Disconnect electrical connector from switch, then remove switch using suitable socket.
3. Reverse procedure to install.

TRANSMISSION REPLACE

BUICK

1. Disconnect battery ground cable.
2. Remove oil lever dipstick and bolt from upper end of oil filler tube.
3. Raise and properly support vehicle.
4. Remove detent cable retaining bolt from transmission, then disconnect detent cable from link (T.V. cable on 200C transmission). Plug hole to avoid entry of dirt or loss of fluid.
5. Disconnect transmission cooler lines, and remove catalytic converter bracket, if necessary.
6. Remove flywheel inspection cover, then the flywheel to converter bolts.
7. If equipped with console shift, disconnect shift control cable from transmission. If equipped with column shift, remove cotter pin and disconnect manual shift linkage.
8. Disconnect speedometer cable and remove propeller shaft.
9. Remove transmission support to mount bolts, and transmission support to frame bolts. Support engine, then raise transmission with a jack and remove support.
10. Lower transmission slightly and remove the engine to transmission bolts.
11. Carefully lower transmission using care to avoid damaging the detent

cable and shift linkage.

12. Reverse procedure to install.

1980–81 DEVILLE & BROUGHAM WITH DIESEL ENGINE

1. From inside vehicle, hold sleeve and pull cable outward, then lift snap lock.
2. Remove transmission oil level dipstick and upper dipstick tube retaining bolt.
3. Raise vehicle, then remove detent cable (T.V. cable on 200C transmission) retaining bolt.
4. Remove detent cable from link and plug hole.
5. Disconnect transmission cooler line at transmission.
6. Remove catalytic converter support bracket.
7. Support engine, then remove flywheel cover and three bolts attaching converter to flywheel.

NOTE: Mark flywheel and converter so they can be installed in the same position.

8. Disconnect speedometer cable, then remove cotter pin from shift linkage.
9. Remove propeller shaft.
10. Remove transmission support attaching bolts, then raise transmission using a suitable jack and remove support.
11. Lower transmission slightly and remove transmission to engine attaching bolts.
12. Move transmission rearward and carefully lower from vehicle.

NOTE: Use tool No. J-21366 to hold converter in position.

13. Reverse procedure to install.

CHEVROLET

Exc. Chevette & 1982–83 Camaro

1. Disconnect battery ground cable and the detent cable from carburetor. Remove filler tube and air cleaner.
2. On vehicles with air conditioning, remove five heater core cover screws from heater assembly. Disconnect electrical connector and, with hoses attached, place heater core cover aside.
3. Raise vehicle and remove propeller shaft.
4. Disconnect speedometer cable, electrical lead to case, oil cooler pipes and the shift linkage.
5. Support transmission with a suitable jack and remove the four rear transmission support bolts.
6. Remove nuts securing catalytic converter bracket to support.
7. Disconnect exhaust pipe at rear of catalytic converter, then at the manifold. Remove exhaust pipe catalytic converter and converter bracket as an assembly.
8. On all models, remove torque convert-

er under pan.

9. Remove converter to flywheel bolts.
10. Lower transmission slightly and remove engine to transmission bolts.
11. Raise transmission and move rearward, then lower from vehicle.
12. Reverse procedure to install.

Chevette

1. Disconnect battery ground cable then disconnect detent downshift cable from bracket.
2. Remove air cleaner and dipstick, then on vehicles with air conditioning, remove the 5 heater core cover retaining screws, disconnect connector and place heater core cover assembly aside.
3. Raise and support vehicle and remove propeller shaft.
4. Disconnect speedometer cable, electrical lead, oil cooler lines, and shift control linkage.
5. Support transmission with suitable jack and remove the crossmember retaining bolts.
6. Remove converter to bracket retaining nuts, then disconnect exhaust pipes from rear of catalytic converter and from exhaust manifolds and remove catalytic converter and converter bracket as an assembly.
7. Remove converter dust shield and remove converter to flywheel bolts.
8. Lower transmission slightly and remove transmission to engine bolts.
9. Raise transmission, then support engine with jack and lower and remove transmission from vehicle.

NOTE: Use converter holding tool J-5384, or keep rear of transmission lower than the front to prevent the converter from sliding out.

10. Before installing transmission, place two inch blocks between rack and pinion housing assembly and oil pan to align engine and transmission.
11. Reverse removal procedure to install and torque converter to flywheel bolts to 30–40 ft. lbs. (40–54 N-m).

1982–83 Camaro

1. Disconnect battery ground cable, then remove air cleaner.
2. Disconnect T.V. cable from carburetor, then remove filler tube.
3. Raise and support vehicle.
4. Remove prop. shaft and disconnect catalytic converter to transmission bracket.
5. Disconnect speedometer cable and T.C.C. electrical connector.
6. Remove torque arm to transmission bolts.

NOTE: When arm is disconnected from transmission, rear spring force will cause torque arm to move toward the floor pan. When disconnecting the arm, carefully place a piece of wood between the floor pan and torque arm to avoid personal injury and damage to the floor pan.

7. Remove flywheel cover and converter to flywheel attaching bolts. Mark fly-

wheel and converter for reference.

8. Support transmission with a suitable jack, then remove transmission rear mount bolt and crossmember.
9. Lower transmission slightly and remove T.V. cable and oil cooler lines.
10. Support engine using tool BT-6424 or equivalent and remove transmission to engine bolts.
11. Remove transmission from vehicle.
12. Reverse procedure to install.

OLDSMOBILE

1. Disconnect battery ground cable and the detent cable (T.V. cable on 200C transmission). from carburetor or accelerator lever. Remove filler tube.
2. Raise vehicle and disconnect detent cable, shift linkage and oil cooler pipes.
3. Remove catalytic converter support bracket and flywheel cover pan.
4. Remove flywheel to converter bolts.
5. Disconnect speedometer cable and remove propeller shaft.
6. Remove transmission support to transmission bolts and the transmission support to frame bolts.
7. Support and raise transmission with a suitable jack, then remove support.
8. Lower transmission slightly and remove engine to transmission bolts.
9. Move transmission rearward and lower from vehicle.
10. Reverse procedure to install.

PONTIAC

Exc. 1000 & 1982–83 Firebird

1. Disconnect battery ground cable.
2. Disconnect detent cable (T.V. cable on 200C transmission) from carburetor, then remove dipstick and oil filler tube from transmission.
3. Raise and support vehicle.
4. Remove detent cable retaining bolt and cable and plug opening.
5. Disconnect transmission cooler lines and speedometer cable from transmission.
6. Disconnect shift linkage from selector lever. If equipped with console, remove spring clip and detent cable from transmission bracket.
7. Remove catalytic converter support bracket.
8. Remove flywheel cover and then the flywheel to converter bolts.
9. Remove propeller shaft.
10. Remove transmission support to transmission mount bolts and transmission support to mount bolts.
11. Raise transmission with a suitable jack and remove support, then lower transmission and remove transmission to engine bolts.
12. Remove transmission. Do not damage oil cooler lines and detent cable.
13. Reverse procedure to install.

1000

Refer to "Transmission, Replace" under "Chevette" for procedure.

1982–83 Firebird

Refer to "Transmission Replace" under "1982–83 Camaro" for procedure.

Turbo Hydra-Matic 200-4R Automatic Transmission

INDEX

TRANSMISSION IDENTIFICATION

The transmission identification number is stamped on the left hand side of the transmission.

             Code

BUICK

	Code
1981 V6-252 Electra & LeSabre	BY, BM
V8-307 Electra	OG
1982 V6-252 Electra & LeSabre	BY
V8-307 Electra & LeSabre	OG
V8-350① Electra & LeSabre	OM
1983 V6-231 Regal	BR
V6-252 Electra & LeSabre	BY
V8-307 Electra & LeSabre	OG
V8-350① Electra, LeSabre & Regal	OM
1984 V6-231 Regal	BQ
V6-252 Electra, LeSabre & Regal	BY, BT
V6-262 ① Regal	OF
V8-305 Regal	HG
V8-307 Electra & LeSabre	OG, OJ
V8-350① Electra, LeSabre & Regal	OM
1985 V6-231 Regal	BQ
V8-307 LeSabre	OG, OJ
V8-350① LeSabre	OM

CADILLAC

	Code
1981 V6-252 Brougham & DeVille	BY
1982 V6-252 Brougham & DeVille	BY
V8-250 Brougham & DeVille	AA
V8-350① Eldorado & Seville	AL
1983 V8-250 Fleetwood & DeVille	AA, AP
V8-350① Fleetwood & DeVille	OM
1984 V8-250 Fleetwood & DeVille	AA, AP

	Code
1985 V8-250 Fleetwood & DeVille	AP
V8-350① Fleetwood & DeVille	OM

CHEVROLET

	Code
1981 V8-305 Impala & Caprice	CU
1982 V8-267 Impala & Caprice	CQ
V8-305 Impala & Caprice	CR
V8-350① Impala & Caprice	OM
1983 V8-350① Impala & Caprice	OM
1984 V6-229 Monte Carlo	CH
V8-305 Monte Carlo	CQ, CR
V8-350① Impala, Caprice, & Monte Carlo	OM
1985 V6-262① Monte Carlo	CH
V8-305 Monte Carlo	CQ, CR
V8-350 Impala & Caprice	OM

OLDSMOBILE

	Code
1981 V6-252 88	BY
V8-307 98	OG
1982 V6-252 98	BY
V8-307 88 & 98	OG
V8-350① 88, 98 & Custom Cruiser	OM
1983 V6-252 98	BY
V8-307 88, 98, Custom Cruiser & Cutlass	OZ, OG
V8-350① 88, 98 & Custom Cruiser	OM
1984 V6-262① Cutlass	OY
V8-305 Cutlass	HG
V8-307 88 & Cutlass	OG, OZ
V8-350① Cutlass	OM

PONTIAC

	Code
1981 V8-307 Catalina & Bonneville	OG
1983 V8-350① Parisienne	OM
1984 V8-305 Bonneville & Grand Prix	CR
V8-350① Bonneville, Grand Prix & Parisienne	OM

	Code
1985 V8-305 Bonneville & Grand Prix	CR
V8-350① Parisienne	OM

①—Diesel engine

DESCRIPTION

This transmission is a fully automatic unit consisting primarily of a three-element hydraulic torque converter with a converter clutch, a compound planetary gear set and an overdrive unit, **Fig. 1.** Five multiple-disc clutches and a band provide the friction elements required to obtain the desired function of the compound planetary gear set and the overdrive unit.

The torque converter couples the engine to the overdrive unit and planetary gears through oil and provides torque multiplication. The combination of the compound planetary gear set and the overdrive unit provides four forward ratios and one reverse. Fully automatic changing of the gear ratios is determined by vehicle speed and engine torque.

The hydraulic system in this transmission is pressurized by a variable capacity vane type pump to provide the working pressure required to operate the friction elements and automatic controls.

TROUBLESHOOTING

NO DRIVE

1. Low fluid level.
2. Manual linkage maladjusted.
3. Low fluid pressure.
   a. Plugged or restricted oil filter.
   b. Cut or missing oil filter O-ring seals.
   c. Faulty pressure regulator valve.
   d. Damaged pump rotor tangs.
   e. Porosity in oil filter to pump intake bore.
4. Springs missing in overdrive unit roller clutch.

Fig. 1   THM 200-4R cross-sectional view

5. Overdrive unit rollers galled or missing.
6. Forward Clutch.
   a. Forward clutch does not apply—piston cracked, seals missing, damaged; clutch plates burned; snap ring out of groove.
   b. Missing or damaged forward clutch oil seal rings; leak in feed circuits; pump to case gasket improperly positioned or damaged.
   c. Stuck or missing clutch housing ball check.
   d. Cup plug leaking or missing in the rear of the forward clutch shaft in the clutch apply passage.
7. Lo and reverse roller clutch springs missing.
8. Lo and reverse roller clutch rollers galled or missing.

HIGH OR LOW OIL PRESSURE

1. Throttle valve cable misadjusted, binding, unhooked, broken, or wrong link.
2. Damaged or leaking throttle valve assembly.
   a. Throttle lever and bracket assembly binding, unhooked or improperly positioned.
   b. Binding throttle valve or plunger valve.
3. Pressure regulator valve binding.
4. Throttle valve boost valve

   a. Valve binding.
   b. Wrong valve (causing low oil pressure only)
5. Reverse boost valve binding.
6. Manual valve unhooked or improperly positioned.
7. Pressure relief valve ball missing or spring damaged.
8. Pump.
   a. Slide stuck.
   b. Slide seal damaged or missing.
   c. Decrease air bleed orifice missing or damaged causing high oil pressure.
   d. Decrease air bleed orifice plugged causing low oil pressure.
9. Throttle valve limit valve binding.
10. Line bias valve binding in open position causing high oil pressure.
11. Line bias valve binding in closed position causing low oil pressure.
12. Incorrect orifices or passages in control valve assembly spacer plate or case.

1-2 SHIFT ONLY AT FULL THROTTLE

1. Throttle valve cable binding, unhooked, broken, or improperly adjusted.
2. Throttle lever and bracket assembly binding or unhooked.
3. Throttle valve exhaust ball lifter or #5 ball binding, improperly positioned, or unhooked.
4. #5 ball sealed causing full throttle

valve pressure regardless of throttle valve position.
5. Throttle valve and plunger binding.
6. Control valve body gaskets leaking, damaged, or incorrectly installed.
7. Porous case assembly.

NO 1-2 SHIFT

1. Governor and governor feed passages.
   a. Plugged governor oil feed orifice in spacer plate.
   b. Check balls missing in governor assembly.
   c. Missing or leaking inner governor cover rubber O-ring seal.
   d. Governor shaft seal missing or damaged.
   e. Stripped governor driven gear.
   f. Governor weights binding on pin.
   g. Governor driven gear not engaged with governor shaft.
2. Control valve assembly
   a. 1-2 shift, Lo 1st/Detent, or 1-2 throttle valve stuck in downshift position.
   b. Spacer plate gaskets improperly positioned.
3. Case
   a. Case channels porous or 2nd oil feed hole undrilled.
   b. Excessive leakage between case bore and intermediate band apply rings.
   c. Intermediate band anchor pin missing or unhooked from band.

d. Broken or missing band.
4. Intermediate servo assembly.
   a. Missing servo cover oil seal.
   b. Porosity in serve; cover, inner piston, or outer piston.
   c. Incorrect intermediate band apply pin.
   d. Incorrect usage of cover and piston.
5. 1-2 accumulator.
   a. Loose 1-2 accumulator housing bolts.
   b. Damaged 1-2 accumulator housing face.
   c. Missing or damaged accumulator plate.

NO 2-3 SHIFT

1. Control valve assembly and spacer plate.
   a. 2-3 shift valve or 2-3 throttle valve stuck in the downshift position.
   b. Leaking, damaged or incorrectly installed valve body gaskets.
   c. Reverse/3rd check ball not seating, damaged or missing.
2. Case channels porous.
3. Center support.
   a. Plugged or undrilled center support direct clutch feed passage.
   b. Damaged steel oil seal rings on center support.
4. Direct clutch.
   a. Inner oil seal ring on piston damaged or missing.
   b. Center oil seal ring on direct clutch hub damaged or missing.
   c. Check ball and/or retainer damaged or missing from direct clutch piston.
   d. Damaged or missing direct clutch piston or housing.
   e. Damaged or missing direct clutch plates.
   f. Direct clutch backing plate snap ring not in groove.
   g. Release spring guide improperly located, preventing piston check ball from seating in retainer.
5. Intermediate servo assembly (third clutch accumulator oil passages).
   a. Broken or missing servo to case oil seal ring on intermediate servo piston.
   b. Intermediate servo and/or capsule missing or damaged.
   c. Plugged or undrilled exhaust hole in case between servo piston seal rings.
   d. Bleed orifice cup plug missing from intermediate servo pocket in case.

NO DRIVE IN R OR SLIPS IN R

1. Binding or improperly adjusted throttle valve cable.
2. Improperly adjusted manual linkage.
3. Binding throttle valve.
4. Throttle valve limit valve binding.
5. Binding line bias valve.
6. Reverse boost valve binding in pressure regulator bore.
7. Reverse/3rd or Lo/Reverse check ball missing or seat in spacer plate damaged.

8. Reverse clutch.
   a. Cracked piston, or missing inner or outer seals.
   b. Clutch plates burned.
   c. Missing or damaged reverse oil seal in case.
   d. Missing clutch plate or wave plate.
9. Center support.
   a. Loose or missing center support attaching bolts.
   b. Blocked or undrilled passages.
   c. Porosity.
10. Direct clutch housing.
    a. Cracked housing or piston.
    b. Missing or damaged inner or outer piston seal.
    c. Missing or damaged check ball in either the direct clutch housing or the piston.
    d. Plates burned.
11. Plugged Lo/Reverse overrun clutch orifice in spacer plate.

DRIVE IN NEUTRAL

1. Manual linkage improperly adjusted or disconnected.
2. Forward clutch.
   a. Clutch does not release.
   b. Sticking exhaust check ball.
   c. Plates burned together.
3. Case cross leaking to forward clutch passage (D4).

SLIPPING 1-2 SHIFT

1. Low fluid level.
2. Spacer plate gaskets damaged or incorrectly installed.
3. Accumulator valve.
   a. Valve sticking in valve body causing low 1-2 accumulator pressure.
   b. Weak or missing spring.
4. 1-2 accumulator piston.
   a. Leaking seal, broken or missing spring.
   b. Leak between piston and pin.
   c. Binding 1-2 accumulator piston.
   d. Damaged 1-2 accumulator piston bore.
5. Intermediate band apply pin.
   a. Incorrect selection of apply pin.
   b. Excessive leakage between apply pin and case.
   c. Apply pin feed hole not completely drilled.
6. Intermediate servo assembly.
   a. Porosity in piston.
   b. Damaged or missing cover to servo oil seal ring.
   c. Leak between servo apply pin and case.
7. Improperly adjusted throttle valve cable.
8. Throttle valve binding, causing low throttle valve pressure.
9. Binding throttle valve limit valve.
10. Line bias valve sticking, causing low line pressure.
11. Worn or burned intermediate band.
12. Case porosity in 2nd clutch passage.

ROUGH 1-2 SHIFT

1. Throttle valve cable binding or improperly adjusted.
2. Binding throttle valve to throttle valve plunger.

3. Binding throttle valve limit valve.
4. Binding accumulator valve.
5. Binding line bias valve.
6. Intermediate servo assembly.
   a. Incorrect selection apply pin.
   b. Damaged or missing servo piston to case oil seal ring.
   c. Bleed cup plug missing in case.
7. 1-2 accumulator.
   a. Oil ring damaged.
   b. Piston stuck.
   c. Broken or missing spring.
   d. Damaged bore.
8. 1-2 shift check ball #8 missing or sticking.

SLIPPING 2-3 SHIFT

1. Low fluid level.
2. Improperly adjusted throttle valve cable.
3. Binding throttle valve.
4. Spacer plate and gaskets.
   a. Direct clutch orifice partially blocked in spacer plate.
   b. Gaskets out of position or damaged.
5. Intermediate servo assembly.
   a. Damaged or missing servo to case oil seal ring.
   b. Damaged piston or servo bore.
   c. Intermediate servo orifice bleed cup plug in case missing.
   d. Case porous in the servo bore area.
6. Direct clutch feed.
   a. Direct clutch feed channels porous.
   b. Loose case to support bolts causing leakage.
   c. Cracked direct clutch piston or housing.
   d. Cut or missing piston seals.
   e. Burned direct clutch plates.
   f. Check ball in piston and/or housing missing, damaged, or leaking.
   g. Check ball capsule damaged.
   h. Release spring guide improperly located preventing check ball from seating in piston.
7. Center support.
   a. Channels cross feeding, leaking, or restricted.
   b. Damaged or missing oil seal rings.

ROUGH 2-3 SHIFT

1. Missing or improperly positioned throttle valve cable.
2. Throttle valve and plunger.
   a. Throttle valve plunger binding.
   b. Throttle valve binding.
3. Throttle valve limit valve binding.
4. Intermediate servo assembly exhaust hole undrilled or plugged between intermediate servo piston seals, preventing intermediate servo piston from completing its stroke.
5. 3-2 exhaust check ball #4 missing or improperly positioned.
6. 3rd accumulator check ball #2 missing or improperly positioned.

SLIPPING 3-4 SHIFT

1. Low fluid level.
2. Control valve assembly and spacer plate.
   a. Gaskets of space plate damaged

or incorrectly installed.
  b. Accumulator valve sticking causing low 3-4 accumulator pressure.
  c. Weak or missing accumulator valve spring.
3. 3-4 accumulator.
  a. Piston stuck.
  b. Damaged bore or oil ring.
4. Center support porosity.
5. Loose center support attaching bolts.
6. Fourth clutch piston surface or seals damaged.
7. Improper clutch plate usage.
8. Burned fourth clutch plates.
9. Case.
  a. Porosity.
  b. 1-2 accumulator housing bolts loose.
  c. 3-4 accumulator piston seal damaged.
  d. 3-4 accumulator leaking between the piston and pin.
  e. 3-4 accumulator bore damaged.

ROUGH 3-4 SHIFT

1. Throttle valve cable improperly positioned or missing.
2. Throttle valve and plunger.
  a. Throttle valve plunger binding.
  b. Throttle valve binding.
3. Throttle valve limit valve binding.
4. 3-4 accumulator.
  a. Piston stuck.
  b. Bore damaged.
5. Fourth clutch piston binding.

NO CONVERTER CLUTCH APPLICATION

1. Electrical problem.
  a. 12 volts not being supplied to clutch solenoid.
  b. Defective solenoid.
  c. Damaged electrical connector.
  d. Defective pressure switch.
  e. Wire grounded.
2. Converter clutch shift valve or throttle valve stuck.
3. Pump Assembly.
  a. Plugged converter signal oil orifice in pump.
  b. Damaged or missing solenoid O-ring.
  c. Orifice cup plug missing in oil cooler passage in pump.
  d. Damaged or improperly positioned pump to case gasket.
  e. Converter clutch application valve stuck.
  f. Cup plug missing from application passage.

ROUGH CONVERTER CLUTCH APPLICATION

1. Damaged converter clutch pressure plate.
2. Damaged or missing check ball in end of turbine shaft.

CONVERTER CLUTCH DOES NOT RELEASE

1. Converter clutch apply valve stuck.
2. Damaged converter.
3. Missing cup plug in pump release passage.

4. Missing or damaged turbine shaft end seal.
5. Hole not drilled through turbine shaft.

FIRST, SECOND & THIRD SPEED ONLY, NO 3-4 SHIFT

1. Control valve assembly and spacer plate.
  a. 3-4 shift valve or 3-4 throttle valve stuck.
  b. Plugged spacer plate orifice.
2. Center support.
  a. Plugged or undrilled oil passages.
  b. Loose or missing center support attaching bolts.
  c. Cracked or damaged fourth clutch piston.
  d. Damaged, missing or improperly assembled fourth clutch piston seals.
  e. Improper plate usage.
  f. Burned fourth clutch plates.
  g. Binding overrun clutch plates.
3. Case porosity.
4. Orifice cup plug missing in 3-4 accumulator passage in case.
5. Leakage between accumulator piston and pin.
6. 3-4 accumulator bore damaged.

NO ENGINE BRAKING IN L1

1. Improperly adjusted manual linkage.
2. D-3 orifice in spacer plate plugged.
3. Control valve body gaskets leaking, damaged, or incorrectly installed.
4. D-2 oil pipe leaking or out of position.
5. L1 overrun clutch valve binding in valve body.
6. L1/Reverse check ball #10 improperly positioned or missing.
7. L1/Detent check ball #9 improperly positioned or missing.
8. PT/D-3 check ball #3 improperly positioned or missing.
9. Turbine shaft and overrun clutch. No manual 3rd or 2nd should also be a complaint with the following:
  a. Plugged or undrilled D-3 oil passage in turbine shaft.
  b. D-3 oil passage not drilled through in overrun clutch hub.
  c. Missing or damaged oil seals in the overrun clutch piston.
  d. Burned overrun clutches.
  e. Overrun clutch backing plate snap ring out of groove.
10. Case porosity.
11. L1/Reverse clutch assembly.
No reverse should also be a complaint with any of the following conditions:
  a. Broken or missing piston seals.
  b. Clutch housing snap ring out of case.
  c. Cracked/porous piston or housing.
  d. Missing or damaged cup plug or rubber seal between case and L1/Reverse clutch housing.

NO ENGINE BRAKING IN L2

1. Manual linkage improperly adjusted.
2. Valve body gaskets leaking, damaged, or improperly installed.
3. Leaking or out of position D-2 oil

pipe.
4. Plugged D-3 orifice in spacer plate.
5. PT/D-3 check ball #3 improperly positioned or missing.
6. Porous case.
7. Missing or damaged intermediate servo cover to case oil seal ring.
8. Intermediate band off anchor pin.
9. Broken or burned intermediate band.
10. D-3 oil passage not drilled through in overrun clutch hub.
11. Missing or damaged oil seals in the overrun clutch piston.
12. Undrilled or plugged D-3 oil hole in turbine shaft.
13. Burned overrun clutches.
14. Overrun clutch backing plate snap ring out of groove.

NO ENGINE BRAKING IN D

1. Manual linkage improperly adjusted.
2. Plugged D-3 orifice in spacer plate.
3. Leaking, damaged, or incorrectly installed valve body gaskets.
4. PT/D-3 check ball #3 improperly positioned or missing.
5. Undrilled or plugged D-3 oil passage in turbine shaft.
6. D-3 oil hole not drilled through in overrun clutch hub.
7. Missing or damaged oil seals in the overrun clutch piston.
8. Burned overrun clutches.
9. Overrun clutch backing plate snap ring out of groove.

WILL NOT HOLD IN PARK

1. Manual linkage improperly adjusted.
2. Internal linkage.
  a. Parking pawl binding in case.
  b. Damaged actuator rod, spring, or plunger.
  c. Broken parking pawl.
  d. Loose or damaged parking bracket.
  e. Missing or improperly positioned manual shaft to case pin.
3. Inside detent lever and pin assembly.
  a. Loose nut.
  b. Worn or damaged hole in lever.
4. Manual detent roller and spring assembly.
  a. Roller assembly to valve body bolt loose.
  b. Pin or roller damaged, improperly positioned, or missing.

NO PART THROTTLE DOWNSHIFTS

1. Binding throttle valve.
2. Throttle valve limit valve binding.
3. Plugged or undrilled spacer plate hole.
4. Improperly positioned or damaged valve body gaskets.
5. Throttle valve modulator downshift valve stuck.
6. Improperly set throttle valve cable.

NO PART THROTTLE 4-3 DOWNSHIFT

On selected models with a part throttle passage in the throttle plunger bushing.
1. Throttle plunger bushing passages not

Fig. 2   Self adjusting throttle valve linkage

NOTE: An early change to a darker color from the usual red color and or a strong odor that is usually associated with overheated fluid is normal and should not be considered as a positive sign of required maintenance of unit failure.

CAUTION: When adding fluid, do not overfill, as foaming and loss of fluid through the vent may occur as the fluid heats up. Also, if fluid level is too low, complete loss of drive may occur especially when cold, which can cause transmission failure.

Fig. 3   Column mounted shift linkage adjustment

open.
2. 3-4 throttle valve bushing passages not open.
3. PT/D-3 check ball #3 incorrectly positioned or missing.
4. Improperly positioned or damaged valve body gaskets.
5. Improperly set throttle valve cable.
6. Throttle valve limit valve binding.

LOW OR HIGH SHIFT POINT

1. Binding or improperly adjusted throttle valve cable.
2. Throttle valve limit valve binding.
3. Throttle valve binding.
4. Throttle valve modulator upshift valve binding.
5. Throttle valve modulator downshift valve binding.
6. Improperly positioned, leaking, or damaged valve body gaskets.
7. Throttle valve plunger binding.
8. 1-2, 2-3, or 3-4 throttle valves binding in bushings.
9. Pressure regulator valve binding.
10. Throttle valve exhaust ball #5 and lifter improperly positioned, unhooked, or missing.
11. Throttle lever and bracket assembly.
    a. Binding, unhooked, or loose at mounting valve body bolt.
    b. Not positioned at the throttle valve plunger bushing pin locator.
12. Broken or missing governor shaft to cover seal ring.
13. Broken or missing governor cover gasket.
14. Porous case.

MAINTENANCE

To check fluid, drive vehicle for at least 15 minutes to bring fluid to operating temperature (200° F.). With vehicle on a level surface and engine idling in Park and parking brake applied, the level on the dipstick should be at the "F" mark. To bring the fluid level from the ADD mark to the FULL mark requires 1 pint of fluid. If vehicle cannot be driven sufficiently to bring fluid to operating temperature, the level on the dipstick should be between the two dimples on the dipstick with fluid temperature at 70° F.

If additional fluid is required, use only Dexron II automatic transmission fluid.

Every 100,000 miles, the oil should be drained, the oil pan removed, the screen cleaned and fresh fluid added. For vehicles subjected to more severe use such as heavy city traffic especially in hot weather, prolonged periods of idling or towing, this maintenance should be performed every 15,000 miles.

DRAINING BOTTOM PAN

1. Remove front and side oil pan attaching bolts, then loosen the rear oil pan attaching bolts.
2. Carefully pry oil pan loose and allow fluid to drain into a suitable container.
3. Remove the oil pan and gasket, then remove the screen attaching bolts and remove screen.
4. Thoroughly clean oil screen and oil pan with solvent.
5. Install oil screen using a new gasket, then install oil pan using a new gasket and torque attaching bolts to 10–13 ft. lbs.
6. Add approximately 3 quarts of fluid, then with engine idling and parking brake applied, move selector lever through each range and return selector lever to PARK.
7. Check fluid level and add fluid as required to bring level between the two dimples on the dipstick.

ADJUSTMENTS

THROTTLE VALVE LINKAGE

Models Equipped With Diesel Engine
1. Remove cruise control rod on vehicles equipped with cruise control.
2. Disconnect throttle valve linkage from throttle assembly.
3. Loosen lock nut on pump rod, then shorten rod by rotating several turns.
4. Rotate throttle lever assembly to full throttle position and secure in this position.
5. Lengthen pump rod by rotating in opposite direction as described in step 3 until injection pump lever contacts full throttle stop.
6. Release throttle lever assembly and tighten pump rod lock nut.
7. Disconnect pump rod from throttle lever assembly.
8. Connect throttle valve linkage to throttle assembly.
9. Depress metal locking tab on upper

end of cable and hold in this position.
10. Position slider through fitting and away from lever assembly until slider contacts metal fitting.
11. Release metal tab, then rotate throttle lever assembly to full throttle position and release.
12. Connect pump rod to lever assembly, then connect cruise control throttle rod, if equipped.
13. On models equipped with cruise control, adjust servo throttle rod until minimum amount of slack is present. Install clip into first hole closest to bellcrank that is within servo bail.

Models Equipped With Gasoline Engine, Manual Type Linkage
1. With engine off, disconnect throttle valve linkage retaining lock.
2. Rotate throttle lever to wide open position and hold in this position.
3. Connect throttle valve linkage retaining lock.

Self Adjusting Linkage, All Models
1. With engine off, depress locking tab and move slider rearward through fitting until slider contacts fitting, **Fig. 2.**
2. Release locking tab, then move carburetor throttle lever to wide open position and release.
3. Check cable for sticking or binding, then test vehicle for proper operation.
4. If transmission does not shift properly, raise and support vehicle and remove transmission oil pan. Inspect throttle lever and bracket assembly on valve body for damage. Check to ensure that throttle valve exhaust valve rod is not worn or damaged. Check to ensure that lifter spring holds lifter rod against bottom of valve body and that throttle valve plunger is not sticking.

MANUAL LINKAGE

Column Mounted
1. Position transmission shift lever in Neutral.
2. Position transmission manual valve lever in Neutral detent.
3. With clamp spring washer and screw assembled onto equalizer lever and control rod, hold clamp against equal-

izer lever, then snug tighten clamp-screw against control rod, **Fig. 3.**

Console Mounted

1. Position console shift lever in Park position.
2. Position transmission manual valve lever in Park detent.
3. Position pin, **Fig. 4,** until pin fits loosely in transmission lever, then tighten attaching nut.

IN-VEHICLE REPAIRS

INTERMEDIATE SERVO, REPLACE

1. Remove intermediate servo cover retaining ring, using a small screwdriver.
2. Remove servo cover and discard seal ring.
3. Remove servo piston and band apply pin assembly.
4. Reverse procedure to install.

SPEEDOMETER DRIVEN GEAR, REPLACE

1. Disconnect speedometer cable.
2. Remove bolt, retainer, speedometer driven gear and the O-ring seal.
3. Reverse procedure to install.

REAR OIL SEAL, REPLACE

1. Remove propeller shaft.
2. Pry seal from extension housing with a suitable tool.
3. Drive new oil seal into extension housing, using a suitable tool.
4. Install propeller shaft.

VALVE BODY, REPLACE

1. Drain transmission oil pan.
2. Remove oil pan and filter.
3. Remove screw and washer securing T.V. cable to transmission and disconnect the cable.
4. Remove throttle lever and bracket assembly. Use caution not to bend throttle lever link.
5. Disconnect electrical connectors at the 4-3 pressure switch and the 4th clutch pressure switch.
6. Remove solenoid attaching bolts, clips and solenoid assembly.
7. Remove manual detent roller and spring assembly.
8. Remove valve body retaining bolts while supporting valve body. Secure manual valve and remove valve body. Use caution not to lose the three check balls.
9. Reverse procedure to install. Torque valve body bolts to 12 ft. lbs.

1-2 & 3-4 ACCUMULATOR, REPLACE

1. Remove valve body.

Fig. 4 Console mounted shift linkage adjustment

2. While supporting 1-2 accumulator housing, remove housing retaining bolts. Then, remove housing and gasket.
3. Support valve body spacer plate, gaskets and accumulator plate to prevent loss of the eight check balls and the 3-4 accumulator spring piston and pin located in the case. Remove remaining retaining bolt on accumulator plate.

NOTE: The intermediate band anchor pin may become dislodged after removing spacer plate and gaskets.

4. Reverse procedure to install.

GOVERNOR, REPLACE

1. Drain transmission oil pan.
2. Remove oil pan and filter.
3. Remove governor attaching bolts, cover and gasket. The governor may come out with the cover. Also, it may be necessary to rotate output shaft counterclockwise while removing governor.
4. Reverse procedure to install.

TRANSMISSION
REPLACE

1981 CADILLAC

1. Disconnect battery ground cable.
2. Remove transmission oil level dipstick. Remove upper bolt on dipstick tube.
3. Raise and support vehicle.
4. Disconnect throttle valve cable from retainer.

5. Disconnect transmission cooler lines from transmission.
6. Remove flywheel under cover. Remove three flywheel to converter attaching bolts. It may be necessary to remove catalytic converter support bracket to gain access to bolts. Mark flywheel and converter for reference during installation.
7. Support engine with suitable jack, then disconnect speedometer cable.
8. Disconnect manual shift linkage from transmission.
9. Mark driveshaft and companion flange for reference during installation, then remove driveshaft.
10. Remove transmission crossmember to transmission mount bolts. Remove transmission crossmember to frame bolts.
11. Raise transmission with suitable jack and remove crossmember.
12. Lower transmission slightly, then remove transmission to engine mounting bolts.
13. Lower transmission and remove from vehicle. Use caution not to drop torque converter as transmission is being removed. Install suitable converter holding tool to secure converter.
14. Reverse procedure to install.

EXC. 1981 CADILLAC

1. Disconnect battery ground cable and remove air cleaner.
2. Disconnect throttle valve cable from carburetor.
3. Remove transmission oil level dipstick. Remove upper bolt on dipstick tube.
4. Raise and support vehicle.
5. Mark driveshaft and companion flange for reference during installation, then remove driveshaft.
6. Disconnect speedometer cable and manual shift linkage from transmission.
7. Disconnect torque converter clutch solenoid electrical connector.
8. Remove flywheel under cover. Mark flywheel and converter for reference during installation. Remove three flywheel to converter attaching bolts.
9. Remove catalytic converter support bracket bolts and the tunnel strap.
10. Remove transmission crossmember to transmission mount bolts. Remove transmission crossmember to frame bolts.
11. Support transmission with suitable jack, then move crossmember rearward.
12. Lower transmission slightly and disconnect throttle valve cable and oil cooler lines.
13. Support engine with suitable jack, then remove engine to transmission mounting bolts.
14. Lower jack and remove transmission from vehicle. Use caution not to drop torque converter as transmission is removed. Install suitable converter holding tool to secure converter.
15. Reverse procedure to install.

Turbo Hydra-Matic 250, 250C, 350, 350C Automatic Transmission

INDEX

TRANSMISSION IDENTIFICATION

A production day and shift built number, transmission model and model year are stamped on the 1-2 accumulator cover, which is located on the middle lower right side of the transmission case.

Code

BUICK

1980 Century & Regal . 7JE, 7KC, 7KH, 7KJ, 7KS, 7KT, 7KV, 7TB, 7KH
Electra & LeSabre 7KD, 7KJ, 7KN, 7LA, 7TB, 7WB, 7WC, TW6
Skyhawk 7KA
1981 V6-231 Century & Regal ....KD, KT, WK
V6-231 LeSabre & Estate Wag. .... KD
V6-252 LeSabre, Estate Wag. & Electra .... KK
V6-307 LeSabre & Estate Wag. ....LB, XA, XL
V6-350 LeSabre & Estate Wag. .... LA, LD
1982 V6-231 Estate Wagon, LeSabre & Regal .... KA
V6-231 Regal Turbo .... KL
V6-231 Regal .... WK
V6-252 Regal 4 Barrel Carb. .... KE

V6-252 Estate Wagon & LeSabre 4 Barrel Carb. ..... KK
V8-307 Estate Wagon & LeSabre XL
V8-350 Regal Diesel ...... LB, WX
V8-350 Estate Wagon & LeSabre Diesel............ LD
V8-350 Estate Wagon & LeSabre Diesel............ WT
1983 V6-231 LeSabre & Regal ...... KA
V6-231 Regal .... WK
V6-252 Regal .... KE
V8-350 Estate Wagon & LeSabre (Diesel) .... LJ
V8-350 Regal (Diesel) .... LB
1984 V6-231 Regal .... WK

CADILLAC

1982 V8-350 Brougham & DeVille Diesel................... WT

CHEVROLET

1980 Chevrolet, Malibu & Monte Carlo 7KD, 7JE, 7JS, 7WD, 7WL
Malibu & Monte Carlo ... 7JJ, 7JK, 7JN, 7KC, 7KJ
Camaro ..7JD, 7JJ, 7JK, 7JL, 7KF
Chevrolet ... 7JE, 7KH, 7TZ, 7WC, 7WH
Corvette 7JC, 7TW
Monza 7KA
1981 V6-229 Malibu & Monte Carlo................... WP
V6-229 Camaro .... JC, XP

V6-229 Chevrolet, Malibu & Monte Carlo .... XP
V6-231 Malibu & Monte Carlo ....KD, KTM WK, XX
V6-231 Chevrolet ....KD
V8-267 Malibu, Monte Carlo & Chevrolet .... XS
V8-267 Camaro, Chevrolet, Malibu & Monte Carlo ...... WC
V8-305 Malibu & Monte Carlo .... WD, XK
V8-305 Camaro, Chevrolet ... WD
V8-350 Malibu & Monte Carlo............... WE
V8-350 Chevrolet LA, LD, WS, WW
V8-350 Corvette .... JD
1982 V6-229 Caprice, Impala, Malibu & Monte Carlo WD, XP
V6-231 Caprice, Impala, Malibu & Monte Carlo ..... KA
V6-231 Malibu & Monte Carlo.................. WK
V8-267 Caprice, Impala, Malibu & Monte Carlo ... WC
V8-267 Caprice, Impala, Malibu & Monte Carlo ... XS
V8-305 Malibu & Monte Carlo............... WD, XK
V8-350 Malibu & Monte Carlo (Diesel) .... LB, WX
V8-350 Caprice & Impala Diesel............LD, WT
1983 V6-229 Caprice & Impala ... XP
V6-231 Caprice & Impala ...... KA
V6-231 Malibu & Monte Carlo................... WK

CHEVROLET—Continued

V8-305 Caprice & Impala ...... XK
V8-305 Malibu & Monte
Carlo .... WD, WE
V8-350 Caprice & Impala
(Diesel) .... LD, LJ
V8-350 Malibu & Monte
Carlo (Diesel) .... LB
1984 V6-229 Caprice & Impala ..... XP
V6-229 Monte Carlo .... XE
V6-231 Monte Carlo ....CQ
V8-305 Caprice & Impala① ...WW
V8-305 Monte Carlo① ....WS
V8-305 Caprice, Impala &
Monte Carlo② .... XK

OLDSMOBILE

1979 V6-231 Cutlass .... KE
V6-231 Omega, Calif. .... KX
V6-231 Omega, Exc. Calif. .... KE
V6-231 88 Exc. Sta. Wag. .... KC
V6-231 Starfire (2.56 Axle) ... KA
V6-231 Starfire (2.93 Axle) .... KL
V8-260 Cutlass & 88 Exc.
Sta. Wag. .... LD
V8-301 88 Exc. Sta. Wag .....MA
V8-305 Cutlass.............. JC
V8-305 Omega, Exc. Calif.
& Hi Alt................. JC
V8-305 Starfire .... WC
V8-350 (Chev. Built) Cut-
lass & Omega............. JD
V8-350 (Olds. Built) Cutlass
Exc. Hi Alt. .... LA
V8-350 (Olds. Built) 88 Exc.
Sta. Wag. Exc. Hi Alt....... LA
V8-350 (Olds. Built) 88 Exc.
Sta. Wag., Hi Alt. .... LH
V8-350 (Olds. Built) 88 Sta.
Wag., Exc. Hi Alt. & Calif. ... LH
V8-350 (Diesel) Cutlass
Sta. Wag., Exc. Calif. &
Hi Alt. .... LS
V8-350 (Diesel) Cutlass
Sta. Wag., 88 Exc. Sta.
Wag. & 98 Exc. Hi Alt. .... LJ
V8-403 88 Sta. Wag. (2.41
or 3.08 Axle) LC
V8-403 88 Sta. Wag. Hi Alt. ... LE
V8-403 88 Sta. Wag. (3.23
Axle) Exc. Hi Alt. .... LK
V8-403 88 Sta. Wag., Exc.
Calif. & Hi Alt...............LW
1980 V6-231 Cutlass & 88 Exc.
Sta. Wagon............. KH, KS
V6-231 Cutlass .... KC
V6-231 Starfire .... KA
V8-260 Cutlass.......... LC, LD
V8-305 Cutlass ... JE, JK, WD, WL
V8-305 88 Exc. Sta. Wagon ... TT
V8-305 88 Sta. Wagon .... WA
V8-350 Cutlass .... LJ
V8-350 88 .... LA
V8-350 88 Wagon, Exc.
Diesel .... TY
V8-350 88 Wagon, Diesel ... WC
1981 V6-231 Cutlass.......... WK, XX
V6-231 88 & 98 .... KD
V8-260 Cutlass LC
V8-267 Cutlass .... WC
V8-307 Cutlass & 88 & 98 XL
V8-350 88 & 98 .... LA, LD

1982 V6-231 Cutlass............. WK
V6-231 Cutlass & 88 .... KA
V8-260 Cutlass & 88 .... LA
V8-307 Cutlass C3
V8-307 Cutlass & 88 XL
V8-350 Cutlass (Diesel) ...... LB
V8-350 88 (Diesel) .... LD
V8-350 88 & 98 (Diesel) ..... WT
1983 V6-231 Cutlass............. WK
V6-231 Cutlass & 88 .... KA
V8-307 Cutlass & 88 XL
V8-350 Cutlass (Diesel) ...... LB
V8-350 88 (Diesel) .... LJ
1984 V6-231 Cutlass............. WK

PONTIAC

1979 V6-231 Full size, Exc. Hi
Alt. .... KC
V6-231 Firebird & Phoenix,
Exc. Hi Alt. .... KX
V6-231 LeMans, Exc. Sta.
Wagon & Grand Prix ...... KE
V6-231 Sunbird, Exc. Calif. ... KL
V6-231 Sunbird, Exc. Hi Alt. ... KA
V8-301 Firebird, Exc. Calif.
& Hi Alt. .... ME, MJ
8-301 Bonneville, Catalina
& LeMans, Exc. Sta.
Wagon, Calif. or Hi Alt.. MA, MP
V8-305 Firebird, Calif. &
Phoenix, Exc. Hi Alt........ JC
V8-305 Phoenix (with Opt.
Axle), Exc. Hi Alt.......... TA
V8-305 Sunbird, Exc. Hi Alt. .. WD
V8-350 Full size, Hi Alt. ...... LH
V8-350 Firebird & LeMans
Sta. Wag., Hi Alt. Phoe-
nix, Calif. & Hi Alt. .... JD
V8-350 Full size, Calif. .... LA
V8-350 Bonneville & Catali-
na, Exc. Calif. & Hi Alt....... KH
V8-350 Phoenix (with Opt.
Axle), Calif. & Hi Alt. .... TR
V8-403 Full size, Calif. ..... LC, LK
V8-403 Full size, Hi Alt. ...... LE
1980 Firebird..................... MC
Full size .... TB
Grand Prix .... MD, TB
LeMans, Grand Am ...HD, MD, TB
1981 V6-231 LeMans & Grand
Prix .... WK, XX
V6-231 LeMans, Bonneville
& Catalina .... KD
V6-231 Firebird .... KY
V6-265 LeMans & Grand
Prix LC
V8-301 LeMans ....MA
V8-350 Bonneville &
Catalina .... LA, LD
1982 V6-231 Bonneville & Grand
Prix .... KA, WK
V6-252 Bonneville & Grand
Prix 4 Barrel Carb. .... KE
V8-350 Bonneville & Grand
Prix Diesel Exc. Calif. ...LB, WX
1983 V6-229 Parisienne ....XD, XH
V6-231 Bonneville & Grand
Prix .... KA, KC, WK
V8-305 Parisienne ....XD, XH
V8-305 Bonneville & Grand
Prix .... WD, XK
V8-350 Parisienne (Diesel) ... WH
V8-350 Bonneville & Grand
Prix (Diesel) .... LB

1984 V6-231 Bonneville & Grand
Prix .... WK
V8-305 Bonneville & Grand
Prix .... XK
①—350C transmission
②—250C transmission

DESCRIPTION

The 1980–82 Turbo Hydra-Matic 250, 250C, 350 & 350C, **Figs. 1 through 4,** are fully automatic three-speed transmissions consisting of a three-element torque converter and a compound planetary gear set. The 1983–85 series Turbo Hydra-Matic 250C & 350C transmissions have a four-element hydraulic torque converter and a planetary gear set. The Turbo Hydra-Matic 350 transmission has four multiple-disc clutches, two roller clutches and a band to provide the required friction elements to obtain the desired function of the planetary gear set. The Turbo Hydra-Matic 250 transmission uses an adjustable intermediate band in place of the intermediate clutch found in the Turbo Hydra-Matic 350. Also, the Turbo Hydra-Matic 250 has three multiple-disc clutches and one roller clutch.

The friction elements couple the engine to the planetary gears through oil pressure, providing three forward speeds and one reverse.

The three element torque converter is of welded construction and is serviced as an assembly. The unit consists of a pump or driving member, a turbine or driven member and a stator assembly. When required, the torque converter supplements the gears by multiplying engine torque. In addition, the 250C and 350C transmissions are equipped with a locking torque converter. The converter clutch assembly consists of a three element torque converter with a converter clutch. The converter clutch is splined to the turbine assembly and, when operated, applies against the converter cover, providing a mechanical direct drive coupling of the engine to the planetary gears. When the converter clutch is released the assembly operates as a normal torque converter.

TROUBLESHOOTING GUIDE

NO DRIVE IN DRIVE RANGE

1. Low oil level (check for leaks).
2. Manual control linkage improperly adjusted.
3. Low oil pressure due to blocked strainer, defective pressure regulator, pump assembly or pump drive gear. See that tangs have not been damaged by converter. Check case for porosity in intake bore.
4. Check control valve assembly to be sure manual valve has not been disconnected from inner lever.
5. Forward clutch may be stuck or damaged. Check pump feed circuits to forward clutch, including clutch drum ball check.
6. Roller clutch assembly broken or damaged.

Fig. 1 Cutaway view of Turbo Hydra-Matic 350 transmission

OIL PRESSURE HIGH OR LOW

High Pressure
1. Vacuum line or fittings leaking.
2. Vacuum modulator.
3. Modulator valve.
4. Pressure regulator.
5. Oil pump.

Low Pressure
1. Vacuum line or fittings obstructed.
2. Vacuum modulator.
3. Modulator valve.
4. Pressure regulator.
5. Governor.
6. Oil pump.

1-2 SHIFT AT FULL THROTTLE ONLY

1. Detent valve may be sticking or linkage may be misadjusted.
2. Vacuum line or fittings leaking.
3. Control valve body gaskets leaking, damaged or incorrectly installed. Detent valve train or 1-2 valve stuck.
4. Check case for porosity.

FIRST SPEED ONLY, NO 1-2 SHIFT

T.H.M. 250 & 350
1. Governor valve may be sticking.
2. Driven gear in governor assembly loose, worn or damaged. If driven gear

shows damage, check output shaft drive gear for nicks or rough finish.
3. Control valve governor feed channel blocked or gaskets leaking. 1-2 shift valve train stuck closed.
4. Check case for blocked governor feed channels or for scored governor bore which will allow cross pressure leak. Check case for porosity.
5. Intermediate clutch or seals damaged.
6. Intermediate roller clutch damaged.

T.H.M. 250
1. Intermediate servo piston seals damaged, missing or installed improperly.
2. Intermediate band improperly adjusted.
3. Intermediate servo apply rod broken.

1ST & 2ND ONLY, NO 2-3 SHIFT

1. Control valve 2-3 shift train stuck. Valve body gaskets leaking, damaged or improperly installed.
2. Pump hub-to-direct clutch oil seal rings broken or missing.
3. Direct clutch piston seals damaged. Piston ball check stuck or missing.

NO FIRST SPEED

T.H.M. 250
1. Intermediate band adjusted too tightly.

2. 1-2 shift valve stuck in upshift position.

T.H.M. 350
1. Excessive number of clutch plates in intermediate clutch pack.
2. Incorrect intermediate clutch piston.

MOVES FORWARD IN NEUTRAL

1. Manual linkage misadjusted.
2. Forward clutch not releasing.

NO FORWARD OR REVERSE OPERATION

1. Fatigue failure of forward clutch housing due to excessive pinion pin runout in output carrier.

NO DRIVE IN REVERSE OR SLIPS IN REVERSE

1. Low oil level.
2. Manual linkage misadjusted.
3. Modulator valve stuck.
4. Modulator and reverse boost valve stuck.
5. Pump hub-to-direct clutch oil seal rings broken or missing.
6. Direct clutch piston seal cut or missing.
7. Low and reverse clutch piston seal cut or missing.

Fig. 2   Cutaway view of Turbo Hydra-Matic 250 transmission

Fig. 3   Cross-sectional view of Turbo Hydra-Matic 250C transmission

A HOUSING COVER ASSEMBLY, CONVERTER
B SPACER, TURBINE THRUST
C PRESSURE PLATE ASSEMBLY
D SPRING, PRESSURE PLATE
E TURBINE ASSEMBLY
F STATOR ASSEMBLY
G THRUST BEARING ASSEMBLY
H CONVERTER PUMP ASSEMBLY

*THE TORQUE CONVERTER CLUTCH ASSEMBLY CANNOT BE DISASSEMBLED.

Fig. 4 Torque converter clutch 250C & 350C transmission

8. Number 1 check ball missing.
9. Control valve body gaskets leaking or damaged.
10. 2-3 valve train stuck in upshifted position.
11. 1-2 valve train stuck in upshifted position.
12. Intermediate servo piston or pin stuck so intermediate band is applied.
13. Low and reverse clutch piston out or seal damaged.
14. Direct clutch plates burned—may be caused by stuck ball check in piston.
15. Forward clutch not releasing.

SLIPS IN ALL RANGES

1. Low oil level.
2. Vacuum modulator valve defective or sticking.
3. Filter assembly plugged or leaking.
4. Pressure regulator valve stuck.
5. Pump to case gasket damaged.
6. Check case for cross leaks or porosity.
7. Forward clutch slipping.

SLIPS 1-2 SHIFT

T.H.M. 250 & 350
1. Low oil level.
2. Vacuum modulator assembly defective.
3. Modulator valve sticking.
4. Pump pressure regulator valve defective.
5. 1-2 accumulator oil ring damaged or missing. Case bore damaged.
6. Pump to case gasket mispositioned or damaged.
7. Check for case porosity.
8. Intermediate clutch piston seals damaged. Clutch plates burned.

T.H.M. 250
1. Intermediate servo piston seals damaged or missing.
2. Burned intermediate band.

T.H.M. 350
1. 2-3 accumulator oil ring damaged or missing.

ROUGH 1-2 SHIFT

T.H.M. 250 & 350
1. Vacuum modulator, check for loose fittings, restrictions in line or defective modulator assembly.
2. Modulator valve stuck.
3. Valve body regulator or boost valve stuck.
4. Pump to case gasket mispositioned or damaged.
5. Check case for porosity.
6. Check 1-2 accumulator assembly for damaged oil rings, stuck piston, broken or missing spring, or damaged case bore.

T.H.M. 250
1. Intermediate band improperly adjusted.
2. Improper or broken servo spring.

T.H.M. 350
1. Burned intermediate clutch plates.
2. Improper number of intermediate clutch plates.

SLIPS 2-3 SHIFT

1. Low oil level.
2. Modulator valve or vacuum modulator assembly defective.
3. Pump pressure regulator valve or boost valve; pump to case gasket mispositioned.
4. Check case for porosity.
5. Direct clutch piston seals or ball check leaking.

ROUGH 2-3 SHIFT

1. High oil pressure. Vacuum leak, modulator valve sticking or pressure regulator or boost valve inoperative.
2. 2-3 accumulator piston stuck, spring broken or missing.

NO ENGINE BRAKING IN 2nd SPEED

1. Intermediate servo or 2-3 accumulator oil rings or bores leaking or accumulator piston stuck.
2. Intermediate band burned or broken.
3. Low oil pressure: Pressure regulator and/or boost valve stuck.

NO ENGINE BRAKING IN 1ST SPEED

1. Manual low control valve assembly stuck.
2. Low oil pressure: Pressure regulator and/or boost valve stuck.
3. Low and reverse clutch piston inner seal damaged.

NO PART THROTTLE DOWNSHIFT

1. Oil pressure: Vacuum modulator assembly, modulator valve or pressure regulator valve train malfunctioning.
2. Detent valve and linkage sticking, disconnected or broken.
3. 2-3 shift valve stuck.

NO DETENT DOWNSHIFTS

1. 2-3 valve stuck.
2. Detent valve and linkage sticking, disconnected or broken.

LOW OR HIGH SHIFT POINTS

1. Oil pressure: Check engine vacuum at transmission end of modulator pipe.
2. Vacuum modulator assembly, vacuum line connections at engine and transmission, modulator valve, pressure regulator valve train.
3. Check governor for sticking valve, restricted or leaking feed holes, damaged pipes or plugged feed line.
4. Detent valve stuck open.
5. 1-2 or 2-3 valve train sticking.
6. Check case for porosity.

NO HOLD IN PARK

1. Manual linkage misadjusted.

2. Parking brake lever and actuator assembly defective.
3. Parking pawl broken or inoperative.
4. Defective or improperly installed inner lever and actuating rod assembly.
5. Parking lock bracket loose, burred or rough edges, or improperly installed.
6. Parking pawl disengaging spring missing, broken or installed improperly.

BURNED FORWARD CLUTCH PLATES

1. Check ball in clutch drum damaged, stuck or missing.
2. Clutch piston cracked, seals damaged or missing.
3. Low line pressure.
4. Pump cover oil seal rings missing, broken or undersize; ring groove oversize.
5. Transmission case valve body face not flat or porosity between channels.

BURNED INTERMEDIATE CLUTCH PLATES

T.H.M. 350
1. Intermediate clutch piston seals damaged or missing.
2. Low line pressure.
3. Transmission case valve body face not flat or porosity between channels.

BURNED INTERMEDIATE BAND

T.H.M. 250
1. Intermediate servo piston seals damaged or missing.
2. Low line pressure.
3. Transmission case valve body face not flat or porosity between channels.

BURNED DIRECT CLUTCH PLATES

1. Restricted orifice in vacuum line to modulator.
2. Check ball in clutch drum damaged, stuck or missing.
3. Defective modulator.
4. Clutch piston cracked, seals damaged or missing.
5. Transmission case valve body face not flat or porosity between channels.

NOISY TRANSMISSION

NOTE: Before checking transmission for noise, ensure noise is not coming from water pump, alternator or any belt driven accessory.

Park, Neutral & All Driving Ranges
1. Low fluid level.
2. Plugged or restricted screen.
3. Damaged screen to valve body gasket.
4. Porosity in valve body intake area.
5. Transmission fluid contaminated with water.

6. Porosity at transmission case intake port.
7. Improperly installed case to pump gasket.
8. Pump gears damaged.
9. Driving gear assembled backwards.
10. Crescent interference in pump.
11. Damaged or worn pump oil seals.
12. Loose converter to flywheel bolts.
13. Damaged converter.

1st, 2nd And/Or Reverse Gear
1. Planetary gears or thrust bearings damaged.
2. Damaged input or output ring gear.

Acceleration In Any Gear
1. Transmission case or transmission oil cooler lines contacting underbody.
2. Broken or loose engine mounts.

Squeal At Low Vehicle Speed
1. Speedometer driven gear shaft seal requires lubrication or replacement.

CONVERTER CLUTCH APPLIED IN ALL RANGES, ENGINE STALLS WHEN TRANSMISSION PUT IN GEAR

1. Converter clutch apply valve in auxiliary valve body stuck in apply position.

CONVERTER CLUTCH APPLIES ERRATICALLY

1. Vacuum hose leak.
2. Vacuum switch malfunction.
3. Release oil orifice at pump blocked or restricted.
4. Turbine shaft O-ring damaged or missing.
5. Converter malfunction, clutch pressure plate warped, etc.
6. O-ring at solenoid damaged or missing.
7. Solenoid bolts loose.

CONVERTER CLUTCH APPLIES AT VERY LOW OR VERY HIGH 3RD GEAR SPEEDS

1. Governor switch malfunction.
2. Governor malfunction.
3. High line pressures.
4. Converter clutch valve sticking or binding.
5. Solenoid malfunction.

CONVERTER CLUTCH APPLIED AT ALL TIMES IN 3RD GEAR

1. Governor pressure switch shorted to ground.
2. Ground wire from solenoid shorted to case.

MAINTENANCE

Fluid should be checked every 6,000 miles with engine idling, selector lever in neutral position, parking brake set and transmission at operating temperature. Use only General Motors Dexron transmis-

sion fluid when adding oil. Do not overfill.
Every 100,000 Miles, remove drain plug, then drain transmission oil sump. Add 2½ quarts on vehicles equipped with THM 250 units and 3 quarts on vehicles equipped with THM 350 units. After replacing plug, check fluid and add enough fluid to bring level to ½ inch below Add mark.

NOTE: A revised type Dexron fluid is used in these transmissions. An early change to a darker color from the usual red color and or a strong odor that is usually associated with overheated fluid is normal, and should not be treated as a positive sign of needed maintenance or failure.

The normal maintenance schedule for drain and refill of this type fluid is every 15,000 miles under severe operating conditions, such as trailer towing. Under normal operating conditions, drain and refill every 100, 000 miles.

MANUAL LINKAGE
ADJUST

BUICK

Console Shift, 1980—81 Century, 1980—85 Electra, LeSabre & Regal
1. Place selector lever in Park position.
2. Place transmission lever in Park position.
3. Position pin to obtain a free pin fit in the transmission lever and torque nut to 15–25 ft. lbs.
4. Check for proper operation.

Column Shift 1980—85
1. Loosen adjusting clamp bolt.
2. Place selector lever against Neutral stop.
3. Place transmission in Neutral.
4. Tighten clamp bolt to 17–23 ft. lbs.

CHEVROLET

Console Shift 1980—81 Camaro, Malibu & Monte Carlo
1. Loosen swivel screw so rod is free to move in swivel, Fig. 5.
2. Place transmission control lever in Drive and loosen pin in transmission lever, so it moves in the slot.
3. Move transmission lever counter-clockwise to L1 detent and then three detents clockwise to Drive position. Tighten nut on transmission lever to 20 ft. lbs.
4. Place transmission control lever in Park and ignition switch in the Lock position and pull lightly against lock stop, then tighten swivel screw to 20 ft. lbs. Check for proper operation.

Column Shift, 1980—85 All
1. Place transmission lever in Neutral by moving lever counter-clockwise to L1 detent then clockwise three detent positions to Neutral.
2. Place selector lever in Neutral as determined by mechanical stop on steering column. Do not use indicator as reference.
3. Assemble swivel, spring washer and screw to lever assembly then tighten screw to 20 ft. lbs., **Fig. 6**

Fig. 5 Manual linkage adjustment. Camaro, Malibu & Monte Carlo

Fig. 6   Column shift linkage, 1980—85 intermediates (top) & full size (bottom)

Fig. 7   Self adjusting throttle valve cable

OLDSMOBILE

Console Shift

1. Loosen shift rod clamp screw and pin in transmission manual lever. Place shift handle and transmission manual lever in Park position.
2. With rod held lightly against Park stop, tighten screw in clamp at lower end of shift rod.
3. Move pin to give "free pin" fit in manual lever and tighten nut.

Column Shift

1. Loosen shift rod clamp screw and place outer lever in the Neutral position. Hold column shift lever in Neutral position and tighten clamp. Check operation.

PONTIAC

Console Shift

1. Disconnect shift cable at transmission lever.
2. Adjust back drive, as outlined under "Back Drive, Adjust" procedure.
3. Unlock ignition switch, move transmission lever two detents counterclockwise, then place transmission shift lever against Neutral stop.
4. Assemble cable to transmission lever, torque nut to 20 ft. lbs.

Column Shift

With shift rod clamp and screw loosely assembled to shift rod, set transmission outer lever in Park position. Check to see that steering column lever is in Park position and tighten clamp on shift rod.

BACK DRIVE
ADJUST

1. Disconnect lower rod at transmission lever.
2. Move transmission lever to Park position.
3. Place transmission selector lever in Park position.
4. Attach lower rod to transmission lever and check for proper operation.

NOTE: Any inaccuracies in the above adjustments may result in premature failure of the transmission due to operation without the controls in full detent. Such operation results in reduced oil pressure and in turn partial engagement of the affected clutches.

T.V. OR DETENT CABLE
ADJUST

MODELS EQUIPPED WITH DIESEL ENGINE

1. Remove cruise control rod on vehicles equipped with cruise control.
2. Disconnect throttle valve linkage from throttle assembly.
3. Loosen lock nut on pump rod, then shorten rod by rotating several turns.
4. Rotate throttle lever assembly to full throttle position and secure in this position.
5. Lengthen pump rod by rotating in opposite direction as described in step 3 until injection pump lever contacts full throttle stop.
6. Release throttle lever assembly and tighten pump rod lock nut.
7. Disconnect pump rod from throttle lever assembly.
8. Connect throttle valve linkage to throttle assembly.
9. Depress metal locking tab on upper end of cable and hold in this position.
10. Position slider through fitting and away from lever assembly until slider contacts metal fitting.
11. Release metal tab, then rotate throttle lever assembly to full throttle position and release.
12. Connect pump rod to lever assembly, then connect cruise control throttle rod, if equipped.
13. On models equipped with cruise control, adjust servo throttle rod until minimum amount of slack is present. Install clip into first hole closest to bellcrank that is within servo bail.

MODELS EQUIPPED WITH GASOLINE ENGINE

1. With engine off, depress locking tab and move slider rearward through fitting until slider contacts fitting, **Fig. 7.**
2. Release locking tab, then move carburetor throttle lever to wide open position and release.
3. Check cable for sticking or binding, then test vehicle for proper operation.
4. If transmission does not shift properly, raise and support vehicle and remove transmission oil pan. Inspect throttle lever and bracket assembly on valve body for damage. Check to ensure that throttle valve exhaust valve rod is not worn or damaged. Check to ensure that lifter spring holds lifter rod against bottom of valve body and that throttle valve plunger is not sticking.

INTERMEDIATE BAND
ADJUST

TURBO HYDRA-MATIC 250

Since the Turbo Hydra-Matic 250 transmission uses an intermediate band instead of a clutch (used in the Turbo Hydra-Matic 350 transmission) to control the operation of the planetary gear sets, it is necessary to adjust the intermediate band as follows:

1. Loosen adjusting screw lock nut, located on case right side, ½ turn.
2. Torque adjusting screw to 30 inch pounds, then back off screw 3 turns.
3. Torque adjusting screw lock nut to 15 foot pounds while holding adjusting screw in position.

Fig. 8 Vacuum switch location.

Fig. 9 Auxiliary valve body solenoid

T.H.M. 250C & 350C TORQUE CONVERTER CLUTCH SWITCH ADJUSTMENTS

LOW VACUUM SWITCH

1. Disconnect vacuum and electrical connectors from low vacuum switch, **Fig. 8.**
2. Connect a suitable test light to either terminal of vacuum switch. Connect a suitable jumper cable from the other terminal to a good ground.
3. Connect remaining lead of test light to power side of removed vacuum switch connector.
4. Attach suitable vacuum pump to vacuum port of switch.
5. Turn ignition on, then actuate vacuum pump. On V6-231, 252 engines, test light should remain off until vacuum pump gauge reads 5.5–6.5 in. Hg. On V8-265, 301 engines the test light should remain off until vacuum gauge reads 6.5–7.5 in. Hg. On V8-350 gas engines, test light should remain off until vacuum gauge reads 7.5–8.5 in. Hg. On V8-350 diesel engines, test light should remain off until vacuum gauge reads 5–6 in. Hg.
6. Decrease vacuum slowly. Light should remain on until vacuum drops to .3–1.3 in. Hg. on V6-231, 252 engines, 1.2–2.2 in. Hg. on V8-265, 301 engines, 1.5–2.5 in. Hg. on V8-350 gas engines and 3.5–4.5 in. Hg. on V8-350 diesel engines. Decreasing vacuum beyond above values should cause light to go out.
7. If above results cannot be obtained, switch is defective and must be replaced.
8. The point at which light comes on and the point at which light goes out must have at least 4 in. of vacuum difference.

HIGH VACUUM SWITCH

NOTE: The high vacuum switch must be adjusted anytime the throttle rod, transmission vacuum valve and high idle speed adjustments are changed.

1. Disconnect high vacuum switch electrical connector, **Fig. 8.**
2. Connect the leads of a suitable test light across the terminals of the high vacuum switch.
3. Energize fast idle solenoid by disconnecting pink and green wire from coolant switch and operate engine at high idle speed, then remove cap from back of high vacuum switch.
4. Before adjustment is performed, the test light must be on, indicating that the switch contacts are closed. If test light is off, close the switch contacts by turning switch adjusting screw clockwise until contacts close.
5. Adjust vacuum switch by turning adjusting screw counterclockwise until switch contact just opens and test light goes off. Turn adjusting screw counterclockwise an additional 1/8–3/16 turn.
6. Reinstall cap on back of vacuum switch and reconnect high vacuum switch and coolant switch electrical connectors.

IN-VEHICLE REPAIRS

VALVE BODY ASSEMBLY

Without Locking Clutch

1. Remove oil pan and strainer.
2. Remove retaining pin to disconnect downshift actuating lever bracket, remove valve body attaching bolts and detent roller and spring assembly.
3. Remove valve body assembly while disconnecting manual control valve link from range selector inner lever.

CAUTION: Do not drop valve.

4. Remove manual valve and link from valve body assembly.
5. Reverse procedure to install.

With Locking Clutch

1. Remove oil pan and filter.
2. Remove detent roller spring assembly from valve body, then disconnect solenoid wires from governor pressure switch and case electrical connector.
3. Remove solenoid attaching bolts, then the solenoid.
4. Remove manual shaft retaining clip and slide manual shaft outward.
5. Remove valve body attaching bolts, then the valve body.
6. Remove auxiliary valve body attaching bolts, then the auxiliary valve body from the valve body.
7. Reverse procedure to install.

AUXILIARY VALVE BODY & SOLENOID

1. Remove oil pan and filter.
2. Remove solenoid wire clip, then disconnect solenoid electrical connectors.
3. Remove two solenoid attaching bolts, then the solenoid, **Fig. 9.**
4. Reverse procedure to install.

AUXILIARY VALVE BODY AND VALVE

1. Remove solenoid as outlined above.
2. Remove retaining bolts, then the auxiliary valve body.
3. Remove apply valve retaining pin, retainer, spring, then the apply valve, **Fig. 10.**
4. Reverse procedure to install.

GOVERNOR PRESSURE SWITCH

1. Drain transmission fluid from pan, then remove pan.
2. Disconnect electrical connector from switch, then remove switch using suitable socket.
3. Reverse procedure to install.

Fig. 10 Auxiliary valve body & valve

Fig. 11 Intermediate clutch accumulator piston removal

GOVERNOR

1. Remove governor cover retainer and cover.
2. Remove governor.

INTERMEDIATE CLUTCH ACCUMULATOR PISTON ASSEMBLY

1. Remove two oil pan bolts adjacent to accumulator piston cover, install compressor on pan lip and retain with these two bolts, **Fig. 11.**
2. Compress intermediate clutch accumulator piston cover and remove retaining ring piston cover and O ring from case.
3. Remove spring and intermediate clutch accumulator piston.

VACUUM MODULATOR & MODULATOR VALVE ASSEMBLY

1. Disconnect vacuum hose from modulator stem and remove vacuum modulator screw and retainer.
2. Remove modulator and its O-ring.
3. Remove modulator valve from case.

EXTENSION HOUSING OIL SEAL

1. Remove propeller shaft.
2. Pry out lip seal with screwdriver or small chisel.

MANUAL SHAFT, RANGE SELECTOR INNER LEVER & PARKING LINKAGE ASSEMBLIES

1. Remove oil pan and strainer.
2. Remove manual shaft to case retainer and unthread jam nut holding range selector inner lever to manual shaft.
3. Remove jam nut and remove manual shaft from range selector inner lever and case. Do not remove manual shaft lip seal unless replacement is required.
4. Disconnect parking pawl actuating rod from range selector inner lever and remove bolt from case.
5. Remove bolts and parking lock bracket.

6. Remove pawl disengaging spring.
7. If necessary to replace pawl or shaft, clean up bore in case and remove shaft retaining plug, shaft and pawl.

TRANSMISSION

REPLACE

BUICK

1. Disconnect battery ground cable.
2. Raise car and remove propeller shaft. If necessary, disconnect exhaust crossover pipe. On Turbo 350 units, remove catalytic converter support bracket, if equipped.
3. Place suitable jack under transmission and fasten transmission securely to jack.
4. Remove vacuum line from vacuum modulator.
5. Loosen cooler line nuts and separate cooler lines from transmission.
6. Remove detent cable from accelerator or carburetor lever assembly. Do not bend cable. Remove plastic guide from bracket and slide cable out through slot.
7. Remove detent cable from detent valve link.
8. Remove crossmember.
9. Disconnect speedometer cable, shift linkage and filler pipe. Remove filler pipe.
10. Support engine at oil pan.
11. Remove transmission flywheel cover pan.
12. Mark flywheel and converter for reassembly and remove three flywheel to converter bolts.
13. Be sure transmission is supported by transmission jack and remove transmission case to engine block bolts.
14. Move transmission rearward to provide clearance between converter and crankshaft. Install converter holding tool, lower transmission and remove.

CADILLAC

1. Disconnect negative battery cable and disconnect detent cable at upper end, then remove top two transmission to engine bolts.
2. Raise and support vehicle.

3. Disconnect transmission linkage and remove speedometer drive cable at transmission, then, using suitable tools, disconnect oil cooler lines at transmission and cap lines and plug connector holes. Move oil cooler lines aside.
4. Disconnect vacuum pipe hose from modulator and position out of way, then remove propeller shaft and lower flexplate inspection cover.
5. Remove the three converter to flexplate attaching bolts, rotating converter and flexplate for bolt accessibility. Do not pry on flexplate ring gear or transmission case.
6. Place suitable jack under rear of engine, then remove four bolts from tunnel strap and remove strap.
7. Remove two rear engine mount to extension housing bolts, then position suitable jack under transmission and raise it sufficiently to take load off rear engine support and remove converter bracket.
8. Remove one bolt from strut support to crossmember, then remove two bolts from each side of rear engine support and slide support back out of position. Support will hang from parking brake cable and exhaust pipe.
9. Remove rear engine support crossmember and remove four remaining transmission housing to engine attaching bolts, lowering engine and transmission, if necessary, to gain access.
10. Disengaging transmission case from locating dowels on engine, move transmission toward rear of car.
11. Install converter holding clamp, J-21366, or equivalent, on front of transmission case and lower transmission from car.
12. Reverse procedure to install.

CHEVROLET

1. Disconnect negative battery cable and raise car.
2. Remove propeller shaft, disconnect speedometer cable, detent cable, modulator vacuum line and oil cooler lines. Disconnect catalytic converter support bracket from transmission.
3. Disconnect shift linkage.

4. Support transmission with suitable jack and remove crossmember.
5. Remove converter under pan.
6. Remove converter to flywheel bolts.
7. loosen exhaust pipe to manifold bolts approximately ¼ inch. Lower transmission until jack is barely supporting transmission.

NOTE: On V8 engines, care must be taken not to lower the rear of the transmission too far as the distributor housing may be forced against firewall causing damage to the distributor.

8. Remove transmission to engine mounting bolts and remove oil filler tube at transmission.
9. Raise transmission to its normal position, support engine with jack and slide transmission rearward from engine and lower it away from vehicle.
10. Reverse procedure to install.

OLDSMOBILE

1. Disconnect battery ground cable.
2. Disconnect detent cable from accelerator or carburetor lever assembly.
3. Remove transmission oil level dipstick. Remove catalytic converter support bracket, if equipped.

4. Raise car and remove detent cable from link. Plug hole.
5. Disconnect oil cooler lines at transmission.
6. Remove flywheel cover pan and mark converter and flywheel for reassembly. Remove three flywheel to converter bolts.
7. Disconnect vacuum modulator line. Remove speedometer clip and driven gear. Plug hole.
8. Disconnect shift linkage.
9. Remove propeller shaft.
10. Support transmission with a suitable jack and remove crossmember.
11. Lower transmission slightly and remove transmission to engine bolts.
12. Remove oil level indicator tube and clip holding detent cable to tube.
13. Lower transmission being careful not to damage cooler lines, detent cable, modulator line and shift linkage.
14. Reverse procedure to install.

PONTIAC

1. Disconnect battery ground cable and release parking brake.
2. Raise car and remove propeller shaft. Remove catalytic converter support bracket, if equipped.
3. Disconnect speedometer cable, vacuum hose at modulator, detent cable at

transmission and shift linkage.

NOTE: When removing detent cable, be careful not to bend it.

4. Support transmission with a suitable jack and remove crossmember.
5. Remove converter dust pan, mark flywheel and converter for reassembly and remove flywheel to converter bolts. Make sure converter hub is free of converter.
6. Disconnect transmission filler pipe at engine and remove pipe from transmission.
7. Lower transmission and engine to gain access to cooler line fitting nuts and disconnect cooler lines. On some models it may be necessary to loosen the exhaust system.
8. With transmission in lowered position, remove the transmission to engine bolts.
9. Raise transmission to its normal position, support engine and slide transmission rearward and lower it away from car.

NOTE: When lowering transmission, keep rear of transmission lower than the front so as not to lose the converter.

10. Reverse procedure to install.

Turbo Hydra-Matic 325-4L Automatic Transmission

INDEX

TRANSMISSION IDENTIFICATION

This transmission may be identified by a model tag attached to the transmission on the left side of the converter housing.

ALL
1982   AJ, AL, AM, BJ, OE, OK

ELDORADO, RIVIERA, SEVILLE & TORONADO
1983   AJ, AL, BE, BJ, OE, OK
1984   AE, AJ, AL, BE, BJ, OE, OK, OQ
1985   AB, AE, AJ, AL, BJ, OE, OK, OQ

DESCRIPTION

The Turbo Hydra-Matic 325-4L transmission, **Fig. 1,** is a fully automatic front wheel drive unit consisting of a four-element torque converter with converter clutch, three compound planetary gear sets and an overdrive unit. Five multiple disc clutches, two roller clutches and a band provide the friction elements required to obtain the desired function of the compound planetary gear sets and the overdrive unit. The combination of the compound planetary gear sets and the overdrive unit provides four forward ratios and

one reverse. Changing of the gear ratios is fully automatic in relation to vehicle speed and engine torque.

The torque converter couples the engine to the overdrive unit and planetary gears through oil and hydraulically provides torque multiplication. It consists of a pump or driven member, a turbine or driven member and a stator assembly. With the engine running, the converter pump acts as a centrifugal pump, picking up oil at its center and discharging it at the rim located between the blades. The shape of the converter pump blades causes the oil to leave the pump spinning in a clockwise direction towards the turbine blades. As the oil strikes the turbine blades, it creates a force which enables the turbine to turn. After the oil has imparted its force to the turbine, it follows the contour of the turbine shell and blades and leaves the turbine in a counter-clockwise direction, or opposite engine rotation. If this oil is allowed to enter the inner section of the converter pump, it will hinder the ability of the pump to deliver oil with any force due to the opposing rotation of pump blades to oil flow. To prevent this from happening, a stator assembly is added to redirect the oil returning from the turbine and change its rotation back to that of the converter pump blades. The stator is located between the pump and turbine and is mounted on a one-way roller clutch which allows it to rotate clockwise, but not counterclockwise. The clockwise flow of oil is used to assist the engine in turning the converter pump. This increases the force of the oil driving the turbine and results in the multiplication of torque from the engine. As turbine and vehicle speed increase, the stator becomes inactive and torque multiplication ceases. At this point, the converter is acting as a fluid coupling, since the converter pump and turbine are turning at approximately the same speed.

The converter clutch provides a direct mechanical coupling of the engine to the transmission. This mechanical coupling prevents the slippage that occurs in conventional torque converters and results in improved fuel economy. The application and release of the converter clutch is determined by a series of controls and by drive range selection.

The hydraulic system in this transmission is pressurized by a gear-type pump to provide the working pressures required to operate the friction elements and automatic controls.

Fig. 1 Cross-sectional view of Turbo Hydra-Matic 325-4L transmission

TROUBLESHOOTING

FLUID LEAK

1. Broken sealant bead around bottom pan and sprocket cover.
2. Improperly torqued oil pan attaching bolts.
3. Cracked sprocket cover.
4. Distorted sealing surface.
5. Missing or damaged T.V. cable or filler pipe seal.
6. Interference between T.V. cable and engine mount.
7. Damaged manual shaft seal assembly.
8. Damaged governor cover, servo cover and speedometer gear O-ring seal.
9. Incorrectly torqued or cross threaded pressure taps and cooler line fittings.
10. Damaged case gasket or low attaching bolt torque.
11. Leaking converter welded seam.
12. Damaged square cut pump seal or low pump attaching bolt torque.
13. Improperly seated governor oil cup plug.

FLUID LEAK FROM VENT

1. High fluid level.

2. Blocked drive sprocket support drain holes.
3. Contaminated fluid.
4. Overheating engine.

HIGH OR LOW FLUID PRESSURE

1. Improper fluid level.
2. Broken, disconnected, binding or misadjusted T.V. cable.
3. Misassembled T.V lever and bracket assembly or binding roll pin.
4. Stuck or binding throttle valve and plunger.
5. Stuck, binding or misassembled pressure regulator valve.
6. Stuck, binding or misassembled pressure regulator valve.
7. Stuck, binding or misassembled reverse boot valve and bushing.
8. Stuck, binding or misassembled M.T.V. valve and bushing.
9. Missing pressure relief valve ball or, distorted spring.
10. Stuck or binding T.V. limit or line bias valve.
11. Clogged oil filter, cracked pickup tube or damaged filter O-ring seal.
12. Damaged gears in oil pump assembly.

NO DRIVE IN D

1. Low Fluid Level.
2. Low oil pressure.
3. Misadjusted manual linkage.
4. Broken torque converter stator roller clutch.
5. Damaged overdrive roller clutch springs or rollers.
6. Damaged overdrive carrier assembly pinions, sun gear or internal gear.
7. Damaged oil pump assembly gears.
8. Broken drive link assembly, sprockets or bearings.
9. Damaged forward clutch assembly piston seals, misassembled clutch, cracked piston, damaged input shaft seals, clutch plates, release springs and/or retainer.
10. damaged input and reaction carrier assembly pinions, sun gear or integral gear.
11. Broken forward clutch input shaft.

1ST SPEED ONLY, NO 1-2 SHIFT

1. Binding governor weights, broken or bent springs, blocked valve body spacer plate/gaskets, worn or damaged drive or driven gear, damaged

seals, blocked case passages or damaged governor oil seal.
2. Stuck 1-2 shift, Lo/1st detent or 1-2 throttle valve.
3. Damaged or burned intermediate band, missing anchor band or misassembled band.
4. Short intermediate servo assembly pin, wrong piston/cover combination or damaged seal.
5. Loose 1-2, 3-4 accumulator housing attaching bolts, mispositioned or blocked spacer plate, damaged gasket or porous housing.

1-2 SHIFT AT FULL THROTTLE ONLY

1. Disconnected or misadjusted T.V. cable or bent T.V. link.
2. Misassembled T.V. lever and bracket assembly.
3. Broken or missing T.V. link.
4. Stuck or binding throttle valve or plunger.
5. Mispositioned or blocked spacer plates and gaskets.
6. Low governor pressure.

1ST & 2ND SPEEDS ONLY, NO 2-3 SHIFT

1. Stuck or binding 2-3 shift valve or throttle valve or mispositioned or blocked spacer plate.
2. Porous case or interconnected passages.
3. Unseated #7 pellet and spring in case cover, porosity or interconnected case cover passages, damaged gasket or improperly torqued case cover attaching bolts.
4. Loose driven sprocket support attaching bolts, mispositioned, cut or leaking oil seal rings or damaged sprocket support gasket.
5. Missing or leaking #6 check ball.
6. Misassembled direct clutch assembly, damaged pistons or seals or damaged ball capsule.
7. Worn governor driven gear, unseated check ball, binding weights or damaged springs.

NO REVERSE OR SLIPS IN REVERSE

1. Misadjusted manual link.
2. Damaged Lo and reverse clutch pistons and seals or cup plug and seal.
3. Misassembled direct clutch, damaged piston seals or ball capsule damaged.
4. Binding or stuck reverse boot valve.
5. Leaking reverse oil pipe.
6. Missing or leaking #6 check ball.
7. Missing or leaking #10 check ball.
8. Mispositioned or damaged Spacer plate.
9. Leaking case cover reverse passage.

DRIVE IN NEUTRAL

1. Misadjusted manual linkage.
2. Leak into D4 oil passage.
3. Fused clutch plates or stuck ball capsule.

SLIPPING 1-2 SHIFT

1. Low fluid level.
2. Mispositioned or blocked spacer plate and gaskets.
3. Loose 1-2 accumulator piston housing bolts, porous housing, damaged stuck or binding 1-2 piston or seal.
4. Damaged or burned intermediate band lining.
5. Incorrect intermediate servo apply pin, porosity, damaged piston or seal.
6. Sticking or binding pressure regulator valve.
7. Binding or stuck line bias, throttle valve or plunger.
8. Misadjusted T.V. cable.
9. Leaking case cover 2nd oil passage.

ROUGH 1-2 SHIFT

1. Misadjusted or binding T.V. cable.
2. Binding or stuck throttle valve or plunger, or T.V. limit valve, line bias valve or accumulator.
3. Incorrect intermediate servo apply pin or missing piston bleed orifice.
4. Damaged, binding or stuck 1-2 accumulator piston.
5. Missing or leaking #8 check ball.
6. Missing or blocked servo bleed orifice.

SLIPPING 2-3 SHIFT

1. Low fluid level.
2. Misadjusted T.V. cable.
3. Mispositioned or blocked spacer plate/gaskets.
4. Leaking #7 pellet and spring.
5. Damaged servo piston seal rings.
6. Missing or blocked servo bleed orifice.
7. Leak in 3rd clutch passage.
8. Damaged direct clutch ball capsule, piston, housing and seal, misassembled direct clutch or burned clutch plates.

ROUGH 2-3 SHIFT

1. Misadjusted T.V. cable.
2. Binding or stuck throttle valve or plunger.
3. Binding or stuck T.V. limit or line bias valve.
4. Binding or stuck M.T.V. up valve.

NO 3-4 SHIFT

1. Stuck or binding shift valve or 3-4 throttle valve.
2. Damaged 4th clutch piston or seals, or 4th feed O-ring seal missing or leaking.
3. Leaking 3-4 accumulator circuit.
4. Mispositioned or blocked spacer plate/gaskets.
5. Binding governor weights, broken or bent springs, blocked valve body spacer plate/gaskets, worn or damaged drive or driven gear, damaged seals, blocked case passages or damaged governor oil seal.

SLIPPING 3-4 SHIFT

1. Damaged accumulator housing piston or seal or loose housing bolts.

2. Binding or stuck accumulator valve.
3. Internal leak, damaged 4th clutch piston seal, damaged O-ring, or loose 4th clutch clutch housing bolts.

ROUGH 3-4 SHIFT

1. Misadjusted T.V. cable.
2. Binding or stuck throttle valve or plunger.
3. Damaged or stuck 3-4 accumulator valve or missing or weak spring.

NO CONVERTER CLUTCH APPLY

1. Stuck converter clutch shift valve.
2. Open solenoid.
3. Sticking or binding converter clutch apply valve or spring.
4. Leaking converter clutch signal pipe or plugged screen.
5. Shorted electrical wire or pinched wire.

ROUGH CONVERTER CLUTCH APPLY

1. Plugged converter clutch apply valve bushing orifice.

NO CONVERTER CLUTCH RELEASE

1. Stuck converter clutch apply valve (in apply position).

NO ENGINE BRAKING IN MANUAL RANGES

1. Misadjusted manual linkage.
2. Mispositioned, damaged or plugged spacer plate or gaskets.
3. Binding or stuck 4-3 control valve.
4. Leaking D2 signal pipe.
5. Leaking or missing #3 check ball.
6. Binding or stuck Lo overrun clutch valve.
7. Missing #10 check ball.
8. Missing or leaking #9 check ball.
9. Damaged overrun clutch pistons, seals or clutch plates.
10. Blocked turbine shaft oil passages.

NO PART THROTTLE DOWNSHIFTS

1. Sticking or binding T.V. valve or plunger.
2. Mispositioned or blocked spacer plates or gaskets.
3. Misadjusted T.V. cable.
4. Binding or stuck T.V. modulator downshift valve.

NO HOLD IN PARK

1. Misadjusted manual linkage.
2. Damaged, mispositioned or misassembled internal linkage.

HIGH OR LOW SHIFT POINTS

1. Misadjusted or damaged T.V. cable.
2. Sticking or binding T.V. limit valve.
3. Sticking or binding throttle valve or plunger.

'COLD' READING IS ABOVE 'FULL' MARK

Fig. 2   Transmission oil dipstick level

FLAT FLANGE

R.T.V. Sealant must be around inside of bolt holes.

RAISED RIB

Typical Oil Pan — Cutaway Section

Fig. 4   Raised rib sealing flange

1/16" BEAD R.T.V. SEALANT

DEPRESSED RIBS

These Designs OK for R.T.V. Sealant
Typical Oil Pan — Cutaway Section

Fig. 3   Flat or depressed rib sealing flange

4. Sticking or binding T.V. modulator upshift or downshift valves.
5. Mispositioned or binding spacer plates or gaskets.
6. Unhooked, mispositioned or misassembled T.V. lever and bracket assembly.
7. Damaged or leaking governor assembly or cover.

MAINTENANCE

CHECKING FLUID LEVEL

To check fluid level, drive vehicle at least 15 miles to allow fluid to reach normal operating temperature (190°–200° F). With vehicle on level surface, parking brake applied and engine running at slow idle, move selector lever through each range, then into Park position. The level on the dipstick should be at the Full Hot mark. To bring fluid level from the Add to Full mark requires only one pint of fluid. If vehicle cannot be driven sufficiently to bring fluid to normal operating temperature, the level on the dipstick should be approximately ½ inch above the Full mark with fluid temperature at 65–85° F., **Fig. 2.**

If additional fluid is required, use Dexron II, or equivalent, automatic transmission fluid.

NOTE: The transmission fluid now being used may appear to be darker or have a stronger odor. This is normal and not a positive sign of required transmission maintenance or transmission failure.

CAUTION: An overfilled transmission can cause foaming and loss of fluid through the vent, resulting in slippage and/or transmission failure. A low fluid level can also cause slippage, particularly when the transmission is cold or the vehicle is driven on a steep hill.

Every 100,000 miles, the transmission fluid should be drained, the oil pan removed, the screen cleaned and fresh fluid added. For vehicles subjected to more severe use such as heavy city traffic, where temperatures reach 90° F, or prolonged periods of idle or towing, this maintenance should be performed every 15,000 miles.

CHANGING FLUID

1. Raise and support vehicle, then position drain pan under transmission oil pan.

2. Remove front and side oil pan attaching bolts, then loosen rear bolts approximately four turns.
3. Carefully pry transmission oil pan loose with screwdriver and allow fluid to drain.
4. Remove remaining bolts, pan and gasket.
5. Drain remaining fluid from pan, clean with solvent and dry with compressed air.
6. Remove transmission screen, clean thoroughly with solvent and dry with compressed air.

NOTE: Paper or felt type filters should be replaced.

7. Install new gasket and O-ring onto screen assembly. Lubricate O-ring with petroleum jelly.
8. Install transmission screen, then position new gasket onto pan and install pan. Torque pan attaching bolts to 12 ft. lbs.

NOTE: Some THM 325-4L transmissions may be built using R.T.V. (Room Temperature Vulcanizing) silicone sealant in place of standard gaskets. If oil pan or side cover is equipped with flat or depressed rib flanges, **Fig. 3,** use, a ⅟₁₆ inch bead of R.T.V. sealant to seal surfaces. If pan or side cover is equipped with a raised rib flange, **Fig. 4,** conventional gaskets must be used.

9. Lower vehicle and add approximately 5 qts. of Dexron II type transmission fluid through filler tube.
10. Apply parking brake, start engine and allow to idle. Do not race engine.
11. Move selector lever through each range, then position lever in Park and check fluid level.

IN-VEHICLE ADJUSTMENTS

SHIFT CONTROL CABLE, ADJUST

NOTE: The following procedure applies to all models except Cadillac. For shift control adjustment on Cadillac models, refer to "Manual Linkage, Adjust."

1. Position steering column shift lever in neutral gate notch, then loosen attaching nut at column lever, **Fig. 5.**
2. Set transmission lever in neutral detent, then move pin to give "free pin" fit in column lever and torque attaching nut two to 20 ft. lbs.
3. Check that starter will not crank in any position except Neutral or Park. Adjust neutral start switch, if necessary.

MANUAL LINKAGE, ADJUST

1. Position steering column shift lever in neutral, then place transmission (A) in neutral, **Fig. 6.**
2. Assemble linkage as shown in figure.
3. Hold clamp (B) flush against transmission control equalizer shaft assembly (C), then finger tighten screw (D) against Rod (E).
4. Torque screw to 20 ft. lbs., noting not to exert force in either direction on shafts (E) or (C).

THROTTLE VALVE (T.V.) CABLE, ADJUST

Self-Adjusting Type
1. Depress lock tab, then move slider in direction away from carburetor throttle body, **Fig. 7.**
2. Release lock tab and open carburetor lever to full throttle stop position to automatically adjust T.V. cable.

Manual Type, With Gasoline Engine
1. Pushing upward, unlock T.V. cable snap-lock button, **Fig. 8.**
2. Rotate carburetor lever to wide open throttle position and hold.
3. Pushing downward, lock T.V. cable snap lock-button, then release carburetor throttle lever.

Manual Type, With Diesel Engine
1. Remove cruise control rod from bellcrank, if equipped.
2. Unlock T.V. cable snap-lock button, then disconnect T.V. cable and throttle

Fig. 5   Shift control cable adjustment

Fig. 6   Manual shift linkage adjustment

Fig. 7   Adjusting T.V. cable. Self-adjusting type

rod from bell crank, **Fig. 9.**
3. Rotate bell crank to full throttle stop and hold in this position.
4. Pull throttle rod and pump lever to full throttle stop position, **Fig. 10,** then adjust throttle rod to meet bell crank. Do not connect throttle rod to bell crank at this time.
5. Release bell crank, then reconnect T.V. cable.
6. Rotate and hold bell crank to full throttle stop, then lock T.V. cable snap-lock button.
7. Reconnect throttle and cruise control rods.

NOTE: If bell crank full throttle stop is not obtained when accelerator pedal is com-

pletely depressed, all full throttle adjustments must be made by completely depressing the accelerator pedal instead of rotating the bell crank by hand.

IN-VEHICLE REPAIRS
VALVE BODY, REPLACE

1. Drain transmission fluid and remove oil pan and screen.
2. Remove screw and disconnect T.V. cable from transmission.
3. Remove throttle lever and bracket assembly, then disconnect converter clutch wiring connections.
4. Remove oil transfer pipes and hold-down brackets.
5. Support valve body and remove retaining bolts.
6. Remove valve body, noting location of check ball.

NOTE: If accumulator housing is removed, support spacer plate during removal and note location of check balls in spacer plate and accumulator housing.

7. Reverse procedure to install. Torque valve body retaining bolts to 10 ft. lbs.

NOTE: Intermediate band anchor pin must locate on intermediate band, or damage to transmission may result.

INTERMEDIATE SERVO, REPLACE

1. Install tool No. J-28493 on transmission case and tighten bolt to depress servo cover.
2. Using a small screwdriver, remove servo cover retaining ring, then remove tool.

Fig. 8   Adjusting T.V. cable. Manual type (gasoline engine)

Fig. 9   Disconnecting T.V. cable & throttle rod

Fig. 10   Adjusting throttle rod

3. Remove servo cover, then remove servo piston and band apply pin assembly.
4. Reverse procedure to install.

SPEEDOMETER GEARS, REPLACE

1. Disconnect speedometer cable, then remove driven gear attaching bolt, retainer and driven gear.
2. Remove governor cover attaching screws and governor cover.
3. Remove governor and speedometer drive gear assembly.
4. Remove speedometer drive gear from governor assembly.
5. Reverse procedure to install.

PRESSURE REGULATOR VALVE, REPLACE

1. Drain transmission fluid and remove oil pan and screen.
2. Push in on pressure regulator valve, and compress valve spring with a small screwdriver.
3. Remove retaining ring, then slowly release spring tension and remove pressure regulator valve.

TRANSMISSION
REPLACE

EXC. MODELS WITH TURBOCHARGED ENGINE

1. Disconnect battery ground cable, then the speedometer cable.
2. Remove air cleaner assembly, then disconnect T.V. cable from bellcrank (diesel engine) or carburetor throttle lever (gasoline engine).
3. Support engine with suitable engine holding fixture.
4. Remove top and the two left upper final drive-to-transmission attaching bolts.
5. Remove remaining accessible engine-to-transmission bolts.
6. Raise and support vehicle, then remove starter.
7. Disconnect converter clutch electrical connections from transmission.
8. Disconnect and plug transmission cooler lines, then remove flywheel inspection cover.
9. On vehicles equipped with V-8 engines, disconnect "Y" pipe from left exhaust pipe.
10. Disconnect right exhaust pipe from exhaust manifold.
11. On all gasoline engine equipped vehicles, disconnect catalytic converter hanger bolts.
12. Lower and support exhaust system approximately five inches, then remove crossmember attaching bolts and the crossmember.
13. Position a suitable transmission jack under transmission, then remove the three remaining final drive-to-transmission bolts.
14. Remove torque converter-to-flywheel attaching bolts, then disconnect shift linkage from transmission.
15. Remove final drive-support bracket bolt and the right transmission mount-through, and bracket bolts.
16. Remove left transmission mount-through bolt, then the lower support bracket-to-transmission bolt.
17. Raise transmission about two inches and remove remaining upper bracket-to-transmission bolts and the last engine-to-transmission bolt.
18. Carefully lower transmission while disengaging the final drive.
19. Install torque converter holding fixture and remove transmission from vehicle.
20. Reverse procedure to install. Torque starter mounting bolts to 30 ft. lbs., transmission mount-to-frame nut to 40 ft. lbs., transmission-to-engine attaching bolts to 35 ft. lbs., flywheel-to-converter bolts to 35 ft. lbs., final drive-to-transmission bolts to 30 ft. lbs. and final drive-support bracket bolt to 35 ft. lbs.

MODELS WITH TURBOCHARGED ENGINE

1. Disconnect battery ground cable, then the speedometer cable.
2. Remove heated air pipe.
3. Remove turbocharger assembly, then the four top engine-to-transmission attaching bolts.
4. Remove top final drive-to-transmission bolt and two final drive-to-engine attaching bolts, then loosen retaining bracket at engine.
5. Support engine with a suitable engine holding fixture, then raise and support vehicle.
6. Disconnect shift linkage from transmission.
7. Disconnect and cap transmission cooler lines, then remove remaining final drive-to-transmission bolts.
8. Remove final drive cover, then disconnect right output shaft bearing support from engine.
9. Turn wheels to gain clearance between final drive and steering linkage, then separate final drive from transmission. Support final drive unit.
10. Remove outlet pipe/converter assembly which was disconnected when turbocharger was removed.
11. Remove starter and the two remaining transmission-to-engine attaching bolts.
12. Disconnect converter cover and position aside.
13. Remove flex plate-to-converter attaching bolts, then position transmission jack under transmission.
14. Remove both transmission mount-through bolts, then the right-mount bracket from transmission.
15. Remove left-mount brackets from both frame and transmission by pulling out inner fender liner and removing attaching bolts through access holes in frame.
16. Separate transmission from engine, then carefully lower and remove from vehicle.
17. Reverse procedure to install. Torque starter mounting bolts to 30 ft. lbs., transmission mount-to-frame nut to 40 ft. lbs., transmission-to-engine attaching bolts to 35 ft. lbs., flywheel-to-converter bolts to 35 ft. lbs., final drive-to-transmission bolts to 30ft. lbs. and final drive-support bracket bolt to 35 ft. lbs.

Turbo Hydra-Matic 400 Automatic Transmission

INDEX

TRANSMISSION IDENTIFICATION

An identification plate is attached to the transmission. The plate indicates year of production, code letters, and serial number.

Code

BUICK

1980		
	LeSabre	BB
	Electra	BB, OB

CADILLAC

1980	Fleetwood Coupe, Fleetwood Brougham, DeVille	AB, AD, AE
1981	DeVille & Brougham①③	AE
	DeVille & Brougham②③	AD
	DeVille & Brougham④	AB

OLDSMOBILE

| 1980 | V8-305 98 | OA |
| | V8-350 98 | OB |

①—With 2.28 axle ratio.
②—With 2.73 axle ratio.
③—Except California.
④—California.

GENERAL DESCRIPTION

This transmission, **Fig. 1**, is a fully automatic unit consisting of a three-element hydraulic torque converter and a compound planetary gear set. Three multiple-disc clutches, two one-way clutches, and two bands provide the friction elements required to obtain the desired functions of the planetary gear set.

The torque converter, the multiple-disc clutches and the one-way clutches couple the engine to the planetary gears through oil pressure, providing three forward speeds and reverse. The torque converter, when required, supplements the gears by multiplying engine torque.

TORQUE CONVERTER

The torque converter is of welded construction and is serviced as an assembly. The unit is made up of two vaned sections, or halves, that face each other in an oil-filled housing. The pump half of the converter is connected to the engine and the turbine half is connected to the transmission.

When the engine makes the converter pump revolve, it sends oil against the turbine, making it revolve also. The oil then returns in a circular flow back to the converter pump, continuing this flow as long as the engine is running.

STATOR

The converter also has a smaller vaned section, called a stator, that funnels the oil back to the converter pump through smaller openings, at increased speed. The speeded up oil directs additional force to the engine-driven converter pump, thereby multiplying engine torque. In other words, without the stator, the unit is nothing more than a fluid coupling.

EXTERNAL CONTROLS

The external control connections to the transmission are:
1. Manual linkage to select the desired operating range.
2. Engine vacuum to operate the vacuum modulator unit.
3. An electrical signal to operate an electric detent solenoid.

VACUUM MODULATOR

A vacuum modulator is used to sense engine torque input to the transmission automatically. The vacuum modulator transmits this signal to the pressure regulator, which controls line pressure, so that all torque requirements of the transmission are met and proper shift spacing is obtained at all throttle openings.

DETENT SOLENOID

The detent solenoid is activated by an electric switch at the carburetor. When the throttle is opened sufficiently to close this switch, the solenoid in the transmission is activated, causing a downshift at speeds below 70 mph. At lower speeds, downshifts will occur at lesser throttle openings without use of the electric switch.

TROUBLESHOOTING GUIDE

OIL PRESSURE HIGH OR LOW

1. Vacuum line or fittings clogged or leaking.
2. Vacuum modulator.
3. Modulator valve.
4. Pressure regulator.
5. Oil pump.
6. Governor.

NO DRIVE IN DRIVE RANGE

1. Low oil level (check for leaks).
2. Manual control linkage not adjusted properly.
3. Low oil pressure. Check for blocked strainer, defective pressure regulator, pump assembly or pump drive gear. See that tangs have not been damaged by converter.
4. Check control valve assembly to see if manual valve has been disconnected from manual lever pin.
5. Forward clutch may be struck or damaged. Check pump feed circuits to forward clutch including clutch drum ball check.
6. Sprag or roller clutch assembled incorrectly.

1-2 SHIFT AT FULL THROTTLE ONLY

1. Detent switch may be sticking or defective.
2. Detent solenoid may be stuck open, loose or have leaking gasket.
3. Control valve assembly may be leaking, damaged or incorrectly installed.
4. Porous transmission case.

CONVERTER PUMP
STATOR SHAFT
FORWARD CLUTCH
PUMP ASSEMBLY
DIRECT CLUTCH
INTERMEDIATE CLUTCH
FRONT BAND
OUTPUT SHAFT
INTERMEDIATE SPRAG
REAR BAND
ROLLER CLUTCH
SPEEDOMETER DRIVE GEAR
SPEEDOMETER DRIVEN GEAR
SUN GEAR
PLANET PINIONS
SUN GEAR SHAFT
MAINSHAFT
FILTER ASSEMBLY
VALVE BODY ASSEMBLY
MANUAL SHAFT
STATOR ASSEMBLY
TURBINE
STATOR ROLLER CLUTCH
TURBINE SHAFT

Fig. 1   Cutaway view of transmission assembly

1ST SPEED ONLY—NO 1-2 SHIFT

1. Governor valve may be sticking.
2. Driven gear in governor assembly loose, worn or damaged.
3. The 1-2 shift valve in control valve assembly stuck closed. Check governor feed channels for blocks, leaks, and position. Also check control valve body gaskets for leaks and damage.
4. Intermediate clutch plug in case may be leaking or blown out.
5. Check for porosity between channels and for blocked governor feed channels in case.
6. Check intermediate clutch for proper operation.

NO 2-3 SHIFT—1ST & 2ND ONLY

1. Detent solenoid may be stuck open.
2. Detent switch may not be properly adjusted.
3. Control valve assembly may be stuck, leaking, damaged, or incorrectly installed.
4. Check direct clutch case center support for broken, leaking or missing oil rings.

5. Check clutch piston seals and piston ball check in clutch assembly.

MOVES FORWARD IN NEUTRAL

1. Manual control linkage improperly adjusted.
2. Forward clutch does not release.
3. Oil pump.
4. Internal linkage.

NO DRIVE IN REVERSE OR SLIPS IN REVERSE

1. Check oil level.
2. Manual control linkage improperly adjusted.
3. Vacuum modulator assembly may be defective.
4. Vacuum modulator valve sticking.
5. Strainer may be restricted or leaking at intake.
6. Regulator or boost valve in pump assembly may be sticking.
7. Control valve assembly may be stuck, leaking or damaged.
8. Rear servo and accumulator may have damaged or missing servo piston seal ring.

9. Reverse band burned out or damaged. Determine that apply pin or anchor pins engage properly.
10. Direct clutch may be damaged or may have stuck ball check in piston.
11. Forward clutch does not release.
12. Low-reverse ball check missing from case.

SLIPS IN ALL RANGES & ON STARTS

1. Check oil level.
2. Vacuum modulator defective.
3. Modulator valve sticking.
4. Strainer assembly plugged or leaking at neck.
5. Pump assembly regulator or boost valve sticking.
6. Leaks from damaged gaskets or cross leaks from porosity of case.
7. Forward and direct clutches burned.

SLIPS 1-2 SHIFT

1. Incorrect oil level.
2. Vacuum modulator valve sticking.
3. Vacuum modulator defective.
4. Pump pressure regulator valve defective.

5. Porosity between channels in case.
6. Control valve assembly.
7. Pump-to-case gasket may be mispositioned.
8. Intermediate clutch plug in case may be missing or leaking excessively.
9. Intermediate clutch piston seal missing or damaged.
10. Intermediate clutch plates burned.
11. Front or rear accumulator oil ring may be damaged.

SLIPS 2-3 SHIFT

1. Items 1 through 6 under Slips 1-2 Shift will also cause 2-3 shift slips.
2. Direct clutch plates burned.
3. Oil seal rings on direct clutch may be damaged permitting excessive leaking between tower and bushing.

ROUGH 1-2 SHIFT

1. Modulator valve sticking.
2. Modulator assembly defective.
3. Pump pressure regulator or boost valve stuck or inoperative.
4. Control valve assembly loosened from case, damaged or mounted with wrong gaskets.
5. Intermediate clutch ball missing or not sealing.
6. Porosity between channels in case.
7. Rear servo accumulator assembly may have oil rings damaged, stuck piston, broken or missing spring or damaged bore.

ROUGH 2-3 SHIFT

1. Items 1, 2 and 3 under Rough 1-2 Shift will also cause rough 2-3 shift.
2. Front servo accumulator spring broken or missing. Accumulator piston may be sticking.

NO ENGINE BRAKING IN 2ND SPEED

1. Front servo or accumulator oil rings may be leaking.
2. Front band may be broken or burned out.
3. Front bank not engaged on anchor pin and/or servo pin.

NO ENGINE BRAKING IN LO RANGE

1. Low-reverse check ball may be missing from control valve assembly.
2. Rear servo may have damaged oil seal ring, bore or piston.
3. Rear servo apply pressure, leaking.
4. Rear band broken, burned out or not engaged on anchor pins or servo pin.

NO PART THROTTLE DOWNSHIFTS

1. Vacuum modulator assembly.
2. Modulator valve.
3. Regulator valve train.
4. Control valve assembly has stuck 3-2 valve or broken spring.

NO DETENT DOWNSHIFTS

1. Detent switch needs fuse, connections tightened or adjustment.
2. Detent solenoid may be inoperative.
3. Detent valve train in control valve assembly malfunctioning.

LOW OR HIGH SHIFT POINTS

1. Oil pressure. Check vacuum modulator assembly, vacuum line connections, modulator valve, and pressure regulator valve train.
2. Governor may have sticking valve or feed holes that are leaking, plugged or damaged.
3. Detent solenoid may be stuck open or loose.
4. Control valve assembly. Check detent, 3-2, and 1-2 shift valve trains, and check spacer plate gaskets for positioning.
5. Check case for porosity, missing or leaking intermediate plug.

NO HOLD IN PARK

1. Manual control linkage improperly adjusted.
2. Internal linkage defective; check for chamfer on actuator rod sleeve.
3. Parking pawl broken or inoperative

NOISY TRANSMISSION

1. Pump noises caused by high or low oil level.
2. Cavitation due to plugged strainer, porosity in intake circuit or water in oil.
3. Pump gears may be damaged.
4. Gear noise in low gear of Drive Range.
5. Transmission contacting body.
6. Defective planetary gear set.
7. Clutch noises during application can be worn or burned clutch plates.

FORWARD CLUTCH PLATES BURNED

1. Check ball in clutch housing damaged, stuck or missing.
2. Clutch piston cracked, seals damaged or missing.
3. Low line pressure.
4. Manual valve mispositioned.
5. Restricted oil feed to forward clutch.
6. Pump cover oil seal rings missing, broken or undersize; ring groove oversize.
7. Case valve body face not flat or porosity between channels.
8. Manual valve bent and center land not properly ground.

INTERMEDIATE CLUTCH PLATES BURNED

1. Constant bleed orifice in center support missing.
2. Rear accumulator piston oil ring damaged or missing.
3. 1-2 accumulator tralve stuck in control valve assembly.
4. Intermediate clutch piston seal damaged or missing.
5. Center support bolt loose.
6. Low line pressure.
7. Intermediate clutch plug in case missing.
8. Case valve body face not flat or porosity between channels.
9. Manual valve bent and center land not ground properly.

DIRECT CLUTCH PLATES BURNED

1. Restricted orifice in vacuum line to modulator.
2. Check ball in direct clutch piston damaged, stuck or missing.
3. Defective modulator bellows.
4. Center support bolt loose.
5. Center support oil rings or grooves damaged or missing.
6. Clutch piston seals damaged or missing.
7. Front and rear servo pistons and seals damaged.
8. Manual valve bent and center land not cleaned up.
9. Case valve body face not flat or porosity between channels.
10. Intermediate sprag clutch installed backwards.
11. 3-2 valve, 3-2 spring or 3-2 spacer pin installed in wrong location in 3-2 valve bore.

MAINTENANCE
CHECKING & ADDING FLUID

Fluid level should be checked at every engine oil change. The full ("F") and "ADD" marks on the transmission dipstick are one pint apart and determine the correct fluid level at normal operating temperature (170° F.). Careful attention to transmission oil temperature is necessary as proper fluid level at low operating temperatures will be below the "ADD" mark on the dipstick. Proper fluid level at higher operating temperatures will rise above the "F" mark.

Fluid level must always be checked with the car on a level surface, and with the engine running to make certain the converter is full. To determine proper fluid level, proceed as follows:

1. Operate engine at a fast idle for about 1½ minutes with selector lever in park ("P") position.
2. Reduce engine speed to slow idle and check fluid level.
3. With engine running add Dexron fluid as required.

NOTE: Cadillac uses an extended-life Dexron transmission fluid. With this new fluid, strainer replacement and fluid change is now recommended at 100,000 miles under normal operating conditions and 50,000 miles under severe or abnormal service such as trailer towing.

This recommendation applies only to the improved fluid and its availability for service. If the new fluid is not available, the former fluid can be used but then the 24,000 mile maintenance rule will apply. Buick and Oldsmobile models: a revised

AUTOMATIC TRANSMISSIONS/TRANSAXLES

type Dexron fluid is used in these transmissions. An early change to a darker color from the usual red color and or a strong odor that is usually associated with overheated fluid is normal, and should not be treated as a positive sign of needed maintenance or unit failure.

The normal maintenance schedule for drain and refill of this type fluid remains unchanged at 24,000 miles under normal service and 12,000 miles under severe operating conditions, such as trailer towing.

CAUTION: Do not overfill as foaming might occur when the fluid heats up. If fluid level is too low, especially when cold, complete loss of drive may result after quick stops. Extremely low fluid level will result in damage to transmission.

DRAINING BOTTOM PAN ONLY

1. Disconnect filler tube at bottom pan and allow fluid to drain. Remove and discard filler tube O-ring.
2. Use a new O-ring on filler tube and install tube on pan.
3. Lower car and add three quarts of Dexron transmission fluid through filler tube when replacing intake pipe and strainer assembly. When just draining bottom pan, add only two quarts.
4. Operate engine at a fast idle for about 1½ minutes with selector lever in park ("P") position.
5. Reduce engine speed to slow idle and check fluid level. Then add fluid as required to bring it to the proper level.

ADDING FLUID TO FILL DRY TRANSMISSION AND CONVERTER

1. Add seven quarts of fluid through filler tube.
2. Operate engine at a fast idle for about 1½ minutes with selector lever in park ("P") position.
3. Reduce engine speed to slow idle and add three more quarts of fluid.
4. Check fluid level and add as required to bring it to the proper level.

BACK DRIVE LINKAGE
ADJUST

Adjust back drive at trunnion so that:
1. Transmission is in full detent in each selector position.
2. With key in Run position and transmission in Reverse, key cannot be removed and steering wheel is not locked.
3. With key in Lock position and transmission in Park, key can be removed and steering wheel is locked.

MANUAL LINKAGE
ADJUST

BUICK COLUMN SHIFT

1. Loosen shift rod adjusting clamp

Fig. 2   Manual linkage adjustment. 1980–81 Cadillac except Seville

bolts.
2. Place selector lever against Neutral stop.
3. Place transmission lever in Neutral.
4. Tighten clamp bolt to 17–23 ft. lbs.

BUICK CONSOLE SHIFT

1. Place selector lever and transmission lever in Park position.
2. Position pin to obtain "Free pin" fit in transmission lever and torque nut to

15–25 ft. lbs.
3. Adjust back drive as outlined previously.

CADILLAC

1. Loosen nut or screw on shift rod trunnion, **Fig. 2.**
2. Pull trunnion lever upward to Park position, then downward to the third (Neutral) step.
3. Place steering column selector lever

Fig. 3   Shift linkage adjustment. Oldsmobile full size (typical)

Fig. 4 Shift linkage. Oldsmobile intermediates (typical)

Fig. 5 Detent switch adjustment. 1980—81 Cadillac

in Neutral position.

4. Tighten the shift rod trunnion nut or screw.
5. Check for proper operation.

OLDSMOBILE

Column Shift

1. Loosen shift rod clamp bolt and place transmission outer lever in Neutral position, **Figs. 3 and 4.**
2. Push on shift rod until selector lever is against Neutral position stop in upper steering column.
3. Tighten bolt in clamp on lower end of shift rod to 20 ft. lbs.
4. Check for proper operation.

DOWNSHIFT SWITCHES

BUICK

Push switch lever all the way towards dash. Final adjustment is made automatically the first time accelerator pedal is depressed to floor.

CADILLAC

1. Remove air cleaner.
2. Make certain carburetor is adjusted to specification and that linkage is at low speed idle setting.
3. Loosen two mounting screws and insert a #42 drill through calibrating hole below lower wire terminal extending through to carburetor side of switch, **Fig. 5.** Adjust position of switch so that lever just touches the carburetor adapter plate arm.

4. Tighten mounting screws and remove drill.
5. Install air cleaner.

OLDSMOBILE

1. Push plunger of switch forward until flush with switch housing.
2. Push accelerator pedal to wide open position to set switch.
3. Energizing of switch can be checked with a test light.

IN CAR REPAIRS

Services outlined in this section can be performed without removing the transmission from the vehicle.

PRESSURE REGULATOR VALVE

NOTE: A solid type pressure regulator valve must be used only in a pump cover with a "Squared Off" (machined) pressure regulator boss, **Fig. 6.** A pressure regulator valve with oil holes and an orifice cup plug may be used with either type pump.

1. Remove bottom pan and strainer.
2. Using a screwdriver or steel rod, compress regulator boost valve bushing against pressure regulator spring, **Fig. 7.**

CAUTION: Pressure regulator spring is under extreme pressure and will force valve bushing out of bore when snap ring is removed if valve bushing is not held securely.

3. Continue to exert pressure on valve bushing and remove snap ring. Gradually release pressure on valve bushing until spring force is exhausted.
4. Carefully remove regulator boose valve bushing and valve, and pressure regulator spring. Be careful not to drop parts as they will fall out if they are not held.
5. Remove pressure regulator valve and spring retainer. Remove spacers if present.
6. Reverse procedure to install.

CONTROL VALVE BODY

1. Remove bottom pan and strainer.
2. Disconnect pressure switch lead wire.
3. Remove control valve body attaching screws and detent roller spring assembly. Do not remove solenoid attaching screws.
4. Remove control valve body and governor pipes. If care is used in removing control valve body, the six check balls will stay in place above spacer plate.
5. Remove governor pipes and manual valve from control valve body.
6. Reverse procedure to install.

GOVERNOR

1. Remove governor cover and discard gasket.
2. Withdraw governor from case.
3. Reverse procedure to install, using a new gasket.

MODULATOR & MODULATOR VALVE

1. Remove modulator attaching screw and retainer.
2. Remove modulator assembly from case and discard O-ring seal.
3. Remove modulator valve from case.
4. Reverse procedure to install, using a new O-ring seal.

AUTOMATIC TRANSMISSIONS/TRANSAXLES

Fig. 6   Pressure regulator identification

PUMP COVER

FOR IDENTIFICATION - SQUARED OFF PRESSURE REG. BOSS.

Fig. 7   Removing and installing pressure regulator valve

SNAP RING PLIERS J-5403

BUSHING
SNAP RING
STEEL ROD

sion.
6. Remove transmission crossmember.
7. Remove detent electrical connector from transmission case.
8. Disconnect speedometer cable.
9. Disconnect shift linkage from transmission.
10. Remove transmission filler pipe.
11. Support engine at oil pan.
12. Remove flywheel cover pan.
13. Mark flywheel and converter pump for reassembly in same position, then remove three converter pump-to-flywheel bolts.
14. Remove transmission-to-engine bolts.
15. Move transmission rearward to provide clearance between converter pump and crankshaft. Install a suitable holding tool to secure converter. Then lower and remove transmission.
16. Reverse above procedure to install.

PARKING LINKAGE

1. Remove bottom pan and oil strainer.
2. Unthread jam nut holding detent lever to manual shaft.
3. Remove manual shaft retaining pin from case.
4. Remove manual shaft and jam nut from case.
5. Remove O-ring seal from manual shaft.
6. Remove parking actuator rod and detent lever assembly.
7. Remove parking pawl bracket, pawl return spring and pawl shaft retainer.
8. Remove parking pawl shaft, O-ring seal and parking pawl.
9. Reverse procedure to install, using new seals and gasket.

REAR SEAL

1. Remove propeller shaft.
2. Pry out seal with screwdriver.
3. Install new seal with a suitable seal driver.
4. Install propeller shaft.

TRANSMISSION
REPLACE

BUICK

1. Raise and support front and rear of car. Remove propeller shaft.
2. Disconnect exhaust crossover pipe, if necessary.
3. Place suitable jack under transmission.
4. Remove vacuum line from vacuum modulator.
5. Separate cooler lines from transmis-

CADILLAC

1. Disconnect battery ground cable and raise vehicle.
2. Disconnect transmission shift linkage, speedometer cable, downshift connector, and the Track Master electrical connector, if equipped.
3. Disconnect and plug oil cooler lines from transmission and position aside. Also, plug transmission ports.
4. Disconnect vacuum line from vacuum modulator and position aside.
5. Remove propeller shaft.
6. Remove lower flywheel housing cover and the three converter to flywheel attaching bolts.

NOTE: This is accomplished by inserting a heavy screwdriver in open slot under one of the converter weld nuts and rotating the converter with a 1¼ inch deep socket until the bolts are accessible. Do not pry on ring gear or transmission case to rotate converter as damage may result.

7. Support rear of engine with a suitable jack.
8. Remove two nuts from tunnel strap, then the strap.
9. Remove two rear engine mounts to extension housing screws.
10. Support transmission with a suitable jack and raise transmission slightly, releasing load from rear engine support crossmember, and remove shim.
11. Remove rear engine support crossmember bolts, then the space from crossmember right side.
12. Disconnect exhaust pipe from manifold and remove rear engine support crossmember.
13. Remove engine to transmission bolts.

NOTE: It may be necessary to slightly lower the engine and transmission to gain access to the upper attaching bolts.

14. Move transmission rearward, disengaging transmission case from engine locating dowels, and install a suitable converter holding tool.
15. Lower transmission from vehicle.
16. Reverse procedure to install. Torque engine to transmission case bolts to 35 ft. lbs. and the converter to flywheel bolts to 30 ft. lbs.

OLDSMOBILE

1. Remove flywheel cover and torque converter attaching bolts.
2. Mark flywheel and converter so they can be installed in same position.
3. Support engine at rear.
4. Disconnect solenoid wires and manual shift linkage at side of transmission.
5. Disconnect oil cooler lines, vacuum modulator line and oil filler pipe.
6. Disconnect parking brake cable.
7. Before removing propeller shaft, scribe marks on drive shaft and companion flange for correct assembly.
8. Disconnect exhaust pipe bracket from rear of crossmember and catalytic converter support bracket from transmission, if necessary.
9. Support transmission, then remove crossmember.
10. Unfasten transmission from engine.
11. Move transmission away from engine, then, before removing transmission, fasten a suitable piece of strap iron to housing to prevent converter from falling out as transmission is removed.

GM Front Wheel Drive Turbo Hydra-Matic 325 Automatic Transmission

INDEX

Fig. 1 Sectional view of Turbo Hydra-Matic 325 automatic transmission

TRANSMISSION IDENTIFICATION

This transmission may be identified by the following codes located on the serial number plate attached to the left side of the converter housing.

BUICK

	Code
1980 Riviera	BJ, OJ, OK, OL, OM
1981 Riviera V6-231	BJ
Riviera V6-252	BE
Riviera V8-307	OH
Riviera V8-350 Diesel	OK

CADILLAC

1980 Eldorado & Seville	AF, AJ, AK
1981 Eldorado & Seville	AG, OK

OLDSMOBILE

1980 Toronado V8-305	OH
Toronado V8-350①	OJ
Toronado V8-350②	OK
1981 Toronado V6-252	BE
Toronado V8-307	OH
Toronado V8-350 Diesel	OK

①—Except diesel engine.
②—Diesel engine.

GENERAL DESCRIPTION

This transmission is a fully automatic front wheel drive unit consisting primarily of a three-element hydraulic torque converter and a compound planetary gear set, **Fig. 1.** Three multiple disc clutches, a roller clutch and a band provide the friction elements required to obtain the desired function of the compound planetary gear set. The compound planetary gear set provides three forward speeds and reverse.

The torque converter couples the engine to the planetary gears through oil and provides torque multiplication. It consists of a pump or driving member, a turbine or driven member and a stator assembly. The stator is mounted on a one-way roller clutch which allows the stator to turn clockwise but not counterclockwise.

The torque converter housing is filled with oil and rotates at engine speed. The converter pump is an integral part of the converter housing, therefore the pump blades rotating at engine speed set the oil within the converter into motion and direct it to the turbine causing the turbine to rotate. As the oil passes through the turbine it travels in such a direction that if it were not redirected by the stator it would strike the rear of the converter pump blades and impede its pumping action. Therefore at low turbine speeds, the oil is redirected by the stator to the converter pump in such a manner that it actually assists the converter pump to deliver power or multiply engine torque. As turbine speed increases, the direction of the oil leaving the turbine changes and flows against the rear side of the stator vanes in a clockwise direction. Since the stator is now impeding the smooth flow of oil, its roller clutch releases and it revolves freely on its shaft. Once the stator becomes inactive, there is no further multiplication of torque within the converter. At this point the converter is acting as a fluid coupling since the converter pump and turbine are being driven at about the same speed, or at a one-to-one ratio.

The hydraulic system in this transmission is pressurized by a gear type pump to provide the working pressures required to operate the friction elements and automatic controls.

TROUBLESHOOTING

Refer to **Figs. 2 through 9** for transmission trouble. Also, refer to the following for causes of low oil pressure, high oil pressure, burned direct clutch, burned forward clutch, burned low-reverse clutch and burned intermediate band.

CAUSES OF LOW OIL PRESSURE

1. Low oil level.
2. Throttle valve system (pressure low in neutral and drive, low to normal in intermediate and reverse):
   a. Throttle valve cable sticking or incorrectly adjusted.
   b. Incorrect cable or link being used.
   c. Throttle valve stuck.
   d. Throttle valve shift valve stuck.
3. Clogged oil screen or O-ring seal missing, leaking or damaged.
4. Control valve assembly bolts loose.
5. Pressure regulator stuck or wrong size.
6. Control valve assembly:
   a. Check balls no. 1 and/or no. 3 missing or out of place.
   b. Control valves stuck.
   c. 1-2 accumulator piston missing, seal damaged, leaking or missing.
   d. Internal leaks.
7. Damaged pump gears.
8. Line boost passage blocked.
9. Lo-Reverse clutch housing to case

seal cup plug leaking (low oil pressure in reverse).

CAUSES OF HIGH OIL PRESSURE

1. Throttle valve system (pressure high in neutral and drive, normal to high in intermediate and reverse):
   a. Throttle valve cable misadjusted or sticking.
   b. Incorrect link or cable being used.
   c. Throttle valve stuck.
   d. Throttle valve shift valve stuck.
2. Pressure regulator valve stuck or wrong size.
3. Control valve assembly valves stuck.
4. Reverse boost orifice in spacer plate plugged (high pressure in reverse only).
5. Line pressure control orifice in pump cover restricted or not drilled.
6. Internal pump or case leaks.

CAUSES OF BURNED DIRECT CLUTCH

1. Case and cover assembly:
   a. Leaking or damaged seal rings on drive sprocket support.
   b. Driven sprocket support sleeve loose or mispositioned.
   c. Cup plug leaking or missing.
   d. No. 6 check ball missing or mispositioned.
   e. Low oil pressure. Refer to "Causes of Low Oil Pressure."
   f. Channels blocked or interconnected.
   g. No. 7 check ball missing from case cover.
2. Direct clutch assembly:
   a. Seals cut, missing or rolled out of groove.
   b. Apply ring missing, incorrect apply ring, or incorrect number of clutch plates used.
   c. Exhaust ball capsule in piston or housing damaged and not sealing. Refer to "Causes of Low Oil Pressure".
   d. Spring guide located over check ball preventing ball from seating.
3. Intermediate servo assembly:
   a. Incorrect servo piston or cover used.
   b. Servo bore scored or damaged.
   c. Servo orifice bleed plug missing.
4. Control valve assembly:
   a. Control valve assembly to case bolts loose.
   b. Sealing surface on control valve assembly, spacer place, case and/ or gasket damaged and leaking.
   c. Porosity in control valve assembly and/or case channels.

CAUSES OF BURNED FORWARD CLUTCH

1. Case and case cover assembly:
   a. Pump to case cover face damaged.
   b. Leaking or damaged seal rings on driven sprocket support.
   c. Driven sprocket support sleeve loose or mispositioned.
   d. Cup plugs leaking or missing.

   e. No. 6 check ball missing or mispositioned.
   f. Low oil pressure. Refer to "Causes of Low Oil Pressure."
   g. Channels blocked or interconnected.
2. Forward clutch assembly:
   a. Seal rings on input shaft damaged or missing.
   b. Cup plug in input shaft damaged or missing.
   c. Input shaft feed passage or orifice restricted.
   d. Housing exhaust ball capsule damaged or missing.
   e. Input shaft passages interconnected.
   f. Housing or shaft seal surface damaged.
   g. Piston seals missing or damaged.
   h. Apply ring missing, wrong apply ring or incorrect number of clutch plates used.
   i. Piston damaged or leaking.
3. Control valve assembly and case:
   a. Control valve assembly to case bolts loose.
   b. Sealing surface on control valve assembly, spacer plate, case or gaskets damaged or leaking.
   c. Porosity between channels in control valve or case.

CAUSES OF BURNED LO-REVERSE CLUTCH

1. Pump assembly:
   a. Leaking seal rings on drive sprocket support.
   b. Driven sprocket sleeve loose or mispositioned.
   c. Cup plug leaking or missing.
   d. No. 6 check ball missing or mispositioned in case.
   e. Reverse feed passage restricted or leaking.
   f. Low oil pressure. Refer to "Causes of Low Oil Pressure".
2. Lo-reverse clutch assembly:
   a. Housing seal area damaged.
   b. Piston or seals damaged.
   c. Apply ring missing, wrong apply ring used, or incorrect number of clutch plates used.
3. Control valve assembly:
   a. Reverse boost valve sticking.
   b. Check balls missing or mispositioned.
4. Case assembly;
   a. Lo-reverse clutch housing to case plug assembly hole restricted, damaged or not seated properly.

CAUSES OF BURNED INTERMEDIATE BAND

1. Band anchor pin missing or not engaged in band.
2. Band not properly aligned or apply pin not engaged.
3. Intermediate servo assembly:
   a. Incorrect size piston or cover.
   b. Seals missing or damaged.
   c. Incorrect band apply pin.
4. Leak in clutch apply system.
5. Control valve assembly:
   a. 1-2 accumulator piston missing or seal leaking.

Fig. 2   THM 325 Trouble-shooting chart, Part 1 of 8

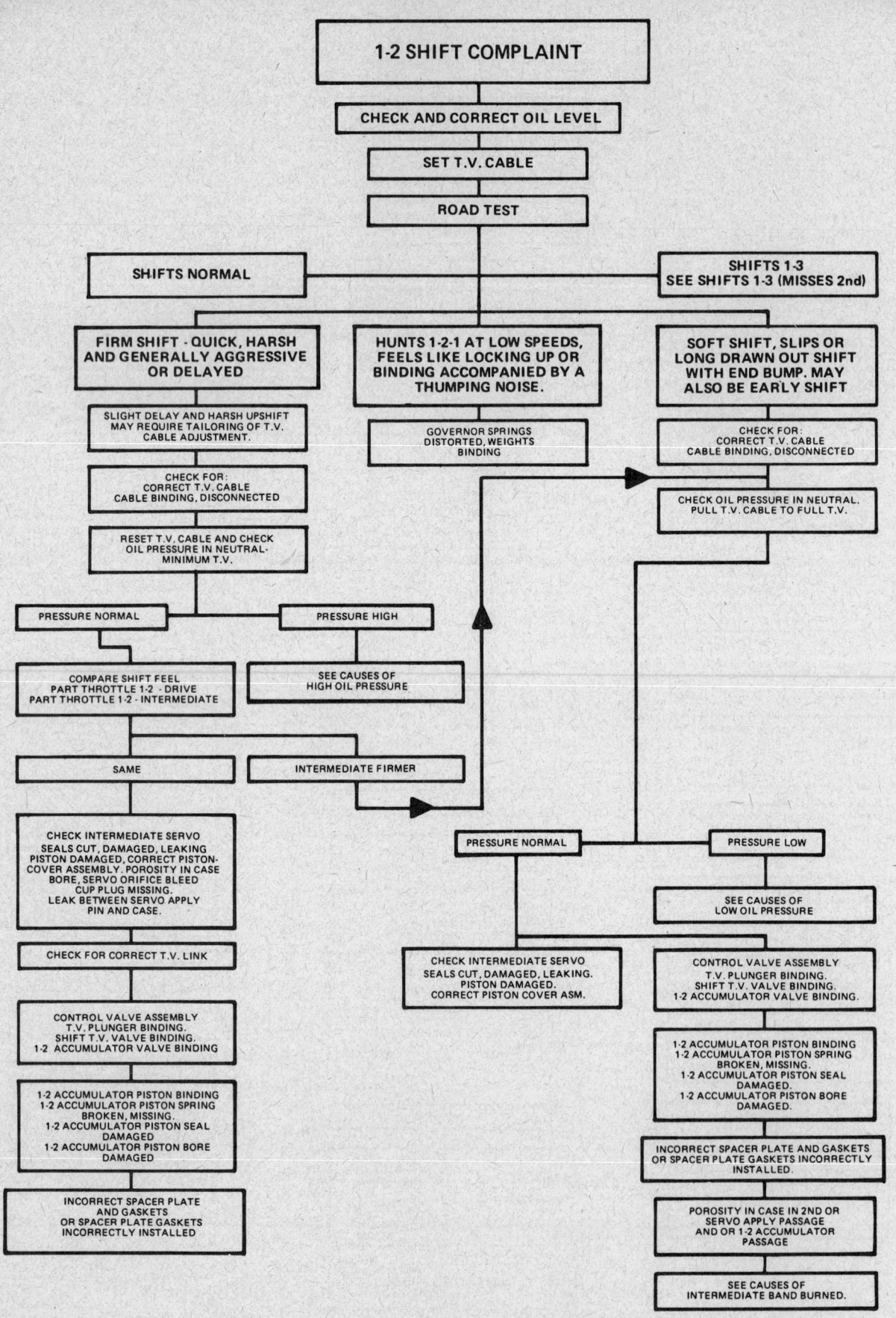

Fig. 3   THM 325 Trouble-shooting chart, Part 2 of 8

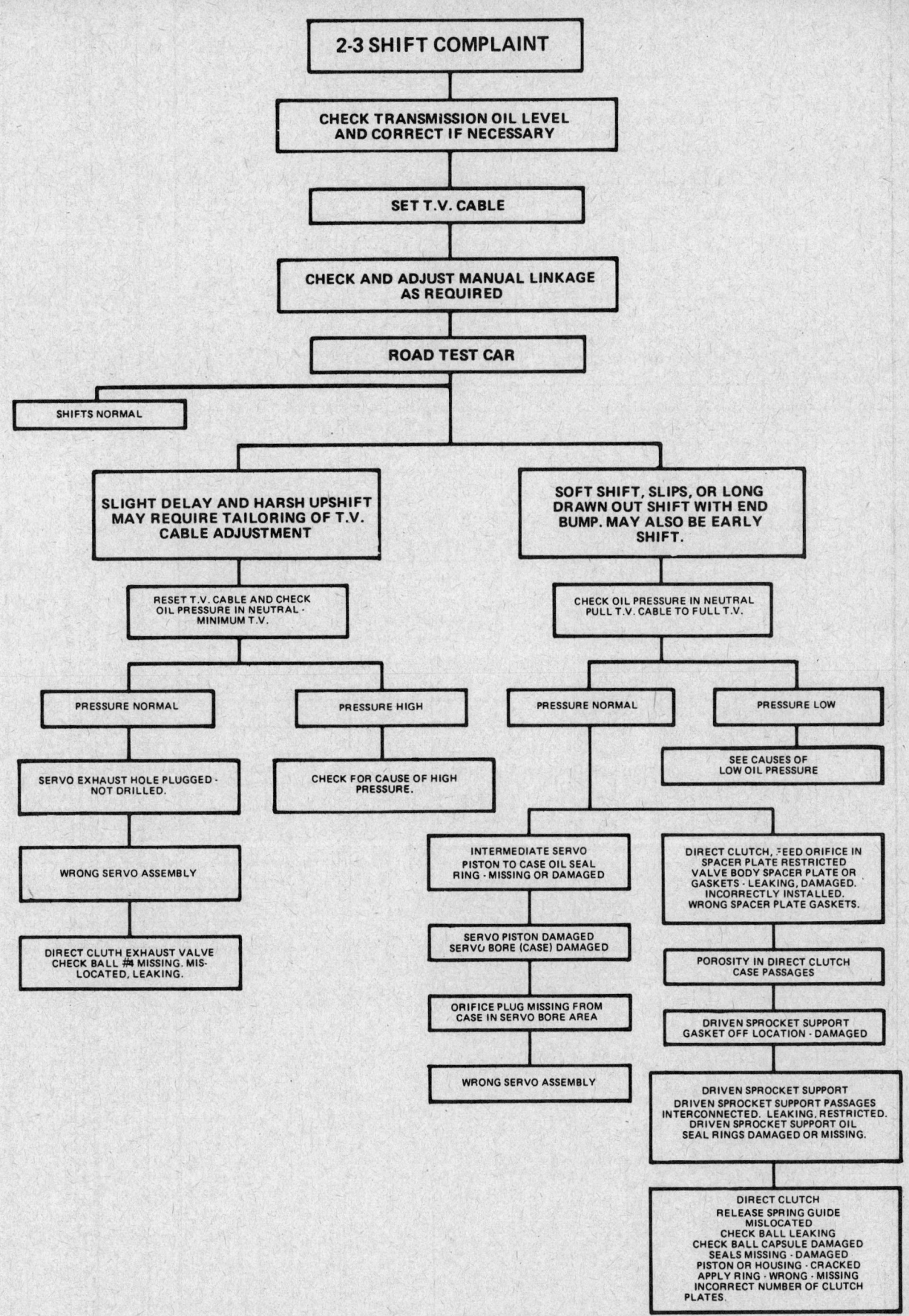

Fig. 4   THM 325 Trouble-shooting chart, Part 3 of 8

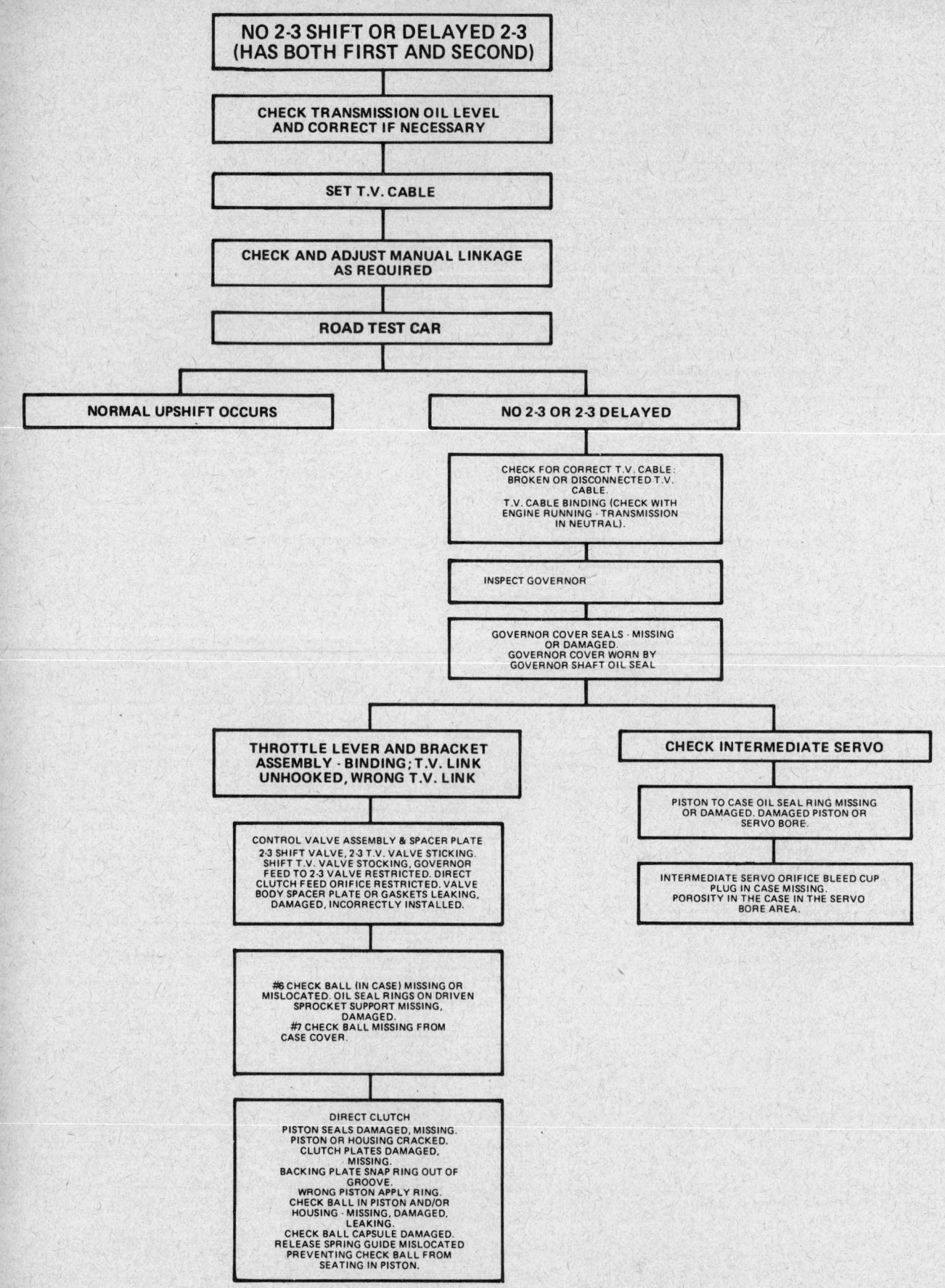

NO 2-3 SHIFT OR DELAYED 2-3 (HAS BOTH FIRST AND SECOND)

CHECK TRANSMISSION OIL LEVEL AND CORRECT IF NECESSARY

SET T.V. CABLE

CHECK AND ADJUST MANUAL LINKAGE AS REQUIRED

ROAD TEST CAR

NORMAL UPSHIFT OCCURS

NO 2-3 OR 2-3 DELAYED

CHECK FOR CORRECT T.V. CABLE: BROKEN OR DISCONNECTED T.V. CABLE. T.V. CABLE BINDING (CHECK WITH ENGINE RUNNING · TRANSMISSION IN NEUTRAL).

INSPECT GOVERNOR

GOVERNOR COVER SEALS · MISSING OR DAMAGED. GOVERNOR COVER WORN BY GOVERNOR SHAFT OIL SEAL

THROTTLE LEVER AND BRACKET ASSEMBLY · BINDING; T.V. LINK UNHOOKED, WRONG T.V. LINK

CHECK INTERMEDIATE SERVO

CONTROL VALVE ASSEMBLY & SPACER PLATE 2-3 SHIFT VALVE, 2-3 T.V. VALVE STICKING. SHIFT T.V. VALVE STOCKING, GOVERNOR FEED TO 2-3 VALVE RESTRICTED. DIRECT CLUTCH FEED ORIFICE RESTRICTED. VALVE BODY SPACER PLATE OR GASKETS LEAKING, DAMAGED, INCORRECTLY INSTALLED.

PISTON TO CASE OIL SEAL RING MISSING OR DAMAGED. DAMAGED PISTON OR SERVO BORE.

INTERMEDIATE SERVO ORIFICE BLEED CUP PLUG IN CASE MISSING. POROSITY IN THE CASE IN THE SERVO BORE AREA.

#6 CHECK BALL (IN CASE) MISSING OR MISLOCATED. OIL SEAL RINGS ON DRIVEN SPROCKET SUPPORT MISSING, DAMAGED. #7 CHECK BALL MISSING FROM CASE COVER.

DIRECT CLUTCH PISTON SEALS DAMAGED, MISSING. PISTON OR HOUSING CRACKED. CLUTCH PLATES DAMAGED, MISSING. BACKING PLATE SNAP RING OUT OF GROOVE. WRONG PISTON APPLY RING. CHECK BALL IN PISTON AND/OR HOUSING · MISSING, DAMAGED, LEAKING. CHECK BALL CAPSULE DAMAGED. RELEASE SPRING GUIDE MISLOCATED PREVENTING CHECK BALL FROM SEATING IN PISTON.

Fig. 5   THM 325 Trouble-shooting chart, Part 4 of 8

NO DRIVE

A "NO DRIVE" COMPLAINT CAN BE REPORTED UNDER SEVERAL
CONDITIONS OR IN DIFFERENT OPERATING RANGES. SELECT
FROM THE FOLLOWING CONDITIONS THE ONE THAT
BEST REPRESENTS THE PROBLEM:

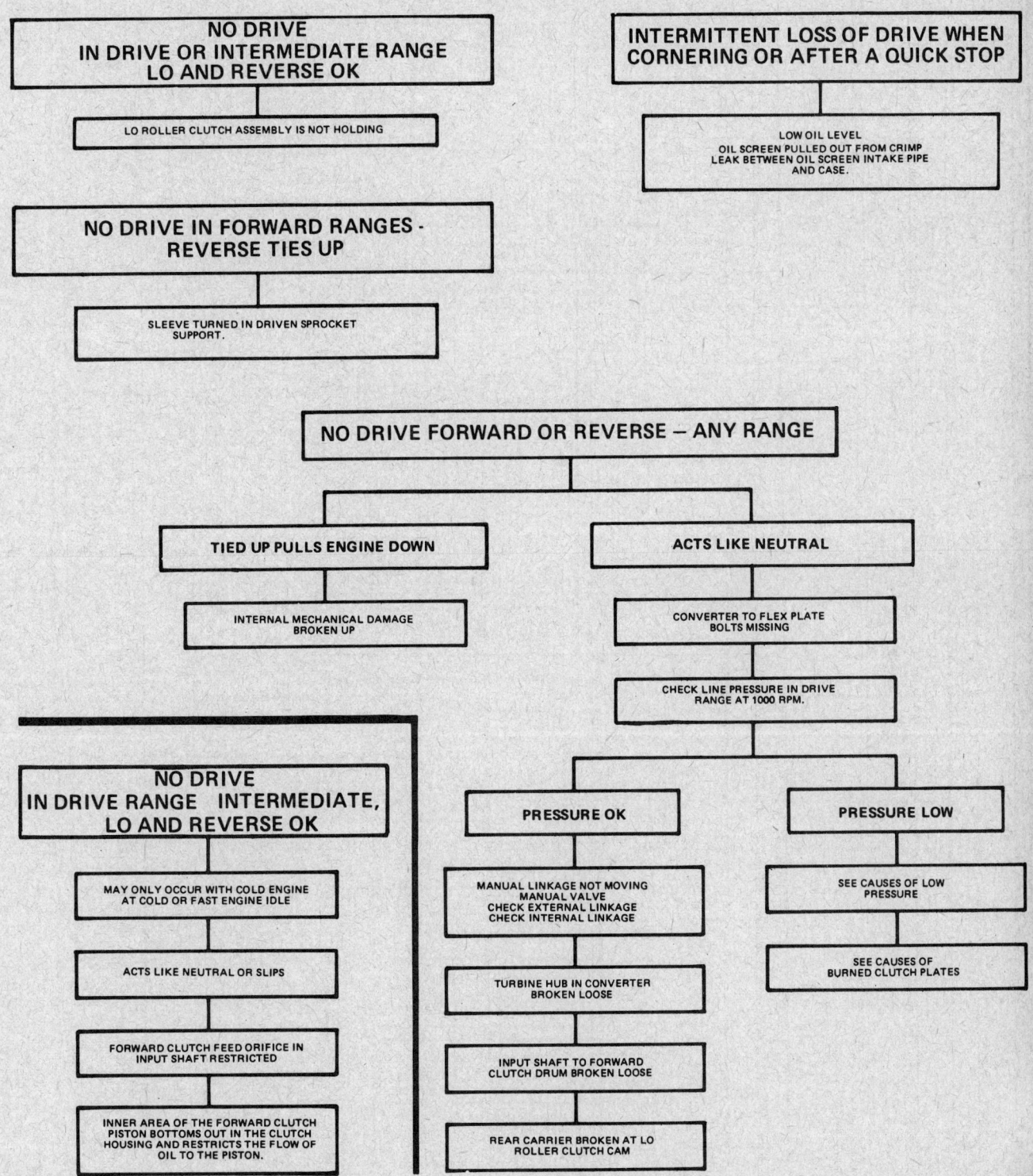

Fig. 6   THM 325 Trouble-shooting chart, Part 5 of 8

Fig. 7   THM 325 Trouble-shooting chart, Part 6 of 8

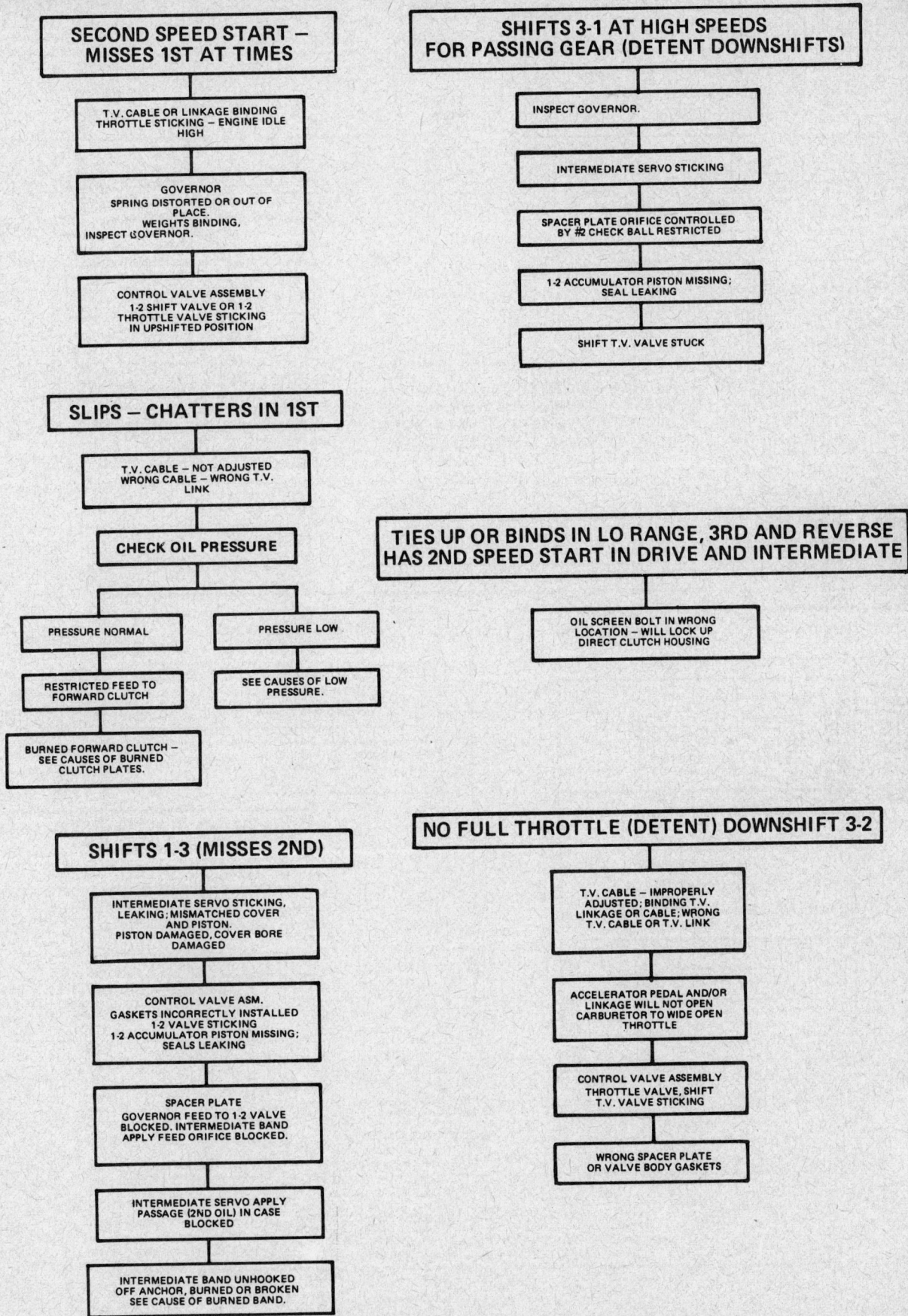

SECOND SPEED START – MISSES 1ST AT TIMES

T.V. CABLE OR LINKAGE BINDING THROTTLE STICKING – ENGINE IDLE HIGH

GOVERNOR SPRING DISTORTED OR OUT OF PLACE. WEIGHTS BINDING, INSPECT GOVERNOR.

CONTROL VALVE ASSEMBLY 1-2 SHIFT VALVE OR 1-2 THROTTLE VALVE STICKING IN UPSHIFTED POSITION

SLIPS – CHATTERS IN 1ST

T.V. CABLE – NOT ADJUSTED WRONG CABLE – WRONG T.V. LINK

CHECK OIL PRESSURE

PRESSURE NORMAL

PRESSURE LOW

RESTRICTED FEED TO FORWARD CLUTCH

SEE CAUSES OF LOW PRESSURE.

BURNED FORWARD CLUTCH – SEE CAUSES OF BURNED CLUTCH PLATES.

SHIFTS 1-3 (MISSES 2ND)

INTERMEDIATE SERVO STICKING, LEAKING; MISMATCHED COVER AND PISTON. PISTON DAMAGED, COVER BORE DAMAGED

CONTROL VALVE ASM. GASKETS INCORRECTLY INSTALLED 1-2 VALVE STICKING 1-2 ACCUMULATOR PISTON MISSING; SEALS LEAKING

SPACER PLATE GOVERNOR FEED TO 1-2 VALVE BLOCKED. INTERMEDIATE BAND APPLY FEED ORIFICE BLOCKED.

INTERMEDIATE SERVO APPLY PASSAGE (2ND OIL) IN CASE BLOCKED

INTERMEDIATE BAND UNHOOKED OFF ANCHOR, BURNED OR BROKEN SEE CAUSE OF BURNED BAND.

SHIFTS 3-1 AT HIGH SPEEDS FOR PASSING GEAR (DETENT DOWNSHIFTS)

INSPECT GOVERNOR.

INTERMEDIATE SERVO STICKING

SPACER PLATE ORIFICE CONTROLLED BY #2 CHECK BALL RESTRICTED

1-2 ACCUMULATOR PISTON MISSING; SEAL LEAKING

SHIFT T.V. VALVE STUCK

TIES UP OR BINDS IN LO RANGE, 3RD AND REVERSE HAS 2ND SPEED START IN DRIVE AND INTERMEDIATE

OIL SCREEN BOLT IN WRONG LOCATION – WILL LOCK UP DIRECT CLUTCH HOUSING

NO FULL THROTTLE (DETENT) DOWNSHIFT 3-2

T.V. CABLE – IMPROPERLY ADJUSTED; BINDING T.V. LINKAGE OR CABLE; WRONG T.V. CABLE OR T.V. LINK

ACCELERATOR PEDAL AND/OR LINKAGE WILL NOT OPEN CARBURETOR TO WIDE OPEN THROTTLE

CONTROL VALVE ASSEMBLY THROTTLE VALVE, SHIFT T.V. VALVE STICKING

WRONG SPACER PLATE OR VALVE BODY GASKETS

Fig. 8   THM 325 Trouble-shooting chart, Part 7 of 8

```
┌────────────────────────────┐          ┌────────────────────────────┐
│       NO OVERRUN            │          │  NO OVERRUN BRAKING IN      │
│   BRAKING IN INTERMEDIATE   │          │       LO (L1)               │
│       1-2 UPSHIFTS OK       │          │       REVERSE OK            │
└────────────┬───────────────┘          └────────────┬───────────────┘
             │                                        │
   ┌─────────────────────┐                  ┌─────────────────────────┐
   │  INTERMEDIATE BOOST  │                  │  CHECK AND ADJUST MANUAL │
   │    VALVE STICKING    │                  │   LINKAGE AS REQUIRED    │
   └──────────┬──────────┘                   └────────────┬────────────┘
             │                                            │
   ┌─────────────────────┐                  ┌─────────────────────────┐
   │ #1 OR #3 CHECK BALL  │                  │  CONTROL VALVE ASSEMBLY  │
   │  MISSING OR LEAKING  │                  │ LO OVERRUN CLUTCH VALVE  │
   └─────────────────────┘                  │ STICKING OR SPRING MISSING│
                                            └─────────────────────────┘
```

CAUTION: BEFORE CHECKING TRANSMISSION FOR WHAT IS BELIEVED TO BE "TRANS. NOISE," MAKE CERTAIN THE NOISE IS NOT FROM THE WATER PUMP, ALTERNATOR, AIR CONDITIONER, POWER STEERING, ETC. THESE COMPONENTS CAN BE ISOLATED BY REMOVING THE PROPER BELT AND RUNNING THE ENGINE NOT MORE THAN TWO MINUTES AT ONE TIME.

TRANSMISSION NOISY

PARK, NEUTRAL & ALL DRIVING RANGES

PUMP CAVITATION
OIL LEVEL LOW
PLUGGED OR RESTRICTED SCREEN
DAMAGED SCREEN "O" RING SEAL
POROSITY IN CASE INTAKE AREA
WATER IN OIL.
POROSITY OR VOIDS AT TRANS.
INTAKE PORT.

PUMP ASSEMBLY
GEARS DAMAGED
DRIVING GEAR ASSEMBLED
BACKWARDS
CRESCENT INTERFERENCE.

CONVERTER
LOOSE BOLTS (CONVERTER TO
FLEX PLATE)
CONVERTER DAMAGE
CRACKED OR BROKEN FLEX PLATE

DURING ACCELERATION — ANY GEAR

TRANSMISSION OR COOLER LINES
GROUNDED TO UNDERBODY.
MOTOR MOUNTS LOSE OR BROKEN

325 MODEL ONLY—DRIVE LINK ASSEMBLY,
WORN OR DAMAGED, MAY SOUND
LIKE POPCORN POPPING.

SQUEAL AT LOW CAR SPEED, ESPECIALLY HOT

SPEEDOMETER DRIVEN GEAR SHAFT
SEAL —
SEAL REQUIRES LUBRICATION OR
REPLACEMENT

IF SPEEDOMETER DRIVEN GEAR
SHAFT APPEARS TWISTED, CHECK
FOR PRESENCE OF ENGINE COOLANT
IN TRANSMISSION.

FIRST, SECOND AND/OR REVERSE

PLANETARY GEAR SET
1. THOROUGHLY CLEAN, DRY & INSPECT CLOSELY. THE ROLLER THRUST
   BEARINGS AND THRUST RACES FOR A PITTING OR ROUGH CONDITION.
2. INSPECT GEARS FOR DAMAGE, WEAR, PITTING AND PINIONS FOR TILT.

Fig. 9   THM 325 Trouble-shooting chart, Part 8 of 8

Fig. 10 Manual linkage

Fig. 11 Downshift linkage adjustment

b. 1-2 accumulator valve sticking.
6. Case cover no. 7 check ball missing or not seating properly.

MAINTENANCE
ADDING OIL

To check fluid, drive vehicle for at least 15 minutes to bring fluid to operating temperature (190°–200° F.). With vehicle on a level surface and engine idling in Park and parking brake applied, the level on the dipstick should be at the Full Hot mark. To bring the fluid level from the ADD mark to the FULL mark requires one pint of fluid. If vehicle cannot be driven sufficiently to bring fluid to operating temperature, the level on the dipstick should be between the two dimples on the dipstick with fluid temperature at 65°–85° F.

If additional fluid is required, use only Dexron II automatic transmission fluid.

NOTE: An early change to a darker color from the usual red color and or a strong odor that is usually associated with overheated fluid is normal and should not be considered as a positive sign of required maintenance or unit failure.

CAUTION: When adding fluid, do not over fill, as foaming and loss of fluid through the vent may occur as the fluid heats up. Also, if fluid level is too low, complete loss of drive may occur especially when cold, which can cause transmission failure.

Every 100,000 miles, the oil should be drained, the oil pan removed, the screen cleaned and fresh fluid added. For vehicles subjected to more severe use such as heavy city traffic especially in hot weather, prolonged periods of idling or towing, this maintenance should be performed every 15,000 miles.

CHANGING OIL

1. Raise vehicle and position drain pan under transmission pan.
2. Loosen rear pan attaching bolts approximately four turns.
3. Carefully pry transmission pan loose with a screwdriver and allow fluid to drain.
4. Remove pan attaching bolts, pan and pan gasket.
5. Drain remaining fluid from pan, then clean pan with solvent and dry with compressed air.
6. Remove transmission screen. Remove O-ring seal from intake pipe or case bore.
7. Thoroughly clean screen assembly with solvent and dry with compressed air.
8. Install O-ring on intake pipe, then install screen retainer.
9. Install gasket on pan, then install pan and torque attaching bolts to 12 ft. lbs.
10. Lower vehicle and add approximately 5 qts. of Dexron II type transmission fluid through filler tube.
11. Start engine and operate at idle speed, then move selector lever through each range.
12. Place transmission in Park position and check fluid level.

MANUAL LINKAGE
ADJUST

1. Loosen transmission control shaft rod clamp, **Fig. 10.**
2. Place shift lever in Neutral position.
3. Place transmission lever in Neutral position.
4. While holding clamp flush against control equalizer shaft assembly, tighten screw against rod finger tight.
5. Tighten clamp screw to 20 ft. lbs. No force should be exerted on in either direction on the rod or equalizer shaft assembly when tighten clamp screw.
6. Check neutral start switch adjustment and adjust as necessary.

DOWNSHIFT CABLE
ADJUST

1. After assembling cable to transmission install cable fitting into engine bracket.
2. Install cable terminal on carburetor lever.
3. Open carburetor lever to full throttle stop position to automatically adjust slider on cable to the correct setting, **Fig. 11.**
4. Release carburetor lever.
5. If cable readjustment is necessary, depress and hold metal tab and move slider back through fitting in direction away from carburetor lever until slider stops against fitting, **Fig. 11.** Release metal lock tab and repeat steps 3 and 4.

IN-VEHICLE REPAIRS
VALVE BODY, REPLACE

1. Drain transmission fluid and remove oil pan and screen.

2. Remove screw and disconnect downshift cable.
3. Remove throttle lever and bracket assembly. Use care not to bend throttle lever link.
4. Remove manual detent roller and spring assembly.
5. Support valve body and remove attaching bolts.
6. While holding manual valve with fingers, remove valve body spacer plate and gaskets together to prevent dropping of four check balls located in valve body and fifth check ball located on spacer plate.

NOTE: After removing valve body, intermediate band anchor pin and reverse clutch cup plug may come out.

7. Place valve body on bench with spacer plate side facing upward and remove check ball from spacer plate.
8. Reverse procedure to install. Torque valve body attaching bolts to 8 ft. lbs.

NOTE: Intermediate band anchor pin must locate on intermediate band or damage to transmission may result.

INTERMEDIATE SERVO, REPLACE

1. Install tool No. J-28493 on transmission case and tighten bolt to depress servo cover.
2. Using a small screwdriver, remove servo cover retaining ring, then remove tool.
3. Remove servo cover, then remove servo piston and band apply pin assembly.
4. Reverse procedure to install.

SPEEDOMETER GEARS, REPLACE

1. Disconnect speedometer cable, then remove driven gear attaching bolt, retainer and driven gear.
2. Remove governor cover attaching screws and governor cover.
3. Remove governor and speedometer drive gear assembly.
4. Remove speedometer drive gear from governor assembly.
5. Reverse procedure to install.

PRESSURE REGULATOR VALVE, REPLACE

1. Drain transmission fluid and remove oil pan and screen.
2. Push in on pressure regulator valve, compress valve spring with a small screwdriver.
3. Remove retaining ring, then slowly release spring tension and remove pressure regulator guide.

DRIVE LINK BELT OR SPROCKETS

Refer to Cadillac Section, Eldorado and Seville Drive Link Belt, for removal and installation procedures.

TRANSMISSION
REPLACE

1. Disconnect battery ground cable.
2. Disconnect speedometer cable and downshift cable from transmission.
3. Support engine with a suitable holding fixture.

4. Remove three upper final drive to transmission attaching bolts.
5. Remove five transmission to engine mounting bolts and the dipstick tube assembly.
6. Raise and support vehicle.
7. Remove splash shield.
8. Disconnect starter wiring and remove the starter.
9. Disconnect transmission oil cooler lines from transmission.
10. Loosen but do not remove torque converter cover screw nearest dipstick tube brace and remove all other screws and cover.
11. Remove the two nuts and bolts securing left hand exhaust pipe to the crossover pipe, then slide the flanges apart for clearance.
12. Support transmission with a suitable jack.
13. Remove the three remaining final drive to the transmission bolts.
14. Remove the remaining transmission to engine bolt and loosen the final drive support bracket.
15. Remove three flywheel to converter bolts.
16. Disconnect shift control linkage at transmission.
17. Remove left and right hand transmission mounts.
18. Slowly lower transmission and move rearward to disengage splines from final drive unit. With transmission lowered install a suitable converter holding tool.
19. Reverse procedure to install. Torque bolts as follows:

Ft. Lbs.
Starter mounting bolts 30
Transmission mount to frame nut 40
Transmission to engine bolts 35
Flywheel to converter bolts 35
Final drive to transmission bolts 30

Turbo Hydra-Matic 700-R4 Automatic Transmission

INDEX

TRANSMISSION IDENTIFICATION

Transmission identification code can be located in one of two positions: right rear pan to case mounting flange or right side transmission to engine mounting flange. The second and third digits of the transmission identification code denotes transmission model.

CHEVROLET

		Code
1982	V8-267 Caprice, Impala	Y4, YL
	V8-305 Caprice, Impala	Y3, YK
	V8-350 Corvette	YA
1983	4-151 Camaro	PQ
	V6-173 Camaro	YF
	V8-305 Camaro	YG, YP
	V8-305 Caprice, Impala	YK
1984	4-151 Camaro	PQ
	V6-173 Camaro	YF
	V8-305 Camaro	YG, YP
	V8-305 Caprice, Impala	YK
	V8-350 Corvette	Y9, YW
1985	4-151 Camaro	PQ
	V6-173 Camaro	YX
	V6-262 Caprice, Impala	YT
	V8-305 Camaro	YP, YZ
	V8-305 Caprice, Impala	YK
	V8-350 Corvette	YC

PONTIAC

		Code
1983	4-151 Firebird	PQ
	V6-173 Firebird	YF, YH
	V8-305 Firebird	YG, YP
	V6-305 Parisienne	YK
1984	4-151 Firebird	PQ
	V6-173 Firebird	YF
	V8-305 Firebird	YG, YP
	V8-305 Parisienne	YK
1985	4-151 Firebird	PQ
	V6-173 Firebird	YX
	V6-262 Parisienne	YT
	V8-305 Firebird	YP, YZ
	V8-305 Parisienne	YK

DESCRIPTION

The model 700-R4, **Fig. 1**, is a fully automatic transmission consisting of a 3-element hydraulic torque converter with the addition of a converter clutch.

Also two planetary gear sets, five multiple-disc type clutches, two roller or one-way clutches and a band are used which provide the friction elements to produce four forward speeds, the last of which is overdrive.

The torque converter, through oil, couples the engine power to the gear sets and hydraulically provides additional torque multiplication when required. Also, through the converter clutch, the converter drive and driven members operate as one unit when applied, providing mechanical drive from the engine through the transmission.

The gear ratio changes are fully automatic in relation to the vehicle speed and engine torque. Vehicle speed and engine torque are directed to the transmission providing the proper gear ratio for maximum efficiency and performance at all throttle openings.

A hydraulic system pressurized by a variable capacity vane-type pump, provides the operating pressure required for the operation of the friction elements and automatic controls.

TROUBLESHOOTING GUIDE

OIL PRESSURE HIGH OR LOW

1. Pump assembly pressure regulator valve binding, dirty or damaged spring.
2. T.V. and reverse boost plug and bushing are dirty, sticking, damaged or incorrectly assembled.
3. Pump assembly pressure relief ball not seated or damaged.
4. Pump assembly slide sticking.
5. Pump assembly not regulating.
6. Excess rotor clearance in pump assembly.
7. Manual valve not engaged or damaged.
8. T.V. exhaust valve binding or damaged.
9. Throttle lever and bracket assembly, misassembled, binding, damaged or check valve missing.
10. Valve body throttle valve or plunger sticking.
11. Valve body T.V. limit valve sticking.
12. Throttle link, not engaged, damaged, incorrect, burr on upper end or hanging on T.V. sleeve.
13. Filter, restricted has missing O-ring or hole in intake pipe.

HIGH OR LOW SHIFT POINTS

1. T.V. cable binding or not set.
2. Improper external linkage travel.
3. Binding throttle valve or plunger.
4. T.V. modulator up or down valve sticking.
5. Valve body gaskets or spacer plate mispositioned or damaged.
6. T.V. limit valve sticking.
7. Pump assembly, sticking pressure regulator valve, T.V. boost valve.
8. Pump slide sticking.

FIRST SPEED ONLY—NO UPSHIFT

1. Sticking governor valve.
2. Governor driven gear is damaged.
3. Governor driven gear retainer pin missing.
4. Nicks or burrs on output shaft.
5. Correct governor retainer pin in case (longer or shorter).
6. Burrs on governor sleeve.
7. Burrs on governor case.
8. Governor weights and springs damaged.

Fig. 1   700-R4 automatic transmission

9. 1-2 shaft valve sticking.
10. Valve body gaskets or spacer plate are mispositioned.
11. Valve body pad—porosity and/or damaged lands.
12. Restricted or damaged governor screen.
13. 2-4 servo apply passages, servo apply pin and pin hole in case, restricted or damaged.
14. Damaged or missing servo piston seals.
15. 2-4 band assembly burned, band anchor pin not engaged.
16. 2-4 band assembly apply end broken.

SLIPS IN FIRST GEAR

1. Forward clutch plates burned.
2. Porosity—forward clutch piston.
3. Forward clutch seals cut or damaged.
4. Damaged forward clutch housing.
5. Forward clutch internal leak.
6. Forward clutch housing check ball damage.
7. Low oil or oil pressure.
8. Accumulator valve sticking.
9. Valve body lands or interconnected passages damaged.
10. Valve body gasket, spacer plate damaged or mispositioned.
11. Binding internal T.V. linkage.
12. 1-2 accumulator piston assembly, piston or bore porous.
13. 1-2 accumulator piston assembly seals cut or damaged.
14. Leak between piston and pin.
15. Missing or broken accumulator spring.

1-2 FULL THROTTLE SHIFTS ONLY

1. T.V. cable not connected.
2. T.V. cable too long or short.
3. Throttle lever bracket assembly misassembled or binding.
4. Missing exhaust check valve.
5. Throttle link not connected, burr on upper end or hanging on T.V. sleeve.
6. Throttle valve or plunger hanging or sticking in full open position.
7. Inter-connected passages-pump, case or valve body restricted or damaged.

1-2 SLIP OR ROUGH

1. Throttle lever and bracket assembly damaged or incorrectly installed.
2. Throttle valve or bushing sticking.
3. Sticking 1-2 shift valve train.
4. Valve body gasket or spacer plate mispositioned.
5. Sticking line bias valve.
6. Sticking accumulator valve.
7. Sticking T.V. limit valve.
8. Incorrect 2-4 servo apply pin.
9. 2-4 servo oil seal rings or seals damaged.
10. 2-4 servo bores, damaged.
11. 2-4 servo oil passages, restricted or missing.
12. 2nd accumulator piston seal damaged.
13. Accumulator spring, missing.
14. 2nd accumulator bores, damaged.
15. 2nd accumulator piston, porous.
16. 2nd accumulator oil passages, re-

stricted or missing.
17. Burned 2-4 band.

2-3 SLIP OR ROUGH

1. 2-3 shift valve train, sticking.
2. Accumulator valve sticking.
3. Valve body gasket or spacer plate mispositioned.
4. Throttle valve sticking.
5. T.V. limit valve sticking.
6. 3-4 clutch plates burned or excessive clutch plate travel.
7. 3-4 piston seals cut or damaged.
8. 3-4 piston porosity.
9. 3-4 piston exhaust ball open.
10. Apply passages restricted.
11. 3-4 clutch check ball capsule damaged or misassembled.

3-4 SLIP OR ROUGH

1. 3-4 accumulator spring missing.
2. 3-4 piston porosity.
3. Accumulator feed passages restricted.
4. 3-4 accumulator piston oil seal ring broken.
5. Accumulator case bore damaged.
6. Servo band apply incorrect.
7. Servo piston seals damaged or missing.
8. Servo piston bores damaged.
9. Servo piston porosity.
10. 3-4 clutch burned. (Refer to 2-3 slip for other clutch diagnosis.)
11. 2-4 band burned.
12. Valve body 2-3 shift valve train sticking.
13. Accumulator valve sticking.
14. Valve body gaskets or spacer plate mispositioned.

15. Valve body throttle valve sticking.
16. T.V. limit valve sticking.

NO REVERSE OR SLIPS IN REVERSE

1. Forward clutch will not release.
2. Manual linkage improperly adjusted.
3. Pump assembly reverse boost plug sticking.
4. Valve body gaskets or spacer plate mispositioned.
5. Lo reverse clutch piston seals cut or damaged.
6. Low reverse clutch apply passages restricted or missing.
7. Lo reverse clutch plates burned.
8. Lo reverse clutch cover plate loose or cover plate gasket damaged.
9. Reverse input clutch plates burned.
10. Reverse input clutch piston seals cut or damaged.
11. Reverse input clutch apply passage restricted or missing.
12. Reverse input clutch housing exhaust ball and capsule damaged.

NO PART THROTTLE DOWNSHIFT

1. Binding external or internal linkage.
2. Valve body T.V. modulator downshift valve binding.
3. Valve body throttle valve binding.
4. Valve body throttle valve bushing. Feed hole restricted or missing.
5. Valve body check ball #3 mispositioned.

NO OVERRUN BRAKING MANUAL 3-2-1

1. External manual linkage not properly adjusted.
2. Overrun clutch plates burned.
3. Overrun clutch inner or outer piston seals damaged.
4. Overrun clutch piston exhaust ball sticking or missing.
5. Overrun clutch piston porosity.
6. Valve body gaskets or spacer plate mispositioned or orifice holes plugged.
7. Valve body 4-3 sequence valve sticking.
8. Valve body check balls 3, 9 or 10 mispositioned.
9. Turbine shaft oil feed passages restricted or missing.
10. Turbine shaft oil seal ring damaged.
11. Turbine shaft plug missing.

NO CONVERTER CLUTCH APPLY

1. 12 volts not being supplied to the transmission.
2. Defective transmission outside electrical connector.
3. Defective inside electrical connectors, wiring harness, solenoid.
4. Defective electrical ground inside transmission.
5. Defective pressure switch or improper connection.
6. Solenoid not grounded.

7. Valve body converter clutch shift or throttle valve sticking.
8. Valve body casting or spacer plate in converter clutch valve area is mispositioned or damaged.
9. Converter clutch apply valve stuck or installed backwards.
10. Pump assembly signal oil orifice restricted or missing.
11. Pump assembly O-ring on solenoid damaged or missing.
12. Pump-to-case gasket damaged or mispositioned.
13. Pump assembly cup plug missing from apply passage.
14. Pump assembly orifice plug missing from cooler input passage.
15. High or uneven bolt torque on cover to body.
16. Converter clutch stop valve or retainer ring not installed properly.

CONVERTER SHUDDER

1. Converter clutch pressure plate damaged.
2. Check ball on end of turbine shaft damaged.
3. Sticking converter clutch shift valve in valve body.
4. Sticking converter clutch apply valve in valve body.
5. Restricted converter clutch apply passage.
6. Low oil or oil pressure.
7. Engine not tuned properly.

NO CONVERTER RELEASE

1. Converter clutch apply valve stuck in open position.
2. O-ring or check ball in end of turbine shaft damaged.
3. Internal converter damaged.

DRIVES IN NEUTRAL

1. Forward clutch burned or not releasing.
2. Manual linkage or manual valve incorrectly set, or disconnected internal linkage.
3. Interconnected case passages.

NO PARK OR WILL NOT HOLD IN PARK

1. Actuator rod assembly bent or damaged.
2. Actuator rod spring binding, or improper crimp.
3. Parking lock pawl return spring damaged, or not assembled properly.
4. Actuator rod is not attached to inside detent lever.
5. Parking brake bracket damaged or bolts not torqued.
6. Inside detent lever nut not torqued.
7. Detent roller improperly installed or damaged.
8. Parking lock pawl binding or damaged.
9. Parking lock pawl interference with lo reverse piston.

NOTE: Be careful to always check oil level, T.V. cable and oil pressure following each troubleshooting procedure.

MAINTENANCE

Fluid level should be checked at every engine oil change. Frequency of change for transmission fluid is dependent on the type of driving conditions in which the vehicle is used. If the transmission is subjected to severe service such as: use in heavy city traffic when the outside temperature regularly reaches 90° F., use in very hilly or mountainous areas, commercial use such as taxi or delivery service, the fluid should be changed every 15,000 miles. Otherwise, change the fluid every 100,000 miles, using Dexron II or equivalent automatic transmission fluid. To check fluid at operating temperature (190°–200° F.), which is obtained only after 15 miles of highway-type driving:
1. Apply parking brake and block wheels.
2. Place selector lever in park and start but do not race, engine. Move selector lever through each range.
3. Check fluid immediately with selector lever in park, engine running at slow idle, and vehicle on level surface. Fluid level should be at full hot mark.

CHANGING FLUID

1. Raise and support vehicle.
2. Place drain pan under transmission oil pan, loosen pan bolts on front of pan, pry carefully with screwdriver to loosen oil pan, and allow fluid to drain.
3. Remove remaining oil pan bolts, oil pan, and gasket.
4. Drain fluid from pan, then clean pan and dry thoroughly with compressed air.
5. Remove oil filter to valve body bolt, then remove filter and gasket, replace with new filter and gasket and install filter attaching bolt. Torque to specification.
6. Install new gasket on oil pan, then install oil pan and torque bolts to 8 ft. lbs.
7. Lower vehicle and add five quarts of automatic transmission fluid through filler tube.
8. With selector lever in park and parking brake applied, start engine and let idle. Do not race engine.
9. Move selector lever through each range, return to park position, check fluid, and add additional fluid to bring level between dimples on dipstick.

ADDING FLUID TO FILL DRY TRANSMISSION AND CONVERTER

1. Add 11½ quarts of transmission fluid through filler tube.
2. Place selector lever in park, depress accelerator to place carburetor on fast idle cam, and move selector lever through each range. Do not race engine.
3. With selector lever in park, engine running at idle (1–3 minutes), and vehicle on level surface, check fluid level and add additional fluid to bring level between dimples on dipstick.

MANUAL LINKAGE
ADJUST

CAMARO & FIREBIRD

1. Loosen manual lever attaching screw, **Fig. 2**.
2. Place transmission manual shaft in neutral position.
3. Place console shift lever in neutral position.
4. Position shift cable pin so that it is centered in manual lever slot, then torque attaching bolts to 12–18 ft. lbs.

CAPRICE, IMPALA & PARISIENNE

1. Loosen Swivel clamp screw.
2. Position shift lever in neutral gate.
3. Position transmission lever in neutral detent.
4. While holding swivel clamp flush against equalizer lever, tighten swivel clamp screw, **Fig. 3**.

NOTE: Do not exert force in either direction on rod or equalizer lever while tightening swivel clamp screw.

CORVETTE

1982
1. Place selector lever (A) in "PARK" position, **Fig. 4**.
2. Place transmission lever (C) in "PARK" position by rotating lever clockwise to last detent position.
3. Connect cable (B) to levers (A) and (C).

1984
1. Attach cable (1), **Fig. 5**, to top of steering column lock lever by routing cable through retaining bracket and seating cable retaining clip firmly in place.
2. Press cable connector firmly over pin on steering column lock lever.

SHIFT CABLE ADJUSTMENT PROCEDURE

1. ASSEMBLE MANUAL LEVER TO TRANS. MANUAL SHAFT AND POSITION TRANSMISSION MANUAL SHAFT IN NEUTRAL POSITION. POSITION CONSOLE SHIFTER LEVER IN NEUTRAL.
2. WITH SHIFT CABLE ATTACHED TO MANUAL LEVER MOVE PIN TO GIVE "FREE PIN" FIT IN MANUAL LEVER SLOT AND TIGHTEN ATTACHING NUT TO SPECIFIED TORQUE.

5 N·M

5 N·M

16-24 N·M (12-18 FT LBS)

16-24 N·M (12-18 FT LBS)

20-27 N·M (15-20 FT LBS)

Fig. 2   Shift linkage adjustment. Camaro & Firebird

3. Place lock lever in locked position and move shifter assembly park lever to Park position.
4. Apply rearward tension to shift lever (3) to hold it against park stop.
5. Pull adjusting key (5) up on cable and install cable to park lock lever pin on shifter. Secure cable with retainer (2).

NOTE: Secure retainer in slot in bracket portion of shifter assembly, then push adjusting key down to lock in place.

1985
1. Place shift control lever in park position.
2. Loosen cable pin retaining nut at transmission lever, **Fig. 6**.
3. Place transmission lever in Park position by rotating lever clockwise to last detent position.
4. Torque cable pin attaching nut at transmission lever as shown, **Fig. 6**.

T.V. CABLE
ADJUST

The T.V. cable should not be thought of as an automatic downshift cable. It controls line pressures, shift points, shift feel, part throttle downshifts, and detent downshifts. The function of the cable is similar to the combined functions of a vacuum modulator and detent downshift cable. The T.V. cable operates the throttle lever and bracket assembly, **Figs. 7 and 8**.

1. Stop engine.
2. Depress re-adjust tab and move slider through fitting, away from lever assembly, until slider stops against fitting. Release re-adjust tab.
3. Open carburetor lever to full throttle stop position to automatically adjust cable, then release carburetor lever and check cable for sticking or binding.
4. Road test vehicle. If delayed or only full throttle shifts still occur, proceed as follows:
   a. Remove oil pan and inspect throttle lever and bracket assembly, **Fig. 9**.
   b. Check T.V. exhaust valve lifter rod for distortion, or binding in control valve assembly or spacer plate.
   c. Make sure T.V. exhaust check ball moves up and down in conjunction with lifter.

STEERING COLUMN

TRANSMISSION

LEVER MUST BE HELD OUT OF PARK WHEN TORQUING NUT. IMPACT TOOL MUST NOT BE USED

EQUALIZER LEVER

LEVER

SWIVEL CLAMP

ROD

SPRING

SCREW

Fig. 3   Column shift manual linkage. Caprice, Impala & Parisienne

LEVER A

LEVER C

CABLE B

Fig. 4   Manual linkage. 1982 Corvette

Fig. 5 Manual linkage. 1984 Corvette

d. Make sure lifter spring holds lifter rod up against control valve assembly.
e. Make sure T.V. plunger is not stuck.
f. Inspect transmission for correct throttle lever to cable link, **Fig. 10.**

SERVO ASSEMBLY
REPLACE

1. On 1984-85 Corvette models, raise and support vehicle, then disconnect exhaust system and remove propeller shaft and torque arm.
2. On all models, remove two oil pan bolts and install tool J-29714 or equivalent, on oil pan flange to depress servo cover.
3. Remove servo cover retaining ring, then remove tool.
4. Remove cover, and seal ring which may be in case.
5. Remove servo piston and bore-apply pin assembly.

6. Reverse procedure to install.

SPEEDOMETER DRIVEN GEAR
REPLACE

1. Disconnect speedometer cable.
2. Remove retainer bolt, retainer, speedometer driven gear, and O-ring seal.
3. Reverse procedure to install, using new O-ring and adjusting fluid level.

REAR OIL SEAL
REPLACE

1. Remove driveshaft, and tunnel strap, if equipped.
2. Using suitable tool, pry out lip oil seal.
3. Coat outer casting of new oil seal with suitable sealer and drive into place with installer J-21426.
4. Install tunnel strap if used, then install driveshaft.

GOVERNOR
REPLACE

1. Raise and support vehicle, then if necessary, remove exhaust system.
2. Remove governor cover from case using extreme care not to damage cover. If cover is damaged, it must be replaced.
3. Remove governor.
4. Reverse procedure to install and check fluid level.

CONTROL VALVE ASSEMBLY
REPLACE

1. Drain and remove oil pan and remove filter and gasket.
2. Disconnect electrical connectors at valve body.
3. Remove detent spring and roller assembly from valve body and remove valve body to case bolts.
4. Remove valve body assembly while disconnecting manual control valve link from range selector inner lever and removing throttle lever bracket from T.V. link.
5. Reverse procedure to install. Torque bolts to 8 ft. lbs. and replenish fluid.

TRANSMISSION
REPLACE

CAMARO & FIREBIRD

1. Remove air cleaner assembly and disconnect T.V. cable at upper end.
2. Raise and support vehicle.
3. Remove torque arm clamp from transmission.
4. Place a wooden block between floor pan and torque arm and disconnect torque arm from rear axle.
5. Remove propeller shaft, then disconnect speedometer cable and T.V. cable from transmission.
6. Disconnect transmission cooler lines and shift linkage.
7. Remove exhaust bracket, then the upper-to-lower support bolts.

Fig. 6 Manual Linkage. 1985 Corvette

Fig. 7 T.V. cable & linkage

Fig. 8 Throttle lever & bracket assembly

Fig. 9 Throttle lever & bracket assembly alignment

Fig. 10 Throttle lever to cable link

8. Support transmission with a suitable jack and remove transmission rear lower support.
9. Remove flywheel cover, then mark relationship between flywheel and converter and remove torque converter attaching bolts.
10. Remove transmission-to-engine attaching bolts and carefully lower transmission from vehicle.
11. Reverse procedure to install.

CAPRICE, IMPALA & PARISIENNE

1. Remove air cleaner assembly, then, disconnect T.V. cable at its upper end. Remove transmission oil dipstick and bolt holding dipstick tube, if accessible.
2. Raise and support vehicle and remove driveshaft.
3. Disconnect speedometer cable, shift linkage, and all electrical leads at

transmission as well as any clips that retain the leads to the transmission case.
4. Remove flywheel cover, mark flywheel and torque converter to maintain original balance. Remove torque converter to flywheel bolts and/or nuts.
5. Disconnect catalytic converter support bracket.
6. Remove transmission support to transmission mount bolt and transmission support to frame bolts and insulators, if used.
7. Position a suitable jack under transmission, raise transmission slightly, and slide transmission support rearward.
8. Lower transmission to gain access to oil cooler lines and T.V. cable attachments, disconnect oil cooler lines and T.V. cable, and cap all openings.
9. Support engine with suitable tool, remove transmission to engine bolts, and disconnect transmission assembly.

10. Install torque converter holding tool J-21366 or equivalent, and remove transmission assembly from vehicle.
11. Reverse procedure to install.

CORVETTE

1. Disconnect battery ground cable.
2. Remove air cleaner assembly and disconnect T.V. cable at upper end.
3. Raise and support vehicle.
4. Remove exhaust system components as necessary.
5. Remove flywheel inspection cover, then mark relationship between flywheel and converter and remove torque converter attaching bolts.
6. Disconnect shift cable and all electrical connectors from transmission, then position suitable jack under transmission.
7. Support engine with suitable jack, then disconnect torque arm from transmission and rear axle.
8. Pry engine and transmission toward left side of vehicle and remove torque arm and propeller shaft.
9. Disconnect cooler lines and T.V. cable from transmission.
10. Remove transmission-to-engine attaching bolts and carefully lower transmission from vehicle.
11. Reverse procedure to install.

Automatic Overdrive Unit, 1984–85 Corvette

INDEX

DESCRIPTION

The automatic overdrive unit used on the 1984–85 Corvette, **Fig. 1,** and the 4-speed manual transmission is essentially a combination of two separate transmission units. The first unit is a conventional 4-speed (83mm) manual system with a 1.1 ratio in 4th gear. On 1984 models, the second unit is a two-speed overdrive system electronically controlled by the ECM which operates with a 1.1 or .68 to 1 ratio. On 1985 models, the second unit is a two speed overdrive system electronically controlled by the ECM which operates with a 1.1 and a .68 to 1 ratio or 1.1 and a .59 to 1 ratio. The two-speed or overdrive unit performs its functions using a planetary gear set in combination with two sets of clutch components.

The ECM is programmed to control the shift solenoid and the overdrive unit. The overdrive mode cannot occur when the transmission is in first gear. It can occur when the transmission is in the remaining three gears.

The hydraulic circuit, **Fig. 2,** consists of a gerotor type pump on the overdrive unit output shaft, a shift valve, solenoid, accumulator valve and a pressure relief valve located in the valve body assembly. In the normal (direct drive) mode, fluid circulates from the pump through a 90–110 psi pressure relief valve and through the cooler lines then back to the pan or sump. When the overdrive switch is closed by the ECM, the solenoid plunger is activated, opening the shift valve passage for fluid flow into the piston. When the solenoid de-energizes, the shift valve returns to its original position.

TROUBLESHOOTING

Refer to **Fig. 3** for automatic overdrive unit troubleshooting procedure.

IN-VEHICLE ADJUSTMENTS

PARK LOCK CABLE, ADJUST

1. Lift adjusting key upward and release cable, **Fig. 4.**
2. Place steering column lock lever into lock park position.
3. Place transmission shift lever into Reverse.
4. Insert a .060 inch feeler gauge against reverse stop, then pull reverse lever until reverse pawl contacts feeler gauge.
5. Push adjusting key downward to set cable.
6. Remove feeler gauge and pull back on shift lever.
7. Ensure reverse pawl hits reverse stop and locks shifter lever in Reverse.

T.V. CABLE, ADJUST

1. Depress and hold metal lock tab, **Fig. 5.**
2. Move slider back, away from throttle body lever until slider contacts fitting.
3. Release metal lock tab.
4. Rotate throttle lever to the Full throttle stop position to obtain a minimum of one click adjustment.

IN-VEHICLE SERVICE

SIDE COVER, REPLACE

1. Place transmission shift lever into 2nd gear.
2. Raise and support vehicle.
3. Disconnect electrical connector(s) from side cover switch(s).
4. Remove switch(s) from side cover.
5. Remove shift levers from shifter shafts.
6. Remove side cover attaching bolts, then the side cover.
7. Reverse procedure to install.

SHIFTER ASSEMBLY

Removal

1. Disconnect battery ground cable.
2. Disconnect electrical connector from power seat switch(s).
3. Remove left seat from vehicle.
4. Remove knob from shift lever.
5. Remove console cover attaching screws, then the console cover.
6. Remove glove compartment lock and left side panel from console.
7. Remove shifter cover.
8. Disconnect three rods from shifter.
9. Disconnect park lock cable from shifter.
10. Remove shifter cross bolt and shifter mounting bracket.
11. Remove shifter mounting bolt from body panel, then the shifter assembly from vehicle.

Installation

1. Position shifter into underbody and install mounting bolt. Torque bolt to 40–51 ft. lbs.
2. Position mounting bracket onto shifter and install bracket bolts. Torque cross bolt to 15–22 ft. lbs. Torque mounting bracket to underbody mount bolt to 10–15 ft. lbs.
3. Install three shifter rods onto shifter assembly.
4. Install park lock cable onto shifter. Adjust park lock cable as described previously.
5. Reverse removal steps 1 through 7 for remaining installation procedure.

T.V. CABLE, REPLACE

Refer to **Figs. 6 and 7** for T.V. cable routing and attachments. Refer to "T.V. Cable, Adjust" for adjustment procedure.

OIL FILTER, REPLACE

1. Disconnect battery ground cable.
2. Raise and support vehicle.
3. Position a suitable drain pan under overdrive unit oil pan. Remove oil pan attaching bolts from front and side of pan.
4. Loosen rear pan attaching bolts approximately 4 turns.
5. Carefully pry oil pan loose, allowing fluid to drain.
6. Remove remaining pan attaching bolts.
7. Drain fluid from oil pan. Clean oil pan with a suitable solvent and dry thoroughly with compressed air.
8. Remove filter from overdrive unit.
9. Install a new filter.
10. During oil pan installation, note the following:
    a. Apply a bead of RTV sealant number 1052366 or equivalent, onto oil pan flange and install oil pan onto overdrive housing.

1. PICKUP TUBE	19. BEARING, THRUST	34. HOUSING ASS'Y
2. LEVER ARM ASSEMBLY	20. NUT, LOCK	35. SHAFT ASS'Y
3. LEVER CAM	TORQUE TO 16-18 FT. LBS.	36. BEARING, THRUST
4. SEAL, "QUAD"	21. CARRIER-BRG. ASS'Y	37. CLUTCH, STOP
5. FITTING	22. SCREWS, C.S.	38. SCREW, 6m x 12mm lg.
6. SEAL, 'O' RING	TORQUE TO 18-20 FT. LBS.	TORQUE TO 6-8 FT. LBS.
7. PLATE, THRUST	23. RING, RETAINING	39. DISC, CLUTCH (4)
8. PLATE, ADAPTOR	24. SCREWS, C.S.	40. PLATE, CLUTCH (4)
9. PISTON-ACCUM. ASS'Y	25. PLATE, FINGER PRES.	41. PLATE, VALVE
10. WASHER, THRUST	26. CLUTCH HUB ASS'Y	42. GASKET, VALVE
11. GEAR, PLANET	27. PLATE, SEL. CLUTCH	43. VALVE BODY ASS'Y
12. SEAL, "QUAD"	28. DISC, CLUTCH (5)	44. SCREW, HEX. 6m x 45mm
13. WASHER, THRUST	29. PLATE, CLUTCH (4)	TORQUE TO 6-8 FT. LBS.
14. WASHER, THRUST	30. PLATE, BEARING	45. BALL, 5/16" STEEL
15. WASHER, THRUST	31. WASHER, THRUST	46. GROMMET
16. GEAR, SUN	32. SCREW, ALLEN 6m x 40mm	47. OIL FILTER
17. SEAL, INPUT	TORQUE TO 6-8 FT. LBS.	48. OIL PAN
18. BEARING, THRUST	33. SEAL, OUTPUT	

Fig. 1 Cross sectional view of overdrive unit. 1985 similar

Fig. 2 Overdrive unit hydraulic circuit

NOTE: The RTV sealant must be wet when installing oil pan onto overdrive housing. RTV sealant should be applied around inside of bolt holes, **Fig. 8.**

   b. Install magnet onto oil pan as shown in **Fig. 8.**
   c. Install oil pan attaching bolts. Torque bolts to 6–8 ft. lbs.
11. Fill overdrive unit with Dexron II automatic transmission fluid.

VALVE BODY, REPLACE

1. Disconnect battery ground cable.
2. Disconnect T.V. cable from throttle body lever.
3. Remove transmission oil pan and filter assembly as described previously.
4. Disconnect tan colored electrical connector from low pressure cut-off switch.
5. Disconnect T.V. cable from T.V. lever, then remove bolt retaining T.V. cable to valve body.
6. Remove remaining 7 valve body to transmission case attaching bolts.
7. Remove valve body and spacer plate assembly from overdrive unit.

NOTE: Care must be taken when removing valve body to prevent loss of the 2 check balls, **Fig. 9.** One check ball is spring loaded under the valve body. The other is located under the transmission case above the separator plate.

8. To install valve body reverse removal procedure and note the following:
   a. Remove T.V. cable attaching bolt from overdrive case. Install tool No. J-34671-1 or equivalent into T.V. cable bore, then hook T.V. cable onto top step, **Fig. 10.**
   b. Unhook T.V. cable from top step, then connect T.V. cable onto lower step.
   c. Position tool No. J-34671-2 or equivalent, between piston and solenoid bracket, **Fig. 11.** Adjust screw/bolt on T.V. lever until bolt contacts cam stop.

OVERDRIVE SOLENOID, REPLACE

1. Disconnect battery ground cable.
2. Remove transmission oil pan and filter assembly as described previously.
3. Disconnect T.V. cable from throttle body lever.
4. Remove valve body as described previously.
5. Using tool No. J-34529 or equivalent, compress shift valve spring, then remove retaining pin.
6. Using tool No. J-34529 or equivalent, compress relief valve springs, then remove retaining pin.
7. Remove solenoid valve body attaching bolts.
8. Remove solenoid valve and check ball assembly from valve body.
9. Reverse procedure to install.

PRESSURE SWITCH, REPLACE

1. Disconnect battery ground cable.
2. Remove transmission oil pan and filter assembly as described previously.
3. Disconnect electrical connectors from pressure switch.
4. Remove switch from valve body.
5. Reverse procedure to install.

OVERDRIVE UNIT OUTPUT SEAL, REPLACE

1. Disconnect battery ground cable.
2. Remove propeller shaft as follows:
   a. Raise and support vehicle.
   b. Disconnect AIR pipe from catalytic converter.
   c. Disconnect AIR pipe clamps from exhaust pipe.
   d. Disconnect oxygen sensor lead.
   e. Remove muffler to support hanger attaching bolts.
   f. Disconnect exhaust pipes from exhaust manifolds.
   g. Remove bolts attaching support beam at the axle and transmission.
   h. Mark relationship of propeller shaft to companion flange. Remove trunnion bearing straps, then the rear universal joint. Tape bearings caps to trunnion to prevent bearing loss.
   i. Slide slip yoke from transmission and remove propeller shaft.

CONDITION	PROBABLE CAUSE	CORRECTION
Overdrive Inop	a. Insufficient Lubricant b. Speedometer Inop c. Blown Fuse d. Temperature Gage Inop e. Console Switch f. 1st Gear Switch at Side Cover Check for (12 volts with Ign. On) g. Solenoid Inop Check for (12 volts at O/D Connector—Engine at operating temp.—wheels off the ground shift trans from 1st into 2nd gear at 12-15 MPH—solenoid should energize at this point) h. Solenoid Check Ball Missing i. Low Pressure Switch j. Shift Valve Inop k. Pressure Regulator Valve Inop l. Drive Pin Broken or Missing in Pump	a. Fill to correct level b. Replace speedometer sensors. Replace speedometer drive or driven gears. c. Replace fuse d. Replace gage or sending unit e. Replace switch or repair wires f. Replace switch or repair wires g. Replace solenoid or repair wires. h. Install check ball i. Replace switch j. Free up valve or replace valve body k. Free up valve or replace valve body l. Replace pin or pump gears
No Overdrive in 2nd Gear	a. 2nd Gear Switch at Side Cover	a. Replace switch or repair wires
No Overdrive in 3rd or 4th Gear	a. 3rd/4th Gear Switch at Side Cover	a. Replace switch or repair wires
Overdrive in All Gears	a. Solenoid Plunger Stuck b. Solenoid Exhaust Hole Plugged c. Shift Valve Stuck	a. Replace Solenoid b. Clear exhaust passage c. Free up shift valve or replace valve body
Harsh Up Shifts	a. T.V. Misadjusted b. Stuck T.V. Valve c. Stuck Accumulator Piston d. Accumulator Seal Damaged	a. Adj. T.V. cable at valve body and Carb. b. Free up valve or replace valve body c. Free up or replace d. Replace seal
Harsh Down Shifts	a. T.V. Misadjusted b. Stuck T.V. Valve c. Accumulator Check Ball missing at Valve Body	a. Adj. T.V. cable at valve body and carb b. Free up valve or replace valve body c. Install check ball
Soft Up Shift	a. T.V. Misadjusted b. Stuck T.V. Valve c. O/D Clutch Plates Burn't	a. Adj. T.V. cable at valve body and Carb b. Free up valve or replace valve body c. Replace clutch plates and disc's

Fig. 3 Overdrive unit troubleshooting chart (Part 1 of 2)

CONDITION	PROBABLE CAUSE	CORRECTION
Soft Downshift	a. T.V. Misadjusted b. Stuck T.V. Valve	a. Adj. T.V. cable at valve body and Carb b. Free up valve or replace valve body
No Downshift	a. E.C.M., throttle position switch	a. Repair or replace E.C.M. or throttle position switch
Slips on Upshift	a. Direct Clutch Plates Burn't b. Excessive Clutch Pack Clearance	a. Replace direct clutch plates and disc's b. Adjust clutch pack clearance
Delayed Upshifts	a. Accumulator Check Ball Missing at Valve Body	a. Install check ball
Chatters on Upshifts	a. Piston Seals Damaged b. Direct Clutch Plates Burn't c. Low mainline pressure	a. Replace seals b. Replace direct clutch plates and disc's c. Check lines for restrictions. Check pump.
O/D Overheats	a. Insufficient Lubricant b. Stuck Cooler Valve c. Cooler Line Restriction d. Restriction in Radiator	a. Fill to correct level b. Free up cooler valve or replace valve c. Flush lines or replace d. Flush radiator or replace
No Reverse	a. Direct Clutch Plates Burn't	a. Replace direct clutch plates and disc's
Noisy in Direct Drive	a. Front Carrier Bearing b. Thrust Bearing in Direct Clutch	a. Replace carrier cover b. Replace thrust bearing
Noisy in Overdrive	a. Pinion Roller Bearings b. Pinion Gears (scored, chipped or burn't) c. Input Sun Gear (scored, chipped or burn't) d. Output Sun Gear (scored, chipped or burn't)	a. Replace carrier cover or housing b. Replace pinion gears c. Replace input sun gear d. Replace output sun gear
No Direct Drive	a. Sprag Damaged	a. Replace Sprag Clutch

Fig. 3   Overdrive unit troubleshooting chart (Part 2 of 2)

3. Using a suitable tool, remove seal from overdrive output shaft.
4. Coat new seal lip with automatic transmission fluid.
5. Using tool No. J-21426 or equivalent, install new seal onto overdrive output shaft seal groove.
6. Reverse removal steps 1 and 2 for remaining installation procedure.

OVERDRIVE UNIT
REPLACE

NOTE: Transmission and overdrive unit are removed as an assembly.

1. Disconnect battery ground cable.
2. Remove air cleaner assembly from engine.
3. Disconnect T.V. cable from left TBI unit.
4. Remove distributor cap and position aside.
5. Raise and support vehicle.
6. Disconnect AIR pipe from catalytic converter. Disconnect AIR pipe clamps from exhaust pipe. Disconnect oxygen sensor lead. Remove muffler to support hanger attaching bolts. Disconnect exhaust pipes from exhaust manifolds.
7. Position a suitable jack under transmission.
8. Remove bolts attaching driveline beam at axle and transmission.
9. Remove driveline beam from vehicle.
10. Mark relationship of the propeller shaft to the axle campanion flange. Remove trunnion bearing straps, then disconnect rear universal joint from axle. Slide propeller shaft slip yoke out from the overdrive unit and remove shaft from the vehicle.
11. Disconnect fluid cooler lines from overdrive unit.
12. Disconnect T.V. cable from overdrive unit.
13. Disconnect shift linkage from shift cover.
14. Disconnect electrical connector from side cover switches, back-up light switch and overdrive unit. Disconnect speedometer cable.
15. Place a suitable jack under engine oil pan with a block of wood placed between jack and pan.
16. Lower transmission slightly.
17. Remove transmission to bellhousing attaching bolts.
18. Slide transmission and overdrive unit rearward to disengage input shaft from clutch.
19. Lower transmission and overdrive unit from vehicle.
20. Remove (7) transmission to overdrive unit attaching bolts and separate overdrive unit from transmission.
21. Reverse procedure to install.

Fig. 4 Park lock cable, adjust

OVERDRIVE UNIT OVERHAUL
OVERDRIVE UNIT CASE DISASSEMBLE

1. Disconnect battery ground cable.
2. Remove overdrive unit from vehicle as described previously.
3. Remove overdrive case filler plug and drain oil from case.
4. Remove retaining bolt and bracket assembly from speedometer sensor and driven gear, **Fig. 12.**
5. Remove (3) ⅛ inch pipe plugs from rear of overdrive unit case.
6. Install (3) pressure plate retaining bolts part No. J-34681 or equivalent into case. Turn bolts until bolt heads are flush with case surface. Turn bolts 2 additional turns by rotating each bolt one turn at a time.

NOTE: This sequence must be followed to prevent pressure plate damage.

7. Remove (4) Allen head bolts retaining adapter plate to overdrive case.
8. Using a plastic hammer, tap adapter plate and separate from overdrive case.
9. Position overdrive unit into a suitable working fixture, and remove large accumulator/piston snap ring.
10. Using a suitable Allen wrench, remove accumulator/piston assembly, **Fig. 13.**
11. Remove carrier and bearing assembly.
12. Remove finger pressure plate.
13. Remove (4) overdrive clutches, (4) composition, (4) steel and (1) clutch stop plate, **Fig. 12.**
14. Remove direct clutch plates, (5) composition, (5) steel and (1) steel bearing plate, **Fig. 12.**
15. Measure each selective clutch plate in the direct clutch set and record readings obtained. The selective clutch plates are used to control the clutch set clearance. When replacing the clutch plates, replace each selective plate with one of the same size.

Fig. 5 T.V. cable, adjust

Fig. 6   T.V. cable routing & attachments. 1984

from output sun gear, **Fig. 12.**

18. Rotate hub to gain access to the pump housing bolts, then remove pump housing attaching bolts.
19. Remove output shaft assembly, **Fig. 12.**
20. Remove pressure plate and springs as follows:
    a. Position tool J-21420-2 or equivalent onto pressure plate with bolt from tool No. J-23327 through center of plate, **Fig. 14.**
    b. Position tool No. J-23327 or equivalent onto rear of overdrive unit case and install retaining nut.
    c. Remove (3) retaining bolts part No. J-34681 from rear of case.
    d. Loosen retaining nut on tool J-23327 bolt to relieve spring tension.
21. Remove cooler valve attaching bolts, then the cooler valve.
22. Remove oil pan attaching bolts, then pry pan from case.
23. Remove oil filter and tube from valve body, **Fig. 15.**
24. Remove T.V. cable assembly from overdrive unit.
25. Remove valve body attaching bolts, then the valve body from overdrive unit case.

16. Inspect overdrive and direct clutch plates as follows:
    a. Inspect composition plates for pitting, flaking wear, glazing, cracking and for chips or metal particles imbedded in lining. If composition plate shows any of these conditions, replace as required.

    b. Inspect steel plates for discoloration. If plate surface is smooth and an uneven color smear is indicated, replace plate. If severe heat (hot) spot discoloration or surface scuffing is indicated, replace plate(s).

17. Remove thrust washer and bearing

VALVE BODY DISASSEMBLE

1. Using tool J-34529 or equivalent, relieve shift valve spring tension, then remove pin, spring and valve, **Fig. 15.**
2. Using tool J-34529 or equivalent, relieve relief valve spring tension, then remove pin, spring and valve.
3. Disconnect electrical connector from pressure switch.
4. Remove solenoid attaching bolts, then the solenoid and check ball.
5. Disconnect remaining electrical connectors from pressure switch, then remove switch from valve body.
6. To assemble valve body, reverse disassembly procedure. Coat all components with clean automatic transmission fluid.

NOTE:

1. INSTALL THE OIL PAN ON HOUSING WHILE R.T.V. SEALANT IS WET.

    PAN AND HOUSING FLANGE SURFACE MUST BE DRY AND FREE OF OIL FILM.

Fig. 7   T.V. cable routing & attachments. 1985

Fig. 8   Magnet & RTV sealant location

Fig. 9 Valve body components

Fig. 10 Hooking T.V. cable onto throttle setting gauge

Fig. 11 Positioning tool J-34671-2 between piston & solenoid bracket

1. TRANSMISSION (Less Overdrive Unit)
2. BOLT, Trans. to Overdrive
3. WASHER, Trans. to Overdrive Bolt Lk.
4. BRACKET, TBI Harness Clip
5. GASKET, Adapter Plate
6. SCREW, Adapter Plate
7. PIN, Dowel
8. PLATE, Adapter
9. "O" RING, Adapter Plt.
10. RING, Accum. Piston Ret.
11. SEAL, Input Sun Gr. Oil
12. BEARING, Annular
13. NUT, Carrier Brg. Lk.
14. CARRIER, Planetary Gear
15. WASHER, Input Sun Gr. Thrust
16. BEARING, Input Sun Gr. Thrust
17. WASHER, Input Sun Gr. Thrust (Selective)
18. GEAR, Input Sun
19. CUP, Brg.
20. WASHER, Planetary Gr. Thrust
21. GEAR, Planetary
22. CUP, Brg.
23. RING, Accum. Piston Ret.
24. SEAL, Accum. Piston
25. SEAL, Accum. Piston
26. PISTON, Accum. Cushion
27. SPRING, Accum. Piston
28. SEAL, Accum. Piston
29. PISTON, Accum.
30. WASHER, Optt. Shf. Thrust
31. BEARING, Optt. Shf. Trust
32. SHAFT, Optt.
33. PLATE, Planetary Gear Thrust
34. PLATE, Clu. Drum
35. BOLT, Clu. Drum
36. RACE, Inner
37. SPRAG, Dir. Clu.
38. HUB, Dir. Clu.
39. DRUM, Dir. Clu
40. PLATE, Dir. Clu. Inr. Driven (Selective)
41. PLATE, Dir. Clu.
42. PLATE, Dir. Clu. Driven
43. PLATE, Dir. Clu. Press
44. BEARING, Dir. Clu.
45. PISTON, Overdrive Clu.
46. PLATE, Overdrive Clu. Driven
47. PLATE, Overdrive Clu.
48. TUBE, Overdrive Vent
49. PLATE, Overdrive Clu. Press
50. WASHER, Dir. Clu. Thrust
51. PISTON, Overdrive Dir. Clu.
52. SPRING, Overdrive Dir. Clu. Otr.
53. SPRING, Overdrive Dir. Clu. Inr.
54. WASHER, Overdrive Dir. Clu. Hub Thrust
55. BEARING, Overdrive Dir. Clu. Hub Thrust
56. CUP, Pump Brg.
57. SCREW, Overdrive Pump & Optt. Shf.
58. HOUSING, W/Brg., Overdrive Pump (Gerotor)
59. PUMP, Overdrive Oil (Gerotor)
60. PIN, Oil Pump Drive
61. SPOOL, Pump (Gerotor)
62. "O" RING, Overdrive Oil Pump
63. "O" RING, Overdrive Oil Pump
64. SCREW, Overdrive Pump Spool (Gerotor)
65. CLIP, Speedo Drive Gr.
66. GEAR, Speedo Drive
67. CASE, Overdrive
68. PLUG, Headless Slotted
69. SEAL, Overdrive Optt. Shf. Oil
70. BUSHING, Case
71. WIRE, Overdrive Vlv. Body Press Sw.
72. PLUG, Sq. Hd. Filler
73. CONNECTOR, Overdrive Sol. Elec.
74. "O" RING, Overdrive Sol. Elec. Conn.
75. GROMMET, Overdrive Oil Screen Tube
76. SCREEN, Overdrive Oil
77. MAGNET, Overdrive Oil Pan
78. PAN, Overdrive Oil
79. BOLT, Overdrive Oil Pan
80. FITTING, Oil Cooler

Fig. 12 Disassembled view of overdrive unit (part 1 of 2). 1985 similar

Fig. 12 Disassembled view of overdrive unit (part 2 of 2). 1985 similar

Fig. 13 Removing piston/accumulator assembly

Fig. 14 Removing or installing pressure plate

1. SOLENOID
2. SOLENOID CHECK BALL
3. PRESSURE SWITCH
4. END PLUG
5. PIN
6. END PLUG
7. SHIFT VALVE
8. PISTON BUSHING (T.V.)
9. PISTON
10. VALVE BODY
11. T.V. VALVE
12. SPRING
13. END PLUG
14. PIN
15. SPRING
16. PIN
17. RELIEF VALVE
18. INNER SPRING
19. OUTER SPRING
20. PIN
21. PICKUP TUBE

Fig. 15 Disassembled view of valve body

OUTPUT SHAFT

Disassemble
1. Remove speedometer gear retainer clip and gear, **Fig. 16.**
2. Remove pump cover attaching screws, then the cover.
3. On 1985 models, remove oil seal from pump cover.
4. On all models, Mark pump gears for assembly. Tilt pump housing downward, then rotate pump housing until gears slide out.
5. Remove drive pin from output shaft.
6. Remove pump housing from output shaft.

7. Remove thrust washer from pump housing, then the thrust bearing and washer from clutch hub.
8. Remove clutch hub from output shaft.
9. Remove sprag clutch from output shaft.

Assembly
1. Coat all components before assembling with clean automatic transmission fluid.
2. Install sprag clutch onto output shaft. Lip on sprag clutch cage must face rearward or toward the oil grooves on the clutch hub.

3. Install clutch hub onto output shaft. Oil grooves on hub must face sprag clutch.
4. Install thrust washer and bearing onto clutch hub.
5. Install thrust washer onto pump housing.
6. Install pump housing onto output shaft, then pin in output shaft.
7. Install pump gears into pump housing. Gears must be installed in same direction as removed. Align marks placed on gears during disassembly.
8. On 1985 models, install oil seal in pump cover.
9. On all models, Place pump cover onto pump housing. Align cover bolt holes, then install bolts. Torque bolts to 6–8 ft. lbs.
10. Install speedometer gear and retaining clip into output shaft.
11. Install new O-rings into pump cover.

CARRIER HOUSING DISASSEMBLE

1. Remove nuts attaching carrier cover, then the cover.
2. Remove thrust washer, thrust bearing, selective washer and input sun gear, **Fig. 17.**
3. Remove pinion gears.
4. Remove steel thrust plate from carrier housing.
5. To assemble carrier housing, reverse disassembly procedure.

ACCUMULATOR/PISTON DISASSEMBLE

1. Remove snap ring retaining accumulator onto piston, **Fig. 18.**
2. Remove accumulator and (24) springs from piston.
3. Remove (2) O-rings from accumulator.
4. Remove (2) O-rings from piston.
5. To assemble accumulator/piston assembly, reverse disassembly procedure. Coat new O-rings with clean automatic transmission fluid before installing.

OVERDRIVE UNIT CASE ASSEMBLE

1. Install pressure plate springs into transmission case pockets as shown in **Fig. 19.**
2. Position pressure plate on top of the springs. Ensure springs are seated into pockets of pressure plate.
3. Position plate tool No. J-21420-2 or equivalent, onto top of pressure plate with bolt of tool No. J-23327 through center of the plate. Position tool No. J-23327 onto rear of case and install retaining nut. Tighten nut on tool until pressure plate is drawn approximately ⅛ inch below overdrive clutch plate step.
4. Install (3) pressure plate attaching bolts. Remove tools J-21420-2 and J-23327 from case.

Fig. 16 Output shaft assembly. 1985 similar

1. CARRIER BASE
2. THRUST PLATE
3. PINION GEARS (4)
4. PINION THRUST WASHERS (4)
5. CARRIER COVER
6. INPUT SUN GEAR
7. SELECTIVE THRUST WASHER
8. THRUST BEARING
9. THRUST WASHER

Fig. 17 Carrier assembly

Fig. 18 Piston/accumulator assembly

Fig. 19 Pressure plate spring installation

Fig. 20 Direct clutch set (pack) assembly

Fig. 21 Overdrive clutch set (pack) assembly

Fig. 22 Aligning pinion gears

Fig. 23 Pinion thrust washer

Fig. 24 Measuring overdrive unit end-play

Fig. 25 Measuring distance from top of bar to adapter plate assembly

Fig. 26 Measuring distance from top of bar to bearing seat

5. Install output shaft assembly into case. Ensure O-rings are properly positioned on pump cover.
6. Install pump attaching bolts. Torque bolts to 10–12 ft. lbs.
7. Install thrust bearing onto output sun gear.
8. Install tanged direct clutch washer with tabs facing pressure plate, **Fig. 20.**
9. Install direct clutch thrust bearing.
10. Install direct clutch thrust washer. The thrust washer will have a tooth missing from its outer edge. The side of the thrust washer with the circular grind pattern must face the thrust bearing. The side with the grind pattern can be identified by notch ground into the tooth, **Fig. 20.**
11. Install (1) composition clutch disc and then a selective clutch plate.

NOTE: Selective clutch plates come in 5 sizes from .080–.120 inch.

12. Alternate the remaining clutch discs and plates until all (5) plates and discs are installed.
13. Install lower portion of the carrier assembly onto the direct clutch set. Shift the carrier until all clutch plates are engaged.
14. Install steel overdrive stop clutch plate, then alternate with a disc and a plate until all (4) plates and discs are installed, **Fig. 21.**

15. Install finger pressure plate.
16. Install carrier thrust plate with tabs facing sprag clutch.
17. Install (2) pinion gears with index mark on gears facing inward or toward each other. Install the other (2) pinion gears with index mark 90° off from the first (2) gears, **Fig. 22.**
18. Install output sun thrust washer onto rear of input sun gear.
19. Install input sun gear.

NOTE: If the input sun gear spreads the pinion gears while installing, the pinion gears are not aligned properly.

20. Install selective thrust washer with oil grooves on washer facing input sun gear.
21. Install thrust bearing onto input sun gear.
22. Install carrier thrust washer onto cover.
23. Install (4) pinion gear thrust washers onto carrier cover, **Fig. 23.**
24. Install carrier cover.
25. Install new attaching nuts. Torque nuts to 6–8 ft. lbs.
26. Measure overdrive unit end-play as follows:
    a. Position straight edge J-34673 or equivalent, across face of overdrive unit as shown in **Fig. 24.** Using depth micrometer J-34672 or equivalent, measure distance from bearing to the top of the bar.

b. Measure thickness of bar (J-34673) with a 0 to 1 micrometer and subtract this reading from reading obtained from micrometer (J-34672). Note reading obtained.
    c. Place straight edge J-34673 or equivalent across rear of adapter plate as shown in **Fig. 25.** Use depth micrometer J-34672 or equivalent and measure distance from top of the bar to adapter plate mounting surface. Note reading obtained.
    d. Measure distance from top of the bar to bearing seat in adapter plate as shown in **Fig. 26.**
    e. Subtract reading obtained in step 26d from reading obtained in step 26c and note difference.
    f. Subtract difference from step 26d from step 26a and b.
    g. The difference should be .000 ± .003 inch. If not, remove carrier cover and install a correct size input sun selective thrust washer.

NOTE: Selective thrust washers are available in 8 sizes, from .123–.158 inch.

27. Install accumulator and piston assembly.
28. Install large snap ring onto the front of the overdrive unit as shown in **Fig. 27.**
29. Using tool No. J-34523 or equivalent, install new seal onto adapter plate, **Fig. 28.**

Fig. 27 Snap ring installation

Fig. 28 Installing new seal onto adapter plate

Fig. 29 Install air line adapter onto overdrive unit case

Fig. 30 Measuring clutch set (pack) clearance

Fig. 31 Valve body check ball location

Fig. 32 T.V. lever adjustment

30. Install adapter plate. Torque adapter plate bolts to 18–20 ft. lbs.
31. On 1985 models, proceed as follows:
   a. Remove seal protector, then install speedometer gear and sensor.
   b. Using tool J-21426 or equivalent, install new output seal.
   c. Install valve body as previously described.
   d. Install oil filter on pickup tube.
   e. Apply a bead of RTV sealant No. 1052366 or equivalent, onto oil pan flange. Install oil pan with RTV wet and torque bolts to 6–8 ft. lbs.
32. On all models, remove first ⅛ inch pipe plug from left side of the overdrive unit. Install air line fitting J-34742 or equivalent into plug hole and tighten, **Fig. 29.**
33. Measure clutch pack clearance as follows:
   a. Loosen pressure plate attaching bolts evenly until spring pressure is released.
   b. Position dial indicator J-8001 or equivalent onto rear of overdrive unit as shown in **Fig. 30.**
   c. Apply a minimum of 100 psi to the air line fitting (J-34742) and note dial indicator reading. Dial indicator reading obtained should be .050–.070 inch. If not, replace direct

clutch selective clutch plates. The selective clutch plates are available in 5 sizes in .010 inch increments from .080–.120 inch. If dial indicator reading obtained is within specified limit, remove clutch pack retaining bolts.
34. Coat the (3) ⅛ inch pipe plugs with a suitable anti-seize compound and install plugs. Torque plugs to 7–9 ft. lbs.
35. Remove air line adapter. Coat plug with a suitable anti-seize compound and install plug. Torque plug to 9–12 ft. lbs.
36. On 1984 models, Install speedometer gear and sensor.
37. Install new output seal onto case.
38. Install valve body as follows:
   a. Install check ball into overdrive case as shown in **Fig. 31.**
   b. Position new gaskets, one on each side of separator plate.
   c. Install separator plate onto valve body.
   d. Install valve body onto overdrive unit case. Torque valve body to case bolts to 6–8 ft. lbs.
   e. Install T.V. cable, retaining clip and bolt.
   f. Install T.V. lever. Connect T.V. cable onto lever.
   g. Install tool No. J-34671-1 or equiv-

alent, into T.V. cable bore located on side of case. Place hook onto T.V. cable, setting the cable onto high step of gauge (J-34671-1). Position cam stop onto valve body as close to the lever as possible and install retaining bolt. Set hook on T.V. cable onto lower step of the gauge (J-34671-1). Place tool No. J-34671-2 or equivalent, between piston and solenoid bracket as shown in **Fig. 32.** Adjust screw/bolt on T.V. lever until bolt contacts cam stop.
39. Install pick-up tube and oil filter onto valve body.
40. Apply a bead of RTV sealant No. 1052366 or equivalent, onto oil pan flange. Install oil pan with RTV wet.
41. Install magnet into oil pan as shown in **Fig. 8.**
42. Install oil pan bolts. Torque bolts to 6–8 ft. lbs.
43. On all models, install overdrive unit onto transmission reverse housing. Guide idler shaft onto adapter plate and into idler gears. Align splines on mainshaft with splines on input sun gear. Slide units together and install overdrive unit case to transmission reverse housing attaching bolts. Torque bolts to 34–36 ft. lbs.

GM FRONT WHEEL DRIVE AXLES

INDEX

DESCRIPTION

The front wheel drive system, **Figs. 1 and 2,** consists of a final drive unit, left and right hand output shafts and drive axles. On Eldorado, Riviera, Seville and Toronado models, the output shafts are splined to the side gears and are retained by a retaining ring. Each drive axle, **Figs. 3 and 4,** consists of an axle shaft, with a ball type constant velocity joint at the outboard end and a tri-pot joint at the inboard end. On 1980–84 Citation, Omega, Phoenix, Skylark and 1982–84 Cavalier, Celebrity, Century, Cimarron, Cutlass Ciera, Firenza, 2000, Skyhawk and 6000 models, two different types of drive axle design are used. Both designs use the same ball type constant velocity joint at the outboard end. One design uses a ball type constant velocity joint at the inboard end, **Fig. 5,** the other design uses a tri-pot joint at the inboard end, **Figs. 4 and 6.** Both designs incorporate male splines which lock on the transaxle gears with snap rings, except for the left side inboard joint used with the automatic transaxles. The left side inboard joint used on automatic transaxle models utilizes a female spline which installs over a transaxle stub shaft. On 1985 Cavalier, Celebrity, Century, Cimarron, Citation, Cutlass Ciera, DeVille, Electra, Firenza, Fleetwood, Omega, Phoenix, Skyhawk, Skylark, 98, 2000 & 6000 models, a ball type constant velocity is used at the outboard end, while a tri-pot type joint is used at the inboard end, **Fig. 4.** Snap rings are used to lock the male splines of the axle shafts into the transaxle gears, except for the left side inboard joint used with the automatic transaxles. The left side inboard joint used on automatic transaxle models utilizes a female spline which installs over a transaxle stub shaft. On 1985 Nova models, a ball type constant velocity joint is used at the outboard end, while a tri-pot type joint is used at the inboard end. Snap rings are used to lock the male splines of the axle shafts into the transaxle gears, **Fig. 4.**

DRIVE AXLE
REPLACE

EXC. ELDORADO, RIVIERA, SEVILLE, TORONADO; 1982 CAVALIER, CIMARRON, FIRENZA, 2000, SKYHAWK; 1985 NOVA

NOTE: On models equipped with tri-pot joints on inboard axles, care must be taken not to over extend joints. When either or both ends are disconnected, over extending the tri-pot joint could result in internal joint separation.

Removal

1. Remove hub nut, then raise and support vehicle and remove wheel and tire assembly.
2. On vehicles equipped with ball type constant velocity inboard joints, **Fig. 5,** install axle shaft boot seal protector J-28712, **Fig. 2,** on inboard and outboard seals. On vehicles equipped with tri-pot inboard joints, **Figs. 4 and 6,** install axle boot seal protector J-

Fig. 1 Front wheel drive components. 1980–85 Eldorado, Riviera, Seville & Toronado

28712 on outboard seal and J-33162 on inboard seal, **Fig. 2.**

3. Disconnect brake line clip at strut.
4. Remove disc brake caliper and caliper support.
5. Mark cam bolt to ensure proper camber alignment during installation.
6. Remove bolts attaching steering knuckle to strut.
7. Using tool J-28468 or J-33008 and J-2619-01, **Fig. 2,** disengage snap rings retaining drive axles.
8. Separate steering knuckle from strut.
9. Carefully pull drive axles from transaxle. On vehicles equipped with tri-pot inboard joints, **Figs. 4 and 6,** do not over extend joints.
10. Using tool J-28733, remove axle shaft from hub and bearing assembly.

Installation

1. Loosely install drive axle to steering knuckle and transaxle.
2. Loosely attach steering knuckle to strut bracket.
3. Install disc brake caliper, torque attaching bolts to 30 ft. lbs.
4. Install drive axle to steering knuckle. The drive axle is an interference fit. Install hub nut, when shaft begins to rotate, insert a brass drift in slot on rotor to prevent shaft from turning. It will take approximately 70 ft. lbs. of torque to seat axle shaft.
5. Apply load on hub by lowering vehicle on jack stand. Align cam bolt alignment marks, then torque nut to 140 ft. lbs.
6. Using a screwdriver in groove provided on inner retainer, install axle shaft on transaxle, **Fig. 2.** Tap on screwdriver until axle shaft is seated in transaxle.
7. Connect brake line clip to strut bracket, then install wheel and tire assembly and lower vehicle.
8. Torque hub nut to 225 ft. lbs. on 1980–82 models and to 185 ft. lbs. on 1983–85 models.

1982 CAVALIER, CIMARRON, FIRENZA, 2000 & SKYHAWK

NOTE: On models equipped with tri-pot joints on inboard axles, care must be taken not to over extend joints. When either or both ends are disconnected, over extending the tri-pot joint could result in internal joint separation.

Removal

1. Remove hub nut, then raise and support vehicle and remove wheel and tire assembly.
2. On vehicles equipped with ball type constant velocity inboard joints, **Fig. 5,** install axle shaft boot seal protector J-28712, **Fig. 2,** on inboard and outboard seals. On vehicles equipped with tri-pot inboard joints, **Figs. 4 and 6,** install axle boot seal protector J-28712 on outboard seal and J-33162 on inboard seal, **Fig. 2.**
3. Remove disc brake caliper, rotor and caliper support.

Fig. 2   Front wheel drive components. 1984–85 Citation & Skylark; 1980–84 Citation, Omega, Phoenix & Skylark; 1982–85 Cavalier, Celebrity, Century, Cimarron, Cutlass Ciera, Firenza, 2000, Skyhawk & 6000 (similar to 1985 Nova)

NOTE: Prior to beginning next step, it is suggested to mark cam bolt to ensure proper camber alignment during installation.

4. Remove strut to steering knuckle attaching bolts, then separate steering knuckle from strut bracket.
5. Using tool J-28468 or J-33008 with extension J-29794, remove axle shaft from transaxle, **Fig. 2.**
6. Using tool J-28733, remove axle shaft from hub and bearing assembly.

Key No.	Part Name
1	RACE, C.V. JOINT OUTER
2	CAGE, C.V. JOINT
3	RACE, C.V. JOINT INNER
4	RING, SHAFT RETAINING
5	BALL (6)
6	RETAINER, SEAL
7	SEAL, C.V. JOINT
8	CLAMP, SEAL RETAINING
9	SHAFT, AXLE (LH)
10	SEAL, TRI-POT JOINT
11	SPIDER, TRI-POT JOINT
12	ROLLER, NEEDLE
13	BALL, TRI-POT JOINT (3)
14	RETAINER, BALL & NEEDLE (3)
15	HOUSING ASSY, TRI-POT (LH)
16	HOUSING ASSY, DAMPER & TRI-POT (RH)
17	SHAFT, AXLE (RH)
18	RING, SPACER
19	RING, RACE RETAINING

Fig. 3   Exploded view of drive axle. 1980–84, Eldorado, Riviera, Seville & Toronado

Key No.	Part Name
1 – RACE, C.V. JOINT OUTER	15 – HOUSING ASM, TRI-POT
2 – CAGE, C.V. JOINT	16 – HOUSING ASM, DAMPER & TRI-POT (RH)
3 – RACE, C.V. JOINT INNER	17 – SHAFT, AXLE (RH)
4 – RING, SHAFT RETAINING	18 – RING, SPACER
5 – BALL (6)	19 – RING, RACE RETAINING
6 – PROTECTOR, CLAMP (2)	20 – CLAMP, SEAL RETAINING
7 – SEAL, C.V. JOINT	21 – RETAINER, NEEDLE
8 – CLAMP, SEAL RETAINING	22 – RING, NEEDLE RETAINER
9 – SHAFT, AXLE (LH)	23 – RING, JOINT RETAINING
10 – SEAL, TRI-POT JOINT	24 – HOUSING, TRI-POT (RH)
11 – SPIDER, TRI-POT JOINT	25 – SHAFT ASM, DAMPER &
12 – ROLLER, NEEDLE	26 – RING, DEFLECTOR
13 – BALL, TRI-POT JOINT (3)	27 – BUSHING, TRILOBAL TRI-POT
14 – RETAINER, BALL & NEEDLE (3)	

Fig. 4   Exploded view of drive axle with tri-pot inboard joint. 1985 models

Installation

1. Loosely install drive axle to steering knuckle and transaxle.
2. Loosely attach steering knuckle to strut bracket.
3. Remove one hub to steering knuckle attaching bolt and install a longer bolt through hub cutout to prevent hub from turning. Install hub nut and washer and torque to 70 ft. lbs.
4. Remove long bolt and install original hub and bearing to steering knuckle attaching bolt. Torque bolts to 63 ft. lbs.
5. Install disc brake caliper and rotor. Torque caliper attaching bolts to 21–35 ft. lbs.
6. Using a screwdriver in groove provided on inner retainer, install axle shaft into transaxle, **Fig. 2.** Tap on screwdriver until axle shaft is seated in transaxle.
7. Torque steering knuckle to strut bracket attaching bolts to 140 ft. lbs.
8. Install wheel and tire and lower vehicle.

9. Torque hub nut to 185 ft. lbs.

1985 NOVA
Removal
1. Remove hub nut cotter pin, the the hub nut and washer.
2. Loosen wheel lug nuts, then raise and support vehicle.
3. Remove wheel and tire assembly, then lower control arm to ball joint attaching nuts and bolts.
4. Using tool J-24319-01, remove tie rod end from steering knuckle.
5. Remove brake caliper support-to-steering knuckle attaching bolts, then the caliper. Support caliper to prevent brake hose damage.
6. Remove rotor, then using tool J-25287, push axle assembly from hub, **Fig. 7.**
7. Using tools J-2619-01 and J-35762, pull axle assembly from transaxle.

NOTE: When removing axle assembly, do not pull on axle shaft. To prevent axle boot damage, do not allow them to contact any

parts during removal.

Installation

NOTE: Prior to installing axle assembly, inspect knuckle inner grease seal. Replace if distorted or worn. Also check for foreign material at hub bearing area

1. Install axle assembly into transaxle. Use a long brass drift and hammer positioned on the tri-pot housing ribs to drive in.
2. Install axle into wheel hub, then lower control arm to ball joint. Torque ball joint nuts and bolts to 47 ft. lbs.
3. Install tie rod end. Torque nut to 38 ft. lbs.
4. Install rotor, then the brake caliper. Torque attaching bolts to 65 ft. lbs.
5. Install tire and wheel assembly, then drive axle nut and washer.
6. Lower vehicle to floor, then torque lug nuts to 76 ft. lbs. and drive axle nut to 137 ft. lbs.
7. Install nut cap and cotter pin.

Key No.	Part Name
1	RACE, C.V. JOINT OUTER
2	CAGE, C.V. JOINT
3	RACE, C.V. JOINT INNER
4	RING, RACE RETAINING
5	BALL (6)
6	RETAINER, SEAL
7	SEAL, C/V JOINT
8	CLAMP, SEAL RETAINING
9	SHAFT, AXLE (LH)
10	SEAL, D/O JOINT
11	RING, BALL RETAINING
12	BALL (6)
13	RACE, D/O JOINT INNER
14	RACE, D/O JOINT
15	RACE, D/O JOINT OUTER
16	RING, JOINT RETAINING
17	RACE, D/O JOINT OUTER
18	SHAFT, AXLE (RH)
19	SLINGER

AUTOMATIC TRANSAXLE
(LH SIDE ONLY)

Fig. 5   Exploded view of drive axle with ball type constant velocity inboard joint. 1980—84 Citation, Omega, Phoenix & Skylark; 1982—84 Cavalier, Celebrity, Century, Cimarron, Cutlass Ciera, Firenza, 2000, Skyhawk & 6000

RIGHT HAND DRIVE AXLE, OUTPUT SHAFT & SEAL
REPLACE

ELDORADO, RIVIERA, SEVILLE & TORONADO

Removal
1. Disconnect battery ground cable.
2. Raise front of vehicle and place jack stands under front frame horns.
3. Remove wheel and tire assembly.
4. Remove cotter pin, nut and shield from tie rod pivot, then using puller J-24319, detach tie rod end from steering knuckle.
5. Install drive shaft seal protector J-28712, then remove cotter pin, nut and washer from drive axle, then remove six screws attaching drive axle to output shaft.

NOTE: To prevent axle shaft from rotating when removing nut or attaching screws, insert a drift through opening on top of caliper into corresponding rotor vane.

6. Remove cotter pin and nut from upper ball joint stud nut, then remove brake hose clip from stud and loosely reinstall nut.

7. Using a hammer and brass drift, rap on steering knuckle to free upper ball joint stud. Use care not to damage brake hose or steering knuckle.
8. Remove nut and separate upper ball joint from steering knuckle.
9. Guide drive axle out of steering knuckle and remove from vehicle.
10. Remove two screws attaching battery cable retainer to support and remove two screws attaching output support to engine, then rotate support downward.
11. Remove front nut and bolt from right hand frame brace, then pivot brace outward to provide clearance.
12. Using a plastic mallet, drive on flange end of output shaft until shaft releases from retaining ring, then remove output shaft and support. Use care not to damage output shaft seal surfaces or splines.
13. Using a suitable pry bar, pry output shaft seal out of housing. Pry at two or three different places to avoid cocking seal. Use care not to damage housing.

Installation
1. Using tool No. J-28518, install output shaft seal. Rotate tool to maintain proper alignment when installing seal.

2. Apply wheel bearing grease between lips of seal.
3. Index splines of output shaft with splines of side gear in final drive assembly, then install shaft by tapping on flange end with a soft faced mallet until retaining ring snaps into shaft groove. Ensure shaft is securely locked into position.

NOTE: When installing output shaft, use care not to damage seal.

4. Align output shaft support and engine block attaching screw holes, then install two support attaching screws. Torque screws to 50 ft. lbs.
5. Install two screws attaching battery cable retainer to support.
6. Guide drive axle into position and install splined end axle into steering knuckle.
7. Position upper ball joint stud into steering knuckle, then place brake hose clip on stud and install stud nut. Torque stud nut to 60 ft. lbs., then install cotter pin. The nut may be tightened an additional 1/6 turn to align cotter pin slots.
8. Install six screws attaching output shaft to drive axle. Torque screws to 60 ft. lbs.
9. Install drive axle washer, nut, retainer and cotter pin. Torque nut to 175 ft.

1 — RACE, C.V. JOINT OUTER
2 — CAGE, C.V. JOINT
3 — RACE, C.V. JOINT INNER
4 — RING, SHAFT RETAINING
5 — BALL (6)
6 — RETAINER, SEAL
7 — SEAL, C.V. JOINT
8 — CLAMP, SEAL RETAINING
9 — SHAFT, AXLE (LH)
10 — SEAL, TRI-POT JOINT
11 — SPIDER, TRI-POT JOINT
12 — ROLLER, NEEDLE
13 — BALL, TRI-POT JOINT (3)
14 — RING, JOINT RETAINING
15 — HOUSING ASSY, TRI-POT (LH)
16 — HOUSING ASSY, TRI-POT (RH)
17 — SHAFT, AXLE (RH)
18 — RING, SPACER
19 — RING, RACE RETAINING
20 — CLAMP, SEAL RETAINING
21 — RETAINER, NEEDLE
22 — RING, NEEDLE RETAINER

Fig. 6 Exploded view of drive axle with tri-pot inboard joint. 1980—84 Citation, Omega, Phoenix & Skylark; 1982—84 Cavalier, Celebrity, Century, Cimarron, Cutlass Ciera, Firenza, 2000, Skyhawk & 6000

lbs. Align cotter pin slot by rotating retainer and bend cotter pin so that retainer is held snugly.
10. Install tie rod pivot on steering knuckle. Torque nut to 44 ft. lbs. The nut may be tightened an additional ⅛ turn to align cotter pin slots.

Fig. 7 Pushing axle assembly from hub. 1985 Nova

TOOL J-25287

11. Install right hand frame brace bolt and nut. Torque belt to 50 ft. lbs.
12. Install front wheel and tire assembly, then lower vehicle and connect battery ground cable.
13. Check output shaft seal for leakage.

LEFT HAND DRIVE AXLE, OUTPUT SHAFT & SEAL
REPLACE
ELDORADO, RIVIERA, SEVILLE & TORONADO
Removal
1. Raise front of vehicle and place jack stands under front frame horns.
2. Remove wheel and tire assembly.
3. Remove cotter pin, nut and shield from tie rod pivot, then using puller J-24319, detach tie rod end from steering knuckle.
4. Remove cotter pin, nut and washer from drive axle, then remove six

screws attaching drive axle to output shaft.

NOTE: To prevent drive axle from rotating when removing nut or attaching screws, insert a drift through opening on top of caliper into corresponding rotor vane.

5. Remove cotter pin and nut from upper ball joint stud nut, then remove brake hose clip from stud and loosely reinstall nut.
6. Using a hammer and brass drift, rap on steering knuckle to free upper ball joint stud. Use care not to damage brake hose or steering knuckle.
7. Remove nut and separate upper ball joint from steering knuckle.
8. Guide drive axle out of steering knuckle and remove from vehicle.
9. Remove front nut and bolt from left hand frame brace, then pivot brace outward to provide clearance.
10. Using a hammer and brass drift, drive on flange end of output shaft until shaft releases from retaining ring, then remove output shaft.
11. Using a suitable pry bar, pry output shaft seal from housing. Pry at two or

Fig. 8 Outer constant velocity joint seal removal & installation. 1980–84 models

three locations to avoid cocking seal. Use care not to damage housing.

Installation

1. Using tool No. J-28518, install output shaft seal. Rotate tool to maintain proper alignment when installing seal.
2. Apply wheel bearing grease between lips of seal.
3. Index splines of output shaft with splines of side gear in final drive assembly then install shaft by tapping center of flange end with a soft faced mallet until retaining ring snaps into shaft groove. Ensure shaft is securely locked into position.

NOTE: When installing output shaft, use care not to damage seal.

Fig. 9 Outer constant velocity joint seal removal & installation. 1985 models

Fig. 10   Outer constant velocity joint disassembly & assembly. 1980—85 models

Fig. 11   Inner tri-pot seal removal & installation. 1980—84 Eldorado, Riviera, Seville & Toronado

Fig. 12   Inner tri-pot seal removal & installation. 1980—84 Citation, Omega, Phoenix & Skylark; 1982—84 Cavalier, Celebrity, Century, Cimarron, Cutlass Ciera, Firenza, 2000, Skyhawk & 6000

4. Guide drive axle into position and install splined end into steering knuckle.

5. Position upper ball joint stud into steering knuckle, then place brake hose clip on stud and install nut. Torque nut to 60 ft. lbs., then install cotter pin. The nut may be tightened an additional 1/6 turn to align cotter pin slots.

6. Install six screws attaching output shaft to drive axle. Torque screws to 60 ft. lbs.

7. Install drive axle water nut, retainer and cotter pin. Torque nut to 175 ft. lbs. and bend cotter pin so that retainer is held snugly.

8. Install tie rod pivot on steering knuckle. Torque nut to 44 ft. lbs. The nut may be tightened an additional 1/6 turn

to align cotter pin slots.

9. Install left hand frame brace bolt and nut. Torque bolt to 50 ft. lbs.

10. Install wheel and tire assembly, then lower vehicle and check output shaft seal for leakage.

RIGHT HAND OUTPUT SHAFT SUPPORT BEARING
REPLACE

ELDORADO, RIVIERA, SEVILLE & TORONADO

1. Remove right hand output shaft as described under Right Hand Drive Axle,

Output Shaft and Seal, Replace.

2. Remove three screws securing bearing retainer to support.

3. Install tool No. J-22912 between flange end of output shaft and flat area of shaft support, with flat surface of tool against flat area of shaft support. Position assembly on a suitable press and press shaft support, bearing, retainer and slinger from output shaft.

4. Remove bearing from output shaft support.

5. Lubricate output shaft support and bearing, then position bearing into support.

6. Pack bearing with wheel bearing grease, then install retainer and three attaching screws.

7. Place assembled components and

REMOVE

1. Cut seal retaining clamps.
2. Remove parts as shown.

INSTALL

1. Flush grease from housing and repack housing with approx. half of grease furnished with new seal.
2. Put remainder of grease in seal.
3. Install parts as shown. Use tool J-34773 to secure seal retaining clamp. Torque to specifications.

TRI-POT HOUSING (DESIGN TYPE A)
SHAFT RETAINING RING
SPIDER ASSEMBLY
CLAMP PROTECTOR Used on some models
Pry tabs 2 places both sides.
TRILOBAL TRI-POT BUSHING
TRI-POT HOUSING (DESIGN TYPE B)
SPACER RING
CLAMP PROTECTOR
SEAL RETAINING CLAMP
TRI-POT JOINT SEAL
AXLE
Seal groove
SEAL RETAINING CLAMP

SEAL RETAINING CLAMPS
Side cutters

Drive Axle Boot Clamp Tool J-34773
SEAL RETAINING CLAMPS
Breaker Bar
Torque wrench Torque to 95 N·m (70 ft/lbs) Both clamps

REMOVE AND INSTALL SEAL RETAINING CLAMP

SPACER RING
Slide ring back on axle shaft
NOTICE: Be sure spacer ring is seated in groove at reassembly

SHAFT RETAINING RING
Remove from axle shaft then slide spider assembly off axle
SPIDER ASSEMBLY
SPACER RING
Snap ring pliers J-8059

REMOVE AND INSTALL SPIDER ASSEMBLY

Fig. 13   Inner tri-pot seal removal & installation. 1985 models

REMOVE

1. Remove parts as shown.

INSTALL

1. Flush grease from joint. Repack joint with approx. half of grease provided.
2. Put remainder of grease in seal.
3. Install parts as shown. Use tool J-22610 to secure seal retaining clamp.

RETAINING RING
JOINT ASSEMBLY
RACE RETAINING RING
SEAL RETAINER
SEAL
Seal groove
Coat inside of seal lip with grease
SEAL RETAINING CLAMP
AXLE SHAFT

SEAL RETAINER
SEAL RETAINING CLAMP
Side cutters
Brass drift lightly tap evenly all around retainer

REMOVE CLAMP AND RETAINER

RACE RETAINING RING
Snap ring pliers J-8059. Spread retaining-ring ears apart and pull shaft out.

REMOVE JOINT ASSEMBLY

Push assembly onto shaft until retaining ring is seated in groove

Arbor press
SEAL RETAINER

INSTALL JOINT ASSEMBLY   **INSTALL SEAL RETAINER**

Fig. 14   Inner constant velocity joint seal removal & installation. 1980—84 Citation, Omega, Phoenix & Skylark; 1982—84 Cavalier, Celebrity, Century, Cimarron, Cutlass Ciera, Firenza, 2000, Skyhawk & 6000

Fig. 15 Inner constant velocity joint removal & installation. 1980–84 Citation, Omega, Phoenix & Skylark; 1982–84 Cavalier, Celebrity, Century, Cimarron, Cutlass Ciera, Firenza, 2000, Skyhawk & 6000

Fig. 16 Deflector ring removal & installation. 1985 models exc. Nova

shaft, then position
...s and output shaft on a
...ess. Using a standard 1¼ in. inside
diameter pipe, press bearing and
assembled components onto shaft.
8. Check to ensure bearing and support
rotate smoothly, then install right hand
output shaft.

OUTER CONSTANT VELOCITY JOINT & SEAL
REPLACE

All Models

For removal and installation procedures
refer to **Figs. 8, 9 and 10.**

INNER TRI-POT SEAL
REPLACE

1980—84 ELDORADO, RIVIERA, SEVILLE & TORONADO

For removal and installation procedures
refer to **Fig. 11.**

1980—84 CITATION, OMEGA, PHOENIX & SKYLARK; 1982—84 CAVALIER, CELEBRITY, CENTURY, CIMARRON, CUTLASS CIERA, FIRENZA, 2000, SKYHAWK & 6000

For removal and installation procedures,
refer to **Fig. 12.**

1985 MODELS

For removal and installation procedures,

refer to **Fig. 13.**

INNER CONSTANT VELOCITY JOINT & SEAL
REPLACE

1980—84 CITATION, OMEGA, PHOENIX & SKYLARK; 1982—84 CAVALIER, CELEBRITY, CENTURY, CIMARRON, CUTLASS CIERA, FIRENZA, 2000, SKYHAWK & 6000

For removal and installation procedures,
refer to **Figs. 14 and 15.**

DEFLECTOR RING
REPLACE

1985 MODELS EXC. NOVA

For removal and installation procedures,
refer to **Fig. 16.**

FINAL DRIVE
REPLACE

EXC. ELDORADO, RIVIERA, SEVILLE & TORONADO

On these models, the final drive unit is
an integral component of the transaxle
assembly.

ELDORADO, RIVIERA, SEVILLE & TORONADO

1. Disconnect battery ground cable.
2. Raise front of vehicle and position jack stands under front frame horns.
3. Remove right and left hand frame brace front attaching bolts, then position braces to provide clearance.
4. Position drain pan under final drive cover, then loosen cover and allow lubricant to drain.
5. Remove final drive cover attaching screws, cover and gasket.
6. Remove screws attaching right and left output shafts to drive axles. Separate output shaft flanges from drive axles to permit clearance of final drive assembly with shafts installed.
7. Remove two screws attaching battery cable retainer to right hand output shaft support, then remove two screws securing support to engine. Rotate support downward to provide clearance for removal.
8. Remove final drive to transmission attaching screws that secures rear of final drive shield, then loosen support bracket screws that secure front of shield and remove shield.
9. Remove five remaining final drive to transmission attaching screws.
10. Remove screws attaching final drive support bracket to engine block.
11. Using tool J-24319, disconnect steering linkage intermediate shaft from pitman and idler arms. Push linkage forward to ensure adequate clearance for final drive assembly removal.
12. Slide final drive assembly forward, off transmission splined shaft and remove unit with output shafts attached. Use care not to damage output shaft seal or splines.
13. Reverse procedure to install. Torque final drive to transaxle attaching bolts to 30 ft. lbs., support bracket bolts to 50 ft. lbs. and output shaft to drive shaft attaching bolts to 60 ft. lbs.

DECIMAL & MILLIMETER EQUIVALENTS

INCH	INCH	MM
1/64	.015625	.397
1/32	.03125	.794
3/64	.046875	1.191
1/16	.0625	1.587
5/64	.078125	1.984
3/32	.09375	2.381
7/64	.109375	2.778
1/8	.125	3.175
9/64	.140625	3.572
5/32	.15625	3.969
11/64	.171875	4.366
3/16	.1875	4.762
13/64	.203125	5.159
7/32	.21875	5.556
15/64	.234375	5.953
1/4	.25	6.350
17/64	.265625	6.747
9/32	.28125	7.144
19/64	.296875	7.541
5/16	.3125	7.937
21/64	.328125	8.334
11/32	.34375	8.731

INCH	INCH	MM
23/64	.359375	9.128
3/8	.375	9.525
25/64	.390625	9.922
13/32	.40625	10.319
27/64	.421875	10.716
7/16	.4375	11.113
29/64	.453125	11.509
15/32	.46875	11.906
31/64	.484375	12.303
1/2	.5	12.700
33/64	.515625	13.097
17/32	.53125	13.494
35/64	.546875	13.890
9/16	.5625	14.287
37/64	.578125	14.684
19/32	.59375	15.081
39/64	.609375	15.478
5/8	.625	15.875
41/64	.640625	16.272
21/32	.65625	16.669
43/64	.671875	17.065

INCH	INCH	MM
11/16	.6875	17.462
45/64	.703125	17.859
23/32	.71875	18.265
47/64	.734375	18.653
3/4	.75	19.050
49/64	.765625	19.447
25/32	.78125	19.884
51/64	.796875	20.240
13/16	.8125	20.637
53/64	.828125	21.034
27/32	.84375	21.431
55/64	.859375	21.828
7/8	.875	22.225
57/64	.890625	22.622
29/32	.90625	23.019
59/64	.921875	23.415
15/16	.9375	23.812
61/64	.953125	24.209
31/32	.96875	24.606
63/64	.984375	25.003
1		25.400

Special Service Tools

Throughout this manual references are made to and illustrations may depict the use of special tools required to perform certain jobs. These special tools can generally be ordered through the dealers of the make vehicle being serviced. It is also suggested that you check with local automotive supply firms as they also supply tools manufactured by other firms that will assist in the performance of these jobs. The vehicle manufacturers special tools are supplied by:

American Motors & General Motors . . . . Service Tool Division
Kent-Moore Corporation
29784 Little Mack
Roseville, Michigan 48066

Chrysler Corp. . . . . Miller Special Tools
A Division of Utica Tool Co.
32615 Park Lane
Garden City, Michigan 48135

Ford Motor Co. . . . . Owatonna Tool Company
Owatonna, Minnesota 55060

Flasher Locations

Car	1980		1981		1982		1983		1984		1985–86	
	TSF	HWF	TSF	HWF	TSF	HWF	TSF	HWF	TSF	HWF	TSF	HWF
American Motors	12	3	12	3	12	3	12	3	12	3	12	3
Buick—Rear Wheel Drive	3	3	3	3	3	3	3	3	3	3	3	3
1980–85 Buick Skylark & 1982–86 Century	6	15	6	15	6	15	6	15	6	15	6	15
Cadillac—Rear Wheel Drive	6	4	6	4	6	4	6	4	6	4	6	4
Cadillac Seville & Eldorado, 1980–85	6	4	6	4	6	4	6	4	6	4	6	4
Cadillac Fleetwood (1985–86) & DeVille (1985–86); 1986 Eldorado & Seville	—	—	—	—	—	—	—	—	—	—	5	6
Calais, 1985–86 Grand AM & Somerset Regal; 1986 Skylark	—	—	—	—	—	—	—	—	—	—	6	3
Camaro & Firebird	4	3	4	3	6	6	6	6	6	6	6	6
Capri & Mustang	4	14	4	14	4	14	4	14	4	14	4	14
Cavalier, Cimarron, 2000, 1982–86 Skyhawk, Firenza & 1984–86 Sunbird	—	—	—	—	5	3	5	3	5	3	5	3
Chev. Malibu & Monte Carlo	3	3	3	3	3	3	3	3	3	3	3	3
Chevette & 1000	13	3	13	3	13	3	13	3	13	3	13	3
Chevrolet Full Size	3	3	3	3	3	3	3	3	3	3	3	3
Chevrolet Citation & Celebrity	6	15	6	15	6	15	6	15	6	15	6	15
Chevrolet Nova	—	—	—	—	—	—	—	—	—	—	3	3
Chrysler, Imperial & 1980–81 LeBaron	7①	6①	7①	6①	3	3	3	3	3	3	3	3
Chrysler E Class, Executive, 1982–86 LeBaron, 1983–86 New Yorker, Town & Country	—	—	—	—	4	5	4	5	4	5	4	5
Chrysler LeBaron GTS & Dodge Lancer	—	—	—	—	—	—	—	—	—	—	10	10
Chrysler Laser	—	—	—	—	—	—	—	—	3	3	3	3
Cordoba & Mirada	5	5	5	5	3	3	3	3	—	—	—	—
Corvette	3	3	3	3	3	3	—	—	7	7	7	7
Cougar, LTD II & Thunderbird	4	4	4	②	4	②	4	4	4	4	4	4
Dodge & Plymouth Full Size	7	6	7	6	—	—	—	—	—	—	—	—
Dodge & Plymouth Intermed.	3	3	3	3	3	3	3	3	3	3	3	3
Dodge Aries, 400, 600 & Plymouth Reliant, Caravelle	—	—	3	3	4	5	4	5	4	5	4	5
Dodge Daytona	—	—	—	—	—	—	—	—	—	—	3	3
Horizon, Omni & 1983–86 Charger & Turismo	3	3	3	3	3	3	3	3	3	3	3	3
Escort, EXP, LN7 & Lynx	—	—	4	5	4	5	4	5	4	5	4	5
Ford & Mercury Full Size	5	5	5	5	5	5	5	5	5	5	5	5
Fairmont, Zephyr & 1983–86 LTD & Marquis	4	4	4	14	4	14	4	4	4	4	4	4
Ford Pinto & Mercury Bobcat	6	6	—	—	—	—	—	—	—	—	—	—
Ford Tempo & Mercury Topaz	—	—	—	—	—	—	—	—	5	5	5	5
Granada, Monarch & Versailles	10	4	4	14	4	14	—	—	—	—	—	—
Grand Am (Exc. 1985–86), Grand Prix, LeMans & 1982–86 Bonneville	3	3	3	3	3	3	3	3	3	3	3	3
Lincoln	5	5	5	5	5③	5③	5③	5③	5	5	5	5
Oldsmobile (Exc. 1985–86 98 & 1986 88)	3	3	3	3	3	3	3	3	3	3	3	3
Oldsmobile Cutlass (Exc. Ciera, 1984–86 Cruiser)	3	3	3	3	3	3	3	3	3	3	3	3
Olds. Omega, Cutlass Ciera & 1984–86 Cruiser	6	15	6	15	6	15	6	15	6	15	6	15
Oldsmobile Toronado	3	3	3	3	6	4	6	4	6	4	6	4
Pontiac Full Size, 1980–81, 1983–86	3	3	3	3	—	—	3	3	3	3	3	3
Pont. Phoenix & 6000	6	15	6	15	6	15	6	15	6	15	6	15
Pontiac Fiero	—	—	—	—	—	—	—	—	5	16	5	16

TSF: Turn Signal Flasher.   HWF: Hazard Warning Flasher.

①—Location 3 on LeBaron. Location 5 on Imperial.   ②—Location 14 on Cougar. Location 4 on Cougar XR7 & Thunderbird.   ③—Location 4 on Lincoln Continental.